Ellen Nugent Berlinguette
2005 Folio Books

PENGUIN BOOKS

SHAKESPEARE'S WORDS

'*Shakespeare's Words* is one of the very few works of reference that deserves a place on the shelves of all Shakespeare lovers and for that matter all lovers of the English language. In all too many cases explanation of Shakespeare's words – both those that have become obsolete and those that have changed in meaning – have been passed down from editor to editor since the nineteenth century. David and Ben Crystal, by contrast, have returned to first principles and in so doing produced the most comprehensive guide to Shakespeare's astonishing linguistic inventiveness that has ever been compiled'
Professor Jonathan Bate, author of *The Genius of Shakespeare*

'A fascinating place to browse ... it takes into account all kinds of scholarly developments ... [The authors] have carried out their work admirably. Their procedures are clear and helpful ... The strongest impression you carry away from *Shakespeare's Words* is how rich his language is'
John Gross, author of *After Shakespeare, Sunday Telegraph*

'This is what everybody who loves Shakespeare – amateur or professional – has been looking for. A clear and accurate guide to the astonishing vocabulary of the world's number one writer ... an inexhaustible feast of illumination'
Michael Wood, historian and broadcaster

'Magnificent ... a huge work of user-friendly scholarship ... When foxed and flummoxed, there's nothing for it but this excellent glossary'
Economist

'Fascinating ... this splendid book ... will be the trusted companion of students, teachers and editors of Shakespeare for decades to come, and the foundation on which all future Shakespeare dictionaries will be obliged to build ... *Shakespeare's Words* will have a vital part to play in returning our attention to the texts as dramatic poetry, as startling masterpieces of form and phrasing'
Kiernan Ryan, *The Times Higher Education Supplement*

David Crystal
Ben Crystal

Shakespeare's Words

A Glossary and Language Companion

With Preface by
STANLEY WELLS

PENGUIN BOOKS

PENGUIN BOOKS

Published by the Penguin Group
Prnguin Books Ltd, 80 Strand, London WC2R ORL, England
Penguin Putnam Inc., 275 Hudson Street, New York, New York 10014, USA
Penguin Books Australia Ltd, 250 Camberwell Road, Camberwell, Victoria 3124, Australia
Penguin Books Canada Ltd, 10 Alcorn Avenue, Toronto, Ontario, Canada, M4V 3B2
Penguin Books India (P) Ltd, 11, Community Centre, Panchsheel Park, New Delhi – 110 017, India
Penguin Books (NZ) Ltd, Cnr Rosedale and Airborne Roads, Albany, Auckland, New Zealand
Penguin Books (South Africa) (Pty) Ltd, 24 Sturdee Avenue, Rosebank 2196, South Africa

Penguin Books Ltd, Registered Offices: 80 Strand, London W2R ORL, England
www.penguin.com

First published 2002
7

Typeset in Minion and Scala Sans
Typeset by Mendip Communications Ltd, Frome, Somerset
Printed by WS Bookwell, Finland

Contents

Preface

STANLEY WELLS

The appearance of a comprehensive and up-to-date glossary of Shakespeare will be greeted with rejoicing by Shakespeare students and scholars all over the world. Throughout the twentieth century anyone concerned with Shakespeare's language has had to rely essentially on out-of-date works deriving from the nineteenth century. A standard work of reference has been Alexander Schmidt's two-volume *Shakespeare-Lexicon* and *Quotation Dictionary* dating from as far back as 1874, reprinted as recently as 1987 and still in print. A product of German philological scholarship, it contains over 50,000 quotations illustrating verbal usages, and is still of value, especially to editors. But Schmidt's work, rooted in the scholarship of its day, was completed without the benefit of the great *Oxford English Dictionary*, conceived in 1857 but which began to appear only in 1884, by which time the editors had got as far as 'ant'. The dictionary crawled to completion only in 1928, since when there have been a number of supplementary volumes. One of the compilers of the *OED* was Charles Talbot Onions (1873–65), but his handy *Shakespeare Glossary* appeared in 1911, well before the parent work was completed. His glossary, too, to which the Crystals pay tribute, is still in print, in the not very comprehensive revision by Robert D. Eagleson of 1986.

In the long period since the origination of Schmidt's and Onions's works, attitudes to Shakespeare's text and to his language have changed, his readership has broadened, and the needs of readers have evolved alongside changes in the English language itself. At the same time great strides have been made in the study of Shakespeare's language. Freudian-influenced criticism has revealed layers of wordplay unsuspected by the Victorians. Specialized areas of Shakespeare's vocabulary, such as his use of sea terms, of legal, military and theatrical terminology, of proverbs, oaths, and the Bible, have been subjected to close scrutiny. Eric Partridge's pioneering *Shakespeare's Bawdy*, first printed in a limited edition in 1947 and also still in print, has been followed by other studies of what one critic called the 'less decent language of Shakespeare's time' which had been largely neglected by the compilers of *OED*, most recently and most valuably by Gordon Williams's three-volume *Dictionary of Sexual Language and Imagery in Shakespearean and Stuart Literature* (1997) and its offshoot *A Glossary of Shakespeare's Sexual Language* (1998).

During this period too, generations of scholarly editors and critics have diligently investigated the connotations and registers of particular words and groups of words, and the Shakespeare canon itself has enlarged with the addition of the collaborative play *The Two Noble Kinsmen* and of *Edward III*, parts at least of which are now generally allowed to have been written by Shakespeare. The preparation of an easily accessible and comprehensive reference work which would subsume these studies has long been devoutly to be wished, and the heroic task undertaken by David and Ben Crystal – the one an eminent linguist and lexicographer, the other an actor as well as a scholar, bringing with him a theatrical perspective – fills a yawning gap in Shakespeare reference shelves. And it is no mere clone of earlier works of the kind. Its innovative features bear witness to the freshness of thought that has gone into it. The list of one hundred Frequently Encountered Words provides an excellent basic foundation for the beginner. The glossary panels devoted to areas of the text such as Stage directions, Greetings, Money, and Archaisms form quick-reference guides to specific topics; some of them, such as those on Verb forms and Comparison, Functional shifts, and Plurals even extend to grammatical usage, though the authors disclaim any overall attempt to explicate Shakespearian grammar. Most original of all are the 'Shakespearian Circles' which go well beyond the authors' basic remit in providing diagrammatic representations of the circles in which various groups of characters in the plays move. Acting as supplements to the conventional character lists, these, with their accompanying plot synopses, offer help with the interlocking worlds of each play. It is fascinating to see how complex are the circles of some plays, such as *Henry VI Parts 1 and 2*, and how relatively simple are others, such as *The Two Gentlemen of Verona*, *The Merchant of Venice*, and *Twelfth Night*.

Every so often it is suggested that the time has come for Shakespeare to be translated into modern English. Though it is true that those who read the plays in foreign translation have the advantage over modern readers in that part of the work of comprehension has been done for them by the translator, the ambitious scope of the present study should not cause readers to suppose that Shakespeare is a closed book to all but readers who have undertaken laborious study of the language in which he wrote and of his particular use of it. As David and Ben Crystal acknowledge, 'it is perfectly possible to go to a Shakespeare play, with little or no awareness of Early Modern English vocabulary, and have a great time.' In the theatre, difficulties experienced on the page can melt away in the mediating solvent of the actors' understanding. For all that, the experience of seeing the plays, and of reading them and the poems, can be profoundly enhanced through an awareness of the endless fecundity of Shakespeare's linguistic resourcefulness such as this book can stimulate.

Introduction

Shakespeare continues to attract a staggering number of new editions, critical commentaries, and discursive essays, but the supportive linguistic literature has been surprisingly sparse. When we were researching the need for this book, we found very little that might be classed as 'high-quality Shakespearian lexicography'. On the other hand, we found a great deal that could be described as 'low-quality lexical commercialism', especially on the Web, in the form of selective word-lists providing crude approximations to the meanings of Elizabethan words, and generalizing about meanings in ways that were often misleading. The tools of enquiry that all students of literature have a right to demand from linguists – in the form of dictionaries, glossaries, thesauri, and concordances – are still remarkably few, by comparison with the literary energy that has been expended on the canon. And there seems to be no let-up in the demand for additional resources, as expressed by teachers, academics, students, actors, journalists, and others, anxious to develop their awareness of Shakespeare's language.

'Onions', of course, is the splendid exception. Having spent three years on the present book with the benefit of modern technology, we cannot but doff our caps in admiration at Charles Talbot Onions' remarkable feat of compilation, *A Shakespeare Glossary*, first published in 1911, revised in 1919, and enlarged in a further revision by Robert D. Eagleson in 1986. Both the present authors have lived with this book in the literary and theatrical parts of their professional lives, and they have benefited repeatedly from its content – in the first author's case, for some forty years. But when you live with someone for so long, you find out their weaknesses as well as their strengths; and our personal marginalia identifying omissions of coverage and inadequacies of treatment reinforce our feeling that there is a need for a fresh work.

All dictionaries should be regularly revised, to take account of new findings and methods, and Shakespeare is no exception. The texts are available to study in ways that were not possible before, and new texts have begun to attract attention: in the present case, our corpus includes the vocabulary of *The Two Noble Kinsmen* and *King Edward III*, which Onions, for example, does not include. The *Oxford English Dictionary* (*OED*), which Onions himself helped to create, is now available on CD-ROM and on the Internet, making it much more practicable to carry out large-scale focused projects of a lexical kind. We have thesaurus and concordance material from the fine project by Marvin Spevack to aid us. And between Hilda Hulme's *Explorations in Shakespeare's Language* (1962) – being

written when the first author was one of her students – and Frank Kermode's *Shakespeare's Language* (2000), we have a wealth of individual lexical studies to inform our judgements as lexicographers.

It is, one must always remember, a matter of judgement. Lexicographers are as human and as creative as anyone else – as the comparison of any two dictionaries will show, with thousands of differences of coverage and treatment. To refer again to Onions: his judgements, made on the basis of an intuition shaped by the lexicon of Victorian England and an educational system in which Latin, in particular, played a major part, will be very different from ours, a century later, where the arrival of new meanings has made old ones less accessible (e.g. *portal*), and where we have different intuitions about what counts as a 'difficult' word. The contrast between our coverage and that of Onions is striking: we include many words that he omitted – a random dozen is *behest*, *beshrew*, *betimes*, *cellarage*, *commonweal*, *contumely*, *disrelish*, *lineaments*, *incontinency*, *saws*, *surfeit*, and *wormwood* – in all, as we guess from comparing a few pages, some 3,000 items. On the other hand, Onions, fascinated as he was with word origins, contains much more on the etymology and cultural history of certain words.

It is not just lexicographers who rely on their intuitions. Editors do too, and in our reading of the notes accompanying the various editions of the plays we have been struck by the remarkable range of opinion about what editors judge to be a word 'worth glossing'. Some plays in the Penguin series have twice as many glossed lexical items as others; and marked variations are found in other series. Similarly, there are personal practices in relation to lexical explanation. Some editions rely on individual sources: one, for example, relates virtually all its lexical observations to Onions; another only to the senses of the *OED*. We have been repeatedly struck by the number of difficult words which are not glossed at all – a manifestation, we feel, of the same sort of limitations as everyone encounters when they read an instruction manual written by specialists. It is difficult for an editor to remember just how difficult some words are, with familiarity increasingly breeding contentment. With thirty-five years separating the ages of the two authors of this book, we found the same problem: the first author's mark-up of the difficult words in a play would be far exceeded by those identified by the second author – and when this happened, we would always err on the side of inclusiveness. Doubtless some people will query why some words are in this book, thinking them 'too easy'; our only defence is that not everyone finds them so.

This is, of course, why we have extended the traditional coverage of a dictionary to include the appendices we have selected. In the days when a Classical background and Latin were a routine part of secondary schooling, there would not have been a need to include some of the features listed there. Regrettably even French words cannot be taken for granted any more, in some parts of the world. We have accordingly been eclectic. We know that Shakespeare is read virtually everywhere; but we also know that not all readers will be familiar with British local geography, so we have added appendices on locational names (Appendices VIII and IX). The same principle applies to some of the panels: for example, we include in our PLANTS panel (p.330) some terms which are still in use, but which will be unfamiliar to people from parts of the world where these plants are not known.

On the other hand, a dictionary is not a substitute for editorial notes, which focus on extracting the full meaning of a word in its individual context, and examining its resonance for the passage or text as a whole. Dictionaries do not particularize in this way; rather, they attempt to make generalizations about the meaning of words. They therefore have to ignore many of the sense associations, plays on words, etymological echoes, quibbles, and other effects that comprise the linguistic identity of a word in its full context. There is no place in a dictionary for the kind of extended discussion of a word like *prone* (such as occurs in Frank Kermode's insightful appreciation), teasing out its implications. At the same time, when there is a chance to draw attention to the complexity of a lexical situation, it is incumbent on the lexicographer to do so. We therefore regularly alert readers to the existence of other meanings than the one which is the focus of a particular entry, using three types of parenthetic information at the end of examples.

- The 'also' convention. For example, a quotation assigned to sense 2 of a headword might be followed by '[also: sense 4]'. This means that editorial practice generally finds sense 2 the primary sense, but sense 4 is definitely relevant in this context.
- The 'or' convention. This convention recognizes the fact that editorial opinion is divergent. If a quotation in sense 2 is followed by '[or: sense 4]' it means that our example could just as easily have been placed under sense 4, editorial opinions differing on the point.
- The 'pun' convention. If we give a quotation in sense 2 and follow it with '[pun: 63, sense 4]', we mean that in line 63 the word is punned in sense 4. The use of '[bawdy pun]' is also needed, from time to time.

It is not our intention to give the sense of a difficult passage as a whole – that is the job of the textual edition. However, from time to time, especially when sentence structure is difficult to follow, we have found it useful to add a further parenthetic explanatory gloss following the quotation, preceded by 'i.e.'. In such ways, our dictionary makes more of a bow in the direction of editorial practice than is usual in glossaries, and we see this as one of its strengths.

OUR PROCEDURE

We did not base our book on any previous compilation. Rather, we took a set of texts and worked through them from scratch, word by word. As this was a book commissioned by Penguin, the obvious choice for primary material was the *New Penguin Shakespeare*, under the general editorship of T. J. B. Spencer and associate editorship of Stanley Wells. This provided us with virtually all our primary data; the unfortunate absence in that series of a text for *Cymbeline* was made good by the use of the Arden edition (editor J.M. Nosworthy), and we used Giorgio Melchiori's edition of *King Edward III* from the New Cambridge Shakespeare.

Our procedure was straightforward. We went through each text and highlit any word whose form or meaning we felt to be 'difficult', either because it was an Elizabethan usage no longer current or because it would pose a problem to a modern readership despite its continued currency. Thus under the first heading we would highlight *fardel* and *tainture*; and under the second *importune* and *ordure*. We were particularly sensitive to those words which have developed a modern sense which is different from the earlier one (the so-called 'false friends'), such as *doubt* [= fear], *supervisor* [= onlooker] and *revolting* [= rebellious], and in such cases we sometimes add an example of the modern usage in order to point the contrast with the obsolete one (as in the case of *rheumatic*).

Any word identified by the Penguin series editors as a problem case, for whatever reason, was automatically included in our coverage; and to avoid the biases of those editors, we carried out the same exercise on all the words singled out for special comment in volumes from two other series. Often, this would make us encounter variants which the Penguin editors had chosen not to include, and we would add these to our corpus too. In particular, we tried to include all First Folio and significant early Quarto variants where these presented more than just an alternative spelling or printer's error. However, we did not go beyond these basic sources, and we certainly did not try to include the hundreds of individual emendations made by the pantheon of editors over the centuries. As it was, the book ended up with 21,263 entries.

With just a few exceptions, every instance of a problematic item was logged separately, regardless of the number of times it appeared. This eventually produced a very large corpus of 47,365 entries. We knew we could never fit all these examples into a single book; but the reasons for covering the texts in such detail were twofold. First, it enabled us to scrutinize all the examples of a word before deciding which one to put into the book: where there was a choice, we have selected the example which illustrates a word meaning most clearly. And secondly, it was always our intention to make the entire corpus available electronically (through a website and CD: for information, consult www.shakespeareswords.com). But, for the book, we restricted ourselves as a rule to one quotation illustrating each word, or distinct sense of a word – just occasionally allowing ourselves the luxury of two or three quotations, where it proved necessary to focus on different aspects of usage (alternative spellings, for example).

We then give up to five other line-references to the word from the corpus, choosing examples which we feel illustrate the diversity of the usage in the clearest way. The aim of multiple examples is to provide enough illustration for a reader to begin to develop a confident intuition about Shakespearian English. That is why we give several examples even in cases where the usage is not especially complex. *Hold 8* [= 'stop, cease'] is a case in point. Following up the examples listed would illustrate a range of usage from the single 'Hold, sir' through the double emphasis of 'Hold, Richard, hold' to the fivefold reiteration of the Messenger in *Two Noble Kinsmen*, as well as its use in a sentence ('we cannot hold') and governing a pronoun ('Hold thee'). In this way one 'gets to know the word' more intimately than if just a single example were given.

In a few exceptional cases we chose not to log every instance of a problematic word's occurrence, partly on grounds of economy and partly on grounds of pedagogy.

- There are several cases where a particular word is used several times in quick succession, in exactly the same sense, within a speech or piece of dialogue. In such cases, we included the first usage only. An example is Falstaff's rising from the dead at the end of *Henry 4 Part 1* (V.iv.110 ff.), where he uses the word *counterfeit* nine times in a dozen lines. We included just one instance, on the grounds that any reader who might use the glossary to check on this word would find that the one look-up would suffice for the whole sequence. On the other hand, if the word were to be used a few pages later, we would once again include it in the database, on the grounds that a reader might value the reminder. This is also the way text editors work.
- There are also a number of words which are used so frequently in the texts that it makes no sense to keep a running check on them by collecting and presenting all instances of their use. A glossary is not a concordance. Examples include such words as *anon*, *apparel*, and *arrant*. On the other hand, it is important that readers become aware of what these words mean as quickly as possible, in their encounter with Shakespeare, as time spent on them will be repaid many times over, as they encounter the texts. We therefore selected 100 of these 'frequently encountered words' (FEW, p.xxi) and gave them special treatment before the A–Z section of the book. They all have their individual place in alphabetical order, of course; but instead of giving just a single example in full, as is our procedure for most entries, we give FEW words a fuller illustration, showing them being used in a variety of grammatical contexts.
- We also handle grammatical words differently in the A–Z section. These are prepositions, conjunctions, pronouns, and a few other forms whose function is more to help build a sentence structure than to convey the content of an utterance. In such cases, we restrict ourselves to a single example of the distinctive usage. A glossary is not a grammar either.

- The alphabetical arrangement of the headword list is for the most part letter-by-letter – strict alphabetical order. However, we make an exception in the case of phrasal verbs and associated idioms – such as *put apart*, *put back*, *put by*, etc. – where it would be silly not to respect the parallels in the way these verbs are used. As a consequence of this decision some lexical items appear out of strict alphabetical order: *putter-on*, for example, is placed after *put upon* in the A–Z listing.
- We treat all the senses of a word-form under the same heading, regardless of whether they belong to different etymological paths or not. This is an important difference from, say, Onions' approach. He has *bay* [= part of a house] and *bay* [= noise of a dog] as completely different headwords, on the grounds that they have distinct etymological origins. We simply recognize them as different senses of the headword *bay*. We find that there are too many cases of uncertain etymology and too many cases where the meaning distinction is unclear for the etymological principle to be consistently implemented.
- We distinguish headwords according to their different grammatical functions – their word-class, or part-of-speech. Many words appear in more than one word-class; indeed, this is one of the features of Shakespeare's style (see p.191). A word like *wanton* is used as noun, adjective, verb, and adverb. When a form appears in several functions, we give noun (*n.*) uses first, then adjective (*adj.*), then verb (*v.*), then adverb (*adv.*), then others (see p.xvii for a complete list of abbreviations).
- We do not generally include elided forms (see p.146) as headwords – forms where a letter (or letters) has been replaced by an apostrophe, such as *o'er*, *e'en*, and *'lege* [= allege]. In such cases, the headword is shown in its full form, to enable readers to find it easily. The alternative, to put words beginning with *o'er-* at *oe-* and those with *over-* at *ov* – the procedure followed by Onions, for example, though not by the *OED* – we find highly confusing. In the quotations, of course, the presence of elided words is shown as they appear in the texts.
- We give only occasional guidance about the pronunciation of a headword. The question of how words were pronounced in Early Modern English is contentious, as is the issue of whether we should represent an older version or a modern equivalent. There can also be several variations in a word's pronunciation, according to the demands of the metre. We have therefore restricted our guidance to just a few cases (such as *disme*, *foison*, *guerdon*) where we felt an indication of the general character of a pronunciation would be helpful.

HEADWORDS

By *headword* we mean any item in bold face – what in lexicology is often referred to as a *lexical item* or *lexeme*. This is often a single word, but sometimes it is two words (e.g. *come near*, *give over*) or a series of words (e.g. *come cut and long tail*). The following points should be noted in relation to the way we handle lexical items as headwords.

SENSES

The 21,263 entries in the A–Z section group themselves under 13,626 headwords. Just over 10,000 of these are single-sense entries; but the remainder have anything from two to twenty-two senses. Some of the very common verbs have a remarkable semantic range, just as they do today – *break*, *pass*, and *draw*, for example, with *take* achieving the highest number, just as it does in modern English dictionaries.

When a headword has more than one sense, there are several ways in which the senses might be ordered. A historical dictionary, for example, puts the oldest senses first. In our case we felt a more useful criterion was frequency: senses which occurred most often in the texts were put first, to give users a better chance of having their enquiry quickly answered. A good example is *favour*, where we distinguish nine senses, illustrated by sixty-three textual examples; but thirty-eight of these examples illustrate *favour* in the sense of 'facial appearance' or 'looks', so this is given as sense 1. Semantically related senses then follow; and generally we aim to keep clusters of related senses together. On the other hand, there are many cases where neither frequency nor any kind of semantic logic provides a principled way of ordering senses; and in such cases we have no alternative but to list them arbitrarily.

We have, on the whole, opted for recognizing sense distinctions, when these are warranted, even if the distinctions are on occasion somewhat fine. This is because we want our dictionary to preserve as many of the nuances of individual contexts as possible. It would be perfectly possible to group the various adjectival senses of *wanton*, for example, into just two or three types; but we give twelve. We recognize some quite restricted senses of the word, accordingly, such as its sense of 'equivocal' in the collocation of 'wanton words' in *Twelfth Night*, or the sense of 'badly behaved' in the collocation of 'wanton boys' in *King Lear*. But we feel this level of discrimination is ultimately more useful than lumping together all such examples into a general-purpose entry with some vague sense of, say, 'irresponsible'. In this way, we believe our approach is closer to the approach of text editors, who pay a great deal of attention to individual nuance. Indeed, our procedure, relying as it does on the observations of many individual editors, could hardly be otherwise.

DEFINITIONS

We were scrupulous in checking the sense of each word against the range of usages listed in the *OED*, insofar as this is possible. It is not uncommon to find editors ascribing a sense to a Shakespearian word which, on the best evidence, would not have been available in Elizabethan times. Although the first recorded usage of a word or sense is never an infallible guide – most words will have been in spoken currency for several years before they turn up in a written text – there is none the less something unsettling when we see words being ascribed senses whose first recorded use in the *OED* is a generation or so after Shakespeare's death, or even later. We recommend standing on the shoulders of the *OED* editors at all times, for one can definitely see so much further as a result. On the other hand, this kind of checking is extremely time-consuming, especially for those words which have dozens of potentially relevant senses. It is the main reason why our own project took so long to complete.

At the same time, one must use the *OED* resource critically. To begin with, not all of Shakespeare's word-forms are listed in that work (especially a number of compounds, such as *after-*

hours, and various prefixed forms) and some of Shakespeare's usages conflate several of the senses that the *OED* distinguishes. But the point is a more general one. No dictionary should be treated as god: all dictionaries are compiled by people who have good days and bad days (we have first-hand experience, in this respect), and whose definitional results range from brilliant to inadequate. We quickly found that we had to devise our own procedure for definitions. The single-synonym approach used in several glossary lists is patently inadequate when we are dealing with someone whose vocabulary is so allusive; and the long list of glosses which the *OED* gives to many word meanings introduces a degree of irrelevance which we need to eliminate. We needed something in between.

In the event we opted for a system which we call *lexical triangulation* – adapting a standard mapping technique to linguistic use. For most headwords we have provided three glosses. Because there are no such things as perfect synonyms, each gloss provides a slightly different slant on the sense of the headword we are trying to capture and thus enables us to focus more sharply on the word's semantic 'core'. *Bale*, for example, is glossed as 'sorrow, pain, misfortune'; *fardel* as 'burden, load, bundle'. To provide a concrete analogy from the world of lighting: one torch shone at a person highlights one side of the face, but a combination of three torches from different angles produces a brightly lit subject. Our hope is that after reflecting on all three glosses, it will be possible to see the meaning of a word more clearly, and develop a sharper sense of where it is located in the semantic scheme of things. The approach works best when comparing a succession of senses within a single headword, where the extra words bring the contrasts in meaning into sharper relief.

We have found this approach illuminating, and we hope others do too. Offering a series of glosses gives people a choice when paraphrasing a piece of text – something which both students and editors need to do. Our three glosses are sometimes very close in meaning, but each word has its individual aesthetic properties and linguistic associations (collocations) which could make it the synonym of choice for someone engaged in interpreting a text. It also allows people to reflect on the direction in which a piece of textual interpretation should go: Hamlet's *fardel* is more in the direction of 'burden'; Autolycus's is more 'bundle'. In many cases, it is not a question of choice: two or three of the nuances turn out to be equally relevant – or indeed, as editorial notes frequently say, the whole point of the usage is to see the interaction between the constituent senses. We have frequently been struck by the way in which multiple glosses suggest directions of interpretation which had not previously occurred to us, and we hope that the approach will prove to be a helpful editorial tool.

No lexical approach works perfectly all the time with an author whose vocabulary is as diverse as Shakespeare's, and in several cases the triangulation technique is simply irrelevant. Sometimes it is impossible or undesirable to do anything other than give a single gloss for a headword, especially for very specific and concrete entities, such as the name of a plant. Faced with *daffadilly*, all we need to know is that it means 'daffodil', and no other glosses are necessary. Similarly, *lip* is glossed as 'kiss', *upreared* as 'standing on end', and *seniory* as 'seniority'. And of course, for a book we are always constrained by length. Many items turn out to require not single-word but longer two-word glosses, such as *shore* **3** meaning 'waterside dump, sewage channel', and if two of these provided the degree of precision required, we would drop our search for a third item. Sometimes we had to drop the synonym search completely, and go for whole phrases or sentences to explain a meaning. Words like *harpy* and *country base* need descriptions and explanations rather than lexical equivalents. There are many variants in our glossing practice, accordingly; but the majority of our definitions conform to the triangulation model, as a glance at any page of the A–Z section will show.

Finally, in relation to definitions, we sometimes have to acknowledge lexicographical defeat, in the form of such comments as 'unclear meaning'. It is well recognized that several Shakespearian words have senses which are either hotly disputed or totally opaque, and we have tried to reflect this in our label. But when we call a word or usage 'unclear' or 'debated', it refers to any of three possibilities: (i) nobody has a clue what the item means; (ii) some people think they know but are uncertain; (iii) an individual editor is strongly in favour of a particular meaning, but another editor – equally strongly – disagrees. In short, our label is no more than a warning to readers: it identifies a word which needs a fuller discussion than a glossary can provide. In such cases, readers need to go to the editorial notes of individual editions for a full grasp of the situation.

QUOTATIONS

All examples of Shakespearian usage are treated in the same way.
- They begin with a *text identifier*, using one of the abbreviations listed on p.XIX.
- This is followed by a line reference, using the corpus texts described above. Where a quotation involves more than one line of text, the line reference is to the line containing the headword. For readers using this glossary in relation to other editions than our chosen texts, some variation is of course to be expected, especially in the prose sections of plays, where – depending on the typographical setting – a line reference may differ by several lines. Paying attention to the context (see below) can be a useful means of quick location in such cases.
- Care needs also to be taken with those editions where significantly different editorial decisions have been made about scene divisions (such as the opening scenes of *Cymbeline*) or about the balance of content taken from Folio and Quarto texts. Where we include variant forms used by editors other than those found in our text corpus, we give the line reference to our corpus edition, but put the variant into the quotation, noting the alternative in following parentheses.
- Words which appear in stage directions are given the line number of the first line of speech following the direction.
- We provide context for each quotation, in the form of information in square brackets immediately following the line reference. The context tells you who is speaking to whom, and – where this is unclear from the quotation –

about whom or what. Many quotations contain such context-dependent words as *he*, *that*, and *there* (what linguists refer to as *deictic* forms), and these make it difficult to develop a full sense of what is being said. It is all very well illustrating the use of *hallow* [= bless] by 'I will hallow thee for this thy deed' (**2H6** IV.x.65), but the quotation means so much more when you know the context – '[Iden to his sword, of killing Cade]'. We therefore give as much context as is needed to make a quotation self-contained. We have also found these contexts helpful in providing a mnemonic for recalling the location of the word being glossed, in the setting of a play.
- Certain other contextual conventions are used (see p.XVII for a complete list). In particular, when a character is the only person on stage, we use the convention illustrated by: '[Hamlet alone]'. When a character is speaking to himself/herself, and other people are on stage, we use the convention: '[Hamlet to himself]'. When characters speak to each other so that others should not hear them, we use the *aside* convention from the texts themselves, as illustrated by: '[Smith aside to his companions]'.

CROSS-REFERENCES

Finally, entries make limited use of cross-referencing, always signalled by the ✎ symbol. Cross-references are of three kinds:
- a cross-reference to an alternative headword, where information can be found, used especially in cases of spelling variants, as in: *bankrout* (*n.*), *bankerout* ✎ bancrout (*n.*)
- a cross-reference to a semantically related word, as in: *bate* ✎ abate; *best* ✎ meanest
- a cross-reference to a panel, appendix, or the FEW (Frequently Encountered Words) section, in which other information of the same kind is collected: ✎ DAYS AND DATES, p.630; ✎ FEW, p.xxi

ENVOI

This book is not a guide to Shakespeare's language as a whole. In particular, it contains little information about pronunciation and grammar. Its focus is exclusively on vocabulary, and on those aspects of usage which influence its choice and form (such as the topics covered in the panels). It is moreover a book written for a particular purpose, to aid those who want to explore the richness of meaning found in the texts. It contains a great deal of detail. But we would not want the existence of our glossary to be interpreted as support for the view that Shakespeare's language is intrinsically difficult or impenetrable, as we see stated in the media from time to time.

It is perfectly possible to go to a Shakespeare play, with little or no awareness of Early Modern English vocabulary, and have a great time. There are many stretches of text where the vocabulary is virtually identical with that used today, and many more where the presence of the occasional 'difficult word' is not noticed because the context makes the meaning of the utterance perfectly clear. Even when the distinctive vocabulary begins to pile up, as in some of the more complex poetic passages, the quality of the acting can transcend the limitations of lexical obscurity. We are reminded of our experience of operas sung in a foreign language (in the days before surtitles) where we have been profoundly moved despite the unintelligibility. There are actually very few passages in Shakespeare where the combination of alien grammar and vocabulary makes the text comparable to it being in a foreign language. Some of the insult sequences are perhaps the nearest (such as Doll's 'basket-hilt stale juggler'), but such utterances never leave the audience in any doubt as to their pragmatic force.

On the other hand, there are many many places where our appreciation of what is happening in a play can be immensely increased by a sharpened awareness of the language used. We have found this ourselves, in the dual experience of reading the texts as literature and as being involved in the texts as drama. Since beginning to write this book, we have between us watched several dozen plays at the various seasons at Stratford, the Globe, the National, and elsewhere, and we have noticed the way our lexical investigations have increased our sensitivity to so much of what we see happening on stage. In particular, the second author has repeatedly found that his work on the book has added a fresh dimension to his work as an actor. We therefore hope that other people using this book will also find their enjoyment of the plays, as literature or drama, enhanced by its use.

ACKNOWLEDGEMENTS

It remains only to thank those people who have assisted us in bringing this book to fruition. Our commissioning editor at Penguin, Martin Toseland, has been an invaluable source of wise advice throughout. Tony McNicholl provided us with the software support we needed to maintain our database, and wrote the programme which translated our database into XML, thus enabling the publisher to set the book directly from our disk. But above all we have to acknowledge the immense amount of help we have received from Hilary Crystal, who input the vast majority of the textual examples, making innumerable suggestions in the process, and saving us thereby an incalculable amount of time. To her, in her dual authorial relationship as wife and mother, this book is affectionately dedicated.

David Crystal
Ben Crystal

Abbreviations, symbols, and conventions

SYMBOLS AND ABBREVIATIONS

adj.	adjective
adv.	adverb
c.	[in Appendices] century
c.	[in Appendices] circa [= about]
conj.	conjunction
det.	determiner
F	Folio (see below)
f.	feminine [in French, Latin, Spanish, and Italian grammar]
ff.	[in line references] and following lines
int.	interjection
m.	masculine [in French, Latin, Spanish, and Italian grammar]
n.	noun
nt.	neuter [in Latin grammar]
part.	particle
prep.	preposition
pron.	pronunciation
Q	Quarto (see below)
QQ	Quartos
v.	verb
>	[in panels] becomes, develops into
☞	see, see also
?	[in panels] unclear meaning or usage
=	equivalent term or meaning
/	marks a shared word in a headword: **call on / upon**
	marks a line break in a quotation: *this rough magic / I here abjure*
...	marks omitted words in a quotation: *we'll ... take upon's the mystery of things*
( )	contain grammatical information
[ ]	contain stylistic and explanatory matter in definitions
	contain alternative prepositions in definitions (see below)
	contain contextual matter before a quotation (see below)
	contain clarifying grammatical words within a quotation (see below)
	contain textual alternatives following a quotation (see below)
	contain clarificatory matter following a quotation (see below)

PRONUNCIATION SYMBOLS USED

Vowels		Consonants	
Symbol	*As in*	*Symbol*	*As in*
a	hat	b	buy
ah	calm	ch	chop
aw	saw	d	day
ay	say	f	fee
ee	see	g	go
er	sir	h	hay
i	hit	j	joy
iy	mine	k	key
oo	do	l	lay
oy	boy	m	me
u	put	n	no
uh	hut	p	pay
		r	ray
		s	so
		sh	shoe
		t	too
		th (voiceless)	thin
		th (voiced)	this
		v	vow
		w	we
		y	you
		z	zoo
		zh	illusion

' indicates a following stressed syllable

ENTRY CONVENTIONS

WITHIN DEFINITIONS

The preposition convention

Where the modern use of a word requires a different following preposition from the one given in the quotation, the modern preposition is given in parentheses.

adjunct *(adj.)* attendant [upon], inevitable result [of] **KJ** III.iii.57 [Hubert to King John, of obeying him] *Though that my death were adjunct to my act … I would do it*

In other words: the Shakespearian usage is 'adjunct to', but modern usage requires *attendant upon* rather than *attendant to* and *inevitable result of* rather than *inevitable result to*.

 This convention is also used in cases where the selected quotation does not actually contain a preposition, but the definition requires one to make the gloss work.

reason *(v.)* **9** argue rationally [about], debate the pros and cons [of] **KL** II.iv.259 [Lear to Regan] *reason not the need!;* **Cym** IV.ii.14; **Ham** II.ii.264; **JC** V.i.96; **KL** I.ii.105

Here the parenthesis also signals that some of the other examples listed do not need the preposition to make the gloss work. The *Hamlet* quotation, for example, is:

Ham II.ii.264 [Hamlet to Rosencrantz and Guildenstern] *I cannot reason.*

WITHIN CONTEXTS

The 'alone' convention

In specifying the context of a quotation, we need to indicate when a character is the only person on stage.

Tem V.i.51 [Prospero alone] *this rough magic / I here abjure*

The 'himself/herself' convention

In specifying the context of a quotation, we need to indicate when a character is speaking to himself/herself while not being the only person on stage.

Oth V.ii.101 [Othello to himself] *th'affrighted globe / Should yawn at alteration*

WITHIN QUOTATIONS

Capitalization convention

In quotations we retain the capital letters and punctuation of the quotation as it appears in the selected text, including line-initial capitals in poetry, but we do not include sentence-ending marks unless they are crucial for meaning (as in the case of some question marks and exclamation marks).

Omitted text conventions

Ellipsis dots (…) show that text has been omitted; items in square brackets are grammatical words which clarify the sense and enable us to keep the quotation as short as possible.

catch *(v.)* **3** catch up with, overtake **Tem** V.i.316 [Prospero to Alonso] *[I'll] promise you … sail so expeditious, that shall catch / Your royal fleet far off*

AFTER QUOTATIONS

The additional reference convention

When a series of additional references follows the chief quotation, the text references are in alphabetical order, and we conflate scenes and lines from the same play.

fancy *(n.)* love, amorousness, infatuation **TNK** V.iv.118 [Theseus to Palamon, of Emilia] *you first saw her, and / Even then proclaimed your fancy;* **Luc** 200; **MA** III.ii.35; **MND** I.i.155; **TC** IV.iv.24; **TNK** IV.ii.52

fardel *(n.)* burden, load, bundle **WT** IV.iv.750 [Autolycus to Shepherd] *The fardel there, what's i'th' fardel?;* **Ham** III.i.76; **WT** IV.iv.703, IV.iv.713, V.ii.3, and V.ii.114

In other words: in the second example, the *Winter's Tale* references are to IV.iv.703, 713, V.ii.3, 114

The F/Q convention

Reference to a word in the First Folio is indicated by the abbreviation F; to later Folios, by the use of an additional number: F2, F3, etc. Reference to unspecified Quarto texts is indicated by the abbreviation Q, or QQ if more than one; to a specific Quarto, by a numeral, Q1, Q2, etc. The variant form then follows.

denotement *(n.)* indication, sign, clue **Oth** III.iii.122 [Othello to Iago, of Iago's pauses] *in a man that's just, / They're close denotements … / That passion cannot rule* [Q1; F *dilations*]

In other words: the item in the quotation is from the Q1 text of *Othello*; the First Folio equivalent is *dilations*.

The 'first/second instance' convention

When two uses of the same headword need to be distinguished in a single quotation, these are identifed using the convention 'first instance' … 'second instance'.

fine *(n.)* **2** ending, termination **KJ** V.iv.38 [Melun to Pembroke, Salisbury, and Bigot, of their executions] *Paying the fine of rated treachery / Even with a treacherous fine of all your lives* [second instance; first instance, sense 3]

In other words: it is the second instance of *fine* in the quotation which has the meaning of 'ending'; the first instance has a different sense, which can be found at sense 3.

The 'pun' convention

When a word motivates a pun in a later line, or a pun refers back to a word in a previous line, the reference is given in parentheses after the quotation.

sconce *(n.)* **2** shelter, screen, guard **CE** II.ii.37 [Dromio of Syracuse to Antipholus of Syracuse] *An you use these blows long I must get a sconce for my head* [pun: 34, sense 1]

In other words: in line 34, the word *sconce* is used in sense 1 [i.e. in the sense of 'head'].

The 'also' convention

When a quotation is followed by *also* and another sense number, we mean that the sense referred to is definitely relevant in this context.

augury *(n.)* **2** discernment, prescience, prophetic skill **TG** IV.iv.65 [Proteus to disguised Julia] *if my augury deceive me not* [also: sense 1]

In other words: refer to *augury* sense 1, where the meaning of 'omens, premonition, divining the future' must also be noted for this quotation.

The 'or' convention

When a quotation is followed by *or* and another sense number, we mean that the sense referred to is an alternative reading for the word in this context.

tainted *(adj.)* **3** disgraced, discredited, dishonoured **H8** IV.ii.14 [Griffith to Katherine, of Wolsey] *a man sorely tainted* [or: sense 2]

In other words: refer to *tainted* sense 2, where the sense given there ('corrupted, dishonourable, depraved') is preferred by some editors.

The 'i.e.' convention

When a quotation is followed by i.e., the following words act as a paraphrase of all or part of the quotation, or add some additional information to make sense of the quotation.

bedfellow *(n.)* intimate companion **TNK** V.iii.44 [Emilia to herself, of Arcite] *mercy and manly courage / Are bedfellows in his visage* [i.e. are seen together in his face]

bear *(v.)* **8** bring forth, produce, yield **AC** IV.vi.7 [Caesar to all] *the three-nooked world / Shall bear the olive freely* [i.e. the olive-branch of peace]

TEXT ABBREVIATIONS

AC	Antony and Cleopatra
AW	All's Well That Ends Well
AY	As You Like It
CE	The Comedy of Errors
Cor	Coriolanus
Cym	Cymbeline
E3	King Edward III
Ham	Hamlet
1H4	Henry IV Part 1
2H4	Henry IV Part 2
H5	Henry V
1H6	Henry VI Part 1
2H6	Henry VI Part 2
3H6	Henry VI Part 3
H8	Henry VIII
JC	Julius Caesar
KJ	King John
KL	King Lear
LL	Love's Labour's Lost
Lover	A Lover's Complaint
Luc	The Rape of Lucrece
MA	Much Ado About Nothing
Mac	Macbeth
MM	Measure for Measure
MND	A Midsummer Night's Dream
MV	The Merchant of Venice
MW	The Merry Wives of Windsor
Oth	Othello
PassP	The Passionate Pilgrim
Per	Pericles
Phoen	The Phoenix and Turtle
R2	Richard II
R3	Richard III
RJ	Romeo and Juliet
Sonn	Sonnets
Tem	The Tempest
Tim	Timon of Athens
Tit	Titus Andronicus
TC	Troilus and Cressida
TG	The Two Gentlemen of Verona
TN	Twelfth Night
TNK	The Two Noble Kinsmen
TS	The Taming of the Shrew
Venus	Venus and Adonis
WT	The Winter's Tale

List of Glossary Panels

Frequently Encountered Words (FEW)

Several of the content-carrying words in Shakespeare are used so often that the provision of a small set of references, as in the A–Z section of this book, has little point. We find it more helpful to approach these words in the manner of a language-teaching phrase-book, singling them out and giving them a somewhat fuller illustration, so that readers can more easily develop an intuition about how they are used. We have selected 100 of these words, in particular senses, in the list below, and chosen quotations for them which illustrate several grammatical contexts. We like to think of these words as a preliminary word-list which captures some of the character of basic Early Modern English vocabulary. Readers who familiarize themselves with these items will be many times repaid by a smoother reading of the texts.

It is important to note that a number of these words are also used in other, less frequent, senses in Shakespearian English. We make a reference to any such senses after each entry below. These senses will all be found in their alphabetical place in the A–Z section.

A further example of each of the words and senses in the list is also given in the A–Z section, with a cross-reference back to these pages.

afeard *(adj.)*
afraid, frightened, scared
Cym IV.ii.94 [Cloten to Guiderius] *Art not afeard?*
1H6 IV.vii.93 [Lucy to all] *A phoenix that shall make all France afeard*
Mac I.iii.95 [Ross to Macbeth] *Nothing afeard of what thyself didst make*
MND III.i.107 [Bottom alone, of his companions] *This is a knavery of them to make me afeard*

anon *(adv.)*
soon, shortly, presently
Ham III.ii.272 [Hamlet to Ophelia] *You shall see anon how the murderer gets the love of Gonzago's wife*
1H4 II.iv.31 [Prince Hal to Poins, of Francis the drawer] *do thou never leave calling 'Francis!', that his tale to me may be nothing but 'Anon'*

apace *(adv.)*
quickly, speedily, at a great rate
AY III.iii.1 [Touchstone to Audrey] *Come apace*
E3 III.i.37 [King John to all, of his confederates] *are marching hither apace*
RJ III.ii.1 [Juliet alone] *Gallop apace, you fiery-footed steeds*

apparel *(n.)*
clothes, clothing, dress
Ham III.ii.45 [Hamlet to Players] *one suit of apparel*

Ham I.iii.72 [Polonius to Laertes] *For the apparel oft proclaims the man*
☞ apparel *(v.)*

arrant *(adj.)*
downright, absolute, unmitigated
Ham III.i.129 [Hamlet to Ophelia] *We are arrant knaves all*
H5 IV.vii.2 [Fluellen to Gower, of the French behaviour] *'tis as arrant a piece of knavery ... as can be offert*
KL II.iv.50 [Fool to Lear] *Fortune, that arrant whore*

attend (on/upon) *(v.)*
await, wait for, expect
Cor I.x.30 [Aufidius to First Soldier] *I am attended at the cypress grove*
Cym II.iii.36 [Cymbeline to Cloten] *Attend you here the door of our stern daughter?*
E3 IV.v.6 [King John to Charles] *Silence attends some wonder*
TG III.i.186 [Valentine alone] *Tarry I here, I but attend on death*
☞ attend *(v.)* 2–8

aught *(n.)*
anything; [together with a negative word] nothing
Ham III.iii.60 [Claudius alone, as if to the King of England] *if my love thou holdest at aught*
Ham V.ii.357 [Horatio to Fortinbras] *If aught of woe or wonder*
TG V.iv.20 [Proteus to Silvia] *Though you respect not aught your servant doth*

avaunt *(int.)*
begone, go away, be off
2H4 I.ii.89 [Falstaff to Servant] *Hence! Avaunt!*
KL III.vi.63 [Edgar as Poor Tom, to imaginary dogs] *Avaunt, you curs!*
Mac III.iv.92 [Macbeth to Banquo's ghost] *Avaunt, and quit my sight!*

aye *(adv.)*
always, ever, for eternity
Cym IV.iv.27 [Belarius to Arviragus and Guiderius] *aye hopeless / To have the courtesy your cradle promised*
R2 V.ii.40 [York to Duchess of York, of Bolingbroke] *Whose state and honour I for aye allow*

base *(adj.)*
1 dishonourable, low, unworthy
AY II.vii.79 [Jaques to Duke Senior] *what is he of basest function*
AY III.ii.64 [Touchstone to Corin] *civet is of a baser birth than tar*
E3 III.iii.183 [King Edward to Prince Edward, of the latter's heart] *never base affections enter there*

1H6 V.v.49 [Suffolk to all] *Disgrace not so your king / That he should be so abject, base, and poor / To choose for wealth*

2 low-born, lowly, plebeian, of lower rank

Cor I.i.155 [Menenius to First Citizen] *one o'th' lowest, basest, poorest / Of this most wise rebellion*

Ham V.ii.60 [Hamlet to Horatio] *'Tis dangerous when the baser nature comes / Between … mighty opposites*

1H6 I.ii.80 [Pucelle to Dauphin, of Our Lady] *Willed me to leave my base vocation*

KL I.ii.10 [Edmund alone] *Why brand they us / With 'base'?*

TNK II.iii.2 [Gaoler's Daughter alone] *I am base, / My father the mean keeper of his prison*

3 poor, wretched, of low quality

1H6 I.i.137 [Third Messenger to all] *A base Walloon … / Thrust Talbot with a spear into the back*

1H6 IV.vi.21 [Talbot to John Talbot, as if to Orleans] *Contaminated, base, / And misbegotten blood I spill of thine*

TNK III.iii.44 [Palamon to Arcite] *Base cousin, / Darest thou break first?*

☛ base *(adj.)* 4–6, base *(n.)*

bawd *(n.)*

pimp, procurer, pander, go-between

Ham III.i.112 [Hamlet to Ophelia] *transform honesty from what it is to a bawd*

R2 V.iii.66 [York to King Henry, of Aumerle] *So shall my virtue be his vice's bawd*

become *(v.)*

1 be fitting, befit, be appropriate to

AY I.i.74 [Orlando to Oliver] *I will no further offend you than becomes me for my good*

1H6 V.iii.170 [Suffolk to Reignier] *Set this diamond safe / In golden palaces, as it becomes*

R2 II.i.140 [King Richard to all, as if to John of Gaunt] *let them die that age and sullens have; / For both hast thou, and both become the grave*

2 grace, honour, dignify

AC I.i.49 [Antony to and of Cleopatra] *Whom everything becomes*

Cor I.iii.10 [Volumnia to Virgilia, of Martius] *considering how honour would become such a person*

1H6 IV.vii.23 [Talbot to dead John Talbot] *O thou whose wounds become hard-favoured Death*

☛ become *(v.)* 3–5

befall *(v.)*

1 happen, occur, take place, turn out

AY IV.iii.103 [Oliver to Rosalind and Celia disguised] *Lo, what befell!*

2H4 I.i.177 [Morton to Lord Bardolph] *What hath then befallen, / Or what hath this bold enterprise brought forth*

2H6 V.iii.33 [Warwick to all] *more such days as these to us befall!*

MND V.i.153 [Snout as Wall to all] *In this same interlude it doth befall / That I … present a wall*

2 happen to, come to

E3 II.ii.23 [Derby to King Edward] *Befall my sovereign all my sovereign's wish*

R2 II.i.129 [John of Gaunt to King Richard] *My brother Gloucester … / Whom fair befall in heaven*

R3 I.iii.281 [Queen Margaret to Buckingham] *fair befall thee and thy noble house!*

R3 I.iv.16 [Clarence to Keeper] *a thousand heavy times … / That had befallen us*

☛ befall of *(v.)*

belike *(adv.)*

probably, presumably, perhaps, so it seems

CE IV.i.25 [Antipholus of Ephesus to Angelo] *Belike you thought our love would last too long*

Ham III.ii.302 [Hamlet to Horatio, of Claudius and the play] *belike he likes it not*

beshrew, 'shrew *(v.)*

curse, devil take, evil befall

Cym II.iii.141 [Innogen to Pisanio, of the ring] *'Shrew me, / If I would lose it for a revenue / Of any king's in Europe*

2H6 III.i.184 [Gloucester to his enemies] *Beshrew the winners*

MND II.ii.60 [Hermia to Lysander] *much beshrew my manners and my pride / If Hermia meant to say Lysander lied*

Oth IV.iii.77 [Desdemona to Emilia] *Beshrew me, if I would do such a wrong*

☛ beshrew *(v.)* 2

bethink *(v.)*,

past form **bethought** call to mind, think about, consider, reflect

MV I.iii.29 [Shylock to Bassanio] *that I may be assured, I will bethink me*

R2 II.iii.8 [Northumberland to Bolingbroke] *I bethink me what a weary way / From Ravenspurgh to Cotswold will be found*

TN III.iv.289 [Sir Toby to Viola as Cesario, of Sir Andrew] *he hath better bethought him of his quarrel*

☛ bethink *(v.)* 2–4

brave *(adj.)*

fine, excellent, splendid, impressive

AY III.iv.36 [Celia to Rosalind, of Orlando] *O, that's a brave man! He writes brave verses, speaks brave words, swears brave oaths … all's brave that youth mounts and folly guides*

Ham II.ii.300 [Hamlet to Rosencrantz and Guildenstern] *this brave o'erhanging firmament*

1H4 IV.i.7 [Hotspur to Douglas] *a braver place / In my heart's love hath no man than yourself*

Tem III.ii.97 [Caliban to Stephano, of Prospero] *He has brave utensils*

☛ brave *(adj.)* 2–3, *(n.)*, *(v.)*

brow *(n.)*

appearance, aspect, countenance

Ham III.iii.7 [Claudius to Rosencrantz and Guildenstern, of the danger seen in Hamlet] *doth hourly grow / Out of his brows*

LL IV.iii.225 [Berowne to King, of Rosaline] *What peremptory eagle-sighted eye / Dares look upon the heaven of her brow*

LL IV.iii.183 [Berowne to all] *When shall you hear that I / Will praise … / A gait, a state, a brow*

☛ brow *(n.)* 2–6

chide *(v.)*,

past form **chid** scold, rebuke, reprove

AC I.iv.30 [Caesar to Lepidus, of Antony] *to confound such time … 'tis to be chid / As we rate boys*

AY III.v.64 [Phebe to Rosalind as Ganymede, of Silvius] *I pray you chide a year together; I had rather hear you chide than this man woo*

AY IV.i.32 [Rosalind as Ganymede to Jaques] *almost chide God for making you that countenance you are*

☛ chide *(v.)* 2–4

colours *(n.)*

battle-flags, ensigns, standards, banners

Cym I.v.18 [Iachimo to all, of Posthumus' banishment] *the approbation of those that weep this lamentable divorce under her colours*

E3 IV.vii.2 [Prince Edward to King John] *Thy bloody ensigns are my captive colours*

1H6 IV.ii.56 [Talbot to all] *God and Saint George … / Prosper our colours in this dangerous fight!*
☞ colours (n.) 2–4

commend (v.)

convey greetings, present kind regards
MM I.iv.88 [Isabella to Lucio] *Commend me to my brother*
MV III.ii.232 [Salerio to Bassanio] *Signor Antonio / Commends him to you*
MW I.iv.152 [Fenton to Mistress Quickly, of Anne] *If thou seest her before me, commend me*
TG II.iv.121 [Proteus to Valentine] *Your friends … have them much commended*
☞ commend (v.) 2–6, (n.)

content (adj.)

agreeable, willing, ready
1H6 V.i.70 [King to Talbot] *are you not content?* [Talbot] *Content, my liege? Yes*
1H6 V.viii.165 [Suffolk to himself] *I could be well content / To be mine own attorney in this case*
☞ content (adj.) 2–3, (n.), (v.)

corse (n.)

corpse, dead body
Ham V.i.163 [First Clown to Hamlet] *we have many pocky corses nowadays*
1H6 I.i.62 [Bedford to First Messenger] *What sayest thou, man, before dead Henry's corse?*

counterfeit (v.)

1 copy, imitate, simulate
E3 II.i.256 [Countess to King Edward] *He that doth clip or counterfeit your stamp / Shall die*
1H6 II.iv.62 [Richard to Somerset] *Meantime your cheeks do counterfeit our roses*
2 pretend, feign, make believe
AY III.v.17 [Phebe to Silvius] *Now counterfeit to swoon*
AY IV.iii.167 [Rosalind as Ganymede to Oliver, of her fainting] *a body would think this was well counterfeited*
Cor II.iii.100 [Coriolanus to Fourth Citizen] *I will counterfeit the bewitchment of some popular man*
☞ counterfeit (n.), (adj.)

course (n.)

course of action, way of proceeding
Cym III.iv.113 [Pisanio to Innogen] *I have considered of a course*
R2 II.i.213 [York to King Richard] *by bad courses may be understood / That their events can never fall out good*
☞ course (n.) 2–8, (v.)

crave (v.)

beg, entreat, request
CE I.ii.26 [First Merchant to Antipholus of Syracuse] *I crave your pardon*
1H6 I.i.159 [Third Messenger to Bedford] *The Earl of Salisbury craveth supply*
1H6 II.iii.12 [Messenger to Countess] *according as your ladyship desired, / By message craved, so is Lord Talbot come*
☞ crave (v.) 2–3

cuckold (n.)

[mocking name] man with an unfaithful wife
AW II.ii.24 [Clown to Countess, of his answer] *As fit as … the cuckold to his horn*
Ham IV.v.120 [Laertes to Claudius] *Cries cuckold to my father*

MW II.ii.297 [Ford alone, of himself] *Fie, fie, fie! Cuckold, cuckold, cuckold!*
Oth III.iii.165 [Iago to Othello] *That cuckold lives in bliss / Who certain of his fate loves not his wronger*
☞ cuckold (v.)

discover (v.)

reveal, show, make known
Cym III.v.96 [Cloten to Pisanio] *Discover where thy mistress is*
MA I.ii.10 [Antonio to Leonato] *the Prince discovered to Claudio that he loved my niece*
TN II.v.154 [Malvolio to himself] *Daylight and champain discovers not more!*
☞ discover (v.) 2–6

envious (adj.)

malicious, spiteful, vindictive, full of enmity
1H6 III.i.196 [Exeter alone, of the peers' agreement] *So will this base and envious discord breed*
MM III.ii.137 [disguised Duke to Lucio, of the Duke] *he shall appear to the envious a scholar*
R2 III.iii.65 [Bolingbroke to all, of King Richard as the sun] *he perceives the envious clouds are bent / To dim his glory*
TNK II.i.319 [Palamon to Gaoler] *Devils take 'em / That are so envious to me!*
☞ envy (n.)

fain (adv.)

[usually with *would*] gladly, willingly
Ham II.ii.131 [Polonius to Claudius, of being faithful] *I would fain prove so*
Ham IV.vii.190 [Laertes to Claudius] *I have a speech o'fire that fain would blaze*
☞ fain (adj.), (v.)

false (adj.)

treacherous, traitorous, perfidious
Ham IV.v.112 [Gertrude to all] *this is counter, you false Danish dogs!*
1H6 IV.i.63 [Gloucester to all, of Burgundy] *such false dissembling guile*
R2 I.iii.106 [First Herald to all, of Bolingbroke] *On pain to be found false and recreant*
☞ false (adj.) 2–8, (n.), (adv.)

fare (v.)

get on, manage, do, cope
Cym III.i.82 [Cloten to Lucius] *if you fall in the adventure, our crows shall fare the better for you*
1H6 II.v.4 [Mortimer to Gaolers] *So fare my limbs with long imprisonment*
E3 IV.vi.1 [Artois to Prince Edward] *How fares your grace?*
TS Induction.ii.100 [Sly to Page dressed as Sly's wife] *I fare well*
☞ fare (v.) 2, (n.)

field (n.)

field of battle, battleground, field of combat
H5 III.ii.9 [Pistol to Nym and Bardolph] *sword and shield, / In bloody field, / Doth win immortal fame*
H5 IV.vi.2 [King Henry to all] *yet keep the French the field*
1H6 V.iii.12 [Pucelle to the spirits] *Help me this once, that France may get the field* [i.e. win the battle]
☞ field (n.) 2–4

forbear (v.)

1 stop, cease, desist
AY II.vii.88 [Orlando to all] *Forbear, and eat no more*
1H6 III.i.106 [Gloucester to his fighting servants] *Let me persuade you to forbear awhile*
3H6 IV.i.6 [Somerset to Richard and George] *forbear this talk*
TG III.i.202 [Proteus to Launce] *Villain, forbear*
2 leave alone, avoid, stay away [from]
AC III.xiii.107 [Antony to Cleopatra] *Have I … / Forborne the getting of a lawful race*
AY II.vii.128 [Orlando to Duke Senior] *forbear your food a little while*
R3 IV.iv.118 [Queen Margaret to Queen Elizabeth] *Forbear to sleep the nights*
➤ forbear (v.) 3–4

forsooth (adv.)

in truth, certainly, truly, indeed
AC V.ii.278 [Clown to Cleopatra, responding to her 'get thee gone'] *Yes, forsooth*
1H4 I.iii.138 [Hotspur to Worcester and Northumberland, of King Henry] *He will forsooth have all my prisoners*
MND III.ii.230 [Helena to Hermia] *wherefore doth Lysander … tender me forsooth affection*
MW III.ii.5 [Robin to Mistress Page] *I had rather, forsooth, go before you like a man*

forswear (v.)

1 swear falsely, perjure [oneself], break one's word
MND I.i.240 [Helena alone] *As waggish boys in game themselves forswear, / So the boy love is perjured everywhere*
RJ III.v.196 [Capulet to Juliet] *I'll not be forsworn*
TG II.v.2 [Launce to Speed] *Forswear not thyself*
2 abandon, renounce, reject, give up
1H4 II.ii.15 [Falstaff as if alone, of Poins] *I have forsworn his company hourly*
3H6 III.ii.153 [Richard to himself] *love forswore me in my mother's womb*
LL V.ii.410 [Berowne to Rosaline, of his rhetorical words] *I do forswear them*
3 deny, repudiate, refuse to admit
1H4 V.ii.38 [Worcester to Hotspur, of King Henry] *now forswearing that he is forsworn* [first instance]
MA V.i.162 [Don Pedro to Benedick, quoting Beatrice on Benedick] *he swore a thing to me on Monday night, which he forswore on Tuesday morning*
RJ I.v.52 [Romeo to himself, of seeing Juliet] *Did my heart love till now? Forswear it, sight!*

fright (v.)

frighten, scare, terrify
Cor I.ix.5 [Cominius to Martius] *where ladies shall be frighted / And … hear more*
H5 V.ii.226 [King Henry to Katherine] *when I come to woo ladies I fright them*
MW II.i.129 [Page to Ford, of Nym] *Here's a fellow frights English out of his wits*
Per V.iii.3 [Pericles to Diana, of himself] *frighted from my country*

gage (n.)

pledge, challenge [usually, a glove or gauntlet thrown down]
H5 IV.i.203 [King Henry to Williams] *Give me any gage of thine, and I will wear it in my bonnet*
R2 IV.i.34 [Fitzwater to Aumerle] *There is my gage, Aumerle, in gage to thine*
➤ gage (v.)

gentle (adj.)

well-born, honourable, noble
Cor II.iii.96 [Coriolanus to Fourth Citizen, of the people] *'Tis a condition they account gentle*
1H6 III.ii.135 [Talbot to Burgundy, of Bedford] *A gentler heart did never sway in court*
1H6 IV.i.44 [Talbot to all] *a hedge-born swain / That doth presume to boast of gentle blood*
Oth III.iv.118 [Desdemona to Cassio] *thrice-gentle Cassio!*
R2 II.iii.45 [Bolingbroke to Percy] *I thank thee, gentle Percy*
➤ gentle (adj.) 2–5, (n.), (adv.)

glass (n.)

mirror, looking-glass
CE V.i.418 [Dromio of Ephesus to Dromio of Syracuse] *Methinks you are my glass*
Cym IV.i.8 [Cloten alone] *it is not vain-glory for a man and his glass to confer in his own chamber*
Ham III.i.154 [Ophelia alone, of Hamlet] *The glass of fashion*
➤ glass (n.) 2–4, (v.)

habit (n.)

dress, clothing, costume
Cym V.i.30 [Posthumus alone] *Let me make men know / More valour in me than my habits show*
H5 III.vi.111 [Montjoy to King Henry] *You know me by my habit*
KJ I.i.210 [Bastard alone, of himself] *not alone in habit and device*
TG II.vii.39 [Lucetta to Julia] *in what habit will you go along?*
➤ habit (n.) 2–4

haply (adv.)

perhaps, maybe, by chance, with luck
CE V.i.284 [Egeon to Duke] *Haply I see a friend will save my life*
Ham IV.i.40 [Claudius to Gertrude] *So haply slander … may miss our name*

heavy (adj.)

sorrowful, sad, gloomy
R3 I.iv.74 [Clarence to Keeper] *My soul is heavy*
RJ I.i.137 [Montague to Benvolio, of Romeo] *Away from light steals home my heavy son*
TG IV.ii.136 [disguised Julia to Host] *it hath been the longest night / That e'er I watched, and the most heaviest*
➤ heavy (adj.) 2–10

hie (v.)

hasten, hurry, speed
AW IV.iv.12 [Helena to Widow and Diana] *My husband hies him home*
CE III.ii.155 [Antipholus of Syracuse to Dromio of Syracuse] *Go, hie thee presently*
Ham I.i.155 [Horatio to Marcellus and Barnardo] *Th'extravagant and erring spirit hies / To his confine*

humour (n.)

mood, disposition, frame of mind, temperament [as determined by bodily fluids]
AY III.ii.19 [Touchstone to Corin, of a shepherd's life] *it fits my humour well*
CE II.ii.7 [Antipholus of Syracuse to Dromio of Syracuse] *Is your merry humour altered?*
R2 V.v.10 [Richard alone] *these same thoughts people this little world, / In humours like the people of this world*
TNK V.ii.36 [Doctor to Wooer, of the Gaoler's Daughter] *The melancholy humour that infects her*
➤ humour (n.) 2–6, (v.); humours, p.230

ill *(adj.)*

bad, adverse, unfavourable

    AC II.ii.162 [Antony to Caesar, of Pompey] *I must thank him only, / Lest my remembrance suffer ill report*

    R2 III.iv.80 [Queen Isabel to Gardener] *how / Camest thou by this ill tidings?*

    ☛ ill *(adj.)* 2–6, *(v.)*, *(adv.)*

ill *(adv.)*

badly, adversely, unfavourably

    1H6 IV.i.74 [King to Talbot, of Burgundy] *Let him perceive how ill we brook his treason*

    R2 V.iii.98 [York to King Henry] *Ill mayst thou thrive if thou grant any grace*

    ☛ ill *(adv.)* 2, *(adj.)*

intent *(n.)*

intention, purpose, aim

    AW I.iii.213 [Countess to Helena] *Had you not lately an intent ... / To go to Paris?*

    KL II.i.63 [Edmund to Gloucester, of Edgar] *I dissuaded him from his intent*

    LL V.ii.753 [Berowne to the ladies, of their beauty] *fashioning our humours / Even to the opposed end of our intents*

    R3 I.i.149 [Richard alone] *if I fail not in my deep intent*

issue *(n.)*

1 child(ren), offspring, family, descendant

    1H6 II.v.94 [Mortimer to Richard] *thou seest that I no issue have*

    KL I.i.66 [Lear to Gonerill] *To thine and Albany's issues / Be this perpetual*

    Mac III.i.64 [Macbeth alone] *For Banquo's issue have I filed my mind*

2 outcome, result, consequence(s)

    H5 V.ii.12 [Queen Isabel to King Henry] *happy be the issue ... / Of this good day*

    Oth III.iii.217 [Iago to Othello] *I am to pray you, not to strain my speech / To grosser issues*

    WT V.iii.128 [Hermione to Perdita] *I ... have preserved / Myself to see the issue*

    ☛ issue *(n.)* 3–4, *(v.)*

knave *(n.)*

scoundrel, rascal, rogue

    Ham V.i.135 [Hamlet to Horatio, of the First Clown] *How absolute the knave is!*

    1H4 II.ii.83 [Falstaff to Travellers] *bacon-fed knaves*

    ☛ knave *(n.)* 2–3

lief, had as *(adj.)*

should like just as much

    Ham III.ii.3 [Hamlet to the Players] *I had as lief the town crier spoke my lines*

    1H4 IV.ii.18 [Falstaff alone] *I press ... such a commodity of warm slaves as had as lief hear the devil as a drum*

like *(adj.)*

same, similar, alike, equal

    Ham I.ii.212 [Horatio to Hamlet] *These hands are not more like*

    Cym IV.ii.237 [Arviragus to Guiderius] *use like note and words*

    3H6 I.i.75 [York to all, of battles previously won] *Why should I not now have the like success?*

    LL IV.ii.84 [Costard to Holofernes, of the one most likely to be pierced] *he that is likest to a hogshead*

    ☛ like *(n.)*, *(adj.)* 2, *(v.)*, *(adv.)*

like *(adv.)*

likely, probable / probably

    AY I.ii.17 [Celia to Rosalind] *nor none is like to have*

    Ham II.ii.348 [Hamlet to Rosencrantz] *it is most like*

    ☛ like *(adv.)* 2–4, *(n.)*, *(adj.)*, *(v.)*

livery *(n.)*

uniform, costume, special clothing

    2H4 V.v.12 [Falstaff to Shallow] *if I had had time to have made new liveries*

    MND I.i.70 [Theseus to Hermia] *examine well your blood, / Whether ... / You can endure the livery of a nun*

    ☛ livery *(n.)* 2–3, *(v.)*

mark *(v.)*

note, pay attention to, take notice of

    Cor V.iii.92 [Coriolanus to Volscians] *Aufidius, and you Volsces, mark*

    Ham II.ii.15 [Polonius to Reynaldo] *do you mark this, Reynaldo*

    2H4 I.ii.123 [Falstaff to Lord Chief Justice] *the disease of not listening, the malady of not marking*

    Mac IV.iii.169 [Ross to Macduff] *Where sighs and groans ... / Are made, not marked*

    ☛ mark *(n.)* 2, *(n.)*

marvellous *(adv.)*

very, extremely, exceedingly

    MND III.i.2 [Quince to all] *here's a marvellous convenient place for our rehearsal*

    R3 III.v.1 [stage direction] *Enter Richard ... and Buckingham, in rotten armour, marvellous ill-favoured*

meet *(adj.)*

fit, suitable, right, proper

    Ham I.v.107 [Hamlet alone] *meet it is I set it down*

    Ham I.v.171 [Hamlet to Horatio and Marcellus] *As I perchance hereafter shall think meet*

    H5 I.ii.255 [Ambassador to King Henry, of the Dauphin] *He therefore sends you, meeter for your spirit, / This tun of treasure*

    2H6 I.iii.158 [Gloucester to King] *I say ... York is meetest man / To be your Regent*

    Mac V.i.16 [Doctor to Gentlewoman, of telling him what she has seen] *'tis most meet you should*

    ☛ meet *(adj.)* 2, *(v.)*, *(adv.)*

mere *(adj.)*

complete, total, absolute, utter

    AY II.vii.166 [Jaques to all] *second childishness, and mere oblivion*

    Cym IV.ii.92 [Cloten to Guiderius] *to thy mere confusion, thou shalt know / I am son to th' queen*

    TS Induction.i.21 [First Huntsman to Lord, of a hound following a scent] *He cried upon it at the merest loss*

    ☛ mere *(adj.)* 2, *(adv.)*

merely *(adv.)*

completely, totally, entirely

    AW IV.iii.20 [Second Lord to First Lord, of themselves] *Merely our own traitors*

    AY III.ii.383 [Rosalind as Ganymede to Orlando] *Love is merely a madness*

    ☛ merely *(adv.)* 2–3

methinks(t), methought(s) *(v.)*

it seems / seemed to me

    AW II.iii.251 [Lafew to Parolles] *Methinkst thou art a general offence*

    Ham V.ii.98 [Hamlet to Osrick] *But yet methinks it is very sultry*

Ham V.ii.5 [Hamlet to Horatio] *Methought I lay / Worse than the mutines in the bilboes*
WT I.ii.154 [Leontes to Hermione] *methoughts I did recoil / Twenty-three years*

morn (n.)
morning, dawn
Ham I.iii.41 [Laertes to Ophelia] *the morn and liquid dew of youth*
Mac IV.iii.4 [Macduff to Malcolm] *Each new morn / New widows howl*
MM II.iv.71 [Isabella to Angelo] *my morn prayer*
Tem V.i.307 [Prospero to Alonso] *In the morn, / I'll bring you to your ship*

morrow (n.)
morning
1H4 II.i.33 [Gadshill to Carriers] *Good morrow, carriers*
2H4 III.i.32 [Warwick to King Henry IV] *Many good morrows to your majesty!*
H5 IV.Chorus.33 [Chorus, of King Henry and his soldiers] *Bids them good morrow*
MW II.ii.32 [Mistress Quickly to Falstaff] *Give your worship good morrow*

office (n.)
task, service, duty, responsibility
MA V.iv.14 [Leonato to Antonio] *You know your office*
MND II.ii.8 [Titania to Fairies] *Sing me now asleep; / Then to your offices*
Tem I.ii.312 [Prospero to Miranda, of Caliban] *He … serves in offices / That profit us*
TN III.iv.317 [First Officer to Second Officer, of Antonio] *This is the man; do thy office*
☛ office (n.) 2–8, (v.)

oft (adv.)
often
AC IV.xiv.139 [Anthony to Guards] *I have led you oft*
Cym V.v.249 [Cornelius to Cymbeline] *The queen, sir, very oft importuned me / To temper poisons for her*

ope (v.)
open
CE III.i.73 [Antipholus of Ephesus to Dromio of Ephesus] *I'll break ope the gate*
Ham I.iv.50 [Hamlet to Ghost] *why the sepulchre … / Hath oped his ponderous and marble jaws*
Tem V.i.49 [Prospero alone] *graves at my command / Have waked their sleepers, oped, and let 'em forth*

owe (v.)
own, possess, have
AW III.ii.119 [Helena alone] *all the miseries which nature owes*
KL I.iv.119 [Fool to Lear] *Lend less than thou owest*
Mac I.iii.75 [Macbeth to Witches] *Say from whence / You owe this strange intelligence*
R3 IV.iv.142 [Queen Elizabeth to King Richard] *The slaughter of the prince that owed that crown*
☛ owe (n.) 2–3

parle, parley (n.)
negotiation, meeting [between enemies under a truce, to discuss terms]
E3 I.ii.22 [King David to Lorraine] *we with England will not enter parley*
H5 III.iii.2 [King Henry to Citizens of Harfleur] *This is the latest parle we will admit*

1H6 III.iii.35 [Pucelle to all, of Burgundy] *Summon a parley; we will talk with him*
TS I.i.114 [Hortensio to Gremio] *the nature of our quarrel yet never brooked parle*
☛ parley (n.) 2–3, (v.)

pate (n.)
head, skull
CE II.i.78 [Adriana to Dromio of Ephesus] *Back, slave, or I will break thy pate across*
Cym II.i.7 [First Lord to Cloten, of Cloten's bowling opponent] *You have broke his pate with your bowl*

peradventure (adv.)
perhaps, maybe, very likely
AY I.i.49 [Celia to Rosalind, of Touchstone] *Peradventure this is not Fortune's work*
E3 V.i.22 [King Edward to Calais Citizens] *You, peradventure, are but servile grooms*
KJ V.vi.31 [Hubert to Bastard, of King John] *The King / Yet speaks, and peradventure may recover*

perchance (adv.)
perhaps, maybe
CE IV.i.39 [Antipholus of Ephesus to Angelo] *Perchance I will be there as soon as you*
KJ IV.i.114 [Arthur to Hubert, of the fire] *it perchance will sparkle in your eyes*
☛ perchance (adv.) 2

perforce (adv.)
1 forcibly, by force, violently
CE IV.iii.94 [Courtesan alone, of Antipholus of Syracuse] *He rushed into my house and took perforce / My ring away*
R2 II.iii.120 [Bolingbroke to York] *my rights and royalties / Plucked from my arms perforce*
2 of necessity, with no choice in the matter
E3 III.i.182 [Mariner to King John, of the navies] *we perforce were fain to give them way*
R2 V.ii.35 [York to Duchess of York] *The hearts of men, they must perforce have melted*

physic (n.)
medicine, healing, treatment
AW II.i.185 [King to Helena] *thy physic I will try*
2H4 IV.v.16 [Prince Henry to Clarence, of King Henry IV] *If he be sick with joy, he'll recover without physic*
MM IV.vi.7 [Isabella to Mariana, of the Duke speaking against her] *'tis a physic / That's bitter to sweet end*
RJ II.iii.48 [Romeo to Friar, of Juliet] *Both our remedies / Within thy help and holy physic lies*
☛ physic (n.) 2, (v.)

place (n.)
position, post, office, rank
3H6 III.i.52 [King to himself] *To strengthen and support King Edward's place*
Mac I.iv.37 [King to all] *Sons, kinsmen, thanes, / And you whose places are the nearest*
Oth I.iii.235 [Othello to Duke] *I crave fit disposition for my wife, / Due reference of place and exhibition*
Per V.i.19 [Helicanus to Lysimachus] *what is your place?*
☛ place (n.) 2–6, (v.)

post (n.)

express messenger, courier

2H4 II.iv.351 [Peto to Prince Henry] *there are twenty weak and wearied posts / Come from the north*

2H6 III.ii.282 [stage direction] *Enter a Post*

3H6 V.i.1 [Warwick to all] *Where is the post that came from valiant Oxford?*

Mac I.iii.97 [Ross to Macbeth] *As thick as hail / Came post with post*

☞ post (n.) 2–3, (v.), (adv.)

power (n.)

armed force, troops, host, army

Cor I.ii.9 [Aufidius to all, reading a letter about the Romans] *They have pressed a power*

1H6 II.ii.33 [Burgundy to all, of the French] *We'll follow them with all the power we have*

1H6 V.i.5 [Alençon to Charles] *keep not back your powers in dalliance*

R2 III.ii.211 [King Richard to all] *That power I have, discharge*

☞ power (n.) 2–9

prate (v.)

prattle, chatter, blather

CE II.ii.202 [Luciana to Dromio of Syracuse] *Why pratest thou to thyself*

Cor I.i.46 [First Citizen to all] *Why stay we prating here?*

Ham V.i.276 [Hamlet to Laertes] *if thou prate of mountains*

☞ prate (n.)

present (adj.)

immediate, instant

Cor III.i.211 [Brutus to all] *Martius is worthy / Of present death*

Ham V.i.291 [Claudius to Laertes] *We'll put the matter to the present push*

☞ present (adj.) 2–7, (n.), (v.)

presently (adv.)

immediately, instantly, at once

CE III.ii.155 [Antipholus of Syracuse to Dromio of Syracuse] *Go, hie thee presently*

TNK II.i.277 [Gaoler to Arcite] *you must presently to th'Duke*

☞ presently (adv.) 2

purpose (n.)

intention, aim, plan

KL I.iv.235 [Gonerill to Lear] *understand my purposes aright*

Mac II.ii.52 [Lady Macbeth to Macbeth] *Infirm of purpose!*

MM V.i.310 [Escalus to disguised Duke] *we will know his purpose*

☞ purpose (n.) 2–3, (v.)

quoth (v.)

said

AW I.iii.83 [Clown to Countess] *One in ten, quoth'a!*

AY II.i.51 [First Lord to Duke Senior, of Jaques] *''Tis right,' quoth he*

CE II.i.62 [Dromio of Ephesus to Adriana] *''Tis dinner-time,' quoth I*

1H4 II.i.49 [Chamberlain to Gadshill] *At hand, quoth pick-purse*

rail (v.)

rant, rave, be abusive [about]

CE IV.iv.72 [Antipholus of Ephesus to Dromio of Ephesus, of Adriana] *Did not her kitchen-maid rail, taunt, and scorn me?*

H5 II.ii.41 [King Henry to Exeter] *Enlarge the man committed yesterday / That railed against our person*

R2 V.v.90 [Richard as if to his horse] *Why do I rail on thee*

TN I.v.89 [Olivia to Malvolio] *There is no slander in an allowed fool, though he do nothing but rail*

remembrance (n.)

memory, bringing to mind, recollection

AW I.iii.129 [Countess to herself] *our remembrances of days fore-gone*

Cym III.i.2 [Lucius to Cymbeline, of Caesar] *whose remembrance yet / Lives in men's eyes*

LL V.ii.805 [Princess to King] *For the remembrance of my father's death*

sad (adj.)

serious, grave, solemn

MA I.iii.56 [Borachio to Don John] *comes me the Prince and Claudio … in sad conference*

MA III.ii.15 [Leonato to Benedick] *methinks you are sadder [than you were]*

MND II.i.51 [Puck to Fairy] *The wisest aunt telling the saddest tale / Sometime for threefoot stool mistaketh me*

MV I.i.1 [Antonio to Salerio and Solanio] *In sooth I know not why I am so sad*

scape, 'scape (v.)

escape, avoid

1H4 II.ii.59 [Prince Hal to all, of the travellers] *if they scape from your encounter, then they light on us*

MW III.v.107 [Falstaff to Ford as Brook] *It was a miracle to 'scape suffocation*

several (adj.)

separate, different, distinct

AC I.v.62 [Alexas to Cleopatra] *twenty several messengers*

Cor I.viii.1 [stage direction] *Enter Martius and Aufidius at several doors*

E3 I.i.168 [Prince Edward to all] *Then cheerfully forward, each a several way*

LL V.ii.125 [Boyet to Princess, of the King's party knowing their ladies] *By favours several which they did bestow*

MND V.i.407 [Oberon to all] *Every fairy take his gait, / And each several chamber bless*

☞ several (adj.) 2–3, (n.)

something (adv.)

somewhat, rather

Cym I.ii.17 [Innogen to Posthumus] *I something fear my father's wrath*

Ham I.iii.121 [Polonius to Ophelia] *Be something scanter of your maiden presence*

2H4 I.ii.189 [Falstaff to Lord Chief Justice] *I was born [with] … something a round belly*

KL I.i.20 [Gloucester to Kent, of Edmund] *this knave came something saucily to the world*

Tem III.i.58 [Miranda to Ferdinand] *I prattle / Something too wildly*

☞ something (adv.) 2

sport (n.)

recreation, amusement, entertainment

AY I.ii.23 [Rosalind to Celia] *I will [be merry], coz, and devise sports*

AY I.ii.124 [Touchstone to Le Beau] *what is the sport … that the ladies have lost?*

Ham III.ii.227 [Second Player as Queen, to her King] *Sport and repose lock from me day and night*

1H6 II.ii.45 [Burgundy to all] *I see our wars / Will turn unto a peaceful comic sport*

LL V.ii.153 [Princess to Boyet] *There's no such sport as sport by sport o'erthrown*
➤ sport *(n.)* 2–4, *(v.)*

still *(adv.)*
constantly, always, continually
Ham III.i.175 [Claudius to Polonius, of Hamlet] *his brains still beating*
1H4 V.ii.6 [Worcester to Vernon, of King Henry] *He will suspect us still*
➤ still *(adv.)* 2, *(adj.)*, *(v.)*

straight *(adv.)*
straightaway, immediately, at once
E3 IV.iv.72 [Herald to Prince Edward, of King John] *He straight will fold his bloody colours up*
1H6 IV.iv.40 [Somerset to Lucy] *I will dispatch the horsemen straight*

suit *(n.)*
formal request, entreaty, petition
CE IV.i.69 [Second Merchant to Officer, of Angelo] *arrest him at my suit*
Cor V.iii.135 [Volumnia to Coriolanus, of the Romans and Volsces] *our suit / Is that you reconcile them*
➤ suit *(n.)* 2–4, *(v.)*

sup *(v.)*
have supper
1H4 I.ii.191 [Prince Hal to Poins, of Eastcheap] *There I'll sup*
2H4 II.ii.139 [Prince Henry to Bardolph, of Falstaff] *Where sups he?*
Oth V.i.117 [Iago to Emilia] *Go know of Cassio where he supped tonight*
➤ sup *(n.)* 2–3

undone *(adj.)*
ruined, destroyed, brought down
Oth V.i.54 [Cassio to Iago] *I am spoiled, undone by villains!*
RJ III.ii.38 [Nurse to Juliet] *We are undone, lady*
WT IV.iv.450 [Shepherd to Florizel] *You have undone a man of fourscore three*

visage *(n.)*
face, countenance
MV III.ii.59 [Portia to Bassanio, of the Trojan wives] *With bleared visages come forth to view / The issue of th'exploit*
RJ I.iv.29 [Mercutio to Romeo] *Give me a case to put my visage in*
➤ visage *(n.)* 2

voice *(n.)*
vote, official support
Cor II.iii.76 [Coriolanus to Second Citizen] *Your good voice, sir. What say you?*
Cor II.iii.155 [First Citizen to Sicinius, of Coriolanus] *He has our voices*
➤ voice *(n.)* 2–5, *(v.)*

want *(v.)*
lack, need, be without

Ham I.ii.150 [Hamlet alone, of Gertrude] *a beast that wants discourse of reason / Would have mourned longer*
1H6 I.i.143 [Bedford to Third Messenger, of Talbot] *such a worthy leader, wanting aid*
➤ want *(v.)* 2–4, *(n.)*

warrant *(v.)*
assure, promise, guarantee, confirm
AW III.v.65 [Widow to Diana, of Helena] *I warrant, good creature, wheresoe'er she is, / Her heart weighs sadly*
AY I.ii.192 [Charles to Duke] *I warrant your grace*
Ham III.iii.29 [Polonius to Claudius, of Gertrude and Hamlet] *I'll warrant she'll tax him home*
1H6 II.v.95 [Mortimer to Richard] *thou seest that … my fainting words do warrant death*
TNK III.vi.68 [Palamon to Arcite] *I'll warrant thee I'll strike home*
➤ warrant *(n.)* 2–6, *(n.)*

wench *(n.)*
girl, lass
Tem I.ii.139 [Prospero to Miranda] *Well demanded, wench*
Tem I.ii.480 [Prospero to Miranda] *Foolish wench!*
TNK II.iii.12 [Gaoler's Daughter alone, of Palamon] *I pitied him, / And so would any young wench*

wit *(n.)*
1 intelligence, wisdom, good sense
CE II.ii.93 [Antipholus of Syracuse to Dromio of Syracuse] *thou didst conclude hairy men plain dealers, without wit*
1H6 I.ii.73 [Pucelle to Dauphin] *I am by birth a shepherd's daughter, / My wit untrained in any kind of art*
2 mental sharpness, acumen, quickness, ingenuity
AY IV.i.151 [Rosalind as Ganymede to Orlando] *Make the doors upon a woman's wit, and it will out at the casement*
AY V.i.11 [Touchstone to himself] *we that have good wits have much to answer for*
➤ wit *(n.)* 3–6, *(v.)*

wont *(v.)*
be accustomed, used [to], be in the habit of
CE II.ii.162 [Luciana to Antipholus of Syracuse] *When were you wont to use my sister thus?*
CE IV.iv.35 [Dromio of Ephesus to Antipholus of Ephesus, of beating] *I bear it on my shoulders, as a beggar wont her brat* [i.e. habitually does to her child]
1H6 I.i.14 [Regnier to all] *Talbot is taken, whom we wont to fear*
3H6 II.vi.76 [Warwick to dead Clifford] *swear as thou wast wont*
➤ wont *(n.)*

wot *(v.)*
learn, know, be told
AC I.v.22 [Cleopatra to Charmian, as if to Antony's horse] *wot'st thou whom thou mov'st?*
1H6 IV.vi.32 [Talbot to John Talbot] *too much folly is it, well I wot*
1H6 IV.vii.55 [Lucy to Charles, of the word 'submission'] *We English warriors wot not what it means*
R3 II.iii.18 [Third Citizen to others] *Stood the state so? No, no, good friends, God wot!*
WT III.ii.75 [Hermione to Leontes] *the gods themselves, / Wotting no more than I, are ignorant*

A–Z GLOSSARY

'a *(v.)* contracted form of 'have' ☛ **VERB FORMS**, p.481

'a *(pron.)* contracted form of 'he' **AW** IV.v.79 [Lafew to Countess, of Bertram] *'A will be here tomorrow* ☛ **ELISION**, p.146

a *(prep.)* **1** variant form of 'at' **2H4** II.iv.227 [Doll to Falstaff] *when wilt thou leave fighting a-days, and foining a-nights;* **TS** V.i.4 [Biondello to Lucentio] *I'll see the church a your back* ☛ a-night *(adv.)*

2 variant form of 'by' **Cor** I.iii.58 [Valeria to Volumnia and Virgilia, of Young Martius] *A my word, the father's son!* [F]

3 variant form of 'in' **1H6** I.ii.102 [Charles to Pucelle] *Then come, a God's name;* **TNK** III.vi.256 [Palamon to Theseus] *I'll be cut a-pieces / Before I take this oath!* ☛ abed *(adv.)*; afield *(adv.)*; a-row *(adv.)*; a-tilt *(adv.)*

4 variant form of 'of' **CE** II.i.11 [Luciana to Adriana, of men having more freedom than women] *Because their business still lies out a'door* [F adore]

5 variant form of 'on' **Ham** II.ii.386 [Hamlet to Rosencrantz] *'A Monday morning, 'twas then, indeed;* **2H4** II.iv.269 [Falstaff to Doll] *I shall receive money a-Thursday* ☛ afire *(adv.)*; afoot *(adv.)*; a-height *(adv.)*; a-high *(adv.)*; a-life *(adv.)*

6 variant form of 'to' **2H4** IV.iii.112 [Falstaff alone] *skill in the weapon is nothing without sack, for that sets it a-work;* **MND** II.ii.7 [Titania to the Fairies] *Sing me now asleep*

a *(int.)* variant form of 'ah' ☛ **EXCLAMATIONS**, p.158

a *(part.)* particle used in front of a proper name, as a supportive war-cry **TNK** V.iii.66 [stage direction] *crying 'A Palamon!';* **1H6** I.i.128; **3H6** IV.viii.51 ☛ **A- AS A PARTICLE**, p.2

-a *(suffix)* syllable often used to make up the rhythm in a song **TNK** III.v.63 [Gaoler's Daughter singing, of the George Alow] *he met with brave gallants of war / By one, by two, by three-a* ☛ **SINGING**, p.402

abandon *(v.)* banish, exile, keep away **TS** Induction.ii.114 [Page as Sly's wife to Sly] *Being all this time abandoned from your bed*

abase *(v.)* lower, cast down **2H6** I.ii.15 [Duchess to Gloucester] *We'll ... never more abase our sight so low / As to vouchsafe one glance unto the ground;* **R3** I.ii.246

abate *(v.)* **1** lessen, lower, diminish **Ham** IV.vii.114 [Claudius to Laertes] *There lives within the very flame of love / A kind of wick or snuff that will abate it;* **Cym** I.v.65; **H5** III.ii.23; **Tit** I.i.46; **TS** Induction.i.135 ☛ bate *(v.)* 1

2 shorten, lessen, reduce **MND** III.ii.432 [Helena to herself, as if addressing the night] *Abate thy hours*

3 deprive, strip, dispossess **KL** II.iv.154 [Lear to Regan, of Gonerill] *She hath abated me of half my train*

4 blunt, put an end to **R3** V.v.35 [Richmond to all, praying to God] *Abate the edge of traitors* [i.e. of their swords]; **2H4** I.i.117

5 set aside, except, bar **LL** V.ii.540 [Berowne to King, of five actors taking nine parts] *Abate throw at novum, and the whole world again / Cannot pick out five such*

abated *(adj.)* humbled, abject, subdued **Cor** III.iii.132 [Coriolanus to Plebeians] *Your ignorance ... deliver you / As most abated captives*

abatement *(n.)* **1** lessening, decrease, diminution **KL** I.iv.59 [Third Knight to Lear] *There's a great abatement of kindness appears;* **Ham** IV.vii.119; **TN** I.i.13; **TNK** I.i.225

2 means remaining, reduced amount [of money] **Cym** V.iv.21 [Posthumus alone, of the way usurers treat their victims] *letting them thrive again / On their abatement*

abed, a-bed *(adv.)* in bed **Mac** II.i.12 [Banquo to Macbeth] *The King's a-bed;* **Oth** III.i.30 [Iago to Cassio] *You have not been abed then?* ☛ a *(prep.)* 3; slug-abed *(n.)*

abed / to bed, brought delivered of a child **Tit** IV.ii.62 [Nurse to Aaron, of Tamora] *she is brought abed;* **Tit** IV.ii.152 [Aaron to Demetrius and Chiron, of Muly] *His wife but yesternight was brought to bed*

abhominable *(adj.)* abominable [from the mistaken etymology 'ab homine'] **LL** V.i.24 [Holofernes to Nathaniel, of Armado's pronunciation] *This is abhominable, which he would call 'abominable'* ➤ abominable *(adj.)*

abhomination *(n.)* variant spelling of 'abomination' ➤ abomination *(n.)*

abhor *(v.)* **1** loathe, abominate, regard with disgust **TN** II.v.192 [Maria to all, of Olivia's dislike of yellow] *'tis a colour she abhors;* **Cor** I.iv.32; **Cym** IV.iii.357; **Tim** IV.iii.20, 399, V.iv.75
2 disgust, horrify, revolt **Oth** IV.ii.161 [Desdemona to Iago] *I cannot say 'whore': / It does abhor me now I speak the word;*
3 reject, protest against, refuse **H8** II.iv.81 [Queen Katherine to Wolsey] *I utterly abhor, yea, from my soul / Refuse you for my judge*

A- AS A PARTICLE

Many words in Shakespearian texts begin with *a-* used as a grammatical particle (an element which affects the meaning of other words but without any dictionary meaning itself). The commonest use is before a verb ending in *-ing* (*coming, going*), to which it is usually shown linked with a hyphen. Historically a form of *on*, it came to be used as a particle emphasizing various aspects of the verb's durative meaning, such as the repeated nature of an action or the length of time it takes. On this basis, to be 'a-feasting' is, as it were, 'to be engaged in the time-consuming activity of feasting' (**MW** II.iii.80). The meaning is often reinforced by accompanying temporal adverbs, as in the Scrivener's complaint about the time it took him to write out Lord Hastings' indictment (**R3** III.vi.7):

Eleven hours I have spent to write it over ...
The precedent was full as long a-doing

For activities which are not by nature durative, such as *kill*, the use of *a-* can be particularly dramatic, as in Othello's wish to extend the time-frame for Cassio's death (**Oth** IV.i.177): 'I would have him nine years a-killing!' And the form can be used with various ironic overtones. Its repetitive or habitual implication can add a sense of routine or ordinariness to an activity, thereby conveying a demeaning effect when used with reference to activities which are very serious in nature: *a-dying* (**R2** II.i.90), *a-praying* (**Ham** III.iii.73), *a-hanging* (**KL** V.iii.272).

Often the role of the particle seems little more than to add an extra syllable to make up the metre of a line. Because *sleeping*, for example, already implies duration, little is added semantically by the addition of *a-*, so that its function in Apemantus's Grace (**Tim** I.ii.66) is purely metrical:

Or a harlot for her weeping,
Or a dog that seems a-sleeping.

Other examples of *a-* particle usage include:

Item	Location	Item	Location
a-bat-fowling	**Tem** II.i.188	a-hunting	**TNK** III.vi.108
a-begging	**TNK** III.vi.238	a-making	**Ham** I.iii.119
a-billing	**Venus** 366	a-maying	**TNK** III.i.1
a-birding	**MW** III.iii.218	a-mending	**TC** I.iii.159
a-bleeding	**MV** II.v.24	a-repairing	**LL** III.i.188
a-breeding	**LL** I.i.97	a-ripening	**H8** III.ii.357
a-brewing	**MV** II.v.17	a-rolling	**H8** V.iii.104
a-capering	**MV** I.ii.58	a-shaking	**Luc** 452
a-coming	**LL** V.ii.581	a-shouting	**JC** I.ii.221
a-doting	**Sonn** 20.10	a-sleeping	**Tim** I.ii.66
a-ducking	**AC** III.vii.64	a-swearing	**Ham** III.iii.91
a-going	**H8** I.iii.50	a-turning	**PassP** VII.16
a-growing	**R3** II.iv.19	a-weeping	**2H4** II.iv.272
a-hooting	**LL** IV.ii.60	a-wooing	**Oth** III.iii.71

A second use of *a-* as a particle occurs in front of adjectives, where it commonly adds a degree of extra intensity or emphasis: to be 'a-hungry' typically implies a somewhat greater strength of the condition than to be simply 'hungry': *a-cold* (**KL** III.iv.80, and often so used by Poor Tom), *a-hungry* (**MW** I.i.251) or *an-hungry* (**Cor** I.i.203). Here too the particle can be a useful way of adding an extra metrical beat to a line, as in **R3** IV.iv.86 [Queen Margaret to Queen Elizabeth]: 'One heaved a-high to be hurled down below'.

These uses of *a-* should be distinguished from *a-* as a prefix (a meaningful element attached to the front of a word). Here *a-* represents the unstressed form of a preposition in front of a noun, usually joined to the rest the word by a hyphen (*a-bed*, **Cym** III.iii.33), sometimes printed solid with it (*abed*), and occasionally left spaced (as in the First Folio printing, *a bed*). It is most commonly found as a variant of *on* (and replaced by *o'* in some text editions), as in these examples from *Pericles*: *a-land* (II.i.28), *a-th'land* (II.i.33), *a-shipboard* (III.i.1).

abhorred *(adj.)* horrifying, disgusting, abominable **Tem** I.ii.273 [Prospero to Ariel, of Sycorax] *thou wast a spirit too delicate / To act her earthy and abhorred commands;* **Ham** V.i.184; **KJ** IV.ii.224; **KL** V.iii.208; **Mac** V.vi.20; **Tem** I.ii.351

abhorring *(n.)* **1** abhorrence, disgust, loathing **Cor** I.i.166 [Martius to First Citizen] *He that will give good words to thee will flatter / Beneath abhorring*
2 object of disgust, something to be loathed **AC** V.ii.60 [Cleopatra to Proculeius] *let the waterflies / Blow me into abhorring!*

abide *(v.)* **1** endure, undergo, face **Cym** III.iv.185 [Innogen to Pisanio, of their plan] *I … will abide it with / A prince's courage;* **2H4** II.iii.36; **3H6** II.v.75, IV.iii.59; **MND** III.ii.422
2 wait for, await, look out for **3H6** I.iv.29 [York to his enemies] *I am your butt, and I abide your shot;* **R2** V.vi.22
3 stay, remain, stop [in a position] **E3** IV.iii.29 [Charles to Villiers, of Villiers' oath] *that doth bind thee to abide;* **Mac** III.i.139; **Tem** V.i.12; **Tim** V.i.2; **Tit** V.ii.137
4 stay a short while, pause before moving on **WT** IV.iii.90 [Clown to Autolycus] *There's no virtue whipped out of the court: they cherish it to make it stay there; and yet it will no more but abide* [or: put up with having to stay]
5 live, dwell, reside **Tim** V.i.2 [Painter to Poet, of Timon] *it cannot be far where he abides;* **Sonn** 27.5
6 pay the penalty for, suffer for, take the consequences of **JC** III.i.94 [Brutus to all] *let no man abide this deed / But we the doers;* **JC** III.ii.115 ☛ **aby** *(v.)*

abiliment *(n.)* ☛ **habiliment** *(n.)*

ability *(n.)* **1** strength, bodily power **Oth** I.iii.25 [First Senator to Duke, of Cyprus] *it … altogether lacks th'abilities / That Rhodes is dressed in;* **WT** II.iii.163
2 action one is capable of **Oth** III.iii.2 [Desdemona to Cassio] *I will do / All my abilities in thy behalf*
3 means, resources, funds **TN** III.iv.334 [Viola as Cesario to Antonio] *Out of my lean and low ability, / I'll lend you something;* **2H4** I.iii.45

abject *(n.)* servile subject, low-placed reject **R3** I.i.106 [Richard to Brakenbury] *We are the Queen's abjects*

abject *(adj.)* mean-spirited, despicable, contemptible **2H6** V.i.25 [York to himself, of Buckingham's questions] *I am so angry at these abject terms;* **1H6** V.v.49; **2H6** II.v.11, IV.i.105; **H8** I.i.127; **TC** III.iii.128

abjectly *(adv.)* contemptibly, in a degrading way, with a low opinion **Tit** II.iii.4 [Aaron alone] *Let him that thinks of me so abjectly / Know that this gold must coin a stratagem*

abjure *(v.)* swear to abandon, solemnly reject **Tem** V.i.51 [Prospero alone] *this rough magic / I here abjure;* **KL** II.iv.203; **TN** I.ii.40; **TS** I.i.33

able *(adj.)* **1** powerful enough, sufficient, capable of dealing [with] **AW** I.i.63 [Countess to Bertram] *Be able for thine enemy*
2 strong, vigorous, powerful **AW** IV.v.79 [Lafew to Countess, of the King] *His highness comes post from Marcellus, of as able body as when he numbered thirty;* **2H4** I.i.43; **H8** II.ii.140

able *(v.)* strengthen, fortify, give power to **KL** IV.vi.169 [Lear to all] *None does offend … I'll able 'em* [or: vouch for]

aboard *(adv.)* ☛ clap her aboard; lay aboard; lay knife aboard

abode *(n.)* **1** delay, procrastination **MV** II.vi.21 [Lorenzo to all] *your patience for my long abode*
2 staying, remaining, lingering **AC** I.i.176 [Enobarbus to Antony, of the business to be done] *especially that of Cleopatra's, which wholly depends on your abode;* **Oth** IV.ii.224
3 dwelling-place, lodging, residence **TS** IV.v.38 [Katherina to Vincentio] *where is thy abode?;* **Cym** I.vii.53; **TG** IV.iii.23

abode *(v.)* predict, forebode, portend **3H6** V.vi.45 [King to Richard, of Richard's birth] *The night-crow cried, aboding luckless time;* **H8** I.i.93

abodement *(n.)* foreboding, omen, premonition **3H6** IV.vii.13 [Edward to Richard] *abodements must not now affright us*

abominable, abhominable *(adj.)* inhuman, unnatural, loathsome **1H6** I.iii.87 [Winchester to Gloucester] *Abominable Gloucester, guard thy head*

abomination *(n.)* **1** hatefulness, repugnance, disgusting state **Luc** 704 *Drunken Desire must vomit his receipt / Ere he can see his own abomination*
2 disgusting vice, shameful act **AC** III.vi.94 [Maecenas to Octavia, of Antony] *most large / In his abominations*

abortive *(n.)* abortion of nature, abnormality **KJ** III.iv.158 [Cardinal Pandulph to Lewis the Dauphin, of the people reacting to natural phenomena] *they will … call them meteors, prodigies and signs, / Abortives, presages*

abortive *(adj.)* **1** monstrous, defective, unnatural **R3** I.iii.227 [Queen Margaret to Richard] *Thou elvish-marked, abortive, rooting hog!;* **LL** I.i.104; **R3** I.ii.21
2 monstrously ill-timed, abhorrent and untimely **2H6** IV.i.60 [Suffolk to Lieutenant] *allay this thy abortive pride*

abound *(v.)* be wealthy, prosper, thrive **H8** I.i.83 [Abergavenny to Buckingham and Norfolk, of his kinsmen] *never / They shall abound as formerly*

about *(adv.)* **1** about your business, into action **Ham** II.ii.586 [Hamlet to himself] *About, my brains;* **2H4** I.ii.244; **JC** III.ii.205; **MW** V.v.55
2 in the process of planning, up to **MW** I.iii.35 [Falstaff to Nym and Pistol] *I will tell you what I am about* [pun: 38]
3 round, in circumference **MW** I.iii.38 [Falstaff to Nym and Pistol] *I am in the waist two yards about* [pun: 35]
4 indirectly, irregularly **KJ** I.i.170 [Bastard to Queen Eleanor, of being conceived illegitimately] *Something about, a little from the right*

about *(prep.)* **1** concerned with **1H6** II.i.70 [Charles to all] *I was employed … / About relieving of the sentinels*
2 in the company of **1H6** III.i.38 [Winchester to all, of Gloucester] *No one but he should be about the King*

above *(adv.)* **1** upstairs **CE** II.ii.217 [Adriana to Antipholus of Syracuse] *I'll dine above with you today;* **MW** II.ii.71
2 in addition, as well **Ham** II.ii.126 [Polonius to Claudius and Gertrude, of Hamlet] *And more above hath his solicitings … / All given to mine ear*

above *(prep.)* beyond **1H6** I.i.121 [Third Messenger to Winchester] *valiant Talbot, above human thought, / Enacted wonders*

abram *(adj.)* dark brown, golden brown [from 'auburn'] **Cor** II.iii.18 [Third Citizen to First Citizen] *our heads are some brown, some black, some abram, some bald*

abridge *(v.)* **1** shorten, cut short **TG** III.i.245 [Proteus to Valentine] *thy staying will abridge thy life;* **JC** III.i.104
2 deprive, debar, dispossess **MV** I.i.126 [Bassanio to Antonio] *Nor do I now make moan to be abridged / From such a noble rate*

abridgement *(n.)* **1** pastime, short entertainment, means of shortening the time **MND** V.i.39 [Theseus to Philostrate] *what abridgement have you for this evening?*
2 curtailment, cutting off, shortening **H5** V.Chorus.44 [to audience] *Then brook abridgement, and your eyes advance;* **Ham** II.ii.419
3 summary, outline, synopsis **Cym** V.v.383 [Cymbeline to all] *This fierce abridgement / Hath to it circumstantial branches*

abroach *(adv.)* afoot, astir, in motion **RJ** I.i.104 [Montague to Benvolio] *Who set this ancient quarrel new abroach?;* **2H4** IV.ii.14; **R3** I.iii.324

abroad *(adv.)* **1** in the outside world, freely at large, elsewhere, everywhere **KL** II.i.7 [Curan to Edmund] *You have heard of the news abroad;* **1H6** II.iii.15; **3H6** V.vi.86; **Tem** V.i.167; **TNK** II.i.152; **WT** IV.iv.252
2 around, about, on the move **E3** II.ii.21 [Derby to Audley] *the king is now abroad;* **Cym** IV.ii.101, 130; **LL** I.i.186

3 away from home, out of the house **KL** I.ii.167 [Edmund to Edgar] *If you do stir abroad, go armed;* **2H4** I.ii.94, 96; **3H6** V.i.96; **MV** III.iii.10; **TNK** IV.i.110

4 wide apart **2H6** III.ii.172 [Warwick to Suffolk, of dead Gloucester] *His hands abroad displayed*

5 widely scattered, all over the place **Tit** IV.i.104 [Titus to Marcus] *The angry northern wind / Will blow these sands like Sibyl's leaves abroad*

abrogate *(v.)* do away with, put an end to, abstain from **LL** IV.ii.54 [Nathaniel to Holofernes] *so it shall please you to abrogate scurrility*

abrook *(v.)* brook, endure, bear **2H6** II.iv.10 [Gloucester to his men, of the Duchess] *ill can thy noble mind abrook / The abject people gazing on thy face / With envious looks*

abruption *(n.)* breaking-off, interruption, hesitation **TC** III.ii.64 [Troilus to Cressida, of her broken speech] *What makes this pretty abruption?*

absent *(adj.)* of absence **R2** II.iii.79 [Berkeley to Bolingbroke] *I come ... to know what pricks you on / To take advantage of the absent time* [i.e. of King Richard]

Absey book *(n.)* [pron: aybee'see] ABC, child's primer **KJ** I.i.196 [Bastard alone, of questioning a traveller] *then comes answer like an Absey book* [i.e. automatically]

absolute *(adj.)* **1** perfect, complete, incomparable **TNK** II.i.26 [Gaoler to Gaoler's Daughter, of Palamon and Arcite] *They are famed to be a pair of absolute men;* **AC** I.ii.2; **Cor** V.v.139; **Ham** V.ii.107; **MM** V.i.54; **MW** III.iii.58

2 certain, definite, positive **Per** I.v.19 [Simonides alone, of Thaisa] *how absolute she's in't;* **Cym** IV.ii.106

3 resolved, positive, settled in mind **MM** III.i.5 [disguised Duke to Claudio] *Be absolute for death*

4 precise, literal, particular **Ham** V.i.135 [Hamlet to Horatio, of the First Clown] *How absolute the knave is!*

5 unrestricted, unconditional, without restraint **1H4** IV.iii.50 [Blunt to Hotspur] *You shall have ... pardon absolute for yourself;* **Cor** III.i.116; **Tem** I.ii.109

6 inflexible, uncompromising, intransigent **Cor** III.ii.39 [Volumnia to Coriolanus] *You are too absolute*

7 curt, peremptory, blunt **Mac** III.vi.40 [Lord to Lennox, of the messenger] *with an absolute 'Sir, not I,' / The cloudy messenger turns me his back*

abstenious *(adj.)* abstemious **Tem** IV.i.53 [Prospero to Ferdinand] *Be more abstenious* [F]

abstract *(n.)* **1** summary, digest **Ham** II.ii.522 [Hamlet to Polonius, of the players] *they are the abstract and brief chronicles of the time* [Q2; F,Q1 *Abstracts*]; **E3** II.i.82; **R3** IV.iv.28

2 list, register, inventory **MW** IV.ii.58 [Mistress Ford to Mistress Page, of hiding-places known to Ford] *he hath an abstract for the remembrance of such places;* **AW** IV.iii.85

3 epitome, embodiment, personification **AC** I.iv.9 [Caesar to Lepidus, of Antony] *A man who is the abstract of all faults / That all men follow;* **KJ** II.i.101

4 [unclear meaning] something removed, withdrawal; abridgement **AC** III.vi.61 [Octavia to Caesar, of Antony] *I begged / His pardon for return.* [Caesar:] *Which soon he granted, / Being an abstract 'tween his lust and him* [F] ➤ **obstruct** *(n.)*

absurd *(adj.)* tasteless, insipid, incongruous **Ham** III.ii.70 [Hamlet to Horatio] *let the candied tongue lick absurd pomp*

abuse *(n.)* **1** deception, hoax, fraud **2H6** V.i.92 [York to King] *Why hast thou broken faith with me, / Knowing how hardly I can brook abuse?;* **Ham** IV.vii.49; **1H6** II.iii.66, IV.i.69; **MM** V.i.203, 245; **MW** V.iii.7 ➤ **self-abuse** *(n.)*

2 offence, wrong, insult, transgression **3H6** III.iii.188 [Warwick to Lewis] *Did I let pass th'abuse done to my niece?;* **E3** V.i.49; **2H6** II.i.40; **3H6** IV.i.13; **RJ** III.i.193; **Sonn** 121.10

3 flouting, violation, improper use **H5** II.Chorus.32 [Chorus] *we'll digest / Th'abuse of distance*

4 corrupt practice, wicked way **Venus** 792 *O strange excuse, / When reason is the bawd to lust's abuse!;* **JC** II.i.115; **MM** II.i.42

abuse *(v.)* **1** deceive, mislead, fool, cheat **Oth** III.iii.264 [Othello alone, of Desdemona] *She's gone: I am abused;* **Cym** IV.ii.351; **Ham** II.ii.601; **KL** IV.vii.77; **MA** V.ii.88; **Tem** V.i.112 ➤ **abused** *(adj.)* 1

2 misuse, maltreat, treat badly, wrong **MW** I.i.3 [Shallow to Evans, of Falstaff] *he shall not abuse Robert Shallow, Esquire;* **AW** V.iii.292, 296; **Cym** II.i.57; **2H6** V.i.172; **KL** III.vii.90; **R3** I.iii.52 ➤ **abused** *(adj.)* 2

3 misapply, employ badly **LL** II.i.213 [Princess to all, of their witticisms] *here 'tis abused;* **Sonn** 82.14

4 demean, do wrong to, dishonour **KL** V.i.11 [Edmund to Regan, of her suspicion] *That thought abuses you;* **AC** V.ii.43; **1H6** IV.v.41; **H8** I.iii.28; **Oth** IV.ii.13; **Per** I.i.38

5 malign, revile, scorn **Tim** II.ii.52 [Varro's Servant to Caphis and Isidore's Servant, of Apemantus] *he'll abuse us!*

abused *(adj.)* **1** deceived, misled, fooled, cheated **KL** IV.i.22 [Gloucester to Old Man, as if to Edgar] *The food of thy abused father's wrath!* ➤ **abuse** *(v.)* 1

2 maltreated, wronged, violated **KL** IV.vii.15 [Cordelia to the gods, of Lear] *Cure this great breach in his abused nature* ➤ **abuse** *(v.)* 2

abuser *(n.)* betrayer, deceiver, corrupter **Oth** I.ii.78 [Brabantio to Othello] *I ... do attach thee / For an abuser of the world*

abusing *(adj.)* harmful, damaging, injurious **R3** III.vii.198 [Buckingham to Richard] *draw forth your noble ancestry / From the corruption of abusing times*

aby *(v.)* suffer for, pay for, atone for **MND** III.ii.175 [Demetrius to Lysander] *Disparage not the faith thou dost not know, / Lest to thy peril thou aby it dear;* **MND** III.ii.335

abysm *(n.)* abyss, chasm, gulf **AC** III.xiii.147 [Antony to Thidias] *my good stars ... / Have empty left their orbs and shot their fires / Into th'abysm of hell;* **Sonn** 112.9; **Tem** I.ii.50

academe *(n.)* academy, place of learning **LL** I.i.13 [King to all] *Our court shall be a little academe* [F *Achademe*]; **LL** IV.iii.294 [F, Q], 328

accent *(n.)* **1** talk, speech, utterance, words **KJ** V.vi.14 [Hubert to Bastard] *pardon me / That any accent breaking from thy tongue / Should 'scape the true acquaintance of mine ear;* **1H4** I.i.3; **Luc** 566; **RJ** II.iv.29; **Sonn** 69.7

2 language, tongue **JC** III.i.113 [Cassius to all, of the re-enactment of Caesar's assassination] *In states unborn, and accents yet unknown*

3 sound, voice quality, way of talking **KJ** I.i.86 [Queen Eleanor to King John, of the Bastard resembling King Richard] *The accent of his tongue affecteth him;* **TC** I.iii.53

4 attempt at speaking, inarticulate sound **Luc** 1719 [of Lucrece] *after many accents and delays, / Untimely breathings, sick and short assays, / She utters this*

accent, second echo, reverberation **H5** II.iv.126 [Exeter to Dauphin, of King Henry] *caves and womby vaultages of France / Shall ... return your mock / In second accent of his ordinance*

accept *(adj.)* decisive, approved, agreed **H5** V.ii.82 [French King to King Henry] *we will suddenly / Pass our accept and peremptory answer*

acceptable *(adj.)* welcome, pleasing, gratifying **E3** I.ii.39 [Lorraine to King David] *I ... will return / Your acceptable greeting to my king*

accepted *(adj.)* acceptable **TC** III.iii.30 [Calchas to all, of Cressida] *her presence / Shall quite strike off all service I have done / In most accepted pain*

accessary *(n.)* assistant, helper, collaborator **AW** II.i.35 [Second Lord to Bertram] *I am your accessary*

accessary *(adj.)* as an accessory, offering support **Luc** 1658 [Lucrece to Collatine, of her mind] *that never was inclined / To accessary yieldings*

accidence *(n.)* inflections of Latin grammar **MW** IV.i.16 [Mistress Page to Evans, of William] *ask him some questions in his accidence*

accident *(n.)* **1** occurrence, event, happening **MND** IV.i.67 [Oberon to Puck] *think no more of this night's accidents;* **1H4** I.ii.205; **Ham** IV.vii.120; **MA** II.i.166; **Oth** I.i.143; **Tem** V.i.250, 306
2 chance, fortune, fate **Cym** V.v.76 [Lucius to Cymbeline] *Consider, sir, the chance of war, the day / Was yours by accident;* **Cym** V.v.278; **Oth** IV.i.269; **Sonn** 124.5

accidental *(adj.)* happening by chance, fortuitous **MM** III.i.152 [Isabella to Claudio] *Thy sin's not accidental, but a trade;* **Luc** 326

accite *(v.)* **1** cite, summon, call **2H4** V.ii.141 [King Henry V to all] *Our coronation done, we will accite ... all our state;* **Tit** I.i.27
2 arouse, induce, excite **2H4** II.ii.56 [Prince Henry to Poins, of being thought a hypocrite] *what accites your most worshipful thought to think so?*

accommodate *(v.)* **1** furnish, equip **2H4** III.ii.65 [Bardolph to Shallow] *a soldier is better accommodated than with a wife;* **KL** IV.vi.81
2 aid, help, give an advantage **Cym** V.iii.32 [Posthumus to Lord, of the youths' situation] *Accommodated by the place*

accommodation *(n.)* amenity, convenience, comfort **MM** III.i.14 [disguised Duke to Claudio] *all th'accommodations that thou bear'st / Are nursed by baseness*

accomplement *(n.)* equipment, military trappings **E3** IV.vi.39 [Philip to King John, of their army] *Arrayed and fenced in all accomplements*

accomplice *(n.)* associate, partner, aide **1H6** V.ii.9 [Scout to Charles] *Success unto our valiant general, / And happiness to his accomplices!*

accomplish *(v.)* **1** equip, provide, furnish **H5** IV.Chorus.12 [Chorus] *The armourers, accomplishing the knights;* **MV** III.iv.61; **R2** II.i.177
2 get possession of, gain, obtain **3H6** III.ii.152 [Richard alone, of the idea of him bewitching ladies] *more unlikely / Than to accomplish twenty golden crowns!*
3 perform, do, carry out **TS** Induction.i.110 [Lord to Servant, of Page behaving as a woman] *Such as he hath observed in noble ladies / Unto their lords, by them accomplished*

accomplishment *(n.)* fulfilment, consummation **Luc** 716 [of Tarquin's rape of Lucrece] *Who this accomplishment so hotly chased*

accompt ✒ account *(n./v.)*

accord *(n.)* **1** harmony, agreement **H5** V.ii.345 [French King to King Henry, of the treaty between France and England] *this dear conjunction / Plant ... Christian-like accord / In their sweet bosoms;* **AY** I.i.60; **TS** III.i.71
2 agreement, assent, consent **Ham** I.ii.123 [Claudius to his court] *This gentle and unforced accord of Hamlet / Sits smiling to my heart;* **CE** II.i.25; **TC** I.iii.238

accord *(v.)* agree, assent, consent **E3** II.ii.26 [Derby to King Edward] *The emperor ... hath accorded to your highness' suit;* **AY** V.iv.130; **H5** II.i.86; **Lover** 3

accordant *(adj.)* sympathetic, ready to agree, responsive **MA** I.ii.12 [Antonio to Leonato, of the Prince and Hero] *if he found her accordant*

according *(adj.)* agreeing, assenting **RJ** I.ii.19 [Capulet to Paris, of Juliet] *within her scope of choice / Lies my consent and fair according voice*

according *(adv.)* accordingly **MM** V.i.479 [Duke to Barnadine] *thou art said to have a stubborn soul ... / And squar'st thy life according*

according as *(prep.)* according to **E3** II.ii.31 [Audley to King Edward] *I have ... levied those horse and foot / According as your charge*

accordingly *(adv.)* correspondingly, suitably, properly **AW** II.v.8 [Bertram to Lafew, of Parolles] *he is very great in knowledge, and accordingly valiant*

accost *(v.)* approach, make up to, pay court to **TN** I.iii.53 [Sir Toby to Sir Andrew, of Maria] *'Accost' is front her, board her, woo her, assail her;* **TN** I.iii.46

accosting *(n.)* [unclear meaning] making of advances, coming on **TC** IV.v.59 [Ulysses to Nestor] *these encounterers, so glib of tongue, / That give accosting welcome ere it comes* [F, Q *a coasting*] ✒ coasting *(adj.)*

account, accompt *(n.)* **1** reckoning, judgement [especially by God] **Ham** I.v.78 [Ghost to Hamlet] *No reckoning made, but sent to my account / With all my imperfections on my head;* **Mac** V.i.37 [Lady Macbeth as if to Macbeth, while sleepwalking] *none can call our power to accompt;* **E3** II.ii.164; **LL** V.ii.200; **MM** II.iv.58; **Oth** I.iii.5 ✒ count *(n.)* 1
2 reckoning, debt, sum owing **Tim** II.ii.138 [Flavius to Timon] *At many times I brought in my accounts;* **R2** I.i.130
3 reckoning, count, estimate **R3** V.iii.11 [King Richard to Norfolk, of the numbers of the enemy] *our battalia trebles that account*
4 number, collection, assortment **RJ** V.i.45 [Romeo alone, of an apothecary] *about his shelves / A beggarly account of empty boxes*
5 expectation, precedent, normal explanation **WT** II.iii.197 [Lord to Leontes, of Cleomenes and Dion's return from the oracle] *their speed / Hath been beyond accompt*

account / accompt, cast make calculations, do arithmetic **2H6** IV.ii.81 [Smith to Cade, of the Clerk] *he can write and read and cast accompt*

account, accompt *(v.)* **1** reckon, judge, consider **MV** IV.i.414 [Portia as Balthasar to Antonio] *I delivering you am satisfied, / And therein do account myself well paid;* **Cym** I.vii.80; **KJ** III.i.122
2 take account of, esteem, appreciate **TG** II.i.58 [Valentine to Speed, of Silvia] *I account of her beauty*

accountant *(adj.)* accountable, responsible, answerable **MM** II.iv.86 [Angelo to Isabella, of Claudio] *his offence is ... / Accountant to the law;* **Oth** II.i.284

accouter, accoutre *(v.)* attire, equip, array **MV** III.iv.63 [Portia to Nerissa] *When we are both accoutered like young men;* **JC** I.ii.105

accoutrement *(n.)* formal embellishment, special trappings **MW** IV.ii.4 [Falstaff to Mistress Ford, of repaying her] *not only ... in the simple office of love, but in all the accoutrement, complement, and ceremony of it;* **KJ** I.i.211

accoutrements, accoustrements *(n.)* clothes, outfit, attire **TS** III.iii.118 [Petruchio to Baptista] *I can change these poor accoutrements;* **AY** II.ii.367

accuse *(n.)* accusation, charge **2H6** III.i.160 [Gloucester to King York ... / By false accuse doth level at my life

accuse *(v.)* object to, find fault with, impugn **H8** II.iv.122 [Campeius to all, of Queen Katherine] *Stubborn to justice, apt to accuse it, and / Disdainful to be tried by't*

accustom *(n.)* custom, habit, routine **WT** IV.iv.12 [Perdita to Florizel] *our feasts / In every mess have folly, and the feeders / Digest it with accustom* [F *a Custome*] [i.e. they are used to it]

ace *(n.)* one [lowest score on a dice] **Cym** II.iii.2 [First Lord to Cloten] *Your lordship is ... the most coldest that ever turned up ace;* **MND** V.i.299 ✒ ames-ace *(n.)*, deuce-ace *(n.)*

acerb, acerbe *(adj.)* bitter, sour, tart **Oth** I.iii.345 [Iago to Roderigo, of Othello] *The food that to him now is as luscious as locusts shall be to him shortly as acerbe as the coloquintida* [Q1; F *bitter*]

achieve *(v.)* **1** gain, obtain, procure **Cor** I.ix.33 [Cominius to Martius] *all / The treasure in this field achieved;* **AW** I.i.44; **Oth** II.i.61; **Sonn** 67.3; **TNK** III.i.112; **TS** I.i.153
2 accomplish an intention, perform successfully **Cor** IV.vii.23 [Aufidius to Lieutenant, of Coriolanus] *he ... does achieve as soon / As draw his sword*
3 finish off, bring to an end, kill **H5** IV.iii.91 [King Henry to Montjoy, of the French] *Bid them achieve me, and then sell my bones* [also: sense 1]

achievement (*n.*) feat, accomplishment, successful action **2H4** IV.v.189 [King Henry IV to Prince Henry, of getting the crown] *all the soil of the achievement goes / With me into the earth;* **TC** I.ii.293

acknow on (*v.*) admit to, confess, acknowledge **Oth** III.iii.316 [Iago to Emilia, of his taking Desdemona's handkerchief] *Be not acknown on't* [F, Q2; Q1 *not you known*]

aconitum (*n.*) variety of highly poisonous plant, aconite **2H4** IV.iv.48 [King Henry IV to Clarence, of his brothers] *the united vessel of their blood, / Mingled with venom of suggestion ... / Shall never leak, though it do work as strong / As aconitum* ☞ **PLANTS**, p.330

acquaintance (*n.*) friends, companions, associates **TS** I.i.34 [Tranio to Lucentio] *Balk logic with acquaintance that you have*

acquit (*adj.*) rid, free, relieved **MW** I.iii.22 [Falstaff to Nym, of Bardolph] *I am glad I am so acquit of this tinderbox* ☞ quit (*adj.*) 2

acquit (*v.*) **1** release, free, discharge **TN** III.iv.211 [Viola as Cesario to Olivia] *I will acquit you* [i.e. from your contract]; **2H4** Epilogue.17
2 pay back, requite, settle the score with **H5** II.ii.144 [King Henry to all, of the traitors] *God acquit them of their practices!;* **MV** V.i.138
3 play one's part, discharge one's responsibility **R3** V.v.3 [Derby to Richmond] *well hast thou acquit thee;* **AY** I.i.120
4 atone for, pay for, do penance for **Luc** 1071 [Lucrece to herself] *I ... with my trespass never will dispense, / Till life to death acquit my forced offence*

acquittance (*n.*) **1** satisfaction, settlement, discharge **Oth** IV.ii.190 [Roderigo to Iago, of Desdemona] *she hath... returned me expectations and comforts of sudden respect and acquittance* [Q1; F *acquaintance*]
2 acquittal, exoneration, excusing **Ham** IV.vii.1 [Claudius to Laertes] *Now must your conscience my acquittance seal;* **Cym** V.iv.171
3 written discharge, final receipt **LL** II.i.161 [Princess to Boyet, of the money owing] *you can produce acquittances / For such a sum*

acquittance (*v.*) acquit, discharge, exonerate **R3** III.vii.232 [Richard to all, of being made to accept the kingship] *Your mere enforcement shall acquittance me / From all the impure blots and stains thereof*

across (*adv.*) **1** folded, crossed **Luc** 1662 [of Collatine] *With sad set eyes and wretched arms across;* **JC** II.i.240
2 from side to side, all the way across **TN** V.i.173 [Sir Andrew to Olivia, of Sebastian] *He's broke my head across*
3 [of a lance] not straight, obliquely; awry, amiss **AW** II.i.67 [Lafew to King, responding to his 'so I had broke thy pate'] *Good faith, across!*

act (*n.*) **1** activity, action, performance **Cym** V.v.265 [Cymbeline to Innogen] *mak'st thou me a dullard in this act?;* **Ham** I.iii.26; **KJ** III.i.274; **MV** I.iii.80, IV.i.19; **WT** V.ii.77
2 action (upon a person), effect **Ham** I.ii.205 [Horatio to Hamlet, of the sentinels] *distilled / Almost to jelly with the act of fear;* **AC** II.ii.119; **Cym** I.vi.22; **Oth** III.iii.325
3 progress, operation, action **Oth** I.i.152 [Iago to Roderigo] *the Cyprus wars, / Which even now stand in act*
4 event, deed, happening **Oth** V.ii.367 [Lodovico to all] *This heavy act with heavy heart relate*
5 performance, staging, production **Mac** I.iii.127 [Macbeth to himself] *Two truths are told / As happy prologues to the swelling Act / Of the imperial theme*
6 play interval, interlude **MND** III.ii.463 [stage direction, of the lovers] *They sleep all the act* [F]

act (*v.*) **1** act out, perform, enact **TNK** V.iii.14 [Theseus to Pirithous] *Nature now / Shall make and act the story;* **AC** IV.ii.45; **Tem** I.ii.273
2 enact, enforce, bring about **2H6** V.i.103 [York to and of the King] *Here is a hand ... to act controlling laws;* **RJ** III.ii.16
3 commit adultery, be promiscuous **MW** IV.ii.100 [Mistress Page to Mistress Ford] *We do not act that often jest and laugh*

Actaeon (*n.*) cuckold **MW** III.ii.39 [Ford alone] *I will ... divulge Page himself for a secure and wilful Actaeon* ☞ **CLASSICAL MYTHOLOGY**, p.613

action (*n.*) **1** campaign, military action, strategy **MA** I.i.6 [Leonato to Messenger] *How many gentlemen have you lost in this action;* **AC** III.vii.68; **Cor** IV.vii.7, V.vi.48; **2H4** I.iii.37, IV.i.190
2 engagement, combat, fighting **TC** IV.v.113 [Agamemnon to all, of Hector and Ajax] *They are in action;* **2H6** V.ii.26; **Oth** I.iii.180; **TNK** I.i.173, ii.97
3 encounter, engagement, exploit **1H4** II.iv.20 [Prince Hal to Poins] *thou hast lost much honour that thou wert not with me in this action* [drinking]; **2H4** I.iii.153
4 law-suit, legal proceeding, litigation **Cym** III.iii.150 [Innogen to Cloten, of her words] *If you will make't an action, call witness to't;* **2H4** II.i.1, 149, V.i.74; **Oth** I.iii.70; **TS** III.ii.233
5 course of action, enterprise; or: trial, legal process **WT** II.i.121 [Hermione to her Ladies] *This action I now go on / Is for my better grace*
6 performance, acting, theatre presentation **Per** III.Chorus.55 [Gower alone, of his story] *action may / Conveniently the rest convey*
7 performance, exercises, acts **Ham** III.i.48 [Polonius to Ophelia] *'Tis too much proved, that with devotion's visage / And pious action we do sugar o'er / The devil himself;* **MW** I.iii.42
8 movement, demeanour, gesture **Ham** III.ii.17 [Hamlet to Players] *Suit the action to the word, the word to the action;* **Ham** III.iv.129; **H5** III.i.6; **JC** II.ii.223; **Mac** V.i.28; **MW** IV.v.109

action-taking (*adj.*) taking legal action, litigious **KL** II.ii.15 [disguised Kent to Oswald, describing him] *a lily-livered, action-taking ... rogue*

actor (*n.*) doer, performer **MM** II.ii.41 [Angelo to Isabella] *To fine the faults whose fine stands in record, / And let go by the actor;* **AW** II.iii.23; **Luc** 608

actual (*adj.*) active, involving specific activity **Oth** IV.ii.152 [Desdemona to Iago, of her offending Othello] *Either in discourse of thought or actual deed;* **Mac** V.i.12

acture (*n.*) action, performance, process of acting **Lover** 185 [of the woman's offences] *Love made them not, with acture they may be, / Where neither party is nor true nor kind*

adage (*n.*) proverb, saying, maxim **3H6** I.iv.126 [York to Queen] *the adage must be verified;* **Mac** I.vii.45

adamant (*n.*) legendary substance of great hardness and magnetism **MND** II.i.195 [Helena to Demetrius] *You draw me, you hard-hearted adamant;* **1H6** I.iv.52; **TC** III.ii.177

addiction (*n.*) inclination, leaning, bent **H5** I.i.54 [Canterbury to Ely, of King Henry] *his addiction was to courses vain;* **Oth** II.ii.5

addition (*n.*) **1** title, name **MW** II.ii.283 [Ford alone, of the names of various devils] *they are devils' additions, the names of fiends;* **AW** II.iii.126; **Oth** IV.i.104, ii.162; **TC** I.iii.244, III.ii.92 ☞ sur-addition (*n.*)
2 attribute, mark of honour, distinction [as if added to a coat of arms] **Cor** I.ix.71 [Coriolanus to Cominius] *I mean ... / To undercrest your good addition* **AW** II.ii.3; **KL** II.ii.22, V.iii.69, 299; **Mac** III.i.99; **TC** V.v.141
3 external honour, distinctive style **KL** I.i.136 [Lear to Cornwall and Albany] *Only we shall retain / The name and all th'addition to a king*
4 polite form of address, style of address **Ham** II.i.47 [Polonius to Reynaldo] *According to the phrase or the addition / Of man and country*
5 exaggeration, overstatement **Ham** IV.iv.17 [Captain to Hamlet] *Truly to speak, and with no addition*
6 advantage, credit, plus **Oth** III.iv.190 [Cassio to Bianca, of Othello] *[I] think it no addition ... / To have him see me womaned*

addle (*adj.*) addled, rotten, putrid **TC** I.ii.133 [Pandarus to Cressida, of Troilus and Helen] *he esteems her no more than I esteem an addle egg;* **RJ** III.i.23

address (*v.*) **1** prepare, make ready, poise to act **AY** V.iv.153 [Jaques de Boys to all] *Duke Frederick ... / Addressed a mighty power;* **Ham** I.ii.216; **H5** III.iii.58; **Mac** II.ii.24; **MND** V.i.106; **WT** IV.iv.53
2 dress, array, attire **Per** II.iii.94 [Simonides to Knights] *in your armours, as you are addressed* [i.e. as you are]
3 direct, apply, turn **MND** II.ii.149 [Lysander to himself] *all my powers, address your love and might / To honour Helen and to be her knight;* **LL** V.ii.92; **MW** III.v.122; **TN** I.iv.15
4 make a formal address **KL** I.i.190 [Lear to Burgundy] *We first address toward you*

adhere (*v.*) **1** agree, suit, fit the circumstances **MW** II.i.57 [Mistress Ford to Mistress Page, of Falstaff's words and actions] *they do no more adhere and keep place together;* **Mac** I.vii.52
2 belong, be relevant, relate **WT** IV.i.28 [Time to audience] *A shepherd's daughter, / And what to her adheres, which follows after, / Is th'argument of Time*

adieu (*int.*) ☞ **FAREWELLS**, p.170

adjourn (*v.*) postpone, defer, put off **Cym** V.iv.78 [First Brother as if to Jove, of Posthumus] *why hast thou thus adjourned / The graces for his merits due*

adjudge (*v.*) **1** sentence, condemn **CE** I.i.147 [Duke to Egeon] *thou art adjudged to the death;* **MM** V.i.400
2 award, grant, bestow **3H6** IV.vi.34 [George to Warwick] *the heavens in thy nativity / Adjudged an olive branch;* **Tit** V.iii.143

adjunct (*n.*) **1** annex, addendum, extra function **LL** IV.iii.294 [F/Q additional lines] [Berowne to all] *Learning is but an adjunct to ourself*
2 aid, aide-memoire, assistant **Sonn** 122.13 *To keep an adjunct to remember thee, / Were to import forgetfulness in me*

adjunct (*adj.*) **1** attendant [upon], inevitable result [of] **KJ** III.iii.57 [Hubert to King John, of obeying him] *Though that my death were adjunct to my act ... I would do it;* **Luc** 133
2 connected, associated, annexed **Sonn** 91.5 *And every humour hath his adjunct pleasure*

admirable (*adj.*) wondrous, marvellous, extraordinary **MND** V.i.27 [Hippolyta to Theseus, of the events of the night] *strange and admirable;* **KL** I.ii.126; **MW** II.ii.218; **WT** IV.iv.204

admirable (*adv.*) wonderfully **Cym** II.iii.17 [Cloten to musicians, of their playing to Innogen] *a wonderful sweet air, with admirable rich words to it*

admiral (*n.*) admiral's ship, flagship **E3** III.i.73 [Mariner to King John, of the English fleet] *on the top gallant of the admiral;* **AC** III.x.2; **E3** III.i.148; **1H4** III.iii.25

admiration (*n.*) **1** amazement, astonishment, wonder **Ham** I.ii.192 [Horatio to Hamlet, while telling him of the Ghost] *Season your admiration for a while;* **Cym** I.vii.38; **Ham** III.ii.334; **H5** II.ii.108; **Tem** III.i.38; **WT** V.ii.11
2 object of wonder, marvel, phenomenon **AW** II.i.88 [King to Lafew, of Helena] *Bring in the admiration*

admire (*v.*) **1** marvel, wonder, be astonished [at] **2H6** III.i.12 [Queen to the King, of Gloucester] *all the court admired him for submission;* **Cor** I.ix.5; **H5** III.vii.123; **Sonn** 123.5; **Tem** V.i.154; **TN** III.iv.149
2 revere, marvel at, respect **TS** I.i.29 [Tranio to Lucentio, of moral discipline] *we do admire / This virtue*

admired (*adj.*) **1** wonderful, amazing, remarkable **Mac** III.iv.109 [Lady Macbeth to Macbeth] *You have ... broke the good meeting / With most admired disorder;* **Cym** I.i.32
2 regarded with admiration, wondered at **Tem** III.i.37 [Ferdinand to Miranda] *Admired Miranda! / Indeed, the top of admiration* [also: sense 1]; **AC** II.ii.124; **3H6** I.iv.130; **RJ** I.i.83; **Tim** V.i.49

admiring (*adj.*) marvelling, filled with wonder **WT** V.iii.41 [Leontes to Paulina, of Hermione's statue] *There's magic in thy majesty, which has / My evils conjured to remembrance, and / From thy admiring daughter took the spirits*

admit (*v.*) **1** permit, allow, grant **CE** I.i.15 [Duke to Egeon, of the decree] *To admit no traffic to our adverse towns;* **Cor** V.vi.20; **Ham** III.i.108; **KJ** II.i.200; **Tem** I.ii.152; **TN** I.ii.46
2 consent to keep company with, have to do with **2H4** II.iv.247 [Falstaff to Doll, of Poins] *such other gambol faculties 'a has ... for the which the Prince admits him*
3 include, take into account **AC** V.ii.140 [Cleopatra to Caesar, of her list of valuables] *Not petty things admitted*
4 be compatible with, be capable of **TC** IV.iv.9 [Cressida to Pandarus] *My love admits no qualifying dross*

admittance (*n.*) **1** fashion, acceptance, vogue **MW** III.iii.54 [Falstaff to Mistress Ford] *Thou hast the right arched beauty of the brow that becomes ... any tire of Venetian admittance*
2 entry into society, social presence, admissibility **MW** II.ii.218 [Ford to Falstaff] *Now, Sir John ... you are a gentleman of excellent breeding ... of great admittance* [also: sense 1]
3 permission to enter **LL** II.i.80 [Princess to Boyet, of her request to see the King] *Now, what admittance, lord?*

admonish (*v.*) inform, forewarn, notify **1H6** V.iii.3 [Pucelle alone] *Now help ... ye choice spirits that admonish me*

admonishment (*n.*) warning, caution **1H6** II.v.98 [Richard to Mortimer] *Thy grave admonishments prevail with me;* **TC** V.iii.2

admonition (*n.*) warning, cautioning, exhortation **MM** III.ii.184 [Escalus to Mistress Overdone] *Double and treble admonition, and still forfeit in the same kind?*

ado (*n.*) fuss, business, to-do **KL** IV.v.2 [Oswald to Regan, of Albany's going to battle] *with much ado;* **MA** title; **MV** I.i.7; **RJ** III.iv.23; **Tit** II.i.98; **Venus** 694

adoptedly (*adv.*) through adoption **MM** I.iv.47 [Isabella to Lucio, of Juliet, responding to 'Is she your cousin?'] *Adoptedly, as school-maids change their names / By vain though apt affection*

adoption (*n.*) association, relationship **Ham** I.iii.62 [Polonius to Laertes] *Those friends thou hast, and their adoption tried, / Grapple them unto thy soul*

adoptious (*adj.*) adopted, appropriated, taken up **AW** I.i.171 [Helena to Parolles] *a world / Of pretty, fond, adoptious christendoms* [i.e. nicknames]

adoring (*n.*) reverence, expression of respect [towards] **Tim** I.i.143 [stage direction] *The Lords rise from table, with much adoring of Timon*

adorning (*n.*) adornment, decoration, ornamentation **AC** II.ii.213 [Enobarbus to Agrippa and Maecenas, of Cleopatra] *Her gentlewomen ... made their bends adornings*

adulterate (*adj.*) adulterous **CE** II.ii.149 [Adriana to Antipholus of Syracuse] *I am possessed with an adulterate blot;* **E3** II.i.111; **Ham** I.v.42; **Luc** 1645; **R3** IV.iv.69; **Sonn** 121.5

adulterate (*v.*) commit adultery, fornicate **KJ** III.i.56 [Constance to Arthur, of fortune] *She adulterates hourly with thine uncle John*

advance (*v.*) **1** raise, lift up, upraise **Cor** II.i.154 [Volumnia to Menenius, of Coriolanus' arm] *Which, being advanced, declines, and then men die;* **H5** II.ii.192; **1H6** I.vi.1; **R3** V.iii.265; **Tem** I.ii.409, IV.i.177
2 display, present, promote **MW** III.iv.79 [Fenton to Mistress Page] *against all checks, rebukes, and manners, / I must advance the colours of my love;* **MND** III.ii.128; **RJ** V.iii.96; **Tim** I.ii.168
3 be active, go forward **TNK** I.ii.112 [Palamon to Arcite] *Our hands advanced before our hearts* [i.e. our hearts are not in our actions]

advanced (*adj.*) raised up, held high, uplifted **TN** II.v.31 [Fabian to Sir Andrew and Sir Toby, of Malvolio] *how he jets under his advanced plumes!;* **Cor** I.vi.61; **TC** IV.v.188

advancement (*n.*) preferment, elevation, progress **Ham** III.ii.67 [Hamlet to Horatio] *what advancement may I hope from thee;* **2H4** V.v.82; **1H6** II.v.69; **KL** II.iv.195; **WT** IV.iv.829

ADDRESS FORMS

When people directly address each other with courtesy or affection, they may choose to use a proper noun (*Jane, Jones, Mrs Smith*) or a common noun (*darling, sir*) — or of course a combination of the two (*darling Jane*). Proper nouns may be informally shortened (*Katherine* > *Kate*) or adapted (*Edward* > *Ned, Yedward*), but there are far more possibilities using common nouns. The language of endearment is explicitly recognized by Falstaff as he addresses his companions (**1H4** II.iv.271): '*gallants, lads, boys, hearts of gold, all the titles of good fellowship*'.

The naming practice performs a variety of expressive functions, shading from courtesy through endearment into sarcasm and insult, and the exact nuance can be deduced only by taking careful note of who the personalities are and the context in which they are speaking. The following list illustrates some of the distinctive expressions in Shakespearian English, when used in direct address. A few may still be heard today, especially in regional dialects.

Item	Location	Personalities	Gloss
bawcock	**WT** I.ii.121	Leontes to Mamillius [father to child]	fine fellow, dear lad [often in parody]
	TN III.iv.112	Sir Toby to Malvolio [aristocrat to steward]	
	H5 III.ii.25	Pistol to Fluellen [soldier to officer]	
biddy	**TN** III.iv.115	Sir Toby to Malvolio [aristocrat to steward]	chicken [childish affectation]
bully	**MW** II.iii.18	Host to Doctor Caius [companions]	dear, excellent [encouragement, warm companionship]
	MND III.i.7	Quince to Bottom [co-actors]	
	Tem V.i.258	Stephano to Caliban [master to servant]	
captain	**1H6** V.iii.97	Margaret to Suffolk [nobles]	[to a senior person of no particular rank; also, familiar address to non-soldier]
	Tim II.ii.77	Page to Fool [acquaintances]	
	WT I.ii.122	Leontes to Mamillius [father to son]	
chuck	**Oth** III.iv.49	Othello to Desdemona [spouses]	chick, chicken [between spouses, to children; also in parody]
	LL V.i.105	Armado to Holofernes [aristocrat to schoolmaster]	
	TN III.iv.113	Sir Toby to Malvolio [aristocrat to steward]	
dame	**Mac** IV.ii.65	Messenger to Lady Macduff	lady, mistress [formally polite]
	AC IV.iv.29	Antony to Cleopatra [lovers]	
	TS II.i.23	Baptista to Katherina [father to daughter]	girl [as reprimand]
	2H6 I.ii.42	Gloucester to Duchess [husband to wife]	woman [as reprimand]
father	**TS** IV.v.45	Katherina to Vincentio	[respectful to an old man]
	Cor V.i.3	Menenius reporting Coriolanus' words to him	
gallant	**MA** III.ii.14	Benedick to all [fellow-lords]	fine gentleman [often ironic or sarcastic]
	MW III.ii.1	Mistress Page to Robin [lady of the house to a page]	
	1H6 III.ii.41	Pucelle to the English [enemies]	
gentle	**WT** IV.iv.46	Florizel to Perdita [lovers]	dearest, dear one [polite intimate]
gentles	**H5** II.Chorus.35	Chorus to audience	ladies and gentlemen [formally polite, regardless of rank]
	LL II.i.211	Princess to all	
	MND V.i.126	Quince to the play audience	
gentleman	**TN** III.i.76	Sir Toby to Viola as Cesario [knight to gentleman]	sir [formally polite, regardless of social rank]
	MND III.i.179	Bottom to Peaseblossom [Queen's consort to fairy attendant]	
	RJ II.ii.100	Juliet to Romeo [lovers]	[conveying sincerity]
gentlewoman	**TG** IV.iv.105	Julia to Silvia [as if messenger to lady]	madam [formally polite]
	RJ II.iv.107	Mercutio to Nurse [noble to member of household]	[mock polite]
goodman	**LL** IV.ii.37	Holofernes to Dull [schoolmaster to constable]	mister, master [dignified, respectful]
	RJ I.v.77	Capulet to Tybalt [head of family to nephew]	[as a reprimand]
	Ham V.i.14	Second Clown to First Clown	[mock politeness]
gossip	**MW** IV.ii.8	Mistress Page to Mistress Ford [friends]	friend, neighbour [usually, woman to woman]
heart	**Cym** I.ii.43	Innogen to Posthumus [lovers]	sweetheart
	RJ I.i.184	Romeo to Benvolio [friends]	dear friend
	RJ I.v.88	Capulet to all [host to guests]	dear friends

ADDRESS FORMS – *continued*

Item	Location	Personalities	Gloss
lady	MA II.i.283	Claudio to Beatrice [lord to a lady at court]	madam [very formal; also, as 'my lady']
	Oth III.iv.36	Othello to Desdemona [spouses]	
	TN V.i.256	Sebastian to Olivia [lovers]	
liege	R2 II.i.147	Northumberland to Richard [lord to king]	lord, sovereign [subject to king; usually 'my liege']
lordings	2H6 I.i.143	Gloucester to all [lord to other lords]	my lords, gentlemen
master	TN IV.ii.27	Sir Toby to Feste as Sir Topas [aristocrat to parson]	[dignified term for a professional person; sometimes applied inappropriately by lower classes, e.g. to a sergeant or yeoman]
	2H4 II.i.i	Hostess to Fang [lady to sergeant]	
	MV II.ii.43	Launcelot to Gobbo [of himself]	
masters	1H6 I.i.152	Bedford to all [lord to other lords]	sirs, gentlemen [formally polite; condescending to social inferiors; often as 'my masters']
	Ham II.ii.420	Hamlet to Players	
	TS I.ii.18	Grumio calling the inhabitants of a house	
mouse	LL V.ii.19	Rosaline to Katharine [friends]	little one [playful, usually to a woman]
	Ham III.iv.184	[Hamlet imagining] Claudius to Gertrude [spouses]	
	TN I.v.58	Feste to Olivia [fool to employer]	
signor, signior	MA V.i.110	Claudio to Benedick [lord to lord]	sir [friendly approach; also as 'good signor'; not restricted to Italy]
	MND IV.i.16	Bottom to Cobweb [Queen's consort to fairy attendant]	
	1H6 III.ii.67	Alençon to Talbot [enemies]	[mock friendliness]
sir	TN IV.ii.17	Sir Toby to Feste as Sir Topas [aristocrat to parson]	[respectful title for a priest, clerk, or other professional; often mock use]
	WT I.ii.135	Leontes to Mamillius [father to son]	
sirs	AC IV.xv.84	Cleopatra to Charmian and Iras	[unusual use to women]
sirrah	KL I.ii.78	Lear to Edmund [father to son]	sir [authoritative]
	TS I.ii.19	Petruchio to Grumio [master to servant]	[authoritative]
	KJ II.i.140	Bastard to Austria [aristocratic adversaries]	[contemptuous]
	KL I.iv.114	Fool to Lear [fool to master]	[familiar]
	Mac IV.ii.31	Lady Macduff to Son [mother to son]	[playful]
sweet	TNK I.i.217	Theseus to Hippolyta [engaged couple]	sweetheart [between spouses and lovers]
	MV II.vi.44	Lorenzo to Jessica [lovers]	
	TG II.iv.152	Valentine to Proteus [good companions]	dear friend [uncommon between men]
sweetheart sweet heart	MW IV.ii.10	Mistress Page to Mistress Ford [friends]	dear
	AW II.iii.266	Parolles to Bertram [friends]	dear friend
	TN III.iv.29	Malvolio to Olivia [as a lover]	darling
	2H4 II.iv.178	Pistol to his sword	darling [with mock affection]
sweeting	Oth II.iii.246	Othello to Desdemona [spouses]	darling
	TS IV.iii.36	Petruchio to Katherina [as lover]	
wench	TS III.ii.237	Petruchio to Katherina [as spouse]	lass, girl [affectionate to wife, daughter, or sweetheart]
	TNK II.i.181	Emilia to Woman [mistress to maid]	
	Tem I.ii.139	Prospero to Miranda [father to daughter]	
worship, your	MA V.i.319	Dogberry to Leonato [constable to governor]	[great respect; also used for mock effect]
	MW II.ii.39	Mistress Quickly to Falstaff [housekeeper to knight]	
	Cor II.i.88	Menenius to Brutus and Sicinius [friend of Coriolanus to enemies]	

➤ COUSIN, p.106

advantage (*n.*) **1** right moment, favourable opportunity 2H6 I.i.240 [York alone] *I will … when I spy advantage, claim the crown;* Cor IV.i.43; 1H4 II.iv.527; H5 III.vi.118; Mac V.iv.11; Tem III.iii.14 ☛ vantage (*n.*) 1

2 advantageous position, place of vantage, superiority AC IV.xi.4 [Caesar to all] *To the vales, / And hold our best advantage;* Ham I.ii.21; 1H6 IV.iv.19; KJ II.i.40; R2 III.iii.42; Sonn 64.6 ☛ vantage (*n.*) 2

3 benefit, gain, advancement, profit MM III.i.246 [disguised Duke to Isabella] *refer yourself to this advantage;* 1H4 I.i.27; 2H6 III.i.25; KJ II.i.206, 577; MV II.vii.19; MW II.iii.103 ☛ vantage (*n.*) 3

4 interest, bonus, addition 1H4 II.v.532 [Prince Hal to Peto] *The money shall be paid back again with advantage;* AW I.iii.98; KJ III.iii.22; MV I.iii.67; TG II.iv.66

5 addition, enhancement, exaggeration H5 IV.iii.50 [King Henry to all, of a survivor of the battle] *he'll remember, with advantages, / What feats he did that day*

advantage, on that to gain those benefits, receiving those advantages 1H6 IV.vi.44 [John Talbot to Talbot, of the benefits of fleeing] *On that advantage, bought with such a shame*

advantage (*v.*) **1** benefit, help, aid TG III.ii.42 [Duke to Proteus, of Valentine] *your good word cannot advantage him;* H5 IV.v.277; JC III.i.242; MM III.i.255; Tem I.i.32; Venus 950

2 enrich, augment, add value to R3 IV.iv.323 [King Richard to Queen Elizabeth] *The liquid drops of tears that you have shed / Shall come again … / Advantaging their love*

3 ☛ vantage (*n./v.*)

advantageable (*adj.*) advantageous, profitable, beneficial H5 V.ii.88 [King Henry to Council members, of altering the treaty] *as your wisdoms best / Shall see advantageable for our dignity*

advantageous (*adj.*) providing advantage, opportune, timely TC V.iv.21 [Diomedes to Troilus] *advantageous care / Withdrew me from the odds of multitude*

adventure (*n.*) **1** venture, enterprise, issue, hazard TNK III.vi.119 [Palamon to Arcite] *I will no more be hidden, nor put off / This great adventure to a second trial;* CE II.ii.226; Cym III.i.82; 1H4 V.ii.95; 3H6 IV.ii.18; KJ V.v.22

2 experience, fortune, chance AY II.iv.41 [Rosalind, as if to Silvius] *searching of thy wound, / I have by hard adventure found mine own*

adventure, at randomly, on the spur of the moment TNK I.iii.75 [Emilia to Hippolyta] *had mine ear / Stolen some new air, or at adventure hummed one*

adventures, at all whatever might happen, regardless of the risks H5 IV.i.113 [Bates to disguised King Henry, of the King wishing himself in the Thames] *so I would he were, and I by him, at all adventures, so we were quit here*

adventure (*v.*) venture, dare, chance, risk R3 I.iii.115 [Richard to Queen Elizabeth] *I dare adventure to be sent to the Tower;* Cym I.vii.172; 1H4 I.ii.169; 2H6 III.ii.350; TG III.i.120; WT II.iii.161

adventurous (*adj.*) risk-taking, imprudently bold, rashly daring Per I.i.36 [Antiochus to Pericles] *princes … adventurous by desire;* Tit V.iii.111

adversary (*n.*) intentional substitute for 'emissary' MW II.iii.85 [Host to Caius] *I will be thy adversary toward Anne Page*

adverse (*adj.*) **1** unfavourable, harmful, hostile 1H6 I.i.54 [Bedford, as if to the spirit of Henry V] *Combat with adverse planets in the heavens!;* AW V.i.26

2 opposing, opposite, other E3 IV.vi.50 [King John to all] *The twentieth part / Of those that live are men enow to quail / The feeble handful on the adverse part*

3 hostile, belligerent, antagonistic CE I.i.15 [Duke to Egeon, of the decree] *To admit no traffic to our adverse towns;* KJ IV.ii.172

adversity (*n.*) piece of perversity, quibbler TC V.i.12 [Patroclus to Thersites] *Well said, adversity!*

advertise, advertize (*v.*) **1** make aware, inform, notify; warn TNK III.i.58 [Arcite to Palamon] *you have been well advertised / How much I dare;* 2H6 IV.ix.23; 3H6 II.i.115, IV.v.9, V.iii.18; R3 IV.iv.499

2 make known, instruct, inform about MM I.i.41 [Duke to Angelo] *I do bend my speech / To one that can my part in him advertise*

advertisement (*n.*) **1** advice, warning, instruction 1H4 IV.i.36 [Hotspur to Worcester, of Northumberland] *Yet doth he give us bold advertisement;* AW III.iii.208; MA V.i.32

2 news, information, notification 1H4 III.ii.172 [King Henry to all, of Blunt's report] *this advertisement is five days old*

advertising (*adj.*) attending, attentive, mindful MM V.i.380 [Duke to Isabella] *I was then / Advertising and holy to your business*

advice (*n.*) **1** consideration, reflection, deliberation MV II.ii.6 [Gratiano to Portia as Balthasar] *My Lord Bassanio upon more advice / Hath sent you here this ring;* Cym I.i.87; H5 II.i.43; 2H6 II.ii.68; MM V.i.461; TG III.i.73

2 judgement, opinion, warning TNK III.i.60 [Arcite to Palamon] *you've seen me use my sword / Against th'advice of fear;* Mac IV.ii.68

3 forethought, discretion, wisdom AW III.iv.19 [Countess to Rynaldo, of Helena] *you did never lack advice so much / As letting her pass so*

4 medical opinion Luc 907 [Lucrece as if to opportunity] *Advice is sporting while infection breeds*

advise, avise (*v.*) **1** consider, take thought, reflect KL II.i.27 [Edmund to Edgar] *Advise yourself;* CE V.i.214; RJ III.v.191; TN IV.ii.94

2 warn, counsel, caution KL V.i.2 [Edmund to a gentleman] *Know of the Duke if … he is advised by aught / To change the course;* AW III.v.25; 1H4 IV.iii.5; 2H6 II.iv.36; KL III.vii.9; MW I.i.154

3 inform, be aware, apprise TG III.i.122 [Duke to Valentine] *Advise me where I may have such a ladder;* 2H4 I.i.172; H5 II.Chorus.12; H8 I.ii.107; MM II.ii.132; TS I.i.183

advised, avised (*adj.*) **1** calculated, premeditated, intentional R2 I.iii.188 [King Richard to Bolingbroke and Mowbray] *never by advised purpose meet / To plot;* KJ IV.ii.214

2 agreed, in accord, determined Luc 1849 [of the lords and Brutus swearing revenge] *When they had sworn to this advised doom;* 2H6 II.i.47

3 judicious, wise, prudent H5 I.ii.179 [Exeter to all] *Th'advised head defends itself at home;* 2H6 V.ii.47; MV I.i.142; Sonn 49.4

advisedly (*adv.*) **1** attentively, watchfully, carefully Venus 457 [of Venus, and Adonis' expression] *This ill presage advisedly she marketh;* Luc 1527

2 wisely, prudently, judiciously Luc 1816 *Brutus … armed his long-hid wits advisedly / To check the tears in Collatinus' eyes*

3 deliberately, intentionally, with full awareness MV V.i.253 [Antonio to Portia, of Bassanio] *your lord / Will never more break faith advisedly;* Luc 180

advocation (*n.*) advocacy, pleading, entreating Oth III.iv.119 [Desdemona to Cassio] *My advocation is not now in tune*

aedile (*n.*) ☛ ROMAN HISTORY, p.377

aerial (*adj.*) airy, sky-clear Oth II.i.39 [Montano to all] *throw out our eyes for brave Othello, / Even till we make the main and th'aerial blue / An indistinct regard* [F *Eriall*]

aery (*n.*) brood [of a bird of prey], nestful R3 I.iii.269 [Queen Margaret to Richard] *Your aery buildeth in our aery's nest;* Ham II.ii.338; KJ V.ii.149; R3 I.iii.263

afar off (*adv.*) indirectly, in a roundabout way WT II.i.104 [Leontes to Lords, of Hermione] *He who shall speak for her is afar off guilty / But that he speaks* [i.e. shows a degree of guilt simply by speaking]; MW I.i.193

afeard (*adj.*) afraid, frightened, scared Ham V.ii.293 [Hamlet to Laertes] *I am afeard you make a wanton of me* ☛ FEW, p.xxi

affect (*n.*) **1** desire, passion, appetite LL I.i.149 [Berowne to King] *every man with his affects is born;* Oth I.iii.260

2 affection, warm feeling, regard **R2** I.iv.30 [King Richard to Aumerle, of people's feelings about Bolingbroke] *to banish their affects with him*

affect *(v.)* **1** incline to, like, favour, be drawn to **KL** I.i.1 [Kent to Gloucester] *I thought the King had more affected the Duke of Albany than Cornwall;* **Cor** IV.vi.32; **1H6** V.i.7; **2H6** III.i.375; **TS** I.i.40; **WT** IV.iv.417 ☛ affected *(adj.)* 1

2 love, like, be fond of **TNK** IV.iii.61 [Doctor to Gaoler, of the Gaoler's Daughter] *Understand you she ever affected any man ere she beheld Palamon?;* **1H6** V.v.57; **LL** I.ii.85, 161; **MA** I.i.275; **TG** III.i.82; **TNK** II.iii.2

3 assume, display, put on, practise in an artificial way **AW** I.i.51 [Countess to Helena, of ceasing her tears] *lest it be rather thought you affect a sorrow than to have't;* **Cor** V.iii.149; **KL** II.ii.94; **MM** I.i.4; **TC** V.v.178; **Tim** IV.iii.200

4 imitate, copy, mimic **TNK** I.ii.45 [Palamon to Arcite] *What need I / Affect another's gait;* **KJ** I.i.86

5 cultivate, aim at, seek out **Cor** II.ii.20 [First Officer to Second Officer, of Coriolanus] *to seem to affect the malice and displeasure of the people;* **Cor** III.iii.1; **Cym** V.v.38; **2H6** IV.vii.91; **LL** IV.ii.55; **MM** I.i.72

affectation *(n.)* ☛ affection *(n.)* 8

affected *(adj.)* **1** disposed, inclined, minded **R3** III.i.171 [Buckingham to Catesby] *sound thou Lord Hastings / How he doth stand affected to our purpose;* **KL** II.i.97; **LL** III.i.23; **MW** III.iv.89; **TG** I.iii.60; **TS** I.i.26 ☛ affect *(v.)* 1

2 devoted, totally in love [with] **TG** II.i.79 [Valentine to Speed, of Silvia] *I stand affected to her;* **LL** II.i.218; **Venus** 157

affectedly *(adv.)* fancifully, artificially, intricately **Lover** 48 [of letters] *With sleided silk, feat and affectedly / Enswathed*

affecting *(adj.)* affected, full of mannerism **MW** II.i.132 [Page to himself, of Nym] *I never heard such a drawling, affecting rogue* [F *drawling-affecting*]

affection *(n.)* **1** fancy, inclination, desire **1H4** III.ii.30 [King Henry to Prince Hal] *let me wonder … / At thy affections;* **Cor** I.i.102, 175; **Oth** I.i.36; **RJ** I.i.126; **TNK** I.iii.72; **TS** I.ii.72

2 emotion, feeling **JC** II.i.20 [Brutus alone, of Caesar] *I have not known when his affections swayed / More than his reason;* **Cor** II.iii.230; **E3** V.i.51; **Tem** I.ii.482; **TN** I.i.37; **TNK** I.i.229

3 desire, passion, lustful feeling **AC** III.xiii.7 [Enobarbus to Cleopatra, of Antony] *The itch of his affection;* **AC** I.v.12, 17; **Luc** 271; **MM** I.i.10; **Oth** IV.iii.97; **WT** I.ii.138

4 love, devotion **E3** II.i.134 [King Edward to Lodowick, of the Countess] *Her beauty hath no match but my affection;* **AC** III.xi.67; **MW** IV.v.10; **Tem** I.ii.449; **TG** I.i.3; **TNK** III.vi.269

5 object of affection **TNK** II.ii.266 [Palamon to Arcite] *I would quickly teach thee / What 'twere to filch affection from another!*

6 disposition, character, state of mind **WT** V.ii.36 [Third Gentleman to all, of Perdita] *the affection of nobleness which nature shows above her breeding;* **Lover** 97; **Mac** IV.iii.77

7 partiality, biased feeling **RJ** III.i.177 [Lady Capulet to Prince, of Benvolio] *Affection makes him false*

8 affectation, posing, artificiality **LL** V.i.4 [Nathaniel to Holofernes] *Your reasons at dinner have been … witty without affection;* **Ham** II.ii.442; **LL** V.ii.407

affection *(v.)* have affection for, love **MW** I.i.211 [Evans to Slender, of Anne] *can you affection the 'oman?*

affectioned *(adj.)* affected, pretentious, self-willed **TN** II.iii.141 [Maria to Sir Toby, of Malvolio] *he is … an affectioned ass*

affeered *(adj.)* [legal] assured, confirmed, settled **Mac** IV.iii.34 [Macduff to Malcolm, as if to Macbeth] *wear thou thy wrongs, / The title is affeered* [F *affear'd*]

affiance *(n.)* **1** confidence, trust, faith **2H6** III.i.74 [Queen to King, of the King's loyalty to Gloucester] *what's more dangerous than this fond affiance?;* **H5** II.ii.127

2 marriage contract, solemn promise to each other **Cym** I.vii.163 [Iachimo to Innogen] *I have spoke this to know if your affiance / Were deeply rooted*

affiance *(v.)* betroth, engage, promise solemnly **MM** III.i.215 [disguised Duke to Isabella, of Mariana] *Angelo … was affianced to her by oath;* **MM** V.i.225

affine *(v.)* bind by ties, obligate, make beholden **Oth** II.iii.212 [Montano to Iago] *If partially affined or leagued in office*

affined *(adj.)* **1** related, connected, affiliated **TC** I.iii.25 [Agamemnon to all] *In fortune's love … the artist and unread, / The hard and soft, seem all affined and kin*

2 constrained, bound, obliged **Oth** I.i.39 [Iago to Roderigo, of Othello] *be judge yourself / Whether I in any just term am affined / To love the Moor*

affinity *(n.)* kinship, relationship, connections **Oth** III.i.45 [Emilia to Cassio, of Montano] *he you hurt is of great fame in Cyprus, / And great affinity* [i.e. relations of high rank]

afflict *(v.)* be made to suffer, torment, persecute **E3** IV.ii.78 [King Edward to Captain, of the burgesses of Calais] *yield themselves, upon their knees, / To be afflicted, hanged, or what I please*

affliction *(n.)* afflicted one, someone in great distress **KJ** III.iv.36 [King Philip to Constance] *O fair affliction, peace!*

afford *(v.)* **1** have to offer, be capable of supplying **TS** V.ii.14 [Petruchio to Baptista] *Padua affords nothing but what is kind;* **Sonn** 79.11; **TS** Induction.i.102

2 grant, permit, allow **AW** IV.i.47 [First Lord to Parolles, of the simple stratagems Parolles wants to use to show his bravery] *We cannot afford you so* [i.e. we cannot let you off so easily]

3 fulfil naturally, offer routinely **TS** V.ii.13 [Baptista to Petruchio, of the hospitality] *Padua affords this kindness*

affray *(v.)* scare, startle, frighten away **RJ** III.v.33 [Juliet to Romeo, of the lark] *arm from arm that voice doth us affray*

affright *(v.)* frighten, terrify, scare **R3** V.iii.309 [King Richard to himself] *Let not our babbling dreams affright our souls;* **Cor** I.i.167; **H5** Prologue.14; **2H6** IV.i.32; **Per** I.i.30; **R3** I.iv.64

affrighted *(adj.)* alarmed, frightened, terrified **Oth** V.ii.101 [Othello to himself] *th'affrighted globe / Should yawn at alteration*

affront *(n.)* assault, attack, onslaught **Cym** V.iii.87 [Second Captain to First Captain] *a fourth man … / That gave th'affront*

affront *(v.)* **1** come face to face with, meet, confront **WT** V.i.75 [Paulina to Cleomenes, of Leontes' promise not to marry again] *Unless another, / As like Hermione as is her picture, / Affront his eye;* **Cym** IV.iii.29; **Ham** III.i.31

2 equal, put in balance, set face to face **TC** III.ii.164 [Troilus to Cressida] *my integrity and truth to you / Might be affronted with the match and weight / Of such a winnowed purity in love*

affy *(v.)* **1** have faith, place trust **Tit** I.i.50 [Bassianus to Marcus] *I do affy / In thy uprightness and integrity*

2 engage, betroth, espouse **2H6** IV.i.80 [Lieutenant to Suffolk] *daring to affy a mighty lord / Unto the daughter of a worthless king;* **TS** IV.iv.49

afield, a-field *(adv.)* **1** on the field of battle **TC** V.iii.67 [Hector to Priam] *Aeneas is a-field;* **TC** I.i.107

2 in the field **1H6** V.iv.30 [Shepherd to Pucelle] *thou didst keep my lambs a-field* ☛ a *(prep.)* 3

afire *(adj.)* on fire, burning **RJ** III.iii.133 [Friar to Romeo, of his wit] *Like powder in a skilless soldier's flask / I set afire by thine own ignorance;* **Tem** I.ii.212 ☛ a *(prep.)* 5

afoot *(adv.)* **1** on foot **1H4** II.ii.34 [Falstaff to Prince Hal] *I'll not bear my own flesh so far afoot again;* **1H4** II.ii.46, 78, iii.87, iv.346; **2H6** V.ii.8; **TC** V.v.21 ☛ a *(prep.)* 5

2 on the go, in existence **KL** II.iv.210 [Lear to all, of France] *I could as well be brought / To knee his throne and … pension beg / To keep base life afoot;* **MM** IV.v.3

3 astir, on the move, up and about **Tit** IV.ii.29 [Aaron to himself, of Tamora] *were our witty Empress well afoot*

4 in foot-soldiers, by way of infantry **AW** IV.iii.157 [First Soldier to Parolles, reading] *Demand of him what strength they are a-foot* ☛ foot *(n.)*

afore (adv.) in front, ahead **Oth** V.i.128 [Iago to Emilia] *Will you go on afore?*

afore (prep.) **1** before, in front of **TNK** I.i.197 [Hippolyta to Theseus] *hang / Your shield afore your heart*
2 before, ahead of **KL** I.v.4 [Lear to Kent] *If your diligence be not speedy I shall be there afore you*
3 in the presence of **Tem** IV.i.7 [Prospero to Ferdinand, of Miranda] *Here, afore heaven, / I ratify this my rich gift* **➤** **SWEARING**, p.435

afore (conj.) before, sooner than **2H4** II.iv.200 [Hostess to all] *I'll forswear keeping house afore I'll be in these tirrits and frights!*

Afric (n.) Africa **Cor** I.viii.3 [Aufidius to Martius] *Not Afric owns a serpent I abhor / More than thy fame and envy;* **Cym** I.ii.98

Afric (adj.) African **TC** I.iii.370 [Ulysses to Nestor, of Achilles] *we were better parch in Afric sun / Than in the pride and salt scorn of his eyes*

afront, a-front (adv.) abreast, side by side in front **1H4** II.iv.195 [Falstaff to all, of the robbers] *These four came all afront*

after (adj.) **1** [nautical] second, following, further **Oth** I.iii.35 [Messenger to all] *The Ottomites ... toward the isle of Rhodes, / Have there injointed with an after fleet* [i.e. in the rear]
2 future, later, following **E3** II.ii.197 [King Edward to Countess] *fame, / Which after ages shall enrich thee with;* **AC** V.ii.286

after (adv.) **➤** have after (v.)

after (prep.) **1** according to **Ham** II.ii.528 [Hamlet to Polonius] *Use every man after his desert, and who shall 'scape whipping?*
2 at the rate of **MM** II.i.230 [Pompey to Escalus, of Vienna] *I'll rent the fairest house in it after threepence a bay*

after that (conj.) after **1H6** II.ii.32 [Burgundy to all, of the Dauphin and Pucelle] *After that things are set in order here, / We'll follow them*

after-debt (n.) unpaid bill after goods have been received, outstanding debt **AW** IV.iii.221 [First Soldier reading Parolles' letter, of Bertram] *He ne'er pays after-debts*

after-dinner (n.) period following dinner, afternoon **MM** III.i.33 [Duke to Claudio] *Thou hast ... as it were an after-dinner's sleep*

after-eye (v.) gaze after, follow with the eye **Cym** I.iv.16 [Innogen to Pisanio, of Posthumus] *Thou shouldst have made him / As little as a crow, or less, ere left / To after-eye him*

after-hours (n.) subsequent time, later moments **R3** IV.iv.293 [King Richard to Queen Elizabeth] *Men shall deal unadvisedly sometimes, / Which after-hours gives leisure to repent;* **RJ** II.vi.2

after-inquiry (n.) divine interrogation after death, last judgement **Cym** V.iv.184 [First Gaoler to Posthumus] *you must ... jump the after-inquiry on your own peril*

after-loss (n.) later blow, knock given after others have been suffered **Sonn** 90.4 *Join with the spite of fortune, make me bow, / And do not drop in for an after-loss*

after-love (n.) later gratitude, future loyalty **R2** V.iii.34 [King Henry to Aumerle] *To win thy after-love I pardon thee;* **TG** III.i.95

after-meeting (n.) follow-up meeting **Cor** II.ii.37 [Menenius to all] *the main point of this our after-meeting*

after-nourishment (n.) later sustenance **Per** I.ii.13 [Pericles alone] *the passions of the mind ... / Have after-nourishment and life by care*

after-supper (n.) period of time immediately after dessert [eaten after the main course of the evening meal] **R3** IV.iii.31 [King Richard to Tyrrel] *Come to me ... at after-supper;* **MND** V.i.34

after-times (n.) hereafter, future, time to come **2H4** IV.ii.51 [Prince John to Hastings] *You are too shallow ... / To sound the bottom of the after-times*

afterward (adv.) afterwards **MW** I.i.120 [Slender to Falstaff, of Falstaff's friends] *They ... afterward picked my pocket;* **AW** I.iii.112; **CE** I.ii.28; **MA** V.iv.118; **MM** V.i.470

a-fume (adj.) **➤** fume (n.) 1

again (adv.) **1** in return, back [in response] **AY** III.v.132 [Phebe to Silvius] *I marvel why I answered not again;* **AC** III.xiii.103; **AW** II.ii.66; **CE** I.ii.85; **1H6** V.iii.160; **MND** V.i.180
2 back [to a former position] **AC** III.xiii.103 [Antony to all, of Thidias] *Being whipped, / Bring him again;* **AW** II.ii.66; **TS** II.i.216

again (prep.) against, facing **E3** I.ii.79 [Countess alone, of the Scots] *Turned hence again the blasting north-east wind*

against, 'gainst (prep.) **1** in the face of **AW** I.iii.169 [Countess to Helena] *Invention is ashamed / Against the proclamation of thy passion*
2 exposed to **KJ** V.iv.25 [Melun to Salisbury] *even as a form of wax / Resolveth from his figure 'gainst the fire;* **Cor** I.ix.30
3 opposite, directed against **1H6** III.ii.15 [Master Gunner to Boy, of the overlooking English position] *A piece of ordnance 'gainst it I have placed*
4 in front of, close to **JC** I.iii.20 [Casca to Cicero] *Against the Capitol I met a lion*
5 contrary to **TNK** III.i.60 [Arcite to Palamon] *you've seen me use my sword / Against th'advice of fear*
6 in preparation for, in anticipation of **Sonn** 49.1 *Against that time ... / When I shall see thee frown on my defects*
7 with respect to **TNK** II.ii.36 [Third Countryman to the others] *Do we all hold against the maying?*
8 by the time of **Ham** I.i.159 [Marcellus to Horatio, of the cockerel] *ever 'gainst that season comes / Wherein our Saviour's birth is celebrated, / This bird of dawning singeth all night long*
9 just before **Ham** II.ii.481 [First Player to all present] *as we often see, against some storm, / A silence in the heavens*

against, 'gainst (conj.) in anticipation of the time when **RJ** IV.i.113 [Friar to Juliet, of taking the potion] *In the meantime, against thou shalt awake, / Shall Romeo by my letters know our drift*

agate (n.) dwarf, midget [as of a tiny figure carved in an agate-seal] **2H4** I.ii.16 [Falstaff to Page] *I was never manned with an agate till now;* **MA** III.i.65

agazed (adj.) astounded, astonished, amazed **1H6** I.i.126 [Third Messenger to all, of Talbot] *All the whole army stood agazed on him*

age (n.) **1** whole life, lifetime, days **1H6** V.v.63 [Suffolk to all] *what is wedlock bound a hell, / An age of discord;* **Cor** III.i.7, IV.vi.52; **1H6** IV.v.46; **TG** III.i.74
2 mature years, old age **TG** I.iii.15 [Panthino to Antonio, of Proteus not having travelled] *Which would be great impeachment to his age;* **H8** III.ii.456; **JC** III.i.93; **R3** IV.iv.172, V.iii.263; **Sonn** 62.14
3 seniority, status as elder brother **Tit** I.i.8 [Saturninus to his followers] *Nor wrong mine age with this indignity* [i.e. of having his claim called in question]

aged (adj.) experienced, accomplished, mature **Tim** V.iii.8 [Soldier alone, of his captain] *An aged interpreter, though young in days*

agent (n.) sense, organ, faculty **Venus** 400 [Venus to Adonis, of a lover and his mistress] *when his glutton eye so full hath fed, / His other agents aim at like delight*

aggravate (v.) **1** add weight to, magnify, increase **MW** II.ii.270 [Falstaff to Ford as Brook, of Ford] *I will aggravate his style*
2 make more grievous, make worse, exacerbate **E3** II.i.442 [Warwick to Countess] *sin doth ten times aggravate itself, / That is committed in a holy place*
3 intensify; malapropism for 'moderate' **2H4** II.iv.157 [Hostess to Pistol] *I beseek you now, aggravate your choler;* **MND** I.ii.76

agitation (n.) movement, motion, activity [physical, not mental] **Mac** V.i.11 [Doctor to Gentlewoman, of Lady Macbeth's sleepwalking] *slumbery agitation*

aglet (n.) (plural) tiny shining ornaments worn on a dress, spangles **TNK** III.iv.2 [Gaoler's Daughter alone] *The little stars and all, that look like aglets*

aglet-baby (n.) [unclear meaning] small ornamental figure forming the tag of a lace **TS** I.ii.78 [Grumio to Hortensio, of Petruchio] *marry him to a puppet or an aglet-baby*

agnize (v.) acknowledge, recognize, confess **Oth** I.iii.229 [Othello to Duke] *I do agnize / A natural and prompt alacrity / I find in hardness*

agone (adv.) ago, past **TN** V.i.195 [Feste to Sir Toby, of the surgeon] *he's drunk, Sir Toby, an hour agone*; **TG** III.i.85

agony (n.) anguish, great distress; or: death-struggle **R3** I.iv.42 [Keeper to Clarence, of Clarence's nightmare] *Awaked you not in this sore agony?*

agood (adv.) in earnest, in a heartfelt way **TG** IV.iv.162 [disguised Julia to Silvia, of Julia] *I made her weep agood*

agot (n.) ☞ agate (n.)

agree (v.) **1** accord, fit in with, match **2H6** I.i.110 [Gloucester to Cardinal, of King Reignier] *whose large style / Agrees not with the leanness of his purse*
2 become harmonious, be reconciled **TS** V.ii.1 [Lucentio to all] *At last, though long, our jarring notes agree*

ague (n.) fever, sickness, shaking [as caused by a fever] **Tem** II.ii.65 [Stephano to himself] *This is some monster of the isle with four legs, who hath got ... an ague*; **1H4** III.i.65; **JC** II.ii.113; **Mac** V.v.4; **MV** I.i.23; **Tem** II.ii.92, 133

agued (adj.) shivering, shaking [as with a fever] **Cor** I.iv.38 [Martius to his troops] *faces pale / With flight and agued fear!*

ague-fit (n.) feverish fit, fit of shaking **R2** III.ii.190 [King Richard to all] *This ague-fit of fear is overblown*

ague-proof (adj.) immune to fevers, resistant to sickness **KL** IV.vi.104 [Lear to all] *I am not ague-proof* [F; Q *argue-proofe*]

a-height (adv.) on high, aloft **KL** IV.vi.58 [Edgar to Gloucester] *Look up a-height* ☞ a (prep.) 5

a-high (adv.) on high, aloft **R3** IV.iv.86 [Queen Margaret to Queen Elizabeth] *One heaved a-high to be hurled down below* ☞ a (prep.) 5

a-hold (adv.) [nautical] close to the wind [to hold steady] **Tem** I.i.48 [Boatswain to the Mariners, of the ship] *Lay her a-hold, a-hold!*

aid (n.) ☞ pray in aid

aidance (n.) aid, assistance, help **Venus** 330 *the heart hath treble wrong / When it is barred the aidance of the tongue*; **2H6** III.ii.165

aidant (adj.) helpful, assisting, beneficial **KL** IV.iv.17 [Cordelia to Doctor, as if to the herbs of the earth] *Be aidant and remediate* [F; Q *beaydant*]

ail (v.) prevent, obstruct, stop **TNK** II.ii.37 [Fourth Countryman to the others] *What should ail us?*

aim (n.) **1** guess, conjecture, surmise **JC** I.ii.162 [Brutus to Cassius] *What you would work me to, I have some aim*; **TG** III.i.28
2 target, object, goal **MM** I.iii.5 [Duke to Friar Thomas] *a purpose / More grave and wrinkled than the aims and ends / Of burning youth*; **2H4** III.ii.259; **R3** IV.iv.89; **TG** V.iv.102

aim, cry [archery] show applause, shout approval [of] **MW** III.ii.40 [Ford alone, of his plans] *to these violent proceedings all my neighbours shall cry aim*; **KJ** II.i.196

aim, give one [archery] guide one's efforts, help one's aim **Tit** V.iii.148 [Lucius to Romans] *give me aim awhile, / For nature puts me to a heavy task*

aim (v.) guess, conjecture, surmise **TG** III.i.45 [Proteus to Duke, of accosting Valentine] *do it so cunningly / That my discovery be not aimed at*; **Ham** IV.v.9; **2H6** II.iv.58; **3H6** III.ii.68; **R3** I.iii.65

aim at (v.) judge, consider, rate **MA** III.ii.86 [Don John to Claudio] *aim better at me by that I now will manifest*

air (n.) **1** melody, tune, strain **Tem** I.ii.394 [Ferdinand to himself] *This music crept by me upon the waters, / Allaying both their fury and my passion / With its sweet air*; **MND** I.i.183; **Tem** I.ii.423, V.i.58; **TNK** I.iii.75
2 manner, style, fashion **Tim** V.i.22 [Painter to Poet] *Promising is the very air o'th' time*; **WT** IV.iv.726

3 likeness, bearing, demeanour **WT** V.i.127 [Leontes to Florizel] *Your father's image is so hit in you, / His very air*
4 fresh air, open air **Ham** II.ii.206 [Polonius to Hamlet] *Will you walk out of the air, my lord?*; **Tim** IV.ii.13
5 breeze, light wind **Ham** I.iv.41 [Hamlet to Ghost] *Bring with thee airs from heaven or blasts from hell*
6 vapour, mist, exhalation **KL** II.iv.159 [Lear to Regan, of Gonerill] *Strike her young bones, / You taking airs, with lameness!*

air, take become known, spread about **TN** III.iv.130 [Maria to Sir Toby and Fabian, of Malvolio] *pursue him now, lest the device take air, and taint* [i.e. people get wind of it]

air (v.) **1** exercise, take the air, provide with fresh air **Cym** I.ii.41 [Innogen to Posthumus] *Were you but riding forth to air yourself*; **Tem** IV.i.70; **WT** IV.iv.759
2 bring into public view, expose, show **Cym** II.iv.96 [Iachimo to Posthumus] *I beg but leave to air this jewel*

air abroad live abroad, experience foreign climates **WT** IV.ii.5 [Camillo to Polixenes] *I have for the most part been aired abroad*

air-braving (adj.) lofty, challenging the air **1H6** IV.ii.13 [Talbot to the French] *your stately and air-braving towers*

air-drawn (adj.) drawn through the air; or: drawn in the air **Mac** III.iv.61 [Lady Macbeth to Macbeth] *This is the air-drawn dagger which you said / Led you to Duncan*

airy (adj.) carried by the wind, widely acknowledged **TC** I.iii.144 [Ulysses to all, of Achilles] *Having his ear full of his airy fame* [or: elevated]

alablaster (n.) alabaster [fine white material derived from limestone] **MV** I.i.84 [Gratiano to Antonio, of a man] *Sit, like his grandsire cut in alablaster*

alablaster (adj.) white, smooth [as alabaster] **R3** IV.iii.11 [Tyrrel alone, of the Princes] *girdling one another / Within their alablaster innocent arms*; **Venus** 363

alack (int.) ☞ REGRETS, p.367

a-land (adv.) on shore, on land **Per** II.i.28 [First Fisherman to Third Fisherman, responding to 'I marvel how the fishes live in the sea'] *Why, as men do a-land* **Per** III.ii.67

alarm, alarum, 'larm, 'larum (n.) **1** call to arms, call to battle, signal to begin fighting **Cor** I.iv.9 [Martius to Messenger] *Then shall we hear their 'larum, and they ours*; **1H6** I.iv.99 [Talbot to all] *Whence cometh this alarum and the noise?*; **TNK** I.iv.81 [Palamon, praying to Venus] *[who] hast the might ... [to] turn th'alarm to whispers*; **Cor** II.ii.74; **E3** V.i.11; **2H4** III.i.17; **1H6** I.iii.18; **R3** I.i.7 ☞ STAGE DIRECTIONS, p.417
2 attack, assault **Venus** 424 [Adonis to Venus, of her approach] *To love's alarms it will not ope the gate*; **Mac** V.ii.4
3 disturbance, turbulence, trouble, loud noise **TS** I.i.126 [Hortensio to Gremio, of Katherina] *Though it pass your patience and mine to endure her loud alarums*; **Tem** I.ii.205; **TS** I.ii.204
4 alarm, agitation, excited feeling **1H6** V.v.85 [King to all] *I feel ... / Such fierce alarums both of hope and fear*; **Ham** II.ii.507; **MW** III.v.67
5 arousal, incitement, encouragement **Oth** II.iii.24 [Iago to Cassio, of Desdemona] *when she speaks, is it not an alarum to love?*; **Venus** 424
6 tumult, uproar, hubbub **Tit** I.i.150 [Lucius to Titus, of their dead] *And with loud 'larums welcome them to Rome*

alarum (v.) arouse, urge on, incite **Mac** II.i.53 [Macbeth alone] *withered Murder, / Alarumed by his sentinel the wolf ... / Moves like a ghost*

alarum (n.) ☞ alarm (n.)

alarum-bell, 'larum-bell (n.) warning bell **2H4** III.i.17 [King Henry IV alone, as if to sleep] *why ... leavest the kingly couch / A watch-case, or a common 'larum-bell?*; **Mac** II.iii.71 [Macduff to all] *Ring the alarum-bell! Murder and treason*; **Mac** V.v.51

alarumed (adj.) galvanized, activated, stirred to action **KL** II.i.52 [Edmund to Gloucester, of Edgar] *he saw my best alarumed spirits / Bold in the quarrel's right*

alas (*int.*) ☛ EXCLAMATIONS, p.158; REGRETS, p.367

albeit (*conj.*) although E3 I.ii.164 [King Edward to Countess] *albeit my business urgeth me, / It shall attend, while I attend on thee*

Albion (*n.*) England 2H6 I.iii.43 [Queen to Suffolk] *Is this ... the royalty of Albion's king?*

alchemy, alchymy (*n.*) wondrous transformation, miraculous transmutation Sonn 33.4 [of the sun] *Gilding pale streams with heavenly alchymy*; Sonn 114.4

alderliefest (*adj.*) most beloved, dearest of all 2H6 I.i.28 [Queen to King] *mine alderliefest sovereign*

ale (*n.*) ale-house, tavern TG II.v.51 [Launce to Speed] *go to the ale with a Christian*

ale, small ☛ beer / ale, small

aleven (*adj.*) eleven MV II.ii.150 [Launcelot to himself] *aleven widows and nine maids is a simple coming-in for one man* [F, Q; a *leuen*]

ale-wife (*n.*) ale-house keeper, barmaid TS Induction.ii.20 [Sly to Lord] *Marian Hacket, the fat ale-wife of Wincot*; 2H4 II.ii.78

aliad (*n.*) ☛ oeillade (*n.*)

a-life (*adv.*) dearly, greatly, on my life WT IV.iv.258 [Mopsa to Clown] *I love a ballad in print a-life, for then we are sure they are true* ☛ a (*prep.*) 5

alike (*adv.*) the same, in the same way 1H6 II.i.55 [Pucelle to Charles] *At all times will you have my power alike?*; Tit II.iii.146

alive (*adv.*) with the living, of present concern JC IV.iii.194 [Brutus to Cassius] *Well, to our work alive*

all (*adv.*) **1** exclusively, totally, altogether KL I.i.104 [Cordelia to Lear] *I shall never marry like my sisters, / To love my father all*; KL I.i.100; Tim I.i.143
  2 alone, only, solely AW III.ii.68 [Countess to Helena, of Bertram] *I do wash his name out of my blood / And thou art all my child*
  3 [intensifying use] quite, so TS III.ii.102 [Tranio as Lucentio to Petruchio] *what occasion of import / Hath all so long detained you*

all- (*as adv. in compounds*) completely, wholly, altogether ☛ all-amazed; all-worthy; amort

all- (*as noun in compounds with -ing or -ed forms*) everyone, everything ☛ all-cheering; all-ending; all-hating; all-licensed; all-obeying; all-watched

all (*conj.*) although R3 IV.iv.226 [Queen Elizabeth to King Richard] *Thy head, all indirectly, gave direction*

all, but in all told, altogether 1H6 IV.i.20 [Talbot to all] *at the Battle of Patay, / When, but in all, I was six thousand strong*

all is one; that's / it's all one it makes no difference, it's one and the same, it doesn't matter MA V.i.49 [Leonato to Don Pedro] *Are you so hasty now? Well, all is one*; TN I.v.124 [Sir Toby to himself] *Well, it's all one*; TNK V.iv.83 [Wooer to Gaoler's Daughter] *That's all one; I will have you*; AW IV.iii.137; TC I.i.79; TNK II.ii.31, V.ii.15, 30 ☛ DISCOURSE MARKERS, p.127

all my best ☛ best, in all my

all of all sum of everything LL V.i.103 [Armado to Holofernes] *The very all of all*

all-abhorred (*adj.*) hated by everyone 1H4 V.i.16 [King Henry to Worcester] *Will you again unknit / The churlish knot of all-abhorred war*

all-amazed (*adj.*) completely dumbfounded TS III.ii.160 [Gremio to Tranio as Lucentio, of Petruchio] *he ... swore so loud / That all-amazed the priest let fall the book* ☛ amazed (*adj.*)

allay (*n.*) means of lessening, source of abatement WT IV.ii.8 [Camillo to Polixenes, of Leontes] *the penitent King ... hath sent for me; to whose feeling sorrows I might be some allay*

allay (*v.*) **1** subside, abate, diminish, quell Tem I.ii.393 [Ferdinand to himself] *This music crept by me upon the waters, / Allaying both their fury and my passion*; 2H6 IV.i.60; 3H6 I.iv.146; KL I.ii.161; MV II.ii.173; Tem I.ii.2

  2 spoil, dilute, qualify AC II.v.50 [Cleopatra to Messenger] *I do not like 'But yet'; it does allay / The good precedence*

allaying (*adj.*) diluting, watering down Cor II.i.45 [Menenius to Sicinius and Brutus] *I am ... one that loves a cup of hot wine with not a drop of allaying Tiber in't*

allayment (*n.*) modifying agent, countermeasure, mitigation Cym I.vi.22 [Queen to Cornelius, of his drugs] *I will ... apply / Allayments to their act*; TC IV.iv.8

all-cheering (*adj.*) invigorating everything RJ I.i.134 [Montague to Benvolio] *so soon as the all-cheering sun / Should in the farthest East begin to draw / The shady curtains from Aurora's bed*

allege (*v.*) advance, produce, bring forward H8 II.i.13 [First Gentleman to Second Gentleman, of Buckingham] *He ... alleged / Many sharp reasons to defeat the law*

alleged (*adj.*) cited in court, proposed, offered H8 II.iv.225 [King Henry to all] *the sharp thorny points / Of my alleged reasons*

allegiant (*adj.*) loyal, faithful, stemming from allegiance H8 III.ii.176 [Wolsey to King Henry] *I / Can nothing render but allegiant thanks*

all-ending (*adj.*) bringing an end to everything, doom-laden E3 IV.iv.9 [Prince Edward to Audley] *no hope to us but sullen dark / And eyeless terror of all-ending night*; R3 III.i.78

all-hail (*n.*) acclamation, salutation, praise Cor V.iii.139 [Volumnia to Coriolanus, of the Romans and Volsces] *each in either side / Give the all-hail to thee*

Allhallond Eve (*n.*) ☛ DAYS AND DATES, p.630

All-hallow (*adj.*) All Saints' Day; period of fine weather in late autumn 1H4 I.ii.156 [Prince Hal to Falstaff] *Farewell, All-hallow summer!* [i.e.brightness in old age] ☛ DAYS AND DATES, p.630

all-hating (*adj.*) hating everything, hateful R2 V.v.66 [Richard alone] *love to Richard / Is a strange brooch in this all-hating world*

alliance (*n.*) **1** kinship, relationship, friendship TNK V.iv.86 [Palamon to Arcite] *O miserable end of our alliance*; 1H6 II.v.53 ☛ ally (*n.*)
  2 marriage RJ II.iii.87 [Friar to Romeo] *For this alliance may so happy prove / To turn your households' rancour to pure love*; MA II.i.293

allicholy, allycholly (*adj./n.*) malapropism for 'melancholy' TG IV.ii.26 [Host to disguised Julia] *methinks you're allycholly*; MW I.iv.148

allied (*adj.*) related, connected TG IV.i.49 [Third Outlaw to Valentine] *An heir, and near allied unto the Duke*; MM III.ii.97

alligant (*adj.*) malapropism for 'elegant' or 'eloquent' MW II.ii.66 [Mistress Quickly to Falstaff, of courtiers' letters to Mistress Ford] *in such alligant terms*

all-licensed (*adj.*) allowed to do anything, given free range KL I.iv.196 [Gonerill to Lear] *this your all-licensed fool*

all-obeying (*adj.*) obeyed by everyone AC III.xiii.77 [Cleopatra to Thidias, of Caesar] *kneel, / Till from his all-obeying breath I hear / The doom of Egypt*

all-oblivious forgetting everything Sonn 55.9 *'Gainst death and all-oblivious enmity / Shall you pace forth*

allot (*v.*) destine, appoint, assign 1H6 V.iii.55 [Suffolk to Margaret] *Thou art allotted to be ta'en by me*

allottery (*n.*) share, portion, allocation AY I.i.68 [Orlando to Oliver] *the poor allottery my father left me by testament*

allow (*v.*) **1** acknowledge, commend, receive [with praise] TNK II.iv.4 [Theseus to Arcite] *you run the best and wrestle / That these times can allow* [i.e. you are the best runner and wrestler]; Cor III.iii.45; TC III.ii.89
  2 approve, sanction, encourage KL II.iv.186 [Lear to all, as if to the heavens] *if your sweet sway / Allow obedience*; Luc 1845; Sonn 19.11, 112.4

3 acknowledge, grant, admit **TN** I.ii.60 [Viola to Captain, of Orsino] *I can sing / And speak to him in many sorts of music / That will allow me very worth his service;* **Cym** III.iii.17; **2H4** I.iii.5; **MW** II.ii.220; **TN** IV.ii.57

4 bestow, legally assign **Tim** V.i.160 [First Senator to Timon] *thou shalt be met with thanks, / Allowed with absolute power;* **MV** IV.i.300

5 permit to indulge, surrender, give over **KL** III.vii.104 [Second Servant to Third Servant, of Edgar as Poor Tom] *his roguish madness / Allows itself to anything*

allowance (*n.*) **1** acknowledgement, admission, confirmation **Cor** III.ii.57 [Volumnia to Coriolanus, of his words to the people] *syllables / Of no allowance to your bosom's truth;* **Ham** III.ii.27; **TC** I.iii.377; **TNK** V.iv.54

2 permission, approval, sanction **KL** I.iv.204 [Gonerill to Lear, of his knights' behaviour] *you protect this course and put it on / By your allowance;* **H8** III.ii.322; **KL** II.ii.104; **Oth** I.i.128

3 regard, respect, reputation **Oth** II.i.49 [Cassio to Montano, of Othello's pilot] *Of very expert and approved allowance;* **TC** I.iii.136

allowed (*adj.*) **1** approved, acknowledged, granted **Oth** I.iii.222 [Duke to Othello, of the person in charge in Cyprus] *we have there a substitute of most allowed sufficiency;* **H8** I.ii.83

2 licensed, authorized, permitted **TN** I.v.89 [Olivia to Malvolio] *There is no slander in an allowed fool;* **LL** I.ii.124, V.ii.478

all-thing (*adv.*) completely, altogether, wholly **Mac** III.i.13 [Lady Macbeth to Macbeth, of Banquo] *If he had been forgotten / It had been … all-thing unbecoming*

all-too-timeless (*adj.*) all too hasty **Luc** 44 [of Tarquin] *some untimely thought did instigate / His all-too-timeless speed*

allure (*v.*) entice, attract, tempt **Cym** I.vii.46 [Iachimo to Innogen] *Sluttery … / Should make desire vomit emptiness, / Not so allured to feed;* **Cym** II.iv.34; **Tim** IV.iii.142

allurement (*n.*) temptation, enticement, charm **AW** IV.iii.209 [Parolles to First Soldier, of his advice to Diana] *to take heed of the allurement of one Count Rossillion*

allusion (*n.*) riddle, wordplay, figure **LL** IV.ii.42 [Holofernes to Dull, of his answer to Dull's riddle] *Th'allusion holds in the exchange*

all-watched (*adj.*) maintaining watchfulness throughout **H5** IV.Chorus.38 [Chorus, of King Henry] *Nor doth he dedicate one jot of colour / Unto the weary and all-watched night*

all-worthy (*adj.*) wholly excellent **Cym** III.v.95 [Pisanio to Cloten] *O, my all-worthy lord!*

ally (*n.*) relative, relation, kinsman **RJ** III.i.109 [Romeo to himself, of Mercutio] *the Prince's near ally* ➤ **alliance** (*n.*)

allycholly (*adj./n.*) ➤ allicholy (*adj./n.*)

Almain German **Oth** II.iii.77 [Iago to Cassio, of the Englishman] *he sweats not to overthrow your Almaine* ➤ **WORLD**, p.634

almanac (*n.*) calendar, register **AC** I.ii.150 [Enobarbus to Antony, of Cleopatra] *We cannot call her winds and waters sighs and tears; they are greater storms and tempests than almanacs can report;* **CE** I.ii.41

alms (*n.*) charity, good deed, meritorious act **MA** II.iii.159 [Don Pedro to Claudio, of Benedick] *it were an alms to hang him*

alms-basket (*n.*) basket containing offerings to be given out for charity **LL** V.i.38 [Costard to Mote, of Holofernes and Nathaniel] *they have lived long on the alms-basket of words!*

alms-deed (*n.*) almsgiving, act of charity **3H6** V.v.79 [Queen as if to Richard] *murder is thy alms-deed*

alms-drink, alms drink (*n.*) dregs of drink given away in charity; or drink taken in charity [to foster reconciliation] **AC** II.vii.5 [First Servant to Second Servant, of Lepidus] *They have made him drink alms drink*

almsman (*n.*) person living through charitable offerings **R2** III.iii.149 [King Richard to Aumerle] *I'll give … / My gay apparel for an almsman's gown*

aloe (*n.*) bitterness, painful experience **Lover** 273 [of love] *sweetens in the suff'ring pangs it bears, / The aloes of all forces, shocks and fears*

aloft (*adv.*) ➤ **STAGE DIRECTIONS**, p.417

aloft (*prep.*) above, over **KJ** IV.ii.139 [King John to Bastard, of the bad news] *now I breathe again / Aloft the flood*

alone (*adj.*) unique, matchless, having no equal **TG** II.iv.165 [Valentine to Proteus, of Silvia] *She is alone;* **TC** I.ii.16

alone (*adv.*) only, solely, uniquely **TNK** IV.ii.37 [Emilia alone] *Palamon, thou art alone / And only beautiful;* **AC** IV.vi.30; **Cor** I.ii.27; **Ham** I.iii.11; **KJ** III.i.64

alone, let [one] **1** leave it to [one], you can rely on [one] **TNK** III.v.31 [Nell to Schoolmaster, of his request to dance well] *Let us alone, sir;* **Tit** I.i.452, IV.iii.113; **TNK** IV.i.145

2 pay no attention to [one], have nothing to do with [one] **TNK** IV.i.127 [Gaoler's Daughter to First Friend, of the other women] *I laugh at 'em, / And let 'em all alone*

along (*adv.*) at full length, stretched out, prostrate **RJ** V.iii.3 [Paris to Page] *Under yon yew trees lay thee all along;* **AY** II.i.30; **Cor** V.vi.57; **JC** III.i.115

along (*prep.*) throughout the whole length of **AY** II.i.32 [First Lord to all] *the brook that brawls along this wood*

along / 'long of (*prep.*) on account of **Cor** V.iv.29 [Menenius to Sicinius, of Coriolanus' return for revenge] *all this is 'long of you*

aloof (*adv.*) a short distance away, to one side **3H6** II.i.17 [Richard to Edward, of a bear] *encompassed round with dogs, / Who having pinched a few and made them cry, / The rest stand all aloof and bark at him;* **2H6** I.i.225; **MND** II.ii.32; **MV** III.ii.42; **RJ** V.iii.26, 282; **TNK** V.i.137 ➤ **STAGE DIRECTIONS**, p.417

alter (*v.*) change, exchange **TN** II.v.152 [Malvolio reading the letter, of Olivia] *She that would alter services with thee* [i.e. change social positions]

altering (*adj.*) afflicting, health-affecting **WT** IV.iv.396 [disguised Polixenes to Florizel, of Florizel's father] *Is he not stupid / With age and altering rheums?*

altogether (*adv.*) entirely, wholly, exclusively **E3** III.iii.57 [King John to King Edward] *[thou] Dost altogether live by pilfering;* **MW** I.ii.7

alway (*adv.*) always **3H6** V.vi.64 [Richard to himself, of the King's blood] *may such purple tears be alway shed / From those that wish the downfall of our house!;* **2H4** I.ii.216

amain (*adv.*) **1** in all haste, at full speed **CE** I.i.93 [Egeon to Duke] *Two ships from far, making amain to us;* **E3** III.i.78, IV.v.121; **2H6** III.i.282, IV.i.114; **3H6** II.v.133; **LL** V.ii.542

2 forcefully, with all one's might **1H6** I.i.128 [Third Messenger to all, of Talbot] *His soldiers … 'A Talbot!' cried out amain;* **TC** V.viii.13

amaze (*n.*) amazement, extreme astonishment **LL** II.i.232 [Boyet to Princess, of the King] *His face's own margin did quote such amazes*

amaze (*v.*) **1** confuse, perplex, bewilder **Ham** II.ii.562 [Hamlet alone] *and amaze indeed / The very faculties of eyes and ears;* **AY** I.ii.102; **KJ** IV.ii.140; **R2** V.ii.85, iii.23; **TS** IV.v.54; **Venus** 684 ➤ amazed (*adj.*)

2 alarm, dismay, scare **1H4** V.v.5 [Prince Hal to King Henry] *I beseech your majesty, make up, / Lest your retirement do amaze your friends;* **MW** V.v.17; **Per** I.iv.87

3 appal, overwhelm, terrify **1H6** IV.vii.84 [Lucy to all, of Talbot] *Were but his picture left amongst you here, / It would amaze the proudest of you all;* **JC** I.ii.128; **MM** V.i.377

amazed (*adj.*) dumbfounded, stunned, thunderstruck, overwhelmed **KL** III.vi.33 [disguised Kent to Lear] *Stand you not so amazed;* **KJ** II.i.226, 356, IV.ii.137, V.i.51; **MW** III.iii.110; **Oth** IV.ii.237; **RJ** III.i.134 ➤ amaze (*v.*) 1

amazement (*n.*) **1** alarm, apprehension, fear **Tem** I.ii.14 [Prospero to Miranda] *Be collected. / No more amazement;* **Per** I.ii.26; **TC** II.ii.211, V.iii.85; **Tem** I.ii.198

2 bewilderment, perplexity, distraction **MM** IV.ii.197 [disguised Duke to Provost] *Put not yourself into amazement how these things should be;* **Ham** III.iv.113; **KJ** V.i.35; **TC** V.iii.85

3 overwhelming wonder **Ham** III.ii.334 [Rosencrantz to Hamlet, of Gertrude] *your behaviour hath struck her into amazement and admiration;* **Tem** I.ii.198

amazing *(adj.)* dreadful, terrifying, stupefying **R2** I.iii.81 [John of Gaunt to Bolingbroke] *let thy blows … / Fall like amazing thunder*

Amazonian *(adj.)* **1** resembling a female warrior [of the mythical Amazonian race]; warlike **3H6** I.iv.114 [York to Queen] *To triumph, like an Amazonian trull, / Upon their woes whom Fortune captivates!*

2 Amazon-like; beardless, hairless **Cor** II.ii.89 [Cominius to all, of Coriolanus] *with his Amazonian chin* ☞ **CLASSICAL MYTHOLOGY**, p.613

ambassage, ambassy *(n.)* ☞ embassage, embassy *(n.)*

amber *(n.)* any amber-coloured substance or material **E3** II.i.117 [King Edward to Lodowick, of the Countess] *Her hair … doth make more fair / The yellow amber*

amble *(v.)* walk in an unnatural way **Ham** III.i.145 [Hamlet to Ophelia, of women] *You jig and amble*

ambling *(n.)* affected way of walking, tripping along **RJ** I.iv.11 [Romeo to Benvolio] *I am not for this ambling*

ambling *(adj.)* walking in an affected way, pretentiously strolling **R3** I.i.17 [Richard alone] *I … want love's majesty / To strut before a wanton ambling nymph*

ambuscado *(n.)* ambush, ambuscade **RJ** I.iv.84 [Mercutio to Romeo, of Queen Mab visiting a soldier] *then dreams he … / Of breaches, ambuscados*

ameer *(n.)* [jocular address] emir [hereditary Arab ruler] **MW** II.i.202 [Host to all] *Will you go, Ameers?* [F *An-heires*] ☞ mynheer *(n.)*

amend *(v.)* **1** cure, heal, improve **Cym** IV.ii.12 [Innogen to all] *I am ill, but your being by me / Cannot amend me;* **1H4** III.i.174; **2H4** I.ii.125; **LL** IV.iii.74; **Lover** 214

2 get better, recover, revive, heal **Mac** IV.iii.145 [Doctor to Malcolm, of the English king curing sick people] *at his touch … / They presently amend;* **Tem** V.i.115

3 make better, ameliorate, lessen the evil of **TN** I.v.44 [Feste to all] *sin that amends is but patched with virtue;* **Cym** V.v.216

amendment *(n.)* recovery, recuperation, improvement **AW** I.i.11 [Countess to Lafew] *What hope is there of his majesty's amendment?;* **R3** I.iii.33; **TS** Induction.ii.127

amends *(n.)* recovery, cure, improvement in health **TS** Induction.ii.96 [Sly to all, of his apparent recovery] *Now Lord be thanked for my good amends*

amerce *(v.)* penalize, punish financially **RJ** III.i.190 [Prince to Montague] *I'll amerce you with so strong a fine*

ames-ace *(n.)* double ace [the lowest throw at dice] **AW** II.iii.77 [Lafew to Parolles] *I had rather be in this choice than throw ames-ace for my life* ☞ ace *(n.)*

amiable *(adj.)* **1** amorous, loving, tender **MW** II.ii.226 [Ford as Brook to Falstaff] *lay an amiable siege to the honesty of this Ford's wife;* **MA** III.iii.146

2 beloved, desirable, lovable **Oth** III.iv.59 [Othello to Desdemona, of his mother's handkerchief] *'Twould make her amiable and subdue my father / Entirely to her love;* **MA** V.iv.48; **MND** IV.i.2

amiss *(n.)* **1** misfortune, calamity, adversity **Ham** IV.v.18 [Gertrude to herself] *Each toy seems prologue to some great amiss*

2 fault, offence, misdeed **Sonn** 35.7 *Myself corrupting, salving thy amiss;* **Sonn** 151.3

amiss *(adj.)* deficient [in mind], deranged **TNK** IV.iii.27 [Doctor to Gaoler, of the Gaoler's Daughter] *How prettily she's amiss!*

amiss *(adv.)* wrongly, improperly, in an unseemly way **E3** II.i.17 [Lodowick alone, of King Edward] *If he did blush, 'twas red immodest shame, / To vail his eyes amiss;* **E3** II.i.21; **Sonn** 59.3

among *(adv.)* from time to time, every now and then **TNK** IV.iii.87 [Doctor to Wooer, of the Gaoler's Daughter] *drink to her, and still among intermingle your petition of grace* ☞ ever among

amorous *(adj.)* expressing love **MA** I.i.304 [Don Pedro to Claudio, of Hero] *I'll … take her hearing prisoner with the force / And strong encounter of my amorous tale;* **AW** V.iii.68

amort *(adj.)* dispirited, spiritless, dejected **1H6** III.ii.124 [Talbot to Burgundy, of the Bastard's taunts] *What, all amort?;* **TS** IV.iii.36

ample *(adj.)* full, complete, absolute **2H4** IV.i.161 [Hastings to Westmorland] *Hath the Prince John a full commission, / In very ample virtue of his father;* **KJ** V.ii.112; **TC** III.iii.89

ample *(adv.)* well, fully, completely **AW** III.v.42 [Widow to Helena] *I know your hostess / As ample as myself;* **Tim** I.ii.128

amplify *(v.)* augment, increase, extend **Cym** I.vi.17 [Queen to Cornelius, of her drug-making] *is't not meet / That I did amplify my judgement in / Other conclusions?*

an *(det.)* ☞ **AN**, panel

anatomize, annothanize *(v.)* dissect, reveal, lay open **KL** III.vi.75 [Lear to all] *let them anatomize Regan;* **AY** IV.iii.31; **AY** I.i.145, II.vii.56; **LL** IV.i.70; **Luc** 1450

anatomy *(n.)* **1** skeleton, skin and bones **CE** V.i.239 [Antipholus of Ephesus to Duke, of Pinch] *A mere anatomy, a mountebank;* **KJ** III.iv.40; **RJ** III.iii.106; **TNK** V.i.115

2 body, cadaver, corpse **RJ** III.iii.106 [Romeo to Friar] *tell me, / In what vile part of this anatomy / Doth my name lodge?;* **TN** III.ii.60

anchor *(n.)* anchorite, hermit, recluse **Ham** III.ii.229 [Second Player as Queen, to her King] *An anchor's cheer in prison be my scope*

anchor *(v.)* **1** concentrate, fix attention, home in **MM** II.iv.4 [Angelo alone] *my invention … / Anchors on Isabel;* **Cym** V.v.394

2 embed, sink, fix firmly **R3** IV.iv.232 [Queen Elizabeth to King Richard] *My tongue should to thy ears not name my boys / Till that my nails were anchored in thine eyes*

anchorage anchor, anchors **Tit** I.i.76 [Titus to all, of a ship] *the bay / From whence at first she weighed her anchorage*

anchoring *(adj.)* riding at anchor **KL** IV.vi.18 [Edgar to Gloucester] *yon tall anchoring bark*

ancient, aunchient *(n.)* **1** ensign, standard-bearer **1H4** IV.ii.23 [Falstaff alone, of his soldiers] *my whole charge consists of ancients;* **H5** III.vi.12 [Fluellen to Gower] *There is an aunchient lieutenant there at the pridge;* **2H4** II.iv.67; **H5** II.i.3; **Oth** I.i.33

2 flag, standard, ensign **1H4** IV.ii.30 [Falstaff alone, of his soldiers] *ten times more dishonourable-ragged than an old fazed ancient*

3 most experienced, senior officers **KL** V.i.32 [Albany to all] *Let's then determine / With th'ancient of war on our proceeding*

ancient, aunchient *(adj.)* **1** long-established, long-standing **H5** IV.i.67 [Fluellen to Gower] *It is the greatest admiration in the universal world, when the true and aunchient prerogatives and laws of the wars is not kept;* **RJ** I.i.104 [Montague to Benvolio] *Who set this ancient quarrel new abroach?;* **Cor** II.i.220, IV.i.3; **1H6** II.iv.93; **R2** I.i.9; **TS** I.ii.46

2 former, earlier, past **1H6** V.iii.27 [Pucelle alone] *My ancient incantations are too weak;* **Cor** V.ii.7; **2H6** IV.vii.25; **KL** IV.i.43; **TNK** III.iii.11

3 time-worn, experienced, renowned **MA** III.iii.39 [Dogberry to First Watchman] *you speak like an ancient and most quiet watchman;* **Cym** V.iii.15

4 aged, very old, venerable **Cym** V.iv.30 [stage direction] *Enter … an ancient matron;* **RJ** I.i.92; **TS** IV.ii.61, V.i.64

ancientry *(n.)* **1** decorum, old-fashioned formality, ancient dignity **MA** II.i.68 [Beatrice to Hero, of a wedding] *full of state and ancientry*

2 old people, elderly **WT** III.iii.61 [Shepherd to himself, of the offences of young people] *getting wenches with child, wronging the ancientry, stealing*

AN

The general rule for the use of the indefinite article in modern English is: *a* is followed by a consonant; *an* is followed by a vowel. But a problem is caused by certain sounds which display properties of both consonants and vowels – in particular, the 'semi-vowels' /oo/ and /y/, as heard at the beginning of *wet* and *yet* respectively. These are articulated in the same way as vowels (they are really very short versions of /u/ and /i/), but within the structure of a word they take up one of the positions used by consonants, at the beginning of a syllable, as in *b-et, s-et, w-et, y-et*.

Shakespearian English shows several cases where the modern rule does not operate. There are instances where *an* is used before /y/:

Items	Examples
an eunuch	Cor III.ii.114
an union	Ham V.ii.266
an urinal	TG II.i.37
an usurer	MA II.i.174
an usurped	Oth I.iii.337
an universal	JC I.i.44

And a case where it is used before /oo/:

Item	Example
an one	AC I.ii.115

There are also several instances where *an* is used before /h/ in ways that would not be heard today. In modern English, /h/ is used as a consonant, so that we say *a horse*, not *an horse*. There is a contemporary usage trend where some people use *an* before *h*-words beginning with an unstressed first syllable, as in *an historic occasion*, but the crucial point is that this does not apply to words where the first syllable is stressed; people today do not (yet) say *an history book*. However, in Shakespearian English we do find *an* also used when the *h*-word is monosyllabic or begins with a stressed syllable:

Items	Examples
an habit	Ham V.ii.187
an habitation	2H4 I.iii.89
an hair	Tem I.ii.30
an hand	Per II.ii.36
an hasty-witted body	TS V.ii.40
an heretic	WT II.iii.114
an heroical	TC III.iii.248
an host	AC II.v.88
an hostess	TC III.iii.252
an house	2H4 I.iii.58
an humble	E3 II.i.233
an humour	H5 II.i.52
an hundred	Cor IV.v.111
an hypocrite	MM V.i.41

and, an (*conj.*) **1** if, even if **KL** I.iv.177 [Lear to Fool] *And you lie, sirrah, we'll have you whipped;* **TS** I.i.127 [Hortensio to Gremio] *there be good fellows in the world, an a man could light on them*
2 as if **H5** II.iii.11 [Hostess to Bardolph, of Falstaff] *'A ... went away an it had been any christom child*
3 if, whether **MND** V.i.190 [Bottom as Pyramus] *To spy an I can hear my Thisbe's face*

an if (*conj.*) if **Ham** I.v.176 [Hamlet to Horatio and Marcellus] *We could, an if we would*

andiron (*n.*) ornamental iron support in a fireplace **Cym** II.iv.88 [Iachimo to Posthumus, of Innogen's room] *Her andirons ... were two winking Cupids / Of silver*

angel (*n.*) **1** demon, evil spirit, attendant spirit **Mac** V.vi.53 [Macduff to Macbeth] *the angel whom thou still hast served*
2 ministering spirit, person who can perform a helpful office **TS** IV.ii.61 [Biondello to Tranio] *I spied / An ancient angel coming down the hill;* **JC** III.ii.182
3 gold coin [with the angel Michael depicted] **MW** I.iii.49 [Falstaff to Pistol, of Ford] *He hath a legion of angels;* **2H4** I.ii.167; **KJ** II.i.590 ☞ **MONEY**, p.286

angerly (*adv.*) angrily, grouchily, testily **TG** I.ii.62 [Julia alone] *How angerly I taught my brow to frown;* **KJ** IV.i.81; **Mac** III.v.1

angle (*n.*) **1** fishing rod, line, hook **AC** II.v.10 [Cleopatra to Charmian] *Give me mine angle;* **Ham** V.ii.66; **TNK** IV.i.59; **WT** IV.ii.45
2 corner, nook, spot **Tem** I.ii.223 [Ariel to Prospero, of Ferdinand] *I left cooling of the air with sighs / In an odd angle of the isle*

an-heires (*n.*) ☞ mynheer (*n.*)

an-hungry (*adj.*) hungry **Cor** I.i.203 [Martius to Menenius, of the citizens] *They said they were an-hungry*

a-night (*adv.*) at night **AY** II.iv.44 [Touchstone to Rosalind, of when he was in love] *coming a-night to Jane Smile* ☞ a (*prep.*) 1

annexion (*n.*) addition, attachment, supplement **Lover** 208 [of gifts to the woman] *Their kind acceptance, weepingly beseeched, / With th'annexions of fair gems enriched*

annexment (*n.*) appendage, adjunct, attachment **Ham** III.iii.21 [Rosencrantz to Claudius] *Each small annexment, petty consequence*

annothanize (*v.*) ☞ anatomize (*v.*)

annoy (*n.*) **1** trouble, vexation, distress **Venus** 497 [Venus to Adonis] *But now I lived, and life was death's annoy;* **3H6** V.vii.45; **Sonn** 8.4; **Tit** IV.i.49; **Venus** 599
2 injury, harm, hurt **R3** V.iii.157 [Ghosts of the Princes to Richmond] *Good angels guard thee from the boar's annoy!*

annoy (*v.*) harm, molest, hurt, injure **2H6** III.i.67 [King to all] *the care you have of us, / To mow down thorns that would annoy our foot, / Is worthy praise;* **Cym** IV.iii.34; **H5** II.ii.102; **JC** I.iii.22, II.i.160; **TS** I.i.181

annoyance (*n.*) **1** injury, harmfulness, danger **Mac** V.i.72 [Doctor to Gentlewoman, of Lady Macbeth] *Remove from her the means of all annoyance;* **KJ** V.i.150
2 discomfort, irritation, hurt **KJ** IV.i.93 [Arthur to Hubert, of Hubert's eyes] *O heaven, that there were ... / Any annoyance in that precious sense*

anon (*adv.*) **1** soon, shortly, presently **Ham** III.ii.250 [Hamlet to Claudius] *You shall see anon* ☞ FEW, p.xxi
2 [after 'now'] at another time, presently **LL** IV.ii.6 [Holofernes to Nathaniel, of an apple] *who now hangeth like a jewel ... and anon falleth like a crab;* **WT** III.iii.90

anon, ever and every now and then, at regular intervals **LL** V.ii.101 [Boyet to Princess, of the King's party] *ever and anon they made a doubt;* **1H4** I.iii.37

anon, still and continually **KJ** IV.i.47 [Arthur to Hubert] *I ... / Still and anon cheered up the heavy time*

anon, till for a little while **AC** II.vii.39 [Pompey aside to Menas] *Forbear me till anon*

answer *(n.)* **1** favourable reply, acceptance **Ham** V.ii.166 [Osrick to Hamlet] *if your lordship would vouchsafe the answer* [i.e. accept the challenge; pun: 167]; **H5** IV.vii.133

2 interrogation, cross-examination, appearance in court, trial **H8** IV.ii.14 [Griffith to Katherine, of Wolsey] *the stout Earl Northumberland / Arrested him at York, and brought him forward … to his answer;* **Cor** III.i.176; **2H4** II.i.30; **2H6** II.i.198; **R2** IV.i.159

3 recompense, requital, response **Cym** IV.iv.13 [Belarius to Guiderius and Arviragus, of Cloten's death] *may drive us to a render … and so extort from's that / Which we have done, whose answer would be death;* **AC** II.vii.99; **H5** IV.vii.133

4 retaliation, armed response **Cym** V.iii.79 [Posthumus alone, of the Roman slaughter] *great the answer be / Britons must take;* **Cym** IV.ii.161; **KL** II.ii.14

5 [fencing] return hit **TN** III.iv.270 [Sir Toby to Sir Andrew, of Viola as Cesario] *on the answer, he pays you as surely as your feet hits the ground they step on;* **Ham** V.ii.263

6 accountability, responsibility, liability, penalty **JC** I.iii.114 [Cassius to Casca] *I know / My answer must be made;* **H5** II.ii.143; **MM** II.iv.73; **Tim** V.iv.63

answer *(v.)* **1** answer back, make a rejoinder **AY** III.v.132 [Phebe to Silvius, of Rosalind as Ganymede] *I marvel why I answered not again;* **Cym** IV.ii.215

2 explain, excuse, answer satisfactorily **2H6** III.i.133 [Suffolk to Gloucester] *these faults are easy, quickly answered;* **2H6** IV.vii.39

3 satisfy, discharge, requite **AY** II.vii.100 [Orlando to all] *He dies that touches any of this fruit / Till I and my affairs are answered;* **Cym** I.v.160; **1H6** IV.i.62; **MW** I.i.108; **Tem** II.i.190; **TN** III.iii.29

4 suffer the consequences [for], be accountable [for] **JC** III.ii.81 [Antony to all] *The noble Brutus / Hath told you Caesar was ambitious … grievously hath Caesar answered it;* **AC** V.ii.178; **Cor** III.i.162; **1H4** IV.ii.8; **R3** IV.ii.92; **TN** III.iv.324

5 cope with, face, encounter **KL** III.iv.98 [Lear to Edgar as Poor Tom] *Thou wert better in a grave than to answer with thy uncovered body this extremity of the skies;* **Cor** I.iv.54; **2H4** IV.v.196; **JC** IV.i.47; **Tim** IV.iii.232

6 engage with, encounter, meet [in fight] **Cor** I.ii.19 [First Senator to Aufidius] *We never yet made doubt but Rome was ready / To answer us;* **AC** III.xiii.36; **KJ** V.vi.60; **TC** I.i.126

7 pay, repay, requite **CE** IV.i.60 [Second Merchant to Antipholus of Ephesus] *say whe'er you'll answer me or no;* **CE** I.i.62, 83; **Luc** 83

8 give in return, repay **3H6** II.vi.55 [Warwick to Richard] *Measure for measure must be answered;* **Cor** V.vi.67

9 respond, react **AW** II.ii.51 [Countess to Clown] *you would answer very well to a whipping* [also: be suited to]; **JC** V.i.6, 24; **TC** I.iii.171

10 live up to, correspond to, be equal to **Cym** IV.ii.192 [Guiderius to Belarius] *All solemn things / Should answer solemn accidents;* **CE** III.i.20; **2H6** IV.x.51; **MA** V.i.12; **MM** III.ii.244; **R3** I.iii.193

11 act along with, sustain, respond to **Cym** V.iii.91 [Posthumus to First Captain, of himself] *Who had not now been drooping here if seconds / Had answered him;* **Cor** I.iii.258; **E3** III.iii.153; **TC** IV.iv.131

12 fulfil, meet, satisfy **MA** II.i.334 [Leonato to Claudio, of a week until the marriage] *a time too brief … to have all things answer my mind;* **Cym** V.v.451; **Tem** I.ii.367

13 return, respond to, requite **MW** IV.iv.10 [Fenton to Host] *the dear love I bear to fair Anne Page, / Who mutually hath answered my affection*

14 account for, justify, defend **Ham** III.iv.177 [Hamlet to Gertrude, of Polonius] *I … will answer well / The death I gave him;* **Cym** III.v.72; **Ham** IV.i.16; **KJ** IV.ii.89; **Oth** I.i.120; **Oth** V.ii.151

15 go along with, belong with **Cym** III.iv.172 [Pisanio to Innogen, of her male disguise] *Fore-thinking this, I have already fit … doublet, hat, hose, all / That answer to them*

16 reflect, mirror, correspond to **H5** IV.Chorus.8 [Chorus, of the two army camps] *Fire answers fire*

answerable *(adj.)* corresponding, commensurate, proportionate **TS** II.i.352 [Gremio to Baptista, of his estate] *all things answerable to this portion;* **Oth** I.iii.341

anthem *(n.)* song of mourning, hymn of grief **Phoen** 21 *Here the anthem doth commence;* **2H4** I.iii.191; **TG** III.i.240; **Venus** 839

anthropophaginian *(n.)* man-eater, cannibal **MW** IV.v.8 [Host to Simple, of Falstaff] *He'll speak like an Anthropophaginian unto thee*

antic, antick(e), antique *(n.)* **1** grotesque figure, grinning jester, buffoon **1H6** IV.vii.18 [Talbot to Servant, as if to Death] *Thou antic Death, which laughest us here to scorn;* **H5** III.ii.31; **MA** I.i.63; **R2** III.ii.162; **TC** V.iii.86; **TS** Induction.i.99

2 bizarre dance, fantastic spectacle, grotesque entertainment **TNK** IV.i.75 [Wooer to all, reporting the Gaoler's Daughter's words] *we'll dance an antic 'fore the Duke;* **LL** II.i.106, 140; **Luc** 459

antic, antick(e), antique *(adj.)* **1** fantastic, bizarre, weird **Ham** I.v.172 [Hamlet to Horatio and Marcellus] *I perchance hereafter shall think meet / To put an antic disposition on;* **AY** II.i.31; **Mac** IV.i.129; **RJ** I.v.56, II.iv.28; **Sonn** 19.10

2 ancient, olden, former **Cor** II.iii.118 [Coriolanus alone] *The dust on antique time would lie unswept;* **AY** II.iii.57; **E3** IV.iv.27; **H5** V.Chorus.26; **Sonn** 59.7, 68.9, 106.7

3 old-fashioned, old-world, antiquated **TN** II.iv.3 [Orsino to Viola as Cesario] *That old and antique song we heard last night;* **MND** V.i.3; **Sonn** 17.12

antic, antick(e), antique *(v.)* make grotesque figure of, make fools of **AC** II.vii.123 [Caesar to Antony] *The wild disguise hath almost / Anticked us all*

anticly, antiquely *(adv.)* grotesquely, like a buffoon, in an antic manner **MA** I.i.96 [Antonio to Leonato, of boys like Claudio and Don Pedro] *That … / Go anticly, show outward hideousness*

antiquary *(adj.)* ancient, olden, former **TC** II.iii.248 [Ulysses to Ajax] *Here's Nestor, / Instructed by the antiquary times*

antique Roman ancient Roman [i.e. viewing suicide as an honourable option] **Ham** V.ii.335 [Horatio to Hamlet] *I am more an antique Roman than a Dane*

antiquity *(n.)* old age, seniority **2H4** I.ii.186 [Lord Chief Justice to Falstaff] *Is not … every part about you blasted with antiquity?;* **AW** II.iii.208 ; **Sonn** 62.10

antre *(n.)* cave, cavern **Oth** I.iii.139 [Othello to all] *of antres vast and deserts idle … / It was my hint to speak*

apace *(adv.)* quickly, speedily, at a great rate **AY** III.ii.192 [Rosalind to Celia, of who is writing the verses] *tell me who is it quickly, and speak apace* ➤ FEW, p.xxi

apaid *(adj.)* ➤ appaid *(adj.)*

apart *(adv.)* away from here; or: separately **Mac** III.i.137 [Macbeth to Murderers, of killing Banquo] *Resolve yourselves apart*

apathaton *(n.)* ➤ epitheton *(n.)*

ape *(n.)* **1** mimic, imitator, impersonator **WT** V.ii.98 [Third Gentleman to all, of the sculptor of Hermione's statue] *he … would beguile Nature of her custom, so perfectly he is her ape;* **Cym** II.ii.31; **LL** V.ii.325

2 fool, idiot, jackass **MA** V.i.91 [Antonio to and of Claudio and Don Pedro] *Boys, apes, braggarts, Jacks;* **Cym** IV.ii.193; **2H4** II.v.211, IV.v.123

ape-bearer *(n.)* showman with a performing monkey **WT** IV.iii.92 [Autolycus to Clown, of the supposed robber] *He hath been since an ape-bearer*

a-pieces *(adv.)* ➤ a *(prep.)* 3

apish *(adj.)* **1** silly, foolish, trifling **AY** III.ii.393 [Rosalind as Ganymede to Orlando] *[I would be] fantastical, apish, shallow*

2 ape-like in copying, stupidly imitative **KL** I.iv.166 [Fool to Lear, of wise men] *Their manners are so apish*

apology *(n.)* formal justification, explanation **LL** V.i.129 [Holofernes to Armado, of Mote as Hercules] *His enter and exit shall be strangling a snake; and I will have an apology for that purpose*

apoplexed *(adj.)* paralysed, benumbed **Ham** III.iv.74 [Hamlet to Gertrude] *that sense / Is apoplexed*

apoplexy *(n.)* paralysis, torpor, total breakdown **Cor** IV.v.230 [First Servingman to Second Servingman] *Peace is a very apoplexy, lethargy;* **2H4** I.ii.108, IV.iv.130

aporne *(n.)* apron **2H6** II.iii.74 [Peter to Robin] *an if I die, I give thee my aporne* [F]

apostrophus *(n.)* mark of elision **LL** IV.ii.119 [Holofernes to Nathaniel, of reading Berowne's letter to Rosaline] *You find not the apostrophus, and so miss the accent* [F *apostraphas*]

apothecary, pothecary *(n.)* one who prepares and sells medicinal drugs **2H6** III.iii.17 [Cardinal to his visions] *bid the apothecary / Bring the strong poison that I bought of him;* **Per** III.ii.9 [Cerimon to Second Servant] *Give this to the pothecary;* **KL** IV.vi.130; **RJ** V.i.37, iii.289

appaid, apaid *(adj.)* pleased, satisfied, contented **Luc** 914 [Lucrece as if to opportunity, of sin] *He gratis comes, and thou art well appaid*

appal *(v.)* turn pale, terrify, dismay **Ham** II.ii.561 [Hamlet alone] *Make mad the guilty and appal the free;* **1H6** I.ii.48; **TC** V.v.15

apparel *(n.)* clothes, clothing, dress **AY** II.iv.5 [Rosalind as Ganymede to Celia as Aliena] *disgrace my man's apparel* ➤ FEW, p.xxi

apparel *(v.)* **1** clothe, dress up, trick out **E3** II.i.411 [Warwick to Countess] *Thus have I … / Apparelled sin in virtuous sentences;* **CE** III.ii.12; **1H6** II.iv.22; **2H6** IV.ii.69; **MA** IV.i.225; **TS** III.ii.89
2 cover, put a hat on **LL** V.i.93 [Armado to Holofernes] *I beseech thee, apparel thy head*

apparent *(n.)* heir-apparent, closest in line **3H6** II.ii.64 [Prince to King, of his sword] *I'll draw it as apparent to the crown;* **WT** I.ii.177

apparent *(adj.)* **1** plainly visible, conspicuous, evident, obvious **R3** III.v.30 [Richard to Buckingham, of Hastings] *his apparent open guilt omitted;* **E3** III.iii.22; **1H6** I.i.3, IV.i.26; **R2** I.i.13, IV.i.124; **WT** I.ii.270
2 certain, inevitable, evident **TG** III.i.116 [Duke to Valentine, of a high chamber] *one cannot climb it / Without apparent hazard of his life;* **1H6** IV.v.44

apparently *(adv.)* blatantly, openly, flagrantly **CE** IV.i.79 [Angelo to Officer] *I would not spare my brother in this case / If he should scorn me so apparently*

appeach *(v.)* denounce, inform against, impeach **R2** V.ii.102 [York to Duchess of York, of Aumerle] *Were he twenty times my son / I would appeach him;* **AW** I.iii.186; **R2** V.ii.79

appeal *(n.)* accusation, charge of treason **R2** IV.i.45 [Percy to Aumerle, of Fitzwater] *His honour is as true / In this appeal as thou art all unjust;* **AC** III.v.10; **R2** I.i.4, IV.i.79

appeal *(v.)* **1** accuse, denounce, impeach **R2** I.i.27 [King Richard to Mowbray and Bolingbroke] *you come, / Namely, to appeal each other of high treason;* **R2** I.i.9, iii.21
2 allege, accuse, charge **R2** I.i.142 [Mowbray to King Richard, of Bolingbroke's charges] *As for the rest appealed*

appear *(v.)* **1** be plain, become apparent **Cor** I.i.22 [Aufidius to all, of their plans] *which in the hatching, / It seemed, appeared to Rome;* **Cor** IV.ii.9 [F]; **H5** I.ii.88
2 reveal, disclose, show **Cym** III.iv.147 [Pisanio to Innogen] *if you could … but disguise / That which, t'appear itself, must not yet be / But by self-danger*
3 present oneself as, have the character of **Per** II.i.142 [Pericles to Fishermen, of his armour] *with it I may appear a gentleman*

appearance *(n.)* likeness, semblance **2H4** I.i.128 [Morton to Northumberland, of Douglas] *whose well-labouring sword / Had three times slain th'appearance of the King*

appearer *(n.)* one who arrives on the scene **Per** V.iii.18 [Pericles to Cerimon] *Reverend appearer*

appease *(v.)* pacify, subdue, made obedient **2H6** IV.iv.42 [Queen to all] *were the Duke of Suffolk now alive, / These Kentish rebels would be soon appeased!*

appellant *(n.)* accuser [of treason], challenger, denouncer **R2** I.iii.4 [Lord Marshal to Aumerle] *The Duke of Norfolk … / Stays but the summons of the appellant's trumpet;* **2H6** II.iii.49, 57; **R2** I.i.34

appendix *(n.)* appendage, accompaniment, hanger-on **TS** IV.iv.100 [Biondello to Lucentio, of Bianca] *you come with your appendix*

apperil *(n.)* peril, risk, danger **Tim** I.ii.32 [Apemantus to Timon] *Let me stay at thine apperil*

appertain *(v.)* pertain, relate **KL** I.i.284 [Gonerill to Regan] *it is not little I have to say of what most nearly appertains to us both;* **JC** II.i.282

appertaining *(adj.)* related, relevant, appropriate **RJ** III.i.62 [Romeo to Tybalt] *the reason that I have to love thee / Doth much excuse the appertaining rage / To such a greeting;* **Tem** III.i.96

appertainings *(n.)* trappings, belongings, appurtenances **Lover** 115 [of the man] *His real habitude gave life and grace / To appertainings and to ornament*

appertainments *(n.)* appurtenances, trappings, prerogatives **TC** II.iii.79 [Agamemnon to Patroclus, of Achilles] *we lay by / Our appertainments, visiting of him*

appertinent *(n.)* appurtenance, accompaniment **H5** II.ii.87 [King Henry to all, of Cambridge] *To furnish him with all appertinents / Belonging to his honour*

appertinent *(adj.)* appertaining, belonging, relating **2H4** I.ii.173 [Falstaff to Lord Chief Justice] *all the other gifts appertinent to man … are not worth a gooseberry;* **LL** I.ii.16

appetite *(n.)* **1** desire, longing, inclination, fancy **TN** II.iv.96 [Orsino to Viola as Cesario, of women] *their love may be called appetite;* **Oth** II.iii.337; **Sonn** 147.4; **TC** I.iii.120; **TN** I.i.3; **Venus** 34
2 sexual desire, passion **TC** II.ii.182 [Hector to Paris and Troilus, of laws] *To curb those raging appetites that are / Most disobedient and refractory;* **Cym** I.vii.43; **Lover** 166; **Luc** 9; **Sonn** 56.2

applause *(n.)* acclamation, shout of approval **Tit** I.i.233 [Marcus to all, of creating Saturninus emperor] *With voices and applause of every sort;* **JC** I.ii.132

apple *(n.)* pupil, centre **MND** III.ii.104 [Oberon to himself, as if to the flower, of Demetrius] *Flower of this purple dye … / Sink in apple of his eye;* **LL** V.ii.475

apple-john *(n.)* kind of apple with a shrivelled skin [associated with midsummer (St John's) day] **1H4** III.iii.4 [Falstaff to Bardolph] *I am withered like an old apple-john;* **2H4** II.iv.1

appliance *(n.)* **1** remedy, cure, treatment **Ham** IV.iii.10 [Claudius to his attendants] *Diseases desperate grown / By desperate appliance are relieved;* **AW** II.i.113; **H8** I.i.124; **TNK** IV.iii.98
2 compliance, subservience; or: means, expedient **MM** III.i.92 [Isabella to Claudio] *Thou art too noble to conserve a life / In base appliances*

application *(n.)* **1** treatment, remedy, healing method **AW** I.ii.74 [King to Bertram, of doctors] *[they] have worn me out / With several applications*
2 analogy, allusion, reference **E3** II.i.163 [King Edward to Lodowick, of the Countess] *in this application to the sun, / Bid her be free and general as the sun*

apply *(v.)* **1** conform, bend, adapt **AC** V.ii.126 [Caesar to Cleopatra] *If you apply yourself to our intents;* **MW** II.ii.229
2 pursue, practise, devote oneself to **TS** I.i.19 [Lucentio to Tranio] *that part of philosophy / Will I apply that treats of happiness / By virtue specially to be achieved*
3 be directed, be given, attend well to **Mac** III.ii.30 [Macbeth to Lady Macbeth] *Let your remembrance apply to Banquo*
4 interpret, expound **JC** II.ii.80 [Caesar to Decius, of Calphurnia's dream] *these does she apply for warnings and portents*

appoint *(v.)* **1** arm, equip, furnish **1H6** IV.ii.21 [General to Talbot] *the Dauphin, well appointed, / Stands with the snares of war to tangle thee;* **3H6** II.i.113 [Q only]; **Tit** IV.ii.16; **TNK** III.vi.134; **WT** IV.iv.589

2 grant, provide, assign **E3** IV.ii.31 [King Edward to Derby, of the poor Frenchmen] *Command that victuals be appointed them;* **JC** IV.i.30; **MW** II.i.192

3 destine, assign, arrange **TNK** V.i.151 [Emilia praying to Diana] *a husband I have 'pointed, / But do not know him;* **Luc** 879

4 ordain, set up, establish **WT** I.ii.326 [Leontes to Camillo, of his doubts about Hermione] *Dost think I am so muddy ... / To appoint my self in this vexation*

5 agree, arrange, make an appointment **MW** III.ii.49 [Slender to Ford] *We have appointed to dine with Mistress Anne;* **Tit** IV.iv.102

6 determine, resolve, purpose **Mac** II.iii.50 [Macbeth to Lennox, of the King's going forth] *he did appoint so*

7 direct, order, instruct **TS** IV.iv.98 [Biondello to Lucentio] *My master hath appointed me to go to Saint Luke's;* **MW** IV.ii.88

appointment (*n.*) **1** equipment, effects, weaponry **TNK** III.i.40 [Palamon to Arcite] *I'll prove it ... with these hands, / Void of appointment, that thou liest;* **Ham** IV.vi.16; **1H4** I.ii.173; **R2** III.iii.53; **TNK** I.iv.15

2 purpose, design, intention **AW** II.v.67 [Bertram to Helena] *my appointments have in them a need / Greater than shows itself at the first view;* **AC** IV.x.8

3 order, direction, arrangement **KJ** II.i.296 [King John to Bastard, of the plain] *where we'll set forth / In best appointment all our regiments;* **H8** II.ii.132

4 preparation, arrangement, coming to terms **MM** III.i.63 [Isabella to Claudio] *your best appointment make with speed*

apprehend (*v.*) **1** seize, arrest, lay hold of **KL** I.ii.79 [Gloucester to Edmund, of Edgar] *I'll apprehend him;* **H5** II.ii.2; **3H6** III.i.71; **MW** IV.v.107; **Oth** I.ii.77; **TN** V.i.84

2 seize upon, snatch at, lay hold of **1H4** I.iii.207 [Worcester to Northumberland, of Hotspur] *He apprehends a world of figures here;* **Tim** I.i.211

3 be apprehensive about, fear **MM** IV.ii.139 [Provost to disguised Duke, of Barnardine] *A man that apprehends death no more dreadfully but as a drunken sleep;* **E3** IV.iv.64; **TC** III.ii.72

4 imagine, conceive, invent **MND** V.i.5 [Theseus to Hippolyta, of lovers' imaginings] *that apprehend / More than cool reason ever comprehends;* **MND** V.i.19

5 perceive the significance, discern, grasp the matter [of] **MA** II.i.72 [Leonato to Beatrice] *you apprehend passing shrewdly;* **TC** III.iii.124

6 view, see, look **Cym** III.iii.17 [Belarius to Guiderius and Arviragus, of his viewpoint] *To apprehend thus, / Draws us a profit from all things we see* [i.e. to see things in this way]

apprehension (*n.*) **1** powers of comprehension, understanding **H5** III.vii.132 [Constable to Orleans] *If the English had any apprehension, they would run away;* **Cor** II.iii.223; **Ham** II.ii.306, IV.i.11

2 conception, grasping by the mind, awareness **R2** I.iii.300 [Bolingbroke to John of Gaunt] *the apprehension of the good / Gives but the greater feeling to the worse;* **Cym** IV.ii.110; **LL** IV.ii.68; **MM** III.i.81; **Tim** I.i.210

3 sharpness of mind, quickness of uptake **MA** III.iv.61 [Beatrice to Margaret] *How long have you professed apprehension?*

4 perception, auditory reception **MND** III.ii.178 [Hermia to all] *Dark night that from the eye his function takes / The ear more quick of apprehension makes*

5 opinion, notion, view **1H6** II.iv.102 [Richard to Somerset, of the slur against his father] *I'll note you in my book of memory / To scourge you for this apprehension;* **1H4** IV.i.66; **Oth** III.iii.138

6 arrest, seizure, laying hold **KL** III.v.18 [Cornwall to Edmund, of Gloucester] *he may be ready for our apprehension;* **3H6** III.ii.122

apprehensive (*adj.*) quick-learning, perceptive, ever alert **AW** I.ii.60 [King to Bertram] *younger spirits, whose apprehensive senses / All but new things disdain;* **2H4** IV.iii.98; **JC** III.i.67

apprenticehood (*n.*) apprenticeship **R2** I.iii.271 [Bolingbroke to John of Gaunt] *Must I not serve a long apprenticehood / To foreign passages*

approach (*n.*) **1** arrival, coming **1H6** II.i.9 [Talbot to the others] *Burgundy, / By whose approach the regions of Artois, / Walloon, and Picardy are friends to us* [i.e. by arriving in support]

2 advances, amorous attention **TG** V.iv.31 [Silvia to Proteus] *By thy approach thou makes me most unhappy*

3 advance, attack, offensive **Tim** V.i.162 [First Senator to Timon, of his help] *So soon we shall drive back / Of Alcibiades th'approaches wild;* **H5** II.iv.9; **KJ** V.ii.131; **Tim** V.ii.4

approach (*v.*) arrive, come, turn up **Cym** II.iv.39 [Iachimo to Posthumus, of Lucius] *He was expected then, / But not approached*

approacher (*n.*) one who approaches **TNK** V.ix.9 [Palamon to his knights] *We ... beguile / The gout and rheum, that in lag hours attend / For grey approachers* [i.e. those approaching death]

approbation (*n.*) **1** expression of approval, pleasurable confirmation, ready sanctioning **Cor** II.iii.250 [Sicinius to Citizens] *revoke / Your sudden approbation;* **Cor** I.i.99, iii.144; **Cym** I.v.17; **H8** I.ii.71; **Per** IV.iii.26

2 proof, confirmation, attestation **Cym** I.v.121 [Iachimo to Posthumus] *Would I had put my estate ... on th'approbation of what I have spoke!;* **MM** V.i.243; **TN** III.iv.178; **WT** II.i.177

3 acceptance as a novice, probationary period **MM** I.ii.177 [Claudio to Lucio] *This day my sister should the cloister enter, / And there receive her approbation*

4 proving true, putting to the test, support **H5** I.ii.19 [King Henry to Canterbury] *many now in health / Shall drop their blood in approbation / Of what your reverence shall incite us to*

approof (*n.*) **1** proven quality, undoubted character **AW** II.v.2 [Lafew to Bertram, of Parolles] *I hope your lordship thinks not him a soldier. [Bertram] Yes ... and of very valiant approof;* **AC** III.ii.27

2 approval, approbation, sanction **MM** II.iv.174 [Isabella alone, of mouths] *That bear in them one and the selfsame tongue, / Either of condemnation or approof*

3 proof, affirmation, attestation **AW** I.ii.50 [Bertram to King, of his father] *So in approof lives not his epitaph / As in your royal speech* [i.e. what you have said attests to him more truthfully than does his epitaph]

appropriation (*n.*) special attribute, particular feature **MV** I.ii.39 [Portia to Nerissa, of the Neopolitan prince and his horse] *he makes it a great appropriation to his own good parts that he can shoe him himself*

approve (*v.*) **1** prove, confirm, corroborate, substantiate **KL** II.iv.178 [Regan to Cornwall, of the trumpet-call announcing Goneril] *This approves her letter;* **AW** III.vii.13; **Ham** I.i.29; **MA** IV.i.297; **Oth** II.iii.58; **WT** IV.ii.27

2 endorse, support, accept as true **Oth** I.iii.11 [Duke to Senators] *the main article I do approve / In fearful sense;* **Per** II.i.51

3 put to the proof, test, try **TS** I.i.7 [Lucentio to and of Tranio] *My trusty servant well approved in all;* **1H4** IV.i.9; **2H4** I.ii.191; **Oth** II.iii.303

4 commend, praise, show to be worthy **Sonn** 42.8 *for my sake even so doth she abuse me, / Suff'ring my friend for my sake to approve her* **Ham** V.ii.134; **Oth** IV.iii.18

5 prove guilty, convict **Oth** II.iii.205 [Othello to all, of the brawl] *he that is approved in this offence ... / Shall lose me*

approved (*adj.*) tested, tried, established, proven **MA** II.i.351 [Don Pedro to all, of Benedick] *he is ... of approved valour;* **CE** V.i.103; **1H4** I.i.54; **MA** IV.i.42; **R2** I.iii.44; **Tit** V.i.1

approver (*n.*) tester, someone who subjects others to the proof **Cym** II.iv.25 [Posthumus to Philario, of the British] *Their discipline ... will make known / To their approvers they are people such / That mend upon the world*

appurtenance (*n.*) usual accompaniment, accessory **Ham** II.ii.370 [Hamlet to Rosencrantz and Guildenstern] *Th'appurtenance of welcome is fashion and ceremony*

apricock (*n.*) apricot **MND** III.i.161 [Titania to Fairies, of Bottom] *Feed him with apricocks;* **R2** III.iv.29; **TNK** II.i.292

apron-man (*n.*) aproned worker, tradesman **Cor** IV.vi.97 [Menenius to Brutus and Sicinius] *You and your apron-men*

apt (*adj.*) **1** fit, ready, prepared **KL** IV.ii.65 [Albany to Gonerill, of his hands] *They are apt enough to dislocate and tear / Thy flesh and bones;* **Ham** I.v.31; **H5** II.ii.86; **JC** III.i.160; **MM** V.i.495; **TN** I.iv.35

2 prompt, quick, ready **H8** II.v.122 [Campeius to all] *The Queen is obstinate, / Stubborn to justice, apt to accuse it, and / Disdainful to be tried by't*

3 natural, predictable, plausible, to be expected **Oth** II.i.278 [Iago alone, of Desdemona and Cassio] *That she loves him, 'tis apt and of great credit;* **Cym** V.v.445; **Oth** V.iv.176

4 likely, inclined, prone **TNK** IV.ii.97 [Pirithous to Theseus, comparing Palamon's knight to Arcite's] *[he is] apter / To make this cause his own;* **JC** II.ii.97; **RJ** III.iii.157

5 yielding, compliant, submissive **Cor** III.ii.29 [Volumnia to Coriolanus] *I have a heart as little apt as yours;* **H5** V.ii.281

6 impressionable, susceptible **JC** V.iii.68 [Messala as if to Error] *Why dost thou show to the apt thoughts of men / The things that are not?;* **Tim** I.i.136; **Venus** 354

aptly (*adv.*) easily, readily **Per** V.ii.5 [Gower alone] *you aptly will suppose / What pageantry ... / The regent made in Mytilene;* **Ham** III.iv.166; **Lover** 88; **TN** III.iv.189; **Venus** 716

aqua-vitae (*n.*) spirits, alcohol, strong drink, brandy **TN** II.v.189 [Sir Toby to Maria, of whether her plan is working] *Like aqua-vitae with a midwife;* **CE** IV.i.90; **MW** II.ii.289; **RJ** III.ii.88, IV.v.16; **WT** IV.iv.782

Aquilon (*n.*) north wind **TC** IV.v.9 [Ajax to trumpeter] *Blow ... till thy sphered bias cheek / Outswell the colic of puffed Aquilon*

Arabian bird phoenix [mythical bird, of which only one existed at any time] **Cym** I.vii.17 [Iachimo to himself, of Innogen] *If she be furnished with a mind so rare, / She is alone th'Arabian bird;* **AC** III.ii.12

araise (*v.*) raise from the dead, awake from the grave **AW** II.i.76 [Lafew to King] *a medicine / That ... / Is powerful to araise King Pippen*

arbitrament, arbitrement (*n.*) **1** deciding of a dispute, determination, settlement **KL** IV.vii.94 [Gentleman to disguised Kent] *The arbitrament is like to be bloody;* **Cym** I.v.47; **H5** IV.i.155; **R3** V.iii.90; **TN** III.iv.255

2 decision, judgement, verdict **TNK** V.iii.107 [Theseus to Emilia, of Arcite] *The gods by their divine arbitrament / Have given you this knight*

3 adjudication, judicious examination **1H4** IV.i.70 [Worcester to Hotspur] *we of the offering side / Must keep aloof from strict arbitrement*

arbitrator (*n.*) **1** one who brings to a conclusion, resolver **1H6** II.v.28 [Mortimer to Gaolers] *now the arbitrator of despairs, / Just Death;* **TC** IV.v.225

2 arbiter, umpire **Luc** 1017 [Lucrece to herself] *Out, idle words ... / Unprofitable sounds, weak arbitrators!*

arbour (*n.*) bower, shady retreat **E3** II.i.61 [King Edward to Lodowick] *in the summer arbour sit by me;* **2H4** V.iii.2

arch (*n.*) chief, master, lord **KL** II.i.58 [Gloucester to Edmund] *The noble Duke, my master, / My worthy arch and patron*

arch (*adj.*) chief, principal, pre-eminent **R3** IV.iii.2 [Tyrrel alone, of killing the Princes] *The most arch deed of piteous massacre [i.e. heinous deed];* **3H6** II.ii.2; **KL** II.i.58

arch-mock (*n.*) chief mockery, main jibe **Oth** IV.i.70 [Iago to Othello] *O, 'tis ... the fiend's arch-mock, / To lip a wanton in a secure couch, / And to suppose her chaste!* ▸ **mock** (*n.*) 1

ardently (*adv.*) burningly, intensely, passionately **TNK** I.i.126 [Emilia to Third Queen] *Your sorrow beats so ardently upon me*

argal, argo (*adv.*) [variants of Latin 'ergo'] therefore **Ham** V.i.19 [First Clown to Second Clown] *Argal, he that is not guilty of his own death shortens not his own life;* **2H6** IV.ii.29 [Bevis to Holland, of the rebels] *Argo, their web of life is spun* ▸ **LATIN**, p.643; **ergo** (*adv.*)

argentine (*adj.*) clothed in silver **Per** V.i.248 [Pericles as if to Diana] *goddess argentine*

argosy (*n.*) large merchant ship **MV** V.i.276 [Portia to Antonio] *three of your argosies / Are richly come to harbour;* **3H6** II.vi.36; **MV** I.i.9, I.iii.18, III.i.92; **TS** II.i.367

argue (*v.*) **1** indicate, betoken, be evidence of **1H6** II.v.7 [Mortimer to Gaolers, of his hair] *these grey locks ... / Argue the end of Edmund Mortimer;* **Ham** V.i.11; **2H6** III.iii.30; **3H6** II.i.25; **Luc** 65; **RJ** II.iii.29

2 examine, discuss the pros and cons of **H8** II.i.168 [First Gentleman to Second Gentleman] *We are too open here to argue this*

argument (*n.*) **1** subject of conversation, subject-matter, topic **MA** I.i.236 [Don Pedro to Benedick] *thou wilt prove a notable argument;* **AW** II.iii.7; **1H4** II.ii.93; **H5** III.vii.34; **KL** II.i.8; **TN** II.v.146

2 story, subject, plot **1H4** II.iv.274 [Prince Hal to Falstaff, of his suggestion for a play] *the argument shall be thy running away;* **Ham** II.ii.354, III.ii.148, 242; **WT** IV.i.29

3 subject, point, theme, target **KL** I.i.215 [France to Lear, of Cordelia] *she whom even but now was ... / The argument of your praise;* **AY** III.i.3; **MA** III.iii.11; **Mac** II.iii.117; **MND** III.ii.242; **R2** I.i.12

4 discussion, debate, dialogue **MA** II.iii.51 [Don Pedro to Balthasar] *if thou wilt hold longer argument, / Do it in notes;* **AW** III.v.58; **KJ** I.i.36; **LL** V.ii.84

5 quarrel, dispute, point of contention **TNK** V.i.70 [Palamon to his knights] *our argument is love;* **H5** III.i.21; **KJ** IV.i.54; **TC** I.i.94 [or: sense 8]

6 proof, evidence, demonstration **TN** III.ii.10 [Fabian to Sir Andrew, of Olivia] *This was a great argument of love in her toward you;* **E3** IV.vii.11; **1H6** IV.i.46; **2H6** I.i.32, III.i.241; **MW** II.ii.236

7 proposition, logical deduction **Tim** III.v.23 [Alcibiades to Senators, of his friend] *He did behove his anger, ere 'twas spent, / As if he had but proved an argument*

8 cause, reason [for a dispute] **AY** I.ii.268 [Le Beau to Orlando] *Grounded upon no other argument;* **Ham** IV.iv.54; **H5** IV.i.139; **TC** I.i.94, IV.v.26

9 power of reasoning, keenness in debate **MA** III.i.96 [Ursula to Hero, of Benedick] *For ... argument and valour, / Goes foremost in report through Italy*

arithmetic (*n.*) calculation, computation, reckoning **Cor** III.i.244 [Cominius to Coriolanus] *'tis odds beyond arithmetic [i.e. they are by far greater in numbers];* **Ham** V.ii.114; **RJ** III.i.102

arithmetician (*n.*) theoretician, academic **Oth** I.i.19 [Iago to Roderigo, of Cassio] *a great arithmetician*

arm (*n.*) **1** strong arm [in attack]; or, might, power **AC** I.v.23 [Cleopatra to Charmian, of Antony] *the arm / And burgonet of men [i.e. pre-eminent attacker]*

2 ▸ **arms** (*n.*)

arm (*v.*) **1** prepare, get ready **Ham** III.iii.24 [Claudius to Rosencrantz and Guildenstern] *Arm you ... to this speedy voyage;* **MND** I.i.117

2 prepare for action, put armour on **AW** I.ii.11 [King to First Lord, of Austria] *He hath armed our answer [to Florence]*

3 give your arm to **TNK** V.iii.135 [Theseus to Arcite, of Emilia] *Arm your prize*

4 take into one's arms, lift up **Cym** IV.ii.400 [Lucius to soldiers, of Cloten's body] *come, arm him*

armado (*n.*) armada, fleet, navy **E3** III.i.64 [Mariner to King John] *The proud armado of King Edward's ships;* **CE** III.ii.144; **KJ** III.iv.2

armed (*adj.*) **1** armoured, mail-clad, furnished with defences **Mac** III.iv.100 [Macbeth to Banquo's ghost] *Approach thou like ... / The armed rhinoceros;* **2H4** II.ii.118; **KJ** V.ii.156

2 provided, ready, prepared [for] **3H6** IV.i.127 [Edward to all, of his enemies] *Yet am I armed against the worst can happen;* **LL** I.i.22

3 with arms **TNK** IV.ii.85 [Messenger to Theseus, of one of Arcite's knights] *his shoulders broad and strong, / Armed long and round [also: pun on 'well-armed']*

arm-gaunt *(adj.)* [unclear meaning] in fine condition; with gaunt limbs; with armoured trappings **AC** I.v.48 [Alexas to Cleopatra, of Antony] *he ... soberly did mount an arm-gaunt steed* [F *Arme-gaunt*]

armigero *(n.)* esquire [entitled to bear heraldic arms] **MW** I.i.9 [Slender to Evans, of Shallow] *who writes himself Armigero - in any bill, warrant, quittance, or obligation*

ARCHAISMS

Many words used in Shakespearian English seem archaic to us today, and are sometimes consciously used as archaisms in such genres as poetry, historical novels, and comic books. The use of *forsooth, zounds, by my troth,* and the like adds an (often artificial) element of antique colouring to an otherwise modern text. Some of the forms will also still be heard in regional dialects.

Archaisms were also around in Shakespeare's time, usually items taken from Chaucer and his contemporaries, or popularized by later writers with a historical consciousness, such as Spenser. The instances typically occur in cases where characters are reading texts where an older style of language has been contrived, such as a love-letter, scroll, or play script; but they also turn up in certain types of character (such as schoolmasters) and in the speech of such bombastic personalities as Pistol (in *Henry V*) and Don Armado (in *Love's Labour's Lost*). Archaisms are most notable in Shakespeare's poems, and in the Chorus monologues of the medieval poet Gower in *Pericles*; these include several instances of a *y-* prefix before verbs, a remnant of the Old English *ge-* form used chiefly as a past-time marker in past participles. Further examples are given under individual entries in the A–Z section.

Item	Gloss	Example
clepe	call	**Venus** 993 [of Venus and death] *She clepes him king of graves*
eke	also, moreover, too	**MND** III.i.88 [Flute as Thisbe, of Pyramus] *Most brisky juvenal, and eke most lovely Jew*
eyne	eyes	**Luc** 1229 *the maid with swelling drops 'gan wet / Her circled eyne*
forthy	therefore, for this reason	**Per** II.Chorus.19 [Gower alone, of Helicanus] *forthy he strive / To killen bad*
hight	is called	**LL** I.i.168 [King to Berowne, of the Spanish visitor] *that Armado hight*
hild	held	**Luc** 1257 *let it not be hild / Poor women's faults, that they are so fulfill'd / With men's abuses!*
iwis	assuredly, certainly, truly	**MV** II.ix.68 [Arragon, reading the portrait's schedule] *There be fools alive iwis, / Silvered o'er*
ne	nor	**Per** II.Chorus.36 [Gower alone, of Pericles] *Ne aught escapend but himself*
sain	said	**LL** III.i.81 [Armado to Mote, of the word 'envoy'] *it is an epilogue or discourse to make plain / Some obscure precedence that hath tofore been sain*
shoon	shoes	**Ham** IV.v.26 [Ophelia singing] *And his sandal shoon*
speken	speak	**Per** II.Chorus.12 [Gower alone] *each man / Thinks all is writ he speken can*
tofore	earlier, beforehand	**LL** III.i.81 [Armado to Mote] *Some obscure precedence that hath tofore been sain*
wight	person, human being	**H5** II.i.57 [Pistol to Nym] *O braggart vile, and damned furious wight!*
writ	gospel, holy writ	**Per** II.Chorus.12 [Gower alone, of Pericles] *each man / Thinks all is writ he speken can* [i.e. everything he says is as true as the gospel]
y-clad	decked out, clothed	**2H6** I.i.33 [King to and of Queen] *Her words y-clad with wisdom's majesty*
yclept	called	**LL** V.ii.594 [Holofernes to audience] *Judas I am, yclept Maccabaeus*
y-ravished	entrance, enrapture, carry away with joy	**Per** III.Chorus.35 [Gower alone, of the news that Pericles is a king] *this ... / Y-ravished the regions round*
y-slacked	reduce to inactivity, quieten down	**Per** III.Chorus.1 [Gower alone] *Now sleep y-slacked hath the rout*

arming (*n.*) establishment, confirmation, substantiation **AW** IV.iii.61 [First Lord to Second Lord, as to whether Bertram has heard the news of Helena's supposed death] *Ay … to the full arming of the verity*

armipotent (*adj.*) mighty in arms, powerful in arms **AW** IV.iii.231 [Second Lord to Bertram, of Parolles] *This is … the armipotent soldier;* **LL** V.ii.642; **TNK** V.i.54

armour (*n.*) suit of armour **TNK** III.vi.3 [Palamon alone, of Arcite] *with him bring / Two swords and two good armours* ☛ **BODY-ARMOUR, p.48**

arms (*n.*) **1** weapons, armaments **R2** II.ii.50 [Green to Queen Isabel] *The banished Bolingbroke … with uplifted arms is safe arrived;* **1H6** I.i.46; **2H6** IV.ix.29, V.i.18; **KL** IV.ii.17; **TC** III.iii.270
  2 coat of arms **2H6** IV.i.42 [Whitmore to Suffolk] *my arms torn and defaced;* **1H6** I.i.80; **2H6** I.i.254
  3 armour, mail, protective covering **R2** III.ii.115 [Scroop to King Richard] *Boys … clap their female joints / In stiff unwieldy arms*

arms' end, at at the point of a sword **TG** V.iv.57 [Proteus to Silvia] *I'll woo you like a soldier, at arms' end*

aroint (*v.*) be gone, away with you **KL** III.iv.118 [Edgar as Poor Tom to all, as if to the nightmare] *aroint thee, witch;* **Mac** I.iii.6

a-row (*adv.*) one after the other, in succession **CE** V.i.170 [Messenger to Adriana] *My master and his man are both broke loose, / Beaten the maids a-row* ☛ **a** (*prep.*) 3

arraign (*v.*) **1** accuse, charge, indict **Ham** IV.v.94 [Claudius to Gertrude, of the rumours flying around] *necessity, of matter beggared, / Will nothing stick our person to arraign / In ear and ear*
  2 put on trial, indict **KL** III.vi.46 [Lear to all, of Gonerill] *Arraign her first;* **KL** III.vi.20, V.iii.157
  3 examine, interrogate, probe **MM** II.iii.21 [disguised Duke to Juliet] *I'll teach you how you shall arraign your conscience*

arraignment (*n.*) trial, interrogation, examination **TNK** I.iii.66 [Emilia to Hippolyta] *No more arraignment* [i.e. no further argument needed]

arrant (*adj.*) downright, absolute, unmitigated **Ham** I.v.124 [Hamlet to Horatio and Marcellus] *There's never a villain dwelling in all Denmark - / But he's an arrant knave* ☛ **FEW, p.xxi**

arras (*n.*) tapestry hanging **1H4** III.iii.97 [Falstaff to Prince Hal] *I fell asleep here, behind the arras;* **Cym** II.ii.26; **Ham** III.iii.28; **1H4** II.iv.485; **MA** I.iii.57; **MW** III.iii.85

arras (*adj.*) made of Arras tapestry fabric **TS** II.i.344 [Gremio to Baptista, of his possessions] *In cypress chests my arras counterpoints*

array (*n.*) **1** attire, clothes, clothing, dress **AY** V.ii.69 [Rosalind as Ganymede to Orlando] *put you in your best array;* **AY** IV.iii.144; **1H6** I.iii.55; **KL** III.iv.79; **TS** IV.iii.176
  2 readiness for combat, warlike state **E3** II.ii.6 [Audley to Derby, of the troops] *[I] bring them hither / In fair array before his majesty;* **E3** III.iii.43, 227

array (*v.*) clothe, dress, attire **MM** III.ii.23 [disguised Duke to Pompey] *I drink, I eat, array myself, and live;* **KL** IV.vii.20

arrearage (*n.*) arrears, overdue payment, outstanding amount **Cym** II.iv.13 [Philario to Posthumus, of Cymbeline] *I think / He'll … send th'arrearages*

arrest (*n.*) order to obey the law, summons to stop **Ham** II.ii.67 [Voltemand to Claudius, of the Norwegian king] *sends out arrests / On Fortinbras*

arrest (*v.*) **1** impound, confiscate, appropriate **MW** V.v.114 [Ford as if to Brook, of Falstaff's behaviour] *His horses are arrested for it*
  2 seize, take hold of, lay hold upon **MM** II.iv.134 [Angelo to Isabella] *I do arrest your words* [i.e. I take you at your word]; **LL** II.i.160

arrivance (*n.*) arriving, landing **Oth** II.i.42 [Third Gentleman to all] *every minute is expectancy / Of more arrivance* [Q; F *Arriuancie*]

arrive (*v.*) reach, arrive at **JC** I.ii.110 [Cassius to Brutus] *ere we could arrive the point proposed;* **Cor** I.iii.180; **3H6** V.iii.8; **Luc** 781

arrive at end up with, obtain **Tim** IV.iii.508 [Timon to Flavius, of Flavius betraying him] *Thou mightst have sooner got another service; / For many so arrive at second masters*

arrogancy (*n.*) arrogance **H8** II.iv.110 [Queen Katherine to Wolsey] *your heart / Is crammed with arrogancy, spleen, and pride*

arrouse (*v.*) sprinkle, bedew, water **TNK** V.v.104 [Theseus to Palamon] *The blissful dew of heaven does arrouse you*

art (*n.*) **1** knowledge, learning, scholarship, science **1H6** I.ii.73 [Pucelle to Dauphin] *I am by birth a shepherd's daughter, / My wit untrained in any kind of art;* **AW** II.i.118, 158; **LL** II.i.45; **Mac** IV.iii.143; **Per** II.iii.82; **TS** I.i.2 ☛ **liberal arts**
  2 accomplishment, achievement, skill **Cym** V.v.339 [Belarius to Cymbeline, of his boys] *those arts they have, as I / Could put into them;* **Lover** 145; **Mac** I.iv.12; **Sonn** 29.7; **Tit** IV.iv.109
  3 skill, knack, dexterity **Ham** IV.vii.96 [Claudius to Laertes, of Lamord] *He … gave you such a masterly report / For art and exercise in your defence*
  4 knowledge, mastery, acquisition **KL** IV.vi.222 [Edgar to Gloucester, of himself] *Who, by the art of known and feeling sorrows, / Am pregnant to good pity*
  5 practical application, knowledge drawn from experience **H5** I.i.51 [Canterbury to Ely] *the art and practic part of life / Must be the mistress to this theoric*
  6 magic, enchantment, trickery **Tem** I.ii.1 [Miranda to Prospero] *If by your art … you have / Put the wild waters in this roar, allay them;* **1H6** I.i.15; **MND** II.ii.110; **Tem** I.ii.25, 28, 291, 372, IV.i.41, 120, Epilogue.14
  7 artifice, artificial conduct; or, wile, trick **Cym** III.iii.46 [Belarius to Guiderius and Arviragus] *Did you but know … the art o'th' court;* **JC** IV.i.37; **Lover** 174; **Sonn** 125.11
  8 rhetorical art, verbal artistry **Ham** II.ii.95 [Gertrude to Polonius] *More matter, with less art;* **MM** I.ii.183; **RJ** II.iv.88; **Sonn** 66.9; **Tim** V.i.83

art (*v.*) ☛ **VERB FORMS, p.481**

artere, artire (*n.*) [early spelling of 'artery'] sinew, ligament, tendon **Ham** I.iv.82 [Hamlet to Horatio and Marcellus] *each petty artere in this body* [reading of F *artire;* Q1 *Artiue;* Q2 *arture*]

article (*n.*) **1** clause, term, provision **Oth** III.iii.22 [Desdemona to Cassio] *If I do vow a friendship, I'll perform it / To the last article;* **AC** II.ii.86; **Ham** I.i.94; **H5** V.ii.78, 94; **2H6** I.i.215; **3H6** I.i.180
  2 item, particular, point of substance **R2** IV.i.232 [Richard to Northumberland, of the latter's offences] *There shouldst thou find one heinous article;* **KJ** II.i.111; **Tem** II.i.195
  3 condition, stipulation, requirement **Cor** II.iii.195 [Sicinius to Citizens, of Coriolanus] *his surly nature, / Which easily endures not article / Tying him to aught*
  4 character, nature, designation **MW** II.i.49 [Mistress Page to Mistress Ford] *thou shouldst not alter the article of thy gentry*
  5 importance, moment, significance **Ham** V.ii.116 [Hamlet to Osrick, of Laertes] *I take him to be a soul of great article*

articulate (*v.*) **1** negotiate, deal, come to terms **Cor** I.ix.76 [Cominius to Lartius] *Send us to Rome / The best, with whom we may articulate*
  2 speak about, spell out, express in words **1H4** V.i.72 [King Henry to Worcester] *These things indeed you have articulate*

artificer (*n.*) workman, artisan, craftsman **KJ** IV.ii.201 [Hubert to King John] *Another lean unwashed artificer / Cuts off his tale and talks of Arthur's death*

artificial (*adj.*) **1** showing creative artistry, artistically skilful **MND** III.ii.203 [Helena to Hermia] *We … like two artificial gods / Have with our needles created both one flower;* **Tim** I.i.38
  2 hypocritical, feigned, phony **3H6** III.ii.184 [Richard alone] *I can … wet my cheeks with artificial tears*
  3 skilful, accomplished, capable **Per** V.i.71 [Lysimachus to Marina, of Pericles] *If that thy prosperous and artificial feat / Can draw him but to answer thee*

4 produced by the black arts **Mac** III.v.27 [Hecat to Witches, of a vaporous drop] *distilled by magic sleights / Shall raise such artificial sprites*

artire *(n.)* ☞ artere *(n.)*

artist *(n.)* **1** scholar, intellectual, learned person **TC** I.iii.24 [Agamemnon to all] *In fortune's love … the artist and unread, / The hard and soft, seem all affined and kin*
2 medical practitioner, physician **AW** II.iii.10 [Lafew to Parolles, of the King] *To be relinquished of the artists*

artless *(adj.)* uncontrolled, unskilful **Ham** IV.v.19 [Gertrude to herself] *So full of artless jealousy is guilt*

arts-man *(n.)* man of learning, scholar **LL** V.i.76 [Armado to Holofernes] *Arts-man, preambulate*

as *(prep.)* on **RJ** V.iii.247 [Friar to Prince] *I writ to Romeo / That he should hither come as this dire night* [or: with intensifying function]

as *(conj.)* **1** as if **Ham** IV.v.105 [Messenger to Claudius, of Laertes] *The rabble call him lord, / And, as the world were now but to begin, … / They cry 'Choose we!'*
2 because **Ham** V.ii.330 [Hamlet to all] *Had I but time - as this fell sergeant, Death, / Is strict in his arrest - O, I could tell you*
3 for what **1H6** III.iv.35 [Vernon to Basset, of Somerset] *thy lord I honour as he is*
4 if **TS** Induction.i.107 [Lord to Servant, of his Page dressed as a woman] *Tell him from me - as he will win my love*
5 so that **Ham** V.ii.40 [Hamlet to Horatio] *An earnest conjuration from the King … / As love between them like the palm might flourish*
6 such as, for instance, to wit **Ham** V.ii.147 [Osrick to Hamlet] *rapiers and poniards, with their assigns, as girdle, hangers, and so*
7 that [following 's' or 'such'] **3H6** I.i.234 [Queen to King] *Thou hast … given unto the house of York such head / As thou shalt reign but by their sufferance*

as yet ☞ yet *(adv.)*

ascribe *(v.)* dedicate, attribute, assign **1H6** III.iv.11 [Talbot to King] *this arm … / Ascribes the glory of his conquest got / First to my God and next unto your grace*

ash *(n.)* spear, lance [made of ash] **Cor** IV.v.111 [Aufidius to Coriolanus, of the latter's body] *whereagainst / My grained ash an hundred times hath broke*

aside *(adv.)* ☞ STAGE DIRECTIONS, p.414

asinico *(n.)* ☞ assinico *(n.)*

ask *(v.)* **1** demand, require, call for **2H6** I.ii.90 [Hume to himself, of the Duchess' plans] *The business asketh silent secrecy;* **TS** II.i.114
2 request, suggest, propose **Per** II.iii.99 [Simonides to all, of the dancing] *this was well asked*

askance, askaunce *(v.)* turn aside, divert **Luc** 637 [Lucrece to Tarquin] *how are they wrapped in with infamies / That from their own misdeeds askance their eyes!*

askance, askaunce *(adv.)* **1** sideways, surreptitiously, with a side glance **Venus** 342 [of Adonis and Venus] *For all askance he holds her in his eye*
2 with disdain, maliciously, scornfully **TS** II.i.241 [Petruchio to Katherina] *thou canst not look askance;* **Sonn** 110.6

askant, askaunt *(prep.)* aslant, across **Ham** IV.vii.166 [Gertrude to Claudius and Laertes] *There is a willow grows askant the brook* [Q2; F *aslant*]

aspect *(n.)* **1** [of a human face] look, appearance, expression **TNK** V.iii.45 [Emilia to herself] *Palamon / Has a most menacing aspect;* **CE** II.ii.120; **Cor** V.vi.32; **1H6** II.iii.19; **R2** I.iii.209; **R3** I.ii.154
2 [of objects] sight, appearance **R2** I.iii.127 [King Richard to Bolingbroke and Mowbray] *our eyes do hate the dire aspect / Of civil wounds;* **CE** III.ii.143; **E3** III.i.67; **KJ** II.i.250
3 gaze, look **H5** III.i.9 [King Henry to all] *lend the eye a terrible aspect;* **AC** I.v.33; **1H4** III.ii.82; **H8** III.ii.369; **Luc** 14

4 [astrology] influential phase, direction of alignment **WT** II.i.107 [Hermione to all] *I must be patient till the heavens look / With an aspect more favourable;* **CE** II.ii.32; **KL** II.ii.104; **Sonn** 26.10; **TC** I.iii.92 ☞ COSMOS, p.102

aspersion *(n.)* sprinkling, shower, spray **Tem** IV.i.18 [Prospero to Ferdinand and Miranda] *No sweet aspersion shall the heavens let fall / To make this contract grow*

aspic *(n.)* type of venomous snake, asp **AC** V.ii.349 [First Guard to Dolabella] *This is an aspic's trail;* **AC** V.ii.292; **Oth** III.iii.447

aspicious *(adj.)* malapropism for 'suspicious' [or 'auspicious'] **MA** III.v.43 [Dogberry to Leonato] *our watch … have indeed comprehended two aspicious persons*

aspire *(v.)* **1** ascend, rise up, climb [to] **MW** V.v.97 [Fairies singing, of lust] *whose flames aspire … higher and higher;* **Luc** 5; **RJ** III.i.117; **Venus** 150
2 rise up, tower, be tall **Per** I.iv.5 [Dionyza to Cleon] *who digs hills because they do aspire / Throws down one mountain to cast up a higher*

asprey *(n.)* osprey **Cor** IV.vii.34 [Aufidius to Lieutenant, of Coriolanus] *I think he'll be to Rome / As is the asprey to the fish* [F]

asquint *(adv.)* with prejudice, in a distorted manner **KL** V.iii.73 [Gonerill to Regan, of her remark] *That eye that told you so looked but asquint*

assail *(v.)* **1** attack, assault, address **3H6** I.i.65 [Clifford to King] *Let us assail the family of York;* **Ham** I.i.31; **2H6** IV.ii.165
2 approach with offers of love, woo with vigour, attempt to seduce **Sonn** 41.6 *Beauteous thou art, therefore to be assailed;* **Cym** II.iii.38; **TN** I.iii.54

assailing *(adj.)* wooing, loving, amorous **RJ** I.i.213 [Romeo to Benvolio, of Rosaline] *She will not … bide th'encounter of assailing eyes*

assault *(n.)* attack, temptation, snare **MM** III.i.186 [disguised Duke to Isabella] *The assault that Angelo hath made to you;* **Ham** II.i.35; **MA** II.iii.117

assay *(n.)* **1** effort, attempt **Ham** III.iii.69 [Claudius alone] *Make assay. / Bow, stubborn knees;* **Luc** 1720; **Mac** IV.iii.143
2 attack, attempt, trial **Ham** II.ii.71 [Voltemand to Claudius] *never more / To give th'assay of arms against your majesty;* **Ham** II.i.65
3 assault, attack, incursion **H5** I.ii.151 [King Henry to Canterbury, of attacks by the Scots] *Galling the gleaned land with hot assays*
4 test, trial, measure **MM** III.i.164 [disguised Duke aside to Claudio, of Angelo and Isabella] *he hath made an assay of her virtue;* **Oth** I.iii.18; **Tim** IV.iii.405
5 evidence, proof, indication **KL** V.iii.141 [Edmund to Edgar] *thy tongue some 'say of breeding breathes*

assay *(v.)* **1** attempt, try, venture **AY** I.iii.127 [Rosalind to Celia] *what if we assayed to steal / The clownish fool;* **CE** I.ii.97; **E3** III.iv.12; **Ham** IV.vii.151; **2H6** IV.v.8; **Per** I.i.60
2 try, test the mettle of, put to the proof **AW** III.vii.44 [Helena to Widow] *tonight / Let us assay our plot;* **1H4** V.iv.33; **Lover** 156; **MM** I.iv.76; **Venus** 608
3 challenge, tempt, win over **Ham** III.i.14 [Gertrude to Rosencrantz and Guildenstern, of Hamlet] *Did you assay him / To any pastime?*
4 make advances to, accost, address proposals to **MW** II.i.24 [Mistress Page alone, of Falstaff's letter] *he dares in this manner assay me?;* **MM** I.i.180

assemblance *(n.)* appearance, display, composition **2H4** III.ii.252 [Falstaff to Shallow] *Care I for the limb, the thews, the stature, bulk, and big assemblance of a man?*

assigns *(n.)* accessories, appurtenances, trappings **Ham** V.ii.147 [Osrick to Hamlet] *rapiers and poniards, with their assigns*

assinico, asinico, assenego *(n.)* [pron: asi'neekoh] little ass, donkey, dolt **TC** II.i.44 [Thersites to Ajax] *an assinico may tutor thee*

assist (*v.*) accompany, attend, escort **Tem** I.i.52 [Gonzalo to all] *The King and Prince at prayers, let's assist them;* **Cor** V.vi.156; **WT** V.i.113

assistance (*n.*) associates, partners, aides **Cor** IV.vi.33 [Sicinius to Brutus, of Coriolanus] *affecting one sole throne / Without assistance*

assistant (*adj.*) in attendance, standing by, available **Ham** I.iii.3 [Laertes to Ophelia] *as the winds give benefit / And convoy is assistant, do not sleep / But let me hear from you*

associate (*n.*) companion, fellow-traveller **Ham** IV.iii.44 [Claudius to Hamlet] *Th'associates tend, and everything is bent / For England*

associate (*v.*) accompany, escort, join with **RJ** V.ii.6 [Friar John to Friar Laurence] *One of our order, to associate me / Here in this city visiting the sick;* **Cor** IV.vi.77

assubjugate (*v.*) reduce to subjugation, demean, debase **TC** II.iii.190 [Ulysses to Agamemnon, of Ajax] *[he must not] assubjugate his merit ... / By going to Achilles*

assume (*v.*) **1** acquire, adopt, take on **Ham** III.iv.161 [Hamlet to Gertrude] *Assume a virtue;* **Ham** I.ii.244; **MV** II.ix.51
2 attain, achieve, reach **Cym** V.v.320 [Belarius to Cymbeline, of himself] *He it is that hath / Assumed this age*
3 undertake, enter, choose **Per** I.i.62 [Pericles to all] *Like a bold champion I assume the lists*

assurance (*n.*) **1** security, certainty, confidence **MND** III.i.18 [Bottom to all] *for the more better assurance, tell them that I ... am not Pyramus, but Bottom the weaver;* **MA** II.ii.45; **Mac** IV.i.82; **Tem** I.ii.45; **TN** II.ii.8; **TNK** V.i.134
2 confirmation, pledge, guarantee **TN** I.v.173 [Viola as Cesario to Olivia] *give me modest assurance if you be the lady of the house;* **Ham** III.iv.63; **3H6** IV.i.140; **TN** III.iii.26; **TS** II.i.380, III.ii.133, IV.ii.118, iv.49
3 claim, title, securing [of] **KJ** II.i.471 [Queen Eleanor to King John, of a marriage between Lewis the Dauphin and Blanche] *by this knot thou shalt so surely tie / Thy now unsured assurance to the crown*
4 safety, security **R3** IV.iv.496 [King Richard to Derby, of Derby's son] *his head's assurance is but frail*

assure (*v.*) **1** settle, convey, leave [to] **TNK** II.i.8 [Gaoler to Wooer] *what I have ... I will assure upon my daughter;* **TS** II.i.336, 372
2 guarantee, make safe against risks **MV** I.iii.29 [Shylock to Bassanio] *that I may be assured, I will bethink me*
3 assign, pledge, guarantee **Sonn** 92.2 *For term of life thou art assured mine*

assured (*adj.*) **1** certain, definite, sure **KL** IV.vii.56 [Lear to all] *Would I were assured / Of my condition;* **KJ** II.i.534; **KL** III.vi.93; **MV** I.iii.27; **Tim** V.i.95
2 betrothed, engaged **KJ** II.i.535 [Austria to Lewis and Blanche, of kissing] *I am well assured / That I did so when I was first assured;* **CE** III.ii.149; **Cym** I.vii.73

astonish, 'stonish (*v.*) **1** fill with wonder, amaze, astound **H5** V.i.37 [Gower to Fluellen, of Pistol] *you have astonished him;* **1H6** V.v.2; **2H6** V.i.146; **JC** I.iii.56
2 stun, dumbfound, strike dumb with dismay **Sonn** 86.8 [of his rival] *neither he, nor his compeers by night / Giving him aid, my verse astonished;* **Ham** III.iv.335; **Luc** 1730; **Venus** 825

astringer (*n.*) keeper of goshawks **AW** V.i.6 [stage direction] *Enter a Gentleman, Astringer to the King*

astronomer (*n.*) astrologer **Cym** III.ii.27 [Innogen to Pisanio, of Posthumus] *learned indeed were that astronomer / That knew the stars as I his characters;* **TC** V.i.88

astronomical (*adj.*) astrological, interpreting the heavens **KL** I.ii.149 [Edgar to Edmund] *How long have you been a sectary astronomical?*

astronomy (*n.*) knowledge of astrology **Sonn** 14.2 *Not from the stars do I my judgement pluck, / And yet methinks I have astronomy*

asunder (*adv.*) separated, apart from each other **2H6** I.iv.50 [Buckingham to guards, of Jourdain, Southwell, and Bolingbroke] *let them be clapped up close, / And kept asunder*

at (*prep.*) **1** in **2H4** I.i.135 [Morton to Northumberland, of his report] *This is the news at full*
2 to **1H6** IV.i.105 [Vernon to King, of Basset and the white rose] *he first took exceptions at this badge*

Ates (*n.*) discord, strife, destruction **LL** V.ii.685 [Berowne to all] *More Ates, more Ates! Stir them on* ☞ **GODS AND GODDESSES**, p.620

athwart (*adv.*) **1** thwartingly, perversely, going against one's plans **1H4** I.i.36 [Westmorland to King Henry, of their plans] *all athwart there came / A post from Wales*
2 askew, awry, out of the normal course **MM** I.iii.30 [Duke to Friar Thomas] *quite athwart / Goes all decorum*

athwart (*prep.*) across **AY** III.iv.38 [Celia to Rosalind, of Orlando] *[he] swears brave oaths, and breaks them bravely ... athwart the heart of his lover;* **LL** IV.iii.133

a-tilt (*adv.*) as if jousting **2H6** I.iii.49 [Queen to Suffolk] *Thou rannest a-tilt in honour of my love* [F]

atomy (*n.*) **1** atom, mote, speck **AY** III.ii.225 [Celia to Rosalind] *It is as easy to count atomies as to resolve the propositions of a lover;* **AY** III.v.13
2 mite, tiny being **RJ** I.iv.57 [Mercutio to Romeo, of Queen Mab] *she comes ... / Drawn with a team of little atomies* [F; Q1 *atomi*]; **2H4** V.iv.29

atone (*v.*) **1** unite, join, reconcile **R2** I.i.202 [King Richard to Bolingbroke and Mowbray] *Since we cannot atone you;* **AC** II.ii.106; **AY** V.iv.107; **Cor** IV.vi.73; **Cym** I.v.37; **Oth** IV.i.231
2 appease, allay, assuage **Tim** V.iv.58 [Alcibiades to Senators] *to atone your fears / With my more noble meaning*

atonement (*n.*) reconciliation, appeasement, harmony **R3** I.iii.36 [Buckingham to Queen Elizabeth, of King Edward] *he desires to make atonement / Between the Duke of Gloucester and your brothers;* **2H4** IV.i.219; **MW** I.i.31

attach (*v.*) **1** arrest, seize, apprehend **CE** IV.i.74 [Angelo to Antipholus of Ephesus] *pay this sum for me, / Or I attach you by this officer;* **CE** IV.i.6; **2H4** IV.ii.109; **Oth** I.ii.77; **R2** II.iii.155; **WT** V.i.181
2 seize, take hold of, grip **Tem** III.iii.6 [Alonso to Gonzalo] *I ... am myself attached with weariness;* **2H4** II.ii.3; **LL** IV.iii.351; **TC** V.ii.164
3 arrest, seize by warrant **1H6** II.iv.96 [Richard to Somerset] *My father was attached, not attainted* [i.e. not convicted of treason]; **H8** I.i.95

attachment (*n.*) seizure, arrest, confinement **TC** IV.ii.5 [Troilus to Cressida] *Sleep ... give as soft attachment to thy senses / As infants' empty of all thought!*

attain (*v.*) obtain, acquire, gain **2H6** I.iv.70 [York to all] *these oracles / Are hardly attained and hardly understood*

attainder (*n.*) **1** accusation, allegation, denunciation **R2** IV.i.24 [Aumerle to all, of Bagot] *mine honour soiled / With the attainder of his slanderous lips;* **H8** II.i.41; **LL** I.i.155
2 dishonourable stain, foul slur **R3** III.v.32 [Richard to Buckingham, of Hastings] *He lived from all attainder of suspects*

attaint (*n.*) **1** disgrace, dishonour, corruption **TC** I.ii.25 [Alexander to Cressida, of Ajax] *There is no man hath ... an attaint but he carries some stain of it;* **CE** III.ii.16; **Luc** 825; **Sonn** 82.2
2 stain, infection, corruption **Venus** 741 [Venus to Adonis] *The marrow-eating sickness whose attaint / Disorder breeds by heating of the blood*
3 condemnation, accusation **KL** V.iii.83 [Albany to Edmund, of Gonerill] *I arrest thee ... and, in thy attaint, / This gilded serpent* [Q; F *arrest*] ☞ **attainder** (*n.*)
4 sign of weariness, suggestion of fatigue **H5** IV.Chorus.39 [Chorus, of King Henry] *he ... overbears attaint / With cheerful semblance*

attaint (*v.*) **1** affect, touch, strike **E3** IV.vi.26 [King John alone] *[I] find myself attainted / With strong surprise of weak and yielding fear;* **1H6** V.v.81; **PassP** XVIII.46 ☞ attainted (*adj.*)

2 taint [by treason], corrupt **1H6** II.ii.92 [Somerset to Richard] *standest not thou attainted, / Corrupted, and exempt from ancient gentry?;* **1H6** II.iv.96; **LL** V.ii.812 [F]; **Sonn** 88.7

3 accuse of treason, condemn **2H6** II.iv.59 [Gloucester to Duchess] *I must offend before I be attainted*

attainture (*n.*) conviction, condemnation, sentence **2H6** I.ii.106 [Hume to himself, of the Duchess] *her attainture will be Humphrey's fall*

attask, attax (*v.*) take to task, blame **KL** I.iv.340 [Gonerill to Albany] *You are much more attasked for want of wisdom / Than praised for harmful mildness* [F *at task for*; Q *alapt* and other readings]

attempt (*n.*) **1** exploit, undertaking, enterprise **1H4** III.ii.13 [King Henry to Prince Hal, of Hal's behaviour] *Such poor, such bare, such lewd, such mean attempts;* **Cym** III.iv.184; **1H4** IV.vi.61; **JC** I.iii.136; **KJ** V.ii.111

2 attack, assault **Mac** III.vi.39 [Lord to Lennox, of Macbeth] *he / Prepares for some attempt of war;* **MM** III.i.256

attempt (*v.*) **1** endeavour, venture, strive [for] **Cor** V.vi.75 [Coriolanus to all] *prosperously I have attempted;* **Cym** I.v.109; **Tim** I.i.130

2 attack, assail, subdue **KL** II.ii.120 [Oswald to Cornwall, of disguised Kent] *got praises of the King / For him attempting who was self-subdued*

3 tempt, persuade, win over **MM** IV.ii.184 [disguised Duke to Provost] *neither my coat, integrity, nor persuasion can with ease attempt you;* **MV** IV.i.418; **MW** IV.ii.200

4 undertake, perform, carry out **JC** V.iii.40 [Cassius to Pindarus] *I swore thee ... whatsoever I did bid thee do, / Thou shouldst attempt it*

attemptable (*adj.*) capable of being seduced **Cym** I.v.58 [Frenchman to Iachimo, of a woman] *more fair, virtuous ... less attemptable*

attend (*v.*) **1** await, wait for, expect **Cor** III.ii.138 [Cominius to Coriolanus] *The Tribunes do attend you* ☞ FEW, p.xxi

2 serve, follow, wait [on/upon] **Ham** II.ii.269 [Hamlet to Rosencrantz and Guildenstern] *I am most dreadfully attended;* **AY** I.ii.155, IV.i.166; **1H6** V.i.55; **KJ** IV.iii.25; **KL** I.i.33

3 serve at court, wait on royalty **Cym** III.iii.22 [Belarius to Guiderius and Arviragus] *this life / Is nobler than attending for a check;* **Cym** III.vii.56; **H8** V.ii.1

ATTENTION SIGNALS

Catching someone's attention is an important interaction strategy, and in Shakespearian English several linguistic devices are used which either no longer exist in modern Standard English or (as in the case of *behold* and *hark*) are used with archaic resonance. Some of these are general-purpose calls of the 'hello' type, such as *ho* (**Ham** I.i.14) and *what, ho* (**Ham** III.ii.62); but others involve distinctive lexical items.

Look!

behold	**Ham** I.i.126 [Horatio to Barnardo and Marcellus, of the Ghost] *Soft, behold, lo, where it comes again!*
lo	**1H6** IV.vii.17 [Servant to Talbot] *O my dear lord, lo where your son is borne!*

Listen!

hark	**TS** I.i.84 [Lucentio aside to Tranio] *Hark, Tranio, thou mayst hear Minerva speak*
hark you	**Ham** II.ii.380 [Hamlet to Rosencrantz and Guildenstern] *Hark you, Guildenstern - and you too - at each ear a hearer*

Be quiet!

buzz	**TNK** III.v.80 [Gaoler's Daughter to Schoolmaster] *You are a fool. Tell ten; I have posed him. Buzz!*
husht	**Per** I.iii.8 [Thaliard alone, to himself] *Husht! Here comes the lord of Tyre*
let be	**Ham** V.ii.218 [Hamlet to Horatio] *Let be* [as Claudius and others enter]
mum	**TS** I.ii.160 [Hortensio aside to Grumio] *Grumio, mum!*
peace	**TN** II.v.33 [Sir Toby to Sir Andrew] *Peace, I say!*
soft	**Ham** III.i.88 [Hamlet to himself, ending his monologue upon seeing Ophelia] *Soft you now, / The fair Ophelia!* [☞ 'behold' above]

Soft is also used in the sense of 'not so fast' (☞ A–Z entry at *soft* (*adv.*) **2**) and as a discourse marker (☞ p.127).

Pay attention!

audience	**Cor** III.iii.40 [Aedile to Plebeians] *List to your Tribunes. Audience!*
good now	**Ham** I.i.70 [Marcellus to Horatio and Barnardo] *Good now, sit down, and tell me he that knows*
hear ye	**1H4** I.ii.132 [Falstaff to Poins] *Here ye, Yedward, if I tarry at home and go not, I'll hang you for going*
mark	**Ham** IV.v.28 [Ophelia to all] *Pray you, mark*

Mark is also used in various ways to do with 'paying attention': ☞ A–Z entries at *mark* (*v.*).

4 accompany, follow closely, go with **TG** V.i.10 [Silvia to Eglamour] *I fear I am attended by some spies;* **Cym** III.iii.77; **Ham** III.iii.22; **H5** II.iv.29; **R2** IV.i.198; **Tem** I.ii.423

5 wait, tarry, postpone **E3** I.ii.165 [King Edward to Countess] *[my business] shall attend, while I attend on thee* [first instance; second instance = wait upon]

6 regard, consider **TN** I.iv.27 [Orsino to Viola as Cesario, of his message to Olivia] *She will attend it better in thy youth;* **AC** II.ii.64; **1H4** I.iii.208; **Luc** 818; **RJ** III.i.196

7 listen [to], pay attention [to] **E3** IV.v.10 [Charles to King John] *Our men … / Look on each other, as they did attend / Each other's words;* **Cor** I.ix.4; **Ham** IV.v.99; **3H6** II.i.167; **Per** I.i.70; **Tem** I.ii.78

8 see to, look after, apply oneself to **AC** IV.vi.27 [Soldier to Enobarbus] *I must attend mine office;* **AW** I.i.4; **1H6** I.i.173; **MW** V.v.40

attendance (*n.*) **1** diligent service, dutiful ministration, assiduous attention **KL** II.iv.238 [Gonerill to Lear, of Regan] *Why might not you … receive attendance / From those that she calls servants;* **R3** III.vii.55; **TNK** III.i.110

2 attention, consideration, notice **E3** II.i.77 [King Edward to Lodowick] *the touch of sweet concordant strings / Could force attendance in the ears of hell*

attent (*adj.*) attentive, heedful, intent **Per** III.Chorus.11 [Gower alone] *Be attent;* **Ham** I.ii.193

attest (*n.*) evidence, witness, testimony **TC** V.ii.124 [Troilus to Ulysses] *there is a credence in my heart … / That doth invert th'attest of eyes and ears*

attest (*v.*) **1** vouch for, be evidence of, testify to **H5** Prologue.16 [Chorus] *a crooked figure may / Attest in little place a million;* **TN** V.i.156

2 call as witnesses **TC** II.ii.133 [Paris to all] *I attest the gods, your full consent / Gave wings to my propension*

attire (*n.*) head-dress **MA** III.i.102 [Hero to Ursula] *I'll show thee some attires;* **RJ** IV.iii.1

attired (*adj.*) wrapped, clothed, swathed **MA** IV.i.142 [Benedick to Leonato] *I am so attired in wonder, / I know not what to say;* **Luc** 1601

attirement (*n.*) outfit, clothing, garment **E3** III.iii.178 [King Edward to the heralds] *bring forth / A strong attirement for the Prince my son* [i.e. a suit of armour]

attorney (*n.*) **1** substitute, deputy, agent **CE** V.i.100 [Adriana to Abbess] *I … will have no attorney but myself*

2 advocate, mediator, promoter **R3** IV.iv.413 [King Richard to Queen Elizabeth, of her daughter] *Be the attorney of my love to her;* **AW** II.ii.20; **Venus** 335

attorney (*v.*) carry out by a substitute, peform by proxy **WT** I.i.27 [Camillo to Archidamus, of Leontes and Polixenes] *their encounters … hath been royally attorneyed with interchange of gifts*

attorney, by by proxy [as opposed to 'in person'] **R3** V.iii.84 [Derby to Richmond] *I, by attorney, bless thee from thy mother;* **AY** IV.i.85

attorneyed (*adj.*) bound, acting as advocate **MM** V.i.382 [Duke to Isabella] *I am still / Attorneyed at your service*

attorney general (*n.*) legally appointed deputy **R2** II.i.203 [York to King Richard, of Hereford] *If you … / Call in the letters patents that he hath / By his attorneys general to sue / His livery*

attorneyship (*n.*) legal practices, arrangement between lawyers **1H6** V.v.56 [Suffolk to all] *Marriage is a matter of more worth / Than to be dealt in by attorneyship*

attribute (*n.*) reputation, credit, honour **Per** IV.iii.18 [Dionyza to Cleon] *for an honest attribute;* **Ham** I.iv.22; **TC** II.iii.115

attribution (*n.*) praise, credit, recognition **1H4** IV.3 [Hotspur to Douglas] *Such attribution should the Douglas have*

attributive (*adj.*) attaching excellence, ascribing worth **TC** II.ii.59 [Hector to Troilus] *the will dotes that is attributive / To what infectiously itself affects* [Q]

atwain, a twain (*adv.*) in two, into two parts **Lover** 6 [of a maid] *Tearing of papers, breaking rings a twain;* **KL** II.ii.72

auburn (*adj.*) yellow-brown, light brown **TG** IV.iv.186 [disguised Julia alone, of Silvia] *Her hair is auburn;* **TNK** IV.ii.125

audaciously (*adv.*) boldly, fearlessly, confidently **LL** V.ii.104 [Boyet to Princess, reporting the King's words to Mote] *fear not thou, but speak audaciously*

audience (*n.*) **1** hearing, attention, reception **AY** III.ii.231 [Celia to Rosalind] *Give me audience;* **Ham** I.iii.93; **JC** III.i.2; **LL** V.ii.313; **Lover** 278; **TNK** I.ii.83 ☞ **ATTENTION SIGNALS**, p.26

2 audience-chamber, presence **AC** II.ii.78 [Caesar to Antony] *you … with taunts / Did gibe my missive out of audience*

audit (*n.*) account, reckoning [especially: in the face of God] **Ham** III.iii.82 [Hamlet to himself, of his father] *And how his audit stands, who knows save heaven?;* **Cym** V.iv.27; **H8** III.ii.141; **Lover** 230; **Sonn** 4.12, 49.4, 126.11

auditor (*n.*) official of the Exchequer, royal accounts officer **1H4** II.i.58 [Chamberlain to Gadshill] *a kind of auditor, one that hath abundance of charge too*

auditory (*n.*) assembly of listeners, audience **Tit** V.iii.95 [Lucius to all] *gracious auditory, be it known to you*

auger-hole (*n.*) hole drilled by an auger; tiny spot **Mac** II.iii.119 [Donalbain to Malcolm] *our fate, / Hid in an auger-hole, may rush and seize us*

aught (*n.*) anything, [with negative word] nothing **Ham** III.i.96 [Hamlet to Ophelia] *I never gave you aught* ☞ **FEW**, p.xxi

augmentation (*n.*) additional detail, fuller account **TN** III.ii.75 [Maria to Sir Toby, of Malvolio] *He does smile his face into more lines than is in the new map with the augmentation of the Indies*

augur, augure (*n.*) **1** augury, prophecy, divination **Mac** III.iv.123 [Macbeth to Lady Macbeth] *Augurs and understood relations have … brought forth / The secret'st man of blood* [F *Augures*]

2 augurer, soothsayer, fortune-teller **Sonn** 107.6 *the sad augurs mock their own presage;* **Phoen** 7

augurer (*n.*) Roman religious official who intepreted and foretold events **Cor** II.i.1 [Menenius to Sicinius and Brutus] *The augurer tells me we shall have news tonight;* **JC** II.ii.37 ☞ **ROMAN HISTORY**, p.377

auguring (*adj.*) prophetic, presaging, forecasting **AC** II.i.10 [Pompey to Menecrates] *My powers are crescent, and my auguring hope / Says it will come to th'full*

augury (*n.*) **1** omens, premonition, divining the future **Ham** V.ii.213 [Hamlet to Horatio] *We defy augury*

2 discernment, prescience, prophetic skill **TG** IV.iv.65 [Proteus to disguised Julia] *if my augury deceive me not* [also: sense 1]

auld (*adj.*) old **Oth** II.iii.91 [Iago singing] *take thine auld cloak about thee* [Q2; F *awl'd*; Q1 *owd*]

aunchient ☞ ancient (*n./adj.*)

aunt (*n.*) **1** old woman, gossip **MND** II.i.51 [Puck to Fairy] *The wisest aunt telling the saddest tale / Sometime for threefoot stool mistaketh me*

2 mistress, whore, prostitute **WT** IV.iii.11 [Autolycus singing] *the thrush and the jay, / Are summer songs for me and my aunts / While we lie tumbling in the hay*

auricular (*adj.*) audible, hearable, perceived by the ear **KL** I.ii.92 [Edmund to Gloucester] *by an auricular assurance have your satisfaction* [F; Q *aurigular*]

auspicious (*adj.*) smiling, cheerful, happy **Ham** I.ii.11 [Claudius to all] *With an auspicious and a dropping eye*

austerely (*adv.*) seriously, sternly, severely **Tem** IV.i.1 [Prospero to Ferdinand] *If I have too austerely punished you, / Your compensation makes amends;* **CE** IV.ii.2

austerity (*n.*) severity, harshness, strictness **Cor** IV.vii.44 [Aufidius to Lieutenant, of Coriolanus] *commanding peace / Even with the same austerity and garb / As he controlled the war* [i.e. severe manner]

authentic (*adj.*) **1** respectable, entitled to esteem **MW** II.ii.219 [Ford as Brook to Falstaff] *you are a gentleman ... authentic in your place and person*
2 valid, authoritative, credible **TC** I.iii.108 [Ulysses to all, of the organization of society] *by degree, stand in authentic place*; **TC** III.ii.179
3 qualified, accredited, authorized **AW** II.iii.12 [Lafew to Parolles] *To be relinquished ... Of all the learned and authentic fellows*

author (*n.*) **1** creator, originator, instigator **Ham** IV.v.81 [Claudius to Gertrude, of Hamlet] *he most violent author / Of his own just remove*; **3H6** IV.vi.18; **Luc** 1244; **TC** III.ii.179; **Tit** I.i.438; **Venus** 1006
2 authority, source, informant **Per** I.Chorus.20 [Gower alone] *I tell you what mine authors say*

authority (*n.*) **1** right to command, position of power **AC** II.vi.95 [Enobarbus to Menas] *If our eyes had authority*; **E3** III.i.30; **KL** I.iv.30; **Tim** II.ii.143
2 power, right, prerogative **KL** I.iii.18 [Gonerill to Oswald, of Lear] *That still would manage those authorities / That he hath given away!*
3 authoritative influence, dictatorial opinion **Ham** IV.ii.16 [Hamlet to and of Rosencrantz] *a sponge ... that soaks up the King's countenance, his rewards, his authorities*; **E3** II.i.444
4 those in authority, the ruling class **Cor** I.i.15 [First Citizen to all] *What authority surfeits on would relieve us*
5 dominion, influence **Oth** I.iii.322 [Iago to Roderigo] *the power and corrigible authority ... lies in our wills*

authorize (*v.*) vouch for, approve, speak with authority **Mac** III.iv.65 [Lady Macbeth to Macbeth] *A woman's story at a winter's fire, / Authorized by her grandam*

avail (*n.*) advantage, benefit, aid **E3** IV.iv.119 [Prince Edward to Third Herald, of Philip] *he ... knows no prayers for my avail*; **AW** III.i.22

avail (*v.*) **1** benefit, profit, prosper **MM** III.i.235 [Isabella to disguised Duke, of Mariana's situation] *how out of this can she avail?*
2 be of use to, help, advantage **Luc** 1273 [Lucrece to Maid, of the Maid weeping] *it small avails my mood*; **1H6** I.i.47, III.i.181

avaunt (*n.*) order to be gone, farewell **H8** II.iii.10 [Anne to Old Lady, of Queen Katherine] *after this process, / To give her the avaunt*

avaunt (*int.*) begone, go away, be off **MW** I.iii.76 [Falstaff to Nym and Pistol] *Rogues, hence, avaunt!* ➤ FEW, p.xxi

ave (*n.*) acclamation, ovation, welcoming shout **MM** I.i.70 [Duke to Angelo, of the people] *I do not relish well / Their loud applause and aves vehement*

Ave-Marie (*n.*) [of a rosary] Hail Mary **2H6** I.iii.54 [Queen to Suffolk, of the King] *all his mind is bent to holiness, / To number Ave-Maries on his beads*; **3H6** II.i.161

aver (*v.*) provide, furnish, affirm **Cym** V.v.203 [Iachimo to Cymbeline, of the evidence against Innogen] *averring notes / Of chamber-hanging, pictures*

avert (*v.*) redirect, turn away **KL** I.i.211 [Lear to France] *I ... beseech you / T'avert your liking a more worthier way / Than on a wretch*

avise, avised ➤ advise (*v.*)

avoid (*v.*) **1** be off, be gone, go away **AC** V.ii.242 [Cleopatra to Guardsman, of the Clown] *Avoid, and leave him*; **CE** IV.iii.48; **2H6** I.iv.39; **Tem** VI.i.142
2 leave, quit, clear out [of] **Cor** IV.v.25 [Third Servingman to Coriolanus] *Pray you avoid the house*; **Cor** IV.v.33; **H8** V.i.86
3 repudiate, deny, reject **MM** III.i.198 [disguised Duke to Isabella, of Angelo] *he will avoid your accusation*; **AY** V.iv.94; **TC** II.ii.66

avoirdupois (*n.*) weight, state of heaviness **2H4** II.iv.249 [Falstaff to Doll, of Prince Harry and Poins] *the weight of a hair will turn the scales between their avoirdupois* [F *Haber-de-pois*]

avouch (*n.*) assurance, guarantee **Ham** I.i.57 [Horatio to Barnardo, of the Ghost] *the sensible and true avouch / Of mine own eyes*

avouch (*v.*) **1** declare, assert, affirm **MW** II.i.125 [Nym to Page, of Falstaff's plan] *I avouch 'tis true*; **H5** V.ii.232; **KL** V.i.44; **Mac** V.v.47; **MND** I.i.106; **R3** I.iii.114
2 justify, warrant, defend **H5** V.i.69 [Gower to Pistol] *Will you mock at an ancient tradition ... and dare not avouch in your deeds any of your words?*; **Mac** III.i.119; **MM** IV.ii.180

avouchment (*n.*) [affirmation] misuse of 'avouch' [sense 1] **H5** IV.viii.36 [Fluellen to King Henry] *I hope your majesty is pear me testimony and witness, and will avouchment, that this is the glove of Alençon*

await for (*v.*) expect, anticipate, look out for **1H6** I.i.48 [Bedford to all] *Posterity, await for wretched years*

awake (*v.*) arouse, prompt, force into action **Tim** II.ii.24 [Caphis to Timon] *My master is awaked by great occasion / To call upon his own*

award (*v.*) adjudge, ordain, decree **R3** II.i.14 [King Edward to Hastings and Rivers, of God] *Lest He ... / Confound your hidden falsehood and award / Either of you to be the other's end*

away with (*v.*) get on with, bear, endure **2H4** III.ii.196 [Shallow to Falstaff, of Jane Nightwork] *She never could away with me*

awd (*adj.*) dialect form of 'old' **LL** V.ii.12 [Dull to Holofernes, misunderstanding him] *'Twas not an awd grey doe, 'twas a pricket* [F *hauld*]

awe (*n.*) **1** reverence, respect, esteem **R2** I.i.118 [King Richard to Mowbray] *by my sceptre's awe I make a vow* [i.e. the reverence owed to my sceptre]; **Tim** IV.i.17
2 fear, terror, dread **1H6** I.i.39 [Winchester to Gloucester] *Thy wife is proud; she holdeth thee in awe* [i.e. she tyrannizes you]
3 subjection, restraint, dread **2H6** I.i.90 [Gloucester to all] *debating to and fro / How France and Frenchmen might be kept in awe?*; **JC** II.i.52

awe (*v.*) **1** repress through dread, constrain in fear **E3** II.ii.132 [Countess to King Edward] *your mightiness / Will overbear and awe these dear regards*
2 control, restrain, master **R2** V.v.91 [Richard as if to his horse] *thou, created to be awed by man*

aweary, a-weary (*adj.*) weary, tired **AW** IV.v.54 [Lafew to Clown] *I begin to be aweary of thee*; **AW** I.iii.43; **JC** IV.iii.94; **Mac** V.v.49; **MV** I.ii.1; **RJ** II.v.25

awed (*adj.*) awe-struck, daunted, intimidated **Venus** 69 [of Adonis] *Pure shame and awed resistance made him fret*

aweless (*adj.*) **1** inspiring no awe, lacking in respect **R3** II.iv.52 [Queen Elizabeth to all] *Insulting tyranny begins to jut / Upon the innocent and aweless throne* [F; Q *lawlesse*]
2 fearless, unintimidated **KJ** I.i.266 [Bastard to Lady Faulconbridge] *The aweless lion could not wage the fight*

awful (*adj.*) **1** awe-inspiring, worthy of respect **2H6** V.i.98 [York to King] *Thy hand is made to grasp a palmer's staff, / And not to grace an awful princely sceptre*; **3H6** II.i.153; **Per** II.Chorus.4; **R2** III.iii.76; **TG** IV.i.46; **TS** V.ii.108
2 full of awe [towards someone], respectful, reverential **R2** III.iii.76 [King Richard to his opponents] *how dare thy joints forget / To pay their awful duty to our presence?*

awhile (*adv.*) a short time, briefly **Ham** V.i.218 [Hamlet to Horatio] *Couch we awhile*; **TNK** IV.ii.70

awkward (*adj.*) **1** unfavourable, contrary, adverse **2H6** III.ii.83 [Queen to King, of her journey to England] *twice by awkward wind from England's bank / Drove back again*
2 perverse, inept, wrong-headed **H5** II.iv.85 [Exeter to French King, of the English claim] *'Tis no sinister nor no awkward claim*

a-work *(adv.)* at work, in action **KL** III.v.6 [Cornwall to Edmund] *a provoking merit set a-work by a reprovable badness*

awry *(adv.)* mistakenly, wrongly, erroneously **2H6** II.iv.58 [Gloucester to Duchess] *Thou aimest all awry;* **R2** II.ii.21

axletree, axle-tree *(n.)* **1** wooden beam acting as the pivot for a cart wheel **1H4** III.i.126 [Hotspur to Glendower] *I had rather hear … a dry wheel grate on the axle-tree*
2 pivot, spindle, axis [around which the heavenly bodies revolve] **TC** I.iii.66 [Ulysses to Agamemnon and Nestor] *a bond of air, strong as the axletree / On which the heavens ride*

ay *(adv.)* yes ➤ **RESPONSES**, p.373

ay *(int.)* ah ➤ **REGRETS**, p.367

aye *(adv.)* always, ever, for eternity **Ham** III.ii.210 [First Player, as King, to his Queen] *This world is not for aye* ➤ FEW, p.xxi

ayword *(n.)* ➤ nayword *(n.)*

azure, azured *(adj.)* coloured blue, bright blue [as of an uncloudy sky] **Cym** II.ii.22 [Iachimo to himself, of Innogen's eyelids] *white and azure laced;* **Cym** IV.ii.222; **E3** IV.v.115; **Tem** V.i.43

baby *(n.)* doll **Cor** III.ii.115 [Coriolanus to Volumnia] *the virgin voice / That babies lulls asleep!* [i.e. as a child lulls dolls asleep] ➤ **clout** *(n.)* 1

baccare, backare *(v.)* [mock Latin] back, stand back, give place **TS** II.i.73 [Gremio to Petruchio] *Baccare! You are marvellous forward*

bacchanal *(n.)* **1** dance in honour of Bacchus [god of wine] **AC** II.vii.102 [Enobarbus to Antony] *Shall we dance now the Egyptian bacchanals*
  2 devotee of Bacchus **MND** V.i.48 [Theseus to Philostrate, of a proposed entertainment] *The riot of the tipsy Bacchanals* ➤ **GODS AND GODDESSES**, p.620

bachelor *(n.)* **1** unmarried person [man or woman] **MA** II.i.42 [Beatrice to Leonato, of Saint Peter] *he shows me where the bachelors sit*
  2 young man **RJ** I.v.112 [Nurse to Romeo, of Juliet] *Marry, bachelor, / Her mother is the lady of the house*

back *(n.)* support, back-up, reserve **Ham** IV.vii.152 [Claudius to Laertes] *this project / Should have a back or second*

back, to the through and through **Tit** IV.iii.48 [Titus to Marcus] *we are … / But metal, Marcus, steel to the very back*

back *(v.)* **1** support, help, back up **3H6** I.iv.73 [Queen to York] *Where are your mess of sons to back you now?*; **3H6** IV.i.41, 43; **Luc** 352, 622
  2 ride, mount, sit on **TNK** III.i.21 [Arcite alone] *two such steeds might well / Be by a pair of kings backed*; **Cym** V.v.428; **1H4** II.iii.74; **Venus** 419

backare *(v.)* ➤ **baccare** *(v.)*

backbite *(v.)* slander, revile, speak badly [of someone] **2H4** V.i.28 [Shallow to Davy, of Falstaff] *Use his men well, … for they are arrant knaves, and will backbite*

backfriend *(n.)* false friend, someone who gives a pat on the back in an apparently friendly way **CE** IV.ii.37 [Dromio of Syracuse to Adriana, of the officer] *A backfriend, a shoulder-clapper*

backing *(n.)* backing up, being in support **1H4** II.iv.145 [Falstaff to Prince Hal, of Hal's behaviour] *Call you that backing of your friends?*; **3H6** II.ii.69

backside *(n.)* back streets, lesser-used thoroughfares **Cym** I.iii.11 [Second Lord aside, of Cloten] *His steel was in debt, it went o'th' backside the town* [i.e. kept out of the way, as if to avoid creditors]

backsword *(adj.)* sword-like stick with a basketwork hilt, used in fencing practice **2H4** III.ii.63 [Shallow to Bardolph, of Falstaff] *I knew him a good backsword man*

back-trick *(n.)* type of backwards dance leap **TN** I.iii.116 [Sir Andrew to Sir Toby] *I think I have the back-trick* [with bawdy pun: 'trick' = 'whore']

backward *(n.)* past portion, earlier part, bygone period **Tem** I.ii.50 [Prospero to Miranda] *What seest thou else / In the dark backward and abysm of time?*

backwardly *(adv.)* unfavourably, in a lowly manner; also: in reverse order of priority **Tim** III.iii.19 [Sempronius to Servant, of giving money to Timon] *does he think so backwardly of me now / That I'll requite it last?*

bacon *(n.)* porker, fat one; also: rustic **1H4** II.ii.89 [Falstaff to Travellers] *On, bacons, on!*

bacon-fed *(adj.)* [= fed on bacon] rustic, peasant, hillbilly **1H4** II.ii.83 [Falstaff to Travellers] *whoreson caterpillars, bacon-fed knaves*

bad *(adj.)* worthless, lowly, of no value **3H6** V.vi.91 [Richard alone, of the succession] *Counting myself but bad till I be best* ➤ **worse** *(adj.)*; **worst** *(n./adj.)*

bade *(v.)* ➤ **bid** *(v.)*

badge *(n.)* **1** outward sign, symbol, mark **R2** V.ii.33 [York to Duchess of York, of Richard] *His face still combating with tears and smiles, / The badges of his grief and patience*; **LL** V.ii.749; **Sonn** 44.14

2 livery, insignia of employment **Tem** V.i.267 [Prospero to lords, of Stephano and Trinculo] *Mark but the badges of these men*
3 crest, emblem **2H6** V.i.201 [Clifford to Warwick] *Might I but know thee by thy house's badge*; **2H6** V.i.202

badge, (*v.*) mark [as if by a badge], stain **Mac** II.iii.99 [Lennox to Malcolm, of the King's attendants] *Their hands and faces were all badged with blood*

baffle (*v.*) **1** [of a knight] publicly disgrace, treat with infamy **R2** I.i.170 [Mowbray to King Richard] *I am disgraced, impeached, and baffled here*; **1H4** I.ii.101; **TN** II.v.156
2 treat shamefully, expose to ridicule **TN** V.i.367 [Olivia to Malvolio] *How have they baffled thee!*; **2H4** V.iii.105

bag (*n.*) money-bag, purse **2H6** I.iii.126 [Cardinal to Gloucester] *the clergy's bags / Are lank and lean with thy extortions*; **KL** II.iv.48; **TS** I.ii.175

baggage (*n.*) good-for-nothing woman, harlot **TS** Induction.i.3 [Sly to Hostess] *Y'are a baggage*; **RJ** III.v.156

bagpipe (*n.*) windbag, verbose speaker **1H4** I.ii.76 [Falstaff to Prince Hal] *the drone of a Lincolnshire bagpipe* [unclear meaning]

bail (*n.*) security for release, guarantee of freedom **AW** V.iii.293 [Diana to Widow] *fetch my bail*; **AW** V.iii.283

bail (*v.*) **1** confine, enclose **Sonn** 133.10 *my friend's heart let my poor heart bail*
2 obtain release for, give freedom to **Luc** 1725 [of Lucrece's soul after stabbing herself] *That blow did bail it from the deep unrest / Of that polluted prison where it breathed*

bailiff (*n.*) sheriff's officer who serves writs, carries out arrests, etc **WT** IV.iii.93 [Autolycus to Clown, of the supposed robber] *He hath been … a process-server, a bailiff*

bait (*n.*) **1** morsel, snack, titbit **TC** V.viii.20 [Achilles to Myrmidons, of Hector] *My half-supped sword … / Pleased with this dainty bait, thus goes to bed*
2 temptation, lure, enticement **Cym** III.iv.58 [Innogen to Pisanio, as if to Posthumus] *All good seeming [shall be] … / But worn a bait for ladies*

bait (*v.*) **1** harass, persecute, torment **Cor** IV.ii.43 [Sicinius to Brutus, of Volumnia] *Why stay we to be baited / With one that wants her wits?*; **2H6** V.i.148; **Mac** V.vi.68; **R2** IV.i.237; **R3** I.iii.108; **WT** II.iii.92
2 tempt, entice, lure **CE** II.i.94 [Adriana to Luciana, of those enticing her husband] *Do their gay vestments his affections bait?*; **MV** III.i.48
3 drink, take refreshment **H8** V.iv.80 [Lord Chamberlain to Porter and Man] *here ye lie baiting of bombards* [or: harass]

baiting-place (*n.*) bear-baiting pit **2H6** V.i.150 [Clifford to York, of Warwick and Salisbury] *We'll bait thy bears to death … / If thou darest bring them to the baiting-place*

bake (*v.*) harden, make solid **Tem** I.ii.256 [Prospero to Ariel] *To do me business in the veins o'th' earth / When it is baked with frost*; **KJ** III.iii.43; **RJ** I.iv.90

baked meats (*n.*) pies, pastries **RJ** IV.iv.5 [Capulet to a servant] *Look to the baked meats*; **Ham** I.ii.180

balance (*v.*) add weight to, make up for **2H6** V.i.9 [York to himself] *I cannot give due action to my words, / Except a sword or sceptre balance it*

balance (*n.*) **1** scales **MV** IV.i.252 [Portia as Balthasar to Shylock] *Are there balance here to weigh / The flesh?*
2 weighing pan of a pair of scales **R2** III.iv.87 [Gardener to Queen Isabel] *In your lord's scale is nothing but himself … / But in the balance of great Bolingbroke / Besides himself are all the English peers*

bald (*adj.*) **1** trivial, foolish, witless **1H4** I.iii.64 [Hotspur to King Henry, of a lord] *This bald unjointed chat of his*; **CE** II.iii.117; **Cor** III.i.164
2 bare-headed [as a sign of respect] **Cor** IV.v.201 [Third Servingman to First Servingman, of Coriolanus] *no question asked him by any of the senators but they stand bald before him*

baldric, baldrick (*n.*) leather shoulder belt, strap [for holding a bugle, sword, etc] **MA** I.i.223 [Benedick to Claudio] *I will … hang my bugle in an invisible baldrick*; **TNK** IV.ii.86 [Messenger to Theseus, of one of Arcite's knights] *on his thigh a sword / Hung by a curious baldric* ☛ **WEAPONS**, p.491

bale (*n.*) sorrow, pain, misfortune **Cor** I.i.161 [Menenius to First Citizen] *Rome and her rats are at the point of battle; / The one side must have bale* [F: *baile*]

baleful (*adj.*) deadly, mortal, malignant **2H6** III.ii.48 [King to Suffolk] *Thou baleful messenger, out of my sight!*; **1H6** V.iv.122; **3H6** II.i.97; **RJ** II.iii.4

balk (*v.*) ☛ **baulk** (*v.*)

ball (*n.*) **1** royal golden orb **H5** IV.i.253 [King Henry alone, of being king] *'Tis not the balm, the sceptre, and the ball*; **Mac** IV.i.120
2 eyeball; also: cannon-ball **H5** V.ii.17 [Queen Isabel to King Henry] *Your eyes which hitherto have borne in them … / The fatal balls of murdering basilisks*

ballad (*v.*) make the subject of a song **AC** V.ii.216 [Cleopatra to Iras] *scald rhymers / Ballad us out o'tune*

ballasting (*n.*) weight [in rank], balance, sway **Cym** III.vii.50 [Innogen to herself, then as if to Posthumus, of Arviragus and Guiderius being her brothers] *would it had been so … then had my prize / Been less, and so more equal ballasting / To thee, Posthumus*

ballet (*n.*) ☛ **chanson** (*n.*)

ballow (*n.*) cudgel, stick **KL** IV.vi.241 [Edgar to Oswald, adopting a country accent] *I'ce try whether your costard or my ballow be the harder* [F; QQ *bat, battero*, etc]

balm (*n.*) **1** fragrant oil used for anointing, consecrated oil **R2** III.ii.55 [Richard to Aumerle] *Not all the water in the rough rude sea / Can wash the balm off from an anointed king*; **2H4** IV.v.115; **H5** IV.i.253; **3H6** III.i.17; **R2** IV.i.206
2 soothing ointment, salve; soothing treatment **TC** I.i.62 [Troilus to Pandarus] *instead of oil and balm, / Thou lay'st in every gash that love hath given me / The knife that made it*; **Tim** V.iv.16
3 aromatic plant, fragrant herb **MW** V.v.62 [Mistress Quickly as Queen of Fairies to all, of Windsor Castle] *The several chairs of order look you scour / With juice of balm*

balm (*v.*) **1** soothe, relieve, heal **KL** III.vi.96 [disguised Kent to Lear] *This rest might yet have balmed thy broken sinews*; **TS** Induction.i.46
2 embalmed, anointed with fragrant oil **Per** III.ii.63 [Cerimon to all, of Thaisa's body] *balmed and entreasured / With full bags of spices!*

balmy (*adj.*) **1** fragrant, delicious, sweet-smelling **Oth** V.ii.16 [Othello to himself, as if to Desdemona] *O balmy breath, that dost almost persuade / Justice to break her sword!*
2 soothing, healing, restorative **Oth** II.iii.251 [Othello to Desdemona] *'tis the soldiers' life / To have their balmy slumbers waked with strife*; **Sonn** 107.9

balsam (*n.*) balm, soothing ointment, healing agent **Tim** III.v.111 [Alcibiades alone] *Is this the balsam that the usuring Senate / Pours into captains' wounds?*

balsamum (*n.*) balm, balsam, aromatic oil **CE** IV.i.90 [Dromio of Syracuse to Antipholus of Ephesus] *I have bought … the balsamum*

ban (*n.*) curse, malediction **KL** II.iii.19 [Edgar alone, of beggars] *Sometimes with lunatic bans … / Enforce their charity*; **Ham** III.ii.267; **Tim** IV.i.34

ban (*v.*) **1** curse, damn, revile **2H6** III.ii.333 [Suffolk to Queen] *You bade me ban, and will you bid me leave*; **2H6** II.iv.25; **Luc** 1460; **PassP** XVIII.32; **Venus** 326
2 excommunicate, pronounce anathema **2H6** III.ii.319 [Suffolk to Queen] *every joint should seem to curse and ban*

bancrout, bankrout, bankerout (*n./adj./v.*) bankrupt **R2** II.i.257 [Willoughby to Ross and Northumberland] *The King's grown bancrout like a broken man*; **LL** I.i.27; **MV** IV.i.122; **R2** II.i.151; **RJ** III.ii.57; **Sonn** 67.9

band (*n.*) **1** bond, obligation, tie **1H4** III.ii.157 [Prince Hal to King Henry] *the end of life cancels all bands* [F]; **AW** IV.ii.56; **Ham** I.ii.24, III.ii.169; **MA** III.i.114; **R2** I.i.2

2 bond, promissory note, legal deed requiring payment **CE** IV.ii.49 [Adriana to Dromio of Syracuse, of Antipholus of Ephesus] *was he arrested on a band?* [pun: 50, sense 6]; **AC** III.i.26; **CE** IV.iii.32

3 body of men, troop **1H6** II.i.1 [stage direction] *Enter a French Sergeant of a Band*; **AC** III.xii.25; **Cor** I.i.26, vi.53; **Cym** IV.iv.11; **E3** I.i.142

4 company, society, fellowship **TNK** V.i.162 [Emilia praying to Diana] *grant / The file and quality I hold I may / Continue in thy band*

5 bond, shackle, chain **Tem** Epilogue.9 [Prospero alone, to audience] *release me from my bands*; **E3** III.iii.164; **3H6** I.i.186; **R2** II.ii.71; **Venus** 225, 363

6 neckband, collar, ruff **CE** IV.ii.50 [Dromio of Syracuse to Adriana, of Antipholus of Ephesus' arrest] *Not on a band, but on a stronger thing* [pun: 49, sense 2]

bandetto, banditto (*adj.*) bandit **2H6** IV.i.137 [Suffolk to the soldiers] *A Roman sworder and banditto slave / Murdered sweet Tully*

ban-dog (*n.*) chained dog, tethered hound **2H6** I.iv.17 [Bolingbroke to Duchess, of the middle of the night] *The time when screech-owls cry and ban-dogs howl*

bandy (*v.*) **1** exchange, swap, send to and fro **KL** I.iv.83 [Lear to Oswald] *Do you bandy looks with me*; **AY** V.i.54; **3H6** I.iv.49; **KL** II.iv.170; **LL** V.ii.29; **TS** V.ii.171

2 band together, make a league, fight **E3** IV.vi.10 [Prince Edward to Artois] *A fig for feathered shafts / When feathered fowls do bandy on our side!*; **Tit** I.i.315

3 drive, strike, toss back **RJ** II.v.14 [Juliet alone, of Nurse] *My words would bandy her to my sweet love*

bandying (*n.*) verbal strife, exchange of words **RJ** III.i.87 [Romeo to Tybalt and Mercutio] *the Prince expressly hath / Forbid this bandying in Verona streets*; **1H6** IV.i.190

bane (*n.*) **1** ruin, woe, destruction **Mac** V.iii.59 [Macbeth to Doctor] *I will not be afraid of death and bane / Till Birnan forest come to Dunsinane*; **Cym** V.iii.58; **2H6** V.i.120; **TC** V.ii.92; **Tit** V.iii.72; **Venus** 372

2 murderer, killer, destroyer **E3** III.iv.103 [King Edward to Prince Edward, of his sword] *warm / With blood of those that fought to be thy bane*

3 poison [from 'ratsbane'] **MM** I.ii.128 [Claudio to Lucio] *rats that ravin down their proper bane*

bane (*v.*) poison, kill, put down **MV** IV.i.46 [Shylock to Duke, of a rat] *And I be pleased to give ten thousand ducats / To have it baned?*

bang (*n.*) knock, blow, thump **JC** III.iii.18 [Second Plebeian to Cinna, of his reply] *You'll bear me a bang for that* [i.e. you'll get a thump]

bank (*n.*) **1** coast, shore **1H4** III.i.42 [Glendower to Hotspur] *the sea / That chides the banks of England, Scotland, Wales*; **2H6** III.ii.83; **MV** V.i.11; **Sonn** 56.11; **Tem** I.ii.390; **TNK** I.i.212 ➤ sea-bank (*n.*)

2 river bank **TNK** III.i.8 [Arcite alone] *We challenge too the bank of any nymph*; **JC** I.i.45; **TNK** V.iii.99

3 ant-hill **E3** III.iv.41 [Audley to King Edward] *The snares of French, like emmets on a bank*

bank (*v.*) [unclear meaning] put in a bank, win; pass by [as in a boat] **KJ** V.ii.104 [Lewis the Dauphin to Cardinal Pandulph, of the English] *Have I not heard these islanders shout out / 'Vive le roi!' as I have banked their towns?*

banket (*n.*) ➤ banquet (*n.*)

bankrout, bankerout (*n.*) ➤ bancrout (*n.*)

banneret (*n.*) **1** standard of a knight entitled to lead his own body of troops **E3** IV.iv.19 [Audley to Prince Edward, of the French army] *the banners, bannerets, / And new-replenished pendants cuff the air*

2 small banner, ornamental streamer **AW** II.iii.202 [Lafew to Parolles] *the scarfs and the bannerets about thee*

banning (*adj.*) cursing, chiding **1H6** V.iii.42 [Richard to Pucelle] *Fell banning hag!*; **Oth** II.i.11

banquet, banket (*n.*) **1** refreshments, light meal, dessert **Tim** I.ii.152 [Timon to Ladies] *there is an idle banquet attends you*; **AC** I.ii.12; **RJ** I.v.122; **TNK** III.i.109; **TS** V.ii.1, 9

2 appetizer, first course, hors d'oeuvres **TNK** I.i.186 [First Queen to Theseus, of his marriage] *Thou shalt remember nothing more than what / That banquet bids thee to*

banquet, running light meal taken hurriedly, quickly served repast **H8** I.iv.12 [Sands to Lovell, of the ladies] *a running banquet … / I think would better please 'em*; **H8** V.iv.64

bar (*n.*) **1** obstruction, barrier, obstacle **MV** II.vii.45 [Morocco to himself] *The watery kingdom … is no bar / To stop the foreign spirits*; **JC** I.iii.96; **MA** II.i.4; **MV** III.ii.119

2 lock, barrier, barricade **Sonn** 48.2 *Each trifle under truest bars to thrust*

3 objection, impediment **R3** I.ii.234 [Richard alone, of the difficulties of wooing Anne] *Having … these bars against me*; **MV** III.ii.19; **MW** III.iv.7; **TS** I.i.133

4 tribunal, judgement place **R3** V.iii.200 [King Richard alone] *All several sins … / Throng to the bar, crying all 'Guilty! Guilty!'*; **H5** V.ii.27

bar (*v.*) **1** prevent, obstruct, block **Cor** III.i.148 [Coriolanus to Brutus] *Purpose so barred, it follows / Nothing is done to purpose*; **Cym** I.v.108; **R3** IV.iv.400; **TS** Induction.ii.134

2 keep out, exclude, prohibit **AY** V.iv.122 [Hymen, to all] *I bar confusion*; **Ham** I.ii.14

3 forbid, deny, deprive [of] **Venus** 330 *the heart hath treble wrong / When it is barred the aidance of the tongue*; **Venus** 784

barbarism (*n.*) **1** rudeness, churlishness **E3** I.ii.9 [Countess to herself] *forced by rough insulting barbarism*

2 lack of culture, uncivilized ignorance **LL** I.i.112 [Berowne to King] *I have for barbarism spoke more / Than for that angel knowledge you can say*

3 savagery, people in the most uncivilized state **R2** V.ii.36 [York to Duchess of York, of Richard] *barbarism itself [must] have pitied him*

Barbary cock-pigeon type of pigeon from the Barbary coast; [reputedly of Eastern men] man who jealously safeguards his wife **AY** IV.i.139 [Rosalind as Ganymede to Orlando] *I will be more jealous of thee than a Barbary cock-pigeon over his hen* ➤ **WORLD**, p.634

Barbary hen guinea hen; or: prostitute **2H4** II.iv.96 [Falstaff to Hostess, of Pistol] *He'll not swagger with a Barbary hen* ➤ **WORLD**, p.634

barbed (*adj.*) armoured with barbs, protectively covered **R2** III.iii.117 [Northumberland to King Richard, of Bolingbroke] *His glittering arms he will commend to rust, / His barbed steeds to stables*; **R3** I.i.10

barber-monger (*n.*) frequenter of the barber-shop **KL** II.ii.29 [disguised Kent to Oswald] *you whoreson cullionly barber-monger*

bare (*n.*) bareness, unadorned state **Lover** 95 *that termless skin / Whose bare out-bragged the web it seemed to wear*

bare (*adj.*) **1** mere, simple **Ham** III.i.76 [Hamlet alone] *he himself might his quietus make / With a bare bodkin*; **TG** II.iv.44

2 threadbare, shabby, ragged **TNK** I.ii.15 [Palamon to Arcite, of what he sees in Thebes] *Scars and bare weeds*; **AW** IV.v.95; **TG** II.iv.43

3 worthless, wretched; or: barefaced, shameless **1H4** III.ii.13 [King Henry to Prince Hal, of Hal's behaviour] *Such poor, such bare, such lewd, such mean attempts*; **Cor** V.i.20; **1H4** I.iii.107; **Venus** 188

4 gaunt, lean, needy **RJ** V.i.68 [Romeo to Apothecary] *Art thou so bare and full of wretchedness / And fearest to die?*; **1H4** IV.ii.67

5 unsheathed, exposed **Oth** V.i.2 [Iago to Roderigo] *Wear thy good rapier bare*

6 unprotected, defenceless, without covering **Tim** IV.iii.266 [Timon to Apemantus, comparing his former associates to leaves] *have with one winter's brush / Fell from their boughs, and left me open, bare, / For every storm that blows*

bare (v.) shave, trim **MM** IV.ii.172 [disguised Duke to Provost] *Shave the head, and tie the beard, and say it was the desire of the penitent to be so bared before his death*

bare-bone (n.) skinny person, fleshless one **1H4** II.iv.319 [Prince Hal to Falstaff] *Here comes lean Jack, here comes bare-bone*

bare-boned (adj.) like a skeleton, fleshless **Luc** 1761 [Lucretius, of Lucrece] *that fair fresh mirror ... / Shows me a bare-boned death by time outworn*

bare-gnawn (adj.) totally consumed, worn away to nothing **KL** V.iii.120 [Edgar to all] *my name is lost, / By treason's tooth bare-gnawn and canker-bit*

barely (adv.) in bareness, exposed, without covering **AW** IV.ii.19 [Diana to Bertram] *You barely leave our thorns to prick ourselves*

bareness (n.) gauntness, leanness, thin condition **1H4** IV.ii.69 [Falstaff to Westmorland, responding to the criticism that his men are 'bare'] *And for their bareness I am sure they never learned that of me*

barful (adj.) full of hindrances, with impediments **TN** I.iv.41 [Viola to herself, of her task in wooing Olivia] *a barful strife!*

baring (n.) removal, shaving off **AW** IV.i.48 [Parolles to himself] *the baring of my beard*

bark, barque (n.) ship, vessel **Ham** IV.iii.43 [Claudius to Hamlet] *The bark is ready;* **CE** I.i.117; **E3** I.i.118; **Mac** I.iii.24; **Tit** I.i.74; **WT** V.ii.65

bark (v.) strip the bark from, tear away **MM** III.i.75 [Isabella to Claudio, of his agreement to Angelo's proposal] *[it] Would bark your honour from that trunk you bear* ☞ **barked** (adj.)

bark about (v.) encrust, form a crust [cover as with tree-bark] **Ham** I.v.71 [Ghost to Hamlet] *And a most instant tetter barked about ... / All my smooth body* [Q1, Q2 bark'd; F bak'd]

barked (adj.) stripped, peeled bare, destroyed **AC** IV.xii.23 [Antony alone] *this pine is barked / That overtopped them all*

barky (adj.) bark-covered **MND** IV.i.43 [Titania to sleeping Bottom] *the female ivy so / Enrings the barky fingers of the elm*

barley-break (n.) type of country game in which a couple occupies a den [nicknamed 'hell'] in the centre of a [barley] field, and tries to catch other couples, who may separate [break] when about to be caught **TNK** IV.iii.30 [Gaoler's Daughter to herself] *sometime we go to barley-break, we of the blessed* [i.e. I know what hell is like]

barley broth (n.) ale [as given to horses] **H5** III.v.19 [Constable to all, of the English] *Can sodden water ... their barley broth / Decoct their cold blood to such valiant heat?*

barm (n.) froth on the top of fermenting ale **MND** II.i.38 [Fairy to Puck] *Are not you he / That ... sometime make the drink to bear no barm* [i.e. stop the fermentation process]

barn, barne (n.) child, baby **WT** III.iii.68 [Shepherd to himself, of Perdita] *Mercy on's, a barne! A very pretty barne;* **AW** I.iii.25; **MA** III.iv.43

barn (v.) store up in a barn, gather in **Luc** 859 [Lucrece to herself, of a sick miser] *he sits, / And useless barns the harvest of his wits*

barnacle (n.) species of goose [believed to begin life as a shellfish] **Tem** IV.i.248 [Caliban to Stephano and Trinculo] *We shall ... all be turned to barnacles*

barren (adj.) **1** unresponsive, dull, apathetic **Ham** III.ii.40 [Hamlet to Players] *some quantity of barren spectators*
2 stupid, empty-headed, dull **TN** I.v.79 [Malvolio to Olivia, of Feste] *I marvel your ladyship takes delight in such a barren rascal;* **CE** II.i.91; **MND** III.ii.13

barrenness (n.) area [of skin] worn dry and bare **CE** III.ii.127 [Dromio of Syracuse to Antipholus of Syracuse, of where Scotland is to be found in the kitchen wench] *I found it by the barrenness, hard in the palm of the hand*

barren-spirited (adj.) dull-minded, lacking the spirit to respond **JC** IV.i.36 [Antony to Octavius, of Lepidus] *A barren-spirited fellow*

barricado (n.) barricade, rampart, barrier **TN** IV.ii.36 [disguised Feste to Malvolio, of his cell] *it hath bay windows transparent as barricadoes;* **E3** V.i.134; **WT** I.ii.204

barricado (v.) fortify, defend, protect [as with a barricade] **AW** I.i.112 [Helena to Parolles, of virginity and man] *how may we barricado it against him?*

barrow (n.) barrowful, cartload **MW** III.v.4 [Falstaff alone] *Have I lived to be carried in a basket like a barrow of butcher's offal?*

Bartholomew boar-pig pig sold at the annual London fair held on St Bartholomew's day **2H4** II.iv.226 [Doll to Falstaff] *Thou whoreson little tidy Bartholomew boar-pig* ☞ **DAYS AND DATES**, p.630

Bartholomew-tide (n.) St Bartholomew's day **H5** V.ii.303 [Burgundy to King Henry] *maids, well summered and warm kept, are like flies at Bartholomew-tide* ☞ **DAYS AND DATES**, p.630

base (n.) **1** basis, foundation, cause **TN** V.i.73 [Antonio to Orsino] *I confess, on base and ground enough, / [myself to be] Orsino's enemy*
2 foundation, supporting structure **TC** IV.v.212 [Ulysses to Hector] *I wonder now how yonder city stands / When we have here her base and pillar by us;* **Sonn** 125.3
3 pedestal **JC** III.ii.189 [Antony to all] *Even at the base of Pompey's statue ... great Caesar fell*
4 [plural] type of knee-length skirt worn by a knight on horseback **Per** II.i.162 [Pericles to Fishermen] *I yet am unprovided / Of a pair of bases*
5 ☞ **bid the base**

base (adj.) **1** dishonourable, low, unworthy **1H6** V.ii.18 [Pucelle to all] *Of all base passions, fear is most accursed* ☞ **FEW**, p.xxi
2 low-born, lowly, plebeian, of lower rank **1H6** III.ii.68 [Talbot to French lords] *Base muleteers of France!* ☞ **FEW**, p.xxi
3 poor, wretched, of low quality **WT** IV.iv.94 [disguised Polixenes to Perdita] *we marry / A gentler scion to the wildest stock, / And make conceive a bark of baser kind / By bud of nobler race* ☞ **FEW**, p.xxi
4 non-precious, worthless, of low value **Ham** IV.i.26 [Gertrude to Claudius] *like some ore / Among a mineral of metals base*
5 low-lying, lowland **R2** II.iv.20 [Salisbury alone, of King Richard] *I see thy glory like a shooting star / Fall to the base earth;* **Luc** 664; **R2** III.iii.191

base (v.) ☞ **bass** (v.)

base-born (adj.) of low birth, lowborn, plebeian **2H6** IV.viii.46 [Clifford to the rebels] *Better ten thousand base-born Cades miscarry;* **2H6** I.iii.81; **3H6** II.ii.143

base-court (n.) [of a castle] lower courtyard, servants' courtyard **R2** III.iii.176 [Northumberland to King Richard, of Bolingbroke] *in the base-court he doth attend;* **R2** III.iii.180

baseless (adj.) unsubstantial, lacking a foundation **Tem** IV.i.151 [Prospero to Ferdinand] *the baseless fabric of this vision*

basely (adv.) dishonourably, shamefully, ignominiously **E3** III.iii.115 [King John to King Edward] *ere I basely will resign my crown;* **AC** IV.xv.55; **1H4** V.ii.82; **1H6** V.v.17; **R2** II.i.241, 253; **TNK** III.vi.267

baseness (n.) **1** socially inferior trait, plebeian quality **Oth** III.iv.27 [Desdemona to Emilia] *but my noble Moor / Is ... made of no such baseness / As jealous creatures are;* **Ham** V.ii.34; **KL** I.ii.10; **MM** III.i.15
2 debasement, lowly state, humiliation **WT** II.iii.78 [Paulina to Antigonus, of Leontes calling the baby a bastard] *that forced baseness / Which he has put upon't;* **AC** IV.xiv.77; **WT** IV.iv.729

3 cowardice, degenerateness, degradation **AC** IV.xiv.57 [Antony to Eros] *the gods* / *Detest my baseness;* **Cor** III.ii.123; **Cym** III.iv.89; **MW** II.ii.20; **TN** V.i.144

4 lowly activity, contemptible work **Tem** III.i.2 [Ferdinand alone] *Some kinds of baseness* / *Are nobly undergone;* **H8** I.ii.67 [F]; **Tem** III.i.12

base viol (*n.*) ➤ **bass viol** (*n.*)

bashful (*adj.*) easily intimidated, readily daunted **3H6** I.i.41 [Warwick to all] *The bloody parliament shall this be called* / *Unless Plantagenet ... be king,* / *And bashful Henry deposed*

basilisk (*n.*) **1** mythical serpent which killed with its look **R3** I.ii.150 [Anne to Richard, of her eyes] *Would they were basilisks to strike thee dead!;* **Cym** IV.ii.107; **2H6** III.ii.52, 324; **3H6** III.ii.187; **WT** I.ii.388

2 type of large cannon **1H4** II.iii.55 [Lady Percy to Hotspur] *thou hast talked* / *Of ... basilisks;* **H5** V.ii.17 ➤ **WEAPONS**, p.491

basis (*n.*) **1** base, foot, foundation **H5** IV.iii.28 [Constable to Dauphin] *Though we upon this mountain's basis by* / *Took stand for idle speculation;* **TC** I.iii.75; **Tem** II.i.122

2 pedestal **JC** III.i.115 [Brutus to all, of Caesar] *That now on Pompey's basis lies along*

basket-hilt (*n.*) sword hilt with protective steel basketwork **2H4** II.iv.127 [Doll to Pistol] *you basket-hilt stale juggler, you!* [i.e. inept swordsman] ➤ **WEAPONS**, p.491

bass, base (*v.*) utter with bass voice, proclaim resonantly **Tem** III.iii.101 [Alonso to Gonzalo, of a sound] *pronounced* / *The name of Prosper: it did bass my trespass*

bass viol, base viol (*n.*) stringed instrument resembling a cello **CE** IV.iii.23 [Dromio of Syracuse to Antipholus of Syracuse, of the officer] *he that went like a bass viol in a case of leather* ➤ **viol** (*n.*)

bastard (*n.*) **1** low-born person **JC** V.iv.2 [Cato to all, of people holding up their heads] *What bastard doth not?*

2 hybrid, cross-breed, mixed variety **WT** IV.iv.83 [Perdita to disguised Polixenes] *streaked gillyvors,* / *Which some call Nature's bastards;* **WT** IV.iv.99

3 variety of sweet Spanish wine **1H4** II.iv.71 [Prince Hal to Francis] *your brown bastard is your only drink;* **1H4** II.iv.26; **MM** III.ii.3

bastard (*adj.*) **1** illegitimate, spurious, unauthorized **CE** III.ii.19 [Luciana to Antipholus of Syracuse] *Shame hath a bastard fame, well managed;* **MV** III.v.11; **Sonn** 68.3

2 inferior, low, of little value **TG** III.i.310 [Launce to Speed, of his love's 'nameless virtues'] *That's as much as to say, bastard virtues*

bastardizing (*n.*) being conceived as a bastard **KL** I.ii.132 [Edmund alone] *I should have been that I am had the maidenliest star in the firmament twinkled on my bastardizing* [i.e. I would have been no different even if ...] [F; Q *bastardy*]

bastardly (*adj.*) malapropism for 'dastardly' **2H4** II.i.47 [Hostess to Falstaff] *thou bastardly rogue*

bastardy (*n.*) condition of illegitimacy **JC** II.i.138 [Brutus to all] *every drop of blood* / *That every Roman bears ...* / *Is guilty of a several bastardy,* / *If he do break the smallest particle* / *Of any promise*

baste (*v.*) sew loosely, tack together, stitch up **MA** I.i.266 [Benedick to Don Pedro] *the guards are but slightly basted*

bastinado cudgelling, beating with a stick [esp. on the soles of the feet] **AY** V.i.53 [Touchstone to William] *I will deal in poison with thee, or in bastinado;* **1H4** II.iv.329; **KJ** II.i.463

bat (*n.*) cudgel, staff, stick **Cor** I.i.54 [Menenius to citizens] *Where go you* / *With bats and clubs?;* **Cor** I.i.159; **KL** IV.vi.241 [Q]; **Lover** 64

batch (*n.*) ➤ **botch** (*n.*) 2

bate (*n.*) discord, strife, quarrel **2H4** II.iv.244 [Falstaff to Doll, of why Prince Harry loves Poins] *'a ... breeds no bate with telling of discreet stories*

bate (*v.*) **1** abate, modify, lessen **MA** II.iii.176 [Claudio to Don Pedro, of Beatrice] *she will die ... rather than she will bate one breath of her accustomed crossness;* **Cym** III.ii.55; **H5** III.ii.25; **LL** I.i.6; **MV** IV.i.72; **Tim** III.iii.27 ➤ **abate** (*v.*) 1

2 [of quantities] lessen, reduce, deduct **AW** II.iii.220 [Lafew to Parolles, of the insults Parolles deserves] *I will not bate thee a scruple;* **2H4** Epilogue.14; **Per** IV.ii.48; **Tem** I.ii.250

3 except, omit, leave out of consideration **Tem** II.i.102 [Sebastian to Antonio, of the incomparable excellence of Alonso's daughter] *Bate, I beseech you, widow Dido;* **AW** II.i.13; **MND** I.i.190

4 omit, lose, leave out **Cor** II.ii.138 [Sicinius to Coriolanus, of the people] *neither will they bate* / *One jot of ceremony;* **Ham** V.ii.23; **Tem** III.iii.86; **TNK** I.i.220

5 lose weight, diminish in size **1H4** III.iii.2 [Falstaff to Bardolph] *Do I not bate?;* **MV** III.iii.32

6 [falconry] beat the wings, flutter **1H4** IV.i.99 [Vernon to Hotspur, of Prince Hal and his companions] *All plumed like estridges that with the wind* / *Bated;* **H5** III.vii.109; **RJ** III.ii.14; **TS** IV.i.182

bate-breeding (*adj.*) mischief-making, discord-raising **Venus** 655 [Venus to Adonis, of solicitude] *this bate-breeding spy* ➤ **breed-bate** (*n.*)

bated (*adj.*) abated, lowered, diminished **MV** I.iii.121 [Shylock to Antonio] *in a bondman's key,* / *With bated breath and whispering humbleness;* **KJ** V.iv.53

bateless (*adj.*) unable to be blunted, permanently sharp **Luc** 9 [of Tarquin] *This bateless edge on his keen appetite*

bat-fowling (*n.*) catching birds roosting at night, by hitting them with a club **Tem** II.i.188 [Sebastian to Gonzalo] *go a-bat-fowling*

batler, batlet (*n.*) wooden club [used for beating clothes being washed] **AY** II.iv.45 [Touchstone to Rosalind and Celia, of Jane Smile] *I remember the kissing of her batler* [F1; F2 *batlet*]

battalia (*n.*) large body of troops arrayed for battle, marshalled force **R3** V.iii.11 [King Richard to Norfolk, of the numbers of the enemy] *our battalia trebles that account* [F; Q *battalion*]; **Ham** IV.v.80

batten (*v.*) glut oneself, grow fat on **Cor** IV.v.34 [Coriolanus to Third Servingman] *go and batten on cold bits;* **Ham** III.iv.68

battery (*n.*) **1** assault, bombardment, blitz **1H6** I.iv.65 [Salisbury to Gargrave and Glansdale] *Let me have your express opinions* / *Where is best place to make our battery next;* **AC** II.vii.107; **Cor** V.iv.21; **Cym** I.v.20; **H6** III.i.37; **Per** V.i.44

2 breach, entry **Per** V.i.44 [Lysimachus to a Lord, of Marina and Pericles] *She ... would allure,* / *And make a battery through his deafened ports;* **3H6** III.i.37; **Venus** 426

battle (*n.*) **1** army, fighting force, battalion **H5** IV.Chorus.9 [Chorus] *Fire answers fire, and through their paly flames* / *Each battle sees the other's umbered face;* **AC** III.ix.2; **E3** IV.v.33; **1H6** IV.vii.13; **KL** III.ii.23; **Mac** V.vi.4

2 battle array, war formation, ranks of soldiers **R3** V.iii.89 [Derby to Richmond] *Prepare thy battle early in the morning;* **Cor** I.vi.51; **H5** IV.iii.69; **3H6** V.iv.66; **R3** V.iii.293; **Venus** 619

3 hostile encounter, force **E3** III.i.121 [King John, as if to the French forces] *with the sulphur battles of your rage* / *The English fleet may be dispersed* [i.e. the hellfire ferocity of your anger]

4 single combat, individual fight **R2** I.i.92 [Bolingbroke to King Richard] *I say, and will in battle prove ...* / *That all the treasons ...* / *Fetch from false Mowbray*

5 ➤ **strike** (*v.*) 1

battled (*adv.*) in battalions, with deployed troops **E3** IV.iv.14 [Audley to Prince Edward, of the French king] *His party stronger battled than our whole*

batty (*adj.*) bat-like **MND** III.ii.365 [Oberon to Puck, of the Athenians] *o'er their brows death-counterfeiting sleep* / *With leaden legs and batty wings doth creep*

bauble (*n.*) **1** toy, plaything **Oth** IV.i.135 [Cassio to Iago, of Bianca] *thither comes the bauble and … falls me thus about my neck;* **Cym** III.i.28; **Tit** V.i.79
  2 piece of rubbish, worthless trifle **Cym** III.ii.20 [Pisanio alone, of the letter] *Senseless bauble;* **Cym** III.iii.23; **TS** IV.iii.82
  3 decorated rod of office, fool's staff **AW** IV.v.28 [Clown to Lafew] *I would give his wife my bauble … to do her service* [with bawdy pun]; **RJ** II.iv.90

bauble (*adj.*) like a toy, paltry, insignificant **TC** I.iii.35 [Nestor to Agamemnon, of a calm sea] *How many shallow bauble boats dare sail / Upon her patient breast*

baubling, bawbling (*adj.*) contemptible, trifling, piddling **TN** V.i.51 [Orsino to Viola as Cesario, of Antonio] *A baubling vessel was he captain of*

baulk (*v.*) **1** refuse, ignore, shirk, let slip **Luc** 696 [of the well-fed hound and hawk] *Make slow pursuit, or altogether balk / The prey;* **TN** III.ii.23
  2 argue over, quibble about **TS** I.i.34 [Tranio to Lucentio] *Balk logic with acquaintance that you have*
  3 fall on ridges between furrows; pile up in mounds **1H4** I.i.69 [King Henry to Westmorland] *Ten thousand bold Scots … / Balked in their own blood*

bavian (*n.*) baboon, ape **TNK** III.v.1 [stage direction] *Enter … six Countrymen, one dressed as a bavian;* **TNK** III.v.33, 131

bavin (*adj.*) [made of] firewood, kindling wood **1H4** III.ii.61 [King Henry to Prince Hal] *The skipping King, he ambled up and down, / With … rash bavin wits, / Soon kindled and soon burnt*

bawcock (*n.*) [fine bird] fine fellow, good chap **WT** I.ii.121 [Leontes to Mamillius] *Why, that's my bawcock;* **H5** III.ii.25, IV.i.44; **TN** III.iv.112 ☛ **ADDRESS FORMS**, p.8

bawd (*n.*) pimp, procurer, pander, go-between **Tim** II.ii.64 [Apemantus to Caphis] *Poor rogues and usurers' men, bawds between gold and want!* ☛ **FEW**, p.xxi

bawdry (*n.*) bawdiness, lewdness, obscenity **AY** III.iii.87 [Touchstone to Audrey] *we must be married, or we must live in bawdry;* **Ham** II.ii.498

bawdy (*adj.*) filthy, obscene, abominable **Ham** II.ii.577 [Hamlet alone, of Claudius] *Bloody, bawdy villain!*

bawdy-house (*n.*) brothel **1H4** III.iii.98 [Falstaff to Prince Hal] *This house is turned bawdy-house;* **1H4** III.iii.16, 156; **2H4** II.iv.141; **H5** II.i.33; **Per** IV.v.7

bay (*n.*) **1** [hunting] last stand, point of capture **R2** II.iii.127 [Bolingbroke to York, of Aumerle] *He should have found his uncle Gaunt a father / To rouse his wrongs and chase them to the bay;* **PassP** XI.iv.233; **R3** IV.iv.42; **Tit** V.iii.56; **Venus** 877
  2 baying, barking, howling **Tit** II.ii.3 [Titus to all] *Uncouple here, and let us make a bay;* **1H6** IV.ii.52
  3 leaf of the bay-tree [used as a herb; symbol of triumph] **H8** IV.ii.83 [stage direction] *wearing on their heads garlands of bays;* **Per** IV.vi.149 [Bawd to Marina] *my dish of chastity with rosemary and bays!*
  4 fame, renown [i.e. laurel wreath] **TNK** Prologue.20 [of Chaucer] *the witless chaff … / That blasts my bays* [i.e. destroys my renown]
  5 living area divided off within a house, gable-end **MM** II.i.231 [Pompey to Escalus, of Vienna] *I'll rent the fairest house in it after threepence a bay*

bay (*v.*) **1** bring to bay, drive to a last stand **MND** IV.i.112 [Hippolyta to Theseus, of Hercules and Cadmus] *they bayed the bear / With hounds of Sparta;* **2H4** I.ii.80; **JC** III.i.204
  2 bark at, howl at **Cym** V.v.223 [Posthumus to all, of virtue] *set / The dogs o' th' street to bay me;* **JC** IV.iii.27

bay about (*v.*) bring to bay, surround **JC** IV.i.49 [Octavius to Antony] *we are at the stake, / And bayed about with many enemies*

be (*v.*) **1** be alive, live **Per** V.i.181 [Marina to Pericles] *If good King Pericles be;* **Ham** III.i.56

  2 become, come to be **TNK** III.vi.244 [Emilia to Theseus] *do men prune / The straight young boughs that blush with thousand blossoms / Because they may be rotten?*
  3 intend, purpose, be determined **1H6** I.i.153 [Bedford to all] *Bonfires in France forthwith I am to make*
  4 represent, speak for **Cor** III.i.64 [Volumnia to Coriolanus] *I am in this / Your wife, your son, these Senators, the nobles*

be off (*v.*) doff the hat **Cor** II.iii.99 [Coriolanus to Fourth Citizen, of the people] *I will … be off to them most counterfeitly*

beached (*adj.*) having a beach, shingly, sandy **MND** II.i.85 [Titania to Oberon] *the beached margent of the sea;* **Tim** V.i.214

beachy (*adj.*) pebble-covered, shingly **2H4** III.i.50 [King Henry IV to Warwick and Surrey] *The beachy girdle of the ocean*

bead (*n.*) **1** tiny thing, smallest of objects **MND** III.ii.330 [Lysander to Hermia] *Get you gone, you dwarf … / You bead, you acorn*
  2 drop of liquid, tear-drop **KJ** II.i.171 [Constance to all] *with these crystal beads heaven shall be bribed;* **JC** III.i.284
  3 [plural] rosary beads **R2** III.iii.147 [King Richard to Aumerle] *I'll give my jewels for a set of beads;* **CE** II.i.197; **2H6** I.i.27, iii.54; **3H6** II.i.161; **R3** III.vii.92

beadle (*n.*) **1** parish constable **2H6** II.i.137 [Mayor to an attendant] *go fetch the beadle hither straight;* **2H4** V.iv.1; **H8** V.iv.65; **KL** IV.vi.161
  2 punisher, chastiser, castigator **H5** IV.i.164 [disguised King Henry to Williams, of God] *War is His beadle;* **KJ** II.i.188; **LL** III.i.172

beadsman (*n.*) almsman, pensioner [who prays for others] **TG** I.i.18 [Proteus to Valentine] *I will be thy beadsman;* **R2** III.ii.116

beak (*n.*) bow, prow, front **Tem** I.ii.196 [Ariel to Prospero, of the ship] *Now on the beak, / Now in the waist* ☛ **SHIPS**, p.397

beam (*n.*) **1** wooden roller in a loom **MW** V.i.21 [Falstaff to Ford as Brook] *I fear not Goliath with a weaver's beam* [i.e. the biblical description of Goliath's spear]
  2 balance, scales, counterpoise **2H6** II.i.200 [King to all, of Justice] *Whose beam stands sure, whose rightful cause prevails;* **AW** II.iii.154; **Oth** I.iii.323
  3 cross-bar [on a scales] **Ham** IV.v.159 [Laertes to Ophelia] *thy madness shall be paid with weight / Till our scale turn the beam* [i.e. tilt the balance]
  4 large wooden staff, lance, club **TC** V.v.9 [Agamemnon to Diomedes] *Margarelon / Hath Doreus prisoner, / And stands colossus-wise, waving his beam*
  5 large object, huge thing **LL** IV.iii.160 [Berowne to all, of his friends seeing a mote in each other's eye] *But I a beam do find in each of three* ☛ mote (*n.*)
  6 reach, range, line [of the eye, thought of as emitting beams of light] **Cor** III.ii.5 [Coriolanus to Nobles] *the precipitation might down stretch / Below the beam of sight;* **Sonn** 114.8

bear (*v.*), past forms **bore, borne 1** behave, look, conduct [oneself] **MM** I.iii.47 [Duke to Friar Thomas] *instruct / How I may formally in person bear me / Like a true friar;* **E3** II.i.19; **1H6** II.iv.14; **2H6** I.i.182; **3H6** II.ii.13; **Tem** I.ii.426
  2 carry on, manage, conduct [an affair] **Cor** IV.vii.21 [Aufidius to Lieutenant, of Coriolanus] *he bears all things fairly;* **Cor** IV.vii.15; **Ham** IV.iii.7; **1H6** II.iv.86; **MA** II.iii.216; **TNK** III.i.90
  3 control, manage, take charge of **R3** II.ii.128 [Buckingham to Rivers] *Where every horse bears his commanding rein*
  4 bear in mind, keep note of **2H4** II.ii.16 [Prince Henry to Poins] *What a disgrace is it to me … to bear the inventory of thy shirts*
  5 sustain, carry through, keep going **Ham** I.iii.67 [Polonius to Laertes, of a quarrel] *being in, / Bear't that th'opposed may beware of thee;* **AW** III.iii.5; **H5** I.ii.213; **Luc** 1132; **Tim** I.i.181
  6 tolerate, endure, put up with **2H6** II.i.150 [King to God, of Simpcox] *seest thou this, and bearest so long?;* **Cor** III.i.33; **2H4** II.iv.58, V.iii.29; **2H6** II.iii.41; **Tim** III.v.40
  7 keep, present, show **1H6** II.iv.13 [Warwick to all] *Between two blades, which bears the better temper;* **E3** IV.iv.30; **1H4** IV.i.20; **2H4** III.ii.229; **Lover** 19; **MA** I.i.63

8 bring forth, produce, yield **AC** IV.vi.7 [Caesar to all] *the three-nooked world / Shall bear the olive freely* [i.e. the olive-branch of peace]

9 take, carry **Oth** I.iii.23 [First Senator to Duke, of the Turk taking Cyprus] *So may he with more facile question bear it;* **2H4** IV.i.133

10 carry [a rider], support **H5** III.vii.43 [Orleans to Dauphin, of his horse] *Your mistress bears well* [with bawdy pun]

11 steer, sail towards **TNK** IV.i.151 [Gaoler's Daughter to Gaoler, of her imagined wood] *Bear for it, master*

12 carry away, take as a companion **Tim** IV.i.32 [Timon alone, as if to Athens] *Nothing I'll bear from thee / But nakedness;* **Tim** I.i.135

13 escort, accompany, go along with **TC** III.iii.30 [Agamemnon to all, of Antenor] *Let Diomedes bear him*

14 be endowed with, have, possess **TC** III.iii.4 [Calchas to all] *through the sight I bear in things to come, / I have abandoned Troy*

bear away (*v.*) leave, sail away **CE** IV.i.88 [Dromio of Syracuse to Antipholus of Ephesus] *there's a bark of Epidamnum / That stays but till her owner comes aboard, / And then she bears away*

bear back (*v.*) move back, go back **JC** III.ii.169 [Plebeians to each other] *Stand back! Room! Bear back!*

bear down (*v.*) overwhelm, put down, overcome **MV** IV.i.211 [Bassanio to all] *malice bears down truth;* **2H4** I.i.11; **Tit** II.i.30

bear hard bear ill will towards, feel resentment against **JC** I.ii.310 [Cassius alone] *Caesar doth bear me hard, but he loves Brutus;* **JC** II.i.215, III.i.157

bear in hand 1 abuse, take advantage of, delude, deceive **Ham** II.ii.67 [Voltemand to Claudius, of old Fortinbras] *his sickness, age, and impotence / Was falsely borne in hand;* **MA** IV.i.299; **Mac** III.i.80; **TS** IV.ii.3

2 profess, pretend, purport **Cym** V.v.43 [Cornelius to Cymbeline, of the Queen] *Your daughter, whom she bore in hand to love … she did confess / Was as a scorpion*

3 encourage with false hopes, foster expectation in **2H4** I.ii.35 [Falstaff to Page, of his tailor] *A rascally yea-forsooth knave, to bear a gentleman in hand, and then stand upon security!*

bear off (*v.*) ward off, keep away, repel **Tem** II.ii.18 [Trinculo to himself] *Here's neither bush nor shrub, to bear off any weather at all*

bear out (*v.*) **1** endure, weather, cope [with] **E3** II.i.364 [Warwick alone, of King Edward] *I'll say his greatness may bear out the shame;* **Oth** II.i.19; **Sonn** 116.12; **TN** I.v.19

2 help out, support, back up **2H4** V.i.42 [Davy to Shallow] *if I cannot once or twice in a quarter bear out a knave against an honest man, I have little credit with your worship*

3 support, authorize, sanction **KJ** IV.i.6 [Executioner to Hubert, of dealing with Arthur] *I hope your warrant will bear out the deed*

4 undertake, carry on, conduct **2H4** IV.v.214 [King Henry IV to Prince Henry, of foreign wars] *action hence borne out / May waste the memory of the former days*

bear up (*v.*) **1** stay upright, not fall down **Tem** III.ii.2 [Stephano to Trinculo and Caliban] *bear up and board 'em* [i.e. drink up]

2 sustain, support, uphold **MM** IV.i.47 [disguised Duke to Isabella, of the plan] *'Tis well borne up*

bearard (*n.*) ☛ **bearherd** (*n.*)

beard (*v.*) defy, affront, oppose openly **1H6** I.iii.44 [Winchester to Gloucester] *I beard thee to thy face;* **Ham** II.ii.423; **1H4** IV.i.12; **1H6** I.iii.45; **2H6** IV.x.36

beard, in one's to one's face, openly **H5** III.ii.69 [Fluellen to Gower, of Macmorris being an ass] *I will verify as much in his beard*

bearer (*n.*) possessor, owner, holder **TC** III.iii.104 [Achilles to Ulysses] *The beauty that is borne here in the face / The bearer knows not* **2H4** IV.v.30; **H8** I.iii.15

bearherd, bear-herd, bearard, bearward, berrord (*n.*) bear-keeper, bear-handler [for dancing or baiting] **2H6** V.i.210 [Clifford to Warwick] *from thy burgonet I'll rend thy bear … / Despite the bearard that protects the bear;* **2H4** I.ii.171; **2H6** V.i.149; **MA** II.i.35; **TS** Induction.ii.19

bearing (*n.*) carrying of hardships, enduring of woes **KL** III.vi.105 [Edgar alone] *the mind much sufferance doth o'erskip / When grief hath mates, and bearing fellowship;* **Tim** III.v.47

bearing (*adj.*) child-bearing, of labour **Per** III.iv.6 [Thaisa to Cerimon] *I was shipped at sea … / Even on my bearing time*

bearing-cloth (*n.*) christening-garment, baptismal shawl **1H6** I.iii.42 [Gloucester to Winchester] *Thy scarlet robes as a child's bearing-cloth / I'll use to carry thee out of this place;* **WT** III.iii.111

bearward (*n.*) ☛ **bearard** (*n.*)

beast (*n.*) mere animal **H5** III.vii.23 [Dauphin to Orleans, of his horse] *all other jades you may call beasts*

beastly (*adj.*) beast-like, brutish, abominable **Cym** III.iii.40 [Arviragus to Belarius] *We are beastly;* **Cym** I.vii.153; **KL** II.ii.67

beastly (*adv.*) like an animal, in a beastly manner **TNK** III.iii.6 [Arcite to Palamon] *You shall not die thus beastly;* **AC** I.v.50; **Cym** V.iii.27; **TC** V.v.5; **TS** IV.ii.34

beat (*v.*) **1** hammer away, ponder furiously **Tem** I.ii.176 [Miranda to Prospero] *For still 'tis beating in my mind, your reason / For raising this sea-storm?;* **Ham** III.i.175; **KL** III.iv.14; **Tem** V.i.246

2 strike **Ham** I.i.39 [Barnardo to Horatio and Marcellus] *The bell then beating one;* **TNK** III.iv.7

3 drive, force, impel **TS** Induction.ii.28 [Lord to Sly, of his kindred] *beaten hence by your strange lunacy;* **KJ** II.i.88; **TS** Induction.ii.84

4 beat the wings, flap wildly **TS** IV.i.182 [Petruchio alone] *kites / That bate and beat and will not be obedient*

beat on / upon (*v.*) be obsessed by, be preoccupied with **2H6** II.i.20 [Cardinal to Gloucester] *thine eyes and thoughts / Beat on a crown;* **TNK** IV.iii.77

beaten (*adj.*) well-tried, well-trodden **Ham** II.ii.269 [Hamlet to Rosencrantz and Guildenstern] *in the beaten way of friendship*

beating (*adj.*) battering, thumping, blow-by-blow **MW** II.ii.27 [Falstaff to Pistol] *[you] will ensconce … your bold beating oaths, under the shelter of your honour!*

beauty (*v.*) beautify, embellish, adorn **Ham** III.i.51 [Claudius to himself] *The harlot's cheek, beautied with plastering art*

beauty-waning (*adj.*) of fading looks, of diminishing beauty **R3** III.vii.184 [Buckingham to Richard, of King Edward's wife] *A beauty-waning and distressed widow*

beaver (*n.*) visor of a helmet, face-guard **H5** IV.ii.42 [Grandpré to all, of the English army] *Big Mars … faintly through a rusty beaver peeps;* **Ham** I.ii.230; **2H4** IV.i.118; **R3** V.iii.50; **TC** I.iii.296 ☛ **BODY-ARMOUR**, p.48

because (*conj.*) so that, in order that **TS** I.i.181 [Tranio to Lucentio, of Baptista and Bianca] *has he closely mewed her up, / Because she will not be annoyed with suitors*

bechance (*v.*) happen to, befall **3H6** I.iv.6 [York alone, of his sons] *God knows what hath bechanced them;* **Luc** 976; **MV** I.i.38; **TG** I.i.61

beck (*n.*) **1** beckoning, command, call **3H6** I.i.68 [King to all, of the house of York] *they have troops of soldiers at their beck;* **AC** III.xi.60; **Ham** III.i.125; **Sonn** 58.5; **TS** Induction.ii.33

2 bow, curtsy, gesture of respect **Tim** I.ii.236 [Apemantus to Timon, of the lords] *Serving of becks and jutting-out of bums!*

beck (*v.*) beckon, nod, call **AC** IV.xii.26 [Antony alone, of Cleopatra] *This grave charm, / Whose eye becked forth my wars;* **KJ** III.iii.13

becking (*n.*) beckoning, calling. nodding [to action] **TNK** I.ii.116 [Arcite to Palamon] *let us follow / The becking of our chance*

beckon (*v.*) make a significant gesture to, signal **Oth** IV.i.131 [Othello to himself] *Iago beckons me* [Q; F *becomes*]

beckoning (*n.*) signal, significant gesture, meaningful sign **TNK** III.v.128 [Schoolmaster to Theseus, of a host and hostess] *with a beckoning / Informs the tapster to inflame the reckoning*

become *(v.)* **1** be fitting, befit, be appropriate to TNK V.iii.50 [Emilia to herself, of Palamon] *Melancholy / Becomes him nobly* ☞ FEW, p.xxi

2 grace, honour, dignify E3 IV.vi.60 [Audley to Esquire, of Prince Edward] *in the crimson bravery of my blood / I may become him with saluting him* ☞ FEW, p.xxi

3 put a good front on, give a pleasing appearance to CE III.ii.11 [Luciana to Antipholus of Syracuse] *Look sweet, speak fair, become disloyalty;* AC II.ii.244

4 bear, handle, present AC III.xii.34 [Caesar to Thidias] *Observe how Antony becomes his flaw*

5 come to (be), to be found, reach 3H6 II.i.10 [Richard to Edward, of York] *I cannot joy, until I be resolved / Where our right valiant father is become;* 3H6 IV.iv.25

becomed *(adj.)* becoming, befitting, appropriate RJ IV.ii.26 [Juliet to Capulet, of Paris] *I ... gave him what becomed love I might*

becoming *(n.)* grace, quality, befitting action AC I.iii.96 [Cleopatra to Antony] *my becomings kill me when they do not / Eye well to you*

bedashed *(adj.)* dashed about, bespattered, splashed about R3 I.ii.163 [Richard to Anne] *all the standers-by had wet their cheeks / Like trees bedashed with rain*

bedazzle *(v.)* confuse by dazzling TS IV.v.46 [Katherina to Vincentio, of her eyes] *That have been so bedazzled with the sun*

bed-blotting *(adj.)* polluting the marriage bed E3 II.i.457 [Warwick to Countess] *When thou convert'st from honour's golden name / To the black faction of bed-blotting shame* [i.e. the hellish sect of adulterers]

bedded *(adj.)* **1** smooth-lying, laid flat Ham III.iv.122 [Gertrude to Hamlet] *Your bedded hair ... / Start up and stand an end*

2 smoothed, dressed; or: fixed in a setting Lover 37 *A thousand favours ... / Of amber crystal and of bedded jet*

bedew *(v.)* moisten with drops, wet with tears 1H6 I.i.104 [Third Messenger to the nobles] *your laments, / Wherewith you now bedew King Henry's hearse;* 2H4 IV.v.114

bedfellow *(n.)* intimate companion TNK V.iii.44 [Emilia to herself, of Arcite] *mercy and manly courage / Are bedfellows in his visage* [i.e. are seen together in his face]

bed-hanger *(n.)* hanging tapestry for a four-poster bed 2H4 II.i.145 [Falstaff to Hostess] *for thy walls, a pretty slight drollery ... is worth a thousand of these bed-hangers and these fly-bitten tapestries*

bedim *(v.)* make dim, cover with cloud Tem V.i.41 [Prospero alone] *I have bedimmed / The noontide sun*

Bedlam *(n./adj.)* colloquial form of Bethlehem Hospital for the insane, in London 2H6 V.i.131 [Clifford to all, of York] *To Bedlam with him!* KL II.iii.14 [Edgar alone] *The country gives me proof and precedent / Of Bedlam beggars* ☞ LONDON, p.631

bedlam *(n.)* mad beggar, madman/woman, lunatic KL III.vii.102 [Second Servant to Third Servant, of Gloucester] *Let's ... get the Bedlam / To lead him where he would;* KJ II.i.183 ☞ Tom o'Bedlam *(n.)*

bedlam *(adj.)* mad, crazed, frantic 2H6 V.i.132 [King to Clifford, of York] *a bedlam and ambitious humour / Makes him oppose himself against his king;* H5 V.i.18; 2H6 III.i.51

bed-presser *(n.)* sluggard, lazy fellow 1H4 II.iv.238 [Prince Hal to Falstaff] *This sanguine coward, this bed-presser*

bedred *(adj.)* ☞ bedrid *(adj.)*

bedrench *(v.)* drench thoroughly, soak, saturate R2 III.iii.46 [Bolingbroke to Northumberland, of impending battle] *such crimson tempest should bedrench / The fresh green lap of fair King Richard's land*

bedrid, bed-rid, bedred *(adj.)* bed-ridden, confined to bed through infirmity WT IV.iv.398 [disguised Polixenes to Florizel, of Florizel's father] *Lies he not bed-rid?;* Ham I.ii.29; LL I.i.136; Luc 975

bed-right *(n.)* consummation, conjugal rights Tem IV.i.96 [Iris to Ceres] *no bed-right shall be paid / Till Hymen's torch be lighted*

bed-swerver *(n.)* person unfaithful to the marriage-bed, adulterer/adulteress WT II.i.93 [Leontes to Lords, of Hermione] *she's / A bed-swerver*

bed-vow *(n.)* marriage vow Sonn 152.3 *In act thy bed-vow broke and new faith torn*

bedward, to showing the way towards bed Cor I.vi.32 [Martius to Cominius] *in heart / As merry as when our nuptial day was done, / And tapers burned to bedward!*

beefs *(n.)* fat cattle, oxen 2H4 III.ii.316 [Falstaff alone, of Shallow] *And now has he land and beefs;* MV I.iii.164

beef-witted *(adj.)* beef-brained, thick-headed, brainless TC II.i.13 [Thersites to Ajax] *thou mongrel beef-witted lord!*

beer / ale, small **1** weak beer, beer of poor quality 2H6 IV.ii.63 [Cade to all] *I will make it felony to drink small beer;* 2H4 II.ii.6; TS Induction.ii.1, 74

2 trivialities, trifles, matters of little consequence Oth II.i.157 [Iago to Desdemona, of a deserving woman] *To suckle fools and chronicle small beer*

beesome *(adj.)* ☞ bisson *(adj.)*

beest *(v.)* ☞ VERB FORMS, p.481

beest-eating *(adj.)* eating the milk produced after the birth of a calf [considered undrinkable, except by rustics] TNK III.v.130 [Schoolmaster to Theseus] *the beest-eating clown*

beetle *(n.)* sledgehammer, heavy ram 2H4 I.ii.230 [Falstaff to himself, of commending the Lord Chief Justice to Westmorland] *If I do, fillip me with a three-man beetle* [i.e. needing three men to wield it]

beetle *(adj.)* overhanging, prominent, bushy RJ I.iv.32 [Mercutio to Romeo, of his mask] *Here are the beetle brows shall blush for me*

beetle *(v.)* overhang, project [like threatening eyebrows] Ham I.iv.71 [Horatio to Hamlet] *the cliff / That beetles o'er his base into the sea* [F; Q1 *beckles*; Q2 *bettles*]

beetle-headed *(adj.)* thick-headed, doltish TS IV.i.143 [Petruchio to Katherina, of Servant] *A whoreson, beetle-headed, flap-eared knave!*

befall *(v.)*, past forms **befallen, befell** **1** happen, occur, take place, turn out 2H6 III.ii.402 [Suffolk to Queen] *let me stay, befall what may befall!* ☞ FEW, p.xxi

2 happen to, come to 3H6 II.i.10 [First Keeper to Second Keeper] *I'll tell thee what befell me on a day* ☞ FEW, p.xxi

befall of *(v.)* become of, happen to CE I.i.124 [Duke to Egeon, of his family] *What have befallen of them and thee till now*

before *(adv.)* **1** ahead, in advance TG II.iv.184 [Proteus to Valentine] *Go on before;* KL I.v.1; Mac I.iv.17; MV V.i.117; R3 I.i.144; Tem V.i.58

2 in the front TS III.ii.55 [Biondello to Tranio as Lucentio, of Petruchio's horse] *near-legged before;* Mac V.vi.85

3 just now, a little while ago Cym III.vi.16 [Innogen alone] *even before, I was / At point to sink, for food*

4 [in relation to God] in support, on one's side H5 I.ii.308 [King Henry to all] *God before, / We'll chide this Dauphin at his father's door*

before-breach *(n.)* previous breaking, earlier violation H5 IV.i.165 [disguised King Henry to Williams, of war] *here men are punished for before-breach of the King's laws* ☞ breach *(n.)* **1**

beforehand *(adv.)* in advance, at an earlier point KJ V.vii.111 [Bastard to all] *let us pay the time but needful woe, / Since it hath been beforehand with our griefs*

before-time *(adv.)* formerly, previously, earlier Cor I.vi.24 [Cominius to Messenger, of Martius] *I have / Before-time seen him thus*

befortune *(v.)* befall, happen, come upon TG IV.iii.41 [Eglamour to Silvia] *I wish all good befortune you*

beg (v.) **1** become a beggar **TNK** III.ii.23 [Gaoler's Daughter alone] *Myself to beg, if I prized life so much / As to deny my act* [i.e. if I save my life through lying, I would be forced to live as a beggar]

2 plead to put in care; treat as a fool **LL** V.ii.490 [Costard to Berowne] *You cannot beg us, sir*

beget (v.), past form **begot 1** give birth to, father, conceive **KL** I.i.96 [Cordelia to Lear] *You have begot me;* **AY** I.i.55; **Cym** V.iv.201; **H5** III.i.23; **TG** III.i.287

2 produce, engender, give rise to **R3** IV.iii.26 [Tyrrel to King Richard] *If to have done the thing you gave in charge / Beget your happiness, be happy;* **Cym** V.iv.123; **3H6** II.v.91; **Tem** I.ii.94; **TG** III.i.97; **WT** V.i.132

3 get, occasion, breed [for] **Luc** 1005 [Lucrece as if to time] *The mightier man, the mightier is the thing / That makes him honoured or begets him hate*

4 obtain, develop, nurture **Ham** III.ii.7 [Hamlet to Players] *you must acquire and beget a temperance*

beggar (v.) **1** reduce to beggary, impoverish, make destitute **MV** II.vi.19 [Gratiano to Salerio, of a ship returning] *Lean, rent, and beggared by the strumpet wind;*

2 rate as worthless, esteem to be of no value **TC** II.ii.92 [Troilus to all] *why do you now … / Beggar the estimation which you prized / Richer than sea and land?*

3 impoverish, exhaust, drain **Sonn** 67.10 [of his friend] *Why should he live … / Beggared of blood to blush through lively veins;* **Ham** IV.v.93

4 use up all the resouces of, exhaust **AC** II.ii.203 [Enobarbus to all, of Cleopatra] *For her own person, / It beggared all description*

beggared (adj.) impoverished, destitute, depleted **H5** IV.ii.41 [Grandpré to all, of the English army] *Big Mars seems bankrupt in their beggared host;*

beggar-fear (n.) fear that a beggar would show **R2** I.i.189 [Bolingbroke to King Richard] *Shall I … with pale beggar-fear impeach my height* [F, Q1; *beggar-face* Q2–5]

beggarly (adj.) **1** destitute, impoverished, poverty-stricken **Oth** IV.ii.157 [Desdemona to Iago, of Othello] *though he do shake me off / To beggarly divorcement;* **RJ** V.i.45

2 in the manner of a beggar, effusive **AY** II.v.26 [Jaques to Amiens, of a beggar] *he renders me the beggarly thanks*

beggary (n.) beggarliness, niggardliness, meanness **AC** I.i.15 [Antony to Cleopatra] *There's beggary in the love that can be reckoned;* **Cym** I.vii.115

begird (v.), past form **begirt** surround, encircle, besiege **E3** I.i.129 [Montague to King Edward, of the Scottish king] *the tyrant hath begirt with siege / The castle of Roxborough;* **E3** III.iv.119 ➤ **gird** (v.) **1**

begnaw (v.) gnaw away, eat away, chew **R3** I.iii.221 [Queen Margaret to Richard] *The worm of conscience still begnaw thy soul!;* **Cor** II.i.178; **TS** III.ii.54

beguild (v.) [unclear meaning] beguile **Luc** 1544 [Lucrece to herself] *To me came Tarquin armed to beguild / With outward honesty* ➤ **beguile** (v.) **1**

beguile (v.) **1** cheat, deceive, trick **1H4** III.iii.66 [Hostess to Falstaff] *you owe me money … and now you pick a quarrel to beguile me of it;* **AC** III.vii.77; **1H6** I.ii.65; **KL** V.iii.152; **R2** IV.i.280; **WT** V.ii.97

2 deprive by deception, cheat out of **TC** IV.iv.34 [Troilus to Cressida] *injury of chance … rudely beguiles our lips / Of all rejoindure;* **LL** I.i.77

3 charm, captivate, bewitch **Oth** IV.i.97 [Iago to himself] *'tis the strumpet's plague / To beguile many and be beguiled by one;* **E3** II.i.79; **KL** II.ii.108; **Luc** 1404; **Oth** I.iii.66; **Venus** 1144

4 charm away, while away, pass pleasantly **R2** II.iii.11 [Northumberland to Bolingbroke] *your company … hath very much beguiled / The tediousness and process of my travel;* **AW** IV.i.21; **Ham** III.ii.236; **TN** III.iii.42

5 coax, draw from, charm from **Oth** I.iii.155 [Othello to all, of Desdemona] *I … often did beguile her of her tears*

6 divert attention from, disguise **Oth** II.i.121 [Desdemona to herself] *I do beguile / The thing I am by seeming otherwise;* **Tit** IV.i.35

beguiling (n.) deception, deceit, trickery **Lover** 170 [of the woman] *For further I could say this man's untrue, / And knew the patterns of his foul beguiling*

behalf (n.), especially: **in behalf (of) 1** advantage, interest, benefit **KJ** I.i.7 [Chatillon to King John, of Philip of France's claim] *in right and true behalf / Of thy deceased brother Geoffrey's son;* **AW** IV.iii.310; **AY** V.iv.203; **3H6** II.i.114

2 name, right, title **R3** III.iv.19 [Hastings to all, of Richard] *in the Duke's behalf I'll give my voice;* **1H4** I.iii.47; **Tim** III.i.18

3 respect, aspect, consideration **KJ** II.i.264 [King Philip to Hubert] *shall your city call us lord / In that behalf which we have challenged it;* **LL** II.i.27

behaviour (n.) **1** person, embodiment, personification **KJ** I.i.3 [Chatillon to King John] *Thus … speaks the King of France, / In my behaviour*

2 courtly behaviour, fine manners, etiquette **LL** V.ii.337 [Berowne to all, of Boyet] *Behaviour, what wert thou / Till this man showed thee*

behest (n.) command, bidding, decree **Cym** V.iv.122 [Sicilius to all, of Jupiter] *Let us with care perform his great behest;* **Luc** 852; **RJ** IV.ii.19

behind (adv.) **1** still to come, to follow **MM** V.i.536 [Duke to all] *we'll show / What's yet behind, that's meet you all should know;* **MM** V.i.526; **TC** I.ii.63

2 in the back **Cym** V.iii.12 [Posthumus to Lord] *the strait pass was dammed / With dead men, hurt behind* [i.e. through running away]

behindhand (adj.) backward, tardy, sluggish **WT** V.i.150 [Leontes to Florizel] *these thy offices, / So rarely kind, are as interpreters / Of my behindhand slackness!*

behold (v.) observe, regard, maintain **TC** II.iii.117 [Agamemnon to Patroclus, of Achilles' virtues] *Not virtuously of his own part beheld*
➤ **ATTENTION SIGNALS**, p.26

beholden (adj.) indebted, under an obligation **Tit** V.iii.33 [Tamora to Titus] *We are beholden to you;* **Tit** I.i.399

beholding (n.) **1** regard, attention, contemplation **TC** III.iii.91 [Achilles to Patroclus, of the lords] *who do … find out / Something not worth in me such rich beholding / As they have often given*

2 sight **KL** III.vii.8 [Cornwall to Edmund] *the revenges we are bound to take upon your traitorous father are not fit for your beholding;* **Cor** I.iii.9; **Per** V.i.223

beholding (adj.) beholden, obliged, indebted **R3** III.i.107 [York to Richard, of Prince Edward] *he is more beholding to you than I;* **MM** IV.iii.157; **MV** I.iii.102; **MW** I.i.254; **Per** II.v.25; **TG** IV.iv.170

behoof (n.) benefit, advantage **2H6** IV.vii.73 [Say to the rebels] *This tongue hath parleyed unto foreign kings / For your behoof;* **Lover** 165; **TNK** I.iv.31

behoofeful (adj.) ➤ **behoveful** (adj.)

behove (n.) benefit, advantage, gain **Ham** V.i.63 [First Clown, singing] *To contract - O - the time for - a - my behove*

behove (v.) **1** befits, be appropriate to, be due to **WT** IV.iv.253 [Autolycus to Clown] *there are cozeners abroad: therefore it behoves men to be wary;* **Ham** I.iii.97; **2H6** I.i.180; **WT** I.ii.395

2 moderate the need for, keep under control **Tim** III.v.22 [Alcibiades to Senators, of his friend] *He did behove his anger, ere 'twas spent* [F *behoove*]

behoveful, behoofeful (adj.) needful, necessary, useful **RJ** IV.iii.8 [Juliet to Lady Capulet] *We have culled such necessaries / As are behoveful for our state tomorrow* [F *behoouefull;* Q1 *behoofeful*]

behowl (v.) howl at, bay, cry out to **MND** V.i.362 [Puck to himself] *Now … the wolf behowls the moon* [F, Q *Beholds*]

being (n.) **1** lodging, dwelling-place **Cym** I.vi.54 [Queen to Pisanio, of Posthumus] *to shift his being / Is to exchange one misery with another*

2 physical existence, life **TG** III.i.57 [Valentine to Duke] *My health and happy being at your court;* **Cym** I.i.38; **Ham** II.i.96; **Oth** I.ii.21; **Tim** IV.iii.247; **TS** I.i.11

being that *(conj.)* since, seeing that **MA** IV.i.247 [Leonato to Benedick] *Being that I flow in grief, / The smallest twine may lead me*

belch *(v.)* give vent to, discharge, emit **Cym** III.v.135 [Cloten alone, of Innogen's words] *the bitterness of it I now belch from my heart*

belching *(adj.)* spouting, spurting **Per** III.i.62 [Pericles to dead Thaisa] *the belching whale / And humming water must o'erwhelm thy corpse;* **TC** V.v.23

beldam, beldame *(n.)* **1** grandmother, aged matron **1H4** III.i.29 [Hotspur to Glendower] *unruly wind … which for enlargement striving / Shakes the old beldam earth;* **Luc** 953

2 old woman, crone **KJ** IV.ii.185 [Hubert to King John, of five moons seen] *Old men and beldams in the streets / Do prophesy upon it dangerously;* **Luc** 1458

3 hag, witch, loathsome old woman **Mac** III.v.2 [Hecat to Witches, in response to 'You look angerly'] *Have I not reason, beldams;* **2H6** I.iv.41

be-lee *(v.)* ☞ lee *(v.)*

belie *(v.)* **1** slander, tell lies about **MA** V.i.67 [Leonato to Claudio] *I say thou hast belied mine innocent child;* **AW** IV.iii.260; **Cym** V.ii.2; **1H4** I.iii.112; **Oth** V.ii.134; **Sonn** 130.14

2 fill with lies, deceive, delude **Cym** III.iv.37 [Pisanio to Innogen, of slander] *whose breath … doth belie / All corners of the world;* **Luc** 1533; **PassP** XVIII.25

belief *(n.)* opinion, awareness, impression **1H6** II.iii.30 [Talbot to Messenger, of the Countess] *she's in a wrong belief* [i.e. she's labouring under a misapprehension]

belike *(adv.)* probably, presumably, perhaps, so it seems **Ham** III.ii.148 [Ophelia to Hamlet] *Belike this show imports the argument of the play* ☞ FEW, p.xxi

bell *(n.)* death-knell **TNK** V.iii.6 [Emilia to Pirithous] *each stroke … sounds more like / A bell than blade*

bellman *(n.)* bell-ringer who announces an impending death [as of a condemned prisoner] **Mac** II.ii.3 [Lady Macbeth alone, of an owl] *the fatal bellman / Which gives the stern'st good-night*

bell-wether *(n.)* leading sheep of a flock [wearing a bell]; cuckold [of a ram, because horned] **MW** III.v.100 [Falstaff to Ford as Brook] *I suffered … an intolerable fright to be detected with a jealous rotten bell-wether;* **AY** I.ii.76

belly *(n.)* womb, uterus **WT** I.ii.204 [Leontes to himself] *No barricado for a belly* [i.e. there is no way of barricading a womb]

belly doublet ☞ great-belly *(adj.)*; thin-belly *(adj.)*

belly-god *(n.)* someone who makes a god of his belly, guzzler **E3** III.iii.155 [King John to the French] *what's this Edward but a belly-god*

belly-pinched *(adj.)* pinched with hunger, starving **KL** III.i.13 [Gentleman to disguised Kent, of the stormy night] *wherein … / The lion and the belly-pinched wolf / Keep their fur dry*

belock *(v.)* lock up, hold tight, intertwine **MM** V.i.208 [Mariana to Angelo, of her hand] *which … / Was fast belocked in thine*

belong *(v.)* be the duty of, pertain to **MA** III.iii.38 [First Watchman to Dogberry] *we know what belongs to a watch*

belonging *(n.)* **1** attribute, capability, personal quality **MM** I.i.29 [Duke to Angelo] *Thyself and thy belongings / Are not thine own so proper as to waste / Thyself upon thy virtues*

2 equipment, trappings **Cor** I.ix.61 [Cominius to all, of Martius] *My noble steed … I give him, / With all his trim belonging*

beloving *(adj.)* loving, devoted **AC** I.ii.24 [Soothsayer to Charmian] *You shall be more beloving than beloved*

bemadding *(adj.)* making mad, maddening **KL** III.i.38 [disguised Kent to Gentleman] *how unnatural and bemadding sorrow / The King hath cause to plain*

bemeet *(v.)* meet with, encounter **KL** V.i.20 [Albany to Regan] *well be-met*

bemete, be-mete *(v.)* measure; also: mete out punishment **TS** IV.iii.111 [Petruchio to Tailor] *I shall so bemete thee with thy yard*

bemoaning *(adj.)* lamenting, plaintive, sorrowful **E3** IV.vii.26 [Audley to Prince Edward] *thy sweet bemoaning speech to me / Is as a mournful knell to one dead sick*

bemock *(v.)* mock at, taunt, flout **Cor** I.i.255 [Sicinius to Brutus, of Martius] *Bemock the modest moon*

bemocked-at *(adj.)* mocked, scorned, derided **Tem** III.iii.64 [Ariel to Alonso, Sebastian, and Antonio, of their swords] *with bemocked-at stabs / Kill the still-closing waters*

bemoil *(v.)* cover with dirt, bemire **TS** IV.i.67 [Grumio to Curtis, of Katherina's fall from her horse] *how she was bemoiled*

bemonster, be-monster *(v.)* make monstrous, deform, pervert **KL** IV.ii.63 [Albany to Gonerill] *Be-monster not thy feature*

bench *(n.)* governing body, court of justice **Cor** III.i.106 [Coriolanus to Senators, of Sicinius] *who puts his 'shall', / His popular 'shall', against a graver bench / Than ever frowned in Greece;* **Cor** III.i.166

bench *(v.)* **1** take a seat on the bench **KL** III.vi.38 [Lear to Fool, of Edgar as Poor Tom] *Bench by his side*

2 give a position of honour, place in authority **WT** I.ii.314 [Leontes to Camillo] *whom I from meaner form / Have benched and reared to worship*

bencher *(n.)* jurist, magistrate, statesman **Cor** II.i.77 [Brutus to Menenius] *you are … a perfecter giber for the table than a necessary bencher in the Capitol*

bench-hole *(n.)* privy hole, lavatory **AC** IV.vii.9 [Scarus to Antony, of the enemy] *We'll beat 'em into bench-holes*

bend *(n.)* **1** movement, bending motion, posture **AC** II.ii.213 [Enobarbus to Agrippa and Maecenas, of Cleopatra] *Her gentlewomen … made their bends adornings*

2 glance, gaze, turning in a particular direction **JC** I.ii.123 [Cassius to Brutus, of Caesar] *that same eye whose bend doth awe the world*

bend *(v.)* **1** aim, direct, level, turn **Per** II.v.47 [Pericles to Simonides, of Thaisa] *[I] … bent all offices to honour her;* **Cor** I.ii.16; **Ham** III.iv.118; **KL** V.ii.74; **MM** I.i.40; **TNK** III.i.31

2 turn, direct one's steps, proceed **CE** V.i.152 [Adriana to Duke, of Antipholus and Dromio of Syracuse] *madly bent on us;* **AW** III.ii.54; **Ham** I.ii.115; **1H4** V.v.36; **Tem** IV.i.174; **WT** V.i.164

3 change, alter, turn in a new direction **Cym** I.vi.81 [Queen alone, of Innogen] *Except she bend her humour* [i.e. change her mind]; **Sonn** 116.4

4 [of brows] knit, wrinkle, frown **1H6** V.iii.34 [Richard to Pucelle] *See how the ugly witch doth bend her brows;* **3H6** V.ii.22; **KJ** IV.ii.90; **R2** II.i.170

5 give way, bow, submit **Oth** I.iii.233 [Othello to Duke] *Most humbly … bending to your state;* **E3** I.i.74; **JC** I.ii.117; **TC** III.iii.71; **TNK** I.i.229

bend up *(v.)* exert, strain, wind up **H5** III.i.16 [King Henry to all] *bend up every spirit / To his full height!;* **Mac** I.vii.79

bending *(adj.)* **1** overhanging, jutting, curved **KL** IV.i.72 [Gloucester to Edgar as Poor Tom] *There is a cliff whose high and bending head / Looks fearfully in the confined deep*

2 bowing, reverential, respectful **R3** IV.iv.95 [Queen Margaret to Queen Elizabeth] *Where be the bending peers that flattered thee?;* **H5** Epilogue.2; **TC** I.iii.236

beneath *(adj.)* lower, earthly **Tim** I.i.45 [Poet to Painter, of his poem about Timon] *Whom this beneath world doth embrace and hug / With amplest entertainment*

benediction *(n.)* **1** blessing, spiritual gift **KL** IV.vii.58 [Cordelia to Lear] *hold your hand in benediction o'er me;* **WT** IV.iv.598

2 blessing, happiness, prosperity **KL** IV.iii.43 [disguised Kent to Gentleman, of Cordelia and Lear] *his own unkindness / That stripped her from his benediction;* **Cym** V.v.351; **KL** II.ii.159

benefactor *(n.)* malapropism for 'malefactor' **MM** II.i.49 [Elbow to all, of Froth and Pompey] *I … do bring in here before your good honour two notorious benefactors*

benefice *(n.)* ecclesiastical living, church appointment **RJ** I.iv.81 [Mercutio to Romeo, of Queen Mab visiting a parson] *Then he dreams of another benefice*

benefit *(n.)* **1** agency, help, means **Cym** IV.ii.342 [Captain to Lucius, of the arrival of the new troops] *With the next benefit o'th' wind* [i.e. with the next advantageous wind]; **CE** I.i.91

2 privilege, right, prerogative **1H6** IV.i.100 [Basset to King] *I crave the benefit of law of arms*

3 profit, gain, return **CE** I.ii.25 [First Merchant to Antipholus of Syracuse, of the merchants] *Of whom I hope to make much benefit*

4 bounty, benefaction, bestowal of rights [from a feudal lord] **1H6** V.iv.152 [Richard to Charles] *accept the title thou usurpest, / Of benefit proceeding from our king;* **R3** III.vii.195

5 quality, advantage, gift **R3** III.vii.195 [Buckingham to Richard] *take to your royal self / This proffered benefit of dignity;* **AY** IV.i.30

benet, be-net *(v.)* ensnare, enmesh, catch in a net **Ham** V.ii.29 [Hamlet to Horatio] *Being thus be-netted round with villainies*

benevolence *(n.)* forced loan, imposed contribution **R2** II.i.250 [Willoughby to Northumberland and Ross] *daily new exactions are devised, / As blanks, benevolences, and I wot not what*

benison *(n.)* blessing, benediction **Mac** II.iv.40 [Old Man to Ross] *God's benison go with you;* **KL** I.i.265, IV.vi.225; **Per** II.Chorus.10

bent *(n.)* **1** direction, turning, inclination **WT** I.ii.179 [Leontes to Hermione, of her and Polixenes] *To your own bents dispose you;* **H5** V.ii.16; **JC** II.i.210; **RJ** II.ii.143; **TC** I.iii.252; **TNK** IV.ii.33

2 disposition, constitution, temperament **MA** IV.i.184 [Benedick to Friar, of the Princes] *Two of them have the very bent of honour*

3 degree, capacity, extent [to which a bow can be bent] **Ham** III.ii.391 [Hamlet to himself] *They fool me to the top of my bent* [i.e. to my utmost limit]; **Ham** II.ii.30; **MA** III.ii.218; **TN** II.iv.37

4 curve, bend, arch **AC** I.iii.36 [Cleopatra to Antony] *Eternity was in our lips and eyes, / Bliss in our brows' bent*

bent *(adj.)* **1** determined, intent, resolved **2H6** III.i.162 [Buckingham to King, of the traitors] *A sort of naughty persons, lewdly bent;* **Ham** IV.iii.44; **KJ** II.i.422; **Mac** III.iv.133; **Sonn** 90.2; **Tit** IV.iv.64

2 inclined, willing, ready **KJ** II.i.422 [King John to Hubert, of Hubert's proposal] *We are bent to hear*

3 ready for firing, tensioned for action **TNK** V.iii.42 [Emilia to herself, of Arcite] *his eye / Is like an engine bent;* **AW** V.iii.10

4 frowning, angry, glowering **TNK** III.i.101 [Palamon to Arcite] *do the deed with a bent brow;* **PassP** XVIII.25

benumbed *(adj.)* paralysed, deprived of strength **TC** II.ii.180 [Hector to Paris and Troilus, of passion] *great minds, of partial indulgence / To their benumbed wills, resist the same*

ben venuto *(n.)* warm welcome **TS** I.ii.279 [Hortensio to Petruchio] *I shall be your ben venuto;* **LL** IV.ii.155

bepaint *(v.)* cover over, colour, tinge **RJ** II.ii.86 [Juliet to Romeo] *would a maiden blush bepaint my cheek / For that which thou hast heard me speak tonight;* **Venus** 901

bepray *(v.)* pray **LL** V.ii.692 [Costard to Armado] *I bepray you, let me borrow my arms again*

bequeath *(n.)* bequest, legacy **E3** IV.vii.55 [Audley to Prince Edward] *lay thy consent / To this bequeath in my last testament*

bequeath *(v.)* resign, give up, assign, hand over **KJ** I.i.149 [Queen Eleanor to Bastard, of Robert Faulconbridge] *Wilt thou … / Bequeath thy land to him, and follow me?*

berattle *(v.)* rattle away on, fill with clamour **Ham** II.ii.341 [Rosencrantz to Hamlet, of the child players] *These … so berattle the common stages* [reading of F *be-ratled*]

beray *(v.)* stain, defile, disfigure **Tit** II.iii.222 [Martius to Quintus] *Lord Bassianus lies berayed in blood*

bereave *(v.)* **1** take away [from], deprive, deny, rob **TNK** II.i.279 [Gaoler to Palamon] *I must awhile bereave you / Of your fair cousin's company;* **2H6** III.i.85; **3H6** II.v.68; **Luc** 373, 835; **MV** III.ii.175; **Tit** II.iii.282

2 plunder, ravage, devastate **E3** IV.vii.24 [Prince Edward to Audley] *What hungry sword hath so bereaved thy face*

bereaved *(adj.)* deprived, robbed, stolen **KL** IV.iv.9 [Cordelia to Doctor, of Lear] *What can man's wisdom / In the restoring his bereaved sense?*

berhyme, be-rime *(v.)* celebrate in rhyme, put into rhyme **RJ** II.iv.40 [Mercutio to Benvolio, of Laura] *she had a better love to berhyme her;* **AY** III.ii.171

Bermoothes *(n.)* Bermuda **Tem** I.ii.229 [Ariel to Prospero] *fetch dew / From the still-vexed Bermoothes* ☛ **WORLD**, p.634

berrord *(n.)* ☛ **bearherd** *(n.)*

bescreen *(v.)* hide from sight, cover up **RJ** II.ii.52 [Juliet to hidden Romeo] *What man art thou that, thus bescreened in night*

beseech *(n.)* beseeching, entreaty, petition **TC** I.ii.293 [Cressida alone, stating a maxim] *Achievement is command; ungained, beseech*

beseech *(v.)* ☛ **POLITENESS**, p.340

beseek *(v.)* dialect form or malapropism for 'beseech' **2H4** II.iv.157 [Hostess to Pistol] *I beseek you now, aggravate your choler*

beseem *(v.)* befit, be fitting [for], be seemly [for] **1H6** III.i.19 [Gloucester to Winchester] *Thou art … wanton, more than well beseems / A man of thy profession;* **CE** V.i.110; **E3** III.iv.76; **3H6** IV.vii.83; **R2** IV.i.116; **TG** II.vii.43

beseeming *(n.)* appearance, look **Cym** V.v.410 [Posthumus to Cymbeline, of Belarius, Arviragus and Guiderius] *I am, sir, / The soldier that did company these three / In poor beseeming*

beseeming *(adj.)* ☛ **grave-beseeming** *(adj.);* ill-beseeming *(adj.);* well-beseeming *(adj.).*

beset *(v.)* set upon, assail, besiege **TG** V.iii.11 [Third Outlaw to First Outlaw] *The thicket is beset;* **Luc** 444; **TG** II.iv.47

beshrew, 'shrew *(v.)* **1** curse, devil take, evil befall **CE** II.i.49 [Dromio of Ephesus to Adriana, of Antipholus of Syracuse] *Beshrew his hand;* **WT** I.ii.281 [Camillo to Leontes] *'Shrew my heart* ☛ **FEW**, p.xxi; **SWEARING**, p.435

2 blame, censure, take to task, wish mischief on **RJ** V.iii.25 [Friar Laurence alone, of Juliet] *She will beshrew me much that Romeo / Hath had no notice of these accidents;* **LL** V.ii.46

beside *(prep.)* by the side of **Mac** V.vi.39 [Malcolm to Seyward] *We have met with foes / That strike beside us* [i.e. to miss us]

beside *(adv.)* **1** to the side, from that path **TNK** III.ii.34 [Gaoler's Daughter alone] *Each errant step beside is torment* [i.e. away from the way to a grave]

2 passing by, to one side **Venus** 981 [of tears in Venus' eyes] *Yet sometimes falls an orient drop beside*

3 besides, in addition **3H6** II.i.174 [Warwick to all, of the King] *to London all the crew are gone, / To frustrate both his oath and what beside / May make against the house of Lancaster;* **1H6** V.i.15

4 otherwise, else **LL** II.i.11 [Boyet to Princess, of her beauty given by Nature] *When she did starve the general world beside* [i.e. apart from you]

besides *(prep.)* beside, beyond **Cym** II.iv.149 [Philario to Iachimo, of Posthumus threatening to act] *Quite besides / The government of patience!*

besiege *(n.)* siege, besieging **E3** II.i.413 [Countess to Warwick, of the King's suit] *Unnatural besiege!*

beslubber *(v.)* besmear, bedaub, spread thickly **1H4** II.iv.303 [Bardolph to Prince Hal, of blood] *[Falstaff persuaded us] to beslubber our garments with it*

besmear *(v.)* **1** smear over, bedaub **JC** III.i.107 [Brutus to all] *let us … besmear our swords;* **KJ** III.i.236; **TN** V.i.49

2 defile, sully, tarnish **MV** V.i.219 [Bassanio to Portia] *My honour would not let ingratitude / So much besmear it;* **H8** I.ii.124

besmirch (*v.*) discolour, sully, stain **Ham** I.iii.15 [Laertes to Ophelia, of Hamlet] *And now no soil nor cautel doth besmirch / The virtue of his will;* **H5** IV.iii.110

besom (*n.*) sweeping-brush, broom **2H6** IV.vii.28 [Cade to Say] *I am the besom that must sweep the court clean of such filth as thou art*

besonian, bezonian (*n.*) scoundrel, rogue, low fellow **2H6** IV.i.136 [Suffolk to the soldiers] *Great men oft die by vile Besonians;* **2H4** V.iii.113

besort (*n.*) retinue, entourage, suitable company **Oth** I.iii.236 [Othello to Duke] *I crave fit disposition for my wife … / With such accommodation and besort / As levels with her breeding*

besort (*v.*) befit, suit, be suitable for **KL** I.iv.247 [Gonerill to Lear, of his entourage] *the remainders … be such men as may besort your age*

bespeak (*v.*), past forms **bespake, bespoke** **1** ask for, order, request **1H4** I.ii.128 [Poins to Prince Hal and Falstaff] *I have bespoke supper tomorrow night in Eastcheap;* **CE** III.ii.179, IV.i.61, iv.134; **MV** III.i.116; **TN** III.iii.41

2 ask, request, entreat **CE** V.i.233 [Antipholus of Ephesus to Duke] *fairly I bespoke the officer / To go in person with me to my house*

3 speak for, arrange for, claim **E3** I.ii.44 [King David to Douglas, of the Countess] *first I do bespeak her for myself;* **KL** V.iii.90

4 address, speak to **TN** V.i.186 [Viola as Cesario to Sir Andrew] *I bespake you fair, and hurt you not;* **Ham** II.ii.140; **1H6** IV.vi.21; **R2** V.ii.20

bespice (*v.*) season with a spice; poison **WT** I.ii.316 [Leontes to Camillo, of Polixenes] *thou, / His cupbearer … mightst bespice a cup / To give mine enemy a lasting wink*

bespoke (*v.*) ☛ **bespeak** (*v.*)

best (*n.*) **1** victory, triumph, success **3H6** V.iii.20 [Edward to all, of their success] *having now the best at Barnet field*

2 best period, heyday, high point **KL** I.ii.47 [Gloucester, reading Edgar's letter] *makes the world bitter to the best of our times* [i.e. while we are in our prime of life]

3 highest ranking person, most eminent person **Tem** I.ii.430 [Ferdinand to Miranda] *I am the best of them that speak this speech;* **R2** IV.i.31; **Tit** IV.iv.33 ☛ **meanest** (*n.*)

4 leading citizens **Cor** I.ix.76 [Cominius to Lartius] *Send us to Rome / The best, with whom we may articulate*

Best, the (*n.*) Jesus Christ **WT** I.ii.419 [Polixenes to Camillo] *my name / Be yoked with his that did betray the Best!*

best, at the **1** as well as one can, in the best possible way **3H6** III.i.8 [First Keeper to Second Keeper] *aim we at the best;* **Oth** I.iii.171; **Tim** I.i.149

2 at the highest point, in the best state **RJ** I.v.119 [Benvolio to Romeo] *The sport is at the best*

best, in all my as far as I can, to the best of my ability **Ham** I.ii.120 [Hamlet to Gertrude] *I shall in all my best obey you*

best, in the even at best **Ham** I.v.27 [Ghost to Hamlet] *Murder most foul, as in the best it is*

best (*adj.*) **1** most appropriate, most suitable **Mac** III.iv.5 [Macbeth to all] *Our hostess keeps her state; but in best time / We will require her welcome*

2 noblest, most eminent **2H6** IV.x.36 [Cade to Iden] *Brave thee? Ay, by the best blood that ever was broached*

best, thou wert / you were you are best advised **Oth** V.ii.160 [Othello to Emilia] *Peace, you were best;* **JC** III.iii.12; **Tem** I.ii.366; **TN** I.v.28

bestained (*adj.*) stained all over, marked with stains **KJ** IV.iii.24 [Salisbury to Bastard, of King John] *We will not line his thin bestained cloak / With our pure honours*

best-boding (*adj.*) most favourable, most promising **TNK** V.iii.77 [Emilia to herself] *Palamon / Had the best-boding chance* [i.e. because his picture lay above her heart]

best-conditioned (*adj.*) best-natured, of finest character **MV** III.ii.293 [Bassanio to Portia, of Antonio] *The best-conditioned and unwearied spirit / In doing courtesies*

bestead, bested (*adj.*) situated, prepared, placed **2H6** II.iii.56 [York to all, of Peter] *I never saw a fellow worse bestead … than is the appellant*

bestir (*v.*) arouse, rouse, make active **KL** II.ii.50 [disguised Kent to Oswald] *you have so bestirred your valour;* **Tem** I.i.4

best-moving (*adj.*) most persuasive **LL** II.i.29 [Princess to Boyet] *we single you / As our best-moving fair solicitor*

bestow (*v.*) **1** give, provide, grant **H5** II.i.10 [Bardolph to Nym, of him and Pistol] *I will bestow a breakfast to make you friends;* **Cor** II.iii.206; **E3** II.ii.143; **Ham** IV.i.4; **KL** I.i.163; **TS** I.i.50

2 give as a gift [to], present [with] **TN** III.iv.2 [Olivia to herself, of Viola as Cesario] *How shall I feast him? What bestow of him?;* **TC** V.iv.26

3 give in marriage, match **AY** V.iv.7 [Rosalind as Ganymede, to Duke Senior] *if I bring in your Rosalind, / You will bestow her on Orlando here?;* **TS** IV.iv.35

4 accommodate, lodge, quarter **Ham** II.ii.521 [Hamlet to Polonius] *will you see the players well bestowed?;* **E3** IV.vii.60; **KL** II.iv.284, IV.vii.285; **Mac** III.i.29; **MW** IV.v.98

5 place, locate, position **Ham** III.i.44 [Polonius to Claudius] *We will bestow ourselves;* **Ham** III.i.33

6 stow away, dispose of **Tem** V.i.299 [Alonso to Stephano and Trinculo] *bestow your luggage where you found it;* **AW** I.iii.220; **CE** I.ii.78; **Ham** III.iv.177, IV.iii.12; **MW** IV.ii.43

7 give out, distribute, deliver **JC** I.iii.151 [Cinna to Cassius] *I will hie, / And so bestow these papers as you bade me*

8 carry, bear, acquit, conduct **TG** III.i.87 [Duke to Valentine] *How and which way I may bestow myself;* **AY** IV.iii.87; **2H4** II.ii.163; **H5** IV.iii.68; **KJ** III.i.225

9 spend, employ, devote [to] **JC** V.v.61 [Octavius to Strato] *wilt thou bestow thy time with me?*

bestowing (*n.*) **1** use, function, employment **TC** III.ii.35 [Troilus alone] *all my powers do their bestowing lose*

2 giving, benevolence, philanthropy **H8** IV.ii.56 [Griffith to Katherine, of Wolsey] *in bestowing, madam, / He was most princely*

bestraught (*adj.*) bereft of wits, mad, out of one's mind **TS** Induction.ii.24 [Sly to Lord] *What! I am not bestraught*

bestrew (*v.*) **1** strew, scatter, sprinkle **TS** Induction.ii.39 [Lord to Sly] *Say thou wilt walk; we will bestrew the ground;* **TS** Induction.i.54

2 cover, lie spread over **Tem** IV.i.20 [Prospero to Ferdinand and Miranda] *discord shall bestrew / The union of your bed*

bestride (*v.*) **1** stand over, protect, safeguard **1H4** V.i.122 [Falstaff to Prince Hal] *if thou see me down in the battle and bestride me;* **CE** V.i.192; **2H4** I.i.207; **2H6** V.iii.9; **Mac** IV.iii.4

2 mount, ride, sit upon **Cym** IV.iv.38 [Arviragus to Belarius and Guiderius] *I … bestride a horse;* **H5** V.ii.92, 97

3 stride across, step across **Cor** IV.v.121 [Aufidius to Coriolanus] *when I first my wedded mistress saw / Bestride my threshold*

4 straddle, stand over with legs astride **JC** I.ii.134 [Cassius to Brutus, of Caesar] *he doth bestride the narrow world / Like a Colossus;* **AC** V.ii.82

best-tempered (*adj.*) most skilfully crafted, of the finest quality [as of metal] **2H4** I.i.115 [Morton to Northumberland, of Percy] *his death … took fire and heat away / From the best-tempered courage in his troops;* **TNK** I.iii.10

betake (*v.*) **1** go, take oneself off, make one's way **E3** III.iv.8 [Lorraine to King John, of the Genoese] *they betook themselves to flight;* **2H6** IV.viii.63; **LL** I.i.230; **Per** I.iii.114; **TNK** III.i.82; **WT** III.ii.207

2 resort, have recourse, commit oneself **TN** III.iv.216 [Sir Toby to Viola as Cesario] *That defence thou hast, betake thee to't*; **PassP** VIII.12; **RJ** I.iv.34; **TN** III.iv.226

3 entrust, commit, give in charge **AW** IV.i.73 [First Soldier to Parolles] *betake thee to thy faith*

beteem, beteene (*v.*) allow, permit, let, grant **Ham** I.ii.141 [Hamlet alone, of King Hamlet] *so loving to my mother / That he might not beteem the winds of heaven / Visit her face too roughly* [Q2; F *beteene*]; **MND** I.i.131

beteene (*v.*) ☞ beteem (*v.*)

bethink (*v.*), past form **bethought** **1** call to mind, think about, consider, reflect **E3** III.iii.88 [King Edward to King John] *Bethink thyself how slack I was at sea*; **Ham** I.iii.90 [Polonius to Ophelia, on the subject of Hamlet] *well bethought* ☞ FEW, p.xxi

2 remember, recollect **MM** V.i.453 [Duke to all] *I have bethought me of another fault*; **3H6** I.iv.91

3 resolve, decide, have a mind **KL** II.iii.6 [Edgar alone] *I ... am bethought / To take the basest and most poorest shape*; **JC** IV.iii.249

4 devise, plan, think up **3H6** III.iii.39 [Lewis to Queen] *with patience calm the storm, / While we bethink a means to break it off*

bethinking (*n.*) reflection, rumination, considering **Venus** 1024 [Venus to love] *Trifles unwitnessed with eye or ear / Thy coward heart with false bethinking grieves*

bethought (*v.*) ☞ bethink (*v.*)

bethump (*v.*) thump soundly, pound, lambaste **KJ** II.i.466 [Bastard to himself, of Hubert's speech] *I was never so bethumped with words / Since I first called my brother's father dad!*

betide (*v.*) **1** happen (to), befall, come (to) **R3** I.ii.17 [Anne to dead Henry VI, of Richard] *More direful hap betide that hated wretch*; **Cym** IV.iii.40; **R2** III.ii.91; **R3** II.iv.71; **Tem** I.ii.31; **TG** IV.iii.40

2 happen, take place, befall **R2** V.i.42 [Richard to Queen Isabel] *tell thee tales / Of woeful ages long ago betid*; **3H6** IV.vi.88

betime (*v.*) [unclear meaning] betide, befall, be appropriate **LL** IV.iii.358 [King to all] *No time shall be omitted / That will betime and may by us be fitted* [F, Q be time]

betime (*adv.*) **1** early, at an early hour **AC** IV.iv.20 [Antony to Soldier] *To business that we love we rise betime*; **Ham** IV.v.49; **TNK** V.ii.58

2 in good time, early on **2H6** III.i.285 [Post to all, of rebellion in Ireland] *Send succours, lords, and stop the rage betime*

3 at once, immediately **KJ** IV.iii.98 [Bastard to Salisbury] *Put up thy sword betime*

betimes (*adv.*) **1** early in the morning, at an early hour **Mac** III.iv.132 [Macbeth to Lady Macbeth] *I will tomorrow - / And betimes I will - to the Weird Sisters*; **1H4** II.iv.532; **MM** IV.iii.44; **Oth** I.iii.370, II.iii.320; **TN** II.iii.2

2 early in life **Ham** IV.iii.217 [Hamlet to Horatio] *what is't to leave betimes?* [i.e. what does an early death matter]

3 speedily, soon, in a short time **WT** I.ii.297 [Camillo to Leontes, of Leontes' suspicions] *be cured / Of this diseased opinion, and betimes*; **AC** IV.iv.27; **2H6** III.i.297; **Mac** IV.iii.162; **R2** II.i.36; **R3** III.i.199

4 at once, forthwith, right now **MV** III.i.19 [Solanio to Salerio] *Let me say amen betimes lest the devil cross my prayer*; **Cym** V.ii.17; **3H6** IV.viii.62, V.iv.45; **JC** II.i.116

betossed (*adj.*) tossed about, shaken up **RJ** V.iii.76 [Romeo to himself] *What said my man when my betossed soul / Did not attend him as we rode?*

betray (*v.*) **1** deceive, seduce, mislead **Oth** V.ii.6 [Othello to himself, of Desdemona] *she must die, else she'll betray more men*; **AC** II.v.11; **Mac** I.iii.124; **MW** V.iii.20; **Tim** IV.iii.148; **Tit** V.ii.147

2 disclose the secrets of, reveal the indiscretions of **TNK** V.i.103 [Palamon praying to Venus] *I never at great feasts / Sought to betray a beauty* [i.e. a beautiful woman]

3 give up, expose, lay open [especially: to punishment] **CE** V.i.90 [Adriana to Luciana, of the Abbess] *She did betray me to my own reproof*; **AY** IV.i.6; **H8** III.i.56; **MW** III.iii.183

betrim (*v.*) trim about, array, embellish **Tem** IV.i.65 [Iris to Ceres] *Thy banks with pioned and twilled brims, / Which spongy April at thy hest betrims*

better (*n.*) readier, more willing **TG** III.ii.19 [Duke to Proteus] *the good conceit I hold of thee ... / Makes me the better to confer with thee*

better (*adj.*) higher-born, of greater social rank **Tem** I.ii.19 [Prospero to Miranda] *I am more better / Than Prospero, master of a full poor cell* ☞ good (adj.) 9

better (*v.*) excel, outstrip, have an advantage over **Per** IV.vi.159 [Marina to Boult, of Pander and Bawd] *they do better thee in their command*; **Sonn** 91.8

bettered (*adj.*) more skilful, held to be better **Ham** V.ii.257 [Claudius to Hamlet, of Laertes] *since he is bettered* [F *better'd*; Q2 *better*]

betumbled (*adj.*) disarranged, disordered, disturbed **Luc** 1037 [of Lucrece] *from her betumbled couch she starteth*

between (*n.*) interim, interval, meantime **WT** III.iii.60 [Shepherd alone, of the age between 10 and 23] *for there is nothing in the between but getting wenches with child*

betwixt (*prep.*) between **AY** I.i.46 [Orlando to Oliver] *were there twenty brothers betwixt us*

bevel (*adj.*) crooked, slanting, sloping **Sonn** 121.11 *I may be straight though they themselves be bevel*

bevy (*n.*) **1** company, circle, coterie **Ham** V.ii.185 [Hamlet to Horatio, of Osrick] *many more of the same bevy* [F; Q2 *breede*]

2 company [of maidens], gathering **TNK** IV.i.71 [Wooer to all, reporting the Gaoler's Daughter's words] *I'll bring a bevy, / A hundred black-eyed maids*; **H8** I.iv.4

beware (*v.*) take care of, have a care for **1H6** I.iii.47 [Gloucester to Winchester] *Priest, beware your beard*

bewasted (*adj.*) wasted away **R2** I.iii.221 [John of Gaunt to King Richard] *My ... time-bewasted light / Shall be extinct*

beweep (*v.*) **1** weep over, wet with tears **KL** I.iv.299 [Lear to Gonerill, as if to his eyes] *Old fond eyes, / Beweep this cause again*; **R3** I.iii.327, iv.247, II.ii.49; **Sonn** 29.2; **Tim** V.i.156

2 drowned in tears, wet with tears **Ham** IV.v.39 [Ophelia singing] *flowers, / Which bewept to the ground did not go*

bewet (*adj.*) wet through **Tit** III.i.146 [Titus to Marcus, of Lucius] *His napkin with his true tears all bewet / Can do no service on her sorrowful cheeks*

bewhore (*v.*) call a whore, make a whore of **Oth** IV.ii.114 [Emilia to Iago, of Othello and Desdemona] *my lord hath so bewhored her*

bewitchment (*n.*) magical appeal, ability to charm **Cor** II.iii.100 [Coriolanus to Fourth Citizen] *I will counterfeit the bewitchment of some popular man*

bewray (*v.*) **1** betray, reveal, expose **3H6** I.i.211 [Exeter to King] *Here comes the Queen, whose looks bewray her anger*; **Cor** V.iii.95; **1H6** IV.i.107; **3H6** III.iii.97; **KL** I.i.106; **Tit** II.iv.3

2 show, unmask, make known **KL** III.vi.109 [Edgar alone] *thyself bewray / When false opinion ... / In thy just proof repeals and reconciles thee*

bezonian (*n.*) ☞ besonian (*n.*)

bias (*n.*) **1** [weighting in a bowl causing it to run obliquely] inclination, tendency, leaning **KL** I.ii.111 [Gloucester to Edmund] *the King falls from bias of nature* [i.e. loses his natural affection]; **KJ** II.i.574; **LL** IV.ii.109; **TN** V.i.257; **TS** V.v.25

2 indirectness, obliqueness **Ham** II.i.65 [Polonius to Reynaldo] *With windlasses and with assays of bias* [i.e. indirect attempts]

bias (*adj.*) swollen like the biased side of a bowl **TC** IV.v.8 [Ajax to trumpeter] *Blow ... till thy sphered bias cheek / Outswell the colic of puffed Aquilon*

bias (*adv.*) awry, wrong, amiss **TC** I.iii.15 [Agamemnon to all, of their war efforts] *trial did draw / Bias and thwart, not answering the aim*

bias-drawing (*n.*) turning away from the truth, crooked dealing **TC** IV.v.169 [Agamemnon to Hector] *faith and troth, / Strained purely from all hollow bias-drawing*

bibble-babble (*n.*) chatter, gabble, empty talk **TN** IV.ii.97 [disguised Feste to Malvolio] *leave thy vain bibble-babble;* **H5** IV.i.70

bid (*v.*), past form **bade** 1 command, order, enjoin, tell **TN** I.v.47 [Feste to Olivia] *The lady bade take away the fool;* **AY** I.ii.58; **JC** I.ii.106; **Tem** I.ii.194; **TN** III.i.104; **TS** I.ii.37

2 invite, ask, entice **AY** V.ii.69 [Rosalind as Ganymede to Orlando] *put you in your best array, bid your friends;* **Tit** I.i.341; **TNK** I.i.186

3 pray, entreat, beg, ask **H5** II.iii.21 [Hostess to all, of Falstaff] *'a bade me lay more clothes on his feet;* **Mac** I.vi.13; **RJ** I.iii.79; **TC** IV.v.180; **Tim** I.i.80; **Tit** IV.iv.106

4 offer, challenge **3H6** V.i.77 [Warwick to all, of George and his army] *Of force enough to bid his brother battle;* **3H6** V.i.63

biddy (*n.*) chicken; chickabiddy [as childish form] **TN** III.iv.115 [Sir Toby to Malvolio] *Ay, biddy, come with me* ☛ **ADDRESS**, p.8

bide (*v.*) 1 endure, suffer, undergo **TN** II.iv.93 [Orsino to Viola as Cesario] *There is no woman's sides / Can bide the beating of so strong a passion;* **KL** III.iv.29; **R3** IV.iv.304; **Sonn** 58.7, 139.8; **TN** II.v.123

2 face, await, undergo **E3** III.iii.141 [King John to the French] *your intended force must bide the touch* [i.e. test its quality - as gold is tested using a touchstone]; **1H4** IV.iv.10; **3H6** II.iii.83; **TN** I.v.59

3 remain, persist, continue in being **TG** III.i.236 [Proteus to Valentine, of the Duke and Silvia] *to close prison he commanded her, / With many bitter threats of biding there;* **CE** II.i.110; **Lover** 33

4 abide, dwell, live **Cym** III.iv.130 [Innogen to Pisanio] *What shall I do the while? Where bide?*

bide upon (*v.*) insist on, dwell on, maintain **WT** I.ii.242 [Leontes to Camillo, thinking he has been deceived by Camillo] *To bide upon't: thou art not honest*

biding (*n.*) 1 place of rest, dwelling-place **Luc** 550 [of a black cloud] *some gentle gust doth get, / Which blow these pitchy vapours from their biding*

2 place to stay, dwelling **KL** IV.vi.224 [Edgar to Gloucester] *I'll lead you to some biding*

bid the base / **bass** challenge someone to a chase [from 'prisoner's base', a boy's chasing game] **TG** I.ii.97 [Lucetta to Julia] *I bid the bass for Proteus;* **Venus** 303

bifold, by-fold (*adj.*) twofold, double **TC** V.ii.147 [Troilus to Ulysses] *Bifold authority, where reason can revolt / Without perdition* [F *By foule*]

big (*adj.*) 1 pregnant [with], swollen **WT** II.i.61 [Leontes to all, of Hermione] *let her sport herself / With that she's big with;* **Cym** I.i.39; **2H4** I.Induction.13; **JC** III.i.282

2 loud, vocal, noisy **KL** V.iii.206 [Edgar to Albany] *Whilst I was big in clamour*

3 arrogant, haughty, proud **H8** I.i.119 [Wolsey to Secretary] *Buckingham / Shall lessen this big look;* **AW** I.iii.92

big (*adv.*) 1 threateningly, violently, menacingly **1H4** IV.i.58 [Hotspur to all] *If that the devil and mischance look big / Upon the maidenhead of our affairs;* **TS** III.ii.227

2 strongly, forcefully, with depth **R2** III.i.114 [Scroop to King Richard] *Boys with women's voices / Strive to speak big* [i.e. like men]; **Tim** I.i.33

biggen (*n.*) nightcap **2H4** IV.v.28 [Prince Henry to himself, of King Henry IV's sleep] *Yet not so sound … / As he whose brow with homely biggen bound / Snores out the watch of night*

bigger-looked (*adj.*) of more daunting appearance **TNK** I.i.215 [Theseus to Artesius] *we shall find / The moiety of a number for a business / More bigger-looked*

bigness (*n.*) large size, good bulk **2H4** II.iv.239 [Falstaff to Doll, of why Prince Harry loves Poins] *Because their legs are both of a bigness*

bilbo (*n.*) sword [from Bilbao, noted for its flexibility] **MW** I.i.150 [Pistol to Falstaff, of Slender] *I combat challenge of this latten bilbo* [i.e. swordsman]; **MW** III.v.101 ☛ **WEAPONS**, p.491

bilboes (*n.*) shackles, fetters, manacles **Ham** V.ii.6 [Hamlet to Horatio] *Methought I lay / Worse than the mutines in the bilboes* [F; Q2 *bilbo*]

bile (*n.*) ☛ **byle** (*n.*)

bill (*n.*) 1 [applied to various kinds of long-handled spear-like weapon] halberd; bill-hook **MA** III.iii.41 [Dogberry to First Watchman] *have a care that your bills be not stolen;* **2H6** IV.x.11; **KL** IV.vi.91; **MA** III.iii.172; **R2** III.ii.118 ☛ **WEAPONS**, p.491

2 notice, label, proclamation, placard **AY** I.ii.114 [Rosalind to Le Beau, of the young wrestlers] *With bills on their necks;* **JC** IV.iii.171; **MA** I.i.36

3 note, document, memorandum **TS** IV.iii.141 [Grumio to Petruchio, of the list of features of a gown] *Error i'th' bill* [also: legal indictment]; **JC** V.ii.1

4 inventory, list, catalogue **MND** I.ii.1 [Quince to all] *I will draw a bill of properties;* **Mac** III.i.99

5 dispatch, written order **JC** V.ii.1 [Brutus to Messala] *give these bills / Unto the legions on the other side*

6 bill of exchange, money order **MW** I.i.10 [Slender to Evans, of Shallow] *who writes himself Armigero - in any bill, warrant, quittance, or obligation*

7 promissory note **2H6** IV.vii.119 [Dick to Cade] *when shall we … take up commodities upon our bills?* [i.e. on credit; pun: sense 1]

bill (*v.*) stroke beaks together [= show affection] **AY** III.iii.74 [Touchstone to Jaques] *as pigeons bill, so wedlock would be nibbling*

billet (*n.*) thick stick, cudgel **MM** IV.iii.53 [Barnadine to disguised Duke] *they shall beat out my brains with billets*

billet (*v.*) enrol, enter in a list **Cor** IV.iii.40 [Volsce to Roman] *The centurions and their charges distinctly billeted*

billing (*n.*) kissing, caressing [as doves] **TC** III.ii.56 [Pandarus to Troilus and Cressida] *What, billing again?*

bind (*v.*), past form **bound** 1 pledge, vow, be under obligation **KL** I.ii.2 [Edmund alone, of Nature] *to thy law / My services are bound;* **AW** II.ii.52

2 oblige, make grateful, indebt **TNK** I.i.37 [Emilia to Third Queen] *What woman I may stead that is distressed / Does bind me to her*

bind in (*v.*) make fast, secure, surround **E3** IV.iv.36 [Audley to Prince Edward, of King John] *the valley for our flight / The king binds in;* **R2** II.i.61, 63

bind up (*v.*) prevent, keep away, impede **AC** II.ii.94 [Antony to Caesar] *when poisoned hours had bound me up / From mine own knowledge* [i.e. from knowing myself]

bird (*n.*) 1 young bird, fledgeling, nestling **1H4** V.i.60 [Worcester to King Henry] *you used us so / As that ungentle gull the cuckoo's bird / Useth the sparrow;* **3H6** II.i.91; **Tit** III.iii.154

2 object of prey, quarry **TS** V.ii.46 [Bianca to Petruchio] *Am I your bird? I mean to shift my bush*

bird-bolt, burbolt (*n.*) short blunt-headed arrow for shooting birds **MA** I.i.39 [Beatrice to Messenger, of Benedick] *my uncle's fool … challenged him at the bird-bolt* [i.e. at an elementary level of archery]; **LL** IV.iii.22; **TN** I.v.87

birding (*n.*) hunting small birds **MW** III.v.42 [Mistress Quickly to Falstaff, of Mistress Ford] *Her husband goes this morning a-birding;* **MW** III.iii.218, IV.ii.53

birdlime (*n.*) sticky substance spread on branches to snare birds **Oth** II.i.125 [Iago to Desdemona] *my invention / Comes from my pate as birdlime does from frieze* [i.e. with great difficulty] ☛ **lime** (*n.*) 1, (*v.*) 1

birth (*n.*) 1 royal birth, noble ancestry **1H6** V.v.68 [Suffolk to all, of Margaret] *Her peerless feature, joined with her birth, / Approves her;* **KJ** II.i.430; **MA** II.i.150; **TN** IV.iii.31

2 nature, kind, natural character **RJ** II.iii.16 [Friar alone, of natural things] *Nor aught so good but, strained from that fair use, / Revolts from true birth*

3 [astrology] horoscope, fortune, destiny **2H6** IV.i.34 [Suffolk to Whitmore] *A cunning man did calculate my birth*

birth-child *(n.)* native, local inhabitant **Per** IV.iv.41 [Gower alone] *The earth … / Hath Thetis' birth-child on the heavens bestowed* [i.e. one born in the sea]

birthdom *(n.)* kingdom of birth, birthright, native land **Mac** IV.iii.4 [Macduff to Malcolm] *Let us … / Bestride our down-fallen birthdom*

birthright *(n.)* inherited qualities, naturally endowed traits **AW** I.i.62 [Countess to Bertram] *thy goodness / Share with thy birthright!*

bisson *(adj.)* **1** blear-eyed, half-blind **Cor** II.i.60 [Menenius to Brutus and Sicinius, of himself] *What harm can your bisson conspectuities glean out of this character* [F: *beesome*]
2 blinding, dazzling **Ham** II.ii.504 [First Player to all, of the Queen] *Run barefoot up and down, threatening the flames / With bisson rheum*

bit *(n.)* morsel, scrap, titbit **LL** I.i.26 [Longaville to all] *dainty bits / Make rich the ribs* **Tim** II.ii.170

bit *(adj.)* marked, scarred **E3** IV.iv.128 [Prince Edward to Audley] *Thyself are busy and bit with many broils*

bite *(v.)* **1** erode, wear down, eat away at **Tem** III.iii.108 [Gonzalo to Adrian, of Alonso, Antonio and Sebastian] *Their great guilt … / Now 'gins to bite the spirits*
2 speak bitterly, inveigh, carp **TC** II.ii.33 [Helenus to Troilus] *No marvel though you bite so sharp at reasons, / You are so empty of them*

bite one's thumb [gesture of insult or defiance] insert the thumb nail into the mouth, making it click againt the upper teeth upon release **RJ** I.i.51 [Sampson to Gregory, of Montague's men] *I will bite my thumb at them*

bite one's tongue stay silent, repress speech **2H6** I.i.228 [York to himself] *York must sit and fret and bite his tongue;* **3H6** I.iv.47

biting *(adj.)* severe, painful, brutal **2H6** IV.vii.14 [Holland aside to Smith, of Cade's 'my mouth shall be the parliament of England'] *Then we are like to have biting statutes, unless his teeth be pulled out*

bitter *(adj.)* sharp, shrewd, keen **TS** V.ii.45 [Petruchio to Bianca] *Have at you for a bitter jest or two* [F *better*]

bitumed *(adj.)* smeared with pitch [bitumen] **Per** III.i.71 [Second Sailor to Pericles] *we have a chest … caulked and bitumed ready;* **Per** III.ii.55

blab *(v.)* **1** prattle, utter innocently **Tit** III.i.83 [Marcus to Lucius and Titus, of Lavinia's tongue] *that delightful engine of her thoughts, / That blabbed them with such pleasing eloquence*
2 talk indiscreetly, betray secrets **TN** I.ii.64 [Captain to Viola] *When my tongue blabs, then let mine eyes not see;* **TC** III.ii.122; **Venus** 126
3 betray, reveal **2H6** III.i.154 [Gloucester to King] *Beaufort's red sparkling eyes blab his heart's malice*

blabber *(v.)* babble, mumble **Ham** III.ii.49 [Hamlet to Players, of a clown at a play] *blabbering with his lips* [in Q1 only]

blabbing *(adj.)* revealing secrets, tell-tale, indiscreet **2H6** IV.i.1 [Lieutenant to all] *The gaudy, blabbing, and remorseful day / Is crept into the bosom of the sea*

black *(n.)* **1** black clothes **WT** I.ii.132 [Leontes to Mamillius, of women saying that he and his son are alike] *were they false / As o'er-dyed blacks … yet were it true* [i.e. clothes made unwearable by over-dying] ☛ **devil wear black**
2 dark complexion **Sonn** 127.1 *In the old age black was not counted fair*

black *(adj.)* **1** dark-complexioned, swarthy **TG** V.ii.10 [Thurio to Proteus] *my face is black;* **MA** III.i.63; **Oth** II.i.130; **TG** III.i.103, IV.iv.153, V.ii.12
2 deadly, doomladen, of death **JC** IV.i.17 [Octavius to Antony] *who should be pricked to die / In our black sentence and proscription*
3 wicked, slanderous, calumnious **H8** I.iii.58 [Lord Chamberlain to Lovell, of Wolsey's nobility] *He had a black mouth that said other of him*

blackamoor *(n.)* black-skinned African, negro **LL** V.ii.158 [stage direction] *Enter blackamoors with music;* **TC** I.i.79; **Tit** IV.ii.51

black-cornered *(adj.)* full of dark places to hide **Tim** V.i.42 [Painter to Poet] *When the day serves, before black-cornered night, / Find what thou wantest by free and offered light*

bladder *(n.)* **1** vessel derived from animals used for storing liquid **RJ** V.i.46 [Romeo alone, of an apothecary] *about his shelves / A beggarly account of empty boxes, / Green earthen pots, bladders*
2 [of the body] cavity, vessel **TC** V.i.20 [Thersites to Patroclus] *the rotten diseases of the south … bladders full of imposthume* [in Q only]
3 air-filled bag **H8** III.ii.359 [Wolsey alone] *I have ventured, / Like little wanton boys that swim on bladders*

blade *(n.)* greenness, immaturity, early days **AW** V.iii.6 [Countess to King, of Bertram's behaviour] *Natural rebellion done i'th' blade of youth*

bladed *(adj.)* many-bladed, abounding in shoots **Mac** IV.i.54 [Macbeth to Witches] *Though bladed corn be lodged and trees blown down;* **MND** I.i.211

blain *(n.)* blister, inflamed sore **Tim** IV.i.28 [Timon alone] *Itches, blains, / Sow all th'Athenian bosoms*

blame *(n.)* **1** fault, sin, offence **AW** V.iii.36 [Bertram to King] *My high-repented blames … pardon to me*
2 blameworthiness, culpability, guilt **R3** V.i.29 [Buckingham to Officers] *Wrong hath but wrong, and blame the due of blame;* **Sonn** 129.3

blame *(adj.)* blameworthy, culpable, guilty **CE** IV.i.47 [Angelo to Antipholus of Ephesus, of the Second Merchant] *I, too blame, have held him here too long;* **Tim** I.ii.26 ☛ **wilful-blame**

blame, to to be blamed, blameworthy **KL** I.ii.42 [Edmund to Gloucester, of the letter] *The contents … are to blame;* **H8** IV.ii.101; **KL** II.ii.156; **RJ** III.v.169; **TS** IV.iii.48; **Venus** 992

blameful *(adj.)* guilty, blameworthy, shameful **2H6** III.ii.212 [Suffolk to Warwick] *Thy mother took into her blameful bed / Some stern untutored churl*

blank *(n.)* **1** bull's-eye, target centre; or, line of sight **KL** I.i.159 [Kent to Lear] *let me still remain / The true blank of thine eye;* **Ham** IV.i.42; **Oth** III.iv.124; **WT** II.iii.5
2 ☛ **blank charter; lots to blanks**

blank *(v.)* make pale, blanch, drain (colour) **Ham** III.ii.230 [Second Player, as Queen, to her King] *Each opposite that blanks the face of joy*

blank charter, blank *(n.)* promisory document with the amount to pay left open **R2** I.iv.48 [King Richard to Green, of his regents] *Our substitutes at home shall have blank charters;* **R2** II.i.250; **TC** III.iii.231

blaspheme *(v.)* slander, defame, defile **Mac** IV.iii.108 [Macduff to Malcolm, as if to Scotland] *the truest issue of thy throne / By his own interdiction … does blaspheme his breed*

blast *(n.)* storm, rage, angry breath **Luc** 869 [Lucrece to herself] *Unruly blasts wait on the tender spring;* **Luc** 1335; **Mac** I.vii.22

blast *(v.)* **1** blight, wither, destroy **2H4** I.ii.186 [Lord Chief Justice to Falstaff] *Is not … every part about you blasted with antiquity?;* **AC** III.x.4; **Ham** III.i.161; **3H6** V.vii.21; **Luc** 49; **TG** I.i.48
2 destroy, ruin, lay waste **TNK** II.i.79 [Palamon to Arcite, of their swords] *These hands shall never draw 'em out like lightning / To blast whole armies more*
3 come to grief, be destroyed, fail **Ham** IV.vii.153 [Claudius to Laertes] *this project / Should have a back or second, that might hold / If this did blast in proof*

blasted *(adj.)* blighted, withered; accursed, malevolent **Mac** I.iii.76 [Macbeth to Witches] *why / Upon this blasted heath you stop our way;* **AC** III.xiii.105; **R3** III.iv.69; **Tim** IV.iii.534

blasting *(adj.)* **1** blighting, withering, destructive **Lover** 72 *The injury of many a blasting hour*

2 defaming, maligning, discrediting **MM** V.i.122 [Duke to Isabella, of Angelo] *Shall we thus permit / A blasting and a scandalous breath to fall / On him so near us?*

blastment (*n.*) blight, withering **Ham** I.iii.42 [Laertes to Ophelia] *And in the morn and liquid dew of youth / Contagious blastments are most imminent*

blaze, blaze forth (*v.*) proclaim, divulge, make known **RJ** III.iii.151 [Friar to Romeo, of Mantua] *Where thou shalt live till we can find a time / To blaze your marriage;* **Venus** 219 [of Venus] *Red cheeks and fiery eyes blaze forth her wrong*

blazon (*n.*) **1** armorial bearing, banner showing a coat-of-arms **MW** V.v.64 [Mistress Quickly as Queen of Fairies to all, of Windsor Castle] *Each fair instalment, coat, and several crest, / With loyal blazon, evermore be blest;* **TN** I.v.282
2 description, representation, delineation **MA** II.i.272 [Don Pedro to Beatrice] *I think your blazon to be true;* **Sonn** 106.5 [also: sense 3]; **TNK** III.i.47
3 revelation, divulging, publication **Ham** I.v.21 [Ghost to Hamlet] *But this eternal blazon must not be / To ears of flesh and blood;* **Sonn** 106.5 [also: sense 2]

blazon (*v.*) proclaim, display [as in a coat of arms] **Cym** IV.ii.170 [Belarius alone, as if to Nature] *thou thyself thou blazon'st / In these two princely boys;* **RJ** II.vi.26; **Tit** IV.iv.18

blazoned (*adj.*) painted, adorned, depicted **Lover** 217 [of jewels] *each several stone / With wit well blazoned*

blazoning (*adj.*) praising, proclaiming, boasting **Oth** II.i.63 [Cassio to Montano, of Desdemona] *One that excels the quirks of blazoning pens*

bleak (*adj.*) **1** exposed, windswept, desolate **Per** III.ii.13 [First Gentleman to Cerimon] *Our lodgings, standing bleak upon the sea*
2 pale, pallid, sickly **AW** I.i.103 [Helena to herself, of Parolles' evils] *they take place when virtue's steely bones / Looks bleak i'th' cold wind*
3 cold, chill, icy **KJ** V.vii.40 [King John to all] *none of you will … entreat the north / To make his bleak winds kiss my parched lips*

blear (*v.*) deceive, delude, fool **TS** V.i.106 [Lucentio to Baptista, of his marriage] *While counterfeit supposes bleared thine eyne*

bleared (*adj.*) blear-eyed, tear-dimmed **Cor** II.i.197 [Brutus to Sicinius, of Coriolanus] *the bleared sights / Are spectacled to see him;* **MV** III.ii.59

bleed (*v.*) lose blood, as a means of healing **2H4** IV.i.57 [Archbishop to Westmorland] *we are all diseased … / And we must bleed for it*

bleeding (*n.*) bloodshed; blood-letting [in medicine] **TNK** III.i.114 [Arcite to Palamon] *I am persuaded this question … / By bleeding must be cured*

bleeding (*adj.*) **1** bloody, blood-soaked, bloodstained **JC** III.i.168 [Brutus to Antony, of killing Caesar] *yet see you but our hands / And this the bleeding business they have done* **KJ** II.i.304; **Mac** V.ii.4
2 unhealed, uncured, undecided **Cor** II.i.72 [Menenius to Brutus and Sicinius] *you … dismiss the controversy bleeding, the more entangled by your hearing*

blench (*n.*) sidelong glance, turning aside **Sonn** 110.7 *These blenches gave my heart another youth*

blench (*v.*) **1** flinch, start, shrink **Ham** II.ii.595 [Hamlet alone, of Claudius] *If 'a do blench;* **TC** I.i.30, II.ii.69
2 swerve, turn aside, give way **MM** IV.v.5 [Duke to Friar Peter] *Though sometimes you do blench from this to that, / As cause doth minister;* **WT** I.ii.333

blend (*adj.*) blended, mingled, intermixed **Lover** 215 *The heaven hued sapphire and the opal blend / With objects manifold*

blent (*adj.*) blended, mixed, applied [as of painting] **TN** I.v.228 [Viola as Cesario to Olivia, of Olivia's face] *'Tis beauty truly blent;* **MV** III.ii.181

bless (*v.*) **1** guard, protect, safeguard **WT** IV.iv.266 [Dorcas to herself] *Bless me from marrying a usurer!;* **Cor** I.iii.46; **MA** V.i.141; **R3** III.iii.4
2 wound, hurt, beat; also: consecrate **CE** II.i.79 [Dromio of Ephesus to Adriana, of Antipholus of Syracuse, reacting to her threat to break his pate 'across'] *he will bless that cross with other beating*
3 ☞ **GREETINGS**, p.206; **POLITENESS**, p.340

blessed, blest (*adj.*) **1** lucky, fortunate, happy **Tem** I.ii.61 [Miranda to Prospero, of their coming to the island] *blessed was't we did?;* **Cor** V.iii.52
2 happy, glad, joyful **Cor** II.ii.56 [Brutus to Menenius, of his role with Sicinius] *Which the rather / We shall be blessed to do*
3 capable of blessing, full of happiness **MV** IV.i.183 [Portia as Balthasar to Shylock, of mercy] *It is twice blest, / It blesseth him that gives and him that takes*
4 curative, therapeutic, endowed with healing properties **Per** III.ii.34 [Cerimon to First Gentleman] *[I have] made familiar / To me … the blest infusions / That dwells in vegetives*

blessed (*adv.*) blessedly, happily **Sonn** 92.13 *But what's so blessed fair that fears no blot, / Thou mayst be false, and yet I know it not*

blessedly (*adv.*) luckily, fortunately, happily **Tem** I.ii.63 [Prospero to Miranda] *were we … blessedly holp hither*

blind (*adj.*) **1** sheer, utter, downright **Cor** V.vi.118 [Aufidius to Lords, of Coriolanus] *Will you be put in mind of his blind fortune* [or: sense 3]
2 dark, black **R3** V.iii.62 [King Richard to Catesby, of Derby] *bid him bring his power … lest his son George fall / Into the blind cave of eternal night;* **Luc** 675; **R3** III.vii.128 [Q]; **TC** III.ii.185 [or: sense 3]
3 heedless, reckless, headstrong **R3** I.iv.255 [Clarence to Murderers] *are you yet to your own souls so blind / That you will war with God by murdering me;* **H5** III.iii.34; **TN** V.i.226 [or: sense 3]

blind (*v.*) make blind, deprive of sight **TNK** V.iii.146 [Hippolyta to all] *Infinite pity / That four such eyes should be so fixed on one / That two must needs be blind for't* [i.e. by death]

blindness (*n.*) concealment, disguise, camouflage **CE** III.ii.8 [Luciana to Antipholus of Syracuse] *Muffle your false love with some show of blindness*

blind-worm (*n.*) slow-worm **Mac** IV.i.16 [Second Witch to Witches] *Adder's fork, and blind-worm's sting*

blinking (*adj.*) blind, sightless **AW** I.i.172 [Helena to Parolles] *a world … / That blinking Cupid gossips*

blister (*n.*) burn-mark **Ham** III.iv.45 [Hamlet to Gertrude, of her imagined forehead] *And sets a blister there* [i.e. as if branded as a whore]

blister (*v.*) raise blisters on [as if branded on the forehead as a whore]; tarnish, stain **MM** II.iii.12 [Provost to disguised Duke, of Juliet] *Who … / Hath blistered her report*

blistered (*adj.*) ornamented with puffs, displaying slashes to show the lining **H8** I.iii.31 [Lovell to Lord Chamberlain, of French-influenced fashion] *Short blistered breeches*

blithe (*adj.*) merry, happy, joyful **MA** II.iii.65, 73 [Balthasar singing] *be you blithe and bonny;* **Per** III.Chorus.8

bloat (*adj.*) bloated, flabby, swollen [with excess] **Ham** III.iv.183 [Hamlet to Gertrude] *[do not] Let the bloat King tempt you again to bed* [Q2 *blowt*; F *blunt*]

block (*n.*) **1** blockhead **TG** II.v.23 [Launce to Speed] *What a block art thou;* **Cor** V.ii.75; **Per** III.ii.89; **WT** I.ii.225
2 [of hats] style, fashion, shape, mould **MA** I.i.71 [Beatrice to Messenger, of Benedick's faith] *it ever changes with the next block;* **KL** IV.vi.184

blockish (*adj.*) thick, obtuse, stupid **TC** I.iii.375 [Ulysses to Nestor] *by device let blockish Ajax draw / The sort to fight with Hector*

blood (n.) **1** passion, feeling, strong emotion [especially sexual] **MV** I.ii.18 [Portia to Nerissa] *The brain may devise laws for the blood;* **AY** V.iv.56; **Ham** I.iii.16; **MA** IV.i.57; **MM** V.i.469; **Oth** I.iii.324

2 anger, temper, passion **2H4** IV.iv.63 [King Henry IV to Clarence, of Prince Henry] *When rage and hot blood are his counsellors;* **Oth** II.iii.199; **TC** II.ii.116, V.i.45; **Tim** III.v.11

3 man of fire, hot-blooded fellow, spirited youth **KJ** II.i.461 [Bastard to himself, of Hubert] *What cannoneer begot this lusty blood?;* **JC** IV.iii.260; **LL** V.ii.704; **MA** III.iii.129

4 spirit, vigour, mettle **1H4** III.i.175 [Worcester to Hotspur, of Hotspur's behaviour] *Though sometimes it show greatness, courage, blood;* **AC** I.ii.191; **1H4** V.ii.78; **MV** V.i.74

5 disposition, temper, mood **Cym** I.i.1 [First Gentleman to Second Gentleman] *our bloods / No more obey the heavens;* **2H4** II.iii.30, IV.iv.38, V.ii.129; **MA** I.i.122; **Oth** I.iii.123

6 blood relationship, kinship **TNK** II.i.227 [Palamon to Arcite] *Friendship, blood, / And all the ties between us I disclaim;* **AY** II.iii.37; **1H4** I.iii.144; **MM** II.i.146; **TN** V.i.207

7 nobility, breeding, gentility, good parentage **KL** III.i.40 [disguised Kent to Gentleman] *I am a gentleman of blood and breeding;* **AW** I.i.60; **E3** II.i.416; **H5** IV.viii.89; **R2** II.i.9; **WT** I.ii.73, 330

8 hereditary rights, appropriate rank, rightful title **1H6** III.i.161 [King to all] *our pleasure is / That Richard be restored to his blood;* **1H6** II.iv.128, III.i.162

9 life-blood, spirit **KJ** IV.ii.99 [Pembroke to King John, of Arthur] *That blood which owed the breadth of all this isle, / Three foot of it doth hold;* **RJ** III.i.183

10 vital fluid, life-giving juice **R2** III.iv.59 [Gardener to First Man, of fruit trees] *being overproud in sap and blood;* **Sonn** 11.3; **Tim** IV.iii.431

11 blood-letting, bleeding **TNK** V.i.64 [Arcite praying to Mars] *[who] healest with blood / The earth when it is sick*

12 colouring, healthy complexion, blushing **MA** IV.i.120 [Leonato to Friar, of Hero] *could she here deny / The story that is printed in her blood?;* **AC** I.iv.52; **LL** IV.iii.261; **MA** IV.i.35

blood, in [hunting] full of life, in fine condition **1H6** IV.ii.48 [Talbot to all] *If we be English deer, be then in blood;* **Cor** I.i.157, IV.v.218; **LL** IV.ii.4

blood (v.) bleed, yield blood **LL** II.i.121 [Rosaline to Berowne, of his heart] *let it blood*

blood-boltered (adj.) with hair matted with blood, with tangled bloody knots of hair **Mac** IV.i.122 [Macbeth to himself] *the blood-boltered Banquo smiles upon me*

blood-drinking (adj.) **1** bloodthirsty, eager for bloodshed **1H6** II.iv.108 [Richard to Somerset] *this pale and angry rose, / As cognizance of my blood-drinking hate*

2 draining the blood away [from the face] **2H6** III.ii.63 [Queen to King] *I would ... / Look pale as primrose with blood-drinking sighs*

blood-sized (adj.) blood-soaked, smeared with blood **TNK** I.i.99 [Second Queen to Hippolyta, of Theseus] *if he i'th' blood-sized field lay swollen* ➤ over-sized (adj.)

bloody (adj.) **1** blood-thirsty, warlike, ferocious **MV** III.iii.34 [Antonio to Solanio, of Shylock] *my bloody creditor;* **2H4** IV.i.34; **H5** II.iv.51; **Mac** IV.i.78; **TN** III.iv.218, 260, V.i.68

2 able to cause bloodshed **1H6** IV.ii.8 [Talbot to the French] *I'll withdraw me and my bloody power;* **AW** III.i.190; **Mac** II.iii.138; **TN** III.iii.33

3 involving bloodshed **Mac** II.iv.22 [Ross to Macduff, of the King's murder] *Is't known who did this more than bloody deed?;* **Tim** III.v.1

4 portending bloodshed; or: blood-red, scarlet **Cor** II.i.70 [Menenius to Brutus and Sicinius] *you ... set up the bloody flag against all patience;* **H5** I.ii.101; **1H6** II.iv.61; **JC** V.i.14

5 blood-containing **AY** III.v.7 [Silvius to Phebe, of an executioner] *he that dies and lives by bloody drops;* **KJ** IV.ii.210

6 in the blood, in the veins **MW** V.v.95 [Fairies, singing] *Lust is but a bloody fire*

bloody-minded (adj.) bloodthirsty, ready to shed someone's

blood **2H6** IV.i.36 [Suffolk to Whitmore, of Suffolk's horoscope] *Yet let not this make thee be bloody-minded;* **3H6** II.vi.33

bloomed (adj.) covered with blossom, in bloom **TNK** III.i.3 [Arcite alone, of Theseus and Hippolyta] *This is a solemn rite / They owe bloomed May*

blossoms (n.) prime, peak, full flowering [as of a plant] **WT** V.ii.123 [Autolycus to himself, of Shepherd and Clown] *Here come those ... already appearing in the blossoms of their fortune;* **Ham** I.v.76

blot (n.) stain, disgrace, blemish **TS** V.ii.138 [Katherina to Widow, of her frown] *It blots thy beauty;* **CE** II.ii.149; **KJ** II.i.114; **LL** IV.iii.239; **Sonn** 36.3; **TG** V.iv.109

blot (v.) **1** slander, defile, blacken **KJ** II.i.132 [Queen Eleanor to Arthur, of Constance] *There's a good mother, boy, that blots thy father*

2 erase, wipe out, obliterate **E3** II.i.173 [King Edward to Lodowick, of what Lodowick has written] *Blot, blot, good Lod'wick;* **Luc** 1299

3 obscure, darken, cloud **Venus** 184 [of Adonis] *His louring brows o'erwhelming his fair sight, / Like misty vapours when they blot the sky*

blot out (v.) cross out, erase, obliterate **3H6** II.ii.92 [Edward to Queen, of the King] *[you] Have caused him ... / To blot out me, and put his own son in*

blow (n.) [fencing] stab, firm stroke **3H6** III.ii.23 [Richard aside to George, of Lady Grey] *Fight closer, or, good faith, you'll catch a blow* [F; Q *clap*] [also: receive a sexual assault]

blow (v.) **1** blossom, bloom, flower **TNK** II.i.193 [Emilia to Woman, of a rose = maid] *How modestly she blows;* **E3** IV.iv.138; **LL** V.ii.293; **TG** I.i.46; **TNK** I.i.11, II.i.198

2 deposit eggs [in], pollute, contaminate **Tem** III.i.63 [Ferdinand to Miranda] *to suffer / The flesh-fly blow my mouth;* **AC** V.ii.60; **LL** V.ii.409; **Oth** IV.ii.66

3 swell to bursting, break, shatter **AC** IV.vi.34 [Enobarbus alone, of Antony's generosity] *This blows my heart*

4 puff up, swell, inflate **TN** II.v.42 [Fabian to Sir Toby and Sir Andrew, of Malvolio] *Look how imagination blows him;* **TC** I.iii.317

5 breathe hot breath [on] **3H6** II.v.3 [King alone] *the shepherd, blowing of his nails*

6 blow up, explode on **H8** V.iv.46 [Man to Porter, of a brassworker] *he stands there like a mortar-piece, to blow us*

blow one's nail / nails twiddle one's thumbs, wait patiently **TS** I.i.107 [Gremio to Hortensio, of waiting for Bianca] *Love is not so great ... but we may blow our nails together, and fast it fairly out;* **LL** V.ii.902

blow wind in the breech feel the wind [we leave behind], run to keep up [with us] **TNK** II.ii.47 [Second Countryman to the others] *All the boys in Athens / Blow wind i'th' breech on's!*

blown (adj.) **1** in full flower, in its bloom **Ham** III.i.160 [Ophelia alone, of Hamlet] *That unmatched form and feature of blown youth;* **AC** III.xiii.39, IV.iv.25; **Ham** III.iii.81; **LL** V.ii.297; **MA** IV.i.56 ➤ half-blown (adj.); unblown (adj.)

2 swollen; or, wind-driven **Per** V.i.254 [Pericles to Helicanus] *Toward Ephesus / Turn our blown sails;* **Cor** V.iv.46

3 swollen, inflated with pride **H5** IV.i.247 [King Henry alone, as if to greatness] *Thinks thou the fiery fever will go out / With titles blown from adulation?;* **1H4** IV.i.47; **KL** IV.iv.27

4 inflamed, swollen, distended **AC** V.ii.347 [Dolabella to Caesar, of Cleopatra] *Here, on her breast, / There is a vent of blood, and something blown;* **WT** IV.iv.787

5 whispered, hinted, insinuated **Oth** III.iii.180 [Othello to Iago, of jealousy] *such exsufflicate and blown surmises* [or: blown up]

blowt (adj.) ➤ bloat (adj.)

blowze (n.) red-faced lass **Tit** IV.ii.72 [Aaron to the baby] *Sweete blowze, you are a beauteous blossom, sure*

blubbered (*adj.*) tear-stained, disfigured with weeping [no comic overtones] TNK I.i.180 [First Queen to Theseus] *what wilt thou think / Of rotten kings or blubbered queens*; 2H4 II.iv.384

blue (*adj.*) [of eyes] dark-circled, shadow-rimmed AY III.ii.358 [Rosalind to Orlando, of his appearance] *a blue eye and sunken, which you have not*; Luc 1587

bluebottle (*adj.*) blue-coated, blue-uniformed 2H4 V.iv.19 [Doll to First Beadle] *you bluebottle rogue*

blue-cap (*n.*) [contemptuous] one who wears a blue bonnet; Scotsman 1H4 II.iv.350 [Falstaff to Prince Hal, of Douglas] *he is there too … and a thousand blue-caps more*

blunt (*adj.*) 1 stupid, obtuse, dull-witted E3 I.ii.17 [Countess to herself] *I'll … list their babble, blunt and full of pride*; 2H4 I.Induction.18; 2H6 IV.i.67; TG II.vi.41

2 plain-spoken, unceremonious, forthright 3H6 III.ii.83 [George aside to Richard, of Edward] *He is the bluntest wooer in Christendom*; E3 I.ii.146; KJ I.i.71; Luc 1300

3 rough, unrefined, uncivilized 3H6 IV.viii.2 [Warwick to all] *Edward from Belgia, / With … blunt Hollanders, / Hath passed in safety through the narrow seas*; Luc 1504

4 rough, harsh, unsparing 3H6 V.i.86 [George to Warwick] *trowest thou … / That Clarence is so harsh, so blunt, unnatural*; Venus 884

blur (*n.*) blot, stain, blemish Luc 222 [Tarquin to himself, of his intention] *This blur to youth*

blur (*v.*) blot, stain, defame Luc 522 [Tarquin to Lucrece] *Thy issue blurred with nameless bastardy*

blurt (*v.*) mouthe in contempt, scoff, mock E3 IV.vi.45 [Charles to all] *the world will blurt and scorn at us*

blurt at (*v.*) treat with contempt, scorn, look down on Per IV.iii.34 [Dionyza to Cleon] *my child … was blurted at*

blushing (*adj.*) 1 glowing, rosy-coloured, lustrous H8 III.ii.354 [Wolsey alone, of a man's rise and fall] *And bears his blushing honours thick upon him*; R2 III.iii.63

2 modest, self-effacing, unassuming 1H4 V.ii.61 [Vernon to Hotspur, of Prince Hal] *He made a blushing cital of himself*

bluster (*n.*) storm, tempest, rough blast WT III.iii.4 [Mariner to Antigonus] *the skies look grimly, / And threaten present blusters*; Tim V.iv.41

blusterer (*n.*) braggart, boaster, swaggerer Lover 58 [of the reverend man] *Sometime a blusterer that the ruffle knew / Of Court of City*

blustering (*adj.*) turbulent, buffeted, tempestuous KJ V.i.21 [Cardinal Pandulph to King John] *My tongue shall hush again this storm of war / And make fair weather in your blustering land*

blusterous (*adj.*) blustery, rough, stormy Per III.i.28 [Pericles to Marina] *a more blusterous birth had never babe*

board (*n.*) 1 table, mealtimes CE III.ii.18 [Luciana to Antipholus of Syracuse, of Adriana] *'Tis double wrong to truant with your bed / And let her read it in thy looks at board*; Oth III.iii.24

2 table Cym III.vii.23 [disguised Innogen to all, of her money] *I would have left it on the board*; 2H6 IV.i.57

board (*v.*) 1 accost, address, approach, tackle MA II.i.128 [masked Beatrice to masked Benedick, of Benedick] *I would he had boarded me*; AW V.iii.211; Ham II.ii.170; MW II.i.83; TN I.iii.54; TS I.ii.94

2 [nautical] get on board Tem II.ii.3 [Stephano to Trinculo and Caliban] *bear up and board 'em* [i.e. drink up]

boast off (*v.*) boast about, extol, sing praises of Tem IV.i.9 [Prospero to Ferdinand, of Miranda] *Do not smile at me that I boast her off* [F *of*]

bob (*n.*) jest, jibe, taunt AY II.vii.55 [Jaques to Duke Senior] *seem senseless of the bob* [i.e. pretend to ignore the jibe]

bob (*v.*) 1 swindle, cheat, get by deception Oth V.i.16 [Iago to himself, of Roderigo] *gold and jewels, that I bobbed from him / As gifts to Desdemona*; TC III.i.67

2 knock, bump, bang MND II.i.49 [Puck to Fairy, of an old woman] *when she drinks, against her lips I bob;*

3 punch, strike, buffet R3 V.iii.335 [King Richard to his army, of the enemy] *these bastard Britains, whom our fathers / Have … beaten, bobbed, and thumped*; TC II.i.68

bobtail (*adj.*) with a docked tail KL III.vi.69 [Edgar as Poor Tom to all] *bobtail tike, or trundle-tail*

bode (*v.*) 1 forebode, portend, predict, augur Oth IV.iii.56 [Desdemona to Emilia] *Mine eyes do itch: / Does that bode weeping?*; Ham I.i.69; 2H6 I.ii.31; 3H6 II.i.39; MA III.iii.82; Oth V.ii.244

2 promise, predict, forecast Tem III.i.71 [Ferdinand to Miranda] *If [I speak] hollowly, invert / What best is boded me to mischief*; TC V.ii.194

bodement (*n.*) omen, portent, augury TC V.iii.80 [Troilus to all, of Andromache or Cassandra] *This foolish, dreaming, superstitious girl / Makes all these bodements*; Mac IV.i.95

bodge (*v.*) ☛ **budge** (*v.*) 2

boding (*adj.*) ominous, full of foreboding TNK I.i.20 [Boy singing to all] *The boding raven*; 2H6 III.ii.327; Oth IV.i.22; Venus 647

bodkin (*n.*) 1 dagger [or other pointed weapon] Ham III.i.76 [Hamlet alone] *he himself might his quietus make / With a bare bodkin*

2 small sharply pointed implement for piercing WT III.iii.83 [Clown to Shepherd, of the effect of the storm] *betwixt the firmament and it [the sea] you cannot thrust a bodkin's point*

3 hair-pin, pin-shaped ornament LL V.ii.608 [Dumaine to Holofernes, of the latter's face] *The head of a bodkin*

4 ☛ SWEARING, p.435

body (*n.*) 1 anyone, anybody, one AY IV.iii.166 [Rosalind as Ganymede to Oliver] *a body would think this was well counterfeited*

2 corporate body, collective mass [of people] Per III.iii.21 [Cleon to Pericles] *the common body … would force me to my duty*; AC I.iv.44; Cor II.iii.180

3 group, ensemble, company TNK III.v.20 [Schoolmaster to all] *Cast yourselves in a body decently*

4 main part, chief element TNK III.v.120 [Schoolmaster to Theseus] *The body of our sport, of no small study*

5 length and breadth, extent KJ IV.ii.112 [Messenger to King John] *never such a power … / Was levied in the body of a land*

6 person, individual MM IV.iv.20 [Angelo alone, of Isabella] *A deflowered maid, / And by an eminent body*; 2H4 V.ii.90; TS V.ii.40

body forth (*v.*) make available to the mind, give mental shape to MND V.i.14 [Theseus to Hippolyta] *imagination bodies forth / The forms of things unknown*

bodykins (*int.*) ☛ SWEARING, p.435

boggle (*v.*) start with fright, shy away, become alarmed AW V.iii.232 [King to Bertram] *You boggle shrewdly*

boggler (*n.*) waverer, vacillator, mind-changer AC III.xiii.110 [Antony to Cleopatra] *You have been a boggler ever*

Bohemian-Tartar (*n.*) barbarian, savage beast MW IV.v.18 [Host to Falstaff, of Simple] *Here's a Bohemian-Tartar tarries the coming down of thy fat woman*

boiled (*adj.*) receiving a sweating treatment [for venereal disease] Cym I.vii.125 [Iachimo to Innogen] *Such boiled stuff / As well might poison poison!*

boiled-brain (*n.*) hothead, maniac, headstrong fellow WT III.iii.62 [Shepherd to himself] *would any but these boiled brains of nineteen and two-and-twenty hunt this weather?*

boisterous (*adj.*) 1 violent, fierce, savage AY II.iii.32 [Orlando to Adam] *with a base and boisterous sword enforce / A thievish living*; AY IV.iii.32; E3 I.ii.75; 3H6 II.i.70; Oth I.iii.225; R2 I.i.4

2 tumultuous, violent, tempestuous E3 III.iv.79 [Prince Edward to all] *My painful voyage on the boist'rous sea*; Ham III.iii.22; 2H4 IV.v.191; R3 II.iii.44

3 irritable, painful, irritating **KJ** I.iv.94 [Arthur to Hubert, of his eyes] *feeling what small things are boisterous there, / Your vile intent must needs seem horrible*

4 painful, hurtful, rough on the feelings **RJ** I.iv.26 [Romeo to Mercutio, of love] *It is too rough, / Too rude, too boisterous, and it pricks like thorn*

boisterous *(adv.)* violently, fiercely, forcefully **KJ** IV.i.75 [Arthur to executioners] *what need you be so boisterous-rough?*

boisterously *(adv.)* forcefully, violently, roughly **KJ** III.iv.136 [Cardinal Pandulph to Lewis the Dauphin] *A sceptre snatched with an unruly hand / Must be as boisterously maintained as gained*

bold *(adj.)* **1** confident, certain, sure **Cym** II.iv.2 [Posthumus to Philario, of Innogen] *I am bold her honour / Will remain hers;* **AW** V.i.5; **1H4** IV.i.36; **LL** II.i.28; **Oth** II.i.51; **Tit** V.i.13

2 overconfident, presumptuous, audacious, impudent **TG** V.iv.163 [Valentine to Duke] *I dare be bold / With our discourse to make your grace to smile;* **1H6** III.i.63; **2H6** I.iii.91; **H8** V.iii.84; **KL** I.iv.238; **TNK** Epilogue.11

3 shameless, immodest, outspoken, coarse **WT** II.i.94 [Leontes to Lords, of Hermione] *she's / A bed-swerver, even as bad as those / That vulgars give bold'st titles;* **H8** V.iii.85; **TNK** V.i.124

4 ready, unafraid, prepared **TNK** III.ii.20 [Gaoler's Daughter alone] *Be bold to ring the bell* [i.e. death knell]

bold, be / make presume, venture, take the liberty **MA** III.ii.7 [Don Pedro to Claudio] *I will only be bold with Benedick for his company* [i.e. I'll ask only him to come with me]; **MW** II.ii.152

bold *(v.)* make bold, hearten, encourage **KL** V.i.26 [Albany to Edmund, of the war] *this business … / Not bolds the King*

bolden *(v.)* embolden, make bold, encourage **H8** I.ii.55 [Queen Katherine to King Henry] *I am much too venturous / In tempting of your patience, but am boldened / Under your promised pardon*

boldened *(adj.)* emboldened, made brave **AY** II.vii.92 [Duke Senior to Orlando] *Art thou thus boldened, man, by thy distress*

boldness *(n.)* confidence, assurance, certainty **MM** IV.ii.152 [disguised Duke to Provost] *in the boldness of my cunning I will lay myself in hazard*

bolin *(n.)* [nautical] bow-line, rope for steadying a sail **Per** III.i.43 [First Sailor to the crew] *Slack the bolins there!*

bollen *(adj.)* swollen, puffed out, inflamed **Luc** 1417 [of people in a painting of Troy] *Here one being thronged bears back, all bollen and red*

bolster *(v.)* lie on the same bolster, share a pillow **Oth** III.iii.396 [Iago to Othello, of Desdemona and Cassio] *Damn them then / If ever mortal eyes do see them bolster / More than their own!*

bolt *(n.)* **1** [short and thick, crossbow] arrow **MND** II.i.165 [Oberon to Puck] *Yet marked I where the bolt of Cupid fell;* **AY** V.iv.62; **Cym** IV.ii.300; **H5** III.vii.119; **MW** III.iv.24 ☛ shaft *(n.)*

2 fetter, shackle, iron fastening **Cym** V.v.10 [Posthumus alone, to the Gods] *give me / The penitent instrument to pick that bolt;* **Cym** V.iv.198; **MM** V.i.343

3 thunderbolt **MM** II.ii.115 [Isabella to Angelo, of the heavens] *with thy sharp and sulphurous bolt / Splits the unwedgeable and gnarled oak;* **Cor** V.iii.152; **Tem** V.i.46

BODY-ARMOUR

A small number of terms relating to a suit of armour are found in Shakespeare, especially in the history plays; several are used together in **TNK** III.vi.53ff, when Arcite and Palamon arm each other.

Headgear

Term	Example	Gloss
beaver	**Ham** I.i.230	lower part of a helmet's face-guard, normally lifted except when fighting
burgonet	**AC** I.v.24	light helmet from Burgundy, used by foot-soldiers
casque	**TNK** III.vi.62	general term for all kinds of helmet
crest	**KJ** II.i.317	helmet [originally, the plume of feathers on a helmet]
helm	**TC** I.ii.233	helmet
helmet	**R2** I.iii.119	[as in modern English]
sallet	**2H6** IV.x.10	small round helmet, often lacking a visor

Body parts

Term	Example	Gloss
brace	**Per** II.i.128	piece of armour protecting the arms; or: coat of armour
buckle	**TNK** III.vi.61	as in modern English, but here for linking pieces of armour
corslet	**Cor** V.iv.20	piece of armour protecting the torso
cuishes, cushes, cuisses	**1H4** IV.i.105	piece of armour protecting the front of the thigh
gauntlet	**Ham** V.ii.218	armoured glove protecting the hand and wrist
gorget	**TC** I.iii.174	piece of armour protecting the throat
grand guard	**TNK** III.vi.58	piece of tournament armour giving additional protection to the breast and left shoulder
mail	**E3** I.ii.29	coat made of small interlinked steel rings (chain-mail)
shoulder-piece	**TNK** IV.ii.127	piece of armour protecting the shoulder
vantbrace, vambrace	**TC** I.iii.297	piece of armour protecting the fore-arm

☛ **WEAPONS**, p.491

bolt (v.) sift, separate out **WT** IV.iv.361 [Florizel to disguised Polixenes] *the fanned snow that's bolted / By th'northern blasts twice o'er*

bolted (adj.) refined, carefully sifted, polished **Cor** III.i.320 [Menenius to Sicinius, of Coriolanus] *He ... is ill schooled / In bolted language;* **H5** II.ii.137

bolter (n.) sifting-cloth, sieve, strainer **1H4** III.iii.69 [Falstaff to Hostess, of what bakers' wives have done to his shirts] *They have made bolters of them*

bolting (n.) [of flour] sifting **TC** I.i.19 [Pandarus to Troilus] *you must tarry the bolting*

bolting-hutch (n.) sifting-bin [used in filtering flour from bran] **1H4** II.iv.438 [Prince Hal (as King) to Falstaff (as Hal), of Falstaff] *Why dost thou converse with ... that bolting-hutch of beastliness*

bombard, bumbard (n.) large leather wine-jug **Tem** II.ii.21 [Trinculo to himself] *Yond same black cloud ... looks like a foul bombard that would shed his liquor;* **1H4** II.iv.439; **H8** V.iv.80

bombast, bumbast (n.) wool padding, stuffing; also: high-flown language, empty words **1H4** II.iv.320 [Prince Hal to Falstaff] *How now my sweet creature of bombast;* **LL** V.ii.776

bombast, bumbast (adj.) bombastic, padded-out, waffly **Oth** I.i.13 [Iago to Roderigo, of Othello and Iago's mediators] *he ... / Evades them with a bombast circumstance*

bona-roba (n.) high-class prostitute, good quality bit of stuff **2H4** III.ii.200 [Shallow to Falstaff, of Jane Nightwork] *She was then a bona-roba;* **2H4** III.ii.22 ☞ **ITALIAN**, p.647

bond (n.) 1 deed, contract, pledge **Mac** IV.i.83 [Macbeth to himself] *I'll make assurance double sure, / And take a bond of fate;* **CE** IV.i.13; **2H4** I.ii.31; **MND** III.ii.267; **MV** I.iii.65; **TN** III.i.20
  2 duty, commitment, obligation **KL** I.i.93 [Cordelia to Lear] *I love your majesty / According to my bond* [i.e. filial duty]; **AC** I.iv.84; **Cym** V.i.7; **MM** V.i.8; **Tim** I.i.148
  3 tie, binding, obligation **Cor** V.iii.25 [Coriolanus to himself] *All bond and privilege of nature, break;* **Sonn** 87.4, 117.4
  4 [physical] tie, restraint, constraint **MND** III.ii.268 [Demetrius to Lysander] *I perceive / A weak bond holds you* [pun: 267, sense 1]
  5 shackle, chain, fetter **E3** IV.v.120 [King John to Salisbury, of Prince Edward and his men] *Hooped with a bond of iron round about* [Q1; Q2 band]; **Cym** V.iv.28

bondage (n.) 1 condition of being bound, constraint, oppression **1H6** V.iii.112 [Margaret to Suffolk] *To be a queen in bondage is more vile / Than is a slave in base servility;* **1H6** V.iii.111; **KL** I.ii.49
  2 binding up, tying up, wrapping up **Cym** V.v.306 [Belarius to the guard, of Guiderius] *Let his arms alone, / They were not born for bondage;* **WT** IV.iv.234
  3 binding power, obligatory force **Cym** II.iv.111 [Posthumus to Iachimo] *The vows of women / Of no more bondage be to where they are made / Than they are to their virtues*

bondmaid (n.) slave girl **TS** II.i.2 [Bianca to Katherina, who has tied her hands] *wrong me not ... / To make a bondmaid and a slave of me*

bondman (n.) bondsman, serf, slave **CE** V.i.288 [Egeon to Antipholus of Ephesus] *is not that your bondman Dromio?;* **AC** III.xiii.149; **CE** V.i.141; **2H6** I.iii.125; **JC** I.iii.101; **MV** I.iii.120

bondslave (n.) slave, bondsman, person in a condition of servitude **Oth** I.ii.99 [Brabantio to all, of Othello's affair] *if such actions may have passage free, / Bondslaves and pagans shall our statesmen be;* **R2** I.i.114; **TN** II.v.184

bone (n.) 1 body, physique, bodily frame **TC** III.iii.172 [Ulysses to Achilles] *High birth, vigour of bone ... are subjects all / To envious and calumniating time;* **Venus** 294
  2 [weaving] bobbin made of bone **TN** II.iv.45 [Orsino to Viola as Cesario, of a song] *the free maids that weave their thread with bones, / Do use to chant it*
  3 (plural) man, person **KJ** I.i.78 [Bastard to King John, of his father] *Fair fall the bones that took the pains for me!*

  4 (plural) pieces of bone [used as a musical instrument] **TNK** III.v.87 [Gaoler's Daughter to Schoolmaster] *let him play / Chi passa o'th' bells and bones;* **MND** IV.i.29

bone-ache (n.), **Neapolitan bone-ache** [pain in the bones from Naples] syphilis, venereal disease **TC** II.iii.18 [Thersites alone] *the vengeance on the whole camp - or rather, the Neopolitan bone-ache;* **TC** V.i.20 [Q]

bonnet (n.) hat, cap **Venus** 339 [of Adonis] *with his bonnet hides his angry brow;* **AY** III.ii.363; **Cor** III.ii.73; **E3** V.i.78; **Ham** V.ii.93; **H5** IV.i.204 ☞ **CLOTHING**, p.79

bonnet (v.) take off the hat, remove the bonnet [in respect or flattery] **Cor** II.ii.26 [Second Officer to First Officer, of Corio-lanus] *his ascent is not by such easy degrees as those who, having been supple and courteous to the people, bonneted*

bonny (adj.) 1 strong, stalwart, strapping **AY** II.iii.8 [Adam to Orlando, of Charles] *The bonny prizer of the humorous Duke;* **E3** I.ii.26
  2 fine, beautiful, splendid **2H6** V.ii.12 [York to Warwick, of Clifford's horse] *the bonny beast he loved so well;* **E3** I.ii.57, 70, III.i.179; **MA** II.iii.65, 73; **TS** II.i.184

book (n.) 1 book-learning, scholarship, erudition **2H6** IV.vii.67 [Say to the rebels] *my book preferred me to the King;* **H8** I.i.122; **MA** IV.i.165; **Tem** III.i.94
  2 deed, charter, set of indentures **1H4** III.i.258 [Glendower to Mortimer] *By this our book is drawn* [i.e. by this time]; **1H4** III.i.217 ☞ **drawn** (v.)
  3 Bible, prayer-book **1H4** II.iv.48 [Francis to Prince Hal] *I'll be sworn upon all the books in England;* **2H4** II.i.100; **LL** IV.iii.248; **MW** I.i.141
  4 writing tablet **JC** I.ii.126 [Cassius to Brutus, of Caesar] *bade the Romans ... write his speeches in their books* [or: volume]
  5 writing, written composition **Sonn** 23.9 *O let my books be then the eloquence / And dumb presagers of my speaking breast*
  6 (plural) good books, favour, regard **MA** I.i.72 [Messenger to Beatrice, of Benedick] *the gentleman is not in your books*

book, by the expertly, as if following a manual **RJ** I.v.110 [Juliet to Romeo] *You kiss by th'book*

book, without off by heart, by rote **TN** I.iii.25 [Sir Toby to Maria, of Sir Andrew] *He ... speaks three or four languages word for word without book;* **RJ** I.ii.59; **TC** II.i.18; **TN** II.iii.142 ☞ **con** (v.)

book (v.) record, list, register **H5** IV.vii.71 [Montjoy to King Henry] *I come to thee for charitable licence, / That we may ... book our dead;* **Sonn** 117.9

bookish (adj.) of mere book-learning, obtained only from books, scholarly **2H6** I.i.257 [York to himself, of Lancaster] *Whose bookish rule hath pulled fair England down;* **Oth** I.i.24

book-man (n.) scholar, student **LL** II.i.213 [Princess to all, of their jesting] *This civil war of wits were much better used / On Navarre and his book-men*

book-mate (n.) fellow student, scholarly associate **LL** IV.i.101 [Boyet to Princess, of Armado] *one that makes sport / To the prince and his book-mates*

book-oath (n.) ☞ **book** (n.) 3

boon (n.) petition, entreaty, request **TG** V.iv.151 [Valentine to Duke] *grant one boon that I shall ask of you;* **Cym** V.v.97, 135; **3H6** III.ii.46; **Per** V.ii.3; **R3** II.i.97; **TG** V.iv.24

boor (n.) peasant, rustic **WT** V.ii.155 [Clown to Shepherd, of swearing] *Let boors and franklins say it, I'll swear it*

boorish (n.) coarse vernacular, uncultured speech **AY** V.i.47 [Touchstone to William] *the society - which in the boorish is 'company'*

boot (n.) 1 good, advantage, profit **AC** IV.i.9 [Maecenas to Caesar, of Antony] *Make boot of his distraction;* **1H6** IV.vi.52; **KL** V.iii.299; **MM** II.iv.11; **TS** V.ii.175; **WT** IV.iv.633
  2 alternative, choice, better way **R2** I.i.164 [King Richard to Mowbray] *We bid: there is no boot*

3 additional element, something added to the bargain **R3** IV.iv.65 [Queen Margaret to Duchess of York] *Young York he is but boot;* **TC** IV.v.40

4 booty, plunder, spoils **1H4** II.i.83 [Gadshill to Chamberlain, of Gadshill's companions and the commonwealth] *they ... make her their boots;* **H5** I.iii.194; **KL** IV.vi.226; **TNK** I.ii.70

5 riding-boot **TG** V.ii.6 [Thurio to Proteus, of his leg] *I'll wear a boot to make it somewhat rounder*

boot (*v.*) **1** help, serve, benefit, be useful [to] **R2** I.iii.174 [King Richard to Mowbray] *It boots thee not to be compassionate;* **3H6** I.iv.125; **Per** I.ii.20; **R2** III.iv.18; **TG** I.i.28; **WT** III.ii.24

2 benefit, increase, compensate **AC** II.v.71 [Cleopatra to Messenger] *I will boot thee with what gift beside / Thy modesty can beg*

3 put on one's boots **2H4** V.iii.132 [Falstaff to Shallow] *Boot, boot, Master Shallow!*

boot, to in addition, as well **Mac** IV.iii.37 [Macduff to Malcolm] *I would not be the villain that thou think'st / For the whole space that's in the tyrant's grasp, / And the rich East to boot;* **1H4** III.ii.97; **KL** IV.vi.226; **R3** V.iii.302; **Sonn** 135.2; **TC** I.ii.239 ☛ SWEARING, p.435

boots, give someone the make fun of someone, make a fool of someone **TG** I.i.27 [Proteus to Valentine] *give me not the boots*

boot-hose (*n.*) over-stocking covering the whole of the lower leg **TS** III.ii.65 [Biondello to Baptista, of Petruchio's man] *with a linen stock on one leg and a kersey boot-hose on the other* ☛ hose (*n.*)

bootless (*adj.*) useless, worthless, fruitless, unavailing **R3** III.iv.102 [Lovel to Hastings] *'Tis bootless to exclaim;* **3H6** I.iv.20; **MV** III.iii.20; **Per** V.i.30; **Tem** I.ii.35; **Venus** 422

bootless (*adv.*) fruitlessly, uselessly, unsuccessfully, in vain **1H4** III.i.63 [Glendower to all, of Bolingbroke] *thrice ... have I sent him / Bootless home;* **H5** III.iii.24; **JC** III.i.75; **MND** II.i.37

bo-peep (*n.*) peep-bo, peek-a-boo [a game played with babies] **KL** I.iv.173 [Fool to Lear] *That such a king should play bo-peep* [i.e. become a child]

border (*v.*) keep within bounds, contain, confine **KL** IV.ii.33 [Albany to Gonerill] *That nature which contemns its origin / Cannot be bordered certain in itself*

bordering (*adj.*) on the border **E3** I.i.127 [Montague to King Edward, of the Scottish king] *He made invasion of the bordering towns*

bore (*n.*) **1** cavity, aperture, hole **Cym** III.ii.58 [Innogen to Pisanio] *Love's counsellor should fill the bores of hearing*

2 bore-hole, auger hole **Cor** IV.vi.88 [Cominius to Brutus and Sicinius] *Your franchises ... confined / Into an auger's bore*

3 calibre, size [of a gun] **Ham** IV.vi.25 [Hamlet to Horatio, by letter] *[my words will be] much too light for the bore of the matter* [i.e. no match for the enormity of the issue]

bore (*v.*) fool, trick, cheat **H8** I.i.128 [Buckingham to Norfolk, of Wolsey] *He bores me with some trick*

boresprit (*n.*) bowsprit; boom extending from the bow to which the lower edge of the front sail is fastened **Tem** I.ii.200 [Ariel to Prospero] *On the ... boresprit would I flame distinctly* [F *Bore-spritt*] ☛ SHIPS, p.397

borne (*adj.*) behaved, conducted, mannered **TC** II.iii.235 [Ulysses to all, of Ajax] *If he were ... surly borne*

borrow (*n.*) borrowing, loan, allowance **WT** I.ii.39 [Hermione to Polixenes] *of your royal presence I'll adventure / The borrow of a week*

borrowed (*adj.*) assumed, pretended, feigned **Per** IV.iv.24 [Gower alone, of the dumb show] *This borrowed passion stands for true old woe* **H5** II.iv.79; **KJ** I.i.4; **Luc** 1549; **RJ** VI.i.104, V.iii.248

bosky (*adj.*) bushy, full of thickets **Tem** IV.i.81 [Ceres to Iris] *with each end of thy blue bow dost crown / My bosky acres*

bosom (*n.*) **1** heart, inner person **Mac** II.i.28 [Banquo to Macbeth] *So I ... still keep / My bosom franchised and allegiance clear;* **AW** I.iii.121; **2H4** I.i.158; **KJ** IV.iii.32; **RJ** V.i.3; **TN** I.v.215

2 inward thoughts, personal counsel **WT** IV.iv.560 [Camillo to Florizel, of Leontes] *he shall not perceive / But that you have your father's bosom there / And speak his very heart;* **JC** V.i.7; **KJ** III.iii.53; **RJ** III.v.241

3 warm-heartedness, tender affection **WT** I.ii.113 [Leontes to himself, of Hermione and Polixenes] *This entertainment / May ... derive a liberty / From heartiness, from bounty, fertile bosom;* **Lover** 127; **Tim** I.ii.123

4 wish, desire **MM** IV.iii.133 [disguised Duke to Isabella, of Angelo] *you shall have your bosom on this wretch*

5 stomach, gut; or: being, person **2H4** I.iii.98 [Archbishop to all, as if to the people] *didst thou disgorge / Thy glutton bosom of the royal Richard;* **Cor** III.i.131

6 surface **KJ** IV.i.3 [Hubert to Executioner] *When I strike my foot / Upon the bosom of the ground, rush forth;* **RJ** II.ii.32; **TC** I.iii.112; **Tim** I.i.69

7 depths **R3** I.i.4 [Richard alone] *all the clouds that loured upon our house / In the deep bosom of the ocean buried;* **KJ** II.i.410; **LL** IV.iii.29

8 pocket on the front of a woman's dress **TG** I.ii.114 [Julia alone, of Proteus' name on a shred of torn letter] *Poor wounded name, my bosom, as a bed, / Shall lodge thee*

bosom, in one's privately, intimately **MA** I.i.302 [Don Pedro to Claudio] *in her bosom I'll unclasp my heart*

bosom, of one's in one's confidence, entrusted with one's secrets **KL** IV.v.26 [Regan to Oswald, of Gonerill] *I know you are of her bosom*

bosom (*adj.*) intimate, confidential, close **MV** III.iv.17 [Portia to Lorenzo] *this Antonio, / Being the bosom lover of my lord*

bosom up (*v.*) take to heart, keep in mind **H8** I.i.112 [Norfolk to Buckingham] *Bosom up my counsel*

bosomed (*adj.*) intimate, close **KL** V.i.13 [Regan to Edmund, of Gonerill] *I am doubtful that you have been conjunct / And bosomed with her*

bossed (*adj.*) ornamented, studded **TS** II.i.346 [Gremio to Baptista, of his possessions] *Turkey cushions bossed with pearl*

botch (*n.*) **1** flaw, blemish, clumsy result **Mac** III.i.133 [Macbeth to Murderers, of killing Banquo] *leave no rubs and botches in the work*

2 tumour, boil, ulcer **TC** V.i.5 [Achilles to Thersites] *Thou crusty botch of nature* [F, Q *batch*]

botch (*v.*) clumsily patch together, fumble with **Ham** IV.v.10 [Gentleman to Gertrude, of people's reaction to Ophelia's speech] *They ... botch the words up fit to their own thoughts;* **H5** II.ii.115; **Tim** IV.iii.287

botch up (*v.*) clumsily contrive, make a mess of **TN** IV.i.55 [Olivia to Sebastian, of Sir Toby] *hear thou ... how many fruitless pranks / This ruffian hath botched up*

botcher (*n.*) mender of old clothes, tailor who does repairs, patcher-up **TN** I.v.42 [Feste to Olivia, of a dishonest man] *let the botcher mend him;* **AW** IV.iii.182; **Cor** II.i.83

botchy (*adj.*) enveloped in sores [botches], tumour-covered **TC** II.i.6 [Thersites to Ajax, of Agamemnon as a boil] *Were not that a botchy core?*

both (*adv.*) the following set [of nouns - not restricted to two] **KL** I.i.49 [Lear to his daughters] *we will divest us both of rule, / Interest of territory, cares of state*

both-sides (*adj.*) two-faced, double-dealing, hypocritical **AW** IV.iii.217 [Bertram to all, of Parolles] *Damnable both-sides rogue!*

bots (*n.*) stomach worm affecting horses **1H4** II.i.9 [Second Carrier to First Carrier, of the damp] *that is the next way to give poor jades the bots;* **Per** II.i.119; **TS** III.ii.54 ☛ SWEARING, p.435

bottle (*n.*) **1** bundle, truss [of hay] **TNK** V.ii.62 [Gaoler's Daughter to Gaoler, of a horse's dowry] *Some two hundred bottles!* **MND** IV.i.32

2 wicker basket **MA** I.i.237 [Benedick to Don Pedro] *hang me in a bottle like a cat*

bottle-ale *(adj.)* dissolute, degenerate, low **2H4** II.iv.126 [Doll to Pistol] *Away, you bottle-ale rascal*; **TN** II.iii.27

bottled *(adj.)* bottle-shaped, hunched, swollen **R3** IV.iv.81 [Queen Elizabeth to Queen Margaret, of Richard] *That bottled spider*; **R3** I.iii.241

bottom *(n.)* **1** essence, gist, main point **AW** III.vii.29 [Widow to Helena] *Now I see / The bottom of your purpose*; **Cor** IV.v.204

2 total extent, basis, foundation **1H4** IV.i.50 [Hotspur to all, of using all their forces at once] *therein should we read / The very bottom and the soul of hope*; **MM** I.i.78

3 lowest point, nadir **2H6** V.ii.78 [Queen to King] *If you be ta'en, we then should see the bottom / Of all our fortunes*; **AW** III.vi.33

4 depths **Cym** IV.ii.204 [Belarius to Arviragus and Guiderius] *O melancholy, / Who ever yet could sound thy bottom*; **2H4** IV.ii.51; **Luc** 1109 ☞ sound *(v.)* 2

5 valley, hollow, dell **AY** IV.iii.79 [Celia as Aliena to Oliver] *West of this place, down in the neighbour bottom*; **1H4** III.i.101; **Venus** 236

6 [nautical: keel, hull] ship, vessel **H5** III.Chorus.12 [Chorus] *behold the threaden sails ... / Draw the huge bottoms through the furrowed sea*; **KJ** II.i.73; **MV** I.i.42; **TN** V.i.54

7 bobbin, ball **TS** IV.iii.132 [Grumio to Petruchio] *beat me to death with a bottom of brown thread*

bottom *(v.)* **1** reach a lower level than, probe more deeply than **Cym** III.iv.117 [Innogen to Pisanio] *I have heard I am a strumpet, and mine ear ... can take no greater wound, / Nor tent, to bottom that*

2 [of wool] wind into a ball; focus, concentrate **TG** III.ii.53 [Thurio to Proteus, of Silvia's love] *You must provide to bottom it on me*

bottomless *(adj.)* inexhaustible, unfathomable, infinite **Luc** 701 *O deeper sin than bottomless conceit / Can comprehend in still imagination!*

boughs *(n.)* leaves, foliage **Tit** I.i.77 [Titus to all, of himself] *bound with laurel boughs*

bought and sold ☞ buy and sell

bounce *(n.)* explosion, detonation, gun-shot **KJ** II.i.462 [Bastard to himself, of Hubert] *He speaks plain cannon - fire and smoke and bounce* ☞ **SOUNDS**, p.410

bounce *(v.)* move with a sudden bound **PassP** VI.13 [of Adonis and Cytherea, by the river] *He, spying her, bounced in*

bouncing *(adj.)* beefy, hefty, strapping **TNK** III.v.26 [Second Countryman to all] *[here's] bouncing Barbary*

bound *(n.)* **1** limit, boundary, confine, barrier **Ham** IV.vii.127 [Claudius to Laertes] *Revenge should have no bounds*; **CE** II.i.17; **1H4** V.iv.89; **KJ** III.i.23; **R3** V.i.20; **TN** I.iv.21

2 territory, region, domain **KL** I.i.63 [Lear to Gonerill, of the map] *Of all these bounds ... / We make thee lady*; **CE** I.i.134; **E3** II.ii.12; **1H6** I.i.54; **Tim** V.iv.61

3 (plural) extent, land, area [within boundaries] **AY** II.iv.80 [Corin to all, of his master's lands] *his flocks, and bounds of feed / Are now on sale*; **AY** III.v.107

bound *(adj.)* **1** obliged, indebted, under an obligation **MW** VI.vi.54 [Fenton to Host] *So shall I evermore be bound to thee*; **Cym** III.v.49, IV.ii.46; **1H6** II.i.37, iv.128; **3H6** II.v.3; **TNK** V.ii.42

2 obliged, required, forced **RJ** I.ii.1 [Capulet to Paris] *Montague is bound as well as I, / In penalty alike*; **AC** II.v.114; **KL** III.vii.10

3 indentured, contracted **Tim** IV.i.10 [Timon alone] *Bound servants, steal*

4 ready, prepared **Ham** I.v.6 [Hamlet to Ghost] *Speak. I am bound to hear* [Ghost's response puns: sense 1]; **AW** II.i.114; **KL** III.vii.7

bound *(v.)* **1** limit, confine, submit **R2** V.ii.38 [York to Duchess of York, of Richard's fate] *heaven hath a hand in these events, / To whose high will we bound our calm contents*

2 contain, enclose, confine **KJ** II.i.431 [Hubert to King John and King Philip] *If love ambitious sought a match of birth, / Whose veins bound richer blood than Lady Blanche?*; **JC** IV.iii.219; **KJ** II.i.442; **TC** IV.v.129

3 determine, mark out, define **TNK** I.ii.103 [Palamon to Arcite] *our fate, / Who hath bounded our last minute* [i.e. decided how long we have to live]

4 bounce, rebound **AW** II.iii.295 [Parolles to Bertram, of his decision to go to the wars] *Why, these balls bound* [i.e. now you're playing a good game]; **R2** I.ii.58

bounded *(adj.)* confined, enclosed, operating within limits **TC** I.iii.111 [Ulysses to all] *the bounded waters / Should lift their bosoms higher than the shores*

bounden *(v.)* indebted, obliged, grateful **KJ** III.iii.29 [Hubert to King John] *I am much bounden to your majesty*; **AY** I.ii.275

bounding *(adj.)* limiting, containing, confining **Luc** 1119 [of a river] *Who, being stopped, the bounding bank o'erflows*

bounteous *(adj.)* open-hearted, full of warm feeling **Oth** III.iii.467 [Othello to Iago] *I greet thy love ... with acceptance bounteous*; **Ham** I.iii.93; **MM** V.i.440

bounteously *(adv.)* very well, liberally, generously **TN** I.ii.53 [Viola to Captain] *I'll pay thee bounteously*

bounty *(n.)* **1** great generosity, gracious liberality, munificence **RJ** II.ii.133 [Juliet to Romeo] *My bounty is as boundless as the sea, / My love as deep*; **AW** IV.iii.9; **E3** I.ii.148; **MV** III.iv.9; **Tim** II.ii.238; **WT** I.ii.113

2 special gift, present **AC** IV.vi.22 [Soldier to Enobarbus] *Antony / Hath after thee sent all thy treasure, with / His bounty overplus*; **TG** I.i.142

3 act of kindness, good turn **Per** II.i.144 [Pericles to Fishermen] *I'll pay your bounties*; **Tim** I.ii.121, II.ii.178, II.ii.80

bourn *(n.)* **1** frontier, destination, boundary **Ham** III.i.79 [Hamlet alone, of death] *from whose bourn / No traveller returns*; **AC** I.i.16; **KL** IV.vi.57; **Per** IV.iv.4; **TC** II.iii.246; **WT** I.ii.134

2 limit of property, land boundary **Tem** II.i.155 [Gonzalo to Alonso, of the imaginary commonwealth] *Contract, succession, / Bourn ... none*

bout *(n.)* **1** fight, round, contest **TN** III.iv.298 [Sir Toby to Sir Andrew, of Viola as Cesario] *The gentleman will ... have one bout with you*; **Ham** IV.vii.157; **1H6** I.v.4, III.i.56

2 round, turn of the floor, division of a dance **MA** II.i.77 [masked Don Pedro to masked Hero] *will you walk a bout with your friend?* [F *about*]; **RJ** I.v.18

bow *(n.)* **1** yoke **AY** III.iii.72 [Touchstone to Jaques] *the ox hath his bow*

2 bowman, archer **E3** IV.vi.14 [Prince Edward to Artois] *command our bows / To hurl away their pretty-coloured yew*

bow *(v.)* **1** make to bend, cause to bend **Cor** V.vi.25 [Aufidius to Conspirators, of Coriolanus' flattery] *to this end / He bowed his nature*; **H5** I.ii.14; **Per** IV.ii.83; **TNK** III.vi.226; **TS** II.i.150

2 retreat, yield, turn away **1H6** IV.v.29 [John Talbot to Talbot] *if I bow, they'll say it was for fear*

bow-back *(n.)* arched back **Venus** 619 [Venus to Adonis, of a boar] *On his bow-back he hath a battle set / Of bristly pikes*

bowed *(adj.)* bent, crooked **H8** II.iii.36 [Old Lady to Anne, of being a queen] *a threepence bowed would hire me*

bowels *(n.)* **1** depths, core, interior **TNK** V.i.164 [Emilia to all, of Diana] *from the bowels of her holy altar*

2 feelings, sensitivity, heart **TC** II.i.48 [Thersites to Ajax] *thou thing of no bowels*; **TC** II.ii.11

3 offspring, children **MM** III.i.29 [disguised Duke to Claudio] *thine own bowels, which do call thee sire*

bower *(n.)* arbour, leafy glade; or: lady's chamber, boudoir **Cor** III.ii.92 [Volumnia to Coriolanus] *I know thou hadst rather / Follow thine enemy in a fiery gulf / Than flatter him in a bower*

bower *(v.)* enclose, fence in **RJ** III.ii.81 [Juliet as if to Nature, of Romeo] *thou didst bower the spirit of a fiend / In mortal paradise of such sweet flesh*

bowget *(n.)* ☞ budget *(n.)*

bow hand (n.) hand which holds a bow LL IV.i.134 [Maria to Boyet, of his remark] *Wide o'the bow hand!* [i.e. shooting too far to one side; wide of the mark]

bowling, bowline (n.) [nautical] rope which keeps the edge of a sail steady TNK IV.i.147 [Gaoler's Daughter to all] *The wind's fair; top the bowling* ☛ SHIPS, p.397

box-tree type of ornamental thick shrub TN II.v.15 [Maria to all] *Get ye all three into the box-tree*

boy (n.) **1** fellow, rogue, wretch CE III.i.62 [Dromio of Syracuse to Adriana] *your town is troubled with unruly boys;* Cor V.vi.101 ☛ ADDRESS FORMS, p.8
2 servant, slave, menial TS Induction.i.12 [Sly alone, as if to the Hostess] *I'll not budge an inch, boy*
3 child 1H4 V.iv.75 [Falstaff to Prince Hal] *Nay, you shall find no boy's play here*

boy (v.) represent by a boy, reduce to a boy-actor level [boys played the female parts in Shakespeare's time] AC V.ii.220 [Cleopatra to Iras] *I shall see / Some squeaking Cleopatra boy my greatness*

boy-queller (n.) ☛ queller (n.)

brabble (n.) **1** brawl, noisy quarrel, fracas TN V.i.62 [First Officer to Orsino, of Antonio] *Here in the streets ... / In private brabble did we apprehend him;* Tit II.i.62
2 quibbling, nit-picking, noisy disputing H5 IV.viii.65 [Fluellen to Williams] *keep you out of prawls, and prabbles, and quarrels, and dissensions* MW IV.i.46 ☛ WELSH, p.649

brabbler (n.) braggart, brawler, quarreller KJ V.ii.162 [Lewis the Dauphin to and of Bastard] *We hold our time too precious to be spent / With such a brabbler*

brace (n.) **1** group of two, couple, pair RJ V.iii.295 [Prince to Capulet and Montague] *I ... / Have lost a brace of kinsmen;* Cor II.iii.60, III.i.243; 3H6 II.v.129; Tem V.i.126 ☛ NUMBERS, p.299
2 state of readiness, defence, preparation Oth I.iii.24 [First Senator to Duke, of Cyprus] *For that it stands not in such warlike brace [as Rhodes]*
3 cord, strap, thong E3 II.i.57 [King Edward to Lodowick] *bid the drummer learn ... the lute, / Or hang him in the braces of his drum*
4 armoured covering for the arms; or: coat of armour Per II.i.128 [Pericles to Fishermen, of his armour] *[my father] pointed to this brace* ☛ BODY-ARMOUR, p.48

braced (adj.) with tightened skin, stretched KJ V.ii.169 [Bastard to Lewis the Dauphin] *even at hand a drum is ready braced*

bracelet (n.) manacle, fetter, handcuff TNK II.v.8 [Gaoler's Daughter alone, of Palamon] *His iron bracelets are not off*

brach (n.) hound [which hunts by scent], bitch 1H4 III.i.230 [Hotspur to Lady Percy, of listening to a Welsh song] *I had rather hear Lady my brach howl in Irish;* KL I.iv.111, III.vi.68; TC II.i.113 [F, Q *brooch*]; TS Induction.i.16

brag (n.) boast, bragging claim Cym V.v.176 [Iachimo to Cymbeline] *our brags / Were cracked of kitchen-trulls*

brag (v.) talk with pride [about], sound off [about] TG IV.i.69 [Second Outlaw to Valentine] *Thou shalt not live to brag what we have offered;* Cym V.iii.93; RJ I.v.67

braggardism, braggartism (n.) bragging, boasting TG II.iv.162 [Proteus to Valentine] *what braggardism is this?* [F *bragadisme*]

bragged (adj.) bragging, boastful, vaunting Cor I.viii.12 [Aufidius to Martius] *Wert thou the Hector / That was the whip of your bragged progeny, / Thou shouldst not scape me here*

bragging (adj.) threatening, menacing, challenging KJ V.i.50 [Bastard to King John] *outface the brow / Of bragging horror*

bragless (adj.) without vain boast, without gloating TC V.ix.5 [Ajax to all, of Achilles' killing of Hector] *If it be so, yet bragless let it be; / Great Hector was a man as good as he*

braid (adj.) [unclear meaning] twisted, deceitful AW IV.ii.73 [Diana alone] *Frenchmen are so braid* [or: licentious; loose]

braid (v.) upbraid, reproach, disparage Per I.i.94 [Pericles to Antiochus, of the latter's sin] *'Twould braid yourself too near for me to tell it*

braided (adj.) plaited, woven, divided into locks Venus 271 [of Adonis' horse] *his braided hanging mane / Upon his compassed crest now stand on end*

brain (n.) (plural) witticisms, clever remarks MA V.iv.102 [Benedick to all] *if a man will be beaten with brains, 'a shall wear nothing handsome about him*

brain (v.) **1** understand, comprehend, grasp Cym V.iv.147 [Posthumus alone] *such stuff as madmen / Tongue, and brain not*
2 murder, dash the brains out of MM V.i.393 [Duke to Isabel, of Claudio] *It was the swift celerity of his death ... / That brained my purpose*

brained (adj.) furnished with a brain, addle-brained Tem III.ii.6 [Trinculo to Stephano, of the others on the island] *If th'other two be brained like us, the state totters*

brainish (adj.) deluded, distracted, deranged Ham IV.i.11 [Gertrude to Claudius, of Hamlet] *in this brainish apprehension kills / The unseen good old man*

brainsick, brain-sick (adj.) **1** mad, foolish, frantic Luc 175 [of fear] *Beaten away by brain-sick rude desire*
2 foolish, addle-headed 1H6 IV.i.111 [King to all] *what madness rules in brainsick men*

brain-sickly (adv.) foolishly, in such an addle-headed way Mac II.ii.46 [Lady Macbeth to Macbeth] *You do unbend your noble strength, to think / So brain-sickly of things*

brake (n.) **1** bush, thicket MND II.i.227 [Demetrius to Helena] *I'll run from thee and hide me in the brakes;* 3H6 III.i.1; H8 I.ii.75; PassP IX.10; TNK III.i.1; Venus 237, 876
2 entanglement, snare, restriction MM II.i.39 [Escalus to Angelo] *Some run from brakes of office* [unclear meaning] [F *brakes of Ice*]

bran (n.) husk, inedible part of grain Cym IV.ii.27 [Belarius to himself] *Nature hath meal, and bran* [i.e. has both good and bad]

branch (n.) division, section, part [of an argument] CE V.i.106 [Abbess to Adriana] *It is a branch and parcel of mine oath;* Cym V.v.384; Ham V.i.11; LL I.i.21; MV II.ii.58

branched embroidered, brocaded TN II.v.46 [Malvolio to himself] *in my branched velvet gown*

branchless (adj.) maimed, disfigured, cut down AC III.iv.24 [Antony to Octavia] *better I were not yours / Than yours so branchless*

brand (n.) **1** ornamental flaming torch [associated with Cupid] Sonn 153.1 *Cupid laid by his brand and fell asleep;* Cym II.iv.91; Sonn 154.2
2 mark of infamy, stigma, disgrace Cor III.i.302 [Menenius to Sicinius, of Coriolanus' life] *to lose it by his country / Were to us ... / A brand to th'end o'th' world*

brand (v.) mark indelibly, make conspicuous AC IV.xiv.76 [Antony to Eros, of himself in Rome] *the wheeled seat / Of fortunate Caesar ... branded / His baseness that ensued*

brandish (v.) make shine, cause to flash 1H6 I.i.3 [Bedford to all, as if to comets] *Brandish your crystal tresses in the sky*

brass (n.) brazenness, effrontery, impudence LL V.ii.395 [Berowne to all] *Can any face of brass hold longer out?*

brass, braze (v.) harden (like brass) KL I.i.10 [Gloucester to Kent, of Edmund] *I have so often blushed to acknowledge him that now I am brazed to it;* Ham III.iv.38

brassy (adj.) hard as brass, unfeeling, impenetrable MV IV.i.31 [Duke to Shylock, of Antonio's losses] *Enow to ... pluck commiseration of his state / From brassy bosoms and rough hearts of flint*

brat (n.) child [not always with contemptuous connotation] 1H6 V.iv.84 [Richard to Pucelle] *Strumpet, thy words condemn thy brat and thee;* 3H6 I.iii.4, V.v.27; R3 I.iii.193, III.v.106; Tit V.i.28

brave *(n.)* boast, bravado, blustering threat **E3** I.i.115 [Lorraine to King Edward] *It is not … any English brave, / Afflicts me so;* **1H6** III.ii.123; **KJ** V.ii.159; **Tit** II.i.30; **TS** III.i.15

brave *(adj.)* **1** fine, excellent, splendid, impressive **Cor** II.ii.5 [First Officer to Second Officer, of Coriolanus] *That's a brave fellow* ➤ FEW, p.xxi

2 noble, worthy, excellent **JC** V.iii.80 [Titinius alone] *Why didst thou send me forth, brave Cassius?;* **AC** I.v.38; **Cor** IV.ii.38; **1H4** V.ii.86; **H8** IV.i.40; **Tit** IV.ii.135

3 audacious, daring, bold **2H6** IV.viii.19 [Cade to Buckingham and Clifford] *are ye so brave?;* **3H6** IV.i.96; **MV** III.iv.65

4 defiant, insolent, impudent **Cor** IV.v.18 [Second Servingman to Coriolanus] *Are you so brave?;* **Tit** II.i.45

brave *(v.)* **1** challenge, defy, confront, provoke **AC** IV.iv.5 [Antony to Eros] *If fortune be not ours today, it is / Because we brave her;* **E3** II.i.148; **2H6** IV.x.34; **R3** IV.iii.57; **Sonn** 12.14; **TS** IV.iii.109, 123 [also: sense 2]

2 make splendid, adorn, brighten up **R3** V.iii.280 [King Richard to Ratcliffe, of the sun] *He should have braved the east an hour ago;* **TS** IV.iii.123 [also: sense 1]

3 swagger, act boastfully, show off **Tit** II.i.26 [stage direction] *Enter Chiron and Demetrius braving;* **Tit** IV.ii.120

bravely *(adv.)* **1** splendidly, worthily, excellently **Cym** II.iv.73 [Iachimo to Posthumus, of Innogen's tapestry] *A piece of work / So bravely done;* **AY** III.iv.38; **H5** III.vi.72; **Mac** V.vi.36; **Tem** III.iii.84

2 showily, with great display, with a fine flourish **H5** IV.iii.69 [Salisbury to King Henry] *The French are bravely in their battles set;* **KJ** V.v.4; **MND** V.i.146; **Tit** IV.viii.112

3 in fine clothes, splendidly dressed **TS** I.ii.216 [stage direction] *Enter Tranio, bravely dressed as Lucentio;* **KL** IV.vi.198; **TS** IV.iii.54

bravery *(n.)* **1** finery, fine clothes, rich dress **E3** IV.vi.59 [Audley to Esquire, of Prince Edward] *in the crimson bravery of my blood / I may become him with saluting him;* **AY** II.vii.80; **TS** III.iii.57

2 splendour, fine display, ostentation **TNK** IV.ii.154 [Pirithous to Theseus] *There shall want no bravery;* **MM** I.iii.10; **Sonn** 34.4

3 display, manifestation, extravagance **Ham** V.ii.79 [Hamlet to Horatio, of Laertes] *the bravery of his grief*

4 bravado, show of daring, swaggering display **Oth** I.i.101 [Brabantio to Roderigo] *Upon malicious bravery dost thou come / To start my quiet* [Q; F *knauerie*]

5 defiant character, threatening appearance **Cym** III.i.19 [Queen to Cymbeline] *Remember … / The natural bravery of your isle*

braving *(adj.)* defiant, daring, boasting **R2** II.iii.111 [York to Bolingbroke] *here art come … / In braving arms against thy sovereign!;* **AW** II.i.3; **E3** IV.iv.15; **R2** II.iii.142

brawl *(n.)* type of French dance **LL** III.i.8 [Mote to Armado] *will you win your love with a French brawl?*

brawl *(v.)* **1** quarrel, squabble, contend **E3** II.ii.48 [King Edward to Lodowick, of the drum] *Poor sheepskin, how it brawls with him that beateth it!;* **2H4** I.iii.70; **TS** IV.i.192

2 [of streams] run noisily **AY** II.i.32 [First Lord to all] *an oak whose antick root peeps out / Upon the brook that brawls along this wood*

brawl down *(v.)* destroy with uproar, force down with clamour **KJ** II.i.383 [Bastard to King John and King Philip, of firing their cannon] *Till their soul-fearing clamours have brawled down / The flinty ribs of this contemptuous city*

brawling *(adj.)* clamorous, noisy, tumultuous **MM** IV.i.9 [Mariana to Boy, of the disguised Duke] *Here comes a man of comfort, whose advice / Hath often stilled my brawling discontent;* **RJ** I.i.176

brawn *(n.)* **1** muscle, fleshy part of the body **Cym** IV.ii.311 [Innogen alone, of the dead body she believes to be Posthumus] *The brawns of Hercules*

2 muscular arm, sturdy limb **Cor** IV.v.123 [Aufidius to Coriolanus] *I had purpose / Once more to hew thy target from thy brawn;* **TC** I.iii.297

3 fattened boar, stuffed pig [ready for eating] **2H4** I.i.19 [Lord Bardolph to Northumberland, of Falstaff] *Harry Monmouth's brawn*

brawn-buttock *(n.)* fleshy buttock, well-rounded bottom **AW** II.ii.17 [Clown to Countess, of his answer] *It is like a barber's chair that fits all buttocks … the brawn-buttock, or any buttock*

braze *(v.)* ➤ brass *(v.)*

brazen *(adj.)* **1** everlasting, imperishable, impenetrable **3H6** II.iii.40 [Edward to Warwick, praying] *Thy brazen gates of heaven may ope;* **3H6** II.iv.4; **LL** I.i.2

2 made of brass, very strong, powerful **Ham** I.i.73 [Marcellus to Horatio and Barnardo, of the activities in Denmark] *such daily cast of brazen cannon;* **E3** V.i.135; **2H6** III.ii.89

brazen-faced *(adj.)* shameless, unblushing, unabashed **KL** II.ii.25 [disguised Kent to Oswald] *What a brazen-faced varlet art thou*

brazier *(n.)* brass-worker **H8** V.iv.40 [Man to Porter, of a man] *he should be a brazier by his face*

breach *(n.)* **1** disregarding, breaking **Ham** I.iv.16 [Hamlet to Horatio, of Claudius' revels] *it is a custom / More honoured in the breach than the observance* ➤ before-breach *(n.)*

2 outbreak, uprising, insurrection **2H6** III.i.288 [Cardinal to all, of rebellion in Ireland] *A breach that craves a quick expedient stop!*

3 tear, gap, hole **KJ** IV.ii.32 [Pembroke to King John] *patches set upon a little breach / Discredit more in hiding of the fault / Than did the fault;* **TC** IV.v.245; **Venus** 1175

4 surf, breaking waves **TN** II.i.20 [Sebastian to Antonio] *you took me from the breach of the sea*

bread *(n.)* ➤ SWEARING, p.435

bread-chipper *(n.)* menial who cuts away the crust of a loaf **2H4** II.iv.310 [Prince Henry to Falstaff] *To dispraise me, and call me pantler, and bread-chipper* [Q; F *chopper*]

break *(v.)* **1** speak, exchange **MA** II.i.132 [masked Beatrice to masked Benedick, of Benedick] *he'll but break a comparison or two on me;* **CE** III.i.75

2 broach a matter, speak **MA** I.i.288 [Don Pedro to Claudio, of Hero] *I will break with her and with her father;* **H8** V.i.47; **JC** II.i.150; **MA** I.i.305, ii.14, II.i.142, 275, III.ii.68

3 [of jokes] crack, make **TC** I.iii.148 [Ulysses to all, of Patroclus] *the livelong day / Breaks scurril jests;* **MA** II.iii.229; **TS** IV.v.72

4 open, begin, get on with **Tit** V.iii.19 [Marcus to Lucius and Saturninus] *break the parle*

5 reveal, disclose, impart **H5** V.ii.242 [King Henry to Katherine] *break thy mind to me in broken English;* **AC** I.ii.178; **1H4** III.i.138; **1H6** I.iii.81; **TG** I.iii.44, III.i.59

6 break one's promise, not keep one's word **MW** III.i.50 [Slender to Ford, of Anne] *I would not break with her for more money than I'll speak of;* **Cor** IV.vi.49; **2H4** Epilogue.11; **MV** I.iii.133, III.i.105; **TNK** III.iii.45

7 interrupt, break in on, cut in on **MW** III.iv.22 [Shallow to Mistress Quickly, of Fenton and Anne] *Break their talk;* **AC** IV.xiv.31; **2H4** IV.v.70; **TC** III.i.50

8 crack, split, beat **CE** I.ii.79 [Antipholus of Syracuse to Dromio of Ephesus] *I shall break that merry sconce of yours;* **CE** II.ii.228; **1H4** III.i.231; **MW** I.i.116

9 burst, rupture **Ham** IV.iv.28 [Hamlet to Captain] *th'imposthume … / That inward breaks, and shows no cause without / Why the man dies;* **TNK** I.ii.73

10 wring, twist, squeeze **1H4** II.iii.90 [Lady Percy to Hotspur] *I'll break thy little finger, Harry*

11 graze, bruise, cut open **RJ** I.iii.39 [Nurse to Lady Capulet, of Juliet] *she broke her brow;* **AY** II.iv.54; **TS** II.i.142

12 disband, disperse, demobilize **AW** IV.iv.11 [Helena to Widow and Diana] *The army breaking, / My husband hies him home*

13 wane, fall away, fail **AY** V.iv.56 [Touchstone to Duke Senior] *as marriage binds and blood breaks*

14 wear out, exhaust **1H4** II.ii.13 [Falstaff, as if alone] *If I travel but four foot … I shall break my wind* [i.e. be out of breath]; **E3** II.ii.49

15 burst open, break through **Ham** IV.v.113 [Claudius to all] *The doors are broke;* **E3** IV.v.58

16 escape, break free, get away **R2** II.i.281 [Northumberland to Ross and Willoughby] *The son of Richard Earl of Arundel / That late broke from the Duke of Exeter;* **Luc** 1270

17 fail to keep, default on **MV** I.iii.160 [Shylock to Bassanio, of Antonio] *If he should break his day;* **AW** II.i.187

18 go bankrupt, become insolvent **Tim** IV.ii.5 [First Servant to Flavius, of Timon's household] *Such a house broke!;* **RJ** III.i.57; **Venus** 336

19 train, discipline, mould **TS** II.i.147 [Baptista to Hortensio as Licio, of Katherina] *thou canst not break her to the lute;* **CE** III.i.77

break in (*v.*) burst in, enter abruptly **2H6** I.iv.40 [stage direction] *Enter the Duke of York and the Duke of Buckingham ... and break in*

break off (*v.*) **1** bring to an end, relieve **3H6** III.iii.39 [Lewis to Queen] *with patience calm the storm, / While we bethink a means to break it off*
2 stop talking, finish a discussion **2H6** III.i.325 [Cardinal to all] *And so break off, the day is almost spent;* **2H6** II.ii.77

break out (*v.*) rush out, come out **TNK** III.v.19 [Schoolmaster to all, of the Duke] *then do you ... / Break comely out before him;* **KJ** IV.ii.101, V.vi.24; **TC** V.ii.52

break up (*v.*) **1** break, open [a seal] **WT** III.ii.130 [Leontes to Officer] *Break up the seals and read;* **MW** II.iv.10
2 burst open, break through **1H6** I.iii.13 [Gloucester to his men, of the Tower] *Break up the gates*
3 break out of, rise up from **2H6** I.iv.18 [Bolingbroke to Duchess, of the middle of the night] *The time when ... ghosts break up their graves*
4 cut up, carve **LL** IV.i.59 [Princess to Boyet, of a sealed letter] *you can carve - / Break up this capon*

breaking (*n.*) bankruptcy, insolvency **Tim** V.i.9 [Poet to Painter, of Timon] *Then this breaking of his has been but a try for his friends?*

break-neck (*n.*) total ruin, destruction, disaster **WT** I.ii.363 [Camillo to himself, of poisoning Polixenes] *to do't or no is certain / To me a break-neck*

break-promise (*n.*) promise-breaker **AY** IV.i.178 [Rosalind as Ganymede to Orlando] *I will think you the most pathetical break-promise*

break-vow (*n.*) breaker of promises **KJ** II.i.569 [Bastard alone, of commodity] *That daily break-vow*

breast (*n.*) **1** singing voice, pair of lungs **TN** II.iii.18 [Sir Andrew to Sir Toby, of Feste] *the fool has an excellent breast*
2 heart **Mac** IV.iii.113 [Macduff to Malcolm] *O my breast, / Thy hope ends here!*

breath (*n.*) **1** utterance, speech, voice **MA** V.i.250 [Leonato to Borachio, of Hero] *Art thou the slave that with thy breath hast killed / Mine innocent child?;* **AW** II.i.148; **1H6** V.v.7; **Mac** V.iii.27; **MV** II.ix.90; **Tem** V.i.157
2 voice, song, sound **MND** II.i.151 [Oberon to Puck, of a mermaid] *Uttering such dulcet and harmonious breath;* **TN** II.iii.52
3 suggestion, persuasion, judgement **Tim** IV.iii.250 [Timon to Apemantus, reacting to the notion that he should want to die] *Not by his breath that is more miserable*
4 life, spirit, living and breathing existence **WT** V.i.83 [Paulina to Leontes, of when he may marry again] *That / Shall be when your first queen's again in breath;* **Per** II.i.6; **RJ** V.iii.229; **Tim** I.ii.46
5 vigour, spirit, energy **Ham** V.ii.265 [Claudius to all] *The King shall drink to Hamlet's better breath* [i.e. power of breathing]
6 easy breathing, power to breathe **CE** IV.i.57 [Antipholus of Ephesus to Angelo] *now you run this humour out of breath* [i.e. you go too far]
7 breathing-space, respite **R3** IV.ii.24 [Buckingham to King Richard] *Give me some little breath, some pause;* **KJ** III.iv.134; **TC** II.iii.111

8 breather, exercising, breath of fresh air **TC** II.iii.111 [Patroclus to Agamemnon, of the visit] *for your health and your digestion sake, / An after-dinner's breath;* **TC** IV.v.92

breathe (*v.*) **1** speak, utter, talk **R2** III.iv.82 [Gardener to Queen Isabel] *Little joy have I / To breathe this news;* **Ham** I.iii.130; **1H4** I.i.3; **KJ** IV.ii.36; **R2** I.i.173; **Tim** V.iii.7
2 catch breath, pause, rest **Cor** I.vi.1 [Cominius to Soldiers] *Breathe you, my friends;* **E3** III.iv.16, V.i.239; **1H4** V.iv.14, 46; **3H6** I.ii.13, iv.108, II.iii.2, vi.31, V.iii.16
3 allow to breathe, rest **2H4** I.i.38 [Travers to Northumberland] *A gentleman ... / That stopped by me to breathe his bloodied horse;* **TS** Induction.i.15
4 exercise, exhaust, tire out **AW** II.iii.253 [Lafew to Parolles] *thou wast created for men to breathe themselves upon thee*

breathe out (*v.*) speak, utter **3H6** I.iv.43 [Clifford to York] *So desperate thieves ... / Breathe out invectives 'gainst the officers*

breathed (*adj.*) strong-winded, well-exercised **TS** Induction.ii.47 [First Servingman to Sly] *thy greyhounds are as swift / As breathed stags;* **LL** V.ii.651; **Tim** I.i.10 ☛ **well-breathed** (*adj.*)

breathed (*adv.*) exercised, extended, exerted **AY** I.ii.205 [Orlando to Duke Frederick] *I am not yet well breathed;* **AC** III.xiii.177

breather (*n.*) **1** living being, creature, man alive **AY** III.ii.272 [Orlando to Jaques] *I will chide no breather in the world but myself;* **Sonn** 81.12
2 speaker, utterer **MM** IV.iv.26 [Angelo alone, of his authority] *That no particular scandal once can touch / But it confounds the breather*

breathing (*n.*) **1** words, utterance, expression **AC** I.iii.14 [Antony to Cleopatra] *I am sorry to give breathing to my purpose*
2 delay, interval, pause **Luc** 1720 [of Lucrece] *after many accents and delays, / Untimely breathings, sick and short assays;* **MA** II.i.336
3 exercise, exertion, active employment **AW** I.ii.17 [Second Lord to King, of the gentry] *who are sick / For breathing and exploit;* **Per** II.iii.100
4 blowing, exhalation, blast **Cym** I.iv.36 [Innogen to Pisanio, of Cymbeline's anger] *like the tyrannous breathing of the north*

breathing (*adj.*) **1** verbal, word-of-mouth **MV** V.i.141 [Portia to Antonio] *I scant this breathing courtesy*
2 living, active, lively **R3** I.i.21 [Richard alone, of himself] *sent before my time / Into this breathing world;* **KJ** II.i.419
3 exercise **Ham** V.ii.171 [Hamlet to Osric] *it is the breathing time of the day with me* [i.e. time for exercise]

breathing while (*n.*) breathing-space, short space of time **R3** I.iii.60 [Richard to all] *His royal grace ... / Cannot be quiet scarce a breathing while;* **Venus** 1142

breathless (*adj.*) lifeless, dead **2H6** III.ii.132 [King to Warwick, of Gloucester] *view his breathless corpse*

breech (*n.*) **1** breeches, trousers [representing the authority of the husband] **3H6** V.v.24 [Richard to Queen] *That you might ... ne'er have stolen the breech from Lancaster;* **2H6** I.iii.144
2 buttocks, behind **TNK** II.ii.47 [Second Countryman to the others] *All the boys in Athens / Blow wind i'th' breech on's!* [or: sense 1]
3 ☛ blow wind in the breech

breech (*v.*) **1** flog, whip on the behind **MW** IV.i.73 [Evans to William] *If you forget your quis, your quaes, and your quods, you must be preeches [mistake for 'breeched']* ☛ **WELSH**, p.649
2 cover [as if with breeches] **Mac** II.iii.113 [Macbeth to all, of the King's attendants] *their daggers / Unmannerly breeched with gore*

breeching (*adj.*) subject to be flogged; novice, beginner **TS** III.i.18 [Bianca to Hortensio as Licio and Lucentio as Cambio] *I am no breeching scholar in the schools*

breed (*n.*) **1** lineage, inheritance, stock **Cym** IV.ii.25 [Belarius to himself, of Arviragus] *breed of greatness!;* **JC** I.ii.150; **Mac** IV.iii.108; **R2** II.i.45
2 children, offspring **Sonn** 12.14 *nothing 'gainst Time's scythe can make defence / Save breed to brave him, when he takes thee thence*

3 sort, kind, type **Ham** III.ii.323 [Guildenstern to Hamlet, of Hamlet's response] *this courtesy is not of the right breed;* **LL** V.ii.266; **MV** I.iii.131

breed (*v.*), past form **bred 1** raise, bring up, support **AY** I.i.4 [Orlando to Adam, of his father] *charged my brother on his blessing to breed me well;* **Cym** I.i.42, II.iii.113; **WT** III.iii.47

2 cherish, nurture, bring into existence **Sonn** 112.13 *You are so strongly in my purpose bred*

3 develop, go on, happen **WT** I.ii.374 [Polixenes to Camillo, of Leontes] *what is breeding / That changes thus his manners*

4 increase, grow, multiply **1H6** III.i.196 [Exeter alone, of the peers' agreement] *So will this base and envious discord breed*

breed out (*v.*) exhaust through breeding, become degenerate **H5** III.v.29 [Dauphin to all] *Our madams mock at us, and plainly say / Our mettle is bred out;* **Tim** I.i.254

breed-bate (*n.*) trouble-maker, one who makes mischief **MW** I.iv.12 [Mistress Quickly to herself, of Rugby] *no tell-tale, nor no breed-bate* ☛ *bate-breeding* (*adj.*)

breeder (*n.*) **1** father, source, originator, author **3H6** III.iii.43 [Queen to Lewis, of Warwick] *see where comes the breeder of my sorrow!;* **TNK** Prologue.10

2 child-bearer, female **3H6** II.i.42 [Richard to Edward] *You love the breeder better than the male*

breeding (*n.*) **1** raising, upbringing **AW** II.iii.113 [Bertram to King, of Helena] *She had her breeding at my father's charge;* **AY** III.ii.28; **Ham** V.i.90; **H8** IV.iii.134; **KL** I.i.8; **WT** IV.iv.577

2 education, proper training **Cym** IV.iv.26 [Belarius to and of Arviragus and Guiderius] *Who find in my exile the want of breeding* [i.e. lack of a good education]

3 ancestry, parentage, noble lineage **2H4** V.iii.107 [Shallow to Pistol] *I know not your breeding;* **Cym** V.iii.17; **WT** IV.iv.714

breese, breeze (*n.*) gadfly **TC** I.iii.48 [Nestor to Agamemnon] *The herd hath more annoyance by the breese / Than by the tiger;* **AC** III.x.14

brew (*v.*) dilute, water down **TC** IV.iv.7 [Cressida to Pandarus, of her affection] *If I could ... brew it to a weak and colder palate*

brewage (*n.*) [drink] brew, concoction, mixture **MW** III.v.29 [Falstaff to Bardolph] *I'll no pullet-sperm in my brewage*

brewed (*adj.*) matured, made up, ready to appear **Mac** II.iii.120 [Donalbain to Malcolm] *Our tears are not yet brewed*

brew-house (*n.*) outhouse used for brewing liquor **MW** III.iii.9 [Mistress Ford to John and Robert] *be ready here hard by in the brew-house*

briar (*n.*) thorn, prickly branch **AY** I.iii.12 [Rosalind to Celia] *O, how full of briars is this working-day world!;* **TNK** II.i.197

bribed (*adj.*) stolen, thieved, poached **MW** V.v.24 [Falstaff to Mistress Ford and Mistress Page] *Divide me like a bribed buck, each a haunch*

briber (*n.*) price paid, incentive, inducement **Tim** III.v.62 [Alcibiades to Second Senator, of his friend] *His service done / At Lacedaemon and Byzantium / Were a sufficient briber for his life*

bridal (*n.*) wedding, marriage **Oth** III.iv.146 [Desdemona to Emilia] *we must think men are not gods, / Nor of them look for such observancy / As fits the bridal*

bride (*n.*) bridegroom, spouse **RJ** III.v.145 [Capulet to Lady Capulet, of Paris and Juliet] *we have wrought / So worthy a gentleman to be her bride*

bride (*v.*) **1** marry, wed **TNK** V.i.109 [Palamon praying to Venus] *I knew a man / Of eighty winters ... who / A lass of fourteen brided*

2 play the bride **TS** III.ii.250 [Tranio as Lucentio to all] *Shall sweet Bianca practise how to bride it?*

bride-habited (*adj.*) dressed as a bride **TNK** V.i.150 [Emilia praying to Diana] *I am bride-habited, / But maiden-hearted*

bridehouse (*n.*) house where a wedding is held **TNK** I.i.22 [Boy singing of birds] *May [not] on our bridehouse perch or sing*

bridle (*v.*) curb, restrain, keep control of **3H6** IV.iv.19 [Lady Grey to Rivers, of her unborn child] *This is it that makes me bridle passion*

brief (*n.*) **1** summary, short account **AW** V.iii.137 [Gentleman to King, of Diana's letter] *she told me, / In a sweet verbal brief, it did concern / Your highness with herself* **AC** V.iii.138; **KJ** II.i.103; **MND** V.i.42

2 summary; contract **AW** II.iii.178 [King to Bertram, of Bertram's marriage] *whose ceremony / Shall seem expedient on the now-born brief* [unclear meaning]

3 letter, dispatch, message **1H4** IV.iv.1 [Archbishop to Sir Michael] *bear this sealed brief ... to the Lord Marshal*

4 epitome, embodiment **E3** II.i.82 [King Edward to Lodowick] *[write] To one ... / Whose body is an abstract or a brief, / Contains each general virtue;* **KJ** II.i.103

brief (*adj.*) **1** quick, speedy, swift, expeditious **KL** V.iii.243 [Edmund to Albany] *Quickly send - / Be brief in it - to the castle;* **AC** IV.xv.90; **R3** II.i.43, IV.iii.57; **TS** III.i.65

2 [unclear meaning] rife, widespread; pressing, urgent **KJ** IV.iii.152 [Bastard to Hubert] *A thousand businesses are brief in hand*

brief (*adv.*) **1** in short, briefly, in sum **Per** III.Chorus.39 [Gower alone, of Pericles] *Brief, he must .. depart to Tyre;* **AY** IV.iii.151; **TNK** V.i.118

2 hurriedly, rapidly, in a rush **RJ** III.iii.174 [Romeo to Friar, of going to Juliet] *But that a joy past joy calls out on me, / It were a grief so brief to part with thee*

brief, in quickly, speedily, expeditiously **TG** I.i.126 [Proteus to Speed] *open the matter in brief*

brief and the long / tedious, the the long and the short **AW** II.iii.28 [Parolles to Lafew, of the King's cure] *'tis very strange, that is the brief and the tedious of it;* **H5** III.ii.114

briefly (*adv.*) **1** quickly, soon, in a moment **Per** III.Chorus.12 [Gower alone] *time that is so briefly spent;* **AC** IV.iv.10; **Cym** V.v.106; **Per** III.i.53

2 a little while ago, a short time past **Cor** I.vi.16 [Cominius to Messenger] *briefly we heard their drums*

briefness (*n.*) speedy action, promptness **Per** V.ii.15 [Gower alone] *In feathered briefness sails are filled;* **KL** II.i.18

brim (*n.*) edge, border, margin **Tem** IV.i.64 [Iris to Ceres] *Thy banks with pioned and twilled brims*

brimmed (*adj.*) filled to the brim, brimful **TNK** V.i.47 [Arcite to his knights] *a cistern / Brimmed with the blood of men*

brinded (*adj.*) streaked, striped, tabby **Mac** IV.i.1 [First Witch to Witches] *Thrice the brinded cat hath mewed*

brine (*n.*) **1** salt water [i.e. tears] **Luc** 796 [Lucrece to herself] *I ... must sit and pine, / Seasoning the earth with showers of silver brine;* **Lover** 17; **RJ** II.iii.65; **TN** I.i.31; **TNK** I.iii.22, III.ii.28

2 sea water, sea **Tem** III.ii.66 [Caliban to Stephano, of Trinculo] *He shall drink naught but brine;* **Tem** I.ii.211

brine-pit (*n.*) salt-pit **Tem** I.ii.338 [Caliban to Prospero, of the island] *The fresh springs, brine-pits, barren place and fertile*

bring (*v.*) **1** accompany, conduct, escort **R2** I.iii.304 [John of Gaunt to Bolingbroke] *I'll bring thee on thy way;* **AC** III.xii.25; **JC** III.ii.49; **MA** III.ii.3; **MM** I.i.61; **TG** I.i.55

2 lead, go, conduct [someone] **TNK** I.v.11 [Third Queen to her dead husband] *This funeral path brings to your household's grave*

3 persuade, induce, cause **TNK** IV.iii.93 [Doctor to Wooer, of their plan for the Gaoler's Daughter] *This may bring her to eat*

4 train, bring up, rear **TNK** V.ii.54 [Gaoler to Gaoler's Daughter, of her horse] *Having these virtues, / I think he might be brought to play at tennis*

5 bring forth, give birth to **WT** II.i.148 [Antigonus to Leontes] *I have three daughters ... Fourteen they shall not see / To bring false generations;* **Sonn** 32.11

6 inform, report, tell **AC** IV.xiii.10 [Cleopatra to Mardian, of Antony] *bring me how he takes my death to the monument;* **Ham** V.ii.192

7 derive, receive, acquire 1H6 II.v.77 [Mortimer to Richard, of Lionel] *he / From John of Gaunt doth bring his pedigree*

bring about (*v.*) complete, bring the end to [a period of time] 3H6 II.v.27 [King alone] *How many hours brings about the day;* R2 I.iii.220

bring away (*v.*) fetch, bring along KL II.ii.137 [Cornwall to his attendants] *Come, bring away the stocks*

bring down (*v.*) reduce, lower Tim IV.iii.87 [Timon to Timan-dra] *bring down rose-cheeked youth / To the tub-fast and the diet*

bring forth (*v.*) **1** express, utter, voice TC I.iii.242 [Aeneas to Agamemnon] *The worthiness of praise distains his worth / If that he praised himself bring the praise forth*
2 put on display, set up in public AC V.ii.219 [Cleopatra to Iras] *Antony / Shall be brought drunken forth*

bring in (*v.*) **1** reinstate, appoint to a position Oth III.iii.74 [Desdemona to Othello, of Cassio] *to have so much to do / To bring him in?*
2 tavern call for food and drink 1H4 I.ii.36 [Prince Hal to Falstaff] *a purse of gold ... spent with crying 'Bring in!'*

bring off (*v.*) rescue, save, deliver TNK I.iii.41 [Hippolyta to Emilia, of Theseus and Pirithous] *Yet fate hath brought them off;* H8 III.ii.220; TC V.vi.25

bring out (*v.*) **1** deprive, divest, dispossess AW V.ii.46 [Parolles to Lafew] *bring me in some grace, for you did bring me out;* AW V.ii.49
2 ☞ STAGE DIRECTIONS, p.417

bring up (*v.*) raise, breed, rear AW IV.iv.19 [Helena to Widow] *heaven / Hath brought me up to be your daughter's dower*

bringing-forth (*n.*) achievement, accomplishment, public deed MM III.ii.136 [disguised Duke to Lucio, of the Duke] *Let him be but testimonied in his own bringings-forth*

bringing up (*n.*) upbringing, breeding 1H4 II.iv.483 [Falstaff to Prince Hal] *If I become not a cart as well as another man, a plague on my bringing up!* [also: being summonsed]

brinish (*adj.*) salt, bitter 3H6 III.i.41 [King to himself, of the Queen] *To hear and see ... / her brinish tears;* Lover 284; Luc 1213; Tit III.i.97

brisk (*adv.*) sprucely, smartly, finely dressed 1H4 I.iii.53 [Hotspur to all, of a lord] *he made me mad / To see him shine so brisk*

brisky (*adj.*) brisk, lively, sprightly MND III.i.88 [Flute as Thisbe, of Pyramus] *Most brisky juvenal*

Britain (*n.*) Breton, person from Brittany R3 V.iii.334 [King Richard to his army, of the enemy] *these bastard Britains;* R3 V.iii.318

Britain (*adj.*) living in Brittany, from Brittany R3 IV.iv.521 [Fourth Messenger to King Richard] *The Britain navy is dispersed by tempest;* R3 IV.iii.40

Brittaine (*n.*) ☞ WORLD, p.634

broach (*v.*) **1** start, bring out, open up AC I.ii.174 [Enobarbus to Antony] *the business you have broached here cannot be without you;* AC I.ii.172; 3H6 II.ii.159
2 raise, introduce into conversation H8 II.iv.149 [Wolsey to King Henry, of the divorce] *whether ever I / Did broach this business to your highness;* TS I.ii.83
3 draw out, set flowing, cause to spurt out [by piercing] 3H6 II.iii.16 [Richard to Warwick] *Thy brother's blood the thirsty earth hath drunk, / Broached with the steely point of Clifford's lance;* 1H6 III.iv.40; 2H6 IV.x.36; Tim II.ii.182
4 pierce, impale, spit Tit IV.ii.84 [Demetrius to Aaron, of Aaron's baby] *I'll broach the tadpole on my rapier's point* H5 V.Chorus.32; MND V.i.146; TNK I.iii.20

broached (*adj.*) newly begun, freshly started 1H4 V.i.21 [King Henry to Worcester, of the latter's standing] *a portent / Of broached mischief to the unborn times*

broad (*adj.*) **1** widespread, far-reaching, widely diffused Mac III.iv.22 [Macbeth to First Murderer, of Fleance's escape] *I'had else been ... / As broad and general as the casing air*
2 unrestrained, free, boisterous Ham III.iv.2 [Polonius to Gertrude, of Hamlet] *his pranks have been too broad to bear with*
3 plain, candid, frank Mac III.vi.21 [Lennox to Lord] *from broad words ... / Macduff lives in disgrace*
4 high and mighty, arrogant TC I.iii.190 [Nestor to all] *Ajax ... bears his head / In such a rein, in full as proud a place / As broad Achilles*
5 plain, evident, obvious RJ II.iv.84 [Romeo to Mercutio, responding to 'an ell broad'] *I stretch it out for that word 'broad', which, added to the goose, proves thee far and wide a broad goose*

broad (*adv.*) **1** completely, fully Ham III.iii.81 [Hamlet to himself, of his father] *With all his crimes broad blown* [i.e. in full bloom]; Tit II.ii.17
2 plainly, candidly, freely Tim III.iv.64 [Second Varro's Servant to First Varro's Servant] *Who can speak broader than he that has no house to put his head in?*

broad-fronted (*adj.*) with a broad forehead or face AC I.v.29 [Cleopatra to Charmian, as if to Julius Caesar] *Broad-fronted Caesar*

brock (*n.*) badger; [contemptuous] stinker, dirty rat TN II.v.102 [Sir Toby as if to Malvolio] *hang thee, brock!*

brogue (*n.*) poor person's roughly made shoe Cym IV.ii.214 [Arviragus to Belarius and Guiderius] *I ... put / My clouted brogues from off my feet*

broil (*n.*) **1** turmoil, confused fighting, battle Cor III.i.33 [Sicinius to Coriolanus] *Stop, / Or all will fall in broil;* E3 IV.iv.128; 1H6 I.i.53; 3H6 V.v.1; Mac I.ii.6; Oth I.iii.87
2 quarrel, row, disturbance 1H6 III.i.92 [Gloucester to his servants] *leave this peevish broil;* 2H6 IV.viii.43; KL V.i.30; R3 I.iv.60

broil (*v.*) **1** subject to great heat; also: be engaged in a struggle H8 IV.i.56 [First Gentleman to Third Gentleman] *Where have you been broiling?*
2 bask, glow, warm [from] TC I.iii.379 [Ulysses to Nestor, of praising Ajax] *that will physic the great Myrmidon [Achilles], / Who broils in loud applause*

broke (*v.*) bargain, negotiate, trade AW III.v.70 [Widow to Helena, of Bertram] *He ... brokes with all that can ... / Corrupt the tender honour of a maid*

broken (*adj.*) **1** disjointed, fragmentary, disconnected WT V.ii.9 [First Gentleman to Autolycus, of the events in court] *I make a broken delivery of the business;* H5 V.ii.243; TC IV.iv.47; TNK IV.iii.6
2 interrupted, disturbed, disrupted H8 I.iv.61 [Wolsey to all] *You have now a broken banquet*
3 fragmentary, left-over KL II.ii.13 [disguised Kent to Oswald, describing him] *an eater of broken meats*
4 fallen out, with the relationship in pieces TG II.v.17 [Speed to Launce, of Proteus and Julia] *are they broken?*
5 bankrupt, ruined, insolvent Cym V.iv.19 [Posthumus to Gaolers] *I know you are more clement than vile men, / Who of their broken debtors take a third*
6 broken in [as a horse]; or: in pieces [as of teeth] AW II.iii.59 [Lafew to Parolles, of the Lords] *I'd give bay curtal and his furniture / My mouth no more were broken than these boys'* [i.e. if I were as young as them]
7 arranged for different groups of instruments TC III.i.49 [Pandarus to Paris] *here is good broken music;* AY II.ii.131; H5 V.ii.240

broker, broker-between (*n.*) go-between, intermediary, agent TG I.ii.41 [Julia to Lucetta, of Lucetta delivering Proteus' letter] *a goodly broker!;* Ham I.iii.127; 2H6 I.ii.101; 3H6 IV.i.63; KJ II.i.568; Lover 173

broker-lackey (*n.*) abject go-between, pander [sic] TC V.x.33 [Troilus to Pandarus] *Hence, broker-lackey!*

broking *(adj.)* acting as a broker, bargain-dealing **R2** II.i.293 [Northumberland to Ross and Willoughby] *we shall … / Redeem from broking pawn the blemished crown*

brooch *(n.)* jewel, ornament **R2** V.v.66 [Richard alone] *love to Richard / Is a strange brooch in this all-hating world;* **Ham** IV.vii.92; **LL** V.ii.614; **TC** II.i.113

brooch *(v.)* adorn, beautify, display as an ornament **AC** IV.xv.25 [Cleopatra to Antony] *Not th'imperious show / Of the full-fortuned Caesar ever shall / Be brooched with me*

brood *(n.)* children, offspring **Tem** III.i.106 [Caliban to Stephano, of Miranda] *She will … bring thee forth brave brood;* **2H4** III.ii.82

brooded *(adj.)* [unclear meaning] full of brooding **KJ** III.iii.52 [King John to Hubert] *in despite of brooded watchful day, / I would into thy bosom pour my thoughts*

brood, on brooding, moping **Ham** III.i.166 [Claudius to Polonius, of Hamlet] *his melancholy sits on brood*

brook *(v.)* **1** endure, tolerate, put up with **R3** I.i.125 [Richard to Hastings] *How hath your lordship brooked imprisonment?;* **AY** I.i.125; **1H4** V.iv.65; **1H6** IV.i.74; **3H6** V.vi.27; **TG** V.iii.4
2 allow, permit, bear **2H6** I.i.168 [Cardinal to all] *This weighty business will not brook delay;* **1H4** IV.i.62; **H5** V.Chorus.44; **2H6** V.i.110; **TS** I.i.114
3 enjoy, find, feel about **R2** III.ii.2 [Aumerle to King Richard] *How brooks your grace the air*

broom-grove *(n.)* grove of broom [a yellow-flowered shrub] **Tem** IV.i.66 [Iris to Ceres] *thy broomgroves, / Whose shadow the dismissed bachelor loves*

broomstaff *(n.)* broomstick **H8** V.iv.54 [Man to Porter, of the attacking apprentices] *they came to th'broomstaff to me* [i.e. fought at close quarters]

brother *(n.)* **1** kinsman, relative, relation **AC** III.ii.1 [Agrippa to Enobarbus, of Antony and Caesar] *What, are the brothers parted?;* **1H6** I.iii.40 ☞ FAMILY, p.168
2 equal, fellow, peer **KL** V.iii.62 [Albany to Edmund] *I hold you but a subject of this war, / Not as a brother;* **KL** V.iii.67
3 fellow-councillor, close adviser **H8** V.i.106 [King Henry to Cranmer] *You a brother of us, / It fits we thus proceed*

brother, second younger son **2H4** II.ii.63 [Poins to Prince Henry] *The worst that they can say of me is that I am a second brother* [i.e. who has to make his own way in the world]

brother, sworn companion-in-arms, devoted friend **H5** II.i.11 [Bardolph to Nym, of them and Pistol] *we'll be all three sworn brothers to France;* **Cor** II.iii.95; **2H4** III.ii.310; **H5** III.ii.44; **MA** I.i.67; **R2** V.i.20

brotherhood *(n.)* guild, fraternity, society **TC** I.iii.104 [Ulysses to all] *communities, / Degrees in schools, and brotherhoods in cities*

brought abed / to bed ☞ abed / to bed, brought

brow *(n.)* **1** appearance, aspect, countenance **Ham** I.ii.4 [Claudius to his court] *our whole kingdom / To be contracted in one brow of woe* ☞ FEW, p.xxi
2 bold front, confidence, effrontery **KJ** V.i.49 [Bastard to King John] *outface the brow / Of bragging horror*
3 eyebrow **RJ** V.i.39 [Romeo alone, of an apothecary] *with overwhelming brows;* **AW** I.i.93; **E3** II.ii.19; **1H4** I.iii.18; **H5** III.i.11; **3H6** V.ii.22
4 forehead [often plural, referring to the two prominences of the forehead] **R3** V.v.6 [Derby to Richmond, of the crown] *to grace thy brows withal;* **LL** V.ii.392; **Per** V.i.108; **R3** I.i.5; **WT** I.ii.119
5 height, peak, pinnacle **2H6** V.iii.4 [York to all, of Salisbury] *like a gallant in the brow of youth;* **KJ** II.i.38
6 overlooking shore, high-lying coast **Oth** II.i.53 [Fourth Gentleman to Montano] *on the brow o'th' sea / Stand ranks of people*

brow-bind *(v.)* wreathe around the brow **Cor** II.ii.96 [Cominius to all, of Coriolanus] *for his meed / Was brow-bound with the oak*

brown *(adj.)* **1** bronze-coloured, burnished **2H6** IV.x.11 [Cade alone] *many a time, but for a sallet, my brain-pan had been cleft with a brown bill*
2 brunette, brown-haired **TNK** III.iii.39 [Arcite to Palamon] *A pretty brown wench 'tis*
3 of dark complexion, sunburnt, burnished **TC** I.ii.94 [Pandarus to Cressida, of Troilus] *for a brown favour*

browny *(adj.)* brownish **Lover** 85 [of the man] *His browny locks did hang in crooked curls*

browse *(v.)* feed upon, nibble at, eat [as animals] **Cym** III.vii.11 [Guiderius to Belarius and Arviragus, of the cold meat] *we'll browse on that;* **AC** I.iv.66

bruise *(v.)* **1** squeeze, crush, put pressure on **H5** III.vi.120 [Montjoy as if French King to King Henry] *we thought not good to bruise an injury till it were full ripe* [or: hit back at a wrong]
2 crush, smash, destroy **Tim** III.v.4 [Second Senator to First Senator, of Alcibiades' friend] *The law shall bruise him;* **MM** II.i.6

bruising *(adj.)* crushing, damaging, crippling **R3** V.iii.111 [Richmond to God, praying for his forces] *Put in their hands Thy bruising irons of wrath*

bruit *(n.)* news, rumour, tidings **3H6** IV.vii.64 [Richard to Edward, of his being proclaimed king] *The bruit thereof will bring you many friends;* **TC** V.ix.4; **Tim** V.i.191

bruit *(v.)* report, announce, proclaim **Mac** V.vii.32 [Macduff to himself] *By this great clatter one of greatest note / Seems bruited;* **E3** III.i.9; **Ham** I.ii.127; **2H4** I.i.114; **1H6** II.iii.67

brunt *(n.)* shock, violence, ferocity **Cor** II.ii.98 [Cominius to all] *in the brunt of seventeen battles*

brush *(n.)* hostile meeting, collision, forceful encounter **Tim** IV.iii.265 [Timon to Apemantus, comparing his former associates to leaves] *have with one winter's brush / Fell from their boughs* [i.e. with a single storm]; **2H6** V.iii.3; **TC** V.iii.34

bubble *(n.)* empty thing, pretty sham, deceptive show **AW** III.vi.5 [First Lord to Bertram, of Parolles] *[he is] a bubble;* **AY** II.vii.153

bubukle, bubuncle *(n.)* [malapropism for 'bubo' and 'carbunkle'] inflamed swelling **H5** III.vi.99 [Fluellen to King Henry, of Bardolph] *his face is all bubukles*

buck *(n.)* laundry, quantity of soiled clothes **2H6** IV.ii.45 [Smith aside to his companions, of Cade's wife] *she washes bucks here at home* [bawdy pun: young men]; **MW** III.i.148

buck-basket *(n.)* basket for dirty laundry **MW** III.v.79 [Falstaff to Ford as Brook, of Mistress Page and Mistress Ford] *they conveyed me into a buck-basket;* **MW** III.iii.2, v.131, V.v.112

bucket *(n.)* beam, yoke [for hoisting or carrying] **2H4** III.ii.257 [Falstaff to Shallow, of Wart] *'A shall … come off and on swifter than he that gibbets on the brewer's bucket*

bucking *(n.)* washing, laundry **MW** III.iii.123 [Mistress Page to Mistress Ford, of Falstaff] *throw foul linen upon him, as if it were going to bucking*

buckle *(v.)* **1** prepare for battle, engage in warfare **E3** III.i.126 [King John to Philip] *thou hear'st what thund'ring terror 'tis / To buckle for a kingdom's sovereignty*
2 grapple, engage, fight at close quarters **1H6** I.ii.95 [Charles to Pucelle] *In single combat thou shalt buckle with me* [with bawdy pun]; **1H6** IV.iv.5, V.iii.28
3 hold together, fasten [as with a buckle] **TNK** I.iii.57 [Emilia to Hippolyta, of Theseus' and Pirithous' love] *More buckled with strong judgement*

buckle in *(v.)* enclose, limit, circumscribe **AY** III.ii.128 [Celia reading, of a man] *the stretching of a span / Buckles in his sum of age*

buckler *(n.)* small round shield **MA** V.ii.17 [Benedick to Margaret] *I give thee the bucklers* [i.e. I give in!]; **1H4** I.iii.227; **2H4** I.ii.1; **RJ** I.i.1 ☞ WEAPONS, p.491

buckler *(v.)* **1** exchange, grapple, couple; catch or ward off [blows] **3H6** I.iv.50 [Clifford to York] *I will … buckler with thee blows* [F; Q *buckle*]

2 shield, protect, defend **2H6** III.ii.216 [Warwick to Suffolk] *the guilt of murder bucklers thee;* **3H6** III.iii.99; **TS** III.ii.238

buckram, buckrom (*n./adj.*) **1** rough cloth, coarse linen **1H4** II.iv.188 [Falstaff to all, of the robbers] *two rogues in buckram suits* [and throughout the scene]; **1H4** I.ii.177
　2 stiff, starched, stuck-up **2H6** IV.vii.22 [Cade to Say] *thou buckram lord!*

buck-washing (*n.*) process of washing very dirty clothing in an alkaline mix [buck] **MW** III.iii.147 [Mistress Ford to Ford] *You were best meddle with buck-washing* [i.e. you are a fine person to interfere with this task]

bud out (*v.*) develop, spring forth, turn out **H8** I.i.94 [Norfolk to Buckingham, of the threat of division between England and France] *Which is budded out? / For France hath flawed the league*

budge, bodge (*v.*) **1** flinch, shrink, move away **Cor** I.vi.44 [Martius to Cominius, of the soldiers] *The mouse ne'er shunned the cat as they did budge / From rascals worse than they;* **1H4** II.iv.347
　2 give way, retreat **3H6** I.iv.19 [York alone] *we charged again: but, out, alas! / We budged again* [F *bodg'd*]; **JC** IV.iii.44

budger (*n.*) flincher, shrinker, mover away **Cor** I.viii.5 [Martius to Aufidius] *Let the first budger die the other's slave*

budget (*n.*) tool-bag, pouch **WT** IV.iii.20 [Autolycus singing] *If tinkers may have leave to live, / And bear the sow-skin budget* [F *bowget*]

buff (*n.*) [of a uniform] stout ox-hide leather **CE** IV.ii.36 [Dromio of Syracuse to Adriana, of the officer] *a fellow all in buff;* **CE** IV.ii.45

buff jerkin close-fitting jacket made of buff worn by constables and soldiers **1H4** I.ii.42 [Prince Hal to Falstaff] *is not a buff jerkin a most sweet robe of durance?* ➤ **jerkin** (*n.*)

buffet (*n.*) blow, stroke, knock **AC** I.iv.20 [Caesar to Lepidus, of Antony] *To … stand the buffet / With knaves that smells of sweat;* **1H4** II.iii.33

buffet (*v.*) **1** beat, strike, cuff **CE** II.ii.167 [Adriana to Dromio of Syracuse, of Antipholus of Syracuse] *thou didst return … / That he did buffet thee*
　2 fight, struggle, deal blows **H5** II.v.139 [King Henry to Katherine] *I might buffet for my love*
　3 beat back, contend with **JC** I.ii.107 [Cassius to Brutus, of the torrent] *we did buffet it / With lusty sinews*

bug (*n.*) **1** bogey, bugbear, imaginary terror **WT** III.ii.91 [Hermione to Leontes] *The bug which you would fright me with I seek;* **Ham** V.ii.22; **3H6** V.ii.2; **TS** I.ii.208
　2 object of terror, terrifying force **Cym** V.iii.51 [Posthumus to Lord, of the Britons] *are grown / The mortal bugs o'th' field* [also: sense 1]

bugbear (*n.*) hobgoblin, bogeyman **TC** IV.ii.33 [Pandarus to Cressida, of Troilus] *A bugbear take him!*

bugle (*adj.*) bead-like, beady, glittering **AY** III.v.47 [Rosalind as Ganymede to Phebe] *Your bugle eyeballs*

bugle-bracelet (*n.*) bracelet adorned with ornamental tube-shaped glass beads **WT** IV.iv.224 [Autolycus singing] *Bugle-bracelet, necklace-amber*

building (*n.*) **1** position, fixed place, location **Per** II.i.157 [Pericles to Fishermen, of his armour] *This jewel holds his building on my arm*
　2 build, construction **Sonn** 80.12 [of a rival poet] *I am a worthless boat, / He of tall building and of goodly pride*
　3 edifice, construction **TC** IV.ii.102 [Cressida to Pandarus] *the strong base and building of my love;* **Cor** I.i.192

bulk (*n.*) **1** body, trunk, frame **Ham** II.i.95 [Ophelia to Polonius, of Hamlet's sigh] *it did seem to shatter all his bulk;* **Luc** 467; **R3** I.iv.40; **TC** IV.iv.127
　2 weight, magnitude, capacity **MM** IV.iv.24 [Angelo alone] *my authority bears a credent bulk*

3 projecting part of a building, structure for displaying goods at the front of a shop **Oth** V.i.1 [Iago to Roderigo] *stand behind this bulk;* **Cor** II.i.202

bull-beef (*n.*) joint of beef [reputed to give strength] **1H6** I.ii.9 [Alençon to all, of the English] *They want their porridge and their fat bull-beeves*

bullet (*n.*) cannon-ball **KJ** II.i.227 [King John to Hubert] *instead of bullets wrapped in fire;* **KJ** II.i.412

bully (*n./adj.*) [especially as a warm form of address] fine fellow, good friend **MND** III.i.7 [Quince to Bottom] *What sayest thou, Bully Bottom?;* **H5** IV.i.48; **MND** IV.ii.18; **MW** I.ii.6, 11, II.iii.16, 26; **Tem** V.i.258 ➤ **ADDRESS FORMS**, p.8

bully rook (*n.*) merry comrade, good mate, old rogue **MW** I.iii.2 [Host to Falstaff] *What says my bully rook?;* **MW** II.i.180

bulwark (*n.*) **1** rampart, fortification **1H6** I.iv.67 [Glansdale to Salisbury, of where to mount the assault] *here, at the bulwark of the bridge;* **1H6** II.i.27
　2 shelter, safeguard, means of escape **H5** IV.i.160 [disguised King Henry to Williams, of soldiers] *some, making the wars their bulwark, that have before gored the gentle bosom of peace with pillage*

bum-baily, bum-bailiff (*n.*) bailiff, sheriff's officer [who catches people by sneaking up behind them] **TN** III.iv.174 [Sir Toby to Sir Andrew, of Viola as Cesario] *Scout me for him at the corner of the orchard like a bum-baily*

bumbard (*n.*) ➤ **bombard** (*n.*)

bumbast (*n.*) ➤ **bombast** (*n.*)

bunch-backed (*adj.*) hunch-backed **R3** I.iii.245 [Queen Margaret to Queen Elizabeth, of Richard] *this poisonous bunch-backed toad;* **R3** IV.iv.81

bung (*n.*) pickpocket; also: hole-stopper [penis] **2H4** II.iv.124 [Doll to Pistol] *you filthy bung, away!*

buoy up (*v.*) surge, swell, rise up **KL** III.vii.59 [Gloucester to Regan] *The sea … would have buoyed up / And quenched the stelled fires*

bur, burr (*n.*) **1** prickly, clinging seedpod **H5** V.ii.52 [Burgundy to King Henry and the French King] *nothing teems / But hateful docks, rough thistles, kecksies, burs* ➤ **PLANTS**, p.330
　2 [prickly, clinging seedpod] thing difficult to shake off **AY** I.iii.13 [Celia to Rosalind, of the briars] *They are but burs … thrown upon thee in holiday foolery*
　3 clinger, person difficult to shake off **TC** III.ii.109 [Pandarus to Troilus, of Cressida's kindred] *they are burs … they'll stick where they are thrown;* **MND** III.ii.260

burbolt (*n.*) ➤ **bird-bolt** (*n.*)

burden, burthen (*n.*) **1** refrain, chorus **AY** III.ii.240 [Celia to Rosalind] *I would sing my song without a burden;* **Tem** I.ii.380; **TG** I.ii.85; **TNK** IV.iii.11; **WT** IV.iv.196
　2 bass accompaniment [in a song] **TS** I.ii.67 [Petruchio to Hortensio] *wealth is burden of my wooing dance;* **MA** III.iv.40
　3 birth, state of pregnancy **CE** V.i.344 [Abbess to Egeon] *a wife once called Aemilia, / That bore thee at a burden two fair sons;* **KJ** III.i.90; **Sonn** 59.4, 97.7; **WT** IV.iv.262
　4 capacity, load, weight **AW** II.iii.204 [Lafew to Parolles] *the scarfs and the bannerets about thee did manifoldly dissuade me from believing thee a vessel of too great a burden;* **TC** I.iii.71
　5 load, pile [here: of hair] **Tim** IV.iii.146 [Timon to Phrynia and Timandra] *thatch / Your poor thin roofs with burdens of the dead* [i.e. hair taken from the dead]

burden, burthen (*v.*) **1** load down, weigh down **Sonn** 102.11 *wild music burthens every bough;* **Tem** V.i.199; **Venus** 419
　2 charge, accuse, lay on **CE** V.i.209 [Adriana to Duke, of Antipholus of Ephesus] *So befall my soul / As this is false he burdens me withal;* **TS** II.i.202

burdened, burthened (*adj.*) burdensome, heavy, oppressive **R3** IV.iv.111 [Queen Margaret to Queen Elizabeth] *Now thy proud neck bears half my burdened yoke*

burdenous (*adj.*) burdensome, onerous, oppressive R2 II.i.260 [Ross to Northumberland, of King Richard] *His burdenous taxations*

burden-wise (*adv.*) in the manner of a musical accompaniment Luc 1133 [Lucrece as if to the nightingale] *burden-wise I'll hum on Tarquin still*

burdock (*n.*) variety of weedy plant KL IV.iv.4 [Cordelia to Doctor, of Lear] *Crowned with … burdock* [F *Hardokes*; Q *hordocks*] **PLANTS**, p.330

burgher (*n.*) citizen, inhabitant, denizen AY II.i.23 [Duke Senior to his Lords, of the deer and the forest] *Being native burghers of this desert city*; MV I.i.10

burgomaster (*n.*) borough-master, town official 1H4 II.i.77 [Gadshill to Chamberlain] *I am joined with … Burgomasters*

burgonet (*n.*) [type of] small light helmet 2H6 V.i.200 [Clifford to Warwick] *I'll write upon thy burgonet*; AC I.v.24; E3 IV.iv.83; 2H6 V.ii.204, 208 ✷ **BODY-ARMOUR**, p.48

burial (*n.*) **1** burial service, funeral solemnities Ham V.i.230 [Priest to Laertes] *the bringing home / Of bell and burial* [i.e. with tolling bell and religious rites]
2 grave, tomb, burial chamber MV I.i.29 [Salerio to Antonio, of a ship] *docked in sand, / Vailing her high-top lower than her ribs / To kiss her burial*

burly-boned (*adj.*) hulking, big-bodied 2H6 IV.x.55 [Cade as if to his sword, of Iden] *if thou … cut not out the burly-boned clown in chines of beef*

burn (*v.*) **1** warm up, spice up TN II.iii.183 [Sir Toby to Sir Andrew] *I'll go burn some sack*
2 infect [with venereal disease] 2H4 II.iv.334 [Falstaff to Prince Henry, of Doll] *she's in hell already, and burns poor souls*
3 suffer from venereal disease CE IV.iii.57 [Dromio of Syracuse to Antipholus of Syracuse] *Ergo, light wenches will burn*
4 waste, fritter away MW II.i.50 [Mistress Ford to Mistress Page] *We burn daylight*; RJ I.iv.43

burnet (*n.*) ✷ **PLANTS**, p.330

burning zone ✷ zone, burning

burnt (*adj.*) mulled, heated MW III.i.100 [Host to all] *let burnt sack be the issue*; MW II.i.197

burr (*n.*) ✷ bur (*n.*)

burst (*n.*) bursting out, violent outbreak TNK V.i.62 [stage direction] *with a short thunder as the burst of a battle*

burst (*adj.*) broken, shattered, rent in two Oth I.i.88 [Iago to Brabantio] *Your heart is burst*; TS I.v.72

burst (*v.*) **1** break, smash TS Induction.i.6 [Hostess to Sly] *You will not pay for the glasses you have burst?*
2 crack, split open 2H4 III.ii.311 [Falstaff alone, of John of Gaunt and Shallow] *he burst his head for crowding among the marshal's men*

burthen (*n.*) earlier spelling of 'burden' ✷ burden (*n.*)

bury (*v.*) **1** abandon forever, consign to oblivion, eliminate JC IV.iii.157 [Brutus to Cassius, of his drink] *In this I bury all unkindness*; 3H6 III.iii.129, IV.i.55; TNK VI.i.126
2 conceal, hide, make inaccessible R2 IV.i.328 [Abbot of Westminster to Aumerle] *You shall … take the Sacrament / To bury mine intents* [i.e. so that you will not divulge my plans]

bush (*n.*) tavern sign-board, advertisement AY V.iv.198 [Rosalind as Epilogue] *If it be true that good wine needs no bush, 'tis true that a good play needs no epilogue*

business (*n.*) **1** deed, action, affair, task Tem I.ii.315 [Prospero to Caliban] *There's other business for thee*; 1H4 III.ii.177; KL I.ii.178; Tem I.ii.367; TNK III.i.90
2 mission, errand, purpose Tem III.iii.70 [Ariel to Alonso, Sebastian, and Antonio] *that's my business to you*; RJ II.ii.16
3 important matter, serious concern Cym V.v.23 [Cymbeline to Cornelius and Ladies] *There's business in these faces*

4 event, happening, occurrence Tem I.ii.451 [Prospero to himself, of Ferdinand meeting Miranda] *this swift business / I must uneasy make*; Tem I.ii.407
5 concern, uneasiness, distress R2 II.ii.75 [Queen Isabel to Green, of York] *full of careful business are his looks!*

buskined (*adj.*) wearing high hunting boots [buskins] MND II.i.71 [Titania to Oberon, of Hippolyta] *Your buskined mistress*

busky (*adj.*) bosky, bushy, shrub-covered 1H4 V.i.2 [King Henry to Prince Hal] *How bloodily the sun begins to peer / Above yon busky hill* [F; Q1 *bulky*]

buss (*n.*) kiss 2H4 II.iv.263 [Falstaff to Doll] *Thou dost give me flattering busses*

buss (*v.*) kiss wantonly, smack against KJ III.iv.35 [Constance as if to death] *I will think thou smilest / And buss thee as thy wife*; Cor III.ii.75; TC IV.v.220

bustling (*adj.*) confused, agitated, excited JC II.iv.18 [Portia to Lucius] *I heard a bustling rumour like a fray*

busy (*adj.*) **1** always engaged, active, constantly occupied R3 I.iii.144 [Rivers to Richard] *in those busy days … / We followed then our lord, our sovereign king*; E3 IV.iv.128
2 interfering, meddlesome, busy-bodying Ham III.iv.34 [Hamlet to dead Polonius] *Thou findest to be too busy is some danger*; Oth III.iii.251, IV.ii.130

but (*adv.*) **1** merely, only E3 I.i.93 [Prince Edward to Lorraine] *I hold thy message but as scurrilous*; CE IV.i.33; Ham V.ii.318; 3H6 III.i.80; Oth IV.i.87
2 just Venus 497 [Venus to Adonis] *But now I lived, and life was death's annoy; / But now I died, and life was lively joy*; Ham I.i.81; MV III.i.76; TS I.i.249

but (*conj.*) **1** except, otherwise than Ham IV.vii.16 [Claudius to Laertes, of Gertrude] *She is so conjunctive to my life and soul / That … / I could not but by her*
2 except that, only with the result that Ham I.ii.126 [Claudius to his court] *No jocund health that Denmark drinks today / But the great cannon to the clouds shall tell*
3 that MA I.iii.29 [Don John to Conrade] *it must not be denied but I am a plain-dealing villain*
4 unless, if … not AY III.ii.46 [Corin to Touchstone] *You told me you salute not at the court but you kiss your hands*
5 without AY III.v.6 [Silvius to Phebe] *The common executioner … / Falls not the axe upon the humbled neck / But first begs pardon*

butcherly (*adv.*) brutally, cruelly, savagely 3H6 II.v.89 [Father to himself, of the war] *What stratagems, how fell, how butcherly … / This deadly quarrel daily doth beget!*

butchery (*n.*) slaughter-house AY II.iii.27 [Adam to Orlando] *this house is but a butchery*

butler (*n.*) servant in charge of the wine-cellar WT IV.iv.56 [Shepherd to Perdita] *When my old wife lived, upon / This day she was both pantler, butler, cook*

butt (*n.*) **1** goal, aim, target [as in archery] 3H6 I.iv.29 [York to his enemies] *I am your butt, and I abide your shot*; H5 I.ii.186; Oth V.ii.265
2 large cask, barrel Tem III.ii.1 [Stephano to Trinculo and Caliban] *When the butt is out we will drink water*; TC V.i.25; Tem II.ii.119, 131
3 ramshackle boat, tub, hulk Tem I.ii.146 [Prospero to Miranda] *A rotten carcass of a butt*
4 buttock, bottom TS V.ii.40 [Bianca to Gremio] *Head and butt!*

butt-end (*n.*) fag-end, final part, remaining piece R3 II.ii.110 [Richard to himself, of the Duchess of York's blessing] *make me die a good old man! / That is the butt-end of a mother's blessing*

butter (*v.*) spread butter on KL II.iv.124 [Fool to Lear, of the foolish woman] *'Twas her brother that in pure kindness to his horse buttered his hay* [i.e. did something just as foolish - because horses would not eat greasy hay]

butter-woman (*n.*) [woman who deals in butter, dairymaid] chatterer, gabbler **AW** IV.i.40 [Parolles to himself] *Tongue, I must put you into a butter-woman's mouth;* **AY** III.ii.94

buttery *(n.)* store-room [for provisions], liquor-store **TS** Induction.i.100 [Lord to Servant, of the Players] *take them to the buttery*

buttery bar ledge by the hatch of a buttery [liquor store] **TN** I.iii.67 [Maria to Sir Andrew] *bring your hand to the buttery bar and let it drink*

button *(n.)* **1** bud **Ham** I.iii.40 [Laertes to Ophelia] *The canker galls the infants of the spring / Too oft before their buttons be disclosed;* **TNK** III.i.6

2 knob at the top of a cap or hat **Ham** II.ii.229 [Guildenstern to Hamlet] *On Fortune's cap we are not the very button* [i.e. summit, high point] ☞ **CLOTHING**, p.79

buttons, in one's [unclear meaning] very plain, easy to see **MW** III.ii.63 [Host to Page, of Fenton as a suitor for Anne] *'Tis in his buttons he will carry't*

buttoned *(adj.)* fitted out with buttons, studded, bossed **E3** I.ii.32 [King David to Lorraine, of the Scots soldiers] *never shall [they] ... from their buttoned tawny leathern belts / Dismiss their biting whinyards*

butt-shaft *(n.)* blunt-headed arrow **RJ** II.iv.16 [Mercutio to Benvolio, of Romeo] *the very pin of his heart cleft with the blind bow-boy's butt-shaft;* **LL** I.ii.169

buxom *(adj.)* lively, cheerful, bright **Per** I.Chorus.23 [Gower alone, of Antiochus' daughter] *So buxom, blithe, and full of face;* **H5** III.vi.25

buy *(v.)* pay for, suffer the consequences of **MND** III.ii.426 [Demetrius to Puck, who is copying Lysander's voice] *Thou shalt buy this dear / If ever I thy face by daylight see;* **3H6** V.i.68

buy and sell, past form **bought and sold** betray, exploit, treat treacherously **CE** III.i.72 [Dromio of Ephesus to Antipholus of Ephesus] *It would make a man mad as a buck to be so bought and sold;* **1H6** IV.iv.13; **H8** I.i.192; **KJ** V.iv.10; **R3** V.iii.306; **TC** II.i.45

buy out *(v.)* **1** redeem, pay ransom to / for **CE** I.ii.5 [First Merchant to Antipholus of Syracuse, of Egeon] *not being able to buy out his life*

2 get rid of, cancel by making a payment **1H4** IV.ii.33 [Falstaff alone, of his men] *such have I to fill up the rooms of them as have bought out their services;* **Ham** III.iii.60; **KJ** I.i.164

3 make up for, cancel out **Tim** III.v.17 [Alcibiades to Senators, of his friend's lack of cowardice] *An honour in him which buys out his fault*

buzz *(n.)* rumour, whisper, report **KL** I.iv.322 [Gonerill to Albany, of Lear and his knights] *Each buzz, each fancy ... / He may enguard his dotage with their powers;* **TS** II.i.206

buzz *(v.)* **1** spread, move about, send **E3** IV.vi.20 [King John alone] *swift-starting fear / Hath buzzed a cold dismay through all our army;* **2H6** I.i.99; **3H6** V.vi.86

2 spread false rumours **3H6** II.vi.95 [Warwick to Edward, of their enemies] *look to have them buzz to offend thine ears;* **Tit** IV.iv.7

buzz *(int.)* ☞ **ATTENTION SIGNALS**, p.26; **EXCLAMATIONS**, p.158; **RESPONSES**, p.373

buzzard *(n.)* **1** ignoramus, stupid person; also: inferior kind of hawk **TS** II.i.206 [Katherina to Petruchio, of his play on words] *Well ta'en, and like a buzzard* [pun: 208, sense 2]

2 [unclear meaning] night-flying insect; cockchafer **TS** II.i.208 [Katherina to Petruchio, responding to the notion of a buzzard catching a turtle-dove] *Ay, for a turtle, as he takes a buzzard* [pun: 207, sense 1]

buzzer *(n.)* rumour-monger, gossiper **Ham** IV.v.91 [Claudius to Gertrude, of Laertes] *wants not buzzers to infect his ear*

buzzing *(n.)* rumour, busy murmuring **H8** II.i.148 [Second Gentleman to First Gentleman] *A buzzing of a separation / Between the King and Katherine?*

by *(adv.)* **1** near by, close at hand **TN** IV.iii.24 [Olivia to Sebastian] *go with me and with this holy man / Into the chantry by;* **2H4** II.iv.86; **H5** IV.ii.28; **LL** V.i.94; **Sonn** 154.9; **Venus** 259

2 aside, out of the way **KJ** IV.iii.94 [Salisbury to Bastard] *Stand by, or I shall gall you*

by *(prep.)* **1** according to **AC** III.iii.39 [Cleopatra to Charmian, of the Messenger's opinion of Octavia] *methinks, by him, / This creature's no such thing*

2 at the house of **JC** II.i.218 [Brutus to Metellus, of Ligarius] *go along by him*

3 as a result of, because of **3H6** IV.iv.12 [Lady Grey to Rivers] *Fell Warwick's brother and by that our foe*

4 concerning, about **AW** V.iii.237 [King to Parolles, of Bertram and Diana] *By him and by this woman here what know you?*

5 compared with **AC** II.ii.186 [Enobarbus to Maecenas, of rumours of a feast] *This was but as a fly by an eagle*

6 on **AY** III.ii.411 [Rosalind as Ganymede to Orlando] *Go with me ... and by the way you shall tell me where in the forest you live*

7 with regard to **AW** III.vii.11 [Helena to Widow, of trust] *you cannot, / By the good aid that I of you shall borrow, / Err in bestowing it*

8 ☞ **SWEARING**, p.435

by that *(conj.)* by the fact that **TNK** III.vi.198 [Emilia to Theseus] *By that you would have pity in another*

by and by *(adv.)* **1** immediately, straightaway, directly **RJ** III.i.170 [Benvolio to Prince] *Tybalt fled / But by and by comes back to Romeo;* **Ham** III.ii.390; **MM** V.ii.67; **MW** IV.i.7; **RJ** III.i.170; **Tem** II.i.15

2 shortly, soon, before long **H5** II.ii.2 [Exeter to Bedford, of the conspirators] *They shall be apprehended by and by;* **1H4** I.ii.37; **2H6** I.iii.2; **MM** III.i.157; **TN** III.iv.171; **WT** IV.iv.504

by any means certainly, indeed **TNK** II.ii.51 [Second Countryman to the others, of the Schoolmaster] *By any means, our thing of learning says so*

by-dependance *(n.)* side-issue, incidental point **Cym** V.v.391 [Cymbeline to all, of his questions] *These ... should be demanded / And all the other by-dependances*

by-drinking *(n.)* drinking between meals **1H4** III.iii.72 [Hostess to Falstaff] *You owe money here ... for your diet, and by-drinkings*

by-fold *(adj.)* ☞ **bifold** *(adj.)*

by-gone *(adj.)* that has just gone by, yesterday **WT** I.ii.32 [Hermione to Leontes, of all being well in Bohemia] *this satisfaction / The by-gone day proclaimed* [i.e. yesterday]

byle, bile *(n.)* older forms of 'boil' **KL** II.iv.218 [Lear to Gonerill] *Thou art a byle, / A plague-sore* [F; Q bile]

by-past *(adj.)* former, elapsed, previous **Lover** 158 *who ever ... forced examples 'gainst her own content / To put the by-past perils in her way?*

by-peep *(v.)* peep sideways, look aside **Cym** I.vii.108 [Iachimo to Innogen] *by-peeping in an eye / Base and illustrous*

by-room *(n.)* side-room, private room **1H4** II.iv.28 [Prince Hal to Poins] *do thou stand in some by-room while I question my puny drawer*

by-word *(n.)* object of scorn, model of cowardice **3H6** I.i.42 [Warwick to all, of the King] *whose cowardice / Hath made us by-words to our enemies*

cabilero (*n.*) gallant, fine fellow **2H4** V.iii.58 [Shallow to all] *I'll drink to Master Bardolph, and to all the cabileros about London* [Q; F *Cauileroes*] ⤖ cavaliero (*adj.*)

cabin (*n.*) **1** small room, hut, shelter **PassP** XIV.3 [Pilgrim, of his love] *She ... daffed me to a cabin hanged with care;* **TN** I.v.257
   2 den, hole, cave **Venus** 637 [Venus to Adonis, of a boar] *O, let him keep his loathsome cabin still;* **Venus** 1038

cabin (*v.*) **1** dwell, lodge, take shelter in **Tit** IV.ii.178 [Aaron to the baby] *I'll make you ... cabin in a cave*
   2 cage, pen in, shut up in limiting bounds **Mac** III.iv.23 [Macbeth to First Murderer] *now I am cabined, cribbed, confined*
   3 be confined, be shut up [in a soldier's tent] **TNK** I.iii.35 [Hippolyta to Emilia, of Theseus and Pirithous] *They two have cabined / In many ... a corner*

cabinet (*n.*) **1** private apartment, intimate chamber **E3** II.i.62 [King Edward to Lodowick, of the arbour] *Make it our counsel house or cabinet*
   2 dwelling, lodging **Venus** 854 [of the lark] *From his moist cabinet mounts up on high;* **Luc** 442

cable (*n.*) scope, reach **Oth** I.ii.17 [Iago to Othello, of Brabantio] *[he will] put upon you what restraint and grievance / That law ... / Will give him cable*

cacodemon (*n.*) evil spirit **R3** I.iii.143 [Queen Margaret to herself, of Richard] *Thou cacodemon!*

caddis (*n.*) tape made of worsted yarn **WT** IV.iv.209 [Servant to Clown, of what Autolycus has for sale] *He hath ... inkles, caddisses, cambrics, lawns*

caddis-garter (*adj.*) garter made of coloured worsted yarns **1H4** II.iv.68 [Prince Hal to Francis, of the vintner] *Wilt thou rob this ... caddis-garter, smooth-tongue Spanish pouch?*

cade (*n.*) cask, barrel [containing 500 herrings] **2H6** IV.ii.32 [Dick aside to his companions, of Cade's explanation of his name] *Or rather of stealing a cade of herrings*

cadent (*adj.*) falling, dropping, descending **KL** I.iv.282 [Lear to the goddess Nature, of any child of Gonerill's] *With cadent tears fret channels in her cheeks* [F; Q *accent*]

caduceus (*n.*) [pron: ka'dyoosius] heraldic wand [in the case of Mercury, entwined with two serpents] **TC** II.iii.12 [Thersites alone, as if to Mercury] *lose all the serpentine craft of thy caduceus*

cage (*n.*) **1** basket, frame **RJ** II.iii.3 [Friar alone] *I must up-fill this osier cage of ours / With baleful weeds*
   2 pen, lock-up, small prison compound **2H6** IV.ii.49 [Dick aside to his companions, of Cade] *his father had never a house but the cage*

'cagion, 'casion (*n.*) dialect version of 'occasion' [= cause] **KL** IV.vi.235 [Edgar to Oswald, adopting a country accent] *'Chill not let go, zir, without vurther 'cagion*

Cain-coloured, cane-coloured (*adj.*) reddish-yellow **MW** I.iv.22 [Simple to Mistress Quickly, of Slender] *He hath ... a Cain-coloured beard* [F; Q *kane colored*] ⤖ **RELIGIOUS PERSONALITIES AND BEINGS**, p.625

caitiff (*n.*) [sympathetic or contemptuous] miserable wretch, wretched creature **MM** II.i.166 [Elbow to Pompey] *O thou caitiff;* **AW** III.ii.114; **MM** V.i.53; **Oth** IV.i.108; **R3** IV.iv.101; **Tim** IV.iii.236

caitiff (*adj.*) wretched, miserable, worthless **MM** V.i.88 [Isabella to Duke, of Angelo] *I went / To this pernicious caitiff deputy;* **R2** I.ii.53; **RJ** V.i.52

cake (*n.*) compressed pack, flattened bundle **RJ** V.i.47 [Romeo alone, of an apothecary] *about his shelves ... old cakes of roses / Were thinly scattered* [i.e. of rose petals, for scent]

caked (*adj.*) solidified, coagulated, clotted **Tim** II.ii.221 [Timon to Flavius, of the Senators] *Their blood is caked, 'tis cold, it seldom flows*

calculate (*v.*) perform calculations, make estimates **JC** I.iii.65 [Cassius to Casca] *Why old men, fools, and children calculate*

calculate one's birth cast a horoscope, foretell an event 2H6 IV.i.34 [Suffolk to Whitmore] *A cunning man did calculate my birth*

calendar *(n.)* **1** record, register, history AW I.iii.4 [Steward to Countess] *the calendar of my past endeavours*
 2 paradigm, yardstick, standard Ham V.ii.109 [Osrick to Hamlet, of Laertes] *he is the card or calendar of gentry*

calf *(n.)* fool, dolt, idiot Ham III.ii.114 [Hamlet to Polonius] *kill so capital a calf;* Ham V.i.114

caliver *(n.)* type of lightweight musket 1H4 IV.ii.19 [Falstaff alone] *a commodity of warm slaves … such as fear the report of a caliver worse than a struck fowl;* 2H4 III.ii.262 ☛ **WEAPONS**, p.491

calkin *(n.)* raised edge of a horse-shoe [which prevents the horse slipping] TNK V.iv.55 [Pirithous to Palamon] *the calkins / Did rather tell [the paving stones] than trample*

call *(n.)* decoy, lure, enticement KJ III.iv.174 [Cardinal Pandulph to Lewis the Dauphin, of a few French soldiers in England] *they would be as a call / To train ten thousand English to their side*

call *(v.)* **1** speak out, give voice Per V.i.244 [Diana to Pericles] *To mourn thy crosses, with thy daughter's, call*
 2 reckon, say to be Mac I.iii.38 [Banquo to Macbeth] *How far is't called to Forres?* [i.e. how far is it?]

call on / upon *(v.)* **1** call to account, challenge, requite AC I.iv.28 [Caesar to Lepidus, of Antony] *If he filled / His vacancy with his voluptuousness, / Full surfeits and the dryness of his bones / Call on him for't*
 2 make a call on, claim repayment of Tim II.ii.25 [Caphis to Timon] *My master is awaked by great occasion / To call upon his own;* 1H4 V.i.129

call to *(v.)* call on, make a visit Tim I.ii.218 [Timon to Third Lord] *I'll tell you true, I'll call to you*

call up *(v.)* arouse, prompt, bring to mind Cor II.iii.193 [Sicinius to Citizens] *As cause had called you up* [i.e. as occasion demanded]

callet, callot *(n.)* **1** slut, drab, harlot 2H6 I.iii.81 [Queen to Suffolk, of the Duchess of Gloucester] *Contemptuous base-born callet as she is;* 3H6 II.ii.145; Oth IV.ii.120
 2 scold, nag WT II.iii.90 [Leontes to and of Paulina] *A callat / Of boundless tongue* [or: sense 1]

calling *(n.)* **1** name, designation AY I.ii.221 [Orlando to Rosalind and Celia, of his birth] *I … would not change that calling / To be adopted heir to Frederick* [or: sense 2]
 2 vocation, profession, high station in life 1H6 III.i.32 [Winchester to all] *how haps it I seek not to advance / Or raise myself, but keep my wonted calling?;* Per IV.ii.37

calm *(n.)* **1** calm sea H8 III.i.166 [Wolsey to Queen Katherine] *I know you have … / A soul as even as a calm*
 2 malapropism for 'qualm' [feeling of nausea] 2H4 II.iv.36 [Hostess to Falstaff, of Doll] *Sick of a calm;* 2H4 II.iv.37

calm *(v.)* becalm, come to a halt, delay 2H6 IV.ix.33 [King to all, of a ship] *having 'scaped a tempest, / Is straightway calmed and boarded with a pirate;* Oth I.i.30

calumniate *(v.)* deal with slanders, handle defamation TC V.ii.126 [Troilus to Ulysses, of eyes and ears] *As if those organs had deceptious functions, / Created only to calumniate*

calumniating *(adj.)* slandering, defaming, reviling TC III.iii.174 [Ulysses to Achilles] *High birth, vigour of bone … are subjects all / To envious and calumniating time*

calumnious *(adj.)* slanderous, defamatory, disparaging Ham I.iii.38 [Laertes to Ophelia] *Virtue itself 'scapes not calumnious strokes*

calve *(v.)* [of humans compared to animals] bring forth Cor III.i.239 [Coriolanus to Menenius, of the Plebeians] *I would they were … not Romans, as they are not, / Though calved i'th' porch o'th' Capitol*

calves'-guts *(n.)* violin strings Cym II.iii.28 [Cloten to Musicians, of their music not affecting Innogen] *it is a vice in her ears, which horse-hairs, and calves'-guts … can never amend*

cambric *(n.)* fine linen from Cambray, Flanders WT IV.iv.209 [Servant to Clown, of what Autolycus has for sale] *He hath … inkles, caddisses, cambrics, lawns;* Cor I.iii.85; Per IV.Chorus.24

camlet, chamblet *(n.)* garment made of fine cloth H8 V.iv.88 [Porter to one in the crowd] *You i'th' camlet* [F *Chamblet*]

camp *(v.)* accommodate, lodge, put up AC IV.viii.33 [Antony to Cleopatra, of his army] *Had our great palace the capacity / To camp this host*

camping *(adj.)* living in an army camp, tent-dwelling AW III.iv.14 [Steward reading Helena's letter, of Bertram] *I … sent him forth / From courtly friends, with camping foes to live*

can *(v.)* **1** be skilled [in], have ability [in] Ham IV.vii.83 [Claudius to Laertes, of the French] *And they can well on horseback;* Cym IV.ii.392; H8 IV.iii.173; Phoen 14; Tem IV.i.27; TG II.iv.163
 2 ☛ 'gan *(v.)*

canakin, cannakin *(n.)* little can, small drinking vessel Oth II.iii.64 [Iago singing] *And let me the canakin clink*

canary, canaries *(n.)* **1** variety of sweet wine from the Canary Islands TN I.iii.77 [Sir Toby to Sir Andrew] *thou lack'st a cup of canary;* 2H4 II.iv.26; MW III.i.80
 2 lively Spanish dance AW II.i.74 [Lafew to King] *a medicine [that can] … make you dance canary*
 3 malapropism, probably for 'quandary' MW II.ii.62 [Mistress Quickly to Falstaff, of Mistress Ford] *The best courtier of them all … could never have brought her to such a canary;* MW II.ii.59

canary *(v.)* dance in the style of the canary LL III.i.11 [Mote to Armado, of a tune] *canary to it with your feet* ☛ canary *(n.)* 2

cancel *(v.)* end, terminate JC I.iii.102 [Casca to Cassius] *So every bondman in his own hand bears / The power to cancel his captivity*

cancel of *(v.)* [unclear word-class] put an end to, wipe out Per I.i.114 [Antiochus to Pericles] *We might proceed to cancel of your days* [Q *counsell*]

cancelled *(adj.)* made null and void, invalidated RJ III.iii.98 [Romeo to Nurse, of Juliet] *what says / My concealed lady to our cancelled love?;* Sonn 30.7

candidatus *(n.)* ☛ **ROMAN HISTORY**, p.377

candied *(adj.)* **1** made of ice, crystallized, glistening Tim IV.iii.227 [Apemantus to Timon] *the cold brook, / Candied with ice;* Tem II.i.284
 2 sugared, honeyed, flattering Ham III.ii.70 [Hamlet to Horatio] *let the candied tongue lick absurd pomp*

candle-case *(n.)* container for candles TS III.ii.45 [Biondello to Tranio as Lucentio, of Petruchio's clothes] *a pair of boots that have been candle-cases*

candle-mine *(n.)* mine of candle-fat 2H4 II.iv.295 [Prince Henry to Falstaff] *You whoreson candle-mine*

candle-waster *(n.)* burner of midnight oil, someone who wastes candles by reading late at night MA V.i.18 [Leonato to Antonio] *make misfortune drunk / With candle-wasters*

candy *(adj.)* sugary, syrupy, honeyed 1H4 I.iii.247 [Hotspur to Northumberland and Worcester] *what a candy deal of courtesy* [Q; F *caudie*]

cane-coloured *(adj.)* ☛ Cain-coloured *(adj.)*

cangenet *(n.)* ☛ canzonet *(n.)*

canker *(n./adj.)* **1** grub that destroys plant buds and leaves, cankerworm, parasite TG I.i.43 [Proteus to Valentine] *in the sweetest bud / The eating canker dwells;* Ham I.iii.39; 2H4 II.ii.88; MND II.ii.3; RJ II.iii.26; Sonn 35.4, 99.12
 2 cancer, ulcer, blight, corruption 2H6 I.iii.18 [Gloucester to Duchess] *Banish the canker of ambitious thoughts!;* E3 I.ii.27; Ham V.ii.69; KJ V.ii.14; Tem I.ii.416; Tim IV.iii.50
 3 wild-rose, dog-rose [that grows wildly] MA I.iii.25 [Don John to Conrade] *I had rather be a canker in a hedge*

canker (*v.*) decay, become corrupt, grow malignant **Tem** IV.i.192 [Prospero to himself, of Caliban] *as with age his body uglier grows, / So his mind cankers*

canker-bit (*adj.*) worm-eaten, eaten away by canker grubs **KL** V.iii.120 [Edgar to all, of his name] *By treason's tooth bare-gnawn and canker-bit*

canker-bloom (*n.*) blossom of the wild rose **Sonn** 54.5 *The canker-blooms have full as deep a dye / As the perfumed tincture of the roses* [or: wild poppies]

canker-blossom (*n.*) grub that destroys the blossom [of love] **MND** III.ii.282 [Hermia to Helena] *you canker-blossom*

cankered (*adj.*) **1** rusted, corroded, tarnished **RJ** I.i.95 [Prince to all, of Verona's citizens] *old partisans ... / Cankered with peace*; **2H4** IV.v.73
2 corrupted, rotten to the core **Cor** IV.v.94 [Coriolanus to Aufidius] *I will fight / Against my cankered country*; **1H4** I.iii.135
3 malignant, malicious, bad-tempered **RJ** I.i.95 [Prince to all, of Verona's citizens] *wield old partisans ... to part your cankered hate*; **KJ** II.i.194

cankering (*adj.*) decaying, corrupting, destroying **Venus** 767 [Venus to Adonis] *Foul cankering rust the hidden treasure frets*

canker-sorrow (*n.*) gnawing grief, all-consuming sorrow **KJ** III.iv.82 [Constance to Cardinal Pandulph, of Arthur] *But now will canker-sorrow eat my bud*

cannibally (*adv.*) in the manner of a cannibal **Cor** IV.v.195 [Second Servingman to First Servingman, of Coriolanus and Aufidius] *An he had been cannibally given, he might have boiled and eaten him too*

cannoneer (*n.*) gunner, artilleryman **Ham** V.ii.270 [Claudius to all] *The trumpet to the cannoneer without*

canon (*n.*) **1** law, decree, rule **Cor** I.x.26 [Aufidius to First Soldier, of Coriolanus] *Where I find him, were it ... / Against the hospitable canon, would I / Wash my fierce hand in's heart*; **Ham** I.ii.132; **LL** I.i.251; **TNK** I.ii.55
2 scriptural canon, Bible **AW** I.i.144 [Parolles to Helena] *self-love ... is the most inhibited sin in the canon*

canon, from the out of order, improper, inappropriate **Cor** III.i.90 [Cominius to Coriolanus, of Sicinius' words] *'Twas from the canon*

canonize (*v.*) glorify, immortalize, exalt **TC** II.ii.203 [Troilus to all] *fame in time to come canonize us*

canonized (*v.*) buried with the Church's rites, consecrated by Christian burial **Ham** I.iv.47 [Hamlet to Ghost] *tell / Why thy canonized bones, hearsed in death, / Have burst their cerements*

canopy (*n.*) **1** sky, firmament **Ham** II.ii.299 [Hamlet to Rosencrantz and Guildenstern] *This most excellent canopy, the air, look you*; **Cor** IV.v.40
2 covering above a bed **RJ** V.iii.13 [Paris as if to Juliet] *thy canopy is dust and stones*; **TS** II.i.345

canopy (*v.*) curtain, veil, cover [as if by a canopy] **Cym** II.ii.21 [Iachimo to himself, of Innogen's eyes] *now canopied / Under these windows*; **Sonn** 12.6; **TN** I.i.42

canstick (*n.*) candlestick **1H4** III.i.125 [Hotspur to Glendower] *I had rather hear a brazen canstick turned ... / And that would set my teeth nothing on edge, / Nothing so much as mincing poetry* [Q; F *Candlestick*]

cantherizing (*n.*) cauterizing, burning with a hot iron **Tim** V.i.131 [Timon as if to the sun, of the Senators] *For each true word a blister, / and each false / Be as a cantherizing to the root o'th' tongue*

cantle (*n.*) segment, corner, slice **AC** III.x.6 [Scarus to Enobarbus] *The greater cantle of the world is lost / With very ignorance*; **1H4** III.i.96

canton (*n.*) song, ballad, verse **TN** I.v.259 [Viola as Cesario to Olivia] *[I would] Write loyal cantons of contemned love*

canvas-climber (*n.*) mariner climbing to trim the sails, sailor **Per** IV.i.62 [Marina to Leonine, of the storm] *from the ladder-tackle washes off / A canvas-climber*

canvass (*v.*) toss about [as if in a canvas sheet], beat, thrash **2H4** II.iv.220 [Doll to Falstaff] *I'll canvass thee between a pair of sheets*; **1H6** I.iii.36

canzonet (*n.*) poem, short song **LL** IV.ii.120 [Holofernes to Nathaniel, of Berowne's letter to Rosaline] *Let me supervise the canzonet* [F *cangenet*]

cap (*n.*) **1** removal of a cap, respectful salutation **Cor** II.i.64 [Menenius to Brutus and Sicinius] *You are ambitious for poor knaves' caps and legs*
2 [raising of a cap] salute, respect, approval **Cym** III.iii.25 [Belarius to Guiderius and Arviragus] *Such gain the cap of him that makes him fine* [i.e. of his tailor]
3 chief, supremo, doyen **Tim** IV.iii.360 [Apemantus to Timon] *Thou art the cap of all the fools alive*

capable (*adj.*) **1** sensitive, receptive, responsive **TC** III.iii.307 [Thersites to Achilles, of taking a letter to Ajax] *Let me carry another to his horse, for that's the more capable creature*; **AY** III.v.23; **Ham** III.iv.128; **KJ** II.i.476; **R3** III.i.155
2 comprehensive, exhaustive, capacious **Oth** III.iii.456 [Othello to Iago, of his bloody thoughts] *a capable and wide revenge / Swallow them up*
3 able to inherit, entitled to possess property **KL** II.i.84 [Gloucester to Edmund] *I'll work the means / To make thee capable*

capable of **1** appreciative of, able to take in **AW** I.i.94 [Helena alone, of Bertram] *[my heart is] too capable / Of every line and trick of his sweet favour*; **Ham** III.ii.11; **KJ** II.i.476; **WT** IV.iv.760
2 open to, subject to, susceptible to **2H4** I.i.172 [Morton to Northumberland, of Percy] *You were advised his flesh was capable / Of wounds and scars*; **H8** V.iii.11; **KJ** III.i.12; **Tem** I.ii.353

capacity (*n.*) intelligence, understanding, capability **TN** II.v.115 [Malvolio to himself, of the meaning of the letter] *this is evident to any formal capacity*; **MND** V.i.105; **TNK** III.v.8

cap and knee (*n.*) cap in hand and bended knee [in order to be deferential] **1H4** IV.iii.68 [Hotspur to Blunt] *The more and less came in with cap and knee*

cap-and-knee (*adj.*) sycophantic, flattering, obsequious **Tim** III.vi.97 [Timon to Lords] *Cap-and-knee slaves*

cap-a-pe, cap-a-pie (*adv.*) [pron: kapa'pay] from head to foot, from top to toe **Ham** I.ii.200 [Horatio to Hamlet, of the Ghost] *a figure like your father, / Armed at point exactly, cap-a-pe* [reading of F *Cap a Pe*; Q1,Q2 *Capapea*]; **WT** IV.iv.731 [Autolycus to Shepherd] *I am courtier cap-a-pie*

caparison (*n.*) **1** trappings, adornments, trimmings **Cor** I.ix.12 [Lartius to and of Martius] *Here is the steed, we the caparison*; **Venus** 286
2 dress, outfit, clothing **WT** IV.iii.27 [Autolycus alone] *With die and drab I purchased this caparison*

caparison (*v.*) put the trappings on, equip, harness **R3** V.iii.290 [King Richard to a servant] *Caparison my horse!*

caparisoned (*adj.*) dressed, decked out, arrayed **AY** III.ii.189 [Rosalind to Celia] *I am caparisoned like a man*; **TS** III.ii.63

caper (*v.*) **1** be lively, show high spirits **MW** III.ii.60 [Host to Page, of Fenton] *He capers*
2 dance with joy, leap with delight **TN** I.iii.133 [Sir Toby to Sir Andrew] *Let me see thee caper*; **LL** V.ii.113; **MV** I.ii.58; **Tem** V.i.238
3 engage in a dancing contest **2H4** I.ii.193 [Falstaff to Lord Chief Justice] *he that will caper with me for a thousand marks*

caper, cut a perform a leap in which the feet are kicked together in the air **Per** IV.ii.102 [Boult to Bawd, of Veroles] *He offered to cut a caper at the proclamation*; **TN** I.iii.114

capering (*adj.*) prancing, cavorting, frolicsome **E3** IV.iv.100 [Prince Edward to Second Herald, of Normandy] *So tell the cap'ring boy*

capital *(adj.)* **1** main, chief, principal **H5** V.ii.96 [King Henry to Queen Isabel, of Katherine] *She is our capital demand;* **1H4** III.ii.110 **2** mortal, deadly, fatal **TNK** I.i.123 [Emilia to Third Queen] *I would buy you / T'instruct me 'gainst a capital grief* **3** worthy of the death penalty, punishable by death **Per** II.iv.5 [Helicanus to Escanes, of incest] *this heinous capital offence;* **Cor** III.iii.81, V.iii.104; **Ham** IV.vii.7

capitulate *(v.)* **1** bargain, parley, treat **Cor** V.iii.82 [Coriolanus to Volumnia] *Do not bid me … capitulate / Again with Rome's mechanics* **2** sign articles of agreement **1H4** III.ii.120 [King Henry to Prince Hal] *Percy, Northumberland, … / Capitulate against us and are up*

capocchia *(n.)* simpleton, dolt, fool **TC** IV.ii.31 [Pandarus to and of Cressida] *A poor capocchia, hast not slept tonight?*

capon *(n.)* **1** chicken, castrated cockerel [bred for eating] **TG** IV.iv.9 [Launce alone, of his dog and Silvia] *he steps me to her trencher and steals her capon's leg;* **AY** II.vii.155; **1H4** II.iv.444; **LL** IV.i.59; **MA** V.i.150 **2** castrated cockerel; so: fool, dolt [as term of abuse] **Cym** II.i.23 [Second Lord to himself, of Cloten] *You are cock and capon too;* **CE** III.i.32

capriccio *(n.)* [Italian] caprice, whim, fancy **AW** II.iii.291 [Parolles to Bertram] *Will this capriccio hold in thee*

capricious *(adj.)* fanciful, witty, ingenious **AY** III.iii.6 [Touchstone to Audrey] *I am here with thee and thy goats, as the most capricious poet, honest Ovid, was among the Goths* [also: pun on 'goat-like, lascivious' (Latin *caper* = goat), reinforced by 'goats / Goths' having similar pronunciations]

captain *(n.)* commander, chief, leader **Oth** II.i.74 [Cassio to Montano, of Desdemona] *our great Captain's Captain;* **AC** III.i.9, 21; **1H6** IV.ii.3; **3H6** IV.vii.30; **R2** I.iv.99; **RJ** II.iv.20 ✷ **ADDRESS FORMS**, p.8

captain *(adj.)* principal, pre-eminent, chief **Sonn** 52.8 [of feasts] *Like stones of worth they thinly placed are / Or captain jewels in the carcanet*

captain-general *(n.)* commander-in-chief **TC** III.iii.277 [Achilles to Patroclus] *the magnanimous and most illustrious captain-general of the Grecian army, Agamemnon*

captainship *(n.)* leadership, command **Tim** V.i.159 [First Senator to Timon] *so please thee … of our Athens, thine and ours, to take / The captainship*

captious *(adj.)* capacious, spacious, roomy **AW** I.iii.197 [Helena to Countess] *in this captious and intenable sieve / I still pour in the waters of my love*

captivate *(v.)* make captive, capture, imprison **LL** III.i.123 [Armado to Costard] *Thou wert immured, restrained, captivated, bound* **1H6** II.iii.41, V.iii.107; **3H6** I.iv.115; **Venus** 281

captive *(adj.)* imprisoning, confining, incarcerating **E3** III.iii.164 [King John to French, of the English] *bind ye them in captive bands*

captive *(v.)* capture, take captive **H5** II.iv.55 [French King to all] *all our princes captived by the hand / Of … Edward*

captivity *(n.)* those made captive, prisoners **1H6** IV.vii.3 [Talbot to Servant] *Triumphant Death, smeared with captivity* [i.e. with the blood of captives]

car *(n.)* carriage, cart, chariot [often of the sun god] **AC** IV.viii.29 [Antony to Cleopatra, of the armour for Scarus] *He has deserved it, were it carbuncled / Like holy Phoebus' car;* **3H6** II.vi.13; **MND** I.ii.31; **R3** V.iii.20; **TG** III.i.154; **TN** II.v.63

carack *(n.)* ✷ carrack *(n.)*

caract *(n.)* ✷ charact *(n.)*

carat *(n.)* worth, value, quality **2H4** IV.v.162 [Prince Henry to King Henry IV, as if to the crown] *Other, less fine in carat, is more precious*

caraway *(n.)* carraway seeds, or a delicacy containing carraway seeds **2H4** V.iii.3 [Shallow to Falstaff] *we will eat a last year's pippin of mine own graffing, with a dish of caraways*

carbonado, carbinado *(n.)* grilled piece of meat **1H4** V.iii.58 [Falstaff alone, of Hotspur] *let him make a carbonado of me;* **Cor** IV.v.194

carbonado *(v.)* slash, cut [as if preparing meat for grilling] **KL** II.ii.35 [disguised Kent to Oswald] *I'll so carbonado your shanks*

carbonadoed *(adj.)* **1** cut, slashed, hacked about **AW** IV.v.98 [Clown to Lafew, of Bertram] *it is your carbonadoed face* **2** scored across for grilling, made ready for broiling **WT** IV.iv.263 [Autolycus to Mopsa, of a ballad] *how a usurer's wife … longed to eat adders' heads and toads carbonadoed*

carbuncle *(n.)* **1** fiery red precious stone **Cor** I.iv.57 [Lartius as if to Martius] *A carbuncle entire, as big as thou art, / Were not so rich a jewel;* **CE** III.ii.142; **Cym** V.v.189; **Ham** II.ii.461 **2** tumour, growth, lump **KL** II.iv.219 [Lear to Gonerill] *Thou art a boil … or embossed carbuncle*

carbuncled *(adj.)* set with precious stones **AC** IV.viii.28 [Antony to Cleopatra, of the armour for Scarus] *He has deserved it, were it carbuncled / Like holy Phoebus' car*

carcanet *(n.)* jewelled necklace **CE** III.i.4 [Antipholus of Ephesus to Angelo, of Adriana] *I lingered with you at your shop / To see the making of her carcanet;* **Sonn** 52.8

card *(n.)* [compass-card, on which the 32 points of the compass are marked] model, accurate guide **Ham** V.ii.109 [Osrick to Hamlet, of Laertes] *he is the card or calendar of gentry;* **Mac** I.iii.17

card, by the *(n.)* [of a compass-card] with minute precision **Ham** V.i.136 [Hamlet to Horatio] *We must speak by the card*

card *(v.)* mix, mingle, adulterate **1H4** III.ii.62 [King Henry to Prince Hal] *The skipping King … carded his state* [i.e. degraded it by mixing with all kinds of people]

cardecue *(n.)* [French: quart d'ecu] quarter of a crown **AW** V.ii.32 [Lafew to Parolles] *There's a cardecue for you;* **AW** IV.iii.270 ✷ **MONEY**, p.286

carder *(n.)* one who combs out impurities in wool **H8** I.ii.33 [Norfolk to King Henry] *The clothiers all … have put off / The spinsters, carders, fullers, weavers*

cardinally *(adv.)* malapropism for 'carnally' **MM** II.i.77 [Elbow to Escalus, of his wife] *if she had been a woman cardinally given*

cardmaker *(n.)* instrument for combing wool **TS** Induction.ii.18 [Sly to Lord] *Am not I … by education a cardmaker*

care *(n.)* **1** attentiveness, heedfulness, diligence **1H6** II.v.97 [Mortimer to Richard] *be wary in thy studious care;* **CE** II.ii.3; **KJ** IV.ii.117; **Per** I.ii.48; **Sonn** 112.9; **TC** V.iv.21 **2** responsibility, duty, matter of concern **2H4** IV.v.136 [King Henry IV to Prince Henry, as if to England] *What wilt thou do when riot is thy care?;* **Cym** V.v.83; **RJ** II.v.178; **Sonn** 48.7; **Tim** III.iv.116; **WT** IV.iv.352 **3** remedy, healing, restoration **1H6** III.iii.3 [Pucelle to all] *Care is no cure, but rather corrosive* **4** anxiety, worry, solicitude [about] **Oth** I.iii.54 [Brabantio to Duke] *nor doth the general care / Take hold on me;* **CE** I.i.43; **Cor** III.i.137; **Cym** V.v.100; **Per** I.ii.13; **R2** III.ii.95, IV.i.195 **5** sorrow, grief, trouble **Cym** IV.ii.297 [Innogen alone, of the body of Cloten] *These flowers are like the pleasures of the world; / This bloody man, the care on't;* **Cym** IV.ii.205; **R2** IV.i.193; **Tim** V.iii.206 **6** sorrowing, grieving, lamentation **1H6** III.iii.3 [Pucelle to all] *Care is no cure* **7** desire, inclination, concern **RJ** III.v.23 [Romeo to Juliet] *I have more care to stay than will to go*

care, take you/thou no don't worry **AC** V.ii.267 [Cleopatra to Clown, of the snake] *Take thou no care; it shall be heeded;* **1H6** I.iv.21

care (*v.*) feel concern, be anxious, trouble oneself **2H6** III.i.173 [Cardinal to King, of himself and his associates] *those that care to keep your royal person / From treason's secret knife;* **Per** I.ii.15; **TC** V.i.61

care for (*v.*) want, like, wish **TNK** III.vi.58 [Arcite to Palamon] *You care not for a grand guard?*

career (*n.*) **1** [of a horse in a combat] charge, gallop, course **H5** III.iii.23 [King Henry to citizens of Harfleur, of wickedness] *When down the hill he holds his fierce career;* **LL** V.ii.482; **MA** V.i.133; **R2** I.ii.49
2 racecourse, horse-racing track **MW** I.i.165 [Bardolph to Evans] *And so conclusions passed the careers* [i.e. matters got out of hand]
3 gambol, capering, nimble movement **H5** II.i.121 [Nym to Pistol, of King Henry] *he passes some humours and careers*
4 rapid course, height, full swing **MA** II.iii.234 [Benedick alone] *Shall quips and sentences ... awe a man from the career of his humour;* **WT** I.ii.286

careful (*adj.*) **1** anxious, concerned, worried **CE** I.i.79 [Egeon to Duke] *My wife, more careful for the latter-born;* **CE** V.i.299; **H5** IV.i.224; **H8** I.ii.130; **Sonn** 143.1; **Tit** IV.iv.84
2 provident, caring, solicitous **RJ** III.v.107 [Lady Capulet to Juliet] *thou hast a careful father, child;* **Tit** V.iii.21
3 painstaking, serious-minded, attentive **TN** IV.ii.9 [Feste alone] *to be said an honest man and a good housekeeper goes as fairly as to say a careful man and a great scholar*
4 protecting; watchful, acting as a safeguard **Per** I.ii.81 [Pericles to Helicanus] *I ... fled / Under the covering of a careful night*

carefully (*adv.*) considerately, attentively **Ham** I.i.6 [Francisco to Barnardo] *You come most carefully upon your hour;* **Tit** IV.iii.28

careless (*adj.*) **1** carefree, unconcerned, untroubled **MW** V.v.52 [Evans as a Satyr to all, of a maid] *Sleep she as sound as careless infancy;* **AY** II.i.52; **TS** IV.ii.79
2 casual, informal, free and easy **TC** V.v.40 [Ulysses to all, of Troilus] *Engaging and redeeming of himself / With such a careless force and forceless care;* **TNK** I.iii.73
3 inattentive, preoccupied, distracted **AY** III.ii.365 [Rosalind as Ganymede to Orlando, of his appearance] *everything about you [should be] demonstrating a careless desolation;* **TNK** I.iii.29
4 negligent, improvident, neglectful **E3** III.ii.19 [First Citizen to First Frenchman, of what happens to the carefree grasshopper] *When frozen cold hath nipped his careless head;* **Tit** I.i.89
5 reckless, thoughtless, heedless **Venus** 556 *careless lust stirs up a desperate courage*
6 uncared-for, untended **Mac** I.iv.12 [Malcolm to King, of the way Cawdor approached death] *To throw away the dearest thing he owed / As 'twere a careless trifle;* **AW** II.iii.162

carelessly (*adv.*) **1** in a carefree way, without concern **Tim** III.v.34 [First Senator to Alcibiades] *He's truly valiant that can ... make his wrongs his outsides, / To wear them, like his raiment, carelessly;* **AY** I.i.112
2 in little esteem, in low regard **RJ** III.iv.25 [Capulet to Paris, of Tybalt's recent death] *It may be thought we held him carelessly ... if we revel much*
3 in a negligent manner, without taking proper military precautions **3H6** IV.i.14 [Warwick to George, of Edward] *Thy brother being carelessly encamped ... / We may surprise and take him*

carelessness (*n.*) indifference, inattention, unconcern [about public opinion] **Cor** II.ii.14 [Second Officer to First Officer, of Coriolanus] *his noble carelessness*

care-tuned (*adj.*) adjusted to sorrow, grief-attuned **R2** III.ii.92 [Scroop to King Richard] *More health and happiness betide my liege / Than can my care-tuned tongue deliver him*

carl, carle (*n.*) [disparaging] churl, peasant, low fellow **Cym** V.ii.4 [Iachimo alone, of disguised Posthumus] *[how] could this carl ... have subdued me / In my profession?*

carlot (*n.*) peasant, rustic, churl **AY** III.v.107 [Silvius to Phebe, of Rosalind as Ganymede] *he hath bought the cottage and the bounds / That the old carlot once was master of*

carman (*n.*) carter, carrier, wagoner **MM** II.i.243 [Pompey to Escalus] *let carman whip his jade;* **2H4** III.ii.306

carnal (*adj.*) bloody, murderous **R3** IV.iv.56 [Queen Margaret to Duchess of York, of Richard] *this carnal cur / Preys on the issue of his mother's body*

carnation (*adj.*) flesh-coloured, pink [as of carnations] **LL** III.i.142 [Costard to Berowne] *how much carnation ribbon may a man buy for a remuneration?*

carol (*n.*) **1** festival song, dancing song **AY** V.iii.27 [Pages singing, of country folk] *This carol they began that hour*
2 song of joy **MND** II.i.102 [Titania to Oberon] *No night is now with hymn or carol blessed*

carouse (*n.*) toast, long draught, cup filled to the brim to be downed in one go **AC** IV.viii.34 [Antony to Cleopatra] *we all would ... drink carouses to the next day's fate;* **TS** I.ii.274

carouse (*v.*) drink at length, imbibe long draughts **AC** IV.xii.12 [Antony to Scarus, of the two sides] *They cast their caps up and carouse together;* **Oth** II.iii.49; **TS** III.ii.170, 224

carper (*n.*) fault-finder, cynic, cavilling critic **Tim** IV.iii.210 [Apemantus to Timon] *Shame not these woods / By putting on the cunning of a carper*

carpet (*n.*) tapestry, piece of embroidered fabric **Per** IV.i.16 [Marina to herself, of Lychorida] *marigolds / Shall as a carpet hang upon thy grave*

carpet (*adj.*) for exploits 'on the carpet' [relating to the court, appropriate to a drawing room] not 'in the field' **TN** III.iv.231 [Sir Toby to Viola as Cesario, of Sir Andrew] *He is knight dubbed with unhatched rapier and on carpet consideration* [i.e. for non-military service]

carpet-monger (*n.*) frequenter of [carpeted] boudoirs, ladies' man **MA** V.ii.32 [Benedick alone, of famous lovers] *a whole bookful of these quondam carpet-mongers*

carrack, carack (*n.*) galleon, large merchant ship, also fitted out for war **TNK** III.iv.14 [Gaoler's Daughter alone] *then would I make / A carrack of a cockleshell;* **CE** III.ii.144; **Oth** I.ii.50

carriage (*n.*) **1** bearing, demeanour, manner of behaviour **CE** III.ii.14 [Luciana to Antipholus of Syracuse] *Teach sin the carriage of a holy saint;* **AC** I.iii.85; **1H4** II.iv.413; **LL** V.iii.306; **MA** I.iii.27; **TN** III.iv.73
2 conduct, management, course of action **H8** III.ii.161 [Wolsey to Queen Katherine] *you may ... / Grow from the King's acquaintance, by this carriage;* **TC** II.iii.130; **WT** III.i.17
3 import, significance, purport **Ham** I.i.94 [Horatio to Marcellus and Barnardo, of King Hamlet's legal agreement with old Fortinbras] *by the same covenant / And carriage of the article designed*
4 carrying, conveyance, removal **Cym** III.iv.189 [Pisanio to Innogen] *Lest ... I be suspected of / Your carriage from the court*
5 burden, load **MW** II.ii.168 [Ford as Brook to Falstaff, of Ford's bag of money] *take all, or half, for easing me of the carriage;* **Tem** V.i.3
6 wagon, gun-carriage **KJ** V.vii.90 [Salisbury to Bastard, of Lewis the Dauphin] *many carriages he hath dispatched / To the sea-side*
7 loop attached to a belt for holding a sword **Ham** V.ii.148 [Osric to Hamlet, of the swords] *Three of the carriages ... are very dear to fancy* ☛ **WEAPONS**, p.491

carrier (*n.*) messenger, courier, go-between **Tit** IV.iii.86 [Titus to Clown] *art not thou the carrier?;* **MW** II.ii.131

carrion (*n.*) **1** carcass, wretch, worthless beast **MM** II.ii.167 [Angelo alone] *I ... / Do as the carrion does, not as the flower;* **H5** IV.ii.37; **JC** II.i.130; **MV** III.i.32; **MW** III.iii.181; **RJ** III.v.156
2 dead putrifying flesh, rotting carcass **E3** III.i.440 [Warwick to Countess] *The freshest summer's day doth soonest taint / The loathed carrion that it seems to kiss;* **Ham** II.ii.182; **2H4** IV.iv.80; **2H6** V.ii.11

carrion (*adj.*) **1** loathsome, vile, disgusting, corrupting **MV** IV.i.41 [Shylock to Duke] *why I rather choose to have / A weight of carrion flesh*; **MV** II.vii.63 [or: sense 3]

2 preying on rotting flesh **RJ** III.iii.35 [Romeo to Friar, of his banishment] *More validity, / More honourable state, more courtship lives / In carrion flies than Romeo*

3 lean as carrion, skeleton-like; or: putrefying **JC** III.i.275 [Antony alone, of Caesar's murder] *this foul deed shall smell above the earth / With carrion men, groaning for burial*;

carry (*v.*) **1** secure, obtain, gain **Cor** II.ii.4 [Second Officer to First Officer, of the election] *Coriolanus will carry it*; **AW** III.vii.19; **Cor** II.i.230, V.vi.43

2 sustain, support, hold one's own **Ham** V.ii.188 [Hamlet to Horatio, of Osrick and his associates] *a ... yeasty collection, which carries them through and through the most fanned and winnowed opinions*

3 wear; also: bear the weight of **1H6** II.i.24 [Burgundy to all, of Pucelle] *underneath the standard of the French / She carry armour as she hath begun* [with bawdy pun: carry someone's weight]

4 endure, put up with **RJ** IV.v.117 [Peter to First Musician] *I will carry no crotchets* ☞ coals, carry

5 carry out, manage, conduct **KL** V.iii.37 [Edmund to Captain] *carry it so / As I have set it down*; **H8** I.ii.134; **MA** II.iii.211; **MM** III.i.257; **MND** III.ii.240; **TNK** I.i.162

6 take, lead, conduct **MW** I.i.119 [Slender to Falstaff, of Falstaff's friends] *They carried me to the tavern*; **MW** I.i.220

7 conduct, comport, present **AW** IV.iii.103 [Bertram to Second Lord, of Parolles] *How does he carry himself?*; **H8** II.iv.143

8 maintain, keep going, carry on with **TN** III.iv.136 [Sir Toby to Fabian and Maria, of their plot] *We may carry it thus for our pleasure*

9 move on, take forward **AC** III.vii.75 [Canidius to Soldier] *This speed of Caesar's / Carries beyond belief*

10 carry off, get away with **AW** IV.i.26 [Parolles to himself, of lying] *It must be a very plausive invention that carries it*; **Oth** I.i.68

11 wield, exercise, exert **KL** I.i.303 [Gonerill to Regan] *If our father carry authority with such disposition as he bears*

12 [archery] send, shoot **2H4** III.ii.45 [Shallow to Silence, of Double] *'A would have ... carried you a forehand shaft a fourteen and fourteen and a half*

carry it (*away*) [from a falconry term 'to fly away with the game'] win the day, have the advantage, succeed **Ham** II.ii.359 [Hamlet to Rosencrantz and Guildenstern, of the players] *Do the boys carry it away?*; **MW** III.ii.63 [Host to Page, of Fenton as a suitor for Anne] *He will carry't*; **LL** III.i.138; **RJ** I.i.73; **TC** II.ii.2, 216; **TNK** III.i.78

carry-tale (*n.*) tell-tale, tale-bearer **LL** V.ii.463 [Berowne to all, of Boyet] *Some carry-tale ... / Told our intents before*; **Venus** 657

cart (*n.*) chariot, carriage **Ham** III.ii.164 [First Player] *Phoebus' cart* [i.e. the sun]

cart (*v.*) drive around in a cart [usual punishment for a prostitute] **TS** I.i.55 [Gremio to Baptista, of courting Katherina] *To cart her rather*; **AY** III.ii.104

carve (*v.*) **1** be a generous hostess; or: speak in a charmingly affected way **MW** I.iii.41 [Falstaff to Pistol, of Mistress Ford] *She discourses, she carves, she gives the leer of invitation*; **LL** V.ii.323

2 serve food to, wait on **TNK** IV.iii.86 [Doctor to Wooer, of the Gaoler's Daughter] *Desire to eat with her, carve her* [i.e. serve her up food with ceremony] [Q *crave*]

3 choose, select [as of a slice of meat] **Ham** I.iii.20 [Laertes to Ophelia, of Hamlet] *He may not, as unvalued persons do, / Carve for himself* [i.e. follow his own inclinations]; **Oth** II.iii.167

4 cut up, prepare **JC** II.i.173 [Brutus to all, of Caesar] *Let's carve him as a dish fit for the gods*

5 cut up meat at table **LL** IV.i.58 [Princess to Boyet, of a sealed letter] *you can carve - / Break up this capon* [also: make courtly gestures]

6 design, make up, shape artistically **MA** II.iii.17 [Benedick alone, of Claudio] *now will he lie ten nights awake carving the fashion of a new doublet*; **TS** IV.iii.89

carver, be one's own be a law unto oneself **R2** II.iii.143 [York to all, of Bolingbroke] *But in this kind to come, in braving arms, / Be his own carver ... it may not be*

case (*n.*) **1** state, plight, situation, circumstance **RJ** IV.v.98 [Nurse to Musicians] *well you know this is a pitiful case*; **AC** III.xiii.54; **AY** V.iv.201; **3H6** V.iii.32; **RJ** III.iii.85; **WT** I.ii.352

2 question, issue, subject **Cym** I.vii.42 [Iachimo to Innogen] *For idiots in this case of favour, would / Be wisely definite*; **1H6** V.iii.166; **3H6** IV.v.18

3 fit state, state of readiness **Tem** III.ii.25 [Trinculo to Caliban] *I am in case to justle a constable*

4 case-law, precedent **2H6** I.iii.202 [Gloucester to King, of how to handle the accusations of treachery] *if I may judge by case* [Q only]

5 outer covering, surface appearance **Sonn** 108.9 *eternal love in love's fresh case / Weighs not the dust and injury of age*; **MM** II.iv.13; **TN** V.i.163

6 suit, overall, outer garment **1H4** I.ii.177 [Poins to Prince Hal] *I have cases of buckram for the nonce*; **CE** IV.iii.23

7 skin, hide, coat **E3** I.i.98 [Warwick to Lorraine, of the King of France] *Bid him leave off the lion's case he wears*; **WT** IV.iv.808

8 mask, disguise, covering **RJ** I.iv.29 [Mercutio to Romeo] *Give me a case to put my visage in*; **LL** V.ii.273, 387

9 holder, covering, receptacle **MA** II.i.85 [masked Hero to masked Don Pedro] *God defend the lute should be like the case!* [i.e. the face to be like the mask]; **AC** IV.xv.88; **2H4** III.ii.315; **KL** IV.vi.145; **WT** V.ii.12

10 set, chest, box **H5** III.ii.4 [Nym to Bardolph] *I have not a case of lives*

case, on the [legal] in relation to this particular case **CE** IV.ii.42 [Dromio of Syracuse to Adriana, of Antipholus of Ephesus' arrest] *he is 'rested on the case*

case (*v.*) **1** cover, protect, enclose **Cym** V.iii.22 [Posthumus to Lord, of the youths] *With faces ... fairer / Than those for preservation cased*; **CE** II.i.85

2 hide, conceal, cover up **TC** III.iii.187 [Ulysses to Achilles] *If thou wouldst not ... case thy reputation in thy tent*

3 put on a mask, cover up **1H4** II.ii.51 [Bardolph to all] *Case ye, case ye*

4 flay, skin **AW** III.vi.96 [Second Lord to Bertram, of Parolles] *We'll make you some sport with the fox ere we case him*

cased (*adj.*) **1** enclosed in a case, in a setting **Per** V.i.110 [Pericles to himself, of Thaisa compared to Marina] *Her eyes as jewel-like, and cased as richly*

2 caged; or: living **KJ** III.i.259 [Cardinal Pandulph to King Philip] *thou mayst hold ... / A cased lion by the mortal paw* [F]

casement (*n.*) **1** window [on hinges and able to be opened] **KL** I.ii.60 [Edmund to Gloucester, of the letter] *I found it thrown in at the casement of my closet*; **AW** II.iii.213; **AY** IV.i.151; **MV** II.v.30, 33; **MW** I.iv.2; **R2** V.ii.14

2 moveable section of a window, light **MND** III.i.50 [Bottom to Quince] *may you leave a casement of the Great Chamber window ... open*

cashier (*v.*) **1** rob, fleece, relieve of money **MW** I.i.164 [Bardolph to Evans, of Slender] *And being fap, sir, was ... cashiered*

2 discharge, dismiss [from service] **MW** I.iii.6 [Host to Falstaff] *Discard, bully Hercules, cashier*

cashiered (*adj.*) dismissed, sacked, discarded **Tim** III.iv.61 [First Varro's Servant to Second Varro's Servant, of Flavius] *What does his cashiered worship mutter?*

casing (*adj.*) encasing, surrounding, enveloping **Mac** III.iv.22 [Macbeth to First Murderer, of Fleance's escape] *I had else been ... / As broad and general as the casing air*

'casion (*n.*) ☞ *'cagion* (*n.*)

cask (*n.*) casket, jewel-box **2H6** III.ii.409 [Suffolk to Queen] *A jewel, locked into the woefullest cask / That ever did contain a thing of worth*

casque, caske (*n.*) helmet **H5** Prologue.13 [Chorus] *the very casques / That did affright the air at Agincourt*; **Cor** IV.vii.43; **R2** I.iii.81; **TC** V.ii.173; **Tit** III.i.169 [F]; **TNK** III.vi.62 ☞ WEAPONS, p.491

cassock (*n.*) military cloak, long coat **AW** IV.iii.166 [Parolles to First Soldier, of the French army] *half of the which dare not shake the snow from off their cassocks lest they shake themselves to pieces*

cast (*n.*) **1** throw [of a dice], stroke **R3** V.iv.9 [King Richard to Catesby] *Slave, I have set my life upon a cast*; **1H4** IV.i.47

2 casting, founding **Ham** I.i.73 [Marcellus to Horatio and Barnardo, of the activities in Denmark] *such daily cast of brazen cannon* [Q2, Q1 *cost*]

3 tinge, shade, hue **Ham** III.i.85 [Hamlet alone] *the native hue of resolution / Is sicklied o'er with the pale cast of thought*

cast (*adj.*) made by casting [i.e. as for a statue] **AY** III.iv.14 [Celia to Rosalind, of Orlando] *He hath bought a pair of cast lips of Diana*

cast (*v.*) **1** calculate, reckon, estimate **2H6** IV.ii.81 [Smith to Cade, of the Clerk] *he can write and read and cast accompt*; **AC** II.vi.54; **Ham** II.i.115; **2H4** I.i.166; **TNK** V.i.56

2 arrange, dispose, organize **TNK** III.v.20 [Schoolmaster to all] *Cast yourselves in a body decently*

3 exclude, bar, proscribe **1H6** V.iv.146 [Charles to Winchester] *I'll rather keep / That which I have than ... / Be cast from possibility of all*; **Cym** V.iv.60

4 cast off, discard, dismiss, reject **Oth** I.i.150 [Iago to Roderigo, of Othello] *the state ... / Cannot with safety cast him*; **Oth** II.iii.265, V.iii.323; **TN** II.v.144

5 dismiss, discharge, release **Oth** II.iii.14 [Iago to Cassio] *Our General cast us thus early for the love of his Desdemona*

6 cast up, throw up, regurgitate **Per** II.i.58 [Second Fisherman to Pericles] *What a drunken knave was the sea to cast thee in our way!*; **Tem** II.i.255; **Tim** IV.iii.41

7 give, bestow [as a dowry] **TNK** II.i.2 [Gaoler to Wooer] *something I may cast to you*

8 [wrestling] throw down, make fall **Mac** II.iii.38 [Porter to Macduff, of drink] *I requited him for his lie and ... I made a shift to cast him* [also: sense 6]

cast away (*v.*) **1** cast off, discard, throw away **AY** IV.i.171 [Rosalind as Ganymede to Orlando] *'Tis but one cast away* [i.e. just one woman abandoned]; **H8** I.ii.48

2 ruin, waste carelessly, squander **TNK** V.ii.20 [Doctor to Gaoler] *Ne'er cast your child away for honesty* [i.e. don't let a concern for chastity be the ruin of her]

3 destroy, ruin **2H6** I.iii.199 [Horner to King, of Peter] *do not cast away an honest man for a villain's accusation*; **KJ** V.v.13; **MV** III.i.92

cast by (*v.*) throw aside, put to one side **RJ** I.i.93 [Prince to all, of the quarrel] *made Verona's ancient citizens / Cast by their grave-beseeming ornaments*

cast the water inspect the urine; diagnose the disease **Mac** V.iii.50 [Macbeth to Doctor] *cast / The water of my land, find her disease*

cast up (*v.*) vomit, throw up, regurgitate **H5** III.ii.53 [Boy alone, of Nym and Bardolph] *Their villainy goes against my weak stomach, and therefore I must cast it up*

Castalion (*n.*) [unclear meaning] Castilian [Spanish]; Castalian [sacred spring on Mt Parnassus] **MW** II.iii.30 [Host to Caius] *Thou art a Castalion-King-Urinal* [F; Q *castallian*]

castaway (*n.*) lost soul, reject, outcast **Luc** 744 [of Lucrece] *She there remains a hopeless castaway*; **R3** II.ii.6

castaway (*adj.*) rejected, cast off, discarded **AC** III.vi.40 [Caesar to Octavia] *That ever I should call thee castaway!*

casted (*adj.*) cast off, thrown aside, abandoned **H5** IV.i.23 [King Henry to Erpingham] *when the mind is quickened, out of doubt / The organs ... newly move / With casted slough*

castigation (*n.*) self-discipline, self-correction, self-denial **Oth** III.iv.41 [Othello to Desdemona] *Much castigation, exercise devout*

casual (*adj.*) accidental, subject to mischance **Cym** I.v.88 [Iachimo to Posthumus] *Your ring may be stolen ... so your brace of unprizable estimations, the one is but frail and the other casual*

casually (*adv.*) accidentally, by mischance **Cym** II.ii.140 [Innogen to Pisanio, of her jewel] *that too casually / Hath left mine arm*

casualty (*n.*) **1** chance occurrence, uncertainty, precariousness **KL** IV.iii.44 [disguised Kent to Gentleman, of Cordelia and Lear] *his own unkindness ... turned her / To foreign casualties*; **Per** V.i.92

2 mischance, misfortune, disaster **MV** II.ix.30 [Arragon to himself] *the martlet / Builds in the weather on the outward wall, / Even in the force and road of casualty*

cat (*n.*) civet cat [source of some perfumes] **KL** III.iv.102 [Lear to Edgar as Poor Tom] *Thou owest ... the cat no perfume*; **AY** III.ii.65

Cataian, Cathayan (*n.*) [from *Cathay* = China] scoundrel, rogue, villain **MW** II.i.135 [Page to himself, of Nym] *I will not believe such a Cataian*; **TN** II.iii.73

catalogue (*n.*) list, register, roll-call **Mac** III.i.91 [Macbeth to Murderers] *in the catalogue ye go for men, / As hounds and greyhounds ... are clept / All by the name of dogs*

cat-a-mountain, cat o'mountain (*adj./n.*) mountain-cat, wildcat, panther **MW** II.ii.25 [Falstaff to Pistol] *[you] will ensconce your rags, your cat-a-mountain looks ... under the shelter of your honour!*; **Tem** IV.i.262

cataplasm (*n.*) poultice, plaster, emollient **Ham** IV.vii.142 [Laertes to Claudius, of a poison] *no cataplasm so rare ... can save the thing from death / That is but scratched withal*

catastrophe (*n.*) **1** conclusion, end-point, expiration **AW** I.ii.57 [King to Bertram] *the catastrophe and heel of pastime*; **2H4** I.i.58; **LL** IV.i.78 [or: sense 2]

2 denouement, final event in a drama **KL** I.ii.133 [Edmund to himself, of Edgar] *pat he comes, like the catastrophe of the old comedy*; **LL** IV.i.78

catch (*n.*) musical round **Tem** III.ii.127 [Trinculo to Stephano] *This is the tune of our catch*; **Tem** III.ii.118; **TN** II.iii.17, 56, 59, 89, 92

catch (*v.*) **1** seize, get hold of, capture **RJ** IV.v.48 [Lady Capulet to herself, of Juliet's life] *cruel death hath catched it from my sight*; **3H6** III.ii.179; **KJ** I.i.173; **Mac** I.v.16, vii.3; **MND** III.ii.30

2 catch up with, overtake **Tem** V.i.316 [Prospero to Alonso] *[I'll] promise you ... sail so expeditious, that shall catch / Your royal fleet far off*

3 receive, take, incur **Tim** II.ii.214 [Flavius to Timon, reporting the Senators] *a noble nature / May catch a wrench*

4 catch the attention of, attract the notice of **H8** II.iii.77 [Lord Chamberlain to himself, of Anne] *Beauty and honour in her are so mingled / That they have caught the King*; **Sonn** 143.6

catch at (*v.*) **1** snatch at, pluck at, grab hold of **AC** V.ii.215 [Cleopatra to Iras] *Saucy lictors / Will catch at us like strumpets*

2 grasp, gather, infer **AC** II.ii.45 [Caesar to Antony] *You may be pleased to catch at mine intent / By what did here befall me*

catch the air struggle for breath **2H6** III.ii.371 [Vaux to Queen, of Beaufort's sickness] *That makes him gasp, and stare, and catch the air*

catching (*adj.*) contagious, infectious **TNK** I.ii.45 [Palamon to Arcite] *Affect another's gait, which is not catching / Where there is faith*

catechize (*v.*) **1** ask questions of **KJ** I.i.192 [Bastard alone] *I suck my teeth and catechize / My picked man of countries*

2 question systematically, cross-examine, interrogate **TN** I.v.57 [Feste to Olivia, of proving her a fool] *I must catechize you for it*; **Oth** III.iv.16

cate-log (*n.*) [idiosyncratic pronunciation of] catalogue, inventory, register **TG** III.i.271 [Launce alone, of his love] *Here is the cate-log of her condition*

cater-cousins (*n.*) good friends, people on the best of terms **MV** II.ii.120 [Gobbo to Bassanio, of Shylock and Launcelot] *His master and he … are scarce cater-cousins*

caterpillar (*n.*) parasite, exploiter, sponger **2H6** IV.iv.37 [First Messenger to King, of the rebels] *All scholars, lawyers, courtiers, gentlemen, / They call false caterpillars*; **R2** II.iii.165, III.iv.47

cates (*n.*) **1** (plural) delicacies, choice foodstuffs **1H6** II.iii.78 [Talbot to Countess] *we may / Taste of your wine and see what cates you have*; **E3** III.i.124; **1H4** III.i.157; **Per** II.iii.29
  2 provisions, food, victuals **CE** III.i.28 [Antipholus of Ephesus to Balthasar] *though my cates be mean, take them in good part*

catling (*n.*) catgut string **TC** III.iii.304 [Thersites to Achilles, of music in Ajax] *none, unless the fiddler Apollo get his sinews to make catlings on*

cat o'mountain (*n.*) ☛ cat-a-mountain (*n.*)

caudie (*n.*) ☛ candy (*n.*)

caudle (*n.*) type of medicinal warm gruel, potion **2H6** IV.vii.83 [Cade to Say] *Ye shall have a hempen caudle* [i.e. the medicine of the hangman's rope] [F4; F1 *candle*]; **LL** IV.iii.172

caudle (*v.*) provide a warm medicinal drink for **Tim** IV.iii.227 [Apemantus to Timon] *Will the cold brook … caudle thy morning taste, / To cure thy o'ernight's surfeit?*

cause (*n.*) **1** reason, motive, ground **KL** IV.iv.215 [Gentleman to Edgar] *the Queen on special cause is here*; **CE** II.i.33; **2H4** I.iii.1; **KL** IV.iii.51, vii.75; **TNK** III.vi.120, Epilogue.12
  2 explanation **KJ** III.iv.156 [Cardinal Pandulph to Lewis the Dauphin, of the people reacting to natural phenomena] *they will pluck away his natural cause / And call them meteors, prodigies and signs*
  3 occasion, circumstance **Cor** IV.i.41 [Cominius to Coriolanus] *if the time thrust forth / A cause for thy repeal*; **Cor** I.vi.83, II.iii.193
  4 affair, business, subject **Mac** III.i.33 [Macbeth to Banquo] *tomorrow … we shall have cause of state / Craving us jointly*; **H5** I.i.45; **JC** V.i.48; **LL** V.ii.787; **Tit** II.iv.9; **TS** IV.iv.26
  5 court case, legal action, matter before the court **Cor** II.i.74 [Menenius to Brutus and Sicinius, of the people] *All the peace you make in their cause*; **Cor** II.i.66; **2H6** IV.vii.81; **H8** V.iii.121; **KL** IV.vi.109
  6 (duelling) one of the situations or grounds set out in the code of honour which justifies a duel **AY** V.iv.49 [Touchstone to Jaques] *the quarrel was upon the seventh cause*; **LL** I.ii.171; **RJ** II.iv.25
  7 matter of concern, apprehension **2H4** I.iii.26 [Archbishop to Lord Bardolph, of uncertain aid] *It was young Hotspur's cause at Shrewsbury* [Q; F *case*]
  8 disease, illness, sickness **Cor** III.i.234 [First Senator to Coriolanus, of the mutiny] *Leave us to cure this cause*; **AW** II.i.111

'cause (*conj.*) because ☛ ELISION, p.146

causeless (*adj.*) **1** outside the normal course of nature, inexplicable by natural causes **AW** II.iii.3 [Lafew to Bertram and Parolles] *we have our philosophical persons to make modern and familiar, things supernatural and causeless*
  2 groundless, unjustified, idle **Venus** 897 [of Venus' senses] *She tells them 'tis a causeless fantasy … that they are afraid*

causeless (*adv.*) for no reason, without justification, groundlessly **2H6** III.i.162 [Gloucester to Queen] *you … / Causeless have laid disgraces on my head*

cautel (*n.*) deceit, trickery, cunning **Ham** I.iii.15 [Laertes to Ophelia, of Hamlet] *Perhaps he loves you now, / And now no soil nor cautel doth besmirch / The virtue of his will*; **Lover** 303

cautelous (*adj.*) **1** crafty, deceitful, wily **Cor** IV.i.33 [Coriolanus to Volumnia, of himself] *be caught / With cautelous baits and practice*
  2 cautious, wary, circumspect **JC** II.i.129 [Brutus to all] *Swear priests and cowards and men cautelous* [or: sense 1]

cavaleiro (*n.*) cabilero (*n.*)

Cavalery (*n.*) cavalier, courtly gentleman **MND** IV.i.22 [Bottom to Mustardseed] *help Cavalery Cobweb to scratch* [F *Caualery*]

cavaliero (*adj.*) gallant, valiant, honourable **MW** II.i.196 [Host to Ford, of Falstaff] *Hast thou no suit against my knight, my guest cavaliero?*; **MW** II.i.181 ☛ cabilero (*n.*)

cavalleria (*n.*) body of fine gentlemen, society of knights **Per** IV.vi.12 [Boult to Bawd, of Marina] *she'll disfurnish us of all our cavalleria* [Q *Caualereea*]

cave (*v.*) live in caves **Cym** IV.ii.138 [Belarius to Guiderius and Arviragus] *It may be heard at court that such as we / Cave here, hunt here*

cave-keeper (*n.*) cave-dweller **Cym** IV.ii.298 [Innogen alone] *I thought I was a cave-keeper*

cave-keeping (*adj.*) cave-dwelling; living in darkness **Luc** 1250 *In men, as in a rough-grown grove, remain / Cave-keeping evils that obscurely sleep*

caveto (*int.*) [summarizing a piece of advice] beware, take care **H5** II.iii.50 [Pistol to all] *Caveto be thy counsellor*

caviary (*n.*) caviare **Ham** II.ii.435 [Hamlet to First Player, of a play] *'Twas caviary to the general* [i.e. only for those with an acquired taste]

cavil (*n.*) quibble, hair-splitting objection **TS** II.i.383 [Tranio as Lucentio to Baptista, of dying before Vincentio] *That's but a cavil. He is old, I young*

cavil (*v.*) dispute over details, raise pointless objections **3H6** I.i.117 [Montague to Richard] *Let's fight it out and not stand cavilling thus*; **1H4** III.i.134; **1H6** V.iv.156; **3H6** III.ii.99; **Luc** 1025, 1093; **TG** I.i.38

'ce (*v.*) dialect version of 'shall' **KL** IV.vi.240 [Edgar to Oswald, adopting a country accent] *I'ce try*

cease (*n.*) ☛ cess (*n.*) 1

cease (*v.*) **1** put off, defer, appease **Tim** II.i.16 [Senator to Caphis, of asking Timon for his money] *Be not ceased / With slight denial*
  2 stop, halt, end **Cym** V.v.255 [Cornelius to Cymbeline] *A certain stuff, which being ta'en would cease / The present power of life*

ceinture (*n.*) belt, girdle **KJ** IV.iii.155 [Bastard to Hubert, of attack from France and unrest in England] *happy he whose cloak and ceinture can / Hold out this tempest* [F *center*]

celerity (*n.*) alacrity, rapidity, swiftness **H5** III.Chorus.2 [Chorus] *Thus with imagined wing our swift scene flies / In motion of no less celerity / Than that of thought*; **AC** I.i.145; **MM** IV.ii.107, V.i.391

cell (*n.*) small humble dwelling **RJ** V.iii.242 [Friar to Prince, of Juliet] *in my cell there would she kill herself*; **RJ** II.ii.192, iv.178; **Tem** I.ii.20, 347

cellarage (*n.*) cellars, basement **Ham** I.v.151 [Hamlet to Horatio and Marcellus, of the Ghost] *You hear this fellow in the cellarage*

cement (*v.*) firmly bring together, unite **AC** II.i.48 [Pompey to Menas, of Antony and Caesar] *the fear of us / May cement their divisions and bind up the petty difference*

censer (*n.*) perfuming vessel with a perforated and ornamented lid **TS** IV.iii.91 [Petruchio to Tailor] *Here's snip and nip and cut and slish and slash, / Like to a censer in a barber's shop*; **2H4** V.iv.18

censor (*n.*) ☛ ROMAN HISTORY, p.377

censure (*n.*) **1** assessment, opinion, judgement, criticism **Ham** I.iii.69 [Polonius to Laertes] *Take each man's censure, but reserve thy judgement*; **1H6** II.iii.10; **Mac** V.iv.14; **Oth** II.iii.187; **Per** II.iv.34; **R3** II.ii.144
  2 condemnation, blame, stricture **AY** IV.i.181 [Rosalind as Ganymede to Orlando] *beware my censure*; **AY** IV.i.7; **Cym** III.iii.55; **H8** III.i.64; **KL** I.iv.205; **MM** III.ii.176
  3 judgement, sentencing **Oth** V.ii.364 [Lodovico to Cassio, of Iago] *To you … / Remains the censure of this hellish villain*; **Cor** V.vi.143

censure (*v.*) **1** judge, think of, give an opinion of [not involving blame] **MA** III.ii.219 [Benedick alone] *I heard how I am censured*; **Cor** II.i.21; **1H6** V.v.97; **2H6** III.i.275; **JC** III.ii.16

2 judge critically, flaw, find fault with **KJ** II.i.328 [Hubert to Heralds, of the armies] *whose equality / By our best eyes cannot be censured*

3 pass judgement on, condemn, pronounce sentence on **TG** I.ii.19 [Lucetta to Julia] *'tis a passing shame / That I ... / Should censure thus on lovely gentlemen;* **KL** V.iii.3; **MM** I.iv.72, II.i.15, 29

center (*n.*) ➤ ceinture (*n.*)

centre (*n.*) **1** centre of the Earth, axis **Ham** II.ii.159 [Polonius to Claudius and Gertrude] *I will find / Where truth is hid, though it were hid indeed / Within the centre;* **MND** III.ii.54; **TC** III.ii.177; **WT** II.i.102

2 Earth [seen as centre of the Ptolemaic universe] **TC** I.iii.85 [Ulysses to Agamemnon] *The heavens themselves, the planets, and this centre / Observe degree, priority, and place* ➤ **COSMOS**, p.102

3 core of being, heart, soul **WT** I.ii.138 [Leontes, probably to himself] *Affection, thy intention stabs the centre;* **RJ** II.i.2; **Sonn** 146.1

century (*n.*) **1** hundred **Cym** IV.ii.391 [disguised Innogen to Lucius, of supposed Posthumus' grave] *when ... I ha' strewed his grave / And on it said a century of prayers*

2 army company of 100 soldiers **Cor** I.vii.3 [Lartius to Lieutenant] *dispatch / Those centuries to our aid;* **KL** IV.iv.6

cerecloth (*n.*) waxed winding-sheet, shroud **MV** II.vii.51 [Morocco to himself, of Portia's lead casket] *it were too gross / To rib her cerecloth in the obscure grave* [F *searecloath*]

cerements (*n.*) waxed shroud, grave-clothes, winding sheet **Ham** I.iv.47 [Hamlet to Ghost] *tell / Why thy canonized bones, hearsed in death, / Have burst their cerements*

ceremonious (*adj.*) scrupulous over formalities, punctilious about ritual **R3** III.i.45 [Buckingham to Cardinal Bourchier] *You are ... / Too ceremonious and traditional;* **R3** III.i.99

ceremony (*n.*) **1** observance, courtesy, regard **JC** IV.ii.21 [Brutus to Lucilius] *When love begins to sicken and decay, / It useth an enforced ceremony*

2 symbol of state, external sign of pomp **H5** IV.i.102 [disguised King Henry to Bates, of the King] *His ceremonies laid by, in his nakedness he appears but a man;* **JC** I.i.65; **MM** II.ii.59

3 sacred token, special symbol **MV** V.i.206 [Portia to Bassanio, of her ring] *What man ... wanted the modesty / To urge the thing held as a ceremony*

4 omen, portent, prognostication **JC** II.i.197 [Cassius to all, of Caesar] *the main opinion he held once / Of fantasy, of dreams, and ceremonies;* **JC** II.ii.13

cere up (*v.*) ➤ sear up (*v.*)

certain (*n.*) number of people, particular members **Cor** II.iii.52 [Coriolanus to Menenius] *Some certain of your brethren roared and ran*

certain (*adj.*) **1** reliable, trustworthy, definite **2H4** I.i.12 [Lord Bardolph to Northumberland] *I bring you certain news from Shrewsbury;* **2H4** III.i.99

2 steady, settled, fixed **MV** IV.i.60 [Shylock to Duke] *a lodged hate and a certain loathing / I bear Antonio;* **TNK** V.iv.21

3 sure, unerring, accurate **MND** II.i.157 [Oberon to Puck, of Cupid] *A certain aim he took*

4 secure, safe **KJ** IV.ii.105 [King John alone] *There is ... / No certain life achieved by others' death*

certainly (*adv.*) firmly, steadfastly, unalterably **1H6** V.i.37 [King to the ambassadors] *are we certainly resolved / To draw conditions of a friendly peace*

certainty (*n.*) **1** truth, facts [about] **Ham** IV.v.142 [Claudius to Laertes] *If you desire to know the certainty / Of your dear father*

2 inevitability, inescapable fact **Cym** IV.iv.27 [Belarius to Arviragus and Guiderius] *The certainty of this hard life*

certes (*adv.*) certainly, assuredly, without doubt **Oth** I.i.16 [Iago to Roderigo, quoting Othello] *Certes ... / I have already chose my officer;* **CE** IV.iv.73; **H8** I.i.48; **LL** IV.ii.160; **Tem** III.iii.31

certificate (*n.*) official document, formal deed **2H4** II.ii.115 [Poins to Prince Henry, of Falstaff's letter] *Why, this is a certificate!*

certify (*v.*) inform, assure, demonstrate to **1H6** II.iii.31 [Talbot to Messenger, of the Countess] *I go to certify her Talbot's here;* **1H6** IV.i.144; **MV** II.viii.10; **R3** III.ii.10

cess (*n.*) **1** cessation, ending, decease **Ham** III.iii.15 [Rosencrantz to Claudius] *The cess of majesty* [Q2; F *cease*]

2 estimation, reckoning, evaluation **1H4** II.i.7 [First Carrier to Ostler, of his horse] *poor jade is wrung in the withers out of all cess* [i.e. to excess]

cesse (*v.*) variant spelling of 'cease' **AW** V.iii.72 [Countess to King] *in me, O nature, cesse*

cestern, cesterne (*n.*) variant spelling of 'cistern' [= water receptacle, vessel, reservoir] **AC** II.v.95 [Cleopatra to Messenger] *So half my Egypt were submerged and made / A cesterne for scaled snakes!* **Mac** IV.iii.63; **Oth** IV.ii.60

chace (*n.*) ➤ chase (*n.*) 4

chafe (*n.*) temper, rage, fury **AC** I.iii.85 [Cleopatra to Charmian, of Antony] *this Herculean Roman does become / The carriage of his chafe*

chafe (*v.*) **1** fret, rage, seethe **MW** V.iii.8 [Mistress Page to Mistress Ford, of Page] *he will chafe at the doctor's marrying my daughter;* **JC** I.ii.101; **KL** II.vi.21; **Tim** I.i.25; **WT** III.iii.86

2 enrage, irritate, anger **TG** III.i.233 [Proteus to Valentine, of Silvia and the Duke] *her intercession chafed him so;* **H8** I.i.123; **TC** I.ii.167; **TS** I.ii.200, II.i.235

3 warm, inflame, rouse **2H6** III.ii.141 [King to himself, of dead Gloucester] *Fain would I go to chafe his paly lips / With twenty thousand kisses;* **TC** Prologue.2

chafed (*adj.*) enraged, irritated, angered **3H6** II.v.126 [Prince to King] *Warwick rages like a chafed bull;* **H8** III.ii.206; **KJ** III.i.259; **Tit** IV.ii.137

chaffless (*adj.*) free from chaff, uncontaminated, unsullied **Cym** I.vii.178 [Iachimo to Innogen, of Posthumus] *The love I bear him / Made me to fan you thus, but the gods made you ... chaffless*

chaffy (*adj.*) [as of chaff] worthless, useless, trashy **TNK** III.i.41 [Palamon to Arcite] *thou liest, and art ... a chaffy lord*

chafing (*n.*) irritation, anger, rage **Venus** 325 *All swoln with chafing, down Adonis sits*

chain (*n.*) chain of office **TN** II.iii.116 [Sir Toby to Malvolio] *rub your chain with crumbs*

chair (*n.*) **1** throne **2H4** IV.v.95 [King Henry IV to Prince Henry] *Dost thou so hunger for mine empty chair;* **3H6** I.i.51, 168, iv.97, II.vi.20, V.v.19; **R3** IV.iv.469, V.iii.252

2 ducal seat **3H6** II.i.90 [Edward to Richard, of York] *His dukedom and his chair with me is left*

3 place of authority **Cor** IV.vii.52 [Aufidius to Lieutenant] *power ... / Hath not a tomb so evident as a chair;* **JC** III.i.64; **MW** V.v.61

chair (*v.*) keep on the throne **Mac** V.iii.21 [Macbeth to himself] *This push / Will chair me ever or dis-seat me now* [F *cheere*]

chair-days (*n.*) old age, days for resting in a chair **2H6** V.ii.48 [Young Clifford to himself, as if to Clifford] *Wast thou ordained ... in thy reverence and thy chair-days, thus / To die in ruffian battle?*

chalice (*n.*) **1** small goblet, tiny tankard **MW** III.v.25 [Falstaff to Bardolph] *Take away these chalices*

2 ceremonial cup, drinking-cup **Ham** IV.vii.159 [Claudius to Laertes, of Hamlet] *I'll have preferred him / A chalice*

chaliced (*adj.*) with cup-shaped blossom **Cym** II.iii.22 [Song] *On chaliced flowers that lies*

challenge (*n.*) **1** claim, demand, assertion **1H6** IV.iv.153 [Richard to Charles] *accept the title thou usurpest, / Of benefit proceeding from our king / And not of any challenge of desert* [i.e. of any rightful claim]

2 legal objection **H8** II.iv.77 [Queen Katherine to Wolsey] *I ... make my challenge / You shall not be my judge*

challenge (v.) **1** demand as a right, claim, call for, insist on LL V.ii.800 [Princess to King] *at the expiration of the year, / Come challenge me;* 3H6 III.iii.86; KL IV.vii.31; LL V.ii.438; R2 II.iii.133; RJ III.v.215

2 reproach, reprove, reprimand Mac III.iv.41 [Macbeth to all, of absent Banquo] *Who may I rather challenge for unkindness / Than pity for mischance*

3 accuse, charge, denounce Tit I.i.343 [Titus alone, of himself] *Dishonoured thus and challenged of wrongs*

challenger (n.) claimant H5 II.iv.95 [Exeter to French King, of King Henry's claim to the French throne] *the native and true challenger;* Ham IV.vii.28

chamber (n.) **1** capital, metropolis, royal residence R3 III.i.1 [Buckingham to Prince Edward] *Welcome … to London, to your chamber*

2 bedchamber, bedroom Per I.i.152 [Antiochus to Thaliard] *you are of our chamber* [i.e. our chamberlain]; AY II.ii.5; Mac I.vii.76, II.ii.19, V.iv.2

3 piece of ordnance, cannon, gun H5 III.Chorus.34 [stage direction] *Alarum, and chambers go off;* 2H4 I.iv.51; H8 I.iv.49

chamber (v.) enclose, lodge, contain R2 I.i.149 [Mowbray to King Richard, of Bolingbroke] *the best blood chambered in his bosom*

chamber-counsel (n.) personal confidences, private conversation WT I.ii.237 [Leontes to Camillo] *I have trusted thee … / With all the nearest things to my heart, as well / My chamber-counsels, wherein … thou / Hast cleansed my bosom*

chamberer (n.) frequenter of ladies' chambers, drawing-room man of fashion Oth III.iii.262 [Othello alone] *I … have not those soft parts of conversation / That chamberers have*

chamberlain (n.) bedchamber attendant Mac I.vii.63 [Lady Macbeth to Macbeth, of the King] *his two chamberlains / Will I with wine and wassail so convince / That memory … / Shall be a-fume;* Tim IV.iii.223

chamber-lye (n.) urine 1H4 II.i.22 [Second Carrier to First Carrier] *your chamber-lye breeds fleas like a loach*

chamblet (n.) ☛ camlet (n.)

champain, champaign (n./adj.) expanse of open countryside KL I.i.64 [Lear to Gonerill] *all these bounds … with champains riched;* Luc 1247; TN II.v.154

champion (n.) warrior, fighter, man of valour Tit I.i.68 [Captain to all, of Titus] *Rome's best champion;* 1H6 III.iv.19; 3H6 V.vii.6; KL V.i.43

champion (adj.) flat and open, like a plain E3 III.iii.116 [King John to King Edward] *This champion field shall be a pool of blood*

champion (v.) challenge, defy, face Mac III.i.71 [Macbeth to himself, of Banquo's children becoming kings] *Rather than so, come fate into the list / And champion me to the utterance!*

chance (n.) **1** event, occurrence, situation [especially, bad] Ham V.ii.328 [Hamlet to all] *You that look pale and tremble at this chance;* Cym IV.iii.35; 2H4 IV.i.81; 3H6 II.v.107; Mac II.iii.88; TS I.i.45

2 outcome, situation TNK V.iii.66 [Emilia to Servant] *What is the chance?* [i.e. what has happened?]; 2H4 III.i.79

3 opportunity, prospect; or: risk Cym I.vi.68 [Queen to Pisanio] *Think what a chance thou changest on* [i.e. if you change sides]

4 possibility, prospect, aspect Oth I.i.73 [Iago to Roderigo, of Brabantio's joy] *throw such chances of vexation on't, / As it may lose some colour*

5 fortune, lot, destiny MV II.i.43 [Morocco to Portia] *bring me unto my chance;* AC I.iii.36; 2H4 III.i.51; KL III.vii.78; Luc 1596; TNK I.ii.116

6 falling out of events, fortuitous circumstance 1H6 V.iv.4 [Shepherd to Pucelle] *now it is my chance to find thee out* [i.e. I have happened to find you]; TC IV.iv.32

7 what may have happened, conceivability, possibility TN I.ii.8 [Captain to Viola] *to comfort you with chance*

8 misfortune, mischance, mishap MA V.i.38 [Leonato to Antonio, of philosophers] *they have … made a push at chance and sufferance*

chance (v.) **1** happen [to], transpire, come about CE I.ii.42 [Antipholus of Syracuse to Dromio of Ephesus] *How chance thou art returned so soon?;* AC III.iv.13; MM I.ii.152; MW V.v.209; Per III.ii.75; WT I.ii.11

2 come by chance, happen to arrive Per V.Chorus.1 [Gower alone] *Marina … chances / Into an honest house*

change (n.) **1** variation, modulation TG IV.ii.66 [Host to disguised Julia] *what fine change is in the music!;* Sonn 76.2

2 variety, assortment, range Cym II.iv.177 [Posthumus alone, of Innogen] *covetings, change of prides, disdain*

3 change of fortune, new circumstances JC V.iii.51 [Messala to Titinius] *It is but change … Octavius / Is overthrown by noble Brutus' power, / As Cassius' legions are by Antony;* AY I.iii.100; TC I.iii.98

4 change of mind, changeableness, caprice Sonn 20.4 *A woman's gentle heart, but not acquainted / With shifting change, as is false women's fashion* JC IV.ii.7; KL I.i.288

5 [dancing] round, turn LL V.ii.209 [masked King to masked Rosaline] *in our measure vouchsafe but one change;* H8 IV.ii.83

change (v.) **1** exchange, trade Per IV.vi.162 [Marina to Boult] *Thou holdest a place / For which the pained'st fiend of hell / Would not in reputation change;* LL V.ii.134, 238; MA IV.i.181; MND II.i.112; R2 III.ii.189; RJ III.v.31

2 substitute, replace, supplant Tem I.ii.82 [Prospero to Miranda, of Antonio's treatment of Prospero's appointees] *or changed 'em, / Or else new formed 'em;* TS III.i.90

3 change sides 3H6 V.i.57 [Edward to Warwick] *Wind-changing Warwick now can change no more*

4 change countenance, turn pale 2H4 IV.v.6 [Clarence to all, of King Henry IV] *His eye is hollow, and he changes much;* Cym I.vii.11; H5 II.ii.73; JC III.i.24; MA V.i.137

5 exchange, replacement [for] TC III.iii.27 [Calchas to all, of Troy and Antenor] *they will almost / Give us a prince of blood … / In change of him* H5 IV.viii.29; MA V.i.181

changeable (adj.) of varying colour [when viewed from different angles], shot TN II.iv.73 [Feste to Orsino] *the tailor make thy doublet of changeable taffeta*

changeful (adj.) changing, variable, unreliable TC IV.iv.96 [Troilus to Cressida] *sometimes … we will tempt the frailty of our powers, / Presuming on their changeful potency*

changeling (n./adj.) **1** child taken by fairies, stolen child MND II.i.23 [Puck to Fairy, of Titania and her attendant] *She never had so sweet a changeling;* MND II.i.120, IV.i.58; WT III.iii.114, IV.iv.683

2 unsightly person [☛ sense 1: an ugly or deformed child left by fairies in exchange for a beautiful one] TNK IV.ii.44 [Emilia alone, of Palamon] *Lie there, Arcite; / Thou art a changeling to him*

3 substitution, changeover, switch Ham V.ii.53 [Hamlet to Horatio] *The changeling never known*

4 waverer, turncoat, fickle thing Cor IV.vii.11 [Aufidius to Lieutenant, of Coriolanus] *his nature / In that's no changeling;* 1H4 V.i.76

changing (adj.) fickle, inconstant, faithless Tit I.i.312 [Saturninus to Titus, of Lavinia] *go give that changing piece / To him that flourished for her with his sword*

channel (n.) **1** course, bed, route KJ II.i.337 [King John to King Philip, comparing his claim to a river] *Whose passage, vexed with thy impediment, / Shall leave his native channel and o'er-swell*

2 open drain, gutter 2H4 II.i.45 [Falstaff to Bardolph, of the Hostess] *Throw the quean in the channel!;* 2H4 II.i.46; 3H6 II.ii.141; Luc 1487

3 narrow inlet, passage into a harbour E3 III.i.161 [Mariner to King John] *Purple the sea, whose channel filled as fast / With streaming gore*

chanson (n.) song Ham II.ii.418 [Hamlet to Polonius] *The first row of the pious chanson will show you more* [F,Q2; Q1 *Ballet*]

chanticleer (n.) rooster [from Chaucer's 'The Nun's Priest's Tale'] Tem I.ii.386 [Ariel singing to Ferdinand] *The strain of strutting chanticleer*

chant it sing out, give tongue **Venus** 869 [of Venus, and Adonis' hounds] *she hears them chant it lustily*

chantry (*n.*) small private chapel **H5** IV.i.294 [King Henry alone, praying] *I have built / Two chantries where the sad and solemn priests / Sing still for Richard's soul;* **TN** IV.iii.24

chaos (*n.*) piece of shapeless matter, amorphous mass **3H6** III.ii.161 [Richard alone] *To disproportion me in every part, / Like to a chaos*

chap (*n.*) ➤ **chaps** (*n.*)

chape (*n.*) metal plate on the sheath of a weapon, especially one covering the dagger-point **AW** IV.iii.142 [First Lord to Bertram, of Parolles] *that had the whole … practice [of war] in the chape of his dagger* ➤ **WEAPONS**, p.491

chapeless (*adj.*) without a sheath **TS** III.ii.47 [Biondello to Tranio as Lucentio, of Petruchio's armoury] *an old rusty sword … with a broken hilt, and chapeless*

chaplain (*n.*) minister, spiritual attendant **E3** II.i.279 [King Edward alone, of the Countess] *are her words sweet chaplains to her beauty?*

chapless, chopless (*adj.*) jawless **RJ** IV.i.83 [Juliet to Friar, of a charnel house] *O'ercovered quite … / With reeky shanks and yellow chapless skulls;* **Ham** V.i.87

chaplet (*n.*) garland, wreath **TNK** I.i.1 [stage direction] *with wheaten chaplets on their heads;* **MND** II.i.110; **TNK** IV.i.73

chapman (*n.*) trader, merchant, dealer **LL** II.i.16 [Princess to Boyet, of beauty] *Not uttered by base sale of chapmen's tongues;* **TC** IV.i.76

chaps, chops (*n.*) **1** jaws **2H6** III.i.259 [Suffolk to Queen, of Gloucester] *Before his chaps be stained with crimson blood;* **AC** III.v.12; **2H4** II.iv.125; **KJ** II.i.352; **Mac** I.ii.22; **Tem** II.ii.85 ➤ **wide-chopped** (*adj.*)

2 crack in the skin, fissure **Tit** V.iii.76 [Marcus to all] *if my frosty signs and chaps of age … / Cannot induce you to attend my words;* **Luc** 1452

3 [jocular] fat cheeks **1H4** I.ii.134 [Poins to Falstaff] *You will, chops?;* **2H4** II.iv.213

charact, caract (*n.*) insignia, badge, distinctive emblem **MM** V.i.56 [Isabella to Duke] *so may Angelo, / In all his dressings, characts … / Be an arch-villain*

character (*n.*) **1** distinctive sign, stamp, trait **E3** III.iii.127 [King Edward to Charles, of Audley] *within his face / Time hath engraved deep characters of age;* **2H4** I.ii.182; **MM** I.i.27, ii.154; **TC** V.ii.167; **TNK** IV.iii.110

2 personality sketch, personal description **Cor** V.iv.26 [Menenius to Sicinius, of Coriolanus] *I paint him in the character* [i.e. describe him accurately]; **Cor** II.i.61; **WT** III.iii.46

3 handwriting, style of writing, lettering **TN** V.i.344 [Olivia to Malvolio] *this is not my writing, / Though … much like the character;* **Cym** III.ii.28; **Ham** IV.vii.50; **MM** V.ii.187; **Per** III.i.65; **WT** V.ii.35

4 letter, letter-shape, graphic symbol **Per** IV.iii.44 [Dionyza to Cleon, of Marina] *her epitaphs / In glittering golden characters;* **Cym** IV.ii.49; **Lover** 174; **MM** V.i.11

5 figure, number **TC** I.iii.325 [Nestor to Ulysses, of Hector's challenge] *The purpose is perspicuous even as substance / Whose grossness little characters sum up*

6 shape, emblem **Lover** 16 [of a handkerchief] *Which on it had conceited characters* [or: sense 3]

7 written record, recorded fact **R3** III.i.81 [Richard to Prince Edward] *without characters fame lives long;* **2H6** I.i.99

8 personal appearance, demeanour **TN** I.ii.52 [Viola to Captain] *this thy fair and outward character*

character (*v.*) inscribe, engrave, write **AY** III.ii.6 [Orlando alone, of the trees] *in their barks my thoughts I'll character;* **E3** II.i.308; **Ham** I.iii.59; **Luc** 807; **Sonn** 108.1; **TG** IV.vii.4

characterless (*adj.*) leaving no trace, lacking any distinctive signs **TC** III.ii.186 [Cressida to Troilus] *When … mighty states characterless are grated / To dusty nothing*

charactery (*n.*) writing, letters, expression **MW** V.v.73 [Mistress Quickly as Queen of Fairies to all] *Fairies use flowers for their charactery;* **JC** II.i.308

chare (*n.*) chore, task, job **AC** V.ii.231 [Cleopatra to Charmian] *when thou hast done this chare;* **AC** IV.xv.74

chare (*v.*) do, accomplish, finish **TNK** III.ii.21 [Gaoler's Daughter alone, of Palamon] *All's chared when he is gone*

charge (*n.*) **1** command, order, injunction, instruction **1H4** I.i.35 [Westmorland to King Henry, of the expedition] *this haste was hot in question, / And many limits of the charge set down;* **E3** II.ii.31; **KJ** IV.ii.75; **Mac** IV.iii.20; **MW** III.iii.6; **TNK** II.i.316 ➤ **give in charge**

2 company, command **H5** IV.iii.6 [Salisbury to all] *I'll to my charge;* **1H4** II.iv.530, III.i.161, iii.184, 198; **2H4** I.ii.62; **JC** IV.ii.48; **R3** V.iii.25

3 task, responsibility, duty **Tem** I.ii.237 [Prospero to Ariel] *thy charge / Exactly is performed;* **AW** III.iii.4; **CE** I.ii.61; **3H6** V.v.20; **Mac** II.ii.6; **Per** III.i.27

4 commission, responsibility, official duty **MA** III.iii.7 [Verges to Dogberry, of the Watch] *give them their charge;* **H5** I.ii.239; **3H6** III.iii.258; **MA** III.iii.1; **R3** I.i.105; **WT** V.i.161

5 responsibility, culpability **R2** I.i.84 [King Richard to Bolingbroke] *What doth our cousin lay to Mowbray's charge?;* **KL** I.i.127

6 accusation, censure, blame **R3** I.iii.325 [Richard alone] *The secret mischiefs that I set abroach / I lay unto the grievous charge of others;* **AY** III.ii.339; **Ham** II.i.28; **1H6** III.i.4; **WT** V.i.194

7 expense, cost, outlay **R2** II.i.159 [King Richard to York, of the Irish wars] *these great affairs do ask some charge;* **CE** V.i.18; **KJ** V.ii.100; **MA** I.i.96; **R3** I.ii.255

8 money entrusted, valuables **1H4** II.i.59 [Chamberlain to Gadshill] *a kind of auditor, one that hath abundance of charge too;* **CE** I.ii.73; **1H4** II.i.47

9 weight, import, moment **RJ** V.ii.18 [Friar Laurence to Friar John, of his letter to Romeo] *The letter was not nice, but full of charge;* **Ham** V.ii.43

charge, in prepared for action, at the ready **2H4** IV.i.118 [Mowbray to Westmorland, of Mowbray's father and Bolingbroke] *Their armed staves in charge*

charge (*v.*) **1** order, command, enjoin **KJ** III.i.151 [King John to Cardinal Pandulph] *Thou canst not … devise a name / So slight, unworthy, and ridiculous, / To charge me to an answer, as the Pope;* **AY** I.i.3; **3H6** V.v.81; **KL** III.vii.51; **Mac** I.iii.77; **Tem** I.ii.453

2 entreat, exhort, enjoin **AW** I.iii.178 [Countess to Helena] *I charge thee … / To tell me truly;* **Cor** IV.vi.114; **MV** V.i.298; **TS** V.i.84

3 entrust, commission, delegate **CE** III.i.8 [Antipholus of Ephesus to Angelo, of Dromio of Ephesus] *I … charged him with a thousand marks*

4 oblige, constrain, compel **TN** II.i.12 [Sebastian to Antonio, of Antonio's propriety] *it charges me in manners the rather to express myself*

5 attack, assail, storm **AC** IV.xi.1 [Caesar to all] *But being charged, we will be still by land* [i.e. unless attacked]; **LL** VI.ii.88; **MA** V.i.134

6 load, heap, pile up **AC** I.ii.4 [Charmian to Alexas] *O that I knew this husband, which you say must charge his horns with garlands!* [F change]

7 overload, overburden, weigh down **Cym** III.iv.43 [Innogen to Pisanio] *If sleep charge Nature* [i.e. if I manage to sleep]; **H5** I.ii.15; **JC** III.iii.2

8 cause expense, burden with a cost **MW** II.ii.160 [Ford as Brook to Falstaff, of acquaintance] *I sue for yours - not to charge you*

9 load [a gun] **2H4** III.ii.254 [Falstaff to Shallow, of Wart] *'A shall charge you, and discharge you, with the motion of a pewterer's hammer*

10 toast, drink a health to **2H4** II.iv.108 [Falstaff to Pistol] *I charge you with a cup of sack* [also: sense 9]

charged (*adj.*) **1** burdened, laden, oppressed **Mac** V.i.50 [Doctor to Gentlewoman, of Lady Macbeth] *The heart is sorely charged;* **H5** I.ii.284

2 loaded; also, given a burden **2H4** II.iv.51 [Falstaff to Doll] *to venture upon the charged chambers bravely*

chargeful *(adj.)* costly, expensive, lavish **CE** IV.i.29 [Angelo to Antipholus of Ephesus, of the chain] *The fineness of the gold, and chargeful fashion*

charge-house *(n.)* school, college **LL** V.i.78 [Armado to Holofernes] *Do you not educate youth at the charge-house on the top of the mountain?*

charging-staff *(n.)* lance used in jousting **TNK** IV.ii.140 [Messenger to Theseus, of one of the knights] *in his hand / He bears a charging staff* ➤ **WEAPONS**, p.491

chariest *(adj.)* most cautious, shyest, most careful **Ham** I.iii.36 [Laertes to Ophelia] *The chariest maid is prodigal enough / If she unmask her beauty to the moon*

chariness *(n.)* careful preservation, strict uprightness **MW** II.i.92 [Mistress Ford to Mistress Page, of Falstaff] *I will consent to act any villainy against him that may not sully the chariness of our honesty*

charitable *(adj.)* kindly, loving, warmhearted **Tim** I.ii.89 [Timon to lords, of the name of friends] *Why have you that charitable title from thousands*

charitably *(adv.)* in all Christian charity **H5** IV.i.138 [Williams to disguised King Henry, of those who die in a battle] *how can they charitably dispose of anything when blood is their argument?*

charm *(n.)* **1** magic spell, enchantment **Tem** V.i.31 [Prospero to Ariel] *My charms I'll break;* **Cor** I.v.21; **MW** II.ii.100; **Oth** I.i.172; **RJ** II.Chorus.6; **Tem** I.ii.467
2 incantation, chant **R3** I.iii.214 [Richard to Queen Margaret, of her cursing] *Have done thy charm*
3 enchantress, witch **AC** IV.xii.25 [Antony alone, of Cleopatra] *This grave charm ... hath at fast and loose / Beguiled me;* **AC** IV.xii.16

charm *(v.)* **1** work magic [on], bewitch, enchant **TN** II.ii.18 [Viola alone, of Olivia] *Fortune forbid my outside have not charmed her!;* **Cym** IV.ii.277; **Ham** I.i.164; **2H6** VI.i.64; **Luc** 1404
2 produce, bring, cause [as by magic] **MND** IV.i.82 [Titania to her attendants] *Music, ho! Music such as charmeth sleep;* **Cym** I.vii.117
3 entreat, implore, conjure **JC** II.i.271 [Portia to Brutus] *I charm you ... / That you unfold to me, your self, your half, / Why you are heavy*
4 overcome, subdue, take over [as if by a charm] **Oth** V.ii.182 [Iago to Emilia] *Go to, charm your tongue* [i.e. be quiet]; **Cym** V.iii.68; **3H6** V.v.31; **Tem** I.ii.467; **TS** IV.ii.58
5 persuade, convince, win over **Cym** V.iii.32 [Posthumus to Lord, of the youths] *more charming, / With their own nobleness;* **Luc** 1681
6 bind, order, tell **TS** I.i.206 [Lucentio to Tranio, of Biondello] *I will charm him first to keep his tongue*

charmed *(adj.)* **1** bewitched, enchanted, placed under a spell **MND** III.ii.376 [Oberon to Puck, of Titania] *I will her charmed eye release / From monster's view;* **Mac** IV.i.9, V.vi.51
2 bewitching, spellbinding, enchanting **Lover** 146 [of the man] *Threw my affections in his charmed power*

charmer *(n.)* enchanter/enchantress, worker of charms **TNK** V.iv.131 [Theseus to the gods] *O you heavenly charmers, / What things you make of us!;* **Oth** III.iv.57

charming *(adj.)* **1** acting as charms, exercising magic power **1H6** V.iii.2 [Pucelle alone] *Now help, ye charming spells and periapts*
2 acting as charms, protecting from evil **Cym** I.iv.35 [Innogen to Pisanio, of her kiss] *set / Betwixt two charming words*

charmingly *(adv.)* enchantingly, delightfully, fascinatingly **Tem** IV.i.119 [Ferdinand to Prospero] *This is a most majestic vision, and / Harmonious charmingly*

charneco *(n.)* variety of sweet Portuguese wine **2H6** II.iii.63 [Second Neighbour to Horner] *here's a cup of charneco*

charnel-house, charnel house *(n.)* bone-store, burial vault **RJ** IV.i.81 [Juliet to Friar] *hide me nightly in a charnel house;* **Mac** III.iv.70

charter *(n.)* **1** right, privilege, prerogative **R3** III.i.54 [Buckingham to Cardinal Bourchier] *You break no privilege nor charter;* **AW** IV.v.89; **AY** II.vii.48; **Cor** I.ix.14; **Sonn** 58.9, 87.3
2 pledge, permission, assurance **Oth** I.iii.243 [Desdemona to Duke] *let me find a charter in your voice*

chartered *(adj.)* licensed, privileged, permitted **H5** I.i.48 [Canterbury to Ely, of King Henry] *when he speaks, / The air, a chartered libertine, is still*

chary *(adj.)* ➤ **chariest** *(adj.)*

chary *(adv.)* carefully, dearly, with cherishing **Sonn** 22.11 *thy heart which I will keep so chary / As tender nurse her babe from faring ill*

chase *(n.)* **1** pursuit, sequence, hunt **AY** I.iii.31 [Celia to Rosalind, of Orlando] *By this kind of chase, I should hate him;* **JC** I.ii.8; **KJ** I.i.223; **MND** II.ii.94; **Sonn** 143.5; **TG** V.iv.15
2 prey, game, victim, quarry **2H6** V.ii.14 [York to Warwick, of Clifford] *Seek thee out some other chase, / For I myself must hunt this deer to death;* **3H6** II.iv.12; **WT** III.iii.56
3 hunting ground, territory **Tit** II.ii.21 [Marcus to Saturninus, of his dogs] *Will rouse the proudest panther in the chase;* **Tit** II.iii.255; **TNK** V.i.131
4 [tennis] forfeited point; also: pursuit **H5** I.ii.267 [King Henry to Ambassador, of the Dauphin] *he hath made a match with such a wrangler / That all the courts of France will be disturbed / With chases* [also: sense 1] [F *Chaces*]

chase *(v.)* harry, harass, persecute **WT** V.i.216 [Florizel to Perdita] *Though Fortune ... / Should chase us, with my father*

chaser *(n.)* pursuer, hunter **Cym** V.iii.40 [Posthumus to Lord] *Then began / A stop i'th' chaser*

chaste *(adj.)* **1** celibate, single, unmarried **MV** I.ii.100 [Portia to Nerissa] *I will die as chaste as Diana;* **RJ** I.i.217
2 of allowed love-making [because married] **TNK** III.vi.200 [Hippolyta to Theseus] *By all the chaste nights I have ever pleased you*
3 pure, stainless, undefiled **Oth** V.ii.2 [Othello to himself, of the 'cause'] *Let me not name it to you, you chaste stars!*

chastisement *(n.)* punishment, retribution, correction **1H6** IV.i.69 [King to Gloucester, of Burgundy] *Why then, Lord Talbot there shall talk with him / And give him chastisement for this abuse;* **MM** V.i.255; **R2** IV.i.22

chat *(n.)* chatter, prattle, idle talk **Luc** 791 [Lucrece to herself] *fellowship in woe doth woe assuage, / As palmers' chat makes short their pilgrimage;* **Tem** II.i.271

chat *(v.)* go on about, gossip about, talk of **Cor** II.i.200 [Brutus to Sicinius, of Coriolanus] *Your prattling nurse ... lets her baby cry / While she chats him*

chattels *(n.)* moveable possessions **H8** III.ii.343 [Suffolk to Wolsey, of lands such as *charmeth* sleep] *To forfeit all your goods, lands, tenements, / Chattels, and whatsoever*

chaudron, chawdron *(n.)* entrails [of a beast] **Mac** IV.i.33 [Third Witch to Witches] *Add thereto a tiger's chaudron / For the ingredience of our cauldron*

chawed *(adj.)* chewed **H5** IV.ii.48 [Grandpré to all, of the English army's horses] *in their pale dull mouths the gimmaled bit / Lies foul with chawed grass*

che *(pron.)* dialect version of 'I' **KL** IV.vi.240 [Edgar to Oswald, adopting a country accent] *keep out, che vor' ye* [i.e. I warrant you]

cheapen *(v.)* bargain for, bid for, settle the price of **Per** IV.vi.9 [Bawd to Pander and Boult, of Marina] *she would make a puritan of the devil if he should cheapen a kiss of her;* **MA** II.iii.30

cheat *(n.)* trick, fraud, deception **WT** IV.iii.118 [Autolycus alone, of his deception] *If I make not this cheat bring out another ... let me be unrolled;* **WT** IV.iii.27

cheater *(n.)* deceiver, sharper, gamester; also: officer who looks after estates forfeited to the crown **Tit** V.i.111 [Aaron to Lucius, of Titus] *I played the cheater for thy father's hand;* **2H4** II.iv.94; **MW** I.iii.64; **Sonn** 151.3

check (*n.*) **1** reprimand, reproof, rebuke **KL** I.iii.21 [Gonerill to Oswald] *Old fools ... must be used / With checks;* **AC** IV.iv.31; **2H4** III.i.64; **MW** III.iv.78; **Oth** I.i.149, III.iii.67, IV.iii.19

2 repulse, reverse, resistance **KJ** V.i.73 [Bastard to King John, of Lewis the Dauphin] *Shall a beardless boy ... brave our fields ... / And find no check?;* **Sonn** 58.7; **TC** I.iii.5

3 restraint, control, counsel of moderation **TS** I.i.32 [Tranio to Lucentio, of moral discipline] *Let's [not] ... so devote to Aristotle's checks / As Ovid be an outcast quite abjured*

4 pause, interruption, stoppage **TC** I.iii.94 [Ulysses to all, of the sun] *posts like the commandment of a king, / Sans check, to good and bad*

check (*v.*) **1** rebuke, scold, reprimand **2H6** I.ii.54 [Duchess to Gloucester] *Next time I'll keep my dreams unto myself, / And not be checked;* **AW** I.i.65; **2H4** I.ii.197; **3H6** III.ii.166; **KL** II.i.140; **R2** V.v.46

2 restrain, stop, hold back **3H6** I.iv.151 [Northumberland to all] *hardly can I check my eyes from tears;* **Sonn** 5.7, 15.6

3 take the reins of, control, manage **KJ** II.i.123 [Queen Eleanor to Constance] *Thy bastard shall be king / That thou mayst be a queen and check the world;* **3H6** II.vi.12; **KJ** III.iv.152

check at (*v.*) **1** turn aside from, shy away from **KL** I.i.150 [Kent to Lear] *check / This hideous rashness;* **Ham** IV.vii.61

2 [falconry] swerve to pounce, turn towards, swoop at **TN** II.v.112 [Sir Toby to Fabian, of Malvolio and the letter's riddle] *with what what the staniel checks at it!;* **TN** III.i.62

checkered (*adj.*) patterned, with varied markings **2H6** III.i.229 [Queen to all, of a snake] *With shining checkered slough*

cheek-roses (*n.*) blushing cheeks **MM** I.iv.16 [Lucio to Isabella] *Hail, virgin, if you be, as those cheek-roses / Proclaim you are no less*

cheer (*n.*) **1** entertainment, fare, food and drink **CE** III.i.66 [Angelo to Antipholus of Ephesus] *Here is neither cheer, sir, nor welcome;* **CE** III.i.19; **Cym** III.vii.39; **MW** III.ii.46; **RJ** IV.v.87; **TS** III.ii.185

2 kind welcome, good reception **Mac** III.iv.32 [Lady Macbeth to Macbeth] *You do not give the cheer*

3 lifestyle, fare, standard of living **Ham** III.ii.229 [Second Player, as Queen, to her King] *An anchor's cheer in prison be my scope*

4 face, look, expression **MV** III.ii.312 [Portia to Bassanio] *show a merry cheer;* **E3** II.ii.101; **1H6** I.ii.48; **MND** III.ii.96; **Tit** I.i.267; **TNK** I.v.4

5 mood, disposition **H8** V.i.142 [King Henry to Cranmer] *Be of good cheer;* **AW** III.ii.64; **Sonn** 97.13; **Tit** II.iii.188; **WT** I.ii.148
☞ **EXCLAMATIONS**, p.158; **GREETINGS**, p.206

6 cheerfulness, mirth, joy **Ham** III.ii.173 [Second Player, as Queen, to her King] *you are so sick of late, / So far from cheer;* **Ham** I.ii.116; **MA** I.iii.66 [or: sense 5]

cheer (*v.*) encourage, urge on, galvanize **3H6** II.ii.78 [Prince to King] *cheer these noble lords;* **H8** I.iv.41; **MND** IV.i.124; **R3** I.iii.5; **Sonn** 15.6; **Venus** 484

cheer up (*v.*) encourage, urge on, egg on **Tim** I.ii.41 [Apemantus to and of Timon, of his guests] *all the madness is he cheers them up to't;* **Luc** 435

cheer thou / you?, how how are you feeling **MV** III.v.65 [Lorenzo to Jessica] *How cheer'st thou, Jessica?*

cheerily (*adv.*) ☞ **EXCLAMATIONS**, p.158

cheerly (*adv.*) **1** cheerfully, brightly, animatedly **Tim** II.ii.219 [Timon to Flavius] *Prithee, man, look cheerly;* **AY** II.vi.13, 17; **H5** II.ii.192; **3H6** V.iv.2; **R2** I.iii.66

2 [cry of encouragement] heartily, with a will **Tem** I.i.5 [Boatswain to Mariners] *Cheerly, cheerly, my hearts;* **1H4** V.iv.43; **RJ** I.v.15, 88; **Tem** I.i.26

chequin (*n.*) type of gold coin [of Italy and Turkey] **Per** IV.ii.24 [Pander to Bawd] *Three or four thousand chequins were as pretty a proportion to live quietly* ☞ **MONEY**, p.286

cherish (*v.*) **1** support, foster, sustain **2H6** I.i.201 [Salisbury to York and Warwick] *And, as we may, cherish Duke Humphrey's deeds;* **TG** V.iv.12; **Tim** III.v.74

2 nourish, cause to grow **3H6** II.vi.19 [Clifford alone] *For what doth cherish weeds but gentle air?;* **KJ** III.i.169; **Luc** 950

3 entertain kindly, look after well **1H4** III.iii.170 [Falstaff to Hostess] *look to thy servants, cherish thy guests*

cherries (*n.*) [metaphor for] lips **TNK** I.i.178 [First Queen to Theseus, of Hippolyta] *Her twinning cherries*

cherry-pit (*n.*) [children's game] throwing cherry-stones into a hole **TN** III.iv.116 [Sir Toby to Malvolio] *'tis not for gravity to play at cherry-pit with Satan*

cherubin (*n.*) **1** cherub, angel; or: cherubim, angels **Cym** II.iv.88 [Iachimo to Posthumus, of Innogen's bedroom] *The roof o'th' chamber / With golden cherubins is fretted;* **Mac** I.vii.22; **MV** V.i.62

2 celestial being, heavenly beauty **Tem** I.ii.152 [Prospero to Miranda] *a cherubin / Thou wast that did preserve me;* **H8** I.i.23; **Lover** 319; **Oth** IV.ii.62; **Sonn** 114.6; **TC** III.ii.67

cherubin (*adj.*) cherubic, angelic **Tim** IV.iii.64 [Timon to Alcibiades, of Phrynia] *Hath in her more destruction than thy sword, / For all her cherubin look*

chevalier (*n.*) knight **1H6** IV.iii.14 [Richard to all, of Talbot] *I ... cannot help the noble chevalier*

chevalry (*n.*) ☞ chivalry (*n.*)

cheverel (*n.*) kid leather [noted for its pliancy] **RJ** II.iv.82 [Mercutio to Romeo] *here's a wit of cheverel, that stretches from an inch narrow to an ell broad!*

cheveril (*adj.*) flexible, yielding, pliant **TN** III.i.12 [Feste to Viola as Cesario] *A sentence is but a cheveril glove to a good wit;* **H8** II.iii.32

chew (*v.*) **1** plan, devise, conceive **H5** II.ii.56 [King Henry to Scroop] *how shall we stretch our eye / When capital crimes, chewed, swallowed, and digested, / Appear before us?*

2 keep repeating, mumble over **MM** II.iv.5 [Angelo alone] *God in my mouth, / As if I did but only chew His name*

chew upon (*v.*) consider, ponder, reflect upon **JC** I.ii.170 [Brutus to Cassius] *chew upon this*

chewet (*n.*) jackdaw, chatterer **1H4** V.i.29 [Prince Hal to Falstaff] *Peace, chewet, peace!* [also: minced-meat dish]

chicken (*n.*) child, little one **TNK** V.iv.94 [Gaoler's Daughter to Gaoler, of Wooer] *Alas, poor chicken, / He was kept down with hard meat and ill lodging;* **Mac** IV.iii.217

chid (*v.*) ☞ chide (*v.*)

chidden (*adj.*) **1** scolded, reproved, rebuked **TC** II.ii.45 [Troilus to Helenus, of the wings of reason] *fly like chidden Mercury from Jove;* **JC** I.ii.183

2 driven along, storm-struck, beaten against **Oth** II.i.12 [Second Gentleman to Montano, of the sea] *The chidden billow seems to pelt the clouds* [F; Q *chiding*]

chide (*v.*), past form **chid 1** scold, rebuke, reprove **TNK** III.i.107 [Arcite to Palamon] *when I spur / My horse, I chide him not*
☞ **FEW**, p.xxi

2 contend with, beat against **1H4** III.i.42 [Glendower to Hotspur] *the sea / That chides the banks of England, Scotland, Wales*

3 quarrel, wrangle, fight **MND** II.i.145 [Titania to Fairies, of herself and Oberon] *We shall chide downright if I longer stay;* **Sonn** III.i

4 brusquely command, drive [away] with harsh words **3H6** II.v.17 [King alone] *my Queen, and Clifford too, / Have chid me from the battle;* **AW** III.vii.42; **KJ** IV.i.86; **MND** III.ii.312; **RJ** IV.i.74; **TG** IV.ii.100

chider (*n.*) quarreller, abusive person **TS** I.ii.225 [Tranio as Lucentio to Petruchio] *I love no chiders*

chiding (*n.*) **1** telling-off, scolding, rebuke **TNK** II.ii.27 [Fourth Countryman to the others] *'tis but a chiding* [i.e. I can only be told off]; **AY** IV.iii.65; **KL** I.iii.1

2 barking, brawling, angry noise **MND** IV.i.114 [Hippolyta to Theseus, of the hounds] *Never did I hear / Such gallant chiding;* **AY** II.i.7

chiding (*adj.*) noisy, brawling, tumultuous **Per** III.i.32 [Pericles to Marina] *Thou hast as chiding a nativity, / As … heaven can make / To herald thee from the womb*; **H8** III.ii.197; **TC** I.iii.54

chief (*n.*) main person **3H6** III.iii.262 [Warwick alone, of Edward] *I was the chief that raised him to the crown*

chief, in chiefly, principally **2H4** IV.i.31 [Westmorland to Archbishop] *Unto your grace do I in chief address / The substance of my speech*; **MM** V.i.218

chief (*adj.*) **1** principal, topmost, pre-eminent **1H6** I.i.177 [Winchester alone] *I intend to … sit at chiefest stern of public weal* [i.e. governing with greatest power]
　　2 finest, best, foremost **1H6** I.i.139 [Third Messenger to all] *all France, with their chief assembled strength* [or: main body]

chief (*adv.*) chiefly, principally **Ham** I.iii.74 [Polonius to Laertes, about wearing appropriate clothes] *And they in France of the best rank and station / Are of a most select and generous chief in that* [unclear meaning]

child (*n.*) **1** baby girl **WT** III.iii.69 [Shepherd to himself, of Perdita] *A boy or a child, I wonder?*
　　2 heir, scion, inheritor **H8** IV.ii.6 [Katherine to Griffith] *Didst thou not tell me … / That the great child of honour, Cardinal Wolsey, / Was dead?*

child, with bulging out **LL** IV.iii.88 [Berowne to himself, of Katharine] *Her shoulder is with child*

child (*v.*) be dealt with by children **KL** III.vi.108 [Edgar alone, of Lear] *He childed as I fathered*

childbed (*adj.*) of being in labour, belonging to confinement **WT** III.ii.102 [Hermione to Leontes, of the way she has been treated] *The childbed privilege denied, which 'longs / To women of all fashion*

child-changed (*adj.*) changed by his children; or: changed into a child **KL** IV.vii.17 [Cordelia to the gods, of Lear] *Th'untuned and jarring senses O wind up / Of this child-changed father*

childhood (*n.*) filial relationship, duty owed to parents **KL** II.iv.173 [Lear to Regan] *Thou better knowest / The offices of nature, bond of childhood*

childing (*adj.*) fertile, fruitful, teeming **MND** II.i.112 [Titania to Oberon] *The childing autumn, angry winter change / Their wonted liveries*

childish (*adj.*) child-like, befitting childhood **WT** IV.iv.399 [disguised Polixenes to Florizel, of Florizel's father] *does [he] nothing / But what he did being childish?* [i.e. when he was a child]

childishness (*n.*) childhood, period of childish behaviour **AY** II.vii.166 [Jaques to all] *last Scene of all … / Is second childishness, and mere oblivion*

childness (*n.*) childish qualities, childishness **WT** I.ii.170 [Polixenes to Leontes, of Florizel] *with his varying childness cures in me / Thoughts that would thick my blood*

chill (*adj.*) sensitive to cold, faint-hearted **AW** IV.v.51 [Clown to Lafew] *the many will be too chill and tender*

'chill (*pron.* + *v.*) dialect version of 'I will' **KL** IV.vi.235 [Edgar to Oswald, adopting a country accent] *'Chill not let go, zir*

chimney (*n.*) fireplace, hearth **Cym** II.iv.80 [Iachimo to Posthumus] *The chimney / Is south the chamber*; **1H4** II.i.21; **MW** V.v.43

chine (*n.*) **1** [of meat] joint, portion, piece **E3** III.iii.159 [King John to the French, of the English] *but scant them of their chines of beef*; **2H6** IV.x.55; **H8** V.iv.26
　　2 ☞ mose in the chine

chinks (*n.*) money-bags, ready money **RJ** I.v.117 [Nurse to Romeo, of Juliet] *he that can lay hold of her / Shall have the chinks*

chip (*n.*) key [of a spinet, harpsichord, etc] **Sonn** 128.10 *those dancing chips, / O'er whom thy fingers walk with gentle gait*

chip bread cut away the crust of a loaf **2H4** II.iv.233 [Falstaff to Doll, of Prince Henry] *'a would ha' chipped bread well*

chirrah (*int.*) [unclear usage; perhaps attempting a greeting in Greek] sirrah **LL** V.i.32 [Armado to Holofernes and Nathaniel] *Chirrah!*

chirurgeonly (*adv.*) like a surgeon **Tem** II.i.142 [Antonio to all, of Sebastian bringing a plaster] *And most chirurgeonly*

chivalry (*n.*) **1** knightly prowess, warlike distinction **Luc** 109 *Collatine's high name, / Made glorious by his manly chivalry*; **3H6** II.i.71; **R2** I.i.203; **TC** IV.iv.147
　　2 knights, men-at-arms **H5** I.ii.157 [Canterbury to King Henry, of England] *When all her chivalry hath been in France*; **2H4** II.iii.20
　　3 knighthood, knightly qualities **TC** I.ii.229 [Pandarus to Cressida, of Troilus] *the prince of chivalry!*; **1H4** V.i.94
　　4 knightly rank [as displayed on a coat-of-arms: a twisted band encircling a helmet] **Per** II.ii.29 [Thaisa to Simonides, of the third knight] *his device a wreath of chivalry*

choice (*n.*) **1** special value, estimation, esteem **AW** III.vii.26 [Helena to Widow, of Bertram] *This ring he holds / In most rich choice*
　　2 picked company, select band **KJ** II.i.72 [Chatillon to King Philip] *a braver choice of dauntless spirits … / Did never float upon the swelling tide*
　　3 ability to choose, skill in choosing **TNK** IV.ii.35 [Emilia alone] *I have no choice*
　　4 abundance, profusion, great supply **1H6** V.v.17 [Suffolk to King, of Margaret] *she is not so divine, / So full replete with choice of all delights*

choice, of picked, specially selected **2H4** I.iii.11 [Hastings to Archbishop] *five-and-twenty thousand men of choice*

choice (*adj.*) **1** chosen, specially worthy, excellent **KL** I.iv.260 [Lear to Gonerill] *My train are men of choice and rarest parts*; **1H6** V.iii.3; **H8** III.i.91; **JC** III.i.163; **TS** I.ii.233
　　2 appropriate, fitting, well-chosen **LL** V.i.15 [Nathaniel to Holofernes] *A most singular and choice epithet*; **H8** I.ii.162

choice-drawn (*adj.*) specially selected, chosen with great care **H5** III.Chorus.24 [Chorus] *who … will not follow / These culled and choice-drawn cavaliers to France?*

choicely (*adv.*) carefully, with great discrimination **2H6** III.i.313 [Cardinal to York] *To Ireland will you lead a band of men, / Collected choicely*

choir, quire (*n.*) **1** company, group, assembly **MND** II.i.55 [Puck to Fairy] *the whole choir hold their hips and laugh*; **2H6** I.iii.87; **Venus** 840
　　2 part of a church where the choir sings **Cym** III.iii.43 [Arviragus to Belarius] *We make a quire … / And sing our bondage freely*

choir, quire (*v.*) **1** sing in tune, make music **Cor** III.ii.113 [Coriolanus to Volumnia] *My throat of war be turned, / Which choired with my drum, into a pipe*
　　2 sing in a choir, sing in chorus **MV** V.i.62 [Lorenzo to Jessica, of the stars as angels] *Still quiring to the young-eyed cherubins*

choke (*v.*) **1** smother, suffocate, stifle **Mac** I.ii.9 [Captain to King, of the battle] *As two spent swimmers that do cling together / And choke their art* [i.e. make swimming impossible]; **Cym** III.v.78
　　2 silence, quieten, still **TNK** V.i.80 [Palamon praying to Venus] *[who] hast the might … to choke Mars's drum*; **TS** II.i.369
　　3 suppress, crush, put down **H8** I.ii.4 [King Henry to Wolsey] *I stood i'th' level / Of a full-charged confederacy, and give thanks / To you that choked it*

choke up (*v.*) smother, suffocate, stifle **E3** II.ii.139 [Countess to King Edward, of the Queen and Salisbury] *It is their lives … / That I would have choked up*; **R2** III.iv.44

choler (*n.*) anger, rage, wrath **2H6** V.i.23 [York to himself] *Scarce can I speak, my choler is so great*; **H5** IV.vii.175; **JC** IV.iii.39; **LL** I.ii.192; **MW** III.iii.78; **R2** I.i.153

choleric (*adj.*) **1** inclined to anger, hot-tempered, irascible **2H6** I.ii.51 [Duchess to Gloucester] *Are you so choleric / With Eleanor, for telling but her dream?*; **JC** IV.iii.43; **KL** I.i.298; **TS** IV.i.160

2 irritable, angry, enraged **CE** II.ii.67 [Dromio of Syracuse to Antipholus of Syracuse, advising him not to eat meat] *Lest it make you choleric*; **CE** II.ii.72; **JC** IV.iii.43; **MM** II.ii.130; **Per** IV.vi.165

3 giving rise to anger, causing bad temper **TS** IV.iii.19 [Grumio to Katherina, of a neat's foot] *I fear it is too choleric a meat*

choose, cannot have no alternative, cannot do otherwise **Cor** IV.iii.33 [Volsce to Roman, of Aufidius] *He cannot choose*; **2H4** III.ii.202; **MV** III.i.104; **Tem** I.ii.186; **TS** Induction.i.40 ☛ **POLITENESS**, p.340

choose forth (*v.*) select, pick out, make a choice **1H6** I.ii.101 [Pucelle to Charles, of her sword] *Out of a great deal of old iron I chose forth*

chop (*v.*) [various readings possible] pounce upon; seize; exchange **TNK** III.i.13 [Arcite alone, as if to Emilia] *In thy rumination / I … might eftsoons come between / And chop on some cold thought!*

chop-fallen downcast, dejected, down in the mouth **Ham** V.i.189 [Hamlet to Horatio, of Yorick] *Not one now to mock your own grinning? Quite chop-fallen?* ☛ **chaps** (*n.*) 1

chopine (*n.*) type of shoe with a high base **Ham** II.ii.426 [Hamlet to one of the players] *your ladyship is nearer to heaven than when I saw you last by the altitude of a chopine*

chopless (*adj.*) ☛ **chapless** (*adj.*)

chop logic (*n.*) ☛ **chopped logic** (*n.*)

chopped, chopt (*adj.*) **1** chapped, chafed, roughened **AY** II.iv.46 [Touchstone to Rosalind and Celia, of Jane Smile] *her pretty chopt hands*; **JC** I.ii.242

2 dried up, fissured, cracked **2H4** III.ii.267 [Falstaff to Wart] *give me always a little, lean, old, chopped, bald shot*; **Sonn** 62.10

chopped logic (*n.*) contentious arguer, disputatious wretch **RJ** III.v.149 [Capulet to Juliet] *How, how, how, how, chopped logic?* [F; Q1 *chop logic*]

chopping (*adj.*) [unclear meaning] equivocating, chopping and changing **R2** V.iii.123 [Duchess of York to York] *The chopping French we do not understand*

choppy (*adj.*) chapped, cracked, rough **Mac** I.iii.43 [Banquo to Witches] *each at once her choppy finger laying / Upon her skinny lips*

chops (*n.*) ☛ **chaps** (*n.*)

chorus (*n.*) character in a play who speaks the prologue and comments on the course of events **Ham** III.ii.254 [Ophelia to Hamlet, after his summary of the play] *You are as good as a chorus*; **H5** Prologue.32; **WT** IV.i

chorus-like (*adv.*) in the manner of a chorus, like a running commentary **Venus** 360 [of Adonis and Venus] *this dumb play had his acts made plain / With tears which chorus-like her eyes did rain* ☛ **chorus** (*n.*)

chosen (*adj.*) **1** choice, outstanding, special **Per** V.i.43 [Lysimachus to Lord, of Marina] *She … with her sweet harmony / And other chosen attractions, would allure*

2 elite, carefully selected **1H6** I.iv.53 [Talbot to all, of the French] *a guard of chosen shot I had* [i.e. marksmen]

chough (*n.*) **1** jackdaw **Tem** II.i.271 [Antonio to Sebastian, of Gonzalo's talking] *I myself could make / A chough of as deep chat* [i.e. train a jackdaw to be as profound]; **AW** IV.i.19; **KL** IV.vi.13; **Mac** III.iv.124; **MND** III.ii.21; **TNK** I.i.20

2 chatterer, prater, prattler **Ham** V.ii.88 [Hamlet to Horatio, of Osrick] *'Tis a chough*

3 rustic, clown **WT** IV.iv.613 [Autolycus to himself, of the Shepherd] *the old man … scared my choughs from the chaff*

'chould (*v.*) dialect version of 'I should' **KL** IV.vi.238 [Edgar to Oswald, adopting a country accent] *'chould ha' bin zwaggered out of my life*

christen (*adj.*) Christian **1H4** II.iv.7 [Prince Hal to Poins, of the drawers] *I … can call them all by their christen names* [Q]; **1H4** II.ii.18

christendom (*n.*) baptismal name, Christian name **AW** I.i.171 [Helena to Parolles] *a world / Of pretty, fond, adoptious christendoms* ☛ **SWEARING**, p.435

Christian (*n.*) ordinary person, normal human being **Ham** III.ii.30 [Hamlet to Players] *having th'accent of Christians*

christom (*adj.*) [malapropism for 'christened' or 'chrism'] in a christening robe, innocent **H5** II.iii.11 [Hostess to Bardolph, of Falstaff] *'A … went away an it had been any christom child*

chronicle (*n.*) **1** story, account, narrative **Tem** V.i.163 [Prospero to Alonso, of his story] *'tis a chronicle of day by day*

2 place in history, historical account **AC** III.xiii.175 [Antony to Cleopatra] *I and my sword will earn our chronicle*

chronicle (*v.*) **1** register, log, put on record [as] **TG** I.i.41 [Valentine to Proteus, of a lover] *he … should not be chronicled for wise*

2 enter into a chronicle, record in history **MND** III.ii.240 [Helena to Hermia] *This sport well carried shall be chronicled*

chrysolite (*n.*) type of semi-precious stone **Oth** V.ii.144 [Othello to Emilia, of Desdemona] *another world / Of one entire and perfect chrysolite*

chuck (*n.*) chicken, chick [usually as a term of endearment] **Mac** III.ii.45 [Macbeth to Lady Macbeth] *Be innocent of the knowledge, dearest chuck, / Till thou applaud the deed*; **AC** IV.v.2; **H5** III.ii.25; **LL** V.i.105, ii.659; **TN** III.iv.113 ☛ **ADDRESS FORMS**, p.8

chuff (*n.*) miser, skinflint; or: churl, clown **1H4** II.ii.88 [Falstaff to Travellers] *ye fat chuffs*

church-like (*adj.*) pious, devout, devotional **2H6** I.i.245 [York to himself, of Lancaster] *Whose church-like humours fits not for a crown*

churl (*n.*) **1** peasant, serf, rustic **Cym** III.vii.37 [Belarius to disguised Innogen, of himself and his sons] *Think us no churls*; **CE** III.i.24; **2H6** III.ii.213; **Tim** I.i.25; **Tit** I.i.489

2 villain, contemptible fellow **Sonn** 32.2 *When that churl Death my bones with dust shall cover*

3 [term of endearment] wretch, miser, villain **Sonn** 1.12 *Within thine own bud buriest thy content, / And, tender churl, mak'st waste in niggarding*; **RJ** V.iii.163

churl (*v.*) turn churlish, become ungracious **Sonn** 69.11 [of observers] *Then churls their thoughts (although their eyes were kind)* [or: with commas, noun use in sense 3]

churlish (*adj.*) **1** rude, blunt, ungracious **H5** IV.i.15 [King Henry to Erpingham] *A good soft pillow for that good white head / Were better than a churlish turf of France*; **AY** V.iv.74; **Ham** V.i.236; **1H6** IV.i.53; **KJ** II.i.519; **Venus** 134

2 violent, rough, harsh **TC** I.ii.21 [Alexander to Cressida, of Ajax] *he is as valiant as the lion, churlish as the bear*; **AY** II.i.7; **KJ** II.i.76, III.i.303; **Venus** 107, 616

3 stiff, hard, unyielding **1H4** V.i.16 [King Henry to Worcester] *Will you again unknit / The churlish knot of all-abhorred war*

4 stingy, miserly, niggardly **AY** II.iv.77 [Corin to Rosalind as Ganymede] *My master is of churlish disposition*

cicatrice (*n.*) scar, scar-like mark **AW** II.i.43 [Parolles to Lords] *Captain Spurio, with his cicatrice … here on his sinister cheek*; **AY** III.v.23; **Cor** II.i.142; **Ham** IV.iii.62

cinder (*n.*) burning coal, flaming ember **2H4** IV.iii.51 [Falstaff to Prince John] *I in the clear sky of fame o'ershine you as much as the full moon doth the cinders of the element* [i.e. the stars]; **AC** V.ii.173

cinquepace (*n.*) five-step capering dance **MA** II.i.66 [Beatrice to Hero] *wooing, wedding, and repenting, is as a Scotch jig, a measure, and a cinquepace*; **Ham** III.ii.50; **TN** I.iii.123

cinque-spotted (*adj.*) having five spots **Cym** II.ii.38 [Iachimo to himself, of Innogen] *On her left breast / A mole cinque-spotted*

cipher (*n.*) figure nought, nonentity, mere nothing **LL** I.ii.55 [Mote to himself, of Armado] *To prove you a cipher*; **AY** III.ii.282; **H5** Prologue.17; **MM** II.ii.39; **WT** I.ii.6

cipher (*v.*) **1** symbolize, represent, portray **Luc** 207 [Tarquin to himself, of his coat of arms] *Some loathsome dash the herald will contrive, / To cipher me how fondly I did dote*; **Luc** 1396

2 decipher, read, spell out **Luc** 811 [Lucrece to herself] *the illiterate that know not how / To cipher what is writ*

circle (*n.*) **1** compass, confines, bounds **KJ** V.ii.136 [Bastard to Lewis the Dauphin, of King John] *[he is] well prepared / To whip this dwarfish war ... / From out the circle of his territories*; **AY** V.iv.34

2 magical circle **AY** II.v.56 [Jaques to Amiens, of a 'ducdame'] *'Tis a Greek invocation, to call fools into a circle*; **H5** V.ii.289; **RJ** II.i.24

3 crown, coronet, diadem **KJ** V.i.2 [King John to Cardinal Pandulph] *Thus have I yielded up into your hand / The circle of my glory*; **AC** III.xii.18

circled (*adj.*) **1** in a circular motion, encircling **RJ** II.ii.110 [Juliet to Romeo, of the moon] *That monthly changes in her circled orb*

2 rounded, circular **Luc** 1229 *the maid with swelling drops 'gan wet / Her circled eyne*

circuit (*n.*) **1** enclosed space, ambit, compass **3H6** I.ii.30 [Richard to York] *How sweet a thing it is to wear a crown; / Within whose circuit is Elysium*; **TNK** III.i.46

2 crown, circlet, diadem **2H6** III.i.352 [York to himself] *the golden circuit on my head*

circummured (*adj.*) walled around **MM** IV.i.27 [Isabella to disguised Duke, of Angelo] *He hath a garden circummured with brick*

circumscribe (*v.*) **1** confine, fence in, hem in **Tit** I.i.71 [Captain to Romans, of Titus] *with fortune is returned / From where he circumscribed with his sword ... the enemies of Rome*

2 restrict, reduce, limit **Ham** I.iii.22 [Laertes to Ophelia, of Hamlet choosing a wife] *must his choice be circumscribed*

circumscription (*n.*) restriction, restraint, constraint **Oth** I.ii.27 [Othello to Iago] *I would not my unhoused free condition / Put into circumscription and confine*

circumstance (*n.*) **1** detail(s), particular(s), specifics **MA** III.ii.91 [Don John to Don Pedro and Claudio, of Hero] *circumstances shortened, ... the lady is disloyal*; **Ham** I.v.127; **1H6** I.i.109; **2H6** I.i.103; **KJ** II.i.77; **RJ** II.v.36

2 circumlocution, verbiage, unnecessary detail **E3** III.i.8 [Lorraine to King John] *not to spend the time in circumstance*; **MV** I.i.154; **Oth** I.i.13; **TS** V.i.23

3 special argument, detailed explanation **TG** III.i.36 [Proteus to Duke, of slander against Valentine] *it must with circumstance be spoken*; **CE** V.i.16; **R3** I.ii.77, 80; **TC** III.iii.114; **TG** I.i.36, 84

4 condition, state, situation **Ham** I.iii.102 [Polonius to Ophelia] *Unsifted in such perilous circumstance*; **Ham** II.ii.157, III.iii.83; **Oth** III.iii.16; **TG** I.i.37

5 pageantry, ceremony, spectacle **WT** V.i.90 [Leontes to Gentleman, of Florizel] *His approach / So out of circumstance and sudden*; **Oth** III.iii.351

circumstanced (*adj.*) governed by circumstances, subject to the situation **Oth** III.iv.197 [Bianca to Cassio] *I must be circumstanced*

circumstantial (*adj.*) full of circumstances, rich in detail **Cym** V.v.384 [Cymbeline to all] *This fierce abridgement / Hath to it circumstantial branches*

circumvent (*v.*) outwit, cheat, get the better of **Ham** V.i.79 [Hamlet to Horatio, of the politician] *one that would circumvent God*

circumvention (*n.*) **1** warning to avoid, chance to outwit **Cor** I.ii.6 [Aufidius to First Senator] *What ever have been thought on in this state / That could be brought to bodily act ere Rome / Had circumvention?*

2 craft, outwitting, getting the better of [someone] **TC** II.iii.15 [Thersites alone, of Ajax's and Achilles' wit] *which ... is so abundant scarce it will not in circumvention deliver a fly from a spider*

cital (*n.*) account, report, mention **1H4** V.ii.61 [Vernon to Hotspur, of Prince Hal] *He made a blushing cital of himself*

cite (*v.*) **1** urge, call on, arouse, summon **3H6** II.i.34 [Edward to Richard, of seeing three suns] *I think it cites us, brother, to the field*; **2H6** III.ii.281; **H8** IV.i.29; **PassP** XIV.15; **TG** I.iv.83

2 be evidence of, confirm, acknowledge **AW** I.iii.205 [Helena to and of the Countess] *Whose aged honour cites a virtuous youth*

cite up (*v.*) call to mind, make reference to **R3** I.iv.14 [Clarence to the Keeper, of himself and Gloucester] *we ... cited up a thousand heavy times / During the wars*; **Luc** 524

citizen (*adj.*) city-bred, city-mannered **Cym** IV.ii.8 [Innogen to all] *I am ... not so citizen a wanton as / To seem to die ere sick*

cittern-head (*n.*) [term of abuse] cittern [type of guitar] with a grotesquely carved head **LL** V.ii.607 [Boyet to Holofernes, of his face] *A cittern-head*

city (*n.*) citizens, city community **Per** V.Epilogue.13 [Gower alone] *to rage the city turn*

City (*adj.*) such as would be found in the City [of London]; formal **Tim** III.vi.68 [Timon to Lords] *Make not a City feast of it, to let the meat cool ere we can agree upon the first place*

civet (*n.*) type of musky perfume [obtained form the civet cat] **KL** IV.vi.130 [Lear to all] *Give me an ounce of civet*; **AY** III.ii.61; III.ii.46

civil (*adj.*) **1** civilized, cultured, refined **Cym** III.vi.23 [Innogen alone] *who's here? / If any thing that's civil, speak*; **AY** III.ii.124; **2H6** IV.vii.56; **Oth** IV.i.64; **TG** V.iv.157; **TN** I.iv.21

2 seemly, decent, well-behaved **TN** III.iv.5 [Olivia to Maria, of Malvolio] *He is sad and civil, / And suits well for a servant with my fortunes*; **2H4** II.vii.87; **H5** I.ii.199; **MA** II.i.270; **RJ** Prologue.4, III.ii.10

3 of civil war **2H4** IV.v.134 [King Henry IV to Prince Henry] *O my poor kingdom, sick with civil blows!*; **AC** I.i.45; **2H4** V.v.109; **2H6** IV.viii.43; **R2** I.iii.128; **RJ** Prologue.4

4 of civil law **MV** V.i.210 [Bassanio to Portia, of her ring] *No woman had it, but a civil doctor*

5 civic, public, city **2H6** I.i.193 [Salisbury to York, of the Irish] *bringing them to civil discipline*; **AC** V.i.16; **2H4** IV.i.42

civility (*n.*) civilized conduct, courteous behaviour, good manners **AY** II.vii.94 [Duke Senior to Orlando] *in civility thou seemest so empty*; **AY** II.vii.97; **MV** II.ii.182; **MW** IV.i.25; **Oth** I.i.132

clack-dish (*n.*) begging bowl with a lid that could be clacked to attract attention **MM** III.ii.120 [Lucio to disguised Duke, of the Duke and a female beggar] *his use was to put a ducat in her clack-dish*

claim (*n.*) demand for service **KJ** V.ii.101 [Lewis the Dauphin to Cardinal Pandulph, of the funders of the conflict] *Who else but I, / And such as to my claim are liable*

clamor, clamour (*n.*) protest, complaint, outcry **KL** I.i.165 [Kent to Lear] *whilst I can vent clamour from my throat*; **KL** IV.iii.31, V.iii.206

clamor, clamour (*v.*) silence, hush, quieten **WT** IV.iv.247 [Clown to Mopsa and Dorcas] *Clamor your tongues, and not a word more*

clangor, clangour (*n.*) clanging, ringing, reverberation **3H6** II.i.18 [Richard to Warwick] *Like to a dismal clangour heard from far*

clap (*v.*) **1** [of two people's hands] strike together, clasp [to seal a bargain] **H5** V.ii.129 [King Henry to Katherine] *Give me your answer ... and so clap hands, and a bargain*; **WT** I.ii.104

2 pat, slap on the back [as an endearment] **R2** V.v.86 [Richard to Groom, of his horse] *This hand hath made him proud with clapping him*

3 enter, strike, place **2H4** III.ii.45 [Shallow to Silence, of Double's archery] *'A would have clapped i'th' clout at twelve score*

4 put smartly, place promptly, set effectively **R2** III.ii.114 [Scroop to King Richard] *Boys with women's voices / Strive to speak big and clap their female joints / In stiff unwieldy arms against thy crown*; **H8** I.iii.18, iv.9, V.iv.79; **RJ** III.i.6

5 [bowls] fix, stick, set **KJ** II.i.583 [Bastard alone, of commodity] *This bawd, this broker ... / Clapped on the outward eye of fickle France*

clap, at a at one stroke, at once **KL** I.iv.291 [Lear to all] *What, fifty of my followers at a clap?*

clap into (*v.*) **1** strike up with, enter briskly into **MA** III.iv.39 [Margaret to Beatrice] *Clap's into 'Light o'love';* **AY** V.iii.10
2 make haste with, get on with **MM** IV.iii.39 [Abhorson to Barnadine] *I would desire you to clap into your prayers*

clap on (*v.*) activate promptly, put on smartly **AC** III.x.19 [Scarus to Enobarbus, of Antony] *Claps on his sea wing;* **MW** II.ii.132

clap to (*v.*) shut tight, slam shut **1H4** II.iv.270 [Falstaff, to Hostess] *Hostess, clap to the doors!;* **Cor** I.iv.53

clap up (*v.*) **1** seal, settle hastily, complete suddenly **KJ** III.i.235 [King Philip to Cardinal Pandulph, of the treaty] *To clap this royal bargain up of peace;* **TS** II.i.318
2 shut up, imprison **2H6** II.iv.49 [Buckingham to guards, of Jourdain, Southwell, and Bolingbroke] *let them be clapped up close;* **AC** IV.ii.17

clap her aboard [as of a ship] board her, jump on board **TNK** II.ii.32 [Second Countryman to First Countryman, of his wife] *Clap her aboard tomorrow night and stow her*

clapper-claw (*v.*) beat up, thrash, scratch **MW** II.iii.59 [Host to Caius, of Evans] *He will clapper-claw thee tightly;* **TC** V.iv.1

clasp (*v.*) cling, hold tight, hang on **Per** IV.i.56 [Marina to Leonine, of Pericles] *clasping to the mast*

clatpole (*n.*) ☞ **clotpoll** (*n.*)

clause (*n.*) premise, assertion, statement **TN** III.i.150 [Olivia to Viola as Cesario] *Do not extort thy reasons from this clause*

claw (*v.*) **1** flatter, preen, set off **LL** IV.i.64 [Dull to Nathaniel, of Holofernes] *If a talent be a claw, look how he claws him with a talent* [also: scratch]
2 flatter, fawn upon, butter up **MA** I.iii.16 [Don John to Conrade] *I ... claw no man in his humour*

clay (*n.*) earth, ground, mud **2H6** III.i.311 [Cardinal to York] *Th'uncivil kerns of Ireland are in arms / And temper clay with blood of Englishmen*

clean (*adj.*) well-built, shapely, comely **TNK** IV.ii.114 [Pirithous to Theseus, of one of Palamon's knights] *all his lineaments / Are as a man would wish 'em, strong and clean*

clean (*adv.*) totally, absolutely, utterly **Cym** III.vi.20 [Innogen alone] *famine, / Ere clean it o'erthrow Nature;* **Cor** III.i.302; **H8** I.iii.29; **JC** I.iii.35; **R2** III.i.10; **Tit** I.i.132

cleanly (*adj.*) **1** clean **WT** I.ii.123 [Leontes to Mamillius] *We must be neat - not neat but cleanly, captain* [i.e. not in the sense of horned cattle]
2 deft, skilful, clever **1H4** II.iv.444 [Prince Hal (as King) to Falstaff (as Hal), of Falstaff] *Wherein neat and cleanly, but to carve a capon and eat it?;* **AY** IV.i.70

cleanly (*adv.*) **1** deftly, cleverly, skilfully **Tit** II.i.94 [Demetrius to Aaron] *hast not thou full often struck a doe / And borne her cleanly by the keeper's nose?*
2 completely, totally, quite **Venus** 694 [Venus to Adonis, of hounds] *Ceasing their clamorous cry till they have singled ... the cold fault cleanly out*

cleanly-coined (*adj.*) cleverly invented, smartly made up **Luc** 1073 [Lucrece as if to Collatine] *I will not ... fold my fault in cleanly-coined excuses*

clean-timbered (*adj.*) well-built, clean-limbed **LL** V.ii.636 [King to all, of Armado as Hector] *I think Hector was not so clean-timbered*

cleap (*v.*) ☞ **clip** (*v.*) 1

clear (*adj.*) **1** pure, spotless, faultless **TNK** I.i.31 [Third Queen to Emilia] *for the sake / Of clear virginity;* **KL** IV.vi.73; **Luc** 11, 382; **Mac** I.vii.18; **MV** II.ix.42; **Tem** III.iii.83

2 innocent, blameless, free from fault, not guilty **3H6** III.iii.183 [Warwick to Lewis, of Edward's marriage] *I am clear from this misdeed of Edward's;* **AC** V.ii.122; **Mac** II.i.28; **MW** III.iii.109; **Per** IV.vi.103; **Tim** III.iii.31
3 serene, cheerful, unclouded **WT** I.ii.343 [Camillo to Leontes] *with a countenance as clear / As friendship wears at feasts;* **MND** III.ii.60; **TS** II.i.172

clear (*adv.*) cheerfully, brightly, with unclouded face **Mac** I.v.69 [Lady Macbeth to Macbeth] *Only look up clear: / To alter favour ever is to fear*

clear all solve all problems **AY** I.i.160 [Oliver alone, of Charles] *this wrestler shall clear all*

clear his own way make his own way; or: prove himself innocent **TNK** III.i.56 [Arcite to Palamon] *Your question's with your equal, who professes / To clear his own way*

clearly (*adv.*) without interference, unobstructedly **KJ** V.v.7 [Lewis the Dauphin to all, of close of the day's battle] *And wound our tottering colours clearly up*

clearness (*n.*) freedom from suspicion, appearance of innocence **Mac** III.i.132 [Macbeth to Murderers] *I require a clearness*

clear-spirited (*adj.*) noble-hearted, of noble soul **TNK** I.ii.74 [Arcite to Palamon] *Clear-spirited cousin*

clearstory (*n.*) ☞ **clerestory** (*n.*)

cleave (*v.*) stick, adhere **3H6** I.iii.50 [Clifford as if to York] *thy son's blood cleaving to my blade*

cleave the pin ☞ **pin** (*n.*) 3

cleave to (*v.*) cling to, adhere to, obey **Tem** IV.i.165 [Ariel to Prospero] *Thy thoughts I cleave to*

clefture (*n.*) fissure, crack, fracture **E3** III.i.164 [Mariner to King John] *the gushing moisture [did] break into / The crannied cleftures of the through-shot planks*

clement (*adj.*) merciful, lenient, compassionate **Cym** V.iv.18 [Posthumus alone, to the gods] *I know you are more clement than vile men*

clepe (*v.*), past form **clept** [archaism] call, name, style **Mac** III.i.93 [Macbeth to Murderers] *Shoughs, water-rugs, and demi-wolves are clept / All by the name of dogs;* **Ham** I.iv.19; **LL** V.i.22; **Venus** 995 ☞ **yclept** (*v.*); **ARCHAISMS**, p.22

clerestory, clearstory (*n.*) upper window [designed for letting in light] **TN** IV.ii.37 [disguised Feste to Malvolio, of his cell] *the clerestories toward the south-north are as lustrous as ebony*

clerk (*n.*) **1** scholar, sage, man of learning **MND** V.i.93 [Theseus to Hippolyta] *Where I have come, great clerks have purposed / To greet me with premeditated welcomes;* **2H6** IV.vii.66; **H8** II.ii.90; **Per** V.Chorus.5
2 cleric, clergyman **1H4** II.i.63 [Gadshill to Chamberlain, of the travellers] *if they meet not with Saint Nicholas' clerks* [i.e. highwaymen]
3 parish clerk, prayer-leader **MA** II.i.98 [masked Margaret to masked Balthasar] *Answer, clerk* [i.e. say Amen]
4 altar-server, assistant **R2** IV.i.173 [Richard to all] *Am I both priest and clerk?*

clerk-like (*adv.*) in the ways of learning, in scholarly ways **WT** I.ii.392 [Polixenes to Camillo] *you are certainly a gentleman, thereto / Clerk-like experienced*

clerkly (*adj.*) scholarly, erudite, full of learning **MW** IV.v.53 [Host to Falstaff] *Thou art clerkly*

clerkly (*adv.*) scholarly, cleverly, adroitly **TG** II.i.102 [Silvia to Valentine, of his letter] *'tis very clerkly done;* **2H6** III.i.179

clew (*n.*) ball of thread **AW** I.iii.177 [Countess to Helena] *you have wound a goodly clew*

client (*n.*) suitor at law **Luc** 1020 [Lucrece as if to her own words] *To trembling clients be you mediators*

climate (*n.*) **1** region, country [without reference to climatic conditions] JC I.iii.32 [Casca to Cicero, of weird happenings] *they are portentous things / Unto the climate that they point upon*; R2 IV.i.130; WT II.iii.178

2 part of the sky KJ II.i.344 [King Philip to King John, of his rule] *That sways the earth this climate overlooks*

climate (*v.*) stay, sojourn, dwell WT V.i.169 [Leontes to Florizel] *The blessed gods / Purge all infection from our air whilst you / Do climate here!*

climatures (*n.*) regions, locality, part of the world Ham I.i.125 [Horatio to Marcellus and Barnardo, of ominous events] *heaven and earth together demonstrated / Unto our climatures and countrymen*

climb (*v.*) reach, attain, achieve TG II.iv.179 [Valentine to Proteus, of Silvia] *I must climb her window*; RJ II.v.74; Tim I.i.79

clime (*n.*) land, region, realm Per IV.iv.6 [Gower alone] *we commit no crime / To use one language in each several clime*; H5 IV.iii.102; 2H6 III.ii.84; MV II.i.10; Oth III.iii.228; R2 V.i.77

cling (*v.*) wither, shrivel, shrink up Mac V.v.40 [Macbeth to Messenger] *Upon the next tree shall thou hang alive / Till famine cling thee*

clinquant glittering with gold or silver, gleaming, sparkling H8 I.i.19 [Norfolk to Buckingham, of the French] *All clinquant, all in gold*

clip (*v.*) **1** embrace, clasp, hug AC V.ii.357 [Caesar to all, of Antony and Cleopatra] *No grave upon the earth shall clip in it / A pair so famous*; AC V.viii.8; Cor I.vi.29; Cym II.iii.133; 2H6 IV.i.6; WT V.ii.52

2 encompass, enclose, surround Oth III.iii.461 [Iago to Othello] *You elements, that clip us round about*

3 cut short, abbreviate, curtail LL V.ii.595 [Dumaine to Berowne, of Holofernes as Judas] *Judas Maccabeus clipped is plain Judas* [pun: 596, sense 1]; KL IV.vii.6

4 pare, cut [as of the edges of a coin] E3 II.i.256 [Countess to King Edward] *He that doth clip or counterfeit your stamp / Shall die* ➤ clipper (*n.*)

5 ➤ clepe (*v.*)

clip about (*v.*) embrace, clasp, hug KJ V.ii.34 [Salisbury to Lewis the Dauphin, as if to England] *Neptune's arms, who clippeth thee about*; Cym V.v.452

clip in (*v.*) bound, surround, encompass 1H4 III.i.41 [Glendower to Hotspur] *Where is he living, clipped in with the sea ... / Which calls me pupil or hath read to me?*

clipper (*n.*) one who clips coins H5 IV.i.222 [disguised King Henry to Bates] *it is no English treason to cut French crowns, and tomorrow the King himself will be a clipper* [pun: decapitate] ➤ clip (*v.*) 4

clip-winged (*adj.*) with wings clipped 1H4 III.i.146 [Hotspur to Mortimer, of Glendower] *Sometime he angers me / With telling me of ... / A clip-winged griffin and a moulten raven*

cloak (*v.*) disguise, conceal, mask E3 II.ii.80 [King Edward to himself] *basest theft is that / Which cannot cloak itself on poverty* [i.e. hide behind the pretext of poverty]

cloak-bag (*n.*) bag for carrying clothes [such as a cloak], portmanteau Cym III.iv.171 [Pisanio to Innogen, of her male disguise] *'Tis in my cloak-bag*; 1H4 II.iv.440

clock and clock, 'twixt from hour to hour, without ceasing Cym III.iv.43 [Innogen to Pisanio] *To weep 'twixt clock and clock*

clock-setter (*n.*) clock-keeper, clock-regulator KJ III.i.324 [Bastard to all] *Old Time the clock-setter, that bald sexton Time*

clod (*n.*) lump, mass, piece of earth MM III.i.124 [Claudio to Isabella, of his body] *This sensible warm motion to become / A kneaded clod*

cloddy (*adj.*) full of clods, clay-filled KJ III.i.80 [King Philip to Constance, of the sun] *Turning ... / The meagre cloddy earth to glittering gold*

clodpole (*n.*) blockhead, thickhead, dolt TN III.iv.186 [Sir Toby to Fabian, of Viola as Cesario receiving Sir Andrew's letter] *he will find it comes from a clodpole*

clog (*n.*) **1** wooden block, heavy piece of wood AW II.v.53 [Bertram to Parolles, of Helena] *Here comes my clog* [also: sense 2]; MA I.iii.31; Oth I.iii.196

2 encumbrance, burden, liability WT IV.iv.674 [Autolycus alone, of Perdita] *The Prince himself is ... stealing away from his father, with his clog at his heels*

3 burden, weight, heaviness R2 V.vi.20 [Percy to King Henry] *The ... Abbot of Westminster / With clog of conscience and sour melancholy*

clog (*v.*) impede, hinder, obstruct [progress] Mac III.vi.43 [Lord to Lennox] *The cloudy messenger ... hums, as who should say 'You'll rue the time / That clogs me with this answer'*

clogging (*adj.*) oppressive, encumbering, hampering R2 I.iii.200 [Bolingbroke to Mowbray] *bear not along / The clogging burden of a guilty soul*

cloistered (*adj.*) confined, restricted [as in a cloister] Mac III.ii.41 [Macbeth to Lady Macbeth] *Ere the bat hath flown / His cloistered flight*

cloistress (*n.*) cloistered nun, member of an enclosed order TN I.i.29 [Valentine to Orsino, of Olivia] *like a cloistress she will veiled walk*

close (*n.*) **1** union, uniting TN V.i.156 [Priest to all, of Olivia and Sebastian] *A contract of eternal bond of love ... / Attested by the holy close of lips*; TG V.iv.118

2 engagement, encounter, confrontation 1H4 I.i.13 [King Henry to all] *Those opposed eyes ... / Did lately meet in the ... furious close of civil butchery*

3 closing cadence, end of a musical theme R2 II.i.12 [John of Gaunt to York] *The setting sun, and music at the close ... is sweetest last* H5 I.ii.182

4 enclosure, yard Tim V.i.203 [Timon to Senators] *I have a tree, which grows here in my close*

close (*adj.*) **1** secret, concealed, hidden TNK III.v.13 [Schoolmaster to all] *there are you / Close in the thicket*; 3H6 IV.v.17; Mac III.v.7; Oth III.iii.122; R3 I.i.158; WT III.iii.120

2 private, secluded, sequestered RJ II.ii.192 [Romeo alone] *Hence will I to my ghostly friar's close cell*; Cym III.v.46; 2H6 II.i.3; MND III.ii.7; R3 V.ii.51; TG I.i.235

3 enclosed, confined, incarcerated Oth V.ii.331 [Lodovico to Othello or Iago] *You shall close prisoner rest*

4 secret, covert, underhanded 2H6 III.iv.73 [Gloucester to himself, of his invitation to parliament] *This is close dealing*; R3 IV.ii.35

5 secretive, tight-lipped, uncommunicative Cym III.v.86 [Cloten to Pisanio] *Close villain, / I'll have this secret from thy heart*; 1H4 II.iii.113; KJ IV.ii.72; MM IV.iii.117; MV II.vi.47

6 closed, shut H8 V.iv.30 [Porter to Servant within] *Keep the door close*; Luc 367

close (*v.*) **1** agree, come to terms, compromise MM V.i.339 [Angelo to Escalus, of the disguised Duke] *Hark how the villain would close now*; Ham II.i.45; 2H4 II.iv.322; JC III.i.202; WT IV.iv.795

2 get to grips, come to close quarters 2H4 II.i.18 [Fang to Hostess, of Falstaff] *If I can close with him, I care not for his thrust*

3 join, unite, combine [again] Mac III.ii.14 [Macbeth to Lady Macbeth, of the snake] *We have scorched the snake, not killed it; / She'll close and be herself*; H5 I.ii.211

4 enclose, include, contain Mac III.i.98 [Macbeth to Murderers, of distinguishing types of dog] *According to the gift which bounteous nature / Hath in him closed* [or: set, as a jewel]; Luc 761

5 embrace, cuddle, hug TG II.v.11 [Launce to Speed, of Proteus and Julia] *they closed in earnest* [also: sense 1]; TC III.ii.47

6 join, clasp RJ II.vi.6 [Romeo to Friar] *Do thou but close our hands with holy words*

close up (*v.*) finally satisfy, put the finishing touches to TS V.ii.9 [Lucentio to all] *My banquet is to close our stomachs up / After our great good cheer*

CLOTHING

Names of Elizabethan items of clothing are frequently found in Shakespearian English, and several of the terms are still in use today with essentially the same meaning (such as *apron, hat, cuff, garters, skirt, stockings*). A number of dress-making terms are brought together in the description of Katherina's dress by the tailor in **TS** IV.iii.120ff.

Term	Example	Male (M) or Female (F)	Gloss
For the head			
bonnet	AY III.ii.363	M	soft brimless head-dress
cap	TS IV.iii.70	F	loose-fitting decorative head-dress
cap	R3 III.vii.35	M	soft brimless head-dress
coif	WT IV.iv.226	M, F	close-fitting cap covering the top, back and sides of the head
corner-cap	LL IV.iii.51	M	cap with (three) corners, mortar-board
coxcomb	MW V.v.137	M	fool's cap, with a crest like a cock's crest
porringer	H8 V.iv.48	M, F	hat shaped like a pudding basin or soup-bowl
statute-cap	LL V.ii.281	M, F	woollen cap ordered (by an Act of 1571) to be worn on Sundays and holy days by all below a certain rank
For the whole or upper body			
doublet	Ham II.i.78	M	close-fitting jacket with short skirt, worn by men
down-sleeves	MA III.iv.19	F	long sleeves to the wrist
frock	Ham III.iv.165	M, F	long coat or tunic; gown, dress
gaberdine	MV I.iii.109	M	loose upper garment of coarse material
half-kirtle	2H4 V.iv.21	F	lower part of a kirtle; skirt
jack	1H4 IV.ii.47	M	sleeveless jacket or tunic, usually of quilted leather
jerkin	TG II.iv.19	M	long close-fitting jacket worn over or in place of a doublet
kirtle	2H4 II.iv.268	F	dress, gown
lace	WT III.ii.171	F	lacing for an undergarment
mantle	JC III.ii.171	M, F	loose sleeveless cloak
rebato	MA III.iv.6	M, F	wing-shaped ornamental collar standing up behind the head
robe	JC II.ii.107	M, F	long loose outer garment extending from neck to ankles
ruff	2H4 II.iv.130	M, F	frill of stiff folded linen, worn around the neck
sea-gown	Ham V.ii.13	F	robe of a coarse material, with a high collar, short sleeves, and mid-leg length
side-sleeves	MA III.iv.19	F	hanging sleeves open from the shoulder and falling away backwards
stomacher	Cym III.iv.85	F	decorative garment used under a bodice to cover the chest and stomach
For the lower body			
codpiece	WT IV.iv.607	M	cloth case or pocket worn by men at the front of breeches or hose
cut	MA III.iv.18	F	ornamental gap in a dress to show the colour underneath
farthingale	TG II.vii.51	F	long skirt extended at the back or on all sides by a framework of hoops
gaskins	TN I.v.23	M	loose-fitting breeches
For the lower body			
hose	AY II.vii.161	M	clothing for the legs and loins; breeches; or: clothing for the leg or lower leg
pantaloon	AY II.vii.159	M	loose fitting breeches, especially as worn by comic stage characters
petticoat	AY II.iv.7	F	long skirt or skirts
round hose	TG II.vii.55	M	breeches puffed out at the hips
ruff	AW III.ii.7	M	flap of a top-boot
slop, slops	2H4 I.ii.29	M	large loose breeches
stock	TN I.iii.128	M	stocking

'Doublet and hose' is a very common locution for typical male attire of the period (as in **AY** II.iv.6).

close *(adv.)* **1** closely, staying near **Ham** IV.v.75 [Claudius to Horatio, of Ophelia] *Follow her close;* **1H4** II.ii.74; **MA** III.iii.105; **Mac** V.i.20; **MM** I.iv.67

2 closely, in a hemmed-in way **E3** III.iv.33 [Derby to King Edward, of Prince Edward] *He's close encompassed with a world of odds!*

3 tightly, in a close-fitting way **TNK** III.vi.57 [Arcite to Palamon, of the armour] *I'll buckle't close;* **1H6** I.iv.9; **Tim** IV.iii.389

4 tightly, close-fistedly, stintingly **Tim** II.ii.144 [Flavius to Timon] *I … 'gainst th'authority of manners prayed you / To hold your hand more close*

5 close together **2H6** I.iii.1 [First Petitioner to all] *let's stand close* [or: sense 6]; **RJ** I.i.107

6 safely, secretly, out of sight **Ham** IV.vii.128 [Claudius to Laertes] *keep close within your chamber;* **Ham** II.i.118; **1H4** II.iv.527; **2H4** I.ii.55; **TN** II.v.19; **TNK** II.v.6

7 securely, in strict confinement **R3** IV.iii.36 [King Richard alone] *The son of Clarence have I pent up close;* **2H6** I.iv.49

closely *(adv.)* **1** secretly, covertly, privately **Ham** III.i.29 [Claudius to Gertrude] *we have closely sent for Hamlet;* **E3** I.ii.16; **KJ** IV.i.132; **LL** IV.iii.135; **RJ** V.iii.255

2 in strict confinement, securely **R3** I.i.38 [Richard alone] *This day should Clarence closely be mewed up;* **TS** I.i.180

closeness *(n.)* solitude, seclusion, retirement **Tem** I.ii.90 [Prospero to Miranda, of himself] *all dedicated / To closeness and the bettering of my mind*

close-stool *(n.)* chamber pot enclosed in a stool, privy **AW** V.ii.17 [Clown to Parolles, of the letter] *A paper from Fortune's close-stool;* **LL** V.ii.574

closet *(n.)* **1** private chamber, study, own room **E3** II.ii.15 [Derby to Audley] *The King is in his closet;* **Cym** I.vi.84; **Ham** II.i.77; **KL** I.ii.61; **Oth** IV.ii.21; **RJ** IV.ii.33

2 private repository for valuables, cabinet **Mac** V.i.6 [Gentlewoman to Doctor, of Lady Macbeth] *I have seen her … unlock her closet;* **JC** III.ii.130; **KL** III.iii.10

3 enclosure surrounding the heart, pericardium **Sonn** 46.6 [of the heart] *A closet never pierced with crystal eyes*

close-tongued *(adj.)* speaking secretly, tight-lipped **Luc** 770 [Lucrece as if to night] *whispering conspirator / With close-tongued treason and the ravisher*

closet-war *(n.)* armchair strategy **TC** I.iii.205 [Ulysses to all, of Achilles' and Ajax' view of military strategy] *They call this bedwork, mappery, closet-war*

closing *(n.)* agreeing, acquiescing, concurring **Tit** V.ii.70 [Tamora to Chiron and Demetrius, of Titus] *This closing with him fits his lunacy*

closure *(n.)* **1** enclosure, bound, limit **R3** III.iii.10 [Rivers, as if to Pomfret Castle] *Within the guilty closure of thy walls / Richard the Second here was hacked to death;* **Sonn** 48.11; **Venus** 782

2 bringing to an end, conclusion, close **Tit** V.iii.133 [Marcus to all, of the Andronici] *[we will] make a mutual closure of our house*

cloth *(n.)* clothing, dress, outfit **Cym** II.iii.122 [Cloten to Innogen, of Posthumus] *a base slave … a squire's cloth* ➤ bearing-cloth *(n.);* foot-cloth *(n.);* state *(n.)*

clothier's yard yard [36 inches / c.90 cm] by which clothiers measured their cloth **KL** IV.vi.88 [Lear to all] *Draw me a clothier's yard* [i.e. pull out the bow to the extent of a full arrow]

cloth-of-gold *(n.)* ➤ tissue *(n.)*

cloth of state ➤ state *(n.)* 9

clotpoll, clotpole, clatpole *(n.)* **1** blockhead, dolt, numskull **TC** II.i.116 [Thersites to all] *I will see you hanged like clotpolls;* **KL** I.iv.46

2 head, pate, noddle **Cym** IV.ii.184 [Guiderius to Belarius] *I have sent Cloten's clotpoll down the stream*

cloud *(n.)* troubled expression, state of gloom **AC** III.ii.51 [Agrippa aside to Enobarbus, of Caesar] *He has a cloud in's face;* **Tim** III.iv.43

clouds, in suspicious, filled with uncertainties **Ham** IV.v.90 [Claudius to Gertrude, of Laertes] *keeps himself in clouds*

cloud *(v.)* defame, blacken, sully **WT** I.ii.280 [Camillo to Leontes, of Hermione] *to hear / My sovereign mistress clouded so*

cloudy *(adj.)* **1** sullen, gloomy, scowling **Mac** III.vi.41 [Lord to Lennox] *The cloudy messenger turns me his back;* **1H4** III.ii.83; **2H6** III.i.155; **R3** II.ii.112; **Venus** 725

2 sorrowful, grief-stricken **Luc** 1084 *cloudy Lucrece shames herself to see*

clout *(n.)* **1** piece of cloth, rag; handkerchief **R3** I.iii.176 [Richard to Queen Margaret, of York] *thou … gav'st the Duke a clout / Steeped in the faultless blood of pretty Rutland;* **AC** IV.vii.6; **Ham** II.ii.504; **KJ** III.iv.58; **RJ** II.iv.201 ➤ swaddling clouts *(n.)*

2 [archery] pin fixing a target, cloth patch at the centre of a target; mark, bull **LL** IV.i.135 [Costard to Maria, of Boyet's remark] *'a must shoot nearer, or he'll ne'er hit the clout;* **2H4** III.ii.45; **KL** IV.vi.92

clouted *(adj.)* metal-studded, hobnailed **Cym** IV.ii.214 [Arviragus to Belarius and Guiderius] *I .. put / My clouted brogues from off my feet;* **2H6** IV.ii.175

cloven *(adj.)* **1** split, cleft apart **Tem** I.ii.277 [Prospero to Ariel, of Sycorax] *she did confine thee … / Into a cloven pine*

2 broken apart, split in pieces **Cor** I.iv.21 [First Senator to Martius, of Aufidius] *List what work he makes / Amongst your cloven army*

clown *(n.)* yokel, rustic, country bumpkin; also: low comic character [in a play] **AY** V.i.46 [Touchstone to William] *Therefore, you clown, … 'abandon the society of this female', or, clown, thou perishest;* **AC** V.ii.241; **AY** V.i.10; **MND** III.i.1; **Tit** IV.iii.77; **WT** III.iii.77

cloy *(v.)* **1** satiate, gorge, satisfy **AC** II.ii.241 [Enobarbus to Maecenas and Agrippa, of Cleopatra] *Other women cloy / The appetites they feed;* **2H4** Epilogue.26; **H5** II.ii.9; **R2** I.iii.296; **R3** IV.iv.62; **Tit** III.i.55

2 scratch with claws **Cym** V.iv.118 [Sicilius to all, of Jupiter] *his royal bird / Prunes the immortal wing, and cloys his beak*

cloyed *(adj.)* **1** bored, overfilled, sated **Cym** I.vi.47 [Iachimo to Innogen] *The cloyed will … / Longs after for the garbage*

2 clogged, crammed, stuffed **Cym** IV.iv.19 [Arviragus to Belarius and Guiderius, of the Britons] *have both their eyes / And ears so cloyed importantly as now* [i.e. filled with matters of importance]

cloyless *(adj.)* never satiating, not glutting **AC** II.i.25 [Pompey to Menas, of Antony] *Epicurean cooks / Sharpen with cloyless sauce his appetite*

cloyment *(n.)* excessive gratification, gorging, satiety **TN** II.iv.98 [Orsino to Viola as Cesario] *No motion of the liver, but the palate, / That suffer surfeit, cloyment, and revolt*

clubs *(int.)* cry calling apprentices to rally round in a fight **Tit** II.i.37 [Aaron to himself, of Chiron and Demetrius arguing] *Clubs, clubs! These lovers will not keep the peace;* **H8** V.iv.50

cluster *(n.)* crowd, mob, throng **Cor** IV.vi.130 [Menenius to Cominius] *Here come the clusters;* **Cor** IV.vi.124

clustering *(adj.)* swarming, thronging, crowded **1H6** IV.vii.13 [Talbot to Servant, of John Talbot] *great rage of heart / Suddenly made him from my side to start / Into the clustering battle of the French*

clutch *(v.)* clench, close **KJ** II.i.589 [Bastard alone, of commodity] *Not that I have the power to clutch my hand / When his fair angels would salute my palm;* **MM** III.ii.45

clyster-pipe *(n.)* enema syringe, douche tube **Oth** II.i.173 [Iago to himself, as if to Cassio] *Yet again your fingers to your lips? Would they were clyster-pipes for your sake!*

coacher *(n.)* [unclear meaning] coach, chariot **AW** II.i.162 [Helena to King] *Ere twice the horses of the sun shall bring / Their fiery coacher his diurnal ring* [F *torcher*]

coach-fellow (*n.*) [one of a team of horses drawing a coach] companion, mate, partner in crime **MW** II.ii.8 [Falstaff to Pistol] *I have grated upon my good friends for three reprieves for you and your coach-fellow Nym*

co-act (*v.*) behave together, carry on **TC** V.ii.120 [Troilus to Ulysses, of Diomedes and Cressida] *if I tell how these two did co-act, / Shall I not lie in publishing a truth?*

coactive (*adj.*) working together, acting in concert **WT** I.ii.141 [Leontes to himself, of lustful desire] *With what's unreal thou coactive art, / And fellow'st nothing*

coagulate (*adj.*) coagulated, clotted, congealed **Ham** II.ii.460 [Hamlet to First Player, quoting lines about Pyrrhus] *o'er-sized with coagulate gore*

coal (*n.*) **1** ember, smouldering fuel **Venus** 338 *Even as a dying coal revives with wind;* **KJ** V.ii.83; **Venus** 387
   2 cinder, piece of charcoal **Cor** IV.vi.139 [Menenius to Citizens, of Coriolanus] *he could burn us all into one coal;* **WT** V.i.68

coals, carry submit to insult, show cowardice; also: do degrading work **RJ** I.i.1 [Sampson to Gregory] *we'll not carry coals;* **H5** III.ii.46

coarse (*adj.*) **1** inferior, low-quality, poor **H8** III.ii.239 [Wolsey to all] *Now I feel / Of what coarse metal ye are moulded*
   2 rough, unrefined **TNK** III.v.8 [Schoolmaster to all] *You their coarse frieze capacities* [i.e. people of limited intelligence]

coarsely (*adv.*) slightingly, disparagingly, derisively **AW** III.v.56 [Diana to Helena, of Parolles and Helena] *There is a gentleman ... / Reports but coarsely of her*

coast (*n.*) **1** quarter, direction, route **2H6** I.ii.93 [Hume to himself] *Yet have I gold flies from another coast*
   2 part of the coast, region **E3** III.i.101 [King John to his confederates] *Here in the middle coast, betwixt you both*

coast (*v.*) **1** travel along the coast **CE** I.i.135 [Egeon to Duke] *I ... coasting homeward came to Ephesus*
   2 move in a roundabout course **H8** III.ii.38 [Lord Chamberlain to Surrey, of Wolsey] *The King in this perceives him how he coasts / And hedges his own way*
   3 make one's way, approach [towards] **Venus** 870 [of Venus, and Adonis' hounds] *all in haste she coasteth to the cry*

coasting (*adj.*) [unclear meaning] approachable, ready, friendly **TC** IV.v.59 [Ulysses to Nestor] *these encounterers, so glib of tongue, / That give a coasting welcome ere it comes* [F, Q] ⟜ accosting (*n.*)

coat (*n.*) **1** coat-of-arms **MW** I.i.15 [Slender to Evans, of Shallow's heirs] *They may give the dozen white luces in their coat;* **Lover** 236; **Luc** 205; **MND** III.ii.213; **MW** V.v.63; **R2** III.i.24
   2 coat-of-mail, surcoat **R2** I.iii.75 [Bolingbroke to John of Gaunt] *with thy blessings steel my lance's point / That it may enter Mowbray's waxen coat;* **1H4** IV.i.100, V.iii.25 [or: sense 1]; **2H4** III.ii.282
   3 monk's habit, clerical garb **MM** IV.ii.183 [disguised Duke to Provost] *neither my coat, integrity, nor persuasion can with ease attempt you*

cobbled (*adj.*) roughly mended, patched, botched **Cor** I.i.194 [Martius to Menenius, of the citizens] *feebling such as stand not in their liking / Below their cobbled shoes*

cobbler (*n.*) bungler, botcher, clumsy workman **JC** I.i.11 [Cobbler to Marullus] *in respect of a fine workman, I am but ... a cobbler* [also: shoe-mender]

cobloaf (*n.*) small round lumpish loaf **TC** II.i.36 [Ajax to Thersites] *Cobloaf!*

cock (*n.*) **1** weathercock **KL** III.ii.3 [Lear to the storm] *spout / Till you have drenched our steeples, drowned the cocks!*
   2 woodcock [known for its foolishness] **WT** IV.iii.34 [Autolycus to himself, of the Clown] *If the springe hold, the cock's mine*
   3 small ship's boat, dinghy **KL** IV.vi.19 [Edgar to Gloucester, of a ship] *her cock, a buoy / Almost too small for sight;* **KL** IV.vi.19

   4 [of a gun] pistol-hammer, cocking-piece **H5** II.i.49 [Pistol to Nym] *I can take, and Pistol's cock is up* [i.e. is ready for firing; with bawdy pun]
   5 tap, spout [of a wine-cask] **Tim** II.ii.167 [Flavius to Timon] *I have retired me to a wasteful cock / And set mine eyes at flow*
   6 softened variant of 'God' ⟜ **SWEARING**, p.435

cock-a-hoop, set [unclear meaning] abandon all restraint, put everything into disorder **RJ** I.v.81 [Capulet to Tybalt] *You will set cock-a-hoop!*

cockatrice (*n.*) murderous serpent, basilisk **R3** IV.i.54 [Duchess of York to herself, of Richard] *A cockatrice hast thou hatched to the world;* **Luc** 540; **RJ** III.ii.47; **TN** III.iv.192

cockered (*adj.*) spoiled, indulged, pampered **KJ** V.i.70 [Bastard to King John, of Lewis the Dauphin] *A cockered silken wanton*

cockerel (*n.*) young cock **Tem** II.i.33 [Antonio to Sebastian, of Adrian] *The cockerel*

cockle (*n.*) **1** variety of weed, darnel **Cor** III.i.70 [Coriolanus to all, of the Citizens] *In soothing them we nourish 'gainst our Senate / The cockle of rebellion;* **LL** IV.iii.359 ⟜ **PLANTS**, p.330
   2 cockleshell, mussel-shell **TNK** IV.i.130 [Gaoler's Daughter to First Friend] *I keep close for all this, / Close as a cockle* [i.e. keep myself to myself]; **Per** IV.iv.2; **TS** IV.iii.66 ⟜ cockle hat

cockled (*adj.*) having a shell **LL** IV.iii.314 [Berowne to all] *Love's feeling is more soft and sensible / Than are the tender horns of cockled snails*

cockle hat hat adorned with a cockle shell [symbol of pilgrimage to the shrine of St James of Compostela] **Ham** IV.v.25 [Ophelia singing] *By his cockle hat and staff* ⟜ cockle (*n.*) 2

cocklight (*n.*) morning cock-crow, dawn **TNK** IV.i.112 [Gaoler's Daughter to her uncle] *For I must lose my maidenhead by cocklight* [with bawdy pun]

cockney (*n.*) **1** squeamish woman, pampered lady **KL** II.iv.117 [Fool to Lear] *Cry to it ... as the cockney did to the eels when she put 'em i'the paste alive* [i.e. telling them to stay down, instead of killing them first]
   2 milksop, sissy, softy **E3** III.iv.114 [King Edward to all, as if to King John] *I hope / Thou know'st King Edward for ... / No love-sick cockney;* **TN** IV.i.14

cockpit (*n.*) theatre pit, theatrical arena **H5** Prologue.11 [Chorus] *Can this cockpit hold / The vasty fields of France?*

cockshut (*n.*) evening twilight [time when poultry were shut away] **R3** V.iii.70 [Ratcliffe to King Richard, of Northumberland] *Much about cockshut time ... / Went through the army*

cock-sure (*adv.*) with complete security, with total confidence **1H4** II.i.87 [Gadshill to Chamberlain] *We steal as in a castle, cock-sure*

cod (*n.*) pod, seed-vessel **AY** II.iv.47 [Touchstone to Rosalind and Celia, of a peascod] *from whom I took two cods*

codding (*adj.*) lecherous, lustful, lascivious **Tit** V.i.99 [Aaron to Lucius, of Chiron and Demetrius] *That codding spirit had they from their mother*

codling (*n.*) unripe apple, half-grown apple **TN** I.v.153 [Malvolio to Olivia, of the age of Viola as Cesario] *as ... a codling when 'tis almost an apple*

codpiece, cod-piece (*n.*) **1** cloth case or pocket worn by a man at the front of breeches or hose; also: what it contains **TG** II.vii.53 [Lucetta to Julia, of her breeches] *You must needs have them with a codpiece;* **KL** III.ii.40; **LL** III.i.181; **MA** III.iii.133; **WT** IV.iv.607 ⟜ **CLOTHING**, p.79
   2 penis **KL** III.ii.27 [Fool, singing to Lear] *The cod-piece that will house / Before the head has any* [i.e. has any covering]; **MM** III.ii.109

coffer (*n.*) **1** box, chest **Oth** II.i.202 [Othello to Iago] *Go to the bay and disembark my coffers;* **Per** III.iv.2
   2 funds, money, wealth **TN** III.iv.337 [Viola as Cesario to Antonio] *there's half my coffer*

coffer up (*v.*) hoard, store away, lay up securely **Luc** 855 [Lucrece to herself] *The aged man that coffers up his gold / Is plagued with cramps*

coffer-lid (*n.*) lid of a treasure-chest **Venus** 1127 [of Venus and Adonis] *She lifts the coffer-lids that close his eyes*

coffin (*n.*) pie-crust, pastry mould **Tit** V.ii.187 [Titus to Chiron and Demetrius] *I'll make a paste, / And of the paste a coffin I will rear* [also: box for the dead] ☞ custard-coffin (*n.*)

cog (*v.*) **1** flatter, fawn, sweet-talk **R3** I.iii.48 [Richard to all] *I cannot … smooth, deceive, and cog;* **Cor** III.ii.133; **MW** III.iii.44, 66
2 cheat, swindle, hoodwink, wheedle **MA** V.i.95 [Antonio to Leonato, of boys like Claudio and Don Pedro] *That lie and cog and flout;* **LL** V.ii.235; **Tim** V.i.93

cogging (*adj.*) deceiving, cheating, double-crossing **Oth** IV.ii.131 [Emilia to Iago] *I will be hanged if … / Some cogging, cozening slave, to get some office, / Have not devised this slander;* **MW** I.i.118, III.i.111; **TC** V.vi.11

cognizance (*n.*) badge, sign, token **1H6** II.iv.108 [Richard to Somerset] *this pale and angry rose, / As cognizance of my blood-drinking hate;* **Cym** II.iv.127; **JC** I.ii.89

cohere (*v.*) agree, accord, hold together **TN** V.i.249 [Viola as Cesario to Sebastian] *Do not embrace me, till each circumstance … do cohere and jump / That I am Viola;* **MM** II.i.11

coherence (*n.*) correspondence, agreement, harmony **2H4** V.i.59 [Falstaff alone, of Shallow] *It is a wonderful thing to see the semblable coherence of his men's spirits and his*

coherent (*adj.*) fitting, accordant, agreeable **AW** III.vii.39 [Widow to Helena] *That time and place … / May prove coherent*

cohort (*n.*) company of soldiers, military division **KL** I.ii.147 [Edmund to Edgar, of a writer] *the effects he writes of succeed unhappily, as of … dissipation of cohorts*

coif, quoif (*n.*) close-fitting cap, nightcap **WT** IV.iv.226 [Autolycus singing] *Golden coifs and stomachers / For my lads to give their dears;* **2H4** I.i.147 ☞ CLOTHING, p.79

coign (*n.*) **1** corner of a building, quoin **Cor** V.iv.1 [Menenius to Sicinius] *See you yond coign o'th' Capitol, yond cornerstone?*
2 projecting corner, prominent position **Mac** I.vi.7 [Banquo to King, of the martlet] *no … / Buttress, nor coign of vantage, but this bird / Hath made his pendent bed and procreant cradle*
3 corner [of the earth] **Per** III.Chorus.17 [Gower alone] *the four opposing coigns*

coil (*n.*) turmoil, disturbance, fuss **Ham** III.i.67 [Hamlet alone] *When we have shuffled off this mortal coil* [i.e. the bustle of life]; **E3** IV.vi.11; **MA** III.iii.91; **Tem** I.ii.207; **TG** I.i.99; **TNK** II.iii.18

coin (*v.*) **1** create, make [as in minting a coin] **Tit** II.iii.5 [Aaron alone] *this gold must coin a stratagem;* **Cym** V.v.23; **MM** II.iv.45
2 create fantasies, fabricate, fantasize **TNK** V.iii.39 [Doctor to Gaoler, of the Gaoler's Daughter] *How her brain coins!*

coinage (*n.*) **1** invention, fabrication, concoction **Ham** III.iv.138 [Gertude to Hamlet, of the Ghost] *This is the very coinage of your brain;* **TNK** I.iii.76
2 means of making money **1H4** IV.ii.8 [Falstaff to Bardolph] *I'll answer the coinage*

coining (*n.*) making coins **KL** IV.vi.83 [Lear to all] *they cannot touch me for coining. I am the King himself* [Q; F *crying*]

coistrel (*n.*) groom, low fellow, knave **TN** I.iii.37 [Sir Toby to Maria] *He's a coward and a coistrel that will not drink to my niece* [F *Coystrill*] ☞ custrel (*n.*)

co-join (*v.*) ☞ conjoin (*v.*)

cold (*n.*) coldness, chill **H8** IV.ii.98 [Patience to Griffith, of Katherine] *How pale she looks? / And of an earthy cold?* [F]

cold (*adj.*) **1** chaste, modest, lacking sensual passion **TNK** V.i.137 [Emilia praying to Diana] *O sacred, shadowy, cold, and constant queen;* **Cym** V.v.181; **Ham** IV.vii.171; **TC** IV.iv.26; **TNK** III.i.13, V.i.93

2 unruffled, impassive, unimpassioned **Cym** II.iii.2 [First Lord to Cloten] *Your lordship is … the most coldest that ever turned up ace*
3 empty, bare, lacking life **1H4** II.iv.316 [Prince Hal to Bardolph, of the meaning of Bardolph's exhalations] *Hot livers, and cold purses*
4 indifferent, unenthusiastic, uninterested **2H6** III.i.224 [Queen to all, of the King] *Henry my lord is cold in great affairs;* **KJ** III.i.317
5 ineffective, unattended to, coldly received **MV** II.vii.73 [Morocco to himself, reading the inscription] *your suit is cold;* **TG** IV.iv.178
6 calm, cool, deliberate **2H4** V.ii.98 [Lord Chief Justice to King Henry V] *After this cold consideration sentence me;* **2H4** III.ii.123; **JC** III.i.213; **MM** IV.iii.98; **R2** I.i.47
7 hopeless, apathetic, miserable **TNK** II.i.309 [Palamon to Gaoler, of Arcite and Emilia] *if he lose her then, he's a cold coward;* **Cym** III.i.76; **3H6** III.iii.133; **JC** V.iii.4
8 gloomy, depressed, dispirited **Cym** II.iii.3 [Cloten to First Lord, of dicing] *It would make any man cold to lose*
9 bad, unwelcome, disagreeable **2H6** II.i.235 [York to himself] *Anjou and Maine both given unto the French! / Cold news for me;* **2H4** V.i.31; **3H6** III.iii.133; **R3** IV.iv.534

coldly (*adv.*) **1** calmly, coolly, objectively, rationally **CE** V.i.273 [Duke to all, of Antipholus of Ephesus] *If he were mad, he would not plead so coldly;* **KJ** II.i.53; **MA** III.ii.117; **RJ** III.i.51; **TNK** II.i.240
2 lightly, with indifference, unenthusiastically **KJ** V.iii.13 [Messenger to King John] *The French fight coldly;* **Ham** IV.iii.64
3 in a cold form, as cold dishes **Ham** I.ii.181 [Hamlet to Horatio] *The funeral baked meats / Did coldly furnish forth the marriage tables*

cold-moving (*adj.*) cool, chilling, distant **Tim** II.ii.217 [Flavius to Timon, of the Senators] *With certain half-caps and cold-moving nods / They froze me into silence*

coldness (*n.*) indifference, apathy, passionless quality **3H6** II.i.121 [Warwick to Edward and Richard, of battle] *the coldness of the King … / That robbed my soldiers of their heated spleen*

coleagued (*adj.*) ☞ colleagued (*adj.*)

collar, colour (*n.*) noose, hangman's halter **RJ** I.i.4 [Gregory to Sampson] *while you live, draw your neck out of collar;* **2H4** V.v.90 ☞ colours, fear no

collars of esses chains made of S-shaped links [part of the insignia of knighthood] **H8** IV.i.37 [stage direction, of what Dorset and Surrey are wearing] *Collars of Esses*

collateral (*adj.*) **1** [astronomy, of the movement of the spheres] parallel, side by side **AW** I.i.87 [Helena alone, of Bertram] *In his bright radiance and collateral light / Must I be comforted*
2 indirect, subordinate, accessory **Ham** IV.v.206 [Claudius to Laertes] *by direct or by collateral hand*

colleagued, coleagued (*adj.*) joined, supported, in league **Ham** I.ii.21 [Claudius to his court, of young Fortinbras' ambitions] *Colleagued with this dream of his advantage* [Q2 *coleagued*]

collect (*v.*) **1** see, perceive, pick up **2H6** III.i.35 [Queen to King, of Gloucester] *The reverent care I bear unto my lord / Made me collect these dangers in the Duke*
2 gather in evidence **H8** I.ii.130 [Wolsey to Surveyor] *relate what you … have collected / Out of the Duke of Buckingham*

collected (*adj.*) composed, self-possessed, cool **Tem** I.ii.13 [Prospero to Miranda] *Be collected*

collection (*n.*) **1** deduction, inference, gathering of meaning **Cym** V.v.433 [Posthumus to Lucius, of the letter left by Jupiter] *whose containing / Is so from sense in hardness, that I can / Make no collection of it;* **Ham** IV.v.9
2 accumulation [i.e. of words and phrases] **Ham** V.ii.188 [Hamlet to Horatio] *a kind of yeasty collection*

collied (*adj.*) **1** clouded, blackened, muddied **Oth** II.iii.200 [Othello to all] *passion, having my best judgement collied, / Assays to lead the way* [F; Q *coold*]
2 blackened, darkened, murky **MND** I.i.145 [Lysander to Hermia, of love] *Brief as the lightning in the collied night*

collier (*n.*) coalman, coal-vendor **RJ** I.i.2 [Gregory to Sampson, of not 'carrying coals'] *For then we should be colliers;* **LL** IV.iii.265; **TN** III.iv.117

collop (*n.*) [piece of flesh] offspring, flesh and blood **1H6** V.iv.18 [Shepherd to Pucelle] *God knows thou art a collop of my flesh;* **WT** I.ii.137

collusion (*n.*) malapropism for 'allusion' **LL** IV.ii.43 [Dull to Holofernes, mispraising him] *the collusion holds in the exchange*

coloquintida (*n.*) bitter-apple, colocynth **Oth** I.iii.345 [Iago to Roderigo, of Othello] *The food that to him now is as luscious as locusts shall be to him shortly as acerbe as the coloquintida*

colossus-wise (*adv.*) like a colossus, with legs astride **TC** V.v.9 [Agamemnon to Diomedes] *Margarelon / Hath Doreus prisoner, / And stands colossus-wise, waving his beam*

colour (*n.*) **1** pretext, pretence **2H6** III.i.236 [Cardinal to all, of Gloucester] *we want a colour for his death;* **AC** I.iii.32; **2H4** I.ii.248; **Luc** 267; **TG** IV.ii.3; **WT** IV.iv.552
  2 good ground, convincing reason, excuse **MW** IV.ii.151 [Ford to all, of his search for Falstaff] *If I find not what I seek, show no colour for my extremity;* **H8** I.i.178; **JC** I.ii.29
  3 semblance, outward appearance, character **1H6** II.iv.34 [Warwick to all] *without all colour / Of base insinuating flattery;* **Ham** III.iv.131; **1H4** III.ii.100; **H5** I.ii.17; **TNK** I.ii.39
  4 suitable appearance, appropriate character **AW** II.v.59 [Bertram to Helena, of his intention to leave] *Which holds not colour with the time*
  5 type, kind, nature **AY** I.ii.95 [Celia to Le Beau] *Sport? Of what colour?;* **KL** II.ii.136
  6 ☛ **colours** (*n.*)

colour (*v.*) **1** disguise, conceal, cloak **Ham** II.ii.280 [Hamlet to Rosencrantz and Guildenstern] *there is a kind of confession in your looks, which your modesties have not craft enough to colour;* **1H4** I.iii.108; **Luc** 92; **MM** II.i.210
  2 explain, make plausible, excuse **Ham** III.i.45 [Polonius to Ophelia] *Read on this book, / That show of such an exercise may colour / Your loneliness*
  3 dye, stain a new colour **WT** II.ii.20 [Paulina to herself] *Here's such ado to make no stain a stain / As passes colouring* [i.e. it exceeds the dyer's skill] [also: sense 2, i.e. it exceeds all belief]; **Cym** V.i.2; **TS** IV.i.120

colourable (*adj.*) capable of being interpreted in many ways, conveniently plausible **LL** IV.ii.148 [Holofernes to Nathaniel] *I do fear colourable colours*

coloured (*adj.*) complexioned, with colour in one's cheeks **1H6** IV.iii.37 [General to Talbot] *These eyes that see thee now well coloured*

colours (*n.*) **1** battle-flags, ensigns, standards, banners **E3** II.ii.100 [King Edward to Prince Edward] *Let's with our colours sweet the air of France* ☛ **FEW**, p.xxi
  2 colour-ensigns, standard-bearers **Ham** V.ii.356 [stage direction] *Enter Fortinbras ... with his train of drum, colours, and attendants*
  3 emblems, badges **1H6** III.iv.29 [Vernon to Basset] *you ... / Disgracing of these colours that I wear;* **1H4** V.iv.26

colours, fear no fear no enemy, fear nothing **TN** I.v.5 [Feste to Maria] *He that is well hanged in this world needs to fear no colours* [pun: 'collar']; **2H4** V.v.91 ☛ **collar** (*n.*)

colt (*n.*) **1** foolish youth, callow ass **MV** I.ii.38 [Portia to Nerissa, of the Neopolitan prince] *that's a colt indeed* [pun: horse]
  2 whore, wanton, lascivious thing **LL** III.i.29 [Mote to Armado] *The hobby-horse is but a colt*

colt (*v.*) **1** trick, dupe, fool **1H4** II.ii.36 [Falstaff to Prince Hal] *What a plague mean ye to colt me thus? [Prince Hal] ... thou art not colted, thou art uncolted* [pun: horse]
  2 have sexual intercourse **Cym** II.iv.133 [Posthumus to Philario, of Innogen and Iachimo] *She hath been colted by him* [also: sense 1]

colt's tooth youthful inclinations, sportive impulses **H8** I.iii.48 [Lord Chamberlain to Sands] *Your colt's tooth is not cast yet?*

co-mate (*n.*) companion, fellow, comrade **AY** II.i.1 [Duke Senior to all] *Now my co-mates and brothers in exile*

comb (*n.*) honeycomb **E3** II.i.284 [King Edward alone, of the Countess] *O, that I were a honey-gathering bee, / To bear the comb of virtue from this flower;* **2H4** IV.iv.79

combat (*n.*) duel, trial by duel **2H6** I.iii.216 [King to all] *the day of combat shall be the last of the next month;* **Ham** I.i.84; **1H6** IV.i.78; **2H6** I.iii.206; **MW** I.i.150; **TC** I.iii.335

combinate (*adj.*) betrothed, contracted, promised **MM** III.i.224 [disguised Duke to Isabella, of Mariana and Angelo] *she lost ... her combinate husband*

combination (*n.*) alliance, league, treaty **H8** I.i.169 [Buckingham to Norfolk, of Wolsey and the treaty] *The articles o'th' combination drew / As himself pleased;* **Ham** III.iv.61; **TN** V.i.380

combine (*v.*) **1** bind, constrain, oblige **MM** IV.iii.143 [disguised Duke to Isabella] *I am combined by a sacred vow / And shall be absent*
  2 unite in harmony, be at one **RJ** II.iii.56 [Romeo to Friar, of his heart and Juliet's] *all combined, save what thou must combine / By holy marriage;* **AY** IV.iv.147

combustion (*n.*) tumult, confusion, disorder **Mac** II.iii.55 [Lennox to Macbeth, of unnatural events] *prophesying ... / Of dire combustion and confused events*

combustious (*adj.*) combustible, flammable, inflammable **Venus** 1162 [Venus to dead Adonis, of love] *It shall be ... / As dry combustious matter is to fire*

come (*v.*) **1** become, grow, come to be **AC** I.iv.44 [Caesar to Lepidus] *the ebbed man ... / Comes deared by being lacked;* **Cym** III.ii.17; **Ham** V.i.154
  2 come to pass, happen, turn out **KL** I.iv.6 [Kent alone] *So may it come;* **3H6** V.v.82
  3 speak, talk, express oneself **TS** I.ii.58 [Hortensio to Petruchio] *shall I then come roundly to thee*

come, let it [drinking call] pass it round **2H4** V.iii.52 [Silence singing] *Fill the cup, and let it come*

come about (*v.*) **1** turn out to be true, be fulfilled **RJ** I.iii.46 [Nurse to Lady Capulet] *To see now how a jest shall come about!*
  2 change direction, veer round **MV** II.vi.64 [Antonio to Gratiano] *The wind is come about*

come away (*v.*) come here, come on **1H4** II.i.23 [First Carrier to Ostler] *Come away, and be hanged, come away!*

come by (*v.*) find, acquire, come across **TS** IV.i.7 [Grumio alone, of freezing] *ere I should come by a fire to thaw me;* **Tim** I.i.208

come cut and long tail [whether a horse or dog has its tail docked or not] whatever happens, come what may **MW** III.iv.46 [Slender to Anne, of his maintaining her] *that I will, come cut and long-tail, under the degree of a squire;* **TNK** V.ii.47

come forth (*v.*) come into existence, be displayed **Tim** I.i.26 [Painter to Poet] *When comes your book forth?;* **AC** V.ii.46

come home rebound, come back [on] **LL** V.ii.632 [Dumaine to all, of Armado as Hector] *Though my mocks come home by me, I will now be merry*

come in (*v.*) **1** approach, move towards **Oth** V.i.44 [Lodovico to Gratiano, of those calling for help] *Let's think't unsafe / To come in to the cry without more help;* **2H4** III.ii.274
  2 submit, reconcile, yield **KJ** V.ii.70 [Cardinal Pandulph to Lewis the Dauphin, of King John] *his spirit is come in / That so stood out against the holy church*

come near (*v.*) **1** enter, come in/into **MW** I.iv.128 [Mistress Quickly to Fenton] *Come near the house, I pray you;* **MV** V.i.223; **MW** III.iii.141
  2 begin to understand, start to appreciate **TN** III.iv.65 [Malvolio alone, as if to Olivia] *Do you come near me now;* **RJ** I.v.21

come of (*v.*) descend from **TS** I.i.13 [Lucentio to Tranio, of his father] *Vincentio come of the Bentivolii*

come off (v.) **1** come away, leave **Cym** I.v.148 [Iachimo to Posthumus] *if I come off, and leave her in such honour as you have trust in*
2 escape, get away **AY** I.ii.28 [Celia to Rosalind] *thou mayst in honour come off again*
3 leave the field of combat, disengage **TNK** V.iii.103 [Emilia to Servant, of the combatants] *They are coming off;* **Cor** I.vi.1; **H5** III.vi.72; **KJ** V.v.4
4 turn out, result **Tim** I.i.30 [Poet to Painter, of the picture] *This comes off well and excellent;* **Ham** III.ii.24; **MM** II.i.56; **TG** II.i.103
5 pay up, settle up **MW** IV.iii.11 [Host to Bardolph, of the Germans] *They must come off*

come over (v.) **1** overshadow, overwhelm, exercise influence over **Oth** IV.i.20 [Othello to Iago, of the handkerchief] *O, it comes o'er my memory / As doth the raven o'er the infected house;* **H5** I.ii.268
2 exceed, surpass **MA** V.ii.7 [Benedick to Margaret, of his writing in a high style] *no man living shall come over it* [also: cross, punning on a 'style' over a wall]

come to (v.) achieve, attain, arrive at **MW** II.i.42 [Mistress Ford to Mistress Page, of being 'knighted'] *if it were not for one trifling respect, I could come to such honour;* **2H4** III.ii.246

come up (v.) **1** come forward [from the rear], reach, advance **TNK** III.vi.76 [Arcite to Palamon] *I spurred hard to come up*
2 come into fashion, become trendy **2H6** IV.ii.9 [Holland to Bevis] *I say it was never merry world in England since gentlemen came up*

come upon (v.) approach, descend on **TC** IV.iii.3 [Paris to Troilus, of Cressida and Diomedes] *her delivery to this valiant Greek / Comes fast upon;* **LL** IV.i.120

come what come may come what may, whatever happens **Mac** I.iii.146 [Macbeth to himself] *Come what come may, / Time and the hour runs through the roughest day*

comeddle (v.) ☞ **commeddle** (v.)

comedian (n.) actor, stage-player **TN** I.v.175 [Olivia to Viola as Cesario] *Are you a comedian?*

comely (adj.) graceful, becoming, decent **Cor** IV.vi.27 [Sicinius to Brutus] *This is a happier and more comely time;* **AY** II.iii.14; **Tim** III.v.15

comely (adv.) gracefully, fittingly, decorously **TNK** V.ii.46 [Gaoler's Daughter to Gaoler, of her horse] *He dances very finely, very comely;* **Lover** 65; **TNK** III.v.19

comer (n.) newcomer, arrival, new visitor **TC** III.iii.168 [Ulysses to Achilles, of time] *slightly shakes his parting guest by th'hand, / And … / Grasps in the comer*

comfect (n.) sweetmeat, sugar-plum, comfit **MA** IV.i.311 [Beatrice to Benedick, of Claudio] *Count Comfect*

comfit-maker (n.) confectioner, maker of sweetmeats **1H4** III.i.242 [Hotspur to Lady Percy] *you swear like a comfit-maker's wife*

comfort (n.) **1** encouragement, support, hope **MW** II.i.88 [Mistress Page to Mistress Ford, of Falstaff] *Let's … give him a show of comfort in his suit;* **KL** IV.i.16; **MM** III.i.39
2 happiness, joy, cheerfulness **RJ** III.iii.165 [Romeo to Friar, of Juliet's ring] *How well my comfort is revived by this;* **KJ** V.iii.9; **R3** II.ii.98; **Tem** I.ii.496; **Tim** I.ii.101
3 recovery, relief, cure **Cym** IV.iii.9 [Cymbeline to all, of his troubles] *It strikes me, past / The hope of comfort*
4 clemency, benevolence, mercy **Cym** V.v.404 [Cymbeline to all, of the prisoners] *they shall taste our comfort*

comfort (v.) **1** encourage, condone, countenance **WT** II.iii.56 [Paulina to Leontes, of herself as a loyal servant] *that dares / Less appear so in comforting your evils*
2 assist, help, give aid to **KL** III.v.19 [Edmund to himself, of Gloucester] *If I find him comforting the King;* **Tit** II.iii.209
3 have pity on, console, relieve **LL** IV.ii.45 [Holofernes to Dull] *God comfort thy capacity*

4 take comfort, take heart, console oneself **AY** II.vi.5 [Orlando to Adam] *Live a little, comfort a little, cheer thyself a little*

comfortable (adj.) **1** cheerful, cheery, light-hearted **Tim** III.iv.72 [Servilius to all, of Timon] *His comfortable temper has forsook him;* **AY** II.vi.9; **Cor** I.iii.2; **R3** IV.iv.174
2 comforting, encouraging, reassuring **R2** II.ii.76 [Queen Isabel to York] *for God's sake speak comfortable words;* **AW** I.i.74; **KL** I.iv.303; **Luc** 164; **RJ** V.iii.148; **TN** I.v.213

comic (adj.) amusing, mirthful, causing merriment **1H6** II.ii.45 [Burgundy to all] *I see our wars / Will turn unto a peaceful comic sport*

coming-in, comings-in (n.) income, revenue, yield **MV** II.ii.151 [Launcelot to himself] *eleven widows and nine maids is a simple coming-in for one man;* **H5** IV.i.236

comingle (v.) ☞ **commeddle** (v.)

coming-on (adj.) amenable, agreeable, compliant **AY** IV.i.102 [Rosalind as Ganymede to Orlando] *I will be your Rosalind in a more coming-on disposition*

comma (n.) **1** [subordinate part of a sentence] detail, jot **Tim** I.i.49 [Poet to Painter] *No levelled malice / Infects one comma in the course I hold*
2 pause, interval, interlude **Ham** V.ii.42 [Hamlet to Horatio, quoting from Claudius' letter to England] *As peace should still her wheaten garland wear / And stand a comma 'tween their amities*

command (n.) **1** authority, commanding power **2H4** III.ii.75 [Bardolph to Shallow, of the word 'accommodated'] *a soldier-like word, and a word of exceeding good command*
2 position of authority, superior role **Per** IV.vi.159 [Marina to Boult, of Pander and Bawd] *Neither of these are so bad as thou art, / Since they do better thee in their command*
3 orders, direction **AW** III.vi.46 [Second Lord to Parolles, of the engagement] *That was not to be blamed in the command of the service*
4 troop, body of men, force **Cor** I.vi.84 [Martius to Soldiers] *I shall quickly draw out my command, / Which men are best inclined*

command, at / upon at one's disposal, at one's pleasure **AY** II.vii.126 [Duke Senior to Orlando] *take upon command what help we have;* **MW** IV.iii.10 [Host to Bardolph, of the Germans] *They have had my house a week at command*

command (v.) **1** force, control, drive **3H6** III.i.87 [King to Keepers, of a feather] *Commanded always by the greater gust;* **3H6** II.vi.36; **Venus** 584
2 have at one's disposal, be entrusted with **Ham** III.ii.331 [Hamlet to Guildenstern] *such answer as I can make, you shall command;* **2H6** V.i.49; **Tim** I.ii.102
3 entrust, authorize, delegate **Cym** III.viii.9 [First Senator to all, of the conflict with Britain] *to you the tribunes, / For this immediate levy, he commands / His absolute commission;* **Cor** I.i.260
4 demand [from], order to be given [from] **Cym** I.vi.8 [Cornelius to Queen] *you have / Commanded of me these most poisonous compounds*

commanded (adj.) forced, feigned, contrived **TS** Induction.i.123 [Lord to Servant, of the Page] *if the boy have not a woman's gift / To rain a shower of commanded tears, / An onion will do well*

commander (n.) victor, champion, conqueror **KJ** II.i.314 [English Herald to Hubert, of King John] *Commander of this hot malicious day*

commandment, commandement (n.) **1** command, instruction, order **2H4** V.iii.135 [Falstaff to Shallow] *the laws of England are at my commandment;* **2H4** III.ii.23; **1H6** I.iii.20; **MV** II.ii.28, IV.i.448; **PassP** XX.44
2 control, authority, sovereignty [over] **KJ** IV.ii.92 [King John to Salisbury and Pembroke] *Have I commandment on the pulse of life?*

commeddle, comeddle (v.) mix, blend, mingle together **Ham** III.ii.79 [Hamlet to Horatio] *blood and judgement are so well commeddled* [Q2: F co-mingled]

commence (v.) admit to a university degree; give a good start to, make fit **2H4** IV.iii.114 [Falstaff alone] *learning [is] a mere hoard of gold kept by a devil, till sack commences it and sets it in act and use*

commend (*n.*) **1** commendation, support, praise **MV** II.ix.90 [Messenger to Portia, of Bassanio's messenger] *he bringeth ... commends and courteous breath;* **Per** II.ii.48
2 (plural) greeting, compliment, remembrance **R2** III.i.38 [Bolingbroke to York, of the Queen] *Tell her I send to her my kind commends;* **R2** III.iii.126

commend (*v.*) **1** convey greetings, present kind regards **Cor** III.ii.135 [Coriolanus to Volumnia] *Commend me to my wife* ➤ **FEW**, p.xxi; **FAREWELLS**, p.170
2 commit, entrust, hand over **LL** II.i.114 [Berowne to Rosaline] *I will commend you to mine own heart;* **AW** V.i.31; **E3** IV.iv.105; **R2** III.iii.116; **TG** I.i.17; **WT** II.iii.181
3 present, introduce, bring [for favourable acceptance] **Cym** I.v.125 [Iachimo to Posthumus] *commend me to the court where your lady is;* **Cor** IV.v.147; **H5** IV.vi.23; **MV** IV.i.143; **Per** IV.Chorus.46
4 praise, admire, extol **TN** IV.ii.47 [Malvolio to Olivia, quoting from the letter] *Remember who commended thy yellow stockings;* **AW** IV.iii.80; **AY** II.i.12; **LL** IV.ii.112; **TG** V.ii.39
5 show well, set off to advantage **Ham** I.ii.39 [Claudius to his ambassadors] *and let your haste commend your duty;* **AY** IV.iii.181
6 declare, offer, direct **TG** IV.i.9 [Proteus alone, of Silvia] *to her beauty I commend my vows;* **H8** II.iii.61

commendable (*n.*) praiseworthy, deserving of approval **1H6** IV.vi.57 [Talbot to John Talbot] *commendable proved, let's die in pride*

commendation (*n.*) **1** introduction, approval, endorsement **Cym** I.v.151 [Iachimo to Posthumus] *provided I have your commendation for my more free entertainment*
2 recommendation, commending, praise **AW** IV.iii.78 [Messenger to Second Lord] *letters of commendations to the King*
3 (plural) regards, compliments, greetings **H8** V.ii.118 [Capuchius to Katherine] *The King ... / Sends you his princely commendations;* **TG** I.iii.53

comment (*n.*) **1** observation, consideration **Ham** III.ii.89 [Hamlet to Horatio] *Even with the very comment of thy soul / Observe my uncle* [i.e. with your closest attention]
2 criticism, objection, carping remark **JC** IV.iii.8 [Cassius to Brutus] *it is not meet / That every nice offence should bear his comment*

comment (*v.*) **1** speculate, conjecture, give an opinion **2H6** III.ii.133 [King to Warwick, of Gloucester] *view his breathless corpse, / And comment then upon his sudden death;* **TNK** V.iv.65
2 meditate, ponder, cogitate **Sonn** 89.2 [of being forsaken] *I will comment upon that offence* [or: enlarge upon]

commenting (*n.*) meditation, pondering, cogitation **R3** IV.iii.51 [King Richard to Ratcliffe] *I have learned that fearful commenting / Is leaden servitor to dull delay*

commerce (*n.*) dealings, transactions, intercourse **Ham** III.i.109 [Ophelia to Hamlet] *Could beauty ... have better commerce than with honesty;* **TC** III.iii.205; **TN** III.iv.171

commission (*n.*) **1** warrant, authority [to act] **1H6** V.iv.95 [Winchester to Richard] *I do greet your excellence / With letters of commission from the King;* **AY** IV.i.127; **2H4** III.ii.88; **KL** V.iii.65; **Mac** I.iv.2; **RJ** IV.i.64
2 command, authority, power **Cor** IV.v.141 [Aufidius to Coriolanus] *take / Th'one half of my commission;* **Cor** IV.vii.14
3 authoritative charge, government instruction **H8** I.ii.20 [Queen Katherine to King Henry, of the people] *There have been commissions / Sent down among 'em;* **H8** I.ii.57, 92
4 formal body comprising justices of the peace **KL** III.vi.38 [Lear to disguised Kent] *You are o'the commission*
5 delegation, body of officials **H8** III.ii.320 [Surrey to Wolsey] *you sent a large commission / To Gregory de Cassado, to conclude ... / A league*

commissioner (*n.*) official acting for the king in his absence **H5** II.ii.61 [King Henry to all] *Who are the late commissioners?*

commit (*v.*) **1** sin, transgress, do wrong **TG** V.iv.77 [Proteus to Valentine] *I do as truly suffer / As e'er I did commit*
2 commit adultery, offend, fornicate **KL** III.iv.78 [Edgar as Poor Tom to all] *commit not with man's sworn spouse*
3 send to jail, put in custody, imprison **H8** V.i.146 [King Henry to Cranmer, of the Council] *If they shall chance ... to commit you;* **WT** II.iii.49
4 give in charge, consign, send in confinement **3H6** IV.iv.11 [Lady Grey to Rivers, of Edward] *new committed to the Bishop of York*

commix (*v.*) mix together, mingle, combine **E3** IV.iii.11 [Villiers to Charles] *profit must with honour be commixed;* **Cym** IV.ii.55; **Lover** 28

commixion, commixtion (*n.*) commixture, make-up, physical blending **TC** IV.v.124 [Hector to Ajax] *Were thy commixion Greek and Trojan*

commixture (*n.*) **1** composition, compound, union **3H6** II.vi.6 [Clifford alone, as if to the House of Lancaster] *now I fall, thy tough commixture melts*
2 complexion, mingling of colour **LL** V.ii.296 [Boyet to and of the ladies] *Dismasked, their damask sweet commixture shown, / Are angels vailing clouds, or roses blown*

commodious (*adj.*) accommodating, compliant, obliging **TC** V.ii.197 [Thersites alone, of Patroclus] *the parrot will not do more for an almond than he for a commodious drab*

commodity (*n.*) **1** supply, quantity, stock, consignment **TN** III.i.43 [Feste to Viola as Cesario] *Now Jove, in his next commodity of hair, send thee a beard!;* **1H4** I.ii.82; **MM** IV.iii.5; **MV** I.i.178
2 asset, advantage, benefit **WT** III.ii.92 [Hermione to Leontes] *To me can life be no commodity;* **2H4** I.ii.250; **KL** IV.i.21; **MV** III.i.27
3 profit, gain, proceeds **Per** IV.ii.28 [Pander to Bawd] *our credit comes not in like the commodity*
4 self-interest, desire for gain, expediency **KJ** II.i.573 [Bastard alone] *France ... rounded in the ear / With that ... smooth-faced gentleman, tickling commodity* [and throughout speech]
5 (plural) goods, wares, merchandise **2H6** IV.vii.119 [Dick to Cade] *when shall we ... take up commodities upon our bills?*

common (*n.*) **1** (people) common people, ordinary citizens **2H6** III.i.28 [Queen to King, of Gloucester] *By flattery hath he won the commons' hearts;* **2H4** II.iii.51; **2H6** III.i.374, ii.122, IV.i.100; **H8** I.ii.104; **R2** II.i.246
2 state, people, community **Cor** I.i.149 [Menenius to Citizens] *digest things rightly / Touching the weal o'th' common*
3 common people, ordinary citizens **Cor** III.i.29 [Cominius to Brutus, of Coriolanus] *Hath he not passed the noble and the common?*
4 commonplace, ordinary, average **Cor** IV.i.32 [Coriolanus to Volumnia] *your son / Will ... exceed the common*
5 vernacular, everyday speech **AY** V.i.48 [Touchstone to William, of Audrey] *this female - which in the common is 'woman'*
6 public property, common land, open pasture **CE** II.ii.29 [Antipholus of Syracuse to Dromio of Syracuse] *Your sauciness will ... make a common of my serious hours;* **JC** IV.i.27; **LL** II.i.209

common, in [of land] in common possession, for the whole community **2H6** IV.vii.16 [Cade to all] *henceforward all things shall be in common;* **2H6** IV.ii.64

common (*adj.*) **1** average, usual, general, ordinary **AY** I.iii.113 [Rosalind to Celia] *I am more than common tall* [i.e. of above-average height]; **LL** I.i.57; **TG** V.iv.62; **TS** I.i.35; **Venus** 293
2 of ordinary people, of the masses **TNK** II.i.128 [Arcite to Palamon] *the ways of honour, / That liberty and common conversation ... [might] / Woo us to wander from;* **2H4** IV.iii.33; **Tim** V.i.190
3 indiscriminate, general, affecting everyone **Tim** V.iv.22 [Second Senator to Alcibiades] *We were not all unkind, nor all deserve / The common stroke of war*
4 cheap, vulgar, promiscuous **Cor** II.iii.94 [Coriolanus to Fourth Citizen] *I have not been common in my love;* **AW** V.iii.188

5 below the rank of gentleman, without rank **1H6** IV.i.31 [Gloucester to all, of Falstaff's cowardliness] *this fact was infamous, / And ill beseeming any common man*
6 public, open, outdoor **Per** IV.vi.174 [Marina to Boult] *Empty ... common shores of filth;* **JC** III.ii.251

commonalty (*n.*) common people, community **Cor** I.i.27 [First Citizen to all, of Martius] *He's a very dog to the commonalty;* **H8** I.ii.170

commoner (*n.*) **1** citizen, denizen, member **2H4** IV.iii.108 [Falstaff alone, of the effect of sherry on the body] *the vital commoners, and inland petty spirits, muster me all to their captain, the heart*
2 whore, harlot, prostitute **Oth** IV.ii. 72 [Othello to Desdemona] *O, thou public commoner!;* **AW** V.iii.194

common-hackneyed (*adj.*) made commonplace by habitual exposure, cheapened **1H4** III.ii.40 [King Henry to Prince Hal, of Hal's behaviour] *So common-hackneyed in the eyes of men*

common house (*n.*) brothel **MM** II.i.43 [Elbow to all, of Froth and Pompey] *If these be good people in a commonweal that do nothing but use their abuses in common houses, I know no law*

common-kissing (*adj.*) touching everyone **Cym** III.iv.165 [Pisanio to Innogen, of her cheek] *Exposing it ... to the greedy touch / Of common-kissing Titan* [i.e. the sun that shines on everyone]

commonplace (*n.*) commonplace book, collection, compilation **E3** IV.iv.116 [Prince Edward to Third Herald, of Philip] *render back this commonplace of prayer / To do himself good in adversity*

commonty (*n.*) ☛ comonty (*n.*)

commonweal, commonwealth (*n.*) state, nation, community, body politic **2H6** II.i.186 [Gloucester to Queen] *I have loved my king and commonweal;* **LL** IV.i.41 [Boyet to Princess, of Costard] *Here comes a member of the commonwealth;* **1H4** IV.iii.80; **1H6** III.i.98; **2H6** I.i.187; **MM** II.i.42; **Tem** II.i.150

commotion (*n.*) **1** insurrection, rebellion, sedition **2H6** III.i.358 [York to himself] *I have seduced ... John Cade of Ashford, / To make commotion;* **2H4** II.iv.358; **2H6** III.i.29
2 perturbation, agitation, disturbed excitement **H8** III.ii.112 [Norfolk to King Henry, of Wolsey] *Some strange commotion / Is in his brain;* **TC** II.iii.173

commune (*v.*) **1** talk, converse, discourse **MM** IV.iii.102 [disguised Duke to Provost] *I would commune with you of such things / That want no ear but yours;* **TNK** IV.iii.76; **TS** I.i.101; **WT** II.i.162
2 share, participate [in] **Ham** IV.v.202 [Claudius to Laertes] *I must commune with your grief* [Q2; F *common*]

communicate (*v.*) share [in], partake [of], participate [in] **CE** II.ii.185 [Adriana to Antipholus of Syracuse, of herself] *Whose weakness, married to thy stronger state, / Makes me with thy strength to communicate*

communication (*n.*) discussion, conference, debate **H8** I.i.86 [Buckingham to Abergavenny and Norfolk, of the event] *What did this vanity / But minister communication of / A most poor issue?*

community (*n.*) commonness, familiarity, everyday acquaintance **1H4** III.ii.77 [King Henry to Prince Hal, of the people] *sick and blunted with community*

commutual, comutual (*adj.*) mutual, joint, answering to each other **Ham** III.ii.169 [First Player, as King, to his Queen] *Hymen did our hands, / Unite commutual in most sacred bands*

comonty, commonty (*n.*) malapropism for 'comedy' **TS** Induction.ii.135 [Sly to Lord] *Is not a comonty a Christmas gambold*

compact (*n.*) agreement, contract, covenant **JC** III.i.215 [Cassius to Antony] *what compact mean you to have with us?;* **AY** V.iv.5; **CE** II.ii.170; **Ham** I.i.86

compact (*adj.*) **1** allied, in league, in collusion **MM** V.i.240 [Duke to Mariana and Friar Peter, of Isabella] *Thou foolish friar, and thou pernicious woman, / Compact with her that's gone;* **KL** II.ii.116

2 made up, composed **MND** V.i.8 [Theseus to Hippolyta] *The lunatic, the lover, and the poet / Are of imagination all compact;* **AY** II.vii.5; **CE** III.ii.22; **Luc** 1423; **Tit** V.iii.87; **Venus** 149 ☛ well-compact (*adj.*)

compact (*v.*) **1** consolidate, confirm, strengthen **KL** I.iv.336 [Gonerill to Oswald, of her anxiety] *And thereto add such reasons of your own / As may compact it more*
2 compound, make up firmly, consolidate **Luc** 530 [Tarquin to Lucrece] *The poisonous simple sometime is compacted / In a pure compound*

companion (*n.*) **1** rogue, rascal, fellow **2H6** IV.x.29 [Iden to Cade] *rude companion, whatsoe'er thou be;* **AW** V.iii.250; **CE** IV.v.59; **Cor** V.ii.58; **MND** I.i.15; **Oth** IV.ii.140
2 associate, aide, comrade **AW** II.iii.191 [Lafew to Parolles] *Are you companion to the Count Rossillion?*

companion (*v.*) make a companion of, join in fellowship **AC** I.ii.31 [Charmian to Soothsayer] *companion me with my mistress*

companionship, of belonging to one company, in a single party **Tim** I.i.246 [Messenger to Timon] *'Tis Alcibiades, and some twenty horse, / All of companionship*

company (*n.*) **1** group of people, party, band **1H4** II.i.58 [Chamberlain to Gadshill, of the franklin] *I heard him tell it to one of his company;* **1H4** II.i.46
2 group of followers, band of retainers **Cym** IV.ii.129 [Guiderius to Belarius and Arviragus, of Cloten] *What company / Discover you abroad?;* **Cym** IV.ii.69, 101
3 companion, associate, comrade **H5** I.i.55 [Canterbury to Ely, of King Henry] *his companion was to courses vain, / His companies unlettered, rude, and shallow;* **AW** IV.iii.31; **MND** I.i.219
4 (plural) companionship, fellowship, comradeship **Ham** II.ii.14 [Claudius to Rosencrantz and Guildenstern, of Hamlet] *by your companies / To draw him on to pleasures*

company (*v.*) accompany, keep company with **Cym** V.v.409 [Posthumus to Cymbeline, of Belarius, Arviragus and Guiderius] *I am, sir, / The soldier that did company these three / In poor beseeming*

comparative (*n.*) comparison-maker, insult-dealer; or: rival **1H4** III.ii.67 [King Henry to Prince Hal, of Richard II] *gave his countenance against his name / To ... stand the push / Of every beardless vain comparative*

comparative (*adj.*) **1** as a means of comparison **Cym** II.iii.128 [Innogen to Cloten, of Posthumus] *if 'twere made / Comparative for your virtues to be styled / The under-hangman of his kingdom* [i.e. comparing you on the basis of virtues, you rank as Posthumus' under-hangman]
2 good at making comparisons; insulting, abusive **1H4** I.ii.80 [Falstaff to Prince Hal] *Thou ... art indeed the most comparative rascalliest sweet young prince*

compare (*n.*) comparison, simile, analogy **TN** II.iv.100 [Orsino to Viola as Cesario] *Make no compare / Between that love a woman can bear me / And that I owe Olivia;* **E3** I.ii.156; **Luc** 40; **Sonn** 21.5, 35.6, 130.14; **TC** III.ii.173; **Venus** 8

compare, above beyond comparison **RJ** III.v.239 [Juliet alone, of the Nurse and Romeo] *to dispraise my lord with that same tongue / Which she hath praised him with above compare*

compare (*v.*) vie, rival, compete **Ham** V.ii.137 [Hamlet to Osrick, of Laertes] *lest I should compare with him in excellence;* **2H4** II.iv.161; **MND** II.ii.105

comparison (*n.*) **1** act of comparing, quibbling, equivocation **1H6** V.iv.150 [Richard to Charles] *Standest thou aloof upon comparison?* [i.e. Will this comparison of our two states keep you from agreeing?]
2 jibing allusion, scoffing analogy **MA** II.i.132 [masked Beatrice to masked Benedick, of Benedick] *he'll but break a comparison or two on me;* **LL** V.ii.833
3 superior trait, outshining point **AC** III.xiii.26 [Antony to Ambassador, of Caesar] *I dare him therefore / To lay his gay comparisons apart*

compartner (*n.*) associate, partner **MA** III.iii.1 [stage direction] *Enter Dogberry and his compartner Verges*

compass (*n.*) **1** range, reach, limit, scope **CE** III.i.87 [Balthasar to Antipholus of Ephesus] *you ... draw within the compass of suspect / The unviolated honour of your wife*; **E3** V.i.140; **Ham** III.ii.375; **Oth** IV.ii.218; **R3** I.iii.283; **RJ** IV.i.47
2 circle, circumference, bound **R2** II.i.101 [John of Gaunt to King Richard] *thy crown, / Whose compass is no bigger than thy head*; **R2** III.iv.40
3 circumference, round measurement **TG** II.vii.51 [Julia to Lucetta] *What compass will you wear your farthingale?*
4 circlet, encircling band **MW** V.v.66 [Mistress Quickly as Queen of Fairies to the fairies] *look you sing, / Like to the Garter's compass, in a ring*
5 revolution, circuit of time **Oth** III.iv.71 [Othello to Desdemona, of a sibyl] *that had numbered in the world / The sun to course two hundred compasses* [i.e. years]; **JC** V.iii.25
6 regularity, proportion, measure **1H4** III.iii.20 [Falstaff to Bardolph] *now I live out of all order, out of all compass* [pun: 19, sense 7]
7 moderation, bounds, due limits **1H4** III.iii.19 [Falstaff to Bardolph] *I .... Lived well, and in good compass* [pun: 20, sense 6]

compass (*v.*) **1** accomplish, fulfil, achieve, bring about **MW** III.iii.188 [Ford to his companions, of Falstaff] *Maybe the knave bragged of that he could not compass*; **E3** IV.iii.37; **Oth** I.iii.355; **Per** I.i.25; **Tem** III.ii.58; **TN** I.ii.45
2 win, obtain, attain **H5** IV.i.287 [King Henry alone, praying] *think not upon the fault / My father made in compassing the crown!*; **Luc** 346; **TG** II.iv.212, IV.ii.89
3 surround, trap, ring in **E3** IV.iii.59 [King John to Charles, of Prince Edward] *we have compassed him; he cannot scape*; **1H6** IV.iv.27
4 surround, be in the middle of **Mac** V.vi.95 [Macduff to Malcolm] *I see thee compassed with thy kingdom's pearl* [i.e. the best of your nobles]
5 embrace, enfold **Tem** V.i.180 [Alonso to Ferdinand] *Now all the blessings / Of a glad father compass thee about*; **CE** IV.i.112; **TC** I.iii.276
6 go around, orbit, make a circuit of **MND** IV.i.96 [Oberon to Titania] *We the globe can compass soon*
7 go round with, travel about with; or: obtain, lay hold of **WT** IV.iii.93 [Autolycus to Clown, of the supposed robber] *he compassed a motion of the Prodigal Son*
8 bend into a circle, make to curve round **MW** III.v.101 [Falstaff to Ford as Brook] *I suffered ... to be compassed like a good bilbo in the circumference of a peck*

compassed (*adj.*) curved, rounded, arched **Venus** 272 [of Adonis' horse] *his braided hanging mane / Upon his compassed crest now stand on end*; **TC** I.ii.112; **TS** IV.iii.135

compassion (*v.*) have compassion on, pity, be sorry for **Tit** IV.i.123 [Marcus alone, of Titus] *O heavens, can you hear a good man groan / And not relent, or not compassion him?*

compassionate (*adj.*) full of lamentation, piteously appealing **R2** I.iii.174 [King Richard to Mowbray] *It boots thee not to be compassionate*

compeer (*n.*) companion, associate, fellow **Sonn** 86.7 [of his rival] *neither he, nor his compeers by night / Giving him aid, my verse astonished*

compeer (*v.*) equal, match, be the peer of **KL** V.iii.70 [Regan to Gonerill, of Edmund] *In my rights, / By me invested, he compeers the best*

compelled (*adj.*) **1** constrained, forced, of necessity **MM** II.iv.57 [Angelo to Isabella] *Our compelled sins / Stand more for number than accompt* [i.e. the sins which we cannot help committing]; **H8** II.iii.87
2 enforced, involuntary, unsought **H8** II.iii.87 [Old Lady to Anne] *fie upon / This compelled fortune!*

competence (*n.*) sufficiency, adequate supply **2H4** V.v.69 [King Henry V to Falstaff] *For competence of life I will allow you, / That lack of means enforce you not to evils*

competency (*n.*) **1** means of life, sufficiency **Cor** I.i.137 [Menenius to Citizens, as the belly addressing the other body parts] *From me receive that natural competency / Whereby they live*
2 sufficiency without excess, modest means **MV** I.ii.8 [Nerissa to Portia] *superfluity comes sooner by white hairs, but competency lives longer*

competent, computent (*adj.*) **1** equivalent, sufficient, adequate **Ham** I.i.90 [Horatio to Marcellus and Barnardo] *a moiety competent / Was gaged by our King*
2 to be reckoned with, needing to be settled **TN** III.iv.241 [Sir Toby to Viola as Cesario, of Sir Andrew] *His indignation derives itself out of a very computent injury*

competitor (*n.*) **1** partner, associate, colleague **LL** II.i.82 [Boyet to Princess, of the King] *he and his competitors in oath / Were all addressed to meet you*; **AC** I.iv.3, II.vii.70, V.i.42; **R3** IV.iv.504; **TG** II.vi.35; **TN** IV.ii.10
2 fellow-candidate **Tit** I.i.66 [Bassianus to Tribunes and Senators, of allowing him into the senate house after Saturninus] *Tribunes, and me, a poor competitor*

compile (*v.*) compose, create in writing **Sonn** 78.9 *be most proud of that which I compile*; **LL** IV.iii.132

complain (*v.*) lament, bewail, bemoan **AY** III.iv.43 [Corin to Rosalind and Celia, of Silvius] *the shepherd that complained of love*; **AY** III.ii.28; **Luc** 1839; **R2** III.iv.18; **RJ** II.Chorus.7

complaining (*n.*) **1** grievance, complaint, gripe **Cor** I.i.207 [Martius to Menenius, of the citizens] *They vented their complainings*
2 lamentation, sorrowing, mourning **Cym** IV.ii.375 [Lucius to disguised Innogen] *Thou mov'st no less with thy complaining than / Thy master in bleeding*

complement (*n.*) ☞ compliment (*n.*)

complete, compleat (*adj.*) **1** accomplished, consummate, thorough **2H6** IV.x.53 [Cade to and of Iden] *By my valour, the most complete champion that ever I heard!*; **H8** III.ii.49; **LL** I.i.44; **TC** III.iii.181; **Tim** III.i.10
2 fully equipped, with everything present **Ham** I.iv.52 [Hamlet to Ghost] *dead corse, again in complete steel*; **H8** III.ii.49; **KJ** II.i.433; **MM** I.iii.3; **TC** III.iii.181; **Tim** IV.iii.245

complexion (*n.*) **1** appearance, look, colouring **Ham** II.ii.453 [Hamlet to First Player, quoting lines about Pyrrhus] *this dread and black complexion*; **LL** I.i.79; **R2** III.ii.194; **Tem** I.ii.29; **TN** II.v.26; **WT** I.ii.381
2 constitution, physical make-up, outward appearance **Ham** V.ii.99 [Hamlet to Osrick] *it is very sultry and hot for my complexion*; **Cor** II.i.204; **Per** IV.vi.76; **Venus** 215
3 natural trait, disposition, temperament, nature **MV** III.i.27 [Solanio to Salerio, of birds] *it is the complexion of them all to leave the dam*; **Ham** I.iv.27; **LL** I.ii.76, 81; **MM** III.i.24, 185

complice (*n.*) accomplice, confederate, associate **R2** II.iii.164 [Bolingbroke to York, of Bristol Castle] *held / By Bushy, Bagot, and their complices* **2H4** I.i.163; **2H6** V.i.212; **3H6** IV.iii.45; **R2** III.i.43

compliment, complement (*n.*) **1** example of good manners, instance of proper behaviour **RJ** II.iv.20 [Mercutio to Benvolio, of Tybalt] *he's the courageous captain of compliments* [i.e. the laws of duelling]; **LL** I.i.166, III.i.20
2 ceremony, etiquette, protocol **KL** V.iii.231 [Albany to all, of receiving Kent] *The time will not allow the compliment / Which very manners urges*; **AC** IV.iv.32; **KJ** V.vi.16; **KL** I.i.301; **LL** V.ii.141; **RJ** II.ii.89
3 show, display, exhibition **MW** IV.ii.5 [Falstaff to Mistress Ford, of repaying her] *not only ... in the simple office of love, but in all the accoutrement, complement, and ceremony of it*; **Oth** I.i.64

COMPARISON

There are several interesting differences between the modern system of expressing comparison and the one available to Shakespeare. To express a higher degree, present-day Standard English allows either an inflected form (*bigger, biggest*) or a form consisting of more than one word (a *periphrastic* form), such as *more / most interesting*. Lower degree is always expressed periphrastically (*less / least happy*). The choice with higher degree depends largely on the length of the adjective, with words of one syllable taking an inflection (*bigger, longest*), words of three syllables or more appearing periphrastically (*more / most interesting*), and words of two syllables sometimes going one way (*happier* rather than *more happy*) and sometimes the other (*most proper* rather than *properest*). There are also some special cases: adjectives derived from verb participles, for example, never take an inflectional ending, even if they are only one syllable long (*a most pained expression*, never *a paindest expression*). Adverbs also allow the expression of comparison: *sooner / soonest, more carefully / most carefully*.

Many examples in Shakespearian English work in the same way; but there are several differences. The most noticeable feature is the use of double comparison, where an inflected and a periphrastic form appear together, producing a more emphatic expression:

Double comparatives	Examples	Double superlatives	Examples
more better	MND III.i.18	most boldest	JC III.i.121
more bigger-looked	TNK I.i.215	most bravest	Cym IV.ii.319
more braver	Tem I.ii.440	most coldest	Cym II.iii.2
more corrupter	KL II.ii.100	most despiteful'st	TC IV.i.33
more fairer	E3 II.i.25	most heaviest	TG IV.ii.136
more headier	KL II.iv.105	most poorest	KL II.iii.7
more hotter	AW IV.v.38	most stillest	2H4 III.i.28
more kinder	Tim IV.i.36	most unkindest	JC III.ii.184
more mightier	MM V.i.235	most worst	WT III.ii.177
more nearer	Ham II.i.11		
more nimbler	E3 II.ii.178		
more proudlier	Cor IV.vii.8		
more rawer	Ham V.ii.122		
more richer	Ham III.ii.313		
more safer	Oth I.iii.223		
more softer	TC II.ii.11		
more sounder	AY III.ii.58		
more strong	Cor I.i.69		
more wider	Oth I.iii.107		
more worse	KL II.ii.146		
more worthier	AY III.iii.54		
less happier	R2 II.i.49		

There are also several cases where an inflectional ending is used where today we would use the periphrastic form.

Modern comparative	Shakespearian comparative	Example
more honest	honester	Cor IV.v.50
more horrid	horrider	Cym IV.ii.331
more loath	loather	2H6 III.ii.355
more often	oftener	MM IV.ii.48
more quickly	quicklier	AW I.i.122
more perfect	perfecter	Cor II.i.76
more wayward	waywarder	AY IV.i.150

Modern superlative	Shakespearian superlative	Example
most ancient	ancient'st	WT IV.i.10
most certain	certain'st	TNK V.iv.21
most civil	civilest	2H6 IV.vii.56
most condemned	contemned'st	KL II.ii.141
most covert	covert'st	R3 III.v.33
most daring	daring'st	H8 II.iv.215
most deformed	deformed'st	Sonn 113.10
most easily	easil'est	Cym IV.ii.206

COMPARISON – *continued*

Modern superlative	Shakespearian superlative	Example
most exact	*exactest*	**Tim** II.ii.161
most extreme	*extremest*	**KL** V.iii.134
most faithful	*faithfull'st*	**TN** V.i.112
most foul-mouthed	*foul mouthed'st*	**2H4** II.iv.70
most honest	*honestest*	**AW** III.v.73
most loathsome	*loathsomest*	**TC** II.i.28
most lying	*lyingest*	**2H6** II.i.124
most maidenly	*maidenliest*	**KL** I.i.131
most pained	*pained'st*	**Per** IV.vi.161
most perfect	*perfectest*	**Mac** I.v.2
most ragged	*ragged'st*	**2H4** I.i.151
most rascally	*rascalliest*	**1H4** I.ii.80
most sovereign	*sovereignest*	**1H4** I.iii.56
most unhopeful	*unhopefullest*	**MA** II.i.349
most welcome	*welcomest*	**1H6** II.ii.56
most wholesome	*wholesom'st*	**MM** IV.ii.70

There are rather fewer cases where a periphrastic form is used where today we would use an inflectional ending.

Modern comparative	Shakespearian comparative	Example
greater	*more great*	**1H4** IV.i.77
longer	*more long*	**Cor** V.ii.63
nearer	*more near*	**AW** I.iii.102

And there are a number of cases where modern Standard English would not use a form of comparison at all, but Shakespearian English allows it. They include some words expressing absolute notions (such as *chief*), which today are generally not compared. Several of these forms can still be heard in regional dialects, of course, and some (such as *littlest*, *worser*) are now considered immature or uneducated.

Modern word	Shakespearian comparison	Example
chief	*chiefest*	**1H6** I.i.177
due	*duer*	**2H4** III.ii.296
just	*justest*	**AC** II.i.2
less	*lesser*	**R2** II.i.95
like	*liker*	**KJ** II.i.126
little	*littlest [cf. smallest]*	**Ham** III.ii.181
rather	*ratherest*	**LL** IV.ii.18
very	*veriest*	**1H4** II.ii.23
worse	*worser [cf. less bad]*	**Ham** III.iv.158

Occasionally, both modern English and Shakespearian English have inflected forms, but they are different. This is the case with *farrer* (**TS** IV.ii.73), where we would today say *farther* or *further*. *Elder* is sometimes used where we would today say *older*, as in **Sonn** 22.8, 'How can I then be elder than thou art?'

Lastly, it is important to note that, when an inflected and a periphrastic form co-exist, the choice can be exploited poetically, to suit the demands of the metre. A case in point is **AY** III.v.51–5 [Rosalind to Silvius]:

> You are a thousand times a properer man
> Than she a woman ...
> And out of you she sees herself more proper
> Than any of her lineaments can show her.

This is probably why we find *more sweet* (**AY** II.i.2) alongside *sweeter* (**MV** V.i.100), *more grave* (**TN** I.iv.28) alongside *graver* (**Cor** III.i.106), and so on.

4 accomplishment, finished quality H5 II.ii.134 [King Henry to Scroop, of other men] *are they… / Garnished and decked in modest complement*

complimental *(adj.)* ceremonial, courteous, full of compliments TC III.i.39 [Pandarus to Servant, of Paris] *I will make a complimental assault upon him*

complot *(n.)* plot, conspiracy, covert plan 2H6 III.i.147 [Gloucester to King, of his enemies] *I know their complot is to have my life*; R3 III.i.192, 200; Tit II.iii.265, V.i.65, ii.147

complot *(v.)* plot together, collude R2 I.iii.189 [King Richard to Bolingbroke and Mowbray] *never … meet / To plot, contrive, or complot any ill*; R2 I.i.96

comply *(v.)* **1** satisfy, fulfil, accomplish Oth I.iii.260 [Othello to Duke, of Desdemona's request] *[I] beg it not / To please the palate of my appetite, / Nor to comply with heat … and proper satisfaction*
2 observe the formalities, show polite conduct Ham V.ii.184 [Hamlet to Horatio, of Osric] *'A did comply, sir, with his dug before 'a sucked it*; Ham II.ii.371

compose *(v.)* **1** make up, produce, fashion AW I.ii.21 [King to Bertram] *Frank nature … / Hath well composed thee*; Mac I.vii.73; MND I.i.48; TC V.ii.173
2 reach agreement, make a settlement AC II.ii.15 [Antony to Ventidius] *If we compose well here, to Parthia*

composed *(adj.)* elaborately constructed, well put together TG III.ii.69 [Proteus to Thurio] *sonnets, whose composed rhymes / Should be full-fraught with serviceable vows*

composition *(n.)* **1** constitution, make-up, state [of mind and body] KL II.ii.19 [disguised Kent to Oswald, describing him] *art nothing but the composition of a knave, beggar … and the son and heir of a mongrel bitch*; AW I.i.200; 1H6 III.ii.74; KJ I.i.88; R2 II.i.73; Sonn 45.9
2 putting together, making up KL I.ii.12 [Edmund alone, comparing bastards to others] *Who in the lusty stealth of nature take / More composition and fierce quality* [i.e. has a better make-up]
3 settlement, truce, coming to terms KJ II.i.561 [Bastard alone, of the treaty] *Mad world! Mad kings! Mad composition!*; AC II.vi.58; Cor III.i.3; Mac I.ii.62; MM I.ii.2
4 arrangement, agreement, bargain AW IV.iii.17 [Second Lord to First Lord, of Bertram] *He … thinks himself made in the unchaste composition*
5 agreed settlement, expected arrangement MM V.i.218 [Angelo to Duke, of Mariana] *her promised proportions / Came short of composition*
6 consistency, compatibility, coherence Oth I.iii.1 [Duke to Senators] *There is no composition in these news / That gives them credit*

composture *(n.)* compost, manure Tim IV.iii.443 [Timon to Bandits] *The earth's a thief, / That feeds and breeds by a composture stolen / From general excrement*

composure *(n.)* **1** character, temperament, make-up AC I.iv.22 [Caesar to Lepidus, of Antony's faults] *his composure must be rare indeed / Whom these things cannot blemish*; TC II.iii.237
2 combination, bond, coming together TC II.iii.99 [Nestor to Ulysses] *it was a strong composure a fool could disunite* [Q; F *counsell*]

compound *(n.)* **1** union, combination, association Cor II.i.55 [Menenius to Brutus and Sicinius] *I find the ass in compound with the major part of your syllables* [i.e. there is foolishness in most of what you say]
2 lump, composition, mass 2H4 II.iv.289 [Falstaff to Prince Henry] *Thou whoreson mad compound of majesty*; 1H4 II.iv.119

compound *(adj.)* composed of the elements Ham III.iv.50 [Hamlet to Gertrude] *this solidity and compound mass* [i.e. the Earth]

compound *(v.)* **1** agree, settle TS I.ii.27 [Petruchio to Grumio] *We will compound this quarrel*; Cor V.vi.84; H5 II.i.94; KJ II.i.281; R3 II.i.76; TS II.i.334
2 come to terms, reach an agreement H5 IV.iii.80 [Montjoy to King Henry] *If for thy ransom thou wilt now compound*; H5 IV.vi.33; MM IV.ii.21
3 put together, construct, compose H5 V.ii.205 [King Henry to Katherine] *Shall not thou and I … compound a boy, half French, half English*; Tim IV.iii.35, iii.274
4 mix, mingle, combine Sonn 71.10 *When I … compounded am with clay*; 2H4 V.v.116; KL I.ii.128

compounded *(adj.)* blended, mingled, combined, made up TNK IV.iii.83 [Doctor to Wooer] *make an addition of some other compounded odours, which are grateful to the sense*; Cym III.v.74; H8 I.i.12

comprehend *(v.)* **1** take in, include, incorporate MND V.i.20 [Theseus to Hippolyta, of imagination] *if it would but apprehend some joy, / It comprehends some bringer of that joy*
2 malapropism for 'apprehend' MA III.v.43 [Dogberry to Leonato] *our watch … have indeed comprehended two aspicious persons*; MA III.iii.24

comprimise *(v.)* variant form of 'compromise' KJ V.i.67 [Bastard to King John] *Shall we … make comprimise* [F]

compromise *(n.)* settlement, solution, amicable arrangement 1H6 V.iv.149 [Richard to Charles] *now the matter grows to compromise*; MW I.i.31; R2 II.i.253

compromise *(v.)* reach agreement, come to terms MV I.iii.75 [Shylock to Antonio, of Jacob] *Laban and himself were compromised / That all the eanlings which were streaked and pied / Should fall as Jacob's hire*

compt *(n.)* reckoning, day of judgement Oth V.ii.271 [Othello to dead Desdemona] *When we shall meet at compt / This look of thine will hurl my soul from heaven* [F; Q1 *count*]; AW V.iii.57

compt, in held in trust, subject to account Mac I.vi.26 [Lady Macbeth to King] *Your servants ever / Have … what is theirs, in compt, / To make their audit at your highness' pleasure*

compter *(n.)* ☛ counter *(n.)*

comptible *(adj.)* sensitive, thin-skinned, impressionable TN I.v.168 [Viola as Cesario to Olivia] *I am very comptible, even to the least sinister usage*

comptless *(adj.)* incalculable, inestimable, immeasureable Venus 84 *one sweet kiss shall pay this comptless debt* [Q]

comptroller *(n.)* steward, master of ceremonies H8 I.iii.67 [Lord Chamberlain to Sands] *I was spoke to, with Sir Henry Guilford, / This night to be comptrollers*

compulsatory, compulsative *(adj.)* involving compulsion, subject to force Ham I.i.103 [Horatio to Marcellus and Barnardo, of young Fortinbras' intentions] *to recover of us by strong hand / And terms compulsatory those foresaid lands* [Q; F *compulsative*]

compulsive *(adj.)* driving onward, forcing forward Oth III.iii.451 [Othello to Iago, of the Pontic sea] *Whose icy current and compulsive course / Ne'er feels retiring ebb*; Ham III.iv.87

compunctious *(adj.)* remorseful, conscience-stricken, contrite Mac I.v.43 [Lady Macbeth alone] *Stop up the access and passage to remorse, / That no compunctious visitings of nature / Shake my fell purpose*

computation *(n.)* working out, reasoning, cogitation CE II.ii.4 [Antipholus of Syracuse alone, of Dromio of Syracuse] *the heedful slave / Is wandered forth in care to seek me out / By computation and mine host's report*

computent *(adj.)* ☛ competent *(adj.)*

comutual *(adj.)* ☛ commutual *(adj.)*

con *(v.)* **1** learn by heart, commit to memory TN I.v.167 [Viola as Cesario to Olivia, of her speech] *I have taken great pains to con it*; AY III.ii.264; JC IV.iii.97; MND I.ii.93; TC II.i.17; TN II.iii.141

2 express, offer, give **AW** IV.iii.150 [Bertram to First Lord, of Parolles' telling the truth] *I con him no thanks for't;* **Tim** IV.iii.427

concave *(adj.)* **1** hollow, empty **AY** III.iv.23 [Celia to Rosalind, of Orlando] *I do think him as concave as a covered goblet;* **Lover** 1
2 hollowed out, overhanging **JC** I.i.47 [Marullus to the people, of the Tiber trembling] *To hear the replication of your sounds / Made in her concave shores*

concavity *(n.)* concave quality, curvature, hollowness **H5** III.ii.58 [Fluellen to Gower, of the mines] *The concavities of it is not sufficient*

conceal *(v.)* malapropism for 'reveal' **MW** IV.v.40 [Simple to Host, of things he must not say] *I may not conceal them*

concealed *(adj.)* **1** unrevealed, kept secret, unacknowledged **RJ** III.iii.98 [Romeo to Nurse, of Juliet] *what says / My concealed lady to our cancelled love?* [i.e. with her married status not yet public]
2 hidden, secret, offering a hiding-place **KJ** V.ii.139 [Bastard to Lewis the Dauphin, of the French reaction to the English power] *To dive like buckets in concealed wells*

concealment *(n.)* **1** something to be concealed, secret **TNK** V.i.123 [Palamon praying to Venus] *him I do not love that … names concealments in / The boldest language*
2 secret arts, esoteric knowledge, mystery **1H4** III.i.161 [Mortimer to Hotspur, of Glendower] *he is a worthy gentleman … profited / In strange concealments*

conceit *(n.)* **1** imagination, fancy, wit **Ham** II.ii.550 [Hamlet alone, of the First Player] *Could force his soul so to his own conceit;* **AY** II.vi.7; **Ham** III.iv.115; **1H6** V.v.15; **LL** V.ii.260; **RJ** II.vi.30
2 imagining, brooding, fanciful thinking **WT** III.ii.142 [Servant to Leontes, of Mamillius] *with mere conceit and fear / Of the Queen's speed, is gone;* **CE** IV.iv.64; **Ham** IV.v.45; **Oth** III.iii.323; **R2** II.ii.33; **RJ** IV.iii.37
3 understanding, intelligence, apprehension **2H4** II.iv.236 [Falstaff to Doll, of Poins] *There's no more conceit in him than is in a mallet;* **AY** V.ii.51; **CE** III.ii.34; **LL** V.ii.399; **Per** III.i.16; **Tim** V.iv.77
4 view, opinion, judgement **E3** III.i.105 [King John to Philip] *what is thy conceit, / Touching the challenge that the English make;* **H8** II.iii.74; **MV** III.v.58; **TG** III.ii.17
5 notion, idea, thought **Tim** V.iv.14 [First Senator to Alcibiades] *When they first griefs were but a mere conceit;* **KJ** III.iii.50; **MA** II.i.273; **MV** III.iv.2; **R3** III.iv.49; **TS** V.iii.156
6 design, ingenuity, conception **Tit** IV.ii.30 [Aaron to himself, of Tamora] *She would applaud Andronicus' conceit;* **Ham** V.ii.150; **1H6** IV.i.102; **Luc** 1423; **Oth** III.iii.114
7 trinket, fancy article, bauble **MND** I.i.33 [Egeus to Lysander, of Hermia] *With bracelets of thy hair, rings, gauds, conceits … hast thou filched my daughter's heart*

conceit *(v.)* conceive an idea [of], think, imagine **JC** III.i.192 [Antony to all] *one of two bad ways you must conceit me, / Either a coward, or a flatterer;* **JC** I.iii.162; **Oth** III.iii.148 [F]

conceited *(adj.)* **1** ingenious, clever, well-devised **2H4** V.i.31 [Shallow to Davy, of his sharp response] *Well conceited, Davy* [i.e. very witty]; **Lover** 16; **Luc** 1371; **MW** I.iii.20; **WT** IV.iv.204
2 of the same opinion, minded **TN** III.iv.286 [Fabian to Sir Toby, of Viola as Cesario and Sir Andrew] *He is as horribly conceited of him* [i.e. has just as frightening an idea of him]

conceitless *(adj.)* dense, witless, unintelligent **TG** IV.ii.93 [Silvia to Proteus] *Thinkest thou I am … so conceitless / To be seduced by thy flattery*

conceive *(v.)* **1** understand, comprehend, follow **MM** II.iv.141 [Angelo to Isabella] *Plainly conceive, I love you;* **AC** II.iv.6; **AY** I.ii.256; **RJ** II.iv.48; **TNK** I.i.48; **TS** V.ii.12
2 think, hold an opinion **Cym** II.iii.152 [Innogen to Cloten, of the Queen] *She's my good lady; and will conceive … / But the worst of me;* **H8** I.ii.105
3 imagine, fancy **Oth** IV.ii.94 [Emilia to Desdemona, of Othello] *what does this gentleman conceive?;* **TN** V.i.360; **WT** III.ii.195

4 devise, form, conceptualize **Tim** I.i.75 [Painter to Poet, of a representation of Fortune] *'Tis conceived to scope*
5 begin to feel, take into the mind **3H6** IV.vi.13 [King to Lieutenant] *such a pleasure as incaged birds / Conceive when … / They quite forget their loss of liberty*

conceiving *(n.)* imagination, insight, mental creativity **Cym** III.iii.98 [Belarius alone, of Arviragus] *shows … / His own conceiving*

conception *(n.)* **1** design, plan, notion **TC** I.iii.312 [Ulysses to Nestor] *I have a young conception in my brain;* **H8** I.iii.139; **MM** II.iv.7; **Oth** V.ii.55
2 imagining, supposition, fanciful idea **Oth** III.iv.152 [Emilia to Desdemona, of Othello's mood] *Pray heaven it be … no conception nor no jealous toy / Concerning you;* **JC** I.ii.41
3 thinking, impression, suspicion **KL** I.iv.66 [Lear to Third Knight] *Thou but rememberest me of mine own conception*

conceptious *(adj.)* prolific, teeming, fruitful **Tim** IV.iii.188 [Timon alone, as if to the earth] *Ensear thy fertile and conceptious womb*

concern *(v.)* **1** be important to, be the concern of **Oth** I.iii.22 [First Senator to Duke, of Cyprus] *it more concerns the Turk than Rhodes;* **MM** I.i.77; **MND** I.i.126; **TNK** II.i.257
2 be of importance, be of concern **LL** IV.ii.140 [Holofernes to Jaquenetta] *deliver this paper into the royal hand of the King; it may concern much;* **1H6** V.iii.116; **TG** I.ii.77
3 befit, suit with, accord with **MND** I.i.60 [Hermia to Theseus] *I know not … how it may concern my modesty / In such a presence here to plead my thoughts*

concernancy *(n.)* import, relevance, purpose **Ham** V.ii.121 [Hamlet to Osrick] *The concernancy, sir?* [i.e. of all this talk]

concerning *(n.)* concern, affair, matter **MM** I.i.56 [Duke to Angelo] *We shall write to you, / As time and our concernings shall importune;* **Ham** III.iv.192

conclude *(v.)* **1** decide, resolve, settle **JC** II.ii.93 [Decius to Caesar] *The Senate have concluded / To give this day a crown to mighty Caesar;* **Mac** III.i.140; **R3** I.iii.14; **TC** IV.ii.66
2 come to a decision, make an agreement **Cor** III.i.145 [Coriolanus to Brutus] *where gentry, title, wisdom, / Cannot conclude but by the yea and no / Of general ignorance*
3 come to terms, reach accord [over] **R2** I.i.156 [King Richard to Mowbray and Bolingbroke] *Forget, forgive, conclude, and be agreed;* **Ham** III.iv.202; **1H6** V.i.5; **2H6** I.i.215
4 prove the truth, settle the matter **1H6** V.iv.16 [Richard to all, of Pucelle] *and so her death concludes;* **KJ** I.i.127
5 end, finish, close **KL** IV.vii.42 [Cordelia to Lear, of Lear on the heath] *'Tis wonder that thy life and wits at once / Had not concluded all* [i.e. ended all together at the same time]

conclusion *(n.)* **1** outcome, upshot, final result **Oth** I.iii.326 [Iago to Roderigo] *the blood and baseness of our natures would conduct us to most preposterous conclusions;* **MW** I.i.165
2 inference, deduction, logical conclusion **WT** I.ii.81 [Hermione to Polixenes, of his and Leontes' innocence before meeting their wives] *Of this make no conclusion, lest you say / Your queen and I are devils*
3 riddle, enigma, conundrum **Per** I.i.57 [Antiochus to Pericles] *read the conclusion then*
4 judgement, opinion, power of appraisal **AC** IV.xv.28 [Cleopatra to Antony] *Your wife Octavia, with her modest eyes / And still conclusion*
5 experiment, investigation **AC** V.ii.353 [Caesar to all, of Cleopatra] *She hath pursued conclusions infinite / Of easy ways to die;* **Cym** I.vi.18; **Luc** 1160
6 consummation, resolution, outcome **Oth** III.iii.425 [Othello to Iago, of Cassio's dream] *this denoted a foregone conclusion*

conclusions, try experiment, see what happens **Ham** III.iv.196 [Hamlet to Gertrude] *like the famous ape, / To try conclusions, in the basket creep*

concord *(n.)* harmony, tunefulness **Sonn** 128.4 *when thou gently sway'st / The wiry concord that mine ear confounds*

concordant *(adj.)* **1** agreeing as one, harmonious, of one heart and mind **Phoen** 46 [of the Phoenix and Dove] *How true a twain / Seemeth this concordant one!*
2 harmonious, tuneful, melodious **E3** II.i.76 [King Edward to Lodowick] *the touch of sweet concordant strings*

concupiscible *(adj.)* hotly desiring, sensual, voluptuous **MM** V.i.98 [Isabella to Duke, of Angelo] *his concup'scible intemperate lust*

concupy *(n.)* concubine, mistress; or: concupiscence, lust **TC** V.ii.180 [Thersites to himself, of Troilus attacking Diomedes' helmet] *He'll tickle it for his concupy*

condemn *(v.)* **1** blame, criticize, censure **JC** IV.iii.10 [Brutus to Cassius] *you yourself / Are much condemned to have an itching palm* [i.e. blamed for greed]
2 discredit, disparage **Sonn** 99.6 *The lily I condemned for thy hand*; **AC** V.ii.100

condemned *(adj.)* damned, confounded, blameworthy **Cor** I.viii.15 [Aufidius to his soldiers] *you have shamed me / In your condemned seconds*

condescend *(v.)* agree, consent, assent **1H6** V.iii.17 [Pucelle to the spirits] *I'll lop a member off and give it you … / So you do condescend to help me now*; **1H6** V.iii.119

condign *(adj.)* deserving, well-deserved, fitting **2H6** III.i.130 [Gloucester to York, of some offenders] *I never gave them condign punishment*; **LL** I.ii.25

condition *(n.)* **1** disposition, temper, mood, character **Oth** II.i.243 [Roderigo to Iago, of Desdemona] *she's full of most blessed condition*; **AY** I.ii.253; **H5** IV.i.102; **JC** II.i.254; **MV** II.i.123; **TS** V.ii.166
2 quality, behaviour, attribute, habit **AW** IV.iii.251 [Parolles to First Soldier, of how Dumaine is treated when drunk] *they know his conditions and lay him in straw*; **Cor** II.iii.96; **KJ** III.i.341; **MA** III.ii.61; **R2** II.iii.106; **TG** III.i.271
3 nature, state, circumstances **KL** IV.iii.33 [Kent to Gentleman] *It is the stars … govern our conditions*; **E3** II.i.318; **2H4** V.ii.11; **MM** I.i.53; **R2** II.iii.107; **TN** V.i.355
4 position, social rank, station **Tem** III.i.59 [Ferdinand to Miranda] *I am, in my condition, / A prince*; **E3** II.i.99; **2H4** IV.iii.83; **H5** IV.i.226; **R3** III.vii.142; **Tim** I.i.54
5 state, way of life **Per** III.i.29 [Pericles to Marina] *Quiet and gentle thy conditions!*; **H5** V.i.75; **R3** I.iii.107
6 settlement, terms, pact **Cor** I.x.2 [First Soldier to Aufidius, of the town] *'Twill be delivered back on good condition* [i.e. on favourable terms]; **Tem** I.ii.117, 120; **TG** V.iv.139
7 contract, covenant, agreement **MV** I.iii.145 [Shylock to Antonio, of his bond] *such sum or sums as are / Expressed in the condition*; **AW** IV.iii.30
8 provision, stipulation, proviso **JC** IV.i.4 [Lepidus to Antony and Octavius] *Upon condition Publius shall not live*; **TC** I.ii.75
9 matter, affair, concern **JC** IV.iii.32 [Cassius to Brutus] *I am … abler than yourself / To make conditions* [i.e. to manage affairs]
10 accepted rule, agreed procedure **TC** IV.v.72 [Aeneas to Agamemnon, of Hector] *he'll obey conditions*

condition *(v.)* make subject to a condition **Tim** IV.iii.529 [Timon to Flavius] *Go, live rich and happy, / But thus conditioned: thou shalt build from men*

conditionally *(adv.)* on condition, providing **3H6** I.i.196 [King to York, of yielding the crown] *Conditionally that here thou take an oath / To cease this civil war*

condole *(v.)* **1** lament, grieve, express great sorrow **MND** I.ii.24 [Bottom to Quince, of his part in the play] *I will condole, in some measure*; **Ham** III.ii.145
2 grieve with, express sympathy with **H5** II.i.122 [Pistol to Nym and Hostess, of Falstaff] *Let us condole the knight*

condolement *(n.)* **1** grief, sorrowing, lamenting **Ham** I.ii.93 [Claudius to Hamlet] *But to persever / In obstinate condolement is a course / Of impious stubbornness*
2 [unclear meaning] share-out, tangible expression of thanks **Per** II.i.151 [Second Fisherman to Pericles] *There are certain condolements*

condoling *(adj.)* moving, affecting, poignant **MND** I.ii.37 [Bottom to Quince, of his part in the play] *A lover is more condoling*

conduce *(v.)* **1** lead, tend, contribute **TC** II.ii.169 [Hector to Paris and Troilus] *The reasons you allege do more conduce / To the hot passion of distempered blood*
2 go on, carry on, take place **TC** V.ii.150 [Troilus to Ulysses] *Within my soul there doth conduce a fight / Of this strange nature*

conduct *(n.)* **1** leadership, command **Tit** IV.iv.65 [Aemilius to Saturninus, of the Goths] *They hither march amain, under conduct / Of Lucius*; **AY** V.iv.154; **Cym** IV.ii.340; **KJ** V.ii.129
2 guidance, direction **KL** III.vi.95 [Gloucester to disguised Kent] *follow me, that will to some provision / Give thee quick conduct*; **2H4** V.ii.36; **RJ** III.iii.131
3 conductor, leader, director **RJ** V.iii.116 [Romeo as if to the poison] *Come, bitter conduct, come, unsavoury guide*; **Luc** 313; **Tem** V.i.244
4 care, protection **TN** III.iv.237 [Viola as Cesario to Sir Toby, of Olivia] *I will return again into the house and desire some conduct of the lady*; **1H4** III.i.88
5 escort, attendant, guide **Cym** III.v.8 [Lucius to Cymbeline] *I desire of you / A conduct over land*; **2H6** II.iv.101; **KJ** I.i.29; **R2** IV.i.157; **R3** I.i.45; **RJ** III.i.124

conduct *(v.)* carry, convey, direct **E3** II.ii.50 [King Edward to Lodowick, of the drum] *I will teach it to conduct sweet lines*

conductor *(n.)* leader, commander, chief **KL** IV.vii.88 [Gentleman to Kent, of Cornwall] *Who is conductor of his people?*

conduit *(n.)* **1** channel, passage, vein **CE** V.i.314 [Egeon to Antipholus and Dromio of Ephesus] *all the conduits of my blood froze up*
2 channel, pipe, aqueduct **Cor** II.iii.241 [Brutus to Citizens] *our best water brought by conduits hither*
3 channel, outflowing, water-spout, fountain **E3** III.i.112 [Philip to King John] *I'll make a conduit of my dearest blood*; **RJ** III.v.129; **Tit** II.iv.30; **WT** V.ii.54

confection *(n.)* medicinal preparation, mixture of drugs **Cym** I.vi.15 [Queen to Cornelius] *our great king himself doth woo me oft / For my confections*; **Cym** V.v.246

confectionary *(n.)* sweetmeat factory, sweet-shop, candy-store **Tim** IV.iii.261 [Timon to Apemantus, of himself] *Who had the world as my confectionary*

confederacy *(n.)* **1** alliance, conspiracy, plot, united opposition **1H4** IV.iv.38 [Archbishop to Sir Michael, of King Henry] *he means to visit us, / For he hath heard of our confederacy*; **H8** I.i.3
2 complicity, collusion, connivance **2H6** II.i.163 [Buckingham to King] *A sort of naughty persons … / Under the countenance and confederacy / Of Lady Eleanor*

confederate *(adj.)* acting as an ally, in league **Ham** III.ii.265 [Third Player, as Lucianus] *Confederate season* [F, Q1; Q2 *Considerat*]

confederate *(v.)* ally, enter into a league, conspire **Tem** I.ii.111 [Prospero to Miranda, of Antonio] *confederates … wi'th' King of Naples*

confer *(v.)* chat, talk together, gossip **TS** V.ii.101 [Katherina to Petruchio, of Bianca and Widow] *They sit conferring by the parlour fire*

conference *(n.)* **1** conversation, talk, discourse **Mac** III.i.79 [Macbeth to Murderers, of information about Banquo] *This I made good to you / In our last conference*; **AY** I.ii.247; **CE** V.i.62; **JC** IV.ii.17; **MA** III.i.25; **TS** II.i.245
2 debate, argument, discussion **JC** I.ii.187 [Brutus to Cassius, of Cicero's looks] *Being crossed in conference by some senators*

confess *(v.)* **1** acknowledge, recognize, admit **Tim** I.ii.20 [First Lord to Timon, of his remark] *we always have confessed it;* **Sonn** 36.1
2 be honest, be frank **KJ** I.i.236 [Bastard to Lady Faulconbridge] *Sir Robert could do well - marry, to confess - / Could he get me!*

confession *(n.)* acknowledgement, avowal **Ham** IV.vii.94 [Claudius to Laertes, of Lamord] *He made confession of you;* **TC** I.iii.269

confessor *(n.)* boaster, braggart [of love affairs] **TNK** V.i.105 [Palamon praying to Venus] *I have been harsh / To large confessors*

confidence *(n.)* **1** reliance, trust, faith **1H6** I.ii.97 [Charles to Pucelle] *if thou vanquishest, thy words are true; / Otherwise I renounce all confidence* [i.e. give up any belief in you]; **H8** I.i.167
2 over-confidence, over-assurance, presumption **JC** II.ii.49 [Calphurnia to Caesar] *Your wisdom is consumed in confidence*
3 malapropism for 'conference' **RJ** II.iv.124 [Nurse to Romeo] *I desire some confidence with you;* **MA** III.v.2; **MW** I.iv.155

confident *(adj.)* **1** trusting, trustful, ready to confide **H8** II.i.146 [Second Gentleman to First Gentleman, of revealing a secret] *I am confident;* **Tit** I.i.64
2 trusting, complacent, self-assured **MW** II.i.174 [Ford to Page] *A man may be too confident*

confine *(n.)* **1** territory, region, domain **R2** I.iii.137 [King Richard to Bolingbroke and Mowbray] *[you] Might from our quiet confines fright fair peace;* **2H4** IV.v.124; **JC** III.i.272; **KJ** IV.ii.246; **R2** III.ii.125; **R3** IV.iv.3
2 limit, bound, domain **RJ** III.i.6 [Mercutio to Benvolio] *one of those fellows that, when he enters the confines of a tavern, claps me his sword upon the table;* **KL** II.iv.143
3 confinement, restraint, limitation **Oth** I.ii.27 [Othello to Iago] *I would not my unhoused free condition / Put into circumscription and confine;* **Lover** 265
4 prison, place of confinement **Ham** II.ii.245 [Hamlet to Rosencrantz and Guildenstern] *there are many confines, wards, and dungeons, Denmark being one o'th' worst;* **AC** III.v.11; **Ham** I.i.156; **Tem** IV.i.121

confine *(v.)* **1** enclose, retain, contain **Cym** V.iv.110 [Jupiter to the spirits, of the document given to Posthumus] *wherein / Our pleasure his full fortune doth confine*
2 banish, remove, place under restriction **WT** II.i.194 [Leontes to all, of Hermione] *we thought it good / From our free person she should be confined*

confined *(adj.)* bounded, enclosed, rimmed **KL** IV.i.73 [Gloucester to Edgar as Poor Tom] *There is a cliff whose high and bending head / Looks fearfully in the confined deep* [i.e. between England and France]

confineless *(adj.)* boundless, unlimited, endless **Mac** IV.iii.55 [Malcolm to Macduff] *Macbeth / Will seem as pure as snow ... compared / With my confineless harms*

confiner *(n.)* inhabitant, dweller, resident **Cym** IV.ii.337 [Captain to Lucius] *The senate hath stirred up the confiners / And gentlemen of Italy*

confirm *(v.)* encourage, strengthen, make firm **1H6** V.v.42 [Suffolk to all, of Reignier] *his alliance will confirm our peace;* **TNK** V.ii.14

confirmed *(adj.)* resolute, determined, purposeful **MA** V.iv.17 [Antonio to Leonato, of giving Hero to Claudio] *Which I will do with confirmed countenance;* **Cor** I.iii.60; **MA** II.i.351; **R3** IV.iv.172

confirmity *(n.)* malapropism for 'infirmity' **2H4** II.iv.57 [Hostess to Doll and Falstaff] *you cannot one bear with another's confirmities*

confix *(v.)* fix firmly, fasten, bind **MM** V.i.230 [Mariana to Duke] *Let me ... else forever be confixed here / A marble monument*

conflux *(n.)* confluence, conjunction, flowing together **TC** I.iii.7 [Agamemnon to all] *knots, by the conflux of meeting sap, / Infect the sound pine* [i.e. by flows of sap joining up]

conformable *(adj.)* compliant, submissive, tractable **H8** II.iv.24 [Queen Katherine to King Henry] *I have been to you a true and humble wife, / At all times to your will conformable;* **TS** II.i.271

confound *(v.)* **1** destroy, overthrow, ruin **TNK** V.i.166 [Emilia to all, of Palamon and Arcite] *this battle shall confound / Both these brave knights;* **AC** II.v.92; **LL** V.ii.517; **MV** III.ii.276; **R2** III.iv.60; **RJ** II.vi.13
2 mar, corrupt, spoil **KJ** IV.ii.29 [Pembroke to King John] *When workmen strive to do better than well, / They do confound their skill in covetousness*
3 make as nothing, do away with **Per** V.ii.14 [Gower alone] *The interim ... all confound*
4 challenge, defy, overturn **R3** IV.iv.262 [King Richard to Queen Elizabeth] *Be not so hasty to confound my meaning;* **AW** II.iii.119
5 discomfit, defeat, put to shame **TG** V.iv.73 [Proteus to Valentine] *My shame and guilt confounds me;* **MM** IV.iv.26; **R3** I.i.14
6 amaze, dumbfound, stun **E3** III.iv.105 [King Edward to Prince Edward] *This day thou hast confounded me with joy;* **E3** IV.iv.47; **Ham** II.ii.562; **1H6** V.iii.71; **JC** III.i.86; **Venus** 882
7 mix up, become indistinguishable **CE** I.ii.38 [Antipholus of Syracuse alone, comparing himself to a drop of water] *falling there to find his fellow forth, / Unseen, inquisitive, confounds himself* [or: sense 1]
8 [of time] waste, consume, squander **Cor** I.vi.17 [Cominius to Messenger] *How couldst thou in a mile confound an hour, / And bring thy news so late;* **AC** I.i.45, I.iv.28
9 spend, take up, consume **1H4** I.iii.99 [Hotspur to King Henry, of Mortimer] *He did confound the best part of an hour / In changing hardiment with great Glendower*

confounded *(adj.)* destroyed, ruined, wrecked **KJ** V.vii.58 [King John to Bastard, of his soon-dead body] *all this thou seest is but a clod / And module of confounded royalty;* **H5** III.i.13

confounding *(adj.)* destructive, ruinous, causing total confusion **Tim** IV.i.20 [Timon alone] *Degrees, observances, customs, laws, / Decline to your confounding contraries;* **Tim** IV.iii.393

confusion *(n.)* **1** destruction, overthrow, ruin **Cym** III.i.66 [Lucius to Cymbeline] *War and confusion ... pronounce I 'gainst thee;* **CE** II.ii.189; **Cor** III.i.110; **1H6** V.i.194; **2H6** V.ii.31; **Mac** II.iii.63
2 calamity, disaster, catastrophe **KJ** IV.iii.152 [Bastard to Hubert] *vast confusion waits ... / The imminent decay of wrested pomp;* **RJ** IV.v.65
3 disturbance, distraction, agitation [of the mind] **Ham** III.i.2 [Claudius to Rosencrantz and Guildenstern, of Hamlet] *why he puts on this confusion;* **MV** III.ii.177
4 outburst, disorder, commotion **RJ** IV.v.66 [Friar to all] *Confusion's cure lives not / In these confusions* [second instance]

confusions, try malapropism for 'try conclusions' [= see what happens] **MV** II.ii.33 [Launcelot to himself, of Gobbo] *I will try confusions with him* ☛ **conclusions, try**

confutation rebuttal, refutation, disproof **1H6** IV.i.98 [Basset to King, of Vernon's view] *In confutation of which rude reproach*

confute *(v.)* **1** overcome, confound, bring to nought **MM** V.i.100 [Isabella to Duke] *My sisterly remorse confutes mine honour*
2 disprove, contradict, rebut **1H4** V.iv.125 [Falstaff alone] *Nothing confutes me but eyes, and nobody sees me*

congeal *(v.)* coagulate, curdle, clot **3H6** I.iii.52 [Clifford as if to York] *thy son's blood ... / Shall rust upon my weapon, till thy blood / Congealed with this, do make me wipe off both*

congealed *(adj.)* icy, freezing, hail-filled **2H4** IV.iv.35 [King Henry IV to Clarence, of Prince Henry] *being incensed, he is ... as sudden / As flaws congealed in the spring of day*

congealment *(n.)* congealed mess, clotted blood **AC** IV.viii.10 [Antony to all, of the people] *they with joyful tears / Wash the congealment from your wounds*

congee, congie *(v.)* **1** take ceremonious leave of, pay formal respects upon departure **AW** IV.iii.86 [Bertram to all] *I have congied with the Duke*
2 curtsy reverently, make a formal bow **H8** IV.ii.83 [stage direction: personages in The Vision, of Katherine] *They first congee unto her*

conger (*n.*) type of sea-eel **2H4** II.iv.240 [Falstaff to Doll, of why Prince Harry loves Poins] *'a … eats conger and fennel;* **2H4** II.iv.53

congest (*v.*) collect, gather, bring together **Lover** 258 *I strong o'er them and you o'er me being strong, / Must for your victory us all congest*

congratulate (*v.*) salute, pay respects to **LL** V.i.83 [Armado to Holofernes] *it is the King's most sweet pleasure and affection to congratulate the Princess*

congree (*v.*) accord, come together in agreement **H5** I.ii.182 [Exeter to all] *government … / Put into parts, doth keep in one consent, / Congreeing in a full and natural close, / Like music* [F; Q *congrue*]

congreet (*v.*) greet one another, exchange greetings **H5** V.ii.31 [Burgundy to King Henry and the French King] *face to face … / You have congreeted*

congregation (*n.*) mass, gathering, assemblage **Ham** II.ii.302 [Hamlet to Rosencrantz and Guildenstern] *a foul and pestilent congregation of vapours*

congrue (*v.*) agree, accord, concur **Ham** IV.iii.66 [Claudius alone, as if to the King of England] *By letters congruing to that effect* [Q2; F *coniuring*]

congruent (*adj.*) fitting, apt, suitable **LL** I.ii.13 [Armado to Mote, of calling him 'tender juvenal'] *I spoke it … as a congruent epitheton appertaining to thy young days;* **LL** V.i.87

conject (*v.*) conjecture, speculate, imagine **Oth** III.iii.148 [Iago to Othello] *your wisdom … / From one that so imperfectly conjects, / Would take no notice* [Q1; F *conceits*]

conjectural (*adj.*) suspicious, full of misgiving, speculative **AW** V.iii.114 [King to Bertram] *Thou … makest conjectural fears to come into me* [F *connecturall*]

conjecture (*n.*) **1** surmise, guess, supposition **H8** II.i.41 [First Gentleman to Second Gentleman, of whether Wolsey had a role in Buckingham's downfall] *'Tis likely, / By all conjectures*
 2 supposition, imaginary case **H5** IV.Chorus.1 [Chorus] *Now entertain conjecture of a time / When creeping murmur and the poring dark / Fills the wide vessel of the universe;* **2H4** I.iii.23
 3 suspicion, misgiving, evil doubt **2H4** I.Induction.16 [Rumour alone] *Rumour is a pipe / Blown by surmises, jealousies, conjectures;* **Ham** IV.v.15; **MA** IV.i.104; **WT** II.i.176
 4 forecast, prediction, prognostication **TC** IV.v.250 [Hector to Achilles, of Achilles' survey of him] *As to prenominate in nice conjecture / Where thou wilt hit me dead?*

conjoin (*v.*) **1** unite, join together **1H6** V.ii.12 [Scout to Charles] *The English army … is now conjoined in one;* **E3** III.i.29; **Ham** III.iv.127; **2H4** IV.v.65
 2 make contact, come together **E3** III.i.148 [Mariner to King John, of the navies] *At last conjoined, and by their admiral / Our admiral encountered many shot;* **WT** I.ii.143 [F *co-ioyne*]

conjointly (*adv.*) together, in unison, in conjunction **KJ** II.i.379 [Bastard to King John and King Philip, of Angiers] *Be friends awhile, and both conjointly bend / Your sharpest deeds of malice on this town;* **JC** I.iii.29

conjunct (*adj.*) coupled, conjoined, united **KL** II.ii.116 [Oswald to Cornwall, of disguised Kent] *he, conjunct, … / Tripped me behind* [i.e. in league with the King] [Q; F *compact*]; **KL** V.i.12

conjunction (*n.*) **1** union, uniting, joining together **KJ** III.i.227 [King Philip to Cardinal Pandulph, of King John] *the conjunction of our inward souls / Married in league;* **2H4** V.i.62; **H5** V.ii.344; **H8** III.ii.45; **KJ** II.i.468; **R3** V.v.20
 2 united forces, joint association **1H4** IV.i.37 [Hotspur to Worcester, of Northumberland] *with our small conjunction we should on, / To see how fortune is disposed to us* ☞ **COSMOS**, p.102

conjunctive (*adj.*) closely united, intimately joined, allied **Oth** I.iii.362 [Iago to Roderigo, of Othello] *Let us be conjunctive in our revenge against him;* **Ham** IV.vii.14

conjuration (*n.*) **1** entreaty, injunction, solemn appeal **Ham** V.ii.38 [Hamlet to Horatio] *An earnest conjuration from the King;* **H5** I.ii.29; **R2** III.ii.23; **RJ** V.iii.68
 2 incantation, invocation of spirits **Oth** I.iii.92 [Othello to all, of Brabantio] *I will a round unvarnished tale deliver … what drugs, what charms, / What conjuration … / I won his daughter;* **2H6** I.ii.99

conjure (*v.*) **1** ask solemnly, entreat earnestly, beseech **WT** I.ii.400 [Polixenes to Camillo] *I conjure thee … that thou declare / What incidency thou dost guess of harm / Is creeping toward me;* **CE** IV.iii.67; **Ham** II.ii.283; **KJ** V.ii.269; **Mac** IV.i.49; **Tim** III.vi.11
 2 call up, bring out, produce **1H4** IV.iii.43 [Blunt to Hotspur] *You conjure from the breast of civil peace / Such bold hostility;* **H5** V.ii.288; **Tim** I.i.7
 3 control, constrain [by invoking divine powers] **1H6** I.v.5 [Talbot to Pucelle] *Devil or devil's dam, I'll conjure thee;* **RJ** II.i.26
 4 engage in magic, cast spells, invoke supernatural aid **CE** III.i.34 [Dromio of Syracuse to Dromio of Ephesus] *Dost thou conjure for wenches;* **JC** I.i.145; **Per** IV.vi.145; **RJ** II.i.6; **TC** II.iii.6
 5 put a spell on, charm, bewitch **AY** V.iv.205 [Rosalind, as Epilogue] *My way is to conjure you;* **Ham** V.i.252; **MW** IV.ii.174
 6 expel evil spirits from, exorcise **MA** II.i.235 [Benedick to Don Pedro, of Beatrice] *I would to God some scholar would conjure her;* **H5** II.i.51

conjure up (*v.*) bring about [as if by magic], cause to appear **MND** III.ii.158 [Helena to Lysander and Demetrius] *a manly enterprise - / To conjure tears up in a poor maid's eyes / With your derision;* **H5** V.ii.284; **JC** II.i.323; **TC** V.ii.127

conjured (*adj.*) made powerful by spells, magically influencing **Oth** I.iii.105 [Brabantio to all, of Othello and Desdemona] *with some dram conjured … / He wrought upon her*

conjurer (*n.*) ☞ conjuror (*n.*)

conjuring (*n.*) entreaty, invocation, incantation **TNK** III.vi.201 [Theseus to all] *These are strange conjurings*

conjuror, conjurer (*n.*) exorcist, sorcerer, raiser of spirits **2H6** I.ii.76 [Duchess to Hume] *Hast thou as yet conferred … / With Roger Bolingbroke, the conjuror?;* **CE** IV.iv.45, V.i.177, 243; **2H6** IV.ii.86; **TNK** III.v.85

connectural (*adj.*) ☞ conjectural (*adj.*)

connive at (*v.*) look indulgently on, cooperate with **WT** IV.iv.672 [Autolycus alone] *the gods do this year connive at us, and we may do anything extempore*

consanguineous (*adj.*) related in blood, of the same family **TN** II.iii.76 [Sir Toby to all, of Olivia] *Am I not consanguineous? Am I not of her blood?*

consanguinity (*n.*) kinship, blood relationship **TC** IV.ii.96 [Cressida to Pandarus, of Calchas] *I know no touch of consanguinity*

conscience (*n.*) **1** internal reflection, inner voice, inmost thought **Cym** I.vii.116 [Iachimo to Innogen] *from my mutest conscience to my tongue;* **Cym** II.ii.36; **Ham** III.i.83; **H5** V.i.114; **WT** III.ii.45
 2 real knowledge, internal conviction, true understanding **3H6** I.i.150 [Exeter to York, of the King] *My conscience tells me he is lawful king;* **Oth** IV.iii.58; **Tim** II.ii.180
 3 sense of indebtedness, feeling of obligation **TN** III.iii.17 [Sebastian to Antonio] *were my worth, as is my conscience, firm, / You should find better dealing*

conscience, in my to my mind **WT** III.iii.4 [Mariner to Antigonus] *In my conscience, / The heavens with that we have in hand are angry / And frown upon's;* **Tim** III.iii.17 ☞ **DISCOURSE MARKERS**, p.127

conscionable (*adj.*) [unclear] conscientious, dedicated, scrupulous **Oth** II.i.231 [Iago to Roderigo, of Cassio] *no further conscionable than in putting on the mere form of civil and humane seeming*

consecrate (*adj.*) consecrated, blessed, sanctified **MND** V.i.405 [Oberon to all] *With this field dew consecrate / Every fairy take his gait*

consent (*n.*) **1** agreement, accord, unanimity, compact **Tim** V.i.138 [First Senator to Timon] *The senators with one consent of love / Entreat thee back to Athens;* **Cor** II.iii.22; **2H4** V.i.64; **H5** I.ii.181, 206; **LL** V.ii.460; **Tem** II.i.207
2 opinion, feeling, counsel **1H6** I.ii.44 [Reignier to all, of the English] *By my consent, we'll even let them alone* [i.e. we'd better just leave them alone]; **3H6** IV.vi.36; **Mac** II.i.25; **WT** V.iii.136

consent (*v.*) agree, concur, acquiesce **KJ** IV.iii.125 [Bastard to Hubert, of Arthur's death] *If thou didst but consent / To this most cruel act, do but despair;* **AY** V.i.42, ii.8; **2H4** I.iii.52; **1H6** I.i.5, v.34; **Oth** V.ii.294

consequence (*n.*) **1** course of events, subsequent happenings **Oth** II.iii.58 [Iago alone] *If consequence do but approve my dream*
2 upshot, outcome, sequel **R3** IV.ii.15 [King Richard to Buckingham] *O bitter consequence / That Edward still should live*
3 importance, weighty matter **Cym** II.iii.120 [Cloten to Innogen, of lower marriages] *you are curbed from that enlargement, by / The consequence o'th' crown*

consequence, in this in the following way **Ham** II.i.45 [Polonius to Reynaldo, of an acquaintance of Laertes] *He closes with you in this consequence: / 'Good sir'*

consequently (*adv.*) subsequently, later, then **R2** I.i.102 [Bolingbroke to King Richard, of Mowbray] *he did plot the Duke of Gloucester's death ... / And consequently ... / Sluiced out his innocent soul;* **KJ** IV.ii.240; **TN** III.iv.72

conserve (*n.*) **1** (plural) preserve, store **TS** Induction.ii.7 [Sly to Servingmen] *give me conserves of beef* [i.e. salted beef]
2 (plural) confections, sweetmeats, candied fruits **TS** Induction.ii.3 [Second Servingman to Sly] *Will't please your honour taste of these conserves?*

conserve (*v.*) preserve in sugar, make into a confection **Oth** III.iv.75 [Othello to Desdemona, of her handkerchief] *it was dyed in mummy, which the skilful / Conserved of maidens' hearts*

consider (*v.*) **1** reflect, think carefully, ponder, contemplate **Mac** II.ii.30 [Lady Macbeth to Macbeth, of his inability to say 'Amen'] *Consider it not so deeply;* **Cym** II.iii.18
2 reward, recompense, requite **Cym** II.iii.26 [Cloten to Musicians, of the music] *if this penetrate, I will consider your music the better;* **WT** IV.ii.17, iv.791

considerance (*n.*) consideration, reflection, thought **2H4** V.ii.98 [Lord Chief Justice to King Henry V] *After this cold considerance sentence me*

considerate (*adj.*) **1** considering, thoughtful, reflecting **AC** II.ii.115 [Enobarbus to Antony, of himself] *your considerate stone*
2 deliberate, calculating, wary **R3** IV.ii.30 [King Richard to himself] *None are for me / That look into me with considerate eyes*

consideration (*n.*) **1** moody contemplation, deep reflection **AC** IV.ii.45 [Antony to all] *Let's to supper, come, / And drown consideration;* **KJ** IV.ii.25; **Tim** IV.iii.197
2 spiritual self-examination, meditation, personal reflection **H5** I.i.28 [Canterbury to Ely, of King Henry] *Consideration like an angel came*

considered (*adj.*) with opportunity for careful thought **Ham** II.ii.81 [Claudius to all] *at our more considered time we'll read, / Answer, and think upon this business*

considering (*n.*) consideration, reflection, brooding **H8** II.iv.185 [King Henry to all] *many mazed considerings did throng / And pressed in with this caution*

consign (*v.*) sign jointly, ratify, subscribe **H5** V.ii.90 [King Henry to Council members, of altering the treaty] *as your wisdoms best / Shall see advantageable for our dignity ... / And we'll consign thereto*

consign to (*v.*) **1** agree with, accept, assent to, endorse **2H4** V.ii.143 [King Henry V to all] *God consigning to my good intents;* **H5** V.ii.294

2 comply in the same way as, submit to the same condition as **Cym** IV.ii.275 [Arviragus and Guiderius singing together, to the supposedly dead Innogen] *all lovers must / Consign to thee and come to dust*

consigned (*adj.*) entrusted, committed, delivered **TC** IV.iv.44 [Troilus to Cressida, of time allowing them farewells] *With distinct breath and consigned kisses to them*

consist (*v.*) be disposed [for], be set, insist **Per** I.iv.83 [Cleon to Dionyza, of Pericles] *Welcome is peace if he on peace consist;* **2H4** IV.i.185

consistory (*n.*) **1** ecclesiastical court **H8** II.iv.1 [stage direction] *The Bishops place themselves on each side the court in manner of a consistory;* **H8** II.iv.92
2 council-chamber, meeting-place **R3** II.ii.151 [Richard to Buckingham] *my counsel's consistory*

consolate (*v.*) console, comfort, cheer **AW** III.ii.128 [Helena alone, as if to Bertram] *pitiful rumour may report my flight / To consolate thine ear*

consolation (*n.*) comfort, good cheer, contentment **TS** II.i.190 [Petruchio to Katherina] *Kate of my consolation*

consonancy (*n.*) **1** accord, harmony [of companionship] **Ham** II.ii.284 [Hamlet to Rosencrantz and Guildenstern] *But let me conjure you ... by the consonancy of our youth*
2 consistency, correspondance, accord **TN** II.v.126 [Malvolio to himself, of interpreting the letter] *there is no consonancy in the sequel that suffers under probation*

consonant (*n.*) little thing, nonentity **LL** V.i.50 [Holofernes to Mote] *Quis, quis, thou consonant?*

consort (*n.*) **1** companion, partner, associate **E3** II.i.197 [Countess to King Edward] *What may thy subject do to draw from thee / Thy gloomy consort, sullen melancholy?*
2 company, mob, crew **KL** II.i.96 [Edmund to Regan, of Edgar and Lear's knights] *he was of that consort;* **TG** IV.i.64
3 company of musicians, ensemble **TG** III.ii.84 [Proteus to Thurio] *Visit by night your lady's chamber-window / With some sweet consort* [or: piece of music]; **2H6** III.ii.327

consort (*v.*) accompany, attend, go with **CE** I.ii.28 [First Merchant to Antipholus of Syracuse] *I'll meet with you upon the mart, / And afterward consort you till bedtime;* **JC** V.i.82; **LL** I.i.250, II.i.178; **MND** III.ii.387; **RJ** II.i.31, III.i.130

consorted (*adj.*) **1** conspiring, associated, in league together **R2** V.iii.137 [King Henry to all, of the conspirators] *all the rest of that consorted crew;* **R2** V.v.15
2 attendant, accompanying, united together **Luc** 1609 [of Lucrece] *Collatine and his consorted lords / With sad attention long to hear her words*

conspectuity (*n.*) faculty of sight, insight, vision **Cor** II.i.60 [Menenius to Brutus and Sicinius, of himself] *What harm can your bisson conspectuities glean out of this character*

conspirant (*n.*) conspirator, intriguer, plotter **KL** V.iii.133 [Edgar to Edmund, of Albany] *Conspirant 'gainst this high illustrious prince* [F; Q *Conspicuate*]

conspire (*v.*) practise, contrive, plot **Oth** III.iii.141 [Othello to Iago] *Thou dost conspire against thy friend;* **TC** V.i.59; **TG** I.i.43

constable (*n.*) **1** chief officer of the royal household [in England and France] **H5** II.iv.1 [stage direction] *Enter the French King, ... the Constable and others;* **H8** II.i.102
2 leader of the Watch, chief officer **MA** III.iii.10 [Dogberry to First Watchman] *who think you the most desartless man to be constable?*

constancy (*n.*) **1** consistency, agreement, uniformity **MND** V.i.26 [Hippolyta to Theseus, of the lovers' stories] *grows to something of great constancy;* **JC** II.i.227
2 fortitude, self-control, steadfastness **JC** II.iv.6 [Portia to herself] *O constancy, be strong upon my side*

3 persistance, perseverance, steadfastness **H8** III.ii.2 [Norfolk to all] *If you will now unite in your complaints / And force them with a constancy*

constant *(adj.)* **1** faithful, steadfast, true **TG** V.iv.112 [Proteus to Julia] *were man / But constant, he were perfect!*; **Cor** I.i.237, IV.i.107; **Cym** I.v.57; **H8** III.i.134

2 settled, resolved, decided **KL** I.i.43 [Lear to Cornwall and Albany] *We have this hour a constant will to publish / Our daughters' several dowers*; **JC** III.i.73; **KL** V.i.4; **MV** III.ii.247; **TN** IV.ii.48

3 unmoving, unchanging, fixed **JC** III.i.60 [Caesar to all] *I am constant as the northern star*

4 settled, stable, steady **Tem** II.ii.113 [Stephano to Trinculo] *My stomach is not constant*

constantly *(adv.)* **1** assuredly, firmly, certainly, confidently **MM** IV.i.21 [disguised Duke to Mariana] *I do constantly believe you*; **TC** IV.i.41

2 resolutely, steadfastly, steadily **JC** V.i.91 [Cassius to Messala] *I am fresh of spirit, and resolved / To meet all perils very constantly*; **Cym** III.v.118; **Ham** I.ii.235; **TN** II.iii.140

constellation [the stars were thought to influence people and events] disposition, character, temperament **TN** I.iv.35 [Orsino to Viola as Cesario, of approaching Olivia] *I know thy constellation is right apt / For this affair* ➤ **COSMOS**, p.102

conster *(v.)* **1** explain, inform, give an account **TN** III.i.55 [Feste to Viola as Cesario, of Olivia's household] *I will conster to them whence you come*

2 construe, interpret, read **Oth** IV.i.101 [Iago to himself, of Othello] *his unbookish jealousy must conster / Poor Cassio's smiles … / Quite in the wrong* [Q; F *conserue*]; **Luc** 324; **PassP** XIV.8 ➤ construe *(v.)*

constitution *(n.)* **1** disposition, temperament, mood **MV** III.ii.246 [Portia to herself, of Antonio's letter to Bassanio] *nothing in the world / Could turn so much the constitution / Of any constant man*

2 construction, make-up, frame **TN** I.iii.125 [Sir Toby to Sir Andrew] *I did think by the excellent constitution of thy leg it was formed under the star of a galliard*

constrain *(v.)* **1** force, compel, oblige **1H6** II.i.7 [Sentinel to his colleague] *Thus are poor servitors … / Constrained to watch in darkness*; **Cym** III.v.47, V.v.141; **KL** II.ii.95

2 violate, invade **Tit** V.ii.176 [Titus to Chiron and Demetrius, of Lavinia] *her spotless chastity … you constrained and forced*

constraint *(n.)* compulsion, coercion, enforcing **E3** IV.v.90 [King John to Charles] *My licence lies in me, / And my constraint stands the excuse for thee* [i.e. you are not to blame if I command you]

constringe *(v.)* compress, squeeze, draw together **TC** V.ii.176 [Troilus to Ulysses] *the dreadful spout … / Constringed in mass by the almighty sun*

construction *(n.)* **1** interpretation, reading, explanation **TN** II.iii.168 [Maria to Sir Toby and Sir Andrew, of the letter for Malvolio] *Observe his construction of it*; **Cor** V.vi.21; **Cym** V.v.434, 445; **Mac** I.iv.13; **MW** II.ii.216

2 judgement, consideration, appraisal **H8** Epilogue.10 [of the play] *All the expected good we're like to hear … is only in / The merciful construction of good women*; **TN** III.i.112

construe *(v.)* **1** interpret, take, understand **LL** V.ii.341 [King to Princess] *Construe my speeches better, if you may*; **2H4** IV.i.102; **JC** I.ii.45, iii.34; **Oth** IV.i.101

2 take as, interpret as **TG** I.ii.56 [Julia alone] *maids … say no to that / Which they would have the profferer construe ay*

3 explain, expound **JC** II.i.307 [Brutus to Portia] *All my engagements I will construe to thee*; **MW** I.iii.41; **TS** III.i.30, 40 ➤ conster *(v.)*

consume away *(v.)* waste away, disintegrate, perish **KJ** IV.i.65 [Arthur to Hubert, of the blinding iron] *would drink my tears / And … after that, consume away in rust*

consumed *(adj.)* used up, spent, passed by **AW** V.iii.38 [King to Bertram] *Not one word more of the consumed time*

consummate *(v.)* accomplish, complete, bring to a conclusion **MM** V.i.375 [Duke to Friar Peter, of marrying Angelo to Mariana] *which consummate, / Return him here again*; **KJ** V.vii.95; **Tit** I.i.340

consummation *(n.)* **1** fitting end, crowning fulfilment [of life] **Ham** III.i.63 [Hamlet to himself] *'Tis a consummation / Devoutly to be wished*; **Cym** IV.ii.280

2 end, conclusion, completion **TNK** V.iii.94 [Servant to Emilia] *The combat's consummation is proclaimed / By the wind instruments*

consumption *(n.)* **1** wasting disease, venereal disease **Tim** IV.iii.152 [Timon to Phrynia and Timandra] *Consumptions sow / In hollow bones of man*; **2H4** I.ii.238; **MA** V.iv.96; **Tim** IV.iii.202

2 destruction, being consumed by fire **KL** IV.vi.129 [Lear to all] *There's hell … burning, scalding, stench, consumption* [F; Q *consumation*]

contagion *(n.)* **1** contagious quality, infecting influence **Ham** III.ii.397 [Hamlet alone] *hell itself breathes out / Contagion to this world*; **CE** II.ii.153; **Cor** I.iv.30; **JC** II.i.265; **TN** II.iii.54

2 poison **Ham** IV.vii.146 [Laertes to Claudius, of his sword] *I'll touch my point / With this contagion*; **RJ** V.iii.152

contagious *(adj.)* **1** pestilential, harmful, noxious **MND** II.i.90 [Titania to Oberon] *the winds … have sucked up from the sea / Contagious fogs*; **1H4** I.ii.196; **2H4** V.v.34; **H5** III.iii.31; **2H6** IV.i.7; **KJ** V.iv.33

2 infectious, catchy **TN** II.iii.52 [Sir Toby to all, of Feste] *A contagious breath* [also: bad breath]

contain *(v.)* **1** retain, keep in one's possession **MV** V.i.201 [Portia to Bassanio] *If you had known … your own honour to contain the ring*; **Sonn** 77.9

2 restrain, keep under control **TS** Induction.i.98 [First Player to Lord] *we can contain ourselves*

containing *(n.)* contents, tenor, matter **Cym** V.v.431 [Posthumus to Lucius, of the letter left by Jupiter] *whose containing / Is so from sense in hardness, that I can / Make no collection of it*

contemn *(v.)* despise, scorn, treat with contempt **TG** II.iv.127 [Valentine to Proteus] *I have done penance for contemning Love*; **AC** III.vi.1; **Cor** II.ii.155; **Cym** I.vii.41; **KL** IV.ii.32; **TNK** III.vi.143

contemned *(adj.)* **1** despised, contemptible, despicable **KL** IV.i.1 [Edgar alone, of being Poor Tom] *Yet better thus, and known to be contemned, / Than still contemned and flattered*; **KJ** V.ii.13; **KL** II.ii.141

2 despised, rejected, spurned **TN** I.v.259 [Viola as Cesario to Olivia] *[I would] Write loyal cantons of contemned love*

contemplate *(v.)* pray, meditate, engage in contemplation **3H6** II.v.33 [King alone, of a shepherd's life] *So many hours must I contemplate*

contemplative *(adj.)* vacant, vacuous, mindlessly gazing **TN** II.v.19 [Maria to all, of Malvolio] *this letter will make a contemplative idiot of him*

contempt *(n.)* **1** disobedience, disregard, defiance **TNK** III.vi.115 [Arcite to Palamon] *If you be seen you perish instantly / For breaking prison, and I, … / For my contempt* [i.e. in ignoring Theseus' order of banishment]

2 disgrace, dishonour, scandal **TN** II.v.196 [Maria to all, of Malvolio's behaviour] *it cannot but turn him into a notable contempt*

contemptible *(adj.)* **1** despised, despicable, lowly **1H6** I.ii.75 [Pucelle to Dauphin] *Heaven and Our Lady gracious hath it pleased / To shine on my contemptible estate*

2 scornful, disdainful, full of contempt **MA** II.iii.180 [Don Pedro to Claudio, of Benedick] *the man … hath a contemptible spirit*

contempts *(n.)* malapropism for 'contents' **LL** I.i.187 [Costard to King, of Armado's letter] *the contempts thereof are as touching me*

contemptuous (*adj.*) contemptible, despicable, loathsome **2H6** I.iii.81 [Queen to Suffolk, of the Duchess] *Contemptuous base-born callet as she is*

contend (*v.*) **1** fight, engage in combat, struggle **KL** III.i.4 [Gentleman to disguised Kent, of Lear] *Contending with the fretful elements; AC* II.ii.84; **Cor** IV.v.116; **H5** I.ii.24; **3H6** IV.v.102; **Mac** II.ii.7
2 compete, vie, rival **Per** I.ii.17 [Pericles alone, of Antiochus] *'Gainst whom I am too little to contend; AW* I.i.61; **2H6** III.ii.384; **3H6** II.v.2; **Mac** I.vi.16; **Per** IV.Chorus.30
3 argue, object, protest **Per** II.iii.24 [First Knight to Pericles] *Contend not, sir*
4 make great efforts, strive vigorously **Sonn** 60.4 [of minutes] *In sequent toil all forwards do contend*

contending (*adj.*) struggling, antagonistic, opposed **H5** V.ii.341 [French King to King Henry] *the contending kingdoms / Of France and England; TS* V.ii.158; **Venus** 82

content (*n.*) **1** pleasure, satisfaction, happiness **H8** I.iv.3 [Guilford to ladies, of Wolsey] *This night he dedicates / To fair content, and you; AW* Epilogue.3; **CE** I.ii.33; **Oth** II.i.190; **TNK** V.iv.16; **WT** V.iii.11
2 contentment, peace of mind **3H6** III.i.64 [King to Second Keeper] *my crown is called content; AW* I.ii.4; **H8** II.iii.20; **MW** I.i.232; **Per** III.ii.38; **R3** V.iv.319
3 acceptance, acquiescence **Per** IV.Chorus.46 [Gower alone] *The unborn event / I do commend to your content; Luc* 1503; **MW** IV.v.114; **Oth** III.iv.116; **R2** V.v.23; **Venus** 61
4 substance, matter, meaning **LL** V.ii.515 [Princess to King, of the pageant] *the contents / Dies in the zeal of that which it presents* [i.e. the eagerness of the presenters will murder the subject-matter]; **AY** V.iv.127

content (*adj.*) **1** agreeable, willing, ready **1H6** V.iii.126 [Suffolk to Margaret] *Are ye so content?* [Margaret] *An if my father please, I am content* ➤ FEW, p.xxi; **RESPONSES**, p.373
2 contented, patient, accepting, undisturbed **MA** V.i.92 [Antonio to Leonato] *Hold you content; AY* III.ii.71; **3H6** III.i.67
3 satisfied, calm, easy in mind **MW** I.iv.68 [Mistress Quickly to Caius] *Good master, be content; Cor* III.ii.130; **JC** V.ii.41; **KL** I.iv.310; **R2** V.ii.82

content (*v.*) **1** please, gratify, delight, satisfy **TS** IV.iii.174 [Petruchio to Katherina, of the adder] *his painted skin contents the eye; AY* V.ii.68; **AY** V.ii.111; **Tem** V.i.170; **TG** III.i.93; **TS** I.i.160
2 calm [down], settle, relax **RJ** I.v.65 [Capulet to Tybalt, of Romeo] *Content thee, gentle coz, let him alone; MA* V.i.87; **Oth** I.i.41; **TS** I.i.90, 195
3 take pleasure in, enjoy **TS** I.i.80 [Bianca to Katherina] *content you in my discontent*
4 reward, compensate, recompense **R3** III.ii.110 [Hastings to Priest, of his sermon] *I am in your debt for your last exercise; / Come the next Sabbath, and I will content you; Oth* III.i.1

contented (*adj.*) **1** willing, ready, agreeable **TS** IV.iv.101 [Lucentio alone, of marrying Bianca] *I may and will, if she be so contented; 3H6* III.i.67; **H8** II.iv.227; **Mac** II.iii.131; **R2** IV.i.199
2 not disposed to complain, amenable **TS** IV.i.155 [Katherina to Petruchio] *The meat was well, if you were so contented*
3 calm, easy in mind, restrained **MW** III.iii.156 [Page to Ford] *be contented; KL* III.iv.106

contention (*n.*) quarrel, dispute, strife **Cym** I.v.51 [Frenchman to Iachimo] *'twas a contention in public; 1H4* I.i.60; **2H4** I.i.9; **3H6** I.i.6; **Oth** II.i.92; **TNK** III.vi.253

contentious (*adj.*) hostile, belligerent, quarrelsome **KL** III.iv.6 [Lear to disguised Kent] *this contentious storm / Invades us to the skin*

contentless (*adj.*) discontented, dissatisfied, unhappy **Tim** IV.iii.246 [Apemantus to Timon] *Best state, contentless, / Hath a distracted and most wretched being*

contestation (*n.*) joint action as enemies, shared antagonism **AC** II.ii.47 [Caesar to Antony, of Antony's wife and brother] *their contestation / Was theme for you*

continence (*n.*) self-restraint, self-control, abstemiousness **Tit** I.i.15 [Bassianus to his followers] *The Imperial seat, to virtue consecrate, / To justice, continence, and nobility*

continency (*n.*) **1** moderation, self-restraint, patience **TS** IV.i.169 [Curtis to Grumio, of Petruchio talking to Katherina] *Making a sermon of continency to her*
2 continence, sexual abstinence, self-restraint **MM** III.ii.164 [Lucio to disguised Duke, of Angelo] *This ungenitured agent will unpeople the province with continency*

continent (*n.*) **1** embodiment, summation, digest **MV** III.ii.130 [Bassanio to all] *Here's the scroll, / The continent and summary of my fortune; Ham* V.ii.110; **LL** IV.i.110
2 container, receptacle, enclosure **2H4** II.iv.280 [Prince Henry to Falstaff] *thou globe of sinful continents* [also: areas of the world; contents]; **AC** IV.xiv.40; **Ham** IV.vi.64; **KL** III.ii.58
3 globe, mass **TN** V.i.268 [Viola to Orsino] *all those swearings keep as true in soul / As doth that orbed continent the fire / That severs day from night*
4 dry land **2H4** III.i.47 [King Henry IV to Warwick and Surrey] *the continent, / Weary of solid firmness, melt itself / Into the sea*
5 bank, embankment, course **MND** II.i.92 [Titania to Oberon] *Contagious fogs ... falling in the land, / Hath every pelting river made so proud / That they have overborne their continents; 1H4* III.i.106

continent (*adj.*) **1** chaste, temperate, restrained **WT** III.ii.33 [Hermione to all] *my past life / Hath been as continent, as chaste, as true / As I am now unhappy*
2 restrictive, constraining, enforcing restraint **LL** I.i.251 [King, reading Armado's letter to him] *contrary to thy established proclaimed edict and continent canon*
3 self-restraining, self-controlled, discreet **KL** I.ii.163 [Edmund to Edgar] *I pray you have a continent forbearance; Mac* IV.iii.64

continuance (*n.*) **1** stay, period of time **1H6** II.v.106 [Mortimer to Richard] *thy uncle is removing hence, / As princes do their courts when they are cloyed / With long continuance in a settled place*
2 maintaining, keeping up, carrying on **MV** I.i.125 [Bassanio to Antonio] *I have disabled mine estate / By something showing a more swelling port / Than my faint means would grant continuance; MM* III.i.240
3 lasting nature, permanence, durability **RJ** Prologue.10 [Chorus, of Romeo and Juliet] *the continuance of their parents' rage, / Which ... naught could remove; TN* I.iv.6

continuantly (*adv.*) malapropism for 'incontinently' [= continually] **2H4** II.i.25 [Hostess to Fang and Snare, of Falstaff] *'A comes continuantly to Pie Corner* [F; Q *continually*]

continuate (*adj.*) **1** uninterrupted, undisturbed, unbroken **Oth** III.iv.174 [Cassio to Bianca] *I shall in a more continuate time / Strike off this score of absence* [F; Q1 *convenient*]
2 continuing, long-lasting, enduring **Tim** I.i.11 [Merchant to Jeweller, of Timon] *A most incomparable man, breathed, as it were, / To an untirable and continuate goodness*

continue (*v.*) **1** keep up, maintain, elaborate **TNK** IV.iii.47 [Doctor to Gaoler, of the Gaoler's Daughter] *How she continues this fancy!*
2 retain, carry on with, preserve **MM** IV.iii.82 [Provost to disguised Duke] *how shall we continue Claudio* [i.e. maintain the deception over Claudio]; **H8** II.iv.33
3 happen later, follow after **Tim** II.ii.5 [Flavius alone, of Timon] *[he] Takes no account / How things go from him, nor resumes no care / Of what is to continue*

continuer (*n.*) someone with staying-power, person who keeps going **MA** I.i.134 [Benedick to Beatrice] *I would my horse had ... so good a continuer*

contract (*v.*) **1** draw together, cause to shrink **Ham** I.ii.4 [Claudius to his court] *our whole kingdom / To be contracted in one brow of woe*
2 shorten, reduce, lessen **Ham** V.i.63 [First Clown, singing] *To contract – O – the time for – a – my behove*
3 shrink, shrivel, cripple **Tim** I.i.252 [Apemantus to Alcibiades] *Aches contract and starve your supple joints!*

4 betrothe, engage **MW** V.v.215 [Fenton to all, of Anne] *she and I, long since contracted;* **R3** III.vii.178; **Sonn** 1.5; **WT** IV.iv.387

contracting (n.) marriage contract, betrothal **MM** III.ii.270 [disguised Duke alone] *So disguise shall by th'disguised ... perform an old contracting*

contraction (n.) marriage contract, betrothal **Ham** III.iv.47 [Hamlet to Gertrude] *such a deed / As from the body of contraction plucks / The very soul*

contradict (v.) oppose, go against, thwart **2H6** III.ii.252 [Salisbury to King, of the commons] *Free from a stubborn opposite intent, / As being thought to contradict your liking*

contradiction (n.) answering back, speaking in opposition **Cor** III.iii.27 [Brutus to Sicinius, of Coriolanus] *He hath been used ... to have his worth / Of contradiction* [i.e. to give as good as he gets]

contrariety (n.) **1** oppositeness, contrariness, antagonism **Cor** IV.vi.74 [Menenius to Sicinius, of Coriolanus] *He and Aufidius can no more atone / Than violent'st contrariety*
2 contradiction, inconsistency, discrepancy **1H6** II.ii.58 [Countess to Talbot, of his reply] *How can these contrarieties agree?*

contrarious (adj.) **1** conflicting, contrary, contradictory **MM** IV.i.61 [disguised Duke alone] *Volumes of report / Run with these false and most contrarious quests / Upon thy doings* [or: sense 2]
2 adverse, unfavourable, hostile **1H4** V.i.52 [Worcester to King Henry] *the contrarious winds that held the King / So long in his unlucky Irish Wars*

contrariously (adv.) in opposed ways, following their own inclination **H5** I.ii.206 [Canterbury to all] *many things ... / To one consent, may work contrariously*

contrary (n.) **1** opposite direction, other way **WT** I.ii.372 [Polixenes to Camillo, of Leontes] *Wafting his eyes to th'contrary*
2 opposite condition, opposing state **Tim** IV.iii.20 [Timon alone] *Degrees, observances, customs, laws, / Decline to your confounding contraries;* **Tem** II.i.150
3 opposite side, position as adversary **H8** II.i.15 [First Gentleman to Second Gentleman, of Buckingham] *The King's attorney, on the contrary, / Urged on the examinations*
4 lie, fabrication, false assertion **CE** IV.iv.77 [Adriana to Pinch] *Is't good to soothe him in these contraries?*

contrary (adj.) **1** opposite, opposing, rival **1H6** III.i.81 [Mayor to all] *The Bishop and the Duke of Gloucester's men ... banding themselves in contrary parts;* **H8** III.ii.26; **WT** V.45
2 different, at a distance apart **MW** II.i.192 [Shallow to Page, of Evans and Caius] *My merry host hath ... appointed them contrary places*
3 wrong, incorrect, erroneous **KJ** IV.ii.198 [Hubert to King John, of a tailor] *Standing on slippers which his nimble haste / Had falsely thrust upon contrary feet;* **MV** I.ii.90

contrary (v.) contradict, gainsay, oppose **RJ** I.v.85 [Capulet to Tybalt] *You must contrary me!*

contrary (adv.) **1** in opposite directions, contrarily **Ham** III.ii.221 [First Player, as King, to his Queen] *Our wills and fates do so contrary run;*
2 in a very different direction **1H4** V.v.4 [King Henry to Worcester] *wouldst thou turn our offers contrary?*

contribution (n.) military levy, aid, supplies **JC** IV.iii.204 [Brutus to Cassius, of the local people] *they have grudged us contribution*

contrive (v.) **1** scheme, plot, conspire **1H6** I.iii.34 [Gloucester to Winchester] *Thou that contrived'st to murder our dead lord;* **AW** IV.iii.23; **AY** IV.iii.135; **JC** I.iii.15; **MV** IV.i.349; **R2** I.i.96
2 pass the time, spend, while away **TS** I.ii.273 [Tranio as Lucentio to Hortensio and Gremio, of Bianca] *Please ye we may contrive this afternoon, / And quaff carouses to our mistress' health*

contriver (n.) intriguer, schemer, plotter **JC** II.i.158 [Cassius to all, of Antony] *We shall find of him / A shrewd contriver;* **Mac** III.v.7

contriving (adj.) plotting, skilfully working [on one's behalf] **AC** I.ii.183 [Antony to Enobarbus] *the letters too / Of many our contriving friends in Rome*

control (n.) compulsion, constraint, mastery **KJ** I.i.17 [Chatillon to King John, of what follows the refusal of Philip's demands] *The proud control of fierce and bloody war*

control (v.) **1** curb, restrain, hold back **KL** III.vii.27 [Cornwall to all] *our wrath, which men / May blame but not control;* **E3** V.i.49; **KL** II.iv.241; **Tit** I.i.423, III.i.258
2 overwhelm, overpower **Tem** I.ii.373 [Caliban to himself, of Prospero] *His art is of such power, / It would control my dam's god Setebos;* **Cor** III.i.161; **Luc** 448, 678
3 calm down, gently rebuke **Tit** V.i.26 [Second Goth to Lucius, of Aaron's child] *I heard / The crying babe controlled with this discourse*
4 challenge, take to task **Tem** I.ii.440 [Prospero aside, of Ferdinand] *The Duke of Milan / And his more braver daughter could control thee;* **Luc** 189

controller (n.) **1** steward, household manager **Tit** II.iii.60 [Tamora to Bassianus] *Saucy controller of my private steps*
2 detractor, censorious critic, slanderer **2H6** III.ii.205 [Queen to all, of Warwick] *He dares not calm his contumelious spirit, / Nor cease to be an arrogant controller*

controlment (n.) control, restraint, check **KJ** I.i.20 [King John to Chatillon] *Here have we war for war and blood for blood, / Controlment for controlment;* **MA** I.iii.19; **Tit** II.i.68

controversy (n.) struggle, contending, competitive dispute **JC** I.ii.109 [Cassius to Brutus, of the torrent] *stemming it with hearts of controversy*

contumelious (adj.) contemptuous, arrogant, insolent **2H6** III.ii.204 [Queen to all, of Warwick] *He dares not calm his contumelious spirit;* **1H6** I.iv.39; **Tim** V.i.172

contumeliously (adv.) disgracefully, contemptuously, arrogantly **1H6** I.iii.58 [Mayor to Gloucester and Winchester] *Fie, lords, that you, being supreme magistrates, / Thus contumeliously should break the peace!*

contumely (n.) scorn, insult, abuse **Ham** III.i.71 [Hamlet alone] *the proud man's contumely*

contusion (n.) bruise, injury, lesion **2H6** V.iii.3 [York to all, of Salisbury] *That winter lion, who in rage forgets / Aged contusions and all brush of time* [i.e. the bruises of old age]

convenience (n.) **1** opportunity, occasion, suitable moment **KL** III.vi.97 [disguised Kent to Lear, of Lear's shattered nerves] *Which, if convenience will not allow, / Stand in hard cure*
2 fitness, appropriateness, propriety **AW** III.ii.72 [Second Lord to Countess, of Bertram] *The Duke will lay upon him all the honour / That good convenience claims;* **MM** III.i.249
3 advantage, desirable feature, point of agreement **Oth** II.i.225 [Iago to Roderigo, of the features in a man that would attract Desdemona] *for want of these required conveniences;* **TC** III.iii.7

conveniency (n.) convenience, opportunity, advantage **Oth** IV.ii.177 [Roderigo to Iago] *Every day thou ... keep'st from me all conveniency;* **MV** IV.i.82

convenient (adj.) fitting, suitable, appropriate **KL** IV.v.31 [Regan to Oswald, of Edmund and Gonerill] *more convenient is he for my hand / Than for your lady's;* **Cor** V.iii.192; **1H6** II.iv.4; **2H6** I.iii.206; **Oth** III.iv.174 [Q1]; **R3** IV.iv.443

conveniently (adv.) fittingly, suitably, appropriately **Per** III.-Chorus.56 [Gower alone, of his story] *action may / Conveniently the rest convey;* **MV** II.viii.45

convent (v.) **1** bring together, assemble, convene **Cor** II.ii.53 [Sicinius to First Senator] *We are convented / Upon a pleasing treaty;* **TNK** I.iv.31, v.9
2 summon, call to appear, send for **H8** V.i.52 [Gardiner to Lovell, of Cranmer] *Tomorrow morning to the Council board / He be convented;* **MM** V.i.158; **TN** V.i.379

conventicle (*n.*) **1** meeting-place **E3** II.i.63 [King Edward to Lodowick] *Since green our thoughts, green be the conventicle / Where we will ease us by disburd'ning them*
2 secret meeting, clandestine gathering **2H6** III.i.166 [Gloucester to his enemies] *Myself had notice of your conventicles*

conversant (*adj.*) occupied, concerned, having to do **KJ** IV.iii.70 [Salisbury to all, vowing revenge on Arthur's apparent murder] *Never to be infected with delight, / Nor conversant with ease and idleness*

conversation (*n.*) **1** way of life, behaviour, manners, conduct **AC** II.vi.121 [Enobarbus to Menas] *Octavia is of a holy, cold, and still conversation*; **2H4** V.v.103; **MW** II.i.23; **Per** II.Chorus.9
2 social interaction, society, dealings **Cor** II.i.89 [Menenius to Brutus and Sicinius] *More of your conversation would infect my brain*; **Cym** I.v.100; **Ham** III.ii.65; **Oth** III.iii.261; **R3** III.v.31; **TNK** II.i.128
3 process, interchange, movement **AW** I.iii.229 [Helena to Countess] *the conversation of my thoughts*

converse (*n.*) conversation, discourse, interaction **Ham** II.i.42 [Polonius to Reynaldo] *Your party in converse, him you would sound*; **LL** V.ii.730; **Oth** III.i.37

converse (*v.*) associate, keep company **AY** V.ii.58 [Rosalind as Ganymede to Orlando] *I have … conversed with a magician*; **Cor** II.i.48; **2H4** V.i.61; **2H6** II.i.190; **KL** I.iv.15; **TG** I.iii.31

conversion (*n.*) **1** change for the better, character transformation **AY** IV.iii.137 [Oliver to Celia as Aliena] *I do not shame / To tell you what I was, since my conversion / So sweetly tastes, being the thing I am*
2 newly honoured person, ennobled fellow **KJ** I.i.189 [Bastard alone, of an ennobled person remembering names] *'Tis too respective and too sociable / For your conversion*

convert (*v.*) change, transform, alter **Mac** IV.iii.228 [Malcolm to Macduff] *let grief / Convert to anger*; **Ham** III.iv.129; **Luc** 592, 691; **MA** I.i.114; **R2** V.iii.63; **Sonn** 11.4, 49.7

convertite (*n.*) convert, penitent **KJ** V.i.19 [Cardinal Pandulph to King John] *you are a gentle convertite*; **AY** V.iv.181; **Luc** 743

convey (*v.*) **1** carry off, make away with, take by force **R3** IV.iv.76 [Queen Margaret to all, of Richard] *saints pray, / To have him suddenly conveyed from hence*; **AC** III.xi.52; **Cym** I.i.63; **3H6** IV.vi.81; **MW** I.iii.26; **R2** IV.i.316
2 manage, conduct, carry on [in secrecy] **KL** I.ii.101 [Edmund to Gloucester] *I will … convey the business as I shall find means*; **Mac** IV.iii.71
3 conceal, hide, secrete **Ham** III.iii.28 [Polonius to Claudius] *Behind the arras I'll convey myself*; **MW** III.iii.110
4 pass off, give out, pretend **H5** I.ii.74 [Canterbury to King Henry] *Hugh Capet … / Conveyed himself as th'heir to th'Lady Lingare*

conveyance (*n.*) **1** channel, conduit, medium **Cor** V.i.55 [Menenius to Sicinius] *These pipes and these conveyances of our blood*
2 escort, conduct, convoy **Oth** I.iii.282 [Othello to Duke, of Iago and Desdemona] *To his conveyance I assign my wife*; **Ham** IV.iv.3
3 removal, carrying off, elimination [of] **R3** IV.iv.283 [Queen Elizabeth to King Richard, of her daughter] *thou … / Mad'st quick conveyance with her good aunt Anne!*
4 skill, dexterity, facility **MA** II.i.225 [Benedick to Don Pedro, of Beatrice] *huddling jest upon jest with such impossible conveyance upon me*
5 trickery, cunning, artifice **3H6** III.iii.160 [Queen to Warwick] *I will not hence till … I make King Lewis behold / Thy sly conveyance*
6 bad management, underhand dealing, dishonesty **1H6** I.iii.2 [Gloucester to servingmen, of the Tower] *Since Henry's death, I fear, there is conveyance*
7 [legal] document transferring property **Ham** V.i.108 [Hamlet to Horatio, of a lawyer] *The very conveyances of his lands*

conveyor (*n.*) thief, robber, pilferer **R2** IV.i.316 [Richard to all] *Conveyors are you all*

convict (*v.*) prove guilty, condemn **R3** I.iv.190 [Clarence to Murderers] *who pronounced / The bitter sentence of poor Clarence' death / Before I be convict by course of law?*

convicted (*adj.*) defeated, vanquished, conquered **KJ** III.iv.2 [King Philip to Lewis the Dauphin and Cardinal Pandulph] *A whole armado of convicted sail / Is scattered and disjoined from fellowship* [or: assembled]

convince (*v.*) **1** defeat, overcome, overpower **Mac** IV.iii.142 [Doctor to Malcolm, of the sick people] *Their malady convinces / The great assay of art*; **Cym** I.v.92; **Mac** I.vii.64; **Oth** IV.i.28
2 disprove, confute **Per** I.ii.123 [Pericles to Helicanus] *time … this truth shall ne'er convince*
3 establish, prove, demonstrate **LL** V.ii.741 [King to Princess, of his love] *The holy suit which fain it would convince*
4 convict, prove guilty **TC** II.ii.131 [Paris to Hector and Troilus] *Else might the world convince of levity / As well my undertakings as your counsels*

convive (*v.*) feast together, enjoy a banquet **TC** IV.v.272 [Agamemnon to the Greeks] *go to my tent; / There in the full convive you*

convocation (*n.*) assembly, gathering, parliament **Ham** IV.iii.20 [Hamlet to Claudius] *A certain convocation of politic worms*; **H5** I.i.76

convoy (*n.*) means of transport, method of conveyance **H5** IV.iii.37 [King Henry to all] *he which hath no stomach to this fight … his passport shall be made, / And crowns for convoy put into his purse*; **AW** IV.iii.88, iv.10; **Ham** I.iii.3; **RJ** II.iv.187

convulsion (*n.*) cramp, spasm, contraction **Tem** IV.i.260 [Prospero to Ariel, of Caliban, Stephano and Trinculo] *charge my goblins that they grind their joints / With dry convulsions*

cony (*n.*) rabbit **Cor** IV.v.219 [Third Servingman to First Servingman, of the people] *they will out of their burrows like conies after rain*; **AY** III.ii.327; **3H6** I.iv.62; **Venus** 687

cony-catch (*v.*) **1** rabbit-catch; trick, dupe **TS** V.i.89 [Gremio to Baptista, of the true Vincentio] *Take heed … lest you be cony-catched in this business*
2 take to cheating, become a trickster **MW** I.iii.30 [Falstaff to Nym and Pistol] *I must cony-catch*

cony-catching (*n.*) rabbit-catching; trickery, evasion, knavery **TS** IV.i.38 [Curtis to Grumio] *you are so full of cony-catching*

cony-catching (*adj.*) cheating, swindling **MW** I.i.118 [Slender to Falstaff] *I have matter in my head … against your cony-catching rascals* [F; Q *cogging*]

cool (*v.*) chill with terror, become cold with fear **Mac** V.v.10 [Macbeth to himself] *The time has been my senses would have cooled / To hear a night-shriek*

cooling card card that dashes an opponent's hope of success; barrier, check **1H6** V.iii.84 [Suffolk to himself, of his marriage] *there lies a cooling card*

coop (*v.*) **1** shut in, enclose, confine **3H6** V.i.109 [Warwick to Edward] *I am not cooped here for defence!*
2 enclose, bind in, protect **KJ** II.i.25 [Austria to Arthur, of England's coast] *Whose foot … coops from other lands her islanders*

copatain hat high-crowned hat in the form of a sugar-loaf **TS** V.i.59 [Vincentio to Tranio as Lucentio, of what Tranio is wearing] *a scarlet cloak, and a copatain hat!*

cope (*n.*) sky, heavens, firmament **Per** IV.vi.121 [Boult to Marina, of her chastity] *[it] is not worth a breakfast in the cheapest country under the cope*

cope, cope with (*v.*) **1** encounter, face, have to do [with], come into contact [with] **E3** III.iii.61 [King John to King Edward] *I scorn to cope / With one so much inferior to myself*; **AY** II.i.67; **2H4** IV.ii.95; **Luc** 99; **Oth** IV.i.86; **WT** IV.iv.421

2 be a match for, stand up to TC II.iii.261 [Ulysses to all] *come knights from east to west, … Ajax shall cope the best*

3 give in recompense for MV IV.i.409 [Bassanio to Portia as Balthasar] *Three thousand ducats due unto the Jew / We freely cope your courteous pains withal*

copesmate *(n.)* companion, partner, familiar friend Luc 925 [Lucrece as if to time] *copesmate of ugly Night*

copped *(adj.)* humped, peaked, heaped up in a mound Per I.i.102 [Pericles to Antiochus] *The blind mole casts / Copped hills towards heaven*

copper *(n.)* coin made of copper LL IV.iii.362 [Berowne alone] *our copper buys no better treasure*

copper *(adj.)* copper-coloured TC I.ii.107 [Cressida to Pandarus] *I had as lief Helen's golden tongue had commended Troilus for a copper nose* [i.e. caused by drink or disease]

copulative *(n.)* person being joined in marriage AY V.iv.54 [Touchstone to Duke Senior] *I press in here, sir, amongst the rest of the country copulatives*

copy *(n.)* **1** example, model, pattern AW I.ii.46 [King to Bertram, of Bertram's father] *Such a man / Might be a copy to these younger times;* H5 III.i.24; KJ IV.ii.113; Tim III.iii.32
2 theme, subject, topic CE V.i.62 [Adriana to Abbess, of Antipholus of Ephesus' infidelity] *It was the copy of our conference*
3 original, master-copy Sonn 11.14 *Thou shouldst print more, not let that copy die*
4 [legal] type of tenure, copyhold; also: process of replication Mac III.ii.38 [Lady Macbeth to Macbeth, of Banquo and Fleance] *in them nature's copy's not eterne*

coragio *(int.)* courage Tem V.i.257 [Stephano to Caliban] *Coragio, bully-monster, coragio;* AW II.v.92 ▶ ITALIAN, p.647

Coram *(n.)* malapropism for 'quorum' [part of a legal formula for installing the number of justices needed to constitute a bench] MW I.i.6 [Slender to Shallow, of Shallow] *justice of peace and Coram*

coranto *(n.)* lively dance with quick running steps AW II.iii.42 [Lafew to Parolles, of the King and Helena] *he's able to lead her a coranto;* H5 III.v.33; TN I.iii.122

cord *(n.)* hangman's rope Cym V.v.213 [Posthumus to all] *O, give me cord, or knife, or poison;* Cym V.iv.168

corded *(adj.)* made of ropes TG III.i.40 [Proteus to Duke, of Valentine and Silvia] *he … will ascend / And with a corded ladder fetch her down*

cordial *(n.)* restorative, stimulant, tonic R3 II.i.41 [King Edward to Buckingham] *A pleasing cordial, princely Buckingham, / Is this thy vow unto my sickly heart;* Cym V.v.247; H8 III.i.106; RJ V.i.85; Tit I.i.169

cordial *(adj.)* reviving, invigorating, restorative Cym IV.ii.327 [Innogen alone, of Pisanio] *The drug he gave me, which he said was precious / And cordial to me;* Cym I.vi.64

core *(n.)* enclosed body, contained corpse TC V.viii.1 [Hector alone, as if to a dead soldier within armour] *Most putrefied core, so fair without*

Corinthian *(n.)* true drinking companion 1H4 II.iv.11 [Prince Hal to Poins, of some acquaintances] *They … tell me flatly I am no proud Jack like Falstaff, but a Corinthian*

co-rival *(n./v.)* ▶ corrival *(n./v.)*

corky *(adj.)* dry, withered, sapless KL III.vii.29 [Cornwall to servants, of Gloucester] *Bind fast his corky arms*

cormorant *(n.)* glutton, gorger, insatiable eater R2 II.i.38 [John of Gaunt to York] *Light vanity, insatiate cormorant*

cormorant *(adj.)* greedy, insatiable, all-devouring LL I.i.4 [King to all] *spite of cormorant devouring Time;* Cor I.i.119; TC II.ii.6

corner *(n.)* quarter, corner of the earth [as on a map showing winds] Cym II.iv.28 [Posthumus to Iachimo] *winds of all the corners [have] kissed your sails*

corner-cap *(n.)* cap with (three) corners, mortar-board LL IV.iii.51 [Berowne to himself, as if to Longaville] *Thou makest the triumviry, the corner-cap of society* ▶ CLOTHING, p.79

cornet *(n.)* **1** company of cavalry, troop of horsemen 1H6 IV.iii.25 [Richard to Lucy] *that Somerset, who in proud heart / Doth stop my cornets* [i.e. hold back my cavalrymen]
2 ▶ STAGE DIRECTIONS, p.417

cornuto *(n.)* beast with horns; cuckold MW III.v.65 [Falstaff to Ford as Brook, of Ford] *the peaking cornuto … comes me in the instant of our encounter*

corollary *(n.)* extra one, surplus, supernumerary Tem IV.i.57 [Prospero to Ariel] *Bring a corollary, / Rather than want a spirit* [i.e. bring too many rather than too few]

coronal *(n.)* coronet, circlet H8 IV.i.37 [stage direction] *The old Duchess of Norfolk, in a coronal of gold*

coronet *(n.)* **1** small crown [inferior to one worn by the sovereign] JC I.ii.236 [Casca to Brutus, of offering Caesar a crown] *'twas not a crown neither, 'twas one of these coronets;* 1H6 V.iv.134; KL I.i.33, 139; Tem I.ii.114
2 garland, wreath, circlet [of flowers, etc] KL IV.vi.182 [stage direction, of Lear] *He takes off his coronet of flowers;* MND IV.i.51

corporal *(adj.)* **1** bodily, physical JC IV.i.33 [Antony to Octavius, of his horse] *His corporal motion governed by my spirit;* AW I.ii.24; Mac I.vii.80; MM III.i.83
2 corporeal, material, physical Mac I.iii.80 [Macbeth to Banquo, of the Witches] *what seemed corporal / Melted*

corporate *(n.)* malapropism for 'corporal' 2H4 III.ii.215 [Bullcalf to Bardolph] *Good Master Corporate Bardolph*

corporate *(adj.)* united as if in one body, in unison Tim II.ii.209 [Flavius to Timon, of the Senators] *They answer, in a joint and corporate voice*

corpse *(n.)* body of a man, physical being 2H4 I.i.192 [Morton to Northumberland] *your son had only but the corpse … to fight* [i.e. he had only the bodies of men to fight with]

corpulent *(adj.)* well-made, full-bodied 1H4 II.iv.412 [Falstaff (as King) to Prince Hal, of himself] *A goodly portly man … and a corpulent*

correct *(v.)* punish, chastise, reprimand 2H6 I.iii.196 [Horner to York, of Peter] *I did correct him for his fault;* KJ II.i.87; Per I.iii.22; TC V.vi.3

corrected *(adj.)* chastised, rebuked, reprimanded Cor V.iii.57 [Coriolanus to Volumnia] *Your knees to me? To your corrected son?*

correction *(n.)* punishment, retribution, rebuke TG III.i.372 [Launce alone, of Speed] *I'll … rejoice in the boy's correction;* LL I.i.210; R2 IV.i.77; TC V.vi.5

correctioner *(n.)* one from the House of Correction [the Bridewell] 2H4 V.iv.20 [Doll to First Beadle] *you filthy famished correctioner*

correspondent responsive, receptive, compliant Tem I.ii.297 [Ariel to Prospero] *I will be correspondent to command*

corresponsive *(adj.)* corresponding, equivalent, analogous TC Prologue.18 [Prologue, of the six city gates] *with massy staples / And corresponsive and fulfilling bolts*

corrigible *(adj.)* **1** corrective, controlling, disciplinary Oth I.iii.322 [Iago to Roderigo] *the power and corrigible authority … lies in our wills*
2 submissive, docile, acquiescent AC IV.xiv.74 [Antony to Eros, of himself in Rome] *bending down / His corrigible neck*

corrival, co-rival *(n.)* **1** equal, match, compeer 1H4 I.iii.205 [Hotspur to Northumberland and Worcester, of drowned honour] *he that doth redeem her thence might wear / Without corrival all her dignities*
2 ally, associate, partner 1H4 IV.iv.31 [Archbishop to Sir Michael] *the King hath drawn … many more corrivals and dear men / Of estimation and command in arms*

corrival, co-rival *(v.)* vie with, compete with, be a rival of **TC** I.iii.44 [Nestor to Agamemnon] *Where's then the saucy boat, / Whose weak untimbered sides but even now / Co-rivalled greatness?*

corroborate *(adj.)* [unclear meaning; perhaps a malapropism] strengthened, fortified **H5** II.i.119 [Pistol to Nym, of Falstaff] *His heart is fracted and corroborate*

corrosive *(n.)* painful cure, sharp remedy **2H6** III.ii.403 [Queen to Suffolk] *Though parting be a fretful corrosive, / It is applied to a deathful wound*

corrosive *(adj.)* aggravating, destructive, wasting away **1H6** III.iii.3 [Pucelle to all] *Care is no cure, but rather corrosive*

corrupt *(v.)* **1** ruin, defile, debase **AW** II.iii.115 [Bertram to King, of marrying Helena] *Disdain / Rather corrupt me ever!*
   2 bribe, grease the palms of **TC** IV.iv.71 [Troilus to Cressida] *I will corrupt the Grecian sentinels*

corrupted *(adj.)* tainted [by a crime], deprived of title **1H6** II.iv.93 [Somerset to Richard] *standest not thou attainted, / Corrupted, and exempt from ancient gentry?*

corruptibly *(adv.)* in a corruptible way, causing decomposition **KJ** V.vii.2 [Prince Henry to Salisbury and Bigot, of King John] *The life of all his blood / Is touched corruptibly*

corruption *(n.)* **1** destruction, spoiling, contagion **Ham** I.iv.35 [Hamlet to Horatio, of the way a defect affects a reputation] *Shall in the general censure take corruption / From that particular fault*
   2 decomposition, putrefaction **E3** I.ii.155 [Countess to King Edward, of areas of rich vegetation] *Delve there, and find this issue and their pride / To spring from ordure and corruption's side* [i.e. from the decay of bodies]

corse *(n.)* corpse, dead body **Tim** V.iv.70 [Alcibiades reading Timon's epitaph] *Here lies a wretched corse, of wretched soul bereft* ☛ FEW, p.xxi

corslet *(n.)* ☛ BODY-ARMOUR, p.48

corslet *(v.)* hold tightly, embrace [like a corslet = defensive armour] **TNK** I.i.177 [First Queen to Theseus, of Hippolyta] *her arms … / By warranting moonlight corslet thee*

cost *(n.)* **1** outlay, expense, expenditure **MA** I.i.90 [Don Pedro to Leonato] *The fashion of the world is to avoid cost, and you encounter it;* **AY** II.vii.76; **2H4** I.iii.60; **H5** IV.iii.25; **2H6** IV.vi.3; **RJ** IV.v.6
   2 abundance, richness, costly appearance **E3** I.ii.153 [Countess to King Edward] *the upper turf of earth doth boast / His pride, perfumes, and parti-coloured cost* [Q1; Q2 *coast*]; **Per** II.ii.69
   3 expensive item, costly development **2H4** I.iii.60 [Lord Bardolph to Hastings, of a house-builder] *who, half-through, / Gives o'er, and leaves his part-created cost / A naked subject to the weeping clouds*

cost *(v.)* involve the loss of, deprive one of **3H6** I.i.268 [King to Exeter, of York] *Whose haughty spirit, winged with desire, / Will cost my crown*

costard *(n.)* [jocular: large kind of apple] head **R3** I.iv.156 [First Murderer to Second Murderer, of Clarence] *Take him on the costard with the hilts of thy sword;* **KL** IV.vi.241; **LL** III.i.68; **MW** III.i.14

costermonger *(n.)* [sellers of fruit (originally 'costard-apples') and vegetables] barrow-boy, apple-seller **2H4** I.ii.171 [Falstaff to Lord Chief Justice] *Virtue is of so little regard in these costermongers' times that true valour is turned bearherd*

costliness *(n.)* splendidness, rarity, preciousness **TNK** V.iii.97 [Emilia to herself, of Arcite] *his richness / And costliness of spirit looked through him*

costly *(adj.)* bountiful, lavish, rich **MV** II.ix.94 [Messenger to Portia] *A day in April never came so sweet / To show how costly summer was at hand*

co-supreme *(n.)* joint supreme ruler **Phoen** 51 [of the Phoenix and Dove] *Co-supremes and stars of love* ☛ supreme *(n.)*

cote *(n.)* cottage **AY** II.iv.80 [Corin to all, of his master] *his cote, his flocks … / Are now on sale;* **AY** III.ii.408

cote *(v.)* **1** [from the movement of dogs in hare coursing] overtake, outstrip, pass by **Ham** II.ii.317 [Rosencrantz to Hamlet, of the players] *We coted them on the way;* **E3** IV.iv.24
   2 ☛ quote *(v.)* 1

cot-quean *(n.)* man acting the housewife, meddler in household affairs **RJ** IV.iv.6 [Nurse to Capulet] *Go, you cot-quean, go*

couch *(v.)* **1** conceal, hide, lie hidden **Ham** V.i.218 [Hamlet to Horatio] *Couch we awhile;* **AY** IV.iii.116; **Ham** II.ii.452; **MW** V.ii.1, iii.13, v.48; **Tit** V.ii.38
   2 crouch, lie in ambush, lurk **Per** III.Chorus.6 [Gower alone] *The cat … / Now couches 'fore the mouse's hole;* **AW** IV.i.21
   3 make crouch down, cause to cower **Luc** 506 [of Tarquin's sword] *like a falcon towering in the skies / Coucheth the fowl below with his wings' shade*
   4 go to a lair, find shelter **KL** III.i.12 [Gentleman to disguised Kent, of the stormy night] *wherein the cub-drawn bear would couch;* **Tim** II.ii.177
   5 lay down, rest, repose **RJ** II.iii.34 [Friar to Romeo] *where unbruised youth with unstuffed brain / Doth couch his limbs, there golden sleep doth reign*
   6 lie, sleep, go to bed **MV** V.i.305 [Gratiano to all] *were the day come, I should wish it dark / Till I were couching with the doctor's clerk;* **AC** IV.xiv.51; **TNK** I.i.182
   7 lower, bring down [to attack position] **1H6** III.ii.134 [Talbot to Burgundy, of Bedford] *A braver soldier never couched lance*

couch down *(v.)* crouch, cower, lie down **H5** IV.ii.35 [Constable to Dauphin] *our approach shall so much dare the field / That England shall couch down in fear and yield*

couched *(adj.)* phrased, expressed, put into words **2H6** III.i.179 [Suffolk to all, of Gloucester's speech] *ignominious words, though clerkly couched*

couching *(n.)* bowing, prostration, stooping **JC** III.i.36 [Caesar to Metellus] *These couchings, and these lowly courtesies / Might fire the blood of ordinary men*

couching *(adj.)* [heraldry] lying down, crouching **1H4** III.i.147 [Hotspur to Mortimer, of Glendower] *Sometime he angers me / With telling me of … / A couching lion*

coulter *(n.)* blade fixed in front of a ploughshare **H5** V.ii.46 [Burgundy to King Henry and the French King, of the weeds which have grown in France] *the coulter rusts / That should deracinate such savagery*

council *(n.)* intense debate, dispute, altercation **JC** II.i.67 [Brutus alone] *The genius and the mortal instruments / Are then in council*

counsel *(n.)* **1** advice, guidance, direction **KJ** II.i.395 [Bastard to King John and King Philip, of his advice] *How like you this wild counsel;* **AY** III.ii.350; **E3** I.i.101; **KL** I.iv.319; **Luc** 494; **R2** III.ii.214
   2 opinion, judgement **WT** IV.iv.406 [disguised Polixenes to Florizel, of the latter's wedding] *The father … should hold some counsel / In such a business;* **Cor** I.i.148
   3 resolution, intention, purpose **MA** II.iii.199 [Claudio to Don Pedro, of Beatrice's love] *let her wear it out with good counsel*
   4 plan, purpose, design **Cor** I.ii.2 [First Senator to Aufidius] *they of Rome are entered in our counsels*
   5 secrecy, confidence, privacy **AW** III.vii.9 [Helena to Widow] *to your sworn counsel I have spoken;* **Cym** III.ii.36; **Ham** II.ii.151; **MW** I.i.113; **TNK** III.i.83
   6 confidential matter, private communication **LL** III.i.165 [Berowne to Costard, of Rosaline] *to her white hand see thou do commend / This sealed-up counsel* ☛ counsel-bearer *(n.)*
   7 secret, inmost thought, confidence **MA** III.iii.84 [Dogberry to Watch] *Keep your fellows' counsels and your own;* **Ham** IV.ii.11
   8 private reflection, self-communing **RJ** II.ii.53 [Juliet to hidden Romeo] *What man art thou that, thus bescreened in night, / So stumblest on my counsel?;* **1H4** IV.iii.11

counsel, of one's in one's confidence, privy to one's intentions **AW** IV.iii.43 [First Lord to Second Lord, of Bertram] *you are not altogether of his counsel* [F *councell*]

COSMOS

Shakespearian English involves frequent reference to astrological and astronomical notions. Several terms form part of the general Ptolemaic view of the universe in which the Earth was thought to be the centre of a series of spheres around which the heavenly bodies revolved. A number of heavenly bodies are named, with the Moon, Sun, the known planets, and various constellations all assigned particular roles, as in present-day astrology, and thought to influence a person's destiny, situation, behaviour, and character.

General notions

Term	Example	Gloss
aspect	TC I.iii.92	direction of alignment of heavenly bodies as seen from Earth; especially, the way people are influenced by their relative positions
centre	TC I.iii.85	the Earth, seen as the centre of the Ptolemaic universe
collateral	AW I.i.87	parallel or side-by-side, referring to the relative movement of the spheres
conjunction	2H4 II.iv.258	the apparent coming together of heavenly bodies as seen from Earth
constellation	TN I.iv.35	configurations of stars as seen from Earth
predominant	AW I.i.194	describing a heavenly body in the ascendant, and thus exercising ruling influence
retrograde	AW I.i.195	describing a heavenly body moving in an apparently contrary direction to the order of the zodiacal signs
sphere	AY II.vii.6	celestial globe in which a heavenly body was thought to move; especially, those thought to carry the heavenly bodies around the Earth
stars	Ham I.iv.32	planets and constellations, especially those in the zodiac
trigon	2H4 II.iv.260	a set of three signs of the zodiac in the form of an equilateral triangle
wandering	Ham V.i.252	describing a heavenly body having its own motion

Specific stars, domains, and signs of the zodiac

Term	Example	Gloss
Aries	Tit IV.iii.71	(Ram) first sign of the zodiac
burning zone	Ham V.i.278	the path of the Sun between Cancer and Capricorn
Cancer	TC II.iii.194	fourth sign of the Zodiac, associated with heat
Charles's Wain	1H4 II.i.2	[wagon of Charlemagne] the Plough; Ursa Major
dog-days	H8 V.iv.41	the hottest days of the year; associated with the astrological position of Sirius, the Dog-star
dragon's tail	KL I.ii.129	the intersection of the orbit of the descending Moon and that of the Sun; associated with lechery
equinoctial	TN II.iii.22	celestial equator
Guards	Oth II.i.15	the Guardians; two stars within the Little Bear constellation, Ursa Minor
Hesperus	AW II.i.164	the evening star
house	RJ IV.i.8	one of the twelve divisions of the zodiac
Mars	AW I.i.189	planet particularly associated with martial or aggressive temperaments
Mercury	WT IV.iii.25	planet particularly associated with eloquence, feats of skill, and the commercial world
Pigrogromitus	TN II.iii.22	mock-astrology jargon
Pole	Oth II.i.15	the pole-star, 'ever-fixed'
Queubus	TN II.iii.23	mock-astrology jargon
Saturn	MA I.iii.11	planet particularly associated with melancholic, morose, or vengeful temperaments
Septentrion	3H6 I.iv.136	the seven stars of Ursa Major
Sol	TC I.iii.89	the Sun [here referred to as a 'planet']
Taurus	TN I.iii.130	(Bull) second sign of the zodiac, associated with cuckoldry (through the notion of horns), and also the neck and throat
Ursa Major	KL I.ii.129	the Great Bear; associated with lechery
Vapians	TN II.iii.22	mock-astrology jargon
Venus	2H4 II.iv.258	planet particularly associated with love, beauty, and fertility
Virgo	Tit IV.iii.65	(Virgin) sixth sign of the zodiac, associated with Astraea, goddess of justice

counsel (*v.*) advise, urge **AY** I.ii.250 [Le Beau to Orlando] *I do in friendship counsel you / To leave this place;* **AY** I.ii.165, III.iii.85; **E3** III.iv.13, IV.iv.93

counsel of (*v.*) ☛ cancel of (*v.*)

counsel-bearer (*n.*) carrier of private messages **E3** II.ii.54 [King Edward to Lodowick, of drum parchment] *To be the herald and dear counsel-bearer / Betwixt a goddess and a mighty king* ☛ counsel (*n.*) 6

counsel-giver (*n.*) counsellor, mentor, advisor **E3** IV.vii.13 [Prince Edward to all] *Artois doth bring with him along / The late good counsel-giver to my soul*

counsel-keeper (*n.*) person who keeps secrets **2H4** II.iv.262 [Poins to Prince Henry, of Bardolph] *look whether the fiery trigon his man be not lisping to his master's old tables, his note-book, his counsel-keeper*

counsel-keeping (*adj.*) able to keep secrets **Tit** II.iii.24 [Tamora to Aaron, of the prince and Dido] *curtained with a counsel-keeping cave*

count (*n.*) **1** account, reckoning **TG** II.i.54 [Speed to Valentine, of Silvia's favour] *[it is] out of all count;* **AC** II.vi.54; **E3** IV.vi.56; **RJ** III.v.46; **Sonn** 2.11 ☛ account (*n.*) 1
2 trial, indictment, reckoning **Ham** IV.vii.17 [Claudius to Laertes] *Why to a public count I might not go*
3 age, tally [of years] **TNK** I.iii.53 [Emilia to Hippolyta, of herself and her friend] *when our count / Was each eleven*

count (*v.*) account, consider, regard **LL** II.i.18 [Princess to Boyet] *I am less proud to hear you tell my worth / Than you much willing to be counted wise / In spending your wit in the praise of mine*

count of (*v.*) take account of, esteem, appreciate **TG** II.i.57 [Speed to Valentine, of Silvia] *no man counts of her beauty*

count of, for (*prep.*) on account of **AW** IV.iii.224 [First Soldier reading Parolles' letter] *For count of this, the Count's a fool, I know it*

counted (*adj.*) recognized, accounted, accepted **R3** IV.i.46 [Queen Elizabeth to Dorset, of herself] *Nor mother, wife, nor England's counted Queen*

countenance (*n.*) **1** demeanour, bearing, manner **KL** I.iv.27 [disguised Kent to Lear] *you have that in your countenance which I would fain call master;* **AY** IV.i.32; **1H4** V.i.69; **TS** II.i.226, IV.ii.65; **WT** V.ii.46
2 expression, look, face **Tit** I.i.266 [Saturninus to Tamora] *Clear up ... that cloudy countenance;* **Cor** IV.vi.60; **1H4** II.iv.385; **2H6** III.i.99; **H8** II.iv.26; **Sonn** 86.13
3 appearance, aspect, look **KL** II.ii.88 [disguised Kent to Cornwall, of Oswald] *His countenance likes me not;* **AY** IV.iii.37; **2H6** III.i.5; **TS** V.i.35, 114
4 favourable appearance, support **JC** I.iii.159 [Casca to Cassius, of Brutus] *that which would appear offence in us, / His countenance, like richest alchemy, / Will change to virtue and to worthiness;* **Ham** I.iii.113
5 position, standing, authority **MW** II.ii.6 [Falstaff to Pistol] *I have been content ... you should lay my countenance to pawn* [i.e. use my credit to borrow money]; **1H4** III.ii.65; **KL** I.iv.63
6 favour, patronage, approval **Ham** IV.ii.15 [Hamlet to and of Rosencrantz] *a sponge ... that soaks up the King's countenance;* **Cor** V.vi.40; **Ham** V.i.27; **2H4** V.v.7; **2H6** II.i.163; **MM** V.i.118

countenance, out of **1** disconcerted, abashed **LL** V.ii.272 [Princess to all] *This pert Berowne was out of countenance quite* [also: in a mask]
2 into a disconcerted state **LL** V.ii.604 [Holofernes to Berowne] *I will not be put out of countenance;* **AC** II.ii.182; **LL** V.ii.618

countenance, put in make one feel comfortable, encourage **LL** V.ii.617 [Berowne to Holofernes] *we have put thee in countenance*

countenance (*v.*) **1** approve, support, encourage **2H4** IV.i.35 [Westmorland to Archbishop, of rebellion] *countenanced by boys and beggary;* **2H4** V.i.33, 45

2 honour, grace, pay respect to **TS** IV.i.88 [Curtis calling to servants] *You must meet my master to countenance my mistress* [also: meet, encounter]
3 face up to, confront **Ham** IV.i.32 [Claudius to Gertrude, of Polonius' murder] *this vile deed / We must ... / Both countenance and excuse;* **Mac** II.iii.77

counter, compter (*n.*) **1** round piece of metal used for counting **WT** IV.iii.35 [Clown to himself, of working out the value of wool] *I cannot do't without counters* [F *Compters*]; **Cym** V.iv.171; **TC** II.ii.28
2 imitation coin, something of no value **AY** II.vii.63 [Jaques to Duke Senior] *What, for a counter, would I do, but good?* [i.e. I will give you nothing much in exchange for your reply]
3 [contemptuous] coin, bit of change **JC** IV.iii.80 [Brutus to Cassius, as if to the gods] *When Marcus Brutus grows so covetous, / To lock such rascal counters from his friends ... / Dash him to pieces!*
4 [a term from hunting] taking an opposite path to the prey **2H4** I.ii.89 [Falstaff to Servant] *You hunt counter* [i.e. you're following the wrong scent]; **CE** IV.ii.39; **Ham** IV.v.112

counter-caster (*n.*) [contemptuous] one who works things out with the help of counters, arithmetician **Oth** I.i.31 [Iago to Roderigo, of Cassio] *this counter-caster*

counterchange (*n.*) reciprocation, mutual regard **Cym** V.v.397 [Cymbeline to all] *the counterchange / Is severally in all*

countercheck (*n.*) countering manoeuvre, rebuke **KJ** II.i.223 [King John to Hubert, of himself] *Who painfully, with much expedient march, / Have brought a countercheck before your gates;* **AY** V.iv.78

counterfeit (*n.*) **1** false imitation, spurious image **H8** V.iii.102 [Surrey to all, of King Henry's ring] *'Tis no counterfeit;* **E3** III.iii.83; **1H4** V.iv.477; **KJ** III.i.99; **RJ** II.iv.44; **TC** II.iii.24
2 impostor, pretender, sham **Oth** V.i.43 [Lodovico to Gratiano, of those calling for help] *These may be counterfeits;* **AW** IV.iii.33; **TG** II.iv.12
3 likeness, portrait, image **MV** III.ii.115 [Bassanio to all] *What find I here? / Fair Portia's counterfeit;* **Luc** 1269; **Sonn** 16.8, 53.5; **Tim** V.i.78

counterfeit (*adj.*) **1** pretended, feigned, sham **AY** IV.iii.169 [Oliver to Rosalind as Ganymede, of her fainting] *This was not counterfeit ... [Rosalind] Counterfeit, I assure you;* **AW** IV.iii.98; **H5** III.vi.60, V.i.66; **Tim** IV.iii.113; **TS** V.i.106
2 painted, portrayed, rendered **Ham** III.iv.55 [Hamlet to Gertrude] *The counterfeit presentment of two brothers*

counterfeit (*v.*) **1** copy, imitate, simulate **E3** II.i.13 [Lodowick alone, of King Edward and the Countess] *Why did he then thus counterfeit her looks?* ☛ FEW, p.xxi
2 pretend, feign, make believe **AY** IV.iii.168 [Rosalind as Ganymede to Oliver] *tell your brother how well I counterfeited* ☛ FEW, p.xxi

counterfeited (*adj.*) **1** copied, imitated, mirrored **1H6** V.iii.63 [Suffolk to himself, of the sun] *Twinkling another counterfeited beam*
2 pretended, feigned, sham **2H4** IV.ii.27 [Prince John to Archbishop] *You have taken up, / Under the counterfeited zeal of God, / The subjects of His substitute, my father*

counterfeiting (*n.*) **1** pretending, feigning, acting **AY** IV.iii.181 [Rosalind as Ganymede to Oliver, of Orlando] *commend my counterfeiting to him*
2 role-playing, pretending **3H6** II.iii.28 [Warwick to all] *Why stand we [here] ... / And look upon, as if the tragedy / Were played in jest by counterfeiting actors?*

counterfeitly (*adv.*) feignedly, in a pretended manner **Cor** II.iii.99 [Coriolanus to Fourth Citizen, of the people] *I will ... be off to them most counterfeitly*

countermand (*n.*) contrary command, revoking order **MM** IV.ii.89 [disguised Duke to Provost] *Have you no countermand for Claudio yet;* **R3** II.i.91

countermand (*v.*) **1** contradict, go counter to, oppose **Luc** 276 [Tarquin to himself] *My heart shall never countermand mine eye*

2 prohibit, forbid, prevent **CE** IV.ii.37 [Dromio of Syracuse to Adriana, of the officer] *one that countermands / The passages of alleys*

countermine (*n.*) excavated passage made by fortress defenders to intercept an enemy mine **H5** III.ii.61 [Fluellen to Gower] *th'athversary ... is digt himself four yard under the countermines* ☞ mine (*n.*)

counterpart (*n.*) duplicate, copy, counterfeit **Sonn** 84.11 *Let him but copy what in you is writ ... / And such a counterpart shall fame his wit*

counterpoint (*n.*) counterpane, quilted bed-covering **TS** II.i.344 [Gremio to Baptista, of his possessions] *In cypress chests my arras counterpoints*

counterpoise (*n.*) counterbalance, of equivalent weight **1H4** II.iii.14 [Hotspur alone, reading a letter] *your whole plot [is] too light, for the counterpoise of so great an opposition*

counterpoise (*v.*) **1** equal, match, rival **Cor** II.ii.85 [Cominius to all, of Coriolanus] *The man I speak of cannot in the world / Be singly counterpoised*; **Cor** V.vi.78; **3H6** III.iii.137; **MA** IV.i.26; **Tim** I.i.149

2 counterbalance, compensate, offset **2H6** IV.i.22 [Lieutenant to First and Second Gentlemen, of the proposed ransom] *The lives of those which we have lost in fight / Be counterpoised with such a petty sum!*

counter-reflect (*n.*) reflection back again **TNK** I.i.127 [Emilia to Third Queen, of her sorrow] *it shall make a counter-reflect 'gainst / My brother's heart*

counter-seal (*v.*) provide with an additional seal, countersign **Cor** V.iii.206 [Coriolanus to the ladies] *you shall bear / A better witness back than words, which we ... will have counter-sealed*

countervail (*v.*) counterbalance, match, be equal to **RJ** II.vi.4 [Romeo to Friar, of Juliet] *[sorrow] cannot countervail the exchange of joy / That one short minute gives me in her sight*; **Per** II.iii.56

country (*n.*) district, region, quarter **2H6** IV.ix.21 [King to the former rebels] *I do dismiss you to your several countries*; **1H6** V.iv.9; **3H6** III.i.75; **MW** I.i.203

country base rural boys' chasing game involving running between bases (safe homes) **Cym** V.iii.20 [Posthumus to Lord, of the two youths] *lads more like to run / The country base than to commit such slaughter*

countryman (*n.*) native of a country **E3** IV.vi.43 [Charles to all] *O that I were some other countryman!* [i.e. a citizen of some other country]

country matters sexual intercourse **Ham** III.ii.125 [Hamlet to Ophelia] *Do you think I meant country matters?* [pun on 'cunt']

county (*n.*) **1** [title of rank] count **RJ** III.v.218 [Nurse to Juliet, of Paris] *I think it best you married with the County*; **AW** III.vii.22; **MA** IV.i.310; **MV** I.i.43; **RJ** V.iii.279; **TN** I.v.291

2 territory under the rule of a count **1H6** V.iii.158 [Suffolk to Reignier] *those two counties I will undertake / Your grace shall well and quietly enjoy* [F *countries*]

couple (*v.*) **1** link, join, tie **1H6** IV.vii.20 [Talbot to Servant] *Coupled in bonds of perpetuity, / Two Talbots ... shall 'scape mortality*

2 leash together **TS** Induction.i.16 [Lord to First Huntsman, of his hounds] *couple Clowder with the deep-mouthed brach*

3 pair off, make couples **TNK** III.v.32 [Schoolmaster to all] *Couple then, / And see what's wanting*

4 marry, join [in wedlock] **AY** III.iii.41 [Touchstone to Audrey, of Sir Oliver Martext] *[he] hath promised ... to couple us*

couples, in in pairs, leashed together **WT** II.i.135 [Antigonus to Leontes, of Hermione's innocence] *I'll go in couples with her*

couplement (*n.*) couple, pair **Sonn** 21.5 *And every fair with his fair doth rehearse, / Making a couplement of proud compare / With Sun and Moon*; **LL** V.ii.529

couplet (*n.*) **1** couple, brace **TN** III.iv.369 [Sir Toby to Sir Andrew and Fabian] *We'll whisper o'er a couplet or two of most sage saws*

2 two chicks, pair of young **Ham** V.i.283 [Gertrude to all] *the female dove / When that her golden couplets are disclosed* [Q2; F *Cuplet*]

courage (*n.*) **1** spirit, disposition, nature **3H6** II.ii.57 [Queen to King] *this soft courage makes your followers faint*; **Cor** III.iii.92; **1H6** IV.i.35, V.v.70

2 young man of bravado, man of spirit **Ham** I.iii.65 [Polonius to Laertes] *But do not dull thy palm with entertainment / Of each new-hatched, unfledged courage* [Q1,Q2; F *Comrade*]; **Cym** II.iv.24

3 lust, sexual desire **Venus** 276 [of Adonis' horse] *His eye, which scornfully glisters like fire, / Shows his hot courage and his high desire* [also: sense 1]

4 intention, purpose, inclination **Tim** III.iii.25 [Sempronius to Servant, of Timon] *I'd such a courage to do him good*

courb (*v.*) ☞ curb (*v.*) 2

course (*n.*) **1** course of action, way of proceeding **RJ** V.iii.27 [Romeo to Balthasar] *do not interrupt me in my course* ☞ FEW, p.xxi

2 habit, custom, practise, normal procedure **H5** I.i.24 [Canterbury to Ely, of King Henry and his love of the Church] *The courses of his youth promised it not*; **Ham** III.iii.83; **H5** I.i.54; **Oth** IV.i.281; **TC** I.iii.9, 87; **Tim** III.iii.41

3 bout, engagement, encounter **Cor** I.v.16 [Lartius to Martius] *Thy exercise hath been too violent / For a second course of fight*; **Oth** IV.ii.92

4 gist, scope, tenor **CE** II.ii.170 [Antipholus of Syracuse to Dromio of Syracuse] *What is the course and drift of your compact?*

5 sail attached to the lower yards of a sailing ship **TNK** III.iv.10 [Gaoler's Daughter alone, of a ship] *Up with a course or two*; **Tem** I.i.35, 48 ☞ SHIPS, p.397

6 flowing stream, tributary, watercourse **Per** IV.iii.28 [Cleon to Dionyza] *he did not flow / From honourable courses* [i.e. origins]

7 [in bear-baiting] attack by a set of dogs **KL** III.vii.53 [Gloucester to Regan and Cornwall] *I am tied to the stake, and I must stand the course*; **Mac** V.vi.12

8 Roman festive chase [held to mark Lupercalia] **JC** I.ii.1 [stage direction] *Enter Caesar; Antony, stripped for the course*; **JC** I.ii.4, 25 ☞ DAYS AND DATES, p.630

course, in as a matter of course **MM** III.i.249 [disguised Duke to Isabella, of how she should behave with Angelo] *This being granted in course*

course (*v.*) **1** chase, hunt, pursue **Mac** I.vi.21 [King to Lady Macbeth, of Macbeth] *We coursed him at the heels and had a purpose / To be his purveyor*; **AC** III.xiii.11; **AY** II.i.39; **KL** IV.iv.55; **LL** IV.iii.2

2 hunt hares [or other game] with hounds by sight **TS** Induction.ii.46 [First Servingman to Sly] *Say thou wilt course, thy greyhounds are as swift / As breathed stags*

course over (*v.*) run an eye over, check out, go through **MW** I.iii.60 [Falstaff to Nym and Pistol, of Mistress Page] *she did so course o'er my exteriors*

courser (*n.*) swift horse, sprinter, charger **Per** II.i.159 [Pericles to Fishermen] *I will mount myself / Upon a courser*; **AC** I.ii.194; **2H4** IV.i.117; **H5** III.vii.42; **Tim** I.ii.211; **Venus** 31

coursing (*adj.*) [hare-coursing] chasing, pursuing **H5** I.ii.143 [King Henry to Canterbury, of the Scots] *We do not mean the coursing snatchers only*

court (*n.*) **1** assembly, court occasion **Cym** III.v.50 [Queen to Cymbeline, of not reporting Innogen's reasons] *our great court / Made me to blame in memory*

2 care, custody, minding **Oth** II.iii.210 [Othello to all] *To manage private and domestic quarrel / In night, and on the court and guard of safety*

court (*v.*) pay court, play the suitor [to] **Tit** II.i.91 [Demetrius to Aaron] *Then why should he despair that knows to court it* [i.e. knows how to court]

court-cupboard *(n.)* sideboard, cabinet **RJ** I.v.7 [First Serving-man to Second Servingman] *remove the court-cupboard*

courtesan, courtezan *(n.)* prostitute, strumpet **1H6** III.ii.45 [Burgundy to Pucelle] *Scoff on, vile fiend and shameless courtesan!*; **CE** IV.iii.45; **Cym** III.iv.125; **KL** III.ii.79

courtesy, cur'sy, curtsy *(n.)* **1** courteous service, polite behaviour, good manners **MV** III.i.45 [Shylock to Salerio, of Antonio] *He was wont to lend money for a Christian courtesy* [Q; F *curtsie*]; **AW** III.ii.97; **LL** V.ii.864; **MND** IV.i.20; **MV** V.i.217; **Tim** I.i.254

2 curtsy, bow, gesture of respect **Tim** I.ii.240 [Apemantus to Timon] *Thus honest fools lay out their wealth on curtsies*; **TS** Induction.i.112 [Lord to Servant, of Page behaving as a woman to Sly] *With soft low tongue and lowly courtesy*; **AY** V.iv.215; **JC** III.i.36; **LL** I.ii.61; **RJ** I.iv.72; **TC** II.iii.104

3 salutation, first greeting, expression of courtesy **TN** I.v.200 [Olivia to Viola as Cesario] *Sure, you have some hideous matter to deliver, when the courtesy of it is so fearful*; **AW** III.v.91

4 usage, custom, convention **AY** I.i.43 [Orlando to Oliver] *The courtesy of nations allows you my better*

court-hand *(n.)* legal style of handwriting **2H6** IV.ii.87 [Dick to Cade, of the Clerk] *he can … write court-hand*

court holy-water gracious but empty promises, courtly flattery **KL** III.ii.10 [Fool to Lear] *court holy-water in a dry house is better than this rain-water out o'door*

courtier *(n.)* courter, wooer, pursuer **AC** II.vi.17 [Pompey to Caesar, Antony and Lepidus, of Brutus and his associates] *courtiers of beauteous freedom*

courtlike *(adj.)* courtly, elegant, well-mannered **MW** II.ii.221 [Ford as Brook to Falstaff] *you are a gentleman … generally allowed for your many warlike, courtlike, and learned preparations*

courtly *(adj.)* belonging to the court, connected with the court **E3** IV.iv.122 [Prince Edward to Third Herald, of his words to Philip] *So tell the courtly wanton*; **AW** III.iv.14; **2H6** I.i.27

court of guard *(n.)* guard-house, guard-room **AC** IV.ix.31 [Sentry to all, of Enobarbus' body] *Let us bear him / To th'court of guard*; **AC** IV.ix.2; **1H6** II.i.4; **Oth** II.i.211

courtship *(n.)* court life, courtliness; also: wooing, courting **2H6** I.iii.52 [Queen to Suffolk] *I thought King Henry had resembled thee / In courage, courtship, and proportion*; **AY** III.ii.333; **LL** V.ii.363; **RJ** III.iii.34

cousin *(n.)* any relative beyond the immediate family; often a term of affection to a socially equal friend ☞ **COUSIN**, p.106; **FAMILY**, p.168

cousin-german *(n.)* first cousin **TC** IV.v.121 [Hector to Ajax] *Thou art … / A cousin-german to great Priam's seed* ☞ **cozen-german** *(n.)*

covenant *(n.)* contract, legal agreement, compact **Cym** I.v.140 [Posthumus to Iachimo] *let there be covenants drawn between's*; **Cym** I.v.162, II.iv.50; **Ham** I.i.93; **1H6** V.iv.114, V.v.88; **TS** II.i.127

covent *(n.)* convent, community **H8** IV.ii.19 [Griffith to Katherine, of the abbot of Leicester and Wolsey] *the reverend abbot, / With all his covent, honourably received him*; **MM** IV.iii.127

cover *(v.)* **1** lay the table **2H4** II.iv.10 [Francis to Drawer, of the apple-johns] *cover, and set them down*; **AY** II.v.28; **MV** III.v.49

2 put on one's hat [after it has been removed to show respect] **AY** III.iii.70 [Touchstone to Jaques] *pray be covered*; **AY** V.i.16; **MV** II.ix.44; **R2** III.ii.171

covered *(adj.)* with a cover in place [to show it is not in use] **AY** III.iv.23 [Celia to Rosalind, of Orlando] *I do think him as concave as a covered goblet*

covert *(n.)* shelter, hiding-place, concealed spot **RJ** I.i.125 [Benvolio to Lady Montague, of Romeo] *he was ware of me / And stole into the covert of the wood*; **WT** IV.iv.646

covert *(adj.)* **1** secret, hidden, concealed **JC** IV.i.46 [Antony to Octavius] *How covert matters may be best disclosed*; **MM** V.i.10

2 secretive, sly, deceitful **R3** III.v.33 [Buckingham to Richard, of Hastings] *he was the covert'st sheltered traitor*

covertly *(adv.)* secretly, stealthily, surreptitiously **MA** II.ii.8 [Borachio to Don John, of how to cross Claudio's marriage] *so covertly that no dishonesty shall appear in me*

coverture *(n.)* **1** protective darkness, cover, concealing shade **3H6** IV.ii.13 [Warwick to George, of Edward] *in night's coverture … / We may surprise and take him*

2 shelter, canopied bower, covered retreat **MA** III.i.30 [Ursula to Hero, of Beatrice] *who even now / Is couched in the woodbine coverture*

3 covering, garment **Cor** I.ix.46 [Martius to all, of the flatterer] *let him be made / A coverture for th'wars* [i.e. let a garment be made for him] [F *Ouerture*; disputed reading] ☞ **ovator** *(n.)*, **overture** *(n.)* 2

coward *(adj.)* cowardly **Tim** V.iv.1 [Alcibiades to Trumpeter] *Sound to this coward and lascivious town / Our terrible approach*; **AY** III.v.13; **Per** IV.iii.25; **Sonn** 74.11

coward *(v.)* make cowardly, make fearful **H5** II.ii.75 [King Henry to Cambridge, Scroop, and Grey] *what read you there / That have so cowarded and chased your blood / Out of appearance?*

cowardship *(n.)* cowardice, fearfulness, timidity **TN** III.iv.379 [Sir Toby to Sir Andrew, of Viola as Cesario] *for his cowardship, ask Fabian*

cower *(v.)* bend, crouch, squat **Per** IV.ii.100 [Boult to Bawd] *do you know the French knight, that cowers i'the hams?*

cowish *(adj.)* cowardly, irresolute, timorous **KL** IV.ii.12 [Gonerill to Edmund, of Albany] *It is the cowish terror of his spirit*

cowl-staff *(n.)* thick shoulder-pole used for carrying a heavy container **MW** III.iii.139 [Mistress Ford to John and Robert] *Where's the cowl-staff?*

cox *(n.)* ☞ **SWEARING**, p.435

coxcomb *(n.)* **1** head **TN** V.i.174 [Sir Andrew to Olivia, of Sebastian] *he's given Sir Toby a bloody coxcomb too*; **H5** V.i.40, 52; **KL** II.iv.119; **MW** III.i.81

2 fool's head, fool, simpleton **LL** IV.iii.82 [Browne to himself, of Dumaine] *O most profane coxcomb*; **AW** III.vi.107; **Cor** IV.vi.136; **H5** IV.i.77; **Oth** V.ii.231; **TN** V.i.203

3 fool's cap [with a crest like a cock's crest] **KL** I.iv.95, 97 [Fool to Kent] *Here's my coxcomb … take my coxcomb*; **MW** V.v.137 ☞ **CLOTHING**, p.79

coy *(adj.)* **1** gentle, considerate, solicitous **Luc** 669 [Tarquin to Lucrece] *Yield to my love: if not, enforced hate / Instead of love's coy touch shall rudely tear thee*; **Venus** 112

2 unresponsive, distant, standoffish, disdainful **TNK** V.ii.61 [Gaoler's Daughter to Gaoler, of Palamon's horse] *he is like his master, coy and scornful*; **MA** III.i.35; **TG** I.i.30, III.i.82; **TS** II.i.237; **Venus** 96

coy *(v.)* **1** caress, stroke, pet **MND** IV.i.2 [Titania to Bottom] *sit thee down … / While I thy amiable cheeks do coy*

2 show reluctance, be loath **Cor** V.i.6 [Menenius to Cominius, of Coriolanus] *if he coyed / To hear Cominius speak*

coying *(n.)* ☞ **cunning** *(n.)* 3

coystrill *(n.)* ☞ **coistrel** *(n.)*

coz *(n.)* [abbreviation of] cousin **AY** I.ii.1 [Celia to Rosalind] *sweet my coz, be merry* ☞ **COUSIN**, p.106

cozen *(v.)* cheat, dupe, trick, deceive **R3** IV.iv.223 [Queen Elizabeth to King Richard, of the Princes] *Cousins … by their uncle cozened / Of comfort*; **KL** V.iii.152; **MW** IV.v.75; **Tit** V.iii.100; **TS** V.i.35; **WT** IV.iv.250

cozenage *(n.)* cheating, trickery, deception **CE** I.ii.97 [Antipholus of Syracuse alone, of Ephesus] *They say this town is full of cozenage*; **Ham** V.ii.67; **MW** IV.v.59

cozened *(adj.)* deceived, deluded, tricked **AW** IV.iv.23 [Helena to Widow] *When saucy trusting of the cozened thoughts / Defiles the pitchy night*

cozener (*n.*) cheat, deceiver, fraud **WT** IV.iv.252 [Autolycus to Clown] *there are cozeners abroad;* **1H4** I.iii.251; **KL** IV.vi.164; **MW** IV.v.61; **TNK** III.i.44

cozen-german (*n.*) German confidence trickster; or: first cousin **MW** IV.v.71 [Evans to Host] *there is three cozen-germans* [F *Cozen-Iermans*; Q *cosen-garmombles*] ☞ **cousin-german** (*n.*)

cozening (*adj.*) cheating, deceiving, fraudulent **Oth** IV.ii.131 [Emilia to Iago] *I will be hanged if … / Some cogging, cozening slave, to get some office, / Have not devised this slander;* **MW** IV.ii.161; **R2** II.ii.69

cozier (*n.*) cobbler **TN** II.iii.89 [Malvolio to Sir Toby, Sir Andrew, and Feste] *ye squeak out your coziers' catches*

crab (*n.*) crab-apple, sour apple **MND** II.i.48 [Puck to Fairy] *sometime lurk I in a gossip's bowl / In very likeness of a roasted crab;* **KL** I.v.15; **LL** IV.ii.6, V.ii.914; **Tem** II.ii.164; **TS** II.i.227

crabbed (*adj.*) **1** frustrating, disagreeable, unpleasant **WT** I.ii.102 [Leontes to Hermione, of the time it took to obtain her love] *Three crabbed months had soured themselves to death*
2 irritable, churlish, bad-tempered **Tem** III.i.8 [Ferdinand alone, of Miranda] *she is / Ten times more gentle than her father's crabbed;* **PassP** XII.1
3 harsh, unpalatable, bitter **MM** III.ii.94 [Lucio to disguised Duke, of being severe to lechers] *Something too crabbed that way, friar*

crab-tree (*n./adj.*) crab-apple tree **Cor** II.i.181 [Menenius to Coriolanus] *We have some old crab-trees here at home;* **H8** V.iv.7

crack (*n.*) **1** flaw, defect, deficiency **WT** I.ii.322 [Camillo to Leontes, of Hermione] *I cannot / Believe this crack to be in my dread mistress* **LL** V.ii.415; **Oth** II.iii.315
2 broken voice quality **Cym** IV.ii.236 [Arviragus to Guiderius] *our voices / Have got the mannish crack*
3 young rascal, little rogue **2H4** III.ii.30 [Shallow to Silence, of Falstaff] *when 'a was a crack, not thus high;* **Cor** I.iii.69
4 cannon-shot, explosive charge **Mac** I.ii.37 [Captain to King, of Macbeth and Banquo] *they were / As cannons overcharged with double cracks*

crack (*v.*) **1** sprain, tear, rupture **WT** II.i.44 [Leontes to Lord, of someone who has seen something unpleasant in a drink] *he cracks his gorge, his sides, / With violent hefts;* **Tem** III.i.26
2 split asunder, snap **KL** III.ii.1 [Lear, as if to the elements] *Blow, winds, and crack your cheeks!;* **H8** III.ii.193
3 collapse, break down, fall to pieces **Tem** V.i.2 [Prospero to Ariel] *My charms crack not*
4 drink, empty, knock back **2H4** V.iii.61 [Shallow to Bardolph and Davy] *you'll crack a quart together*
5 boast, trumpet, crow **LL** IV.iii.266 [King to Berowne] *Ethiops of their sweet complexion crack;* **Cym** V.v.177
6 clip [of gold illegally taken from a coin] **Ham** II.ii.427 [Hamlet to one of the players] *your voice, like a piece of uncurrent gold, be not cracked within the ring* [also: break]

crack the wind over-use, over-exert **Ham** I.iii.108 [Polonius to Ophelia] *not to crack the wind of the poor phrase* [i.e. make it get out of breath, an image from making an animal go too fast]

COUSIN

The kinship term, *cousin* - often familiarly abbreviated as *coz* or *cuz* - is very much broader in its Shakespearian use than we find today. In modern English, it is primarily used for the relationship between the children of brothers and sisters (*first cousins*), with some extension permitted, such as for the children of first cousins (*second cousins*, or *cousins once removed*) and their children. But in Shakespeare we find it used for virtually any relative beyond the immediate family, both for blood relatives and relatives through marriage, and often as a term of affection between socially equal people who are not relatives at all, such as monarchs of different countries.

Example	Speaker and addressee	Text	Relationship
AY I.iii.40	Duke Frederick to Rosalind	*You, cousin*	Rosalind is his niece
R2 I.ii.46	Duchess of Gloucester to John of Gaunt	*Our cousin Hereford*	Hereford is her nephew
Ham III.ii.102	Claudius to Hamlet	*How fares our cousin Hamlet?*	Hamlet is his stepson
R3 II.ii.8	Duchess of York to Clarence's children	*My pretty cousins*	The children are her grandchildren
TN I.v.123	Olivia to Feste, of Sir Toby	*seek the crowner, and let him sit o' my coz*	Sir Toby is her uncle
1H4 III.1.49	Mortimer to Hotspur	*Peace, cousin Percy*	Hotspur is his brother-in-law
1H4 III.i.53	Glendower to Hotspur	*I can teach you, cousin, to command the devil*	Hotspur is his son-in-law's sister's husband
1H4 I.i.31	King Henry to Westmoreland	*my gentle cousin*	Westmoreland's wife is Henry's half-sister
RJ III.i.113	Romeo to himself, after marrying Juliet	*Tybalt, that an hour / Hath been my cousin*	Tybalt is Juliet's cousin
1H6 IV.i.114	King to Richard and Somerset	*Good cousins both*	They are kinsmen through different marriages of Henry's great-grandfather
TNK I.i.222	Theseus to Pirithous	*Cousin, I charge you*	They are long-standing comrades

☞ **FAMILY**, p.168

cracked *(adj.)* **1** deteriorated, decayed, flawed **Cym** IV.iv.50 [Belarius to Arviragus and Guiderius, of his life] *No reason I … should reserve / My cracked one to more care* [i.e. damaged by age]
2 broken, crushed, fractured **Cym** V.v.207 [Iachimo to Cymbeline, of Posthumus and Innogen] *he could not / But think her bond of chastity quite cracked;* **1H4** II.iii.96; **KL** I.i.89
3 [of coins] flawed, damaged, blemished **1H4** II.iii.95 [Hotspur to Lady Percy] *We must have bloody noses, and cracked crowns* [pun: sense 2]

cracker *(n.)* boaster, braggart, windbag **KJ** II.i.147 [Austria to all, of the Bastard] *What cracker is this same that deafs our ears*

crack-hemp *(n.)* rogue who deserves to be hanged, gallows-bird **TS** V.i.40 [Vincentio to Biondello] *Come hither, crack-hemp*

cradle *(n.)* **1** place of repose, resting place **Venus** 1185 [Venus to Adonis] *Lo, in this hollow cradle take thy rest;* **MND** III.i.71
2 birthplace, home **Tim** V.iv.40 [First Senator to Alcibiades] *Spare thy Athenian cradle*
3 birth, infancy **Cym** IV.iv.28 [Belarius to Arviragus and Guiderius] *aye hopeless / To have the courtesy your cradle promised*

craft *(n.)* **1** skill, art, ability **R2** I.iv.13 [Aumerle to King Richard, of his heart] *that taught me craft / To counterfeit oppression of such grief*
2 skilful activity, cunning plan **Ham** III.iv.211 [Hamlet to Gertrude] *'tis most sweet / When in one line two crafts directly meet*
3 cunning, deceit, guile **Ham** III.iv.189 [Hamlet to Gertrude] *I essentially am not in madness, / But mad in craft;* **MW** V.v.218; **TC** III.ii.151, IV.iv.102

craft *(v.)* carry out a craft; also: act craftily **Cor** IV.vi.120 [Menenius to Brutus and Sicinius] *You have crafted fair!*

crafty *(adj.)* **1** cunning, devious, wily **Ham** III.i.8 [Guildenstern to Claudius, of Hamlet] *But with a crafty madness keeps aloof;* **KJ** IV.i.53
2 skilfully made, cleverly designed **MA** III.i.22 [Hero to Ursula, of praising Benedick] *Of this matter / Is little Cupid's crafty arrow made*

crafty-sick *(adj.)* pretending sickness **2H4** I.Induction.37 [Rumour] *old Northumberland / Lies crafty-sick*

crafty-swearing *(adj.)* making devious vows **TC** V.iv.9 [Thersites alone, of Nestor and Ulysses] *the policy of those crafty-swearing rascals … is not proved worth a blackberry*

crammed *(adj.)* overfed, stuffed to excess **TC** II.ii.49 [Troilus to Helenus] *Manhood and honour / Should have hare-hearts, would they but fat their thoughts / With this crammed reason*

cramp *(n.)* rheumatic, arthritic **TNK** V.i.110 [Palamon praying to Venus, of an old man] *the aged cramp / Had screwed his square foot round*

cram up *(v.)* force into a small space, stuff in **TC** IV.iv.42 [Troilus to Cressida] *Injurious Time … / Crams his rich thievery up*

crank *(n.)* **1** winding passage, meandering duct **Cor** I.i.135 [Menenius to Citizens, as the belly addressing the other body parts] *through the cranks and offices of man*
2 winding path, twisting street, sidestreet **TNK** I.ii.28 [Arcite to Palamon] *The cranks and turns of Thebes*

crank *(v.)* wind, twist, zigzag **Venus** 682 [Venus to Adonis, of the hunted hare] *He cranks and crosses with a thousand doubles;* **1H4** III.i.94

crannied *(adj.)* cracked, split, holed **E3** III.i.164 [Mariner to King John] *the gushing moisture [did] break into / The crannied cleftures of the through-shot planks* [QQ cranny]; **MND** V.i.156

crants *(n.)* (singular) garland, wreath, chaplet **Ham** V.i.228 [Priest to Laertes, of Ophelia] *Yet here she is allowed her virgin crants* [Q2; F Rites]

crare *(n.)* small trading boat **Cym** IV.ii.205 [Belarius to Arviragus and Guiderius, of melancholy] *to show what coast thy sluggish crare / Might'st easil'est harbour in* [F care]

crasing, crazing *(n.)* grazing, ricochet, rebound **H5** IV.iii.105 [King Henry to Montjoy] *Mark then abounding valour in our English, / That being dead, like to the bullet's crasing, / Break out into a second course of mischief* [F, Q crasing]

crave *(v.)* **1** beg, entreat, request **1H6** II.iii.76 [Talbot to Countess] *Nor other satisfaction do I crave* ☛ FEW, p.xxi
2 need, demand, require **1H6** II.iii.28 [Messenger to Talbot, of the Countess] *my lady craves / To know the cause of your abrupt departure;* **2H6** III.i.288; **JC** II.i.15; **KL** I.i.127; **Tim** II.ii.233; **TNK** V.iii.64
3 wish to know, solicit **TNK** II.i.145 [Arcite to Palamon] *envy of ill men / Crave our acquaintance* [☛ envy *(n.)* 1, 2 for alternative readings]

craven *(n.)* **1** [cock-fighting] cock that shows no fighting spirit **TS** II.i.225 [Katherina to Petruchio] *you crow too like a craven*
2 coward **1H6** IV.i.15 [Talbot to Falstaff] *I vowed … / To tear the Garter from thy craven's leg;* **H5** IV.vii.130

craven *(adj.)* cowardly, spineless, weak-hearted **E3** IV.v.25 [King John to Philip] *Awake thy craven powers, and tell on;* **Ham** IV.iv.40; **1H6** II.iv.87

craven *(v.)* make cowardly, make timorous **Cym** III.iv.79 [Innogen to Pisanio] *Against self-slaughter / There is a prohibition so divine / That cravens my weak hand*

craver *(n.)* beggar, asker, supplicant **Per** II.i.88 [Second Fisherman to Pericles] *I'll turn craver too*

craze *(v.)* crack, break down, shatter **R3** IV.iv.17 [Duchess of York to Queen Elizabeth] *So many miseries have crazed my voice*

crazed *(adj.)* flawed, unsound, impaired **MND** I.i.92 [Demetrius to Lysander] *yield / Thy crazed title to my certain right*

crazy *(adj.)* frail, infirm, fragile **1H6** III.ii.89 [Talbot to Bedford] *We will bestow you in some better place, / Fitter for sickness and for crazy age*

creak *(v.)* make something creak, squeak **AW** II.i.31 [Bertram to Parolles] *Creaking my shoes on the plain masonry*

cream *(v.)* form a frothy layer on the surface **MV** I.i.89 [Gratiano to Antonio] *There are a sort of men whose visages / Do cream and mantle like a standing pond*

creature *(n.)* **1** man, human **KL** IV.vi.158 [Lear to Gloucester] *Thou hast seen … the creature run from the cur?*
2 created being **Per** III.ii.43 [Second Gentleman to Cerimon] *hundreds call themselves your creatures;* **Sonn** 1.1
3 dependant, servant **Tim** I.i.120 [Old Athenian to Timon, of Lucilius] *this thy creature, / By night frequents my house;* **H8** III.ii.36
4 material comfort, drink, liquor **Oth** II.iii.300 [Iago to Cassio] *good wine is a good familiar creature if it be well used;* **2H4** II.ii.11
5 object, instrument, thing **KJ** IV.i.120 [Arthur to Hubert, of fire and iron] *Creatures of note for mercy-lacking uses*

credence *(n.)* faith, confidence, trust **AW** III.iii.2 [Duke to Bertram] *we … lay our best love and credence / Upon thy promising fortune;* **TC** V.ii.122

credent *(adj.)* **1** trustful, believing, credulous **Ham** I.iii.30 [Laertes to Ophelia, of Hamlet] *Then weigh what loss your honour may sustain / If with too credent ear you list his songs;* **Lover** 279
2 believable, credible, trustworthy **MM** IV.iv.24 [Angelo alone] *my authority bears a credent bulk*
3 probable, likely **WT** I.ii.142 [Leontes to himself, of lustful desire] *'tis very credent / Thou mayst co-join with something*

credit *(n.)* **1** credibility, believing, belief **Oth** II.i.278 [Iago alone, of Desdemona and Cassio] *That she loves him, 'tis apt and of great credit;* **JC** III.i.191; **Per** V.iii.77; **Tem** II.i.62, III.iii.26; **WT** V.ii.60
2 trust, faith, belief **Cym** I.vii.157 [Iachimo as if to Posthumus, of Innogen] *The credit that thy lady hath of thee / Deserves thy trust;* **CE** III.ii.22; **KL** II.i.35; **WT** I.ii.157
3 reputation, name, standing, honour **AY** I.i.119 [Charles to Oliver] *I wrestle for my credit;* **AW** I.i.76; **H8** II.ii.265; **Per** IV.ii.28; **TNK** III.vi.223; **TS** IV.ii.107

4 report, news, story **TN** IV.iii.6 [Sebastian alone, of Antonio] *I found this credit / That he did range the town to seek me out*

credit (*v.*) **1** believe, trust, have faith in **2H6** IV.ii.142 [Stafford to the rebels, of Cade] *And will you credit this base drudge's words*
2 do credit to, grace, give esteem to **TS** IV.i.93 [Curtis to Grumio, of the servants and Katherina] *I call them forth to credit her* [pun: 94]

creditor (*n.*) credit [column in an account book] **Cym** V.iv.169 [First Gaoler to Posthumus, of the hangman's rope] *you have no true debitor and creditor but it* [i.e. death cancels all debts] ➤ debitor (*n.*)

credulous (*adj.*) **1** highly receptive, readily accepting [of] **Tit** V.ii.74 [Tamora to Chiron and Demetrius, of Titus accepting her disguise as Revenge] *being credulous in this mad thought;* **MM** II.iv.130
2 over-ready to believe, naively trusting **AW** II.i.115 [King to Helena] *We ... may not be so credulous of cure*

creek (*n.*) winding pathway, narrow lane **CE** IV.ii.38 [Dromio of Syracuse to Adriana, of the officer] *one that countermands / The passages of alleys, creeks*

creep (*v.*) **1** steal into, worm one's way into **Cym** I.v.22 [Iachimo to all, of Posthumus] *how creeps acquaintance?* [i.e. how have you managed to get to know each other?]
2 shuffle along, move cringingly **AC** III.iii.18 [Messenger to Cleopatra, of Octavia] *She creeps*

crescent (*n.*) waxing moon, growing person **MND** V.i.235 [Theseus to Demetrius, of Starveling as Moonshine] *He is no crescent*

crescent (*adj.*) growing, developing, increasing **AC** II.i.10 [Pompey to Menecrates] *My powers are crescent;* **Cym** I.v.2; **Ham** I.iii.11

crescive (*adj.*) growing, increasing, developing **H5** I.i.66 [Ely to Canterbury, of Prince Hal's growth] *Unseen, yet crescive in his faculty*

cresset (*n.*) beacon, blazing torch, fire-basket **1H4** III.i.13 [Glendower to Hotspur] *At my nativity / The front of heaven was full of fiery shapes, / Of burning cressets*

crest (*n.*) **1** [originally the plume of feathers on a] helmet, head-piece **1H6** V.iii.25 [Pucelle alone] *Now the time is come / That France must vail her lofty-plumed crest;* **1H4** V.iv.71; **Mac** V.vi.50; **TC** I.iii.380; **Tit** I.i.367; **Venus** 104
2 [on an animal head or neck] ridge of feathers, ridge of hairs; hackles **Venus** 272 [of Adonis' horse] *his braided hanging mane / Upon his compassed crest now stand on end;* **Cor** IV.v.218; **1H4** I.i.98; **JC** IV.ii.26; **KJ** IV.iii.149
3 heraldic device placed above the shield and helmet in a coat-of-arms **MND** III.ii.214 [Helena to Hermia, of their childhood friendship] *like coats in heraldry ... crowned with one crest;* **KJ** IV.iii.46; **MW** V.v.63; **Sonn** 107.14; **TS** II.i.223

crest-fallen (*adj.*) humbled, abashed, shamed **R2** I.i.188 [Boling-broke to King Richard] *Shall I seem crest-fallen in my father's sight?;* **2H6** IV.i.59

crestless (*adj.*) lacking a heraldic crest **1H6** II.iv.85 [Warwick to Somerset, of Suffolk] *Spring crestless yeomen from so deep a root?*

crest-wounding (*adj.*) harming family honour **Luc** 828 [Lucrece to herself] *O unfelt sore, crest-wounding private scar!*

crew (*n.*) **1** band, company, body of men **Luc** 1731 [of Lucrece's suicide] *astonished with this deadly deed, / Stood Collatine and all his lordly crew;* **R3** I.iv.15; **TG** IV.i.74
2 gang, mob, ring **R2** V.iii.137 [King Henry to all, of the conspirators] *all the rest of that consorted crew*

crewel (*adj.*) made of a thin coloured worsted yarn **KL** II.iv.7 [Fool to Lear, of Kent] *He wears crewel garters* [Q; F *cruell*]

crib (*n.*) **1** hovel, hut, shack **2H4** III.i.9 [King Henry IV alone] *Why rather, sleep, liest thou in smoky cribs*

2 manger, food-box **Ham** V.ii.87 [Hamlet to Horatio, of Osrick] *his crib shall stand at the king's mess*

crib (*v.*) shut up [as in a tiny hovel], confine within a small space **Mac** III.iv.23 [Macbeth to First Murderer] *now I am cabined, cribbed, confined*

crier (*n.*) officer who makes announcements in a court of law **KJ** II.i.134 [Bastard to all, of Austria] *Hear the crier!*

crime (*n.*) **1** sin, offence, wrong-doing **TNK** I.i.3 [Arcite to Palamon] *yet unhardened in / The crimes of nature, let us leave the city;* **CE** II.ii.150; **Ham** II.i.43, III.iii.81; **KL** I.iii.5; **TNK** V.iv.10
2 accusation, charge, denunciation **E3** III.iii.170 [King Edward to the English peers] *let us ... clear us of that scandalous crime;* **Sonn** 120.8

crimeful (*adj.*) laden with crime, criminal, lawless **Luc** 970 [Lucrece as if to time, of Tarquin] *Devise extremes beyond extremity, / To make him curse this cursed crimeful night;* **Ham** IV.vii.7

cringe (*v.*) distort, contort, twist **AC** III.xiii.100 [Antony to servants, of Thidias] *Whip him ... / Till like a boy you see him cringe his face*

cripple (*v.*) ➤ grapple (*v.*)

crisp (*adj.*) **1** shining, bright, clear **Tim** IV.iii.184 [Timon alone, of earth] *With all th'abhorred births below crisp heaven*
2 rippling, undulating, curling with waves **Tem** IV.i.130 [Iris to the nymphs] *Leave your crisp channels;* **1H4** I.iii.105

crisped (*adj.*) stiffly curled **MV** III.ii.92 [Bassanio to himself] *those crisped snaky golden locks, / Which make such wanton gambols with the wind*

critic (*adj.*) censorious, carping, fault-finding **LL** IV.iii.168 [Berowne to all] *To see ... critic Timon laugh at idle toys!*

critical (*adj.*) censorious, judgemental, faultfinding **Oth** II.i.118 [Iago to Desdemona] *I am nothing if not critical;* **MND** V.i.54

croak (*v.*) rumble, growl **KL** III.vi.31 [Edgar as Poor Tom, as if to the devil in his stomach] *Croak not*

crone (*n.*) old hag, withered old woman **WT** II.iii.76 [Leontes to Antigonus, of the baby and Paulina] *Give't to thy crone* [or: old ewe]

crook (*v.*) bend **Ham** III.ii.71 [Hamlet to Horatio] *crook the pregnant hinges of the knee*

crook-back (*n.*) hunchback **3H6** V.v.30 [Prince to all, of Richard] *take away this scolding crook-back rather*

crook-back (*adj.*) hunchbacked **3H6** I.iv.75 [Queen to York, of Richard] *where's that valiant crook-back prodigy*

crooked (*adj.*) **1** malignant, perverse, contrary, devious **2H4** IV.v.184 [King Henry IV to Prince Henry] *God knows ... / By what by-paths and indirect crooked ways / I met this crown;* **H8** V.iii.44; **KJ** III.i.46; **Sonn** 60.7; **TG** IV.i.21; **Venus** 134
2 rounded, curved **H5** Prologue.15 [Chorus] *a crooked figure may / Attest in little place a million* [i.e. an end-placed zero can turn a small figure into a large one]; **Luc** 508; **Sonn** 100.14
3 curling, twisting **Cor** II.i.53 [Menenius to Sicinius and Brutus] *if the drink you give me touch my palate adversely, I make a crooked face at it;* **Cym** V.v.478; **Lover** 85
4 false, wrongful, illegal **H5** I.ii.94 [Canterbury to King Henry, of the French kings] *they ... rather choose to hide them in a net / Than amply to imbare their crooked titles*

crooked-pated (*adj.*) with a twisted head, with a deformed skull **AY** III.ii.78 [Touchstone to Corin] *a crooked-pated, old, cuckoldly ram*

crop (*v.*) **1** cut down, remove, hack off **1H6** II.iv.41 [Vernon to all] *he upon whose side / The fewest roses are cropped from the tree / Shall yield the other;* **E3** III.iii.40; **1H4** V.iv.72; **1H6** I.i.80; **Per** I.i.142; **R3** I.ii.247
2 break off, cut through **Venus** 1175 [of Venus, and Adonis' flower] *She crops the stalk*
3 bear a crop, have a child **AC** II.ii.233 [Agrippa to Enobarbus, of Caesar and Cleopatra] *He ploughed her, and she cropped*

cross (n.) **1** trial, affliction, trouble R3 III.i.4 [Prince Edward to Richard, of the journey] *our crosses on the way / Have made it tedious, wearisome, and heavy;* AY II.iv.10, V.iv.128; KL V.iii.276; R2 II.ii.79; Sonn 34.12, 42.12

2 hindrance, obstacle, stumbling block MA II.ii.4 [Don John to Borachio] *Any bar, any cross, any impediment will be medicinable to me;* Luc 912; TNK III.vi.127

3 coin [referring to the cross stamped on some types of coin] 2H4 I.ii.228 [Lord Chief Justice to Falstaff, rejecting his request for a loan] *You are too impatient to bear crosses* [also: sense 1]; AY II.iv.10; LL I.ii.33

4 crossness; also: sign of the cross CE II.i.79 [Dromio of Ephesus to Adriana, of Antipholus of Syracuse, reacting to her threat to break his pate 'across'] *he will bless that cross with other beating*

cross (adj.) **1** perverse, contrarious, contradictory TS II.i.243 [Petruchio to Katherina] *Nor hast thou pleasure to be cross in talk;* H8 III.ii.214; R3 III.i.126; RJ IV.i.5; Tit II.iii.53

2 forked, zigzag JC I.iii.50 [Cassius to Casca] *the cross blue lightning seemed to open / The breast of heaven;* KL IV.vii.35

3 angry, ill-tempered, outraged E3 III.iii.97 [Prince Edward to King John] *Look not for cross invectives at our hands*

cross (v.) **1** prevent, thwart, forestall LL V.ii.138 [Princess to Katharine, of the King's party] *The effect of my intent is to cross theirs;* Cym III.v.163; MV III.i.19; MW V.v.36; Sonn 90.2; TG II.vi.40

2 contradict, challenge, go against H8 III.ii.234 [Suffolk to Wolsey, of King Henry's words] *Who dare cross 'em;* JC V.i.19; MM IV.ii.164; Per IV.iii.16; TNK IV.i.119; TS IV.v.10

3 afflict, plague, go against TG IV.i.12 [Valentine to Outlaws] *A man I am crossed with adversity;* 1H6 I.iv.72; Luc 968; MA I.iii.62; MM II.ii.159; TS II.i.28

4 cross the path of, intercept, encounter Ham I.i.127 [Horatio to Barnardo and Marcellus, on seeing the Ghost] *I'll cross it, though it blast me;* 1H4 V.iii.2; TNK IV.i.40

5 interrupt, cut in on TS IV.i.64 [Grumio to Curtis] *hadst thou not crossed me, thou shouldst have heard*

6 [of a debt] cancel by crossing through, strike out Tim I.ii.159 [Flavius to himself, of Timon] *When all's spent, he'd be crossed then, an he could* [pun: 157] [i.e. he'd like to have his debts cancelled]

cross (adv.) across, in the middle MA V.i.136 [Claudio to Don Pedro, of Benedick] *give him another staff; this last was broke cross* [i.e. by inept jousting]

cross-gartered (adj.) with garters crossed along the legs TN II.v.149 [Malvolio reading the letter] *Remember who … wished to see thee ever cross-gartered;* TN III.iv.50

cross-gartering (n.) wearing garters crossed along the legs TN III.iv.20 [Malvolio to Olivia] *this does make some obstruction in the blood, this cross-gartering*

crossing (n.) thwarting, opposing, challenging, contradiction 1H4 III.i.33 [Glendower to Hotspur] *of many men / I do not bear these crossings;* Cor III.ii.21

crossly (adv.) adversely, unfavourably, disadvantageously R2 II.iv.24 [Salisbury alone, of King Richard] *crossly to thy good all fortune goes*

cross-row (n.) alphabet R3 I.i.55 [Clarence to Richard, of King Edward] *He … from the cross-row plucks the letter G*

crossway (n.) cross-road MND III.ii.383 [Puck to Oberon] *Damned spirits all / That in crossways and floods have burial*

crotchet (n.) strange notion, perverse idea, whimsical fancy MW II.i.144 [Mistress Ford to Ford] *thou hast some crotchets in thy head now;* MA I.iii.54; MM III.ii.121; RJ IV.v.117

crouch (v.) **1** bend low, bow down, cringe JC IV.i.45 [Brutus to Cassius] *Must I stand and crouch / Under your testy humour?*

2 duck down, lie hidden Tem V.i.90 [Ariel singing] *In a cowslip's bell I lie; / There I crouch when owls do cry;* KJ V.ii.140

crouching (adj.) submissive, cringing, docile Tim V.iv.9 [Alcibiades to Senators] *Now the time is flush, / When crouching marrow in the bearer strong / Cries of itself 'No more'*

crow (n.) **1** crowbar CE III.i.84 [Antipholus of Ephesus to Dromio of Ephesus] *Fetch me an iron crow;* CE III.i.80; RJ V.ii.21, iii.22

2 cockerel KJ V.ii.144 [Bastard to Lewis the Dauphin, of the French] *to thrill and shake / Even at the crying of your nation's crow*

crow, pluck a settle the quarrel, clear up the matter CE III.i.83 [Dromio of Ephesus to Antipholus of Ephesus] *we'll pluck a crow together*

crowflower (n.) ✷ PLANTS, p.330

crowkeeper, crow-keeper (n.) scarecrow, farmer's boy, person who keeps crows away KL IV.vi.87 [Lear to all] *That fellow handles his bow like a crow-keeper;* RJ I.iv.6

crown (n.) **1** type of coin [usually bearing the imprint of a monarch's crown] H5 IV.i.219 [disguised King Henry to Bates] *the French may lay twenty French crowns to one they will beat us* [also: sense 2]; MM I.ii.51 [Lucio to Gentlemen, of the number of their sexual diseases] *A French crown more* [with bawdy pun: syphilis as a French disease]; H5 IV.i.37; LL III.i.139; TC IV.iv.104 ✷ MONEY, p.286

2 head R3 III.ii.43 [Hastings to Catesby] *I'll have this crown of mine cut from my shoulders;* MND I.ii.90 [Quince to Bottom] *Some of your French crowns have no hair at all* [also: French crown = baldness from venereal disease]; 1H4 II.iii.96; Mac I.v.40, III.iv.80; Tem I.ii.233

3 king, monarch, ruler AC V.ii.91 [Cleopatra to Dolabella, of Antony] *In his livery / Walked crowns and crownets*

crown of the sun French gold crown Per IV.ii.107 [Bawd to Boult, of Veroles] *I know he will come … to scatter his crowns of the sun* [also: sexual disease]

crown (v.) **1** endow with honour, invest with special dignity Tim II.ii.186 [Timon to Flavius] *in some sort these wants of mine are crowned, / That I account them blessings*

2 enthrone, give absolute power to 1H4 III.i.210 [Glendower to Mortimer, translating Lady Mortimer] *she will … on your eyelids crown the god of sleep*

crown up (v.) add regal status to, dignify TC III.ii.181 [Troilus to Cressida] *'As true as Troilus' shall crown up the verse, / And sanctify the numbers*

crowner (n.) coroner TN I.v.129 [Olivia to Feste] *Go thou and seek the crowner;* Ham V.i.4, 22

crownet (n.) **1** coronet, crown TC Prologue.6 [Prologue] *Sixty and nine that wore / Their crownets regal from th'Athenian bay / Put forth toward Phrygia;* AC IV.xii.27

2 prince, noble AC V.ii.91 [Cleopatra to Dolabella, of Antony] *In his livery / Walked crowns and crownets*

crownet (adj.) wreathed, entwined, garlanded Ham IV.vii.172 [Gertrude to Claudius and Laertes, of Ophelia] *There on the pendent boughs her crownet weeds / Clambering to hang* [reading of Q2 *cronet;* F *Coronet*]

crudy (adj.) curdy, thick, congealed 2H4 IV.iii.97 [Falstaff alone, of the effect of sherry on the brain] *It … dries me there all the foolish and dull and crudy vapours which environ it*

cruel (n.) [unclear meaning] form of cruelty, cruel creature KL III.vii.64 [Gloucester to Regan, as if speaking to the porter at the gate] *Good porter, turn the key, / All cruels else subscribe*

cruel (adv.) terribly, extremely, exceedingly TNK Epilogue.3 [Speaker to audience] *I am cruel fearful*

crupper (n.) leather saddle-strap on a horse CE I.ii.56 [Dromio of Ephesus to Antipholus of Syracuse] *sixpence … / To pay the saddler for my mistress' crupper;* TS III.ii.59, IV.i.72

crusado, cruzado (n.) Portuguese gold coin [bearing the figure of a cross] Oth III.iv.26 [Desdemona to Emilia, of her handkerchief] *I had rather have lost my purse / Full of crusadoes* ✷ MONEY, p.286

crush (v.) **1** drink down, quaff, knock back RJ I.ii.79 [Servant to Romeo] *I pray come and crush a cup of wine*

2 force the sense of, strain a meaning from **TN** II.v.136 [Malvolio to himself, of the initials in the letter] *to crush this a little, it would bow to me*

crushed (*adj.*) broken-down, subdued, forced out of shape **H5** I.ii.175 [Exeter to all, of England staying at home] *that is but a crushed necessity* [i.e. the necessity does not follow at all]

crust over (*v.*) encrust with sores, cover with scabs **Tim** III.vi.99 [Timon to Lords] *Of man and beast the infinite malady / Crust you quite o'er!*

cruzado (*n.*) ☛ crusado (*n.*)

cry (*n.*) **1** company, pack [as of hounds] **Oth** II.iii.354 [Roderigo to Iago] *I do follow here in the chase, not like a hound that hunts, but one that fills up the cry*; **Cor** III.iii.120, IV.i.150; **Ham** III.ii.286; **MND** IV.i.123
2 [of hounds] noise, call, yelp **Tit** II.ii.11 [stage direction] *Here a cry of hounds*; **TNK** II.ii.54; **Venus** 870, 885
3 acclaim, shout of approval **TC** III.iii.184 [Ulysses to Achilles] *The cry went once on thee*
4 rumour, gossip, common report **Oth** IV.i.124 [Iago to Cassio, of Bianca] *the cry goes that you shall marry her*

cry (*v.*) **1** speak loudly, shout out, proclaim **KL** V.i.48 [Edgar to Albany] *let but the herald cry*; **AW** II.i.17; **Ham** II.ii.437; **H8** I.i.27; **R2** III.ii.102; **WT** I.ii.411 ☛ match (*n.*) 5
2 give tongue, cry out **TS** Induction.i.21 [First Huntsman to Lord, of a hound following a scent] *He cried upon it at the merest loss*; **Ham** IV.v.111; **TN** II.v.120
3 protest, rebel, cry out **Tit** V.ii.160 [Titus to Caius and Valentine, of Chiron and Demetrius] *stop their mouths, if they begin to cry*; **Cor** II.iii.203
4 beg, entreat, implore **Oth** I.iii.273 [Duke to Othello] *Th'affair cries haste, / And speed must answer it*; **AY** III.v.61; **1H6** V.v.53; **KL** III.ii.58; **Lover** 42; **R3** V.iii.225 ☛ POLITENESS, p.340
5 offer for sale, advertise **Per** IV.ii.89 [Boult to Bawd, of Marina] *I have cried her almost to the number of her hairs*; **Per** IV.ii.88

cry aim ☛ aim, cry

cry on (*v.*) shout out, call out about **R3** V.iii.232 [Richmond to Lords, of Richard's victims] *Methought their souls ... cried on victory*; **Ham** V.ii.358; **Oth** V.i.48

cry out (*v.*) **1** [hunting] call like a hound **MW** IV.ii.185 [Ford to his companions] *If I cry out thus upon no trail, never trust me when I open again*
2 be in labour **H8** V.i.67 [King Henry to Lovell, of Anne] *What, is she crying out?*

cry up (*v.*) show to be true, proclaim, announce in public [by] **TNK** I.ii.13 [Palamon to Arcite] *Your advice / Is cried up with example*; **H8** I.i.84

crystal (*n.*) (plural) eyes **H5** II.iii.51 [Pistol to Hostess] *Go, clear thy crystals* [i.e. wipe your eyes]; **Venus** 963

crystal (*adj.*) **1** clear, bright, transparent **R2** I.i.41 [Bolingbroke to Mowbray] *the more fair and crystal is the sky, / The uglier seem the clouds that in it fly*; **Cym** V.iv.81; **Venus** 633, 957
2 bright, gleaming, glittering **1H6** I.i.3 [Bedford to all, as if to comets] *Brandish your crystal tresses in the sky*

crystalline (*adj.*) transparent as crystal, translucent **Cym** V.iv.113 [Jupiter to his eagle] *Mount ... to my palace crystalline*

cub-drawn (*adj.*) drained of milk by cubs, ravenous **KL** III.i.12 [Gentleman to disguised Kent, of the stormy night] *wherein the cub-drawn bear would couch*

cubiculo (*n.*) bedroom, bedchamber **TN** III.ii.50 [Sir Toby to Sir Andrew] *We'll call thee at thy cubiculo*

cubit (*n.*) measure of length or distance [from the length of the forearm: c.20 inches / c.51 cm] **Tem** II.i.262 [Antonio to Sebastian, of the distance between Tunis and Naples] *A space whose ev'ry cubit / Seems to cry out*

cuckold (*n.*) [mocking name] man with an unfaithful wife **MW** V.v.109 [Ford to Falstaff] *Now, sir, who's a cuckold now?* ☛ FEW, p.xxi

cuckold (*v.*) [mocking name] dishonour a man by making his wife unfaithful **Oth** I.iii.363 [Iago to Roderigo, of Othello] *If thou canst cuckold him*; **MW** III.v.126

cuckoldly (*adj.*) [term of abuse] with the character of a cuckold **AY** III.ii.78 [Touchstone to Corin] *a crooked-pated, old, cuckoldly ram* [i.e.with horns]

cuckold-mad (*adj.*) mad through being a cuckold **CE** II.i.58 [Dromio of Ephesus to Adriana, of Antipholus of Syracuse] *I mean not cuckold-mad, / But sure he is stark mad*

cuckold-maker (*n.*) seducer of a married woman **H8** V.iv.25 [Man to Porter] *cuckold or cuckold-maker*

cuckoldy (*adj.*) cuckolded **MW** V.v.110 [Ford as if to Brook] *Falstaff's a knave, a cuckoldy knave*; **MW** II.ii.257 ☛ cuckold (*v.*)

cuckoo-bud (*n.*) [unclear meaning] type of flower, perhaps chosen because its name resembles 'cuckold'; or: buttercup **LL** V.ii.885 [Ver singing] *cuckoo-buds of yellow hue* ☛ PLANTS, p.330

cuckoo-flower (*n.*) variety of wild flower growing at the time of year when cuckoos call **KL** IV.iv.4 [Cordelia to Doctor, of Lear] *Crowned with ... cuckoo-flowers* ☛ PLANTS, p.330

cuffs, go to come to blows **Ham** II.ii.354 [Rosencrantz to Hamlet] *the player went to cuffs in the question*

cuish, cuisse (*n.*) ☛ cush (*n.*)

cull (*v.*) select, pick out, choose **LL** V.i.88 [Holofernes to Armado, of 'posterior'] *The word is well culled*; **1H6** V.iii.10; **3H6** III.i.4; **KJ** II.i.40; **RJ** III.iii.7; **Tit** IV.i.44

cull forth (*v.*) select, pick out, choose **KJ** II.i.391 [Bastard to King John and King Philip, of their conflict] *fortune shall cull forth ... her happy minion / To whom in favour she shall give the day*; **TNK** I.i.169

cull out (*v.*) pick out, choose, decide on **JC** I.i.49 [Marullus to the people] *And do you now cull out a holiday?*

culled (*adj.*) chosen, picked, selected **H5** III.Chorus.24 [Chorus] *who ... will not follow / These culled and choice-drawn cavaliers to France?*; **LL** IV.iii.232

cullion (*n.*) wretch, rascal, rogue **2H6** I.iii.38 [Queen to Petitioners] *Away, base cullions!*; **H5** III.ii.21; **TS** IV.ii.20

cullionly (*adv.*) like a cullion [= rogue], rascally, despicable **KL** II.ii.29 [disguised Kent to Oswald] *you whoreson cullionly barber-monger*

cullison (*n.*) badge, emblem [= cognizance, in heraldry] **Ham** III.ii.49 [Hamlet to Players] *My coat wants a cullison* [Q1 only]

culverin (*n.*) type of small cannon **1H4** II.iii.55 [Lady Percy to Hotspur] *thou hast talked of / Of ... culverin* ☛ WEAPONS, p.491

cumber (*v.*) distress, trouble, burden **E3** II.i.299 [Warwick to King Edward, of Edward's grief] *It shall not cumber long your majesty*; **JC** III.i.264; **Tim** III.vi.47

cunger (*n.*) ☛ conger (*n.*)

cunning (*n.*) **1** skill, ability, expertise **Per** III.ii.26 [Cerimon to First Gentleman] *Virtue and cunning were endowments greater / Than nobleness and riches*; **AC** II.iii.35; **Ham** II.ii.439; **2H6** II.i.130; **Tim** IV.iii.210; **TNK** I.i.43
2 knowledge, awareness, discernment **MM** IV.ii.153 [disguised Duke to Provost] *in the boldness of my cunning I will lay myself in hazard*; **Oth** III.iii.49; **Tim** V.iv.28
3 deviousness, deceit, craftiness, artfulness **RJ** II.ii.101 [Juliet to Romeo] *I'll prove more true / Than those that have more cunning to be strange* [also: sense 1] [Q1; F *coying*]; **AW** V.iii.216; **TN** II.ii.22; **TNK** III.vi.120; **TS** II.i.404
4 [magical] knowledge, art, craft **1H6** III.iii.10 [Charles to Pucelle] *We ... of thy cunning had no diffidence*; **1H6** II.i.50
5 ploy, ruse, clever device **KL** II.i.29 [Edmund to Edgar] *In cunning I must draw my sword upon you* [F; Q *crauing*]

cunning (*adj.*) **1** knowledgeable, skilful, clever **MA** V.i.218 [Don Pedro to Borachio, of Dogberry] *This learned Constable is too cunning to be understood;* **2H6** I.ii.75; **Oth** IV.i.90; **R3** III.i.135; **TC** III.i.28; **TS** I.i.184

2 skilfully made, ingenious **R2** I.iii.163 [Mowbray to King Richard, of his own tongue] *like a cunning instrument cased up* **1H4** II.iv.89; **Oth** V.ii.11, V.ii.329

cunningly (*adv.*) **1** skilfully, cleverly, competently **TNK** III.v.92 [Schoolmaster to all, of the Gaoler's Daughter's dancing] *Persuasively and cunningly!*

2 craftily, artfully, deviously **TNK** II.i.245 [Arcite to Palamon] *Why then would you deal so cunningly*

cup (*v.*) supply with drink, make drunk **AC** II.vii.115 [Boy singing, as if to Bacchus] *Cup us till the world go round*

cupboard (*v.*) stow away, keep in, hoard **Cor** I.i.98 [Menenius to Citizens, of the belly] *it did remain / I'th' midst o'th' body, idle and unactive, / Still cupboarding the viand*

cuplet (*n.*) ☞ **couplet** (*n.*) 2

cur (*n.*) dog, mastiff, watch-dog [without a contemptuous sense] **Mac** III.i.92 [Macbeth to Murderers] *hounds and greyhounds, mongrels, spaniels, curs;* **MV** I.iii.115

curate (*n.*) parish priest, parson **TN** IV.ii.2 [Maria to Feste, of Malvolio] *make him believe thou art Sir Topas the curate;* **LL** V.i.107

curb (*n.*) controlling chain or strap passed under a horse's jaw; check, restraint **AY** III.iii.73 [Touchstone to Jaques] *the horse [hath] his curb;* **Cor** I.i.68; **TNK** V.iv.74

curb (*v.*) **1** bow, bend, stoop **Ham** III.iv.156 [Hamlet to Gertrude] *Virtue itself of vice must pardon beg, / Yea, curb and woo for leave to do him good* [F *courb*]

2 restrain, inhibit, hold back **Cym** II.iii.119 [Cloten to Innogen, of lower marriages] *you are curbed from that enlargement, by / The consequence o'th' crown*

curbed (*adj.*) restrained, controlled **AW** II.iv.43 [Parolles to Helena, of Bertram's forced departure] *Whose want and whose delay is strewed with sweets, / Which they distil now in the curbed time* ☞ **uncurbed** (*adj.*)

curd (*n.*) type of foodstuff derived from milk **3H6** II.v.47 [King alone] *the shepherd's homely curds*

curd (*v.*) congeal, coagulate, curdle **Ham** I.v.69 [Ghost to Hamlet, of the poison] *it doth posset / And curd ... / The thin and wholesome blood;* **AW** I.iii.144

curds and whey foodstuff made of curdled milk **Tit** IV.ii.177 [Aaron to his baby] *I'll make you ... / feed on curds and whey*

curdy (*v.*) congeal, solidify **Cor** V.iii.66 [Coriolanus to Volumnia] *chaste as the icicle / That's curdied by the frost from purest snow*

cure (*n.*) **1** charge, care, office **H8** I.iv.33 [Sands to Lord Chamberlain, of entertaining the ladies] *For my little cure, / Let me alone* [also: sense 2]

2 state of health, condition, soundness **Oth** II.i.51 [Cassio to Montano] *my hopes, not surfeited to death, / Stand in bold cure;* **KL** III.vi.98

cureless (*adj.*) incurable, fatal, without remedy **MV** IV.i.142 [Shylock to Gratiano] *Repair thy wit, good youth, or it will fall / To cureless ruin;* **3H6** II.vi.23; **Luc** 772

curfew (*n.*) evening bell **Tem** V.i.40 [Prospero alone] *you ... that rejoice / To hear the solemn curfew;* **MM** IV.ii.72

curiosity (*n.*) scrupulousness, fastidiousness, painstaking attention to detail **Tim** IV.iii.305 [Apemantus to Timon, of humanity] *When thou wast in thy gilt and thy perfume, they mocked thee for too much curiosity;* **KL** I.i.6, ii.4, iv.69

curious (*adj.*) **1** finely made, skilfully wrought, elaborate **TNK** IV.ii.86 [Messenger to Theseus, of one of Arcite's knights] *on his thigh a sword / Hung by a curious baldric;* **3H6** II.v.53; **KL** I.iv.32; **Lover** 49; **Per** I.iv.43; **Venus** 734

2 exquisite, excellent, fine **Per** I.i.17 [Pericles to all, of Antiochus' daughter's face] *where is read / Nothing but curious pleasures*

3 hidden, subtle, minute **TC** III.ii.64 [Troilus to Cressida] *What too curious dreg espies my sweet lady in the fountain of our love?*

4 careful, fastidious, attentive **AW** I.ii.20 [King to Bertram] *Frank nature, rather curious than in haste, / Hath well composed thee;* **RJ** I.iv.31

5 particular, difficult to satisfy, hard to please **AC** III.ii.35 [Antony to Caesar] *You shall not find, / Though you be ... curious, the least cause / For what you seem to fear;* **Sonn** 38.13; **TS** IV.iv.36

6 worrisome, disquieting, causing anxiety **WT** IV.iv.511 [Florizel to Camillo] *I am so fraught with curious business that / I leave out ceremony*

7 anxious, concerned, apprehensive **Cym** I.vii.191 [Iachimo to Innogen, of his supposed treasures] *I am something curious ... / To have them in safe stowage*

curious-good (*adj.*) finely elaborate, excellently wrought **Luc** 1300 [of parts of Lucrece's letter] *This is too curious-good, this blunt and ill*

curious-knotted (*adj.*) with intricate patterns of flower-beds **LL** I.i.240 [King reading Armado's letter to him] *thy curious-knotted garden*

curiously (*adv.*) **1** skilfully, carefully, proficiently **TS** IV.iii.139 [Tailor reading, of a gown] *The sleeves curiously cut* [also: sense 3]; **MA** V.i.151

2 elaborately, artistically, exquisitely **AW** IV.iii.32 [First Lord to Second Lord, of Bertram's judgement of Parolles] *wherein so curiously he had set this counterfeit*

3 fastidiously, minutely, ingeniously **Ham** V.i.202 [Horatio to Hamlet] *'Twere to consider too curiously to consider so*

curled (*adj.*) with elegantly curled hair, adorned with ringlets **Oth** I.ii.68 [Brabantio to Othello, of Desdemona] *So opposite to marriage that she shunned / The wealthy curled darlings of our nation;* **AC** V.ii.300

curled-pate (*adj.*) curly-headed **Tim** IV.iii.161 [Timon to all, of disease] *Make curled-pate ruffians bald*

currance (*n.*) current, torrent, flow **H5** I.i.34 [Canterbury to Ely, of King Henry] *Never came reformation in a flood / With such a heady currance scouring faults*

current (*n.*) **1** eddy, movement, flow **1H4** II.iii.57 [Lady Percy to Hotspur] *thou hast talked / Of ... all the currents of a heady fight*

2 practice, course, way of behaviour **Ham** III.iii.57 [Claudius alone] *In the corrupted currents of this world;* **MV** IV.i.64

3 circulation, currency **1H4** IV.i.5 [Hotspur to Douglas] *not a soldier of this season's stamp / Should go as general current through the world*

current (*adj.*) **1** [as of a coin] authentic, genuine, valid **R3** I.ii.84 [Anne to Richard] *thou canst make / No excuse current but to hang thyself;* **2H4** II.i.120; **R2** I.iii.231; **R3** I.iii.255; **TNK** I.i.216

2 accepted, genuine, taken at face value **1H4** I.iii.67 [Hotspur to King Henry, of a lord] *let not his report / Come current for an accusation;* **R3** II.i.96

3 valid, correct, true **1H4** II.i.55 [Chamberlain to Gadshill] *It holds current that I told you yesternight*

4 acceptable, up-to-date, fashionable **H8** I.iii.47 [Sands to Lovell and Lord Chamberlain, of his entertaining ladies with music] *have an hour of hearing, and ... / Held current music too*

currier (*n.*) runner, messenger, courier **Mac** I.vii.23 [Macbeth alone] *heaven's cherubin, horsed / Upon the sightless curriers of the air* [i.e. the winds]

currish (*adj.*) mean-spirited, snarling, quarrelsome **TG** IV.iv.47 [Launce to Proteus, of Silvia's reaction to the present of a dog] *she ... tells you currish thanks is good enough for such a present;* **3H6** V.v.26; **MV** IV.i.133, 289; **TS** V.ii.54

curry (*v.*) use flattery, talk fawningly **2H4** V.i.67 [Falstaff alone] *I would curry with Master Shallow that no man could better command his servants*

cursitory (*adj.*) cursory, hurried, superficial **H5** V.ii.77 [French King to King Henry] *I have but with a cursitory eye / O'erglanced the articles*

curst (*adj.*) **1** bad-tempered, quarrelsome, shrewish, cross **MND** III.ii.300 [Helena to Demetrius and Lysander] *I was never curst;* **1H4** II.iii.48; **LL** IV.i.36; **MA** II.i.18; **TN** III.ii.40; **TS** I.i.177

   2 angry, furious, fierce **WT** III.iii.126 [Clown to Shepherd, of bears] *They are never curst but when they are hungry;* **2H6** III.ii.312; **KL** II.i.64; **Venus** 887

curstness (*n.*) ill humour, bad temper **AC** II.ii.25 [Lepidus to Caesar and Antony] *Touch you the sourest points with sweetest terms, / Nor curstness grow to th'matter* [i.e. don't let bad temper enter into it]

cur'sy (*n.*) ➤ *courtesy* (*n.*)

curtail (*v.*) cut short, diminish **R3** I.i.18 [Richard alone, of his appearance] *I … am curtailed of this fair proportion*

curtain (*n.*) banner, ensign **H5** IV.ii.39 [Grandpré to all, of the English army] *Their ragged curtains poorly are let loose*

curtal (*adj.*) with a docked tail; common, household **CE** III.ii.154 [Dromio of Syracuse to Antipholus of Syracuse, of the kitchen wench] *She had transformed me to a curtal dog;* **AW** II.iii.58; **MW** II.i.103; **PassP** XVII.19

curtle-axe (*n.*) cutlass, cutting sword **H5** IV.ii.19 [Constable to Dauphin, of the English army] *Scarce blood enough in all their sickly veins / To give each naked curtle-axe a stain;* **AY** I.iii.115 ➤ WEAPONS, p.491

curtsy, curtsey (*n.*) **1** act of courteous respect, deferential action, bow **2H4** II.i.123 [Falstaff to Lord Chief Justice] *if a man will make curtsy and say nothing, he is virtuous;* **2H4** Epilogue.1; **KL** III.vii.26 ➤ *courtesy* (*n.*)

   2 courtly ceremony, mannered politeness **MA** IV.i.314 [Beatrice to Benedick] *manhood is melted into curtsies*

curtsy, curtsey (*v.*) bow low, do reverence, pay respect **TN** II.v.61 [Malvolio to himself] *Toby approaches, curtsies there to me;* **Luc** 1338; **MV** I.i.13

curvet (*n.*) [horse-riding] type of high leap **AW** II.iii.280 [Parolles to Bertram] *the bound and high curvet / Of Mars's fiery steed*

curvet (*v.*) [of a horse] leap about, act friskily, prance **Venus** 279 [of Adonis' horse] *he rears upright, curvets and leaps;* **AY** III.ii.237

cush, cuish, cuisse (*n.*) armoured thigh-piece **1H4** IV.i.105 [Vernon to all, of Prince Hal] *His cuishes on his thighs* [F, Q *cushes*] ➤ BODY-ARMOUR, p.48

cushing (*n.*) cushion **KL** III.vi.34 [disguised Kent to Lear] *Will you lie down and rest upon the cushings?*

cushion (*n.*) seat of office, judgement seat **Cor** IV.vii.43 [Aufidius to Lieutenant, of Coriolanus' nature] *not moving / From th'casque to th'cushion* [i.e. not taking up a peaceful civic life]; **Cor** III.i.101

custard-coffin (*n.*) crust surrounding a custard tart **TS** IV.iii.82 [Petruchio to Katherina, of the shape of a cap] *A custard-coffin* ➤ *coffin* (*n.*)

custom (*n.*) **1** habit, usual practice, customary usage **Oth** III.iii.121 [Othello to Iago, of Iago's pauses] *such things in a false disloyal knave / Are tricks of custom;* **AY** II.i.2; **Cym** I.v.135; **Ham** III.iv.38; **JC** III.i.269; **KL** I.ii.3

   2 customary tribute [as if by a tenant to a lord] **E3** V.i.79 [Copland to King Edward, of King David] *Receive … the custom of my fraught*

3 trade, business, line of work **WT** IV.iv.97 [Third Gentleman to all, of the sculptor of Hermione's statue] *he … would beguile Nature of her custom, so perfectly he is her ape*

customed (*adj.*) **1** customary, ordinary, usual **KJ** III.iv.155 [Cardinal Pandulph to Lewis the Dauphin, of King John and the people] *no customed event, / But they will pluck away his natural cause / And call them meteors, prodigies and signs*

   2 legally sanctioned, established by custom **2H6** V.i.188 [Salisbury to King] *Who can be bound by any solemn vow… / To wring the widow from her customed right* [i.e. to part of her husband's estate]

customer (*n.*) harlot, prostitute, whore **AW** V.iii.284 [King to Diana] *I think thee now some common customer;* **Oth** IV.i.120

custom-shrunk (*adj.*) down in business, suffering great loss of trade **MM** I.ii.83 [Mistress Overdone to herself] *what with the sweat, what with the gallows, and what with poverty, I am custom-shrunk*

custrel (*n.*) scoundrel, rogue, low fellow **Per** IV.vi.163 [Marina to Boult] *Thou art / The damned doorkeeper to every custrel / That comes inquiring for his Tib* ➤ *coistril* (*n.*)

cut (*n.*) **1** ornamental gap in a dress to show the colour underneath **MA** III.iv.18 [Margaret to Hero, of the Duchess of Milan's gown] *cloth o'gold, and cuts, and laced with silver;* **TS** IV.iii.90 ➤ CLOTHING, p.79

   2 blow, misfortune, disaster **AC** I.ii.167 [Enobarbus to Antony] *If there were no more women but Fulvia, then had you indeed a cut, and the case is to be lamented*

   3 work-horse, nag **TNK** III.iv.22 [Gaoler's Daughter alone, singing, probably of Palamon] *He s' buy me a white cut, forth for to ride;* **1H4** II.i.5; **TN** II.iii.180

cut (*adj.*) ➤ *come cut and long tail; draw cuts*

cut off (*v.*) **1** remove, take away, reduce **KL** II.iv.169 [Lear to Regan] *'Tis not in thee … to cut off my train;* **JC** V.i.9

   2 interrupt, break off **KJ** IV.ii.202 [Hubert to King John, of someone's gossip] *Another lean unwashed artificer / Cuts off his tale and talks of Arthur's death*

   3 put to death, bring to an untimely end **H5** III.vi.104 [King Henry to all, of thieves] *We would have all such offenders so cut off;* **3H6** III.ii.142; **MM** V.i.35

cutpurse (*n.*) pickpocket, thief, robber **WT** IV.iv.668 [Autolycus alone] *To have an open ear, a quick eye, and a nimble hand is necessary for a cutpurse;* **Ham** III.iv.100; **2H4** II.iv.124; **H5** V.i.82; **KL** III.ii.90; **TNK** II.i.267

cutter (*n.*) carver, sculptor, engraver **Cym** II.iv.83 [Iachimo to Posthumus, of the sculpture of Diana] *the cutter / Was as another Nature*

cuttle (*n.*) knife used by pickpockets for cutting purses; bully, cut-throat **2H4** II.iv.126 [Doll to Pistol] *I'll thrust my knife in your mouldy chaps an you play the saucy cuttle with me*

cyme (*n.*) [debated reading] plant-top, head of a plant; drug which induces vomiting **Mac** V.iii.55 [Macbeth to Doctor] *What rhubarb, cyme, or what purgative drug / Would scour these English hence?* [F]

cynic (*n.*) critic, fault-finder **E3** II.i.311 [Warwick to King Edward] *Age is a cynic, not a flatterer;* **JC** IV.iii.131

cypress (*n.*) type of lightweight fabric, gauze cloth, crape material [when black, used in mourning] **TN** III.i.118 [Olivia to Viola as Cesario] *a cypress, not a bosom, / Hides my heart;* **WT** IV.iv.221

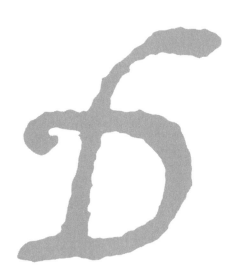

dace *(n.)* type of small fish, used as a bait **2H4** III.ii.319 [Falstaff alone] *If the young dace be a bait for the old pike*

daemon, demon *(n.)* ministering spirit, guardian angel **AC** II.iii.20 [Soothsayer to Antony] *Thy daemon ... thy spirit which keeps thee*

daff *(v.)*, past form **daft** **1** take off, throw off **AC** IV.iv.13 [Antony to Cleopatra, of his armour] *till we do please / To daff't for our repose;* **Lover** 297 ➤ doff *(v.)*

2 put off, deflect, sidetrack **Oth** IV.ii.175 [Roderigo to Iago] *Every day thou daff'st me with some device* [F *dafts*; Q *doffest*]; **MA** V.i.78; **PassP** XIV.3

3 put to one side, thrust aside **MA** II.iii.169 [Don Pedro to Leonato] *I would have daffed all other respects*

daff aside *(v.)* throw off, thrust aside **1H4** IV.i.96 [Hotspur to Vernon, of Prince Hal and companions] *that daffed the world aside*

daffadilly *(n.)* daffodil **TNK** IV.i.73 [Wooer to all, reporting the Gaoler's Daughter's words] *maids ... / With chaplets on their heads of daffadillies*

daintiest *(adj.)* mostly delicious flavour, choicest taste **2H6** III.ii.322 [Suffolk to Queen, of the King and Warwick] *Gall ... the daintiest that they taste!*

daintily *(adv.)* with satisfied palate, relishing the taste **Tit** V.iii.60 [Titus to Saturninus, of Chiron and Demetrius] *both baked in this pie, / Whereof their mother daintily hath fed*

dainty *(n.)* **1** delight, choice pleasure **LL** IV.ii.24 [Nathaniel to Holofernes, of Dull] *he hath never fed of the dainties that are bred in a book*

2 delicacy, choice foodstuff **Venus** 164 [Venus to Adonis] *Dainties [are made] to taste;* **CE** III.i.21; **TS** II.i.189

3 fastidious hesitation, prim response **RJ** I.v.20 [Capulet to ladies] *She that makes dainty, / She, I'll swear, hath corns*

dainty *(adj.)* **1** splendid, fine, excellent **TNK** III.v.73 [Third Countryman to all, of the Gaoler's Daughter] *There's a dainty madwoman;* **Tem** V.i.95; **TNK** III.v.113

2 delicately pretty, of tender beauty **H8** I.iv.94 [King Henry to Lord Chamberlain, of Anne] *she is a dainty one;* **TC** V.ii.83; **Tit** II.i.117, II.ii.26

3 fastidious, scrupulous, refined, particular **1H6** V.iii.38 [Richard to Pucelle, of Charles] *No shape but his can please your dainty eye;* **2H4** IV.i.196; **LL** IV.i.145; **Mac** II.iii.141; **TC** I.iii.145; **TNK** II.ii.40

dainty *(adv.)* beautifully, delightfully, excellently **TNK** II.i.184 [Woman to Emilia, replying to a question about a choice of colour on a skirt] *Dainty, madam.*

dalliance *(n.)* **1** frivolity, idleness, wasteful activity **1H6** V.i.23 [King to Gloucester] *fitter is my study and my books / Than wanton dalliance with a paramour;* **Ham** I.iii.50; **H5** II.Chorus.2; **1H6** V.ii.5

2 idle talk, fooling about, waste of time **CE** IV.i.59 [Second Merchant to Antipholus of Ephesus] *My business cannot brook this dalliance;* **CE** IV.i.48

3 love-talk, flirting, amorous caressing **Tem** IV.i.51 [Prospero to Ferdinand and Miranda] *Do not give dalliance / Too much the rein*

dally *(v.)* **1** deal lightly, play about, tease **TN** II.iv.47 [Orsino to Viola as Cesario, of a song] *It is silly sooth, / And dallies with the innocence of love;* **LL** V.i.98; **Luc** 554; **TN** III.i.14

2 trifle, behave mockingly **R3** II.i.12 [King Edward to Hastings and Rivers] *Take heed you dally not before your King;* **1H4** V.iii.55; **Luc** 1120

3 flirt, be amorous, engage in love-play **Ham** III.ii.256 [Hamlet to Ophelia] *I could interpret between you and your love, if I could see the puppets dallying;* **R3** III.vii.73

4 delay, linger, loiter **KL** III.vi.91 [Gloucester to disguised Kent] *If thou shouldst dally half an hour;* **TS** IV.iv.68

dam *(n.)* mother **Tit** V.ii.144 [Titus to himself, of Tamora, Chiron, and Demetrius] *A pair of cursed hell-hounds and their dam;* **1H6** I.v.5; **3H6** II.ii.135; **MV** IV.i.136; **TNK** V.iii.23; **TS** III.ii.155 ➤ **FAMILY**, p.168

damask *(adj./n.)* light-red, pink [colour of the damask rose] **TNK** IV.i.74 [Wooer to all, reporting the Gaoler's Daughter's words] *With cherry lips and cheeks of damask roses;* **AY** III.v.123; **Cor** II.i.208; **LL** V.ii.296; **PassP** VII.5; **TN** II.iv.111

damasked *(adj.)* having the hue of the damask rose, adorned with colours **Sonn** 130.5 *I have seen roses damasked, red and white*

dame *(n.)* **1** woman, girl **TS** II.i.23 [Baptista to Katherina, of her treatment of Bianca] *Why, how now, dame, whence grows this insolence?;* **2H4** III.ii.112, 224; **1H6** II.i.50; **2H6** I.ii.42 ➤ **ADDRESS FORMS**, p.8
  2 mother, nurse **E3** II.i.422 [Countess to Warwick] *No marvel though the leprous infant die, / When the stern dame envenometh the dug;* **Luc** 1477
  3 lady, mistress, woman of rank **Luc** 21 [of Lucrece] *kings might be espoused to more fame, / But king nor peer to such a peerless dame;* **Luc** 1034; **Mac** IV.ii.65; **MND** V.i.285
  4 mistress of a household, lady of the house **WT** IV.iv.57 [Shepherd to Perdita] *When my old wife lived, upon / This day she was ... / Both dame and servant*

damn *(v.)* condemn, be sinful **Ham** V.ii.68 [Hamlet to Horatio, of Claudius] *is't not to be damned / To let this canker of our nature come / In further evil?*

damnable *(adj.)* deserving damnation, evil, in a state of mortal sin **AY** V.ii.59 [Rosalind as Ganymede to Orlando] *I have ... conversed with a magician, most profound in his art, and yet not damnable;* **AW** IV.iii.25

damosella *(n.)* damsel, young maiden **LL** IV.ii.127 [Holofernes to Jaquenetta, of the letter] *But, damosella virgin, was this directed to you?*

damp *(n.)* fog, mist, vapour **Luc** 778 [Lucrece as if to night] *With rotten damps ravish the morning air;* **AC** IV.ix.13; **AW** II.i.163

Dan, Don *(n.)* [*don*, short form of Latin 'dominus'] master, sir **LL** III.i.177 [Berowne alone] *This Signor Junior, giant-dwarf, Dan Cupid* [Q1 *dan;* F *Don*]; **MA** V.ii.76 [Benedick to Beatrice] *Therefore is it most expedient for the wise, if Don Worm, his conscience, find no impediment to the contrary*

dance *(v.)* set dancing, excite, rouse **Cor** IV.v.119 [Aufidius to Coriolanus] *But that I see the here ... more dances my rapt heart / Than when I first my wedded mistress saw / Bestride my threshold*

dancing-rapier *(n.)* ornamental sword worn in dancing **Tit** II.i.39 [Demetrius to Chiron] *our mother ... / Gave you a dancing-rapier by your side*

dandle *(v.)* pamper, fondle, pet **2H6** I.iii.143 [Duchess to King, of the Queen] *She'll hamper thee, and dandle thee like a baby;* **Tit** IV.ii.160

danger *(n.)* damage, harm, mischief **JC** II.i.17 [Brutus alone, of crowning Caesar] *we put a sting in him / That at his will he may do danger with;* **H8** I.ii.157; **MV** VI.i.38

danger *(v.)* endanger, imperil, risk **AC** I.ii.193 [Antony to Enobarbus, of Pompey] *whose quality, going on, / The sides o'th' world may danger*

danger, in one's within one's power, at one's mercy **MV** IV.i.177 [Portia as Balthasar to Antonio] *You stand within his danger, do you not?*

dangerous *(adj.)* threatening, severe, menacing **Per** I.i.90 [Antiochus to Pericles, of not touching his daughter] *that's an article within our law / As dangerous as the rest;* **1H4** V.i.69; **2H6** II.i.21; **MA** V.i.97; **Tim** IV.iii.495

dangerous *(adv.)* dangerously, mortally, seriously **3H6** I.i.11 [Edward to York] *Lord Stafford's father ... / Is either slain or wounded dangerous*

dank *(adj.)* damp **1H4** II.i.8 [Second Carrier to First Carrier] *Peas and beans are as dank here as a dog*

dankish *(adj.)* dank, damp, humid **CE** V.i.248 [Antipholus of Ephesus to Duke] *in a dark and dankish vault at home*

Dansker *(n.)* Dane **Ham** II.i.7 [Polonius to Reynaldo] *Inquire me first what Danskers are in Paris*

dare *(n.)* daring, boldness, risk **1H4** IV.i.78 [Hotspur to Worcester, of Northumberland's absence] *It lends ... / A larger dare to our great enterprise*

dare *(v.)* **1** challenge, confront, defy **H8** III.ii.307 [Wolsey to Surrey] *I dare your worst objections;* **1H6** I.iii.45; **MND** III.ii.413; **RJ** II.iv.12
  2 present, deliver, inflict **Ham** IV.iv.52 [Hamlet alone] *all that fortune, death, and danger dare*
  3 daze, paralyse with fear, terrify **H5** IV.ii.34 [Constable to Dauphin] *our approach shall so much dare the field / That England shall couch down in fear and yield;* **H8** III.ii.282
  4 disturb, distract **E3** III.iv.59 [King Edward to all] *dare a falcon when she's in her flight, / And ever after she'll be haggard-like*
  5 ➤ durst, that thou

dareful *(adj.)* audacious, bold, full of defiance **Mac** V.v.6 [Macbeth to all, of the besieging troops] *We might have met them dareful, beard to beard* [or adverb use: boldly]

daring-hardy *(adj.)* foolhardy, rashly bold **R2** I.iii.43 [Lord Marshal to Bolingbroke] *no person be so bold / Or daring-hardy as to touch the lists*

dark *(adj.)* **1** sad, melancholic, gloomy **Sonn** 97.3 *What freezings have I felt, what dark days seen!;* **MV** V.i.87; **RJ** III.v.36; **Venus** 182
  2 unfavourable, malignant, evil **TNK** I.iv.1 [First Queen to Theseus] *To thee no star be dark;* **R2** I.i.169
  3 undivulged, secret, unrevealed **KL** I.i.36 [Lear to all] *Meantime we shall express our darker purpose;* **Cym** III.iv.146; **LL** V.ii.19

dark *(v.)* eclipse, obscure, cloud **Per** IV.Chorus.35 [Gower alone, of the praising of Marina] *This so darks / In Philoten all graceful marks*

dark *(adv.)* in the dark **AY** III.v.39 [Rosalind as Ganymede to Phebe] *I see no more in you / Than without candle may go dark to bed*

darken *(v.)* obscure, eclipse, deprive of fame **Cor** IV.vii.5 [Lieutenant to Aufidius] *you are darkened in this action;* **AC** III.i.24; **Cor** II.i.251; **Per** III.ii.28

darking *(n.)* darkening, setting **TC** V.viii.7 [Achilles to Hector] *Even with the vail and darking of the sun / To close the day up, Hector's life is done* [F]

darkling *(adv.)* in the dark, in darkness **KL** I.iv.213 [Fool to Lear] *out went the candle and we were left darkling;* **AC** IV.xv.10; **MND** II.ii.92

darkly *(adv.)* **1** cunningly, subtly, secretly **AW** IV.iii.10 [Second Lord to First Lord] *I will tell you a thing, but you shall let it dwell darkly with you;* **MM** I.ii.277
  2 frowningly, ominously; gloomily **R3** I.iv.172 [Clarence to First Murderer] *How darkly and how deadly dost thou speak!;* **TN** II.i.3
  3 obscurely, cryptically, enigmatically **KJ** IV.ii.232 [King John to Hubert] *When I spake darkly what I purposed;* **LL** V.ii.23

darnel *(n.)* weeds, cockle, tares **1H6** III.ii.44 [Pucelle to the English, of the corn] *'Twas full of darnel;* **H5** V.ii.45; **KL** IV.iv.5
  ➤ **PLANTS**, p.330

darraign *(v.)* array, set in order, prepare **3H6** II.ii.72 [Messenger to all, of the King's enemies] *Darraign your battle, for they are at hand*

dart *(n.)* arrow; or: light spear **E3** IV.iii.138 [Salisbury to King Edward, of the army surrounding Prince Edward] *Here crossbows and deadly wounding darts;* **AC** IV.xiv.70; **Cor** I.vi.61; **2H6** III.i.362; **MM** I.iii.2; **Oth** IV.i.269

dart *(v.)* hurl like an arrow **LL** V.ii.396 [Berowne to Rosaline] *Here stand I, lady; dart thy skill at me;* **Cym** IV.ii.314; **KL** II.iv.160

darting *(adj.)* arrow-shooting **AC** III.i.1 [Ventidius to Silius, as if to the Parthians] *Now, darting Parthia, art thou struck*

dash *(n.)* **1** encounter, sight, meeting **1H6** I.ii.71 [Reignier to all, of Pucelle] *She takes upon her bravely at first dash* [i.e. from the first]
  2 stroke, mark, sign **Luc** 206 [Tarquin to himself, of his coat of arms] *Some loathsome dash the herald will contrive*

3 trace, touch, tinge **WT** V.ii.111 [Autolycus alone] *had I not the dash of my former life in me*

dash (*v.*) **1** cast down, daunt, dishearten **Oth** III.iii.212 [Iago to Othello, of what he has told him] *I see this hath a little dashed your spirits;* **LL** V.ii.578

2 overturn, rescind, frustrate **3H6** II.i.117 [Warwick to Edward and Richard, of the Queen] *she was coming with a full intent / To dash our late decree in parliament*

3 frustrate, spoil, ruin **LL** V.ii.462 [Berowne to all, of the scheme] *Here was a consent, / Knowing aforehand of our merriment, / To dash it like a Christmas comedy*

4 diminish, infringe, destroy **E3** IV.v.74 [Charles to King John] *I hope your highness will not so disgrace me / And dash the virtue of my seal at arms*

dastard (*n.*) coward, sissy, runaway, traitor **1H6** IV.i.19 [Talbot to all, of Falstaff] *This dastard … / Like to a trusty squire did run away;* **1H6** I.ii.23; **2H6** IV.viii.26; **3H6** II.ii.114; **R2** I.i.190

dastard (*adj.*) dastardly, cowardly, despicable **Cor** IV.v.78 [Coriolanus to Aufidius] *The cruelty and envy of the people, / Permitted by our dastard nobles;* **1H6** I.i.144, iv.111

date (*n.*) **1** duration, period of existence **KJ** IV.iii.106 [Hubert to Bigot, of Arthur] *I loved him, and will weep / My date of life out for his sweet life's loss;* **MND** III.ii.373; **R3** IV.iv.255; **RJ** I.iv.108, V.iii.229

2 time, season, fashion **RJ** I.iv.3 [Benvolio to Romeo, of making a formal apology] *The date is out of such prolixity*

3 lifetime, term of existence **Per** III.iv.14 [Cerimon to Thaisa, of Diana's temple] *Where you may abide till your date expire*

4 due date, agreed day [for the end of a contract] **Sonn** 18.4 *Summer's lease hath all too short a date* [i.e. tenancy]; **Luc** 26; **Tim** II.i.22

5 limit, term, endpoint **Sonn** 14.14 *of thee this I prognosticate, / Thy end is Truth's and Beauty's doom and date;* **1H6** IV.vi.9

6 age **CE** I.ii.41 [Antipholus of Syracuse alone, of Dromio of Ephesus] *Here comes the almanac of my true date* [i.e. the proof of how old I am]

dateless (*adj.*) everlasting, eternal, endless **R2** I.iii.151 [King Richard to Mowbray] *The sly slow hours shall not determinate / The dateless limit of thy dear exile;* **RJ** V.iii.115; **Sonn** 30.6, 153.6

daub (*v.*) **1** bedaub, smear, defile **1H4** I.i.6 [King Henry to all] *No more the thirsty entrance of this soil / Shall daub her lips with her own children's blood;* **KL** II.i.64; **R3** III.v.29

2 pretend, fake, pass off **KL** IV.i.51 [Edgar as Poor Tom to himself] *I cannot daub it further* [F; Q *dance*]

daubery, daubry (*n.*) trickery, pretence, deceitful show **MW** IV.ii.165 [Ford to Mistress Ford, of charms and spells] *such daubery as this is beyond our element*

daughter (*n.*) ☞ **FAMILY**, p.168

dauphin, dolphin (*n.*) title of the eldest son of the King of France [between 1349 and 1830] **H5** I.ii.260 [King Henry to all] *We are glad the Dauphin is so pleasant with us* [and throughout the play]; **KJ** II.i.425 [Hubert to King John and King Philip, of Lewis and Blanche] *Look upon the years / Of Lewis the Dolphin and that lovely maid;* **H5** I.ii.289; **1H6** V.iii.37; **KJ** V.i.32

daw (*n.*) **1** jackdaw [as noted for its stupidity]; dolt, fool **1H6** II.iv.18 [Warwick to all] *in these nice sharp quillets of the law … I am no wiser than a daw;* **Cor** IV.v.46; **MA** II.iii.247; **Oth** I.i.66; **TC** I.ii.244; **TN** III.iv.35

2 jackdaw [without any implication] **LL** V.ii.894 [Ver singing, of spring] *When turtles tread, and rooks, and daws*

dawning (*n.*) dawn, daybreak, early morning **Ham** I.i.161 [Marcellus to Horatio, of the cock] *This bird of dawning singeth all night long;* **KL** II.ii.1; **MM** IV.ii.91 ☞ **GREETINGS**, p.206

day (*n.*) **1** day of battle, contest **1H4** V.iv.158 [Prince Hal to Lancaster and Falstaff] *The trumpet sounds retreat, the day is ours;* **E3** III.iii.169; **1H4** V.iii.29; **3H6** IV.vi.86; **KJ** III.iv.116, V.iii.1, iv.5, 14

2 appointed day, fixed date **MV** I.iii.160 [Shylock to Bassanio, of Antonio] *If he should break his day;* **MV** II.viii.25

3 anniversary **2H4** III.ii.180 [Bullcalf to Falstaff] *a cough, sir, which I caught with ringing in the King's affairs upon his coronation day*

4 (plural) time, delay, period of action **Tit** IV.ii.164 [Aaron to Demetrius and Chiron] *see that you take no longer days, / But send the midwife presently to me*

5 time, hour [of day] **Tem** V.i.3 [Prospero to Ariel] *How's the day?*

6 light, brightness **AC** IV.viii.13 [Antony to Cleopatra] *thou day o'th' world*

7 ☞ many a day, for this; nature, days of; young days, of so

days, by every day, day by day **TC** IV.i.10 [Paris to Aeneas] *Diomed a whole week by days / Did haunt you in the field*

day, by the in the morning, by the clock **1H4** II.i.1 [First Carrier, alone] *An it be not four by the day I'll be hanged*

day, these seven years' this past seven years, in a long time **2H6** II.i.2 [Queen to all] *I saw not better sport these seven years' day*

day-bed (*n.*) couch, sofa, divan **TN** II.v.47 [Malvolio to himself] *having come from a day-bed, where I have left Olivia sleeping;* **R3** III.vii.71 [Q]

daylight (*n.*) ☞ burn daylight

day-woman (*n.*) ☞ dey-woman (*n.*)

dazzle (*v.*) grow dim, become unable to see properly **Tit** III.ii.85 [Titus to Young Lucius] *thy sight is young / And thou shalt read when mine begin to dazzle;* **3H6** II.i.25; **Venus** 1064

dead (*adj.*) **1** dying, near to death **2H6** V.ii.4 [Warwick to Clifford] *dead men's cries do fill the empty air*

2 deadly, dire, grave **KJ** V.vii.65 [Salisbury to Bastard, of King John] *You breathe these dead news in as dead an ear*

3 fatal, deadly, mortal **WT** IV.iv.431 [Polixenes to Shepherd] *Though full of our displeasure, yet we free thee / From the dead blow of it;* **R2** IV.i.10

4 deadly, death-dealing, murderous **MND** III.ii.57 [Hermia to Demetrius] *So should a murderer look; so dead, so grim*

5 death-like, lifeless, spiritless **Cym** V.v.259 [Innogen to Cornelius, of taking the drug] *Most like I did, for I was dead;* **2H4** I.i.71; **Oth** II.iii.171; **R2** III.ii.79; **Tem** V.i.230

6 condemned to death, to be put to death **Cym** V.v.299 [Cymbeline to Guiderius] *thou'rt dead;* **MW** IV.ii.40

7 deprived of life, killed **2H6** III.ii.192 [Warwick to Queen] *Who finds the partridge in the puttock's nest, / But may imagine how the bird was dead*

dead-killing (*adj.*) mortal, deadly, fatal **Luc** 540 [of Tarquin] *with a cockatrice' dead-killing eye / He rouseth up himself;* **R3** IV.i.35

deadly (*adj.*) deathly, death-like **KL** V.iii.288 [Kent to Lear] *All's cheerless, dark, and deadly;* **CE** IV.iv.91; **KL** IV.ii.36; **Mac** III.ii.215; **TN** I.v.254; **TNK** I.v.3

deadly (*adv.*) **1** extremely, implacably, to the death **AW** V.iii.117 [King to Bertram, of Helena] *thou didst hate her deadly;* **Cor** II.i.58; **3H6** I.v.84; **MA** V.i.170

2 with a resemblance of death **TNK** I.v.3 [Song] *Our dole more deadly looks than dying*

3 mortally, fatally **TC** V.v.12 [Agamemnon to all] *Amphimachus and Thoas [are] deadly hurt*

deadly-handed (*adj.*) death-dealing, murderous **2H6** V.ii.9 [York to Warwick] *The deadly-handed Clifford slew my steed*

deadly-standing (*adj.*) death-dealing **Tit** II.iii.32 [Aaron to Tamora] *What signifies my deadly-standing eye*

dead men's fingers ☞ **PLANTS**, p.330

deaf (*v.*) deafen **TNK** I.ii.80 [Palamon to Arcite, of Creon] *the echoes of his shames have deafed / The ears of heavenly justice;* **KJ** II.i.147; **LL** V.ii.853

deafing (*n.*) drowning out, blocking out [of sound] **TNK** V.iii.9 [Emilia to Pirithous] *there is / No deafing, but to hear*

deafing (*adj.*) deafening, ear-splitting **2H4** III.i.24 [King Henry IV alone, of waves] *hanging them / With deafing clamour in the slippery clouds* [Q; F *deaff'ning*]

deal (*n.*) amount, quantity JC I.ii.244 [Casca to Brutus] *the rabblement … uttered such a deal of stinking breath;* 1H4 I.iii.247; KL II.ii.118; PassP XVII.17; R2 I.iii.269; Tit III.i.243

deal (*v.*) **1** proceed, behave, conduct oneself R3 IV.iv.292 [King Richard to Queen Elizabeth] *Men shall deal unadvisedly sometimes;* AC III.xi.39; 1H4 II.iv.164; MA V.i.101; Tem V.i.271; TNK II.i.259
2 express oneself, speak KL IV.vii.62 [Lear to Cordelia] *to deal plainly, / I fear I am not in my perfect mind*
3 have dealings, have to do Per IV.vi.23 [Lysimachus to Boult, of a whore] *that a man may deal withal and defy the surgeon*
4 bestow, apportion, grant KL IV.i.65 [Gloucester to Edgar as Poor Tom] *That I am wretched / Makes thee the happier. Heavens deal so still!;* Tim I.ii.222

deal upon (*v.*) deal with, proceed against R3 IV.ii.73 [King Richard to Tyrrel] *Two deep enemies … / Are they that I would have thee deal upon*

deal with (*v.*) make use of, resort to MW I.iii.93 [Nym to Pistol] *I will incense Page to deal with poison*

dear (*adj.*) **1** dire, grievous, hard H5 II.ii.181 [King Henry to the traitors] *God of His mercy give / You … true repentance / Of all your dear offences;* LL V.ii.786; R3 V.ii.21; RJ I.v.118; Sonn 37.3; Tit III.i.255
2 important, major, significant KL III.i.19 [disguised Kent to Gentleman] *I … dare upon the warrant of my note / Commend a dear thing to you;* 1H4 I.i.33, IV.i.34; H5 V.ii.344; KL IV.iii.51; RJ V.ii.19
3 of great worth, valuable, precious Tem III.i.39 [Ferdinand to Miranda, of her name] *the top of admiration, worth / What's dearest to the world;* JC IV.iii.101; LL II.i.9; R2 I.i.130; Sonn 32.11; TC III.iii.128
4 expensive, costly Cor I.i.18 [First Citizen to all, of the authorities] *they think we are too dear;* 1H6 IV.ii.53; LL II.i.10
5 pleasing, delightful, congenial Ham V.ii.149 [Osric to Hamlet] *Three of the carriages … are very dear to fancy*
6 heartfelt, earnest, zealous TG IV.iii.14 [Silvia to Eglamour] *what dear good will / I bear unto … Valentine;* 1H4 V.iv.94; H8 V.iii.119; LL V.ii.853; TC V.ii.9; WT II.iii.149
7 noble, honourable, worthy TNK I.iv.9 [Theseus to Queens, of their dead husbands] *honour them / With treble ceremony; rather than a gap / Should be in their dear rites;* 1H4 III.i.176, IV.iv.31; Per IV.vi.178; TC V.iii.27

dear (*adv.*) **1** direly, grievously, with difficulty 2H4 IV.iii.66 [Colevile to Prince John, of the other rebel leaders] *Had they been ruled by me, / You should have won them dearer than you have*
2 sorely, keenly, bitterly JC III.i.196 [Antony to all, as if to dead Caesar's spirit] *Shall it not grieve thee dearer than thy death, / To see thy Antony making his peace*

deared (*adj.*) loved, endeared, prized AC I.iv.44 [Caesar to Lepidus] *the ebbed man … / Comes deared by being lacked* [F *fear'd*]

dearly (*adv.*) **1** keenly, deeply, intensely AY I.iii.32 [Celia to Rosalind, of Orlando] *my father hated his father dearly;* CE II.i.139; Cym I.vii.13; Ham IV.iii.40
2 beautifully, exquisitely Cym II.ii.18 [Iachimo to himself, of Innogen] *Rubies unparagoned, / How dearly they do't* [i.e. kiss]
3 grievously, at great cost H8 V.iii.30 [Gardiner to the Councillors, of national discord] *as of late days our neighbours, / The upper Germany, can dearly witness;* Cym II.iv.128

dearn, dearne (*adj.*) ➤ dern (*adj.*)

dearness (*n.*) affection, fondness, warmth MA III.ii.88 [Don John to Claudio, of Don Pedro] *in dearness of heart hath holp to effect your ensuing marriage*

dearth (*n.*) **1** scarcity, shortage, lack [of food], famine Cor I.i.70 [Menenius to Citizens] *For the dearth, / The gods, not the patricians, make it;* AC II.vii.19; KL I.ii.144; R2 III.iii.163; Sonn 14.2; TG II.vii.16
2 costliness, high value Ham V.ii.117 [Hamlet to Osric, of Laertes] *his infusion of such dearth and rareness*

death (*n.*) skull, memento mori MV II.vii.63 [Morocco to himself, of the contents of the gold casket] *A carrion Death;* KJ V.i.177 ➤ death's-head (*n.*)

death, take my stake my life 2H6 II.iii.87 [Horner to all, of York] *I will take my death I never meant him any ill*

death-bed (*n.*) grave TNK I.i.11 [Boy singing to all] *Marigolds, on death-beds blowing*

death-boding (*adj.*) full of forebodings about death, deadly ominous Luc 165 *No noise but owls' and wolves' death-boding cries*

deathful (*adj.*) mortal, fatal, deadly 2H6 III.ii.404 [Queen to Suffolk] *Though parting be a fretful corrosive, / It is applied to a deathful wound*

deathlike (*adj.*) deadly, mortal, fatal Per I.i.30 [Antiochus to Pericles] *deathlike dragons here affright thee hard*

death-practised (*adj.*) whose death has been plotted KL IV.vi.276 [Edgar to himself, of Albany] *I'll … / With this ungracious paper strike the sight / Of the death-practised Duke*

death-procuring (*adj.*) fatal, lethal, deadly E3 V.i.146 [Salisbury to King Edward, of the attack on Prince Edward] *Anon the death-procuring knell begins*

death's-head (*n.*) skull, memento mori MV I.ii.48 [Portia to Nerissa] *I had rather be married to a death's-head;* 2H4 II.iv.229 ➤ death (*n.*)

deathsman (*n.*) executioner 2H6 III.ii.217 [Warwick to Suffolk] *I should rob the deathsman of his fee;* 3H6 V.v.67; KL IV.vi.258; Luc 1001

death-token fatal symptom, death-like sign TC II.iii.175 [Ulysses to Agamemnon, of Achilles] *He is so plaguy proud that the death-tokens of it / Cry 'No recovery'*

death-worthy (*adj.*) deserving death Luc 635 [Lucrece to Tarquin] *This guilt would seem death-worthy in thy brother*

debate (*n.*) quarrel, wrangling, strife 2H4 IV.iv.2 [King Henry IV to all] *if God doth give successful end / To this debate;* LL I.i.171; MND II.i.116; Sonn 89.13

debate (*v.*) **1** discuss, argue over, dispute about 3H6 IV.vii.51 [Edward to Montgomery] *we'll debate / By what safe means the crown may be recovered;* AC II.ii.20; AW I.ii.75; 3H6 IV.vii.53; Sonn 15.11
2 decide [by debate], resolve Ham IV.iv.26 [Hamlet to Captain] *twenty thousand ducats / Will not debate the question of this straw*
3 fight, contend, strive Luc 1421 [of people in a painting of Troy] *It seemed they would debate with angry swords*

debatement (*n.*) consideration, deliberation, discussion MM V.i.99 [Isabella to Duke] *after much debatement;* Ham V.ii.45

debile (*adj.*) feeble, weak, puny Cor I.ix.48 [Martius to all] *I have not … foiled some debile wretch;* AW II.iii.33

debitor (*n.*) debtor [debt column in an account book] Cym V.iv.169 [First Gaoler to Posthumus, of the hangman's rope] *you have no true debitor and creditor but it* [i.e. death cancels all debts]; Oth I.i.31 ➤ creditor (*n.*)

debonair (*adj.*) gracious, courtly, of gentle disposition TC I.iii.235 [Aeneas to Agamemnon, of Trojans] *Courtiers as free, as debonair, unarmed, / As bending angels*

deboshed, deboyst (*adj.*) debauched, corrupted, depraved KL I.iv.238 [Gonerill to Lear, of his knights] *Men so disordered, so deboshed and bold* [F; Q *deboyst*]; AW II.iii.137, V.iii.206 [F]; Tem III.ii.25

deboysed (*adj.*) ➤ deboshed (*adj.*)

debt, in constrained by necessity, under obligation Tim III.vi.13 [Lucius to Lucullus] *was I in debt to my importunate business*

debted (*adj.*) in debt, indebted, obligated CE IV.i.31 [Angelo to Antipholus of Ephesus, of the Second Merchant] *I stand debted to this gentleman*

debuty (*n.*) malapropism for 'deputy' [= deputy alderman] 2H4 II.iv.83 [Hostess to Falstaff] *I was before Master Tisick the debuty t'other day*

decay (*n.*) **1** destruction, downfall, ending 2H6 III.i.194 [Gloucester to King] *thy decay I fear;* Cor III.i.78; KJ I.i.28; Luc 808; MW V.v.143; R3 IV.iv.409

2 decline, downturn, falling off **KL** V.iii.286 [Kent to Lear] *from your first of difference and decay;* **Sonn** 15.11

3 destitute person, case of hardship **TNK** I.ii.32 [Palamon to Arcite] *I pity / Decays where'er I find them;* **TNK** I.ii.29

decay (*v.*) be destroyed, become ruined, fail **1H6** I.i.34 [Gloucester to Winchester, of King Henry V] *Had not churchmen prayed, / His thread of life had not so soon decayed;* **AC** II.i.4; **Cym** I.vi.56; **Sonn** 71.12

decayed (*adj.*) ruined, destitute, impoverished **CE** IV.iii.25 [Dromio of Syracuse to Antipholus of Syracuse, of the officer] *he, sir, that takes pity on decayed men and gives them suits of durance*

deceased (*adj.*) past, previous, gone by **2H4** III.i.77 [Warwick to King Henry IV] *There is a history in all men's lives / Figuring the natures of the times deceased*

deceit (*n.*) deception, stratagem, trick **MW** V.v.218 [Fenton to all, of his marriage to Anne] *this deceit loses the name of craft*

deceitful (*adj.*) sham, false, bogus **TS** IV.iv.80 [Biondello to Lucentio, of Baptista] *talking with the deceiving father of a deceitful son*

deceivable (*adj.*) **1** deceptive, illusory **TN** IV.iii.21 [Sebastian alone, of his situation] *There's something in't / That is deceivable*
2 deceitful, insincere **R2** II.iii.84 [York to Bolingbroke] *thy knee, / Whose duty is deceivable and false*

deceive (*v.*) **1** delude, mislead, take in **TC** V.iii.90 [Cassandra to Hector] *Thou dost thyself and all our Troy deceive;* **AY** I.ii.184; **1H4** V.i.11; **3H6** I.i.155; **JC** II.i.105; **Sonn** 4.10
2 disappoint, frustrate, let down **H8** Prologue.17 [of the audience] *they / That come to hear a merry, bawdy play … / Will be deceived*

deceiving (*adj.*) sham, false, bogus **TS** IV.iv.80 [Biondello to Lucentio, of Baptista] *talking with the deceiving father of a deceitful son*

decent (*adj.*) satisfying propriety, observing conformity **H8** IV.ii.145 [Katherine to Capuchius, of her serving-women] *will deserve … / For honesty and decent carriage, / A right good husband*

deceptious (*adj.*) deceptive, misleading, deceiving **TC** V.ii.125 [Troilus to Ulysses, of eyes and ears] *As if those organs had deceptious functions*

decern (*v.*) malapropism for 'concern' **MA** III.v.3 [Dogberry to Leonato] *I would have some confidence with you that decerns you nearly*

decimation (*n.*) killing one in every ten persons **Tim** V.iv.31 [Second Senator to Alcibiades] *By decimation and a tithed death … take thou the destined tenth*

decipher (*v.*) **1** distinguish, make out **CE** V.i.335 [Duke to all, of the two Antipholuses] *Who deciphers them?*
2 discover, detect, find out **1H6** IV.i.184 [Exeter alone, of Richard's heart] *I fear we should have seen deciphered there / More rancorous spite;* **Tit** IV.ii.8
3 make known to, indicate to **MW** V.ii.9 [Shallow to Slender, of Anne's clothes] *The white will decipher her well enough*

decision (*n.*) way of deciding, resolution, trial [by combat] **TNK** V.iii.3 [Emilia to Pirithous] *I had rather see a wren hawk at a fly / Than this decision*

deck (*v.*) cover, adorn, decorate **3H6** III.i.63 [King to Second Keeper] *My crown is in my heart … / Not decked with diamonds and Indian stones;* **H5** Prologue.28; **1H6** I.ii.99; **Tem** III.i.98; **TNK** II.i.77; **TS** I.i.16

deck up (*v.*) array, attire, adorn **RJ** IV.ii.41 [Capulet to Lady Capulet, of Juliet] *help to deck up her*

decking (*n.*) adorning, dressing, attiring **TNK** I.iii.74 [Emilia to Hippolyta, of her friend's choice of dress] *I followed / For my most serious decking*

declare (*v.*) explain, clarify, make plain **1H6** II.v.53 [Richard to Mortimer] *for alliance' sake, declare the cause / My father … lost his head*

declension (*n.*) decline, deterioration, downward course **Ham** II.ii.149 [Polonius to Claudius and Gertrude, of Hamlet] *Fell … by this declension, / Into the madness;* **2H4** II.ii.168; **R3** III.vii.188

decline (*v.*) **1** incline, lean, bend **KL** IV.ii.22 [Gonerill to Edmund] *Decline your head;* **CE** III.ii.44, 142
2 fall, descend, come down **Cor** II.i.154 [Volumnia to Menenius, of Coriolanus' arm] *Which, being advanced, declines, and then men die;* **Cor** I.i.191; **Ham** II.ii.476; **TC** V.v.189
3 sink, fall to a low level **Tim** IV.i.20 [Timon alone] *Degrees, observances, customs, and laws, / Decline to your confounding contraries;* **Ham** I.v.50
4 go systematically through, recite in order **TC** II.iii.51 [Thersites to Achilles] *I'll decline the whole question;* **R3** IV.iv.97

declined (*n.*) vanquished person, someone brought down **TC** IV.v.189 [Nestor to Hector, of Hector's sword] *Not letting it decline on the declined;* **TC** III.iii.76

declined (*adj.*) brought low, in poor fortune; or: fallen away in vigour, in poor condition **AC** III.xiii.27 [Antony to Ambassador, of Caesar] *I dare him … answer me declined, sword against sword*

declining (*adj.*) **1** hanging, bowing, drooping **TS** Induction. i.117 [Lord to Servant, of Page behaving as a woman to Sly] *with declining head into his bosom*
2 falling, sinking, descending **Tim** I.i.91 [Poet to Painter, of friends of one who falls from Fortune] *Not one accompanying his declining foot*

decoct (*v.*) warm up, heat up, inflame **H5** III.v.20 [Constable to all, of the English] *Can sodden water, / A drench for sur-reined jades … / Decoct their cold blood to such valiant heat?*

decorum (*n.*) propriety, seemliness, what is appropriate **AC** I.ii.74 [Iras to Charmian, as if to Isis] *Therefore, dear Isis, keep decorum;* **AC** V.ii.17

decrease (*v.*) malapropism for 'increase' **MW** I.i.230 [Slender to Shallow, of Slender's love for Anne] *heaven may decrease it upon better acquaintance*

decree (*n.*) **1** decision, judgement **Tit** V.ii.11 [Titus to disguised Tamora, Chiron, and Demetrius] *Is it your trick to make me ope the door, / That so my sad decrees may fly away, / And all my study be to no effect?*
2 arrangement, decision, resolve **RJ** III.v.138 [Capulet to Lady Capulet, of Juliet] *Have you delivered to her our decree?*

decree (*v.*) arrange, decide, resolve **RJ** III.iii.146 [Friar to Romeo] *get thee to thy love, as was decreed;* **MA** I.iii.31; **Tit** II.ii.274

dedicate (*adj.*) dedicated, devoted, committed **2H6** V.ii.37 [Young Clifford to himself] *He that is truly dedicate to war / Hath no self-love;* **MM** II.ii.154

dedicated (*adj.*) of dedication, inscribed **Sonn** 82.3 *The dedicated words which writers use / Of their fair subject*

deed (*n.*) performance, action **Tim** V.i.25 [Painter to Poet] *the deed of saying is quite out of use* [i.e. the carrying out of a promise]; **AW** III.vi.88; **Ham** I.ii.27; **KL** I.i.71

deed-achieving (*adj.*) achieved by deeds, won by actions **Cor** II.i.166 [Volumnia to Coriolanus] *By deed-achieving honour newly named*

deedless (*adj.*) performing no deeds, inactive **TC** IV.v.98 [Ulysses to Agamemnon, of Troilus] *firm of word, / Speaking in deeds, and deedless in his tongue* [i.e. not boasting about his prowess]

deem (*n.*) thought, notion, opinion **TC** IV.iv.58 [Cressida to Troilus, of being true] *what wicked deem is this?*

deem (*v.*) judge, estimate, appraise **Cym** V.v.57 [First Brother, to music, of Posthumus] *Innogen, that best / could deem his dignity;* **2H6** III.ii.65

deep (*n.*) depths, middle **JC** IV.iii.224 [Brutus to Cassius] *The deep of night is crept upon our talk;* **MW** IV.iv.38

deep *(adj.)* **1** solemn, weighty, important **1H4** I.iii.188 [Worcester to Hotspur and Northumberland] *to your quick-conceiving discontents / I'll read you matter deep and dangerous;* **Cym** II.iii.90; **Mac** I.iii.125, vii.20; **R3** IV.ii.118

2 learned, profound, erudite **Per** V.Chorus.5 [Gower alone, of Marina] *Deep clerks she dumbs* **2H4** IV.ii.17; **R3** III.vii.74; **Tem** II.i.271

3 large, heavy, serious **Tim** III.iv.32 [First Varro's Servant to Lucius' Servant, of loans to Timon] *'Tis much deep*

4 profound, esoteric, occult **1H4** III.i.46 [Glendower to Hotspur] *bring him out that is but woman's son / Can ... hold me pace in deep experiments*

5 deeply cunning, profound in craft **2H6** III.i.57 [Suffolk to King] *Gloucester is a man / Unsounded yet and full of deep deceit;* **R3** I.iii.223, II.i.38, ii.28

6 subtle, intricate, complex **TNK** I.iii.43 [Hippolyta to Emilia, of Theseus and Pirithous] *Their knot of love, / Tied ... with a finger of so deep a cunning;* **Tit** III.i.214

7 deadly, grave, mortal **R3** IV.ii.71 [King Richard to Tyrrel, of the Princes] *Two deep enemies ... / Are they that I would have thee deal upon*

8 loud, resounding; low-pitched **1H6** II.iv.12 [Warwick to all] *Between two dogs, which hath the deeper mouth*

deep-drawing *(adj.)* displacing great depth of water, heavily-laden **TC** Prologue.12 [Prologue] *the deep-drawing barks do ... disgorge / Their warlike fraughtage*

deep-fet *(adj.)* draw from deep within **2H6** II.iv.33 [Duchess to Gloucester, of herself] *followed with a rabble that rejoice / To ... hear my deep-fet groans*

deeply *(adv.)* **1** profoundly, thoroughly, sincerely **2H4** V.ii.52 [King Henry V to his brothers] *Sorrow so royally in you appears / That I will deeply put the fashion on / And wear it in my heart;* **TN** II.v.41; **TS** IV.iv.42

2 loudly, sonorously, resoundingly **TS** II.i.193 [Petruchio to Katherina] *thy beauty sounded, / Yet not so deeply as to thee belongs;* **Venus** 832

3 solemnly, with great seriousness **Ham** III.ii.235 [First Player, as King, to his Queen, of her vow] *'Tis deeply sworn*

deep-revolving *(adj.)* deeply considering, meditating, pondering **R3** IV.ii.42 [King Richard to himself] *The deep-revolving witty Buckingham / No more shall be the neighbour to my counsels* ➤ revolve *(v.)*

deer *(n.)* animal, beast **KL** III.iv.132 [Edgar as Poor Tom to Gloucester] *mice and rats and such small deer*

deface *(v.)* **1** disfigure, defame, mar **1H6** V.v.29 [Gloucester to King, of his existing engagement] *How shall we then dispense with that contract / And not deface your honour with reproach?*

2 [heraldry] efface, obliterate, blot out **2H6** IV.i.42 [Whitmore to Suffolk] *Broke be my sword, my arms torn and defaced;* **2H6** I.i.100; **MV** III.ii.299

defame *(n.)* disgrace, infamy, dishonour **Luc** 1033 [Lucrece as if to her hand] *if I live, thou liv'st in my defame;* **Luc** 768, 817

defame *(v.)* dishonour, disgrace, make infamous **2H6** III.i.123 [York to Gloucester] *England was defamed by tyranny*

default *(n.)* **1** failure, negligence, oversight **1H6** IV.iv.28 [Lucy to Somerset] *Talbot perisheth by your default;* **1H6** II.i.60

2 offence, fault, misdeed **CE** I.ii.52 [Dromio of Ephesus to Antipholus of Syracuse] *we that know what 'tis to fast and pray / Are penitent for your default today*

3 [unclear meaning] absence, lack, want **AW** II.iii.227 [Lafew to Parolles] *I may say, in the default, 'He is a man I know' [i.e. in the absence of anything better to talk about]*

defeat *(n.)* act of destruction, ruin **Ham** II.ii.568 [Hamlet alone, of his father] *Upon whose ... life / A damned defeat was made [Q2; F debate];* **Ham** V.ii.58; **MA** IV.i.45

defeat *(v.)* **1** refute, resist **H8** II.i.14 [First Gentleman to Second Gentleman, of Buckingham] *He ... alleged / Many sharp reasons to defeat the law*

2 frustrate, bring to nought **MND** IV.i.156 [Egeus to Theseus, of the lovers' actions] *Thereby to have defeated you and me*

3 defraud, deprive **Sonn** 20.11 *a woman wert thou first created, / Till Nature as she wrought thee fell a-doting, / And by addition me of thee defeated*

4 deface, disfigure, disguise **Oth** I.iii.337 [Iago to Roderigo] *defeat thy favour with an usurped beard*

5 destroy, ruin, wreck **Oth** IV.ii.159 [Desdemona to Iago, of Othello] *his unkindness may defeat my life;* **Tim** V.iii.164

defeature *(n.)* disfigurement, defacement, loss of beauty **CE** II.i.98 [Adriana to Luciana, of Antipholus of Ephesus] *Then is he the ground / Of my defeatures;* **CE** V.i.300; **Venus** 736

defect *(n.)* **1** deficiency, shortcoming **Mac** II.i.18 [Macbeth to Banquo] *Being unprepared / Our will became the servant to defect;* **Luc** 151; **Sonn** 149.11

2 malapropism for 'effect' **MV** II.ii.132 [Gobbo to Bassanio] *That is the very defect of the matter;* **MND** III.i.35

defence *(n.)* **1** fencing, swordsmanship, skill of self-defence **Ham** IV.vii.96 [Claudius to Laertes, of Lamord] *He ... gave you such a masterly report / For art and exercise in your defence;* **AY** III.iii.56; **JC** IV.iii.200; **KJ** IV.iii.84; **TN** III.iv.216

2 self-defence, resisting attack **Tim** III.v.56 [Alcibiades to Senators] *To kill, I grant, is sin's extremest gust, / But in defence, by mercy, 'tis most just*

3 arms, armour, means of defence **AC** IV.iv.10 [Antony to Eros] *Go put on thy defences;* **RJ** III.iii.134

defend *(v.)* forbid, prohibit **R2** I.iii.18 [Mowbray to Lord Marshal] *my oath, - / Which God defend a knight should violate!;* **AC** III.iii.42; **1H4** IV.iii.38; **MA** IV.ii.19; **Oth** I.iii.263; **R3** III.vii.80

defendant *(adj.)* defensive, protective **H5** II.iv.8 [French King to Dauphin] *line and new repair our towns of war / With men of courage and with means defendant*

defensible *(adj.)* defendable, capable of providing a defence **H5** III.iii.50 [Governor to King Henry] *we no longer are defensible;* **2H4** II.iii.38

defer *(v.)* waste, put off, delay **1H6** III.ii.33 [Reignier to all] *Defer no time; delays have dangerous ends*

defiance *(n.)* renunciation, disowning, rejection; or: contempt **MM** III.i.146 [Isabella to Claudio] *Take my defiance*

defier *(n.)* **1** challenger, confronter, denouncer **TNK** V.i.120 [Palamon praying to Venus] *I am ... / To those who boast and have not [done what they boast of], a defier*

2 herald declaring war **TNK** I.ii. 107 [Valerius to Arcite] *The intelligence of state came in the instant / With the defier [i.e. Creon heard of the war from his own spies at the same time as Theseus' herald announced it]*

defile *(v.)* make filthy, pollute, dirty **Per** I.iv.37 [Cleon to Dionyza] *houses are defiled for want of use*

define *(v.)* **1** present, set forth, characterize **H5** IV.Chorus.46 [Chorus, of King Henry] *mean and gentle all / Behold, as may unworthiness define, / A little touch of Harry in the night [i.e. insofar as our unworthy efforts can present it]*

2 explain, elucidate, clarify **LL** I.ii.90 [Armado to Mote, of his remark] *Define, define, well-educated infant*

definement *(n.)* description, definition, delineation **Ham** V.ii.112 [Hamlet to Osrick, of Laertes] *his definement suffers no perdition in you*

definitive *(adj.)* decided, final, determined **MM** V.i.424 [Duke to Mariana] *We are definitive*

deformed *(adj.)* deforming, disfiguring; or: deformed, disfigured **CE** V.i.299 [Egeon to Antipholus and Dromio of Ephesus] *careful hours with time's deformed hand / Have written strange defeatures in my face*

defunct *(n.)* dead person, deceased **Cym** IV.ii.358 [Lucius to all] *nature doth abhor to make his bed / With the defunct*

defunction *(n.)* death, decease **H5** I.ii.58 [Canterbury to King Henry] *four hundred one-and-twenty years / After defunction of King Pharamond*

defunctive *(adj.)* to do with dying, funereal **Phoen** 14 *Let the priest in surplice white, / That defunctive music can, / Be the death-divining swan* [i.e. that is well-versed in music for funerals]

defuse *(v.)* ➻ diffuse *(v.)*

defused *(adj.)* ➻ diffused *(adj.)* 1

defy *(v.)* **1** reject, despise, disdain, renounce **PassP** XII.11 [Pilgrim] *Age, I do defy thee;* **AY** V.iv.213; **1H4** I.iii.225; **MV** III.v.65; **MW** II.ii.70; **Per** IV.vi.24
   2 distrust, suspect, doubt **1H4** IV.i.6 [Hotspur to Douglas] *I do defy / The tongues of soothers*

degrade *(v.)* lower in rank, reduce in degree **1H6** IV.i.43 [Talbot to all, of an unworthy knight] *He [should] ... / Be quite degraded*

degree *(n.)* **1** rank, station, standing **E3** IV.v.104 [King John to Salisbury] *Say ... of what degree thou art;* **1H6** V.i.29; **LL** V.ii.504; **R3** III.vii.142; **TN** I.iii.104; **WT** II.i.85
   2 condition, state of being, stage of life **2H4** I.ii.234 [Falstaff to himself, of youth and age] *both the degrees prevent my curses*
   3 step, stage, rung **3H6** II.i.192 [Warwick to Edward] *The next degree is England's royal throne;* **Cor** II.ii.24; **JC** II.i.26; **Tim** IV.iii.254; **TN** I.v.130, III.i.120
   4 measure, extent, amount **KL** I.i.219 [France to Lear, of Cordelia] *her offence / Must be of such unnatural degree;* **Oth** II.i.230; **R2** I.i.80
   5 respect, way, manner **TC** I.ii.70 [Pandarus to Cressida] *nor Hector is not Troilus in some degrees* [i.e. not in any respect]

degree, by little by little, bit by bit **1H6** III.i.194 [Exeter alone] *As festered members rot but by degree*

deify *(v.)* adore as a god, idolize **AY** III.ii.348 [Rosalind as Ganymede to Orlando, of his love poems] *all ... deifying the name of Rosalind* [F2; F1 *defying*]

deign *(v.)* **1** willingly accept, not disdain **AC** I.iv.63 [Caesar to Lepidus, as if to Antony] *Thy palate then did deign / The roughest berry on the rudest hedge;* **TG** I.i.149
   2 be willing, think fit **3H6** IV.vii.39 [Edward to Lord Mayor] *Edward will defend ... all those friends that deign to follow me*

deject *(adj.)* dejected, downcast, cast down **Ham** III.i.156 [Ophelia alone] *I, of ladies most deject and wretched;* **TC** II.ii.50

deject *(v.)* **1** humble, abase, cast down **Tim** IV.iii.9 [Timon alone] *Raise me this beggar and deject that lord* [F *deny't*];
   2 lower, reduce, lessen **TC** II.ii.122 [Troilus to Hector] *We may not ... once deject the courage of our minds, / Because Cassandra's mad*

dejected *(adj.)* cast down, abased, humbled **Per** II.ii.45 [Simonides to Thaisa, of Pericles] *From the dejected state wherein he is, / He hopes by you his fortunes yet may flourish;* **KL** IV.i.3; **MW** V.v.160

delated *(adj.)* reported in detail, detailed, expanded **Ham** I.ii.38 [Claudius to the ambassadors, limiting their power to] *the scope / Of these delated articles* [Q2; F *dilated;* Q1 *related*]

delay *(n.)* set of delaying tactics, procrastination **MW** II.i.89 [Mistress Page to Mistress Ford, of Falstaff] *Let's ... lead him on with a fine-baited delay*

delay *(v.)* quench, subdue, allay **AW** IV.iii.18 [First Lord to Second Lord] *God delay our rebellion!*

deliberate *(adj.)* calculating, carefully considering **MV** II.ix.80 [Portia to Nerissa, of her suitors] *O these deliberate fools!*

delicate *(n.)* delicacy, luxury, delight **3H6** II.v.51 [King alone, of the shepherd's life] *Is far beyond a prince's delicates*

delicate *(adj.)* **1** fine in quality, of exquisite nature, dainty **Tem** I.ii.272 [Prospero to Ariel, of Sycorax] *thou wast a spirit too delicate / To act her earthy and abhorred commands;* **H5** II.iv.40; **Oth** I.iii.20, III.iii.266; **Tem** I.ii.442; **Tim** IV.iii.386
   2 finely wrought, skilfully made, ingenious **Ham** V.ii.150 [Osric to Hamlet] *most delicate carriages*

3 pleasant, delightful, congenial **WT** III.i.1 [Cleomenes to Dion] *The climate's delicate;* **Mac** I.vi.10; **Oth** I.iii.349; **Tem** I.i.44, ii.88; **WT** IV.iv.196
   4 cunning, ingenious, skilful **KL** IV.vi.185 [Lear to all] *It were a delicate stratagem to shoe / A troop of horse with felt;* **AW** IV.v.101; **Cym** V.v.47; **Oth** IV.i.186
   5 pleasure-seeking, voluptuous, self-indulgent **Tem** II.i.46 [Antonio to Sebastian] *Temperance was a delicate wench;* **MA** I.i.282
   6 sensitive, tender, not robust **KL** III.iv.12 [Lear to disguised Kent] *When the mind's free / The body's delicate;* **Ham** IV.iv.48

delight *(n.)* pleasure, enjoyment **2H4** II.iii.29 [Lady Percy to Northumberland, of Percy] *in affections of delight ... / He was the mark and glass, copy and book, / That fashioned others*

delighted *(adj.)* **1** delightful, joyful, pleasing **Oth** I.iii.286 [Duke to Brabantio] *If virtue no delighted beauty lack, / Your son-in-law is far more fair than black*
   2 endowed with delight **MM** III.i.124 [Claudio to Isabella, of what might follow death] *the delighted spirit / To bathe in fiery floods;* **Cym** V.iv.102

delightful *(adj.)* full of delight, experiencing great pleasure **Per** II.i.159 [Pericles to Fishermen] *a courser, whose delightful steps / Shall make the gazer joy to see him tread* [Q *delight*]

deliver *(v.)* **1** report [to], communicate [to], tell, describe **CE** II.ii.173 [Antipholus of Syracuse to Dromio of Syracuse, of Adriana] *her very words / Didst thou deliver to me on the mart;* **JC** III.i.181; **Mac** III.iii.2; **Per** V.iii.63; **TN** V.i.287; **WT** V.ii.26
   2 express one's mind, disburden in speech **Per** V.i.105 [Pericles to himself] *I ... shall deliver weeping* [unclear meaning]
   3 free, release, liberate **TN** V.i.312 [Olivia to Fabian, of Malvolio] *See him delivered;* **AW** I.i.1; **2H4** V.v.39; **MM** IV.vi.11; **R3** I.i.115; **TN** IV.ii.67
   4 hand over, convey, commit to the keeping [of someone] **MM** I.iii.11 [Duke to Friar Thomas] *I have delivered to Lord Angelo ... / My absolute power;* **1H4** V.v.27; **LL** I.i.292; **MV** II.vii.59; **TC** II.ii.3; **TG** IV.iv.70
   5 present, show, display **Cor** V.vi.141 [Aufidius to Lords] *I'll deliver / Myself your loyal servant,* **Cor** V.iii.38; **Per** II.ii.40; **TN** I.ii.43
   6 be born, bring forth **LL** IV.ii.70 [Holofernes to Nathaniel and Dull, of his literary gifts] *These are ... delivered upon the mellowing of occasion;* **CE** I.i.403; **Oth** I.iii.365

deliver up *(v.)* surrender, yield, give up totally **H5** II.iv.103 [Exeter to French King] *Deliver up the crown;* **2H6** I.i.120

deliverance *(n.)* **1** delivery, utterance, reporting **AW** II.v.3 [Lafew to Bertram, of Parolles being an experienced soldier] *You have it from his own deliverance;* **AW** II.ii.82; **3H6** II.i.97
   2 delivery, giving birth **Cym** V.v.371 [Cymbeline to all] *Ne'er mother / Rejoiced deliverance more*

deliverly *(adv.)* nimbly, lightly, sprightly **TNK** III.v.29 [Schoolmaster to the dancers, of their dancing] *carry it sweetly and deliverly*

delivery *(n.)* **1** release, deliverance, freedom **R3** I.iv.249 [Clarence to Murderers, of Richard] *he .. swore with sobs / That he would labour my delivery*
   2 account, statement, narration **WT** V.ii.9 [First Gentleman to Autolycus, of the events in court] *I make a broken delivery of the business*

delver *(n.)* [grave]digger, excavator **Ham** V.i.14 [Second Clown to First Clown] *hear you, Goodman Delver*

demand *(n.)* **1** question, enquiry, request **TC** II.iii.66 [Thersites to Patroclus, responding to 'Why am I a fool?'] *Make that demand to the Creator;* **AW** IV.iii.42; **Ham** II.i.12; **3H6** III.iii.259; **H8** II.iii.52; **KL** I.v.3
   2 condition, request, claim **MW** I.i.210 [Slender to Evans, of Anne] *I will marry her upon any reasonable demands*

demand *(v.)* **1** request to tell, question, ask [about] **Cym** III.vii.64 [Belarius to disguised Innogen] *We'll mannerly demand thee of thy story;* **AW** IV.iii.173; **2H6** II.i.170; **H8** I.i.153; **Oth** V.ii.298; **Tem** I.ii.139

2 ask for, claim **Oth** III.iv.185 [Cassio to Bianca, of the handkerchief] *Ere it be demanded ... I'd have it copied;* **Tit** V.i.160

demean (*v.*) behave, conduct, comport [oneself] **CE** IV.iii.82 [Courtesan alone] *Antipholus is mad, / Else would he never so demean himself;* **CE** V.i.88; **2H6** I.i.186, iii.101; **3H6** I.iv.7

demerit (*n.*) (plural) merits, deserts, deserving **Cor** I.i.270 [Sicinius to Brutus] *Opinion, that so sticks on Martius, shall / Of his demerits rob Cominius;* **Oth** I.ii.22

demesne (*n.*) (plural) territories, lands, dominions **RJ** II.i.20 [Mercutio calling to Romeo] *I conjure thee by Rosaline's ... quivering thigh, / And the demesnes that there adjacent lie;* **Cym** III.iii.70; **RJ** III.v.181

demi-Atlas (*n.*) supporter of half the world **AC** I.v.23 [Cleopatra to Charmian, of Antony] *The demi-Atlas of this earth*

demi-cannon (*n.*) type of large gun **TS** IV.iii.88 [Petruchio to Tailor, of a gown] *A sleeve? 'Tis like a demi-cannon* ➤ **WEAPONS**, p.491

demi-coronal (*n.*) small coronet **H8** IV.i.37 [stage direction, of the Marquis Dorset] *on his head a demi-coronal of gold*

demi-devil (*n.*) half-devil **Oth** V.ii.298 [Othello to all, of Iago] *Will you ... demand that demi-devil / Why he hath thus ensnared my soul and body?;* **Tem** V.i.272

demi-natured (*adj.*) of a shared nature **Ham** IV.vii.86 [Claudius to Laertes, of Lamord] *As had he been incorpsed and demi-natured / With the brave beast*

demi-puppet (*n.*) tiny puppet, dwarf-like creature **Tem** V.i.36 [Prospero alone] *you demi-puppets that / By moonshine do the green, sour ringlets make*

demise (*v.*) transmit, confer, convey **R3** IV.iv.248 [Queen Elizabeth to King Richard] *what state ... / Canst thou demise to any child of mine?*

demi-wolf (*n.*) dog/wolf cross-breed **Mac** III.i.93 [Macbeth to Murderers] *Shoughs, water-rugs, and demi-wolves are clept / All by the name of dogs*

demon (*n.*) ➤ **daemon** (*n.*)

demonstrate (*v.*) manifest, show, display **AY** III.ii.365 [Rosalind as Ganymede to Orlando, of his appearance] *everything about you [should be] demonstrating a careless desolation;* **Ham** I.i.124; **H5** IV.ii.52

demure (*adj.*) grave, serious, sober, solemn **2H4** IV.iii.89 [Falstaff alone, of boys like Prince John] *There's never none of these demure boys come to any proof;* **H8** I.ii.167; **Luc** 1219; **TN** II.v.52

demure (*v.*) look demurely, gaze decorously **AC** IV.xv.29 [Cleopatra to Antony] *Your wife Octavia ... shall acquire no honour / Demuring upon me*

demurely (*adv.*) gently, in a subdued way; or, solemnly **AC** IV.ix.30 [Sentry to all] *The drums / Demurely wake the sleepers;* **MV** II.ii.179

den (*n.*) ➤ **GREETINGS**, p.206

denay (*n.*) denial, refusal, rejection **TN** II.iv.123 [Orsino to Viola as Cesario] *My love can give no place, bide no denay*

denay (*v.*) deny **2H6** I.iii.102 [York to King, of himself] *let him be denayed the Regentship*

denier (*n.*) tenth of a penny [trivial sum, paltry amount] **1H4** III.iii.78 [Falstaff to Hostess] *I'll not pay a denier;* **R3** I.ii.251; **TS** Induction.i.7 ➤ **MONEY**, p.286

denote (*v.*) **1** portray, depict, represent **Ham** I.ii.83 [Hamlet to Gertrude, of his feelings] *'Tis not ... [these] shapes of grief, / That can denote me truly* [F; Q2 *deuote*]; **Oth** IV.i.281

2 mark out, single out, distinguish **MW** IV.vi.39 [Fenton to Host, of Anne's costume] *The better to denote her to the doctor* [F *deuote*]

denotement (*n.*) **1** indication, sign, clue **Oth** III.iii.122 [Othello to Iago, of Iago's pauses] *in a man that's just, / They're close denotements ... / That passion cannot rule* [Q1; F *dilations*] ➤ dilation (*n.*)

2 account, description, making known **Oth** II.iii.308 [Iago to Cassio, of Desdemona] *the contemplation, mark, and denotement of her parts and graces* [F, Q *deuotement*] ➤ devotement (*n.*)

denounce (*v.*) declare, proclaim, announce **KJ** III.i.319 [Cardinal Pandulph to all, of King Philip] *I will denounce a curse upon his head;* **AC** III.vii.5; **KJ** III.iv.159; **R3** I.iii.179

denunciation (*n.*) proclamation, public announcement, official declaration **MM** I.ii.147 [Claudio to Lucio, of Juliet] *we do denunciation lack / Of outward order* [i.e. the publishing of banns]

deny (*v.*) **1** refuse, rebuff, reject **RJ** I.i.157 [Benvolio to Montague, of Romeo] *I'll know his grievance, or be much denied;* **1H6** V.iii.75; **MV** III.iii.26; **R2** II.i.204; **Tim** III.iii.7; **TNK** III.vi.186

2 refuse, decline, scorn **R3** V.iii.344 [Messenger to King Richard, of Derby] *he doth deny to come;* **KL** II.iv.84; **LL** V.ii.228; **RJ** I.v.20; **Tim** IV.iii.533; **TS** II.i.179

3 disallow, forbid, refuse permission [for] **3H6** II.ii.172 [Edward to Queen] *thou deniest the gentle King to speak;* **CE** IV.iv.62; **KL** III.ii.66; **MV** II.ii.166; **R2** I.iii.128; **R3** III.i.35

4 disown, disavow, renounce **1H6** V.iv.20 [Shepherd to Pucelle] *Deny me not;* **CE** III.i.9; **LL** IV.iii.117; **RJ** II.ii.34; **TC** IV.ii.49; **TN** III.iv.378

5 refuse to talk about **Ham** III.iv.346 [Rosencrantz to Hamlet] *if you deny your griefs to your friend*

6 refuse admittance to, keep out **1H4** II.iv.481 [Falstaff to Prince Hal] *If you will deny the sheriff, so; if not, let him enter;* **H5** V.ii.292

depart (*n.*) **1** departure, departing, leave-taking **TG** V.iv.98 [Proteus to disguised Julia, of a ring] *At my depart I gave this unto Julia;* **2H6** I.i.2; **3H6** VI.vi.92; **TNK** I.i.27

2 death, passing away **3H6** II.i.110 [Warwick to Edward and Richard, of York] *Tidings ... / Were brought me of your loss and his depart*

depart (*v.*) separate, part company, take leave of one another **Sonn** 109.3 *As easy might I from myself depart / As from my soul which in thy breast doth lie;* **Cym** I.ii.39; **Tim** I.i.258

depart with (*v.*) part with, give away **TNK** II.i.1 [Gaoler to Wooer] *I may depart with little while I live;* **RJ** I.i.563

depart withal (*v.*) surrender, give up **LL** II.i.147 [King to Princess, of Aquitaine] *Which we much rather had depart withal, / And have the money by our father lent*

departing (*n.*) separation, parting, division **3H6** II.vi.43 [Richard to all, hearing Clifford groan] *A deadly groan, like life and death's departing*

departure (*n.*) death, decease, demise **1H6** IV.ii.41 [General to Talbot, of the drum that sounds like a warning bell] *mine shall ring thy dire departure out*

depend (*v.*) **1** persist, continue, remain hanging **Luc** 1615 [Lucrece to Collatine] *In me moe woes than words are now depending;* **Cym** IV.iii.23

2 have consequences for, menace, hover over **TC** II.iii.19 [Thersites alone, of the Neapolitan bone-ache] *for that ... is the curse depending on those that war for a placket* [Q; F *dependent*]; **RJ** III.i.119

3 lean, rest, recline **Cym** II.iv.91 [Iachimo to Posthumus, of Innogen's room] *Her andirons ... were two winking Cupids ... nicely / Depending on their brands*

depend on / upon (*v.*) **1** serve, wait on, be a dependant of **TC** III.i.4 [Pandarus to Servant, of Paris] *You depend upon him;* **Sonn** 92.4, 101.3

2 serve, support, rely on **TNK** III.i.51 [Arcite to Palamon] *Honour and honesty / I cherish and depend on*

dependant (*n.*) attendant, servant, retainer **KL** I.iv.60 [Third Knight to Lear] *There's a great abatement of kindness appears ... in the general dependants* [i.e. all the servants]

dependant (*adj.*) ➤ depend (*v.*) 2

dependency, dependancy (*n.*) **1** dependence **MM** V.i.62 [Duke to all, of Isabella] *Her madness hath the oddest frame of sense, / Such a dependency of thing on thing*

2 body of dependants **Cym** II.iii.117 [Cloten to Innogen, of the souls of herself and Posthumus] *On whom there is no more dependency / But brats and beggary*

3 submissiveness, willing compliance **AC** V.ii.26 [Proculeius to Cleopatra, of Caesar] *Let me report to him / Your sweet dependency*

depender (*n.*) dependant, one who relies **Cym** I.vi.58 [Queen to Pisanio, of Posthumus] *To be depender on a thing that leans*

deplore (*v.*) tell with grief, express with lamentation **TN** III.i.159 [Viola as Cesario to Olivia] *never more / Will I my master's tears to you deplore*

deploring (*adj.*) mournful, doleful, bewailing **TG** III.ii.85 [Proteus to Thurio, of the musicians] *to their instruments / Tune a deploring dump*

depose (*v.*) **1** swear, take an oath [from] **3H6** I.ii.26 [Richard to York, of the King] *'twas he that made you to depose; **R2** I.iii.30 [King Richard to Lord Marshal, of Bolingbroke] *Depose him in the justice of his cause*

2 testify, bear witness **MM** V.i.196 [Mariana to Duke, of Angelo] *such a time / When, I'll depose, I had him in mine arms*

3 take away, deprive, dispossess **R2** IV.i.191 [Richard to Bolingbroke] *You may my glories and my state depose, / But not my griefs*

depositary (*n.*) trustee, manager of affairs **KL** II.iv.246 [Lear to Regan and Gonerill] *Made you ... my depositaries*

depravation (*n.*) depravity, corruption, moral degeneracy **TC** V.ii.135 [Troilus to Ulysses] *do not give advantage / To stubborn critics, apt, without a theme / For depravation, to square the general sex / By Cressid's rule*

deprave (*v.*) defame, disparage, deride **Tim** I.ii.137 [Apemantus to himself] *Who lives that's not depraved or depraves?; **MA** V.i.95

depraved (*adj.*) slandered, disparaged, defamed **Tim** I.ii.137 [Apemantus to himself] *Who lives that's not depraved or depraves?* ☞ deprave (*v.*)

depress (*v.*) bring low, humble, put down **R2** III.iv.68 [Gardener to First Man, of King Richard] *Depressed he is already*

deprive (*v.*) **1** take away, remove, carry off **Luc** 1752 [Lucretius as if to dead Lucrece] *That life was mine which thou hast here deprived;* **Ham** I.iv.73; **Luc** 1186

2 dispossess, disinherit **KL** I.ii.4 [Edmund alone] *Wherefore should I ... permit / The curiosity of nations to deprive me* [i.e. take away my rights]

deputation (*n.*) **1** delegation, appointment as deputy **AC** III.xiii.74 [Cleopatra to Thidias, of Caesar] *in deputation / I kiss his conquering hand* [i.e. as my representative]; **1H4** IV.i.32, iii.87; **MM** I.i.20

2 position, office, appointment **TC** I.iii.152 [Ulysses to Agamemnon, of Patroclus] *Sometime ... / Thy topless deputation he puts on*

deputed (*adj.*) acting as a symbol of office **MM** II.ii.60 [Isabella to Angelo] *Not the king's crown, nor the deputed sword*

deracinate (*v.*) uproot, pluck up, eradicate **TC** I.iii.99 [Ulysses to all, of disorder in the planets] *Divert and crack, rend and deracinate / The unity and married calm of states;* **H5** V.ii.47

derivation (*n.*) descent, family origins **Per** V.i.89 [Marina to Pericles] *My derivation was from ancestors / Who stood equivalent with mighty kings*

derivative (*n.*) thing proceeding, heritage, inheritance **WT** III.ii.43 [Hermione to Leontes] *for honour, / 'Tis a derivative from me to mine*

derive (*v.*) **1** descend **1H6** II.v.84 [Mortimer to Richard] *Thy father ... derived / From famous Edmund Langley, Duke of York;* **2H4** IV.v.44; **3H6** I.iv.119; **JC** I.ii.322; **MA** IV.i.133 ☞ derived (*adj.*)

2 inherit, fall heir to **AY** I.iii.60 [Rosalind to Duke Frederick] *Treason is not inherited ... / Or, if we did derive it from our friends, / What's that to me?;* **AW** I.i.43

3 explain, justify, give the basis of **TC** II.iii.60 [Achilles to Thersites, of his listing of people who are fools] *Derive this; come*

4 bring down [on], direct [to] **H8** II.iv.32 [Queen Katherine to King Henry] *What friend of mine / That had to him derived your anger did I / Continue in my liking;* **AW** V.iii.263

derived (*adj.*) descended, in lineage **TG** V.iv.147 [Duke to Valentine] *Thou art a gentleman, and well derived;* **MND** I.i.99; **TG** V.ii.23 ☞ derive (*v.*) 1

dern, dearn, dearne (*adj.*) **1** dreary, dark, wild **Per** III.Chorus.15 [Gower alone, of searching for Pericles] *By many a dern and painful perch*

2 dread, dark, sombre **KL** III.vii.62 [Gloucester to Regan] *If wolves had at thy gate howled that dern time* [Q *dearne*; F *stern*]

derogate (*adj.*) degenerate, debased, degraded **KL** I.iv.277 [Lear to the goddess Nature, of Gonerill] *from her derogate body never spring / A babe to honour her*

derogate (*v.*) act in an undignified way, disparage one's rank **Cym** II.i.44 [Second Lord to Cloten] *You cannot derogate*

derogately (*adv.*) disparagingly, in a derogatory way **AC** II.ii.38 [Caesar to Antony] *that I should / Once name you derogately*

derogation (*n.*) loss of dignity, disparagement, detraction **Cym** II.i.42 [Cloten to Lords, of going to see Iachimo] *Is there no derogation in't?*

derry (*int.*) ☞ SINGING, p.402

desart (*n.*) ☞ desert (*n.*)

desartless (*adj.*) underserving, lacking in merit [probably malapropism for 'desertless'] **MA** III.iii.9 [Dogberry to First Watchman] *who think you the most desartless man to be constable?*

descant (*n.*) melodious accompaniment, tuneful variation **E3** II.i.122 [King Edward to Lodowick] *what a world of descant makes my soul / Upon this voluntary ground of love!;* **R3** III.vii.48; **TG** I.ii.94

descant (*v.*) **1** develop a theme about, comment, make remarks **R3** I.i.27 [Richard alone] *I ... descant on mine own deformity;* **PassP** XIV.4

2 sing along in harmony **Luc** 1134 [Lucrece as if to the nightingale] *I'll hum on Tarquin still, / While thou on Tereus descants better skill*

descending (*n.*) descent, family, lineage **Per** V.i.128 [Pericles to Marina] *thou camest / From good descending?* [F *descent*; Q1 *discending*]

descension (*n.*) descent, fall from dignity, degradation **2H4** II.ii.168 [Prince Henry to Poins] *From a god to a bull? A heavy descension!* [F, Q *declension*] ☞ declension (*n.*)

descry (*n.*) sighting, spotting, discovery of what is distant **KL** IV.vi.213 [Gentleman to Edgar, of the French army] *The main descry* [i.e. sighting of the main force] [F; Q *descryes*]

descry (*v.*) **1** catch sight of, make out, espy, discover **E3** III.i.62 [Mariner to King John] *Near to the coast I have descried ... / The proud armado of King Edward's ships;* **AC** III.vii.54; **KL** IV.v.13; **Oth** II.i.4; **Per** V.Epilogue.7; **TS** I.i.229

2 find out, detect, discover **LL** V.ii.389 [King to his friends] *We were descried;* **RJ** V.iii.181

3 reveal, disclose, make known **1H6** I.ii.57 [Bastard to all, of Pucelle] *What's past and what's to come she can descry*

desert, desart (*n.*) **1** deserving, due recompense, right **3H6** III.iii.192 [Warwick to Lewis] *my desert is honour;* **AW** II.iii.152; **E3** V.i.72; **MM** V.i.9; **TG** III.i.159; **Tit** I.i.16

2 worth, merit, deserving **TG** V.iv.160 [Duke to Valentine, of the Outlaws] *Dispose of them as thou knowest their deserts;* **AW** I.iii.195; **R3** III.vii.153; **Sonn** 49.10; **Tim** I.i.68; **Tit** III.i.170

3 worthy deed, meritorious action **1H6** III.iv.25 [King to Talbot] *for these good deserts / We here create you Earl of Shrewsbury;* **KL** II.iv.134; **R2** I.iii.44; **TC** III.iii.172; **TN** III.iv.339

4 cause, deserving, warrant **R3** II.i.68 [Richard to all] *That, all without desert, have frowned on me;* **CE** III.i.112; **TG** II.iv.55; **Tit** I.i.48

5 desolate place, wilderness **AY** II.vii.111 [Orlando to Duke Senior] *in this desert inaccessible;* **TG** V.iv.2; **WT** III.iii.2

desert *(adj.)* desolate, lonely, isolated **Tem** II.i.37 [Adrian to all] *Though this island seem to be desert;* **AY** II.iv.69, IV.iii.142

deserve *(v.)* **1** earn, win, receive **Cym** III.iii.54 [Belarius to Guiderius and Arviragus] *many times, / Doth ill deserve by doing well;*

2 be worthy, be entitled to honour **MA** III.i.115 [Beatrice alone, as if to Benedick] *others say thou dost deserve, and I / Believe it better than reportingly*

3 requite, recompense, pay back **Oth** I.i.184 [Brabantio to Roderigo] *good Roderigo, I'll deserve your pains*

deserved *(adj.)* deserving, meritorious, praiseworthy **AW** II.i.189 [Helena to King] *If I break time … unpitied let me die, / And well deserved;* **Cor** III.i.290

deserving *(n.)* **1** worthiness, desert, merit **2H4** IV.iii.43 [Prince John to Falstaff, of capturing Colevile] *It was more of his courtesy than your deserving;* **AW** I.iii.6, III.v.60; **KL** I.i.30

2 reward, recompense, desert **MM** V.i.474 [Angelo to all, of death] *'Tis my deserving, and I do entreat it;* **KL** III.iii.21, V.iii.302; **Sonn** 87.6

deserving *(adj.)* deserving of gratitude, meritorious **TNK** V.iv.34 [Palamon to his knights, of the Gaoler's Daughter] *more to me deserving / Than I can quite or speak of*

design *(n.)* **1** undertaking, purpose, enterprise **TC** II.ii.195 [Troilus to Hector, of his speech] *there you touched the life of our design;* **AW** III.vi.38; **Cym** II.ii.23; **R2** II.ii.44; **R3** III.iv.24; **WT** IV.iv.499

2 scheme, plan, plot **Tem** I.ii.163 [Prospero to Miranda, of Gonzalo] *being then appointed / Master of this design;* **Cym** II.ii.23, V.v.192; **H8** I.ii.181; **WT** II.i.50

design *(v.)* indicate, designate, mark out **R2** I.i.203 [King Richard to Bolingbroke and Mowbray] *we shall see / Justice design the victor's chivalry*

designed *(adj.)* prearranged, designated **Ham** I.i.94 [Horatio to Marcellus and Barnardo, of King Hamlet's legal agreement with old Fortinbras] *by the same covenant / And carriage of the article designed*

designment *(n.)* undertaking, enterprise, design **Oth** II.i.22 [Third Gentleman to all] *The desperate tempest hath so banged the Turks / That their designment halts;* **Cor** V.vi.35

desire *(n.)* **1** good wishes, regards **Ham** II.ii.60 [Voltemand to Claudius, of Norway's response] *Most fair return of greetings and desires*

2 charm, desirability **Oth** IV.i.94 [Iago to himself, of Bianca] *A housewife, that by selling her desires / Buys herself bread and clothes*

desire *(v.)* **1** request, wish, ask [for] **TC** IV.v.48 [Ulysses to Cressida, of a kiss] *I do desire it;* **AY** V.iv.53; **1H6** II.ii.11; **KL** I.iv.243; **MND** III.i.177; **TN** II.i.34

2 require, command **KJ** I.i.12 [Chatillon to King John, of King Philip] *Desiring thee to lay aside the sword / Which sways usurpingly*

3 invite, welcome, request the presence of **TC** IV.v.150 [Ajax to all, of Hector] *I would desire / My famous cousin to our Grecian tents;* **H5** IV.i.27

desired *(adj.)* liked, admired, esteemed **Oth** II.i.198 [Othello to Desdemona] *you shall be well desired in Cyprus*

desolation *(n.)* **1** despondency, dejection, depression **AY** III.ii.366 [Rosalind as Ganymede to Orlando, of his appearance] *everything about you [should be] demonstrating a careless desolation*

2 barren emptiness, dreary absence **Cym** V.iv.206 [First Gaoler alone, if everyone were good] *O, there were desolation of gaolers and gallowses!*

despatch *(n.)* ☞ dispatch *(n.)*

desperate *(adj.)* **1** despairing, hopeless, without hope **TG** III.ii.5 [Thurio to Duke, of Silvia] *I am desperate of obtaining her;* **Cym** IV.iii.6; **Ham** IV.vii.26; **Sonn** 147.7; **Tim** III.iv.103; **TN** II.ii.8

2 risky, dangerous, hazardous **AY** V.iv.32 [Orlando to Duke Senior, of Ganymede] *[he] hath been tutored in the rudiments / Of many desperate studies;* **1H6** II.i.45; **TS** II.i.320

3 disregarding, careless, reckless **TN** V.i.61 [First Officer to Orsino, of Antonio] *Here in the streets, desperate of shame and state, / In private brabble did we apprehend him;* **AW** II.i.184; **H8** III.i.86; **KL** II.iv.300; **R2** V.iii.20

4 deadly serious, bold, steadfast **RJ** III.iv.12 [Capulet to Paris, of Juliet] *I will make a desperate tender / Of my child's love*

desperately *(adv.)* **1** recklessly, disregarding all risks **R3** I.iv.274 [Second Murderer to himself, of Clarence's murder] *A bloody deed, and desperately dispatched!;* **CE** V.i.140

2 despairingly, in a state of hopelessness **KL** V.iii.290 [Kent to Lear] *Your eldest daughters have fordone themselves, / And desperately are dead;* **MW** II.ii.142

desperation *(n.)* reckless despair, desperate thoughts [of self-destruction] **Ham** I.iv.75 [Horatio to Hamlet, of the Elsinore cliff] *The very place puts toys of desperation … into every brain;* **Tem** I.ii.210

despised *(adj.)* scorned, derided, treated with contempt **1H6** II.v.42 [Mortimer to Richard] *Why didst thou say of late thou wert despised?;* **1H6** II.v.36; **R2** II.iii.94

despite *(n.)* **1** contempt, scorn, disdain **E3** III.iv.97 [Prince Edward to all] *in despite, I carved my passage forth;* **Cor** III.iii.139; **1H6** IV.vii.22; **3H6** II.i.59; **MA** I.i.217; **Oth** IV.ii.115

2 malice, spite, hatred **TN** III.iv.218 [Sir Toby to Viola as Cesario, of Sir Andrew] *full of despite, bloody as the hunter, attends thee at the orchard end;* **1H6** III.ii.52; **Oth** IV.iii.90; **RJ** V.iii.48

3 outrage, shame, wrong **Luc** 1026 [Lucrece to herself] *In vain I spurn at my confirmed despite*

despite, in **1** in spite of [one], as opposed to [one] **Tit** I.i.364 [Titus to all, of Mutius] *would you bury him in my despite?;* **CE** III.i.108; **Cym** IV.i.14

2 no matter what else happens **TS** Induction.i.126 [Lord to Servant, of the Page using an onion] *in a napkin being close conveyed, / Shall in despite enforce a watery eye*

despite *(v.)* spite, anger, wreak malice on **MA** II.ii.28 [Don John to Borachio, of Claudio and Hero] *Only to despite them I will endeavour anything*

despite of *(prep.)* in spite of **MM** I.ii.26 [Lucio to First Gentleman] *thou thyself art a wicked villain, despite of all grace;* **1H6** IV.vi.8

despite of, in *(prep.)* in spite of **MA** II.i.354 [Don Pedro to Claudio and Leonato] *I … will so practise on Benedick that, in despite of his quick wit, …. he shall fall in love with Beatrice*

despiteful *(adj.)* cruel, spiteful, malicious **R3** IV.36 [Anne to all, of her being crowned Richard's queen] *Despiteful tidings!;* **AC** II.vi.22; **AW** III.iv.13; **AY** V.ii.75; **TC** I.iii.33; **Tit** IV.iv.50

despitefully *(adv.)* maliciously, cruelly; or: shamefully **Luc** 670 [Tarquin to Lucrece] *despitefully I mean to bear thee / Unto the base bed of some rascal groom*

despoil *(v.)* deprive, strip, dispossess **2H6** III.iii.10 [King to Duchess of Gloucester] *Despoiled of your honour in your life* [i.e. for the rest of your life]

destiny *(n.)* **1** divine power, fate [one of the three destinies] **TC** IV.v.184 [Nestor to Hector] *I have … seen thee oft, / Labouring for destiny* [i.e. doing the work of the Fates] ☞ **CLASSICAL MYTHOLOGY**, p.613

2 preordained outcome, divine foretelling **Tem** III.iii.54 [Ariel to Alonso, Sebastian, and Antonio] *You are three men of sin, whom destiny … / Hath caused to belch up you*

destitute *(adj.)* abandoned, deserted, forsaken **Luc** 441 [of Lucrece's breast] *Whose ranks of blue veins … / Left their round turrets destitute and pale*

destruction *(n.)* death, slaughter **H5** III.iii.4 [King Henry to citizens of Harfleur] *to our best mercy give yourselves, / Or, like to men proud of destruction, / Defy us to our worst*

detain (*v.*) keep back, withhold, retain **R2** I.i.90 [Bolingbroke to King Richard, of money given to Mowbray] *The which he hath detained for lewd employments* **CE** II.i.107; **KL** I.i.41

detect (*v.*) **1** expose, unmask, uncover **MW** II.ii.295 [Ford alone] *I will … detect my wife;* **Tit** II.iv.27

  2 reveal, betray, show **3H6** II.ii.143 [Richard to Queen] *Shamest thou not, knowing whence thou art extraught, / To let thy tongue detect thy base-born heart?*

  3 accuse, censure, condemn **MM** III.ii.115 [disguised Duke to Lucio] *I never heard the absent Duke much detected for women*

detection (*n.*) exposure, revelation, evidence of unfaithfulness **MW** II.ii.236 [Ford as Brook to Falstaff, of Mistress Ford] *could I come to her with any detection in my hand*

detention (*n.*) failure to pay, withholding payment **Tim** II.ii.43 [Timon to Flavius] *How goes the world that I am thus encountered / With … the detention of long-since-due debts / Against my honour?*

determinate (*adj.*) **1** determined upon, intended, proposed **TN** II.i.9 [Sebastian to Antonio] *my determinate voyage is mere extravagancy*

  2 conclusive, definitive, decisive **Oth** IV.ii.225 [Iago to Roderigo, of a reason for detaining Othello] *none can be so determinate as the removing of Cassio;* **H8** II.iv.176

  3 determined, fixed, decided **Sonn** 87.4 *My bonds in thee are all determinate* [i.e. their time of expiry is fixed by you]

determinate (*v.*) bring to an end, terminate, limit **R2** I.iii.150 [King Richard to Mowbray] *The sly slow hours shall not determinate / The dateless limit of thy dear exile*

determination (*n.*) **1** mind, decision, resolution **MV** I.ii.95 [Nerissa to Portia, of the wooers] *They have acquainted me with their determinations … to return to their home;* **Ham** III.i.169; **MW** III.v.64

  2 ending, termination, endpoint **Sonn** 13.6 *So should that beauty which you hold in lease / Find no determination*

determine (*v.*) **1** make a decision [about], reach a conclusion [about] **MV** IV.i.106 [Duke to all, of Bellario] *Whom I have sent for to determine this;* **AC** V.i.59; **2H4** IV.i.162; **Luc** 1150; **R3** I.iii.15; **RJ** III.i.51

  2 resolve, decide, settle [on] **R3** II.ii.141 [Richard to all] *go we to determine / Who they shall be that straight shall post to Ludlow;* **R3** I.i.30, III.ii.13; **Sonn** 46.11; **TNK** III.v.54

  3 be decided, be concluded, make an end **AC** IV.iii.2 [Second Soldier to First Soldier, of the battle] *It will determine one way;* **Cor** III.iii.43, V.iii.120

  4 put an end to, do away with, terminate **2H4** IV.v.82 [King Henry IV to Warwick, of Prince Henry] *where is he that will not stay so long / Till his friend sickness have determined me?*

  5 come to an end, dissolve, melt **AC** III.xiii.161 [Cleopatra to Antony, of a poisoned hailstone] *as it determines, so / Dissolve my life!*

determined (*adj.*) **1** planned, decided upon, prepared **Tit** V.ii.139 [Tamora aside to Chiron and Demetrius, of telling Saturninus] *How I have governed our determined jest*

  2 appointed, given a limit **1H6** IV.vi.9 [John Talbot to Talbot] *To my determined time thou gavest new date;* **R3** V.i.19

  3 confined, limited, restricted **MM** III.i.73 [Isabella to Claudio] *a restraint … / To a determined scope*

detest (*v.*) **1** renounce, repudiate; or: hate, abhor **TN** V.i.137 [Olivia to Viola as Cesario] *Ay me, detested!*

  2 malapropism for 'protest' **MM** II.i.66 [Elbow to Escalus] *My wife … whom I detest before heaven;* **MW** I.iv.145

detested (*adj.*) detestable, loathsome, hateful **KL** I.ii.77 [Gloucester to Edmund, of Edgar] *Unnatural, detested, brutish villain!;* **R2** II.iii.108

detract (*v.*) take away, subtract, deduct **1H6** V.iv.142 [Charles to the English, of his status as ruler of many French territories] *Shall I … / Detract so much from that prerogative / As to be called the viceroy of the whole?*

detraction (*n.*) slander, calumny, defamation, disparagement **TN** II.v.133 [Fabian as if to Malvolio] *you might see more detraction at your heels than fortunes before you;* **1H4** V.i.138

deuce-ace (*n.*) [gambling] two and one **LL** I.ii.46 [Mote to Armado] *I am sure you know how much the gross sum of deuce-ace amounts to* ➤ **ace** (*n.*)

devest, divest (*v.*) undress, unclothe, disrobe **Oth** II.iii.175 [Iago to Othello, of Cassio and Montano] *in terms like bride and groom / Devesting them for bed*

device (*n.*) **1** plot, stratagem, trick **H8** I.i.204 [Buckingham to Norfolk] *I shall perish / Under device and practice;* **AY** I.i.141; **CE** I.ii.95; **TC** I.iii.375; **Tit** IV.iv.112; **TN** II.iii.155

  2 plan, scheme, intention **MND** I.ii.96 [Quince to all] *if we meet in the city we shall be dogged with company, and our devices known;* **Ham** III.ii.222; **LL** V.i.131; **MV** III.iv.81; **TS** I.i.190

  3 planning, devising, invention **AY** IV.iii.21 [Rosalind as Ganymede to Silvius, of Phebe's letter] *This is a letter of your own device;* **Ham** IV.vii.63

  4 design, ingenuity, work **Cym** I.vii.189 [Iachimo to Innogen] *plate of rare device*

  5 skilful piece of work **Lover** 232 *Lo this device was sent me from a Nun*

  6 mechanism, contrivance, apparatus **Tem** III.iii.54 [stage direction] *with a quaint device, the banquet vanishes*

  7 excuse, evasion, subterfuge **R3** III.vi.11 [Scrivener alone, of Hastings' indictment] *Who is so gross / That cannot see this palpable device?;* **Oth** IV.ii.175

  8 resourcefulness, aspiration, cast of mind **AY** I.i.156 [Oliver alone, of Orlando] *full of noble device;* **Venus** 789

  9 way of thinking, inclination, fancy **Tit** II.i.79 [Aaron to Demetrius and Chiron, of their quarrelling over Lavinia] *you do but plot your deaths / By this device*

  10 show, performance, production **LL** V.ii.661 [Armado to all, of his portrayal of Hector] *I will forward with my device;* **MND** V.i.50; **Tim** I.ii.147

  11 heraldic design, emblematic figure, armorial **Per** II.ii.15 [Simonides to Thaisa] *'Tis now your honour … to entertain / The labour of each knight in his device* [i.e. on his shield]; **E3** IV.iv.27; **KJ** I.i.210

devil (*n.*) diabolical thing, worst possible event **TNK** III.vi.270 [Arcite to Theseus, of Emilia] *I'll … die for her, / Make death a devil* [i.e. even if I endure a horrible death]

devil wear black, let the to hell with mourning! **Ham** III.ii.138 [Hamlet to Ophelia] *let the devil wear black, for I'll have a suit of sables* ➤ **black** (*n.*) **1**

devise (*v.*) **1** ponder, deliberate, think **Cor** I.i.100 [Menenius to Citizens, of the body parts other than the belly] *th'other instruments / Did see and hear, devise, instruct*

  2 invent, imagine, make up [an account] **RJ** III.i.68 [Romeo to Tybalt] *I … love thee better than thou canst devise;* **AC** II.ii.194; **LL** I.ii.177

  3 enlighten, explain [to], resolve [for] **Ham** IV.vii.52 [Claudius to Laertes] *Can you devise me?* [Q2; F *aduise*]

  4 give, assign, confer on **Cor** II.ii.122 [First Senator to Cominius, of Coriolanus] *He cannot but with measure fit the honours / Which we devise him*

  5 provide, prepare, make ready **1H6** I.i.172 [Exeter to all, of the King at Eltham] *for his safety there I'll best devise*

devise on (*v.*) decide upon, resolve, determine **1H6** I.ii.124 [Reignier to Charles] *What devise you on?* [i.e. what have you decided to do?]

devised (*adj.*) invented, fabricated, maliciously made-up **1H4** III.ii.23 [Prince Hal to King Henry] *in reproof of many tales devised*

devoted (*adj.*) **1** devoted, dedicated, addicted **TS** I.i.32 [Tranio to Lucentio, of moral discipline] *so devote to Aristotle's checks / As Ovid be an outcast quite abjured*

2 holy, consecrated, dedicated **R3** I.ii.35 [Anne to all, of Richard] *What black magician conjures up this fiend / To stop devoted charitable deeds?*; **TG** IV.ii.120

devotement *(n.)* worship, reverence **Oth** II.iii.308 [Iago to Cassio, of Desdemona] *the contemplation, mark, and devotement of her parts and graces* [F, Q *deuotement*] ➤ denotement *(n.)*

devotion *(n.)* purpose, object, intent **R3** IV.i.9 [Anne to Queen Elizabeth, of her purpose] *Upon the like devotion as yourselves*

devout *(adj.)* serious, devoted, committed **LL** V.ii.777 [Princess to King, of not treating the lords' approaches seriously] *more devout than this in our respects / Have we not been*

dew *(n.)* dewfall, dampness, moisture **Cor** II.iii.31 [Third Citizen to Second Citizen, of the latter's wit] *being three parts melted away with rotten dews*

dew *(v.)* bedew, moisten, water **MND** II.i.9 [Fairy to Puck] *I serve the Fairy Queen, / To dew her orbs upon the green*; **Mac** V.ii.30; **RJ** V.iii.14

dew-bedabbled *(adj.)* splashed all over with dew **Venus** 703 [Venus to Adonis, of the hare] *Then shalt thou see the dew-bedabbled wretch / Turn, and return*

dewberry *(n.)* species of blackberry **MND** III.i.161 [Titania to Fairies, of Bottom] *Feed him with … dewberries*

dewlap, dewlop *(n.)* folds of loose skin hanging about the neck **MND** II.i.50 [Puck to Fairy] *sometime lurk I in a gossip's bowl … / And on her withered dewlap pour the ale* [F, Q *dewlop*]

dewlapped *(adj.)* with folds of loose skin around the throat **Tem** III.iii.46 [Gonzalo to Alonso] *Who would believe that there were mountaineers / Dewlapped like bulls*; **MND** IV.i.121

dexter *(adj.)* [heraldry] of the right side **TC** IV.v.128 [Hector to Ajax, of Ajax's mixed heritage] *my mother's blood / Runs on the dexter cheek* ➤ sinister *(adj.)*

dexteriously *(adv.)* with dexterity, adroitly, skilfully **TN** I.v.55 [Feste to Olivia, of being able to prove her a fool] *Dexteriously, good madonna*

dexterity *(n.)* agility, adroitness, facility **Ham** I.ii.157 [Hamlet alone, of his mother] *to post / With such dexterity to incestuous sheets*

dey-woman, day-woman *(n.)* dairy-maid **LL** I.ii.125 [Dull to Armado, of Jaquenetta] *she is allowed for the dey-woman* [F *Day-woman*]

diadem *(n.)* crown, sovereign power **3H6** II.i.152 [Warwick to Richard] *this strong right hand of mine / Can pluck the diadem from faint Henry's head*; **1H6** II.v.89; **2H6** I.i.244, ii.7; **3H6** I.iv.104, II.ii.82; **Tit** I.i.6

dial *(n.)* watch, timepiece, pocket sundial **AY** II.vii.33 [Jaques to all, of Touchstone] *I did laugh … / An hour by his dial*; **1H4** V.ii.83; **3H6** II.v.24; **Luc** 327; **Oth** III.iv.171; **Sonn** 77.2

dialect *(n.)* language, manner of speaking **MM** I.ii.182 [Claudio to Lucio, of Isabella] *in her youth / There is a prone and speechless dialect, / Such as move men*

dialogue *(v.)* **1** carry on a dialogue, hold a conversation **Tim** II.ii.55 [Apemantus to Varro's Servant] *Dost dialogue with thy shadow?*

2 express as a dialogue, provide a conversation **Lover** 132 [of the man] *Consent's bewitched, ere he desire have granted, / And dialogued for him what he would say*

diapason *(n.)* harmony an octave below **Luc** 1132 [Lucrece as if to the nightingale] *I at each sad strain will strain a tear, / And with deep groans the diapason bear*

diaper *(n.)* towel, napkin, cloth **TS** Induction.i.55 [Lord to Huntsmen, of servants to attend Sly] *Another bear the ewer, the third a diaper*

dich *(v.)* [perhaps a dialectal form] do it **Tim** I.ii.71 [Apemantus to himself, of his food] *Much good dich thy good heart* [i.e. may the food do to you]

Dick *(n.)* low fellow, jack-in-office **LL** V.ii.464 [Berowne to all, of Boyet] *some Dick … / Told our intents before* ➤ Hob and Dick

diction *(n.)* verbal description, account in words **Ham** V.ii.117 [Hamlet to Osrick, of Laertes] *to make true diction of him*

didst *(v.)* ➤ VERB FORMS, p.481

die *(n.)* one of a pair of dice **R3** V.iv.10 [King Richard to Catesby] *I have set my life upon a cast, / And I will stand the hazard of the die*; **MND** V.i.299; **Tim** V.iv.34; **WT** IV.iii.26

die *(v.)* **1** cease, expire, come to an end **E3** I.i.65 [Lorraine to King Edward, of Guienne] *Or else thy title in that province dies*

2 suffer pain, go through agony **Mac** IV.iii.111 [Macduff to Malcolm] *the queen that bore thee … / Died every day she lived*; **MA** III.ii.62

die by oneself die by one's own hand, commit suicide **Cor** V.ii.100 [Menenius to First Watch] *He that hath a will to die by himself*

die on *(v.)* die fighting, challenge in mortal combat **TG** II.iv.112 [Proteus to Silvia, of her claim to be a worthless mistress] *I'll die on him that says so but yourself*

diet *(n.)* **1** board, daily need **TN** III.iii.41 [Antonio to Sebastian] *I will bespeak our diet*; **Ham** I.i.99; **1H4** III.iii.72

2 food **Oth** III.iii.15 [Cassio to Desdemona] *feed upon some nice and waterish diet*; **AC** V.ii.212; **Tim** III.vi.67

3 therapeutic nutrition, curative regime **Tim** IV.iii.88 [Timon to Timandra] *bring down rose-cheeked youth / To the tub-fast and the diet*; **MM** I.ii.23; **TG** II.i.23

4 way of living, course of life **R3** I.i.139 [Richard to Hastings, of King Edward] *he hath kept an evil diet long*

diet *(v.)* **1** feed, be given food, fatten **1H6** I.ii.10 [Alençon to all, of the English] *they must be dieted like mules*; **Cor** I.ix.51; **Cym** III.iv.182

2 feed to a satisfactory level, condition by feeding **Cor** V.i.58 [Menenius to Sicinius, of Coriolanus] *I'll watch him / Till he be dieted to my request* [i.e. until he will listen favourably]; **Oth** II.i.285

3 limit, restrict, restrain **AW** IV.iii.28 [Second Lord to First Lord, of Bertram] *he is dieted to his hour*; **AW** V.iii.221

dieter *(n.)* dietician, nutritionist, feeder **Cym** IV.ii.51 [Guiderius to Belarius and Arviragus, of disguised Innogen] *he … sauced our broths, as Juno had been sick, / And he her dieter* [i.e. as if ministering to the gods]

differ *(v.)* change character, become different **Tim** III.i.46 [Flaminius to Lucullus] *Is't possible the world should so much differ, / And we alive that lived?*

difference *(n.)* **1** quarrel, disagreement, dispute **H8** I.i.101 [Norfolk to Buckingham, of Wolsey] *The state takes notice of the private difference / Betwixt you and the Cardinal*; **2H4** IV.i.179; **KJ** II.i.355; **KL** II.ii.48; **MV** IV.i.168; **TNK** III.vi.278

2 cause of argument, nature of disagreement **Cym** I.v.50 [Iachimo to Frenchman] *Can we with manners ask what was the difference?*

3 change, variation, shifting **AY** II.i.6 [Duke Senior to all] *The seasons' difference*; **KL** V.iii.286

4 variety, range, assortment **Per** IV.ii.76 [Bawd to Marina] *You shall have the difference of all complexions*

5 choice, alternative, option **KJ** III.i.204 [Lewis the Dauphin to King Philip] *the difference / Is purchase of a heavy curse from Rome, / Or the light loss of England for a friend*

6 distinction, fine quality **Ham** V.ii.107 [Osrick to Hamlet, of Laertes] *full of most excellent differences*

7 distinction, discrimination, contrast [between] **MW** II.i.53 [Mistress Ford to Mistress Page] *as long as I have an eye to make difference of men's liking*

8 class difference, distinction of rank **KL** I.iv.89 [disguised Kent to Oswald] *I'll teach you differences*; **H8** I.i.139

9 [heraldry] variation, distinguishing mark [on a coat-of-arms] **MA** I.i.64 [Beatrice to Leonato, of Benedick's wit] *let him bear it for a difference between himself and his horse*; **Ham** IV.v.184

difference (*n.*) difference, dissimilarity **Cor** V.iv.11 [Menenius to Sicinius] *There is differency between a grub and a butterfly*

different (*adj.*) **1** distinct, individual, separate **KJ** III.iv.60 [Constance to Cardinal Pandulph] *too well I feel / The different plague of each calamity*

2 various, several **Tim** I.i.259 [Timon to Alcibiades] *Ere we depart we'll share a bounteous time / In different pleasures*

differing (*adj.*) different, varying, diverse **TNK** V.iv.74 [Pirithous to Palamon, of Arcite's horse] *When neither curb would crack … nor differing plunges / Disroot his rider*

diffidence (*n.*) distrust, misgiving, lack of confidence **KJ** I.i.65 [Queen Eleanor to Bastard, of his mother] *Thou dost … wound her honour, with this diffidence*; **1H6** III.iii.10; **H6** I.ii.146

diffuse (*v.*) disguise, obscure, make indistinct **KL** I.iv.2 [Kent alone] *I other accents borrow / That can my speech diffuse* [F, Q *defuse*]

diffused (*adj.*) **1** disorderly, mixed-up, jumbled **H5** V.ii.61 [Burgundy to King Henry and the French King] *our house, and ourselves and children … grow like savages … / To swearing and stern looks, diffused attire* [F3; F1 *defus'd*]; **MW** IV.iv.53; **R3** I.ii.78

2 troubled, confused, bewildered **E3** V.i.126 [Salisbury to King Edward] *Our hearts were dead, our looks diffused and wan*

dig (*v.*) **1** dig down, lessen by digging, excavate **Per** I.iv.5 [Dionyza to Cleon] *who dig hills because they do aspire / Throws down one mountain to cast up a higher*

2 ☛ GREETINGS, p.206

digest, disgest (*v.*) **1** digest, swallow **E3** III.i.124 [Philip to King John] *how this echoing cannon shot … disgests my cates!* [i.e. helps my food to go down]; **JC** I.ii.298, IV.iii.47

2 take in, incorporate, assimilate **KL** I.i.128 [Lear to Cornwall and Albany] *With my two daughters' dowers digest the third*; **AW** V.iii.74

3 arrange, organize, order **R3** III.i.200 [Richard to Buckingham] *We may digest our complots in some form*; **AC** II.ii.181; **Ham** II.ii.438

4 understand, interpret, comprehend **Cor** I.i.148 [Menenius to Citizens] *digest things rightly / Touching the weal o'th' common* [F *disgest*]; **Cor** III.i.131

5 endure, brook, put up with **H8** III.ii.53 [Surrey to all] *But will the King / Digest this letter of the Cardinal's?*; **H5** II.Chorus.31; **LL** V.ii.289; **MV** III.v.85; **WT** IV.iv.12

6 dissipate, disperse, get rid of **1H6** IV.i.167 [King to Richard and Somerset] *Go cheerfully together and digest / Your angry choler on your enemies*

dignified (*adj.*) raised in status, invested with dignity **Cym** II.iii.126 [Innogen to Cloten] *thou wert dignified enough / Even to the point of envy*

dignity (*n.*) **1** worth, nobleness, excellence **AC** V.ii.166 [Cleopatra to Caesar] *things of such dignity / As we greet modern friends withal*; **Cym** V.iv.57; **LL** IV.iii.234; **TC** II.ii.55

2 official position, high office, rule **2H6** V.i.194 [York to King] *I am resolved for death and dignity*; **CE** I.i.144; **1H4** I.i.98; **2H4** IV.v.99; **JC** III.i.178; **R3** III.vii.195

3 dignitary, high officer **1H6** I.iii.50 [Gloucester to Winchester] *In spite of Pope or dignities of Church*

digress (*v.*) deviate, diverge, depart **RJ** III.iii.127 [Friar to Romeo] *Thy noble shape is but a form of wax, / Digressing from the valour of a man*; **TS** III.ii.106

digressing (*adj.*) transgressing, offending, wrongdoing **R2** V.iii.65 [King Henry to York, of Aumerle] *thy abundant goodness shall excuse / This deadly blot in thy digressing son*

digression (*n.*) transgression, moral deviation, lapse in proper behaviour **Luc** 202 [Tarquin to himself] *my digression is so vile, so base, / That it will live engraven in my face*; **LL** I.ii.111

dilate (*v.*) **1** relate, describe, enlarge upon **CE** I.i.123 [Duke to Egeon, of his wife and children] *Do me the favour to dilate at full / What have befallen of them and thee till now*

2 relate in full, narrate at length **Oth** I.iii.152 [Othello to all] *I would all my pilgrimage dilate*

dilated (*adj.*) **1** ample, extensive, diffuse **TC** II.iii.247 [Ulysses to Ajax, of his wisdom] *Which, like a bourn, … confines / Thy spacious and dilated parts* [also: large in girth]

2 extended, leisurely, lengthy **AW** II.i.57 [Parolles to Bertram, of the Lords] *take a more dilated farewell*

3 ☛ delated (*adj.*)

dilation (*n.*) accusation, charge, allegation **Oth** III.iii.122 [Othello to Iago, of Iago's pauses] *in a man that's just, / They're close dilations … / That passion cannot rule* [or: delay] [F; Q1 *denotements*] ☛ denotement (*n.*) 1

dild (*v.*) ☛ 'ild (*v.*)

dildo (*n.*) nonsense refrain in a ballad; also: artificial penis **WT** IV.iv.196 [Servant to Clown, of Autolycus' songs] *with such delicate burdens of dildos and fadings*

dilemma (*n.*) choice of action, alternative position **AW** III.vi.69 [Parolles to Bertram] *I will presently pen down my dilemmas*

diligence (*n.*) **1** attentiveness, assiduity, careful service **1H6** V.iii.9 [Pucelle alone, of the arrival of the spirits] *This speedy and quick appearance argues proof / Of your accustomed diligence to me*; **Cym** IV.iii.20; **Ham** V.ii.92; **Tem** I.ii.304

2 diligent person, attentive servant **Tem** V.i.241 [Prospero aside to Ariel] *Bravely, my diligence*

diligent (*adj.*) **1** attentive, heedful, ready to respond **Tem** III.i.42 [Ferdinand to Miranda, of other ladies] *Th'harmony of their tongues hath into bondage / Brought my too diligent ear*; **TS** IV.iii.39

2 assiduous, persistent **Tim** III.iv.41 [Flaminius to Titus] *You are too diligent*; **KL** V.i.53

dim (*adj.*) dull, pale-coloured, lacking lustre **KJ** III.iv.85 [Constance to King Phillip, of Arthur] *he will look as hollow as a ghost, / As dim and meagre as an ague's fit*; **Luc** 403, 1588; **TNK** I.i.9; **WT** IV.iv.120

dimension (*n.*) **1** bodily form, physical frame **TN** V.i.234 [Sebastian to Viola as Cesario] *A spirit I am indeed, / But am in that dimension grossly clad / Which from the womb I did participate*; **TN** I.v.250

2 (plural) parts of the body, organs **MV** III.i.54 [Shylock to Solanio and Salerio] *Hath not a Jew … dimensions, senses, affections, passions?*; **KL** I.ii.7

diminitive (*adj.*) diminutive **Mac** IV.ii.10 [Macduff's Wife to Ross] *the poor wren, / The most diminitive of birds*

diminutive (*n.*) undersized person, very small being **AC** IV.xii.37 [Antony to Cleopatra] *most monster-like be shown / For poor'st diminutives*; **TC** V.i.31

dine (*v.*) have lunch **JC** I.ii.287 [Cassius to Casca] *Will you dine with me tomorrow?*

dint (*n.*) **1** impression, force, mark **Venus** 354 [of Adonis and Venus] *His tend'rer cheek receives her soft hand's print / As apt as new-fall'n snow takes any dint*; **JC** III.ii.195

2 stroke, blow, attack **E3** V.i.52 [King Edward to Queen] *we / As well can master our affections / As conquer other by the dint of sword*

dire (*adj.*) dangerous, dreadful, evil **Ham** III.ii.268 [Third Player, as Lucianus, addressing his drug] *Thy natural magic and dire property*

direct (*adj.*) **1** downright, straightforward, absolute **Tim** IV.iii.20 [Timon alone] *There's nothing level in our cursed natures / But direct villainy*

2 following normal legal procedure; or: immediate **Oth** I.ii.86 [Brabantio to Othello, of Othello's going to prison] *till fit time / Of law and course of direct session / Call thee to answer*

direct (*v.*) delegate, assign, hand over **Per** I.ii.109 [Helicanus to Pericles] *Your rule direct to any*

direction (*n.*) **1** instruction, guidance, counsel **Oth** I.iii.296 [Othello to Desdemona] *I have but an hour / Of love, of worldly matters and direction / To spend with thee*; **MV** II.i.14

2 authoritative guidance, tactical knowledge, capacity for direction **R3** V.iii.16 [King Richard to all] *Call for some men of sound direction*

3 way of proceeding, course of action **Ham** II.i.66 [Polonius to Reynaldo] *By indirections find directions out*

directitude (*n.*) [humorous nonsense word; unclear meaning] discredit **Cor** IV.v.215 [Third Servingman to First Servingman, of Coriolanus] *whilst he's in directitude.* [First Servingman] *Directitude? What's that?*

directive (*adj.*) subject to direction, under the control [of] **TC** I.iii.356 [Nestor to Ulysses, of the powerful effect of good opinion] *In no less working than are swords and bows / Directive by the limbs*

directly (*adv.*) **1** immediately, at once **Mac** V.i.66 [Gentlewoman to Doctor, of Lady Macbeth, in response to 'Will she go now to bed?'] *Directly*; **Ham** III.ii.219; **1H4** II.iii.89

2 straightforwardly, rightly, without evasion **Oth** IV.ii.208 [Iago to Roderigo] *I have dealt most directly in thy affair*; **Cor** IV.v.192; **Cym** III.v.114; **JC** I.i.12, III.iii.9

3 plainly, clearly, evidently **MV** IV.i.356 [Portia as Balthasar to Shylock, of Antonio] *indirectly, and directly too, / Thou hast contrived against the very life / Of the defendant*; **Cym** I.v.155; **Oth** II.i.212, iii.340

4 exactly, rightly, entirely **PassP** II.10 [Pilgrim] *whether that my angel be turned fiend, / Suspect I may, yet not directly tell*; **MV** I.iii.74

direful (*adj.*) dreadful, terrible, frightful **Tem** I.ii.26 [Prospero to Miranda] *The direful spectacle of the wrack*; **Luc** 741; **Mac** I.ii.26; **R3** IV.iv.85; **Tit** V.iii.143; **Venus** 98

dire-lamenting (*adj.*) deeply sorrowing, dreadfully lamenting **TG** III.ii.82 [Proteus to Thurio] *After your dire-lamenting elegies*

direness (*n.*) horror, terror, dread **Mac** V.v.14 [Macbeth to himself] *Direness … / Cannot once start me*

dirge (*n.*) funeral song, song of mourning **TNK** II.v.15 [Gaoler's Daugher alone] *some wenches … will sing my dirge*; **Ham** I.ii.12; **Luc** 1612; **RJ** IV.v.88

dirt (*n.*) [contemptuous] land **Ham** V.ii.89 [Hamlet to Horatio, of Osrick] *spacious in the possession of dirt* [i.e. the owner of many acres]

dirty (*adj.*) repulsive, hateful, abominable **Cym** III.vii.28 [Arviragus to disguised Innogen] *those / Who worship dirty gods*

disable (*v.*) disparage, belittle, devalue **AY** V.iv.73 [Touchstone to Jaques, of a courtier] *he disabled my judgement*; **AY** IV.i.30; **1H6** V.iii.67

disabling (*n.*) disparagement, detraction, belittling **MV** II.vii.30 [Morocco to himself] *to be afeard of my deserving / Were but a weak disabling of myself*

disallow of (*v.*) reject, deny, refuse to admit **KJ** I.i.16 [King John to Chatillon, of King Philip's demands] *What follows if we disallow of this?*

disanimate (*v.*) dishearten, discourage, dispirit **1H6** III.i.185 [Gloucester to King] *The presence of a king engenders love / Amongst his subjects and loyal friends / As it disanimates his enemies*

disannul (*v.*) **1** annul, abolish, cancel **CE** I.i.145 [Duke to Egeon, of his office and oath] *Which princes, would they, may not disannul*

2 make null and void, bring to nothing **3H6** III.iii.81 [Oxford to all, of the succession] *Warwick disannuls great John of Gaunt*

disappointed (*adj.*) unprepared, unequipped **Ham** I.v.77 [Ghost to Hamlet] *Cut off even in the blossoms of my sin, / Unhouseled, disappointed*

disaster (*n.*) **1** inauspicious sight, unfavourable appearance **Ham** I.i.118 [Horatio to Marcellus and Barnardo, of ominous events] *As stars with trains of fire and dews of blood, / Disasters in the sun*

2 unlucky star, unfavourable planet **AW** I.i.170 [Helena to Parolles, of Bertram] *His faith, his sweet disaster*

3 misfortune, instance of bad luck **Mac** III.i.111 [First Murderer to Macbeth, of himself] *So weary with disasters, tugged with fortune*

disaster (*v.*) [astrology] ruin, strike with calamity, bring

misfortune on **AC** II.vii.16 [First Servant to Second Servant] *the holes where eyes should be, which pitifully disaster the cheeks*

disbench (*v.*) unseat, make rise **Cor** II.ii.69 [Brutus to Coriolanus] *I hope / My words disbenched you not*

disbranch (*v.*) remove a branch, cut off, sever **KL** IV.ii.34 [Albany to Gonerill] *She that herself will sliver and disbranch / From her material sap*

disburden (*v.*) unburden, unload, reveal **E3** II.i.64 [King Edward to Lodowick] *Since green our thoughts, green be the conventicle / Where we will ease us by disburd'ning them*

disburse (*v.*) pay out, spend, give away **Luc** 1203 [Lucrece as if to Collatine] *all my fame that lives disbursed be / To those that live and think no shame of me*

discandy (*v.*) dissolve, liquefy, melt away **AC** IV.xii.22 [Antony alone] *The hearts … do discandy, melt their sweets / On blossoming Caesar* ☞ **uncandied** (*adj.*)

discandying (*n.*) dissolving, melting, thawing **AC** III.xiii.165 [Cleopatra to Antony] *By the discandying of this pelleted storm* [F *discandering*]

discase (*v.*) **1** undress, disrobe, strip **WT** IV.iv.629 [Camillo to Autolycus, of Florizel] *discase thee instantly … and change garments with this gentleman*

2 shed a disguise, take off outer garments **Tem** V.i.85 [Prospero to Ariel] *I will discase me*

discern (*v.*) distinguish, make a difference between **KL** IV.ii.52 [Gonerill to Albany] *Who hast not … an eye discerning / Thine honour from thy suffering* [F; Q *deseruing*]

discharge (*n.*) **1** performance, fulfilment, execution **Tem** II.i.258 [Antonio to Sebastian] *what's past is prologue, what to come, / In yours and my discharge*; **TC** IV.iv.40

2 dismissal, permission to leave **E3** II.ii.32 [King Edward to Audley] *Then let those foot trudge hence upon those horse, / According to our discharge, and be gone*

3 payment, settlement, release from all liability **Cym** V.iv.170 [First Gaoler to Posthumus, of the hangman's rope] *of what's past, is, and to come, the discharge*

4 financial settlement, payment of what is owing **2H6** I.iii.167 [York to Suffolk] *My lord of Somerset will keep me here, / Without discharge, money, or furniture*

discharge (*v.*) **1** fulfil, execute, perform **AW** I.iii.117 [Countess to Steward, of his report] *You have discharged this honestly*; **2H6** II.iv.103; **TC** III.ii.85; **Tem** III.i.22

2 play, perform, execute **MND** IV.ii.8 [Quince to Flute, of Bottom] *You have not a man in all Athens able to discharge Pyramus but he*; **Cor** III.ii.106; **MND** I.ii.86, V.i.351

3 give vent to, emit, sound off **H8** I.ii.206 [Surveyor to King Henry, of Buckingham] *He … did discharge a horrible oath*; **Luc** 1605

4 fire off, send forth, get rid of **TNK** II.ii.316 [Palamon to Gaoler] *To discharge my life?* [i.e. kill me]

5 fire [a gun] **2H4** III.ii.255 [Falstaff to Shallow, of Wart] *'A shall charge you, and discharge you, with the motion of a pewterer's hammer*

6 release from service, let go, dismiss **2H4** IV.ii.92 [Prince John to Westmorland] *let our army be discharged too*; **2H4** IV.ii.61; **3H6** IV.ii.109; **TNK** V.i.170

7 eradicate, remove, get rid of **WT** II.iii.11 [Servant to Leontes, of Mamillius] *'Tis hoped his sickness is discharged*

8 pay, reimburse, settle with **CE** IV.i.32 [Angelo to Antipholus of Ephesus, of the Second Merchant] *I pray you see him presently discharged*; **CE** IV.iv.117; **MV** III.ii.273; **Tim** II.ii.14

9 respond to a toast, drink a further health **2H4** II.iv.108 [Falstaff to Pistol] *do you discharge upon mine hostess* [also: sense 5 and bawdy pun]

disciple (*v.*) teach, instruct, train **AW** I.ii.28 [King to Bertram, of Bertram's father] *He … was / Discipled of the bravest* [i.e. trained the bravest; or: trained by the bravest]

DISCOURSE MARKERS

Certain words and phrases play an important role in maintaining the dynamic of conversational interaction and the flow of connected speech in a monologue.

In its basic form, a dialogue contains two elements: X speaks and Y responds.

- Within X, some discourse features show how X is organizing the utterance, and others show X acknowledging Y's presence.
- Within Y's response, there are features which acknowledge what X has just said.

Modern English has changed in many ways from Shakespearian English in this respect (though several expressions remain in use, such as *I trust, well, come come*). The list below illustrates some of the distinctive expressions.

Shakespeare was well aware of the communicative force of discourse markers and related expressions, judging by the sequence in *Comedy of Errors* (IV.iv.67ff.), when Dromio of Ephesus (D) responds to Antipholus of Ephesus (A) by varying the start of each utterance:

A: Dined at home? Thou villain, what sayst thou?
D: Sir, **sooth to say**, you did not dine at home.
A: Were not my doors locked up, and I shut out?
D: **Perdie**, your doors were locked, and you shut out.
A: And did not she herself revile me there?

D: **Sans fable**, she herself reviled you there.
A: Did not her kitchen-maid rail, taunt, and scorn me?
D: **Certes** she did. The kitchen vestal scorned you.
A: And did not I in rage depart from thence?
D: **In verity** you did.

Within X's speech

X draws Y's attention to a point

Item	Location	Example	Gloss
conscience, o'	Per IV.ii.19	there's two unwholesome, o'conscience	[= on my conscience] I'm sure
fear me, I	TN III.i.111	So did I abuse / Myself, my servant, and, I fear me, you	I'm afraid, I fear
good deed	WT I.ii.42	yet, good deed, Leontes, / I love thee	indeed, in truth
good now	WT V.i.19	[Leontes, of the word 'killed' being used against him] Now, good now, / Say so but seldom	please, be so good as
know't	WT I.ii.204	Know't: It will let in and out the enemy	be certain of it
la	Ham IV.v.57	Indeed, la, without an oath. I'll make an end on't	indeed [i.e. an intensifier]
la you	TN III.iv.100	La you, an you speak ill of the devil, how he takes it at heart!	see, look now
law	Per IV.i.77	Believe me, law, / I never killed a mouse, nor hurt a fly	indeed
look you	1H4 I.iii.236	[Hotspur, on being called a fool] Why, look you, I am whipped and scourged with rods	can't you see
prithee, I	CE II.i.55	But say, I prithee, is he coming home?	I beg you ☛ POLITENESS, p.340
protest, I	CE V.i.2	But I protest he had the chain of me	I insist, I'm sure
say	CE II.i.45	Say, is your tardy master now at hand?	tell me
think it	WT I.ii.202	and 'tis powerful, think it, / From east, west, north, and south	be certain of it

X reformulates or adds to a point

nay, more	CE I.i.16	To admit no traffic to our adverse towns. Nay, more: / If any born at Ephesus ...	furthermore
which is more	MW II.ii.74	there has been earls - nay, which is more, pensioners	moreover

X summarizes a point

all, this is for	Ham I.iii.131	This is for all: / I would not ... / Have you ... give words or talk with the Lord Hamlet	to sum up

(continues)

DISCOURSE MARKERS – *continued*

Item	Location	Example	Gloss
concluded, be it	**WT** I.ii.203	*Be it concluded, / No barricado for a belly*	to sum up
few, in	**H5** I.ii.246	*Thus then, in few: / Your highness …*	in a few words
once this	**CE** III.i.89	*Once this: your long experience of her wisdom … / Plead on her part some cause to you unknown*	in short
word, at a	**MW** I.i.100	*He hath wronged me, indeed he hath, at a word, he hath*	in short
word, with a	**1H4** II.iv.251	*Then did we two set on you four, and, with a word, out-faced you from your prize*	in a word

X lets Y know the utterance is about to end

end, there an	**TS** V.ii.97	*The fouler fortune mine, and there an end*	and that's that
even so much	**TC** I.iii.283	[Aeneas reporting Hector] *'… and not worth / The splinter of a lance.' Even so much.* [Agamemnon] *This shall be told our lovers*	this is all I was told to say
fine, in	**AW** IV.iii.51	*in fine, made a groan of her last breath, and now she sings in heaven*	finally, to conclude
soft	**CE** II.ii.118	*But soft - who wafts us yonder?*	stop, hold on

X lets Y know the topic is changing

what though	**AY** III.iii.46	*here we have … no assembly but horn-beasts. But what though? Courage!*	what of it, so what

Within Y's response

Response sentences may be a simple *yea* or *nay*, as well as *yes* or *no* (**RESPONSES**, p.373). But a response may carry an additional nuance.

An alternative or contrast

nay	**MW** IV.iv.74	[Page] *Go, send to Falstaff straight.* [Ford] *Nay, I'll to him again in name of Brook*	rather
nay, but	**Cor** I.i.253	[Brutus] *Marked you his lip and eyes?* [Sicinius] *Nay, but his taunts.*	never mind A, what about B

A stronger degree of affirmation or assurance than 'yes'

e'en so	**Ham** V.i.196	[Hamlet] *Dost thou think Alexander looked o'this fashion i'th' earth?* [Horatio] *E'en so.*	exactly, quite
heart, with all my	**KL** IV.vi.32	[Edgar] *Now fare ye well, good sir.* [Gloucester] *With all my heart.*	I thoroughly agree with you
warrant you, I	**AC** III.iii.47	[Cleopatra] *All may be well enough.* [Charmian] *I warrant you, madam.*	I certainly agree
what else?	**3H6** IV.vi.56	[Warwick] *And all his lands and goods be confiscate.* [George] *What else?*	assuredly, certainly

A stronger degree of denial or rejection than 'no'

let go	**Cor** III.ii.18	[Volumnia] *I would have had you put your power well on / Before you had worn it out.* [Coriolanus] *Let go.*	enough, stop

A confirmation check on what X has just said

pray ye?	**AC** II.vi.111	[Enobarbus] *But she is now the wife of Marcus Antonius.* [Menas] *Pray ye, sir?*	I beg your pardon?

DISCOURSE MARKERS – *continued*

Item	Location	Example	Gloss
say you?	**Ham** IV.v.28	[Gertrude] *Alas, sweet lady, what imports this song?* [Ophelia] *Say you?*	what did you say?
say'st me so?	**TS** I.ii.187	[Petruchio] *I hear no harm.* [Gremio] *No, say'st me so, friend?*	is that what you tell me?

A prompt for X to continue

Item	Location	Example	Gloss
good	**TC** I.ii.14	[Alexander] *They call him Ajax.* [Cressida] *Good, and what of him?*	all right
good, make that	**TN** I.v.6	[Feste] *He that is well hanged in this world needs to fear no colours.* [Maria] *Make that good.*	explain that
have at you	**CE** III.i.51	[Dromio of Ephesus] *Have at you with a proverb …* [Luce] *Have at you with another …*	initiating a mock-hostile exchange
trow	**MA** III.iv.52	[Margaret] *… there's no more sailing by the star.* [Beatrice] *What means the fool, trow?*	I wonder, can one suppose

An acknowledgement that X has made a point

Item	Location	Example	Gloss
go to	**KL** III.iii.7	[Edmund] *Most savage and unnatural!* [Gloucester] *Go to. Say you nothing.*	no more of that
said, you have	**AC** II.vi.106	[Enobarbus] *sure he cannot weep't back again.* [Menas] *Y'have said, sir.*	you have said what has to be said

An acknowledgement of X's attitude

Item	Location	Example	Gloss
come	**H5** IV.i.196	*You'll never trust his word after! Come, 'tis a foolish saying*	come on
may, you	**Cor** II.iii.33	[Third Citizen] *… to help get thee a wife.* [Second Citizen] *You are never without your tricks. You may, you may!*	have your little joke

An expression of unwillingness to continue with X's topic

Item	Location	Example	Gloss
all one, that's / 'tis	**TNK** V.ii.30	[Wooer] *She's eighteen* [Doctor] *She may be - / But that's all one, 'tis nothing to our purpose*	that makes no difference
said, I have	**AC** I.ii.58	[Iras] *Give me particulars.* [Soothsayer] *I have said.*	I have said what I wanted to say
ways, go thy	**AW** IV.v.54	[Clown] *… the broad gate and the great fire.* [Lafew] *Go thy ways. I begin to be aweary of thee.*	no more, be off

An expression of response uncertainty to X

Item	Location	Example	Gloss
O Lord, sir!	**AW** II.ii.40	[Countess] *I pray you, sir, are you a courtier?* [Clown] *O Lord, sir! - There's a simple putting off.*	catch-phrase to fill an awkward silence

Some discourse markers are intended to elicit actions, not further speech, as in modern English (such as saying *take that* before a blow).

Item	Location	Example	Gloss
come your ways	**KL** II.ii.35	*Draw, you rascal! Come your ways!*	come on, then – starting a fight
have with you	**Cor** II.i.262	[Brutus] *Let's to the Capitol …* [Sicinius] *Have with you.*	let's go / I'm with you

discipline (*n.*) **1** military strategy, tactics, training in the art of war **KJ** II.i.39 [King Philip to all] *Call for our chiefest men of discipline*; **E3** II.i.188; **H5** III.ii.70; **1H6** IV.ii.44; **R3** III.vii.16, V.iii.17

2 learning, schooling, course of instruction **TG** III.ii.88 [Duke to Proteus, of his advice] *This discipline shows thou hast been in love*; **TC** II.iii.29; **TS** I.i.30

discipline (*v.*) **1** thrash, trounce, beat **Cor** II.i.121 [Menenius to Volumnia, of Coriolanus] *Has he disciplined Aufidius soundly?*

2 teach, train, instruct **TC** II.iii.241 [Ulysses to Ajax] *he that disciplined thine arms to fight*; **Lover** 261

disclaim (*v.*) disown, repudiate, renounce [connection with] **KL** I.i.113 [Lear to Cordelia] *Here I disclaim all my paternal care*; **KJ** I.i.247; **KL** II.i.51; **R2** I.i.70

disclaiming (*n.*) repudiation, disowning disavowal [of] **Ham** V.ii.235 [Hamlet to Laertes] *Let my disclaiming from a purposed evil*

disclose (*n.*) disclosure, bringing into public view **Ham** III.i.167 [Claudius to Polonius] *And I do doubt the hatch and the disclose / Will be some danger*

disclose (*v.*) **1** hatch, be born **Ham** V.i.283 [Gertrude to all] *the female dove / When that her golden couplets are disclosed*

2 open up, unfold, unclose **Ham** I.iii.40 [Laertes to Ophelia] *The canker galls the infants of the spring / Too oft before their buttons be disclosed*; **Sonn** 54.8

discomfit (*n.*) defeat, overthrow, rout **2H6** V.ii.86 [Young Clifford to King and Queen] *uncurable discomfit / Reigns in the hearts of all our present parts*

discomfit (*v.*) **1** defeat, overthrow, beat **1H4** I.i.67 [King Henry to Westmorland] *The Earl of Douglas is discomfited*; **1H4** III.ii.114; **2H6** V.i.63

2 discourage, disconcert, deject **TS** II.i.163 [Baptista to Hortensio as Licio] *be not so discomfited*

discomfiture (*n.*) rout, overthrow, utter defeat **1H6** I.i.59 [First Messenger to all] *Sad tidings ... / Of loss, of slaughter, and discomfiture*

discomfort (*n.*) **1** sorrow, distress, grief **AC** IV.ii.34 [Enobarbus to Antony, of the servants] *What mean you, sir, / To give them this discomfort?*; **2H4** I.i.104; **Mac** IV.ii.29

2 discouragement, loss of heart **Mac** I.ii.28 [Captain to King] *from that spring whence comfort seemed to come, / Discomfort swells*; **R2** III.ii.65

discomfort (*v.*) **1** discourage, dishearten, dispirit **JC** V.iii.106 [Brutus to Cato, of Cassius] *His funerals shall not be in our camp, / Lest it discomfort us*; **TC** V.x.10

2 trouble, grieve, worry **Ham** III.ii.175 [Second Player as Queen, to her King] *Discomfort you, my lord, it nothing must*

discomfortable (*adj.*) disheartening, soul-destroying, discouraging **R2** III.ii.36 [King Richard to Aumerle] *Discomfortable cousin*

discommend (*v.*) find fault with, disapprove of, criticize **KL** II.ii.107 [disguised Kent to Cornwall] *my dialect which you discommend so much*

discontent (*n.*) **1** discontented person, malcontent, agitator **AC** I.iv.39 [Messenger to Caesar] *to the ports / The discontents repair*; **1H4** V.i.76

2 discontented mind, dissatisfied soul **1H4** I.iii.187 [Worcester to Northumberland and Hotspur] *to your quick-conceiving discontents / I'll read you matter deep and dangerous*

3 discontented thought, feeling of dissatisfaction **Tit** I.i.446 [Tamora aside to Saturninus] *Dissemble all your griefs and discontents*; **Tim** V.i.222

discontented (*adj.*) full of discontent, expressing frustration **Oth** V.ii.310 [Lodovico to all] *here's another discontented paper*

discontenting (*adj.*) discontented, angry, displeased **WT** IV.iv.529 [Camillo to Florizel] *Your discontenting father [I'll] strive to qualify, / And bring him up to liking*

discord (*n.*) vendetta, disagreement, dissension **1H6** IV.iv.22 [Lucy to Somerset, of Talbot] *Let not your private discord keep away / The levied succours that should lend him aid*

discourse (*n.*) **1** conversation, talk, chat **CE** III.ii.169 [Antipholus of Syracuse alone, of Luciana] *Of such enchanting presence and discourse*; **MV** III.v.42; **R3** V.iii.100; **TC** II.ii.117; **Tem** V.i.304; **TG** V.ii.15

2 rationality, faculty of understanding **Ham** IV.iv.36 [Hamlet alone] *He that made us with such large discourse*; **TC** I.ii.253; **TN** IV.iii.12

3 course, process, manner **Oth** IV.ii.152 [Desdemona to Iago, of her offending Othello] *Either in discourse of thought or actual deed*; **Ham** I.ii.150; **TC** II.iii.171

discourse (*v.*) **1** talk, chat, converse **Venus** 145 [Venus to Adonis] *Bid me discourse, I will enchant thine ear*; **Cym** III.iii.38; **H5** III.ii.102; **MND** V.i.165; **TG** V.ii.17; **TNK** III.vi.129

2 relate, talk about, recount **Per** I.iv.18 [Cleon to Dionyza] *I'll then discourse our woes*; **CE** V.i.396; **JC** III.i.295; **MND** IV.ii.26; **R2** V.vi.10; **Tit** V.iii.80

3 sound out, give forth **Ham** III.ii.367 [Hamlet to Guildenstern, of a pipe] *it will discourse most eloquent music*

discourser (*n.*) story-teller, raconteur, narrator **H8** I.i.41 [Norfolk to Buckingham] *the tract of everything / Would by a good discourser lose some life / Which action's self was tongue to*

discover (*v.*) **1** reveal, show, make known **MW** II.ii.177 [Ford as Brook to Falstaff] *I shall discover a thing to you* ✒ FEW, p.xxi

2 recognize, distinguish, discern **MM** IV.ii.168 [Provost to disguised Duke] *Angelo ... will discover the favour*; **Cor** II.i.40; **JC** II.i.75

3 expose, uncover, give away **KL** II.i.65 [Edmund to Gloucester, of Edgar] *with curst speech / I threatened to discover him*

4 find, uncover, come upon **Oth** I.i.179 [Roderigo to Brabantio, of Othello] *I think I can discover him*

5 spy, spot, make out **CE** I.i.92 [Egeon to Duke] *we discovered / Two ships from far, making amain to us*; **AC** IV.xii.2; **Cym** IV.ii.130

6 reconnoitre, scout out **R2** III.iii.33 [Percy to Northumberland, of Worcester] *he ... sent me over by Berkeley to discover / What power the Duke of York had levied there*; **AC** IV.x.8; **Tim** V.ii.1

discoverer (*n.*) scout, spy, patrol **2H4** IV.i.3 [Archbishop to Hastings and Mowbray] *send discoverers forth / To know the numbers of our enemies*

discovery (*n.*) **1** disclosure, admission, revelation **WT** I.ii.441 [Camillo to Polixenes] *I'll put / My fortunes to your service, which are here / By this discovery lost*; **Cor** I.ii.22; **Ham** II.ii.294; **H5** II.ii.162; **TC** V.i.20; **TG** III.i.45

2 revealing, exposure, presentation **Tim** V.i.33 [Poet to Painter, of a poem for Timon] *with a discovery of the infinite flatteries that follow youth and opulency*

3 reconnaisance, reconnoitring, spying **KL** V.i.53 [Edmund to Albany, of the enemy] *Here is the guess of their true strength and forces / By diligent discovery*; **Mac** V.iv.6

4 exploration, travel **AY** III.i.191 [Rosalind to Celia] *One inch of delay more is a South Sea of discovery* [i.e. the delay would seem as long as a voyage to (or in) the South Seas]; **Tem** II.i.247

discredit (*v.*) harm the reputation of, bring into discredit **AC** I.ii.156 [Enobarbus to Antony, of Cleopatra] *not to have been blessed withal would have discredited your travel* [i.e. lose credibility as a traveller through not seeing this wonder]

discreet (*adj.*) discerning, judicious, prudent **RJ** I.i.193 [Romeo to Benvolio, of love] *A madness most discreet*; **Cor** III.i.150

discretion (*n.*) **1** prudence, sound judgement, good sense **Tem** II.i.191 [Gonzalo to Antonio] *I will not adventure my discretion so weakly*; **AY** I.i.136; **Oth** III.iii.34

2 judgement, discernment, awareness **Ham** II.ii.465 [Polonius to Hamlet, of how Hamlet's speech was delivered] *with good accent and good discretion*

discuss (*v.*) disclose, make known, declare **H5** III.ii.60 [Fluellen to Gower] *you may discuss unto the Duke*; **MW** I.iii.87, IV.v.2

disdain (*n.*) vexation, frustration, wounded feeling **TC** I.ii.34 [Alexander to Cressida, of Ajax knocking Hector down] *the disdain and shame whereof hath ever since kept Hector fasting and waking;* **3H6** III.iii.127

disdain (*v.*) despise, scorn, show contempt **Per** V.i.119 [Marina to Pericles, of her history] *it would seem / Like lies disdained in the reporting;* **1H6** V.iii.98

disdained (*adj.*) disdainful, scornful, supercilious **1H4** I.iii.181 [Hotspur to Northumberland and Worcester] *Revenge the jeering and disdained contempt / Of this proud King*

disease (*n.*) **1** lack of ease, distress, trouble **1H6** II.v.44 [Richard to Mortimer, after making him comfortable] *in that ease I'll tell thee my disease*
2 annoyance, grievance, weakness **AY** V.iv.63 [Touchstone to Duke Senior] *According to the fool's bolt, sir, and such dulcet diseases* [i.e. and other silly things]
3 mental illness, disturbance of mind **TS** Induction.i.60 [Lord to Huntsmen, of servants to attend Sly] *Another tell him ... that his lady mourns at his disease;* **KL** I.i.164

disease (*v.*) spoil, trouble, disturb **Cor** I.iii.106 [Volumnia to Valeria, of Virgilia] *As she is now, she will but disease our better mirth*

disedge (*v.*) take the edge off, have appetite satisfied **Cym** III.iv.95 [Innogen to Pisanio, as if to Posthumus] *when thou shalt be disedged by her / That now thou tirest on*

disfigure (*v.*) stand for, disguise, alter the appearance of **MND** III.i.54 [Quince to Bottom, of one of the company] *he comes to disfigure or to present the person of Moonshine*

disfurnish (*v.*) deprive, strip, dispossess **TG** IV.i.14 [Valentine to Outlaws] *if you should here disfurnish me;* **Per** IV.vi.11; **Tim** III.ii.45

disgest (*v.*) ☞ **digest** (*v.*)

disgrace (*n.*) **1** misfortune, calamity, injury **Cor** I.i.92 [First Citizen to Menenius] *you must not think to fob off our disgrace with a tale*
2 disfigurement, marring **Sonn** 33.8 [of clouds hiding the sun] *Stealing unseen to west with this disgrace* **LL** I.i.3

disgrace, in insultingly, with contempt **1H6** IV.vi.20 [Talbot to John Talbot, of Orleans] *I ... in disgrace / Bespoke him thus*

disgrace (*v.*) insult, dishonour, deny respect [to] **MV** III.i.49 [Shylock to Salerio, of Antonio] *He hath disgraced me;* **1H6** III.i.99, iv.29

disgraced (*adj.*) humiliating, shamed, dishonoured **WT** I.ii.188 [Leontes as if to Mamillius] *thy mother plays, and I / Play too - but so disgraced a part, whose issue / Will hiss me to my grave*

disgraceful (*adj.*) lacking in grace, unbecoming, displeasing **1H6** I.i.86 [Bedford to all] *Away with these disgraceful wailing robes!*

disgracious (*adj.*) disliked, out of favour, displeasing **R3** IV.iv.178 [King Richard to Duchess of York] *If I be so disgracious in your eye, / Let me march on;* **R3** III.vii.111

disguise (*n.*) **1** deception, pretence **AW** III.vi.97 [Second Lord to Bertram of Parolles] *When his disguise and he is parted;* **AW** IV.i.75
2 drunkenness, state of intoxication **AC** II.vii.122 [Caesar to Antony] *The wild disguise hath almost / Anticked us all*

dish (*v.*) present on a dish, put in front of one **WT** III.ii.71 [Hermione to Leontes] *for conspiracy, / I know not how it tastes, though it be dished / For me to try how*

dishabit (*v.*) dislodge, remove from the foundations **KJ** II.i.220 [King John to Hubert, of the effect of cannon fire on the city walls] *from their fixed beds of lime / Had been dishabited*

dishclout (*n.*) dishcloth, rag **LL** V.ii.710 [Mote to all, of Armado] *he wore none but a dishclout of Jaquenetta's ... next to his heart;* **RJ** III.v.220

dishonest (*adj.*) **1** undutiful, unreliable, irresponsible **TN** I.v.37 [Olivia to Feste] *you grow dishonest*

2 dishonourable, discreditable, shameful **TN** III.iv.376 [Sir Toby to Sir Andrew, of Viola as Cesario] *A very dishonest, paltry boy;* **MM** V.i.260
3 indecent, unchaste, immodest, lewd **AY** V.iii.4 [Audrey to Touchstone] *I hope it is no dishonest desire to desire to be a woman of the world?;* **H5** I.ii.49; **MW** III.iii.173, IV.ii.96

dishonestly (*adv.*) treacherously **Cym** IV.ii.40 [Guiderius to Arviragus and Belarius, of disguised Innogen] *He said he was ... / Dishonestly afflicted*

dishonesty (*n.*) **1** dishonour, shameful deed, disgraceful action **WT** II.iii.47 [Paulina to Leontes, in response to Leontes' questioning of Antigonus 'Canst not rule her?'] *From all dishonesty he can;* **TN** III.iv.377
2 unchasteness, lewdness, immorality **MW** IV.ii.125 [Mistress Ford to Ford] *if you suspect me in any dishonesty*

dishonour (*n.*) indignity, insulting treatment **JC** IV.iii.108 [Brutus to Cassius] *Do what you will, dishonour shall be humour*

dishonoured (*adj.*) dishonourable, dishonouring, shameful **KL** I.i.228 [Cordelia to Lear] *It is no ... dishonoured step / That hath deprived me of your grace and favour;* **Cor** III.i.60

disinsanity (*n.*) madness, great foolishness **TNK** III.v.2 [Schoolmaster to all] *What tediosity and disinsanity / Is here among ye!*

disjoin (*v.*) disengage, separate [oneself] **JC** II.i.18 [Brutus alone] *Th'abuse of greatness is when it disjoins / Remorse from power;* **KJ** III.i.197, 262, III.iii.3; **Venus** 541

disjoint (*adj.*) disjointed, out of joint, disconnected **Ham** I.ii.20 [Claudius to his court, of young Fortinbras] *thinking ... / Our state to be disjoint*

disjoint (*v.*) fall to pieces, become disjointed **Mac** III.ii.16 [Macbeth to Lady Macbeth] *let the frame of things disjoint*

disjunction (*n.*) separation, division, disunion **WT** IV.iv.526 [Camillo to Florizel, of Perdita] *from the whom ... / There's no disjunction to be made*

dislike (*n.*) **1** displeasure, disapproval, antipathy **3H6** IV.i.73 [Lady Grey to all, of becoming queen] *your dislikes ... / Doth cloud my joys;* **2H6** III.ii.257
2 discord, disagreement, dissension **1H4** V.i.26 [Worcester to King Henry] *I have not sought the day of this dislike;* **KL** I.iv.322; **TC** II.iii.222

dislike (*v.*) **1** upset, displease, offend **Oth** II.iii.43 [Cassio to Iago, of calling the gallants in] *I'll do it, but it dislikes me;* **RJ** II.ii.61
2 disapprove of, take exception to **AY** V.iv.68 [Touchstone to Jaques] *I did dislike the cut of a certain courtier's beard;* **AW** III.ii.121

disliken (*v.*) disguise, make unlike, camouflage **WT** IV.iv.648 [Camillo to Perdita] *disliken / The truth of your own seeming*

dislimn (*v.*) obliterate, efface, blot out **AC** IV.xiv.10 [Antony to Eros] *That which is now a horse, even with a thought / The rack dislimns* [F *dislimes*]

dislodge (*v.*) withdraw, retreat, pull back **E3** I.ii.56 [King David to all] *Dislodge, dislodge! It is the King of England;* **Cor** V.iv.40

disloyal (*adj.*) unfaithful, adulterous, two-timing **MA** III.ii.93 [Don John to Don Pedro and Claudio, of Hero] *the lady is disloyal*

dismal (*adj.*) **1** disastrous, calamitous, devastating **Ham** V.ii.361 [Ambassador to all] *The sight is dismal;* **Ham** II.ii.454; **1H6** I.i.105; **Mac** III.v.21; **RJ** IV.v.113
2 sinister, ominous, malign **Venus** 889 [of Venus hearing the hounds] *This dismal cry rings sadly in her ear;* **AW** V.iii.128; **3H6** II.iii.18, vi.58, V.vi.48; **R3** III.iii.12

dismantle (*v.*) **1** strip off, remove, take away **KL** I.i.217 [France to Lear, of Cordelia] *Commit a thing so monstrous to dismantle / So many folds of favour*
2 deprive, strip, divest **Ham** III.ii.291 [Hamlet to Horatio] *This realm dismantled was / Of Jove himself* [i.e. its strength was removed]
3 remove an outer garment, take off a cloak **WT** IV.iv.648 [Camillo to Perdita] *Dismantle you*

dismasked *(adj.)* unmasked, with mask removed **LL** V.ii.296 [Boyet to and of ladies] *Dismasked, their damask sweet commixture shown*

disme *(n.)* [pron: diym] tenth person killed **TC** II.ii.19 [Hector to Priam, of the war dead] *Every tithe soul 'mongst many thousand dismes / Hath been as dear as Helen* [i.e. of many thousand such individuals]

dismember *(v.)* blow to pieces, divide limb from limb **RJ** III.iii.134 [Friar to Romeo, of his wit] *Like powder in a skilless soldier's flask / Is set afire ... / And thou dismembered with thine own defence*

dismissed *(adj.)* rejected, discarded, spurned **Tem** IV.i.67 [Iris to Ceres] *thy broomgroves, / Whose shadow the dismissed bachelor loves*

dismission *(n.)* **1** rejection, dismissal, repudiation **Cym** II.iii.51 [Queen to Cloten, of Innogen] *you in all obey her, / Save when command to your dismission tends*

 2 discharge from service, permission to leave **AC** I.i.26 [Cleopatra to Antony] *Your dismission / Is come from Caesar*

dismount *(v.)* **1** lower, cast down **Lover** 281 [of the old man] *his wat'ry eyes he did dismount, / Whose sights till then were levelled on my face*

 2 [fencing] draw, remove from the sheath **TN** III.iv.219 [Sir Toby to Viola as Cesario] *Dismount thy tuck*

disnatured *(adj.)* unnatural, aberrant, outlandish **KL** I.iv.280 [Lear to the goddess Nature, of any child of Gonerill's] *it may live / And be a thwart disnatured torment to her*

disorbed *(adj.)* removed from its sphere, knocked out of its orbit **TC** II.ii.46 [Troilus to Helenus, of flying from danger] *like a star disorbed* [i.e. a shooting star]

disordered *(adj.)* disorderly, unruly, riotous **KL** I.iv.238 [Gonerill to Lear, of his knights] *Men so disordered, so deboshed and bold;* **KL** I.iv.252

disparagement *(n.)* disgrace, dishonour, discredit **RJ** I.v.70 [Capulet to Tybalt, of Romeo] *I would not ... / Here in my house do him disparagement;* **CE** I.i.149

disparity *(n.)* inequality, dissimilarity, lack of quality **TNK** V.iii.88 [Emilia to herself, of Palamon and Arcite] *Their nobleness peculiar to them, gives / The prejudice of disparity ... / To any lady breathing* [i.e. makes women feel inferior]

dispark *(v.)* convert [a park] to other uses, change the nature of [a park] **R2** III.i.23 [Bolingbroke to Bushy and Green] *you have ... / Disparked my parks*

dispatch, despatch *(n.)* **1** settlement of business, sorting out of affairs **Cor** I.i.274 [Sicinius to Brutus] *Let's hence and hear / How the dispatch is made;* **AW** III.ii.53, IV.iii.89; **LL** II.i.31, IV.i.5

 2 prompt settlement, speedy handling **H8** V.i.16 [Gardiner to Lovell] *business / That seeks dispatch by day;* **MM** IV.iv.10

 3 hasty removal, speedy concealment **KL** I.ii.33 [Gloucester to Edmund, of the letter] *What needed then that terrible dispatch of it into your pocket?*

 4 sending off, going, departure **Cym** III.viii.16 [First Senator to the tribunes, of their forces] *the words of your commission / Will tie you to the numbers and the time / Of their despatch;* **H5** II.v.6; **Oth** I.iii.46

 5 dismissal, leave to go **Cor** V.iii.180 [Volumnia to Coriolanus] *Yet give us our despatch;* **KL** II.i.124

 6 management, direction, supervision **Mac** I.v.66 [Lady Macbeth to Macbeth] *you shall put / This night's great business into my dispatch;* **Sonn** 143.3; **TN** II.iii.18

dispatch, despatch *(v.)* **1** deal with promptly, settle, get [something] done quickly **AW** IV.iii.84 [Bertram to First Lord] *I have tonight dispatched sixteen businesses;* **AY** III.iii.60; **E3** IV.v.54; **Ham** III.iii.3; **Oth** I.iii.147; **R3** IV.ii.81

 2 deprive, dispossess **Ham** I.v.75 [Ghost to Hamlet] *by a brother's hand / Of life, of crown, of queen at once dispatched;* **KL** IV.v.12

3 kill, put to death, make away with, finish off **RJ** V.i.79 [Apothecary to Romeo, of a poison] *if you had the strength / Of twenty men it would dispatch you straight;* **AC** IV.xiv.104; **E3** II.ii.174; **2H6** III.ii.2; **KJ** IV.i.27; **Tit** IV.ii.85

 4 hurry up, be quick **CE** IV.i.52 [Second Merchant to Angelo] *I pray you, sir, dispatch;* **AC** III.xii.26; **2H4** II.iv.13; **2H6** II.iii.91; **R2** IV.i.242; **WT** IV.iv.636

 5 send away, send off **AW** III.iv.34 [Countess to Steward] *Dispatch the most convenient messenger;* **H5** II.iv.141; **KJ** I.i.99; **TG** I.iii.38, II.vii.88; **Tim** II.i.193

 6 send off, send messengers **WT** II.i.182 [Leontes to Antigonus, of Hermione's guilt] *for a greater confirmation ... I have dispatched in post / To sacred Delphos*

 7 dismiss, get rid of, send away **Oth** IV.iii.8 [Othello to Desdemona] *Dispatch your attendant* [Q; F *dismisse*]; **Per** II.v.14

dispense with *(v.)* **1** disregard, pardon, put up with **Luc** 1704 [Lucrece to all, of the rape] *May my pure mind with the foul act dispense;* **CE** II.i.103; **Luc** 1070; **MM** III.i.138

 2 have done with, do away with, forgo **MM** III.i.157 [disguised Duke to Isabella] *Might you dispense with your leisure;* **MW** II.i.44; **Tim** III.ii.88

 3 gain exemption from, set aside, dissolve **1H6** V.v.28 [Gloucester to King, of his existing engagement] *How shall we then dispense with that contract;* **E3** IV.vii.34; **2H6** V.i.181; **LL** I.i.145

dispersed *(adj.)* rent, shattered, scattered **Luc** 1805 'My daughter' and 'my wife' with clamours filled / The dispersed air*

dispersedly *(adv.)* from various positions, here and there **Tem** I.ii.382, 384 [stage direction] *Burden, dispersedly*

dispiteous *(adj.)* pitiless, merciless **KJ** IV.i.34 [Hubert to himself, of his tears] *Turning dispiteous torture out of door!* [F *dispitious*]

displace *(v.)* **1** remove, banish, get rid of **Mac** III.iv.108 [Lady Macbeth to Macbeth] *You have displaced the mirth;* **Luc** 887

 2 remove from office, lose one's position **2H6** I.i.175 [Somerset to all, of the Cardinal] *If Gloucester be displaced, he'll be Protector*

displant *(v.)* transplant, remove, displace **RJ** III.iii.60 [Romeo to Friar] *Hang up philosophy! / Unless philosophy can ... / Displant a town*

display *(v.)* **1** act, behave, carry on **KL** II.iv.40 [disguised Kent to Lear, of the messenger] *which of late / Displayed so saucily against your highness*

 2 diffuse, spread out, disperse **Luc** 118 *Till sable Night ... / Upon the world dim darkness doth display*

displayed *(adj.)* **1** unfolded, opened, in full bloom **TN** II.iv.39 [Orsino to Viola as Cesario] *women are as roses whose fair flower, / Being once displayed, doth fall that very hour*

 2 extended, stretched, spread **2H6** III.ii.172 [Warwick to Suffolk, of dead Gloucester] *His hands abroad displayed*

 3 [if of the troops] deployed, drawn up; [if of the banners] arrayed, unfurled **KJ** II.i.309 [French Herald to Hubert, of the French army] *Who are at hand, triumphantly displayed*

displeasure *(n.)* **1** injury, wrong, hurt **CE** IV.iv.114 [Adriana to Officer] *Hast thou delight to see a wretched man / Do outrage and displeasure to himself?;* **CE** V.i.142; **E3** V.i.124

 2 being out of favour, discredit; or: discomfort, trouble **Oth** III.i.41 [Emilia to Cassio] *I am sorry / For your displeasure;* **H8** III.ii.392

disponge, dispunge *(v.)* pour out [as from a sponge], rain down, discharge **AC** IV.ix.13 [Enobarbus to himself, as if to the moon] *The poisonous damp of night disponge upon me*

disport *(n.)* diversion, pastime, entertainment **Oth** I.iii.268 [Othello to all] *when ... my disports corrupt and taint my business*

disport *(v.)* entertain, amuse, divert **3H6** IV.v.8 [Richard to Hastings and Stanley, of Edward] *He ... / Comes hunting this way to disport himself;* **Tim** I.ii.133

dispose *(n.)* **1** disposal, control, discretion **TG** II.vii.86 [Julia to Lucetta] *All that is mine I leave at thy dispose;* **CE** I.i.21; **KJ** I.i.263; **TG** IV.i.76

2 disposition, manner, bearing **Oth** I.iii.391 [Iago alone, of Cassio] *He hath a person and a smooth dispose / To be suspected;* **TC** II.iii.162

dispose *(v.)* **1** place, distribute, organize **CE** I.ii.73 [Antipholus of Syracuse to Dromio of Ephesus] *tell me how thou hast disposed thy charge* [i.e. deposited the money]; **E3** V.i.62; **Tim** I.ii.153; **Tit** IV.ii.172
  2 carry out, manage, handle **KJ** III.iv.11 [Lewis the Dauphin to King Philip, of England's victory] *So hot a speed, with such advice disposed … / Doth want example;* **Tem** I.ii.225
  3 control, direct, govern **H5** IV.iii.133 [King Henry to all] *how thou pleasest, God, dispose the day!*
  4 direct, make arrangements for **WT** I.ii.179 [Leontes to Hermione and Polixenes] *To your own bents dispose you;* **Per** I.ii.117
  5 come to terms, make a deal **AC** IV.xiv.123 [Diomedes to Antony, of Cleopatra] *you did suspect / She had disposed with Caesar*
  6 decide, prepare, get ready **E3** III.i.130 [King John to Philip] *[earthquake and lightning] Affrights not more than kings when they dispose / To show the rancour of their high-swoll'n hearts*

dispose of *(v.)* make arrangements for **Tit** IV.ii.172 [Aaron to himself, of his baby] *Now to the Goths … / There to dispose this treasure in mine arms;* **R2** II.ii.117

disposed *(adj.)* **1** arranged, placed, distributed **TNK** IV.ii.122 [Messenger to Theseus, of one of the knight's freckles] *so few and well disposed;* **TC** IV.v.116 ☞ **ill-disposed** *(adj.)*
  2 directed, applied, arranged **H8** I.ii.116 [King Henry to Queen Katherine, of Buckingham's qualities] *When these so noble benefits shall prove / Not well disposed … / They turn to vicious forms*
  3 of a particular disposition, with a turn of mind **2H6** III.i.76 [Queen to King, of Gloucester] *he's disposed as the hateful raven;* **Sonn** 88.1
  4 inclined to be merry, feeling playful **LL** II.i.236 [Princess to Ladies] *Boyet is disposed;* **LL** V.ii.466; **TN** II.iii.80

disposer *(n.)* **1** settler, handler, manager **TNK** III.vi.117 [Arcite to Palamon, of what the world will say] *we had a noble difference, / But base disposers of it* [i.e. we handled it in a dishonourable way]
  2 [unclear meaning] one who makes arrangements, one who can handle [a person] **TC** III.i.84 [Paris to Helen, of where Troilus is to have supper] *with my disposer Cressida;* **TC** III.i.86

disposing *(n.)* disposal, management, control **KJ** V.vii.92 [Salisbury to Bastard, of Lewis the Dauphin] *he hath … put his cause and quarrel / To the disposing of the Cardinal;* **Cor** IV.vii.40; **H8** I.i.43; **Venus** 1040

disposition *(n.)* **1** composure, state of mind, temperament **TN** III.i.132 [Viola as Cesario to Olivia] *Grace and good disposition attend your ladyship;* **AC** I.v.53; **AW** III.vi.41; **AY** III.ii.190; **Ham** I.iv.55; **KL** I.ii.127
  2 natural temperament, normal state of mind **Cor** III.ii.111 [Coriolanus to Volumnia] *Away, my disposition, and possess me / Some harlot's spirit!;* **Ham** I.ii.169; **Mac** III.iv.112; **MM** III.ii.220; **MW** II.i.56; **WT** IV.iv.135
  3 inclination, mood, frame of mind **KL** I.iv.217 [Gonerill to Lear] *put away / These dispositions which of late transport you;* **AY** II.iv.77; **Cor** II.i.13; **Ham** III.i.12; **KL** III.v.5; **MM** I.ii.117
  4 affectation, show of temperament **Ham** I.v.172 [Hamlet to Horatio and Marcellus] *I … shall think meet / To put an antic disposition on*
  5 arrangement, care, management **Oth** I.iii.234 [Othello to Duke] *Most humbly … / I crave fit disposition for my wife*
  6 control, direction, management **TC** IV.i.49 [Paris to Aeneas, of the arrangement to exchange Cressida] *The bitter disposition of the time / Will have it so;* **MM** III.ii.165
  7 aptitude, gift, capacity **AW** I.i.39 [Countess to Lafew, of Helena] *her education promises her dispositions she inherits*

dispossess *(v.)* cause to lose possession **KJ** IV.iii.23 [Salisbury to Bastard] *The King hath dispossessed himself of us*

dispraise *(n.)* disparagement, censure, reproach **LL** IV.iii.262 [Berowne to King, of Rosaline's dark colouring] *red, that would avoid dispraise, / Paints itself black, to imitate her brow;* **TG** III.ii.47; **Tim** I.i.169

dispraise *(v.)* disparage, belittle, denigrate **2H4** II.iv.309 [Prince Henry to Falstaff] *To dispraise me, and call me pantler, and bread-chipper;* **1H4** V.i.59; **H5** V.ii.198; **RJ** III.v.238; **Sonn** 95.7; **TG** III.ii.55

dispraisingly *(adv.)* disparagingly, critically, depreciatingly **Oth** III.iii.72 [Desdemona to Othello] *When I have spoke of you dispraisingly*

disprise, disprize *(v.)* undervalue, disparage, hold in contempt **TC** IV.v.74 [Achilles to Agamemnon, of Hector's response] *A little proudly, and great deal disprizing / The knight opposed* [F; Q *misprising*]

disprized *(adj.)* unvalued, held in contempt, disparaged **Ham** III.i.72 [Hamlet alone] *The pangs of dispriz'd love* [F; Q2 *despiz'd*]

disproperty *(v.)* dispossess, deprive, strip [someone of] **Cor** II.i.240 [Brutus to Sicinius] *Dispropertied their freedoms*

disproportioned *(adj.)* discrepant, inconsistent, incoherent **Oth** I.iii.2 [First Senator to Duke, of the news] *Indeed they are disproportioned*

disprove *(v.)* refute, rebut, prove wrong **Oth** V.ii.171 [Emilia to Iago, of Othello] *Disprove this villain*

dispunge *(v.)* ☞ **disponge** *(v.)*

dispurse *(v.)* disburse, pay out, give away **2H6** III.i.117 [Gloucester to all] *many a pound of mine own proper store … / Have I dispursed to the garrisons*

disputable *(adj.)* disputatious, argumentative, ready to argue **AY** II.v.32 [Jaques to Amiens, of Duke Senior] *He is too disputable for my company*

disputation *(n.)* dialogue, discourse, conversation **H5** III.ii.92 [Fluellen to Macmorris] *I beseech you now … a few disputations with you;* **1H4** III.i.199

dispute *(n.)* disputation, argument, debate **TNK** V.iv.135 [Theseus to the gods] *with you leave dispute / That are above our question*

dispute *(v.)* **1** discuss, consider, deal with [a state of affairs] **RJ** III.iii.64 [Friar to Romeo] *Let me dispute with thee of thy estate;* **WT** IV.iv.397
  2 deal with, handle, struggle against **Mac** IV.iii.219 [Malcolm to Macduff, of the news of Macduff's murdered family] *Dispute it like a man*

disquantity *(v.)* lessen in quantity, reduce, cut down **KL** I.iv.245 [Gonerill to Lear] *Be then desired … / A little to disquantity your train*

disquiet *(adj.)* upset, disturbed, troubled **TS** IV.i.154 [Katherina to Petruchio] *be not so disquiet*

disquietly *(adv.)* uneasily, in a disturbing manner **KL** I.ii.113 [Gloucester to Edmund] *all ruinous disorders follow us disquietly to our graves*

disrelish *(v.)* distaste, disfavour, dislike **Oth** II.i.226 [Iago to Roderigo, of Desdemona] *her delicate tenderness will … disrelish and abhor the Moor*

disroot *(v.)* dislodge, displace, remove **TNK** V.iv.75 [Pirithous to Palamon, of Arcite's horse] *neither curb would crack, girth break, nor differing plunges / Disroot his rider*

disseat, dis-seat *(v.)* **1** unseat, throw, remove **TNK** V.iv.72 [Pirithous to Palamon, of Arcite's horse] *seeks all foul means / Of boisterous and rough jadery to disseat / His lord*
  2 unseat, remove from the throne **Mac** V.iii.21 [Macbeth to himself] *This push / Will chair me ever or dis-seat me now* [F *dis-eate*]

dissemble *(v.)* **1** disguise, cloak, give a deceptive appearance to **R3** II.i.8 [King Edward to Hastings and Rivers] *Dissemble not your hatred;* **PassP** XVIII.28; **Per** II.v.23; **Tit** I.i.446; **TN** IV.ii.4; **TS** IV.iv.42

2 deceive, disguise the truth, pretend 1H6 III.i.141 [Gloucester to all] *So help me God, as I dissemble not;* Cor III.ii.62; E3 IV.iii.70; R3 II.ii.31; Tim V.i.93; Venus 641

dissembled (*adj.*) concealed, pretended, feigned Tit I.i.441 [Tamora to Saturninus, of Titus] *Whose fury not dissembled speaks his griefs*

dissembler (*n.*) hypocrite, deceiver, charlatan R3 I.ii.184 [Anne to Richard] *Arise, dissembler;* MA V.i.53; RJ III.ii.87

dissembling (*n.*) pretence, deceit, dissimulation 3H6 III.iii.119 [Lewis to Warwick] *all dissembling set aside;* AC I.i.79

dissembling (*adj.*) deceitful, hypocritical, false R3 I.i.236 [Richard alone] *no friends to back my suit at all / But … dissembling looks;* AY III.iv.6; CE IV.iv.98; MND II.ii.104; TN V.i.162

dissembly (*n.*) malapropism for 'assembly' MA IV.ii.1 [Dogberry to Verges] *Is our whole dissembly appeared?*

dissension (*n.*) dispute, squabble, quarrel [over] Cor IV.iv.17 [Coriolanus alone] *On a dissension of a doit*

dissentious (*adj.*) quarrelsome, argumentative, fractious Cor I.i.162 [Martius to Citizens] *What's the matter, you dissentious rogues*

dissever (*v.*) divide, split up, separate KJ II.i.388 [Bastard to King John and King Philip, of a united attack on Angiers] *That done, dissever your united strengths;* AW II.i.122; E3 IV.iv.5

dissevered (*adj.*) divided, split, broken E3 I.i.123 [Montague to King Edward, of the league with the Scots] *Cracked and dissevered;* WT V.iii.155

dissipation (*n.*) dispersal, break-up, dissolving KL I.ii.147 [Edmund to Edgar, of a writer] *the effects he writes of succeed unhappily, as of … dissipation of cohorts*

dissolutely (*adv.*) malapropism for 'resolutely' MW I.i.234 [Slender to Shallow] *I am freely dissolved, and dissolutely*

dissolution (*n.*) **1** melting, liquefaction, dissolving MW III.v.106 [Falstaff to Ford as Brook, of himself] *a man of continual dissolution and thaw* [i.e. through sweating]; Luc 355
2 total destruction, disintegration MM III.ii.213 [disguised Duke to Escalus] *there is so great a fever on goodness that the dissolution of it must cure it;* KL I.ii.144; R2 II.i.258

dissolve (*v.*) **1** loosen, release, set free TC V.ii.159 [Troilus to Ulysses] *The bonds of heaven are slipped, dissolved, and loosed;* AW I.ii.66; R2 II.ii.71
2 separate, part, break up MW V.v.216 [Fenton to Mistress Page, of Anne] *she and I … / Are now so sure that nothing can dissolve us;* Cor I.i.202
3 melt, liquefy TG III.ii.8 [Duke to Thurio, of love] *as a figure / Trenched in ice, which with an hour's heat / Dissolves to water;* MND I.i.245; R2 III.ii.108; Venus 565
4 melt into tears, break down in grief KL V.iii.201 [Albany to Edgar] *I am almost ready to dissolve, / Hearing of this*
5 lose influence, reduce to nothing Tem V.i.64 [Prospero to the charmed lords] *The charm dissolves apace*

dissolved (*adj.*) **1** destroyed, ruined; also: annulled E3 II.ii.167 [Countess to King Edward] *Resolved to be dissolved*
2 malapropism for 'resolved' MW I.i.234 [Slender to Shallow] *I am freely dissolved*

dissuade (*v.*) persuade, give advice AC IV.vi.13 [Enobarbus alone] *Alexas … did dissuade / Great Herod to incline himself to Caesar*

distaff (*n.*) device for weaving, spindle KL IV.ii.17 [Gonerill to Edmund] *I must change arms at home and give the distaff / Into my husband's hands;* Cym V.iii.34; TN I.iii.97; WT I.ii.37

distaff-woman (*n.*) woman occupied in spinning R2 III.ii.118 [Scroop to King Richard] *distaff-women manage rusty bills / Against thy seat*

distain (*v.*) **1** dishonour, defile, corrupt E3 II.i.392 [Warwick to Countess] *The King that would distain thee will advance thee;* Luc 786; R3 V.iii.323; TC I.iii.241

2 cast a shadow over, outshine, eclipse Per IV.iii.31 [Dionyza to Cleon, of Marina] *She did distain my child* [Q *disdaine*]

distance (*n.*) **1** [fencing] regulation space to be kept between contestants MW II.i.207 [Shallow to Page, on fencing] *In these times you stand on distance;* MW II.iii.23; RJ II.iv.21
2 [fencing: see sense 1] enmity, discord, dissension Mac III.i.115 [Macbeth to Murderers, of Banquo being his enemy] *in such bloody distance / That every minute of his being thrusts / Against my near'st of life*

distaste (*v.*) **1** dislike, not relish, be averse to KL I.iii.15 [Gonerill to Oswald, of serving Lear negligently] *If he distaste it let him to my sister* [F; Q *dislike*]; TC II.ii.67
2 be distasteful, offend the taste, disgust Oth III.iii.324 [Iago alone] *Dangerous conceits are in their natures poisons, / Which at the first are scarce found to distaste*
3 make distasteful, destroy the relish of TC IV.iv.47 [Troilus to Cressida] *a single famished kiss, / Distasted with the salt of broken tears;* TC II.ii.124

distasteful (*adj.*) showing dislike, displaying aversion Tim II.ii.216 [Flavius to Timon, of the Senators' responses] *After distasteful looks and these hard fractions* [i.e. the Senators found the matter distasteful]

distemper (*n.*) **1** malady, illness, derangement WT I.ii.385 [Camillo to Polixenes] *There is a sickness / Which puts some of us in distemper, but / I cannot name the disease;* Cym III.iv.193; Ham II.ii.55, III.ii.344; MW III.v.71; TNK IV.iii.3
2 disaffection, ill humour, strange behaviour Ham III.ii.344 [Rosencrantz to Hamlet] *what is your cause of distemper?*
3 bad temper, cross mood MW IV.ii.25 [Mistress Page to Mistress Ford, of Ford] *any madness I ever yet beheld seemed but tameness … to this his distemper he is in now;* MW III.iii.204, v.71; WT I.ii.385
4 intoxication, state of drunkenness H5 II.ii.54 [King Henry to all] *little faults, proceeding on distemper, / Shall not be winked at*

distemper (*v.*) disorder, derange, disturb, confuse TNK IV.iii.69 [Doctor to Gaoler and Wooer, of the Gaoler's Daughter] *That intemperate surfeit of her eye hath distempered the other senses;* TN II.i.5; Venus 653

distemperature (*n.*) **1** ailment, disorder, malady Per V.i.25 [Lysimachus to Helicanus, of Pericles] *Upon what ground is his distemperature?;* CE V.i.82; RJ II.iii.36
2 disordered condition, inclement state [of weather] 1H4 I.i.3 [King Henry to all, of the sun] *The day looks pale / At his distemperature;* 1H4 III.i.31; MND II.i.106

distempered (*adj.*) **1** troubled, disturbed, inclement AW I.iii.146 [Countess to Helena, of her tears] *this distempered messenger of wet;* KJ III.iv.154
2 vexed, troubled, ill-humoured KJ IV.iii.21 [Bastard to all] *Once more today well met, distempered lords!;* Ham III.ii.309; Tem IV.i.145; TNK IV.i.119
3 disordered, disturbed, diseased RJ II.iii.29 [Friar to Romeo] *argues a distempered head / So soon to bid good morrow to thy bed;* 2H4 III.i.41; Sonn 153.12; TC II.ii.170; TN I.v.86
4 insane, deranged, lunatic Mac V.ii.15 [Cathness to Menteth, of Macbeth] *He cannot buckle his distempered cause / Within the belt of rule*

distempering (*adj.*) intoxicating, disturbing, disorienting Oth I.i.100 [Brabantio to Roderigo] *Being full of supper and distempering draughts*

distil (*v.*) **1** melt, reduce, dissolve Ham I.ii.204 [Horatio to Hamlet, of the sentinels] *distilled / Almost to jelly with the act of fear* [Q1,Q2 *distill'd;* F *bestil'd*]
2 trickle down, fall in tiny drops Tit III.i.17 [Titus as if to the earth, of his eyes] *I will befriend thee more with rain / That shall distil from these two ancient ruins;* RJ V.iii.15; Tit II.iii.201

distilled (*adj.*) fragrant, scented, aromatic TS Induction.i.46 [Lord to Huntsmen, of Sly] *Balm his foul head in warm distilled waters*

distilling (*adj.*) infusing, penetrative, permeating the body **RJ** IV.i.94 [Friar to Juliet] *this distilling liquor drink thou off* [F; Q1 *distilled*]; **Venus** 66

distilment (*n.*) distillation, extract **Ham** I.v.64 [Ghost to Hamlet] *And in the porches of my ears did pour / The leperous distilment*

distinct (*n.*) separate entity, differentiated thing **Phoen** 27 [of the Phoenix and Dove] *Two distincts, division none*

distinction (*n.*) act of distinguishing, discrimination, differentiation **TC** III.ii.25 [Troilus alone, of being with Cressida] *I do fear besides / That I shall lose distinction in my joys*; **Cym** V.v.385; **TC** I.iii.27

distinctively (*adv.*) distinctly **Oth** I.iii.154 [Othello to all, of Desdemona] *I would all my pilgrimage dilate / Whereof by parcels she had something heard, / But not distinctively* [F2; Q *intentively*; F1 *instinctiuely*] ☛ **intentively** (*adv.*)

distinctly (*adv.*) **1** individually, separately, personally **Tem** I.ii.200 [Ariel to Prospero] *On the topmast, / The yards, and boresprit would I flame distinctly*; **Cor** IV.iii.40
   2 clearly, without confusion **Oth** II.iii.280 [Cassio to Iago] *I remember a mass of things, but nothing distinctly*; **Cor** III.i.205

distinguish (*v.*) **1** call, describe as, dub **TNK** III.v.103 [Schoolmaster to Theseus] *We are a few of those collected here / That ruder tongues distinguish villager*
   2 discern, make out, show distinctly **R2** II.ii.20 [Bushy to Queen Isabel, of perspectives] *eyed awry, / Distinguish form*
   3 discriminate, decide between **TNK** IV.ii.54 [Emilia alone] *having two fair gauds of equal sweetness, / Cannot distinguish*

distinguishment (*n.*) distinguishing, distinction, differentiation **WT** II.i.86 [Leontes to Hermione] *mannerly distinguishment leave out / Betwixt the prince and beggar*

distract (*adj.*) **1** deranged, mad, mentally disturbed **TN** V.i.277 [Olivia to Orsino, of Malvolio] *They say, poor gentleman, he's much distract*; **CE** IV.iii.42; **Ham** IV.v.2; **JC** IV.iii.153; **KL** IV.vi.280; **Tit** III.iii.26
   2 confused, perplexed **E3** IV.vi.5 [Artois to Prince Edward] *The amazed French / Are quite distract with gazing on the crows*
   3 divided, separated, scattered **Lover** 231 [the woman, of her treasures] *to your audit comes / Their distract parcels*

distract (*v.*) **1** divide, separate, draw apart **AC** III.vii.43 [Enobarbus to Antony] *you ... / Distract your army*; **Oth** I.iii.320
   2 drive mad, derange, unbalance **2H4** II.i.105 [Falstaff to Lord Chief Justice, of the Hostess] *poverty hath distracted her*
   3 [unclear meaning] perplex, bewilder **MW** II.ii.130 [Falstaff to himself, of hearing from both Mistress Ford and Mistress Page] *This news distracts me*; **Oth** II.iii.249

distracted (*adj.*) **1** perplexed, confused, agitated **Ham** III.i.5 [Rosencrantz to Claudius, of Hamlet] *He does confess he feels himself distractedly*; **Mac** II.iii.101; **MM** IV.iv.2; **TC** V.iii.192; **Tem** V.i.12; **Tim** III.iv.114
   2 irrational, foolish, unreasonable **Ham** IV.iii.4 [Claudius to his attendants, of Hamlet] *He's loved of the distracted multitude*
   3 divided, torn apart, rent asunder **AW** V.iii.35 [King to Bertram] *to the brightest beams / Distracted clouds give way*

distractedly (*adv.*) disjointedly, erratically, with agitation **TN** II.ii.21 [Viola alone, of Olivia] *she did speak in starts, distractedly*; **Lover** 28

distraction (*n.*) **1** perturbation, agitation, frenzied state **WT** I.ii.149 [Hermione to Leontes] *You look / As if you held a brow of much distraction*; **H8** III.i.112; **MW** III.v.78; **Sonn** 119.8; **TC** V.ii.42; **WT** V.ii.47
   2 madness, derangement, insanity **TN** V.i.311 [Orsino to Olivia, of Malvolio's letter] *This savours not much of distraction*; **Ham** V.ii.223; **Tem** III.iii.91; **TN** V.i.65; **TNK** IV.iii.1
   3 division, small detachment **AC** III.vii.76 [Soldier to Canidius, of Caesar] *His power went out in such distractions as / Beguiled all spies*

distrain (*v.*) seize, confiscate, commandeer **R2** II.iii.130 [Bolingbroke to York] *My father's goods are all distrained and sold*; **1H6** I.iii.61; **R3** V.iii.323

distress (*n.*) hardship, adversity, difficulty **1H6** IV.i.37 [Talbot to all, of Knights of the Garter] *Not fearing death nor shrinking for distress*

distressed (*adj.*) afflicted with hardships, troubled with difficulties **Cym** IV.ii.47 [Belarius to Arviragus and Guiderius, of disguised Innogen] *This youth, howe'er distressed, appears he hath had / Good ancestors*; **1H6** IV.iii.30

distressful (*adj.*) earned through great hardship, gained from toil **H5** IV.i.263 [King Henry alone] *the wretched slave, / Who ... / Gets him to rest, crammed with distressful bread*

distrust (*n.*) **1** lack of confidence, doubt **KJ** V.i.46 [Bastard to King John] *Let not the world see fear and sad distrust / Govern the motion of a kingly eye*
   2 fear for, be anxious about **Ham** III.ii.174 [Second Player, as Queen, to her King] *So far from cheer ... / That I distrust you*

distrustful (*adj.*) hesitant, diffident, lacking confidence **1H6** I.ii.126 [Pucelle to Reignier and Alençon] *distrustful recreants, / Fight till the last gasp*

disturb (*n.*) disturbance **R3** IV.ii.72 [King Richard to Tyrrel, of the princes] *Foes to my rest and my sweet sleep's disturbs* [Q; F *disturbers*]

disvalued (*adj.*) discredited, disparaged, degraded **MM** V.i.219 [Angelo to Duke, of Mariana] *her reputation was disvalued / In levity*

disvouch (*v.*) disavow, contradict, refuse to acknowledge **MM** IV.iv.1 [Escalus to Angelo, of the Duke] *Every letter he hath writ hath disvouched other*

ditch-delivered (*adj.*) born in a ditch **Mac** IV.i.31 [Third Witch to Witches] *babe, / Ditch-delivered by a drab*

ditch-dog (*n.*) dead dog thrown in a ditch **KL** III.iv.126 [Edgar as Poor Tom to Gloucester, of himself] *swallows the old rat and the ditch-dog*

ditcher (*n.*) ditch-maker **Ham** V.i.30 [First Clown to Second Clown] *There is no ancient gentlemen but gardeners, ditchers, and grave-makers*

ditty (*n.*) **1** song **Venus** 836 [of Venus] *She ... sings extemporally a woeful ditty*; **1H4** III.i.119; **MND** V.i.385; **PassP** XIV.19, XX.11; **Tem** I.ii.406
   2 words, lyrics **AY** V.iii.40 [Touchstone to Pages, of their song] *there was no great matter in the ditty*

diurnal (*adj.*) daily **AW** II.i.162 [Helena to King] *Ere twice the horses of the sun shall bring / Their fiery torcher his diurnal ring*

dive-dapper (*n.*) diving waterfowl, dabchick **Venus** 86 *Like a dive-dapper peering through a wave*

divers (*adj.*) different, various, several **1H6** IV.i.25 [Talbot to all] *Myself and divers gentlemen beside / Were there surprised*; **AY** III.ii.299; **H5** I.ii.184; **MV** III.i.103; **R3** I.ii.217; **WT** V.i.201

diverted (*adj.*) turned from its natural course, deviant **AY** II.iii.37 [Orlando to Adam, of Oliver] *the malice / Of a diverted blood*

divest (*v.*) ☛ **devest** (*v.*)

dividable (*adj.*) in a divided state, separated **TC** I.iii.105 [Ulysses to all] *Peaceful commerce from dividable shores* [i.e. countries separated by the sea]

dividant (*adj.*) divisible, distinguishable, separable **Tim** IV.iii.5 [Timon alone, of the sun and moon] *Whose procreation, residence, and birth, / Scarce is dividant*

divide (*n.*) distinguish the qualities, list the attributes [of someone] **Ham** V.ii.113 [Hamlet to Osrick, of Laertes] *to divide him inventorially*

divide (*v.*) **1** share out, distribute, apportion **Lover** 67 [of the reverend man and the woman] *he again desires her ... / Her grievance with his hearing to divide*
   2 share, participate, have a portion **Cor** I.vi.87 [Cominius to Soldiers] *Make good this ostentation, and you shall / Divide in all with us*

divided (*adj.*) **1** broken, stifled, half-smothered **TNK** II.i.41 [Gaoler's Daughter to Gaoler, of Palamon and Arcite] *Yet sometime a divided sigh … will break from one of them*

2 shared, with everyone partaking **Tim** I.ii.47 [Apemantus to himself, of Timon] *The fellow that sits next him … pledges the breath of him in a divided draught*

3 incomplete, imperfect, defective **KJ** II.i.439 [Hubert to all, of Blanche and the Dauphin] *she [has] a fair divided excellence, / Whose fullness of perfection lies in him*
➣ well-divided (*adj.*)

dividual (*adj.*) different, separate [i.e. between man and woman] **TNK** I.iii.82 [Emilia to Hippolyta] *the true love 'tween maid and maid may be / More than in sex dividual* [Q *individuall*]

divination (*n.*) guess, conjecture, prophecy **Venus** 670 [Venus to Adonis, of her heart] *fear doth teach it divination;* **2H4** I.i.88

divine (*n.*) **1** clergyman, priest, parson **MV** I.ii.14 [Portia to Nerissa] *It is a good divine that follows his own instructions;* **Cor** II.iii.57; **E3** IV.iv.115; **MM** III.ii.199; **RJ** III.iii.50

2 high-priest, holy man **WT** III.i.19 [Dion to Cleomenes] *the oracle, / Thus by Apollo's great divine sealed up*

divine (*adj.*) **1** immortal, eternal **R2** I.i.38 [Bolingbroke to Mowbray] *for what I speak … my divine soul answer it in heaven*

2 godlike, sacred, blessed **TC** IV.v.170 [Agamemnon to Hector] *faith and troth … / Bids thee with most divine integrity … welcome*

divine (*v.*) **1** guess, suppose, conjecture **Oth** I.ii.39 [Cassio to Othello, responding to 'What is the matter?'] *Something from Cyprus, as I may divine*

2 make guesses [about], predict the outcome **AC** II.vi.114 [Enobarbus to Menas] *If I were bound to divine of this unity*

3 predict, foretell, prophesy **R2** III.iv.79 [Queen Isabel to Gardener, of King Richard] *Darest thou … / Divine his downfall?*

divinely (*adv.*) piously, spiritually, in a religious manner **R3** III.vii.61 [Catesby to Buckingham, of Richard] *He is within … / Divinely bent to meditation;* **KJ** II.i.237

divineness (*n.*) divinity, perfection, supreme excellence **Cym** III.vii.16 [Belarius to Guiderius and Arviragus, of disguised Innogen] *Behold divineness / No elder than a boy!*

diviner (*n.*) witch, sorceress, magician **CE** III.ii.148 [Dromio of Syracuse to Antipholus of Syracuse, of the kitchen wench] *this drudge or diviner laid claim to me*

divining (*adj.*) prophesying, foreseeing, foretelling **3H6** IV.vi.90 [King to all, of Richmond] *If secret powers / Suggest but truth to my divining thoughts, / This pretty lad will prove our country's bliss*

divinity (*n.*) **1** theology **Oth** II.iii.340 [Iago alone] *How am I then a villain / To counsel Cassio to this parallel course / Directly to his good? Divinity of hell!;* **KL** IV.vi.100

2 divination, divine power, supernatural presence **MW** V.i.3 [Falstaff to Mistress Quickly] *They say there is divinity in odd numbers*

division (*n.*) **1** dissension, discord, disunity **AC** II.i.48 [Pompey to Menas, of Antony and Caesar] *the fear of us / May cement their divisions and bind up the petty difference;* **1H6** IV.i.193; **KL** I.ii.136, 145

2 [music] variation, modulation **1H4** III.i.204 [Mortimer to Lady Mortimer] *ditties highly penned, / Sung by a fair queen … / With ravishing division to her lute;* **Mac** IV.iii.96; **RJ** III.v.29

divorce (*n.*) **1** cause of separation, reason for estrangement **Venus** 932 [Venus as if to death] *Hateful divorce of love;* **Tim** IV.iii.383

2 separating force **H8** II.i.76 [Buckingham to all] *as the long divorce of steel falls on me / Make of your prayers one sweet sacrifice*

divorcement (*n.*) divorce, separation **Oth** IV.ii.157 [Desdemona to Iago, of Othello] *though he do shake me off / To beggarly divorcement*

divulge (*v.*) **1** proclaim, reveal, make publicly known **TN** I.v.249 [Olivia to Viola as Cesario, of Orsino] *[he is] In voices well divulged* [i.e. well spoken of]; **MW** III.ii.38

2 become public, be revealed **Ham** IV.i.22 [Claudius to Gertrude, of Hamlet's supposed madness] *To keep it from divulging let it feed / Even on the pith of life*

dizzy (*v.*) make dizzy, confuse, bewilder **TC** V.ii.177 [Troilus to Ulysses] *the dreadful spout … / Shall dizzy with more clamour Neptune's ear;* **Ham** V.ii.113

dizzy-eyed (*adj.*) dazzling, blinding **1H6** IV.vii.11 [Talbot to Servant, of John Talbot] *Dizzy-eyed fury and great rage of heart / Suddenly made him from my side to start* [i.e. with eyes dazzled by fury]

do (*v.*) **1** describe, depict, report **AY** II.vii.84 [Jaques to Duke Senior, of Touchstone] *Let me see wherein / My tongue hath wronged him: if it do him right, / Then he hath wronged himself*

2 achieve, complete, fulfil **AY** V.iv.167 [Duke Senior to all] *let us do those ends / That here were well begun*

3 organize, arrange, manage **TNK** II.ii.41 [Second Countryman to the others, of the Schoolmaster] *For he does all;* **H8** IV.ii.60

4 convey, deliver, transmit **Oth** III.ii.2 [Othello to Iago, of the pilot] *by him do my duties to the senate;* **WT** V.ii.56

5 perform, play one's part, act **MND** I.ii.64 [Quince to Snug, of playing the lion] *You can do it extempore;* **MA** II.i.104; **MND** I.ii.23; **TC** IV.ii.26; **Tim** III.i.50; **TNK** II.ii.57

6 destroy, consume, reduce to nothing **Luc** 23 [of happiness] *if possessed, as soon decayed and done / As is the morning silver melting dew;* **Venus** 749

7 do harm, cause trouble **Mac** I.iii.10 [First Witch to Witches] *I'll do, I'll do, and I'll do*

8 go on, carry on **Tem** IV.i.239 [Trinculo to Stephano, responding to Stephano choosing fine clothes] *Do, do!;* **TC** II.i.40

dock (*n.*) variety of weedy herb **H5** V.ii.52 [Burgundy to King Henry and the French King, of the fields] *nothing teems / But hateful docks, rough thistles;* **Tem** II.i.146 ➣ **PLANTS**, p.330

doctor (*n.*) **1** scholar, model of intelligence **MA** V.i.195 [Claudio to Don Pedro, of a man 'who leaves off his wit'] *He is then a giant to an ape; but then is an ape a doctor to such a man*

2 learned man, scholar; or: astrologer, physician **R2** I.i.157 [King Richard to Mowbray and Bolingbroke] *Our doctors say this is no month to bleed*

doctrine (*n.*) **1** learning, body of knowledge, science **AW** I.iii.236 [Countess to Helena] *the schools, / Embowelled of their doctrine*

2 precept, lesson **AC** V.ii.31 [Cleopatra to Proculeius] *I hourly learn / A doctrine of obedience;* **LL** IV.iii.326; **RJ** I.i.238

document (*n.*) lesson, lecture, instruction **Ham** IV.v.179 [Laertes to all, of Ophelia's speech] *A document in madness*

do de (*int.*) ➣ **SOUNDS**, p.410

dodge (*v.*) go this way and that, haggle, drag one's feet **AC** III.xi.62 [Antony to Cleopatra] *I must … dodge / And palter in the shifts of lowness*

doer (*n.*) achiever, performer, hero **TNK** II.i.30 [Gaoler to Gaoler's Daughter, of Palamon and Arcite] *I heard them reported in the battle to be the only doers* [i.e. the only ones worth mentioning]

doff (*v.*) throw off, get rid of, do away with **KJ** III.i.128 [Constance to Austria, of his lion skin] *Doff it for shame;* **Mac** IV.iii.188; **RJ** II.ii.47; **TC** V.iii.31; **TS** III.ii.99 ➣ **daff** (*v.*)

dog (*n.*) **1** fellow, individual **R2** V.v.70 [Richard to Groom] *that sad dog / That brings me food*

2 ruthless enemy, merciless beast **Cor** I.i.26 [First Citizen to all, of Martius] *He's a very dog to the commonalty*

dog at, be a be adept at, be experienced in **TN** II.iii.58 [Sir Andrew to Sir Toby] *I am dog at a catch;* **TG** IV.iv.12

dog (*v.*) follow closely, pursue like a dog **TC** V.i.91 [Thersites alone, of Diomedes] *I will rather leave to see Hector than not to dog him* [i.e. I'd rather forgo seeing Hector]

dog-ape (*n.*) [dog-faced] baboon **AY** II.v.24 [Jaques to Amiens] *th'encounter of two dog-apes*

dog-days (*n.*) hottest days of the year [associated with the astrological position of Sirius, the Dog-star] **H8** V.iv.41 [Man to Porter, of a brass-worker] *twenty of the dog-days now reign in's nose* ☞ **COSMOS**, p.102

dogged (*adj.*) **1** fierce, cruel, ferocious **KJ** IV.i.128 [Hubert to Arthur, of his enemies] *I'll fill these dogged spies with false reports;* **KJ** IV.iii.149

2 spiteful, malicious, vindictive **2H6** III.i.158 [Gloucester to King] *dogged York, that reaches at the moon*

dog-hearted (*adj.*) cruel, callous, malevolent **KL** IV.iii.45 [disguised Kent to Gentleman, of Cordelia and Lear] *his own unkindness … gave her dear rights / To his dog-hearted daughters*

dog-weary (*adj.*) dog-tired, exhausted **TS** V.ii.60 [Biondello to Tranio] *I have watched so long / That I'm dog-weary*

doing (*n.*) action, performance, activity **Tit** III.ii.62 [Titus to Marcus, of a fly] *How would he … buzz lamenting doings in the air;* **Cor** I.ix.23, 40; **H8** I.ii.74; **R3** II.ii.90

doit (*n.*) [small Dutch coin = half an English farthing] trivial sum, worthless amount, trifle **Tem** II.ii.31 [Trinculo to himself, of people in England] *they will not give a doit to relieve a lame beggar;* **Cor** V.iv.56; **2H6** III.i.112; **MV** I.iii.137; **Per** IV.ii.48; **Tim** I.i.215 ☞ **MONEY**, p.286

dole (*n.*) **1** grief, sorrow, sadness **Ham** I.ii.13 [Claudius to his court, of himself] *In equal scale weighing delight and dole;* **AY** I.ii.121; **MND** V.i.270; **Per** III.Chorus.42; **TNK** I.v.3

2 share, part, portion, lot **AW** II.ii.168 [Bertram to King] *what dole of honour / Flies where you bid it*

3 delivery, distribution, dealing out **2H4** I.i.169 [Morton to Northumberland] *It was your presurmise / That in the dole of blows your son might drop*

dole, happy man be his destiny, fate, lot **MW** III.iv.63 [Slender to Anne, of whoever wins her] *if it be my luck, so; if not, happy man be his dole* [i.e. good luck to the man who wins you]; **1H4** II.ii.75; **TS** I.i.137; **WT** I.ii.163

dollar (*n.*) ☞ **MONEY**, p.286

dolour (*n.*) sorrow, grief, lamentation **Luc** 1582 *It easeth some, though none it ever cured, / To think their dolour others have endured;* **KL** II.iv.52; **Mac** IV.iii.8; **MM** I.ii.49; **Tem** I.ii.21; **WT** V.ii.86

dolphin (*n.*) ☞ **dauphin** (*n.*)

domestic (*n.*) servant, slave **H8** II.iv.114 [Queen Katherine to Wolsey] *your words, / Domestics to you, serve your will as't please / Yourself pronounce their office*

domestic (*adj.*) **1** internal, to do with home affairs, local **KL** V.i.30 [Gonerill to all] *these domestic and particular broils;* **JC** III.i.263

2 appropriate in the home **Tim** IV.i.17 [Timon alone] *Domestic awe, night-rest, and neighbourhood … / Decline to your confounding contraries*

domination (*n.*) possession, dominion, sovereign territory **KJ** II.i.176 [Constance to Queen Eleanor, of Arthur] *Thou and thine usurp / The dominations, royalties, and rights / Of this oppressed boy*

dominator (*n.*) ruler, lord, sovereign **Tit** II.iii.31 [Aaron to Tamora] *though Venus govern your desires, / Saturn is dominator over mine;* **LL** I.i.217

domineer (*v.*) feast riotously, raise the roof **TS** III.ii.223 [Petruchio to all] *Go to the feast, revel and domineer*

dominical (*n.*) [liturgy] letter printed prominently so as to identify the Sundays in the church year **LL** V.ii.44 [Rosaline to and of Katharine] *My red dominical, my golden letter*

dominie (*n.*) schoolmaster, teacher **TNK** II.ii.40 [Second Country-man to the others] *will the dainty dominie, the schoolmaster, / Keep touch;* **TNK** III.v.134, 147 ☞ **dan** (*n.*)

dominion (*n.*) land, territory, province **E3** IV.ii.11 [Salisbury to Mountford] *The whole dominion of the realm of France;* **Cym** III.ii.41; **E3** II.i.11, IV.i.11; **H8** II.iv.16; **KL** I.i.177

Don (*n.*) ☞ **dan** (*n.*)

donation (*n.*) **1** giving, bestowal, imparting **Cym** V.v.368 [Belarius to Cymbeline, of Guiderius' mole] *It was wise Nature's end, in the donation / To be his evidence now;* **Tim** III.ii.85

2 gift, present, favour **Tem** IV.i.85 [Iris to Ceres] *some donation freely to estate / On the blest lovers*

done (*adj.*) finished with, put off **3H6** IV.i.104 [Post to Edward, of the Queen's message] *my mourning weeds are done*

doom (*n.*) **1** judgement, sentence, decision **AY** I.iii.81 [Duke Frederick to Celia] *Firm and irrevocable is my doom;* **1H6** IV.i.45; **3H6** II.vi.46; **R2** I.iii.148; **Sonn** 145.7; **Tit** III.i.51

2 final destiny, deciding fate, death and destruction **KJ** III.i.311 [Constance to Lewis the Dauphin, of war against England] *alter not the doom / Forethought by heaven;* **AC** III.xiii.78; **MW** V.v.58; **R3** IV.iv.12; **Sonn** 14.14

3 doomsday, day of judgement **RJ** III.ii.67 [Juliet to Nurse] *dreadful trumpet, sound the General Doom;* **Ham** III.iv.51; **Luc** 924; **Mac** II.iii.75, IV.i.116

doom, day of last day of life, death-day **Tit** II.iii.42 [Aaron to Tamora] *This is the day of doom for Bassianus;* **3H6** V.vi.93; **R2** III.ii.189

doom (*v.*) **1** decree, decide, adjudge **Tit** IV.ii.113 [Nurse to all, of Tamora] *The Emperor in his rage will doom her death;* **Cym** V.v.421; **R3** II.i.104; **RJ** III.i.134

2 condemn, pronounce judgement against **Tit** III.i.47 [Titus to Lucius] *tribunes with their tongues doom men to death;* **Cor** I.viii.6; **KJ** IV.iii.39; **R3** III.i.65; **TNK** V.i.156

doomsday (*n.*) death-day, day of judgement **RJ** V.iii.234 [Friar to Prince, of Romeo and Juliet] *their stolen marriage day / Was Tybalt's doomsday;* **1H4** IV.i.134; **R3** V.i.12

door (*n.*) quarter, direction **1H4** III.iii.87 [Falstaff to Prince Hal] *Is the wind in that door, i'faith, must we all march?*

door, out of (*adv.*) **1** outwardly, on the outside **Cym** I.vii.15 [Iachimo to himself, of Innogen] *All of her that is out of door most rich!*

2 out of doors, out of the house **KJ** IV.i.34 [Hubert to himself, of his tears] *Turning dispiteous torture out of door!*

door, within so as not to be heard outside, not so loudly **Oth** IV.ii.143 [Iago to Emilia] *Speak within door* [Q *dores*]

door-keeper (*n.*) procurer, pander, whoremaster **Per** IV.vi.116 [Lysimachus to Boult] *Avaunt, thou damned doorkeeper!;* **Per** IV.vi.163

dormouse (*n.*) sleepy, dozing, slumbering **TN** III.ii.18 [Fabian to Sir Andrew] *awake your dormouse valour*

dost (*v.*) ☞ **VERB FORMS**, p.481

dotage (*n.*) **1** doting, infatuation, excessive affection **MND** IV.i.46 [Oberon to Puck, of Titania] *Her dotage now I do begin to pity;* **AC** I.i.1, ii.118; **MA** II.iii.168, 212; **Oth** IV.i.27

2 feebleness of mind, senility **Tim** III.v.99 [Alcibiades to Senators] *Banish me? / Banish your dotage;* **KL** I.iv.290, 323, II.iv.192

dotant (*n.*) dotard, dullard, one whose mind is impaired by age **Cor** V.ii.43 [First Watch to and of Menenius] *such a decayed dotant*

dotard (*n.*) old fool, senile idiot **MA** V.i.59 [Leonato to Claudio] *I speak not like a dotard nor a fool;* **Cym** I.i.50; **TS** V.i.96; **WT** II.iii.74

dote (*v.*) become deranged, behave foolishly **CE** V.i.195 [Egeon to himself] *Unless the fear of death doth make me dote;* **CE** V.i.330; **LL** V.ii.76; **TC** II.ii.59; **Tit** III.ii.23; **Venus** 837

dote on / upon (*v.*) **1** be infatuated with, idolize **E3** II.i.385 [Warwick to Countess] *The mighty King of England dotes on thee;* **AY** I.ii.132; **E3** II.i.213; **Ham** V.ii.186; **Tem** IV.i.231; **TG** IV.iv.79

2 love dearly, give tender care **AW** II.i.47 [Parolles to Lords] *Mars dote on you for his novices!*

doth (*v.*) ☞ **VERB FORMS**, p.481

doting (*adj.*) foolish, stupid, weak-minded **CE** IV.iv.56 [Antipholus of Ephesus to Pinch] *Peace, doting wizard;* **2H4** IV.iv.126

double (*n.*) sharp turn, doubling back **Venus** 682 [Venus to Adonis, of the hunted hare] *He cranks and crosses with a thousand doubles*

double (*adj.*) **1** equivocal, ambiguous **H8** IV.ii.38 [Katherine to Griffith, of Wolsey] *I'th' presence / He would ... be ever double / Both in his words and meaning*

2 forked, divided **R2** III.ii.21 [King Richard to the earth, of an adder] *Whose double tongue may with a mortal touch / Throw death upon thy sovereign's enemies;* **LL** V.ii.245; **MND** II.ii.9, III.ii.72

3 divided, twofold, dual **Cor** III.i.142 [Coriolanus to Brutus] *This double worship, / Where one part does disdain with cause, the other / Insult without all reason* [i.e. respect paid to two authorities]

4 worth twice the value of the standard coin **MV** II.viii.19 [Solanio to Salerio, impersonating Shylock] *two sealed bags of ducats, / Of double ducats*

5 [of beer] extra strong, very powerful **E3** III.i.26 [King John to all] *Those frothy Dutchmen puffed with double beer;* **2H6** II.iii.64

double (*v.*) **1** repeat, reiterate **R2** I.i.57 [Mowbray to King Richard, of Bolingbroke] *my free speech ... would post until it had returned / These terms of treason doubled down his throat* [F *doubly*]

2 become slurred, thicken, stutter **2H6** II.iii.91 [York to all, of Horner] *Dispatch; this knave's tongue begins to double*

double (*adv.*) **1** doubly, for the second time, twice over **WT** V.iii.107 [Paulina to Leontes, of Hermione] *Do not shun her / Until you see her die again, for then / You kill her double;* **AW** II.iii.237; **Mac** IV.i.82

2 deceptively, deceitfully, in a two-faced way **RJ** II.iv.165 [Nurse to Romeo, of Juliet] *if you should deal double with her, truly it were an ill thing*

double-charge (*v.*) load twice over **2H4** V.iii.123 [Falstaff to Pistol] *I will double-charge thee with dignities*

doubled (*adj.*) redoubled in strength, twice as strong as previously **Cor** II.ii.114 [Cominius to all, of Coriolanus] *his doubled spirit / Requickened what in flesh was fatigate*

double-fatal (*adj.*) yielding two kinds of death **R2** III.ii.116 [Scroop to King Richard] *Thy very beadsmen learn to bend their bows / Of double-fatal yew against thy state* [i.e. death from its poisonous berries or from the bows it makes]

double-man (*n.*) apparition, wraith, spectre **1H4** V.iv.136 [Falstaff to Prince Hal, responding to 'Thou art not what thou seemest'] *No, that's certain, I am not a double-man*

doublet ☞ CLOTHING, p.79

doubt (*n.*) **1** suspicion, apprehension **Oth** III.iii.186 [Othello to Iago, of Desdemona] *Nor from mine own weak merits will I draw / The smallest fear or doubt of her revolt;* **2H4** IV.i.197; **LL** V.ii.101; **Oth** III.iii.426; **PassP** XIV.4

2 danger, risk, fear **Per** I.ii.90 [Pericles to Helicanus, of Antiochus' fear] *To lop that doubt, he'll fill this land with arms;* **Cym** IV.iv.14; **3H6** IV.viii.37; **R2** III.iv.69

3 question, difficulty, hesitation [over] **TG** V.ii.20 [Proteus to Thurio, of Silvia's feelings about Thurio's valour] *she makes no doubt of that;* **H8** II.ii.215

doubt, in without clear meaning, ambiguous **Ham** IV.v.6 [Gentleman to Gertrude, of Ophelia] *she ... speaks things in doubt*

doubt, out of without doubt, unquestionably, indubitably **MW** II.i.72 [Mistress Page to Mistress Ford, of Falstaff's letters] *He will print them, out of doubt*

doubt (*v.*) **1** fear, be afraid [for], feel anxious [for] **2H4** Epilogue.6 [Epilogue] *what indeed I should say will, I doubt, prove mine own marring;* **1H4** I.ii.179; **MA** V.i.117; **Oth** III.iii.19; **R3** III.v.94; **TC** I.ii.276

2 suspect, have suspicions about, fear **RJ** V.iii.44 [Balthasar to himself, of Romeo] *His looks I fear, and his intents I doubt;* **Ham** I.ii.256; **KJ** IV.i.19; **MW** I.iv.40; **Per** I.ii.86; **Tit** II.iii.68

3 ☞ dout (*v.*)

doubtful (*adj.*) **1** fearful, worried, apprehensive **KL** V.i.12 [Regan to Edmund, of Gonerill] *I am doubtful that you have been conjunct ... with her;* **KJ** V.i.36; **Mac** III.ii.7; **MW** IV.v.77; **TN** IV.iii.27; **TS** Induction.i.92

2 dreadful, awful, frightful **CE** I.i.69 [Egeon to Duke, of the light] *Did but convey unto our fearful minds / A doubtful warrant of immediate death*

3 worrisome, disquieting; or: of uncertain outcome **1H6** IV.i.151 [King to all] *Let me be umpire in this doubtful strife;* **3H6** IV.vi.62

doubtfully (*adv.*) **1** ambiguously, hesitatingly, indistinctly **CE** II.i.50 [Luciana to Dromio of Ephesus, of Antipholus] *Spake he so doubtfully thou couldst not feel his meaning?;* **Tim** IV.iii.122

2 dreadfully, awfully, fearfully **CE** II.i.53 [Dromio of Ephesus to Luciana, of Antipholus of Syracuse's blows] *he struck ... so doubtfully that I could scarce understand them*

doubtless (*adj.*) **1** certain, sure, free from doubt **1H4** III.ii.20 [Prince Hal to King Henry] *I am doubtless I can purge / Myself of many* [offences] *I am charged withal*

2 without fear, free from apprehension **KJ** IV.i.129 [Hubert to Arthur] *sleep doubtless and secure / That Hubert ... / Will not offend thee*

doughty-handed (*adj.*) valiant in fighting, formidable in combat **AC** IV.viii.5 [Antony to all] *doughty-handed are you*

dout (*v.*) put out, extinguish **H5** IV.ii.9 [Dauphin to Constable, of the horses] *their hot blood may spin in English eyes / And dout them with superfluous courage* [F *doubt*]; **Ham** IV.vii.191

dowdy (*n.*) unattractive woman, shabbily dressed girl **RJ** II.iv.41 [Mercutio to Benvolio] *Dido [was] a dowdy*

dower (*n.*) dowry, property or wealth given with a wife **KL** I.i.108 [Lear to Cordelia] *Thy truth then be thy dower;* **TG** III.i.78 [Duke to Valentine, of Silvia] *let her beauty be her wedding-dower;* **AW** V.iii.325; **1H6** V.i.44; **MM** I.i.149; **Tem** III.i.54; **TS** IV.iv.45

dower (*v.*) give a dower to, endow **KL** I.i.204 [Lear to Burgundy, of Cordelia] *Dowered with our curse and strangered with our oath* [F; Q *Couered*]

dowerless (*adj.*) lacking a dowry **KL** I.i.256 [France to Lear, of Cordelia] *Thy dowerless daughter;* **KL** II.iv.207

dowlas (*n.*) cheap coarse linen [from Doulas, Brittany] **1H4** III.iii.68 [Falstaff to Hostess, of his shirts] *Dowlas, filthy dowlas*

dowle, dowl (*n.*) small feather, tiny part of a feather **Tem** III.iii.66 [Ariel to Alonso, Sebastian, and Antonio, of what their swords cannot do] *diminish / One dowle that's in my plume*

down (*n.*) downs, undulating hills **Tem** IV.i.81 [Ceres to Iris] *with each end of thy blue bow dost crown / My bosky acres and my unshrubbed down*

down (*v.*) fall, go down, be overthrown **3H6** IV.iii.43 [Edward to all] *I see that Edward needs must down;* **3H6** IV.iv.28, vi.100

down (*adv.*) **1** dead on the ground **RJ** V.iii.209 [Prince to Montague, of Romeo] *thou art early up / To see thy son and heir now early down*

2 in bed **RJ** IV.v.12 [Nurse to Juliet] *What, dressed, and in your clothes, and down again?;* **RJ** III.v.66

down (*int.*) ☞ SINGING, p.402

downfall, down-fall (*n.*) later stages, declining, passing away **3H6** III.iii.104 [Oxford to Warwick, of his father] *in the downfall of his mellowed years*

downfall, down-fall (*adj.*) downfallen **Mac** IV.iii.4 [Macduff to Malcolm] *Let us ... / Bestride our down-fallen birthdom*

down-gyved (*adj.*) hanging down like fetters [gyves] **Ham** II.i.80 [Ophelia to Polonius, of Hamlet] *his stockings fouled, / Ungartered, and down-gyved to his ankle*

down-pillow (*n.*) pillow made of soft feathers **Cym** III.vii.8 [Belarius to Guiderius and Arviragus] *resty sloth / Finds the down-pillow hard*

downright *(adj.)* **1** plain, ordinary, straightforward **MM** III.ii.100 [Lucio to disguised Duke] *this Angelo was not made by man and woman after this downright way of creation;* **H5** V.ii.144; **Oth** I.iii.246
  2 directed straight down, coming from above **2H6** II.iii.90 [Horner to Peter] *have at thee with a downright blow;* **3H6** I.i.12, iv.32; **RJ** III.v.128

downright *(adv.)* **1** straight away, directly **Venus** 645 [Venus to Adonis] *fell I not downright?*
  2 outright, totally, utterly **LL** V.ii.389 [King to his friends, of the ladies] *They'll mock us now downright;* **MND** II.i.145

down-rope *(v.)* trickle down, seep **H5** IV.ii.46 [Grandpré to all, of the English horses] *The gum down-roping from their pale-dead eyes*

down-sleeve *(n.)* ☞ CLOTHING, p.79

down-trod *(adj.)* down-trodden, crushed, oppressed **1H4** I.iii.133 [Hotspur to Northumberland] *I will lift the down-trod Mortimer* [Q; F *downfall*]

downtrodden *(adj.)* oppressed, crushed by tyranny **KJ** II.i.241 [King Philip to Hubert, of Arthur] *For this downtrodden equity we tread / In warlike march these greens*

downy *(adj.)* **1** soft as down, comfort-giving **Mac** II.iii.73 [Macduff to all] *Shake off this downy sleep;* **AC** V.ii.315
  2 fluffy, soft **2H4** IV.v.33 [Prince Henry to himself, of King Henry IV] *By his gates of breath / There lies a downy feather which stirs not* [F *dowlney*; Q *dowlny*]

Dowsabel *(n.)* sweetheart, lady-love **CE** IV.i.111 [Dromio of Syracuse alone] *That is where we dined, / Where Dowsabel did claim me for her husband*

dowset *(n.)* testicles of a deer [considered a culinary delicacy] **TNK** III.v.156 [Schoolmaster to Theseus, of the hunted stag] *May … the ladies eat his dowsets*

doxy *(n.)* beggar's mistress, whore; sweetheart **WT** IV.iii.2 [Autolycus singing] *When daffodils begin to peer, / With heigh, the doxy over the dale*

dozens, by in dozens of different ways **TNK** III.ii.25 [Gaoler's Daughter alone] *Should I try death by dozens*

drab *(n.)* harlot, slut, whore **MM** II.i.223 [Pompey to Escalus] *If your worship will take order for the drabs and the knaves;* **Ham** II.ii.584; **1H6** V.iv.32; **2H6** II.i.152; **Mac** IV.i.31; **TC** V.i.92

drabbing *(n.)* whoring, associating with harlots **Ham** II.i.26 [Polonius to Reynaldo, of Laertes' imagined behaviour] *drinking, fencing, swearing, quarrelling, / Drabbing*

drachma *(n.)* ☞ MONEY, p.286

draff *(n.)* pig-swill, refuse, garbage **1H4** IV.ii.34 [Falstaff alone, of his soldiers] *a hundred and fifty tattered prodigals lately come from swine-keeping, from eating draff and husks;* **MW** IV.ii.101

dragonish *(adj.)* shaped like a dragon **AC** IV.xiv.2 [Antony to Eros] *Sometime we see a cloud that's dragonish*

dragon's tail [astrology] intersection of the orbit of the descending moon and that of the sun [associated with lechery] **KL** I.ii.129 [Edmund alone] *My father compounded with my mother under the Dragon's tail* ☞ COSMOS, p.102

dram *(n.)* **1** tiny amount, small quantity **WT** II.i.138 [Antigonus to Leontes, of Hermione] *every dram of woman's flesh is false, / If she be;* **AW** II.iii.219; **Ham** I.iv.36; **MV** IV.i.6; **Tim** V.i.149; **TN** III.iv.79
  2 [small dose of] poison **Cym** V.v.382 [Cornelius to Cymbeline, of Innogen] *the queen's dram she swallowed;* **RJ** III.v.90; **TNK** I.i.142; **WT** I.ii.320

draught *(n.)* **1** cup of drink **Tim** I.ii.47 [Apemantus to himself, of Timon] *The fellow that sits next him … pledges the breath of him in a divided draught*
  2 privy, cess-pool, sewer **Tim** V.i.100 [Timon to Poet and Painter, of knaves] *drown them in a draught;* **TC** V.i.71

drave *(v.)* drove [past tense of 'drive'] ☞ PAST TENSES, p.319

draw *(v.)* **1** bring together, draw in, gather **KJ** V.vii.113 [Lewis the Dauphin to Cardinal Pandulph] *Before I drew this gallant head of war;* **Cor** II.iii.252; **Ham** IV.v.144; **1H4** IV.i.33; **JC** I.iii.22; **TC** II.ii.72
  2 take up, receive, collect **MV** IV.i.87 [Shylock to Bassanio] *If every ducat … / Were in six parts, and every part a ducat, / I would not draw them;* **2H4** I.iii.109; **KL** I.i.85; **WT** I.ii.248
  3 draw up, draft, frame **1H6** V.i.38 [King to the ambassadors] *are we certainly resolved / To draw conditions of a friendly peace;* **1H4** III.i.76, 135, 217; **MND** I.i.97; **MV** IV.i.391
  4 write out, draw up, present **TS** III.i.68 [Hortensio as Licio to Bianca, of a method of learning scales] *there it is in writing fairly drawn;* **KJ** II.i.103
  5 picture, represent, frame **KJ** II.i.503 [Lewis the Dauphin to King Philip, of Blanche] *I never loved myself / Till now infixed I beheld myself / Drawn in the flattering table of her eye*
  6 pull out, force out **TNK** V.i.114 [Palamon praying to Venus, of an old man] *Torturing convulsions from his globy eyes / Had almost drawn their spheres;* **KL** IV.vi.88
  7 draw out, extend, prolong **Sonn** 28.13 *day doth daily draw my sorrows longer*
  8 proceed, move, progress **TC** I.iii.14 [Agamemnon to all, of their war efforts] *trial did draw / Bias and thwart, not answering the aim*
  9 deploy, position, dispose **E3** II.i.186 [King Edward to Lodowick] *thou know'st not how to draw a battle;* **E3** II.i.193
  10 draw a sword **Cym** I.ii.91 [Pisanio to Queen, of Cloten and Posthumus] *My Lord your son drew on my master;* **RJ** I.i.3, II.iv.156, III.i.8, 66
  11 [archery] draw back a bow-string **Tit** IV.iii.64 [Titus to all] *Now, masters, draw;* **R3** V.iii.340; **Tit** IV.iii.3
  12 withdraw, revoke **2H4** II.i.148 [Falstaff to Hostess] *Go, wash thy face, and draw the action;* **3H6** V.i.25
  13 demand, call forth, extract **KJ** II.i.111 [King John to King Philip, of Philip's right to question him] *To draw my answer from thy articles*
  14 empty, drain, exhaust **Cym** V.iv.166 [First Gaoler to Posthumus, of someone who has spent a lot on drink] *the purse too light, being drawn of heaviness;* **MM** II.i.195
  15 draw liquor [from barrels] **MW** I.iii.10 [Host to Falstaff, of Bardolph] *he shall draw*
  16 drink deep, drain **Tem** II.ii.144 [Trinculo to Caliban] *Well drawn, monster*
  17 carry a burden, drag a load **Oth** IV.i.67 [Iago to Othello] *Think every bearded fellow that's but yoked / May draw with you;* **TC** V.i.44
  18 [hunting] follow prey by the scent **CE** IV.i.39 [Dromio of Syracuse to Adriana, of the officer] *A hound that runs counter, and yet draws dryfoot well*

draw cuts draw straws, cast lots **CE** V.i.423 [Dromio of Syracuse to Dromio of Ephesus] *We'll draw cuts for the senior*

draw forth *(v.)* bring forward, redeem, recover **R3** III.vii.197 [Buckingham to Richard] *draw forth your noble ancestry / From the corruption of abusing times*

draw in *(v.)* hold back, keep in **3H6** IV.iv.21 [Lady Grey to Rivers, of her unborn child] *for this I draw in many a tear*

draw on *(v.)* **1** draw down, bring about **3H6** III.iii.75 [Queen to Lewis, of his sister's marriage to Edward] *Look … that by this league and marriage / Thou draw not on thy danger and dishonour*
  2 bring on, produce **Cym** IV.iv.14 [Belarius to Guiderius and Arviragus, of killing Cloten] *whose answer would be death / Drawn on with torture*
  3 draw in, attract [support] **Ham** V.ii.386 [Horatio to Fortinbras, of Hamlet] *from his mouth whose voice will draw on more* [supporters for Fortinbras]

draw out *(v.)* **1** choose, select, find **Cor** I.vi.84 [Martius to Soldiers] *I shall quickly draw out my command, / Which men are best inclined;* **TNK** I.i.160
  2 extend, prolong, protract **JC** III.i.100 [Brutus to all, of dying] *'tis but the time / And drawing days out, that men stand upon*

draw to head bring to full strength, deploy, mobilize **Cym** III.v.25 [Cymbeline to all, of Lucius] *The powers that he already hath in Gallia / Will soon be drawn to head*

draw toward an end conclude business, end the conversation **Ham** III.iv.217 [Hamlet to Polonius' body] *Come, sir, to draw toward an end with you*

drawer (*n.*) one who draws drink from a cask, tapster, barman **1H4** II.iv.29 [Prince Hal to Poins, of Francis] *stand in some by-room while I question my puny drawer;* **2H4** II.ii.167; **MW** II.ii.155; **RJ** III.i.9

drawn (*adj.*) **1** with sword drawn **MND** III.ii.402 [Puck in Demetrius' voice, to Lysander] *Here, villain, drawn and ready;* **RJ** I.i.69; **Tem** I.i.313
2 [unclear meaning] drawn from cover, hunted; disembowelled; dragged along **1H4** III.iii.112 [Falstaff to Hostess] *There's ... no more truth in thee than in a drawn fox*

drayman (*n.*) man who drives a cart without wheels [a dray] **TC** I.ii.249 [Pandarus to Cressida, of Achilles] *A drayman, a porter, a very camel!*

dread (*adj.*) **1** revered, deeply honoured, held in awe **E3** II.i.218 [Countess to King Edward] *my thrice dread sovereign;* **3H6** III.iii.32; **H8** V.i.121; **Per** I.ii.52; **Tit** V.ii.82; **WT** I.ii.322
2 frightening, terrifying, fearful **Tem** I.ii.206 [Ariel to Prospero, of Neptune] *his dread trident shake;* **Ham** II.ii.453; **KL** II.ii.121; **Luc** 965; **Mac** IV.i.143; **R2** III.iii.134

dread (*v.*) fear, anticipate in fear, be anxious about **MV** IV.i.89 [Shylock to all] *What judgement shall I dread, doing no wrong?;* **AC** IV.xiv.127; **Cym** V.i.15; **3H6** II.vi.92; **PassP** VII.10; **Tit** II.iii.50

dread-bolted (*adj.*) with frightening thunderbolts **KL** IV.vii.33 [Cordelia to Lear] *Was this a face ... / To stand against the deep dread-bolted thunder*

dreadful (*adj.*) **1** inspiring dread, causing fear, daunting **1H6** I.i.110 [Third Messenger to all, of Talbot] *this dreadful lord ... / Was round encompassed and set upon;* **1H6** II.iii.7; **Oth** II.iii.169; **R3** I.i.8; **TC** IV.iv.126, v.4, V.v.14
2 full of dread, fearful, terrified **Ham** I.ii.207 [Horatio to Hamlet, of the sentinels' vision of the Ghost] *This to me / In dreadful secrecy impart they did*

dreadfully (*adv.*) with dread, in great fear **MM** IV.ii.139 [Provost to disguised Duke, of Barnardine] *A man that apprehends death no more dreadfully but as a drunken sleep*

dream (*v.*) concentrate, focus attention **TG** II.iv.170 [Valentine to Proteus] *Forgive me, that I do not dream on thee*

dreg (*n.*) impurity, corruption, defiling matter **Tim** I.ii.238 [Apemantus to Timon] *Friendship's full of dregs;* **Sonn** 74.9; **TC** III.ii.64

dreg (*v.*) [metaphor of] make cloudy [with dregs] **TNK** I.ii.97 [Arcite to Valerius, of a soldier's feelings] *his action's dregged with mind assured / 'Tis bad he goes about* [i.e. hindered if he thinks he's fighting in a bad cause]

drench (*n.*) drink, draught **H5** III.v.19 [Constable to all] *sodden water, / A drench for sur-reined jades*

drench (*v.*) drown, plunge, immerse **1H6** IV.vii.14 [Talbot to Servant, of John Talbot] *in that sea of blood my boy did drench / His over-mounting spirit;* **Venus** 494

drenched (*adj.*) full of drink, drowned **Mac** I.vii.68 [Lady Macbeth to Macbeth, of the King's attendants] *Their drenched natures lies as in a death*

dress (*v.*) **1** prepare, make ready **MW** I.iv.94 [Mistress Quickly aside to Simple, of Caius] *I keep his house; and I ... dress meat;* **AC** V.ii.273; **Cym** III.vii.62; **H5** IV.i.10; **TC** I.iii.166; **TS** IV.iii.40
2 equip, provide, supply [with] **Oth** I.iii.26 [First Senator to Duke, of Cyprus] *it ... altogether lacks th'abilities / That Rhodes is dressed in*
3 [of horses] train, break in; groom **R2** V.v.80 [Groom to Richard] *That horse that I so carefully have dressed!*

4 [of wounds] treat, minister to, care for **Oth** V.i.124 [Iago to all] *let's see poor Cassio dressed;* **TN** V.i.202
5 [of land] cultivate, tend, look after **R2** III.iv.56 [Gardener to Second Man, of King Richard] *what pity is it / That he had not so trimmed and dressed his land / As we this garden!;* **R2** III.iv.73

dresser (*n.*) serving-table, kitchen table **TS** IV.i.149 [Petruchio to servants, of the meat] *How durst you ... bring it from the dresser*

dressing (*n.*) **1** official robes, finery **MM** V.i.56 [Isabella to Duke] *so may Angelo, / In all his dressings ... / Be an arch-villain*
2 reworking, refashioning **Sonn** 123.4 [of Time's pyramids] *They are but dressings of a former sight*

drift (*n.*) **1** plan, intention, aim **RJ** IV.i.114 [Friar to Juliet] *Shall Romeo by my letters know our drift;* **Ham** IV.vii.150; **3H6** I.i.46; **MM** IV.v.4; **TG** II.vi.43, III.i.18
2 direction, progress, course **Tem** V.i.29 [Prospero to Ariel, of the lords] *They being penitent, / The sole drift of my purpose doth extend / Not a frown further;* **CE** II.ii.170; **Ham** III.i.1; **TC** III.iii.113; **Tim** I.i.46
3 shower, deluge, load **KJ** II.i.412 [King Philip to all] *Our thunder from the south / Shall rain their drift of bullets on this town*

drift (*adj.*) driving, strong **TNK** V.iii.100 [Emilia to herself, of Arcite's spirit] *it could / No more be hid ... / Than humble banks can go to law with waters / That drift winds force to raging*

drink (*n.*) drinking-bout, carousing **Tim** III.v.75 [Second Senator to Alcibiades, of his friend] *'Tis inferred to us / His days are foul and his drink dangerous;* **AC** II.vii.103

drink (*v.*) **1** drink down, swallow up **Tim** I.ii.134 [Apemantus to himself] *We ... spend our flatteries to drink those men / Upon whose age we void it up again* [also: drink a health to] ☛ **FAREWELLS**, p.170
2 inhale, take in, suck in **AC** V.ii.213 [Cleopatra to Iras, of the Romans] *In their thick breaths ... shall we be enclouded, / And forced to drink their vapour*

drive (*v.*) **1** carry on, move along **TNK** II.ii.43 [Third Countryman to the others, of the Schoolmaster] *The matter's too far driven between him / And the tanner's daughter to let slip now* [i.e. it's gone too far]
2 hasten, fly, move off quickly **KL** III.vi.89 [Gloucester to disguised Kent] *drive toward Dover*
3 fall, rush, dash **Tit** II.iii.64 [Tamora to Bassianus] *the hounds / Should drive upon thy new-transformed limbs;* **Ham** II.ii.470

drive, let shoot, strike at, aim blows at **1H4** II.iv.219 [Falstaff to all] *three misbegotten knaves ... came at my back and let drive at me;* **E3** IV.vi.29; **1H4** II.iv.191

driven (*adj.*) ☛ thrice-driven (*adj.*)

driving (*adj.*) drifting, driven by the storm **TN** I.ii.11 [Captain to Viola] *When you ... / Hung on our driving boat*

drollery (*n.*) **1** comic picture, cartoon, caricature **2H4** II.i.143 [Falstaff to Hostess] *for thy walls, a pretty slight drollery ... is worth a thousand of these bed-hangers*
2 puppet-show, comic entertainment **Tem** III.iii.22 [Sebastian to all, of the spirits] *A living drollery!*

drooping (*adj.*) **1** failing, decaying, faltering **1H6** IV.v.5 [Talbot to John Talbot] *When sapless age and weak unable limbs / Should bring thy father to his drooping chair* [i.e. his invalid chair]
2 [of the sun] moving downward **2H4** I.Induction.3 [Rumour alone] *from the orient to the drooping west*

drop (*v.*) drift, meander, come casually **Tim** I.ii.1 [stage direction] *Then comes, dropping after all, Apemantus*

dropping (*adj.*) **1** tearful, falling in teardrops, sorrowful **Ham** I.ii.11 [Claudius to his court, of himself] *With an auspicious and a dropping eye*
2 dripping-wet, soaked, drenched **Per** IV.i.63 [Marina to Leonine, of sailors] *with a dropping industry they skip / From stem to stern*

dropsied (*adj.*) puffed up, turgid, pretentious **AW** II.iii.127 [King to Bertram] *Where great additions swell's and virtue none, / It is a dropsied honour*

dropsy (*n.*) type of disease in which the body retains watery fluids **Tem** IV.i.230 [Caliban to Stephano, of Trinculo] *The dropsy drown this fool!*; **1H4** I.iv.439

dross (*n.*) impure matter, tainted substance, rubbish **TC** IV.iv.9 [Cressida to Pandarus] *My love admits no qualifying dross*; **Sonn** 146.11

drossy (*adj.*) worthless, frivolous, foolish **Ham** V.ii.186 [Hamlet to Horatio, of Osrick] *many more of the same bevy that I know the drossy age dotes on*

drouth (*n.*) **1** dry situation, lack of moisture **Per** III.Chorus.8 [Gower alone] *crickets sing … / All the blither for their drouth* **2** drought, thirst **Venus** 544 [of Adonis' lips, and of Venus] *Whose precious taste her thirsty lips well knew, / Whereon they surfeit, yet complain on drouth*

drovier (*n.*) drover, cattle-dealer **MA** II.i.178 [Benedick to Claudio] *that's spoken like an honest drovier*

drowning-mark (*n.*) indication of death by drowning **Tem** I.i.29 [Gonzalo to himself, of Boatswain] *Methinks he hath no drowning-mark upon him*

drowsy (*adj.*) causing sleepiness, sleep-inducing, soporific **RJ** IV.i.96 [Friar to Juliet] *through all thy veins shall run / A cold and drowsy humour*; **Oth** III.iii.328

drudge (*n.*) slave, serf, lackey **TS** IV.i.115 [Petruchio to Grumio] *you whoreson malt-horse drudge!*; **AW** I.iii.45; **2H6** IV.ii.142; **MV** III.ii.103; **Sonn** 151.11; **Tim** IV.iii.255

drug (*n.*) poisonous plant **Tit** I.i.157 [Titus to his dead sons, of the tomb] *Here grow no damned drugs*

drug-damned (*adj.*) damnable for its use of poisons, potion-cursed **Cym** III.iv.15 [Innogen to Pisanio, of Posthumus] *That drug-damned Italy hath out-craftied him*

drum (*n.*) drummer **1H6** I.i.1 [stage direction] *Enter Charles the Dauphin … marching with drum and soldiers*; **AW** V.iii.253; **R3** IV.iv.149 ☛ **STAGE DIRECTIONS**, p.417

drumble (*v.*) dawdle, loiter, move sluggishly **MW** III.iii.139 [Mistress Ford to John and Robert] *Look how you drumble!*

drunk asleep in a drunken stupour, dead drunk **Ham** III.iii.89 [Hamlet to himself, of Claudius] *When he is drunk asleep*

dry (*adj.*) **1** barren, arid, yielding no result **TC** I.iii.329 [Nestor to Ulysses, of Achilles] *were his brain as barren / As banks of Libya - though, Apollo knows, / 'Tis dry enough*; **TN** I.v.36 **2** dried, withered, shrivelled **MA** II.i.105 [masked Ursula to masked Antonio, of Antonio] *Here's his dry hand up and down*; **AY** II.vii.39; **TC** II.iii.221 **3** thirsty, parched, longing **Tem** I.ii.112 [Prospero to Miranda, of Antonio] *So dry he was for sway* [i.e. eager] **4** severe, hard, harsh **CE** II.ii.68 [Dromio of Syracuse to Antipholus of Syracuse, advising him not to eat meat] *Lest it make you choleric, and purchase me another dry basting*

dry-beat (*v.*) cudgel, thrash, beat soundly **RJ** III.i.78 [Mercutio to Tybalt, of his nine lives] *dry-beat the rest of the eight*; **RJ** IV.v.122

dry-beaten (*adj.*) bruised, soundly beaten **LL** V.ii.263 [masked Berowne to all] *By heaven, all dry-beaten with pure scoff!*

dryfoot, dry-foot (*adv.*) [hunting] by following the scent of the feet **CE** IV.ii.39 [Dromio of Syracuse to Adriana, of the officer] *A hound that runs counter, and yet draws dryfoot well*

dry nurse (*n.*) housekeeper **MW** I.ii.3 [Evans to Simple, of Caius' house] *there dwells one Mistress Quickly, which is in the manner of his nurse, or his dry nurse*

dub (*v.*) invest with the status of, style **H5** II.ii.120 [King Henry to Scroop] *to dub thee with the name of traitor*; **R3** I.i.82

ducat (*n.*) ☛ **MONEY**, p.286

ducdame [unclear meaning] probably a nonsense word, explained later by Jaques to mean a 'Greek invocation, to call fools into a circle' **AY** II.v.51 [Jaques, singing] *Ducdame, ducdame, ducdame.*

duck (*v.*) make a brief bow, act in a cringing way **R3** I.iii.49 [Richard to all] *I cannot … / Duck with French nods*; **Tim** IV.iii.18

dudgeon (*n.*) [of a dagger] handle, hilt, haft **Mac** II.i.46 [Macbeth alone, as if to a dagger] *on thy blade and dudgeon, gouts of blood*

due (*n.*) **1** appropriate ritual, propriety **Cym** III.v.11 [Cymbeline to his Lords] *The due of honour in no point omit*; **TNK** V.i.5 **2** justice, rightfulness, validity **H8** V.i.131 [King Henry to Cranmer] *not ever / The justice and the truth o'th' question carries / The due o'th' verdict with it* **3** debt, liability, amount owing **Tim** II.ii.19 [Caphis to Timon] *here is a note of certain dues*; **MV** IV.i.37; **Tim** II.ii.153

due (*adj.*) appropriate, proper, fitting **WT** III.ii.57 [Hermione to Leontes, of his remark] *'tis a saying, sir, not due to me*; **2H6** V.i.8

due (*v.*) endue, grace, endow **1H6** IV.ii.34 [General to Talbot] *This is the latest glory of thy praise / That I, thy enemy, due thee withal*

due (*adv.*) duly, dutifully, fully **2H4** III.ii.296 [Falstaff alone, of Shallow] *every third word a lie, duer paid to the hearer than the Turk's tribute*

duello (*n.*) established duelling code **TN** III.iv.298 [Sir Toby to Sir Andrew, of Viola as Cesario] *The gentleman will … have one bout with you, he cannot by the duello avoid it*; **LL** I.ii.172

dug (*n.*) nipple, teat, breast **R3** II.ii.30 [Duchess of York to Clarence's son, of Richard] *from my dugs he drew not this deceit*; **E3** II.i.422; **Ham** V.ii.184; **2H6** III.ii.393; **RJ** I.iii.27; **Venus** 875

duke it (*v.*) act the duke, play the part of a duke **MM** III.ii.90 [Lucio to disguised Duke] *Lord Angelo dukes it well*

dulcet (*adj.*) sweet, mild, pleasant, agreeable **TS** Induction.i.49 [Lord to Huntsmen, of music] *To make a dulcet and a heavenly sound*; **AY** V.iv.63; **MND** II.i.151; **TN** II.iii.54

dull (*adj.*) **1** dead, lifeless, sluggish, inactive **MM** IV.iv.19 [Angelo alone] *This deed … makes me unpregnant / And dull to all proceedings*; **AW** I.i.215; **Ham** I.v.32; **Oth** I.i.124; **Sonn** 44.1; **TC** II.ii.210 **2** bored, uninterested, inattentive **KJ** III.iv.109 [Lewis the Dauphin to Cardinal Pandulph] *Life is as tedious as a twice-told tale, / Vexing the dull ear of a drowsy man* **3** gloomy, melancholic, sullen **Tem** I.ii.285 [Prospero to Ariel, of Caliban] *Dull thing, I say so*; **KL** V.iii.280; **MA** III.iii.69; **RJ** I.iv.21; **Sonn** 97.13; **Tit** II.i.128 **4** dim, not sharp, lacking keenness **Tit** II.iii.195 [Quintus to Aaron] *My sight is very dull, whate'er it bodes*; **TS** Induction.i.22 **5** insensitive, incapable of sensation **WT** I.ii.296 [Polixenes to Camillo] *Turn then my freshest reputation to / A savour that may strike the dullest nostril / Where I arrive*; **CE** V.i.317 **6** obtuse, stupid **JC** I.iii.57 [Cassius to Casca] *You are dull, Casca*; **Cor** I.ix.6; **Tem** V.i.298; **TG** II.vi.41 **7** [unclear meaning] sleep-inducing, soothing, producing drowsiness **2H4** IV.v.2 [King Henry IV to all] *Let there be no noise made … / Unless some dull and favourable hand / Will whisper music to my weary spirit*

dull (*v.*) **1** make dreary, take the edge off **Sonn** 103.8 [of a face] *That over-goes my blunt invention quite, / Dulling my lines* **2** bore, make weary, be tedious to **Sonn** 102.14 *I would not dull you with my song* **3** stupefy, satisfy to the point of slothfulness **H5** II.iv.16 [Dauphin to French King] *peace itself should not so dull a kingdom*; **H5** II.ii.9 **4** make undiscerning, make insensitive **Ham** I.iii.64 [Polonius to Laertes] *But do not dull thy palm with entertainment / Of each new-hatched, unfledged courage* [i.e. do not give your handshake indiscriminately] **5** blunt, reduce the activity of **Oth** II.iii.377 [Iago alone] *Dull not device by coldness and delay*; **Ham** I.iii.77

dull (*adv.*) heavily, deeply **Cym** II.ii.31 [Iachimo to himself, of Innogen] *sleep, thou ape of death, lie dull upon her*

dullard (*n.*) dimwit, dunce, ignoramus **Cym** V.v.265 [Cymbeline to Innogen] *mak'st thou me a dullard in this act?*

dull-eyed lacking insight, easily deceived **MV** III.iii.14 [Shylock to Antonio] *I'll not be made a soft and dull-eyed fool*

dullness, dulness *(n.)* lethargy, sluggishness, inactivity **Sonn** 56.8 *do not kill / The spirit of love with a perpetual dullness*

dullness, dulness *(adv.)* sleepiness, drowsiness, tiredness **Tem** I.ii.185 [Prospero to Miranda, of her sleeping] *'Tis a good dullness, / And give it way* [i.e. give in to it]; **Oth** I.iii.266

dumb *(adj.)* wordless, silent, mute **1H6** II.iv.26 [Richard to all] *Since you are tongue-tied and so loath to speak / In dumb significants proclaim your thoughts*

dumb *(v.)* make inaudible, reduce to silence **AC** I.v.50 [Alexas to Cleopatra, of Antony's horse] *what I would have spoke / Was beastly dumbed by him* [F *dumbe*]; **Per** V.Chorus.5

dumb-discoursive *(adj.)* silently persuasive, with compelling silent arguments **TC** IV.iv.89 [Troilus to Cressida, of the Greeks' virtues] *in each grace of these / There lurks a still and dumb-discoursive devil*

dump *(n.)* **1** plaintive melody, mournful song **Luc** 1127 *Distress likes dumps, when time is kept with tears;* **MA** II.iii.69; **RJ** IV.v.126; **TG** III.ii.85

2 tune, melody **RJ** IV.v.104 [Peter to Fiddler] *O play me some merry dump to comfort me*

3 (plural) low spirits, feeling of melancholy **TS** II.i.277 [Baptista to Katherina] *In your dumps?;* **Tit** I.i.394

Dun *(n.)* horse's name [involving the lifting of a log 'horse' in a Christmas game called 'drawing dun out of the mire'] **RJ** I.iv.41 [Mercutio to Romeo] *If thou art Dun, we'll draw thee from the mire* [pun: 40 ☛ *dun's the mouse*]

dun *(adj.)* **1** dark, murky, gloomy **Mac** I.v.49 [Lady Macbeth alone] *Come, thick night, / And pall thee in the dunnest smoke of hell;*

2 grey-brown **Sonn** 130.3 [of his mistress] *If snow be white, why then her breasts are dun;* **TN** I.iii.128

dun's the mouse [proverbial] keep quiet, be still **RJ** I.iv.40 [Mercutio to all] *dun's the mouse, the constable's own word!* [pun: 39, 41] ☛ *Dun (n.)*

dung *(n.)* earth, soil, clay **AC** V.ii.7 [Cleopatra to all] *it is great / To do that thing … / Which sleeps, and never palates more the dung* [i.e. taste the produce of the earth]

dungy *(adj.)* dung-like; or, vile, filthy, loathsome **AC** I.i.35 [Antony to Cleopatra] *Our dungy earth alike / Feeds beast as man;* **WT** II.i.157

dup *(v.)* [contraction of 'do up'] open **Ham** IV.v.53 [Ophelia singing] *And dupped the chamber door* [F. dupt]

durance *(n.)* **1** confinement, imprisonment, incarceration **TN** V.i.273 [Viola to Orsino, of the Captain] *He, upon some action, / Is now in durance at Malvolio's suit;* **2H4** V.v.34; **LL** III.i.126; **MM** III.i.70

2 durability, lasting nature; also: type of strong durable cloth **1H4** I.ii.43 [Prince Hal to Falstaff] *is not a buff jerkin a most sweet robe of durance?;* **CE** IV.iii.26

dure *(v.)* endure, bear, withstand **TNK** I.iii.5 [Hippolyta to Pirithous, of Theseus] *I wish him / Excess and overflow of power … / To dure ill-dealing fortune*

durst, that thou you wouldn't dare!, if you dare! **TNK** III.i.57 [Palamon to Arcite, of his threat to fight] *That thou durst, Arcite!* ☛ dare *(v.)*; **PAST TENSES**, p.319

dusky *(adj.)* **1** dark, shadowy **Tem** IV.i.89 [Ceres to Iris, of Venus and her son] *Since they did plot / The means that dusky Dis my daughter got*

2 extinguished, lacking in light **1H6** II.v.122 [Richard alone] *Here dies the dusky torch of Mortimer*

dust *(n.)* speck of dust, particle, iota **R2** II.iii.90 [York to and of Bolingbroke] *Why have those banished and forbidden legs / Dared once to touch a dust of England's ground?;* **AW** V.iii.55; **KJ** III.iv.128, IV.i.92

Dutchman *(n.)* German **AW** II.iii.40 [Lafew to Parolles] *Lustique, as the Dutchman says*

duteous *(adj.)* dutiful, obedient, of allegiance **R2** IV.i.209 [Richard to all] *With mine own breath release all duteous oaths;* **Cym** III.v.155, V.v.86; **KL** IV.vi.253; **Luc** 1360

duty *(n.)* **1** act of loyalty, expression of homage **R2** III.iii.188 [Bolingbroke to all, of King Richard] *show fair duty to his majesty;* **1H6** III.i.172; **3H6** V.vii.28; **H8** I.ii.198; **Oth** III.iii.2; **R2** III.iii.48

2 reverence, due respect, proper attitude **TS** Induction.i.80 [First Player to Lord, of staying the night] *So please your lordship to accept our duty;* **AW** II.i.125; **Ham** I.ii.40; **2H6** I.iii.156; **LL** IV.ii.141; **R3** I.iii.250

3 fitting praise, due respect, proper regard **1H4** V.ii.55 [Vernon to Hotspur, of Prince Hal] *He gave you all the duties of a man*

4 due, desert, deserving **TS** IV.i.32 [Grumio to Curtis] *Do thy duty, and have thy duty* [second instance]

5 debt, obligation, dues **E3** II.i.316 [King Edward to Warwick] *These are the vulgar tenders of false men, / That never pay the duty of their words*

duty, at at one's service, to command **Tim** IV.iii.263 [Timon to Apemantus, of himself] *Who had … / The mouths, the tongues, the eyes, and hearts of men / At duty*

dwell *(v.)* exist, continue, persist **MV** I.iii.152 [Bassanio to Antonio, of taking Shylock's bond] *I'd rather dwell in my necessity;* **AW** IV.iii.10; **MW** III.v.66

dwell on / upon **1** preserve, maintain, pay attention to **RJ** II.ii.88 [Juliet to Romeo] *Fain would I dwell on form;* **MW** II.ii.232

2 wait for, await **E3** II.i.412 [Warwick to Countess, of King Edward] *[I] dwell upon thy answer in his suit*

dying *(adj.)* fading, dying away **TN** I.i.4 [Orsino to all, of the music] *It had a dying fall*

eager *(adj.)* **1** keen, biting **Ham** I.iv.2 [Horatio to Hamlet] *It is a nipping and an eager air*

2 sharp, cutting **R2** I.i.49 [Mowbray to King Richard] *The bitter clamour of two eager tongues;* **3H6** II.vi.68

3 sour, bitter, acid **Ham** I.v.69 [Ghost to Hamlet, of the poison] *like eager droppings into milk* [Q1,Q2; F *Aygre*]; **Sonn** 118.2

4 fierce, angry, savage **1H6** I.ii.38 [Charles to all, of the English] *hunger will enforce them to be more eager* [also: keen to get food]; **E3** I.ii.25

5 impetuous, fierce, impassioned **3H6** I.iv.3 [York alone] *all my followers to the eager foe / Turn back and fly;* **Luc** 1298; **R2** V.iii.74

ean *(v.)* bring forth lambs **3H6** II.v.36 [King alone, of a shepherd's ewes] *So many weeks ere the poor fools will ean*

eaning *(adj.)* lambing **MV** I.iii.84 [Shylock to Antonio, of ewes] *Who … did in eaning time / Fall parti-coloured lambs*

eanling *(n.)* new-born lamb **MV** I.iii.76 [Shylock to Antonio] *all the eanlings which were streaked and pied / Should fall as Jacob's hire*

ear *(n.)* hearing, listening, paying attention **KL** III.iv.89 [Edgar as Poor Tom to all, of himself] *light of ear*

ear, in the within earshot **Ham** III.i.185 [Polonius to Claudius, of the Queen and Hamlet] *in the ear / Of all their conference*

ears, by the at odds, fighting like beasts **AW** I.ii.1 [King to First Lord] *The Florentines and Senoys are by th'ears;* **Cor** I.i.231

ears, over drowned **Tem** IV.i.214 [Stephano to Trinculo] *I will fetch off my bottle, though I be o'er ears for my labour*

ear *(v.)* **1** listen to, hear, give ear to **TNK** III.i.29 [Arcite alone, of Emilia] *I eared her language*

2 plough, break through **AC** I.iv.49 [Messenger to Caesar] *Menecrates and Menas … / Makes the sea serve them, which they ear and wound / With keels of every kind*

3 plough, till, cultivate **R2** III.ii.212 [King Richard to Aumerle] *That power I have, discharge, and let them go / To ear the land;* **AW** I.iii.44

ear-bussing, ear-kissing *(adj.)* ear-kissing, reaching the ear only as rumours **KL** II.i.8 [Curan to Edmund, of the news] *they are yet but ear-bussing arguments* [Q; F *ear-kissing*]

earing *(n.)* ploughing **AC** I.ii.112 [Antony to Messenger] *we bring forth weeds / When our quick winds lie still, and our ills told us / Is as our earing* [i.e. being told harsh truths is good for us – as ploughing is to the earth]

ear-kissing *(adj.)* ☞ ear-bussing *(adj.)*

earl *(n.)* lord, peer, nobleman **RJ** III.iv.21 [Capulet to Lady Capulet, of Juliet and Paris] *She shall be married to this noble earl*

early *(adv.)* at the outset, at first hearing **TNK** V.iv.47 [Pirithous to Palamon] *tidings … / That are most early sweet and bitter* [i.e. when you first hear them] *[disputed reading]*

earn *(v.)* **1** yearn, mourn, grieve **H5** II.iii.3 [Pistol to Hostess] *my manly heart doth earn;* **H5** II.iii.6; **JC** II.ii.129

2 grieve, sadden, wound **R2** V.v.76 [Groom to Richard, of Bolingbroke's coronation] *how it earned my heart when I beheld … that coronation day* [F *yern'd*]

earnest *(n.)* pledge, instalment, deposit, payment in advance **Mac** I.iii.103 [Ross to Macbeth, of the King] *for an earnest of a greater honour, / He bade me from him call thee Thane of Cawdor;* **E3** IV.v.3; **1H6** V.iii.16; **KL** I.iv.94; **Per** IV.ii.42; **Tim** IV.iii.169

earnest *(adj.)* genuine, real, serious **CE** II.ii.24 [Dromio of Syracuse to Antipholus of Syracuse] *now your jest is earnest* [pun: 'deposit for a bargain']

earnest, of genuine, real, serious **AY** IV.iii.170 [Oliver to Rosalind as Ganymede, of her fainting] *it was a passion of earnest* [i.e. for real]

earnest penny guarantee, promise [small sum of money paid to secure a bargain] **E3** III.i.151 [Mariner to King John, of the flagships] *the other [ships], that beheld these twain / Give earnest penny of a further wrack*

earnest-gaping *(adj.)* eagerly peering, gazing with special intensity **2H6** III.ii.105 [Queen to King] *the dusky sky began to rob / My earnest-gaping sight of thy land's view*

earnestly *(adv.)* steadfastly, intently **Tit** V.i.22 [Second Goth to Lucius, of a monastery] *I earnestly did fix mine eye / Upon the wasted building*

earth *(n.)* piece of dirt, beast of the earth **Tem** I.ii.314 [Prospero to Caliban] *Thou earth, thou, speak!*

earth *(v.)* put in the earth, bury, inter **Tem** II.i.238 [Antonio to Sebastian, of Gonzalo] *When he is earthed*

earth-delving *(adj.)* burrowing **Venus** 687 [Venus to Adonis, of the hunted hare] *Sometime he runs … where earth-delving conies keep*

earthly *(adj.)* **1** within the earth, existing in the ground **3H6** I.iv.17 [York alone, quoting Richard] *A sceptre or an earthly sepulchre!*
　2 ☞ **earthy** *(adj.)* **3**

earth-vexing *(adj.)* tormenting earthly life, life-afflicting **Cym** V.v.42 [Sicilius, to music, as if to Jove] *Thou shouldst have … shielded him / from this earth-vexing smart*

earthy *(adj.)* **1** of the earth, made of clay **Tit** I.i.102 [Lucius to Titus, of the tomb] *this earthy prison* [Q1; F *earthly*]; **2H6** III.ii.147
　2 earthly, dwelling in this world **KJ** III.i.147 [King John to Cardinal Pandulph] *What earthy name to interrogatories / Can task the free breath of a sacred king?*
　3 pale, earth-coloured, lifeless as earth **Tit** II.iii.229 [Martius to Quintus, of Bassianus' ring] *Which like a taper in some monument / Doth shine upon the dead man's earthy cheeks* [Q; F *earthly*]
　4 coarse, unrefined, gross **Tem** I.ii.273 [Prospero to Ariel, of Sycorax] *thou wast a spirit too delicate / To act her earthy and abhorred commands;* **CE** III.ii.34

ease *(n.)* **1** comfort, relief, solace **3H6** V.v.72 [George to Queen, of killing her] *I will not do thee so much ease;* **Ham** I.i.132; **TC** V.x.56; **TS** V.ii.178
　2 disuse, neglect, idleness **2H6** III.ii.198 [Suffolk to all, of his sword] *rusted with ease*

ease, at one's in comfort, free from cares **3H6** III.iii.151 [Warwick to Queen] *Henry now lives in Scotland at his ease*

ease, in with ease, easily; or: in sloth **Ham** I.v.33 [Ghost to Hamlet] *the fat weed / That roots itself in ease on Lethe wharf*

easeful *(adj.)* comfortable, relaxing, soothing **3H6** V.iii.6 [Edward to all] *I spy a … cloud. / That will encounter with our glorious sun / Ere he attain his easeful western bed*

easily *(adv.)* in comfort, at ease **Oth** V.i.83 [Iago to all, of Cassio] *O, for a chair / To bear him easily hence!;* **AY** III.ii.310

easiness *(n.)* **1** indifference, unconcern, carelessness **Ham** V.i.67 [Horatio to Hamlet, of the way the First Clown deals with death] *Custom hath made it in him a property of easiness*
　2 gentleness, kindness, indulgence **H8** V.iii.25 [Gardiner to all] *Out of our easiness and childish pity / To one man's honour*

easy *(adj.)* **1** slight, petty, insignificant **2H6** III.i.133 [Suffolk to Gloucester] *these faults are easy, quickly answered;* **Cor** V.iii.41, vi.65; **2H4** V.ii.71; **KJ** III.i.207; **Tit** III.i.197
　2 open, receptive, amenable **WT** IV.iv.502 [Camillo to Florizel] *I would your spirit were easier for advice*
　3 comfortable, restful, agreeable **E3** IV.vii.61 [Prince Edward to all, of Audley] *I will see my friend bestowed / Within an easy litter*
　4 effortless, straightforward, uncomplicated **KJ** I.i.36 [Queen Eleanor to King John, of uniting England and France] *With very easy arguments of love*
　5 loosely fitting, comfortable **AW** V.iii.275 [Lafew to King, of Diana] *This woman's an easy glove*
　6 careless, unconcerned; or: naive, trusting **H8** III.ii.356 [Wolsey alone, of a man's rise and fall] *when he thinks, good easy man, full surely / His greatness is a-ripening*

easy *(adv.)* easily **H5** II.ii.125 [King Henry to and of Scroop, quoting a devil] *I can never win / A soul so easy as that Englishman's;* **AW** V.iii.125; **Mac** II.iii.134; **Sonn** 109.3

easy-held *(adj.)* easily endured, agreeably maintained **1H6** V.iii.139 [Suffolk to Reignier, of Margaret] *her easy-held imprisonment / Hath gained thy daughter princely liberty*

easy-melting *(adj.)* pliable, manipulatable, easily persuaded **3H6** II.i.170 [Warwick to Richard and Edward, of the Queen and her supporters] *Have wrought the easy-melting King like wax*

ebbed *(adj.)* out-of-power, whose fortunes have waned **AC** I.iv.43 [Caesar to Lepidus] *the ebbed man … / Comes deared by being lacked*

ebon *(adj.)* **1** ebony, black **LL** I.i.237 [King reading Armado's letter to him] *the ebon-coloured ink which here thou viewest*
　2 dark, sombre **Venus** 948 [Venus as if to death, of Adonis] *Love's golden arrow at him should have fled, / And not Death's ebon dart, to strike him dead;* **2H4** V.v.37

Ebrew *(adj.)* Hebrew **1H4** II.iv.174 [Falstaff to all, of the robbers] *they were bound … or I am a Jew else: an Ebrew Jew* [i.e. a Jew of Jews]

ech *(v.)* ☞ **eke** *(v.)*

eche *(v.)* increase, add to, supplement **Per** III.Chorus.13 [Gower alone] *time that is so briefly spent / With your fine fancies quaintly eche*

ecstasy *(n.)* **1** fit, bout of madness, frenzied behaviour **CE** IV.iv.49 [Courtesan to all, of Antipholus of Ephesus] *Mark how he trembles in his ecstasy;* **Ham** II.i.102; **MA** II.iii.152; **Mac** III.ii.22; **Oth** IV.i.79; **Tit** IV.i.124
　2 madness, lunacy **Ham** III.iv.139-40 [Gertrude to Hamlet] *This bodiless creation ecstasy / Is very cunning in.* [Hamlet] *Ecstasy?;* **Ham** III.i.161, iv.75
　3 emotion, state of mind, feeling **Venus** 895 [of Venus] *Thus stands she in a trembling ecstasy;* **Lover** 69; **Mac** IV.iii.170

eddy *(n.)* whirlpool **TNK** I.ii.10 [Arcite to Palamon] *bring us to an eddy / Where we should turn or drown*

edge *(n.)* **1** ardour, keen desire **MM** I.iv.60 [Lucio to Isabella, of Angelo] *a man … [who] doth rebate and blunt his natural edge / With profits of the mind;* **Ham** III.ii.259; **R2** I.iii.296; **TS** I.ii.72
　2 keen delight, special enjoyment **Tem** IV.i.29 [Ferdinand to Prospero, of his marriage-day] *The edge of that day's celebration*
　3 stimulus, push, incentive **Ham** III.i.26 [Claudius to Rosencrantz and Guildenstern, of Hamlet] *give him a further edge*
　4 sharpness, keenness **Tit** II.i.26 [Demetrius to Chiron] *thy wits wants edge / And manners to intrude where I am graced*
　5 high and narrow ridge **2H4** I.i.170 [Morton to Northumberland, of Percy] *You knew he walked o'er perils, on an edge, / More likely to fall in than to get o'er*
　6 sword, weapon **AC** II.vi.38 [Pompey to the Triumvirs] *To part with unhacked edges;* **Cor** V.vi.113

edged *(adj.)* sharp, sharpened, cutting **1H6** III.iii.52 [Pucelle to Burgundy] *turn thy edged sword another way;* **H5** III.v.38

edgeless *(adj.)* blunted, useless, ineffective **R3** V.iii.164 [Ghost of Anne to Richard] *think on me, / And fall thy edgeless sword*

edict *(n.)* authority, judgement, valuation **AC** III.xii.32 [Caesar to Thidias] *Make thine own edict for thy pains* [i.e. decide your own recompense]

edify *(v.)* **1** enlighten, instruct, inform **Ham** V.ii.152 [Horatio to Hamlet] *I knew you must be edified by the margent;* **Oth** III.iv.14; **TNK** II.ii.52
　2 profit, gain instruction **TNK** III.v.95 [Schoolmaster to Theseus] *Stay, and edify;* **TNK** III.v.97

education *(n.)* upbringing, nurture, raising **Oth** I.iii.180 [Desdemona to Brabantio] *To you I am bound for life and education*

ee *(n.)* [northern form of] eye **TNK** III.iv.20 [Gaoler's Daughter alone, singing] *And I'll clip my yellow locks, an inch below mine ee*

e'en *(adv.)* ☞ **even** *(adv.)*

effect (*n.*) **1** result, end, outcome, fulfilment **KL** I.i.185 [Kent to Gonerill and Regan] *good effects may spring from words of love;* **AC** V.ii.329; **1H6** V.iv.102; **KL** I.ii.142; **MM** IV.ii.156; **TG** I.i.50

2 purpose, end, intended deed **KJ** IV.i.38 [Arthur to Hubert, of the writing of the warrant to blind him] *Too fairly, Hubert, for so foul effect;* **Ham** III.iv.130; **TC** III.iii.216; **Tit** IV.iii.60

3 sign, mark, token, manifestation **JC** II.i.250 [Portia to Brutus, of his impatience] *Hoping it was but an effect of humour;* **2H4** II.i.129; **KL** II.iv.174; **Mac** V.i.10; **MM** III.i.24; **Sonn** 85.14

4 drift, tenor, import **Ham** I.iii.45 [Ophelia to Laertes] *I shall the effect of this good lesson keep;* **AY** IV.iii.36; **Cym** V.iv.135; **Ham** V.ii.37; **KL** III.i.52

5 benefit, advantage [resulting from an action] **Ham** III.iii.54 [Claudius alone] *I am still possessed / Of those effects for which I did the murder*

6 desire, passion, emotion **Luc** 250 [of Tarquin's evil thoughts] *Which in a moment doth confound and kill / All pure effects* ☞ **affect** (*n.*) **1**

effect (*v.*) **1** cause, produce, bring about **TS** I.i.86 [Hortensio to Baptista] *Sorry am I that our good will effects / Bianca's grief;* **1H6** V.i.15

2 bring into effect, fulfil, show to be true **2H6** III.i.170 [Gloucester to his enemies] *The ancient proverb will be well effected: / 'A staff is quickly found to beat a dog'*

3 carry out, accomplish **Cor** I.ix.18 [Martius to Lartius] *He that has but effected his good will / Hath overta'en mine act*

effectless (*adj.*) ineffective, fruitless, useless **Per** V.i.50 [Helicanus to Lysimachus, of the efforts to revive Pericles] *all effectless;* **Tit** III.i.76

effectual (*adj.*) **1** effective, efficient **TS** III.i.66 [Hortensio as Licio to Bianca, of a method of learning scales] *More pleasant, pithy, and effectual*

2 conclusive, decisive, pertinent **2H6** III.i.41 [Queen to the lords, of Gloucester] *Reprove my allegation if you can; / Or else conclude my words effectual;* **Tit** V.iii.42

3 effective, actual, with full effect **TG** III.i.223 [Proteus to Valentine, of Valentine's sentence of banishment] *Which, unreversed, stands in effectual force*

effectually (*adv.*) **1** in effect, in fact, in reality **Sonn** 113.4 [of the mind's eye] *Seems seeing, but effectually is out*

2 to the purpose, fittingly; or: earnestly **Tit** IV.iv.107 [Aemilius to Saturninus] *Your bidding shall I do effectually*

effeminate (*adj.*) **1** feeble, soft, unmanly **1H6** V.iv.107 [Richard to all] *Shall we at last conclude effeminate peace?;* **1H6** I.i.35; **R2** V.iii.10; **TC** III.iii.218

2 gentle, tender, compassionate **R3** III.vii.210 [Buckingham to Richard] *we know your … effeminate remorse*

effigy (*n.*) likeness, image, portrait **AY** II.vii.197 [Duke Senior to Orlando, of his father] *mine eye doth his effigies witness / Most truly limned and living in your face*

effuse (*n.*) effusion, outflow, pouring out **3H6** II.vi.28 [Clifford alone] *much effuse of blood doth make me faint*

effuse (*v.*) spill, shed **1H6** V.iv.52 [Pucelle to all, of herself] *Whose maiden blood, thus rigorously effused*

effusion (*n.*) spilling, shedding **1H6** V.i.9 [Gloucester to King] *the only means / To stop effusion of our Christian blood;* **H5** III.vi.128; **KJ** V.ii.49

eftest (*adj.*) [unclear malapropism] quickest, most convenient **MA** IV.ii.34 [Dogberry to Sexton, of the way to proceed] *that's the eftest way*

eftsoons (*adv.*) **1** later on, afterwards **Per** V.i.254 [Pericles to Helicanus, of going to Ephesus] *Eftsoons I'll tell thee why*

2 occasionally, from time to time **TNK** III.i.12 [Arcite alone, as if to Emilia] *In thy rumination / I … might eftsoons come between / And chop on some cold thought!*

egal, egall (*adj.*) equal, matched, equivalent **MV** III.iv.13 [Portia to Lorenzo] *companions … / Whose souls do bear an egall yoke of love;* **Tit** IV.iv.4

egally (*adv.*) equally, evenly, commensurately **R3** III.vii.212 [Buckingham to Richard, of Richard's compassion] *Which we have noted in you to your kindred / And egally indeed to all estates*

eggshell (*n.*) something worthless **Ham** IV.iv.53 [Hamlet alone] *Even for an eggshell*

eglantine (*n.*) ☞ **PLANTS**, p.330

egma (*n.*) malapropism for 'enigma' **LL** III.i.70 [Costard to Armado, of cures for his cut shin] *No egma, no riddle, no l'envoy, no salve in the mail*

egregious (*adj.*) **1** significant, extraordinary, exceptional **H5** IV.iv.11 [Pistol to French Soldier] *thou diest on point of fox, / Except … thou do give to me / Egregious ransom*

2 shocking, outrageous, flagrant **AW** II.iii.215 [Parolles to Lafew] *you give me most egregious indignity;* **Cym** V.v.211; **H5** II.i.43

egress and regress [legal] right of leaving and return, freedom to come and go **MW** II.i.200 [Host to Ford] *Thou shalt have egress and regress*

eisel, eisell, esile, eysell (*n.*) vinegar **Ham** V.i.272 [Hamlet to Laertes] *Woo't drink up eisel?* [reading of F, Q2 *Esile*; Q1 *vessels*]; **Sonn** 111.10 *I will drink / Potions of eysell 'gainst my strong infection*

eke, eke out (*v.*) add to, increase, supplement **H5** III.Chorus.35 [Chorus] *Still be kind, / And eke out our performance with your mind;* **AW** II.v.74; **AY** I.ii.183; **MV** III.ii.23

eke (*adv.*) [archaism] also, moreover, too **MND** III.i.88 [Flute as Thisbe, of Pyramus] *Most brisky juvenal, and eke most lovely Jew;* **MW** I.iii.88, II.iii.67; **TNK** III.v.131 ☞ **ARCHAISMS**, p.22

elbow, out at in bad condition **MM** II.i.59 [Pompey to Angelo, of Elbow not speaking] *He cannot, sir. He's out at elbow*

elbow (*v.*) jostle, thrust back, crowd in **KL** IV.iii.42 [disguised Kent to Gentleman, of Lear] *A sovereign shame so elbows him*

eld (*n.*) **1** men of old, people from former times **MW** IV.iv.34 [Mistress Page to all, of Herne the Hunter] *The superstitious idle-headed eld / Received and did deliver to our age / This tale … for a truth*

2 old age, advanced years **MM** III.i.36 [disguised Duke to Claudio, of his youth] *doth beg the alms / Of palsied eld*

elder (*n.*) **1** senior, superior **JC** IV.iii.56 [Cassius to Brutus] *I said an elder soldier, not a better;* **LL** V.ii.602

2 later one, more advanced one **Cym** V.i.14 [Posthumus alone, to the gods] *you some permit / To second ills with ills, each elder worse* [i.e. each worse than the previous one: debated meaning]

3 elder tree **MW** II.iii.26 [Host to Caius, of Caius] *What says … My heart of elder?* [i.e. my man with a soft core, my cowardly one]; **2H4** II.iv.253

elder (*adj.*) greater **AC** III.x.13 [Scarus to Enobarbus, of the advantage in the fight] *ours the elder*

elder-gun (*n.*) pop-gun **H5** IV.i.193 [Williams to disguised King Henry, responding to his 'I will never trust his word after'] *That's a perilous shot out of an elder-gun*

eldest (*adj.*) oldest, longest **Tem** V.i.186 [Alonso to Ferdinand, of Miranda] *Your eld'st acquaintance cannot be three hours;* **CE** I.i.125; **Ham** III.iii.37

elect (*adj.*) chosen, selected, picked out **R2** IV.i.126 [Bishop of Carlisle to all, of King Richard] *the figure of God's majesty / His captain, steward, deputy elect*

elect (*v.*) **1** pick out, choose, select **MM** I.i.18 [Duke to Escalus, of Angelo] *we have … / Elected him our absence to supply;* **E3** I.i.142; **R2** III.i.57

2 acknowledge, choose, accept **1H6** IV.i.4 [Gloucester to the Governor of Paris, of Henry] *take your oath: / That you elect no other king but him*

ELISION

As in modern English, words often appear in a reduced or *elided* form, with the omitted element shown by an apostrophe. The reason for the elision varies: in some cases it enables a word to fit the metrical character of a line or focuses the emphasis within a sentence more sharply; in others it helps to capture the colloquial character of conversational speech or identifies a character's idiosyncratic way of talking. In most cases, the identity of the underlying word is obvious from the context, though some of the more unusual forms can make the reader hesitate – such as Lady Capulet's *thou's* (RJ I.iii.10).

Some patterns are frequent and predictable, and these are listed below: *'tis*, for example, is the regular contraction of *it is* (by contrast with present-day *it's*). The verbs *be, have,* and *do* are commonly contracted with a preceding pronoun in colloquial speech, as in modern English. Often the contracted forms are the same as those used today (e.g. *he's, we'll, let's, o'clock*); but there are several differences, including those listed below.

In some cases, it is only the written form that is distinctive: in modern English we do not usually write *y'are* for 'you are' or *o'doors* for 'of doors', but the colloquial pronunciation of *you are going* or *out of doors* would hardly differ between then and now. The presence or absence of an apostrophe in the texts also varies, depending partly on editorial practice and partly on whether a form might legitimately be considered a word in its own right (as in *squire* vs. *esquire*); for clarity, all forms are written with an apostrophe below.

Elision in grammatical words

Form	Location	Examples

Verbs

have > *ha'*	**Ham** V.i.23	*Will you ha' the truth on't?*
shall > *s'*	**RJ** I.iii.10	*thou's hear our counsel*
wilt > *'t, 'lt*	**Ham** V.i.279	*an thou'lt mouth, / I'll rant as well as thou*
wouldst thou > *woo't*	**Ham** V.i.271	*Woo't weep?*

Pronouns

he > *'a*	**RJ** I.iii.41	*'A was a merry man*
it [after a word] > *'t*	**Ham** V.i.122	*I do not lie in't* [also: to't, for't, is't, on't, etc.]
it [before a word] > *'t*	**Ham** I.i.7	*'Tis now struck twelve* [also: 'twere, 'twill, etc.]
them > *'em*	**Tem** I.ii.330	*each pinch more stinging / Than bees that made'em*
thou > *th'*	**Ham** V.ii.336	*As th'art a man*
us > *'s*	**Mac** I.iii.124	*to betray's*
you > *y'*	**Tim** I.ii.128	*You see ... how ample y'are beloved*

Determiners [articles and other noun specifiers]

his > *'s*	**Mac** II.ii.22	*one did laugh in's sleep* [also: all's, in's, and's]
our > *'r*	**1H4** II.i.44	*By'r lady*
the > *th'*	**Ham** I.ii.9	*our Queen, / Th'imperial jointress to this warlike state*
this > *'s*	**Ham** III.ii.136	*my father died within's two hours*

Prepositions

against > *'gainst*	**1H6** I.iv.15	*A piece of ordnance 'gainst it I have placed*
amidst > *'midst*	**Luc** 566	*'midst the sentence so her accent breaks*
amongst > *'mongst*	**1H6** I.iv.50	*great fear of my name 'mongst them*
before > *'fore*	**1H6** I.iii.22	*prizest him 'fore me*
betwixt > *'twixt*	**Tem** I.ii.240	*The time 'twixt six and now*
in > *'i*	**1H4** II.iv.364	*i'faith*
of > *'o*	**CE** II.i.11	*Because their business still lies out o'door*
on > *'o*	**Tem** I.i.40	*A pox o'your throat*
over > *o'er*	**Mac** I.iii.93	*In viewing o'er the rest*
to > *t'*	**KL** V.iii.185	*t'assume a semblance / That very dogs disclaimed*
with > *wi'*	**RJ** I.iii.33	*To see it tetchy and fall out wi'th' dug*

Conjunction

because > *'cause*	**H8** IV.ii.78	*'Cause the musicians play me that sad note*

ELISION – *continued*

Form	Location	Examples
Adverb		
so > s'	**Cor** IV.vi.122	*never / S'incapable of help*

Elision in word-endings

Adjectives

| -*est* > -'*st* | **Tem** I.i.58 | *gape at wid'st* ☛ **COMPARISON**, p.88 |

Verbs

| -*est* > -'*st* | **Tem** I.ii.333 | *When thou cam'st first, / Thou strok'st me* |

Elision in lexical words

Initial single consonant

| God > 'od | **AY** III.v.43 | *'Od's my little life* ☛ **SWEARING**, p.435 |
| yield > 'ild | **Mac** I.vi.13 | *God 'ield us* |

Initial unstressed syllable

account	**E3** II.ii.164	*The universal sessions call to 'count / This packing evil*
agree	**MM** IV.i.41	*Are there no other tokens ... 'greed concerning her observance?*
anoint	**MND** III.ii.351	*I have 'nointed an Athenian's eyes*
apothecary	**Per** III.ii.9	*Give this to the 'pothecary*
array	**E3** III.iii.227	*orderly disposed, and set in 'ray*
arrest	**CE** IV.ii.45	*[he] is in a suit of buff which 'rested him*
attend	**R2** IV.i.198	*The cares I give, I have, though given away, / They 'tend the crown*
begin	**Cym** II.iii.20	*Phoebus 'gins arise*
behaviour	**TN** III.iv.202	*With the same 'haviour that your passion bears*
belong	**AW** IV.ii.42	*It is an honour 'longing to our house*
concern	**TS** V.i.66	*what 'cerns it you if I wear pearl and gold?*
escape	**1H4** II.iv.160	*I have 'scaped by miracle*
establish	**1H6** V.i.10	*the only means / To ... 'stablish quietness on every side*

Medial single consonant

even > e'en	**TNK** V.iv.100	*e'en very here / I sundered you*
never > ne'er	**RJ** I.v.53	*I ne'er saw true beauty*
over > o'er	**Mac** IV.i.144	*The flighty purpose never is o'ertook*
taken > ta'en	**TN** III.iii.29	*were I ta'en here, it would scarce be answered*
whoever > whoe'er	**1H6** I.iii.7	*Whoe'er he be [also: howe'er, whate'er, soe'er, etc.]*

Medial syllable

| countenance | **Cym** III.iv.13 | *keep that count'nance still* |
| interrogatory | **AW** IV.iii.179 | *let me answer to the particular of the inter'gatories* |

Final single consonant

| give > gi' | **RJ** I.ii.57 | *God gi' good-e'en* |
| have > ha' | **TS** V.ii.180 | *Well, go thy ways, old lad, for thou shalt ha't* |

Final unstressed syllable

| seven | **Mac** I.iii.22 | *Weary sev'n-nights nine times nine* |

elected *(adj.)* chosen, selected, picked out **Cym** III.iv.111 [Innogen to Pisanio] *Th'elected deer before thee*

election *(n.)* choice, preference **AW** II.iii.54 [King to Helena, of the Lords] *Thy frank election make;* **Cym** I.iii.25; **KL** I.i.206; **TC** II.ii.62; **Tit** I.i.186; **TNK** V.i.154

elegancy *(n.)* elegance **LL** IV.i.121 [Holofernes to Nathaniel, of Berowne's letter to Rosaline] *for the elegancy, facility, and golden cadence of poesy, caret*

elegy *(n.)* love-poem, song of lamentation **TG** III.ii.82 [Proteus to Thurio] *After your dire-lamenting elegies*

element *(n.)* **1** (plural) substances from which all material things are made [believed to be earth, water, air, fire] **TN** II.iii.9 [Sir Toby to Sir Andrew] *Does not our lives consist of the four elements?;* **JC** V.v.73; **Oth** II.iii.41; **TC** I.iii.41; **Tem** I.i.21, V.i.318
2 (plural) elements of life, life-forces **AC** II.vii.45 [Antony to Lepidus, of the crocodile] *the elements once out of it, it transmigrates*
3 (plural) forces of nature, atmospheric powers **AC** III.ii.40 [Caesar to Octavia] *The elements be kind to thee;* **Cor** I.x.10; **KL** III.i.4, ii.16; **Oth** II.i.45, III.iii.461
4 substance, raw material, physical matter **Tem** III.iii.62 [Ariel to Alonso, Sebastian, and Antonio] *The elements, / Of whom your swords are tempered;* **AC** V.ii.90; **Luc** 1588; **MA** II.i.317
5 air, sky, heavens **2H4** IV.iii.52 [Falstaff to Prince John] *I in the clear sky of fame o'ershine you as much as the full moon doth the cinders of the element* [i.e. the stars]; **H5** IV.i.101; **JC** I.iii.128; **TN** I.i.27
6 essence, embodiment, heart and soul **Oth** II.iii.53 [Iago alone, of three local men] *The very elements of this warlike isle*
7 place, sphere, station **TN** III.iv.123 [Malvolio to all] *I am not of your element;* **KL** II.v.56
8 sphere of knowledge, proper comprehension **MW** IV.ii.165 [Ford to Mistress Ford, of her maid's aunt's spells] *She works by ... such daubery as this is beyond our element;* **H8** I.i.48

eleven and twenty long just right, perfect [a winning hand in the card game of Thirty-one] **TS** IV.ii.57 [Tranio to Bianca, of Petruchio] *That teacheth tricks eleven and twenty long, / To tame a shrew*

elf *(v.)* tangle, mat, twist **KL** II.iii.10 [Edgar alone] *I'll ... elf all my hairs in knots*

elf-lock *(n.)* hair treated by elves; matted locks **RJ** I.iv.90 [Mercutio to Romeo, of Queen Mab] *That ... bakes the elf-locks in foul sluttish hairs* [F Elklocks; Q1 Elfelocks]

elf-skin *(n.)* shrunken thing, mere nothing **1H4** II.iv.240 [Falstaff to Prince Hal] *you elf-skin* [F elke-skin; Q1 elsskin]

eliad *(n.)* ☞ oeillade *(n.)*

ell *(n.)* measure of length [45 inches / c.114 cm in England] **RJ** II.iv.83 [Mercutio to Romeo] *here's a wit of cheverel, that stretches from an inch narrow to an ell broad;* **CE** III.ii.115; **1H4** III.iii.71

else *(adv.)* **1** otherwise **CE** III.ii.29 [Antipholus of Syracuse to Luciana] *what your name is else I know not;* **Ham** IV.iii.59; **TC** V.ii.59; **Tem** III.iii.81; **Tim** I.ii.158; **TNK** IV.i.110 ☞ **DISCOURSE MARKERS**, p.127
2 elsewhere, in another direction **TG** IV.ii.121 [Proteus to Silvia] *since the substance of your perfect self / Is else devoted, I am but a shadow;* **CE** V.i.50
3 suchlike, others besides **KJ** II.i.276 [Bastard to himself, reacting to King John's estimate of the English numbers] *Bastards and else!*
4 (used after the noun) in addition **Ham** I.iv.33 [Hamlet to Horatio, of a type of person] *His virtues else ... / Shall in the general censure take corruption* [i.e. his other virtues]

elvish-marked *(adj.)* marked out at birth by evil fairies, displaying spite **R3** I.iii.227 [Queen Margaret to Richard] *Thou elvish-marked ... hog!*

emballing *(n.)* investment with the orb [as a mark of sovereignty] **H8** II.iii.47 [Old Lady to Anne, of being a queen] *for little England / You'd venture an emballing* [with bawdy pun]

embark *(v.)* engage in an enterprise, involve in an undertaking **Oth** I.i.150 [Iago to Roderigo, of Othello] *he's embarked / With such loud reason to the Cyprus wars*

embarquement *(n.)* embargo, impediment, prohibition **Cor** I.x.22 [Aufidius to First Soldier] *Embarquements all of fury ... shall [not] lift up / Their rotten privilege and custom 'gainst / My hate to Martius*

embassade *(n.)* embassy, mission [as an ambassador] **3H6** IV.iii.33 [Warwick to Edward] *you disgraced me in my embassade* [F; Q *embassage*]

embassador *(n.)* variant form of 'ambassador' **2H6** III.ii.276 [Suffolk to all of Salisbury] *he was the lord embassador / Sent ... to the King* [F]

embassage, ambassage *(n.)* message, errand, business, mission **R2** III.iv.93 [Queen Isabel as if to mischance] *Doth not thy embassage belong to me;* **E3** I.i.21; **LL** III.i.98; **MA** I.i.259; **R3** II.i.3; **Sonn** 26.3

embassy *(n.)* **1** message [especially via an ambassador] **Sonn** 45.6 *In tender embassy of love to thee;* **H5** I.i.95; **KJ** I.i.6; **LL** II.i.3; **WT** I.i.28
2 ambassadorial role, function as ambassador **LL** I.i.132 [Berowne to King] *here comes in embassy / The French King's daughter;* **KJ** I.i.22, 99; **TC** IV.v.216

embattailed *(adj.)* in battle positions, marshalled for fight **KJ** IV.ii.200 [Hubert to King John] *many thousand warlike French / That were embattailed and ranked in Kent*

embattle *(v.)* deploy, draw up, marshal **H5** IV.ii.12 [Messenger to all] *The English are embattled;* **AC** IV.ix.3; **E3** V.v.31; **MW** II.ii.240

embayed *(adj.)* within a bay, protected by the shore **Oth** II.i.18 [Montano to Second Gentleman] *If that the Turkish fleet / Be not ... embayed, they are drowned*

ember-eve *(n.)* evening before ember-days [church quarterly 3-day period of fasting and prayer] **Per** I.Chorus.6 [Gower alone] *On ember-eves and holidays*

emblaze *(v.)* proclaim publicly, set forth [as on a coat of arms] **2H6** IV.x.69 [Iden to his sword, of Cade's blood] *thou shalt wear it as a herald's coat, / To emblaze the honour that thy master got*

emblem *(n.)* image, symbol, allegory **TNK** II.i.191 [Emilia to Woman, of the rose] *It is the very emblem of a maid*

embody *(v.)* become part of the same body as, unite as **AW** V.iii.173 [Diana to Bertram] *I by vow am so embodied yours*

embolden *(v.)* make more bold, encourage, foster **Tim** III.v.3 [First Senator to Second Senator] *Nothing emboldens sin so much as mercy*

emboss *(v.)* [hunting] run down, drive to exhaustion **AW** III.vi.92 [First Lord to Bertram of Parolles] *we have almost embossed him* [or: box up]

embossed *(adj.)* **1** driven to such extremes, made mad with exhaustion **TS** Induction.i.15 [Lord to First Huntsman, of his hound] *the poor cur is embossed;* **AC** IV.xiii.3
2 foaming, driven forward **Tim** V.i.215 [Timon to Senators, of his grave] *Who once a day with his embossed froth / The turbulent surge shall cover*
3 swollen, bulging, protuberant **1H4** III.iii.155 [Prince Hal to Falstaff] *thou whoreson impudent embossed rascal;* **AY** II.vii.67; **KL** II.iv.219
4 covered as if with ornamental studs **E3** V.i.135 [Salisbury to King Edward, of the army surrounding Prince Edward] *every barricado's open front / Was thick embossed with brazen ordinance*

embound enclose, contain, confine **KJ** IV.iii.137 [Hubert to Bastard, of Arthur's body] *that sweet breath / Which was embounded in this beauteous clay*

embowel *(v.)* disembowel **1H4** V.iv.110 [Falstaff alone, of Prince Hal] *If thou embowel me today, I'll give you leave to powder me and eat me too tomorrow;* **1H4** V.iv.108

embowelled *(adj.)* disembowelled, emptied, drained **AW** I.iii.236 [Countess to Helena] *the schools, / Embowelled of their doctrine;* **R3** V.ii.10

embrace *(v.)* **1** welcome, joyfully accept **Ham** V.ii.246 [Hamlet to Laertes, of Laertes' love] *I embrace it freely;* **Cym** III.iv.178; **2H6** IV.viii.13; **3H6** III.i.24; **TN** II.v.143

2 accept, avail oneself of **Tim** III.i.27 [Lucullus to Flaminius, of Timon] *he would embrace no counsel, take no warning;* **MA** I.i.96

embraced *(adj.)* cherished, joyfully accepted **MV** II.viii.52 [Solanio to Salerio, of Antonio] *let us … quicken his embraced heaviness / With some delight or other*

embracement *(n.)* embrace, clasping, hug **Per** I.i.8 [Antiochus to Pericles, of his daughter] *clothed like a bride / For embracements;* **Cor** I.iii.4; **E3** III.iii.28; **H8** I.i.10; **R3** II.i.30; **Venus** 312

embrasure *(n.)* embrace, clasping **TC** IV.iv.36 [Troilus to Cressida] *injury of chance … forcibly prevents / Our locked embrasures*

embrue *(v.)* ➤ imbrue *(v.)*

eminence *(n.)* **1** superiority, mastery, advantage **TC** II.iii.252 [Ulysses to Nestor] *were your days / As green as Ajax' … / You should not have the eminence of him*

2 special honour, exceptional homage **Mac** III.ii.31 [Macbeth to Lady Macbeth, of Banquo] *Present him eminence both with eye and tongue*

emmet *(n.)* ant **E3** III.iv.41 [Audley to King Edward] *The snares of French, like emmets on a bank*

emmew *(v.)* ➤ enew *(v.)*

empale *(v.)* ➤ impale *(v.)*

empannel *(v.)* ➤ impannel *(v.)*

emperal *(n.)* malapropism for 'emperor' **Tit** IV.iii.93 [Clown to Titus] *I am going … to take up a matter of brawl betwixt my uncle and one of the Emperal's men*

emperial *(adj.)* malapropism for 'imperial' **Tit** IV.iv.40 [Clown to Tamora, of speaking with her] *an your mistress-ship be Emperial*

emperious *(adj.)* ➤ imperious *(adj.)*

empery *(n.)* **1** absolute dominion, sovereignty **H5** I.ii.227 [King Henry to all] *we'll sit / Ruling in large and ample empery / O'er France;* **R3** III.vii.135; **Tit** I.i.19, 204

2 empire, emperor's domain **Cym** I.vii.120 [Iachimo to Innogen] *A lady / So fair, and fastened to an empery / Would make the great'st king double*

emphasis *(n.)* vigorous expression, forceful utterance **Ham** V.i.251 [Hamlet to all, of Laertes] *What is he whose grief / Bears such an emphasis;* **AC** I.v.68

empierce *(v.)* pierce through, transfix, impale **RJ** I.iv.19 [Romeo to Mercutio, of Cupid] *I am too sore empierced with his shaft* [F *enpearced*]

empire *(n.)* emperor **AW** III.ii.31 [Countess as if to Bertram, of his behaviour] *the misprizing of a maid too virtuous / For the contempt of empire* [i.e. that even emperors would not despise her]; **Tit** I.i.186

empiric *(n.)* medical quack, untrained practitioner **AW** II.i.122 [King to Helena] *we must not … prostitute our past-cure malady / To empirics*

empiricutic *(n./adj.)* quackery, imposture; quackish, fraudulent **Cor** II.i.112 [Menenius to Virgilia] *The most sovereign prescription in Galen is but empiricutic* [F *Emperickqutique*]

empleached, impleached *(adj.)* entwined, intertwined, interwoven **Lover** 205 [of locks of hair] *With twisted metal amorously empleached*

employ *(v.)* **1** devote, apply, occupy [oneself] **1H6** III.iii.16 [Alençon to Pucelle] *Employ thee, then, sweet virgin, for our good*

2 make use of, use one's services **AC** III.iii.35 [Cleopatra to Messenger] *I will employ thee back again;* **AY** III.v.96

employment *(n.)* **1** task, service, commission **Cym** III.v.111 [Cloten to Pisanio] *undergo those employments wherein I should have cause to use thee;* **KJ** I.i.198; **LL** IV.iii.134

2 matter, business, affair **TN** II.v.81 [Malvolio to himself, of the letter] *What employment have we here?*

3 use, purpose, end **R2** I.i.90 [Bolingbroke to King Richard, of money given to Mowbray] *The which he hath detained for lewd employments*

empoison *(v.)* **1** poison, corrupt, destroy **MA** III.i.86 [Hero to Ursula] *How much an ill word may empoison liking*

2 give poison, destroy by poison **Cor** V.vi.11 [Aufidius to First Conspirator, of Coriolanus] *As with a man by his own alms empoisoned*

emportment *(n.)* fit of passion, state of emotion **TNK** I.iii.80 [Emilia to Hippolyta] *This rehearsal … comes in / Like old emportment's bastard* [i.e. like someone carried away by their feelings] [Q *importments*]

empty *(adj.)* **1** famished, hungry, having an empty stomach **3H6** I.i.268 [King to Exeter, of York] *Will … like an empty eagle / Tire on the flesh of me and of my son!;* **2H6** III.i.248

2 empty-handed, with nothing to give **Tim** III.vi.38 [Lucullus to Timon] *I returned you an empty messenger*

3 unburdened, idle, unoccupied **JC** IV.i.26 [Antony to Octavius, of Lepidus] *turn him off, / Like to the empty ass, to shake his ears / And graze in commons*

emulate *(adj.)* ambitious, full of jealous rivalry, emulous **Ham** I.i.83 [Horatio to Marcellus and Barnardo, of old Fortinbras] *pricked on by a most emulate pride*

emulation *(n.)* **1** ambitious rivalry, contention, conflict **TC** II.ii.213 [Hector to all, of the Greeks] *I was advertised their great general slept, / Whilst emulation in the army crept;* **1H6** IV.i.113; **JC** II.iii.13; **Luc** 1808; **R3** II.iii.25; **TC** III.iii.156

2 triumph, success, accomplishment **Cor** I.i.212 [Martius to Menenius, of the citizens] *they threw their caps … / Shouting their emulation* [or: rivalling each other in shouting]

emulator *(n.)* disparager, denigrator, belittler **AY** I.i.134 [Oliver to Charles, of Orlando] *an envious emulator of every man's good parts*

emulous *(adj.)* **1** envious, filled with rivalry, greedy for praise **TC** II.iii.228 [Nestor to Ulysses, of Ajax] *He is not emulous, as Achilles is;* **TC** III.iii.189, IV.i.29

2 rivalling, competing, emulating **TC** II.iii.72 [Thersites to Patroclus] *a good quarrel to draw emulous factions and bleed to death upon;* **TNK** V.iii.124

emure *(n.)* ➤ immure *(n.)*

enact *(n.)* purpose, resolve, resolution **Tit** IV.ii.117 [Aaron to Chiron, of his skin colour] *that will betray with blushing / The close enacts and counsels of thy heart*

enact *(v.)* **1** bring about, accomplish, perform **1H6** III.i.117 [Warwick to Gloucester and Winchester] *You see what mischief … / Hath been enacted through your enmity;* **R3** V.iv.2; **Tem** IV.i.121

2 decree, ordain, enter in the records **Luc** 529 [Tarquin to Lucrece] *A little harm done to a great good end / For lawful policy remains enacted;* **1H6** V.v.123; **MV** IV.i.345

enacture *(n.)* performance, fulfilment, execution **Ham** III.ii.207 [First Player, as King, to his Queen] *The violence of either grief or joy / Their own enactures with themselves destroy* [Q2; F *ennactors*]

enamelled *(adj.)* brightly coloured, multi-coloured, kaleidoscopic **TNK** III.i.7 [Arcite alone, of Emilia] *sweeter / Than … / Th'enamelled knacks o'th' mead or garden;* **CE** II.i.109; **MND** II.i.255; **TG** II.vii.28

enamoured [on] *(adj.)* in love [with], delight [in], relish **E3** IV.vii.23 [Prince Edward to Audley] *thou … look'st so merrily upon thy grave / As if thou wert enamoured on thine end*

encaged, incaged *(adj.)* encaged, caged up **Venus** 582 [of Adonis, and Venus' heart] *The which … / He carries thence incaged in his breast;* **3H6** IV.vi.12

encamp (*v.*) form into a camp, settle in a camp **RJ** II.iii.23 [Friar alone] *Two such opposed kings encamp them still / In man as well as herbs - grace and rude will*

encave (*v.*) hide away, conceal **Oth** IV.i.81 [Iago to Othello] *Do but encave yourself*

enchafe (*v.*) heat, excite, anger **Cym** IV.ii.174 [Belarius alone, of Arviragus and Guiderius] *they are … as rough, / (Their royal blood enchafed) as the rud'st wind*

enchafed (*adj.*) angry, furious, enraged **Oth** II.i.17 [Second Gentleman to Montano] *I never did like molestation view / On the enchafed flood*

enchant (*v.*) charm, bewitch, win over **Venus** 145 [Venus to Adonis] *Bid me discourse, I will enchant thine ear;* **1H6** III.iii.40; **Lover** 89; **Oth** I.ii.63

enchanting (*adj.*) bewitching, captivating, holding under a spell **AC** I.ii.129 [Antony alone, of Cleopatra] *I must from this enchanting queen break off;* **Luc** 1521

enchantingly (*adv.*) as if put under a spell **AY** I.i.156 [Oliver alone, of Orlando] *of all sorts enchantingly beloved*

enchased (*adj.*) adorned, decorated, inlaid **2H6** I.ii.8 [Duchess to Gloucester] *King Henry's diadem, / Enchased with all the honours of the world?*

enclog (*v.*) hinder, encumber, impede **Oth** II.i.70 [Cassio to all, of the rocks] *Traitors enscarped to enclog the guiltless keel* [Q; F *enclogge*]

enclose (*v.*) seize, grip, imprison **TNK** III.i.30 [Arcite alone, as if to Palamon, of Emilia] *if / Thou knewest my mistress breathed on me … / What passion would enclose thee;* **1H6** I.i.136

encloud (*v.*) envelop, engulf, surround [as in a cloud] **AC** V.ii.212 [Cleopatra to Iras, of the Romans] *In their thick breaths … shall we be enclouded*

encompass (*v.*) 1 surround, encircle, enclose **3H6** II.i.15 [Richard to Edward, of York] *he bore him … as a bear encompassed round with dogs;* **1H6** I.i.114, III.ii.53; **3H6** II.i.3; **TNK** IV.i.62

2 outwit, catch out, get round **MW** II.ii.149 [Falstaff to himself] *Mistress Ford and Mistress Page, have I encompassed you?*

encompassed (*adj.*) surrounded, encircled, enclosed **E3** IV.v.59 [Captain to King John, of Salisbury and his knights, and of Prince Edward] *sought to break our ranks / And make their way to the encompassed prince*

encompassment (*n.*) talking around [a subject], roundabout means **Ham** II.i.10 [Polonius to Reynaldo] *By this encompassment and drift of question*

encouch (*v.*) enclose, embed, wrap around **E3** II.i.69 [King Edward to Lodowick] *encouch the word / Before and after with such sweet laments*

encounter (*n.*) 1 conversational interaction, discourse style **Ham** V.ii.187 [Hamlet to Horatio] *an habit of encounter*

2 accosting, address, approach **TS** IV.v.54 [Vincentio to and of Katherina] *That with your strange encounter much amazed me;* **TG** II.vii.41

3 behaviour, conduct, manner of meeting **WT** III.ii.48 [Hermione to Leontes] *With what encounter so uncurrent I / Have strained t'appear thus* [i.e. what limits of behaviour have I exceeded that I should now find myself on trial]

4 liaison, intercourse, amorous affair **MM** III.i.252 [disguised Duke to Isabella] *If the encounter acknowledge itself hereafter;* **Ham** II.ii.164; **MA** III.iii.146; **MW** III.v.68

5 skirmish, assault, engagement **LL** V.ii.82 [Boyet to ladies] *Encounters mounted are / Against your peace*

encounter (*v.*) 1 stand opposite, take a partner **Tem** IV.i.137 [Iris to the reapers] *these fresh nymphs encounter every one / In country footing*

2 approach, go to, move towards **TN** III.i.72 [Sir Toby to Viola as Cesario] *Will you encounter the house?;* **MA** I.i.91

3 meet, bump into one another **Tim** III.vi.5 [Lucullus to Lucius, of Timon's motives] *Upon that were my thoughts tiring when we encountered*

4 confront, assail, attack **Tim** II.ii.41 [Timon to Flavius] *How goes the world that I am thus encountered / With clamorous demands*

5 oppose, thwart, defeat **3H6** IV.viii.36 [King to Exeter] *the power that Edward hath in field / Should not be able to encounter mine*

encounter with (*v.*) 1 meet, approach [as an adversary] **Tit** V.ii.2 [disguised Tamora to Chiron and Demetrius, of Titus] *in this strange and sad habiliment, / I will encounter with Andronicus;* **1H6** II.ii.46; **Venus** 672

2 contest, dispute, confront **AW** I.iii.203 [Helena to Countess] *Let not your hate encounter with my love;* **3H6** V.iii.5

encounterer (*n.*) flirt, coquette, tease **TC** IV.v.58 [Ulysses to Nestor, of Cressida] *O, these encounterers, so glib of tongue*

encrimsoned (*adj.*) dyed crimson, made bright red **Lover** 201 *In bloodless white, and the encrimsoned mood*

encumbered (*v.*) folded **Ham** I.v.174 [Hamlet to Horatio and Marcellus] *With arms encumbered thus*

end (*n.*) 1 purpose, aim, design **H8** III.ii.447 [Wolsey to Cromwell] *Let all the ends thou aim'st at be thy country's;* **AY** V.iv.167; **Cym** III.iv.168; **3H6** II.v.39; **Tem** I.ii.89; **TNK** Epilogue.15

2 outcome, result, issue **Mac** III.v.21 [Hecat to Witches] *this night I'll spend / Unto a dismal and a fatal end;* **Cym** III.vii.5; **Ham** III.ii.223; **JC** II.ii.27; **Tem** II.i.4

3 ultimate end, end of all things **KL** V.iii.261 [Kent to all, of seeing Lear and dead Cordelia] *Is this the promised end?* [i.e. the end of the world]

4 death, ending [of life] **Sonn** 14.14 *Thy end is Truth's and Beauty's doom and date;* **2H4** IV.iv.130; **2H6** I.iv.32; **R3** II.i.15; **TNK** III.ii.38

5 scrap, fragment, tag, ending **R3** I.iii.336 [Richard alone] *thus I clothe my naked villainy / With odd old ends stolen forth of Holy Writ;* **MA** I.i.267

6 root cause, source **H8** II.i.40 [Second Gentleman to First Gentleman, of Buckingham's downfall] *The Cardinal is the end of this*

7 **☞** draw toward an end; still an end; **DISCOURSE MARKERS**, p.127

end, an / on upright, vertical **R3** I.iii.303 [Buckingham to all, of Queen Margaret] *My hair doth stand an end to hear her curses;* **TNK** V.iv.67 [Pirithous to Palamon] *the hot horse … comes on end* [i.e. rears up]; **TNK** V.iv.77

end (*v.*) 1 provide an end for, give purpose to **Cor** II.ii.127 [Cominius to all, of Coriolanus] *He … is content / To spend the time to end it* [i.e. as an end in itself]

2 settle, resolve **2H6** II.iii.55 [King to all, of the fight between Horner and Peter] *Here let them end it, and God defend the right!*

3 [harvesting] gather in, bring in **Cor** V.vi.37 [Aufidius to Conspirators, of Coriolanus] *I … help to reap the fame / Which he did end all his*

endamage (*v.*) damage, injure, harm **TG** III.ii.43 [Duke to Proteus, of Valentine] *Your slander never can endamage him;* **1H6** II.i.77

endamagement (*n.*) damage, injury, harm **KJ** II.i.209 [King John to Hubert, of the French armies] *Have hither marched to your endamagement;* **E3** I.i.379

endart (*v.*) embed, bury, send in [as an arrow] **RJ** I.iii.99 [Juliet to Lady Capulet] *no more deep will I endart mine eye / Than your consent gives strength to make it fly*

endeared (*adj.*) 1 attached in honour, bound by affection **Tim** I.ii.231 [Second Lord to Timon] *[we are] So infinitely endeared [to you];* **2H4** II.iii.11; **Tim** III.ii.32

2 made more precious, increased in value **Sonn** 31.1 *Thy bosom is endeared with all hearts / Which I by lacking have supposed dead*

endeavour (v.) try to obtain, strive to procure 1H6 II.v.69 [Mortimer to Richard] *the Percys ... / Endeavoured my advancement to the throne*

ending (adj.) dying, near one's end 2H4 IV.v.80 [King Henry IV to the princes] *This bitter taste / Yields his engrossments to the ending father;* TG III.i.240

endite (v.) deliberate malapropism for 'invite' RJ II.iv.126 [Benvolio to Mercutio, of Nurse and Romeo] *She will endite him to some supper*

endless (adj.) **1** boundless, universal, impenetrable KJ V.vi.12 [Hubert as if to his memory, of not recognizing Bastard] *Thou and endless night / Have done me shame*
  2 never-ending, impossible, unattainable TNK Prologue.22 [of Chaucer] *it were an endless thing ... to aspire to him*

endow (v.) provide with a dowry Tim I.i.143 [Timon to Old Athenian, of his daughter] *How shall she be endowed / If she be mated with an equal husband?*

endowment (n.) endowing of possessions, enriching with property R2 II.iii.138 [Willoughby to York, of Bolingbroke] *Base men by his endowments are made great*

endue (v.) ☛ indue (v.)

endued (adj.) ☛ indued (adj.)

endurance (n.) ☛ indurance (n.)

endure (v.) **1** let, allow, permit TS IV.iii.75 [Katherina to Petruchio] *Your betters have endured me say my mind;* Mac V.iv.9
  2 undergo, suffer, put up with TNK II.v.10 [Gaoler's Daughter alone, of arranging Palamon's escape] *My father / Durst better have endured cold iron than done it* [i.e. being clapped in irons; or, swordfighting]; 1H6 II.iv.10; R3 III.vii.229
  3 live out a life, continue in existence KL V.iii.209 [Edgar to Albany, of Kent discovering who Poor Tom was] *finding / Who 'twas that so endured*

enew (v.) drive into the water MM III.i.94 [Isabella to Claudio, of Angelo] *This outward-sainted deputy ... follies doth enew / As falcon doth the fowl* [F *emmew*]

enfeoff (v.) surrender, abandon, give up completely 1H4 III.ii.69 [King Henry to Prince Hal, of Richard II] *The skipping King ... / Enfeoffed himself to popularity*

enfettered (adj.) placed in fetters, enchained, enslaved Oth II.iii. 335 [Iago alone, of Othello and Desdemona] *His soul is so enfettered to her love*

enfoldings (n.) garments, clothes WT IV.iv.726 [Autolycus to Shepherd] *Seest thou not the air of the court in these enfoldings?*

enforce (v.) **1** emphasize, urge, lay stress upon JC III.ii.39 [Brutus to all, of Caesar] *his offences [are not] enforced, for which he suffered death;* AC V.ii.125; Cor II.iii.218, III.iii.3; MM V.i.265
  2 force, compel, constrain, drive Tem V.i.100 [Prospero to Ariel, of the Mariners] *enforce them to this place;* 2H6 IV.iv.17
  3 act upon by force Luc 303 [of Tarquin and Lucrece's door locks] *Each one by him enforced, retires his ward;* 2H4 IV.i.71; H5 IV.vii.60; JC IV.iii.111
  4 gain by force, exact AY II.iii.32 [Orlando to Adam] *with a base and boisterous sword enforce / A thievish living;* LL III.i.73; Tim V.iv.45
  5 rape, violate, ravish Cym IV.i.17 [Cloten alone, as if to Posthumus] *thy mistress [shall be] enforced*

enforced (adj.) **1** forced, constrained, affected JC IV.ii.21 [Brutus to Lucilius] *When love begins to sicken and decay, / It useth an enforced ceremony;* R3 III.v.9
  2 violated, assaulted, ravished MND III.i.195 [Titania to Fairies, of the moon] *when she weeps, weeps every little flower, / Lamenting some enforced chastity*
  3 violating, shown in an assault Luc 668 [Tarquin to Lucrece] *enforced hate / Instead of love's coy touch shall rudely tear thee*

enforcedly (adv.) under compulsion, out of necessity Tim IV.iii.242 [Apemantus to Timon, of his behaviour] *thou / Dost it enforcedly*

enforcement (n.) **1** enforcing, propulsion 2H4 I.i.120 [Morton to Northumberland] *the thing that's heavy in itself / Upon enforcement flies with greatest speed;* R3 III.vii.232
  2 violation, overcoming AW V.iii.107 [King to Bertram, of Helena's ring] *Confess 'twas hers, and by what rough enforcement / You got it from her;* R3 III.vii.8

enfranched (adj.) enfranchised, freed, liberated AC III.xiii.149 [Antony to Thidias, of Caesar] *he has / Hipparchus, my enfranched bondman* [F]

enfranchise (v.) set free, liberate R3 I.i.110 [Richard to Clarence] *whatso'er you will employ me in ... / I will perform it to enfranchise you;* AC I.i.23; LL III.i.118; TG III.i.124; Tit IV.ii.124; WT II.ii.61

enfranchisement (n.) freedom, liberation, release R2 III.iii.114 [Northumberland to King Richard, of Bolingbroke] *to beg / Enfranchisement immediate on his knees* [i.e. from banishment]; 2H6 V.i.113; JC III.i.57, 81; KJ IV.ii.52; R2 I.iii.90

enfreed (adj.) liberated, released TC IV.i.39 [Paris to Aeneas, of Diomedes] *render him, / For the enfreed Antenor, the fair Cressid*

enfreedom (v.) make free, liberate LL III.i.122 [Armado to Costard, of 'enfranchising' him] *I mean setting thee at liberty, enfreedoming thy person*

engage (v.) **1** pledge, give the guarantee of AY V.iv.163 [Jaques de Boys to all, of his account] *This to be true, / I do engage my life;* CE V.i.162; 1H4 I.i.21, II.iv.499; JC II.i.127; MV III.ii.262
  2 take up a gage, accept a challenge R2 IV.i.56 [Another Lord to Aumerle, of the former's gage] *Engage it to the trial if thou darest;* R2 IV.i.71
  3 enter into combat, make an attack TC V.v.39 [Ulysses to all, of Troilus] *Engaging and redeeming of himself / With such a careless force and forceless care;* AC IV.vii.1
  4 hold as a hostage 1H4 V.ii.43 [Douglas to all] *I have thrown / A brave defiance in King Henry's teeth, / And Westmorland that was engaged did bear it;* 1H4 IV.iii.95
  5 mortgage, put in pawn Tim II.ii.151 [Flavius to Timon, of his land] *'Tis all engaged*

engage to involve in, associate with 2H4 I.i.180 [Lord Bardolph to Northumberland] *We all that are engaged to this loss / Knew that we ventured on such dangerous seas*

engaged (adj.) **1** entangled, involved, trapped Ham III.iii.69 [Claudius alone] *O limed soul, that ... / Art more engaged*
  2 pledged, bound, sworn TC V.iii.68 [Hector to Priam] *I do stand engaged to many Greeks, / Even in the faith of valour, to appear*

engaol (v.) put in gaol, lock up R2 I.iii.166 [Mowbray to King Richard] *Within my mouth you have engaoled my tongue*

engender (v.) produce, develop, generate 3H6 V.iii.13 [George to Edward] *every cloud engenders not a storm;* Tim IV.iii.182; TS IV.i.158

engendered (adj.) devised, hatched, conceived Oth I.iii.397 [Iago alone, of his plan] *It is engendered*

engendering (n.) begetting, breeding, multiplying TC II.iii.157 [Ajax to Agamemnon] *I do hate a proud man as I hate the engendering of toads*

engild (v.) gild, brighten, illuminate MND III.ii.187 [Lysander to Hermia] *Fair Helena, who more engilds the night / Than all yon fiery oes and eyes of light*

engine (n.) **1** plot, device, means, instrument TG III.i.138 [Duke to Valentine, of a ladder] *an engine fit for my proceeding;* AW III.v.19; Oth IV.ii.216; Tit II.i.123
  2 weapon, instrument of warfare Cor V.iv.19 [Menenius to Sicinius, of Coriolanus] *When he walks, he moves like an engine;* Oth III.iii.352; TC I.iii.208; Tem II.i.164; Tit V.iii.85; TNK V.iii.42
  3 instrument, implement, organ Tit III.i.82 [Marcus to Lucius and Titus, of Lavinia's tongue] *that delightful engine of her thoughts;* Venus 367
  4 mechanical device, lever, implement KL I.iv.265 [Lear to Gonerill, of Cordelia's fault] *like an engine, wrenched my frame of nature / From the fixed place*

engineer, enginer (n.) constructor of military works; plotter, contriver **TC** II.iii.8 [Thersites alone] *Then there's Achilles - a rare engineer* [i.e. to undermine defensive walls]; **Ham** III.iv.207 ☞ ingener (n.)

engirt (adj.) surrounded, encircled, hemmed in **E3** IV.iv.90 [Second Herald to and of Prince Edward] *thy youth is so engirt with peril;* **2H6** III.i.200; **Luc** 1173

engirt (v.) encircle, enclose **2H6** V.i.99 [York to King, of the crown] *That gold must round engirt these brows of mine;* **Luc** 221; **Venus** 364

englut (v.) swallow up, gulp down, devour **Oth** I.iii.57 [Brabantio to Duke] *my particular grief … engluts and swallows other sorrows;* **H5** IV.iii.83; **Tim** II.ii.171

engraff, engraft, engrafted (adj.) ☞ ingraft, ingrafted (adj.)

engraffed (adj.) ☞ ingraft (adj.)

engross (v.) **1** get together, collect, gather, seize **MW** II.ii.190 [Ford as Brook to Falstaff, of Mistress Ford] *I have … engrossed opportunities to meet her;* **AC** III.vii.36; **2H4** IV.v.72

2 collect up, appropriate, monopolize **AW** III.ii.65 [Countess to Helena] *If thou engrossest all the griefs are thine / Thou robbest me of a moiety;* **Sonn** 133.6

3 write out in proper legal form **R3** III.vi.2 [Scrivener alone] *Here is the indictment … / Which in a set hand fairly is engrossed*

4 fatten, distend, make bloated **R3** III.vii.75 [Buckingham to Lord Mayor, of Richard] *He is … / Not sleeping, to engross his idle body*

engross up (v.) amass, accumulate, collect together **1H4** III.ii.148 [Prince Hal to King Henry] *Percy is but my factor … / To engross up glorious deeds on my behalf*

engrossing (adj.) all-absorbing, monopolizing **RJ** V.iii.115 [Romeo to sleeping Juliet] *lips … seal with a righteous kiss / A dateless bargain to engrossing death!*

engrossment (n.) stockpiling, accumulation, collecting activity **2H4** IV.v.80 [King Henry IV to the princes] *This bitter taste / Yields his engrossments to the ending father*

enguard (v.) protect, preserve, shield **KL** I.iv.323 [Gonerill to Albany, of Lear] *Each buzz, each fancy … / He may enguard his dotage*

enigmatical (adj.) enigmatic, mysterious, puzzling **MA** V.iv.27 [Benedick to Leonato] *Your answer … is enigmatical*

enjoined (adj.) joined together in a common cause, bound by oath **AW** III.v.93 [Widow to Helena] *Of enjoined pentitents / There's four or five … / Already at my house*

enjoy (v.) **1** possess, have, own **KJ** II.i.240 [King Philip to Hubert, of Arthur and King John] *king o'er him and all that he enjoys;* **Cym** I.v.76

2 indulge, give rein to, continue to practise **AC** II.vi.78 [Pompey to Enobarbus] *Enjoy thy plainness*

3 possess with delight, take pleasure [in], savour **R2** II.iv.14 [Captain to Salisbury] *Rich men look sad, and ruffians dance and leap - / The one in fear to lose what they enjoy, / The other to enjoy by rage and war;* **Sonn** 29.8

4 possess in love, sleep with **TNK** II.iii.30 [Gaoler's Daughter alone, of Palamon] *I would fain enjoy him;* **3H6** III.ii.95

enjoyer (n.) possessor, owner **Sonn** 75.5 [of a miser and his wealth] *proud as an enjoyer*

enjoying (n.) experiencing, benefit, blessing **TNK** II.i.114 [Arcite to Palamon] *the enjoying of our griefs together*

enlard (v.) smear with grease, add fatty juice to **TC** II.iii.193 [Ulysses to Agamemnon, of Ajax going to Achilles] *That were to enlard his [Achilles'] fat-already pride*

enlarge (v.) **1** release, set at large, discharge **E3** III.iii.8 [King Edward to Gobin] *We here enlarge and give thee liberty;* **H5** II.ii.40; **JC** IV.ii.46; **MW** II.ii.215; **Sonn** 70.12; **TN** V.i.275

2 enhance, promote, enrich **2H4** I.i.204 [Morton to Northumberland, of the Archbishop] *He … doth enlarge his rising with the blood / Of fair King Richard*

3 widen, extend, augment **Ham** V.i.222 [Priest to Laertes, of Ophelia] *Her obsequies have been as far enlarged / As we have warranty*

enlargement (n.) **1** release, liberation, freeing **LL** III.i.5 [Armado to Mote, of Costard] *give enlargement to the swain;* **1H4** III.i.28; **1H6** II.v.30; **3H6** IV.vi.5

2 freedom of action, privilege of choice **Cym** II.iii.119 [Cloten to Innogen, of lower marriages] *you are curbed from that enlargement, by / The consequence o'th' crown*

enlighten (v.) light up, throw light upon, illuminate **Sonn** 152.11 *I … to enlighten thee gave eyes to blindness*

enlink (v.) connect, chain, join closely [to] **H5** III.iii.18 [King Henry to citizens of Harfleur, of war] *Do … all fell feats / Enlinked to waste and desolation?*

ennactor (n.) ☞ enacture (n.)

enormity (n.) vice, wickedness, transgression **Cor** II.i.15 [Menenius to Brutus and Sicinius] *In what enormity is Martius poor in that you two have not in abundance?*

enormous (adj.) disorderly, abnormal, monstrous **TNK** V.i.62 [Arcite praying to Mars] *O great corrector of enormous times;* **KL** II.ii.167

enow (adv.) enough **H5** IV.v.19 [Orleans to Constable] *We are enow yet living in the field / To smother up the English in our throngs;* **AC** I.iv.11; **E3** IV.iv.49; **1H6** V.v.56; **Mac** IV.ii.57; **MV** IV.i.29

enpatron (v.) make a patron of, have under one's patronage **Lover** 224 [the woman, of her love-tokens] *Since I their altar, you enpatron me*

enpearce, enpierce (v.) ☞ empierce (v.)

enraged (adj.) **1** passionate, ardent, furiously aroused **Venus** 29 [of Venus] *Being so enraged, desire doth lend her force;* **MA** II.iii.102

2 inflamed, heated, roused **2H4** I.i.144 [Northumberland to Morton] *my limbs, / Weakened with grief, being now enraged with grief, / Are thrice themselves* ☞ enridged (adj.)

enrank (v.) set in ranks, draw up in battle lines **1H6** I.i.115 [Third Messenger to all, of Talbot] *No leisure had he to enrank his men*

enrapt (adj.) enraptured, inspired, carried away **TC** V.iii.65 [Priam to Hector] *I myself / Am like a prophet suddenly enrapt*

enridged (adj.) thrown into ridges, rippling **KL** IV.vi.71 [Edgar to Gloucester, of the imagined fiend] *he had … / Horns welked and waved like the enridged sea* [Q; F enraged]

enring (v.) form a ring round, encircle, surround **MND** IV.i.43 [Titania to Bottom] *the female ivy so / Enrings the barky fingers of the elm*

enrobe (v.) dress in a robe, put a gown on **MV** I.i.34 [Salerio to Antonio, of cargo lost from a wrecked ship] *Enrobe the roaring waters with my silks*

enrol (v.) record, register, legally enter **JC** III.ii.38 [Brutus to all, of Caesar] *The question of his death is enrolled in the Capitol;* **3H6** II.i.172; **LL** I.i.38

enrooted (adj.) entangled by the roots **2H4** IV.i.205 [Archbishop to Mowbray, of King Henry IV] *His foes are so enrooted with his friends*

enround (v.) surround, encircle **H5** IV.Chorus.36 [Chorus, of King Henry] *Upon his royal face there is no note / How dread an army hath enrounded him*

enscarped (adj.) sharp-sided, abruptly shelving **Oth** II.i.70 [Cassio to all, of the rocks] *Traitors enscarped to clog the guiltless keel* [F ensteep'd; Q1 enscerped] ☞ ensteeped (adj.)

enschedule (v.) put in a schedule, write down in a list **H5** V.ii.73 [King Henry to Burgundy, of the English demands] *Whose tenors and particular effects / You have, enscheduled briefly, in your hands*

ensconce, insconce (v.) **1** protect, conceal, shelter **MW** III.iii.84 [Falstaff to Mistress Ford] *I will ensconce me behind the arras;* **AW** II.iii.4; **CE** II.ii.38; **Luc** 1515; **MW** II.ii.25

2 secure, establish oneself firmly **Sonn** 49.9 [of his friend frowning on his defects] *Against that time do I ensconce me here*

enseamed (*adj.*) greasy, slimy **Ham** III.iv.93 [Hamlet to Gertrude] *the rank sweat of an enseamed bed* [F; Q2 *inseemed*]

ensear (*v.*) dry up, wither, make arid **Tim** IV.iii.188 [Timon alone, of the earth] *Ensear thy fertile and conceptious womb*

ensheltered (*adj.*) within shelter, in a safe haven **Oth** II.i.18 [Montano to Second Gentleman] *If that the Turkish fleet / Be not ensheltered … they are drowned*

enshield (*adj.*) shielded, defended **MM** II.iv.80 [Angelo to Isabella] *these black masks / Proclaim an enshield beauty ten times louder / Than beauty could*

ensign (*n.*) **1** standard, banner, flag **Cym** V.v.481 [Cymbeline to all] *let / A Roman, and a British ensign wave / Friendly together*; **JC** V.i.79; **RJ** V.iii.94

2 standard-bearer **JC** V.iii.3 [Cassius to Titinius] *This Ensign here of mine was turning back*

3 symbol, token, emblem **Tit** I.i.255 [Titus to Saturninus, of his sword, chariot, and prisoners] *Mine honour's ensigns humbled at thy feet*

ensinewed, insinewed (*adj.*) joined together in strength **2H4** IV.i.170 [Archbishop to Westmorland] *All members of our cause … / That are ensinewed to this action*

enskied (*adj.*) placed in heaven **MM** I.iv.34 [Lucio to Isabella] *I hold you as a thing enskied and sainted*

enstate (*bv.*) ➤ instate (*v.*)

ensteeped (*adj.*) located underwater, submerged **Oth** II.i.70 [Cassio to all, of the rocks] *Traitors ensteeped to clog the guiltless keel* [F; Q1 *enscerped*] ➤ enscarped (*adj.*)

ensue (*v.*) **1** follow [especially, as a logical outcome] **AY** I.iii.30 [Celia to Rosalind, of the Duke Senior loving Sir Rowland dearly] *Doth it therefore ensue that you should love his son dearly?*; **E3** V.i.91; **Luc** 502; **R2** II.i.197

2 befall, happen, become **WT** IV.i.25 [Time to audience, of Perdita] *What of her ensues / I list not prophesy*

enswathe (*v.*) tie up, bind together **Lover** 49 [of letters] *With sleided silk, feat and affectedly / Enswathed*

entail (*n.*) provision that an estate should pass to an heir **AW** IV.iii.271 [Parolles to First Soldier, of Dumaine] *he will … cut th'entail from all remainders*

entail to (*v.*) **1** bestow on, confer on, transfer to **3H6** I.i.194 [King to York] *I here entail / The crown to thee*; **E3** I.i.59

2 appoint as heir **3H6** I.i.235 [Queen to King, of York] *To entail him and his heirs unto the crown*

entame (*v.*) tame, subdue, quell **AY** III.v.48 [Rosalind as Ganymede to Phebe] *'Tis not your inky brows … / That can entame my spirits to your worship*

enter (*n.*) entrance, entering, arrival **LL** V.i.128 [Holofernes to Armado, of Mote as Hercules] *His enter and exit shall be strangling a snake*

enter (*v.*) **1** enter into, engage in **1H6** III.i.63 [Richard to himself, imagining the lords talking to him] *Must your bold verdict enter talk with lords?*

2 begin, take the first steps in **2H4** II.i.1 [Hostess to Fang] *have you entered the action?*; **2H4** II.i.9

3 recommend [to], introduce [to], admit into society **AC** IV.xiv.113 [Decretas to himself] *This sword but shown to Caesar … / Shall enter me with him*

enter in (*v.*) be acquainted with, be aware of **Cor** I.ii.2 [First Senator to Aufidius] *they of Rome are entered in our counsels*

entered (*adj.*) ➤ man-entered (*adj.*); well-entered (*adj.*)

enterlude (*n.*) ➤ interlude (*n.*)

entertain (*n.*) entertainment, reception, treatment **Per** I.i.120 [Antiochus to Pericles] *your entertain shall be / As doth befit our honour and your worth*

entertain (*v.*) **1** receive, admit, let in **CE** III.i.120 [Antipholus of Ephesus to Angelo] *mine own doors refuse to entertain me*; **2H4** V.ii.54; **Luc** 1629; **Per** II.ii.14; **TC** I.iii.354; **Venus** 969

2 welcome, receive kindly, treat well, show hospitality to **2H6** V.i.4 [York to and of himself] *burn bonfires clear and bright, / To entertain great England's lawful king*; **AY** III.ii.397; **Luc** 842; **R3** I.iv.134; **Tem** IV.i.75; **TS** II.i.244

3 receive, sustain, meet with **AC** II.i.46 [Pompey to Menas, of Antony and Caesar] *they have entertained cause enough / To draw their swords*

4 cherish, harbour, welcome **TC** II.iii.195 [Ulysses to Agamemnon] *add more coals to Cancer when he burns / With entertaining great Hyperion*; **MM** III.i.78; **Tem** I.ii.75

5 hire, employ, maintain, take into service **JC** V.v.60 [Octavius to all] *All that served Brutus, I will entertain them*; **AW** III.iii.88; **Cym** IV.ii.394; **MA** I.iii.54; **RJ** I.ii.256; **TG** IV.iv.67

6 consider, treat, think of **MW** II.i.80 [Mistress Page to Mistress Ford] *I'll entertain myself like one that I am not acquainted withal*

7 admit into consideration, grant as a possibility **RJ** III.i.171 [Benvolio to Prince, of Romeo] *Who had but newly entertained revenge*; **AC** II.vii.63

8 occupy, engage, fill up **MW** II.i.62 [Mistress Ford to Mistress Page, of revenge against Falstaff] *I think the best way were to entertain him with hope*

9 enter upon, engage in, accept **1H6** V.iv.175 [Richard to all] *here we entertain a solemn peace*

10 accept as true, allow, accommodate **CE** II.ii.195 [Antipholus of Syracuse to himself, of Adriana's approach] *Until I know this sure uncertainty, / I'll entertain the offered fallacy*; **H5** IV.Chorus.1

11 treat, deal with, handle **1H6** II.iii.71 [Countess to Talbot] *I am sorry that with reverence / I did not entertain thee as thou art*; **H5** I.ii.111; **1H6** I.iv.38; **KL** I.iv.57; **Tim** I.ii.184

12 maintain, keep up, practise **MV** I.i.90 [Gratiano to Antonio, of some men] *whose visages … do a wilful stillness entertain*; **Luc** 1514; **R2** II.ii.4

13 while away, pass away **Sonn** 39.11 *To entertain the time with thoughts of love*; **Luc** 1361; **R3** I.i.29

entertainer (*n.*) receiver, harbourer, person who considers **Tem** II.i.19 [Gonzalo to Alonso] *When every grief is entertained that's offered, / Comes to th'entertainer*

entertainment (*n.*) **1** treatment, hospitality, reception **Tem** I.ii.466 [Ferdinand to Prospero] *I will resist such entertainment*; **AC** III.xiii.140; **E3** V.i.211; **TN** I.v.207; **TS** III.i.2; **Venus** 1108

2 pleasant reception, favourable welcome **Tim** I.ii.178 [Timon to Flavius, of the senators] *let's be provided to show them entertainment*; **Cor** V.ii.61; **2H4** IV.v.174; **2H6** I.i.70; **Oth** III.iii.248; **TS** II.i.54

3 hospitality, provision for needs **KL** II.iv.201 [Regan to Lear] *I am … out of that provision / Which shall be needful for your entertainment*; **AY** IV.iv.69, IV.iii.144; **MW** I.iii.40

4 treatment, attitude, disposition **Cor** IV.v.10 [Coriolanus alone, of the Servingmen's attitude] *I have deserved no better entertainment / In being Coriolanus*; **Ham** V.ii.200; **Per** IV.ii.52; **WT** I.ii.118

5 manner of reception, way to handle **MM** III.ii.203 [Provost to Escalus, of the disguised Duke and Claudio] *this friar hath … advised him for th'entertainment of death*

6 feast, banquet **Tim** I.ii.144 [Timon to Ladies] *You have … / Set a fair fashion on our entertainment*

7 payroll, service, employment **AW** IV.i.15 [First Lord to all, of Parolles] *He must think us some band of strangers i'th' adversary's entertainment*; **AC** IV.vi.17; **Cor** IV.iii.40

8 [mistaken use] guest, resident **MW** IV.v.69 [Evans to Host] *Have a care of your entertainments*

enthralled (*adj.*) enslaved, made captive **TG** II.iv.132 [Valentine to Proteus] *Love hath chased sleep from my enthralled eyes*; **1H6** V.iii.101

enticing (*adj.*) acting as a decoy, seductive **2H6** I.iii.87 [Suffolk to Queen, of the Duchess of Gloucester] *myself have limed a bush for her, / And placed a quire of such enticing birds / That she will light to listen to the lays*

entire (*adj.*) sincere, genuine, earnest **TS** IV.ii.23 [Tranio as Lucentio to Hortensio] *I have often heard / Of your entire affection to Bianca* [also: complete, total]

entirely (*adv.*) sincerely, heartily **MV** III.ii.225 [Portia to Bassanio, of the arrivals] *They are entirely welcome;* **AW** I.iii.96; **MA** III.i.37

entitle, intitle (*v.*) have a rightful claim [to] **LL** V.ii.807 [Princess to King, of her challenge to him] *If this thou do deny, let our hands part, / Neither entitled in the other's heart* [also: inscribe] [F *intitled;* Q1 *Intiled*]; **Sonn** 37.7

entitule, intitule (*v.*) **1** entitle, grace with the name of **LL** V.i.7 [Nathaniel to Holofernes] *a companion of the King's, who is intituled, nominated, or called Don Adriano de Armado*

2 have a rightful claim, furnish with a title **Luc** 57 [of Lucrece's face] *beauty, in that white entituled / From Venus' doves, doth challenge that fair field*

entomb (*v.*) lay in a tomb, bury, inter **E3** III.iii.171 [King Edward to the English peers] *let us ... clear us of that scandalous crime, / Or be entombed in our innocence;* **Tim** V.iv.66

entrails (*n.*) inside, interior **Tit** II.iii.230 [Martius to Quintus, of Bassianus' ring shining] *And shows the ragged entrails of this pit*

entrance (*n.*) **1** admission, right of entering, entrance-fee **TS** II.i.54 [Petruchio to Baptista, of Hortensio as Licio] *for an entrance to my entertainment / I do present you with a man of mine*

2 arrival, coming in **Per** II.iii.64 [Simonides to Thaisa, of Pericles] *to make his entrance more sweet*

entranced (*adj.*) unconscious, insensible, thrown into a trance **Per** III.ii.93 [Cerimon to all, of Thaisa] *She hath not been entranced above five hours*

entreasured (*adj.*) ☛ intreasured (*adj.*)

entreat, intreat (*n.*) entreaty, supplication, plea **Tit** I.i.486 [Saturninus to Marcus, of Titus' sons] *at my lovely Tamora's entreats, / I do remit these young men's heinous faults;* **R3** III.vii.224[Q]; **Tit** I.i.452

entreat, intreat (*v.*) **1** persuade, prevail upon **2H4** II.i.181 [Falstaff to Gower] *shall I entreat you with me to dinner?;* **AY** I.ii.139, 150; **1H6** V.iii.21; **TC** V.v.265, 274

2 beseech, beg, ask earnestly **E3** I.i.53 [Audley to King Edward] *The Duke of Lorraine ... / Entreats he may have conference with your highness;* **1H6** II.ii.40

3 negotiate, intervene, parley **2H6** IV.iv.9 [King to Buckingham, of the rebels] *I'll send some holy bishop to entreat;* **AY** IV.iii.73; **KL** III.iii.5

4 treat, handle, deal with **TC** IV.iv.112 [Troilus to Diomedes, of Cressida] *Entreat her fair;* **2H6** II.iv.81; **3H6** I.i.271; **R2** III.i.37

entreatment (*n.*) interaction, exchange, discourse **Ham** I.iii.122 [Polonius to Ophelia] *Set your entreatments at a higher rate / Than a command to parle*

entrench, intrench (*v.*) **1** put within a trench **E3** III.iv.87 [Prince Edward to King Edward] *thousands had entrenched me round about* [i.e. surrounded me]; **E3** IV.ii.3; **1H6** I.iv.9

2 gash, make a deep cut in **AW** II.i.44 [Parolles to Lords, of Spurio's cheek] *it was this very sword entrenched it*

entwist (*v.*) clasp with a twist, entwine, wreathe around **MND** IV.i.42 [Titania to Bottom] *So doth the woodbine the sweet honeysuckle / Gently entwist*

enure, inure (*v.*) accustom, habituate, adapt **TN** II.v.143 [Malvolio reading the letter] *to inure thyself to what thou art like to be, cast thy humble slough and appear fresh;* **Lover** 251; **Luc** 321

enurn (*v.*) ☛ inurn (*v.*)

envenom (*v.*) poison, taint, destroy **KJ** III.i.63 [Constance to Salisbury, of King Philip] *Envenom him with words;* **AY** II.iii.15

envenomed (*adj.*) poisoned, infected with venom **Ham** V.ii.315 [Hamlet to all, of Laertes' sword] *The point envenomed too?;* **Ham** V.ii.311; **2H6** III.ii.267

envious (*adj.*) malicious, spiteful, vindictive, full of enmity **AY** II.i.4 [Duke Senior to all] *Are not these woods / More free from peril than the envious court?* ☛ FEW, p.xxi

enviously (*adv.*) spitefully, maliciously, vindictively **Ham** IV.v.6 [Gentleman to Gertrude, of Ophelia] *she ... / Spurns enviously at straws*

envire (*v.*) surround, encircle, beset **E3** II.i.415 [Countess to Warwick] *To have escaped the danger of my foes, / And to be ten times worse envired by friends!* [QQ *inuierd*]

environ (*v.*) surround, envelop, encircle, engulf **1H6** V.iv.90 [Pucelle to all] *darkness and the gloomy shade of death / Environ you;* **3H6** II.i.50; **R3** I.iv.59; **RJ** IV.iii.50; **TG** I.i.16; **Tit** III.i.94

envoy (*n.*) ☛ l'envoy (*n.*)

envy (*n.*) **1** malice, ill-will, enmity **H8** III.i.113 [Wolsey to Queen Katherine] *You turn the good we offer into envy;* **Cor** IV.v.106; **E3** III.ii.12; **MV** IV.i.126; **R2** I.ii.21; **Tem** I.ii.258

2 admiration, desire [to be like], jealousy **Per** IV.Chorus.12 [Gower alone] *envy, oft the wrack / Of earned praise;* **Cor** I.viii.4; **Cym** II.iii.127; **TNK** II.i.144

envy, envy at (*v.*) **1** show malice [towards], hate, regard with ill will **H8** V.iii.112 [Cromwell to all, of Cranmer] *whose honesty the devil / And his disciples only envy at;* **TS** II.i.18 [Bianca to Katherina, of Gremio] *Is it for him you do envy me so?;* **Cor** III.iii.57, 95; **2H6** III.i.206

2 begrudge, resent, object to **KJ** III.iv.73 [Constance to King Philip, of her strands of hair] *now I envy at their liberty*

enwheel (*v.*) encircle, surround, ring **Oth** II.i.87 [Cassio to Desdemona] *the grace of heaven ... / Enwheel thee round*

enwomb (*v.*) be present in the womb [as], be born **AW** I.iii.139 [Countess to Helena] *I ... put you in the catalogue of those / That were enwombed mine*

enwrap (*v.*) absorb, engross, enfold **TN** IV.iii.3 [Sebastian alone] *though 'tis wonder that enwraps me thus, / Yet 'tis not madness*

Ephesian (*n.*) good mate, old drinking companion **2H4** II.ii.143 [Page to Prince Henry, of Falstaff's friends] *Ephesians, my lord, of the old church;* **MW** IV.v.16

epicure (*n.*) **1** [follower of Epicurus] someone who does not believe in divine power or a future life **AC** II.vii.52 [Antony to Caesar, of Lepidus believing that a crocodile transmigrates] *else he is a very epicure*

2 pleasure-seeker, glutton **E3** III.i.25 [King John to all] *in Netherland, / Among those ever-bibbing epicures;* **Mac** V.iii.8

Epicurean (*adj.*) **1** sensual, lecherous, pleasure-seeking **MW** II.ii.273 [Ford alone, of Falstaff] *What a damned Epicurean rascal is this!*

2 devoted to the pleasures of eating, cultivating gluttony **AC** II.i.24 [Pompey to all, of Antony] *Epicurean cooks / Sharpen with cloyless sauce his appetite*

epicurism (*n.*) gluttony, gorging, sensual excess **KL** I.iv.240 [Gonerill to Lear, of her court] *epicurism and lust / Makes it ... like a tavern*

epithet (*n.*) turn of phrase, expression **E3** II.i.30 [King Edward to himself] *With epithets and accents of the Scot;* **LL** V.i.15, ii.171; **MA** V.ii.61; **Oth** I.i.14

epitheton (*n.*) epithet, adjective, description **LL** I.ii.13 [Armado to Mote, of calling him 'tender juvenal'] *as a congruent epitheton appertaining to thy young days* [F *apathaton*]

epitome (*n.*) miniature, abridgement, abstract **Cor** V.iii.68 [Volumnia to Coriolanus, of Young Martius] *This is a poor epitome of yours*

equal (*adj.*) **1** fair, equitable, evenhanded **H8** II.ii.106 [King Henry to and of Campeius and Wolsey] *Two equal men;* **AY** I.i.165; **Cor** I.x.14; **H8** II.iv.18; **TNK** I.iii.32, V.iv.115

2 precise, exact, just **MV** I.iii.146 [Shylock to Antonio, of his bond] *let the forfeit / Be nominated for an equal pound / Of your fair flesh;* **2H4** IV.i.67

3 of the same social position; or: of equivalent fortune **Tim** I.i.144 [Timon to Old Athenian, of his daughter] *How shall she be endowed / If she be mated with an equal husband?*

equal *(v.)* be compared with, be likened to **3H6** V.v.55 [Queen to all, of the killing of the Prince] *They that stabbed Caesar ... / Did not offend ... / If this foul deed were by to equal it*

equal *(adv.)* equally **H8** I.i.159 [Buckingham to Norfolk, of Wolsey] *he is equal ravenous / As he is subtle*

equally *(adv.)* **1** to an equal degree, justly **MA** I.i.12 [Messenger to Leonato, of Claudio's honour] *Much deserved on his part and equally remembered by Don Pedro*
2 with justice, justly, impartially **KL** V.iii.46 [Albany to Edmund, of the captives] *to use them / As we shall find their merits and our safety / May equally determine*

equalness *(n.)* equality **AC** V.i.48 [Caesar to all, of Antony] *our stars, / Unreconciliable, should divide / Our equalness to this*

equinoctial *(n.)* [mock-astronomy] equator [celestial or terrestrial] **TN** II.iii.23 [Sir Andrew to Feste] *thou spok'st of ... the Vapians passing the equinoctial of Queubus*

equinox *(n.)* counterbalance, having one as long as the other **Oth** II.iii.119 [Iago to Montano, of Cassio] *do but see his vice: / 'Tis to his virtue a just equinox*

equipage *(n.)* **1** equipment, fitted-out condition **Sonn** 32.12 [of himself] *A dearer birth than this his love had brought / To march in ranks of better equipage*
2 [unclear meaning] small parts, instalments **MW** II.ii.4 [Pistol to Falstaff] *I will retort the sum in equipage* [Q only]

equity *(n.)* **1** justice, impartiality, fairness **1H4** II.ii.98 [Falstaff to all] *An the Prince and Poins be not two arrant cowards there's no equity stirring;* **2H6** III.i.146; **KL** III.vi.37
2 right, just demand **KJ** II.i.241 [King Philip to Hubert, of Arthur] *For this downtrodden equity we tread / In warlike march these greens before your town*

equivocal *(adj.)* equivocating, quibbling, evasive **AW** V.iii.249 [King to all, of Parolles] *What an equivocal companion is this!*

equivocation *(n.)* ambiguous usage, double-meaning **Ham** V.i.136 [Hamlet to Horatio] *We must speak by the card, or equivocation will undo us;* **Mac** V.v.43

equivocator *(n.)* dealer in ambiguities, trader in double meanings **Mac** II.iii.8 [Porter alone, of someone knocking] *here's an equivocator that could swear in both the scales against either scale;* **Mac** II.iii.11, 29

ere *(prep.)* before **Ham** II.ii.575 [Hamlet alone, of Claudius] *ere this / I should ha' fatted all the region kites / With this slave's offal*

ere *(conj.)* **1** before **Ham** III.ii.339 [Rosencrantz to Hamlet, of Gertrude] *She desires to speak with you in her closet ere you go to bed*
2 rather than **TNK** I.i.95 [Second Queen to Hippolyta] *weep ere you fail*

ere that *(conj.)* before **1H6** III.i.97 [Third Servingman to and of Gloucester] *ere that we will suffer such a prince ... / To be disgraced*

erection *(n.)* malapropism for 'direction' **MW** III.v.37 [Mistress Quickly to Falstaff, of John and Robert] *they mistook their erection*

erewhile *(adv.)* a short time ago, a while before **MND** III.ii.274 [Hermia to Lysander] *I am as fair now as I was erewhile;* **AY** II.iv.86, III.v.105; **LL** IV.i.98

ergo *(adv.)* therefore **TS** IV.iii.126 [Grumio to Tailor] *I bid thy master cut out the gown, but I did not bid him cut it to pieces. Ergo, thou liest;* **AW** I.iii.49; **CE** IV.iii.56; **LL** V.ii.589; **MV** II.ii.52 ☞ **LATIN**, p.643; argal *(adv.)*

eriall *(adj.)* ☞ aerial *(adj.)*

eringo *(n.)* candied sweetmeat from the sea holly [eryngium] believed to be an aphrodisiac **MW** V.v.20 [Falstaff to Mistress Ford] *Let the sky ... hail kissing-comfits, and snow eringoes*

err *(v.)* go astray from duty, turn away **3H6** IV.viii.46 [King to Exeter, of his subjects] *I have not been ... forward of revenge, though they much erred*

errand *(n.)* message, report, news **Cor** V.ii.58 [Menenius to First Watch] *I'll say an errand for you*

errant *(adj.)* wandering, straying, erring **TNK** III.ii.34 [Gaoler's Daughter alone] *which way now? / The best way is the next way to a grave; / Each errant step beside is torment;* **TC** I.iii.9

erring *(adj.)* straying, wandering, drifting **Oth** I.iii.350 [Iago to Roderigo, of Othello's marriage to Desdemona] *a frail vow betwixt an erring barbarian and a super-subtle Venetian;* **AY** III.ii.126; **Ham** I.i.155

erroneous *(adj.)* **1** misguided, mistaken, deluded **R3** I.iv.198 [Clarence to Murderers] *Erroneous vassals!*
2 criminal, wicked, evil **3H6** II.v.90 [Father to himself, of the war] *What stratagems ... / Erroneous, mutinous, and unnatural, / This deadly quarrel daily doth beget!*

error *(n.)* **1** wandering, roaming, straying [from a course] **Oth** V.ii.110 [Othello to Emilia, of the reported murder] *It is the very error of the moon*
2 deceit, falsehood, deception **TC** V.iii.110 [Troilus to Pandarus, of Cressida] *My love with words and errors still she feeds*
3 defect, flaw, blemish **TNK** IV.ii.31 [Emilia alone, of Palamon] *Yet these that we count errors may become him*

erst *(adv.)* **1** formerly, once, before **Tit** V.iii.79 [Marcus to Lucius, of Aeneas] *Speak, Rome's dear friend, as erst our ancestor ... did discourse;* **H5** I.i.48; **2H6** II.iv.13; **Per** I.i.50; **Sonn** 12.6
2 not long ago, just now **AY** III.v.95 [Phebe to Silvius] *Thy company, which erst was irksome to me*

eruption *(n.)* **1** disturbance, outbreak of calamity, turbulence **JC** I.iii.78 [Cassius to Casca, of weird happenings] *A man no mightier than thyself ... / And fearful, as these strange eruptions are;* **Ham** I.i.69; **1H4** III.i.25
2 outburst of merriment, sally of wit **LL** V.i.108 [Armado to Holofernes, of entertainment] *the curate and your sweet self are good at such eruptions*

escape *(n.)* **1** outburst, outbreak, sally **MM** IV.i.62 [disguised Duke alone, of greatness] *thousand escapes of wit / Make thee the father of their idle dream*
2 elopement, running off, stealing away **Oth** I.iii.195 [Brabantio to Desdemona, of other children] *thy escape would teach me tyranny / To hang clogs on them*
3 transgression, misdeed, moral error **Tit** IV.ii.112 [Chiron to all, of Tamora] *Rome will despise her for this foul escape*

eschew *(v.)* avoid, escape, prevent **MW** V.v.229 [Page to Fenton] *What cannot be eschewed must be embraced*

escote *(v.)* pay for, support, maintain **Ham** II.ii.345 [Hamlet to Rosencrantz, of the child players] *How are they escoted?*

esile *(n.)* ☞ eisel *(n.)*

esperance *(n.)* hope, expectation, optimism **TC** V.ii.123 [Troilus to Ulysses] *there is a credence in my heart, / An esperance so obstinately strong;* **KL** IV.i.4

espial *(n.)* spy, watcher, observer **1H6** I.iv.8 [Master Gunner to Boy] *The Prince's espials have informed me;* **Ham** III.i.32; **1H6** IV.iii.6

espouse *(v.)* unite (in marriage), contract **Tit** I.i.245 [Saturninus to Titus, of Lavinia] *will I ... in the sacred Pantheon her espouse;* **H5** II.i.74, IV.vi.26; **2H6** I.i.9, 46; **Luc** 20; **Tit** I.i.331

espy *(v.)* catch sight of, discern, see **Per** V.Chorus.18 [Gower alone] *Lysimachus our Tyrian ship espies;* **KJ** II.i.506; **Lover** 5; **Luc** 361; **TC** III.ii.64; **Tit** II.iii.48

esquire *(n.)* **1** candidate for knighthood, attendant on a knight **H5** I.i.14 [Canterbury to Ely] *Six thousand and two hundred good esquires;* **H5** IV.viii.83
2 gentleman, country squire **2H4** III.ii.56 [Shallow to Bardolph] *I am Robert Shallow, sir, a poor esquire of this county;* **2H6** IV.x.41

essay (n.) trial, testing, proof **KL** I.ii.45 [Edmund to Gloucester, of Edgar's supposed letter] *I hope ... he wrote this but as an essay or taste of my virtue;* **Sonn** 110.8

essence (n.) very life, foundation of being **TG** III.i.182 [Valentine alone, of Silvia] *She is my essence*

essentially (adv.) in fact, really, deep down **Ham** III.iv.188 [Hamlet to Gertrude] *I essentially am not in madness, / But mad in craft*

-est (ending) ☞ **VERB FORMS**, p.481

estate (n.) **1** state, situation, circumstances **H5** IV.i.94 [Williams to disguised King Henry, of Erpingham] *what thinks he of our estate?;* **AC** V.ii.152; **KL** V.iii.207; **MV** I.i.43; **RJ** III.iii.64; **WT** IV.ii.40
2 high rank, standing, status **Ham** V.i.217 [Hamlet to Horatio, of the person about to be buried] *'Twas of some estate;* **E3** II.i.99; **H8** IV.i.37; **Luc** 92; **MV** II.ix.41; **TN** I.v.248
3 degree of rank, place in life, type of person **AW** I.iii.108 [Steward to Countess, of Helena and Bertram] *such difference betwixt their two estates;* **LL** V.ii.834; **R3** III.vii.212; **TS** III.ii.99
4 state, kingdom **Mac** I.iv.38 [King to all] *We will establish our estate upon / Our eldest, Malcolm* [i.e. our succession]; **H8** II.ii.68
5 piece of property **Per** IV.ii.31 [Pander to Bawd] *if in our youths we could pick up some pretty estate*
6 endowment, bestowal **Cor** II.i.109 [Menenius to Virgilia, of a letter from Coriolanus] *It gives me an estate of seven years' health*
7 fortune, prosperity **Tim** III.ii.7 [First Stranger to Lucius, of Timon] *his estate shrinks from him*

estate (v.) endow, settle upon, bestow (up)on **AY** V.ii.11 [Oliver to Orlando] *all the revenue that was old Sir Rowland's will I estate upon you;* **MND** I.i.98; **Tem** IV.i.85; **TNK** II.i.11

esteem (n.) **1** value, estimation, worth **AW** V.iii.1 [King to Countess, of Helena's supposed death] *We lost a jewel of her, and our esteem / Was made much poorer by it;* **Cym** V.v.253; **2H6** III.ii.21
2 reputation, regard, respectability **TS** IV.v.64 [Petruchio to Vincentio, of Bianca] *she is of good esteem*
3 high rank, nobility **1H6** III.iv.8 [Talbot to King] *five hundred prisoners of esteem*

esteem (v.) regard, think, consider **TS** Induction.i.120 [Lord to Servant, of Sly] *Who for this seven years hath esteemed him / No better than a poor and loathsome beggar* [i.e. thought himself]; **1H6** IV.i.5

estimable (adj.) appreciative, full of regard **TN** II.i.24 [Sebastian to Antonio, of Viola's beauty] *I could not with such estimable wonder over-far believe that*

estimate (n.) **1** value, esteem, estimation **Sonn** 87.2 *like enough thou know'st thy estimate;* **AW** II.i.180; **TC** II.ii.55; **Tim** I.i.14
2 reputation, honour, respectability **Cor** III.iii.114 [Cominius to Sicinius] *My dear wife's estimate;* **R2** II.iii.56

estimation (n.) **1** esteem, respect, reputation **Ham** II.ii.333 [Hamlet to Rosencrantz, of the players] *Do they hold the same estimation they did when I was in the city?;* **CE** III.i.102; **Cor** V.ii.59; **LL** I.i.259; **MA** II.ii.22; **Oth** I.iii.271
2 value, worth, high quality **AW** V.iii.4 [King to Countess, of Bertram and Helena] *your son ... lacked the sense to know / Her estimation home*
3 valued object, treasure **TC** II.ii.92 [Troilus to all] *why do you now ... / Beggar the estimation which you prized / Richer than sea and land?;* **Cym** I.v.88
4 guess, conjecture, speculation **1H4** I.iii.266 [Worcester to Hotspur] *I speak not this in estimation, / As what I think might be*
5 estimated amount, reckoning **MV** IV.i.328 [Portia as Balthasar to Shylock, of weighing Antonio's flesh] *if the scale do turn / But in the estimation of a hair*

estridge (n.) type of large hawk, goshawk **AC** III.xiii.196 [Enobarbus alone, of Antony in a fury] *in that mood / The dove will peck the estridge;* **1H4** IV.i.98

etcetera (n.) substitute for an indelicate word, here probably 'vagina' **2H4** II.iv.179 [Pistol to all] *And are etceteras nothings?*

eternal (adj.) immortal, everlasting **Mac** III.i.67 [Macbeth alone] *for Banquo's issue have I ... mine eternal jewel / Given to the common enemy of man* [i.e. my soul]; **3H6** III.iii.124; **Sonn** 38.12

eterne (adj.) eternal, everlasting, for ever **Ham** II.ii.488 [First Player to all present, of Mars' armour] *forged for proof eterne;* **Mac** III.ii.38

eternity (n.) perpetual existence, lasting for ever **2H6** II.iv.90 [Duchess of Gloucester to herself] *Death, at whose name I oft have been afeard, / Because I wished this world's eternity*

eternize (v.) immortalize, make famous for ever **2H6** V.iii.31 [Warwick to all] *Saint Albans battle ... / Shall be eternized in all age to come*

Ethiop, Ethiope (adj./n.) Ethiopian, African, person with a dark countenance **AY** IV.iii.36 [Rosalind as Ganymede to Silvius, of Phebe's letter to Ganymede] *Such Ethiop words, blacker in their effect / Than in their countenance;* **RJ** I.v.46 [Romeo to Servingman, of Juliet] *she hangs upon the cheek of night / As a rich jewel in an Ethiop's ear;* **LL** IV.iii.116; **MA** V.iv.38; **PassP** XVI.16; **TG** II.vi.26 ☞ **WORLD**, p.634

Ethiopian (n.) negro, black-skinned person **WT** IV.iv.361 [Florizel to disguised Polixenes, of Perdita's hand] *as white as ... Ethiopian's tooth*

even (n.) **1** evening **RJ** II.vi.21 [Juliet to Friar] *Good even to my ghostly confessor;* **H5** III.i.20; **Sonn** 28.12, 132.7; **TG** V.ii.42 ☞ **GREETINGS**, p.206
2 plain truth, straightforward explanation **H5** II.i.117 [Nym to all, of Falstaff] *The King hath run bad humours on the knight, that's the even of it*

even (adj.) **1** straightforward, forthright, direct **Ham** II.ii.287 [Hamlet to Rosencrantz and Guildenstern] *be even and direct with me;* **H5** IV.viii.108; **H8** III.i.37; **MA** IV.i.261
2 steady, steadfast, unwavering **JC** II.i.133 [Brutus to all] *do not stain / The even virtue of our enterprise*
3 smooth, without obstacles **R3** III.vii.156 [Richard to Buckingham] *if ... my path were even to the crown;* **2H4** II.iii.2
4 level, horizontal, flat **JC** V.i.17 [Antony to Octavius] *lead your battle softly on / Upon the left hand of the even field;* **H5** V.ii.48; **1H6** IV.ii.12; **KJ** II.i.399, 576
5 real, exact, precise **AW** V.iii.323 [King to all] *Let us ... this story know / To make the even truth in pleasure flow*
6 equal, alike, same **R2** III.iv.36 [Gardener to Second Man] *All must be even in our government;* **AW** II.i.191; **TN** V.i.236

even (v.) **1** make good, settle, put straight **TNK** I.iv.11 [Theseus to Queens] *we will ... even each thing / Our haste does leave imperfect;* **AW** I.iii.3
2 [unclear meaning] keep pace with; or: sort out, reach agreement over **Cym** III.iv.183 [Innogen to Pisanio] *we'll even / All that good time will give us*

even, e'en (adv.) **1** just, exactly **TC** II.i.98 [Thersites to Achilles, agreeing with his observation] *E'en so;* **AY** I.i.80; **Ham** V.i.69, 180; **Venus** 55 ☞ **DISCOURSE MARKERS**, p.127
2 just [now] **Ham** IV.iii.20 [Hamlet to Claudius, of Polonius] *A certain convocation of politic worms are e'en at him;* **1H4** II.iv.192 [Prince Hal to Falstaff, of the robbers] *Thou saidst but two even now;* **KJ** III.i.233; **Tim** II.ii.73; **TNK** IV.ii.47
3 carefully, steadily, circumspectly **1H4** I.iii.279 [Worcester to Hotspur and Northumberland] *bear ourselves as even as we can, / The King will always think him in our debt;* **Tit** IV.iv.8
4 equably, evenly, steadily **KJ** II.i.576 [Bastard alone, of the world] *Made to run even upon even ground* [first instance]; **Cor** IV.vii.37
5 quite, fully, simply **AC** V.ii.154 [Cleopatra to Caesar] *The ingratitude of this Seleucus does / Even make me wild;* **Cor** I.iv.59; **MW** IV.vi.12

even over (*v.*) make sense of, straighten out KL IV.vii.80 [Doctor to Cordelia, of Lear] *it is danger / To make him even o'er the time he has lost*

even to't just go for it Ham II.ii.428 [Hamlet to Players] *We'll e'en to't like French falconers*

even-Christian (*n.*) fellow Christian Ham V.i.28 [First Clown to Second Clown] *pity that great folk should have countenance in this world to drown or hang themselves more than their even-Christian* [F *euen Christian*; Q2 *even-Christen*; Q1 *other people*]

evenly (*adv.*) **1** directly, in a straight line H5 II.iv.91 [Exeter to French King, of King Henry] *you find him evenly derived / From … / Edward the Third;* 1H4 III.i.99
 2 in an even direction, along the same lines MA II.ii.7 [Don John to Borachio, of Claudio] *whatsoever comes athwart his affection ranges evenly with mine*

even-pleached (*adj.*) with branches evenly layered H5 V.ii.42 [Burgundy to King Henry and the French King, of peace] *her hedges even-pleached* ➤ **pleached** (*adj.*) 2

event (*n.*) outcome, issue, consequence 1H6 IV.i.191 [Exeter alone, of the quarrelling lords] *it doth presage some ill event;* KL I.iv.345; MA IV.i.233; TN II.iii.169; TNK I.i.113; TS III.i.126

ever (*adv.*) constantly, continually, at all times R2 II.ii.133 [Bagot to Bushy and Green] *we ever have been near the King;* Per III.i.30

ever among all the while; or: everywhere 2H4 V.iii.22 [Silence singing] *And lusty lads roam here and there … ever among so merrily*

ever and anon ➤ anon, ever and

ever-bibbing (*adj.*) always drinking, tippling E3 III.i.25 [King John to all] *in Netherland, / Among those ever-bibbing epicures*

ever-during (*adj.*) always enduring, everlasting Luc 224 [Tarquin to himself, of his intention] *this surviving shame, / Whose crime will bear an ever-during blame*

everlasting (*adj.*) made of the durable material of an arresting officer's uniform CE IV.ii.33 [Dromio of Syracuse to Adriana, of Antipholus of Ephesus] *A devil in an everlasting garment hath him*

evermore (*adv.*) always, constantly, at all times R2 II.iii.65 [Bolingbroke to Ross and Willoughby] *Evermore thank's the exchequer of the poor*

everywhere (*adv.*) here and there, in many places TNK II.i.152 [Palamon to Arcite] *What a misery / It is to live abroad, and everywhere!*

evidence (*n.*) **1** witness, testimony, avowal AC I.iii.74 [Antony to Cleopatra, of himself] *My precious queen, forbear, / And give true evidence to his love* [i.e. bear true witness]; 2H6 III.ii.21; Luc 1650; MA IV.i.35; R3 I.iv.186
 2 evidence against someone, witnesses for the prosecution KL III.vi.35 [Lear to disguised Kent, of his daughters] *bring in their evidence*

evident (*adj.*) **1** certain, conclusive, definite Cym II.iv.120 [Posthumus to Iachimo, of Innogen] *Render me some corporal sign about her / More evident than this*
 2 inevitable, certain, inescapable Cor V.iii.112 [Volumnia to Coriolanus] *We must find / An evident calamity;* Cor IV.vii.52

evil (*n.*) **1** affliction, misfortune, hardship AY II.vii.133 [Orlando to Duke Senior, of Adam] *Oppressed with two weak evils, age and hunger;* H8 II.i.141; JC II.ii.81; TN II.i.6
 2 malady, illness, disease Cor I.i.177 [Martius to Citizens] *A sick man's appetite, that for / Which would increase his evil;* AY II.vii.67; KJ III.iv.114; WT II.iii.56
 3 [unclear meaning] hovel; privy; brothel MM II.ii.172 [Angelo alone] *Having waste ground enough, / Shall we desire to raze the sanctuary / And pitch our evils there*

Evil, the the king's evil, scrofula [a lymphatic disease] Mac IV.iii.146 [Malcolm to Macduff, of the people's disease] *'Tis called the Evil*

evitate (*v.*) avoid, avert, get away from MW V.v.220 [Fenton to all, of his marriage to Anne] *therein she doth evitate and shun / A thousand irreligious cursed hours*

ewer (*n.*) pitcher containing water for washing hands Tim III.i.7 [Lucullus to himself] *I dreamt of a silver basin and ewer tonight;* TS Induction.i.55, II.i.341

exact (*adj.*) accomplished, highly skilled, expert Tim II.ii.161 [Flavius to Timon] *Call me before th'exactest auditors;* TC I.iii.180

exact (*v.*) enforce payment, take taxes 2H6 IV.vii.64 [Say to the rebels] *When have I aught exacted at your hands, / But to maintain the King, the realm, and you?*

exaction (*n.*) **1** extortionate taxation, exorbitant demand H8 I.ii.47 [Queen Katherine to Wolsey, of taxation] *These exactions … are / Most pestilent to th'hearing;* H8 I.ii.25, 52; R2 II.i.249
 2 exacting, enforcement MV I.iii.161 [Shylock to Bassanio, of Antonio] *what should I gain / By the exaction of the forfeiture?*

exactly (*adv.*) **1** completely, totally, entirely Ham I.ii.200 [Horatio to Hamlet, of the Ghost] *a figure like your father, / Armed at point exactly*
 2 expressly, with great propriety R2 I.i.140 [Mowbray to John of Gaunt] *I … exactly begged / Your grace's pardon*

exalt (*v.*) lift up, upraise JC I.iii.8 [Casca to Cicero] *I have seen / Th'ambitious ocean … be exalted with the threatening clouds*

examination (*n.*) **1** deposition, testimony, statement H8 I.i.116 [Wolsey to Secretary, of Buckingham's surveyor] *Where's his examination?;* H8 II.i.16
 2 malapropism for 'examine' MA III.v.54 [Dogberry to Verges] *We are now to examination these men*

example (*n.*) precedent, parallel case TN II.v.38 [Malvolio to himself, of his marrying Olivia] *There is example for't;* H8 I.ii.90; KJ III.iv.13; Lover 268

example (*v.*) **1** find an example for, provide a model for Tim IV.iii.437 [Timon to Bandits] *I'll example you with thievery* [i.e. give you justification for thieving]; Sonn 84.4; TC I.iii.132
 2 exemplify, illustrate LL III.i.82 [Armado to Mote, of l'envoy] *I will example it;* KJ IV.iii.56
 3 act as a precedent for LL IV.iii.122 [Dumaine to himself] *Ill, to example ill, / Would from my forehead wipe a perjured note*
 4 justify, defend, vindicate LL I.ii.111 [Armado to Mote, of being in love] *I may example my digression by some mighty precedent*

exampled (*adj.*) exemplified, illustrated, instantiated H5 I.ii.156 [Canterbury to King Henry, of England] *hear her but exampled by herself* [i.e. by her own past deeds]

exasperate (*adj.*) enraged, incensed, angered TC V.i.27 [Thersites to Patroclus] *Why art thou then exasperate*

exceed (*v.*) outdo, surpass, excel, be superior TNK III.vi.46 [Palamon to Arcite] *Wilt thou exceed in all;* Luc 229; MA III.iv.16; Per II.iii.16

exceeding (*adj.*) very great, huge, exceptional E3 III.iii.67 [King John to King Edward] *with me have I brought / Exceeding store of treasure;* AW V.i.1; 1H6 IV.iv.41; 2H6 V.i.70

exceeding (*adv.*) exceedingly, extremely, very CE I.i.57 [Egeon to Duke, of the Dromio twins] *their parents were exceeding poor;* 1H4 IV.ii.62; 2H4 V.iii.3; H8 II.i.52; MV I.i.67, II.ii.47

excellency (*n.*) excellence, accomplishment, talent MA II.iii.44 [Don Pedro to Balthasar] *It is the witness still of excellency / To put a strange face on his own perfection*

excellent (*adj.*) **1** [of people] all-excelling, pre-eminent, superlative 1H6 I.ii.110 [Charles to Pucelle] *Excellent Pucelle, if thy name be so;* R3 IV.iv.53
 2 [in a bad or neutral sense] exceptionally great, supreme, extreme KL I.ii.118 [Edmund alone] *This is the excellent foppery of the world;* AC I.i.40; Tit II.iii.7

except (*conj.*) unless 1H6 III.i.114 [Warwick to Gloucester and Winchester] *Yield … / Except you mean with obstinate repulse / To slay your sovereign*

EXCLAMATIONS

Shakespearian English has some distinctive ways of expressing attitudes in short exclamatory sentences, and some (e.g. *come, come*, **1H4** IV.iii.16) are still used today. As with modern English, there are more expressing negative emotions (contempt, disdain, disgust, impatience, indignation, etc.) than positive ones (cheerfulness, delight, assurance, etc.). In some cases, words are used whose meaning is totally dependent on the context, as interpreted by the actor, sometimes permitting a wide range of possible tones of voice: these are *a* or *ah* (**2H4** II.i.49), *ha* (**MM** II.ii.164), and *hum* (**Ham** II.ii.586). Sometimes a vocalization is associated with a particular character, such as Henry VIII's use of *ha* (**H8** III.ii.61). Expressions of regret are grouped separately: ◆ **REGRETS**, p.367.

Negative attitudes

alas	**3H6** V.i.109	*Alas, I am not cooped here for defence!*	usually regret, but here more indignation
blessed fig's end	**Oth** II.i.244	[Roderigo] *she's full of most blessed condition.* [Iago] *Blessed fig's end!*	worthlessness – cf. modern 'my foot!'
buzz	**Ham** II.ii.392	[Polonius] *The actors are come hither, my lord.* [Hamlet] *Buzz, buzz*	impatience or contempt, when being told something already known
fico for, a	**MW** I.iii.27	*'Steal'? Foh, / A fico for the phrase!*	contempt, often expressed in a gesture [using the thumb between the first and second fingers]
fie	**Venus** 611	*'Fie, fie,' he says, 'you crush me'*	disgust, indignation, shame
fie on	**CE** V.i.27	*Fie on thee, wretch*	disgust, indignation, shame
fig for, a	**2H6** II.iii.67	*a fig for Peter!*	contempt, often expressed in a gesture [as for 'fico']
foh	**Ham** II.ii.585	*Fie upon't, foh!*	disgust, abhorrence
go to	**Ham** I.iii.11	*Ay, 'fashion' you may call it. Go to, go to*	impatience – cf. modern 'come, come' [see also below]
hanged, be	**H8** V.iv.17	*How got they in, and be hanged?*	impatience, irritation
how	**KL** I.i.94	*How, how, Cordelia! Mend your speech a little*	surprise, irritation – cf. modern 'what?'
how now	**LL** IV.iii.198	*How now, what is in you?*	surprise, reproach
hoyday	**R3** IV.iv.459	*Hoyday, a riddle!*	contemptuous surprise, impatience
marry come up	**RJ** II.v.62	*Are you so hot? Marry come up, I trow*	impatience, surprise, shock [real or affected]
marry trap with you	**MW** I.i.155	*I will say 'Marry trap with you'*	contempt, insult [unclear meaning]
me, O	**Cor** II.iii.53	*O me, the gods! / You must not speak of that*	shock, horrified surprise – cf. modern 'goodness me'
much	**2H4** II.iv.129	*God's light, with two points on your shoulder? Much!*	scornful disbelief, incredulity
out	**TS** IV.i.133	*Out, you rogue! You pluck my foot awry*	impatience, irritation
out, alas	**3H6** I.iv.19	*we charged again; but, out alas! / We budged again*	disgust, reproach, indignation, regret
out on	**CE** II.i.68	*I know not thy mistress. Out on thy mistress!*	indignation, reproach
out upon it	**TNK** II.iii.5	*To marry him is hopeless; / To be his whore is witless. Out upon't!*	frustration, irritation

except, except against *(v.)* **1** take exception to, object to, repudiate **R2** I.i.72 [Bolingbroke to Mowbray] *I … lay aside my high blood's royalty, / Which fear, not reverence, makes thee to except*; **TG** II.iv.153 [Valentine to Proteus] *thou wilt except against my love*; **TN** I.iii.6

2 object to, take exception to **TG** I.iii.83 [Proteus alone, of Antonio] *with … mine own excuse / Hath he excepted most against my love*; **JC** II.i.281; **Sonn** 147.8

exception *(n.)* **1** (often plural) objection, dislike, disapproval **TG** V.ii.3 [Proteus to Thurio, of Silvia] *she takes exceptions at your person*; **H5** IV.vii.23; **1H6** IV.i.105; **3H6** III.ii.46; **TG** I.iii.81; **TN** I.iii.4

2 resentment, sense of grievance **AW** I.ii.40 [King to Bertram, of Bertram's father] *his honour … knew the true minute when / Exception bid him speak*; **Ham** V.ii.225

exceptless *(adj.)* making no exceptions, indiscriminate **Tim** IV.iii.498 [Timon as if to the gods] *Forgive my general and exceptless rashness*

excess *(n.)* usury, interest **MV** I.iii.59 [Antonio to Shylock] *I neither lend nor borrow / By taking nor by giving of excess*

exchange *(n.)* **1** change, transposition **LL** IV.ii.42 [Holofernes to Dull, of his answer to Dull's riddle] *Th'allusion holds in the exchange* [i.e. of names in the riddle]

EXCLAMATIONS – *continued*

pah	Ham V.i.197	*And smelt so? Pah!*	disgust, abhorrence
peace	AY II.iv.62	*Peace, fool, he's not thy kinsman*	reproach, impatience
pish	Oth IV.i.41	*It is not words that shakes me thus! Pish!*	contempt, impatience, disgust [here, very strong]
pooh	Ham I.iii.101	*Affection? Pooh!*	scorn, contempt, impatience
pow waw	Cor II.i.136	*[Virgilia] The gods grant them true. [Volumnia] True? Pow waw!*	ridicule, scorn – cf. modern 'bow wow'
push	Tim III.vi.108	*Push! Did you see my cap?*	contempt, impatience [cf. pish]
rope, a	1H6 I.iii.53	*Winchester goose! I cry a rope, a rope!*	derision, contempt, anger
tailor	MND II.i.54	*Down topples she, / And 'Tailor' cries*	[unclear meaning, said when falling] shock, surprise
tilly-vally	TN II.iii.77	*Am I not of her blood! Tilly-vally!*	impatience – cf. modern 'nonsense!'
tush	Ham I.i.29	*Tush, tush, 'twill not appear*	disparagement, disbelief, contempt
tut	RJ I.i.197	*Tut, I have left myself*	impatience, dissatisfaction
when	JC II.i.5	*When, Lucius, when? Awake, I say!*	impatience
when, ay	1H4 II.i.40	*[Gadshill] I pray thee lend me thine [lantern] [Second Carrier] Ay, when? Canst tell?*	derision
when, nay	3H6 V.i.49	*Nay, when? Strike now, or else the iron cools*	impatience

Positive attitudes

cheer, good	TNK I.i.233	*Good cheer, ladies; / Now turn we towards your comfort*	reassurance, encouragement
cheerily	E3 IV.vii.44	*Cheerily, bold man, thy soul is all too proud / To yield her city*	encouragement, support
content	TS V.ii.70	*[Hortensio responding to Petruchio's proposal] Content. What's the wager?*	agreement, satisfaction
fair befall	R3 III.v.46	*Now fair befall you!*	good wishes
good as the best	Tim V.i.22	*[Poet] I must ... tell him of an intent that's coming toward him. [Painter] Good as the best*	strong affirmation – cf. modern 'that's splendid'
good now	AC I.ii.27	*Good now, some excellent fortune!*	entreaty, acquiescence, surprise
go to	TS V.i.123	*Fear not, Baptista, we will content you, go to*	reassurance – cf. modern 'don't worry' [see also above]
heigh	Tem I.i.5	*Heigh, my hearts!*	encouragement
heigh-ho, hey-ho	AY II.vii.181	*Hey-ho, sing hey-ho, unto the green holly*	joy, delight
said, well	Tit IV.iii.64	*[Titus to Lucius, of his archery] O, well said, Lucius!*	praise – cf. modern 'well done'
summer's day	E3 I.ii.81	*O summer's day; see where my cousin comes*	relief, delight

Some of these items have other functions: ☞ **ATTENTION SIGNALS**, p.26; **DISCOURSE MARKERS**, p.127; **POLITENESS**, p.340.

---

2 transformation, altered appearance **MV** II.vi.35 [Jessica to Lorenzo, of her male clothing] *I am much ashamed of my exchange*

excite (*v.*) incite, stir up, move **TN** II.v.159 [Malvolio to himself] *every reason excites to this, that my lady loves me*; **Cym** V.v.346; **Mac** V.ii.5

excitement (*n.*) incentive, encouragement, exhortation **TC** I.iii.182 [Ulysses to all] *All our ... / Achievements, plots, orders, preventions, / Excitements to the field*; **Ham** IV.iv.58

exclaim (*n.*) exclamation, outcry, protest **R3** I.ii.52 [Anne to Richard, of the earth] *thou hast ... / Filled it with cursing cries and deep exclaims*; **R2** I.ii.2; **R3** IV.iv.135; **TC** V.iii.91; **Tit** IV.i.85

exclaim (*v.*) complain, protest, make an outcry **R3** III.iv.102 [Lovel to Hastings] *'Tis bootless to exclaim*

exclaim against / on (*v.*) decry, cry out against, rail at **Ham** II.ii.349 [Hamlet to Rosencrantz, of the child players] *their writers do them wrong to make them exclaim against their own succession*; **Luc** 741 [of Lucrece] *She stays, exclaiming on the direful night*; **Luc** 757; **Oth** II.iii.301; **TNK** I.ii.86

exclaim on / upon (*v.*) accuse, blame, denounce [loudly] **1H6** IV.iv.30 [Lucy to Somerset] *York ... upon your grace exclaims* [i.e. York blames you]; **1H6** V.iii.134 [Reignier to Suffolk] *I am a soldier and unapt to weep / Or to exclaim on fortune's fickleness*; **1H6** III.iii.60; **MV** III.ii.174; **R3** III.iii.15; **Venus** 930

exclamation *(n.)* **1** loud reproach, outcry, clamorous complaint **KJ** II.i.558 [King John to King Philip, of Constance] *I trust we shall … in some measure satisfy her so / That we shall stop her exclamation;* **H8** I.ii.52; **Luc** 705; **R3** IV.iv.154

2 malapropism for 'acclamation'; complaint, outcry **MA** III.v.24 [Dogberry to Leonato] *I hear as good exclamation on your worship as of any man in the city*

excrement *(n.)* outgrowth [of hair] **LL** V.i.98 [Armado to Holofernes, of the King] *with his royal finger thus dally with my excrement, with my mustachio;* **CE** II.ii.84; **Ham** III.iv.122; **MV** III.ii.87; **WT** IV.iv.709

excursion *(n.)* sortie, sally, bout of fighting **1H6** III.ii.36 [stage direction] *Enter Talbot in an excursion from within the town;* **H5** IV.iv.1; **2H6** V.ii.72 ☞ **STAGE DIRECTIONS**, p.417

excuse *(n.)* pardon, dispensation, exoneration **E3** IV.v.91 [King John to Charles] *thy licence lies in me, / And my constraint stands the excuse for thee;* **Cor** I.iii.103; **Luc** 235; **TS** Induction.ii.123

excuse *(v.)* **1** explain, give reasons [for] **CE** III.i.92 [Balthasar to Antipholus of Ephesus, of Adriana] *she will well excuse / Why at this time the doors are made against you;* **MND** V.i.347

2 seek to decline, beg to get out of **TG** I.iii.71 [Antonio to Proteus, of his being sent to the court] *Excuse it not*

execration *(n.)* curse, imprecation, denunciation **2H6** III.ii.305 [Suffolk to Queen] *Cease, gentle Queen, these execrations;* **E3** III.iii.98; **TC** II.iii.7

execute *(v.)* **1** carry out, fulfil, perform **MV** III.i.65 [Shylock to Solanio and Salerio] *The villainy you teach me I will execute;* **Cor** IV.v.223; **E3** II.ii.146; **2H6** III.i.256; **Tem** I.ii.104; **TNK** IV.iii.71

2 implement, activate, bring into operation **TC** V.vii.6 [Achilles to Myrmidons] *In fellest manner execute your arms;* **Oth** II.iii.222

execution *(n.)* **1** action, performance, doing **KL** I.i.137 [Lear to Cornwall and Albany] *the sway, / Revenue, execution of the rest … be yours;* **Cor** III.iii.21; **2H4** IV.vii.71; **Oth** III.iii.463; **TNK** IV.iii.98; **WT** I.ii.260

2 exercising, putting into operation **3H6** II.ii.111 [Richard to Northumberland] *scarce I can refrain / The execution of my big-swollen heart / Upon that Clifford;* **2H4** IV.i.212; **MM** I.i.59

3 satisfaction, accomplishment **2H4** IV.i.172 [Archbishop to Westmorland] *All members of our cause … / Acquitted by a true substantial form / And present execution of our wills*

4 killing, slaying, slaughter **TC** V.v.38 [Ulysses to all, of Troilus] *who hath done today / Mad and fantastic execution;* **1H6** III.ii.35; **Mac** I.ii.18; **Tit** II.iii.36

executor *(n.)* **1** agent, doer, performer **Tem** III.i.13 [Ferdinand alone, of his work] *such baseness / Had never like executor* [i.e. never had such a performer]

2 executioner **H5** I.ii.203 [Canterbury to all, of honey-bees] *The sad-eyed justice … / Delivering o'er to executors pale / The lazy yawning drone*

3 disposer of remains **H5** IV.ii.49 [Grandpré to all, of the English army] *their executors, the knavish crows, / Fly o'er them all*

exempt *(adj.)* removed, cut off, excluded, debarred **AY** II.i.15 [Duke Senior to all] *this our life, exempt from public haunt;* **CE** II.ii.180; **1H6** II.v.93; **3H6** III.iii.127; **Tim** IV.ii.31

exequies *(n.)* funeral rites, burial ceremonies **1H6** III.ii.133 [Talbot to Burgundy, of Bedford] *see his exequies fulfilled in Rouen*

exercise *(n.)* **1** habitual activity, usual occupation, employment **AY** I.i.67 [Orlando to Oliver] *such exercises as may become a gentleman;* **Ham** II.ii.297; **Per** I.iv.38; **WT** I.ii.166

2 manly sport, martial practice **TG** I.iii.32 [Panthino to Antonio, of Proteus at the emperor's court] *There shall he … be in eye of every exercise / Worthy his youth;* **2H4** IV.v.75; **3H6** IV.vi.85; **KJ** IV.ii.60; **TC** IV.iv.77; **WT** IV.ii.32

3 skilful practice, facility **Ham** IV.vii.96 [Claudius to Laertes, of Lamord] *He … gave you such a masterly report / For art and exercise in your defence*

4 religious practice, spiritual observance **R3** III.vii.63 [Catesby to Buckingham, of Richard] *in no worldly suits would he be moved / To draw him from his holy exercise;* **Ham** III.i.45; **Oth** III.iv.41; **WT** III.ii.239

5 sermon, homily, religious discourse **R3** III.ii.109 [Hastings to Priest] *I am in your debt for your last exercise*

exercise *(v.)* **1** work, practise, perform [a function] **Tem** I.ii.328 [Prospero to Caliban] *Urchins / Shall … / All exercise on thee*

2 engage in manly sports, practise the martial arts **TNK** II.i.72 [Palamon to Arcite] *O, never / Shall we two exercise … / Our arms again*

exeunt *(v.)* [Latin] they exit ☞ **STAGE DIRECTIONS**, p.417; **LATIN**, p.643

exhalation *(n.)* **1** meteor, shooting star **H8** III.ii.226 [Wolsey alone] *I shall fall / Like a bright exhalation in the evening;* **JC** I.i.44; **KJ** III.iv.153

2 fiery emanation, flaming body **1H4** II.iv.313 [Bardolph to Prince Hal] *Do you behold these exhalations?*

3 outpouring, discharge **E3** III.i.128 [King John to Philip] *when the exhalations of the air / Breaks in extremity of lightning flash*

exhale *(v.)* **1** cause to flow, draw out, draw up **R3** I.ii.58 [Anne to Richard, of Henry VI's wounds] *'tis thy presence that exhales this blood;* **LL** IV.iii.68; **R3** I.ii.165; **RJ** III.v.13

2 draw forth [a sword] **H5** II.i.59 [Pistol to Nym] *The grave doth gape, and doting death is near: / Therefore exhale!*

exhaled *(adj.)* dragged from a proper course; also: drawn up as a vapour **1H4** V.i.19 [King Henry to Worcester] *Will you … be no more an exhaled meteor*

exhaust *(v.)* draw out, elicit, extract **Tim** IV.iii.120 [Timon to Alcibiades, of babies] *Whose dimpled smiles from fools exhaust their mercy*

exhibit *(v.)* **1** submit for inspection, produce for consideration, propose **MW** II.i.26 [Mistress Page alone] *I'll exhibit a bill in the parliament for the putting down of men;* **1H6** III.i.153; **MM** IV.iv.9

2 malapropism for 'inhibit'; or: manifest, demonstrate **MV** II.iii.10 [Launcelot to Jessica] *Adieu! Tears exhibit my tongue*

exhibiter, exhibitor *(n.)* proposer, introducer, mover **H5** I.i.74 [Canterbury to Ely, of King Henry] *swaying more upon our part / Than cherishing th'exhibiters against us*

exhibition *(n.)* **1** allowance, pension, maintenance **Oth** I.iii.235 [Othello to Duke] *I crave fit disposition for my wife, / Due reference of place and exhibition;* **Cym** I.vii.122; **KL** I.ii.25; **TG** I.iii.69

2 gift, present, offer **Oth** IV.iii.73 [Emilia to Desdemona, of infidelity] *I would not do such a thing for … any petty exhibition*

3 malapropism for 'commission' **MA** IV.ii.5 [Verges to Dogberry] *we have the exhibition to examine*

exigent *(n.)* **1** end, extremity, last state **1H6** II.v.9 [Mortimer to Gaolers, of his eyes] *These eyes … / Wax dim, as drawing to their exigent*

2 time of necessity, critical moment **JC** V.i.19 [Antony to Octavius, of his orders] *Why do you cross me in this exigent?* **AC** IV.xiv.63

exion *(n.)* idiosyncratic form of 'action' **2H4** II.i.28 [Hostess to Fang and Snare, of Falstaff] *since my exion is entered*

exorciser *(n.)* spirit-raiser, one who conjures spirits **Cym** IV.ii.276 [Guiderius singing, to the supposedly dead Innogen] *No exorciser harm thee!* [F *Exorcisor*]

exorcism *(n.)* calling up of spirits, conjuration **2H6** I.iv.4 [Bolingbroke to Hume, of the Duchess of Gloucester] *Will her ladyship behold and hear our exorcisms?*

exorcist *(n.)* one who calls up spirits **AW** V.iii.302 [King to all] *Is there no exorcist / Beguiles the truer office of mine eyes?;* **JC** II.i.323

expect *(n.)* expectation, anticipation **TC** I.iii.70 [Agamemnon to Ulysses] *be't of less expect / That matter needless … / Divide thy lips*

expect *(v.)* await, wait for **1H6** V.iii.145 [Suffolk to Reignier] *here I will expect thy coming;* **2H6** IV.ix.12; **LL** IV.i.84; **MV** V.i.49; **TG** I.i.54

expectance (*n.*) expectant state, watchful anticipation **TC** IV.v.146 [Aeneas to Hector and Ajax] *There is expectance here from both the sides / What further you will do*

expectancy (*n.*) expectation, hope for the future, source of hope **Oth** II.i.41 [Third Gentleman to all] *every minute is expectancy / Of more arrivance;* **Ham** III.i.153

expectation (*n.*) **1** anticipation, hopefulness **H5** III.iii.44 [Governor to King Henry] *Our expectation hath this day an end;* **2H4** V.ii.31; **JC** I.i.41; **TNK** III.i.14
2 situation of being expected **Mac** III.iii.10 [Second Murderer to all] *The rest that are within the note of expectation, / Already are i'the court* [i.e. on the list of guests]

expecter (*n.*) person awaiting news **TC** IV.v.156 [Hector to Aeneas] *signify this loving interview / To the expecters of our Trojan part*

expedience (*n.*) **1** speed, haste, dispatch **H5** IV.iii.70 [Salisbury to King Henry] *The French … will with all expedience charge on us;* **R2** II.i.287
2 rapid departure, hasty expedition, urgent enterprise **AC** I.ii.179 [Antony to Enobarbus] *I shall break / The cause of our expedience to the Queen;* **1H4** I.i.33

expedient (*adj.*) speedy, rapid, expeditious **R2** I.iv.39 [Green to King Richard] *for the rebels which stand out in Ireland, / Expedient manage must be made;* **E3** IV.iv.10; **2H6** III.i.288; **KJ** II.i.60, 223; **R3** I.ii.216

expediently (*adv.*) expeditiously, promptly, speedily **AY** III.i.18 [Duke Frederick to all, of the appropriation of Oliver's lands] *Do this expediently*

expedition (*n.*) **1** haste, speedy action, prompt dispatch **H5** II.ii.191 [King Henry to all] *Let us deliver / Our puissance into the hand of God, / Putting it straight in expedition;* **2H4** IV.iii.34; **Mac** II.iii.107; **TG** I.iii.37, III.i.164; **Tim** V.ii.3
2 prompt departure, sudden leaving **WT** I.ii.458 [Polixenes to Camillo] *Good expedition be my friend*
3 warlike enterprise, setting out for war **R3** IV.iii.54 [King Richard to Ratcliffe] *fiery expedition be my wing;* **JC** IV.iii.168; **R3** IV.iv.136
4 ready learning, awareness, insight **H5** III.ii.75 [Fluellen to Gower] *Captain Jamy is … of great expedition and knowledge in th'aunchient wars*

expeditious (*adj.*) speedy, sudden, quickly needed **KJ** I.i.49 [King John to Queen Eleanor, of the war] *Our abbeys and our priories shall pay / This expeditious charge*

expend (*v.*) **1** spend, employ, use **2H6** III.i.150 [Gloucester to King, of his enemies] *if my death might make this island happy … / I would expend it with all willingness;* **Ham** II.ii.23
2 spend, use up, squander **Per** III.ii.28 [Cerimon to First Gentleman, of nobleness and riches] *Careless heirs / May the two latter darken and expend*

expense (*n.*) **1** extravagance, expenditure, spending **MW** III.iv.5 [Fenton to Anne, of Page] *he doth object … my state being galled with my expense, / I seek to heal it only by his wealth;* **MW** II.ii.136; **Sonn** 94.6
2 spending, using up, laying out **KL** II.i.99 [Regan to all, of Edgar and Gloucester] *To have th'expense and waste of his revenues*
3 loss, using up, expending **Sonn** 30.8 *I … moan th'expense of many a vanished sight*

experience (*n.*) learning, expertise, knowledge **AW** I.iii.218 [Helena to Countess, of her father's prescriptions] *such as his reading / And manifest experience had collected*

experiment (*n.*) investigation, inquiry, exploration **MW** IV.ii.32 [Mistress Page to Mistress Ford, of Ford and Page] *[he] hath drawn him and the rest of their company from their sport, to make another experiment of his suspicion;* **1H4** III.i.46

experimental (*adj.*) on the basis of experience, often observed **MA** IV.i.164 [Friar to Leonato] *my observations, / Which with experimental seal doth warrant / The tenor of my book*

expert (*adj.*) experienced, tried and tested **1H6** III.ii.126 [Talbot to Burgundy, of Rouen] *Now will we take some order in the town / Placing therein some expert officers;* **Oth** II.i.49

expiate (*adj.*) reached, fully arrived **R3** III.iii.23 [Ratcliffe to Rivers] *The hour of death is expiate*

expiate (*v.*) extinguish, bring to an end **Sonn** 22.4 *when in thee time's furrows I behold, / Then look I death my days should expiate*

expiation (*n.*) purification, atonement **Tit** I.i.37 [Marcus to Saturninus and Bassianus, of Titus] *He [hath] … / To the monument of the Andronici / Done sacrifice of expiation*

expire (*v.*) end, conclude, terminate **KJ** V.v.36 [Melun to Pembroke, Salisbury, and Bigot] *Even this ill night, your breathing shall expire;* **RJ** I.iv.109

expired (*adj.*) ended, finished, dead **1H6** II.v.31 [Mortimer to Gaolers, of Richard] *I would his troubles likewise were expired*

exploit (*n.*) **1** act, deed, enterprise **R3** IV.ii.35 [King Richard to a Page] *Know'st thou not any whom corrupting gold / Will tempt unto a close exploit of death?*
2 military action, martial undertaking **AW** I.ii.17 [Second Lord to King, of the gentry] *who are sick / For breathing and exploit;* **AW** IV.i.37; **2H6** I.i.194; **R3** V.iii.331

exposition (*n.*) malapropism for 'disposition' [= inclination] **MND** IV.i.38 [Bottom to Titania] *I have an exposition of sleep come upon me*

expositor (*n.*) expounder, explainer, interpreter **LL** II.i.72 [Rosaline to Princess, of Berowne's tongue] *conceit's expositor*

expostulate (*v.*) **1** expound, debate, discourse **3H6** II.v.135 [Exeter to King] *stay not to expostulate, make speed;* **Ham** II.ii.86; **TG** III.i.251
2 remonstrate, plead, argue at length **Oth** IV.i.204 [Othello to Iago, of Desdemona] *I'll not expostulate with her, lest her body and beauty unprovide my mind again*

expostulation (*n.*) protestation, reproof, remonstration **TC** IV.iv.59 [Troilus to Cressida] *we must use expostulation kindly*

exposture (*n.*) exposure, laying open **Cor** IV.i.36 [Volumnia to Coriolanus] *Determine on some course / More than a wild exposture to each chance*

exposure (*n.*) unprotected state, defensive weakness, vulnerability **TC** I.iii.195 [Nestor to all, of Ajax] *[he] sets Thersites … / To weaken and discredit our exposure*

express (*adj.*) **1** explicit, specific, clear **1H6** I.iii.20 [Woodville to Gloucester, of Winchester] *From him I have express commandment / That thou nor none of thine shall be let in;* **KJ** IV.ii.234
2 considered, firm, precise **1H6** I.iv.64 [Salisbury to all] *Let me have your express opinions / Where is best place to make our battery next*
3 well-formed, well-designed, exact **Ham** II.ii.305 [Hamlet to Rosencrantz and Guildenstern, of the nature of man] *in form and moving how express and admirable*
4 fixed, final, irrevocable **TNK** III.vi.229 [Emilia to Theseus] *If such vows / Stand for express will* [i.e. represent your final decision]

express (*v.*) show, reveal, display **MM** II.iv.136 [Angelo to Isabella] *If you be one [a woman], as you are well expressed / By all external warrants;* **Ham** I.iii.71; **2H6** I.i.18; **KL** IV.iii.17; **TN** I.i.13; **TS** II.i.77

expressure (*n.*) **1** expression, picture, image **TC** III.iii.204 [Ulysses to Achilles, of the mystery in the soul of a state] *Which hath an operation more divine / Than breath or pen can give expressure to;* **MW** V.v.67
2 expression, attitude, look **TN** II.iii.150 [Maria to Sir Toby, of Malvolio] *by … the expressure of his eye*

expulse (*v.*) expel, drive out, banish **1H6** III.iii.25 [Alençon to all, of England] *For ever should they be expulsed from France;* **E3** III.ii.48

exquisite (*adj.*) **1** special, excellent, particularly valuable **Tim** III.ii.29 [Lucius to Servilius, of Timon] *my very exquisite friend;* **Cym** I.vii.190

2 ingenious, abstruse, far-fetched **TN** II.iii.136 [Sir Toby to Sir Andrew, of beating Malvolio for being a puritan] *Thy exquisite reason, dear knight?*

exsufflicate *(adj.)* inflated, swollen, puffed up **Oth** III.iii.180 [Othello to Iago, of jealousy] *such exsufflicate and blown surmises*

extant *(n.)* **1** in existence, living, existing **TNK** II.i.202 [Palamon to Arcite, of Emilia] *She is all the beauty extant;* **Ham** III.ii.271

2 current, present, immediate **TC** IV.v.168 [Agamemnon to Hector] *in this extant moment, faith and troth ... / Bids thee ... welcome*

extemporal *(n.)* extempore, improvised, impromptu **E3** IV.iv.115 [Prince Edward to Third Herald, of Philip] *I think him no divine extemporal* [i.e. improvising cleric]

extemporal *(adj.)* extempore, unplanned, improvised **LL** IV.ii.50 [Holofernes to Nathaniel] *will you hear an extemporal epitaph on the death of the deer?;* **1H6** III.i.6; **LL** I.ii.176

extemporally *(adv.)* in an improvised way, impromptu **Venus** 836 [of Venus] *She ... sings extemporally a woeful ditty;* **AC** V.ii.217

extempore *(adj./adv.)* without preparation, improvised, for the occasion **1H4** II.iv.273 [Falstaff to all] *Shall we have a play extempore?;* **TS** II.i.257; **WT** IV.iv.673

2 spontaneously, involuntarily, without thinking **1H4** II.iv.309 [Prince Hal to Bardolph] *ever since thou hast blushed extempore;* **MND** I.ii.64

extend *(v.)* **1** exaggerate, magnify, blow up **Cym** I.i.25 [First Gentleman to Second Gentleman, of Posthumus] *I do extend him ... within himself* [i.e. overpraise him only insofar as he deserves it]; **AC** V.ii.62; **Cym** I.v.19

2 stretch, push so far, give scope to **Oth** II.i.97 [Cassio to Iago] *Let it not gall your patience ... / That I extend my manners;* **Cym** II.iii.59

3 seize upon, take possession of **AC** I.ii.102 [Messenger to Antony] *Labienus ... hath with his Parthian force / Extended Asia*

4 show, offer, permit **KJ** IV.i.119 [Arthur to Hubert] *you do lack / That mercy which fierce fire and iron extends*

5 [unclear meaning] react to; evaluate; enlarge in scope **TC** III.iii.120 [Ulysses to Achilles, of man's abilities] *Nor doth he of himself know them for aught / Till he behold them formed in th'applause / Where they're extended*

extend *(adj.)* racked, stretched **AW** II.i.173 [Helena to King] *extended / With vildest torture let my life be ended*

extent *(n.)* **1** [of politeness] extending, showing, exercise of behaviour **Ham** II.ii.372 [Hamlet to Rosencrantz and Guildenstern] *my extent to the players, which I tell you must show fairly outwards;* **Tit** IV.iv.3

2 appropriation, seizure of property authorized by writ **AY** III.i.17 [Duke Frederick to all, of Oliver] *let my officers ... / Make an extent upon his house and lands*

3 assault, attack, onslaught **TN** IV.i.52 [Olivia to Sebastian] *Let thy fair wisdom, not thy passion, sway / In this uncivil and unjust extent / Against thy peace*

extenuate *(v.)* mitigate, lessen, tone down **Oth** V.ii.338 [Othello to all] *Speak of me as I am: nothing extenuate;* **AC** V.ii.125; **JC** III.ii.38; **MA** IV.i.48; **MND** I.i.120; **TC** II.ii.188

extenuation *(n.)* excuse, mitigation, remission **1H4** III.ii.22 [Prince Hal to King Henry] *such extenuation let me beg*

exteriorly *(adv.)* on the outside, superficially **KJ** IV.ii.257 [Hubert to King John, of his appearance] *Which, howsoever rude exteriorly, / Is yet the cover of a fairer mind*

extermine *(v.)* destroy, end, exterminate **AY** III.v.89 [Silvius to Phebe] *By giving love, your sorrow and my grief / Were both extermined*

extern *(n.)* exterior, outward appearance **Sonn** 125.2 *I bore the canopy, / With my extern the outward honouring*

extern *(adj.)* external, outward, exterior **Oth** I.i.64 [Iago to Roderigo] *when my outward action doth demonstrate / The native act and figure of my heart / In compliment extern*

extinct *(adj.)* extinguished, put out, quenched **R2** I.iii.222 [John of Gaunt to King Richard] *My ... time-bewasted light / Shall be extinct with age* [i.e. by age]; **Ham** I.iii.118; **TNK** V.iii.20

extincted *(adj.)* extinguished, quenched, stifled **Oth** II.i.81 [Cassio to Montano, of Othello] *That he may ... / Give renewed fire to our extincted spirits*

extincture *(n.)* extinction, quenching **Lover** 294 *cold modesty hot wrath: / Both fire from hence, and chill extincture hath*

extinguish *(v.)* eclipse, put in the shade **1H6** V.iii.192 [Suffolk alone, of Margaret] *Bethink thee on her ... natural graces that extinguish art*

extirp *(v.)* root out, eradicate, eliminate **1H6** III.iii.24 [Charles to Pucelle, of England] *should that nation ... be extirped from our provinces;* **MM** III.ii.97

extirpate *(v.)* remove, eliminate, drive away **Tem** I.ii.125 [Prospero to Miranda, of Antonio] *he... / Should presently extirpate me and mine / Out of the dukedom*

extolment *(n.)* praising, praise, extolling **Ham** V.ii.115 [Hamlet to Osrick] *in the verity of extolment*

extort *(v.)* **1** torture, abuse, wring **MND** III.ii.160 [Helena to Lysander and Demetrius] *None of noble sort / Would ... extort / A poor soul's patience*

2 extract with force, wring out **TN** III.i.150 [Olivia to Viola as Cesario] *Do not extort thy reasons from this clause: / For that I woo, thou therefore hast no cause*

extorted *(adj.)* ill-gotten, gained by evil means **Ham** I.i.138 [Horatio to Ghost] *if thou hast uphoarded in thy life / Extorted treasure in the womb of earth*

extracting *(adj.)* distracting, preoccupying, disconcerting **TN** V.i.278 [Olivia to all, of Malvolio] *A most extracting frenzy of mine own / From my remembrance clearly banished his*

extraught *(adj.)* descended, derived, extracted **3H6** II.ii.142 [Richard to Queen] *Shamest thou not, knowing whence thou art extraught, / To let thy tongue detect thy base-born heart?*

extravagancy *(n.)* wandering, drifting, roving about **TN** II.i.10 [Sebastian to Antonio] *my determinate voyage is mere extravagancy*

extravagant *(adj.)* vagrant, straying, roaming **Ham** I.i.155 [Horatio to Marcellus and Barnardo] *Th'extravagant and erring spirit hies / To his confine;* **LL** IV.ii.67; **Oth** I.i.137; **TNK** IV.iii.72

extreme *(n.)* **1** extremity, outermost area **2H4** IV.iii.105 [Falstaff alone, of the effect of sherry on the blood] *makes it course from the inwards to the parts' extremes*

2 highest degree, largest kind **3H6** III.ii.115 [Richard to George, of Edward's marrying being 'a ten day wonder'] *By so much is the wonder in extremes* [i.e. of the greatest kind]

3 hardship, tribulation, privation **Luc** 969 [Lucrece as if to time] *Devise extremes beyond extremity, / To make him curse this cursed crimeful night;* **1H6** IV.i.38

4 intense emotion, violent passion **TNK** IV.ii.101 [Pirithous to Theseus, of one of Palamon's knights] *a settled valour, / Not tainted with extremes, runs through his body;* **RJ** IV.i.62

5 outrageous behaviour, extravagance, exaggeration **WT** IV.iv.6 [Perdita to Florizel] *To chide at your extremes it not becomes me;* **Tit** III.i.214

extremity *(n.)* **1** utmost degree, greatest amount **WT** V.ii.18 [First Gentleman to Autolycus, of Leontes' and Camillo's reactions] *joy or sorrow: but in the extremity of the one it must needs be;* **CE** I.i.142; **Ham** III.ii.178; **KL** V.iii.205; **R2** II.ii.72

2 conclusion, outcome, very end **E3** IV.iii.18 [Villiers to Charles, reacting to his refusal to grant Salisbury a passport] *Why, then I know the extremity, my lord: / I must return to prison*

3 utmost severity, extreme intensity, hardship **H8** V.i.19 [Lovell to Gardiner] *The Queen's in labour ... in great extremity;* **Cym** III.iv.17; **Ham** II.ii.190; **KL** III.iv.99; **Luc** 969; **RJ** II.Chorus.14

4 extreme urgency, absolute necessity, crisis **Cor** IV.i.4 [Coriolanus to Volumnia] *You were used / To say extremities was the trier of spirits;* **Cor** III.ii.41

5 ridiculous behaviour, embarrassing conduct **MW** IV.ii.68 [Falstaff to Mistress Ford and Mistress Page] *devise something. Any extremity rather than a mischief;* **MW** IV.ii.151

exufflicate *(adj.)* ☞ exsufflicate *(adj.)*

eyas *(n.)* [young hawk taken from the nest for the purpose of training] one whose training is complete **Ham** II.ii.338 [Rosencrantz to Hamlet, of the child players] *an eyrie of children, little eyases* [F *Yases*]

eyas-musket *(n.)* young male sparrow-hawk **MW** III.iii.20 [Mistress Ford to Robin] *How now, my eyas-musket*

eye *(n.)* **1** sight, view, presence **KL** IV.iv.8 [Cordelia to soldiers, of Lear] *bring him to our eye;* **AC** III.ix.2; **H8** I.i.30; **Mac** III.i.124; **MV** I.i.137; **TN** II.ii.15

2 look, glance, gaze **Tem** I.ii.442 [Prospero to himself, of Ferdinand and Miranda] *At the first sight / They have changed eyes;* **AC** III.xiii.156; **1H4** I.iii.141; **Oth** II.i.38

3 supervision, appearance, presence **Mac** IV.iii.186 [Ross to Malcolm] *Your eye in Scotland / Would create soldiers*

4 hint, tinge, slight shade **Tem** II.i.58 [Sebastian to Antonio, of the ground] *With an eye of green in't*

5 eye-socket **R2** II.i.270 [Northumberland to Ross and Willoughby] *Even through the hollow eyes of death / I spy life peering*

6 [bowls] hollow in the side of a bowl **KJ** II.i.583 [Bastard alone, of commodity] *This bawd, this broker ... / Clapped on the outward eye of fickle France* [i.e. making France's eye swerve (towards it)]

eye, in his in front of him, in his presence **Ham** IV.iv.6 [Fortinbras to his captain, of Claudius] *We shall express our duty in his eye*

eyes, in the in one's sight, in front of one **AC** II.ii.212 [Enobarbus to Agrippa and Maecenas, of Cleopatra] *Her gentlewomen ... tended her i'th' eyes*

eye *(v.)* **1** look, appear, seem **AC** I.iii.97 [Cleopatra to Antony] *my becomings kill me when they do not / Eye well to you*

2 look at, stare at, regard **Cym** V.v.114 [Cymbeline to disguised Innogen, of Iachimo] *Wherefore ey'st him so?;* **Cym** V.v.124

3 watch carefully, pay attention to **TC** V.vii.7 [Achilles to Myrmidons] *Follow me, sirs, and my proceedings eye*

eye-glass *(n.)* lens of the eye **WT** I.ii.268 [Leontes to Camillo] *your eye-glass / Is thicker than a cuckold's horn*

eyeless *(adj.)* blind, sightless, unseeing **E3** IV.iv.9 [Prince Edward to Audley] *no hope to us but sullen dark / And eyeless terror of all-ending night;* **KL** III.i.8

eye-offending *(adj.)* which hurts the eyes **TN** I.i.31 [Valentine to Orsino, of Olivia] *she will ... water once a day her chamber round / With eye-offending brine*

eye-strings *(n.)* muscles of the eye [thought to break at the point when a dear sight is lost] **Cym** I.iv.17 [Innogen to Pisanio] *I would have broke mine eye-strings*

eyne *(n.)* [archaism] eyes **Per** III.Chorus.5 [Gower alone] *The cat, with eyne of burning coal;* **AY** IV.iii.51; **LL** V.ii.206; **Lover** 15; **Luc** 643; **MND** II.ii.105 ☞ ARCHAISMS, p.22

eyrie *(n.)* ☞ aerie *(n.)*

eysell *(n.)* ☞ eisel *(n.)*

fable (*v.*) speak falsely, lie, fabricate **TNK** III.v.104 [Schoolmaster to Theseus] *to say verity, and not to fable;* **1H6** IV.ii.42 ☛ **DISCOURSE MARKERS**, p.127

fabric (*n.*) building, edifice **Cor** III.i.246 [Cominius to Coriolanus] *manhood is called foolery when it stands / Against a falling fabric;* **WT** I.ii.429

fabulous (*adj.*) mythical, fabricated, invented **1H6** II.iii.17 [Countess to Talbot] *I see report is fabulous and false*

face (*n.*) **1** appearance, outward show, look **TNK** III.i.108 [Arcite to Palamon] *content and anger / In me have but one face* [i.e. I look the same whether pleased or angry]; **AC** III.xiii.5; **1H4** IV.iii.82; **JC** V.i.10; **KJ** V.ii.88; **LL** V.ii.395
   2 representation, image; skull **LL** V.ii.609 [Berowne to Holofernes, of the latter's face] *A death's face in a ring*

face (*v.*) **1** countenance, condone, cover over **R2** IV.i.284 [Richard, as to the mirror] *Is this the face which faced so many follies*
   2 confront impudently, defy **TS** V.i.109 [Vincentio to all, of Tranio] *That faced and braved me in this matter so;* **TS** IV.iii.123
   3 bully, intimidate, turn **TN** IV.ii.93 [Malvolio to Feste, of his enemies] *They ... do all they can to face me out of my wits;* **H5** III.vii.79
   4 cover over, put a false face on **1H4** V.i.74 [King Henry to Worcester, of the rebels' arguments] *To face the garment of rebellion / With some fine colour that may please the eye*
   5 deceive, show a false face **1H6** V.iii.142 [Suffolk to Reignier] *Fair Margaret knows / That Suffolk doth not flatter, face, or feign*
   6 exclude, expel; or: deny [to one's face] **TN** V.i.86 [Antonio to Orsino, of Viola as Cesario] *his false cunning ... / Taught him to face me out of his acquaintance*
   7 brazen out, carry through shamelessly **TS** II.i.398 [Tranio alone, of his bid as Lucentio against Gremio for Bianca] *I have faced it with a card of ten* [i.e. of ten pips]
   8 trim with braid, adorn **TS** IV.iii.121 [Grumio to Tailor] *Thou hast faced many things* [also: sense 2; pun: 123]

face down (*v.*) confront with impudence, persist in contradicting **CE** III.i.6 [Antipholus of Ephesus to Angelo, of Dromio of Ephesus] *here's a villain that would face me down*

face out (*v.*) brazen out, carry through shamelessly **TS** II.i.282 [Katherina to Baptista, of Petruchio] *That thinks with oaths to face the matter out;* **H5** III.ii.33

face-royal (*n.*) majestic face, face like a king **2H4** I.ii.22 [Falstaff to Page, of Prince Henry] *he will not stick to say his face is a face-royal* [pun: 24, royal (*adj.*) 2]

facile (*adj.*) easy, smooth, effortless **Oth** I.iii.23 [First Senator to Duke, of the Turk taking Cyprus] *So may he with more facile question bear it*

facinerious (*adj.*) extremely wicked, villainous, criminal **AW** II.iii.28 [Parolles to Lafew, of the King's cure] *he's of a most facinerious spirit that will not acknowledge it [to be the very hand of heaven]*

facing (*n.*) trimming, adorning, decking out **MM** III.ii.9 [Pompey to Elbow, of a userer's garment] *furred with fox and lamb skins too, to signify that craft ... stands for the facing*

fact (*n.*) evil deed, wicked act, crime **2H6** I.iii.171 [Warwick to all, of Somerset's behaviour] *a fouler fact / Did never traitor in the land commit;* **Luc** 349; **Mac** III.vi.10; **MM** V.i.431; **Tim** III.v.16; **WT** III.ii.84

fact, in the in the act, red-handed **2H6** II.i.168 [Buckingham to King, of the conspirators] *Whom we have apprehended in the fact*

faction (*n.*) **1** party, group, set [of people] **1H6** II.iv.125 [Warwick to Richard] *this brawl today, / Grown to this faction in the Temple garden;* **E3** II.i.458; **Ham** V.ii.232; **1H4** IV.i.67; **R3** V.iii.13; **TG** V.i.36
   2 forming into a group **TC** II.iii.99 [Nestor to Ulysses, of Ajax and Achilles] *their fraction is more our wish than their faction*
   3 quarrel, squabble, dissension **AC** I.iii.48 [Antony to Cleopatra] *Equality of two domestic powers / Breed scrupulous faction;* **TC** III.iii.190; **Tim** III.v.74

4 insult, dissension, abuse **AY** V.i.54 [Touchstone to William] *I will bandy with thee in faction*

factionary (*n.*) activist, partisan, champion **Cor** V.iii.29 [Menenius to First Watch] *always factionary on the party of your general*

factious (*adj.*) **1** sectarian, partisan, arising from factions **TC** II.ii.210 [Hector to all] *I have a roisting challenge sent amongst / The dull and factious nobles of the Greeks*; **1H6** IV.i.113, 190; **2H6** II.i.39; **TC** III.ii.191

2 ready to form a faction **R3** I.iii.127 [Richard to Queen Elizabeth] *you and your husband Grey / Were factious for the house of Lancaster*; **JC** I.iii.118; **R3** II.i.20

3 rebellious, seditious **3H6** I.i.74 [King to York] *Thou factious Duke of York, descend my throne*; **2H6** V.i.135

factor (*n.*) agent, representative, broker **1H4** III.ii.147 [Prince Hal to King Henry] *Percy is but my factor ... / To engross up glorious deeds on my behalf*; **AC** I.vi.10; **CE** I.i.42; **Cym** I.vii.188; **R3** III.vii.133, IV.iv.72

faculty (*n.*) function, power, capability **Sonn** 122.6 *so long as brain and heart / Have faculty by nature to subsist*; **AW** I.iii.221; **H8** I.ii.73; **JC** I.iii.67; **Mac** I.vii.17; **TNK** IV.iii.71

fade (*v.*) decay, decompose, become corrupt **Tem** I.ii.400 [Ariel singing to Ferdinand, of Alonso] *Nothing of him that doth fade, / But doth suffer a sea-change*

fadge (*v.*) **1** succeed, be suitable, turn out well **LL** V.i.140 [Armado to Holofernes, of the pageant] *We will have, if this fadge not, an antic*

2 turn out, end up, come off **TN** II.ii.33 [Viola alone, of the situation] *How will this fadge?*

fading (*n.*) nonsense refrain in a ballad [with allusion to sexual energy] **WT** IV.iv.197 [Servant to Clown, of Autolycus' songs] *with such delicate burdens of dildos and fadings*

fail (*n.*) **1** failure [to comply with], lack **WT** II.iii.169 [Leontes to Antigonus, of his command] *the fail / Of any point in't shall not only be / Death to thyself, but to thy lewd-tongued wife*; **H8** I.ii.145, II.iv.198; **TNK** I.ii.105; **WT** V.i.27

2 failure, fault, wrong **Cym** III.iv.65 [Innogen to Pisanio, as if to Posthumus] *Goodly and gallant shall be false and perjured / From thy great fail*

fail (*v.*) **1** fall short, let down, disappoint **Cor** V.iii.90 [Volumnia to Coriolanus] *if you fail in our request* [i.e. fail to grant]; **2H6** II.i.51

2 die out, come to an end **2H6** II.ii.56 [Warwick to all, of Henry's line of succession] *Till Lionel's issue fails, his should not reign*

fain (*adj.*) **1** obliged, forced, compelled **MM** IV.iii.169 [Lucio to disguised Duke, of making a woman pregnant] *I was fain to forswear it*; **E3** III.i.182; **2H4** II.i.140; **MM** IV.iii.151; **MW** II.ii.24; **TG** I.ii.120

2 satisfied, well pleased, glad **KL** IV.vii.38 [Cordelia to Lear, of Lear on the heath] *wast thou fain ... / To hovel thee with swine and rogues*; **1H6** III.ii.114

3 fond, inclined [to], apt [to] **2H6** II.i.8 [King to all] *man and birds are fain of climbing high*

fain (*v.*) be glad, be delighted, rejoice **3H6** IV.vii.31 [Hastings to all, of the Lord Mayor] *The good old man would fain that all were well*

fain (*adv.*) gladly, willingly **Ham** II.ii.153 [Polonius to Claudius and Gertrude] *I would fain know that* ☞ **FEW**, p.xxi

faint (*adj.*) **1** feeble, half-hearted **KL** I.iv.67 [Lear to Third Knight] *I have perceived a most faint neglect of late*; **Cor** IV.ii.52; **Tim** III.iii.26

2 faint-hearted, timorous, fearful **3H6** II.i.152 [Warwick to Richard] *this strong right hand of mine / Can pluck the diadem from faint Henry's head*; **3H6** V.iv.51; **KJ** V.v.4; **RJ** III.iii.15

3 weak, fatigued, lacking in strength **3H6** I.iv.23 [York alone, of his enemies] *I am faint and cannot fly their fury*; **2H4** I.i.108; **H5** I.i.16; **3H6** II.vi.28

4 inadequate, lacking, in short supply **MV** I.i.125 [Bassanio to Antonio] *I have disabled mine estate / By something showing a more swelling port / Than my faint means would grant continuance*

5 pale, lightly coloured **MND** I.i.215 [Hermia to Helena] *often you and I / Upon faint primrose beds were wont to lie*

faint (*v.*) **1** lose courage, show fear, lose heart, take fright **3H6** II.ii.57 [Queen to King] *this soft courage makes your followers faint*; **R3** V.iii.173; **Sonn** 80.1; **TC** II.ii.143; **TNK** III.vi.121; **Venus** 569

2 make faint, depress **H8** II.iii.103 [Anne to Old Lady, of her advancement] *it faints me / To think what follows*

faintly (*adv.*) **1** hardly, scarcely, very slightly **KL** I.ii.171 [Edmund to Edgar] *I have told you what I have seen and heard but faintly*

2 timidly, half-heartedly, without conviction **KJ** IV.ii.227 [King John to Hubert] *I faintly broke with thee of Arthur's death*; **Cor** V.i.67; **Oth** IV.ii.112; **R2** V.iii.102

3 weakly, feebly, faintheartedly **1H6** I.ii.8 [Charles to all] *Otherwhiles the famished English ... / Faintly besiege us*; **R2** I.iii.281; **RJ** I.iv.7; **Venus** 482

4 like a coward, fearfully **Luc** 740 [of Tarquin] *He faintly flies, sweating with guilty fear*

faintness (*n.*) cowardice, fearfulness, timidity **1H6** IV.i.107 [Vernon to King, of Basset] *Pronouncing that the paleness of this flower / Bewrayed the faintness of my master's heart*

fair (*n.*) **1** fair face, beauty **Venus** 1086 [of Adonis] *sun and sharp air / Lurked like two thieves to rob him of his fair*; **AY** III.ii.91; **Lover** 206; **MND** I.i.182; **RJ** II.Chorus.3; **Sonn** 18.7

2 fortune, happiness, favour **R3** I.iii.281 [Queen Margaret to Buckingham] *fair befall thee and thy noble house!*; **KJ** I.i.78; **R2** II.i.129; **R3** III.v.46; **TC** III.i.43; **TS** V.ii.110

fair (*adj.*) **1** handsome, good-looking, beautiful **Sonn** 127.1 *In the old age black was not counted fair*; **LL** IV.i.11; **TC** I.i.68; **Tem** IV.i.24; **TNK** V.ii.44; **TS** II.i.17

2 good, elegant, fine **TNK** V.iii.56 [Gaoler's Daughter to Gaoler, of her horse's ability to write] *A very fair hand*; **TC** III.i.45

3 pale, of light complexion **Tit** III.i.203 [Aaron to himself] *Let fools do good, and fair men call for grace*; **TG** V.ii.9

4 fine, pleasing, splendid, excellent **E3** II.ii.6 [Audley to Derby, of the troops] *[I] bring them hither / In fair array before his majesty*; **Cor** IV.vi.119; **Sonn** 78.2; **TC** III.i.43 [second instance]; **TG** I.i.50; **Tim** III.v.64

5 appropriate, courteous, pleasing **R2** III.iii.188 [Bolingbroke to all, of King Richard] *show fair duty to his majesty*; **TC** I.iii.219, III.i.44 [second instance], 48; **Tim** I.i.190

6 plausible, flattering, seductive **TC** III.i.47 [Helen to Pandarus] *you are full of fair words*; **1H6** III.iii.18; **LL** II.i.29; **Mac** I.vii.81

7 virtuous, honourable, upright **Tim** III.v.18 [Alcibiades to Senators, of his friend] *with a noble fury and fair spirit ... / He did oppose his foe*; **Luc** 346; **TC** III.i.44, ii.93; **Tim** III.ii.55

8 fortunate, favoured **AC** I.ii.18 [Soothsayer to Charmian] *You shall be yet far fairer than you are*; **R2** IV.i.21; **TC** III.ii.46

9 favourable, unobstructed, clear **LL** IV.i.10 [Forester to Princess, of a vantage point for hunting] *A stand where you may make the fairest shoot* [pun: 11, sense 1]

10 legitimate, lawful, proper **WT** II.i.150 [Antigonus to Leontes, of Antigonus' daughters] *I had rather glib myself than they / Should not produce fair issue*; **KJ** V.ii.4; **RJ** I.iii.15

11 healthy, sound, fit **AY** I.i.11 [Orlando to Adam, of Oliver's horses] *they are fair with their feeding*; **Sonn** 45.12

12 clean, unsoiled, not dirty **Cor** I.ix.68 [Coriolanus to Cominius] *when my face is fair you shall perceive / Whether I blush or no*; **TS** IV.i.44

fair (*v.*) make good-looking, beautify **Sonn** 127.6 *Fairing the foul with Art's false borrowed face*

fair (*adv.*) **1** kindly, encouragingly, courteously **2H4** V.ii.33 [Clarence to Lord Chief Justice] *you must now speak Sir John Falstaff fair, / Which swims against your stream of quality*; **CE** IV.iv.150; **Ham** IV.i.36; **3H6** II.i.271; **R2** III.iii.128; **TC** IV.iv.112

2 well, in a good hand, elegantly [like a clerk] **KJ** IV.i.37 [Hubert to Arthur, of the warrant to blind him] *Is it not fair writ?*; **Ham** V.ii.32, 34

3 tidily, neatly, becomingly **2H6** III.ii.11 [Suffolk to Murderers] *Have you laid fair the bed?*

4 in fine array, brightly laid out **E3** IV.v.43 [King John to Philip, of the French] *So many fair against a famished few*

5 well, nobly, beautifully **Cym** V.iv.49 [Sicilius, to music, of Posthumus] *Great nature, like his ancestry, / moulded the stuff so fair;* **1H4** III.i.136; **Venus** 744

6 successfully, promisingly, favourably **1H4** V.v.43 [King Henry to all] *since this business so fair is done, / Let us not leave till all our own be won;* **TC** I.iii.372

7 fully, quite, wholly **KJ** I.i.69 [Bastard to Queen Eleanor, of Robert proving his illegitimacy] *'a pops me out / At least from fair five hundred pound a year;* **TS** IV.ii.3

8 in full view **TC** IV.v.235 [Hector to Achilles] *Stand fair, I pray thee; let me look on thee*

fair hour time of youth, favourable opportunity [as a young man] **Ham** I.ii.62 [Claudius to Laertes, of his return to France] *Take thy fair hour*

fair weather ☛ weather, make fair

fairest-boding (adj.) most favourable, most encouraging **R3** V.iii.228 [Richmond to Lords, of his rest] *The sweetest sleep, and fairest-boding dreams*

fair-faced (adj.) attractive, appealing, presenting a good prospect **KJ** II.i.417 [Hubert to King John and King Philip] *I shall show you peace and fair-faced league*

fairing (n.) gift, present **LL** V.ii.2 [Princess to her ladies] *we shall be rich ere we depart / If fairings come thus plentifully in*

fairly (adv.) **1** cordially, warmly, becomingly **Tim** I.ii.183 [Timon to Second Servant, of a gift of horses] *I shall accept them fairly;* **Ham** II.ii.373; **R2** III.i.37; **TS** I.i.108

2 neatly, elegantly, handsomely, beautifully **TS** I.ii.143 [Gremio to Lucentio as Cambio, of books] *I'll have them very fairly bound;* **R3** III.vi.2; **Sonn** 5.4; **TC** III.iii.33; **TS** III.ii.60

3 bountifully, handsomely, generously **AY** V.iv.164 [Duke Senior to Jaques de Boys] *Thou offerest fairly to thy brothers' wedding*

4 promisingly, favourably, propitiously **AC** II.ii.150 [Antony to Caesar, of the marriage proposal] *this good purpose, that so fairly shows*

5 fully, completely, entirely **Tim** I.ii.174 [Timon to First Servant, of the arrival of the senators] *They are fairly welcome;* **RJ** II.v.45; **TC** III.i.44; **TNK** IV.i.27

6 free from foul play, in a healthy state **R3** IV.iv.352 [Queen Elizabeth to King Richard, of her daughter] *how long fairly shall her sweet life last?*

fairness (n.) **1** beauty, loveliness, comeliness **Cym** V.v.168 [Iachimo to Cymbeline, of Italian women] *that hook of wiving, / Fairness, which strikes the eye*

2 honesty, uprightness, fair dealing **Cor** I.ix.72 [Coriolanus to Cominius] *I mean . . . / To undercrest your good addition / To th'fairness of my power* [i.e. as honorably as I can]

fair-play, fair play (n.) chivalrous action, honourable conduct **KJ** V.ii.118 [Bastard to Lewis the Dauphin] *According to the fair play of the world, / Let me have audience*

fair-play (adj.) chivalrous, courtly, full of honour **KJ** V.i.67 [Bastard to King John] *Shall we, upon the footing of our land, / Send fair-play orders and make compromise*

fairy (n.) **1** enchantress, captivator **AC** IV.viii.12 [Antony to Scarus, of Cleopatra] *To this great fairy I'll commend thy acts*

2 malignant spirit [as well as its modern sense] **Cym** II.ii.9 [Innogen as if to the gods] *From fairies and the tempters of the night, / Guard me;* **CE** IV.iii.35

faith (n.) **1** promise, assurance, pledge **TNK** III.vi.1 [Palamon alone] *About this hour my cousin gave his faith / To visit me again;* **TC** V.iii.69; **TNK** III.vi.1; **WT** IV.iv.35, 457, 474

2 constancy, fidelity, loyalty **MA** II.i.165 [Claudio alone] *beauty is a witch / Against whose charms faith melteth into blood;* **AC** III.xiii.43; **2H4** IV.i.191; **H8** III.i.53; **TC** V.ii.67; **TNK** IV.ii.46

3 religious belief **TNK** I.ii.66 [Palamon to Arcite, of Creon] *almost puts / Faith in a fever* [i.e. sickly] ☛ **SWEARING**, p.435

4 reliability, dependability, trustworthiness **H8** II.i.143 [First Gentleman to Second Gentleman] *You do not doubt my faith, sir?;* **1H4** II.i.32; **TC** IV.v.168

5 self-confidence, self-assurance **TNK** I.ii.46 [Palamon to Arcite] *What need I / Affect another's gait, which is not catching / Where there is faith* [also: sense 3]

faith (v.) believe, trust, credit **KL** II.i.69 [Edmund to Gloucester, as if Edgar to Edmund] *would the reposal / Of any trust ... in thee / Make thy words faithed?*

faith-breach (n.) breach of faith, treason, treachery **Mac** V.ii.18 [Angus to all, of Macbeth] *Now minutely revolts upbraid his faith-breach*

faitour, faitor (n.) cheat, imposter, fraud **2H4** II.iv.155 [Pistol to Page] *Down, faitours!* [F *Fates*]

falchion (n.) curved broadsword **Luc** 1046 [Lucrece to herself] *I feared by Tarquin's falchion to be slain;* **3H6** I.iv.12; **KL** V.iii.274; **LL** V.ii.612; **Luc** 176; **R3** I.ii.94 ☛ **WEAPONS**, p.491

fall (n.) **1** low level, low ebb **Tim** II.i.210 [Flavius to Timon, of the Senators] *now they are at fall, want treasure*

2 mistake, fault, lapse **H5** II.ii.139 [King Henry to Scroop] *thy fall hath left a kind of blot / To mark the full-fraught man and best endued / With some suspicion;* **MW** I.i.235

3 cadence, lowering of tune **TN** I.i.4 [Orsino to all, of the music] *It had a dying fall*

4 setting, closing [of the day] **E3** V.i.27 [Second Citizen to King Edward] *The sun ... that in the western fall / Beholds us now low brought through misery*

5 wrestling bout **AY** I.i.118 [Charles to Oliver, of Orlando] *hath a disposition ... to try a fall;* **AY** I.iii.25

fall (v.) **1** drop, descend, let fall **Oth** IV.i.246 [Othello to Desdemona] *If that the earth could teem with woman's tears, / Each drop she falls would prove a crocodile;* **AY** II.v.5; **CE** II.ii.134; **JC** IV.ii.26; **MND** V.i.141; **R3** V.iii.136

2 befall, fall on, come to **AC** III.vii.39 [Enobarbus to Antony, of Caesar] *No disgrace / Shall fall you for refusing him at sea;* **KJ** I.i.78

3 happen, occur, come to pass **1H6** II.i.59 [Pucelle to all] *Had your watch been good, / This sudden mischief never could have fallen;* **H8** II.i.141; **JC** V.i.104

4 work out, happen, turn out **E3** V.i.212 [King Edward to King John, of John's reception in England] *Howe'er it falls, it cannot be so bad / As ours hath been since we arrived in France;* **Ham** IV.vii.69; **JC** III.i.146, 243; **Oth** III.iii.235

5 fall short, fail, do not live up to **TNK** III.vi.236 [Emilia to Theseus, of his oath] *if ye fall in't;* **TNK** III.vi.272

6 sin, trespass, commit wrong **Cym** V.i.13 [Posthumus alone, of people who have died] *that's love, / To have them fall no more*

7 discharge, issue, run **Luc** 653 [Lucrece to Tarquin] *Thou art ... a sea ... / And lo, there falls into thy boundless flood / Black lust*

fall away (v.) be thin, emaciate, waste away **TNK** III.vi.66 [Palamon to Arcite] *Am I fallen much away?*

fall foul fall out, quarrel, come into conflict **2H4** II.iv.164 [Pistol to Hostess] *Shall we fall foul for toys?*

fall from (v.) desert, forsake, renounce **KJ** III.i.320 [King Philip to King John] *England, I will fall from thee;* **3H6** III.iii.209

fall off (v.) **1** withdraw, step aside, move back **H8** IV.i.64 [Third Gentleman to First and Second Gentlemen, of Queen Anne] *The rich stream / Of lords and ladies ... fell off / A distance from her*

2 become estranged, withdraw from allegiance **Tim** V.i.57 [Poet to Timon] *Hearing you were retired, your friends fall'n off;* **KJ** V.v.11

fall on (v.) join a fray, attack in force **H8** V.iv.53 [Man to Porter, of club-wielding apprentices] *They fell on; I made good my place*

fall out (v.) turn out, happen, come to pass **RJ** III.iv.1 [Capulet to Paris] *Things have fallen out, sir, so unluckily*

fall over (*v.*) defect, revolt, go over **KJ** III.i.127 [Constance to Austria] *dost thou now fall over to my foes?*

fall to (*v.*) begin to do, abandon oneself to **TS** I.i.38 [Tranio to Lucentio, of mathematics and metaphysics] *Fall to them as you find your stomach serves you;* **TNK** V.iv.66

fall to, fall to it (*v.*) set to work, begin eating **R2** V.v.98 [Keeper to Richard, of the food] *will't please you to fall to?;* **Tim** I.ii.69 [Apemantus, at the close of his grace] *So fall to't*

fallacy (*n.*) delusion, misconception, error **CE** II.ii.195 [Antipholus of Syracuse to himself, of Adriana's approach] *Until I know this sure uncertainty, / I'll entertain the offered fallacy*

fallen-off (*adj.*) mutinous, rebellious, insubordinate **Cym** III.viii.6 [First Senator to all] *the legions now in Gallia are / Full weak to undertake our wars against / The fall'n-off Britons*

falliable (*adj.*) malapropism for 'infallible' **AC** V.ii.257 [Clown to Cleopatra] *But this is most falliable, the worm's an odd worm*

falling-from (*n.*) falling away, desertion, defection **Tim** IV.iii.402 [First Bandit to others, of Timon] *the falling-from of his friends, drove him into this melancholy*

falling in (*n.*) reconciliation, coming together **TC** III.i.100 [Helen to Pandarus, of Paris and Cressida] *Falling in after falling out may make them three*

fallow (*n.*) area of arable land, ploughed field **H5** V.ii.54 [Burgundy to King Henry and the French King] *our vineyards, fallows, meads, and hedges … / grow to wildness*

fallow (*adj.*) **1** unsown, uncultivated **H5** V.ii.44 [Burgundy to King Henry and the French King, of peace] *her fallow leas / The darnel, hemlock, and rank fumitory / Doth root upon*

2 fawn-coloured, pale brown **MW** I.i.83 [Slender to Page] *How does your fallow greyhound, sir?*

false (*n.*) false person, deceiver **TC** III.ii.188 [Cressida to Troilus] *let memory, / From false to false, among false maids in love, / Upbraid my falsehood!* [first two instances]; **TN** II.ii.29

false (*adj.*) **1** treacherous, traitorous, perfidious **1H6** II.iv.74 [Somerset to Richard] *Where false Plantagenet dare not be seen* ➤ FEW, p.xxi

2 disloyal, faithless, inconstant, unfaithful **Oth** IV.ii.38 [Othello to Desdemona] *Heaven truly knows that thou art false as hell;* **AC** IV.xv.44; **Sonn** 92.14; **TC** IV.ii.56; **TNK** V.v.92; **WT** II.i.138 ➤ secret-false (*adj.*)

3 sham, spurious, not genuine, artificial **Tim** I.ii.239 [Apemantus to Timon] *Methinks false hearts should never have sound legs;* **AY** III.v.73; **E3** II.i.315; **1H6** II.iii.17; **MA** III.iv.85; **Tim** IV.iii.516

4 wrong, mistaken **2H6** III.i.193 [Gloucester to King] *Ah, that my fear were false;* **AC** IV.iv.7; **CE** V.i.179

5 defective, weak, inadequate **WT** IV.iii.105 [Autolycus to Clown] *I am no fighter. I am false of heart that way;* **H5** V.ii.218

6 illegitimate, bastard **WT** II.i.148 [Antigonus to Leontes, of Antigonus' daughters] *Fourteen they shall not see / To bring false generations*

7 unfair, unjust, double-crossing **TG** IV.i.28 [Valentine to Outlaws, of why he was banished] *I killed a man … / But yet I slew him manfully in fight, / Without false vantage*

8 [of an instrument or voice] out of tune **JC** IV.iii.289 [Lucius to Brutus, of his instrument] *The strings … are false;* **Venus** 780

false (*v.*) make false, betray, corrupt **Cym** II.iii.68 [Cloten alone, of the women attending on Innogen] *'tis gold / Which … makes / Diana's rangers false themselves* [or: adjectival use]

false (*adv.*) **1** slanderously, faithlessly, with such calumny **2H6** III.i.184 [Gloucester to and of his enemies] *Beshrew the winners, for they played me false!;* **Cym** III.iv.116

2 unfairly, with a trick, cheatingly **Tem** V.i.172 [Miranda to Ferdinand, of their chess game] *you play me false*

3 wrongly, erroneously, in error **MA** IV.i.235 [Friar to Leonato] *if all aim but this be levelled false;* **TG** IV.ii.11

false fire discharge of blank cartridges **Ham** III.ii.275 [Hamlet to all, of Claudius] *What, frighted with false fire?*

false-boding (*adj.*) wrongly prophesying **R3** I.iii.246 [Hastings to Queen Margaret] *False-boding woman, end thy frantic curse*

false-faced (*adj.*) hypocritical, sanctimonious **Cor** I.ix.44 [Martius to all] *let courts and cities be / Made all of false-faced soothing*

false-heart (*adj.*) false-hearted, treacherous **2H6** V.i.143 [York to Clifford] *I am thy king, and thou a false-heart traitor*

falsehood (*n.*) **1** disloyalty, treachery, faithlessness **3H6** IV.iv.8 [Lady Grey to Rivers, of Edward] *betrayed by falsehood of his guard;* **H8** II.iv.97; **Tem** I.ii.95

2 delusion, deception, illusion **TNK** IV.iii.91 [Doctor to Wooer, of the Gaoler's Daughter] *It is a falsehood she is in, which is with falsehoods to be combated*

falsely (*adv.*) treacherously, deceitfully, dishonestly **AW** V.iii.113 [King to Bertram, of Bertram's denial about Helena's ring] *Thou speakest it falsely;* **Cor** III.i.60; **2H6** I.iii.186; **LL** I.i.76

false-play (*v.*) play unfairly **AC** IV.xiv.19 [Antony to Eros, of Cleopatra] *she … has / Packed cards with Caesar, and false-played my glory / Unto an enemy's triumph*

falsing (*adj.*) deceptive, playing false **CE** II.ii.102 [Antipholus of Syracuse to Dromio of Syracuse, of Dromio's reasons] *not sure in a thing falsing*

fame (*n.*) **1** reputation, renown, character **2H4** II.iv.73 [Hostess to Doll] *I am in good name and fame with the very best;* **CE** III.i.19; **1H6** III.ii.76; **2H6** V.ii.60; **Luc** 1203; **TC** I.iii.144

2 report, account, description **Per** V.Epilogue.11 [Gower alone, of Cleon] *when fame / Had spread his cursed deed;* **AC** II.ii.168; **1H6** II.iii.67; **H8** I.iv.66; **TNK** IV.ii.153

fame (*v.*) make famous, celebrate the fame of **Sonn** 84.11 *Let him but copy what in you is writ … / And such a counterpart shall fame his wit*

famed (*adj.*) reputed, celebrated, renowned **3H6** IV.vi.26 [Warwick to King] *Your grace hath still been famed for virtuous;* **JC** I.ii.152

familiar (*n.*) **1** close friend, intimate associate **LL** V.i.91 [Armado to Holofernes] *the King is a noble gentleman, and my familiar;* **Tim** IV.ii.10

2 attendant spirit, personal demon **2H6** IV.vii.100 [Cade to the rebels, of Say] *He has a familiar under his tongue;* **1H6** III.ii.122, V.iii.10; **LL** I.ii.166

familiar (*adj.*) **1** friendly, congenial, welcoming **Oth** II.iii.300 [Iago to Cassio] *good wine is a good familiar creature if it be well used;* **JC** IV.ii.16; **MW** I.iii.42

2 close to a family, domestic **MW** I.i.18 [Evans to Shallow, of the luce / louse] *It is a familiar beast to man*

3 unduly intimate, too close **KL** V.i.16 [Regan to Edmund, of Gonerill] *Be not familiar with her*

familiarity (*adj.*) malapropism for 'familiar' **2H4** II.i.97 [Hostess to Falstaff, of a neighbour] *didst thou not … desire me to be no more so familiarity with such poor people*

familiarly (*adv.*) as a member of the same family, with intimate acquaintance **R3** IV.iv.316 [King Richard to Queen Elizabeth] *The King … / Familiarly shall call thy Dorset brother*

famous (*adj.*) **1** notorious, infamous, well-known **AC** I.iv.48 [Messenger to Caesar] *Menecrates and Menas, famous pirates*

2 memorable, glorious, bringing renown **E3** I.i.146 [King Edward to Prince Edward] *we do commence / A famous war*

famous (*v.*) make famous, become celebrated **Sonn** 25.9 *The painful warrior famoused for worth*

famously (*adv.*) gloriously, with renown **R3** II.iii.19 [Third Citizen to other Citizens, of Henry VI's reign] *then this land was famously enriched / With politic grave counsel;* **Cor** I.i.35

fan (*v.*) winnow, blow upon [to separate good from bad] **Cym** I.vii.177 [Iachimo to Innogen, of Posthumus] *The love I bear him / Made me to fan you thus*

fanatical (*adj.*) extravagant, flamboyant, over-the-top **LL** V.i.18 [Holofernes to Nathaniel, of Armado] *I abhor such fanatical phantasimes*

FAMILY

Most Shakespearian kinship terms look the same as their modern counterparts. The chief exceptions are the terms for grandparents, *grandam* (**KJ** II.i.159) and *grandsire* (**MW** I.i.54) alongside *grandmother* and *grandfather*; *stepdame* (**Cym** I.vii.1) alongside *stepmother*; and *sire* and *dam* are also used as a contemptuous way of referring to a father and mother, as in Queen Margaret's insult to Richard, 'thou art neither like thy sire nor dam' (**3H6** II.ii.135). But the familiar terms regularly have a wider range of application.

Same generation

Brother and *sister* are used to include in-laws and step-siblings.

Example	People involved	Text	Relationship
KL IV.ii.15	Gonerill of Cornwall	*my brother*	Cornwall is her brother-in-law
R3 V.iii.95	Derby to Richmond	*thy brother, tender George*	George is his step-brother
R2 II.ii.90	York of the Duchess of Gloucester	*my sister Gloucester*	the Duchess is his sister-in-law

Generation above

Mother and *father* are used to include in-laws and step-parents, though *daughter-in law* (**AW** I.iii.162), *father-in-law* (**R3** I.iv.49), and *stepmother* (**Cym** I.ii.2) also occur.

Cym V.v.270	Cymbeline to Innogen, of the Queen	*thy mother*	the Queen is her stepmother
R3 V.ii.5	Richmond of Stanley	*our father Stanley*	Stanley is his stepfather

In the following case, *father-in-law* is itself being used in a broader sense.

R3 V.iii.82	Richmond to Derby	*noble father-in-law*	Derby is his stepfather

Generation below

Son and *daughter* are used to include in-laws and step-children.

Cym I.ii.1	Queen to Innogen	*you shall not find me, daughter*	Innogen is her stepdaughter
2H4 II.iii.1	Northumberland to Lady Percy	*gentle daughter*	Lady Percy is his daughter-in-law
R3 II.i.19	King Edward to Lord Dorset	*son Dorset*	Dorset is his stepson
KL I.i.41	Lear to Cornwall	*our son of Cornwall*	Cornwall is his son-in-law

Nephew and *niece* includes other relatives alongside the modern use.

TC I.ii.12	Alexander to Cressida, of Ajax	*nephew to Hector*	Ajax is Hector's first cousin
R3 IV.i.1	Duchess of York of Lady Margaret	*my niece Plantagenet*	Lady Margaret is her granddaughter

Cousin has the widest application of all: ☛ **COUSIN**, p.106.

---

fancy *(n.)* **1** love, amorousness, infatuation **TNK** V.iv.118 [Theseus to Palamon, of Emilia] *you first saw her, and / Even then proclaimed your fancy;* **Luc** 200; **MA** III.i.35; **MND** I.i.155; **TC** IV.iv.24; **TNK** IV.ii.52

2 sweetheart, love, lover **Lover** 197 *Look here what tributes wounded fancies sent me;* **Lover** 61; **Oth** III.iv.63

3 imagination, creativity, inventiveness **Ham** V.i.182 [Hamlet to Horatio, of Yorick] *A fellow of ... most excellent fancy;* **AC** II.ii.206; **H5** III.Chorus.7; **MND** V.i.25; **Per** III.Chorus.13; **TNK** V.iii.103

4 imagination, mind, mental state **WT** V.iii.60 [Paulina to Leontes, of Hermione's statue] *No longer shall you gaze on't, lest your fancy / May think anon it moves;* **H8** IV.ii.94, V.i.60; **MA** III.i.95; **Tem** V.i.59

5 imagining, flight of fancy, fanciful thought **TS** Induction.i.42 [Lord to Huntsmen, of Sly's reaction to his transformation] *Even as a flattering dream or worthless fancy;* **E3** IV.iii.83; **KL** I.iv.322; **Oth** IV.ii.25; **Tem** IV.i.122; **WT** III.ii.179

6 fancifulness, flamboyance, showiness **LL** I.i.168 [King to Berowne, of Armado] *This child of fancy;* **Ham** I.iii.71

7 whim, inclination, caprice **MA** III.ii.30 [Don Pedro to Claudio, of Benedick] *a fancy that he hath to strange disguises;* **AW** IV.i.17; **MA** III.ii.34; **MM** II.ii.151; **TNK** III.ii.2; **TS** III.ii.66

8 impromptu composition, musical invention **2H4** III.ii.307 [Falstaff alone, of Shallow's tunes] *'A ... sware they were his fancies or his good-nights*

fancy (*v.*) like, love, admire **TN** II.v.25 [Malvolio to himself, of Olivia] *should she fancy, it should be one of my complexion;* **2H6** I.iii.92; **TC** V.ii.168; **TG** III.i.67; **TS** II.i.12

fancy-monger (*n.*) love-dealer, trader in love **AY** III.ii.349 [Rosalind as Ganymede to Orlando, of the man carving 'Rosalind' in trees] *If I could meet that fancy-monger* ➤ **fancy** (*n.*) 1

fancy-sick (*adj.*) love-sick, infatuated, pining **MND** III.ii.96 [Oberon to Puck, of Helena] *All fancy-sick she is* ➤ **fancy** (*n.*) 1; **sick** (*adj.*) 1

fane (*n.*) 1 temple **Cor** I.x.20 [Aufidius to First Soldier] *nor fane nor Capitol … shall lift up / Their rotten privilege and custom 'gainst / My hate to Martius*
  2 oracle, temple-voice **Cym** IV.ii.242 [Guiderius to Arviragus] *notes of sorrow out of tune are worse / Than priests and fanes that lie*

fang (*v.*) seize, take hold of **Tim** IV.iii.23 [Timon alone] *Destruction fang mankind* [F *phang*]

fangled (*adj.*) fashion-conscious, novelty-obsessed, trendy **Cym** V.iv.134 [Posthumus alone] *our fangled world*

fanned (*adj.*) well-sifted, tested, considered **Ham** V.ii.189 [Hamlet to Horatio] *the most fanned and winnowed opinions* [i.e. most tried and tested views] [reading of F *fond*; Q2 *prophane*]

fantasied (*adj.*) full of strange fancies **KJ** IV.ii.144 [Bastard to King John, of the English] *I find the people strangely fantasied*

fantastic (*n.*) showy dresser, fop, dandy **MM** [list of characters in the play] *Lucio, a Fantastic*

fantastic (*adj.*) 1 extravagant, fanciful, ingenious **Ham** IV.vii.168 [Gertrude to Claudius and Laertes, of Ophelia] *fantastic garlands did she make;* **TG** II.vii.47; **Venus** 850
  2 imagined, existing only in the mind **R2** I.iii.299 [Bolingbroke to John of Gaunt] *thinking on fantastic summer's heat*

fantastical (*adj.*) 1 fanciful, imaginative, full of wild ideas **WT** IV.iv.747 [Clown to Shepherd, of Autolycus] *He seems to be the more noble in being fantastical;* **MA** II.iii.20; **MM** III.ii.88; **Oth** II.i.217; **TN** I.i.15; **TNK** IV.iii.13
  2 imaginary, unreal, illusory **Mac** I.iii.52 [Banquo to Witches] *Are ye fantastical, or that indeed / Which outwardly ye show?;* **Mac** I.iii.138

fantastically (*adv.*) fancifully, grotesquely, bizarrely **KL** IV.vi.80 [stage direction] *Enter Lear fantastically dressed with wild flowers;* **H5** II.iv.27

fantastico (*n.*) absurdity, person of wild ideas **RJ** II.iv.28 [Mercutio to Benvolio] *The pox of such antic, lisping, affecting fantasticoes* ➤ **phantasime** (*n.*)

fantasy (*n.*) 1 imagining, delusion, hallucination **Ham** I.i.23 [Marcellus to Barnardo, of the Ghost] *Horatio says 'tis but our fantasy;* **JC** II.i.197, 231; **MND** II.i.258, V.i.5
  2 imagination, inventiveness, mental creativity **2H4** V.ii.13 [Lord Chief Justice to Warwick, of his fate] *Which cannot look more hideously upon me / Than I have drawn it in my fantasy;* **MW** V.v.51
  3 imagination, mind, thought **JC** III.ii.2 [Cinna to himself] *I dreamt tonight that I did feast with Caesar, / And things unluckily charge my fantasy*
  4 whim, caprice, fancy **Oth** III.iii.296 [Emilia alone, of Iago] *but to please his fantasy;* **KJ** V.vii.18
  5 ardent desire, amorous fancy **AY** II.iv.27 [Silvius to Corin] *How many actions most ridiculous / Hast thou been drawn to by thy fantasy?;* **AY** V.ii.89; **MND** I.i.32; **MW** V.v.93

fap (*adj.*) drunk **MW** I.i.164 [Bardolph to Evans, of Slender] *being fap, sir, was … cashiered*

far (*adj.*) farther, more distant **JC** III.i.168 [Antony to all] *press not so upon me; stand far off;* **JC** V.iii.11; **WT** IV.iv.428

far (*adv.*) 1 to great lengths, very highly **Cym** I.i.24 [Second Gentleman to First Gentleman, of Posthumus] *You speak him far;* **Cym** V.v.309
  2 very greatly, deeply **Tim** I.ii.170 [First Lord to Timon] *I am so far already in your gifts*

farborough (*n.*) malapropism for 'thirdborough' [= parish officer] **LL** I.i.182 [Dull to Berowne, of the King] *I am his grace's farborough* [Q1; F *tharborough*] ➤ **thirdborough** (*n.*)

farce, force (*v.*) stuff, cram **TNK** IV.iii.7 [Gaoler to Doctor, of the Gaoler's Daughter's speech] *the name Palamon lards it, that she farces every business withal;* **TC** V.i.55 [Thersites alone, of Menelaus] *malice forced with wit* [Q *faced*]; **Mac** V.v.5; **TC** II.iii.220

farced (*adj.*) spiced up, stuffed with flattery **H5** IV.i.256 [King Henry alone] *The farced title running fore the king*

fardel (*n.*) burden, load, bundle **WT** IV.iv.750 [Autolycus to Shepherd] *The fardel there, what's i'th' fardel?;* **Ham** III.i.76; **WT** IV.iv.703, 713, V.ii.3, 114

fare (*n.*) 1 food, provision **KJ** V.vii.35 [King John to Prince Henry, in reply to 'How fares your majesty?'] *Poisoned - ill fare!* [also: fortune]
  2 happening, state of things, cheer **3H6** II.i.95 [Warwick to Richard and Edward] *What fare? What news abroad?* [i.e. what's happening?]

fare (*v.*) 1 get on, manage, do, cope **Tem** V.i.253 [Prospero to Alonso] *How fares my gracious sir?* ➤ **FEW**, p.xxi
  2 go, happen, turn out **TNK** V.iv.45 [Palamon to all] *How do things fare?;* **2H6** IV.vii.109; **3H6** II.v.1; **MA** IV.ii.220

fare … well ➤ **FAREWELLS**, p.170

farewell (*int.*) ➤ **FAREWELLS**, p.170

far-fet (*adj.*) cunning, scheming, devious **2H6** III.i.293 [Somerset to all, of York] *with all his far-fet policy*

farm (*v.*) lease out, rent out, let **R2** I.iv.45 [King Richard to Green] *We are enforced to farm our royal realm;* **Ham** IV.iv.20

farm, in farmed out, to let, rented out **R2** II.i.256 [Ross to Northumberland and Willoughby] *The Earl of Wiltshire hath the realm in farm*

farrer (*adv.*) farther, further **TS** IV.ii.73 [Tranio as Lucentio to Pedant] *Travel you farrer on, or are you at the farthest?* [F *farre*]

farrow (*n.*) [of pigs] litter, young, piglet **Mac** IV.i.64 [First Witch to Witches] *Pour in sow's blood that hath eaten / Her nine farrow*

farthingale (*n.*) long skirt extended at the back by a framework of hoops **TG** IV.iv.36 [Launce to his dog] *When didst thou see me … make water against a gentlewoman's farthingale?;* **MW** III.iii.60; **TG** II.vii.51 ➤ **CLOTHING**, p.79

fartuous (*adj.*) malapropism for 'virtuous' **MW** II.ii.94 [Mistress Quickly to Falstaff, of Mistress Page] *she's as fartuous a civil modest wife … as any is in Windsor*

fashion (*n.*) 1 manner, way, mode, appearance **JC** I.iii.34 [Cicero to Casca] *men may construe things after their fashion* [i.e. in their own way]; **Ham** I.iii.111; **2H4** IV.iv.54; **JC** III.iii.133; **Tim** I.i.144
  2 conventional behaviour, conformity, customary use **H5** IV.i.82 [King Henry alone, of Fluellen] *Though it appear a little out of fashion, / There is much care and valour in this Welshman;* **AY** III.ii.248; **CE** I.i.74; **Ham** II.ii.371, III.i.176; **Oth** II.i.200
  3 fad, modish behaviour, whim **Ham** I.iii.6 [Laertes to Ophelia, of Hamlet's love] *Hold it a fashion and a toy in blood;* **Ham** I.iii.112
  4 observance, style, latest practice **1H6** II.iv.76 [Richard to Somerset] *I scorn thee and thy fashion* [i.e. of wearing the red rose]; **JC** IV.i.39
  5 workmanship, craftsmanship, execution **CE** IV.i.29 [Angelo to Antipholus of Ephesus, of the chain] *The fineness of the gold, and chargeful fashion*
  6 kind, type, sort **WT** III.ii.103 [Hermione to Leontes, of the way she has been treated] *The childbed privilege denied, which 'longs / To women of all fashion;* **AY** II.ii.56; **TG** V.iv.61
  7 title, name, character **H8** IV.ii.159 [Capuchius to Katherine, of her request] *I will, / Or let me lose the fashion of a man!*
  8 (plural) horse disease affecting the nose and mouth [farcy] **TS** III.ii.51 [Biondello to Tranio as Lucentio, of Petruchio's horse] *infected with the fashions*

FAREWELLS

Several words and phrases can be used to say farewell or to bring a conversation to a close, either gently or abruptly. Most are no longer used (*good night* is the chief exception), or are used only in certain contexts (e.g. 'make my farewells'). Modern English *goodbye* is also present, in a variety of spellings; its modern form is an early 19th-century development.

Keyword	Location	Example

A simple farewell

adieu	**Ham** I.v.91	*Adieu, adieu, adieu*
fare	**2H4** III.ii.289	*Fare you well, gentle gentlemen* [also: *thee, ye*]
farewell	**Ham** II.i.74	*Farewell*
God bye [= God be with you]	**1H6** III.ii.73	*God bye, my lord*
	Ham II.i.69	*God bye ye*
	Ham II.ii.546	*God bye to you*
	AY III.ii.250	*God buy you*
	Oth I.iii.187	*God bu'y! I have done*

A farewell with time of day

even	**Cor** II.i.88	*Good e'en to your worships*
morrow	**KL** II.ii.156	*Give you good morrow!*
night	**Ham** III.iv.218	*Good night, mother*
	Ham I.i.16	*Give you good night*

A farewell with kind regards

commend	**Ham** V.ii.178	*I commend my duty to your lordship*
	Ham I.v.183	*I do commend me to you*
	CE I.ii.32	*I commend you to your own content* [i.e. wish you all you wish yourself]
	RJ II.iv.208	*Commend me to thy lady*

A farewell with concern for well-being

keep	**2H4** III.ii.288	*God keep you!*
merry	**RJ** I.ii.79	*Rest you merry*
save	**Ham** II.ii.221	*God save you, sir!*

A dismissal

drink	**R3** III.ii.105	*There, drink this for me* [thanking a messenger]
even	**RJ** III.v.172	*O, God-i-good-e'en!*
leave	**TN** II.iv.71	*Give me now leave, to leave thee* [very courteous dismissal]
way, ways	**TNK** III.v.59	*Go thy ways* [i.e. on your way]
	TN III.i.131	*There lies your way*

There is some overlap with expressions used in greeting: ☛ **GREETINGS**, p.206.

fashion (*v.*) **1** form, shape, make [into] **1H6** III.iii.65 [Pucelle to Burgundy] *When Talbot hath set footing once in France, / And fashioned thee that instrument of ill;* **Cor** II.iii.224; **2H4** II.iii.32; **KL** I.ii.180; **MA** I.iii.27

2 mould, transform, change the fashion of **JC** II.i.220 [Brutus to Metellus, of Ligarius] *Send him but hither, and I'll fashion him*

3 arrange, contrive, manage **MA** II.ii.42 [Borachio to Don John] *I will so fashion the matter that Hero shall be absent;* **1H4** I.iii.291; **JC** II.i.30; **MND** III.ii.194; **MV** I.iii.90; **Oth** IV.ii.234

fashion in (*v.*) frame, work in, introduce **TC** IV.iv.64 [Troilus to Cressida] *'be thou true,' say I, to fashion in / My sequent protestation*

fashion-monging (*adj.*) fashion-following, dealing in fashions, dandified **MA** V.i.94 [Antonio to Leonato, of Claudio and Don Pedro] *Scambling, out-facing, fashion-monging boys*

fast (*n.*) fasting, hunger **Venus** 55 *as an empty eagle, sharp by fast, / Tires with her beak on feathers, flesh and bone;* **Ham** II.ii.147

fast (*adj.*) **1** constant, firm, steadfast **2H6** V.ii.21 [York to Clifford] *thou art so fast mine enemy;* **Cym** I.vii.138; **3H6** IV.i.119, V.ii.3; **Oth** I.iii.357

2 firm, fixed, definite **KL** I.i.38 [Lear to all] *'tis our fast intent / To shake all cares and business from our age*

3 bound, assured, promised **MM** I.ii.146 [Claudio to Lucio, of Juliet] *She is fast my wife / Save that we do denunciation lack / Of outward order* ☛ hand-fast (*adj.*)

4 locked up, firmly bolted **H8** V.ii.3 [Cranmer to himself, of the Council Chamber door] *All fast?*; **3H6** IV.vii.10

5 close, very near [to] **TNK** II.v.6 [Gaoler's Daughter alone, of a cedar tree] *Fast by a brook*; **2H6** III.ii.189

6 fast asleep **RJ** IV.v.1 [Nurse to herself, of Juliet] *Fast, I warrant her, she*

fast (*v.*) **1** starve, stay empty, go without [food] **1H6** III.ii.42 [Pucelle to the English] *I think the Duke of Burgundy will fast / Before he'll buy again at such a rate*; **WT** IV.iv.597

2 do penance **Ham** I.v.11 [Ghost to Hamlet] *And for the day confined to fast in fires*

fast (*adv.*) **1** constantly, firmly, steadfastly **Sonn** 11.1 *As fast as thou shalt wane, so fast thou grow'st* [second instance]

2 tightly, firmly, securely **MM** V.i.208 [Mariana to Angelo] *This is the hand which … / Was fast belocked in thine*; **Sonn** 134.8

fast and loose type of cheating game [in which people bet on whether the end of a coiled rope is fastened or not]; not playing fairly **LL** III.i.101 [Costard to Mote] *To sell a bargain well is as cunning as fast and loose*; **AC** IV.xii.28; **LL** I.ii.151

fast out (*v.*) pass a period of abstinence **TS** I.i.108 [Gremio to Hortensio, of waiting for Bianca] *we may blow our nails together, and fast it fairly out*

fasten (*v.*) fix the idea, establish, inculcate **JC** V.i.11 [Antony to Octavius, of the enemy] *They could … come down / With fearful bravery, thinking by this face / To fasten in our thoughts that they have courage*

fastened (*adj.*) determined, steadfast, confirmed **KL** II.i.76 [Gloucester to Edmund, of Edgar] *O strange and fastened villain!*

fasting (*adj.*) caused by abstinence, hunger-induced **LL** IV.iii.120 [Dumaine to himself, of sending a token to Katharine] *That shall express my true love's fasting pain*

fastly (*adv.*) readily, quickly **Lover** 61 [of the woman] *A reverend man … / Towards this afflicted fancy fastly drew*

fat (*n.*) **1** plenty, wealth, abundance **R3** V.iii.259 [Richmond to his soldiers] *Your country's fat shall pay your pains the hire*

2 vat, wine cask, barrel **AC** II.vii.113 [Boy singing, as if to Bacchus] *In thy fats our cares be drowned*

fat (*adj.*) **1** hefty, substantial, full-bodied **1H4** II.i.68 [Gadshill to Chamberlain] *If I hang, I'll make a fat pair of gallows*

2 gross, heavy, dull **TN** V.i.107 [Olivia to Orsino, of his love-suit] *It is as fat and fulsome to mine ear / As howling after music*

3 fertile, rich, productive **2H4** IV.iv.54 [King Henry IV to Clarence] *Most subject is the fattest soil to weeds*

4 stuffy, fusty, close **1H4** II.iv.1 [Prince Hal to Poins] *come out of that fat room*

fat (*v.*) fatten, feed up, nourish **Tit** III.i.202 [Aaron to himself] *how this villainy / Doth fat me with the very thoughts of it*; **Ham** IV.iii.21; **TC** II.ii.48; **Tit** IV.ii.177 [F]; **TNK** III.vi.12

fatal (*adj.*) **1** ominous, full of foreboding, doom-laden **Mac** II.i.36 [Macbeth alone, as if to a dagger] *Art thou not, fatal vision, sensible / To feeling as to sight?*; **3H6** II.v.98, vi.56, IV.ii.21; **JC** V.i.87; **Mac** II.ii.3; **Tit** II.iii.97

2 decreed by fate, of destiny **1H6** I.iv.77 [Talbot to all, of Salisbury's wounding] *Accursed fatal hand / That hath contrived this woeful tragedy!*

3 death-dealing, death-boding **TN** III.iv.261 [Fabian to Viola as Cesario, of Sir Andrew] *He is … the most skilful, bloody, and fatal opposite that you could possibly have found in any part of Illyria*; **H5** II.iv.13; **3H6** I.iv.22, V.vi.16; **Tit** II.iii.202

fatal-plotted (*adj.*) containing a deadly plot **Tit** II.iii.47 [Aaron to Tamora, of a letter] *give the King this fatal-plotted scroll*

fate (*n.*) destiny, fortune **AC** IV.viii.34 [Antony to Cleopatra] *we all would … drink carouses to the next day's fate*; **AC** III.xiii.169; **Tim** III.v.14

fated (*adj.*) fateful, controlling our destiny **AW** I.i.213 [Helena alone] *The fated sky / Gives us free scope*

father (*n.*) **1** old man, venerable sir **TS** IV.v.48 [Katherina to Vincentio] *I perceive thou art a reverend father*; **KL** IV.vi.72; **Lover** 71; **Mac** II.iv.4; **MV** II.ii.56; **Tim** I.i.114 ✎ **ADDRESS FORMS**, p.8

2 stepfather **Ham** III.iv.10 [Gertrude to Hamlet] *thou hast thy father much offended* ✎ **FAMILY**, p.168

3 father of the Church, early Christian writer **LL** IV.ii.146 [Nathaniel to Holofernes] *as a certain father saith*; **LL** IV.ii.32

father (*v.*) **1** show one's paternal origin, resemble one's father **MA** I.i.102 [Don Pedro to all, of Beatrice] *the lady fathers herself*

2 be dealt with by a father **KL** III.vi.108 [Edgar alone, of Lear] *He childed as I fathered*

fatherly (*adv.*) in a paternal manner, with a father's love **Cym** II.iii.33 [Cloten to Second Lord, of Cymbeline] *he cannot choose but take this service I have done fatherly*

fathom (*n.*) calibre, ability, depth **Oth** I.i.153 [Iago to Roderigo, of Othello and the state] *Another of his fathom they have none / To lead their business*

fatigate (*adj.*) fatigued, weary, tired **Cor** II.ii.115 [Cominius to all, of Coriolanus] *his doubled spirit / Requickened what in flesh was fatigate*

fatness (*n.*) grossness, bloatedness **Ham** III.iv.154 [Hamlet to Gertrude] *in the fatness of these pursy times*

fat-witted (*adj.*) thick-witted, slow, dull **1H4** I.ii.2 [Prince Hal to Falstaff] *Thou art so fat-witted with drinking of old sack*

faucet-seller (*n.*) seller of taps for wine-barrels **Cor** II.i.66 [Menenius to Brutus and Sicinius] *You wear out a good wholesome forenoon in hearing a cause between an orange-wife and a faucet-seller*

fault (*n.*) **1** sin, offence, crime **H5** IV.i.286 [King Henry alone, praying] *think not upon the fault / My father made in compassing the crown!*; **2H6** III.i.47; **3H6** I.iv.106; **KL** I.i.15; **MM** V.i.453; **Tim** III.v.1

2 mistake, error, blunder **KJ** IV.ii.30 [Pembroke to King John] *oftentimes excusing of a fault / Doth make the fault the worser by th'excuse*; **2H6** I.iii.197; **3H6** III.ii.164; **MM** II.i.40, V.i.460; **TG** IV.iv.13

3 failing, weakness **H5** II.Chorus.20 [Chorus, as if to England] *thy fault France hath in thee found out*; **JC** I.iii.45; **MM** II.i.28; **MW** III.iii.206

4 misfortune, mischance, bad luck **Per** IV.ii.70 [Marina to Bawd, of Leonine] *The more my fault / To 'scape his hands where I was like to die*

5 [hunting] break in a line of scent, loss of scent **Venus** 694 [Venus to Adonis, of hounds] *Ceasing their clamorous cry till they have singled … the cold fault cleanly out*; **TN** II.v.125; **TS** Induction.i.18

fault of, for (*prep.*) in default of, in the absence of **RJ** II.iv.119 [Romeo to Nurse, of his name] *I am the youngest of that name, for fault of a worse*

faultful (*adj.*) sinful, culpable, wicked **Luc** 715 [of Tarquin] *this faultful lord of Rome*

faulty (*adj.*) guilty, blameworthy, culpable **2H6** III.ii.202 [Suffolk to Warwick] *Say, if thou darest … / That I am faulty in Duke Humphrey's death*

favour (*n.*) **1** [facial] appearance, countenance, features, looks **Cym** V.v.93 [Cymbeline to Lucius, of disguised Innogen] *His favour is familiar to me*; **AY** IV.iii.87; **Ham** V.i.191; **1H4** III.ii.136; **MA** II.i.84; **TC** IV.v.213

2 appearance, look, aspect **KJ** V.iv.50 [Salisbury to Melun, of returning his allegiance to King John] *I do love the favour and the form / Of this most fair occasion*; **JC** I.iii.129

3 charm, attractiveness, gracefulness **TG** II.i.52 [Valentine to Speed, of Silvia] *her beauty is exquisite, but her favour infinite*; **Cym** I.vii.42; **Ham** IV.v.189; **Oth** IV.iii.20

4 friendship, good will, friendly regard **WT** I.ii.365 [Polixenes to Camillo] *methinks / My favour here begins to warp*; **Ham** V.ii.78; **1H6** III.iii.34

5 mark of favour, gift, token [often a love-token] **LL** V.ii.773 [Princess to King] *We have received … / Your favours;* **AW** V.iii.74; **KL** IV.ii.21; **Lover** 36; **MND** VI.i.48; **TNK** II.i.65

6 token worn as a mark of identity or friendship **H5** IV.vii.149 [King Henry to Fluellen, of a glove] *wear thou this favour for me, and stick it in thy cap;* **1H4** V.iv.95

7 gesture or token of regard, bow, curtsy **R2** IV.i.168 [Richard to all, of them as former subjects] *I well remember / The favours of these men* [or: sense 1]; **TNK** III.v.30

8 pardon, leave, kind indulgence **Mac** I.iii.149 [Macbeth to all] *Give me your favour* ➤ POLITENESS, p.340

9 leniency, kindness, clemency **WT** II.iii.178 [Leontes to Antigonus, of taking the baby far away] *leave it … to its own protection / And favour of the climate;* **2H6** IV.vii.62

favoured (*adj.*) ➤ hard-favoured (*adj.*); ill-favoured (*adj.*); well-favoured (*adj.*)

favourite (*n.*) follower, supporter, ally **3H6** I.i.56 [King to Northumberland and Clifford, of York] *you both have vowed revenge / On him, his sons, his favourites, and his friends;* **1H6** IV.i.190

fawn (*v.*) revel, gloat, show delight **Luc** 421 *As the grim lion fawneth o'er his prey*

fazed (*adj.*) frayed, unravelled, tattered **1H4** IV.ii.30 [Falstaff alone, of his soldiers] *ten times more dishonourable-ragged than an old fazed ancient* [Q; F *fac'd*]

fealty (*n.*) [feudal obligation of obedience] duty of loyalty, allegiance, fidelity **Tit** I.i.260 [Saturninus to Romans] *forget your fealty to me;* **Cym** V.v.73; **E3** I.i.79; **2H6** V.i.50; **R2** V.ii.45; **TG** II.iv.89

fear (*n.*) **1** awe, reverence, dread **TNK** V.i.149 [Emilia praying to Diana] *lend thine ear … to my petition / Seasoned with holy fear*

2 apprehension, dread **3H6** IV.vi.62 [King to Warwick and George, of the Queen and Prince] *till I see them here, by doubtful fear / My joy of liberty is half eclipsed*

3 object of dread, thing to be feared **2H4** IV.v.195 [King Henry IV to Prince Henry, of rebellion against the crown] *All these bold fears / Thou seest with peril I have answered;* **1H4** I.iii.86

4 formidableness, ability to inspire fear **3H6** II.vi.5 [Clifford alone, as if to the House of Lancaster] *My love and fear glued many friends to thee*

5 frightfulness, terrifying appearance **Cym** III.iv.9 [Innogen to Pisanio] *Put thyself / Into a haviour of less fear*

6 duty, solicitude, obligation **Ham** III.iii.8 [Guildenstern to Claudius] *Most holy and religious fear it is*

fear (*v.*) **1** frighten, scare, terrify, daunt **3H6** V.ii.2 [Edward to himself] *Warwick was a bug that feared us all;* **AC** II.vi.24; **2H4** IV.iv.121; **MV** II.i.9; **TNK** III.vi.129; **Venus** 1094

2 fear for, worry about, be anxious about **1H4** IV.i.24 [Messenger to Worcester, of Northumberland] *He was much feared by his physicians;* **AW** III.v.28; **3H6** III.iii.24; **MV** III.ii.29; **Tim** II.ii.15; **Venus** 642

3 doubt, mistrust **2H6** I.iv.5 [Hume to Bolingbroke, of the Duchess of Gloucester] *Fear you not her courage;* **Ham** III.iv.7; **3H6** I.ii.60; **TN** V.i.218; **TNK** III.iii.51

feared (*adj.*) infused with fear, full of fear, frightened **H5** I.ii.155 [Canterbury to King Henry, of England] *She hath been then more feared than harmed;* **Cym** II.iv.6

fearful (*adj.*) **1** timid, timorous, frightened, full of fear **3H6** I.i.25 [Warwick to York] *This is the palace of the fearful King;* **CE** I.i.68; **3H6** I.i.178; **H8** VI.i.87; **TNK** Epilogue.3; **Venus** 677

2 causing fear, awe-inspiring, terrifying, alarming **R3** V.iii.98 [Derby to Richmond] *The leisure and the fearful time / Cuts off the ceremonious vows of love;* **Cym** III.iv.44; **E3** III.ii.33; **JC** I.iii.78; **R3** I.i.11; **TN** I.v.200

fearfully (*adv.*) frighteningly, terrifyingly **KL** IV.i.73 [Gloucester to Edgar as Poor Tom] *There is a cliff whose high and bending head / Looks fearfully in the confined deep* [or: timorously, if envisaged as a person] [F; Q *firmely*]

fear-surprised (*adj.*) made helpless by fear, overcome by fear **Ham** I.ii.203 [Horatio to Hamlet, of the Ghost] *Thrice he walked / By their oppressed and fear-surprised eyes*

feast-finding (*adj.*) searching out feasts [at which to entertain the company] **Luc** 817 [Lucrece to herself] *Feast-finding minstrels tuning my defame*

feasting (*adj.*) jubilant, sumptuous, festive **RJ** V.iii.86 [Romeo to dead Paris, of Juliet] *her beauty makes / This vault a feasting presence full of light*

feat (*n.*) **1** achievement, skill, accomplishment **Per** V.i.71 [Lysimachus to Marina, of Pericles] *If that thy prosperous and artificial feat / Can draw him but to answer thee;* **TNK** II.iv.13

2 action, deed, conduct **TNK** III.i.45 [Palamon to Arcite] *give me language such / As thou hast showed me feat* [i.e. suit your words to your actions]; **H8** I.i.61; **TNK** V.i.43

3 [wicked] deed, action, crime **H5** III.iii.17 [King Henry to citizens of Harfleur, of war] *Do … all fell feats / Enlinked to waste and desolation?;* **Ham** IV.vii.6

feat (*adj.*) **1** adept, deft, graceful **Cym** V.v.88 [Lucius to Cymbeline, of disguised Innogen] *never master had / A page … / So feat, so nurse-like*

2 becoming, neat, well fitting **Tem** II.i.278 [Antonio to Sebastian] *look how well my garments sit upon me, / Much feater than before*

feat (*v.*) show a model of behaviour **Cym** I.i.49 [First Gentleman to Second Gentleman, of Posthumus' role with the courtiers] *to th' more mature / A glass that feated them*

feat (*adv.*) neatly, prettily, elegantly **Lover** 48 [of letters] *With sleided silk, feat and affectedly / Enswathed*

feather (*n.*) kind, type, disposition **Tim** I.i.104 [Timon to Messenger] *I am not of that feather to shake off / My friend when he must need me*

feathered (*adj.*) winged, fleet, swift **Per** V.ii.15 [Gower alone] *In feathered briefness sails are filled*

featly (*adv.*) gracefully, skilfully, nimbly **WT** IV.iv.178 [disguised Polixenes to Shepherd, of Perdita] *She dances featly;* **Tem** I.ii.379

feature (*n.*) physical appearance, bodily shape, looks **AC** II.v.112 [Cleopatra to Alexas, of the Messenger] *bid him / Report the feature of Octavia;* **AY** III.iii.3; **Ham** III.i.160; **R3** I.i.19; **Tem** III.i.52; **TG** II.iv.71

fecks (*n.*) ➤ SWEARING, p.435

fedary, federary, feodary (*n.*) confederate, accomplice, accessory **WT** II.i.90 [Leontes to Lords, of Hermione] *she's a traitor, and Camillo is / A fedary with her* [F *Federarie*]; **MM** II.iv.122

fee (*n.*) **1** value, worth **Ham** I.iv.65 [Hamlet to Horatio] *I do not set my life at a pin's fee*

2 payment, reward, recompense **MND** III.ii.113 [Puck to Oberon, of Lysander] *Pleading for a lover's fee;* **R3** I.ii.169; **Venus** 393

3 possession, property **TNK** I.i.198 [Hippolyta to Theseus] *that neck / Which is my fee*

4 dependent creature, beneficiary, vassal **Tim** III.vi.79 [Timon as if to the gods] *The rest of your fees … what is amiss in them, you gods, make suitable for destruction*

fee, in in absolute possession, as freehold **Ham** IV.iv.22 [Captain to Hamlet, of the land being fought over] *should it be sold in fee*

fee (*v.*) **1** pay, recompense **3H6** I.iv.92 [Queen to York] *Thou wouldst be fee'd, I see, to make me sport*

2 purchase, procure, secure **MV** III.i.116 [Shylock to Tubal] *fee me an officer;* **MW** II.ii.190

fee'd (*adj.*) paid by a fee, hired, bribed **Mac** III.iv.131 [Macbeth to Lady Macbeth, of his courtiers] *There's not a one of them, but in his house / I keep a servant fee'd;* **TN** I.v.273

feeble (*v.*) make feeble, weaken **Cor** I.i.193 [Martius to Menenius, of the citizens] *feebling such as stand not in their liking*

feed (*n.*) pasture, grazing land **AY** II.iv.80 [Corin to all, of his master's lands] *his flocks, and bounds of feed / Are now on sale*

feeder (*n.*) **1** servant, parasite, lackey **Tim** II.ii.164 [Flavius to Timon] *When all our offices have been oppressed / With riotous feeders;* **AC** III.xiii.109

2 servant; or: shepherd **AY** II.iv.96 [Corin to Celia as Aliena and Rosalind as Ganymede] *I will your very faithful feeder be*

feeding (*n.*) grazing-ground, pasturage **WT** IV.iv.171 [Shepherd to disguised Polixenes, of Florizel] *They call him Doricles, and boasts himself / To have a worthy feeding* [i.e. a valuable landed estate]

fee-farm (*n.*) [legal] state of tenure granted in perpetuity **TC** III.ii.49 [Pandarus to Troilus] *How now, a kiss in fee-farm!* [i.e. apparently never-ending]

fee-grief (*n.*) individual sorrow, personal distress **Mac** IV.iii.196 [Macduff to Ross, of Ross's news] *What concern they? / The general cause, or is it a fee-grief / Due to some single breast?*

feel (*v.*) **1** react to, be affected by **KL** IV.ii.13 [Gonerill to Edmund, of Albany] *He'll not feel wrongs / Which tie him to an answer*

2 experience, live through [something] **Cym** III.iii.46 [Belarius to Guiderius and Arviragus] *Did you but know the city's usuries, / And felt them knowingly;* **Cor** III.iii.129

3 test, discover, sound out **H5** IV.i.121 [disguised King Henry to Bates, of his comments about the King] *you speak this to feel other men's minds;* **KL** I.ii.87

feeling (*n.*) **1** sensibility, intuition, understanding **Ham** V.i.65 [Hamlet to Horatio, of the First Clown] *Has this fellow no feeling of his business?*

2 experience, sensibility, sense of awareness [of the consequences] **Cym** V.v.68 [Cymbeline to all, of Innogen] *it was folly in me, thou mayst say, / And prove it in thy feeling*

feeling (*adj.*) **1** deeply felt, heartfelt, acutely sensed **WT** IV.ii.7 [Camillo to Polixenes, of Leontes] *to whose feeling sorrows I might be some allay;* **KL** IV.vi.222; **RJ** III.v.74

2 capable of sensation **Venus** 892 [of Venus' heart] *With cold-pale weakness numbs each feeling part*

feeling-painful (*adj.*) painfully felt, heartfelt **Luc** 1679 [Lucrece to Collatine] *My woe too sensible thy passion maketh / More feeling-painful*

feelingly (*adv.*) **1** pertinently, aptly, to the point **TN** II.iii.152 [Maria to Sir Toby, of Malvolio] *he shall find himself most feelingly personated;* **MM** I.ii.34

2 in ways that reach the senses **AY** II.i.11 [Duke Senior to all] *counsellors / That feelingly persuade me what I am;* **KL** IV.vi.150

fee-simple, fee simple (*n.*) private estate [belonging to the owner and his heirs for ever]; permanent lease, full possession **2H6** IV.x.24 [Cade to himself, of Iden] *Here's the lord of the soil come to seize me for a stray, for entering his fee-simple without leave;* **AW** IV.iii.270; **Lover** 144; **RJ** III.i.31; **TC** V.i.20 [Q]

fee simple, in complete possession **MW** IV.ii.198 [Mistress Page to Mistress Ford, of Falstaff] *If the devil have him not in fee simple, with fine and recovery, he will never ... attempt us again*

feeze (*v.*) ☞ **pheeze** (*v.*)

feign (*v.*) **1** depict, imagine, conjure up **Tim** I.i.226 [Apemantus to Poet, of Timon] *Look in thy last work, where thou hast feigned him a worthy fellow;* **3H6** I.ii.31

2 make appear, put on a demeanour **RJ** II.v.16 [Juliet alone] *old folks, many feign as they were dead*

feigned (*adj.*) **1** sham, pretended, spurious **Tit** IV.iv.21 [Saturninus to all, of Titus] *his feigned ecstasies / Shall be no shelter to these outrages;* **R3** V.i.21

2 deceptive, contrived in order to deceive **Cym** V.v.279 [Pisanio to Cymbeline] *By accident, / I had a feigned letter of my master's / Then in my pocket*

feigning (*n.*) pretentiousness, posturing, courtly display **TN** III.i.96 [Olivia to Viola as Cesario] *'Twas never merry world / Since lowly feigning was called compliment*

felicitate (*adj.*) made happy, joyful, ecstatic **KL** I.i.75 [Regan to Lear] *I am alone felicitate / In your dear highness' love*

felicity (*n.*) happiness, bliss, joy **Ham** V.ii.341 [Hamlet to Horatio] *Absent thee from felicity awhile*

fell (*n.*) **1** skin, hide **KL** V.iii.24 [Lear to Cordelia, of their enemies] *The good-years shall devour them, flesh and fell* [i.e. totally]; **Mac** V.v.11

2 fleece **AY** III.ii.50 [Corin to Touchstone, of the ewes] *their fells you know are greasy*

fell (*adj.*) **1** cruel, fierce, savage **Luc** 766 [Lucrece as if to and of night] *Black stage for tragedies and murders fell;* **Cym** IV.ii.109; **3H6** II.v.89; **R2** I.iii.302; **TC** IV.v.269; **TNK** III.ii.15

2 mighty, terrible **Tit** V.iii.99 [Lucius to all, of Chiron and Demetrius] *For their fell faults our brothers were beheaded;* **Cor** IV.v.18; **Ham** V.ii.330; **2H4** IV.v.206; **Mac** IV.ii.71; **Sonn** 74.1

3 deadly, destructive, virulent **Tim** IV.iii.62 [Timon to Alcibiades, of Phrynia] *This fell whore of thine*

fell (*adv.*) fiercely, savagely, brutally **Ham** V.ii.61 [Hamlet to Horatio] *Between the pass and fell incensed points / Of mighty opposites*

fell-lurking (*adj.*) savagely waiting, fierce in attendance **2H6** V.i.146 [York to Clifford, of Warwick and Salisbury] *with the very shaking of their chains / They may astonish these fell-lurking curs*

fellow (*n.*) **1** companion, associate **TS** I.i.127 [Hortensio to Gremio] *there be good fellows in the world, an a man could light on them;* **3H6** IV.iii.55; **KL** III.i.48; **MV** I.i.51; **Tem** II.i.279

2 counterpart, match, equal **CE** I.ii.37 [Antipholus of Syracuse alone, comparing himself to a drop of water] *That in the ocean seeks another drop, / Who, falling there to find his fellow forth ... confounds himself;* **Cym** III.iv.92; **Tim** I.i.81; **TN** III.iv.78

3 spouse, husband/wife **Tem** III.i.84 [Miranda to Ferdinand] *To be your fellow / You may deny me*

4 servant, attendant, hireling **LL** I.ii.145 [Costard to Armado] *I am more bound to you than your fellows*

5 fellow-servant, colleague **Cor** IV.v.2 [First Servingman alone] *I think our fellows are asleep;* **Tim** IV.iii.18, 25; **TS** I.i.220

6 practitioner, specialist, expert **AW** II.iii.12 [Lafew to Parolles] *To be relinquished ... Of all the learned and authentic fellows*

7 keeper, warden, forester **MW** V.v.26 [Falstaff to Mistresses Ford and Page] *I will keep ... my shoulders for the fellow of this walk*

8 worthless individual, good-for-nothing **TNK** II.i.226 [Palamon to Arcite, of Emilia] *Thou art ... a fellow / False as thy title to her;* **AC** III.xiii.123; **MM** V.i.266

fellow (*v.*) share in, become a partner of **WT** I.ii.142 [Leontes to himself, of lustful desire] *With what's unreal thou coactive art, / And fellow'st nothing*

fellowly (*adj.*) companiable, sympathetic, of fellowship **Tem** V.i.64 [Prospero to charmed Gonzalo] *Mine eyes, ev'n sociable to the show of thine, / Fall fellowly drops*

fellowship (*n.*) partnership, membership, participation **Ham** III.ii.286 [Hamlet to Horatio, of the play before Claudius] *Would not this... get me a fellowship in a cry of players, sir?;* **Tim** V.ii.12

felly (*n.*) piece of curved wood forming part of a wheel rim **Ham** II.ii.493 [First Player to all present, of Fortune] *Break all the spokes and fellies from her wheel* [reading of F *Fallies*; Q2 *follies*]

felonious (*adj.*) wicked, criminal, iniquitous **2H6** III.i.129 [Gloucester to York] *a bloody murderer / Or foul felonious thief that fleeced poor passengers*

female (*adj.*) womanish, weak, delicate **R2** III.ii.114 [Scroop to King Richard] *Boys ... clap their female joints / In stiff unwieldy arms*

femitar, femiter (*n.*) ☞ **fumiter** (*n.*)

fen (*n.*) marshland, swamp **Cor** IV.i.30 [Coriolanus to Volumnia] *I go alone, / Like to a lonely dragon that his fen / Makes feared and talked of more than seen;* **Tem** I.ii.322, II.i.51, II.i.2

fence (*n.*) **1** fencing ability, skill at swordplay **MA** V.i.75 [Leonato to Don Pedro, of fighting Claudio] *Despite his nice fence and his active practice;* **2H6** II.i.51, iii.78; **KJ** II.i.290; **MW** I.i.265

2 defence, barrier, protection **3H6** IV.i.44 [Hastings to Montague] *Let us be backed with God and with the seas / Which He hath given for fence impregnable;* **MA** V.i.84

3 protect, shield, defend **Per** I.ii.31 [Pericles alone] *the tops of trees / Which fence the roots they grow by;* **3H6** II.vi.75, III.iii.98; **Luc** 63

fenced *(adj.)* fortified, furnished, equipped **E3** IV.vi.39 [Philip to King John, of their army] *Arrayed and fenced in all accomplements*

fennel *(n.)* fragrant herb used as a sauce for fish **2H4** II.iv.240 [Falstaff to Doll, of why Prince Harry loves Poins] *'a ... eats conger and fennel* ☛ **PLANTS**, p.330

fenny *(adj.)* fen-living, marshland-dwelling **Mac** IV.i.12 [Second Witch to Witches] *Fillet of a fenny snake / In the cauldron boil and bake*

fen-sucked *(adj.)* rising from marshes **KL** II.iv.162 [Lear to Regan, of Gonerill] *Infect her beauty, / You fen-sucked fogs drawn by the powerful sun*

feodory *(n.)* accomplice, confederate, accessory **Cym** III.ii.21 [Pisanio alone, of the letter] *Senseless bauble, / Art thou a feodary for this act*

fere *(n.)* spouse, partner, wife / husband **Tit** IV.i.88 [Marcus to all, of Lucrece] *the woeful fere / And father of that chaste dishonoured dame;* **TNK** V.i.116

fern-seed *(n.)* seed from the fern [thought to confer invisibility] **1H4** II.i.90 [Chamberlain to Gadshill] *I think you are more beholding to the night than to fern-seed for your walking invisible;* **1H4** II.i.88

ferret *(adj.)* ferret-like, red, blazing **JC** I.ii.185 [Brutus to Cassius] *Cicero / Looks with such ferret and such fiery eyes*

ferret *(v.)* worry [like a ferret], hunt after **H5** IV.iv.29 [Pistol to Boy, of French Soldier] *I'll fer him, and firk him, and ferret him*

fertile *(adj.)* abundant, profuse, rich **TN** I.v.244 [Viola as Cesario to Olivia, of Orsino's love] *With adorations, fertile tears;* **WT** I.ii.113

ferula *(n.)* cane, rod, stick [for punishment] **TNK** III.v.111 [Schoolmaster to Theseus] *I ... humble with a ferula the tall ones*

fervency *(n.)* enthusiasm, ardour, fervour **AC** II.v.18 [Charmian to Cleopatra] *your diver / Did hang a salt fish on his hook, which he / With fervency drew up*

fescue *(n.)* [device for indicating letters to young readers] pointer, rod, stick **TNK** II.ii.34 [Third Countryman to First Countryman, of his wife] *do but put / A fescue in her fist, and you shall see her / Take a new lesson out*

fester *(v.)* corrupt, putrify, rot **RJ** IV.iii.43 [Juliet alone, of the tomb where she will wake] *Where bloody Tybalt, yet but green in earth, / Lies festering;* **Cor** I.ix 30; **H5** IV.iii.88; **Sonn** 94.14

festinate *(adj.)* speedy, hasty, hurried **KL** III.vii.10 [Cornwall to Edmund] *Advise the Duke ... to a most festinate preparation* [F *festiuate;* Q *festuant*]

festinately *(adv.)* quickly, speedily, in a hurry **LL** III.i.5 [Armado to Mote, of Costard] *bring him festinately hither*

festival *(adj.)* light-hearted, befitting a holiday **MA** V.ii.40 [Benedick alone] *I cannot woo in festival terms*

fet *(v.)* **1** fetch **R3** II.ii.121 [Buckingham to all] *Forthwith from Ludlow the young Prince be fet* [F; Q *fetcht*]

2 derive, draw **H5** III.i.18 [King Henry to all] *you noblest English, / Whose blood is fet from fathers of war-proof!*

fetch *(n.)* **1** dodge, stratagem, contrivance **KL** II.iv.85 [Lear to Gloucester, of Regan's excuses] *Mere fetches* [F; Q *Iustice*]; **Ham** II.i.38

2 type of fodder crop; vetch, tare **Tem** IV.i.61 [Iris to Ceres] *thy rich leas / Of ... fetches*

fetch *(v.)* **1** escort, accompany, conduct **JC** II.ii.59 [Decius to Caesar] *I come to fetch you to the Senate House;* **JC** II.ii.108

2 take, perform, make **Cym** I.ii.12 [Queen to Innogen] *I'll fetch a turn about the garden;* **MV** V.i.73

3 trace, find the origin of **2H4** II.ii.112 [Prince Henry to Poins, of every man] *they will be kin to us, or they will fetch it from Japhet*

4 derive, stem **R2** I.i.97 [Bolingbroke to King Richard] *all the treasons ... in this land / Fetch from false Mowbray;* **H5** II.ii.116

5 rescue, save, deliver **MM** II.iv.93 [Angelo to Isabella, of any influential person] *Could fetch your brother from the manacles / Of the all-binding law*

fetch about *(v.)* change tack, move in a roundabout way **KJ** IV.ii.24 [Salisbury to King John, of his second coronation] *It makes the course of thoughts to fetch about*

fetch in *(v.)* **1** surround, close in upon, capture **AC** IV.i.14 [Caesar to Maecenas, of Antony] *Within our files there are ... / Enough to fetch him in*

2 bring in, involve **H8** I.i.80 [Buckingham to Abergavenny, of Wolsey] *[he] Must fetch him in he papers* [i.e. he requires the presence of whoever he puts on his list]

3 lead on, take in, trick into a confession **MA** I.i.206 [Claudio to Don Pedro] *You speak this to fetch me in*

fetch off *(v.)* **1** rescue, get back, retrieve **AW** III.vi.17 [Second Lord to Bertram, of Parolles] *let him fetch off his drum;* **AW** III.vi.38; **Cor** I.iv.64; **Tem** IV.i.213

2 do away with, make an end of, kill **WT** I.ii.334 [Camillo to Leontes, of Polixenes] *I ... will fetch off Bohemia* [also: sense 1]

3 fleece, trick, get the better of **2H4** III.ii.291 [Falstaff alone, of Shallow and Silence] *I will fetch off these justices*

fetter *(v.)* restrain, overcome, suppress **MM** III.i.70 [Isabella to Claudio] *There is a devilish mercy in the judge ... that will free your life, / But fetter you till death;* **MA** V.i.25; **Tit** V.iii.6; **TN** III.i.152

fettle *(v.)* make ready, put in order **RJ** III.v.153 [Capulet to Juliet] *fettle your fine joints 'gainst Thursday next*

fever *(v.)* throw into a fever, cause to shiver **AC** III.xiii.138 [Antony to Thidias] *Henceforth / The white hand of a lady fever thee*

feverous *(adj.)* feverish, restless **TC** III.ii.34 [Troilus alone] *My heart beats thicker than a feverous pulse;* **MM** III.i.78

few, in *(a)* in few words, in short, in brief **Tem** I.ii.144 [Prospero to Miranda, of Antonio's agents] *In few, they hurried us aboard a bark;* **Ham** I.iii.126; **2H4** I.i.112; **H5** I.ii.246; **MM** III.i.229; **TS** I.ii.51

fewness and truth in few words and in truth **MM** I.iv.39 [Lucio to Isabella] *Fewness and truth, 'tis thus*

fia *(int.)* ☛ **via** *(int.)*

fichew, ficho *(n.)* ☛ **fitchew** *(n.)*

fico *(n.)* fig **MW** I.iii.27 [Pistol to Nym, of the word 'steal'] *A fico for the phrase!* ☛ **EXCLAMATIONS**, p.158

fidelity, by my upon my word of honour **MW** IV.ii.144 [Shallow to Ford] *By my fidelity, this is not well*

fidiuse *(v.)* [jocular form of 'Aufidius'] treated as Aufidius was treated **Cor** II.i.126 [Menenius to Volumnia] *I would not have been so fidiused for all the chests in Corioles*

fie *(int.)* ☛ **EXCLAMATIONS**, p.158

fie away *(v.)* be off, begone **TN** II.iv.52 [Feste singing] *Fie away, fie away, breath!*

field *(n.)* **1** field of battle, battleground, field of combat **Ham** V.ii.396 [Fortinbras to all] *Such a sight as this / Becomes the field* ☛ **FEW**, p.xxi

2 duelling place **RJ** III.i.57 [Mercutio to Tybalt, of Romeo] *go before to field, he'll be your follower!;* **TN** II.iii.124

3 field officer, general **LL** III.i.184 [Browne alone, of Cupid] *And I to be a corporal of his field* [i.e. a subordinate under his command]

4 wasteland, wilderness **KL** III.iv.107 [Fool to Lear] *a little fire in a wild field;* **E3** III.iii.22

field, in engaged in military operations, in military array **AC** II.i.17 [Menas to all] *Caesar and Lepidus / Are in the field*

field-bed *(n.)* bed out in the open, bed on the ground **RJ** II.i.40 [Mercutio as if to Romeo] *This field-bed is too cold for me to sleep*

fielded (*adj.*) in the battle-field, engaged in battle **Cor** I.iv.12 [Martius to Messenger, as if to Mars] *I prithee, make us quick in work, … / To help our fielded friends!*

fiend (*n.*) monster, malign being, evil foe **Venus** 638 [Venus to Adonis, of a boar] *Beauty hath nought to do with such foul fiends*

fierce (*adj.*) **1** ardent, active, vigorous **LL** V.ii.842 [Rosaline to Berowne] *With all the fierce endeavour of your wit;* **KL** I.ii.12

2 wild, lively, violent **MND** IV.i.68 [Oberon to Puck, of the Athenians] *May all to Athens back again repair / And think no more of this night's accidents / But as the fierce vexation of a dream;* **H8** I.i.54

3 drastic, severe, extreme **Cym** V.v.383 [Cymbeline to all] *This fierce abridgement / Hath to it circumstantial branches;* **Tim** IV.ii.30

fiery (*adj.*) **1** ardent, spirited, animated **2H4** IV.iii.98 [Falstaff alone, of the effect of sherry on the brain] *makes it … full of nimble, fiery, and delectable shapes;* **R3** IV.iii.54

2 spreading like fire **Ham** IV.iii.42 [Claudius to Hamlet] *this deed … must send thee hence / With fiery quickness*

fiery (*adv.*) brightly, conspicuously, brilliantly **Ham** V.ii.251 [Hamlet to Laertes] *Your skill shall, like a star … / Stick fiery off indeed*

fife (*n.*) fife-player **MV** II.v.29 [Shylock to Jessica] *the vile squealing of the wry-necked fife*

fift (*adj*) variant spelling of 'fifth' **KJ** IV.ii.184 [Hubert to King John, of five moons seen] *the fift did whirl about / The other four in wondrous motion* [F]

fifteen, fifteenth (*n.*) tax of a fifteenth part levied on personal property **2H6** I.i.131 [Gloucester to all, of the Queen] *Suffolk should demand a whole fifteenth / For costs and charges in transporting her!;* **2H6** IV.vii.19 [Messenger to Cade, of Say] *he that made us pay one-and-twenty fifteens*

fig (*n.*) ➤ **EXCLAMATIONS**, p.158

fig (*v.*) **1** word used along with a rude gesture [of the thumb between the first two fingers of a fist] **2H4** V.iii.118 [Pistol to Falstaff] *When Pistol lies, do this, and fig me* ➤ **figo** (*n.*)

2 ➤ **jig** (*v.*)

fight (*n.*) screen raised for protecting the crew during a sea-battle **MW** II.ii.132 [Pistol to himself] *up with your fights*

fight out (*v.*) fight to the very end **Tit** V.iii.101 [Lucius to all, of Titus] *basely cozened / Of that true hand that fought Rome's quarrel out*

figo (*n.*) word used along with a rude gesture [of the thumb between the first two fingers of a fist] **H5** IV.vi.60 [Pistol to disguised King Henry] *The figo for thee then!;* **H5** III.vi.56 ➤ **fig** (*v.*) 1

figure (*n.*) **1** form, design, shape, conception **2H4** I.iii.43 [Lord Bardolph to Hastings, of building] *when we see the figure of the house, / Then must we rate the cost of the erection;* **KJ** V.iv.25; **Oth** I.i.63; **Sonn** 98.11; **TC** III.iii.123; **Tim** V.i.152

2 figure of speech, device, piece of rhetoric **1H4** I.iii.207 [Worcester to Northumberland, of Hotspur] *He apprehends a world of figures here;* **AY** V.i.40; **Ham** II.ii.98; **LL** I.i.54; **TNK** III.v.15; **TS** I.ii.112

3 copy, image, likeness **R2** IV.i.125 [Bishop of Carlisle to all, of King Richard] *shall the figure of God's majesty … / Be judged by subject and inferior breath;* **Cym** V.v.25; **MM** I.i.16; **TG** III.ii.6; **TNK** II.i.87

4 face; or: body **TNK** V.iii.59 [Emilia to herself] *yet may Palamon wound Arcite to / The spoiling of his figure*

5 portrayal, rendering, presentation **Tem** III.iii.84 [Prospero to Ariel] *Bravely the figure of this harpy hast thou / Performed;* **AW** III.i.12; **RJ** V.iii.301

6 role, part, character **Cym** III.iii.96 [Belarius alone, comparing Arviragus to Guiderius] *in as like a figure / Strikes life into my speech*

7 parallel, comparison, analogy **H5** IV.vii.31 [Fluellen to Gower] *there is figures in all things;* **H5** IV.vii.42

8 fancy, imagining, phantasm **MW** IV.ii.204 [Mistress Page to Mistress Ford, of telling their husbands about Falstaff] *to scrape the figures out of your husband's brains;* **JC** II.i.231

9 astrological diagram, horoscope **MW** IV.ii.165 [Ford to Mistress Ford, of her maid's aunt] *She works by charms, by spells, by th'figure*

10 writing system, type of orthography **Tim** V.iii.7 [Soldier alone] *Our captain hath in every figure skill*

figure (*v.*) **1** symbolize, represent, portray **MND** I.i.237 [Helena to herself, of Cupid] *Wings and no eyes figure unheedy haste;* **2H4** IV.i.45; **Lover** 199; **MM** I.ii.52; **Sonn** 108.2

2 reproduce, look like, shape like **E3** III.i.72 [Mariner to King John, of the English fleet] *Figuring the horned circle of the moon;* **2H4** III.i.77

3 foretell, reveal, disclose **3H6** II.i.32 [Richard to Edward, of seeing three suns] *In this the heaven figures some event*

figure over (*v.*) cover with a pattern, embellish, ornament **KJ** V.ii.53 [Lewis the Dauphin to Salisbury, of Salisbury's tears] *this effusion … makes me more amazed / Than had I seen the vaulty top of heaven / Figured quite o'er with burning meteors*

figured (*adj.*) **1** decorated, ornamented, adorned with designs **R2** III.iii.150 [King Richard to Aumerle] *I'll give … / My figured goblets for a dish of wood*

2 signalled, indicated by gestures **PassP** IV.10 [of Adonis and Cytherea] *he refused to take her figured proffer*

filbert (*n.*) hazel-nut **Tem** II.ii.168 [Caliban to Stephano] *I'll bring thee / To clust'ring filberts*

file (*n.*) **1** rank of soldiers, formation **Tim** V.ii.1 [Third Senator to Messenger, of Alcibiades] *Are his files / As full as thy report?;* **AC** IV.i.12; **AW** III.iii.9; **Cor** II.i.22; **H8** I.ii.42; **Mac** III.i.101

2 register, list, roll **H8** I.i.75 [Buckingham to Abergavenny, of Wolsey] *He makes up the file / Of all the gentry;* **2H4** I.iii.10; **Mac** III.i.94, V.ii.8

3 body, number **MM** III.ii.130 [Lucio to disguised Duke] *the greater file of the subject held the Duke to be wise*

4 rank, status, standing **TNK** V.i.161 [Emilia praying to Diana] *grant / The file and quality I hold I may / Continue in thy band* [i.e. my status as a virgin]

file (*v.*) **1** keep pace, stay in line **H8** III.ii.171 [Wolsey to King Henry] *My endeavours / Have ever come too short of my desires, / Yet filed with my abilities* [F *fill'd*]

2 polish, hone, refine **Tit** II.i.123 [Aaron to Demetrius and Chiron, of Tamora] *she shall file our engines with advice*

3 defile, corrupt, taint **Mac** III.i.64 [Macbeth alone] *for Banquo's issue have I filed my mind*

filed (*adj.*) refined, smooth, polished **PassP** XVIII.8 [Pilgrim, advising a lover] *Smooth not thy tongue with filed talk;* **Sonn** 85.4 *precious phrase by all the Muses filed;* **LL** V.i.10

fill (*n.*) (plural) shafts of a cart **TC** III.ii.44 [Pandarus to Cressida] *an you draw backward, we'll put you i'th' fills*

fill up (*v.*) **1** equal, measure, make the sum of **LL** V.ii.193 [Boyet to masked lords] *How many inches doth fill up one mile*

2 swell, increase, make full **1H4** III.ii.116 [King Henry to Prince Hal, of Douglas] *Thrice hath this Hotspur … made a friend of him, / To fill the mouth of deep defiance up*

3 satisfy, fulfil, meet **KJ** II.i.556 [King John to King Philip, of Constance] *I trust we shall, / If not fill up the measure of her will, / Yet in some measure satisfy her;* **MV** IV.i.158

fillet (*n.*) head-band **Lover** 33 [of the woman's hair] *Some in her threaden fillet still did bide*

fill-horse (*n.*) draught-horse, horse which goes between shafts **MV** II.ii.88 [Gobbo to Launcelot] *Thou hast got more hair on thy chin than Dobbin my fill-horse has on his tail*

fillip, fillop (*v.*) strike smartly against, tap against, touch **Cor** V.iii.59 [Coriolanus to Volumnia] *let the pebbles on the hungry beach / Fillip the stars* [F *Fillop*] [i.e. rise up against]; **2H4** I.ii.230; **TC** IV.v.45

filly *(adj.)* female **MND** II.i.46 [Puck to Fairy] *Neighing in likeness of a filly foal*

film *(n.)* gossamer, fine thread **RJ** I.iv.66 [Mercutio to Romeo, of Queen Mab] *Her whip, of cricket's bone; the lash, of film*

film *(v.)* film over, cover up **Ham** III.iv.148 [Hamlet to Gertrude, of her reaction to his behaviour] *It will but skin and film the ulcerous place*

filth *(n.)* **1** vile creature, foul animal **KL** IV.ii.39 [Albany to Gonerill] *Filths savour but themselves*
2 whore, slut, harlot **Tim** IV.i.6 [Timon alone] *To general filths / Convert o'th' instant, green virginity*

filthy *(adj.)* nasty, contemptible, disgusting **Tim** I.i.201 [Apemantus to Timon, of the Painter] *he's but a filthy piece of work*; **TS** IV.iii.65

find *(v.)* **1** find out, see through **H5** IV.i.252 [King Henry alone, of greatness] *I am a king that find thee*; **AW** II.iii.204, iv.31, V.ii.42
2 search through, sift, probe **Cym** IV.ii.204 [Belarius to Arviragus and Guiderius] *O melancholy, / Who ever yet could sound thy bottom, find / The ooze*
3 discover, perceive, discern **Cor** III.iii.129 [Coriolanus to Plebeians] *Your ignorance - which finds not till it feels*
4 find the truth about, discover the reason for **TNK** III.vi.49 [Arcite to Palamon] *You'll find it* [i.e. find it true]; **Ham** III.i.186
5 furnish, provide, supply **H5** I.ii.72 [Canterbury to King Henry, of Hugh Capet] *To find his title with some shows of truth*
6 expect, receive, meet with **2H4** V.ii.30 [Prince John to Lord Chief Justice] *Though no man be assured what grace to find, / You stand in coldest expectation*

find forth *(v.)* seek out, encounter, meet with **CE** I.ii.37 [Antipholus of Syracuse alone, comparing himself to a drop of water] *That in the ocean seeks another drop, / Who, falling there to find his fellow forth ... confounds himself*

find out *(v.)* **1** discover, find, come upon **3H6** III.ii.178 [Richard to and of himself] *like one lost in a thorny wood ... / Not knowing how to find the open air, / But toiling desperately to find it out*; **1H6** V.iv.4; **2H6** III.ii.407; **JC** I.iii.134; **R2** II.iii.144
2 detect, perceive, grasp **1H6** II.iv.21 [Richard to Warwick] *The truth appears so naked on my side / That any purblind eye may find it out*
3 inquire into, follow up **MW** II.i.119 [Ford to himself, of Falstaff's approaches to his wife] *I will find out this*

finder *(n.)* jury-member who determines if someone is insane, ascertainer **TN** III.iv.139 [Sir Toby to Maria] *we will bring the device to the bar, and crown thee for a finder of madmen*

fine *(n.)* **1** outcome, final result, conclusion **MA** I.i.226 [Benedick to Claudio] *the fine is ... I will live a bachelor*; **AW** IV.iv.35; **Ham** V.i.104
2 ending, termination **KJ** V.iv.38 [Melun to Pembroke, Salisbury, and Bigot, of their executions] *Paying the fine of rated treachery / Even with a treacherous fine of all your lives* [second instance; first instance, sense 3]
3 punishment, penalty, retribution **Cor** V.vi.65 [First Lord to Aufidius, of Coriolanus] *What faults he made before the last ... / Might have found easy fines*; **KJ** V.iv.37; **MM** II.ii.40
4 tax, levy **1H6** I.iii.64 [Winchester to Mayor, of Gloucester] *O'ercharging your free purses with large fines*
5 [legal] fee, contracted amount **CE** II.ii.81 [Dromio of Syracuse to Antipholus of Syracuse] *to pay a fine for a periwig*
6 [legal] agreement to transfer land possession **MW** IV.ii.199 [Mistress Page to Mistress Ford, of Falstaff] *If the devil have him not in fee simple, with fine and recovery, he will never ... attempt us again* [i.e. with everything transferred to him]; **CE** II.ii.79; **Ham** V.i.103

fine, in in the end, finally, in conclusion **1H6** I.iv.34 [Talbot to all, of his ransom] *In fine, redeemed I was as I desired*; **AW** III.vii.19, 33; **Ham** II.ii.69, IV.vii.132; **KL** II.i.47 ➤ **DISCOURSE MARKERS**, p.127

fine *(adj.)* **1** graceful, exquisitely formed **Tem** I.ii.495 [Prospero aside to Ariel] *Thou hast done well, fine Ariel!*; **Tem** I.ii.317, 421
2 finely clothed, smartly dressed **TS** II.i.310 [Petruchio to Baptista] *I will be sure my Katherine shall be fine*; **MA** I.i.226; **Tem** V.i.262; **TS** V.i.58
3 handsome [as modern use] **Ham** V.i.105 [Hamlet to Horatio, of a lawyer] *his fine pate* [pun: *(n.)*, sense 6]
4 artificially beautiful, showily decorative **Ham** II.ii.444 [Hamlet to First Player, of a play's style] *very much more handsome than fine*
5 refined, sophisticated, cultivated **1H4** IV.i.2 [Hotspur to Douglas] *If speaking truth / In this fine age were not thought flattery*
6 subtle, intricate **AW** V.iii.266 [King to Parolles] *thou art too fine in thy evidence*; **MM** I.i.36
7 clear, pure **TC** IV.iv.3 [Cressida to Pandarus] *The grief is fine, full perfect, that I taste*
8 sensitive, responsive, reactive **Ham** IV.v.163 [Laertes to all] *Nature is fine in love*; **WT** I.ii.226
9 powdery [as modern use] **Ham** V.i.105 [Hamlet to Horatio] *full of fine dirt* [pun: *(n.)*, sense 6]

fine *(v.)* **1** pledge, stake, wager **H5** IV.vii.67 [King Henry to Montjoy] *Know'st thou not / That I have fined these bones of mine for ransom?*
2 bring to an end, complete, conclude **Luc** 936 [Lucrece as if to time] *Time's office is to fine the hate of foes*
3 punish, impose a penalty [on] **MM** III.i.118 [Claudio to Isabella, of Angelo] *Why would he for the momentary trick / Be perdurably fined?*; **MM** II.ii.40

fine-baited *(adj.)* full of attractive temptations, enticingly baited **MW** II.i.89 [Mistress Page to Mistress Ford, of Falstaff] *Let's ... lead him on with a fine-baited delay*

fineless *(adj.)* boundless, unlimited, infinite **Oth** III.iii.171 [Iago to Othello] *riches fineless is as poor as winter, / To him that ever fears he shall be poor*

finely *(adv.)* nicely, delicately, subtly **TS** IV.iii.20 [Grumio to Katherina, of satisfying her hunger] *How say you to a fat tripe finely broiled?*; **MM** I.i.35; **MW** III.v.26, V.iii.20

finger *(v.)* steal, pinch, pilfer **Ham** V.ii.15 [Hamlet to Horatio, of Rosencrantz and Guildenstern] *I ... / Fingered their packet*

finical *(adj.)* nit-picking, fussy, over-particular **KL** II.ii.16 [disguised Kent to Oswald, describing him] *finical rogue* [Q *superfinicall*]

finish *(v.)* die, come to an end **Cym** V.v.413 [Posthumus to Iachimo] *I had you down, and might / Have made you finish*; **Cym** V.v.36

finny *(adj.)* provided with fins **Per** II.i.48 [Pericles to himself, of the Fishermen] *from the finny subject of the sea / These fishers tell the infirmities of men* [Q *fenny*]

firago *(n.)* virago, hero, fighter **TN** III.iv.268 [Sir Toby to Sir Andrew, of Viola as Cesario] *I have not seen such a firago*

fire *(n.)* **1** ardour, fervour, burning passion **AW** III.vii.26 [Helena to Widow, of Bertram yielding his ring] *in his idle fire, / To buy his will it would not seem too dear*
2 disease, infection **Tim** IV.iii.143 [Timon to Phrynia and Timandra, of a reformer] *Let your close fire predominate his smoke* [or: sense 1]
3 will o' the wisp **MND** III.i.103 [Puck to the fleeing rustics] *Sometime a horse I'll be ... sometime a fire*
4 lightning, thunderbolt **Tem** I.ii.5 [Miranda to Prospero] *the sea, mounting to th'welkin's cheek, / Dashes the fire out*
5 sun **AC** I.iii.68 [Antony to Cleopatra] *By the fire / That quickens Nilus' slime, I go from hence / Thy soldier-servant*
6 ➤ false fire

fire *(v.)* set on fire, ignite, inflame **R2** III.iii.42 [King Richard to Aumerle, of the sun] *He fires the proud tops of the eastern pines*; **Cym** I.vii.104

fire hence / out (v.) drive away by fire KL V.iii.23 [Lear to Cordelia] *He that parts us shall bring a brand from heaven / And fire us hence like foxes;* PassP II.14 [Pilgrim] *The truth I shall not know, but live in doubt, / Till my bad angel fire my good one out*

firebrand (n.) 1 piece of wood kindled in the fire 2H4 II.ii.85 [Page to Prince Henry] *Althaea dreamt she was delivered of a firebrand*
2 will-o'-the-wisp, moving light Tem II.ii.6 [Caliban alone, of Prospero's spirits] *But they'll [not] … lead me, like a firebrand, in the dark*

fire-drake (n.) fiery being, dragon, man with a fiery nose H8 V.iv.43 [Man to Porter, of a brass-worker] *That fire-drake did I hit three times on the head*

fire-ill (n.) burning disease [possibly: pox] TNK III.v.53 [First Countryman to all, of the missing woman] *A fire-ill take her*

fire-new (adj.) fresh from the fire, brand-new, freshly minted LL I.i.176 [Berowne to all, of Armado] *A man of fire-new words;* KL V.iii.130

firing (n.) firewood, fuel Tem II.ii.177 [Caliban singing] *Nor fetch in firing / At requiring* [i.e. when told to]

firk (v.) beat, trounce, whip H5 IV.iv.29 [Pistol to Boy, of French Soldier] *I'll fer him, and firk him, and ferret him*

firm (adj.) 1 constant, steadfast, resolute AC I.v.43 [Alexas to Cleopatra, quoting Antony] *Say the firm Roman to great Egypt sends / This treasure of an oyster*
2 stable, secure, settled R2 III.iv.42 [First Man to Gardener, of their garden] *Showing as in a model our firm estate*

first (n.) 1 beginning, outset, start KL V.iii.286 [Kent to Lear] *from your first of difference and decay;* Mac V.ii.11; TS III.ii.213
2 [heraldry] first tincture in a blazon MND III.ii.213 [Helena to Hermia, of themselves] *Two of the first, like coats in heraldry*

first, at at once, immediately, from the start AY II.vii.95 [Orlando to Duke Senior] *You touched my vein at first;* Cym I.v.98; 1H6 II.i.51

first, upon our on our first raising the matter Ham II.ii.61 [Voltemand to Claudius, of old Fortinbras] *Upon our first, he sent out to suppress / His nephew's levies*

first (adv.) 1 at first Ham IV.ii.18 [Hamlet to Rosencrantz and Guildenstern, comparing them to an apple] *first mouthed, to be last swallowed*
2 already, before, previously Per IV.iv.20 [Gower alone, of Pericles] *This king to Tarsus … / To fetch his daughter home, who first is gone*

first and last, at to one and all, from beginning to end Mac III.iv.1 [Macbeth to all] *At first / And last, the hearty welcome*

first-conceived (adj.) first perceived, previously heard 2H6 III.ii.44 [King to all, of Suffolk previously sounding like a raven] *thinks he that the chirping of a wren … / Can chase away the first-conceived sound?*

firstling (n.) 1 first result, opening event TC Prologue.27 [Prologue, of the wars] *our play / Leaps o'er the vaunt and firstlings of those broils*
2 first product, first fruits Mac IV.i.146 [Macbeth to himself] *From this moment / The very firstlings of my heart shall be / The firstlings of my hand* [i.e. my first thoughts will be turned immediately into actions]

fisher (n.) fisherman RJ I.ii.40 [Servant alone] *It is written that … the fisher [should meddle] with his pencil and the painter with his nets;* CE I.i.116; Per II.i.49; Venus 526

fisnomy (n.) physiognomy, face, countenance AW IV.v.38 [Clown to Lafew, of the devil] *his fisnomy is more hotter in France than there*

fist (v.) strike [with the fist], punch, knock 2H4 II.i.20 [Fang to Hostess, of Falstaff] *An but fist him once, an 'a come but within my vice*

fisting (n.) punching, knock, boxing Per IV.vi.165 [Marina to Boult] *To the choleric fisting of every rogue / Thy ear is liable*

fistula (n.) type of ulcer, abscess AW I.i.33 [Lafew to Bertram, of the King's illness] *A fistula*

fit (n.) 1 fever, attack, seizure Mac III.iv.20 [Macbeth to First Murderer, hearing that Fleance has escaped] *Then comes my fit again;* Cor III.ii.33; E3 I.ii.162; 2H4 I.i.142; KJ III.iv.114; TNK V.ii.10
2 spasm, short burst TC III.i.56 [Paris to Pandarus] *you say so in fits* [also: short musical snatches]
3 grimace, facial twitch H8 I.iii.7 [Lord Chamberlain to Sands, of the effect of France upon the English] *A fit or two o'th' face*
4 conflict, beating, turmoil Cym I.iv.12 [Pisanio to Innogen, of Posthumus] *the fits and stirs of's mind;* Mac IV.ii.17
5 stage, period, hours H8 I.i.78 [Queen Katherine to Campeius and Wolsey] *I feel / The last fit of my greatness*

fit (adj.) 1 suited, fitting, appropriate H8 II.ii.115 [King Henry to Wolsey, of Gardiner] *I find him a fit fellow;* AW III.v.12; CE IV.iii.95; Cor I.i.130; KL I.i.97; TN III.iv.170
2 ready, prepared, made suitable Cym III.iv.170 [Pisanio to Innogen, of her male disguise] *Fore-thinking this, I have already fit … doublet, hat, hose, all / That answer to them;* 2H6 II.iii.54
3 in a proper state, in the right circumstances Cor I.iii.45 [Volumnia to Gentlewoman] *Tell Valeria / We are fit to bid her welcome* [or: sense 2]

fit (v.) 1 suit, befit, be suitable [for] RJ I.v.75 [Tybalt to Capulet, of frowning at the sight of Romeo] *It fits when such a villain is a guest;* AY III.ii.19; Ham II.ii.26; 1H6 III.i.57; TN III.iii.39; TNK V.iii.8
2 belong together, match Ham IV.v.180 [Laertes to all, of Ophelia's speech] *thoughts and remembrance fitted*
3 adapt, conform, accommodate Cor II.ii.140 [Menenius to Coriolanus] *Pray you go fit you to the custom;* Cym III.iv.194, V.v.55; KJ III.iii.26
4 supply [with what is fit], satisfy MA I.i.298 [Don Pedro to Claudio] *I will fit thee with the remedy;* AW II.i.90; Cym V.v.21; MA II.iii.40; TNK V.ii.11
5 fit out, equip, provide Tit IV.i.113 [Titus to Young Lucius] *go with me into mine armoury. … I'll fit thee;* Tit V.ii.85
6 be fit, be in satisfactory condition TNK IV.iii.36 [Arcite to Palamon] *if you feel yourself not fitting yet* [i.e. in sufficient shape]
7 employ, use, make serve LL V.ii.358 [King to all] *No time shall be omitted / That will betime and may by us be fitted*
8 find a fitting punishment, be revenged upon TNK III.v.59 [Fourth Countryman to all, as if to the missing woman] *I'll fit thee*
9 force out of place by a convulsion Sonn 119.7 *How have mine eyes out of their spheres been fitted / In the distraction of this madding fever!*

fit it harmonize, go well together LL IV.i.130 [Costard to Maria, of Rosaline and Boyet's repartee] *How both did fit it!*

fit (adv.) suitably, fittingly, appropriately AW I.i.101 [Helena to herself, of Parolles] *these fixed evils sit so fit in him;* AW II.ii.19

fitchew, fichew, ficho (n.) polecat, skunk; also: prostitute KL IV.vi.122 [Lear to all] *The fitchew nor the soiled horse goes to't / With a more riotous appetite* [F; Q *fichew*]; Oth IV.i.146 [Cassio to Iago, of Bianca] *'Tis such another fitchew!* [F; Q1 *ficho*]; TC V.i.57

fitful (adj.) full of fits, marked by paroxysms Mac III.ii.23 [Macbeth to Lady Macbeth, of the King] *After life's fitful fever he sleeps well*

fitly (adv.) 1 justly, fittingly, aptly Cor IV.ii.34 [Volumnia to Brutus, of Coriolanus] *Cats that can judge as fitly of his worth / As I can;* Cor I.i.110; KL I.i.200; Per II.i.30
2 at the right time, at a suitable moment KL I.ii.166 [Edmund to Edgar] *I will fitly bring you to hear my lord speak;* Tim III.iv.111

fitment (n.) 1 preparation, appropriate state Cym V.v.410 [Posthumus to Cymbeline, of taking a soldier's role] *'twas a fitment for / The purpose I then followed*
2 fitting action, duty, what is called for Per IV.vi.6 [Bawd to Pander and Boult, of Marina] *she should do for clients her fitment*

fitness (*n.*) **1** proper behaviour, appropriate conduct H8 II.iv.231 [Campeius to King Henry] *'tis a needful fitness / That we adjourn this court till further day;* KL IV.ii.63
2 inclination, readiness Ham V.ii.196 [Hamlet to Lord, of Claudius] *If his fitness speaks, mine is ready;* Cym IV.i.6
3 state of readiness, being properly prepared TC I.iii.202 [Ulysses to all, of military strategy] *how many hands shall strike, / When fitness calls them on*

fives (*n.*) (plural) horse disease affecting the parotid glands [the strangles] TS III.ii.53 [Biondello to Tranio as Lucentio, of Petruchio's horse] *past cure of the fives*

fix (*v.*) make firm, secure Cor I.viii.4 [Aufidius to Martius] *Fix thy foot* [i.e. take a sure foothold]

fixed (*adj.*) **1** certain, indisputable, definite Tim I.i.9 [Jeweller to Merchant, of Timon's worthiness] *that's most fixed*
2 rooted, established, in place KL III.iv.8 [Lear to disguised Kent] *where the greater malady is fixed / The lesser is scarce felt*
3 painted, made fast, finished off WT V.iii.47 [Paulina to Perdita, of Hermione's statue] *The statue is but newly fixed, the colour's / Not dry*
4 gritted, grinding, grated 2H6 III.ii.313 [Suffolk to Queen, of his curses] *Delivered strongly through my fixed teeth*

fixture (*n.*) way of placing, setting down MW III.iii.58 [Falstaff to Mistress Ford] *the firm fixture of thy foot* [i.e. on the ground]

fixure (*n.*) **1** fixture, position, attitude WT V.iii.67 [Leontes to all, of Hermione's statue] *The fixure of her eye has motion in't*
2 stability, fixed position, settled state TC I.iii.101 [Ulysses to all, of disorder in the planets] *rend ... / The unity and married calm of states / Quite from their fixure!*

flag (*n.*) reed, rush; also: variety of iris AC I.iv.45 [Caesar to Lepidus, of the people] *This common body, / Like to a vagabond flag upon the stream, / Goes to and back*

flag, set up the bloody declare war, engage in battle Cor II.i.71 [Menenius to Brutus and Sicinius] *you ... set up the bloody flag against all patience*

flagging (*adj.*) drooping, pendulous, sluggish 2H6 IV.i.5 [Lieutenant to all, of the dragons pulling Hecate's chariot] *with their drowsy, slow, and flagging wings*

flake (*n.*) lock of hair KL IV.vii.30 [Cordelia to Lear] *Had you not been their father, these white flakes / Did challenge pity of them*

flaky (*adj.*) streaked with light R3 V.iii.87 [Derby to Richmond] *flaky darkness breaks within the east*

flame (*v.*) **1** inflame, excite; or: convey by flaming Tem I.ii.198 [Ariel to Prospero] *in every cabin / I flamed amazement*
2 blaze, shine, flash Tem I.ii.200 [Ariel to Prospero] *On the topmast, / The yards, and boresprit would I flame distinctly*

flamen (*n.*) priest serving a particular deity Cor II.i.205 [Brutus to Sicinius] *Seld-shown flamens / Do press among the popular throngs;* Tim IV.iii.156 ☛ ROMAN HISTORY, p.377

flaming (*adj.*) extravagant, high-flown, vividly elaborate TC I.ii.105 [Cressida to Pandarus] *too flaming a praise for a good complexion* [also: glowing]

flanker (*n.*) soldier deployed on the flanks of an army E3 II.i.187 [King Edward to Lodowick] *These wings, these flankers, and these squadrons*

flap-dragon (*n.*) tiny sweetmeat, small cake LL V.i.42 [Costard to Mote] *Thou art easier swallowed than a flap-dragon* ☛ flap-dragons (*n.*)

flap-dragon (*v.*) swallow like a flap-dragon WT III.iii.95 [Clown to Shepherd, of the ship] *to see how the sea flap-dragoned it*

flap-dragons (*n.*) [game of bravado] snap-dragons: small burning objects floating on liquor, which have to be avoided while drinking; or: edible objects floating on burning liquor, to be seized and eaten 2H4 II.iv.241 [Falstaff to Doll, of why Prince Harry loves Poins] *'a ... drinks off candles' ends for flap-dragons*

flap-eared (*adj.*) with long hanging ears TS IV.i.143 [Petruchio to Katherina, of Servant] *A whoreson, beetle-headed, flap-eared knave!*

flap-mouthed (*adj.*) with wide loosely hanging lips Venus 920 [of a hound] *Another flap-mouthed mourner*

flare (*v.*) blow in the air, stream loosely MW IV.vi.42 [Fenton to Host, of Anne's costume] *quaint in green she shall be loose enrobed, / With ribands pendent, flaring 'bout her head*

flash (*v.*) **1** break out suddenly, move abruptly KL I.iii.5 [Gonerill to Oswald, of Lear] *He flashes into one gross crime or other*
2 make a display, show off, shine out [as] Tim II.i.32 [Senator to Caphis, of Timon] *Lord Timon will be left a naked gull, / Which flashes now a phoenix*

flask (*n.*) powder-flask, case for carrying gunpowder RJ III.iii.132 [Friar to Romeo, of his wit] *Like powder in a skilless soldier's flask / Is set afire by thine own ignorance;* LL V.ii.613

flat (*n.*) **1** low-lying land, plain, swampy ground Cym III.iii.11 [Belarius to Guiderius and Arviragus] *I'll tread these flats;* Ham IV.v.102; Tem II.ii.2
2 shoal, sandbank MV III.i.5 [Salerio to Solanio] *the Goodwins ... a very dangerous flat;* MV I.i.26

flat (*adj.*) **1** downright, plain, basic TS V.i.32 [Petruchio to Vincentio, suspecting him of being an imposter] *this is flat knavery;* MA II.i.203
2 stale, insipid, unpalatable TC IV.i.63 [Diomedes to Paris, of Menelaus] *He ... would drink up / The lees and dregs of a flat tamed piece*
3 feeble, dull, deficient H5 Prologue.9 [Chorus] *The flat unraised spirits that hath dared / On this unworthy scaffold to bring forth / So great an object*

flat-long (*adj.*) with the flat side of a sword; ineffectively Tem II.i.184 [Antonio to Sebastian, of Gonzalo's reaction to their laughing at him] *What a blow was there given!* [Sebastian] *An it had not fall'n flat-long*

flatly (*adv.*) **1** plainly, straight, bluntly TS I.ii.76 [Grumio to Hortensio, of Petruchio] *he tells you flatly what his mind is*
2 in a prone position Venus 463 [of Venus] *she flatly falleth down*

flatness (*n.*) completeness, absoluteness, limitless nature WT III.ii.121 [Hermione to all, of her father] *That he did but see / The flatness of my misery*

flatter (*v.*) **1** extenuate, gloss over, mitigate 1H6 V.v.25 [Gloucester to King, of his proposed mariage to Margaret] *So should I give consent to flatter sin*
2 deceive, beguile 3H6 III.ii.143 [Richard alone, of his distance from the crown] *I chide the means that keeps me from it ... / Flattering me with impossibilities;* Sonn 87.13

flatter up (*v.*) pamper, indulge, mollycoddle LL V.ii.809 [King to Princess] *To flatter up these powers of mine with rest*

flatter with / withal (*v.*) **1** encourage, foster [false] hope 1H6 II.i.51 [Charles to Pucelle] *Didst thou at first, to flatter us withal, / Make us partakers of a little gain;* TN I.v.293 [Olivia to Malvolio, of Viola as Cesario] *Desire him not to flatter with his lord*
2 try to please, ingratiate oneself with R2 II.i.88 [King Richard to John of Gaunt] *Should dying men flatter with those that live?*

flattering (*adj.*) superficially attractive, appealing, enticing 2H6 I.i.161 [Cardinal to all, of Gloucester] *for all this flattering gloss, / He will be found a dangerous Protector*

flattering-sweet (*adj.*) sweetly appealing, enticingly delightful RJ II.ii.141 [Romeo alone] *all this is but a dream, / Too flattering-sweet to be substantial*

flattery (*n.*) pleasing plausibility, gratifying deception, self-delusion LL IV.iii.284 [Dumaine to Berowne, of breaking their oaths honourably] *some flattery for this evil;* Oth IV.i.130; Sonn 42.14; Tit III.i.252

flaunt (*n.*) finery, ostentatious clothing, trappings WT IV.iv.23 [Perdita to Florizel, of Polixenes] *how / Should I, in these my borrowed flaunts, behold / The sternness of his presence?*

flaw *(n.)* **1** gust, squall, blast **2H4** IV.iv.35 [King Henry IV to Clarence, of Prince Henry] *being incensed, he is ... as sudden / As flaws congealed in the spring of day;* **Cor** V.iii.74; **Ham** V.i.212; **2H6** III.i.354; **Per** III.i.39; **Venus** 456
2 burst of passion, upsurge of feelings **MM** II.iii.11 [Provost to disguised Duke, of Juliet] *falling in the flaws of her own youth*
3 fragment, tiny piece **KL** I.iv.280 [Lear to Regan and Gonerill] *this heart / Shall break into a hundred thousand flaws*
4 lapse, fault, error **AC** III.xii.34 [Caesar to Thidias] *Observe how Antony becomes his flaw*

flaw *(v.)* make a crack in, break, damage **H8** I.ii.21 [Queen Katherine to King Henry, of the people] *There have been commissions / Sent down among 'em which hath flawed the heart / Of all their loyalties;* **H8** I.i.95

flawed *(adj.)* cracked, broken **KL** V.iii.194 [Edgar to Albany, of Gloucester] *his flawed heart ... / Burst smilingly*

flax-wench *(n.)* female flax worker **WT** I.ii.277 [Leontes to Camillo, of Hermione] *My wife ... deserves a name / As rank as any flax-wench that puts to / Before her troth-plight*

flayed *(adj.)* stripped, skinned, undressed **WT** IV.iv.637 [Camillo to Autolycus, of Florizel] *The gentleman is half flayed already*

fleckled *(adj.)* dappled, flecked, speckled **RJ** II.iii.190 [Romeo alone] *darkness fleckled like a drunkard reels / From forth day's pathway made by Titan's wheels*

fledge *(adj.)* **1** covered with down, displaying growth **2H4** I.ii.20 [Falstaff to Page, of Prince Henry] *the Prince your master, whose chin is not yet fledge*
2 grown large enough for flight, ready to fly **MV** III.i.27 [Solanio to Salerio, of Jessica] *Shylock for his own part knew the bird was fledged* [F; Q *flidge*]

fleece *(v.)* plunder, rob, strip of possessions **2H6** III.i.129 [Gloucester to York] *a ... foul felonious thief that fleeced poor passengers*

fleer *(n.)* sneer, mockery, jeering **Oth** IV.i.82 [Iago to Othello, of Cassio] *mark the fleers, the gibes, and notable scorns / That dwell in every region of his face* [F; Q1 *Ieeres* = jeers]

fleer *(v.)* jeer, grin scornfully, laugh mockingly **RJ** I.v.57 [Tybalt to himself, of Romeo] *dares the slave / Come hither ... / To fleer and scorn at our solemnity?*; **LL** V.ii.109; **MA** V.i.58

fleering *(adj.)* sneering, jeering, scornfully laughing **JC** I.iii.117 [Casca to Cassius, of himself] *such a man / That is no fleering tell-tale*

fleet *(n.)* dancing company, group, assembly **MA** II.i.128 [masked Beatrice to masked Benedick, of Benedick] *I am sure he is in the fleet*

fleet *(adj.)* swift, nimble, active **TS** Induction.ii.47 [First Servingman to Sly] *thy greyhounds are as swift / As breathed stags, ay, fleeter than the roe;* **LL** V.ii.261; **TS** Induction.i.24

fleet *(v.)* **1** turn, pass, change **MV** III.ii.108 [Portia to herself] *How all the other passions fleet to air;* **2H6** II.iv.4
2 [of souls] leave, pass away, fly off **KJ** II.i.285 [King John to all] *God forgive the sin of all those souls / That ... shall fleet;* **Cym** V.iii.25; **MV** IV.i.135
3 idle away, while away **AY** I.i.111 [Charles to Oliver, of Duke Senior's noblemen] *many ... fleet the time carelessly*
4 be afloat, be under sail **AC** III.xiii.171 [Antony to Cleopatra] *our severed navy too / Have knit again, and fleet*

fleeting *(adj.)* **1** changeable, inconstant, fickle **R3** I.iv.55 [Clarence to Keeper, of himself] *false, fleeting, perjured Clarence;* **AC** V.ii.240
2 swift-moving, speedy **E3** I.i.118 [King Edward to all] *our fleeting bark is under sail*

fleet-winged *(adj.)* swift of flight **Luc** 1216 *fleet-winged duty with thought's feathers flies*

flesh *(n.)* meat **2H4** V.iii.19 [Silence singing] *praise God for the merry year, / When flesh is cheap and females dear;* **Per** II.i.81

flesh *(v.)* **1** [of a sword] use for the first time in battle **1H4** V.iv.128 [Prince Hal to Lancaster] *full bravely hast thou fleshed / Thy maiden sword;* **H5** II.iv.50; **1H6** IV.vii.36
2 initiate, introduce [to bloodshed] **KJ** V.i.71 [Bastard to King John, of Lewis the Dauphin] *Shall a beardless boy ... flesh his spirit in a warlike soil;* **KL** II.ii.43
3 plunge into the flesh **E3** IV.iii.34 [King Edward to all] *Edward's sword must flesh itself in such / As wilful stubborness hath made perverse*
4 [give a piece of the kill to a hound to stimulate its desire to hunt further] reward, stimulate, excite **AW** V.iii.15 [Second Lord to First Lord, of Bertram and Diana] *this night he fleshes his will in the spoil of her honour;* **2H4** IV.v.133

fleshed *(adj.)* **1** well used to bloodshed, hardened **R3** IV.iii.6 [Tyrrel alone, of the Princes' killers] *they were fleshed villains;* **2H4** I.i.149; **H5** III.iii.11
2 blooded, initiated into fighting **TN** IV.i.38 [Sir Toby to Sebastian] *you are well fleshed*

flesh-fly *(n.)* fly that lays its eggs in dead flesh **Tem** III.i.63 [Ferdinand to Miranda] *to suffer / The flesh-fly blow my mouth*

fleshly *(adj.)* made of flesh, mortal **KJ** IV.ii.245 [King John to Hubert, of himself] *in the body of this fleshly land*

fleshment *(n.)* first achievement, successful accomplishment **KL** II.ii.121 [Oswald to Cornwall, of disguised Kent] *in the fleshment of this dread exploit / Drew on me here again* [F; Q *flechuent*]

fleshmonger *(n.)* fornicator, pander, pimp **MM** V.i.331 [Lucio to disguised Duke] *was the Duke a fleshmonger*

fleur-de-lis, flower-de-luce *(n.)* heraldic lily [royal symbol of France] **E3** III.i.79 [King John to all, of King Edward] *Dare he already crop the fleur-de-lis?;* **H5** V.ii.208 [King Henry to Katherine] *What say'st thou, my fair flower-de-luce?;* **1H6** I.ii.99 [Pucelle to Charles] *here is my keen-edged sword, / Decked with five flower-de-luces on each side;* **E3** III.ii.43; **1H6** I.i.80; **2H6** V.i.11

flewed *(adj.)* with large cheek folds [flews], chapped **MND** IV.i.119 [Theseus to Hippolyta] *My hounds are bred out of the Spartan kind; / So flewed, so sanded*

flexible *(adj.)* yielding, pliable, easily moved **3H6** I.iv.141 [York to Queen] *Women are soft, mild, pitiful, and flexible*

flexure *(n.)* bending [the knee or head], bowing **TC** II.iii.105 [Ulysses to Nestor, of the elephant] *his legs are legs for necessity, not for flexure;* **H5** VI.i.248

flidge *(adj.)* ➤ fledge *(adj.)* 2

flight *(n.)* **1** company, host, multitude **Ham** V.ii.354 [Horatio to dead Hamlet] *flights of angels sing thee to thy rest!*
2 archery contest, flight-shooting **MA** I.i.37 [Beatrice to Messenger, of Benedick] *He ... challenged Cupid at the flight*
3 [of arrows] power of flight, size and weight **MV** I.i.141 [Bassanio to Antonio, of arrows] *when I had lost one shaft, / I shot his fellow of the self-same flight*

flighty *(adj.)* swiftly conceived, quickly vanishing **Mac** IV.i.144 [Macbeth to himself] *The flighty purpose never is o'ertook / Unless the deed go with it*

flinch *(v.)* fall short, give way, turn aside **AW** II.i.187 [Helena to King] *If I ... flinch in property / Of what I spoke*

fling *(n.)* **1** dig, gibe, taunt **1H6** III.i.64 [Richard to himself, of his need to hold his tongue] *Else would I have a fling at Winchester*
2 dash off, go away in a rush **Tim** IV.ii.45 [Flavius alone, of Timon] *He's flung in rage from this ingrateful seat / Of monstrous friends*

flint *(n.)* **1** type of hard stone, flintstone **E3** IV.vi.37 [Philip to King John, of Prince Edward and his men] *Some twenty naked starvelings with small flints / Hath driven back a puissant host of men;* **AC** IV.ix.16; **Cym** III.vii.7; **E3** III.iii.182, IV.vi.14
2 flint-like, hard, merciless **2H4** IV.iv.33 [King Henry IV to Clarence, of Prince Henry] *being incensed, he is flint;* **R2** V.i.3

flint-heart *(adj.)* hard-hearted, hard-boiled **E3** II.i.72 [King Edward to Lodowick, of his writing] *[it may] make a flint-heart Scythian pitiful*

flinty *(adj.)* hard, harsh, tough **Oth** I.iii.228 [Othello to all, of custom] *Hath made the flinty and steel couch of war / My thrice-driven bed of down;* **2H6** II.iv.9; **KJ** II.i.384; **Tim** IV.iii.487

flirt *(v.)* scorn, jeer at, scoff at **TNK** I.ii.18 [Palamon to Arcite, of a soldier] *now flirted / By peace for whom he fought*

flirt-gill *(n.)* fast girl, loose woman **RJ** II.iv.150 [Nurse to Romeo, of Mercutio] *I am none of his flirt-gills*

flock *(n.)* tuft of wool **1H4** II.i.6 [First Carrier to Ostler] *put a few flocks in the point*

flood *(n.)* **1** sea, deep, waves, rushing water **3H6** II.v.9 [King alone] *Sometime the flood prevails, and then the wind;* **E3** III.i.170; **Ham** I.iv.69; **MND** II.i.127; **Oth** II.i.2; **TC** I.i.104

2 river, stream, rushing water **JC** I.i.103 [Cassius to Brutus, reporting Caesar's challenge] *Leap in with me into this angry flood;* **KJ** V.iv.53; **Lover** 44; **Luc** 653; **R3** I.iv.45; **TNK** IV.i.95

3 sea voyage **Per** III.Chorus.45 [Gower alone, of Pericles' voyage] *half the flood / Hath their keel cut*

4 time of flowing in, influx **JC** IV.iii.217 [Brutus to Cassius] *There is a tide in the affairs of men, / Which, taken at the flood, leads on to fortune*

flood, in at its height, in its prime **TC** I.iii.300 [Nestor to Aeneas, of Hector] *his youth in flood*

flote *(n.)* sea, waves **Tem** I.ii.234 [Ariel to Prospero] *the rest o'th' fleet ... are upon the Mediterranean flote* [or, especially with a comma after 'Mediterranean': afloat]

flour *(n.)* fine essence, best part **Cor** I.i.143 [Menenius to Citizens, as the belly addressing the other body parts] *all / From me do back receive the flour of all, / And leave me but the bran* [F *Flowre*]

flourish *(n.)* **1** fanfare **R3** IV.iv.149 [King Richard to the trumpeters] *A flourish* ☛ **STAGE DIRECTIONS**, p.417

2 [of language] eloquence, fine words, rhetorical embellishment **LL** II.i.14 [Princess to Boyet] *my beauty, though but mean, / Needs not the painted flourish of your praise;* **LL** IV.iii.236

3 ornamentation, decoration, adornment **Ham** V.ii.176 [Hamlet to Osrick] *after what flourish your nature will;* **Ham** II.ii.91; **R3** I.iii.240, IV.iv.82

flourish *(v.)* **1** embellish, adorn, add lustre to **MM** IV.i.74 [disguised Duke to Mariana, of Angelo] *the justice of your title to him / Doth flourish the deceit*

2 thrive, prosper, display triumph **Tit** I.i.41 [Marcus to Saturninus and Bassianus] *Renowned Titus, flourishing in arms*

flourish with *(v.)* wave, brandish, shake about **TNK** V.i.82 [Palamon praying to Venus] *[who] canst make / A cripple flourish with his crutch;* **Tit** I.i.313

flout *(n.)* insult, jibe, taunt **LL** V.ii.833 [Rosaline to Berowne, of the world's view of him] *Full of comparisons and wounding flouts;* **LL** V.ii.269

flout *(v.)* insult, abuse, mock **CE** I.ii.91 [Antipholus of Syracuse to Dromio of Ephesus] *wilt thou flout me thus unto my face;* **1H6** IV.i.75; **MA** V.iv.100; **Mac** I.ii.51; **R3** II.i.80; **TS** II.i.29

flout at *(v.)* mock, jeer, scoff **AY** I.ii.44 [Celia to Rosalind] *Nature hath given us wit to flout at Fortune;* **MA** V.iv.105; **Tit** III.i.244

flouting *(adj.)* mocking, scoffing, scornful **MA** I.i.171 [Benedick to Claudio] *do you play the flouting Jack*

flouting-stock *(n.)* vlouting-stock *(n.)*

flow *(n.)* flowing **Tim** II.ii.168 [Flavius to Timon] *I have ... set mine eyes at flow;* **H8** I.i.152; **Tim** V.iv.76

flow *(v.)* **1** move, travel, run **Tim** I.ii.53 [Second Lord to Timon, of a circulating cup] *Let it flow this way*

2 [of water] rise to a great height **Tem** II.i.226 [Antonio to Sebastian] *I'll teach you how to flow*

flower-de-luce *(n.)* ☛ fleur-de-lis *(n.)*

floweret *(n.)* small flower **1H4** I.i.8 [King Henry to all, of England] *No more shall trenching war ... bruise her flowerets with the armed hoofs / Of hostile paces;* **MND** IV.i.54

flowering *(adj.)* flourishing, vigorous, in full bloom **1H6** II.v.56 [Mortimer to Richard, of his imprisonment] *hath detained me all my flowering youth*

flowing *(adj.)* bountiful, abundant, copious **H8** II.iii.62 [Lord Chamberlain to Anne] *the King's majesty ... / Does purpose honour to you no less flowing / Than Marchioness of Pembroke*

flush *(adj.)* **1** lusty, vigorous, full of life **Ham** III.iii.81 [Hamlet to himself, of Claudius] *'A took my father grossly ... / With all his crimes broad blown, as flush as May;* **AC** I.iv.52

2 ripe, set, ready **Tim** V.iv.8 [Alcibiades to Senators] *Now the time is flush* [i.e. for battle]

flushing *(n.)* reddening, redness **Ham** I.ii.155 [Hamlet alone, of his mother's grief] *Ere yet the salt of most unrighteous tears / Had left the flushing in her galled eyes / She married*

flux *(n.)* **1** stream, flow, flood **AY** II.i.52 [First Lord to Duke Senior, quoting Jaques] *thus misery doth part / The flux of company*

2 discharge, flow **AY** III.ii.65 [Touchstone to Corin] *civet is ... the very uncleanly flux of a cat* [i.e. from the cat's anal gland]

fluxive *(adj.)* flowing, streaming, tearful **Lover** 50 [of the woman's letters] *These often bathed she in her fluxive eyes*

fly *(n.)* parasite, flatterer, hanger-on **RJ** II.iv.32 [Mercutio to Benvolio] *these strange flies, these fashion-mongers ... who stand so much on the new form*

fly *(v.)* **1** leave, run away [from], flee **AY** I.iii.98 [Celia to Rosalind] *devise with me how we may fly;* **Cor** I.x.19; **1H6** I.i.97; **2H6** II.i.159; **R3** V.iii.186; **Tem** V.i.35

2 flock, rush, hasten **1H6** I.i.96 [Exeter to all] *The Dauphin crowned king? All fly to him?*

3 storm out, attack furiously **1H6** I.i.98 [Gloucester to all] *We will not fly but to our enemies' throats*

4 hawk, hunt with hawks **2H6** II.i.1 [Queen to all] *for flying at the brook, / I saw not better sport these seven years' day* [i.e. hunting water-fowl]

fly-blowing *(n.)* having flies deposit their eggs **Tem** V.i.284 [Trinculo to Alonso] *I shall not fear fly-blowing* [i.e. flies will not come near me because I am so wet]

flying-off *(n.)* desertion, defection, forsaking **KL** II.iv.86 [Lear to Gloucester, of Regan's excuses] *The images of revolt and flying-off*

fob off *(v.)* put off with a trick, get rid of, dispose of **Cor** I.i.92 [First Citizen to Menenius] *you must not think to fob off our disgrace with a tale*

foh *(int.)* ☛ **EXCLAMATIONS**, p.158

foil *(n.)* **1** sword, rapier **H5** IV.Chorus.50 [Chorus] *With four or five most vile and ragged foils;* **Ham** II.ii.395, IV.vii.135, V.ii.248; **MA** V.ii.13 ☛ **WEAPONS**, p.491

2 check, repulse, setback, defeat **1H6** III.iii.11 [Charles to Pucelle] *One sudden foil shall never breed distrust;* **E3** III.i.142; **1H6** V.iii.23; **Tem** III.i.46

3 setting, background which sets something off to advantage [dull metal sets off a gem] **R3** V.iii.251 [Richmond to his soldiers, of King Richard] *A base foul stone, made precious by the foil / Of England's chair;* **Ham** V.ii.249; **1H4** I.ii.213; **Lover** 153; **R2** I.iii.266; **TNK** IV.ii.26

4 flaw, blemish, disgrace **AC** I.iv.24 [Caesar to Lepidus] *yet must Antony / No way excuse his foils when we do bear / So great weight in his lightness*

foil *(v.)* **1** defeat, overcome; throw [in wrestling] **Cor** I.ix.48 [Martius to all] *I have not ... foiled some debile wretch;* **AY** I.i.122; **3H6** V.iv.42; **Sonn** 25.10; **TC** I.iii.372; **Venus** 114

2 dishonour, demean, degrade **E3** III.iii.77 [King Edward to King John, of John's taunts] *If thou have uttered them to foil my fame;* **Cym** II.i.120

3 frustrate, baulk, disappoint **PassP** VII.15 [Pilgrim, of his love] *She framed the love, and yet she foiled the framing*

foin (*n.*) sword-thrust **KL** IV.vi.245 [Edgar to Oswald] *no matter vor your foins*

foin (*v.*) [fencing] thrust, lunge **2H4** II.i.16 [Hostess to Snare, of Falstaff] *He will foin like any devil* [with bawdy pun]; **MW** II.iii.21

foining (*n./adj.*) [fencing] thrusting, lunging **MA** V.i.84 [Antonio to Claudio] *I'll whip you from your foining fence*; **2H4** II.iv.227

foison, foizon (*n.*) **1** [pron: ˈfoyzn] abundance, plenty, profusion **AC** II.vii.20 [Antony to Lepidus, of those estimating the flow of the Nile] *They know … if dearth / Or foison follow*; **Mac** IV.iii.88; **Sonn** 53.9; **Tem** II.i.166, IV.i.110
2 harvest, crop **TNK** V.i.53 [Arcite praying to Mars] *whose breath blows down / The teeming Ceres' foison*; **MM** I.iv.43

fold (*v.*) hide, swathe, wrap up **Luc** 1073 [Lucrece as if to Collatine] *I will not … fold my fault in cleanly-coined excuses*

fold in (*v.*) enfold, envelop, encompass **Cor** III.iii.68 [Coriolanus to Sicinius] *The fires i'th' lowest hell fold in the people*

folded (*adj.*) hidden, veiled, concealed **CE** III.ii.36 [Antipholus of Syracuse to Luciana] *Lay open to my earthy gross conceit … / The folded meaning of your words' deceit*

follow (*v.*) **1** seek after, pursue, strive for, court **Tim** I.i.40 [Painter to Poet, of Timon] *How this lord is followed!*; **AC** V.i.36; **TNK** Prologue.2, III.vi.145
2 act as a follower, be an attendant [on] **KL** II.iv.257 [Gonerill to Lear] *What need you five-and-twenty … / To follow*; **JC** V.v.66
3 treat, serve, attend **AC** V.ii.151 [Cleopatra to Caesar] *behold, / How pomp is followed!*
4 imitate, copy; take as a model [in fashion] **TNK** I.ii.50-1 [Palamon to Arcite] *Why am I bound / By any genereous bond to follow him / Follows his tailor* [i.e. he who follows his tailor's advice]
5 aim at, relate to, pertain to **AW** II.i.99 [King to Helena] *does your business follow us?*

follower (*n.*) second, attendant **RJ** III.i.57 [Mercutio to Tybalt, of Romeo] *go before to field, he'll be your follower!*

folly (*n.*) wantonness, lewdness **TC** V.ii.19 [Cressida to Diomedes] *tempt me no more to folly*; **Luc** 851; **MW** II.ii.233; **Oth** V.ii.133

folly-fallen (*adj.*) falling into folly, stooping to foolishness **TN** III.i.66 [Viola alone] *wise men, folly-fallen, quite taint their wit*

fond (*adj.*) **1** foolish, stupid, mad **R3** III.iv.81 [Hastings to himself, of his imminent execution] *I, too fond, might have prevented this*; **1H6** V.iii.81; **KL** IV.vii.60; **MND** II.ii.94; **Tit** II.iii.172; **WT** IV.i.18
2 foolish, trifling, frivolous **AW** V.iii.178 [Bertram to Lafew, of Diana] *this is a fond and desperate creature*; **AW** I.i.171; **Ham** I.v.99; **MM** II.ii.149; **MND** III.ii.114; **Oth** I.ii.196
3 tender, loving, affectionate **Oth** III.iii.442 [Othello to Iago] *All my fond love thus do I blow to heaven*; **Luc** 284; **R2** V.i.101; **RJ** IV.v.82
4 infatuated, doting, passionate **E3** II.i.293 [King Edward alone] *I cannot beat / With reason and reproof fond love away*; **Cym** [or: sense 5, 6]; **MM** II.ii.187; **MND** II.i.266; **Oth** III.iv.156; **RJ** II.ii.98
5 eager [for], desirous [of] **Cor** V.iii.162 [Volumnia to Coriolanus, of herself] *she, poor hen, fond of no second brood*; **Sonn** 84.14; **TNK** I.ii.46
6 obsessed [with] **KJ** III.iv.92 [King Philip to Constance] *You are as fond of grief as of your child*; **Cym** I.i.37
7 credulous, naive, gullible **CE** II.i.116 [Luciana to Adriana] *How many fond fools serve mad jealousy!*
8 ☛ fanned (*adj.*)

fond (*v.*) dote, be infatuated **TN** II.ii.34 [Viola alone, of Orsino's love for Olivia] *I, poor monster, fond as much on him*

fond (*adv.*) foolishly, stupidly **AW** I.iii.70 [Clown singing, of the sacking of Troy] *Fond done, done fond*

fondling (*n.*) [term of endearrment] foolish one, dear pet **Venus** 229 [Venus to Adonis] *Fondling … I have hemmed thee here*

fondly (*adv.*) foolishly, stupidly, madly **R2** III.iii.185 [Northumberland to Bolingbroke, of King Richard] *Sorrow and grief of heart / Makes him speak fondly*; **CE** IV.ii.56; **3H6** II.ii.38; **KJ** II.i.258; **R3** III.vii.146; **TS** V.ii.31

fondness (*n.*) foolish affection, naive devotion **AW** I.iii.165 [Countess to Helena] *My fear hath catched your fondness*; **H8** III.i.131; **MM** II.iv.28

fool (*n.*) **1** [term of endearment or pity] dear, darling, innocent creature **KL** V.iii.303 [Lear to all, of Cordelia] *And my poor fool is hanged!* [or: sense 4]; **3H6** II.v.36; **LL** II.i.119; **Tit** III.ii.20; **TS** III.ii.156; **WT** II.i.118
2 simple creature, poor thing **AY** II.i.22 [Duke Senior to all, of the deer] *it irks me the poor dappled fools … [should] / Have their round haunches gored*
3 simpleton, born idiot, insane person **JC** I.iii.65 [Cassius to Casca] *Why old men, fools, and children calculate*; **AW** IV.iii.184
4 [professional] clown, jester **MND** IV.i.208 [Bottom to himself] *man is but a patched fool*; **AC** I.i.13
5 plaything, pawn, puppet **Ham** I.iv.54 [Hamlet to Ghost] *we fools of nature*; **TC** V.ii.33

fool (*adj.*) foolish, silly **MV** II.ix.26 [Arragon to himself] *the fool multitude that choose by show*; **MV** I.i.102

fool and feather foolishness and foppery [feathered plumes] **H8** I.iii.25 [Lovell to Lord Chamberlain, of French-influenced Englishmen] *They must … leave those remnants / Of fool and feather that they got in France*

fool-begged (*adj.*) foolish, idiotic, silly **CE** II.i.41 [Adriana to Luciana] *if thou live to see like right bereft, / This fool-begged patience in thee will be left*

foolish (*adj.*) **1** like an idiot, lacking in sense **R3** IV.ii.54 [King Richard to Catesby, of Edward Plantagenet] *The boy is foolish*
2 roguish, lewd; or: ridiculous **1H4** II.iv.397 [Falstaff (as King) to Prince Hal] *a foolish hanging of thy nether lip*

foolish-compounded (*adj.*) composed of folly **2H4** I.ii.7 [Falstaff to Page] *The brain of this foolish-compounded clay, man*

foot (*n.*) **1** foot-soldiers, infantry **AC** IV.x.4 [Antony to Scarus] *our foot / Upon the hills … / Shall stay with us*; **E3** II.ii.30; **1H4** III.iii.184; **2H4** II.i.172; **1H6** IV.i.165; **R3** V.iii.295
2 step, degree, foothold **KJ** I.i.182 [Bastard alone, of his advancement] *A foot of honour better than I was* [also: measure of land]
3 foothold, position, presence **KL** III.i.32 [disguised Kent to Gentleman, of the French] *have secret feet / In some of our best ports*
4 moving the feet, running away, flight **1H4** V.v.20 [Prince Hal to King Henry, of Douglas] *when he saw … all his men / Upon the foot of fear* [i.e. flying in panic]

foot, at close behind, closely **Ham** IV.iii.56 [Claudius to attendants, of Hamlet] *Follow him at foot*

foot, on **1** in employment, taking place, under way **WT** I.i.3 [Archidamus to Camillo] *my services are now on foot*; **2H4** I.iii.37; **KJ** III.iv.169; **MW** IV.vi.22
2 [hunting] roused, up for pursuit **Venus** 679 [Venus to Adonis] *when thou hast on foot the purblind hare, / Mark … / How he outruns the wind*; **E3** III.iv.121

foot (*v.*) **1** pace, walk about **MW** II.i.115 [Pistol to Ford] *thieves do foot by night*; **KL** III.i.115
2 gain a foothold, land **H5** II.iv.143 [Exeter to Dauphin, of King Henry] *he is footed in this land already*; **KL** III.iii.12, vii.45
3 seize with talons, clutch with claws **Cym** V.iv.116 [Sicilius to all] *the holy eagle / Stooped, as to foot us*
4 kick, boot **MV** I.iii.115 [Shylock to Antonio] *You, that did … foot me as you spurn a stranger cur / Over your threshold*; **Cym** III.v.145

foot it dance away, tread lively **RJ** I.v.27 [Capulet to ladies] *Give room! and foot it, girls*; **Tem** I.ii.379

footboy (*n.*) boy attendant, page-boy, servant on foot [accompanying a rider], **H8** V.iii.139 [King Henry to Councillors, of Cranmer] *to let this man … wait like a lousy footboy / At chamber door;* **1H6** III.ii.69; **H8** V.ii.24; **TS** III.ii.68

footcloth, foot-cloth (*n.*) stately ornamental cloth worn over the back of a horse **2H6** IV.i.54 [Suffolk to Lieutenant] *Hast thou not … / Bare-headed plodded by my foot-cloth mule* [i.e. the mule which carried the cloth]; **2H6** IV.iv.43

footcloth, foot-cloth (*adj.*) equipped with long trappings **R3** III.iv.84 [Hastings to himself] *Three times today my footcloth horse did stumble*

footing (*n.*) **1** support, surface, foundation, foothold **WT** III.iii.107 [Clown to Shepherd, of helping the ship] *there your charity would have lacked footing;* **1H4** I.iii.191; **KJ** V.i.66
 2 landing, disembarking, setting foot on shore **Oth** II.i.76 [Cassio to Montano, of Iago] *Whose footing here anticipates our thoughts / A se'nnight's speed*
 3 footfall, strides **MV** V.i.24 [Jessica to Lorenzo] *I hear the footing of a man;* **TC** I.iii.156
 4 footprint, track, trail **Venus** 148 [Venus to Adonis] *I will … / Dance on the sands, and yet no footing seen*
 5 foot, step **Venus** 722 [Venus to Adonis] *if thou fall … / The earth, in love with thee, thy footing trips*
 6 dance, measure **Tem** IV.i.138 [Iris to the reapers] *these fresh nymphs encounter every one / In country footing*

footing, set set foot **H8** III.i.183 [Queen Katherine to Campeius and Wolsey, of herself] *when she set footing here;* **2H6** III.ii.87; **TC** II.ii.156

foot-landraker (*n.*) roaming footpad, highwayman who travels on foot **1H4** II.i.74 [Gadshill to Chamberlain] *I am joined with no foot-landrakers*

footman (*n.*) **1** foot-soldier, infantryman **AC** III.vii.44 [Enobarbus to Antony, of the army] *which doth most consist / Of war-marked footmen;* **E3** I.i.140
 2 footpad, highwayman who robs on foot **WT** IV.iii.63 [Clown to Autolycus, asking who robbed him] *a horseman or a footman?*

footsteps (*n.*) footpath, pathway, steps **KJ** I.i.216 [Bastard alone, of deceit] *For it shall strew the footsteps of my rising*

fop (*n.*) fool, buffoon, jackass **KL** I.ii.14 [Edmund alone] *creating a whole tribe of fops*

fopped (*adj.*) duped, cheated, hoodwinked **Oth** IV.ii.194 [Roderigo to Iago, of Iago's behaviour] *I … begin to find myself fopped in it*

foppery (*n.*) **1** folly, foolishness, stupidity **MM** I.ii.132 [Lucio to Claudio] *I had as lief have the foppery of freedom as the mortality of imprisonment;* **KL** I.ii.118; **MV** II.v.34
 2 foolish prank, hoax, deceit **MW** V.v.124 [Falstaff to all] *the sudden surprise of my powers, drove the grossness of the foppery into a received belief … that they were fairies*

foppish (*adj.*) foolish, silly, stupid **KL** I.iv.164 [Fool to Lear] *Fools had ne'er less grace in a year, / For wise men are grown foppish*

for (*prep.*) **1** as **E3** II.i.266 [Countess to King Edward] *Adam … was honoured for a married man*
 2 by **TS** I.i.186 [Tranio to Lucentio] *for my hand, / Both our inventions meet and jump in one*
 3 despite **1H6** I.iii.46 [Gloucester to his men, of the Tower] *Draw, men, for all this privileged place*
 4 in return for **CE** IV.iii.69 [Courtesan to Antipholus of Syracuse] *Give me the ring of mine you had at dinner, / Or for my diamond the chain you promised*
 5 instead of **Ham** V.i.226 [Priest to Laertes, of the dead Ophelia] *For charitable prayers … pebbles should be thrown on her*
 6 on account of **Ham** I.iv.24 [Hamlet to Horatio, of some men] *for some vicious mole of nature in them*
 7 on behalf of **TNK** I.i.38 [Theseus to First Queen] *Deliver you for all*

8 regarding, as for **1H6** V.i.41 [Gloucester to Armagnac ambassador] *for the proffer of my lord your master, / I have informed his highness so at large*

for (*conj.*) **1** as for **TNK** III.vi.168 [Arcite to Theseus, of Emilia] *For scorning thy edict, … ask that lady / Why she is fair*
 2 because **TS** I.i.92 [Baptista to all, of Bianca] *And for I know she taketh most delight / In music … / Schoolmasters will I keep within my house*
 3 since **TNK** II.i.326 [Gaoler to Palamon] *for you are dangerous, / I'll clap more irons on you*
 4 whereas **E3** III.iii.25 [Prince Edward to King Edward] *Yet those that would submit we kindly pardoned, / For who in scorn refused our proffered peace / Endured the penalty of sharp revenge*

for all (*conj.*) although **MW** I.i.252 [Slender to Simple] *for all you are my man, go wait upon my cousin Shallow*

for and (*conj.*) and [emphatic] **Ham** V.i.93 [First Clown, singing] *A pickaxe and a spade, a spade, / For and a shrouding sheet*

for why, forwhy (*adv.*) **1** why, for what reason **TNK** III.v.12 [Schoomaster to all] *ye are all dunces! / Forwhy, here stand I*
 2 for which reason, because of this **TS** III.ii.166 [Gremio to Tranio as Lucentio, of Katherina's trembling and Petruchio] *For why, he stamped and swore;* **Tit** III.i.229

for why (*conj.*) for which **Oth** I.iii.254 [Desdemona to Duke, of Othello] *The rites for why I love him are bereft me* [F]

forage (*n.*) preying, raging **LL** IV.i.92 [Boyet reading Armado's letter to Jaquenetta, of the Nemean lion] *he from forage will incline to play*

forage (*v.*) **1** range abroad, go out and about **KJ** V.i.59 [Bastard to King John] *Forage, and run / To meet displeasure farther from the doors*
 2 plunder, pillage, ravage **E3** IV.iii.81 [King John to Charles, of King Edward] *we shall drive him hence / And forage their country as they have done ours*
 3 eat greedily, glut oneself [on] **Venus** 554 [of Venus] *With blindfold fury she begins to forage;* **H5** I.ii.110

foragement (*n.*) foraging act, scavenging **E3** II.i.397 [Warwick to Countess] *The lion doth become his bloody jaws, / And grace his foragement by being mild*

forbear (*v.*) **1** stop, cease, desist **2H6** III.ii.46 [King to Suffolk] *Lay not thy hands on me; forbear, I say* ☞ **FEW**, p.xxi
 2 leave alone, avoid, stay away [from] **KL** I.ii.158 [Edmund to Edgar, of Gloucester] *forbear his presence* ☞ **FEW**, p.xxi
 3 control oneself, have patience [for] **AC** I.iii.73 [Antony to Cleopatra] *My precious queen, forbear;* **CE** II.i.31; **1H6** III.i.52; **KL** II.iv.104; **MV** III.ii.3; **TG** II.vii.14
 4 withdraw, leave, give way **WT** V.iii.85 [Paulina to Leontes] *Either forbear, / Quit presently the chapel, or resolve you / For more amazement;* **AC** V.ii.175; **Cym** I.i.68; **Per** II.iv.41

forbearance (*n.*) **1** patience, restraint, moderation **Cym** II.iii.97 [Innogen to Cloten] *one of your great knowing / Should learn … forbearance;* **Cym** II.iv.162; **MM** IV.i.22
 2 absence, abstention, staying away **R2** IV.i.120 [Bishop of Carlisle to and of all] *true noblesse would / Learn him forbearance from so foul a wrong;* **KL** II.ii.164
 3 refusal, reluctance [to be involved] **1H6** II.iv.19 [Richard to Warwick] *here is a mannerly forbearance*

forbod (*v.*) [past tense of 'forbid'] forbade **Luc** 1648 [Lucrece to Collatine, of Tarquin] *My bloody judge forbod my tongue to speak* [Q]

force (*n.*) **1** energy, power, conviction **TNK** I.i.201 [Emilia to Theseus, of Hippolyta] *If you grant not / My sister her petition in that force* [i.e. with the same vigour]
 2 physical strength, might, vigour **TC** V.v.40 [Ulysses to all, of Troilus] *Engaging and redeeming of himself / With such a careless force and forceless care;* **WT** IV.iv.371

3 opposition, resistance, strength 1H6 II.i.32 [Talbot to all, of the French] *if it chance the one of us do fail, / The other yet may rise against their force;* Cor I.x.14; 2H6 I.i.208

4 compelling weight, power to convince 1H6 III.i.159 [King to Gloucester] *And those occasions, uncle, were of force*

5 [of weather] violence, turbulence, stress MV II.ix.30 [Arragon to himself] *like the martlet / Builds in the weather on the outward wall, / Even in the force and road of casualty*

force (*v.*) **1** hesitate, scruple, care for LL V.ii.440 [Princess to King] *Your oath once broke, you force not to forswear;* Luc 1021

2 reinforce, strengthen, augment Mac V.v.5 [Macbeth to all, of the besieging troops] *Were they not forced with those that should be ours / We might have met them dareful* [F]

3 make happen, compel, bring about H5 II.Chorus.32 [Chorus] *we'll digest / Th'abuse of distance, force a play*

4 urge, press, enforce H8 III.ii.2 [Norfolk to all] *If you will now unite in your complaints / And force them with a constancy;* Cor III.ii.51; MM III.i.113

5 violate, ravish, rape Luc 1657 [Lucrece to Collatine, of her mind] *That was not forced*

6 ☛ farce (*v.*)

force, of necessarily, of necessity, whether one will or not LL I.i.145 [King to all, of their oaths] *We must of force dispense with this decree;* 1H4 I.iii.120; JC IV.iii.201; MV IV.i.418; WT IV.iv.420

force perforce with violent compulsion 2H6 I.i.256 [York to himself, of Lancaster] *force perforce I'll make him yield the crown;* 2H4 IV.i.114, iv.46; KJ III.i.142

forced (*adj.*) **1** enforced, imposed, constrained WT II.iii.78 [Paulina to Antigonus, of Leontes calling the baby a bastard] *that forced baseness / Which he has put upon't!;* JC IV.iii.203

2 strained, uneasy, unnatural WT IV.iv.41 [Florizel to Perdita] *With these forced thoughts ... darken not / The mirth o'th' feast*

3 unnatural, contrived, brought about by violence Ham V.ii.377 [Horatio to the Ambassadors and Fortinbras] *deaths put on by cunning and forced cause* [F forc'd; Q2 for no]

forceless (*adj.*) **1** effortless, easygoing, nonchalant TC V.v.40 [Ulysses to all, of Troilus] *Engaging and redeeming of himself / With such a careless force and forceless care*

2 frail, fragile, delicate Venus 152 [Venus to Adonis, of primroses] *These forceless flowers like sturdy trees support me*

fordo (*v.*) **1** wreck, destroy, ruin Oth V.i.129 [Iago to himself] *This is the night / That either makes me, or fordoes me quite;* Ham II.i.103

2 put an end to, kill, destroy KL V.iii.289 [Kent to Lear] *Your eldest daughters have fordone themselves* [F fore-done; Q foredoome]; Ham V.i.217; KL V.iii.253

'fore (*prep.*) **1** before H5 IV.i.256 [King Henry alone] *The farced title running fore the king*

2 in the face of Cor IV.iv.3 [Coriolanus alone, of Antium] *Many an heir / Of these fair edifices 'fore my wars / Have I heard groan and drop*

3 shortened form of 'afore' ☛ SWEARING, p.435

fore-advise (*v.*) previously advise, instruct earlier Cor II.iii.190 [Sicinius to Citizens] *As you were fore-advised*

fore-bemoaned (*adj.*) previously lamented Sonn 30.11 *I ... tell o'er / The sad account of fore-bemoaned moan*

forecast (*n.*) forethought, prudence, foresight 3H6 V.i.42 [Richard to all] *Alas, that Warwick had no more forecast*

foredone (*adj.*) exhausted, tired out, worn out MND V.i.364 [Puck to himself] *the heavy ploughman snores / All with weary task foredone*

fore-end (*n.*) early part, initial period Cym III.iii.73 [Belarius to Guiderius and Arviragus] *in all / The fore-end of my time* [i.e. my early years]

forego (*v.*) perform before, carry out in the past TNK I.i.172 [Theseus to Queens, of his marriage] *it more imports me / Than all the actions that I have foregone*

foregoer (*n.*) forebear, predecessor, ancestor AW II.iii.136 [King to Bertram] *Honours thrive / When rather from our acts we them derive / Than our foregoers*

foregone (*adj.*) previous, prior, earlier Sonn 30.9 *Then can I grieve at grievances foregone;* AW I.iii.129; Oth III.iii.425

forehand, fore-hand (*n.*) **1** upper hand, superiority, advantage H5 IV.i.273 [King Henry alone, of a wretched slave] *but for ceremony, such a wretch ... / Had the fore-hand and vantage of a king*

2 leading power, mainstay, linchpin TC I.iii.143 [Ulysses to all, of Achilles] *whom opinion crowns / The sinew and the forehand of our host*

forehand, fore-hand (*adj.*) **1** beforehand, previously committed MA IV.i.48 [Claudio to Leonato, of Hero] *You will say she did embrace me as a husband, / And so extenuate the 'forehand sin*

2 [archery] shooting straight ahead 2H4 III.ii.46 [Shallow to Silence, of Double] *'A would have ... carried you a forehand shaft a fourteen and fourteen and a half* [i.e. he could shoot an arrow nearly 300 yards]

forehead (*n.*) **1** commanding countenance, assurance, audacity 2H4 I.iii.8 [Mowbray to Archbishop] *we should advance ourselves / To look with forehead bold and big enough / Upon the power and puissance of the King;* TC III.i.105

2 ☛ teeth and forehead of, to the

forehorse, fore-horse (*n.*) foremost horse, leader [in a team of horses] TNK I.ii.59 [Palamon to Arcite] *Either I am / The fore-horse in the team;* AW II.i.30

foreknow (*v.*) know in advance, have previous knowledge KJ IV.ii.154 [Peter of Pomfret to King John, of his prophecy] *Foreknowing that the truth will fall out so*

foreknowing (*n.*) knowing in advance, foreknowledge Ham I.i.135 [Horatio to Ghost] *If thou art privy to thy country's fate, / Which happily foreknowing may avoid, / O, speak!*

forenoon (*n.*) part of the day before noon AC I.ii.28 [Charmian to Soothsayer] *Let me be married to three kings in a forenoon and widow them all;* Cor II.i.65; MM II.ii.160

forepast, fore-past (*adj.*) **1** past, previous, former E3 IV.iv.129 [Prince Edward to Audley] *stratagems forepast with iron pens / Are texted in thine honourable face*

2 previously passed, already accumulated AW V.iii.121 [King to all] *My fore-past proofs ... / Shall tax my fears of little vanity*

fore-rank (*n.*) first section H5 V.ii.97 [King Henry to Queen Isabel, of Katherine] *She is our capital demand, comprised / Within the fore-rank of our articles*

fore-recited (*adj.*) previously reported H8 I.ii.127 [King Henry to Queen Katherine, of the Surveyor] *Bid him recount / The fore-recited practices*

forerun (*v.*) forecast, foreshadow, be the precursor of R2 II.iv.15 [Captain to Salisbury, of abnormalities of nature] *These signs forerun the death or fall of kings;* 2H4 IV.iv.82; LL I.iii.356; MM V.i.8; R2 III.iv.28; RJ V.i.53

foresaid (*adj.*) aforesaid H8 I.i.190 [Buckingham to Norfolk, of the King of France] *he would ... break the foresaid peace;* KJ III.i.145; LL II.v.154; MM II.i.103

foresay (*v.*) predict, foretell Cym IV.ii.146 [Arviragus to Belarius and Guiderius] *Let ordinance / Come as the gods foresay it*

foresee (*v.*) provide in advance for, make provision for Tim IV.iii.160 [Timon to all, of removing the nose] *Of him that, his particular to foresee, / Smells from the general weal*

foreshow (*v.*) display, indicate, show forth Per IV.iv.86 [Marina to Leonine] *your looks foreshow / You have a gentle heart*

foreskirt (*n.*) front skirts H8 II.iii.98 [Old Lady to Anne] *honour's train / Is longer than his foreskirt*

forespent (*adj.*) previously shown, earlier displayed Cym II.iii.58 [Cymbeline to Queen, of Lucius] *his goodness forespent on us;* H5 II.iv.36

fore-spurrer (n.) one who has ridden ahead **MV** II.ix.95 [Messenger to Portia, of Bassanio's messenger] *A day in April never came so sweet / To show how costly summer was at hand, / As this for-spurrer comes before his lord*

forestall (v.) **1** prevent, stop, intercept, waylay **TC** IV.v.230 [Achilles to Ulysses] *I shall forestall thee;* **Ham** III.iii.49; **LL** V.ii.473; **TC** I.iii.199

2 deprive, bar, deny **Cym** III.v.70 [Queen to herself, of Cymbeline] *may / This night forestall him of the coming day!*

forestalled (adj.) [unclear meaning] certain to be refused **2H4** V.ii.38 [Lord Chief Justice to Prince John, Clarence, and Gloucester] *never shall you see that I will beg / A ragged and forestalled remission*

foretell (v.), past form **foretold 1** tell earlier, say beforehand **Tem** IV.i.149 [Prospero to Ferdinand] *These our actors, / As I foretold you, were all spirits*

2 forewarn, alert, give notice **3H6** IV.vii.12 [Richard to Edward, of the gates of York] *men that stumble at the threshold / Are well foretold that danger lurks within*

forethink (v.) anticipate, foresee, predict **1H4** III.ii.38 [King Henry to Prince Hal] *the soul of every man / Prophetically do forethink thy fall;* **Cym** III.iv.170; **KJ** III.i.312

fore-vouched (adj.) previously declared, earlier affirmed **KL** I.i.220 [France to Lear] *your fore-vouched affection / Fall into taint*

foreward (n.) vanguard, front line [of soldiers] **R3** V.iii.294 [King Richard to Norfolk] *My foreward shall be drawn out all in length*

forfeit (n.) **1** someone defeated and in danger of death **TC** IV.v.187 [Nestor to Hector] *I have … seen thee scorning forfeits and subduements* [i.e. refusing to take an easy victim]

2 [unclear meaning] list of penalties for bad behaviour **MM** V.i.319 [disguised Duke to Escalus] *the strong statutes / Stand like the forfeits in a barber's shop*

forfeit (v.) sin, transgress, do wrong **MM** III.ii.184 [Escalus to Mistress Overdone] *Double and treble admonition, and still forfeit in the same kind?*

forfeiter (n.) defaulter, person guilty of breaking an agreement **Cym** III.ii.38 [Innogen to Pisanio, as if to the seal on her letter] *Though forfeiters you cast in prison, yet / You clasp young Cupid's tables*

forfeiture (n.) forfeit, penalty **MV** IV.i.122 [Shylock to Bassanio, of Antonio] *To cut the forfeiture from that bankrupt there;* **MV** I.iii.161, III.iii.22; **Tim** II.ii.34

forfend (v.) forbid **Tit** I.i.437 [Tamora to Saturninus] *The gods of Rome forfend / I should be author to dishonour you;* **1H6** V.iv.65; **3H6** IV.i.21 [Q]; **R2** IV.i.129; **TC** I.iii.302 [Q]; **WT** IV.iv.527

forfended (adj.) forbidden, prohibited, denied **KL** V.i.11 [Regan to Edmund, of Albany and Gonerill] *have you never found my brother's way / To the forfended place?* [i.e. made love to Gonerill]

forge (v.) **1** invent, contrive, devise **Tit** V.ii.71 [Tamora to Chiron and Demetrius, of Titus] *Whate'er I forge to feed his brain-sick humours / Do you uphold*

2 cause to fashion, lead to contrive **H8** I.ii.181 [Surveyor to King Henry, of Buckingham] *'twas dangerous / For him to ruminate on this so far, until / It forged him some design*

forged (adj.) **1** false, counterfeit, spurious **1H6** III.i.192 [Exeter alone] *This late dissension grown betwixt the peers / Burns under feigned ashes of forged love;* **1H6** IV.i.102

2 fabricated, invented, falsified **Ham** I.v.37 [Ghost to Hamlet] *by a forged process of my death*

forgery (n.) **1** fictitious account, invention, fabrication **Ham** II.i.20 [Polonius to Reynaldo, of Laertes] *And there put on him / What forgeries you please;* **Ham** IV.vii.88; **PassP** I.4

2 deceit, deception, lying **3H6** III.iii.175 [Lewis to Warwick, of Edward's letter] *to soothe your forgery and his, / Sends me a paper to persuade me patience?*

forget (v.) **1** neglect, disregard, give no thought to **H8** II.i.29 [First Gentleman to Second Gentleman, of Buckingham's words] *all / Was either pitied in him or forgotten;* **Cym** III.iv.162, 165

2 behave inappropriately, lose sight of one's position **Oth** II.iii.182 [Othello to Cassio] *How comes it, Michael, you are thus forgot?*

3 lose one's sense of identity **TS** Induction.i.39 [Lord to Huntsmen, of transforming sleeping Sly] *Would not the beggar then forget himself?*

forgetfulness (n.) neglect, disregard, lack of proper attention **Tim** V.i.142 [Second Senator to Timon, of the senators] *They confess / Toward thee forgetfulness too general-gross*

forgetive (adj.) good at forging thoughts, inventive, creative **2H4** IV.iii.98 [Falstaff alone, of the effect of sherry on the brain] *It … makes it apprehensive, quick, forgetive*

forging (adj.) counterfeiting, making false copies **Venus** 729 [Venus to Adonis] *Cynthia for shame obscures her silver shine, / Till forging Nature be condemned of treason*

forgive (v.) excuse, let off **TN** I.v.185 [Olivia to Viola as Cesario] *I forgive you the praise*

forgo (v.) lose, part with, give up **1H6** IV.i.149 [King to all, of the loss of France through English quarrelling] *let us not forgo / That for a trifle that was bought with blood!*

fork (n.) **1** forked tongue **Mac** IV.i.16 [Second Witch to Witches] *Adder's fork, and blind-worm's sting;* **MM** III.i.16

2 barbed arrow-head **KL** I.i.144 [Kent to Lear, of the arrow] *though the fork invade / The region of my heart*

3 (plural) legs **KL** IV.vi.119 [Lear to all] *yon simpering dame, / Whose face between her forks presages snow*

forked (adj.) **1** two-horned **Oth** III.iii.273 [Othello alone, of being a cuckold] *this forked plague is fated to us / When we do quicken;* **TC** I.ii.165; **WT** I.ii.185

2 having two legs **KL** III.iv.104 [Lear to Edgar as Poor Tom] *Unaccommodated man is no more but such a poor, bare, forked animal as thou art*

3 cleft, twin-peaked **AC** IV.xiv.5 [Antony to Eros] *we see … / A vapour sometime like … / A forked mountain*

4 barbed, sharp-pointed **AY** II.i.24 [Duke Senior to all, of the deer] *with forked heads / Have their round haunches gored*

forlorn (n.) outcast, refugee, forsaken person **3H6** III.iii.26 [Queen to Lewis] *Henry … [is] forced to live in Scotland a forlorn*

forlorn (adj.) **1** wretched, abandoned, destitute **2H6** IV.i.65 [Whitmore to Lieutenant, of Suffolk] *Speak, captain, shall I stab the forlorn swain?;* **Cym** V.v.406; **2H6** II.iv.45; **KL** IV.vii.39

2 meagre, puny, scrawny **2H4** III.ii.301 [Falstaff alone, of Shallow] *'A was so forlorn that his dimensions to any thick sight were invincible*

3 life-endangering, risk-taking **1H6** I.ii.19 [Charles to all] *for the honour of the forlorn French*

form (n.) **1** image, likeness, shape **MV** II.vii.61 [Portia to Morocco, of the gold casket] *if my form lie there, / Then I am yours;* **Ham** III.ii.24; **H5** III.vi.68; **LL** II.i.67; **MM** II.iv.126; **RJ** III.iii.126

2 imprinted shape, impressed image **TN** II.ii.30 [Viola alone] *How easy is it for the proper false / In women's waxen hearts to set their forms;* **Ham** I.v.100; **LL** II.i.223

3 pattern, shaping, outcome, order **KJ** V.iv.50 [Salisbury to Melun, of returning his allegiance to King John] *I do love the favour and the form / Of this most fair occasion;* **2H4** III.i.83; **KJ** V.vii.26; **LL** V.ii.517

4 orderly manner, good arrangement **R3** V.iii.24 [Richmond to all] *I'll draw the form and model of our battle* [i.e. the military formation]; **2H4** IV.i.20; **JC** II.i.20; **KJ** III.iv.101; **R3** III.i.200

5 way of behaving, behaviour, code of conduct **JC** IV.ii.40 [Cassius to Brutus] *this sober form of yours hides wrongs;* **Cor** III.i.323; **Ham** III.i.154; **2H4** IV.i.34; **LL** V.ii.325; **RJ** II.iv.34

6 formal procedure, due process, formality **KL** III.vii.25 [Cornwall to all, of Gloucester] *we may not pass upon his life / Without the form of justice;* **2H4** IV.v.119; **LL** V.ii.517; **MM** V.i.56; **RJ** II.ii.88; **TC** I.iii.87

7 position, rank, status **WT** I.ii.313 [Leontes to and of Camillo] *whom I from meaner form / Have benched and reared to worship;* **Cor** II.ii.142; **MM** II.iv.12

8 physical appearance, outward appearance **Tem** I.ii.412 [Miranda to Prospero, of Ferdinand] *It carries a brave form;* **Ham** III.iv.127; **KL** II.iv.75; **Tim** I.i.17; **TN** V.i.232; **WT** II.i.69

9 physical expression, outward behaviour **H5** II.ii.116 [King Henry to Scroop] *All other devils ... / Do botch and bungle up damnation / With patches, colours, and with forms;* **Ham** II.ii.554

10 substance, essence, true meaning **1H4** I.iii.208 [Worcester to Northumberland, of Hotspur] *He apprehends a world of figures here, / But not the form of what he should attend;* **Sonn** 43.6

11 bench **LL** II.i.204 [Costard to Berowne, of Jaquenetta] *I was seen ... sitting with her upon the 'form'* [pun: sense 6]; **JC** III.ii.260

formal *(adj.)* **1** normal, sane, rational **AC** II.v.41 [Cleopatra to Messenger] *Thou shouldst come like a Fury crowned with snakes, / Not like a formal man;* **CE** V.i.105; **TN** II.v.115

2 stock, regular, conventionally portrayed **R3** III.i.82 [Richard to himself] *like the formal Vice, Iniquity, / I moralize two meanings in one word*

3 punctilious, stiff, standing on ceremony **TS** III.i.59 [Lucentio as Cambio to Hortensio as Licio] *Are you so formal, sir?*

4 external, outward, surface **JC** II.i.227 [Brutus to all, of their intentions] *bear it as our Roman actors do, / With untired spirit and formal constancy*

former *(adj.)* forward, advance, foremost **JC** V.i.79 [Cassius to Messala] *on our former ensign / Two mighty eagles fell, and there they perched*

fornicatress *(n.)* woman guilty of fornication **MM** II.ii.23 [Angelo to Provost, of Juliet] *See you the fornicatress be removed*

forsake *(v.)* **1** refuse, decline, reject **AW** II.iii.55 [King to Helena, of the Lords] *Thou hast power to choose, and they none to forsake;* **1H6** IV.ii.14

2 leave, depart [from] **H8** II.i.89 [Buckingham to Lovell] *My vows and prayers / Yet are the King's and, till my soul forsake, / Shall cry for blessings on him;* **H8** II.i.132

forseal *(v.)* [unclear usage] seal up close, forestall, prevent **WT** I.ii.337 [Camillo to Leontes, of keeping Hermione] *thereby forsealing / The injury of tongues in courts and kingdoms / Known and allied to yours* [F *for sealing*] **☞** seal *(v.)* 7

forslow *(v.)* be slow, delay, put off **3H6** II.iii.56 [George to all] *Forslow no longer*

forsooth *(adv.)* in truth, certainly, truly, indeed **Oth** I.i.19 [Iago to Roderigo, of Cassio] *And what was he? / Forsooth, a great arithmetician* **☞** FEW, p.xxi; **SWEARING**, p.435

forspeak *(v.)*, past form **forspoke** oppose, speak against, object to **AC** III.vii.3 [Cleopatra to Enobarbus] *Thou hast forspoke my being in these wars*

forspent *(adj.)* exhausted, worn out **3H6** II.iii.1 [Warwick alone] *Forspent with toil ... I lay me down a little while to breathe;* **2H4** I.i.37

forswear *(v)*, past forms **forsworn, forswore** **1** swear falsely, perjure [oneself], break one's word **KJ** III.i.101 [Constance to King Philip] *You are forsworn* **☞** FEW, p.xxi

2 abandon, renounce, reject, give up **TG** III.ii.4 [Thurio to Duke, of Silvia] *she hath ... / Forsworn my company* **☞** FEW, p.xxi

3 deny, repudiate, refuse to admit **CE** V.i.10 [Angelo to Second Merchant, of Antipholus of Syracuse] *that self chain about his neck / Which he forswore most monstrously to have* **☞** FEW, p.xxi

forswearing *(n.)* perjury, oath-breaking **R3** I.iv.205 [Second Murderer to Clarence, of God] *vengeance doth He hurl on thee / For false forswearing*

forsworn *(adj.)* perjured, falsely swearing **R2** IV.i.52 [Another Lord to Aumerle] *forsworn Aumerle* **☞** forswear *(v.)* 1

forted *(adj.)* fortified, reinforced, strengthened **MM** V.i.12 [Duke to Angelo, of Angelo's deserving] *it deserves ... / A forted residence*

forth *(adv.)* **1** away from home, out **CE** II.ii.220 [Adriana to Dromio of Syracuse] *if any ask you for your master, / Say he dines forth;* **Tim** II.ii.17

2 forward **AY** I.ii.69 [Touchstone to Rosalind and Celia] *Stand you both forth now;* **TNK** I.i.162

3 straight, directly **Tim** I.i.50 [Poet to Painter, of his poem] *flies an eagle flight, bold and forth on*

forth *(prep.)* out of **1H6** I.ii.54 [Bastard to all, of Pucelle] *A holy maid ... is to raise this tedious siege / And drive the English forth the bounds of France*

forthcoming *(adj.)* **1** producable in court, available as evidence / as a witness **TS** V.i.84 [Tranio as Lucentio to Baptista, of Vincentio] *I charge you see that he be forthcoming;* **2H6** I.iv.52

2 in custody, awaiting trial **2H6** II.i.174 [Cardinal to Gloucester, of the Duchess] *Your lady is forthcoming yet at London*

forthright *(n.)* straight path, direct course **Tem** III.iii.3 [Gonzalo to all] *Here's a maze trod indeed, / Through forthrights and meanders;* **TC** III.iii.158

forthy *(adv.)* [archaism] therefore, for this reason **Per** II.Chorus.19 [Gower alone, of Helicanus] *forthy he strive / To killen bad* **☞** ARCHAISMS, p.22

fortitude *(n.)* strength, might, power **Oth** I.iii.220 [Duke to Othello, of Cyprus] *the fortitude of the place is best known to you;* **1H6** II.i.17

fortunate *(adj.)* **1** bringing good fortune, lucky, favourable **TNK** III.vi.146 [Palamon to Theseus, of Emilia] *That fortunate bright star*

2 favoured by fortune, successful **3H6** IV.vi.25 [King to Warwick] *thou art fortunate in all thy deeds;* **1H6** V.ii.21

fortune *(n.)* **1** good fortune, success **KJ** III.i.333 [Blanche to King Philip] *Father, I may not wish the fortune thine;* **Cym** IV.i.10; **2H4** I.i.23; **Mac** III.i.77; **TNK** II.i.291; **TS** I.i.16

2 wealth, possessions, substance **WT** IV.iv.587 [Camillo to Florizel, of Sicilia] *I think you know my fortunes / Do all lie there;* **AC** II.v.49; **Oth** III.iv.20

3 chance, fate, [one's] lot **3H6** V.v.6 [Somerset to Edward] *[I'll] stoop with patience to my fortune;* **1H6** IV.iv.39; **3H6** II.ii.83; **Oth** III.iii.260; **TS** III.ii.23, V.ii.97

4 lucky chance, good luck **MV** II.ix.19 [Arragon to himself] *Fortune now / To my heart's hope!;* **Cor** V.vi.118; **RJ** III.iii.144; **TNK** II.i.306

fortune *(v.)* happen, chance, occur **TG** V.iv.170 [Valentine to Duke] *you will wonder what hath fortuned*

forward *(adj.)* **1** ready, eager, inclined **R3** III.ii.46 [Catesby to Hastings, of Richard and the crown] *[he] hopes to find you forward / Upon his party for the gain thereof;* **E3** II.i.301; **Ham** III.i.7; **3H6** IV.viii.46; **H8** IV.i.9

2 prepared, at an advanced stage of readiness **Cym** III.v.29 [Cymbeline to Queen, of the danger from Lucius] *Our expectation that it would be thus / Hath made us forward;* **1H4** II.ii.45

3 spirited, eager, lively **R2** IV.i.72 [Fitzwater to Surrey] *How fondly dost thou spur a forward horse!;* **2H4** I.i.173

4 insistent, demanding, eager **2H6** III.ii.253 [Salisbury to King, of the commons' will for Suffolk] *mere instinct of love and loyalty ... / Makes them thus forward in his banishment;* **TS** II.i.73

5 chief, foremost, leading **E3** III.iii.206 [Prince Edward to all] *My gracious father, and ye forward peers* [or: sense 1]

6 in the front line, in forward position **AW** III.ii.113 [Helena alone, of Bertram] *Whoever charges on his forward breast, / I am the caitiff that do hold him to't*

7 promising, early-maturing, precocious **3H6** I.i.203 [King to York] *long live thou and these thy forward sons!;* **AY** III.iii.11; **3H6** II.ii.58; **MA** I.iii.52; **R3** III.i.155; **TG** I.i.45

8 early, premature **R3** III.i.94 [Richard to himself, of Prince Edward] *Short summers lightly have a forward spring;* **Ham** I.iii.8; **Sonn** 99.1

forward (*v.*) go forward, advance, set out on foot 3H6 IV.vii.81 [Edward to all] *We'll forward towards Warwick*

forward (*adv.*) [go] onward, ahead TNK III.v.97 [Theseus to Schoolmaster] *Well, sir, go forward;* TNK III.v.16

forward top forelock, hair at the front of the head AW V.iii.39 [King to Bertram] *Let's take the instant by the forward top* [i.e. take time by the forelock]

forwardness (*n.*) state of readiness, preparedness, zeal Cym IV.ii.342 [Lucius to Captain, of the arrival of the new troops] *This forwardness / Makes our hopes fair;* 3H6 IV.v.23, V.iv.65

forwardness (*adj.*) rashness, boldness, over-eagerness AY I.ii.140 [Duke Frederick to all, of Orlando] *his own peril on his forwardness*

forwearied (*adj.*) worn out, exhausted KJ II.i.233 [King John to Hubert, of himself] *Forwearied in this action of swift speed*

foster-nurse (*n.*) nurse who brings up someone else's child as her own KL IV.iv.12 [Doctor to Cordelia] *Our foster-nurse of nature is repose*

foster up (*v.*) bring up, nurse, nourish KJ V.ii.75 [Cardinal Pandulph to Lewis the Dauphin, of the French might] *like a lion fostered up at hand, / It may lie gently at the foot of peace* [i.e. reared by hand]

foul (*adj.*) **1** plain-looking, unattractive, ugly Venus 133 [Venus to Adonis] *Were I hard-favoured, foul, or wrinkled-old;* AC I.ii.73; AY III.iii.35; Oth II.i.138; TS I.ii.68; Venus 773
  2 false, hypocritical, shameful Per IV.iv.23 [Gower alone] *See how belief may suffer by foul show;* TS Induction.ii.15
  3 detestable, vile, loathsome TS V.ii.158 [Katherina to Widow, of a disobedient wife] *What is she but a foul contending rebel;* AY III.iii.33; Tim III.v.75
  4 dirty, miry, muddy MW III.iii.122 [Mistress Page to Mistress Ford, of Falstaff] *throw foul linen upon him, as if it were going to bucking;* AY V.iv.60; 1H4 II.i.85; TNK I.i.58; TS IV.i.2, 59
  5 harsh, rough, hard Venus 573 *Foul words and frowns must not repel a lover*
  6 [of a pistol-barrel after firing] dirty, clogged H5 II.i.53 [Nym to Pistol] *If you grow foul with me … I will scour you with my rapier* [i.e. if you shoot your mouth off at me]

fouled (*adj.*) filthy, dirtied Ham II.i.79 [Ophelia to Polonius, of Hamlet] *his stockings fouled*

foulness (*n.*) **1** dishonesty, wickedness, bad reputation H8 III.ii.183 [King Henry to Wolsey, of loyalty] *The honour of it / Does pay the act of it, as … / The foulness is the punishment*
  2 immorality, impurity, depravity KL I.i.227 [Cordelia to Lear, of the cause of her situation] *It is no vicious blot, murder or foulness*
  3 plainness, unattractiveness AY III.iii.36 [Touchstone to Audrey] *praised be the gods for thy foulness;* AY III.v.66

foundation (*n.*) charitable institution MA V.i.304 [Dogberry to Leonato, after receiving recompense] *God save the foundation!;* Cym III.vi.7

founded (*adj.*) firmly based, secure, stable Mac III.iv.21 [Macbeth to First Murderer, of Fleance's escape] *I had else been perfect … founded as the rock*

founder (*v.*) make lame, cause to break down 2H4 IV.iii.35 [Falstaff to Prince John] *I have foundered nine score and odd posts;* Tem IV.i.30; TNK V.ii.50

fount (*n.*) spring, stream Luc 850 [Lucrece to herself] *Why should … toads infect fair founts with venom mud?;* H8 I.i.154

fountain (*n.*) spring, source, well Oth IV.ii.58 [Othello to Desdemona] *The fountain from the which my current runs;* Mac II.iii.95

foutre (*n.*) [strong rude expression of contempt] fuck 2H4 V.iii.115 [Pistol to Shallow] *A foutre for thine office!;* 2H4 V.iii.99

fowl (*n.*) bird Phoen 10 *From this session interdict / Every fowl of tyrant wing* [i.e. bird of prey]

fox (*n.*) type of sword [perhaps with a fox-like engraving on it] H5 IV.iv.9 [Pistol to French Soldier] *thou diest on point of fox*

foxship (*n.*) [quality of a fox] low cunning, slyness, ingratitude Cor IV.ii.18 [Volumnia to Sicinius, of Coriolanus] *Hadst thou foxship / To banish him*

fracted (*adj.*) broken H5 II.i.119 [Pistol to Nym, of Falstaff] *His heart is fracted and corroborate;* Tim II.i.22

fraction (*n.*) **1** fragment, scrap, shred TC V.ii.161 [Troilus to Ulysses, of Cressida] *The fractions of her faith … are bound to Diomed;* Tim II.ii.216
  2 quarrelling, discord, dissension TC II.iii.98 [Nestor to Ulysses, of Ajax and Achilles] *their fraction is more our wish than their faction*

fragment (*n.*) scrap of food, left-over Cym V.iii.44 [Posthumus to Lord, of the Britons] *Like fragments in hard voyages became / The life o' th' need;* AC III.xiii.117; TC V.i.8

frailty (*n.*) **1** moral weakness, shortcoming, liability to give in to temptation Ham I.ii.146 [Hamlet alone] *Frailty, thy name is woman;* MW II.i.216; Oth IV.iii.100; Sonn 121.7
  2 body, frame Mac II.iii.123 [Banquo to all] *when we have our naked frailties hid / That suffer in exposure, let us meet*

frame (*n.*) **1** framework, structure, construction 1H6 II.iii.53 [Talbot to Countess, of what his body represents] *were the whole frame here … / Your roof were not sufficient to contain't;* Ham II.ii.298; Mac III.ii.16; Sonn 24.3; TN I.i.34; TNK III.v.112
  2 plan, established order, scheme of things MA IV.i.126 [Leonato to Hero, of his having had just one child] *Chid I for that at frugal Nature's frame?*
  3 order, definite form, regular shape Ham III.ii.317 [Guildenstern to Hamlet] *put your discourse into some frame;* Ham I.ii.20; LL III.i.188
  4 framing, plotting, contriving MA IV.i.187 [Benedick to Friar, of Don John] *Whose spirits toil in frame of villainies*
  5 nature, frame of mind, disposition Tim I.i.72 [Poet to Painter, of the people in his poem] *One do I personate of Lord Timon's frame* [also: build]

frame (*v.*) **1** fashion, make, form, create MV I.i.51 [Solanio to Antonio] *Nature hath framed strange fellows in her time;* H5 IV.iii.14; Per IV.ii.133; Sonn 5.1; TG III.ii.76; Tim V.i.121
  2 adapt, adjust, shape, accommodate 3H6 III.ii.185 [Richard alone] *I can … frame my face to all occasions;* AC V.ii.55; Cor III.ii.84; Cym II.iii.45; Sonn 118.6; TS I.i.224
  3 arrange, organize, plan KL I.ii.98 [Gloucester to Edmund] *Frame the business after your own wisdom;* 2H4 IV.i.178; MA I.iii.23; Tim IV.iii.263
  4 prepare, make ready, prime MM III.i.256 [disguised Duke to Isabella, of Mariana] *The maid will I frame and make fit*
  5 direct one's steps, shape a course, betake oneself Per I.Chorus.32 [Gower alone, of Antiochus' daughter] *[her] beauty … / Made many princes thither frame / To seek her*
  6 perform, manage, carry out AC II.ii.216 [Enobarbus to Agrippa and Maecenas, of those making the sails swell on Cleopatra's barge] *those flower-soft hands, / That yarely frame the office*

framed (*adj.*) designed, properly planned, well-prepared WT V.i.91 [Leontes to Gentleman, of Florizel's arrival] *'Tis not a visitation framed, but forced / By need and accident*

frampold (*adj.*) disagreeable, bad-tempered, moody MW II.ii.87 [Mistress Quickly to Falstaff, of Mistress Ford and Ford] *she leads a very frampold life with him;* TNK III.v.58

franchise (*n.*) **1** right, liberty, freedom Cor IV.vi.87 [Cominius to Brutus and Sicinius] *Your franchises, … confined / Into an auger's bore*
  2 free exercise, freedom to implement Cym III.i.57 [Cymbeline to Lucius, of the British laws crushed by Caesar] *whose repair, and franchise, / Shall … be our good deed*

franchised (*adj.*) free from evil, upright Mac II.i.28 [Banquo to Macbeth] *So I … still keep / My bosom franchised and allegiance clear*

Francisco (*n.*) Frenchman **MW** II.iii.25 [Host to and of Caius] *Is he dead, my Francisco?* [F; Q *francoyes*]

francoyes (*n.*) ☞ Francisco (*n.*)

frank (*n.*) pig-sty **2H4** II.ii.140 [Prince Henry to Bardolph, of Falstaff] *Doth the old boar feed in the old frank?*

frank (*adj.*) **1** generous, liberal, bounteous **RJ** II.ii.131 [Juliet to Romeo, of withdrawing her love] *But to be frank and give it thee again;* **AW** I.ii.20; **Cor** I.i.130; **KL** III.iv.20; **Oth** III.iv.44; **Sonn** 4.4

2 free, unconstrained, unrestricted **AW** II.iii.54 [King to Helena, of the Lords] *Thy frank election make*

frank up (*v.*) shut up in a sty, put in an enclosure **R3** I.iii.313 [Richard to Queen Elizabeth, of Clarence] *He is franked up to fatting for his pains;* **R3** IV.v.3

franklin (*n.*) landowner ranking below the gentry, rich free-holder, yeoman **Cym** III.ii.78 [Innogen to Pisanio, of her riding-suit] *no costlier than would fit / A franklin's housewife;* **1H4** II.i.55; **WT** V.ii.156

frankly (*adv.*) **1** freely, without restraint, unrestrictedly **TC** I.iii.253 [Agamemnon to Aeneas] *Speak frankly as the wind;* **TC** V.viii.19; **Tim** II.ii.184

2 freely, unconditionally, unreservedly **MM** III.i.109 [Isabella to Claudio, of her life] *I'd throw it down for your deliverance / As frankly as a pin;* **Tit** I.i.423

3 with no ill-will, openly, without rancour **Ham** V.ii.247 [Hamlet to Laertes] *I … will this brothers' wager frankly play*

frantic (*adj.*) mad, insane, frenzied, out of one's senses **Tit** V.iii.63 [Saturninus to Titus, of killing Tamora] *Die, frantic wretch, for this accursed deed;* **AY** I.iii.47; **1H6** III.ii.5; **R3** IV.iv.68; **Tit** IV.iv.59; **TS** III.ii.12

fraud (*n.*) **1** delusion, deception, trick **E3** IV.v.55 [King John to Philip, of the French] *at once dispatch / This little business of a silly fraud*

2 trickery, stratagem, artifice **3H6** IV.iv.33 [Lady Grey to Rivers, of sanctuary] *There shall I rest secure from force and fraud*

3 faithlessness, deceitfulness, insincerity **1H6** IV.iv.36 [Lucy to Somerset] *The fraud of England … / Hath now entrapped the noble-minded Talbot*

fraudful fraudulent, treacherous, deceitful **2H6** III.i.81 [Queen to King, of Gloucester] *the welfare of us all / Hangs on the cutting short that fraudful man*

fraught (*n.*) **1** freight, cargo, goods **TN** V.i.58 [First Officer to Orsino] *this is that Antonio / That took the Phoenix, and her fraught from Candy;* **E3** III.iv.81, V.i.79; **Tit** I.i.74 [Q1]

2 burden, load **Oth** III.iii.446 [Othello to Iago, as if to his heart] *Swell, bosom, with thy fraught*

fraught (*adj.*) filled, laden, packed **MV** II.viii.30 [Salerio to Solanio, of the English channel] *there miscarried / A vessel of our country richly fraught;* **E3** IV.iv.105; **KL** I.iv.216; **TC** Prologue.4

fraught (*v.*) burden, weigh down, encumber **WT** IV.iv.511 [Florizel to Camillo] *I am so fraught with curious business that / I leave out ceremony;* **Cym** I.i.57; **PassP** XVII.16

fraughtage (*n.*) luggage, freight, cargo **CE** IV.i.88 [Dromio of Syracuse to Antipholus of Ephesus, of a ship] *Our fraughtage, sir, / I have conveyed aboard;* **TC** Prologue.13

fraughting (*adj.*) forming the cargo, making up the freight **Tem** I.ii.13 [Miranda to Prospero, of the doomed ship] *The fraughting souls within her*

fray (*v.*) frighten, terrify, scare [by] **TC** III.ii.30 [Pandarus to Troilus, of Cressida] *She … fetches her wind so short, as if she were frayed with a sprite*

free (*adj.*) **1** liberal, lavish, generous **Tim** III.iv.81 [Timon to all] *Have I been ever free, and must my house / Be my retentive enemy, my gaol?;* **Ham** I.iii.93; **1H6** I.iii.64; **2H6** IV.vii.117; **MM** V.i.385; **TC** IV.v.100

2 generous, magnanimous **WT** II.ii.44 [Emilia to Paulina, of the plan to take the baby to Leontes] *your free undertaking cannot miss / A thriving issue;* **TN** I.v.87

3 noble, honourable, worthy **TN** I.v.249 [Olivia to Viola as Cesario, of Orsino] *[he is] free, learned, and valiant;* **2H6** III.i.223; **Oth** II.iii.310; **TNK** II.i.235; **WT** IV.iv.545

4 free of worry, untroubled, carefree **KL** III.iv.11 [Lear to disguised Kent] *When the mind's free / The body's delicate;* **H8** III.i.32; **KL** III.vi.103, IV.i.80; **Oth** III.iii.337; **TN** II.iv.45

5 innocent, guiltless **H8** II.iv.99 [Wolsey to Queen Katherine, of King Henry] *If he know / That I am free of your report;* **AY** II.vii.85; **Ham** II.ii.561, III.i.251; **Oth** III.iii.253; **WT** II.iii.30

6 direct, free from legal constraint **R2** II.iii.135 [Bolingbroke to York] *I lay my claim / To my inheritance of free descent*

7 on the loose, unconfined, unrestricted **JC** II.i.79 [Brutus alone, as if to conspiracy] *Sham'st thou to show thy dangerous brow by night, / When evils are most free?*

8 open, unobstructed, unimpeded **Cym** I.vii.68 [Iachimo to Innogen, of Posthumus] *laughs from's free lungs;* **Tim** I.i.46

9 frank, undisguised, open **Mac** I.iii.155 [Macbeth to Banquo] *let us speak / Our free hearts each to other;* **Cor** II.iii.199, III.i.73, V.vi.26; **MM** I.i.77

10 freely given, willing, unconstrained **3H6** IV.vi.36 [George to Warwick] *I yield thee my free consent;* **Ham** IV.iii.63; **MM** IV.iii.89; **R2** I.iii.88; **Sonn** 125.10

11 uninfected, free from disease **MM** I.ii.43 [Second Gentleman to First Gentleman] *thou art tainted or free*

12 [unclear meaning] not in formal marching order; quick **TC** V.x.30 [Troilus to drummers] *Strike a free march to Troy!*

free (*v.*) **1** absolve, acquit, clear **Cor** IV.vii.47 [Aufidius to Lieutenant, of Coriolanus] *I dare so far free him*

2 remove, get rid of, relieve **Cym** III.vii.52 [Guiderius to Belarius and Arviragus, of disguised Innogen's distress] *Would I could free't!*

free (*adv.*) freely, in a liberal way **Mac** II.i.19 [Macbeth to Banquo] *Being unprepared / Our will became the servant to defect, / Which else should free have wrought*

freedom (*n.*) **1** concession, privilege, permission **JC** III.i.54 [Brutus to Caesar] *Desiring thee that Publius Cimber may / Have an immediate freedom of repeal*

2 ☞ use thy freedom

freely (*adv.*) **1** without conditions, unreservedly **Tim** I.ii.9 [Timon to Ventidius, of the loan] *I gave it freely ever*

2 gladly, willingly, readily **Tim** I.i.114 [Timon to Old Athenian, of a request to hear him] *Freely, good father*

freeness (*n.*) generosity, liberality, benevolence **Cym** V.v.422 [Cymbeline to all, of Posthumus] *We'll learn our freeness of a son-in-law*

freestone (*n.*) greyish-yellow, browny-yellow [as of limestone or sandstone] **AY** IV.iii.26 [Rosalind as Ganymede to Silvius, of Phebe] *she has a leathern hand, / A freestone-coloured hand*

French crown ☞ crown (*n.*) 1, 2

French-crown-colour (*adj.*) light yellow coloured [as the French crown coin] **MND** I.ii.88 [Bottom to Quince, of his beard for the play] *your French-crown-colour beard*

frenzy (*n.*) distraction, agitation, delirium **TN** V.i.278 [Olivia to Orsino, of Malvolio] *A most extracting frenzy of mine own / From my remembrance clearly banished his;* **KJ** IV.ii.122; **Luc** 1675; **Tit** IV.i.17, iv.12; **TS** Induction.ii.131

frequent (*adj.*) **1** familiar, in habitual company **Sonn** 117.5 *I have frequent been with unknown minds*

2 addicted, inclined, disposed **WT** IV.ii.32 [Camillo to Polixenes, of Florizel] *he is … less frequent to his princely exercises than formerly he hath appeared*

fresh (*n.*) freshwater stream, fresh spring **Tem** III.ii.67 [Caliban to Stephano, of Trinculo] *I'll not show him / Where the quick freshes are*

fresh (*adj.*) **1** young, lovely, blooming **TS** IV.v.29 [Petruchio to Katherina, of Vincentio] *Hast thou beheld a fresher gentlewoman?*; **WT** IV.iv.548

2 bright, blooming, gay **E3** II.i.439 [Warwick to Countess] *The freshest summer's day*

3 refreshed, invigorated, renewed **1H6** III.iii.86 [Charles to Burgundy] *Thy friendship makes us fresh*; **TC** V.vi.20

4 ready, eager, hungry **TN** I.i.9 [Orsino to all, as if to love] *how quick and fresh art thou*

fret (*n.*) **1** ridge for guiding the fingers on the neck of a lute [or similar instrument] **TS** II.i.149 [Hortensio as Licio to Baptista, of teaching Katherina the lute] *I did but tell her she mistook her frets* [pun: 152, sense 2]

2 irritation, annoyance, vexation **TS** II.i.152 [Hortensio as Licio to Baptista, of teaching Katherina the finger-positions on the lute] *'Frets, call you these?' quoth she* [pun: 149, sense 1]

fret (*v.*) **1** wear out, eat away, erode **R2** III.iii.167 [King Richard to Aumerle, of their shed tears] *they have fretted us a pair of graves / Within the earth* [i.e. made for us through wearing away]; **H8** III.ii.105; **KL** I.iv.282; **TS** II.i.321; **Venus** 767

2 decay, fester, ferment **MW** III.v.104 [Falstaff to Ford as Brook] *I suffered ... to be stopped in, like a strong distillation, with stinking clothes that fretted in their own grease*

3 chafe, be vexed, worry **1H4** II.ii.2 [Poins to Prince Hal, of Falstaff] *he frets like a gummed velvet* [i.e. a fabric which wears out quickly]; **MV** IV.i.77

4 distress oneself, worry, express discontent **Mac** V.v.25 [Macbeth to himself] *Life's but a ... poor player / That struts and frets his hour upon the stage*

5 struggle, chafe, move in turmoil **H5** IV.vii.77 [Montjoy to King Henry, of the French dead] *their wounded steeds / Fret fetlock-deep in gore*

6 rage, rampage **Venus** 621 [Venus to Adonis, of a boar] *His eyes like glow-worms shine when he doth fret*; **Luc** 648

7 adorn elaborately, decorate ornately [as a carved ceiling] **Ham** II.ii.301 [Hamlet to Rosencrantz and Guildenstern] *this majestical roof fretted with golden fire*; **Cym** II.iv.88; **JC** II.i.104

fretful (*adj.*) **1** angry, irritated, ill-tempered **KL** III.i.4 [Gentleman to disguised Kent, of Lear] *Contending with the fretful elements*; **Ham** I.v.20

2 irritating, aggravating, gnawing **2H6** III.ii.403 [Queen to Suffolk] *Though parting be a fretful corrosive, / It is applied to a deathful wound*

fretted (*adj.*) chequered, mixed; or, distressed **AC** IV.xii.8 [Scarus alone, of Antony] *His fretted fortunes give him hope and fear*

fretting (*n.*) impatience, vexation, frustration **1H6** I.i.16 [Reignier to all, of Salisbury] *he may well in fretting spend his gall*

fretting (*adj.*) intermittently blowing, squalling **3H6** II.vi.35 [Edward to all] *a sail, filled with a fretting gust, / [doth] Command an argosy to stem the waves* [also: nagging]

friend (*n.*) **1** lover, sweetheart, suitor **LL** V.ii.823 [Maria to Longaville] *At the twelvemonth's end / I'll change my black gown for a faithful friend*; **Cym** I.v.66; **MW** III.iii.109; **RJ** III.v.77; **TG** IV.vi.30; **TNK** II.i.16

2 relation, relative, kinsman **1H6** V.iv.9 [Pucelle to Shepherd] *Thou art no father nor no friend of mine*; **AW** I.iii.190; **AY** I.iii.60; **2H4** III.ii.103; **Per** V.i.125; **RJ** III.v.75

3 well-wisher, favourer **MW** I.iv.135 [Mistress Quickly to Fenton, of Anne] *she is ... one that is your friend*

friend, at as a friend, in friendship **WT** V.i.139 [Florizel to Leontes, of Polixenes] *from him [I] / Give you all greetings that a king, at friend, / Can send his brother*

friend, to as a friend, friendly **Mac** IV.iii.10 [Malcolm to Macduff] *what I can redress, / As I shall find the time to friend, I will*; **AW** V.iii.182

friend (*v.*) **1** befriend, sustain, assist **TNK** I.iv.2 [Second Queen to Theseus] *Both heaven and earth / Friend thee for ever*; **Cym** III.iii.46; **H5** IV.v.17; **H8** I.ii.140; **TC** I.ii.79

2 befriend, become intimate **Cym** I.v.103 [Iachimo to Posthumus, of Innogen] *had I admittance, and opportunity to friend*

friending (*n.*) friendliness, friendship, affection **Ham** I.v.185 [Hamlet of himself, to Horatio and Marcellus] *t'express his love and friending to you*

friendly (*adv.*) in a friendly way **Tit** I.i.222 [Titus to Tribunes, of their votes] *Will ye bestow them friendly on Andronicus?*; **Tit** IV.ii.40

friendship (*n.*) friendly act, favour, act of kindness **Tim** IV.iii.71 [Alcibiades to Timon] *What friendship may I do thee?*; **KL** III.ii.62

frieze (*n.*) type of rough woollen cloth **Oth** II.i.125 [Iago to Desdemona] *my invention / Comes from my pate as birdlime does from frieze* [i.e. with great difficulty]; **MW** V.v.137; **TNK** III.v.8

fright (*v.*), past form **frighted** frighten, scare, terrify **KJ** V.i.58 [Bastard to King John, of John's enemies] *shall they seek the lion in his den, / And fright him there?* ☞ **FEW**, p.xxi

frighted (*adj.*) frightened, terrified, scared **Luc** 1149 *the poor frighted deer that stands at gaze*; **1H4** I.i.2, III.i.37; **WT** IV.iv.117

frightful (*adj.*) frightening, terrifying, full of horror **2H6** III.ii.326 [Suffolk to Queen, of the King and Warwick] *Their music frightful as the serpent's hiss*; **R3** IV.iv.170

frippery (*n.*) second-hand clothes shop **Tem** IV.i.226 [Trinculo to Caliban] *We know what belongs to a frippery*

frisk (*n.*) lively movement, caper, jig **TNK** III.v.30 [Schoolmaster to the dancers, of their dancing] *now and then a favour and a frisk*

friskin (*n.*) antic, friskiness, playful action **TNK** IV.iii.79 [Doctor to Wooer, of the Gaoler's Daughter] *other objects ... become the pranks and friskins of her madness* [i.e. what makes her madness play tricks and jump about]

frivolous (*adj.*) **1** silly, paltry, trivial **TS** V.i.23 [Petruchio to Pedant as Vincentio] *leave frivolous circumstances*

2 groundless, insufficient, paltry **3H6** I.i.27 [Richard to York] *Your oath ... is vain and frivolous* [i.e. without legal weight]; **1H6** IV.i.112

frock (*n.*) dress, gown, costume **Ham** III.iv.165 [Hamlet to Gertrude, of custom] *He likewise gives a frock or livery / That aptly is put on* ☞ **CLOTHING**, p.79

frolic (*adj.*) frolicsome, merry, frisky **MND** V.i.377 [Puck to himself] *we fairies ... / Now are frolic*

frolic (*v.*) be joyful, make merry **TS** IV.iii.178 [Petruchio to Katherina] *therefore frolic*

from (*prep.*) **1** away from **TNK** V.vii.103 [Doctor to Wooer, of Gaoler's Daughter] *You must not from her* [i.e. leave her]; **Tim** IV.iii.529

2 contrary to **JC** II.i.196 [Cassius to all, of Caesar's belief in superstition] *Quite from the main opinion he held once / Of fantasy*

front (*n.*) **1** forehead, face **R3** I.i.9 [Richard alone] *Grim-visaged war hath smoothed his wrinkled front*; **AC** I.i.6; **Ham** III.iv.57; **KJ** II.i.356; **KL** II.ii.106

2 forelock **Oth** III.i.48 [Emilia to Cassio] *To take the safest occasion by the front*

3 beginning, start, opening **Sonn** 102.7 *Philomel in summer's front doth sing*; **WT** IV.iv.3

4 ☞ head and front

front of heaven sky **1H4** III.i.35 [Glendower to Hotspur] *at my birth / The front of heaven was full of fiery shapes*

front (*v.*) **1** confront, face, meet **1H4** II.ii.58 [Prince Hal to all] *you four shall front them in the narrow lane*; **AC** I.iv.79; **Cor** V.ii.40; **2H4** IV.i.25; **1H6** IV.vii.26; **TN** I.iii.53

2 oppose, confront, be hostile to **AC** II.ii.65 [Antony to Caesar] *... / Could not with graceful eyes attend those wars / Which fronted mine own peace*

3 march in the front rank, be in the forefront **H8** I.ii.42 [Wolsey to King Henry] *I … front but in that file / Where others tell steps with me*

frontier (*n.*) **1** confrontation, defiance, challenge **1H4** I.iii.18 [King Henry to Worcester] *majesty might never yet endure / The moody frontier of a servant brow*
  2 fortified outwork, barrier against attack **1H4** II.iii.54 [Lady Percy to Hotspur] *thou hast talked / Of … frontiers*
  3 border fortress, frontier town **Ham** IV.iv.16 [Hamlet to Captain, of his army] *Goes it against the main of Poland, sir, / Or for some frontier?*

fronting (*adj.*) confronting, facing **2H4** IV.iv.66 [King Henry IV to Clarence, of Prince Henry] *with what wings shall his affections fly / Towards fronting peril and opposed decay!*

frontlet (*n.*) forehead, ornamental headband [of frowns] **KL** I.iv.185 [Lear to Gonerill] *What makes that frontlet on?*

frosty (*adj.*) hoary, white-haired **2H6** V.i.167 [King to Salisbury, of loyalty] *If it be banished from the frosty head, / Where shall it find a harbour in the earth?*

froth (*n.*) insubstantial thing, empty moment **Luc** 212 [Tarquin to himself, of raping Lucrece] *a froth of fleeting joy*

froth (*v.*) make beer foam up [so that not so much is sold] **MW** I.iii.14 [Host to Bardolph] *Let me see thee froth and lime*

froward (*adj.*) **1** perverse, obstinate, wilful, ungovernable **TS** I.ii.89 [Hortensio to Petruchio, of Katherina] *she is … shrewd and froward;* **E3** III.iii.31; **1H6** III.i.18; **3H6** IV.vii.83; **PassP** IV.14; **Venus** 562
  ➤ toward (*adj.*) 1
  2 adverse, unfavourable, contrary **E3** III.i.134 [King John, as if to Fortune] *change the froward winds*

frown (*n.*) **1** fierce look, severe face **Tem** V.i.127 [Prospero aside to Sebastian and Antonio] *I here could pluck his highness' frown upon you;* **Cym** V.iii.28
  2 brow, forehead **WT** II.iii.100 [Paulina to all, of the baby] *The trick of's frown*

fructify (*v.*) bear fruit, become fruitful **LL** IV.ii.29 [Nathaniel to Holofernes, of Dull] *we thankful should be … for those parts that do fructify in us more than he*

fruit (*n.*) dessert, last course **Ham** II.ii.52 [Polonius to Claudius] *My news shall be the fruit* [Q2; F *Newes*]

fruitful (*adj.*) **1** fertile, productive of children **AC** I.ii.53 [Charmian to Iras] *if an oily palm be not a fruitful prognostication, I cannot scratch mine ear*
  2 abundant, overflowing, prolific **Ham** I.ii.80 [Hamlet to Gertrude, of his grief] *the fruitful river in the eye*
  3 generous, bountiful, liberal **H8** I.iii.56 [Lovell to Lord Chamberlain, of Wolsey] *That churchman bears … / A hand as fruitful as the land that feeds us;* **Oth** II.iii.331
  4 promising, full of potential, talented **Cym** V.iv.55 [First Brother, to music, of Posthumus] *where was he / That could stand up his parallel, / or fruitful object be*

fruitfully (*adv.*) plentifully, amply, abundantly **KL** IV.vi.264 [Edgar, reading Gonerill's letter] *time and place will be fruitfully offered*

fruitfulness (*n.*) liberality, generosity, of a giving nature **Oth** III.iv.38 [Othello to Desdemona, of her moist hand] *This argues fruitfulness and liberal heart*

fruitless (*adj.*) barren, sterile, useless **E3** I.ii.14 [Countess to herself] *in the barren, bleak, and fruitless air*

frush (*v.*) smash, strike violently **TC** V.vi.29 [Hector to a Greek soldier, of his fine armour] *I'll frush it, and unlock the rivets all*

frustrate (*adj.*) unsuccessful, thwarted, fruitless **Tem** III.iii.11 [Alonso to Gonzalo] *the sea mocks / Our frustrate search on land;* **AC** V.i.2

frustrate (*v.*) annul, make null and void, render ineffectual **3H6** II.i.174 [Warwick to all, of the King] *to London all the crew are gone, / To frustrate … his oath*

frutify (*v.*) malapropism for 'certify' **MV** II.ii.123 [Launcelot to Bassanio] *my father, being I hope an old man, shall frutify unto you*

fry (*n.*) **1** young fish **AW** IV.iii.216 [Parolles to First Soldier, of Bertram] *who is a whale to virginity, and devours up all the fry it finds;* **Venus** 526
  2 brood, offspring, progeny **H8** V.iv.35 [Porter to Man] *what a fry of fornication is at door!;* **Mac** IV.ii.84

fry (*v.*) burn with lust; or: burn in hell **TC** V.ii.57 [Thersites to himself] *Fry, lechery, fry!*

fub (*v.*) fob off, cheat, rob **1H4** I.ii.59 [Falstaff to Prince Hal] *[shall there be] resolution thus fubbed as it is with the rusty curb of old Father Antic the law?* [Q; F *fobb'd*]

fub off (*v.*) fob off, put off **2H4** II.i.32 [Hostess to Fang and Snare, of Falstaff] *[I] have been fubbed off … from this day to that day*

fugitive (*n.*) **1** exile, refugee, deserter **1H6** III.iii.67 [Pucelle to Burgundy] *And thou be thrust out like a fugitive?*
  2 vagabond, vagrant, beggar **E3** III.iii.52 [King John to King Edward] *I condemn thee for a fugitive;* **E3** III.iii.154

fulfil (*v.*) **1** perform, execute, carry out **1H6** III.ii.133 [Talbot to Burgundy, of Bedford] *see his exequies fulfilled in Rouen*
  2 fill up, make complete **Luc** 1258 *let it not be hild / Poor women's faults that they are so fulfilled / With men's abuses*

fulfilling (*adj.*) fitting exactly, well-complementing **TC** Prologue.18 [Prologue, of the six city gates] *with massy staples / And corresponsive and fulfilling bolts*

full (*n.*) fullness, entire range, complete scope **TC** III.iii.241 [Achilles to Patroclus, of Hector] *to behold his visage / Even to my full of view*

full, at in detail, at full length **Ham** IV.iii.65 [Claudius alone, as if to the King of England] *Our sovereign process, which imports at full, / By letters*

full, in the to the full, amply **TC** IV.v.272 [Agamemnon to the Greeks] *go to my tent; / There in the full convive you*

full (*adj.*) **1** whole, entire, complete **AY** III.ii.4 [Orlando alone, as if to Diana] *Thy huntress' name that my full life doth sway;* **Cym** V.iv.110; **H8** II.iv.108
  2 ideal, perfect, complete **KL** I.iv.3 [Kent alone] *my good intent / May carry through itself to that full issue / For which I razed my likeness;* **AC** III.xiii.87; **Oth** I.i.67
  3 unrestrained, unlimited, copious **Per** I.iv.22 [Cleon to Dionyza, of Tarsus] *A city on whom plenty held full hand*
  4 food-filled, stomach-swollen **AC** I.iv.27 [Caesar to Lepidus, of Antony] *If he filled / His vacancy with his voluptuousness, / Full surfeits and the dryness of his bones / Call on him for't*

full (*adv.*) **1** fully, completely, properly **KL** I.iv.334 [Gonerill to Oswald, of Regan] *Inform her full of my particular fear;* **1H6** V.v.17; **2H6** I.i.66; **MA** I.i.101; **TC** IV.v.3; **TNK** I.i.220
  2 very, exceedingly, extremely **Tem** I.ii.20 [Prospero to Miranda] *I am … master of a full poor cell;* **AW** I.i.103; **1H4** V.iii.29; **H8** I.i.133; **MM** V.i.157; **Oth** I.ii.10

full-acorned (*adj.*) fed full of acorns **Cym** II.iv.168 [Posthumus alone, of Iachimo's seduction] *Like a full-acorned bear*

fullam, fulham (*n.*) type of loaded dice **MW** I.iii.80 [Pistol to Nym] *gourd and fullam holds, / And high and low beguiles the rich and poor* [i.e. high and low numbers on the dice]

full-charged (*adj.*) fully loaded **H8** I.ii.3 [King Henry to Wolsey] *I stood i'th' level / Of a full-charged confederacy*

fuller (*n.*) cleanser and thickener of cloth **H8** I.ii.33 [Norfolk to King Henry] *The clothiers all … have put off / The spinsters, carders, fullers, weavers*

full-fortuned (*adj.*) replete with good fortune, full of success **AC** IV.xv.24 [Cleopatra to Antony] *Not th'imperious show / Of the full-fortuned Caesar ever shall / Be brooched with me*

full-fraught (*adj.*) filled to the brim, jam-packed **TG** III.ii.70 [Proteus to Thurio] *sonnets, whose composed rhymes / Should be full-fraught with serviceable vows;* **H5** II.ii.139

full-gorged *(adj.)* allowed to eat her fill **TS** IV.i.177 [Petruchio alone, of Katherina as a falcon] *till she stoop she must not be full-gorged*

full-hearted *(adj.)* full of courage, totally confident **Cym** V.iii.7 [Posthumus to Lord, of the Romans] *the enemy full-hearted*

fulness *(n.)* prosperity, affluence, situation of plenty **Cym** III.vi.12 [Innogen alone] *To lapse in fulness / Is sorer than to lie for need*

fulsome *(adj.)* **1** distasteful, nauseating, repulsive **R3** V.iii.133 [Ghost of Clarence to Richard] *I that was washed to death with fulsome wine;* **KJ** III.iv.32; **Oth** IV.i.36; **TN** V.i.107
  2 randy, lustful, lascivious **MV** I.iii.83 [Shylock to Antonio, of Jacob's sticks] *He stuck them up before the fulsome ewes*

fume *(n.)* **1** harmful vapour [rising from the stomach to the brain] **Tem** V.i.67 [Prospero to himself, of the King's company] *the ignorant fumes that mantle / Their clearer reason;* **Cym** IV.ii.301; **Mac** I.vii.66
  2 fit of anger, furious mood **2H6** I.iii.148 [Buckingham to Cardinal, of the Duchess of Gloucester] *her fume needs no spurs;* **Venus** 316

fume *(v.)* be in a rage, show anger **TS** II.i.152 [Hortensio as Licio to Baptista, of Katherina and the frets on a lute] *'Frets, call you these?' quoth she, 'I'll fume with them.'*

fumiter *(n.)* fumitory [variety of weed] **KL** IV.iv.3 [Cordelia to Doctor, of Lear] *Crowned with rank fumiter* [F *Femitar;* Q *femiter*] ☛ **PLANTS**, p.330

fumitory *(n.)* variety of weed **H5** V.ii.45 [Burgundy to King Henry and the French King, of peace] *her fallow leas / The darnel, hemlock, and rank fumitory / Doth root upon* ☛ **PLANTS**, p.330

function *(n.)* **1** activity, action, performance **Mac** I.iii.140 [Macbeth to himself] *My thought … / Shakes so my single state of man / That function is smothered in surmise* [i.e. my imaginings take away my power to act]; **Ham** II.ii.553
  2 ability to exercise the faculties, natural powers **Oth** II.iii. *338* [Iago alone, of Othello and Desdemona] *her appetite shall play the god / With her weak function* [with bawdy pun]
  3 office, occupation, calling **TN** IV.ii.6 [Feste alone, of his priestly disguise] *I am not tall enough to become the function well;* **AY** II.vii.79; **Cor** IV.v.34, vi.9; **Oth** IV.ii.26; **TN** V.i.159

furbished *(adj.)* gleaming, shining; or: refurbished, refitted **Mac** I.ii.32 [Captain to King] *the Norweyan lord, surveying vantage, / With furbished arms and new supplies of men, / Began a fresh assault*

furious *(adj.)* **1** passionate, uproarious, excitable **AC** III.xiii.194 [Enobarbus alone, of Antony] *To be furious / Is to be frighted out of fear* [i.e. raging with anger]; **Cym** II.iii.5
  2 cruel, malevolent **H5** III.vi.26 [Pistol to Fluellen] *giddy Fortune's furious fickle wheel*

furnace *(v.)* send out as if from a furnace **Cym** I.vii.66 [Iachimo to Innogen, of Posthumus' companion] *He furnaces / The thick sighs from him*

furnish *(v.)* **1** provide, supply, possess **CE** IV.i.34 [Antipholus of Ephesus to Angelo] *I am not furnished with the present money;* **AW** I.i.67; **H5** II.iii.87; **JC** III.i.66; **MV** I.iii.55; **Tem** III.i.140
  2 provide for, prepare, make ready **AW** II.iii.288 [Bertram to Parolles, of the King] *His present gift / Shall furnish me to those Italian fields;* **MV** I.i.182
  3 dress, clothe, equip, fit out **AY** III.ii.238 [Celia to Rosalind, of Orlando] *He was furnished like a hunter;* **AY** V.iv.204; **MA** III.i.103; **RJ** IV.ii.35; **TG** II.vii.85; **TNK** II.iv.45
  4 endow, equip, have qualities **Cym** I.vii.16 [Iachimo to himself, of Innogen] *If she be furnished with a mind so rare;* **Cym** I.v.7; **1H6** IV.ii.39

furnish out *(v.)* provide food for, supply the needs of **Tim** III.iv.115 [Flavius to Timon] *There is not so much left to furnish out / A moderate table*

furnished *(adj.)* equipped, fitted out, outfitted **Per** II.ii.52 [Second Lord to Simonides, of Pericles] *he comes / To an honoured triumph strangely furnished;* **1H4** IV.i.97; **H8** II.ii.3; **WT** IV.iv.585

furnishing *(n.)* decoration, surface factor, window-dressing **KL** III.i.29 [disguised Kent to Gentleman, of Albany and Cornwall's reasons] *perchance, these are but furnishings*

furniture *(n.)* **1** furnishing, fittings, embellishments **H8** II.i.99 [Vaux to servants, of Buckingham's barge] *fit it with such furniture as suits / The greatness of his person*
  2 trappings, harness **AW** II.iii.58 [Lafew to Parolles] *I'd give bay curtal and his furniture / My mouth no more were broken than these boys'* [i.e. I'd give away my horse and trappings if I were as young as them]
  3 outfit, dress, costume **TS** IV.iii.176 [Petruchio to Katherina, of her clothes] *this poor furniture and mean array*
  4 equipment, matériel **E3** III.i.6 [King John to all, of King Edward] *How hast thou heard that he provided is / Of martial furniture;* **1H4** III.iii.199; **2H6** I.iii.167

furred *(adj.)* made of fur, fur-lined **2H6** IV.ii.45 [Smith aside to his companions, of Cade's wife] *not able to travel with her furred pack*

furrow-weed *(n.)* weed growing in the furrows of ploughed fields **KL** IV.iv.3 [Cordelia to Doctor, of Lear] *Crowned with rank fumiter and furrow-weeds* ☛ **PLANTS**, p.330

further *(adj.)* **1** future, eventual **2H6** III.i.138 [Suffolk to Gloucester] *I … commit you to my lord Cardinal / To keep until your further time of trial*
  2 another **H8** II.iv.232 [Campeius to King Henry] *'tis a needful fitness / That we adjourn this court till further day*

furtherance *(n.)* aid, assistance, help **Per** II.i.155 [Pericles to Fishermen] *By your furtherance I am clothed in steel;* **E3** IV.i.5; **1H6** V.iii.21

fury *(n.)* **1** inspiration, frenzy, zeal **Oth** III.iv.72 [Othello to Desdemona, of her handkerchief] *A sibyl … / In her prophetic fury sewed the work*
  2 impetuous way, fierce passion **MW** II.i.83 [Mistress Page to Mistress Ford, of Falstaff] *unless he know some strain in me that I know not myself, he would never have boarded me in this fury*
  3 fit of madness **Tit** IV.i.24 [Young Lucius to Marcus, of Lavinia] *my noble aunt … would not but in fury fright my youth*

fury-innocent *(n.)* [unclear usage] anyone in a calm state of mind; anyone passion-free **TNK** I.iii.79 [Emilia to Hippolyta] *This rehearsal - / Which fury-innocent wots well* [Q] ☛ **innocent** *(n.)*

furze *(n.)* spiny shrub, gorse **Tem** IV.i.180 [Ariel to Prospero, of Stephano, Trinculo, and Caliban following] *through … sharp furzes;* **Tem** I.i.62

fust *(v.)* become musty, grow mouldy **Ham** IV.iv.39 [Hamlet alone, of the Creator] *gave us not … reason / To fust in us unused*

fustian *(n.)* **1** type of coarse cloth [of cotton and flax] **TS** IV.i.42 [Grumio to Curtis] *the serving-men in their new fustian*
  2 bombast, nonsense, gibberish **Oth** II.iii.273 [Cassio to Iago, of himself] *And discourse fustian with one's own shadow!*

fustian *(adj.)* **1** high-flown, made up in a ridiculous way **TN** II.v.107 [Fabian to Sir Toby] *A fustian riddle!;*
  2 bombastic, ranting, blustering **2H4** II.iv.184 [Doll to all, of Pistol] *I cannot endure such a fustian rascal*

fustilarian *(n.)* [unclear meaning] smelly old woman **2H4** II.i.58 [Page to Hostess] *You fustilarian!*

fusty *(adj.)* musty, mouldy, stale-smelling **Cor** I.ix.7 [Cominius to Martius] *the fusty plebeians;* **TC** I.iii.161, II.i.101

fut *(n.)* ☛ **SWEARING**, p.435

futurely *(adv.)* in the future, hereafter **TNK** I.i.174 [Theseus to Queens, of his marriage] *it more imports me / Than all the actions that I have foregone / Or futurely can cope*

FUNCTIONAL SHIFT

One of the most distinctive features of the English language, since the loss of inflectional endings in the early Middle Ages, is the formation of new words by changing their word class, or part of speech – a process variously known as *functional shift* or *word-class conversion*. In Shakespearian English the process is copiously illustrated, and includes many vivid and dramatic instances of linguistic creativity. In several cases (asterisked below), no earlier instances of the word, or of one of its usages, are recorded by the *Oxford English Dictionary* (*OED*), and it can safely be assumed that a good proportion of these are Shakespearian creations.

Virtually any word class can be converted, and the texts show examples going in different directions.

Item	Location	Example	Comment
askance*	**Luc** 637	*they … from their own misdeeds askance their eyes*	adverb to verb
beseech*	**TC** I.ii.293	*Achievement is command; ungained, beseech*	verb to noun
here*	**KL** I.i.261	*Thou losest here, a better where to find*	adverb to noun
impair*	**TC** IV.v.103	*he … / Nor dignifies an impair thought with breath*	verb to adjective
kingdom*	**TC** II.iii.173	*Kingdomed Achilles in commotion rages*	noun to adjective
third	**TNK** I.ii.96	*what man / Thirds his own worth*	adjective to verb
where	**KL** I.i.261	*Thou losest here, a better where to find*	adverb to noun

Among the commoner types are adjectives used as verbs, generally expressing the notion of 'to make [adjective]' - for example, *dumbed by him* = 'made dumb by him'.

coy	**Cor** V.i.6	*if he coyed / To hear Cominius speak*	
craven*	**Cym** III.iv.79	*There is a prohibition so divine / That cravens my weak hand*	
demure*	**AC** IV.xv.29	*Your wife … shall acquire no honour / Demuring upon me*	
dumb*	**AC** I.v.50	*what I would have spoke / Was beastly dumbed by him*	in transitive use
happy*	**Sonn** 6.6	*That use is not forbidden usury, / Which happies those that pay the willing loan*	
muddy*	**AW** V.ii.4	*I am … muddied in Fortune's mood*	
safe	**AC** I.iii.55	*that which most with you should safe my going, / Is Fulvia's death*	
tardy*	**WT** III.ii.160	*the good mind of Camillo tardied / My swift command*	

The commonest form of conversion is noun to verb, with certain types of noun particularly involved. Most are concrete and specific in meaning, referring to people, their attributes, functions, and contexts. Indeed, one of the creative reasons for conversion is to find more vivid ways of expressing everyday notions, or of avoiding abstract locutions, as when *lip a wanton* replaces the mundane 'kiss', or *godded me* replaces 'treat as a god'. It is very unusual to find an abstract noun converted to a verb, though a few examples are given at the end of the following list, which groups noun conversions into broad semantic types. Most of the usages can be glossed as 'make … into', 'treat … as', 'use … for', 'act as…', and suchlike: for example, *she Phebes me* = 'she treats me as Phebe'.

Names of people

Kate*	**TS** III.ii.244	*Petruchio is Kated*
Phebe*	**AY** IV.iii.40	*She Phebes me*

Types of people, gods, animals, and other animate beings

boy	**AC** V.ii.220	*Some squeaking Cleopatra boy my greatness*
bride	**TS** III.ii.250	*Shall sweet Bianca practise how to bride it?*
child	**KL** III.vi.108	*he childed as I fathered*
companion*	**AC** I.ii.31	*companion me with my mistress*
duke	**MM** III.ii.90	*Lord Angelo dukes it well*
father	**KL** III.vi.108	*He childed as I fathered*
friend	**Cym** II.iii.46	*be friended / With aptness of the season*
god	**Cor** V.iii.11	*This last old man … godded me indeed*
jade*	**AC** III.i.34	*We have jaded out o'th' field*

(continues)

FUNCTIONAL SHIFT – *continued*

Item	Location	Example	Comment
lackey	AC I.iv.46	This common body ... / Goes to and back, lackeying the varying tide	
out-villain*	AW IV.iii.265	He hath out-villained villainy	
prince	Cym III.iii.85	Nature prompts them / In simple and low things to prince it	
queen*	WT IV.iv.446	I'll queen it no inch farther	
spaniel	AC IV.xii.21	The hearts / That spanieled me at heels	
stranger*	KL I.i.204	Dowered with our curse and strangered with our oath	
uncle*	R2 II.iii.86	uncle me no uncle	in sense of 'address as uncle'
virgin*	Cor V.iii.48	my true lip / Hath virgined it e'er since	
woman	AW III.ii.50	the first face of neither ... / Can woman me unto't	

Parts of the body

Item	Location	Example	Comment
arm*	Cym IV.ii.400	come, arm him	in sense of 'take in one's arms'
brain*	Cym V.iv.147	such stuff as madmen / Tongue, and brain not	in sense of 'conceive in the brain'
ear	TNK III.i.29	I eared her language	
eye	AC I.iii.97	my becomings kill me when they do not / Eye well to you	
jaw*	TNK III.ii.7	I reck not if the wolves would jaw me	
knee*	Cor V.i.5	fall down, and knee / The way into his mercy	in transitive use in sense of 'bow'
lip*	AC II.v.30	a hand that kings have lipped	
tongue*	Cym V.iv.147	such stuff as madmen / Tongue	in sense of 'utter'
womb	WT IV.iv.487	all the sun sees or / The close earth wombs	

Clothing

Item	Location	Example	Comment
buckle	TNK I.iii.57	Theirs [is] ... / More buckled with strong judgement	
corslet*	TNK I.i.177	her arms ... shall / By warranting moonlight corslet thee	
glove*	2H4 I.i.147	A scaly gauntlet ... / Must glove this hand	

Descriptions of the body and its behaviour, feelings, or well-being

Item	Location	Example	Comment
ballad*	AC V.ii.216	scald rhymers / Ballad us out o'tune	in transitive use
bass*	Tem III.iii.101	it did bass my trespass	in sense of 'utter'
choir/quire*	MV V.i.62	Still quiring to the young-eyed cherubins	
compassion*	Tit IV.i.123	can you hear a good man groan / And ... not compassion him	
dialogue*	Tim II.ii.55	Dost dialogue with thy shadow?	
dower*	KL I.i.204	Dowered with our curse	
fever*	AC III.xiii.138	Henceforth / The white hand of a lady fever thee	
joy	TNK IV.ii.63	Two greater and two better never yet / Made mothers joy	
lethargy*	KL I.iv.225	his discernings are lethargied	
looks*	Cym V.v.94	Thou hast looked thyself into my grace	in sense of 'bring by looks into a certain condition'
medicine	Cym IV.ii.243	Great griefs medicine the less	
pageant*	TC I.iii.151	he pageants us	
re, fa*	RJ IV.v.117	I'll re you, I'll fa you	
sermon*	Tim II.ii.177	Come, sermon me no further	first since an isolated usage in the early Middle Ages
word*	Cym IV.ii.240	I'll word it with thee	first since an isolated usage in the early Middle Ages

Places where people live and die, and the objects they live with

Item	Location	Example	Comment
barn*	Luc 859	he sits, / And useless barns the harvest of his wits	
bench*	KL III.vi.38	thou ... / Bench by his side	in sense of 'seat on a bench'
canopy*	Cym II.ii.21	th'enclosed lights, now canopied under these windows	

FUNCTIONAL SHIFT – *continued*

Item	Location	Example	Comment
chapel*	TNK I.i.50	give us the bones ... that we may chapel them	
couch	TNK I.i.182	if thou couch / But one night with her	
cupboard	Cor I.i.98	[of the belly] Still cupboarding the viand	
grave	R2 III.ii.140	Those whom you curse ... lie full low, graved in the hollow ground	
hinge*	Tim IV.iii.212	Be thou a flatterer now ... Hinge thy knee	
hovel	KL IV.vii.39	wast thou fain ... to hovel thee with swine	
label*	TN I.v.235	every particle and utensil labelled to my will	
oar*	Tem II.i.120	he ... oared / Himself with his food arms	
office*	Cor V.ii.60	a Jack guardant cannot office me from my son	in transitive use
property*	TN IV.ii.91	They have here propertied me	
sepulchre*	TG IV.ii.114	Go to thy lady's grave and call hers thence; / Or, at the least, in hers sepulchre thine	
skiff*	TNK I.iii.37	they have skiffed torrents	
sty	Tem I.ii.342	here you sty me / In this hard rock	
urn*	TNK I.i.44	He will not suffer us to burn their bones, / To urn their ashes	in sense of 'deposit in an urn'
window*	AC IV.xiv.72	wouldst thou be windowed in great Rome	

The environment

Item	Location	Example	Comment
bower*	RJ III.ii.81	thou didst bower the spirit of a fiend / In mortal paradise	
cave	Cym IV.ii.138	it may be heard at court that such as we cave here, hunt here	in intransitive use
climate*	WT V.i.169	whilst you do climate here	
mud*	Tem V.i.151	myself were mudded in that oozy bed	
shore*	WT IV.iv.831	If he think it fit to shore them again	in sense of 'put ashore'

Abstract notions

Item	Location	Example	Comment
fortune	AC I.ii.75	keep decorum, and fortune him accordingly	
grace	R2 II.iii.86	grace me no grace	
necessity*	AW V.iii.85	if her fortunes ever stood necessitied to help	not in OED
scandal	JC I.ii.76	if you know / That I do fawn on men ... / And after scandal them	in sense of 'revile'

gaberdine *(n.)* cloak, cape, loose upper garment **MV** I.iii.109 [Shylock to Antonio] *You … spit upon my Jewish gaberdine;* **Tem** II.ii.38, 109 ☛ **CLOTHING**, p.79

gad *(n.)* engraving tool, stylus **Tit** IV.i.102 [Titus to Marcus, of Lavinia's writing] *I … with a gad of steel will write these words*

gad, upon the suddenly, as if pricked with a gad [= goad] **KL** I.ii.26 [Gloucester to himself, of Lear's actions] *All this done / Upon the gad?*

gage *(n.)* pledge, challenge [usually, a glove or gauntlet thrown down] **R2** IV.i.46 [Percy to Aumerle] *there I throw my gage* ☛ FEW, p.xxi

gage, rest under remain as challenges **R2** IV.i.86 [Bolingbroke to Aumerle] *These differences shall all rest under gage / Till Norfolk be repealed.*

gage *(v.)* **1** pledge, contract, stake **Luc** 144 *one for all or all for one we gage;* **Ham** I.i.91; **1H4** I.iii.171
  2 pledge, bind, commit **TC** V.i.38 [Achilles to Patroclus, of a letter] *gaging me to keep / An oath that I have sworn;* **Luc** 1351; **MV** I.i.130

gain *(v.)* restore, regain, improve **Cym** IV.ii.167 [Arviragus to Belarius, of disguised Innogen] *to gain his colour / I'd let a parish of such Clotens blood*

gaingiving *(n.)* misgiving, apprehension, qualm **Ham** V.ii.209 [Hamlet to Horatio, of his feelings] *it is such a kind of gain-giving as would perhaps trouble a woman* [F; Q2 *gamgiuing*]

gainsay *(v.)* **1** contradict, say the contrary, forbid **3H6** V.iv.74 [Queen to her followers] *what I should say / My tears gainsay;* **2H4** I.i.91; **TC** IV.v.132
  2 deny, refuse **3H6** IV.vii.73 [Montgomery to all, throwing down his gauntlet] *whoso'er gainsays King Edward's right, / By this I challenge him to single fight*
  3 deny, renounce, disown **H8** II.iv.96 [Wolsey to Queen Katherine, of King Henry] *If it be known to him / That I gainsay my deed;* **WT** III.ii.55

gainsaying *(n.)* denial, refusal **WT** I.ii.19 [Leontes to Polixenes, asking him to stay longer] *I'll no gainsaying* [i.e. I won't be refused]

'gainst *(prep.)* ☛ against *(prep.)*

gait *(n.)* **1** manner of walking, bearing, movement **Tem** IV.i.102 [Ceres to Iris, of Juno] *I know her by her gait;* **AC** III.iii.17; **KL** V.iii.173; **MND** V.i.358; **TNK** I.ii.45; **WT** IV.iv.727
  2 proceedings, course, doings, steps **TN** I.iv.15 [Orsino to Viola as Cesario, of Olivia] *address thy gait unto her;* **Ham** I.ii.31; **Luc** 1081; **MND** V.i.406; **Tim** V.iv.73

gale *(n.)* wind, breeze **Tem** V.i.315 [Prospero to Alonso] *I'll … promise you calm seas, auspicious gales;* **E3** III.i.77; **KL** II.ii.77

gall *(n.)* **1** bile [reputed for its bitterness] **Mac** I.v.46 [Lady Macbeth alone] *Come to my woman's breasts / And take my milk for gall;* **E3** III.iii.72; **2H4** I.ii.177; **Luc** 889; **PassP** XVII.16; **TC** I.iii.193
  2 bitterness, spitefulness, vindictiveness **MM** III.ii.178 [disguised Duke alone] *What king … / Can tie the gall up in the slanderous tongue?;* **H5** II.ii.30; **KL** I.iv.267; **RJ** I.v.92; **TC** V.v.30; **TNK** I.i.120
  3 spirit of anger, venom, ability to be angry **Ham** II.ii.574 [Hamlet alone] *For it cannot be / But I am pigeon-livered and lack gall / To make oppression bitter;* **1H6** I.ii.16; **H8** I.i.152; **Oth** IV.iii.91; **TC** I.iii.237; **TN** III.ii.46
  4 irritation, annoyance **KL** I.iv.113 [Lear to Fool] *A pestilent gall to me!* [i.e. source of irritation]
  5 sore, pain, painful spot **LL** V.ii.237 [masked Berowne to masked Princess] *Thou grievest my gall*
  6 bitter substance exuded by oak-trees **Cym** I.ii.32 [Posthumus to Innogen] *I'll drink the words you send / Though ink be made of gall*

gall *(v.)* **1** vex, annoy, irritate **1H4** I.iii.226 [Hotspur to Northumberland and Worcester] *All studies here I solemnly defy, / Save how to gall and pinch this Bolingbroke;* **Cor** II.iii.194; **2H4** I.ii.232; **MM** II.ii.102; **Oth** I.i.149; **WT** I.ii.316

2 chafe, rub, make sore **2H4** I.ii.149 [Lord Chief Justice to Falstaff] *I am loath to gall a new-healed wound;* **Ham** V.i.139; **MW** III.iv.5; **Per** IV.i.54; **R2** V.v.94

3 injure, harm, wound **2H4** IV.i.89 [Westmorland to Archbishop] *Wherein have you been galled by the King?;* **Ham** I.iii.39; **H5** I.ii.151; **H8** III.ii.207; **KJ** IV.iii.94

4 graze, scratch **Tit** IV.iii.71 [Marcus to Titus] *The Bull, being galled, gave Aries such a knock;* **Ham** IV.vii.146; **TS** V.ii.60

5 scoff, jeer, mock **H5** V.i.71 [Gower to Pistol, of Fluellen] *I have seen you gleeking and galling at this gentleman twice or thrice*

gallant (*n.*) **1** fine gentleman, man of fashion **LL** V.ii.363 [Princess to King, of the Russian visitors] *Trim gallants, full of courtship and of state;* **AY** I.ii.187; **1H6** III.ii.41; **MA** III.iv.87; **R2** V.iii.15; **Tem** I.ii.414 ➤ **ADDRESS FORMS**, p.8

2 man-of-war, warship **TNK** III.v.64 [Gaoler's Daughter singing] *well hailed, you jolly gallants*

3 flag flown on the rear mast of a ship **E3** III.i.73 [Mariner to King John, of the English fleet] *on the top gallant of the admiral* ➤ **SHIPS**, p.397

gallant (*adj.*) **1** fine, splendid, grand **H8** III.ii.49 [Suffolk to all, of Anne] *She is a gallant creature;* **JC** V.i.3; **Tit** I.i.320, 403, IV.ii.163

2 showy, fancy, ostentatious **AW** IV.iii.101 [Second Lord to Bertram, of Parolles] *poor gallant knave*

gallant of war (*n.*) man-of-war, warship **TNK** III.v.62 [Gaoler's Daughter singing, of the George Alow] *he met with brave gallants of war*

gallantry (*n.*) gallants, nobility, gentry **TC** III.i.133 [Paris to Pandarus, of those on the battlefield] *all the gallantry of Troy*

gallant-springing (*adj.*) finely growing, developing well **R3** I.iv.224 [First Murderer to Clarence] *gallant-springing brave Plantagenet, / That princely novice, was struck dead by thee*

galled (*adj.*) **1** sore, swollen, inflamed **AY** II.vii.50 [Jaques to Duke Senior] *they that are most galled with my folly;* **Ham** I.ii.155, III.ii.252; **R3** IV.iv.52; **TC** V.x.55; **TNK** III.v.128

2 fretted, chafed, battered **Luc** 1440 [of Trojans in a painting of Troy] *their ranks began / To break upon the galled shore;* **H5** III.i.12

gallery (*n.*) long large room used for walks, exercise, etc **H8** V.i.86 [King Henry to all] *Avoid the gallery*

galliard (*n.*) type of lively, high-spirited dance **TN** I.iii.113 [Sir Toby to Sir Andrew] *What is thy excellence in a galliard?;* **H5** I.ii.253; **TN** I.iii.121

galliass (*n.*) heavily built warship using sails and oars [larger than a galley] **TS** II.i.371 [Tranio as Lucentio to Gremio, of his father's ships] *two galliasses / And twelve tight galleys*

gallimaufry (*n.*) complete mixture, whole assembly, every sort **MW** II.i.108 [Pistol to Ford, of Falstaff's women] *He loves the gallimaufry;* **WT** IV.iv.326

galloglass, gallowglass (*n.*) axe-wielding Irish soldier **2H6** IV.ix.26 [Messenger to King] *a mighty power / Of gallowglasses and stout kerns / Is marching hitherward in proud array;* **Mac** I.ii.13

gallow (*v.*) frighten, scare, startle **KL** III.ii.44 [disguised Kent to Lear] *The wrathful skies / Gallow the very wanderers of the dark*

Galloway nag small strong riding horse [from Galloway, Scotland]; prostitute **2H4** II.iv.185 [Pistol to all] *Know we not Galloway nags?* [i.e. we know a whore when we see one]

gallows (*n.*) someone who deserves to be hanged **LL** V.ii.12 [Katharine to Rosaline, of Cupid] *a shrewd unhappy gallows;* **Tem** I.i.30

gambol (*n.*) leap, caper, antic **TNK** III.v.76 [Third Countryman to all, of the Gaoler's Daughter] *she'll do the rarest gambols*

gambol (*adj.*) playful, sportive, spirited **2H4** II.iv.245 [Falstaff to Doll, of Poins] *such other gambol faculties 'a has that show a weak mind and an able body*

gambol (*v.*) shy away, leap away **Ham** III.iv.145 [Hamlet to Gertrude] *I the matter will re-word, which madness / Would gambol from*

gambold (*n.*) frolic, entertainment, pastime **TS** Induction.ii.136 [Sly to Lord] *Is not a comonty a Christmas gambold*

gamboys (*n.*) ➤ viol-de-gamboys (*n.*)

game (*n.*) **1** hunting practice, sporting routine **LL** IV.ii.163 [Holofernes to Nathaniel, of hunting] *The gentles are at their game;* **3H6** IV.v.11

2 quarry, object of the chase **3H6** V.v.14 [Huntsman to Edward] *this way lies the game;* **Cym** III.iii.98; **3H6** III.i.14; **TC** V.vii.12

3 game of love, amorous play **TC** IV.v.63 [Ulysses to Nestor, of those like Cressida] *Set them down / For … daughters of the game;* **Oth** II.iii.19

4 gambling **Ham** III.iii.91 [Hamlet to himself, of Claudius] *When he is … / At game*

gamesome (*adj.*) sportive, merry, playful **TS** II.i.239 [Petruchio to Katherina] *thou art pleasant, gamesome;* **Cym** I.vii.60; **JC** I.ii.28

gamester (*n.*) **1** gambler, adventurer **LL** I.ii.42 [Mote to Armado] *You are a gentleman and a gamester;* **TS** II.i.393

2 one drawn to amorous sport, one who plays the game, prostitute **AW** V.iii.188 [Bertram to King, of Diana] *She … was a common gamester to the camp;* **Per** IV.vi.71

3 fun-lover, frolicsome fellow **H8** I.iv.45 [Anne to Sands] *You are a merry gamester*

4 athlete [contemptuous], fun-lover **AY** I.i.153 [Oliver alone, of Orlando] *Now will I stir this gamester*

gamoth, gamouth (*n.*) ➤ gamut (*n.*)

gamut (*n.*) musical scale **TS** III.i.65 [Hortensio as Licio to Bianca, of playing the lute] *I must begin … / To teach you gamut in a briefer sort* [F *gamoth*]

'gan, can (*v.*) began **Luc** 1228 *the maid with swelling drops 'gan wet / Her circled eyne;* **2H4** I.i.129; **Lover** 177; **PassP** XVI.6; **Per** III.Chorus.36; **Venus** 95 ➤ **ELISION**, p.146

gap (*n.*) entrance, access-point, position of opportunity **H8** V.i.36 [Lovell to Gardiner] *Cromwell … / Stands in the gap and trade of more preferments*

gape (*v.*) long, be eager, yearn **RJ** II.Chorus.2 [Chorus] *old desire doth in his deathbed lie, / And young affection gapes to be his heir;* **E3** III.i.15

gaping (*n.*) bawling, shouting, yelling **H8** V.iv.3 [Porter to servants within] *Ye rude slaves, leave your gaping*

gaping (*adj.*) with mouth open [as on a dish prepared for eating] **MV** IV.i.47 [Shylock to Duke] *Some men there are love not a gaping pig*

gar (*n.*) French pronunciation of 'God' ➤ **SWEARING**, p.435

garb (*n.*) manner, style, fashion **Ham** II.ii.372 [Hamlet to Rosencrantz and Guildenstern] *let me comply with you in this garb;* **Cor** IV.vii.44; **KL** II.ii.95; **Oth** II.i.297

garbage (*n.*) offal, entrails **Ham** I.v.57 [Ghost to Hamlet] *So lust … / Will sate itself in a celestial bed / And prey on garbage*

garboil (*n.*) trouble, disturbance, commotion **AC** I.iii.61 [Antony to Cleopatra, of Fulvia] *at thy sovereign leisure read / The garboils she awaked;* **AC** II.ii.71

garden-house (*n.*) small building in a garden [often used for lovers' assignations] **TNK** IV.iii.55 [Gaoler's Daughter to herself] *th'other [woman] curses a suing fellow and her garden-house;* **MM** V.i.210

gardon (*n.*) error for 'guerdon' [= reward] **LL** III.i.166 [Costard to Berowne, of his 'guerdon'] *Gardon, O sweet gardon!* [F] ➤ guerdon (*n.*) 1

garland (*n.*) **1** wreath of victory **2H4** V.ii.84 [Lord Chief Justice to King Henry V] *wearing now the garland;* **2H4** IV.v.201; **R3** III.ii.40; **TNK** V.i.44

2 pride, glory, hero **AC** IV.xv.64 [Cleopatra to all, of dead Antony] *withered is the garland of the war;* **Cor** I.i.182

garner (*n.*) granary, corn storehouse **Tem** IV.i.111 [Ceres singing] *Barns and garners never empty;* **Cor** I.i.248

garner (*v.*) store up, lay up, deposit **Oth** IV.ii.56 [Othello to Desdemona] *there where I have garnered up my heart*

garnish (*n.*) outfit, adornment, trimming **MV** II.vi.45 [Lorenzo to Jessica, of her attire] *Even in the lovely garnish of a boy*

garnish (*v.*) provide with a good supply [of words] **MV** III.v.64 [Lorenzo to Jessica, of Launcelot] *many fools … / Garnished like him, that for a tricksy word / Defy the matter* [or: dressed up]

gaskins (*n.*) loose-fitting trousers, wide breeches **TN** I.v.23 [Maria to Feste, of his points] *if both break, your gaskins fall* ➤ **CLOTHING**, p.79

gast (*v.*) frighten, alarm, scare **KL** II.i.54 [Edmund to Gloucester, of Edgar] *gasted by the noise I made*

gastness (*n.*) terror, dread, frightened look **Oth** V.i.106 [Iago to all, of Bianca] *Do you perceive the gastness of her eye?* [F; Q *ieastures* = gestures]

gate (*n.*) **1** way, road, path **KL** IV.vi.237 [Edgar to Oswald, adopting a country accent] *go your gate* [i.e. be on your way]
2 entrance, doorway, portal **Cym** III.iii.2 [Belarius to Guiderius and Arviragus] *this gate / Instructs you how t'adore the heavens* [i.e. because its height makes you bow as you pass through it]

gather (*v.*) **1** infer, work out [for oneself], guess at **KL** IV.v.32 [Regan to Oswald] *You may gather more*; **1H6** II.v.96
2 collect one's thoughts **Ham** II.ii.108 [Polonius to Claudius and Gertrude] *Now gather, and surmise*
3 gain information, collect knowledge **AW** IV.i.81 [First Soldier to Parolles] *The General … will lead thee on / To gather from thee*

gaud (*n.*) gaudy toy, showy plaything, trinket **MND** I.i.33 [Egeus to Lysander, of Hermia] *With bracelets of thy hair, rings, gauds, conceits … hast thou filched my daughter's heart*; **KJ** III.iii.36; **MND** IV.i.166; **TC** III.iii.176; **TNK** IV.ii.53; **TS** II.i.3

gaudy (*adj.*) **1** bright, brilliant, shining **Venus** 1088 [of Adonis' bonnet] *Under whose brim the gaudy sun would peep*; **LL** V.ii.797; **Luc** 272; **Sonn** 1.10
2 festive, joyful, merry **AC** III.xiii.182 [Antony to Cleopatra] *Let's have one other gaudy night*
3 paltry, showy, tastelessly ornate **TNK** II.i.157 [Palamon to Arcite] *I … am sufficient / To tell the world 'tis but a gaudy shadow*

gauntlet (*n.*) ➤ **BODY-ARMOUR**, p.48

gawded (*adj.*) made-up, prepared with cosmetics, adorned **Cor** II.i.209 [Brutus to Sicinius, of Roman women] *the war of white and damask in / Their nicely gawded cheeks*

gay (*adj.*) showy, pretentious, gaudy **AC** III.xiii.26 [Antony to Ambassador, of Caesar] *I dare him therefore / To lay his gay comparisons apart*

gaze, at [of a deer] in an expectant stance, with intent look **Luc** 1149 *the poor frighted deer that stands at gaze*

gaze (*v.*) viewing, observation, direction of looking **Oth** I.iii.19 [First Senator to Duke, of the Turkish attack] *'Tis a pageant / To keep us in false gaze* [i.e. looking the wrong way]

gear (*n.*) **1** business, affair, matter **2H6** III.i.91 [York to himself, of his poor situation] *I will remedy this gear ere long*; **MV** I.i.110, II.ii.154; **RJ** II.iv.98; **TC** I.i.6; **Tit** IV.iii.53
2 equipment, furnishing **TC** III.ii.209 [Pandarus alone] *Cupid grant all tongue-tied maidens here / Bed, chamber, and Pandar to provide this gear!*
3 stuff, substance **RJ** V.i.60 [Romeo to Apothecary, of poison] *such soon-speeding gear / As will disperse itself through all the veins*
4 attire, dress, clothes **LL** V.iii.303 [Rosaline to Princess, of their previous visitors] *Disguised like Muscovites in shapeless gear*

geck (*n.*) dupe, sucker, fool **TN** V.i.341 [Malvolio to Olivia] *Why have you suffered me to be … made the most notorious geck and gull / That e'er invention played on?*; **Cym** V.iv.67

geld (*v.*), past forms **gelded, gelt** **1** castrate, spay **MV** V.i.144 [Gratiano to Nerissa, of her ring] *Would he were gelt that had it for my part*; **MM** II.i.219; **TNK** IV.i.132; **WT** II.i.147

2 deprive, strip, dispossess **R2** II.i.237 [Ross to Willoughby, of Bolingbroke] *Bereft and gelded of his patrimony*; **1H4** III.i.106; **LL** II.i.149; **WT** IV.iv.607

gelding (*n.*) castrated horse; horse that is placid in temperament **MW** II.ii.289 [Ford alone] *I will rather trust … a thief to walk my ambling gelding … than my wife with herself*

gem (*n.*) jewel, treasure, pride **Ham** IV.vii.93 [Laertes to Claudius, of Lamord] *the brooch indeed / And gem of all the nation*

geminy (*n.*) pair, couple, brace **MW** II.ii.9 [Falstaff to Pistol] *I have grated upon my good friends for three reprieves for you and your coach-fellow Nym, or else you had looked through the grate, like a geminy of baboons* [i.e. like twin baboons]

gender (*n.*) **1** kind, sort, type **Oth** I.iii.320 [Iago to Roderigo, of their bodies as a garden] *supply it with one gender of herbs or distract it with many*
2 offspring, brood **Phoen** 18 [of the crow] *thy sable gender mak'st / With the breath thou giv'st and tak'st*

gender, general common people, general public **Ham** IV.vii.18 [Claudius to Laertes, of Hamlet] *the great love the general gender bear him*

gender (*v.*) copulate, beget, engender **Oth** IV.ii.61 [Othello to Desdemona] *a cistern for foul toads / To knot and gender in!*

general (*n.*) **1** ordinary people, general public, populace **Ham** II.ii.436 [Hamlet to First Player, of a play] *'Twas caviary to the general* [i.e. unpalatable to those lacking a taste for it]; **JC** I.ii.12; **MM** II.iv.27; **TC** I.iii.342
2 leader, chief **RJ** V.iii.219 [Prince to all] *then will I be general of your woes*
3 (plural) general points, group features **TC** I.iii.180 [Ulysses to all, of Patroclus' imitations] *All our abilities … / Severals and generals of grace exact*

general, in by everyone **TC** IV.v.21 [Ulysses to all, of Cressida being kissed just by Agamemnon] *Yet is the kindness but particular, / 'Twere better she were kissed in general* [also: by all the Generals]

general (*adj.*) **1** common, of everyone, public **Ham** II.ii.560 [Hamlet alone, of the First Player] *And cleave the general ear with horrid speech*; **Cor** III.i.146; **2H6** V.ii.43; **JC** V.v.71; **LL** II.i.11; **Tit** II.iii.183 ➤ **gender, general**
2 all-embracing, universal, comprehensive **Tim** IV.iii.257 [Timon to Apemantus] *thou wouldst have plunged thyself / In general riot*; **KJ** IV.iii.17; **Mac** III.iv.22; **Tim** II.ii.205, IV.iii.444
3 joint, common, communal **2H4** IV.i.167 [Archbishop to Westmorland, of the schedule] *this contains our general grievances*; **H8** II.ii.94; **TC** I.iii.322; **Tit** II.iii.59
4 open to all, universally benevolent **E3** II.i.164 [King Edward to Lodowick, of the Countess] *in this application to the sun, / Bid her be free and general as the sun*

general-gross (*adj.*) palpably evident to all **Tim** V.i.142 [Second Senator to Timon, of the senators] *They confess / Toward thee forgetfulness too general-gross* ➤ **gross** (*adj.*) 1

generally (*adv.*) universally, without exception, in the eyes of all **AW** I.i.7 [Lafew to Bertram, of the King] *He that so generally is at all times good*; **AW** II.iii.37; **H8** II.i.47; **R2** II.ii.131

generation (*n.*) **1** family, progeny **R2** V.v.8 [Richard alone, of his brain and soul] *these two beget / A generation of still-breeding thoughts*; **2H4** V.ii.49; **KL** I.i.117; **Tem** III.iii.34; **WT** II.i.148
2 posterity, procreation, humankind **Per** III.iii.25 [Cleon to Pericles, of breaking a promise] *The gods revenge it upon me and mine / To the end of generation*
3 genealogy, line of descent **TC** III.i.128 [Pandarus to himself, of Paris and Helen] *Is this the generation of love? Hot blood, hot thoughts, and hot deeds?*
4 breed, class, pedigree **Tim** I.i.203 [Apemantus to Painter] *Thy mother's of my generation. What's she, if I be a dog?*
5 [unclear meaning] world, human race **MM** IV.iii.87 [disguised Duke to Provost] *Ere twice the sun hath made / His journal greeting to yond generation*

generative *(adj.)* male, capable of generation **MM** III.ii.105 [Lucio to disguised Duke, of Angelo] *he is a motion generative* ☞ ungenerative *(adj.)*

generosity *(n.)* nobility, aristocracy **Cor** I.i.209 [Martius to Menenius, of the petition granted to the Citizens] *a strange one, / To break the heart of generosity*

generous *(adj.)* well-bred, mannerly, noble-minded **Oth** III.iii.277 [Desdemona to Othello] *Your dinner, and the generous islanders / By you invited, do attend your presence;* **Ham** IV.vii.134; **KL** I.ii.8; **MM** IV.vi.13; **TC** II.ii.156; **TNK** III.i.54

genius *(n.)* **1** soul, spirit, being **2H4** III.ii.303 [Falstaff alone, of Shallow] *'A was the very genius of famine;* **TN** III.iv.128
    2 spirit, angel **Tem** IV.i.27 [Ferdinand to Prospero] *the strong'st suggestion / Our worser genius can* [i.e. that any evil spirit could make]
    3 attendant spirit, guardian spirit **Mac** III.i.55 [Macbeth alone, of Banquo] *under him / My genius is rebuked;* **JC** II.i.66; **TC** IV.iv.49
    4 alter ego, second self **CE** V.i.333 [Duke to all, of the two Antipholuses] *One of these men is genius to the other*

gennet *(n.)* ☞ jennet *(n.)*

gentility *(n.)* **1** nobility, good birth **TNK** I.i.25 [First Queen to Theseus] *For pity's sake and true gentility's;* **AY** I.i.19
    2 good manners, polite behaviour **LL** I.i.127 [Berowne to Longaville, of a decree] *A dangerous law against gentility!*

gentle *(n.)* **1** [polite intimate address] dear one **WT** IV.iv.46 [Florizel to Perdita] *Be merry, gentle* ☞ **ADDRESS FORMS**, p.8
    2 (plural) ladies and gentlemen, gentlefolk **H5** Prologue.8 [Chorus] *pardon, gentles all;* **H5** II.Chorus.35; **LL** II.i.211; **MND** V.i.126, 419
    3 (plural) gentlemen **LL** IV.ii.162 [Holofernes to Nathaniel, of the lords] *The gentles are at their game;* **MW** III.ii.82; **TS** III.ii.92

gentle *(adj.)* **1** well-born, honourable, noble **R2** IV.i.228 [Richard to Northumberland] *Gentle Northumberland* ☞ **FEW**, p.xxi
    2 courteous, friendly, kind **LL** V.ii.626 [Holofernes to Berowne, of their insults] *This is not generous, not gentle, not humble;* **JC** II.i.279; **KJ** III.iii.19; **MW** I.iv.135; **R3** III.iv.20; **Tem** Epilogue.11
    3 refined, discriminating, sophisticated **LL** IV.iii.236 [Berowne to King, of praising Rosaline] *Lend me the flourish of all gentle tongues;* **Mac** I.vi.3; **WT** IV.iv.93
    4 peaceful, calm, free from violence **KJ** III.i.251 [King Philip to Cardinal Pandulph] *impose / Some gentle order;* **Sonn** 48.11; **TC** IV.i.12
    5 made peaceful, become violence-free **Mac** III.iv.75 [Macbeth to Lady Macbeth] *Blood hath been shed ere now, i'the olden time, / Ere humane statute purged the gentle weal*

gentle *(v.)* elevate, ennoble, dignify **H5** IV.iii.63 [King Henry to all, of those who may die in the battle] *be he ne'er so vile, / This day shall gentle his condition*

gentle *(adv.)* courteously, kindly **TC** IV.v.287 [Ulysses to Troilus] *As gentle tell me, of what honour was / This Cressida* [i.e. be so kind as to tell me]

gentle-hearted *(adj.)* noble-hearted **3H6** I.iv.176 [Queen to York, as she stabs him] *here's to right our gentle-hearted King*

gentleman *(n.)* someone of high birth, nobleman **R2** III.i.27 [Bolingbroke to Bushy and Green] *leaving me no sign ... / To show the world I am a gentleman*

gentleman in arms *(n.)* gentleman bearing a coat-of-arms **R2** III.ii.202 [Scroop to Richard] *all your southern gentlemen in arms / Upon his [Bolingbroke's] party* [or: gentlemen are bearing arms]

gentleman of a company non-ranking volunteer with a status higher than that of a private **1H4** IV.ii.24 [Falstaff alone, of his soldiers] *my whole charge consists of ancients, corporals, lieutenants, gentlemen of companies;* **H5** II.i.39

gentleness *(n.)* nobility, good breeding, courtesy **MND** II.ii.138 [Helena to Lysander] *I thought you lord of more true gentleness;* **JC** I.ii.33; **LL** V.ii.730; **TC** I.ii.254, IV.i.21; **Tit** I.i.240

gentlewoman *(n.)* woman of good breeding, well-born lady **TS** IV.iii.70 [Katherina to Petruchio, of a cap] *gentlewomen wear such caps as these;* **AW** IV.iii.13; **2H4** II.iv.297; **MM** III.i.220; **WT** III.iii.71 ☞ **ADDRESS FORMS**, p.8

gently *(adv.)* **1** like a gentleman, honourably, with dignity **3H6** II.vi.45 [Edward to Richard, of someone groaning] *If friend or foe, let him be gently used;* **JC** IV.ii.31; **R2** I.i.79; **TNK** III.i.36; **WT** IV.iv.791
    2 generously, nobly, befittingly **WT** IV.iv.791 [Autolycus to Clown and Shepherd, of Polixenes] *Being something gently considered, I'll bring you where he is aboard* [i.e. being rather well bribed; or: being regarded as something of a gentleman]
    3 quietly, tamely, without a fight **Mac** V.vi.34 [Seyward to Malcolm] *The castle's gently rendered;* **Tem** I.ii.298

gentry *(n.)* **1** courtesy, gentlemanliness, good breeding **Ham** V.ii.109 [Osric to Hamlet, of Laertes] *he is the card or calendar of gentry;* **Ham** II.ii.22; **Luc** 569
    2 social rank, breeding, level in society **MW** II.i.49 [Mistress Page to Mistress Ford] *thou shouldst not alter the article of thy gentry*
    3 position of gentleman, high rank **1H6** II.iv.93 [Somerset to Richard] *standest not thou attainted, / Corrupted, and exempt from ancient gentry?;* **Cor** III.i.144; **WT** I.ii.393

George *(n.)* badge [of the Order of the Garter] displaying St George and the dragon **2H6** IV.i.29 [Suffolk to Whitmore] *Look on my George; I am a gentleman;* **R3** IV.iv.369

german, germane *(n.)* near relative, blood relation **Oth** I.i.114 [Iago to Brabantio] *you'll have coursers for cousins, and jennets for germans*

german, germane *(adj.)* **1** near related, closely akin **Tim** IV.iii.342 [Timon to Apemantus, of being a leopard] *thou wert german to the lion;* **TNK** V.i.9; **WT** IV.iv.769
    2 appropriate, connected, pertinent **Ham** V.ii.155 [Hamlet to Osric] *The phrase would be more germane to the matter* [i.e. because cannons were mounted on 'carriages']

germen *(n.)* seed, life-forming elements **Mac** IV.i.58 [Macbeth to Witches] *though the treasure / Of nature's germens tumble all together* [F *Germaine*]; **KL** III.ii.8

gest *(n.)* **1** feat, deed, exploit **AC** IV.viii.2 [Antony to all] *let the Queen know of our gests*
    2 stage [in a journey], point in time **WT** I.ii.41 [Hermione to Polixenes, of Leontes in Bohemia] *I'll give him my commission / To let him there a month behind the gest / Prefixed for's parting*

gesture *(n.)* demeanour, attitude, manner **H5** IV.Chorus.25 [Chorus, of the English] *their gesture sad, / Investing lank-lean cheeks and war-worn coats;* **AY** V.ii.60

get *(v.)* **1** beget, conceive, breed **TS** II.i.403 [Tranio as Lucentio alone] *Fathers commonly / Do get their children;* **3H6** II.ii.133; **Mac** I.iii.66; **Oth** I.iii.189; **Sonn** 7.14; **Tem** I.ii.319
    2 win, gain, obtain victory in **3H6** I.iv.1 [York alone] *The army of the Queen hath got the field;* **1H6** V.iii.12; **H8** V.v.65
    3 acquire, gain, earn **Tim** I.i.126 [Old Athenian to Timon, of his daughter] *On whom I may confer what I have got*
    4 make money, get wealth, earn a living **Per** IV.ii.26 [Bawd to Pander] *Is it a shame to get when we are old?*
    5 work hard for **AY** III.ii.69 [Corin to Touchstone] *I earn that I eat, get that I wear*

get within *(v.)* [fencing] get inside the guard of, get within the defences of **CE** V.i.34 [Adriana to all, of Antipholus of Syracuse] *Some get within him*

getter *(n.)* begetter **Cor** IV.v.231 [First Servingman to Second Servingman] *Peace is ... a getter of more bastard children than war's a destroyer of men*

getting *(n.)* **1** begetting, procreation, breeding **MA** II.i.297 [Beatrice to Don Pedro, of a husband] *I would rather have one of your father's getting;* **AC** III.xiii.107; **MM** III.ii.111
    2 covetousness, acquiring things **H8** IV.ii.55 [Griffith to Katherine, of Wolsey] *though he were unsatisfied in getting*

ghastly *(adj.)* **1** full of fear, frightened **Tem** II.i.314 [Alonso to Antonio and Sebastian] *Wherefore this ghastly looking?*; **JC** I.iii.23 **2** terrifying, terrible, deathly **Sonn** 27.11 [of a jewel] *hung in ghastly night*

ghost *(n.)* **1** spirit, soul **1H6** I.i.52 [Bedford, as if to the spirit of Henry V] *thy ghost I invocate*; **KL** V.iii.311 ☞ yield the ghost **2** dead body, corpse **2H6** III.ii.161 [Warwick to Suffolk] *Oft have I seen a timely-parted ghost*; **Ham** I.iv.85

ghost *(v.)* haunt, appear as a ghost **AC** II.vi.13 [Pompey to Caesar, Antony and Lepidus] *Julius Caesar, / Who at Philippi the good Brutus ghosted*

ghostly *(adj.)* spiritual, holy **RJ** II.ii.192 [Romeo alone] *Hence will I to my ghostly Friar's close cell*; **3H6** III.ii.107; **MM** IV.iii.46; **RJ** II.iii.41, vi.21, III.iii.50

giantess *(n.)* she-giant **MW** II.i.74 [Mistress Page to Mistress Ford] *I had rather be a giantess and lie under Mount Pelion*

gib *(n.)* tom-cat **Ham** III.iv.191 [Hamlet to Gertrude] *who that's but a queen … / Would from a paddock, from a bat, a gib, / Such dear concernings hide?*

gib *(adj.)* castrated **1H4** I.ii.74 [Falstaff to Prince Hal] *I am as melancholy as a gib cat*

gibbet *(v.)* [unclear meaning] hang [as on a gibbet] **2H4** III.ii.256 [Falstaff to Shallow, of Wart] *'A shall … come off and on swifter than he that gibbets on the brewer's bucket*

gibbet-maker *(n.)* person who constructs gibbets **Tit** IV.iii.80 [Clown to Titus, of Jupiter] *Ho, the gibbet-maker?*

gibe *(n.)* scoff, taunt, jeer **MW** III.iv.227 [Evans to Caius, of Host] *A lousy knave, to have his gibes and his mockeries*; **Cym** III.iv.160; **MW** IV.v.74

gibe *(v.)* scoff, jeer, ridicule **AC** II.ii.78 [Caesar to Antony] *you … with taunts / Did gibe my missive out of audience*

giber *(n.)* joker, wit, comedian **Cor** II.i.77 [Brutus to Menenius] *you are … a perfecter giber for the table than a necessary bencher in the Capitol*

gibing *(adj.)* scoffing, taunting, jeering **LL** V.ii.847 [Rosaline to Berowne, of his challenge] *that's the way to choke a gibing spirit*; **1H4** III.ii.66

gibingly *(adv.)* sarcastically, tauntingly, in a mocking manner **Cor** II.iii.224 [Sicinius to Citizens, of Coriolanus] *Th'apprehension of his present portance, / Which most gibingly, ungravely, he did fashion*

giddily *(adv.)* **1** lightly, carelessly, inconsequentially **TN** II.iv.83 [Orsino to Viola as Cesario, of Olivia] *The parts that fortune hath bestowed upon her … I hold as giddily as fortune* **2** madly, foolishly, insanely **MA** III.iii.128 [Borachio to Conrade, of fashion] *how giddily 'a turns about all the hot bloods between fourteen and five-and-thirty*

giddiness *(n.)* rashness, foolishness, madness **AY** V.ii.5 [Oliver to Orlando, of falling in love] *Neither call the giddiness of it in question*

giddy *(adj.)* **1** frivolous, flighty, fickle, irresponsible **3H6** IV.viii.5 [Warwick to all, of Edward] *many giddy people flock to him*; **AY** III.ii.336; **Cor** I.i.266; **H5** I.i.145; **2H6** II.iv.21; **TN** II.iv.33 **2** foolish, stupid, ill-considered **2H4** I.iii.89 [Archbishop to all] *An habitation giddy and unsure / Hath he that buildeth on the vulgar heart*; **KJ** III.i.292 **3** bewildered, confused, nonplussed **KJ** IV.ii.131 [King John to Messenger] *Thou hast made me giddy / With these ill tidings* **4** mad, crazy, insane **R3** II.iii.5 [Second Citizen to First Citizen, of King Edward's death] *I fear 'twill prove a giddy world* [F; Q *troublous*] **5** wild with rage, mad with anger **1H6** III.i.83 [Mayor to all, of the rioters] *many have their giddy brains knocked out* **6** swaying, quaking, dizzying **E3** III.i.127 [King John to Philip] *The earth, with giddy trembling when it shakes*; **2H4** III.i.18; **MV** III.ii.144; **R3** I.iv.17; **TC** III.ii.16

giddy-paced whirling, moving at a bewildering pace **TN** II.iv.6 [Orsino to Viola as Cesario] *these most brisk and giddy-paced times*

gift *(n.)* **1** quality, accomplishment, talent **MW** I.i.58 [Shallow to Evans, of Anne] *She has good gifts*; **TN** I.iii.28; **TS** I.i.105 **2** giving, imparing, bestowal **Tim** I.ii.139 [Apemantus to himself] *Who dies that bears not one spurn to their graves / Of their friends' gift?*

gig *(n.)* spinning-top **LL** V.i.63 [Holofernes to Mote] *Go whip thy gig*; **LL** IV.iii.165

gig, gidge *(v.)* ☞ jig *(v.)*

giglot *(n.)* harlot, strumpet, wanton **MM** V.i.344 [Escalus to Provost, of Isabella and Mariana] *Away with those giglots*; **1H6** IV.vii.41

giglot *(adj.)* whore-like, fickle, giddy **Cym** III.i.32 [Queen to Cymbeline, of Cassibelan] *who was once at point / (O giglot fortune!) to master Caesar's sword*

gild *(v.)*, past forms **gilt, gilded** **1** cover, coat, smear **Mac** II.ii.56 [Lady Macbeth to Macbeth] *I'll gild the faces of the grooms withal* [i.e. with blood]; **E3** IV.iv.99; **KJ** I.i.316 **2** bring colour to, brighten, illuminate **TG** V.i.1 [Eglamour alone] *The sun begins to gild the western sky*; **Cym** V.v.34; **1H4** V.iv.157; **Sonn** 20.6, 28.12; **Tem** V.i.280 **3** enrich, adorn, beautify **KJ** II.i.491 [King John to King Philip, of Blanche's dowry] *all that we upon this side the sea … / Find liable to our crown and dignity, / Shall gild her bridal bed* **4** supply with money, enrich **MV** II.vi.49 [Jessica to Lorenzo] *I will … gild myself / With some more ducats*

gild over *(v.)* smooth over, cover the defect of **2H4** I.ii.151 [Lord Chief Justice to Falstaff] *Your day's service at Shrewsbury hath a little gilded over your night's exploit on Gad's Hill*

gilded *(adj.)* **1** glittering, gold-coloured, tinged with gold **KL** V.iii.13 [Lear to Cordelia] *we'll … laugh / At gilded butterflies*; **AC** I.iv.62; **Cym** V.v.4; **KL** IV.vi.112, V.iii.85 **2** gold-bearing, supplied with money **Ham** III.iii.58 [Claudius alone] *Offence's gilded hand may shove by justice* [i.e. judges may be bribed]

gillyvor *(n.)* gillyflower, clove-scented pink **WT** IV.iv.98 [disguised Polixenes to Perdita] *make your garden rich in gillyvors*; **WT** IV.iv.82 ☞ **PLANTS**, p.330

gilt *(n.)* **1** gold, money **H5** II.Chorus.26 [Chorus, of the traitors] *Have, for the gilt of France … / Confirmed conspiracy with fearful France* **2** **H5** IV.iii.110 [King Henry to Montjoy] *Our gayness and our gilt are all besmirched*; **Tim** IV.iii.304

gilt *(adj.)* **1** coated, glazed **LL** V.ii.644 [Dumaine to all, of Mars' gift to Hector] *A gilt nutmeg* **2** coated with gold **2H4** IV.iii.49 [Falstaff to Prince John] *if you do not all show like gilt two-pences to me* [i.e. forged so as to look like half-crowns]

gilt *(v.)* ☞ gild *(v.)*

gimmaled *(adj.)* jointed, hinged, linked **E3** I.ii.29 [King David to Lorraine, of the Scots soldiers] *never shall [they] … lay aside their jacks of gimmaled mail* [QQ *Gymould*]; **H5** V.ii.47

gimmers *(n.)* gimmals, mechanical joints, connecting links **1H6** I.ii.41 [Reignier to all, of the English] *I think by some odd gimmers or device / Their arms are set like clocks, still to strike on*

gin *(n.)* snare, trap **3H6** I.iv.61 [Clifford to all, of York] *so strives the woodcock with the gin*; **E3** IV.iii.21; **2H6** III.i.262; **Mac** IV.ii.36; **MW** IV.ii.111; **TN** II.v.83 ☞ ging *(n.)*

gin, 'gin *(v.)* begin [to] **PassP** XIII.3 [of beauty] *A flower that dies when first it 'gins to bud*; **Cor** II.i.113; **Cym** II.iii.20; **Mac** I.ii.25, V.v.49; **Tem** III.iii.108

ging *(n.)* gang, company, whole household **MW** IV.ii.111 [Ford to all] *There's a knot, a ging, a pack, a conspiracy against me* [F2; F *gin*]

gipe *(n.)* jibe, scoff, jest **H5** IV.vii.47 [Fluellen to Gower, of Falstaff] *he was full of jests, and gipes, and knaveries, and mocks*

gird *(n.)* **1** rebuke, reproof, reproach **1H6** III.i.132 [Warwick to King, of Winchester] *The Bishop hath a kindly gird*

2 taunt, gibe, dig **TS** V.ii.58 [Lucentio to Tranio, of his remark] *I thank thee for that gird*

gird (*v.*) **1** encircle, surround, ring **TNK** II.ii.81 [Arcite alone] *who knows / Whether my brows may not be girt with garlands;* **H5** I.ii.152 ➤ **begird** (*v.*)
2 mock, taunt, laugh [at] **Cor** I.i.254 [Brutus to Sicinius, of Martius] *Being moved, he will not spare to gird the gods;* **2H4** I.ii.6
3 ➤ **girt** (*v.*)

gird in (*v.*) encircle, surround, ring **3H6** IV.viii.20 [Warwick to all] *My sovereign ... / Like to his island girt in with the ocean*

gird up (*v.*) tie round, truss up **Sonn** 12.7 *And Summer's green all girded up in sheaves*

girded (*adj.*) besieged, blockaded, encircled **H5** III.Chorus.27 [Chorus] *Behold the ordnance on their carriages, / With fatal mouths gaping on girded Harfleur*

girdle (*n.*) **1** waist **Tim** III.iv.91 [Timon to Servants, of his bills] *Knock me down with 'em; cleave me to the girdle;* **KL** IV.vi.126
2 belt **E3** IV.v.94 [Charles to King John] *Shall I not give my girdle from my waist;* **Cym** III.i.81; **1H4** III.iii.149; **2H4** I.ii.38; **LL** IV.v.51; **MND** II.i.175 ➤ **WEAPONS**, p.491

girdle, turn one's find an outlet for anger, put up with it **MA** V.i.139 [Claudio to Don Pedro, of Benedick's anger] *he knows how to turn his girdle*

girt, gird (*v.*) invest, equip, provide **1H6** III.i.173 [King to Richard] *I girt thee with the valiant sword of York;* **2H6** I.i.63

girth (*n.*) **1** circumference, perimeter **TNK** V.i.56 [Arcite praying to Mars] *The masoned turrets, that both makest and breakest / The stony girths of cities* [i.e. fortified walls]
2 saddle-securing belt around the body of a horse **TNK** V.iv.74 [Pirithous to Palamon, of Arcite's horse] *When neither curb would crack, girth break*

give (*v.*) **1** grant, allow, bestow **Ham** I.v.142 [Hamlet to Horatio and Marcellus] *Give me one poor request;* **Cor** IV.iv.25; **Mac** I.iii.118
2 deal out, make, carry out **Cym** V.iii.87 [Second Captain to First Captain] *a fourth man ... / That gave th'affront*
3 dispose, mind, incline **Cor** IV.v.195 [Second Servingman to First Servingman, of Coriolanus] *An he had been cannibally given*
4 consider, account, hold [in mind] **WT** III.ii.94 [Hermione to Leontes] *The crown and comfort of my life, your favour, / I do give lost, for I do feel it gone*
5 suggest, prompt, intimate **Cor** IV.v.153 [Second Servingman to First Servingman, of Coriolanus] *my mind gave me his clothes made a false report of him;* **H8** V.iii.109
6 portray, report, represent **AC** I.iv.40 [Messenger to Caesar, of Pompey] *men's reports / Give him much wronged;* **Cor** I.ix.54
7 display, show, bear arms of **MW** I.i.15 [Slender to Evans, of Shallow's ancestors] *They may give the dozen white luces in their coat;* **TN** I.v.29
8 call, nickname **RJ** IV.v.114 [First Musician to Peter] *Then will I give you the serving-creature;* **RJ** IV.v.112
9 give up, renounce **KJ** I.i.146 [Bastard to Queen Eleanor, of his land] *I would give it every foot to have this face*
10 give forth, emit, flow **Tim** IV.iii.487 [Timon to Flavius, of mankind] *whose eyes do never give / But thorough lust and laughter*
11 ➤ **FAREWELLS**, p.170

give away (*v.*) sacrifice, renounce, abandon **Oth** III.iii.28 [Desdemona to Cassio, of herself] *thy solicitor shall rather die / Than give thy cause away*

give back (*v.*) retire, yield, back off **TG** V.iv.127 [Valentine to Thurio] *give back, or else embrace thy death*

give fire begin firing, shoot, discharge **2H4** II.iv.177 [Pistol to Hostess] *let the fiend give fire!*

give in (*v.*) provide, supply, furnish **Ham** III.ii.64 [Claudius alone] *we ourselves compelled ... / To give in evidence*

give in charge give orders, command, direct **E3** II.ii.16 [Derby to Audley, of King Edward] *he gave in charge / Till after dinner none should interrupt him;* **1H6** II.i.3.1; **2H6** II.iv.80; **3H6** IV.i.32; **R3** IV.iii.25

give life bring up, raise, nurture **TNK** II.iv.7 [Arcite to Theseus, of his sporting skills] *[my father] to these gentle uses gave me life*

give off (*v.*) **1** cease, leave the area **AC** IV.iii.26 [First Soldier to all, of the music] *Let's see how it will give off*
2 give up, yield, relinquish **KJ** V.i.27 [King John alone] *Did not the prophet / Say ... / My crown I should give off?*

give out (*v.*) **1** report, assert, make known **1H6** IV.iii.3 [Messenger to Richard, of the scouts who followed the Dauphin] *They ... give it out / That he is marched to Bordeaux;* **Cym** V.v.312; **MA** II.i.191; **Tem** V.i.223; **TNK** II.i.5
2 proclaim, announce, herald **WT** V.i.85 [Gentleman to Leontes, of the arrival] *One that gives out himself Prince Florizel;* **Mac** IV.iii.192
3 estimate, predict of **2H4** IV.i.23 [Mowbray to Archbishop, of the King's forces] *The just proportion that we gave them out*
4 surrender, give up, stop using **2H6** IV.viii.24 [Cade to rebels] *I thought ye would never have given out these arms till you had recovered your ancient freedom*

give over (*v.*) **1** desert, leave, abandon **Tim** III.iii.13 [Sempronius to Servant, of Timon] *His friends, like physicians, / Thrice give him over;* **1H4** III.iii.35; **MND** III.ii.130; **Tem** II.i.12; **Tit** IV.ii.48; **TS** I.ii.104
2 retire, give up a trade, abandon a way of life **Per** IV.ii.33 [Pander to Bawd] *the sore terms we stand upon with the gods will be strong with us for giving o'er;* **Per** IV.ii.25
3 cease, finish, leave off **Luc** 1567 [of Lucrece ripping a painting of Sinon] *At last she smilingly with this gives o'er;* **Cym** II.iii.15; **Per** IV.ii.25

give thanks say grace before meals **TS** IV.i.145 [Petruchio to Katherina] *Will you give thanks, sweet Kate*

give up (*v.*) give in, yield, succumb **Cym** II.ii.46 [Iachimo to himself, of Innogen's book] *here the leaf's turned down / Where Philomel gave up*

give way (*v.*) **1** yield to, succumb to, submit to **Tem** I.ii.186 [Prospero to Miranda, of her sleeping] *'Tis a good dullness, / And give it way;* **2H6** V.vii.76
2 keep out of the way [of], steer clear [of] **Tim** IV.iii.355 [Apemantus to Timon, of a plague of company] *I will fear to catch it, and give way;* **TN** III.iv.193 [Fabian to Sir Toby, of Viola as Cesario and Olivia] *Give them way till he take leave*

given (*adj.*) disposed, inclined, minded **JC** I.ii.196 [Antony to Caesar, of Cassius] *He is a noble Roman, and well given;* **2H6** III.i.72

giving out (*n.*) suggestion, intimation, utterance **Ham** I.v.178 [Hamlet to Horatio and Marcellus] *Or such ambiguous giving out;* **MM** I.iv.54; **Oth** IV.i.128

glad (*n.*) gladness, joy, delight **Per** II.Chorus.38 [Gower alone, of Pericles] *Fortune ... / Threw him ashore, to give him glad*

glad (*v.*) **1** gladden, brighten, cause to rejoice **Per** II.iii.21 [Simonides to Knights] *Your presence glads our days;* **3H6** IV.vi.93; **H8** II.iv.196; **Per** I.Chorus.4, iv.28; **Tit** I.i.169
2 make a gladness of **Per** I.i.10 [Antiochus to Pericles, of his daughter] *Nature this dowry gave; to glad her presence* [i.e. to make her presence in this world a delight (either to herself or to others); or: her existence enhanced Nature]

gladding (*n.*) delighting, making joyful **H8** V.i.71 [Suffolk to King Henry, of Queen Anne's labour] *With gentle travail, to the gladding of / Your highness with an heir!*

glade (*n.*) opening, path, gap **TNK** IV.i.64 [Wooer to Gaoler] *Through a small glade cut by the fishermen*

gladly (*adv.*) willingly, happily, pleasureably **Cor** I.ix.6 [Cominius to Martius] *where ladies shall be frighted / And, gladly quaked, hear more*

glaive (*n.*) long-handled blade, spear **E3** III.iv.89 [Prince Edward to King Edward, of the French] *lay as thick upon my battered crest / As on an anvil with their ponderous glaives*

glance (*n.*) hit, innuendo, riposte **AY** II.vii.57 [Jaques to Duke Senior] *the squandering glances of the fool*

glance (v.) **1** touch, have an impact Per III.iii.6 [Cleon to Pericles] *Your shakes of fortune … glance / Full wonderingly on us*; KL V.iii.146
2 miss the mark, be ineffective MW V.v.227 [Falstaff to all] *though you have ta'en a special stand to strike at me, … your arrow hath glanced*
3 turn, move, pass MM V.i.307 [Escalus to disguised Duke, of Angelo] *to glance from him / To th'Duke himself, to tax him with injustice*; Sonn 76.3

glance at (v.) **1** allude to, refer to, mention in passing CE V.i.66 [Adriana to Abbess, of Antipholus' infidelity] *In company I often glanced at it*; JC I.ii.317
2 pick on, snipe at, cast aspersions on MND II.i.75 [Oberon to Titania] *How canst thou … / Glance at my credit with Hippolyta, / Knowing I know thy love to Theseus?*

glance away (v.) bounce off, ricochet off TS V.ii.61 [Petruchio to Hortensio, of Tranio's remark] *the jest did glance away from me*

glanders (n.) horse disease affecting the nostrils and jaws TS III.ii.50 [Biondello to Tranio as Lucentio, of Petruchio's horse] *possessed with the glanders*

glass (n.) **1** mirror, looking-glass AY III.v.54 [Rosalind as Ganymede to Silvius, of Phebe] *'Tis not her glass but you that flatters her* ☛ FEW, p.xxi
2 magic mirror, crystal ball MM II.ii.95 [Angelo to Isabella, of the law] *like a prophet / Looks in a glass that shows … future evils*; Mac IV.i.118
3 [sand of the] hourglass Tem I.ii.240 [Prospero to Ariel, of the time after noon] *At least two glasses*; AW II.i.165; 1H6 IV.ii.35; Sonn 126.2; TNK V.i.18; WT IV.i.16
4 eye-ball Cor III.ii.117 [Coriolanus to Volumnia] *schoolboys' tears take up / The glasses of my sight!* [i.e. fill my eyes]; R2 I.iii.208; Venus 1129

glass (v.) enclose in glass LL II.i.230 [Boyet to Princess, of jewels in crystal] *tendering their own worth from where they were glassed*

glass eyes spectacles KL IV.vi.171 [Lear to all] *Get thee glass eyes*

glass-faced (adj.) mirror-faced, self-reflecting Tim I.i.60 [Poet to Painter, of Timon's followers] *from the glass-faced flatterer / To Apemantus*

glass-gazing (adj.) admiring oneself in the mirror KL II.ii.16 [disguised Kent to Oswald, describing him] *glass-gazing … rogue*

glassy (adj.) **1** as if made of glass, translucent Luc 102 [of Lucrece and Tarquin's eyes] *[she could not] read the subtle shining secrecies / Writ in the glassy margents of such books*
2 [unclear meaning] frail as glass, brittle; or: mirroring, reflecting [divinity] MM II.ii.120 [Isabella to Angelo, of man] *Most ignorant of what he's most assured, / His glassy essence*

glaze (v.) stare, glare, gaze JC I.iii.21 [Casca to Cicero] *I met a lion, / Who glazed upon me*

glean (v.) collect, scrape together, gather up AY III.v.102 [Silvius to Phebe] *To glean the broken ears after the man / That the main harvest reaps*; Ham IV.ii.19; H8 III.ii.284

gleaned (adj.) stripped, depleted, emptied H5 I.ii.151 [King Henry to Canterbury, of attacks by the Scots] *Galling the gleaned land with hot assays* [i.e. the land which had no defenders]

gleek (n.) taunt, gibe, insult 1H6 III.ii.123 [Talbot to Burgundy] *Now where's the Bastard's braves and Charles his gleeks?*; RJ IV.v.112

gleek (v.) make a pointed joke, jest, gibe MND III.i.139 [Bottom to Titania] *I can gleek upon occasion*; H5 V.i.70

glib (adj.) smooth, suave, oily Tim I.i.55 [Poet to Painter] *As well of glib and slipp'ry creatures as / Of grave and austere quality, tender down / Their services to Lord Timon*

glib (v.) geld, castrate WT II.i.149 [Antigonus to Leontes, of his daughters] *I had rather glib myself than they / Should not produce fair issue*

glimpse (n.) trace, tinge, pinch TC I.ii.25 [Alexander to Cressida, of Ajax] *There is no man hath a virtue that he hath not a glimpse of*

glister (v.) glitter, sparkle, gleam KJ V.i.54 [Bastard to King John] *Away, and glister like the god of war*; TNK VI.i.69; Venus 275; WT III.ii.168

glistering (n.) brilliance, sparkle, shining nature WT IV.i.14 [Time to audience] *I … make stale / The glistering of this present*

glistering (adj.) glittering, shining, sparkling Tem IV.i.193 [stage direction] *Enter Ariel, loaden with glistering apparel*; H5 II.ii.117; H8 II.iii.21; R2 III.iii.178; Tit II.i.7

globe (n.) head, brain Ham I.v.97 [Hamlet alone] *whiles memory holds a seat / In this distracted globe*

globy (adj.) globular, bulging, protruding TNK V.i.113 [Palamon praying to Venus, of an old man] *Torturing convulsions from his globy eyes / Had almost drawn their spheres*

glooming (adj.) gloomy, dark, dismal RJ V.iii.305 [Prince to all] *A glooming peace this morning with it brings*

glorify (v.) add glory to, increase the splendour of KJ II.i.442 [Hubert to King John and King Philip, of Lewis the Dauphin and Blanche] *two such silver currents, when they join, / Do glorify the banks that bound them in*

glorious (adj.) seeking glory, eager for renown Cym I.vii.7 [Innogen alone] *most miserable / Is the desire that's glorious*; Per I.Chorus.9

glory (n.) **1** splendour, magnificence, brilliance E3 II.i.399 [Warwick to Countess] *The King will in his glory hide thy shame*; E3 II.i.449, ii.71; Sonn 60.7
2 boastful spirit, vaingloriousness LL IV.i.31 [Princess to all] *Glory grows guilty of detested crimes*; KJ II.i.350
3 exalted person, majesty, celebrity E3 II.i.453 [Warwick to Countess] *every glory that inclines to sin*

glose (v.) speak flatteringly, talk smoothly R2 II.i.10 [John of Gaunt to York] *He that no more must say is listened more / Than they whom youth and ease have taught to glose*

gloss (n.) **1** deceptive appearance, plausibility 1H6 IV.i.103 [Vernon to King, of Basset] *he seem with forged quaint conceit / To set a gloss upon his bold intent*; E3 I.i.78; 2H6 I.i.161; H8 V.iii.71; Mac I.vii.34; Tim I.i.15
2 brightness, freshness, shine, lustre TNK I.i.5 [Arcite to Palamon] *before we further / Sully our gloss of youth*; 1H6 IV.iv.6; Tem II.i.66
3 marginal comment, superficial wordplay LL IV.iii.346 [Longaville to all, of Berowne's comments] *Lay these glosses by* [F *glozes*]

glover (n.) glove-maker, leather-worker MW I.iv.20 [Mistress Quickly to Simple, of Slender] *Does he not wear a great round beard like a glover's paring-knife?*

glow (v.) blush, redden, flush Ham III.iv.49 [Hamlet to Gertrude] *Heaven's face does glow* [i.e. with shame]; AC II.ii.209

gloze (n.) ☛ **gloss** (n.) 3

gloze (v.) **1** speak fair words, flatter, talk plausibly Per I.i.111 [Antiochus to himself, of Pericles] *I will gloze with him*; R2 II.i.10; Tit IV.iv.35
2 gloss, interpret H5 I.ii.40 [Canterbury to King Henry, of the Salic land] *the French unjustly gloze / To be the realm of France*
3 expound, comment upon, give a commentary TC II.ii.166 [Hector to Paris and Troilus] *you … on the cause and question now in hand / Have glozed, but superficially*

glue (v.) attach, join, bring together 3H6 II.vi.5 [Clifford alone, as if to the House of Lancaster] *My love and fear glued many friends to thee*

glut (v.) swallow up, devour, engulf Tem I.i.58 [Gonzalo to all, of the Boatswain] *He'll be hanged yet, / Though every drop of water … gape at wid'st to glut him*

glutton (n.) rich man in the Dives and Lazarus parable 2H4 I.ii.33 [Falstaff to Page, of his tailor] *Let him be damned like the glutton!*
☛ **RELIGIOUS PERSONALITIES AND BEINGS**, p.625

glutton *(adj.)* gluttonous, voracious, greedy **2H4** I.iii.98 [Archbishop to all, as if to the people] *didst thou disgorge / Thy glutton bosom of the royal Richard*

gnarl *(v.)* snarl, growl **2H6** III.i.192 [Gloucester to King] *wolves are gnarling who shall gnaw thee first*

gnarling *(adj.)* snarling, growling **R2** I.iii.292 [John of Gaunt to Bolingbroke] *gnarling sorrow hath less power to bite*

go *(v.)* **1** walk, travel on foot **Cym** IV.ii.294 [Innogen alone] *I have gone all night;* **1H4** I.ii.14; **KL** I.iv.120; **TG** IV.ii.20; **Tim** IV.iii.46

2 go off, set about, proceed **Per** I.iii.13 [Helicanus to Lords, of Pericles] *he's gone to travel*

3 come, accompany, stay **Tit** IV.i.27 [Young Lucius to Lavinia] *if my uncle Marcus go, / I will most willingly attend your ladyship*

4 live, exist, breathe **TNK** Prologue.11 [of Chaucer] *a poet never went / More famous*

5 pass as current, be valued **AW** II.iii.130 [King to Bertram, of character] *The property by what it is should go, / Not by the title;* **2H4** I.ii.170; **TC** IV.ii.23

6 be [like], suggest, present itself **TNK** II.iv.21 [Emilia to all, of Arcite] *His mother was a wondrous handsome woman; / His face methinks goes that way* [i.e. indicates that conclusion]

7 join, follow, be in tune **MA** I.i.173 [Benedick to Claudio] *in what key shall a man take you to go in the song?*

8 be pregnant, be with child **TNK** IV.i.124 [Gaoler's Daughter to First Friend, of his sister and Palamon] *if she sees him once, she's gone;* **2H4** V.iv.9; **H8** VI.i.77; **R3** II.v.85

9 [unclear meaning] enjoy a sexual relationship **AC** I.ii.65 [Charmian to Iras, as if to Isis, of Alexas] *O, let him marry a woman that cannot go*

go about *(v.)* **1** endeavour, set to work, start trying **MND** IV.i.205 [Bottom alone] *Man is but an ass if he go about to expound this dream;* **MA** I.iii.11; **Venus** 319; **WT** IV.iv.696

2 take in hand, make busy, set in motion **2H6** II.i.142 [Simpcox to Gloucester] *You go about to torture me in vain*

3 be evasive, talk in a roundabout way **AW** I.iii.183 [Countess to Helena] *Go not about*

go about with *(v.)* get the better of, set to work on **MA** IV.ii.26 [Dogberry to Sexton, of Conrade] *I will go about with him*

go along come along, come with me **MND** I.i.123 [Theseus to Demetrius and Egeus] *go along*

go before *(v.)* **1** anticipate, forestall **AY** IV.i.129 [Rosalind as Ganymede to Orlando] *There's a girl goes before the priest*

2 surpass, outdo, be superior to **Cym** V.ii.8 [Iachimo alone, of disguised Posthumus] *If that thy gentry, Britain, go before / This lout;* **Cym** I.v.69

go beyond *(v.)* exceed, surpass, transcend **TNK** III.vi.206 [Hippolyta to Theseus] *you swore I went beyond all women*

go even agree, give assent [to] **Cym** I.v.42 [Posthumus to Frenchman, of himself] *rather shunned to go even with what I heard*

go forward *(v.)* **1** go ahead, take place, come to pass **3H6** III.iii.58 [Queen to herself, of a marriage between Edward and Lady Bona] *If that go forward, Henry's hope is done*

2 carry on, keep it up **TS** I.i.160 [Lucentio to Tranio, of his advice] *Go forward, this contents*

go off *(v.)* die, pass away, depart **Mac** V.vi.75 [Seyward to Malcolm, of their comrades] *Some must go off;* **AC** IV.xiii.6

go on *(v.)* go forward, press ahead **TNK** V.i.41 [Arcite to his knights, of what to ask from Mars] *the speed also - to go on*

go over *(v.)* read through, look over **LL** IV.i.98 [Princess to Boyet, of Armado's writing style] *Else your memory is bad, going o'er it erewhile* [also: climb over (a stile)]

go through *(v.)* **1** do what is undertaken, keep one's word **TNK** II.ii.31 [First Countryman to the others, of his wife] *I'll go through, let her mumble;* **MM** II.i.258

2 haggle at length, carry out a piece of bargaining **Per** IV.ii.41 [Boult to Bawd, of Marina] *I have gone through for this piece you see*

go thy / your ways ☞ ways, go thy / your 4

go to *(v.)* **1** accord with, correspond to, match **MW** II.i.56 [Mistress Ford to Mistress Page, of Falstaff] *I would have sworn his disposition would have gone to the truth of his words*

2 get moving, get to work, come on **Tem** IV.i.252 [Stephano to Caliban, of the clothing] *Go to, carry this!*

3 ☞ **DISCOURSE MARKERS**, p.127; **EXCLAMATIONS**, p.158

go to it **1** copulate, engage in sexual intercourse **Per** IV.vi.70 [Lysimachus to Marina] *Did you go to't so young?;* **KL** IV.vi.122

2 ☞ to it

go under *(v.)* seem to be, appear **AW** III.v.20 [Mariana to Diana, of soldiers] *their promises ... are not the things they go under*

go up *(v.)* be sheathed, be put away **JC** V.i.52 [Octavius to all, of his drawn sword] *When think you that the sword goes up again?*

go whistle ☞ whistle, go

gobbet *(n.)* piece of raw flesh **2H6** IV.i.85 [Lieutenant to Suffolk] *overgorged / With gobbets of thy mother's bleeding heart;* **2H6** V.ii.58

god *(v.)* make a god of, idolize **Cor** V.iii.11 [Coriolanus to Aufidius, of Menenius] *This last old man ... godded me indeed*

God *(n.)* ☞ **FAREWELLS**, p.170; **GREETINGS**, p.206; **POLITENESS**, p.340; **SWEARING**, p.435

goer-between *(n.)* go-between **TC** III.ii.199 [Pandarus to Cressida and Troilus] *let all pitiful goers-between be called ... after my name* ☞ broker-between *(n.)*

gog *(n.)* [softened form of 'God'] ☞ **SWEARING**, p.435

going *(n.)* walking, going at one's usual pace **TG** III.i.367 [Launce to Speed] *thou hast stayed so long that going will scarce serve the turn*

going out *(n.)* expedition, journey, excursion **H8** I.i.73 [Buckingham to Abergavenny] *Upon this French going out*

gold *(n.)* **1** money [not only gold coins] **AY** II.iv.59 [Celia to Rosalind and Touchstone] *question yond man / If he for gold will give us any food*

2 golden state, object made of gold **2H6** V.i.99 [York to King, of the crown] *That gold must round engirt these brows of mine;* **Cor** V.vi.64

golden *(adj.)* resplendent, dazzling, richly dressed **1H4** IV.iii.73 [Hotspur to Blunt, of King Henry] *The more and less ... followed him / Even at the heels in golden multitudes*

goldenly *(adv.)* excellently, splendidly **AY** I.i.6 [Orlando to Adam, of his brother Jaques] *report speaks goldenly of his profit*

gone *(adj.)* lost, ruined, brought down **R3** IV.iii.20 [Tyrrel alone, of the Princes' killers] *both are gone with conscience and remorse;* **LL** V.ii.669; **WT** IV.iv.815

good *(n.)* **1** goodwill, goodness **H8** IV.ii.60 [Griffith to Katherine, of the fall of Wolsey's foundation at Ipswich] *Unwilling to outlive the good that did it*

2 good fellow **Per** II.Chorus.9 [Gower alone, of Pericles] *The good in conversation ... / Is still at Tarsus;* **Tim** I.i.3, 15; **Tim** II.ii.75

3 interest, advantage, benefit **Cor** II.i.234 [Sicinius to Brutus, of Coriolanus] *It shall be to him then as our good wills, / A sure destruction*

good, do prosper, succeed, triumph **2H6** IV.iii.14 [Dick to Cade] *If we mean to thrive and do good, break open the gaols*

good, do one **1** make prosper, enable to succeed **MA** I.i.269 [Claudio to Don Pedro] *your highness now may do me good;* **2H6** I.ii.77; **3H6** III.ii.38

2 be of use, provide assistance to **2H6** III.i.219 [King to all, of Gloucester] *myself ... / Look after him, and cannot do him good*

good *(adj.)* **1** [intensifying use] real, genuine **AY** I.i.26 [Celia to Rosalind] *love no man in good earnest;* **Tim** II.ii.232

2 kind, benevolent, generous **Tim** I.i.242 [Timon to Apemantus] *it thou wert not sullen, I would be good to thee;* **Tim** III.i.24

3 kind, friendly, sympathetic **LL** V.ii.274 [Rosaline to all] *The King was weeping-ripe for a good word*

4 amenable, tractable, manageable **TS** I.i.127 [Hortensio to Gremio, of a husband for Katherina] *there be good fellows in the world, an a man could light on them*

5 honest, virtuous, honourable **Cor** II.i.58 [Menenius to Brutus and Sicinius, of their supporters] *they lie deadly that tell you have good faces*

6 seasonable, appropriate, proper **CE** II.ii.70 [Antipholus of Syracuse to Dromio of Syracuse] *learn to jest in good time*

7 just, right, commendable **2H6** II.i.28 [Suffolk to Gloucester, of malice] *no more than well becomes / So good a quarrel*

8 intended, right, proper **RJ** I.iv.46 [Mercutio to Romeo] *Take our good meaning*

9 high-ranking, highborn, distinguished **R2** I.i.40 [Bolingbroke to Mowbray] *Thou art ... a miscreant, / Too good to be so* ➤ **better** (adj.)

10 rich, wealthy, substantial **Cor** I.i.15 [First Citizen to all] *We are accounted poor citizens, the patricians good;* **1H4** IV.ii.15; **MV** I.iii.12

good, 'tis very well **Tit** I.i.412 [Saturninus to Bassianus] *'Tis good, sir. You are very short with us*

good (adv.) [intensifying use] really, genuinely **1H4** III.iii.44 [Falstaff to Bardolph] *the sack that thou hast drunk me would have bought me lights as good cheap at the dearest chandler's in Europe*

good-conceited (adj.) cleverly devised, ingeniously composed **Cym** II.iii.16 [Cloten to musicians, of their playing to Innogen] *a very excellent good-conceited thing*

good deed (adv.) in truth, in reality **WT** I.ii.42 [Hermione to Leontes] *yet, good deed, Leontes, / I love thee not a jar o'th' clock behind / What lady she her lord* ➤ **DISCOURSE MARKERS**, p.127

good-den / e'en / even / morrow ➤ **GREETINGS**, p.206; **FAREWELLS**, p.170

good-faced (adj.) smooth-faced, pretty **WT** IV.iii.112 [Autolycus to Clown] *good-faced sir .. sweet sir*

good life comfortable position, respectable way of life **MW** III.iii.112 [Mistress Page to Mistress Ford] *defend your reputation, or bid farewell to your good life for ever* ➤ **song of good life**

goodly (adj.) **1** splendid, excellent, fine **Tim** III.iii.28 [Servant alone, as if to Sempronius] *Your lordship's a goodly villain;* **AC** II.vii.35; **Lover** 137; **MA** III.iii.171; **Per** V.i.17; **Tem** V.i.260

2 good-looking, handsome, attractive, comely **Tem** V.i.182 [Miranda to all] *How many goodly creatures are there here!;* **2H4** IV.i.20; **KL** IV.iii.17; **MV** I.iii.99; **Per** IV.i.9; **WT** II.ii.26

goodman (adj.) **1** title for a person under the rank of gentleman, yeoman **RJ** I.v.77 [Capulet to Tybalt] *What, goodman boy!;* **KL** II.ii.42, IV.i.57; **LL** I.i.295, IV.i.36, V.i.142 ➤ **ADDRESS FORMS**, p.8

2 husband **TS** Induction.ii.104 [Sly to Page dressed as his wife] *I am your goodman*

goodness (n.) **1** natural kindness, generosity, bounty **H8** III.i.159 [Wolsey to Queen Katherine] *For goodness' sake, consider what you do;* **H8** Prologue.23; **Tim** I.i.11, ii.16

2 excellence, virtue, good qualities **TNK** II.v.35 [Pirithous to Arcite, of Emilia] *pray observe her goodness*

3 benefit, advantage, successful outcome **KL** V.i.7 [Regan to Edmund] *You know the goodness I intend upon you;* **Mac** IV.iii.136

4 piece of luck, good fortune **TNK** II.i.117 [Palamon to Arcite] *'Tis a main goodness, cousin, that our fortunes / Were twinned together*

good-night, good night (n.) **1** night-time serenade **2H4** III.ii.307 [Falstaff alone, of Shallow's tunes] *'A ... sware they were his fancies or his good-nights*

2 [as farewell] we bid each other a last farewell **WT** I.ii.411 [Camillo to Polixenes] *mark my counsel ... or both yourself and me / Cry lost, and so good night*

good now ➤ **ATTENTION SIGNALS**, p.26; **DISCOURSE MARKERS**, p.127; **POLITENESS**, p.340

good-presaging (adj.) favourable, propitious, auspicious **E3** III.iii.209 [Prince Edward to all, of the honour done to him] *cheers my ... strength / With comfortable good-presaging signs* [Q2]

goodwife (n.) mistress of a house, Mrs **2H4** II.i.91 [Hostess to Falstaff] *Did not goodwife Keech the butcher's wife come in then;* **MW** II.ii.33

good-year / goodyear, what the [expression of impatience] what the deuce **2H4** IV.iv.172 [Hostess to Pistol, of Hiren] *What the goodyear, do you think I would deny her?;* **2H4** II.iv.57; **MA** I.iii.1; **MW** I.iv.119 ➤ **SWEARING**, p.435

good-years (n.) [unclear meaning] good times to come **KL** V.iii.24 [Lear to Cordelia, of their enemies] *The good-years shall devour them, flesh and fell*

goose (n.) **1** prostitute, whore **LL** III.i.120 [Costard to Armado, of his release] *I smell some l'envoy, some goose in this;* **LL** IV.iii.73; **RJ** II.iv.73 ➤ **Winchester goose** (n.)

2 simpleton, dolt, bungler **AY** III.iv.40 [Celia to Rosalind, of Orlando] *as a puisny tilter that spurs his horse but on one side breaks his staff like a noble goose*

3 smoothing iron **Mac** II.iii.14 [Porter alone, of someone at the door] *Come in, tailor; here you may roast your goose*

goose (adj.) stupid, foolish, idiotic **Mac** V.iii.12 [Macbeth to Servant] *Where got'st thou that goose look?*

goose pen (n.) goose-quill, quill-pen **TN** III.ii.47 [Sir Toby to Sir Andrew] *though thou write with a goose pen, no matter*

goosequill (n.) pen made from a goose quill **Ham** II.ii.342 [Rosencrantz to Hamlet] *many wearing rapiers are afraid of goosequills* [i.e. are afraid of being ridiculed]

gorbellied (adj.) pot-bellied, fat-paunched **1H4** II.ii.87 [Falstaff to Travellers] *Hang ye, gorbellied knaves, are ye undone?*

Gordian knot apparently unsolvable problem, extreme difficulty **H5** I.i.46 [Canterbury to Ely, of King Henry] *Turn him to any cause of policy, / The Gordian knot of it he will unloose;* **Cym** II.ii.34

gore-blood (n.) gory blood, clotted blood **RJ** III.ii.56 [Nurse to Juliet, of Tybalt's body] *all bedaubed in blood, / All in gore-blood*

gored (adj.) deeply wounded, bleeding **TC** III.iii.228 [Achilles to Patroclus] *My fame is shrewdly gored;* **KL** V.iii.318

gorge (n.) **1** throat, stomach **Venus** 58 [of an eagle feeding] *Till either gorge be stuffed or prey be gone;* **WT** II.i.44

2 stomach contents **Oth** II.i.226 [Iago to Roderigo, of Desdemona] *her delicate tenderness will ... begin to heave the gorge* [i.e. feel disgusting]; **Ham** V.i.184; **Tim** IV.iii.41

gorget (n.) piece of armour for protecting the throat **TC** I.iii.174 [Ulysses to all, of Patroclus impersonating Nestor] *with a palsy fumbling on his gorget / Shake in and out the rivet* ➤ **BODY-ARMOUR**, p.48

gosling (n.) beginner, greenhorn, novice **Per** IV.ii.81 [Bawd to Marina] *Marry, whip the gosling* [i.e. confound the kid!]; **Cor** V.iii.35

gospelled (adj.) converted to the gospel, Christian **Mac** III.i.87 [Macbeth to Murderers, of Banquo] *Are you so gospelled, / To pray for this good man*

goss (n.) gorse, spiny shrub **Tem** IV.i.180 [Ariel to Prospero, Stephano, Trinculo, and Caliban following] *through ... pricking goss*

gossamer (n.) fine thread of a spider's web **RJ** II.vi.18 [Friar to himself] *A lover may bestride the gossamers / That idles in the wanton summer air*

gossip (n.) **1** godparent, baptismal sponsor **H8** V.v.12 [King Henry to Godparents] *My noble gossips;* **CE** V.i.406; **TG** III.i.268; **WT** II.iii.41

2 friend, neighbour **MW** IV.ii.8 [Mistress Page to Mistress Ford] *What ho, gossip Ford;* **2H4** II.i.92; **MV** III.i.6; **RJ** II.i.11 ➤ **ADDRESS FORMS**, p.8

3 tattler, chatterer, idle talker **Tit** IV.ii.149 [Aaron to Demetrius, of the Nurse] *A long-tongued, babbling gossip?;* **R3** I.i.83; **RJ** III.v.171

4 old woman, gossiping woman **MND** II.i.47 [Puck to Fairy] *sometime lurk I in a gossip's bowl;* **RJ** III.v.174

gossip (v.) **1** be a close companion, talk together **MND** II.i.125 [Titania to Oberon, of the mother of her attendant] *Full often hath she gossiped by my side;* **CE** V.i.408

2 act as a godparent, be a sponsor **AW** I.i.172 [Helena to Parolles] *a world … / That blinking Cupid gossips*

gossiping (*n.*) merry-making, joyful meeting **CE** V.i.420 [Dromio of Ephesus to Dromio of Syracuse, of the others] *Will you walk in to see their gossiping?*; **KJ** V.ii.59

gossip-like (*adj.*) gossiping, tattling, chattering **MA** V.i.179 [Benedick to Claudio] *I will leave you now to your gossip-like humour*

got (*v.*) ☞ get (*v.*)

gourd (*n.*) type of loaded dice **MW** I.iii.80 [Pistol to Nym] *gourd and fullam holds, / And high and low beguiles the rich and poor* [i.e. high and low numbers from the dice]

gout (*n.*) drop, spot, trace **Mac** II.i.46 [Macbeth alone, as if to a dagger] *on thy blade and dudgeon, gouts of blood*

govern (*v.*) **1** restrain, control, hold in check **Luc** 602 [Lucrece to Tarquin] *kings like gods should govern every thing*; **KL** V.iii.159
2 guide, direct, lead **Sonn** 113.2 *mine eye is in my mind, / And that which governs me to go about / Doth part his function*; **Tit** V.ii.139

governess (*n.*) ruler, mistress **Luc** 443 [of the veins on Lucrece's breasts] *the quiet cabinet / Where their dear governess and lady lies*; **MND** II.i.103

government (*n.*) **1** control, charge, management **1H4** IV.i.19 [Hotspur to Messenger, of Northumberland's army] *Under whose government come they along?*; **Cym** II.iv.150; **1H6** II.i.64; **MM** IV.ii.133; **MND** V.i.123; **RJ** IV.i.102
2 self-control, self-discipline, moral conduct **3H6** I.iv.132 [York to Queen, of women] *'Tis government that makes them seem divine*; **1H4** III.i.178; **H8** II.iv.138; **Luc** 1400; **MM** III.i.195; **Oth** III.iii.254

governor (*n.*) tutor, mentor **1H6** I.i.171 [Exeter to all, of himself and Henry VI] *Being ordained his special governor*

gown (*n.*) **1** loose upper garment worn by men **Per** II.i.79 [First Fisherman to Pericles] *I have a gown here!*; **3H6** IV.iii.29; **Per** II.i.164; **Tem** IV.i.227
2 dressing-gown, nightgown **RJ** I.i.75 [stage direction] *Enter old Capulet in his gown*; **2H4** III.i.181; **JC** II.iii.229

grace (*n.*) **1** honour, favour, recognition, respect **1H6** I.iv.7 [Master Gunner to Boy] *Something I must do to procure me grace*; **AW** V.ii.46; **1H4** V.iv.156; **2H4** V.v.6; **JC** III.ii.58; **R2** III.iii.181
2 virtue, good quality **H8** I.ii.122 [King Henry to Queen Katherine, of Buckingham] *he … / Hath into monstrous habits put the graces / That once were his*; **2H4** V.v.55; **H5** I.ii.243; **R3** II.iv.13; **RJ** II.iii.11; **TC** I.iii.180
3 personal duty, sense of propriety **Cym** I.ii.67 [Cymbeline to Innogen, of her feelings] *Past grace? obedience?*; **MW** II.ii.109
4 gracefulness, charm, elegance **TNK** III.vi.69 [Emilia to Servant, of Palamon] *He looked all grace and success*; **AW** V.iii.216; **LL** V.ii.848; **Oth** IV.iii.20; **Per** IV.Chorus.9; **TG** IV.ii.41
5 favour, good will **R3** II.i.78 [Queen Elizabeth to King Edward] *take our brother Clarence to your grace*; **AC** III.xii.19; **2H4** IV.iv.28; **KL** II.iv.181; **Tem** V.i.296; **Tim** III.v.95
6 pardon, clemency **1H4** V.i.106 [King Henry to Worcester, of the rebels] *And will they take the offer of our grace*
7 success, favourable outcome, fortune **TNK** V.i.108 [Theseus to Palamon, of Mars] *to Arcite gave / The grace of the contention*; **MND** II.ii.95; **R3** III.iv.96; **TG** III.i.146
8 means of salvation, divine favour **LL** I.i.150 [Berowne to King] *every man with his affects is born, / Not by might mastered, but by special grace*; **Cym** I.ii.68; **TC** III.i.15; **Tim** II.ii.91
9 grace before meals, prayer of thanksgiving **LL** IV.ii.153 [Holofernes to Nathaniel] *if before repast it shall please you to gratify the table with a grace*; **Tim** I.ii.61; **Tit** IV.iii.99
10 procedure, attitude, affectation **2H4** II.i.192 [Falstaff to Lord Chief Justice] *This is the right fencing grace, my lord*; **MV** III.iv.65
11 model of beauty, exquisite being [as one of the Three Graces] **TC** I.ii.236 [Pandarus to Cressida, of Troilus] *Had I a sister were a grace, or a daughter a goddess, he should take his choice* ☞ **GODS AND GODDESSES**, p.620

12 herb of grace **AC** IV.ii.38 [Antony to Enobarbus, of the servants' tears] *Grace grow where those drops fall!* [also: sense 8]

grace (*v.*) **1** favour, add merit to, do honour to **1H6** II.iv.81 [Somerset to Suffolk] *We grace the yeoman by conversing with him*; **AW** I.i.79; **H5** III.vi.67; **JC** III.i.58; **R2** V.vi.51; **Sonn** 132.11
2 gain honour, get credit **AY** I.i.139 [Oliver to Charles, of Orlando] *if he do not mightily grace himself on thee* [i.e. by defeating you]
3 give credit to, lend plausibility to **KJ** IV.ii.62 [Pembroke to King John, of Arthur's imprisonment] *That the time's enemies may not have this / To grace occasions*
4 show mercy to, reprieve **E3** II.i.397 [Warwick to Countess] *The lion doth become his bloody jaws, / And grace his foragement by being mild*

graced (*adj.*) **1** stately, dignified, gracious **KL** I.iv.242 [Gonerill to Lear, of her court] *more like a tavern or a brothel / Than a graced palace*; **Mac** III.iv.40 ☞ well-graced (*adj.*)
2 honoured, favoured **TG** I.iii.58 [Proteus to Antonio, of Valentine] *daily graced by the Emperor*

graceful (*adj.*) **1** full of grace, virtuous, upright **WT** V.i.170 [Leontes to Florizel] *You have a holy father, / A graceful gentleman*
2 favourable, friendly, approving **AC** II.ii.64 [Antony to Caesar] *I … / Could not with graceful eyes attend those wars / Which fronted mine own peace*

graceless (*adj.*) wicked, ungodly, immoral **KJ** IV.iii.58 [Bastard to all, of Arthur's apparent murder] *The graceless action of a heavy hand*; **E3** II.i.374, 430; **2H6** IV.iv.38; **TS** V.ii.159

gracious (*adj.*) **1** filled with divine grace, godly, devout **Mac** III.i.65 [Macbeth alone, of Banquo's sons] *For them the gracious Duncan have I murdered*; **KJ** III.iv.81, 96
2 holy, sanctified **Ham** I.i.165 [Marcellus to Horatio, of Christmas night] *So hallowed and so gracious is that time*; **Sonn** 79.3
3 blessed, happy, joyful **Cym** V.v.402 [Innogen to Belarius] *You … did relieve me, / To see this gracious season*; **Ham** V.ii.85
4 in favour, enjoying grace, esteemed **3H6** III.iii.117 [Lewis to Warwick, of Edward] *is he gracious in the people's eye?*; **AY** I.ii.175; **Tit** I.i.11
5 showing favour, displaying benevolence **Sonn** 10.11 *Be, as thy presence is, gracious and kind*; **Sonn** 7.1; **Tit** I.i.81
6 good, virtuous, well-behaved **WT** IV.ii.26 [Polixenes to Camillo, of Florizel] *Kings are no less unhappy, their issue not being gracious, than they are in losing them when they have approved their virtues*
7 acceptable, righteous, full of favour **TC** II.ii.126 [Troilus to Hector, of a quarrel] *Which hath our several honours all engaged / To make it gracious*
8 pleasing, agreeable, inspired **TN** II.iii.21 [Sir Andrew to Feste] *thou wast in very gracious fooling last night*
9 delightful, lovely, charming **TG** III.i.356 [Launce to Speed, of wealth] *that word makes the faults gracious*; **Cor** II.i.168; **MA** IV.i.106; **MND** IV.i.215; **MV** III.ii.76
10 graceful, elegant, attractive **Sonn** 135.7 *Shall will in others seem right gracious*; **TN** I.v.251

graciously (*adv.*) through divine grace, in all holiness **MM** II.iv.77 [Isabella to Angelo] *Let me be ignorant, and in nothing good / But graciously to know I am no better*; **Per** IV.vi.56

gradation (*n.*) **1** step-by-step progress, steady steps **MM** IV.iii.98 [disguised Duke alone] *By cold gradation … / We shall proceed with Angelo*
2 seniority, relative rank, career advancement **Oth** I.i.37 [Iago to Roderigo] *Preferment goes by letter and affection, / And not by old gradation, where each second / Stood heir to th'first*

graff (*n.*) **1** grafted plant **Per** V.i.57 [Lysimachus to Helicanus] *God / For every graff would send a caterpillar*
2 graft, shoot, scion **Luc** 1062 [Lucrece as if to Collatine] *This bastard graff shall never come to growth*

graff (v.) graft **AY** III.ii.113 [Rosalind to Touchstone] *I'll graff it with you, and then I shall graff it with a medlar* ☛ **graft** (v.)

graffing (n.) grafting **2H4** V.iii.3 [Shallow to Falstaff] *we will eat a last year's pippin of mine own graffing*

graft (v.) insert, implant, make grow **WT** I.ii.246 [Leontes to Camillo] *thou art … / A servant grafted in my serious trust / And therein negligent; **AW** I.ii.54; **2H6** III.ii.214; **R2** III.iv.101; **R3** III.vii.126 ☛ **graff** (v.)

grafter (n.) tree from which a graft has been taken **H5** III.v.9 [Dauphin to all, of the English] *Shall a few sprays of us … / Spirt up so suddenly into the clouds, / And overlook their grafters?*

grain, in inherent, ingrained, indelible **TN** I.v.227 [Olivia to Viola as Cesario, of her face] *'Tis in grain … 'twill endure wind and weather; **CE** III.ii.111

grained (adj.) **1** straight-grained, tough, strong **Cor** IV.v.111 [Aufidius to Coriolanus, of the latter's body] *whereagainst / My grained ash an hundred times hath broke; **Lover** 64

2 furrowed, lined, wrinkled **CE** V.i.312 [Egeon to Antipholus and Dromio of Ephesus] *this grained face of mine*

3 ingrained, indelible, fast-dyed **Ham** III.iv.91 [Gertrude to Hamlet] *such black and grained spots* [F; Q2 *greeued*]

gramercy, gramercies (int.) great thanks **Tit** I.i.498 [Saturninus to Titus, of hunting with him] *Be it so, Titus, and gramercy too; **Tim** II.ii.71 ☛ **POLITENESS**, p.340

grand (adj.) chief, pre-eminent, great **AC** III.i.9 [Silius to Ventidius] *thy grand captain, Antony*

grandam (n.) grandmother **KJ** I.i.168 [Queen Eleanor to Bastard] *I am thy grandam; **LL** V.ii.17; **Mac** III.iv.65; **MV** II.ii.184; **R3** IV.iv.299; **TC** I.iii.299 ☛ **FAMILY**, p.168

grand guard piece of tournament armour protecting the chest and left shoulder **TNK** III.vi.58 [Arcite to Palamon] *You care not for a grand guard?* ☛ **WEAPONS**, p.491

grandjuror (n.) person who has served on a grand jury **1H4** II.ii.90 [Falstaff to Travellers] *You are grandjurors, are ye?* [i.e. men of substance]

grandsire (n.) **1** grandfather **Tit** V.iii.160 [Lucius to Young Lucius] *Thy grandsire loved thee well; **MV** I.i.84; **MW** I.i.54; **RJ** II.iv.31; **TC** IV.v.196; **Tit** III.i.49 ☛ **FAMILY**, p.168

2 old man, aged person **TS** IV.v.50 [Petruchio to Vincentio] *good old grandsire; **Ham** II.ii.462

grandsire (adj.) long-established, old-fashioned **RJ** I.iv.37 [Romeo to all] *I am proverbed with a grandsire phrase*

grange (n.) country house, farmhouse **Oth** I.i.107 [Brabantio to Roderigo] *My house is not a grange; **MM** III.i.265; **WT** IV.iv.301

grant (n.) **1** consent, permission, approval **3H6** III.iii.130 [Bona to Lewis, of marrying Edward] *Your grant, or your denial, shall be mine*

2 granting, gift, reason for agreeing to a request **MA** I.i.296 [Don Pedro to Claudio] *The fairest grant is the necessity* [i.e. what meets a need]

3 granting of titles, conveyance of land **H5** V.ii.330 [Exeter to King Henry, of the French King] *having any occasion to write for matter of grant*

grant (v.) **1** acknowledge, confess, affirm **Cym** V.v.15 [Cymbeline to Belarius, Arviragus and Guiderius] *you, the liver, heart, and brain of Britain, / By whom (I grant) she lives*

2 submit, yield, assent **3H6** I.i.245 [Queen to King, of entailing the succession to York] *The soldiers should have tossed me on their pikes / Before I would have granted to that act*

granted (adj.) acknowledged, admitted, recognized **Cym** II.i.46 [Second Lord to himself, of Cloten] *You are a fool granted*

grapple (v.) join, fasten, bind **KJ** V.ii.36 [Salisbury to Lewis the Dauphin, as if to England] *Neptune's arms, who clippeth thee about, / Would … grapple thee unto a pagan shore* [F *cripple*]

grasp (n.) embrace, clasp **TC** IV.ii.13 [Troilus to Cressida, of night] *With venomous wights she … flies the grasps of love*

grasp in (v.) embrace, clasp in the arms **TC** III.iii.168 [Ulysses to Achilles, of time] *slightly shakes his parting guest by th'hand, / And … / Grasps in the comer*

grass (v.) graze, feed, eat pasture **2H6** IV.ii.65 [Cade to all] *in Cheapside shall my palfrey go to grass*

grate (n.) **1** grating, grill, lattice **1H6** I.iv.60 [Salisbury to all, of the French] *Here, through this grate, I count each one; **1H6** I.iv.10

2 prison bars, grating, cage **MW** II.ii.9 [Falstaff to Pistol] *else you had looked through the grate, like a geminy of baboons*

grate (v.) **1** harass, irritate, aggravate **AC** I.i.18 [Antony to Messenger, of the news] *Grates me!; **Ham** III.i.3

2 wear away, pulverise, erode through the rubbing away of time **TC** III.ii.186 [Cressida to Troilus] *When … mighty states characterless are grated / To dusty nothing*

grate on / upon (v.) pester, harass, make heavy demands on **2H4** IV.i.90 [Westmorland to Archbishop] *What peer hath been suborned to grate on you; **MW** II.ii.6

grateful (adj.) pleasing, agreeable, gratifying **TS** II.i.76 [Gremio to Baptista] *this is a gift very grateful; **TNK** IV.iii.84

gratify (v.) **1** reward, repay, show gratitude for **MV** IV.i.403 [Duke to Antonio, of Portia as Balthasar] *gratify this gentleman; **Cor** II.ii.38; **Cym** II.iv.7; **Oth** V.ii.212; **Per** I.iv.101; **TS** I.ii.270

2 please, oblige, favour **LL** IV.ii.153 [Holofernes to Nathaniel] *if before repast it shall please you to gratify the table with a grace*

gratillity (n.) humorous version of 'gratuity' **TN** II.iii.25 [Feste to Sir Andrew] *I did impetticoat thy gratillity*

gratis (adv.) for nothing, without payment **MW** II.ii.16 [Falstaff to Pistol] *Thinkest thou I'll endanger my soul gratis?; **Cor** III.i.125; **Ham** II.ii.322; **2H4** IV.iii.68; **Luc** 914; **MV** III.iii.2

gratulate (adj.) gratifying, pleasing, to be rejoiced at **MM** V.i.526 [Duke to Escalus] *There's more behind that is more gratulate*

gratulate (v.) greet, welcome, salute **R3** IV.i.10 [Anne to Queen Elizabeth, of her purpose] *To gratulate the gentle princes; **E3** I.ii.87; **Tim** I.ii.123; **Tit** I.i.224

grave (n.) (plural) greave, leg-armour **2H4** IV.i.50 [Westmorland to Archbishop, of war] *Turning your books to graves, your ink to blood*

grave (adj.) **1** respected, revered, wise **E3** III.iii.128 [King Edward to Charles, of Audley] *these grave scholars of experience; **Mac** III.i.21; **MM** I.iii.5; **Tem** I.ii.189; **WT** V.iii.1

2 important, dignified, serious **AC** II.vii.118 [Caesar to Antony] *Our graver business / Frowns at this levity **Cor** II.i.57; **1H6** V.i.54; **WT** I.ii.173

3 deadly, destructive, baneful **AC** IV.xii.25 [Antony alone, of Cleopatra] *This grave charm … hath at fast and loose / Beguiled me*

grave (v.) **1** bury, inter, entomb **Tim** IV.iii.167 [Timon to all] *And ditches grave you all!; **R2** III.ii.140

2 engrave, inscribe [in], cut into **Venus** 376 [Venus to Adonis, of her heart] *being steeled, soft sighs can never grave it; **Luc** 755

grave-beseeming (adj.) suitably dignified, sober-looking **RJ** I.i.93 [Prince to all, of the quarrel] *made Verona's ancient citizens / Cast by their grave-beseeming ornaments*

graved (adj.) **1** graven, carved, engraved **MV** II.vii.36 [Morocco to himself, of the gold casket] *Let's see once more this saying graved in gold*

2 furrowed, engraved [with lines] **TNK** V.iii.46 [Emilia to herself, of Palamon] *his brow / Is graved* [also, play on 'graves' for his enemies]

gravel (n.) stones, deposits **TC** V.i.19 [Thersites to Patroclus] *diseases of the south … loads o'gravel i'th' back, lethargies*

gravelled (v.) perplexed, at a loss, stumped **AY** IV.i.67 [Rosalind to Ganymede to Orlando] *when you were gravelled for lack of matter*

graven (adj.) engraved, inscribed, sculpted **Sonn** 100.10 [of his friend's face] *If Time have any wrinkle graven there*

gravity *(n.)* **1** respectability, authority, dignified position H8 III.i.73 [Queen Katherine to and of Campeius and Wolsey] *such men of gravity and learning;* CE II.ii.177; JC II.i.149; LL V.ii.74; Sonn 49.8; TN III.iv.116

2 old age, the aged, the elderly 1H4 II.iv.287 [Falstaff to Hostess] *What doth gravity out of his bed at midnight?;* TNK V.i.85

3 wisdom, sage advice RJ III.v.174 [Capulet to Nurse] *Utter your gravity o'er a gossip's bowl*

grease *(n.)* sweat, melted fat TNK IV.iii.36 [Gaoler's Daughter to herself, of hell] *there shall we be put in a cauldron of lead and usurers' grease* [i.e. because userers were punished by being boiled in oil]

greasily *(adv.)* indecently, smuttily, in a vulgar way LL IV.i.138 [Maria to Costard] *you talk greasily*

great *(adj.)* **1** important, weighty, serious 2H6 III.ii.299 [King to Warwick] *I have great matters to impart to thee*

2 of high rank, eminent TNK IV.ii.92 [Pirithous to Theseus, comparing Palamon's knight to Arcite's] *I guess he is a prince too, / And if it may be, greater*

3 valiant, noble, honourable KL I.i.46 [Lear to all, of France and Burgundy] *Great rivals in our youngest daughter's love;* TNK IV.ii.118

4 high, full TC IV.iii.1 [Paris to all] *It is great morning* [i.e. broad daylight]; AW III.iii.2; Cym IV.ii.61

5 full of emotion R2 II.i.228 [Ross to Northumberland] *My heart is great;* 2H4 IV.iii.109; R3 V.iii.348; TS V.ii.170

6 pregnant, prolific Tim IV.iii.190 [Timon alone, as if to the earth] *Go great with tigers, dragons, wolves, and bears*

great way complete, total, absolute AW I.i.100 [Helena to herself, of Parolles] *I ... / Think him a great way fool*

great-belly *(adj.)* with lower part padded H5 IV.vii.46 [Fluellen to Gower, of Falstaff] *the fat knight with the great-belly doublet* ➤ thin-belly *(adj.)*

greatly *(adv.)* nobly, honourably Ham IV.iv.55 [Hamlet alone] *But greatly to find quarrel in a straw;* H5 Epilogue.5

greatness *(n.)* **1** power, might, authority AY I.iii.87 [Duke Frederick to Rosalind] *in the greatness of my word, you die*

2 nobility of mind, dignity of spirit AC V.i.64 [Caesar to Proculeius, of Cleopatra] *Give her what comforts / The quality of her passion shall require, / Lest in her greatness, by some mortal stroke, / She do defeat us*

grece, grise, grize *(n.)* step, degree, grade Tim IV.iii.16 [Timon alone] *every grise of fortune / Is smoothed by that below;* TN III.i.121 [Viola as Cesario to Olivia, of pity being akin to love] *No, not a grize* [i.e. not a bit]; TNK II.i.28 [Gaoler's Daughter to Gaoler, of Palamon and Arcite] *they stand a grece above the reach of report* [Q *greise*]

gree *(v.)* ➤ agree *(v.)*; ELISION, p.146

greediness *(n.)* eagerness, keenness, enthusiasm WT V.ii.100 [Third Gentleman to all, of the main protagonists going to Paulina's house] *Thither with all greediness of affection are they gone, and there they intend to sup*

Greek, foolish / merry buffoon, merry person, silly joker TC I.ii.110 [Cressida to Pandarus, of Helen loving Troilus more than Paris] *Then she's a merry Greek indeed;* TN IV.i.17 [Sebastian to Feste] *I prithee, foolish Greek, depart from me;* TC IV.iv.55

Greekish *(adj.)* Greek, Grecian TC V.i [Achilles to Patroclus, of Hector] *I'll heat his blood with Greekish wine tonight;* TC I.iii.221, III.iii.211, IV.v.130, 185, V.iv.6

green *(n.)* **1** greenery, grass, vegetation MND II.i.99 [Titania to Oberon] *the quaint mazes in the wanton green / For lack of tread are undistinguishable;* Sonn 12.7, 68.11; Tem V.i.37

2 grass-covered land, grassy mound KJ II.i.242 [King Philip to Hubert, of Arthur] *For this downtrodden equity we tread / In warlike march these greens before your town;* Per IV.i.14

green *(adj.)* **1** fresh, recent, new RJ IV.iii.42 [Juliet alone, of the tomb] *Where bloody Tybalt, yet but green in earth, / Lies festering;* Ham I.ii.2; 2H4 II.i.95; H5 V.ii.40; 2H6 III.i.287; TS IV.v.47

2 youthful, inexperienced, immature AC I.v.74 [Cleopatra to Charmian] *My salad days, / When I was green in judgement;* KJ III.iv.145; Oth II.i.239; PassP IV.2; Tim IV.i.7; Venus 806

3 weak, undeveloped R3 II.ii.127 [Buckingham to Rivers] *the estate is green and yet ungoverned;* R3 II.i.135; WT III.ii.179

greenly *(adv.)* **1** like an inexperienced youth, timidly, sheepishly H5 V.ii.142 [King Henry to Katherine] *I cannot look greenly, nor gasp out my eloquence*

2 unskilfully, like an amateur Ham IV.v.84 [Claudius to Gertrude, of Polonius] *we have done but greenly / In hugger-mugger to inter him*

green-sickness *(n.)* **1** type of illness supposed to affect lovesick young women AC III.ii.6 [Enobarbus to Agrippa] *Lepidus ... is troubled / With the green-sickness;* 2H4 IV.iii.92

2 sexual squeamishness, sickly naivety Per IV.vi.13 [Pander to Boult, of Marina] *the pox upon her green-sickness for me!*

green-sickness *(adj.)* affected by green-sickness RJ III.v.156 [Capulet to Juliet] *Out, you green-sickness carrion!*

greet *(v.)* **1** address, offer a salutation, acknowledge in words Ham IV.vi.6 [Horatio alone] *from what part of the world / I should be greeted* [i.e. by letter]; Per II.iv.19

2 please, gratify, satisfy Per IV.iii.38 [Dionyza to Cleon, of Marina's supposed murder] *It greets me as an enterprise of kindness;* Per V.ii.9

3 bewail, lament, weep for TN II.iv.60 [Feste singing] *not a friend greet / My poor corpse*

greeting *(n.)* address, speech , discourse R2 I.i.36 [Bolingbroke to Mowbray] *mark my greeting well*

greise *(n.)* ➤ grece *(n.)*

grey *(adj.)* **1** aged, senescent, very old TNK V.iv.9 [Palamon to his knights] *We ... beguile / The gout and rheum, that in lag hours attend / For grey approachers* [i.e. old people approaching death]; 1H4 II.iv.441

2 blue Tit II.ii.1 [Titus to all] *The hunt is up, the morn is bright and grey;* 2H4 II.iii.19

3 [of eyes] grey-blue, blue-tinged Venus 140 [Venus to Adonis] *Mine eyes are grey and bright;* RJ II.iv.42; TG IV.iv.189

gride *(v.)* pierce, wound, stab Tit II.iii.260 [Saturninus to Tamora] *[I am] gride with killing grief* [F *grieu'd*; Q1 *griude*] [debated reading]

grief *(n.)* **1** grievance, complaint, hurt, injury 1H4 IV.iii.42 [Blunt to Hotspur] *The King hath sent to know / The nature of your griefs;* AC II.ii.104; H8 III.i.92; JC IV.ii.42; Per II.iv.23; TC I.iii.2

2 pain, torment, distress 1H4 V.i.132 [Falstaff alone] *Can honour ... take away the grief of a wound?;* 2H4 I.ii.116; KJ IV.i.48; Mac IV.iii.174; Sonn 34.9; Tim V.iv.75

grief-shot *(adj.)* grief-stricken, inconsolable Cor V.i.45 [Menenius to Brutus, of Coriolanus] *Return me ... grief-shot / With his unkindness*

grievance *(n.)* **1** distress, suffering, pain TG I.ii.17 [Proteus to Valentine] *Commend thy grievance to my holy prayers;* Lover 67; Sonn 30.9; TG III.ii.86, IV.iii.37

2 cause of annoyance, painful constraint, source of sorrow RJ I.i.157 [Benvolio to Montague, of Romeo] *I'll know his grievance;* 2H4 IV.i.196; Oth I.ii.15

grieve *(v.)* vex, hurt, trouble TS II.i.37 [Baptista alone] *Was ever gentleman thus grieved as I?;* CE II.i.38; Per II.iv.19

grieved *(adj.)* aggrieved, wronged, ill-used H8 I.ii.104 [Wolsey aside to Secretary] *The grieved commons / Hardly conceive of me;* MA IV.i.87

grievous *(adj.)* heavy, grave, serious H8 V.i.98 [King Henry to Cranmer] *I have, and most unwillingly, of late / Heard many grievous ... complaints of you;* E3 III.iv.49

grievous *(adv.)* very, extremely 1H4 IV.i.16 [Messenger to Hotspur, of Northumberland] *He cannot come, my lord, he is grievous sick;* R2 I.iv.54

GREETINGS

The commonest modern English greetings are not found in Shakespearian English: *hello* and *hi* did not enter the language until the 19th century; and although expressions with *how* are widespread, they are generally different in form. Greetings may also be different in range of application: *good even*, for example, might be said any time after noon.

Keyword	Location	Example

A greeting with an enquiry about health or well-being

cheer	**TS** IV.iii.37	*Mistress, what cheer?*
how	**Ham** IV.vii.162	*How, sweet Queen!*
	Ham V.i.82	*How dost thou, sweet lord?*
	Ham IV.v.41	*How do you, pretty lady?*
	AY I.ii.144	*How now, daughter and cousin?*
	TS IV.iii.36	*How fares my Kate?*
well	**Ham** II.ii.379	*Well be with you, gentlemen*
	TS I.ii.161	*you are well met, Signor Hortensio*

A greeting with a divine invocation

bless	**MW** II.iii.16	*Bless thee, bully doctor!*
	Ham IV.vi.7	*God bless you, sir*
	MV II.ii.110	*God bless your worship!*
mercy	**KJ** I.i.185	*God 'a' mercy, fellow* [= God have mercy on you (somewhat patronizing)]
save	**TS** I.ii.160	*God save you, Signor Gremio*
	MW II.iii.17	*Save you, Master Doctor Caius!*
speed	**R3** II.iii.6	*Neighbours, God speed!*

A greeting for a time of day

dawning	**KL** II.ii.1	*Good dawning to thee, friend*
day	**Tim** I.i.1	*Good day, sir*
	Tim III.iv.6	*Good day at once* [= to one and all]
	Tim III.vi.1	*The good time of day to you, sir*
morrow	**Ham** V.i.81	*Good morrow, sweet lord!*
	MW II.iii.19	*Give you good morrow, sir*
	MW II.ii.32	*Give your worship good morrow*
	RJ II.iv.106	*God ye good-morrow, gentlemen*
even [= evening]	**AY** IV.i.13	*Good even, Audrey*
	AY V.i.14	*God ye good even, William*
	MW II.i.182	*Good even and twenty, good Master Page* [i.e. twenty times over]
	RJ I.ii.56	*Good-e'en, good fellow*
	RJ I.ii.57	*God gi' good-e'en*
	LL IV.i.42	*God dig-you-den all!*
	KJ I.i.185	*Good den, Sir Richard*

A greeting to monarchs

befall	**R2** I.i.20	*Many years of happy days befall / My gracious sovereign*
greeting	**AC** V.ii.9	*Caesar sends greeting to the Queen of Egypt*
hail	**KL** II.iv.122	*Hail to your grace*
peace	**KJ** II.i.84	*Peace be to France*
save	**R2** II.ii.41	*God save your majesty*
welcome	**AC** II.ii.28	*Welcome to Rome*

Some of these expressions are also used in leave-taking: ➤ **FAREWELLS**, p.170.

grievously *(adv.)* **1** sorrowfully, deeply, with great grief **TG** III.ii.14 [Duke to Proteus, of Valentine] *My daughter takes his going grievously;* **Oth** V.i.53

2 seriously, greatly **JC** III.ii.81 [Antony to all, of Caesar being ambitious] *grievously hath Caesar answered it;* **KJ** IV.iii.134; **MW** IV.iv.20

griffin *(n.)* fabulous beast, part lion part eagle **MND** II.i.232 [Helena to Demetrius] *The dove pursues the griffin;* **1H4** III.i.146

grim-looked *(adj.)* grim-looking, forbidding **MND** V.i.167 [Bottom as Pyramus] *O grim-looked night, O night with hue so black*

grim-visaged *(adj.)* with a stern face **R3** I.i.9 [Richard alone] *Grim-visaged war hath smoothed his wrinkled front*

grin *(v.)* bare the teeth, grimace, snarl **Venus** 459 *as the wolf doth grin before he barketh;* **2H6** III.i.18, iii.24, IV.i.77; **3H6** I.iv.56

grind *(v.)* **1** torment, afflict, plague **Tem** IV.i.259 [Prospero to Ariel, of Caliban, Stephano and Trinculo] *charge my goblins that they grind their joints / With dry convulsions*

2 whet, sharpen, stimulate **Sonn** 110.11 *Mine appetite I never more will grind / On newer proof, to try an older friend*

gripe *(n.)* **1** grip, hold, grasp **Mac** III.i.61 [Macbeth alone, of the Witches] *they … put a barren sceptre in my gripe* [F]; **Cym** I.vii.106, III.i.41; **H8** V.iii.100

2 vulture, eagle **Luc** 543 [of Lucrece held by Tarquin] *Like a white hind under the gripe's sharp claws*

gripe *(v.)* clutch, grasp, seize **MW** I.iii.80 [Pistol to Nym, as if to Falstaff] *Let vultures gripe thy guts!;* **1H4** V.i.57; **3H6** I.iv.171; **KJ** IV.ii.190; **Per** I.i.50; **R2** II.i.189

griping *(adj.)* voracious, grasping, devouring **E3** III.i.89 [Mariner to King John, of the French fleet] *as when the empty eagle flies / To satisfy his hungry griping maw*

grise *(n.)* **1** step, stair **Oth** I.iii.198 [Duke to Brabantio] *Let me … lay a sentence / Which as a grise or step may help these lovers / Into your favour*

2 ☞ *grece (n.)*

grisled *(adj.)* grisly, frightening, horrible **Per** III.Chorus.47 [Gower alone] *the grisled north / Disgorges such a tempest forth*

grisly *(adj.)* grim, ghastly, menacing **1H6** I.iv.47 [Talbot to all, of the French] *My grisly countenance made others fly*

grize *(n.)* ☞ *grece (n.)*

grizzle *(n.)* sprinkling of grey hairs **TN** V.i.163 [Orsino to Viola as Cesario] *What wilt thou be / When time hath sowed a grizzle on thy case?*

grizzled *(adj.)* grey, sprinkled with grey hairs **AC** III.xiii.17 [Antony to Ambassador] *To the boy Caesar send this grizzled head;* **Ham** I.ii.240

groan *(v.)* utter groans during childbirth **TNK** III.vi.245 [Emilia to Theseus, of Palamon and Arcite] *The goodly mothers that have groaned for these*

groaning *(adj.)* crying out in labour **MM** II.ii.15 [Provost to Angelo] *What shall be done … with the groaning Juliet?*

groat *(n.)* ☞ **MONEY,** p.286

groom *(n.)* **1** servingman, servant, male attendant **Mac** II.ii.50 [Lady Macbeth to Macbeth] *smear / The sleepy grooms with blood;* **H8** IV.i.172; **Luc** 671; **Mac** II.ii.5; **Tit** V.ii.163; **TS** III.i.151 [also: sense 3]

2 fellow, character, creature **TS** IV.i.111 [Petruchio to Servants] *You logger-headed and unpolished grooms!;* **E3** V.i.22; **2H6** IV.i.130, ii.116; **KL** II.iv.212; **Per** IV.vi.189

3 bridegroom **Cym** V.iii.42 [Guiderius to disguised Innogen] *Were you a woman … / I should woo hard, but be your groom in honesty;* **TS** III.ii.151 [also: sense 1]

gross *(n.)* overall total, whole amount **MV** III.ii.158 [Portia to Bassanio, of her qualities] *which to term in gross, / Is an unlessoned girl;* **Ham** I.i.68

gross, by / by the in large quantities, wholesale **LL** V.ii.319 [Berowne to all, of Boyet selling wit] *we that sell by gross … / Have*

not the grace to grace it with such show; **WT** IV.iv.208 [Servant to Clown, of Autolycus] *He hath … points more than all the lawyers in Bohemia can learnedly handle, though they come to him by th'gross*

gross *(adj.)* **1** plain, striking, evident, obvious **H5** II.ii.103 [King Henry to Scroop] *the truth of it stands off as gross / As black and white;* **E3** II.i.143; **MM** I.ii.154; **MW** III.ii.177; **Oth** III.iii.401; **Tim** III.v.39 ☞ *general-gross (adj.)*

2 large, big, huge **KL** IV.vi.14 [Edgar to Gloucester] *The crows and choughs … / Show scarce so gross as beetles;* **1H4** II.iv.222; **LL** V.ii.268; **Oth** III.iii.217

3 whole, total, entire **AY** IV.i.180 [Rosalind as Ganymede to Orlando] *chosen out of the gross band of the unfaithful;* **2H4** II.i.82; **LL** I.ii.45

4 excessively large, coarsely luxuriant **Ham** I.ii.136 [Hamlet alone, of the world] *Things rank and gross in nature / Possess it merely*

5 heavy, weighty, bulky **Venus** 150 [Venus to Adonis, of love] *Not gross to sink, but light;* **Ham** IV.iv.46; **1H4** II.iv.496

6 bad, inferior, poor **LL** IV.iii.315 [Berowne to all] *Love's tongue proves dainty Bacchus gross in taste;* **AC** V.ii.212; **H5** III.i.24; **Luc** 1655; **MV** II.vii.50; **Sonn** 82.13

7 coarse, vulgar, unrefined **Ham** IV.vii.170 [Gertrude to Claudius and Laertes] */ That liberal shepherds give a grosser name;* **2H4** IV.iv.73; **H5** II.ii.132; **LL** I.i.29; **MW** III.iii.38

8 vile, abhorrent, wicked **Oth** V.ii.309 [Cassio to Othello, of Iago's plots] *Most heathenish and most gross!;* **KL** I.i.5; **Luc** 1315; **RJ** II.iv.163; **Sonn** 151.6; **WT** I.ii.301

9 dull, obtuse, ignorant **TN** II.v.156 [Malvolio to himself] *I will wash off gross acquaintance;* **CE** III.ii.34; **E3** III.i.19; **H5** IV.i.275; **R3** III.vi.10 ☞ *palpable-gross (adj.)*

10 earthly, lowly **MM** II.ii.87 [Isabella to Angelo] *Shall we serve heaven / With less respect than we do minister / To our gross selves?*

gross *(adv.)* plainly, obviously, explicitly **MM** II.iv.82 [Angelo to Isabella] *I'll speak more gross: / Your brother is to die*

grossly *(adv.)* **1** openly, blatantly, brazenly **AC** III.x.28 [Canidius to all, of Antony] *he has given example for our flight / Most grossly by his own;* **CE** II.ii.178; **H5** II.ii.107; **KJ** V.ii.94; **KL** I.i.291; **Oth** III.iii.392

2 obviously, plainly, palpably **AW** I.iii.173 [Countess to Helena, of Helena's love for Bertram] *thine eyes / See it so grossly shown in thy behaviours;* **Sonn** 99.5

3 materially, physically, with substance **MV** V.i.65 [Lorenzo to Jessica, of harmony in immortal souls] *whilst this muddy vesture of decay / Doth grossly close it in, we cannot hear it;* **TN** V.i.234

4 stupidly, senselessly, foolishly **R3** IV.i.79 [Anne to Queen Elizabeth, of Richard] *my woman's heart / Grossly grew captive to his honey words;* **KJ** III.i.163; **MM** III.i.18, V.i.469

5 in a state of excess, with great sins unabsolved **Ham** III.iii.80 [Hamlet to himself, of Claudius] *'A took my father grossly*

6 coarsely, indelicately, indecently **MV** V.i.266 [Portia to Gratiano] *Speak not so grossly*

grossness *(n.)* **1** flagrant nature, obviousness, enormity **MW** V.v.124 [Falstaff to all] *the sudden surprise of my powers, drove the grossness of the foppery into a received belief … that they were fairies;* **MV** III.ii.80; **TC** I.iii.325; **TN** II.ii.68

2 material nature, bodily form **MND** III.i.151 [Titania to Bottom] *I will purge thy mortal grossness*

3 unrefined nature, deplorable standard, coarseness **R3** III.i.46 [Buckingham to Cardinal Bourchier, of seizing York from sanctuary] *Weigh it but with the grossness of this age*

ground *(n.)* **1** reason, cause, source **Per** V.i.25 [Lysimachus to Helicanus, of Pericles] *Upon what ground is his distemperature?;* **CE** II.i.97; **E3** II.i.58; **R3** I.iii.68; **WT** II.i.159

2 foundation, basis, root **TNK** I.iii.56 [Emilia to Hippolyta, of Theseus' and Pirithous' love] *Theirs has more ground;* **AW** III.vii.3; **LL** IV.iii.294 [F, Q]; **TS** III.i.71

3 advantage, upper hand, edge **2H4** II.iii.53 [Lady Percy to Northumberland, of the rebels] *If they get ground and vantage of the King;* **Cym** I.v.101

4 face of the earth, globe **1H4** IV.i.11 [Douglas to Hotspur, of Hotspur] *No man so potent breathes upon the ground / But I will beard him*

5 land, country **Ham** I.i.15 [Horatio to Francisco, identifying himself and Marcellus] *Friends to this ground*

6 green, surface, lawn **Cor** V.ii.20 [Menenius to First Watch] *Like to a bowl upon a subtle ground*

7 valley, area of low-lying countryside **PassP** IX.8 [of Cytherea and Adonis] *She, silly queen, … / Forbade the boy he should not pass those grounds*

8 bottom [as of the sea] **2H4** IV.i.17 [Mowbray to Archbishop, of Northumberland] *Thus do the hopes we have in him touch ground / And dash themselves to pieces;* **1H4** I.iii.202; **2H4** IV.iv.40

9 background, surface, setting **1H4** I.ii.210 [Prince Hal alone] *like bright metal on a sullen ground;* **Luc** 1074

10 [music] constant bass rhythm underneath a descant, foundation **E3** II.i.123 [King Edward to Lodowick] *what a world of descant makes my soul / Upon this voluntary ground of love!;* **R3** III.vii.48

grounded (*adj.*) firmly established, deep-rooted, strongly founded **R3** I.iii.29 [Derby to Queen Elizabeth, of the Countess of Richmond] *her weakness … proceeds / From wayward sickness, and no grounded malice;* **Sonn** 62.4

groundlings (*n.*) audience standing in a theatre courtyard **Ham** III.ii.10 [Hamlet to Players] *split the ears of the groundlings*

ground-piece (*n.*) [unclear meaning] painting used as a teaching-aid **TNK** I.i.122 [Emilia to Third Queen] *If that you were / The ground-piece of some painter* ☛ **piece** (*n.*) 1

grovelling (*adj.*) prone, prostrate, lying flat **KJ** II.ii.305 [French Herald to Hubert, of the English] *Many a widow's husband grovelling lies*

grow (*v.*) **1** arise, come into existence **CE** IV.i.8 [Angelo to Second Merchant] *Even just the sum that I do owe to you / Is growing to me by Antipholus;* **CE** IV.iv.119, 132; **WT** I.ii.431

2 approach, move, draw **1H6** V.iv.149 [Richard to Charles] *now the matter grows to compromise;* **JC** II.i.107

grow to (*v.*) be an integral part of, become one with **2H4** I.ii.87 [Falstaff to Servant] *I lay aside that which grows to me?;* **MV** II.ii.15

grow unto (*v.*) cling to, stick to, be one with **Ham** IV.vii.84 [Claudius to Laertes, of Lamord] *He grew unto his seat;* **Cym** I.iv.1

grow upon (*v.*) take liberties with, trouble; also: grow up [too fast] **AY** I.i.80 [Oliver alone, of Orlando] *Begin you to grow upon me?*

grub (*n.*) maggot, worm **RJ** V.iii.126 [Friar to Balthasar] *What torch is yond that vainly lends his light / To grubs and eyeless skulls?*

grub up (*v.*) dig up, uproot **H8** V.i.23 [Gardiner to Lovell, of Queen Anne as a plant] *I wish it grubbed up now*

grudge (*n.*) murmuring, complaining, reluctance **Tem** I.ii.249 [Ariel to Prospero] *I have … served / Without or grudge or grumblings*

grudge (*v.*) grumble, complain, be discontented **TNK** III.v.297 [Theseus to all, of the loser] *nor shall he grudge to fall;* **1H6** III.i.178

grudging (*adj.*) resentful, embittered, aggrieved **1H6** IV.i.141 [King to all, of the French] *How will their grudging stomachs be provoked / To wilful disobedience;* **R3** II.i.9

grumble (*v.*) mutter, mumble, growl **KL** III.iv.42 [disguised Kent to Edgar as Poor Tom] *What art thou that dost grumble there i'the straw?*

grumbling (*adj.*) querulous, discontented, carping **3H6** I.iv.76 [Queen to York, of Richard] *with his grumbling voice*

guard (*n.*) **1** protection, keeping, custody **Cor** I.x.25 [Aufidius to First Soldier, of Coriolanus] *Where I find him, were it / At home upon my brother's guard* [i.e. under my brother's protection]; **CE** V.i.149; **MV** I.iii.172

2 safeguard, escort, safe conduct **TC** V.ii.187 [Aeneas to Troilus] *Ajax, your guard, stays to conduct you home*

3 period of watch **AC** IV.vi.23 [Soldier to Enobarbus] *The messenger / Came on my guard*

4 [fencing] defensive position, posture of defence **MM** I.iii.51 [Duke to Friar Thomas, of Angelo] *Stands at a guard with envy*

5 trimming, trapping, adornment **LL** IV.iii.56 [Berowne to himself] *rhymes are guards on wanton Cupid's hose;* **2H4** I.ii.148; **MA** I.i.266; **MM** III.i.100 ☛ **velvet-guard** (*n.*)

guard (*v.*) **1** safeguard, protect, justify **Sonn** 49.12 *this my hand, against myself uprear / To guard the lawful reasons on thy part*

2 escort, accompany [under guard] **2H4** IV.ii.122 [Prince John to guards, of Archbishop, Hastings, and Mowbray] *Some guard these traitors to the block of death*

3 adorn, ornament, deck out **KJ** IV.ii.10 [Salisbury to King John] *To guard a title that was rich before* ☛ **guarded** (*adj.*)

guardage (*n.*) guardianship, protection, keeping **Oth** I.ii.70 [Brabantio to Othello, of Desdemona] *Run from her guardage to the sooty bosom / Of such a thing as thou*

guardant (*n.*) guard, protector, keeper **1H6** IV.vii.9 [Talbot to Servant, of John Talbot] *when my angry guardant stood alone;* **Cor** V.ii.60

guarded (*adj.*) ornamented, trimmed, tricked out **MV** II.ii.144 [Bassanio to servant, of Launcelot] *Give him a livery / More guarded than his fellows';* **2H4** IV.i.34; **MA** I.i.265 ☛ **guard** (*v.*) 3

gudgeon (*n.*) type of fish used as a bait; credulity, gullibility **MV** I.i.102 [Gratiano to Antonio] *fish not with this melancholy bait / For this fool gudgeon, this opinon*

guerdon (*n.*) [pron: ˈgerdn] reward, recompense **MA** V.iii.5 [Claudio, reading from a scroll about Hero] *Death, in guerdon of her wrongs, / Gives her fame;* **LL** III.i.165

guerdon (*v.*) reward, recompense **3H6** III.iii.191 [Warwick to Lewis] *am I guerdoned at the last with shame?;* **2H6** I.iv.45

guess (*n.*) conjecture, opinion, view **Sonn** 69.10 [of observers] *They look into the beauty of thy mind, / And that in guess they measure by thy deeds;* **AW** II.i.150; **JC** I.i.3

guess (*v.*) **1** assume, surmise, suppose **TNK** III.i.109 [Arcite to Palamon, of the banquet] *you must guess / I have an office there* [i.e. as you can imagine]; **Cor** I.i.17

2 recall, remember, bring to mind **3H6** IV.i.90 [Edward to the Post, of the French response] *Tell me their words as near as thou canst guess them*

guessingly (*adv.*) as conjecture, by guesswork **KL** III.vii.47 [Gloucester to all] *I have a letter guessingly set down*

guestwise (*adv.*) in the manner of a guest, as a visitor **MND** III.ii.171 [Demetrius to Lysander, of Hermia] *My heart to her but as guestwise sojourned*

guide (*n.*) guidance, direction, conduct **Tim** I.i.247 [Timon to Messenger, of Alcibiades' company] *give them guide to us*

guider (*n.*) guide, scout **Cor** I.vii.7 [Lartius to Lieutenant] *Our guider, come; to th'Roman camp conduct us*

guidon (*n.*) pennant, flag **H5** IV.ii.58 [Constable to Dauphin] *I stay but for my guidon*

guilder (*n.*) ☛ **MONEY**, p.286

guile (*n.*) cunning, deceit, treachery **1H6** IV.i.63 [Gloucester to all, of Burgundy] *such false dissembling guile*

guiled (*adj.*) treacherous, deceiving, full of guile **MV** III.ii.97 [Bassanio to himself] *ornament is but the guiled shore / To a most dangerous sea*

guileful (*adj.*) full of guile, deceitful, devious **Tit** V.i.104 [Aaron to Lucius, of Quintus and Martius] *I trained thy brethren to that guileful hole;* **1H6** I.i.77

guiltless (*adj.*) of innocent people **2H6** IV.vii.95 [Say to Cade] *These hands are free from guiltless bloodshedding*

guilty (*adj.*) **1** shameful, culpable, reprehensible **TNK** III.i.90 [Palamon to Arcite] *dares any / So noble bear a guilty business?*

2 responsible [for], answerable [for] **KL** I.ii.120 [Edmund alone] *we make guilty of our disasters the sun, the moon, and stars*

guinea-hen *(n.)* trollop, courtesan, prostitute **Oth** I.iii.312 [Iago to Roderigo] *Ere I would say I would drown myself for the love of a guinea-hen*

guise *(n.)* way, custom, practice **Mac** V.i.19 [Gentlewoman to Doctor, of Lady Macbeth] *This is her very guise;* **Cym** V.i.32; **2H6** I.iii.40; **Tim** IV.iii.468; **Venus** 1177

gules *(adj.)* [heraldry] red **Tim** IV.iii.60 [Timon to Alcibiades] *With man's blood paint the ground gules;* **Ham** II.ii.455

gulf *(n.)* **1** whirlpool **H5** II.iv.10 [French King to Dauphin] *England his approaches makes as fierce / As waters to the sucking of a gulf;* **CE** II.ii.135; **Ham** III.iii.16; **H5** IV.iii.82; **3H6** V.vi.25

2 abyss, chasm, pit **Cor** III.ii.91 [Volumnia to Coriolanus] *thou hadst rather / Follow thine enemy in a fiery gulf / Than flatter him in a bower;* **Cor** I.i.96

3 huge stomach, voracious gut **Mac** IV.i.23 [Third Witch to Witches] *maw and gulf / Of the ravined salt sea shark*

gull *(n.)* **1** dupe, fool, simpleton **H5** III.vi.66 [Gower to Fluellen, of Pistol] *'tis a gull, a fool, a rogue;* **Oth** V.ii.162; **R3** I.iii.327; **TN** III.ii.65, V.i.204, 341

2 trick, hoax, deception **MA** II.iii.120 [Benedick to himself, of what the others are saying] *I should think this is a gull*

3 unfledged bird **1H4** V.i.60 [Worcester to King Henry] *you used us so / As that ungentle gull the cuckoo's bird / Useth the sparrow;* **Tim** II.i.31

gull *(v.)* deceive, dupe, trick **H5** II.ii.121 [King Henry to Scroop] *that same demon that hath gulled thee thus;* **Sonn** 86.10; **TN** III.iii.130

gull-catcher *(n.)* fool-trapper, trickster **TN** II.v.180 [Fabian to Sir Toby, of Maria] *Here comes my noble gull-catcher*

gum *(n.)* **1** substance used as incense in ceremonies **TNK** I.v.4 [Song] *Balms and gums and heavy cheers*

2 sticky secretion, mucus **H5** IV.ii.46 [Grandpré to all, of the English horses] *The gum down-roping from their pale-dead eyes*

gun-stone *(n.)* cannon-ball, bullet, projectile **H5** I.ii.283 [King Henry to Ambassador, of the Dauphin] *this mock of his/ Hath turned his balls to gun-stones*

gurnet *(n.)* type of fish with a disproportionately large head [thus used as an insult] **1H4** IV.ii.12 [Falstaff alone] *If I be not ashamed of my soldiers, I am a soused gurnet*

gust *(n.)* **1** outburst, violent blast **Tim** III.v.55 [Alcibiades to Senators] *To kill, I grant, is sin's extremest gust* [or: sense 3]

2 rush of wind **Cor** I.vi.5 [Cominius to Soldiers] *By interims and conveying gusts we have heard / The charges of our friends* [i.e. the noise carried by the wind]

3 relish, taste, inclination **TN** I.iii.28 [Maria to Sir Toby, of Sir Andrew] *he hath the gift of a coward to allay the gust he hath in quarrelling;* **Sonn** 114.11

gust *(v.)* taste; realize, know of **WT** I.ii.219 [Leontes to himself, of the talk of people around him] *'Tis far gone / When I shall gust it last*

guttered *(adj.)* gullied, furrowed, jagged **Oth** II.i.69 [Cassio to all] *The guttered rocks ... do omit / Their mortal natures*

gyve *(n.)* **1** (plural) fetters, shackles **RJ** II.ii.179 [Juliet to Romeo, of a captive bird] *Like a poor prisoner in his twisted gyves;* **Cym** V.iv.14; **1H4** IV.ii.39; **Lover** 242; **MM** V.ii.11; **TNK** III.ii.14

2 (plural) handicaps, defects **Ham** IV.vii.21 [Claudius to Laertes, of the public's behaviour towards Hamlet] *Convert his gyves to graces*

gyve *(v.)* fetter, shackle, ensnare **Oth** II.i.167 [Iago to himself, as if to Cassio] *I will gyve thee in thine own courtship*

ha' (*v.*) contracted form of 'have' **3H6** IV.v.27 [Richard to all] *let's ha' no more ado*

ha (*int.*) ☛ EXCLAMATIONS, p.158; RESPONSES, p.373

haberdasher (*n.*) dealer in small articles relating to clothing **H8** V.iv.46 [Man to Porter] *a haberdasher's wife of small wit*

haberdepois (*n.*) ☛ avoirdupois (*n.*)

habiliment, abiliment (*n.*) (usually plural) clothes, dress, attire, outfit **TG** IV.i.13 [Valentine to Outlaws] *My riches are these poor habiliments;* **Tit** V.ii.1 [disguised Tamora to Chiron and Demetrius] *in this strange and sad habiliment;* **AC** III.vi.17; **R2** I.iii.28; **TS** IV.iii.166

habit (*n.*) **1** dress, clothing, costume **TS** V.i.65 [Tranio as Lucentio to Vincentio] *you seem a sober ancient gentleman by your habit* ☛ FEW, p.xxi
 2 covering, guise, adorning **MM** II.iv.13 [Angelo alone] *O place … / How often dost thou with thy case, thy habit, / Wrench awe from fools;* **Oth** I.iii.108
 3 behaviour, bearing, demeanour **MV** II.ii.177 [Gratiano to Bassanio] *If I do not put on a sober habit, … never trust me more;* **AY** III.ii.288; **E3** I.ii.146; **LL** V.ii.758; **TN** V.i.213
 4 routine, settled practice, regular behaviour **TG** V.iv.1 [Valentine alone] *How use doth breed a habit in a man!;* **Ham** V.ii.187

habited (*adj.*) clothed, dressed, clad **Tem** IV.i.139 [stage direction] *Enter certain Reapers, properly habited;* **H8** I.iv.64, V.v.1; **Tit** II.iii.57; **WT** IV.iv.543

habitude (*n.*) character, disposition, temperament **Lover** 114 [of the man] *His real habitude gave life and grace / To appertainings and to ornament*

hack (*v.*) [unclear meaning] be promiscuous, go whoring **MW** II.i.48 [Mistress Page to Mistress Ford] *These knights will hack;* **MW** IV.i.61

hackney (*n.*) prostitute, harlot, whore **LL** III.i.30 [Mote to himself, of Armado] *and your love perhaps a hackney*

hackneyed (*adj.*) ☛ common-hackneyed (*adj.*)

hade land (*n.*) strip of land left unploughed in a field **2H4** V.i.12 [Davy to Shallow] *shall we sow the hade land with wheat?* [Q; F head-land]

hadst (*v.*) ☛ VERB FORMS, p.481

hag (*n.*) **1** witch, sorceress **1H6** III.ii.52 [Talbot to Pucelle] *Foul fiend of France and hag of all despite*
 2 malicious sprite, wicked fairy **RJ** I.iv.92 [Mercutio to Romeo, of Queen Mab] *This is the hag, when maids lie on their backs, / That presses them*

hag-born (*adj.*) born of a witch **Tem** I.ii.283 [Prospero to Ariel, of Caliban] *A freckled whelp, hag-born*

haggard (*n.*) [falconry] wild hawk **MA** III.i.36 [Hero to Ursula, of Beatrice] *I know her spirits are as coy and wild / As haggards of the rock;* **TN** III.i.62; **TS** IV.i.179, ii.39

haggard (*adj.*) wild, unmanageable, untrainable **Oth** III.iii.257 [Othello alone, of Desdemona] *If I do prove her haggard … / I'd whistle her off*

haggard-like (*adj.*) wild, unmanageable, untrainable **E3** III.iv.60 [King Edward to all] *dare a falcon when she's in her flight, / And ever after she'll be haggard-like* [Q2; Q1 huggard]

haggish (*adj.*) like a hag, ugly, repulsive **AW** I.ii.29 [King to Bertram, of Bertram's father] *on us both did haggish age steal on*

haggle (*v.*) mangle, hack, lacerate **H5** IV.vi.11 [Exeter to King Henry, of York] *all haggled over*

hag-seed (*n.*) witch-child **Tem** I.ii.365 [Prospero to Caliban] *Hag-seed, hence!*

hail (*int.*) ☛ GREETINGS, p.206

hair (*n.*) **1** character, nature, kind **1H4** IV.i.61 [Worcester to Hotspur] *The quality and hair of our attempt / Brooks no division;* **MW** II.iii.36

2 jot, iota, trace **2H4** I.ii.23 [Falstaff to Page, of Prince Henry's face] *God may finish it when He will, 'tis not a hair amiss yet* [also: hair of the beard]; **TC** III.ii.182

3 [product stuffed with hair] tennis-ball **H5** III.vii.13 [Dauphin to Orleans, of his horse] *He bounds from the earth as if his entrails were hairs*

hair, against the against the grain, contrary to inclination **TC** I.ii.27 [Alexander to Cressida, of Ajax] *He is … merry against the hair;* **RJ** II.iv.93

hair / hair's breadth, to a in every little detail, in full, exactly **MW** IV.ii.3 [Falstaff to Mistress Ford] *I profess requital to a hair's breadth;* **TC** III.i.141 [Paris to Pandarus, of remembering Troilus' excuse] *To a hair*

hair-worth (*n.*) hair's worth **TNK** V.iv.51 [Pirithous to Palamon] *a steed … owing / Not a hair-worth of white* [i.e. not as much as a single white hair]

halberd (*n.*) **1** long-handled weapon ending in a combination of axe-blade and spearhead **R3** I.ii.40 [Richard to Gentleman] *Advance thy halberd higher than my breast* ☞ **WEAPONS**, p.491

2 person armed with a halberd **R3** I.iii.1 [stage direction] *Enter the corse of Henry the Sixth, with halberds to guard it;* **R3** V.i.1

halcyon (*n.*) kingfisher **1H6** I.ii.131 [Pucelle to all] *Expect Saint Martin's summer, halcyon days* [i.e. a period of peace and calm]; **KL** II.ii.76

hale (*v.*) **1** drag, pull, haul **1H6** V.iv.64 [Pucelle to all] *ye hale me to a violent death;* **AC** II.v.65; **2H4** V.v.35; **MA** I.iii.57; **Per** IV.i.55; **TN** III.ii.58

2 molest, drag about, push around **TS** V.i.97 [Vincentio to all] *Thus strangers may be haled and abused*

half (*n.*) other half, wife **JC** II.i.274 [Portia to Brutus] *That you unfold to me, your self, your half, / Why you are heavy*

half, be one's go half-shares with one, share the stake with one **TS** V.ii.77 [Baptista to Lucentio] *I'll be your half Bianca comes*

half-blooded (*adj.*) of only one noble parent; bastard **KL** V.iii.81 [Albany to Edmund] *Half-blooded fellow*

half-blown (*adj.*) half-blossomed **KJ** III.i.54 [Constance to Arthur] *Of nature's gifts thou mayst with lilies boast / And with the half-blown rose* ☞ **blown** (*adj.*) 1

half-cap (*n.*) half removal of the cap by way of negligent courtesy **Tim** II.ii.217 [Flavius to Timon, of the Senators] *With certain half-caps and cold-moving nods / They froze me into silence*

half-cheek (*n.*) profile, side-view **LL** V.ii.614 [Berowne to Holofernes, of the latter's face] *Saint George's half-cheek in a brooch*

half-cheeked (*adj.*) [horse-riding] with broken side-rings [cheeks]; or: halfway up the cheeks **TS** III.ii.55 [Biondello to Tranio as Lucentio, of Petruchio's horse] *with a half-cheeked bit*

half-face (*n.*) profile, side-view **KJ** I.i.92 [Bastard to himself, of Robert] *he hath a half-face like my father*

half-faced (*adj.*) **1** thin-faced, with a pinched look **2H4** III.ii.257 [Falstaff to Shallow] *this same half-faced fellow Shadow*

2 [of a coin] showing a monarch's profile; also: clipped, imperfect **KJ** I.i.94 [Bastard to himself] *A half-faced groat*

3 imperfect, incomplete, defective **1H4** I.iii.206 [Hotspur to Northumberland and Worcester] *But out upon this half-faced fellowship!*

4 with only half the face visible **2H6** IV.i.98 [Lieutenant to Suffolk, of the house of York] *Burns with revenging fire, whose hopeful colours / Advance our half-faced sun*

half-kirtle (*n.*) skirt [lower part of a kirtle] **2H4** V.iv.21 [Doll to First Beadle] *if you be not swinged I'll forswear half-kirtles* ☞ **kirtle** (*n.*)

half-part (*n.*) half each, fair shares **Per** IV.i.95 [Third Pirate to others, of capturing Marina] *Half-part, mates*

half-pence (*n.*) fragment, tiny piece, bit **MA** II.iii.142 [Leonato to Claudio, of Beatrice] *she tore the letter into a thousand half-pence*

half-sight (*n.*) someone half-blind **TNK** V.iii.95 [Emilia to herself] *Half-sights saw / That Arcite was no babe*

half-supped (*adj.*) with supper interrupted, half-satisfied **TC** V.viii.19 [Achilles to Myrmidons] *My half-supped sword … / Pleased with this dainty bait, thus goes to bed*

half-sword, at at the length of a small-sized sword, at close quarters **1H4** II.iv.159 [Falstaff to Prince Hal, of the robbery] *I am a rogue if I were not at half-sword with a dozen of them* ☞ **WEAPONS**, p.491

half-worker (*n.*) co-worker, co-operator, collaborator **Cym** II.iv.154 [Posthumus alone] *women / Must be half-workers*

half-world (*n.*) hemisphere, half of the globe **Mac** II.i.49 [Macbeth alone] *Now o'er the one half-world / Nature seems dead*

halidom, by my (*n.*) ☞ **SWEARING**, p.435

hall (*n.*) guild, company, profession **TC** V.x.48 [Pandarus alone] *As many as be here of Pandar's hall*

halloing (*n.*) ☞ **hallowing** (*n.*)

halloo (*v.*) ☞ **hallow** (*v.*)

hallow (*v.*) bless, glorify, honour as holy **2H6** IV.x.65 [Iden to his sword, of killing Cade] *I will hallow thee for this thy deed*

hallow, holloa, hollow (*v.*) **1** shout, yell, cry out **TN** I.v.261 [Viola as Cesario to Olivia] *[I would] Hallow your name to the reverberate hills;* **R2** IV.i.54 [Another Lord to Aumerle] *I … spur thee on with full as many lies / As may be hollowed in thy treacherous ear;* **TNK** II.i.102, iv.11, III.ii.8; **WT** III.iii.75 ☞ **holla** (*v.*)

2 follow with shouts, call after **Cor** I.viii.7 [Aufidius to Martius] *If I fly, Martius, / Holloa me like a hare*

hallowed (*adj.*) ☞ **well-hallowed** (*adj.*)

hallowed verge magic circle, charmed ring **2H6** I.iv.21 [Bolingbroke to Duchess of Gloucester, of the spirits] *Whom we raise / We will make fast within a hallowed verge*

hallowing, hallooing, halloing, holloaing (*n.*) shouting, hallooing, crying out **2H4** I.ii.190 [Falstaff to Lord Chief Justice] *For my voice, I have lost it with hallooing* [F, Q *hallowing*]; **MV** V.i.43 [Lorenzo to Launcelot] *Leave holloaing, man!;* **TG** V.iv.13 [Valentine alone] *What halloing and what stir is this today?;* **TNK** III.i.1 [stage direction] *Noise and hallowing as of people a-maying*

halt (*v.*) limp, proceed lamely **R3** I.i.23 [Richard to himself] *dogs bark at me as I halt by them;* **Ham** II.ii.325; **2H4** I.ii.248; **Tem** IV.i.11; **Tim** IV.i.24; **TN** V.i.189

halter (*n.*) **1** rope with a noose [for hanging] **Tit** V.i.47 [Lucius to soldiers, of Aaron] *A halter … Hang him on this tree;* **1H4** II.iv.318; **KL** I.iv.317, III.ii.52; **Oth** IV.ii.135

2 rope, noose [for leading a beast] **2H6** IV.ix.10 [stage direction] *Enter multitudes, with halters about their necks;* **2H6** IV.ix.11

haltered (*adj.*) with a noose around it **AC** III.xiii.130 [Antony to Cleopatra] *A haltered neck which does the hangman thank / For being yare about him*

halting (*n.*) hesitation, wavering, faltering **Cym** III.v.93 [Cloten to Pisanio] *Come nearer: / No further halting*

halting (*adj.*) **1** hesitating, limping, faltering **MA** V.iv.87 [Claudio to all, of Benedick] *A halting sonnet of his own pure brain*

2 wavering, dilatory, shifting **KJ** V.ii.174 [Bastard to Lewis the Dauphin, of Cardinal Pandulph] *this halting legate here*

hammer (*v.*) think hard, deliberate, ponder **TG** I.iii.18 [Antonio to Panthino] *Nor needest thou much importune me to that / Whereon this month I have been hammering*

hammer of (*v.*) think hard about, ponder on **WT** II.ii.49 [Emilia to Paulina] *I'll presently / Acquaint the Queen of your most noble offer, / Who but today hammered of this design*

hammer out (*v.*) puzzle out, work hard at, work out **R2** V.v.5 [Richard alone, of the direction of his thinking] *I'll hammer it out;* **2H6** I.ii.47

hamper (*v.*) impede, obstruct, fetter **2H6** I.iii.143 [Duchess to King, of the Queen] *She'll hamper thee, and dandle thee like a baby*

hams (n.) thighs, legs RJ II.iv.52 [Mercutio to Romeo] *such a case as yours constrains a man to bow in the hams*; Ham II.ii.201; Per IV.ii.100

hand (n.) **1** ability, skill [with the hand] TNK IV.i.138 [Gaoler's Daughter to First Friend, of Palamon] *he'll tickle it up / In two hours, if his hand be in* [i.e. if he is in good form]
2 agency, means, aid KJ II.i.302 [French Herald to Hubert, of Arthur] *Who by the hand of France this day hath made / Much work for tears in many an English mother*; Ham V.v.206
3 care, escort, keeping E3 II.ii.109 [King Edward to Lodowick] *fetch the Countess hither in thy hand*
4 handiwork, job, work H8 V.iv.69 [Lord Chamberlain to Porter and Man] *You've made a fine hand* [i.e. made a fine job of this!]; Cor IV.vi.119
5 handwriting R3 III.vi.2 [Scrivener alone] *Here is the indictment … / Which in a set hand fairly is engrossed*; JC I.ii.313; R2 V.iii.52; TNK V.ii.56 ☛ court-hand (n.)
6 signature, written authorization KJ IV.ii.215 [Hubert to King John, of Arthur's death warrant] *Here is your hand and seal for what I did*; R2 IV.i.25; WT IV.iv.281

hand, at at the start of a race JC IV.ii.23 [Brutus to Lucilius] *hollow men, like horses hot at hand, / Make gallant show and promise of their mettle*

hand, at / in any in any case, at any rate AW III.vi.39 [First Lord to Bertram, of Parolles] *let him fetch off his drum in any hand*; TS I.ii.224 [Petruchio to Tranio as Lucentio, of Katherina] *Not her that chides, sir, at any hand*; TS I.ii.144

hand, in to deal with, here present TN I.iii.62 [Sir Andrew to Maria] *do you think you have fools in hand?*

hand, out of 1 at once, immediately, straight away 3H6 IV.vii.63 [Richard to Edward] *we will proclaim you out of hand*; E3 IV.ii.55; 1H6 III.ii.102; Tit V.ii.77
2 finished with, off one's hands 2H4 III.i.103 [King Henry IV to Warwick and Surrey] *were these inward wars once out of hand, / We would … unto the Holy Land*

hands, of all on every side LL II.iii.217 [Berowne to all, of being in love] *of all hands must we be forsworn*

hand (v.) lay hands on, handle, have to do with Tem I.i.23 [Boatswain to Gonzalo] *we will not hand a rope more*; WT IV.iv.345

handfast, hand-fast (n.) marriage contract, betrothal Cym I.vi.78 [Queen alone, of Pisanio and Innogen] *the remembrancer of her to hold / The hand-fast to her lord* ☛ fast (adj.) 3

handfast, in held fast, in custody, under arrest WT IV.iv.764 [Autolycus to Shepherd] *If that shepherd be not in handfast, let him fly*

hand-in-hand (adj.) claiming equality, equally balanced Cym I.v.67 [Iachimo to Posthumus] *a kind of hand-in-hand comparison*

handkercher (n.) handkerchief AW V.iii.319 [Lafew to Parolles] *lend me a handkercher*; AY IV.iii.98, V.ii.26; Cor II.i.256; H5 III.ii.48; KJ IV.i.42

handsaw (n.) heron [probably a variant of 'heronshaw', i.e. a young heron] Ham II.ii.378 [Hamlet to Guildenstern] *I know a hawk from a handsaw*

handsome (adj.) **1** naturally graceful, artlessly elegant Ham II.ii.443 [Hamlet to First Player, of a play's style] *very much more handsome than fine*
2 proper, fitting, appropriate TNK IV.i.79 [Wooer to all, of the Gaoler's Daughter] *she must … see the house made handsome* [i.e. tidy]; MA IV.ii.83; TNK IV.i.9

handsomely (adv.) **1** beautifully, elegantly, attractively Tem V.i.294 [Prospero to Caliban, of his cell] *trim it handsomely*; WT IV.iv.746
2 conveniently, opportunely, readily to hand Tit II.iii.268 [Saturninus reading a letter, of Bassianus] *if we miss to meet him handsomely*

handsomeness (n.) graciousness, courtesy, decent behaviour TC II.i.15 [Ajax to Thersites] *I will beat thee into handsomeness!*

handy-dandy choose, make your choice [from the children's game: choosing which hand holds an object] KL IV.vi.154 [Lear to Gloucester, of a justice and a thief] *change places and, handy-dandy, which is the justice, which is the thief?*

hang (v.) suspend, hold off, put off 2H4 IV.i.211 [Archbishop to Mowbray] *this land … hangs resolved correction in the arm / That was upreared to execution*

hang off (v.) leave hold, stop clinging MND III.ii.260 [Lysander to Hermia] *Hang off, thou cat, thou burr!*

hang the lip ☛ lip, hang the

hang together (v.) keep in one piece, carry on existing MW III.ii.12 [Ford to Mistress Page, of Mistress Ford] *as idle as she may hang together, for want of company*

hanged (adj.) decorated with hangings, furnished with tapestries PassP XIV.3 [Pilgrim, of his love] *She … daffed me to a cabin hanged with care*

hanger (n.) ☛ WEAPONS, p.491

hanging (n.) wall-covering, tapestry, curtain 2H6 V.iii.12 [Richard to York] *like rich hangings in a homely house*; TNK III.v.126

hanging (adj.) gloomy, morose, melancholy MM IV.ii.30 [Pompey to Abhorson] *a good favour you have, but that you have a hanging look* [pun: being hung]

hangman (n.) rascal, rogue, reprobate MA III.ii.10 [Don Pedro to Claudio, of Cupid and Benedick] *the little hangman dare not shoot at him*

hangman (adj.) fit for the hangman, infernal, diabolical TG IV.iv.53 [Launce to Proteus] *the hangman boys in the market-place* [F *Hangmans boyes*]

Hannibal (n.) malapropism for 'cannibal' MM II.i.167 [Elbow to Pompey] *thou wicked Hannibal!*

hap (n.) **1** fortune, lot, fate 1H6 I.vi.10 [Charles to all] *More blessed hap did ne'er befall our state*; 2H6 III.i.314; 3H6 II.iii.9; Luc 42; R3 I.iii.17; TS I.ii.266
2 luck, chance, accident Tim III.ii.25 [Servilius to himself, of Lucius] *See, by good hap, yonder's my lord*; AC II.iii.33; CE I.i.114; LL II.i.196; MA III.i.105
3 happening, event, occurrence H8 Epilogue.13 [of men] *'tis ill hap / If they hold when their ladies bid 'em clap*; RJ III.iii.171

hap (v.) happen, take place, come to pass Oth V.i.127 [Iago to Emilia] *tell my lord and lady what hath happed*; Cor III.i.24; 1H6 III.i.31; Per I.Chorus.22; Sonn 9.3; TS I.iv.103

hapless (adj.) luckless, unfortunate, unlucky E3 IV.iii.71 [Charles, reading a prophecy] *that shall be the hapless dreadful day*; CE I.i.141; 1H6 III.i.203; 3H6 V.vi.15; Luc 1045; TG I.i.32

haply (adv.) perhaps, maybe, by chance, with luck Ham III.i.172 [Claudius to Polonius, of Hamlet] *Haply the seas … shall expel / This something-settled matter in his heart* ☛ FEW, p.xxi; happily (adv.) 1

happen (v.) happen to, befall E3 IV.iii.65 [Charles to King John] *I have a prophecy … / Wherein is written what success is like / To happen us in this outrageous war*

happily (adv.) **1** perhaps, by chance, maybe 2H6 III.i.306 [Queen to York, of Somerset losing France] *Thy fortune, York … / Might happily have proved far worse than his*; Ham II.ii.383; MM IV.ii.92; Oth III.iii.236; Per I.iv.92; TS IV.iv.54 ☛ haply (adv.)
2 opportunely, propitiously, with good fortune TS I.ii.210 [Gremio to Hortensio, of Lucentio as Cambio] *This gentleman is happily arrived … for his own good and yours*; H8 V.i.85, ii.8; KJ V.vii.101; TS IV.iv.19
3 fittingly, appropriately, aptly H8 IV.ii.10 [Katherine to Griffith, of how Wolsey died] *If well, he stepped before me happily / For my example*

happiness *(n.)* **1** good luck, success, good fortune **TNK** II.ii.82 [Arcite alone, of Emilia] *happiness prefer me to a place / Where I may ever dwell in sight of her;* **MA** I.i.120; **Oth** III.iv.104; **Tim** I.i.79

2 felicity, aptness, appropriateness [of expression] **Ham** II.ii.209 [Polonius to himself, of Hamlet] *A happiness that often madness hits on*

3 pleasing demeanour, felicitous manner **MA** II.iii.182 [Don Pedro to Claudio, of Benedick] *He hath ... a good outward happiness*

happy *(adj.)* **1** fortunate, lucky, favoured **AC** IV.v.1 [Soldier to Antony] *The gods make this a happy day to Antony!;* **1H6** V.iii.115; **H8** IV.ii.147; **KL** IV.vi.72; **RJ** III.iii.137; **TG** III.i.57

2 opportune, appropriate, propitious, favourable **JC** II.ii.60 [Caesar to Decius] *you are come in very happy time / To bear my greeting to the senators;* **Ham** V.ii.199; **2H4** IV.ii.79; **KJ** V.i.63; **MA** IV.i.279; **Tit** III.iii.23

3 accomplished, favoured, proficient **Cym** III.iv.176 [Pisanio to Innogen, of Lucius] *tell him / Wherein you're happy;* **H8** Prologue.24; **TG** IV.i.33

4 well-chosen, felicitous, fitting **LL** V.ii.370 [Rosaline to King, of the Russian visitors] *They did not bless us with one happy word*

happy time, in **1** well met **AW** V.i.6 [Helena to Gentleman] *In happy time!;* **Oth** III.i.30

2 coming just at the right time **RJ** III.v.111 [Juliet to Lady Capulet, of her father's good news] *Madam, in happy time!* ☞ time, in good 2

happy *(v.)* make happy, delight, content **Sonn** 6.6 [of storing beauty] *That use is not forbidden usury, / Which happies those that pay the willing loan*

harbinger *(n.)* forerunner, herald, precursor **Mac** V.vi.10 [Macduff to all, of the trumpets] *Those clamorous harbingers of blood and death;* **CE** III.ii.12; **Ham** I.i.122; **MND** III.ii.380; **Phoen** 5; **TNK** I.i.8

harbour *(n.)* shelter, refuge, safe lodging **Tim** V.iv.53 [Second Senator to Alcibiades] *all thy powers / Shall make their harbour in our town till we / Have sealed thy full desire;* **Luc** 768

harbour *(v.)* lodge, stay, shelter **CE** III.ii.157 [Antipholus of Syracuse to Dromio of Syracuse] *I will not harbour in this town tonight;* **3H6** IV.vii.78; **TG** III.i.140, 149

harbourage *(n.)* shelter, refuge, haven **Per** I.iv.100 [Pericles to Cleon] *[we] look for ... harbourage for ourself, our ships, and men;* **KJ** II.i.234

hard *(adj.)* **1** strong, tough, powerful **1H4** I.ii.179 [Prince Hal to Poins, of their companions] *but I doubt they will be too hard for us;* **Cor** IV.v.190; **3H6** V.i.70; **LL** I.i.244, IV.i.139

2 hardened, toughened **2H6** IV.ii.20 [Bevis to Holland] *there's no better sign of a brave mind than a hard hand;* **Tim** IV.iii.270

3 painful, harrowing, tough **AY** II.iv.41 [Rosalind, as if to Silvius] *searching of thy wound, / I have by hard adventure found mine own;* **AY** III.iv.307; **Cym** V.iii.44; **Sonn** 133.6; **TN** III.i.112

4 unpleasant, harsh, cruel **KL** III.iv.142 [Gloucester to Lear, of Gonerill and Regan] *all your daughters' hard commands;* **KL** III.iii.63; **MW** I.iii.42; **TNK** III.i.106

5 bad, poor, inadequate **TG** II.vii.81 [Julia to Lucetta, of Proteus] *do him not that wrong / To bear a hard opinion of his truth;* **TNK** V.ii.95

6 difficult, not easy [to obtain] **Ham** I.ii.60 [Polonius to Claudius, of Laertes] *Upon his will I sealed my hard consent;* **KL** III.vi.98

7 tough, unfeeling, unsentimental **WT** I.ii.153 [Leontes to Hermione] *sometimes Nature will betray its folly ... and make itself a pastime / To harder bosoms!*

8 pressing, persistent, unremitting **Venus** 559 [of Adonis and Venus] *faint and weary, with her hard embracing*

hard *(adv.)* **1** close, near **KL** II.ii.61 [disguised Kent to Lear] *hard by here is a hovel;* **AY** III.v.75; **E3** III.iii.13; **3H6** I.i.51; **MW** III.ii.9; **TN** I.iii.102

2 earnestly, vigorously, energetically **AY** III.v.76 [Rosalind as Ganymede to Silvius, of Phebe] *Shepherd, ply her hard;* **Cym** III.vii.42; **TG** II.iv.47

3 badly, poorly, ill **TNK** Epilogue.5 [Speaker to audience, of none of the audience smiling] *Then it goes hard;* **Ham** III.iv.208; **1H4** I.iii.264; **TG** I.i.85; **TS** IV.ii.80

4 with difficulty, not easily **Oth** I.ii.10 [Iago to Othello, of Roderigo] *he prated / And spoke such scurvy and provoking terms / Against your honour, / That ... / I did full hard forbear him;* **AY** III.ii.304

hard-a-keeping *(adj.)* too hard to keep **LL** I.i.65 [Berowne to King] *having sworn too hard-a-keeping oath*

hard-favoured *(adj.)* ugly, unattractive, unsightly, hideous **TG** II.i.46 [Speed to Valentine, of Silvia] *Is she not hard-favoured, sir?;* **AY** III.iii.26; **H5** III.i.8; **1H6** IV.vii.23; **3H6** V.v.78; **Venus** 133 ☞ well-favoured *(adj.)*

hardiment *(n.)* display of valour, daring deed **1H4** I.iii.100 [Hotspur to King Henry, of Mortimer] *He did confound the best part of an hour / In changing hardiment with great Glendower;* **Cym** V.v.75; **TC** IV.v.28

hardiness *(n.)* boldness, daring, audacity, courage **Cym** III.vi.22 [Innogen alone] *hardness ever / Of hardiness is mother;* **H5** I.ii.221

hardly *(adv.)* **1** with great difficulty, only with difficulty **AC** V.i.74 [Caesar to all] *you shall see / How hardly I was drawn into this war;* **1H6** III.ii.40; **2H6** V.i.92; **KJ** V.vi.42; **R2** II.iv.2; **TG** II.i.103

2 severely, harshly, badly **H8** I.ii.105 [Wolsey aside to Secretary] *The grieved commons / Hardly conceive of me;* **Cym** III.iii.8; **2H4** II.ii.41

hardness *(n.)* **1** hardship, adversity, harsh situation **Oth** I.iii.231 [Othello to Duke] *I do agnize / A natural and prompt alacrity / I find in hardness;* **Cym** III.vi.21

2 difficulty of understanding **Cym** V.v.432 [Posthumus to Lucius, of the letter left by Jupiter] *whose containing / Is so from sense in hardness, that I can / Make no collection of it*

hardoke *(n.)* ☞ burdock *(n.)*

hard-ruled *(adj.)* difficult to manage, obstreperous **H8** III.ii.101 [Wolsey to himself, of Anne] *that she should lie i'th' bosom of / Our hard-ruled King*

hardy *(adj.)* bold, daring, forward **TNK** I.i.204 [Emilia to Theseus] *nor be so hardy / Ever to take a husband;* **TN** II.ii.9

hare-heart *(n.)* heart as timid as a hare **TC** II.ii.48 [Troilus to Helenus] *Manhood and honour / Should have hare-hearts, would they but fat their thoughts / With this crammed reason*

hark *(v.)* ☞ ATTENTION SIGNALS, p.26

harlot *(n.)* prostitute, whore **Ham** IV.v.120 [Laertes to Claudius] *That drop of blood that's calm proclaims me bastard, ... brands the harlot;* **CE** V.i.205; **Cor** III.ii.112; **RJ** II.iv.42

harlot *(adj.)* lewd, lascivious, licentious **WT** II.iii.4 [Leontes to himself, of Polixenes] *the harlot-king / Is quite beyond mine arm*

harlotry *(n.)* **1** harlot, whore **Oth** IV.ii.232 [Iago to Roderigo, of Cassio] *He sups tonight with a harlotry* [F; Q1 *harlot*]

2 [affectionate] little wretch, baggage **RJ** IV.iv.14 [Capulet to Nurse, of Juliet] *A peevish self-willed harlotry it is;* **1H4** III.i.193

harlotry *(adj.)* trashy, tawdry, third-rate **1H4** II.iv.388 [Hostess to all, of Falstaff pretending to be king] *he doth it as like one of these harlotry players as ever I see!*

harm *(n.)* **1** injury, hurt, pain **1H6** IV.vii.30 [Talbot to Servant] *My spirit can no longer bear these harms;* **Cor** I.ix.56; **E3** II.i.314; **1H6** IV.vii.46; **Mac** IV.iii.55

2 misfortune, affliction, trouble **CE** I.i.65 [Egeon to Duke] *A league ... had we sailed / Before the always wind-obeying deep / Gave any tragic instance of our harm;* **AY** III.ii.71; **3H6** V.iv.2; **KJ** III.i.39; **R3** II.ii.103

harmful (*adj.*) perilous, dangerous, full of harm **2H6** III.ii.262 [Salisbury to King, of a serpent approaching the sleeping King] *It were but necessary you were waked, / Lest, being suffered in that harmful slumber, / The mortal worm might make the sleep eternal*

harmless (*adj.*) innocent, causing no harm **Luc** 1723 [of Lucrece] *she sheathed in her harmless breast / A harmful knife;* **3H6** II.i.62; **TNK** IV.iii.3

harness (*n.*) **1** armour **Tim** I.ii.51 [Apemantus to all] *Great men should drink with harness on their throats;* **AC** IV.viii.15; **Mac** V.v.52; **TC** V.iii.31

2 armed men, men-at-arms, armament **1H4** III.ii.101 [King Henry to Prince Hal, of Hotspur] *He doth fill fields with harness in the realm*

harness (*v.*) dress in armour, arm, equip **TC** I.ii.8 [Alexander to Cressida, of Hector] *Before the sun rose he was harnessed light*

harnessed (*adj.*) armoured, armed **KJ** V.ii.132 [Bastard to Lewis the Dauphin, of the French invasion] *This harnessed masque and unadvised revel*

harp (*v.*) guess, express in words, give voice to **Mac** IV.i.73 [Macbeth as if to First Apparition] *Thou hast harped my fear aright*

harper (*n.*) harpist, minstrel **LL** V.ii.405 [Berowne to Rosaline] *Nor woo in rhyme, like a blind harper's song*

harpy (*n.*) mythical rapacious bird, half woman, half vulture [symbolizing divine retribution] **Per** IV.iii.46 [Cleon to Dionyza] *Thou art like the harpy;* **MA** II.i.248; **Tem** III.iii.54, 84

harrow (*v.*) disturb, distress, vex **Ham** I.i.44 [Horatio to Marcellus and Barnardo, of the Ghost] *It harrows me with fear and wonder* [F; Q1 *horrors*]

harrow up (*v.*) disturb, distress, vex **Ham** I.v.16 [Ghost to Hamlet] *I could a tale unfold whose lightest word / Would harrow up thy soul*

harry (*v.*) mistreat, harass, ill-use **AC** III.iii.39 [Cleopatra to Charmian, of the Messenger] *I repent me much / That so I harried him*

hart (*n.*) male deer **Cym** II.iv.27 [Posthumus to Iachimo] *The swiftest harts have posted you by land;* **Cym** V.iii.24

harvest-home (*n.*) **1** close of the harvesting season **1H4** I.iii.34 [Hotspur to King Henry, of a lord's chin] *Showed like a stubble-land at harvest-home*

2 gathering-in, moment of success **MW** II.ii.262 [Falstaff to Ford as Brook, of Ford] *the cuckoldy-rogue's coffer - and there's my harvest-home*

hast (*v.*) ☞ VERB FORMS, p.481

haste (*v.*) hurry, speed up, accelerate **RJ** IV.i.11 [Paris to Friar, of Juliet] *her father … in his wisdom hastes our marriage;* **MV** II.ii.105

haste-post-haste (*adj.*) with all possible speed, very prompt, most expeditious **Oth** I.ii.37 [Cassio to Othello] *The Duke … requires your haste-post-haste appearance* ☞ post-haste (*adj.*)

hasty (*adj.*) rash, impetuous, impulsive **3H6** IV.i.18 [Richard to Edward] *hasty marriage seldom proveth well;* **Cym** IV.ii.165; **3H6** IV.viii.2

hasty-witted (*adj.*) quick-witted, quick-thinking **TS** V.ii.40 [Bianca to Gremio] *An hasty-witted body / Would say your head and butt were head and horn*

hatch (*n.*) **1** hatching [as from an egg] **2H4** III.i.82 [Warwick to King Henry IV, of prophecies] *Such things become the hatch and brood of time;* **Ham** III.i.167

2 lower part of a door, half-door, gate **KL** III.vi.72 [Edgar as Poor Tom to all] *Dogs leapt the hatch and all are fled;* **CE** III.i.33; **KJ** I.i.171, V.ii.138

3 (plural) movable deck planks **R3** I.iv.17 [Clarence to Keeper, of Richard] *we paced along / Upon the giddy footing of the hatches;* **MW** II.i.86; **R3** I.iv.13; **Tem** I.ii.230

hatched (*adj.*) inlaid, streaked, ornamented **TC** I.iii.65 [Ulysses to Agamemnon] *venerable Nestor, hatched in silver* [i.e. with hair streaked with silver]

hatched (*adv.*) with the upper half closed **Per** IV.ii.31 [Pander to Bawd] *'twere not amiss to keep our door hatched*

hatchet (*n.*) executioner's axe **2H6** IV.vii.84 [Cade to Say] *Ye shall have … the help of hatchet*

hatchment (*n.*) [heraldry] tablet displaying a person's coat-of-arms **Ham** IV.v.214 [Laertes to Claudius, of Polonius] *No trophy, sword, nor hatchment o'er his bones*

hateful (*adj.*) **1** full of hate **2H6** II.iv.23 [Duchess to Gloucester, of the crowd] *hide thee from their hateful looks;* **R2** II.ii.137

2 repulsive, obnoxious, incompatible [with] **KJ** III.iii.47 [King John to Hubert, of merriment] *A passion hateful to my purposes;* **RJ** II.ii.55

hath (*v.*) ☞ VERB FORMS, p.481

haught (*adj.*) haughty, arrogant, high-and-mighty **R2** IV.i.253 [Richard to Northumberland] *thou haught, insulting man;* **2H6** I.iii.66; **3H6** II.i.168; **R3** II.i.28

haughty (*adj.*) high-minded, aspiring, lofty **1H6** IV.i.35 [Talbot to all] *Knights of the Garter were … full of haughty courage;* **1H6** II.v.79, III.iii.78

haunch (*n.*) latter end, hind part **2H4** IV.iv.92 [King Henry IV to Westmorland] *thou art a summer bird, / Which ever in the haunch of winter sings / The lifting up of day*

haunt (*n.*) **1** public places, society, company **AC** IV.xiv.54 [Antony alone] *Dido and her Aeneas shall want troops, / And all the haunt be ours;* **Ham** IV.i.18

2 frequent resort, regular visit **AY** II.i.15 [Duke Senior to all] *this our life, exempt from public haunt*

haunt (*v.*) **1** frequent, visit habitually **Mac** I.vi.9 [Banquo to King, of the martlet] *Where they most breed and haunt I have observed / The air is delicate;* **LL** I.i.160

2 pursue, afflict, beset **H5** II.iv.52 [French King to all, of the English] *That haunted us in our familiar paths;* **Per** III.iii.6

hautboy (*n.*) type of musical instrument; oboe **AC** IV.iii.13 [stage direction] *Music of hautboys under the stage;* **2H4** III.ii.315; **2H6** I.i.1 ☞ STAGE DIRECTIONS, p.417

have (*v.*) **1** understand, grasp, comprehend **Ham** III.ii.105 [Claudius to Hamlet] *I have nothing with this answer;* **Ham** III.ii.105; **TNK** V.ii.33

2 be given **3H6** IV.iv.10 [Lady Grey to Rivers] *as I further have to understand*

3 take, convey; or: have to do [with] **WT** IV.iv.790 [Autolycus to Clown and Shepherd] *Tell me … what you have to the King*

4 ☞ lief, had as

have after (*v.*) let's follow **Ham** I.iv.89 [Horatio to Marcellus, of the departure of Hamlet and the Ghost] *Have after*

have at (*v.*) let's face, let's see **TNK** Epilogue.10 [Speaker to audience] *Have at the worst can come, then!* [i.e. let's see the worst you can do]

have-at-him (*n.*) thrust **H8** II.ii.83 [Norfolk aside to Suffolk, of the situation continuing] *If it do, / I'll venture one have-at-him* ☞ have at you

have at it let's try it, let's have a go at it **WT** IV.iv.294 [Autolycus to Dorcas and Mopsa, of singing a ballad together] *Have at it with you*

have at [someone] [said at the start of a fencing attack or other confrontation] I come at, let me at [a person] **2H6** IV.ii.113 [Cade to himself, of Stafford] *Now have at him!;* **TS** V.ii.45 [Petruchio to Bianca] *Have at you for a bitter jest or two;* **2H4** I.ii.194; **2H6** II.iii.89; **H8** V.iii.113; **LL** IV.iii.288; **TNK** III.vi.131 ☞ have-at-him (*n.*); DISCOURSE MARKERS, p.127

have done put an end to, stop **CE** I.ii.72 [Antipholus of Syracuse to Dromio of Ephesus] *have done your foolishness*

have to I'll move forward to, I'll go onwards to **TS** IV.v.78 [Hortensio alone] *Have to my widow!*

have to't let's go at it, let's renew the fight **TS** I.i.136 [Hortensio to Gremio, of suspending enmity until a husband is found for Katherina] *then have to't afresh*

have with you I'll join you, I'll be with you **AY** I.ii.245 [Rosalind to Celia] *Have with you;* 1H6 II.iv.114; MW II.i.146; TNK II.ii.27 **☞** **FAREWELLS**, p.170

haven (*n.*) harbour, port **Cym** I.ii.102 [Pisanio to Innogen, of Posthumus] *he would not suffer me / To bring him to the haven;* **Cym** I.iv.1; **Per** I.ii.49

haver (*n.*) possessor, holder, displayer **Cor** II.ii.83 [Cominius to all] *valour is the chiefest virtue and / Most dignifies the haver*

having (*n.*) 1 fortune, estate, means **MW** III.ii.66 [Page to Host, of Fenton as a suitor for Anne] *The gentleman is of no having;* **Mac** I.iii.55; **Oth** IV.iii.90; **Tim** V.i.16; **TN** III.iv.335; **WT** IV.iv.714
  2 accomplishment, quality, gift **Lover** 235 [of a nun] *Whose rarest havings made the blossoms dote*

haviour (*n.*) behaviour, manner, demeanour **Cym** III.iv.9 [Innogen to Pisanio] *Put thyself / Into a haviour of less fear;* **Ham** II.ii.12; **MW** I.iii.73; **R2** I.iii.77; **RJ** II.ii.99; **TN** III.iv.202

havoc (*n.*) [in fighting and hunting: calling for] total slaughter, general devastation **JC** III.i.273 [Antony alone, of Caesar's spirit] *Shall … / Cry havoc and let slip the dogs of war;* **Cor** III.i.273; **Ham** V.iii.358; **KJ** II.i.357

hawk (*v.*) 1 hunt with hawks **2H6** I.ii.58 [Messenger to Gloucester] *Saint Albans, / Where as the King and Queen do mean to hawk*
  2 clear the throat noisily **AY** V.iii.10 [First Page to all, of beginning a song] *without hawking, or spitting*

hawk at (*v.*) pursue, attack, chase **TNK** V.iii.2 [Emilia to Pirithous] *I had rather see a wren hawk at a fly / Than this decision;* **Mac** II.iv.13

hawking (*adj.*) hawk-like, sharp, alert **AW** I.i.93 [Helena alone, of Bertram] *his hawking eye*

hawthorn-bud (*n.*) young dandy, budding courtier **MW** III.iii.67 [Falstaff to Mistress Ford] *I cannot cog … like a many of these lisping hawthorn-buds that come like women in men's apparel*

hay (*n.*) 1 hay-making, harvest **3H6** IV.viii.61 [Edward to all] *The sun shines hot; and, if we use delay, / Cold biting winter mars our hoped-for hay*
  2 type of winding country dance **LL** V.i.148 [Dull to Holofernes] *I will play on the tabor to the Worthies, and let them dance the hay*
  3 [fencing] home thrust, thrust through **RJ** II.iv.26 [Mercutio to Benvolio] *Ah, the immortal passado! the punto reverso! the hay!*

hazard (*n.*) 1 risk, peril, danger **TG** III.i.116 [Duke to Valentine, of a high chamber] *one cannot climb it / Without apparent hazard of his life;* **AC** III.vii.47; **E3** IV.vii.52; **2H4** IV.i.15; **H5** III.vii.84; **MM** IV.ii.153
  2 [gambling] chance, fortune; throw [of dice] **R3** V.iv.10 [King Richard to Catesby] *I will stand the hazard of the die;* **1H4** IV.i.48; **JC** V.i.68; **MV** II.i.45; **Tim** V.iv.34; **TNK** II.i.120
  3 [royal tennis] opening in a court where a ball is unplayable [and thus a winning point is scored] **H5** I.ii.264 [King Henry to Ambassador, of the Dauphin] *We will in France … play a set / Shall strike his father's crown into the hazard* [i.e. put his crown in danger]

hazard, come / go to play dice, gamble **H5** III.vii.82 [Rambures to all] *Who will go to hazard with me for twenty prisoners?* [pun: 84, sense 1]; **MV** II.ix.18

hazard, in in peril, at risk **MM** IV.ii.153 [disguised Duke to Provost] *in the boldness of my cunning I will lay myself in hazard;* **Cor** II.iii.255

hazards, upon all against any odds **KJ** V.vi.7 [Hubert to unrecognized Bastard] *I will upon all hazards well believe / Thou art my friend*

hazard (*v.*) 1 expose to danger, put at risk **AW** II.i.183 [King to Helena, of her life] *Thou this to hazard needs must intimate / Skill infinite;* **Oth** II.iii.134; **Tim** III.v.38, IV.iii.337; **TNK** II.i.258

2 expose to risk, take one's chance [of] **MV** II.vii.9 [Morocco, reading about the lead casket] *Who chooseth me must give and hazard all he hath;* **MV** III.ii.2
  3 put into the hands of, make dependent on **AC** III.xii.19 [Ambassador to Caesar, of Cleopatra] *of thee craves / The circle of the Ptolemies for her heirs, / Now hazarded to thy grace*

he (*n.*) man, person **RJ** V.i.67 [Apothecary to Romeo, of poison] *Mantua's law / Is death to any he that utters them;* **3H6** I.i.46, II.ii.97; **TS** III.ii.233

head (*n.*) 1 fighting force, army, body of troops **1H4** IV.iv.25 [Sir Michael to Archbishop] *there is … a head / Of gallant warriors;* **1H6** I.iv.100 [Messenger to Talbot] *the French have gathered head;* **Cor** II.ii.86; **Cym** IV.ii.139; **1H4** III.i.60; **3H6** II.i.140; **KJ** V.ii.113
  2 power, strength, scope **3H6** I.i.233 [Queen to King] *Thou hast … given unto the house of York such head / As thou shalt reign but by their sufferance;* **2H4** I.iii.17, III.i.72; **KJ** I.i.579; **TS** I.ii.246
  3 commander, officer, captain **AC** IV.i.10 [Caesar to Maecenas] *Let our best heads / Know that tomorrow the last of many battles / We mean to fight*
  4 leader, chief, director **2H6** II.i.165 [Buckingham to King] *Lady Eleanor … / The ringleader and head of all this rout*
  5 advancing crowd of insurgents, uprising **Ham** IV.v.103 [Messenger to Claudius] *Laertes, in a riotous head, / O'erbears your officers*
  6 headway, progress, advance **E3** IV.iv.10 [Audley to Prince Edward, of the French] *This sudden, mighty, and expedient head;* **Oth** I.iii.271
  7 surface, surge, swell **1H4** I.iii.105 [Hotspur to King Henry, of the Severn] *hid his crisp head in the hollow bank;* **MV** II.vii.44
  8 headland, cape, promontory **AC** III.vii.51 [Antony to all] *will we … from th'head of Actium / Beat th'approaching Caesar*
  9 source, origin, fountainhead **R2** III.iii.108 [Northumberland to King Richard, of Bolingbroke and Richard] *Currents that spring from one most gracious head;* **AW** I.iii.167; **Ham** I.i.106
  10 category, topic, heading **Tim** III.v.28 [First Senator to Alcibiades] *Your words have took such pains as if they laboured / To … set quarrelling / Upon the head of valour*
  11 arrow-head **AY** II.i.24 [Duke Senior to all, of the deer] *with forked heads / Have their round haunches gored* **☞** **WEAPONS**, p.491
  12 **☞** take head from; turn head

head, at head on [with an enemy] **Tit** V.i.102 [Aaron to Lucius, of himself] *As true a dog as ever fought at head*

head, of the first [of deer] with antlers first developed **LL** IV.ii.10 [Nathaniel to Holofernes, of a deer] *it was a buck of the first head*

head, take the act without restraint, make a rush forward **R2** III.iii.14 [York to Northumberland, of dropping the title 'King' for Richard] *he would / Have been so brief with you to shorten you, / For taking so the head, your whole head's length* [also, pun: title]

head, to one's to one's face, frankly, openly **MA** V.i.62 [Leonato to Claudio] *Know, Claudio, to thy head, / Thou hast so wronged mine innocent child;* **MM** III.iii.141; **MND** I.i.106

head and front height and breadth, greatest extent **Oth** I.iii.80 [Othello to all, of his marriage to Desdemona] *The very head and front of my offending / Hath this extent, no more*

headborough (*n.*) parish officer, town constable **MA** III.v.1 [stage direction] *Enter … Dogberry and the Headborough, Verges* **☞** thirdborough (*n.*)

headed (*adj.*) having come to a head, full-grown, matured **AY** II.vii.67 [Duke Senior to Jaques] *all th'embossed sores and headed evils / That thou … hast caught*

heading (*n.*) beheading **MM** II.i.226 [Escalus to Pompey, of the possible outcome] *It is but heading and hanging*

headlong (*adv.*) head downwards, without ceremony **2H6** IV.x.78 [Iden to dead Cade] *Hence will I drag thee headlong by the heels*

head-lugged (*adj.*) pulled along by the ears; or: baited, tormented **KL** IV.ii.42 [Albany to Gonerill, of Lear] *Whose reverence even the head-lugged bear would lick* ➤ **lugged** *(adj.)*

headly *(adj.)* ➤ **heady** *(adj.)* 1

headpiece *(n.)* 1 head-covering **KL** III.ii.25 [Fool to Lear] *He that has a house to put's head in has a good headpiece* [also: sense 2]
2 brain, intellect **WT** I.ii.227 [Leontes to Camillo, of Hermione persuading Polixenes to stay] *Not noted, is't, / But ... By some severals / Of headpiece extraordinary?*

headstall *(n.)* part of a horse's bridle that goes over the head **TS** III.ii.56 [Biondello to Tranio as Lucentio, of Petruchio's horse] *with ... a headstall of sheep's leather*

heady *(adj.)* 1 violent, weighty, raging **H5** III.iii.32 [King Henry to citizens of Harfleur] *the filthy and contagious clouds / Of heady murder, spoil, and villainy* [F *headly*]; **1H4** II.iii.57; **H5** I.i.34
2 reckless, headstrong, impulsive **KL** II.iv.105 [Lear to Gloucester] *I ... am fallen out with my more headier will*

heady-rash *(adj.)* hasty-headed, full of reckless thoughts **CE** V.i.216 [Antipholus of Ephesus to Duke] *Nor heady-rash provoked with raging ire* ➤ **rash** *(adj.)* 3

health *(n.)* 1 toast, salutation in drink **AC** II.vii.83 [Pompey to all] *This health to Lepidus!*; **AC** II.vi.131; **2H4** V.iii.24; **RJ** I.iv.85; **Tim** I.ii.52, 55; **TN** I.iii.35
2 well-being, benevolence **Ham** I.iv.40 [Hamlet to Ghost] *Be thou a spirit of health or goblin damned*
3 well-being, prosperity **Ham** IV.vii.80 [Claudius to Laertes, of old age] *his sables and his weeds, / Importing health and graveness*
4 well-being, deliverance **CE** I.i.152 [Duke to Egeon] *I'll limit thee this day / To seek thy health by beneficial help* [F: *helpe*]
5 well-being, safety **JC** IV.iii.36 [Cassius to Brutus] *Have mind upon your health*

healthful *(adj.)* healthy, wholesome, fit [in health] **Ham** III.iv.142 [Hamlet to Gertrude] *My pulse as yours doth temperately keep time / And makes as healthful music*; **AW** II.iii.47; **CE** I.i.115; **H8** I.i.3; **JC** II.i.319

heap *(n.)* company, host, multitude **R3** II.i.54 [Richard to and of all] *this princely heap*; **JC** I.iii.23

heap, on a in ruins **Tim** IV.iii.102 [Alcibiades to Timon] *When I have laid proud Athens on a heap*

heaps, on in a mass, all together **TC** III.ii.26 [Troilus alone, of battle] *when they charge on heaps*

hear on *(v.)* listen further to **Tim** I.i.80 [Poet to Painter] *Nay, sir, but hear me on*

hearer *(n.)* playgoer, audience **H8** Prologue.24 [of the audience] *you are known / The first and happiest hearers of the town*

hearing *(n.)* news, report, spectacle **TS** V.ii.181 [Vincentio to all, of Katherina's speech] *'Tis a good hearing when children are toward*; **Cym** III.i.4

hearken *(v.)* 1 listen [to], pay attention [to] **Tem** I.ii.122 [Prospero to Miranda] *This King of Naples ... hearkens my brother's suit*; **Tem** III.ii.38 [Caliban to Stephano] *Wilt thou be pleased to hearken once again to the suit I made to thee?*; **2H4** II.iv.274; **Venus** 868
2 be on the lookout, await an opportunity **TS** IV.v.53 [Baptista to Tranio as Lucentio] *old Gremio is hearkening still*

hearken after *(v.)* 1 inquire into, find out about **MA** V.i.203 [Claudio to Don Pedro, of Borachio and Conrade] *Hearken after their offence*
2 hanker for, be attracted to **LL** I.i.214 [Costard to Berowne] *Such is the sinplicity of man to hearken after the flesh* [Q; F *simplicitie*]

hearken for *(v.)* 1 look forward to, lie in wait for **1H4** V.iv.51 [Prince Hal to King Henry] *they did me too much injury / That ever said I hearkened for your death*
2 desire, be attracted to **TS** I.ii.257 [Petruchio to Tranio as Lucentio, of Bianca] *The youngest daughter whom you hearken for*

hearsed *(v.)* coffined, placed in a hearse **Luc** 657 [Lucrece to Tarquin] *Thy sea within a puddle's womb is hearsed*; **Ham** I.iv.47; **MV** III.i.81

heart *(n.)* 1 courage, spirit, valour **Cor** II.iii.203 [Brutus to Citizens] *had your bodies / No heart among you?*; **AC** III.xiii.198; **KL** V.iii.131; **TS** IV.v.77, V.ii.170; **WT** IV.iii.105
2 spirit, soul, essence **Tim** I.i.280 [First Lord to Second Lord, of Timon] *He outgoes / The very heart of kindness*; **Cor** I.vi.55; **H8** I.ii.1 ➤ **DISCOURSE MARKERS**, p.127
3 utmost, maximum **TNK** III.i.4 [Arcite alone, of the rite they owe May] *the Athenians pay it / To th'heart of ceremony* [i.e. with as much ceremony as possible]
4 [term of endearment] sweetheart, beloved, love **Cym** I.ii.43 [Innogen to Posthumus, of her diamond] *take it, heart* ➤ **ADDRESS FORMS**, p.8
5 [term of endearment] dear friend **RJ** I.i.184 [Romeo to Benvolio, of his 'I rather weep'] *Good heart, at what?*
6 (plural) grand-hearted lads, fine companions **MND** IV.ii.23 [Bottom to all] *Where are these hearts?*; **Tem** I.i.5, 26

heart, for my for my life **TS** I.ii.38 [Petruchio to Hortensio, of Grumio knocking at the gate] *I ... could not get him for my heart to do it*

heart, in [in making a toast] in good spirits, in a spirit of fellowship **Tim** I.ii.52 [Timon to a lord] *My lord, in heart!*

heart, out of in poor condition, lacking in strength; also: lacking inclination **1H4** III.iii.6 [Falstaff to Bardolph] *I shall be out of heart shortly*

hearted *(adj.)* 1 heartfelt, spirited, full of vigour **Oth** I.iii.361 [Iago to Roderigo] *My cause is hearted*; **AC** III.xiii.177
2 seated in the heart, heart-centred **Oth** III.iii.445 [Othello to Iago] *Yield up, O love, thy crown and hearted throne / To tyrannous hate!*

hearten up *(v.)* encourage, cheer up, animate **Luc** 295 [of Tarquin] *heartens up his servile powers*

heartless *(adj.)* cowardly, gutless, spiritless **RJ** I.i.65 [Tybalt to Benvolio] *art thou drawn among these heartless hinds?*; **Luc** 471, 1392

heartlings ➤ **SWEARING**, p.435

heart-offending *(adj.)* heart-damaging **2H6** III.ii.60 [Queen to King, of Gloucester] *Might liquid tears or heart-offending groans ... recall his life*

heart-whole *(adj.)* with affections uncommitted, with the heart uninvolved **AY** IV.i.43 [Rosalind as Ganymede to Orlando, of the late-arriving suitor] *I'll warrant him heart-whole*

hearty *(adj.)* loving, devoted, sincere **AC** IV.ii.38 [Antony to all] *My hearty friends*

heat *(n.)* 1 anger, rage, passion **Cor** III.i.63 [First Senator to Coriolanus, of his speaking again] *Not in this heat, sir, now*; **Ham** III.iv.4, IV.v.156
2 urgency, intensity, force **Oth** I.ii.40 [Cassio to Othello] *It is a business of some heat*
3 desire, passion, libido **MM** III.i.37 [disguised Duke to Claudio, of being old] *Thou hast neither heat, affection, limb, nor beauty*
4 normal body temperature **TN** I.v.127 [Feste to Olivia, of a drunken man] *One draught above heat makes him a fool*

heat, in the while feeling heated, while worked up **KL** I.i.306 [Gonerill to Regan] *We must do something, and i'th' heat* [i.e. strike while the iron is hot]

heat *(v.)* race over, speed across **WT** I.ii.96 [Hermione to Leontes] *You may ride's / With one soft kiss a thousand furlongs ere / With spur we heat an acre*

heated *(adj.)* angry, inflamed, enraged, aroused **TNK** IV.ii.82 [Messenger to Theseus, of one of Arcite's knights] *as a heated lion, so he looks*; **3H6** II.i.123

heath *(n.)* heather **Tem** I.i.62 [Gonzalo alone, of being on dry land] *Long heath, brown furze, anything*

heave *(n.)* deep sigh, heaving [of the chest] **Ham** IV.i.1 [Claudius to Gertrude] *These profound heaves / You must translate*

heave (*v.*) **1** raise, lift up **AC** II.vii.13 [Second Servant to First Servant] *a partisan I could not heave;* **Cym** V.v.157; **2H6** IV.x.49; **Tit** IV.i.40

2 throw, toss, cast **Luc** 586 [Lucrece to Tarquin] *My sighs like whirlwinds labour hence to heave thee;* **Luc** 413

heave up (*v.*) raise, lift up **Venus** 351 [of Venus and Adonis] *With one fair hand she heaveth up his hat;* **2H6** I.ii.13

heaved-up (*adj.*) raised, lifted up **Luc** 111 [of Lucrece] *Her joy with heaved-up hand she doth express;* **Luc** 638 ☛ up-heave (*v.*)

heaven (*n.*) ☛ heavens (*n.*)

heavenly (*adj.*) **1** beautiful, delightful, sublime **TNK** IV.ii.32 [Emilia alone] *Narcissus was a sad boy, but a heavenly*

2 divine, celestial **TNK** V.iv.131 [Theseus to gods] *O you heavenly charmers, / What things you make of us!*

heavens (*n.*) **1** powers above, will of heaven **2H6** V.ii.73 [King to Queen] *Can we outrun the heavens?*

2 [covering over the rear of a stage] sky **1H6** I.i.1 [Bedford to all] *Hung be the heavens with black*

heavily (*adv.*) sorrowfully, sadly, gloomily **R3** I.iv.1 [Keeper to Clarence] *Why looks your grace so heavily today?;* **Mac** IV.iii.182; **R3** II.iii.40; **Sonn** 30.10; **Tem** IV.i.139

heaviness (*n.*) **1** sadness, grief, sorrow **2H4** IV.ii.82 [Archbishop to Mowbray] *Against ill chances men are ever merry, / But heaviness foreruns the good event;* **E3** V.i.130; **Luc** 1283; **MV** II.viii.52; **RJ** III.iv.11; **Tem** V.i.200

2 sleepiness, drowsiness **Tem** I.ii.307 [Miranda to Prospero] *The strangeness of your story put / Heaviness in me*

heaving (*n.*) groan, deep sigh **WT** II.iii.35 [Paulina to Lords, of Leontes] *'Tis such as you, / That ... do sigh / At each his needless heavings*

heaving (*adj.*) swelling, aroused, agitated **TC** II.ii.197 [Troilus to Hector] *the performance of our heaving spleens*

heavy (*adj.*) **1** sorrowful, sad, gloomy **3H6** I.iv.160 [York to Queen, of his son's murder] *if thou tellest the heavy story right ... the hearers will shed tears* ☛ FEW, p.xxi

2 grave, serious, weighty **1H4** I.iii.65 [Lady Percy to Hotspur] *Some heavy business hath my lord in hand;* **Ham** III.iii.84; **KL** IV.vi.147; **MM** I.iv.65; **RJ** III.iii.157; **TG** I.ii.84

3 pressing, weighty, overpowering **Tem** II.i.197 [Sebastian to Alonso, of the latter's feeling sleepy] *Do not omit the heavy offer of it*

4 weary, exhausted, worn out **MND** V.i.363 [Puck to himself] *the heavy ploughman snores;* **Cym** V.iv.165; **R3** III.i.5; **Tem** II.i.192

5 weighed down, burdened, laden **TC** IV.i.67 [Diomedes to Paris, of Menelaus] *he as you, each heavier for a whore*

6 tedious, tiresome, uninteresting **Venus** 156 [Venus to Adonis, of love] *may it be / That thou should think it heavy unto thee?*

7 slow-moving, sluggish, laggard **AC** III.vii.38 [Enobarbus to Antony, of Caesar's navy] *Their ships are yare; yours, heavy;* **MND** V.i.358

8 gloomy, dark, overcast **Oth** V.i.42 [Lodovico to Gratiano] *It is a heavy night;* **MM** IV.i.34

9 troublesome, iniquitous, heinous **2H4** IV.iii.55 [Prince John to Falstaff, responding to 'let desert mount'] *Thine's too heavy to mount* [also: heavy in weight]

10 brutal, oppressive, wicked **KJ** IV.iii.58 [Bastard to all, of Arthur's apparent murder] *The graceless action of a heavy hand*

heavy-gaited (*adj.*) ponderously walking, clumsy-moving **R2** III.ii.15 [King Richard to the earth, of his foes] *let ... heavy-gaited toads, lie in their way*

hebona (*n.*) poisonous plant [identity not known, perhaps henbane] **Ham** I.v.62 [Ghost to Hamlet] *With juice of cursed hebona in a vial* [Q1,Q2; F *hebenon*] ☛ PLANTS, p.330

hectic (*n.*) wasting fever, persistent fever **Ham** IV.iii.68 [Claudius alone, as if to the King of England] *like the hectic in my blood*

hedge (*v.*) **1** deviate from a straight path, shift direction **H8** III.ii.39 [Lord Chamberlain to Surrey, of Wolsey] *The King in this perceives him how he coasts / And hedges his own way;* **TC** III.iii.158

2 evade, be devious, prevaricate **MW** II.ii.24 [Falstaff to Pistol] *I myself sometimes ... am fain to shuffle, to hedge*

3 protect, surround **Ham** IV.v.125 [Claudius to all] *There's such divinity doth hedge a king*

hedge in (*v.*) restrict, confine, limit **JC** IV.iii.30 [Cassius to Brutus] *You forget yourself, / To hedge me in* [i.e. limit my authority]

hedge out (*v.*) exclude, keep out, shut out **TC** III.i.59 [Helen to Pandarus, of his attempt to talk to Paris alone] *this shall not hedge us out*

hedge-pig (*n.*) hedgehog **Mac** IV.i.2 [Second Witch to Witches] *Thrice, and once the hedge-pig whined*

hedge-priest (*n.*) [contemptuous] roadside cleric, uneducated priest **LL** V.ii.538 [Berowne to King, counting off the Worthies] *The pedant, the braggart, the hedge-priest, the fool, and the boy*

heed (*n.*) **1** consideration, care, attention **Cor** V.vi.62 [Aufidius to Lords] *have you with heed perused / What I have written to you?;* **H5** V.ii.80; **H8** III.ii.82; **TNK** III.vi.232

2 that which one heeds; or: guardian **LL** I.i.82 [Berowne to King, of a woman's eye] *Who dazzling so, that eye shall be his heed*

heedful (*adj.*) **1** careful, mindful, watchful **Luc** 495 [Tarquin to Lucrece] *Will is deaf, and hears no heedful friends;* **AW** I.iii.220

2 attentive, receptive, alert **3H6** III.iii.63 [Warwick to Bona, of Edward] *fame, late entering at his heedful ears*

heedfully (*adv.*) **1** attentively, carefully, conscientiously **Tem** I.ii.78 [Miranda to Prospero, of how she is listening to him] *most heedfully;* **TG** II.vi.11

2 with anxious attention, apprehensively **Luc** 454 [of Lucrece woken by Tarquin] *heedfully doth view / The sight which makes supposed terror true*

heedless (*adj.*) careless, slack, inattentive **TS** IV.i.152 [Petruchio to servants] *You heedless jolt-heads*

heel (*n.*) end, completion, termination **AW** I.ii.57 [King to Bertram] *the catastrophe and heel of pastime;* **AC** II.ii.163

heels, at close behind, in close pursuit **TNK** I.i.221 [Pirithous to Theseus] *I'll follow you at heels*

heels, by the in the stocks, in irons **2H4** I.ii.124 [Lord Chief Justice to Falstaff] *To punish you by the heels would amend the attention of your ears*

heels, out at penniless, destitute, in desperate straights **MW** I.iii.28 [Falstaff to Nym and Pistol] *I am almost out at heels*

heels, take my take to my heels, run away **CE** I.ii.94 [Dromio of Ephesus to Antipholus of Syracuse] *I'll take my heels*

heft (*n.*) heaving, retching **WT** II.i.45 [Leontes to Lord, of someone who has seen something unpleasant in a drink] *he cracks his gorge, his sides, / With violent hefts*

heigh (*int.*) ☛ EXCLAMATIONS, p.158; REGRETS, p.367; SING-ING, p.402

height (*n.*) **1** maximum, highest amount, utmost degree **TC** V.i.3 [Achilles to Patroclus, of Hector] *let us feast him to the height;* **Ham** I.iv.21; **H8** I.ii.214; **Tim** III.v.88

2 rank, high birth, high degree **R2** I.i.189 [Bolingbroke to King Richard] *Shall I ... with pale beggar-fear impeach my height*

3 [navigation] altitude, elevation **Sonn** 116.8 [of a star] *Whose worth's unknown, although his height be taken*

heightened (*adj.*) exalted, elevated, raised up **Cor** V.vi.22 [Aufidius to Third Conspirator, of Coriolanus] *being so heightened, / He watered his new plants with dews of flattery*

heighth (*n.*) variant spelling of 'height' **KJ** IV.iii.46 [Salisbury to Bastard, of finding Arthur's body] *This is the very top, / The heighth, the crest, or crest unto the crest, / Of murder's arms* [F]

heinous (*adj.*) calamitous, terrible, severe **KJ** III.iv.90 [Cardinal Pandulph to Constance] *You hold too heinous a respect of grief;* **KJ** IV.iii.56

heinously (*adv.*) atrociously, shockingly, dreadfully **1H4** III.iii.187 [Falstaff to Prince Hal] *I am heinously unprovided*

heir (*n.*) offspring, progeny, fruit **R2** II.ii.63 [Queen Isabel to Green] *Bolingbroke [is] my sorrow's dismal heir;* **2H4** IV.i.198

heir general (*n.*) heir from either male or female lines **H5** I.ii.66 [Canterbury to King Henry, of Pepin] *as heir general, being descended / Of Blithild*

hell-hated (*adj.*) hated as hell is hated **KL** V.iii.145 [Edmund to Edgar] *I ... / With the hell-hated lie o'erwhelm thy heart*

hell-kite (*n.*) kite from hell, hellish savage **Mac** IV.iii.217 [Macduff to Ross, of Macbeth] *O hell-kite!* ☛ **kite** (*n.*)

helm (*n.*) **1** helmet **R3** V.iii.352 [King Richard to his army] *Victory sits on our helms;* **AW** III.iii.7; **Cor** IV.v.128; **KL** IV.ii.57; **Oth** I.iii.269; **TC** I.ii.233
   2 helmsman, guide, pilot **Cor** I.i.75 [Menenius to Citizens] *you slander / The helms o'th' state*
   3 covering of hair **KL** IV.vii.36 [Cordelia to Lear, of Lear on the heath] *To watch, poor perdu, / With this thin helm?*

helm (*v.*) guide, steer, direct **MM** III.ii.134 [disguised Duke to Lucio, of himself] *the business he hath helmed*

help (*n.*) treatment, cure, relief **CE** V.i.160 [Adriana to Duke, of Antipholus] *Let him be brought forth, and borne hence for help*

help, at in our favour, ready to help **Ham** IV.iii.43 [Claudius to Hamlet] *the wind at help* [i.e. in the right quarter]

help (*v.*) restore, succour, cure **Cym** III.vi.4 [Innogen alone] *I should be sick, / But that my resolution helps me*

helpless (*adj.*) unavailing, useless, unprofitable **R3** I.ii.13 [Anne to dead Henry VI] *in these windows that let forth thy life / I pour the helpless balm of my poor eyes;* **CE** II.i.39; **Luc** 1027; **Venus** 604

hem (*n.*) edge, margin, shore **Tim** IV.v.66 [Soldier to Alcibiades, of Timon] *Entombed upon the very hem o'th' sea*

hem (*v.*) **1** enclose, surround, confine **Venus** 229 [Venus to Adonis] *Fondling ... I have hemmed thee here;* **Venus** 1022
   2 make a noise like 'hmm' or 'ahem' **Ham** IV.v.5 [Gentleman to Gertrude, of Ophelia] *she ... hems, and beats her heart* ☛ **SOUNDS**, p.410

hem away (*v.*) remove, clear away [with a cough or 'hem'] **AY** I.iii.18 [Celia to Rosalind, of burs] *Hem them away* [pun on 'bur', something sticking in the throat]

hem (*int.*) **1** [drinking call] make a noise like 'ahem'; clear the throat **2H4** III.ii.212 [Shallow to Falstaff] *Our watchword was 'Hem, boys!'* **1H4** II.iv.16
   2 make a noise like 'hmm' **MA** V.i.16 [Leonato to Antonio, of another wronged person] *cry 'hem!' when he should groan* [i.e. in hesitation]

hemlock (*n.*) variety of poisonous plant **KL** IV.iv.4 [Cordelia to Doctor, of Lear] *Crowned with ... hardokes, hemlock;* **H5** V.ii.45 ☛ **PLANTS**, p.330

hempen (*adj.*) **1** made of hemp **2H6** IV.vii.83 [Cade to Say] *Ye shall have a hempen caudle* [i.e. the medicine of the hangman's rope]
   2 in clothing made of hemp, rustically attired **MND** III.i.70 [Puck to himself, of the rustics] *What hempen homespuns have we swaggering here*

hempseed (*n.*) malapropism for 'homicide' **2H4** II.i.56 [Hostess to Falstaff] *thou hempseed!*

hence (*adv.*) **1** away from here, from this place **Ham** IV.iii.57 [Claudius to all, of Hamlet] *I'll have him hence tonight* ☛ **HENCE, THENCE, AND WHENCE**, p.219
   2 in the next world **Ham** III.ii.232 [Second Player, as Queen, to her King] *Both here and hence pursue me lasting strife*

henceforth (*adv.*) from now on, from this time forth **AY** I.ii.31 [Celia to Rosalind, of Fortune] *that her gifts may henceforth be bestowed equally* ☛ **HENCE, THENCE, AND WHENCE**, p.219

henceforth, from from now on, from this time forth **AY** I.ii.23 [Rosalind to Celia, agreeing] *From henceforth I will*

hence-going (*n.*) departure, leaving **Cym** III.ii.64 [Innogen to Pisanio] *from our hence-going / And our return*

henchman (*n.*) squire, page of honour **MND** II.i.121 [Oberon to Titania] *I do but beg a little changeling boy / To be my henchman*

hent (*n.*) clutch, grasp **Ham** III.iii.88 [Hamlet to himself] *Up, sword, and know thou a more horrid hent* [or: occasion, if variant of 'hint']

hent (*v.*) **1** grasp, take hold of **WT** IV.iii.122 [Autolycus singing] *Jog on, jog on, the footpath way, / And merrily hent the stile-a*
   2 reach, arrive at, occupy **MM** IV.vi.14 [Friar Peter to Isabella and Mariana] *The generous and gravest citizens / Have hent the gates*

herald (*n.*) messenger, carrier, emissary **R3** I.i.72 [Clarence to Richard] *there is no man secure / But ... night-walking heralds* [i.e. thieves]

herald (*adj.*) message-bearing, acting as a herald **TG** III.i.144 [Duke reading Valentine's letter to Silvia] *My herald thoughts in thy pure bosom rest them*

heraldry (*n.*) heraldic devices, armorial bearings **Ham** II.ii.454 [Hamlet to First Player, quoting lines about Pyrrhus] *this dread and black complexion smeared / With heraldry more dismal* [i.e. with colours changed from black to red]

herb (*n.*) plant **R3** II.iv.13 [York to Duchess of York, quoting Richard] *Small herbs have grace* ☛ **PLANTS**, p.330

herb of grace (*n.*) ☛ **PLANTS**, p.330

herblet (*n.*) little herb **Cym** IV.ii.287 [Belarius to dead Cloten and supposedly dead Innogen] *These herblets shall [wither]*

herb-woman (*n.*) woman who sells herbs **Per** IV.vi.81 [Lysimachus to Marina, of Bawd] *your herb-woman*

herdman (*n.*) herdsman **Venus** 456 [of Adonis' mouth] *Like a red morn, that ever yet betokened ... / Gusts and foul flaws to herdmen and to herds*

here (*adv.*) ☛ **HERE, THERE, AND WHERE**, p.220

hereafter (*adj.*) future, forthcoming, later **1H6** II.ii.10 [Talbot to all] *hereafter ages may behold / What ruin happened;* **E3** V.i.229; **R3** IV.iv.390

hereafter (*adv.*) **1** after this, in time to come **Ham** I.v.171 [Hamlet to Horatio and Marcellus] *As I perchance hereafter shall think meet*
   2 at some time in the future **Mac** V.v.17 [Macbeth to Seyton, of hearing the news of Lady Macbeth's death] *She should have died hereafter* [debated meaning: she would have died at some time in any case] ☛ **HERE, THERE, AND WHERE**, p.220

here-approach (*n.*) arrival here **Mac** IV.iii.133 [Malcolm to Macduff] *before thy here-approach, / Old Seyward with ten thousand warlike men ... was setting forth*

herein (*adv.*) in here, in this [matter, situation, etc] **Ham** I.ii.14 [Claudius to all] *Nor have we herein barred / Your better wisdoms* ☛ **HERE, THERE, AND WHERE**, p.220

here-remain (*n.*) stay, visit, sojourn **Mac** IV.iii.148 [Malcolm to Macduff, of the English king curing the sick] *Which often since my here-remain in England / I have seen him do*

heritage (*n.*) inheritance, legacy **AW** I.iii.24 [Clown to Countess] *Service is no heritage* [i.e. a servant's life does not yield a good future for his children]

hermit (*n.*) one who prays for another, beadsman **Mac** I.vi.20 [Lady Macbeth to King, of the honours the King has bestowed] *For those of old ... / We rest your hermits*

Herod of Jewry out-and-out villain **MW** II.i.19 [Mistress Page to herself, of Falstaff] *What a Herod of Jewry is this!*

heroical (*adj.*) **1** heroic **LL** IV.i.67 [Boyet reading Armado's letter to Jaquenetta] *have commiseration on thy heroical vassal;* **H5** II.iv.59
   2 appropriate to the character of a hero **TC** III.iii.192 [Ulysses to Achilles] *'gainst your privacy / The reasons are more potent and heroical;* **TC** III.iii.248

hest (*n.*) command, behest, order **Tem** I.ii.274 [Prospero to Ariel, of Sycorax] *Refusing her grand hests;* **1H4** II.iii.64; **LL** V.ii.65; **Tem** III.i.37, IV.i.65

hewgh (*int.*) ☛ **SOUNDS**, p.410

HENCE, THENCE, AND WHENCE

This set of adverbs still has some literary use, though *whence* is now rare, having been replaced in modern English by 'where from'. *Hence* is the most complex form, having meanings of place, time, and result (the latter common in modern formal English), and also entering into the occasional compound formation, such as *hence-going* [= departure] (**Cym** III.ii.64). Other constructions belonging to this set (e.g. *whenceforth*) were used in Early Modern English, but are not found in Shakespeare.

Item	Location	Example	Gloss
hence	**AY** II.vii.3	*he is but even now gone hence*	(away) from here, from this place
	CE III.i.122	*I'll meet you at that place some hour hence*	from now, from this point in time
	Lover 110	*controversy hence a question takes*	as a result, therefore
henceforth	**RJ** III.v.241	*Thou and my bosom henceforth shall be twain*	from this time forth; from now on
henceforward	**2H6** IV.vii.16	*henceforward all things shall be in common*	from now on
thence	**Tem** I.ii.394	*Thence I have followed it*	(away) from there, from that place
whence	**1H6** I.iv.99	*Whence cometh this alarum and the noise?*	from which / what place, from where [also: from what source / origin]
whencesoever	**R2** II.iii.22	*It is my son ... / Sent from my brother Worcester whencesoever*	from whatever place, from somewhere or other

Several of these forms were sometimes used with a redundant preposition.

hence, from	**R2** III.iii.6	*Richard not far from hence hath hid his head*	
henceforth, from	**1H4** I.iii.5	*I will from henceforth rather be myself*	
thence, from	**CE** IV.iv.147	*Fetch our stuff from thence*	
whence, from	**CE** III.i.37	*Let him walk from whence he came*	
whence, of	**MM** III.ii.206	*Of whence are you?*	

☞ HERE, THERE, AND WHERE, p.220; **HITHER, THITHER, AND WHITHER**, p.224

hey, hey-ho (*int.*) **☞ SINGING**, p.402

heyday (*n.*) excited state, youthful wildness **Ham** III.iv.70 [Hamlet to Gertrude] *The heyday in the blood is tame*

hick (*v.*) hiccup [from drinking] **MW** IV.i.61 [Mistress Quickly to Mistress Page, of Evans and William] *He teaches him to hick and to hack*

hide (*v.*) disregard, overlook, put out of sight **LL** V.ii.727 [Princess to King] *excuse or hide / The liberal opposition of our spirits*

hideous (*adj.*) terrifying, frightful, horrifying **Sonn** 5.6 *For never resting time leads summer on / To hideous winter;* **Ham** I.iv.54, II.ii.474; **Sonn** 12.2

hie (*v.*) hasten, hurry, speed **CE** I.i.90 [Dromio of Ephesus to Antipholus of Syracuse] *hie you home to dinner* **☞ FEW**, p.xxi

Hiems (*n.*) winter [personified] **MND** II.i.109 [Titania to Oberon] *we see ... on old Hiems' thin and icy crown / An odorous chaplet of sweet summer buds;* **LL** V.ii.880

high (*adj.*) **1** very great, extreme **Tim** IV.iii.432 [Timon to Bandits, of drinking wine] *Till the high fever seethe your blood to froth;* **3H6** II.i.59; **Luc** 19; **Oth** V.ii.94; **R3** III.vii.154; **Tim** IV.iii.246

2 important, major, special **1H6** I.vi.26 [Charles to all, of Pucelle] *Her ashes ... / Transported shall be at high festivals;* **2H4** IV.vi.3; **H8** I.i.61; **JC** I.ii.169; **KL** III.vi.109

3 noble, dignified, aristocratic **3H6** I.iv.72 [Queen to York] *Was't you that ... made a preachment of your high descent?;* **AC** V.ii.364; **TC** Prologue.2

4 proud, haughty, grand **R2** I.iv.2 [Richard to Aumerle] *How far brought you high Hereford on his way?* [Aumerle] *I brought high Hereford, if you call him so, / But to the next highway;* **AC** III.xiii.126; **H8** I.i.107; **Tem** V.i.25

5 lofty, elevated, grand **1H6** I.i.93 [Charles to Pucelle] *Thou hast astonished me with thy high terms;* **H8** Prologue.3

6 sophisticated, elevated, superior **Tem** III.iii.89 [Prospero to Ariel] *My high charms work*

7 built-up, raised **2H4** I.ii.37 [Falstaff to Page] *The whoreson smoothy-pates do now wear nothing but high shoes and bunches of keys at their girdles*

high (*adv.*) fully, altogether **TN** I.i.15 [Orsino to all, of love] *it alone is high fantastical;* **AW** V.iii.10; **Oth** IV.ii.240

high-battled (*adj.*) in charge of great armies **AC** III.xiii.29 [Enobarbus to himself] *like enough, high-battled Caesar will / Unstate his happiness*

high-born (*adj.*) noble, lofty, grand **LL** I.i.170 [King to Berowne, of Armado] *For interim to our studies shall relate / In high-born words the worth of many a knight*

high-coloured (*adj.*) flushed, red-faced **AC** II.vii.4 [Second Servant to First Servant] *Lepidus is high-coloured*

high-cross (*n.*) cross in a town centre **TS** I.i.130 [Gremio to Hortensio, of a fate better than marrying Katherina] *to be whipped at the high-cross every morning*

high-day (*n.*) day of celebration, festival day, holiday **Tem** II.ii.182 [Caliban to Stephano] *Freedom, high-day!*

HERE, THERE, AND WHERE

A particularly productive kind of word-formation in Early Modern English was to use the adverbs *here*, *there*, and *where* as the first elements of compounds, the second element being a preposition, or occasionally another adverb. Not all the possible combinations are found in Shakespeare: the list below gives those which are present, in their chief meanings, some of which of course are still in use today (e.g. *thereabouts*, *therefore*).

Item	Location	Example	Gloss
+about			
hereabout	**Oth** V.i.57	*I think that one of them is hereabout*	around here
hereabouts	**RJ** V.i.38	*I do remember an apothecary, / And hereabouts 'a dwells*	around here
thereabout	**Ham** II.ii.445	*[of a tale] thereabout of it especially when he speaks of Priam's daughter*	about that part, concerning the matter
thereabouts	**AW** IV.iii.171	*Five or six thousand horse … or thereabouts*	approximately, about that [place, number, time, etc.]
whereabout	**Mac** II.i.58	*The very stones prate of my whereabout*	whereabouts
whereabout	**1H4** II.iii.107	*I must not have you henceforth question me / Whither I go, nor reason whereabout*	about what, on what business
+after			
hereafter	**Cor** III.ii.85	*thou wilt frame / Thyself, forsooth, hereafter theirs*	after this, in time to come
thereafter	**2H4** III.ii.56	*[Shallow] How a score of ewes now? [Silence] Thereafter as they be*	conforming to the matter
+against			
whereagainst	**Cor** IV.v.110	*that body, whereagainst / My grained ash an hundred times hath broke*	against which place
+at			
thereat	**KL** IV.ii.75	*[of a servant] bending his sword / To his great master; who, thereat enraged, / Flew on him*	thereupon, because of that
whereat	**Cor** V.vi.134	*Thou hast done a deed whereat valour will weep*	at which
+by			
hereby	**LL** I.ii.130	*[Armado] I will visit thee at the lodge. [Jaquenetta] That's hereby*	nearby, close by
hereby	**R3** I.iv.94	*[of giving up Clarence] I will not reason what is meant hereby*	by this, from this circumstance
thereby	**AY** II.vii.48	*And thereby hangs a tale*	by that, through that
whereby	**TS** II.i.266	*by this light whereby I see your beauty*	by which
+fore			
therefore	**Tem** IV.i.22	*Therefore take heed*	for that reason
wherefore	**KJ** V.i.44	*But wherefore do you droop?*	why
+in			
herein	**Ham** II.ii.76	*[of a paper] an entreaty, herein further shown*	in here, in this [matter/situation, etc.]
therein	**Ham** II.ii.79	*[of a paper] such regards of safety and allowance / As therein are set down*	in there, in that [matter/situation, etc.]
wherein	**Sonn** 24.3	*My body is the frame wherein 'tis held*	in which
wherein	**AY** III.ii.214	*Wherein went he? [i.e. in what clothes]*	in what [condition, matter, etc.]

HERE, THERE, AND WHERE – *continued*

Item	Location	Example	Gloss
+into			
whereinto	Oth III.iii.136	*where's that palace whereinto foul things / Sometimes intrude not?*	in which
+of			
hereof	TS IV.v.75	*go along and see the truth hereof*	of this, concerning this
thereof	R3 I.iii.307	*I repent / My part thereof that I have done to her*	of that, concerning that
whereof	TC I.iii.14	*every action ... / Whereof we have record*	of which, about which
whereof	Tim II.ii.175	*The breath is gone whereof this praise is made*	by means of which, through which
+on			
thereon	3H6 III.iii.116	*[of Edward being the true king] Thereon I pawn my credit and mine honour*	on that, upon that [place, subject, etc.]
whereon	Ham III.iv.125	*Whereon do you look?*	on what
whereon	Mac IV.i.137	*Infected be the air whereon they ride*	on which
whereon	Tem I.ii.127	*Whereon, a treacherous army levied*	whereupon
+out			
whereout	TC IV.v.245	*I may give the local wound a name, / And make distinct the very breach whereout / Hector's great spirit flew*	out of which, from which
+soever / somever			
wheresoever, wheresoe'er	MND II.ii.96	*Happy is Hermia, wheresoe'er she lies*	wherever
wheresomever	H5 II.iii.7	*Would I were with him, wheresome'er he is*	wherever
+through			
wherethrough, where-through	Sonn 24.11	*windows to my breast, where-through the Sun / Delights to peep*	through which
+to			
hereto	Cor II.ii.64	*A kinder value of the people than / He hath hereto prized them at*	hitherto, up to this time
thereto	TN V.i.83	*His life I gave him, and did thereto add / My love*	besides, in addition
thereto	H5 V.ii.90	*Anything in or out of our demands, / And we'll consign thereto*	to that [matter/place/time, etc.]
whereto	MND III.ii.256	*whereto tends all this?*	in what/which direction
whereto	Ham III.iii.46	*Whereto serves mercy / But to confront the visage of offence?*	for what purpose, to what end
whereto	KL V.viii.138	*To prove upon thy heart, whereto I speak, / Thou liest*	to which
+tofore			
heretofore	E3 I.i.46	*my breast, / Which heretofore was racked in ignorance*	before now, formerly
wheretofore	E3 IV.iii.49	*And wheretofore I loved thee as Villiers, / Hereafter I'll embrace thee as myself*	while until now

(continues)

HERE, THERE, AND WHERE – *continued*

Item	Location	Example	Gloss
+until [generally = unto]			
whereuntil	LL V.ii.492	*we know whereuntil it doth amount*	to which/what
+unto			
thereunto	H8 I.iii.27	*With all their honourable points of ignorance / Pertaining thereunto*	to that [place/matter, etc.]
whereunto	Cym III.iv.108	*[of the court] whereunto I never / Purpose return*	to which
+upon			
hereupon	LL I.ii.56	*I will hereupon confess I am in love*	upon this point, in relation to this matter
thereupon	2H4 IV.ii.68	*And thereupon I drink unto your grace*	upon that, on that basis
whereupon	R2 II.ii.58	*[on some being proclaimed traitors] whereupon the Earl of Worcester / Hath broken his staff*	for which reason, on which account
whereupon	1H4 IV.iii.42	*The King hath sent to know ... where-upon / You conjure from the breast of civil peace / Such bold hostility*	why, on what ground
whereupon	Sonn 20.6	*Gilding the object whereupon it gazeth*	upon which
+with			
therewith	Oth I.ii.88	*How may the Duke be therewith satisfied*	with that, along with that, by means of that
wherewith	1H6 I.i.102	*An army have I mustered in my thoughts / Wherewith already France is overrun*	with which / what

☞ HENCE, THENCE, AND WHENCE, p.219; HITHER, THITHER, AND WHITHER, p.224; YON WORDS, p.507

high-day *(adj.)* befitting a holiday MV II.ix.98 [Portia to Messenger, of Bassanio's messenger] *Thou spend'st such high-day wit in praising him*

high-engendered *(adj.)* coming from the heavens, brought into being from above KL III.ii.23 [Lear to the storm] *join / Your high-engendered battles 'gainst a head / So old and white as this*

higher *(adj.)* [unclear meaning] upper, northern AW II.i.12 [King to Lords] *Let higher Italy ... see that you come / Not to woo honour, but to wed it*

higher *(adv.)* **1** further, longer MW V.v.105 [Mistress Page to all] *I pray you ... hold up the jest no higher*
  2 [unclear meaning] further afield AW IV.iii.41 [Second Lord to First Lord, of Bertram] *Will he travel higher*

high-judging *(adj.)* judging from on high KL II.iv.223 [Lear to Gonerill] *tell tales of thee to high-judging Jove*

high-lone *(adv.)* upright by oneself, without support RJ I.iii.37 [Nurse to Lady Capulet, of Juliet as a baby] *she could stand high-lone*

highly *(adv.)* **1** greatly, crucially, in an important way Tit IV.iii.28 [Publius to Marcus, of Titus] *it highly us concerns / By day and night t'attend him carefully;* R3 III.i.180
  2 ambitiously, to be in a high position Mac I.v.18 [Lady Macbeth alone, of Macbeth] *What thou wouldst highly / That wouldst thou holily*

3 in high style, in an elevated manner 1H4 III.i.202 [Mortimer to Lady Mortimer] *thy tongue / Makes Welsh as sweet as ditties highly penned*

high-minded *(adj.)* arrogant, haughty, imperious 1H6 I.v.12 [Talbot to himself, of Pucelle] *this high-minded strumpet*

highmost, high-most *(adj.)* highest, topmost RJ II.v.9 [Juliet alone] *Now is the sun upon the highmost hill / Of this day's journey;* Sonn 7.9

high-pitched *(adj.)* high-aspiring Luc 41 [of Tarquin] *envy ... did sting / His high-pitched thoughts*

high-proof *(adj.)* tested to the highest level, of proven strength MA V.i.122 [Claudio to Benedick, of himself and Don Pedro] *we are high-proof melancholy*

high-repented *(adj.)* bitterly repented AW V.iii.36 [Bertram to King] *My high-repented blames ... pardon me*

high-resolved *(adj.)* highly determined Tit IV.iv.64 [Aemilius to Saturninus, of the Goths] *with a power / Of high-resolved men*

high-sighted *(adj.)* high-flying, soaring beyond view JC II.i.118 [Brutus to all] *So let high-sighted tyranny range on*

high-stomached *(adj.)* proud, haughty, stubborn R2 I.i.18 [Richard to John of Gaunt, of Bolingbroke and Mowbray] *High-stomached are they both*

hight *(v.)* [archaism] is called **LL** I.i.248 [King reading Armado's letter to him, of a man] *Which, as I remember, hight Costard;* **LL** I.i.168; **MND** V.i.138; **Per** IV.Chorus.18 ☛ **ARCHAISMS**, p.22

high-vaunting *(adj.)* boastful, bragging, loud-mouthed **E3** IV.vii.3 [Prince Edward to Charles] *you, high-vaunting Charles of Normandy*

high-viced *(adj.)* full of great wickedness **Tim** IV.iii.110 [Timon to Alcibiades] *when Jove / Will o'er some high-viced city hang his poison / In the sick air*

high-witted *(adj.)* quick-witted **Tit** IV.iv.35 [Tamora to herself] *thus it shall become / High-witted Tamora to gloze with all*

high-wrought *(adj.)* extremely rough, highly turbulent **Oth** II.i.2 [First Gentleman to Montano, of the sea] *it is a high-wrought flood*

hild *(v.)* [archaism] held **Luc** 1257 *let it not be hild / Poor women's faults that they are so fulfilled / With men's abuses* ☛ **ARCHAISMS**, p.22

hilding *(n.)* good-for-nothing, worthless individual **RJ** III.v.168 [Capulet to Lady Capulet, of Juliet] *Out on her, hilding!;* **AW** III.vi.3; **Cym** II.iii.122; **RJ** II.iv.42; **TNK** III.v.43; **TS** II.i.26

hilding *(adj.)* good-for-nothing, worthless **2H4** I.i.57 [Lord Bardolph to Northumberland, of a gentleman] *He was some hilding fellow that had stolen / The horse he rode on;* **H5** IV.ii.27

hind *(n.)* **1** boor, fellow, rustic, peasant **2H6** III.ii.271 [Suffolk to Salisbury] *the commons, rude unpolished hinds;* **CE** III.i.77; **Cym** V.iii.77; **1H4** II.iii.17; **2H6** IV.iv.33; **LL** I.i.113
2 servant, domestic, worker **AY** I.i.17 [Orlando to Adam, of Oliver] *he lets me feed with his hinds;* **MW** III.v.90
3 female deer **MND** II.i.232 [Helena to Demetrius] *the mild hind / Makes speed to catch the tiger;* **JC** I.iii.106; **TC** III.ii.192

hinder legs *(n.)* hind legs **Venus** 698 [Venus to Adonis, of the hare] *Stands on his hinder legs with listening ear*

hindmost *(adj.)* last to arrive, last in order **2H6** III.i.2 [King to all, of Gloucester] *'Tis not his wont to be the hindmost man*

hinge *(v.)* bend, make flexible **Tim** IV.iii.212 [Apemantus to Timon] *Hinge thy knee*

hint *(n.)* **1** opportunity, moment, chance **Oth** I.iii.141 [Othello to all] *of antres vast and deserts idle … / It was my hint to speak;* **AC** III.iv.9, xi.18; **Cym** V.v.172; **Oth** I.iii.165
2 occasion, circumstance, experience **Tem** II.i.3 [Gonzalo to Alonso] *Our hint of woe / Is common;* **Tem** I.ii.134

hip, of the with the hips, using his hip **TNK** II.ii.71 [First Countryman to the others, of Arcite] *This fellow has a vengeance trick o'th' hip* [i.e. in wrestling]

hip, have on / upon the [wrestling] at a disadvantage, in an unfavourable position **MV** IV.i.331 [Gratiano to Shylock] *Now, infidel, I have you on the hip!;* **MV** I.iii.43; **Oth** II.i.296

hipped *(adj.)* with an injured hip, lame **TS** III.ii.48 [Biondello to Tranio as Lucentio, of Petruchio] *his horse hipped*

hire *(n.)* wages, payment, earnings **Cym** II.iv.129 [Posthumus to Iachimo] *take thy hire;* **AY** II.iii.39; **Cor** I.iii.38; **2H6** III.ii.225

history *(n.)* **1** story, tale, narrative **TS** Induction.ii.139 [Page as Sly's wife to Sly, of a comedy] *It is a kind of history;* **3H6** V.vi.28; **KL** I.i.236
2 history-play, chronicle, stage drama **WT** III.ii.35 [Hermione to Leontes, of the indictment against her] *which is more / Than history can pattern, though devised / And played to take spectators;* **AY** II.vii.165

history *(v.)* recount, narrate, relate **2H4** IV.i.201 [Archbishop to Mowbray, of King Henry IV] *therefore will he … keep no tell-tale to his memory / That may repeat and history his loss / To new remembrance*

histy *(adj.)* ☛ yeasty *(adj.)*

hit *(n.)* shot, stroke **RJ** I.i.208 [Romeo to Benvolio, responding to 'a right fair mark … is soonest hit'] *Well, in that hit you miss*

hit *(v.)* **1** hit the mark with, get at, reach **LL** IV.i.119 [Boyet to Maria, of Rosaline] *Have I hit her now?;* **AW** V.iii.195; **2H6** IV.ii.19
2 match, fall in [with], coincide [with] **Mac** III.vi.1 [Lennox to Lord] *My former speeches have but hit your thoughts;* **H8** I.ii.84; **Tim** III.i.6
3 agree, be in accord; or: strive, aim **KL** I.i.302 [Gonerill to Regan] *let us hit together* [Q; F *sit*]

hit it words of a song refrain [used in **LL** IV.i.126] **LL** IV.i.122 [Rosaline to Boyet] *Shall I come upon thee with an old saying … as touching the hit it?*

hither *(adv.)* here, to this place / time / end **Ham** II.ii.318 [Rosencrantz to Hamlet, of the players] *And hither are they coming* ☛ **HITHER, THITHER, AND WHITHER**, p.224

hitherto *(adv.)* **1** to this point, up to here **1H4** III.i.70 [Mortimer to all, of the division of land] *England, from Trent and Severn hitherto, / By south and east is to my part assigned* ☛ **HITHER, THITHER, AND WHITHER**, p.224
2 to this extent **Ham** III.ii..216 [First Player, as King, to his Queen] *And hitherto doth love on fortune tend*
3 up to now **Ham** I.ii.247 [Hamlet to Horatio, Marcellus, and Barnardo, of the Ghost] *If you have hitherto concealed this sight*

hive *(n.)* beehive-shaped head-covering **Lover** 8 [of the woman] *Upon her head a plaited hive of straw*

hoar *(adj.)* **1** grey-white, hoary **Tim** IV.iii.36 [Timon alone, of gold] *This yellow slave / Will …. / Make the hoar leprosy adored;* **Ham** IV.vii.167; **TNK** I.i.20
2 mouldy, musty, rotten **RJ** II.iv.130 [Mercutio to Romeo, of Nurse] *a hare … in a lenten pie, that is something stale and hoar ere it be spent* [also: whore]

hoar *(v.)* make white with disease **Tim** IV.iii.156 [Timon to all] *Hoar the flamen, / That scolds against the quality of flesh*

Hob and Dick every Tom, Dick, and Harry **Cor** II.iii.115 [Coriolanus alone] *To beg of Hob and Dick that does appear / Their needless vouches?*

hobby-horse *(n.)* **1** harlot, whore, prostitute **WT** I.ii.276 [Leontes to Camillo] *My wife's a hobby-horse* [F *Holy-Horse*]; **LL** III.i.28; **Oth** IV.i.154
2 buffoon, clown, joker **MA** III.ii.66 [Benedick to Leonato, of the others] *I have studied … wise words to speak to you, which these hobby-horses must not hear*

hob, nob give or take, come what may **TN** III.iv.235 [Sir Toby to Viola as Cesario, of Sir Andrew] *Hob, nob! is his word*

hodge-pudding *(n.)* stuffing made of many ingredients **MW** V.v.150 [Ford to all, of Falstaff] *a hodge-pudding?*

hogshead *(n.)* large cask, barrel [of wine] **WT** III.iii.91 [Clown to Shepherd, of the ship] *anon swallowed with yeast and froth, as you'd thrust a cork into a hogshead;* **1H4** II.iv.5; **2H4** II.iv.62; **LL** IV.ii.85; **Tem** IV.i.251

hoise *(v.)* **1** hoist **R3** IV.iv.527 [Fourth Messenger to King Richard, of Richmond] *He … / Hoised sail, and made his course again for Britain* [F *Hois'd*; Q *Hoist*]
2 heave up, remove by force **2H6** I.i.167 [Buckingham to Somerset] *We'll quickly hoise Duke Humphrey from his seat*

hoist *(v.)* launch; or: make go aloft **Tem** I.ii.148 [Prospero to Miranda, of reaching the ship with Antonio's agents] *There they hoist us*

hold *(n.)* **1** stronghold, castle, fortress **3H6** I.i.52 [Messenger to York] *fortify your hold, my lord;* **2H4** I.Induction.35; **KJ** V.vii.19
2 cell **MM** IV.iii.85 [disguised Duke to Provost, of Claudio and Barnadine] *Put them in secret holds*
3 guard, custody, confinement **R2** III.iv.83 [Gardener to Queen Isabel] *King Richard he is in the mighty hold / Of Bolingbroke;* **R3** IV.v.3; **TS** I.ii.117
4 shelter, refuge, sanctuary **Cym** III.vi.18 [Innogen alone] *'tis some savage hold;* **Cym** III.iii.20

hold *(v.)* **1** keep, maintain, observe **TNK** III.vi.228 [Emilia to Theseus] *That oath was rashly made, and in your anger; / Your reason will not hold it;* **AW** I.i.76; **1H4** III.ii.17; **KL** I.iii.27; **R3** III.ii.104; **Tem** II.i.65

2 keep, preserve, conserve **TG** V.iv.130 [Valentine to Thurio] *Verona shall not hold thee* [i.e. keep you safe]; **MA** I.i.84; **Oth** V.ii.330; **Per** II.ii.22

3 stand firm, continue, carry on **JC** I.ii.288 [Casca to Cassius, of dining with him] *Ay, if I be alive, and your mind hold;* **AC** II.v.92; **Ham** V.ii.173; **2H4** IV.i.217; **KL** I.iii.27; **MW** V.i.1

4 bear, tolerate, endure **Cor** III.ii.80 [Volumnia to Coriolanus] *humble as the ripest mulberry / That will not hold the handling;* **KL** II.iv.193; **TS** I.i.106

5 apply, be apt, remain valid **1H4** I.ii.30 [Prince Hal to Falstaff, of Falstaff's comparison] *Thou sayest well, and it holds well, too;* **MW** I.iii.80

6 survive, last out [until] **Ham** V.i.164 [First Clown to Hamlet] *we have many pocky corses nowadays that will scarce hold the laying in* [i.e. into the ground]

7 stay unbroken, hold out [in a fight] **TNK** III.vi.91 [Palamon to Arcite, of his sword] *if it but hold, I ask no more;* **TNK** III.vi.15; **TS** II.i.146

8 stop, cease, hold on **3H6** V.v.43 [Edward to Richard] *Hold, Richard, hold; for we have done too much;* **AY** V.i.12; **3H6** I.iv.54; **JC** V.iii.85; **KL** V.iii.153; **TNK** V.iv.40

9 withhold, hold back **H8** Epilogue.14 [of men] *'tis ill hap / If they hold when their ladies bid 'em clap;* **JC** II.i.201; **KJ** II.i.282

10 consider, regard, esteem, value [as] **Oth** I.iii.384 [Iago alone, of Othello] *He holds me well;* **Cym** IV.iii.16; **3H6** II.ii.109; **H8** I.iii.47; **MA** III.ii.87; **TNK** III.vi.89

11 avail, profit, benefit **AW** III.ii.91 [First Lord to Countess, of Parolles] *The fellow has a deal of that too much / Which holds him much to have* [i.e. he makes a good profit from his behaviour]

12 hold property, own land **2H6** IV.vii.115 [Cade to all] *Men shall hold of me in capite*

13 wager, offer as a bet **TS** III.ii.80 [Biondello to Baptista] *I hold you a penny;* **AW** III.ii.9

hold hands with be equal to, be comparable to **KJ** II.i.494 [King John to King Philip, of Blanche] *she in beauty, education, blood, / Holds hand with any princess of the world*

hold in *(v.)* keep silence, keep one's mouth shut **1H4** II.ii.78 [Gadshill to Chamberlain] *I am joined … with Burgomasters and great O-yeas, such as can hold in* [also: stick together; hold fast to a quarry]

hold it out keep it up **MW** IV.ii.126 [Ford to Mistress Ford, of her protestation of innocence] *Hold it out*

hold off *(v.)* be reticent, keep distance **Ham** II.ii.291 [Hamlet to Rosencrantz and Guildenstern] *hold not off* [i.e. speak freely]

HITHER, THITHER, AND WHITHER

'-ither' words all have the implication 'to a place / time / end', the selection of the meaning of location, time, or consequence depending on the context. *Hither, thither,* and *whither* are typically locational; most uses of *hitherto* are temporal. All uses of *hitherward(s)* and *thitherward* are locational. There is a close link between *whither* and *thither,* as seen in such pairings as 'Whither I go, thither shall you go too' (**1H4** II.iii.118). Context also motivates the choice between a static and a dynamic interpretation of place - 'whither away', in particular, carries a more dynamic force, as in 'Whither away so fast?' (**R3** II.iii.1).

Item	Location	Example	Gloss
hither and hither-			
hither	AY I.i.148	*I am heartily glad I came hither to you*	here, to this place
hitherto	1H6 III.iii.9	*We have been guided by thee hitherto*	up to now, thus far
hitherto	1H4 III.i.70	*England, from Trent and Severn hitherto, / By south and east is to my part assigned*	to this place, to this point
hitherto	Ham III.ii.216	*And hitherto doth love on fortune tend*	to this extent
hitherward	KL IV.iv.21	*The British powers are marching hitherward*	in this direction, towards this place
hitherwards	1H4 IV.i.92	*The Earl of Westmoreland seven thousand strong / Is marching hitherwards*	in this direction, towards this place
thither and thither-			
thither	Ham IV.iii.32	*In heaven. Send thither to see*	there, to that place
thither	AY I.i.161	*Nothing remains but that I kindle the boy thither*	to that end
thitherward	AW III.ii.52	*We met him thitherward*	in that direction, towards that place
whither and -whither			
whither	H8 V.i.6	*Whither so late?*	to which place, to whatever place
whither	Per IV.vi.124	*Whither would you have me?*	to what result, for what purpose
somewhither	Tit IV.i.11	*Somewhither would she have thee go with her*	somewhere

➤ **HERE, THERE, AND WHERE,** p.220; **HENCE, THENCE, AND WHENCE,** p.219

hold on (*v.*) carry on, go on with **E3** II.i.50 [King Edward to Lodowick] *bid the lords hold on their play at chess*

hold out (*v.*) sustain, maintain, keep up **3H6** II.vi.24 [Clifford alone] *No way to fly, nor strength to hold out flight;* **TN** IV.i.5

hold up (*v.*) **1** continue, keep going, carry on **MW** V.v.105 [Mistress Page to all] *hold up the jest no higher;* **Ham** V.i.31; **MA** II.iii.124; **MND** III.ii.239

2 support, uphold, sustain **3H6** I.i.46 [Warwick to York] *The proudest he that holds up Lancaster;* **2H4** I.iii.17, IV.ii.35; **KJ** II.i.364

hold-door (*adj.*) brothel door-keeping **TC** V.x.52 [Pandarus alone] *Brethren and sisters of the hold-door trade*

hold-fast (*adj.*) firmly grasping **Luc** 555 [of a cat] *in his hold-fast foot the weak mouse panteth*

holding (*n.*) **1** logic, maintaining, consistency **AW** IV.ii.27 [Diana to Bertram] *This has no holding, / To swear by him whom I protest to love / That I will work against him*

2 leasehold, tenure, grant of occupation **KJ** V.i.3 [Cardinal Pandulph to King John, of the crown] *Take again / From this my hand, as holding of the Pope / Your sovereign greatness and authority*
3 refrain, chorus **AC** II.vii.109 [Enobarbus to all] *The holding every man shall beat as loud / As his strong sides can volley*

holding up (*n.*) ability to maintain, power of sustaining **MM** III.i.262 [disguised Duke to Isabella, of his plan] *It lies much in your holding up*

holding-anchor (*n.*) [nautical] largest anchor; most stabilizing factor **3H6** V.iv.4 [Queen to all, of their situation] *The cable broke, the holding-anchor lost*

hole (*n.*) large pit in the ground **JC** II.i.205 [Decius to all] *unicorns may be betrayed with trees, / And ... elephants with holes*

holidam / holidame, by my ☞ **SWEARING**, p.435

holiday (*adj.*) refined, select, genteel **1H4** I.iii.45 [Hotspur to King Henry, of a lord] *With many holiday and lady terms / He questioned me* ☞ **speak holiday**

holiday time (*n.*) best time, prime **MW** II.i.2 [Mistress Page alone] *have I 'scaped love-letters in the holiday time of my beauty, and am I now a subject for them?*

holla, holloa (*v.*) halloo, shout, call out [to] **Venus** 973 [of Venus] *she hears some huntsman holloa* [Q1 hallow]; **1H4** I.iii.220; **KL** III.i.55

holla, holloa (*int.*) whoa, stop [to a horse] **Venus** 284 [of Adonis' horse] *What recketh he his rider's ... flattering 'Holla';* **AY** III.ii.237; **KL** V.iii.72 ☞ **hallow** (*v.*)

holland (*n.*) fine linen fabric **1H4** III.iii.70 [Hostess to Falstaff, of shirt material] *holland of eight shillings an ell!;* **2H4** II.ii.22

holloa (*int. / v.*) ☞ **holla** (*int. / v.*)

hollow (*adj.*) **1** empty, false, insincere **2H6** III.ii.66 [Queen to King, of Gloucester] *it is known we were but hollow friends;* **Ham** III.ii.218; **1H6** III.i.137; **2H6** III.i.43; **JC** IV.ii.23; **TC** IV.v.169

2 empty, wanting, insubstantial **TC** I.iii.80 [Ulysses to all] *look how many Grecian tents do stand / Hollow upon this plain*

hollow (*v.*) ☞ **hallow** (*v.*)

hollowly (*adv.*) insincerely, hypocritically, deceitfully **MM** II.iii.23 [disguised Duke to Juliet, of her penitence] *I'll ... try your penitence, if it be sound, / Or hollowly put on;* **Tem** III.i.70

hollowness (*n.*) insincerity, hypocrisy, lip-service **KL** I.i.154 [Kent to Lear] *Nor are those empty-hearted whose low sounds / Reverb no hollowness;* **KL** I.ii.112

holp (*v.*) past form of 'help' ☞ **PAST TENSES**, p.319

holy (*adj.*) **1** virtuous, upright, of great excellence **TG** IV.ii.40 [Musicians' song, of Silvia] *Holy, fair, and wise is she;* **Cym** III.iv.179; **TG** IV.ii.5

2 of holiness; also: full of holes **CE** II.i.80 [Dromio of Ephesus to Adriana, of his master, reacting to her threat to break his pate 'across'] *An he will bless that cross with other beating, / Between you I shall have a holy head*

holy-ale (*n.*) rural festival **Per** I.Chorus.6 [Gower alone] *On ember-eves and holy-ales* [Q *Holidayes*]

holy-cruel (*adj.*) cruel by being holy **AW** IV.ii.32 [Bertram to Diana] *Be not so holy-cruel*

holy-horse (*n.*) ☞ **hobby-horse** (*n.*) 1

holy tie marriage **TNK** Prologue.6 [of a play's 'marriage day'] *after holy tie and first night's stir*

homage (*n.*) **1** act of homage, acknowledgement of allegiance **TN** I.v.202 [Viola as Cesario to Olivia] *I bring ... no taxation of homage*

2 submission, servility, respectful acknowledgement **2H6** III.ii.224 [Warwick to Suffolk, of the latter begging his pardon] *after all this fearful homage done*

homager (*n.*) one who owes homage, vassal **AC** I.i.31 [Cleopatra to Antony] *that blood of thine / Is Caesar's homager*

home (*adv.*) **1** fully, thoroughly, unsparingly **KL** III.iii.11 [Gloucester to Edmund] *These injuries the King now bears will be revenged home;* **AW** V.iii.4; **Cor** III.iii.1; **Ham** III.iii.29; **Mac** I.iii.119; **WT** V.iii.4

2 into the heart of the enemy, to the target **Oth** V.i.2 [Iago to Roderigo] *Wear thy good rapier bare, and put it home;* **Cor** I.iv.38; **LL** V.i.57

3 to the end, to the finish **WT** I.ii.248 [Leontes to Camillo] *thou art ... a fool / That see'st a game played home*

4 bluntly, to the point, forthrightly **AC** I.ii.106 [Antony to Messenger] *Speak to me home;* **Cor** IV.ii.48; **Oth** II.i.162

5 directly, forthwith, right away **CE** IV.iii.92 [Courtesan alone, of Antipholus] *My way is now to hie home to his house*

6 [nautical] back into the ship, away from its hold **WT** I.ii.214 [Camillo to Leontes, of Polixenes] *You had much ado to make his anchor hold: / When you cast out, it still came home*

7 ☞ **lay home**

homely (*adj.*) **1** plain, simple, ordinary **2H6** V.iii.12 [Richard to York] *like rich hangings in a homely house;* **Cym** III.vii.6; **3H6** II.v.22; **RJ** II.iii.51; **WT** IV.iii.38, iv.331

2 plain-looking, unattractive, ugly **TG** II.iv.96 [Valentine to Thurio] *Upon a homely object Love can wink;* **CE** II.i.89; **WT** IV.iv.423

3 fating my humble parentage **AW** II.v.75 [Helena to Bertram] *[I shall] seek to eke out that / Wherein toward me my homely stars have failed / To equal my great fortune*

homespun (*n.*) wearer of home-made clothing, rustic, yokel **MND** III.i.70 [Puck to himself, of the rustics] *What hempen homespuns have we swaggering here*

homicide (*n.*) killer of men, murderer, slayer **1H6** I.ii.25 [Reignier to all] *Salisbury is a desperate homicide*

honest (*adj.*) **1** chaste, pure, virtuous **Oth** IV.ii.64 [Desdemona to Othello] *I hope my noble lord esteems me honest;* **AW** IV.ii.11; **AY** III.iii.23; **MW** I.iv.135; **TNK** V.ii.21; **WT** II.i.68

2 honourable, respectable, upright **RJ** III.i.62 [Nurse to Juliet] *O courteous Tybalt, honest gentleman!;* **Cor** V.iii.166; **Ham** III.i.122; **LL** V.ii.672; **R3** IV.iv.360; **TS** III.ii.25

3 genuine, real, true **2H4** V.i.44 [Davy to Shallow, of Visor] *The knave is mine honest friend;* **Ham** I.v.138; **MA** II.i.178; **MM** III.ii.148

4 innocent, well-intentioned, innocuous **MA** III.i.84 [Hero to Ursula] *I'll devise some honest slanders / To stain my cousin with*

honestly (*adv.*) honourably, commendably, worthily **Tim** V.i.14 [Painter to Poet, of visiting Timon] *It will show honestly in us*

honesty (*n.*) **1** virtue, chastity **AY** III.iii.27 [Touchstone to Audrey] *honesty coupled to beauty is to have honey a sauce to sugar;* **AW** I.iii.90; **3H6** III.ii.72; **MW** I.iii.46; **Tit** II.iii.135; **WT** II.i.155

2 honour, integrity, uprightness **AW** I.i.19 [Countess to Lafew, of Helena's father] *whose skill was almost as great as his honesty;* **Cym** III.vii.42; **JC** IV.iii.67; **KL** I.ii.351; **MA** II.i.351; **Oth** V.ii.243

3 generosity, liberality, hospitality **Tim** III.i.28 [Lucullus to Flaminius, of Timon] *Every man has his fault, and honesty is his*

4 decency, decorum, good manners **TN** II.iii.86 [Malvolio to Sir Toby, Sir Andrew, and Feste] *Have you no wit, manners, nor honesty;* **Ham** II.ii.203

honeyseed *(n.)* malapropism for 'homicide' **2H4** II.i.50 [Hostess to Falstaff] *thou honeyseed rogue!*

honey-stalk *(n.)* clover flower [harmful to sheep when eaten too much] **Tit** IV.iv.91 [Tamora to Saturninus, of enchanting Titus with words] *more dangerous / Than baits to fish, or honey-stalks to sheep*

honeysuckle *(adj.)* malapropism for 'homicidal' **2H4** II.i.48 [Hostess to Falstaff] *thou honeysuckle villain*

honour *(n.)* **1** fame, renown, glory **Cym** I.i.29 [First Gentleman to Second Gentleman, of Sicilius] *who did join his honour / Against the Romans*; **Mac** III.iv.39; **Oth** V.ii.243; **Tit** I.i.7; **TNK** III.vi.130
 2 credit, good name, reputation **TC** IV.v.287 [Ulysses to Troilus] *of what honour was / This Cressida in Troy?*; **AW** IV.ii.45; **Ham** III.i.42; **Per** II.ii.16; **TN** V.i.333
 3 noble rank, position of dignity, title of renown **KL** V.iii.127 [Edgar to Edmund, of the right to draw his sword] *it is the privilege of mine honours*; **Cor** II.i.190; **MW** I.i.42; **WT** II.ii.50
 4 object of honour, source of distinction **AW** IV.ii.42 [Bertram to Diana, of his ring] *It is an honour 'longing to our house*

honourable *(adj.)* **1** honest, upright, dignified **WT** II.i.111 [Hermione to Lords] *I have / That honourable grief lodged here which burns / Worse than tears drown*
 2 noble, distinguished, illustrious **2H6** IV.ii.46 [Cade to all] *am I of an honourable house*

honoured *(adj.)* honourable, dignified, virtuous **Ham** I.iv.16 [Hamlet to Horatio, of Claudius' revels] *it is a custom / More honoured in the breach than the observance*; **Cor** III.i.72; **KL** I.i.9

honour-owing honour-owning, honourable **H5** IV.vi.9 [Exeter to King Henry, of York] *by his bloody side, / Yoke-fellow to his honour-owing wounds, / The noble Earl of Suffolk also lies*

hood *(n.)* [unclear meaning] head-covering, bonnet **RJ** IV.iv.13 [Capulet alone, of Lady Capulet saying she will keep an eye on him] *A jealous hood* [i.e. a jealous woman] ☞ jealous-hood *(n.)*

hooded *(adj.)* [falconry] concealed, masked **H5** III.vii.108 [Constable to Orleans, of the Dauphin] *'Tis a hooded valour, and when it appears it will bate*

hoodman *(n.)* blind man [a call in Blind Man's Buff] **AW** IV.iii.117 [First Lord to Bertram, of Parolles] *Hoodman comes*

hoodman-blind *(n.)* blind-man's buff **Ham** III.iv.78 [Hamlet to Gertrude] *What devil was't / That thus hath cozened you at hoodman-blind?* [F; Q1 *hob-man*; Q2 *hodman*]

hoodwink *(v.)* **1** blindfold, cover one's eyes **AW** III.vi.22 [First Lord to Bertram, of Parolles] *We will bind and hoodwink him*; **RJ** I.iv.4
 2 deceive, delude **Mac** IV.iii.72 [Macduff to Malcolm] *the time you may so hoodwink*
 3 cover up, hide from sight **Tem** IV.i.206 [Caliban to Stephano] *the prize I'll bring thee to / Shall hoodwink this mischance*

hoodwinked *(adj.)* blindfolded, made unable to see **AW** IV.i.80 [First Soldier to Parolles] *hoodwinked as thou art*; **Cym** V.ii.16

hook *(n.)* **1** bait, lure, temptation **Cym** V.v.167 [Iachimo to Cymbeline, of Italian women] *that hook of wiving, / Fairness, which strikes the eye*
 2 pike, bill-hook **1H4** II.iv.331 [Falstaff to Prince Hal, of Glendower] *he of Wales that … swore the devil his true liegeman upon the cross of a Welsh hook*

hook *(v.)* attach, secure, make fast [as with a hook] **WT** II.iii.7 [Leontes to himself, of Hermione] *she / I can hook to me*

hook on *(v.)* stay close behind **2H4** II.i.161 [Falstaff to Bardolph] *Hook on, hook on!*

hoop *(n.)* circular shape, bent posture **Tem** I.ii.259 [Prospero to Ariel, of Sycorax] *who with age and envy / Was grown into a hoop*

hoop *(v.)* **1** encircle, enclose, enfold **WT** IV.iv.436 [Polixenes to Perdita, of Florizel] *if ever henceforth thou … hoop his body more with thy embraces*
 2 ☞ whoop *(v.)*

hope *(n.)* **1** likelihood, possibility **MW** III.iii.183 [Mistress Ford to Mistress Page, of Falstaff] *Shall we … give him another hope to betray him to another punishment?*
 2 prospect, expectation **Luc** 605 [Lucrece to Tarquin] *If in thy hope thou dar'st do such outrage, / What dar'st thou not when once thou art a king?* [i.e. as heir to a throne]

hope *(v.)* expect, anticipate, envisage **AC** II.i.38 [Menas to Pompey] *I cannot hope / Caesar and Antony shall well greet together*; **Cym** II.iii.152

hopeful *(adj.)* **1** promising, giving hope of success **RJ** I.ii.15 [Capulet to Paris, of Juliet] *She's the hopeful lady of my earth*; **H8** III.ii.419
 2 hoped-for, anticipated **Tit** II.iii.49 [Aaron to Tamora, of Bassianus and Lavinia] *Here comes a parcel of our hopeful booty*

hopeless *(adj.)* **1** despairing, without hope **3H6** I.iv.42 [Clifford to York] *So desperate thieves, all hopeless of their lives*; **CE** I.i.136; **Cym** IV.iv.27
 2 beyond hope, impossible to hope for **TNK** II.iii.4 [Gaoler's Daughter alone, of Palamon] *To marry him is hopeless*

hor-dock *(n.)* ☞ burdock *(n.)*

horn *(n.)* **1** (plural) outgrowths imagined to be on the head of a cuckold **AC** I.ii.4 [Charmian to Alexas] *O that I knew this husband, which you say must charge his horns with garlands!* ☞ cuckold *(n.)*
 2 horned beast **LL** IV.i.112 [Boyet to Rosaline, of the Princess while hunting] *My lady goes to kill horns* [pun: cuckold]
 3 type of wind instrument **MA** I.iii.58 [Benedick to himself] *a horn for my money* [i.e. I prefer war/sport to music]; **Cor** III.i.95
 4 drinking-horn **KL** III.vi.74 [Edgar as Poor Tom to himself] *thy horn is dry*

horn-beast *(n.)* horned animal **AY** III.iii.46 [Touchstone to Audrey, of the forest] *here we have … no assembly but horn-beasts* [pun on horns, suggesting a cuckold]

hornbook, horn-book *(n.)* [teaching device] leaf of paper, protected by a piece of thin horn, showing the letters of the alphabet and other information **LL** V.i.45 [Mote to Armado, of Holofernes] *He teaches boys the horn-book*

horning *(n.)* giving horns, making a cuckold **Tit** II.iii.67 [Lavinia to Tamora] *'Tis thought you have a goodly gift in horning*

horn-mad *(adj.)* [as of horned beasts] furious, enraged, raving mad **MA** I.i.249 [Claudio to Benedick] *thou wouldst be horn-mad*; **CE** II.i.57; **MW** I.iv.48, III.v.140

horn-maker *(n.)* maker of cuckolds **AY** IV.i.56 [Orlando to Rosalind as Ganymede] *Virtue is no horn-maker* ☞ cuckold *(n.)*

horologe *(n.)* clock, dial, timepiece **Oth** II.iii.125 [Iago to Montano, of Cassio] *He'll watch the horologe a double set, / If drink rock not his cradle*

horrible *(adv.)* extremely, exceedingly, terribly **1H4** II.iv.359 [Falstaff to Prince Hal] *art thou not horrible afeard?*; **KL** IV.vi.3

horrid *(adj.)* horrifying, frightful, terrifying **H5** IV.Chorus.28 [Chorus, of the English] *So many horrid ghosts*; **Cym** IV.ii.331; **Ham** II.ii.560; **H5** III.vi.76; **TN** III.iv.195

horridly *(adv.)* dreadfully, frightfully, terrifyingly **Ham** I.iv.55 [Hamlet to Ghost] *So horridly to shake our disposition*

horse *(n.)* cavalry, horse soldiers **Tim** I.i.245 [Messenger to Timon] *'Tis Alcibiades, and some twenty horse*; **AC** III.i.33; **E3** V.i.136; **2H4** II.i.172; **JC** IV.ii.29; **R3** V.iii.295

horse *(v.)* **1** sit astride [as on a horse], straddle **Cor** II.i.203 [Brutus to Sicinius] *ridges horsed / With variable complexions*
 2 mount, put on top of **WT** I.ii.288 [Leontes to Camillo, of Hermione and Polixenes] *Is whispering nothing? … Horsing foot on foot?*

horse-drench *(n.)* dose of horse medicine **Cor** II.i.113 [Menenius to Virgilia, of a prescription] *of no better report than a horse-drench*

horse-hairs *(n.)* bow-strings **Cym** II.iii.28 [Cloten to Musicians, of their music not affecting Innogen] *it is a vice in her ears, which horse-hairs … can never amend*

hose *(n.)* [pair of] breeches **TG** II.vii.55 [Lucetta to Julia] *A round hose ... now's not worth a pin;* **AW** II.iii.248; **AY** II.vii.161; **H5** III.vii.51; **LL** IV.iii.56; **Mac** II.iii.14 ☞ boot-hose *(n.)*; **CLOTHING**, p.79

hospitable *(adj.)* offering hospitality, affording welcome **Cor** I.x.26 [Aufidius to First Soldier] *Against the hospitable canon* [i.e. the law of hospitality]

host *(n.)* **1** army, armed multitude **H5** IV.Chorus.32 [Chorus, of King Henry] *forth he goes and visits all his host;* **AC** IV.viii.33; **Cym** IV.ii.352; **E3** IV.i.16; **1H6** IV.iv.31; **3H6** II.i.206
  2 inn, lodging, place of shelter **KL** V.ii.2 [Edgar to Gloucester] *take the shadow of this tree / For your good host;* **CE** V.i.411

host *(v.)* lodge, stay, put up **E3** I.ii.166 [King Edward to his lords, of the Countess's castle] *here will I host tonight;* **AW** III.v.93; **CE** I.ii.9

hostler *(n.)* ostler, stableman, groom **Cor** III.iii.32 [Coriolanus to Menenius, of being calm] *Ay, as an hostler*

hot *(adj.)* **1** hot-tempered, angry, passionate **TS** II.i.287 [Petruchio to Baptista, of Katherina] *She is not hot, but temperate as the morn;* **H5** IV.ii.8; **KL** II.iv.99; **MV** V.i.74; **R3** III.iv.37; **RJ** III.v.175
  2 enthusiastic, ardent, eager, keen **R3** I.iii.310 [Richard to Queen Elizabeth] *I was too hot to do somebody good;* **2H4** IV.iii.119; **KL** V.iii.67; **RJ** II.v.62; **TC** II.iii.171; **WT** II.iii.32
  3 lecherous, lustful, hot-blooded **TC** III.i.128 [Pandarus to himself, of Paris and Helen] *Is this the generation of love? Hot blood, hot thoughts, and hot deeds;* **AC** III.xiii.118; **Cym** V.v.180; **MW** V.v.11; **Oth** III.iii.400; **Tem** IV.i.98
  4 active, vigorous **WT** IV.iii.67 [Clown to Autolycus] *If this be a horseman's coat, it hath seen very hot service;* **1H4** I.i.34; **H5** III.ii.3; **H8** V.i.175; **KJ** III.v.11
  5 fast, hasty **H8** I.i.133 [Norfolk to Buckingham] *Anger is like / A full hot horse;* **Cym** V.v.322; **JC** IV.ii.23
  6 feverish, heated, burning **1H4** II.iv.316 [Prince Hal to Bardolph, of the meaning of Bardolph's exhalations] *Hot livers, and cold purses*

hot-blooded *(adj.)* lecherous, passionate, lustful **MW** V.v.2 [Falstaff to himself] *the hot-blooded gods assist me!*

hot-house *(n.)* brothel; bath-house **MM** II.i.64 [Elbow to Angelo, of Pompey's mistress] *she professes a hot-house, which I think is a very ill house too*

hotly *(adv.)* **1** angrily, passionately, fiercely **Venus** 178 [of Venus and Adonis] *Titan ... / With burning eye did hotly overlook them;* **TNK** V.i.105
  2 ardently, desperately, avidly **KL** IV.vi.163 [Lear to an imaginary beadle and whore] *Thou hotly lusts to use her in that kind / For which thou whipp'st her*
  3 urgently, eagerly, fervently **Oth** I.ii.44 [Cassio to Othello] *You have been hotly called for*

hour *(n.)* **1** time, moment **MA** II.ii.30 [Borachio to Don John] *find me a meet hour to draw Don Pedro and the Count Claudio alone;* **H8** I.ii.162; **MA** IV.i.279
  2 [time of] appointment, engagement, meeting **MV** II.vi.2 [Salerio to Gratiano, of Lorenzo] *His hour is almost past;* **2H6** II.i.176
  3 (plural) fixed time, timetable **TS** I.i.103 [Katherina as if to Baptista] *shall I be appointed hours;* **CE** III.i.2
  4 ☞ fair hour

hour, in an at the same time **TN** II.i.17 [Sebastian to Antonio, of his father] *He left behind him myself and a sister, both born in an hour*

hourly *(adj.)* **1** continual, constant, regular **Cym** I.ii.20 [Innogen to Posthumus] *I shall here abide the hourly shot / Of angry eyes*
  2 constantly, hour by hour **KJ** III.i.56 [Constance to Arthur, of fortune] *She adulterates hourly with thine uncle John* [also: like a whore]

house *(n.)* **1** inn, tavern **1H4** II.i.10 [Second Carrier to First Carrier] *This house is turned upside down since Robin Ostler died;* **1H4** II.i.15; **MM** I.ii.95; **R3** III.v.77; **TG** IV.ii.134; **TS** Induction.ii.89

2 household, family **H5** V.ii.56 [Burgundy to King Henry and the French King] *our houses and ourselves and children / Have lost ... / The sciences*
  3 ancestry, lineage, family **MM** II.iv.112 [Isabella to Angelo] *Ignomy in ransom and free pardon / Are of two houses;* **E3** II.i.263; **1H4** II.iii.3
  4 school of instruction, training school **RJ** II.iv.24 [Mercutio to Benvolio, of Tybalt] *A gentleman of the very first house*
  5 [astrology] heavenly domain [one of twelve divisions of the heavens] **RJ** IV.i.8 [Paris to Friar] *Venus smiles not in a house of tears*
  ☞ **COSMOS**, p.102
  6 housing, sheath, place of rest **RJ** V.iii.203 [Capulet to Lady Capulet] *This dagger hath mista'en, for, lo, his house / Is empty on the back of Montague*

house *(v.)* pursue into a house, drive into a house **CE** V.i.188 [Adriana to all, of Antipholus] *Even now we housed him in the abbey here;* **CE** V.i.272

house of profession brothel, whorehouse **MM** IV.iii.2 [Pompey alone] *I am as well acquainted here as I was in our house of profession*

house-clog *(n.)* prison-restraint, shackle, fetter **TNK** III.i.43 [Palamon to Arcite] *Had I a sword, / And these house-clogs away*

household *(n.)* family, house, dynasty **1H6** IV.vi.38 [Talbot to his son] *In thee thy mother dies, our household's name*

household *(adj.)* **1** throughout the house **3H6** IV.vi.14 [King to Lieutenant, of caged birds] *after many moody thoughts, / At last by notes of household harmony / They quite forget their loss of liberty*
  2 domesticated, house-trained **TS** II.i.271 [Petruchio to Katherina, of his intentions] *bring you from a wild Kate to a Kate / Conformable as other household Kates*

housekeeper, house-keeper *(n.)* **1** householder, hospitable person **TN** IV.ii.8 [Feste alone] *to be said an honest man and a good housekeeper goes as fairly as to say a careful man and a great scholar*
  2 domestic watchdog, housedog **Mac** III.i.96 [Macbeth to Murderers, of dogs] *The valued file / Distinguishes the swift, the slow, the subtle, / The house-keeper*
  3 stay-at-home person **Cor** I.iii.52 [Valeria to Volumnia and Virgilia] *You are manifest housekeepers*

house-keeping *(n.)* hospitality, maintaining a welcoming household **LL** II.i.104 [Princess to King] *I hear your grace hath sworn out house-keeping;* **2H6** I.i.189

housewife, huswife *(n.)* [pron: ˈhusif] hussy, wanton, minx **H5** V.i.76 [Pistol alone] *Doth fortune play the housewife with me now?;* **TN** I.iii.98 [Sir Toby to Sir Andrew] *I hope to see a huswife take thee between her legs* [also: woman who keeps house]; **AC** IV.xv.44; **2H4** III.ii.306; **Oth** II.i.111, IV.i.94

housewifery *(n.)* housekeeping, household management **Oth** II.i.111 [Iago to Emilia and Desdemona] *you are ... players in your housewifery;* **H5** II.iii.58

hovel *(v.)* find poor shelter [as in a hovel] **KL** IV.vii.39 [Cordelia to Lear, of Lear on the heath] *wast thou fain ... / To hovel thee with swine and rogues*

hovel-post door-post of a hovel **MV** II.ii.62 [Launcelot to Gobbo] *Do I look like a cudgel or a hovel-post* ☞ post *(n.)*

hovering *(adj.)* wavering, hesitating, uncertain **WT** I.ii.302 [Leontes to Camillo] *I hate thee, / Pronounce thee ... a hovering temporizer*

how *(adv.)* how much?, at what rate? **2H4** III.ii.47 [Shallow to Silence] *How a score of ewes now?;* **2H4** III.ii.37; **Per** IV.vi.18

how *(int.)* ☞ **EXCLAMATIONS**, p.158; **GREETINGS**, p.206; **POLITENESS**, p.340

howbeit *(adv.)* nevertheless, however ☞ **HOW AND HOW-**, p.228

howbeit *(conj.)* however **H5** I.ii.91 [Canterbury to King Henry, of the French] *Howbeit they would hold up this Salic law*

howbeit that *(conj.)* although **Oth** II.i.279 [Iago alone, of Othello] *The Moor – howbeit that I endure him not – / Is of a constant, loving, noble nature*

however, howe'er *(adv.)* whatever **Ham** IV.iii.70 [Claudius alone] *Howe'er my haps, my joys were ne'er begun* ➤ **HOW AND HOW-**, p.228

howlet *(n.)* ➤ owlet *(n.)*

howsomever, howsome'er, how ... some'er *(adv.)* however, howsoever, in whatever way [+ subordinate clause] **Ham** I.v.84 [Ghost to Hamlet] *But howsomever thou pursues this act;* **Ham** I.v.170 [Hamlet to Horatio and Marcellus] *How strange or odd some'er I bear myself;* **Ham** III.ii.405 [Hamlet alone, of Gertrude] *How in my words somever she be shent* ➤ **HOW AND HOW-**, p.228

hox *(v.)* hamstring, disable, cripple **WT** I.ii.244 [Leontes to Camillo] *thou art a coward, / Which hoxes honesty behind*

hoy *(n.)* small coastal vessel **CE** IV.iii.40 [Dromio of Syracuse to Antipholus of Syracuse] *then were you hindered by the sergeant to tarry for the hoy Delay*

hoyday *(int.)* ➤ **EXCLAMATIONS**, p.158

hue *(n.)* appearance, complexion **Sonn** 82.5 *Thou art as fair in knowledge as in hue;* **Sonn** 20.7, 104.11; **Tit** I.i.264, II.iii.73; **Venus** 747

hue and cry *(n.)* general pursuit [of a felon] **MW** IV.v.83 [Host to Bardolph] *Hue and cry, villain, go!;* **1H4** II.iv.492

hug *(v.)* bed down, curl up, lie close **KJ** V.ii.142 [Bastard to Lewis

---

HOW AND HOW-

How has always had a variety of interrogative and exclamatory uses, either alone or in combination with other words (as with modern *how about, how come?*). Several present-day uses are to be found in Shakespearian English: then as now, *how* was used to express manner ('I know how to curse', **Tem** I.ii.364) and extent ('How high a pitch his resolution soars!', **R2** I.i.109), and it was used in enquiries after health in similar ways to today. *However* was also often used in the modern way. Among the differences of expression are some correlative constructions ('I'll take the sacrament on't, how and which way you will', **AW** IV.ii.135), the use of *how now* as a greeting or exclamation (➤ **GREETINGS**, p.206; **EXCLAMATIONS**, p.158), and *how-* used as an element in compound forms. The chief differences are shown below, with examples of the compound uses as adverb and as conjunction.

how

Location	Example	Gloss
MM II.i.71	[Elbow] *My wife, sir, whom I detest ...* [Escalus] *How? Thy wife!*	what? [as exclamation]
TS IV.iii.20	*How say you to a fat tripe finely broiled?*	what? [as interrogation]
MA III.i.59	*I never yet saw man, / How wise, how noble*	however, to whatever extent
2H6 V.i.73	*How art thou called?*	what, with what name
2H4 III.ii.37	*How a good yoke of bullocks at Stamford fair?*	at what rate?, at what price?

how-

Item	Location	Example	Gloss
howbeit (adv.)	**Cor** I.ix.69	*Howbeit, I thank you*	nevertheless, however
howbeit (conj.)	**H5** I.ii.91	*Howbeit they would hold up this Salic law / To bar your highness*	although, though
howbeit that (conj.)	**Oth** II.i.279	*The Moor - howbeit that I endure him not*	although, though
however, howe'er (conj.)	**Ham** IV.iii.70	*Howe'er my haps, my joys were ne'er begun*	whatever
however, howe'er (conj.)	**KL** IV.ii.66	*Howe'er thou art a fiend, / A woman's shape doth shield thee*	although, however much
howsoever, howsoe'er (adv.)	**MND** V.i.27	[of the story] *But howsoever, strange and admirable*	in any case, at any rate
howsoever, howsoe'er (adv.)	**KJ** IV.ii.257	*my form, / Which, howsoever rude exteriorly, / Is yet the cover of a fairer mind*	to whatever extent, in whatever degree
howsoever, howsoe'er (conj.)	**Tem** V.i.158	*howsoe'er you have / Been justled from your senses*	to whatever extent, in whatever degree
how ... soever, how ... soe'er (adv.)	**LL** I.i.189	*How low soever the matter, I hope in God for high words*	to whatever extent, in whatever degree
howsomever, howsome'er (conj.)	**AW** I.iii.56	*howsome'er their hearts are severed in religion*	in whatever way, although

the Dauphin, of how the French will have to behave] To hug with swine

huge *(adj.)* great, important, of high rank **Tim** I.ii.48 [Apemantus to himself] *If I were a huge man, I should fear to drink at meals*

hugger-mugger, in secretly, stealthily, furtively **Ham** IV.v.85 [Claudius to Gertrude, of Polonius] *we have done but greenly / In hugger-mugger to inter him*

hugy *(adj.)* huge, immense, enormous **E3** II.i.403 [Warwick to Countess] *can one drop of poison harm the sea, / Whose hugy vastures can digest the ill*

hulk *(n.)* ship, vessel **2H4** II.iv.63 [Doll to Hostess, of Falstaff] *You have not seen a hulk better stuffed in the hold;* **1H6** V.v.6; **TC** II.iii.263

hulk *(adj.)* hugely ungraceful, clumsily large **2H4** I.i.19 [Lord Bardolph to Northumberland, of Falstaff] *the hulk Sir John*

hull *(v.)* lie, float, drift [with sails furled] **TN** I.v.196 [Viola as Cesario to Maria] *I am to hull here a little longer;* **H8** II.iv.199; **R3** IV.iv.438

hum *(v.)* **1** murmur approval, make encouraging noises **TNK** III.v.15 [Schoolmaster to all, of the Duke] *he hears, and nods, and hums*

2 say 'hum' [as a sign of displeasure, dissatisfaction, impatience, etc] **Cor** V.i.50 [Menenius to Sicinius, of Coriolanus] *to bite his lip / And hum at good Cominius, much unhearts me;* **Cor** V.iv.21; **Mac** III.vi.42; **TC** I.iii.165 ☛ **EXCLAMATIONS**, p.158

human *(adj.)* **1** worldly, secular, mundane **2H4** IV.iii.120 [Falstaff alone, of possible sons] *the first human principle I would teach them should be to forswear thin potations* [Q *humane*]

2 tender, delicate, gentle **E3** II.i.79 [King Edward to Lodowick] *the strains of poets' wit / Beguile and ravish soft and human minds*

humane *(adj.)* **1** polite, courteous, refined **TC** IV.i.21 [Aeneas to Diomedes] *In humane gentleness, / Welcome to Troy!;* **Oth** II.i.233

2 civil, benevolent **Mac** III.iv.75 [Macbeth to Lady Macbeth] *Blood hath been shed ere now, i'the olden time, / Ere humane statute purged the gentle weal*

humanely *(adv.)* out of fellow feeling, as fellow human beings **Cor** I.i.18 [First Citizen to all, of obtaining food from the authorities] *If they would yield us but the superfluity while it were wholesome, we might guess they relieved us humanely*

humanity *(n.)* human potential, manhood **1H6** II.iii.52 [Talbot to Countess] *what you see is but the smallest part / And least proportion of humanity* [i.e. of my substance = my army]

human-kindness *(n.)* natural feelings, human qualities **Mac** I.v.15 [Lady Macbeth alone, of Macbeth] *Yet do I fear thy nature: / It is too full o'the milk of human-kindness / To catch the nearest way* [F *humane*] [i.e. the softer side of humanity]

humble *(adj.)* **1** polite, well-mannered, civil **LL** V.ii.732 [Princess to King] *A heavy heart bears not a humble tongue*

2 lowly, ignoble, low **TS** III.i.87 [Hortensio alone, of Bianca's possible preference for Lucentio as Cambio] *if thy thoughts … be so humble*

3 low-lying **TNK** V.iii.99 [Emilia to herself, of Arcite's spirit] *it could / No more be hid … / Than humble banks can go to law with waters*

humble-bee *(n.)* bumble-bee **LL** III.i.83 [Armado to Mote] *The fox, the ape, and the humble-bee;* **AW** IV.v.6; **TC** V.x.42

humble-visaged *(adj.)* with humble faces **LL** II.i.34 [Princess to Boyet, of the King] *we attend, / Like humble-visaged suitors, his high will*

humidity *(n.)* **1** moisture, dampness, vapours **Tim** IV.iii.2 [Timon alone, as if to the sun] *draw from the earth / Rotten humidity*

2 bundle of fluids **MW** III.iii.38 [Mistress Ford to Mistress Page, of Falstaff] *We'll use this unwholesome humidity*

humming *(adj.)* murmuring **Per** III.i.63 [Pericles to dead Thaisa] *humming water … must o'erwhelm thy corpse*

humorous *(adj.)* **1** capricious, moody, temperamental **H5** II.iv.28

[Dauphin to French King, of King Henry] *a vain, giddy, shallow, humorous youth;* **AY** IV.i.18; **Ham** II.ii.322; **2H4** IV.iv.34; **LL** III.i.172; **TC** II.iii.128

2 humid, damp, moist **RJ** II.i.31 [Benvolio to Mercutio, of Romeo] *he hath hid himself among these trees / To be consorted with the humorous night*

humour *(n.)* **1** mood, disposition, frame of mind, temperament [as determined by bodily fluids] **MW** I.i.125 [Nym to all] *That's my humour* ☛ FEW, p.xxi; **HUMOURS**, p.230

2 fancy, whim, inclination, caprice **KJ** IV.ii.209 [King John to Hubert] *It is the curse of kings to be attended / By slaves that take their humours for a warrant;* **1H4** I.ii.69; **H5** II.i.52; **JC** II.i.56; **Tim** I.ii.157; **Venus** 850

3 style, method, way, fashion **R3** I.ii.227 [Richard alone, of Anne] *Was ever woman in this humour wooed?;* **2H4** IV.iv.158; **H5** II.iii.57; **MW** I.iii.78, II.i.120; **TN** II.v.51

4 sentiment, turn of phrase, manner of expression **MW** I.iii.59 [Nym to himself, of Pistol's remark] *I thank thee for that humour;* **MW** I.iii.20, 47, 51; **Tit** IV.iv.19

5 secretion, fluid, juice **RJ** IV.i.96 [Friar to Juliet, of taking the potion] *presently through all thy veins shall run / A cold and drowsy humour;* **1H4** IV.iv.438; **H5** II.i.116; **MA** III.ii.25

6 dampness, vapour, moisture **JC** II.i.262 [Portia to Brutus] *is it physical / To walk unbraced and suck up the humours / Of the dank morning?*

humour *(v.)* like the mood of, find enjoyable, indulge **MW** I.iii.51 [Nym to Falstaff and Pistol] *Humour me the angels;* **JC** I.ii.312; **LL** III.i.11

humoured *(adj.)* expressing a particular disposition; lying, treacherous **MW** II.i.122 [Nym to Page, of Mistress Page] *I should have borne the humoured letter to her*

humour-letter *(n.)* letter displaying a particular sentiment **MW** I.iii.72 [Nym to Falstaff] *Here, take the humour-letter*

Hungarian *(adj.)* [pun on 'hungry'] beggarly, thievish **MW** I.iii.19 [Pistol to Bardolph] *O base Hungarian wight!*

hungerly *(adj.)* sparse, meagre **TS** III.ii.174 [Gremio to Tranio as Lucentio, of the sexton] *his beard grew thin and hungerly*

hungerly *(adv.)* hungrily, greedily, avidly **Oth** III.iv.101 [Emilia to Desdemona, of men] *They eat us hungerly;* **Tim** I.i.257

hungry *(adj.)* barren, sterile, unfertile **Cor** V.iii.58 [Coriolanus to Volumnia] *let the pebbles on the hungry beach / Fillip the stars* [uncertain meaning]

hungry-starved *(adj.)* dying with hunger, famished **1H6** I.v.16 [Pucelle to the French] *cheer up thy hungry-starved men*

hunt *(n.)* game, quarry that has been killed **Cym** III.vii.62 [Belarius to Arviragus and Guiderius] *we'll go dress our hunt*

hunt's-up *(n.)* daybreak song to wake huntsmen [or a newly married wife] **RJ** III.v.34 [Juliet to Romeo, of the lark] *arm from arm that voice doth us affray, / Hunting thee hence with hunt's-up to the day*

hurdle *(n.)* cart, frame [as used for dragging traitors to execution] **RJ** III.v.155 [Capulet to Juliet] *go with Paris to Saint Peter's Church, / Or I will drag thee on a hurdle thither*

hurly *(n.)* commotion, uproar, turmoil **2H4** III.i.25 [King Henry IV alone, of a storm] *with the hurly death itself awakes;* **KJ** III.iv.169; **TS** IV.i.189

hurly-burly *(n.)* commotion, uproar, turmoil **Mac** I.i.3 [Second Witch to First Witch, in response to 'When shall we three meet again?'] *When the hurly-burly's done;* **1H6** I.iii.57

hurly-burly *(adj.)* hectic, turbulent, stormy **1H4** V.i.78 [King Henry to Worcester] *discontents, / Which gape and rub the elbow at the news / Of hurly-burly innovation*

hurricano *(n.)* water-spout **KL** III.ii.2 [Lear to the storm] *You cataracts and hurricanoes, spout;* **TC** V.ii.175

hurry *(n.)* commotion, excitement, activity **TNK** II.i.18 [Gaoler to Gaoler's Daughter] *So soon as the court hurry is over*

HUMOURS

In early accounts of human physiology, a person's physical and mental disposition was thought to be governed by a combination of fluids, or *humours*, within the body. Four humours were recognized: *blood, phlegm, choler* (also called *yellow bile*), and *melancholy* (also called *black bile* or *black choler*). The notion transferred readily into a range of senses to do with temperament, mood, inclination, and manner of action (☞ humour *(n.)* 2–4), regarded as permanent or alterable features of behaviour. They often referred to a particular facet of behaviour, such as manner of expression – most fully exploited in the character of Nym in **MW** and **H5**. The original physical sense of *humour* as a physical secretion is also still found in Early Modern English (☞ humour *(n.)* 5–6).

Good health was thought to come from having the four humours in balance; but characters often display the predominance of one or the other, and their actions are interpreted accordingly. For example, if a character was hot-tempered, he or she would be thought to have an excess of *choler*: Lear (**KL**), Petruchio (**TS**), Gloucester (**2H6**), and Cassius (**JC**) are examples of people at some point described as choleric. 'You are altogether governed by humours', complains Lady Percy of her hot-headed husband (**1H4** III.i.228). *Blood, choler*, and *melancholy* are terms used in the plays; *phlegm* is not, though its functions are indirectly referred to, as in the example below. The term is misapplied by Mistress Quickly (**MW** I.iv.73) when she describes Dr Caius as a 'phlegmatic' (she means 'choleric').

☞ **BLOOD** *(n.)* **1–5, CHOLER** *(n.),* **CHOLERIC** *(adj.),* **MELANCHOLY** *(n.)*

Humour	Typical disposition	Seen in character	Example
blood	optimistic, passionate, amorous, courageous	Hotspur (as described by his wife)	In military rules, humours of blood, / He was the mark and glass, copy and book, / That fashioned others (**2H4** II.iii.30)
phlegm	dull, indifferent, indolent, apathetic, idle	Falstaff and his companions (as described by Prince Hal)	I know you all, and will awhile uphold / The unyoked humour of your idleness, (**1H4** I.ii.194)
choler	angry, irascible, bad-tempered	Cassius (as described by Brutus)	Go show your slaves how choleric you are … Must I stand and crouch / Under your testy humour? (**JC** IV.iii.43)
melancholy	sad, gloomy, sullen, depressed	Jaques (as described by Rosalind)	They say you are a melancholy fellow. [Jaques] I am so: I do love it better than laughing (**AY** IV.i.3)

hurt *(n.)* **1** wound, injury, scar **Tim** III.v.110 [Alcibiades alone] *I myself / Rich only in large hurts*
  2 attack, offence, [causing] damage **E3** III.i.172 [Mariner to King John] *All shifts were tried, both for defence and hurt*

hurt *(adj.)* wounded, injured **Ham** V.ii.318 [Claudius to all] *I am but hurt*

hurtle *(v.)* sound violently, resound harshly **JC** II.ii.22 [Calphurnia to Caesar] *The noise of battle hurtled in the air*

hurtless *(adj.)* without hurting, harmlessly **KL** IV.vi.167 [Lear to all] *the strong lance of justice hurtless breaks*

hurtling *(n.)* tumult, violent conflict **AY** IV.iii.132 [Oliver to Rosalind and Celia disguised, of Orlando's fight with the lion] *in which hurtling / From miserable slumber I awaked*

husband *(n.)* houskeeper, steward, domestic manager **TS** V.i.60 [Vincentio to Tranio as Lucentio] *While I play the good husband at home, my son and my servant spend all at the university;* **2H4** V.iii.11; **H8** III.ii.142; **MM** III.ii.67

husband *(v.)* **1** manage, handle, look after **TS** Induction.i.66 [Lord to Huntsmen, of transforming Sly] *It will be pastime passing excellent, / If it be husbanded with modesty*
  2 tend, improve, cultivate **2H4** IV.iii.117 [Falstaff alone, of Prince Henry's cold blood] *he hath like lean, sterile, and bare land manured, husbanded, and tilled*
  3 make the most of, thrive well with **MW** IV.vi.52 [Host to Fenton] *husband your device*

husband-friend *(n.)* husband as well as lover **RJ** III.v.43 [Juliet to Romeo] *Art thou gone so, love-lord, aye husband-friend?* [F; separated by comma in F2]

husbandry *(n.)* **1** thrift, good economy, careful management **Mac** II.i.4 [Banquo to Fleance] *There's husbandry in heaven: / Their candles are all out;* **Cor** IV.vii.22; **Ham** I.iii.77; **MV** III.iv.25; **Sonn** 13.10
  2 household work, chores **2H4** III.ii.113 [Mouldy to Falstaff] *My old dame will be undone now for one to do her husbandry and her drudgery* [also: acting as a husband]
  3 industriousness, diligence, eagerness to work **Per** III.ii.19 [Second Gentleman to Cerimon, of the storm] *That is the cause we trouble you so early; / 'Tis not our husbandry*
  4 farming, land management **Sonn** 3.6 *where is she so fair whose uneared womb / Disdains the tillage of thy husbandry?*

hush *(adj.)* hushed, silent, quiet **Ham** II.ii.484 [First Player to all present] *the orb below / As hush as death*

husht *(int.)* ☞ **ATTENTION SIGNALS**, p.26

huswife *(n.)* ☞ housewife *(n.)*

Hydra-headed *(adj.)* many-headed, multifarious, manifold **H5** I.i.35 [Canterbury to Ely, of King Henry] *never Hydra-headed wilfulness / So soon did lose his seat*

hyen *(n.)* hyena **AY** IV.i.144 [Rosalind as Ganymede to Orlando] *I will laugh like a hyen*

hyperbolical *(adj.)* outrageous, immoderate, intemperate **TN** IV.ii.25 [disguised Feste to the fiend in Malvolio] *Out, hyperbolical fiend*

hysterica passio [Latin: hysterical passion] hysteria **KL** II.iv.55 [Lear to himself] *Hysterica passio, down, thou climbing sorrow!*

ice *(n.)* [metaphor for] cold contempt **TNK** I.ii.34 [Palamon to Arcite, of destitutes] *That sweating in an honourable toil / Are paid with ice to cool 'em*

ides *(n.)* [Roman calendar] half-way point in a month **JC** I.ii.18 [Soothsayer to Caesar] *Beware the ides of March;* **JC** II.i.40, III.i.1, IV.iii.18, V.i.113

idiot *(n.)* jester, clown, fool **KJ** III.iii.45 [King John to Hubert] *that idiot, laughter*

idle *(adj.)* **1** useless, barren, worthless **R3** III.i.103 [York to Richard] *You said that idle weeds are fast in growth;* **AC** V.ii.50; **AW** IV.iii.210; **KL** I.ii.49; **LL** I.i.296; **Sonn** 122.3

2 mad, crazy, lunatic **KJ** V.vii.4 [Prince Henry to Salisbury and Bigot, of King John] *his pure brain ... / Doth by the idle comments that it makes / Foretell the ending of mortality;* **AW** III.vii.26; **CE** II.ii.218; **Ham** III.iv.12; **KL** I.iii.17; **TS** Induction.ii.12

3 foolish, stupid, empty-headed **AY** V.vii.49 [Rosalind as Ganymede to Orlando] *I will weary you then no longer with idle talking;* **AW** II.v.49; **LL** V.ii.854; **WT** III.ii.179

4 foolish, superstitious, fanciful **RJ** I.iv.97 [Mercutio to Romeo, of dreams] *the children of an idle brain*

5 trifling, unimportant, trivial **Tim** I.ii.152 [Timon to Ladies] *there is an idle banquet attends you;* **2H4** IV.i.189; **LL** IV.iii.168; **Oth** I.ii.95; **TN** III.iii.47

6 frivolous, capricious, wanton **Tem** II.i.170 [Antonio aside to Sebastian, of the subjects in Gonzalo's commonwealth not marrying] *all idle - whores and knaves;* **R3** I.i.31

7 empty, unoccupied, inactive **2H4** II.ii.122 [Prince Henry, reading Falstaff's letter] *Repent at idle times as thou mayst;* **R2** III.iv.66

8 careless, inattentive, lax **Tim** IV.iii.27 [Timon alone] *I am no idle votarist;* **Ham** II.ii.138

9 bored, jaded, wearied **MW** III.ii.12 [Ford to Mistress Page, of Mistress Ford] *as idle as she may hang together, for want of company*

10 inactive, unmoving, inert **KL** IV.vi.21 [Edgar to Gloucester, of the waves] *That on th'unnumbered idle pebble chafes*

11 uninhabited, empty; or: barren, sterile **Oth** I.iii.139 [Othello to all] *of antres vast and deserts idle ... / It was my hint to speak*

idle-headed *(adj.)* ignorant, foolish, superstitious **MW** IV.iv.34 [Mistress Page to all, of Herne the Hunter] *The superstitious idle-headed eld / Received and did deliver to our age / This tale ... for a truth*

idleness *(n.)* pastime, foolishness, silly diversion **TN** I.v.59 [Olivia to Feste] *for want of other idleness, I'll bide your proof*

idly *(adv.)* **1** foolishly, crazily, frivolously **R2** III.iii.171 [King Richard to Aumerle] *I talk but idly;* **CE** IV.iv.127; **2H4** II.ii.28; **2H6** III.i.255; **KJ** V.i.72

2 without paying attention, casually **Tim** I.i.20 [Poet to Painter, of his poem] *A thing slipped idly from me* [F *idlely*]; **KJ** IV.ii.124

3 indifferently, half-heartedly, unenthusiastically **R2** V.ii.25 [York to Duchess of York] *the eyes of men, / After a well graced actor leaves the stage, / Are idly bent on him that enters next*

if *(conj.)* **1** as long as **TNK** V.ii.15 [Doctor to Wooer, of having no singing voice] *That's all one, if ye make a noise*

2 ☞ an if *(conj.)*

if for *(conj.)* because **KL** I.i.224 [Cordelia to Lear] *If for I want that glib and oily art / To speak and purpose not*

if that *(conj.)* if **1H6** I.iii.28 [Servingmen to Woodville, of the Tower gates] *we'll burst them open if that you come not quickly*

ignobly *(adv.)* dishonourably, shamefully, badly **1H6** II.v.35 [Richard to Mortimer, of himself] *thus ignobly used;* **KL** III.vii.35

ignomy *(n.)* ignominy, dishonour, shame **TC** V.x.33 [Troilus to Pandarus] *Ignomy and shame / Pursue thy life;* **MM** II.iv.111; **Tit** IV.ii.114

ignorance *(n.)* **1** negligence, obtuseness, lack of understanding **KL** IV.v.9 [Regan to Oswald, of Gloucester] *It was great ignorance ... / To let him live;* **Cor** III.i.98, iii.129, IV.vi.106, V.ii.39

2 ignoramus, example of ignorance **TC** III.iii.312 [Thersites alone, of Ajax] *I had rather be a tick in a sheep than such a valiant ignorance*

ignorant *(n.)* [those who are] unaware, unconscious **Ham** II.ii.562 [Hamlet alone] *Confound the ignorant* [i.e. of the crime]

ignorant *(adj.)* **1** dull, unwitting, simple-minded **Cor** II.iii.218 [Sicinius to Citizens] *on a safer judgement all revoke / Your ignorant election;* **Cor** II.iii.173
　2 that keeps one in ignorance **WT** I.ii.397 [Polixenes to Camillo, of what Camillo knows] *imprison't not / In ignorant concealment*

'ild, 'ield, dild *(v.)* [form of 'yield'] reward, repay, requite **AY** III.iii.68 [Touchstone to Jaques] *God 'ild you for your last company;* **Ham** IV.v.42 [Ophelia to Claudius, responding to 'How do you?'] *Well, God dild you!* [Q2; F *dil'd*; Q1 *yeeld*] **Mac** I.vi.13 [King to Lady Macbeth] *Herein I teach you / How you shall bid 'God 'ield us' for your pains* [F *God-eyld*] ➤ **POLITENESS**, p.340

ill *(n.)* **1** wrong, injury, harm, evil **RJ** IV.v.94 [Friar to all] *The heavens do lour upon you for some ill;* **AC** I.ii.130; **H5** IV.i.181; **2H6** I.ii.19; **Luc** 91; **Tem** I.ii.353
　2 trouble, affliction, misfortune **E3** IV.v.123 [King John to Salisbury, of King Edward] *tell the king this is not all his ill;* **R2** III.iii.170 [Richard to Aumerle, of their imagined fate] *Would not this ill do well?;* **AC** I.ii.111
　3 illness, malady, affliction **TNK** V.iv.26 [Palamon to Gaoler, of the Gaoler's Daughter] *her kind of ill / Gave me some sorrow;* **Sonn** 147.3

ill *(adj.)* **1** bad, adverse, unfavourable **1H6** IV.vi.191 [Exeter alone, of the quarrelling lords] *it doth presage some ill event* ➤ **FEW**, p.xxi
　2 evil, wicked, immoral **Tem** I.ii.458 [Miranda to Prospero, of Ferdinand] *There's nothing ill can dwell in such a temple;* **H8** IV.ii.43; **R2** I.i.93; **R3** I.iv.214; **Tem** I.ii.459; **TNK** II.i.144
　3 poor, inadequate, miserable **RJ** IV.ii.3 [Servingman to Capulet, of hiring cooks] *You shall have none ill, sir;* **JC** IV.ii.7; **TNK** V.ii.95
　4 sick, indisposed, unwell **R2** II.i.92 [King Richard to John of Gaunt] *I breathe, and see thee ill.* [John of Gaunt] *... I see thee ill; / Ill in myself to see* [i.e. with poor power of sight in myself] [pun: 94, *(n.)* sense 1]; **AC** I.iii.72; **Ham** V.ii.206
　5 annoyed, cross, vexed **MW** II.i.33 [Mistress Page to Mistress Ford] *You look very ill* [taken in 34 to mean 'unattractive']
　6 unskilful, inexpert, unskilled **Ham** II.ii.119 [Hamlet to Ophelia, in his letter] *I am ill at these numbers;* **H8** III.ii.142; **Luc** 1300

ill *(adv.)* **1** badly, adversely, unfavourably **CE** II.ii.177 [Adriana to Antipholus of Syracuse] *How ill agrees it with your gravity / To counterfeit thus grossly with your slave* ➤ **FEW**, p.xxi
　2 imperfectly, poorly, to ill effect **AW** IV.ii.27 [Diana to Bertram] *would you believe my oaths / When I did love you ill?;* **2H6** II.i.34

ill-annexed *(adj.)* badly added, adversely attached **Luc** 874 [Lucrece to herself] *We have no good that we can say is ours / But ill-annexed Opportunity / Or kills his life or else his quality*

ill-beseeming *(adj.)* unseemly, inappropriate, unbecoming **3H6** I.iv.113 [York to Queen] *How ill-beseeming is it in thy sex / To triumph;* **2H4** IV.i.84; **RJ** I.v.74, III.iii.113 ➤ **well-beseeming** *(adj.)*

ill-boding *(adj.)* inauspicious, predicting evil, prophesying doom **1H6** IV.vi.6 [Talbot to John Talbot] *O, malignant and ill-boding stars!;* **3H6** II.vi.59

ill-breeding *(adj.)* mischief-making, discontented **Ham** IV.v.15 [Horatio to Gertrude, of Ophelia] *she may strew / Dangerous conjectures in ill-breeding minds*

ill-composed *(adj.)* made up of wicked elements **Mac** IV.iii.77 [Malcolm to Macduff] *there grows / In my most ill-composed affection such / A staunchless avarice*

ill-dispersing *(adj.)* evil-scattering, spreading wickedness **R3** IV.i.52 [Duchess of York to all] *O ill-dispersing wind of misery!*

ill-disposed *(adj.)* **1** badly arranged, poorly presented **H5** IV.Chorus.51 [Chorus] *four or five most vile and ragged foils, / Right ill-disposed in brawl ridiculous* ➤ **disposed** *(adj.)*
　2 indisposed, unwell, under the weather **TC** II.iii.76 [Patroclus to Agamemnon, of Achilles] *Within his tent, but ill-disposed*

ill-divining *(adj.)* giving premonitions of harm, ominously prophesying **RJ** III.v.54 [Juliet to Romeo] *I have an ill-divining soul!*

ill-erected *(adj.)* built for wicked ends **R2** V.i.2 [Queen Isabel to her attendants] *This is the way / To Julius Caesar's ill-erected Tower*

ill-favoured *(adj.)* ugly, unattractive, unsightly **MW** I.i.278 [Slender to Anne, of bears] *they are very ill-favoured rough things;* **AY** III.v.53; **MW** III.iv.32; **R3** III.v.1; **TG** II.vii.54; **TS** I.i.59

ill-favouredly *(adv.)* **1** badly, unpleasingly, offensively **H5** IV.ii.38 [Grandpré to all, of the English army] *Yon island carrions ... / Ill-favouredly become the morning field;* **AY** III.ii.255; **MW** III.v.63
　2 with plain features, unattractively **AY** I.ii.38 [Celia to Rosalind, of Fortune] *those that she makes honest she makes very ill-favouredly*

ill-inhabited *(adj.)* badly housed, poorly accommodated **AY** III.iii.8 [Jaques to himself, of Touchstone] *O knowledge ill-inhabited*

ill-left *(adj.)* badly equipped; or, left in disorder **R2** II.iii.153 [York to all] *my power is weak and all ill-left*

illness *(n.)* wickedness, evil conduct, badness **Mac** I.v.18 [Lady Macbeth alone, of Macbeth] *Thou wouldst be great ... but without / The illness should attend it*

ill-nurtured *(adj.)* ill-bred, badly brought up **2H6** I.ii.42 [Gloucester to Duchess] *Ill-nurtured Eleanor!*

ill-roasted *(adj.)* badly cooked **AY** III.ii.35 [Touchstone to Corin] *thou art damned, like an ill-roasted egg all on one side*

ill-seeming *(adj.)* of ugly appearance, unpleasant to look at **TS** V.ii.142 [Katherina to Widow, of an angry woman] *like a fountain troubled, / Muddy, ill-seeming, thick, bereft of beauty*

ill-sorted *(adv.)* badly matched, in bad company **2H4** II.iv.145 [Doll to all, of the word 'occupy'] *which was an excellent good word before it was ill-sorted*

ill-spirited *(adj.)* evil-hearted, wickedly minded **1H4** V.v.2 [King Henry to Worcester] *Ill-spirited Worcester, did not we send grace ... to all of you?*

ill-ta'en *(adj.)* [ill-taken] unfounded, unwarranted, badly grounded **WT** I.ii.460 [Polixenes to Camillo, of Hermione] *part of his theme, but nothing / Of his ill-ta'en suspicion!*

ill-tempered *(adj.)* unbalanced, with elements of mood [humours] badly mixed **JC** IV.iii.114 [Cassius to Brutus] *Hath Cassius lived / To be but mirth and laughter to his Brutus, / When grief and blood ill-tempered vexeth him?* [pun: 115]

ill-tuned *(adj.)* harsh-sounding, unmelodious **KJ** III.i.197 [King Philip to Constance] *It ill beseems this presence to cry aim / To these ill-tuned repetitions*

illume *(v.)* light up, illuminate, brighten **Ham** I.i.37 [Barnardo to Horatio, identifying a star] *Had made his course t'illume that part of heaven*

illusion *(n.)* deception, delusion, deceit **H8** I.ii.178 [Surveyor to King Henry] *I told my lord the Duke, by th'devil's illusions / The monk might be deceived;* **Mac** III.v.28; **MND** III.ii.98

illustrate *(adj.)* illustrious, resplendent, renowned **LL** V.i.115 [Holofernes to Nathaniel, of Armado] *this most gallant, illustrate, and learned gentleman;* **LL** IV.i.67

illustrate *(v.)* show, indicate, make evident **TNK** II.iv.22 [Hippolyta to all, of Arcite] *But his body / And fiery mind illustrate a brave father*

illustrous *(adj.)* lack-lustre, dull, dim **Cym** I.vii.109 [Iachimo to Innogen] *by-peeping in an eye / Base and illustrous*

ill-weaved *(adj.)* poorly woven **1H4** V.iv.87 [Prince Hal to dead Hotspur] *Ill-weaved ambition, how much art thou shrunk*

ill-well *(adv.)* wickedly well, cruelly accurately **MA** II.i.104 [masked Ursula to masked Antonio] *You could never do him so ill-well unless you were the very man*

ill-wresting *(adj.)* twisting the truth, turning to disadvantage **Sonn** 140.11 *this ill-wresting world is grown so bad*

image (*n.*) **1** embodiment, instance, form **TS** Induction.i.33 [Lord to sleeping Sly] *Grim death, how foul and loathsome is thine image!;* **E3** III.iii.202; **2H4** V.ii.74; **2H6** I.iii.174; **KL** II.iv.86; **MW** IV.vi.17

2 effigy, statue, sculpture **JC** I.i.68 [Flavius to Marullus, of the statues] *let no images / Be hung with Caesar's trophies;* **1H4** IV.i.100; **2H6** I.iii.58; **MA** II.i.8; **MM** III.ii.43; **WT** V.iii.57

3 personal likeness, semblance **3H6** V.iv.54 [Oxford to Prince, of his grandfather] *long mayst thou live / To bear his image;* **R3** I.ii.50

4 appearance, aspect, countenance **TN** III.iv.353 [Antonio to Second Officer, of Viola as Cesario] *to his image, which methought did promise / Most venerable worth, did I devotion*

5 idea, conception, mental picture **MM** III.i.260 [Isabella to disguised Duke, of his plan] *The image of it gives me content already*

6 representation, depiction, portrayal **Ham** III.ii.248 [Hamlet to Claudius] *This play is the image of a murder done in Vienna*

imagery (*n.*) decorated cloth, painted fabric **R2** V.ii.16 [York to Duchess of York] *all the walls / With painted imagery*

imaginary (*adj.*) imaginative, creative, of the imagination **H5** Prologue.18 [Chorus] *let us … / On your imaginary forces work*

imagination (*n.*) **1** delusion, fancy, imagining **MW** III.iii.203 [Page to Ford, of Ford's suspicion] *what devil suggests this imagination?;* **KL** IV.vi.282

2 thought, soul-searching, introspection **MA** IV.i.223 [Friar to Leonato, of Hero and Claudio] *Th'idea of her life shall … creep / Into his study of imagination*

imagine (*v.*) **1** guess, think, consider **E3** III.iii.93 [King Edward to King John] *Imagine, Valois, whether I intend / To skirmish not for pillage, but for the crown*

2 conceive, devise, plan **2H6** I.ii.19 [Gloucester to Duchess] *when I imagine ill / Against my king and nephew*

imagined (*adj.*) **1** of imagination, conceived in the mind **H5** III.Chorus.1 [Chorus] *Thus with imagined wing our swift scene flies*

2 all imaginable, as much as can be conceived **MV** III.iv.52 [Portia to Balthasar, of garments] *Bring them, I pray thee, with imagined speed / Unto the traject, to the common ferry*

imbar, imbare (*v.*) [unclear meaning] bar, exclude; reveal, demonstrate **H5** I.ii.94 [Canterbury to King Henry, of the French kings] *they … rather choose to hide them in a net / Than amply to imbar their crooked titles* [F *imbarre;* Q *imbace*]

imbecility (*n.*) physical weakness, feebleness, puniness **TC** I.iii.114 [Ulysses to all] *Strength should be lord of imbecility*

imbrue, embrue (*v.*) pierce, stab, stain with blood **MND** V.i.336 [Flute as Thisbe] *Come blade, my breast imbrue;* **2H4** II.iv.191

imitation (*n.*) artificiality, unoriginal notion **JC** IV.i.37 [Antony to Octavius, of Lepidus] *one that feeds / On objects, arts, and imitations*

immanity (*n.*) enormous barbarity, atrocious cruelty **1H6** V.i.13 [King to Gloucester] *It was both impious and unnatural / That such immanity and bloody strife / Should reign among professors of one faith*

immask (*v.*) hide, disguise, cover [as with a mask] **1H4** I.ii.178 [Poins to Prince Hal] *I have cases of buckram for the nonce, to immask our noted outward garments*

immaterial (*adj.*) flimsy, slight, of little substance **TC** V.i.28 [Thersites to Patroclus] *thou idle immaterial skein of sleave-silk*

immediacy (*n.*) position closest to the sovereign, being next in standing **KL** V.iii.66 [Regan to Albany, of Edmund's acting for her] *The which immediacy may well stand up / And call itself your brother* [F; Q *imediate*]

immediate (*adj.*) **1** close in succession, proximate, direct **Ham** I.ii.109 [Claudius to Hamlet] *You are the most immediate to our throne;* **AW** II.iii.131; **2H4** IV.v.43

2 cherished, nearest the heart **Oth** III.iii.155 [Iago to Othello] *Good name in man and woman … / Is the immediate jewel of their souls*

immediately (*adv.*) directly, instantly, without delay **MND** I.i.45 [Egeus to Theseus, of Hermia's punishment for her actions] *according to our law / Immediately provided in that case*

imminence (*n.*) impending evil, approaching peril **TC** V.x.13 [Troilus to Aeneas] *I … dare all imminence that gods and men / Address their dangers in*

immodest (*adj.*) **1** arrogant, insolent, shameless **E3** III.iii.103 [Prince Edward to King John] *all the immodest poison of thy throat;* **1H6** IV.i.126

2 improper, immoderate, inordinate **WT** III.ii.101 [Hermione to Leontes, of the way she has been treated] *with immodest hatred / The childbed privilege denied*

immoment (*adj.*) unimportant, trifling, of no consequence **AC** V.ii.166 [Cleopatra to Caesar] *I some lady trifles have reserved, / Immoment toys*

immure (*n.*) wall **TC** Prologue.8 [Prologue, of Troy] *within whose strong immures / The ravished Helen … / With wanton Paris sleeps* [F emures]

immured (*adj.*) walled up, enclosed, confined **LL** III.i.122 [Armado to Costard] *Thou wert immured, restrained, captivated, bound;* **E3** II.i.178; **LL** IV.iii.304; **MV** II.vii.52; **Sonn** 84.3

imp (*n.*) child, scion, son **2H4** V.v.43 [Pistol to King Henry V] *The heavens thee guard and keep, most royal imp of fame!;* **H5** IV.i.45; **LL** I.ii.5, V.ii.584

imp out (*v.*) [of a falcon's wing] repair, insert feathers into **R2** II.i.292 [Northumberland to Ross and Willoughby] *we shall … / Imp out our drooping country's broken wing*

impaint (*v.*) depict, portray, paint a picture of **1H4** V.i.80 [King Henry to Worcester] *never yet did insurrection want / Such water-colours to impaint his cause*

impair (*adj.*) [unclear meaning] unworthy, dishonourable; harmful, injurious **TC** IV.v.103 [Ulysses to Agamemnon, of Troilus] *Nor dignifies an impair thought with breath* [F; Q *impare*]

impale, empale (*v.*) encircle, enclose, ring **3H6** III.iii.189 [Warwick to Lewis, of Edward] *Did I impale him with the regal crown?;* **3H6** III.ii.171; **TC** V.vii.5

impall (*v.*) enfold, wrap in [as if with a pall = robe] **E3** III.iii.180 [King Edward to Prince Edward] *with this armour I impall thy breast*

impannel, empannel (*v.*) enrol, oblige to appear in a court **Sonn** 46.9 *To 'cide this title is impannelled / A quest of thoughts* [i.e. to decide this claim]

impart (*v.*) **1** tell, make known, communicate **Ham** I.i.170 [Horatio to Barnardo and Marcellus] *Let us impart what we have seen tonight / Unto young Hamlet;* **Cym** V.v.446; **Ham** III.ii.337, V.ii.91

2 bestow, give, grant **Ham** I.ii.112 [Claudius to Hamlet] *no less nobility of love … / Do I impart toward you*

3 provide, yield, make available **Luc** 1039 [of Lucrece's room] *this no-slaughterhouse no tool imparteth / To make more vent for passage of her breath*

impartial (*adj.*) indifferent, disinterested, detached **Venus** 748 [Venus to Adonis] *favour, savour, hue and qualities, / Whereat th'impartial gazer late did wonder*

impartment (*n.*) communication, imparting of information **Ham** I.iv.59 [Horatio to Hamlet, of the Ghost] *As if it some impartment did desire / To you alone*

impasted (*adj.*) made into a paste, crusted **Ham** II.ii.457 [Hamlet to First Player, quoting lines about Pyrrhus] *Baked and impasted with the parching streets*

impatience (*n.*) **1** anger, rage, fury **1H6** IV.vii.8 [Talbot to Servant, of John Talbot] *he … did commence / Rough deeds of rage and stern impatience;* **Cor** V.vi.146; **KJ** IV.iii.32

2 lack of composure, failure to bear suffering well **R3** II.ii.38 [Duchess of York to Queen Elizabeth] *What means this scene of rude impatience?*

impatient (*adj.*) **1** angry, irate, incensed **1H6** II.i.54 [Pucelle to Charles] *Wherefore is Charles impatient with his friend?;* **TS** Induction.i.97

2 frustrated, restless, eagerly longing **LL** II.i.224 [Boyet to Princess, of the King] *His tongue, all impatient to speak and not see*

impawn (*v.*) **1** pledge as security, put in pawn, commit **H5** I.ii.21 [King Henry to Canterbury] *take heed how you impawn our person;* **1H4** IV.iii.108; **WT** I.ii.436

2 wager, pledge, stake **Ham** V.ii.160 [Hamlet to Osrick, of what has been wagered] *Why is this all impawned* [F *impon'd*]; **Ham** V.ii.146

impeach (*n.*) **1** charge, accusation, indictment **CE** V.i.270 [Duke to all] *what an intricate impeach is this!*

2 disparagement, reproach [to], detraction [from] **3H6** I.iv.60 [Northumberland to Clifford] *ten to one is no impeach of valour*

impeach (*v.*) **1** accuse, charge, challenge **R2** I.i.170 [Mowbray to Richard] *I am disgraced, impeached, and baffled here;* **CE** V.i.29; **KJ** II.i.116; **RJ** V.iii.226; **Sonn** 125.14

2 discredit, disparage, call into question **MND** II.i.214 [Demetrius to Helena] *You do impeach your modesty too much;* **1H4** I.iii.74; **MV** III.ii.278, iii.29; **R2** I.i.189

impeachment (*n.*) **1** charge, accusation, indictment **R3** II.ii.22 [Boy to Duchess of York, of Clarence] *the King … / Devised impeachments to imprison him*

2 discredit, reproach, detriment **TG** I.iii.15 [Panthino to Antonio, of Proteus not having travelled] *Which would be great impeachment to his age*

3 impediment, hindrance, obstacle **H5** III.vi.140 [King Henry to Montjoy] *I … could be willing to march on to Calais / Without impeachment*

impediment (*n.*) obstruction, hindrance, obstacle **Cor** II.iii.227 [Brutus to Citizens, of Coriolanus] *we laboured, / No impediment between, but that you must / Cast your election on him* [i.e. as long as there was no problem in the meantime]; **Cor** I.i.70

imperator (*n.*) emperor, absolute ruler, sovereign **E3** II.ii.40 [King Edward to himself, of the Countess] *She is as imperator over me;* **LL** III.i.182

imperceiverant (*adj.*) [unclear meaning] unperceptive, undiscerning **Cym** IV.i.14 [Cloten alone, of Innogen and Posthumus] *this imperceiverant thing loves him in my despite* [F *imperseuerant*] ► imperseverant (*adj.*)

imperfect (*adj.*) **1** unfinished, incomplete **KL** IV.iii.3 [Gentleman to disguised Kent, of the reason for France's departure] *Something he left imperfect in the state*

2 faulty, lacking in character **Cor** II.i.46 [Menenius to Brutus and Sicinius, of himself] *said to be something imperfect in favouring the first complaint* [i.e. without listening to the other side]

3 unclear, equivocal, inexplicit **Mac** I.iii.69 [Macbeth to Witches] *Stay, you imperfect speakers!*

imperial (*n.*) emperor, imperial personage **TG** II.iii.4 [Launce alone] *[I] am going … to the Imperial's court*

imperial (*adj.*) commanding, authoritative, unquestioned **TC** I.iii.187 [Nestor to all, of Achilles and Patroclus] *Who … opinion crowns / With an imperial voice*

imperious, emperious (*adj.*) imperial, majestic, sovereign **Tit** I.i.253 [Titus to Saturninus, of his sword, prisoner, and chariot] *Presents well worthy Rome's imperious lord;* **AC** IV.xv.23; **Ham** V.i.209; **2H4** III.i.20; **1H6** III.i.44; **Venus** 996

imperiously (*adv.*) majestically, with a commanding manner **Venus** 265 [of Adonis' horse] *Imperiously he leaps, he neighs, he bounds*

imperseverant (*adj.*) [unclear meaning] stubborn, obstinate **Cym** IV.i.14 [Cloten alone, of Innogen and Posthumus] *this imperseverant thing loves him in my despite* [F *imperseuerant*] ► imperceiverant (*adj.*)

impertinency (*n.*) irrelevance, nonsense, senselessness **KL** IV.vi.175 [Edgar to all, of Lear] *O matter and impertinency mixed*

impertinent (*adj.*) **1** irrelevant, beside the point **Tem** I.ii.138 [Prospero to Miranda, of his explanation] *without the which, this story / Were most impertinent*

2 malapropism for 'pertinent' **MV** II.ii.126 [Launcelot to Bassanio] *the suit is impertinent to myself*

impetticoat, impetticos (*v.*) pocket up **TN** II.iii.25 [Feste to Sir Andrew] *I did impetticoat thy gratillity* [F *impeticos*]

impious (*adj.*) lacking reverence towards God, wicked, irreligious **1H6** V.i.12 [King to Gloucester] *It was both impious and unnatural / That such immanity and bloody strife / Should reign among professors of one faith;* **Cym** III.iii.6; **H5** III.iii.15; **Per** IV.iii.17

impiteous (*adj.*) impetuous, violent, pitiless **Ham** IV.v.102 [Messenger to Claudius] *The ocean … / Eats not the flats with more impiteous haste* [reading of F, Q2 *impittious*]

impleached (*adj.*) ► empleached (*adj.*)

implement (*n.*) furnishing, instrument, chattel **Tim** IV.ii.16 [Flavius to Second Servant, of the servants] *All broken implements of a ruined house*

implorator (*n.*) one who implores or entreats, supplicator **Ham** I.iii.129 [Polonius to Ophelia, of Hamlet's vows] *mere implorators of unholy suits*

imply (*v.*) insinuate, suggest the involvement of **2H4** IV.ii.24 [Prince John to Archbishop] *you … / Imply the countenance and grace of heaven* [Q; F *Employ*]

import (*n.*) importance, significance, consequence **TG** III.i.55 [Duke to Valentine, of Valentine's letters] *Be they of much import?;* **1H6** I.i.91; **Oth** III.iii.313; **RJ** V.i.19; **TS** III.iii.101

import (*v.*) **1** signify, mean, suggest **KL** IV.v.6 [Regan to Oswald, of Edmund] *What might import my sister's letter to him?;* **Ham** IV.vii.80; **MM** V.i.108; **Oth** III.iii.30; **Sonn** 122.14; **Tim** V.ii.11

2 be of importance to, concern, matter to **TC** IV.ii.50 [Aeneas to Pandarus, of Troilus] *It doth import him much to speak with me;* **AC** I.ii.122; **Ham** V.ii.21; **KL** IV.iii.4; **LL** IV.i.60; **TNK** I.i.172

3 involve as a consequence, carry along **AC** II.ii.138 [Agrippa to Caesar and Antony] *all great fears, which now import their dangers, / Would … be nothing*

4 portend, signify, predict **1H6** I.i.2 [Bedford to all] *Comets, importing change of times and states;* **RJ** V.i.28

5 represent, depict, indicate **Ham** III.ii.148 [Ophelia to Hamlet] *Belike this show imports the argument of the play;* **Ham** III.ii.124

importance (*n.*) **1** import, subject-matter **WT** V.ii.18 [First Gentleman to Autolycus, of Leontes' and Camillo's reactions] *the wisest beholder that knew no more but seeing could not say if th'importance were joy or sorrow;* **Cym** I.v.39

2 urgent request, urging, encouragement **TN** V.i.361 [Fabian to Olivia] *Maria writ / The letter at Sir Toby's great importance;* **KJ** II.i.7

importancy (*n.*) importance, significance **Oth** I.iii.20 [First Senator to Duke] *When we consider / Th'importancy of Cyprus to the Turk*

important (*adj.*) urgent, pressing, demanding, importunate **MA** II.i.62 [Beatrice to Hero] *If the Prince be too important;* **AW** III.vii.21; **CE** V.i.138; **Ham** III.iv.109

importantly (*adv.*) with matters of importance **Cym** IV.iv.19 [Arviragus to Belarius and Guiderius, of the Britons] *have both their eyes / And ears so cloyed importantly as now*

importing (*adj.*) expressing significance, full of import **AW** V.iii.136 [Gentleman to King, of Helena] *Her business looks in her / With an importing visage*

importing (*prep.*) concerning, regarding, relating to **Ham** I.ii.23 [Claudius to his court, of young Fortinbras] *He hath not failed to pester us with message / Importing the surrender of those lands*

importless (*adj.*) trivial, unimportant, insignificant **TC** I.iii.71 [Agamemnon to Ulysses] *be't of less expect / That matter needless, of importless burden, / Divide thy lips*

importment (*n.*) **1** [unclear meaning] importance, significance **TNK** I.iii.80 [Emilia to Hippolyta] *This rehearsal … comes in / Like old importment's bastard* [i.e. falsifying its real meaning]
2 ☞ emportment (*n.*)

importunacy (*n.*) importunity, urgent solicitation, pressing entreaty **Tim** II.ii.46 [Flavius to Caphis and other Servants] *Your importunacy cease till after dinner;* **TG** IV.ii.108

importunate (*adj.*) persistent, pressing, insistent **Tim** II.i.28 [Senator to Caphis] *Put on a most importunate aspect;* **Ham** IV.v.2; **LL** V.i.94; **Oth** IV.i.26; **Tim** III.vi.13; **WT** IV.ii.1

importune (*v.*) **1** urge, press **Ham** I.iii.110 [Ophelia to Polonius, of Hamlet] *he hath importuned me with love / In honourable fashion;* **CE** IV.i.2; **E3** II.i.371; **Sonn** 142.10; **Tem** II.i.130; **Tim** II.i.16
2 beg [for], ask persistently [for] **R3** II.ii.14 [Boy to Duchess of York, of Clarence's death] *God will revenge it, whom I will importune / With earnest prayers;* **AY** I.i.86; **Cym** V.v.249; **LL** II.i.32; **MM** V.i.430

importuned (*adj.*) beseeching, pleading, imploring **KL** IV.iv.26 [Cordelia to herself, as if to Lear] *great France / My mourning and importuned tears hath pitied* [F *importun'd*; Q *important*]

importunity (*n.*) persistent solicitation, troublesome persistence **MV** IV.i.158 [Clerk reading Bellario's letter, of Portia as Balthasar] *He is furnished with my opinion which … comes with him at my importunity;* **Ham** I.iii.32; **Oth** III.iii.249

impose (*n.*) imposition, command, imposed duty **TG** IV.iii.8 [Eglamour to Silvia] *According to your ladyship's impose, / I am thus early come*

impose (*v.*) subject, put **MA** V.i.260 [Claudio to Leonato] *Impose me to what penance your invention / Can lay upon my sin*

imposition (*n.*) **1** order, charge, comand **MV** III.iv.33 [Portia to Lorenzo] *I do desire you / Not to deny this imposition;* **AW** IV.iv.29; **Luc** 1697; **MV** I.ii.98
2 extra burden, additional demand **TNK** I.iv.44 [Theseus to all, of different events] *Hath set a mark which nature could not reach to / Without some imposition*
3 imposed penalty, burden, weight **WT** I.ii.74 [Polixenes to Hermione, of his and Leontes' sinless early life] *the imposition cleared / Hereditary ours* [i.e. with the hereditary burden of our original sin being cleared away]
4 accusation, charge, imputation **MM** I.ii.187 [Lucio to Claudio, of encouraging Isabella's powers to persuade] *which else would stand under grievous imposition*

impossible (*adj.*) incredible, inconceivable, preposterous **MA** II.i.124 [masked Beatrice to masked Benedick, of Benedick] *his gift is in devising impossible slanders;* **MA** II.i.225

imposthume (*n.*) abscess, putrid swelling **Venus** 743 [Venus to Adonis] *Surfeits, imposthumes, grief and damned despair, / Swear Nature's death for framing thee so fair;* **Ham** IV.iv.27; **TC** V.i.20 [Q]

imposture (*n.*) impostor, fraud **Per** V.i.179 [Marina to Pericles] *It may be / You think me an imposture*

impotence (*n.*) helplessness, powerlessness, decrepitude **Ham** II.ii.66 [Voltemand to Claudius, of the Norwegian king] *his sickness, age, and impotence*

impotent (*adj.*) helpless, powerless, decrepit **LL** V.ii.843 [Rosaline to Berowne] *your task shall be … / To enforce the pained impotent to smile;* **Ham** I.ii.29

imprese (*n.*) crest, heraldic device, emblem **R2** III.i.25 [Bolingbroke to Bushy and Green] *you have … / Razed out my imprese*

impress (*n.*) **1** conscription, enforced service **AC** III.vii.36 [Enobarbus to Antony] *Your mariners are muleters, reapers, people / Engrossed by swift impress;* **Ham** I.i.75; **TC** II.i.97
2 impression, stamp, sense **TG** III.ii.6 [Duke to Thurio] *This weak impress of love is as a figure / Trenched in ice*

impress (*v.*) **1** conscript, enlist, force into service **1H4** I.i.21 [King Henry to all, of Christ] *under whose blessed cross / We are impressed and engaged to fight;* **Mac** IV.i.94

2 imprint, engrave, stamp [as by a seal] **AW** I.iii.128 [Countess to herself] *love's strong passion is impressed in youth;* **LL** II.i.222

impressed (*adj.*) conscripted, forced to enlist **KL** V.iii.51 [Edmund to Albany] *turn our impressed lances in our eyes*

impression (*n.*) **1** shape, resemblance, appearance **3H6** III.ii.162 [Richard to and of himself] *Like to … an unlicked bear-whelp / That carries no impression like the dam*
2 indentation, depth of presence **Cor** V.iii.51 [Coriolanus to Volumnia, as he kneels] *Of thy deep duty more impression show / Than that of common sons*

impressure (*n.*) imprint, impression, indentation, stamp **TC** IV.v.131 [Hector to Ajax, of his limbs] *Wherein my sword had not impressure made / Of our rank feud;* **AY** III.v.23; **TN** II.v.92

imprimis (*adv.*) in the first place **TS** IV.i.59 [Grumio to Curtis] *Imprimis, we came down a foul hill;* **2H6** I.i.43; **TG** III.i.271; **TS** IV.iii.130

improper (*adj.*) unfitting, unsuitable, inappropriate **KL** V.iii.219 [Edgar to Albany, of Kent and Lear] *did him service / Improper for a slave*

improve (*v.*) employ to advantage, make good use of **JC** II.i.159 [Cassius to all, of Antony] *you know his means, / If he improve them, may well stretch so far / As to annoy us all*

improvident (*adj.*) shortsighted, lacking foresight, careless **1H6** II.i.58 [Pucelle to Charles] *Improvident soldiers!;* **MW** II.ii.275

impudency (*n.*) impudence, effrontery, presumption **LL** V.i.5 [Nathaniel to Holofernes] *Your reasons at dinner have been … audacious without impudency*

impudent (*adj.*) shameless, immodest, unblushing **TC** III.iii.217 [Patroclus to Achilles] *A woman impudent and mannish grown / Is not more loathed than an effeminate man / In time of action*

impugn (*v.*) call into question, dispute the validity of **2H6** III.i.281 [York to all] *It skills not greatly who impugns our doom*

imputation (*n.*) reputation, prestige, estimation **TC** I.iii.339 [Nestor to Ulysses, of Hector's challenge] *Our imputation shall be oddly poised / In this willed action;* **Ham** V.ii.140; **2H4** V.i.66

impute (*v.*) regard, consider, reckon **Sonn** 83.9 [of his lack of words] *This silence for my sin you did impute*

in (*v.*) gather in, bring in, harvest **AW** I.iii.45 [Clown to Countess] *He that ears my land … gives me leave to in the crop*

in (*adv.*) **1** in prison **2H4** V.v.38 [Pistol to Falstaff] *For Doll is in*
2 in the same situation **LL** IV.iii.18 [Berowne alone, of the other votaries and being in love] *I would not care a pin if the other three were in*
3 in an inebriated state, drunk **AC** II.vii.33 [Enobarbus to Lepidus, responding to 'I'll ne'er out'] *Not till you have slept; I fear me you'll be in till then*
4 ☞ STAGE DIRECTIONS, p.417

in (*prep.*) **1** at **TNK** V.iv.126 [Theseus to all] *give grace unto / The funeral of Arcite, in whose end / The visages of bridegrooms we'll put on* [= at the end of which]
2 by **AW** II.iv.32 [Clown to Parolles] *Did you find me in your self*
3 into **2H4** I.ii.48 [Page to Falstaff, of Bardolph] *He's gone in Smithfield to buy your worship a horse*
4 of **Cor** II.ii.13 [Second Officer to First Officer, of the people] *for Coriolanus neither to care whether they love or hate him manifests the true knowledge he has in their disposition*
5 on **E3** II.i.199 [King Edward to Countess] *I am blunt, and cannot strew / The flowers of solace in a ground of shame*
6 within **2H4** I.iii.7 [Mowbray to Archbishop] *I … would be better satisfied / How in our means we should advance ourselves*

in-a-door (*adv.*) indoors **KL** I.iv.124 [Fool to Lear] *keep in-a-door*

inaidible (*adj.*) unable to be assisted, incapable of being helped **AW** II.i.119 [King to Helena] *labouring art can never ransom nature / From her inaidible estate*

incaged (*adj.*) ☞ encaged (*adj.*)

incapable (*adj.*) insensible, unconscious, incomprehending **R3** II.ii.18 [Duchess of York to Clarence's children] *Incapable and shallow innocents*; **Ham** IV.vii.178

incapable of (*adj.*) unable to take in, unable to hold **Sonn** 113.13 *Incapable of more, replete with you, / My most true mind thus maketh mine untrue*

incardinate (*adj.*) malapropism for 'incarnate' **TN** V.i.178 [Sir Andrew to Olivia, of Sebastian] *he's the very devil incardinate*

incarnadine (*v.*) redden, turn blood-red **Mac** II.ii.62 [Macbeth alone] *my hand will … / The multitudinous seas incarnadine, / Making the green one red*

incarnation (*n.*) malapropism for 'incarnate' **MV** II.ii.24 [Launcelot alone, of Shylock] *the Jew is the very devil incarnation*

incense (*v.*) incite, urge, set on **MA** V.i.224 [Borachio to Don Pedro] *your brother incensed me to slander the Lady Hero*; **KL** II.iv.301; **R3** III.i.152; **Tem** III.iii.75; **WT** V.i.61 ☛ **insense** (*v.*)

incensed (*adj.*) inflamed, angered, enraged **2H4** I.iii.14 [Hastings to Archbishop, of Northumberland] *whose bosom burns / With an incensed fire of injuries*; **Ham** V.ii.61; **H8** I.ii.65; **KJ** III.i.238; **LL** V.ii.694; **Per** V.i.143

incensement (*n.*) anger, wrath, fury **TN** III.iv.233 [Sir Toby to Viola as Cesario, of Sir Andrew] *his incensement at this moment is … implacable*

incensing (*adj.*) anger-arousing, inflaming with wrath **AW** V.iii.25 [King to Lafew, of Bertram's offence] *deeper than oblivion we do bury / Th'incensing relics of it*

incertain (*adj.*) **1** uncertain, doubtful, dubious **Tim** IV.iii.244 [Apemantus to Timon] *Willing misery / Outlives incertain pomp*; **2H4** I.iii.24; **JC** V.i.95; **MM** III.i.130
  2 uncertain, needing guidance, in a doubtful state **AW** III.i.15 [Second Lord to Duke] *I have found / Myself in my incertain grounds to fail*; **WT** V.i.29

incertainty (*n.*) uncertainty **Sonn** 107.7 *Incertainties now crown themselves assured*; **Sonn** 115.11; **WT** III.ii.167

incessantly (*adv.*) instantly, immediately, without delay **Tit** IV.iv.113 [Saturninus to Tamora, of Titus] *go incessantly, and plead to him* [F *successantly*; Q1 *sucessantly*] ☛ **successantly** (*adv.*)

inch, at an very closely, instantly ready [to act] **2H6** I.iv.41 [York to Duchess of Gloucester] *Beldam, I think we watched you at an inch*

inches, by very gradually, bit by bit, by small degrees **TC** II.i.48 [Thersites to Ajax] *I will begin at thy heel, and tell what thou art by inches*; **Cor** V.iv.38

inches, even to his every inch of him, from top to toe **TC** IV.v.111 [Ulysses to Agamemnon, of Aeneas knowing Troilus] *one that knows the youth / Even to his inches*

incharitable (*adj.*) uncharitable **Tem** I.i.41 [Sebastian to Boatswain] *you bawling, blasphemous, incharitable dog!*

inch-meal (*adv.*) inch by inch, little by little **Tem** II.ii.3 [Caliban alone, of Prospero] *make him / By inch-meal a disease!*

incidency (*n.*) incident, event, occurrence **WT** I.ii.403 [Polixenes to Camillo] *I conjure thee … that thou declare / What incidency thou dost guess of harm / Is creeping toward me*

incident (*adj.*) likely to happen, applicable, natural **Tim** IV.i.21 [Timon alone] *Plagues incident to men, / Your potent and infectious fevers heap / On Athens*; **Tim** V.i.198; **WT** IV.iv.125

incision (*n.*) blood-letting **LL** IV.iii.95 [Berowne as if to Dumaine, of Katharine as a fever] *then incision / Would let her out in saucers*

incite (*v.*) urge, prompt, summon **Cym** III.viii.6 [First Senator to all, of the conflict with Britain] *we do incite / The gentry to this business*; **H5** I.ii.20

incivil (*adj.*) uncivil, unmannerly, discourteous **Cym** V.v.292 [Guiderius to Cymbeline, of Cloten being a prince] *A most incivil one*

inclination (*n.*) character, temperament, disposition **3H6** III.ii.76 [Lady Grey to Edward] *this merry inclination / Accords not with the sadness of my suit*; **AC** II.v.113

incline (*v.*) turn, be disposed, desire **LL** IV.i.92 [Boyet reading Armado's letter to Jaquenetta, of the Nemean lion] *he from forage will incline to play*

incline to (*v.*) lean towards, favour, support **KL** III.iii.12 [Gloucester to Edmund] *We must incline to the King*; **1H6** V.i.154

inclining (*n.*) **1** favour, partiality, indulgence **AW** III.vi.35 [Second Lord to Bertram, of Parolles] *your inclining cannot be removed*
  2 party, following, faction **Oth** I.ii.82 [Othello to Brabantio] *Hold your hands, / Both you of my inclining and the rest*

inclining (*adj.*) compliant, sympathetic, submissive **Oth** II.iii.330 [Iago alone] *'tis most easy / Th'inclining Desdemona to subdue / In any honest suit*

inclip (*v.*) embrace, enclose, enfold **AC** II.vii.68 [Menas to Pompey] *Whate'er the ocean pales, or sky inclips*

include (*v.*) conclude, settle, bring to a close **TG** V.iv.161 [Duke to Valentine] *we will include all jars / With triumphs* [or: enclose, shut in]

inclusive (*adj.*) **1** comprehensive, all-embracing, extensive **AW** I.iii.221 [Helena to Countess, of her father's prescriptions] *notes whose faculties inclusive were / More than they were in note*
  2 enclosing, encircling, encompassing **R3** IV.i.58 [Anne to herself, of the crown] *the inclusive verge / Of golden metal*

income (*n.*) arrival, advent, entrance **Luc** 334 [Tarquin to himself] *Pain pays the income of each precious thing*

incomprehensible (*adj.*) boundless, infinite, beyond comprehension **1H4** I.ii.184 [Poins to Prince Hal, of Falstaff] *The virtue of this jest will be the incomprehensible lies that this same fat rogue will tell us*

inconsiderate (*n.*) unthinking person, ignorant being **LL** III.i.76 [Armado to Mote, of Costard] *Doth the inconsiderate take salve for l'envoy and the word 'l'envoy' for a salve?*

inconsiderate (*adj.*) thoughtless, precipitate, reckless **KJ** II.i.67 [Chatillon to King Philip, of English soldiers] *Rash, inconsiderate, fiery voluntaries*

incontinence (*n.*) lacking self-restraint, indulgence [in the pleasures of the flesh] **TNK** I.ii.7 [Arcite to Palamon] *And here to keep in abstinence we shame / As in incontinence* [i.e. as shameful to abstain from evil as to commit it]

incontinency (*n.*) lack of sexual restraint, sexual indulgence, infidelity **Cym** III.iv.48 [Innogen to Pisanio, as if to Iachimo of Posthumus] *Thou didst accuse him of incontinency*; **Cym** II.iv.127; **Ham** II.i.30

incontinent (*adj.*) unchaste, unable to restrain oneself **Tim** IV.i.3 [Timon alone] *Matrons, turn incontinent*; **AY** V.ii.37; **TC** V.i.94

incontinent (*adv.*) immediately, forthwith, at once **Oth** IV.iii.11 [Desdemona to Emilia, of Othello] *He says he will return incontinent*; **AY** V.ii.37; **R2** V.vi.48

incontinently (*adv.*) immediately, at once, forthwith **Oth** I.iii.302 [Roderigo to Iago] *I will incontinently drown myself*

inconvenience (*n.*) harm, troublesome disadvantage **1H6** I.iv.14 [Master Gunner to Boy, of the overlooking English position] *To intercept this inconvenience, / A piece of ordnance 'gainst it I have placed*; **H5** V.ii.66

inconvenient (*adj.*) unsuitable, inappropriate, out of place **AY** V.ii.63 [Rosalind as Ganymede to Orlando] *if it appear not inconvenient to you*

incony (*adj.*) fine, darling, rare **LL** IV.i.143 [Costard alone, of the repartee] *most incony vulgar wit*; **LL** III.i.133

incorporal (*adj.*) incorporeal, insubstantial, immaterial **Ham** III.iv.119 [Gertrude to Hamlet] *And with th'incorporal air do hold discourse?* [Q2; F *corporall*]

incorporate *(adj.)* united in one body, combined in one entity **Venus** 540 [of Venus and Adonis] *Incorporate then they seem; face grows to face;* **CE** II.ii.131; **H5** V.ii.358; **JC** I.iii.135; **MND** III.ii.208; **Tit** I.i.465

incorporate *(v.)* make one body [of], unite **JC** II.i.273 [Portia to Brutus] *that great vow / Which did incorporate and make us one;* **RJ** II.vi.37

incorpsed *(adj.)* made into one body, incorporated, fused **Ham** IV.vii.86 [Claudius to Laertes, of Lamord] *As had he been incorpsed and demi-natured / With the brave beast*

incorrect *(adj.)* behaving in a contrary way, uncorrected **Ham** I.ii.95 [Claudius to Hamlet, of the latter's grief] *It shows a will most incorrect to heaven*

increase *(n.)* **1** produce, growth, yield, crop **Venus** 169 [Venus to Adonis] *Upon the earth's increase why shouldst thou feed;* **2H6** III.ii.385; **3H6** II.ii.164; **MND** II.i.114; **Tit** V.ii.190

2 offspring, descendants, procreation **Venus** 791 [Adonis to Venus, of her approach to him] *You do it for increase;* **Cor** III.iii.114

increaseful *(adj.)* productive, fruitful, multiplying **Luc** 958 [Lucrece as if to time] *Time's glory is ... / To cheer the ploughman with increaseful crops*

incredulous *(adj.)* incredible, unbelievable **TN** III.iv.80 [Malvolio alone] *no incredulous or unsafe circumstance ... can come between me and the full prospect of my hopes*

Ind *(n.)* Indies **AY** III.ii.84 [Rosalind, reading] *From the east to western Ind* ☛ **WORLD**, p.634

indent *(n.)* indentation, gouge, recess **1H4** III.i.100 [Hotspur to all, of the river] *It shall not wind with such a deep indent*

indent *(v.)* **1** move in a zigzag, double back **Venus** 704 [Venus to Adonis, of the hare] *Then shalt thou see the dew-bedabbled wretch / Turn, and return, indenting with the way*

2 bargain, covenant, make an agreement **1H4** I.iii.86 [King Henry to all] *Shall we ... indent with fears*

indented *(adj.)* sinuous, zigzag, undulating **AY** IV.iii.113 [Oliver to Rosalind and Celia disguised, of the snake] *it unlinked itself / And with indented glides did slip away*

indenture *(n.)* **1** (plural) [legal] joint agreement, articles of agreement **1H4** III.i.135 [Hotspur to all] *Are the indentures drawn?;* **Ham** V.i.108; **1H4** III.i.76, 254

2 contract, agreement **KJ** II.i.20 [Austria to Arthur, kissing him] *As seal to this indenture of my love;* **1H4** II.iv.46; **Per** I.iii.8, IV.vi.175

index *(n.)* prologue, preface, table of contents **R3** IV.iv.85 [Queen Margaret to Queen Elizabeth] *I called thee ... / The flattering index of a direful pageant;* **Ham** III.iv.53; **R3** II.ii.149; **TC** I.iii.343

Indian *(adj.)* dark-complexioned, dark-haired **MV** III.ii.99 [Bassanio to himself] *ornament is but ... the beauteous scarf / Veiling an Indian beauty*

indict *(v.)* charge, convict, accuse **Ham** II.ii.441 [Hamlet to First Player] *no matter in the phrase that might indict the author of affectation*

indictment *(n.)* legal document containing a charge **2H4** IV.i.126 [Mowbray to Westmorland] *by indictment and by dint of sword;* **2H4** II.iv.338; **R3** III.vi.1

indifferency *(n.)* **1** impartiality, moderation, equity **KJ** II.i.579 [Bastard alone, of the world] *This sway of motion, this commodity, / Makes it take head from all indifferency*

2 ordinariness, average character **2H4** IV.iii.20 [Falstaff to himself] *An I had but a belly of any indifferency*

indifferent *(adj.)* **1** impartial, unbiased, neutral **R2** II.iii.115 [Bolingbroke to York] *Look on my wrongs with an indifferent eye;* **H5** I.i.72; **H8** II.iv.17; **TG** III.i.44

2 unconcerned, without a preference **TNK** III.vi.60 [Arcite to Palamon] *I am indifferent* [i.e. I don't mind]

3 average, ordinary, typical **Tim** I.i.31 [Painter to Poet, of the praise of his picture] *Indifferent* [i.e. it's not too bad]; **Ham** II.ii.227

4 not different, identical, same **TS** IV.i.82 [Grumio to Curtis, of the servants' clothes] *their garters of an indifferent knit*

indifferent *(adv.)* **1** moderately, tolerably, reasonably **TN** I.v.236 [Olivia to Viola as Cesario, of her features] *two lips, indifferent red;* **Ham** III.i.122, V.ii.97; **H5** IV.vii.31; **TC** I.i.223

2 equally, alike, correspondingly **TS** I.ii.178 [Hortensio to Gremio] *I'll tell you news indifferent good for either*

indifferently *(adv.)* **1** impartially, equally, alike **JC** I.ii.87 [Brutus to Cassius, of honour and death] *I will look on both indifferently;* **Cor** II.ii.16; **Tit** I.i.433

2 to some extent, fairly well **Ham** III.ii.35 [First Player to Hamlet, of their performing style] *I hope we have reformed that indifferently*

indigest *(n.)* shapeless mass, confused situation **KJ** V.vii.26 [Salisbury to Prince Henry, of King John] *you are born / To set a form upon that indigest / Which he hath left so shapeless and so rude*

indigest *(adj.)* shapeless, deformed, crude **Sonn** 114.5 *To make of monsters, and things indigest, / Such cherubins as your sweet self resemble*

indigested *(adj.)* improperly formed, uncompleted **2H6** V.i.157 [Clifford to Richard] *heap of wrath, foul indigested lump;* **3H6** V.vi.51

indign *(adj.)* unworthy, shameful, dishonourable **Oth** I.iii.270 [Othello to all] *Let ... all indign and base adversities / Make head against my estimation!*

indirect *(adj.)* **1** roundabout, devious, oblique **R3** I.iv.221 [Clarence to Murderers, of God] *He needs no indirect or lawless course / To cut off those that have offended Him*

2 deceitful, not straightforward, dishonest **R3** III.i.31 [Buckingham to Hastings, of Queen Elizabeth] *what an indirect and peevish course / Is this of hers!*

indirection *(n.)* **1** roundabout means, indirect approach **Ham** II.i.66 [Polonius to Reynaldo] *By indirections find directions out*

2 devious means, malpractice **JC** IV.iii.75 [Brutus to Cassius] *I had rather coin my heart ... than to wring / From the hard hands of peasants their vile trash / By any indirection;* **KJ** III.i.276

indirectly *(adv.)* **1** wrongfully, unjustly, illegitimately **H5** II.iv.94 [Exeter to French King, of King Henry] *Your crown and kingdom, indirectly held / From him;* **KJ** II.i.49

2 inattentively, distractedly, away from the point **1H4** I.iii.65 [Hotspur to King Henry] *I answered indirectly*

indiscretion *(n.)* lack of judgement, recklessness **Ham** V.ii.8 [Hamlet to Horatio] *Our indiscretion sometime serves us well*

indisposition *(n.)* unwillingness, reluctance, disinclination **Tim** II.ii.135 [Timon to Flavius] *Perchance some single vantages you took / When my indisposition put you back* [i.e. my reluctance to talk about the subject put you off]

indistinguishable *(adj.)* shapeless, misshapen, disfigured **TC** V.i.26 [Patroclus to Thersites] *you whoreson indistinguishable cur*

indistinguished, undistinguished *(adj.)* limitless, unimaginable, beyond apprehension **KL** IV.vi.270 [Edgar to all, of Gonerill] *O indistinguished space of woman's will!* [Q2 vndistinguisht]

indite *(v.)* **1** write, compose, set down **LL** IV.i.95 [Princess to Boyet, of Armado] *What plume of feathers is he that indited this letter?*

2 malapropism for 'invite' **2H4** II.i.26 [Hostess to Fang and Snare, of Falstaff] *he is indited to dinner to the Lubber's Head*

individable *(adj.)* indivisible [with no changes in the location of action on stage]; or: unclassifiable **Ham** II.ii.398 [Polonius to Hamlet, of the players' productions] *scene individable, or poem unlimited*

indrenched *(adj.)* drowned, immersed, submerged **TC** I.i.52 [Troilus to Pandarus, of his hopes] *Reply not in how many fathoms deep / They lie indrenched*

indubitate *(adj.)* certain, undoubted, undeniable **LL** IV.i.68 [Boyet reading Armado's letter to Jaquenetta] *most illustrate King Cophetua set eye upon the pernicious and most indubitate beggar Zenelophon*

induce (*v.*) move, persuade, prevail upon **Cor** I.ix.16 [Martius to Lartius] *induced / As you have been - that's for my country*

inducement (*n.*) **1** influential reason, persuasive cause **H8** II.iv.169 [King Henry to all, of the divorce] *Then mark th'inducement*
2 temptation, bad influence, persuasiveness **AW** III.ii.89 [Countess to Lords, of Parolles] *My son corrupts a well-derived nature / With his inducement*

induction (*n.*) opening scene [of a play], initial step, preparation **R3** I.i.32 [Richard alone] *Plots have I laid, inductions dangerous;* **1H4** III.i.2; **2H4** [opening scene]; **R3** IV.iv.5; **TS** [opening scene]

indue, endue (*v.*) **1** endow, furnish, provide **Cor** II.iii.139 [Menenius to Coriolanus] *the Tribunes / Endue you with the people's voice;* **KJ** IV.ii.43 [King John to Pembroke and Salisbury, of reasons for his second coronation] *more, more strong, when lesser is my fear, / I shall indue you with;* **LL** V.ii.639; **TN** I.v.92
2 introduce, lead, bring **Oth** III.iv.142 [Desdemona to Emilia] *let our finger ache, and it endues / Our healthful members even to that sense / Of pain* [F; Q *indue*]

indued, endued (*adj.*) endowed, supplied [with appropriate qualities] **CE** II.i.22 [Luciana to Adriana, of men] *Indued with intellectual sense and souls;* **Ham** IV.vii.179; **H5** II.ii.139

indurance, endurance (*n.*) distressing delay, hardship **H8** V.i.121 [King Henry to Cranmer] *I should have ta'en some pains ... to have heard you / Without indurance further* [F] [or: duress, imprisonment]; **Per** V.i.136

indurate (*adj.*) callous, hardened, obstinate **3H6** I.iv.142 [York to Queen] *Thou [art] stern, indurate, flinty* [Q; F *obdurate*]

industrious (*adj.*) **1** devoted, zealous, attentive **1H4** I.i.62 [King Henry to Westmorland, of Blunt] *Here is a dear, a true industrious friend*
2 ingenious, skilful, clever **KJ** II.i.376 [Bastard to King John and King Philip, of the people of Angiers] *they gape and point / At your industrious scenes and acts of death*

industriously (*adv.*) intentionally, deliberately, purposely **WT** I.ii.256 [Camillo to Leontes] *In your affairs ... if industriously / I played the fool, it was my negligence*

industry (*n.*) **1** toil, labour, exertion **3H6** V.iv.11 [Queen to all] *the ship splits on the rock, / Which industry and courage might have saved;* **Cym** III.vii.4
2 diligence, earnestness, steady application **Cym** III.v.112 [Cloten to Pisanio] *undergo those employments wherein I should have cause to use thee with a serious industry*
3 laborious gallantry, assiduity in service to a lady **LL** IV.i.87 [Boyet reading Armado's letter to Jaquenetta] *Thine in the dearest design of industry*

inequality (*n.*) [unclear meaning] difference of rank, social disparity; injustice, partiality **MM** V.i.65 [Isabella to Duke] *do not banish reason ... / For inequality*

inevitable unavoidable, unable to be averted **TN** III.iv.270 [Sir Toby to Sir Andrew, of Viola as Cesario] *he gives me the stuck-in with such a mortal motion that it is inevitable*

inexecrable (*adj.*) inexorable, unmoveable, relentless; or: execrable, accursed, damnable **MV** IV.i.128 [Gratiano to Shylock] *be thou damned, inexecrable dog*

inexorable (*adj.*) merciless, relentlessly severe **3H6** I.iv.154 [York to Queen, of her] *more inexorable ... than tigers of Hyrcania*

infallible (*adj.*) unquestionable, definite, certain **LL** IV.i.63 [Boyet reading Armado's letter to Jaquenetta] *that thou art fair is most infallible;* **MM** III.ii.106

infallibly (*adv.*) accurately, precisely, faithfully **Ham** V.ii.120 [Osrick to Hamlet, of Laertes] *Your lordship speaks most infallibly of him*

infamonize (*v.*) brand with infamy, defame **LL** V.ii.675 [Armado to Costard] *Dost thou infamonize me among potentates?*

infamy (*n.*) bad report, terrible reputation **TG** II.vii.64 [Lucetta to Julia] *never dream on infamy, but go;* **1H6** IV.i.143

infant (*n.*) young plant [figurative use] **Ham** I.iii.39 [Laertes to Ophelia] *The canker galls the infants of the spring*

infect (*v.*) affect, influence, stir **KJ** IV.iii.69 [Salisbury to all, vowing revenge on Arthur's apparent murder] *Never to be infected with delight;* **Cor** V.vi.72

infected (*adj.*) affected, artificial, put on **Tim** IV.iii.203 [Apemantus to Timon] *This is in thee a nature but infected, / A poor unmanly melancholy;* **Lover** 323

infection (*n.*) **1** contamination, rottenness, bad influence **Tem** II.ii.1 [Caliban alone] *All the infections that the sun sucks up;* **2H6** III.ii.287
2 malapropism for 'affection' **MV** II.ii.115 [Gobbo to Bassanio, of Launcelot] *He hath a great infection, sir, as one would say, to serve;* **MW** II.ii.112

infer (*v.*) **1** adduce, bring up, put forward **R3** III.v.74 [Richard to Buckingham] *Infer the bastardy of Edward's children;* **3H6** II.ii.44, III.i.49; **R3** III.vii.12, IV.iv.343; **Tim** III.v.74
2 imply, demonstrate, illustrate **2H4** V.v.14 [Falstaff to Shallow, of their clothes] *this poor show doth better; this doth infer the zeal I had to see him*

infest (*v.*) harass, trouble, assail **Tem** V.i.246 [Prospero to Alonso] *Do not infest your mind with beating on / The strangeness of this business*

infinite (*n.*) **1** infinity, infinite quantity, eternity **TG** II.vii.70 [Julia to Lucetta] *instances of infinite of love, / Warrant me welcome to my Proteus;* **MA** II.iii.103
2 immensity, magnitude, vastness **TC** II.ii.29 [Troilus to Hector, of Priam] *Will you with counters sum / The past-proportion of his infinite* [i.e. his extraordinary greatness which defies calculation]

infinitive (*adj.*) malapropism for 'infinite' **2H4** II.i.23 [Hostess to Fang and Snare, of Falstaff] *he's an infinitive thing upon my score*

infirmity (*n.*) **1** defect, flaw, weakness **KL** I.i.202 [Lear to Burgundy, of Cordelia] *Will you with those infirmities she owes ... / Take her*
2 indisposition, illness, malady **Cym** III.v.47 [Queen to Cymbeline, of Innogen's seclusion] *Whereto constrained by her infirmity*

infix (*v.*) implant, fasten onto **AW** V.iii.47 [Bertram to King] *the impression of mine eye infixing*

infixed (*adj.*) captured, caught, firmly held **KJ** II.i.502 [Lewis the Dauphin to King Philip, of Blanche] *I never loved myself / Till now infixed I beheld myself / Drawn in the flattering table of her eye*

inflame (*v.*) increase, raise, charge extra **TNK** III.v.129 [Schoolmaster to Theseus, of a host and hostess] *with a beckoning / Informs the tapster to inflame the reckoning*

inflamed (*adj.*) **1** fervent, glowing, ardent **KL** I.i.255 [France to Cordelia] *'Tis strange that from their cold'st neglect / My love should kindle to inflamed respect*
2 engulfed with fire **KJ** V.i.7 [King John to Cardinal Pandulph, of the French] *stop their marches 'fore we are inflamed*

inflammation (*n.*) inflamed senses, heated condition [through drinking] **2H4** IV.iii.94 [Falstaff alone, of boys like Prince John] *They are generally fools and cowards - which some of us should be too, but for inflammation*

inflict (*v.*) afflict, trouble, plague **Per** V.i.58 [Lysimachus to Helicanus] *God / For every graff would send a caterpillar, / And so inflict our province*

infliction (*n.*) being inflicted, implementation, enforcement **MM** I.iii.28 [Duke to Friar Thomas] *our decrees, / Dead to infliction, to themselves are dead*

infold (*v.*) enfold, wrap up, conceal **MV** II.vii.69 [Morocco reading from the scroll] *Gilded tombs do worms infold;* **RJ** III.iii.74; **Venus** 225

inform (*v.*) **1** report, relate, tell **Cor** I.vi.42 [Martius to Cominius, of the Messenger] *He did inform the truth*

2 provide evidence, bring a charge **Ham** IV.iv.32 [Hamlet alone] *How all occasions do inform against me* [i.e. accuse me]

3 invest with, inspire in, impart to **Cym** I.ii.10 [Queen to Posthumus, of Cymbeline] *'twere good / You leaned unto his sentence, with what patience / Your wisdom may inform you*

4 take form, appear in a shape **Mac** II.i.48 [Macbeth alone, as if to a dagger] *It is the bloody business which informs / Thus to mine eyes*

informal *(adj.)* demented, mentally disturbed **MM** V.i.234 [Angelo to Duke, of Isabella and Mariana] *These poor informal women*

information *(n.)* **1** item of information, piece of intelligence **H8** V.iii.110 [Cromwell to all, of Cranmer] *In seeking tales and informations / Against this man*

2 source of knowledge, informant **Cor** IV.vi.54 [Menenius to Brutus, of a slave] *reason with the fellow … / Lest you shall chance to whip your information*

infortunate *(adj.)* unfortunate **2H6** IV.ix.18 [King to former rebels] *Henry, though he be infortunate, / Assure yourselves, will never be unkind;* **KJ** II.i.178

infuse *(v.)* **1** fill, imbue, pervade **TS** Induction.ii.15 [Lord to and of Sly] *that a mighty man of such descent … / Should be infused with so foul a spirit!*

2 pour into, shed on, radiate upon **1H6** I.ii.85 [Pucelle to Dauphin, of Our Lady] *With those clear rays which she infused on me / That beauty am I blessed with which you may see*

infusion *(n.)* **1** mixture of qualities, combination of attributes **Ham** V.ii.116 [Hamlet to Osrick, of Laertes] *his infusion of such dearth and rareness*

2 natural characteristic, tincture, liquid extract **Per** III.ii.34 [Cerimon to First Gentleman] *[I have] made familiar / To me … the blest infusions / That dwells in vegetives*

ingaged *(adj.)* engaged [to her]; or, not promised [to anyone else] **AW** V.iii.96 [Bertram to Lafew, of the woman who threw him a ring] *she … thought / I stood ingaged*

ingener *(n.)* inventor, designer, creator **Oth** II.i.65 [Cassio to Montano, of Desdemona] *One that … in th'essential vesture of creation / Does tire the ingener* [F *tyre the Ingeniuer*; Q1 *bear all excellency*] ☛ **engineer** *(n.)*

ingenious *(adj.)* **1** alert, fully conscious, intelligent, capable **KL** IV.vi.279 [Gloucester to Edgar] *I stand up and have ingenious feeling / Of my huge sorrows;* **Ham** V.i.244; **LL** IV.ii.77; **R3** III.i.155

2 intellectual, refined, in liberal arts **TS** I.i.9 [Lucentio to Tranio] *Here let us … haply institute / A course of learning and ingenious studies*

3 [unclear meaning] lacking all ability, stupid **AW** V.ii.23 [Clown to Lafew, of Parolles] *he looks like a poor, decayed, ingenious, foolish, rascally knave*

4 skilfully constructed, cleverly invented **Cym** IV.ii.186 [Belarius to Guiderius] *My ingenious instrument … it sounds*

ingeniously *(adv.)* honestly, with all sincerity, without reserve **Tim** II.ii.226 [Timon to Flavius] *Ingeniously I speak, / No blame belongs to thee*

inglorious *(adj.)* shameful, humiliating, ignominious **KJ** V.i.65 [Bastard to King John, of peace with France] *O inglorious league!*

ingot *(n.)* **1** bar of precious metal, gold bar **MM** III.i.26 [disguised Duke to Claudio, of an ass] *whose back with ingots bows*

2 coin, piece **TNK** I.ii.17 [Palamon to Arcite] *th'martialist, who did propound / To his bold ends honour and golden ingots*

ingraft, engraffed *(adj.)* **1** ingrafted, ingrained, deep-rooted **Oth** II.iii.135 [Montano to Iago, of Cassio] *one of an ingraft infirmity;* **TNK** IV.iii.48 [Doctor to Gaoler, of the Gaoler's Daughter] *'Tis not an engraffed madness* ☛ **long-ingraffed** *(adj.)*

2 closely attached, associated [with] **2H4** II.ii.59 [Poins to Prince Henry] *you have been so lewd, and so much engraffed to Falstaff*

ingraft, engraft *(v.)* graft in, insert new growth into **Sonn** 15.14 [of Time] *As he takes from you, I engraft you new*

ingrafted, engrafted *(adj.)* **1** deep-rooted, firmly implanted **JC** II.i.184 [Cassius to Brutus, of Antony] *in the ingrafted love he bears to Caesar*

2 closely fastened, firmly fixed **Sonn** 37.8 [of qualities] *I make my love engrafted to this store*

ingrate *(adj.)* ungrateful, unthankful, unappreciative **1H4** I.iii.135 [Hotspur to Northumberland] *this ingrate and cankered Bolingbroke;* **Cor** V.ii.82; **KJ** V.ii.151; **TN** V.i.111; **TS** I.ii.267

ingrateful *(adj.)* **1** ungrateful, unappreciative **Tit** V.i.12 [First Goth to Lucius, of Titus] *Whose high exploits and honourable deeds / Ingrateful Rome requites with foul contempt;* **Cor** II.iii.10; **H5** II.ii.95; **KJ** V.vii.43; **Tim** IV.ii.45; **WT** III.ii.185

2 unacceptable, displeasing, disagreeable **Cor** II.ii.30 [Second Officer to First Officer, of the people's attitude to Coriolanus] *a kind of ingrateful injury*

ingratitude *(n.)* act of ingratitude, ungrateful response **TC** III.iii.147 [Ulysses to Achilles, of oblivion] *A great-sized monster of ingratitudes*

ingredience *(n.)* composition, ingredients, contents **Mac** IV.i.34 [Third Witch to Witches] *Add thereto a tiger's chaudron / For the ingredience of our cauldron;* **Mac** I.vii.11; **Oth** II.iii.298

inhabit *(v.)* lodge, dwell, reside **TG** V.iv.7 [Valentine alone, as if to Silvia] *thou that dost inhabit in my breast*

inhabitable *(adj.)* uninhabitable, unlivable **R2** I.i.65 [Mowbray to Richard] *were I tied to run afoot / Even to … any other ground inhabitable*

inhearse *(v.)* bury, place in a coffin **Sonn** 86.3 [of his rival's verses] *That did my ripe thoughts in my brain inhearse, / Making their tomb the womb wherein they grew?*

inhearsed *(adj.)* as if in a coffin **1H6** IV.vii.45 [Burgundy to all, of John Talbot] *See where he lies inhearsed in the arms / Of the most bloody nurser of his harms*

inherent *(adj.)* fixed, irremovable, permanent **Cor** III.ii.123 [Coriolanus to Volumnia] *Lest I … teach my mind / A most inherent baseness*

inherit *(v.)* **1** receive, obtain, come into possession [of] **Tit** I.iii.3 [Aaron alone, of his supposed lack of sense] *To bury so much gold under a tree / And never after to inherit it;* **LL** I.i.73; **MW** II.i.68; **R2** II.i.83; **RJ** I.ii.30

2 secure, win, gain possession of **TG** III.ii.87 [Proteus to Thurio, of singing love-songs to Silvia] *This, or else nothing, will inherit her*

3 realize, come to fruition **Cor** II.i.191 [Volumnia to Coriolanus] *I have lived / To see inherited my very wishes*

4 put in possession of, provide [with] **R2** I.i.85 [King Richard to Bolingbroke, of Mowbray's charge] *It must be great that can inherit us / So much as of a thought of ill in him*

5 possess, hold power over **KL** IV.vi.126 [Lear to all] *to the girdle do the gods inherit* [i.e. as far down as the waist]

6 occupy, inhabit, live on **Tem** IV.i.154 [Prospero to Ferdinand] *the great globe itself, / Yea, all which it inherit*

inheritance *(n.)* acquiring, obtaining, winning **Cor** III.ii.68 [Volumnia to Coriolanus] *show our general louts / How you can frown, than spend a fawn upon 'em / For the inheritance of their loves*

inheritor *(n.)* owner, possessor, acquirer **LL** II.i.5 [Boyet to Princess, of her visit to the King] *To parley with the sole inheritor / Of all perfections that a man may owe;* **Ham** V.i.109

inheritrix *(n.)* female inheritor, heiress **H5** I.ii.51 [Canterbury to King Henry] *no female / Should be inheritrix in Salic land*

inhibited *(adj.)* prohibited, forbidden, proscribed **Oth** I.ii.79 [Brabantio to Othello] *a practiser / Of arts inhibited;* **AW** I.i.143

inhibition *(n.)* formal prohibition, official ban [from playing in the city] **Ham** II.ii.331 [Rosencrantz to Hamlet, of the players] *I think their inhibition comes by the means of the late innovation*

inhooped *(adj.)* [cock-fighting] kept within a hoop [to make birds fight] **AC** II.iii.39 [Antony alone, of Caesar] *his quails ever / Beat mine, inhooped, at odds*

iniquity (*n.*) piece of wickedness, little devil **Per** IV.vi.23 [Lysimachus to Boult] *wholesome iniquity have you* [with comma after 'iniquity': sinner]

initiate (*adj.*) novice, beginner's, as of one newly initiated **Mac** III.iv.142 [Macbeth to Lady Macbeth] *My strange and self-abuse / Is the initiate fear that wants hard use*

injoint (*v.*) unite, join up, come together **Oth** I.iii.35 [Messenger to all] *The Ottomites ... toward the isle of Rhodes, / Have there injointed with an after fleet*

injunction (*n.*) order, directive, command **Tem** III.i.11 [Ferdinand alone, of having to carry out his task] *Upon a sore injunction;* **KL** III.iv.143

injurious (*adj.*) **1** causing injury, harmful, offending, unjust **TG** I.ii.106 [Julia alone] *Injurious wasps, to feed on such sweet honey, / And kill the bees;* **Cym** III.i.48; **3H6** III.iii.101; **Sonn** 44.2, 63.2; **TC** IV.iv.41
2 insulting, slanderous, offensive **3H6** III.iii.78 [Warwick to Queen] *Injurious Margaret!;* **Cor** III.iii.69; **Cym** IV.ii.86; **2H6** I.iv.47

injury (*n.*) **1** grievance, wrong, complaint **2H4** I.iii.14 [Hastings to Archbishop, of Northumberland] *whose bosom burns / With an incensed fire of injuries;* **Cor** V.i.65; **1H4** I.ii.50; **KJ** II.i.187; **TC** IV.iv.32
2 insult, affront, slight **MND** II.i.147 [Oberon as if to Titania] *Thou shalt not from this grove / Till I torment thee for this injury;* **3H6** IV.i.107; **MM** V.i.254; **MND** III.ii.148
3 taunting, injuring, injuriousness **KJ** II.i.188 [Constance to King John, of Queen Eleanor] *Her injury [is] the beadle to her sin*
4 sore, abscess, boil **H5** III.vi.120 [Montjoy as if French King to King Henry] *we thought not good to bruise an injury till it were full ripe* [or: hit back at a wrong]

injury (*v.*) injure, wrong, do injustice to **RJ** III.i.67 [Romeo to Tybalt] *I do protest I never injuried thee* [Q2; F, Q1 injured]

inkhorn (*adj.*) pedantic, book-scribbling **1H6** III.i.99 [Third Servingman to Gloucester, of the King] *To be disgraced by an inkhorn mate*

inkle (*n.*) kind of linen tape, yarn **LL** III.i.136 [Costard alone] *What's the price of this inkle?;* **Per** V.Chorus.8; **WT** IV.iv.209

inland (*adj.*) **1** internal, inner **2H4** IV.iii.108 [Falstaff alone, of the effect of sherry on the body] *the vital commoners, and inland petty spirits, muster me all to their captain, the heart*
2 cultured, brought up in society, not rustic **AY** III.i.333 [Rosalind to Orlando, of her uncle] *who was in his youth an inland man*

inland (*adv.*) in civilized society, not rustic **AY** II.vii.97 [Orlando to Duke Senior] *yet am I inland bred / And know some nurture*

inlay (*v.*) furnish, provide, take one's place in **Cym** V.v.353 [Belarius to Cymbeline, of the children] *they are worthy / To inlay heaven with stars*

inly (*adj.*) inward, internal, heartfelt **TG** II.vii.18 [Julia to Lucetta] *Didst thou but know the inly touch of love;* **3H6** I.iv.171

inly (*adv.*) inwardly, deep within **Tem** V.i.200 [Gonzalo to all] *I have inly wept;* **E3** I.ii.147; **H5** IV.Chorus.24

innocency (*n.*) innocence **1H4** IV.iii.63 [Hotspur to Blunt, of King Henry] *beg his peace / With tears of innocency and terms of zeal;* **E3** III.iii.171; **2H4** V.ii.39; **KJ** IV.iii.110; **MM** III.ii.9

innocent (*n.*) simpleton, dimwit, mental defective **TNK** IV.i.41 [Gaoler to Wooer, of the Gaoler's Daughter] *as if she were a fool, / An innocent;* **AW** IV.iii.184; **TNK** I.iii.79

innocent (*adj.*) silly, half-witted, foolish **MA** V.ii.37 [Benedick alone] *I can find out no rhyme to 'lady' but 'baby' - an innocent rhyme*

innovation (*n.*) **1** revolution, disturbance, commotion **Oth** II.iii.36 [Cassio to Iago, of the effect of drink] *behold what innovation it makes here;* **1H4** V.i.78

2 new fashion; or: insurrection **Ham** II.ii.332 [Rosencrantz to Hamlet, of the players] *I think their inhibition comes by the means of the late innovation* [i.e. the using of boy actors; or: the insurrection of the Earl of Essex]

innovator (*n.*) revolutionary, radical, rebel **Cor** III.i.174 [Sicinius to Coriolanus, of the people] *in whose name myself / Attach thee as a traitorous innovator*

innumerable (*adj.*) incalculable, countless, immense **H8** III.ii.326 [Surrey to Wolsey] *you have sent innumerable substance ... / To furnish Rome*

inobled (*adj.*) ☞ mobled (*adj.*)

inoculate (*v.*) engraft, graft into **Ham** III.i.118 [Hamlet to Ophelia] *virtue cannot so inoculate our old stock* [F; Q2 euocutat]

inordinate (*adj.*) immoderate, intemperate, excessive **Luc** 94 [of Tarquin] *nothing in him seemed inordinate;* **1H4** III.ii.12; **Oth** II.iii.298 ☞ unordinate (*adj.*)

inquire (*n.*) inquiry, enquiry **Per** III.Chorus.22 [Gower alone] *Fame answering the most strange inquire*

inquire forth (*v.*) seek out, ask after one's whereabouts **TG** II.iv.184 [Proteus to Valentine] *I shall inquire you forth*

inquisition (*n.*) inquiry, search, questioning **Tem** I.ii.35 [Miranda to Prospero] *You have often ... left me to a bootless inquisition;* **AY** II.ii.20

inquisitive (*adj.*) eager for information, seeking knowledge **CE** I.i.126 [Egeon to Duke] *My youngest boy ... became inquisitive / After his brother;* **CE** I.ii.38

insane (*adj.*) causing madness, producing insanity **Mac** I.iii.83 [Banquo to Macbeth] *have we eaten on the insane root / That takes the reason prisoner?*

insanie (*n.*) frenzy, madness, lunacy **LL** V.i.25 [Holofernes to Nathaniel, of Armado's pronunciation] *It insinuateth me of insanie* [F, Q1 infamie]

insatiate, unsatiate (*adj.*) insatiable, never satisfied, voracious **Tit** V.i.88 [Lucius to all, of Tamora] *O most insatiate and luxurious woman!;* **R2** II.i.38; **R3** III.v.86, vii.7

insconce (*v.*) ☞ ensconce (*v.*)

inscroll (*v.*) enter on a scroll, inscribe **MV** II.vii.72 [Morocco reading from the scroll] *Had you been as wise as bold ... / Your answer had not been inscrolled*

insculp (*v.*) carve, engrave **MV** II.vii.57 [Morocco to himself] *A coin that bears the figure of an angel / Stamped in gold - but that's insculped upon*

insculpture (*n.*) inscription, engraving **Tim** V.iv.67 [Soldier to Alcibiades, of Timon] *on his grave-stone this insculpture*

inseemed (*adj.*) ☞ enseamed (*adj.*)

insense (*v.*) make understand, inform **H8** V.i.43 [Gardiner to Lovell, of Cranmer] *I have / Incensed the lords o'th' Council that he is ... / A most arch heretic* [F incenst]

insensible (*adj.*) incapable of being perceived by the senses **1H4** V.i.137 [Falstaff alone, of the word 'honour'] *'Tis insensible, then?*

inseparate (*adj.*) undivided, united, conjoined **TC** V.ii.151 [Troilus to Ulysses] *a thing inseparate / Divides more wider than the sky and earth*

insert again put in place of, substitute [with] **LL** IV.ii.19 [Holofernes to Nathaniel, of Dull's misunderstanding] *after his ... unconfirmed fashion - to insert again my haud credo for a deer*

inshell (*v.*) draw in, withdraw within a shell **Cor** IV.vi.45 [Menenius to Sicinius, of Aufidius' horns] *Which were inshelled when Martius stood for Rome*

inship (*v.*) put on board a ship, embark **1H6** V.i.49 [King to Gloucester, of the ambassadors] *see them ... brought to Dover, where inshipped, / Commit them to the fortune of the sea*

insinewed (*adj.*) ☞ ensinewed (*adj.*)

insinuate (*v.*) **1** curry favour, work subtly [on], ingratiate oneself **Tit** IV.ii.38 [Demetrius to Chiron and Aaron] *to see so great a lord / Basely insinuate and send us gifts;* **AY** V.iv.203; **R3** I.iv.150; **Venus** 1012

2 behave subtly, follow an indirect route **WT** IV.iv.730 [Autolycus to Shepherd] *Think's thou, for that I insinuate, to toaze from thee thy business, I am therefore no courtier?*

3 spread subtly, convey with cunning **E3** III.iii.80 [King Edward to King John] *slyly to insinuate with the world ... thy vicious and deformed cause*

4 turn, introduce [to], instil [with] **LL** V.i.25 [Holofernes to Nathaniel, of Armado's pronunciation] *It insinuateth me of insanie*

insinuating (*adj.*) ingratiating, fawning, obsequious **1H6** II.iv.35 [Warwick to all] *without all colour / Of base insinuating flattery;* **Oth** IV.ii.130

insinuation (*n.*) **1** beginning, instilling, suggestion **LL** IV.ii.14 [Holofernes to Nathaniel, of Dull's misunderstanding] *a kind of insinuation, as it were*

2 ingratiation, worming their way in **Ham** V.ii.59 [Hamlet to Horatio, of Rosencrantz and Guildenstern] *Their defeat / Does by their own insinuation grow*

insisture (*n.*) [unclear meaning] steady continuance, constancy, regularity **TC** I.iii.87 [Ulysses to all, of the heavens] *Observe ... / Insisture, course, proportion, season, form*

insociable (*adj.*) **1** unsociable, lacking the benefits of society **LL** V.ii.794 [Princess to King, of living in a hermitage] *this austere insociable life*

2 intolerable, impossible to associate with **LL** V.i.18 [Holofernes to Nathaniel, of Armado] *I abhor ... such insociable and point-device companions*

insolence (*n.*) overbearing pride, haughtiness, presumptuous arrogance **2H6** II.i.31 [Gloucester to Suffolk] *England knows thine insolence;* **2H6** I.i.173, iii.120; **TS** II.i.23

insolent (*adj.*) proud, haughty, arrogant **2H6** III.i.7 [Queen to King, of Gloucester] *will ye not observe ... / How insolent of late he is become*

insomuch (*conj.*) insofar as **E3** III.iii.58 [King John to King Edward] *insomuch thou hast infringed thy faith ... / I hold thee for a false pernicious wretch*

inspiration (*n.*) supernatural power, inspired means **CE** II.ii.176 [Antipholus of Syracuse to Dromio of Syracuse, of Adriana] *How can she thus then call us by our names? - Unless it be by inspiration*

inspired (*adj.*) coming from God, of divine origin **AW** I.i.148 [Helena to King] *Inspired merit so by breath is barred*

instalment (*n.*) stall, seat where someone is installed **MW** V.v.63 [Mistress Quickly as Queen of Fairies to all, of Windsor Castle] *Each fair instalment, coat, and several crest, / With loyal blazon, evermore be blest!*

instance (*n.*) **1** sign, evidence, proof **2H4** III.i.99 [Warwick to King Henry IV] *I have received / A certain instance that Glendower is dead;* **CE** I.i.65; **2H6** III.ii.159; **MA** II.ii.38; **MM** IV.iii.128; **MW** II.ii.236

2 illustration, example, case **AY** II.vii.157 [Jaques to all] *the justice, ... / Full of wise saws and modern instances;* **AY** III.ii.49; **TC** I.iii.77, V.ii.156, x.40; **TN** IV.iii.12

3 reason, motive, cause **R3** III.ii.25 [Hastings to Messenger, of Stanley] *Tell him his fears are shallow, without instance;* **Ham** III.ii.192; **H5** II.ii.119

4 moment, point in time **LL** V.ii.802 [Princess to King, of his return to claim her] *I will ... till that instance, shut / My woeful self up in a mourning house* [Q1; F *instant*]

5 presence, appearance; or: urgency **2H4** IV.i.83 [Archbishop to Westmorland] *the examples / Of every minute's instance, present now, / Hath put us in these ill-beseeming arms*

instant, at an at the same time, simultaneously **MW** IV.iv.3 [Page to Mistress Page, of Falstaff] *did he send you both these letters at an instant?*

instant, on the this very instant, as soon as possible **Tim** IV.i.7 [Timon alone] *To general filths / Convert o'th' instant, green virginity*

instant (*adj.*) **1** immediate, direct **1H4** IV.iv.20 [Archbishop to Sir Michael] *I fear the power of Percy is too weak / To wage an instant trial with the King;* **TC** III.iii.153

2 imminent, impending, close at hand **2H4** I.iii.37 [Lord Bardolph to Hastings] *this present quality of war, / Indeed, the instant action*

3 urgent, pressing, imperative **Tim** III.i.19 [Flaminius to Lucullus, of Timon] *having great and instant occasion to use fifty talents;* **Tim** III.ii.36

4 immediately raisable, quickly mobilized **Cor** V.i.38 [Sicinius to Menenius] *the instant army we can make*

instant (*adv.*) immediately, instantly, at once **Tim** II.ii.235 [Timon to Flavius, of five talents] *give't these fellows / To whom 'tis instant due;* **Ham** I.v.94

instantly (*adv.*) at once, simultaneously, in a moment **1H4** V.ii.64 [Vernon to Hotspur, of Prince Hal] *As if he mastered ... a double spirit / Of teaching and of learning instantly*

instate, enstate (*v.*) endow, invest, bestow **MM** V.i.421 [Duke to Mariana, of Angelo's possessions] *We do instate and widow you with all*

insteeped (*adj.*) steeped, immersed, soaked **H5** IV.vi.12 [Exeter to King Henry, of Suffolk] *York ... / Comes to him, where in gore he lay insteeped*

instinct (*n.*) impulse, prompting, urge **2H6** III.ii.250 [Salisbury to King, of the commons] *mere instinct of love and loyalty ... / Makes them thus forward*

institute (*v.*) **1** appoint, name, place in office **1H6** IV.i.162 [King to Richard] *we institute your grace / To be our Regent*

2 begin, introduce, set up **TS** I.i.8 [Lucentio to Tranio] *Here let us ... haply institute / A course of learning*

institution (*n.*) custom, usage, practice **MM** I.i.10 [Duke to Escalus] *Our city's institutions ... [you are] pregnant in*

instruction (*n.*) **1** advice, good direction, counsel **MM** II.iii.38 [disguised Duke to Juliet, of Claudio] *I am going with instruction to him;* **Cym** I.vi.47

2 prompting, suggestion, insinuation **MM** III.ii.235 [disguised Duke to Escalus, of Claudio] *Yet had he framed to himself, by the instruction of his frailty, many deceiving promises of life*

3 precept, prompting, conviction **Cor** III.ii.53 [Volumnia to Coriolanus] *speak / To th'people, not by your own instruction*

4 basis in fact, knowledge, information **Oth** IV.i.41 [Othello to Iago] *Nature would not invest herself in such shadowing passion without some instruction*

5 lesson, education, direction **Cor** I.iv.22 [Lartius to Martius, of the Roman army] *Their noise be our instruction*

instrument (*n.*) **1** agent, means, method **3H6** IV.vi.18 [King to Warwick, of God and his freedom] *He was the author, thou the instrument;* **AW** V.iii.202; **Mac** III.i.80; **Tem** III.iii.55

2 agent, servant, retainer **TNK** I.i.163 [Theseus to Artesius] *forth and levy / Our worthiest instruments;* **TNK** I.ii.68

3 organ, faculty, functioning part **Cor** I.i.99 [Menenius to Citizens, of the body parts other than the belly] *th'other instruments / Did see and hear, devise, instruct;* **JC** I.i.66; **Oth** I.iii.267

4 weapon, armament **Mac** IV.iii.238 [Malcolm to Macduff] *Macbeth / Is ripe for shaking, and the powers above / Put on their instruments* [or: encourage their agents]

insubstantial (*adj.*) lacking substance, imaginary, unreal **Tem** IV.i.155 [Prospero to Ferdinand, of the spirits] *this insubstantial pageant faded*

insufficience (*n.*) insufficiency, inadequacy, deficiencies **WT** I.i.14 [Archidamus to Camillo] *We will give you sleepy drinks, that your senses, unintelligent of our insufficience, may, though they cannot praise us, as little accuse us*

insult (v.) be insolent, show scorn, triumph scornfully 3H6 I.iv.124 [York to Queen, of her father] *Hath that poor monarch taught thee to insult?*; **AY** III.v.36; **Cor** III.i.144; **Sonn** 107.12; **Tit** III.ii.71

insulter (n.) triumphant boaster, scorner, exulter **Venus** 550 [of Adonis' lips] *Paying what ransom the insulter willeth*

insulting (adj.) scornfully boasting, contemptuously exulting 3H6 I.iii.14 [Rutland to Clifford, of a lion] *so he walks, insulting o'er his prey*; 1H4 V.iv.53; 3H6 II.i.167; R3 II.iv.51

insultment (n.) insult, contempt, derision **Cym** III.v.142 [Cloten alone, of Posthumus] *my speech of insultment ended on his dead body*

insuppressive (adj.) insuppressible, irrepressible, indomitable **JC** II.i.134 [Brutus to all] *do not stain ... th'insuppressive mettle of our spirits*

inteemable (adj.) [debated meaning] unable to be poured out **AW** I.iii.197 [Helena to Countess] *in this captious and inteemible sieve / I still pour in the waters of my love* [F *intemible*] ☞ **intenable** (adj.)

integrity (n.) 1 unity, wholeness, oneness **Cor** III.i.159 [Coriolanus to Brutus] *Your dishonour ... bereaves the state / Of that integrity which should become't*
2 undivided devotion, wholehearted sincerity **TG** III.ii.77 [Proteus to Thurio, of displaying his feelings in poetry] *frame some feeling line / That may discover such integrity*

intellect (n.) purport, meaning, contents **LL** IV.ii.132 [Holofernes to Jaquenetta] *I will look again on the intellect of the letter*

intellectual (adj.) which gives intellect, intelligent **E3** II.i.236 [Countess to King Edward] *As easy may my intellectual soul / Be lent away*

intelligence (n.) 1 information, news, communication **R2** III.iii.1 [Bolingbroke to all] *by this intelligence we learn / The Welshmen are dispersed*; **Cym** IV.ii.347; 1H4 V.v.10; **KL** II.i.21; **MW** III.v.77; **TC** V.ii.195
2 spying, espionage, secretly obtained information **H8** I.i.153 [Buckingham to Norfolk, of Wolsey] *by intelligence ... I do know / To be corrupt and treasonous*; 1H4 IV.iii.98; H5 II.Chorus.12; R3 I.i.55
3 source of information, secret service **KJ** IV.ii.116 [King John to Messenger] *where hath our intelligence been drunk?*
4 communication, discourse, conversation **AY** I.iii.45 [Rosalind to Duke Frederick] *If with myself I hold intelligence*

intelligencer (n.) 1 messenger, informant, bringer of news **2H4** IV.ii.20 [Prince John to and of Archbishop] *The very opener and intelligencer / Between the grace, the sanctities, of heaven / And our dull workings*
2 secret agent, spy, operative **R3** IV.iv.71 [Queen Margaret to Duchess of York, of Richard] *hell's black intelligencer*

intelligencing (adj.) spying, acting as go-between **WT** II.iii.68 [Leontes to Paulina, of her] *A most intelligencing bawd!*

intelligent (adj.) 1 bearing intelligence, giving inside information **KL** III.vii.11 [Cornwall to Edmund] *Our posts shall be swift and intelligent betwixt us* [F; Q *intelligence*]; **KL** III.i.25, v.10
2 communicative, forthcoming, candid **WT** I.ii.378 [Polixenes to Camillo, of Leontes' change in attitude] *Do you know and dare not / Be intelligent to me?*

intemperance (n.) wild behaviour, lack of restraint **1H4** III.ii.156 [Prince Hal to King Henry] *I do beseech your majesty may salve / The long-grown wounds of my intemperance* [Q; F *intemperature*] ☞ **intemperature** (n.)

intemperate (adj.) excessive, immoderate, inordinate **MM** V.i.98 [Isabella to Duke, of Angelo] *his concup'scible intemperate lust*; **TNK** IV.iii.69

intemperature (n.) intemperance, licentiousness **1H4** III.ii.156 [Prince Hal to King Henry] *I do beseech your majesty may salve / The long-grown wounds of my intemperature* [F; Q *intemperance*] ☞ **intemperance** (n.)

intenable (adj.) [debated meaning] unable to retain **AW** I.iii.197 [Helena to Countess] *in this captious and intenable sieve / I still pour in the waters of my love* [F *intemible*] ☞ **inteemable** (adj.)

intend (v.) 1 pretend, convey, purport, profess **MA** II.ii.32 [Borachio to Don John] *intend a kind of zeal both to the Prince and Claudio*; **Luc** 121; **R3** III.v.8, vii.44; **Tim** II.ii.215; **TS** IV.i.189
2 tend, incline, be predisposed **2H4** I.ii.8 [Falstaff to Page] *The brain of this foolish-compounded clay, man, is not able to invent anything that intends to laughter more than I invent*
3 mean, imply, suggest **2H4** IV.i.164 [Westmorland to Hastings, of the authority to negotiate] *That is intended in the general's name*; **AC** II.ii.44
4 plan, arrange, organize **MW** IV.vi.38 [Fenton to Host, of Anne] *Her mother hath intended ... / That quaint in green she shall be loose enrobed*
5 be determined to make, plan to take **Sonn** 27.6 *my thoughts ... / Intend a zealous pilgrimage to thee*; **Per** I.iii.116
6 plan to go, direct one's course **1H4** IV.i.92 [Vernon to Hotspur] *The King himself ... is set forth, / Or hitherwards intended speedily*; 3H6 II.v.139
7 [translation of French 'entendre'] understand **MW** I.iv.45 [Caius to Mistress Quickly] *Do intend vat I speak?*

intended (adj.) extended, enlarged, increased in power **E3** III.iii.141 [King John to the French] *now's the time / That your intended force must bide the touch*

intendment (n.) intent, intention, purpose **AY** I.i.125 [Charles to Oliver, of Orlando] *you might stay him from his intendment*; H5 I.ii.144; **Oth** IV.ii.203; **Venus** 222

intent (n.) intention, purpose, aim **RJ** V.iii.154 [Friar to Juliet] *A greater power than we can contradict / Hath thwarted our intents* ☞ **FEW**, p.xxi

intention (n.) intensity, forceful purpose, powerful direction **WT** I.ii.138 [Leontes to himself] *Affection, thy intention stabs the centre*

intentively (adv.) paying continuous attention, with unbroken interest **Oth** I.iii.154 [Othello to all, of Desdemona] *I would all my pilgrimage dilate / Whereof by parcels she had something heard, / But not intentively* [Q; F1 *instinctiuely*; F2 *distinctiuely*] ☞ **distinctively** (adv.)

intercept (v.) 1 prevent, stop, get rid of **1H6** I.iv.14 [Master Gunner to Boy, of the overlooking English position] *To intercept this inconvenience, / A piece of ordnance 'gainst it I have placed*
2 interrupt, break in on, cut off **Tit** III.i.40 [Titus to Lucius, of stones] *For that they will not intercept my tale*

intercession (n.) 1 prayer, plea, entreaty **TNK** V.i.45 [Arcite to his knights, of Mars] *Our intercession, then, / Must be to him*; **RJ** II.iii.50
2 break, interlude, intermission **E3** V.i.237 [King Edward to all] *we do proclaim a rest, / An intercession of our painful arms*

interchange (v.) swap, exchange, substitute 3H6 IV.vii.3 [Edward to all] *I shall interchange / My waned state for Henry's regal crown*

interchangeably (adv.) in turn, in exchange, reciprocally **R2** I.i.146 [Mowbray to Richard] *I ... interchangeably hurl down my gage*; 1H4 III.i.77; **R2** V.ii.98

interchangement (n.) interchange, exchange **TN** V.i.157 [Priest to Olivia, of her marriage] *Strengthened by interchangement of your rings*

interdict (v.) forbid, prohibit, debar **Phoen** 9 *From this session interdict / Every fowl of tyrant wing*

interdiction (n.) prohibition, debarring, forbidding **Mac** IV.iii.107 [Macduff to Malcolm, as if to Scotland] *the truest issue of thy throne / By his own interdiction stands accused*

interess (v.) admit, give a share, lay claim **KL** I.i.85 [Lear to Cordelia] *to whose young love / The vines of France and milk of Burgundy / Strive to be interessed* [F *interest*]

interest (*n.*) **1** valid claim [on], rights of possession [to] **KL** I.i.50 [Lear to his daughters] *we will divest us both of rule, / Interest of territory;* **Cym** I.iv.30; **1H4** III.ii.98; **KJ** V.ii.89; **Luc** 1797; **TNK** III.vi.297
  2 property, share, legal right **Luc** 1067 [Lucrece as if to Collatine, of herself] *thou shalt know thy interest was not bought / Basely with gold*
  3 possession, right, title **Luc** 1619 [Lucrece to Collatine] *in the interest of thy bed / A stranger came*
  4 personal involvement, special concern **RJ** III.i.188 [Prince to Montague] *I have an interest in your hate's proceeding*

interim (*n.*) interval, break, interlude **Sonn** 56.9 *Let this sad interim like the ocean be / Which parts the shore;* **LL** I.i.169

interims, by at intervals, from time to time **Cor** I.vi.5 [Cominius to Soldiers] *By interims and conveying gusts we have heard / The charges of our friends*

interjoin (*v.*) unite, join with one another **Cor** IV.iv.22 [Coriolanus alone] *fellest foes … shall grow dear friends / And interjoin their issues*

interlace (*v.*) insert, introduce, weave into a design **Luc** 1390 [of a painting of Troy] *the painter interlaces / Pale cowards marching on with trembling paces*

interlude, enterlude (*n.*) short play, theatrical performance [staged to fill an interval] **TN** V.i.370 [Feste to Malvolio] *I was one, sir, in this interlude, one Sir Topas;* **KL** V.iii.90; **MND** I.ii.5, V.i.153

intermission (*n.*) **1** interval of time, delay, interruption **Mac** IV.iii.231 [Macduff to Malcolm] *gentle heavens, / Cut short all intermission*
  2 respite, pause, rest **MV** III.ii.199 [Gratiano to Bassanio] *intermission / No more pertains to me, my lord, than you;* **AY** II.vii.32
  3 interruption; or: pausing **KL** II.iv.32 [disguised Kent to Lear, of the messenger] *Delivered letters, spite of intermission* [i.e. despite interrupting me; or: despite his breathless pausing]

intermissive (*adj.*) intermittent, recurrent; or, temporarily interrupted **1H6** I.i.88 [Bedford to all] *Wounds will I lend the French … / To weep their intermissive miseries*

intermit (*v.*) withhold, suspend, keep back **JC** I.i.54 [Marullus to people] *Pray to the gods to intermit the plague / That needs must light on this ingratitude*

interpret (*v.*) provide a dialogue [as does a puppeteer on behalf of the puppets] **Tim** I.i.35 [Poet to Painter, of someone in his picture for Timon] *To th'dumbness of the gesture / One might interpret;* **Ham** III.ii.255

interpretation (*n.*) rendering, treatment, execution **Cor** V.iii.69 [Volumnia to Coriolanus, of Young Martius] *This is a poor epitome of yours, / Which by th'interpretation of full time / May show like all yourself* [i.e. in the fullness of time]

interpreter (*n.*) commentator, observer, pundit **H8** I.ii.82 [Wolsey to King Henry] *What we oft do best, / By sick interpreters, once weak ones, is / Not ours, or not allowed*

interrogatory (*n.*) interrogation, questioning, inquisition **AW** IV.iii.180 [Parolles to First Soldier] *let me answer to the particular of the inter'gatories;* **Cym** V.v.393; **KJ** III.i.147; **MV** V.i.298

interruption resistance, hindrance, obstruction **KJ** III.iv.9 [King Philip to Cardinal Pandulph, of King John] *And bloody England into England gone, / O'erbearing interruption, spite of France*

intertangled (*adj.*) intertwined, entwined, interlaced **TNK** I.iii.59 [Emilia to Hippolyta, of Theseus and Pirithous] *Their intertangled roots of love*

intertissued (*adj.*) interwoven **H5** IV.i.255 [King Henry alone] *The intertissued robe of gold and pearl*

intervallum (*n.*) interval, break between sessions **2H4** V.i.74 [Falstaff alone, of Prince Henry] *'a shall laugh without intervallums*

interview (*n.*) face-to-face meeting **TC** IV.v.155 [Hector to Aeneas] *signify this loving interview / To the expecters of our Trojan part*

intestate (*adj.*) leaving no will, lacking inheritance **R3** IV.iv.128 [Queen Elizabeth to Duchess of York, of words] *Airy succeeders of intestate joys* [Q; F *intestine*]

intestine (*adj.*) internal, civil, domestic **CE** I.i.11 [Duke to Egeon] *the mortal and intestine jars / 'Twixt thy seditious countrymen and us;* **1H4** I.i.12

intil (*prep.*) to **Ham** V.i.73 [First Clown singing] *age … hath shipped me intil the land* [F; Q2 *into*]

intimate (*v.*) refer to, communicate, inform of **LL** II.i.129 [King to Princess] *your father here doth intimate / The payment of a hundred thousand crowns*

intimation (*n.*) intrusion, expression, suggestion **LL** IV.ii.13 [Holofernes to Nathaniel, of Dull's misunderstanding] *Most barbarous intimation!*

intitle (*v.*) ☛ **entitle** (*v.*)

intitule (*v.*) ☛ **entitule** (*v.*)

into (*prep.*) against **Tem** I.ii.100 [Prospero to Miranda, of Antonio] *like one / Who having into truth, by telling of it … he did believe / He was indeed the Duke*

intolerable (*adj.*) excessive, exorbitant, exceedingly great **MW** V.v.152 [Page to all, of Falstaff] *Old, cold, withered, and of intolerable entrails?;* **1H4** II.iv.526

intolerable (*adv.*) excessively, exceedingly, extremely **TS** II.ii.88 [Hortensio to Petruchio, of Katherina] *she is intolerable curst*

intreasured, entreasured (*adj.*) safely stored up, kept as in a treasury **2H4** III.i.81 [Warwick to King Henry IV] *the main chance of things / As yet not come to life, who in their seeds / And weak beginning lie intreasured;* **Per** III.ii.63 [Cerimon to all, of Thaisa's body] *balmed and entreasured / With full bags of spices!*

intreat (*n./v.*) ☛ **entreat** (*n./v.*)

intrench (*v.*) ☛ **entrench** (*v.*)

intrenchant (*adj.*) uncuttable, incapable of being gashed **Mac** V.vi.48 [Macbeth to Macduff] *As easy mayst thou the intrenchant air / With thy keen sword impress, as make me bleed*

intrinse (*adj.*) intricate, involved; or: inward, secret **KL** II.ii.73 [disguised Kent to Cornwall, of Oswald] *the holy cords … / Which are t'intrinse t'unloose* [F *intrince*; Q *intrench*]

intrinsicate (*adj.*) intricate, complicated, entangled **AC** V.ii.303 [Cleopatra to asp] *With thy sharp teeth this knot intrinsicate / Of life at once untie*

intrusion (*n.*) breaking in, forced entry **CE** II.ii.189 [Adriana to Antipholus of Syracuse] *moss, / Who, all for want of pruning, with intrusion / Infect thy sap;* **CE** III.i.103

inundation (*n.*) outpouring, overflowing, flood **KJ** V.ii.48 [Lewis the Dauphin to Salisbury, of a lady's tears] *Being an ordinary inundation;* **KJ** V.i.12

inure (*v.*) ☛ **enure** (*v.*)

inurn (*v.*) entomb, bury, inter **Ham** I.iv.49 [Hamlet to Ghost] *the sepulchre / Wherein we saw thee quietly inurn'd* [F; Q1, Q2 *interr'd*]

invectively (*adv.*) vehemently, passionately, in an abusive way **AY** II.i.58 [First Lord to Duke Senior, of Jaques] *most invectively he pierceth through / The body of country*

invent (*v.*) create, compose, write creatively **Sonn** 38.1 *How can my Muse want subject to invent, / While thou dost breathe;* **AY** IV.iii.29

invention (*n.*) **1** inventiveness, imagination, creative faculty **H5** Prologue.2 [Chorus] *O for a Muse of fire, that would ascend / The brightest heaven of invention;* **AY** II.v.44; **LL** IV.ii.157; **MA** V.i.270; **MW** III.v.78; **Oth** II.i.124
  2 mind, thought, imagination **MM** II.iv.3 [Angelo alone] *my invention … / Anchors on Isabel*
  3 novelty, fresh creation, innovation **Per** I.iv.40 [Cleon to Dionyza] *palates … / Must have inventions to delight the taste;* **TN** III.ii.42; **TS** III.i.79

4 composition, written exposition **TN** V.i.331 [Malvolio to Olivia, of the letter] *say 'tis not your seal, not your invention;* **Luc** 1302

5 plan, scheme, stratagem **KL** I.ii.20 [Edmund alone] *if this letter speed / And my invention thrive;* **1H6** III.i.5; **3H6** IV.i.35; **TN** V.i.342; **TS** I.i.187

6 fiction, fabrication, contrivance **AW** IV.i.26 [Parolles to himself, of his lying] *It must be a very plausive invention that carries it;* **AW** III.vi.90; **Mac** III.i.32

7 concoction, trumped-up charge **Cor** III.ii.143 [Coriolanus to Cominius, of the Tribunes] *Let them accuse me by invention*

8 devising excuses, capacity for evasion **AW** I.iii.168 [Countess to Helena, of loving Bertram] *Invention is ashamed / Against the proclamation of thy passion / To say thou dost not* [i.e. in the face of your evident feelings]

inventorially *(adv.)* as in an inventory, one by one, in detail **Ham** V.ii.113 [Hamlet to Osric, of Laertes] *to divide him inventorially*

inventory *(n.)* detailed list, itemization **Cor** I.i.19 [First Citizen to all, of the authorities] *The leanness that afflicts us ... is as an inventory to particularize their abundance*

invest *(v.)* **1** clothe, dress, adorn **Tem** II.i.230 [Antonio to Sebastian, of Sebastian's purpose] *If you but knew ... How, in stripping it, / You more invest it*

2 empower, install in office, give authority **2H4** IV.iv.6 [King Henry IV to all] *Our substitutes in absence [are] well invested*

3 envelop, permeate, infuse **H5** IV.Chorus.26 [Chorus, of the English] *their gesture sad, / Investing lank-lean cheeks and war-worn coats*

4 besiege, put pressure on **Ham** I.iii.83 [Polonius to Laertes] *The time invests you* [Q2; F *inuites*]

investments *(n.)* (plural) garments, clothes, clothing **2H4** IV.i.45 [Westmorland to Archbishop] *You ... / Whose white investments figure innocence;* **Ham** I.iii.128

inveterate *(n.)* long-standing, deep-rooted **Tem** I.ii.122 [Prospero to Miranda] *This King of Naples, being an enemy / To me inveterate;* **KJ** V.ii.14; **R2** I.i.14

invised *(adj.)* hidden, unseen, invisible **Lover** 212 [of a diamond] *'twas beautiful and hard, / Whereto his invised properties did tend*

invisible *(adj.)* unforeseeable, unseeable, hidden **Ham** IV.iv.50 [Hamlet alone, of Fortinbras] *Makes mouths at the invisible event*

inviting *(n.)* invitation **Tim** III.vi.10 [Lucullus to Lucius, of Timon] *He hath sent me an earnest inviting*

invocate *(v.)* invoke, call upon, entreat **R3** I.ii.8 [Anne to dead Henry VI] *I invocate thy ghost;* **E3** II.i.65; **1H6** I.i.52

invocation *(n.)* entreaty, supplication **KJ** III.iv.42 [Constance to King Philip] *that fell anatomy ... / Which scorns a modern invocation* [also: incantation]

inward *(n.)* intimate friend, close acquaintance **MM** III.ii.124 [Lucio to disguised Duke, of the Duke] *I was an inward of his*

inward *(adj.)* **1** intimate, closely associated **R3** III.iv.8 [Buckingham to all, of Richard] *Who is most inward with the noble Duke?*

2 secret, private, undisclosed **MA** IV.i.10 [Friar to Claudio and Hero] *If either of you know any inward impediment;* **LL** V.i.92

3 internal, domestic, civil **2H4** III.i.103 [King Henry IV to Warwick and Surrey] *were these inward wars once out of hand, / We would ... unto the Holy Land*

inward *(adv.)* internally, inside **Sonn** 62.4 [of self-love] *It is so grounded inward in my heart;* **Ham** IV.iv.28

inwardness *(n.)* attachment, intimacy, close friendship **MA** IV.i.243 [Benedick to Leonato] *you know my inwardness and love / Is very much unto the Prince*

ireful *(adj.)* wrathful, angry, furious **3H6** II.v.132 [Queen to King, of Edward and Richard] *bloody steel grasped in their ireful hands;* **CE** V.i.151; **1H6** IV.vi.16; **3H6** II.i.57; **Venus** 628

irk *(v.)* bother, trouble, distress **AY** II.i.22 [Duke Senior to all] *it irks me the poor dappled fools ... [should] / Have their round haunches gored*

irksome *(adj.)* hateful, offensive, loathsome **AY** III.v.95 [Phebe to Silvius] *Thy company, which erst was irksome to me*

iron *(n.)* **1** iron weapon, steel, sword **TN** IV.i.38 [Sir Toby to Sebastian] *put up your iron;* **Cor** I.v.6; **TC** II.iii.16; **TNK** II.v.10

2 armour **AC** IV.iv.3 [Antony to Eros] *put thine iron on* [i.e. on me]

iron *(adj.)* in armour, mail-clad **2H4** IV.ii.8 [Prince John to Archbishop] *to see you here an iron man* [also: stern, harsh]

iron age age of cruelty, time of wickedness **KJ** IV.i.60 [Arthur to Hubert, of being blinded] *none but in this iron age would do it!*

iron-witted *(adj.)* dull-witted, obtuse, dense **R3** IV.ii.28 [King Richard to himself] *I will converse with iron-witted fools*

irreconciled *(adj.)* unabsolved, not reconciled with God **H5** IV.i.148 [disguised King Henry to Williams] *if a servant ... be assailed by robbers, and die in many irreconciled iniquities*

irrecoverable *(adj.)* beyond redemption, past recovery **2H4** II.iv.327 [Falstaff to Prince Henry] *The fiend hath pricked down Bardolph irrecoverable*

irregular *(adj.)* lawless, disorderly, unruly **1H4** I.i.40 [Westmorland to King Henry] *to fight / Against the irregular and wild Glendower;* **KJ** V.iv.54

irregulous *(adj.)* unruly, lawless, uncontrollable **Cym** IV.ii.315 [Innogen alone, as if to Pisanio] *Conspired with that irregulous devil, Cloten*

irremovable *(adj.)* immovable, inflexible, adamant **WT** IV.iv.504 [Camillo to himself, of Florizel] *He's irremovable, / Resolved for flight*

irresolute *(adj.)* unresolved, undecided, unaccomplished **H8** I.ii.209 [Surveyor to King Henry, of Buckingham] *he would outgo / His father by as much as a performance / Does an irresolute purpose*

issue *(n.)* **1** child(ren), offspring, family, descendant **WT** II.iii.93 [Leontes to Paulina, of Perdita] *This brat is none of mine: / It is the issue of Polixenes* ➤ **FEW**, p.xxi

2 outcome, result, consequence(s) **R3** III.vii.53 [Richard to Buckingham, of his proposal] *No doubt we'll bring it to a happy issue* ➤ **FEW**, p.xxi

3 yield, product, result **E3** I.ii.154 [Countess to King Edward, of areas of rich vegetation] *Delve there and find this issue and their pride / To spring from ordure and corruption's side*

4 action, deed, proceeding **JC** III.i.294 [Antony to Servant, of the conspirators] *shall I try, / In my oration, how the people take / The cruel issue of these bloody men;* **Cym** II.i.47

issue *(v.)* **1** descend, born **1H6** V.iv.38 [Pucelle to all, of herself] *issued from the progeny of kings;* **Tem** I.ii.59

2 come forth, sally out **Cor** I.vi.10 [Messenger to Cominius] *The citizens of Corioles have issued / And given to Lartius and to Martius battle*

issueless *(adj.)* childless, without an heir **Sonn** 9.3 *if thou issueless shalt hap to die;* **WT** V.i.173

itching palm avaricious disposition, desire for personal gain **JC** IV.iii.10 [Brutus to Cassius] *you yourself / Are much condemned to have an itching palm*

item *(n.)* **1** entry, detail, point **Cym** I.v.6 [Iachimo to all, of Posthumus' endowments] *I to peruse him by items* [i.e. point by point]

2 [legal] particular point **TG** III.i.274 [Launce alone, of his love] *Item: She can milk;* **2H6** I.i.49; **H8** III.ii.320

iterance *(n.)* repetition, reiteration **Oth** V.ii.149 [Othello to Emilia, on her repeating 'My husband!'] *What needs this iterance, woman?* [F; Q *iteration*]

iteration *(n.)* **1** cliche, repeated assertion, endless repetition **TC** III.ii.174 [Troilus to Cressida, of lovers] *when their rhymes ... / Want similes, truth tired with iteration*
   2 ability to quote scripture **1H4** I.ii.90 [Falstaff to Prince Hal] *thou hast damnable iteration*

ivory *(adj.)* white **Tim** I.i.73 [Poet to Painter, of Timon] *Whom Fortune with her ivory hand wafts to her;* **Luc** 464

iwis *(adv.)* [archaism] assuredly, certainly, truly **TS** I.i.62 [Katherina to Hortensio, of marriage] *Iwis it is not halfway to her heart;* **MV** II.ix.68; **Per** II.Chorus.2; **R3** I.iii.101 ☛ **ARCHAISMS**, p.22

jack (*n.*) **1** jacket, tunic, coat [usually of quilted leather] **E3** I.ii.29 [King David to Lorraine, of the Scots soldiers] *never shall [they] … lay aside their jacks of gimmaled mail;* **1H4** IV.ii.47 ➧ **CLOTHING**, p.79

2 figure of a man who strikes a bell on the outside of a clock **R3** IV.ii.113 [King Richard to Buckingham] *like a Jack thou keep'st the stroke / Betwixt thy begging and my meditation;* **R2** V.v.60 ➧ minute-jack (*n.*)

3 key [in a harpsichord, virginal, etc; strictly, part of the key mechanism] **Sonn** 128.5 *I envy those jacks that nimble leap / To kiss the tender inward of thy hand*

Jack (*n.*) **1** Jack-in-office, ill-mannered fellow, lout, knave **1H4** V.iv.137 [Falstaff to all] *if I be not Jack Falstaff, then am I a Jack;* **Cor** V.ii.60; **1H4** III.iii.84; **MA** I.i.171; **R3** I.iii.72; **TS** II.i.158 ➧ minute-jack (*n.*)

2 Jack o'lantern, trickster, practical joker **Tem** IV.i.197 [Stephano to Caliban] *your fairy … has done little better than played the Jack with us*

3 serving-man **TS** IV.i.43 [Grumio to Curtis, of preparations in the house] *Be the Jacks fair within* [also: leather-drinking vessel]

Jack-a-Lent (*n.*) [jocular; male figure used as an Aunt Sally during Lent] puppet, poppet, doll **MW** III.iii.24 [Mistress Page to Robin] *You little Jack-a-Lent, have you been true to us?;* **MW** V.v.127

jackanapes, jackanape, jack'nape (*n.*) upstart, buffoon, monkey **H5** V.ii.141 [King Henry to Katherine] *I could … sit like a jackanapes;* **MW** I.iv.107 [Caius to Simple] *I will teach a scurvy jackanape priest to meddle or make;* **MW** I.i.105 [Caius to Simple] *You, jack'nape, give-a this letter to Sir Hugh;* **AW** III.v.84; **Cym** II.i.3; **MW** II.iii.76

jack-dog (*n./adj.*) mongrel, currish, mutt-like **MW** II.iii.57 [Caius to Host, of Evans] *Scurvy jack-dog priest!;* **MW** III.i.76

Jack-sauce (*n.*) saucy knave, impudent fellow **H5** IV.vii.138 [Fluellen to King Henry, of Williams' challenger] *If he be perjured … his reputation is as arrant a villain and a Jack-sauce as ever his black shoe trod upon God's ground*

Jack-slave (*n.*) knavish slave, villainous fellow **Cym** II.i.20 [Cloten to Lords] *every Jack-slave hath his bellyful of fighting*

jade (*n.*) **1** worn-out horse, hack, worthless nag **TS** IV.i.1 [Grumio alone] *fie on all tired jades;* **AW** II.iii.282; **E3** IV.iv.97; **H5** III.v.19; **R2** III.iii.179; **TNK** V.iv.81

2 [contemptuous] wretch, worthless individual **KJ** II.i.385 [Bastard to King John and King Philip, of the men of Angiers] *I'd play incessantly upon these jades;* **TS** II.i.201

jade (*v.*) **1** drive like worn-out hacks **AC** III.i.34 [Ventidius to Silius] *The ne'er-yet-beaten horse of Parthia / We have jaded out o'th' field*

2 deceive, dupe, make a fool of **H8** III.ii.280 [Surrey to all, of Wolsey] *To be thus jaded by a piece of scarlet;* **TN** II.v.158

jaded (*adj.*) low-bred, ignoble, contemptible **2H6** IV.i.52 [Suffolk to Lieutenant] *King Henry's blood … / Must not be shed by such a jaded groom* [Q jady]

jadery (*n.*) behaviour typical of an ill-tempered hack **TNK** V.iv.72 [Pirithous to Palamon, of Arcite's horse] *seeks all foul means / Of boisterous and rough jadery to disseat / His lord* ➧ jade (*n.*) 1

jady (*adj.*) ➧ jaded (*adj.*)

jakes (*n.*) lavatory, privy, latrine **KL** II.ii.64 [disguised Kent to Cornwall, of Oswald] *I will … daub the wall of a jakes with him*

jangle (*v.*) wrangle, squabble, argue **LL** II.i.211 [Princess to all] *Good wits will be jangling*

jar (*n.*) **1** conflict, quarrel, dissension **CE** I.i.11 [Duke to Egeon] *the mortal and intestine jars / 'Twixt thy seditious countrymen and us;* **1H6** I.i.44; **Venus** 100

2 discord, disharmony, disagreement **TC** I.iii.117 [Ulysses to all, of right and wrong] *Between whose endless jar justice resides;* **AY** II.vii.5; **TG** V.iv.161

3 tick **WT** I.ii.43 [Hermione to Leontes] *I love thee not a jar o'th' clock behind / What lady she her lord*

jar / jars, at in / into conflict, in / into a state of dissension **2H6** I.i.251 [York to himself] *Watch [till] … Humphrey with the peers be fallen at jars;* **2H6** IV.viii.40 [Clifford to the rebels] *whilst you live at jar, / The fearful French … / Should make a start o'er seas and vanquish you?*

jar (v.) **1** quarrel, wrangle, disagree [over] **1H6** III.i.70 [King to Gloucester and Winchester] *what a scandal is it to our crown / That two such noble peers as ye should jar;* **Tit** II.i.103

2 grate, sound discordantly **TG** IV.ii.65 [disguised Julia to Host, of the music] *it jars so;* **2H6** II.i.55; **TS** III.i.38

3 [unclear meaning] make tick; strike; make discordant **R2** V.v.51 [Richard alone] *My thoughts are minutes, and with sighs they jar / Their watches on unto mine eyes*

jaunce (n.) jaunt, fatiguing journey **RJ** II.v.26 [Nurse to Juliet] *What a jaunce have I!* [F, Q1 *iaunt*]

jaunce (v.) jaunt, trudge about, run around **RJ** II.v.52 [Nurse to Juliet] *Beshrew your heart for sending me about / To catch my death with jauncing up and down!* [F *iaunting*]

jauncing (adj.) prancing, romping, gambolling **R2** V.v.94 [Richard to Groom] *I bear a burden like an ass, / Spurred, galled, and tired by jauncing Bolingbroke*

jaundice (n.) sallowness, yellowness [as a sign of envy or jealousy] **TC** I.iii.2 [Agamemnon to all] *What grief hath set the jaundice on your cheeks?*

jaunt (n.) ☞ jaunce (n./v.)

jaw (v.) bite, eat, devour **TNK** III.ii.7 [Gaoler's Daughter alone] *I reck not if the wolves would jaw me*

jay (n.) [bird of bright plumage] showy woman, whore **MW** III.iii.39 [Mistress Ford to Mistress Page, of Falstaff] *We'll teach him to know turtles from jays* [i.e. faithful women from unfaithful ones]; **Cym** III.iv.50

jealous (adj.) **1** suspicious, mistrustful, wary, watchful **KL** I.iv.68 [Lear to Third Knight, of their neglect] *which I have rather blamed as mine own jealous curiosity;* **Luc** 800; **R3** III.i.36; **TG** III.i.28; **TS** IV.v.76; **Venus** 321

2 doubtful, uncertain, apprehensive **JC** I.ii.161 [Brutus to Cassius] *That you do love me, I am nothing jealous*

3 anxious, uneasy, worried [about] **H5** IV.i.278 [Erpingham to King Henry] *your nobles, jealous of your absence, / Seek through your camp to find you;* **TN** IV.iii.27

4 vigilant, zealous, solicitous **AY** II.vii.152 [Jaques to all] *a soldier, … / Jealous in honour* [i.e. sensitive to matters concerning his honour]

jealous-hood (n.) [unclear meaning] state of being jealous **RJ** IV.iv.13 [Capulet alone, of Lady Capulet saying she will keep an eye on him] *A jealous-hood* [i.e. typical female jealousy] ☞ hood (n.)

jealousy (n.) **1** suspicion, mistrust, apprehension **2H4** I.Induction.16 [Rumour alone] *Rumour is a pipe / Blown by surmises, jealousies, conjectures;* **AC** II.ii.137; **Ham** II.i.113; **H5** II.ii.126; **MA** II.ii.44; **Mac** IV.iii.29

2 suspicious nature, apprehensive state of mind **Oth** III.iii.146 [Iago to Othello] *my nature's plague … of my jealousy / Shapes faults that are not*

3 concern, anxiety, solicitude **TN** III.iii.8 [Antonio to Sebastian, of his reason for following him] *jealousy what might befall your travel, / Being skill-less in these parts;* **Venus** 649

jean (n.) type of twilled cotton cloth [= unsophisticated, unrefined] **TNK** III.v.8 [Schoolmaster to all] *ye jean judgements* [i.e. you simpletons]

jennet, gennet (n.) small Spanish horse **E3** IV.iv.91 [Second Herald to Prince Edward] *The Duke of Normandy … / By me hath sent a nimble-jointed jennet;* **Oth** I.i.114; **Venus** 260

jerk (n.) stroke, thrust, sally **LL** IV.ii.124 [Holofernes to Nathaniel, of Ovid's family name 'Naso' (= nose)] *for smelling out … the jerks of invention*

jerkin (n.) male upper garment, close-fitting jacket [often made of leather] **MW** I.iii.16 [Falstaff to Bardolph] *An old cloak makes a new jerkin;* **TC** III.iii.265; **Tem** IV.i.236; **TG** II.iv.19 ☞ CLOTHING, p.79; buff jerkin; leathern-jerkin (adj.)

jess (n.) [falconry] short strap fastened to a hawk's legs [to which the leash is attached] **Oth** III.iii.258 [Othello alone, of Desdemona] *If I do prove her haggard, / Though that her jesses were my dear heart-strings, / I'd whistle her off*

jest (v.) **1** make believe, act, play parts **Ham** III.ii.244 [Hamlet to Claudius, of the players] *they do but jest*

2 amuse oneself, go to an entertainment **R2** I.iii.95 [Mowbray to King Richard] *As gentle and as jocund as to jest / Go I to fight*

jest, break a play a practical joke **TS** IV.v.72 [Vincentio to Petruchio, of his companions] *Like pleasant travellers, to break a jest / Upon the company you overtake*

jest upon (v.) mock, scoff at, trifle with **CE** II.ii.28 [Antipholus of Syracuse to Dromio of Syracuse] *Your sauciness will jest upon my love*

jet (n.) type of black coal **2H6** II.i.111 [Simpcox to Gloucester, of Gloucester's gown] *coal-black as jet*

jet (v.) strut, swagger, parade **TN** II.v.31 [Fabian to Sir Andrew and Sir Toby, of Malvolio] *how he jets under his advanced plumes!;* **Cym** III.iii.5; **Per** I.iv.26

jet upon (v.) encroach on, usurp, trespass upon **R3** II.iv.51 [Queen Elizabeth to all] *Insulting tyranny begins to jet / Upon the innocent and aweless throne* [F *Iutt;* Q *iet*]; **Tit** II.i.64 ☞ jut (v.)

jew (n.) [unclear meaning] jewel; juvenal; Jew **LL** III.i.133 [Costard alone, of Armado] *my incony jew!*

jewel (n.) **1** fine ornament, costly adornment **Per** II.ii.12 [Simonides to Thaisa] *jewels lose their glory if neglected;* **CE** II.i.109

2 miniature in a jewelled setting **TN** III.iv.204 [Olivia to Viola as Cesario] *wear this jewel for me, 'tis my picture*

jig (n.) lively song; frivolous dance **LL** IV.iii.166 [Berowne to all] *To see … profound Solomon to tune a jig;* **MA** II.i.65; **TN** I.iii.122

jig (v.) move jerkily [as in a jig] **Ham** III.i.145 [Hamlet to Ophelia, of women] *You jig and amble* [Q2 *gig;* F *gidge;* Q1 *fig*]

jig off (v.) sing in the style of a jig **LL** III.i.10 [Mote to Armado] *to jig off a tune at the tongue's end*

jigging (adj.) moving in the manner of a jig **JC** IV.iii.135 [Brutus to Cassius, of the Poet] *What should the wars do with these jigging fools?*

jig-maker (n.) comic performer, jester **Ham** III.ii.134 [Hamlet to Ophelia] *your only jig-maker* [i.e. your champion jester]

Jill (n.) serving-maid **TS** IV.i.44 [Grumio to Curtis, of preparations in the house] *Be the Jacks fair within, the Jills fair without* [also: leather drinking-vessel]

Jockey (n.) [pet name] little Jack, Jacky **R3** V.iii.305 [King Richard, reading from a letter to Norfolk] *Jockey of Norfolk, be not so bold*

jocund (adj.) merry, joyful, cheerful **Tem** III.ii.118 [Caliban to all] *Let us be jocund!;* **Mac** III.ii.40; **R3** V.iii.233; **RJ** III.v.9; **TN** V.i.130

jog (v.) move on, go off, be away **TS** III.ii.210 [Katherina to Petruchio] *You may be jogging whiles your boots are green*

John-a-dreams (n.) dreamer, idle muser **Ham** II.ii.565 [Hamlet alone] *I … peak / Like John-a-dreams*

join (v.) **1** encounter, come together, meet in conflict **3H6** II.i.120 [Warwick to Edward and Richard, of fighting the Queen] *Our battles joined, and both sides fiercely fought;* **1H4** V.i.85; **3H6** II.i.15; **R3** V.iii.313

2 link up, unite, combine **3H6** IV.viii.62 [Richard to all, of Warwick] *Away betimes, before his forces join*

3 ally, unite, associate **Cym** I.i.29 [First Gentleman to Second Gentleman, of Sicilius] *who did join his honour / Against the Romans*

joinder (n.) joining, union, uniting **TN** V.i.155 [Priest to Olivia, of her marriage] *Confirmed by mutual joinder of your hands*

join-stool, joined-stool (n.) ☞ joint-stool (n.)

joint (*n.*) limb, body part **1H4** IV.i.83 [Hotspur to all] *yet all our joints are whole;* **TC** IV.v.233

joint, out of disordered, disorganized, out of order **Ham** I.v.188 [Hamlet to himself] *The time is out of joint*

joint (*v.*) unite, combine, join together **AC** I.ii.93 [Messenger to Antony, of Fulvia and Lucius] *jointing their force 'gainst Caesar;* **Cym** V.iv.142

jointress (*n.*) woman holding a property right from her deceased husband, dowager **Ham** I.ii.9 [Claudius to his court, of Gertrude] *our Queen, / Th'imperial jointress to this warlike state*

joint ring (*n.*) finger-ring made in two separable parts **Oth** IV.iii.71 [Emilia to Desdemona, of infidelity] *I would not do such a thing for a joint ring*

joint-stool, join-stool, joined-stool (*n.*) well-made stool [by a joiner] [also used in phrases of ridicule] **KL** III.vi.51 [Fool to imagined Gonerill] *I took you for a joint-stool* [proverbial: excuse me for not seeing you]; **RJ** I.v.6 [First Servingman to Second Servingman] *Away with the joint-stools;* **2H4** II.iv.242; **TS** II.i.198

jointure (*n.*) marriage settlement, part of a husband's estate due to his widow **3H6** III.iii.136 [Lewis to Warwick, of marriage between Edward and Bona] *forthwith shall articles be drawn / Touching the jointure that your king must make;* **AY** IV.i.49; **MW** III.iv.49; **RJ** V.iii.297; **TS** II.i.363

jollity (*n.*) sexual pleasure, carnal enjoyment **CE** II.ii.95 [Dromio of Syracuse to Antipholus of Syracuse, of hairy men's wit] *he loseth it in a kind of jollity*

jolly (*adj.*) **1** amorous, lustful, licentious **Cym** I.vii.67 [Iachimo to Innogen, of Posthumus] *the jolly Briton … laughs;* **R3** IV.iii.43
  2 [intensifier] very, extremely; or: arrogant, overbearing **TS** III.ii.212 [Katherina to Petruchio] *'Tis like you'll prove a jolly surly groom*

jolthead, jolt-head (*n.*) blockhead, dolt, numskull **TS** IV.i.152 [Petruchio to servants] *You heedless joltheads;* **TG** III.i.285

jordan (*n.*) chamber-pot **2H4** II.iv.33 [Falstaff to Will] *empty the jordan;* **1H4** II.i.21

journal (*adj.*) daily, diurnal, routine **MM** IV.iii.87 [disguised Duke to Provost] *Ere twice the sun hath made / His journal greeting to yond generation;* **Cym** IV.ii.10

journey-bated (*adj.*) weakened by travel, tired-out **1H4** IV.iii.26 [Hotspur to Vernon] *So are the horses of the enemy / In general journey-bated and brought low*

journeyman (*n.*) **1** employed craftsman, contracted artisan **R2** I.iii.274 [Bolingbroke to John of Gaunt] *I was a journeyman to grief*
  2 common workman, hireling **Ham** III.ii.33 [Hamlet to Players, of players he has seen] *some of Nature's journeymen*

jovial (*adj.*) majestic, like Jove [Jupiter] **Cym** V.v.105 [Jupiter to all, of Posthumus] *Our Jovial star reigned at his birth* [i.e. the planet Jupiter]; **Cym** IV.ii.311; **KL** IV.vi.199

jowl (*v.*) dash, knock, thrust **Ham** V.i.76 [Hamlet to Horatio, of the skull held by the First Clown] *How the knave jowls it to the ground;* **AW** I.iii.54

joy (*n.*) [unclear meaning] delight, bliss [for Mary, as the mother of Jesus]; or: darling, pet **2H4** II.iv.47 [Doll to Falstaff] *Yea, Mary's joys, our chains and our jewels* [F *I marry*; Q *Yea, joy*]

joy (*v.*) **1** feel joy, be happy, rejoice **RJ** II.ii.116 [Juliet to Romeo] *I joy in thee;* **AC** IV.vi.20; **3H6** II.i.77; **KJ** III.iv.107; **R3** IV.iv.93; **Sonn** 45.13
  2 add joy to, enjoy, gladden, brighten **R2** V.vi.26 [King Henry to Carlisle] *Choose out some secret place, some reverent room … and with it joy thy life;* **2H6** III.ii.365; **2H6** IV.ix.1; **Per** I.i.9; **R3** II.iv.59
  3 derive enjoyment from, delight in **Tit** II.iii.83 [Lavinia to Bassianus, of Tamora and Aaron] *let her joy her raven-coloured love;* **R3** II.iv.59

joyed (*adj.*) overjoyed, delighted, full of rejoicing **Cym** V.v.425 [Arviragus to Posthumus, of the latter becoming a brother to he and Guiderius] *Joyed are we that you are*

judge (*v.*) **1** suppose, consider, think **2H6** III.ii.67 [Queen to King, of Gloucester] *It may be judged I made the Duke away;* **TG** I.ii.139, III.i.25
  2 establish, determine, decide upon **MW** I.i.85 [Page to Slender, of his greyhound losing] *It could not be judged, sir*

judgement (*n.*) **1** opinion, estimation, assessment **KL** I.i.152 [Kent to Lear] *Answer my life my judgement* [i.e. I stake my life on my opinion] **AW** I.ii.61; **Ham** III.ii.96; **KL** I.iv.57; **Sonn** 131.12; **TG** IV.iv.148
  2 knowledge, understanding, wisdom **Cym** I.vi.17 [Queen to Cornelius, of her drug-making] *is't not meet / That I did amplify my judgement in / Other conclusions?*
  3 reason, discernment, good sense **Ham** IV.v.86 [Claudius to Gertrude, of Ophelia] *Divided from herself and her fair judgement;* **Cor** II.iii.204; **Ham** III.ii.79
  4 discretion, good sense, tact **TNK** III.v.37 [Schoolmaster to the man dressed as a baboon] *when you bark do it with judgement*
  5 expert, critic, judge **TC** I.ii.192 [Pandarus to Cressida, of Antenor] *he's one o'th' soundest judgements in Troy whosoever;* **TNK** III.v.8
  6 guide, leader, director **E3** II.ii.70 [King Edward alone] *love hath eyes as judgement to his steps*
  7 judgement day **Sonn** 55.13 *till the judgement that yourself arise, / You live in this;* **KL** I.iv.16

judicious (*adj.*) **1** judicial, according to the law **Cor** V.vi.127 [Second Lord to the assembly, of Coriolanus] *His last offences to us / Shall have judicious hearing*
  2 appropriate, fitting, proper **KL** III.iv.71 [Lear to disguised Kent] *Judicious punishment!*

Jug (*n.*) pet-name for Joan; sweetheart, mistress **KL** I.iv.221 [Fool to Gonerill] *Whoop, Jug, I love thee!*

juggle (*v.*) play conjuring tricks; have sex **1H6** V.iv.68 [Richard to all, of Pucelle] *She and the Dauphin have been juggling*

juggle (*v.*) deceive, cheat, trick **H8** I.iii.1 [Lord Chamberlain to Sands] *Is't possible the spells of France should juggle / Men into such strange mysteries?*

juggle with (*v.*) deceive, cheat, trick **Ham** IV.v.132 [Laertes to Claudius] *I'll not be juggled with*

juggler (*n.*) **1** sorcerer, conjuror, magician **CE** V.i.240 [Antipholus of Ephesus to Duke, of Pinch] *A threadbare juggler and a fortune-teller*
  2 trickster, deceiver, fraud **MND** III.ii.282 [Hermia to Helena] *you juggler;* **2H4** II.iv.127

juggling (*n.*) deceiving, cheating, trickery **TC** II.iii.70 [Thersites to Patroclus] *Here is such patchery, such juggling, and such knavery!*

juggling (*adj.*) deceiving, cheating, full of trickery **Mac** V.vi.58 [Macbeth to Macduff, of evil spirits] *be these juggling fiends no more believed / That palter with us in a double sense;* **KJ** III.i.169; **TC** V.ii.25

jump (*n.*) venture, risk, hazard **AC** III.viii.6 [Caesar to Taurus] *Our fortune lies / Upon this jump*

jump (*v.*) **1** agree, coincide, tally **R3** III.i.11 [Richard to Prince Edward, of a man's outward show] *which … / Seldom or never jumpeth with the heart;* **1H4** I.ii.68; **MV** II.ix.32; **Oth** I.iii.5; **TN** V.i.249; **TS** I.i.187
  2 risk, hazard, imperil **Mac** I.vii.7 [Macbeth alone, of his achieving success] *We'd jump the life to come;* **Cor** III.i.154; **Cym** V.iv.184

jump (*adv.*) exactly, precisely **Oth** II.iii.375 [Iago alone, of Othello] *I'll … bring him jump when he may Cassio find / Soliciting his wife;* **Ham** I.i.65, V.ii.369; **TNK** I.ii.40

junket (*n.*) delicacy, sweetmeat, confection **TS** III.ii.247 [Baptista to all] *there wants no junkets at the feast*

jure (*v.*) make a juror of **1H4** II.ii.90 [Falstaff to Travellers] *You are grandjurors, are ye? We'll jure ye, faith*

just (*n.*) joust, tournament **R2** V.ii.52 [York to Aumerle] *Do these justs and triumphs hold?*

just *(adj.)* **1** accurate, exact, precise H5 IV.vii.114 [King Henry to heralds] *Bring me just notice of the numbers dead;* 2H4 IV.i.23; KL III.i.37; MA II.i.333; Mac V.iv.14; MV IV.i.324

2 proper, true Per II.ii.48 [First Lord to Simonides, of Pericles] *He had need mean better than his outward show / Can any way speak in his just commend*

3 justifiable, legitimate AY IV.iii.130 [Oliver to Rosalind and Celia disguised] *nature, stronger than his just occasion* [i.e. the perfect excuse]

4 equal, even 2H4 IV.i.224 [Westmorland probably to Archbishop, of Prince John] *Pleaseth your lordship / To meet his grace just distance 'tween our armies?* [i.e. midway]

5 honourable, loyal, faithful Ham III.ii.64 [Hamlet to Horatio] *thou art e'en as just a man;* JC III.ii.86; KL III.v.9; TC V.iii.20

6 truthful, honest AW V.iii.236 [King to Parolles, of Bertram's displeasure] *Which on your just proceeding I'll keep off*

just *(adv.)* **1** exactly, precisely AW IV.ii.69 [Diana alone, of Bertram] *My mother told me just how he would woo;* CE IV.i.7; 2H6 I.iv.60; Mac III.iii.4; RJ III.iii.86; TC I.iii.164

2 quite so, correct AY III.ii.257 [Orlando, replying to Jaques' question] *Yes, just;* 2H4 III.ii.80; JC I.ii.54; MA II.i.24; MM V.i.200; Tit IV.ii.24

just-dooming *(adj.)* rightly-judging, justly-ordaining E3 III.iv.18 [King Edward alone] *Just-dooming heaven … / That hast this day given way unto the right*

justice *(n.)* judge, magistrate AW V.ii.33 [Lafew to Parolles] *Let the justices make you and Fortune friends;* AY V.iv.95

justicer *(n.)* judge KL IV.ii.79 [Albany to all, as if to the heavens] *This shows you are above, / You justicers* [F *Iustices*]; Cym V.v.214; KL III.vi.21, 55

justify *(v.)* **1** affirm, acknowledge, corroborate WT V.iii.145 [Leontes to Camillo, of Paulina or Camillo, and himself and Polixenes] *whose worth and honesty / Is richly noted, and here justified / By us, a pair of kings;* Per V.i.218; WT I.ii.278

2 prove, confirm, demonstrate Tem V.i.128 [Prospero aside to Sebastian and Antonio] *I here could … justify you traitors;* AW IV.iii.53; Cym II.iv.79; H8 I.ii.6; TNK III.i.64

3 excuse, exonerate, clear 2H6 II.iii.16 [Gloucester to Duchess] *I cannot justify whom the law condemns;* MM V.i.159; Sonn 139.1; WT I.i.9

justle *(v.)* jostle, hustle, elbow Tem V.i.158 [Prospero to Alonso] *howsoe'er you have / Been justled from your senses;* Tem III.ii.25

justling *(adj.)* jostling, clashing, chaotic 1H4 IV.i.18 [Hotspur to Messenger, of Northumberland] *how has he the leisure to be sick / In such a justling time?*

justly *(adv.)* exactly, precisely, closely 2H4 IV.i.67 [Archbishop to Westmorland] *I have in equal balance justly weighed / What wrongs our arms may do, what wrongs we suffer;* AY I.ii.232; Per V.i.87; RJ III.ii.78

jut *(v.)* push, shove, knock; or: strut, swagger, parade R3 II.iv.51 [Queen Elizabeth to all] *Insulting tyranny begins to jut / Upon the innocent and aweless throne* [F *Iutt*; Q *iet*] ☞ jet upon *(v.)*

jutty *(n.)* projection, protrusion [of a building] Mac I.vi.6 [Banquo to King, of the martlet] *no jutty, frieze … but this bird / Hath made his pendent bed and procreant cradle*

jutty *(v.)* jut out over, project over H5 III.i.13 [King Henry to all] *As fearfully as doth a galled rock / O'erhang and jutty his confounded base*

juvenal *(n.)* youth, young man LL I.ii.8 [Armado to Mote] *my tender juvenal;* 2H4 I.ii.19; LL III.i.64; MND III.i.88

kam *(adj.)* crooked, misleading, perverse **Cor** III.i.302 [Sicinius to Brutus, of Menenius' argument] *This is clean kam*

kecksie *(n.)* variety of hollow-stalked plant **H5** V.ii.52 [Burgundy to King Henry and the French King] *nothing teems / But hateful docks, rough thistles, kecksies, burs* ☞ **PLANTS**, p.330

keech *(n.)* lump of congealed fat **H8** I.i.55 [Buckingham to Norfolk, of Wolsey] *such a keech ... with his very bulk*

keel *(v.)* cool **LL** V.ii.909 [Hiems singing, of winter] *While greasy Joan doth keel the pot* [i.e. to prevent it boiling over]

keen *(adj.)* **1** sharp, cutting, severe **MND** III.ii.323 [Helena to Demetrius and Lysander, of Hermia] *when she is angry she is keen and shrewd;* **Ham** III.ii.257
  2 perceptive, sensitive, shrewd **MM** II.i.5 [Escalus to Angelo] *Let us be keen and rather cut a little / Than fall, and bruise to death* [also: sense 1]

keep *(n.)* keeping, custody, care **TS** I.ii.116 [Hortensio to Petruchio, of Bianca] *in Baptista's keep my treasure is*

keep *(v.)* **1** lodge, live, dwell **MM** III.i.10 [disguised Duke to Claudio] *this habitation where thou keep'st;* **1H6** III.i.47; **LL** IV.i.99; **MV** III.iii.19; **Per** II.i.131; **TC** II.i.117
  2 stay within, remain inside **3H6** I.i.207 [Warwick to all] *I'll keep London with my soldiers;* **Cym** II.iii.81; **1H6** III.ii.69; **LL** IV.iii.300; **Tem** I.i.14; **Tim** III.iv.73
  3 guard, watch, tend **2H4** I.i.1 [Lord Bardolph alone] *Who keeps the gate here, ho?;* **AW** I.i.144; **Ham** IV.v.117; **1H6** II.i.63; **Tit** I.i.12; **TNK** II.v.39
  4 keep up, maintain, carry on **RJ** V.iii.16 [Paris as if to Juliet] *The obsequies that I for thee will keep / Nightly shall be to strew thy grave and weep;* **CE** III.i.61; **H5** I.ii.274; **H8** I.iii.10; **JC** I.ii.159; **MM** I.iii.10
  5 look after, watch over, maintain **Cym** III.vii.9 [Belarius to the cave] *Poor house, that keep'st thyself!* [i.e. contains no-one]; **AY** IV.iii.82; **TS** I.i.193, II.i.251
  6 continue, carry on, remain **Per** IV.i.21 [Dionyza to Marina] *Why do you keep alone?;* **E3** II.ii.372; **Ham** II.ii.337; **Tem** II.i.264; **Tim** I.ii.234; **Venus** 678
  7 stay on, remain on **H5** IV.vi.2 [King Henry to Exeter] *yet keep the French the field;* **Cym** I.iv.10
  8 detain, hold in custody, be guarded **2H6** III.i.138 [Suffolk to Gloucester] *I ... commit you to my lord Cardinal / To keep until your further time of trial*
  9 protect, defend, preserve **2H6** III.i.173 [Cardinal to King, of himself and his associates] *those that care to keep your royal person / From treason's secret knife;* **3H6** V.ii.15
  10 look to, attend to, follow **MM** IV.v.3 [Duke to Friar Peter] *keep your instruction*
  11 restrain, control, discipline **TG** IV.iv.10 [Launce alone] *'tis a foul thing when a cur cannot keep himself in all companies!*
  12 celebrate, solemnize **TNK** V.ii.74 [Wooer to Gaoler's Daughter] *I am content, / If we shall keep our wedding there*

keep back *(v.)* prevent, restrain, forcibly hold back **3H6** IV.vii.56 [Montgomery to Edward] *I'll ... keep them back that come to succour you*

keep below stairs remain a servant **MA** V.ii.10 [Margaret to Benedick] *shall I always keep below stairs?*

keep down *(v.)* prevent from growing, keep small **TNK** V.ii.95 [Gaoler's Daughter to Gaoler, of Wooer] *Alas, poor chicken, / He was kept down with hard meat and ill lodging*

keep fair quarter with play fair over, behave honourably over, have a proper regard to **CE** II.i.108 [Adriana to Luciana, of her husband] *So he would keep fair quarter with his bed*

keep on *(v.)* go ahead, go on, carry on **Tim** II.ii.39 [Timon to Lords] *I do beseech you, good my lords, keep on;* **MW** I.i.288

keep touch *(v.)* keep [one's] promise, prove reliable **TNK** II.ii.41 [Second Countryman to the others] *will the dainty dominie, the schoolmaster, / Keep touch;* **TNK** III.iii.53

keep your way keep going, don't stop **MW** III.ii.1 [Mistress Page to Robin] *Nay, keep your way, little gallant;* **H8** II.iv.128

keeper *(n.)* **1** gaoler, warden, custodian **1H6** II.v.1 [Mortimer to Gaolers] *Kind keepers of my weak decaying age;* **1H6** II.v.17, 120; **3H6** II.i.111; **KJ** III.iii.64; **Tim** I.ii.67

2 nurse, carer **2H4** I.i.143 [Northumberland to Morton] *as the wretch … breaks like a fire / Out of his keeper's arms;* **RJ** V.iii.89

3 protecting spirit, guardian angel **Tem** III.iii.21 [Alonso to all] *Give us kind keepers, heavens!*

keisar *(n.)* kaiser, emperor **MW** I.iii.9 [Host to Falstaff] *Thou'rt an emperor - Caesar, Keisar, and Pheazar*

ken *(n.)* range of sight, view, visible distance **Luc** 1114 *'Tis double death to drown in ken of shore;* **Cym** III.vi.6; **2H4** IV.i.149; **2H6** III.ii.113

ken *(v.)* **1** see, make out, espy **2H6** III.ii.101 [Queen to King] *As far as I could ken thy chalky cliffs;* **E3** III.i.65; **TNK** IV.i.150

2 know, understand, be aware of **TNK** V.i.100 [Palamon praying to Venus] *would not [reveal secrets], / Had I kenned all that were* [i.e. all that existed]

3 know, be acquainted with **TC** IV.v.14 [Ulysses to Agamemnon, of Diomedes] *I ken the manner of his gait;* **MW** I.iii.34

kennel *(n.)* **1** street drain, gutter **2H6** IV.i.71 [Lieutenant to Suffolk] *kennel, puddle, sink, whose filth and dirt / Troubles the silver spring where England drinks;* **TS** IV.iii.98

2 pack, mob **1H6** IV.ii.47 [Talbot to all] *A little herd of England's timorous deer, / Mazed with a yelping kennel of French curs!*

kennel *(v.)* go outside to the dog-house **KL** I.iv.110 [Fool to Lear] *Truth's a dog must to kennel*

kerchief *(n.)* cloth head-covering, scarf **MW** III.iii.55 [Mistress Ford to Falstaff, of her favoured headwear] *A plain kerchief;* **JC** II.i.315; **MW** IV.ii.67

kern *(n.)* lightly armed Irish foot-soldier **R2** II.i.156 [King Richard to York, of the Irish] *We must supplant those rough rug-headed kerns;* **H5** III.vii.51; **2H6** III.i.310, 361, IV.ix.26; **Mac** I.ii.13, 30, V.vi.27

kernel *(n.)* seed, pip **Tem** II.i.94 [Antonio to Sebastian, of an imaginary apple] *sowing the kernels of it in the sea*

kersey *(n./adj.)* coarsely woven plain woollen cloth **MM** I.ii.33 [First Gentleman to Lucio] *a list of an English kersey;* **TS** III.ii.64

kersey *(adj.)* plain, simple, ordinary **LL** V.ii.413 [Berowne to Rosaline] *my wooing mind shall be expressed / In russet yeas and honest kersey noes*

kettle *(n.)* kettledrum **Ham** V.ii.269 [Claudius to all] *let the kettle to the trumpet speak*

key *(n.)* **1** tone, voice, style of expression **MV** I.iii.120 [Shylock to Antonio] *in a bondman's key, / With bated breath and whispering humbleness;* **TNK** I.i.94

2 accord, rapport, mind **MND** III.ii.206 [Helena to Hermia, of their friendship] *Both warbling of one song, both in one key*

key-cold *(adj.)* cold as a metal key **R3** I.ii.5 [Anne to dead Henry VI] *Poor key-cold figure of a holy king;* **Luc** 1774

kibe *(n.)* chilblain, inflamed heel **KL** I.v.9 [Fool to Lear] *If a man's brains were in's heels, were't not in danger of kibes?;* **Ham** V.i.139; **MW** I.iii.29; **Tem** II.i.281

kick at *(v.)* spurn, scorn, reject with contempt **Cor** II.ii.122 [Cominius to all, of Coriolanus] *Our spoils he kicked at*

kickshaw *(n.)* **1** trifle, triviality, worthless distraction **TN** I.iii.109 [Sir Toby to Sir Andrew, of revelling] *Art thou good at these kickshawses*

2 fancy dish **2H4** V.i.24 [Shallow to Davy] *a joint of mutton, and any pretty little tiny kickshaws*

kicky-wicky *(n.)* [jocular] girl-friend, wife **AW** II.iii.278 [Parolles to Bertram] *He wears his honour in a box unseen / That hugs his kicky-wicky here at home* [F2 *kicksie-wicksie*]

kid-fox *(n.)* crafty young cub **MA** II.iii.40 [Claudio to Don Pedro, of Benedick] *We'll fit the kid-fox with a pennyworth* [i.e. we'll pay him well for hiding so craftily]

kidney *(n.)* constitution, nature, type **MW** III.v.105 [Falstaff to Ford as Brook] *a man of my kidney*

kill *(v.)* **1** satisfy, allay, subdue, put an end to **AW** V.iii.21 [King to Lafew, of Bertram] *the first view shall kill / All repetition;* **TG** I.ii.68

2 put down, outdo, master **TS** IV.i.166 [Peter to Nathaniel, of Petruchio and Katherina] *He kills her in her own humour*

3 break, distress, grieve **1H6** V.iv.2 [Shepherd to Pucelle] *this kills thy father's heart outright*

kiln-hole *(n.)* fire-hole of a kiln, oven **MW** IV.ii.54 [Mistress Page to Falstaff] *Creep into the kiln-hole;* **WT** IV.iv.245

kind *(n.)* **1** nature, reality, character, disposition **JC** I.iii.64 [Cassius to Casca] *Why birds and beasts from quality and kind … change from their ordinance;* **AY** III.ii.99; **Luc** 1147; **Tem** II.i.166; **TG** III.i.90; **Tit** II.i.116

2 manner, way, state **1H4** I.iii.119 [King Henry to Hotspur] *you shall hear in such a kind from me / As will displease you;* **KL** IV.vi.163; **MA** II.i.59; **MM** III.ii.185; **R2** II.iii.142; **TC** II.iii.127

3 role, part **AC** V.ii.262 [Clown to Cleopatra] *the worm will do his kind;* **Tem** III.i.89

4 mode of action, business, matter **TC** I.iii.285 [Agamemnon to Aeneas, of the Greek response to Aeneas' challenge] *If none of them have soul in such a kind;* **TG** III.ii.56

5 breed, lineage, stock, family **TG** II.iii.2 [Launce alone, of weeping] *all the kind of the Launces have this very fault;* **MND** IV.i.118; **Per** V.i.67; **R2** IV.i.141

6 nature, close natural relationship **Ham** I.ii.65 [Hamlet to himself, of his relationship to Claudius] *A little more than kin, and less than kind;* **MV** I.iii.84

7 respect, regard, particular **MND** I.i.54 [Theseus to Hermia] *in this kind, wanting your father's voice, / The other [Demetrius] must be held the worthier;* **AY** II.i.27

kind *(adj.)* **1** showing natural feeling, acting by nature **Sonn** 143.12 *And play the mother's part, kiss me, be kind;* **Ham** IV.v.148; **2H6** I.i.18; **Luc** 1423; **MA** I.i.25; **MV** I.iii.139

2 loving, affectionate, fond **CE** I.i.44 [Egeon to Duke, of his problems] *Drew me from kind embracements of my spouse;* **AW** V.iii.308; **2H6** I.i.19; **KJ** V.vii.108; **Tit** I.i.64; **TS** V.ii.14

3 friendly, agreeable, pleasant **MV** II.v.44 [Shylock to Jessica, of Launcelot] *The patch is kind enough, but a huge feeder;* **Tem** I.ii.309; **Tim** II.ii.222; **TNK** I.i.38

4 gracious, full of courtesy **Per** V.i.140 [Pericles to Marina] *Thy name, my most kind virgin?;* **TG** IV.ii.43; **Tim** I.ii.145

5 generous, liberal, benevolent **Tim** III.ii.55 [Lucius to Servilius] *I have no power to be kind;* **Tim** IV.ii.40

6 happy, good, favourable **Tem** III.i.69 [Ferdinand to Miranda] *O heaven … crown what I profess with kind event*

kind *(adv.)* kindly, lovingly, with affection **Tim** I.ii.221 [Timon to lords] *I take all and your several visitations / So kind to heart*

kindle *(v.)* **1** stir up, incite, provoke **AY** I.i.161 [Oliver alone, of Orlando] *Nothing remains but that I kindle the boy thither*

2 [of a female animal] be born, deliver **AY** III.ii.328 [Rosalind to Orlando] *As the cony that you see dwell where she is kindled*

kindless *(adj.)* inhuman, unnatural, monstrous **Ham** II.ii.578 [Hamlet alone, of Claudius] *lecherous, kindless villain!*

kindly *(adj.)* **1** natural, proper **MA** IV.i.72 [Claudio to Leonato, of Hero] *by that fatherly and kindly power / That you have in her;* **2H4** IV.v.84

2 friendly, good-natured, well-disposed **AC** II.v.78 [Cleopatra to Charmian] *kindly creatures / Turn all to serpents!;* **Tim** II.ii.222

3 fitting, suitable **1H6** III.i.132 [Warwick to King, of Winchester] *The Bishop hath a kindly gird*

kindly *(adv.)* **1** in accordance with human nature, expressing normal humanity **R3** II.ii.24 [Boy to Duchess of York, of Richard] *he … kindly kissed my cheek;* **AY** II.iii.53; **TG** II.iv.38

2 with natural affection, with compassion **Tem** V.i.24 [Prospero to Ariel] *shall not myself … be kindlier moved than thou art* [also: sense 1]

3 lovingly, gently, affectionately **TC** IV.iv.59 [Troilus to Cressida] *we must use expostulation kindly*; **1H6** II.v.40; **TNK** II.v.29

4 naturally, spontaneously, convincingly **TS** Induction.i.64 [Lord to Huntsmen, of reacting to transformed Sly] *do it kindly, gentle sirs*; **RJ** II.iv.54

kindly, and by all means, in any case **TS** Induction.i.13 [Sly alone, of the thirdborough] *Let him come, and kindly*

kindness (*n.*) **1** kind nature, natural courtesy, natural affection **1H6** II.ii.50 [Talbot to Burgundy] *when a world of men / Could not prevail with all their oratory / Yet hath a woman's kindness overruled*; **Per** IV.iii.38

2 feelings of kinship **TS** V.ii.5 [Lucentio to Bianca, of welcoming his father] *While I with self-same kindness welcome thine* [also: sense 3]; **AY** IV.iii.129

3 friendship, affection, good will **TN** II.i.35 [Sebastian to Antonio] *my bosom is full of kindness*; **R3** IV.ii.22

4 kind act, fond display **Per** IV.vi.6 [Bawd to Pander and Boult, of Marina] *she should ... do me the kindness of our profession*

kindred (*n.*) matching character, resemblance [to one another] **TS** III.ii.49 [Biondello to Tranio as Lucentio, of Petruchio's horse] *with an old mothy saddle and stirrups of no kindred*

kine (*n.*) cattle, cows **1H4** II.iv.459 [Falstaff (as Hal) to Prince Hal (as King), of himself] *If to be fat is to be hated, then Pharoah's lean kine are to be loved*

kingdomed (*adj.*) constituted as a kingdom **TC** II.iii.173 [Ulysses to Agamemnon] *Kingdomed Achilles in commotion rages, / And batters down himself*

kirtle (*n.*) dress, gown **2H4** II.iv.268 [Falstaff to Doll] *What stuff wilt have a kirtle of?*; **PassP** XIX.11 ➧ **half-kirtle** (*n.*)

kiss (*v.*) fraternize, associate, consort **AC** II.vi.96 [Enobarbus to Menas] *If our eyes had authority, here they might take two thieves kissing* [i.e. take into custody]

kissing-comfit (*n.*) perfumed sweetmeat for sweetening the breath **MW** V.v.20 [Falstaff to Mistress Ford] *Let the sky ... hail kissing-comfits*

kitchen (*v.*) entertain in the kitchen **CE** V.i.416 [Dromio of Syracuse to Dromio of Ephesus] *There is a fat friend at your master's house / That kitchened me for you today at dinner*

kitchen-trull kitchen-maid, serving-girl **Cym** V.v.177 [Iachimo to Cymbeline] *our brags / Were cracked of kitchen-trulls*

kite (*n.*) bird of prey; thieving bird [of ill omen; also, strong term of abuse] **JC** V.i.84 [Cassius to Messala] *ravens, crows, and kites / Fly o'er our heads*; **KL** I.iv.259 [Lear to Gonerill] *Detested kite*; **AC** III.xiii.89; **H5** II.i.73; **Mac** III.iv.72; **TS** IV.i.181; **WT** II.iii.185

knack (*n.*) trifle, knick-knack, ornament **WT** IV.iv.346 [disguised Polixenes to Florizel] *I was wont / To load my she with knacks*; **MND** I.i.34; **TNK** III.i.106; **TS** IV.iii.67; **WT** IV.iv.439

knap (*v.*) **1** hit, knock, rap **KL** II.iv.118 [Fool to Lear, of the woman and the eels] *She knapped 'em o'the coxcombs with a stick* [F; Q *rapt*]

2 bite into, nibble at, peck at **MV** III.i.9 [Solanio to Salerio, of Report] *I would she were as lying a gossip in that as ever knapped ginger*

knave (*n.*) **1** scoundrel, rascal, rogue **AY** I.ii.70 [Touchstone to Celia and Rosalind] *swear by your beards that I am a knave* ➧ FEW, p.xxi

2 servant, menial, lackey **Oth** I.i.126 [Roderigo to Brabantio] *a knave of common hire, a gondolier*; **AC** V.ii.3; **MW** III.v.90; **Oth** I.i.45

3 boy, lad, fellow **JC** IV.iii.239 [Brutus to Lucius, of his sleeping] *Poor knave, I blame thee not*; **AC** IV.xiv.12; **KL** I.i.20, iv.96; **LL** III.i.141

knavery (*n.*) **1** roguish trick, roguery, trickery **TN** IV.ii.67 [Sir Toby to Feste] *I would we were well rid of this knavery*; **AW** I.iii.12; **AY** I.ii.72; **MND** III.i.106; **TC** II.iii.71; **TS** I.ii.136

2 treachery, trap, trickery **Oth** I.iii.388 [Iago alone, of Cassio] *To get his place and to plume my will / In double knavery*; **Ham** III.iv.206; **H8** V.ii.32

3 showy adornment, trumpery, ornamentation **TS** IV.iii.58 [Petruchio to Katherina, of clothes] *With amber bracelets, beads, and all this knavery*

knavish (*adj.*) rascally, mischievous, roguish **LL** V.ii.97 [Boyet to Princess, of the King's party] *Their herald is a pretty knavish page*; **Ham** III.ii.250, IV.ii.23

kneaded (*adj.*) compressed, compacted, moulded **MM** III.i.124 [Claudio to Isabella, of his body] *This sensible warm motion to become / A kneaded clod* [i.e. an unfeeling lump of earth]

knee (*n.*) bending of a knee, right to be knelt before **Tim** IV.iii.37 [Timon alone, of gold] *This yellow slave / Will ....place thieves, / And give them title, knee, and approbation* ➧ cap and knee, with

knee (*v.*) **1** go on one's knees, kneel **Cor** V.i.5 [Menenius to all, of Coriolanus] *knee / The way into his mercy*

2 kneel before, beg, supplicate **KL** II.iv.209 [Lear to all, of France] *I could as well be brought / To knee his throne*

knee-crooking (*adj.*) bowing, kneeling, genuflecting **Oth** I.i.45 [Iago to Roderigo] *You shall mark / Many a duteous and knee-crooking knave*

knell (*n.*) **1** death-knell, omen of death **Cor** V.iv.21 [Menenius to Sicinius, of Coriolanus] *He ... talks like a knell*

2 death-knell, mourning song **AW** V.iii.67 [King to Bertram, of his reflections on the past situation] *Be this sweet Helen's knell*

knight (*n.*) devotee, servant, follower [male or female] **AW** I.iii.111 [Steward to Countess, of Helena's thoughts about herself] *Dian no queen of virgins, that would suffer her poor knight surprised without rescue*; **MA** V.iii.13

knight-errant (*n.*) adventurer; night-sinner **2H4** V.iv.22 [First Beadle to Doll] *come, you she knight-errant*

knight of the battle one whose knighthood was conferred after prowess on the battlefield **Cym** V.v.20 [Cymbeline to Belarius, Arviragus and Guiderius] *Arise my knights o'th' battle*

knit (*n.*) style, pattern, type **TS** IV.i.82 [Grumio to Curtis, of the servants' clothes] *their garters of an indifferent knit*

knit (*adj.*) ➧ **well-knit** (*adj.*)

knit (*v.*) **1** unite, join, make one **KJ** II.i.398 [King John to King Philip] *shall we knit our powers / And lay this Angiers even with the ground*; **KJ** III.i.226

2 relate, join in blood **1H6** V.i.17 [Gloucester to King] *The Earl of Armagnac, near knit to Charles* [i.e. closely related]

knit, knit up (*v.*) **1** tie, fasten [by means of a knot] **KJ** IV.i.42 [Arthur to Hubert] *When your head did but ache, / I knit my handkercher about your brows*; **TG** II.vii.45 [Julia to Lucetta, of her hair] *I'll knit it up in silken strings / With twenty odd-conceited true-love knots*; **MW** II.i.68; **Tit** II.iv.10

2 entangle, tie up, catch up **Tem** III.iii.90 [Prospero to Ariel] *these, mine enemies, are all knit up / In their distractions*

knock (*n.*) hard blow, harsh stroke, buffet **H5** III.ii.3 [Nym to Bardolph] *the knocks are too hot*; **R3** V.iii.5; **WT** IV.iii.28

knock (*v.*) strike, beat, hit **TG** II.iv.7 [Speed to Valentine, of Thurio] *'Twere good you knocked him*; **TC** IV.ii.34

knock it strike up **H8** I.iv.108 [King Henry to all] *Let the music knock it*

knoll (*v.*) toll, ring, peal **AY** II.vii.115 [Orlando to all] *If ever been where bells have knolled to church*; **AY** II.vii.122; **TNK** I.i.134

knot (*n.*) **1** company, band, assembly **R3** III.iii.5 [Grey to Ratcliffe, of him and his associates] *A knot you are of damned bloodsuckers*; **JC** III.i.117; **MW** III.ii.46, IV.ii.111; **R3** III.i.182; **Tim** III.vi.89

2 intertwining of arms **Tit** III.ii.4 [Titus to Marcus] *unknit that sorrow-wreathen knot*

3 marriage-tie, bond of wedlock **R3** IV.iii.42 [King Richard to himself, of Richmond marrying King Edward's daughter] *And by that knot looks proudly on the crown*

4 intricately designed flower-bed **R2** III.iv.46 [First Man to the Gardener, of England as a garden] *Her knots disordered*

knot *(v.)* gather together, assemble, congregate **Oth** IV.ii.61 [Othello to Desdemona] *a cistern for foul toads / To knot and gender in!*

knot-grass *(n.)* species of creeping weed **MND** III.ii.329 [Lysander to Hermia] *You minimus of hindering knot-grass made*

knotty-pated *(adj.)* block-headed, dull-witted **1H4** II.iv.223 [Prince Hal to Falstaff] *thou knotty-pated fool*

know *(v.)* **1** acknowledge, remember, think [of] **Tim** III.v.91 [Alcibiades to Senators] *I do beseech you know me;* **MND** I.i.68; **Tim** I.ii.193; **TNK** III.vi.253 ☛ **DISCOURSE MARKERS**, p.127

2 recognize **3H6** II.v.70 [Son to himself, of killing his father] *pardon, father, for I knew not thee;* **2H4** II.iv.185; **JC** II.i.255; **TNK** IV.i.140

3 be acquainted, meet before **AC** II.vi.83 [Menas to Enobarbus] *You and I have known, sir;* **Cym** I.v.33

4 find out, ascertain, learn [from] **TN** III.iv.248 [Viola as Cesario to Sir Toby] *do me this courteous office, as to know of the knight what my offence to him is;* **Tim** II.ii.2

5 see through, find out about **AW** III.vi.12 [Second Lord to Bertram, of Parolles] *It were fit you knew him;* **AW** I.iii.100

6 unravel, get to understand **CE** II.ii.194 [Antipholus of Syracuse to himself, of Adriana's approach] *Until I know this sure uncertainty, / I'll entertain the offered fallacy*

7 have sexual knowledge of, have intercourse with **MM** V.i.186 [Mariana to Duke] *I have known my husband;* **MA** IV.i.46

knowing *(n.)* **1** knowledge, awareness, understanding **Tim** III.ii.68 [First Stranger to Second and Third Strangers, of Lucius] *in my knowing / Timon has been this lord's father*

2 knowledge of the world, experience, savoir-faire **Cym** II.iii.96 [Innogen to Cloten] *one of your great knowing / Should learn ... forbearance;* **Cym** I.v.27

knowing *(adj.)* knowledgeable, intelligent, perceptive **Ham** IV.vii.3 [Claudius to Laertes] *you have heard, and with a knowing ear*

knowingly *(adv.)* with knowledge, with worldly experience **Cym** III.iii.46 [Belarius to Guiderius and Arviragus] *Did you but know the city's usuries, / And felt them knowingly;* **AW** I.iii.245

knowledge *(n.)* **1** familiar territory, world of acquaintance **H5** III.vii.131 [Orleans to Constable, of King Henry] *to mope with his fat-brained followers so far out of his knowledge*

2 carnal knowledge, intimate acquaintance **Cym** II.iv.51 [Iachimo to Posthumus] *Had I not brought / The knowledge of your mistress home*

known *(adj.)* well-acquainted, familiar to each other **WT** IV.iv.66 [Shepherd to Perdita] *bid / These unknown friends to's welcome, for it is / A way to make us better friends, more known*

kyth *(n.)* ☛ tithe *(n.)*

la *(int.)* ☞ **EXCLAMATIONS**, p.158

label *(n.)* **1** document, sheet of writing **Cym** V.v.431 [Posthumus to Lucius] *I found / This label on my bosom*
2 codicil, appendix, additional clause **RJ** IV.i.57 [Juliet to Friar] *ere this hand ... / Shall be the label to another deed*

label *(v.)* attach as a codicil, affix as a supplementary note **TN** I.v.235 [Olivia to Viola as Cesario, of her beauty] *It shall be inventoried, and every particle and utensil labelled to my will*

labour *(n.)* **1** service, effort, hard work **KL** I.iv.7 [Kent alone, to himself] *thy master ... / Shall find thee full of labours*
2 hard work, physical toil [with pun on childbirth] **TNK** IV.ii.129 [Messenger to Theseus, of a knight's arms] *Which speaks him prone to labour*

labour *(v.)* work hard for, try to bring about, urge **R3** I.iv.249 [Clarence to Murderers, of Richard] *he ... swore with sobs / That he would labour my delivery*

labour for *(v.)* **1** progress towards, approach **Tim** III.iv.8 [Philotus to Lucius' Servant, of the time] *Labouring for nine*
2 do the work of, exert oneself on behalf of **TC** IV.v.184 [Nestor to Hector] *I have ... seen thee oft, / Labouring for destiny*

laboured *(adj.)* **1** hard-worked, exhausted by toil **KJ** II.i.232 [King John to Hubert, of himself] *whose laboured spirits ... / Craves harbourage*
2 carefully fashioned, produced with great skill **Per** II.iii.17 [Simonides to Pericles, of art] *you are her laboured scholar*

labouring *(adj.)* aspiring, striving, showing endeavour **AW** II.i.118 [King to Helena] *labouring art can never ransom nature / From her inaidible estate*

laboursome *(adj.)* laborious, assiduous, hard-working **Cym** III.iv.166 [Pisanio to Innogen] *forget / Your laboursome and dainty trims*; **Ham** I.ii.59

lace *(n.)* lacing of stays, bodice-string **WT** III.ii.171 [Paulina to all] *O cut my lace, lest my heart, cracking it, / Break too!*; **AC** I.iii.71; **R3** IV.i.33

lace *(v.)* ornament, trim, bedeck [as if with lace] **Sonn** 67.4 [of his friend] *sin by him advantage should achieve, / And lace itself with his society?*

lack *(v.)* miss, be no longer here **Cor** IV.i.15 [Coriolanus to Volumnia] *I shall be loved when I am lacked*

lacks of, it it is a little before **Ham** I.iv.3 [Horatio to Hamlet and Marcellus] *I think it lacks of twelve*

lackey *(n.)* **1** footman, minion, flunky **AY** III.ii.287 [Rosalind to Celia, of Orlando] *I will speak to him like a saucy lackey*; **AW** IV.iii.282; **H5** III.vii.108, IV.i.265; **H8** V.ii.17; **TS** III.ii.63
2 hanger-on, camp follower **H5** IV.iv.73 [Boy alone] *I must stay with the lackeys, with the luggage of our camp*; **H5** V.ii.24

lackey *(adj.)* servile, menial, abject **R3** V.iii.318 [King Richard to his army, of the enemy] *A scum of Britains and base lackey peasants* [or: hanger-on]

lackey *(v.)* move about aimlessly [as does a lackey] **AC** I.iv.46 [Caesar to Lepidus, of the people] *This common body ... / Goes to and back, lackeying the varying tide*

lack-linen *(adj.)* badly dressed, disreputable **2H4** II.iv.120 [Doll to Pistol] *you poor, base, rascally, cheating, lack-linen mate!*

lack-lustre *(adj.)* sombre, solemn, grave **AY** II.vii.21 [Jaques to all, of Touchstone's watch] *looking on it, with lack-lustre eye*

lad *(n.)* serving-man, man of low birth [not necessarily young] **KL** I.iv.137 [Lear replying to Fool] *No, lad*

ladder-tackle *(n.)* rope-ladder in the rigging **Per** IV.i.61 [Marina to Leonine, of the storm] *from the ladder-tackle washes off / A canvas-climber*

lade *(v.)* drain, bail, empty **3H6** III.ii.139 [Richard alone, of someone wanting to cross the sea to reach a far-off shore] *he'll lade it dry to have his way*

lading (n.) cargo, freight, merchandise **MV** III.i.3 [Salerio to Solanio] *Antonio hath a ship of rich lading wracked on the narrow seas;* **Per** I.ii.49; **Tit** I.i.75

lady (n.) aristocrat, noble **1H4** III.i.247 [Hotspur to Lady Percy] *Swear me, Kate, like a lady as thou art* ☞ **ADDRESS FORMS**, p.8

lady (adj.) lady-like, effeminately delicate, aristocratic **1H4** I.iii.45 [Hotspur to King Henry, of a lord] *With many holiday and lady terms / He questioned me*

lady-smock (n.) cuckoo-flower **LL** V.ii.884 [Ver singing] *lady-smocks all silver-white* ☞ **PLANTS**, p.330

lag (adj.) **1** late-coming, last, closing **TNK** V.iv.8 [Palamon to his knights] *We … beguile / The gout and many, that in lag hours attend / For grey approachers* [i.e. in the last days of life]; **H8** I.iii.35
  2 late, lagging behind, tardy **R3** II.i.92 [Richard to King Edward, of Clarence's countermand] *That came too lag to see him buried*

lag of lagging behind, lingering after **KL** I.ii.6 [Edmund alone] *I am some twelve or fourteen moonshines / Lag of a brother* [i.e. younger than]

lagging (adj.) lingering, dragging, drawn-out **R2** I.iii.214 [Bolingbroke to King Richard] *Four lagging winters and four wanton springs*

lakin (n.) ☞ **SWEARING**, p.435

lam-damn (v.) [unclear meaning] beat the hell out of, thrash without pity **WT** II.i.143 [Antigonus to Leontes, of whoever has convinced Leontes that Hermione is an adultress] *Would I knew the villain! / I would lam-damn him* [F *Land-damne*]

lame (adj.) unsatisfactory, mediocre, faulty **E3** I.i.76 [King Edward to Lorraine, of the King of France] *His lame unpolished shifts are come to light*

lame (v.) give the appearance of lameness to, make deficient [by comparison] **Cym** V.v.163 [Iachimo to Cymbeline, of Italian women] *for feature, laming / The shrine of Venus;* **WT** V.ii.55

lamely (adv.) imperfectly, defectively; also: haltingly, in a lame manner **R3** I.i.22 [Richard alone, of himself] *sent before my time / Into this breathing world … so lamely;* **TG** II.i.86

lamentable (adj.) sorrowful, mournful, sad **KJ** III.i.22 [Constance to Salisbury] *Why holds thine eye that lamentable rheum*

lamentably (adv.) mournfully, dolefully, sorrowfully **WT** IV.iv.192 [Clown to Servant, of his liking a ballad] *a very pleasant thing indeed, and sung lamentably*

lamp (n.) eye **CE** V.i.316 [Egeon to Antipholus and Dromio of Ephesus] *Yet hath … / My wasting lamps some fading glimmer left*

lampass (n.) horse disease affecting the mouth **TS** III.ii.51 [Biondello to Tranio as Lucentio, of Petruchio's horse] *troubled with the lampass*

lance (n.) lancer, horse soldier armed with a lance **E3** V.i.113 [Salisbury to King Edward] *A troop of lances met us on the way;* **KL** V.iii.51

lance, break a engage in a jousting contest **1H6** III.ii.50 [Pucelle to Bedford] *will you … Break a lance, / And run a-tilt at death within a chair?*

lanch (v.) pierce, stab, wound **R3** IV.iv.225 [Queen Elizabeth to King Richard, of the Princes] *Whose hand soever lanched their tender hearts, / Thy head … gave direction* [i.e. whoever's was the hand]

land (n.) **1** tract of land, plot **CE** IV.ii.38 [Dromio of Syracuse to Adriana, of the officer] *one that countermands / The passages of alleys, creeks, and narrow lands*
  2 lawn, soil, ground **LL** V.ii.309 [Princess to ladies] *Whip to our tents, as roes runs o'er the land;* **Tem** IV.i.130

land-damn (v.) ☞ lam-damn (v.)

landed (adj.) possessed of land, having property **MW** IV.iv.84 [Mistress Page alone] *Slender, though well landed, is an idiot*

land-fish (n.) fish living on land; unnatural being **TC** III.iii.263 [Thersites to Achilles, of Ajax] *He's grown a very land-fish*

landman (n.) fighter on land [as opposed to sea] **AC** IV.iii.12 [Second Soldier to all] *I have an absolute hope / Our landmen will stand up*

land-service (n.) military service done on land **AC** II.vi.94 [Enobarbus to Menas] *I deny my land service;* **2H4** I.ii.136; **WT** III.iii.92

lane (n.) path, passage, way **Cym** V.ii.12 [Belarius to Arviragus and Guiderius] *The lane is guarded;* **Cym** V.iii.7, 13; **3H6** I.iv.9; **TNK** I.iv.19

languish (n.) wasting disease, drooping sickness **AC** V.ii.42 [Cleopatra to Proculeius] *death … / That rids our dogs of languish*

languish (v.) pass [time] in languishing, waste **Cym** I.vii.72 [Iachimo to Innogen, of Posthumus' companion] *will's free hours languish for / Assured bondage*

languishment (n.) longing, pain, grief [caused by love] **E3** II.i.94 [King Edward to Lodowick, of the Countess] *how full of languishment / Her beauty makes me;* **Luc** 1130, 1141; **Tit** II.i.110

languor (n.) distress, sorrow, affliction **Tit** III.i.13 [Titus to Tribunes and Senators] *in the dust I write / My heart's deep languor*

lank (adj.) shrunken, loose, slack **2H6** I.i.127 [Cardinal to Gloucester] *the clergy's bags / Are lank and lean with thy extortions*

lank (v.) grow thin, become shrunken **AC** I.iv.71 [Caesar to Lepidus, as if to Antony] *all this … / Was borne so like a soldier that thy cheek / So much as lanked not*

lank-lean (adj.) gaunt, haggard, wasted **H5** IV.Chorus.26 [Chorus, of the English] *their gesture sad, / Investing lank-lean cheeks and war-worn coats*

lantern (n.) light-filled arena, brilliantly lit place **RJ** V.iii.84 [Romeo to dead Paris, of Juliet's tomb] *A grave? O, no, a lantern*

lanthorn (n.) lantern **MND** V.i.233 [Starveling as Moonshine] *This lanthorn doth the horned moon present;* **E3** II.ii.90; **2H4** I.ii.46

lap (v.) wrap, swathe, enfold, clad **R3** II.i.117 [King Edward to all, of Clarence] *he did lap me / Even in his garments;* **Cym** V.v.361; **Mac** I.ii.56; **PassP** XX.24

lapse (n.) fall, moral decline **AW** II.iii.162 [King to Bertram] *I will throw thee from my care for ever / Into the staggers and the careless lapse / Of youth and ignorance*

lapse (v.) **1** do wrong, sin, transgress **Cym** III.vi.12 [Innogen alone] *To lapse in fulness / Is sorer than to lie for need*
  2 apprehend, seize, detain **TN** III.iii.37 [Antonio to Sebastian] *if I be lapsed in this place, / I shall pay dear*

lapsing (n.) slipping, collapsing, failing **Cor** V.ii.19 [Menenius to First Watch] *all the size that verity / Would without lapsing suffer*

lapwing (n.) type of plover [bird with wily methods of escaping the notice of predators; associated with amorous intrigue] **MA** III.i.24 [Hero to Ursula] *look where Beatrice, like a lapwing, runs;* **MM** I.iv.32

lard (v.) **1** strew, deck, cover **Ham** IV.v.38 [Ophelia singing] *Larded all with sweet flowers;* **Ham** V.ii.20
  2 mix in, intermix, intermingle **MW** IV.vi.14 [Fenton to Host, of Anne's letter] *The mirth whereof so larded with my matter / That neither singly can be manifested / Without the show of both;* **TC** V.i.54
  3 permeate, saturate, pepper **TNK** IV.iii.7 [Gaoler to Doctor, of the Gaoler's Daughter's speech] *the name Palamon lards it* [i.e. is brought into it]
  4 enrich [with blood], saturate **H5** IV.vi.8 [Exeter to King Henry, of York] *brave soldier, doth he lie, / Larding the plain*
  5 fatten, build up **Tim** IV.iii.12 [Timon alone] *It is the pasture lards the wether's sides*
  6 drip fat on, enrich with fat **1H4** II.ii.107 [Prince Hal to Poins] *Falstaff sweats to death, / And lards the lean earth as he walks along*

larder (n.) pantry, provision room **H8** V.iv.5 [Servant within to Porter] *I belong to th'larder*

large (n.) full-grown version **KJ** II.i.101 [King Philip to King John, of Arthur's resemblance to John's brother] *This little abstract doth contain that large / Which died in Geoffrey*

large (*adj.*) **1** generous, bountiful, liberal, lavish **2H4** IV.i.184 [Hastings to Mowbray] *If we can make our peace / Upon such large terms;* **KL** I.i.52, 131; **Mac** III.ii.11; **WT** IV.iv.147

2 frank, free, unrestrained **TC** III.ii.152 [Cressida to Troilus] *I ... fell so roundly to a large confession, / To angle for your thoughts*

3 widespread, general, extensive **Tim** IV.iii.128 [Timon to Alcibiades] *Make large confusion*

4 licentious, coarse **MA** II.iii.195 [Don Pedro to Leonato, of Benedick] *some large jests he will make;* **AC** III.vi.93; **MA** IV.i.50

5 grandiose, impressive sounding **KL** I.i.184 [Kent to Gonerill and Regan] *your large speeches may your deeds approve;* **2H6** I.i.109; **TNK** V.i.105

6 high, great, extensive **JC** IV.iii.25 [Brutus to Cassius] *shall we now ... sell the mighty space of our large honours / For so much trash;* **TC** I.iii.223

7 general, broad; or: powerfully built, robust **KJ** I.i.88 [Queen Eleanor to King John] *Do you not read some tokens of my son / In the large composition of this man?*

large, at **1** at length, in full, thoroughly **2H6** III.i.172 [Buckingham to King, of the conspiracy] *more at large your grace shall understand;* **CE** V.i.396; **2H4** IV.iv.101; **1H6** II.v.59; **MND** V.i.150; **Per** V.i.59

2 in general, as a whole **LL** I.i.153 [Browne to King] *to the laws at large I write my name*

large-handed (*adj.*) grasping, rapacious, avaricious **Tim** IV.i.11 [Timon alone, of servants] *Large-handed robbers your grave masters are*

largely (*adv.*) **1** fully, at length **MA** V.iv.69 [Friar to Don Pedro and Claudio] *I'll tell you largely of fair Hero's death*

2 abundantly, amply, greatly **2H4** I.iii.12 [Hastings to Archbishop] *our supplies live largely in the hope / Of great Northumberland*

largess (*n.*) free gift, generous present **TS** I.ii.148 [Gremio to Lucentio as Cambio, of the fee Baptista will pay] *I'll mend it with a largess;* **H5** IV.Chorus.43

lark's-heels (*n.*) ☞ PLANTS, p.330

'larum (*n.*) ☞ alarum (*n.*)

'larum-bell (*n.*) ☞ alarum-bell (*n.*)

lash (*v.*) scourge, punish, flog **CE** II.i.15 [Luciana to Adriana] *headstrong liberty is lashed with woe*

lass-lorn (*adj.*) jilted, forsaken by a sweetheart **Tem** IV.i.68 [Iris to Ceres] *thy broomgroves, / Whose shadow the dismissed bachelor loves, / Being lass-lorn*

last (*n.*) **1** last part, end **Tem** I.ii.170 [Prospero to Miranda] *hear the last of our sea-sorrow;* **JC** III.ii.12

2 last thing to be done, final action **Tim** III.vi.90 [Timon to Lords] *This is Timon's last*

3 end, conclusion, final test **Mac** V.vi.71 [Macbeth to Macduff] *Yet will I try the last* [i.e. fight to the end]

4 last time **AW** V.iii.79 [Lafew to Bertram, of Helena] *The last that e'er I took her leave at court*

5 wooden model of the foot, for shaping shoes **RJ** I.ii.40 [Servant alone] *It is written that the shoemaker should meddle with his yard and the tailor with his last* [with bawdy pun]

last (*adj.*) latest, current, present **AY** III.iii.69 [Touchstone to Jaques] *God 'ild you for your last company*

last ☞ first and last, at

last (*v.*) remain, stay, persist as **LL** V.ii.798 [Princess to King, of his love surviving a year in a hermitage] *But that it bear this trial, and last love*

last (*adv.*) at last **Ham** IV.ii.19 [Hamlet to Rosencrantz and Guildenstern, comparing them to an apple] *first mouthed, to be last swallowed*

lasting (*adj.*) unceasing, ongoing, everlasting **RJ** IV.v.45 [Lady Capulet to herself, of Juliet's supposed death] *Most miserable hour that e'er time saw / In lasting labour of his pilgrimage!*

lastly (*adv.*) in the end, finally **TNK** II.i.108 [Palamon to Arcite] *we shall die ... lastly, / Children of grief and ignorance*

latch (*v.*) **1** catch, receive, take hold of **Mac** IV.iii.195 [Ross to Malcolm and Macduff] *I have words / That would be howled out in the desert air, / Where hearing should not latch them;* **Sonn** 113.6

2 catch, nick **KL** II.i.51 [Edmund to Gloucester, of Edgar] *With his prepared sword he ... latched mine arm* [F; Q lanch't]

3 fasten, secure; or: moisten [leach] **MND** III.ii.36 [Oberon to Puck] *hast thou yet latched the Athenian's eyes / With the love juice*

late (*adj.*) **1** recent, not long past **1H6** III.i.191 [Exeter alone] *This late dissension grown betwixt the peers;* **Ham** II.ii.332; **3H6** IV.v.3; **H8** II.i.147; **R2** I.i.4; **Venus** 469

2 recently appointed **H5** II.ii.61 [King Henry to all] *Who are the late commissioners?;* **H5** II.iv.31

3 former, previous **H8** III.ii.33 [First Gentleman to Second Gentleman, of Katherine] *the late marriage made of none effect*

late (*adv.*) recently, a little while ago / before **1H6** III.ii.132 [Talbot to Burgundy] *The noble Duke of Bedford, late deceased;* **Ham** II.ii.505; **3H6** II.v.93; **KL** III.iv.161; **R3** III.i.99; **Venus** 1026

late, of recently, a little while ago **TG** V.ii.32 [Duke to Proteus and Thurio] *Which of you saw Sir Eglamour of late?;* **Cor** III.i.42; **1H6** II.v.42; **H8** I.ii.97; **LL** V.ii.361; **MM** IV.ii.71

lated (*adj.*) belated, benighted, overtaken by the night **Mac** III.iii.6 [First Murderer to all] *Now spurs the lated traveller apace / To gain the timely inn;* **AC** III.xi.3

lately (*adv.*) **1** recently, of late **2H4** Epilogue.8 [Epilogue] *I was lately here in the end of a displeasing play;* **AW** I.i.28; **AY** II.ii.14; **KL** III.iv.161; **Tem** II.ii.35; **TN** V.i.150

2 formerly, within recent times **E3** IV.vii.1 [Prince Edward to King John] *John in France, and lately John of France*

late-sacked (*adj.*) recently pillaged **Luc** 1740 [of Lucrece's body lying in blood] *Who like a late-sacked island vastly stood / Bare and unpeopled in this fearful flood*

latest (*n.*) last part, final bit **Tim** IV.ii.23 [Flavius to Servants] *The latest of my wealth I'll share amongst you*

latest (*adj.*) last, final **3H6** II.i.108 [Warwick to Edward and Richard, of Wakefield] *Where your brave father breathed his latest gasp;* **Cor** V.iii.11; **2H4** IV.v.182; **H5** III.iii.2; **1H6** IV.iii.33; **TNK** V.iv.29

late-walking (*n.*) going out with whores late at night **MW** V.v.143 [Falstaff to all] *This is enough to be the decay of lust and late-walking through the realm*

lath (*n.*) **1** thin wood **TN** IV.ii.125 [Feste singing, of Vice] *with dagger of lath, in his rage and wrath;* **1H4** II.iv.132; **2H6** IV.ii.1; **RJ** I.iv.5

2 toy sword, stage weapon **Tit** II.i.41 [Demetrius to Chiron] *have your lath glued within your sheath / Till you know better how to handle it*

latten (*adj.*) made of thin brass, tin-plate **MW** I.i.150 [Pistol to Falstaff, of Slender] *I combat challenge of this latten bilbo*

latter (*adj.*) **1** last, dying, final **3H6** IV.vi.43 [King to all] *[I] will ... in devotion spend my latter days;* **1H6** II.v.38

2 recent, of one's later days **Tim** V.iv.74 [Alcibiades as if to Timon, of the sentiments in his epitaph] *These well express in thee thy latter spirits*

latter-born (*n.*) second-born, younger [twin] **CE** I.i.79 [Egeon to Duke] *My wife, more careful for the latter-born*

latter day last day, day of judgement **H5** IV.i.133 [Williams to disguised King Henry] *all those legs, and arms, and heads, chopped off in a battle, shall join together at the latter day*

lattice (*n.*) lattice-work, criss-cross adornment; also: tavern symbol **2H4** II.ii.75 [Page to Prince Henry, of Bardolph] *'A calls me e'en now ... through a red lattice;* **AW** II.iii.212

laud (*n.*) **1** praise, homage, honour **2H4** IV.v.234 [King Henry IV to Warwick] *Laud be to God!;* **Luc** 622, 887; **TC** III.iii.179; **TNK** V.i.58

2 song of praise, hymn **Ham** IV.vii.177 [Gertrude to Claudius and Laertes, of Ophelia] *she chanted snatches of old lauds* [Q2; F, Q1 tunes]

laud (*v.*) praise, honour, give homage to **Cym** V.v.477 [Cymbeline to all] *Laud we the gods*

laughter (*n.*) laughing-stock, object of scorn **JC** I.ii.72 [Cassius to Brutus] *Were I a common laughter*

launch (*v.*) lance [to let out infection] **AC** V.i.36 [Caesar to all] *we do launch / Diseases in our bodies*

laund (*n.*) clearing [in a wood], glade, grassy space **3H6** III.i.2 [First Keeper to Second Keeper] *through this laund anon the deer will come*; **TNK** III.i.2; **Venus** 813

launder (*v.*) wash, bathe **Lover** 17 [of the woman crying into a handkerchief] *Laund'ring the silken figures in the brine*

laundry (*n.*) laundress **MW** I.ii.4 [Evans to Simple, of Caius' house] *there dwells one Mistress Quickly, which is in the manner of … his laundry, his washer, and his wringer*

laurel (*adj.*) **1** of the bay tree [as a symbol of victory] **Tit** I.i.77 [Titus to all, of himself] *bound with laurel boughs*
  2 renowned, famed **E3** III.iii.190 [Derby to Prince Edward] *Be still adorned with laurel victory* [i.e. crowned with a laurel wreath]

lave (*v.*) wash, bathe, soak **TS** II.i.341 [Gremio to Baptista, of Bianca] *Basins and ewers to lave her dainty hands*; **Mac** III.ii.33; **Tit** IV.ii.102

lavish (*adj.*) **1** effusive, unrestrained, exuberant **1H6** II.v.47 [Richard to Mortimer, of Somerset] *he used his lavish tongue / And did upbraid me with my father's death*; **E3** II.i.307
  2 undisciplined, impetuous, wild **Mac** I.ii.59 [Ross to King, of Macbeth defeating Norway] *Curbing his lavish spirit*; **2H4** IV.iv.64

lavishly (*adv.*) unrestrainedly, in an undisciplined way **2H4** IV.ii.57 [Prince John to Archbishop, of King Henry IV] *My father's purposes have been mistook, / And some about him have too lavishly / Wrested his meaning and authority*

lavolt, lavolta (*n.*) lively, high-leaping dance **H5** III.v.33 [Britaine to all, of the French women] *They … teach lavoltas high and swift corantos*; **TC** IV.iv.85

law (*n.*) charge, accusation, case [against] **H8** II.i.14 [First Gentleman to Second Gentleman, of Buckingham] *He … alleged / Many sharp reasons to defeat the law*

law, by in court, with legal proceedings **TS** Induction.i.12 [Sly alone, of the thirdborough] *I'll answer him by law*

law, go to sue, fight against, argue with **TNK** V.iii.99 [Emilia to herself, of Arcite's spirit] *it could / No more be hid … / Than humble banks can go to law with waters*

law (*int.*) ☞ **EXCLAMATIONS**, p.158

lawful (*adj.*) excusable, allowable, justifiable **Ham** III.i.32 [Claudius to Gertrude, of Ophelia] *Her father and myself, lawful espials*

lawn (*n.*) [type of] fine linen **WT** IV.iv.220 [Autolycus singing] *Lawn as white as driven snow*; **E3** II.i.56; **Luc** 259; **Oth** IV.iii.72; **Venus** 590; **WT** IV.iv.209

lay (*n.*) **1** song **Per** V.Chorus.4 [Gower alone, of Marina] *she dances / As goddess-like to her admired lays*; **Ham** IV.vii.182; **2H6** I.iii.88; **PassP** XIV.18; **Sonn** 98.5; **TNK** V.i.89
  2 wager, stake, bet **Oth** II.iii.314 [Iago to Cassio] *my fortunes against any lay worth naming*; **Cym** I.v.144; **2H6** V.ii.27

lay (*adj.*) unclerical, secular, worldly **H8** I.iv.11 [Sands to Lovell, of Wolsey] *had the Cardinal / But half my lay thoughts in him*

lay (*v.*) **1** apply, place, put **Ham** III.iv.146 [Hamlet to Gertrude] *Lay not that flattering unction to your soul*; **2H6** IV.viii.57; **H8** I.i.84, V.iv.77
  2 attribute, ascribe, impute **R2** I.i.84 [King Richard to Bolingbroke] *What doth our cousin lay to Mowbray's charge?*; **AC** II.ii.59, V.ii.129; **Ham** IV.i.17; **R3** I.iii.96, 325
  3 put forward, present, use **MW** II.ii.6 [Falstaff to Pistol] *I have been content … you should lay my countenance to pawn* [i.e. use my patronage to borrow money]

4 set up, arrange, devise **MW** III.iii.178 [Mistress Page to Mistress Ford, of the extent of Ford's jealousy] *I will lay a plot to try that*; **1H4** II.i.53; **KJ** III.iv.146
  5 put on a surface in layers, add layers of colour to **Sonn** 101.7 *Beauty [needs] no pencil, beauty's truth to lay*
  6 allay, reduce, moderate **TC** IV.iv.52 [Pandarus to himself] *Rain, to lay this wind, or my heart will be blown up by the root*
  7 keep down, make subside **TG** II.iii.30 [Launce alone] *see how I lay the dust with my tears*
  8 flatten, bring down, lay low **3H6** V.vii.21 [Richard to himself, of the baby prince and Edward] *I'll blast his harvest, if your head were laid*
  9 bring down, inflict **Cym** IV.iii.325 [Innogen alone, of Pisanio and Cloten] *malice and lucre in them / Have laid this woe here*
  10 appease, prevent from walking **RJ** II.i.26 [Mercutio to Benvolio, of Romeo] *To raise a spirit in his mistress' circle / Of some strange nature, letting it there stand / Till she had laid it* [with bawdy pun]
  11 circulate with warrants for arrest **2H6** IV.x.4 [Cade alone] *all the country is laid for me*
  12 wager, stake, bet **Cym** I.v.124 [Iachimo to Posthumus] *I will lay you ten thousand ducats to your ring*; **Cym** I.ii.105; **Ham** V.ii.162, 164; **H5** IV.i.218; **LL** I.i.295
  13 [nautical] steer away from the shore **Tem** I.i.49 [Boatswain to Mariners] *Lay her off!*; **Tem** I.i.48

lay aboard (*v.*) attack at close quarters, lay alongside **2H6** IV.i.25 [Whitmore to all] *I lost mine eye in laying the prize aboard*

lay about (*v.*) strike out, fight hard **TC** I.ii.56 [Pandarus to Cressida, of Hector] *He'll lay about him today*; **E3** III.i.176

lay apart (*v.*) set aside, put away **AY** IV.iii.45 [Rosalind as Ganymede, reading from Phebe's letter to Ganymede] *thy godhead laid apart*

lay by (*v.*) **1** lay aside, set aside, disregard **AW** V.i.15 [Helena to Gentleman] *goaded with most sharp occasions / Which lay nice manners by*; **Cym** III.vii.57; **TC** II.iii.78
  2 [highwaymen] stand and deliver; put down your weapons **1H4** I.ii.35 [Prince Hal to Falstaff] *a purse of gold … got with swearing 'Lay by!'*

lay down (*v.*) **1** lose, relinquish, sacrifice **2H6** IV.i.16 [Master to First Gentleman, of his ransom] *A thousand crowns, or else lay down your head*
  2 formulate, work out, estimate **2H4** I.iii.35 [Hastings to all] *it never yet did hurt / To lay down likelihoods and forms of hope*; **H5** I.ii.137; **MA** IV.i.234

lay for (*v.*) waylay, ambush, seize **Tim** III.v.116 [Alcibiades alone] *I'll cheer up / My discontented troops, and lay for hearts*

lay home talk severely, rebuke, berate **Ham** III.iv.1 [Polonius to Gertrude, of Hamlet] *Look you lay home to him*

lay knife aboard make a claim, establish a position **RJ** II.iv.197 [Nurse to Romeo, of Paris wooing Juliet] *there is a nobleman in town … that would fain lay knife aboard*

lay on / upon (*v.*) **1** set to, set about, undertake vigorously **WT** IV.iii.39 [Clown to himself, of Perdita] *my father hath made her mistress of the feast, and she lays it on*; **H5** V.ii.140; **Tem** III.ii.153
  2 inflict blows, beat soundly **E3** III.iv.88 [Prince Edward to King Edward, of the French] *lay as thick upon my battered crest / As on an anvil with their ponderous glaives*; **KJ** II.i.146 [Bastard to Austria] *I'll … lay on that shall make your shoulders crack*

lay out (*v.*) expend, spend, use up **Cym** II.iii.86 [Innogen to Cloten] *You lay out too much pains / For purchasing but trouble*; **1H4** IV.ii.5; **Tim** I.ii.240; **TNK** I.ii.111

lay to (*v.*) bring into action, put to work **Tem** IV.i.250 [Stephano to Caliban] *lay to your fingers*

lay unto (*v.*) add to, place along with **TNK** V.i.133 [Palamon praying to Venus, of her token] *being laid unto / Mine innocent true heart, arms in assurance / My body*

lay up (*v.*) **1** consign, put away, allocate **TNK** II.i.60 [Arcite to Palamon, of his imprisonment] *to that destiny have patiently / Laid up my hour to come* [i.e. the rest of my life]
  2 stow away, pack away, store **2H4** V.i.78 [Falstaff alone, of Prince Henry] *you shall see him laugh till his face be like a wet cloak ill laid up!*

lay upon (*v.*) bestow on, impose on **H8** I.i.78 [Buckingham to Abergavenny, of Wolsey and the gentry] *To whom as great a charge as little honour / He meant to lay upon*

layer-up (*n.*) preserver, storer, upholder **H5** V.ii.228 [King Henry to Katherine] *old age, that ill layer-up of beauty, can do no more spoil upon my face*

laying on (*n.*) vigorous attack, dealing of blows **TC** I.ii.207 [Pandarus to Cressida, of the marks on Hector's helmet] *there's laying on*

lazar (*n.*) leper, diseased person **TC** V.i.61 [Thersites alone] *I care not to be the louse of a lazar so I were not Menelaus;* **H5** I.i.15; **TC** II.iii.32

lazar (*adj.*) leprous **H5** II.i.73 [Pistol to Nym] *from the powdering tub of infamy / Fetch forth the lazar kite of Cressid's kind*

lazar-like (*adj.*) like leprosy, leprous **Ham** I.v.72 [Ghost to Hamlet] *And a most instant tetter barked about, / Most lazar-like … / All my smooth body*

lea (*n.*) meadow, field **Tem** IV.i.60 [Iris to Ceres] *thy rich leas / Of wheat;* **H5** V.ii.44; **Tim** IV.iii.194

lead (*n.*) **1** leaden coffin lining **1H6** I.i.64 [Bedford to Messenger, of Henry V] *the loss of those great towns / Will make him burst his lead and rise from death*
  2 cauldron [of molten lead] **WT** III.ii.175 [Paulina to Leontes] *What studied torments, tyrant, hast for me? … Boiling / In leads or oils?*
  3 (plural) lead-covered flat roofs **R3** III.vii.54 [Buckingham to Richard] *Go, go, up to the leads!;* **Cor** II.i.203, II.vi.83

lead (*v.*) **1** put lead weights on **TNK** I.i.116 [Third Queen to Emilia] *he that will fish / For my least minnow, let him lead his line*
  2 govern, dominate, direct **3H6** II.vi.34 [Edward to all] *Some troops pursue the bloody-minded Queen, / That led calm Henry;* **KJ** III.i.163

lead away (*v.*) lead astray, seduce, tempt **Sonn** 96.11 *How many gazers mightst thou lead away, / If thou wouldst use the strength of all thy state!*

leaden (*adj.*) **1** burdensome, heavy, cumbersome **JC** IV.iii.266 [Brutus to himself, as if to slumber] *Layest thou thy leaden mace upon my boy;* **1H6** IV.vi.12
  2 heavy, dull, spiritless **Venus** 34 [of Adonis] *With leaden appetite, unapt to toy;* **JC** III.i.173; **LL** IV.iii.297

leading (*n.*) leadership, command, generalship **1H4** IV.iii.17 [Vernon to all] *Being men of such great leading as you are*

leaf (*n.*) petal **1H6** IV.i.92 [Basset to King, of the red rose] *the sanguine colour of the leaves*

league (*n.*) **1** compact, alliance, treaty, bond of friendship **KJ** V.i.65 [Bastard to King John, of peace with France] *O inglorious league!;* **E3** IV.ii.1; **2H6** I.i.96; **Luc** 287; **MW** III.ii.23; **Tit** V.iii.23
  2 [measure of distance] c.3 miles [c.5 km] **CE** I.i.63 [Egeon to Duke] *A league from Epidamnum had we sailed;* **CE** I.i.101; **Tem** I.ii.145

league (*v.*) **1** bind together, ally, confederate **Oth** II.iii.212 [Montano to Iago] *If partially affined or leagued in office* [i.e. not prepared to testify against a fellow-officer]
  2 join, link, intertwine **Cym** IV.ii.213 [Arviragus to Belarius and Guiderius, of disguised Innogen] *His arms thus leagued*

leaguer (*n.*) military camp **AW** III.vi.24 [First Lord to Bertram, of Parolles] *he is carried into the leaguer of the adversaries*

leak (*v.*) urinate, piss **1H4** II.i.21 [Second Carrier to First Carrier] *we leak in your chimney*

leaked (*adj.*) sprung a leak, full of holes **Tim** IV.ii.19 [Third Servant to Flavius] *Leaked is our bark*

leaking (*adj.*) issuing forth, rising, surging **E3** III.ii.58 [Third Frenchman to all, of the burning cities] *as the leaking vapour in the wind / Turned but aside*

lean (*adj.*) **1** slight, mean, poor **AC** II.ii.19 [Lepidus to Caesar and Antony] *let not / A leaner action rend us;* **CE** II.ii.94; **TN** III.iv.334
  2 barren, unproductive **2H4** IV.iii.116 [Falstaff alone, of Prince Henry's cold blood] *he hath like lean, sterile, and bare land manured, husbanded, and tilled;* **1H4** II.ii.107

lean (*v.*) **1** depend, appertain [to], relate [to] **Ham** IV.iii.59 [Claudius to attendants] *everything is sealed and done / That else leans on the affair*
  2 need support, incline towards a fall **Cym** I.vi.58 [Queen to Pisanio, of Posthumus] *To be depender on a thing that leans*

lean unto (*v.*) accept, be well-disposed towards **Cym** I.i.9 [Queen to Posthumus, of Cymbeline] *'twere good / You leaned unto his sentence*

lean-looked (*adj.*) lean-looking, gaunt **R2** II.iv.11 [Captain to Salisbury] *lean-looked prophets whisper fearful change*

leap (*v.*) **1** jump into, throw oneself into **TNK** II.i.272 [Arcite to Palamon] *I'll throw my body out, / And leap the garden*
  2 rejoice, enthuse, exult **E3** II.ii.13 [Audley to Derby] *doth his highness leap to hear these news?;* **Venus** 1026

leaping-house (*n.*) brothel, whorehouse **1H4** I.ii.9 [Prince Hal to Falstaff, of Falstaff's need to know the time] *Unless … dials [were] the signs of leaping-houses*

learn (*v.*) **1** teach, instruct [not a regional dialect usage as in modern English] **Tem** I.ii.365 [Caliban to Miranda] *The red plague rid you / For learning me your language!;* **AY** I.i.5; **Cym** I.vi.12; **MA** IV.i.28; **Oth** I.iii.181; **RJ** III.ii.12
  2 be edified, receive instruction [from] **JC** IV.iii.54 [Brutus to Cassius] *I shall be glad to learn of noble men*
  3 inform of, tell about **TC** II.i.20 [Ajax to Thersites] *learn me the proclamation;* **TC** II.i.90

learned (*adj.*) wise, erudite, sagacious **Cor** III.i.99 [Coriolanus to Senators] *If you are learned, / Be not as common fools*

learning (*n.*) **1** scholarship, learned opinion **H8** II.ii.137 [King Henry to Wolsey and Campeius] *The most convenient place that I can think of / For such receipt of learning is Blackfriars*
  2 field of education, domain of instruction **Cym** I.i.43 [First Gentleman to Second Gentleman, of Posthumus] *The king … / Puts to him all the learnings that his time / Could make him the receiver of*

lease, out by let out to others, not under one's full ownership **TG** V.ii.29 [Proteus to Thurio, of Thurio's possessions] *they are out by lease*

leash (*n.*) [hunting] set of three, trio **1H4** II.iv.7 [Prince Hal to Poins] *I am sworn brother to a leash of drawers*

leasing (*n.*) **1** lie, falsehood, untruth **Cor** V.ii.22 [Menenius to First Watch, of Coriolanus] *I … in his praise / Have almost stamped the leasing* [i.e. given falsehood the stamp of truth]
  2 skill in lying, ability to lie **TN** I.v.92 [Feste to Olivia] *Now Mercury endue thee with leasing*

least (*n.*) lowest estimate **Tim** V.ii.2 [Messenger to Third Senator, of Alcibiades' numbers] *I have spoke the least*

least, at ultimately, in the final analysis **2H4** I.iii.47 [Lord Bardolph to Hastings, if a building costs too much] *What do we then but draw anew the model / In fewer offices, or at least desist / To build at all?*

least, at the at the lowest estimate, at any rate **LL** IV.ii.9 [Nathaniel to Holofernes] *the epithets are sweetly varied, like a scholar at the least*

least, of the too small; or: inferior **TNK** III.vi.64 [Arcite to Palamon, of the gauntlets] *Those are o'th' least*

leather-coat (*n.*) russet apple [with a rough skin] **2H4** V.iii.40 [Davy to Bardolph] *There's a dish of leather-coats for you*

leathern *(adj.)* **1** leather-like **AY** IV.iii.25 [Rosalind as Ganymede to Silvius, of Phebe] *she has a leathern hand*; **E3** I.ii.32; **Venus** 392
  2 clothed in animal skins **E3** II.ii.115 [King Edward alone, of the Countess] *The register of all rarieties / Since leathern Adam*

leathern-jerkin *(adj.)* wearing a leather jacket **1H4** II.iv.67 [Prince Hal to Francis, of the vintner] *Wilt thou rob this ... leathern-jerkin ... Spanish pouch?* ☞ **jerkin** *(n.)*

leave *(n.)* **1** permitting, allowance, availability **Tim** II.ii.132 [Timon to Flavius] *I might so have rated my expense / As I had leave of means*
  2 leave-taking, permission to depart **Mac** IV.iii.236 [Malcolm to Macduff] *go we to the King; our power is ready; / Our lack is nothing but our leave*
  3 ☞ **FAREWELLS**, p.170; **POLITENESS**, p.340

leave *(v.)* **1** cease, stop, give up **H8** IV.ii.94 [Katherine to Griffith] *Bid the music leave*; **Cor** IV.ii.52; **Ham** III.iv.67; **3H6** II.ii.168; **Luc** 148; **TG** II.vi.17
  2 abandon, forsake, relinquish **H8** II.ii.3 [Katherine to Griffith] *My legs like loaden branches bow to th'earth, / Willing to leave their burden*; **CE** II.i.41; **MW** II.ii.22; **TG** IV.iv.71
  3 part with, lose, forsake **MV** V.i.150 [Gratiano to Portia, of the words on his ring] *Love me, and leave me not*; **MV** V.i.172
  4 spare, leave alive **TC** V.v.26 [Nestor to all, of Hector] *Here, there, and everywhere, he leaves and takes*
  5 break off, stop, interrupt oneself **Venus** 715 [Venus to Adonis] *Where did I leave?*
  6 pass by, go past **AY** IV.iii.81 [Celia as Aliena to Oliver] *The rank of osiers ... / Left on your right hand brings you to the place*

leave off *(v.)* give up, abandon, leave alone **AW** I.iii.236 [Countess to Helena, of the King's illness] *the schools ... have left off / The danger to itself* [i.e. left it to look after itself]

leaven *(n.)* [baking] fermenting element, infusing mixture, adulteration **TC** II.i.14 [Ajax to Thersites] *Speak, then, you vinewd'st leaven*; **Cym** III.iv.63

leavened *(adj.)* carefully considered, well-thought-out **MM** I.i.51 [Duke to Angelo] *We have with leavened and prepared choice / Proceeded to you*

leavening *(n.)* process of fermentation in dough **TC** I.i.21 [Pandarus to Troilus] *you must tarry the leavening*

leavy *(adj.)* leafy, covered with foliage **Mac** V.vi.1 [Malcolm to all] *Your leavy screens throw down*

lecher *(v.)* copulate, play the part of a lecher **KL** IV.vi.113 [Lear to all] *the small gilded fly / Does lecher in my sight*

lecture *(n.)* **1** lesson, instructive example **Ham** II.i.67 [Polonius to Reynaldo] *my former lecture and advice*; **Cor** II.iii.234; **Luc** 618
  2 classroom lesson **TS** I.i.145 [Gremio to Lucentio as Cambio, of Bianca] *see you read no other lectures to her*; **TS** III.i.8, 23

lee *(n.)* ☞ **lees** *(n.)*

lee *(v.)* cut off from the wind, make helpless **Oth** I.i.30 [Iago to Roderigo] *I ... must be leed and calmed / By debitor and creditor* [Q *led*; F *be-leed*]

leech *(n.)* physician, healer **Tim** V.iv.84 [Alcibiades to Senators] *make each / Prescribe to other, as each other's leech*

leer *(n.)* **1** complexion, countenance, look **Tit** IV.ii.118 [Aaron to Chiron, of skin colour] *Here's a young lad framed of another leer*; **AY** IV.i.60
  2 glance, look, eye **MW** I.iii.41 [Falstaff to Pistol, of Mistress Ford] *She discourses, she carves, she gives the leer of invitation* [i.e. the come-hither look]

leer *(v.)* look sideways, cast a side glance, smile disarmingly **LL** V.ii.480 [Browne to Boyet] *You leer upon me, do you?*; **2H4** V.v.6; **TC** V.i.86

lees *(n.)* (plural) dregs, remains, remnants **Mac** II.iii.92 [Macbeth to all] *The wine of life is drawn, and the mere lees / Is left this vault to brag of*; **TNK** I.iv.29

leese *(v.)* lose, fail to preserve **Sonn** 5.14 *flowers distilled though they with winter meet, / Leese but their show; their substance still lives sweet*

leet *(n.)* local court of justice, manorial court **TS** Induction.ii.86 [First Servingman to Sly, of the hostess of the house] *And say you would present her at the leet*; **Oth** III.iii.139

leg *(n.)* **1** bending of a knee, genuflection, obeisance **1H4** II.iv.381 [Prince Hal to Falstaff] *Well, here is my leg*; **AW** II.ii.10; **Cor** II.i.64; **R2** III.iii.175; **Tim** I.ii.237; **TN** II.iii.19
  2 [unclear meaning] supporting member **Tim** III.vi.80 [Timon as if to the gods] *the Senators of Athens, together with the common leg of people*

legate *(n.)* papal representative **H8** III.ii.311 [Surrey to Wolsey] *without the King's assent or knowledge / You wrought to be a legate*

legatine, legative *(adj.)* as a legate **H8** III.ii.339 [Suffolk to Wolsey] *those things you have done of late / By your power legatine within this kingdom / Fall into th'compass of a praemunire* [F *Legatiue*]

'lege *(v.)* allege **TS** I.ii.28 [Grumio to Hortensio, of Petruchio] *'tis no matter ... what he 'leges in Latin*

legend *(n.)* probably a malapropism for 'legion' **MW** I.iii.49 [Falstaff to Nym and Pistol, of Ford] *He hath a legend of angels* [F]

legerity *(n.)* lightness, nimbleness, alacrity **H5** IV.i.23 [King Henry to Erpingham] *The organs ... newly move / With casted slough and fresh legerity*

legion *(n.)* army, power, force **E3** IV.iv.63 [Prince Edward to Audley, of King John] *that same king / Hath but the puissant legion of one king*

legitimation *(n.)* legitimacy **KJ** I.i.248 [Bastard to Lady Faulconbridge] *Legitimation, name, and all is gone*

leiger *(n.)* ☞ **lieger** *(n.)*

leisure *(n.)* opportunity, moment, available time **CE** V.i.376 [Antipholus of Syracuse to Luciana] *What I told you then / I hope I shall have leisure to make good*; **AW** I.i.209; **H8** III.ii.140; **KJ** II.i.58; **Sonn** 58.4; **TS** IV.iii.59

leisure, by only after careful consideration, but slowly **Tit** I.i.304 [Saturninus to Titus] *I'll trust by leisure him that mocks me once, / Thee never*

leman *(n.)* lover, paramour, sweetheart **TN** II.iii.24 [Sir Andrew to Feste] *I sent thee sixpence for thy leman*; **2H4** V.iii.46; **MW** IV.ii.154

lend *(v.)* give, grant, bestow [on] **JC** III.ii.74 [Antony to all] *Friends, Romans, countrymen, lend me your ears*; **Ham** IV.v.210; **2H6** I.i.19; **KJ** I.i.84; **MM** III.ii.230; **R2** I.iii.146

lending *(n.)* **1** (plural) something lent, borrowing **KL** III.iv.105 [Lear to himself, as if to his clothes] *Off, off, you lendings!* [i.e. things provided by the beasts]
  2 (plural) advance of money to soldiers [in lieu of regular pay] **R2** I.i.89 [Bolingbroke to King Richard] *eight thousand nobles / In name of lendings for your highness' soldiers*

length *(n.)* **1** range, reach, scope **Per** I.i.168 [Thaliard to Antiochus, of Pericles] *if I can get him within my pistol's length*
  2 stride, distance [in leaping] **TNK** V.v.57 [Pirithous to Palamon] *the horse / Would make his length a mile* [i.e. it seemed capable of strides a mile long]
  3 length of time, duration left in life, delay **AC** IV.xiv.46 [Antony alone] *now / All length is torture*

length, at in the end, in the long term **Tim** II.ii.154 [Flavius to Timon] *And at length / How goes our reck'ning?*

length *(v.)* lengthen, prolong **PassP** XIV.30 *good day, of night now borrow; / Short night, to-night, and length thyself to-morrow*

lengthened *(adj.)* prolonged, lasting throughout life **Cym** V.iii.13 [Posthumus to Lord] *cowards living / To die with lengthened shame*

lenity *(n.)* mildness, gentleness, mercifulness **H5** III.vi.109 [King Henry to Fluellen] *when lenity and cruelty play for a kingdom / the gentler gamester is the soonest winner*; **Cor** III.i.99; **H5** III.ii.25; **1H6** V.iv.125; **3H6** II.vi.22; **RJ** III.i.123

lenten *(adj.)* **1** made in Lent [without meat] **RJ** II.iv.129 [Mercutio to Romeo, of Nurse] *a hare ... in a lenten pie, that is something stale and hoar ere it be spent*
2 dismal, meagre, scanty **TN** I.v.8 [Maria to Feste] *A good lenten answer!*; **Ham** II.ii.316

l'envoy *(n.)* explanation, exposition, address **LL** III.i.69 [Armado to Mote, of his riddle] *Come, thy l'envoy - begin*

leperous, leprous *(adj.)* infected, poisoned, leprosy-like **E3** II.i.421 [Countess to Warwick] *No marvel though the lep'rous infant die*; **Ham** I.v.64

lesson *(v.)* **1** instruct, teach, advise **TG** II.vii.5 [Julia to Lucetta] *I do conjure thee ... / To lesson me*; **Cor** II.iii.176; **R3** I.iv.243
2 discipline, admonish, teach a lesson to **AC** III.xii.13 [Ambassador to Caesar, of Antony] *He lessons his requests*

lest *(conj.)* unless, in case **E3** I.i.99 [Warwick to Lorraine, of the King of France] *Bid him leave off the lion's case he wears, / Lest, meeting with the lion in the field, / He chance to tear him piecemeal for his pride*

let *(n.)* hindrance, obstacle, snag **E3** II.ii.135 [Countess to King Edward] *remove those lets / That stand between your highness' love and mine*; **H5** V.ii.65; **Luc** 330, 646; **TNK** III.v.155

let *(v.)* **1** hinder, prevent, stand in the way **TG** III.i.113 [Valentine to Duke, of the Duke's lady] *What lets but one may enter at her window?*; **CE** II.i.105; **Ham** I.iv.85; **Luc** 328; **TN** V.i.246
2 allow to stay, let remain **WT** I.ii.41 [Hermione to Polixenes, of Leontes in Bohemia] *I'll give him my commission / To let him there a month behind the gest / Prefixed for's parting*
3 refrain, omit, keep from **Luc** 10 [of Lucrece] *Collatine unwisely did not let / To praise ... that sky of his delight* [i.e. Lucrece]

let-alone *(n.)* power to interfere, ability to hinder **KL** V.iii.80 [Albany to Gonerill] *The let-alone lies not in your good will*

let alone ☛ alone, let

let be ☛ ATTENTION SIGNALS, p.26

let blood 1 slaughter, kill, massacre **JC** III.i.152 [Antony to all] *I know not ... / Who else must be let blood*; **Cym** IV.ii.168
2 bleed [as a medical treatment] **TC** II.iii.210 [Ajax to all, of Achilles] *I'll let his humours' blood*

let down *(v.)* lose, forfeit, give up **TNK** II.i.251 [Arcite to Palamon] *shall I stand still / And let mine honour down* [i.e. allow myself to be dishonoured]

let fall *(v.)* lower, debase, fail to live up to **TNK** Prologue.15 [of Chaucer's story] *If we let fall the nobleness of this*

let go ☛ DISCOURSE MARKERS, p.127

let out *(v.)* lend, make a loan of **Tim** III.v.108 [Alcibiades alone, of the Senators] *they have told their money and let out / Their coin upon large interest*

lethargy *(n.)* **1** unnatural drowsiness, harmful torpor **TC** V.i.19 [Thersites to Patroclus] *diseases of the south ... lethargies, cold palsies*
2 coma, state of unconsciousness **Oth** IV.i.53 [Iago to Cassio] *The lethargy must have his quiet course*

lethargy *(v.)* affect with lethargy, dull, subdue **KL** I.iv.225 [Lear to all, of himself] *his discernings / Are lethargied*

lethe *(n.)* death, oblivion, life-blood **JC** III.i.206 [Antony to dead Caesar, and his killers] *Signed in thy spoil, and crimsoned in thy lethe* [F *Lethee*]

Lethe'd *(adj.)* oblivious, all-forgetting, stuporous **AC** II.i.27 [Pompey to Menas, of Antony] *That sleep and feeding may prorogue his honour / Even till a Lethe'd dullness*

letter *(n.)* **1** [letter of] influence, recommendation, introduction **Oth** I.i.36 [Iago to Roderigo] *Preferment goes by letter and affection*
2 lettering, written form **LL** V.ii.40 [Rosaline to Princess, of Berowne's verses] *Much in the letters, nothing in the praise*

3 (plural) sophisticated learning, great scholarship **Tem** II.i.153 [Gonzalo to Alonso, of the imaginary commonwealth] *Letters should not be known*; **2H4** IV.i.44
4 (plural) study, learning, knowledge **Per** IV.Chorus.8 [Gower alone, of Marina] *trained / In music's letters*

letter, affect *(v.)* practise alliteration **LL** IV.ii.55 [Holofernes to Nathaniel, of his epitaph] *I will something affect the letter, for it argues facility*

letters patent *(n.)* open documents issued by the sovereign which conferred an office, privilege, right, etc **H8** III.ii.250 [Wolsey to all, of the seal given to him] *the King ... / Tied it by letters patents*

lettered *(adj.)* learned, literate, educated **LL** V.i.44 [Armado to Holofernes] *are you not lettered?*

level *(n.)* **1** [archery] direct aim, target, range **WT** III.ii.80 [Hermione to Leontes] *My life stands in the level of your dreams, / Which I'll lay down*; **Lover** 309; **Sonn** 117.11
2 line of fire **H8** I.ii.2 [King Henry to Wolsey] *I stood i'th' level / Of a full-charged confederacy*; **AW** II.i.156; **RJ** III.iii.103

level *(adj.)* **1** steady, steadfast, constant **2H4** II.i.112 [Lord Chief Justice to Falstaff] *It is not a confident brow ... can thrust me from a level consideration*; **Tim** IV.iii.19; **TN** II.iv.31
2 straight, direct **Ham** IV.i.42 [Claudius to Gertrude] *As level as the cannon to his blank*
3 accessible, readily achievable **2H4** IV.iv.7 [King Henry IV to all] *everything lies level to our wish*
4 plain, obvious, manifest **Ham** IV.v.153 [Claudius to Laertes, of his guiltlessness] *It shall as level to your judgement 'pear / As day does to your eye*

level *(v.)* aim, direct, target **MA** IV.i.235 [Friar to Leonato] *if all aim but this be levelled false*; **Lover** 282; **R3** IV.iv.203

level at *(v.)* **1** aim for, have as a target **Per** II.iii.113 [Simonides to Knights, of love] *that's the mark I know you level at*; **2H4** III.i.259; **2H6** III.i.160; **3H6** II.ii.19; **Per** I.i.165; **Sonn** 121.9
2 guess correctly, rightly anticipate **AC** V.ii.334 [Caesar to Dolabella, of Cleopatra] *She levelled at our purposes*; **MV** I.ii.36

level with *(v.)* fit, suit, be in keeping with **Oth** I.iii.237 [Othello to Duke] *I crave fit disposition for my wife ... / With such accommodation and besort / As levels with her breeding*

levelled *(adj.)* targetted, directed, aimed **Lover** 22 [of the woman] *Sometimes her levelled eyes their carriage ride, / As they did batt'ry to the spheres intend*; **Tim** I.i.48

leviathan *(n.)* sea-monster, whale **MND** II.i.174 [Oberon to Puck] *be thou here again / Ere the leviathan can swim a league*; **H5** III.iii.26; **TG** III.ii.80

levied *(adj.)* raised, mustered, drawn up **1H6** IV.iv.31 [Lucy to Somerset, of York] *Swearing that you withhold his levied host / Collected for this expedition*; **1H6** IV.iv.23

levity *(n.)* licentiousness, wantonness, immorality **MM** V.i.220 [Angelo to Duke, of Mariana] *her reputation was disvalued / In levity*

levy *(n.)* recruitment of soldiers, conscription of men **Mac** III.ii.22 [Macbeth to Lady Macbeth, of the King] *Nor steel, nor poison, / Malice domestic, foreign levy, nothing / Can touch him further*; **Cor** V.vi.67; **Cym** III.viii.9; **Ham** II.ii.62

levy *(v.)* **1** enlist, conscript, muster **1H6** IV.iii.11 [Richard to all] *my promised supply / Of horsemen that were levied for this siege*; **AC** III.vi.67; **E3** II.i.30; **1H6** II.v.88; **KL** V.iii.104; **Tem** I.ii.128
2 [unclear meaning] level, purpose, intend **Per** II.v.50 [Pericles to Simonides] *Never did thought of mine levy offence*

lewd *(adj.)* **1** improper, unseemly **R2** I.i.90 [Bolingbroke to King Richard, of money given to Mowbray] *The which he hath detained for lewd employments*; **1H4** III.ii.13; **2H4** II.ii.58; **TS** IV.iii.65
2 wicked, vile, evil **1H6** III.i.15 [Gloucester to Winchester] *Thy lewd, pestiferous, and dissentious pranks*; **MA** V.i.317

3 ignorant, foolish, ill-mannered **R3** I.iii.61 [Richard to all, of King Edward] *you ... trouble him with lewd complaints*

4 lascivious, unchaste, lustful **R3** III.vii.71 [Buckingham to Lord Mayor, of Richard] *He is not lulling on a lewd love-bed*

lewdly *(adv.)* **1** wickedly, evilly, mischievously **2H6** II.i.162 [Buckingham to King, of the traitors] *A sort of naughty persons, lewdly bent;* **1H4** II.iv.416

2 stupidly, foolishly **TNK** IV.ii.35 [Emilia alone] *I have lied so lewdly / That women ought to beat me*

lewdness *(n.)* **1** foolishness, absurd behaviour **H8** I.iii.35 [Lovell to Lord Chamberlain, of French-influenced Englishmen back in France] *They may ... 'oui' away / The lag end of their lewdness*

2 obscenity, carnality, lascivious behaviour **Ham** I.v.54 [Ghost to Hamlet] *But virtue as it never will be moved, / Though lewdness court it in a shape of heaven*

lewdster *(n.)* debaucher, profligate, lascivious individual **MW** V.iii.21 [Mistress Page to Mistress Ford, of Falstaff] *Against such lewdsters and their lechery, / Those that betray them do no treachery*

lewd-tongued *(adj.)* foul-mouthed, scurrilous, abusive **WT** II.iii.171 [Leontes to Antigonus, of his command] *the fail / Of any point in't shall not only be / Death to thyself, but to thy lewd-tongued wife*

liable *(adj.)* **1** subject, legally bound **JC** II.ii.104 [Decius to Caesar] *reason to my love is liable;* **KJ** II.i.490, V.ii.101

2 legally belonging, in her ownership **E3** I.ii.46 [King David to Douglas, of the Countess's jewels] *Those are her own, still liable to her*

3 fitting, apt, suitable **KJ** IV.ii.226 [King John to Hubert] *Finding thee ... / Apt, liable to be employed in danger;* **LL** V.i.87

libbard *(n.)* leopard **LL** V.ii.544 [Boyet to all, of Costard] *With libbard's head on knee*

libel *(n.)* **1** false statement, damaging attack [on women] **TNK** V.i.101 [Palamon praying to Venus] *nor would [I] the libels read / Of liberal wits*

2 defamatory poster, slanderous leaflet **R3** I.i.33 [Richard alone] *Plots have I laid, inductions dangerous, / By drunken prophecies, libels, and dreams*

liberal *(adj.)* **1** overgenerous, licentious **MV** II.ii.172 [Bassanio to Gratiano, of his characteristics] *where thou art not known, why there they show / Something too liberal;* **MV** V.i.226; **Oth** III.iv.38; **TG** III.i.338

2 coarse, licentious, promiscuous **1H6** V.iv.82 [Warwick to all, of Pucelle] *It's sign she hath been liberal and free;* **Ham** IV.vii.170; **MA** IV.i.90; **Oth** II.i.161; **TNK** IV.i.102

3 free-and-easy, unrestrained **LL** V.ii.728 [Princess to King] *excuse or hide / The liberal opposition of our spirits*

4 indiscreet, imprudent **R2** II.i.229 [Ross to Northumberland] *My heart ... must break with silence / Ere't be disburdened with a liberal tongue*

5 noble, tasteful, refined **3H6** I.ii.43 [York to Edward, of Kentishmen] *they are ... / Witty, courteous, liberal, full of spirit;* **2H6** IV.vii.58; **LL** II.i.168

6 fanciful, lavish **Ham** V.ii.150 [Osrick to Hamlet] *Three of the carriages ... of very liberal conceit* [or: sense 5]

liberal *(adv.)* freely, unrestrainedly **Oth** V.ii.218 [Emilia to Iago] *I will speak as liberal as the north*

liberal arts the trivium [grammar, logic, rhetoric] and quadrivium [arithmetic, geometry, music, astronomy] **Tem** I.ii.73 [Prospero to Miranda, of Milan] *for the liberal arts / Without a parallel* ➤ **art** *(n.)* 1

liberal-conceited *(adj.)* lavishly ingenious **Ham** V.ii.159 [Hamlet to Osrick] *three liberal-conceited carriages*

libertine *(n.)* **1** debaucher, reprobate, dissolute **AY** II.vii.65 [Duke Senior to Jaques] *thou thyself hast been a libertine;* **MA** II.i.125

2 free spirit, unconfined wanderer **H5** I.i.48 [Canterbury to Ely, of King Henry] *when he speaks, / The air, a chartered libertine, is still*

liberty *(n.)* **1** unrestrained act, improper licence, reckless freedom **1H4** V.ii.71 [Hotspur to Vernon, of Prince Hal] *Never did I hear / Of any prince so wild a liberty;* **CE** I.ii.102; **Sonn** 41.1; **Tim** IV.i.25

2 liberation, deliverance **Ham** III.ii.346 [Rosencrantz to Hamlet] *You do surely bar the door upon your own liberty* [i.e. release from madness]

3 (plural) rights, prerogatives, privileges **Per** I.ii.112 [Pericles to Helicanus, of Antiochus] *should he wrong my liberties in my absence?;* **Cor** III.ii.214

4 permission, leave, consent **1H6** III.iv.42 [Basset to Vernon] *I'll ... crave / I may have liberty to venge this wrong*

5 plays not written according to traditional rules of drama; also: district not subject to a sheriff's legal order [i.e. more suitable for theatres] **Ham** II.ii.400 [Polonius to Hamlet, of the players] *For the law of writ and the liberty, these are the only men*

licence *(n.)* **1** authority to act, freedom of action **E3** IV.v.90 [King John to Charles] *thy licence lies in me;* **MM** II.iv.145

2 licentiousness, immorality, promiscuity **MM** III.ii.195 [Escalus to Mistress Overdone, of Lucio] *That fellow is a fellow of much licence*

lictor *(n.)* ➤ **ROMAN HISTORY**, p.377

lid *(n.)* ➤ **SWEARING**, p.435

lie *(n.)* accusation of lying, charge of falsehood **WT** V.ii.130 [Clown to Autolycus] *Give me the lie, do, and try whether I am not now a gentleman born;* **Ham** II.ii.571; **R2** IV.i.53 ➤ throat, lie in one's

lie *(v.)* **1** live, dwell, reside, lodge **TG** IV.ii.133 [disguised Julia to Host] *where lies Sir Proteus?;* **AW** III.v.30; **2H4** II.ii.270; **JC** III.i.286; **R2** III.iii.25; **TS** IV.iv.56

2 lie in prison, take the place [of] **R3** I.i.115 [Richard to Clarence] *I will deliver you, or else lie for you* [also: tell lies for]

3 be encamped, be quartered **1H6** I.ii.6 [Charles to all] *At pleasure here we lie, near Orleans*

4 sleep, go to bed **3H6** III.ii.69 [Edward to Lady Grey] *I aim to lie with thee;* **MV** V.i.262; **TN** III.i.8

5 hang, depend, hinge **TNK** II.ii.230 [Arcite to Palamon, of his love for Emilia] *if the lives of all my name lay on it;* **E3** III.iv.120; **TNK** III.vi.90

6 be obligatory, be incumbent **Cor** III.ii.52 [Volumnia to Coriolanus] *Because that now it lies you on to speak / To th'people* [i.e. incumbent on you]

lie, give the deceive; [wrestling] lay someone out; make urinate **Mac** II.iii.33 [Porter to Macduff, of drink] *it ... equivocates him in a sleep and giving him the lie, leaves him*

lie by *(v.)* settle down, lay to rest **H8** III.i.11 [Gentlewoman singing] *Even the billows of the sea, / Hung their heads, and then lay by*

lie low *(v.)* be killed, find oneself dead **MA** V.i.52 [Antonio to all, of Leonato] *If he could right himself with quarrelling, / Some of us would lie low*

lie under *(v.)* be subject to, suffer the consequence of **MA** IV.i.167 [Friar to Leonato, of Hero] *If this sweet lady lie not guiltless here / Under some biting error;* **TC** II.i.134

lief *(adj.)* dear, beloved, cherished **2H6** III.i.164 [Gloucester to Queen, of the King] *you ... have stirred up / My liefest liege to be mine enemy*

lief, had as should like just as much **AY** I.i.136 [Oliver to Charles, of Orlando] *I had as lief thou didst break his neck as his finger* ➤ **FEW**, p.xxi

liege *(n.)* lord, sovereign **AY** I.ii.146 [Rosalind to Duke Frederick] *Ay, my liege, so please you* ➤ **ADDRESS FORMS**, p.8

liegeman *(n.)* vassal, subject, follower **E3** I.i.64 [Lorraine to King Edward] *Thou mayst be sworn true liegeman to our king;* **Ham** I.i.15; **1H4** II.iv.331; **1H6** V.iv.128; **WT** II.iii.173

lieger, leiger (*n.*) resident ambassador, representative, envoy **Cym** I.vi.80 [Queen alone, of Pisanio and Innogen] *I have given him that, / Which if he take, shall quite unpeople her / Of liegers for her sweet* [i.e. remove all those who represent her husband]; **MM** III.i.62 [Isabella to Claudio, of his going to heaven] *Where you shall be an everlasting leiger*

lieu of, in (*prep.*) in return for, in recompense for **AY** II.iii.65 [Orlando to Adam] *thou prunest a rotten tree / That cannot so much as a blossom yield / In lieu of all thy pains and husbandry*

lieu whereof, in in recompense for this **KJ** V.iv.44 [Melun to Pembroke, Salisbury, and Bigot, of his warning] *In lieu whereof, I pray you bear me hence*

lieutenantry (*n.*) use of subordinates, office of lieutenants **AC** III.xi.39 [Antony to Eros, of Octavius] *He alone / Dealt on lieutenantry*; **Oth** II.i.169

life (*n.*) **1** living being, person **MA** IV.i.224 [Friar to Leonato, of Hero] *every lovely organ of her life / Shall come apparelled in more precious habit*; **2H4** I.i.141

2 means of life, way of survival **2H4** V.v.69 [King Henry V to Falstaff] *For competence of life I will allow you, / That lack of means enforce you not to evils*; **Cym** V.iii.45

3 continued existence, survival **Ham** V.ii.22 [Hamlet to Horatio] *such bugs and goblins in my life* [i.e. if I should be allowed to live]

☛ SWEARING, p.435

4 energy, spirit, liveliness **Tem** III.iii.87 [Prospero to Ariel] *with good life / And observation strange, my meaner ministers / Their several kinds have done*; **AC** I.ii.191

5 ☛ give life

life, for one's of a capital nature **2H4** I.ii.134 [Lord Chief Justice to Falstaff] *I sent for you, when there were matters against you for your life*

life, to the convincingly, in a faithful manner **Cor** III.ii.106 [Coriolanus to Volumnia] *You have put me now to such a part which never / I shall discharge to th'life*

lifelings (*n.*) **☛ SWEARING**, p.435

life-rendering (*adj.*) life-giving [to its young], self-sacrificing **Ham** IV.v.148 [Laertes to Claudius, of Polonius' friends] *like the kind life-rendering pelican / Repast them with my blood*

lifter (*n.*) thief **TC** I.ii.118 [Cressida to Pandarus, of Troilus] *Is he so young a man, and so old a lifter* [pun: 117, capable of lifting weights]

lifting up (*n.*) dawning, arrival, arising **2H4** IV.iv.93 [King Henry IV to Westmorland] *thou art a summer bird, / Which ever in the haunch of winter sings / The lifting up of day*

liggens (*n.*) **☛ SWEARING**, p.435

light (*n.*) **1** ability to see clearly, power of vision **TG** II.i.68 [Speed to Valentine] *[if only] your own eyes had the lights they were wont to have*

2 inkling, foresight, glimmering **KJ** IV.iii.61 [Salisbury to Bastard, of Arthur's apparent murder] *We had a kind of light what would ensue*

3 sign, signal, indication **TN** V.i.334 [Malvolio to Olivia] *tell me ... / Why you have given me such clear lights of favour?*

4 help, enlightenment, information **TG** III.i.49 [Duke to Proteus, of Valentine] *he shall never know / That I had any light from thee of this*

5 (plural) eyes **Cym** II.ii.21 [Iachimo to himself, of Innogen] *under-peep her lids, / To see th'enclosed lights*

light (*adj.*) **1** promiscuous, licentious, immoral, wanton **LL** IV.iii.361 [Berowne alone] *Light wenches may prove plagues to men forsworn*; **CE** IV.iii.52; **E3** II.ii.91; **2H4** II.iv.290; **MA** III.iv.41; **MM** V.i.278

2 joyful, merry, light-hearted **RJ** IV.ii.46 [Capulet to Lady Capulet] *My heart is wondrous light*; **Cym** V.iv.165; **2H4** IV.ii.85; **LL** V.ii.15; **Luc** 1434; **TS** II.i.203

3 easy, ready, effortless **Tem** I.ii.452 [Prospero to himself, of Ferdinand meeting Miranda] *this swift business / I must uneasy make, lest too light winning / Make the prize light* [first instance; second instance: sense 5]

4 minor, slight, of little value **Tem** I.ii.490 [Ferdinand to himself, of Prospero] *this man's threats / To whom I am subdued, are but light to me*; **Ham** IV.vi.25; **H5** II.ii.89; **R2** II.iv.86

5 [of counterfeit coins] of less weight, worthless, cheap **Oth** II.iii.168 [Othello to all] *He that stirs next ... / Holds his soul light*; **Cym** V.iv.25; **2H4** I.ii.167; **Oth** II.iii.271 [Q]; **RJ** II.vi.20; **Tem** I.ii.453

6 facile, frivolous, of no consequence **RJ** II.ii.99 [Juliet to Romeo] *thou mayst think my 'haviour light*; **AC** I.ii.177; **AW** II.ii.82; **KL** III.iv.89; **LL** V.ii.19; **TN** V.i.337

light (*v.*) **1** alight, descend, fall, come to rest **Per** IV.ii.68 [Bawd to Marina] *You are light into my hands*; **Ham** III.vi.60, V.ii.349; **KL** III.iv.65; **2H6** I.iii.88; **MV** IV.i.38

2 dismount, descend, alight **1H4** I.i.63 [King Henry to Westmorland, of Blunt] *new lighted from his horse*; **H8** I.i.9; **JC** V.iii.31; **R2** I.i.82

3 give light to, show the way to **Mac** V.v.22 [Macbeth to himself] *all our yesterdays have lighted fools / The way to dusty death*

light (*adv.*) **1** slightly, as of little value **Sonn** 88.1 *When thou shalt be disposed to set me light*

2 lightly, without heavy equipment **TC** I.ii.8 [Alexander to Cressida, of Hector] *Before the sun rose he was harnessed light* [or: quickly]

light on (*v.*) come across, meet with, chance upon **TS** I.i.110 [Gremio to Hortensio, of Bianca] *if I can by any means light on a fit man to teach her*; **KL** III.i.54; **TS** I.i.127, ii.165

lighten (*v.*) **1** flash lightning **1H6** I.iv.97 [stage direction] *it thunders and lightens*

2 enlighten, send spiritual illumination to **2H4** II.i.193 [Lord Chief Justice to Falstaff] *the Lord lighten thee, thou art a great fool*

lighten forth (*v.*) flash out, send down as lightning **R2** III.iii.69 [York to all, of Richard] *his eye ... lightens forth / Controlling majesty*

light-foot (*adj.*) light-footed **R3** IV.iv.440 [King Richard to Ratcliffe] *Some light-foot friend post to the Duke of Norfolk*

lightless (*adj.*) dark, hidden, yielding no light **Luc** 1555 [Lucrece to herself, of a painting of Sinon] *Such devils steal effects from lightless hell*; **Luc** 4

lightly (*adv.*) **1** readily, easily **H5** II.ii.89 [King Henry to all, of Cambridge] *this man / Hath, for a few light crowns, lightly conspired*; **CE** IV.iv.5; **TG** III.i.142

2 commonly, often, invariably **R3** III.i.94 [Richard to himself, of Prince Edward] *Short summers lightly have a forward spring*

3 slightly, in small degree **Cor** IV.i.29 [Coriolanus to Volumnia] *Believe't not lightly*

lightness (*n.*) **1** irresponsibility, levity, frivolity, fickleness **3H6** III.i.88 [King to Keepers, of a feather] *Such is the lightness of you common men*; **AC** I.iv.25; **TS** IV.ii.24

2 lewdness, wantonness, licentiousness **MM** II.ii.170 [Angelo alone] *Can it be / That modesty may more betray our sense / Than woman's lightness*; **2H4** I.ii.45

3 lightheadedness, faintness, dizziness **Ham** II.ii.149 [Polonius to Claudius and Gertrude, of Hamlet] *Fell ... into a weakness, / Thence to a lightness*

like (*n.*) identity, equivalent, counterpart **AW** I.i.219 [Helena alone] *The mightiest space in fortune nature brings / To join like likes* [i.e. to bring together people of the same kind]; **Cym** I.i.21

like (*adj.*) **1** same, similar, alike, equal **Ham** IV.vii.115 [Claudius to Laertes] *And nothing is at a like goodness still* **☛ FEW**, p.xxi

2 like-minded, harmonious **Tim** I.ii.102 [Timon to lords] *what a precious comfort 'tis to have so many like brothers commanding one another's fortunes!*

like *(v.)* **1** please, suit **TG** IV.ii.54 [Host to disguised Julia] *The music likes you not;* **Ham** V.ii.259; **H8** V.iii.148; **KL** II.ii.88; **R3** III.iv.49; **Tem** IV.i.239 ☛ **POLITENESS**, p.340

2 love **TS** II.i.267 [Petruchio to Katherina] *Thy beauty that doth make me like thee well;* **CE** III.ii.7

3 find, think of **TNK** V.ii.101 [Gaoler to Doctor, of the Gaoler's Daughter] *How did you like her?* [i.e. her medical condition]

4 resemble, look like, take after **3H6** V.vi.82 [Richard alone] *this word 'love' … / Be resident in men like one another / And not in me* [i.e. in men who resemble one another]

5 liken, make like, make resemble **1H6** IV.vi.48 [John Talbot to Talbot] *like me to the peasant boys of France;* **2H4** II.i.88

6 thrive, look, do **2H4** III.ii.83 [Shallow to Falstaff] *you like well, and bear your years very well*

7 be impressed [by], make a choice **Ham** IV.iii.5 [Claudius to his attendants] *the distracted multitude, / Who like not in their judgement but their eyes*

like of *(v.)* admire, enjoy, derive pleasure from **Tem** III.i.57 [Miranda to Ferdinand] *Nor can imagination form a shape, / Besides yourself, to like of;* **LL** I.i.107

like *(adv.)* **1** likely, probable / probably **Ham** II.ii.152 [Gertrude to Claudius, agreeing] *It may be, very like* ☛ **FEW**, p.xxi

2 alike, in the same way, identically **Sonn** 132.12 *And suit thy pity like in every part*

3 equally, similarly, also **Tem** III.iii.67 [Ariel to Alonso, Sebastian, and Antonio] *My fellow ministers / Are like invulnerable;* **CE** I.i.83

4 nearly, almost **AY** V.iv.46 [Touchstone to all] *I have had four quarrels, and like to have fought one* [i.e. came near to fighting one]

like, great very likely **2H6** III.i.379 [York alone, of Cade] *Say that he thrive, as 'tis great like he will*

like as *(conj.)* as if **Ham** I.i.217 [Horatio to Hamlet, of the Ghost] *It … did address / Itself to motion like as it would speak*

likelihood *(n.)* **1** future, promise, potential **1H4** III.ii.45 [King Henry to Prince Hal] *And left me … / A fellow of no mark nor likelihood*

2 indication, sign, ground **Oth** I.iii.108 [Duke to Brabantio, of the arguments against Othello] *these thin habits and poor likelihoods / Of modern seeming*

3 likely outcome, probability **1H4** I.i.58 [Westmorland to King Henry, of the two sides] *by discharge of their artillery, / And shape of likelihood, the news was told* [i.e. the way events were shaping]

likely *(adj.)* promising, hopeful; or: seemly, good-looking **MV** II.ix.92 [Messenger to Portia, of Bassanio's messenger] *I have not seen / So likely an ambassador of love*

likeness *(n.)* appearance, look **KL** I.iv.4 [Kent alone] *my good intent / May carry through itself to that full issue / For which I razed my likeness*

liking *(n.)* **1** desire, will, pleasure **Venus** 248 [of Adonis' dimples] *these round enchanting pits, / Opened their mouths to swallow Venus' liking;* **2H6** III.ii.252

2 approving, consent, acquiescence **WT** IV.iv.530 [Camillo to Florizel] *Your discontenting father [I'll] strive to qualify, / And bring him up to liking*

3 bodily shape, good condition **MW** II.i.53 [Mistress Ford to Mistress Page] *I shall think the worse of fat men as long as I have an eye to make difference of men's liking;* **1H4** III.iii.5 ☛ **well-liking** *(adj.)*

4 lustful affection, sexual attraction **Per** I.Chorus.25 [Gower alone, of Antiochus' daughter] *With whom the father liking took*

lily *(adj.)* lily-white **Tit** II.iv.44 [Marcus to Lavinia] *those lily hands;* **Luc** 386

lily-tincture *(n.)* lily-white colouring **TG** IV.iv.152 [disguised Julia to Silvia, of Julia] *air hath … pinched the lily-tincture of her face*

limb *(n.)* **1** member, branch **2H4** V.ii.135 [King Henry V to his brothers] *let us choose such limbs of noble counsel*

2 functioning organ, strength of limb **MM** III.i.37 [disguised Duke to Claudio, of being old] *Thou hast neither heat, affection, limb, nor beauty*

limbeck *(n.)* retort, distilling apparatus, alembic **Sonn** 119.2 *Siren tears / Distilled from limbecks foul as hell within;* **Mac** I.vii.67

limber *(adj.)* limp, floppy, weak **WT** I.ii.47 [Hermione to Polixenes] *You put me off with limber vows*

limb-meal *(adv.)* limb from limb, to pieces **Cym** II.iv.147 [Posthumus to Philario, of Innogen] *O, that I had her here, to tear her limb-meal!*

limbo *(n.)* prison, confinement, incarceration **CE** IV.ii.32 [Dromio of Syracuse to Adriana, of Antipholus of Ephesus] *He's in Tartar limbo*

limbo patrum [Latin: temporary home of departed spirits between heaven and hell] gaol, imprisonment **H8** V.iv.63 [Man to Porter, of the attacking youths] *I have some of 'em in Limbo Patrum*

lime *(n.)* **1** birdlime **Mac** IV.ii.36 [Macduff's wife to her son] *Poor bird, thou'dst never fear / The net nor lime;* **Tem** IV.i.245; **TG** III.ii.68 ☛ **birdlime** *(n.)*

2 lime-juice [added to wine to improve its sparkle] **1H4** II.iv.120 [Falstaff to Francis] *here's lime in this sack too*

lime *(v.)* **1** trap, snare, catch [as if by using birdlime] **3H6** V.vi.13 [King to Richard] *The bird that hath been limed in a bush, / With trembling wings misdoubteth every bush;* **AW** III.v.23; **3H6** V.vi.17; **Luc** 88; **MA** III.i.104; **TN** III.iv.75

2 add birdlime to **2H6** I.iii.86 [Suffolk to Queen, of the Duchess of Gloucester] *myself have limed a bush for her* [i.e. set a trap]; **2H6** II.iv.54

3 cement, bind, fuse **3H6** V.i.84 [George to Warwick] *I will not ruinate my father's house, / Who gave his blood to lime the stones together*

4 mix wine with lime [to add to its sparkle] **MW** I.iii.14 [Host to Bardolph] *Let me see thee froth and lime* [Q; F *liue*]

limed *(adj.)* trapped, ensnared [as with birdlime] **Ham** III.iii.68 [Claudius alone] *O limed soul* ☛ **birdlime** *(n.)*

limekiln *(n.)* limestone-like deposit, white lump **TC** V.i.20 [Thersites to Patroclus] *the rotten diseases of the south … limekilns i'th' palm* [in Q only]

lime-twig *(n.)* twig smeared with birdlime **2H6** III.iii.16 [Cardinal as if to Death, of Gloucester's hair] *Like lime-twigs set to catch my winged soul* ☛ **birdlime** *(n.);* twig *(n.)*

limit *(n.)* **1** prescribed time, fixed period **R3** III.iii.7 [Ratcliffe to all] *The limit of your lives is out;* **E3** IV.iv.147; **MM** III.i.217; **R2** I.iii.151; **WT** III.ii.105

2 permitted extent, bounds [of allegiance] **1H4** IV.iii.39 [Blunt to Hotspur] *out of limit and true rule / You stand against anointed majesty*

3 delimited territory, precinct, bounded region **1H4** III.i.69 [Mortimer to all, of the map] *The Archdeacon hath divided it / Into three limits very equally;* **Sonn** 44.4; **Venus** 235

4 ground, territory **AW** I.i.139 [Parolles to Helena] *virginity … should be buried in highways out of all sanctified limit*

5 bank, edge, boundary **R2** III.ii.109 [Scroop to Richard, comparing a river] *So high above his limits swells the rage / Of Bolingbroke*

6 duty, assignment, responsibility **1H4** I.i.35 [Westmorland to King Henry, of the expedition] *this haste was hot in question, / And many limits of the charge set down*

limit *(v.)* appoint, specify, fix the limit of **CE** I.i.151 [Duke to Egeon] *I'll limit thee this day / To seek thy health by beneficial help;* **R3** V.iii.25

limitation *(n.)* allotted time, appointed period **Cor** II.iii.138 [Menenius to Coriolanus] *You have stood your limitation;* **JC** II.i.283

limited *(adj.)* **1** appointed, designated, nominated **Mac** II.iii.49 [Macduff to Macbeth, of waking the King] *I'll make so bold to call, / For 'tis my limited service;* **KJ** V.ii.123; **MM** IV.ii.161

2 with exclusive membership, limited-entry Tim IV.iii.430 [Timon to Bandits] *there is boundless theft / In limited professions*

limiter *(n.)* arbiter, judge [of the limits of life] TNK V.i.30 [Arcite to Palamon] *hoist we / The sails, that must these vessels port even where / The heavenly limiter pleases*

limn out *(v.)* paint, draw, portray Venus 290 *Look when a painter would surpass the life / In limning out a well-proportioned steed*

limned *(v.)* portrayed, reproduced, painted AY II.vii.198 [Duke Senior to Orlando, of his father] *mine eye doth his effigies witness / Most truly limned and living in your face*

line *(n.)* **1** degree, rank, station TC I.iii.88 [Ulysses to all, of the heavens] *Observe ... / Insisture, course, proportion, season, form, / Office, and custom, in all line of order;* 1H4 I.iii.166; 1H4 III.ii.85

2 line of descent, lineage, pedigree H5 II.iv.88 [Exeter to French King, of King Henry] *He sends you this most memorable line*

3 derived power, scope, warrant MM I.iv.56 [Lucio to Isabella, of the Duke] *Upon his place, / And with full line of his authority, / Governs Lord Angelo*

4 conduct, way of behaving, course of action MW IV.ii.20 [Mistress Page to Mistress Ford] *your husband is in his old lines again*

5 lineament, distinctive feature AW V.iii.49 [Bertram to King, of a woman's face] *Which warped the line of every other favour;* Cym IV.ii.104

6 prepared written statement 1H6 III.i.1 [Winchester to Gloucester] *Comest thou with deep premeditated lines?*

7 stroke, paint, lines of makeup E3 III.iii.81 [King Edward to King John] *with a strumpet's artificial line / To paint thy vicious and deformed cause*

8 equator H8 V.iv.43 [Man to Porter, of a brass-worker] *all that stand about him are under the line*

9 lime tree, linden tree Tem IV.i.193 [Prospero to Ariel, carrying clothes] *hang them on this line;* Tem IV.i.235

line and level, by very methodically, with great precision Tem IV.i.239 [Trinculo to Stephano] *We steal by line and level*

line *(v.)* **1** strengthen, support, fortify 1H4 II.iii.86 [Lady Percy to Hotspur] *my brother Mortimer ... hath sent for you / To line his enterprise;* 2H4 I.iii.27; H5 II.iv.7; Mac I.iii.111; TNK IV.ii.127

2 draw, sketch, delineate AY III.ii.88 [Rosalind reading] *All the pictures fairest lined / Are but black to Rosalind*

3 cram, stuff, fill AY II.vii.155 [Jaques to all] *the justice, ... with good capon lined*

4 be given a lining AY III.ii.101 [Touchstone to Rosalind] *Wintered garments must be lined* [also: copulate (of dogs)]

lineal *(adj.)* lineally descended, in the direct line, hereditary KJ V.vii.102 [Bastard to Prince Henry] *may your sweet self put on / The lineal state and glory of the land!;* E3 I.i.36; 2H4 IV.v.47; H5 I.ii.82; KJ II.i.85; R2 III.iii.113

lineament *(n.)* **1** line, feature, characteristic, attribute MA V.i.14 [Leonato to Antonio] *In every lineament, branch, shape, and form;* MV III.iv.15; RJ I.iii.84

2 (plural) parts of the body, form, shape TNK IV.ii.113 [Pirithous to Theseus, of one of Palamon's knights] *all his lineaments / Are as a man would wish 'em*

3 personal appearance, distinctive quality R2 III.i.9 [Bolingbroke to Bushy and Green] *You have misled ... / A happy gentleman in blood and lineaments*

lined *(adj.)* filled, stuffed Tim IV.i.14 [Timon alone] *Son of sixteen, / Pluck the lined crutch from thy old limping sire;* TNK II.i.5

line-grove *(n.)* grove of lime trees Tem V.i.10 [Ariel to Prospero] *In the line-grove which weather-fends your cell*

linen *(adj.)* pale, pallid, bleached Mac V.iii.16 [Macbeth to Servant] *Those linen cheeks of thine / Are counsellors to fear*

ling, old [person resembling] salted cod AW III.ii.13 [Clown to Countess] *Our old lings ... o'th' country are nothing like your old ling ... o'th' court*

linger *(v.)* **1** delay, put off, keep waiting MND I.i.4 [Theseus to Hippolyta, of the moon] *She lingers my desires;* TC V.x.9

2 prolong, draw out, extend Oth IV.ii.224 [Iago to Roderigo, of Othello] *he goes into Mauritania ... unless his abode be lingered here by some accident;* R2 II.ii.72

3 stay on [in town], wait around MW III.ii.52 [Shallow to all] *We have lingered about a match between Anne Page and my cousin Slender*

linger out *(v.)* prolong, draw out Sonn 90.8 *Give not a windy night a rainy morrow, / To linger out a purposed overthrow*

lingering *(adj.)* long-drawn-out, protracted, lengthy 1H6 I.i.74 [Messenger to all, of the generals] *One would have lingering wars with little cost;* 2H4 I.i.156

lining *(n.)* material which lies inside, contents R2 I.iv.61 [King Richard to Bushy, of John of Gaunt] *The lining of his coffers shall make coats / To deck our soldiers*

link *(n.)* **1** light, lamp, flare 1H4 III.iii.42 [Falstaff to Bardolph, of Bardolph's nose] *Thou hast saved me a thousand marks in links and torches*

2 blacking [from a burnt torch] TS IV.i.120 [Grumio to Petruchio] *There was no link to colour Peter's hat*

linsey-woolsey *(n.)* [mix of flax and wool] verbal mish-mash, nonsense AW IV.i.11 [First Lord to First Soldier] *what linsey-woolsey hast thou to speak to us again?*

linstock *(n.)* stick holding a lit match for firing a cannon H5 III.Chorus.33 [Chorus alone] *the nimble gunner / With linstock now the devilish cannon touches;* 1H6 I.iv.57

lip *(v.)* kiss AC II.v.30 [Cleopatra to Messenger, of her hand] *that kings / Have lipped;* Oth IV.i.71

lip, bite one's make an angry facial gesture Cor V.i.49 [Menenius to Sicinius, of Coriolanus] *Yet to bite his lip / And hum at good Cominius much unhearts me*

lip, hang the look vexed, pout, sulk TC III.i.136 [Helen to Paris, of Pandarus (or Troilus)] *He hangs the lip at something*

lip, make a curl a lip, mock, sneer Cor II.i.110 [Menenius to Virgilia] *I will make a lip at the physician*

Lipsbury *(n.)* [unclear meaning; perhaps: 'lips-town'] space between the lips, jaws KL II.ii.8 [disguised Kent to Oswald] *If I had thee in Lipsbury pinfold I would make thee care for me* [i.e. trapped between my teeth]

liquor *(n.)* **1** [alcoholic] drink Ham V.i.60 [First Clown to Second Clown] *fetch me a stoup of liquor;* AY II.iii.49; 2H4 III.i.53; Tem V.i.280

2 liquid Tit V.ii.198 [Titus to Lavinia, of Chiron's and Demetrius' blood] *Let me go grind their bones to powder small, / And with this hateful liquor temper it;* H8 I.i.144; Tem II.ii.21

liquor *(v.)* **1** grease, oil MW IV.v.90 [Falstaff to himself] *If it should come to the ear of the court how I have been transformed ... they would ... liquor fishermen's boots with me*

2 lubricate, make drunk 1H4 II.i.86 [Gadshill to Chamberlain, of the commonwealth] *justice hath liquored her* [also: sense 1; bribe]

liquorish *(adj.)* pleasantly tasting, appetising Tim IV.iii.195 [Timon alone, of the earth's produce] *Whereof ingrateful man with liquorish draughts / And morsels unctuous greases his pure mind*

lisp *(v.)* **1** talk in an affected way, speak with affectation LL V.ii.323 [Berowne to all, of Boyet] *'A can carve too, and lisp;* Ham III.i.145

2 talk in a loving voice 2H4 II.iv.261 [Poins to Prince Henry, of Bardolph] *look whether the fiery trigon his man be not lisping to his master's old tables*

3 put on a foreign accent AY IV.i.30 [Rosalind as Ganymede to Jaques] *Look you lisp and wear strange suits*

list *(n.)* **1** (usually plural) combat arena at a tournament R2 I.iii.32 [Lord Marshal to Bolingbroke] *wherefore comest thou hither / Before King Richard in his royal lists?;* 1H6 V.v.32; 2H6 II.iii.50; Mac III.i.70; Per I.i.62; Venus 595

2 muster, troop, band, recruitment **KL** V.iii.110 [Herald to all] *If any man of quality or degree within the lists of the army*; **Ham** I.i.98, ii.32

3 boundary, limit, confines **1H4** IV.i.51 [Hotspur to all, of using all their forces at once] *therein should we read … / The very list, the very utmost bound / Of all our fortunes*; **AW** II.i.51; **Ham** IV.v.101; **H5** V.ii.267; **MM** I.i.6; **Oth** IV.i.75

4 limit, objective **TN** III.i.75 [Viola as Cesario to Sir Toby, of Olivia] *she is the list of my voyage*

5 wish, desire, inclination **Oth** II.i.104 [Iago to Desdemona, of Emilia's speech] *I find it still when I have list to sleep*

6 cloth edging, border material **MM** I.ii.33 [First Gentleman to Lucio] *I had as lief be a list of an English kersey as be piled*; **MM** I.ii.29; **TS** III.ii.66

list (*v.*) **1** wish, like, please **MA** III.iv.75 [Margaret to Beatrice] *I am not such a fool to think what I list*; **E3** IV.v.93; **1H6** I.v.22; **Luc** 1008; **Tem** III.ii.16; **TS** IV.v.7

2 listen **Ham** I.v.22 [Ghost to Hamlet] *List, list, O, list!*; **2H6** I.iii.90; **KJ** II.i.468; **TC** V.iii.18; **TS** II.i.356; **WT** IV.iv.538

3 listen to, pay attention to **R2** I.iii.124 [Richard to all] *list what with our council we have done*; **Cor** I.iv.20; **E3** I.ii.17; **Ham** I.iii.30; **KL** V.iii.179; **Oth** II.i.211

4 care, choose, desire **WT** IV.i.26 [Time to audience, of Perdita] *What of her ensues / I list not prophesy*; **TS** III.ii.164

listen (*v.*) listen to, pay attention to, hear **JC** IV.i.41 [Antony to Octavius] *Listen great things*; **R2** II.i.9

listen after (*v.*) look out for, keep a watch on **2H6** I.iii.147 [Buckingham to Cardinal] *I will … listen after Humphrey, how he proceeds*; **2H4** I.i.29

lither (*adj.*) yielding, submissive, compliant **1H6** IV.vii.21 [Talbot to Servant] *Two Talbots, winged through the lither sky, … shall 'scape mortality*

litigious (*adj.*) quarrelsome, contentious, marred by disputes **Per** III.iii.3 [Pericles to Cleon] *Tyrus stands / In a litigious peace*

litter (*n.*) **1** [transportable] bed, couch **KJ** V.iii.16 [King John to his servants] *To my litter straight; / Weakness possesseth me, and I am faint*; **E3** IV.vii.61; **KL** III.vi.88

2 animal straw, rushes, bedding **KJ** V.ii.140 [Bastard to Lewis the Dauphin, of French reaction to English power] *To crouch in litter of your stable planks*

litter (*v.*) [comparing humans to animals] bring forth, be born **Tem** I.ii.282 [Prospero to Ariel, of Caliban and Sycorax] *the son that she did litter here*; **Cor** III.i.238; **WT** IV.iii.25

little (*n.*) small achievement, slight accomplishments **Cor** I.ix.51 [Martius to all] *As if I loved my little should be dieted / In praises sauced with lies*

little, in on a small scale, in miniature **TN** III.iv.85 [Sir Toby to Fabian, of Malvolio] *If all the devils of hell be drawn in little … yet I'll speak to him*; **AY** III.ii.136; **Ham** II.ii.365; **Lover** 90

little, in a in brief, shortly **H8** II.i.11 [First Gentleman to Second Gentleman, of Buckingham's trial] *I'll tell you in a little*

little (*adj.*) **1** in little, microcosmic, miniature **R2** II.i.45 [John of Gaunt to York, of England] *this little world*

2 [of voices] small, tiny **MND** III.i.121 [Bottom singing to himself] *The wren with little quill*

3 thin, lean, skinny **TG** V.ii.5 [Proteus to Thurio, of Thurio's leg] *it is too little*

little-seeming (*adj.*) [difficult meaning] of no account; or: who refuses to acknowledge appearances **KL** I.i.198 [Lear to Burgundy, of Cordelia] *that little-seeming substance*

live (*adj.*) ☛ well to live (*adj.*)

live (*v.*) **1** be active, live on, make a home **1H4** V.ii.20 [Worcester to Vernon, of Hotspur] *All his offences live upon my head*

2 stay afloat, avoid destruction **TN** I.ii.14 [Captain to Viola] *a strong mast, that lived upon the sea*

liveless (*adj.*) spelling variant of 'lifeless' **AY** I.ii.240 [Orlando to Rosalind and Celia] *that which here stands up / Is but a quintain, a mere liveless block* [F *liuelesse*]

livelihood (*n.*) liveliness, animation, vivacity **Venus** 26 [of Adonis] *his sweating palm, / The precedent of pith and livelihood*; **AW** I.i.49; **R3** III.iv.55

lively (*adj.*) **1** living, breathing **Tit** III.i.105 [Titus to Lavinia, of his reaction if he had seen her plight in a picture] *what shall I do, / Now I behold thy lively body so?*

2 life-giving, enlivening, invigorating **Venus** 498 [Venus to Adonis] *But now I died, and death was lively joy*

3 lifelike, striking, vivid **AY** V.iv.27 [Duke Senior to all] *I do remember in this shepherd boy / Some lively touches of my daughter's favour*

liver (*n.*) **1** part of the body thought to be at the seat of the passions [especially sexual desire] **MV** III.ii.86 [Bassanio to himself, of cowards] *have livers white as milk*; **AY** III.ii.403; **1H4** II.iv.316; **Luc** 47; **MA** IV.i.229; **TN** II.i.38

2 living creature, inhabitant, being **Cym** III.iv.142 [Innogen to Pisanio] *prithee think / There's livers out of Britain*

livery (*n.*) **1** uniform, costume, special clothing **2H6** IV.ii.70 [Cade to all, of when he is king] *I will apparel them all in one livery* ☛ FEW, p.xxi

2 badge, token, recognizable image **MV** II.i.2 [Morocco to Portia, of his complexion] *The shadowed livery of the burnished sun*

3 service, following, entourage **AC** V.ii.90 [Cleopatra to Dolabella, of Antony] *In his livery / Walked crowns and crownets*

4 ☛ sue one's livery

livery (*v.*) array in a livery, dress up **Lover** 105 [of the man] *His rudeness so with his authorized youth, / Did livery falseness in a pride of truth*

living (*n.*) possessions, means of support, livelihood **MV** V.i.286 [Antonio to Portia] *you have given me life and living*; **KL** I.iv.107; **MV** III.ii.156; **Tim** I.ii.225, IV.iii.520; **WT** IV.iii.95

living (*adj.*) real, genuine, not put on **AY** III.ii.400 [Rosalind as Ganymede to Orlando] *I drave my suitor from his mad humour of love to a living humour of madness*

lo (*int.*) ☛ ATTENTION SIGNALS, p.26

loach (*n.*) type of small fish **1H4** II.i.22 [Second Carrier to First Carrier] *your chamber-lye breeds fleas like a loach*

load (*n.*) burden, imputation **JC** IV.i.20 [Antony to Octavius, of Lepidus] *we lay these honours on this man, / To ease ourselves of divers slanderous loads*

loaden (*adj.*) laden, weighed down **H8** IV.ii.2 [Katherine to Griffith] *My legs like loaden branches bow to th'earth*

loathly (*adj.*) loathsome, hateful., disgusting **2H4** IV.iv.122 [Gloucester to all] *The people … do observe / Unfathered heirs and loathly births of nature*; **Tem** IV.i.21

loathly (*adv.*) with such loathing, with detestation **KL** II.i.48 [Edmund to Gloucester, of Edgar] *Seeing how loathly opposite I stood / To his unnatural purpose*

loathness (*n.*) **1** loathing, repulsion, dislike **Tem** II.i.132 [Sebastian to Alonso, of Alonso's daughter] *Weighed between loathness and obedience*

2 unwillingness, reluctance, disinclination **AC** III.xi.18 [Antony to attendants] *look not sad, / Nor make replies of loathness*

lob (*n.*) clown, country lout, yokel **MND** II.i.16 [Fairy to Puck] *Farewell, thou lob of spirits*

lob down (*v.*) hang, droop, sag **H5** IV.ii.45 [Grandpré to all, of the English army] *their poor jades / Lob down their heads*

lobby (*n.*) ante-room, corridor **Tim** I.i.83 [Poet to Painter, of Timon's associates in his poem] *his lobbies fill with tendance* ☛ voiding lobby (*n.*)

lock (*n.*) shackle, hobble, fetter **Cym** V.iv.1 [First Gaoler to Posthumus] *you have locks upon you*; **Cym** V.iv.8

lock (v.) keep captive, keep away, detain **Tim** I.ii.252 [Apemantus to Timon] *I'll lock thy heaven from thee;* **TNK** I.i.176

lock forth (v.) lock out, lock the door against **CE** IV.iv.93 [Antipholus of Ephesus to Adriana] *wherefore didst thou lock me forth today?*

lockram (n.) type of Breton linen fabric **Cor** II.i.201 [Brutus to Sicinius] *The kitchen malkin pins / Her richest lockram 'bout her reechy neck*

locust (n.) [unclear meaning] fruit of the carob tree, locust-bean **Oth** I.iii.344 [Iago to Roderigo, of Othello] *The food that to him now is as luscious as locusts shall be to him shortly as acerbe as the coloquintida*

lodestar (n.) guiding star, beacon **MND** I.i.183 [Helena to Hermia] *Your eyes are lodestars;* **Luc** 179

lodge (v.) 1 sleep, lie, remain **2H6** I.i.78 [Gloucester to all, of Henry V] *Did he so often lodge in open field;* **3H6** I.i.32, IV.iii.13
2 beat down, flatten, make level **Mac** IV.i.54 [Macbeth to Witches] *Though bladed corn be lodged and trees blown down;* **2H6** III.ii.176; **R2** III.iii.162
3 harbour, entertain, foster **2H4** IV.v.207 [King Henry IV to Prince Henry, of his supporters] *by whose power I well might lodge a fear / To be again displaced;* **R3** I.i.66

lodged (adj.) deep-rooted, inveterate, ingrained **MV** IV.i.60 [Shylock to Duke] *a lodged hate and a certain loathing / I bear Antonio*

lodging (n.) room, chamber, living quarters **R2** I.ii.68 [Duchess of Gloucester to John of Gaunt, of Pleshey] *what shall good old York there see / But empty lodgings*

loggats (n.) type of game [in which sticks are thrown to lie near a target stake] **Ham** V.i.91 [Hamlet to Horatio] *Did these bones cost no more the breeding but to play at loggats with them?*

loggerhead (n.) blockhead, numbskull, dolt **LL** IV.iii.202 [Berowne to Costard] *you whoreson loggerhead;* **1H4** II.iv.4; **RJ** IV.iv.21

logger-headed (adj.) thick-headed, stupid, doltish **TS** IV.i.111 [Petruchio to Servants] *You logger-headed and unpolished grooms!*

loiterer (n.) idler, layabout, vagabond **TG** III.i.289 [Launce to Speed] *O illiterate loiterer!*

loll (v.) hang down loosely, thrust out **Cym** V.iii.8 [Posthumus to Lord, of the Romans] *Lolling the tongue with slaught'ring* [i.e. with their tongues hanging out]

loneliness (n.) being alone, solitariness **Ham** III.i.46 [Polonius to Ophelia] *That show of such an exercise may colour / Your loneliness* [F; Q2 *lowlines*]

lonely (adj.) isolated, secluded, standing apart **WT** V.iii.18 [Paulina to Leontes, of Hermione's statue] *I keep it / Lonely, apart*

long (v.) 1 belong, pertain, relate **AW** IV.ii.42 [Bertram to Diana, of his ring] *It is an honour 'longing to our house;* **H5** II.iv.80; **H8** I.ii.32; **MM** II.ii.59; **TS** IV.iv.7
2 belong to, be part of **Per** II.Chorus.40 [Gower alone] *this longs the text*

'long of (prep.) 1 on account of **1H4** IV.iii.33 [Richard to Lucy, of the French] *we lose, they daily get; / All 'long of this vile traitor Somerset*
2 ➤ along of (prep.)

longing (adj.) prompted by longing, full of yearning **TG** II.vii.85 [Julia to Lucetta] *take a note of what I stand in need of / To furnish me upon my longing journey*

long-ingraffed (adj.) long-implanted, long-engrafted, habitual **KL** I.i.296 [Gonerill to Regan, of Lear] *must we look from his age to receive not alone the imperfections of long-ingraffed condition* [F; Q *ingraffed*] ➤ ingraft (adj.) 1

longly (adv.) for a long time, constantly, persistently **TS** I.i.162 [Tranio to Lucentio, of Bianca] *you looked so longly on the maid*

long-staff (n.) long cudgel, quarterstaff **1H4** II.i.74 [Gadshill to Chamberlain] *I am joined with … no long-staff sixpenny strikers*

long-tongued (adj.) chattering, prattling **Tit** IV.ii.149 [Aaron to Demetrius, of the Nurse] *A long-tongued, babbling gossip?;* **3H6** II.ii.102

loo (int.) ➤ SOUNDS, p.410

loof (v.) luff, bring into the wind **AC** III.x.17 [Scarus to Enobarbus, of Cleopatra's ship] *She once being loofed*

look (v.) 1 expect, anticipate, hope, await the time **Tit** III.i.200 [Aaron to Titus] *Look by and by to have thy sons with thee;* **H8** V.i.117; **KL** I.i.295; **R2** I.iii.243; **Sonn** 22.4; **Tem** V.i.293
2 find, seek, look for **AY** II.v.30 [Amiens to Jaques, of Duke Senior] *He hath been all this day to look you;* **KL** III.iii.13; **MW** IV.ii.76; **TNK** IV.ii.52; **WT** IV.iv.355
3 take care, see, be sure **2H4** I.ii.209 [Falstaff to Lord Chief Justice] *look you pray, all you that kiss my lady Peace at home;* **Ham** I.iii.59; **MW** V.v.61
4 look likely, promise, tend **Cor** III.iii.29 [Brutus to Sicinius, of Coriolanus] *he speaks / What's in his heart, and that is there which looks / With us to break his neck*
5 be prepared, expect, count on **2H4** IV.ii.116 [Prince John to Archbishop, Hastings, and Mowbray] *look to taste the due / Meet for rebellion;* **3H6** II.vi.95
6 face, turn towards **Cym** V.iii.37 [Posthumus to Lord, of the youths' effect on the Britons] *'gan to look / The way that they did;* **Cym** III.v.32
7 change one's state through one's looks **Cym** V.v.94 [Cymbeline to disguised Innogen] *Thou hast looked thyself into my grace*

look about (v.) be on the look-out, be wary **KL** IV.vii.92 [disguised Kent to Gentleman] *'Tis time to look about*

look after (v.) 1 follow with the eye, look with favour on **2H6** III.i.219 [King to all, of Gloucester] *myself … / Look after him, and cannot do him good;* **MW** II.i.136
2 watch closely, keep an eye on, police **MM** I.ii.143 [Lucio to Claudio] *Is lechery so looked after?*

look against (v.) look at directly **MW** II.ii.234 [Ford as Brook to Falstaff, of Mistress Ford] *She is too bright to be looked against*

look beyond (v.) exaggerate, find too much in **2H4** IV.iv.67 [Warwick to King Henry IV, of Prince Henry] *you look beyond him quite*

look for (v.) 1 expect, hope for, anticipate **TS** IV.ii.117 [Tranio as Lucentio to Pedant, of Vincentio] *My father is here looked for every day;* **Cym** II.iv.170; **KL** II.iv.227; **R2** I.vi.161; **TS** IV.iv.16
2 wait for, be on the lookout for **AC** II.i.20 [Pompey to Menas, of Caesar and Lepidus] *I know they are in Rome together, / Looking for Antony*
3 be watchful for, look after **E3** III.ii.25 [First Citizen to First Frenchman, of his dependents] *[we] Must look in time to look for them and us* [i.e. make sure we allow time to protect them]

look on (v.) 1 respect, hold in esteem, regard highly **3H6** V.vii.22 [Richard to himself] *I am not looked on in the world*
2 observe, be a witness to **H8** I.i.205 [Brandon to Buckingham] *I am sorry / To see you ta'en from liberty, to look on / The business present*

look out (v.) 1 show, appear, manifest **AC** V.i.50 [Caesar to all, of the Egyptian] *The business of this man looks out of him;* **TC** IV.v.56; **Tim** III.ii.75
2 seek out, find by looking **Tim** III.ii.61 [Lucius to Servilius] *I'll look you out a good turn*

look through (v.) become visible, show clearly **TNK** V.iii.97 [Emilia to herself, of Arcite] *his richness / And costliness of spirit looked through him;* **Ham** IV.vii.150

look to it beware, be on your guard **2H6** I.i.154 [Cardinal to all] *Look to it, lords*

look unto (v.) attend to, take care of **TS** Induction.i.26 [Lord to First Huntsman, of the hounds] *look unto them all*

look up (*v.*) be cheerful, take courage **WT** V.i.214 [Florizel to Perdita] *Dear, look up;* **H8** III.iii.50; **2H4** IV.iv.113

look upon (*v.*) **1** turn towards, look in the direction of **WT** IV.iv.819 [Autolycus to Clown] *I will but look upon the hedge, and follow you* [i.e. relieve myself]

2 look on, act like a spectator **3H6** II.iii.27 [Warwick to all] *Why stand we [here] … / And look upon, as if the tragedy / Were played in jest by counterfeiting actors?*

3 take notice of, turn towards **TS** IV.i.178 [Petruchio alone, of Katherina as a falcon] *she never looks upon her lure*

look how (*conj.*) just as **R3** I.ii.203 [Richard to Anne] *Look how my ring encompasseth thy finger, / Even so thy breast encloseth my poor heart*

look what (*conj.*) whatever **TG** I.iii.74 [Antonio to Proteus] *Look what thou wantest shall be sent after thee;* **MA** I.i.297; **R3** I.iii.113, IV.iv.291; **Sonn** 9.9, 37.13; **TS** IV.iii.188

look when (*conj.*) whenever, as soon as **MND** III.ii.124 [Lysander to Helena] *Look when I vow, I weep;* **CE** II.i.12; **R3** I.iii.289, III.i.194

look whom (*conj.*) whomsoever **Sonn** 11.11 [of nature] *Look whom she best endowed, she gave the more*

loon (*n.*) ▶ **lown** (*n.*)

loop (*n.*) **1** loop-hole, opening, avenue **1H4** IV.i.71 [Worcester to Hotspur] *[we] Must … stop all sight-holes, every loop from whence / The eye of reason may pry in upon us*

2 metal ring, pivot, prop **Oth** III.iii.362 [Othello to Iago, of Desdemona's infidelity] *so prove it / That the probation bear no hinge nor loop / To hang a doubt on*

looped (*adj.*) full of holes **KL** III.iv.31 [Lear to himself, as if to wretches everywhere] *Your looped and windowed raggedness* [Q; F *lop'd*]

loose (*n.*) [archery] moment of release, crucial point **LL** V.ii.737 [King to Princess, of time] *often at his very loose decides / That which long process could not arbitrate*

loose (*adj.*) **1** casual, lax, careless **TC** III.iii.41 [Ulysses to all, of Achilles] *Lay negligent and loose regard upon him;* **H8** II.i.127; **LL** V.ii.848; **TC** IV.iv.45

2 immoral, improper, contemptible **KJ** III.i.292 [Cardinal Pandulph to King Philip, of maintaining a treaty with England] *arm thy constant and thy nobler parts / Against these giddy loose suggestions*

3 flirtatious, unconstrained, uninhibited **LL** V.ii.761 [Berowne to ladies, of their conduct] *Which parti-coated presence of loose love / Put on by us*

4 ▶ **fast and loose**

loose (*v.*) **1** [archery] shoot an arrow **Tit** IV.iii.59 [Titus to Marcus] *loose when I bid*

2 release, let out, set free **2H6** III.ii.89 [Queen to King, of the god of winds] *he that loosed them forth their brazen caves*

3 revoke, cancel **MV** IV.i.24 [Duke to Shylock] *Thou wilt … loose the forfeiture*

loose shot marksman not attached to a company **H8** V.iv.55 [Man to Porter, of the attacking apprentices] *a file of boys behind 'em, loose shot, delivered such a shower of pebbles*

loose-bodied (*adj.*) loose-fitting **TS** IV.iii.130 [Tailor reading] *Imprimis, a loose-bodied gown* [also: fit for a prostitute]

loosely (*adv.*) negligently, with laxity, carelessly **2H4** II.ii.7 [Poins to Prince Henry, of small beer] *a prince should not be so loosely studied as to remember so weak a composition*

loose-wived (*adj.*) with an unfaithful wife **AC** I.ii.73 [Iras to Charmian] *it is a heart-breaking to see a handsome man loose-wived*

lop (*n.*) [of a tree] lopped off branch **H8** I.ii.96 [King Henry to Wolsey, of the taxation] *we take / From every tree lop, bark, and part o'th' timber*

lop (*v.*) remove, eliminate, get rid of **Per** I.ii.90 [Pericles to Helicanus, of Antiochus' fear] *To lop that doubt, he'll fill this land with arms*

lord (*v.*) make a lord, ennoble, elevate **Tem** I.ii.97 [Prospero to Miranda, of Antonio] *being thus lorded*

lording (*n.*) **1** young lord, young gentleman **WT** I.ii.62 [Hermione to Polixenes, of he and Leontes as boys] *You were pretty lordings then?;* **PassP** XV.1

2 (plural) my lords, gentlemen **2H6** I.i.143 [Gloucester to all] *Lordings, farewell* ▶ **ADDRESS FORMS**, p.8

lordship (*n.*) **1** function of being a lord **AW** V.iii.156 [King to Bertram, of wives] *you fly them as you swear them lordship* [i.e. swear to marry them]

2 lord's estate **2H6** IV.vii.4 [Cade to Dick, in response to 'I have a suit unto your lordship'] *Be it a lordship, thou shalt have it for that word*

lose (*v.*) **1** part with, let go of, give up **TNK** V.iii.136 [Theseus to Arcite, of Emilia] *I know you will not lose her;* **AW** V.ii.44; **H8** IV.i.96, ii.102

2 waste, throw away, give unprofitably **MW** II.i.220 [Ford alone, of Mistress Ford] *If I find her honest, I lose not my labour;* **Cor** II.iii.57; **TG** I.i.67

3 lose sight of, forget **H8** II.i.57 [Buckingham to the people, before his execution] *Hear what I say, and then go home and lose me;* **MND** I.i.114; **TN** II.ii.20

4 miss, lose out on, be deprived of **TNK** V.iii.1 [Pirithous to Emilia, of the contest] *Will you lose this sight?;* **TNK** V.vii.97, 101

5 harm, damage **KL** I.i.115 [Gloucester to Edmund, of Edgar] *find out this villain … it shall lose thee nothing* [i.e. you will gain by it]

6 ruin the reputation of, destroy the credibility of **Sonn** 88.8 *thou in losing me shalt win much glory;* **KL** I.i.233

7 spend, pass through, while away **2H6** V.ii.46 [Young Clifford to himself, as if to his father] *Wast thou ordained … / To lose thy youth in peace*

8 perplex, bewilder, overwhelm [by] **Ham** IV.vii.53 [Laertes to Claudius, of Hamlet's letter] *I am lost in it*

lose oneself (*v.*) roam about, wander around **CE** I.ii.30 [Antipholus of Syracuse to First Merchant] *I will go lose myself*

losel, lozel (*n.*) worthless fellow, rogue, scoundrel **WT** II.iii.108 [Leontes to Antigonus] *losel, thou art worthy to be hanged*

losing (*adj.*) involving some degree of loss **MV** IV.i.62 [Shylock to Duke, of Antonio] *I follow thus / A losing suit against him*

loss (*n.*) **1** perdition, destruction **WT** II.iii.191 [Antigonus to the baby] *Poor thing, condemned to loss!;* **KL** III.vi.93

2 ruin, detriment, deprivation [of honour] **Cym** III.v.158 [Pisanio alone, as if to Cloten] *Thou bid'st me to my loss*

3 losing, defeat, overthrow **TN** V.i.55 [Orsino to Viola as Cesario, of Antonio] *very envy and the tongue of loss / Cried fame and honour on him* [i.e. the voice of those defeated]

lost (*adj.*) **1** ruined, perished, destroyed **Tem** IV.i.203 [Trinculo to Caliban, of Stephano's threat to be displeased with him] *Thou wert but a lost monster;* **WT** V.iii.135

2 prevented, missed, forestalled **3H6** III.i.7 [First Keeper to Second Keeper] *my shoot is lost*

3 groundless, idle, unwarranted **Oth** V.ii.267 [Othello to Gratiano] *Do you go back dismayed? 'Tis a lost fear*

lot (*n.*) result of casting lots **AC** II.vi.62 [Pompey to Antony] *take the lot*

lot, by by chance **Ham** II.ii.415 [Hamlet to Polonius] *As by lot, God wot*

lots to blanks [in a lottery] drawing of a winning ticket rather than a blank ticket **Cor** V.ii.10 [Menenius to Second Watch] *it is lots to blanks / My name hath touched your ears* [i.e. the chances are]

lottery (*n.*) **1** odds, chance, probability **AW** I.iii.85 [Clown to Countess] *An we might have a good woman born but one every blazing star … 'twould mend the lottery well* [i.e. improve the odds against finding a good woman]

2 chance, turn of events **JC** II.ii.119 [Brutus to all] *So let high-sighted tyranny range on / Till each man drop by lottery*

3 prize, allotment, award **AC** II.ii.248 [Maecenas to Agrippa and Enobarbus, of Antony] *Octavia is / A blessed lottery to him*

loud (*n.*) loudness, volume **Cym** III.v.44 [Attendant to Cymbeline, of Innogen] *there's no answer / That will be given to th'loud of noise we make*

loud (*adj.*) **1** heard everywhere, resounding **TNK** I.ii.76 [Arcite to Palamon, of Creon] *we may nothing share / Of his loud infamy*
2 hectic, noisy, clamorous **KJ** V.iv.14 [Melun to Pembroke, Salisbury, and Bigot] *if the French be lords of this loud day*
3 clamorous, loudly supported; or: pressing, urgent **Oth** I.i.151 [Iago to Roderigo, of Othello] *he's embarked / With such loud reason to the Cyprus wars*
4 windy, stormy, blustery **WT** III.iii.10 [Mariner to Antigonus] *'tis like to be loud weather*

lour, lower (*v.*) frown, scowl, look dark and threatening **CE** II.i.86 [Luciana to Adriana] *Fie, how impatience loureth in your face;* **R2** I.iii.235; **R3** I.i.3, V.iii.284; **RJ** IV.v.94; **Sonn** 149.7

louring (*adj.*) **1** gloomy, threatening, dark **E3** IV.vii.17 [Prince Edward to Philip] *Too bright a morning brings a louring day;* **RJ** II.v.6
2 frowning, scowling, angry **Venus** 183 [of Adonis] *His louring brows o'erwhelming his fair sight*

louse (*v.*) become lice-infested **KL** III.ii.29 [Fool to Lear, of the subject of his song] *The head and he shall louse*

lousy (*adj.*) contemptible, vile, despicable **2H6** IV.i.50 [Suffolk to Lieutenant] *Obscure and lousy swain*

lout (*v.*) mock, ridicule; or: delay, hold up **1H6** IV.iii.13 [Richard to all, of Somerset] *I am louted by a traitor villain*

love (*n.*) **1** mistress, lover, paramour **3H6** III.ii.88 [Edward to himself, of Lady Grey] *she shall be my love or else my queen;* **3H6** III.ii.95
2 very dear friend **MV** IV.i.274 [Antonio to Bassanio, of Portia] *bid her be judge / Whether Bassanio had not once a love* **Sonn** 13.1
3 act of kindness, affectionate deed **KJ** IV.i.49 [Arthur to Hubert] *What good love may I perform for you?;* **Ham** I.ii.251
4 expression of love, love-vow **KL** V.iii.89 [Albany to Regan] *If you will marry, make your loves to me*

loves, of all for love's sake **MW** II.i.111 [Mistress Quickly to Falstaff] *Mistress Page would desire you to send her your little page, of all loves*

love (*v.*) **1** be friend to, be attractive to **LL** IV.iii.334 [Berowne to all, of renouncing their oath] *for love's sake, a word that loves all men* [second instance]
2 ☛ POLITENESS, p.340

love-book (*n.*) book dealing with matters of love, courtship manual **TG** I.i.19 [Valentine to Proteus] *on a love-book pray for my success?*

love-day (*n.*) day for settling disputes **Tit** I.i.494 [Saturninus to Tamora] *This day shall be a love-day* [also: for love-making]

love-feat (*n.*) act of courtship, exploit prompted by love **LL** V.ii.124 [Boyet to Princess, of the King's party] *every one his love-feat will advance / Unto his several mistress* [F, Q1]

love-lay (*n.*) love-song **E3** II.i.97 [King Edward to Lodowick] *who but women do our love-lays greet?*

lovely (*adj.*) loving, amorous **TS** III.ii.122 [Petruchio to Baptista, of Kate as his bride] *And seal the title with a lovely kiss;* **PassP** IV.3; **TG** I.ii.19

love-prate (*n.*) love-chatter, amorous talk **AY** IV.i.186 [Celia to Rosalind] *You have simply misused our sex in your love-prate*

lover (*n.*) companion, comrade, dear friend **JC** III.ii.13 [Brutus to all] *Romans, countrymen, and lovers, hear me for my cause;* **Cor** V.ii.14; **2H4** IV.iii.13; **MV** III.iv.17; **TC** III.iii.214; **TNK** V.v.123

lovered (*adj.*) provided with a lover **Lover** 320 *Who young and simple would not be so lovered*

loveshaft (*n.*) love-causing arrow **MND** II.i.159 [Oberon to Puck, of Cupid] *he ... loosed his loveshaft smartly from his bow*

love-shaked (*adj.*) lovesick, in such a fever of love **AY** III.ii.352 [Orlando to Rosalind] *I am he that is so love-shaked*

love-springs (*n.*) young shoots of love, youthful growth of love **CE** III.ii.3 [Luciana to Antipholus of Syracuse] *Shall ... / Even in the spring of love thy love-springs rot?*

love-suit (*n.*) wooing, courtship **Sonn** 136.4 *Thus far for love, my love-suit sweet fulfil* ☛ suit (*n.*)

loving (*adj.*) friendly, loyal, staunch **3H6** II.i.179 [Warwick to Edward] *all the friends that thou ... / Amongst the loving Welshmen canst procure*

low (*n.*) lowly person **2H4** III.i.30 [King Henry IV alone] *Then happy low, lie down!*

low (*adj.*) **1** humble, lowly, inferior **MV** I.iii.40 [Shylock to himself, of Antonio] *in low simplicity / He lends out money gratis;* **AY** II.iii.68; **KL** II.i.140, iii.17; **WT** I.ii.227
2 short, small **MA** I.i.161 [Benedick to Claudio, of Hero] *she's too low for a high praise;* **AY** IV.iii.88; **TNK** II.i.50
3 gentle, mild, not shrill **AC** III.iii.12 [Cleopatra to Messenger, of Octavia] *Is she shrill-tongued or low?;* **TNK** Induction.i.112

low (*adv.*) humbly, in a lowly manner **3H6** IV.vi.20 [King to Warwick] *I may conquer Fortune's spite / By living low*

low country lower regions of the body **2H4** II.ii.21 [Prince Henry to Poins] *the rest of thy low countries have made a shift to eat up thy holland* [also: Netherlands]

low-crooked (*adj.*) low-bending, profound **JC** III.i.43 [Caesar to Metellus] *sweet words, / Low-crooked curtsies and base spaniel fawning*

lower (*v.*) ☛ lour (*v.*)

lowering (*adj.*) ominous, threatening, gloomy **2H6** III.i.206 [King to all, as if to Gloucester] *What lowering star now envies thy estate*

lowliness (*n.*) appearance of humility, apparent meekness **JC** II.i.22 [Brutus alone] *lowliness is young ambition's ladder*

lowly (*adj.*) **1** humble, modest, submissive **TN** III.i.96 [Olivia to Viola as Cesario] *'Twas never merry world / Since lowly feigning was called compliment;* **E3** V.i.77; **2H6** III.i.127; **TS** Induction.i.112
2 laid low, prostrate; or: little, tiny **1H6** III.iii.47 [Pucelle to Burgundy] *As looks the mother on her lowly babe*

lown, loon (*n.*) rogue, sluggard; worthless idiot **Mac** V.iii.11 [Macbeth to Servant] *thou cream-faced loon!;* **Oth** II.iii.87 [Iago singing, of King Stephen] *he called the tailor lown;* **Per** IV.vi.16

lowness (*n.*) degradation, abasement, decline **KL** III.iv.68 [Lear to disguised Kent, of Edgar as Poor Tom] *Nothing could have subdued nature / To such a lowness but his unkind daughters*

low-spirited (*adj.*) ignoble, abject, cowardly **LL** I.i.241 [King reading Armado's letter to him, of Costard] *There did I see that low-spirited swain*

loyal (*adj.*) legitimate **KL** II.i.83 [Gloucester to Edmund] *Loyal and natural boy*

lozel (*n.*) ☛ losel (*n.*)

lubber (*n.*) clumsy dolt, blundering lout **TC** III.iii.139 [Ulysses to Achilles, of the lords] *They clap the lubber Ajax on the shoulder;* **KL** I.iv.90; **TG** II.v.40; **TN** IV.i.13

lubberly (*n.*) clumsy, loutish, oafish **MW** V.v.181 [Slender to Page] *I came ... to marry Mistress Anne Page, and she's a great lubberly boy*

luce (*n.*) [heraldry] pike [type of fish] **MW** I.i.15 [Slender to Evans, of Shallow's heirs] *They may give the dozen white luces in their coat* [mispronounced by Evans as 'louse' in 17]

lucky (*adj.*) fortunate, successful, prosperous **H5** II.ii.184 [King Henry to all] *We doubt not of a fair and lucky war;* **AC** III.xiii.179; **2H6** III.i.291; **MA** V.iii.32

- LY

Several adverbs which in modern English would end in *-ly* appear without the suffix in Shakespearian English. In most cases, adverb forms with the *-ly* are also found at that time - *nobly*, for example, in **RJ** III.v.181, *damnably* in **1H4** IV.ii.12; but *audible* (see below) is a case where the *-ly* form seems not to have entered English until later (earliest *Oxford English Dictionary* citation, 1635).

Item	Location	Example
according	**MM** V.i.479	*thou art said to have a stubborn soul … / And squar'st thy life according*
audible	**MM** V.i.405	*The very mercy of the law cries out / Most audible*
bountiful	**Cor** II.iii.101	*I will … give it bountiful*
damnable	**WT** III.ii.185	*That did but show thee … damnable ingrateful*
dear	**MND** III.ii.175	*Lest to thy peril thou aby it dear*
dishonourable	**1H4** IV.ii.30	*ten times more dishonourable-ragged than an old fazed ancient*
easy	**Sonn** 109.3	*As easy might I from myself depart*
equal	**H8** I.i.159	*he is equal ravenous / As he is subtle*
exceeding	**CE** I.i.57	*their parents were exceeding poor*
frantic	**Sonn** 147.10	*I am … frantic mad with evermore unrest*
grievous	**1H4** IV.i.16	*he is grievous sick*
loose	**MW** IV.vi.41	*she shall be loose enrobed*
marvellous	**MA** IV.ii.25	*A marvellous witty fellow*
noble	**AC** II.ii.102	*'Tis noble spoken*
singular	**2H4** III.ii.108	*Very singular good, in faith*
treacherous	**1H6** I.v.30	*Sheep run not half so treacherous from the wolf*
unfortunate	**1H6** I.iv.4	*Howe'er unfortunate I missed my aim*
willing	**H8** IV.ii.130	*most willing, madam*

The opposite effect can also be seen: some adverbs were formed from nouns with the *-ly* suffix, such as *angerly* (**KJ** IV.i.81) and *hungerly* (**Oth** III.iv.101), which today have developed alternative forms (*angrily*, *hungrily*).

lucre *(n.)* **1** gain, acquisition, procurement **1H6** V.iv.141 [Charles to the English, of the French territories] *for lucre of the rest unvanquished*
2 profit, financial gain **Cym** IV.ii.324 [Innogen alone, of Pisanio and Cloten] *malice and lucre in them / Have laid this woe here*

luggage *(n.)* stuff, trappings, goods **Tem** V.i.299 [Alonso to Stephano and Trinculo] *bestow your luggage where you found it*; **Tem** IV.i.231

lugged *(adj.)* [of bears] baited **1H4** I.ii.74 [Falstaff to Prince Hal] *I am as melancholy as a … lugged bear* ☛ **head-lugged** *(adj.)*

lull *(v.)* loll, recline, lounge **R3** III.vii.71 [Buckingham to Lord Mayor, of Richard] *He is not lulling on a lewd love-bed*

lumpish *(adj.)* despondent, dejected, in low spirits **TG** III.ii.62 [Duke to Proteus, of Silvia] *she is lumpish, heavy, melancholy*

lunatic *(adj.)* hallucinating, suffering from delusions **TS** Induction.i.61 [Lord to Huntsmen, of Sly] *Persuade him that he hath been lunatic*

lune *(n.)* frenzied fit, tantrum, mad outburst **WT** II.ii.30 [Paulina to Emilia, of Leontes] *These dangerous, unsafe lunes i'th' King*; **TC** II.iii.129

lurch *(v.)* rob, cheat **Cor** II.ii.99 [Cominius to all, of Coriolanus] *He lurched all swords of the garland*; **MW** II.ii.24

lure *(n.)* [falconry] baited apparatus for recalling a hawk **TS** IV.i.178 [Petruchio alone, of Katherina as a falcon] *she never looks upon her lure*

lurk *(v.)* **1** keep hidden, stay out of sight **KL** III.vi.113 [Edgar alone, to himself] *Lurk, lurk!*
2 idle, loiter, loaf **3H6** IV.ii.15 [Warwick to George, of Edward] *His soldiers lurking in the towns about*

lust *(n.)* desire, pleasure, delight **Luc** 1384 [of Trojans in a painting of Troy] *Gazing upon the Greeks with little lust*; **TC** IV.iv.131

lust-breathed *(adj.)* inspired by lust, driven by passion **Luc** 3 *From the besieged Ardea all in post … / Lust-breathed Tarquin leaves the Roman host*

lust-dieted *(adj.)* pleasure-gorged, self-indulgent **KL** IV.i.66 [Gloucester to Edgar as Poor Tom, as if to the heavens] *Let the superfluous and lust-dieted man … feel your power quickly*

lustful *(adj.)* lust-arousing **TS** Induction.ii.37 [Lord to Sly] *We'll have thee to a couch / Softer and sweeter than the lustful bed*

lustihood *(n.)* lustiness, youthful vigour, robustness **TC** II.ii.50 [Troilus to Helenus] *reason and respect / Make livers pale and lustihood deject*; **MA** V.i.76

lustily *(adv.)* vigorously, heartily, with a will **TG** IV.ii.25 [Thurio to Musicians] *Let's tune, and to it lustily awhile*

lustique *(adj.)* lusty, lively, sportive **AW** II.iii.40 [Lafew to Parolles, of the King] *Lustique, as the Dutchman says*

lustre *(n.)* **1** light, glory, brilliance **Tim** I.ii.146 [Timon to Ladies, of the feast] *You have added worth unto't and lustre*; **AC** I.iii.28
2 gleam, glimmer, flash **LL** IV.iii.86 [Holofernes to Nathaniel, of Costard's remark] *A good lustre of conceit in a turf of earth*

lusty *(adj.)* **1** vigorous, strong, robust, eager **KJ** II.i.322 [English Herald to Hubert] *like a jolly troop of huntsmen come / Our lusty English*; **E3** I.i.143; **2H4** II.i.3; **JC** II.i.78; **R2** V.iii.19; **Venus** 31 ☛ **over-lusty** *(adj.)* **1**
2 merry, cheerful, lively **TS** II.i.160 [Petruchio to Baptista, of Katherina] *it is a lusty wench*; **AY** II.ii.52; **E3** II.ii.73; **2H4** III.ii.15; **RJ** I.iv.113; **TNK** II.ii.46 ☛ **over-lusty** *(adj.)* **2**
3 pleasing, pleasant, agreeable **E3** II.i.54 [King Edward alone, of Lodowick] *[This fellow] hath a lusty and persuasive spirit*; **AY** III.v.121

4 tasty, flavourful, well-flavoured **TNK** III.iii.27 [Palamon to Arcite, of venison] *'Tis a lusty meat*
5 lustful, sensual, sexful **AY** IV.ii.18 [Lords, singing] *The horn, the horn, the lusty horn;* **RJ** I.ii.26

luxurious *(adj.)* lustful, lecherous, lascivious **Mac** IV.iii.58 [Malcolm to Macduff, of Macbeth] *I grant him bloody, / Luxurious;* **H5** IV.iv.20; **MA** IV.i.39; **TC** V.iv.8; **Tit** V.i.88

luxuriously *(adv.)* lustfully, lecherously, lasciviously **AC** III.xiii.120 [Antony to Cleopatra] *what hotter hours ... you have / Luxuriously picked out*

luxury *(n.)* lust, lechery, lasciviousness **Ham** I.v.83 [Ghost to Hamlet] *A couch for luxury and damned incest;* **H5** III.v.6; **Lover** 314; **MW** V.v.94; **R3** III.v.79; **TC** V.ii.56

lym *(n.)* [doubtful reading] bloodhound **KL** III.vi.68 [Edgar as Poor Tom to all] *Hound or spaniel, brach or lym*

mace (*n.*) staff of office, official sceptre **CE** IV.iii.27 [Dromio of Syracuse to Antipholus of Syracuse, of the officer] *he that sets up his rest to do more exploits with his mace than a morris-pike*

Machiavel (*n.*) master of intrigue, political schemer **MW** III.i.93 [Host to all] *Am I a Machiavel?*

machination (*n.*) plotting, intrigue, scheming **KL** I.ii.112 [Gloucester to Edmund] *Machinations, hollowness … and all ruinous disorders follow us;* **KL** V.i.46

machine (*n.*) **1** body, human frame **Ham** II.ii.123 [Hamlet's salutation in his letter to Ophelia] *Thine evermore, most dear lady, whilst this machine is to him*
  2 show, entertainment; or: device **TNK** III.v.112 [Schoolmaster to Theseus] *I … / Do here present this machine, or this frame*

maculate (*adj.*) impure, spotted, stained **TNK** V.i.145 [Emilia praying to Diana] *[who] never yet / Beheld thing maculate;* **LL** I.ii.88

maculation (*n.*) stain, sport, defilement **TC** IV.iv.63 [Troilus to Cressida] *there's no maculation in thy heart* [i.e. of faithlessness]

mad (*adj.*) **1** wild, uncontrollable, excitable, high-spirited **TNK** II.i.180 [Emilia to Woman] *Men are mad things;* **Cor** IV.ii.9; **1H4** II.i.75; **LL** II.i.243; **MW** I.iv.64; **TNK** III.v.24
  2 wild, faithless, inconstant **Oth** IV.iii.26 [Desdemona to Emilia, of her mother's maid] *he she loved proved mad*
  3 angry, furious, beside oneself **3H6** I.iv.89 [Queen to York] *Thou shouldst be mad*
  4 strange, bizarre, weird **TNK** III.iii.22 [Arcite to Palamon] *Is't not mad lodging, / Here in the wild woods*

mad (*v.*) **1** madden, exasperate, infuriate **R2** V.v.61 [Richard alone] *This music mads me;* **CE** IV.iv.124, V.i.84; **KL** IV.ii.43; **Tit** III.i.104
  2 madden, excite, provoke **AW** V.iii.213 [Bertram to King, of Diana] *Madding my eagerness with her restraint*

madam (*n.*) high-ranking lady **H5** III.v.28 [Dauphin to all] *Our madams mock at us;* **H8** I.i.23

mad-bred (*adj.*) produced by madness **2H6** III.i.354 [York to himself, of the crown] *Do calm the fury of this mad-bred flaw*

madcap (*n.*) mad-brained fellow, lunatic **KJ** I.i.84 [King John to Queen Eleanor, of the Bastard] *what a madcap hath heaven lent us here!;* **TG** II.v.7

madcap (*adj.*) reckless, impulsive, wildly behaved **1H4** IV.i.95 [Hotspur to Vernon] *The nimble-footed madcap Prince of Wales;* **LL** II.i.201; **TS** II.i.281

madded (*adj.*) maddened **Cym** IV.ii.313 [Innogen alone, as if to Pisanio] *All curses madded Hecuba gave the Greeks … be darted on thee!*

madding (*n.*) maddening, incensing, provocation **Cym** II.ii.37 [Iachimo to himself, of Innogen's stolen bracelet] *this will witness outwardly … / To th'madding of her lord*

madding (*adj.*) **1** becoming mad, frenzied **2H6** III.ii.117 [Queen to King, of Ascanius] *When he to madding Dido would unfold / His father's acts*
  2 driving one mad, provoking madness **Sonn** 119.8 *How have mine eyes out of their spheres been fitted / In the distraction of this madding fever!*

made (*adj.*) **1** resolved, framed, decided **KL** IV.vii.9 [Kent to Cordelia] *Yet to be known shortens my made intent*
  2 with success assured, with fortune made **MND** IV.ii.17 [Snug to all] *If our sport had gone forward, we had all been made men;* **TNK** III.v.77 [First Countryman to all] *We are made, boys!;* **TNK** III.v.75, 157

made up, made-up (*adj.*) **1** accomplished, consummate, out-and-out **Tim** V.i.96 [Timon to Poet and Painter, of a knave] *Yet remain assured / That he's a made-up villain*
  2 finished off, put together **R3** I.i.21 [Richard alone, of himself] *sent before my time / Into this breathing world, scarce half made up*

madonna (*n.*) my lady, madam **TN** I.v.52 [Feste to Olivia] *Good madonna, give me leave to prove you a fool*

madrigal *(n.)* song, pleasant tune **PassP** XIX.8 [Pilgrim] *By shallow rivers, by whose falls / Melodious birds sing madrigals*

maggot-pie *(n.)* magpie **Mac** III.iv.124 [Macbeth to Lady Macbeth] *Augurs and understood relations have / By maggot-pies … brought forth / The secret'st man of blood*

magic *(n.)* special power **Ham** III.ii.268 [Third Player, as Lucianus, addressing his drug] *Thy natural magic and dire property*

magistrate *(n.)* member of the government, leader of the community **2H6** IV.ii.18 [Holland to Bevis] *should we be magistrates;* **1H6** I.iii.57

magnanimious *(adj.)* of great spirit, nobly valiant **AW** III.vi.61 [Bertram to Parolles] *be magnanimious in the enterprise*

magnanimity *(n.)* greatness of spirit, nobleness of heart **3H6** V.iv.41 [Prince to all, of the effect of the Queen's words on a coward] *Infuse his breast with magnanimity*

magnanimous *(adj.)* valiant, heroic, courageous **H5** III.vi.6 [Fluellen to Gower] *The Duke of Exeter is as magnanimous as Agamemnon;* **2H4** III.ii.158

magnificent *(adj.)* grand, stately, majestic **LL** I.i.188 [King to Berowne, Dumaine, and Longaville] *A letter from the magnificent Armado*

magnifico *(n.)* Venetian leader **MV** III.ii.280 [Salerio to Bassanio, of Shylock] *the magnificoes / Of greatest port have all persuaded with him*

maid *(n.)* **1** human, mortal [woman] **Tem** I.ii.428 [Ferdinand to Miranda] *My prime request … is … / If you be maid or no?;* **Tem** I.ii.429
    2 virgin, unmarried woman **TN** V.i.260 [Sebastian to Olivia] *You are betrothed both to a maid and man;* **AY** III.ii.208; **TNK** V.iv.33
    3 handmaid, servant, attendant **Tem** III.i.84 [Miranda to Ferdinand] *I am your wife, if you will marry me. / If not, I'll die your maid* [or: sense 2]
    4 young fish **MM** I.ii.92 [Pompey to Mistress Overdone, of a Prisoner] *there's a woman with maid by him*

maiden *(adj.)* **1** unblemished, unstained, not put to use **KJ** IV.ii.252 [Hubert to King John] *This hand of mine / Is yet a maiden and an innocent hand*
    2 befitting chastity **H8** IV.ii.169 [Katherine to Patience] *strew me over / With maiden flowers;* **Luc** 408
    3 untried, untested, uninitiated [in battle] **1H6** IV.vii.38 [Pucelle to all, as if to John Talbot] *Thou maiden youth, be vanquished by a maid*
    4 without bloodshed **TC** IV.v.87 [Achilles to Aeneas] *A maiden battle, then?*

maidenhead *(n.)* **1** virginity **TS** III.ii.224 [Petruchio to all, of Katherina] *Carouse full measure to her maidenhead;* **2H4** II.iv.74; **H8** II.iii.23; **RJ** I.i.24; **TC** IV.ii.23; **TNK** IV.i.112
    2 opening stage, first step **1H4** IV.i.59 [Hotspur to all] *If that the devil and mischance look big / Upon the maidenhead of our affairs*

maidhood *(n.)* maidenhood **Oth** I.i.173 [Brabantio to Roderigo] *Is there not charms / By which the property of youth and maidhood / May be abused?* [F; Q *manhood*]

maid-pale *(adj.)* fragile as a young girl, delicate **R2** III.iii.98 [King Richard to his opponents, of the effect of future battles on England] *Change the complexion of her maid-pale peace / To scarlet indignation*

mail *(n.)* **1** armour, chain mail, piece of armour **TC** III.iii.152 [Ulysses to Achilles, of past honour] *Quite out of fashion, like a rusty mail / In monumental mockery;* **E3** I.ii.29 ✪ **BODY-ARMOUR**, p.48
    2 wallet, pouch, travel bag **LL** III.i.71 [Costard to Armado, of cures for his cut shin] *No egma, no riddle, no l'envoy, no salve in the mail*

mail up *(v.)* wrap up, envelop, encase **2H6** II.iv.31 [Duchess to Gloucester] *Methinks I should not thus be led along, / Mailed up in shame*

mailed *(adj.)* mail-clad, armoured **1H4** IV.i.116 [Hotspur to all] *The mailed Mars shall on his altar sit*

maim *(n.)* wound, injury, mutilation **2H6** II.iii.41 [Queen to all, of Gloucester] *That bears so shrewd a maim;* **Cor** IV.v.89

maim *(v.)* make powerless, undermine, subvert **H8** III.ii.312 [Surrey to Wolsey, of Wolsey becoming a legate] *by which power / You maimed the jurisdiction of all bishops*

maimed *(adj.)* incomplete, deficient, wanting **Ham** V.i.215 [Hamlet to Horatio] *with such maimed rites*

main *(n.)* **1** open sea, ocean **KJ** II.i.26 [Austria to Arthur, of England] *hedged in with the main;* **MV** V.i.97; **Oth** II.i.3, 39; **R3** I.iv.20; **Sonn** 80.8
    2 mainland **KL** III.i.6 [Gentleman to disguised Kent, of Lear] *Bids the wind … swell the curled waters 'bove the main*
    3 central part, chief part **Ham** IV.iv.15 [Hamlet to Captain, of his army] *Goes it against the main of Poland*
    4 main concern, chief point **2H6** I.i.206 [Salisbury to York and Warwick] *let's make haste away, and look unto the main;* **Ham** II.ii.56
    5 broad expanse, open view **Sonn** 60.5 *Nativity once in the main of light / Crawls to maturity*
    6 strength, force, full might **TC** II.iii.259 [Ulysses to all] *Tomorrow / We must with all our main of power stand fast;* **Oth** II.i.13
    7 [gambling] stake, bet, throw **1H4** IV.i.47 [Hotspur to all] *Were it good … To set so rich a main / On the nice hazard of one doubtful hour?* [also: army]

main *(adj.)* **1** very great, major, considerable **TNK** II.i.117 [Palamon to Arcite] *'Tis a main goodness, cousin, that our fortunes / Were twinned together;* **2H6** I.i.208; **H8** II.ii.6, III.ii.215, IV.i.31
    2 leading, chief, pre-eminent **AC** I.i.192 [Antony to Enobarbus, of Pompey] *who, high in name and power, / Higher than both in blood and life, stands up / For the main soldier*
    3 firm, strong, solid **JC** II.i.196 [Cassius to all, of Caesar's belief in superstition] *Quite from the main opinion he held once / Of fantasy*

main *(v.)* maim, cripple **2H6** IV.ii.153 [Cade to Dick, of the sale of Maine] *thereby is England mained and fain to go with a staff*

main-course *(n.)* principal sail of a ship, mainsail **Tem** I.i.35 [Boatswain to Mariners] *Bring her to try with main-course* ✪ **SHIPS**, p.397

mainly *(adv.)* **1** greatly, very much, mightily **1H4** II.iv.195 [Falstaff to all, of the robbers] *These four came all afront, and mainly thrust at me;* **Ham** IV.vii.9; **TC** IV.v.84
    2 entirely, completely, totally **KL** IV.vii.65 [Lear to Cordelia] *I am mainly ignorant / What place this is;* **TNK** V.ii.8

mainport *(n.)* [unclear meaning] tribute, offering **Cym** IV.iv.16 [Posthumus alone, of making satisfaction] *If of my freedom 'tis the mainport* [F *maine part*]

mainsail *(n.)* ✪ **SHIPS**, p.397

maintain *(v.)* **1** defend, justify, support **Sonn** 121.13 [of rumour-mongers] *Unless this general evil they maintain;* **LL** V.ii.881; **TNK** III.i.53
    2 afford, stand the cost of **TS** V.i.67 [Tranio as Lucentio to Vincentio, of his attire] *I thank my good father, I am able to maintain it*

main-top *(n.)* top of a ship's mainmast **Cym** IV.ii.320 [Innogen alone, of how she believes Pisanio to have caused Posthumus' death] *From this most bravest vessel of the world / Struck the main-top!* ✪ **SHIPS**, p.397

majestical *(adj.)* **1** majestic, regal, kingly **1H6** IV.vii.39 [Pucelle to all, of John Talbot] *with a proud majestical high scorn;* **Ham** I.i.144; **LL** V.ii.102
    2 grand, stately **LL** V.i.11 [Holofernes to Nathaniel, of Armado] *his gait [is] majestical*

major *(n.)* major premiss, proposition **1H4** II.iv.481 [Falstaff to Prince Hal] *I deny your major*

majority (*n.*) pre-eminence, superiority, supremacy 1H4 III.ii.109 [King Henry to Prince Hal, of Douglas] *Whose high deeds … / Holds from all soldiers chief majority*

make (*n.*) ☞ mate and make

make (*v.*) **1** do, have to do MW IV.ii.49 [Mistress Page to Falstaff] *what make you here?*; AY I.i.27, III.ii.215; R2 V.iii.88; RJ V.iii.280; Tim III.v.47

2 do, perform, carry out MW II.i.218 [Ford to himself, of Mistress Page and Falstaff] *She was in his company at Page's house, and what they made there I know not* [i.e. what they got up to]; AY IV.iii.62; Cor V.vi.64; H8 I.iv.46; KL V.iii.94

3 create, bring about, produce AC I.ii.16 [Soothsayer to Charmian] *I make not, but foresee*; TNK V.iii.14

4 prove effective, be of avail 3H6 II.i.175 [Warwick to all, of the King] *to London all the crew are gone, / To frustrate both his oath and what beside / May make against the house of Lancaster*; RJ V.iii.225

5 bring success [to], prosper Tem II.ii.30 [Trinculo to himself, of Caliban in England] *There would this monster make a man*; TNK II.ii.21, III.v.101

6 come, proceed, approach H8 I.iv.55 [Servant to Lord Chamberlain, of people outside] *They've left their barge and landed, / And hither make*; 3H6 IV.v.10

7 become, form, make up TS I.i.244 [Lucentio to Tranio, of Bianca] *To make one among these wooers*

8 raise, acquire, procure Oth I.iii.349 [Iago to Roderigo] *Make all the money thou canst*; 2H4 I.i.214; JC IV.i.44; Oth I.iii.353; R3 IV.iv.450

9 give, provide H8 I.iii.52 [Lord Chamberlain to Lovell, of Wolsey] *This night he makes a supper*; MW I.i.56

10 bring the total to 1H4 IV.ii.6 [Bardolph to Falstaff] *This bottle makes an angel*

11 draw up, arrange, agree to 2H6 IV.i.10 [Lieutenant to all, of the captives] *Here shall they make their ransom on the sand*; JC IV.iii.32

12 matter, count, signify AC II.vi.116 [Menas to Enobarbus] *I think the policy of that purpose made more in the marriage than the love of the parties*

13 consider, regard, treat [as] Tit II.i.81 [Demetrius to Aaron, of wooing Lavinia] *Why makes thou it so strange?*; AW V.iii.5

14 make out, discern, detect Cym I.iv.14 [Innogen to Pisanio, of Posthumus] *Thou shouldst have made him / As little as a crow*

15 make fast, shut, close AY IV.i.150 [Rosalind as Ganymede to Orlando] *Make the doors upon a woman's wit, and it will out at the casement*; CE III.i.93

16 eat, finish, complete Cym III.vii.24 [disguised Innogen to all] *so soon / As I had made my meal*

17 ☞ bold, make; lip, make a; mouths, make

make away (*v.*) put an end to, do away with Tit II.iii.208 [Aaron to himself, of fetching Saturninus to find Quintus and Martius] *That he thereby may have a likely guess / How these were they that made away his brother*; 2H6 III.i.167; Sonn 11.8; Tim I.ii.103; Tit II.iii.189, IV.ii.166

make forth (*v.*) advance, come forward JC V.i.25 [Antony to Octavius, of Brutus and Cassius] *Make forth; the Generals would have some words*

make from (*v.*) [unclear meaning] avoid, beware; or: let go, release KL I.i.143 [Lear to Kent] *The bow is bent and drawn; make from the shaft*

make good 1 justify, vindicate, confirm TN I.v.6 [Maria to Feste, of his remarks] *Make that good*; MV I.iii.91; TNK I.i.226; WT II.iii.60

2 perform well, succeed in carrying out TS I.i.74 [Baptista to Gremio and Hortensio] *that I may soon make good / What I have said - Bianca, get you in*; 2H6 V.i.122; Tim I.ii.195; TS Induction.i.17

3 hold, secure, make sure of Cor I.v.12 [Martius to Lartius] *take / Convenient numbers to make good the city*; Cym V.iii.23; KL I.i.172

make in (*v.*) go in, make [one's] way through TNK IV.i.94 [Wooer to all, of the Gaoler's Daughter] *I made in to her*

make nothing of treat as worthless, deal with contemptuously KL III.i.9 [Gentleman to disguised Kent, of Lear's hair] *the impetuous blasts … / Catch in their fury and make nothing of*

make on (*v.*) **1** make of, compose, form KL III.vi.53 [Lear to all, as if to Regan] *whose warped looks proclaim / What store her heart is made on*

2 make much of Cor IV.v.198 [Third Servingman to First Servingman, of Coriolanus] *he is so made on here within as if he were son and heir to Mars*

make one join in the action, take part MW II.i.42 [Shallow to Page] *if I see a sword out, my finger itches to make one*; LL V.i.146

make out (*v.*) go, go out TN II.v.58 [Malvolio to himself, of Sir Toby] *Seven of my people … make out for him*

make to (*v.*) move towards, go in the direction of JC III.i.18 [Brutus to Cassius, of Popilius] *Look how he makes to Caesar*; JC V.iii.29

make up (*v.*) **1** advance to the front, move forward, press on 1H4 V.iv.57 [King Henry to Prince Hal] *Make up to Clifton*; E3 IV.vi.48; 1H4 V.iv.4; KJ III.ii.5

2 contribute, add up, help to produce WT II.i.179 [Leontes to Antigonus, of the supposed adultery of Hermione and Polixenes] *all other circumstances / Made up to th'deed - doth push on this proceeding*

3 agree, conclude, make good KJ II.i.541 [King Philip to all, of Constance's reaction to the alliance] *this match made up / Her presence would have interrupted much*

4 reconcile, settle, arrange KL I.i.206 [Burgundy to Lear, of Lear's offer of Cordelia] *Election makes not up in such conditions* [i.e. it is not possible to choose]; TNK II.ii.33

5 create, cause the formation of KJ III.i.106 [Constance to King Philip, of the treaty] *our oppression hath made up this league* [i.e. your oppression of us]

6 conclude, finish, end E3 I.ii.156 [Countess to King Edward] *to make up my all too long compare*

make whole put right, bring to agreement KJ I.i.35 [Queen Eleanor to King John, of enmity between England and France] *This might have been prevented and made whole*

makeless (*adj.*) mateless, husbandless Sonn 9.4 *The world will wail thee like a makeless wife* [also: matchless]

make-peace (*n.*) peacemaker R2 I.i.160 [John of Gaunt to King Richard] *To be a make-peace shall become my age*

making (*n.*) physical appearance, bodily form, build MND II.i.32 [Fairy to Puck] *Either I mistake your shape and making quite*; CE IV.ii.22

malady of France venereal disease H5 V.i.78 [Pistol alone] *News have I that my Doll is dead i'th' spital / Of malady of France*

malapert (*adj.*) impudent, saucy, impertinent R3 I.iii.254 [Queen Margaret to Dorset] *you are malapert*; 3H6 V.v.32; TN IV.i.43

malcontent (*n.*) discontented individual, trouble-maker E3 III.i.13 [Charles to all] *England was wont to harbour malcontents*; MW I.iii.95; TG II.i.19

malcontent (*adj.*) discontented, disaffected, dissatisfied 3H6 IV.i.10 [Edward to George] *you stand pensive, as half-malcontent*; E3 II.ii.15; 3H6 V.vi.60

male (*n.*) father, parent, begetter 3H6 V.vi.15 [King to Richard, of himself and his son] *the hapless male to one sweet bird*

malediction (*n.*) cursing, invective, denunciation KL I.ii.145 [Edmund to Edgar, of a writer] *the effects he writes of succeed unhappily, as of … maledictions against king and nobles*

malefaction (*n.*) evil-doing, criminal act Ham II.ii.590 [Hamlet alone, of guilty people] *They have proclaimed their malefactions*

malice (*n.*) hostility, hatred, ill-will, enmity Oth I.iii.267 [Iago to Cassio] *a punishment more in policy than in malice*; Cor II.i.220, ii.20; R2 I.i.9, 14; Tim IV.iii.454

malicious (*adj.*) **1** wicked, evil-minded, of ill will TNK III.vi.132 [Theseus to Palamon and Arcite] *What ignorant and mad malicious traitors / Are you* [or: sense 2]

2 violent, hostile, wrathful KJ II.i.314 [English Herald to Hubert, of King John] *Commander of this hot malicious day*; Ham I.i.147

maliciously (*adv.*) violently, virulently, ragingly **WT** I.ii.321 [Camillo to Leontes, of poisoning Polixenes] *I could do this, and that with no rash potion, / But with a lingering dram that should not work / Maliciously, like poison*

malign (*v.*) deal maliciously with, be hostile to **Per** V.i.88 [Marina to Pericles] *wayward fortune did malign my state*

malignancy (*n.*) evil influence, inauspicious character **TN** II.i.4 [Sebastian to Antonio] *The malignancy of my fate might perhaps distemper yours*

malkin (*n.*) wench, drab, slut **Cor** II.i.200 [Brutus to Sicinius] *The kitchen malkin pins / Her richest lockram 'bout her reechy neck;* **Per** IV.iii.34

mallard (*n.*) wild drake **AC** III.x.19 [Scarus to Enobarbus, of Antony] *like a doting mallard*

mallecho (*n.*) [unclear meaning] mischief, misdeed **Ham** III.ii.146 [Hamlet to Ophelia] *this is miching mallecho* [F *malicho*; Q1, Q2 *Mallico*]

mallow (*n.*) variety of wild plant **Tem** II.i.146 [Sebastian aside to Antonio, of what Gonzalo might plant] *Or docks, or mallows* ☛ **PLANTS**, p.330

malmsey (*n.*) variety of strong sweet red wine **R3** I.iv.157 [First Murderer to Second Murderer, of Clarence] *throw him into the malmsey-butt;* **LL** V.ii.233

malmsey-nose (*adj.*) nose the colour of malmsey **2H4** II.i.37 [Hostess to Fang and Snare, of Bardolph] *that arrant malmsey-nose knave* ☛ **malmsey** (*n.*)

malthorse, malt-horse (*n./adj.*) heavy brewer's horse; so: drudge, idiot **TS** IV.i.115 [Petruchio to Grumio] *you whoreson malt-horse drudge!;* **CE** III.i.32

maltworm, malt-worm (*n.*) drinker [of malt-liquor], drunkard, inebriate **1H4** II.i.76 [Gadshill to Chamberlain] *I am joined with ... none of these mad mustachio purple-hued maltworms;* **2H4** II.iv.329

mammer (*v.*) stammer, hesitate, mutter **Oth** III.iii.70 [Desdemona to Othello] *I wonder in my soul / What you would ask me that I should deny, / Or stand so mammering on?*

mammet (*n.*) doll, puppet **RJ** III.v.185 [Capulet to Lady Capulet, of Juliet] *A whining mammet;* **1H4** II.iii.95

mammock (*v.*) tear to shreds, rip to pieces **Cor** I.iii.66 [Valeria to Volumnia and Virgilia, of Young Martius and a butterfly] *O, I warrant, how he mammocked it*

man (*n.*) **1** human nature, humanity [as opposed to beasts] **KL** II.iii.8 [Edgar alone] *That ever penury, in contempt of man, / Brought near to beast* [i.e. despising human claims to be superior to beasts]
2 manhood, maturity, adulthood **Cym** IV.ii.110 [Belarius to Arviragus, of Cloten] *Being scarce made up ... to man* [i.e. he is mentally undeveloped]
3 manliness, courage, valour **KL** II.iv.41 [disguised Kent to Lear] *Having more man than wit about me* [i.e. more courage than discretion]
4 servant, attendant, lackey **TS** I.i.1 [stage direction] *Enter Lucentio and his man Tranio;* **R3** I.i.80
5 agent, representative **2H6** I.iii.16 [First Petitioner to Queen, of his petition] *Mine is ... against John Goodman, my lord Cardinal's man*

man (*v.*) **1** employ, exert, send out **Oth** V.ii.268 [Othello to Gratiano] *Man but a rush against Othello's breast, / And he retires*
2 attend, serve, wait on [by] **2H4** I.ii.16 [Falstaff to Page] *I was never manned with an agate till now;* **2H4** I.ii.52
3 [falconry] tame, make tractable **TS** IV.i.179 [Petruchio alone, of Katherina as a falcon] *Another way I have to man my haggard*

manage (*n.*) **1** management, handling, control [especially of a horse, as a result of training] **AY** I.i.11 [Orlando to Adam, of Oliver's horses] *they are taught their manage;* **1H4** II.iii.51; **H8** V.iii.24; **Per** IV.vi.60; **RJ** III.i.143; **TNK** V.iv.69

2 management, direction, administration **Tem** I.ii.70 [Prospero to Miranda, of Antonio] *I ... to him put / The manage of my state;* **MV** III.iv.25; **R2** I.iv.39; **TC** III.iii.25
3 government, rulers **KJ** I.i.37 [Queen Eleanor to King John, of the enmity between England and France] *the manage of two kingdoms must / With fearful bloody issue arbitrate*
4 gallop at full speed **LL** V.ii.482 [Boyet to Berowne, of recent events] *Full merrily / Hath this brave manage, this career, been run*

manage (*v.*) **1** wield, handle, use **R2** III.ii.118 [Scroop to King Richard] *distaff-women manage rusty bills / Against thy seat;* **2H4** III.ii.265, 273; **TG** III.i.247
2 conduct, carry on **Oth** III.iii.209 [Othello to Iago] *To manage private and domestic quarrel*
3 [of horses] ride, handle, put through one's paces **Venus** 598 [of Adonis approaching Venus] *He will not manage her, although he mount her*

manager (*n.*) employer, user, handler **LL** I.ii.175 [Armado alone, of his sword] *your manager is in love*

man at arms, man-at-arms (*n.*) fully equipped soldier, heavily armed warrior **3H6** V.iv.42 [Prince to all, of the effect of the Queen's words on a coward] *make him, naked, foil a man at arms*

mandate (*n.*) command, order **Ham** III.iv.205 [Hamlet to Gertrude, of Rosencrantz and Guildenstern] *They bear the mandate*

mandragora (*n.*) mandrake plant [seen as a narcotic] **Oth** III.iii.327 [Iago to himself, as if to Othello] *Not poppy, nor mandragora ... / Shall ever medicine thee to that sweet sleep / Which thou owed'st yesterday;* **AC** I.v.4 ☛ **PLANTS**, p.330

mandrake (*n.*) **1** variety of poisonous plant [thought to emit a lethal shriek when pulled from the ground] **2H6** III.ii.310 [Suffolk to Queen] *Would curses kill, as doth the mandrake's groan;* **RJ** IV.iii.47
2 variety of poisonous plant [whose long forked root was thought to resemble a man's legs and private parts; thus, with aphrodisiac properties] **2H4** III.ii.304 [Falstaff alone, of Shallow] *the whores called him mandrake*
3 noisy growth, dwarf **2H4** I.ii.14 [Falstaff to Page] *Thou whoreson mandrake* ☛ **PLANTS**, p.330

man-entered (*adj.*) entered into manhood **Cor** II.ii.97 [Cominius to all, of Coriolanus] *His pupil age / Man-entered thus*

mangle (*v.*) wound, gash, hack **Oth** V.i.79 [Iago to Cassio] *may you suspect / Who they should be that have thus mangled you?*

manhood (*n.*) manliness, courage, valour **TNK** I.i.72 [First Queen to Thesus] *I hope ... / Some god hath put his mercy in your manhood;* **TNK** III.i.64, v.36

manifest (*adj.*) clear, evident, obvious **MM** V.i.299 [disguised Duke to Escalus] *The Duke's unjust / Thus to retort your manifest appeal;* **AW** I.iii.218; **Cor** I.iii.52

manifested (*adj.*) plain, apparent, unmistakeable **MM** IV.ii.156 [disguised Duke to Provost, of his remarks about Claudio] *To make you understand this in a manifested effect*

manifoldly (*adv.*) in manifold ways, each in its own way **AW** II.iii.203 [Lafew to Parolles] *the scarfs and the bannerets about thee did manifoldly dissuade me from believing thee a vessel of too great a burden*

manikin (*n.*) little man, puppet **TN** III.ii.51 [Fabian to Sir Toby, of Sir Andrew] *This is a dear manikin to you*

mankind (*n.*) man-like woman, virago; or: mad, furious, infuriated **Cor** IV.ii.16 [Sicinius to Volumnia] *Are you mankind?*

mankind (*adj.*) man-like, mannish **WT** II.iii.67 [Leontes to Paulina] *A mankind witch!*

manly (*adv.*) heroically, bravely, gallantly **TNK** III.i.79 [Palamon to Arcite] *brave souls in shades / That have died manly*

manner (*n.*) **1** (plural) proper behaviour, good conduct, forms of politeness **Oth** II.i.98 [Cassio to Iago] *Let it not gall your patience ... / That I extend my manners;* **AY** III.ii.39; **1H6** II.ii.54; **KJ** II.i.127; **TNK** III.v.52

2 (plural) morals, character, way of behaving **Tem** V.ii.291 [Prospero to all, of Caliban] *He is as disproportioned in his manners / As in his shape;* **AW** I.i.60; **AY** III.ii.40; **Tim** IV.iii.200

3 (plural) ways of life, social conditions **CE** I.ii.12 [Antipholus of Syracuse to Dromio of Syracuse] *I'll view the manners of the town*

4 character, nature, quality **2H4** IV.iv.123 [Gloucester to all] *The seasons change their manners*

5 fashion, usage, custom **LL** V.ii.365 [Rosaline to King, of the Princess] *My lady, to the manner of the days, / In courtesy gives undeserving praise*

6 [legal] act, work, deed **LL** I.i.200 [Costard to Berowne, of being caught with Jaquenetta] *I was taken with the manner* [i.e. caught in the act]

7 [legal] thing stolen, stolen goods **1H4** II.iv.308 [Prince Hal to Bardolph] *thou stolest a cup of sack eighteen years ago, and wert taken with the manner* [i.e. caught in the act]

manner, in as it were, in a manner of speaking **R2** III.i.11 [Bolingbroke to Bushy and Green, of Richard] *You have in manner with your sinful hours / Made a divorce betwixt his Queen and him*

mannerly *(adj.)* **1** well-mannered, courteous, genteel **1H6** II.iv.19 [Richard to Warwick] *here is a mannerly forbearance;* **WT** II.i.86

2 seemly, decent, modest **RJ** I.v.98 [Juliet to Romeo] *you do wrong your hand too much, / Which mannerly devotion shows in this*

mannerly *(adv.)* politely, courteously, with good manners **Cym** III.vii.64 [Belarius to disguised Innogen] *We'll mannerly demand thee of thy story*

mannish *(adj.)* **1** of a man, adult, mature **Cym** IV.ii.236 [Arviragus to Guiderius] *our voices / Have got the mannish crack*

2 masculine, macho **AY** I.iii.119 [Rosalind to Celia, of their male disguise] *As many other mannish cowards have*

man of arms, man-of-arms *(n.)* soldier, fighting man **1H6** I.iv.30 [Talbot to all] *with a baser man-of-arms by far … they would have bartered me*

man of wax faultless, perfect [as of a wax model] **RJ** I.iii.77 [Nurse to Juliet, of Paris] *why, he's a man of wax*

manor *(n.)* country house, mansion, estate **AW** III.ii.9 [Clown to Countess] *I knew a man … hold a goodly manor for a song;* **H8** I.i.84

man-queller *(n.)* ☞ queller *(n.)*

mansion *(n.)* dwelling-place, home, lodging [not necessarily stately] **Sonn** 95.9 *Oh what a mansion have those vices got / Which for their habitation chose out thee;* **Sonn** 146.6

mansionry *(n.)* place of habitation; or: building place **Mac** I.vi.5 [Banquo to King] *The temple-haunting martlet, does approve / By his loved mansionry that the heaven's breath / Smells wooingly here* [F Mansonry]

mantle *(n.)* **1** loose sleeveless cloak **JC** III.ii.171 [Antony to all, of Caesar's cloak] *You all do know this mantle;* **Ham** I.i.167; **TNK** I.i.63 ☞ **CLOTHING**, p.79

2 surface vegetable matter, covering **KL** III.iv.127 [Edgar as Poor Tom to Gloucester, of himself] *drinks the green mantle of the standing pool*

mantle *(v.)* **1** cover, conceal, obscure **Tem** V.i.67 [Prospero to himself, of the King's company] *the ignorant fumes that mantle / Their clearer reason*

2 cover with a coating, form a scum **MV** I.i.89 [Gratiano to Antonio] *There are a sort of men whose visages / Do cream and mantle like a standing pond*

mantled *(adj.)* covered, surfaced **Tem** IV.i.182 [Ariel to Prospero, of Stephano, Trinculo, and Caliban] *I left them / I'th' filthy mantled pool beyond your cell* [i.e. slime-covered]

many *(n.)* multitude, throng **2H4** I.iii.91 [Archbishop to all, as if to the common people] *O thou fond many, with what loud applause / Didst thou beat heaven with blessing Bolingbroke*

many a day, for this during these past few days **Ham** III.i.91 [Ophelia to Hamlet] *How does your honour for this many a day?*

map *(n.)* **1** outline, picture, image **R3** II.iv.54 [Queen Elizabeth to all] *I see, as in a map, the end of all;* **Luc** 402; **Sonn** 68.1

2 epitome, embodiment, incarnation **2H6** III.i.203 [King to all, as if to Gloucester] *in thy face I see / The map of honour, truth, and loyalty;* **E3** III.iii.218; **R2** V.i.12; **Sonn** 68.13

mappery *(n.)* mere map-making **TC** I.iii.205 [Ulysses to all, of Achilles' and Ajax' view of military strategy] *They call this bed-work, mappery, closet-war*

mar *(v.)* ruin, harm, injure, damage **TS** IV.iii.113 [Petruchio to Tailor, of Katherina] *thou hast marred her gown;* **AY** I.i.30; **JC** III.ii.198; **KL** I.i.95; **Tem** I.i.13; **WT** IV.iv.476

marble *(adj.)* enduring, solid [as marble] **E3** III.iv.90 [Prince Edward to all] *marble courage still did underprop;* **WT** V.iii.88

marbled *(adj.)* shining like marble; reminiscent of marble **Tim** IV.iii.192 [Timon alone, of the earth's new monsters] *whom thy upward face / Hath to the marbled mansion all above / Never presented*

marcantant *(n.)* malapropism of Italian 'mercatante', merchant **TS** IV.ii.63 [Biondello to Tranio, of the man he has seen] *a marcantant or a pedant*

march *(n.)* **1** sequence, rhythmical movement **E3** II.ii.63 [King Edward alone] *my arms … shall meet my foe / In a deep march of penetrable groans*

2 border region, frontier **H5** I.ii.140 [Canterbury to King Henry] *They of those marches … / Shall be a wall sufficient to defend / Our inland*

March-chick *(n.)* precocious youth, presumptuous youngster **MA** I.iii.52 [Don John to Borachio, probably of Claudio] *A very forward March-chick!*

marchpane *(n.)* marzipan **RJ** I.v.8 [First Servingman to Second Servingman] *save me a piece of marchpane*

mare *(n.)* goblin that causes nightmares [by sitting on the sleeper's chest] **2H4** II.i.74 [Hostess to Falstaff] *I will ride thee a-nights like the mare*

mare, ride the wild type of schoolboy game involving one boy leaping on top of others **2H4** II.iv.242 [Falstaff to Doll, of why Prince Harry loves Poins] *'a … rides the wild mare with the boys*

mare's dead, whose what's the fuss, what's going on **2H4** II.i.41 [Falstaff to all] *How now, whose mare's dead? What's the matter?*

margent *(n.)* **1** margin [of a page, where an explanatory note would be found] **Ham** V.ii.153 [Horatio to Hamlet] *I knew you must be edified by the margent* [i.e. need to have something explained]; **Luc** 102; **RJ** I.iii.87

2 margin, edge, border **Lover** 39 [of the woman by the river] *Upon whose weeping margent she was set;* **LL** II.i.232; **MND** II.i.85

mark *(n.)* **1** target, goal, aim **2H6** I.i.241 [York to himself, of the crown] *that's the golden mark I seek to hit;* **2H4** II.iii.31; **LL** IV.i.111; **MA** II.i.226; **Sonn** 116.5; **Tim** V.iii.10

2 reach, aim, range **AC** III.vi.87 [Caesar to Octavia] *You are abused / Beyond the mark of thought;* **Cor** II.ii.87

3 shot at a target **LL** IV.i.131 [Maria to Costard, of Rosaline and Boyet's repartee] *A mark marvellous well shot, for they both did hit it* [bawdy pun: 133]

4 notable sight, object of serious attention **TNK** I.iv.20 [Theseus to all, of Palamon and Arcite] *they were a mark / Worth a god's view;* **MM** V.i.320; **WT** IV.iv.8

5 (plural) insignia, regalia **Cor** II.iii.140 [Menenius to Coriolanus] *in th'official marks invested*

6 birthmark, discolouration, blemish **MND** V.i.402 [Oberon to all, of the Athenians] *Nor mark prodigious … / Shall upon their children be*

7 mark used as a signature by an illiterate person **2H6** IV.ii.95 [Cade to Clerk] *Dost thou use to write thy name? Or hast thou a mark to thyself*

8 ☞ **MONEY**, p.286

9 ☞ **POLITENESS**, p.340

mark (*v.*) **1** note, pay attention to, take notice of **Ham** III.ii.156 [Ophelia to Hamlet] *I'll mark the play* ☛ FEW, p.xxi; **ATTENTION SIGNALS**, p.26
   2 destine, brand, designate **3H6** II.ii.137 [Queen to Richard] *thou art … / Marked by the destinies to be avoided;* **1H4** III.i.38; **2H6** IV.ii.115; **3H6** II.vi.40

market (*n.*) **1** purchase, spending opportunity, outlay **TN** III.iii.47 [Antonio to Sebastian] *your store, / I think, is not for idle markets*
   2 marketing [i.e. profitable use] **Ham** IV.iv.34 [Hamlet alone] *What is a man, / If his chief good and market of his time / Be but to sleep*
   3 opportunity to make a profit **TNK** Epilogue.9 [Speaker to audience] *hiss, and kill / Our market*

market-man (*n.*) man who trades in a market **1H6** V.v.54 [Suffolk to all] *So worthless peasants bargain for their wives, / As market-men for oxen*

marking (*n.*) noting, notice, attending [to] **LL** I.i.274 [Costard to King, of the proclamation] *I do confess much of the hearing of it, but little of the marking of it*

markman (*n.*) marksman **RJ** I.i.206 [Romeo to Benvolio, of his guess about Romeo's love] *A right good markman*

marl (*n.*) clay, earth, loam **MA** II.i.55 [Beatrice to Leonato] *a clod of wayward marl*

marmoset (*n.*) type of small monkey **Tem** II.ii.167 [Caliban to Stephano] *I [will] … instruct thee how / To snare the nimble marmoset*

married (*adj.*) joined in harmony, well-proportioned **RJ** I.iii.84 [Lady Capulet to Juliet, of Paris] *Examine every married lineament*

marring (*n.*) harm, detriment, loss **2H4** Epilogue.6 [Epilogue] *what indeed I should say will, I doubt, prove mine own marring*

marrow (*n.*) **1** rich and nutritious substance derived from bone cavities **TNK** III.v.6 [Schoolmaster to all] *the very plum-broth / And marrow of my understanding laid upon ye* [i.e. the very best of my intellect]
   2 spirit, courage, strength **Tim** V.iv.9 [Alcibiades to Senators] *When crouching marrow in the bearer strong / Cries of itself 'No more'*

marry (*v.*) **1** join together, unite **KL** V.iii.227 [Edmund to all, of the deaths] *All three / Now marry in an instant;* **2H4** V.i.62
   2 be a marriage dowry for **AW** III.vii.35 [Helena to Widow, of Diana] *To marry her I'll add three thousand crowns*

marry (*int.*) by Mary **AY** I.i.30 [Orlando to Oliver] *Marry, sir, I am helping you* ☛ **SWEARING**, p.435; **EXCLAMATIONS**, p.158

marshal (*v.*) conduct, lead, steer **Ham** III.iv.206 [Hamlet to Gertrude, of Rosencrantz and Guildenstern] *They must … marshal me to knavery*

mart (*n.*) **1** market **CE** I.ii.27 [First Merchant to Antipholus of Syracuse] *I'll meet with you upon the mart;* **CE** I.ii.74, II.i.5, III.i.12; **MV** III.i.42; **Per** IV.iv.4
   2 bargaining, buying and selling, trading **Ham** I.i.74 [Marcellus to Horatio and Barnardo, of activities in Denmark] *foreign mart for implements of war;* **TS** II.i.320

mart (*v.*) **1** do business, bargain, make a deal **WT** IV.iv.349 [disguised Polixenes to Florizel, of Autolycus] *you have let him go / And nothing marted with him;* **Cym** I.vii.151
   2 sell, market, traffic in **JC** IV.iii.11 [Brutus to Cassius] *you yourself / Are much condemned … / To sell and mart your offices for gold / To undeservers*

martial (*adj.*) **1** warlike, valiant, brave **1H6** I.iv.74 [Talbot to Salisbury] *How farest thou, mirror of all martial men?;* **AY** I.iii.118; **1H6** II.i.21
   2 military, warlike, combat **E3** III.i.6 [King John to all, of King Edward] *How hast thou heard that he provided is / Of martial furniture*

martialist (*n.*) soldier, military man [i.e. follower of Mars] **E3** III.iii.174 [King Edward to Prince Edward] *As ancient custom is of martialists;* **TNK** I.ii.16

martlemas (*n.*) [idiosyncratic] case of plenty, fullness of being **2H4** II.ii.96 [Poins to Bardolph, of Falstaff] *how doth the martlemas your master?* ☛ **DAYS AND DATES**, p.630

martlet (*n.*) house-martin [which often builds its nest in churches] **Mac** I.vi.4 [Banquo to King] *This guest of summer, / The temple-haunting martlet;* **MV** II.ix.28

martyr (*v.*) **1** mutilate, torture, disfigure **Tit** III.i.81 [Lucius to Lavinia] *who hath martyred thee?;* **Tit** III.i.107
   2 slay, slaughter, butcher **Tit** V.i.179 [Titus to Demetrius and Chiron] *Hark … how I mean to martyr you*

martyred (*adj.*) mutilated, tortured, disfigured **Tit** III.ii.36 [Titus to Marcus, of Lavinia] *I can interpret all her martyred signs*

marvel (*n.*) astonishment, amazement, surprise **WT** V.i.187 [Lord to Leontes] *I speak amazedly, and it becomes / My marvel and my message;* **Cym** III.i.10

marvel (*adj.*) strange, remarkable **TS** IV.ii.86 [Tranio as Lucentio to Pedant, of not hearing of the danger to him] *'Tis marvel*

marvel (*v.*) wonder, be curious **1H6** II.i.48 [Alençon to all] *Here cometh Charles, I marvel how he sped;* **AW** II.v.58; **KL** IV.ii.1

marvellous (*adv.*) very, extremely, exceedingly **Ham** III.ii.309 [Guildenstern to Hamlet, of Claudius] *Is in his retirement marvellous distempered* ☛ FEW, p.xxi

Mary-bud (*n.*) marigold bud **Cym** II.iii.23 [Song] *winking Mary-buds begin to ope their golden eyes* ☛ **PLANTS**, p.330

masculine (*adj.*) manly, virile, macho **1H6** II.i.22 [Burgundy to all, of Pucelle] *Pray God she prove not masculine ere long*

mash (*v.*) [brewing] ferment, mix **Tit** III.ii.38 [Titus to Marcus, of Lavinia drinking her tears] *Brewed with her sorrow, mashed upon her cheeks*

mask (*n.*) barrier worn to protect the complexion against the sun **TC** I.ii.262 [Cressida to Pandarus, of her defences] *my mask to defend my beauty*

mask (*v.*) take part in a masque **RJ** I.v.38 [Capulet to Cousin Capulet] *then we masked*

masoned (*adj.*) formed with masonry; or: mason-built **TNK** V.i.55 [Arcite praying to Mars] *who dost pluck / With hand armipotent … / The masoned turrets*

masonry (*n.*) stonework, floor **AW** II.i.31 [Bertram to Parolles] *Creaking my shoes on the plain masonry*

masque (*n.*) masquerade, pageant, show **KJ** V.ii.132 [Bastard to Lewis the Dauphin, of the French invasion] *This harnessed masque and unadvised revel*

masque (*v.*) ☛ **mask** (*v.*)

masquing (*adj.*) elaborate, grotesque, suitable for use in a masque **TS** IV.iii.87 [Petruchio to Tailor, of a gown] *What masquing stuff is here?*

mass (*n.*) **1** size, numbers, large amount **Ham** IV.iv.47 [Hamlet alone] *this army of such mass and charge*
   2 service, liturgy, divine celebration **RJ** IV.i.38 [Juliet to Friar] *shall I come to you at evening mass?*

massy (*adj.*) massive, heavy, colossal **Tem** III.iii.68 [Ariel to Alonso, Sebastian, and Antonio] *Your swords are now too massy for your strengths;* **E3** II.i.137; **Ham** III.iii.17; **MA** III.iii.134; **TC** Prologue.17, II.iii.16

mast (*n.*) fruit of forest trees, edible produce **Tim** IV.iii.421 [Timon to Bandits] *The oaks bear mast* [i.e. acorns]

master (*n.*) **1** teacher, school-master **TS** III.i.52 [Bianca to Lucentio as Cambio] *I must believe my master;* **PassP** XV.2; **TS** IV.ii.7
   2 ☛ **ADDRESS FORMS**, p.8

master (*v.*) own, possess, have at one's disposal **Sonn** 106.8 *Even such a beauty as you master now;* **Luc** 863; **MV** V.i.174

master-cord (*n.*) main sinew **H8** III.ii.106 [Surrey to Norfolk, of Wolsey's apparent anger] *I would 'twere something that would fret the string, / The master-cord on's heart!*

masterdom (*n.*) supremacy, dominion, command **Mac** I.v.68 [Lady Macbeth to Macbeth, of their plan] *Which shall ... / Give solely sovereign sway and masterdom*

masterless (*adj.*) abandoned, lacking an owner **RJ** V.iii.142 [Friar to himself] *What mean these masterless and gory swords*

masterly (*adj.*) of one's skill, of one's mastery **Ham** IV.vii.95 [Claudius to Laertes, of Lamord] *He ... gave you such a masterly report / For art and exercise in your defence*

masterly (*adv.*) from experience, in a masterly way **TN** II.iv.22 [Orsino to Viola as Cesario] *Thou dost speak masterly*

mastership (*n.*) [ironic use] senior citizen, leading light **E3** IV.ii.79 [King Edward to Captain, of the burgesses of Calais] *you may inform their masterships;* **TG** III.i.277

mastic (*adj.*) gummy, resinous, sticky **TC** I.iii.73 [Agamemnon to Ulysses] *When rank Thersites opes his mastic jaws*

match (*n.*) **1** bargain, contract, agreement **MV** III.i.40 [Shylock to Salerio, of Antonio] *There I have another bad match;* **AW** V.iii.30; **Cor** II.iii.79; **Cym** III.vii.3; **TS** II.i.323; **Venus** 586

2 appointment, assignation, rendezvous **MM** V.i.209 [Mariana to Angelo] *This is the body / That took away the match from Isabel*

3 matching, equality **KJ** II.i.430 [Hubert to King John and King Philip] *If love ambitious sought a match of birth, / Whose veins bound richer blood than Lady Blanche?* [also: suitable marriage]

4 game, contest, competition **R2** III.iii.165 [King Richard to Aumerle] *shall we ... make some pretty match with shedding tears*

5 victory, success, triumph **RJ** II.iv.69 [Romeo to Mercutio] *Swits and spurs, swits and spurs! or I'll cry a match*

6 opponent, rival, foe **2H6** V.ii.10 [York to Warwick, of Clifford] *match to match I have encountered him*

7 robbery, operation, enterprise **1H4** I.ii.107 [Falstaff to Prince Hal] *Now shall we know if Gadshill have set a match!*

match (*v.*) **1** join in marriage, make a match **TN** I.iii.103 [Sir Toby to Sir Andrew, of Olivia] *she'll not match above her degree;* **2H6** I.i.129; **3H6** III.iii.210; **MA** II.i.57; **RJ** III.v.179; **TS** IV.iv.32

2 compare, equate, make equal **Tim** I.i.5 [Poet to Painter] *What strange, / Which manifold record not matches?;* **Oth** III.iii.235

mate (*n.*) **1** companion, associate, comrade **R3** I.iii.339 [Richard to Murderers] *my hardy, stout, resolved mates!;* **AC** V.i.43; **1H6** I.ii.92; **KL** III.vi.105; **TG** V.iv.14

2 fellow, individual **2H4** II.iv.120 [Doll to Pistol] *you poor, base, rascally, cheating, lack-linen mate!;* **E3** III.iii.53; **1H6** III.i.99; **TS** I.i.58

mate (*v.*) **1** astound, amaze, confound **Mac** V.i.74 [Doctor to Gentlewoman, of Lady Macbeth] *My mind she has mated, and amazed my sight* [also: bewildered]

2 check, frustrate, hinder **Venus** 909 [of Venus] *Her more than haste is mated with delays*

3 be a match for, cope with **H8** III.ii.274 [Wolsey to Surrey] *I ... / Dare mate a sounder man than Surrey can be*

4 checkmate, overcome, finish off **2H6** III.i.265 [Suffolk to all] *that is good deceit / Which mates him first that first intends deceit*

mate and make husband and wife **KL** IV.iii.34 [disguised Kent to Gentleman, of Lear's daughters] *one self mate and make could not beget / Such different issues*

mated (*adj.*) bewildered, confused **CE** V.i.282 [Duke to all] *I think you are all mated, or stark mad;* **CE** III.ii.54

material (*adj.*) **1** full of matter, containing substance **AY** III.iii.29 [Jaques to himself, of Touchstone] *A material fool!;* **KL** IV.ii.35

2 relevant, pertinent, germane **Cym** I.vii.207 [Iachimo to Innogen] *I have outstood my time, which is material / To th'tender of our present*

matin (*n.*) morning **Ham** I.v.89 [Ghost to Hamlet] *The glow-worm shows the matin to be near*

matron (*n.*) married woman **Tim** IV.i.3 [Timon alone] *Matrons, turn incontinent;* **Cor** II.i.255; **Cym** V.iv.30; **Tim** IV.iii.113

matter (*n.*) **1** subject-matter, content, substance **Tem** II.i.90 [Antonio to Sebastian, of Gonzalo] *What impossible matter will he make easy next?;* **AY** III.v.137; **H8** III.ii.21; **KL** III.v.14; **RJ** III.ii.83; **TN** III.iv.141

2 significance, import, meaning **KL** I.i.55 [Gonerill to Lear] *I love you more than word can wield the matter* [i.e. more than words can say]; **Ham** IV.i.1; **MV** III.v.65; **Tem** II.i.234

3 stuff, soul, substance **WT** II.iii.98 [Paulina to all, of the baby] *the whole matter / And copy of the father;* **KJ** IV.i.64

4 affair(s), business, real issue **2H6** I.iii.33 [Suffolk to Peter] *We'll hear more of your matter before the King;* **Oth** I.i.84 [Brabantio to Roderigo] *What is the matter there?;* **3H6** III.iii.258; **H8** I.i.126; **LL** I.i.198; **TN** I.v.203; **WT** V.ii.103

5 reason, cause, ground **2H4** I.ii.134 [Lord Chief Justice to Falstaff] *I sent for you, when there were matters against you for your life;* **AC** II.ii.57; **2H4** I.Induction.15; **Ham** II.ii.441; **MW** I.i.116; **TS** I.i.33

6 means, capacity, wherewithal **MW** V.v.135 [Falstaff to all, of his brain] *it wants matter to prevent so gross o'erreaching as this;* **MA** I.i.258

7 pus, discharge, fluid [from a wound] **LL** III.i.117 [Costard to Armado, of his broken shin] *Till there be more matter in the shin;* **KJ** III.iv.167; **MW** I.i.117 ; **TC** II.i.8 [also: sense 1]

matter, to the relevant, pertinent, apposite **MM** V.i.90 [Isabella to Duke, of her description of Angelo] *The phrase is to the matter*

mattock (*n.*) tool for loosening hard ground **RJ** V.iii.22 [Romeo to Balthasar] *Give me that mattock and the wrenching iron;* **RJ** V.iii.22 [stage direction], 185; **Tit** IV.iii.11

mature (*adj.*) ready, ripe, set **Cor** IV.iii.22 [Roman to Volsce, of the nobles' discontent] *This ... is almost mature for the violent breaking out;* **KL** IV.vi.274

maugre (*prep.*) [pron: ˈmawguh] in spite of **Tit** IV.ii.109 [Aaron to Demetrius, of the baby] *This maugre all the world I will keep safe;* **KL** V.iii.129; **TN** III.i.148

maund (*n.*) wicker basket **Lover** 36 [of the woman] *A thousand favours from a maund she drew*

maw (*n.*) belly, stomach; throat, gullet **E3** III.i.89 [Mariner to King John, of the French fleet] *as when the empty eagle flies / To satisfy his hungry griping maw;* **H5** II.i.46; **KJ** V.vii.37; **MM** III.ii.20; **Tim** III.iv.53; **Venus** 602

may (*v.*) to take part in May-day festivities **TNK** III.i.1 [stage direction] *Noise and hallowing as of people a-maying*

may, you go on, carry on **Cor** II.iii.34 [Second Citizen to Third Citizen] *You are never without your tricks. You may, you may!* **☛** **DISCOURSE MARKERS**, p.127

maying (*n.*) May-day festivities **TNK** II.ii.36 [Third Countryman to the others] *Do we all hold against the maying?* [i.e. to take part in the maying]

maze (*n.*) **1** arrangement of paths, network of tracks **Tem** V.i.242 [Alonso to all] *This is as strange a maze as e'er men trod;* **MND** II.i.99

2 chance wandering about, labyrinthine business **TS** I.ii.54 [Petruchio to Hortensio] *I have thrust myself into this maze, / Haply to wive*

maze (*v.*) confuse, bewilder, perplex **1H6** IV.ii.47 [Talbot to all] *A little herd of England's timorous deer, / Mazed with a yelping kennel of French curs!*

mazed (*adj.*) bewildered, confused, perplexed **H8** II.iv.185 [King Henry to all] *many mazed considerings did throng / And pressed in with this caution;* **MND** II.i.113

mazzard (*n.*) [jocular] skull, head, bowl **Oth** II.iii.148 [Cassio to Montano] *I'll knock you o'er the mazzard;* **Ham** V.i.88

me (*int.*) **☛** **REGRETS**, p.367

meacock (*adj.*) spiritless, languid, docile **TS** II.i.306 [Petruchio to all] *A meacock wretch can make the curstest shrew*

mead (*n.*) meadow **TS** V.ii.138 [Katherina to Widow, of her frown] *It blots thy beauty as frosts do bite the meads;* **H5** V.ii.54; **KL** I.i.65; **MND** II.i.83; **Tit** II.iv.54; **Venus** 636

meagre (*adj.*) **1** lean, gaunt, emaciated **2H6** III.ii.162 [Warwick to Suffolk, of a dead body] *Of ashy semblance, meagre, pale, and bloodless;* **E3** III.iii.202
2 thin, slight, scrawny **TNK** IV.ii.27 [Emilia alone, of Palamon] *He's swarth and meagre*
3 barren, poor-quality, unproductive **KJ** III.i.80 [King Philip to Constance, of the sun] *Turning … / The meagre cloddy earth to glittering gold*

meal (*n.*) flour, edible part of grain **Cym** IV.ii.27 [Belarius to himself] *Nature hath meal, and bran* [i.e. has both good and bad]

meal (*v.*) stain, spot, blemish **MM** IV.ii.80 [disguised Duke to Provost, of Angelo] *Were he mealed with that / Which he corrects*

mealy (*adj.*) powdery, scaly, grainy **TC** III.iii.79 [Achilles to Patroclus] *men, like butterflies, / Show not their mealy wings but to the summer*

mean (*n.*) **1** means, way, method **2H6** IV.viii.67 [Buckingham to rebels] *we'll devise a mean / To reconcile you all unto the King;* **AC** IV.vi.35; **H8** V.iii.146; **Luc** 1045; **Oth** III.i.36; **TG** III.i.38
2 means, agent, cause **R3** I.iii.89 [Richard to Queen Elizabeth] *You may deny that you were not the mean / Of my Lord Hastings' late imprisonment* [F; Q *cause*]
3 (plural) manner, mode, method **Ham** IV.v.213 [Laertes to Claudius, of Polonius] *His means of death;* **MM** II.iv.48
4 (plural) resources, wherewithal, wealth **Tim** II.ii.172 [Flavius to Timon] *What heart, head, sword, force, means, but is Lord Timon's?;* **AW** I.v.35; **AY** II.vii.73; **KL** I.i.20; **MM** II.ii.24; **Tim** V.iv.20
5 (plural) capacity, capability, potential **JC** I.ii.158 [Cassius to all, of Antony] *you know his means, / If he improve them, may well stretch so far / As to annoy us all*
6 mediation, intercession, intervention **Cym** II.iv.3 [Philario to Posthumus, of Cymbeline] *What means do you make to him?*
7 means of access, passage **Ham** II.vi.14 [Hamlet to Horatio, by letter] *give these fellows some means to the King;* **AW** V.i.35
8 moderation, measure, limit **1H6** I.ii.121 [Reignier to Alençon, of Charles] *Shall we disturb him, since he keeps no mean?* [i.e. seems to have no self-control, with bawdy pun]
9 (plural) obstacles, intervening factors **3H6** III.ii.141 [Richard alone, of the crown] *I chide the means that keeps me from it*
10 middle, midway **MV** I.ii.7 [Nerissa to Portia] *It is no mean happiness … to be seated in the mean* [second instance]
11 middle-part singer, tenor, alto **WT** IV.iii.42 [Clown to himself, of the shearer singers] *they are most of them means and basses;* **LL** V.ii.328; **TG** I.ii.95
12 ☛ by any means

means, make take pains, make efforts **TG** V.iv.138 [Duke to Thurio, of Silvia] *To make such means for her as thou hast done, / And leave her on such slight conditions;* **R3** V.iii.249

mean (*adj.*) **1** of low rank, inferior in position, less important **3H6** III.ii.97 [Lady Grey to Edward] *I am too mean to be your queen;* **H5** III.i.29; **1H6** IV.vi.23; **2H6** II.i.180; **R3** IV.i.52; **Tit** II.i.73 ☛ meaner (*n.*), meanest (*n.*)
2 lowly, humble, poor **TS** IV.iii.176 [Petruchio to Katherina, of her clothes] *this poor furniture and mean array;* **AC** IV.xv.74; **Cor** IV.i.v.1; **Cym** II.iii.132; **R2** I.iii.33; **Tem** III.i.4 ☛ meanest (*n.*)
3 unworthy, insignificant, unimportant **3H6** I.iii.19 [Rutland to Clifford] *I am too mean a subject for thy wrath;* **AW** III.v.59; **Cym** II.ii.29; **2H6** III.ii.146; **TC** II.iii.193; **TS** V.iii.31 [first instance]
4 average, moderate, middling **LL** II.i.13 [Princess to Boyet] *my beauty, though but mean, / Needs not the painted flourish of your praise;* **MV** I.ii.7; **TS** V.iii.32

mean space in the meantime, meanwhile **E3** III.i.94 [King John to all] *Mean space, my lords, 'tis best we be dispersed*

mean (*v.*) **1** intend, purpose, mean to act **Cor** I.ix.56 [Cominius to Martius] *we'll put you - / Like one that means his proper harm - in manacles;* **AW** IV.iii.25; **1H6** V.i.39; **KL** III.vii.76; **MW** III.iv.82; **WT** I.ii.146
2 intend for, have in mind for **TNK** Epilogue.14 [Speaker to audience] *If the tale we have told … any way content ye, / For to that honest purpose it was meant ye*
3 lament, mourn, make complaint **MND** V.i.315 [Demetrius to Lysander, of Thisbe] *And thus she means, videlicet*

mean-apparelled (*adj.*) humbly dressed, in poor clothes **TS** III.ii.70 [Tranio as Lucentio to Baptista, of Petruchio] *oftentimes he goes but mean-apparelled*

mean-born (*adj.*) low-born, of humble birth **2H6** III.i.335 [York to himself] *Let pale-faced fear keep with the mean-born man*

meander (*n.*) crooked path, winding way **Tem** III.iii.3 [Gonzalo to all] *Here's a maze trod indeed, / Through forthrights and meanders*

meaner (*n.*) lower ranking, less eminent **AC** II.v.83 [Cleopatra to herself] *These hands do lack nobility, that they strike / A meaner than myself* ☛ mean (*adj.*) **1**

meanest (*n.*) lowest ranking, least eminent **2H6** IV.viii.36 [Clifford to rebels, of Cade] *Will he … make the meanest of you earls and dukes?;* **Tit** IV.iv.33 ☛ best (*n.*) **3**; mean (*adj.*) **1**

meaning (*n.*) design, intention, purpose **3H6** IV.vii.60 [Edward to all] *'tis wisdom to conceal our meaning;* **AW** III.vii.45; **H5** I.ii.241; **KL** V.iii.4; **R3** III.v.54; **Tim** V.iv.59

meanly (*adv.*) **1** humbly, in a lowly manner **R3** IV.iii.37 [King Richard alone, of Clarence] *His daughter meanly have I matched in marriage;* **Cym** III.iii.82
2 tolerably, moderately well, well enough **LL** V.ii.328 [Berowne to all, of Boyet] *he can sing / A mean most meanly*

meanly, not not a little, in no small degree **CE** I.i.59 [Egeon to Duke] *My wife, not meanly proud of two such boys*

measles (*n.*) scabs; or: lepers **Cor** III.i.78 [Coriolanus to First Senator] *those measles / Which we disdain should tetter us*

measurable (*adj.*) fitting, apt, suitable **LL** V.i.87 [Holofernes to Armado] *The posterior of the day … is liable, congruent, and measurable for the afternoon*

measure (*n.*) **1** extent, size, amount, quantity, mass **3H6** II.i.105 [Warwick to Edward and Richard] *to add more measure to your woes;* **AC** III.iv.8; **Cor** V.i.47; **H5** V.ii.136; **JC** III.i.150; **Oth** IV.iii.72
2 limit, moderation, extent not to be exceeded **AC** I.i.2 [Philo to Demetrius] *this dotage of our general's / O'erflows the measure;* **MA** I.i.1, 2, 3, II.i.63; **R2** III.iv.8
3 due proportion, appropriate degree, full quantity **Mac** V.vi.112 [Malcolm to all] *What's more to do … / We will perform in measure, time, and place;* **3H6** II.iii.32
4 range, reach, scope **TG** V.iv.128 [Valentine to Thurio] *Come not within the measure of my wrath*
5 [of drink] vessel-full, tot **Oth** II.iii.28 [Iago to Cassio] *Cyprus gallants that would fain have a measure to the health of black Othello;* **TS** III.ii.224
6 course of action, means **KL** IV.vii.3 [Cordelia to Kent, of recompensing him] *My life will be too short / And every measure fail me;* **AC** III.iv.35; **TC** I.iii.202; **Tim** V.iv.4
7 punishment, treatment, retribution **TNK** IV.iii.33 [Gaoler's Daughter to herself, of souls in hell] *O, they have shrewd measure;* **MM** III.ii.232
8 slow stately dance, graceful movement **RJ** I.v.50 [Romeo to himself, of Juliet] *The measure done, I'll watch her place of stand;* **AW** II.i.56; **AY** V.iv.43; **H5** V.ii.135; **MA** II.i.65; **WT** IV.iv.727
9 accompaniment, background melody **KJ** III.i.304 [Blanche to Lewis the Dauphin] *Shall braying trumpets and loud churlish drums … be measures to our pomp?*
10 metre, poetic skill **H5** V.ii.134 [King Henry to Katherine, of using verse] *I have neither words nor measure*

11 pattern of movement, regular course, routine **MV** II.vi.11 [Gratiano to Salerio] *Where is the horse that doth untread again / His tedious measures with the unbated fire / That he did pace them first?*

measure, with liberally, abundantly, lavishly **AY** V.iv.176 [Duke Senior to all] *With measure heaped in joy;* **Cor** II.ii.121

measure *(v.)* **1** pass through, travel over, traverse **MV** III.iv.84 [Portia to Nerissa] *we must measure twenty miles today;* **KJ** V.v.3; **LL** V.ii.186; **R2** III.ii.125; **TG** II.vii.10

2 apportion, dispense, give out **RJ** I.iv.10 [Benvolio to Romeo, of the Capulets] *We'll measure them a measure and be gone* [first instance]

3 judge, appraise **Venus** 524 [Adonis to Venus] *Measure my strangeness with my unripe years;* **2H4** V.ii.65

4 check that the length of two weapons is the same [before beginning a duel] **AY** V.iv.84 [Touchstone to Jaques, of himself and a courtier] *we measured swords and parted;* **MW** I.i.115

measure back *(v.)* retrace, travel back, cover the distance **Tem** II.i.264 [Antonio to Sebastian] *How shall that Claribel / Measure us back to Naples?*

measuring *(n.)* task of checking measurement **MW** II.i.191 [Shallow to Page, of Evans and Caius] *My merry host hath had the measuring of their weapons* [i.e. has been appointed umpire]

meat *(n.)* **1** food, nourishment **JC** I.ii.148 [Cassius to Brutus] *Upon what meat doth this our Caesar feed, / That he is grown so great?;* **Cym** III.vii.22; **2H6** IV.x.37; **RJ** I.i.22; **Tim** III.iv.51; **TS** IV.iii.9

2 edible part **KL** I.iv.157 [Fool to Lear] *I have cut the egg i'the middle and eat up the meat*

3 foodstuff, fodder, scraps **KL** II.ii.13 [disguised Kent to Oswald, describing him] *an eater of broken meats*

mechanic *(n.)* workman, handicraftsman **Cor** V.iii.83 [Coriolanus to Volumnia] *Do not bid me ... capitulate / Again with Rome's mechanics* [i.e. rabble]

mechanic *(adj.)* **1** common, vulgar, commonplace **AC** V.ii.209 [Cleopatra to Iras] *Mechanic slaves ... shall / Uplift us to the view;* **AC** IV.iv.32

2 worker, labouring **H5** I.ii.200 [Canterbury to all, of honey-bees] *The poor mechanic porters crowding in / Their heavy burdens*

mechanical *(n.)* manual worker, craftsman, menial **2H6** I.iii.191 [York to Horner] *Base dunghill villain and mechanical;* **JC** I.i.3; **MND** III.ii.9

mechanical *(adj.)* common, servile, menial **MW** II.ii.265 [Falstaff to Ford as Brook, of Ford] *Hang him, mechanical salt-butter rogue!;* **2H4** V.v.36

medal *(n.)* miniature portrait, pendant, charm **WT** I.ii.307 [Leontes to Camillo, of Hermione and Polixenes, in response to 'Who does infect her?'] *Why, he that wears her like her medal, hanging / About his neck*

meddle *(v.)* **1** fight, engage in combat, exchange blows **TN** III.iv.245 [Sir Toby to Viola as Cesario] *meddle you must ... or forswear to wear iron about you*

2 busy oneself, concern oneself **RJ** I.ii.39 [Servant alone] *It is written that the shoemaker should meddle with his yard* [with bawdy pun]

meddle or make interfere, butt in **MW** I.iv.107 [Caius to Simple, of Evans] *I will teach a scurvy jackanape priest to meddle or make;* **MA** III.iii.51

meddle with *(v.)* enter into, mingle with **Tem** I.ii.22 [Miranda to Prospero] *More to know / Did never meddle with my thoughts*

meddling *(adj.)* interfering, intruding **2H6** III.iii.21 [King to God, of the Cardinal] *beat away the busy meddling fiend / That lays strong siege unto this wretch's soul*

medicinable *(adj.)* **1** medicinal, healing, curative, restorative **TC** I.iii.91 [Ulysses to all, of the sun] *whose med'cinable eye / Corrects the ill aspects of planets evil;* **MA** II.ii.5; **Oth** V.ii.347; **TC** III.iii.44

2 curable, able to be healed **Cym** III.ii.33 [Innogen to Pisanio] *Some griefs are med'cinable;* **E3** II.i.323

medicine *(n.)* **1** healing, effective remedy **RJ** II.iii.20 [Friar alone] *Within the infant rind of this weak flower / Poison hath residence, and medicine power*

2 physician, doctor **WT** IV.iv.584 [Florizel to Camillo] *Preserver of my father, now of me, / The medicine of our house;* **AW** II.i.72

3 love potion **1H4** II.ii.18 [Falstaff, as if alone, of Poins] *If the rascal have not given me medicines to make me love him, I'll be hanged ... I have drunk medicines*

4 poison **KL** V.iii.97 [Gonerill to herself] *I'll ne'er trust medicine* [F; Q *poyson*]

medicine *(v.)* cure, heal, relieve **Cym** IV.ii.243 [Belarius to Guiderius and Arviragus] *Great griefs, I see, med'cine the less; for Cloten / Is quite forgot*

medicine potable elixir believed to be of special efficacy because derived from gold **2H4** IV.v.163 [Prince Henry to King Henry IV, as if to the crown] *Other, less fine in carat, is more precious, / Preserving life in medicine potable*

meditance *(n.)* meditation, reflection, contemplation **TNK** I.i.136 [First Queen to Theseus] *your first thought is more / Than others' laboured meditance*

meditate *(v.)* contemplate, plan, deliberate **1H6** II.iv.60 [Somerset to Richard, of the location of his argument] *Here in my scabbard, meditating that / Shall dye your white rose in a bloody red*

meditation *(n.)* **1** thought, thinking **Ham** I.v.30 [Hamlet to Ghost] *with wings as swift / As meditation;* **TNK** III.v.93

2 prayer, spiritual contemplation **2H6** III.iii.33 [King to Warwick] *let us all to meditation*

medlar *(n.)* **1** apple-like fruit eaten when its flesh has begun to decay [also: pun on 'meddler'] **Tim** IV.iii.306 [Apemantus to Timon] *There's a medlar for thee* [pun: 309, sense 2]; **AY** III.ii.114, 116

2 whore, prostitute **MM** IV.iii.170 [Lucio to disguised Duke] *They would else have married me to the rotten medlar*

medlar *(adj.)* variety of tree [whose fruit were thought to resemble female genitalia] **RJ** II.i.34 [Mercutio to Benvolio, of Romeo] *Now will he sit under a medlar tree* ➤ **PLANTS**, p.330

meed *(n.)* **1** reward, prize, recompense **R3** I.iv.231 [Clarence to Murderers] *If you are hired for meed, go back again;* **Cor** II.ii.95; **LL** I.i.257; **MW** II.ii.197; **TG** V.iv.23; **TNK** V.iii.16

2 merit, worth, excellence **3H6** IV.viii.38 [King to Exeter] *My meed hath got me fame;* **Ham** V.ii.141; **3H6** I.i.36

3 gift, service, benefaction **Tim** I.i.282 [Second Lord to First Lord, of Timon] *No meed but he repays / Sevenfold above itself;* **Tit** V.iii.65

meet *(adj.)* **1** fit, suitable, right, proper **Ham** V.i.95 [First Clown, singing] *For such a guest is meet* ➤ **FEW**, p.xxi; **unmeet** *(adj.)*

2 even, quits, revenged [on] **MA** I.i.43 [Leonato to Beatrice, of Benedick] *he'll be meet with you*

meet *(v.)* **1** fight with, meet in battle **Cor** I.iv.3 [Martius to Messenger] *Say, has our general met the enemy?;* **Cym** IV.ii.160

2 come together for love **MW** V.v.117 [Mistress Ford to Falstaff] *we could never meet*

3 begin, start, keep **TNK** III.i.98 [Arcite to Palamon] *Enter your muset, lest this match between's / Be crossed ere met* [i.e. be over before it starts]

meet with *(v.)* fit in with, suit, agree with **Tim** IV.iii.468 [Flavius to himself] *How rarely does it meet with this time's guise, / When man was wished to love his enemies!*

meet *(adv.)* suitably, fittingly, appropriately **AW** V.iii.330 [King to all] *All yet seems well, and if it end so meet*

meetly *(adj.)* quite good, moderate, reasonable **AC** I.iii.81 [Cleopatra to Antony] *You can do better yet; but this is meetly*

meetness *(n.)* fitness, readiness **Sonn** 118.7 *I ... sick of welfare found a kind of meetness*

meiny (*n.*) **1** multitude, crowd, throng **Cor** III.i.66 [Coriolanus to all, of the Citizens] *The mutable, rank-scented meiny*

2 household retinue, followers **KL** II.iv.34 [disguised Kent to Lear, of Regan and Cornwall] *They summoned up their meiny* [F; Q *men*]

melancholy (*n.*) ill-temper, sullenness [thought to be the result of too much 'black bile' in the blood] **KJ** III.iii.42 [King John to Hubert] *if that surly spirit, melancholy, / Had baked thy blood*

melancholy (*adj.*) dark, dismal, gloomy **AY** II.vii.112 [Orlando to Duke Senior] *Under the shade of melancholy boughs*

mell (*v.*) get involved, associate, copulate **AW** IV.iii.223 [First Soldier reading Parolles' letter] *Men are to mell with, boys are not to kiss* [i.e. men like Parolles are the ones to love, not boys like Bertram]

mellowed (*adj.*) mature, advancing **3H6** III.iii.104 [Oxford to Warwick, of his father] *in the downfall of his mellowed years*

melting (*adj.*) **1** moving, affecting, causing tenderness **2H4** IV.iv.32 [King Henry IV to Clarence, of Prince Henry] *He hath ... a hand / Open as day for melting charity* [F; Q *meeting*]

2 soft-hearted, tender-hearted, pitying **3H6** I.iv.174 [Queen to Northumberland, of York] *Think but upon the wrong he did us all, / And that will quickly dry thy melting tears*

member (*n.*) **1** sharer, participant, partaker **H5** IV.i.274 [King Henry alone] *The slave, a member of the country's peace*

2 limb, piece of a body **1H6** V.iii.15 [Pucelle to spirits] *I'll lop a member off and give it you*; **TC** IV.v.130

memorial (*adj.*) of remembrance, of recollection **TC** V.ii.83 [Cressida as if to Troilus' sleeve] *Thy master ... takes my glove, / And gives memorial dainty kisses to it*

memorize (*v.*) make memorable, cause to be remembered **Mac** I.ii.41 [Captain to King, of Macbeth and Banquo] *they meant to ... memorize another Golgotha*; **H8** III.ii.52

memory (*n.*) **1** memorial, remembrance **Cor** V.vi.155 [Aufidius to all, of Coriolanus] *he shall have a noble memory*; **AY** II.iii.3; **Cor** IV.v.74, V.i.17

2 history, memorial record **2H6** I.i.98 [Gloucester to all, of the contract between the King and Queen] *Blotting your names from books of memory*; **TNK** II.v.16

3 reminder, memento **KL** IV.vii.7 [Cordelia to Kent, of his disguise] *These weeds are memories of those worser hours*; **Sonn** 77.6

memory, of remembered, not forgotten **Ham** V.ii.383 [Fortinbras to Horatio] *I have some rights of memory in this kingdom*

mend (*n.*) remedy, way of improving **TC** I.i.69 [Pandarus to Troilus, of Cressida] *if she be fair, 'tis the better for her; an she be not, she has the mends in her own hands* [i.e. by using cosmetics]

mend (*v.*) **1** amend, improve, make better, put right **KL** I.i.94 [Lear to Cordelia] *Mend your speech a little*; **AC** I.iii.82; **AY** II.iv.91; **Tim** V.i.87; **TN** I.v.69; **TS** IV.i.162

2 increase the value of, make more excellent **Tim** I.i.176 [Jeweller to Timon] *You mend the jewel by the wearing it*; **Sonn** 78.11

3 do better, pull oneself together **Cor** I.iv.38 [Martius to his troops] *Mend and charge home*

4 supplement, augment **Tim** IV.iii.284 [Apemantus to Timon, offering him food] *Here, I will mend thy feast*; **CE** IV.iii.59; **TS** I.ii.148

mended (*adj.*) improved, made better **Cym** I.v.44 [Posthumus to Frenchman, of himself] *upon my mended judgement ... my quarrel was not altogether slight*

merchandise (*v.*) commercialise, turn into merchandise **Sonn** 102.3 *That love is merchandised whose rich esteeming / The owner's tongue doth publish everywhere*

merchant (*n.*) **1** dealer, purveyor **1H6** II.iii.56 [Countess to Talbot, of his reply] *This is a riddling merchant for the nonce* [or: sense 2]

2 fellow, character, lad **RJ** II.iv.142 [Nurse to Romeo, of Mercutio] *what saucy merchant was this that was so full of his ropery?*

3 merchant-ship **Tem** II.i.5 [Gonzalo to Alonso] *The masters of some merchant ... / Have just our theme of woe*

merchant-marring (*adj.*) capable of damaging a merchant-ship **MV** III.ii.271 [Bassanio to Salerio, of Antonio] *not one vessel scape the dreadful touch / Of merchant-marring rocks?*

mercy (*n.*) compassion, forgiveness, pardon **AY** III.v.61 [Rosalind as Ganymede to Phebe, of Silvius] *Cry the man mercy* [i.e. beg his pardon] ☞ POLITENESS, p.340; SWEARING, p.435

mere (*adj.*) **1** complete, total, absolute, utter **Ham** V.i.280 [Gertrude to all] *This is mere madness* ☞ FEW, p.xxi

2 sole, personal, particular **MM** V.i.152 [Friar Peter to Duke, of Friar Lodowick] *Upon his mere request*; **KL** IV.i.20

mere (*adv.*) **1** totally, absolutely **AW** III.v.54 [Helena to Diana, answering a question] *Ay, surely, mere the truth* [i.e. that's nothing but the truth]

2 exclusively, purely, solely **1H6** IV.vii.54 [Lucy to Charles] *Submission, Dauphin. 'Tis a mere French word*; **TC** III.iii.107

mered (*adj.*) [unclear meaning] sole, entire; particular, specific **AC** III.xiii.10 [Enobarbus to Cleopatra, of Antony] *he being / The mered question*

merely (*adv.*) **1** completely, totally, entirely **Ham** I.ii.137 [Hamlet alone, of the world] *Things rank and gross in nature / Possess it merely* ☞ FEW, p.xxi

2 purely, for no other reason than **H8** II.i.162 [First Gentleman to Second Gentleman, of Wolsey's action] *And merely to revenge him on the Emperor*; **R2** II.i.243

3 only, nothing more than **MM** V.i.451 [Isabella to Duke] *Thoughts are no subjects, / Intents but merely thoughts*; **H8** I.iii.6

meridian (*n.*) highpoint, culmination, climax **H8** III.ii.224 [Wolsey alone] *from that full meridian of my glory / I haste now to my setting*

merit (*n.*) **1** desert, deserving, inner worth **KL** V.iii.45 [Albany to Edmund, of the captives] *to use them / As we shall find their merits and our safety / May equally determine*; **AC** V.ii.178; **LL** IV.i.21

2 reward, just desert **R2** I.iii.156 [Mowbray to Richard] *A dearer merit ... / Have I deserved* [i.e. a better reward]; **KL** III.v.6; **TNK** V.i.128

3 good works [yielding reward from God] **1H4** I.ii.107 [Falstaff to Prince Hal] *if men were to be saved by merit*; **AW** II.i.148

4 deserving person, righteous individual **Ham** III.i.74 [Hamlet alone] *the spurns / That patient merit of th'unworthy takes*

5 meritorious service **AC** II.vii.55 [Menas aside to Pompey] *If for the sake of merit thou wilt hear me*

mermaid (*n.*) siren **CE** III.ii.45 [Antipholus of Syracuse to Luciana] *O, train me not, sweet mermaid, with thy note*; **CE** III.ii.172

merry (*adj.*) **1** facetious, droll, jocular **Ham** III.ii.131 [Ophelia to Hamlet] *You are merry, my lord*; **3H6** II.ii.76; **Tim** III.ii.25

2 hilarious, uproarious, hysterical **TS** Induction.i.95 [Lord to First Player] *Lest ... / You break into some merry passion* [i.e. a fit of merriment]

3 in good spirits, well **JC** II.iv.45 [Portia to Lucius, of Brutus] *commend me to my lord; / Say I am merry*

4 [of winds] favourable, helpful, advantageous **CE** IV.i.91 [Dromio of Syracuse to Antipholus of Ephesus] *the merry wind / Blows fair from land*; **E3** II.ii.77

mervailous (*adj.*) marvellous, amazing, remarkable **H5** II.i.44 [Pistol to Nym] *The 'solus' in thy most mervailous face!*

mess (*n.*) **1** company, group, gang of four **LL** V.ii.361 [Princess to King] *A mess of Russians left us but of late*; **3H6** I.iv.73; **LL** IV.iii.205

2 small group of people eating together **WT** I.ii.227 [Leontes to Camillo, of Hermione persuading Polixenes to stay] *Lower messes / Perchance are to this business purblind?*; **WT** IV.iv.11

3 dining company, banqueting table **KJ** I.i.190 [Bastard alone, of a traveller] *He and his toothpick at my worship's mess*; **Ham** V.ii.88

4 serving of food, dish **Tim** IV.iii.423 [Timon to Bandits, of food] *Nature on each bush / Lays her full mess before you*; **KL** I.i.117; **Oth** IV.i.199; **TS** IV.iv.70

5 small quantity, little bit **2H4** II.i.93 [Hostess to Falstaff, of a neighbour] *coming in to borrow a mess of vinegar*

message, of on the business of carrying a message, as messenger **2H6** IV.i.114 [Suffolk to Lieutenant] *I go of message from the Queen to France*

messenger (*n.*) **1** pursuivant, officer **AY** I.ii.57 [Celia to Touchstone] *Were you made the messenger?* [i.e. were you sent to arrest me?]

2 malapropism for 'message' **MW** II.ii.92 [Mistress Quickly to Falstaff] *I have another messenger to your worship*

met (*int.*) ☞ **GREETINGS**, p.206

metal (*n.*) substance, material, fabric **R3** IV.iv.302 [King Richard to Queen Elizabeth, of his future children] *They are as children ... / Even of your metal;* **MA** II.i.52

metal of India pure gold **TN** II.v.14 [Sir Toby to Maria] *How now, my metal of India?* [pun: mettle]

metamorphose (*v.*) transform, alter one's disposition, change one's shape **TG** I.i.66 [Proteus alone, as if to Julia] *thou hast metamorphosed me;* **TG** II.i.28

metamorphosed (*adj.*) turned into stone, transformed, petrified **E3** IV.v.37 [Philip to King John] *our soldiers ... stand like metamorphosed images*

metaphysical (*adj.*) supernatural, transcending the laws of nature **Mac** I.v.27 [Lady Macbeth alone, of Macbeth and the crown] *Which fate and metaphysical aid doth seem / To have thee crowned withal*

mete (*v.*) **1** appraise, measure, evaluate **2H4** IV.iv.77 [Warwick to King Henry IV, of Prince Henry's followers] *their memory / Shall as a pattern or a measure live / By which his grace must mete the lives of other*

2 aim, level **LL** IV.i.133 [Boyet to Maria] *Let the mark have a prick in't, to mete at if it may be*

meteor (*n.*) aurora, luminous emanation, atmospheric effect **RJ** III.v.13 [Juliet to Romeo] *Yond light is not daylight ... / It is some meteor that the sun exhales;* **KJ** III.iv.157, V.ii.53

mete-yard (*n.*) measuring rod, yard-stick **TS** IV.iii.148 [Grumio to Tailor] *give me thy mete-yard*

metheglin (*n.*) [mi'theglin] strong spiced Welsh mead **MW** V.v.157 [Evans to all, of Falstaff] *given to ... taverns, and sack, and wine, and metheglins;* **LL** V.ii.233

methinks(t), methought(s) (*v.*) it seems /seemed to me **Ham** III.ii.240 [Gertrude to Hamlet] *The lady doth protest too much, methinks;* **Ham** V.i.62 [First Clown, singing] *Methought it was very sweet* ☞ **FEW**, p.xxi

method (*n.*) **1** exposition, thesis, expressed content **1H6** III.i.13 [Gloucester to Winchester] *Think not ... / That therefore I ... am not able / Verbatim to rehearse the method of my pen*

2 table of contents, summary arrangement **TN** I.v.217 [Viola as Cesario to Olivia, responding to 'In what chapter of his bosom?'] *To answer by the method, in the first of his heart* [i.e. to reply to you using the same approach]

methought (*v.*) ☞ methinks (*v.*)

metre (*n.*) verse, poem, composition **R2** II.i.19 [York to John of Gaunt] *Lascivious metres, to whose venom sound / The open ear of youth doth always listen*

metre (*adj.*) metrical, doggerel **1H4** III.i.124 [Hotspur to Glendower] *I had rather be a kitten and cry 'mew' / Than one of these same metre ballad-mongers*

mettle, mettell (*n.*) **1** spirit, temperament, disposition **KL** I.i.69 [Regan to Lear] *I am made of that self mettle as my sister;* **Ham** I.i.96; **JC** I.ii.293, IV.ii.24; **Mac** I.vii.73; **R2** I.ii.23

2 spirit, vigour, zest **1H4** V.iv.23 [Prince Hal to King Henry, of Lancaster] *this boy / Lends mettle to us all!;* **AC** I.i.143; **1H4** IV.iii.22; **H5** III.i.27; **JC** II.i.134; **TC** I.iii.258

3 substance, matter **AY** II.vii.82 [Jaques to Duke Senior] *the mettle of my speech;* **Tim** IV.iii.180

mew (*v.*) coop up, confine, shut up **MND** I.i.71 [Theseus to Hermia, of a nun] *For aye to be in shady cloister mewed;* **R3** I.i.132

mew up (*v.*) coop up, confine, shut up **R3** I.i.38 [Richard alone] *This day should Clarence closely be mewed up;* **KJ** IV.ii.57; **R3** I.iii.138; **RJ** III.iv.11; **TS** I.i.87, 180

mewl (*v.*) mewl [like a cat]; or: cry feebly **AY** II.vii.145 [Jaques to all] *the infant, / Mewling and puking in the nurse's arms*

micher (*n.*) truant, absentee, malingerer **1H4** II.iv.401 [Falstaff (as King) to Prince Hal] *Shall the blessed sun of heaven prove a micher, and eat blackberries?*

miching (*adj.*) [unclear meaning] sneaking, skulking, lurking **Ham** III.ii.146 [Hamlet to Ophelia] *this is miching mallecho* [F, Q1; Q2 *munching*]

mickle (*adj.*) great, much, large **1H6** IV.vi.35 [Talbot to John Talbot] *Tomorrow I shall die with mickle age;* **CE** III.i.45; **E3** V.i.194; **2H6** V.i.174; **PassP** XV.9; **RJ** II.iii.11

microcosm (*n.*) little world **Cor** II.i.59 [Menenius to Brutus and Sicinius] *the map of my microcosm* [i.e. my face]

middle earth (*n.*) earth, seen as midway between heaven and hell **MW** V.v.80 [Evans as a Satyr to all, of Falstaff] *I smell a man of middle earth*

mid-season (*n.*) noon, middle of the day **Tem** I.ii.239 [Ariel to Prospero, of the time] *Past the mid-season*

mighty (*adj.*) influential, important, leading **TS** II.i.104 [Baptista to Tranio as Lucentio, of Vincentio] *A mighty man of Pisa*

milch (*adj.*) **1** milking, in milk **Venus** 875 *Like a milch doe, whose swelling dugs do ache*

2 [milky] moist, tearful **Ham** II.ii.515 [First Player to all present] *Would have made milch the burning eyes of heaven*

milch-kine (*n.*) dairy-milk cows **TS** II.i.350 [Gremio to Baptista] *I have a hundred milch-kine to the pail;* **MW** IV.iv.31

militarist (*n.*) soldier, warrior **AW** IV.iii.140 [First Lord to Bertram] *this is Monsieur Parolles, the gallant militarist*

milk-livered (*adj.*) chicken-hearted, cowardly **KL** IV.ii.50 [Goner-ill to Albany] *Milk-livered man!*

milk-pap (*n.*) nipple, teat **Tim** IV.iii.116 [Timon to Alcibiades] *those milk-paps / That ... bore at men's eyes*

milky (*adj.*) **1** of the colour of milk; white-haired **Ham** II.ii.476 [First Player to all present, of Pyrrhus' sword] *declining on the milky head / Of reverend Priam*

2 weak, timorous, feeble **Tim** III.i.54 [Flaminius alone] *Has friendship such a faint and milky heart / It turns in less than two nights?*

millioned (*adj.*) numbered by the million **Sonn** 115.5 [of time] *whose millioned accidents / Creep in 'twixt vows* [or: million]

mill-sixpence (*n.*) sixpence made in a coin-making mill **MW** I.i.144 [Slender to all] *seven groats in mill-sixpences*

mimic (*n.*) burlesque actor, performer, thespian **MND** III.ii.19 [Puck to Oberon, of Bottom] *forth my mimic comes*

mince (*v.*) **1** play down, soften, make little of **AC** I.ii.106 [Antony to Messenger] *mince not the general tongue;* **Oth** I.iii.241

2 walk like a lady, walk with delicate short steps **MW** V.i.8 [Falstaff to Mistress Quickly] *Hold up your head, and mince*

3 suggest by walking pretentiously, give an affected impression of **KL** IV.vi.120 [Lear to all] *yon simpering dame, ... / That minces virtue*

4 chop into pieces, cut into tiny bits **Tim** IV.iii.123 [Timon to Alcibiades, of a baby] *mince it sans remorse;* **Ham** II.ii.512

minced (*adj.*) cut up into little pieces for baking **TC** I.ii.256 [Cressida to Pandarus, of the qualities that 'spice and season a man'] *Ay, a minced man* [also: displaying affected mannerisms]

mincing (*n.*) affected movement, pretentious manner **H8** II.iii.31 [Old Lady to Anne] *Saving your mincing* [i.e. despite your affectation]

mincing (*adj.*) affected, pretentious, daintily moving 1H4 III.i.128 [Hotspur to Glendower] *I had rather hear a brazen canstick turned ... / And that would set my teeth nothing on edge, / Nothing so much as mincing poetry*

mind (*n.*) **1** inclination, desire, wish Cym IV.ii.147 [Belarius to Guiderius and Arviragus] *I had no mind / To hunt this day;* H8 IV.i.8; JC I.ii.288; TG I.ii.137; Tim IV.ii.50; TS V.ii.169
   2 intention, purpose, intent RJ V.ii.4 [Friar Laurence to Friar John, of Romeo] *if his mind be writ, give me his letter;* Cym III.iv.145; 1H6 II.ii.59; H8 I.ii.161; Tim I.ii.161; TS I.ii.77
   3 character, disposition, spirit AW I.i.40 [Countess to Lafew] *an unclean mind carries virtuous qualities;* TG V.iii.13
   4 feeling, presentiment, misgiving JC III.i.144 [Cassius to Brutus, of Antony] *have I a mind / That fears him much*

mind (*v.*) **1** intend, have a mind 3H6 IV.i.64 [George to Edward] *I shortly mind to leave you;* 3H6 IV.i.8, 139; Per II.iv.3
   2 put in mind, remind WT III.ii.223 [Paulina to Leontes] *Let me be punished, that have minded you / Of what you should forget;* H5 IV.iii.13, 84
   3 think of, call to mind H5 IV.Chorus.53 [Chorus to audience] *sit and see, / Minding true things by what their mockeries be;* RJ IV.i.13; TNK IV.i.37
   4 pay attention to, take notice of TS I.i.246 [Lord to Sly] *you do not mind the play*
   5 purpose, intend, hold an opinion Sonn 11.7 *If all were minded so, the times should cease*

minded (*adj.*) ☛ bloody-minded (*adj.*); high-minded (*adj.*); motley-minded (*adj.*); well-minded (*adj.*)

mine (*n.*) **1** source of supply, abundant store AC IV.vi.32 [Enobarbus alone, as if to Antony] *Thou mine of bounty;* TNK II.ii.133
   2 excavated passage under a fortress wall H5 III.ii.55 [Gower to Fluellen] *you must come presently to the mines* ☛ countermine (*n.*)

mine (*v.*) undermine, sap, subvert AY I.i.18 [Orlando to Adam, of Oliver] *he ... mines my gentility with my education;* Ham III.iv.149

mineral (*n.*) **1** mine, mineral deposit Ham IV.i.26 [Gertrude to Claudius] *like some ore / Among a mineral of metals base*
   2 substance, poison, toxin Cym V.v.50 [Cornelius to Cymbeline, of the Queen] *she had / For you a mortal mineral;* Oth I.ii.74

mingle (*v.*) join, unite, combine 2H4 V.ii.132 [King Henry V to his brothers, of his temperament] *it shall mingle with the state of floods, / And flow henceforth in formal majesty;* WT IV.iv.457

minikin (*adj.*) shrill; or: dainty, tiny KL III.vi.43 [Edgar as Poor Tom, as if to a shepherd] *for one blast of thy minikin mouth*

minimus (*n.*) tiniest of creatures, insignificant being MND III.ii.329 [Lysander to Hermia] *You minimus of hindering knot-grass made*

minion (*n.*) **1** darling, favourite, select one TN V.i.123 [Orsino to Olivia, of Viola as Cesario] *this your minion, whom I know you love;* CE II.i.87; Cym II.iii.40; 3H6 II.ii.84; KJ II.i.392; Mac I.ii.19
   2 hussy, jade, minx TS II.i.13 [Katherina to Bianca] *Minion, thou liest;* CE III.i.59; 2H6 I.iii.136; Oth V.i.33; RJ III.v.151; Tit II.iii.124

minister (*n.*) messenger, agent, servant Tem III.iii.62 [Ariel to Alonso, Sebastian, and Antonio] *I and my fellows / Are ministers of Fate;* Ham I.iv.39; 1H6 V.iv.93; H8 I.i.108; Mac V.vi.107; Oth V.ii.8

minister (*v.*) **1** provide, supply, give TN V.iv.82 [Malvolio to Olivia, of Feste] *unless you laugh and minister occasion to him, he is gagged;* 2H6 I.i.31; H8 I.i.86; Oth II.i.261; Tem II.i.177
   2 prompt, suggest, indicate MM IV.v.6 [Duke to Friar Peter] *hold you ever to our special drift, / Though sometimes you do blench from this to that, / As cause doth minister*
   3 act, govern, officiate Tim IV.i.6 [Timon alone] *Slaves and fools / Pluck the grave wrinkled Senate from the bench, / And minister in their steads*

minnow (*n.*) [variety of fish] insignificant object LL I.i.241 [King reading Armado's letter to him, of Costard] *There did I see that ... base minnow of thy mirth;* Cor III.i.89

minority (*n.*) under-age period, earlier youth, childhood LL V.i.128 [Holofernes to Armado, of Mote] *He shall present Hercules in minority;* AW IV.v.70

minstrel (*n.*) [derisive term for] musician RJ IV.v.113 [Peter to Musicians, of their refusing to play] *I will give you the minstrel*

minstrelsy (*n.*) **1** noisy playing and singing, musical rowdiness Tim II.ii.166 [Flavius to Timon] *when every room / Hath blazed with lights and brayed with minstrelsy*
   2 court singer LL I.i.174 [King to all, of Armado] *I will use him for my minstrelsy*

minute, by the minute by minute, continually AC III.i.20 [Ventidius to Silius, of Sossius' renown] *Which he achieved by th'minute;* Cym V.v.51

minute-jack (*n.*) mind-changing villain, fickle lout Tim III.vi.97 [Timon to Lords] *Cap-and-knee slaves, vapours, and minute-jacks!* ☛ jack (*n.*) 2

minutely (*adj.*) taking place minute by minute Mac V.ii.18 [Angus to all, of Macbeth] *Now minutely revolts upbraid his faith-breach* [or: adverb use, every minute]

mirable (*adj.*) wonderful, marvellous TC IV.v.142 [Hector to Ajax] *Neoptolemus so mirable*

miracle (*v.*) make a wonder of, show miraculous Cym IV.ii.29 [Belarius to himself, of Arviragus] *I'm not their father, yet who this should be, / Doth miracle itself, loved before me* [i.e. this must be someone really special if they should love him more than me]

mire (*v.*) sink in the mire, get bogged down Tim IV.iii.149 [Timon to Phrynia and Timandra] *Paint till a horse may mire upon your face*

mirror (*n.*) supreme example, paragon, model of excellence H5 II.Chorus.6 [Chorus, of King Henry] *the mirror of all Christian kings;* 1H6 I.iv.74; 3H6 III.iii.84

mirth (*n.*) **1** merry-making, pleasure-seeking Per II.iii.7 [Simonides to Knights] *Prepare for mirth, for mirth becomes a feast;* MW II.ii.215; WT I.i.166
   2 joke, diversion, sport AC I.iv.18 [Caesar to Lepidus, of Antony] *To give a kingdom for a mirth;* MW V.vi.14

misadventure (*n.*) misfortune, mishap, tragic accident RJ V.i.29 [Balthasar to Romeo] *Your looks are pale and wild and do import / Some misadventure;* RJ V.iii.188

misadventured (*adj.*) unfortunate, calamitous, disastrous RJ Prologue.7 [Chorus, of Romeo and Juliet] *Whose misadventured piteous overthrows / Doth with their death bury their parents' strife*

Misanthropos (*n.*) man-hater Tim IV.iii.54 [Timon to Alcibiades] *I am Misanthropos, and hate mankind*

misbecome (*v.*) appear unbecoming to, be unseemly to LL V.ii.763 [Browne to ladies, of their conduct] *if [we] ... / Have misbecomed our oaths and gravities;* 2H4 V.ii.100; H5 II.iv.118

misbecomingly (*adv.*) unbecomingly, unattractively, unfittingly TNK V.iii.54 [Emilia to herself, of Palamon] *Those darker humours that / Stick misbecomingly on others*

misbegot (*adj.*) misbegotten, illegitimate, bastard Tim III.v.29 [First Senator to Alcibiades] *set quarrelling / Upon the head of valour; which indeed / Is valour misbegot*

misbegotten (*adj.*) illegitimate, bastard 1H6 IV.vi.22 [Talbot to his son, as if to Orleans] *Contaminated, base, / And misbegotten blood I spill of thine*

miscall (*v.*) misname, call by a wrong name TC V.iv.20 [Diomedes to Troilus] *Thou dost miscall retire;* R2 I.iii.263

miscarry (*v.*) **1** come to harm, perish, meet death 1H6 IV.iii.16 [Richard to all, of Talbot] *If he miscarry, farewell wars in France;* 2H6 IV.viii.46; KL V.i.5; R3 V.i.5; TN III.iv.63; TNK V.iii.101
   2 come to harm, be lost, be destroyed MV III.ii.315 [Bassanio, reading Antonio's letter] *my ships have all miscarried;* MV II.viii.29
   3 go wrong, fail, be unsuccessful Cor I.i.264 [Brutus to Sicinius] *what miscarries / Shall be the general's fault;* 2H4 V.ii.46; KJ V.v.3; Oth V.i.6; RJ V.iii.267; TC I.iii.351

4 be scarce, fail, become unproductive **LL** IV.i.113 [Boyet to Rosaline] *if thou marry, / Hang me by the neck if horns that year miscarry*

5 [of letters] go astray, fall into the wrong hands **H8** III.ii.30 [Suffolk to all] *The Cardinal's letters to the Pope miscarried;* **LL** IV.ii.138

mischance (*n.*) misfortune, calamity, mishap **3H6** III.iii.8 [Queen to Lewis] *now mischance hath trod my title down;* **Ham** III.ii.238; **1H6** IV.vi.49; **2H6** III.ii.284; **RJ** V.iii.221; **TG** V.iii.3

mischief (*n.*) **1** catastrophe, calamity, misfortune **1H6** V.iii.39 [Pucelle to Richard] *A plaguing mischief light on Charles and thee!;* **2H4** IV.ii.47; **H8** II.i.66; **Mac** I.v.48; **MW** IV.ii.69; **Per** I.iv.8

2 wicked action, evil deed, harmful scheme **RJ** V.i.35 [Romeo alone] *O mischief, thou art swift / To enter in the thoughts of desperate men;* **1H6** III.ii.39; **H8** V.i.49; **JC** V.i.51; **Tit** III.i.272, V.i.65

3 harm, injury, damage **1H6** III.i.116 [Warwick to Gloucester and Winchester] *You see what mischief … / Hath been enacted through your enmity;* **KL** I.ii.161, I.vii.81; **Tit** V.i.110

4 disease, ailment, misfortune **MA** I.iii.12 [Don John to Conrade] *thou … goest about to apply a moral medicine to a mortifying mischief;* **Tim** IV.iii.169

mischief (*v.*) hurt, injure, do harm to **Tim** IV.iii.471 [Flavius to himself] *Grant I may ever love, and rather woo / Those that would mischief me than those that do!*

mischievous (*adj.*) harmful, damaging, injurious **JC** II.i.33 [Brutus alone, of Caesar as a serpent's egg] *Which, hatched, would, as his kind, grow mischievous*

misconster (*v.*) misconstrue, misinterpret, take wrongly **E3** V.i.215 [King John to King Edward, of his visit to England] *Of this I was foretold, / But did misconster what the prophet told;* **AY** I.ii.254; **1H6** II.iii.72; **MV** II.ii.175; **R3** III.v.60

misconstruction (*n.*) misunderstanding, misinterpretation **KL** II.ii.115 [Oswald to Cornwall, of disguised Kent] *It pleased the King his master very late / To strike at me upon his misconstruction*

miscreant (*n.*) **1** villain, wretch, rascal **R2** I.i.39 [Bolingbroke to Mowbray] *Thou art a traitor and a miscreant;* **1H6** III.iv.44, V.iii.44

2 unbeliever, heretic **KL** I.i.161 [Lear to Kent] *O vassal, miscreant!* [F; Q *recreant*] ☛ **recreant** (*n.*) 3

miscreate (*adj.*) wrongly created, illegitimate **H5** I.ii.16 [King Henry to Canterbury] *God forbid … / That you should … nicely charge your understanding soul / With opening titles miscreate*

misdemean (*v.*) behave improperly, misconduct **H8** V.iii.14 [Lord Chancellor to Cranmer] *you … / Have misdemeaned yourself*

misdo (*v.*) do wrongly, transgress **E3** II.i.395 [Warwick to Countess] *What mighty men misdo, they can amend*

misdoubt (*n.*) suspicion, mistrust, doubtfulness **2H6** III.i.332 [York to himself] *steel thy fearful thoughts, / And change misdoubt to resolution;* **2H4** IV.i.204

misdoubt (*v.*) **1** distrust, suspect, have misgivings about **MW** II.i.173 [Ford to Page] *I do not misdoubt my wife;* **3H6** V.vi.14; **LL** IV.iii.192; **R3** III.ii.86

2 disbelieve, doubt the reality [of] **AW** III.vii.1 [Helena to Widow] *If you misdoubt me that I am not she;* **AC** III.vii.62; **AW** I.iii.120

misdread (*n.*) dread of evil, fear of harm **Per** I.ii.12 [Pericles alone] *the passions of the mind, / That have their first conception by misdread*

miser (*n.*) wretch, miserable being **1H6** V.iv.7 [Pucelle to Shepherd] *Decrepit miser!*

misery (*n.*) complete poverty, destitution, beggary **Cor** II.ii.125 [Cominius to all, of Coriolanus] *He covets less / Than misery itself would give*

misgive (*v.*) **1** make one feel uneasy, cause one to be apprehensive **MW** V.v.206 [Page to Ford] *My heart misgives me;* **3H6** IV.vi.94; **TNK** II.ii.70

2 have misgivings, have a bad feeling **E3** III.i.137 [King John to himself, on seeing the Mariner] *My heart misgives;* **Oth** III.iv.87

3 be uneasy about, feel apprehension about **RJ** I.iv.106 [Romeo to Benvolio] *my mind misgives / Some consequence*

misgoverned (*adj.*) unruly, unrestrained **R2** V.ii.5 [Duchess of York to York] *rude misgoverned hands from windows' tops / Threw dust and rubbish on King Richard's head*

misgovernment (*n.*) misconduct, wicked behaviour **MA** IV.i.97 [Don John to Hero] *I am sorry for thy much misgovernment*

misgraffed (*adj.*) badly grafted, ill-matched, unsuited **MND** I.i.137 [Lysander to Hermia] *The course of true love never did run smooth; / But either it was different in blood … / Or else misgraffed in respect of years*

mishap (*n.*) evil, misfortune, calamity **1H6** I.i.23 [Exeter to all] *Shall we curse the planets of mishap;* **CE** I.i.142

mishaved (*adj.*) badly behaved **RJ** III.iii.143 [Friar to Romeo] *like a mishaved and sullen wench, / Thou pouts upon thy fortune* [Q2; F *mishaped*; Q1 *misbehau'd*]

mislike (*n.*) dislike, distaste, displeasure **3H6** IV.i.24 [Edward to Richard and George] *Setting your scorns and your mislike aside*

mislike (*v.*) dislike, be displeased with **MV** II.i.1 [Morocco to Portia] *Mislike me not for my complexion;* **AC** III.xiii.147; **2H6** I.i.138; **TNK** III.vi.259

misordered (*adj.*) disordered, confused, troubled **2H4** IV.ii.33 [Archbishop to Prince John] *The time misordered doth … / Crowd us and crush us to this monstrous form*

misplace (*v.*) put words in the wrong place **MM** II.i.85 [Escalus to Angelo, of Elbow] *Do you hear how he misplaces?*

misprised (*adj.*) mistaken, misguided, erroneous **MND** III.ii.74 [Demetrius to Hermia] *You spend your passion on a misprised mood*

misprision (*n.*) **1** mistake, error, misunderstanding, misconception **MA** IV.i.183 [Friar to all] *There is some strange misprision in the Princes;* **1H4** I.iii.26; **LL** IV.iii.96; **MND** II.ii.90; **Sonn** 87.11; **TN** I.v.50

2 contempt, scorn, disdain **AW** II.iii.151 [King to Bertram, of Helena] *That dost in vile misprision shackle up / My love and her desert* [or: error]

misprize (*v.*) despise, undervalue, scorn **AY** I.i.159 [Oliver alone] *I am altogether misprized;* **AY** I.ii.169; **MA** III.i.52

misprizing (*n.*) despising, slighting, holding in contempt **AW** III.ii.30 [Countess as if to Bertram, of his behaviour] *the misprizing of a maid too virtuous / For the contempt of empire*

misproud (*adj.*) wrongly proud, arrogant, high and mighty **3H6** II.vi.7 [Clifford alone, as if to the House of Lancaster] *now I fall, thy tough commixture melts, / Impairing Henry, strengthening misproud York*

misreport (*v.*) speak badly of, slander **MM** V.i.148 [Friar Peter to Duke, of Friar Lodowick] *a man that never yet / Did … misreport your grace*

miss (*n.*) wrong-doing, misbehaviour, misdeed **Venus** 53 [of Adonis and Venus] *He saith she is immodest, blames her miss*

miss (*v.*) **1** forgo, do without, go without **Tem** I.ii.311 [Prospero to Miranda, of Caliban] *We cannot miss him;* **Cor** I.i.229

2 fail to meet, let down **MW** III.v.51 [Falstaff to Mistress Quickly, of Mistress Ford] *I will not miss her*

3 be unsuccessful, be inadequate **RJ** Prologue.14 [Chorus] *What here shall miss, our toil shall strive to mend*

missed (*adj.*) lost, missing, forgotten **Sonn** 122.8 *thy record never can be missed*

misshapen (*adj.*) gone awry, badly directed **RJ** III.iii.131 [Friar to Romeo] *Thy wit, that ornament to shape and love, / Misshapen in the conduct of them both*

mis-sheathe (*v.*) sheathe wrongly **RJ** V.iii.205 [Capulet to Lady Capulet, of Romeo's dagger] *it mis-sheathed in my daughter's bosom*

missing (*n.*) absence, disappearance, non-attendance [at court] **Cym** V.v.275 [Pisanio to Cymbeline] *Lord Cloten, / Upon my lady's missing, came to me*

missingly *(adv.)* by being aware of absence, with a sense of loss **WT** IV.ii.31 [Camillo to Polixenes, of Florizel] *I have missingly noted he is of late much retired from court* [or: regretfully]

missive *(n.)* messenger, emissary, courier **AC** II.ii.78 [Caesar to Antony] *you ... with taunts / Did gibe my missive out of audience*

misspeak *(v.)* speak inaccurately, express badly **KJ** III.i.4 [Constance to Salisbury, of the marriage treaty] *thou hast misspoke, misheard*

mist *(n.)* confused state, state of uncertainty **CE** II.ii.226 [Antipholus of Syracuse to himself] *I'll ... in this mist at all adventures go*

mistake *(v.)* **1** misunderstand, take wrongly, misconceive **H5** III.ii.129 [Gower to Fluellen and Macmorris] *you will mistake each other;* **1H6** II.iii.73; **H8** I.i.195; **R2** III.iii.15; **Sonn** 87.10; **Tim** I.ii.8

2 act in error, perform the wrong action **RJ** V.iii.203 [Capulet to Lady Capulet] *This dagger hath mista'en, for, lo, his house / Is empty on the back of Montague;* **Tim** III.ii.22

3 wrongly deliver, take to the wrong person **LL** IV.i.107 [Princess to Costard, of Berowne] *Thou hast mistaken his letter;* **LL** IV.vi.60

4 offend, transgress (against) **R2** III.iii.17 [York to Bolingbroke] *Take not, good cousin, further than you should, / Lest you mistake the heavens are over our heads* [pun: 15, sense 1]

mistempered *(adj.)* **1** disordered, diseased, deranged **KJ** V.i.12 [King John to Cardinal Pandulph, of the English unrest] *This inundation of mistempered humour / Rests by you only to be qualified*

2 tempered for wickedness, made with evil intent **RJ** I.i.87 [Prince to all] *Throw your mistempered weapons to the ground* [also: intemperately used]

mistful *(adj.)* misty, tearful **H5** IV.vi.34 [King Henry to Exeter] *I must perforce compound / With mistful eyes, or they will issue too* [F *mixtfull*]

misthink *(v.)* think ill of, have a bad opinion about **3H6** II.v.108 [King to himself, of deaths in battle] *How will the country for these woeful chances / Misthink the King and not be satisfied!*

misthought *(adj.)* misjudged, thought ill of **AC** V.ii.176 [Cleopatra to Caesar] *we, the greatest, are misthought / For things that others do*

mistreading *(n.)* misdeed, transgression, faulty step **1H4** III.ii.11 [King Henry to Prince Hal] *thou art only marked ... / To punish my mistreadings*

mistrust *(n.)* suspicion, distrust, strong doubt **2H6** III.i.242 [Suffolk to all, of Gloucester] *we have but trivial argument, / More than mistrust, that shows him worthy death*

mistrust *(v.)* suspect the existence of, apprehend, anticipate **3H6** V.vi.38 [King to Richard] *many a thousand, / Which now mistrust no parcel of my fear ... / Shall rue the hour that ever thou wast born*

mistrustful *(adj.)* fearful, intimidating, raising concern **Venus** 826 [of Venus] *'stonished as night-wanderers often are, / Their light blown out in some mistrustful wood*

misuse *(n.)* misbehaviour, transgression, impropriety **Oth** IV.ii.108 [Desdemona alone, of Othello] *How have I been behaved, that he might stick / The smallest opinion on my least misuse?* [F; Q1 *abuse*]

misuse *(v.)* **1** disgrace, deride, abuse **MW** IV.ii.97 [Mistress Page to Mistress Ford, of Falstaff] *We cannot misuse him enough;* **AY** IV.i.186; **MA** II.i.219

2 deceive, delude, fool **MA** II.ii.25 [Borachio to Don John] *Proof enough to misuse the Prince*

mitigate *(v.)* **1** moderate, reduce the severity of **MV** IV.i.200 [Portia as Balthasar to Shylock] *I have spoke thus much / To mitigate the justice of thy plea*

2 appease, pacify, calm **1H6** III.i.88 [King to Gloucester] *mitigate this strife*

mitigation *(n.)* lowering, softening, quietening **TN** II.iii.89 [Malvolio to Sir Toby, Sir Andrew, and Feste] *ye squeak out your coziers' catches without any mitigation or remorse of voice*

mo, moe *(adj.)* more [in number] **Mac** V.iii.35 [Macbeth to Seyton] *Send out moe horses, skirr the country round;* **Lover** 47 [of the woman] *she ... / Found yet mo letters;* **Cym** III.i.37; **2H4** I.ii.5 [F *more*]; **MA** II.iii.68; **Oth** IV.iii.54; **WT** IV.iv.271 [F]

moan *(n.)* **1** grief, lamentation, sorrow, complaint **1H6** II.iii.43 [Countess to Talbot] *Thy mirth shall turn to moan;* **Ham** IV.v.198; **MV** III.iii.23; **PassP** XX.7; **R3** II.ii.113; **Sonn** 44.12

2 plaintiveness, mournfulness, melancholy **Per** IV.Chorus.27 [Gower alone, of Marina] *She sung, and made the night-bird mute, / That still records with moan*

mobled *(adj.)* with face muffled up, veiled **Ham** II.ii.500 [First Player to all present] *who ... had seen the mobled Queen* [Q1, Q2; F *inobled*]

mock *(n.)* **1** act of mockery, mocking remark, derisive action, scornful irony **Tit** IV.iv.58 [Saturninus as if to Titus] *For this proud mock I'll be thy slaughterman;* **H5** I.ii.282; **JC** II.i.96; **LL** V.ii.832; **MA** III.i.79; **Tem** III.ii.84 ☞ **arch-mock** *(n.)*

2 mockery, derision, ridicule **Oth** I.i.69 [Brabantio to Othello] *t'incur a general mock*

mock *(v.)* **1** make fun of, ridicule **Ham** II.ii.541 [Hamlet to First Player, of Polonius] *and look you mock him not* [or: sense 2]; **MW** V.iii.19

2 imitate, mimic, copy **WT** V.iii.20 [Paulina to Leontes, of Hermione's statue] *prepare / To see the life as lively mocked as ever / Still sleep mocked death*

3 deceive, delude, mislead **Mac** I.vii.81 [Macbeth to Lady Macbeth] *Away, and mock the time with fairest show;* **MW** V.iii.18; **Sonn** 61.4

4 disprove, defy, disppoint **2H4** V.ii.126 [King Henry V to his brothers, of King Henry IV] *with his spirits sadly I survive / To mock the expectation of the world*

mocked, well make a jocular riposte, evade an argument using flattery **Tim** I.i.177 [Timon to Jeweller] *Well mocked*

mockery *(n.)* subject of ridicule, object of derision **Cym** V.iii.56 [Posthumus to Lord, of the victory] *Will you rhyme upon't, / And vent it for a mock'ry*

mockery *(adj.)* mocking, derisive **LL** V.ii.139 [Princess to Katharine, of the King's party] *They do it but in mockery merriment*

mocking *(n.)* imitation, representation, impression **Tim** I.i.36 [Painter to Poet, of someone in the picture for Timon] *It is a pretty mocking of the life*

model *(n.)* **1** replica, image, copy **R2** I.ii.28 [Duchess of Gloucester to John of Gaunt] *thy wretched brother ... / Who was the model of thy father's life;* **Ham** V.ii.50; **H8** IV.ii.132

2 microcosm, miniature, tiny replica **H5** II.Chorus.16 [Chorus] *O England! model to thy inward greatness;* **R2** III.ii.153

3 ground-plan, layout, outline **R3** V.iii.24 [Richmond to all] *I'll draw the form and model of our battle;* **2H4** I.iii.42; **R2** V.i.11

4 design, blueprint, ground-plan **MA** I.iii.42 [Don John to Borachio] *Will it serve for any model to build mischief on?*

modern *(adj.)* ordinary, trite, commonplace, everyday **Mac** IV.iii.170 [Ross to Macduff and Malcolm, of Scotland] *where violent sorrow seems / A modern ecstasy;* **AC** V.ii.167; **AW** V.iii.216; **KJ** III.iv.42; **RJ** III.ii.120; **Sonn** 83.7

modest *(adj.)* **1** moderate, reasonable, mild, limited **TS** II.i.286 [Petruchio to Baptista, of Katherina] *she's not froward, but modest as the dove;* **AW** II.i.128; **H8** V.iii.69; **KL** I.iv.24; **MA** I.i.21; **TN** I.v.173

2 moderate, uninflated, free from exaggeration **KL** IV.vii.5 [Kent to Cordelia] *All my reports go with the modest truth*

3 decorous, seemly, not offending modesty **MA** II.i.347 [Hero to Don Pedro] *I will do any modest office;* **MA** IV.i.35

modestly *(adv.)* without exaggeration, in due measure **JC** I.ii.69 [Cassius to Brutus] *I, your glass, / Will modestly discover to yourself / That yourself which you yet know not of;* **TC** IV.v.222

modesty *(n.)* **1** moderation, restraint, discipline **H8** IV.ii.74 [Katherine to Griffith] *With thy religious truth and modesty;* **Ham** II.ii.439, III.ii.19, V.ii.204; **JC** III.i.213; **MV** V.i.205; **TS** Induction.i.92

2 propriety, protocol, seemly behaviour **H8** II.ii.135 [King Henry to Gardiner, of a letter] *Deliver this with modesty to th'Queen;* **MM** III.ii.241; **TN** II.i.11, V.i.333

3 feelings of shame, sense of propriety **Ham** II.ii.280 [Hamlet to Rosencrantz and Guildenstern] *there is a kind of confession in your looks, which your modesties have not craft enough to colour*

4 chastity, virtue, propriety **Tem** III.i.53 [Miranda to Ferdinand] *by my modesty, / The jewel in my dower*

modicum (*n.*) limited quantity, tiny amount **TC** II.i.67 [Thersites to Achilles, of Ajax] *what modicums of wit he utters!*

module (*n.*) image, pattern, model, empty pretence **KJ** V.vii.58 [King John to Bastard, of his soon-dead body] *all this thou seest is but a clod / And module of confounded royalty;* **AW** IV.iii.98

moe (*adj.*) ☞ mo (*adj.*)

moiety (*n.*) **1** share, portion, part **WT** II.iii.8 [Leontes to himself, of Hermione] *say that she were gone … a moiety of my rest / Might come to me again;* **AW** III.ii.66; **1H4** III.i.92; **MV** IV.i.26; **Sonn** 46.12; **TC** II.ii.108

2 half, equal share **H8** I.ii.12 [King Henry to Queen Katherine, of her request] *Half your suit / Never name to us … / The other moiety ere you ask is given;* **AC** V.i.19; **Cym** I.v.105; **H5** V.ii.213; **R3** I.iii.249; **WT** III.ii.38

moist (*adj.*) **1** damp, dripping, dewy **Venus** 854 [of the lark] *From his moist cabinet mounts up on high;* **Tim** IV.iii.224

2 watery, rheumy **2H4** I.ii.182 [Lord Chief Justice to Falstaff] *Have you not a moist eye, a dry hand*

moist (*v.*) moisten **AC** V.ii.281 [Cleopatra to Iras] *Now no more / The juice of Egypt's grape shall moist this lip*

moist star the Moon [because of its influence on the tides] **Ham** I.i.118 [Horatio to Barnardo and Marcellus] *the moist star / Upon whose influence Neptune's empire stands*

moldwarp (*n.*) mole [animal] **1H4** III.i.143 [Hotspur to Mortimer, of Glendower] *Sometime he angers me / With telling me of the moldwarp*

mole (*n.*) blemish, fault **Ham** I.iv.24 [Hamlet to Horatio, of certain men who have] *some vicious mole of nature in them*

molest (*v.*) vex, annoy, bother **Tit** V.ii.9 [Titus to all] *Who doth molest my contemplation?;* **Tem** II.i.285

molestation (*n.*) disturbance, distress, upset **Oth** II.i.16 [Second Gentleman to Montano] *I never did like molestation view / On the enchafed flood*

mollification (*n.*) appeasement, placating, pacifying **TN** I.v.197 [Viola as Cesario to Olivia, of Maria] *Some mollification for your giant*

mome (*n.*) blockhead, fool, dolt **CE** III.i.32 [Dromio of Syracuse to Dromio of Ephesus] *Mome, malthorse, capon, coxcomb, idiot, patch*

moment (*n.*) **1** importance, weight, consequence **Cym** I.vii.182 [Iachimo to Innogen] *a small request, / And yet of moment too;* **Ham** III.i.86; **1H6** I.ii.5; **3H6** I.ii.22

2 cause, motive, consideration **AC** I.ii.143 [Antony to Enobarbus, of Cleopatra] *I have seen her die twenty times upon far poorer moment*

moment, on the immediately, instantly **Tim** I.i.82 [Poet to Painter, of Timon's associates in his poem] *on the moment / Follow his strides*

momentany (*adj.*) momentary, transitory, fleeting **MND** I.i.143 [Lysander to Hermia, of choosing to love] *War, death, or sickness did lay siege to it, / Making it momentany as a sound*

monarchize (*v.*) perform the role of a monarch, play a king's part **R2** III.ii.165 [King Richard to all, of a king as a buffoon] *Allowing him a breath, a little scene, / To monarchize*

monarcho (*n.*) vain hanger-on at court, pretentious absurdity **LL** IV.i.100 [Boyet to Princess, of Armado] *A phantasime, a Monarcho*

monopoly (*n.*) exclusive trading right granted by the sovereign **KL** I.iv.151 [Fool to Lear] *If I had a monopoly out they would have part on't*

monsieur (*n.*) French gentleman **H8** I.iii.21 [Lord Chamberlain to Lovell] *I would pray our monsieurs / To think an English courtier may be wise, / And never see the Louvre*

monster (*n.*) **1** marvel, monstrosity, prodigy **Mac** V.vi.64 [Macduff to Macbeth] *We'll have thee, as our rarer monsters are, / Painted upon a pole;* **AC** IV.xii.36; **H5** II.ii.85

2 cuckold, victim of adultery **Ham** III.i.139 [Hamlet to Ophelia] *For wise men know well enough what monsters you make of them*

monster (*v.*) **1** make a monster of **KL** I.i.220 [France to Lear, of Cordelia's offence] *Must be of such unnatural degree / That monsters it*

2 describe as something wonderful, make into an unnatural marvel **Cor** II.ii.75 [Coriolanus to Menenius] *To hear my nothings monstered*

monstrous (*adj.*) unnatural, outlandish, aberrant **2H6** IV.x.64 [Iden to himself] *Is't Cade that I have slain, that monstrous traitor?;* **2H4** IV.ii.34; **3H6** III.ii.164; **H8** I.ii.122; **JC** II.i.81; **Tim** V.i.86

monstrous (*adv.*) exceedingly, wonderfully, extraordinarily **MND** I.ii.48 [Bottom to Quince] *I'll speak in a monstrous little voice;* **AW** II.i.184

monstruosity (*n.*) monstrosity, extraordinary nature **TC** III.ii.79 [Troilus to Cressida] *This is the monstruosity in love, lady, that the will is infinite, and the execution confined*

montant (*n.*) [fencing] upward thrust **MW** II.iii.24 [Host to Caius, in answer to 'Vat be you all … come for?'] *to see thee pass … thy montant*

monument (*n.*) **1** memory, memorial, remembrance **2H6** IV.iii.10 [Cade to Dick, of Stafford's coat of mail] *This monument of the victory will I bear;* **2H6** I.i.100, III.i.342; **MA** V.ii.72; **R3** I.i.6; **Tim** IV.iii.462

2 portent, warning, sign **TS** III.ii.94 [Petruchio to all, of their stares] *As if they saw some wondrous monument*

3 tomb, burial chamber **H8** II.i.94 [Buckingham to Lovell, of King Henry] *when old time shall lead him to his end, / Goodness and he fill up one monument!*

4 effigy, carved figure, statue **Luc** 391 [of Lucrece] *like a virtuous monument she lies;* **AW** IV.ii.6; **Cym** II.ii.32

monumental (*adj.*) **1** serving as a moment, providing a memorial **TC** III.iii.153 [Ulysses to Achilles, of past honour] *Quite out of fashion, like a rusty mail / In monumental mockery*

2 kept as a memento, serving as a token **AW** IV.iii.16 [Second Lord to First Lord, of Bertram and Diana] *He hath given her his monumental ring*

mood (*n.*) **1** anger, fury, frenzy, fit of temper **TG** IV.i.51 [Second Outlaw to Valentine] *a gentleman / Who, in my mood, I stabbed unto the heart;* **AW** V.ii.4; **CE** II.i.179; **Cor** I.iii.67; **MND** III.ii.74

2 frame of mind, mental state **Luc** 1273 [Lucrece to Maid, of her maid's tears] *it small avails my mood;* **Ham** IV.v.3

3 mode, manner, variety **Ham** I.ii.82 [Hamlet to Gertrude, of his feelings] *all forms, moods, shapes of grief*

4 tune, tune, key **2H4** IV.v.199 [King Henry IV to Prince Henry] *now my death / Changes the mood* [or: sense 2]

moody (*adj.*) **1** angry, wrathful, rancorous, sullen **1H6** III.i.124 [Warwick to Winchester] *the Duke / Hath banished moody discontented fury;* **1H4** I.iii.18, V.i.81; **R3** V.i.7; **RJ** III.i.12; **Tem** I.ii.244

2 melancholy, sombre, gloomy **AC** II.v.1 [Cleopatra to all, of music] *moody food / Of us that trade in love;* **3H6** V.vi.13

moody-mad (*adj.*) wild with rage, furiously angry **1H6** IV.ii.50 [Talbot to all] *moody-mad and desperate stags*

moon, below the of this world, not spiritual **H8** III.ii.134 [King Henry to Norfolk, of Wolsey] *His thinkings are below the moon, not worth / His serious considering*

mooncalf (*n.*) monstrosity, misshapen creature, monster **Tem** II.ii.132 [Stephano to Caliban] *How now, mooncalf?*; **Tem** II.ii.104, III.ii.20

moonish (*adj.*) changeable, fickle, capricious **AY** III.ii.392 [Rosalind as Ganymede to Orlando] *I, being but a moonish youth*

moonshine (*n.*) **1** moonlight **KL** II.ii.29 [disguised Kent to Oswald] *I'll make a sop o'the moonshine of you* [i.e. while the moon is still out]
 2 month **KL** I.ii.5 [Edmund alone] *I am some twelve or fourteen moonshines / Lag of a brother* [i.e. younger than]

moonshine in the water nothing, a thing of naught **LL** V.ii.208 [masked Rosaline to masked King] *Thou now requests but moonshine in the water*

mop (*n.*) grimace, pout **Tem** IV.i.47 [Ariel to Prospero, of the spirits] *Each one ... / Will be here with mop and mow*

mope (*v.*) act aimlessly, be in a daze, wander about **H5** III.vii.130 [Orleans to Constable, of King Henry] *to mope with his fat-brained followers so far out of his knowledge*; **Ham** III.iv.82

moped (*adj.*) bewildered, confused, in a daze **TNK** III.ii.25 [Gaoler's Daughter alone] *I am moped; / Food took I none these two days*

moping (*adv.*) in a daze, bewilderedly **Tem** V.i.240 [Boatswain to Alonso] *we ... were brought moping hither*

mopping (*n.*) grimacing, making faces **KL** IV.i.60 [Edgar as Poor Tom to Gloucester] *Flibberdigibbet, [prince] of mopping and mowing*

moral (*n.*) **1** hidden meaning, import, significance **H5** III.vi.32 [Fluellen to Pistol, of Fortune] *she is painted also with a wheel, to signify to you, which is the moral of it, that she is turning*; **MA** III.iv.71; **TC** IV.iv.106
 2 symbolic figure, allegory **H5** III.vi.37 [Fluellen to Pistol] *Fortune is an excellent moral*

moral (*adj.*) **1** full of moral sentiments, arguing the pros and cons **KL** IV.ii.58 [Gonerill to Albany] *thou, a moral fool*
 2 pointing a moral, allegorical **Tim** I.i.93 [Painter to Poet] *A thousand moral paintings I can show*

MONEY

Money terms can be grouped into three main categories: English, foreign, and terms expressive of tiny amounts. The pre-1971 *pound* (£) consisted of 20 *shillings* (*s*), with each shilling consisting of 12 *pence* (*d*), and each *penny* consisted of two *halfpennies* or four *farthings*. In Shakespeare's day, coins of several different intermediate denominations were in circulation. References to foreign coins were usually notional, suggestive of large amounts or small amounts, rather than conveying any precise value; the equivalent English values of the time, which are added below, are at best approximate. The terms which express the idea of a tiny amount are given with a quotation to illustrate the sense.

English

Small value amounts

Unit	Example	Value
obolus / ob	1H4 II.iv.524	halfpenny
halfpence	AY III.ii.341	silver halfpenny
three farthings	LL III.i.135	coin of this value
penny	LL III.i.137	coin of this value
twopence	MW I.i.145	silver coin of this value
threepence	H8 II.iii.36	coin of this value
groat	2H4 I.ii.237	fourpenny piece
mill-sixpence	MW I.i.144	sixpence made in a stamping mill
sixpence	2H4 I.ii.25	coin of this value
tester	MW I.iii.82	sixpenny piece
testril	TN II.iii.32	sixpenny piece
shilling	2H6 IV.vii.19	coin of this value

Large value amounts

Unit	Example	Value
angel	CE IV.iii.40	gold coin; value: between 6s 8p and 10s at various times; design displayed Archangel Michael
noble	1H6 V.iv.23	gold coin; value: third of a pound, 6s 8d
royal	R2 V.v.67	gold coin; value: 10s
Harry ten shillings	2H4 III.ii.216	half-sovereign coin from the reign of Henry VII; value: 5s
pound	MW V.v.123	[as in modern English]

Foreign

Unit	Example	Value
chequin	Per IV.ii.24	gold coin of Italy and Turkey; equivalent English value: about 8s
crown	AY I.i.2	gold coin, of varying value in different countries; English coin, value: 5s

moral (*v.*) moralize, sermonize **AY** II.vii.29 [Jaques to all, of Touchstone] *When I did hear / The motley fool thus moral on the time* [or, used as adjective: being moralistic]

moralise, moralize (*v.*) **1** explain, interpret **TS** IV.iv.78 [Lucentio to Biondello, of Tranio's signs] *I pray thee moralize them; Luc 104*

2 draw lessons from, interpret morally **AY** II.i.44 [Duke Senior to First Lord, of Jaques' reactions to the deer] *Did he not moralize this spectacle?; R3* III.i.83

3 teach by example, use illustration to make a point **Venus** 712 [Venus to Adonis] *Unlike myself thou hear'st me moralize*

moraller (*n.*) moralizer, self-critic **Oth** II.iii.290 [Iago to Cassio] *you are too severe a moraller*

more (*n.*) additional amount, extra quantity **TN** V.i.134 [Viola as Cesario to Olivia, of loving Orsino] *More by all mores than e'er I shall love wife* [i.e. more than any comparison can suggest]

more (*adj.*) **1** greater **Cor** III.i.124 [Volumnia to Coriolanus] *it is my more dishonour;* **CE** II.ii.181; **1H4** IV.i.45; **KJ** II.i.34; **Luc** 332; **Venus** 78

2 older **LL** IV.ii.40 [Holofernes to Dull] *The moon was a month old when Adam was no more*

more (*adv.*) ☛ **DISCOURSE MARKERS, p.127**

more above ☛ above (*adv.*) 2

more and less **1** men of high and low rank **2H4** I.i.209 [Morton to Northumberland, of the Archbishop] *more and less do flock to follow him;* **1H4** IV.iii.68; **Mac** V.iv.12; **Sonn** 96.3

2 great and small **Ham** V.ii.351 [Hamlet to Horatio, of Fortinbras] *tell him, with th'occurrents, more and less*

more-having (*n.*) having more, amassing, acquiring **Mac** IV.iii.81 [Malcolm to Macduff] *my more-having would be as a sauce / To make me hunger more*

moreover (*adv.*) as well as the fact, besides the fact **Ham** II.ii.2 [Claudius to Rosencrantz and Guildenstern] *Moreover that we much did long to see you*

morisco (*n.*) morris dancer **2H6** III.i.365 [York to himself, of Cade] *I have seen / Him caper upright like a wild Morisco*

morn (*n.*) morning, dawn **Ham** I.i.167 [Horatio to Marcellus and Barnardo] *the morn in russet mantle clad* ☛ **FEW, p.xxi**

MONEY – *continued*

Unit	Example	Value
crusado	**Oth** III.iv.26	Portuguese gold coin; equivalent English value: about 3s
dollar	**Mac** I.ii.65	[= thaler] German silver coin; also in other countries with varying value; equivalent English value: about 5s
drachma	**JC** III.ii.243	Greek silver coin of varying but significant value, also used in surrounding countries [cf. below]
ducat	**MV** I.iii.1	gold (sometimes silver) coin used in several European countries, with varying value; equivalent English value: between a fifth and a third of a pound (in Italy, about 3s 6d)
guilder	**CE** I.i.8	gold coin used in parts of Europe
mark	**H8** V.i.170	accounting unit in England; value: two-thirds of a pound (13s 4d); name of a coin, in some countries
talent	**Tim** I.i.99	high-value accounting unit in some ancient countries; equivalent English value unclear: perhaps £200

Tiny amounts

Unit	Example	Value
cardecue	**AW** IV.iii.270 *for a cardecue he will see the fee-simple of his salvation*	[= quart d'ecu] French silver coin of little value; equivalent English value: about 8d
denier	**1H4** III.iii.78 *I'll not pay a denier*	French copper coin of little value, twelfth of a sou (which was a twentieth of a livre); equivalent English value, tenth of a penny
doit	**MV** I.iii.137 *I would ... take no doit / Of usance for my moneys*	Dutch coin of little value; equivalent English value, half a farthing
drachma	**Cor** I.v.5 *See here these movers that do prize their hours / At a cracked drachma*	coin assumed to be of small value [cf. above]
eightpenny	**1H4** III.iii.104 [of a ring] *A trifle, some eightpenny matter*	conventional expression for a trivial amount
forty pence	**H8** II.iii.89 *Is it bitter? Forty pence, no*	proverbial for a small sum; the standard amount of a bet or fee
solidare	**Tim** III.i.43 *Here's three solidares for thee*	not a known coin; perhaps derived from the solidus (Roman gold coin); expressive of a paltry sum

morris *(n.)* morris dance **TNK** V.vii.49 [Gaoler's Daughter to Gaoler, of her horse] *He'll dance the morris twenty mile an hour;* **AW** II.ii.23; **TNK** II.i.329, III.v.107

morris, nine men's area marked out in squares for playing nine men's morris [a type of open-air game using nine 'men' on each side] **MND** II.i.98 [Titania to Oberon] *The nine men's morris is filled up with mud*

morris-pike *(n.)* type of pike [thought to be of Moorish origin] **CE** IV.iii.27 [Dromio of Syracuse to Antipholus of Syracuse, of the officer] *he that sets up his rest to do more exploits with his mace than a morris-pike* ☛ **pike** *(n.)* 1

morrow *(n.)* morning **1H4** II.iv.534 [Peto to Prince Hal] *Good morrow, good my lord* ☛ **FEW**, p.xxi; **GREETINGS**, p.206

morsel *(n.)* dish, mouthful, piece of flesh **MM** III.ii.51 [Lucio to Pompey] *How doth my dear morsel, thy mistress?;* **Tem** II.i.291

mort *(n.)* death, dying moment **WT** I.ii.118 [Leontes to himself, of Hermione and Polixenes] *to sigh, as 'twere / The mort o'th' deer*

mortal *(adj.)* **1** fatal, deadly, lethal **Mac** I.v.39 [Lady Macbeth alone] *Come, you spirits / That tend on mortal thoughts, unsex me here;* **AC** V.i.64; **Cym** V.v.50; **Oth** III.iv.111; **TN** III.iv.255; **WT** III.ii.146
2 human, subject to death, characterized by mortality **Ham** III.i.67 [Hamlet alone] *what dreams may come / When we have shuffled off this mortal coil;* **H8** II.iv.228; **Luc** 13; **Mac** IV.i.99; **R2** I.i.177; **Tem** V.i.188

mortal *(adv.)* fatally, lethally, destructively **Cor** V.iii.190 [Coriolanus to Volumnia, of himself] *Most dangerously you have with him prevailed, / If not most mortal to him;* **MM** II.ii.123

mortality *(n.)* **1** mortal nature, human life **Mac** II.iii.90 [Macbeth to all] *from this instant / There's nothing serious in mortality;* **Cym** IV.i.15; **H5** IV.iii.107; **KJ** V.vii.5; **MM** III.i.175
2 death **1H6** IV.v.32 [John Talbot to Talbot] *Here on my knee I beg mortality;* **1H6** IV.vii.22; **MM** IV.ii.142
3 deadliness, mortification, deadly situation **MM** I.ii.133 [Lucio to Claudio] *I had as lief have the foppery of freedom as the mortality of imprisonment*

mortally *(adv.)* **1** of human origin **Per** V.i.103 [Marina to Pericles] *I was mortally brought forth*
2 grievously, bitterly, intensely **Per** III.iii.6 [Cleon to Pericles] *Your shakes of fortune … haunt you mortally*

mortal-staring *(adj.)* with death-like glare, lethally penetrating **R3** V.iii.91 [Derby to Richmond] *put thy fortune to th' arbitrement / Of … mortal-staring war*

mortar-piece *(n.)* type of small high-firing cannon **H8** V.iv.46 [Man to Porter, of a brass-worker] *he stands there like a mortar-piece, to blow us* ☛ **piece** *(n.)* 7; **WEAPONS**, p.491

mortgage *(v.)* pledge, contract, bind **Sonn** 134.2 *I myself am mortgaged to thy will*

mortified *(adj.)* **1** deadened, dead to feeling, numbed **JC** II.i.324 [Ligarius to Brutus] *Thou, like an exorcist, hast conjured up / My mortified spirit;* **KJ** II.iii.15; **Mac** V.ii.5
2 dead to earthly pleasures, insensible to worldly desires **LL** I.i.28 [Dumaine to King, of himself] *Dumaine is mortified*
3 dying to sin, put under subjection **H5** I.i.26 [Canterbury to Ely, of King Henry] *his wildness, mortified in him, / Seemed to die too*

mortifying *(adj.)* killing, deadly, lethal **MA** I.iii.12 [Don John to Conrade] *thou … goest about to apply a moral medicine to a mortifying mischief*

mortise *(v.)* fit together, join tightly [like pieces of wood] **Ham** III.iii.20 [Rosencrantz to Claudius] *ten thousand lesser things / Are mortised and joined together*

mose in the chine [unclear meaning] be in the final stages of the glanders **TS** III.ii.50 [Biondello to Tranio as Lucentio, of Petruchio's horse] *possessed with the glanders and like to mose in the chine*

most *(adj.)* maximum, utmost **MM** IV.i.43 [Isabella to disguised Duke] *my most stay / Can be but brief;* **Sonn** 85.10

mot *(n.)* motto, words on a device **Luc** 830 [Lucrece to herself, of Collatine's reproach] *Tarquin's eye may read the mot afar*

mote *(n.)* speck of dust, tiny particle, trifle **H5** IV.i.174 [disguised King Henry to Williams] *should every soldier … wash every mote out of his conscience;* **E3** II.i.437; **Ham** I.i.112; **KJ** IV.i.91; **Luc** 1251; **Per** IV.iv.21 ☛ **beam** *(n.)* 5

mother *(n.)* **1** ☛ **FAMILY**, p.168
2 womanish qualities **H5** IV.vi.31 [Exeter to King Henry] *all my mother came into mine eyes / And gave me up to tears*

mother-wit natural intelligence **TS** II.i.257 [Petruchio to Katherina, of his repartee] *It is extempore, from my mother-wit*

motion *(n.)* **1** inner movement, inward prompting, natural impulse, imagining **MV** V.i.86 [Lorenzo to Jessica, of a man without music] *The motions of his spirit are dull as night;* **AC** II.iii.14; **AW** III.i.13; **JC** II.i.64; **LL** IV.ii.68; **Oth** I.iii.95
2 emotion, inclination, desire, impulse **TN** II.iv.18 [Orsino to Viola as Cesario, of lovers] *Unstaid and skittish in all motions else;* **KJ** I.i.212, IV.ii.255; **Tim** II.i.3; **TN** II.iv.97
3 power to act normally, reaction, faculties **Oth** I.ii.75 [Brabantio to Othello, of Desdemona] *thou hast … / Abused her delicate youth with drugs or minerals / That weakens motion;* **MM** III.i.123
4 cause, prompting, provocation **Cor** II.i.48 [Menenius to Brutus and Sicinius, of himself] *hasty and tinder-like upon too trivial motion;* **Cym** II.iv.172; **H8** I.i.153
5 urging, prompting, encouragement **Cor** II.ii.51 [First Senator to Tribunes] *We do request … / Your loving motion toward the common body;* **CE** I.i.60; **MW** III.ii.31
6 proposal, proposition, suggestion, offer **MM** V.i.532 [Duke to Isabel] *I have a motion much imports your good;* **AW** V.iii.262; **1H6** V.i.7; **MW** III.iv.62; **TS** I.i.246; **TS** I.ii.177
7 act of moving, movement, stirring **LL** V.ii.216 [masked King to masked Rosaline] *The music plays; vouchsafe some motion to it;* **AW** II.iii.232; **2H4** IV.iii.33; **H8** I.ii.86; **Luc** 1326; **Oth** II.iii.168
8 orbit, rhythm of movement **CE** III.ii.24 [Luciana to Antipholus of Syracuse, of women] *We in your motion turn*
9 expression, grimace; or: agitation, emotion **1H4** II.iii.62 [Lady Percy to Hotspur] *in thy face strange motions have appeared*
10 [fencing] attack, execution **KL** II.i.49 [Edmund to Gloucester, of Edgar] *in fell motion / With his prepared sword he charges home;* **Ham** IV.vii.100, 156; **TN** III.iv.270
11 puppet-show **WT** IV.iii.93 [Autolycus to Clown, of the supposed robber] *he compassed a motion of the Prodigal Son;* **MM** III.ii.105; **TG** II.i.89
12 bowel movement **MW** III.i.95 [Host to all, of Caius] *he gives me the potions and the motions*

motion *(v.)* advocate, propose, promote **1H6** I.iii.63 [Winchester to Mayor, of Gloucester] *One that still motions war and never peace*

motive *(n.)* **1** cause, mover, instigator **Tim** V.iv.27 [Second Senator to Alcibiades] *Nor are they living / Who were the motives that you first went out;* **Oth** IV.ii.42
2 inspiration, incentive, mover **Mac** IV.iii.27 [Malcolm to Macduff] *Why in that rawness left you wife and child, / Those precious motives*
3 instrument, agent, moving organ **TC** IV.v.57 [Ulysses to Nestor, of Cressida] *her wanton spirits look out / At every joint and motive of her body;* **AW** IV.iv.20; **R2** I.i.193
4 impulse, prompting, incitement **Ham** V.ii.239 [Laertes to Hamlet] *nature, / Whose motive in this case should stir me*

motley *(n.)* **1** distinctive dress of a fool **TN** I.v.52 [Feste to Olivia] *I wear not motley in my brain;* **AY** II.vii.34, 58; **KL** I.iv.144
2 fool **AY** III.iii.71 [Jaques to Touchstone] *Will you be married, motley?;* **Sonn** 110.2

motley *(adj.)* in the distinctive [multicoloured] dress of a fool **AY** II.vii.43 [Jaques to Duke Senior] *I am ambitious for a motley coat;* **AY** II.vii.13; **H8** Prologue.16

motley-minded *(adj.)* muddle-headed, foolish-minded **AY** V.iv.40 [Jaques to Duke Senior, of Touchstone] *this is the motley-minded gentleman*

mould (*n.*) **1** soil, earth, clay **H5** III.ii.22 [Pistol to Fluellen] *Be merciful, great Duke, to men of mould!*; **E3** III.iii.30, V.i.171; **TC** I.iii.293

2 nature, frame, character **TS** I.i.60 [Hortensio to Katherina] *No mates for you / Unless you were of gentler, milder mould*

3 model, pattern, paradigm **Ham** III.i.154 [Ophelia alone, of Hamlet] *the mould of form*

mould (*v.*) model, shape, fashion **TS** IV.iii.64 [Petruchio to Haberdasher, of a cap] *this was moulded on a porringer*

mould up (*v.*) go to create, help to form **H8** V.v.26 [Cranmer to all, of Princess Elizabeth] *All princely graces / That mould up such a mighty piece as this*

moulten (*adj.*) having moulted **1H4** III.i.146 [Hotspur to Mortimer, of Glendower] *Sometime he angers me / With telling me of … / A clip-winged griffin and a moulten raven*

mount (*v.*) **1** ascend, rise up, climb **2H6** III.i.22 [Queen to King, of Gloucester] *should you fall, he is the next will mount*; **2H4** IV.iii.54; **H5** IV.i.104; **Tit** II.i.13

2 cause to boil, make rise **H8** I.i.144 [Norfolk to Buckingham] *The fire that mounts the liquor till't run o'er*

mount, on conspicuously, for all to see **Ham** IV.vii.28 [Laertes to Claudius, of Ophelia] *Stood challenger, on mount*

mountain (*adj.*) pre-eminent, larger than life **H5** II.iv.57 [French King to all, of the Black Prince] *his mountain sire, on mountain standing*

mountaineer (*n.*) [often contemptuous] mountain-dweller, native of the mountains **Cym** IV.ii.100 [Cloten to Guiderius] *Yield, rustic mountaineer*; **Cym** IV.ii.71, 120, 370; **Tem** III.iii.45

mountain-foot (*n.*) foothills **TG** V.ii.46 [Duke to all] *meet with me / Upon the rising of the mountain-foot / That leads toward Mantua*

mountain-squire (*n.*) squire of barren land **H5** V.i.34 [Fluellen to Pistol] *You called me yesterday mountain-squire* ☞ **squire** (*n.*) 5

mountant (*adj.*) mounting, rising, always being lifted up **Tim** IV.iii.136 [Timon to Phrynia and Timandra] *Hold up, you sluts, / Your aprons mountant*

mountanto (*n.*) [directional thrust in fencing] fencer, duellist **MA** I.i.28 [Beatrice to Messenger, of Benedick] *is Signor Mountanto returned from the wars, or no?*

mountebank (*n.*) itinerant quack, travelling drug-seller, charlatan **Ham** IV.vii.140 [Laertes to Claudius] *I bought an unction of a mountebank*; **CE** I.ii.101, V.i.239; **Oth** I.iii.61

mountebank (*v.*) win over by plausible trickery **Cor** III.ii.132 [Coriolanus to Volumnia, of the people] *I'll mountebank their loves*

mounted (*adj.*) exalted, high, lofty **TNK** I.iv.4 [Theseus to Queens] *Th'impartial gods, who from the mounted heavens / View us*

mounting (*adj.*) ambitious, aspiring, rising **KJ** I.i.206 [Bastard alone] *worshipful society … fits the mounting spirit like myself*

mournful (*adj.*) heartbreaking, distressing, causing sorrow **1H6** II.ii.16 [Talbot to all, of Salisbury] *The treacherous manner of his mournful death*

mourningly (*adv.*) in a spirit of mourning **AW** I.i.28 [Lafew to Countess, of de Narbon] *The King very lately spoke of him … mourningly*

mouse (*n.*) ☞ **ADDRESS FORMS**, p.8

mouse (*v.*) tear, bite, rend **KJ** II.i.354 [Bastard to King John and King Philip, of death] *now he feasts, mousing the flesh of men*

mouse-hunt (*n.*) mouse-hunter; prowler, pursuer of women **RJ** IV.iv.11 [Lady Capulet to Capulet] *you have been a mouse-hunt in your time*

mouth (*n.*) **1** utterance, expression, voice **RJ** V.iii.216 [Prince to all] *Seal up the mouth of outrage for a while*; **H8** I.i.137

2 mouthpiece, spokesman **3H6** V.v.18 [Prince to Edward] *Suppose that I am now my father's mouth*

3 bark, baying, howl **1H6** II.iv.12 [Warwick to all] *Between two dogs, which hath the deeper mouth*

mouths, make make faces, grimace, show scorn **Ham** IV.iv.50 [Hamlet alone, of Fortinbras] *Makes mouths at the invisible event*

mouth (*v.*) **1** take into the mouth **Ham** IV.ii.18 [Hamlet to Rosencrantz] *an apple … first mouthed, to be last swallowed*

2 join mouths, kiss erotically, snog **MM** III.ii.172 [Lucio to disguised Duke, of the Duke] *he would mouth with a beggar*

mouthed (*adj.*) open-mouthed, yawning, gaping **Sonn** 77.6 *The wrinkles which thy glass will truly show / Of mouthed graves*

mouth-friend (*n.*) friend in word only; or: friend won by feeding **Tim** III.vi.89 [Timon to Lords] *You knot of mouth-friends!*

mouth-honour (*n.*) honour shown in words not deeds **Mac** V.iii.27 [Macbeth to himself, of what will come his way] *mouth-honour, breath / Which the poor heart would fain deny and dare not*

movable, moveable (*n.*) (plural) personal possessions, private effects, pieces of property **R3** IV.ii.89 [Buckingham to King Richard] *I claim … the movables / Which you have promised I shall possess*; **R3** III.i.195

move (*v.*) **1** arouse, affect, stir [by emotion] **TS** II.i.194 [Petruchio to Katherina] *Myself am moved to woo thee for my wife*; **KJ** III.i.217; **KL** I.iv.271; **Lover** 101; **TC** VII.37; **Tim** I.i.34

2 move to anger, provoke, exasperate **JC** IV.iii.58 [Cassius to Brutus] *When Caesar lived, he durst not thus have moved me*; **AC** II.ii.4; **Per** II.ii.71; **RJ** IV.v.95; **TN** III.iv.109; **Venus** 623

3 encourage, instigate, prompt **AC** II.i.42 [Menas to Pompey, of Antony and Caesar, respectively] *His brother warred upon him - although, I think, / Not moved by Antony*; **Cym** V.v.343; **Ham** III.ii.192; **H8** V.i.100; **RJ** III.i.12; **Tim** V.ii.13

4 appeal, urge, exhort **AW** I.ii.6 [King to First Lord] *the Florentine will move us / For speedy aid*; **CE** II.ii.190; **JC** I.ii.166; **TC** III.iii.216

5 persuade, influence, talk encouragingly to **RJ** III.iv.2 [Capulet to Paris, of Juliet] *we have had no time to move our daughter*; **R3** III.vii.139

6 raise an issue [with], mention a matter [to] **H8** II.iv.209 [King Henry to Lincoln] *You remember / How under my oppression I did reek / When I first moved you*; **H8** II.iv.217

7 raise, bring up, introduce **TC** II.iii.81 [Agamemnon to Patroclus, of Achilles] *perchance he think / We dare not move the question of our place*

8 shake one's resolve, alter one's position **TS** I.ii.71 [Petruchio to Hortensio, of marrying a rich wife whatever her qualities] *She moves me not, or not removes at least / Affection's edge in me*

9 woo, make a proposal to, make a move towards **TG** I.ii.27 [Julia to Lucetta, of Proteus] *he … hath never moved me*

moveable (*n.*) ☞ **movable** (*n.*)

moved (*adj.*) **1** upset, agitated, distressed **Tem** IV.i.146 [Prospero to Ferdinand] *You do look … in a moved sort*; **MW** I.iv.89; **WT** I.ii.150

2 aroused, provoked, exasperated **RJ** I.i.88 [Prince to all] *hear the sentence of your moved prince*; **H8** V.i.46; **TC** IV.iv.128

3 in a bad temper, angered, exasperated **TS** V.ii.141 [Katherina to Widow] *A woman moved is like a fountain troubled*; **TC** I.ii.5

mover (*n.*) active fellow, operator **Cor** I.v.4 [Martius to Lartius, of the Roman soldiers] *See here these movers that do prize their hours / At a cracked drachma*

moving (*n.*) power to move, affecting, stirring **E3** II.i.73 [King Edward to Lodowick] *For so much moving hath a poet's pen*

mow (*n.*) derisive grimace, pout, mocking expression **Tem** III.iii.84 [stage direction] *the shapes … dance with mocks and mows*; **Cym** I.vii.41; **Ham** II.ii.363; **Tem** IV.i.47

mow (*v.*) grimace, pout, make mouths **Tem** II.ii.9 [Caliban alone, of Prospero's spirits] *like apes, that mow and chatter at me*

mowing (*n.*) grimacing, making mouths **KL** IV.i.61 [Edgar as Poor Tom to Gloucester] *Flibberdigibbet, [prince] of mopping and mowing*

moy (n.) [misunderstanding of French 'moi'] type of coin; measure of goods H5 IV.iv.14 [Pistol to French Soldier] *I will have forty moys*

much (adj.) **1** great, flagrant, brazen MA IV.i.97 [Don John to Hero] *I am sorry for thy much misgovernment*
2 serious, of great matter 1H6 IV.i.192 [Exeter alone] *'Tis much when sceptres are in children's hands*
3 hard, difficult R3 III.vii.92 [Buckingham to Lord Mayor] *When holy ... men / Are at their beads, 'tis much to draw them thence* [F; Q *hard*]

much (adv.) **1** very Tim III.iv.32 [First Varro's Servant to Lucius' Servant, of loans to Timon] *'Tis much deep; Ham IV.v.13*
2 very largely, to a great extent LL V.ii.472 [Berowne to his companions, of his summary of events] *Much upon this 'tis* [i.e. this is roughly what happened]

much (int.) ➤ EXCLAMATIONS, p.158

mud (v.) **1** bury in mud Tem V.i.151 [Alonso to Prospero] *I wish / Myself were mudded in that oozy bed / Where my son lies; Tem I.iii.104*
2 muddy, make foul Luc 577 [Lucrece to Tarquin] *Mud not the fountain that gave drink to thee*

muddied (adj.) **1** covered in mud, made filthy AW V.ii.4 [Parolles to Clown] *I am ... muddied in Fortune's mood; AW V.ii.21*
2 stirred up, disturbed, agitated Ham IV.v.82 [Claudius to Gertrude] *the people muddied, / Thick and unwholesome in their thoughts*

muddy (adj.) **1** made of clay, resembling mud MV V.i.64 [Lorenzo to Jessica, of harmony in immortal souls] *whilst this muddy vesture of decay / Doth grossly close it in, we cannot hear it*
2 dirty, foul 2H4 II.iv.53 [Doll to Falstaff] *Hang yourself, you muddy conger*
3 dull-witted, muddle-headed 1H4 II.i.98 [Gadshill to Chamberlain] *Farewell, you muddy knave; WT I.ii.325*
4 at a loss, confused, all at sea TNK III.v.121 [Schoolmaster to Theseus] *I first appear, though rude, and raw, and muddy* [or: sense 3]
5 [of a young deer] sluggish, lazy 2H4 II.iv.39 [Doll to Falstaff] *A pox damn you, you muddy rascal* ➤ rascal (n.)

muddy-mettled (adj.) sluggish, dull-spirited Ham II.ii.564 [Hamlet alone, of himself] *A dull and muddy-mettled rascal*

muffle (v.) hide, conceal, camouflage CE III.ii.8 [Luciana to Antipholus of Syracuse] *Muffle your false love with some show of blindness*

muffled (adj.) blindfolded, covered up MM V.i.483 [Duke to Provost] *What muffled fellow's that?; AW IV.iii.115; RJ I.i.171*

muleter, muleteer (n.) mule-driver AC III.vii.35 [Enobarbus to Antony] *Your mariners are muleters, reapers; 1H6 III.ii.68* [Talbot to French lords] *Base muleteers of France!*

mulled (adj.) stupefied, dull, numb Cor IV.v.231 [First Servingman to Second Servingman] *Peace ... is mulled, deaf, sleepy*

multiplied (adj.) many-headed, myriad, multiple Cor III.i.131 [Coriolanus to Brutus, of the Citizens] *How shall this bosom multiplied digest / The Senate's courtesy?*

multipotent (adj.) most powerful TC IV.v.129 [Hector to Ajax] *by Jove multipotent*

multitude (n.) large numbers, great host TC V.iv.22 [Diomedes to Troilus] *advantageous care / Withdrew me from the odds of multitude* [i.e. the risk of being outnumbered]

multitudinous (adj.) **1** myriad, innumerable; or: containing multitudes [of creatures] Mac II.ii.62 [Macbeth alone] *my hand will ... / The multitudinous seas incarnadine, / Making the green one red*
2 belonging to the multitude Cor III.i.156 [Coriolanus to all] *beseech you ... pluck out / The multitudinous tongue*

mum (adj.) silent, mute, saying nothing R3 III.vii.3 [Buckingham to Richard] *The citizens are mum; MM V.i.285*

mum (int.) be quiet, shush TS I.ii.160 [Hortensio aside to Grumio] *Grumio, mum!; MA II.i.109; Tem III.ii.51; TS I.i.73* ➤ ATTENTION SIGNALS, p.26

mumble (v.) grumble [beneath the breath], complain, mutter TNK II.ii.31 [First Countryman to the others, of his wife] *I'll go through, let her mumble*

mumble-news (n.) tale-bearer, tattler, gossip LL V.ii.464 [Berowne to all, of Boyet] *Some mumble-news ... / Told our intents before*

mummer (n.) actor in a dumb-show Cor II.i.70 [Menenius to Brutus and Sicinius] *you make faces like mummers*

mummy (n.) **1** dead flesh, pulp MW III.v.16 [Falstaff alone, on his size if he had swelled in the river] *I should have been a mountain of mummy*
2 preparation made from mummies Oth III.iv.74 [Othello to Desdemona, of her handkerchief] *it was dyed in mummy*

mundane (adj.) worldly, earthly Per III.ii.69 [Cerimon reading Pericles' scroll, of Thaisa] *This queen, worth all our mundane cost*

muniment (n.) support, furnishing, provision Cor I.i.116 [First Citizen to Menenius, of the body parts] *With other muniments and petty helps / In this our fabric*

mural (n.) [disputed reading] wall MND V.i.203 [Theseus to all, on exit of Snout as Wall] *Now is the mural down between the two neighbours* [F *morall down*] ➤ mure (n.)

murder, murther (n.) wound, gash [serious enough to cause death] Mac III.iv.80 [Macbeth to Lady Macbeth, of dead men] *now they rise again / With twenty mortal murders on their crowns*

murder, murther (v.) tear off, mangle, destroy 2H4 II.iv.130 [Pistol to Doll] *God let me not live but I will murder your ruff for this* ➤ murther (n./v.)

murdering-piece (n.) type of weapon which scatters lethal projectiles Ham IV.v.96 [Claudius to Gertrude, of the rumours against him] *Like to a murderous-piece, in many places / Gives me superfluous death* ➤ piece (n.) 7; WEAPONS, p.491

mure (n.) wall 2H4 IV.iv.119 [Clarence to Warwick, of King Henry IV] *Th'incessant care and labour of his mind / Hath wrought the mure that should confine it in / So thin that life looks through and will break out; MND V.i.203* [F *morall*] ➤ mural (n.)

murmur (n.) rumour, hearsay, gossip TN I.ii.32 [Captain to Viola, of Orsino being in love] *then 'twas fresh in murmur*

murrain (n.) plague, pestilence Tem III.ii.80 [Trinculo to Stephano] *A murrain on your monster; Cor I.v.3; TC II.i.19* ➤ SWEARING, p.435

murrion (adj.) infected with plague [murrain], diseased MND II.i.97 [Titania to Oberon] *crows are fatted with the murrion flock*

murther (n./v.) variant spelling of 'murder' AW I.i.138 [Parolles to Helena] *virginity murthers itself; Venus 906* ➤ murder (n./v.)

muscadel (n.) type of strong sweet wine TS III.ii.171 [Gremio to Tranio as Lucentio, of Petruchio drinking] *quaffed off the muscadel*

muse (v.) **1** wonder, be surprised R3 I.iii.304 [Rivers to Buckingham, of Queen Margaret] *I muse why she's at liberty; Cor III.ii.7; 2H4 IV.i.165; 2H6 III.i.1; KJ III.i.317; TG I.iii.64*
2 wonder at, marvel at Tem III.iii.37 [Alonso to all] *I cannot too much muse / Such shapes;*
3 wonder, speculate, ponder TG I.ii.161 [Speed to Valentine] *Why muse you, sir?; AW II.v.65; 3H6 III.ii.109*
4 complain, deplore, be astonished E3 III.iii.47 [King John to King Edward] *John, the true King of France, / Musing thou shouldst encroach upon his land*
5 grumble, moan MW V.v.231 [Mistress Page to all] *Well, I will muse no further*

muset, musit (n.) [of a hare] hiding place, lair Venus 683 [Venus to Adonis, of the hunted hare] *The many musits through the which he goes / Are like a labyrinth to amaze his foes; TNK III.i.97*

mushrump (*n.*) mushroom **Tem** V.i.39 [Prospero alone] *you whose pastime / Is to make midnight mushrumps*

music (*n.*) **1** musicians, players **MV** V.i.98 [Nerissa to Portia, of hearing music] *It is your music, madam, of the house;* **H8** IV.i.91, ii.94; **MV** V.i.53; **TNK** III.v.31
 2 ☛ ply his music

musit (*n.*) ☛ muset (*n.*)

musk-cat (*n.*) musk-deer [from which musk is obtained]; sweetly scented creature **AW** V.ii.20 [Clown to Lafew, of Parolles] *Here is … not a musk-cat*

muss (*n.*) type of children's game in which players scramble for things thrown on the ground **AC** III.xiii.91 [Antony to all, of how kings would respond to his call] *Like boys unto a muss*

mussel-shell (*n.*) empty-head, gaping idiot [with mouth open like a mussel-shell] **MW** IV.v.25 [Falstaff to Simple, answering his question] *Ay, marry, was it, mussel-shell*

mustachio (*n.*) moustache **LL** V.i.99 [Armado to Holofernes, of the King] *with his royal finger thus dally with my excrement, with my mustachio*

mustachio (*adj.*) moustached, bewhiskered **1H4** II.i.75 [Gadshill to Chamberlain] *I am joined with … none of these mad mustachio purple-hued maltworms*

muster (*n.*) **1** (plural) enlistment of soldiers, mobilizing of troops **KL** IV.ii.16 [Gonerill to Edmund, of Cornwall] *Hasten his musters;* **2H4** I.Induction.12
 2 (plural) groups of soldiers, ranks **AC** I.i.3 [Philo to Demetrius, of Antony] *Those his goodly eyes, / That o'er the files and musters of the war / Have glowed like plated Mars*

muster (*v.*) **1** assemble, gather together [at], rush **MM** II.iv.20 [Angelo alone] *Why does my blood thus muster to my heart;* **2H4** IV.iii.109; **Luc** 442
 2 recruit, enlist, enroll **Cym** IV.iv.10 [Belarius to Guiderius and Arviragus] *we being … not mustered / Among the bands*
 3 display, illustrate, exhibit **AW** II.i.53 [Parolles to Bertram, of the Lords] *they … do muster true gait*

muster-file (*n.*) official list of men **AW** IV.iii.164 [Parolles to First Soldier] *the muster-file … amounts not to fifteen thousand poll*

mutability (*n.*) fickleness, inconstancy, caprice **Cym** II.iv.178 [Posthumus alone] *Nice longing, slanders, mutability*

mutation (*n.*) changeableness, instability, vacillation **Cym** IV.ii.133 [Belarius to Guiderius and Arviragus, of Cloten] *his honour* [or: humour] */ Was nothing but mutation*

mute (*n.*) **1** actor with no words to say, silent spectator **Ham** V.ii.329 [Hamlet to all] *You … / That are but mutes or audience to this act*
 2 dumb servant [as in a Turkish court] **TN** I.ii.63 [Captain to Viola, of Orsino] *Be you his eunuch, and your mute I'll be*

mutine (*n.*) mutineer, rebel **KJ** II.i.378 [Bastard to King John and King Philip] *Do like the mutines of Jerusalem, / Be friends awhile;* **Ham** V.ii.6

mutine (*v.*) rebel, revolt, mutiny **Ham** III.iv.84 [Hamlet to Gertrude, of the sense of shame] *If thou canst mutine in a matron's bones*

mutiny (*n.*) **1** riot, civil disturbance, state of discord **RJ** I.v.80 [Capulet to Tybalt] *You'll make mutiny among my guests!;* **1H6** IV.i.131; **2H6** III.ii.128; **JC** III.ii.123; **LL** I.i.167; **TC** I.iii.96
 2 rebellion, revolt, quarrel **H8** III.ii.120 [King Henry to Norfolk, of Wolsey] *There is a mutiny in's mind;* **3H6** I.iv.77; **Tit** IV.i.84

mutton (*n.*) **1** sheep **MV** I.iii.164 [Shylock to Bassanio] *flesh of muttons, beefs, or goats;* **AY** III.ii.53
 2 prostitute, courtesan **TG** I.i.97 [Speed to Proteus, of Julia] *I, a lost mutton, gave your letter to her, a laced mutton;* **MM** III.ii.171

mutual (*adj.*) **1** common, general, omnipresent **MND** IV.i.116 [Hippolyta to Theseus, of the hounds barking] *every region near / Seemed all one mutual cry;* **MV** V.i.77; **R3** II.ii.113; **Tit** V.iii.133; **Venus** 1018
 2 intimate, private, innermost **2H6** I.i.25 [Queen to King] *The mutual conference that my mind hath had* [with you] *… / Makes me the bolder to salute my king / With ruder terms*
 3 well-matched, complementary **1H4** I.i.14 [King Henry to all] *Those opposed eyes … / Shall now, in mutual well-beseeming ranks, / March all one way;* **AC** I.i.37
 4 with parts united, well-ordered **Tit** V.iii.70 [Marcus to all] *let me teach you how to knit again / This scattered corn into one mutual sheaf*

mutuality (*n.*) intimacy, familiar exchange, intimate dealing **Oth** II.i.253 [Iago to Roderigo] *When these mutualities so marshal the way, hard at hand comes … th'incorporate conclusion* [Q; F *mutabilities*]

mutually (*adv.*) all together, jointly **MW** V.v.99 [Fairies singing, of Falstaff] *Pinch him, fairies, mutually*

mynheer (*n.*) [Dutch] gentleman **MW** II.i.202 [Host to all] *Will you go, mynheers?* [F *An-heires*] ☛ ameer (*n.*)

mystery (*n.*) **1** trade, office, occupation **Tim** IV.iii.455 [First Bandit to others, of Timon] *'Tis in the malice of mankind that he thus advises us, not to have us thrive in our mystery;* **MM** IV.ii.26; **Oth** IV.ii.29; **Tim** IV.i.18
 2 mastery, art, skill **AW** III.vi.59 [Bertram to Parolles] *your mystery in stratagem*
 3 way of behaving **H8** I.iii.2 [Lord Chamberlain to Sands] *Is't possible the spells of France should juggle / Men into such strange mysteries?*
 4 secret matter, inexplicable essence **TC** III.iii.201 [Ulysses to Achilles] *There is a mystery … in the soul of state;* **Ham** III.ii.374

nail *(n.)* **1** [measure of cloth] sixteenth of a yard [c.6 cm] **TS** IV.iii.107 [Petruchio to Tailor] *Thou yard, three-quarters, half-yard, quarter, nail*
2 ☞ blow one's nails

naked *(adj.)* **1** defenceless, undefended, unarmed **H8** III.ii.457 [Wolsey to Cromwell, of God] *He would not in mine age / Have left me naked to mine enemies;* **Cor** I.x.20; **3H6** V.ii.256; **Oth** V.ii.256; **R2** I.ii.31; **Tim** II.i.31
2 stripped of all belongings, without means **Ham** IV.vii.43 [Hamlet to Claudius, by letter] *I am set naked on your kingdom*
3 exposed, unprotected, laid open **2H4** I.iii.61 [Lord Bardolph to Hastings, of someone who stops a building project] *[who] leaves his part-created cost / A naked subject to the weeping clouds*
4 exposed to view **Cor** II.ii.135 [Coriolanus to Menenius, of the people] *I cannot / Put on the gown, stand naked, and entreat them* [or, wearing only an outer garment]
5 bare, austere, unfurnished **LL** V.ii.790 [Princess to King] *go with speed / To some forlorn and naked hermitage*

name *(n.)* **1** reputation, fame, renown **E3** IV.iv.69 [Herald to Prince Edward] *If thou call forth a hundred men of name;* **Ham** V.ii.338; **2H4** II.iv.73; **MA** I.i.7; **Per** IV.vi.178; **TNK** V.iii.27
2 honour, credit, glory **Cor** II.i.130 [Volumnia to Menenius, of Cominius] *he gives my son the whole name of the war*
3 famous name, luminary, celebrity **2H4** IV.i.152 [Westmorland to Mowbray] *Our battle is more full of names than yours;* **Cor** IV.vi.127
4 title of rank, formal appellation **Cor** V.i.12 [Cominius to Menenius, of Coriolanus] *He ... forbade all names*
5 kingly title, dignified rank **1H4** III.ii.65 [King Henry to Prince Hal] *The skipping King ... gave his countenance against his name*
6 rightful claimant, legitimate authority **KJ** III.i.147 [King John to Cardinal Pandulph] *What earthy name to interrogatories / Can task the free breath of a sacred king?*
7 legitimate title **AC** I.ii.37 [Charmian to Soothsayer] *belike my children shall have no names* [i.e. they will be bastards]
8 family, stock, kin **TNK** II.i.230 [Arcite to Palamon, of his love for Emilia] *if the lives of all my name lay on it*
9 signature [representing a pledge] **E3** IV.v.75 [Charles to King John, of Salisbury] *He hath my never broken name to show* [i.e. I have never broken my promise before]

name *(v.)* **1** give particulars of, speak about, describe **KL** I.i.71 [Regan to Lear, of Gonerill] *I find she names my very deed of love;* **E3** IV.iv.52
2 appoint, choose, designate [to an office] **Mac** II.iv.31 [Macduff to Ross, of Macbeth] *He is already named*

nameless *(adj.)* **1** inexpressible, beyond words; or, too small to be worth describing **TG** III.i.309 [Speed reading Launce's paper, of his love's virtues] *She hath many nameless virtues*
2 bearing no legitimate name **Luc** 522 [Tarquin to Lucrece] *Thy issue blurred with nameless bastardy*

nap *(n.)* surface texture of a fabric, pile **2H6** IV.ii.5 [Bevis to Holland] *I tell thee, Jack Cade the clothier means to dress the commonwealth, and turn it, and set a new nap upon it*

napkin *(n.)* **1** handkerchief **Oth** III.iii.284 [Othello to Desdemona] *Your napkin is too little;* **AY** IV.iii.94; **Ham** V.ii.282; **3H6** I.iv.79; **Lover** 15; **Tit** III.i.140
2 square piece of cloth **1H4** IV.ii.41 [Falstaff alone] *the half shirt is two napkins tacked together*

napless *(adj.)* threadbare, worn, frayed **Cor** II.i.226 [Brutus to Sicinius] *The napless vesture of humility* [F *Naples*]

narrow *(adj.)* limited, very small, poor **AC** III.iv.8 [Antony to Octavia, of Caesar paying him terms of honour] *most narrow measure lent me*

narrowly *(adv.)* carefully, with close attention **Per** IV.ii.3 [Pander to Boult] *Search the market narrowly;* **MA** V.iv.114; **TS** III.ii.138

narrow-prying *(adj.)* inquisitive, snooping, meddlesome **TS** III.ii.145 [Tranio to Lucentio] *We'll overreach … / The narrow-prying father Minola*

native *(n.)* origin, source, root **Cor** III.i.129 [Coriolanus to Brutus, of the Citizens] *Th'accusation … could never be the native / Of our so frank donation*

native *(adj.)* **1** natural, habitual, normal **RJ** IV.i.97 [Friar to Juliet, of taking the potion] *no pulse / Shall keep his native progress, but surcease;* **KJ** II.i.337, III.iv.83; **LL** IV.iii.261
2 innate, inborn, instinctive **Oth** I.i.63 [Iago to Roderigo] *when my outward action doth demonstrate / The native act and figure of my heart*
3 by reason of birth **3H6** III.iii.190 [Warwick to Lewis] *Did I put Henry from his native right?*
4 closely related, connected by birth **AW** I.i.219 [Helena alone] *To … kiss like native things*

native *(adv.)* in a natural way **LL** I.ii.101 [Mote to Armado, of a lady] *still her cheeks possess the same / Which native she doth owe*

nativity *(n.)* **1** birth **1H6** V.iv.27 [Shepherd to Pucelle] *cursed be the time / Of thy nativity!*
2 conjunction of stars at birth, horoscope **3H6** IV.vi.33 [George to Warwick] *the heavens in thy nativity / Adjudged an olive branch*
3 country of birth **AY** IV.i.31 [Rosalind as Ganymede to Jaques] *be out of love with your nativity*

natural *(n.)* congenital idiot, half-wit, fool **AY** I.ii.51 [Celia to Rosalind, of Touchstone] *Fortune … hath sent this natural for our whetstone;* **AY** I.ii.47, III.ii.30; **RJ** II.iv.89; **Tem** III.ii.32

natural *(adj.)* **1** feeling proper affection, having normal feelings **Mac** IV.ii.9 [Macduff's wife to Ross, of Macduff] *He wants the natural touch;* **H5** II.Chorus.19; **KL** II.i.83; **MM** I.iv.60
2 personal, formed by nature **Cym** II.ii.28 [Iachimo to himself, of Innogen] *some natural notes about her body;* **Cym** III.v.137
3 legitimate, by birthright, rightful **3H6** I.i.82 [Clifford to Warwick, of Exeter] *Whom should he follow but his natural king?*
4 related by blood **AY** I.i.135 [Oliver to Charles, of Orlando] *me, his natural brother;* **Tim** IV.iii.384
5 inherent, intrinsic **Ham** III.ii.268 [Third Player, as Lucianus, addressing his drug] *Thy natural magic and dire property*
6 lacking artifice, reflecting the reality of the world **Tim** V.i.83 [Timon to Poet] *thou art even natural in thine art* [also: reflecting one's own nature]

natural *(adv.)* like a half-wit, idiotically **TN** I.iii.26 [Maria to Sir Toby, of Sir Andrew's gifts] *He hath indeed all, most natural;* **TN** II.iii.82

natural fool born fool, simpleton by nature **KL** IV.vi.192 [Lear to all] *I am even / The natural fool of fortune*

naturalize *(v.)* familiarize, accustom, enlighten **AW** I.i.205 [Parolles to Helena] *my instruction shall serve to naturalize thee*

nature *(n.)* **1** natural feelings, natural affection **Ham** I.v.81 [Ghost to Hamlet, of his murder] *If thou hast nature in thee, bear it not;* **Ham** III.iii.32; **1H6** III.iii.59; **Tem** V.i.76
2 natural powers, normal state [of mind and body] **Mac** V.i.9 [Doctor to Gentlewoman, of Lady Macbeth's sleepwalking] *A great perturbation in nature;* **Cym** V.v.257; **KL** IV.iv.12; **Mac** II.ii.7; **Tim** IV.iii.177; **TNK** I.iv.43
3 human nature **KL** III.iv.3 [disguised Kent to Lear] *The tyranny of the open night's too rough / For nature to endure;* **AC** I.iii.16; **Ham** III.ii.19; **Mac** IV.iii.67; **Per** III.ii.24; **Tim** V.iv.77
4 mortal life, natural life **AW** IV.iii.238 [Parolles to First Soldier] *I would repent out the remainder of nature;* **Cym** V.v.151; **Ham** I.v.12; **2H4** V.ii.4; **Mac** III.iv.27; **Tim** IV.iii.269
5 personality, innate disposition, character **Mac** III.i.49 [Macbeth alone, of Banquo] *in his royalty of nature / Reigns that which would be feared;* **AW** V.iii.207; **Ham** III.iv.169; **KL** II.i.114; **MM** III.i.166; **Tim** IV.iii.203

6 natural order, ungoverned state, way of the world [often personified] **MM** I.i.36 [Duke to Angelo] *Nature never lends / The smallest scruple of her excellence;* **AW** II.i.118; **Cor** IV.vii.35; **KL** I.ii.11; **MA** III.i.63; **TNK** IV.ii.7
7 function, capacity, role **Tim** IV.iii.45 [Timon alone, of gold] *I will make thee / Do thy right nature;* **AY** III.i.16
8 ☞ days of nature

naught, nought *(n.)* **1** nothing **Tem** I.ii.18 [Prospero to Miranda] *thee … naught knowing / Of whence I am;* **AC** III.v.21; **AY** I.i.33; **1H6** I.ii.135; **2H6** III.i.307; **WT** II.i.177
2 wickedness, immorality, sinfulness **R3** I.i.99 [Richard to Brakenbury, of Mistress Shore] *He that doth naught with her … / Were best he do it secretly;* **MND** IV.ii.14
3 ruin, disaster, catastrophe **AC** III.x.1 [Enobarbus alone] *Naught, naught, all naught!* [or: adjectival use]

naught, nought *(adj.)* **1** worthless, useless, of no value **AC** IV.xv.77 [Cleopatra to all] *All's but naught;* **AY** I.ii.63, III.i.15; **H8** Epilogue.5; **Venus** 993
2 improper, offensive, naughty **KL** II.iv.129 [Lear to Regan, of Gonerill] *Thy sister's naught;* **Ham** III.ii.156
3 bad, wicked, sinful **RJ** III.ii.87 [Nurse to Juliet, of men] *All forsworn, all naught, all dissemblers;* **Cym** V.v.271; **Mac** IV.iii.224
4 lost, ruined, brought to nothing **Cor** III.i.230 [Menenius to Coriolanus] *Be gone, away! / All will be naught else*
5 damaging, harmful, hurtful **E3** I.i.169 [Prince Edward to all] *In great affairs 'tis naught to use delay*

naughtily *(adv.)* wickedly, immorally **TC** IV.ii.37 [Cressida to Troilus, of her last remark] *You smile and mock me, as if I meant naughtily*

naughty *(adj.)* **1** wicked, evil, vile **MV** V.i.91 [Portia to Nerissa, of a candle flame] *So shines a good deed in a naughty world;* **1H4** II.iv.420; **H8** V.i.138; **JC** I.i.15; **MA** V.i.284; **MM** I.i.74
2 bad, nasty, horrible **KL** III.iv.106 [Fool to Lear] *'tis a naughty night to swim in;* **AW** V.iii.253; **TC** II.ii.32

nave *(n.)* **1** [of wheels] hub, pivot **2H4** II.iv.250 [Prince Henry to Poins, of Falstaff] *Would not this nave of a wheel have his ears cut off?* [pun: knave]; **Ham** II.ii.494
2 navel **Mac** I.ii.22 [Captain to King, of Macbeth killing Macdonwald] *he unseamed him from the nave to the chops*

navel *(n.)* very heart, nerve centre **Cor** III.i.123 [Coriolanus to all, of the Citizens] *Even when the navel of the state was touched, / They would not thread the gates*

navigation *(n.)* shipping, vessels **Mac** IV.i.53 [Macbeth to Witches] *though the yesty waves / Confound and swallow navigation up*

nay *(n.)* denial, refusal, rejection **PassP** XVII.8 [Pilgrim, of his love] *Where her faith was firmly fixed in love, / There a nay is placed without remove*

nay *(adv.)* ☞ **DISCOURSE MARKERS**, p.127; **EXCLAMATIONS**, p.158; **RESPONSES**, p.373

nayward *(n.)* contrary, denial, disbelief **WT** II.i.64 [Hermione to Leontes, of Leontes' accusation] *I'll be sworn you would believe my saying, / Howe'er you lean to th'nayward*

nayword, nay-word *(n.)* **1** password, watchword **MW** V.ii.5 [Slender to Page, of Anne] *we have a nay-word how to know one another;* **MW** II.ii.122
2 byword, proverb **TN** II.iii.130 [Maria to Sir Toby, of Malvolio] *If I do not gull him into a nayword* [F an ayword] [i.e. make a catch-phrase of him for stupidity]

ne *(conj.)* [archaism] nor **Per** II.Chorus.36 [Gower alone, of Pericles] *Ne aught escapend but himself* ☞ **ARCHAISMS**, p.22

neaf *(n.)* fist, clenched hand **2H4** II.iv.181 [Pistol to Falstaff] *I kiss thy neaf;* **MND** IV.i.19

Neapolitan bone-ache ☞ bone-ache *(n.)*

near *(adj.)* **1** close to the throne [in order of succession], near relation **Mac** I.iv.37 [King to all] *Sons, kinsmen, thanes, / And you whose places are the nearest;* **2H4** IV.v.212; **2H6** III.i.21; **KJ** II.i.424 [F]; **R3** II.iii.25
2 intimate, familiar **H8** II.ii.133 [Wolsey to Campeius, of Gardiner] *I will have none so near else*
3 personal, private **Tim** III.vi.10 [Lucullus to Lucius, of Timon's invitation] *which many my near occasions did urge me to put off*
4 closely affecting, intimately touching **Mac** III.i.117 [Macbeth to Murderers, of Banquo] *every minute of his being thrusts / Against my near'st of life* [i.e. like a sword entering my vital parts]

near *(adv.)* **1** closely, intimately, seriously **Tim** I.ii.176 [Flavius to Timon] *vouchsafe me a word. It does concern you near;* **1H6** III.i.58; **Oth** II.iii.214; **Per** I.i.94; **R3** IV.iii.49; **TG** III.i.60
2 to the point, to the purpose **Cym** III.v.92 [Cloten to Pisanio] *Come nearer: / No further halting*
3 a short distance away **Tim** II.ii.128 [Flavius to Servants] *Pray you, walk near. I'll speak with you anon*

near *(prep.)* **1** in attendance on **TNK** III.i.18 [Arcite alone, of Emilia] *She … / Hath made me near her*
2 intimate with, closely connected with **2H4** V.i.66 [Falstaff alone] *If I had a suit to Master Shallow, I would humour his men with the imputation of being near their master*

near-legged *(adj.)* knock-kneed **TS** III.ii.55 [Biondello to Tranio as Lucentio, of Petruchio's horse] *near-legged before*

nearly *(adv.)* closely, particularly, especially **Mac** IV.ii.67 [Messenger to Macduff's wife] *I doubt some danger does approach you nearly;* **KL** I.i.284; **MND** I.i.126

nearness *(n.)* intimacy, close relationship **TNK** V.i.10 [Theseus to Palamon and Arcite] *You … come / To blow that nearness out that flames between ye*

neat *(n.)* ox, cow, cattle **WT** I.ii.125 [Leontes to Mamillius] *the steer, the heifer, and the calf / Are all called neat;* **1H4** II.iv.241; **JC** I.i.25; **MV** I.i.112; **Tem** II.ii.69; **TS** IV.iii.17

neat *(adj.)* **1** posh, elegant, trim, refined **TG** I.ii.10 [Lucetta to Julia, of Eglamour] *a knight well-spoken, neat, and fine;* **KL** II.ii.39
2 dainty, elegant, tasty **Cym** IV.ii.49 [Guiderius to Belarius and Arviragus, of disguised Innogen] *But his neat cookery!*
3 clean, spotless, smart **WT** I.ii.123 [Leontes to Mamillius] *We must be neat* [pun: 125 with noun sense]

neat-herd *(n.)* cowherd, cattleman **Cym** I.ii.80 [Innogen to Cymbeline] *Would I were / A neat-herd's daughter;* **WT** IV.iv.323

neb *(n.)* mouth, beak **WT** I.ii.183 [Leontes to himself, of Hermione and Polixenes] *How she holds up the neb, the bill to him!*

necessaries *(n.)* travelling necessities, personal luggage **Ham** I.iii.1 [Laertes to Ophelia] *My necessaries are embarked*

necessary *(adj.)* **1** inevitable, unavoidable, certain **AY** III.iii.47 [Touchstone to Audrey] *As horns are odious, they are necessary;* **Ham** III.ii.202; **2H4** III.i.83
2 providing a useful service, indispensable **Cor** II.i.77 [Brutus to Menenius] *you are … a perfecter giber for the table than a necessary bencher in the Capitol*

necessitied *(adj.)* in dire need [of], brought into necessity **AW** V.iii.85 [King to Bertram, of Helena] *if her fortunes ever stood / Necessitied to help*

necessity *(n.)* **1** inevitability, constrained outcome **2H4** IV.i.102 [Westmorland to Mowbray] *Construe the times to their necessities*
2 unavoidable event **2H4** III.i.88 [King Henry IV to Warwick, of historical events] *Are these things then necessities?;* **WT** IV.iv.38

neck *(n.)* throat **AC** III.xiii.161 [Cleopatra to Antony, of hail] *the first stone / Drop in my neck*

neck of, in the *(prep.)* immediately afterwards **1H4** IV.iii.92 [Hotspur to Blunt, of King Henry] *he deposed the King, / Soon after that deprived him of his life, / And in the neck of that tasked the whole state*

need *(n.)* time of necessity, needy situation, emergency **RJ** V.i.53 [Romeo alone, of earlier thinking about poison] *this same thought did but forerun my need;* **AW** II.iv.49; **Cym** V.iii.45

need, for a if necessary, if need be, at a pinch **Ham** II.ii.538 [Hamlet to First Player] *You could for a need study a speech;* **3H6** I.iii.67; **R3** III.v.84

need *(v.)* be necessary, be needful **3H6** I.iv.125 [York to Queen, of insulting him] *It needs not, … proud Queen;* **TC** V.i.12

need *(adv.)* ☞ **needs** *(adv.)*

needful *(adj.)* **1** necessary, needed, indispensable **TC** IV.iv.138 [Troilus to Cressida] *To our own selves bend we our needful talk;* **Cym** IV.iii.8; **1H6** IV.iii.18; **H8** II.iv.231
2 full of need, needing reinforcements **3H6** II.i.146 [Warwick to Edward, of George] *he was lately sent … / With aid of soldiers to this needful war*

needless *(adj.)* **1** unnecessary, pointless, superfluous **Cor** II.iii.116 [Coriolanus alone] *To beg of Hob and Dick that does appear / Their needless vouches?*
2 not needed, unused, superfluous **KJ** V.v.5 [Lewis the Dauphin to all, of saying good night to the retreating English] *with a volley of our needless shot*
3 not lacking, having no need **AY** II.i.46 [First Lord to Duke Senior, of the deer] *weeping into the needless stream* [i.e. not needing any more water]

needly *(adv.)* of necessity, unavoidably **RJ** III.ii.117 [Juliet to herself] *sour woe delights in fellowship / And needly will be ranked with other griefs*

needs *(adv.)* of necessity, necessarily **MV** III.iv.14 [Portia to Lorenzo, of good friends] *There must be needs a like proportion / Of lineaments, of manners, and of spirit*

needy *(adj.)* **1** unworthy, deficient, inadequate **E3** III.iii.53 [King John to King Edward] *I condemn thee for … a needy mate*
2 needed, necessary **Per** I.iv.95 [Pericles to all] *our ships … / Are stored with corn to make your needy bread*

neele *(n.)* needle **Per** V.Chorus.5 [Gower alone, of Marina] *with her neele [she] composes / Nature's own shape;* **Per** IV.Chorus.23

ne'er-offence *(n.)* [unclear meaning] non-offence **Cym** V.v.335 [Belarius to Cymbeline] *Your pleasure was my ne'er-offence* [F *neere offence*]

neeze *(v.)* sneeze **MND** II.i.56 [Puck to Fairy, of the reaction to his antics] *the whole choir hold their hips and laugh … and neeze*

negation *(n.)* denial, dissent, contradiction **TC** V.ii.130 [Troilus to Ulysses] *my negation hath no taste of madness*

negative *(adj.)* denying, refusing to believe **WT** I.ii.274 [Leontes to Camillo] *If thou wilt confess - / Or else impudently negative / To have nor eyes, nor ears, nor thought*

neglect *(n.)* disregard, inattention **AY** V.iv.179 [Jaques to Jaques de Boys] *The Duke hath … thrown into neglect the pompous court?* [i.e. rejected]

neglect *(v.)* **1** cause to be neglected **R3** III.iv.24 [Richard to all] *I trust / My absence doth neglect no great design;* **LL** V.ii.750
2 disregard, slight, give little respect [to] **H8** III.ii.11 [Suffolk to all, of Wolsey] *Which of the peers / Have uncontemned gone by him, or at least / Strangely neglected?*

neglected *(adj.)* underrated, underestimated, undervalued **H5** II.iv.13 [French King to all] *examples / Left by the fatal and neglected English / Upon our fields*

neglectingly *(adv.)* neglectfully, negligently, carelessly **1H4** I.iii.51 [Hotspur to King Henry] *I … / Out of my grief and my impatience / Answered neglectingly*

neglection *(n.)* negligence, neglect, disregard **Per** III.iii.20 [Cleon to Pericles, of Marina] *If neglection / Should therein make me vile;* **1H6** IV.iii.49; **TC** I.iii.127

negligence *(n.)* disregard, neglect, indifference Ham IV.v.136 [Laertes to Claudius] *both the worlds I give to negligence* [i.e. I care nothing about this world or the next]

negligent *(adj.)* through neglecting to act, due to negligence AC III.vi.81 [Caesar to Octavia] *we in negligent danger* ☛ wilful-negligent *(adj.)*

neighbour *(adj.)* **1** neighbouring, nearby, adjacent LL V.ii.94 [Boyet to Princess] *I stole into a neighbour thicket by;* AY IV.iii.79
2 nearby, not far away, accessible E3 I.ii.24 [King David to Lorraine, of the English] *[we will] burn their neighbour towns*

neighbour *(v.)* be close, be well acquainted [with] KL I.i.119 [Lear to Cordelia, of savages] *shall to my bosom / Be as well neighboured;* Ham II.ii.12

neighbourhood *(n.)* **1** neighbourly conduct, neighbourliness Tim IV.i.17 [Timon alone] *Domestic awe, night-rest, and neighbourhood ... / Decline to your confounding contraries;* H5 I.ii.154, V.ii.345
2 friendly relations, close alliance E3 III.i.40 [Bohemia to King John] *as league and neighbourhood / Requires*

neither *(adv.)* for all that, nevertheless Ham V.ii.114 [Hamlet to Osrick, of Laertes] *to divide him inventorially would dizzy th'arithmetic of memory, and yet but yaw neither*

nephew *(n.)* **1** cousin 1H6 II.v.64 [Mortimer to Richard] *Henry the Fourth ... / Deposed his nephew Richard*
2 grandson Oth I.i.113 [Iago to Brabantio] *you'll have your nephews neigh to you* ☛ FAMILY, p.168

nerve *(n.)* **1** sinew, ligament, muscle Mac III.iv.101 [Macbeth to Banquo's ghost] *my firm nerves / Shall never tremble;* AC IV.viii.21; Cym III.iii.94; Ham I.iv.83; Sonn 120.4; Tem I.ii.485
2 strength, vigour, forcefulness TNK I.ii.69 [Palamon to Arcite, of Creon] *who only attributes / The faculties of other instruments / To his own nerves and act*

nervy *(adj.)* muscular, sinewy, vigorous Cor II.i.153 [Volumnia to Menenius, of Coriolanus] *Death ... in's nervy arm doth lie*

nether *(adj.)* **1** lower, bottom Oth V.ii.43 [Desdemona to Othello] *why gnaw you so your nether lip?;* 1H4 II.iv.398; Oth V.iii.37
2 belonging to the earth, earthly, worldly KL IV.ii.79 [Albany to all, of the gods] *that these our nether crimes / So speedily can venge*

nether-stock *(n.)* stocking for the lower leg 1H4 II.iv.113 [Falstaff to all] *I'll sew nether-stocks, and mend them and foot them too;* KL II.iv.10 ☛ stock *(n.)* 3

neuter *(adj.)* neutral, taking neither side R2 II.iii.158 [York to all] *I do remain as neuter*

never-daunted *(adj.)* never dispirited, never overcome with fear 2H4 I.i.110 [Morton to Northumberland, of Monmouth] *whose swift wrath beat down / The never-daunted Percy to the earth*

never-surfeited *(adj.)* never filled to excess Tem III.iii.56 [Ariel to Alonso, Sebastian, and Antonio] *You are three men of sin, whom destiny ... the never-surfeited sea / Hath caused to belch up you* ☛ surfeited *(adj.)*

NEGATIVES

Feste, attempting to impress Orsino with some complex word-play, observes 'if your four negatives make your two affirmatives ...' (TN V.i.20). This supposed rule endeared itself greatly to prescriptive grammarians in later centuries, who tried to impose it on the whole of English, despite the fact that the strict mathematical logic was used only in a few formal styles of expression. They were largely successful. It is now said to be 'bad grammar' to use a double negative within a single clause in standard English unless one is being logically precise.

In Shakespearian English we often find sequences of negative words whose sole function is to intensify the negative meaning of an utterance. (This is how the rule continues to operate in regional dialects today where, for example, *I've **not** got any money* is strengthened by *I've **not** got **no** money*, and further strengthened by *I've **not** got **no** money **neither**.*) A range of negative forms is involved, such as *no, not, none, neither, never, nowhere,* and *nothing,* as well as words with negative implication, such as *deny.* When Richard accuses Queen Elizabeth of Hastings' imprisonment, he uses two negatives to make his point, 'You may deny that you were not the mean / Of my Lord Hastings' late imprisonment' (R3 I.iii.89). There is no 'cancelling out' of meanings here, nor in any of the examples below.

Double

AY I.ii.16	*You know my father hath no child but I, **nor none** is like to have*
CE IV.ii.17	*I **cannot nor** I will not hold me still*
Ham V.i.131	[Hamlet] *What man dost thou dig it for?* [First Clown] *For no man, sir.* [Hamlet] *What woman then?* [First Clown] *For **none neither**.*
Ham III.i.164	***Nor** what he spake ... / Was **not** like madness*
MW IV.ii.149	[Ford] *he's not here I seek for.* [Page] *No, **nor nowhere** else but in your brain*
Tem III.ii.18	[Stephano] *We'll not run ...* [Trinculo] ***Nor** go **neither**; but you'll lie like dogs, and yet say **nothing neither***

Triple

AY I.ii.26	*love no man in good earnest, **nor no** further in sport **neither***
LL V.i.144	[Holofernes] *Thou hast spoken no word all this while.* [Dull] ***Nor** understood **none neither**, sir*
TN III.i.156	[Viola, of her heart] *And that no woman has, **nor never none** / Shall mistress be of it, save I alone*

☛ RESPONSES, p.373

new *(adv.)* **1** newly, freshly, recently, just **RJ** I.i.161 [Benvolio to Romeo, of the time of day] *But new struck nine;* **Ham** III.iv.60; **1H4** I.iii.33; **Tim** I.ii.76

2 immediately, just **KJ** III.i.233 [King Philip to Cardinal Pandulph, of the treaty] *even before this truce, but new before*

new-added *(adj.)* reinforced, supplemented, augmented **JC** IV.iii.207 [Brutus to Cassius, of the local people] *The enemy ... / By them shall make a fuller number up, / Come on refreshed, new-added*

new-apparelled *(adj.)* in a change of clothing **CE** IV.iii.14 [Dromio of Syracuse to Antipholus of Syracuse] *have you got the picture of old Adam new-apparelled?* [possibly: got the officer out of uniform, and thus got rid of him]

new-begot *(adj.)* newly acquired, freshly obtained **1H6** I.i.79 [Messenger to nobles] *Let not sloth dim your honours new-begot*

new-conceived *(adj.)* in early pregnancy **TNK** IV.ii.128 [Messenger to Theseus, of a knight's arms] *Gently they swell, like women new-conceived*

new-dated *(adj.)* of recent date **2H4** IV.i.8 [Archbishop to Hastings and Mowbray] *I have received / New-dated letters from Northumberland*

new-delivered *(adj.)* lately freed, freshly released **R3** I.i.121 [Richard to himself] *who comes here? The new-delivered Hastings?*

new-devised *(adj.)* newfangled, freshly invented **LL** I.ii.61 [Armado to Mote, of ransoming desire] *to any French courtier for a new-devised curtsy*

new-enkindled *(adj.)* freshly lit **KJ** IV.iii.163 [Bastard to King John, of Bigot and Salisbury] *With eyes as red as new-enkindled fire*

new-fallen *(adj.)* newly become due, recently acquired **1H4** V.i.44 [Worcester to King Henry] *You swore to us ... / That you did ... claim no further than your new-fallen right*

new-fangled *(adj.)* fond of novelty, distracted by new things **AY** IV.i.140 [Rosalind as Ganymede to Orlando] *more new-fangled than an ape*

new-fire *(v.)* rekindle, ignite again **Sonn** 153.9 *at my mistress' eye Love's brand new-fired*

new-fired *(adj.)* rekindled, inflamed anew **JC** II.i.332 [Ligarius to Brutus] *with a heart new-fired I follow you*

new-found *(adj.)* recently invented, freshly created **TG** IV.iv.127 [Silvia to disguised Julia, of Proteus' lines] *they are ... full of new-found oaths*

new-replenished *(adj.)* repeatedly blown out by the wind to their full length **E3** IV.iv.20 [Audley to Prince Edward, of the French army] *the banners, bannerets, / And new-replenished pendants cuff the air*

new-store *(v.)* freshly populate, supply with new children **H5** III.v.31 [Dauphin to all, of the French women] *they will give / Their bodies to the lust of English youth, / To new-store France with bastard warriors* ➤ **store** *(v.)*

new-ta'en *(adj.)* [new-taken] freshly caught, just captured **TC** III.ii.32 [Pandarus to Troilus, of Cressida] *she fetches her breath as short as a new-ta'en sparrow*

new-trimmed *(adj.)* newly fitted out **H8** I.ii.80 [Wolsey to King Henry, of ravenous fishes] *do a vessel follow / That is new-trimmed*

new-trothed *(adj.)* recently engaged **MA** III.i.38 [Hero to Ursula, of Beatrice being in love] *So says the Prince and my new-trothed lord*

new-tuned *(adj.)* freshly coined, fashionable **H5** III.vi.75 [Gower to Fluellen, of men like Pistol's boasts about the wars] *which they trick up with new-tuned oaths*

next *(adj.)* nearest, shortest, most direct **WT** III.iii.120 [Shepherd to Clown] *Home, home, the next way;* **AW** I.iii.58; **1H4** II.i.9; **TNK** III.ii.33

next morning tomorrow morning **Tim** II.ii.28 [Timon to Caphis] *I prithee but repair to me next morning*

nice *(adj.)* **1** fastidious, particular, fussy, overscrupulous **H5** V.ii.270 [King Henry to Katherine] *the nice fashion of your country in denying me a kiss;* **AW** V.i.15; **2H4** II.iii.40; **LL** V.ii.219; **TG** III.i.82; **TNK** V.ii.77

2 fine, precise, particular, subtle **3H6** IV.vii.58 [Richard to Edward] *wherefore stand you on nice points?;* **1H6** II.iv.17; **LL** V.ii.232; **Lover** 97; **MV** II.i.14; **TC** IV.v.250

3 critical, delicate, uncertain **1H4** IV.i.48 [Hotspur to all] *Were it good ... To set so rich a main / On the nice hazard of one doubtful hour?*

4 minutely detailed, carefully accurate **Luc** 1412 [of people in a painting of Troy] *Some high, some low, the painter was so nice;* **Mac** IV.iii.174

5 trivial, unimportant, slight **RJ** III.i.154 [Benvolio to Prince, of Tybalt] *Romeo ... bid him bethink / How nice the quarrel was;* **AW** IV.iii.89; **2H4** IV.i.189; **JC** IV.iii.8; **Oth** III.iii.15; **R3** III.vii.174

6 foolish, stupid **2H4** I.i.145 [Northumberland to the crutch he uses] *Hence, therefore, thou nice crutch!* [or: unmanly]

7 whimsical, capricious, temperamental **TS** III.i.78 [Bianca to Hortensio as Licio, of his idiosyncratic musical scale] *I am not so nice / To change true rules for odd inventions*

8 adept, skilful, dexterous **MA** V.i.75 [Leonato to Don Pedro, of fighting Claudio] *Despite his nice fence and his active practice*

9 lustful, lecherous, lascivious, wanton **LL** III.i.21 [Mote to Armado, of his examples] *these betray nice wenches;* **Cym** II.iv.178

nicely *(adv.)* **1** scrupulously, punctiliously, meticulously, fastidiously **H5** V.ii.94 [Queen Isabel to King Henry] *Haply a woman's voice may do some good, / When articles too nicely urged be stood on;* **KL** II.ii.102, V.iii.142; **Per** IV.vi

2 subtly, triflingly, fancifully **TN** III.i.14 [Viola as Cesario to Feste] *They that dally nicely with words may quickly make them wanton;* **H5** I.ii.15; **R2** II.i.84

3 carefully, skilfully, ingeniously **Cor** II.i.209 [Brutus to Sicinius, of Roman women] *the war of white and damask in / Their nicely gawded cheeks;* **Cym** II.iv.90

niceness *(n.)* coyness, fastidiousness, excessive scruple **Cym** III.iv.157 [Pisanio to Innogen] *change ... fear, and niceness ... into a waggish courage;* **TNK** V.ii.19

nicety *(n.)* coyness, shyness, reserve **MM** II.iv.162 [Angelo to Isabella] *Lay by all nicety and prolixious blushes*

nick *(n.)* **1** nick of time, critical moment **TNK** III.v.74 [Third Countryman to all, of the Gaoler's Daughter] *Comes i'th' nick;* **Oth** V.ii.313

2 reckoning, count, estimation **TG** IV.ii.73 [Host to disguised Julia, of Proteus and Silvia] *he loved her out of all nick*

nick *(v.)* [unclear meaning] cut through, maim; do out of, cheat of; mark with foolishness **AC** III.xiii.8 [Enobarbus to Cleopatra, of Antony] *The itch of his affection should not then / Have nicked his captainship*

nickname *(v.)* invent names for, misname **LL** V.ii.349 [Princess to King] *You nickname virtue – 'vice' you should have spoke;* **Ham** III.i.145

niece *(n.)* ➤ **FAMILY**, p.168

niggard *(n.)* miser, mean person, skinflint **Mac** IV.iii.180 [Macduff to Ross] *Be not a niggard of your speech;* **CE** II.i.84; **H8** I.i.70; **Sonn** 4.5

niggard *(adj.)* **1** miserly, parsimonious, sparing **Luc** 79 [of Collatine and Lucrece] *The niggard prodigal that praised her so;* **Sonn** 72.8; **Tim** V.iv.77

2 grudging, reluctant, unwilling **Ham** III.i.13 [Rosencrantz to Gertrude, of Hamlet] *Niggard of question* [i.e. unwilling to start a conversation]

niggard *(v.)* **1** begrudge, hoard, use sparingly **E3** I.ii.123 [Countess to King Edward] *now niggard not thy state;* **TNK** I.iv.32

2 put off, fob off, stint **JC** IV.iii.226 [Brutus to Cassius] *nature must obey necessity, / Which we will niggard with a little rest*

niggarding (*n.*) hoarding, begrudging, acting in a mean manner **Sonn** 1.12 *Within thine own bud buriest thy content, / And tender churl mak'st waste in niggarding*

niggardly (*adj.*) mean-minded, tight-fisted, miserly **TN** II.v.4 [Sir Toby to Fabian, of Malvolio] *Wouldst thou not be glad to have the niggardly, rascally sheep-biter come by some notable shame?;* **H5** II.iv.46

niggardly (*adv.*) sparingly, grudgingly, slightly **MW** II.ii.191 [Ford as Brook to Falstaff, of Mistress Ford] *I have … fee'd every slight occasion that could but niggardly give me sight of her*

nigh (*adj.*) near, close **3H6** V.i.8 [Warwick to Somerville] *how nigh is Clarence now?;* **Cym** III.iv.150; **3H6** V.ii.5; **Mac** IV.ii.72

nigh (*adv.*) nearly, almost **2H6** III.ii.82 [Queen to King, of his sorrow for Gloucester] *Was I for this nigh wrecked upon the sea*

nigh (*prep.*) near **Tem** I.ii.216 [Prospero to Ariel] *was not this nigh shore?*

night (*n.*) **1** evening **1H4** III.i.78 [Mortimer to all, of the sealing of their agreement] *A business that this night may execute*
   2 darkness, blackness **KJ** V.vi.12 [Hubert as if to his memory, of not recognizing Bastard] *Thou and endless night / Have done me shame*

night, at at nightfall, this evening **2H4** V.v.93 [Falstaff to all] *I shall be sent for soon at night;* **MW** II.ii.270

night-bird (*n.*) nightingale, bird that sings at night **Per** IV.Chorus.26 [Gower alone, of Marina] *She sung, and made the night-bird mute* [Q *night bed*]

nighted (*adj.*) **1** dark, black as night **Ham** I.ii.68 [Gertrude to Hamlet] *cast thy nighted colour off* [Q2; F *nightly*]
   2 blacked-out, overtaken by night **KL** IV.v.13 [Regan to Oswald, of Gloucester] *Edmund, I think, is gone … to dispatch / His nighted life*

nightgown, night-gown (*n.*) dressing-gown **Oth** I.i.161 [stage direction] *Enter Brabantio in his night-gown;* **2H4** III.i.1; **JC** II.ii.1; **MA** III.iv.17; **Mac** V.i.5; **Oth** IV.iii.33

nightly (*adj.*) **1** of the night, active at night **MND** V.i.360 [Theseus to all] *A fortnight hold we this solemnity / In nightly revels and new jollity;* **TG** II.iv.130; **Tit** II.iii.97
   2 ☞ **nighted** (*adj.*)

nightly (*adv.*) at night, during the night **MW** V.v.65 [Mistress Quickly as Queen of Fairies to all] *nightly, meadow-fairies, look you sing*

night-oblations (*n.*) evening devotions **Per** V.iii.70 [Pericles to Diana] *I … / Will offer night-oblations to thee*

night-rule (*n.*) night-time activity, nocturnal diversion **MND** III.ii.5 [Oberon to Puck] *What night-rule now about this haunted grove?*

night-walking (*adj.*) secret, going about by night **R3** I.i.72 [Clarence to Richard] *there is no man secure / But … night-walking heralds*

nill (*v.*) will not **TS** II.i.264 [Petruchio to Katherina] *will you, nill you, I will marry you;* **Ham** V.i.17; **PassP** XIV.8; **Per** III.Chorus.55

nimble (*adj.*) sudden, swift, rapid **KL** IV.vii.34 [Cordelia to Lear, of Lear on the heath] *In the most terrible and nimble stroke / Of quick cross lightning*

nimble-pinioned (*adj.*) swift-winged **RJ** II.v.7 [Juliet alone] *Therefore do nimble-pinioned doves draw love*

nimble-set (*adj.*) agile, athletic **TNK** IV.ii.125 [Messenger to Theseus, of one of the knights] *tough and nimble-set, / Which shows an active soul*

nimbly (*adj.*) bracingly, in an invigorating way **Mac** I.vi.2 [King to all] *the air / Nimbly and sweetly recommends itself / Unto our gentle senses*

nine-fold (*n.*) set of nine attendants **KL** III.iv.116 [Edgar as Poor Tom to all, of St Withold] *He met the nightmare and her nine-fold*

ninny (*n.*) simpleton, fool **Tem** III.ii.63 [Caliban to Trinculo] *What a pied ninny's this!*

nip (*v.*) **1** press, enforce, compel **Per** V.i.233 [Pericles to all, of the music] *It nips me into listening*
   2 [as of pinching off the buds on a plant] cut short one's growth, check one's development **Tit** IV.iv.70 [Saturninus to all, of the news of Lucius' attack] *These tidings nip me*

nit (*n.*) little fellow; shrimp, gnat **TS** IV.iii.108 [Petruchio to Tailor] *Thou flea, thou nit, thou winter-cricket;* **LL** V.i.149

Nob (*n.*) familiar form of Robert **KJ** I.i.147 [Bastard to Queen Eleanor] *I would not be Sir Nob in any case!* [also: knob]

noble (*n.*) **1** nobility **Cor** III.i.29 [Cominius to Brutus, of Coriolanus] *Hath he not passed the noble and the common?*
   2 English gold coin, worth 6s. 8d [= c.£0.33] **R2** I.i.88 [Bolingbroke to King Richard] *Mowbray hath received eight thousand nobles* ☞ **MONEY**, p.286

noble (*adj.*) **1** of good breeding, high-born **KL** V.iii.163 [Edmund to Edgar] *If thou'rt noble, / I do forgive thee*
   2 valuable, precious, notable **AC** V.ii.168 [Cleopatra to Caesar] *say / Some nobler token I have kept apart*

nobleness (*n.*) nobility, aristocratic rank **Per** III.ii.27 [Cerimon to First Gentleman] *Virtue and cunning were endowments greater / Than nobleness and riches*

noblesse (*n.*) nobility, nobleness **R2** IV.i.119 [Bishop of Carlisle to and of all] *true noblesse would / Learn him forbearance from so foul a wrong* [Q1; F *noblenesse*]

nod (*n.*) fool, simpleton, idiot **TC** I.ii.196 [Cressida to Pandarus, of Troilus] *Will he give you the nod?* [also: head movement of recognition]

nod (*v.*) call with a nod, beckon **AC** III.vi.66 [Caesar to Octavia, of Antony] *Cleopatra / Hath nodded him to her*

noddy (*n.*) fool, simpleton, buffoon **TG** I.i.113 [Proteus to Speed, of what has just been said] *that's noddy*

noise (*n.*) **1** report, rumour, news **KL** III.vi.109 [Edgar alone] *Mark the high noises;* **TC** I.ii.12
   2 band, company of musicians **2H4** II.iv.11 [Francis to Drawer] *see if thou canst find out Sneak's noise*
   3 musical sounds, melodious noises **Tem** III.ii.136 [Caliban to Stephano and Trinculo] *the isle is full of noises, / Sounds, and sweet airs;* **AC** IV.iii.13; **Mac** IV.i.105

noise (*v.*) rumour, spread about, noise abroad **Tim** IV.iii.404 [Second Bandit to others, of Timon] *It is noised he hath a mass of treasure;* **H8** I.ii.105

noise it clamour, cry out, make a loud noise **AC** III.vi.96 [Maecenas to Octavia] *Antony … gives his potent regiment to a trull / That noises it against us*

noiseless (*adj.*) peaceful, tranquil, quiet **KL** IV.ii.56 [Gonerill to Albany] *France spreads his banners in our noiseless land*

noisome (*adj.*) noxious, harmful, evil **MA** V.ii.49 [Beatrice to Benedick] *foul breath is noisome;* **Cym** I.vi.26; **1H6** I.v.23; **R2** III.iv.38

nole (*n.*) noddle, head **MND** III.ii.17 [Puck to Oberon, of Bottom] *An ass's nole I fixed on his head*

nominate (*v.*) **1** name, specify, designate [as] **MV** I.iii.146 [Shylock to Antonio, of his bond] *let the forfeit / Be nominated for an equal pound / Of your fair flesh;* **LL** I.i.15, V.i.8
   2 give names to, mention by name **2H6** II.i.128 [Gloucester to all, of 'blind' Simpcox's ability to name colours] *suddenly to nominate them all, it is impossible;* **AY** V.iv.85

nomination (*n.*) **1** naming, mention, reference **LL** IV.ii.133 [Holofernes to Jaquenetta, of re-reading the letter] *for the nomination of the party writing to the person written unto;* **Ham** V.ii.126
   2 appointing, specifying, designation **R3** III.iv.5 [Derby to all, of the coronation date] *It … wants but nomination*

nonage (*n.*) minority, period of legal infancy R3 II.iii.13 [Second Citizen to other Citizens, of Prince Edward as a ruler] *in his nonage ... / No doubt shall ... govern well*

nonce, for the for that purpose, for the occasion 1H4 I.ii.177 [Poins to Prince Hal] *I have cases of buckram for the nonce;* Ham IV.vii.159; 1H6 II.iii.56

non-come (*n.*) malapropism for 'nonplus' [= state of perplexity] MA III.v.57 [Dogberry to Verges] *Here's that shall drive some of them to a non-come*

none (*adj.*) no H8 IV.i.33 [First Gentleman to Second Gentleman, of Katherine] *the late marriage made of none effect* [i.e. null and void]

none of you, will have nothing to do with WT II.i.3 [Mamillius to First Lady] *I'll none of you*

nonny, non, nony (*int.*) ☛ SINGING, p.402

nonpareil (*n.*) person without equal, unique one, paragon Tem III.ii.101 [Caliban to Stephano, of Prospero and Miranda] *He himself / Calls her a nonpareil;* AC III.ii.11; Cym II.iv.160; Mac III.iv.18; TN I.v.243

non-regardance (*n.*) failure to respect, contempt, disdain TN V.i.119 [Orsino to Olivia] *Since you to non-regardance cast my faith*

non-suit (*v.*) reject the suit of, refuse Oth I.i.16 [Iago to Roderigo, of Othello] *he ... / Non-suits my mediators*

nook-shotten (*adj.*) crookedly shaped, corner-ridden H5 III.v.14 [Britaine to all] *To buy a slobbery and a dirty farm / In that nook-shotten isle of Albion*

nor ... nor (*prep.*) neither...nor RJ III.i.193 [Prince to Montague] *Nor tears nor prayers shall purchase out abuses*

north (*n.*) north wind KJ V.vii.39 [King John to all] *entreat the north / To make his bleak winds kiss my parched lips;* Cym I.iv.36; Oth V.ii.218 [F]

northern star (*n.*) pole-star JC III.i.60 [Caesar to all] *I am constant as the northern star*

Norweyan (*adj.*) Norwegian Mac I.ii.51 [Ross to King, of Fife] *Where the Norweyan banners flout the sky;* Mac I.ii.31, iii.94

nose (*v.*) smell Ham IV.iii.35 [Hamlet to Claudius, of Polonius' body] *you shall nose him as you go up the stairs;* Cor V.i.28

nose-herb (*n.*) scented plant, herb for smelling [as opposed to eating] AW IV.v.16 [Lafew to Clown] *They are not herbs ... they are nose-herbs* ☛ PLANTS, p.330

notable (*adj.*) 1 noted, notorious, conspicuous, infamous MM V.i.266 [Escalus to Lucio, of Friar Lodowick] *We shall find this friar a notable fellow;* TN II.v.196
2 observable, noticeable, perceptible Oth IV.i.82 [Iago to Othello, of Cassio] *mark the fleers, the gibes, and notable scorns / That dwell in every region of his face*

notary (*n.*) 1 noter, observer, witness Luc 765 [Lucrece as if to night] *Dim register and notary of shame*
2 clerk authorized to draw up contracts MV I.iii.141 [Shylock to Antonio] *Go with me to a notary*

note (*n.*) 1 attention, notice, regard TNK I.iv.19 [Theseus to all, of Palamon and Arcite] *I fixed my note / Constantly on them;* Cor I.ix.48; Cym IV.iv.20; JC I.ii.180; Mac III.ii.44; WT V.ii.42
2 knowledge, information, intimation TC IV.i.44 [Paris to Aeneas, of Troilus] *give our friend of him note of our approach;* H8 I.ii.48; Tem II.i.252
3 characteristic, trait, distinctive feature Cym II.ii.28 [Iachimo to himself, of Innogen] *some natural notes about her body;* MW I.i.156; TNK V.iv.53
4 sign, mark, token TC II.iii.124 [Agamemnon to Patroclus, of Achilles] *we think him ... in self-assumption greater / Than in the note of judgement;* H5 IV.Chorus.14; H8 I.i.63; WT V.ii.11
5 observation, record, description AC III.iii.23 [Charmian to Cleopatra, of the Messenger] *Three in Egypt / Cannot make better note;* Cym V.v.203

6 instruction, indication, direction Cym I.ii.102 [Pisanio to Innogen, of Posthumus] *left these notes / Of what commands I should be subject to;* AW I.iii.221
7 reputation, distinction, standing Cym I.vii.22 [Innogen reading a letter, of Iachimo] *He is one of the noblest note;* AW I.iii.152, 222; Cym III.iii.58; LL III.i.22; Lover 233
8 list, record, roll WT IV.iii.45 [Clown to himself] *I must have ... mace; dates - none, that's out of my note;* Mac III.iii.10; TS I.ii.142
9 memorandum TS IV.iii.127 [Tailor to Grumio] *here is the note of the fashion to testify;* AW IV.iii.126
10 bill, invoice, account 2H4 V.i.15 [Davy to Shallow] *Here is now the smith's note for shoeing and plough-irons;* MV III.ii.140; Tim II.ii.19
11 melody, tune, music, song AY II.v.43 [Jaques to all] *I'll give you a verse to this note;* CE III.ii.45; Cym IV.ii.241; E3 II.i.34; H8 IV.ii.78; TG I.ii.81
12 reproach, stigma, mark of disgrace R2 I.i.43 [Bolingbroke to Mowbray] *the more to aggravate the note, / With a foul traitor's name stuff I thy throat;* LL V.ii.75; Luc 208

note (*v.*) 1 observe, pay attention [to], take special note [of] MA I.i.154 [Benedick to Claudio, of Hero] *I noted her not;* AY III.ii.245; JC V.iii.22; Mac III.iv.55; Sonn 99.13; TN IV.iii.35
2 notice, perceive, observe Tim III.i.31 [Lucullus to Flaminius] *I have noted thee always wise;* Luc 414
3 show, indicate, intimate Ham I.v.178 [Hamlet to Horatio and Marcellus] *to note / That you know aught of me*
4 brand with disgrace, stigmatize, publicly discredit JC IV.iii.2 [Cassius to Brutus] *You have condemned and noted Lucius Pella / For taking bribes here of the Sardians*

noted (*adj.*) 1 recognizable, well-known, familiar KJ IV.ii.21 [Salisbury to King John] *the antique and well noted face / Of plain old form is much disfigured;* 1H4 I.ii.178; Sonn 76.6; WT V.iii.145
2 closely observed, taken note of TC V.ii.12 [Thersites to himself, of Cressida] *any man may sing her, if he can take her clef: she's noted* [also: well-known; notorious]
3 stigmatized, disgraced, discredited Tit II.iii.86 [Lavinia to Bassianus, of Saturninus] *these slips have made him noted long*

notedly (*adv.*) particularly, especially, definitely MM V.i.330 [disguised Duke to Lucio, responding to 'do you remember what you said of the Duke?'] *Most notedly*

not-fearing (*adj.*) fearless, unafraid, courageous Cym II.iv.19 [Posthumus to Philario, of the Romans] *landed / In our not-fearing Britain*

nothing (*n.*) 1 [state of] nothingness, oblivion, extinction Tim V.i.186 [Timon to Senators] *nothing brings me all things;* H8 III.ii.208; MND V.i.301
2 nonsense, emptiness, rubbish Tem II.i.175 [Alonso to Gonzalo] *Thou dost talk nothing to me;* Ham IV.v.7; KL I.iv.127
3 insignificance, unimportance, triviality TNK V.ii.30 [Doctor to Wooer] *that's all one, 'tis nothing to our purpose* [i.e. that's irrelevant]; WT IV.iv.609
4 no-one, nobody KL II.ii.163 [disguised Kent alone] *Nothing almost sees miracles / But misery* [i.e. hardly anyone but the wretched sees miracles]
5 no point, no particular KL V.iii.95 [Albany to Edmund] *thou art in nothing less / Than I have here proclaimed thee;* Ham IV.v.13

nothing (*adv.*) not at all, in any / no way H8 I.i.207 [Buckingham to Norfolk] *It will help me nothing / To plead mine innocence;* Cym IV.iii.14, iv.15

nothing, all the world to the odds are a million to one RJ III.v.214 [Nurse to Juliet] *Romeo is banished; and all the world to nothing / That he dares ne'er come back to challenge you*

nothing-gift (*n.*) gift of no value Cym III.vii.58 [Innogen to herself, of great men] *laying by / That nothing-gift of differing multitudes* [i.e. flattery]

notice (*n.*) 1 information, intelligence, notification H5 IV.vii.114 [King Henry to heralds] *Bring me just notice of the numbers dead;* 2H4 I.iii.85; JC III.ii.272; LL I.i.264

NUMBERS

In just a few cases, numbers and numerical expressions differ from those found in modern English. In counting above 100, the *and* is sometimes omitted: thus we find 'one hundred twenty-six' (**H5** IV.viii.82) and 'a hundred fifty' (**E3** V.i.174) alongside 'a hundred and seven' (**Oth** I.iii.3) and 'a hundred and fifty' (**MW** III.iv.49).

Item	Example	Gloss
brace	**TNK** III.i.20	pair
thrice	**AY** I.i.54	3 times
twain	**TNK** III.v.143	2

Counting in units and tens

two and twenty	**1H4** I.i.68	22
three and twenty	**WT** III.iii.59	23
four and twenty	**1H4** III.iii.73	24
five and twenty	**AY** V.i.19	25
two and thirty	**TS** I.ii.32	32
three and thirty	**JC** V.i.53	33
five and thirty	**Tem** III.ii.13	35
two and forty	**RJ** IV.i.105	42
two and fifty	**1H6** IV.vii.73	52

Counting in twenties

half a score	**TS** I.ii.109	10
score	**Cym** III.ii.69	20
score or two	**R3** I.ii.256	20–40
three or four score	**1H4** II.iv.5	60–80
fourscore	**AY** II.iii.71	80
eight score eight	**Oth** III.iv.170	168
nine score and odd	**2H4** IV.iii.35	±180
nine score and seventeen	**MM** IV.iii.5	197
twelve score	**MW** III.ii.30	240 [firing distance in yards]
fourteen	**2H4** III.ii.46	280 [archery distance in yards]
fourteen and a half	**2H4** III.ii.46	290 [archery distance in yards]
threescore thousand	**E3** IV.iii.62	60,000 [army size]

Indefinite numbers

Item	Example	Quotation	Gloss
twice and once	**2H4** V.iii.38	*I have been merry twice and once ere now*	many times
two or three	**Per** II.iv.17	*Enter two or three Lords*	a few
three	**AC** III.iii.22	*Three in Egypt / Cannot make better note*	very few
four	**Tim** V.i.218	*Lips, let four words go by, and language end*	an indefinite number – two or three
and twenty	**TNK** V.ii.107	[Daughter] *Shall we kiss too?* [Wooer] *A hundred times.* [Daughter] *– And twenty*	many more
hundred	**TG** IV.iv.142	*I have wept a hundred several times*	a lot

---

2 recognition, official acknowledgement **KL** II.iv.244 [Regan to Lear, of his knights] *to no more / Will I give place or notice*

notify *(v.)* notice, take note, observe **MW** II.ii.80 [Mistress Quickly to Falstaff, of Mistress Ford] *she gives you to notify that her husband will be absence from his house between ten and eleven*

notion *(n.)* understanding, awareness, intellect **KL** I.iv.224 [Lear to all, of himself] *his notion weakens;* **Cor** V.vi.107; **Mac** III.i.82

notorious *(adj.)* notable, out-and-out, evident **Oth** V.ii.237 [Montano to Gratiano, of Iago] *'Tis a notorious villain*

not-pated *(adj.)* crop-headed, short-haired **1H4** II.iv.68 [Prince Hal to Francis, of the vintner] *Wilt thou rob this ... not-pated ... Spanish pouch?*

nourish *(n.)* nurse, nursemaid **1H6** I.i.50 [Bedford to all] *Our isle be made a nourish of salt tears*

nourished *(adj.)* nurse, care for, bring up **Tit** V.i.60 [Lucius to Aaron] *Thy child shall live, and I will see it nourished*

no-verb *(n.)* word of warning; or: non-existing word **MW** III.i.96 [Host to all, of Evans] *he gives me the proverbs and the no-verbs*

novice (*n.*) recruit, rookie, greenhorn **AW** II.i.47 [Parolles to Lords] *Mars dote on you for his novices!*

novum (*n.*) game of dice in which throws of nine and five were significant **LL** V.ii.540 [Berowne to King, of the Worthies] *Abate throw at novum* [possibly: a throw of five might count as nine, as with the players in the pageant]

now (*adv.*) just now **Per** I.ii.95 [Pericles to Helicanus] *thyself art one, / Who now reprovedst me*

noyance (*n.*) harm, damage, injury **Ham** III.iii.13 [Rosencrantz to Claudius] *The single and peculiar life is bound … / To keep itself from noyance*

nullity (*n.*) non-event, mere nothing, blank **TNK** III.v.55 [School-master to all] *Our business is become a nullity, / Yea, and a woeful and a piteous nullity*

numb (*adj.*) paralysed, immobile **1H6** II.v.13 [Mortimer to Gaolers, of his feet] *whose strengthless stay is numb*

number (*n.*) **1** (plural) verses, lines **LL** IV.iii.55 [Longaville to himself, of his verses] *These numbers will I tear, and write in prose;* **Ham** II.ii.119; **LL** IV.ii.121; **Sonn** 17.6, 79.3; **TC** III.ii.181
2 (plural) metre, versification **TN** II.v.99 [Malvolio to himself, of the lines of Oliva's supposed letter] *The numbers altered;* **RJ** II.iv.38

number (*v.*) put into verses **AC** III.ii.17 [Enobarbus to Agrippa] *Think, speak, cast, write, sing, number*

numbered (*adj.*) enumerated, counted **Cym** I.vii.36 [Iachimo to Innogen] *the twinned stones / Upon the numbered beach* [F]

numbering (*n.*) estimation, evaluation, assessment **LL** V.ii.35 [Rosaline to Princess, of Berowne's verses] *The numbers true, and, were the numbering too, / I were the fairest goddess on the ground*

numbering (*adj.*) counting out, measuring **R2** V.v.50 [Richard alone] *now hath time made me his numbering clock* [i.e. clock with numbered hours marked on it]

nuncio (*n.*) messenger, emissary **TN** I.iv.28 [Orsino to Viola as Cesario, of his message to Olivia] *She will attend it better in thy youth / Than in a nuncio's of more grave aspect*

nuncle (*n.*) child-like shortening of 'mine uncle'; guardian, master **KL** I.iv.104 [Fool to Lear] *How now, nuncle!* [and throughout the Fool's part]

nurse (*n.*) nourisher, feeder **TS** Induction.ii.131 [Lord to Sly] *melancholy is the nurse of frenzy*

nurse (*v.*) nourish, take care of **Tit** V.i.84 [Aaron to Lucius] *To save my boy, to nurse and bring him up* [F, Q1 *nourish*]

nurser (*n.*) fosterer, encourager, nourisher **1H6** IV.vii.46 [Burgundy to all, of John Talbot] *See where he lies inhearsed in the arms / Of the most bloody nurser of his harms* [i.e. of the harm he has inflicted]

nursery (*n.*) **1** nursing, loving care, ministering **KL** I.i.124 [Lear to Kent, of Cordelia] *I … thought to set my rest / On her kind nursery*
2 training-ground, prep school **AW** I.ii.16 [Second Lord to King, of the war] *It well may serve / A nursery to our gentry*

nurture (*n.*) manners, culture, good upbringing **AY** II.vii.98 [Orlando to Duke Senior] *yet am I inland bred / And know some nurture*

nuthook, nut-hook (*n.*) constable, beadle, officer **2H4** V.iv.7 [Doll to First Beadle] *Nut-hook, nut-hook, you lie!;* **MW** I.i.155

nuzzle up (*v.*) rear, bring up, nurture **Per** I.iv.42 [Cleon to Dionyza] *mothers … to nuzzle up their babes / Thought naught too curious*

nyas eyas, hawk nestling, young hawk **RJ** II.ii.167 [Romeo to Juliet] *My nyas?* [F *Neece*]

nymph (*n.*) beauty, damsel, siren **R3** I.i.17 [Richard alone] *I … want love's majesty / To strut before a wanton ambling nymph;* **MND** IV.i.126

O *(n.)* **1** circle, orb, sphere **AC** V.ii.81 [Cleopatra to Dolabella] *A sun and moon, which ... lighted / The little O o'th' earth;* **MND** III.ii.188
 2 cipher, zero, nought **KL** I.iv.188 [Fool to Lear] *Now thou art an O without a figure* [i.e. without a number before it to make it significant]
 3 spot, pimple **LL** V.ii.45 [Rosaline to and of Katharine] *O that your face were not so full of O's*
 4 sorrowful exclamation **RJ** III.iii.91 [Nurse to Romeo] *Why should you fall into so deep an O?*

O *(int.)* **1** vocalization used before a direct address [to a person, thing, concept, etc] **RJ** I.i.178 [Romeo to Benvolio] *O heavy lightness;* **TC** V.ii.181 [Troilus to himself] *O false Cressid!*
 2 oh [used in emphatic emotion] **TNK** II.i.71 [Palamon to Arcite] *O, never / Shall we two exercise ... / Our arms again*

o' *(prep.)* **1** of **H8** V.i.131 [King Henry to Cranmer] *not ever / The justice and the truth o'th' question carries / The due o'th' verdict with it*
 2 on **Tim** IV.i.7 [Timon alone] *To general filths / Convert o'th' instant, green virginity*

oaf *(n.)* ☛ ouph *(n.)*

oak *(n.)* crown of oak leaves [awarded to a victorious soldier] **TNK** IV.ii.137 [Messenger to Theseus, of one of the knights] *About his head he wears the winner's oak;* **Cor** II.ii.96

oar *(v.)* move as with an oar **Tem** II.i.120 [Francisco to Alonso, of Ferdinand] *he ... oared / Himself with his good arms in lusty stroke / To th' shore*

oath *(n.)* promise, undertaking **AY** I.ii.20 [Celia to Rosalind] *when I break that oath*

oathable *(adj.)* oath-worthy, fit to take an oath **Tim** IV.iii.136 [Timon to Phrynia and Timandra] *You are not oathable*

ob *(n.)* obolus, halfpenny **1H4** II.iv.524 [Peto to Prince Hal, reading from Falstaff's papers] *Item bread ... ob.* ☛ **MONEY**, p.286

obdurate *(adj.)* stubborn, obstinate, inflexible **Venus** 199 [Venus to Adonis] *Art thou obdurate, flinty, hard as steel?;* **Luc** 429 ☛ indurate *(adj.)*

obedience *(n.)* obeisance, act of submission **2H4** IV.v.147 [Prince Henry to King Henry IV, while kneeling] *Let me no more from this obedience rise*

obedient *(adj.)* of obedience, dutiful **AW** II.iii.159 [King to Bertram] *Do thine own fortunes that obedient right*

obeisance *(n.)* bow, curtsy, respectful salutation **TS** Induction-i.106 [Lord to Servant, of behaving to his Page dressed as a woman] *call him 'madam', do him obeisance*

obey *(v.)* respond to, be affected by **MW** III.iii.180 [Mistress Page to Mistress Ford, of Falstaff] *His dissolute disease will scarce obey this medicine*

object *(n.)* **1** spectacle, sight, object of attention **JC** IV.i.37 [Antony to Octavius, of Lepidus] *one that feeds / On objects, arts, and imitations;* **Cor** I.i.19; **3H6** II.ii.4; **KL** II.iii.17; **Luc** 806; **TC** II.ii.41; **Tit** III.i.64
 2 objection, protestation **Tim** IV.iii.123 [Timon to Alcibiades] *Swear against objects* [i.e. take an oath not to be moved by protest]

object *(v.)* urge, adduce, bring up **1H6** II.iv.116 [Warwick to Richard, of Somerset's faction] *This blot that they object against your house;* **1H6** III.i.7; **3H6** V.v.89; **R3** II.iv.17

objected *(adj.)* [legal sense] urged as an objection, brought forward in argument **1H6** II.iv.43 [Somerset to Vernon] *it is well objected*

objection *(n.)* **1** accusation, charge, allegation **2H6** I.iii.153 [Gloucester to all] *As for your spiteful false objections, / Prove them;* **1H6** IV.i.129; **H8** III.ii.307
 2 offer, proposal, claim **E3** II.ii.121 [King Edward to Countess] *art thou come / To speak ... yea / To my objection in thy beauteous love?*

oblation *(n.)* offering, gift **Lover** 223 [the woman, of her treasures] *these of force must your oblations be;* **Sonn** 125.10

obligation (*n.*) bond, agreement, legal document 2H6 IV.ii.87 [Dick to Cade, of the Clerk] *he can make obligations, and write court-hand;* MW I.i.10

obliged (*adj.*) contracted, bound by marriage MV II.vi.7 [Salerio to Gratiano] *ten times faster Venus' pigeons fly / To seal love's bonds new-made than they are wont / To keep obliged faith unforfeited*

oblique (*adj.*) indirectly resembling TC V.i.52 [Thersites alone, of Menelaus as a transformation of Jupiter] *the primitive statue and oblique memorial of cuckolds* [i.e. an indirect reminder, Jupiter not being himself a cuckold]

obliquy (*n.*) [unclear meaning] oblique, obliquity; deviance, perversity Tim VI.iii.18 [Timon alone] *All's obliquy; / There's nothing level in our cursed natures / But direct villainy* [F *obliquie*]

oblivion (*n.*) forgetfulness, inability to recall Ham IV.iv.40 [Hamlet alone] *whether it be / Bestial oblivion*

obloquy (*n.*) disgrace, reproach, slander AW IV.ii.44 [Bertram to Diana, of his ring] *Which were the greatest obloquy i'th' world / In me to lose;* 1H6 II.v.49; Luc 523

obscene (*adj.*) disgusting, offensive, repulsive LL I.i.236 [King reading Armado's letter to him, of seeing Costard and Jaquenetta] *I did encounter that obscene and most preposterous event*

obscenely (*adv.*) malapropism possibly for 'seemly' MND I.ii.100 [Bottom to all, of the wood] *there we may rehearse most obscenely*

obscure (*v.*) 1 conceal, protect, hide AY V.iv.34 [Orlando to Duke Senior] *a great magician, / Obscured in the circle of this forest*
  2 live in obscurity, overshadow, eclipse 1H6 II.v.26 [Mortimer to Gaolers] *hath Richard been obscured, / Deprived of honour and inheritance*

obscured (*adj.*) disguised, covert, incognito KL II.ii.166 [disguised Kent alone] *my obscured course* [i.e. way of life]

obsequious (*adj.*) 1 dutiful [without suggesting servility]; appropriate after a death Tit V.iii.151 [Lucius to Marcus, of Titus' body] *draw you near / To shed obsequious tears upon this trunk;* Ham I.ii.92; 3H6 II.v.118; Sonn 31.5, 125.9
  2 devoted, compliant, ready to please MW IV.ii.2 [Falstaff to Mistress Ford] *I see you are obsequious in your love;* MM II.iv.28

obsequiously (*adv.*) as a mourner, with proper regard for the dead R3 I.ii.3 [Anne to bearers] *I ... obsequiously lament / Th'untimely fall of virtuous Lancaster*

obsequy (*n.*) funeral rite, burial ceremony 3H6 I.iv.147 [York to Queen] *These tears are my sweet Rutland's obsequies;* Cym IV.ii.282; 2H6 III.ii.146; Phoen 12; RJ V.iii.16; Tit I.i.163

observance (*n.*) 1 proper attention, attentiveness, heed MW II.ii.189 [Ford as Brook to Falstaff, of Mistress Ford] *I have ... followed her with a doting observance;* AY III.ii.227, V.ii.91, 93; TC II.iii.163
  2 honour, dutiful ceremony, due respect TC I.iii.31 [Nestor to Agamemnon] *With due observance of thy godlike seat;* AW II.v.74; TNK II.iv.51, V.i.69
  3 powers of observation AC III.iii.22 [Messenger to Cleopatra, of her asking if his description of Octavia is certain] *Or I have no observance;* AW III.ii.5; Luc 1385
  4 compliance, carrying out what has to be done MM IV.i.41 [disguised Duke to Isabella, of Mariana] *Are there no other tokens ... 'greed concerning her observance?*

observancy (*n.*) proper attention, tender attentiveness Oth III.iv.145 [Desdemona to Emilia, of men] *we must ... / Nor of them look for such observancy / As fits the bridal* [F; Q *observances*]

observant (*n.*) ingratiating attendant, obsequious servant KL II.ii.101 [Cornwall to all] *twenty silly-ducking observants*

observation (*n.*) 1 observance, rite, customary practice MND IV.i.103 [Theseus to his attendants] *now our observation is performed;* KJ I.i.208
  2 observance, careful attention, heed Tem III.iii.88 [Prospero to Ariel] *with good life / And observation strange, my meaner ministers / Their several kinds have done*

3 observed truth, maxim AY II.vii.41 [Jaques to Duke Senior, of Touchstone] *he hath strange places [in his brain] crammed / With observation*

observe (*v.*) 1 humour, gratify, indulge 2H4 IV.iv.30 [King Henry IV to Clarence, of Prince Henry] *he is gracious, if he be observed;* 2H4 IV.iv.36, 49; JC IV.iii.45; TNK V.ii.13
  2 honour, wait upon, show all courtesy to TNK II.iv.35 [Pirithous to Arcite, of Emilia] *pray observe her goodness*
  3 perceive, see through, be aware of AW I.iii.131 [Countess to herself, of Helena] *I observe her now*
  4 take notice of, interpret, examine scientifically Tim III.iv.18 [Titus to Philotus] *I'll show you how t'observe a strange event*

observed (*n.*) one demanding respect, deserving of honour Ham III.i.155 [Ophelia alone, of Hamlet] *Th'observed of all observers*

observing (*adj.*) compliant, deferential, obsequious TC II.iii.127 [Agamemnon to Patroclus, of Achilles] *[we] underwrite in an observing kind / His humorous predominance*

observingly (*adv.*) observantly, perceptively, with proper observation H5 IV.i.5 [King Henry to Bedford and Gloucester] *There is some soul of goodness in things evil, / Would men observingly distil it out*

obstacle (*adj.*) [rustic error for] obstinate 1H6 V.iv.17 [Shepherd to Pucelle] *Fie, Joan, that thou wilt be so obstacle!*

obstinate (*adj.*) unyielding, inflexible, hard-hearted Cor V.iii.26 [Coriolanus to himself] *Let it be virtuous to be obstinate*

obstruct (*n.*) [debated meaning] obstruction, impediment, hindrance AC III.vi.61 [Caesar to Octavia, of her and Antony] *Being an obstruct 'tween his lust and him* [F *abstract*] ▶ **abstract** (*n.*) 4

obstruction (*n.*) 1 obstacle, difficulty, hindrance TN II.v.115 [Malvolio to himself, of interpreting the letter] *There is no obstruction in this*
  2 deathly state, rigor mortis MM III.i.122 [Claudio to Isabella] *to die ... / To lie in cold obstruction and to rot*

occasion (*n.*) 1 circumstance, opportunity R3 II.ii.148 [Buckingham to Richard] *I'll sort occasion ... / To part the Queen's proud kindred from the Prince;* Ham I.iii.54; 1H6 IV.i.130; KL I.iii.25; Oth II.i.235; TN I.v.82
  2 ground, reason, cause, matter 3H6 I.iii.44 [Rutland to Clifford] *when I give occasion of offence, / Then let me die;* Cym IV.ii.187; E3 V.i.198; 2H4 I.iii.86; Oth IV.i.58; RJ III.i.41
  3 need, want, requirement Tim II.ii.196 [Timon to Servants, of the Lords] *my occasions have found time to use 'em toward a supply of money;* AW IV.i.14; Cym V.v.87; KJ II.i.82; MV I.i.151
  4 course of events, state of affairs Mac II.ii.70 [Lady Macbeth to Macbeth] *Get on your nightgown, lest occasion call us / And show us to be watchers;* E3 V.i.129; KJ IV.ii.125; TS III.ii.101
  5 political opportunity, expedient circumstance AC II.vi.129 [Enobarbus to Menas, of Antony] *He married but his occasion here*
  6 occurrence, action, manifestation Lover 86 *every light occasion of the wind*

occident (*n.*) west Cym IV.ii.372 [disguised Innogen to Lucius] *I may wander / From east to occident;* R2 III.iii.67

occidental (*adj.*) western, westerly; sunset AW II.i.163 [Helena to King] *Ere twice in murk and occidental damp / Moist Hesperus hath quenched his sleepy lamp*

occulted (*adj.*) hidden, concealed Ham III.ii.90 [Hamlet to Horatio, of Claudius] *If his occulted guilt / Do not itself unkennel*

occupation (*n.*) 1 handicraft, trade, employment JC I.ii.264 [Casca to Brutus] *An I had been a man of any occupation;* AC IV.iv.17; Cor IV.i.14, vi.98; Tem II.i.157
  2 calling, habit, business KL II.ii.90 [disguised Kent to Cornwall] *'tis my occupation to be plain*

occupy (*v.*) fornicate, have sexual dealings [with] 2H4 II.iv.144 [Doll to all] *the word 'occupy', which was an excellent good word before it was ill-sorted;* RJ II.iv.97

occurrent (*n.*) incident, event, occurrence Ham V.ii.351 [Hamlet to Horatio, of Fortinbras] *tell him, with th'occurrents, more and less*

'od shortened form of 'God' ☞ SWEARING, p.435

odd (*n.*) ☞ odds (*n.*)

odd (*adj.*) **1** eccentric, peculiar, unusual LL V.i.13 [Holofernes to Nathaniel, of Armado] *He is too picked, too spruce, too affected, too odd;* TC IV.v.41; TS III.i.79, ii.69
2 singular, unique, individual TC IV.v.42 [Menelaus to Cressida] *Every man is odd* [pun: 41, sense 1; not even]
3 alone, single, solitary TC IV.v.44 [Cressida to Menelaus, of losing Helen to Paris] *you are odd, and he is even with you*
4 casual, chance, or other Oth II.iii.122 [Iago to Montano, of Cassio] *On some odd time of his infirmity*
5 occasional; or: extra Ham V.ii.174 [Hamlet to Osrick] *I will gain nothing but my shame and the odd hits* [i.e. my fortuitous hits on Laertes; or: the three additional hits from Laertes]
6 isolated, out of the way Tem I.ii.223 [Ariel to Prospero, of Ferdinand] *I left cooling of the air with sighs / In an odd angle of the isle*

odd (*adv.*) at odds, at variance TC IV.v.265 [Ajax to Achilles, of Hector] *The general state, I fear, / Can scarce entreat you to be odd with him*

odd-conceited (*adj.*) elaborately odd, ingeniously devised TG II.vii.46 [Julia to Lucetta, of her hair] *I'll knit it up in silken strings / With twenty odd-conceited true-love knots*

odd-even (*adj.*) between 12 and 1, around midnight Oth I.i.124 [Roderigo to Brabantio] *At this odd-even and dull watch o'th' night*

oddly (*adv.*) unequally, unevenly; or: unusually, in a peculiar way TC I.iii.339 [Nestor to Ulysses, of Hector's challenge] *Our imputation shall be oddly poised / In this willed action*

odds (*n. plural*) **1** superiority, advantage, edge Tit V.ii.19 [Titus to disguised Tamora] *Thou hast the odds of me;* AY I.i.148; 2H6 IV.x.42; R2 III.iv.89; TS IV.iii.150
2 inequalities, unfavourable circumstances E3 IV.iv.64 [Prince Edward to Audley] *Then apprehend no odds, / For one to one is fair equality;* E3 III.iv.33; 3H6 II.i.147; TC V.iv.22
3 differences, distinctions, inequalities AC IV.xv.66 [Cleopatra to all, of dead Antony] *young boys and girls / Are level now with men. The odds is gone*
4 quarrel, disagreement, strife Oth II.iii.179 [Iago to Othello] *I cannot speak / Any beginning to this peevish odds;* MW III.i.50; Tim IV.iii.43
5 probability, likelihood, odds-on Cym V.ii.9 [Iachimo alone, as if to the British] *the odds / Is that we scarce are men and you are gods;* TNK II.iii.1

odoriferous (*adj.*) odorous, sweet-smelling, fragrant KJ III.iv.26 [Constance as if to death] *Thou odoriferous stench!;* LL IV.ii.124

odour (*n.*) perfume, fragrance, scent TNK IV.iii.83 [Doctor to Wooer] *make an addition of some other compounded odours, which are grateful to the sense*

oeillade (*n.*) [pron: 'iliad, uh'yahd'] amorous glance, look of love, ogle KL IV.v.25 [Regan to Oswald, of Gonerill] *She gave strange oeillades ... / To noble Edmund* [F *Eliads;* Q *aliads];* MW I.iii.55

o'er- (*beginning a word*) ☞ located in alphabetical position as 'over-'

of (*prep.*) **1** about 1H6 I.i.73 [First Messenger to all] *whilst a field should be dispatched and fought, / You are disputing of your generals*
2 against H5 II.iii.26 [Nym to Hostess, of Falstaff] *They say he cried out of sack*
3 by AY II.i.50 [First Lord to Duke Senior, of Jaques and a stag] *being there alone, / Left and abandoned of his velvet friend*
4 between TNK II.i.54 [Gaoler's Daughter to Gaoler] *Lord, the difference of men!*
5 for AC I.i.62 [Demetrius to Philo] *I will hope / Of better deeds tomorrow*
6 from JC IV.iii.54 [Brutus to Cassius] *I shall be glad to learn of noble men*

7 in TNK I.iii.23 [Hippolyta to Pirithous, of herself and Emilia] *if / You stay to see of us such spinsters, we / Should hold you here for ever*
8 in the form of Cor I.ix.10 [Cominius to Martius] *Yet cam'st thou to a morsel of this feast, / Having fully dined before*
9 on Ham II.ii.290 [Hamlet to himself, of Rosencrantz and Guildenstern] *I have an eye of you*
10 out of AY IV.i.78 [Orlando to Rosalind as Ganymede, referring back to his question 'Who could be out, being before his beloved mistress?'] *What, of my suit?*
11 with KJ V.ii.59 [Lewis the Dauphin to Salisbury, of people unlike him] *Full warm of blood, of mirth, of gossiping*

off (*adj.*) beside the point, irrelevant Cor II.ii.58 [Menenius to Brutus, of the latter's remarks] *That's off, that's off!*

off (*adv.*) **1** off the ship, ashore AC II.vii.118 [Caesar to Antony] *Let me request you off*
2 off-stage TNK III.i.96 [stage direction] *They wind horns off* ☞ STAGE DIRECTIONS, p.417

offal (*n.*) dross, waste, refuse JC I.iii.109 [Cassius to Casca] *What trash is Rome, / What rubbish, and what offal*

off-cap (*v.*) doff the cap, take off the hat [in respect] Oth I.i.10 [Iago to Roderigo, of Othello] *Three great ones of the city ... / Off-capped to him* [F *Off-capt;* Q *Oft capp'd*]

offence (*n.*) **1** damage, injury, harm 1H6 IV.i.75 [King to Talbot, of Burgundy] *Let him perceive ... what offence it is to flout his friends;* 1H6 I.ii.49; JC IV.iii.199; KL I.iv.207; MND II.ii.23; Oth II.iii.260 [Q]
2 opposition, hostility, antagonism 1H6 V.v.96 [King to Gloucester] *banish all offence;* AC IV.xv.45; KJ II.i.250
3 offensive matter, object of annoyance JC II.i.268 [Portia to Brutus] *You have some sick offence within your mind;* Cor V.i.28
4 [in fencing] attacking stroke, offensive action TNK V.iii.63 [Emilia to herself, of Palamon and Arcite] *[they] might / Omit a ward or forfeit an offence / Which craved that very time*

offenceful (*adj.*) sinful, wrongful, full of offence MM II.iii.26 [disguised Duke to Juliet] *your most offenceful act / Was mutually committed?*

offenceless (*adj.*) incapable of causing offence, harmless Oth II.iii.267 [Iago to Cassio] *one would beat his offenceless dog to affright an imperious lion*

offend (*v.*) **1** harm, hurt, pain MV IV.i.140 [Shylock to Gratiano] *Thou but offend'st thy lungs to speak so loud;* KL I.i.304; Oth II.iii.193; TC V.iii.4
2 wrong, sin against, abuse Oth V.ii.59 [Desdemona to Othello] *I never did / Offend you in my life*
3 assail, attack, fall upon CE I.i.90 [Egeon to Duke] *the sun ... / Dispersed those vapours that offended us*

offendress (*n.*) female offender AW I.i.139 [Parolles to Helena] *virginity ... should be buried in highways out of all sanctified limit, as a desperate offendress against nature*

offer (*n.*) offering, proposal, invitation, inducement KJ V.vii.84 [Salisbury to Bastard, of the Dauphin] *Cardinal Pandulph ... brings from him such offers of our peace / As we with honour and respect may take;* H8 III.ii.4; Tem II.i.197

offer (*v.*) **1** attempt, start, try, make a move 1H6 III.i.1 [stage direction] *Gloucester offers to put up a bill;* Cor II.ii.64; H5 II.i.36; H8 II.iv.121; MW III.i.68; RJ III.iii.108
2 dare, presume, venture TC II.iii.61 [Thersites to Achilles] *Agamemnon is a fool to offer to command Achilles;* 2H4 IV.i.217; KJ IV.ii.94; TS V.i.56; WT IV.iv.773
3 bring an offering, make a donation 2H6 II.i.91 [Simpcox to Queen, reporting St Alban's words] *offer at my shrine, and I will help thee*
4 bring gifts, give presents AY V.iv.164 [Duke Senior to Jaques de Boys] *Thou offerest fairly to thy brothers' wedding*
5 make, opt for, declare TS V.ii.161 [Katherina to Widow, of women] *To offer war where they should kneel for peace*

offering (*n.*) ritual, oblation, sacrificial rite Mac II.i.52 [Macbeth alone] *Witchcraft celebrates / Pale Hecat's offerings*

offering *(adj.)* challenging, taking the offensive 1H4 IV.i.69 [Worcester to Hotspur] *we of the offering side / Must keep aloof from strict arbitrement*

office *(n.)* **1** task, service, duty, responsibility WT II.ii.31 [Paulina to Emilia, of telling Leontes about the new baby] *The office / Becomes a woman best* ➤ FEW, p.xxi

2 role, position, place, function MV II.ix.41 [Arragon to himself] *O that estates, degrees, and offices / Were not derived corruptly;* AC II.iii.1; 2H4 V.iii.122; LL V.ii.350; PassP XIV.16; TNK III.i.111

3 officialdom, people who hold office Ham III.i.73 [Hamlet alone] *The insolence of office;* H8 I.i.44

4 performance, business, intrigue MA II.i.161 [Claudio alone] *Friendship is constant ... / Save in the office and affairs of love;* H5 V.ii.355; TNK V.i.122

5 service, sympathy, kindness MW III.i.46 [Page to Evans] *We are come to do you a good office;* MM V.i.361; MW I.i.94; R2 II.ii.136; WT II.iii.188, V.i.148

6 room, apartment, living area 2H4 I.iii.47 [Lord Bardolph to Hastings, of building] *we ... draw anew the model / In fewer offices*

7 (plural) kitchen, buttery, serving-room Oth II.ii.8 [Herald, reading aloud] *All offices are open;* Tim II.ii.163

8 (plural) servants' quarters, service rooms Mac II.i.14 [Banquo to Macbeth, of the King] *He hath ... sent forth great largess to your offices;* Cor I.i.135; R2 I.ii.69

office *(v.)* **1** officiously withhold, use petty authority to block Cor V.ii.60 [Menenius to First Watch] *a Jack guardant cannot office me from my son Coriolanus*

2 carry out the work for, act as servants to AW III.ii.126 [Helena alone, of staying where she is] *no, although ... angels officed all*

office-badge *(n.)* symbol of office 2H6 I.ii.25 [Gloucester to Duchess] *this staff, mine office-badge in court*

officed *(adj.)* **1** functional, working, serviceable Oth I.iii.267 [Othello to all] *light-winged toys / Of feathered Cupid seel with wanton dullness / My speculative and officed instruments* [F; Q *active*]

2 playing a role, having a function WT I.ii.172 [Leontes to Polixenes, of Mamillius compared to Florizel] *So stands this squire / Officed with me* [i.e. he carries out the same office with me]

officer *(n.)* **1** constable TS V.i.82 [Tranio as Lucentio to all] *Call forth an officer;* 1H4 II.ii.105

2 executioner, hangman, gaoler Cym V.iv.177 [First Gaoler to Posthumus, of a condemned man] *I think he would change places with his officer*

3 (plural) household, servants Ham IV.v.104 [Messenger to Claudius] *Laertes, in a riotous head, / O'erbears your officers*

officer of arms *(n.)* herald, pursuivant TNK III.vi.135 [Theseus to Palamon and Arcite] *making battle ... / Without my leave and officers of arms*

officious *(adj.)* **1** meddlesome, interfering, overzealous Cor I.viii.14 [Aufidius to his soldiers] *Officious and not valiant, you have shamed me;* H8 III.ii.237

2 obliging, attentive, diligent Tit V.ii.200 [Titus to all] *be everyone officious / To make this banquet;* WT II.iii.158

oft *(adv.)* often Ham I.iii.72 [Polonius to Laertes] *the apparel oft proclaims the man* ➤ FEW, p.xxi

often *(adj.)* frequent, numerous, continuous E3 III.iv.91 [Prince Edward to all] *my weary arms, with often blows*

oftentimes *(adv.)* often, frequently, on many occasions TS III.ii.70 [Tranio as Lucentio to Baptista, of Petruchio] *oftentimes he goes but mean-apparelled;* 1H4 III.i.24; KJ IV.ii.30; TG III.i.26

oft-subdued *(adj.)* often-defeated, frequently subjugated 1H6 I.v.32 [Talbot to the English] *As you fly from your oft-subdued slaves*

oft-times *(adv.)* often, frequently, on many occasions Cym I.vii.62 [Innogen to Iachimo, of Posthumus] *He did incline to sadness, and oft-times / Not knowing why*

oil *(n.)* **1** [vat of] boiling oil WT III.ii.175 [Paulina to Leontes] *What studied torments, tyrant, hast for me? ... Boiling / In leads or oils?*

2 smoothness, glibness, ingratiating manner TNK III.i.103 [Palamon to Arcite] *be rough with me, and pour / This oil out of your language*

oily *(adj.)* moist, clammy, greasy AC I.ii.53 [Charmian to Iras] *if an oily palm be not a fruitful prognostication, I cannot scratch mine ear*

old *(n.)* old people, elders TC II.ii.105 [Cassandra to all] *Virgins and boys, mid-age and wrinkled old ... / Add to my clamour*

old *(adj.)* **1** olden, ancient, bygone TN II.iv.43 [Orsino to Viola as Cesario, of a song] *it is old and plain;* Sonn 127.1; TN II.iv.48

2 hackneyed, worn-out, stale TN I.v.105 [Olivia to Feste] *you see ... how your fooling grows old;* Oth II.i.136

3 degenerate, lapsed, unregenerate R2 V.iii.145 [Duchess of York to Aumerle] *Come, my old son. I pray God make thee new*

4 plenty of, abundant, more than enough Tem I.ii.369 [Prospero to Caliban] *I'll rack thee with old cramps;* 2H4 II.iv.19; MA V.ii.87; Mac II.iii.2; MV IV.ii.15; MW I.iv.5

5 normal, usual, commonplace KL III.vii.100 [Third Servant to Second Servant, of Regan] *If she live long, / And in the end meet the old course of death*

6 experienced, practised, skilled TN I.iii.112 [Sir Andrew to Sir Toby] *I will not compare with an old man;* RJ III.iii.94

olive *(n.)* olive-branch [symbol of peace] 2H4 IV.iv.87 [Westmorland to King Henry IV] *Peace puts forth her olive everywhere;* Tim V.iv.82; TN I.v.202

Olympian *(n.)* athlete in the Olympic games; or: Olympian god TC IV.v.194 [Nestor to Hector] *I have seen thee ... / When that a ring of Greeks have hemmed thee in, / Like an Olympian wrestling*

omen *(n.)* calamity, ominous event, disaster Ham I.i.123 [Horatio to Marcellus and Barnardo, of unnatural events] *prologue to the omen coming on*

ominous *(adj.)* fateful, portentous TC V.iii.6 [Andromache to Hector] *My dreams will sure prove ominous to the day;* Ham II.ii.452

omit *(v.)* neglect, disregard, forget about 2H4 IV.iv.27 [King Henry IV to Clarence, of Prince Henry] *omit him not;* Cor III.i.146; JC IV.iii.218; MM IV.iii.71; Tem II.i.197; TG II.iv.63

on *(adv.)* [go] onward, forward 1H4 IV.i.37 [Hotspur to Worcester, of Northumberland] *with our small conjunction we should on*

on *(prep.)* **1** against RJ III.iii.101 [Nurse to Romeo, of Juliet] *she ... then on Romeo cries*

2 at CE V.i.210 [Luciana to Duke, of Adriana] *Ne'er may I look on day nor sleep on night / But she tells to your highness simple truth* [second instance]

3 because of TNK IV.i.50 [Gaoler to Wooer, of the Gaoler's Daughter's madness] *Either this was her love to Palamon, / Or fear of my miscarrying on his 'scape*

4 from 1H6 I.v.6 [Talbot to Pucelle] *Blood will I draw on thee*

5 in Tit II.iii.223 [Martius to Quintus] *Lord Bassianus lies berayed in blood, / All on a heap*

6 in the name of 1H6 I.vi.28 [Charles to all] *No longer on Saint Denis will we cry*

7 of KL I.iv.102 [Fool to disguised Kent, of Lear] *this fellow has banished two on's daughters*

8 onto Cor II.ii.93 [Cominius to all, of Coriolanus] *Tarquin's self he met, / And struck him on his knee*

9 on top of Ham V.ii.389 [Horatio to Fortinbras, of a council meeting] *let this same be presently performed ... lest more mischance / On plots and errors happen*

once *(adv.)* **1** once and for all, in a word MA I.i.297 [Don Pedro to Claudio] *'Tis once, thou lovest;* Cor II.iii.1; H8 I.ii.82; KJ I.i.74; MA V.i.200 ➤ DISCOURSE MARKERS, p.127

2 ever, at any time Mac V.v.15 [Macbeth to himself] *Direness ... / Cannot once start me;* AC V.ii.54; Ham I.v.121; Sonn 135.6; Tim I.ii.248, V.i.54

3 one day, some time 2H4 V.iii.59 [Davy to Shallow] *I hope to see London once ere I die;* JC IV.iii.189; RJ I.iii.62

4 some time, at a convenient point **MW** III.iv.96 [Fenton to Mistress Quickly, of Anne] *I pray thee once tonight / Give my sweet Nan this ring*

once, at *(adv.)* all together, jointly, collectively **1H4** I.iii.290 [Worcester to Northumberland and Hotspur] *our powers at once … shall happily meet* **3H6** IV.viii.31; **H8** III.i.110; **R2** V.ii.16; **Tim** III.iv.6

one *(pron.)* ☛ all is one

oneyer *(n.)* ☛ onyer *(n.)*

onixe *(n.)* ☛ union *(n.)*

only *(adj.)* **1** outstanding, peerless, pre-eminent **1H6** IV.vii.77 [Lucy to all] *Is Talbot slain, the Frenchmen's only scourge*; **Ham** III.ii.134; **2H4** II.i.142; **TNK** II.i.30

2 sole, exclusive **Cor** I.ix.36 [Cominius to Martius, of Martius' share of the treasure] *to be ta'en forth / Before the common distribution at / Your only choice*; **3H6** IV.i.45

3 habitual, typical; or: mere **AY** V.iii.12 [First Page to all, of noisy behaviour before singing] *the only prologues to a bad voice*

only *(adv.)* **1** especially, particularly **1H6** I.iv.97 [Talbot to all] *Wretched shall France be only in my name* [i.e. just to hear my name]

2 as a sole exception, excepting **KL** I.i.135 [Lear to Cornwall and Albany] *Only we shall retain / The name and all th'addition to a king*

3 alone, solely, exclusively **JC** V.v.56 [Strato to Messala] *For Brutus only overcame himself*; **TS** II.i.355

onset *(n.)* **1** start, beginning, commencement **Tit** I.i.241 [Saturninus to Titus] *And for an onset … / Lavinia will I make my empress*

2 attack, assault **KJ** II.i.326 [Hubert to Heralds] *we might behold … the onset and retire / Of both your armies*

onset, give the make a beginning with, start acting on **TG** III.ii.94 [Thurio to Proteus] *I have a sonnet that will serve the turn / To give the onset to thy good advice*

onyer, oneyer *(n.)* [unclear meaning] officer with financial responsibility **1H4** II.i.77 [Gadshill to Chamberlain] *I am joined … with Burgomasters and great onyers* [Qo, Q1 *Oneyres*; F *Oneyers*]

ope *(v.)* open **Ham** IV.v.147 [Laertes to Claudius] *thus wide I'll ope my arms* ☛ FEW, p.xxi

open *(adj.)* **1** public, exposed to general view **H8** II.i.168 [First Gentleman to Second Gentleman] *We are too open here to argue this*; **CE** IV.iv.65; **MM** II.i.125; **MW** I.iii.23

2 public, widely frequented, fashionable **H5** I.i.59 [Canterbury to Ely, of King Henry] *never noted in him … any sequestration, / From open haunts and popularity*

3 exposed, open to the elements **Tim** IV.iii.266 [Timon to Apemantus, comparing his former associates to leaves] *Fell from their boughs, and left me open, bare, / For every storm that blows*

4 displayed, made visible **Luc** 1248 [of women] *Their smoothness, like a goodly champaign plain, / Lays open all the little worms that creep*; **KL** III.i.34

5 easy to get through; or: give too much of a view **TNK** II.i.318 [Gaoler to Palamon] *The windows are too open*

6 generous, liberal, freely giving **Tim** V.i.56 [Poet to Timon] *Having often of your open bounty tasted*; **2H4** IV.iv.32; **TC** V.ii.25

open *(v.)* **1** reveal, uncover, disclose **WT** IV.iv.733 [Autolycus to Shepherd] *I command thee to open thy affair*; **Cym** V.v.58; **Ham** II.ii.18; **Per** I.ii.87, V.i.132; **TG** I.i.126

2 announce, communicate, divulge **E3** II.ii.14 [Derby to Audley, of the news] *I have not yet found time to open them*; **Cym** V.v.42

3 [hunting] bark at finding a scent **MW** IV.ii.186 [Ford to his companions] *If I cry out thus upon no trail, never trust me when I open again*

open *(adv.)* out in the open, in public **TN** III.iii.38 [Sebastian to Antonio] *Do not then walk too open*

open-arse *(n.)* [rustic bawdy, from the shape of the fruit] medlar fruit **RJ** II.i.38 [Mercutio as if to Romeo, of Romeo's mistress] *O that she were / An open-arse*

opener *(n.)* interpreter, elucidator, expositor **2H4** IV.ii.20 [Prince John to and of Archbishop] *The very opener and intelligencer / Between the grace, the sanctities, of heaven / And our dull workings*

operance *(n.)* operation, action, activity **TNK** I.iii.63 [Emilia to Hippolyta] *elements / That … effect / Rare issues by their operance*

operant *(adj.)* active, vital, potent, functioning **Ham** III.ii.184 [First Player, as King, to his Queen] *My operant powers their functions leave to do*; **Tim** IV.iii.25

operation *(n.)* **1** effect, force, influence, power **AC** IV.xv.26 [Cleopatra to Antony] *If knife, drugs, serpents, have / Edge, sting, or operation*; **E3** II.i.404; **KL** I.i.111; **RJ** III.i.8

2 plan, active thought, working idea **MW** I.iii.84 [Nym to Pistol] *I have operations which be humours of revenge*

operative *(adj.)* effective, efficacious, capable of working **KL** IV.iv.14 [Doctor to Cordelia, of providing Lear with rest] *that to provoke in him / Are many simples operative*

opinion *(n.)* **1** public opinion, popular judgement **Oth** I.iii.222 [Duke to Othello] *opinion … throws a more safer voice on you*; **Cor** I.i.269; **2H4** V.i.128; **Luc** 937; **MV** I.i.91; **Per** II.ii.55

2 reputation, character, honour **1H4** V.iv.47 [King Henry to Prince Hal] *Thou hast redeemed thy lost opinion*; **1H4** IV.i.77; **JC** II.i.145; **Oth** II.iii.189; **TC** IV.iv.102; **Tit** I.i.419

3 gossip, suspicion, malicious rumour **Oth** IV.ii.108 [Desdemona alone, of Othello] *How have I been behaved, that he might stick / The smallest opinion on my least misuse?*; **TNK** III.i.240

4 judgement, conviction, belief **JC** II.ii.6 [Caesar to Servant] *Go bid the priests do present sacrifice, / And bring me their opinions of success*; **1H6** II.iv.52; **TNK** III.vi.240

5 arrogance, self-conceit, hubris **LL** V.i.5 [Nathaniel to Holofernes] *Your reasons at dinner have been … learned without opinion*; **1H4** III.i.179; **TC** III.iii.264

opinioned *(adj.)* malapropism for 'pinioned' **MA** IV.ii.65 [Dogberry to Verges, of Conrade and Borachio] *let them be opinioned*

oppose *(v.)* **1** display, exhibit, present **H8** IV.i.67 [Third Gentleman to First and Second Gentlemen, of Queen Anne] *opposing freely / The beauty of her person to the people*; **2H6** IV.x.43

2 compare, draw a parallel between **Tit** I.i.135 [Demetrius to Chiron] *Oppose not Scythia to ambitious Rome*

3 place in opposition, set up as resistance **TC** I.iii.333 [Nestor to Ulysses, of Hector's challenge] *Who may you else oppose … / If not Achilles?*; **MV** IV.i.10; **Tim** III.iv.80

opposed *(adj.)* **1** opposite, facing **1H4** III.i.106 [Mortimer to Hotspur, of the river] *Gelding the opposed continent as much / As on the other side it takes from you*; **MV** II.ix.62; **TC** IV.v.94

2 hostile, malevolent **2H4** IV.iv.66 [King Henry IV to Clarence, of Prince Henry] *with what wings shall his affections fly / Towards fronting peril and opposed decay!*

3 hostile, of conflicting forces **1H4** I.i.9 [King Henry to all] *Those opposed eyes … / Shall now … / March all one way*

opposeless *(adj.)* unable to be resisted, unchallengeable **KL** IV.vi.38 [Gloucester to himself, as if to the gods] *To quarrel with your great opposeless wills*

opposing *(adj.)* opposite, antipodal **Per** III.Chorus.17 [Gower alone] *the four opposing coigns*

opposite *(n.)* **1** opponent, adversary, antagonist **KL** V.iii.43 [Albany to Edmund] *You have the captives / Who were the opposites of this day's strife*; **Cor** II.ii.22; **2H4** I.iii.55; **2H6** V.iii.22; **MM** III.ii.156; **TN** III.iv.261

2 opposing force, adversity **Ham** III.ii.230 [Second Player, as Queen, to her King] *Each opposite that blanks the face of joy*

opposite *(adj.)* opposed, hostile, adverse, antagonistic [to] **R3** IV.iv.402 [King Richard to Queen Elizabeth] *Be opposite all planets of good luck / To my proceeding*; **2H6** III.ii.251; **KJ** III.i.254; **KL** II.i.48; **R3** IV.iv.216; **Tim** I.i.277 ☛ wilful-opposite *(adj.)*

opposition *(n.)* **1** presenting for combat, contesting, encounter **Ham** V.ii.168 [Osrick to Hamlet] *the opposition of your person in trial;* **Cym** IV.i.13; **LL** V.ii.728

2 counter-proposal, alternative proposition **E3** II.ii.144 [King Edward to Countess] *Thy opposition is beyond our law*

oppress *(v.)* **1** dominate, overwhelm, crush **TNK** V.i.22 [Palamon to Arcite] *were't one eye / Against another, arm oppressed by arm, / I would destroy th'offender* [i.e. one arm against the other]

2 crowd out, throng, overwhelm **Tim** II.ii.163 [Flavius to Timon] *When all our offices have been oppressed / With riotous feeders*

3 trouble, distress, worry **Cym** V.iv.99 [Jupiter to all] *Be not with mortal accidents oppress;* **AW** I.iii.142

oppressed *(adj.)* distressed, troubled, burdened **Ham** I.ii.203 [Horatio to Hamlet, of the Ghost and the observers] *Thrice he walked / By their oppressed and fear-surprised eyes*

oppression *(n.)* **1** misfortune, distress, difficulty **AC** IV.vii.2 [Agrippa to all] *our oppression / Exceeds what we expected;* **R2** I.iv.14

2 weight, burden, pressure **R2** III.iv.31 [Gardener to First Man, of the apricots] *Which … make their sire / Stoop with oppression of their prodigal weight*

oppugnancy *(n.)* opposition, conflict, contention **TC** I.iii.111 [Ulysses to all, of disorder] *Each thing meets / In mere oppugnancy*

opulency *(n.)* opulence, affluence, wealth **Tim** V.i.34 [Poet to Painter, of a poem for Timon] *with a discovery of the infinite flatteries that follow youth and opulency*

or *(conj.)* before **Ham** V.ii.30 [Hamlet to Horatio] *Or I could make a prologue to my brains*

or … or *(conj.)* either … or **JC** V.v.3 [Clitus to Brutus, of Statilius] *he is or ta'en or slain*

or ever *(conj.)* **1** before **Ham** I.ii.147 [Hamlet alone, of Gertrude] *or e'er those shoes were old / With which she followed my poor father's body*

2 that ever **Ham** I.ii.183 [Hamlet to Horatio, of Gertrude's wedding-day] *Would I had met my dearest foe in heaven / Or ever I had seen that day*

orange-tawny *(adj.)* dull yellowish brown **MND** I.ii.87 [Bottom to Quince, of his beard for the play] *your orange-tawny beard*

orange-wife *(n.)* woman who sells oranges **Cor** II.i.66 [Menenius to Brutus and Sicinius] *You wear out a good wholesome forenoon in hearing a cause between an orange-wife and a faucet-seller*

oration *(n.)* petition, supplication **Tit** IV.iii.115 [Titus to Marcus, of a knife] *fold it in the oration*

orator *(n.)* advocate, spokesman, champion **CE** III.ii.10 [Luciana to Antipholus of Syracuse] *Be not thy tongue thy own shame's orator*

oratory *(n.)* eloquence, persuasiveness **1H6** II.ii.49 [Talbot to Burgundy] *when a world of men / Could not prevail with all their oratory*

orb *(n.)* **1** sphere, planet, star, heavenly body **KL** I.i.111 [Lear to Cordelia] *By all the operation of the orbs / From whom we do exist;* **Cym** I.vii.35; **MV** V.i.60

2 sphere, orbit, circle **RJ** II.ii.110 [Juliet to Romeo, of the moon] *That monthly changes in her circled orb;* **AC** III.xiii.146; **Cym** V.v.372; **1H4** V.i.17; **Per** I.ii.122; **Tim** IV.iii.2

3 earth, world **Ham** II.ii.483 [First Player to all present] *the orb below /As hush as death*

4 rounded mass, ring, crown **E3** IV.iv.18 [Audley to Prince Edward, of the hill where the French army stands] *an orb / Aloft the which the banners, bannerets, / And new-replenished pendants cuff the air*

5 fairy ring, circle **MND** II.i.9 [Fairy to Puck] *I serve the Fairy Queen, / To dew her orbs upon the green*

orbed *(adj.)* rounded, orb-like, spherical **Lover** 25 [of the woman's eyes] *Sometimes diverted their poor balls are tied / To th'orbed earth;* **Ham** III.ii.165; **TN** V.i.268

orchard *(n.)* garden **RJ** II.ii.63 [Juliet to Romeo] *The orchard walls are high and hard to climb;* **Ham** I.v.35; **JC** III.ii.249; **KJ** V.vii.10; **TN** III.iv.174; **TS** II.i.111

ordain *(v.)* **1** appoint, establish, institute **1H6** IV.i.33 [Talbot to all, of the Garter] *When first this Order was ordained;* **1H6** I.i.171; **TS** III.i.10

2 fate, destine, decree **2H6** V.ii.45 [Young Clifford to himself, as if to his father] *Wast thou ordained … / To die in ruffian battle?*

order *(n.)* **1** arrangement, disposition, direction **H5** III.ii.63 [Gower to Fluellen] *The Duke of Gloucester, to whom the order of the siege is given;* **JC** I.ii.25; **KJ** III.i.251; **MM** II.i.225; **TC** IV.v.70; **TS** I.ii.124

2 prescribed practice, regular procedure **TN** I.iii.8 [Maria to Sir Toby] *you must confine yourself within the modest limits of order;* **Ham** V.ii.224; **KL** I.iv.18; **MM** I.ii.148

3 agreement, arrangement, entente **1H4** III.i.67 [Glendower to all] *shall we divide our right / According to our threefold order taken?;* **KJ** V.ii.4

4 injunction, command, dictate **WT** IV.i.10 [Time to audience] *Let me pass / The same I am ere ancient'st order was*

5 manner, process, method **TS** III.i.63 [Hortensio as Licio to Bianca, of playing the lute] *To learn the order of my fingering;* **2H6** III.ii.129

6 formation, formal array **2H6** IV.ii.178 [Dick to Cade, of the enemy] *They are all in order, and march toward us;* **2H4** IV.iv.100

7 rank, status **H8** IV.i.26 [First Gentleman to Second Gentleman] *The Archbishop / Of Canterbury, accompanied with other / Learned and reverend fathers of his order*

8 order of knighthood **MW** V.v.61 [Mistress Quickly as Queen of Fairies to all, of Windsor Castle] *The several chairs of order look you scour / With juice of balm* [i.e. seats belonging to the knights of the Order of the Garter]

order, out of rebellious, insubordinate, disobedient **2H6** IV.ii.179 [Cade to Dick] *are we in order when we are most out of order*

order, take make arrangements **2H6** III.i.320 [York to all] *Provide me soldiers, lords, / Whiles I take order for mine own affairs;* **CE** V.i.146; **1H6** III.i.126; **2H6** III.i.274; **MM** II.i.223; **Oth** V.ii.73

order *(v.)* **1** arrange, plan, organize **Tem** I.ii.29 [Prospero to Miranda] *I have with such provision in mine art / So safely ordered*

2 dispose, deal with, treat **JC** V.v.79 [Octavius to all, of Brutus] *Within my tent his bones tonight shall lie, / Most like a soldier, ordered honourably*

ordered *(adj.)* organized, prepared, ready **Cym** II.iv.21 [Posthumus to Philario] *Our countrymen / Are men more ordered than when Julius Caesar / Smiled at their lack of skill*

ordering *(n.)* management, direction, regulation **KJ** V.i.77 [King John to Bastard] *Have thou the ordering of this present time*

orderly *(adv.)* according to the rules, properly, in the prescribed way **TS** II.i.45 [Gremio to Petruchio, of addressing Baptista] *You are too blunt, go it orderly;* **R2** I.iii.9; **TG** I.i.122

ordinance *(n.)* **1** appointed place in nature **JC** I.iii.66 [Cassius to Casca, of weird happenings] *Why all these things change from their ordinance*

2 providence, divine will, what is ordained **Cym** IV.ii.145 [Arviragus to Belarius and Guiderius] *Let ordinance / Come as the gods foresay it*

3 decree, divine rule, injunction **KL** IV.i.67 [Gloucester to Edgar as Poor Tom, as if to the heavens] *the superfluous and lust-dieted man / That slaves your ordinance*

4 usage, practice, course **H5** II.iv.83 [Exeter to French King] *honours that pertain / By custom and the ordinance of times / Unto the crown of France*

5 rank, position, standing [in the state] **Cor** III.ii.12 [Coriolanus to Nobles] *one but of my ordinance stood up / To speak of peace or war*

6 ☛ **ordnance** *(n.)*

ordinant *(adj.)* providential, directing, in control **Ham** V.ii.48 [Hamlet to Horatio] *even in that was heaven ordinant* [Q2; F *ordinate*]

ordinary *(n.)* **1** routine, norm, usual procedure **AY** III.v.42 [Rosalind as Ganymede to Phebe] *I see no more in you than in the ordinary / Of nature's sale-work*

2 regular meal, standard fare, meal-time **AW** II.iii.200 [Lafew to Parolles] *I did think thee for two ordinaries to be a pretty wise fellow;* **AC** II.ii.230

ordinary *(adj.)* everyday, commonplace, regularly experienced **KJ** V.ii.48 [Lewis the Dauphin to Salisbury, of a lady's tears] *Being an ordinary inundation*

ordinate *(adj.)* ☛ **ordinant** *(adj.)*

ordnance, ordinance *(n.)* cannon, artillery **H5** III.Chorus.26 [Chorus alone, of the English army] *Behold the ordnance on their carriages;* **E3** V.i.135; **Ham** V.ii.264; **1H6** I.iv.15; **KJ** II.i.218; **TS** I.ii.201

ordure *(n.)* filth, dirt, dung **H5** II.iv.39 [Constable to Dauphin] *As gardeners do with ordure hide those roots;* **E3** I.ii.155

ore *(n.)* precious metal **Ham** IV.i.25 [Gertrude to Claudius] *like some ore / Among a mineral of metals base*

organ *(n.)* **1** agent, instrument, means **Ham** IV.vii.69 [Laertes to Claudius] *I might be the organ;* **MM** I.i.20

2 feature, trait, facet **MA** IV.i.224 [Friar to Leonato, of Hero] *every lovely organ of her life*

3 musical instrument **Ham** III.ii.376 [Hamlet to Rosencrantz and Guildenstern] *there is much music … in this little organ*

orgulous *(adj.)* proud, haughty, arrogant **TC** Prologue.2 [Prologue] *The princes orgulous … / Have to the port of Athens sent their ships*

orient *(n.)* eastern part of the sky [where the sun rises] **Sonn** 7.1 *Lo, in the Orient when the gracious light / Lifts up his burning head*

orient *(adj.)* **1** lustrous, brilliant, bright **R3** IV.iv.322 [King Richard to Queen Elizabeth, of her tears] *transformed to orient pearl;* **AC** I.v.41; **MND** IV.i.53; **PassP** X.3; **Venus** 981

2 eastern; sunrise, dawn **E3** V.i.29 [Second Citizen to King Edward] *The sun … / Did in the orient purple of the morn / Salute our coming forth*

oriental *(adj.)* brilliant, glowing, radiant **E3** II.i.11 [Lodowick alone, of the Countess's colouring] *her oriental red*

orifex *(n.)* orifice, opening, aperture **TC** V.ii.154 [Troilus to Ulysses, of the division in Cressida] *the spacious breadth of this division / Admits no orifex for a point as subtle / As Ariachne's broken woof to enter*

original *(n.)* point of origin, cause, source **2H4** I.ii.116 [Falstaff to Lord Chief Justice, of apoplexy] *It hath it original from much grief;* **MND** II.i.117

orison *(n.)* prayer, plea **Ham** III.i.89 [Hamlet to Ophelia] *in thy orisons / Be all my sins remembered; Cym* I.iv.32; **E3** IV.iv.78; **H5** II.ii.53; **3H6** I.iv.110; **RJ** IV.iii.3

ornament *(n.)* **1** special quality, distinction **E3** II.i.86 [King Edward to Lodowick] *every ornament that thou wouldst praise;* **1H4** III.i.120

2 (plural) robes, garments, attire **1H6** V.i.54 [Winchester to Legate, of his promise of money] *For clothing me in these grave ornaments;* **RJ** I.i.93

ort *(n.)* scrap, fragment, fraction **Tim** IV.iii.401 [First Bandit to others, of Timon's gold] *It is some poor fragment, some slender ort of his remainder;* **Luc** 985; **TC** V.ii.161

orthography *(n.)* **1** speaker of high-flown phrases, stylistically polished person **MA** II.iii.19 [Benedick alone, of Claudio] *He was wont to speak plain … now is he turned orthography*

2 correct spelling **LL** V.i.19 [Holofernes to Nathaniel, of Armado] *I abhor … such rackers of orthography*

osier *(n.)* willow **AY** IV.iii.80 [Celia as Aliena to Oliver] *The rank of osiers by the murmuring stream;* **LL** IV.ii.108; **PassP** V.4, VI.5

osier *(adj.)* made of willow **RJ** II.iii.3 [Friar alone] *I must up-fill this osier cage of ours / With baleful weeds*

ostent *(n.)* display, show, manifestation **MV** II.ii.183 [Gratiano to Bassanio, of his future behaviour] *Like one well studied in a sad ostent / To please his grandam;* **H5** V.Chorus.21; **MV** II.viii.44; **Per** I.ii.25

ostentation *(n.)* **1** public show, display, exhibition **R2** II.iii.94 [York to Bolingbroke] *Frighting … villages with war / And ostentation of despised arms;* **AC** III.vi.52; **Cor** I.vi.86; **2H4** II.ii.47; **LL** V.i.106; **MA** IV.i.203

2 ceremony, ritual **Ham** IV.v.215 [Laertes to Claudius, of Polonius] *No noble rite nor formal ostentation*

3 pretentiousness, false show, showing off **LL** V.ii.409 [Berowne to Rosaline, of his rhetorical words] *these summer flies / Have blown me full of maggot ostentation*

other *(adv.)* otherwise, in any other way **Mac** I.vii.77 [Lady Macbeth to Macbeth, of how their plan will be received] *Who dares receive it other*

othergates *(adv.)* otherwise, differently, in another way **TN** V.i.191 [Sir Andrew to Viola as Cesario, of Sir Toby] *if he had not been in drink, he would have tickled you othergates than he did*

otherwhere *(adv.)* elsewhere, somewhere else **H8** II.ii.58 [Lord Chamberlain to Norfolk and Suffolk] *The King has sent me otherwhere;* **CE** II.i.30, 104

otherwhiles *(adv.)* at various times, on occasion **1H6** I.ii.7 [Charles to all] *Otherwhiles the famished English … / Faintly besiege us*

ouch *(n.)* ornament, gem; also: sore **2H4** II.iv.48 [Falstaff to Doll] *your brooches, pearls, and couches*

ought *(v.)* past form of 'owe' ☛ **PAST TENSES**, p.319

oui away *(v.)* chatter away in French **H8** I.iii.34 [Lovell to Lord Chamberlain, of French-influenced Englishmen back in France] *They may … 'oui' away / The lag end of their lewdness* [F *wee*]

ounce *(n.)* lynx **MND** II.ii.36 [Oberon to Titania, of what she might see] *Be it ounce or cat or bear*

ouph, oaf *(n.)* elf, elfen child, changeling **MW** V.v.57 [Mistress Quickly as Queen of Fairies to all] *Strew good luck, ouphes, on every sacred room;* **MW** IV.iv.48

ousel, woosel *(n./adj.)* blackbird **MND** III.i.118 [Bottom singing to himself] *The ousel cock so black of hue;* **2H4** III.ii.7

out *(v.)* drop out, quit **2H4** V.iii.65 [Shallow to Bardolph, of Davy] *The knave will stick by thee, … 'a will not out*

out *(adv.)* **1** in error, at fault, wrong **TNK** I.ii.26 [Arcite to Palamon] *Are you not out?* [i.e. mistaken] **LL** IV.i.134; **WT** II.i.72

2 at a loss, put out, nonplussed; unable to remember one's lines **Cor** V.iii.41 [Coriolanus to himself] *I have forgot my part and I am out;* **AY** III.ii.244, IV.i.68, 74; **LL** V.ii.152, 173

3 angry, out of sorts **JC** I.i.16 [Cobbler to Flavius] *be not out with me* [pun: 17, sense 9]

4 fallen out, in a state of unfriendliness **MV** III.v.29 [Jessica to Lorenzo] *Launcelot and I are out*

5 in arms, in rebellion **Mac** IV.iii.183 [Ross to Macduff] *there ran a rumour / Of many worthy fellows that were out*

6 at an end, finished **Tim** III.vi.16 [Lucius to Lucullus, of Timon] *I am sorry, when he sent to borrow of me, that my provision was out* [i.e. exhausted]; **AC** IV.ix.32; **AW** I.i.58; **Ham** V.ii.190; **Luc** 356; **Sonn** 113.4

7 fully, completely, outright, totally **Tem** I.ii.41 [Prospero to Miranda] *then thou wast not / Out three years old;* **Cor** IV.v.124; **E3** II.ii.49

8 out of pocket **TN** II.iii.178 [Sir Andrew to Sir Toby] *If I cannot recover your niece, I am a foul way out* [or: sense 3]

9 out at heels, with worn shoes **JC** I.i.17 [Cobbler to Flavius] *if you be out, sir, I can mend you* [pun: 16, sense 3]

10 out-of-date, not in vogue [for] **RJ** I.iv.3 [Benvolio to Romeo, of making a formal apology] *The date is out of such prolixity*

11 into public circulation, out to interest **AW** I.i.145 [Parolles to Helena, of virginity] *Out with't!*

12 away from home, abroad **KL** I.i.31 [Gloucester to Kent, of Edmund] *He hath been out nine years*

13 out in the field, away fighting **TNK** II.i.23 [Gaoler's Daughter to Gaoler, of Palamon and Arcite] *'twere pity they should be out*

14 ☛ EXCLAMATIONS, p.158

out *(prep.)* **1** out of **2H4** II.ii.23 [Prince Henry to Poins] *those [babies] that bawl out the ruins of thy linen*

2 outside **Tim** IV.i.38 [Timon alone] *The gods confound … / Th'Athenians both within and out that wall*

3 [unclear meaning] without **H8** I.i.79 [Buckingham to Abergavenny, of Wolsey] *his own letter, / The honourable board of Council out, / Must fetch him in he papers* [i.e. without consulting the Council]

out of *(prep.)* **1** beyond, outside **H8** I.ii.114 [King Henry to Queen Katherine, of Buckingham] *he may furnish and instruct great teachers, / And never seek for aid out of himself*

2 free from **1H4** IV.i.135 [Douglas to Hotspur] *I am out of fear / Of death or death's hand for this one half year*

3 outside of **LL** III.i.139 [Costard alone, of 'remuneration'] *I will never buy and sell out of this word*

out of suits with out of favour with **AY** I.ii.234 [Rosalind to Orlando, of herself] *one out of suits with fortune* [i.e. no longer clothed by fortune]

out-brag *(v.)* surpass in beauty, excel in pride **Lover** 95 *that termless skin / Whose bare out-bragged the web it seemed to wear*

outbrave *(v.)* **1** surpass in bravery, outdo in daring **MV** II.i.28 [Morocco to Portia] *I would … / Outbrave the heart most daring on the earth*

2 outdo in beauty, excel in splendour **Sonn** 94.12 *But if that flower with base infection meet, / The basest weed outbraves his dignity*

outbreast *(v.)* outsing, surpass in voice **TNK** V.iii.127 [Theseus to Emilia, of two nightingales] *by and by outbreasted, that the sense / Could not be judge between 'em*

out-breathed *(adj.)* put out of breath, winded **2H4** I.i.108 [Morton to Northumberland, of Percy] *mine eyes saw him in bloody state … wearied and out-breathed*

outburn *(v.)* burn away, incinerate, be consumed **PassP** VII.14 [Pilgrim, of his love] *She burnt out love, as soon as straw out-burneth*

out-crafty *(v.)* artfully outwit, surpass in cunning **Cym** III.iv.15 [Innogen to Pisanio, of Posthumus] *That drug-damned Italy hath out-craftied him*

outdare *(v.)* **1** overcome by daring, outbrave **1H4** V.i.40 [Worcester to King Henry] *It was myself, my brother, and his son, / That … boldly did outdare / The dangers of the time*

2 exceed in daring, dare more than **Cor** I.iv.55 [Lartius to First Soldier, of Martius] *O noble fellow! / Who sensibly outdares his senseless sword*

outdared *(adj.)* overcome by daring, cowed, outbraved; or: excessively daring, brazen, unabashed **R2** I.i.190 [Bolingbroke to King Richard, of Mowbray] *this outdared dastard*

outdure *(v.)* endure, outlast, survive **TNK** III.vi.10 [Palamon alone] *I feel myself … able once again / To outdure danger*

outdwell *(v.)* stay beyond **MV** II.vi.3 [Gratiano to Salerio, of Lorenzo] *it is marvel he outdwells his hour*

outface *(v.)* **1** defy, intimidate, overcome by confronting **2H6** IV.x.44 [Iden to Cade] *See if thou canst outface me with thy looks;* **KJ** II.i.97, V.i.49; **KL** II.ii.11; **PassP** I.8

2 put down, overcome, put to shame **R2** IV.i.285 [Richard, as to a mirror] *Is this the face … / That was at last outfaced by Bolingbroke?;* **LL** V.ii.620

3 present a bold front, maintain a defiant image **AY** I.iii.120 [Rosalind to Celia, of their male disguise] *As many other mannish cowards have / That do outface it with their semblances* [i.e. bluff it out]

outgo *(v.)* **1** outdo, outstrip, surpass **Tim** I.i.279 [First Lord to Second Lord, of Timon] *He outgoes / The very heart of kindness;* **Cym** II.iv.84; **H8** I.ii.207; **TNK** III.vi.79

2 outdistance, go faster than **AC** III.ii.61 [Caesar to Octavia] *the time shall not / Outgo my thinking on you*

out-jest *(v.)* overcome with the force of jokes **KL** III.i.16 [Gentleman to disguised Kent, of the Fool] *who labours to out-jest / His [Lear's] heart-struck injuries*

outlive *(v.)* survive, live longer **Tit** II.iii.132 [Tamora to Chiron, of Lavinia] *Let not this wasp outlive, us both to sting*

outlook *(v.)* outstare, overcome by facing up to **KJ** V.ii.115 [Lewis the Dauphin to Cardinal Pandulph, of his army] *I … culled these fiery spirits from the world / To outlook conquest and to win renown*

out-night *(v.)* outdo in making references to the night **MV** V.i.23 [Jessica to Lorenzo] *I would out-night you, did nobody come*

out-paramour *(v.)* have more lovers than **KL** III.iv.88 [Edgar as Poor Tom to all, of himself] *I … in woman out-paramoured the Turk* [i.e. the Grand Sultan]

outpeer *(v.)* surpass, outrival, exceed **Cym** III.vii.59 [Innogen to herself, of Arviragus and Guiderius] *Great men … / Could not outpeer these twain*

outrage *(n.)* **1** violence, hostility, fury **R3** II.iv.64 [Duchess of York to all] *O preposterous / And frantic outrage;* **CE** I.i.6

2 passionate expression, emotional outcry **RJ** V.iii.216 [Prince to all] *Seal up the mouth of outrage for a while;* **1H6** IV.i.126; **R3** I.iii.276

outrageous *(adj.)* **1** excessively fierce, extremely violent **Tit** III.iii.13 [Titus to Lavinia] *When thy poor heart beats with outrageous beating;* **E3** IV.iii.65

2 temperamental, capricious, volatile **Ham** III.i.58 [Hamlet to himself] *The slings and arrows of outrageous fortune*

outrun *(v.)* escape, avoid, elude **2H6** V.ii.73 [King to Queen] *Can we outrun the heavens?;* **3H6** I.ii.14

outscorn *(v.)* ☛ **outstorm** *(v.)*

outsell *(v.)* exceed in value, surpass **Cym** II.iv.102 [Iachimo to Posthumus, of Innogen] *Her pretty action did outsell her gift;* **Cym** III.v.75

outside *(n.)* **1** appearance, look, outside show **TN** II.ii.18 [Viola alone, of Olivia] *Fortune forbid my outside have not charmed her!;* **AY** I.iii.118; **Tim** I.i.163

2 (plural) mere external thing, outward form **Tim** III.v.33 [First Senator to Alcibiades] *He's truly valiant that can … make his wrongs his outsides, / To wear them, like his raiment, carelessly*

outsleep *(v.)* sleep beyond [a time], sleep in **MND** V.i.355 [Theseus to all] *I fear we shall outsleep the coming morn*

outspeak *(v.)* far exceed, more than warrant **H8** III.ii.127 [King Henry to Norfolk, of Wolsey's inventory] *I find at such proud rate that it outspeaks / Possession of a subject* [i.e. he has more than befits someone who is not a king]

outsport *(v.)* make merry beyond the bounds of, revel beyond the limits of **Oth** II.iii.3 [Othello to Cassio] *Let's teach ourselves that honourable stop, / Not to outsport discretion*

outstand *(v.)* outstay, remain beyond **Cym** I.vii.207 [Iachimo to Innogen] *I have outstood my time*

out-storm *(v.)* rage more violently than a storm **KL** III.i.10 [Gentleman to disguised Kent, of Lear] *Strives … to out-storm / The to-and-fro conflicting wind and rain* [Q outscorn]

outstretch *(v.)* stretch out out to the end, strain beyond the limit **Tim** V.iii.3 [Soldier alone, reading Timon's epitaph] *Timon is dead, who hath outstretched his span*

outstretched *(adj.)* **1** over-inflated, puffed up, swollen [by ambition] **Ham** II.ii.263 [Hamlet to Rosencrantz and Guildenstern] *Then are our … outstretched heroes the beggars' shadows*

2 opened wide, fully distended **MM** II.iv.153 [Isabella to Angelo] *with an outstretched throat I'll tell the world / What man thou art*

outstrike (v.) surpass in striking, deal a swifter blow than **AC** IV.vi.36 [Enobarbus alone, of his heart] *If swift thought break it not, a swifter mean / Shall outstrike thought*

outswear (v.) **1** conquer by swearing, swear to do without **LL** I.ii.62 [Armado to Mote] *methinks I should outswear Cupid*
2 outdo in swearing **MV** IV.ii.17 [Portia to Nerissa, of Bassanio and Gratiano] *we'll outface them, and outswear them too*

outsweeten (v.) exceed in sweetness **Cym** IV.ii.224 [Arviragus to Belarius and Guiderius, as if to disguised Innogen] *The leaf of eglantine … / Outsweetened not thy breath*

out-tongue (v.) speak more loudly than, be more persuasive than **Oth** I.ii.19 [Othello to Iago, of Brabantio] *My services … / Shall out-tongue his complaints* ➤ **tongue** (v.)

outvenom (v.) be more poisonous than, exceeds in venom **Cym** III.iv.36 [Pisanio to Innogen, of slander] *whose tongue / Outvenoms all the worms of Nile*

out-vie (v.) outbid, outdo, better **TS** II.i.378 [Tranio as Lucentio to Baptista, of bidding for Bianca] *Gremio is out-vied*

out-wall (n.) external appearance, outer clothing **KL** III.i.45 [disguised Kent to Gentleman] *I am much more / Than my out-wall*

outward (n.) outward show, external appearance, demeanor **Cym** I.i.23 [First Gentleman to Second Gentleman, of Posthumus] *I do not think / So fair an outward … / Endows a man, but he*; **Lover** 80; **Sonn** 69.5; **TC** III.ii.160

outward (adj.) **1** external, surface, superficial **MV** III.ii.73 [Bassanio to himself] *So may the outward shows be least themselves*; **Cor** I.vi.77; **Cym** I.i.9; **JC** I.ii.91; **KL** IV.iv.10
2 acting as an external observer, looking from outside **AW** III.i.11 [Second Lord to Duke, of giving an opinion] *like a common and an outward man*
3 formal, official, public **MM** I.ii.148 [Claudio to Lucio, of Juliet] *we do denunciation lack / Of outward order* [i.e. the publishing of banns]

outwear (v.) **1** wear away, spend, pass **LL** II.i.23 [Princess to Boyet, of the King's vow to allow no women to the court] *Till painful study shall outwear three years*
2 use up, waste the time of **H5** IV.ii.61 [Constable to all] *The sun is high, and we outwear the day*
3 outlast, last the whole length of **Venus** 841 [of Venus] *Her song was tedious, and outwore the night*

outwork (v.) excel in workmanship, transcend **AC** II.ii.206 [Enobarbus to Agrippa and Maecenas, of Cleopatra] *O'erpicturing that Venus where we see / The fancy outwork nature*

outworth (v.) outvalue, be more powerful than **H8** I.i.122 [Buckingham to Norfolk and Abergavenny] *A beggar's book / Outworths a noble's blood*

ovator (n.) one who receives an ovation **Cor** I.ix.46 [Martius to all, of the flatterer] *let him be made / An ovator for th'wars* [i.e. let him be given an ovation for what he has done in war] [F *Ouerture*; disputed reading] ➤ **coverture** (n.) 3; **overture** (n.) 2

over (adj.) observing, overseeing, spying **WT** IV.iv.650 [Camillo to Perdita] *I do fear eyes over*

over and over head over heels **Cor** I.iii.63 [Valeria to Volumnia and Virgilia, of Young Martius] *over and over he comes*

overbear (v.) **1** overwhelm, overcome, overpower **Ham** IV.v.104 [Messenger to Claudius] *Laertes, in a riotous head, / O'erbears your officers*; **H5** IV.Chorus.39; **KJ** III.iv.9; **MA** II.iii.152; **Mac** IV.iii.64; **Per** V.i.194
2 overrule, overcome, put down **Tit** IV.iv.2 [Saturninus to all] *Was ever seen / An emperor in Rome thus overborne*; **E3** II.i.132; **1H6** III.i.53; **3H6** III.ii.166; **KJ** V.ii.37; **MND** IV.i.178

overblow (v.) **1** blow over, pass away, abate **Tem** II.ii.108 [Trinculo to Stephano] *Is the storm overblown?*; **2H6** I.iii.150; **R2** III.iii.190; **R3** II.iv.61; **TS** V.ii.3

2 blow away, blow off **H5** III.iii.31 [King Henry to citizens of Harfleur] *the cool and temperate wind of grace / O'erblows the filthy and contagious clouds*

over-boots (adj.) (plural) boot-deep, following a reckless course **TG** I.i.25 [Valentine to Proteus] *you are over-boots in love* ➤ **over-shoes** (adj.)

overbulk (v.) outgrow, dominate, tower over **TC** I.iii.320 [Ulysses to Nestor, of Achilles' pride] *[it] must or now be cropped / Or, shedding, breed a nursery of like evil / To overbulk us all*

overbuy (v.) exceed in worth, pay too much for **Cym** I.ii.77 [Innogen to Cymbeline, of Posthumus] *he … overbuys me / Almost the sum he pays* [i.e. the amount he suffers is far more than I am worth]

overcharged (adj.) **1** overburdened, overtaxed, overwrought **2H6** III.ii.376 [Vaux to Queen, of the Cardinal] *whispers to his pillow … / The secrets of his overcharged soul*; **3H6** V.v.78; **MND** V.i.85; **Sonn** 23.8; **WT** III.ii.148
2 overburdened, overstocked, overfilled **TG** I.i.101 [Speed to Proteus, of Julia being compared to a sheep] *If the ground be overcharged, you were best stick her*
3 overloaded, filled too full of powder **2H6** III.ii.331 [Queen to Suffolk, of his curses] *like an overcharged gun, recoil / And turns the force of them upon thyself*

overcloyed (adj.) overfilled, satiated, stuffed to busting **R3** V.iii.319 [King Richard to his army, of the enemy] *A scum of Britains … / Whom their o'ercloyed country vomits forth*

overcome (v.) suddenly come over, swiftly pass across **Mac** III.iv.110 [Macbeth to Lady Macbeth, of Banquo's ghost] *Can such things be, / And overcome us like a summer's cloud*

overcount (v.) outnumber, exceed in number **AC** II.vi.26 [Antony to Pompey] *At land thou know'st / How much we do o'ercount thee* [pun: 27, cheat]

overcover (v.) cover up, bury **RJ** IV.i.82 [Juliet to Friar] *hide me nightly in a charnel house, / O'ercovered quite with dead men's rattling bones*

over-crow (v.) overpower, overwhelm, triumph over **Ham** V.ii.347 [Hamlet to Horatio] *The potent poison quite o'er-crows my spirit*

overdo (v.) outdo, surpass, surpass **Ham** III.ii.13 [Hamlet to Players, of a player] *whipped for o'erdoing Termagant*

over-dusted (adj.) covered over with dust **TC** III.iii.179 [Ulysses to Achilles] *all … give to dust that is a little gilt / More laud than gilt o'er-dusted* [i.e. consigned to oblivion]

over-dyed (adj.) dyed over with another colour **WT** I.ii.132 [Leontes to Mamillius, of women saying that he and his son are alike] *were they false / As o'er-dyed blacks … yet were it true*

over-eaten (adj.) eaten away all over, gnawed at on all sides **TC** V.ii.163 [Troilus to Ulysses, of Cressida] *The … greasy relics / Of her o'er-eaten faith, are bound to Diomed*

over-eye (v.) watch, observe; or: look too much at **TS** Induction.i.93 [Lord to First Player, of Sly] *over-eyeing of his odd behaviour*; **LL** IV.iii.78

over-far (adv.) too far, to too great an extent **TN** II.i.24 [Sebastian to Antonio, of Viola's beauty] *I could not with such estimable wonder over-far believe that*

over-flourished (adj.) heavily embellished, richly decorated **TN** III.iv.361 [Antonio to First Officer] *the beauteous evil / Are empty trunks o'erflourished by the devil*

overflow (v.) **1** flood, become inundated **Tit** III.i.220 [Titus to Marcus] *When heaven doth weep, doth not the earth o'erflow?*; **Tit** III.i.228
2 overwhelm, destroy, defeat **AW** IV.iii.24 [Second Lord to First Lord] *he that in this action contrives against his own nobility, in his proper stream o'erflows himself*

3 pour out, overflow with **MW** II.ii.147 [Falstaff alone, of being given a drink by Ford as Brook] *Such Brooks are welcome to me, that o'erflows such liquor*

over-fly (*v.*) fly past, overtake in flight **Venus** 324 [of the jennet and Adonis' horse] *mad, unto the wood they hie them, / Out-stripping crows that strive to over-fly them*

overfraught (*adj.*) too heavily laden, overburdened **Mac** IV.iii.210 [Malcolm to Macduff] *the grief that does not speak / Whispers the o'erfraught heart and bids it break*

overgalled (*adj.*) badly swollen, heavily inflamed **TC** V.iii.55 [Troilus to Hector, of Priam and Hecuba] *Their eyes o'ergalled with recourse of tears*

overglance (*v.*) glance over, cast the eye over **LL** IV.ii.130 [Holofernes to Jaquenetta] *I will overglance the superscript;* **H5** V.ii.78

overgo (*v.*) **1** exceed, surmount, go beyond **R3** II.ii.61 [Duchess of York to Queen Elizabeth] *what cause have I … / To overgo thy woes;* **Sonn** 103.7

2 travel through, pass over, traverse **LL** V.ii.196 [masked Rosaline to masked Berowne] *Of many weary miles you have o'ergone*

overgone (*adj.*) worn out, overcome, exhausted **3H6** II.v.123 [King to himself, of the Father and Son who killed their Son and Father] *Sad-hearted men, much overgone with care*

overgorged (*adj.*) gorged to excess, overfed, glutted **2H6** IV.i.84 [Lieutenant to Suffolk] *overgorged / With gobbets of thy mother's bleeding heart*

over-great (*adj.*) imperious, high-handed, excessive **H8** I.i.222 [Buckingham to all] *My surveyor is false. The o'er-great Cardinal / Hath showed him gold*

over-green (*v.*) cover over, gloss over, whitewash **Sonn** 112.4 *So you o'er-green my bad, my good allow?*

overgrown (*adj.*) covered with growth [i.e. hair] **Cym** IV.iv.33 [Guiderius to Belarius] *yourself / So out of thought, and thereto so o'ergrown* [or: grown out of memory]

overhear (*v.*) hear told over, hear again **LL** V.ii.95 [Boyet to Princess] *I … overheard what you shall overhear*

overhold (*v.*) overestimate, overvalue, rate too highly **TC** II.iii.132 [Agamemnon to Patroclus, of Achilles] *if he overhold his price so much, / We'll none of him*

overjoy (*n.*) excess of happiness, great rejoicing **2H6** I.i.31 [Queen to King, of her speech] *ruder terms, such as my wit affords, / And overjoy of heart doth minister*

over-laboured (*adj.*) overworked, overburdened, exhausted by work **Cym** II.ii.11 [Iachimo to himself] *man's o'er-laboured sense / Repairs itself by rest*

overleap (*v.*) **1** pass over, pass by , skip **Cor** II.ii.134 [Coriolanus to Menenius, of talking to the people] *Let me o'erleap that custom*

2 leap over, jump across **Mac** I.iv.50 [Macbeth to himself, of Cumberland's elevation] *That is a step / On which I must fall down, or else o'erleap*

3 leap too far, overshoot **Mac** I.vii.27 [Macbeth alone] *Vaulting ambition which o'erleaps itself*

overleather (*n.*) leather in the upper part of a shoe **TS** Induction.ii.11 [Sly to Servingmen] *such shoes as my toes look through the overleather*

over-leaven (*v.*) leaven too much, pervade, imbue to excess **Ham** I.iv.29 [Hamlet to Horatio] *some habit that too much o'er-leavens / The form of plausive manners*

overlive (*v.*) survive, outlive, outlast **2H4** IV.i.15 [Archbishop to Hastings and Mowbray, of Northumberland's hopes] *That your attempts may overlive the hazard / And fearful meeting of their opposite*

overlook (*v.*) **1** look over, peruse, read through **TG** I.ii.50 [Julia alone] *I would I had o'erlooked the letter;* **Ham** IV.vi.14; **H5** II.iv.90; **KL** V.i.50; **MND** II.ii.127

2 rise above, look down on **Tit** II.i.8 [Aaron alone, of the sun] *overlooks the highest-peering hills;* **H5** III.v.9; **Venus** 178

3 inspect, superintend, oversee **R3** III.v.17 [Richard to Catesby] *o'erlook the walls;* **Per** I.ii.48

4 bewitch, subject to magic **MV** III.ii.15 [Portia to Bassanio, of his eyes] *They have o'erlooked me and divided me;* **MW** V.v.83

5 overflow, rise above, exceed **KJ** V.iv.55 [Salisbury to Melun, of the once rebel lords as a river] *Stoop low within those bounds we have o'erlooked*

overlooking (*n.*) **1** perusal, inspection, scrutiny **KL** I.ii.39 [Edmund to Gloucester, of the letter] *I find it not fit for your o'erlooking*

2 guardianship, looking after, custody **AW** I.i.38 [Countess to Lafew, of Helena] *bequeathed to my overlooking*

over-lusty (*adj.*) **1** too vigorous, over-active **KL** II.iv.9 [Fool to Lear] *When a man's over-lusty at legs, then he wears wooden nether-stocks* ➤ **lusty** (*adj.*) 1

2 over-cheerful, excessively merry **H5** IV.Chorus.18 [Chorus] *secure in soul, / The confident and over-lusty French / Do the low-rated English play at dice* ➤ **lusty** (*adj.*) 2

overmaster (*v.*) **1** overcome, control, master completely **Ham** I.v.140 [Hamlet to Horatio and Marcellus] *For your desire to know what is between us, / O'ermaster't as you may*

2 usurp, take by force, hold in one's power **KJ** II.i.109 [King Philip to King John, of Arthur] *Which owe the crown that thou o'ermasterest*

overmatched (*adj.*) outnumbered, faced with superior strength **3H6** I.iv.64 [York to and of his enemies] *So true men yield, with robbers so o'ermatched;* **1H6** IV.iv.11

overmatching (*adj.*) overwhelming, of superior power **3H6** I.iv.21 [York alone] *I have seen a swan … spend her strength with overmatching waves*

overmount (*v.*) transcend, rise above, soar higher than **H8** II.iii.94 [Old Lady to Anne, of her advancement] *With your theme I could / O'ermount the lark* [i.e. sing louder than the lark]

over-mounting (*adj.*) mounting too high, over-ambitious **1H6** IV.vii.15 [Talbot to Servant, of John Talbot] *in that sea of blood my boy did drench / His over-mounting spirit*

overname (*v.*) name in succession, read through the list of **MV** I.ii.34 [Portia to Nerissa, of the suitors] *I pray thee overname them*

overnight (*n.*) previous evening, night before **Tim** IV.iii.228 [Apemantus to Timon] *Will the cold brook … caudle thy morning taste, / To cure thy o'ernight's surfeit?*

overnight, at last night, yesterday evening **AW** III.iv.23 [Steward to Countess, of Helena's letter] *If I had given you this at overnight*

over-office (*v.*) ➤ **overreach** (*v.*) 3

overparted (*adj.*) unequal to the part, having too difficult a part to play **LL** V.ii.581 [Costard to all, of Nathaniel's ability to play his role] *for Alisander … a little o'erparted*

overpass (*v.*) spend, pass, live out **1H6** II.v.117 [Richard to Mortimer] *In prison hast thou spent a pilgrimage, / And like a hermit overpassed thy days*

overpast (*adj.*) past, now ended, former **R3** IV.iv.396 [Queen Elizabeth to King Richard, of time to come] *that thou hast / Misused ere used, by times ill-used o'erpast* [Q; F repast]

overpeer (*v.*) **1** look down on, look out over, overlook **3H6** V.ii.14 [Warwick alone, of the cedar] *Whose top branch over-peered Jove's spreading tree;* **1H6** I.iv.11; **MV** I.i.12

2 rise above, tower over **Ham** IV.v.101 [Messenger to Claudius] *The ocean, overpeering of his list;* **Cor** II.iii.120

overperch (*v.*) fly over, surmount **RJ** II.ii.66 [Romeo to Juliet] *With love's light wings did I o'erperch these walls*

overpicture (*v.*) surpass, outdo, excel **AC** II.ii.205 [Enobarbus to Agrippa and Maecenas, of Cleopatra] *O'erpicturing that Venus where we see / The fancy outwork nature*

overplus (n.) surplus, excess, superfluity AC III.vii.50 [Antony to all] *Our overplus of shipping will we burn*; Sonn 135.2

overplus (adj.) additional , extra, further AC IV.vi.22 [Soldier to Enobarbus] *Antony / Hath after thee sent all thy treasure, with / His bounty overplus*

overpost (v.) pass over, disregard, overlook [of] 2H4 I.ii.152 [Lord Chief Justice to Falstaff, of the exploit at Gad's Hill] *You may thank th'unquiet time for your quiet o'erposting that action* ➤ post over (v.)

overpressed (adj.) overpowered, overwhelmed, overcome Sonn 139.8 *thy might / Is more than my o'erpressed defence can bide?*; Cor II.ii.91; Per III.ii.82

over-prize (v.) overvalue, overrate, overestimate Tem I.ii.92 [Prospero to Miranda, of his studies] *which … / O'er-prized all popular rate* [i.e. were more valuable than people rate them]

overproud (adj.) excessively swollen, too luxuriant R2 III.iv.59 [Gardener to First Man, of fruit trees] *being overproud in sap and blood*

over-rank (adj.) over-ripe; rotten, corrupted TNK V.i.63 [Arcite praying to Mars] *Shaker of o'er-rank states* ➤ rank (adj.) 3

overraught (v.) ➤ overreach (v.)

overreach, over-reach (v.), past form **overraught** 1 outwit, outdo, cheat E3 V.i.26 [King Edward to Calais Citizens] *you cannot overreach us thus*; Tit V.ii.143; TS III.ii.144
  2 overtake, come up with, pass by Ham III.i.17 [Rosencrantz to Gertrude] *certain players / We o'er-raught on the way*
  3 get the better of, has the advantage of Ham V.i.78 [Hamlet to Horatio, of a skull] *This might be the pate of a politician, which this ass now o'erreaches* [Q2 ore-reaches; F o'er-offices = lord it over]

overreaching (n.) deception, exaggeration, fabrication MW V.v.135 [Falstaff to all, of his brain] *it wants matter to prevent so gross o'erreaching as this*

over-read (v.) read over, read through KL I.ii.38 [Edmund to Gloucester] *a letter from my brother that I have not all o'er-read*; 2H4 III.i.2; JC III.i.4

over-red (v.) cover over with blood, redden over Mac V.iii.14 [Macbeth to Servant] *Go prick thy face and over-red thy fear*

overridden (adj.) ridden too hard, exhausted after too much riding E3 III.iii.162 [King John to the French, of the English] *they are as resty-stiff / As 'twere a many overridden jades*

over-ride (v.) outride, outstrip 2H4 I.i.30 [Lord Bardolph to Northumberland, of Travers] *I over-rode him on the way*

overrule (v.) prevail, overcome, win over 1H6 II.ii.50 [Talbot to Burgundy] *when a world of men / Could not prevail with all their oratory / Yet hath a woman's kindness overruled*

overrun (v.) 1 review, go over, make an overview of 3H6 I.iv.45 [York to Clifford] *in thy thought o'errun my former time*
  2 flow over, stream down TS Induction.ii.64 [First Servingman to Sly, of his supposed wife's tears] *Like envious floods o'errun her lovely face*

overscutched (adj.) [unclear meaning] well-beaten, often whipped 2H4 III.ii.306 [Falstaff alone, of Shallow] *'A … sung those tunes to the overscutched housewives that he heard the carmen whistle*

oversee (v.) be executor of, officially look after Luc 1205 [Lucrece as if to Collatine] *Thou … shalt oversee this will*

overseen (adj.) betrayed, deceived, deluded Luc 1206 [Lucrece as if to Collatine] *Thou … shalt oversee this will; / How was I overseen that thou shalt see it!*

overset (v.) 1 overthrow, overcome, defeat 2H4 I.i.185 [Lord Bardolph to Northumberland] *since we are o'erset, [we] venture again*
  2 overturn, capsize, overwhelm RJ III.v.136 [Capulet to Juliet] *The winds, thy sighs … / Without a sudden calm will overset / Thy tempest-tossed body*

overshade (v.) overshadow, cast a gloom over WT I.ii.457 [Polixenes to Camillo] *Fear o'ershades me*; 3H6 II.vi.62

overshine, over-shine (v.) 1 outshine, surpass, excel 2H4 IV.iii.50 [Falstaff to Prince John] *I in the clear sky of fame o'ershine you*
  2 shine upon, light up, illuminate 3H6 II.i.38 [Edward to Richard, of York's three sons] *Should … join our lights together / And over-shine the earth*

overshoes, over-shoes (adj.) (plural) shoe-deep, following a reckless course TG I.i.24 [Proteus to Valentine, of Leander] *he was more than over-shoes in love* [i.e. completely immersed in love]; ➤ over-boots (adj.)

overshoes, over-shoes (adv.) deep enough to cover the shoes CE III.ii.108 [Dromio of Syracuse to Antipholus of Syracuse, of the kitchen wench] *She sweats a man may go overshoes in the grime of it* [i.e. because of the amount of sweat]

overshoot (v.) 1 [miss a target by shooting too high] go astray in aim, wide of the mark JC III.ii.151 [Antony to all, of Caesar's will] *I have o'ershot myself to tell you of it*; H5 III.vii.121; LL I.i.140, IV.iii.158
  2 shoot ahead of, run out of reach of Venus 680 [Venus to Adonis, of the hunted hare] *Mark … to overshoot his troubles, / How he outruns the wind*

over-sized (adj.) painted over, smeared [i.e. covered with a substance resembling size] Ham II.ii.460 [Hamlet to First Player, quoting lines about Pyrrhus] *o'er-sized with coagulate gore* ➤ blood-sized (adj.)

overskip (v.) pass over without noticing, jump lightly over KL III.vi.104 [Edgar alone] *the mind much sufferance doth o'erskip*

overslip (v.) pass by unnoticed, slip past TG II.ii.9 [Proteus to Julia] *when that hour o'erslips me in the day / Wherein I sigh not*; Luc 1576

oversnow (v.) snow over, make white with snow Sonn 5.8 *Beauty o'ersnowed and bareness everywhere*

overspent (adj.) spent, finished, at an end E3 V.i.61 [King Edward to all] *We would, till gloomy winter were o'erspent, / Dispose our men in garrison a while*

overstain (v.) cover with stains, smear over KJ III.i.236 [King Philip to Cardinal Pandulph, of French and English hands] *they were besmeared and overstained / With slaughter's pencil*

overstare (v.) outstare, face down MV II.i.27 [Morocco to Portia] *I would o'erstare the sternest eyes that look*

overstink (v.) stink worse than, drown the smell of Tem IV.i.184 [Ariel to Prospero, of Stephano, Trinculo, and Caliban] *the foul lake / O'erstunk their feet*

overstrawed (adj.) strewn about, sprinkled over Venus 1143 [Venus to dead Adonis, of love] *The bottom poison, and the top o'erstrawed / With sweets that shall the truest sight beguile*

oversway (v.) prevail upon, override, overturn JC II.i.203 [Decius to all, of Caesar] *If he be so resolved, / I can o'ersway him*; Ham V.i.224; LL V.ii.67; Sonn 65.2; Venus 109

overswear (v.) swear over again TN V.i.266 [Viola to Orsino, of her previous attestations] *all those sayings will I overswear*

over-swell (v.) flood, inundate, overflow JC IV.iii.159 [Cassius to Lucius] *Fill, Lucius, till the wine o'erswell the cup*; H5 II.ii.89; KJ II.i.337

overtake (v.) 1 accomplish, achieve, fulfil Mac IV.i.144 [Macbeth to himself] *The flighty purpose never is o'ertook / Unless the deed go with it*
  2 catch up to, come up with KL IV.i.42 [Gloucester to Old Man] *If for my sake / Thou wilt o'ertake us hence a mile or twain / I'the way toward Dover*
  3 surpass, outdo, rival Cor I.ix.19 [Martius to Lartius] *He that has but effected his good will / Hath overta'en mine act*
  4 drunkenly overcome, overpowered by drink Ham II.i.58 [Polonius to Reynaldo, of Laertes] *there o'ertook in's rouse*

over-teemed (adj.) excessively productive, exhausted by child-bearing **Ham** II.ii.506 [First Player to all present, of Hecuba] *About her lank and all o'er-teemed loins*

overthrow (*v.*) defeat, destroy, vanquish **1H6** V.iv.105 [Richard to all] *So many … / That in this quarrel have been overthrown*

overthrown (*adj.*) ruined, disgraced, brought into disrepute **MW** III.iii.90 [Mistress Page to Mistress Ford] *you're overthrown*

overtop (*v.*) excel, surpass, go beyond the (normal) level of **TC** III.iii.164 [Ulysses to Achilles, of others] *what they do in present, / Though less than yours in past, must o'ertop yours;* **H8** II.iv.88

over-topping getting above oneself, becoming too ambitious **Tem** I.ii.81 [Prospero to Miranda, of people in court] *who t'advance, and who / To trash for over-topping*

overtrip (*v.*) skip over, pass lightly over **MV** V.i.7 [Jessica to Lorenzo] *In such a night / Did Thisbe fearfully o'ertrip the dew*

overture (*n.*) **1** disclosure, revelation **TN** I.v.201 [Viola as Cesario to Olivia] *I bring no overture of war;* **KL** III.vii.88; **WT** II.i.172
2 opening, aperture **Cor** I.ix.46 [Martius to all, of the flatterer] *let him be made / An overture for th'wars* [i.e. the one who leads the attack] [disputed reading] ☞ coverture (*n.*) 3, ovator (*n.*)

overvalue (*v.*) exceed in value **Cym** I.v.106 [Iachimo to Posthumus] *I dare … pawn the moiety of my estate, to your ring, which in my opinion o'ervalues it something*

over-walk (*v.*) walk over, cross by walking **1H4** I.iii.190 [Worcester to Northumberland and Hotspur] *to o'er-walk a current roaring loud / On the unsteadfast footing of a spear*

overwatch (*v.*) stay up late, remain awake **MND** V.i.356 [Theseus to all] *I fear we shall outsleep the coming morn / As much as we this night have overwatched*

overwatched (*adj.*) wearied from too much watching, exhausted from lack of sleep **JC** IV.iii.239 [Brutus to Lucius] *thou art o'erwatched;* **KL** II.ii.168

overweathered (*adj.*) weather-worn, storm-damaged **MV** II.vi.18 [Gratiano to Salerio, of a ship returning] *With over-weathered ribs and ragged sails*

overween (*v.*) **1** presume too much, go too far **Tit** II.i.29 [Chiron to Demetrius] *thou dost overween in all;* **2H4** IV.i.147; **3H6** III.ii.144
2 presume, venture, take the liberty **WT** IV.ii.8 [Camillo to Polixenes, of Leontes] *to whose feeling sorrows I might be some allay - or I o'erween to think so*

overweening (*adj.*) arrogant, overambitious, high and mighty **TN** II.v.29 [Sir Toby to Sir Andrew and Fabian, of Malvolio] *Here's an overweening rogue!;* **E3** III.i.58; **2H6** III.i.159; **R2** I.i.147; **R3** V.iii.329; **TG** III.i.157

overweigh (*v.*) outweigh, exceed, prevail over **MM** II.iv.170 [Angelo to Isabella] *my false o'erweighs your true;* **Ham** III.ii.27; **MM** II.iv.157; **TNK** II.iv.19

overwhelming (*adj.*) overhanging, bulging, protruding **RJ** V.i.39 [Romeo alone, of an apothecary] *with overwhelming brows*

overworn (*adj.*) **1** faded, worn out, worse for wear **R3** I.i.81 [Richard to Clarence, of Queen Elizabeth] *The jealous o'erworn widow;* **Sonn** 63.2; **Venus** 135
2 used up, spent **Venus** 866 [of Venus] *Musing the morning is so much o'erworn*

over-wrested (*adj.*) overstrained, overdone, over-the-top **TC** I.iii.157 [Ulysses to Agamemnon, of Patroclus] *Such … o'er-wrested seeming / He acts thy greatness in*

over-wrestle (*v.*) surpass, outdo, exceed **TNK** I.iv.45 [Theseus to all, of different events] *sickness in will / O'er-wrestling strength in reason* [? = a sick person's will-power can exceed a strong-person's force of reason as to what is possible] [Q *Or wrastling*]

owe (*v.*) **1** own, possess, have **AW** II.v.79 [Helena to Bertram] *I am not worthy of the wealth I owe* ☞ FEW, p.xxi
2 repay, compensate, pay back **Cor** III.i.241 [Menenius to Coriolanus] *One time will owe another;* **MA** V.iv.52
3 have in store for, hold towards **Cor** V.vi.139 [Aufidius to Lords, of Coriolanus] *the great danger / Which this man's life did owe you*

owlet, howlet (*n.*) young owl, owl **Mac** IV.i.17 [Second Witch to Witches] *Lizard's leg and howlet's wing;* **TNK** III.v.68

ox (*n.*) fool, dupe **MW** V.v.120 [Ford to Falstaff, replying to Falstaff's 'I am made an ass'] *Ay, and an ox too*

O-yea (*n.*) [unclear meaning] public crier [who shouts Oyez, 'Hear ye'] **1H4** II.i.77 [Gadshill to Chamberlain] *I am joined … with Burgomasters and great O-yeas* [unclear reading] [Qo, Q1 *Oneyres;* F *Oneyers*]

oyes, oyez (*n.*) hear ye [town crier's 'Oyez'] **MW** V.v.41 [Mistress Quickly as Queen of Fairies to Pistol as Hobgoblin] *Crier Hobgoblin, make the fairy oyes;* **TC** IV.v.143

pace *(n.)* **1** way of walking, gait **Per** V.i.111 [Pericles to himself, of Marina] *In pace another Juno;* **R2** V.ii.10; **Venus** 294

2 obedient movement, trained walk **AW** IV.v.65 [Countess to Lafew, of the Clown] *he has no pace, but runs where he will*

pace *(v.)* **1** [horse-training] break in, teach one paces, properly train **H8** V.iii.22 [Gardiner to the Councillors] *those that tame wild horses / Pace 'em not in their hands to make 'em gentle;* **Per** IV.vi.59

2 train to move, control the course of **MM** IV.iii.131 [disguised Duke to Isabella] *pace your wisdom / In that good path that I would wish it go;* **AC** II.ii.68

3 move on, proceed, pass on **WT** IV.i.23 [Time to audience] *I … with speed so pace / To speak of Perdita*

pacify *(v.)* stay quiet; or: malapropism for 'satisfy' [= be assured] **2H4** II.iv.78 [Hostess to Falstaff] *pacify yourself, Sir John*

pack *(n.)* **1** gang, group, circle, confederacy **R3** III.iii.4 [Grey to Ratcliffe, of him and his associates] *God bless the Prince from all the pack of you!;* **CE** IV.iv.100; **KL** V.iii.18; **MW** IV.ii.111

2 knapsack, back-pack, bundle **2H6** IV.ii.45 [Smith aside to his companions, of Cade's wife] *not able to travel with her furred pack* [with bawdy pun]

pack *(v.)* **1** take [oneself] off, be off, depart **E3** IV.v.109 [King John to Salisbury] *Then to Calais pack;* **2H6** III.ii.111; **H8** I.iii.33; **KL** II.iv.76; **MV** II.ii.9; **TS** II.i.177

2 plot, scheme, intrigue **Cym** III.v.81 [Cloten to Pisanio] *are you packing, sirrah?;* **Ham** III.iv.212

3 enter into a private arrangement, make a secret deal **Tit** IV.ii.154 [Aaron to Demetrius and Chiron, of Muly] *Go pack with him and give the mother gold*

4 arrange, rig, shuffle cheatingly **AC** IV.xiv.19 [Antony to Eros, of Cleopatra] *she … has / Packed cards with Caesar*

5 load up, load with goods **1H4** II.i.3 [First Carrier, alone] *yet our horse not packed;* **2H4** IV.v.77

packed *(adj.)* in league, acting as an accomplice **MA** V.i.286 [Leonato to Don Pedro, of Margaret] *Who I believe was packed in all this wrong;* **CE** V.i.219

packhorse *(n.)* work-horse, drudge, toiler **R3** I.iii.121 [Richard to Queen Elizabeth, of King Edward] *I was a packhorse in his great affairs;* **Luc** 928

packing *(n.)* plotting, contriving, underhand dealing **TS** V.i.107 [Gremio to all] *Here's packing, with a witness, to deceive us all;* **KL** III.i.26

packing *(adj.)* furtive, underhand, plotting **E3** II.ii.165 [Countess to King Edward] *The universal sessions calls to 'count / This packing evil*

packthread, pack-thread *(n.)* twine used for tying up bundles, string **RJ** V.i.47 [Romeo alone, of an apothecary] *about his shelves … / Remnants of packthread;* **TS** III.ii.61

paction *(n.)* compact, agreement, treaty **H5** V.ii.357 [Queen Isabel to King Henry and Katherine] *never may ill office, or fell jealousy … / Thrust in between the paction of these kingdoms* [F *Pation*]

paddle *(v.)* toy [with], play wantonly [with], fondle **Ham** III.iv.186 [Hamlet to Gertrude, of Claudius] *paddling in your neck with his damned fingers;* **Oth** II.i.247; **WT** I.ii.115

paddock, padock *(n.)* toad **Ham** III.iv.191 [Hamlet to Gertrude] *[who would] from a paddock … / Such dear concernings hide?;* **Mac** I.i.8

pagan *(n.)* prostitute, whore **2H4** II.ii.147 [Prince Henry to Page, of Doll] *What pagan may that be?*

pagan *(adj.)* unbelieving, faithless, doubting **1H4** II.iii.30 [Hotspur alone, to the writer of a letter he is reading] *What a pagan rascal is this*

page *(v.)* follow like a page **Tim** IV.iii.225 [Apemantus to Timon] *Will these moist trees … page thy heels*

pageant *(n.)* show, scene, spectacle, tableau **R2** IV.i.320 [Abbot of Westminster to all] *A woeful pageant have we here beheld;* **AC** IV.xiv.8; **AY** II.vii.139; **2H6** I.ii.67; **MND** III.ii.114; **TC** III.iii.272

pageant (*v.*) imitate as if in a play, impersonate, parody TC I.iii.151 [Ulysses to all, of Patroclus] *He pageants us*

pain (*n.*) effort, endeavour, exertion, labour R3 V.iii.259 [Richmond to his soldiers] *Your country's fat shall pay your pains the hire;* Cym III.iii.50; 2H6 I.iv.43; MV II.ii.172; Per III.ii.24; Tem I.ii.242

pain of, in (*prep.*) on pain of, under the penalty of 2H6 III.ii.257 [Salisbury to King] *In pain of your dislike, or pain of death*

pained (*adj.*) tormented, distressed, persecuted Per IV.vi.161 [Marina to Boult] *the pained'st fiend of hell;* LL V.ii.843

painful (*adj.*) **1** painstaking, diligent, laborious TS V.ii.148 [Katherina to Widow, of her husband's role] *commits his body / To painful labour;* Cor V.v.71; E3 IV.ii.44; Per III.Chorus.15; Sonn 25.9; Tem III.i.1 [or: sense 2]
  2 suffering from pain, causing hurt E3 V.i.230 [Prince Edward to King Edward, of future ages] *when they read / The painful traffic of my tender youth;* Tem III.i.1
  3 inflicting pain, harmful, afflicting E3 V.i.237 [King Edward to all] *we do proclaim a rest, / An intercession of our painful arms* [also: sense 1]
  4 arduous, gruelling, taxing H5 IV.iii.111 [King Henry to Montjoy] *Our gayness and our gilt are all besmirched / With rainy marching in the painful field*

painfully (*adv.*) diligently, taking great pains LL I.i.74 [Berowne to King, of delights] *As painfully to pore upon a book;* KJ I.i.223; Tim V.ii.1

paint (*v.*) adorn, beautify, enhance Sonn 62.14 *Painting my age with beauty of thy days;* Ham V.i.190; JC III.i.63; TNK II.i.193

paint out (*v.*) display, depict fully, portray MA III.ii.98 [Don John to Claudio, of Hero] *The word is too good to paint out her wickedness*

painted (*adj.*) **1** colourful, multicoloured TS IV.iii.174 [Petruchio to Katherina, of the adder] *his painted skin contents the eye;* AY II.i.3; TC III.ii.13; TNK II.i.65
  2 unreal, artificial, superficial R3 IV.iv.83 [Queen Margaret to Queen Elizabeth] *I called thee ... poor shadow, painted queen;* LL IV.iii.237; R3 I.iii.240; Tim IV.ii.36
  3 feigned, counterfeit, disguised H8 V.iii.71 [Gardiner to Cranmer] *Your painted gloss discovers, / To men that understand you, words and weakness;* Ham III.i.53; KJ III.i.105
  4 depicted, represented [as on a sign] Tem II.ii.28 [Trinculo to himself, of Caliban] *had [I] but this fish painted, not a holiday fool there but would give a piece of silver*
  5 frozen, motionless [as in a painting] Ham II.ii.478 [First Player to all present] *So as a painted tyrant Pyrrhus stood*

painting (*n.*) **1** cosmetics, paint [for the face], beautifying Sonn 83.1 *I never saw that you did painting need;* Cym III.iv.51; Ham III.i.143; H8 I.i.26; LL IV.iii.257, 261
  2 paint, pigment, colour WT V.iii.83 [Paulina to Leontes, of kissing Hermione's statue] *You'll ... stain your own [lips] / With oily painting*

pair of, a few, two or three Ham III.iv.185 [Hamlet to Gertrude] *a pair of reechy kisses*

pair of stairs flight of stairs AY V.ii.36 [Rosalind as Ganymede to Orlando, of Celia as Aliena and Oliver] *have they made a pair of stairs to marriage*

pair-taunt-like (*adv.*) like a winning hand in the card game 'post and pair' LL V.ii.67 [Rosaline to Princess, of Berowne] *So pair-taunt-like would I o'ersway his state / That he should be my fool* [F *pertaunt-like*]

pajock (*n.*) [unclear meaning] savage, degenerate; or, peacock Ham III.ii.293 [Hamlet to Horatio] *now reigns here / A very, very - pajock* [reading of F *Paiocke;* Q2 *paiock*]

palate (*v.*) **1** relish, enjoy AC V.ii.7 [Cleopatra to all] *it is great / To do that thing ... / Which sleeps, and never palates more the dung;* TC IV.i.60

2 present a flavour to, savour of Cor III.i.104 [Coriolanus to Senators, of them and the Tribunes] *both your voices blended, the great'st taste / Most palates theirs* [i.e. the dominant voices will be from the people rather than the patricians]

pale (*n.*) **1** fence, paling, enclosure 1H6 IV.ii.45 [Talbot to all] *How we are parked and bounded in a pale;* CE II.i.100; Ham I.iv.28; H8 V.iv.89; TC II.iii.246; Venus 230
  2 fenced land, park, enclosure MND II.i.4 [Fairy to Puck, in response to 'whither wander you?'] *Over park, over pale*
  3 paleness, pallor [of the cheeks] Venus 589 [of Venus] *a sudden pale ... / Usurps her cheek;* WT IV.iii.4

pale (*adj.*) wan, fearful, pale-hearted H5 II.Chorus.14 [Chorus] *The French ... with pale policy / Seek to divert the English purposes;* AY I.iii.102; H5 V.ii.342; Mac III.ii.50

pale (*v.*) **1** enclose, surround, encompass AC II.vii.68 [Menas to Pompey] *Whate'er the ocean pales, or sky inclips;* 3H6 I.iv.103
  2 dim, make pale Ham I.v.90 [Ghost to Hamlet] *The glow-worm ... 'gins to pale his uneffectual fire*

pale in (*v.*) fence in, hem in, enclose Cym III.i.20 [Queen to Cymbeline, of Britain] *ribbed and paled in / With rocks unscaleable and roaring waters;* H5 V.Chorus.10

paled (*adj.*) pale, white, colourless Lover 198 *paled pearls and rubies red as blood* [Q *palyd*]

pale-visaged (*adj.*) pale-faced KJ V.ii.154 [Bastard to rebel lords] *your own ladies and pale-visaged maids, / Like Amazons, come tripping after drums*

palfrey (*n.*) horse for everyday riding H5 III.vii.26 [Dauphin to Orleans, of his horse] *It is the prince of palfreys;* 2H6 IV.i.65; Tit V.ii.50; Venus 384

palisado (*n.*) palisade, defensive position using pointed stakes 1H4 II.iii.54 [Lady Percy to Hotspur] *thou hast talked / Of ... palisadoes*

pall (*v.*) **1** fail, miscarry, abort Ham V.ii.9 [Hamlet to Horatio] *Our indiscretion sometime serves us well / When our deep plots do pall* [reading of F *paule;* Q2 *fall*]
  2 wrap, cover, drape Mac I.v.49 [Lady Macbeth alone] *Come, thick night, / And pall thee in the dunnest smoke of hell*

palled (*adj.*) decayed, weakened, enfeebled AC II.vii.81 [Menas to himself, as if to Pompey] *I'll never follow thy palled fortunes more*

pallet (*n.*) bed, straw mattress 2H4 III.i.10 [King Henry IV alone, of people sleeping] *in smoky cribs, / Upon uneasy pallets*

palliament (*n.*) robe, gown [of someone aspiring to Roman consulship] Tit I.i.185 [Marcus to Titus] *This palliament of white and spotless hue*

palm (*n.*) **1** palm leaf as a symbol of victory JC I.ii.131 [Cassius to Brutus, of Caesar] *it doth amaze me / A man of such a feeble temper should ... bear the palm alone;* Cor III.i.117
  2 praise, honour, esteem TC III.i.154 [Helen to Paris, of Hector] *what he shall receive of us in duty / Gives us more palm in beauty than we have;* TC II.iii.189

palmer (*n.*) pilgrim Luc 791 [Lucrece to herself] *fellowship in woe doth woe assuage, / As palmers' chat makes short their pilgrimage;* AW III.v.34; 2H6 V.i.97; R2 III.iii.151; RJ I.v.100

palmy (*adj.*) flourishing, triumphant Ham I.i.113 [Horatio to Barnardo and Marcellus, comparing Denmark to ancient Rome] *In the most high and palmy state of Rome* [i.e. worthy to bear the palm of triumph]

palpable (*adj.*) evident, obvious, apparent Ham V.ii.275 [Osrick to all] *A hit, a very palpable hit;* E3 III.i.143; R3 III.vi.11

palpable-gross (*adj.*) obviously clumsy, plainly ignorant MND V.i.357 [Theseus to all] *This palpable-gross play hath well beguiled / The heavy gait of night* ☞ **gross** (*adj.*) 9

palsy (*n.*) shaking fit, tremor, paralysis TC V.i.19 [Thersites to Patroclus] *diseases of the south ... lethargies, cold palsies, and the like*

palsy *(adj.)* palsied, trembling, shaking **TC** I.iii.174 [Ulysses to all, of Patroclus impersonating Nestor] *with a palsy fumbling on his gorget*

palter *(v.)* prevaricate, deal evasively [with], quibble **JC** II.i.126 [Brutus to all, of their group] *secret Romans that have spoke the word, / And will not palter;* **AC** III.xi.63; **Mac** V.vi.59; **TC** II.iii.230, V.ii.49

paltering *(n.)* evasiveness, equivocation, trickery **Cor** III.i.58 [Cominius to all] *This paltering / Becomes not Rome*

paly *(adj.)* **1** pallid, bloodless, colourless **2H6** III.ii.141 [King to himself, of dead Gloucester] *Fain would I go to chafe his paly lips / With twenty thousand kisses*
2 pale, faint **H5** IV.Chorus.8 [Chorus] *Fire answers fire, and through their paly flames, / Each battle sees the other's umbered face*

pamphlet *(n.)* document, text **1H6** III.i.2 [Winchester to Gloucester] *Comest thou … / With written pamphlets studiously devised?*

pander *(v.)* gratify, act as a sexual go-between for **Ham** III.iv.89 [Hamlet to Gertrude] *reason panders will* [F; Q2 *pardons*]

pander, pandar *(n.)* pimp, procurer, go-between **TC** III.ii.201 [Pandarus to Cressida and Troilus] *Let … all brokers-between [be called] Pandars!;* **Cym** III.iv.31; **H5** IV.v.14; **KL** II.ii.19; **MW** V.v.165; **WT** II.i.46

panderly *(adj.)* pimping, procuring, go-between **MW** IV.ii.111 [Ford to John and Robert] *O you panderly rascals!*

pang *(v.)* afflict with pangs, torture, torment **H8** II.iii.15 [Anne to Old Lady, of losing pomp] *'tis a sufferance panging / As soul and body's severing;* **Cym** III.iv.97

pantaloon *(n.)* old man, dotard [i.e. one wearing pantaloons = breeches] **TS** III.i.36 [Lucentio as Cambio to Bianca, of Gremio] *we might beguile the old pantaloon;* **AY** II.vii.159; **TS** I.i.46 ➤ CLOTHING, p.79

pantler *(n.)* servant in charge of the bread, pantryman **2H4** II.iv.233 [Falstaff to Doll, of Prince Henry] *'A would have made a good pantler;* **Cym** II.iii.123; **2H4** II.iv.310; **WT** IV.iv.56

panyn *(n.)* ➤ pavin *(n.)*

pap *(n.)* teat, nipple **LL** IV.iii.23 [Browne to himself, of Cupid and the King] *Thou hast thumped him with thy bird-bolt under the left pap*

paper *(n.)* **1** piece of writing, composition **Sonn** 38.4 *Thine own sweet argument, too excellent, / For every vulgar paper to rehearse*
2 paper replacement for money **Tim** I.ii.246 [Apemantus to Timon] *I fear me thou wilt give away thyself in paper shortly* [i.e. in promissory notes]

paper *(v.)* put down on paper, write down **H8** I.i.80 [Buckingham to Abergavenny, of Wolsey] *[he] Must fetch him in he papers* [i.e. he requires the presence of whoever he puts on his list]

parable *(n.)* indirect means, oblique utterance, similitude **TG** II.v.35 [Launce to Speed, of whether Julia and Proteus will marry] *Thou shalt never get such a secret from me but by a parable*

paradox *(n.)* statement going against accepted belief, absurdity **Oth** II.i.136 [Desdemona to Iago] *These are old fond paradoxes;* **Ham** III.i.114; **TC** I.iii.184

paragon *(v.)* **1** compare, match, place side by side **AC** I.v.71 [Cleopatra to Charmian] *I will give thee bloody teeth / If thou with Caesar paragon again / My man of men;* **H8** II.iv.230
2 surpass, excel, transcend **Oth** II.i.62 [Cassio to Montano, of Othello] *he hath achieved a maid / That paragons description*

paramour *(n.)* **1** lover **1H6** V.i.23 [King to Gloucester] *fitter is my study and my books / Than wanton dalliance with a paramour;* **1H6** III.ii.53, V.iii.82; **RJ** V.iii.105
2 malapropism for 'paragon' **MND** IV.ii.12 [Quince to Flute, of Bottom] *he is a very paramour for a sweet voice*

paraquito *(n.)* parakeet, parrot **1H4** II.iii.88 [Lady Percy to Hotspur] *Come, come, you paraquito, answer me*

parcel *(n.)* **1** part, piece, portion, bit **MW** II.i.213 [Evans to Slender] *divers philosophers hold that the lips is parcel of the mouth;* **AC** III.xiii.32; **CE** V.i.106; **Cor** I.ii.32; **1H4** III.ii.159; **Tit** II.iii.49
2 detail, particular, specific point **2H4** IV.ii.36 [Archbishop to Prince John] *I sent your grace / The parcels and particulars of our grief*
3 small group, company, party **AW** II.iii.51 [King to Helena] *This youthful parcel / Of noble bachelors;* **LL** V.ii.160; **MV** I.ii.102

parcel *(v.)* [debated meaning] increase, add to the list of **AC** V.ii.163 [Cleopatra to Caesar] *mine own servant should / Parcel the sum of my disgraces by / Addition of his envy*

parcel-bawd *(n.)* part-time pimp **MM** II.i.61 [Elbow to Angelo, of Pompey] *A … parcel-bawd; one that serves a bad woman*

parcel-gilt *(adj.)* partly gilded **2H4** II.i.84 [Hostess to Falstaff] *Thou didst swear to me upon a parcel-gilt goblet*

parcelled *(adj.)* particular, related to individual cases **R3** II.ii.81 [Duchess of York to herself, of Clarence's children and Queen Elizabeth] *Their woes are parcelled, mine is general*

parcelling *(n.)* dividing up, itemizing, listing **E3** IV.iv.41 [Prince Edward to Audley, of the French] *Thy parcelling this power hath made it more*

parch *(v.)* dry up, shrivel up **3H6** I.iv.87 [Queen to York] *Hath thy fiery heart so parched thine entrails / That not a tear can fall for Rutland's death?*

parchment-bottom *(n.)* [descriptive of a] drum **E3** II.ii.49 [King Edward to Lodowick, of the drum] *break the thund'ring parchment-bottom out*

pard *(n.)* panther, leopard **TC** III.ii.192 [Cressida to Troilus] *As false / As … / Pard to the hind;* **AY** II.vii.151; **MND** II.ii.37; **Tem** IV.i.262

pardon *(n.)* permission, consent, approval **Ham** I.ii.56 [Laertes to Claudius] *your gracious leave and pardon;* **AC** III.vi.60; **Ham** III.ii.325, IV.vii.45; **3H6** IV.i.87; **LL** IV.ii.100 ➤ POLITENESS, p.340

pardon *(v.)* excuse, give permission to **TG** III.ii.98 [Duke to Proteus] *I will pardon you* [i.e. give you leave to go]; **3H6** IV.i.89; **MA** II.i.112

parfect *(v.)* malapropism probably for 'perform' or 'present' **LL** V.ii.500 [Costard to Berowne] *I am, as they say, but to parfect one man in one poor man – Pompion* [Q1; F *perfect*]

parish top *(n.)* whipping-top kept for parishioners' use [of unclear purpose] **TN** I.iii.39 [Sir Toby to Maria, of anyone not drinking to his niece] *till his brains turn o'the toe, like a parish top*

paritor *(n.)* summoning officer for an ecclesiastical court **LL** III.i.183 [Berowne alone, of Cupid] *Sole imperator and great general / Of trotting paritors*

park *(n.)* hunting ground **3H6** IV.v.3 [Richard to Hastings and Stanley] *this chiefest thicket of the park;* **3H6** V.ii.24; **MND** II.i.4; **MW** V.i.10; **Tit** III.i.88

park *(v.)* enclose, contain, shut in [as if in a park] **1H6** IV.ii.45 [Talbot to all] *How we are parked and bounded in a pale*

park-ward *(n.)* direction of Windsor Great Park **MW** III.i.5 [Simple to Evans, of where Simple has looked for Caius] *the pittie-ward, the park-ward, every way* ➤ pittie-ward *(n.)*

parle, parley *(n.)* **1** negotiation, meeting [between enemies under a truce, to discuss terms] **1H6** III.iii.37 [Burgundy to all] *Who craves a parley with the Burgundy?;* **3H6** V.i.16 [Edward to trumpeter] *Go, trumpet, to the walls and sound a parle* ➤ FEW, p.xxi
2 argument, altercation, exchange **TNK** III.iii.10 [Arcite to Palamon] *No more of these vain parleys;* **Mac** II.iii.79
3 talk, conversation, discourse **TG** I.ii.5 [Julia to Lucetta] *the … gentlemen / That every day with parle encounter me*

parle, parley *(v.)* **1** discuss terms, treat, negotiate with **KJ** II.i.78 [Chatillon to King Philip, of the English] *They are at hand – / To parley or to fight;* **2H6** IV.iv.13, vii.72; **TG** IV.i.60

2 talk, discuss, enter into conversation LL V.ii.122 [Boyet to Princess, of the King's party] *Their purpose is to parley, court, and dance* [F *parlee*]; Ham I.iii.123; KJ IV.ii.238; LL II.i.5

parling *(adj.)* speaking, parleying Luc 100 [of Lucrece and Tarquin's eyes] *she … / Could pick no meaning from their parling looks*

parlous *(adj.)* **1** perilous, dangerous, hazardous MND III.i.12 [Snout to Bottom] *a parlous fear!*; AY III.ii.41
2 shrewd, sharp, wily R3 II.iv.35 [Queen Elizabeth to York] *A parlous boy!*; R3 III.i.154

parlously *(adv.)* astoundingly, amazingly, exceedingly TNK II.ii.53 [Second Countryman to the others, of the Schoolmaster] *he himself will edify the Duke / Most parlously*

parmacity *(n.)* spermaceti [medicinal substance from the sperm-whale] 1H4 I.iii.57 [Hotspur to King Henry] *the sovereignest thing on earth / Was parmacity for an inward bruise*

parricide *(n.)* **1** patricide, murder of a father Mac III.i.31 [Macbeth to Banquo, of Malcolm and Donalbain] *not confessing / Their cruel parricide*
2 patricide, father-murderer KL II.i.45 [Edmund to Gloucester, of Edgar] *I told him the revenging gods / 'Gainst parricides did all the thunder bend*

parrot *(n.)* nonsense, rubbish, without understanding Oth II.iii.272 [Cassio to Iago, of himself] *Drunk! And speak parrot!*

parrot-teacher *(n.)* chatterer, babbler, empty talker MA I.i.130 [Benedick to Beatrice] *you are a rare parrot-teacher*

part *(n.)* **1** quality, attribute, gift, accomplishment [of mind or body] MW II.ii.103 [Falstaff to Mistress Quickly] *Setting the attraction of my good parts aside*; Cym III.v.72; H8 II.iii.27; KL I.iv.260; LL II.i.44; TN I.iv.34
2 side, camp, party 3H6 II.v.66 [Son to himself] *My father … / Came on the part of York*; Cym I.ii.96; E3 IV.vi.50; 1H6 I.i.94; KJ II.i.359; RJ I.i.114
3 remnant, fragment, vestige KL IV.vi.39 [Gloucester to himself, as if to the gods] *My snuff and loathed part of nature should / Burn itself out*; 2H6 V.ii.87
4 action, conduct, behaviour 2H4 IV.v.65 [King Henry IV to all, of Prince Henry] *This part of his conjoins with my disease, / And helps to end me*; JC I.iii.54; LL V.ii.735; MV IV.i.92; Tim V.i.7
5 territory, region, province 2H6 I.i.65 [King to York] *We here discharge your grace from being Regent / I'the parts of France*; MM II.iv.28

part *(v.)* **1** depart [from], leave, quit R2 III.i.3 [Bolingbroke to Bushy and Green] *your souls must part your bodies*; CE V.i.221; H8 IV.i.92; Mac V.vi.91; Per V.iii.38; Tim IV.ii.21
2 divide, share, split up TNK V.i.17 [Theseus to Palamon and Arcite] *betwixt ye / I part my wishes*; H8 V.ii.27; JC V.v.81; MV II.ii.138; Tim I.ii.46; WT I.ii.18
3 cleave, break, tear KJ IV.iii.146 [Bastard to Hubert] *England now is left / To tug and scamble and to part by th'teeth / The unowed interest of proud-swelling state*; 3H6 I.iv.69
4 distinguish between, differentiate LL I.ii.7 [Armado to Mote] *How canst thou part sadness and melancholy*

part, part of *(adv.)* partly, in some measure H8 III.i.24 [Queen Katherine to Wolsey and Campeius] *Your graces find me here part of a housewife*; Sonn 113.3 *that which governs me to go about, / Doth part his function, and is partly blind* [i.e. partly carries out its role]

part away *(v.)* depart, leave H8 III.i.97 [Campeius to Queen Katherine] *if the trial of the law o'ertake ye / You'll part away disgraced*

partake *(v.)* **1** make known, impart, communicate WT V.iii.132 [Paulina to all] *your exultation / Partake to everyone*; Per I.i.153
2 take sides, take the part of Sonn 149.2 *I against myself with thee partake*

partaker *(n.)* ally, supporter, associate 1H6 II.iv.100 [Richard to Somerset, of the slur against his father] *For your partaker Pole, and you yourself, / I'll … scourge you for this apprehension*

part-created *(adj.)* partly built 2H4 I.iii.60 [Lord Bardolph to Hastings, of someone who stops a building project] *[who] leaves his part-created cost / A naked subject to the weeping clouds*

parted *(adj.)* **1** divided, unfocused, indistinct MND IV.i.188 [Hermia to all, of recent events] *Methinks I see these things with parted eye, / When everything seems double*
2 gifted, endowed, accomplished TC III.iii.96 [Ulysses to Achilles, of man] *how dearly ever parted … / Cannot make boast to have that which he hath*

partial *(adj.)* **1** disposed, minded, inclined CE I.i.4 [Duke to Egeon] *I am not partial to infringe our laws*
2 biased, prejudiced, self-interested KL I.iv.308 [Albany to Gonerill] *I cannot be so partial*; TC II.ii.179
3 of partiality, alleging bias R2 I.iii.241 [John of Gaunt to Richard] *A partial slander sought I to avoid*

partial, in with partiality, in a biased manner MM II.i.31 [Angelo to Escalus] *When I … do so offend, / Let mine own judgement pattern out my death / And nothing come in partial* [i.e. to argue in my favour]

partialize *(v.)* make partial, bias, make one-sided R2 I.i.120 [King Richard to Mowbray, of Bolingbroke] *Such neighbour nearness to our sacred blood / Should nothing privilege him, nor partialize / The unstooping firmness of my upright soul*

partially *(adv.)* with partiality, in a biased way Luc 634 [Lucrece to Tarquin, of men] *Their own transgressions partially they smother*; Oth II.iii.212

participate *(v.)* take, receive, share in TN V.i.235 [Sebastian to Viola as Cesario] *A spirit I am indeed, / But am in that dimension grossly clad / Which from the womb I did participate* [i.e. my body is as solid now as it was then]

participation *(n.)* association, companionship, fellowship 1H4 III.ii.87 [King Henry to Prince Hal] *thou hast lost thy princely privilege / With vile participation*

parti-coated *(adj.)* motley, of many forms LL V.ii.761 [Berowne to ladies, of their jests] *Which parti-coated presence of loose love / Put on by us*

parti-coloured *(adj.)* variegated, diverse, multi-coloured MV I.iii.85 [Shylock to Antonio, of ewes] *Who … did in eaning time / Fall parti-coloured lambs*; E3 I.ii.153

particular *(n.)* **1** individual issue, point of detail 2H4 IV.ii.36 [Archbishop to Prince John] *I sent your grace / The parcels and particulars of our grief*; AW III.vii.179; Ham II.ii.239; 2H4 IV.v.90
2 individual person, self AC IV.ix.20 [Enobarbus to himself, as if to Antony] *Forgive me in thine own particular*; Cor II.iii.42; KL II.iv.287; TC II.ii.9
3 private matter, personal business AC I.iii.54 [Antony to Cleopatra] *My more particular … / Is Fulvia's death*; Sonn 91.7; Tim IV.iii.160
4 intimacy, personal relationship Cor V.i.3 [Menenius to all, of Cominius] *his general, who loved him / In a most dear particular*; H8 III.ii.189
5 (plural) details, full account Tem V.i.135 [Alonso to Prospero] *Give us particulars of thy preservation*

particular, for your as far as you are concerned, in your case Cor IV.vii.13 [Lieutenant to Aufidius] *I mean for your particular*

particular, on my in my own case, as far as I am concerned AW II.v.61 [Bertram to Helena] *The ministration and required office / On my particular* [i.e. the duties and responsibilities relating to me as a husband]

particular *(adj.)* **1** personal, special, private KL V.i.30 [Gonerill to all] *these domestic and particular broils*; Cor V.ii.66; Ham I.ii.75; MM IV.iv.25; TC IV.v.20; Tim V.ii.8
2 detailed, specific, precise Ham II.i.12 [Polonius to Reynaldo] *come you more nearer / Than your particular demands will touch it*

particularity *(n.)* personal matter, individual issue 2H6 V.ii.44 [Young Clifford to himself] *Now let … / Particularities and petty sounds / To cease!*; H5 III.ii.126

particularize (v.) give details of, itemize **Cor** I.i.20 [First Citizen to all, of the authorities] *The leanness that afflicts us … is as an inventory to particularize their abundance*

particularly (adv.) **1** in person, individually **Cor** IV.v.69 [Coriolanus to Aufidius, of himself] *who hath done / To thee particularly … / Great hurt*
2 by singling out any one individual **Tim** I.i.47 [Poet to Painter, of his poem] *My free drift / Halts not particularly* [i.e. my meaning does not stop to focus on individuals]

parti-eyed (adj.) [unclear meaning] with eyes of mixed colours; bleeding **KL** IV.i.10 [Edgar to himself, of Gloucester] *My father, parti-eyed!* [F *poorlie, leed*]

parting (n.) departure, leave-taking, setting-out **TG** II.iii.11 [Launce alone, of leaving his family] *A Jew would have wept to have seen our parting*

partisan (n.) weapon with a long handle and a broad head, sometimes with a projection at the side **Ham** I.i.141 [Marcellus to Horatio, of the Ghost] *Shall I strike it with my partisan?*; **AC** II.vii.13; **Cym** IV.ii.399; **RJ** I.i.72 ☛ **WEAPONS**, p.491

partition (n.) **1** separation, distinction **2H4** IV.i.194 [Mowbray to Hastings] *our corn shall seem as light as chaff, / And good from bad find no partition*; **Cym** I.vii.37
2 wall, dividing structure; also: section of a learned book **MND** V.i.164 [Demetrius to Theseus, of the Wall] *It is the wittiest partition that ever I heard discourse*

partly (adv.) slightly, in some measure, a little **JC** V.i.89 [Cassius to Messala, of birds being a bad omen] *I but believe it partly*; **Cym** IV.ii.64; **Oth** I.i.123; **TC** III.i.18

partner (n.) co-sponsor at a christening **H8** V.iii.167 [King Henry to Cranmer, of the christening] *You shall have two noble partners with you*; **H8** V.v.5

partner (v.) associate, equate, match **Cym** I.vii.121 [Iachimo to Innogen] *A lady / So fair … to be partnered / With tomboys*

party (n.) **1** side, faction, camp **1H6** II.iv.123 [Warwick to Richard] *in signal of my love to thee … / Will I upon thy party wear this rose*; **Cor** I.i.232, V.ii.29; **KJ** III.i.1.29; **TC** II.ii.157
2 litigant, disputant, side **Cor** II.i.69 [Menenius to Brutus and Sicinius] *When you are hearing a matter between party and party*
3 side, part, function **R2** III.iii.115 [Northumberland to King Richard, of Bolingbroke's recall] *Which on thy royal party granted once* [i.e. if granted on your majesty's part]
4 participant, accessory, supporter **Cor** V.vi.14 [Second Conspirator to Aufidius] *If you do hold the same intent wherein / You wished us parties*; **1H4** III.i.1; **WT** I.ii.383, II.iii.21
5 person, fellow **Tem** III.ii.59 [Stephano to Caliban, of Prospero] *Canst thou bring me to the party?*; **2H4** I.ii.4; **LL** IV.ii.133, V.ii.668
6 side, position, viewpoint **1H6** II.iv.32 [Somerset to all, of his supporters] *Let him that … dare maintain the party of the truth*

party-verdict (n.) share in a joint decision **R2** I.iii.234 [Richard to John of Gaunt] *Thy son is banished upon good advice / Whereto thy tongue a party-verdict gave*

pash (n.) head **WT** I.ii.128 [Leontes to Mamillius] *Thou want'st a rough pash and the shoots that I have / To be full like me*

pash (v.) strike, smash, knock **TC** II.iii.201 [Ajax to all, of Achilles] *I'll pash him o'er the face* [F; Q *push*]

pashed (adj.) smashed, battered, crushed **TC** V.v.10 [Agamemnon to Diomedes, of Margarelon] *[he] stands colossus-wise … / Upon the pashed corpses of the kings*

pass (n.) **1** [fencing] swordthrust, lunge **Ham** V.ii.292 [Hamlet to Laertes] *pass with your best violence*; **Ham** IV.vii.137, V.ii.61
2 bout, exchange, round [in fencing] **Ham** V.ii.163 [Osrick to Hamlet] *in a dozen passes*; **MW** II.i.207; **TN** III.iv.268
3 passage, crossing, thoroughfare **H5** II *Chorus*.39 [Chorus] *charming the narrow seas / To give you gentle pass*; **Cym** V.iii.11; **Ham** II.ii.77

4 sally, witty stroke, quip **Tem** IV.i.244 [Stephano to Trinculo] *'Steal by line and level' is an excellent pass of pate* [i.e. a very clever piece of wit]
5 standing, reputation, estimation **AW** II.v.53 [Bertram to Parolles, of Lafew] *common speech / Gives him a worthy pass*
6 issue, end, outcome **Sonn** 103.11 *For to no other pass my verses tend / Than of your graces and your gifts to tell*
7 predicament, juncture, critical point **KL** III.iv.60 [Lear to disguised Kent and Fool, of Edgar as Poor Tom] *has his daughters brought him to this pass?*; **CE** III.i.17; **TS** V.ii.123
8 [unclear meaning] trespass; course of action; trickery **MM** V.i.367 [Angelo to Duke] *your grace … / Hath looked upon my passes*

pass (v.) **1** surpass, go beyond, outdo **LL** IV.iii.239 [Berowne to King, of Rosaline] *She passes praise*; **Ham** I.ii.85; **MW** I.i.277, IV.ii.115; **RJ** I.i.236; **TS** I.i.125
2 pass muster, stand up well **MW** I.iii.47 [Nym to Pistol] *The anchor is deep. Will that humour pass?*
3 be approved [by], be ratified [by] **Cor** III.i.29 [Cominius to Brutus, of Coriolanus] *Hath he not passed the noble and the common?*; **H8** V.iii.59
4 advance, move on, proceed **JC** I.ii.24 [Caesar to Cassius, of Soothsayer] *Let us leave him. Pass*; **H8** II.iv.130
5 move outside, go beyond **Tim** V.iv.60 [Alcibiades to Senators] *not a man / Shall pass his quarter*
6 pass through, traverse **JC** I.i.42 [Marullus to people] *To see great Pompey pass the streets of Rome*
7 confirm, ratify, affirm **TS** IV.iv.45 [Baptista to Pedant as Vincentio] *if you … pass my daughter a sufficient dower*; **TS** IV.ii.118
8 transact, complete, carry through **TS** IV.iv.57 [Tranio as Lucentio to Baptista, of the marriage arrangements] *We'll pass the business privately and well*
9 go through, go over **Mac** III.i.79 [Macbeth to Murderers] *I … passed in probation with you / How you were borne in hand*
10 use, show, employ **H5** II.i.121 [Nym to Pistol, of King Henry] *he passes some humours and careers*; **MW** II.iii.23
11 let pass, omit, avoid **Cor** II.iii.137 [Coriolanus to Menenius, of addressing the people] *Please you / That I may pass this doing*
12 experience, feel **MW** I.i.154 [Nym to Slender] *Be advised, sir, and pass good humours* [i.e. make the best of it]
13 care, heed, trouble oneself about **2H6** IV.ii.120 [Cade to rebels, of the Staffords] *As for these silken-coated slaves, I pass not*
14 endure, undergo, experience **TC** II.ii.140 [Paris to all] *Were I alone to pass the difficulties … / Paris should ne'er retract what he hath done*
15 represent, impersonate, perform **LL** V.i.122 [Holofernes to Nathaniel, of Costard] *this swain … shall pass Pompey the Great*
16 pass over, ignore, disregard **Oth** II.ii.240 [Iago to Othello] *some strange indignity / Which patience could not pass*; **KJ** II.i.258; **MM** IV.v.12
17 pass sentence, adjudicate **MM** II.i.19 [Angelo to Escalus, of the jury] *passing on the prisoner's life*; **KL** III.vii.24
18 pass away, pass from life, die **KL** IV.vi.47 [Edgar to and of Gloucester] *Thus might he pass indeed. Yet he revives*; **2H6** III.iii.25

pass upon (v.) [unclear meaning] jest at; impose on; pass judgement upon **TN** III.i.41 [Viola as Cesario to Feste] *an thou pass upon me, I'll no more with thee*

passable (adj.) veritable, real, tolerable **Cym** I.iii.8 [First Lord to Cloten, of Cloten's opponent] *his body's a passable carcass, if he be not hurt*

passado (n.) forward thrust, lunge **RJ** III.i.83 [Mercutio to Tybalt] *Come, sir, your passado!*; **LL** I.ii.172; **RJ** II.iv.25

passage (n.) **1** incident, occurrence, event, happening **RJ** Prologue.9 [Chorus, of Romeo and Juliet] *The fearful passage of their death-marked love*; **Cym** III.iv.93; **Ham** IV.vii.111; **1H4** III.i.8; **H8** II.iv.165; **TNK** IV.iii.97
2 passing, progress, moving on **1H6** II.v.108 [Richard to Mortimer] *would some part of my young years / Might but redeem the passage of your age!*; **KJ** II.i.336

3 passing on, extending, line of descent **H5** I.i.86 [Canterbury to Ely, of King Henry] *The severals and unhidden passages / Of his true titles to some certain dukedoms*

4 passing away, departure from life, death **Ham** III.iii.86 [Hamlet to himself, of Claudius] *To take him in the purging of his soul, / When he is fit and seasoned for his passage;* **Ham** V.ii.392

5 traffic, passing to and fro, movement of people **CE** IV.ii.38 [Dromio of Syracuse to Adriana, of the officer] *one that countermands / The passages of alleys;* **CE** III.i.99; **Oth** V.i.37

6 journey, travelling, wandering **R2** I.iii.272 [Bolingbroke to John of Gaunt] *Must I not serve a long apprenticehood / To foreign passages*

7 combat, contest, fight [= passage of arms] **TNK** V.iv.114 [Theseus to all] *in the passage / The gods have been most equal;* **H5** III.vi.90

8 expression, turn of phrase **AW** I.i.18 [Countess to Lafew, of her husband's death] *O that 'had', how sad a passage 'tis!* [also: sense 1, 4]

passant *(adj.)* [heraldry] walking, with three paws on the ground and one raised **MW** I.i.18 [Evans to Shallow, of Shallow's coat of arms] *It agrees well, passant* [also, without comma: well enough]

passed *(adj.)* recently uttered, just expressed **2H6** III.ii.221 [Warwick to Suffolk] *I would … / Make thee beg pardon for thy passed speech*

passenger *(n.)* wayfarer, traveller, passer-by **TG** IV.i.72 [Valentine to Outlaws] *Provided that you do no outrages / On … poor passengers;* **2H6** III.i.129; **R2** V.iii.9; **TG** IV.i.1, V.iv.15; **Venus** 91

passing *(adj.)* **1** unsurpassed, extreme, pre-eminent **3H6** V.i.106 [Warwick to George] *O passing traitor;* **Ham** I.ii.17, II.i.71

2 ringing to mark a death **Venus** 702 [Venus to Adonis, of the hare hearing the hounds] *his grief may be compared … / To one sore sick that hears the passing-bell*

passing *(adv.)* very, exceedingly, extremely **TS** II.i.236 [Petruchio to Katherina] *I find you passing gentle;* **Cor** I.i.201; **Ham** II.ii.411; **MND** II.i.20; **TG** IV.iv.145; **Venus** 297

passion *(n.)* **1** powerful feeling, overpowering emotion [often opposed to 'reason'] **1H6** V.ii.18 [Pucelle to all] *Of all base passions, fear is most accursed;* **AY** I.ii.246; **Ham** III.ii.204; **JC** I.ii.40; **LL** IV.iii.200; **Venus** 967

2 emotional state, mental condition **Tem** IV.i.143 [Ferdinand to Miranda] *Your father's in some passion / That works him strongly;* **CE** V.i.47; **JC** I.ii.48; **KJ** IV.ii.79; **Per** I.ii.11; **Tim** III.v.21

3 suffering, torment, deep grief **Tit** I.i.109 [Tamora to Titus, of herself] *A mother's tears in passion for her son;* **AC** V.i.63; **Luc** 1317; **Tem** I.ii.393; **TN** II.iv.4

4 fit of anger, feeling of rage **WT** IV.iv.493 [Florizel to Camillo, of Polixenes] *cast your good counsels / Upon his passion;* **CE** V.i.151; **H8** I.i.149; **Mac** III.iv.90; **Tim** III.i.56; **TNK** III.i.31

5 passionate outburst, emotional passage **2H4** I.i.161 [Lord Bardolph to Northumberland] *This strained passion doth you wrong;* **AC** III.x.5; **Ham** III.ii.9; **KJ** V.ii.263; **MV** II.viii.12; **Tit** III.i.216

passion *(v.)* experience deep feeling, be profoundly moved, grieve **TG** IV.iv.164 [disguised Julia to Silvia] *'twas Ariadne passioning / For Theseus' perjury;* **LL** I.i.252; **Tem** V.i.24; **Venus** 1059

passionate *(v.)* express with great emotion **Tit** III.ii.6 [Titus to Marcus, of himself and Lavinia] *want our hands / And cannot passionate our tenfold grief / With folded arms*

passionate *(adj.)* **1** impassioned, vehement, excessively emotional **2H6** I.i.102 [Cardinal to Gloucester] *what means this passionate discourse;* **KJ** II.i.544

2 compassionate, inclined to pity, tender-hearted **R3** I.iv.119 [Second Murderer to First Murderer] *I hope this passionate humour of mine will change* [F; Q *holy*]

passport *(n.)* **1** document providing details **Per** III.ii.64 [Cerimon to all, of Thaisa's body] *A passport too!*

2 licence given to an inmate of an institution to travel abroad as

a beggar **AW** III.ii.55 [Helena to Countess, of Bertram's letter] *here's my passport*

passy-measures *(adj.)* dancing with slow pace **TN** V.i.197 [Sir Toby to Feste, of the surgeon] *he's a rogue and a passy-measures pavin* [also: beyond all proportion] [i.e. his slowness is beyond belief]

past *(prep.)* incapable of **AW** II.i.158 [Helena to King] *My art is not past power*

paste *(n.)* pastry, doughy mixture **R2** III.ii.154 [King Richard to all] *that small model of the barren earth / Which serves as paste and cover to our bones;* **KL** II.iv.118; **Tit** V.ii.186

pastern *(n.)* hoof, leg **H5** III.vii.12 [Dauphin to Orleans] *I will not change my horse with any that treads but on four pasterns*

pastime *(n.)* pleasure, delight, enjoyment **AW** I.ii.57 [King to Bertram] *the catastrophe and heel of pastime, / When it was out*

pastor *(n.)* shepherd, herdsman **R2** III.iii.100 [Richard to his opponents, of the effect of future battles on England] *bedew / Her pastor's grass with faithful English blood*

pastoral *(n.)* pastoral play, theatrical event on a rural theme **WT** IV.iv.134 [Perdita to Florizel] *I play as I have seen them do / In Whitsun pastorals*

past-proportion *(n.)* immeasurableness, quantity beyond compare **TC** II.ii.29 [Troilus to Hector, of Priam] *Will you with counters sum / The past-proportion of his infinite* [i.e. his extraordinary greatness which defies calculation]

pastry *(n.)* pastry-making part of the kitchen **RJ** IV.iv.2 [Nurse to Lady Capulet] *They call for dates and quinces in the pastry*

past-saving *(adj.)* beyond redemption, incapable of salvation **AW** IV.iii.137 [Bertram to Lords, of Parolles] *What a past-saving slave is this!*

pasture *(n.)* nurture, rearing, upbringing **H5** III.i.27 [King Henry to yeomen] *show us here / The mettle of your pasture*

pasty *(n.)* meat-pie **Tit** V.ii.188 [Titus to Chiron and Demetrius] *I'll … make two pasties of your shameful heads*

pat *(adv.)* **1** neatly, opportunely, aptly **Ham** III.iii.73 [Hamlet to himself] *Now might I do it pat;* **H8** II.iii.84; **KL** I.ii.133

2 spot on, on the dot, very timely **MND** III.i.2 [Quince to Bottom, in answer to 'Are we all met?'] *Pat, pat*

3 precisely, just, exactly **MND** V.i.183 [Bottom to Theseus, of the play's outcome] *it will fall pat as I told you*

patch *(n.)* fool, clown; rogue, knave **MV** II.v.44 [Shylock to Jessica, of Launcelot] *The patch is kind enough, but a huge feeder;* **CE** III.i.36; **LL** IV.iii.31; **Mac** V.iii.15; **MND** III.ii.9; **Tem** III.ii.63

patch *(v.)* **1** fabricate, make up [as in patchwork] **AC** II.ii.56 [Antony to Caesar, of the reasons suggested for enmity] *If you'll patch a quarrel, … / It must not be with this*

2 patch over, cover up **MA** V.i.17 [Leonato to Antonio] *Patch grief with proverbs*

3 blotch, mark, cover over **KJ** III.i.47 [Constance to Arthur] *If thou [wert] … / Patched with foul moles and eye-offending marks*

patch up *(v.)* invent in haste, fabricate, make **AC** II.ii.60 [Caesar to Antony] *You patched up your excuses*

patched *(adj.)* wearing a patchwork costume, multi-coloured **MND** IV.i.207 [Bottom to himself] *man is but a patched fool*

patchery *(n.)* roguery, knavery, tricks **TC** II.iii.70 [Thersites to Patroclus] *Here is such patchery, such juggling, and such knavery!;* **Tim** V.i.94

pate *(n.)* head, skull **CE** I.ii.82 [Dromio of Ephesus to Antipholus of Syracuse] *I have some marks of yours upon my pate* ➤ **FEW**, p.xxi

paten *(n.)* dish on which the bread is placed during the Mass; shining circle **MV** V.i.59 [Lorenzo to Jessica] *the floor of heaven / Is thick inlaid with patens of bright gold*

patent *(n.)* **1** privilege, right, title **MND** I.i.80 [Hermia to Theseus, on being a nun] *So will I grow … / Ere I will yield my virgin patent up / Unto his lordship [Demetrius];* **Sonn** 87.8

PAST TENSES

Verbs in English have one inflected form for expressing past time, the *past tense*, which is typically formed by adding -*ed* to the base form of the verb: *I walk* > *I walked*, *they ask* > *they asked*. There are some 300 irregular past tenses in modern English, ranging from the 'slightly' irregular *I say* > *I said* to the fundamentally different *I go* > *I went*, the types correlating with the grammatical situation in Old English, where there were several distinctive verb classes.

A related form, seen in *I have asked*, is often called the *past participle* – but many modern texts avoid this term, because the form is by no means restricted to the expression of past time; in particular, the same form is used in *passive* constructions, such as *I am asked*, *I was asked*, and *I will be asked* (where present, past, and future times are expressed). The regular formation adds -*ed*, but -*en* is also common, as in *I have taken* and *I was taken*, and this book therefore uses -*en forms* as a conventional way of referring to the class as a whole, whether regular or irregular. A related context is when an -*en* form is used as an adjective, as in *the castle was attacked* > *the attacked castle*, and examples are included in the -*en* lists below.

Verb forms have changed greatly since Old English (as they continue to do, illustrated by modern usage variation between *sweat* and *sweated*), and in Shakespearian English we see several distinctive forms. As with all patterns of change, old forms for a while co-exist alongside new ones, and sometimes convey different nuances of meaning; an example is the Princess's observation that 'None are so surely caught, when they are catched, / As wit turned fool' (**LL** V.ii.69), where *catched* conveys a more dynamic sense than *caught*. The following list illustrates only those forms which display some difference between Shakespearian and modern English. It does not include forms where the difference seems to be one of spelling only, such as *chopt* for *chopped* (**AY** II.iv.46).

Irregular > Regular

Past tenses

In Shakespeare	Modern English	Example
durst, I	dared	**TNK** II.ii.76
fast, I	fasted	**Cym** IV.ii.347
holp, I	helped	**2H6** V.iii.8
lift, he	lifted	**1H6** I.i.16
ought, you [F]	owed	**1H4** III.iii.132
sweat, service	sweated	**AY** II.iii.58

-en forms

engraven, it will live	engraved	**Luc** 203
fell, by violence	felled	**E3** III.iv.25
fretten, they are	fretted	**MV** IV.i.77
graft, her royal stock	grafted	**R3** III.vii.126
heat, though	heated	**KJ** IV.i.61
holp, you have	helped	**Cor** III.i.275
sweaten, that's	sweated / sweat	**Mac** IV.i.64

Regular > Irregular

Past tenses

bended, his eyes	bent	**Ham** II.i.100
betted, John o'Gaunt	bet	**2H4** III.ii.44
catched, he	caught	**Cor** I.iii.63
digged, Adam	dug	**Ham** V.i.37
shaked, I	shook/shaken	**Tem** II.i.324
showed, hast	shown	**TNK** III.i.45
sicked, Edward	sickened	**2H4** IV.iv.128

-en forms

beated, shows me	beaten	**Sonn** 62.10
becomed, would have	become	**Cym** V.v.407
blowed, would have	blown	**H5** III.ii.88
builded, keep it	built	**AC** III.ii.30
love-shaked, is	love-shaken	**AY** III.ii.352

(continues)

PAST TENSES – *continued*

In Shakespeare	Modern English	Example
misshaped trunk	misshapen	**3H6** III.ii.170
quitted, having	quit	**WT** V.i.191
splitted, was	split	**CE** I.i.104
waked, I am	woken	**CE** IV.iv.32

Irregular stays irregular

Past tenses

awaked, I	awoke	**AY** IV.iii.133
bare, Caesar	bore	**1H6** I.ii.139
bestrid, he	bestrode	**Cor** II.ii.90
brake, tidings	broke	**1H4** I.i.48
drave, I	drove	**AY** III.ii.399
drive, a troubled mind	drove	**RJ** I.i.120
forbod, my judge	forbade	**Luc** 1648
o'erstunk, the lake	overstank	**Tem** IV.i.184
shore, grief	sheared	**Oth** V.ii.205
spake, he	spoke	**Ham** III.i.164
sprung, the origin	sprang	**Ham** III.i.179
strook, [it]	struck	**Luc** 262
sware, he	swore	**2H4** III.ii.307
writ, I	wrote	**AY** V.ii.73

-en forms

arose, are	arisen	**CE** V.i.389
awaked, was	awoken	**R3** IV.i.84
beat, are	beaten	**Cor** I.iv.30
bidden, he is	bid	**MA** III.iii.31
bore, he hath	borne	**Ham** V.i.183 [F *borne*]
broke, the doors are	broken	**Ham** IV.v.113
chid, should have	chided	**CE** IV.i.50
chose, have you	chosen	**Cor** II.iii.154
droven, we had	driven	**AC** IV.vii.5
eat, hath	eaten	**R2** V.v.85
forbid, am	forbidden	**Ham** I.v.13
forgot, you have	forgotten	**CE** III.ii.i
forsook, have	forsaken	**Cor** IV.v.79
froze, be	frozen	**CE** V.i.314
hid, hear faults	hidden	**Per** I.ii.61
holden, [to be]	held	**2H6** II.iv.71
lien, hath	lain	**Ham** V.i.170 [F *laine*]
loaden with kisses	laden	**TNK** II.i.85
mistook, purposes	mistaken	**Ham** II.ii.378
o'ertook, was	overtaken	**Ham** II.i.58
rid, hath	ridden	**MND** V.i.119
sawn, was	sown	**Lover** 91
shook, I have	shaken	**R2** IV.i.163
shore, you have	shorn	**MND** V.i.332
smit, have	smitten	**Tim** II.i.23
smote, [been]	smitten	**Cor** III.i.317
spoke to, would be	spoken	**Ham** I.i.45
stole, have	stolen	**JC** II.i.238
stricken, hath	struck	**JC** II.i.192
strove, have I	striven	**H8** II.iv.30

PAST TENSES – *continued*

In Shakespeare	Modern English	Example
strucken, hath	struck	**CE** I.ii.45
strucken deer	stricken	**Ham** III.ii.280
sung, she	sang	**TNK** IV.i.63
swam, you have	swum	**AY** IV.i.33
took, is	taken	**1H6** I.i.145
unbegot, children	unbegotten	**R2** III.iii.88
undertook, to be	undertaken	**Oth** V.ii.308
unspoke, leave	unspoken	**KL** I.i.236
well-foughten field	well-fought	**H5** IV.vi.18
writ, we have	written	**Ham** I.ii.27
wrote, hath	written	**Cym** III.v.2

Many past forms derived from Latin, mostly ending in *-ated* in modern English, are found without the ending.

confiscate, [are]	confiscated	**CE** I.i.21
consecrate, this body	consecrated	**CE** II.ii.141
consummate, be	consummated	**MA** III.ii.1
contaminate, should be	contaminated	**CE** II.ii.142
contract, was he	contracted	**R3** III.vii.178
convict, I be	convicted	**R3** I.iv.190
create, there	created	**MND** V.i.395
dedicate, are	dedicated	**MM** II.ii.154
delineate, see	delineated	**E3** II.ii.86
exasperate, hath	exasperated	**Mac** III.vi.38
excommunicate, stands	excommunicated	**E3** II.i.334
situate, there's	situated	**CE** II.i.16
subjugate, will be	subjugated	**E3** III.ii.28
suffocate, may he be	suffocated	**2H6** I.i.122
unite, the arms	united	**E3** III.i.75

For archaic verbs in Shakespeare's time: ☞ **ARCHAISMS**, p.22.

---

2 carte blanche, formal permission **Oth** IV.i.196 [Iago to Othello, of Desdemona] *If you are so fond over her iniquity, give her patent to offend;* **AW** IV.v.64

path (*n.*) way, course of action **TNK** V.ii.22 [Doctor to Gaoler, of the Gaoler's Daughter] *if she will be honest, / She has the path before her* [i.e. marriage]

path (*v.*) pursue one's course, go on one's way **JC** I.iii.1 [Brutus alone, as if to conspiracy] *if thou path, thy native semblance on*

pathetical (*adj.*) **1** pathetic, touching, moving **LL** IV.i.149 [Costard alone, of Mote] *it is a most pathetical nit!;* **LL** I.ii.93
  2 pathetic, miserable, deplorable **AY** IV.i.177 [Rosalind as Ganymede to Orlando] *I will think you the most pathetical break-promise*

patience (*n.*) **1** leave, permission, indulgence **1H6** II.iii.77 [Talbot to Countess] *Nor other satisfaction do I crave / But only, with your patience, that we may / Taste of your wine;* **Ham** III.ii.117; **R3** IV.i.15
  ☞ **POLITENESS**, p.340
  2 endurance, fortitude, composure **KL** IV.iii.16 [Gentleman to disguised Kent, of Cordelia] *patience and sorrow strove / Who should express her goodliest*

patient (*adj.*) calm, serene, of quiet mind **Cor** III.i.85 [Coriolanus to Menenius] *Were I as patient as the midnight sleep;* **KL** IV.vi.80

patient (*v.*) be patient, calm, quieten **Tit** I.i.124 [Titus to Tamora] *Patient yourself, madam*

patiently (*adv.*) **1** with endurance, with fortitude **KL** IV.vi.36 [Gloucester to himself, as if to the gods] *I … / Shake patiently my great affliction off*
  2 calmly, with quiet expectation **TC** V.ix.7 [Agamemnon to all] *March patiently along*

patrician (*n.*) ☞ **ROMAN HISTORY**, p.377

patrimony (*n.*) estate, inheritance, property **KL** V.iii.76 [Regan to Edmund] *Take thou my soldiers, prisoners, patrimony;* **TS** IV.iv.22

patron (*n.*) **1** defender, protector, lord and master **Tit** I.i.68 [Captain to Romans, of Titus] *Patron of virtue;* **3H6** V.i.27
  2 supporter, advocate **Tit** I.i.1 [Saturninus to senators] *Noble patricians, patrons of my right*

patronage (*v.*) protect, uphold, defend **E3** III.iii.214 [Prince Edward to all, of his use of his gifts] *To patronage the fatherless and poor;* **1H6** III.i.48, iv.32

pattern (*n.*) **1** picture, model, specimen, example **KL** III.ii.37 [Lear to himself] *I will be the pattern of all patience;* **E3** IV.ii.12; **1H6** V.v.65; **Luc** 1350; **R3** I.ii.54; **Sonn** 19.12
  2 precedent, previous example **KJ** III.iv.16 [King Philip to Lewis the Dauphin] *Well could I bear that England had this praise, / So could find some pattern of our shame;* **Tit** V.iii.43

pattern (*v.*) **1** parallel, match, equal **WT** III.ii.35 [Hermione to Leontes, of the indictment against her] *which is more / Than history can pattern, though devised / And played to take spectators*

2 show a model, give a precedent **Luc** 629 [Lucrece to Tarquin] *When patterned by thy fault foul sin may say / He learned to sin, and thou didst teach the way?*

pattern out (*v.*) be a pattern for, act as a precedent for **MM** II.i.30 [Angelo to Escalus] *When I … do so offend, / Let mine own judgement pattern out my death*

paunch (*v.*) stab in the paunch, wound in the stomach **Tem** III.ii.91 [Caliban to Stephano, of Prospero] *There thou mayst … paunch him with a stake*

pause (*n.*) hesitation, delay **Ham** III.i.68 [Hamlet alone] *what dreams may come / When we have shuffled off this mortal coil / Must give us pause* [i.e. make us hesitate]; **Ham** IV.iii.9

pause, in hesitating, not proceeding, pausing **Ham** III.iii.42 [Claudius alone] *I stand in pause where I shall first begin*

pause (*v.*) delay, take time to consider **CE** II.i.32 [Adriana to and of Luciana] *No marvel though she pause* [i.e. no wonder she delays]

pause upon (*v.*) deliberate about, take time to consider **1H4** V.v.15 [King Henry to all] *Bear Worcester to the death, and Vernon too. / Other offenders we will pause upon*

pauser (*adj.*) prompting a pause, circumspect **Mac** II.iii.108 [Macbeth to all] *The expedition of my violent love / Outrun the pauser reason* [or, with comma after pauser: one who pauses, delayer]

pausingly (*adv.*) with pauses, hesitantly, haltingly **H8** I.ii.168 [Surveyor to King Henry, of Buckingham's monk] *with demure confidence / This pausingly ensued*

paved (*adj.*) with a paved base, pebbled **MM** V.i.432 [Duke to Mariana, of Isabella] *Her brother's ghost his paved bed would break;* **MND** II.i.84

pavement (*n.*) paved surface, thoroughfare **TC** III.iii.162 [Ulysses to Achilles, of a fallen horse] *Lie there for pavement to the abject rear*

pavilion (*n.*) ceremonial tent **TC** I.iii.305 [Agamemnon to Aeneas] *To our pavilion shall I lead you first;* **AC** II.ii.204; **LL** V.ii.652; **TC** Prologue.15

pavilioned (*adj.*) in ceremonial tents **H5** I.ii.129 [Westmorland to King Henry, of the English nobles] *Whose hearts have left their bodies here in England / And lie pavilioned in the fields of France*

pavin (*n.*) type of stately dance, pavane **TN** V.i.197 [Sir Toby to Feste, of the surgeon] *he's a rogue and a passy-measures pavin* [F *panyn*] [i.e. his slowness is beyond belief]

pawn (*n.*) pledge, surety, forfeit **KL** I.i.155 [Kent to Lear] *My life I never held but as a pawn / To wage against thine enemies;* **KJ** V.ii.141; **MW** III.i.101; **TG** I.iii.47, II.iv.89; **WT** IV.iv.802

pawn (*v.*) stake, pledge, risk **3H6** III.iii.116 [Warwick to Lewis, of Edward's right to be king] *Thereon I pawn my credit;* **Luc** 156; **MV** III.v.77; **TC** I.iii.301; **Tim** I.i.151; **WT** II.iii.165

pawn down (*v.*) stake, pledge, risk **KL** I.i.86 [Edmund to Gloucester, of Edgar] *I dare pawn down my life for him*

pax (*n.*) tablet bearing an image of the Crucifixion, used as a symbol of peace within the Mass **H5** III.vi.39 [Pistol to Fluellen, of Bardolph] *he hath stolen a pax, and hanged must 'a be;* **H5** III.vi.44

pay (*n.*) reward, payment **TNK** V.iii.32 [Theseus to Emilia] *You … must needs be by / To give the service pay* [i.e. to reward the labour of the winner]

pay (*v.*) **1** repay, requite, recompense **H8** III.ii.182 [King Henry to Wolsey, of loyalty] *The honour of it / Does pay the act of it;* **KJ** III.iii.22; **Per** II.i.144; **Tem** V.i.70

2 punish, pay back, retaliate against **TNK** III.vi.52 [Palamon to Arcite] *With all the justice of affection / I'll pay thee soundly;* **H5** IV.iv.192; **TN** III.iv.270

3 kill, settle with, discharge **1H4** II.iv.187 [Falstaff to all, of the robbers] *Two I am sure I have paid;* **1H4** II.iv.214, V.iii.46, iv.113

4 beat, make suffer **MW** IV.v.57 [Falstaff to Host, of the learning he had from the wise woman] *I paid nothing for it neither, but was paid for my learning* [second instance]

peace (*n.*) state of calm, amenable condition **TNK** III.v.88 [Schoolmaster to all, of the Gaoler's Daughter] *fluently persuade her to a peace* [i.e. get her to calm down]

peace (*v.*) be still, keep silent, be calm **KL** IV.vi.102 [Lear to all] *the thunder would not peace at my bidding;* **MW** IV.i.24 ☛ **ATTENTION SIGNALS**, p.26

peaceful (*adj.*) undisturbed, unopposed, untroubled **R2** III.ii.125 [King Richard to Scroop, of his lords] *they have let the dangerous enemy / Measure our confines with such peaceful steps*

peace-parted (*adj.*) who have departed this life in peace **Ham** V.i.234 [Priest to Laertes, of Ophelia] *[sing] such rest to her / As to peace-parted souls*

peach (*v.*) **1** impeach, denounce, accuse **MM** IV.iii.11 [Pompey alone, of Caper's wrongdoing] *some four suits of peach-coloured satin, which now peaches him a beggar* [i.e. denounces him as a beggar]

2 turn informer, give evidence against **1H4** II.ii.43 [Falstaff to Prince Hal] *I'll peach for this*

peak (*v.*) **1** mope about, brood, languish **Ham** II.ii.564 [Hamlet alone] *I … peak / Like John-a-dreams*

2 waste away, grow thin, become emaciated **Mac** I.iii.23 [First Witch to other Witches, of a sailor] *Shall he dwindle, peak, and pine*

peaking (*adj.*) sneaking, skulking, lurking **MW** III.v.65 [Falstaff to Ford as Brook, of Ford] *the peaking cornuto … comes me in the instant of our encounter*

peal (*n.*) discharge, volley, burst **Ham** V.ii.397 [stage direction] *a peal of ordnance is shot off*

pearl (*n.*) cataract [in the eye] **TG** V.ii.13 [disguised Julia to herself, of the proverb 'black men are pearls in beauteous ladies' eyes'] *'Tis true, such pearls as put out ladies' eyes*

peasant (*n.*) servant, fellow, rascal **CE** II.i.81 [Adriana to Dromio of Ephesus] *Hence, prating peasant;* **CE** V.i.231

peasant (*adj.*) **1** base, low, villainous **Ham** II.ii.547 [Hamlet alone] *what a rogue and peasant slave am I!;* **TG** V.ii.35; **TS** IV.i.115

2 country, rural, backwoods **2H4** I.Induction.33 [Rumour alone, of the supposed deaths of the royal family] *This have I rumoured through the peasant towns*

peascod (*n.*) pea-plant, pea-pod **TN** I.v.152 [Malvolio to Olivia, of the age of Viola as Cesario] *as a squash is before 'tis a peascod;* **AY** II.iv.47; **2H4** II.iv.378; **KL** I.iv.195

pease (*n.*) peas **MND** IV.i.36 [Bottom to Titania, rejecting nuts] *I had rather have a handful or two of dried pease;* **Tem** IV.i.61

peat (*n.*) pet, spoilt darling **TS** I.i.78 [Katherina to and of Bianca] *A pretty peat!*

peck (*n.*) **1** heap, quantity, measure [a quarter of a bushel] **MND** IV.i.31 [Bottom to Titania] *a peck of provender*

2 circular vessel capable of holding a peck [quarter bushel] of goods **MW** III.v.102 [Falstaff to Ford as Brook] *I suffered … to be compassed like a good bilbo in the circumference of a peck*

peck (*v.*) pitch, throw, fling **H8** V.iv.89 [Porter to one in the crowd] *get up o'th' rail; / I'll peck you o'er the pales else*

peculiar (*adj.*) particular, private, personal **TNK** V.iii.87 [Emilia to herself, of Palamon and Arcite] *Their nobleness peculiar to them;* **Cym** V.v.83; **Ham** III.iii.11; **Luc** 14; **Oth** III.iii.79; **TC** II.iii.164

pedant (*n.*) schoolmaster, teacher **TN** III.ii.71 [Maria to Sir Toby, of Malvolio's cross-gartering] *Most villainously; like a pedant that keeps a school i'the church;* **LL** III.i.174, V.ii.533; **TS** III.i.4, 46, 85, IV.ii.63

pedantical (*adj.*) pedantic, exaggerated, artificial **LL** V.ii.408 [Berowne to Rosaline] *spruce affection, / Figures pedantical*

pedascule (*n.*) little pedant **TS** III.i.48 [Hortensio as Licio to himself, of Lucentio as Cambio] *Pedascule, I'll watch you better yet*

peeled (*adj.*) tonsured, shaven, bald **1H6** I.iii.30 [Gloucester to Winchester] *Peeled priest, dost thou command me to be shut out?*

peep (*v.*) **1** appear, show one's face **2H6** II.i.41 [Cardinal to Gloucester, of the place to answer the challenge] *where thou darest not peep;* **PassP** XIV.29, XVII.28

2 peer through half-closed eyes **MV** I.i.52 [Solanio to Antonio] *Nature hath framed strange fellows in her time: / Some that will evermore peep through their eyes / And laugh*

peep about (*v.*) emerge into view, look around **JC** I.ii.136 [Cassius to Brutus, of Caesar compared to a Colossus] *we ... / Walk under his huge legs, and peep about / To find ourselves dishonourable graves*

peer (*n.*) mate, companion; wife **Per** I.Chorus.21 [Gower alone, of Antiochus] *This king unto him took a peer*

peer (*v.*) **1** appear, come into sight **H5** IV.vii.83 [King Henry to Montjoy] *a many of your horsemen peer / And gallop o'er the field;* **Luc** 472; **TS** IV.iii.170; **WT** IV.iv.3

2 flow, rise, pour **KJ** III.i.23 [Constance to Salisbury, of his tears] *Like a proud river peering o'er his bounds*

peer out (*v.*) peep out, show oneself **WT** IV.iii.1 [Autolycus singing] *When daffodils begin to peer* [or: appear]; **MW** IV.ii.23

peevish (*adj.*) **1** silly, foolish; or: headstrong, impulsive **H5** III.vii.129 [Orleans to Constable] *What a wretched and peevish fellow is this King of England;* **AY** III.v.110; **1H6** II.iv.76; **3H6** V.vi.18; **Oth** III.iii.88; **TN** I.v.290

2 obstinate, perverse, self-willed [contrast modern sense of 'irritable, morose'] **R3** III.i.31 [Buckingham to Hastings, of Queen Elizabeth] *what an indirect and peevish course / Is this of hers!;* **E3** II.i.23; **Ham** I.ii.100; **KJ** II.i.402; **RJ** IV.ii.14; **TG** V.ii.49

3 fretful, irritable, ill-tempered **Cym** I.vii.54 [Iachimo to Pisanio, of Iachimo's servant] *He's strange and peevish;* **MV** I.i.86

peevish-fond (*adj.*) obstinately foolish **R3** IV.iv.417 [King Richard to Queen Elizabeth] *be not peevish-fond in great designs* [Q; F peevish found]

peg (*n.*) pin on a stringed instrument to which the strings are fastened **Oth** II.i.194 [Iago to himself] *I'll set down the pegs that make this music*

Peg-a-Ramsey (*n.*) [dance tune] name of a spying wife in a contemporary ballad **TN** II.iii.74 [Sir Toby to Maria] *Malvolio's a - Peg-a-Ramsey* ☛ **CONTEMPORARY FIGURES**, p.629

peise (*v.*) **1** weigh down, burden, load **E3** II.i.304 [King Edward to Warwick, as if to the world] *Why dost thou tip men's tongues with golden words, / And peise their deeds with weight of heavy lead;* **MV** III.ii.22 [F]

2 poise, balance, keep in equilibrium **KJ** II.i.575 [Bastard alone, of the world] *who of itself is peised well*

peise down (*v.*) weigh down, burden, load down **R3** V.iii.106 [Richmond to Derby] *I'll strive ... to take a nap, / Lest leaden slumber peise me down tomorrow*

peize (*v.*) ☛ **piece** (*v.*) 4

pelf (*n.*) **1** possessions, property, goods **Tim** I.ii.61 [Apemantus's grace] *I crave no pelf;* **Per** II.Chorus.35

2 treasure, booty, spoil **PassP** XIV.12 [Pilgrim] *'Wander,' a word for shadows like myself, / As take the pain, but cannot pluck the pelf*

pelican (*adj.*) bird reputed to feed her young with her own blood **KL** III.iv.72 [Lear to disguised Kent] *'Twas this flesh begot / Those pelican daughters*

pelicocks (*n.*) ☛ **pillicock** (*n.*)

pellet (*v.*) hit [as if with pellets], pelt **Lover** 18 [of a handkerchief] *That seasoned woe had pelleted in tears*

pelleted (*adj.*) filled with pellets, full of hail **AC** III.xiii.165 [Cleopatra to Antony] *By the discandying of this pelleted storm*

pell-mell (*adv.*) in headlong confusion, in disordered haste **LL** IV.iii.344 [Berowne to all, of the ladies] *Pell-mell, down with them!;* **KL** IV.vi.117

pelt (*v.*) shout angrily, harangue **Luc** 1418 [of people in a painting of Troy] *Another smothered seems to pelt and swear*

pelting (*adj.*) paltry, petty, worthless, insignificant **TC** IV.v.267 [Hector to Achilles] *We have had pelting wars since you refused / The Grecians' cause;* **KL** II.iii.18; **MM** II.ii.112; **MND** II.i.91; **R2** II.i.60; **TNK** II.i.322

pen (*n.*) penmanship, style of handwriting **LL** IV.ii.150 [Nathaniel to Holofernes, of his thoughts on Berowne's verses] *Marvellous well for the pen*

pen (*v.*) shut up, confine; silence **Luc** 681 [of Tarquin gagging Lucrece] *with the nightly linen that she wears / He pens her piteous clamours in her head*

penalty (*n.*) punishable offence, criminal act **E3** II.i.268 [Countess to King Edward] *It is a penalty to break your statutes*

pencil (*n.*) finely-pointed paint-brush **Sonn** 101.7 *Beauty* [needs] *no pencil, beauty's truth to lay;* **KJ** III.i.237; **LL** V.ii.43; **RJ** I.i.40

pencilled (*adj.*) painted, shown in a painting **Tim** I.i.163 [Timon to Painter, of the painting] *these pencilled figures are / Even such as they give out;* **Luc** 1497; **TNK** V.iii.13

pendant (*n.*) long narrow flag, pennon, pennant **E3** IV.iv.20 [Audley to Prince Edward, of the French army] *the banners, bannerets, / And new-replenished pendants cuff the air;* **E3** IV.iv.26

pendent (*adj.*) **1** downhanging, drooping, dangling **MW** IV.vi.42 [Fenton to Host, of Anne's costume] *quaint in green she shall be loose enrobed, / With ribands pendent;* **AC** IV.xiv.4; **Ham** IV.vii.172; **Mac** I.vi.8

2 hanging in space, floating in the air **MM** III.i.129 [Claudio to Isabella] *To be ... blown with restless violence round about / The pendent world*

pendulous (*adj.*) overhanging, suspended overhead **KL** III.iv.64 [Lear to Edgar as Poor Tom] *all the plagues that in the pendulous air / Hang fated o'er men's faults*

penetrable (*adj.*) **1** receptive, susceptible, capable of being affected **R3** III.vii.224 [Richard to all] *I am not made of stone, / But penetrable to your kind entreaties;* **Ham** III.iv.37; **Luc** 559

2 penetrating, piercing **E3** II.ii.63 [King Edward alone] *my arms ... shall meet my foe / In a deep march of penetrable groans*

penetrate (*v.*) pierce the feelings, touch the heart [also: sexual innuendo] **Cym** II.iii.12 [Cloten to First Lord, of music played to Innogen] *they say it will penetrate*

penetrative (*adj.*) penetrating, deeply piercing **AC** IV.xiv.75 [Antony to Eros, of himself in Rome] *his face subdued / To penetrative shame*

penitent (*adj.*) **1** undergoing penance **CE** I.ii.52 [Dromio of Ephesus to Antipholus of Syracuse] *we that know what 'tis to fast and pray / Are penitent for your default today*

2 of penance, of repentance **Cym** V.iv.10 [Posthumus alone, asking the gods for death to set him free] *give me / The penitent instrument to pick that bolt*

penned (*adj.*) specially composed, set down in writing **LL** V.ii.147 [Princess to Rosaline, of the King's party] *Nor to their penned speech render we no grace*

penner (*n.*) pen-case, pen-holder **TNK** III.v.123 [Schoolmaster to and of Theseus] *At whose great feet I offer up my penner* [or: performance as a writer]

penning (*n.*) handwriting, penmanship **KL** IV.vi.139 [Lear to Gloucester] *Read thou this challenge; mark but the penning of it*

pennon (*n.*) streamer, banner, flag **H5** III.v.49 [French King to all] *Bar Harry England, that sweeps through our land / With pennons painted in the blood of Harfleur!*

penn'orth (*n.*) ☛ **pennyworth** (*n.*)

penny (*n.*) ☛ **earnest penny**

penny (*adj.*) cheap **Cym** V.iv.168 [First Gaoler to Posthumus] *O, the charity of a penny cord!*

pennyworth, penn'orth (*n.*) **1** amount, quantity, sum **MV** I.ii.67 [Portia to Nerissa] *you will ... swear that I have a poor pennyworth in the English* [also: sense 2]

2 money's worth, bargain, good value **MA** II.iii.40 [Claudio to Don Pedro, of Benedick] *We'll fit the hid-fox with a pennyworth* [i.e. we'll pay him well for hiding so craftily] [F *kid-fox*]; **TNK** IV.iii.66
3 value, rate, price **2H6** I.i.220 [York to himself] *Pirates may make cheap pennyworths of their pillage* [i.e. squander their gains]
4 small amount, little bit **RJ** IV.v.4 [Nurse to Juliet] *You take your pennyworths now* [i.e. your extra sleep]

pensioner *(n.)* gentleman of the royal bodyguard **MND** II.i.10 [Fairy to Puck, of Titania] *The cowslips tall her pensioners be*; **MW** II.ii.74

pensive *(adj.)* sorrowful, sad, full of melancholy **RJ** IV.v.39 [Friar to Juliet] *My leisure serves me, pensive daughter, now*

pensived *(adj.)* [unclear meaning] pensive, reflective; melancholic; apprehensive **Lover** 219 [of gifts from the woman's suitors] *Of pensived and subdued desires the tender*

pent *(adj.)* imprisoned, closely confined **R3** I.iv.261 [Clarence to Murderers] *pent from liberty, as I am now*; **Cor** III.iii.89; **R3** IV.i.34; **Sonn** 133.13

pent-up *(adj.)* confined without food, ravenous **3H6** I.iii.12 [Rutland to Clifford] *So looks the pent-up lion o'er the wretch*

pent up *(v.)* shut up, confine, lock in **R3** IV.iii.36 [King Richard alone] *The son of Clarence have I pent up close*; **2H6** II.iv.24

penthouse, pent-house *(n.)* covered way, sloping porch, overhanging roof **MA** III.iii.101 [Borachio to Conrade] *Stand thee close ... under this pent-house*; **MV** II.vi.1

penthouse, pent-house *(adj.)* like a lean-to shed **Mac** I.iii.20 [First Witch to other Witches, of a sailor] *Sleep shall neither night nor day / Hang upon his penthouse lid* [i.e. his eyelids will hang over his eyes like the sloping roof of a shed]

penthouse-like *(adj.)* like a projecting roof **LL** III.i.16 [Mote to Armado] *your hat penthouse-like o'er the shop of your eyes*

penurious *(adj.)* poverty-stricken, needy, beggarly **Tim** IV.iii.93 [Alcibiades to Timon, of gold] *The want whereof doth daily make revolt / In my penurious band*

people *(n.)* household, servants **MW** IV.ii.12 [Mistress Ford to Mistress Page, in answer to 'who's at home beside yourself?'] *none but mine own people*

peppercorn *(n.)* [berry of black pepper] tiny thing, mere nothing **1H4** III.iii.8 [Falstaff to Bardolph] *An I have not forgotten what the inside of a church is made of, I am a peppercorn*

pepper-gingerbread *(n.)* hot-spiced gingerbread **1H4** III.i.249 [Hotspur to Lady Percy] *Swear me, Kate ... / A good mouth-filling oath, and leave ... such protest of pepper-gingerbread, / To velvet-guards* [i.e. protestation of brief taste, or effect]

peradventure *(adv.)* perhaps, maybe, very likely **Cor** II.i.87 [Menenius to Brutus and Sicinius, of their predecessors] *peradventure some of the best of 'em were hereditary hangmen* ☞ FEW, p.xxi

perceive *(v.)* receive, get, obtain **TG** I.i.133 [Proteus to Speed, of Julia] *Couldst thou perceive so much from her?* [punned in next line: receive money]

perch *(n.)* measure of land [c.5.5 yards / c.5 m]; distance **Per** III.Chorus.15 [Gower alone] *By many a dern and painful perch*

perchance *(adv.)* **1** perhaps, maybe **Ham** III.i.65 [Hamlet alone] *To sleep - perchance to dream* ☞ FEW, p.xxi
2 by good fortune, by chance **TN** I.ii.6 [Captain to Viola] *It is perchance that you yourself were saved*

perdition *(n.)* **1** ruin, destruction, devastation **H5** III.vi.95 [Fluellen to King Henry] *The perdition of th'athversary hath been very great*; **TC** V.ii.148; **Tem** III.iii.78; **TN** III.iv.281; **WT** IV.iv.375
2 loss, diminution, decrease **Tem** I.ii.30 [Prospero to Miranda] *not so much perdition as an hair*; **Ham** V.ii.112

perdu *(n.)* sentinel exposed to danger, sentry placed in a hazardous position **KL** IV.vii.35 [Cordelia to Lear, of Lear on the heath] *poor perdu*

perdurable *(adj.)* everlasting, long-lasting, enduring **H5** IV.v.7 [Dauphin to all] *O perdurable shame!*; **Oth** I.iii.334

perdurably *(adv.)* eternally, everlastingly, for ever **MM** III.i.118 [Claudio to Isabella, of Angelo] *Why would he for the momentary trick / Be perdurably fined?*

perdy, perdie *(int.)* ☞ SWEARING, p.435

peregrinate *(adj.)* affectedly foreign, cosmopolitan **LL** V.i.14 [Holofernes to Nathaniel, of Armado] *He is ... too peregrinate*

peremptorily *(adv.)* assuredly, positively, decisively **1H4** II.iv.418 [Falstaff (as King) to Prince Hal] *peremptorily I speak it, there is virtue in that Falstaff*

peremptory *(adj.)* **1** determined, resolved, absolutely decided **TS** II.i.131 [Petruchio to Baptista, of Katherina] *I am as peremptory as she proud-minded*; **Cor** III.i.284; **H5** V.ii.82; **KJ** II.i.454; **LL** IV.iii.224; **TG** I.iii.71
2 overbearing, imperious, dictatorial **2H6** II.i.23 [Gloucester to Cardinal] *Is your priesthood grown peremptory?*; **2H6** III.i.8; **3H6** IV.viii.59; **Per** II.v.74

perfect *(adj.)* **1** complete, pure, sheer, utter **Tem** I.i.30 [Gonzalo to himself, of the Boatswain] *his complexion is perfect gallows*; **1H6** V.v.50
2 certain, definite, positive **WT** III.iii.1 [Antigonus to Mariner] *Thou art perfect, then, our ship hath touched upon / The deserts of Bohemia?*; **Cym** III.i.73, IV.ii.118; **KJ** V.vi.6
3 innocent, guiltless, clear **Oth** I.ii.31 [Othello to Iago] *My parts, my title, and my perfect soul / Shall manifest me rightly*
4 clear, in accord with **Ham** V.ii.67 [Hamlet to Horatio, of Claudius] *is't not perfect conscience / To quit him with this arm?*
5 adult, grown up, mature **KL** I.i.73 [Edmund to Gloucester] *sons at perfect age and fathers declined*
6 complete, totally accomplished, well-trained **TG** I.iii.20 [Antonio to Panthino, of Proteus] *he cannot be a perfect man, / Not being tried and tutored in the world*; **TNK** II.iv.15
7 completely prepared, fully made ready **MM** V.i.82 [Duke to Lucio] *when you have / A business for yourself, ... / Be perfect*; **TNK** III.vi.88
8 well aware, fully informed **Mac** IV.ii.66 [Messenger to Macduff's wife] *I am not to you known, / Though in your state of honour I am perfect*
9 in a state of complete satisfaction, totally content **Mac** III.iv.20 [Macbeth to First Murderer, of Fleance's escape] *I had else been perfect*; **Mac** III.i.107; **Tim** I.i.85
10 complete, flawless, unblemished **Tem** III.i.47 [Ferdinand to Miranda] *O you, / So perfect and so peerless*; **Per** V.i.207; **TG** IV.ii.120
11 word-perfect, perfectly accurate **LL** V.ii.556 [Costard to Princess, of his lines] *I hope I was perfect*
12 inform fully, instruct completely **MM** IV.iii.140 [disguised Duke to Isabella, of Mariana and Friar Peter] *Her cause and yours / I'll perfect him withal*; **Per** III.ii.65; **Tem** I.ii.79

perfectness *(n.)* **1** fullness **2H4** IV.iv.74 [Warwick to King Henry IV, of Prince Henry] *like gross terms, / The Prince will, in the perfectness of time, / Cast off his followers*
2 state of being word-perfect **LL** V.ii.174 [masked Berowne to Mote, of his speech] *Is this your perfectness?*

perfidious *(adj.)* treacherous, unfaithful, disloyal **Tem** I.ii.68 [Prospero to Miranda, of Antonio] *that a brother should / Be so perfidious!*; **H8** I.ii.156; **Tem** I.ii.147

perforce *(adv.)* **1** forcibly, by force, violently **AY** I.ii.18 [Celia to Rosalind, of Duke Frederick] *what he hath taken away from thy father perforce* ☞ FEW, p.xxi
2 of necessity, with no choice in the matter **1H6** II.iv.115 [Richard to all] *How I am braved and must perforce endure it!* ☞ FEW, p.xxi

performance *(n.)* discharge, fulfilment, manifestation **TC** II.ii.197 [Troilus to Hector] *the performance of our heaving spleens*

perfume (*n.*) perfumed mistress, fragrant woman **Tim** IV.iii.208 [Apemantus to Timon] *Thy flatterers yet ... / Hug their diseased perfumes*

perfume (*v.*) malapropism for 'perfuse' [= cause to flow through] **2H4** II.iv.27 [Hostess to Doll, of canary] *it perfumes the blood ere one can say 'What's this?'*

perfumer (*n.*) someone employed to make rooms smell sweetly **MA** I.iii.54 [Borachio to Don John] *Being entertained for a perfumer*

periapt (*n.*) amulet, charm, talisman **1H6** V.iii.2 [Pucelle alone] *Now help, ye charming spells and periapts*

peril, at at risk of punishment **KL** III.vii.51 [Regan to Gloucester] *Wast thou not charged at peril*

period (*n.*) **1** full stop, end, ending, conclusion **1H6** IV.ii.17 [General to Talbot] *The period of thy tyranny approacheth;* **AC** IV.ii.25; **E3** II.i.130; **2H4** IV.v.229; **Luc** 380; **Oth** V.ii.353
  2 point of completion, fitting conclusion, consummation **MW** III.iii.42 [Falstaff to Mistress Ford, of meeting her] *This is the period of my ambition;* **KL** V.iii.202; **MW** V.ii.208; **R3** I.ii.237, II.i.44
  3 rhetorical pause, sentence ending, termination **MND** V.i.96 [Theseus to Hippolyta, of clerks] *I have seen them ... / Make periods in the midst of sentences;* **Luc** 565; **TG** II.i.110
  4 end, purpose, goal **H8** I.ii.209 [King Henry to all, of Buckingham] *There's his period, / To sheathe his knife in us;* **KL** IV.vii.96

period (*v.*) end, conclude; [with 'comfort' as object] put an end to; or [with 'comfort' as subject]: come to an end **Tim** I.i.103 [Messenger to Timon, of a letter for Ventidius] *which failing / Periods his comfort* [i.e. if he does not get it, his happiness is over]

perish (*v.*) destroy, wither, become ruined **TNK** IV.iii.23 [Gaoler's Daughter to herself] *We maids that have our livers perished;* **AC** III.i.27; **2H6** III.ii.100

perishing (*adj.*) deadly, destructive, malignant **Cym** IV.ii.60 [Arviragus to Belarius and Guiderius] *Grow, patience! / And let the stinking-elder, grief, untwine / His perishing root, with the increasing vine!*

periwig (*n.*) wig **TG** IV.iv.188 [disguised Julia alone, of Silvia's hair-colour] *I'll get me such a coloured periwig;* **CE** II.ii.81

periwig-pated (*adj.*) bewigged, wearing a wig **Ham** III.ii.9 [Hamlet to Players] *a robustious periwig-pated fellow*

perjure (*n.*) perjurer **LL** IV.iii.45 [Berowne to himself, of Longaville] *he comes in like a perjure, wearing papers*

perk up (*v.*) make smart, deck out, spruce up **H8** II.iii.21 [Anne to Old Lady] *'tis better to be lowly born, / And range with humble livers in content, / Than to be perked up in a glistering grief*

pernicious (*adj.*) destructive, dangerous, ruinous **2H6** III.ii.226 [Warwick to Suffolk] *Pernicious blood-sucker of sleeping men!;* **2H6** II.i.21; **H8** V.iii.19

perniciously (*adv.*) with deep loathing, to the point of destruction **H8** II.i.50 [Second Gentleman to First Gentleman, of Wolsey] *All the commons / Hate him perniciously*

peroration (*n.*) rhetorical speech, oratorical discourse **2H6** I.i.103 [Cardinal to Gloucester] *what means ... / This peroration with such circumstance?*

perpend (*v.*) consider, ponder, reflect **TN** V.i.296 [Feste to Olivia] *perpend, my princess, and give ear;* **AY** III.ii.64; **Ham** II.ii.105; **H5** IV.iv.8; **MW** II.i.108

perplexed (*adj.*) **1** troubled, disturbed, worried **Cym** V.v.108 [Lucius to all, of disguised Innogen] *Why stands he so perplexed?;* **Cym** III.iv.7; **E3** V.i.189
  2 bewildered, distracted, disoriented **KJ** III.i.221 [King Philip to all] *I am perplexed, and know not what to say;* **Oth** V.ii.342

perplexity (*n.*) riddler, source of confusion **LL** V.ii.298 [Princess to Boyet] *Avaunt, perplexity!*

persever (*v.*) **1** persevere, persist, keep at it **Per** IV.vi.103 [Lysimachus to Marina] *Persever in that clear way thou goest;* **AY** V.ii.4; **CE** II.ii.225; **KL** III.v.20; **MND** III.ii.237; **TG** III.ii.28
  2 proceed, carry on **AW** III.vii.37 [Widow to Helena] *Instruct my daughter how she shall persever;* **AW** IV.iii.37; **KJ** I.i.421

persisted (*adj.*) persistent, continual, enduring **AC** V.i.30 [Agrippa to all] *nature must compel us to lament / Our most persisted deeds*

persistive (*adj.*) persisting, long-lasting, persevering **TC** I.iii.21 [Agamemnon to all] *the protractive trials of great Jove / To find persistive constancy in men*

person (*n.*) **1** fine figure, personality **Cor** I.iii.10 [Volumnia to Virgilia, of Martius] *considering how honour would become such a person;* **MND** IV.ii.11; **TC** IV.iv.78
  2 physical appearance, bodily figure **TC** I.ii.193 [Pandarus to Cressida, of Antenor] *he's ... a proper man of person;* **3H6** III.ii.167

personage (*n.*) appearance, demeanour **TN** I.v.150 [Olivia to Malvolio, of Viola as Cesario] *Of what personage and years is he?*

personal (*adj.*) personally engaged, present in person **1H4** IV.iii.88 [Hotspur to Blunt, of King Henry] *When he was personal in the Irish war*

personate (*v.*) **1** describe, represent, delineate **TN** II.iii.152 [Maria to Sir Toby, of Malvolio] *he shall find himself most feelingly personated;* **Tim** I.i.72
  2 stand for, represent, symbolize **Cym** V.v.455 [Soothsayer to Cymbeline] *The lofty cedar ... / Personates thee*

personating (*n.*) representation, symbolic portrayal **Tim** V.i.32 [Poet to Painter, of a poem for Timon] *It must be a personating of himself*

perspective (*n.*) picture in which perspective is altered so as to appear distorted unless seen from a particular angle **AW** V.iii.48 [Bertram to King] *Contempt his scornful perspective did lend me;* **R2** II.ii.18; **TN** V.i.214

perspectively (*adv.*) as if through an optical instrument **H5** V.ii.315 [French King to King Henry, of French cities] *you see them perspectively, the cities turned into a maid* **➤ perspective** (*n.*)

persuade (*v.*) **1** urge, entreat, beseech **Ham** IV.v.170 [Laertes to Ophelia] *Hadst thou thy wits, and didst persuade revenge, / It could not move thus;* **3H6** III.iii.176; **MW** I.i.1
  2 plead, entreat **MV** III.ii.281 [Salerio to Bassanio, of Shylock] *the magnificoes / Of greatest port have all persuaded with him*
  3 convince, be sure, satisfy **TNK** III.i.113 [Arcite to Palamon] *I am persuaded this question ... / By bleeding must be cured*

persuasion (*n.*) **1** conviction, principle, opinion **MND** I.i.156 [Lysander to Hermia, of her argument for patience] *A good persuasion;* **Cym** I.v.111
  2 belief, impression, understanding **MM** IV.i.46 [Isabella to disguised Duke, of her servant] *whose persuasion is / I come about my brother*
  3 evidence, persuasive indication **Tim** III.vi.7 [Lucius to Lucullus, of Timon's lack of money] *It should not be, by the persuasion of his new feasting*
  4 argument, inducement, reason **1H6** III.iii.18 [Pucelle to all] *By fair persuasions, mixed with sugared words*

pert (*adj.*) lively, brisk, sprightly **MND** I.i.13 [Theseus to Philostrate] *Awake the pert and nimble spirit of mirth*

pertain (*v.*) belong, have a right **WT** V.iii.113 [Camillo to Polixenes, of Hermione] *If she pertain to life, let her speak too;* **TNK** III.vi.32

pertly (*adv.*) **1** smartly, quickly, briskly **Tem** IV.i.58 [Prospero to Ariel] *Appear, and pertly*
  2 boldly, audaciously, impudently **TC** IV.v.219 [Ulysses to Hector] *yonder walls, that pertly front your town*

perusal (*n.*) inspection, scrutiny, examination **Ham** II.i.90 [Ophelia to Polonius, of Hamlet] *He falls to such perusal of my face*

peruse (*v.*) **1** inspect, scrutinize, examine **Ham** IV.vii.135 [Claudius to Laertes, of Hamlet] *He ... / Will not peruse the foils*

2 reconnoitre, scout out, survey **1H6** IV.ii.43 [Talbot to all] *Out, some light horsemen, and peruse their wings;* **CE** I.ii.13

perverse (*n.*) obstinate, stubborn, intransigent **E3** IV.ii.35 [King Edward to all] *Edward's sword must flesh itself in such / As wilful stubborness hath made perverse*

pervert (*v.*) **1** divert, turn aside, redirect **Cym** II.iv.151 [Philario to Iachimo, of Posthumus] *Let's follow him, and pervert the present wrath / He hath against himself*
 2 lead astray, seduce, corrupt **AW** IV.iii.13 [Second Lord to First Lord, of Bertram] *He hath perverted a young gentlewoman*

pester (*v.*) obstructing, crowding, clogging **Cor** IV.vi.7 [Sicinius to Brutus] *Dissentious numbers pestering streets*

pestered (*adj.*) afflicted, troubled, plagued **Mac** V.ii.23 [Menteth to all, of Macbeth] *Who then shall blame / His pestered senses to recoil and start*

pestiferous (*adj.*) pestilent, mischievous, pernicious **1H6** III.i.15 [Gloucester to Winchester] *Thy lewd, pestiferous, and dissentious pranks;* **AW** IV.iii.297

pestilence (*n.*) plague, epidemic, fatal disease **R2** I.iii.284 [John of Gaunt to Bolingbroke] *suppose / Devouring pestilence hangs in our air;* **AC** III.x.9

petar (*n.*) bomb, explosive **Ham** III.iv.208 [Hamlet to Gertrude] *For 'tis the sport to have the enginer / Hoist with his own petar* [i.e. blown up by his own device]

petitionary (*adj.*) imploring, suppliant, entreating **AY** III.ii.183 [Rosalind to Celia] *I prithee now with most petitionary vehemence;* **Cor** V.ii.72

petticoat (*n.*) long skirt **AY** I.iii.15 [Celia to Rosalind, of burs] *If we walk not in the trodden paths, our very petticoats will catch them;* **AC** I.ii.169; **AY** III.ii.325; **3H6** V.v.23; **TNK** V.ii.82; **TS** II.i.5 **☞ CLOTHING,** p.79

pettish (*adj.*) petulant, peevish, bad-humoured **TC** II.iii.129 [Agamemnon to Patroclus, of Achilles] *[we] watch / His pettish lunes*

pettitoes (*n.*) trotters, feet **WT** IV.iv.603 [Autolycus to himself, of the Clown] *he would not stir his pettitoes till he had both tune and words*

petty (*adj.*) **1** small, weak, inadequate, insignificant **Cym** I.ii.42 [Innogen to Posthumus] *Such parting were too petty;* **AC** III.xii.8; **Ham** I.iv.82; **1H6** I.i.91
 2 minor, subordinate, inferior **WT** IV.iv.4 [Florizel to Perdita] *This your sheep-shearing / Is as a meeting of the petty gods;* **2H4** IV.iii.108

pew-fellow (*n.*) one who shares a church bench; companion, associate **R3** IV.iv.58 [Queen Margaret to Duchess of York, of Richard and the Duchess] *this carnal cur ... makes her pew-fellow with others' moan!*

pewterer (*n.*) maker of pewter utensils **2H4** III.ii.255 [Falstaff to Shallow, of Wart] *'A shall charge you, and discharge you, with the motion of a pewterer's hammer* [i.e. very rapidly]

phang (*v.*) **☞ fang** (*v.*)

phantasime (*n.*) one full of fancies, extravagantly behaved individual **RJ** II.iv.28 [Mercutio to Benvolio, of Tybalt] *The pox of such antic, lisping, affecting phantasimes* [Q1 *fantasticoes*; F *phantacies*]; **LL** IV.i.100, V.i.18 **☞ fantastico** (*n.*)

phantasma (*n.*) illusion, bad dream, nightmare **JC** II.i.65 [Brutus alone] *Between the acting of a dreadful thing / And the first motion, all the interim is / Like a phantasma or a hideous dream*

pheazar (*n.*) [unclear meaning] vizier, person of great stature **MW** I.iii.9 [Host to Falstaff] *Thou'rt an emperor - Caesar, Keisar, and Pheazar*

pheeze, feeze (*v.*) do for, settle the hash of, fix **TS** Induction.i.1 [Sly to Hostess] *I'll pheeze you, in faith;* **TC** II.iii.203

philosopher (*n.*) one learned in natural philosophy, sage **KL** III.iv.147 [Lear to Gloucester, of Edgar as Poor Tom] *let me talk with this philosopher;* **KL** III.iv.165, 170; **Tim** II.ii.113

philosopher's two stones two hypothetical means of (i) giving eternal youth and (ii) turning base metals into gold **2H4** III.ii.318 [Falstaff alone, of Shallow] *I'll make him a philosopher's two stones to me* [i.e. a source of unbelievable wealth]

philosophy (*n.*) natural philosophy, i.e. science **Ham** I.v.366 [Hamlet to Rosencrantz, of the current situation] *there is something in this more than natural, if philosophy could find it out*

phlegmatic (*adj.*) malapropism for 'choleric' [= angry] **MW** I.iv.73 [Mistress Quickly to Caius] *be not so phlegmatic*

phoenix (*n.*) **1** wonder, marvel, paragon **AW** I.i.165 [Helena to Parolles, of her virginity] *There shall your master have ... / A phoenix*
 2 ☞ CLASSICAL MYTHOLOGY, p.613

phoenix (*adj.*) [unclear meaning] rare, matchless, beautiful **Lover** 93 [of the man] *His phoenix down began but to appear / Like unshorn velvet*

phrase (*n.*) **1** phrasing, language, mode of expression **KL** IV.vi.8 [Gloucester to Edgar] *thou speak'st / In better phrase and matter than thou didst;* **Ham** I.iv.19, II.ii.441; **2H4** III.ii.72
 2 manner, style, way **AC** I.ii.108 [Antony to Messenger] *Rail thou in Fulvia's phrase*

phrase (*v.*) call, name, style **H8** I.i.34 [Norfolk to Buckingham, of the Kings of England and France] *When these suns - / For so they phrase 'em*

phraseless (*adj.*) lacking language to describe **Lover** 225 [the woman to the reverend man] *advance ... that phraseless hand*

physic (*n.*) **1** medicine, healing, treatment **AY** III.ii.344 [Rosalind to Orlando] *I will not cast away my physic but on those that are sick* **☞ FEW,** p.xxi
 2 knowledge of the human body, medical science **LL** II.i.123 [Rosaline to Berowne, of whether bleeding would cure his sick heart] *My physic says ay;* **Cym** V.ii.268

physic (*v.*) **1** cure, correct, dose with medicine **Mac** II.iii.47 [Macbeth to Macduff] *The labour we delight in physics pain;* **AY** I.i.81; **Lover** 259; **TC** I.iii.378; **WT** I.i.37
 2 keep in good health, minister to **Cym** III.ii.34 [Innogen to Pisanio, of the grief of being apart from Posthumus] *it doth physic love*

physical (*adj.*) medicinal, therapeutic, restorative **JC** II.i.262 [Portia to Brutus] *is it physical / To walk unbraced;* **Cor** I.v.18

pia mater (*n.*) membrane covering the brain; brain **TN** I.v.110 [Feste to Olivia, of Sir Toby] *one of thy kin has a most weak pia mater;* **LL** IV.ii.70; **TC** II.i.70

pibble-pabble (*n.*) **☞ bibble-babble** (*n.*)

pick (*n.*) pike **E3** I.ii.52 [Messenger to King David] *The sun ... showed / A field of plate, a wood of picks advanced* **☞ WEAPONS,** p.491

pick (*v.*) **1** throw, pitch, hurl **Cor** I.i.198 [Martius to Menenius, of the citizens] *I'd make a quarry / With thousands of these quartered slaves as high / As I could pick my lance*
 2 extract, make out, detect **MND** V.i.100 [Theseus to Hippolyta, of clerks unable to speak in his presence] *Out of this silence yet I picked a welcome;* **Luc** 100

picked (*adj.*) **1** fastidious, neat, foppish **LL** V.i.13 [Holofernes to Nathaniel, of Armado] *He is too picked, too spruce, too affected;* **KJ** I.i.193
 2 over-refined, fastidious, particular **Ham** V.i.138 [Hamlet to Horatio] *the age is grown so picked*
 3 specially chosen, selected **Tem** V.i.247 [Prospero to Alonso] *At picked leisure ... single I'll resolve you*

picked-hatch, pickt-hatch (*n.*) spiked half-door; house of disrepute, brothel **MW** II.ii.18 [Falstaff to Pistol] *Go ... to your manor of Pickt-hatch, go*

pickers and stealers hands **Ham** III.ii.343 [Hamlet to Rosencrantz] *And do still [love you], by these pickers and stealers*

picking (*adj.*) fastidious, trifling, fussy **2H4** IV.i.196 [Archbishop to Mowbray] *the King is weary / Of dainty and such picking grievances6*

picklock (*n.*) instrument for picking locks **MM** III.ii.15 [Elbow to disguised Duke, of Pompey] *we have found upon him … a strange picklock* [i.e. for chastity belts]

pickpurse, pick-purse (*n.*) pickpocket, purse-stealer **AY** III.iv.21 [Celia to Rosalind, of Orlando] *he is not a pick-purse nor a horse-stealer;* **1H4** II.i.49; **LL** IV.iii.207; **MW** I.i.148

pickthank (*n.*) flatterer, sycophant; tale-bearer, rumour-monger **1H4** III.ii.25 [Prince Hal to King Henry] *in reproof of many tales devised … / By smiling pickthanks*

picture (*n.*) **1** appearance, countenance, visible form **MV** I.ii.68 [Portia to Nerissa, of Falconbridge] *He is a proper man's picture;* **TG** II.iv.207

2 likeness, image, imitation **WT** V.ii.169 [Clown to Autolycus] *the kings and the princes … are going to see the Queen's picture;* **CE** IV.iii.13

3 description **KL** II.i.80 [Gloucester to Edmund, of Edgar] *his picture / I will send far and near*

4 scene, visible position, conspicuous place **WT** IV.iv.600 [Autolycus to himself] *I saw whose purse was best in picture*

picture (*v.*) depict, represent, portray **Cym** V.v.181 [First Gaoler to Posthumus] *Your death has eyes in's head then: I have not seen him so pictured*

pie (*n.*) magpie **3H6** V.vi.48 [King to Richard] *at thy birth … chattering pies in dismal discords sung;* **TNK** I.i.21

piece (*n.*) **1** work (of art), creation **Tim** I.i.28 [Poet to Painter, of his picture] *Let's see your piece; **Tim** I.i.159, 250, V.i.19; **TNK** I.iii.10; **WT** V.ii.94

2 specimen, masterpiece **Ham** II.ii.303 [Hamlet to Rosencrantz and Guildenstern] *What a piece of work is a man;* **AC** I.ii.155; **H8** V.v.26; **KL** IV.iii.5; **R3** I.iii.10

3 [of virtue] model, picture, paragon **Tem** I.ii.56 [Prospero to Miranda] *Thy mother was a piece of virtue;* **AC** III.ii.28; **Per** IV.vi.109

4 accomplishment, forte, skill **TNK** II.v.14 [Arcite to Theseus, of his own horsemanship] *they that knew me / Would say it was my best piece*

5 creature, individual, person, woman **WT** IV.iv.32 [Florizel to Perdita, of the gods] *Their transformations / Were never for a piece of beauty rarer;* **Tit** I.i.312; **TNK** III.v.42

6 kind, type, sort **Tim** III.ii.66 [First Stranger to Second and Third Strangers, of Lucius' behaviour] *just of the same piece / Is every flatterer's spirit*

7 cannon, piece of artillery, fire-arm **Ham** V.ii.275 [stage direction] *A piece goes off;* **Ham** I.iv.7; **2H4** III.ii.273; **MW** IV.ii.53 ➤ mortar-piece (*n.*); murdering-piece (*n.*)

8 coin, piece of money **Tim** III.vi.21 [Lucullus to Lucius, of Timon's request] *A thousand pieces* [i.e. gold coins]; **Cor** III.iii.32; **Cym** V.iv.25

9 wine cask, butt of liquor **TC** IV.i.63 [Diomedes to Paris, of Menelaus] *He … would drink up / The lees and dregs of a flat tamed piece*

10 bit of ground, place **TNK** III.vi.263 [Palamon to Theseus, of Arcite] *I … dare kill this cousin / On any piece the earth has*

piece (*v.*) **1** add to, join to, augment **AC** I.v.45 [Alexas to Cleopatra, quoting Antony] *I will piece / Her opulent throne with kingdoms;* **Cor** II.iii.211; **KL** I.i.199; **Lover** 119; **WT** V.ii.101

2 complete, make up, improve **TNK** V.iv.31 [Palamon to Gaoler, of the Gaoler's Daughter] *to piece her portion / Tender her this*

3 mend, repair, make whole **TS** III.ii.59 [Biondello to Tranio as Lucentio, of Petruchio's horse] *with … one girth six times pieced;* **Oth** I.iii.217

4 prolong, extend, drag out **MV** III.ii.22 [Portia to Bassanio] *I speak too long, but 'tis to piece the time* [F, Q *peize*]

piece out (*v.*) **1** augment, increase, supplement **KL** III.vi.2 [Gloucester to disguised Kent] *I will piece out the comfort with what addition I can;* **JC** II.i.51; **MW** III.ii.30; **TC** III.i.51

2 prolong, extend, drag out **R2** V.i.92 [Richard to Queen Isabel] *piece the way out with a heavy heart;* **MV** III.ii.22

piece up (*v.*) add to, make up, parcel up **WT** V.ii.56 [Polixenes to Leontes] *Let him that was the cause of this have power / To take off so much grief from you as he / Will piece up in himself*

pied (*adj.*) of different colours, multi-coloured **LL** V.ii.883 [Ver singing, of spring] *When daisies pied and violets blue;* **MV** I.iii.76; **Sonn** 98.2; **Tem** III.ii.63

piedness (*n.*) diverse colouring, multi-coloured character **WT** IV.iv.87 [Perdita to disguised Polixenes, of gillyvors] *There is an art which in their piedness shares / With great creating Nature*

pierce (*v.*) **1** move, touch, get through to **MV** IV.i.126 [Gratiano to Shylock] *Can no prayers pierce thee?*

2 see, reach, penetrate **Tem** II.i.246 [Antonio to Sebastian, of the latter's hopes] *even / Ambition cannot pierce a wink beyond*

piercing (*adj.*) **1** moving, touching, poignant **TS** II.i.176 [Petruchio alone, of wooing Katherina] *I'll … say she uttereth piercing eloquence*

2 oppressive, severe, distressing **Cor** I.i.81 [First Citizen to Menenius, of the patricians] *provide more piercing statutes daily to chain up and restrain the poor*

pight (*adj.*) **1** determined, set, fixed **KL** II.i.64 [Edmund to Gloucester, of Edgar's intention] *I … found him pight to do it*

2 pitched, set up **TC** V.x.24 [Troilus as if to the enemy tents] *Thus proudly pight upon our Phrygian plains*

pignut (*n.*) variety of edible nutty root, earth chestnut **Tem** II.ii.165 [Caliban to Stephano] *I … will dig thee pignuts*

pike (*n.*) **1** lance, spear **2H4** II.iv.50 [Falstaff to Doll, of a soldier] *to come off the breach, with his pike bent bravely* ➤ WEAPONS, p.491

2 central spike in a buckler **MA** V.ii.21 [Benedick to Margaret] *you must put in the pikes with a vice* ➤ WEAPONS, p.491

3 defensive stake **1H6** I.i.116 [Third Messenger to all, of Talbot] *He wanted pikes to set before his archers*

4 pitchfork, hayfork **Cor** I.i.21 [First Citizen to all, of the authorities] *Let us revenge this with our pikes*

pilcher (*n.*) **1** pilchard **TN** III.i.33 [Feste to Viola as Cesario] *fools are as like husbands as pilchers are to herrings*

2 [contemptuous] scabbard **RJ** III.i.79 [Mercutio to Tybalt] *Will you pluck your sword out of his pilcher by the ears?*

pilgrimage (*n.*) journey, passage, voyage **R2** I.iii.264 [Bolingbroke to John of Gaunt, of banishment] *an enforced pilgrimage;* **KL** V.iii.194; **MM** II.i.36; **R2** I.iii.230

pill (*v.*) **1** pillage, plunder, rob **Tim** IV.i.12 [Timon alone, of servants] *Large-handed robbers your grave masters are, / And pill by law;* **R2** II.i.246; **R3** I.iii.158

2 [of bark] peel, strip **MV** I.iii.81 [Shylock to Antonio] *The skilful shepherd pilled me certain wands* [F *pil'd*; Q *pyld*]; **Luc** 1167

pill up (*v.*) [unclear meaning] plunder, rob; pile up, accumulate **2H4** IV.v.72 [King Henry IV to princes, of fathers] *they have engrossed and pilled up / The cankered heaps of strange-achieved gold* [F *pyl'd*; Q *pilld*]

pillage (*n.*) plunder, spoil, booty **1H6** IV.vii.41 [Pucelle to all, reporting John Talbot] *Young Talbot was not born / To be the pillage of a giglot wench*

pilled (*adj.*) made bald, with hair removed **MM** I.ii.34 [First Gentleman to Lucio] *be piled, as thou art pilled, for a French velvet* [i.e. because treated for venereal disease] [F *pil'd*]

pilled (*adv.*) poorly, miserably, beggarly **1H6** I.iv.33 [Talbot to all, of his ransom offer] *I … craved death / Rather than I would be so pilled esteemed*

pillicock [slang] penis **KL** III.iv.73 [Edgar as Poor Tom to all] *Pillicock sat on Pillicock Hill* [F; Q *pelicocks*]

pin (*n.*) **1** trifle, triviality, insignificant amount MM III.i.109 [Isabella to Claudio, of her life] *I'd throw it down for your deliverance / As frankly as a pin;* MM II.i.93; MW I.i.108; TC V.ii.23; TG I.i.108, II.vii.55

2 peg [to hold things together] 2H4 III.ii.143 [Falstaff to Shallow, of Wart] *his apparel is built upon his back, and the whole frame stands upon pins*

3 [archery] peg in the middle of a target; centre RJ II.iv.15 [Mercutio to Benvolio, of Romeo] *the very pin of his heart cleft with the blind bow-boy's butt-shaft;* LL IV.i.137

pin and web ☞ web and the pin

pin's fee, a the value of a trifle Ham I.iv.65 [Hamlet to Horatio and Marcellus] *I do not set my life at a pin's fee*

pinch (*n.*) **1** pain, pang, torment Cym I.ii.61 [Innogen to Cymbeline] *There cannot be a pinch in death / More sharp than this is;* Tem V.i.77

2 hardship, extremity, privation KL II.iv.206 [Lear to all] *Necessity's sharp pinch!*

3 tiny bite, slight nip Tem IV.i.233 [Caliban to Stephano and Trinculo, of Prospero] *From toe to crown he'll fill our skins with pinches;* 1H6 IV.ii.49

pinch (*v.*) **1** torment, pain, torture Tem V.i.276 [Caliban to all] *I shall be pinched to death;* 1H4 I.iii.226; 2H4 IV.v.30; H8 II.iii.1; Tem V.i.74; TNK V.iii.133

2 bite, nip 3H6 II.i.16 [Richard to Edward, of a bear] *encompassed round with dogs, / Who having pinched a few and made them cry, / The rest stand all aloof*

3 harass, irritate, annoy AC II.vii.6 [Second Servant to First Servant, of the drinkers] *they pinch one another by the disposition*

4 wear away, eat into, corrode TG IV.iv.152 [disguised Julia to Silvia, of Julia] *air hath ... pinched the lily-tincture of her face*

5 cause trouble, bring into difficulties TS I.i.364 [Tranio as Lucentio to Gremio] *What, have I pinched you*

6 take, squeeze, press WT I.ii.115 [Leontes to himself, of Hermione and Polixenes] *to be ... pinching fingers, / As now they are;* MW IV.vi.44

pinched (*adj.*) tortured, tormented; or: distressed, afflicted; or: reduced to nothing WT II.i.51 [Leontes to Lord, of Camillo] *He has discovered my design, and I / Remain a pinched thing*

pinching (*adj.*) bitingly cold; or narrowly restricting Cym III.iii.38 [Arviragus to Belarius] *How / In this our pinching cave shall we discourse / The freezing hours away?*

pinch-spotted (*adj.*) discoloured with pinch-marks Tem IV.i.261 [Prospero to Ariel, of Caliban, Stephano and Trinculo] *more pinch-spotted make them / Than pard*

pine (*v.*) **1** starve, hunger, waste away Luc 1115 *He ten times pines that pines beholding food;* Luc 905

2 afflict, wear out, cause to waste away R2 V.i.77 [Richard to Northumberland] *I towards the north, / Where shivering cold and sickness pines the clime*

3 torment, trouble, afflict Venus 602 *poor birds, deceived with painted grapes, / Do surfeit by the eye and pine the maw*

pined (*adj.*) made thin with grief, wasted away with sorrow Lover 32 [of the woman's hair] *Hanging her pale and pined cheek beside*

pinfold (*n.*) pound, place for keeping stray animals TG I.i.107 [Proteus to Speed] *I mean the pound - a pinfold;* KL II.ii.8

pining (*adj.*) consuming, wasting, eating away 1H6 III.iii.49 [Pucelle to Burgundy] *see the pining malady of France*

pinion (*n.*) outermost feather, appendage AC III.xii.4 [Dolabella to Caesar, of Antony's messenger] *He sends so poor a pinion of his wing*

pinioned (*adj.*) **1** bound, tied up, secured MW IV.ii.116 [Page to Ford] *You must be pinioned*

2 with arms bound, with wings clipped AC V.ii.53 [Cleopatra to Proculeius] *I / Will not wait pinioned at your master's court*

pink (*adj.*) half-shut, blinking, tiny AC II.vii.112 [Boy, singing] *Plumpy Bacchus with pink eyne!*

pinked (*adj.*) ornamented with perforations, pierced, scalloped H8 V.iv.48 [Man to Porter, of a haberdasher's wife] *that railed upon me till her pinked porringer fell off her head*

pinnace (*n.*) small speedy boat with a single mast 2H6 IV.i.107 [Suffolk to and of Lieutenant] *Being captain of a pinnace;* 2H6 IV.i.9; MW I.iii.75

pioned (*adj.*) [unclear meaning] trenched, furrowed, channelled Tem IV.i.64 [Iris to Ceres] *Thy banks with pioned and twilled brims*

pioneer, pioner (*n.*) **1** sapper, labouring foot-soldier Luc 1380 [of a painting of Troy] *There might you see the labouring pioneer / Begrimed with sweat;* Oth III.iii.343

2 miner, digger, excavator H5 III.ii.84 [Gower to Macmorris] *Have the pioneers given o'er?;* Ham I.v.163

pious (*adj.*) religious, holy; or: dutiful, loyal Mac III.vi.12 [Lennox to Lord, of Macbeth killing the King's attendants] *Did he not straight - / In pious rage - the two delinquents tear*

pip (*n.*) mark on a playing card [as used in the game of 'one-and-thirty'] TS I.ii.33 [Grumio to Hortensio, of Petruchio hitting him] *being perhaps, for aught I see, two and thirty, a pip out* [i.e. he has gone too far; or: he's not quite right in the head]

pipe (*n.*) voice TN I.iv.32 [Orsino to Viola as Cesario] *Thy small pipe / Is as the maiden's organ, shrill and sound*

pipe (*v.*) whistle, look in vain Tit IV.iii.24 [Titus to all] *then we may go pipe for justice*

pipe-wine (*n.*) wine drawn directly from the cask [pipe] MW III.ii.81 [Ford to himself, of Falstaff] *I shall drink in pipe-wine first with him*

piping (*adj.*) shrill-toned, high-pitched [either: of pipes; or: of women and children's voices] R3 I.i.24 [Richard alone] *in this weak piping time of peace*

pirate (*n.*) **1** thief, marauder, plunderer R3 I.iii.157 [Queen Margaret to all] *Hear me, you wrangling pirates*

2 pirate-ship Ham IV.vi.16 [Hamlet to Horatio, by letter] *a pirate of very warlike appointment*

pish (*int.*) ☞ EXCLAMATIONS, p.158

pismire (*n.*) ant 1H4 I.iii.237 [Hotspur to Northumberland and Worcester] *I am ... stung with pismires*

pissing while a very short time; also: with enough time to urinate TG IV.iv.18 [Launce alone, of his dog] *he had not been there ... a pissing while but all the chamber smelt him*

piss o'th' nettle be in a bad temper, show irritation TNK III.v.58 [Fourth Countryman to all, of the missing woman] *Now to be frampold, now to piss o'th' nettle*

pistol (*v.*) shoot with a pistol TN II.v.36 [Sir Andrew to Fabian and Sir Toby, of Malvolio] *Pistol him*

pit (*n.*) hole prepared for hunted animals JC V.v.23 [Brutus to Volumnius] *Our enemies have beat us to the pit*

pitch (*n.*) **1** height [to which a bird of prey soars before swooping] 2H6 II.i.6 [King to Gloucester, of Gloucester's falcon] *what a pitch she flew above the rest!;* 1H6 II.iv.11; JC I.i.73; RJ I.iv.21; Sonn 86.6; Tit II.i.14

2 height, elevation, high aspiration TN I.i.12 [Orsino to all, of love] *naught enters there, / Of what validity and pitch soe'er, / But falls into abatement;* Ham III.i.86 [Q]; 1H6 II.iii.54; R3 III.vii.187

3 black tar-like substance [used to waterproof planks, etc; often, a symbol of defilement] Tem I.ii.3 [Miranda to Prospero] *The sky it seems would pour down stinking pitch;* 1H4 II.iv.405; 2H6 II.i.191; LL IV.iii.3; Oth II.iii.350

pitch (*v.*) **1** set, place LL IV.iii.3 [Berowne alone, probably of Rosaline's eyes] *They have pitched a toil;* Venus 551

2 place oneself, settle, alight TNK II.i.273 [Arcite to Palamon, of Emilia] *I'll ... pitch between her arms to anger thee*

3 provide sharp stakes for 1H6 III.i.103 [First Servingman to Gloucester] *the very parings of our nails shall pitch a field when we are dead*

pitch and pay pay as you go, no credit **H5** II.iii.46 [Pistol to all] *The word is 'Pitch and pay!'*

pitch-ball *(n.)* ball black as pitch **LL** III.i.194 [Berowne alone, of Rosaline] *With two pitch-balls stuck in her face for eyes* ➤ pitch *(n.)* 3

pitched *(adj.)* strategically planned, made ready for combat **Tim** I.ii.227 [Timon to Alcibiades] *all the lands thou hast / Lie in a pitched field;* **E3** III.iii.173; **1H6** IV.ii.23

pitchy *(adj.)* pitch-dark, black, inky, dark **3H6** V.vi.85 [Richard alone, of George] *I will sort a pitchy day for thee;* **AW** IV.iv.24; **1H6** II.ii.2; **Luc** 550; **Venus** 821 ➤ pitch *(n.)* 3

piteous *(adj.)* full of pity, compassionate, tender **Tem** I.ii.14 [Prospero to Miranda] *Tell your piteous heart / There's no harm done;* **Ham** III.iv.129

piteously *(adv.)* so as to excite pity, evoking compassion **Tit** V.i.66 [Aaron to Lucius, of his confession] *villainies, / Ruthful to hear, yet piteously performed*

pitfall *(n.)* bird-trap, fowler's snare **Mac** IV.ii.36 [Macduff's wife to her son] *Poor bird, thou'dst never fear / The net nor lime, the pitfall nor the gin!*

pith *(n.)* **1** strength, toughness, mettle **H5** III.Chorus.21 [Chorus alone] *grandsires, babies, and old women, / Either past or not arrived to pith and puissance;* **Oth** I.iii.83; **Venus** 26

2 essence, central point, main purpose **MM** I.iv.70 [Lucio to Isabella] *that's my pith of business / 'Twixt you and your poor brother;* **TS** I.i.163

3 importance, weight, gravity **Ham** III.i.86 [Hamlet alone] *enterprises of great pitch and moment* [F; Q *pitch*]

pithless *(adj.)* feeble, frail, puny [lacking pith, or marrow] **1H6** II.v.11 [Mortimer to Gaolers, of his arms] *pithless arms, like to a withered vine*

pitiful *(adj.)* compassionate, merciful, tender **3H6** I.iv.141 [York to Queen] *Women are soft, mild, pitiful, and flexible;* **AW** III.ii.127; **3H6** III.ii.32; **JC** III.i.169; **TC** III.ii.198

pitifully *(adv.)* with compassion, by showing mercy **Tim** III.v.53 [Alcibiades to Senators] *As you are great, be pitifully good*

pittance *(n.)* meal, fare, provision **TS** IV.iv.61 [Tranio as Lucentio to Baptista, of the hospitality available at his lodging] *You are like to have a thin and slender pittance*

pittie-ward *(n.)* direction of Windsor Little Park **MW** III.i.5 [Simple to Evans, of where Simple has looked for Caius] *the pittie-ward, the park-ward, every way* ➤ park-ward *(n.)*

pittikins *(n.)* [diminutive form] pity **Cym** IV.ii.293 [Innogen alone] *'Ods pittikins* ➤ **SWEARING**, p.435

pity *(n.)* bad thing, sad fate, calamity [for] **LL** V.ii.495 [Costard to Berowne] *it were pity you should get your living by reck'ning;* **MND** III.i.39

pity *(v.)* be merciful to, assist **KL** III.iii.3 [Gloucester to Edmund, of Lear] *I desired their leave that I might pity him*

pizzle *(n.)* penis **1H4** II.iv.241 [Falstaff to Prince Hal] *you bull's-pizzle*

place *(n.)* **1** position, post, office, rank **KL** II.iv.11 [Lear to disguised Kent] *What's he that hath so much thy place mistook* ➤ **FEW**, p.xxi

2 precedence, proper place **H8** I.ii.10 [King Henry to kneeling Queen Katherine] *Arise, and take place by us;* **AW** I.i.102; **LL** III.i.66; **Tim** III.iii.15

3 dignity, honour, privilege **WT** I.ii.448 [Polixenes to Camillo] *Be pilot to me, and thy places shall / Still neighbour mine*

4 proper place, safe place **AY** II.iii.27 [Adam to Orlando] *This is no place, this house is but a butchery*

5 room, lodging, quarters **KL** II.iv.244 [Regan to Lear, of his knights] *to no more / Will I give place or notice*

6 way, room **JC** IV.iii.201 [Brutus to Cassius] *Good reasons must of force give place to better;* **JC** III.i.10, IV.iii.144; **TC** III.iii.199

place, in present, attending, at hand **MM** V.i.496 [Duke to all, of Lucio] *here's one in place I cannot pardon;* **3H6** IV.vi.103, vi.31; **TS** I.ii.154

place where, in in a suitable place **TS** IV.iii.145 [Tailor to Grumio, of his honesty] *an I had thee in place where, thou shouldst know it*

place *(v.)* **1** establish in office, appoint to a post **E3** I.i.41 [Artois to King Edward] *And place the true shepherd of our commonwealth;* **Tim** IV.iii.36

2 arrange, dispose, express **1H6** III.ii.3 [Pucelle to her soldiers] *be wary how you place your words;* **1H6** V.iii.179

3 arrange the seating, find places **H8** I.iv.20 [Lord Chamberlain to Guildford] *Place you that side*

placed *(adj.)* fixed, set, firm **AC** V.ii.238 [Cleopatra alone] *My resolution's placed*

placket *(n.)* **1** petticoat, apron **WT** IV.iv.606 [Autolycus to himself, of the crowd] *you might have pinched a placket, it was senseless;* **WT** IV.iv.243

2 opening in the front of a skirt or petticoat **LL** III.i.181 [Berowne alone, of Cupid] *Dread prince of plackets;* **KL** III.iv.93; **TC** II.iii.20

plague *(n.)* calamity, affliction, scourge **R2** V.iii.3 [King Henry to all, of his son] *If any plague hang over us, 'tis he;* **KJ** II.iv.60; **KL** I.ii.3, IV.i.46, 63

plague *(v.)* torment, vex, trouble **TC** V.ii.107 [Cressida to Diomedes] *I shall be plagued*

plaguy *(adv.)* confoundedly, insufferably, pestilently **TC** II.iii.175 [Ulysses to Agamemnon, of Achilles] *He is so plaguy proud that the death-tokens of it / Cry 'No recovery.'*

plain *(n.)* open country **TNK** II.ii.54 [Second Countryman to the others, of the Schoolmaster] *Bring him to th'plains, his learning makes no cry*

plain *(adj.)* **1** honest, open, free from deceit **Luc** 1532 [of Lucrece and a painting of Sinon] *signs of truth in his plain face she spied;* **CE** II.ii.93; **LL** V.ii.177

2 simple, homely, unaffected **E3** I.ii.146 [Countess to King Edward] *a country swain, / Whose habit rude and manners blunt and plain / Presageth nought*

3 [bowls] level, flat, even, smooth **AW** II.i.31 [Bertram to Parolles] *Creaking my shoes on the plain masonry;* **Cor** III.i.61; **Tit** V.i.68

plain *(v.)* **1** complain, lament, bewail **KL** III.i.39 [disguised Kent to Gentleman] *how unnatural and bemadding sorrow / The King hath cause to plain*

2 make plain, explain, give utterance to **Per** III.Chorus.14 [Gower alone] *What's dumb in show, I'll plain with speech*

plain *(adv.)* honestly, frankly, openly **3H6** III.ii.69 [Edward to Lady Grey] *To tell thee plain, I aim to lie with thee*

plaining *(n.)* **1** complaining, moaning, lamenting **R2** I.iii.175 [King Richard to Mowbray] *After our sentence plaining comes too late;* **Luc** 559

2 wailing, crying **CE** I.i.73 [Egeon to Duke] *piteous plainings of the pretty babes*

plainly *(adv.)* **1** openly, straightforwardly, without reserve **Cor** V.iii.3 [Coriolanus to Aufidius] *You must report to th'Volscian lords how plainly / I have borne this business*

2 bluntly, frankly, candidly **KL** IV.vii.62 [Lear to Cordelia] *to deal plainly, / I fear I am not in my perfect mind*

plainness *(n.)* plain-speaking, openness, frankness **KL** I.i.129 [Lear to all, of Cordelia] *Let pride, which she calls plainness, marry her;* **KL** I.iv.6; **TN** I.i.148

plainsong *(n.)* **1** simple straightforward melody **H8** I.iii.45 [Sands to Lovell and Lord Chamberlain, of entertaining ladies with music] *An honest country lord, as I am … may bring his plainsong, / And have an hour of hearing* [with bawdy pun]

2 plain truth, bottom line **H5** III.ii.6 [Pistol to Nym] *The plainsong is most just; for humours do abound;* **H5** III.ii.5

plainsong *(adj.)* lacking in ornament, melodically simple **MND** III.i.124 [Bottom singing to himself] *The plainsong cuckoo grey*

PLANTS

Botanical nomenclature in Early Modern English is often different from that used today, both in terms and in meanings. And even in those cases where the names of flowers, herbs, shrubs, and other plants are the same as in modern English, there is sometimes a symbolic association no longer present. The following list illustrates these differences, but excludes plants used as food (lettuce, potato, etc.); distinctive usage here is covered under individual entries in the A–Z section. Clusters of plant names can be found at **Ham** IV.v.176ff, **TNK** I.i.1ff, **WT** IV.iv.73ff, and **MND** II.i.249ff.

Item	Example	Identity	Comment
Flowers			
burnet	H5 V.ii.49	Rosaceae: Sanguisorba; Poterium	flower 'brought sweetly forth' in meadows
carnation	WT IV.iv.82	Caryophyllaceae: Dianthus caryophyllus	one of the 'fairest flowers o'th' season'
clover	H5 V.ii.49	Leguminosae: Trifolium	plant 'brought sweetly forth' in meadows
columbine	Ham IV.v.181	Ranunculaceae: Aquilegia	nectar organs horned in shape; associated with cuckoldry
cowslip	H5 C.ii.49	Primulaceae: Primula veris	flower 'brought sweetly forth' in meadows
crowflower	Ham IV.vii.169	possibly Caryophyllaceae: Lychnis flos-cuculi	unclear meaning; probably the ragged robin; used as part of a 'fantastic garland'
cuckoo-bud	LL V.ii.885	unclear meaning	'of yellow hue'; possibly the buttercup, or an invented name
Cupid's flower	MND IV.i.72	✼ pansy	
daffodil	WT IV.iv.118	Liliaceae: Asphodelus	'That … take / The winds of March with beauty'
daisy	Ham IV.v.184	Compositae: Bellis perennis	common in meadows; associated with unhappy love, dissembling
dead-men's fingers	Ham IV.vii.171	✼ long purple	
Dian's bud	MND IV.i.72	unclear meaning	herb associated with chastity; perhaps artemisia
eglantine	Cym IV.ii.223	Rosaceae: Rosa rubiginosa	sweet briar, known for its sweet smell; it 'out-sweetened not' Innogen's breath
gillyvor	WT IV.iv.82	Caryophyllaceae: Dianthus caryophyllus	gillyflower, clove-scented pink; one of the 'fairest flowers o'th' season'; also called 'nature's bastard'
harebell	TNK I.i.9	Liliaceae: Scilla nutans	wild hyacinth, bluebell; 'dim' and 'azured' (Cym IV.ii.222)
lady-smock	LL V.ii.884	Cruciferae: Cardamine pratensis	cuckoo-flower; 'all silver-white'
lark's-heels	TNK I.i.12	Ranunculaceae: Delphinium consolida	larkspur; described as 'trim'
lily	TG II.iii.19	Liliaceae: usually Lilium candidum	associated with purity, freshness, whiteness; described as 'sweetest, fairest' (Cym IV.iii.201)
long purple	Ham IV.vii.169	possibly Orchidaceae: Orchis mascula	unclear meaning; probably a type of wild orchis; used as part of a 'fantastic garland'; also called 'dead-men's fingers'
love in idleness	MND II.i.168	✼ pansy	
marigold	WT IV.iv.104	Compositae: Calendula officinalis	opens when the sun shines; 'goes to bed with' sun / And with him rises weeping'; one of the 'flowers of middle summer … given / To men of middle age'
Mary-bud	Cym II.iii.23	✼ marigold	bud of a marigold
pansy	Ham IV.v.177	Violaceae: Viola tricolor	associated with 'thoughts' [French: pensées], especially of lovers; also called 'love-in-idleness', 'Cupid's flower'
muskrose	MND II.i.252	Rosaceae: Rosa moschata	wild rambling rose; 'a bank … / Quite overcanopied with luscious woodbine, / With sweet muskroses'

PLANTS – *continued*

Item	Example	Identity	Comment
narcissus	**TNK** II.i.173	Amaryllidaceae: Narcissus poeticus	associated with Narcissus ☛ **CLASSICAL MYTHOLOGY**, p.613
oxlip	**MND** II.i.250	Primulaceae: Primula	'a bank ... / Where oxlips and the nodding violet grows'
pink	**TNK** I.i.4	Caryophyllaceae: Dianthus plumarius	'maiden pinks, of odour faint'
primrose	**TNK** I.i.7	Primulaceae: Primula veris	'first-born child of Ver'; described as 'fair' and 'pale'
rose	**TNK** I.i.1	Rosaceae: Rosa	'Not royal in their smells alone, / But in their hue'; 'the very emblem of a maid' (**TNK** II.i.190); white and red varieties as political symbols in **H6**
sedge	**TG** II.vii.29	general meaning	several species of long grassy plant growing in wet places
violet	**Ham** IV.v.185	Violaceae: Viola odorata	associated with love; proverbial for the transience of life or faithfulness
woodbine	**MND** II.i.251	Caprifoliaceae: Lonicera periclymenum	honeysuckle; 'a bank ... / Quite overcanopied with luscious woodbine'
woodbine	**MND** IV.i.41	possibly Convolvulaceae: Convolvulus	'So doth the woodbine the sweet honeysuckle / Gently entwine'

Herbs and spices

Item	Example	Identity	Comment
carduus benedictus	**MA** III.iv.66	Latin: blessed thistle	medicinal herb; 'the only thing for a qualm'
fennel	**Ham** IV.v.181	Umbelliferae: Foeniculum vulgare	aromatic, used as a condiment; associated with flattery, insincerity
hyssop	**Oth** I.iii.319	Labiatae: Hyssopus officinalis	aromatic herb, used medicinally
lavender	**WT** IV.iv.104	Labiatae: Lavandula vera	known for its perfume; one of the 'flowers of middle summer ... given / To men of middle age'
marjoram	**WT** IV.iv.104	Labiatae: Origanum	one of the 'flowers of middle summer ... given / To men of middle age'; culinary and medicinal properties
mint	**WT** IV.iv.104	Labiatae: Mentha viridis	aromatic plant used in cookery; one of the 'flowers of middle summer ... given / To men of middle age'
nose-herb	**AW** IV.v.16	plant for smelling	distinguished from herbs which can be eaten
rosemary	**Ham** IV.v.176	Labiatae: Rosmarinus officinalis	aromatic shrub; associated with 'remembrance', funerals
samphire	**KL** IV.vi.15	Umbelliferae: Crithmum maritimum	aromatic plant used in pickles
savory	**WT** IV.iv.104	Labiatae: Satureia	herb used as in cookery; one of the 'flowers of middle summer ... given / To men of middle age'
sweet-marjoram	**AW** IV.v.14	Labiatae: Origanum marjorana	aromatic herb used in cookery; [of Helena] 'the sweet-marjoram of the sallet'

Trees and shrubs

Item	Example	Identity	Comment
bay	**Per** IV.vi.149	Lauraceae: Laurus nobilis	bay-tree; also called laurel; associated with fame, reputation
elder	**MW** II.iii.26	Caprifoliaceae: Sambucus nigra	shrub or small tree with elaborate growth; known for its soft wood
herb-grace, herb of grace	**Ham** IV.v.182	☛ rue	

(continues)

PLANTS – *continued*

Item	Example	Identity	Comment
ivy	**CE** II.ii.187	Araliaceae: Hedera helix	climbing shrub; associated with conceal-ment
laurel	**Tit** I.i.75	☛ bay	
line	**Tem** IV.i.192	Tiliaceae: Tilia	lime-tree, linden tree
medlar	**AY** III.iii.114	Rosaceae: Mespilus germanica	fruit-tree; fruit eaten when its flesh has begun to decay ; also, thought to resemble buttocks or female genitalia
plantain	**TNK** I.ii.61	Plantaginaceae: Plantago major	herb for treating wounds
rue	**Ham** IV.v.182	Rutaceae: Ruta graveolens	aromatic shrub, leaves often used medic-inally; associated with repentance, pity; also called 'herb of grace', described as 'sour' (**R2** III.iv.105)
senna	**Mac** V.iii.55	Leguminosae: Cassia	shrub with purgative medicinal properties
sycamore	**Oth** IV.iii.38	Moraceae: Ficus sycomorus	Mediterranean species; different from the English species (as in **LL** V.ii.89)
thyme	**MND** II.i.249	Labiatae: Thymus	aromatic herb; 'a bank where the wild thyme blows'; 'sweet thyme true' (**TNK** I.i.6)
willow	**3H6** III.iii.228	Salicaceae: Salix	associated with grief, unrequited love

Plants viewed as unpleasant

Item	Example	Identity	Comment
aconitum	**2H4** IV.iv.48	Ranunculaceae; Aconitum napellus	highly poisonous plant
burdock [F *hard-okes*]	**KL** IV.iv.4	Compositae: Arctium lappa	type of weed; associated with the 'idle weeds that grow / In our sustaining corn'
bur, burr	**H5** V.ii.52	prickly flower-head	known for its sticky properties; especially associated with the burdock
cockle	**LL** IV.iii.359	Caryophyllaceae: Lychnis githago	corn-weed; associated with the Bible (*Matt* 13)
cuckoo-flower	**KL** IV.iv.4	various species of wild flower which bloom when the cuckoo is heard	here, associated with the 'idle weeds that grow / In our sustaining corn'
darnel	**KL** IV.iv.5	Gramineae: Lolium temulentum	type of weed, associated with the 'idle weeds that grow / In our sustaining corn'
dock	**H5** V.ii.52	Polygonaceae: Rumex obtusifolius	'hateful' weed; one of the plants 'losing both beauty and utility'
fumiter	**KL** IV.iv.3	Fumariaceae: usually Fumaria officinalis	type of weed; described as 'rank'
fumitory	**H5** V.ii.45	Fumariaceae: usually Fumaria officinalis	type of weed; described as 'rank'
furrow-weed	**KL** IV.iv.3	general meaning	weed growing on the furrows of a ploughed field
hardoke	**KL** IV.iv.4	unclear meaning	type of weed, possibly burdock; associated with the 'idle weeds that grow / In our sustaining corn'
hebona	**Ham** I.v.62	unclear meaning	poisonous plant, perhaps henbane
hemlock	**KL** IV.iv.4	Umbelliferae: Conium maculatum	poisonous weed ; associated with rankness and (**Mac** IV.i.25) darkness
kecksies	**H5** V.ii.52	hollow-stemmed weedy plants	associated with plants 'losing both beauty and utility'
mallow	**Tem** II.i.146	Malvaceae: Malva sylvestris	common hairy wild plant
mandrake	**RJ** IV.iii.47	Solanaceae: Mandragora	poisonous plant, whose roots resemble the lower human body; supposedly emits a lethal shriek on being pulled up; also, supposed aphrodisiac properties; as man-dragora (**AC** I.v.4), a narcotic

---

PLANTS – *continued*

Item	Example	Identity	Comment
nettle	**KL** IV.iv.4	Urticaceae: Urtica	stinging weed; associated with pain, poison, ugliness
speargrass	**1H4** II.iv.309	Ranunculaceae: Ranunculus	spearwort; used by beggars and others to make artificial wounds
thistle	**H5** V.ii.52	Compositae: Carduus	one of the plants 'losing both beauty and utility'
wormwood	**Luc** 893	Compositae: Artemisia absinthium	absinthe plant, proverbial for its bitter taste

---

plaint *(n.)* lamentation, expression of sorrow **3H6** II.vi.23 [Clifford alone] *Bootless are plaints*; **3H6** III.i.41; **Luc** 1364; **R2** V.iii.126

plaintful *(adj.)* mournful, full of complaining **Lover** 2 *a hill whose concave womb reworded, / A plaintful story from a sist'ring vale*

planched *(adj.)* boarded, wooden, made of planks **MM** IV.i.29 [Isabella to disguised Duke] *to that vineyard is a planched gate*

planet *(n.)* star **2H6** IV.iv.16 [Queen to herself, of dead Suffolk] *Ruled like a wandering planet over me*

planetary *(adj.)* caused by the bad influence of a planet **Tim** IV.iii.109 [Timon to Alcibiades] *Be as a planetary plague*

plank *(n.)* planking, floor **KJ** V.ii.140 [Bastard to Lewis the Dauphin, of French reaction to English power] *To crouch in litter of your stable planks*

plant *(n.)* foot, sole of the foot **AC** II.vii.2 [First Servant to Second Servant, of the drinkers] *Some o'their plants are ill-rooted already* [punning on the botanical sense]

plant *(v.)* **1** set up, establish, introduce **Mac** V.vi.104 [Malcolm to all] *What's more to do, / Which would be planted newly with the time ... / We will perform*; **AC** I.iii.26; **Venus** 557
2 fix in the ground, set up, place **TNK** III.i.293 [Theseus to all] *in this place, / In which I'll plant a pyramid*
3 install, set up, put in place **3H6** I.i.48 [Warwick to York] *I'll plant Plantagenet*

plantage *(n.)* vegetation, plant-life **TC** III.ii.175 [Troilus to Cressida, of examples of lovers' comparisons] *as plantage to the moon* [i.e. as plants increase in growth at full moon]

plantain *(n.)* variety of medicinal herb **RJ** I.ii.51 [Romeo to Benvolio, of a herbal cure] *Your plantain leaf is excellent for that*; **LL** III.i.71 ➤ **PLANTS**, p.330

plantation *(n.)* colonization, colonial settlement **Tem** II.i.145 [Gonzalo to Alonso] *Had I plantation of this isle* [pun: 146, cultivation]

planting *(n.)* installing, stationing, establishing **E3** I.i.134 [King Edward to Warwick] *the planting of Lord Mountford*

plash *(n.)* pool, puddle, pond **TS** I.i.23 [Lucentio to Tranio, of moving from Pisa to Padua] *as he that leaves / A shallow plash to plunge him in the deep*

plate *(n.)* **1** special tableware, household utensils of value **2H4** II.i.153 [Hostess to Falstaff] *I am loath to pawn my plate*; **2H4** II.i.140; **H8** III.ii.125; **RJ** I.v.7; **Tim** III.ii.21; **TS** II.i.340
2 armour, plate-armour **E3** I.i.52 [Messenger to King David] *The sun ... showed / A field of plate*; **E3** IV.iv.17; **KL** IV.vi.166
3 silver coin, silver piece **AC** V.ii.92 [Cleopatra to Dolabella, of Antony] *realms and islands were / As plates dropped from his pocket*

plated *(adj.)* wearing plate armour, armour-protected **AC** I.i.4 [Philo to Demetrius, of Antony] *Those his goodly eyes, / That o'er the files and musters of the war / Have glowed like plated Mars*; **R2** I.iii.28

platform *(n.)* **1** plan, scheme, strategy **1H6** II.i.77 [Pucelle to all, of the English] *[we must] lay new platforms to endamage them*
2 gun-platform, battery emplacement **Oth** II.iii.114 [Montano to all] *To th'platform*; **Ham** I.ii.252

plausibly *(adv.)* with applause, with total approval **Luc** 1854 *The Romans plausibly did give consent / To Tarquin's everlasting banishment*

plausive *(adj.)* **1** pleasing, praiseworthy, laudable **AW** I.ii.53 [King to Bertram, of Bertram's father] *his plausive words / He scattered not in ears*; **Ham** I.iv.30
2 plausible, convincing, believable **AW** IV.i.26 [Parolles to himself, of his lying] *It must be a very plausive invention that carries it*

play *(n.)* playing, performance **H8** I.iii.45 [Sands to Lovell and Lord Chamberlain, of his entertaining ladies with music] *beaten / A long time out of play* [with bawdy pun]

play *(v.)* **1** display, show, demonstrate **Tem** I.ii.209 [Ariel to Prospero] *Not a soul / But ... played / Some tricks of desperation*
2 play with, amuse oneself with **WT** II.i.52 [Leontes to Lord, of Camillo] *He has discovered my design, and I / remain a pinched thing; yea, a very trick / For them to play at will*
3 play for, make bets about **H5** IV.Chorus.19 [Chorus] *secure in soul, / The confident and over-lusty French / Do the low-rated English play at dice*; **TN** II.v.183
4 stay idle, take a holiday **TNK** II.ii.28 [Fourth Countryman to the others] *Let the plough play today*
5 fence **Ham** IV.vii.104 [Claudius to Laertes] *Your sudden coming o'er to play with you*; **Ham** V.ii.194, 201

play it off [drinking call] finish it off, down it **1H4** II.iv.16 [Prince Hal to Poins, of the tavern drinkers] *when you breathe in your watering they cry 'Hem!' and bid you 'Play it off!'*

play one's prize [fencing] win a game, succeed in a bout **Tit** I.i.402 [Saturninus to Bassianus, of him and his bride] *you have played your prize*

play the wantons ➤ *wantons, play the*

play upon *(v.)* play guns on, aim at; also: torment **KJ** II.i.385 [Bastard to King John and King Philip, of the men of Angiers] *I'd play incessantly upon these jades*

playfere *(n.)* playfellow, playmate, companion **TNK** IV.iii.89 [Doctor to Wooer, of the Gaoler's Daughter] *Learn what maids have been her companions and playferes*

playing day *(n.)* school holiday, day off **MW** IV.i.10 [Mistress Page to Mistress Quickly] *'Tis a playing day*

plea *(n.)* **1** claim, argument, issue **MV** IV.i.200 [Portia as Balthazar to Shylock] *I have spoke thus much / To mitigate the justice of thy plea*; **LL** II.i.7; **MV** III.ii.282
2 quarrel, argument, strife **TNK** III.i.115 [Arcite to Palamon] *I am a suitor / That to your sword you will bequeath this plea*

pleached *(adj.)* **1** intertwined, folded, bound together **AC** IV.xiv.73 [Antony to Eros] *Wouldst thou … see / Thy master thus: with pleached arms*

2 with hedges made of interlaced branches **MA** III.i.7 [Hero to Margaret, of Beatrice] *bid her steal into the pleached bower* ☛ thick-pleached *(adj.)*

plead *(v.)* **1** make a case for, present an argument for **1H6** II.iv.29 [Richard to all, of his supporters] *If he suppose that I have pleaded truth;* **3H6** I.i.103

2 argue, debate, wrangle **1H6** III.i.57 [Warwick to Somerset, of Winchester] *It fitteth not a prelate so to plead*

3 give an oration, hold forth **Luc** 1401 [of a painting of Troy] *There pleading might you see grave Nestor stand*

pleasance *(n.)* pleasure, delight, gratification **PassP** XII.2 *Youth is full of pleasance, Age is full of care;* **Oth** II.iii.283

pleasant *(adj.)* **1** facetious, joking, droll **TS** IV.v.72 [Vincentio to Petruchio, of his companions] *Like pleasant travellers, to break a jest / Upon the company you overtake;* **H5** I.ii.260; **MA** I.i.34; **MM** III.ii.107; **TC** III.i.61; **TS** III.i.56

2 merry, festive, jolly **TS** Induction.ii.128 [Lord to Sly, of the players] *hearing your amendment, / Are come to play a pleasant comedy;* **H8** I.iv.90; **TS** I.ii.46, II.i.239; **WT** IV.iv.191

3 pleasurable, enjoyable, pleasing **KL** V.iii.168 [Edmund to Edgar] *The gods are just, and of our pleasant vices / Make instruments to plague us*

pleasantly *(adv.)* gratifyingly, satisfyingly **TC** IV.v.249 [Hector to Achilles] *Think'st thou to catch my life so pleasantly / As to prenominate in nice conjecture / Where thou wilt hit me dead?*

please *(v.)* requite, satisfy, appease **CE** IV.iv.47 [Adriana to Pinch] *I will please you what you will demand;* **KJ** IV.ii.126 ☛ **POLITENESS**, p.340

please-man *(n.)* yes-man, sycophant, toady **LL** V.ii.463 [Berowne to all, of Boyet] *some please-man … / Told our intents before*

pleasure *(n.)* **1** wish, desire, will **2H6** I.i.56 [Messenger to Gloucester] *'tis his highness' pleasure / You do prepare to ride unto Saint Albans;* **2H6** IV.i.142; **3H6** III.ii.20; **JC** V.iii.247; **Tim** II.i.14; **TS** I.i.81

2 intention, resolution, desire **KL** V.i.4 [Edmund to gentleman, of Albany] *Bring his constant pleasure;* **KL** V.iii.2

3 gratification, whim, caprice **Cym** V.v.335 [Belarius to Cymbeline] *Your pleasure was my ne'er-offence*

4 enjoyment, pleasant occasion, revelry **Tim** I.ii.143 [Timon to Ladies] *You have done our pleasures much grace*

5 pleasure ground, park **JC** III.ii.251 [Antony to all, of Caesar's bequests] *common pleasures, / To walk abroad and recreate yourselves*

pleasure *(v.)* please, gratify, give pleasure to **MW** I.i.227 [Shallow to Slender] *what I do is to pleasure you;* **Tim** III.ii.57

pleat *(n.)* fold, hanging, covering **Luc** 93 [of Tarquin] *Hiding base sin in pleats of majesty*

pleated *(adj.)* ☛ plighted *(adj.)* 2

plebeian, plebeii *(n.)* ☛ **ROMAN HISTORY**, p.377

plebs *(n.)* ☛ tribunal plebs

pledge *(n.)* **1** toast, drinking of a health **Ham** I.iv.12 [Hamlet to Horatio, of Claudius] *The kettledrum and trumpet thus bray out / The triumph of his pledge*

2 guarantor, surety **TS** I.ii.44 [Hortensio to Petruchio] *I am Grumio's pledge;* **2H6** V.i.50; **Tit** III.i.290

3 glove [thrown down], gage **1H6** IV.i.120 [Richard to Somerset] *There is my pledge*

pledge *(v.)* drink a toast to, drink to **2H4** IV.ii.73 [Westmorland to Archbishop] *I pledge your grace;* **2H6** V.iii.53; **2H6** II.iii.66; **Per** II.iii.78; **TNK** III.iii.16, 38

plenteous *(adj.)* generous, liberal, bountiful **Tim** I.ii.123 [Cupid to Timon] *The five best senses … come freely / To gratulate thy plenteous bosom*

pleurisy, plurisy *(n.)* excess, superfluity, superabundance **Ham** IV.vii.116 [Claudius to Laertes] *goodness, growing to a pleurisy;* **TNK** V.i.66

pliant *(adj.)* suitable, opportune, favourable **Oth** I.iii.150 [Othello to all] *I … / Took once a pliant hour*

plight *(n.)* **1** good shape, health, fit condition **TC** III.ii.159 [Troilus to and of Cressida] *To keep her constancy in plight and youth;* **Sonn** 28.1; **TNK** III.i.88

2 pledge, promise, marriage-vow **KL** I.i.101 [Cordelia to Lear] *That lord whose hand must take my plight*

plight *(v.)* betroth, engage **TNK** V.iii.110 [Theseus to Emilia and Arcite] *be plighted with / A love that grows as you decay*

plight one's troth, plight troth **1** make marriage vows **Cym** I.ii.27 [Posthumus to Innogen] *I will remain the loyal'st husband that did e'er plight troth* ☛ troth-plight *(n./adj.)*

2 make a solemn promise [not to do no harm] **KL** III.iv.117 [Edgar as Poor Tom to all, of St Withold and the nightmare] *He … / Bid her alight and her troth plight*

plighted *(adj.)* **1** pledged, promised, engaged **1H6** V.iii.162 [Reignier to Suffolk, of Margaret] *I … / Give thee her hand for sign of plighted faith*

2 folded, hidden; also: solemnly pledged **KL** I.i.280 [Cordelia to her sisters] *Time shall unfold what plighted cunning hides* [F; Q pleated]

plot *(n.)* **1** plan, scheme, stratagem **TC** I.iii.181 [Ulysses to all] *All our … / Achievements, plots, orders, preventions, / Excitements to the field;* **KJ** III.iv.146; **Tem** III.ii.110

2 position, situation, site **KJ** II.i.40 [King Philip to all, of the strategists] *To cull the plots of best advantages*

3 place, spot **Tit** II.i.115 [Aaron to Demetrius and Chiron, of the forest] *many unfrequented plots there are*

4 piece of earth; body **Cor** III.ii.102 [Coriolanus to Volumnia] *were there but this single plot to lose, / This mould of Martius*

pluck *(v.)* **1** draw down, bring down **TNK** V.i.53 [Arcite praying to Mars] *who dost pluck / With hand armipotent … / The masoned turrets;* **JC** II.i.73; **Tem** V.i.127; **TNK** I.i.191, II.ii.17

2 extract, snatch, pull out **Sonn** 14.1 *Not from the stars do I my judgement pluck*

3 tug, yank, pull sharply **TS** IV.i.133 [Petruchio to Servant, on taking off his boots] *You pluck my foot awry*

4 draw, find, select [as from a pack of cards] **AW** I.iii.86 [Clown to Countess, of a good woman] *a man may draw his heart out ere 'a pluck one*

5 ☛ crow, pluck a

pluck away *(v.)* disregard, reject, throw out **KJ** III.iv.156 [Cardinal Pandulph to Lewis the Dauphin, of the people reacting to natural phenomena] *they will pluck away his natural cause / And call them meteors, prodigies and signs*

pluck down *(v.)* **1** tear loose, pull apart **JC** III.ii.259 [Third Plebeian to all] *Pluck down benches*

2 pull down, drag down **TC** III.iii.86 [Achilles to Patroclus, of the slippery nature of honours] *when they fall, … / The love that leaned on them, as slippery too, / Doth one pluck down another*

pluck off *(v.)* come down [in level of aspiration], look lower **H8** II.iii.40 [Old Lady to Anne] *Pluck off a little*

pluck on *(v.)* **1** draw on, pull in, drag in **R3** V.ii.63 [King Richard to himself] *I am in / So far in blood that sin will pluck on sin;* **KJ** III.i.57

2 test, make a trial of **MM** II.iv.147 [Isabella to Angelo] *your virtue hath a licence in't … / To pluck on others*

pluck up *(v.)* take hold, get in control **MA** V.i.196 [Don Pedro to Claudio, as if to himself] *pluck up, my heart, and be sad*

pluck upon *(v.)* bring to ruin, demolish **KL** IV.ii.85 [Gonerill to herself] *May all the building in my fancy pluck / Upon my hateful life*

plucking *(n.)* pulling off, removal **TS** IV.i.134 [Petruchio to Servant, of pulling off one boot awkwardly] *mend the plucking off the other*

plum-broth (*n.*) rich soup made of meat, fruit, and spices, especially eaten at Christmas **TNK** III.v.5 [Schoolmaster to all] *the very plum-broth / And marrow of my understanding laid upon ye* [i.e. the very best of my intellect]

plume up (*v.*) furnish with plumage; put a feather in the cap of **Oth** I.iii.387 [Iago alone, of Cassio] *To get his place and to plume up my will / In double knavery* [F; Q1 *make*]

plume-plucked (*adj.*) humbled, stripped of plumes **R2** IV.i.108 [York to Bolingbroke] *I come to thee / From plume-plucked Richard*

plummet (*n.*) weighted line used for measuring the depth of water **Tem** V.i.56 [Prospero alone] *deeper than did ever plummet sound / I'll drown my book; **MW** V.v.161; **Tem** III.iii.103*

plum porridge [contemptuous, for the type of person who would eat] rich, fruity porridge [= heavy, lumbering individual] **TNK** II.ii.73 [Second Countryman to the others, of Arcite] *hang him, plum porridge!*

plumpy (*adj.*) plump **AC** II.vii.112 [Boy, singing] *Plumpy Bacchus with pink eyne!*

plurisy (*n.*) ➤ pleurisy (*n.*)

ply (*v.*) keep on at, press, urge **AY** III.v.76 [Rosalind as Ganymede to Silvius, of Phebe] *Shepherd, ply her hard;* **3H6** III.ii.50; **Tit** IV.i.15, V.ii.80

ply one's music go one's own way **Ham** II.i.73 [Polonius to Reynaldo, of Laertes] *And let him ply his music* [or: meant literally]

ply one's book study, work at, apply oneself to **TS** I.i.193 [Tranio to Lucentio, of Lucentio's role in Padua] *Keep house and ply his book*

pocket up (*v.*) put up with, endure, swallow **KJ** III.i.200 [Austria to Bastard, of the Bastard's insults] *I must pocket up these wrongs*

pocky (*adj.*) poxy, disease-infected [with syphilis, smallpox] **Ham** V.i.163 [First Clown to Hamlet] *we have many pocky corses nowadays*

poesy (*n.*) poetry **TG** III.ii.72 [Duke to Proteus] *Much is the force of heaven-bred poesy;* **Sonn** 78.4; **Tim** I.i.21

poinst (*v.*) ➤ appoint (*v.*) 2

point (*n.*) **1** sword-point **1H4** II.iv.190 [Falstaff to Prince Hal] *here I lay, and thus I bore my point;* **Ham** V.ii.61; **1H4** II.iv.197, V.iv.20; **Mac** I.ii.58
  2 (usually plural) tagged lace [especially for attaching hose to the doublet] **TS** III.ii.48 [Biondello to Tranio as Lucentio, of Petruchio's clothes] *with two broken points;* **AC** III.xiii.157; **1H4** II.iv.210; **2H4** II.iv.128; **TN** V.i.21; **WT** IV.iv.207
  3 summit, apex, highest point **MND** II.ii.125 [Lysander to Helena] *touching now the point of human skill, / Reason becomes the marshal to my will;* **TC** III.iii.89
  4 decision, conclusion, direction **Cor** IV.vi.127 [Cominius to Brutus and Sicinius, of Coriolanus] *Aufidius, / The second name of men, obeys his points* [i.e. obeys him in every point]
  5 trifle, triviality, minor matter **MND** V.i.118 [Theseus to all, of Quince] *This fellow doth not stand upon points* [i.e. restrict himself to small points] [pun: punctuation mark]
  6 aim, purpose, culmination **KL** IV.vii.96 [Kent alone] *My point and period will be throughly wrought ... as this day's battle's fought*
  7 situation, position, juncture **2H6** I.i.214 [York to himself, of lost regions of France] *the state of Normandy / Stands on a tickle point now they are gone*
  8 finger, hand, pointer **R2** V.v.53 [Richard alone] *my finger, like a dial's point;* **1H4** V.ii.83
  9 [falconry] rising in the air, position [to attack prey] **2H6** II.i.5 [King to Gloucester] *But what a point ... your falcon made*
  10 trumpet call used as a signal in a battle **2H4** IV.i.52 [Westmorland to Archbishop] *Turning ... your tongue divine / To a loud trumpet and a point of war*
  11 saddle-bow, pommel **1H4** II.i.6 [First Carrier to Ostler] *put a few flocks in the point*

points, all / **at all** in every part, in all respects, completely **AY** I.iii.114 [Rosalind to Celia] *Were it not better ... / That I did suit me all points like a man?;* **R2** I.iii.2 [Aumerle to Lord Marshal, responding to 'is Harry Hereford armed?'] *Yea, at all points*

point, at just about, on the point [of] **Cor** III.i.193 [Sicinius to Plebeians] *You are at point to lose your liberties;* **Cym** III.vi.17

point, at / **at a** in readiness, prepared, armed **KL** I.iv.321 [Gonerill to Albany, of Lear] *'Tis politic and safe to let him keep / At point a hundred knights;* **Mac** IV.iii.135 [Malcolm to Macduff] *Old Seyward with ten thousand warlike men, / Already at a point, was setting forth;* **Cym** III.i.31; **Ham** I.ii.200; **KL** III.i.33

point, full full stop, complete halt **2H4** II.iv.179 [Pistol to all] *Come we to full points here?*

point, to exactly, completely, to the letter **Tem** I.ii.194 [Prospero to Ariel] *Hast thou, spirit, / Performed to point the tempest*

point (*v.*) **1** direct, suggest, indicate [to] **Ham** I.v.129 [Hamlet to Horatio and Marcellus] *as your business and desire shall point you;* **LL** II.i.231
  2 ➤ appoint (*v.*)

point forth (*v.*) indicate, suggest, allude to **WT** IV.iv.558 [Camillo to Florizel, of writing down how he is to behave towards Leontes] *The which shall point you forth at every sitting / What you must say;* **Cym** V.v.455

point-blank (*adv.*) **1** straight, with a direct aim **MW** III.ii.30 [Ford alone] *a cannon will shoot point-blank twelve score*
  2 reach, easy range **2H6** IV.vii.23 [Cade to Say] *Now art thou within point-blank of our jurisdiction regal*

point-device, point-devise (*adj.*) immaculate, affectedly precise, trim to the point of perfection **AY** III.ii.367 [Rosalind to Orlando] *you are rather point-device in your accoutrements;* **LL** V.i.18

point-device, point-devise (*adv.*) to the last detail, to the point of perfection **TN** II.v.157 [Malvolio to himself, of the description in the letter] *I will be point-devise the very man*

pointed (*adj.*) ending in a point, coming to a peak **TNK** IV.ii.23 [Emilia alone] *as from a promontory / Pointed in heaven*

pointing-stock (*n.*) object to be pointed at, laughing-stock, butt **2H6** II.iv.46 [Duchess to Gloucester] *I... / Was made a wonder and a pointing-stock / To every idle rascal follower* ➤ stock (*n.*) 4

poise (*n.*) **1** balance of weight, equipoise **MM** II.iv.68 [Angelo to Isabella] *equal poise of sin and charity;* **3H6** II.v.13
  2 weight, heaviness, load **TNK** V.iv.81 [Pirithous to Palamon, of Arcite's horse] *Backward the jade comes o'er, and his full poise / Becomes the rider's load*
  3 weight, importance, gravity **KL** II.i.119 [Regan to Gloucester] *Occasions ... of some poise* [Q; F *prize*]; **Oth** III.iii.82
  4 forceful impact, heavy blow **TC** I.iii.207 [Ulysses to all, of a battering-ram] *the great swing and rudeness of his poise*

poise (*v.*) balance, weigh, make even **TNK** I.i.86 [Second Queen to Hippolyta] *That equally canst poise sternness with pity;* **AW** II.iii.153; **2H6** II.i.199; **Oth** I.iii.324; **RJ** I.ii.94; **TC** IV.i.66

poison, sweet flattery **KJ** I.i.213 [Bastard alone, of himself] *to deliver / Sweet, sweet, sweet poison for the age's tooth*

poke (*n.*) pocket, wallet, bag **AY** II.vii.20 [Jaques to all, of Touchstone] *then he drew a dial from his poke*

poking-stick (*n.*) rod for stiffening the folds of a ruff **WT** IV.iv.228 [Autolycus singing] *Pins and poking-sticks of steel*

Polack (*n.*) Poles, Polish people **Ham** II.ii.63 [Voltemand to Claudius] *a preparation 'gainst the Polack;* **Ham** I.i.63 [Horatio to Marcellus and Barnardo, of King Hamlet] *He smote the sledded Polacks on the ice* [a reading of F *Pollax;* ➤ poleaxe]; **Ham** IV.iv.23

Polack (*adj.*) Polish, in Poland **Ham** V.ii.370 [Horatio to Fortinbras] *You from the Polack wars*

PLURALS

Several nouns appear as plural in Shakespearian English which are singular in modern English, and there are other kinds of number difference, as illustrated in the selection below. Plurality may be shown both by the form of the word (as in modern *boy > boys*) or by its agreement with the verb or determiner (as in *this sheep is > these sheep are*).

The Shakespearian situation is complicated by the existence of forms which might reflect a personal or regional dialect, as well as by usages which may be the result of printing errors. Examples include Shylock's use of *beefs* and *muttons* and the various plurals used by speakers with a Welsh background, such as *disparagements* (☞ **WELSH**, p.649). Examples of the reverse process (singular > plural) can also be found, as in 'their business still lies out o'door' (**CE** II.i.11) alongside 'out of doors' (**Cor** I.iii.72), and 'conquer other by the dint of sword' (**E3** V.i.52), where modern usage would use *others*.

Item	Location	Example	Modern use

Shakespearian plural > Modern singular

Item	Location	Example	Modern use
attires	**AC** V.ii.228	Go fetch my best attires	attire
beefs	**2H4** III.ii.316	now has he land and beefs	beef
behalfs	**TNK** II.ii.53	in our behalfs	behalf
behaviours	**JC** I.ii.42	Which give some soil … to my behaviours	behaviour
companies	**Ham** II.ii.14	by your companies / To draw him on to pleasures	company
courages	**Cym** II.iv.24	Now wing-led with their courages	courage
funerals	**JC** V.iii.105	His funerals shall not be in our camp	funeral
informations	**H8** V.iii.110	In seeking tales and informations	information
kindreds	**TNK** II.i.62	Where are our friends and kindreds?	kindred
moneys	**MV** I.iii.105	you have rated me / About my moneys	money
musics	**Cym** II.iii.38	I have assailed her with musics	music
muttons	**MV** I.iii.164	flesh of muttons, beefs, or goats	mutton
revenges	**Mac** V.ii.3	Revenges burn in them	revenge
sheeps	**LL** II.i.205	Two hot sheeps, marry?	sheep
thunders	**Mac** I.ii.26	Shipwracking storms and direful thunders	thunder

Shakespearian both singular and plural > Modern either singular or plural

Item	Location	Example	Modern use
news	**1H6** I.i.67	These news would cause him once more yield the ghost [plural]	this news [singular]
	1H4 I.i.58	the news was told [singular]	
nuptials	**MND** I.i.124	I must employ you in some business / Against our nuptial [singular]	our nuptials [plural]
	Per V.iii.80	We'll celebrate their nuptials [plural]	
odds	**R2** III.iv.89	with that odds he weighs King Richard down [singular]	those odds [plural]
	MM III.i.41	death we fear, / That makes these odds all even [plural]	
riches	**Sonn** 87.6	for that riches where is my deserving? [singular]	those riches [plural]
	Tim IV.ii.32	riches point to misery and contempt [plural]	
tidings	**R2** III.iv.80	how / Camest thou by this ill tidings [singular]	these tidings [plural]
	KJ IV.ii.132	Thou hast made me giddy / With these ill tidings [plural]	
victuals	**MA** I.i.46	You had musty victual [singular]	victuals [plural]
	Cym III.vi.13	it eats our victuals [plural]	

Shakespearian double plurals > Modern plural

Item	Location	Example	Modern use
gallowses	**Cym** V.iv.207	there were desolation of gaolers and gallowses	gallows
teeths	**JC** V.i.41	You showed your teethes like apes [F]	teeth

For archaic plurals, ☞ **ARCHAISMS**, p.22

Poland *(adj.)* Polish **CE** III.ii.102 [Dromio of Syracuse to Antipholus of Syracuse, of the kitchen wench] *her rags and the tallow in them will burn a Poland winter* [i.e. keep a candle alight all through a Polish winter]

pole *(n.)* [unclear meaning] polestar, guiding star **AC** IV.xv.65 [Cleopatra to all, of dead Antony] *The soldier's pole is fall'n*

poleaxe, pole-axe *(n.)* battle-axe **LL** V.ii.574 [Costard to Nathaniel] *Your lion, that holds his pole-axe sitting on a close-stool, will be given to Ajax*

poleaxe, sledded battle-axe made like a sledge-hammer **Ham** I.i.63 [Horatio to Marcellus, of King Hamlet] *in an angry parle, / He smote the sledded poleaxe on the ice* [a reading of Q1,2 *pollax*, F *Pollax;* ☛ Polack]

polecat *(n.)* [slang] prostitute, courtesan, whore **MW** IV.ii.174 [Ford to Falstaff in disguise as a woman] *Out of my door ... you polecat;* **MW** IV.i.27

pole-clipt *(adj.)* with twined-round poles; hedged in by poles **Tem** IV.i.68 [Iris to Ceres] *thy pole-clipt vineyard*

policy *(n.)* **1** statecraft, statesmanship, diplomacy **TC** I.iii.197 [Ulysses to all, of Achilles and Ajax] *They tax our policy, and call it cowardice;* **2H6** III.i.238; **MA** IV.i.196; **Oth** II.iii.266; **R2** V.i.84; **TN** III.ii.28
    2 stratagem, cunning, intrigue, craft **1H4** I.iii.107 [Hotspur to King Henry] *Never did bare and rotten policy / Colour her working with such deadly wounds;* **AY** V.i.55; **2H6** IV.i.83; **H8** III.ii.259; **KJ** II.i.396; **TS** II.i.285
    3 expediency, shrewdness, self-interest **Tim** III.ii.89 [First Stranger to Second and Third Strangers] *Men must learn now with pity to dispense, / For policy sits above conscience*

politic *(adj.)* **1** prudent, cautious, discreet, shrewd **KL** I.iv.320 [Gonerill to Albany, of Lear] *'Tis politic and safe to let him keep / At point a hundred knights;* **1H6** II.v.101; **Oth** III.iii.13; **R3** I.iii.20; **TC** III.iii.254; **TN** III.v.155
    2 crafty, wily, self-serving **Tim** III.iii.29 [Servant alone] *The devil knew not what he did when he made man politic;* **AY** IV.i.13, V.iv.44; **Ham** IV.iii.20; **MA** V.ii.58; **Tim** III.iii.105
    3 cunning, full of intrigue, wily **AW** IV.i.21 [First Lord to First Soldier, as interpreter] *you must seem very politic;* **MW** III.i.93

politician *(n.)* schemer, intriguer, plotter **KL** IV.vi.172 [Lear to all] *like a scurvy politician seem / To see the things thou dost not;* **Ham** V.i.78; **TN** III.iii.73, III.iii.35

politicly *(adv.)* in a politic manner, strategically, shrewdly **TS** IV.i.174 [Petruchio alone] *Thus have I politicly begun my reign;* **2H6** III.i.341

poll *(n.)* **1** head **2H4** II.iv.254 [Prince Henry to Poins, of Falstaff] *Look whe'er the withered elder hath not his poll clawed like a parrot;* **AW** IV.iii.165; **Ham** IV.v.196
    2 number of persons **Cor** III.i.134 [Coriolanus to Brutus, quoting the Citizens] *We are the greater poll* [i.e. the majority]
    3 voting list, head-count **Cor** III.iii.10 [Sicinius to Aedile] *Have you a catalogue / Of all the voices that we have procured, / Set down by th'poll?*

pollax *(n.)* ☛ poleaxe, sledded

polled *(adj.)* **1** bald, hairless **TNK** V.i.85 [Palamon praying to Venus] *the polled bachelor, ... at seventy thou canst catch*
    2 shorn, cleared, stripped bare **Cor** IV.v.209 [Third Servingman to First Servingman, of Coriolanus] *He will mow all down before him, and leave his passage polled*

Polonian *(n.)* Pole **E3** III.i.34 [King John to all] *Some friends have we ... / The stern Polonian*

poltroon *(n.)* worthless coward, mean-spirited wretch **3H6** I.i.62 [Clifford to King] *Patience is for poltroons*

pomander *(n.)* perfumed ball; or: case containing perfumed substances **WT** IV.iv.595 [Autolycus to himself, of what he has left to sell] *not a ribbon, glass, pomander, brooch ... to keep my pack from fasting*

pomewater *(n.)* variety of large juicy apple **LL** IV.ii.4 [Holofernes to Nathaniel] *The deer was ... ripe as the pomewater*

pommel *(n.)* ornamental knob **LL** V.ii.612 [Boyet to Holofernes, of the latter's face] *The pommel of Caesar's falchion*

pomp *(n.)* **1** pageant, ceremony, procession **KJ** II.i.560 [King John to King Philip, of the marriage] *Go we as well as haste will suffer us / To this unlooked-for, unprepared pomp;* **KJ** III.i.304, IV.ii.9, 173; **MND** I.i.15
    2 greatness, nobility, high estate **2H6** II.iv.41 [Duchess to Gloucester] *To think upon my pomp shall be my hell;* **AC** V.ii.151; **KJ** IV.iii.154; **Tim** IV.iii.244

Pompion *(n.)* [= pumpkin] malapropism for 'Pompey' **LL** V.ii.501 [Costard to Browne] *I am ... but to parfect one man in one poor man - Pompion the Great*

pompous *(adj.)* **1** glorious, magnificent, splendid **Per** III.Chorus.4 [Gower alone] *this most pompous marriage-feast;* **E3** IV.v.14; **R2** IV.i.249
    2 full of pomp, ceremonious, grand **AY** V.iv.179 [Jaques to Jaques de Boys] *The Duke hath ... thrown into neglect the pompous court?*

ponderous *(adj.)* weighty, substantial, profound **WT** IV.iv.521 [Camillo to Florizel] *If your more ponderous and settled project / May suffer alteration;* **KL** I.i.78

poniard *(n.)* dagger **AW** IV.i.74 [First Soldier to Parolles] *seventeen poniards are at thy bosom;* **3H6** II.i.98; **MA** II.i.227; **Tit** II.iii.120 ☛ WEAPONS, p.491

pontifical *(adj.)* worn by a pope, episcopal **1H4** III.ii.56 [King Henry to Prince Hal] *Thus did I keep ... / My presence, like a robe pontifical, / Ne'er seen but wondered at*

poop *(v.)* make a fool of; or: do away with [through venereal disease] **Per** IV.ii.22 [Boult to Pander, of one of their girls and a client] *she quickly pooped him*

poor-John *(n.)* salted hake, dried fish **RJ** I.i.30 [Gregory to Sampson] *'Tis well thou art not fish; if thou hadst, thou hadst been poor-John;* **Tem** II.ii.26

poorly *(adv.)* abjectly, humbly, miserably **R2** III.iii.128 [King Richard to Aumerle] *We do debase ourselves ... / To look so poorly and to speak so fair*

pop *(v.)* arrive unexpectedly, move in suddenly **TC** IV.v.28 [Patroclus to Menelaus, of a kiss] *thus popped Paris in his hardiment, / And parted thus you and your argument* [i.e. Helen]

pop out [informal] disinherit, turn from **KJ** I.i.68 [Bastard to Queen Eleanor, of Robert proving his illegitimacy] *'a pops me out / At least from fair five hundred pound a year*

poperin *(adj.)* ☛ poppering *(adj.)*

popinjay *(n.)* parrot, prattler, chatterer **1H4** I.iii.49 [Hotspur to King Henry, of a lord] *To be so pestered with a popinjay*

poppering / poperin *(adj.)* variety of pear [from Poperinghe, Belgium] **RJ** II.i.38 [Mercutio as if to Romeo, of Romeo's mistress] *O that she were / An open-arse and thou a poppering pear!* [with bawdy pun]

poppy *(n.)* poppy-seed [used as a drug], opium **Oth** III.iii.327 [Iago to himself, as if to Othello] *Not poppy, nor mandragora ... / Shall ever medicine thee to that sweet sleep / Which thou owed'st yesterday*

popular *(adj.)* **1** plebeian, of the common people **H5** IV.i.38 [Pistol to disguised King Henry] *art thou base, common, and popular?;* **Cor** III.i.106
    2 currying favour with the people **Cor** II.iii.100 [Coriolanus to Fourth Citizen] *I will counterfeit the bewitchment of some popular man*

popularity *(n.)* populace, common people, the masses **1H4** III.ii.69 [King Henry to Prince Hal] *The skipping King ... / Enfeoffed himself to popularity;* **H5** I.i.59

populous (*adj.*) numerous, many, abundant **AC** III.vi.50 [Caesar to Octavia] *the dust / Should have ascended to the roof of heaven, / Raised by your populous troops*

poring (*adj.*) through which one needs to peer, eye-straining **H5** IV.Chorus.2 [Chorus] *Now entertain conjecture of a time / When creeping murmur and the poring dark / Fills the wide vessel of the universe*

porpentine (*n.*) porcupine **Ham** I.v.20 [Ghost to Hamlet] *Like quills upon the fretful porpentine;* **2H6** III.i.363; **TC** I.ii.25

porridge (*n.*) meat and vegetable stew or broth [reputed to produce strength] **1H6** I.ii.9 [Alençon to all, of the English] *They want their porridge and their fat bull-beeves;* **CE** II.ii.107; **KL** III.iv.53; **LL** I.i.290

porringer (*n.*) **1** pudding basin, pot [for puddings, soup, etc] **TS** IV.iii.64 [Petruchio to Haberdasher, of a cap] *this was moulded on a porringer*
2 hat shaped like a pudding basin or soup-bowl **H8** V.iv.48 [Man to Porter, of a haberdasher's wife] *that railed upon me till her pinked porringer fell off her head* 🖝 **CLOTHING**, p.79

port (*n.*) **1** portal, entrance, gateway **Tim** V.iv.55 [Alcibiades to Senators] *Descend, and open your uncharged ports;* **Cor** I.vii.1; **KL** II.i.79; **Per** V.i.44; **TC** IV.iv.110; **TNK** V.i.147
2 bearing, demeanour, carriage **H5** Prologue.6 [Chorus] *Then should the warlike Harry … / Assume the port of Mars;* **AC** IV.xiv.52; **2H6** IV.i.19
3 station, position, dignity **TS** III.i.35 [Lucentio as Cambio to Bianca] *my man Tranio … bearing my port;* **MV** III.ii.281
4 style of living, way of life **TS** I.i.200 [Lucentio to Tranio] *Thou shalt … / Keep house, and port, and servants, as I should;* **MV** I.i.124

port (*v.*) carry, bring; or, bring to port **TNK** V.i.29 [Arcite to Palamon] *hoist we / The sails, that must these vessels port*

portable (*adj.*) bearable, supportable, endurable **KL** III.vi.106 [Edgar alone] *How light and portable my pain seems now;* **Mac** IV.iii.89; **TC** I.iii.134

portage (*n.*) **1** portholes, openings **H5** III.i.10 [King Henry to all, of the eye] *Let it pry through the portage of the head / Like the brass cannon*
2 [unclear meaning] life's voyage, journey through life **Per** III.i.36 [Pericles to Marina] *thy loss is more than can / Thy portage quit*

portal (*n.*) door, doorway, gateway **Luc** 309 [of Tarquin] *As each unwilling portal yields him way;* **Ham** III.iv.137

portance (*n.*) behaviour, demeanour, bearing **Oth** I.iii.138 [Othello to all] *I spake of … portance in my travels' history;* **Cor** II.iii.223

portcullis (*v.*) furnish with a portcullis, fortify **R2** I.iii.167 [Mowbray to Richard] *you have engaoled my tongue, / Doubly portcullised with my teeth and lips* [Q1 portculist; F percullist]

portend (*v.*) mean, signify, import **Cym** IV.ii.182 [Belarius alone] *it's strange / What Cloten's being here to us portends;* **Cym** IV.ii.350; **1H4** II.iv.315; **TN** II.v.117

portentous (*adj.*) ominous, threatening, full of foreboding **JC** I.iii.31 [Casca to Cicero, of weird happenings] *they are portentous things;* **Ham** I.i.109

portion (*n.*) **1** dowry, marriage gift, settlement **KL** I.i.242 [Burgundy to Lear] *Give but that portion which yourself proposed;* **TNK** V.iv.31; **TS** II.i.352
2 lot, destiny, fortune **E3** V.i.31 [Second Citizen to King Edward, of the truth of what the citizens have said] *Or may our portion be with damned fiends* [i.e. may we be damned otherwise]

portly (*adj.*) stately, majestic, dignified **RJ** I.v.66 [Capulet to Tybalt, of Romeo] *'A bears him like a portly gentleman;* **1H4** II.iv.412; **MV** I.i.9; **MW** I.iii.57; **Per** I.iv.61; **TC** IV.v.162

pose (*v.*) baffle, confuse, confound **TNK** III.v.80 [Gaoler's Daughter to and of Schoolmaster] *I have posed him;* **MM** II.iv.51

posied (*adj.*) inscribed with a motto **Lover** 45 [of the woman] *she … / Cracked many a ring of posied gold and bone*

position (*n.*) **1** [in logic] affirmation, assertion, hypothesis **TNK** III.v.52 [Schoolmaster to all] *In manners this was false position;* **Oth** II.i.229; **TC** III.iii.112
2 deliberate exposition, statement as a proposition **Oth** III.iii.232 [Iago to Othello, of Desdemona] *I do not in position / Distinctly speak of her*
3 arrangement, ordering, sequence **TN** II.v.117 [Malvolio to himself, of a line in the letter] *what should that alphabetical position portend?*

positive (*adj.*) unconditional, absolute, unqualified **TC** II.iii.64 [Thersites to Achilles] *Patroclus is a fool positive*

possess (*v.*) **1** notify, inform, acquaint **MV** IV.i.35 [Shylock to Duke] *I have possessed your grace of what I purpose;* **Cor** II.i.127; **KJ** IV.ii.203; **MA** V.i.268; **Mac** IV.iii.202; **TC** IV.iv.111
2 fill, imbue **MW** I.iii.93 [Nym to Pistol, of Page] *I will possess him with yellowness;* **H5** VI.i.108; **KJ** III.iii.41; **RJ** V.i.10
3 put in possession, endow **AC** III.xi.21 [Antony to attendants] *I will possess you of that ship and treasure;* **3H6** II.v.57; **R2** I.i.107
4 take possession of, seize **CE** II.ii.186 [Adriana to Antipholus of Syracuse] *If aught possess thee from me, it is dross*

possess it have your way, go for it **AC** II.vii.99 [Caesar to Antony, of the latter's injunction to be a child of the time] *Possess it, I'll make answer*

possessed (*adj.*) **1** mad, crazy, under demonic control **CE** V.i.246 [Antipholus of Ephesus to Duke, of Pinch] *This pernicious slave … / Cries out I was possessed;* **R2** II.i.108
2 propertied, affluent, provided for **MND** I.i.100 [Lysander to Theseus, of Demetrius] *I am … as well derived as he, / As well possessed*

possession (*n.*) **1** actual holding, real ownership, immediate possession **3H6** II.vi.110 [Warwick to all] *Now to London, / To see these honours in possession;* **TS** II.i.122
2 property, estate, belongings **TC** III.iii.5 [Calchas to all] *I have abandoned Troy, left my possession*
3 joint rights, shared ownership **R2** III.i.13 [Bolingbroke to Bushy and Green] *You have … / Broke the possession of a royal bed*
4 possessor, holder, occupier **1H4** III.ii.43 [King Henry to Prince Hal] *Had I so lavish of my presence been … / Opinion, that did help me to the crown, / Had still kept loyal to possession*

posset (*n.*) restorative hot drink, made of milk, liquor, and other ingredients **MW** V.v.168 [Page to Falstaff] *Thou shalt eat a posset tonight at my house;* **Mac** II.ii.6; **MW** I.iv.7

posset (*v.*) curdle, clot, coagulate **Ham** I.v.68 [Ghost to Hamlet, of the poison] *it doth posset / And curd … / The thin and wholesome blood* [F1; Q2 *possesse*]

possibility (*n.*) **1** capability, ability, competence **AW** III.vi.76 [Bertram to Parolles] *I … to the possibility of thy soldiership will subscribe for thee*
2 (plural) financial prospects **MW** I.i.59 [Evans to Shallow, of Anne] *Seven hundred pounds, and possibilities, is goot gifts*

possibility, with within the bounds of possiblity, realistically, practically **Tit** III.i.213 [Marcus to Titus] *speak with possibility, / And do not break into these deep extremes* [F *possibilities*]

possitable (*adj.*) version of 'positively' **MW** I.i.220 [Evans to Slender] *You must speak possitable*

post (*n.*) **1** express messenger, courier **1H4** I.i.37 [Westmorland to King Henry] *yesternight … there came / A post from Wales* 🖝 **FEW**, p.xxi
2 post-horse **RJ** V.i.21 [Balthasar to Romeo, of Juliet's death] *I … presently took post to tell it you;* **2H4** IV.iii.36

post, in in haste, at top speed **RJ** V.iii.273 [Balthasar to Prince, of Romeo] *in post he came from Mantua;* **CE** II.i.63; **3H6** III.iii.222; **Luc** 1; **R2** II.i.296; **WT** II.i.182
3 door-post **TN** I.v.143 [Malvolio to Olivia, of Viola as Cesario] *he says he'll stand at your door like a sheriff's post;* **CE** I.ii.64

post (*v.*) **1** hasten, speed, ride fast **E3** IV.i.35 [Salisbury to Villiers] *take horse and post from hence;* **Ham** I.ii.156; **JC** III.i.287; **KL** III.vii.1; **R2** V.v.59; **TG** II.iii.32

 2 carry rapidly, convey swiftly **Cym** II.iv.27 [Posthumus to Iachimo] *The swiftest harts have posted you by land*

 3 be over, rush past **PassP** XIV.25 [Pilgrim, of his love] *Were I with her, the night would post too soon*

post (*adv.*) in haste, with speed **Per** IV.Chorus.48 [Gower alone] *I carried winged time / Post on the lame feet of my rhyme;* **AW** IV.v.78; **2H4** II.iv.372

post off (*v.*) postpone, put off, defer **3H6** IV.viii.40 [King to Exeter, of his subjects] *I have not ... posted off their suits with slow delays*

post over (*v.*) pass over, disregard, go through with haste **2H6** III.i.255 [Suffolk to all, of how not to behave towards an accused murderer] *His guilt should be but idly posted over / Because his purpose is not executed* ☛ o'erpost (*v.*)

poster (*n.*) fast traveller, speedy rover **Mac** I.iii.32 [Witches chanting, of themselves] *Posters of the sea and land*

posterior (*n.*) [facetious] hind part, later part **LL** V.i.84 [Armado to Holofernes] *in the posteriors of this day;* **LL** V.i.113

posterity (*n.*) family, line of descendants, succession **KJ** II.i.96 [King Philip to King John] *thou hast ... / Cut off the sequence of posterity;* **Mac** III.i.4

postern (*n.*) entrance, side gate, back door **WT** I.ii.464 [Camillo to Polixenes] *It is in mine authority to command / The keys of all the posterns;* **MM** IV.ii.86; **R2** V.v.17; **TG** V.i.9; **WT** II.i.52

posthaste, post-haste (*n.*) great expedition, speed of preparation **Ham** I.i.107 [Horatio to Barnardo and Marcellus, referring to the military preparations taking place in Denmark] *this posthaste and romage in the land*

posthaste, post-haste (*adv.*) at full speed **3H6** II.i.138 [Warwick to Edward and Richard] *[we] In haste, post-haste, are come to join with you;* **R2** I.iv.55 ☛ haste-post-haste (*adj.*); post-post-haste (*adj.*)

post-horse (*n.*) **1** fast horse **RJ** V.i.26 [Romeo to Balthasar] *Get me ink and paper, / And hire posthorses*

 2 pony-express, express horse **2H4** I.Induction.4 [Rumour alone] *Making the wind my post-horse;* **R3** I.i.146

posting (*n.*) haste, speed, rush **AW** V.i.1 [Helena to Widow and Diana] *this exceeding posting day and night / Must wear your spirits low;* **Sonn** 51.4

posting (*adj.*) swift, speeding, hurrying **Cym** III.iv.37 [Pisanio to Innogen, of slander] *whose breath / Rides on the posting winds*

post-post-haste (*adj.*) with all possible speed, extremely speedy **Oth** I.iii.46 [Duke to First Senator, of Marcus Luccicos] *wish him / Post-post-haste dispatch* [or: adverbial interpretation, very speedily] ☛ posthaste (*adj.*)

posture (*n.*) **1** bearing, demeanour, presence **Cor** II.ii.213 [Brutus to Sicinius, of Coriolanus] *As if that whatsoever god ... gave him graceful posture;* **Cym** V.v.165

 2 position, condition, nature **JC** V.i.33 [Cassius to Antony] *The posture of your blows are yet unknown*

posy (*n.*) short piece of poetry [often inscribed inside a ring] **MV** V.i.148 [Gratiano to Portia, of Nerissa's ring] *whose posy was ... 'Love me, and leave me not';* **Ham** III.ii.161; **TNK** IV.i.90

pot (*n.*) stew-pot, cooking-pot **Cor** I.iv.49 [Soldiers to each other, of Martius] *To th'pot, I warrant him*

potation (*n.*) draught, drinking-bout **2H4** IV.iii.122 [Falstaff alone, of possible sons] *the first human principle I would teach them should be to forswear thin potations;* **Oth** II.iii.50

potato (*n.*) sweet potato, yam [regarded as an aphrodisiac] **MW** V.v.19 [Falstaff to Mistress Ford] *Let the sky rain potatoes*

potch (*v.*) poke, thrust, jab **Cor** I.x.15 [Aufidius to First Soldier, of Coriolanus] *I'll potch at him some way*

potency (*n.*) power, authority, command **MM** II.ii.67 [Isabella to Angelo] *I would to heaven I had your potency;* **Cor** II.iii.181; **H8** I.i.105; **KL** I.i.172; **TC** IV.iv.96

potent (*n.*) potentate, ruler **KJ** II.i.358 [Bastard to King John and King Philip] *Back to the stained field, / You equal potents*

potent (*adj.*) **1** powerful, influential **Tem** I.ii.275 [Prospero to Ariel, of Sycorax] *she did confine thee, / By help of her more potent ministers;* **AC** III.vi.95; **AY** V.iv.166; **Ham** II.ii.600; **1H4** VI.i.11; **Tem** V.i.50

 2 capable, accomplished, competent **Oth** II.iii.72 [Iago to Cassio, of England] *where indeed they are most potent in potting*

potential (*adj.*) powerful, mighty, strong **Oth** I.ii.13 [Iago to Othello, of Brabantio] *hath in his effect a voice potential / As double as the Duke's;* **KL** II.i.75

potently (*adv.*) mightily, strongly, powerfully **H8** V.i.134 [King Henry to Cranmer] *You are potently opposed;* **Ham** II.ii.202

pothecary (*n.*) ☛ apothecary (*n.*)

pother (*n.*) fuss, uproar, commotion **Cor** II.i.210 [Brutus to Sicinius] *Such a pother*

potion (*n.*) **1** poison, deadly drink **MND** III.ii.264 [Lysander to Hermia] *O hated potion, hence!* [Q1; F *poison*]

 2 medicine **2H4** I.ii.128 [Falstaff to Lord Chief Justice] *Your lordship may minister the potion of imprisonment to me;* **2H4** I.ii.197

potting (*n.*) drinking, tippling, imbibing **Oth** II.iii.72 [Iago to Cassio, of England] *where indeed they are most potent in potting*

pottle, pottle-pot (*n.*) drinking vessel containing two quarts **2H4** V.iii.63 [Bardolph to Shallow, agreeing that he and Davy will drink a quart] *Yea, sir, in a pottle-pot;* **MW** III.v.26 [Falstaff to Bardolph] *brew me a pottle of sack finely;* **MW** II.ii.74; **MW** II.i.197; **Oth** II.iii.78

pottle-deep (*adj.*) to the bottom of a two-quart vessel **Oth** II.iii.50 [Iago alone] *Roderigo ... hath tonight caroused / Potations pottle-deep*

pouch (*n.*) purse, wallet **1H4** II.iv.69 [Prince Hal to Francis, of the vintner] *Wilt thou rob this ... smooth-tongue Spanish pouch?*

poulter (*n.*) poulterer **1H4** II.iv.426 [Falstaff to Prince Hal] *hang me up by the heals for ... a poulter's hare* [i.e. one hanging up in a poulterer's shop]

pouncet-box (*n.*) small box with a perforated lid for holding snuff or perfume **1H4** I.iii.37 [Hotspur to King Henry, of a lord] *he held / A pouncet-box*

pound (*n.*) **1** pound-weight, weight, load **Cor** III.i.312 [Menenius to Brutus] *This tiger-footed rage ... will too late / Tie leaden pounds to's heels*

 2 (plural) sum of money **H8** II.iii.84 [Old Lady to Anne, of being in court] *nor could [I] / Come pat betwixt too early and too late / For any suit of pounds* [i.e. I could never get the timing right when asking for money]

pound (*v.*) shut up, confine [as animals in a pound] **Cor** I.iv.17 [First Senator to Martius, of the enemy] *We'll break our walls / Rather than they shall pound us up;* **TG** I.i.103

powder (*n.*) gunpowder **RJ** III.iii.132 [Friar to Romeo, of his wit] *Like powder in a skilless soldier's flask / Is set afire by thine own ignorance;* **KJ** II.i.448; **RJ** II.vi.10, V.i.64

powder (*v.*) season with salt, pickle **1H4** V.iv.111 [Falstaff alone, of Prince Hal] *If thou embowel me today, I'll give you leave to powder me and eat me too tomorrow*

powdered (*adj.*) seasoned, salted, well-spiced **MM** III.ii.56 [Lucio to Pompey, of Mistress Overdone] *Ever your fresh whore and your powdered bawd*

powdering-tub (*n.*) sweating-tub for the treatment of venereal disease **H5** II.i.72 [Pistol to Nym] *from the powdering tub of infamy / Fetch forth the lazar kite of Cressid's kind* ☛ tub (*n.*)

POLITENESS

As with other types of emotion, the interpretation of everyday politeness expressions depends partly on context and actor interpretation. For example, most uses of *so please you* are affable, but when Oswald uses it on abruptly leaving Lear (**KL** I.iv.45) it is positively rude, equivalent to 'Excuse me, I'm busy'. The table does not include cases of 'special pleading', such as the highly refined formulae used by aristocrats to each other (e.g. 'an it please your grace', **2H6** II.iv.76) or the formulaic begging expression used by prisoners to passers-by, 'for the Lord's sake' (**MM** IV.iii.18).

Item	Location	Example

When asking or begging for something [modern: please; may I ask]

beseech you	**Cor** I.iii.28	Beseech you, give me leave to retire myself
beseech you, I	**KL** I.iv.234	I do beseech you / To understand my purposes aright
good now	**TNK** III.iii.9	Sit down, and good now, / No more of these vain parleys
pray	**Tem** III.i.24	Pray, give me that
pray, I	**Cor** II.iii.74	Kindly, sir, I pray let me ha't
pray you, I	**AY** II.iv.58	I pray you, one of you question yond man
prithee	**Ham** II.ii.498	Prithee say on
prithee, I	**AY** I.ii.25	[Rosalind] what think you of falling in love? [Celia] Marry, I prithee, do, to make sport withal

When asking for agreement or permission to do something [modern: if you please; by your leave; if you agree; begging your pardon; etc.]

favour, by your	**KL** IV.vi.211	But, by your favour, / How near's the other army?
favour, under	**Tim** III.v.41	My lords, then, under favour – pardon me
leave, by	**Cym** V.v.315	Have at it then, by leave
leave, by your	**MW** I.i.179	[before kissing] By your leave, good mistress
leave, give us	**MW** II.ii.155	Give us leave, drawer [i.e. please leave us]
like you, an it	**MM** II.i.154	First, an it like you, the house is a respected house
like you, so	**Cym** II.iii.53	So like you, sir, ambassadors from Rome
offence, without	**Cym** I.vi.6	But I beseech your grace, without offence … wherefore you have / Commanded of me
pardon, by your	**MA** II.i.314	By your grace's pardon [before leaving]
pardon, under	**LL** IV.ii.100	Under pardon, sir, what are the contents?
patience, by your	**Cor** I.iii.75	[Volumnia] She shall [go out of doors]. [Virgilia] Indeed, no, by your patience
patience, under your	**Tit** II.iii.66	Under your patience, gentle Empress
please it	**MA** I.i.150	Please it your grace lead on? [i.e. may it please]
please you	**CE** I.ii.27	Please you, I'll meet with you upon the mart
please you, may it	**2H6** II.iv.80	So am I given in charge, may't please your grace
please you, so	**AY** I.i.86	So please you, he is here at the door, and importunes access
please you, will it	**MM** IV.i.58	Will't please you walk aside?
vouchsafe	**MA** III.ii.3	I'll bring you thither … if you'll vouchsafe me [i.e. be pleased to agree]

When apologizing [modern: I apologize; I beg your pardon; excuse me]

mercy, cry	**R3** V.iii.225	Cry mercy, lords and watchful gentlemen, / That you have ta'en a tardy sluggard here
mercy, I cry you	**1H6** V.iii.109	[Suffolk] Lady, wherefore talk you so? [Margaret] I cry you mercy, 'tis but quid for quo
mercy, I cry your worships	**MND** III.i.174	I cry your worships mercy, heartily

When softening an offensive remark or dubious subject [modern: pardon my language; excuse my French]

bless us, God	**MND** IV.ii.13	A paramour is – God bless us – a thing of naught
manhood, saving your	**2H4** II.i.25	'A comes continually to Pie Corner – saving your manhoods – to buy a saddle

POLITENESS – continued

Item	Location	Example
mark, bless the	TG IV.iv.18	*he had not been there, bless the mark, a pissing while*
mark, God bless the	MV II.ii.21	*the Jew my master who, God bless the mark, is a kind of devil*
mark, God save the	1H4 I.iii.55	*Of guns, and drums, and wounds, God save the mark! / And telling me*
reverence, saving	Cym IV.i.5	*The rather (saving reverence of the word), for 'tis said a woman's fitness comes by fits*
reverence, saving your	1H4 II.iv.455	*that he is, saving your reverence, a whoremaster*
sir-reverence	CE III.ii.93	*such a one as a man may not speak of without he say 'sir-reverence'*

When thanking [modern: thank you; thanks; many thanks]

God-a-mercy	Ham II.ii.172	[Polonius] *How does my good Lord Hamlet?* [Hamlet] *Well, God-a-mercy*
God dild you	Ham IV.v.42	[Claudius] *How do you, pretty lady?* [Ophelia] *Well, God dild you!* [i.e. God reward you]
gramercy	Tit IV.ii.7	[Young Lucius] *I greet your honours ...* [Demetrius] *Gramercy, lovely Lucius*
gramercies	TS I.i.41	[Tranio] *study what you most affect.* [Lucentio] *Gramercies, Tranio*

➤ EXCLAMATIONS, p.158; FAREWELLS, p.170; GREETINGS, p.206; REGRETS, p.367

---

power (*n.*) **1** armed force, troops, host, army **Ham** IV.iv.9 [Hamlet to Captain] *whose powers are these?*; **1H6** I.iv.103 [Messenger to Talbot, of Pucelle] *Is come with a great power to raise the siege* ➤ FEW, p.xxi

2 single force, one power **E3** IV.iv.44 [Prince Edward to Audley] *Then, all the world - and call it but a power - / Easily ta'en up*; **E3** IV.iv.52

3 authority, government **Cor** I.i.218 [Martius to Menenius, of the rabble] *It will in time / Win upon power*

4 force, strength, might **H8** II.ii.6 [Lord Chamberlain alone, reading a letter about his horses] *a man of my lord Cardinal's, by commission and main power, took 'em from me*; **Cor** I.viii.11

5 exercise of power, authoritative action **2H4** II.i.128 [Lord Chief Justice to Falstaff] *You speak as having power to do wrong*; **KL** I.i.170; **MM** I.i.79

6 (plural) physical faculties, bodily strength **AY** II.vi.8 [Orlando to Adam] *Thy conceit is nearer death than thy powers*

7 control, influence, sway **Cym** IV.i.21 [Cloten alone, of Cymbeline] *my mother, having power of his testiness*; **AC** I.ii.190

8 faculty, function, ability **LL** V.ii.809 [King to Princess] *To flatter up these powers of mine with rest*; **AC** III.xii.36; **2H6** III.ii.41; **LL** IV.iii.307; **MW** V.v.124

9 (usually plural) gods, deities, divinities **Tem** III.iii.74 [Ariel to Alonso, Sebastian, and Antonio] *The powers ... have / Incensed the seas and shores*; **AC** II.i.6; **JC** V.i.106

powers (*n.*) faculties, abilities to act **Ham** III.ii.184 [First Player, as King, to his Queen] *My operant powers their functions leave to do*

powther (*n.*) ➤ **pudder** (*n.*)

pow waw (*int.*) ➤ EXCLAMATIONS, p.158

pox (*n.*) venereal disease; also: plague, or any other disease displaying skin pustules **2H4** I.ii.233 [Falstaff to himself, of young limbs and lechery] *the gout galls the one and the pox pinches the other*; **RJ** II.iv.28 ➤ SWEARING, p.435

prabbles (*n.*) ➤ **pribbles and prabbles**

practic (*adj.*) practical, pragmatic, down-to-earth **H5** I.i.51 [Canterbury to Ely] *the art and practic part of life / Must be the mistress to this theoric*

practice (*n.*) **1** scheme, plot, stratagem, intrigue **H8** III.ii.29 [Surrey to all, of Wolsey] *How came / His practices to light?*; **Ham** V.ii.311; **2H6** III.i.46; **KJ** IV.iii.63; **Oth** III.iv.137; **PassP** XVIII.9

2 trickery, treachery **TN** V.i.350 [Olivia to Malvolio] *This practice hath most shrewdly passed upon thee*; **Cym** V.v.199; **2H6** III.ii.22; **KL** V.iii.149; **MA** IV.i.186; **MM** III.ii.262

3 carrying out, performance, execution [of a plot] **MA** V.i.235 [Borachio to Don Pedro, of his treachery] *[Don John] paid me richly for the practice of it*

4 doings, proceedings, dealings **AC** III.xi.39 [Antony to Eros, of Octavius] *He ... no practice had / In the brave squares of war*; **Ham** II.ii.38; **Per** III.ii.33

5 occupation, profession, line of work **TN** III.i.63 [Viola alone, of Feste] *This is a practice / As full of labour as a wise man's art*; **TS** II.i.164

practisant (*n.*) conspirator, plotter, intriguer **1H6** III.ii.20 [Bastard to all] *Here entered Pucelle and her practisants*

practise (*v.*) **1** plot, scheme, conspire **KJ** I.i.214 [Bastard alone, of himself] *I will not practise to deceive*; **AY** I.i.139; **1H6** II.i.25; **2H6** II.i.166; **KJ** IV.i.20; **TG** IV.i.48

2 put to use, employ **TC** II.ii.109 [Cassandra to all] *Practise your eyes with tears!*

3 engage in, carry on, take up **Per** II.i.67 [Pericles to Second Fisherman, of fishing] *I never practised it*

4 copy, emulate, carry out **2H4** II.iii.23 [Lady Percy to Northumberland, of Percy] *He had no legs that practised not his gait*

practise on / upon (*v.*) **1** plot against **H5** II.ii.99 [King Henry to Scroop] *Wouldst thou have practised on me, for thy use?*; **KL** III.ii.57; **RJ** III.v.210

2 work upon, act craftily with, make to operate **2H4** II.i.113 [Lord Chief Justice to Falstaff, of the Hostess] *You have ... practised upon the easy-yielding spirit of this woman*; **JC** IV.iii.87; **MA** II.i.354; **TS** Induction.i.34

3 try to seduce, carry on with **TNK** V.i.100 [Palamon praying to Venus] *I never practised / Upon man's wife*

practised (*adj.*) studied, well-versed, accomplished **WT** I.ii.116 [Leontes to himself, of Hermione and Polixenes] *making practised smiles / As in a looking glass*

practiser (*n.*) practitioner **AW** II.i.185 [King to Helena] *Sweet practiser, thy physic I will try*

praemunire (*n.*) [pron: preemyu'neeree] writ accusing someone of recognizing the power of the pope [as opposed to the sovereign] **H8** III.ii.340 [Suffolk to Wolsey] *all those things you have done of late ... / Fall into th'compass of a praemunire*

praetor (*n.*) ➤ **ROMAN HISTORY**, p.377

praise (*n.*) **1** praiseworthiness, merit, virtue **TC** II.ii.146 [Priam to Paris] *to be valiant is no praise at all;* **MV** V.i.108
　2 credit, honour, prestige **AC** II.vi.43 [Pompey to Triumvirs] *Though I lose / The praise of it by telling*

praise (*v.*) **1** appraise, test, try out **TG** III.i.335 [Speed reading from Launce's paper, of his love's vices] *She will often praise her liquor* [pun: 337, lauded]
　2 appraise, assess, put a valuation on **TN** I.v.238 [Olivia to Viola as Cesario] *Were you sent hither to praise me?*

prank (*n.*) **1** outrageous deed, excessive behaviour **Oth** III.iii.200 [Iago to Othello] *In Venice they do let God see the pranks / They dare not show their husbands;* **Ham** III.iv.2; **KL** I.iv.234; **Oth** II.i.140; **TN** IV.i.54; **WT** IV.iv.695
　2 malicious act, wicked deed **1H6** III.i.15 [Gloucester to Winchester] *Thy lewd, pestiferous, and dissentious pranks*
　3 trick, frolic, mischief **CE** II.ii.218 [Adriana to Antipholus of Syracuse] *I'll ... shrive you of a thousand idle pranks;* **TNK** V.iii.79

prank (*v.*) dress up, deck out, adorn **Cor** III.i.23 [Coriolanus to Lartius, of Sicinius and Brutus] *they do prank them in authority* [i.e. dress themselves up]; **TN** II.iv.85

prank up (*v.*) dress up, deck out, bedeck **WT** IV.iv.10 [Perdita to Florizel] *me, poor lowly maid, / Most goddess-like pranked up*

prate (*n.*) prattle, chatter, blather **KJ** IV.i.25 [Hubert to himself, of Arthur] *If I talk to him, with his innocent prate / He will awake my mercy;* **1H6** IV.i.124

prate (*v.*) prattle, chatter, blather **Cor** V.iii.159 [Volumnia to and of Coriolanus] *he lets me prate / Like one i'th' stocks* ➤ **FEW**, p.xxi

prater (*n.*) chatterer, idle talker **H5** V.ii.157 [King Henry to Katherine] *A speaker is but a prater*

prating (*adj.*) prattling, chattering, blathering **RJ** II.iv.196 [Nurse to Romeo, of Juliet] *when 'twas a little prating thing;* **CE** I.ii.101; **Ham** III.iv.216; **MV** V.i.164; **R3** III.i.151; **TS** IV.iii.112

pray (*v.*) ➤ **POLITENESS**, p.340; **DISCOURSE MARKERS**, p.127

pray in aid [legal] claim the assistance of someone who has a shared interest in a defence action **AC** V.vii.27 [Proculeius to Cleopatra, of Caesar] *A conqueror that will pray in aid for kindness, / Where he for grace is kneeled to* [i.e. he will ask you to help him to be kind to you]

preachment (*n.*) sermon, discourse, harangue **3H6** I.iv.72 [Queen to York] *Was't you that ... made a preachment of your high descent?*

preambulate (*v.*) walk forth, go in front **LL** V.i.76 [Armado to Holofernes] *Arts-man, preambulate* [F, Q1 *preambulat*]

precedence (*n.*) previous utterance, prior speech **LL** III.i.81 [Armado to Mote, of l'envoy] *it is an epilogue or discourse to make plain / Some obscure precedence that hath tofore been sain;* **AC** II.v.51

precedent (*n.*) **1** example, instance, case **Luc** 1261 [of men abusing women] *The precedent whereof in Lucrece view;* **1H4** II.iv.32; **KL** II.iii.13; **Tit** V.iii.43; **Venus** 26
　2 worthy example, model to be followed [in mediaeval chivalry] **E3** IV.v.103 [King John to Charles] *Dwell'st thou on precedents?;* **R2** II.i.130
　3 original text from which a copy is made **KJ** V.ii.3 [Lewis the Dauphin to Melun, of a treaty with the English lords] *Return the precedent to these lords again;* **R3** III.vi.7

precedent (*adj.*) former, previous, prior **Tim** I.i.137 [Old Athenian to Timon] *Our own precedent passions do instruct us / What levity's in youth;* **AC** IV.xiv.83; **Ham** III.iv.99

precept (*n.*) **1** detailed direction, precise instruction **MM** IV.i.39 [Isabella to disguised Duke, of Angelo] *In action all of precept, he did show me / The way* [unclear meaning]
　2 writ, warrant, court order **2H4** V.i.11 [Davy to Shallow] *those precepts cannot be served*

preceptial (*adj.*) consisting of precepts, full of wise instructions **MA** V.i.24 [Leonato to Antonio] *passion, which before / Would give preceptial medicine to rage*

precinct (*n.*) sector, area of control **1H6** II.i.68 [Charles to all, of Pucelle] *Within her quarter and mine own precinct / I was employed in passing to and fro*

precious (*adj.*) out-and-out, worthless, good-for-nothing **Cym** IV.ii.83 [Cloten to Guiderius] *Thou precious varlet*

precious-dear (*adj.*) dearly precious **TC** V.iii.28 [Hector to Cassandra and Andromache] *the dear man / Holds honour far more precious-dear than life*

preciously (*adv.*) profitably, valuably, usefully **Tem** I.ii.241 [Prospero to Ariel] *The time 'twixt six and now / Must by us both be spent most preciously*

precious-princely (*adv.*) like the precious character of a prince **KJ** IV.iii.40 [Bigot to all, of Arthur's body] *when he doomed this beauty to a grave, / Found it too precious-princely for a grave*

precipitance (*n.*) jumping from a great height, headlong fall **TNK** I.i.142 [Third Queen to Theseus] *Those that with cords, knives, drams, precipitance, / Weary of this world's light* [or: drams' precipitance = rapidly working poisons] [no comma in Q]

precipitate (*v.*) fall headlong, plunge, tumble **KL** IV.vi.50 [Edgar to Gloucester] *Hadst thou been ... / So many fathom down precipitating*

precipitation (*n.*) **1** sheer drop, steepness, precipitousness **Cor** III.ii.4 [Coriolanus to Nobles, of the people] *Let them ... pile ten hills on the Tarpeian rock, / That the precipitation might down stretch / Below the beam of sight*
　2 throwing headlong, hurling down **Cor** III.iii.102 [Sicinius to assembly, of Coriolanus] *we ... banish him our city, / In peril of precipitation / From off the rock Tarpeian*

precise (*adj.*) **1** puritanical, strictly moral, scrupulously correct **MM** I.iii.50 [Duke to Friar Thomas] *Lord Angelo is precise;* **MM** III.i.97
　2 scrupulously pure, strictly observed, unstained **MW** II.ii.22 [Falstaff to Pistol] *it is as much as I can do to keep the terms of my honour precise*

preciseness (*n.*) morality, propriety, rectitude **1H6** V.iv.67 [Warwick to Pucelle] *Is all your strict preciseness come to this?*

precisian (*n.*) strict adviser, spiritual mentor **MW** II.i.5 [Mistress Page alone, reading from Falstaff's letter] *though Love use Reason for his precisian, he admits him not for his counsellor*

pre-contract (*n.*) pre-nuptial agreement **MM** IV.i.71 [disguised Duke to Mariana, of Angelo] *He is your husband on a pre-contract*

precurrer (*n.*) precursor, forerunner **Phoen** 6 [of the screech-owl] *Foul precurrer of the fiend*

precurse (*n.*) forerunner, precursor, heralding **Ham** I.i.121 [Horatio to Marcellus and Barnardo, of unnatural happenings in Denmark] *And even the like precurse of feared events*

predestinate (*adj.*) fated, predestined, predictable **MA** I.i.122 [Benedick to Beatrice] *some gentleman or other shall 'scape a predestinate scratched face*

predicament (*n.*) category, class, division **1H4** I.iii.166 [Hotspur to Northumberland and Worcester] *I descend ... / To show the line and the predicament / Wherein you range* [also: danger]

predict (*n.*) prediction, foretelling **Sonn** 14.8 *say with Princes if it shall go well, / By oft predict that I in heaven find* [i.e. common signs] [debated reading]

predominance (*n.*) ascendancy, predominant influence, authority **Mac** II.iv.8 [Ross to Old Man] *Is't night's predominance or the day's shame / That darkness does the face of earth entomb;* **KL** I.ii.123; **TC** II.iii.128

predominant (*adj.*) [astrology] in the ascendant, ruling **AW** I.i.194 [Parolles to Helena, of Mars] *When he was predominant;* **2H6** III.i.145; **WT** I.ii.202

predominate *(v.)* **1** [astrology] be in the ascendancy, exert a controlling influence MW II.ii.268 [Falstaff to Ford as Brook, of Ford] *I will predominate over the peasant*
2 prevail over, control, dominate Tim IV.iii.143 [Timon to Phrynia and Timandra, of a reformer] *Let your close fire predominate his smoke*

prefer *(v.)* **1** promote, advance, recommend TNK II.ii.82 [Arcite alone, of Emilia] *happiness prefer me to a place / Where I may ever dwell in sight of her;* Cym II.iii.45; H8 IV.i.102; JC III.i.28; MND IV.ii.34; Per II.ii.17
2 present, put forward, introduce TS I.i.97 [Baptista to Gremio and Hortensio, of schoolmasters for Bianca] *Prefer them hither*
3 present, bring forward 1H6 III.i.10 [Gloucester to Winchester] *in writing I preferred / The manner of thy vile outrageous crimes;* Tim III.iv.50
4 place before, offer, present with Ham IV.vii.158 [Claudius to Laertes, of Hamlet] *I'll have preferred him / A chalice* [Q2 prefard; F prepar'd]

preferment *(n.)* advancement, promotion TG I.iii.7 [Panthino to Antonio] *other men ... / Put forth their sons to seek preferment out;* Cym V.iv.208; H8 V.i.36; MV II.ii.135; R3 I.iii.94; WT V.ii.112

prefixed *(adj.)* fixed, settled, prearranged, decided in advance RJ V.iii.253 [Friar to Prince, of Juliet] *At the prefixed hour of her waking;* MM IV.iii.77; TC IV.iii.1; TNK III.vi.304; WT I.ii.42

pre-formed *(adj.)* previously formed, naturally endowed, innate JC I.iii.67 [Cassius to Casca, of weird happenings] *Why all these things change from their ordinance, / Their natures, and pre-formed faculties*

pregnancy *(n.)* quick-wittedness, inventive imagination 2H4 I.ii.172 [Falstaff to Lord Chief Justice] *pregnancy is made a tapster, and his quick wit wasted in giving reckonings*

pregnant *(adj.)* **1** well-disposed, ready, inclined, receptive TC IV.iv.87 [Troilus to Cressida, of fair virtues] *To which the Grecians are most prompt and pregnant;* Ham III.ii.71; KL IV.vi.223; Per IV.Chorus.44; TN III.i.86
2 obvious, clear, evident MM II.i.23 [Angelo to Escalus] *'Tis very pregnant, / The jewel that we find, we stoop and take't;* Cym IV.ii.325; Oth II.i.229
3 very likely, extremely probable AC II.i.45 [Pompey to Menas, of Antony and Caesar] *'Twere pregnant they should square between themselves*
4 meaningful, compelling, convincing Ham II.ii.209 [Polonius to himself, of Hamlet] *How pregnant sometimes his replies are!;* KL II.i.75; WT V.ii.30
5 well-versed, knowledgeable MM I.i.11 [Duke to Escalus] *Our city's institutions ... [you are] pregnant in*
6 resourceful, wily TN II.ii.28 [Viola alone, of her disguise] *I see thou art a wickedness / Wherein the pregnant enemy does much* [i.e. Satan]

prejudicate *(v.)* prejudge, give an influential opinion about AW I.ii.8 [King to First Lord, of Austria] *our dearest friend / Prejudicates the business*

prejudice *(n.)* detriment, damage, misfortune H8 I.i.182 [Buckingham to Norfolk, of Emperor Charles] *His fears were that the interview [might] ... / Breed him some prejudice;* TNK V.iii.88

prejudice *(v.)* injure, harm, damage 1H6 III.iii.91 [Charles to all] *let us ... seek how we may prejudice the foe*

prejudicial *(adj.)* damaging to one's rights, tending to invalidate a claim 3H6 I.i.144 [Warwick to all, of Richard II voluntarily resigning his crown] *Think you 'twere prejudicial to his crown?*

premeditation *(n.)* forecast, outlook 3H6 III.ii.133 [Richard alone, of his place in the succession] *A cold premeditation for my purpose!*

premise *(n.)* **1** condition, stipulation, pledge Tem I.ii.123 [Prospero to Miranda] *in lieu o'th' premises / Of homage*

2 (plural) evidence, circumstances admitted in court H8 II.i.63 [Buckingham to the people, of the law] *'T has done, upon the premises, but justice*

premised *(adj.)* preordained, predestined 2H6 V.ii.41 [Young Clifford to himself] *let the vile world end, / And the premised flames of the last day / Knit earth and heaven together*

prenominate *(adj.)* aforesaid, previously mentioned Ham II.i.43 [Polonius to Reynaldo] *Having ever seen in the prenominate crimes / The youth you breathe of guilty*

prenominate *(v.)* name beforehand, specify in advance TC IV.v.250 [Hector to Achilles] *Think'st thou to catch my life so pleasantly / As to prenominate in nice conjecture / Where thou wilt hit me dead?*

prentice *(n.)* apprentice 2H4 II.ii.169 [Prince Henry to Poins] *From a prince to a prentice?;* AW IV.iii.182; 2H6 I.iii.196, II.iii.71

preordained *(adj.)* intended, normal, appointed TNK IV.iii.71 [Doctor to Gaoler and Wooer, of the Gaoler's Daughter] *[her senses] may return and settle again to execute their preordained faculties*

pre-ordinance *(n.)* pre-ordained law, previously established ordinance JC III.i.38 [Caesar to Metellus, of Metellus' approach] *turn pre-ordinance and first decree / Into the law of children*

preparation *(n.)* **1** equipped military force, force ready for war Oth I.iii.14 [Sailor to Duke] *The Turkish preparation makes for Rhodes;* AC IV.x.1; Cor I.ii.15; Cym IV.iii.29; KL IV.iv.22; Oth I.iii.219
2 expedition, military proceeding KJ IV.ii.111 [Messenger to King John, of France] *never such a power / For any foreign preparation / Was levied in the body of a land*
3 forewarning, prior ceremony MW II.ii.152 [Ford as Brook to Falstaff] *I make bold to press with so little preparation upon you*
4 accomplishment, capacity, achievement MW II.ii.221 [Ford as Brook to Falstaff] *you are a gentleman ... generally allowed for your many warlike, courtlike, and learned preparations*

prepare *(n.)* preparation, readiness 3H6 IV.i.130 [Edward to Pembroke and Stafford] *make prepare for war*

prepare up *(v.)* prepare, put in readiness RJ IV.ii.45 [Capulet to Lady Capulet] *I will walk myself / To County Paris, to prepare up him / Against tomorrow* [F him up]

prepared *(adj.)* drawn, ready for action KL II.i.50 [Edmund to Gloucester, of Edgar] *With his prepared sword he charges home*

preposterous *(adj.)* **1** contrary to the natural order, monstrous, perverted Oth I.iii.326 [Iago to Roderigo] *the blood and baseness of our natures would conduct us to most preposterous conclusions;* 3H6 V.vi.5; R3 II.iv.63; TC V.i.20; TS III.i.9
2 totally out of place, extremely improper LL I.i.236 [King reading Armado's letter to him, of seeing Costard and Jaquenetta] *I did encounter that obscene and most preposterous event*
3 malapropism for 'prosperous' WT V.ii.143 [Clown to Shepherd] *being in so preposterous estate as we are*

preposterously *(adv.)* out of the normal course of events, unnaturally, perversely MND II.ii.121 [Puck to Oberon] *those things do best please me / That befall preposterously;* H5 II.ii.112; MW II.ii.231; Oth I.iii.62; Sonn 109.11

prerogative *(n.)* **1** principle, right, code H5 IV.i.67 [Fluellen to Gower] *It is the greatest admiration in the universal world, when the true and aunchient prerogatifes and laws of the wars is not kept*
2 rights of office, due privilege, pre-eminence Tem I.ii.105 [Prospero to Miranda, of Antonio] *he did believe / He was indeed the Duke ... / With all prerogative*
3 precedence, prior place TS III.i.6 [Hortensio as Licio to Lucentio as Cambio, of teaching Bianca] *give me leave to have prerogative*

prerogatived *(adj.)* privileged, advantaged, favoured Oth III.iii.271 [Othello alone, of great people] *Prerogatived are they less than the base*

presage (*n.*) **1** sign, indication, portent **TN** III.ii.62 [Fabian to Sir Toby, of Sir Andrew and Viola as Cesario] *his opposite the youth bears in his visage no great presage of cruelty;* **KJ** I.i.28, III.iv.158; **Venus** 457

2 foreboding, presentiment, misgiving **R2** II.ii.141 [Bagot to Bushy and Green] *If heart's presages be not vain, / We three here part that ne'er shall meet again;* **Sonn** 107.6

presage (*v.*) **1** signify, indicate **E3** IV.v.21 [King John to Philip] *What fearful words are those thy looks presage?;* **AC** I.ii.49; **E3** I.ii.147; **1H6** IV.i.191; **KL** IV.vi.119; **MV** III.ii.173

2 predict, forecast **RJ** V.i.2 [Romeo alone] *My dreams presage some joyful news at hand;* **3H6** V.i.71; **JC** V.i.78; **MV** I.i.175

presager (*n.*) indicator, interpreter, announcer **Sonn** 23.10 *O let my books be then the eloquence, / And dumb presagers of my speaking breast*

presaging (*adj.*) portending, discerning, insightful **3H6** IV.vi.92 [Somerset to Oxford] *Henry's late presaging prophecy / Did glad my heart with hope of this young Richmond*

prescience (*n.*) **1** foreknowledge, visionary power **Tem** I.ii.180 [Prospero to Miranda] *by my prescience / I find my zenith doth depend upon / A most auspicious star;* **AC** I.ii.22

2 foresight, forethought, planning ahead **Luc** 727 [of Lucrece] *her subjects … / Which in her prescience she controlled still;* **TC** I.iii.199

prescribe (*v.*) limit, restrict, confine **KL** I.ii.24 [Gloucester to himself] *the King gone tonight? prescribed his power?* [F; Q *subscribd*]

prescript (*n.*) order, direction, instruction **AC** III.viii.5 [Caesar to Taurus] *Do not exceed / The prescript of this scroll;* **Ham** II.ii.142

prescript (*adj.*) prescribed, appropriate, laid down **H5** III.vii.44 [Dauphin to Orleans, of his horse bearing him well] *which is the prescript praise and perfection of a good and particular mistress*

prescription (*n.*) legal claim founded on long use **3H6** III.iii.94 [Warwick to Oxford, of the succession] *threescore and two years - a silly time / To make prescription for a kingdom's worth*

presence (*n.*) **1** royal assembly, eminent company **R3** III.iv.64 [Hastings to Richard] *The tender love I bear your grace … / Makes me most forward in this princely presence;* **AC** II.ii.114; **1H6** I.i.21; **H8** IV.ii.37; **KJ** II.i.196; **R3** I.iii.54

2 royal reception chamber **H8** III.i.17 [Gentleman to Queen Katherine] *the two great Cardinals / Wait in the presence;* **2H6** I.iii.109, III.ii.228, 238; **R2** I.iii.289; **RJ** V.iii.86

3 majesty **KJ** II.i.377 [Bastard to King John and King Philip] *Your royal presences, be ruled by me*

4 gracious self, dignity as a person, personal position **KJ** II.i.367 [King John to Hubert, of himself] *Lord of our presence, Angiers, and of you;* **KJ** I.i.137

5 appearance, bearing, demeanour **Per** V.i.64 [Lysimachus to Helicanus, of Marina] *Is't not a goodly presence?;* **LL** V.ii.761; **MV** III.ii.54; **Sonn** 10.11; **TC** III.iii.270

6 attendance, state of being present **R2** IV.i.62 [Fitzwater to Surrey] *You were in presence then* [i.e. you were there]; **2H4** IV.iv.17; **H5** I.ii.2

7 malapropism for 'presents' [= documents] **2H6** IV.vii.26 [Cade to Say] *Be it known unto thee by these presence*

present (*n.*) **1** present time, immediate moment, matter in hand **JC** I.ii.164 [Brutus to Cassius] *For this present, / I would not … / Be any further moved;* **Cor** I.vi.60, III.iii.42; **Cym** IV.iii.8; **JC** I.ii.164; **WT** IV.i.14

2 available means, current resources **TN** III.iv.336 [Viola as Cesario to Antonio] *I'll make division of my present with you*

3 object presented **Per** II.ii.41 [Thaisa to Simonides, of Pericles] *his present is / A withered branch*

4 written document **LL** IV.iii.187 [King to Jaquenetta, of the letter] *What present hast thou there?;* **AY** I.ii.115 [F]

present, from the beside the present point **AC** II.vi.30 [Lepidus to Pompey, of the latter's reference to his house] *this is from the present*

present, on the right now, immediately, forthwith **Tim** I.i.145 [Old Athenian to Timon, of his daughter's dowry] *Three talents on the present; in future, all*

present, this just now, recently **TN** I.v.224 [Olivia to Viola as Cesario, after removing her veil] *such a one I was this present* [i.e. at the last viewing of the picture]

present (*adj.*) **1** immediate, instant **CE** IV.i.5 [Second Merchant to Angelo] *make present satisfaction* ☛ **FEW**, p.xxi

2 pressing, urgent **CE** I.ii.29 [First Merchant to Antipholus of Syracuse] *My present business calls me from you now;* **Tim** III.ii.35

3 imminent, impending, approaching **WT** III.iii.4 [Mariner to Antigonus] *the skies look grimly, / And threaten present blusters*

4 sudden, spur-of-the-moment **AC** II.ii.143 [Agrippa to Caesar and Antony, of his proposal] *'tis a studied, not a present thought*

5 ready, available, immediately accessible **CE** IV.i.34 [Antipholus of Ephesus to Angelo] *I am not furnished with the present money*

6 occurring at this time, taking place now **1H4** IV.i.44 [Hotspur to Worcester, of Northumberland] *His present want / Seems more than we shall find it*

7 remaining, surviving, still existing **2H6** V.ii.87 [Young Clifford to King and Queen] *uncurable discomfit / Reigns in the hearts of all our present parts*

present (*v.*) **1** symbolize, represent, suggest **MA** III.iii.73 [Dogberry to Second Watchman] *you … are to present the Prince's own person;* **2H4** V.ii.79; **3H6** II.v.100

2 put forward [for immediate action] **TNK** I.i.151 [First Queen to Theseus] *that work / Presents itself to th'doing* [i.e. needs to be done now]; **TS** Induction.ii.86

3 show, reveal, manifest **1H4** III.i.177 [Worcester to Hotspur, of Hotspur's behaviour] *oftentimes it doth present harsh rage*

4 act, represent, play the part of **MW** IV.vi.20 [Fenton to Host, of Anne] *Tonight … / Must my sweet Nan present the Fairy Queen*

presentation (*n.*) semblance, display, show **R3** IV.iv.84 [Queen Margaret to Queen Elizabeth] *I called thee … / The presentation of but what I was;* **AY** V.iv.104

presented (*adj.*) **1** displayed, exhibited, paraded **KL** II.iii.11 [Edgar alone] *I'll … with presented nakedness outface / The winds and persecutions of the sky*

2 offered, bestowed, proffered **Venus** 405 [Venus to Adonis] *take advantage on presented joy*

presently (*adv.*) **1** immediately, instantly, at once **Ham** V.ii.387 [Horatio to Fortinbras] *let this same be presently performed* ☛ **FEW**, p.xxi

2 after a short time, soon, before long **Tim** III.vi.36 [Timon to Lords] *We shall to't presently* [i.e. we shall eat soon]; **AC** III.v.7

presentment (*n.*) **1** picture, portrait, depiction **Ham** III.iv.55 [Hamlet to Gertrude] *The counterfeit presentment of two brothers*

2 presentation, bestowal, offering for acceptance **Tim** I.i.27 [Poet to Painter, of his next book] *Upon the heels of my presentment*

preserve (*v.*) keep, maintain, look after **TNK** V.ii.104 [Doctor to Wooer, of the Gaoler's Daughter] *still preserve her in this way*

preserved (*adj.*) kept safe from evil, protected **MM** II.ii.153 [Isabella to Angelo, of what she will offer him] *prayers from preserved souls, / From fasting maids*

press (*n.*) **1** crowd, throng **JC** I.ii.15 [Caesar to all] *Who is it in the press that calls on me?;* **H8** IV.i.78, V.iv.83

2 clothes-press, cupboard, wardrobe **MW** III.iii.199 [Evans to all] *If there be anypody in the house … and in the presses, heaven forgive my sins;* **MW** IV.ii.57

3 commission to raise men **1H4** IV.ii.12 [Falstaff alone] *I have misused the King's press damnably*

press (*v.*) **1** levy, raise, conscript **1H4** IV.ii.14 [Falstaff alone] *I press me none but good householders;* **Cor** I.i.9, III.i.122; **1H4** IV.ii.36; **3H6** II.v.64; **R2** III.ii.58

2 push forward, thrust, come / go boldly **JC** II.iv.15 [Portia to Lucius] *take good note / What Caesar doth, what suitors press to him;* **AY** V.iv.54; **3H6** III.i.19; **H8** II.iv.186; **JC** II.ii.88; **Tit** IV.iii.90

3 oppress, burden, weigh down **Venus** 545 [of Adonis and Venus] *He with her plenty pressed, she faint with dearth;* **Venus** 430; **WT** II.iii.39

4 impress [as a stamp on a coin], imprint, mark **TNK** I.i.109 [Third Queen to Emilia, of her first poor effort at expressing herself] *sorrow wanting form / Is pressed with deeper matter*

5 urge, compel, spur **TNK** I.i.73 [First Queen to Theseus, of a god] *[who will] press you forth / Our undertaker*

press down *(v.)* overburden, weigh down, oppress **CE** IV.ii.64 [Adriana to Luciana] *I am pressed down with conceit*

press-money *(n.)* money paid to recruits when conscripted **KL** IV.vi.87 [Lear to all] *There's your press-money*

pressure *(n.)* impression, stamp, image **Ham** I.v.100 [Hamlet alone] *I'll wipe away … all pressures past;* **Ham** III.ii.24

prest *(adj.)* engaged, made ready, hired **MV** I.i.160 [Antonio to Bassanio] *say to me what I should do … / And I am prest unto it;* **Per** IV.Chorus.45

presume on *(v.)* take insufficiently into account, rely too readily on **Sonn** 22.13 *Presume not on thy heart when mine is slain;* **TC** IV.iv.96

presuppose *(v.)* suggest earlier, previously lay down **TN** V.i.348 [Olivia to Malvolio, of his behaviour] *in such forms which here were presupposed / Upon thee in the letter*

presurmise *(n.)* suspicion beforehand, thought in advance **2H4** I.i.168 [Morton to Northumberland] *It was your presurmise / That in the dole of blows your son might drop*

pretence *(n.)* **1** plan, design, intention, purpose **TG** III.i.47 [Proteus to Duke, of Valentine's plans] *love of you … / Hath made me publisher of this pretence;* **AW** IV.iii.47; **Cor** I.ii.20; **KL** I.ii.88; **Mac** II.iii.128; **WT** III.ii.17

2 pretext, excuse, alleged ground **H8** I.ii.59 [Queen Katherine to King Henry, of taxation] *the pretence for this / Is named your wars in France*

pretend *(v.)* **1** claim, avow, profess **Tit** I.i.45 [Marcus to Saturninus and Bassianus, of the Capitol and Senate] *Whom you pretend to honour and adore;* **Cym** II.iii.112, V.v.250; **3H6** IV.vii.57; **MM** III.i.228

2 intend, design, plan **Luc** 576 [Lucrece to Tarquin] *Reward not hospitality / With such black payment as thou hast pretended;* **1H6** IV.i.6; **Mac** II.iv.24

3 import, imply, mean **1H6** IV.i.54 [Gloucester to all, of Burgundy's letter] *doth this churlish superscription / Pretend some alteration in good will?*

pretended *(adj.)* intended, purposed, proposed **E3** III.iii.105 [Prince Edward to King John] *our pretended quarrel is truly just;* **TG** II.vi.37; **TNK** I.i.210

pretender *(n.)* claimant, suitor, wooer **TNK** V.i.158 [Emilia praying to Diana] *He of the two pretenders that best loves me*

prettily *(adv.)* cleverly, ingeniously; or: charmingly **MND** II.ii.59 [Hermia to Lysander] *Lysander riddles very prettily;* **TNK** IV.iii.27

prettiness *(n.)* pleasantness, agreeableness **Ham** IV.v.189 [Laertes to all, of Ophelia] *Thought and afflictions, passion, hell itself, / She turns to favour and to prettiness*

pretty *(adj.)* **1** clever, ingenious, artful **MV** II.vi.37 [Jessica to Lorenzo] *lovers cannot see / The pretty follies that themselves commit;* **H5** I.ii.177; **R2** III.iii.165; **TC** I.ii.156; **Tim** I.i.36

2 nice, proper, apt **Cor** I.i.88 [Menenius to Citizens] *I shall tell you / A pretty tale;* **AY** III.v.11; **Cym** III.iv.149

3 [of men] fine, good-looking **AY** III.v.113 [Phebe to Silvius, of Rosalind as Ganymede] *It is a pretty youth;* **AY** IV.i.1; **Cor** I.iii.59; **KL** I.iv.96

4 good, excellent, fine **Tim** III.i.15 [Lucullus to Flaminius] *what hast thou there under thy cloak, pretty Flaminius?;* **H5** IV.vi.28

5 fair, considerable, ample **AY** V.i.28 [William to Touchstone] *I have a pretty wit*

6 childish, trifling, naive **Sonn** 41.1 *Those pretty wrongs that liberty commits*

prevail *(v.)* **1** succeed, win, be victor **1H6** II.i.56 [Pucelle to Charles] *Sleeping or waking must I still prevail;* **Cor** I.iii.101

2 succeed in seduction, have one's way [in a sexual encounter] **1H6** IV.v.103 [Suffolk alone] *Thus Suffolk hath prevailed;* **1H6** IV.v.78; **Sonn** 41.8

prevailing *(adj.)* successful, effective, influential **Tit** III.i.26 [Titus to Tribunes and Senators] *let me say… / My tears are now prevailing orators*

prevailment *(n.)* prevailing action, power, influence **MND** I.i.35 [Egeus to Lysander, of Hermia] *With … messengers / Of strong prevailment in unhardened youth - / With cunning hast thou filched my daughter's heart*

prevent *(v.)* **1** forestall, anticipate **Ham** II.ii.294 [Hamlet to Rosencrantz and Guildenstern] *So shall my anticipation prevent your discovery;* **AW** III.ii.22; **1H6** IV.i.71; **2H4** I.ii.234; **3H6** IV.iv.29; **TNK** V.iv.6

2 take steps to thwart, avoid by prompt action **TG** II.ii.40 [Julia to Lucetta] *I would prevent / The loose encounters of lascivious men;* **1H4** IV.iv.35; **JC** II.i.28; **KL** I.i.45; **R2** III.iii.179; **Sonn** 100.14

3 forestall, baffle, confound **KL** III.iv.152 [Edgar as Poor Tom to Lear, replying to 'What is your study?'] *How to prevent the fiend*

4 anticipate, expect, look ahead to **Tim** V.i.201 [Timon to Senators, of the Athenians] *I'll teach them to prevent wild Alcibiades' wrath* [then taken by the Senators as if Timon meant 'avoid']

5 spare, able to avoid **E3** V.i.161 [Queen to all, as if to Prince Edward] *I would thy mother in the sea / Had been prevented of this mortal grief!*

prevention *(n.)* **1** forestalling action, preventive measure **JC** III.i.19 [Cassius to Casca] *be sudden, for we fear prevention;* **2H6** II.iv.57; **JC** II.i.85; **TC** I.iii.181

2 intervention, forestalling, interposing **E3** II.ii.179 [Countess to King Edward] *My resolution is more nimbler far / Than thy prevention can be in my rescue*

prewarn *(v.)* forewarn, forecast, predict **TNK** V.i.51 [Arcite praying to Mars] *whose approach / Comets prewarn*

prey *(n.)* **1** preying, violence, devouring **MND** II.ii.156 [Hermia alone, as if to Lysander] *Methought a serpent ate my heart away, / And you sat smiling at his cruel prey;* **KL** III.v.90

2 booty, spoil, plunder **Venus** 724 [Venus to Adonis] *Rich preys make true men thieves*

prey, in in pursuit of prey **H5** I.ii.169 [Ely to King Henry] *once the eagle England being in prey, / To her unguarded nest the weasel Scot / Comes sneaking*

preyful *(adj.)* desirous of prey, preying **LL** IV.ii.57 [Holofernes to Nathaniel and Dull] *The preyful Princess pierced and pricked a pretty pleasing pricket* [F *prayfull*]

pribbles and prabbles vain chatter and silly quarrelling **MW** I.i.51 [Evans to Shallow] *It were a goot motion if we leave our pribbles and prabbles;* **MW** V.v.158

price *(n.)* value, worth, importance **TC** II.ii.83 [Troilus to Hector, of Helen] *she is a pearl / Whose price hath launched above a thousand ships;* **Cym** I.i.51; **KL** II.i.119; **RJ** IV.i.27; **TNK** V.i.52

price *(v.)* evaluate, value, prize **KL** I.i.70 [Regan to Lear, of Gonerill] *I … price me at her worth* [F *prize*]

prick *(n.)* **1** thorn, prickle, barb **TNK** III.iv.25 [Gaoler's Daughter alone] *O for a prick now, like a nightingale*

2 spike, skewer, prong **KL** II.iii.16 [Edgar alone, of beggars] *Strike in their numbed and mortified bare arms / Pins, wooden pricks*

3 spine **Tem** II.ii.12 [Caliban alone, of Prospero's spirits] *like hedgehogs … mount / Their pricks at my footfall*

4 marker, pointer, indication **TC** I.iii.343 [Nestor to Ulysses, of tables of contents] *although small pricks / To their subsequent volumes*

5 [on a sundial] mark, point, division **Luc** 781 [Lucrece as if to night, of the sun] *Ere he arrive his weary noontide prick;* **3H6** I.iv.34

6 bull's-eye, target, centre spot **LL** IV.i.139 [Costard to Boyet, of Maria] *She's too hard for you at pricks* [with bawdy pun]; **LL** IV.i.133

prick (*v.*) **1** pin, fix, stick **TS** III.ii.66 [Biondello to Baptista, of Petruchio's man's dress] *an old hat, and the humour of forty fancies pricked in't for a feather*

2 urge, incite, motivate **TS** III.ii.69 [Tranio as Lucentio to Baptista, of Petruchio's outfit] *'Tis some odd humour pricks him to this fashion*; **JC** II.i.124

3 spur a horse, ride, gallop **E3** I.ii.48 [Messenger to King David] *as we were pricking on the hills*

4 torment, vex, grieve **RJ** I.iv.28 [Mercutio to Romeo] *Prick love for pricking, and you beat love down*

5 dress up, deck out **2H4** III.ii.152 [Falstaff to Shallow, of Feeble] *if he had been a man's tailor he'd ha' pricked you*

prick down, prick (*v.*) mark (down), put on a list, record in writing **JC** IV.i.1 [Antony to Octavius and Lepidus] *These many then shall die; their names are pricked*; **2H4** IV.iv.327, III.ii.110; **JC** III.i.216, IV.i.3, 16

prick off (*v.*) mark down, pick out, select [for death] **1H4** V.i.130 [Falstaff alone] *how if honour prick me off when I come on*

prick on (*v.*) incite, urge on, spur on **R2** II.iii.78 [Berkeley to Bolingbroke] *I come ... to know what pricks you on*; **Ham** I.i.83; **1H4** V.i.129; **1H6** III.ii.78; **LL** I.i.256; **Oth** III.iii.409

prick out (*v.*) choose, select, mark down **Sonn** 20.13 [of Nature] *she pricked thee out for women's pleasure*

pricked (*adj.*) [of wine] soured, gone off **2H4** III.ii.111 [Mouldy to Falstaff, of being 'pricked' - added to the list] *I was pricked well enough before, an you could have let me alone* [also: vexed, grieved]

pricket (*n.*) two-year-old buck deer **LL** IV.ii.49 [Dull to Holofernes] *'twas a pricket that the Princess killed*; **LL** IV.ii.12

pricksong (*n.*) vocal music written down, printed music **RJ** II.iv.21 [Mercutio to Benvolio, of Tybalt] *He fights as you sing pricksong*

pride (*n.*) **1** splendour, magnificence, pomp **E3** I.ii.148 [Countess to King Edward, of her house] *inly beautified / With bounty's riches and fair hidden pride*; **E3** I.ii.153, 159; **KL** II.iv.180; **Sonn** 80.12, 103.2

2 prime, best condition, fullness of growth **3H6** V.vii.4 [Edward to all] *What valiant foemen ... / Have we mowed down in tops of all their pride!*

3 highest point, culmination, climax **1H4** I.i.60 [Westmorland to King Henry, of the two sides] *in the very heat / And pride of their contention*

4 honour, glory, renown **1H6** IV.vi.57 [Talbot to John Talbot] *commendable proved, let's die in pride*; **1H6** IV.vii.16

5 haughty power, arrogant force **1H6** III.ii.40 [Talbot alone] *hardly we escaped the pride of France*; **1H6** IV.vi.15

6 [of horses] spirit, vigour, mettle **1H4** IV.iii.22 [Vernon to Hotspur] *Your uncle Worcester's horse came but today, / And now their pride and mettle is asleep*

7 sexual desire, lustful excess **Cym** II.iv.177 [Posthumus alone, of Innogen] *covetings, change of prides, disdain* **Oth** III.iii.401 [Iago to Othello, of Desdemona and Cassio] *Were they ... / As salt as wolves in pride* [i.e. on heat]; **Cym** II.iv.177

pride of place highest point reached by a bird of prey before swooping down **Mac** II.iv.12 [Old Man to Ross] *A falcon towering in her pride of place / Was by a mousing owl hawked at and killed*

priest (*n.*) priestess **Per** V.i.241 [Diana to Pericles, of Ephesus] *when my maiden priests are met together*; **Cym** I.vi.133

prig (*n.*) [slang] thief, crook, tinker **WT** IV.iii.98 [Clown to Autolycus, of the supposed robber] *Prig, for my life, prig!*

primal (*adj.*) primaeval, original, earliest **Ham** III.iii.37 [Claudius alone, of his offence] *It hath the primal eldest curse upon't*; **AC** I.iv.41

prime (*n.*) **1** spring, springtime **Sonn** 97.7 *The teeming autumn big with rich increase, / Bearing the wanton burthen of the prime*; **Luc** 332

2 early years, prime of life, fullness of youth **AW** II.i.182 [King to Helena, of her qualities] *all / That happiness and prime can happy call*; **AY** V.iii.35; **R3** IV.iv.171; **Sonn** 70.8; **TG** I.i.49

3 perfection, fullness **AY** V.iii.35 [Pages, singing] *For love is crowned with the prime* [or: sense 2]

prime (*adj.*) **1** first, original, initial **R3** IV.iii.19 [Tyrrel alone, reporting the Princes' killers] *We smothered / The most replenished sweet work of nature / That from the prime creation e'er she framed*; **Per** IV.iii.27

2 principal, chief, foremost **H8** III.ii.162 [King Henry to Wolsey] *Have I not made you / The prime man of the state?*; **H8** I.ii.67; **Tem** I.ii.72, 426

3 chief, dearest, favourite **TNK** I.i.2 [Arcite to Palamon] *Dear Palamon ... our prime cousin*

4 lecherous, randy, lustful **Oth** III.iii.400 [Iago to Othello, of Desdemona and Cassio] *Were they as prime as goats*

primero (*n.*) type of gambling card game **MW** IV.v.93 [Falstaff to himself] *I never prospered since I foreswore myself at primero*; **H8** V.i.7

primest (*n./adj.*) best, finest, most supreme **TNK** III.i.19 [Arcite alone] *this beauteous morn, / The primest of all the year*; **H8** II.iv.229; **TNK** I.i.161, V.iii.70

primitive (*adj.*) original, classical, typical **TC** V.i.51 [Thersites alone, of Menelaus as a transformation of Jupiter] *the primitive statue and oblique memorial of cuckolds*

primogenitive (*n.*) primogeniture; right of inheritance due to the first-born child **TC** I.iii.106 [Ulysses to all] *How could ... / The primogenitive and due of birth ... / But by degree, stand in authentic place?*

primy (*adj.*) in its prime, at its most active **Ham** I.iii.7 [Laertes to Ophelia, of Hamlet's love] *A violet in the youth of primy nature*

prince (*n.*) **1** ruler, monarch, sovereign **1H6** I.i.35 [Gloucester to Winchester] *None do you like but an effeminate prince*

2 person of royal blood [of either sex], noble **1H6** V.iii.114 [Margaret to Suffolk] *princes should be free*; **KJ** V.vii.97

prince (*v.*) behave like a prince, act royally **Cym** III.iii.85 [Belarius alone, of Guiderius and Arviragus] *Nature prompts them / In simple and low things to prince it*

princess (*n.*) paragon, sovereign form, ideal **MND** III.ii.144 [Demetrius to Helena] *let me kiss / This princess of pure white*

principal (*n.*) **1** person chiefly responsible, leading practitioner **WT** II.i.92 [Leontes to Lords, of Hermione and Polixenes] *her most vile principal*

2 mistress, superior, manager **Per** IV.vi.78 [Lysimachus to Marina] *hath your principal made known unto you who I am?*

3 main rafter, joist **Per** III.ii.15 [First Gentleman to Cerimon] *The very principals did seem to rend*

principality (*n.*) spiritual being very high in the hierarchy of angels **TG** II.iv.150 [Valentine to Proteus, of Silvia] *let her be a principality*

princox (*n.*) conceited young fellow, impertinent youth **RJ** I.v.86 [Capulet to Tybalt] *You are a princox, go!*

print (*n.*) imprint, image, stamped impression **LL** II.i.222 [Boyet to Princess, of the King] *His heart, like an agate with your print impressed*; **MA** I.i.188; **MM** IV.iv.130; **Tem** I.ii.352; **WT** II.iii.98

print, in in a precise way, by the letter, very carefully **LL** III.i.168 [Costard to Berowne, of delivering a letter] *I will do it, sir, in print*; **AY** V.iv.87; **TG** II.i.160

printless (*adj.*) making no print, leaving no trace **Tem** V.i.34 [Prospero alone, as if to elves] *ye that on the sands with printless foot / Do chase the ebbing Neptune*

prison (*v.*) imprison, lock up, confine **Sonn** 133.9 *Prison my heart in thy steel bosom's ward*; **Luc** 642

prisonment (*n.*) imprisonment, detention, captivity **TNK** III.i.32 [Palamon to Arcite] *Thou shouldst perceive my passion, if these signs / Of prisonment were off me*; **KJ** III.iv.161

prithee (*int.*) ☛ **POLITENESS**, p.340

private (*n.*) **1** privacy, own company, solitude **TN** III.iv.89 [Malvolio to Fabian] *Let me enjoy my private*

2 private communication, confidential message **KJ** IV.iii.16 [Salisbury to Pembroke, of Melun] *Whose private with me of the Dauphin's love / Is much more general than these lines import*

3 intimate, favourite **Ham** II.ii.233 [Guildenstern to Hamlet, of fortune's relationship to himself and Rosencrantz] *her privates we*

4 ordinary person, someone not holding high position **H5** IV.i.231 [King Henry alone] *what have kings that privates have not too, / Save ceremony*

private (*adj.*) **1** personal, individual, particular **JC** III.i.214 [Antony to all, of Caesar's killers] *What private griefs they have, alas, I know not, / That made them do it*; **1H6** IV.iv.22; **H8** I.i.101; **Tim** V.iv.26

2 secluded, unfrequented, remote **2H6** II.ii.60 [Warwick to Salisbury, of York] *in this private plot be we the first / That shall salute our rightful sovereign*; **AY** III.ii.16

privately (*adv.*) secretly, quietly, covertly **TNK** II.i.46 [Gaoler to Gaoler's Daughter] *The Duke himself came privately in the night*

prived (*adj.*) bereaved, deprived of loved ones **H5** II.iv.107 [Exeter to French King] *the prived maiden's groans* [F *priuy*]

privilege (*n.*) **1** sanctuary, immunity, asylum **KJ** I.i.261 [Bastard to Lady Faulconbridge] *Some sins to bear their privilege on earth*; **1H6** II.iv.86; **Tit** IV.iv.57

2 advantage, superiority, edge **1H6** III.i.122 [Gloucester to Warwick, of Winchester] *I would see his heart out ere the priest / Should ever get that privilege of me*

3 benefit, advantage, licence **1H4** V.ii.18 [Worcester to Vernon, of Hotspur] *My nephew's trespass ... hath ... an adopted name of privilege* [i.e. a nickname allowing him to be rash]

privilege (*v.*) authorize, license, sanction **Sonn** 58.10 *you yourself may privilege your time / To what you will*

privileged (*adj.*) [of a professional fool] allowed to say anything **TC** II.iii.56 [Achilles to Patroclus, of Thersites] *He is a privileged man*

privily (*adv.*) secretly, privately, stealthily **KL** III.iii.13 [Gloucester to Edmund, of Lear] *I will look him and privily relieve him*; **3H6** I.ii.39; **H8** I.i.183; **MM** I.i.67

privity (*n.*) participation, private knowledge **H8** I.i.74 [Buckingham to Abergavenny, of Wolsey] *Why ... took he upon him - / Without the privity o'th' King - t'appoint / Who should attend on him?*

privy 1 privately aware [of], secretly knowledgeable [about] **RJ** V.iii.266 [Friar to Prince, of Juliet] *to the marriage / Her nurse is privy*; **AC** I.ii.42; **Ham** I.i.134; **2H6** III.i.47; **TG** III.i.12

2 informed [of], made aware [of] **3H6** I.ii.46 [York to all] *And yet the King not privy to my drift*

3 private, particular, exclusive **MV** IV.i.351 [Portia as Balthasar to Shylock, of his goods] *the other half / Comes to the privy coffer of the state*

4 secret, personal, private **CE** III.ii.150 [Dromio of Syracuse to Antipholus of Syracuse, of the kitchen wench] *this drudge or diviner ... told me what privy marks I had about me*

5 secret, stealthy, clandestine **R3** III.v.105 [Richard alone] *Now will I go to take some privy order*

privy chamber (*n.*) private room, inner room **H8** I.iv.99 [Wolsey to Lovell] *is the banquet ready / I'th' privy chamber?*

privy-kitchen (*n.*) personal kitchen **2H4** II.iv.328 [Falstaff to Prince Henry, of Bardolph] *his face is Lucifer's privy-kitchen*

prize (*n.*) **1** value, worth, esteem **Cym** III.vii.49 [Innogen to herself, of Arviragus and Guiderius being her brothers] *would it had been so ... then had my prize / Been less* [also: sense 3]

2 advantage, privilege **3H6** II.i.20 [Richard to Edward, of York] *Methinks 'tis prize enough to be his son*; **3H6** I.iv.59

3 captured vessel **2H6** IV.i.8 [Lieutenant to all] *bring forth the soldiers of our prize*; **2H6** IV.i.25

4 [unclear meaning] bargain, contest, valuation **AC** V.ii.183 [Caesar to Cleopatra] *Caesar's no merchant, to make prize with you / Of things that merchants sold* [i.e. to haggle with you]

prize (*v.*) **1** esteem, value, hold **MA** III.i.90 [Ursula to Hero, of Beatrice] *Having so swift and excellent a wit / As she is prized to have*; **Cor** I.v.4; **1H6** I.iii.22; **Oth** IV.i.174

2 think nothing of, care nothing for **Sonn** 143.8 [of a housewife] *Not prizing her poor infant's discontent*; **WT** IV.iv.372

prizer (*n.*) prize-fighter, champion **AY** II.iii.8 [Adam to Orlando, of Charles] *The bonny prizer of the humorous Duke*

probable (*adj.*) **1** provable, demonstrable, attestable **Cym** II.iv.115 [Philario to Posthumus, of Innogen's bracelet] *It may be probable she lost it*; **Tem** V.i.249

2 plausible, believable, likely sounding **AW** III.vi.91 [First Lord to Bertram of Parolles] *[he will] clap upon you two or three probable lies*; **AW** II.iv.49; **Cor** IV.vi.66

3 worthy of belief, sufficient proof **2H6** III.ii.178 [Warwick to Suffolk, of the evidence of dead Gloucester's murder] *The least of all these signs were probable*

probal (*adj.*) reasonable, sure to be approved by **Oth** II.iii.328 [Iago alone] *this advice is free I give, and honest, / Probal to thinking*

probation (*n.*) **1** proof, demonstration **Cym** V.v.363 [Belarius to Cymbeline, of the mantle] *which for more probation / I can with ease produce*; **Ham** I.i.157; **Mac** III.i.79; **MM** V.i.157; **Oth** III.iii.362

2 investigation, examination, testing **TN** II.v.127 [Malvolio to himself, of interpreting the letter] *there is no consonancy in the sequel that suffers under probation*

3 candidature for membership, process of becoming a novice **MM** V.i.72 [Isabella to Duke] *I, in probation of a sisterhood, / Was sent to by my brother*

proceed (*v.*) **1** continue, go on, carry on **1H6** V.iv.162 [Alençon to Charles] *ruthless slaughters as are daily seen / By our proceeding in hostility*

2 behave, pursue a course, conduct oneself **2H6** I.iii.147 [Buckingham to Cardinal] *I will ... listen after Humphrey, how he proceeds*

3 advance through, make progress via **Tim** IV.iii.253 [Timon to Apemantus] *Hadst thou ... proceeded / The sweet degrees that this brief world affords* [also: take (an academic degree)]

4 result, arise, come from **Cym** III.v.59 [Queen alone, of Pisanio having her drug] *I pray his absence / Proceed by swallowing that*

proceeder (*n.*) worker, scholar, student **TS** IV.ii.11 [Hortensio as Licio to Tranio as Lucentio, of Lucentio as Cambio courting Bianca] *Quick proceeders*

proceeding (*n.*) **1** course of action, measures **TG** III.i.138 [Duke to Valentine, of a ladder] *an engine fit for my proceeding*; **KL** V.i.32

2 career, advancement, onward course **JC** II.ii.103 [Decius to Caesar] *my dear dear love / To your proceeding*

3 (plural) conduct, behaviour, actions **TNK** III.i.53 [Arcite to Palamon, of honour and honesty] *with them ... / I'll maintain my proceedings*

4 (plural) line of descent, pedigree **2H6** II.ii.53 [Warwick to all, of the line of succession] *What plain proceedings is more plain than this?*

process (*n.*) **1** progress, course, path **TC** IV.i.9 [Paris to Aeneas] *Witness the process of your speech within*; **H8** II.ii.9; **R2** II.iii.12; **Sonn** 104.6

2 proceedings, dealings **Ham** III.iii.29 [Polonius to Claudius] *Behind the arras I'll convey myself / To hear the process* [i.e. what happens]; **LL** V.ii.738

3 account, report, story **R3** IV.iii.32 [King Richard to Tyrrel, of the Princes] *thou shalt tell the process of their death*; **Ham** I.v.37; **R3** IV.iv.254

4 command, mandate, instructions **Ham** IV.iii.65 [Claudius alone, as if to the King of England] *thou mayst not coldly set / Our sovereign process*; **AC** I.i.28

5 proper legal procedure **Cor** III.i.312 [Menenius to Brutus] *Proceed by process*

process-server *(n.)* officer who serves a summon WT IV.iii.92 [Autolycus to Clown, of the supposed robber] *He hath been … a process-server*

proclaim *(v.)* **1** denounce, make one's wickedness known MM II.iv.151 [Isabella to Angelo] *I will proclaim thee*
2 officially declare to be an outlaw KL II.iii.1 [Edgar alone] *I heard myself proclaimed*

proclaimed *(adj.)* publicly declared [as an outlaw], announced by proclamation KL IV.vi.226 [Oswald to all, of Gloucester] *A proclaimed prize!*

proclamation *(n.)* reputation, favourable account, public standing MM III.ii.135 [disguised Duke to Lucio, of the Duke] *The very stream of his life … [must] give him a better proclamation*

proconsul *(n.)* ☞ ROMAN HISTORY, p.377

procrastinate *(v.)* postpone, defer, put off CE I.i.159 [Egeon to all, of himself] *to procrastinate his lifeless end*

procreant *(n.)* person engaged in procreation, copulator Oth IV.ii.27 [Othello to Emilia] *Leave procreants alone and shut the door*

procreant *(adj.)* for the purpose of procreation Mac I.vi.8 [Banquo to King, of the martlet] *no jutty, frieze … but this bird / Hath made his pendent bed and procreant cradle*

procurator *(n.)* deputy, agent, proxy 2H6 I.i.3 [Suffolk to King] *As procurator to your excellence, / To marry Princess Margaret for your grace*

procure *(v.)* **1** bring, induce, make come RJ III.v.67 [Juliet to herself, of Lady Capulet] *What unaccustomed cause procures her hither?*; PassP XVII.21; RJ II.ii.145
2 contrive, endeavour, take measures 1H6 V.v.88 [King to Suffolk] *procure / That Lady Margaret do vouchsafe to come*
3 contrive for, devise for, bring about 2H6 II.iv.62 [Gloucester to Duchess, of his foes] *All these could not procure me any scathe / So long as I am loyal*

prodigal *(n.)* **1** waster, squanderer, spendthrift TN I.iii.22 [Maria to Sir Toby, of Sir Andrew] *He's a very fool and a prodigal*; 1H4 IV.ii.33; Luc 79; MV III.i.41; TC V.i.29; Tim IV.iii.279
2 [Biblical reference] prodigal son CE IV.iii.18 [Dromio of Syracuse to Antipholus of Syracuse, of the officer] *He that goes in the calf's skin that was killed for the prodigal*

prodigal *(adj.)* **1** wastefully lavish, foolishly extravagant MV II.v.15 [Shylock to Jessica, of going to supper] *I'll go in hate to feed upon / The prodigal Christian*; AY I.i.36; E3 III.iii.123; Ham I.iii.36; H8 V.v.12; LL V.ii.64
2 effusive, lavish, generous LL II.i.9 [Boyet to Princess] *Be now as prodigal of all dear grace / As Nature was in making graces dear*; R2 I.iii.256; Tim II.ii.170; Venus 755
3 excessive, extra, superfluous R2 III.iv.31 [Gardener to First Man, of the apricots] *Which … make their sire / Stoop with oppression of their prodigal weight*

prodigal *(adv.)* lavishly, extravagantly Ham I.iii.116 [Polonius to Ophelia] *I do know, / When the blood burns, how prodigal the soul / Lends the tongue vows*

prodigious *(adj.)* **1** ominous, portentous, promising evil MND V.i.402 [Oberon to all, of the Athenians] *Nor mark prodigious … / Shall upon their children be*; JC I.iii.77; TC V.i.89
2 abnormal, monstrous, unnatural KJ III.i.46 [Constance to Arthur] *If thou [wert] … / Lame, foolish, crooked, swart, prodigious*; R3 I.ii.22; RJ I.v.140
3 malapropism for 'prodigal' TG II.iii.3 [Launce alone] *like the prodigious son*

prodigiously *(adv.)* with monstrous outcome, with unnatural birth KJ III.i.91 [Constance to King Philip, of women hoping not to give birth on the wedding anniversary] *Lest that their hopes prodigiously be crossed*

prodigy *(n.)* **1** omen, portent, sign JC II.i.198 [Cassius to all, of Caesar] *It may be these apparent prodigies … / May hold him from the Capitol today*; 1H4 V.i.20; JC I.iii.28; KJ III.iv.157; Tit I.i.104; TS III.ii.95
2 monster, abnormal birth, ominous monstrosity 3H6 I.iv.75 [Queen to York, of Richard] *where's that valiant crook-back prodigy*; R2 II.ii.64

proditor *(n.)* traitor, betrayer, renegade 1H6 I.iii.31 [Winchester to Gloucester] *thou most usurping proditor*

produce *(v.)* lead them forth, bring them out TNK III.v.135 [Pirithous to Schoolmaster] *Produce!*

proface *(int.)* [polite expression used to someone about to eat or drink] may it do you good, for your benefit 2H4 V.iii.27 [Davy to Page, offering wine] *Proface!*

profane *(adj.)* **1** blasphemous, irreverent, foul-mouthed Cym II.iii.123 [Innogen to Cloten] *Profane fellow*; Oth I.i.115
2 worldly-wise, irreverent, flippant Oth II.i.160 [Desdemona to Cassio, of Iago] *is he not a most profane and liberal counsellor?*

profane *(v.)* **1** misuse, abuse, maltreat 2H4 IV.ii.357 [Prince Henry to Poins] *I feel me much to blame, / So idly to profane the precious time*; Cor I.ix.41
2 desecrate, violate, commit sacrilege R2 III.iii.81 [King Richard to his opponents] *no hand … / Can grip the sacred handle of our sceptre / Unless he do profane, steal, or usurp*

profess *(v.)* **1** declare, avow, affirm KL I.i.72 [Regan to Lear] *I profess / Myself an enemy to all other joys*; H8 II.iv.84; MM IV.ii.97
2 undertake, pledge WT IV.iv.366 [disguised Polixenes to Florizel, of his love] *let me hear / What you profess*; MW IV.ii.3
3 practise, pursue, claim knowledge of MA III.iv.61 [Beatrice to Margaret] *How long have you professed apprehension?*; AY III.ii.387; 1H4 V.ii.91; TC III.iii.269; TS IV.ii.8
4 make profession of, do as an occupation AW II.i.102 [Helena to King, of her father] *In what he did profess, well found*; KL I.iv.11; MM II.i.63; Tem II.i.240
5 profess friendship, declare attachment WT I.ii.456 [Polixenes to Camillo, of himself and Leontes] *a man which ever / Professed to him*; JC I.i.77

professed *(adj.)* with avowed affection, displaying openly declared love KL I.i.272 [Cordelia to her sisters, of Lear] *To your professed bosoms I commit him*

profession *(n.)* **1** avowal of skilled knowledge, declaration of ability to carry out a task AW II.i.83 [Lafew to King, of Helena] *her sex, her years, profession, / Wisdom*
2 solemn vow, sworn declaration KL V.iii.128 [Edgar to Edmund] *it is the privilege of mine honours, / My oath, and my profession*
3 religious calling, profession of faith H8 III.i.157 [Wolsey to Queen Katherine, of doing her harm] *The way of our profession is against it*

professor *(n.)* adherent, devotee, professing Christian H8 III.i.115 [Queen Katherine to Campeius and Wolsey] *Woe upon ye, / And all such false professors!*; WT V.i.108

proffer *(n.)* **1** offer, proposal, proposition 1H6 V.v.137 [Alençon to Winchester] *This proffer is absurd and reasonless*; AW II.i.147; 1H6 V.i.41; PassP IV.10
2 attempt, effort, endeavour E3 IV.iv.146 [Audley to Prince Edward] *If we fear not, then no resolved proffer / Can overthrow the limit of our fate*

proffer *(v.)* **1** make a proposal, put oneself forward PassP XVIII.24 [Pilgrim, advising a lover] *be thou not slack / To proffer, though she put thee back*
2 express, utter, put into words E3 II.i.300 [King Edward to Warwick] *A kind and voluntary gift thou profferest*

profit *(n.)* **1** progress, proficiency, improvement AY I.i.6 [Orlando to Adam, of his brother Jaques] *report speaks goldenly of his profit*; MV II.v.45; Tem I.ii.172

2 furtherance, progress, advancement **Ham** II.ii.24 [Gertrude to Rosencrantz and Guildenstern] *expend your time with us awhile / For the supply and profit of our hope*

3 welfare, well-being, benefit **2H6** I.i.202 [Salisbury to York and Warwick] *cherish Duke Humphrey's deeds / While they do tend the profit of the land*

profit (*v.*) benefit, be of use to, do good to **Tem** I.ii.313 [Prospero to Miranda, of Caliban] *He … serves in offices / That profit us*

profited (*adj.*) proficient, advanced, skilful **1H4** III.i.160 [Mortimer to Hotspur, of Glendower] *he is a worthy gentleman … profited / In strange concealments*

profound (*adj.*) **1** weighty, important **KJ** III.i.318 [Lewis the Dauphin to King Philip] *I muse your majesty doth seem so cold, / When such profound respects do pull you on!*

2 with powerful qualities, with secret powers **Mac** III.v.24 [Hecat to Witches, of the corner of the moon] *There, hangs a vaporous drop profound*

3 complete, utter, total **LL** V.ii.52 [Katharine to Princess, of Dumaine's letter] *Vilely compiled, profound simplicity* [also: wise]

progenitor (*n.*) forefather, ancestor, forebear **1H6** IV.i.166 [King to Richard and Somerset] *sons of your progenitors*

progeny (*n.*) **1** ancestry, descent, parentage **1H6** V.iv.38 [Pucelle to all, of herself] *issued from the progeny of kings;* **Cor** I.viii.12; **1H6** III.iii.61

2 child **LL** V.ii.739 [King to Princess, of her father's death] *the mourning brow of progeny / Forbid the smiling courtesy of love* [i.e. the face of a bereaved child]

prognostication (*n.*) **1** sign, forecast, prediction **AC** I.ii.53 [Charmian to Iras] *if an oily palm be not a fruitful prognostication, I cannot scratch mine ear*

2 weather forecast in the almanac **WT** IV.iv.784 [Autolycus to Clown] *in the hottest day prognostication proclaims*

progress (*n.*) **1** course, movement, changing position **JC** II.i.2 [Brutus alone] *I cannot, by the progress of the stars, / Give guess how near to day*

2 state passage, royal journey **2H6** I.iv.71 [York to all] *The King is now in progress towards Saint Albans;* **Ham** IV.iii.30

progression (*n.*) onward movement, moving along the way **LL** IV.ii.138 [Holofernes to Nathaniel, of Berowne's letter] *which accidentally, or by the way of progression, hath miscarried*

project (*n.*) **1** conception, idea, notion **MA** III.i.55 [Hero to Ursula, of Beatrice] *She cannot love, / Nor take no shape nor project of affection*

2 anticipation, speculation, prospect **2H4** I.iii.29 [Lord Bardolph to Archbishop, of Percy] *Flattering himself in project of a power / Much smaller than the smallest of his thoughts*

project (*v.*) set forth, frame, present **AC** V.ii.121 [Cleopatra to Caesar] *I cannot project mine own cause so well / To make it clear*

projection (*n.*) scheme, plan, design **H5** II.iv.46 [Dauphin to Constable] *a weak and niggardly projection / Doth like a miser spoil his coat with scanting / A little cloth*

prolixious (*adj.*) time-wasting, tedious, protracted **MM** II.iv.162 [Angelo to Isabella] *Lay by all nicety and prolixious blushes*

prolixity (*n.*) long-windedness, tedious exposition **MV** III.i.11 [Solanio to Salerio, of his report] *without any slips of prolixity;* **RJ** I.iv.3

prologue (*n.*) preliminary statement **Ham** V.ii.30 [Hamlet to Horatio] *Or I could make a prologue to my brains* [i.e. before I could decide what to do]

prolong (*v.*) postpone, put off, delay **MA** IV.i.252 [Friar to Hero] *this wedding-day / Perhaps is but prolonged;* **R3** III.iv.45

promise (*v.*) **1** assure, declare [to], tell plainly **RJ** III.iv.6 [Capulet to Paris] *I promise you, but for your company, / I would have been abed an hour ago;* **1H6** IV.i.174; **MM** III.i.179; **R3** II.iii.2

2 add to, reinforce, augment **AW** I.i.39 [Countess to Lafew, of Helena] *her education promises her dispositions she inherits*

3 give one grounds for, lead one to expect **H8** I.i.48 [Norfolk to Buckingham, of the organiser of the celebrations] *One, certes, that promises no element / In such a business*

promise forth have an engagement elsewhere **JC** I.ii.286 [Casca to Cassius, of dining with him] *No, I am promised forth*

promised (*adj.*) previously agreed **Ham** IV.iv.3 [Fortinbras to his captain] *Fortinbras / Craves the conveyance of a promised march*

promotion (*n.*) advancement in life, social betterment **RJ** IV.v.71 [Friar to all, of Juliet] *The most you sought was her promotion;* **KJ** II.i.492

prompt (*adj.*) **1** inclined, disposed, prone **TC** IV.iv.87 [Troilus to Cressida, of fair virtues] *To which the Grecians are most prompt and pregnant*

2 ready and willing, well-disposed **AC** III.xiii.75 [Cleopatra to Thidias, of Caesar] *I am prompt / To lay my crown at's feet;* **Tim** III.i.35

prompt (*v.*) remind, put in mind, make reflect **MA** I.i.283 [Claudio to Don Pedro] *delicate desires, / All prompting me how fair young Hero is;* **Tim** II.ii.146

prompted (*adj.*) eagerly ready, urged on to act **TC** V.ii.178 [Troilus to Ulysses] *my prompted sword / Falling on Diomed*

prompture (*n.*) prompting, instigation, urging **MM** II.iv.178 [Isabella alone, of Claudio] *he hath fall'n by prompture of the blood*

prone (*adj.*) **1** eager, ready **Cym** V.iv.201 [First Gaoler alone, of Posthumus] *I never saw one so prone* [i.e. to die]; **Luc** 684

2 submissive, vulnerable, docile **MM** I.ii.182 [Claudio to Lucio, of Isabella] *in her youth / There is a prone and speechless dialect, / Such as move men*

pronounce (*v.*) **1** deliver, speak, declare **MV** I.ii.10 [Portia to Nerissa, of her words] *Good sentences, and well pronounced;* **Ham** III.ii.318; **H8** III.ii.163

2 tell, narrate, report **Cor** V.vi.58 [Third Conspirator to Aufidius, of Coriolanus] *After your way his tale pronounced* [i.e. told in the way you want]

3 proclaim, officially declare, announce **2H6** IV.viii.8 [Buckingham to Cade] *we … here pronounce free pardon to them all / That will forsake thee*

proof (*n.*) **1** tested strength, proven power of resistance, impenetrability **R2** I.iii.73 [Bolingbroke to John of Gaunt] *Add proof unto mine armour with thy prayers;* **AC** IV.viii.15; **Cym** V.v.5; **2H6** IV.ii.57; **RJ** I.i.210; **Venus** 626

2 experience, actual practice, tried knowledge **TN** III.i.121 [Viola as Cesario to Olivia] *'tis a vulgar proof / That very oft we pity enemies;* **Cym** I.vii.70; **Ham** III.ii.179; **JC** II.i.21; **RJ** I.i.170; **Sonn** 129.11

3 test, trial **1H6** I.i.94 [Charles to Pucelle] *Only this proof I'll of thy valour make;* **E3** II.i.221; **JC** V.i.49; **MA** I.i.43; **Oth** V.i.26; **TNK** V.iii.57

4 evidence, demonstration, testimony **JC** II.i.299 [Portia to Brutus] *I have made strong proof of my constancy;* **1H6** V.iii.8; **H8** II.ii.16; **KL** II.iii.13; **MA** II.i.166; **TN** III.iv.259

5 making good, showing to be loyal **KL** III.vi.111 [Edgar alone to himself, of those who disbelieve him] *In thy just proof repeals and reconciles thee*

6 result, outcome, upshot **TS** IV.iii.43 [Petruchio to Katherina, of his having prepared a meal for her] *all my pains is sorted to no proof;* **Cym** III.i.77

proof, come to turn out well, fulfil one's promise **2H4** IV.iii.90 [Falstaff alone, of men like Prince John] *There's never none of these demure boys come to any proof*

proof (*adj.*) **1** impenetrable, impervious, sound **Cor** I.iv.25 [Martius to his troops] *fight / With hearts more proof than shields;* **Ham** III.iv.39

2 unmoved, impervious, indifferent **WT** IV.iv.834 [Autolycus alone, of the name of rogue] *I am proof against that title*

propagate (*v.*) increase, multiply **Tim** I.i.70 [Poet to Painter, of people at the foot of Fortune's hill] *all kind of natures, / That labour on the bosom of this sphere / To propagate their states*

propagation (*n.*) enlargement, increasing in extent **MM** I.ii.149 [Claudio to Lucio] *Only for propagation of a dower*

propend (*v.*) incline, be disposed, have a propensity **TC** II.ii.191 [Hector to all] *I propend to you / In resolution to keep Helen still*

propension (*n.*) propensity, inclination, cast of mind **TC** II.ii.134 [Paris to all] *your full consent / Gave wings to my propension*

proper (*adj.*) **1** good-looking, handsome, comely **MA** II.iii.181 [Claudio to Don Pedro, of Benedick] *He is a very proper man;* **AY** III.v.55; **JC** I.i.24; **MV** I.ii.68; **Tit** V.ii.50; **TS** I.ii.141

2 very, own **Cym** IV.ii.97 [Cloten to Guiderius] *When I have slain thee with my proper hand;* **AW** IV.iii.314; **E3** II.i.314; **JC** V.iii.96; **MM** V.i.405; **Tem** III.iii.61

3 thorough, absolute, complete **MA** I.iii.48 [Don John to Borachio, of Claudio] *A proper squire!;* **MW** V.i.173; **Mac** III.iv.59

4 personal, private, individual **TN** V.i.316 [Olivia to Orsino] *One day shall crown th'alliance on't … / Here at my house, and at my proper cost;* **AW** IV.ii.49; **2H6** III.i.115; **MM** I.i.30

5 special, particular, specific **JC** I.i.41 [Brutus to Cassius, of his worries] *Conceptions only proper to myself;* **MM** I.ii.128, V.i.110

6 characteristic, typical, normal **Ham** II.i.114 [Polonius to Ophelia] *it is as proper to our age / To cast beyond ourselves;* **KL** IV.ii.60

7 honest, honourable, worthy **2H4** II.ii.148 [Page to Prince Henry, of Doll] *A proper gentlewoman;* **AC** III.iii.37; **AW** IV.iii.208; **Cym** III.iv.63

8 fine, excellent, good **2H4** II.ii.63 [Poins to Prince Henry] *I am a proper fellow of my hands* [i.e. good with my fists]

properly (*adv.*) privately, personally **Cor** V.ii.80 [Coriolanus to Menenius] *I owe / My revenge properly* [i.e. it is my own affair]

propertied (*adj.*) of a quality, having the nature **AC** V.ii.83 [Cleopatra to Dolabella, of Antony] *his voice was propertied / As all the tuned spheres*

property (*n.*) **1** quality, character, nature **R2** III.ii.135 [Scroop to all] *Sweet love … changing his property, / Turns to the sourest and most deadly hate;* **AC** I.i.58; **Ham** II.i.103; **Oth** I.i.173

2 feature, characteristic, particular respect **AW** II.i.187 [Helena to King] *If I … flinch in property / Of what I spoke* [i.e. fall short in any respect]; **Ham** V.i.67; **Phoen** 37

3 means to an end, commercial asset **MW** III.iv.10 [Fenton to Anne, of Page] *he … tells me 'tis a thing impossible / I should love thee but as a property*

4 (*plural*) stage requisites, accessories, props **MND** I.ii.97 [Quince to all, of their play] *I will draw a bill of properties;* **MW** IV.iv.76

property (*v.*) **1** make a property of, treat as an object, exploit **TN** IV.ii.91 [Malvolio to Feste, of his captors] *They have here propertied me;* **KJ** V.ii.79

2 appropriate, take possession of **Tim** I.i.59 [Poet to Painter, of Timon's fortune] *Subdues and properties to his love and tendance / All sorts of hearts*

prophane (*adj.*) ☛ **fanned** (*adj.*)

prophet (*n.*) **1** portent, omen, foretelling **1H6** III.ii.32 [Charles to all, of Pucelle's torch] *A prophet to the fall of all our foes!*

2 soothsayer, seer, prognosticator **R2** II.iv.11 [Captain to Salisbury] *lean-looked prophets whisper fearful change*

propinquity (*n.*) close kinship, blood relationship **KL** I.i.114 [Lear to Cordelia] *Here I disclaim all my paternal care, / Propinquity*

proportion (*n.*) **1** measure, extent, degree, magnitude **E3** II.i.104 [King Edward to Lodowick, of the Countess] *judge what her condition is / By the proportion of her mightiness;* **1H4** IV.iv.15; **H8** V.i.129

2 part, portion, amount **Per** IV.ii.25 [Pander to Bawd] *Three or four thousand chequins were as pretty a proportion to live quietly;* **1H6** II.iii.52

3 weighing up, appropriate measuring **2H4** IV.i.23 [Mowbray to Archbishop, of the King's forces] *The just proportion that we gave them out;* **H5** II.iv.45; **Mac** I.iv.20; **MW** V.v.214

4 natural order, proper relationship **H5** IV.i.141 [Williams to disguised King Henry, of the King] *who to disobey were against all proportion of subjection;* **H5** II.ii.109; **TC** I.iii.87

5 relation, connection, link **2H6** I.i.231 [York to himself] *realms of England, France, and Ireland / Bear that proportion to my flesh and blood / As did the fatal brand Althaea burnt / Unto the Prince's heart of Calydon*

6 size, bulk **1H6** II.iii.20 [Countess to Talbot, of how she had expected Talbot to look] *his grim aspect / And large proportion of his strong-knit limbs*

7 bodily shape, physical form **2H6** I.iii.52 [Queen to Suffolk] *I thought King Henry had resembled thee / In … proportion;* **R3** I.i.18

8 (*plural*) military material, forces and supplies needed for war **H5** I.ii.305 [King Henry to all] *let our proportions for these wars / Be soon collected;* **Ham** I.ii.32; **H5** I.ii.137

9 marriage portion, dowry **MM** V.i.217 [Angelo to Duke, of Mariana] *her promised proportions / Came short of composition*

10 proper rhythm, correct value [of notes] **R2** V.v.43 [Richard alone] *How sour sweet music is / When time is broke, and no proportion kept;* **RJ** II.iv.21

11 malapropism for 'portion' [= share of the estate] **TG** II.iii.3 [Launce alone] *I have received my proportion*

proportionable (*adj.*) proportional, comparable, commensurate [with] **R2** II.ii.124 [Bushy to Bagot and Green] *For us to levy power / Proportionable to the enemy / Is all unpossible*

proportioned (*adj.*) regulated, well-ordered **Luc** 774 [Lucrece as if to night] *Make war against proportioned course of time*

propose (*n.*) conversation, discourse, purposes **MA** III.i.12 [Hero to Margaret, of Beatrice] *There will she hide her, / To listen to our propose* [i.e. to what we have in mind]

propose (*v.*) **1** converse, discourse, hold forth **MA** III.i.3 [Hero to Margaret] *shalt thou find my cousin Beatrice / Proposing with the Prince and Claudio;* **Oth** I.i.25

2 bring up for consideration, set before the mind **TC** II.ii.147 [Paris to Priam, of Helen] *I propose not merely to myself / The pleasures such a beauty brings with it*

3 imagine, contemplate, picture **2H4** V.ii.92 [Lord Chief Justice to King Henry V] *Be now the father and propose a son*

4 face, confront, be ready to meet **Tit** II.i.80 [Chiron to Aaron, of Lavinia] *a thousand deaths / Would I propose to achieve her whom I love*

proposition (*n.*) **1** offer, proposal **TC** I.iii.3 [Agamemnon to all] *The ample proposition that hope makes … / Fails in the promised largeness*

2 question, problem **AY** III.ii.226 [Celia to Rosalind] *It is as easy to count atomies as to resolve the propositions of a lover*

propound (*v.*) set before oneself, propose [as a goal] **TNK** I.ii.16 [Palamon to Arcite] *th'martialist, who did propound / To his bold ends honour and golden ingots*

propriety (*n.*) **1** natural state, normal condition **Oth** II.iii.170 [Othello to all, of the bell] *it frights the isle / From her propriety*

2 proper character, real identity **TN** V.i.145 [Olivia to Viola as Cesario] *it is the baseness of thy fear / That makes thee strangle thy propriety* [also: proprietorship, as a husband]

propugnation (*n.*) defence, justification, vindication **TC** II.ii.137 [Paris to all] *What propugnation is in one man's valour / To stand the push and enmity of those / This quarrel would excite?*

prorogue (*v.*) **1** postpone, delay, defer **RJ** IV.i.48 [Friar to Juliet, of her forthcoming marriage to Paris] *nothing may prorogue it;* **RJ** II.ii.78; **TNK** I.i.196

2 suspend, put on hold, waive **AC** II.i.26 [Pompey to Menas, of Antony] *That sleep and feeding may prorogue his honour / Even till a Lethe'd dullness*

3 prolong, draw out, lengthen **Per** V.i.24 [Helicanus to Lysimachus, of Pericles] *hath not … taken sustenance / But to prorogue his grief*

proscription *(n.)* condemnation JC IV.i.17 [Octavius to Antony] *who should be pricked to die / In our black sentence and proscription;* JC IV.iii.171

prosecute *(v.)* pursue, follow up, seek Tit IV.i.91 [Marcus to all] *we will prosecute by good advice / Mortal revenge upon these traitorous Goths*

prosecution *(n.)* pursuit, chase, hounding AC IV.xiv.65 [Antony to Eros] *Th'inevitable prosecution of / Disgrace and horror*

prospect *(n.)* field of view, vista, outlook Mac I.iii.73 [Macbeth to Witches] *to be king / Stands not within the prospect of belief;* E3 III.iii.117; 2H6 III.ii.324

prosper *(v.)* make prosperous, give success to 1H6 I.i.53 [Bedford, as if to the spirit of Henry V] *Prosper this realm, keep it from civil broils;* KL IV.vi.30; MW V.ii.12

prosperity *(n.)* success, good fortune Cor I.v.23 [Lartius to Martius] *Prosperity be thy page!*; Cor II.i.164; Oth II.i.271

prosperous *(adj.)* **1** profitable, beneficial, leading to a successful outcome Mac III.i.21 [Macbeth to Banquo] *your good advice, / Which still hath been both grave and prosperous;* 1H4 III.i.2; Per V.i.71, 78

2 favourable, happy, showing success RJ IV.i.122 [Friar to Juliet, of taking the potion] *Be strong and prosperous / In this resolve;* Cor II.i.98

3 favourable, sympathetic, well-disposed Oth I.iii.242 [Desdemona to Duke] *To my unfolding lend your prosperous ear;* Tim V.i.181

protect *(v.)* act as escort for, be custodian of 2H6 II.iv.79 [Gloucester to Stanley, of the Duchess] *Must you ... protect my lady here?*

protest *(n.)* protestation, declaration, avowal TC III.ii.173 [Troilus to Cressida, of lovers] *their rhymes, / Full of protest, of oath;* 1H4 III.i.249

protest *(v.)* **1** make protestation, avow, affirm, proclaim Ham III.ii.240 [Gertrude to Hamlet, of the Player Queen] *The lady doth protest too much;* 1H6 IV.ii.19; JC III.i.238; MA IV.i.275; Mac V.ii.11; Tim III.ii.81

2 declare, say, swear MW II.i.197 [Ford to Host, in response to his question] *None, I protest;* RJ II.iv.169

3 profess openly, acknowledge publicly Tim IV.iii.436 [Timon to Bandits] *Do villainy, do, since you protest to do't, / Like workmen*

4 declare love MW III.v.68 [Falstaff to Ford as Brook, of himself and Mistress Ford] *we ... embraced, kissed, protested;* RJ II.iv.174

protestation *(n.)* solemn declaration, affirmation Luc 1844 [of Brutus] *he ... to his protestation urged the rest;* AW V.iii.139; LL I.i.33; TG I.ii.99

protester *(n.)* declarer of friendship, affirmer of affection JC I.ii.74 [Cassius to Brutus] *To stale with ordinary oaths my love / To every new protester*

protract *(v.)* delay, defer, put off, defer Cym IV.ii.232 [Guiderius to Arviragus] *Let us ... not protract with admiration what / Is now due debt*

protractive *(adj.)* protracted, interminable, long-drawn-out TC I.iii.20 [Agamemnon to all] *the protractive trials of great Jove*

proud *(adj.)* **1** fine, splendid, luxurious KL III.iv.79 [Edgar as Poor Tom to all] *set not thy sweet heart on proud array;* H8 III.ii.127; Sonn 98.2

2 courageous, valiant, brave KJ V.i.79 [Bastard to King John] *Our party may well meet a prouder foe;* 3H6 I.i.46

3 high-spirited, high-mettled R3 V.iii.341 [King Richard to his army] *Spur your proud horses hard;* Cor I.i.168; H5 Prologue.27

4 taking pride in, elated by the thought of H5 III.iii.4 [King Henry to citizens of Harfleur] *to our best mercy give yourselves, / Or, like to men proud of destruction, / Defy us to our worst*

5 bulging, swelling TS IV.iii.167 [Petruchio to Katherina] *Our purses shall be proud, our garments poor*

6 swollen, high, in flood KJ III.i.23 [Constance to Salisbury, of his tears] *Like a proud river peering o'er his bounds;* MND II.i.91

proudest *(n./adj.)* eminent, notable, grand MW II.ii.73 [Mistress Quickly to Falstaff, of courtiers' advances to Mistress Ford] *they could never get her so much as sip on a cup with the proudest of them all*

proudly *(adv.)* haughtily, arrogantly, disdainfully 1H6 I.ii.62 [Charles to Reignier, of Pucelle] *Question her proudly;* 2H4 V.ii.130; R3 IV.iii.42

provand *(n.)* provender, provisions, food Cor II.i.243 [Brutus to Sicinius] *camels ... who have their provand / Only for bearing burdens*

prove *(v.)* **1** test, try out, make trial [of] MA I.iii.68 [Don John to Borachio and Conrade] *Shall we go prove what's to be done?*; Cor IV.v.96; KL IV.vi.90; MW I.iii.90; Sonn 26.14; WT I.ii.443

2 find, establish, experience Ham III.i.47 [Polonius to Ophelia] *'Tis too much proved, that with devotion's visage ... we do sugar o'er / The devil himself;* AC I.ii.34; Sonn 72.4; Venus 597

3 demonstrate, establish, show to be true 3H6 III.iii.180 [Queen to Lewis, of Edward's marriage] *This proveth Edward's love and Warwick's honesty!*; Per IV.vi.188; Sonn 2.12, 117.13, 153.7

4 prove to be true, turn out to be the truth TN III.iv.374 [Viola to herself, of Sebastian being alive] *if it prove, / Tempests are kind, and salt waves fresh in love!*; JC V.i.4; TC III.ii.89

5 justify [one's] claim, establish TNK II.v.9 [Theseus to Arcite] *What proves you?* [i.e. to be a gentleman]

provender *(n.)* feed, fodder 1H6 I.ii.11 [Alençon to all, of the English] *they must be dieted like mules / And have their provender tied to their mouths;* TNK V.ii.57

proverb *(v.)* provide with worldly wisdom [by] RJ I.iv.37 [Romeo to all] *I am proverbed with a grandsire phrase*

provide *(v.)* **1** get ready, equip [oneself] AY I.iii.85 [Duke Frederick to Rosalind] *You, niece, provide yourself;* Ham III.iii.7

2 prepare, make ready, plan AC III.iv.36 [Antony to Octavia] *Provide your going;* Tim V.i.31

provided *(adj.)* prepared, ready, provided with necessities KL II.iv.227 [Regan to Lear] *I looked not for you yet, nor am provided / For your fit welcome;* 2H6 I.iv.3; R3 III.iv.44; TG I.iii.72

providence *(n.)* **1** foresight, forethought TC III.iii.196 [Ulysses to Achilles] *The providence that's in a watchful state / Knows almost every grain of Pluto's gold;* Ham IV.i.17

2 direction, fate, destiny JC V.i.106 [Brutus to Cassius] *arming myself with patience / To stay the providence of some high powers / That govern us below*

provincial *(adj.)* subject to local church jurisdiction MM V.i.314 [disguised Duke to Escalus, of the Duke] *His subject am I not, / Nor here provincial*

Provincial *(adj.)* from Provins or Provence [France] Ham III.ii.285 [Hamlet to Horatio] *with two Provincial roses on my razed shoes* [i.e. double rose patterns, made of ribbons]

provision *(n.)* **1** supply of necessities KL III.vi.94 [Gloucester to disguised Kent] *follow me, that will to some provision / Give thee quick conduct;* KL II.iv.200

2 resources, money supply Tim III.vi.15 [Lucius to Lucullus, of Timon] *I am sorry, when he sent to borrow of me, that my provision was out*

3 foresight, advance preparation, looking ahead Tem I.ii.28 [Prospero to Miranda] *I have with such provision in mine art / So safely ordered*

provocation *(n.)* erotic stimulation, inciting lustful thoughts MW V.v.21 [Falstaff to Mistress Ford] *Let there come a tempest of provocation;* Oth II.iii.22

provoke *(v.)* **1** call forth, invite, invoke Tem I.ii.140 [Prospero to Miranda] *My tale provokes that question;* 1H6 II.iii.69; MM III.i.18

2 bring about, induce, engender Tim I.i.24 [Poet to Painter, of inspiration] *Our gentle flame / Provokes itself* [i.e. not needing an external source]; KL IV.iv.13

3 impel, urge on, drive 1H6 V.v.6 [King to Suffolk] *as rigour of tempestuous gusts / Provokes the mightiest hulk against the tide*

4 incite, rouse, urge on **KJ** IV.ii.207 [Hubert to King John, of killing Arthur] *did you not provoke me?*; **AY** I.iii.108
    5 make tremble, cause to shake **2H6** IV.vii.86 [Say to Dick, of his quivering] *The palsy and not fear provokes me*

provost *(n.)* officer in charge of the arrest, custody, and punishment of prisoners **MM** V.i.250 [Friar Peter to Duke, of Friar Lodowick] *Your provost knows the place where he abides*; **MM** I.ii.115

provulgate *(v.)* promulgate, make public, publish abroad **Oth** I.ii.21 [Othello to Iago] *when I know that boasting is an honour, / I shall provulgate*

prune *(n.)* ☛ stewed prune

prune *(v.)* [of birds] trim feathers with the beak, preen **Cym** V.iv.118 [Sicilius to all, of Jupiter] *his royal bird / Prunes the immortal wing*; **1H4** I.i.97; **LL** IV.iii.181

pry *(v.)* spy, peer **Tit** V.i.114 [Aaron to Lucius] *I pried me through the crevice of a wall*

psaltery *(n.)* type of plucked stringed instrument **Cor** V.iv.48 [Second Messenger to Sicinius] *sackbuts, psalteries, and fifes*

public *(adj.)* accepted, authorized, official **E3** V.i.72 [Copland to King Edward, of his behaviour] *No wilful disobedience … / But my desert and public law of arms*

publican *(n.)* tax-collector **MV** I.iii.38 [Shylock to himself, of Antonio] *How like a fawning publican he looks*

publish *(v.)* **1** announce, make public, make generally known **H8** III.ii.68 [Suffolk to all, of King Henry] *Shortly, I believe, / His second marriage shall be published*; **Cym** V.v.479; **2H6** III.ii.17; **KL** I.i.43; **Sonn** 102.4
    2 speak openly of, talk about **TN** II.i.25 [Sebastian to Antonio, of Viola] *thus far I will boldly publish her*
    3 denounce in public, vilify, show up **WT** II.i.98 [Hermione to Leontes, of his accusation of adultery] *How will this grieve you, / When you shall come to clearer knowledge, that / You thus have published me!*

published *(adj.)* proclaimed, publicly announced **KL** IV.vi.232 [Oswald to Edgar] *Wherefore … / Darest thou support a published traitor?*

publisher *(n.)* exposer, divulger, one who makes public **TG** III.i.47 [Proteus to Duke, of Valentine's plans] *love of you … / Hath made me publisher of this pretence*; **Luc** 33

pucelle *(n.)* maid, virgin, girl; also: drab, trollop, slut **1H6** I.iv.107 [Talbot as if to the French] *Pucelle or pussel, Dolphin or dogfish, / Your hearts I'll stamp out* [i.e. virgin or whore]

pudder *(n.)* hubbub, din, uproar **KL** III.ii.50 [Lear to disguised Kent] *the great gods / That keep this dreadful pudder o'er our heads* [F; Q *Powther*]

pudding *(n.)* **1** type of large savoury dish; dumpling, pasty **TG** IV.iv.29 [Launce alone, of his dog] *I have sat in the stocks for puddings he hath stolen*; **AW** II.ii.26; **H5** II.i.83; **Per** II.i.82
    2 stuffing **MW** II.i.29 [Mistress Page alone, of Falstaff] *revenged I will be, as sure as his guts are made of puddings*; **1H4** II.iv.441

puddle *(v.)* make muddy, cloud, muddle **Oth** III.iv.139 [Desdemona to Emilia, of Othello] *some unhatched practice … / Hath puddled his clear spirit*

puddled *(adj.)* muddily stirred up, filthy, foul **CE** V.i.173 [Messenger to Adriana] *Great pails of puddled mire*

pudency *(n.)* modesty, bashfulness, shyness **Cym** II.iv.163 [Posthumus alone, of Innogen's actions] *did it with / A pudency so rosy*

puffed *(adj.)* **1** increased, extended, stuffed **Ham** IV.iv.49 [Hamlet alone, of Fortinbras] *with divine ambition puffed*; **MW** V.v.151
    2 puffed up, swollen (with vanity) **Ham** I.iii.49 [Ophelia to Laertes, of his possible behaviour] *like a puffed and reckless libertine*; **Tim** IV.iii.181

puffing *(adj.)* puffed-out, swollen, swelling **RJ** II.ii.31 [Romeo to himself, of an angel] *When he bestrides the lazy, puffing clouds* [F *lazy-puffing*, Q1 *lasie pacing*]

pugging *(adj.)* [unclear meaning] pulling, thieving, pilfering **WT** IV.iii.7 [Autolycus singing] *The white sheet bleaching on the hedge … / Doth set my pugging tooth an edge* [i.e. taste for pinching things]

puisny *(adj.)* inferior, insignificant, petty **AY** III.iv.39 [Celia to Rosalind, of Orlando] *as a puisny tilter that spurs his horse but on one side breaks his staff*

puissance *(n.)* power, might, force **KJ** III.i.339 [King John to Bastard] *go draw our puissance together*; **2H4** I.iii.9; **H5** II.i.190; **2H6** IV.ii.154; **R3** V.iii.300; **TNK** I.i.155

puissant *(adj.)* powerful, mighty, strong **H5** I.ii.119 [Ely to King Henry] *my thrice-puissant liege*; **3H6** II.i.206 [Messenger to Warwick] *The Queen is coming with a puissant host*; **E3** IV.iv.63; **H5** I.ii.116; **2H6** IV.ix.25; **KL** V.iii.214; **R3** IV.iv.434

puke-stocking *(adj.)* dark-coloured woollen stocking **1H4** II.iv.68 [Prince Hal to Francis, of the vintner] *Wilt thou rob this … puke-stocking … Spanish pouch?*

puling *(n./adj.)* **1** whimpering, whining, complaining **RJ** III.v.184 [Capulet to Lady Capulet, of Juliet] *a wretched puling fool*; **Cor** IV.ii.52; **TC** IV.ii.62
    2 whimperingly, whiningly, complainingly **TG** II.i.24 [Speed to Valentine] *you have learned … to speak puling, like a beggar*

pull *(n.)* wrench, blow, thing torn away **2H6** II.iii.41 [Queen to all, of Gloucester] *two pulls at once - / His lady banished and a limb lopped off*

pull at *(v.)* drink up, swallow, draw in **AW** II.iii.222 [Lafew to Parolles, of the latter being wiser] *thou hast to pull at a smack o'th' contrary* [i.e. you have to swallow some of your own folly before you can become wise]

pull in *(v.)* rein in, bring to a halt **Mac** V.v.42 [Macbeth to himself] *I pull in resolution*

pullet-sperm *(n.)* [contemptuous] poultry-seed, egg **MW** III.v.28 [Falstaff to Bardolph] *I'll no pullet-sperm in my brewage*

pulpit *(n.)* public speaking place, platform, rostrum **JC** III.i.236 [Brutus aside to Cassius] *I will myself into the pulpit first*; **JC** III.i.80, 84, 229, 250, ii.1

pulsidge *(n.)* malapropism for 'pulses' **2H4** II.iv.23 [Hostess to Doll] *Your pulsidge beats as extraordinarily as heart would desire*

pumpion *(n.)* pumpkin **MW** III.iii.38 [Mistress Ford to Mistress Page, of Falstaff] *We'll use … this gross watery pumpion*

pun *(v.)* pound, hammer, batter **TC** II.i.37 [Thersites to Ajax, of Achilles] *He would pun thee into shivers with his fist*

punish *(v.)* afflict, plague, torment **Ham** V.ii.223 [Hamlet to Laertes] *I am punished with a sore distraction*

punk *(n.)* harlot, strumpet, whore **MM** V.i.179 [Lucio to Duke, of Mariana] *she may be a punk*; **AW** II.ii.21; **MM** V.i.519; **MW** II.ii.131

punto *(n.)* [fencing] thrust with the sword-point **MW** II.iii.23 [Host to Caius, in answer to 'Vat be you all … come for?'] *to see thee pass thy punto*

punto reverso *(n.)* [fencing] backhanded thrust **RJ** II.iv.26 [Mercutio to Benvolio] *the punto reverso!*

puny *(adj.)* untried, inexperienced **1H4** II.iv.29 [Prince Hal to Poins, of Francis] *stand in some by-room while I question my puny drawer*; **1H6** IV.vii.36

pupil *(adj.)* of being a pupil, as an apprentice **Cor** II.ii.96 [Cominius to all, of Coriolanus] *His pupil age / Man-entered*

pur *(n.)* [debated meaning] knave in a type of card game [post and pair] **AW** V.ii.19 [Clown to Lafew, of Parolles] *Here is a pur of Fortune's*

purblind *(adj.)* **1** half-blind, dim-sighted **1H6** II.iv.21 [Richard to Warwick] *The truth appears so naked on my side / That any purblind eye may find it out*; **RJ** II.i.12; **TC** I.ii.29; **Venus** 679

2 blind **LL** III.i.176 [Berowne alone, of Cupid] *This wimpled, whining, purblind, wayward boy;* **WT** I.ii.228

purchase (*n.*) **1** proceeds, plunder, booty **1H4** II.i.93 [Gadshill to Chamberlain] *thou shalt have a share in our purchase* [Q; F *purpose*]; **H5** III.ii.42

2 acquisition, prize, spoil **Per** I.ii.72 [Pericles to Helicanus] *I sought the purchase of a glorious beauty;* **R3** III.vii.186

3 profit, purchasing power, gain **1H4** III.iii.40 [Falstaff to Bardolph, of Bardolph's face] *if I did not think thou hadst been … a ball of wildfire, there's no purchase in money*

4 beneficial result, benefit, advantage **Per** I.Chorus.9 [Gower alone, of singing a song] *The purchase is to make men glorious*

5 financial return, earning power **TN** IV.i.22 [Feste to Sebastian] *These wise men that give fools money get themselves a good report - after fourteen years' purchase* [i.e. if they pay well for it]

purchase (*v.*) **1** acquire, obtain, win **R2** I.iii.282 [John of Gaunt to Bolingbroke] *say I sent thee forth to purchase honour;* **AY** III.ii.330; **Cor** II.i.134; **MV** II.ix.43; **Tit** II.iii.275; **TNK** II.iv.26

2 deserve, earn, merit **LL** V.ii.59 [Rosaline to Princess, of their lovers] *They are worse fools to purchase mocking so;* **MA** III.i.70

3 endeavour, strive, exert oneself; *or:* make a bargain, invest **Tim** III.i.48 [Lucius to Servilius] *How unluckily it happened that I should purchase the day before for a little part and undo a great deal of honour!* [i.e. my efforts would gain me only a little bit of honour]

purchase out (*v.*) buy off punishment for **RJ** III.i.193 [Prince to Montague] *Nor tears nor prayers shall purchase out abuses*

purchased (*adj.*) acquired, obtained through one's own conduct **AC** I.iv.14 [Lepidus to Caesar, of Antony] *His faults, in him, seem … hereditary / Rather than purchased*

pure (*adj.*) **1** clear, lucid **KJ** V.vii.2 [Prince Henry to Salisbury and Bigot, of King John] *his pure brain … / Doth by the idle comments that it makes / Foretell the ending of mortality*

2 sheer, utter, total **Per** III.ii.16 [First Gentleman to Cerimon] *Pure suprise and fear / Made me to quit the house*

pure (*adv.*) purely, solely, only **TN** V.i.81 [Antonio to Orsino, of Viola as Cesario] *For his sake / Did I expose myself - pure for his love*

purgation (*n.*) **1** purging, cleansing, clearing away **AY** I.iii.51 [Duke Frederick to Rosalind, of traitors] *If their purgation did consist in words;* **AY** V.iv.43; **Ham** III.ii.315; **LL** III.i.124

2 acquittal, clearing away of guilt **H8** V.iii.152 [Lord Chancellor to King Henry, of Cranmer's proposed imprisonment] *for his … fair purgation to the world;* **WT** III.ii.7

purge (*n.*) purging, cleansing, flushing out of evil **Mac** V.ii.28 [Cathness to all] *pour we in our country's purge / Each drop of us* [i.e. let us be prepared to shed all our blood to help cleanse our country]

purge (*v.*) **1** cleanse, purify, get rid of impurities [in] **TN** I.i.21 [Orsino to all, of Olivia] *she purged the air of pestilence;* **AC** I.iii.53; **KJ** III.i.239; **LL** V.ii.812 [F]; **Mac** V.iii.52; **RJ** I.i.191

2 expel, get rid of, flush out **R2** I.i.153 [Richard to Mowbray and Bolingbroke] *Let's purge this choler without letting blood;* **2H4** IV.i.65; **3H6** V.vi.88; **KJ** II.i.372; **RJ** I.v.107; **WT** V.i.168

3 clear, excuse, exonerate **RJ** V.iii.226 [Friar to Prince] *here I stand, both to impeach and purge / Myself condemned and myself excused;* **H8** V.i.102

4 make up for, be rid [of], compensate **TNK** I.ii.23 [Palamon to Arcite, of Juno] *peace might purge / For her repletion*

5 repent, atone **1H4** V.iv.163 [Falstaff alone] *I'll purge, and leave sack* [*also:* cleanse my body]

6 exude, discharge, void **Ham** II.ii.199 [Hamlet to Polonius, of old men] *their eyes purging thick amber*

purged (*adj.*) purified, refined, clarified **H5** II.ii.136 [King Henry to Scroop, of other men] *Not working with the eye without the ear, / And but in purged judgement trusting neither?*

purger (*n.*) healer, cleanser, purifier **JC** II.i.180 [Brutus to all, of killing Caesar] *We shall be called purgers, not murderers*

purl (*v.*) curl, rise in a twisting way **Luc** 1407 [of Nestor in a painting of Troy] *from his lips did fly / Thin winding breath which purled up to the sky*

purlieu (*n.*) edge, fringe, border [of forest land] **AY** IV.iii.77 [Oliver to Celia and Rosalind disguised] *Where in the purlieus of this forest stands / A sheepcote*

purple (*adj.*) bright-red, blood-coloured, bloody **R2** III.iii.94 [King Richard to his opponents, of Bolingbroke] *He is come to open / The purple testament of bleeding war;* **3H6** I.iv.12, V.vi.64; **R3** IV.iv.277; **RJ** I.i.85; **Venus** 1

purpled (*adj.*) reddened with blood, bloodstained **JC** III.i.158 [Antony to all] *whilst your purpled hands do reek and smoke;* **KJ** II.i.322

purple-hued (*adj.*) purple-faced **1H4** II.i.76 [Gadshill to Chamberlain] *I am joined with … none of these mad mustachio purple-hued maltworms*

purple-in-grain (*adj.*) dyed bright red **MND** I.ii.87 [Bottom to Quince, of his beard for the play] *your purple-in-grain beard*

purport (*n.*) meaning, expression, effect **Ham** II.i.82 [Ophelia to Polonius, of Hamlet] *with a look so piteous in purport*

purpose (*n.*) **1** intention, aim, plan **1H4** IV.iii.111 [Hotspur to Blunt, of King Henry] *in the morning early shall mine uncle / Bring him our purposes* ☛ FEW, p.xxi

2 point at issue, matter in hand **2H4** Epilogue.7 [Epilogue] *But to the purpose, and so to the venture;* **Cym** V.v.178; **Ham** II.ii.278; **JC** III.i.146; **KL** I.iv.176; **RJ** II.v.43

3 outcome, result, end **Cym** IV.ii.345 [Lucius to Soothsayer] *What have you dreamed of late of this war's purpose?;* **E3** I.i.61; **Ham** IV.vii.139

purpose, to effectively, to any effect **Cor** III.i.149 [Coriolanus to Brutus] *Nothing is done to purpose;* **WT** I.ii.89

purpose (*v.*) **1** intend, plan **Tem** II.i.22 [Gonzalo to Sebastian] *You have spoken truer than you purposed;* **Cor** V.iii.119; **Cym** III.iv.109; **2H4** IV.v.155; **KJ** V.vii.86; **MV** IV.i.35

2 intend to do, resolve to act **KL** I.i.225 [Cordelia to Lear] *If for I want that glib and oily art / To speak and purpose not* [i.e. intend not to do what I have said]

3 decide, resolve, determine **JC** II.ii.27 [Caesar to Calphurnia] *What can be avoided / Whose end is purposed by the mighty gods?;* **AY** IV.iii.128

purposed (*adj.*) **1** proposed, intended, contemplated **LL** V.ii.91 [Boyet to Princess, of the approach of the King's party] *to interrupt my purposed rest;* **KL** II.ii.140; **Lover** 118; **Oth** III.iv.113; **Sonn** 90.8

2 planned, premeditated, prearranged **Cor** III.i.38 [Coriolanus to Menenius, of the opposition to his election] *It is a purposed thing, / and grows by plot, / To curb the will of the nobility*

purse (*n.*) **1** resources, funds, available money **Ham** I.iii.70 [Polonius to Laertes] *Costly thy habit as thy purse can buy;* **Cym** I.vii.135; **Tim** I.ii.193

2 bag containing the great seal **H8** I.i.115 [stage direction] *Enter Cardinal Wolsey, the purse borne before him;* **H8** II.iv.1, IV.i.37

purse up (*v.*) take possession of, put into one's keeping **AC** II.ii.192 [Enobarbus to Maecenas, of Cleopatra] *When she first met Mark Antony, she pursed up his heart*

pursent (*v.*) dialect form of 'present' **LL** V.ii.488 [Costard to Berowne, of only three Worthies] *it is vara fine, / For every one pursents three*

pursue (*v.*) **1** proceed with, take forward, continue **TNK** I.iii.25 [Pirithous to Hippolyta and Emilia] *Peace be to you / As I pursue this war*

2 persecute, castigate, hound **MM** V.i.109 [Duke to Isabella, of Angelo] *it imports no reason / That with such vehemency he should pursue / Faults proper to himself*

pursuivant (*n.*) royal messenger, state messenger [with power to execute warrants] **E3** IV.ii.54 [King Edward to Percy] *we'll have a pursuivant dispatched;* **1H6** II.v.5; **2H6** I.iii.32; **H8** V.ii.1, 23; **R3** III.iv.88

pursuivant-at-arms (*n.*) junior officer attending a herald **R3** V.iii.59 [King Richard to Catesby] *Send out a pursuivant-at-arms / To Stanley's regiment*

pursy (*adj.*) **1** flabby, puffed-up, swollen **Ham** III.iv.154 [Hamlet to Gertrude] *in the fatness of these pursy times*
  2 short-winded, puffed out **Tim** V.iv.12 [Alcibiades to Senators] *pursy insolence shall break his wind / With fear and horrid flight*

purveyor (*n.*) steward sent ahead to make preparations for the arrival of someone important **Mac** I.vi.22 [King to Lady Macbeth, of Macbeth] *We coursed him at the heels and had a purpose / To be his purveyor*

push (*n.*) **1** pushing, shoving, thrusting forward **1H4** III.ii.66 [King Henry to Prince Hal, of Richard II] *gave his countenance against his name / To … stand the push / Of every beardless vain comparative*
  2 attack, assault, thrust **JC** V.ii.5 [Brutus to Messala, of the enemy] *sudden push gives them the overthrow;* **MA** V.i.38; **TC** II.ii.138
  3 test, trial **Ham** V.i.291 [Claudius to Laertes] *We'll put the matter to the present push*
  4 extremity, limit, measure **TNK** II.iii.6 [Gaoler's Daughter alone] *What pushes are we wenches driven to / When fifteen once has found us* [i.e. when we've reached the age of 15]
  5 crisis, emergency **Mac** V.iii.20 [Macbeth to himself] *This push / Will chair me ever or dis-seat me now* [or: sense 2]
  6 climactic moment, critical time **WT** V.iii.129 [Paulina to Hermione, of those watching] *Lest they desire upon this push to trouble / Your joys with like relation*

push (*v.*) strike, press hard, thrust **WT** III.ii.2 [Leontes to all] *This sessions … / Even pushes 'gainst our heart*

push-pin (*n.*) type of children's game [the pushing over of a peg to cross the peg of another player] **LL** IV.iii.167 [Berowne to all] *To see … Nestor play at push-pin with the boys*

pusillanimity (*n.*) cowardliness, timidity, fearfulness **2H4** IV.iii.103 [Falstaff alone, of a white and pale liver] *which is the badge of pusillanimity*

pussel (*n.*) ☞ **pucelle** (*n.*)

put (*v.*) **1** force, make, compel **Tit** IV.ii.175 [Aaron to the baby] *it is you that puts us to our shifts;* **AW** II.ii.1; **MM** I.i.5; **Tem** II.i.282
  2 force, press, thrust **MM** II.ii.133 [Angelo to Isabella] *Why do you put these sayings upon me?;* **AY** I.ii.89; **Cor** II.ii.139
  3 impress, urge **Ham** I.iii.94 [Polonius to Ophelia, of the reports he has heard] *If it be so - as so 'tis put on me*
  4 cause, encourage, provoke **Cym** II.iii.104 [Innogen to Cloten] *You put me to forget a lady's manners*
  5 bestow, grant, place officially **Tim** I.ii.199 [Flavius to himself, of Timon] *His land's put to their books* [i.e. entered in their account books]; **Per** IV.vi.89
  6 enlist, call up [as] **2H4** III.ii.163 [Falstaff to Feeble, of Wart] *I cannot put him to a private soldier, that is the leader of so many thousands*

put apart (*v.*) dismiss, send away **WT** II.ii.14 [Gaoler to Paulina] *So please you … / To put apart these your attendants*

put back (*v.*) repulse, reject, refuse **3H6** V.v.80 [Queen as if to Richard] *Petitioners for blood thou ne'er puttest back;* **TC** IV.iv.33; **Tim** II.ii.135

put by (*v.*) **1** thrust aside, reject, set aside **JC** I.ii.220 [Casca to Brutus, of Caesar being offered a crown] *he put it by with the back of his hand;* **JC** I.ii.227, 236, 241
  2 give up, desist from **Oth** II.iii.166 [Othello to all] *put by this barbarous brawl*

put down (*v.*) crush, defeat, put to silence **TN** I.iii.78 [Sir Toby to Sir Andrew] *When did I see thee so put down?;* **TN** I.v.79

put forth (*v.*) **1** set out [from], leave **AC** IV.x.7 [Antony to Scarus, of the enemy] *They have put forth the haven;* **2H4** I.i.186
  2 send abroad, send away **TG** I.iii.7 [Panthino to Antonio] *other men … / Put forth their sons to seek preferment out*
  3 make a show, come forward, promise **Cor** I.i.249 [Martius to Citizens] *Your valour puts well forth*
  4 be in evidence, emerge, be displayed **WT** I.ii.254 [Camillo to Leontes, of a man's failings] *his negligence, his folly, fear … / Sometime puts forth*

put in (*v.*) present a claim, put in a bid **Tim** III.iv.85 [Lucius' Servant to Titus, of his bill] *Put in now, Titus;* **MM** I.ii.100

put off (*v.*) **1** dismiss, brush aside, spurn **AW** II.ii.6 [Countess to Clown, of the court] *you put off that with such contempt;* **H8** II.iv.21; **Tim** III.vi.11
  2 keep away, avert, evade **LL** V.i.111 [Rosaline to Boyet, of evading his question] *Finely put off!;* **Per** I.i.141
  3 pass off, palm off, foist on **AW** II.ii.9 [Clown to Countess] *if God have lent a man any manners he may easily put it off at court*
  4 dismiss, lay off, make redundant **H8** I.ii.32 [Norfolk to King Henry] *The clothiers all … have put off / The spinsters, carders, fullers, weavers*
  5 doff, remove, take off **2H4** II.iv.6 [Drawer to Francis] *The Prince … putting off his hat*

put on (*v.*) **1** instigate, provoke, incite **Oth** II.iii.341 [Iago alone] *When devils will the blackest sins put on;* **Cym** V.i.9; **Ham** V.ii.377; **KL** I.iv.203, II.i.98
  2 push on, urge, encourage **LL** IV.i.114 [Boyet to Rosaline, as a riposte to her 'Finely put off!' = evade] *Finely put on!*
  3 show, manifest, exhibit **LL** I.i.225 [Brutus to all] *Let not our looks put on our purposes;* **JC** I.iii.60; **TC** III.iii.270
  4 put to the test, set to work **Ham** V.ii.391 [Fortinbras to all, of Hamlet] *he was likely, had he been put on, / To have proved most royal*
  5 arrange, appoint, organize **Ham** IV.vii.130 [Claudius to Laertes] *We'll put on those shall praise your excellence*
  6 demand, compel, claim **Oth** II.i.144 [Desdemona to Iago, of a deserving woman] *One that … did justly put on the vouch of very malice itself*

put out (*v.*) disconcert, distract, make one forget one's lines **LL** V.ii.478 [Berowne to Boyet] *You put our page out;* **LL** V.ii.102

put over (*v.*) **1** refer, hand over, direct **KJ** I.i.62 [Bastard to King John, of the truth of his parentage] *I put you o'er to heaven, and to my mother*
  2 display, exhibit, show forth **RJ** IV.v.121 [Second Musician to Peter] *Pray you put up your dagger, and put out your wit*

put stuff to copulate with **Tim** IV.iii.273 [Timon to Apemantus, of his father] *who in spite put stuff / To some she-beggar and compounded thee*

put to (*v.*) **1** set before, make available to **Cym** I.i.43 [First Gentleman to Second Gentleman, of Posthumus] *The king … / Puts to him all the learnings that his time / Could make him the receiver of*
  2 go to work, have sex **WT** I.ii.277 [Leontes to Camillo, of Hermione] *say / My wife's a hobby-horse, deserves a name / As rank as any flax-wench that puts to / Before her troth-plight*

put to it put to the proof, make trial of **WT** I.ii.16 [Leontes to Polixenes] *We are tougher, brother, / Than you can put us to't;* **AW** III.vi.1; **MM** II.ii.90; **Oth** III.iii.468

put together (*v.*) set against each other, oppose in combat **Cym** I.v.38 [Frenchman to Posthumus] *it had been pity you should have been put together*

put up (*v.*) **1** sheathe, put away **Tem** I.ii.470 [Prospero to Ferdinand] *Put thy sword up;* **Tit** II.i.53; **TN** IV.i.38
  2 conceal, hide away, pocket **KL** I.ii.28 [Gloucester to Edmund] *Why so earnestly seek you to put up that letter?;* **LL** IV.i.107
  3 pack up, put away **RJ** IV.v.96 [First Musician to others] *we may put up our pipes and be gone*

4 submit to, put up with **Tit** I.i.436 [Saturninus to Tamora, of pardoning Titus] *be dishonoured openly, / And basely put it up without revenge?* [also: sense 1]

5 make rise from cover, raise **2H6** II.i.44 [Cardinal to Gloucester] *Had not your man put up the fowl so suddenly, / We had had more sport*

put up a bill present a list of accusations **1H6** III.i.1 [stage direction] *Gloucester offers to put up a bill*

put upon (*v.*) provoke into doing, encourage into **Cor** II.i.248 [Sicinius to Brutus, of Coriolanus' insolence reaching the people] *which time shall not want, / If he be put upon't*

put upon / on (*v.*) ascribe to, impute to, attribute to **Ham** II.i.19 [Polonius to Reynaldo, of Laertes] *And there put on him / What forgeries you please;* **Mac** I.vii.70 [Lady Macbeth to Macbeth, of the King] *What cannot you and I ... put upon / His spongy officers*

putter-on (*n.*) instigator, inciter, agitator **WT** II.i.141 [Antigonus to Leontes] *You are abused, and by some putter-on;* **H8** I.ii.24

putter-out (*n.*) investor, lender, speculator **Tem** III.iii.49 [Gonzalo to Alonso] *Each putter-out of five for one* [i.e. guaranteeing a fivefold return for an insured sum, upon successful completion of a foreign journey]

putting-by (*n.*) refusal, rejection, thrusting aside **JC** I.ii.228 [Casca to Brutus, of Caesar refusing a crown] *at every putting-by mine honest neighbours shouted*

putting down (*n.*) suppression, restraint, repression **MW** II.i.27 [Mistress Page alone] *I'll exhibit a bill in the parliament for the putting down of men*

putting on (*n.*) instigation, prompting, urging **Cor** II.iii.251 [Brutus to Citizens, of Coriolanus' election] *Say you ne'er had done't ... but by our putting on;* **MM** IV.ii.114; **Oth** II.i.295

puttock (*n.*) kite; greedy scavenger **Cym** I.ii.71 [Innogen to Cymbeline] *I chose an eagle, / And did avoid a puttock;* **2H6** III.ii.191; **TC** V.i.58

puzzel (*n.*) ☞ pucelle (*n.*)

puzzle (*v.*) **1** bewilder, perplex, baffle **Ham** III.i.80 [Hamlet alone] *the dread of something after death ... puzzles the will;* **TN** IV.ii.43

2 complicate things for, be an embarrassment for **AC** III.vii.10 [Enobarbus to Cleopatra, of the war] *Your presence needs must puzzle Antony*

pyramid (*n.*) obelisk, pillar **TNK** V.iii.80 [Servant to Emilia] *Palamon had Arcite's body / Within an inch o'th' pyramid;* **Sonn** 123.2; **TNK** III.vi.293

pyramides (*n.*) pyramids **AC** V.ii.61 [Cleopatra to Proculeius] *make / My country's high pyramides my gibbet*

pyramis (*n.*) pyramid **1H6** I.vi.21 [Charles to all, of Pucelle] *A statelier pyramis to her I'll rear / Than Rhodope's of Memphis ever was;* **AC** II.vii.35

quaff *(v.)* drink down, take a long draught of **TS** I.ii.274 [Tranio as Lucentio to Hortensio and Gremio, of Bianca] *Please ye we may ... quaff carouses to our mistress' health;* **2H4** IV.v.86

quaff off *(v.)* drain a cup in a long draught **TS** III.ii.171 [Gremio to Tranio as Lucentio, of Petruchio drinking] *quaffed off the muscadel*

quail *(n.)* courtesan, prostitute **TC** V.i.49 [Thersites alone, of Agamemnon] *one that loves quails* [also: the bird as food]

quail *(v.)* **1** overpower, destroy, make an end **MND** V.i.279 [Bottom as Pyramus] *O Fates ... / Quail, crush, conclude, and quell;* **AC** V.ii.85
2 daunt, dishearten, intimidate **E3** IV.vi.49 [King John to all] *The twentieth part / Of those that live are men enow to quail / The feeble handful on the adverse part*
3 fail, slacken, flag **AY** II.ii.20 [Duke Frederick to all, of Celia and Rosalind] *let not search and inquisition quail / To bring again these foolish runaways*

quaint *(adj.)* **1** ingenious, clever, skilful **Tem** III.iii.54 [stage direction] *with a quaint device, the banquet vanishes;* **2H6** III.ii.274; **Tem** I.ii.317
2 artful, cunning **MV** III.iv.69 [Portia to Nerissa, of dressing as men] *I'll ... tell quaint lies;* **1H6** IV.i.102; **TS** III.ii.146
3 intricate, elaborate **MND** II.i.99 [Titania to Oberon] *the quaint mazes in the wanton green / For lack of tread are undistinguishable*
4 pretty, attractive, lovely **TNK** I.i.5 [Boy singing to all] *Daisies smell-less, yet most quaint;* **MND** II.ii.7; **TS** IV.iii.102
5 nice, prim, fastidious **Tit** II.iii.126 [Demetrius to Tamora, of Lavinia] *This minion stood upon her chastity ... / And with that quaint hope braves your mightiness* [F *painted*]

quaint *(adv.)* elaborately, elegantly, finely **MW** IV.vi.41 [Fenton to Host, of Anne's costume] *quaint in green she shall be loose enrobed*

quaintly *(adv.)* **1** subtly, skilfully, ingeniously **TG** III.i.117 [Valentine to Duke] *a ladder, quaintly made of cords;* **Ham** II.i.31; **Per** III.Chorus.13; **TG** II.i.116
2 elaborately, artistically, with skill **MV** II.iv.6 [Solanio to all, of torchbearers] *'Tis vile, unless it may be quaintly ordered;* **3H6** II.v.24

quake *(v.)* cause to quake, make tremble, agitate **Cor** I.ix.6 [Cominius to Martius] *where ladies shall be frighted / And, gladly quaked, hear more*

qualification *(n.)* true condition, character, nature **Oth** II.i.266 [Iago to Roderigo] *will I cause these of Cyprus to mutiny, whose qualification shall come into no true taste again but by the displanting of Cassio*

qualified *(adj.)* **1** endowed with good qualities, accomplished **Cym** I.v.57 [Frenchman to Iachimo, of a woman] *more fair, virtuous ... qualified;* **TS** IV.v.66
2 of such quality, of such a nature, fitting **WT** II.i.113 [Hermione to Lords] *With thoughts so qualified as your charities / Shall best instruct you measure me*

qualify *(v.)* **1** moderate, weaken, diminish **KL** I.ii.159 [Edmund to Edgar, of Gloucester] *forbear his presence until some little time hath qualified the heat of his displeasure;* **Ham** IV.vii.112; **MA** V.iv.67; **MM** IV.ii.80; **MV** IV.i.7; **TC** II.ii.119
2 appease, pacify, calm down **WT** IV.iv.529 [Camillo to Florizel] *Your discontenting father [I'll] strive to qualify, / And bring him up to liking;* **KJ** V.i.13
3 dilute, weaken, mix with water **Oth** II.iii.36 [Cassio to Iago] *I have drunk but one cup tonight, and that was craftily qualified too*

qualifying *(adj.)* moderating, diluting, weakening **TC** IV.iv.9 [Cressida to Pandarus] *My love admits no qualifying dross*

quality *(n.)* **1** nature, disposition, character **KL** II.iv.88 [Gloucester to Lear, of Cornwall] *You know the fiery quality of the Duke;* **AC** I.i.54; **2H4** V.ii.34; **Luc** 1702; **Oth** I.iii.248; **TN** III.i.61
2 accomplishment, capacity, ability **Per** IV.ii.43 [Bawd to Boult, of Marina] *has she any qualities?;* **AW** I.i.41; **Cym** III.v.138; **KL** I.i.5; **MW** V.v.40; **TG** III.i.269

3 rank, standing, position **KL** V.iii.118 [Herald to Edgar] *What are you? / Your name, your quality;* **Cym** I.v.28; **2H4** IV.i.11; **H5** IV.viii.89; **Oth** III.iii.350; **TNK** I.iv.14

4 profession, occupation, business **MM** II.i.57 [Angelo to Elbow, of Pompey and Froth] *What quality are they of?;* **Ham** II.ii.345, 430; **H5** III.vi.135

5 characteristic, feature, property **Tem** I.ii.337 [Caliban to Prospero] *I ... showed thee all the qualities o'th' isle;* **RJ** II.iii.12

6 importance, special significance **Oth** I.iii.279 [Duke to Othello, of an officer] *he shall our commission bring to you, / With such things else of quality and respect / As doth import you* [or: rank]

7 occasion, cause **Tim** III.vi.107 [Lucius to Lords] *Know you the quality of Lord Timon's fury?;* **2H4** I.iii.36; **TC** IV.i.45

8 companions, associates, fraternity **TG** IV.i.58 [First Outlaw to Valentine] *you are ... a man of such perfection / As we do in our quality much want;* **Tem** I.ii.193

9 party, company, side **1H4** IV.iii.36 [Hotspur to Blunt] *you are not of our quality, / But stand against us like an enemy*

qualm *(n.)* **1** sudden sickness, feeling of nausea, fainting attack **MA** III.iv.68 [Margaret to Beatrice, of Carduus Benedictus] *it is the only thing for a qualm;* **LL** V.ii.279

2 sickening fear, sinking feeling **2H6** I.i.53 [Gloucester to King] *Some sudden qualm hath struck me at the heart*

quantity *(n.)* **1** fragment, little piece, tiny amount **TS** IV.iii.110 [Petruchio to Tailor] *Away, thou rag, thou quantity, thou remnant;* **Ham** III.iv.76; **2H4** V.i.56; **KJ** V.iv.23

2 equal amount, same proportion **MND** I.i.232 [Helena to herself] *Things base and vile, holding no quantity, / Love can transpose to form and dignity;* **Ham** III.ii.177

quarrel *(n.)* cause of complaint, reason for hostility, difference, claim **R2** I.iii.13 [Lord Marshal to Mowbray] *say who thou art ... and what thy quarrel;* **2H6** II.iii.53; **H8** II.iii.14; **JC** II.i.28; **Mac** IV.iii.137; **R3** I.iv.207

quarrel *(v.)* quibble, dispute, equivocate **MV** III.v.51 [Lorenzo to Launcelot] *Yet more quarrelling with occasion* [i.e. quibbling at every opportunity]

quarrel at *(v.)* object to; or: start quarrelling at **MW** I.i.270 [Slender to Anne, of bear-baiting] *I shall as soon quarrel at it as any man in England*

quarrel with *(v.)* object to, take exception to, refuse to practise **KJ** V.9 [King John to Cardinal Pandulph, of the English] *Our people quarrel with obedience*

quarrelous *(adj.)* quarrelsome, argumentative, cantankerous **Cym** III.iv.161 [Pisanio to Innogen, of her proposed guise] *quick-answered, saucy, and / As quarrelous as the weasel*

quarry *(n.)* [in hunting] heap of dead, pile of bodies **Cor** I.i.196 [Martius to Menenius, of the citizens] *I'd make a quarry / With thousands of these quartered slaves;* **Ham** V.ii.358; **Mac** IV.iii.206

quarter *(n.)* **1** quarters, lodging, residence **Tim** V.iv.60 [Alcibiades to Senators] *not a man / Shall pass his quarter* [or: military area]; **AW** III.vi.60; **1H6** II.i.68

2 relationships, relations, mutual conduct **Oth** II.iii.174 [Iago to Othello, of Cassio and Montano] *Friends all but now ... / In quarter and in terms*

3 direction, bearing, point [of the compass] **Mac** I.iii.16 [First Witch to other Witches, of the winds] *And the very ports they blow / All the quarters that they know / I'the shipman's card*

4 divide into quarters [on a flag or shield] **E3** III.i.76 [Mariner to King John] *The arms of England and of France unite / Are quartered equally by herald's art;* **E3** IV.iv.28

5 army division, unit of soldiers **E3** IV.iv.50 [Prince Edward to Audley, of the French] *These quarters, squadrons, and these regiments*

6 period of watch **KJ** V.v.20 [Lewis the Dauphin to Messenger] *keep good quarter and good care tonight!;* **AC** IV.iii.25

7 ➤ keep fair quarter with

quarter *(v.)* **1** add a coat-of-arms to a [quarter of] a shield **MW** I.i.22 [Slender to Shallow] *I may quarter, coz?*

2 cut to pieces, hack, mutilate **JC** III.i.268 [Antony alone] *mothers shall but smile when they behold / Their infants quartered with the hands of war;*

quarter day [day marking a quarter of the year, when house tenancies would change] removal day **E3** III.ii.3 [First Frenchman to all] *is it quarter day that you remove, / And carry bag and baggage too?*

quartered *(adj.)* **1** cut into four pieces **Cor** I.i.197 [Martius to Menenius, of the citizens] *I'd make a quarry / With thousands of these quartered slaves;* **KJ** II.i.506, 508

2 belonging to quarters, of an encampment **Cym** IV.iv.18 [Arviragus to Belarius and Guiderius, of the Britons] *when they hear their Roman horses neigh, / Behold their quartered fires*

quartering *(adj.)* for cutting into quarters, dismembering **E3** V.i.37 [King Edward to Calais Citizens] *Your bodies shall ... feel the stroke of quartering steel;* **E3** III.ii.5; **1H6** IV.ii.11

quat *(n.)* pimple, small boil **Oth** V.i.11 [Iago to himself, of Roderigo] *I have rubbed this young quat almost to the sense*

quatch *(adj.)* [unclear meaning] squat, fat, plump **AW** II.ii.17 [Clown to Countess, of types of buttock] *the quatch-buttock*

quean *(n.)* bawd, jade, hussy **2H4** II.i.45 [Falstaff to Bardolph, of the Hostess] *Throw the quean in the channel!;* **AW** II.ii.24; **MW** IV.ii.161

queasy *(adj.)* **1** disgusted, nauseated, upset **AC** III.vi.20 [Agrippa to all, of Rome's reaction to Antony's behaviour] *queasy with his insolence already*

2 easily upset, delicate, fastidious **MA** II.i.355 [Don Pedro to all, of Benedick] *in despite of his quick wit and his queasy stomach*

3 uncertain, hazardous; or: delicate, ticklish **KL** I.ii.17 [Edmund alone] *I have one thing of a queasy question / Which I must act*

queen *(v.)* act as a queen, aspire to being a queen **WT** IV.iv.446 [Perdita to Florizel] *I'll queen it no inch farther*

quell *(n.)* murder, slaying, slaughter **Mac** I.vii.72 [Lady Macbeth to Macbeth, of the King's men] *who shall bear the guilt / Of our great quell*

quell *(v.)* **1** destroy, overcome, vanquish **1H6** I.i.163 [Exeter to all] *to quell the Dauphin utterly*

2 kill, destroy, slay **MND** V.i.279 [Bottom as Pyramus] *O Fates ... / Quail, crush, conclude, and quell*

queller *(n.)* destroyer, killer **2H4** II.i.50 [Hostess to Falstaff] *Thou art ... a man-queller - and a woman-queller;* **TC** V.v.45 [Achilles as if to Hector] *Come, come, thou boy-queller, show thy face*

quench *(v.)* **1** cool down, settle down **Cym** I.vi.47 [Queen to Pisanio, of Innogen] *Dost thou think in time / She will not quench*

2 extinguish, put out, knock out **Mac** II.ii.2 [Lady Macbeth alone, of the King's attendants] *What hath quenched them hath given me fire*

quern *(n.)* hand-mill for grinding corn **MND** II.i.36 [Fairy to Puck] *Are not you he / That ... sometimes labour in the quern*

quest *(n.)* **1** inquiry, pursuit, investigation **MM** IV.i.61 [disguised Duke alone] *Volumes of report / Run with these false and most contrarious quests / Upon thy doings* [F *quest*] [or: with comma after 'false', = *(v.)* search for game, give tongue at the sight of game]

2 jury, body of persons appointed to hold an inquiry **Sonn** 46.10 *To 'cide this title is impannelled / A quest of thoughts*

3 judicial inquiry, official investigation **R3** I.iv.187 [Clarence to Murderers] *What lawful quest have given their verdict up / Unto the frowning judge?*

4 inquest **Ham** V.i.22 [First Clown to Second Clown] *crowner's quest law*

questant *(n.)* seeker, searcher, someone engaged in a quest **AW** II.i.16 [King to Lords] *When / The bravest questant shrinks*

question (*n.*) **1** argument, contention, dispute **TNK** V.i.127 [Palamon praying to Venus] *Give me the victory of this question;* **Ham** V.ii.369; **KL** I.iii.14; **MM** II.iv.90; **MV** IV.i.169; **TNK** III.vi.222

2 point at issue, problem, business **AC** II.ii.44 [Caesar to Antony, of Egypt] *if you there / Did practise on my state, your being in Egypt / Might be my question;* **AC** III.xiii.10; **KL** II.i.17; **2H6** IV.ii.132; **TC** II.iii.81; **WT** I.ii.324

3 consideration, contention **MM** I.i.46 [Duke to Angelo] *Escalus, / Though first in question, is thy secondary;* **Cym** I.i.34; **H5** I.i.5; **RJ** I.i.229

4 debating, discussion, investigation **H5** III.ii.115 [Jamy to Fluellen and Macmorris] *I wad full fain hear some question 'tween you tway;* **1H4** I.i.34; **KL** V.iii.34; **MV** IV.i.73; **Sonn** 12.9; **TC** IV.i.12

5 questioning, interrogation, examination **WT** V.i.197 [Lord to Leontes, of Camillo and the rustics] *I spake with him; who now / Has these poor men in question;* **E3** III.iii.109; **MA** V.iv.6; **MV** V.i.343; **TNK** V.iv.136

6 conversation, discourse, piece of talk **AY** III.iv.32 [Rosalind to Celia] *I met the Duke yesterday and had much question with him;* **2H4** I.i.48; **Ham** III.ii.113; **Oth** I.iii.113; **TNK** I.iii.8; **WT** I.ii.47

7 source [of strife], cause, issue **JC** III.i.37 [Brutus to all, of Caesar] *The question of his death is enrolled in the Capitol;* **Ham** I.i.111

8 fighting, conflict, altercation **Oth** I.iii.23 [First Senator to Duke, of the Turk taking Cyprus] *So may he with more facile question bear it*

question (*v.*) **1** dispute, quarrel [over], call in question **H8** I.ii.99 [King Henry to Wolsey, of the taxation] *To every county / Where this is questioned send our letters with / Free pardon;* **Cym** II.iv.52; **H8** II.iv.50; **MV** IV.i.70

2 converse with, talk away [at / with] **Luc** 122 [of Tarquin] *long he questioned / With modest Lucrece;* **1H4** I.iii.46

3 enquire about, discuss, deliberate **1H6** II.ii.72 [Pucelle to all] *Question ... no further of the case;* **Per** I.iii.11

4 discuss the matter, talk things over **MW** III.i.70 [Host to Shallow, of Caius and Evans] *Disarm them, and let them question*

question, call in discuss, deliberate upon **JC** IV.iii.163 [Brutus to all] *Now sit we close ... / And call in question our necessities*

question, in on trial, under examination **2H4** I.ii.58 [Lord Chief Justice to Servant, of Falstaff] *He that was in question for the robbery?;* **MA** III.iii.173

question, in contempt of without the shadow of a doubt **TN** II.v.88 [Malvolio to himself, of the letter supposedly from Olivia] *It is, in contempt of question, her hand*

question, out of undoubtedly, beyond question, certainly **LL** IV.i.30 [Princess to all] *out of question so it is sometimes; / Glory grows guilty of detested crimes*

questionable (*adj.*) inviting interrogation, of whom questions may be asked **Ham** I.iv.43 [Hamlet to Ghost] *Thou comest in such a questionable shape / That I will speak to thee*

questionless (*adv.*) unquestionably, undoubtedly, most certainly **MV** I.i.176 [Bassanio to Antonio, of wooing Portia] *I should questionless be fortunate;* **Per** V.i.42

questrist (*n.*) one who goes in quest of another, seeker **KL** III.vii.16 [Oswald to Cornwall, of Lear's knights] *Hot questrists after him* [F; Q *questrits*]

quick (*n.*) **1** sensitive parts [of the body], tender flesh **Ham** II.ii.595 [Hamlet alone, of Claudius] *I'll tent him to the quick;* **CE** II.ii.139; **Ham** IV.vii.122; **Tem** V.i.25; **Tit** IV.i.28, iv.36

2 living, those alive **Ham** V.i.247 [Laertes to all] *Now pile your dust upon the quick and dead;* **E3** III.i.156; **Ham** V.i.124

quick (*adj.*) **1** living, vital, full of life **H5** II.ii.79 [King Henry to traitors] *The mercy that was quick in us but late / By your own counsel is suppressed and killed;* **1H6** V.iii.8; **LL** I.ii.28; **MND** I.i.149; **MW** III.iv.84; **Sonn** 45.5, 113.7

2 lively, animated, vivacious **JC** I.ii.293 [Brutus to Cassius, of Casca] *He was quick mettle when he went to school;* **AC** I.ii.111; **H5** III.v.21; **LL** I.i.159; **TC** IV.v.54; **TG** III.i.91

3 quick-witted, inventive, lively **LL** I.ii.29 [Armado to Mote] *thou art quick in answers;* **AC** V.ii.216; **Sonn** 76.2

4 sharp, keen, alert **TG** IV.ii.61 [Host to disguised Julia] *You have a quick ear;* **TN** I.i.9; **TS** V.ii.11; **WT** IV.iv.667

5 vigorous, quick-acting, energetic **R3** I.ii.195 [Queen Margaret to all] *give way, dull clouds, to my quick curses!;* **AW** V.iii.40; **Tim** IV.iii.45

6 alive to possibilities, lively, impatient **3H6** III.ii.144 [Richard alone] *My eye's too quick, my heart o'erweens too much*

7 fresh, invigorating, sharp **Per** IV.i.27 [Dionyza to Marina, of the seashore] *The air is quick there*

8 running, flowing, gushing **Tem** III.ii.67 [Caliban to Stephano, of Trinculo] *I'll not show him / Where the quick freshes are*

9 hasty, hurried **MM** I.i.53 [Duke to Angelo] *Our haste from hence is of so quick condition / That it prefers itself;* **R3** IV.iv.361

10 pregnant, with child **LL** V.ii.673 [Costard to Armado, of Jaquenetta] *She's quick;* **LL** V.ii.678

quick (*adv.*) alive **Ham** V.i.275 [Hamlet to Laertes, of Ophelia] *Be buried quick with her;* **AW** V.iii.301; **R3** I.ii.65; **WT** IV.iv.132

quick-answered (*adj.*) ready with sharp answers **Cym** III.iv.160 [Pisanio to Innogen, of her proposed guise] *Ready in gibes, quick-answered*

quick-conceiving (*adj.*) perceptive, astute, ready to understand **1H4** I.iii.187 [Worcester to Northumberland and Hotspur] *to your quick-conceiving discontents / I'll read you matter deep and dangerous*

quicken (*v.*) **1** revive, rejuvenate, give life [to] **R3** IV.iv.124 [Queen Elizabeth to Queen Margaret] *My words are dull. O, quicken them with thine!;* **AC** I.iii.69; **H5** IV.ii.20; **1H6** IV.vi.13; **MV** II.viii.52; **Tem** III.i.6

2 receive life, be conceived **Oth** III.iii.274 [Othello, alone, of being a cuckold] *this forked plague is fated to us / When we do quicken;* **Oth** IV.ii.66

quickening (*n.*) fresh animation, reviving, return of life **MM** V.i.492 [Duke to Isabella, of Angelo] *Methinks I see a quickening in his eye*

quickening (*adj.*) life-giving, animating **Tim** IV.iii.185 [Timon alone, of the earth] *Whereon Hyperion's quickening fire doth shine*

quicksilver (*n.*) liquid mercury **2H4** II.iv.224 [Falstaff to Doll, of Pistol] *The rogue fled from me like quicksilver*

quiddity (*n.*) subtlety, nicety, quibble **1H4** I.ii.45 [Falstaff to Prince Hal] *What, in thy quips and thy quiddities?;* **Ham** V.i.97

quid for quo [Latin: quid pro quo] tit for tat **1H6** V.iii.109 [Margaret to Suffolk, of her speaking aside, as he has done] *I cry you mercy, 'tis but quid for quo*

quiet (*n.*) calmness, peace of mind, serenity **H8** II.iv.63 [Wolsey to Queen Katherine, of delaying the hearing no longer] *as well / For your own quiet;* **2H4** IV.v.71; **2H6** II.ii.67; **H8** II.ii.73; **TS** II.i.323

quiet (*adj.*) calm, peaceful, relaxed **2H6** I.ii.141 [King to Duchess of Gloucester] *Sweet aunt, be quiet*

quietly (*adv.*) in peace, undisturbed **3H6** I.ii.15 [York to Edward, of the King] *I took an oath that he should quietly reign;* **1H6** V.iii.153, 159

quietness (*n.*) peace, amity, reconciliation **1H6** V.i.10 [Gloucester to King] *the only means / To ... stablish quietness on every side*

quietus (*n.*) discharge, clearing of accounts, release **Ham** III.i.75 [Hamlet alone] *he himself might his quietus make / With a bare bodkin* [i.e. from life]; **Sonn** 126.12

quill (*n.*) musical pipe, voice, note **MND** III.i.121 [Bottom singing to himself] *The wren with little quill*

quill, in the in a body, all together **2H6** I.iii.3 [First Petitioner to all] *My Lord Protector will come this way by and by, and then we may deliver our supplications in the quill*

quillet *(n.)* quibble, equivocation, hair-splitting distinction **2H6** III.i.261 [Suffolk to all, of Gloucester] *do not stand on quillets how to slay him;* **Ham** V.i.97; **1H6** II.iv.17; **LL** IV.iii.286; **Oth** III.i.23; **Tim** IV.iii.156

quilt *(n.)* quilted furnishing, padded covering **1H4** IV.ii.47 [Prince Hal to Falstaff] *How now, quilt?*

quintain *(n.)* heavy post used as a mark for tilting practice **AY** I.ii.240 [Orlando to Rosalind and Celia] *that which here stands up / Is but a quintain, a mere lifeless block*

quintessence *(n.)* purest form, most perfect manifestation **Ham** II.ii.308 [Hamlet to Rosencrantz and Guildenstern, of the nature of man] *this quintessence of dust;* **AY** III.ii.135

quip *(n.)* retort, taunt, gibe **TG** IV.ii.12 [Proteus alone, of Silvia] *notwithstanding all her sudden quips*

quire *(n./v.)* variant spelling of 'choir' ☞ choir *(n./v.)*

quirk *(n.)* **1** trick, turn, peculiarity **TN** III.iv.239 [Viola as Cesario to Sir Toby, of Sir Andrew having a certain type of character] *Belike this is a man of that quirk*
  2 quip, wisecrack, witticism **MA** II.iii.229 [Benedick alone] *I may chance have some odd quirks and remnants of wit broken on me*
  3 extravagant turn of phrase, verbal flourish **Oth** II.i.63 [Cassio to Montano, of Desdemona] *One that excels the quirks of blazoning pens*

quit *(adj.)* **1** away from, out of **H5** IV.i.113 [Bates to disguised King Henry, of the King wishing himself in the Thames] *so I would he were, and I by him, at all adventures, so we were quit here*
  2 freed [from], relieved [of] **2H4** III.ii.232 [Feeble to Bardolph] *he that dies this year is quit for the next;* **Tim** IV.iii.398

quit *(v.)* **1** rid, free, relieve **TNK** III.i.72 [Palamon to Arcite, of his shackles] *Quit me of these cold gyves;* **H5** III.v.47; **2H6** III.ii.218; **3H6** III.iii.128; **H8** V.i.70 ☞ acquit *(adj.)*
  2 remit, release from **MV** IV.i.378 [Antonio to Duke, of Shylock] *To quit the fine for one half of his goods, / I am content;* **CE** I.i.23; **E3** IV.i.24, iii.5; **MM** V.i.480
  3 acquit, absolve, clear **1H4** III.ii.19 [Prince Hal to King Henry] *I would I could / Quit all offences;* **AW** V.iii.297; **AY** III.i.11; **Cym** V.v.167; **2H4** II.iv.337; **H5** II.ii.166
  4 release from service, let go **TN** V.i.318 [Orsino to Viola] *Your master quits you*
  5 pay back, repay, reward **MM** V.i.493 [Duke to Angelo] *your evil quits you well;* **AC** III.xiii.124; **Cor** IV.v.86; **Ham** V.ii.68; **R3** V.iii.263; **RJ** II.iv.188
  6 avenge, requite, take vengeance [on] **KL** III.vii.86 [Gloucester to all, as if to Edmund] *enkindle all the sparks of nature / To quit this horrid act;* **AC** III.xiii.151; **MA** IV.i.198; **MM** V.i.408; **R3** IV.iv.64; **TS** III.i.90
  7 draw level, be quits **Ham** V.ii.263 [Claudius to all] *If Hamlet … quit in answer of the third exchange*
  8 make compensation for, requite **Per** III.i.36 [Pericles to Marina] *thy loss is more than can / Thy portage quit*
  9 answer, respond to, requite **H5** III.ii.100 [Jamy to all] *I sall quit you with gud leve*
  10 acquit, do one's part, bear [oneself] **KL** II.i.30 [Edmund to Edgar] *quit you well*

quite *(v.)* [= requite] reward, repay, recompense **R2** V.i.43 [Richard to Queen Isabel, of old story-tellers] *to quite their griefs / Tell thou the lamentable tale of me;* **TNK** V.iv.35

quite *(adv.)* totally, completely, entirely **1H6** I.i.90 [Second Messenger to nobles] *France is revolted from the English quite;* **1H6** IV.i.43; **RJ** V.i.82

quittal *(n.)* requital, recompense, payment **Luc** 236 [Tarquin to himself, of imagined enmity with Collatine] *this desire / Might have excuse to work upon his wife, / As in revenge or quittal of such strife*

quittance *(n.)* **1** due recompense, repayment, requital **H5** II.ii.34 [King Henry to Grey] *We … shall forget the office of our hand / Sooner than quittance of desert and merit;* **Tim** I.i.285
  2 resistance, retaliation, counterblow **2H4** I.i.108 [Morton to Northumberland, of Percy] *mine eyes saw him in bloody state, / Rendering faint quittance … / To Harry Monmouth*
  3 document certifying a release from debt, receipt of discharge **MW** I.i.10 [Slender to Evans, of Shallow] *who writes himself Armigero - in any bill, warrant, quittance, or obligation*

quittance *(v.)* repay, requite, reciprocate **1H6** II.i.14 [Talbot to all, of the French] *Embrace we then this opportunity, / As fitting best to quittance their deceit;* **E3** V.i.124

quiver *(adj.)* nimble, quick, active **2H4** III.ii.272 [Shallow to Falstaff] *there was a little quiver fellow, and 'a would manage you his piece thus*

quoif *(n.)* ☞ coif *(n.)*

quoit *(v.)* throw, pitch, chuck [like a quoit] **E3** IV.vi.40 [King John to all] *They quoit at us and kill us up* [i.e. throw stones at us]; **2H4** II.iv.187

quondam *(adj.)* former, erstwhile, previous **3H6** III.i.23 [First Keeper to Second Keeper, of the person overheard] *This is the quondam king;* **H5** I.i.75; **3H6** III.iii.153; **LL** V.i.6; **MA** V.ii.32; **TC** IV.v.179

quote *(v.)* **1** closely observe, note, examine **TC** IV.v.233 [Achilles to Hector] *I have with exact view perused thee, Hector, / And quoted joint by joint;* **Ham** II.i.112; **KJ** IV.ii.222; **Luc** 812; **RJ** I.iv.31; **Tit** IV.i.50
  2 note, jot, write **Ham** III.ii.45 [Hamlet to Players, of a type of clown] *gentlemen quote his jests down in their tables* [in Q1 only]
  3 display, indicate, show **LL** II.i.232 [Boyet to Princess, of the King] *His face's own margin did quote such amazes*
  4 regard, consider, interpret **LL** V.ii.781 [Rosaline to Longaville, of the seriousness of the lords' advances] *We did not quote them so*
  5 refer to, cite **LL** IV.iii.85 [Dumaine to himself, of Katharine] *Her amber hairs for foul hath amber quoted* [i.e. her amber-coloured hair makes an amber stone seem ugly when referred to]

quote for *(v.)* regard as, consider to be, mention as **AW** V.iii.205 [Bertram to King, of Parolles] *He's quoted for a most perfidious slave*

quoth *(v.)* said **AY** II.i.47 [First Lord to Duke Senior, of Jaques] *'Poor deer,' quoth he* ☞ FEW, p.xxi

quoth a, quotha *(int.)* did he say?, indeed! **AW** I.iii.83 [Clown to Countess] *One in ten, quoth 'a!;* **Per** II.i.78 [First Fisherman to Pericles] *Die, quotha!;* **2H4** V.iii.16; **MW** II.i.129

quotidian *(n.)* type of fever with attacks every day **AY** III.ii.350 [Rosalind to Orlando, of the writer of love poems] *he seems to have the quotidian of love upon him;* **H5** II.i.114

rabbit-sucker *(n.)* sucking rabbit, baby rabbit 1H4 II.iv.426 [Falstaff to Prince Hal] *hang me up by the heals for a rabbit-sucker*

rabble *(n.)* **1** crowd, pack, mob MW III.v.70 [Falstaff to Ford as Brook, of Ford] *at his heels a rabble of his companions*
2 minions, gang, rest of the mob Tem IV.i.37 [Prospero to Ariel, of the other spirits] *Go bring the rabble*

rabblement *(n.)* rabble 2H6 IV.viii.1 [stage direction] *Enter again Cade and all his rabblement;* JC I.ii.242

race *(n.)* **1** inherited nature, natural disposition Tem I.ii.358 [Miranda to Caliban] *thy vile race ... had that in't which good natures / Could not abide to be with;* MM II.iv.160
2 origin, stock, ancestry AC I.iii.37 [Cleopatra to Antony] *none our parts so poor / But was a race of heaven* [i.e. of heavenly origin]
3 descendants, children, posterity TNK V.iii.117 [Theseus to Emilia, of Palamon] *lest his race / Should show i'th' world too godlike*
4 family, house, dynasty Cym V.iv.83 [Sicilius, to music, as if to Jupiter] *no longer exercise / Upon a valiant race thy harsh ... injuries*
5 herd, host, company MV V.i.72 [Lorenzo to Jessica] *do but note a wild and wanton herd / Or race of youthful and unhandled colts*
6 course, passage KJ III.iii.39 [King John to Hubert] *If the midnight bell / Did ... / Sound on into the drowsy race of night*
7 [of ginger] root WT IV.iii.45 [Clown to himself] *I must have ... a race or two of ginger* ➤ raze *(n.)*

race out *(v.)* raze out, erase, scrape away R2 II.iii.75 [Berkeley to Bolingbroke] *'Tis not my meaning / To race one title of your honour out* [Q; F *raze*]; R2 III.i.25 ➤ raze out *(v.)*

rack *(n.)* **1** clouds, cloud formations Ham II.ii.482 [First Player to all present] *the rack stand still;* AC IV.xiv.10
2 [of clouds] driven accumulation, billowing movement Sonn 33.6 [of the sun] *permit the basest clouds to ride / With ugly rack on his celestial face*
3 shred of cloud, fragment of mist Tem IV.i.156 [Prospero to Ferdinand, of the spirits] *Leave not a rack behind*
4 machine of torture which stretches the limbs MV III.ii.25 [Bassanio to Portia] *Let me choose, / For as I am, I live upon the rack;* KL V.iii.312; TC I.ii.139

rack *(v.)* **1** drive, move with force E3 II.i.4 [Lodowick alone] *inconstant clouds / That rack upon the carriage of the winds*
2 stretch, strain, extend MV I.i.181 [Antonio to Bassanio, of his credit] *That shall be racked even to the uttermost*
3 exaggerate, inflate, increase MA IV.i.218 [Friar to Leonato, of a prized thing lost] *then we rack the value*
4 exhaust by imposing excessive charges, reduce to poverty 2H6 I.iii.126 [Cardinal to Gloucester] *The commons hast thou racked*
5 torment, torture, scourge MM IV.i.64 [disguised Duke alone] *thousand escapes of wit ... rack thee in their fancies;* E3 I.i.46
6 stretch on the rack 2H6 III.i.376 [York to himself, of Cade] *Say he be taken, racked, and tortured;* LL V.ii.812; MM V.i.313

racker *(n.)* torturer, tormentor LL V.i.19 [Holofernes to Nathaniel, of Armado] *I abhor ... such rackers of orthography*

racking *(adj.)* wind-driven, passing like smoke 3H6 II.i.27 [Richard to Edward] *Three glorious suns ... / Not separated with the racking clouds, / But severed*

raddock *(n.)* ➤ ruddock *(n.)*

rag *(n.)* **1** worthless wretch, good-for-nothing creature, beggar R3 V.iii.329 [King Richard to his army, of the enemy] *Lash hence these overweening rags of France;* MW IV.ii.173; Tim IV.iii.272; TS IV.iii.110
2 smallest bit, scrap, farthing CE IV.iv.84 [Dromio of Ephesus to Antipholus of Ephesus] *surely, master, not a rag of money*

rage *(n.)* **1** violent outburst, furious passion 2H4 IV.iv.63 [King Henry IV to Clarence, of Prince Henry] *When rage and hot blood are his counsellors;* KL IV.iii.16; Luc 424, 468
2 warlike ardour, martial spirit 1H4 I.iii.30 [Hotspur to King Henry] *when the fight was done, / When I was dry with rage and extreme toil;* 1H6 IV.vii.8, 11; KJ II.i.265; R2 II.iv.14
3 violence, fighting, conflict 2H6 III.i.285 [Post to all, of rebellion in Ireland] *Send succours, lords, and stop the rage betime*

4 madness, insanity, derangement **KL** IV.vii.78 [Doctor to Cordelia, of Lear] *The great rage ... is killed in him;* **CE** IV.iii.87, V.i.48, 144; **KL** IV.iv.19; **RJ** IV.iii.53

5 folly, rashness, mad jest **LL** V.ii.417 [Berowne to Rosaline, of his verbal slip] *Yet I have a trick / Of the old rage* [or: sense 4]; **MV** II.i.35

rage (*v.*) rave, show signs of madness **KJ** V.vii.11 [Prince Henry to Pembroke, of King John] *Doth he still rage?*

ragged (*adj.*) **1** rough, harsh **Sonn** 6.1 *Then let not winter's ragged hand deface / In thee thy summer ere thou be distilled;* **AY** II.v.14; **2H4** I.i.151; **Tit** II.i.230

2 broken, jagged, fragmented **E3** V.i.204 [King Edward to King John, of the French towns] *That now are turned to ragged heaps of stones;* **H5** IV.Chorus.50; **3H6** V.iv.27; **MW** IV.iv.29; **Tit** V.iii.132; **Venus** 37

3 rough-hewn, dilapidated, rugged **R2** V.v.21 [Richard alone] *my ragged prison walls;* **E3** I.ii.157; **2H4** I.Induction.35; **R3** IV.i.101; **TG** I.ii.121

4 dressed in rags, unkempt, tattered **2H6** IV.iv.32 [First Messenger to King, of Cade] *His army is a ragged multitude;* **2H4** III.ii.140; **Luc** 892

5 beggarly, shabby, abject **2H4** V.ii.38 [Lord Chief Justice to Prince John, Clarence, and Gloucester] *never shall you see that I will beg / A ragged and forestalled remission*

raging (*adj.*) **1** roving, wanton, riotous **Oth** I.iii.327 [Iago to Roderigo] *we have reason to cool our raging motions, our carnal stings;* **R3** III.v.82; **TC** II.ii.182

2 mad, rash, crazy **Tim** II.i.4 [Senator alone, of Timon] *Still in motion / Of raging waste?*

rail (*v.*) rant, rave, be abusive [about] **AY** III.ii.270 [Jaques to Orlando] *we two will rail against our mistress the world* ☞ **FEW**, p.xxi

railer (*n.*) ranter, reviler **3H6** V.v.38 [Edward to Prince, as he stabs him] *Take that, the likeness of this railer here* [i.e. the image of your mother]

railing (*n.*) abuse, insulting speech, vilification **TN** I.v.90 [Olivia to Malvolio] *There is ... no railing in a known discreet man;* **AY** IV.iii.44; **2H6** III.i.172

railing (*adj.*) abusive, derisive, haranguing **TC** V.iv.28 [Thersites to Hector] *I am a rascal, a scurvy railing knave;* **E3** III.iii.98, IV.i.12; **1H4** III.i.154

raiment (*n.*) clothing, clothes, dress **TS** Induction.ii.4 [Third Servingman to Sly] *What raiment will your honour wear today?;* **Cor** V.iii.94; **KL** II.iv.151; **Sonn** 22.6; **Tim** III.v.34; **TS** II.i.5

raise (*v.*) **1** rouse, excite, incite **WT** II.i.198 [Leontes to all, of Hermione's supposed adultery] *this business / Will raise us all*

2 rouse, stir up, call to arms **MW** V.v.203 [Caius to all] *I'll raise all Windsor*

3 rouse, wake up **JC** IV.iii.245 [Brutus to Varro and Claudius] *It may be I shall raise you by and by / On business to my brother Cassius*

4 elevate in rank, advance, promote **Tim** I.i.123 [Old Athenian to Timon, of Lucilius] *my estate deserves an heir more raised / Than one which holds a trencher;* **3H6** II.ii.22

5 put an end to, finish **1H6** I.ii.13 [Reignier to all, of the English] *Let's raise the siege;* **1H6** I.iv.103

raise up (*v.*) stimulate, stir up, excite **MW** V.v.51 [Evans as a Satyr to all, of a maid] *Raise up the organs of her fantasy*

raising (*n.*) rumour-raising, stirring-up, incitement **Cor** IV.vi.61 [Sicinius to Messenger] *'Tis this slave ... his raising, / Nothing but his report*

raisins of the sun sun-dried grapes **WT** IV.iii.47 [Clown to himself] *I must have ... four pound of prunes, and as many of raisins o'th' sun*

rake up (*v.*) bury, cover up **KL** IV.vi.273 [Edgar to dead Oswald] *Here in the sands / Thee I'll rake up*

ram (*n.*) battering-ram **Luc** 464 [of Tarquin's hand on Lucrece's breast] *Rude ram, to batter such an ivory wall*

ramp (*n.*) whore, brazen woman **Cym** I.vii.134 [Iachimo to Innogen, of Posthumus] *Whiles he is vaulting variable ramps*

rampallian (*n.*) ruffian, villain, scoundrel **2H4** II.i.57 [Page to Hostess] *You rampallian!*

ramping (*adj.*) rampant, rearing up **1H4** III.i.147 [Hotspur to Mortimer, of Glendower] *Sometime he angers me / With telling me of ... a ramping cat;* **3H6** V.ii.13; **KJ** III.i.122

rampired (*adj.*) fortified by ramps of earth, strengthened against attack **Tim** V.iv.47 [First Senator to Alcibiades] *Set but thy foot / Against our rampired gates and they shall ope*

rancour (*n.*) bitterness, hatred, malice **R3** III.ii.86 [Derby to Hastings] *This sudden stab of rancour I misdoubt;* **2H6** III.i.144; **Mac** III.i.66

random, at untended, neglected, uncared for **CE** I.i.43 [Egeon to Duke] *the great care of goods at random left*

range (*n.*) battle line, fighting position **AC** III.xiii.5 [Enobarbus to Cleopatra, of the war] *whose several ranges / Frighted each other*

range (*v.*) **1** wander freely, roam, rove **TN** IV.iii.7 [Sebastian alone, of Antonio] *I found this credit / That he did range the town to seek me out;* **AY** I.iii.66; **E3** III.i.187; **Ham** III.iii.2; **Sonn** 109.5; **TS** III.i.89

2 occupy, take up, be placed **1H4** I.iii.167 [Hotspur to Northumberland and Worcester] *I descend ... / To show the line and the predicament / Wherein you range*

3 arrange, lay out, array [in order] **Cor** III.i.205 [Cominius to Plebeians] *That is the way to ... bury all which yet distinctly ranges / In heaps and piles of ruin*

ranged (*adj.*) arranged, ordered; or: spacious, extensive **AC** I.i.34 [Antony to Cleopatra] *Let ... the wide arch / Of the ranged empire fall!*

ranger (*n.*) gamekeeper, forester **Cym** II.iii.68 [Cloten alone] *'tis gold / Which ... makes / Diana's rangers false themselves* [i.e. the women attending on Innogen]

rank (*n.*) **1** row, line, series **AY** IV.iii.80 [Celia as Aliena to Oliver] *The rank of osiers by the murmuring stream;* **Sonn** 122.3

2 position, place **JC** III.i.69 [Caesar to all, of himself] *I do know but one / That unassailable holds on his rank*

3 way of moving, progress **AY** III.ii.94 [Touchstone to Rosalind] *it is the right butter-women's rank to market* [i.e. the rhymes move along ponderously]

4 (plural) troops, forces, army **Tim** V.iv.39 [First Senator to Alcibiades] *Bring in thy ranks, but leave without thy rage*

rank (*adj.*) **1** growing in abundance, excessively luxuriant [often unattractively] **Ham** I.ii.136 [Hamlet alone, of the world] *Things rank and gross in nature / Possess it merely;* **AY** II.vii.46; **Ham** III.iv.153; **H5** V.ii.45, 50; **H8** V.i.52; **Sonn** 118.12 ☞ over-rank (*adj.*)

2 foul-smelling, stinking **MW** III.v.84 [Falstaff to Ford as Brook] *the rankest compound of villainous smell that ever offended nostril;* **AC** V.ii.212; **Ham** III.iii.36; **2H4** III.i.39; **Sonn** 69.12; **TN** II.v.121

3 foul, festering, diseased **RJ** I.i.50 [Benvolio to Romeo] *Take thou some new infection to thy eye, / And the rank poison of the old will die;* **H8** I.ii.186; **JC** III.i.152; **Sonn** 121.12

4 gross, outlandish, coarse **KL** I.iv.199 [Gonerill to Lear, of his retinue] *breaking forth / In rank and not-to-be-endured riots;* **Ham** II.i.20; **Lover** 307; **Oth** II.i.297; **WT** I.ii.277

5 large, serious, grievous **Tem** V.i.132 [Prospero to Antonio] *I do forgive / Thy rankest fault*

6 bloated, swollen, puffed-up **TC** I.iii.318 [Ulysses to Nestor] *the seeded pride / That hath to this maturity blown up / In rank Achilles;* **2H4** IV.i.64

7 lascivious, lustful, lewd **MV** I.iii.77 [Shylock to Antonio] *the ewes being rank, / In end of autumn turned to the rams;* **Cym** II.iv.176; **Oth** III.iii.230

8 full to overflowing, brimful **Venus** 71 *Rain added to a river that is rank / Perforce will force it overflow the bank*

9 high, good, great **Ham** IV.iv.22 [Captain to Hamlet, of the land being fought over] *Nor will it yield ... / A ranker rate* [i.e. of interest]

10 violent, heated, intemperate **TC** IV.v.132 [Hector to Ajax, of his limbs] *Wherein my sword had not impressure made / Of our rank feud* [or: overblown]

11 strong, stout, firm **AY** IV.i.77 [Rosalind as Ganymede to Orlando] *I should think my honesty ranker than my wit* [possible reading]

12 numerous, frequent, abundant **MW** IV.vi.22 [Fenton to Host, of Anne slipping away with Slender] *While other jests are something rank on foot*

rank (*v.*) **1** arrange in ranks, order in rows **Tim** I.i.68 [Poet to Painter, of Fortune's hill] *The base o'th' mount / Is ranked with all deserts*

2 place, class, put down **AC** IV.ix.21 [Enobarbus to himself] *let the world rank me in register / A master-leaver and a fugitive*

3 find, accompany [by] **RJ** III.ii.117 [Juliet to herself] *sour woe delights in fellowship / And needly will be ranked with other griefs*

rank (*adv.*) densely, thickly, completely **TC** I.iii.196 [Nestor to all, of Ajax] *[he] sets Thersites … / To weaken and discredit our exposure, / How rank soever rounded in with danger*

ranked (*adj.*) drawn up in battle order **KJ** IV.ii.200 [Hubert to King John] *many thousand warlike French / That were embattailed and ranked in Kent*

rankle (*v.*) cause a festering wound **R3** I.iii.290 [Queen Margaret to Buckingham, of Richard] *His venom tooth will rankle to the death*; **R2** I.iii.302

rankly (*adv.*) grossly, very much, completely **Ham** I.v.38 [Ghost to Hamlet] *So the whole ear of Denmark / Is … / Rankly abused*

rankness (*n.*) **1** excess, abundance, profusion **H8** IV.i.59 [Third Gentleman to First Gentleman, of the crowd in the Abbey] *I am stifled / With the mere rankness of their joy* [i.e. its exuberance and smell]

2 excessive growth, rebelliousness **AY** I.i.81 [Oliver alone, of Orlando] *I will physic your rankness*; **KJ** V.iv.54

rank-scented (*adj.*) foul-smelling, stinking **Cor** III.i.66 [Coriolanus to all, of the Citizens] *The mutable, rank-scented meiny*

ransack-constraining (*adj.*) that makes plundering unavoidable **E3** III.ii.49 [Third Frenchman to all] *ransack-constraining war / Sits like to ravens upon your houses' tops*

ransacked (*adj.*) violated, ravished, plundered **E3** II.ii.194 [King Edward to Countess, of Lucrece] *whose ransacked treasury hath tasked / The vain endeavour of so many pens*; **TC** II.ii.151

ransom (*n.*) money owing, amount to be paid **Tim** I.i.109 [Timon to Messenger, of Ventidius] *I will send his ransom*

ranting (*adj.*) boisterous, jovial, noisily convivial **MW** II.i.177 [Page to Ford] *Look where my ranting host of the Garter comes*

rap (*v.*) transport, move with rapture **Cym** I.vii.51 [Innogen to Iachimo] *What … / Thus raps you?*

rape (*n.*) abduction, violent seizure **Tit** I.i.407 [Saturninus to Bassianus] *Thou and thy faction shall repent this rape*; **TC** II.ii.149

rapier (*n.*) ☛ WEAPONS, p.491

rapine (*n.*) rape **Tit** V.ii.59 [Titus to disguised Tamora, of disguised Chiron and Demetrius] *So thou destroy Rapine and Murder here*

rapt (*adj.*) **1** absorbed, engrossed, preoccupied **Tim** I.i.19 [Painter to Poet] *You are rapt, sir, in some work*; **TC** III.iii.123; **Tem** I.ii.77

2 enraptured, entranced, thrilled **Cor** IV.v.119 [Aufidius to Coriolanus] *that I see thee here … dances my rapt heart*;

3 carried away with emotion, lost for words **Tim** V.i.62 [Poet to Timon, of his friends' desertion] *I am rapt, and cannot cover / The monstrous bulk of this ingratitude / With any size of words*

rapture (*n.*) **1** seizure, plundering, carrying away **Per** II.i.156 [Pericles to Fishermen] *spite of all the rapture of the sea*

2 fit, seizure, convulsion **Cor** II.i.199 [Brutus to Sicinius] *Your prattling nurse / Into a rapture lets her baby cry*

rare (*adj.*) **1** marvellous, splendid, excellent **TN** III.i.83 [Sir Andrew to himself, of Viola as Cesario] *That youth's a rare courtier*; **AC** II.ii.210; **AY** V.iv.101; **1H6** II.iii.10; **H8** I.ii.111; **Sonn** 56.14

2 unusual, striking, exceptional **WT** IV.iv.32 [Florizel to Perdita, of the gods] *Their transformations / Were never for a piece of beauty rarer*; **AC** V.i.31; **Cym** I.vii.16; **KL** I.i.260; **Mac** V.vi.64; **Tem** IV.i.123

3 profound, special, exquisite **Cym** I.ii.66 [Innogen to Cymbeline] *I am senseless of your wrath; a touch more rare / Subdues all pangs*

4 infrequent, uncommon, few in number **Sonn** 52.5 *Therefore are feasts so solemn and so rare, / Since seldom coming in the long year set*

rarely (*adv.*) **1** splendidly, beautifully, excellently **TNK** II.i.184 [Emilia to Woman] *This is a pretty colour; will't not do / Rarely upon a skirt*; **AC** IV.iv.11; **Cym** II.iv.75; **MA** III.iv.63; **Tim** IV.iii.468; **TNK** III.iv.16

2 exceptionally, outstandingly, unbelievably **AC** V.ii.158 [Cleopatra to Seleucus] *O rarely base!*; **Per** V.i.68; **WT** V.i.149

rareness (*n.*) exceptional character, rarity **Ham** V.ii.117 [Hamlet to Osrick, of Laertes] *his infusion of such dearth and rareness*

rariety (*n.*) rarity, exceptional quality **E3** II.i.114 [King Edward alone, of the Countess] *The register of all rarieties / Since leathern Adam*

rarity (*n.*) exceptional nature, striking quality **Tem** II.i.61 [Gonzalo to all, of their situation] *The rarity of it is - which is indeed almost beyond credit*; **AW** IV.iii.266; **Phoen** 53

rascal (*n.*) **1** worthless wretch, good-for-nothing **2H4** II.iv.124 [Doll to Pistol] *Away, you cutpurse rascal*; **Cor** I.i.157 [also: sense 2]; **2H4** II.iv.184, V.iv.30; **1H6** I.iii.35, IV.ii.49

2 young or inferior deer in a herd; one of the common herd **AY** III.iii.52 [Touchstone to Audrey, of horns] *the noblest deer hath them as huge as the rascal*; **2H4** II.iv.39; **1H6** IV.ii.49

rascal (*adj.*) worthless, good-for-nothing **2H4** II.iv.223 [Falstaff to Doll, of Pistol] *A rascal bragging slave!*; **2H6** II.iv.47, IV.v.51; **JC** IV.iii.80; **Luc** 671; **Tim** IV.iii.430

rased down obliterated, torn down **Sonn** 64.3 *sometime lofty towers I see down rased*

rased, razed (*adj.*) obliterating, erasing **Sonn** 122.7 [of brain and heart] *Till each to rased oblivion yield his part*

rash (*adj.*) **1** sudden, quickly acting, operating immediately **TC** IV.ii.60 [Aeneas to Troilus] *I scarce have leisure to salute you, / My matter is so rash*; **2H4** IV.iv.48; **JC** IV.iii.119; **Luc** 473; **MM** V.i.389; **WT** I.ii.319

2 quickly lit, briefly flaming **1H4** III.ii.61 [King Henry to Prince Hal] *The skipping King, he ambled up and down, / With … rash bavin wits*

3 hasty, impetuous, impulsive **Tem** I.ii.468 [Miranda to Prospero, of Ferdinand] *Make not too rash a trial of him*; **2H6** IV.i.28 ☛ heady-rash (*adj.*)

rash (*v.*) force, drive; or: slash with **KL** III.vii.57 [Gloucester to Regan] *I would not see … thy fierce sister / In his anointed flesh rash boarish fangs* [Q; F stick]

rash (*adv.*) hastily, impetuously, impulsively **Oth** III.iv.79 [Desdemona to Othello] *Why do you speak so startingly and rash?* [F; Q1 rashly]

rash-levied (*adj.*) hastily raised **R3** IV.iii.50 [King Richard to Ratcliffe] *Ely … troubles me more near / Than Buckingham and his rash-levied strength*

rate (*n.*) **1** quantity, amount, instance **TNK** I.iv.29 [Theseus to all, of Palamon and Arcite] *The very lees of such, millions of rates, / Exceed the wine of others* [i.e. are millions of times more valuable]; **2H4** IV.i.22

2 opinion, estimation, view **Tem** II.i.111 [Alonso to Gonzalo, of Alonso's daughter] *My son is lost, and, in my rate, she too*; **Tem** I.ii.92

3 mode of life, style of living **MV** I.i.127 [Bassanio to Antonio] *Nor do I now make moan to be abridged / From such a noble rate*; **H8** III.ii.127

4 worth, value, merit **RJ** V.iii.301 [Montague to Capulet] *There shall no figure at such rate be set / As that of true and faithful Juliet*; **AW** V.iii.91; **MND** III.i.145

5 cost, expense **3H6** II.ii.51 [King to Clifford] *I'll leave my son my virtuous deeds behind … / For all the rest is held at such a rate / As brings a thousand-fold more care to keep;* **H8** I.i.99

6 price, fee **AW** V.iii.217 [Bertram to King, of Diana] *Her infinite cunning … / Subdued me to her rate*

rate *(v.)* **1** berate, reproach, rebuke, scold **2H6** III.ii.56 [Queen to King] *Why do you rate my lord of Suffolk thus?;* **E3** II.ii.77; **2H4** III.i.64; **MV** I.iii.104; **RJ** III.v.169; **TS** IV.i.170

2 reckon, estimate, appraise **2H6** IV.i.30 [Suffolk to Whitmore] *Rate me at what thou wilt, thou shalt be paid;* **AW** II.i.179; **2H4** I.iii.44; **LL** V.ii.774; **MV** II.vii.26; **Tim** I.i.172

3 allot, apportion, assign **AC** III.vi.25 [Caesar to all, of Antony] *having in Sicily / Sextus Pompeius spoiled, we had not rated him / His part o'th' isle*

4 be worth, count as much as **AC** III.xi.69 [Antony to Cleopatra, of her tears] *one of them rates / All that is won and lost*

rate at *(v.)* berate, reproach, rebuke, scold **2H6** III.i.175 [Cardinal to King, of himself and his associates] *If those … / Be thus upbraided, chid, and rated at*

rated *(adj.)* **1** assessed, exposed, evaluated **KJ** V.iv.37 [Melun to Pembroke, Salisbury, and Bigot, of their executions] *Paying the fine of rated treachery*

2 valued, prized, to be reckoned with **1H4** IV.iv.17 [Archbishop to Sir Michael, of Glendower and the other rebels] *Who with them was a rated sinew too*

ratify *(v.)* make metrically correct, bring into proportion **LL** IV.ii.121 [Holofernes to Nathaniel, of Berowne's letter to Rosaline] *Here are only numbers ratified*

rational *(adj.)* endowed with reason **LL** I.ii.113 [Armado to Mote, of Jaquenetta] *that I took in the park with the rational hind Costard*

ratsbane *(n.)* rat poison **2H4** I.ii.40 [Falstaff to Page, of tradesmen] *I had as lief they would put ratsbane in my mouth as offer to stop it with security;* **1H6** V.iv.29; **KL** III.iv.53

Ratolorum *(n.)* malapropism for 'rotulorum' [= of the rolls] **MW** I.i.8 [Slender to Shallow, of Shallow's position as a justice] *and Ratolorum too*

raught *(v.)* ☛ reach *(v.)*

ravel *(v.)* become entangled, get confused **TG** III.ii.52 [Thurio to Proteus, of Silvia's love] *Lest it should ravel, and be good to none*

ravel out *(v.)* unravel, disentangle, make clear **R2** IV.i.227 [Richard to Northumberland] *must I ravel out / My weaved-up follies?;* **Ham** III.iv.187

ravelled *(adj.)* tangled, confused, jumbled up **Mac** II.ii.37 [Macbeth to Lady Macbeth] *Sleep that knits up the ravelled sleave of care*

raven *(v.)* feed ravenously on, devour voraciously **Cym** I.vii.49 [Iachimo to Innogen] *The cloyed will … ravening first the lamb*

raven up *(v.)* feed ravenously on, devour voraciously **Mac** II.iv.28 [Ross to Macduff] *Thriftless ambition that will raven up / Thine own life's means!*

ravenous *(adj.)* rapacious, predatory, insatiable **Tit** V.iii.194 [Lucius to all] *As for that ravenous tiger, Tamora … / No mournful bell shall ring her burial*

ravin *(adj.)* ravenous, starving, devouring **AW** III.ii.117 [Helena alone] *the ravin lion when he roared / With sharp constraint of hunger*

ravin down *(v.)* gobble ravenously, devour voraciously **MM** I.ii.128 [Claudio to Lucio] *rats that ravin down their proper bane*

ravined, ravened *(adj.)* stuffed with prey, glutted **Mac** IV.i.24 [Third Witch to Witches] *maw and gulf / Of the ravined salt sea shark*

ravish *(v.)* **1** entrance, enrapture, carry away with joy **E3** II.i.79 [Edward to Lodowick] *the strains of poets' wit / Beguile and ravish soft and human minds;* **1H6** V.v.15; **2H6** I.i.32; **LL** I.i.165; **MA** II.iii.56; **Per** III.Chorus.35 ☛ **ARCHAISMS**, p.22

2 snatch from, tear from **TNK** II.i.76 [Palamon to Arcite] *Our good swords now … / Ravished our sides;* **KL** III.vii.38

3 seize, despoil, corrupt **Luc** 778 [Lucrece as if to night] *With rotten damps ravish the morning air*

ravished *(adj.)* abducted, carried off by force **TC** Prologue.9 [Prologue] *The ravished Helen … / With wanton Paris sleeps*

raw *(adj.)* unrefined, unskilled, unpolished **R2** II.iii.42 [Percy to Bolingbroke] *I tender you my service, / Such as it is, being tender, raw, and young;* **AY** III.ii.68; **Ham** V.ii.122; **MV** III.iv.77; **Per** IV.ii.51

rawly *(adv.)* immaturely, so young **H5** IV.i.136 [Williams to disguised King Henry, of those who die in a battle] *some upon their children rawly left*

rawness *(n.)* unprotected state, vulnerable situation **Mac** IV.iii.26 [Malcolm to Macduff] *Why in that rawness left you wife and child*

ray *(v.)* **1** disfigure, stain, blemish **TS** III.ii.52 [Biondello to Tranio as Lucentio, of Petruchio's horse] *rayed with the yellows*

2 dirty, soil, make filthy **TS** IV.i.3 [Grumio alone] *Was ever man so rayed?*

raze *(n.)* [of ginger] root **1H4** II.i.26 [Second Carrier to First Carrier] *I have … two razes of ginger, to be delivered* ☛ **race** *(n.)*

raze *(v.)* alter, take away, get rid of **KL** I.iv.4 [Kent alone] *my good intent / May carry through itself to that full issue / For which I razed my likeness*

raze, raze off *(v.)* take off, pluck off **R3** III.ii.11 [Messenger to Hastings, of Stanley] *He dreamt the boar had razed off his helm;* **R3** III.iv.82

raze, raze out erase, obliterate, wipe out **2H4** V.ii.127 [King Henry V to his brothers, of King Henry IV] *with his spirits sadly I survive … to raze out / Rotten opinion;* **Tit** I.i.454 [Tamora aside to Saturninus, of the Andronici] *I'll … raze their faction and their family;* **Cym** V.v.70; **2H6** I.i.99; **MM** I.ii.11; **Per** I.i.18; **TNK** I.i.33 ☛ race out *(v.)*

raze forth *(v.)* erase, delete, remove **Sonn** 25.11 [of a warrior] *After a thousand victories once foiled, / Is from the book of honour razed forth*

razed *(adj.)* **1** cut, slashed, slit **Ham** III.ii.286 [Hamlet to Horatio] *with two Provincial roses on my razed shoes* [i.e. with decorative openings]

2 ☛ rased *(adj.)*

razorable *(adj.)* ready for shaving **Tem** II.i.254 [Antonio to Sebastian] *till newborn chins / Be rough and razorable*

razure *(n.)* erasure, effacement, obliteration **MM** V.i.13 [Duke to Angelo, of Angelo's deserving] *it deserves / A forted residence 'gainst the tooth of time / And razure of oblivion*

reach *(n.)* **1** capacity, capability, power of attainment **Ham** I.iv.56 [Hamlet to Ghost] *With thoughts beyond the reaches of our souls*

2 capacity of mind, penetration **Ham** II.i.64 [Polonius to Reynaldo] *we of wisdom and of reach*

reach *(v.),* past form **raught** **1** equal, match, attain to **TNK** III.vi.80 [Arcite to Palamon] *you outwent me, / Nor could my wishes reach you* [i.e. I could not fulfil my desire to match you]; **LL** IV.ii.41

2 give, hold out **H5** IV.vi.21 [Exeter to King Henry, of York] *He smiled me in the face, raught me his hand;* **TNK** V.v.91

3 carry off, snatch away, take hold of **AC** IV.ix.29 [Sentry to all, of Enobarbus] *The hand of death hath raught him;* **2H6** II.iii.43

reach at *(v.)* reach out for, strive to attain **2H6** I.i.11 [Duchess to Gloucester, of the crown] *reach at the glorious gold;* **3H6** I.iv.68; **R2** I.iii.72

reaching *(adj.)* far-reaching **2H6** IV.vii.75 [Say to Cade] *Great men have reaching hands*

read *(v.)* **1** interpret, discern, make something of **KJ** I.i.87 [Queen Eleanor to King John] *Do you not read some tokens of my son / In the large composition of this man?;* **Cym** III.v.76

2 reckon, consider, take into account **H8** I.i.104 [Norfolk to Buckingham, of Wolsey] *I advise … you read / The Cardinal's malice and his potency / Together*

read to *(v.)* lecture, tutor, coach **1H4** III.i.43 [Glendower to Hotspur] *Where is he living … / Which calls me pupil or hath read to me?*

ready *(adj.)* **1** eager, willing, ready to act **Tit** I.i.154 [Titus as if to the dead] *Rome's readiest champions, repose you here in rest;* **Tim** I.i.47
2 easy, quick, convenient **TS** I.ii.217 [Tranio as Lucentio to all] *which is the readiest way / To the house of Signor Baptista Minola?*
3 alert, vigilant, attentive **Cor** II.ii.114 [Cominius to all, of Coriolanus] *the din of war 'gan pierce / His ready sense*
4 dressed, clothed **Cym** II.iii.80 [Cloten to Lady, of Innogen] *Your lady's person, is she ready?;* **1H6** II.i.39

ready *(adv.)* readily, quickly, speedily **E3** II.i.68 [King Edward to Lodowick] *Talking of grief, to make thee ready groan*

reaped *(adj.)* barbered, clipped, trimmed **1H4** I.iii.33 [Hotspur to King Henry, of a lord] *his chin new reaped*

rear *(v.)* **1** raise, lift up **2H6** III.ii.34 [Somerset to lords, of the King] *Rear up his body;* **3H6** II.vi.86; **Tem** II.i.300; **Tit** III.i.168
2 raise, incite, rouse up **R2** IV.i.145 [Bishop of Carlisle to Bolingbroke] *if you rear this house against this house* [F]
3 raise, lift up, boost **AC** II.i.35 [Pompey to Menas] *But let us rear / The higher our opinion*

rearward *(n.)* **1** rear, behind the main body of troops **1H6** III.iii.33 [Pucelle to all, of Burgundy] *Now in the rearward comes the Duke and his [troops];* **Sonn** 90.6
2 rearguard action **RJ** III.ii.121 [Juliet to Nurse, of mentioning that Romeo is banished] *with a rearward following Tybalt's death*

rearward of, in the *(prep.)* in the rear of, following on behind **2H4** III.ii.305 [Falstaff alone, of Shallow] *'A came ever in the rearward of the fashion;* **MA** IV.i.124

rearward of, on the *(prep.)* following, immediately after **MA** IV.i.124 [Leonato to Hero] *Myself would, on the rearward of reproaches, / Strike at thy life*

reason *(n.)* **1** power of reason, judgement, common-sense [often opposed to 'passion'] **JC** II.i.21 [Brutus alone, of Caesar] *I have not known when his affections swayed / More than his reason;* **Ham** IV.iv.58; **Oth** I.iii.18; **Tem** V.i.155; **Tit** III.i.217; **TNK** III.vi.228
2 reasoning, argument **TC** II.ii.24 [Hector to Priam, of Helen] *What merit's in that reason which denies / The yielding of her up?;* **H8** V.i.50; **TC** II.ii.38, 117
3 reasonable view, sensible judgement, right opinion **3H6** II.ii.93 [Clifford to Edward, of the succession] *And reason too; / Who should succeed the father but the son?;* **2H4** II.ii.46; **KJ** IV.iii.31; **LL** II.ii.168; **MV** III.v.38; **Tim** I.i.12
4 account, version, explanation **AW** III.i.2 [Duke to Lords] *now have you heard / The fundamental reasons of this war;* **AW** III.i.10; **Cor** V.vi.59; **KL** V.iii.83; **Sonn** 89.4
5 observation, remark, point **LL** V.ii.1 [Nathaniel to Holofernes] *Your reasons at dinner have been sharp and sententious;* **AY** I.iii.6; **MM** I.ii.184; **R3** IV.iv.361; **Sonn** 151.8
6 alternative, choice, possibility **TG** II.iv.210 [Proteus alone, of Silvia] *when I look on her perfections, / There is no reason but I shall be blind;* **2H4** III.ii.320
7 reasonable treatment, justified course of action **MW** I.i.196 [Slender to Shallow] *I shall do that that is reason;* **MW** I.i.218; **Tem** III.ii.120; **Tit** I.i.282

reason *(v.)* **1** talk, speak, converse **MV** II.viii.27 [Salerio to Solanio] *I reasoned with a Frenchman yesterday;* **CE** III.ii.53; **Cor** IV.vi.52; **H5** III.vii.35; **R3** II.iii.39, IV.iv.535
2 argue rationally [about], debate the pros and cons [of] **KL** II.iv.259 [Lear to Regan] *reason not the need!;* **Cym** IV.ii.14; **Ham** II.ii.264; **JC** V.i.96; **KL** II.i.105
3 raise, bring up, discuss **TG** II.i.134 [Valentine to Speed] *What are you reasoning with yourself?;* **KL** V.i.28; **RJ** III.i.51

4 argue for, plead for, support **Cor** V.iii.176 [Volumnia to Coriolanus, of Young Martius] *This boy … / Does reason our petition with more strength*

reasonable *(adj.)* **1** endowed with reason, rational **Tem** V.i.81 [Prospero to the charmed company] *the approaching tide / Will shortly fill the reasonable shore*
2 moderate, not excessive, fair-minded **MW** I.i.195 [Slender to Shallow] *you shall find me reasonable*

reave *(v.)*, past form **reft** rob, deprive **AW** V.iii.86 [King to Bertram, of Helena] *Had you that craft to reave her / Of what should stead her most?;* **Per** II.i.84 [Pericles to Thaisa] *[I] … / Was by the rough seas reft of ships and men;* **CE** I.i.129; **Cym** III.iii.103; **E3** III.i.157; **MA** IV.i.194; **Venus** 1174

rebate *(v.)* **1** check, stop, suppress **E3** I.i.40 [Artois to King Edward, of the King of France] *wherein may our duty be more seen / Than striving to rebate a tyrant's pride*
2 subdue, moderate, make dull **MM** I.iv.60 [Lucio to Isabella, of Angelo] *a man … [who] doth rebate and blunt his natural edge / With profits of the mind*

rebato *(n.)* stiff ornamental collar, ruff **MA** III.iv.6 [Margaret to Hero] *I think your other rebato were better* ☞ **CLOTHING**, p.79

rebel *(adj.)* rebellious, uncontrollable, recalcitrant **JC** III.i.40 [Caesar to Metellus] *Be not fond, / To think that Caesar bears such rebel blood*

rebellion *(n.)* revolt of the flesh, lust **AW** IV.iii.18 [First Lord to Second Lord] *God delay our rebellion!*

rebellious *(adj.)* not obeying, disobedient, mutinous **Ham** II.ii.468 [First Player to all present, of Priam] *His antique sword, / Rebellious to his arm;* **AY** II.iii.49

rebound *(n.)* reflection, return, echo **AC** V.ii.104 [Dolabella to Cleopatra, of her grief] *I do feel, / By the rebound of yours, a grief*

rebuke *(n.)* **1** severe blow, violent check **1H4** V.v.1 [King Henry to all] *Thus ever did rebellion find rebuke*
2 insult, shame, reproach **R2** II.i.166 [York to King Richard] *Nor Gaunt's rebukes … / Have ever made me sour my patient cheek* [i.e. the insults suffered by Gaunt]

rebuke *(v.)* repress, put down, check **Mac** III.i.55 [Macbeth alone, of Banquo] *under him / My genius is rebuked;* **H5** III.vi.119; **KJ** II.i.9; **MND** III.ii.43; **Per** I.i.1

rebuse *(v.)* malapropism for 'abuse' **TS** I.ii.7 [Grumio to Petruchio] *Is there any man has rebused your worship?*

recall *(v.)* revoke, annul, nullify **CE** I.i.148 [Duke to Egeon] *passed sentence may not be recalled*

recanter *(n.)* one who retracts, party of withdrawal **Tim** V.i.144 [Second Senator to Timon, of the state] *which doth seldom / Play the recanter*

recanting *(adj.)* causing an action to be retracted, resulting in withdrawal **R2** I.i.193 [Bolingbroke to King Richard] *The slavish motive of recanting fear;* **Tim** I.ii.16

receipt *(n.)* **1** what is received, acquisition, gain **Luc** 703 *Drunken Desire must vomit his receipt / Ere he can see his own abomination;* **Cor** I.i.110
2 reception, receiving venue **H8** II.ii.137 [King Henry to Wolsey and Campeius] *The most convenient place that I can think of / For such receipt of learning is Blackfriars*
3 recipe, formula, prescription **AW** II.i.105 [Helena to King, of her father] *Many receipts he gave me;* **AW** I.iii.239; **1H4** II.i.87
4 sum received, amount obtained **R2** I.i.126 [Mowbray to Bolingbroke] *Three parts of that receipt I had for Calais*

receive *(v.)* **1** consider, believe, regard **TG** V.iv.78 [Valentine to Proteus] *once again I do receive thee honest;* **Ham** II.ii.436; **Mac** I.vii.74; **TN** III.iv.189
2 understand, take in, comprehend **Per** I.i.1 [Antiochus to Pericles] *you have at large received / The danger of the task you undertake?;* **MM** II.iv.82

3 take in, admit, recruit **Cym** IV.iv.5 [Guiderius to Belarius and Arviragus] *the Romans / Must or for Britons slay us or receive us / For barbarous and unnatural revolts*

received *(adj.)* **1** definite, absolute, positive **MW** V.v.125 [Falstaff to all] *the sudden surprise of my powers, drove the grossness of the foppery into a received belief … that they were fairies*
2 fashionable, accepted as a norm, generally adopted **AW** II.i.55 [Parolles to Bertram, of the Lords' behaviour] *under the influence of the most received star;* **WT** IV.i.11

receiving *(n.)* perception, awareness, discernment **TN** III.i.117 [Olivia to Viola as Cesario] *To one of your receiving / Enough is shown*

receptacle *(n.)* repository, storehouse, receiving-chamber **Tit** I.i.95 [Titus to all, of the tomb] *O sacred receptacle of my joys;* **Per** IV.vi.173; **RJ** IV.iii.39; **Tit** II.iii.235

recheat *(n.)* horn call for bringing hounds together **MA** I.i.222 [Benedick to Claudio] *I will have a recheat winded in my forehead*

reck *(v.)* regard, heed, care [for] **TC** V.vi.26 [Troilus as if to Fate] *I reck not though thou end my life today;* **AY** II.iv.78; **Ham** I.iii.51; **TG** IV.iii.40; **TNK** III.ii.7; **Venus** 283

reckless *(adj.)* negligent, thoughtless, careless **3H6** V.vi.7 [King to Richard, of the Lieutenant] *So flies the reckless shepherd from the wolf*

reckon *(v.)* **1** quantify, calculate, measure **AC** I.i.15 [Antony to Cleopatra] *There's beggary in the love that can be reckoned;* **Sonn** 136.8
2 add up, keep count of **Tim** III.iv.57 [Flavius to Lucius' Servant and Titus, of Timon] *I have no more to reckon, he to spend*

reckon up *(v.)* list, enumerate **Sonn** 121.9 *they that level / At my abuses reckon up their own;* **TS** Induction.ii.91

reckon with *(v.)* make a reckoning of, take full account of what is owed to **Mac** V.vi.100 [Malcolm to all] *We shall not spend a large expense of time / Before we reckon with your several loves*

reckoning *(n.)* **1** counting up, enumeration, calculation **LL** I.ii.40 [Armado to Moth] *I am ill at reckoning;* **H5** IV.i.284; **LL** V.ii.496, 793; **RJ** I.i.33; **TC** III.iii.253
2 bill [at an inn], settling of account **Cym** V.iv.158 [First Gaoler to Posthumus, of his hanging] *A heavy reckoning for you;* **AY** III.iv.29; **1H4** I.ii.49, II.iv.100; **2H4** I.ii.173; **TNK** III.v.129
3 assessment of debts, settlement of accounts **Tim** II.ii.155 [Flavius to Timon] *And at length / How goes our reck'ning?*
4 [of personal qualities] rendering of account, settlement of debts **Ham** I.v.78 [Ghost to Hamlet] *No reckoning made, but sent to my account / With all my imperfections on my head;* **1H4** III.ii.152; **Tim** II.ii.155
5 esteem, estimation, distinction **RJ** I.ii.4 [Paris to Capulet, of him and Montague] *Of honourable reckoning are you both*

reclaim *(v.)* **1** subdue, tame, make obedient **RJ** IV.ii.47 [Capulet to Lady Capulet, of Juliet] *My heart is wondrous light, / Since this same wayward girl is so reclaimed;* **2H6** V.ii.54
2 win back, bring back **1H6** III.iv.5 [Talbot to King] *this arm that hath reclaimed / To your obedience fifty fortresses*

reclusive *(adj.)* secluded, cloistered, withdrawn from society **MA** IV.i.240 [Friar to Leonato, of Hero] *you may conceal her … / In some reclusive and religious life*

recognizance *(n.)* **1** token, sign, symbol **Oth** V.ii.213 [Othello to Gratiano, of Desdemona and Cassio] *she did gratify his amorous works / With that recognizance … that I first gave her*
2 bond recognizing a debt **Ham** V.i.102 [Hamlet to Horatio, of the owner of a skull] *a great buyer of land, with his statutes, his recognizances*

recoil *(v.)* **1** fall away, degenerate, give way **Mac** IV.iii.19 [Malcolm to Macduff] *A good and virtuous nature may recoil / In an imperial charge;* **Cym** I.vii.128
2 yield, defer, give in to **Oth** III.iii.234 [Iago to Othello, of Desdemona] *Her will, recoiling to her better judgement*

3 go back in time, return in memory **WT** I.ii.154 [Leontes to Hermione, of Mamillius] *Looking on the lines / Of my boy's face, methoughts I did recoil / Twenty-three years*

recollect *(v.)* gather up, collect, amass **Per** II.i.50 [Pericles to himself, of the Fishermen] *[they] recollect / All that may men approve*

recollected *(adj.)* studied, artificial, refined **TN** II.iv.5 [Orsino to Viola as Cesario] *light airs and recollected terms / Of these most brisk and giddy-paced times*

recomforture *(n.)* consolation, comfort, solace **R3** IV.iv.425 [King Richard to Queen Elizabeth, of her dead children] *they will breed / Selves of themselves, to your recomforture*

recommend *(v.)* **1** commit, commend, consign **Cor** II.ii.149 [Menenius to Tribunes] *We recommend to you, Tribunes of the People, / Our purpose to them;* **TN** V.i.89
2 inform, notify, communicate to **Oth** I.iii.41 [Messenger to First Senator] *Signor Montano … / With his free duty recommends you thus*

recompense *(n.)* **1** payment for services, reward **MW** IV.vi.55 [Fenton to Host] *I'll make a present recompense;* **Cor** III.i.121
2 repayment, return, compensation **1H6** V.iii.19 [Pucelle to spirits] *My body shall / Pay recompense, if you will grant my suit;* **MA** V.iv.83

recompense *(v.)* compensate, redress, make restitution **1H6** III.i.163 [Warwick to King, of Richard] *So shall his father's wrongs be recompensed*

recompt *(v.)* recount, narrate, report **3H6** II.i.96 [Richard to Warwick, of York's death] *if we should recompt / Our baleful news*

reconciled *(adj.)* absolved, confessed, penitent **Lover** 329 *all that borrowed motion seeming owed, / Would … new pervert a reconciled Maid*

reconcilement *(n.)* reconciliation, appeasement, peace **Ham** V.ii.241 [Laertes to Hamlet] *I stand aloof, and will no reconcilement*

record *(n.)* **1** recollection, memory **TN** V.i.243 [Sebastian to Viola as Cesario, of their father's death] *that record is lively in my soul;* **Sonn** 59.5, 122.8
2 witness, confirmation **R2** I.i.30 [Bolingbroke to King Richard] *heaven be the record to my speech!;* **E3** I.i.32
3 recorded history, public remembrance **AC** IV.xiv.99 [Antony to dead Eros] *My queen and Eros / Have by their brave instruction got upon me / A nobleness in record;* **Tim** I.i.5
4 recorder **TNK** V.i.137 [stage direction] *Still music of records*

record *(v.)* sing, warble, chant **Per** IV.Chorus.27 [Gower alone, of Marina] *She sung, and made the night-bird mute, / That still records with moan;* **TG** V.iv.6

recordation *(n.)* **1** remembrance, recollection, commemoration **2H4** II.iii.61 [Lady Percy to Northumberland] *For recordation to my noble husband*
2 committing to memory, solemn recording **TC** V.ii.118 [Troilus to Ulysses] *To make a recordation to my soul / Of every syllable that here was spoke*

recountment *(n.)* account, narrative, relating [of what has happened] **AY** IV.iii.141 [Oliver to Rosalind and Celia disguised, of his meeting with Orlando] *Tears our recountments had most kindly bathed*

recourse *(n.)* **1** opportunity of going, means of access **R3** III.v.108 [Richard alone] *Now will I … give notice that no manner of person / Have any time recourse unto the princes;* **E3** V.i.27; **MW** II.ii.198; **TG** III.i.112
2 repeated flowing, recurrence **TC** V.iii.55 [Troilus to Hector, of Priam and Hecuba] *Their eyes o'ergalled with recourse of tears*

recover *(v.)* **1** revive, restore to health **AW** III.ii.20 [Countess reading Bertram's letter, of Helena] *she hath recovered the King;* **JC** I.i.24; **Per** III.ii.9; **Tem** II.ii.91; **TNK** I.iv.27; **WT** IV.iv.782
2 get hold of, obtain, get **TN** II.iii.177 [Sir Andrew to Sir Toby] *If I cannot recover your niece, I am a foul way out*

3 reach, get to, make **TG** V.i.12 [Eglamour to Silvia, of the forest] *If we recover that, we are sure enough;* **Tem** III.ii.13

4 recall, recollect, bring to mind **E3** III.iv.94 [Prince Edward to all] *I would recover / My gifts you gave me, and my zealous vow*

5 get back; also: cover again **CE** II.ii.78 [Dromio of Syracuse to Antipholus of Syracuse] *There's no time for a man to recover his hair that grows bald by nature*

recovery (*n.*) **1** attainment, gain, restoration **Ham** V.i.104 [Hamlet to Horatio, of a lawyer] *the recovery of his recoveries* [first instance; pun: sense 2]

2 [legal] procedure for transferring property into full ownership **CE** II.ii.80 [Antipholus of Syracuse to Dromio of Syracuse, of a man recovering his hair] *May he not do it by fine and recovery?;* **Ham** V.i.103; **MW** IV.iii.198

recreant (*n.*) **1** coward, faint-hearted individual **1H6** I.ii.126 [Pucelle to Reignier and Alençon] *distrustful recreants, / Fight till the last gasp;* **MND** III.ii.409; **R2** I.ii.53; **TC** I.iii.287

2 deserter, renegade, villain **2H6** IV.viii.26 [Cade to rebels] *you are all recreants and dastards;* **Cor** V.iii.114

3 heretic, unbeliever, apostate **KL** I.i.166 [Lear to Kent] *Hear me, recreant* [F] [or: sense 2] ➤ **miscreant** (*n.*) 2

recreant (*adj.*) cowardly, faint-hearted, craven **KJ** III.i.129 [Constance to Austria] *hang a calf's skin on those recreant limbs;* **2H4** V.iii.92; **Luc** 710; **R2** I.i.144, iii.106

recreate (*v.*) refresh, restore, enjoy **JC** III.ii.252 [Antony to all, of Caesar's bequests] *common pleasures, / To walk abroad and recreate yourselves*

recreation (*n.*) **1** amusement, entertainment, fun **1H4** I.ii.153 [Falstaff to Poins] *the true prince may - for recreation sake - prove a false thief*

2 source of amusement, figure of fun **TN** II.iii.131 [Maria to Sir Toby, of Malvolio] *If I do not ... make him a common recreation*

3 refreshment, pastime, diversion **WT** II.iii.238 [Leontes to all, of Hermione and Mamillius] *Once a day I'll visit / The chapel where they lie, and tears shed there / Shall be my recreation*

rectifier (*n.*) one who puts things right, director **TNK** III.v.108 [Schoolmaster to Theseus] *I that am the rectifier of all*

rector (*n.*) ruler, governor; or: parish priest **AW** IV.iii.57 [First Lord to Second Lord, of Helena] *Her death ... was faithfully confirmed by the rector of the place*

rectorship (*n.*) rule, government, dominion **Cor** II.iii.204 [Brutus to Citizens] *had you tongues to cry / Against the rectorship of judgement?*

recure (*v.*) heal, make whole, restore to health **Venus** 465 *A smile recures the wounding of a frown;* **R3** III.vii.129; **Sonn** 45.9

rede (*n.*) advice, counsel, guidance **Ham** I.iii.51 [Ophelia to Laertes, of someone who does not follow his own advice] *And recks not his own rede*

redeem (*v.*) **1** free, liberate, extricate **KJ** III.iv.71 [Constance to King Philip] *O that these hands could so redeem my son* [i.e. from prison]; **E3** III.iv.35, 63; **1H6** II.v.88; **TC** V.v.39

2 ransom **CE** I.i.8 [Duke to Egeon, of the merchants] *wanting guilders to redeem their lives;* **1H6** I.iv.34

3 [of time lost] get back, buy back, make amends for **1H6** II.v.108 [Richard to Mortimer] *would some part of my young years / Might but redeem the passage of your age!;* **E3** III.ii.18; **1H4** I.ii.215; **Sonn** 100.5

redeliver (*v.*) repeat, relate, report **Ham** V.ii.175 [Osrick to Hamlet] *Shall I re-deliver you e'en so?* [F; Q1, Q2 *deliver*]

redemption (*n.*) **1** rescue, recovery **TNK** V.iii.82 [Servant to Emilia] *Th'assistants made a brave redemption*

2 ransom, means of release [from debt] **CE** IV.ii.46 [Dromio of Syracuse to Adriana, of his master] *Will you send him, mistress, redemption*

red-lattice (*adj.*) [sign of a] tavern, ale-house **MW** II.ii.26 [Falstaff to Pistol] *[you] will ensconce ... your red-lattice phrases, and your bold beating oaths, under the shelter of your honour!*

redoubted (*adj.*) feared, dreaded, revered **R2** III.iii.198 [Bolingbroke to King Richard] *my most redoubted lord;* **E3** V.i.177; **H5** II.iv.14; **1H6** II.i.8; **MV** III.ii.88

redound (*v.*) fall out, contribute, turn out **2H6** IV.ix.47 [Buckingham to King] *I ... doubt not so to deal / As all things shall redound unto your good*

redress (*n.*) **1** relief, assistance, help, comfort **R2** III.ii.32 [Bishop of Carlisle to King Richard] *heaven's offer we refuse, / The proffered means of succour and redress;* **1H6** IV.iii.25, V.iii.18; **3H6** II.i.20; **KJ** III.iv.23; **TNK** II.ii.20

2 remedy, amendment, improvement **KL** I.iv.201 [Gonerill to Lear, of his knights' behaviour] *I had thought ... / To have found a safe redress;* **KL** I.iv.205

redress (*v.*) repair, remedy, put right **PassP** XIII.10 *broken glass no cement can redress;* **3H6** V.v.2

reduce (*v.*) restore, bring back, lead back **R3** II.ii.68 [Queen Elizabeth to all] *All springs reduce their currents to mine eyes;* **H5** V.ii.63; **R3** V.v.36; **TNK** IV.iii.93

reechy (*adj.*) **1** dirty, filthy, squalid **Ham** III.iv.185 [Hamlet to Gertrude] *a pair of reechy kisses;* **Cor** II.i.201

2 begrimed by smoke, discoloured, filthy **MA** III.iii.131 [Borachio to Conrade] *like Pharoah's soldiers in the reechy painting*

reed (*adj.*) reedy, squeaking **MV** III.iv.67 [Portia to Nerissa, of dressing as men] *I'll ... speak between the change of man and boy / With a reed voice*

re-edify (*v.*) rebuild, restore **Tit** I.i.354 [Titus to all, of the tomb] *Which I have sumptuously re-edified;* **R3** III.i.71

reek (*n.*) foggy vapour, steam, fume, smoke **Cor** III.iii.121 [Coriolanus to Plebeians] *You common cry of curs, whose breath I hate / As reek o'th' rotten fens;* **MW** III.iii.74

reek (*v.*) **1** steam, smoke, give off vapour **JC** III.i.158 [Antony to all] *whilst your purpled hands do reek and smoke;* **Cor** II.ii.117; **Cym** I.iii.2; **H5** IV.iii.101; **LL** IV.iii.138; **Sonn** 130.8

2 break into a sweat, perspire **Venus** 555 [of Venus] *Her face doth reek and smoke;* **H8** II.iv.208

reeking (*adj.*) **1** sweaty, heated, perspiring **KL** II.iv.29 [disguised Kent to Lear] *came ... a reeking post, / Stewed in his haste*

2 smeared with blood, freshly bloodstained **E3** III.iv.102 [King Edward to Prince Edward] *with thy sword, yet reeking warm*

reeky (*adj.*) foul-smelling, smoky **RJ** IV.i.83 [Juliet to Friar, of being in a charnel-house] *with dead men's rattling bones, / With reeky shanks and yellow chapless skulls*

reels (*n.*) [plural] revels, revelry, merrymaking **Ham** I.iv.9 [Hamlet to Horatio] *The King doth wake tonight and takes his rouse, / Keeps wassail, and the swaggering upspring reels;* **AC** II.vii.92

reel (*v.*) waver, become unsteady, turn suddenly **Sonn** 7.10 [of the sun in the evening] *Like feeble age he reeleth from the day;* **TNK** V.iv.21

refel (*v.*) refuse, deny, reject **MM** V.i.94 [Isabella to Duke, of Angelo] *he refelled me*

refer (*v.*) **1** entrust, commit, commend **WT** III.ii.114 [Hermione to all] *I do refer me to the oracle;* **MM** III.i.246; **Oth** I.ii.64

2 assign, give, bestow **Cym** I.i.6 [First Gentleman to Second Gentleman, of Cymbeline] *His daughter ... hath referred herself / Unto a poor but worthy gentleman*

reference (*n.*) **1** case for consideration, referring for a decision **AC** V.ii.23 [Proculeius to Cleopatra] *Make your full reference freely to my lord;* **AW** V.iii.29

2 [unclear meaning] designation, appointment, assignment **Oth** I.iii.235 [Othello to Duke] *I crave fit disposition for my wife, / Due reference of place and exhibition*

refigure (*v.*) make a new likeness of, replicate **Sonn** 6.10 *Ten times thyself were happier than thou art, / If ten of thine ten times refigured thee*

refined *(adj.)* civilized, cultivated, sophisticated **R2** IV.i.130 [Bishop of Carlisle to all] *forfend it God / That in a Christian climate souls refined / Should show so heinous ... a deed!*

reflect *(v.)* shine, cast a bright light **Tit** I.i.229 [Titus to Tribunes, of Saturninus] *whose virtues will, I hope, / Reflect on Rome as Titan's rays on earth;* **Luc** 376

reflection *(n.)* return, turning back, retrogression [at the spring equinox] **Mac** I.ii.25 [Captain to King] *the sun 'gins his reflection, / Shipwracking storms and direful thunders*

reflex *(n.)* reflection, image, shadow **RJ** III.v.20 [Romeo to Juliet, of the light in the sky] *'Tis but the pale reflex of Cynthia's brow*

reflex *(v.)* throw, cast, shed **1H6** V.iv.87 [Pucelle to all] *May never glorious sun reflex his beams / Upon the country where you make abode*

reform *(v.)* malapropism for 'inform' **MA** V.i.241 [Dogberry to Don Pedro] *our Sexton hath reformed Signor Leonato of the matter*

reformation *(n.)* radical political change, new government **2H6** IV.ii.61 [Cade to all] *your captain is brave, and vows reformation*

refractory *(adj.)* rebellious, obstinate, umanageable **TC** II.ii.183 [Hector to Paris and Troilus, of laws] *To curb those raging appetites that are / Most disobedient and refractory*

refrain *(v.)* restrain, hold back, keep under control **3H6** II.ii.110 [Richard to Northumberland] *scarce I can refrain / The execution of my big-swollen heart / Upon that Clifford*

reft *(v.)* ☞ reave *(v.)*

refuge *(n.)* resource, last defence, final recourse **1H6** V.iv.69 [Richard to all, of Pucelle] *I did imagine what would be her refuge;* **Cor** V.iii.11; **Luc** 1654

refuge *(v.)* shelter from, take refuge from **R2** V.v.26 [Richard alone, of beggars in the stocks] *refuge their shame / That many have, and others must sit there*

refuse *(n.)* dross, dregs, leavings **Sonn** 150.6 *in the very refuse of thy deeds, / There is such strength and warrantise of skill*

refuse *(v.)* spurn, disown, cast off **RJ** II.ii.34 [Juliet as if to Romeo] *Deny thy father and refuse thy name;* **MA** IV.i.182, ii.60

regard *(n.)* **1** consideration, concern, thought, heed **Mac** III.ii.12 [Lady Macbeth to Macbeth] *Things without all remedy / Should be without regard;* **1H6** IV.v.22; **Luc** 277, 305; **Tim** I.ii.249; **TS** IV.i.112

2 consideration, respect, factor **JC** III.i.224 [Brutus to Antony] *Our reasons are so full of good regard;* **E3** II.ii.132; **Ham** III.i.87; **KL** I.i.239

3 respect, repute, esteem **H5** II.iv.117 [Exeter to Dauphin, in reply to 'What to him from England?'] *Scorn and defiance, slight regard, contempt;* **2H4** I.ii.170; **1H6** IV.i.145; **JC** IV.ii.12; **TC** III.iii.128

4 look, glance, gaze **TN** V.i.209 [Sebastian to Olivia] *You throw a strange regard upon me;* **MM** II.v.20; **TC** III.iii.254; **Tem** III.i.40; **TN** II.v.52, 66

5 view, prospect, sight **Oth** II.i.40 [Montano to all] *throw out our eyes for brave Othello, / Even till we make the main and th'aerial blue / An indistinct regard* [i.e. till our eyes become unable to distinguish sea from sky]

regard *(v.)* **1** take note of, pay heed to, value **TG** III.i.256 [Proteus to Valentine] *Regard thy danger;* **Cor** III.i.67; **2H6** II.i.18, IV.ii.10; **TG** III.i.70; **Tit** V.iii.130

2 esteem, repute, respect **JC** V.iii.88 [Titinius alone, as if to Brutus] *see how I regarded Caius Cassius;* **Cor** V.vi.144

3 gaze upon, look down on, observe **JC** V.iii.21 [Cassius to Pindarus] *Regard Titinius, / And tell me what thou not'st about the field;* **TNK** V.i.15

4 tend, look after, take care of **1H6** III.ii.86 [Talbot to all, of Bedford] *regard this dying prince*

regard, in *(conj.)* insofar as **1H6** V.iv.124 [Winchester to the French] *in regard King Henry gives consent / Of mere compassion and of lenity*

regardfully *(adv.)* respectfully, with great esteem, with high praise **Tim** IV.iii.82 [Timandra to and of Timon] *Is this th' Athenian minion whom the world / Voiced so regardfully?*

regenerate *(adj.)* **1** renegade, degenerate, unnatural **E3** I.i.105 [Lorraine to Artois] *Regenerate traitor*

2 reborn, formed anew **R2** I.iii.70 [Bolingbroke to John of Gaunt] *O thou ... / Whose youthful spirit in me regenerate*

regent *(n.)* ruler, governor, sovereign **LL** III.i.178 [Berowne alone, of Cupid] *Regent of love-rhymes;* **Per** V.i.187; **R2** II.i.109

REGRETS

Several distinctive forms are used to express the range of emotions which include regret, grief, sorrow, lament, and remorse. Some are intensified by being used in conjunction with an emphatic word or phrase, or can be preceded by *O* or *Ah*. A number are used in the Nurse's report of Tybalt's death (**RJ** III.ii.37ff.) and Gertrude's reaction to Ophelia's madness (**Ham** IV.v.27ff.).

Item	Location	Example
alack, 'lack	**AY** IV.iii.53	*Alack, in me what strange effect*
alack the day	**RJ** III.ii.39	*Alack the day! he's gone, he's killed*
alack for woe	**R2** III.iii.70	*alack for woe / That any harm should stain so fair a show!*
alas	**Ham** IV.v.37	*Alas, look here, my lord*
alas the day	**AY** III.ii.212	*Alas the day, what shall I do with my doublet and hose?*
ay me	**Ham** III.iv.52	*Ay me! what news?*
'lack	**Cym** IV.ii.374	*'Lack, good youth!*
out alas	**Tit** II.iii.258	*out alas, here have we found him dead*
well-a-day	**MW** III.iii.93	*O well-a-day, Mistress Ford*
well-a-near	**Per.**III.Chorus.51	*The lady shrieks and, well-a-near, / Does fall in travail*
weraday	**RJ** III.ii.37	*Ah, weraday! He's dead*
woe	**Ham** II.ii.500	*But who, ah woe!, had seen the mobled Queen*

☞ **EXCLAMATIONS**, p.158

regiment (*n.*) rule, regimen, normal state **AC** III.vi.95 [Maecenas to Octavia] *Antony … gives his potent regiment to a trull / That noises it against us;* **TNK** IV.iii.94

region (*n.*) **1** sky, air, heavens **Ham** II.ii.485 [First Player to all present] *the dreadful thunder / Doth rend the region;* **RJ** II.ii.21
2 rank, sphere, social standing **MW** III.ii.67 [Page to Host, of Fenton as a suitor for Anne] *He is of too high a region;* **Cym** V.iv.93

region (*adj.*) in the sky, of the air **Ham** II.ii.576 [Hamlet alone] *all the region kites;* **Sonn** 33.12

register (*n.*) **1** record, catalogue, inventory **AC** IV.ix.21 [Enobarbus to himself] *let the world rank me in register / A master-leaver and a fugitive;* **Lover** 52; **MW** II.ii.181; **Sonn** 123.9
2 registrar, recorder **Luc** 765 [Lucrece as if to night] *Dim register and notary of shame*

register (*v.*) record, formally write down **R3** III.i.75 [Prince Edward to Buckingham, of the origins of the Tower] *say … it were not registered*

regreet (*n.*) fresh greeting, return of salutation **MV** II.ix.89 [Messenger to Portia, of Bassanio's messenger] *he bringeth sensible regreets;* **KJ** III.i.241

regreet (*v.*) greet again, salute upon returning **E3** III.iv.77 [Prince Edward to all] *I regreet you all with hearty thanks;* **R2** I.iii.67, 142, 186

regress (*n.*) ➤ egress and regress

reguerdon (*n.*) recompense, reward, repayment **1H6** III.i.172 [King to Richard] *in reguerdon of that duty done*

reguerdon (*v.*) recompense, reward, repay **1H6** III.iv.23 [King to Talbot] *Yet never have you tasted our reward / Or been reguerdoned with so much as thanks*

regular (*adj.*) established, prescribed, constituted **Tim** V.iv.61 [Alcibiades to Senators] *not a man / Shall … offend the stream / Of regular justice in your city's bounds*

rehearsal (*n.*) story, account, recounting **2H6** I.ii.24 [Duchess to Gloucester, of his dream] *I'll requite it / With sweet rehearsal of my morning's dream;* **TNK** I.iii.78

rehearse (*v.*) **1** relate, recount, give an account of **TS** I.ii.122 [Hortensio to Petruchio, of Katherina's faults] *those defects I have before rehearsed;* **1H6** III.i.13; **Sonn** 38.4, 81.11; **TG** IV.i.25; **WT** V.ii.60
2 pronounce, speak, utter **MND** V.i.387 [Titania to Fairies] *rehearse your song by rote;* **R2** V.iii.127; **Sonn** 71.11
3 repeat, recite, say over again **TG** III.i.346 [Launce to Speed, of the last point made] *Rehearse that once more*

reign (*v.*) have power, exercise influence **Cym** V.v.373 [Cymbeline to Arviragus and Guiderius] *after this strange starting from your orbs, / You may reign in them now!*

rein (*n.*) **1** control, restraint, curb **KL** III.i.27 [disguised Kent to Gentleman, of Albany and Cornwall] *the hard rein which both of them hath borne / Against the old kind King*
2 (plural) loins, kidneys **MW** III.v.21 [Falstaff to Bardolph] *my belly's as cold as if I had swallowed snowballs for pills to cool the reins*

reinforce (*v.*) obtain reinforcements **Cym** V.ii.18 [Lucius to Iachimo] *or betimes / Let's re-inforce, or fly* [F]

reinforcement (*n.*) fresh attack, renewal of force **Cor** II.ii.111 [Cominius to all, of Coriolanus] *with a sudden reinforcement struck / Corioles like a planet*

rejoice (*v.*) gladden, cheer, make joyful **E3** V.i.188 [King Edward to Prince Edward] *As things long lost when they are found again, / So doth my son rejoice his father's heart*

rejoicer (*n.*) cheerer, encourager, consoler **TNK** V.i.121 [Palamon praying to Venus] *I am … / To those who would [love] and cannot, a rejoicer*

rejoicingly (*adv.*) in an exulting manner, with delight **Cym** III.v.146 [Cloten alone, of Innogen] *She hath despised me rejoicingly*

rejoindure (*n.*) reunion, reuniting **TC** IV.iv.35 [Troilus to Cressida] *injury of chance … rudely beguiles our lips / Of all rejoindure*

rejourn (*v.*) put off, postpone, adjourn **Cor** I.i.67 [Menenius to Brutus and Sicinius] *You … rejourn the controversy of threepence to a second day of audience*

relapse (*n.*) [unclear meaning] falling back, return; rebound **H5** IV.iii.107 [King Henry to Montjoy, of the plague released by dead English bodies] *[who] Break out into a second course of mischief, / Killing in relapse of mortality* [i.e. with a deadly second effect]

relation (*n.*) **1** report, account, narration **Mac** IV.iii.173 [Macduff to Ross] *O relation / Too nice and yet too true;* **Cym** II.iv.86; **Per** V.i.123; **TC** III.iii.201; **Tem** V.i.164; **WT** V.iii.130
2 relationship, connection, association **Mac** III.iv.123 [Macbeth to Lady Macbeth] *Augurs and understood relations have … brought forth / The secret'st man of blood* [or: narratives]

relative (*adj.*) pertinent, relevant, substantial **Ham** II.ii.602 [Hamlet alone] *I'll have grounds / More relative than this*

release (*v.*) give up, hand over, transfer **R2** IV.i.209 [Richard to all] *With mine own breath release all duteous oaths;* **2H6** I.i.51

relent (*v.*) yield, give way, give up **Venus** 200 [Venus to Adonis] *stone at rain relenteth* [i.e. eventually wears away]; **MM** III.i.232; **MW** II.ii.29

relenting (*adj.*) soft-hearted, sympathetic, pitying **Luc** 1829 [Brutus to Collatine] *do not steep thy heart / In such relenting dew of lamentations;* **2H6** III.i.227; **R3** IV.iv.431

relic (*n.*) memory, trace, recollection **AW** V.iii.25 [King to Lafew, of Bertram's offence] *deeper than oblivion we do bury / Th'incensing relics of it;* **JC** II.ii.89

relief (*n.*) **1** assistance, help, aid **Cym** III.v.116 [Cloten to Pisanio] *thou shouldst neither want my means for thy relief, nor my voice for thy preferment*
2 refreshment, sustenance, pasture **Venus** 235 [Venus to Adonis, of her body] *Within this limit is relief enough*

relier (*n.*) thing relied upon **Luc** 639 [Lucrece to Tarquin] *to thee, my heaved-up hands appeal, / Not to seducing lust, thy rash relier*

relieve (*v.*) aid, assist, rescue **AW** V.iii.86 [King to Bertram, of Helena's ring] *by this token / I would relieve her;* **AC** V.ii.41; **Cym** V.v.401; **KL** III.iii.13, 17; **TN** III.iv.352

religion (*n.*) **1** religious observance, spiritual duty, obligation **AC** V.ii.199 [Dolabella to Cleopatra] *your command, / Which my love makes religion to obey;* **AY** IV.i.182; **RJ** I.ii.87
2 religious belief; or: fear, superstition **Cym** I.v.133 [Iachimo to Posthumus] *I see you have some religion in you*

religious (*adj.*) **1** devout, conscientious, scrupulous **TN** III.iv.380 [Fabian to Sir Andrew, of Viola as Cesario] *a most devout coward, religious in it!* [i.e. treating cowardice as if it were a religion]; **H8** IV.ii.74; **Sonn** 31.6
2 sacred, solemn, inviolate **Ham** III.iii.8 [Guildenstern to Claudius] *Most holy and religious fear it is / To keep those many many bodies safe / That live and feed upon your majesty*
3 member of a religious order **AY** III.ii.332 [Rosalind to Orlando] *an old religious uncle of mine taught me to speak*

religiously (*adv.*) **1** in accord with religious belief **Tit** I.i.127 [Titus to Tamora, of the dead] *for their brethren slain / Religiously they ask a sacrifice*
2 solemnly, with all due ceremony **KJ** III.i.140 [Cardinal Pandulph to King John, of the Pope] *I … in his name religiously demand / Why thou against the church … / So wilfully dost spurn*
3 reverently, piously, devoutly **LL** IV.ii.146 [Nathaniel to Holofernes, of reading Berowne's letter] *you have done this in the fear of God, very religiously*

relinquish (*v.*) abandon, desert, give up [by] **AW** II.iii.10 [Lafew to Parolles, of the King] *To be relinquished of the artists* [i.e. thought to be incurable]

reliques (*n.*) antiquities, ancient ruins, old places **TN** III.iii.19 [Sebastian to Antonio] *Shall we go see the reliques of this town?*

relish (*n.*) **1** trace, suggestion, hint **Mac** IV.iii.95 [Malcolm to Macduff] *verity, temperance, stableness … / I have no relish of them;* **Ham** III.iii.92; **2H4** I.ii.98

2 liking, taste, inclination **Cor** II.i.182 [Menenius to Coriolanus, of the Tribunes] *We have some old crab-trees here at home that will not / Be grafted to your relish;* **TN** IV.i.59

3 kind, quality, type **H5** IV.i.107 [disguised King Henry to Bates, of the King] *his fears … be of the same relish as ours are*

4 taste, flavour, savour **TC** III.ii.17 [Troilus alone] *Th'imaginary relish is so sweet / That it enchants my sense*

relish (*v.*) **1** have a flavour [of], taste, savour **Cym** III.ii.30 [Innogen to Pisanio, of Posthumus' letter] *Let what is here contained relish … of his content;* **AY** III.ii.227; **Ham** III.i.118; **Per** II.v.61; **TNK** I.ii.77

2 feel, experience, sense **Tem** V.i.23 [Prospero to Ariel] *myself … that relish all as sharply*

3 be acceptable, find favour **WT** V.ii.120 [Autolycus to himself, of Perdita's background] *had I been the finder-out of this secret, it would not have relished among my other discredits*

4 appreciate, like, approve of **Oth** II.i.162 [Cassio to Desdemona, of Iago] *you may relish him more in the soldier than in the scholar;* **WT** II.i.167

5 sing, warble, croon **Luc** 1126 [Lucrece to birds] *Relish your nimble notes to pleasing ears;* **TG** II.i.19

reliver (*v.*) restore, hand over, give up again **MM** IV.iv.5 [Angelo to Escalus, of meeting the Duke at the gates] *why … reliver our authorities there?*

relume (*v.*) relight, rekindle, burn afresh **Oth** V.ii.13 [Othello to himself, of Desdemona] *once put out thy light … / I know not where is that Promethean heat / That can thy light relume* [F re-*Lume*; Q1 *returne*]

remain (*n.*) remainder, rest **Cym** III.i.86 [Cymbeline to Lucius] *All the remain is 'Welcome'* [i.e. all that is left to say]; **Cor** I.iv.64; **JC** V.v.1

remain (*v.*) dwell, live, reside **Cym** IV.iii.14 [Pisanio to Cymbeline, of Innogen] *I nothing know where she remains;* **AY** III.ii.215; **Tem** I.ii.424

remainder (*n.*) **1** balance, amount remaining unpaid **R2** I.i.130 [Mowbray to Bolingbroke] *my sovereign liege was in my debt / Upon remainder of a dear account* [i.e. the balance of a heavy debt]

2 remaining wealth, residue of a fortune **Tim** IV.iii.401 [First Bandit to others, of Timon's gold] *It is some poor fragment, some slender ort of his remainder*

3 rest, remaining people **Cym** I.ii.60 [Posthumus to Innogen] *The gods … bless the good remainders of the court!;* **KL** I.iv.246

4 subsequent heir, person who has a further interest **AW** IV.iii.272 [Parolles to First Soldier, of Dumaine] *he will … cut th'entail from all remainders*

remainder (*adj.*) left-over, remaining, uneaten **AY** II.vii.39 [Jaques to Duke Senior, of Touchstone's brain] *as dry as the remainder biscuit / After a voyage;* **TC** II.ii.71

remand (*v.*) refer, send back, hand over **Tim** V.iv.62 [Alcibiades to Senators, of soldiers who offend] *[they] shall be remanded to your public laws / At heaviest answer* [F *remedied*] ➤ remedy (*v.*)

remarkable (*adj.*) wonderful, extraordinary, exceptional **AC** IV.xv.67 [Cleopatra to all, of dead Antony] *there is nothing left remarkable / Beneath the visiting moon*

remediate (*adj.*) remedial, restorative, healing **KL** IV.iv.17 [Cordelia to Doctor, as if to the herbs of the earth] *Be aidant and remediate*

remedy (*n.*) help, relief, alternative **1H6** V.iii.135 [Suffolk to Reignier] *there is remedy enough;* **1H6** V.iii.132

remedy, no no question, no alternative **MW** II.ii.118 [Mistress Quickly to Falstaff, of Mistress Page] *You must send her your page - no remedy*

remedy (*v.*) hand over for remedy, send for correction **Tim** V.iv.62 [Alcibiades to Senators, of soldiers who offend] *[they] shall be remedied to your public laws / At heaviest answer* [F] ➤ remand (*v.*)

remember (*v.*) **1** remind, bring to someone's mind **Tem** I.ii.243 [Ariel to Prospero] *Since thou dost give me pains, / Let me remember thee what thou has promised;* **H5** V.Chorus.43; **KJ** III.iv.96; **R2** I.iii.269; **R3** II.v.23; **WT** III.ii.228

2 recollect, recall, call to mind **Tem** I.ii.406 [Ferdinand to himself] *This ditty does remember my drowned father;* **AY** III.v.131; **KL** IV.vi.229; **Sonn** 74.12; **Tim** II.ii.233; **TS** IV.ii.96

3 commemorate, acknowledge, reward, recognize **1H4** V.iv.100 [Prince Hal to dead Hotspur] *Thy ignominy sleep with thee in the grave, / But not remembered in thy epitaph;* **Cor** II.i.45; **MA** I.i.12; **Per** II.Chorus.13

4 mention, make known **2H4** V.ii.142 [King Henry V to all] *Our coronation done, we will accite, / As I before remembered, all our state;* **H8** IV.ii.160

remembrance (*n.*) **1** memory, bringing to mind, recollection **AW** V.iii.20 [King to Lafew] *Praising what is lost / Makes the remembrance dear* ➤ FEW, p.xxi

2 reminder **2H4** V.ii.115 [King Henry V to Lord Chief Justice, giving him the sword of justice] *With this remembrance: that you use the same … / As you have done 'gainst me*

3 notice, paying attention **Mac** III.ii.30 [Macbeth to Lady Macbeth] *Let your remembrance apply to Banquo;* **2H4** IV.i.202; **TN** V.i.279

4 love-token, keepsake, memento **Ham** III.i.93 [Ophelia to Hamlet] *I have remembrances of yours;* **MV** IV.i.419; **Oth** III.iii.288, iv.182; **TG** II.ii.5

remembrance (*v.*) mistake for 'remember' **MW** III.iii.224 [Evans to Caius] *remembrance tomorrow on the lousy knave, mine host*

remembrancer (*n.*) official reminder, aide-memoire **Mac** III.iv.36 [Macbeth to Lady Macbeth] *Sweet remembrancer!;* **Cym** I.vi.77

remiss (*adj.*) careless, inattentive, negligent **1H6** IV.iii.29 [Richard to Lucy] *thus we die while remiss traitors sleep;* **Ham** IV.vii.133

remission (*n.*) **1** pardon, forgiveness **Luc** 714 *The guilty rebel for remission prays;* **2H4** V.ii.38; **TG** I.ii.65

2 power to pardon, inclination to forgive **MM** V.i.495 [Duke to all] *I find an apt remission in myself;* **Cor** V.ii.80

remissness (*n.*) negligence, laxity, carelessness **MM** II.ii.96 [Angelo to Isabella] *future evils, / Either now, or by remissness new, conceived* [debatable punctuation]

remit (*v.*) give up, resign, surrender **LL** V.ii.459 [Berowne to Princess, of her and the jewel] *I remit both twain*

remonstrance (*n.*) revelation, display, manifestation **MM** V.i.389 [Duke to Isabella] *I … would not rather / Make rash remonstrance of my hidden power*

remorse (*n.*) **1** pity, regret, sorrow **1H6** V.iv.97 [Winchester to Richard] *the states of Christendom, / Moved with remorse of these outrageous broils;* **Ham** II.ii.489; **3H6** III.i.40; **MA** IV.i.209; **MW** III.v.9; **R3** V.iii.20

2 pity, compassion, tenderness **E3** V.i.34 [King Edward to Calais Citizens] *for yourselves, look you for no remorse;* **KJ** IV.iii.50; **Mac** I.v.42; **MM** II.ii.54; **Tem** V.i.76; **Venus** 257

3 consideration, thoughtfulness for others **TN** II.iii.89 [Malvolio to Sir Toby, Sir Andrew, and Feste] *ye squeak out your coziers' catches without any mitigation or remorse of voice*

remorseful (*adj.*) **1** conscience-stricken, guilty, full of sorrow **R3** I.ii.155 [Richard to Anne, of his eyes] *which never shed remorseful tear;* **AW** V.iii.58; **2H6** IV.i.1

2 compassionate, caring, full of pity **TG** IV.iii.13 [Silvia to Eglamour] *thou art … / Valiant, wise, remorseful*

remotion (*n.*) removal, departure; or: remoteness **Tim** IV.iii.344 [Timon to Apemantus, of being a leopard] *All thy safety were remotion;* **KL** II.iv.109

remove (n.) **1** change of residence, departure **KL** II.iv.4 [Gentleman to Lear, of Regan and Cornwall] *The night before there was no purpose in them / Of this remove;* **AC** I.ii.197; **AW** V.iii.131; **MM** I.i.43
2 exchange, switch, substitution **LL** V.ii.135 [Princess to her ladies, of changing favours] *so shall your loves / Woo contrary, deceived by these removes;* **PassP** XVII.8
3 removal, departure, elimination **Ham** IV.v.82 [Claudius to Gertrude, of Hamlet] *he most violent author / Of his own just remove*
4 removal, raising [of a siege] **Cor** I.ii.28 [Second Senator to Aufidius, of the Romans] *If they set down before's, for the remove / Bring up your army*

remove (v.) go, move off, depart **Mac** V.iii.2 [Macbeth to all] *Till Birnan Wood remove to Dunsinane / I cannot taint with fear;* **AW** V.i.23; **AY** III.iv.51; **1H6** II.v.104; **H8** II.i.42; **KJ** V.ii.33

removed (adj.) **1** remote, secluded, further away **Ham** I.iv.61 [Marcellus to Hamlet, of the Ghost] *It waves you to a more removed ground;* **AY** III.ii.330; **MM** I.iii.8; **WT** V.ii.105
2 estranged, remote, alienated **TN** V.i.87 [Antonio to Orsino, of Viola as Cesario] *[he] grew a twenty years' removed thing / While one would wink*
3 at a remove, not closely involved **1H4** IV.i.35 [Hotspur to Worcester, of Northumberland] *nor did he think it meet / To lay so dangerous and dear a trust / On any soul removed but on his own*
4 degree separated in line of succession **KJ** II.i.186 [Constance to King John, of Queen Eleanor and Arthur] *God hath made ... her the plague / On this removed issue* [i.e. a generation removed from her - her grandson]

removedness (n.) absence [from court], non-attendance **WT** IV.ii.36 [Polixenes to Camillo, of Florizel] *I have eyes under my service which look upon his removedness* [i.e. I have people watching him]

rend (v.) tear apart, lay waste, devastate **MV** II.v.5 [Shylock to Launcelot] *Thou shalt not ... sleep, and snore, and rend apparel out;* **AW** III.vi.45

render (n.) **1** account, declaration, admission **Cym** IV.iv.11 [Belarius to Guiderius and Arviragus] *newness of Cloten's death ... may drive us to a render / Where we have lived;* **Tim** V.i.147
2 rendering up, surrender, account **Sonn** 125.12 *But mutual render only me for thee;* **Cym** V.iv.17

render (v.) **1** give up, surrender, yield **Mac** V.vi.34 [Seyward to Malcolm] *The castle's gently rendered;* **AC** IV.xiv.33; **Lover** 221; **MV** III.iv.49; **Sonn** 126.12
2 exchange, give in return **TC** IV.i.38 [Paris to Aeneas, of Diomedes] *render him, / For the enfreed Antenor, the fair Cressid;* **E3** II.ii.126
3 give back [to], return [to] **AY** I.ii.19 [Celia to Rosalind, of Duke Frederick] *what he hath taken away ... I will render thee again* [i.e. recompense you]; **E3** IV.iv.116
4 declare, state, give an account **Cym** V.v.135 [disguised Innogen to Cymbeline] *My boon is, that this gentleman may render / Of whom he had this ring;* **Cym** V.v.119; **H5** I.ii.239
5 describe, represent, depict [as] **AY** IV.iii.123 [Celia as Aliena to Oliver, of Orlando's view of Oliver] *he did render him the most unnatural / That lived amongst men;* **AW** I.iii.225; **Cym** III.iv.152

render up (v.) give up, surrender, yield **Ham** I.v.4 [Ghost to Hamlet] *I to sulphurous and tormenting flames / Must render up myself*

rendezvous (n.) **1** refuge, retreat, haven **H5** V.i.79 [Pistol alone, of Doll] *there my rendezvous is quite cut off;* **1H4** IV.i.57
2 last resort, final shift **H5** II.i.15 [Nym to Bardolph] *That is my rest, that is the rendezvous of it*

renegado (n.) renegade, turncoat, deserter **TN** III.ii.66 [Maria to Sir Toby and Fabian] *Yond gull Malvolio is turned heathen, a very renegado*

renege (v.) **1** renounce, refuse, abandon **AC** I.i.8 [Philo to Demetrius, of Antony] *His captain's heart ... reneges all temper*

2 deny, refuse, decline **KL** II.ii.76 [disguised Kent to Cornwall, of Oswald] *Renege, affirm ... / With every gale and vary of their masters* [F; Q *Reuenge*]

renew (v.) become new, grow again, regenerate **Tim** IV.iii.69 [Timon to Alcibiades] *renew I could not like the moon; / There were no suns to borrow of*

renouncement (n.) renunciation, denial, abandonment [of the world] **MM** I.iv.35 [Lucio to Isabella] *I hold you as ... / By your renouncement an immortal spirit*

renown (n.) **1** reputation, good name, honour **Cym** V.v.202 [Iachimo to Cymbeline, of Posthumus and Innogen] *By wounding his belief in her renown;* **AW** IV.iii.14, iv.36; **Per** IV.v.35
2 report, hearsay, rumour **Tem** V.i.193 [Ferdinand to Alonso, of Prospero] *Of whom so often I have heard renown*

renown (v.) bring renown to, make famous **TN** III.iii.24 [Sebastian to Antonio] *the memorials and the things of fame / That do renown this city;* **H5** I.ii.118

rent (adj.) torn, shredded, ripped up **LL** IV.iii.218 [King to Berowne, of the torn letter] *did these rent lines show some love of thine?*

rent (v.) rend, tear, pull to pieces **MND** III.ii.215 [Helena to Hermia] *And will you rent our ancient love asunder;* **3H6** III.ii.175; **Mac** IV.iii.168; **R3** I.ii.126

repair (n.) **1** restoration, renewal, recovery **WT** V.i.31 [Dion to Paulina] *What holier than, for royalty's repair ... / To bless the bed of majesty again;* **Cym** III.i.57; **KJ** III.iv.113
2 coming, arrival, approach **Ham** V.ii.212 [Horatio to Hamlet, of the court] *I will forestall their repair hither;* **3H6** V.i.20; **LL** II.i.226; **MM** IV.i.42

repair (v.) **1** come, go, make one's way **Cor** III.ii.148 [Coriolanus to Sicinius] *I'll ... / Repair to th'Senate House;* **3H6** IV.vii.15 [Edward to Richard, of York city] *hither will our friends repair to us;* **Ham** IV.vi.22; **KJ** II.i.554; **MND** IV.i.66; **TG** IV.i.45; **TNK** IV.iii.89
2 restore, renew, revive **AW** I.ii.30 [King to Bertram] *It much repairs me / To talk of your good father;* **Cym** I.ii.63; **2H6** V.iii.5; **3H6** III.iii.193; **MV** II.i.141; **Per** IV.ii.106

repairing (adj.) with power of recovery, with ability to revive **2H6** V.iii.22 [Salisbury to all, of the enemy] *Being opposites of such repairing nature*

repast (n.) food and drink, meal, refreshment **E3** III.i.115 [King John to Philip] *cheer our stomachs with repast;* **LL** IV.ii.152

repast (v.) feed, nourish, supply **Ham** IV.v.149 [Laertes to Claudius, of Polonius' friends] *like the kind life-rendering pelican / Repast them with my blood*

repasture (n.) food, repast, meal **LL** IV.i.94 [Boyet reading Armado's letter to Jaquenetta] *what art thou then? / Food for his rage, repasture for his den*

repeal (n.) recall, return from banishment **Cor** IV.i.41 [Cominius to Coriolanus] *if the time thrust forth / A cause for thy repeal;* **JC** III.i.54; **Luc** 640; **TG** III.i.234

repeal (v.) recall, call back [from exile] **R2** IV.i.87 [Bolingbroke to Aumerle] *These differences shall all rest under gage / Till Norfolk be repealed. Repealed he shall be;* **AW** II.iii.48; **Cor** V.v.5; **2H6** III.ii.349; **Oth** II.iii.347; **TG** V.iv.144

repealing (n.) recall, return from banishmenth **JC** III.i.51 [Metellus to all, of appealing to Caesar] *For the repealing of my banished brother*

repeat (v.) mention, speak of, utter **H8** I.ii.13 [King Henry to Queen Katherine] *Repeat your will, and take it;* **Per** I.iv.31

repeated (adj.) renewed, reiterated, enumerated **Cym** I.vii.4 [Innogen alone] *those repeated vexations*

repetition (n.) **1** recital, narration, relating **Luc** 1285 [Lucrece to Maid, of Tarquin's attack] *If it should be told, / The repetition cannot make it less;* **Cor** I.i.43; **KJ** II.i.197; **R3** I.iii.164
2 going over the past, re-opening of old wounds **AW** V.iii.22 [King to Lafew, of Bertram] *the first view shall kill / All repetition*

repine *(n.)* discontent, vexation, irritation **Venus** 490 [of Adonis' eyes] *clouded with his brow's repine*

repine *(v.)* be discontented, complain, feel dissatisfaction 1H6 V.ii.20 [Pucelle to all] *Let Henry fret and all the world repine;* **Cor** III.i.43

repining *(adj.)* grudging, grumbling **TC** I.iii.243 [Aeneas to Agamemnon] *what the repining enemy commends, / That breath fame blows*

replenished *(adj.)* complete, perfect, consummate **R3** IV.iii.18 [Tyrrel alone, reporting the Princes' killers] *We smothered / The most replenished sweet work of nature;* **LL** II.ii.26; **WT** II.i.79

repletion *(n.)* over-indulgence, excessive living **TNK** I.ii.24 [Palamon to Arcite, of Juno] *peace might purge / For her repletion*

replication *(n.)* **1** reply, answer, response **Ham** IV.ii.12 [Hamlet to Rosencrantz] *what replication should be made by the son of a king?;* **Lover** 122

2 reverberation, echo **JC** I.i.46 [Marullus to the people, of the Tiber trembling] *To hear the replication of your sounds / Made in her concave shores;* **LL** V.ii.15

report *(n.)* **1** reputation, fame, renown **Cym** III.iii.57 [Belarius to Guiderius and Arviragus] *my report was once / First, with the best of note;* **Cor** II.ii.27; **MA** III.i.97; **MM** II.iii.12; **TNK** II.i.28

2 acclamation, acclaim, commendation **1H6** II.iii.43 [Messenger to Talbot, of Talbot himself] *the man / Whose glory fills the world with loud report*

3 account, description **AC** II.ii.51 [Antony to Caesar] *I … have my learning from some true reports / That drew their swords with you* [or: reporter, narrator]; **Sonn** 83.5

4 rumour, gossip, hearsay **1H6** II.iii.17 [Countess to Talbot] *I see report is fabulous and false;* **AC** II.ii.189; **AY** I.i.5; **TNK** II.i.6

report *(v.)* give an account [of], describe in words **Ham** V.ii.333 [Hamlet to Horatio] *Report me and my cause aright / To the unsatisfied;* **Cor** V.iv.25; **Cym** II.iv.83; **KJ** I.i.25; **Per** V.i.129

reportingly *(adv.)* by hearsay, by report **MA** III.i.116 [Beatrice alone, of Benedick] *others say thou dost deserve, and I / Believe it better than reportingly*

reposal *(n.)* reposing, placing, deposit **KL** II.i.67 [Edmund to Gloucester, as if Edgar to Edmund] *would the reposal / Of any trust … in thee / Make thy words faithed?*

repose *(v.)* confidently settle, happily rely **3H6** IV.vi.47 [George to Warwick] *on thy fortune I repose myself;* **AW** III.vi.12; **TG** IV.iii.26

reprehend *(v.)* **1** reprove, censure, rebuke **MND** V.i.419 [Puck to audience] *Gentles, do not reprehend;* **R3** III.vii.27, 112; **Tit** III.ii.69; **Venus** 1065

2 malapropism for 'represent' **LL** I.i.181 [Dull to Berowne, of the King] *I myself reprehend his own person*

reprisal *(n.)* prize, booty, trophy **1H4** IV.i.118 [Hotspur to all, of the King's army] *I am on fire / To hear this rich reprisal is so nigh*

reproach *(n.)* **1** blame, disgrace, shame **2H6** III.ii.69 [Queen to King, of being thought to have been involved in Gloucester's death] *So shall … princes' courts be filled with my reproach;* **E3** II.i.406; **1H6** I.i.97; **Oth** IV.i.47; **Tit** IV.i.93

2 someone deserving of blame, source of disgrace **2H6** II.iv.96 [Duchess to Stanley] *I am but reproach*

3 malapropism for 'approach' **MV** II.v.20 [Launcelot to Shylock] *My young master doth expect your reproach*

reprobance *(n.)* damnation, perdition **Oth** V.ii.208 [Gratiano to dead Desdemona, of her father] *Did he live now, / This sight would make him … fall to reprobance* [F; Q *reprobation*]

reproof *(n.)* **1** disproof, refutation, rebuttal **1H4** III.ii.23 [Prince Hal to King Henry] *in reproof of many tales devised;* **1H4** I.ii.188

2 rebuff, rebuke, censure **TC** I.iii.33 [Nestor to Agamemnon] *In the reproof of chance / Lies the true proof of men;* **Cor** II.ii.32

3 shame, disgrace, reproach **CE** V.i.90 [Adriana to Luciana, of the Abbess] *She did betray me to my own reproof;* **Tim** V.iv.57

reprovable *(adj.)* blameworthy, reprehensible, deserving cen-sure **KL** III.v.6 [Cornwall to Edmund] *a provoking merit set a-work by a reprovable badness*

reprove *(v.)* disprove, rebut, refute, deny **2H6** III.i.40 [Queen to lords, of Gloucester] *Reprove my allegation if you can;* **MA** II.iii.226; **Venus** 787

repugn *(v.)* reject, oppose, deny **1H6** IV.i.94 [Basset to King, of Vernon] *stubbornly he did repugn the truth*

repugnancy *(n.)* resistance, fighting back, opposition **Tim** III.v.46 [Alcibiades to Senators] *Why do fond men … let the foes quietly cut their throats / Without repugnancy?*

repugnant *(adj.)* opposing, resisting, refusing **Ham** II.ii.469 [First Player to all present, of Priam] *His antique sword … / Repugnant to command* [i.e. not following his orders]

repulse *(n.)* refusal, rejection, rebuff **1H6** III.i.114 [Warwick to Gloucester and Winchester] *Except you mean with obstinate repulse / To slay your sovereign*

reputation *(n.)* honour, esteem, integrity **AC** III.xi.49 [Antony to Eros] *I have offended reputation;* **MW** I.iii.73

repute *(v.)* consider, think, reckon **Tit** I.i.369 [Titus to all] *My foes I do repute you every one;* **2H6** V.i.177; **TG** I.vii.59; **Tit** I.i.451; **TS** IV.ii.113

repute of *(v.)* think highly of, hold in esteem **2H6** III.i.48 [Suffolk to Queen, of Gloucester] *reputing of his high descent, / As next the King he was successive heir*

reputed *(adj.)* acknowledged, recognized, accounted **KJ** I.i.136 [Queen Eleanor to and of Bastard] *the reputed son of Coeur-de-lion*

request *(n.)* demand, state of being sought after **Cor** III.i.51 [Volumnia to Coriolanus, of policy] *it shall hold companionship in peace / With honour as in war, since that to both / It stands in like request* [i.e. a combination of honour and policy is equally needed]

requicken *(v.)* revive, reanimate, refresh **Cor** II.ii.115 [Cominius to all, of Coriolanus] *his doubled spirit / Requickened what in flesh was fatigate*

require *(v.)* **1** request, ask, beg **AC** III.xii.12 [Ambassador to Caesar, of Antony] *he … / Requires to live in Egypt;* **Cor** II.ii.154; **H8** II.iv.144; **KL** IV.iii.6; **MW** I.i.93

2 demand, claim, insist on **Tem** V.i.132 [Prospero to Antonio] *I … require / My dukedom of thee*

3 command, summon, demand **H8** III.ii.122 [King Henry to Norfolk, of Wolsey] *Papers of state he sent me to peruse, / As I required*

4 call up, make available **Tem** V.i.51 [Prospero alone] *when I have required / Some heavenly music;* **H5** III.ii.133

5 deserve, merit, justify **WT** III.ii.62 [Hermione to Leontes, of Polixenes] *I do confess / I loved him as in honour he required*

requiring *(n.)* demanding, requesting as a right **H5** II.iv.101 [Exeter to French King, of King Henry] *if requiring fail, he will compel;* **MM** III.i.244; **Tem** II.ii.178

requital *(n.)* recompense, reward, repayment **KJ** II.i.34 [Constance to Austria, of Arthur] *give him strength / To make a more requital to your love;* **AW** V.i.5; **Cor** II.ii.48; **MW** IV.iii.2; **TG** I.i.143

requite *(v.),* past forms **requit, requited** **1** reward, repay, recompense **Ham** I.ii.251 [Hamlet to Horatio and sentinels] *I will requite your loves;* **Tem** III.iii.72 [Ariel to Alonso, Sebastian, and Antonio, of Prospero] *Exposed unto the sea, which hath requit it;* **Cor** IV.ii.12; **3H6** III.i.48; **MA** II.iii.219; **R3** I.iv.68; **Tem** V.i.169

2 avenge, pay back, take vengeance on **Ham** IV.vii.138 [Claudius to Laertes, of Hamlet] *Requite him for your father;* **H8** II.i.46; **Oth** IV.ii.15; **Tit** III.i.295

roundel *(n.)* bat **MND** II.ii.1 [Titania, instructing Fairies] *Come, now a roundel and a fairy song*

re-salute *(v.)* approach again, greet once more **Tit** I.i.329 [Saturninus to all] *I will not re-salute the streets of Rome … till from forth this place / I lead espoused my bride*

rescue (*n.*) **1** [legal] forced removal from custody **Cor** III.i.275 [Sicinius to Menenius] *how comes't that you / Have holp to make this rescue?*; **AC** III.xi.48; **CE** IV.iv.109

2 [cry for help to stop someone escaping] help, assistance **2H4** II.i.54 [Hostess to all] *bring a rescue or two*; **2H4** II.i.53

resemblance (*n.*) likelihood, probability, uncertain prospect **MM** IV.ii.182 [disguised Duke to Provost, of the likelihood that the Duke will agree] *Not a resemblance, but a certainty*

reservation (*n.*) **1** keeping back, leaving aside **KL** I.i.133 [Lear to Cornwall and Albany] *With reservation of an hundred knights*; **Cor** III.iii.130

2 concealment, secrecy, keeping out of sight **AW** I.iii.220 [Helena to Countess, of her father's prescriptions] *In heedfullest reservation to bestow them*; **AW** II.iii.243

reserve (*v.*) preserve, retain, keep **Per** IV.i.39 [Dionyza to Marina] *Reserve / That excellent complexion*; **Ham** III.iv.76; **KL** III.iv.62; **R3** IV.iv.72; **Sonn** 32.7; **Tit** I.i.168

reserved (*adj.*) well-guarded, preserved, sustained **AW** III.v.61 [Helena to Diana, of herself] *all her deserving / Is a reserved honesty*

residence (*n.*) normal place of performance, usual venue [in the city] **Ham** II.ii.329 [Hamlet to Rosencrantz, of the players] *Their residence, both in reputation and profit, was better both ways*

resist (*v.*) revolt, repel, fill with distaste **Per** II.iii.29 [Simonides to himself, of Pericles] *These cates resist me, he but thought upon* [thinking of his qualities makes even the delicacies seem unpalatable by comparison]

resolute (*n.*) desperado, determined character **Ham** I.i.98 [Horatio to Marcellus and Barnardo, of young Fortinbras' actions] *Sharked up a list of lawless resolutes*

resolution (*n.*) **1** determination, courage, firmness of purpose **TS** IV.ii.43 [Hortensio to Tranio as Lucentio] *I take my leave, / In resolution as I swore before*; **1H4** I.ii.59

2 certainty, definiteness, positive knowledge **KL** I.ii.100 [Gloucester to Edmund] *I would unstate myself to be in a due resolution*

resolve (*n.*) **1** constancy, firmness of purpose, steadfastness **1H6** V.v.75 [Suffolk to all, of Margaret] *a lady of so high resolve*

2 decision, resolution, conclusion **3H6** III.i.129 [Lewis to Bona, of marrying Edward] *let us hear your firm resolve*

resolve (*v.*) **1** answer, respond to **3H6** III.ii.19 [Lady Grey to Edward] *May it please your highness to resolve me now*; **E3** II.i.45; **LL** II.i.110; **Per** I.i.72; **R3** IV.ii.26; **Tit** V.iii.35

2 satisfy, free from doubt **3H6** II.i.9 [Richard to Edward, of York] *I cannot joy, until I be resolved / Where our right valiant father is become*; **H5** I.ii.4; **JC** III.ii.180; **MM** IV.ii.202; **Per** V.i.1

3 inform, tell **R3** IV.v.20 [Derby to Urswick, of Richmond] *My letter will resolve him of my mind*; **KL** II.iv.24; **Tem** V.i.248

4 decide, make up one's mind **3H6** I.i.49 [Warwick to York] *Resolve thee, Richard; claim the English crown*; **2H4** II.iii.67; **H5** III.iii.1; **Mac** III.i.137; **Tit** I.i.281; **WT** V.iii.86

5 be certain [of], rest assured, be sure **1H6** I.ii.91 [Pucelle to Dauphin] *Resolve on this: thou shalt be fortunate / If thou receive me for thy warlike mate*

6 decide, determine, settle **E3** III.iii.169 [King Edward to English peers] *let us resolve the day*

7 remove, dispel, clear away **3H6** IV.i.134 [Edward to Hastings and Montague] *Resolve my doubt*; **1H6** V.v.101; **KJ** II.i.371

8 melt, dissolve, transform **Ham** I.ii.130 [Hamlet to himself] *O that this too too sullied flesh would melt, / Thaw, and resolve itself into a dew*; **KJ** V.iv.25; **Lover** 296; **Tim** IV.iii.441

resolved (*adj.*) **1** determined, settled, decided **KJ** V.vi.29 [Hubert to Bastard, of King John's poisoner] *a resolved villain*; **E3** IV.iv.146; **2H4** IV.i.211; **H5** I.ii.223; **2H6** V.i.194; **TG** II.vi.12

2 convinced, satisfied, assured **1H6** III.iv.20 [King to Talbot] *Long since we were resolved of your truth*; **3H6** II.ii.124

resolvedly (*adv.*) freeing from doubt, in a way which will remove all uncertainty **AW** V.iii.329 [King to all] *Of that and all the progress ... / Resolvedly more leisure shall express*

resort (*n.*) **1** visits, visitings, approaches **Ham** II.ii.143 [Polonius to Claudius and Gertrude, on how Ophelia should respond to Hamlet] *she should lock herself from his resort*; **Per** IV.vi.76; **TG** III.i.108; **Tim** I.i.131

2 habitual meeting, regular visiting **MM** I.ii.101 [Mistress Overdone to Pompey] *shall all our houses of resort in the suburbs be pulled down?*

3 crowd, gathering, company **TG** I.ii.4 [Julia to Lucetta] *all the fair resort of gentlemen / That every day with parle encounter me*

resorter (*n.*) regular, frequenter, customer **Per** IV.vi.22 [Lysimachus to Boult] *'tis the better for you that your resorters stand upon sound legs*

resound (*v.*) resounding noise, reverberation **E3** II.ii.59 [King Edward to Lodowick] *we think it an uncivil thing / To trouble heaven with such harsh resounds*

respect (*n.*) **1** consideration, factor, circumstance **KJ** III.i.318 [Lewis the Dauphin to King Philip] *I muse your majesty doth seem so cold, / When such profound respects do pull you on*; **Ham** III.i.68; **MV** V.i.99; **R2** II.i.25; **R3** III.vii.174; **Venus** 911

2 attention, heed, deliberation **Luc** 275 [Tarquin to himself] *Respect and reason wait on wrinkled age!*; **1H4** IV.iii.31; **KJ** IV.ii.214; **LL** V.ii.777; **MV** I.i.74; **TC** II.ii.49

3 regard, admiration, favour, opinion **KJ** III.iii.28 [King John to Hubert] *I am almost ashamed / To say what good respect I have of thee*; **Cym** II.iii.134; **JC** I.ii.59; **KL** I.i.255; **MND** II.i.224; **Per** III.iii.33

4 esteem, status, honour **JC** V.v.77 [Octavius to all, of Brutus] *let us use him, / With all respect and rites of burial*; **AW** III.iii.192; **KJ** V.vii.85; **KL** I.i.248; **Mac** III.vi.29; **MW** III.i.54

5 courtesy, politeness, consideration **Cor** III.i.180 [Menenius to all] *On both sides more respect*; **2H4** II.ii.95; **Luc** 642

6 relevance, pertinence; or: position **Oth** I.iii.279 [Duke to Othello, of an officer] *he shall our commission bring to you, / With such things else of quality and respect / As doth import you*

respect, in in comparison **3H6** V.v.56 [Queen to all, of Caesar and the dead Prince] *He was a man; this, in respect, a child*

respect, upon with consideration, deliberately **KL** II.iv.23 [Lear to disguised Kent] *'tis worse than murder / To do upon respect such violent outrage* [or: to someone deserving of respect]

respect (*v.*) **1** pay attention to, heed **TG** III.i.89 [Valentine to Duke, of the Duke's supposed lady friend] *Win her with gifts, if she respect not words*; **Cym** I.vii.155; **JC** IV.iii.69; **LL** I.ii.172; **R3** I.iv.154; **TNK** I.i.26 ☞ **well-respected** (*adj.*)

2 bear in mind, consider **2H6** III.i.24 [Queen to King, of Gloucester] *Respecting what a rancorous mind he bears*; **CE** IV.iv.39; **MM** IV.i.52; **Venus** 911

3 value, have regard for, prize **TG** V.iv.20 [Proteus to Silvia] *you respect not aught your servant doth*; **MM** III.i.79; **Sonn** 85.13, 149.9; **TG** I.ii.134, IV.iv.191

4 scruple about, have qualms about **TG** V.iv.54 [Proteus to Silvia] *In love, / Who respects friend?*; **R2** II.i.131

respect of, in (*prep.*) **1** in comparison with **JC** I.i.10 [Cobbler to Marullus] *in respect of a fine workman, I am but ... a cobbler*

2 on account of **TG** III.i.315 [Speed reading from Launce's paper, of his love's vices] *She is not to be kissed fasting, in respect of her breath*

respected (*adj.*) malapropism for 'suspected' **MM** II.i.154 [Elbow to Escalus] *the house is a respected house*

respecting (*prep.*) **1** in comparison with **WT** V.i.35 [Paulina to Dion, of Hermione] *There is none worthy, / Respecting her that's gone*

2 with regard to, with reference to **H8** II.iv.180 [King Henry to all, of Queen Katherine] *Respecting this our marriage with the dowager*

respective (*adj.*) **1** careful, attentive, considerate **MV** V.i.156 [Nerissa to Gratiano, of her ring] *You should have been respective and have kept it*; **KJ** I.i.188; **RJ** III.i.123

2 worthy of respect, estimable, inspiring admiration **TG** IV.iv.192 [disguised Julia alone, of Proteus and Silvia] *What should it be that he respects in her / But I can make respective in myself*

respectively (*adv.*) with all respect, graciously **Tim** III.i.8 [Lucullus to Flaminius] *you are very respectively welcome*

respite (*n.*) **1** extent of time, time-scale **MM** IV.ii.157 [disguised Duke to Provost] *I crave but four days' respite;* **H8** II.iv.177; **R3** V.i.19
2 interval, pause, delay **1H6** IV.i.170 [King to all] *Ourself … / After some respite will return to Calais*

respite (*v.*) save, prolong, grant **MM** II.iii.41 [Juliet to Provost] *O injurious love, / That respites me a life whose very comfort / Is still a dying horror*

responsive (*adj.*) suited, corresponding, matched **Ham** V.ii.149 [Osric to Hamlet] *carriages … very responsive to the hilts*

rest (*n.*) **1** [period of] peace, calm, repose **KJ** IV.ii.55 [Pembroke to King John] *If what in rest you have in right you hold* [i.e. if you hold by right what you possess in peace]; **AC** I.iii.53; **KL** I.i.123
2 interval, space, pause **MW** I.iii.25 [Nym to Falstaff] *The good humour is to steal at a minute's rest* [i.e. in the space of a minute]
3 final stake, last resolve **H5** II.i.15 [Nym to Bardolph] *That is my rest, that is the rendezvous of it* ☛ set up one's rest
4 residence, lodging, stay **Ham** II.ii.13 [Claudius to Rosencrantz and Guildenstern] *I entreat you both … / That you vouchsafe your rest here in our court;* **Per** II.Chorus.26

RESPONSES

Yes and *no* are the standard basic ways in modern English of responding to another person or rhetorically to oneself, *yes* expressing such notions as affirmation, assent, and agreement, and *no* such notions as dissent, refusal, and denial. In earlier English, the situation was more complex. *Yes* and *no* were used when the stimulus utterance contained a negative word; and *yea* and *nay* were used when no such word was present. In the following examples from the early scenes of *Hamlet*, both of these usages can be seen (the negative words are highlighted).

Item	Location	Stimulus	Response
yes	Ham I.ii.230	*Then saw you **not** his face?*	*O yes, my lord*
yea	Ham I.v.98	*Remember thee?*	*Yea, from the table of my memory / I'll wipe away all trivial fond records*
no	Ham I.iv.62	*But do **not** go with it*	*No, by no means*
nay	Ham I.ii.77	*Why seems it so particular with thee?*	*'Seems', madam? Nay, it is*

This distinction was already breaking down around 1600: *yes* and *no* were beginning to take over all functions, with *yea* and *nay* becoming restricted to emphatic usage. (They eventually left the standard language altogether, though they are still widely used in regional dialects.)

Hamlet displays the new system alongside the old (though there are few instances of *yes*, as the usual affirmative response in that play is *ay*). An example of a 'self-response' is given as a comparison (I.v.135), along with an example from a different play. In each case, there is no negative word in the stimulus utterance.

Item	Location	Stimulus	Response
yes	Ham I.v.135	*I am sorry they offend you, heartily.*	*Yes, faith, heartily.*
yes	MM II.iii.25	*Love you the man that wronged you?*	*Yes, as I love the woman that wronged him*
ay	Ham I.iv.13	*Is it a custom?*	*Ay, marry, is't*
no	Ham I.v.119	*Good my lord, tell it*	*No, you will reveal it*
no	Ham II.i.108	*have you given him any hard words of late?*	*No, my good lord*

Both new and old negative usages can be seen in quick succession in **Ham** II.ii.334ff.:

Hamlet: *Are they so followed?*
Rosencrantz: *No, indeed are they not.*
Hamlet: *How comes it? Do they grow rusty?*
Rosencrantz: *Nay, their endeavour keeps in the wonted pace.*

All four words had other functions than direct response. *Nay*, for example, could also used as an introductory word, expressive of doubt or reservation, without any direct response being made to the preceding utterance.

Item	Location	Stimulus	Response
nay	Ham I.i.2	*Who's there?*	*Nay, answer me*
nay	Ham II.ii.290	*[aside] Nay then, I have an eye of you*	

A wide range of other words and phrases (e.g. *content, ha, buzz buzz*) could of course also be used as responses:
☛ **DISCOURSE MARKERS**, p.127; **POLITENESS**, p.340; **EXCLAMATIONS**, p.158.

rest (*v.*) **1** remain, stay, stand **1H6** V.v.95 [King to Suffolk] *till you do return / I rest perplexed with a thousand cares;* **AY** I.ii.275; **Ham** III.iii.64; **3H6** IV.viii.22; **MW** IV.vi.48; **R3** III.i.157

2 remain [to be done], be left **1H6** I.iii.70 [Mayor to all] *Naught rests for me in this tumultuous strife / But to make open proclamation;* **E3** III.i.185; **3H6** I.ii.44, III.ii.45, IV.ii.13, V.vii.42; **TS** I.i.243

rest, let so much for, think no further of [someone / something] **2H6** I.ii.90 [Suffolk to Queen, of the Duchess of Gloucester] *So let her rest;* **TS** IV.iii.26

rest under gage ☞ *gage, rest under*

re-stem (*v.*) retrace, go back upon **Oth** I.iii.37 [Messenger to First Senator, of the Ottomites] *they do re-stem / Their backward course* [F; Q2 *resterne*]

restful (*adj.*) quiet, peaceful, free from strife **R2** IV.i.12 [Bagot to Aumerle, reporting Aumerle's words] *Is not my arm of length, / That reacheth from the restful English court / As far as Calais to mine uncle's head?*

resting (*adj.*) stationary, unchanging, stable **JC** III.i.61 [Caesar to all, of the north star] *Of whose true-fixed and resting quality / There is no fellow in the firmament*

restitution (*n.*) recovery, restoration, retrieval **Cor** III.i.16 [Lartius to Coriolanus, of Aufidius] *he would pawn his fortunes / To hopeless restitution* [i.e. beyond all hope of recovery]

restorative (*n.*) healing power, medicinal cordial **Per** I.Chorus.8 [Gower alone, of a song] *lords and ladies … / Have read it for restoratives*

restore (*v.*) have one's titles returned, reinstate **1H6** I.iv.95 [Somerset to Richard] *till thou be restored thou art a yeoman*

restrain (*v.*) **1** withhold, keep back, hold back **Cor** V.iii.167 [Volumnia to Coriolanus] *thou restrain'st from me the duty which / To a mother's part belongs;* **Tim** V.i.146

2 draw tightly, pull taut **TS** III.ii.57 [Biondello to Tranio as Lucentio, of Petruchio's horse's headstall] *being restrained to keep him from stumbling*

restrained (*adj.*) forbidden, prohibited, banned **MM** II.iv.48 [Angelo to Isabella] *'tis all as easy … to put metal in restrained means / To make a false one* [i.e. coin]

restraint (*n.*) **1** captivity, imprisonment, confinement **Cym** I.ii.5 [Queen to Innogen] *Your gaoler shall deliver you the keys / That lock up your restraint;* **KJ** IV.ii.52; **MM** I.ii.123; **TNK** II.i.40

2 prohibition, exclusion, keeping out **CE** III.i.97 [Balthasar to Antipholus of Ephesus, of Adriana] *To know the reason of this strange restraint*

resty (*adj.*) lazy, sluggish **Cym** III.vii.7 [Belarius to Guiderius and Arviragus] *resty sloth / Finds the down-pillow hard;* **Sonn** 100.9; **TC** I.iii.263

resty-stiff (*adj.*) stiff because too rested, sluggish **E3** III.iii.161 [King John to the French, of the English] *they are as resty-stiff / As 'twere a many overridden jades*

resume (*v.*) undertake, take, accept **Tim** II.ii.4 [Flavius alone, of Timon] *[he] Takes no account / How things go from him, nor resumes no care / Of what is to continue*

retail (*v.*) recount, relate in detail, retell **R3** IV.iv.335 [King Richard to Queen Elizabeth, of her daughter] *To whom I will retail my conquest won;* **2H4** I.i.32; **R3** III.i.77

retain (*v.*) employ, take into service **TNK** I.ii.24 [Palamon to Arcite, of Juno] *peace might … retain anew / Her charitable heart;* **H8** I.ii.192

retention (*n.*) **1** means of retaining, way of keeping in mind **Sonn** 122.9 *That poor retention could not so much hold* [i.e. his notebook]

2 limit, restriction, holding back **TN** V.i.79 [Antonio to Orsino, of Viola as Cesario] *His life I gave him, and did thereto add / My love without retention or restraint*

3 [medicine] power to retain emotion **TN** II.iv.95 [Orsino to Viola as Cesario] *no woman's heart / So big to hold so much, they lack retention*

4 place of detention, confinement **KL** V.iii.48 [Edmund to Albany] *I thought it fit / To send the old and miserable King / To some retention*

retentive (*adj.*) confining, constraining, imprisoning **Tim** III.iv.82 [Timon to all] *Have I been ever free, and must my house / Be my retentive enemy, my gaol?;* **JC** I.iii.95

retire (*n.*) retreat, withdrawal **KJ** II.i.326 [Hubert to Heralds] *we might behold … the onset and retire of both your armies;* **Cor** I.vi.3; **1H4** II.iii.53; **H5** IV.iii.86; **3H6** II.i.149; **LL** II.i.220

retire (*v.*) **1** withdraw, take oneself away **Tem** IV.i.161 [Prospero to Ferdinand and Miranda] *retire into my cell / And there repose;* **LL** V.ii.590; **Oth** II.iii.369; **R2** IV.i.96; **RJ** V.iii.11, 21; **Tem** V.i.311

2 retreat, pull back, withdraw **R2** II.ii.46 [Green to Queen Isabel, of King Richard] *he … might have retired his power;* **Cor** I.vi.50; **3H6** I.iv.14; **KJ** V.iii.13

3 draw back, pull back, yield **Luc** 303 [of Tarquin and Lucrece's door locks] *Each one by him enforced, retires his ward*

retired (*adj.*) **1** withdrawn, secluded, cloistered **Tim** V.i.57 [Poet to Timon] *Hearing you were retired, your friends fall'n off;* **Cym** III.v.36; **Tem** I.ii.91; **WT** IV.ii.31

2 retiring, reserved, withdrawn **WT** IV.iv.62 [Shepherd to Perdita] *You are retired, / As if you were a feasted one and not / The hostess of the meeting*

3 retreating, receded, subsiding **KJ** V.iv.53 [Salisbury to Melun, of the rebel lords] *like a bated and retired flood … run on in obedience / Even to our ocean, to our great King John*

retirement (*n.*) **1** retreat, withdrawal, falling back **1H4** V.iv.5 [Prince Hal to King Henry] *I beseech your majesty, make up, / Lest your retirement do amaze your friends*

2 withdrawal, returning [to one's rooms] **Ham** III.ii.309 [Guildenstern to Hamlet] *The King … Is in his retirement marvellous distempered;* **H5** I.i.58

3 something to fall back on **1H4** IV.i.56 [Douglas to all, of Northumberland's absence] *A comfort of retirement lives in this*

retort (*v.*) **1** turn back, return, reflect **RJ** III.i.164 [Benvolio to Prince, of Mercutio's parry] *sends / It back to Tybalt, whose dexterity / Retorts it;* **TC** III.iii.101

2 repay, pay back, recompense **MW** II.ii.4 [Pistol to Falstaff] *I will retort the sum in equipage* [Q only]; **H5** II.i.48

3 reject, refuse, deny **MM** V.i.299 [disguised Duke to Escalus] *The Duke's unjust, / Thus to retort your manifest appeal*

retreat (*n.*) trumpet call signalling retreat **2H4** IV.iii.71 [Westmorland to Prince John] *Retreat is made and execution stayed*

retrograde (*adj.*) **1** [astrology] moving in a contrary direction **AW** I.i.195 [Helena to Parolles, of Mars] *When he was retrograde*

2 contrary, opposed, repugnant **Ham** I.ii.114 [Claudius to Hamlet] *For your intent … / It is most retrograde to our desire*

return (*n.*) response, reaction, repayment **Tim** III.v.83 [Alcibiades to Senators, of his friend] *I'll pawn my victories, all / My honour to you, upon his good returns* [i.e. he will make a good return to you for your mercy]

return (*v.*) **1** answer, report, say in reply [to] **Per** II.ii.4 [Simonides to First Lord, of the knights] *Return them we are ready;* **CE** II.ii.166; **H5** III.iii.123; **R2** I.iii.122, III.iii.121; **TC** I.iii.54

2 send back, respond with **Tim** III.vi.38 [Lucullus to Timon] *I returned you an empty messenger;* **Tim** II.ii.142

3 pass, transfer **Ham** I.i.91 [Horatio to Marcellus and Barnardo] *a moiety competent / Was gaged by our King, which had returned / To the inheritance of Fortinbras, / Had he been vanquisher*

revel (*n.*) revelry, festivity, courtly entertainment **Tem** IV.i.148 [Prospero to Ferdinand] *Our revels now are ended;* **KJ** V.ii.132

revel (*v.*) make merry, riot, hold a party **3H6** I.iv.71 [Queen to York] *Was't you that revelled in our parliament;* **3H6** II.ii.150

revengement (*n.*) revenge, retribution, punishment **1H4** III.ii.7 [King Henry to Prince Hal, of God] *in his secret doom out of my blood / He'll breed revengement and a scourge for me*

revengingly *(adv.)* by way of revenge, in retaliation **Cym** V.ii.4 [Iachimo alone, of Britain] *the air on't / Revengingly enfeebles me*

revenue *(n.)* **1** income, yield, profit **AY** I.i.97 [Charles to Oliver] *lands and revenues enrich the new Duke;* **KL** I.ii.53, II.i.99; **MND** I.i.6; **Tem** I.ii.98

2 possession, tenure, custody **R3** III.vii.157 [Richard to Buckingham, of his right to the crown] *As the ripe revenue and due of birth* [i.e. as something ready to be possessed]

reverb *(v.)* reverberate, re-echo, resound **KL** I.i.154 [Kent to Lear] *Nor are those empty-hearted whose low sounds / Reverb no hollowness*

reverberate *(adj.)* reverberating, resounding, echoing **TN** I.v.261 [Viola as Cesario to Olivia] *[I would] Hallow your name to the reverberate hills*

reverence *(n.)* **1** respected state, venerable condition **MA** V.i.64 [Leonato to Claudio] *I am forced to lay my reverence by;* **2H6** V.ii.48; **KL** IV.ii.42, vii.29; **MA** II.iii.122

2 profound respect, esteem **Cym** IV.ii.247 [Belarius to Arviragus and Guiderius] *reverence ... doth make distinction / Of place 'tween high and low;* **AY** I.i.48; **R2** I.i.54, 72

3 bow, obeisance, salutation **TS** Induction.i.51 [Lord to Huntsmen, of talking to Sly] *with a low submissive reverence*

4 ☛ saving reverence of

reverence, do pay homage, worship, show respect [to] **JC** III.ii.121 [Antony to all, of Caesar] *now lies he there, / And none so poor to do him reverence;* **MV** I.i.13; **TNK** II.i.188

reverence *(v.)* pay homage, hold in respect **1H6** I.iv.140 [Charles to the English, of his territories] *I am ... therein reverenced for their lawful king*

reverend *(adj.)* revered, worthy, respected **CE** V.i.124 [Second Merchant to Angelo] *a reverend Syracusian merchant;* **Ham** II.ii.477; **Lover** 57; **MV** IV.i.160; **TN** III.iv.73; **TS** IV.v.48

reverent *(adj.)* worthy of respect, holy, religious **1H6** V.iii.47 [Suffolk to Margaret] *I will touch thee but with reverent hands;* **2H6** III.i.34; **R2** V.vi.25

reverently *(adv.)* with profound respect, in great esteem **3H6** II.ii.109 [Richard to Northumberland] *I hold thee reverently*

reverse *(n.)* [fencing] back-handed stroke **MW** II.iii.23 [Host to Caius, in answer to 'Vat be you all ... come for?'] *to see thee pass ... thy reverse*

reversion *(n.)* **1** right of succession, situation of reverting to its original owner **R2** I.iv.35 [King Richard to Aumerle, of Bolingbroke] *As were our England in reversion his;* **R2** II.ii.38

2 prospective inheritance, expectation of possession **1H4** IV.i.54 [Douglas to all] *where now remains / A sweet reversion;* **TC** III.ii.90

revert *(v.)* return, go back **Ham** IV.vii.23 [Claudius to Laertes] *my arrows ... / Would have reverted to my bow again*

reverted *(adj.)* revolted, in rebellion, mutinied **CE** III.ii.131 [Dromio of Syracuse to Antipholus of Syracuse, of finding France in the kitchen wench] *In her forehead, armed and reverted, making war against her heir* [F2 *haire*]

review *(v.)* **1** survey again, look once more at **Sonn** 74.5 [of the line of verse] *When thou reviewest this, thou dost review / The very part was consecrate to thee* [first instance]

2 see again, observe once more **Sonn** 74.5 [of the line of verse] *When thou reviewest this, thou dost review / The very part was consecrate to thee* [second instance]

revive *(v.)* **1** refresh, restore, invigorate **AW** IV.iv.34 [Helena to Widow and Diana] *time revives us*

2 come back to life, live again **1H6** I.i.18 [Exeter to all] *Henry is dead and never shall revive*

revokement *(n.)* revoking, revocation, repeal **H8** I.ii.106 [Wolsey aside to Secretary, of the taxation] *let it be noised / That through our intercession this revokement / And pardon comes*

revolt *(n.)* **1** betrayal, change of heart, faithlessness **RJ** IV.i.58 [Juliet to Friar] *ere ... my true heart with treacherous revolt / Turn to another;* **AC** IV.ix.19; **Cym** III.iv.56; **LL** V.ii.74; **Oth** III.iii.186; **Sonn** 92.10

2 rebellion, act of disobedience **Oth** I.i.135 [Roderigo to Brabantio] *Your daughter ... hath made a gross revolt;* **MW** I.iii.94; **Tim** IV.iii.92

3 rebel, revolutionary, malcontent **KJ** V.ii.151 [Bastard to rebel lords] *you ingrate revolts;* **Cym** IV.iv.6; **KJ** V.iv.7

4 revulsion of appetite, distaste, disgust **Cym** I.vii.112 [Iachimo to Innogen] *all the plagues of hell should at one time / Encounter such revolt*

revolt *(v.)* change sides, alter allegiance, desert **1H6** IV.i.64 [King to Gloucester, of Burgundy] *Doth my uncle Burgundy revolt?;* **AC** IV.v.4, vi.9; **2H6** IV.ii.117

revolted *(adj.)* **1** rebellious, insurgent, insubordinate **AC** IV.ix.8 [Enobarbus to himself] *When men revolted shall upon record / Bear hateful memory;* **1H4** I.ii.91; **R2** II.ii.57

2 faithless, disloyal, inconstant **WT** I.ii.199 [Leontes to himself] *Should all despair / That have revolted wives, the tenth of mankind / Would hang themselves;* **MW** III.ii.35; **TC** V.iii.189

3 runaway, truant, delinquent **1H4** IV.ii.28 [Falstaff alone, of those in his command] *revolted tapsters, and ostlers trade-fallen*

revolting *(adj.)* rebellious, mutinous, insurgent **2H6** IV.i.87 [Lieutenant to Suffolk] *The false revolting Normans thorough thee / Disdain to call us lord;* **1H6** I.i.4; **KJ** III.i.257; **R2** III.iii.163

revolution *(n.)* **1** reversal, change, twists and turns [of fortune] **2H4** III.i.46 [King Henry IV to Warwick and Surrey] *O God, that one might read the book of fate, / And see the revolution of the times;* **Ham** V.i.89

2 moving round [a point], revolving round **AC** I.ii.126 [Antony alone] *The present pleasure, / By revolution lowering, does become / The opposite of itself* [i.e. descends as if on the outside of a wheel]

3 twisting and turning of the thoughts **LL** IV.ii.68 [Holofernes to Nathaniel and Dull, of his literary gift] *full of forms, figures, shapes, objects, ideas, apprehensions, motions, revolutions*

revolve *(v.)* consider, ponder, meditate **TN** II.v.139 [Malvolio reading the letter] *If this fall into thy hand, revolve;* **Cym** III.iii.14; **Luc** 127; **R3** IV.iv.123; **TC** II.iii.185 ☛ deep-revolving *(adj.)*

reword, re-word *(v.)* **1** repeat, reiterate, put into words again **Ham** III.iv.144 [Hamlet to Gertrude] *I the matter will re-word*

2 re-echo, resound, reverberate **Lover** 1 *a hill whose concave womb reworded, / A plaintful story*

rhapsody *(n.)* string, miscellany, meaningless heap **Ham** III.iv.49 [Hamlet to Gertrude] *sweet religion makes / A rhapsody of words*

Rhenish *(n.)* Rhineland wine **Ham** V.i.177 [First Clown to Hamlet, of Yorick] *'A poured a flagon of Rhenish on my head once;* **Ham** I.iv.10; **MV** I.ii.90, III.i.37

rhetoric *(n.)* oratory, flowery language **LL** IV.iii.237 [Browne to King] *Fie, painted rhetoric!;* **LL** II.i.215

rheum *(n.)* **1** tears **KJ** IV.i.33 [Hubert to himself, of his tears] *How now, foolish rheum!;* **Cor** V.vi.46; **Ham** II.ii.504; **KJ** IV.iii.108; **MA** IV.i.75

2 watery discharge, seepage [especially of the eyes] **KJ** III.i.22 [Constance to Salisbury] *Why holds thine eye that lamentable rheum;* **AC** III.ii.57; **CE** III.ii.135; **R2** I.iv.8; **TC** V.iii.104

3 catarrh, headcold, coughing and spluttering **Oth** III.iv.51 [Othello to Desdemona] *I have a salt and sorry rheum offends me;* **MM** III.i.31; **TNK** V.iv.8; **WT** IV.iv.396

4 spit, spittle, saliva **MV** I.iii.114 [Shylock to Antonio] *You, that did void your rheum upon my beard;* **H5** III.v.52

rheumatic *(adj.)* **1** with symptoms of rheum [watery discharge], catarrhal, cold-like **Venus** 135 [Venus to Adonis] *Were I ... / O'erworn, despised, rheumatic and cold;* **MND** II.i.105

2 likely to cause rheumatism **MW** III.i.44 [Page to Shallow] *in your doublet and hose this raw rheumatic day?*

3 malapropism for 'choleric' or 'lunatic' **2H4** II.iv.56 [Hostess to Doll and Falstaff] *You are both … as rheumatic as two dry toasts;* **H5** II.iii.35

rheumy *(adj.)* moist, wet, damp **JC** II.i.266 [Portia to and of Brutus] *tempt the rheumy and unpurged air, / To add unto his sickness*

rhymer *(n.)* [disparaging] versifier, rhymester **AC** V.ii.215 [Cleopatra to Iras] *scald rhymers / Ballad us out o'tune;* **Sonn** 38.10

rib *(n.)* rampart, protective wall **R2** III.iii.32 [Bolingbroke to Northumberland] *Go to the rude ribs of that ancient castle*

rib *(v.)* enclose [as if with ribs] **MV** II.vii.51 [Morocco to himself, of Portia's lead casket] *it were too gross / To rib her cerecloth in the obscure grave;* **Cym** III.i.20

ribald *(adj.)* raucously abusive, noisily irreverent **TC** IV.ii.9 [Troilus to Cressida] *the busy day … hath roused the ribald crows*

riband *(n.)* ribbon **Ham** IV.vii.76 [Claudius to Laertes] *A very riband in the cap of youth;* **MW** IV.vi.42; **RJ** III.i.28; **TNK** III.v.28

ribaudred *(adj.)* [unclear meaning] foul, obscene, wanton **AC** III.x.10 [Scarus to Enobarbus, as if to Cleopatra] *You ribaudred nag of Egypt*

rich *(adj.)* **1** high, noble, great **Oth** II.iii.189 [Othello to Montano] *you … spend your rich opinion for the name / Of a night-brawler?;* **Tim** V.iv.77

2 experienced, sophisticated, cultivated **AW** V.iii.17 [Lafew to King, of Helena] *Whose beauty did astonish the survey / Of richest eyes* [or: sense 1]

rich-left *(adj.)* richly endowed, left well-off **Cym** IV.ii.226 [Arviragus to Belarius and Guiderius, of the charitable behaviour of a robin] *sore shaming / Those rich-left heirs, that let their fathers lie / Without a monument!*

richly *(adv.)* **1** nobly, mightily, in a powerful way **Cym** V.v.3 [Cymbeline to all] *the poor soldier that so richly fought*

2 abundantly, fully, amply **WT** V.iii.145 [Leontes to Camillo, of Paulina or Camillo] *whose worth and honesty / Is richly noted*

rid *(v.)* **1** get rid of, destroy, kill **Tem** I.ii.364 [Caliban to Miranda] *The red plague rid you / For learning me your language!;* **3H6** V.iii.21, v.67; **R2** V.iv.11

2 remove from, clear away from **2H6** III.i.233 [Queen to all] *Gloucester should be quickly rid the world*

3 cover, accomplish, get through **Cym** III.ii.68 [Innogen to Pisanio] *How many score of miles may we well rid or / 'Twixt hour, and hour?* [F1; F2 *ride*]

riddle-like *(adv.)* in the manner of a riddle, hiding the truth of a situation **AW** I.iii.212 [Helena to Countess, of her intention to hide her love] *But riddle-like lives sweetly where she dies*

riddling *(adj.)* dealing in riddles, riddle-making **1H6** II.iii.56 [Countess to Talbot, of his reply] *This is a riddling merchant for the nonce*

ride *(v.),* past forms **rid, ridden** **1** control, dominate, tyrannize **CE** II.i.210 [Dromio of Syracuse to Luciana, of Adriana] *she rides me, and I long for grass;* **MW** V.v.136

2 manage, conduct, control **MND** V.i.119 [Lysander to Theseus, of Quince] *He hath rid his prologue like a rough colt;* **H8** II.ii.2

3 press, harass, pursue **2H4** II.i.74 [Hostess to Falstaff] *I will ride thee a-nights like the mare*

4 lie at anchor **Per** V.iii.11 [Pericles as if to Diana, of Mytilene] *'gainst whose shore / Riding*

ridge *(n.)* roof ridge, rooftop **Cor** II.i.203 [Brutus to Sicinius] *ridges horsed / With variable complexions*

ridiculous *(adj.)* in ridicule, derisive **LL** III.i.75 [Armado to Costard] *the heaving of my lungs provokes me to ridiculous smiling!*

riding *(adj.)* horse-racing **Cym** III.ii.72 [Innogen to Pisanio] *I have heard of riding wagers*

riding-rod *(n.)* cane used in riding, switch **KJ** I.i.140 [Bastard to Queen Eleanor, of Robert Faulconbridge] *if my legs were two such riding-rods*

rifle *(v.)* search and rob, plunder **TG** IV.i.4 [Third Outlaw to Valentine] *we'll make you sit, and rifle you;* **Luc** 1050

rift *(v.)* split, cleave, rend apart **WT** V.i.66 [Paulina to Leontes] *I'd shriek, that even your ears / Should rift to hear me;* **Tem** V.i.45

rig *(v.)* fit out, equip, prepare **AC** II.vi.20 [Pompey to Caesar, Antony, and Lepidus, of the reason for his quarrel] *that is it / Hath made me rig my navy*

riggish *(adj.)* licentious, wanton, lascivious **AC** II.ii.245 [Enobarbus to Maecenas and Agrippa, of Cleopatra] *the holy priests / Bless her when she is riggish*

right *(n.)* **1** just claim, rights, title **3H6** I.ii.11 [Richard to York, of the King] *Your right depends not on his life or death;* **CE** II.i.40; **1H4** III.i.66; **3H6** IV.iv.32; **KJ** II.i.282; **Tit** I.i.200

2 justice, rightfulness, justification **3H6** II.ii.62 [King to Prince] *draw thy sword in right;* **3H6** I.i.166, III.i.19, V.i.78; **KL** II.i.53

right *(adj.)* **1** typical, true, classic **MND** III.ii.302 [Helena to Lysander and Demetrius] *I am a right maid for my cowardice!;* **AC** IV.xii.28, III.i.94, 266; **JC** II.ii.20; **TNK** III.vi.215

2 correct [in opinion], right-minded **AC** III.xiii.61 [Cleopatra to Thidias, of Caesar] *He is a god, and knows / What is most right;* **Cor** II.iii.47; **TS** V.ii.108

3 veritable, true, good **MA** III.iii.160 [Second Watchman to the other Watchmen] *Call up the right Master Constable;* **2H4** V.ii.102; **LL** IV.iii.327; **Sonn** 66.7

4 in her right mind, sane, rational **TNK** V.ii.103 [Doctor to Gaoler, of the Gaoler's Daughter] *I'll make her right again;* **TNK** IV.i.45

5 straight, not bent to one side **LL** V.ii.562 [Boyet to Nathaniel as Alexander, of his portrayal] *Your nose says no, you are not; for it stands too right* [i.e. unlike the reported physical description of Alexander]

right *(v.)* set right, vindicate, give redress **WT** II.i.99 [Hermione to Leontes] *You scarce can right me throughly then to say / You did mistake*

right *(adv.)* **1** very, altogether, properly **KL** I.i.97 [Cordelia to Lear] *I return those duties back as are right fit;* **Cym** II.iv.135; **Sonn** 144.3

2 just, precisely **MND** IV.ii.28 [Bottom to all] *I will tell you everything, right as it fell out!;* **CE** V.i.347; **2H6** III.i.40; **TC** I.iii.170

3 correctly, truly, accurately **AY** II.vii.84 [Jaques to Duke Senior, of his tongue attacking a person] *if it do him right, / Then he hath wronged himself* [i.e. if I have done him justice]

4 clearly, unmistakeably, assuredly **KJ** V.iv.60 [Salisbury to Melun] *I do see the cruel pangs of death / Right in thine eye*

right, do one **1** give one satisfaction **MA** V.i.144 [Benedick aside to Claudio, challenging him] *Do me right;* **2H4** V.iii.72

2 support one's cause, take one's part **KJ** II.i.18 [King Philip to and of Arthur] *Who would not do thee right!*

right on straight out, without art **JC** III.ii.224 [Antony to all] *I only speak right on;* **Lover** 26

right out outright, ordinary, out-and-out **Tem** IV.i.101 [Iris to Ceres, of Cupid] *Swears he will … be a boy right out*

right-drawn *(adj.)* drawn in a rightful cause **R2** I.i.46 [Bolingbroke to Mowbray] *What my tongue speaks my right-drawn sword may prove*

righteously *(adv.)* rightly, correctly, truly **AY** I.ii.12 [Celia to Rosalind] *if the truth of thy love to me were so righteously tempered as mine is to thee*

rigol *(n.)* circle, ring **Luc** 1745 [of Lucrece's blood] *About the mourning and congealed face / Of that black blood a watery rigol goes;* **2H4** IV.v.37

rigorously *(adv.)* cruelly, savagely, with severity **1H6** V.iv.52 [Pucelle to all, of herself] *Whose maiden blood, thus rigorously effused*

rigour *(n.)* strength, severity, harshness **2H6** I.iii.194 [York to King, of Horner] *Let him have all the rigour of the law;* **1H6** V.v.5; **3H6** II.i.125; **KL** V.i.22

rim *(n.)* [rim of the belly] midriff, paunch, diaphragm **H5** IV.iv.15 [Pistol to French Soldier] *I will have forty moys, / Or I will fetch thy rim out at thy throat*

ring *(n.)* **1** round, circuit, orbit **AW** II.i.162 [Helena to King] *Ere twice the horses of the sun shall bring / Their fiery torcher his diurnal ring*
2 circle surrounding the sovereign's head [on a coin]; ringing [of the voice] **Ham** II.ii.427 [Hamlet to one of the players] *your voice, like a piece of uncurrent gold, be not cracked within the ring*
3 eye-socket **KL** V.iii.187 [Edgar to Albany, of Gloucester] *Met I my father with his bleeding rings*

ring about *(v.)* encircle, surround, enclose **1H6** IV.iv.14 [Lucy to Somerset, of Talbot] *ringed about with bold adversity*

ring time time for exchanging rings **AY** V.iii.18 [Pages, singing] *In the spring time, the only pretty ring time*

ring-carrier *(n.)* go-between, bawd **AW** III.v.91 [Mariana to all, as if to Parolles] *And [hang you for] your courtesy, for a ring-carrier!*

ringlet *(n.)* fairy dance in a ring, circular dance **Tem** V.i.37 [Prospero alone] *you demi-puppets that / By moonshine do the green, sour ringlets make*; **MND** II.i.86

riot *(n.)* **1** dissipation, wasteful revelry, extravagance **Tim** IV.iii.257 [Timon to Apemantus] *thou wouldst have plunged thyself / In general riot*; **Per** I.iv.54; **Tim** II.ii.3, IV.i.28
2 dissipation, debauchery, wantonness **Sonn** 41.11 *thy beauty, and thy straying youth, / Who lead thee in their riot*; **2H4** IV.iv.62, V.v.65
3 excess, abundance, profusion **Venus** 1147 [Venus to dead Adonis, of love] *It shall be sparing, and too full of riot*

riotous *(adj.)* unrestrained, vociferous, uninhibited **2H6** V.i.64 [Suffolk to Lieutenant] *This hand of mine hath writ in thy behalf, / And therefore shall it charm thy riotous tongue*

ripe *(adj.)* **1** matured, ready for action **JC** III.i.213 [Brutus to Cassius] *Our legions are brim-full, our cause is ripe*; **Ham** V.vii.63; **MV** I.iii.60
2 ready, inclined, well-disposed **TNK** I.iii.91 [Hippolyta to Emilia] *If I were ripe for your persuasion*; **Cor** I.iii.20
3 ready, fully prepared **MND** V.i.42 [Philostrate to Theseus] *There is a brief how many sports are ripe*; **H5** III.vi.121
4 properly considered, fully thought out **R3** III.vii.157 [Richard to Buckingham, of his right to the crown] *As the ripe revenue and due of birth* [i.e. as something ready to be possessed]; **WT** I.ii.332
5 mature, sophisticated, refined **TG** II.iv.68 [Valentine to Duke, of Proteus] *His head unmellowed, but his judgement ripe*; **AY** IV.iii.88, V.i.20; **Per** I.Chorus.12
6 red and full like ripe fruit **MND** III.ii.139 [Demetrius to Helena] *how ripe in show / Thy lips ... tempting grow!*; **KL** IV.iii.20
7 drunk **Tem** V.i.279 [Alonso to lords] *Trinculo is reeling ripe*

ripe *(v.)* ripen, mature **KJ** II.i.472 [Queen Eleanor to King John, of Arthur] *yon green boy shall have no sun to ripe / The bloom that promiseth a mighty fruit*; **AY** II.vii.26; **2H4** IV.i.13; **MND** II.ii.124

ripely *(adv.)* immediately, quickly; or: with full development **Cym** III.v.22 [Cymbeline to all] *It fits us therefore ripely ... be in readiness*

riping *(n.)* ripening, coming to readiness **MV** II.viii.40 [Salerio to Solanio, quoting Antonio to Bassanio] *stay the very riping of the time*

rise *(v.)* **1** get up, get out of bed **TNK** V.ii.58 [Gaoler's Daughter to Gaoler, of her horse] *that ostler / Must rise betime that cozens him*

ROMAN HISTORY

The Roman plays make routine references to political or social roles, using a distinctive vocabulary, and characters in other plays sometimes refer to them. This is standard terminology, encountered whenever writers refer to Classical Rome, and there is no difference between the way Shakespeare would refer to these people and the way any modern English writer would. They are not therefore included in the A–Z section; but as anyone unfamiliar with the period would certainly find them to be 'hard words', the chief items are listed below.

Item	Example	Gloss
aedile [pron: aydiyl]	Cor III.i.172	assistant to the tribunes, with a range of responsibilities (such as public order)
augurer	Cor II.i.1	religious official who interpreted signs (such as the behaviour of birds and the entrails of sacrificial victims) to advise on how affairs should proceed and to predict future events
candidatus	Tit I.i.185	someone standing as a candidate for political office, conventionally dressed in a white toga
censor	Cor II.iii.243	magistrate responsible for the census of citizens and who acted as a watchdog of public morals
centurion	Cor IV.iii.39	commander of a century [a body of *c*.100 men] in the Roman legion
flamen	Cor II.i.205	priest devoted to the service of a particular deity
lictor	Cor II.ii.35	officer attendant on a magistrate, who enforced the sentences given to offenders
patrician	Cor I.i.14	member of one of the elite Roman families, from which leading figures (senators, consuls, etc.) were selected
plebeian	Cor II.i.90	member of the common people [plural: plebeians, plebeii]
praetor	JC I.iii.143	annually elected chief magistrate, subordinate to the consul
proconsul	Cym III.viii.8	provincial commander, carrying out the duties of a consul
senator	JC II.iv.35	member of the governing council
sibyl	1H6 I.ii.56	one of a number of wise women ('the nine sibyls of old Rome') reputed to have powers of prophecy
tribune [of the people]	Cor II.i.1	officer appointed to protect the rights of plebeians

2 ascend, reach the top **1H6** II.i.32 [Talbot to all, of the French] *if it chance the one of us do fail, / The other yet may rise against their force*

rivage *(n.)* coast, shore, bank **H5** III.Chorus.14 [Chorus] *do but think / You stand upon the rivage and behold / A city*

rival *(n.)* partner, associate, companion **Ham** I.i.13 [Barnardo to Francisco] *Horatio and Marcellus, / The rivals of my watch*

rival *(v.)* act as a rival, compete **KL** I.i.191 [Lear to Burgundy] *who … / Hath rivalled for our daughter*

rivality *(n.)* equal partnership, equality of stature **AC** III.v.7 [Eros to Enobarbus, of Lepidus] *Caesar … presently denied him rivality*

rive *(v.)* **1** split, rend, cleave **JC** I.iii.6 [Casca to Cicero] *the scolding winds / Have rived the knotty oaks;* **AC** IV.xiii.5; **Cor** V.iii.153; **JC** IV.iii.84; **TC** I.i.37, iii.316

2 open up, burst from, break out of **KL** III.ii.58 [Lear to disguised Kent, as if to a criminal] *Close pent-up guilts, / Rive your concealing continents*

3 set off, fire, make explode **1H6** IV.ii.29 [General to Talbot] *Ten thousand French have ta'en the sacrament / To rive their dangerous artillery*

rivelled *(adj.)* furrowed, wrinkled **TC** V.i.20 [Thersites to Patroclus] *the rotten diseases of the south … the rivelled fee-simple of the tetter* [in Q only] *[i.e. permanently wrinkled scaly skin]*

rivet *(n.)* bolt for fastening a piece of armour **TC** I.iii.175 [Ulysses to all, of Patroclus impersonating Nestor] *with a palsy fumbling on his gorget / Shake in and out the rivet*

rivo *(int.)* [unclear meaning] exclamation used while drinking **1H4** II.iv.109 [Prince Hal to Poins] *'Rivo!' says the drunkard*

road *(n.)* **1** harbour, anchorage, roadstead **MV** V.i.288 [Antonio to Portia] *my ships / Are safely come to road;* **CE** III.ii.155; **2H4** II.ii.160; **TG** I.i.53, II.iv.185; **TS** II.i.368

2 pathway, route, course **MV** II.ix.30 [Arragon to himself] *the martlet / Builds in the weather on the outward wall, / Even in the force and road of casualty*

3 inroad, raid, incursion **H5** I.ii.138 [King Henry to all, of the Scots] *who will make road upon us;* **Cor** III.i.5

4 period of travel, stage **H8** IV.ii.17 [Griffith to Katherine, of Wolsey] *At last, with easy roads, he came to Leicester*

roadway *(n.)* highway, common way **2H4** II.ii.54 [Prince Henry to Poins] *Never a man's thought in the world keeps the roadway better than thine*

roan *(adj.)* with a coat of mixed colour **R2** V.v.78 [Groom to Richard] *Bolingbroke rode on roan Barbary*

roarer *(n.)* roaring wave, thundering breaker **Tem** I.i.17 [Boatswain to Gonzalo] *What cares these roarers for the name of king?*

roast, rule the has total authority, domineer, be master **2H6** I.i.107 [Gloucester to all, of Suffolk] *the new-made duke that rules the roast* [Q; F *rost*]

robustious *(adj.)* boisterous, noisy, unruly **Ham** III.ii.9 [Hamlet to Players] *a robustious periwig-pated fellow;* **H5** III.vii.144

rod *(n.)* **1** inroad, foray, raid **E3** I.ii.25 [King David to Lorraine, of the English] *[we will] persist / With eager rods beyond their city,* York

2 cane, stick **Tim** II.ii.79 [Apemantus to Page] *Would I had a rod in my mouth, that I might answer thee profitably*

rogue *(n.)* vagrant, vagabond, beggar **KL** IV.vii.39 [Cordelia to Lear, of Lear on the heath] *wast thou fain … / To hovel thee with swine and rogues forlorn*

roguing *(adj.)* living like rogues, villainous, rascally **Per** IV.i.97 [Leonine alone] *These roguing thieves*

roguish *(adj.)* characteristic of vagabonds, wild **KL** III.vii.103 [Second Servant to Third Servant, of Edgar as Poor Tom] *his roguish madness / Allows itself to anything*

roisting *(adj.)* roistering, swaggering, vaunting **TC** II.ii.209 [Hector to all] *I have a roisting challenge sent amongst … the Greeks*

rolled *(adj.)* curled up, coiled **2H6** III.i.228 [Queen to all] *the snake rolled in a flowering bank*

rolling *(adj.)* flashing, expressive **TNK** IV.ii.108 [Pirithous to Theseus, of one of Palamon's knights] *in his rolling eyes sits victory*

romage *(n.)* commotion, turmoil, bustle **Ham** I.i.107 [Horatio to Marcellus and Barnardo] *this posthaste and romage in the land* [in some editions: *rummage*]

Roman *(adj.)* of Rome; sober, serious **AC** I.ii.84 [Cleopatra to Charmian, of Antony] *on the sudden / A Roman thought hath struck him*

Romish *(adj.)* Roman **Cym** I.vii.152 [Innogen to Iachimo, of Cymbeline] *if he shall think it fit / A saucy stranger in his court to mart / As in a Romish stew*

rondure *(n.)* roundness; sphere of the earth and the accompanying heavens **Sonn** 21.8 *With April's first-born flowers and all things rare, / That heaven's air in this huge rondure hems*

ronyon *(n.)* [term of abuse for a woman] mangy creature **Mac** I.iii.6 [First Witch to other Witches, of a sailor's wife] *'Aroint thee, witch!' the rump-fed ronyon cries;* **MW** IV.ii.174

rood *(n.)* ☛ **SWEARING**, p.435

rook *(n.)* ☛ bully rook

rook *(v.)* crouch, cower, squat **3H6** V.vi.47 [King to Richard] *at thy birth … / The raven rooked her on the chimney's top*

rooky *(adj.)* filled with rooks, black, dark **Mac** III.ii.51 [Macbeth to Lady Macbeth] *the crow makes wing to the rooky wood*

room *(n.)* **1** place, space **KJ** III.iv.93 [Constance to King Philip] *Grief fills the room up of my absent child;* **3H6** II.vi.54; **JC** IV.iii.39; **R2** V.v.107, vi.25

2 place, seat **TS** III.ii.249 [Baptista to all] *let Bianca take her sister's room*

3 opportunity, scope, chance **KJ** III.i.180 [Constance to Cardinal Pandulph] *lawful let it be / That I have room with Rome to curse awhile!*

4 position [in line to the throne] **3H6** III.ii.132 [Richard alone, of the future children standing between him and the crown] *To take their rooms, ere I can place myself*

root *(n.)* **1** bottom [of one's heart] **Cor** II.i.178 [Menenius to Coriolanus] *A curse begin at very root on's heart / That is not glad to see thee;* **AC** V.ii.105; **TG** V.v.104

2 vegetable root **Tim** IV.iii.23 [Timon alone] *Earth, yield me roots;* **Tim** I.ii.70, 132

root *(v.)* **1** provide with roots, receive the roots of **TG** II.iv.160 [Valentine to Proteus] *lest the base earth … / Disdain to root the summer-swelling flower*

2 grow, be established, flourish **RJ** I.i.122 [Benvolio to Lady Montague] *the grove of sycamore / That westward rooteth from this city side* [i.e. at the west side of the city]

3 root up, tear out **Tim** V.i.163 [First Senator to Timon, of Alcibiades] *Who like a boar too savage doth root up / His country's peace;* **Venus** 636

rootedly *(adv.)* deep-seatedly, in an entrenched way **Tem** III.ii.96 [Caliban to Stephano, of Prospero's spirits] *They all do hate him / As rootedly as I*

rope *(n.)* [cry of derision, imitating a parrot's cry] hangman's rope, halter **1H6** I.iii.53 [Gloucester to Winchester] *I cry a rope, a rope!;* **Tem** I.i.31 ☛ **EXCLAMATIONS**, p.158

ropery *(n.)* roguery, tricks, rascal ways **RJ** II.iv.143 [Nurse to Romeo, of Mercutio] *what saucy merchant was this that was so full of his ropery?*

rope-trick *(n.)* [unclear meaning] possibly a malapropism of 'rhetoric' or 'rope-rhetoric' [i.e. bombastic rhetoric] **TS** I.ii.110 [Grumio to Hortensio, of Petruchio] *he'll rail in his rope-tricks*

roping *(adj.)* forming rope-like threads, drooping **H5** III.v.23 [Constable to all] *Let us not hang like roping icicles / Upon our houses' thatch*

rosed (*adj.*) rosy, rose-coloured **Tit** II.iv.24 [Marcus to Lavinia, of blood] *Doth rise and fall between thy rosed lips*

rose over colour over like a rose, make rosy **H5** V.ii.291 [Burgundy to King Henry, of Katherine] *being a maid yet rosed over with the virgin crimson of modesty*

rote (*v.*) learn by heart, fix routinely **Cor** III.ii.55 [Volumnia to Coriolanus] *speak … with such words that are but roted in / Your tongue*

rotten (*adj.*) **1** unhealthy, corrupting, unwholesome **Tim** IV.iii.2 [Timon alone, of the sun] *draw from the earth / Rotten humidity;* **Cor** II.iii.31; **Luc** 778; **TC** V.i.17

  2 diseased, infected, liver-rotten **MW** III.v.100 [Falstaff to Ford as Brook] *I suffered … an intolerable fright to be detected with a jealous rotten bell-wether*

  3 flawed, erroneous, corrupt **2H4** V.ii.128 [King Henry V to his brothers] *Rotten opinion, who hath writ me down / After my seeming;* **Cor** I.x.23

  4 rusted, tarnished **R3** III.v.1 [stage direction] *Enter Richard … and Buckingham, in rotten armour*

rough (*adj.*) **1** violent, harsh, cruel **3H6** I.iv.142 [York to Queen] *Thou [art] stern, obdurate, flinty, rough, remorseless;* **2H6** IV.ix.44; **3H6** I.iv.27, II.i.63

  2 arbitrary, severe, strong **Tim** IV.iii.445 [Timon to Bandits] *The laws … in their rough power / Has unchecked theft*

  3 imperfect, unpolished, untidy **Tim** I.i.44 [Poet to Painter, of his poem about Timon] *I have in this rough work shaped out a man*

  4 inadequate, dull, lacking grace **LL** V.ii.306 [Rosaline to Princess, of their visitors] *their rough carriage so ridiculous;* **1H6** V.iii.71

  5 difficult to manage, not thoroughly trained **TS** I.i.55 [Gremio to Baptista, of Katherina] *She's too rough for me;* **TNK** II.iv.47

  6 hairy, shaggy **WT** I.ii.128 [Leontes to Mamillius] *Thou want'st a rough pash and the shoots that I have / To be full like me*

rough-hew (*v.*) hew roughly, give rough shape to **Ham** V.ii.11 [Hamlet to Horatio] *There's a divinity that shapes our ends, / Rough-hew them how we will*

round (*n.*) **1** circle dance, ring **MND** II.i.140 [Titania to Oberon] *If you will patiently dance in our round … go with us;* **Mac** IV.i.129; **MND** III.i.100

  2 circlet, ring, crown **Mac** IV.i.87 [Macbeth to Witches, of the Third Apparition] *That … wears upon his baby brow the round / And top of sovereignty;* **Mac** I.v.26; **MW** IV.iv.49

  3 globe, earth **Venus** 368 [Venus to Adonis] *O fairest mover on this mortal round*

  4 rung **JC** II.i.24 [Brutus alone, of an ambitious young man] *when he once attains the upmost round*

round (*adj.*) **1** blunt, forthright, straight, plain-spoken **TN** II.iii.93 [Malvolio to Sir Toby] *I must be round with you;* **CE** II.i.82; **Ham** III.i.184; **H5** IV.i.198; **KL** I.iv.53; **Oth** I.iii.90

  2 heavy, substantial **H8** V.iv.79 [Lord Chamberlain to Porter and Man] *I'll … on your heads / Clap round fines for neglect;* **MV** I.iii.100

round (*v.*) **1** ring, encircle, surround **R2** III.ii.161 [King Richard to all] *the hollow crown / That rounds the mortal temples of a king;* **AW** I.iii.147; **MND** II.i.50; **R3** V.i.59; **TNK** IV.i.84

  2 become round, grow to full form [in pregnancy] **WT** II.i.16 [First Lady to Mamillius] *The Queen, your mother, rounds apace*

  3 finish off, bring to completeness **Tem** IV.i.158 [Prospero to Ferdinand] *our little life / Is rounded with a sleep*

  4 whisper, murmur, speak privately **WT** I.ii.217 [Leontes to himself, of people around him] *They're here with me already: whispering, rounding;* **KJ** II.i.566; **PassP** XVIII.51

round (*adv.*) openly, roundly, in a straightforward way **Ham** II.ii.139 [Polonius to Claudius and Gertrude] *I went round to work*

roundel (*n.*) dance in a circle **MND** II.ii.1 [Titania to Fairies] *Come, now a roundel and a fairy song*

roundly (*adv.*) **1** plainly, to the point, straight out **1H4** I.ii.22 [Prince Hal to Falstaff, asking for a reply] *Come, roundly, roundly;* **TS** I.ii.58, III.ii.213, IV.iv.103

  2 bluntly, outspokenly; or: fluently, glibly **R2** II.i.122 [King Richard to John of Gaunt] *This tongue that runs so roundly in thy head;* **TC** III.ii.152; **TS** V.ii.21

  3 smartly, briskly, directly **AY** V.iii.10 [First Page to all, of the song] *Shall we clap into't roundly;* **2H4** III.ii.17

roundure (*n.*) roundness, rounded form **KJ** II.i.259 [King Philip to Hubert, of not acknowledging Arthur] *'Tis not the roundure of your old-faced walls / Can hide you from our messengers of war* [F *rounder*]

rouse (*n.*) full draught (of wine), brimful cup, carousing **Ham** I.iv.8 [Hamlet to Horatio] *The King doth wake tonight and takes his rouse;* **Ham** I.ii.127, II.i.58; **Oth** II.iii.60

rouse (*v.*) **1** [hunting] startle from a lair, draw out **3H6** V.i.65 [Edward to Richard] *We'll quickly rouse the traitors;* **Cym** III.iii.98; **1H4** I.iii.196; **Mac** III.ii.53; **R2** II.iii.127; **Venus** 240

  2 raise, lift up **H5** I.ii.276 [King Henry to Ambassador] *When I do rouse me in my throne of France;* **AC** V.ii.283; **2H4** IV.i.116; **Luc** 541

rout (*n.*) **1** band, company, crowd **TNK** III.v.105 [Schoolmaster to Theseus] *We are a merry rout;* **2H6** II.i.165; **Per** III.Chorus.1; **TNK** III.v.149; **TS** III.ii.180

  2 rabble, mob, disorderly crowd **2H4** IV.i.9 [Prince John to Archbishop] *Cheering a rout of rebels with your drum;* **CE** III.i.101; **1H6** IV.i.173; **JC** I.i.78; **Tim** IV.iii.44

  3 brawl, disturbance, riot **Oth** II.iii.204 [Othello to all] *Give me to know / How this foul rout began;* **2H4** IV.i.33

rout, on the put to rout, in disordered flight **2H6** V.ii.31 [Young Clifford to himself, of the battle] *All is on the rout*

rover (*n.*) wanderer, vagabond **WT** I.ii.176 [Leontes to Hermione, of Mamillius and Polixenes] *Next to thyself and my young rover, he's / Apparent to my heart*

row (*n.*) stanza, verse **Ham** II.ii.418 [Hamlet to Polonius] *The first row of the pious chanson will show you more* [F, Q2; Q1 *verse*]

rowel (*n.*) small sharp wheel at the end of a spur **TNK** V.iv.70 [Pirithous to Palamon, of Arcite's horse] *pig-like he whines / At the sharp rowel;* **Cym** IV.iv.39

rowel-head (*n.*) extremity of the spur-wheel **2H4** I.i.46 [Travers to Northumberland, of a gentleman] *he … struck his armed heels / Against the panting sides of his poor jade / Up to the rowel-head*

royal (*adj.*) **1** like a king, majestic **KL** V.iii.174 [Albany to all, of Edgar] *thy very gait did prophesy / A royal nobleness;* **AY** IV.iii.118; **H5** IV.viii.100; **R3** I.ii.244; **TNK** III.i.154

  2 kingly; also: to the value of the English coin worth ten shillings **1H4** I.ii.139 [Falstaff to Prince Hal] *thou camest not of the blood royal, if thou darest not stand for ten shillings;* **1H4** II.iv.283 ☞ **MONEY**, p.286

  3 generous, munificent, bountiful **JC** III.ii.245 [Third Plebeian to all] *O royal Caesar!;* **H8** IV.i.8; **JC** III.i.127

royalize (*v.*) make royal, invest with a majestic character **R3** I.iii.124 [Richard to Queen Elizabeth, of King Edward] *To royalize his blood I spent mine own;* **E3** IV.iv.37

royal merchant merchant prince **MV** III.ii.239 [Gratiano to Salerio] *How doth that royal merchant, good Antonio?;* **MV** IV.i.29

royalty (*n.*) **1** majesty, royal highness **KJ** V.ii.129 [Bastard to Lewis the Dauphin, of King John] *thus his royalty doth speak in me;* **AC** I.iii.91; **H5** III.Chorus.5; **WT** I.ii.15

  2 regal quality, majestic character, lordliness **Mac** III.i.49 [Macbeth alone, of Banquo] *in his royalty of nature / Reigns that which would be feared;* **Cym** IV.ii.178

  3 emblem of royalty, symbol of sovereignty **R3** V.v.4 [Derby to Richmond, of the crown] *this long usurped royalty;* **1H4** IV.iii.55; **KJ** IV.ii.5

  4 right granted by a monarch, royal prerogative **R2** III.iii.113 [Northumberland to King Richard, of Bolingbroke] *His coming hither hath no further scope / Than for his lineal royalties;* **KJ** II.i.176; **R2** II.i.190, iii.119; **Tem** I.ii.110

roynish (*adj.*) vulgar, scurvy, coarse **AY** II.ii.8 [Second Lord to Duke Frederick] *the roynish clown … is also missing*

rub (n.) **1** [bowls] obstacle, impediment, hindrance **Ham** III.i.65 [Hamlet to himself] *there's the rub*; **Cor** III.i.60; **H5** II.ii.188; **H8** II.i.129; **KJ** III.iv.128; **R2** III.iv.4

2 roughness, unevenness, inequality **Mac** III.i.133 [Macbeth to Murderers, of killing Banquo] *leave no rubs and botches in the work*

rub (v.) **1** hinder, impede, sidetrack **KL** II.ii.152 [Gloucester to disguised Kent, of Cornwall] *Whose disposition … / Will not be rubbed nor stopped*

2 irritate, annoy, aggravate **Tem** II.i.140 [Gonzalo to Sebastian] *You rub the sore, / When you should bring the plaster*

3 stir up, encourage, stimulate **TC** II.iii.198 [Nestor to himself, of Ulysses and Ajax] *he rubs the vein of him*

rub on (v.) [bowls] encounter an obstacle which changes the course of a bowl **TC** III.ii.48 [Pandarus to Troilus, of Cressida] *So, so, rub on, and kiss the mistress*

rubbing (n.) hindrance, impediment, forming of obstacles **LL** IV.i.140 [Boyet to Costard, of challenging Maria to bowl] *I fear too much rubbing* [with bawdy pun]

rubbish (n.) litter, debris, waste matter **JC** I.iii.109 [Cassius to Casca] *What trash is Rome, / What rubbish, and what offal*

rubies (n.) lips [red as rubies] **Cym** II.ii.17 [Iachimo to himself, of Innogen] *Rubies unparagoned*

rubious (adj.) ruby-coloured, deep red **TN** I.iv.32 [Orsino to and of Viola as Cesario] *Diana's lip / Is not more smooth and rubious*

ruddock (n.) robin, redbreast **Cym** IV.ii.224 [Arviragus to Belarius and Guiderius] *the ruddock … / With charitable bill* [F *Raddocke*]

rude (adj.) **1** violent, harsh, unkind **2H6** IV.iv.33 [First Messenger to King, of Cade] *His army is a ragged multitude / Of hinds and peasants, rude and merciless*; **CE** V.i.358; **2H4** I.i.159; **KJ** IV.ii.240; **R2** V.v.105; **TC** IV.iv.40

2 rough, wild, harsh-looking **R2** III.iii.32 [Bolingbroke to Northumberland] *Go to the rude ribs of that ancient castle*; **AC** I.iv.64; **KJ** IV.iii.257, V.vii.27; **R3** IV.i.101; **Sonn** 11.10, 113.9

3 [of wind or water] stormy, turbulent, harsh **KL** IV.ii.30 [Albany to Gonerill] *the dust which the rude wind / Blows in your face*; **2H4** III.i.20, 27; **H8** III.ii.364; **MND** II.i.152; **R2** III.iii.54; **TN** V.i.76

4 uncivilized, uncultivated, unrefined **MM** IV.iii.79 [disguised Duke to Provost, of Barnardino] *whiles I / Persuade this rude wretch willingly to die*; **Cym** III.vii.38; **1H4** III.iii.14; **2H6** III.ii.271; **JC** III.i.30; **KJ** I.i.64

5 impolite, offensive **AY** II.vii.93 [Duke Senior to Orlando] *Art thou … a rude despiser of good manners*; **2H4** I.i.196; **2H6** IV.x.29; **H8** IV.ii.103

6 ignorant, unlearned, uneducated **LL** V.i.84 [Armado to Holofernes] *in the posteriors of this day, which the rude multitude call the afternoon*; **H5** I.i.55; **1H6** IV.i.98; **MND** III.ii.9; **R2** III.iv.74

7 amateurish, inexpert, lacking polish **Oth** I.iii.81 [Othello to all] *Rude am I in my speech*; **2H6** III.i.30; **RJ** I.v.51; **Sonn** 32.4; **TC** III.ii.23; **TNK** III.v.121

8 cacophonous, raucous, barbarous **MV** II.ii.168 [Bassanio to Gratiano] *Thou art too wild, too rude and bold of voice*; **KJ** IV.ii.150; **Oth** III.iii.352; **R3** II.ii.38; **TC** I.i.91

9 uncontrolled, unruly, of the flesh **Luc** 175 [of fear] *Beaten away by brain-sick rude desire*; **RJ** II.iii.24

rude-growing (adj.) spreading rough and wild **Tit** II.iii.198 [Quintus to Martius] *What subtle hole is this, / Whose mouth is covered with rude-growing briers?*

rudely (adj.) violent, rough, harsh **Per** III.i.30 [Pericles to Marina] *Thou art the rudeliest welcome to this world*

rudely (adv.) **1** violently, roughly, with great force **Luc** 669 [Tarquin to Lucrece] *enforced hate / Instead of love's coy touch, shall rudely tear thee*; **Cor** IV.v.145; **Luc** 170; **Sonn** 66.6; **TC** IV.iv.34

2 discourteously, boorishly, with ill manners **1H4** III.ii.32 [King Henry to Prince Hal] *Thy place in Council thou hast rudely lost*

3 roughly, clumsily, imperfectly **R3** I.i.16 [Richard alone] *I … am rudely stamped*

rudeness (n.) **1** rough manner, uncouth behaviour **JC** I.ii.297 [Cassius to Brutus, of Casca] *This rudeness is a sauce to his good wit*; **TC** II.i.52

2 violent action, forceful strength **TC** I.iii.207 [Ulysses to all, of a battering-ram] *the great swing and rudeness of his poise*; **Lover** 104

3 roughness, coarse state **Cym** IV.ii.214 [Arviragus to Belarius and Guiderius, of his shoes] *whose rudeness / Answered my steps too loud*

rudesby (n.) ruffian, piece of insolence, unmannerly fellow **TN** IV.i.50 [Olivia to Sir Toby] *Rudesby, be gone!*; **TS** III.ii.10

rudiment (n.) first principles, basic points **TNK** III.v.3 [Schoolmaster to all] *Have my rudiments / Been laboured so long with ye*

rue (v.) pity, grieve for, feel for **2H6** II.iv.24 [Duchess to Gloucester, of the crowd] *in thy closet pent up, rue my shame*; **Tit** I.i.108

ruff (n.) ruffle, flap of a top-boot **AW** III.ii.7 [Clown to Countess, of Bertram] *he will look upon his boot … mend the ruff and sing* ☛ **CLOTHING**, p.79

ruffian (adj.) violent, brutal, villainous **2H4** III.i.22 [King Henry IV alone] *the visitation of the winds, / Who take the ruffian billows by the top*; **2H6** V.ii.49

ruffian (v.) rage, bluster, rampage **Oth** II.i.7 [Montano to First Gentleman, of the wind] *If it hath ruffianed so upon the sea*

ruffle (n.) hustle-and-bustle, flurry, excitement **Lover** 58 [of the reverend man] *Sometime a blusterer, that the ruffle knew / Of Court of City*

ruffle (v.) **1** rage, bluster, storm **KL** II.iv.296 [Gloucester to all] *the bleak winds / Do sorely ruffle* [F; Q *russel*]

2 handle roughly, treat with outrage **KL** III.vii.41 [Gloucester to Regan] *my hospitable favours / You should not ruffle thus*

3 make trouble, cause a disturbance **Tit** I.i.316 [Saturninus to Titus, of Bassianus] *One fit … / To ruffle in the commonwealth of Rome*

ruffle up (v.) stir to anger, enrage **JC** III.ii.229 [Antony to all] *there were an Antony / Would ruffle up your spirits*

ruffling (adj.) frilled, lace-adorned; also: embellishing, gay **TS** IV.iii.60 [Petruchio to Katherina, of the Tailor] *To deck thy body with his ruffling treasure*

rugged (adj.) **1** hairy, shaggy, bristling **Mac** III.iv.99 [Macbeth to Banquo's ghost] *Approach thou like the rugged Russian bear*; **Ham** II.ii.450; **2H6** III.ii.175

2 frowning, wrinkled with irritation **Mac** III.ii.27 [Lady Macbeth to Macbeth] *sleek o'er your rugged looks*

rug-headed (adj.) shaggy-headed, shock-headed **R2** II.i.156 [King Richard to York, of the Irish] *We must supplant those rough rug-headed kerns*

ruin (n.) **1** ruination, destruction, devastation **1H6** III.iii.46 [Pucelle to Burgundy, of France] *the cities and the towns defaced / By wasting ruin of the cruel foe*; **1H6** II.ii.11, V.ii.7; **TC** V.iii.58

2 [metaphor for] destitute, case of hardship **TNK** I.ii.13 [Palamon to Arcite] *What strange ruins … may we perceive / Walking in Thebes?*; **MV** II.ix.48; **TNK** I.ii.27

3 fall, giving way, overthrow **1H6** IV.vii.10 [Talbot to Servant, of John Talbot] *when my angry guardant stood alone, / Tendering my ruin*

4 (plural) remains, remnants, residue **2H4** II.ii.23 [Prince Henry to Poins] *God knows whether those that bawl out the ruins of thy linen shall inherit His kingdom*

ruinate (v.) reduce to ruins, bring to destruction **3H6** V.i.83 [George to Warwick] *I will not ruinate my father's house*; **Luc** 944; **Sonn** 10.7

ruinous (adj.) ruined, decayed, ravaged **Tit** V.i.21 [Second Goth to Lucius] *I strayed / To gaze upon a ruinous monastery*; **TC** V.ii.25; **TG** V.iv.9

rule (n.) **1** principle, order, regulation **TC** V.ii.144 [Troilus to Ulysses, of Cressida] *If there be rule in unity itself, / This is not she*; **JC** V.i.100; **R3** I.ii.68; **TS** III.i.79

2 proper discipline, good management **TC** I.iii.78 [Ulysses to all] *The specialty of rule hath been neglected;* **1H4** IV.iii.39; **Mac** V.ii.16; **MV** IV.i.175

3 government, country, state **3H6** III.iii.76 [Queen to Lewis] *usurpers sway the rule awhile*

rule (*v.*) control, direct, guide **Venus** 673 [Venus to Adonis] *if thou needs wilt hunt, be ruled by me;* **Cor** III.i.36; **1H6** III.iii.8; **2H4** IV.iii.65; **TN** IV.i.63

rumour (*n.*) **1** tumult, din, confusion **JC** II.iv.18 [Portia to Lucius] *I heard a bustling rumour like a fray;* **KJ** V.iv.45

2 talk, report, news **1H6** II.iii.7 [Countess to herself, of Talbot] *Great is the rumour of this dreadful knight*

run (*v.*) **1** pass, spread, bring, cause to flow **MW** I.i.155 [Nym to Slender] *if you run the nuthook's humour on me;* **H5** II.i.116

2 fall, move, come **H8** I.ii.110 [Queen Katherine to King Henry] *I am sorry that the Duke of Buckingham / Is run in your displeasure*

3 follow a course, behave **KJ** III.iii.5 [King Philip to Cardinal Pandulph] *What can go well, when we have run so ill?* [also: sense 4]

4 run away [from battle] **Tem** III.ii.17 [Stephano to Caliban] *We'll not run*

runs the world away, thus that's the way of the world **Ham** III.ii.283 [Hamlet to Horatio] *For some must watch, while some must sleep. / Thus runs the world away*

runagate (*n.*) **1** runaway, vagabond, fugitive **RJ** III.v.89 [Lady Capulet to Juliet, of Romeo] *in Mantua, / Where that same banished runagate doth live;* **Cym** I.vii.137, IV.i.62

2 renegade, turncoat, rebel **R3** IV.iv.464 [King Richard to Derby, of Richmond] *White-livered runagate*

runaway (*n.*) deserter, coward, renegade **R3** V.iii.317 [King Richard to his army, of the enemy] *A sort of vagabonds, rascals, and runaways*

running (*adj.*) running out, emptying **Cym** I.vii.49 [Iachimo to Innogen] *that tub / Both filled and running*

running banquet ⮞ banquet, running

rush (*n.*) **1** reed **AC** III.v.16 [Eros to Enobarbus, of Antony] *He … spurns / The rush that lies before him;* **AY** III.v.356, v.22; **CE** IV.iii.72; **Cym** II.ii.12

2 ring made of rushes, reed ring **AW** II.ii.22 [Clown to Countess, of his answer] *As fit as … Tib's rush for Tom's forefinger*

3 charge, onslaught, attack **Oth** V.ii.268 [Othello to Gratiano] *Man but a rush against Othello's breast, / And he retires*

rush-candle (*n.*) candle made of a rush dipped in tallow-wax [giving poor light] **TS** IV.v.14 [Katherina to Petruchio, of the sun] *if you please to call it a rush-candle … it shall be so for me*

rushling (*adj.*) rustling, swishing **MW** II.ii.65 [Mistress Quickly to Falstaff, of courtiers' dress] *so rushling … in silk and gold*

russel (*v.*) ruffle (*v.*) 1

russet (*adj.*) **1** rustic, homely, simple **LL** V.ii.413 [Berowne to Rosaline] *my wooing mind shall be expressed / In russet yeas and honest kersey noes*

2 reddish-brown [the colour of a rough cloth once worn by country people] **Ham** I.i.167 [Horatio to Marcellus and Barnardo] *the morn in russet mantle clad*

russet-pated (*adj.*) with reddish-brown head; or: grey-headed **MND** III.ii.21 [Puck to Oberon] *russet-pated choughs, many in sort*

rustically (*adv.*) like a rustic, in a countrified way **AY** I.i.6 [Orlando to Adam, of Oliver] *he keeps me rustically at home*

rustle (*v.*) clatter, make a racket **AC** V.ii.319 [stage direction] *Enter the Guard, rustling in*

ruth (*n.*) pity, compassion, sympathy **Sonn** 132.4 [of his lover's eyes] *Looking with pretty ruth upon my pain;* **Cor** I.i.195; **R2** III.iv.106; **TC** V.iii.48

ruthful (*adj.*) piteous, lamentable, woeful **TC** V.iii.48 [Troilus to Hector, of their swords] *Spur them to ruthful work;* **3H6** II.v.95; **Tit** V.i.66

ruthless (*adj.*) unpitying, pitiless, unsparing **2H6** II.iv.34 [Duchess to Gloucester] *The ruthless flint doth cut my tender feet;* **R3** IV.iii.5

rut-time (*n.*) mating season, time for sex **MW** V.v.13 [Falstaff to himself] *Send me a cool rut-time, Jove*

rutting (*n.*) fornication, promiscuity **Per** IV.v.9 [First Gentleman to Second Gentleman] *I am out of the road of rutting for ever*

ruttish (*adj.*) lustful, lascivious, wanton **AW** IV.iii.210 [Parolles to First Soldier, of Bertram] *a foolish idle boy, but for all that very ruttish*

rye-straw (*adj.*) made of straw from the rye plant **Tem** IV.i.136 [Iris to reapers] *your rye-straw hats put on*

's *(det.)* **1** contracted form of 'his' **KL** I.v.29 [Fool to Lear, of why a snail has a house] *Why, to put's head in*
2 contracted form of 'this' **Ham** III.ii.136 [Hamlet to Ophelia] *my father died within's two hours*

's *(pron.)* **1** contracted form of 'us' **AC** III.xiii.114 [Antony to Cleopatra] *the wise gods ... laugh at's*
2 contracted form of 'shall' **RJ** I.iii.10 [Lady Capulet to Nurse] *thou's hear our counsel*

sa *(int.)* ➤ **SOUNDS**, p.410

sable *(n.)* **1** black **Ham** I.ii.242 [Horatio to Hamlet, describing King Hamlet's beard] *A sable silvered*
2 rich fur [from the animal, sable], expensive garment **Ham** III.ii.139 [Hamlet to Ophelia] *I'll have a suit of sables*; **Ham** IV.vii.79

sable *(adj.)* black **Per** V.Chorus.19 [Gower alone, of Pericles' ship] *His banners sable*; **Ham** II.ii.450; **Luc** 117, 1074; **Phoen** 18; **Sonn** 12.4

sack *(n.)* [type of] white wine **2H4** V.iii.14 [Shallow to Falstaff] *I have drunk too much sack at supper*; **1H4** I.ii.3; **MW** II.ii.143; **Tem** II.ii.119; **TN** II.iii.183; **TS** Induction.ii.2

sack *(v.)* plunder, pillage, despoil **RJ** III.iii.107 [Romeo to Friar, of where his name lives in his body] *Tell me, that I may sack / The hateful mansion*

sackbut *(n.)* type of bass trumpet, with a trombone-like slide **Cor** V.iv.48 [Second Messenger to Sicinius] *sackbuts, psalteries, and fifes*

sacred *(adj.)* **1** consecrated, hallowed, sanctified **H5** I.ii.7 [Canterbury to King Henry] *God and His angels guard your sacred throne*; **1H6** I.ii.114; **KJ** III.i.148
2 revered, respected [as if a holy thing] **CE** V.i.133 [Adriana to Duke] *Justice, most sacred Duke, against the Abbess!*; **1H6** IV.vi.40; **TG** III.i.211; **TS** I.i.173
3 accursed, blasphemous **Tit** II.i.120 [Aaron to Demetrius and Chiron, of Tamora] *our Empress with her sacred wit / To villainy and vengeance consecrate* [or: consecrated]

sacrificing *(adj.)* sacrificial **Tit** I.i.147 [Lucius to Titus] *entrails feed the sacrificing fire*

sacring *(adj.)* [in the Mass] rung at the moment of consecration **H8** III.ii.295 [Surrey to Wolsey] *I'll startle you / Worse than the sacring bell*

sad *(adj.)* **1** serious, grave, solemn **H5** IV.i.294 [King Henry alone, praying] *I have built / Two chantries where the sad and solemn priests / Sing still for Richard's soul* ➤ **FEW**, p.xxi
2 dismal, morose, sullen **MND** III.ii.439 [Puck to himself, of Hermia] *Here she comes, curst and sad*; **AC** III.xiii.183; **R2** V.v.70
3 downcast, distressed, mournful, gloomy **MA** I.iii.13 [Don John to Conrade] *I must be sad when I have cause*; **H5** IV.Chorus.25; **3H6** III.ii.110; **MA** I.iii.2, II.i.265
4 dark-coloured, sober-hued **Tit** V.ii.1 [disguised Tamora to Chiron and Demetrius] *in this strange and sad habiliment*

sad-eyed, sad-faced *(adj.)* grave-looking **H5** I.ii.202 [Canterbury to all] *The sad-eyed justice, with his surly hum*; **Tit** V.iii.66 [Marcus to all] *You sad-faced men, people and sons of Rome*

sadly *(adv.)* seriously, gravely, solemnly **MA** II.ii.216 [Benedick alone] *The conference was sadly borne*; **Ham** II.ii.168; **2H4** V.ii.125; **Oth** II.i.32; **R3** V.iii.288; **RJ** I.i.201

sadness *(n.)* seriousness, gravity **Cym** I.vii.62 [Innogen to Iachimo, of Posthumus] *When he was here / He did incline to sadness*; **3H6** III.ii.77

sadness, in / in good in earnest, seriously **AW** IV.iii.198 [Parolles to First Soldier] *In good sadness, I do not know* [i.e. in all honesty]; **RJ** I.i.199 [Benvolio to Romeo] *Tell me in sadness, who is that you love*; **MW** III.v.113, IV.ii.86; **TS** V.ii.63; **Venus** 807

safe *(adj.)* **1** harmless, not dangerous **R2** V.iii.40 [King Henry to Aumerle] *I'll make thee safe!*
2 sure, certain, assured **KL** I.iv.201 [Gonerill to Lear, of his knights' behaviour] *I had thought ... / To have found a safe redress*; **Mac** III.iv.24

3 sound, sensible, level-headed **Cym** IV.ii.131 [Belarius to Guiderius and Arviragus, of Cloten] *in all safe reason / He must have some attendants;* **Cor** II.iii.217

4 sane, sound, mentally balanced **KL** IV.vi.81 [Edgar to himself, of Lear] *The safer sense will ne'er accommodate / His master thus*

5 safely out of the way **Tem** III.i.21 [Miranda to Ferdinand, of Prospero] *He's safe for these three hours;* **TS** IV.iv.79

safe (v.) **1** remove danger from, make one feel secure about **AC** I.iii.55 [Antony to Cleopatra] *My more particular, / And that which most with you should sake my going, / Is Fulvia's death*

2 conduct safely, give safe-conduct to **AC** IV.vi.26 [Soldier to Enobarbus] *Best you safed the bringer / Out of the host*

safe (adv.) trustworthily, in an assured way **Mac** I.iv.28 [Macbeth to King] *doing everything / Safe toward your love and honour*

safeguard (n.) safeguarding, defence, protection **3H6** II.ii.18 [Clifford to King] *doves will ne'er peck in safeguard of their brood;* **Cor** III.ii.68; **MM** V.i.416; **R3** V.iii.260

safeguard, on under safe-conduct, with guarantee of safe passage **Cor** III.i.9 [Lartius to Coriolanus, of Aufidius] *On safeguard he came to me*

safety (n.) **1** prudent course of action, best safeguard **2H6** V.iii.23 [York to all, of the enemy] *I know our safety is to follow them;* **KJ** IV.iii.12; **Mac** III.i.53; **TC** V.iii.94

2 safe keeping, custody **RJ** V.iii.183 [First Watchman to Second Watchman, of Balthasar] *Hold him in safety till the Prince come hither;* **KJ** V.ii.158

3 concern for safety, need for protection **Ham** IV.vii.8 [Laertes to Claudius] *these feats … / As by your safety, greatness, wisdom, all things else, / You mainly were stirred up*

saffron (n.) **1** orange-red dye [for colouring some types of food or drink] **WT** IV.iii.44 [Clown to himself] *I must have saffron to colour the warden pies*

2 saffron-coloured clothing **AW** IV.v.2 [Lafew to Countess, of Parolles] *whose villainous saffron would have made all the unbaked and doughy youth of a nation in his colour*

saffron (adj.) orange-red in colour **Tem** IV.i.78 [Ceres to Iris] *with thy saffron wings;* **CE** IV.v.59

sage (adj.) solemn, grave, dignified **TN** III.iv.369 [Sir Toby to Sir Andrew and Fabian] *We'll whisper o'er a couplet or two of most sage saws;* **Ham** V.i.233

said, I / you have finished speaking, had one's say **WT** III.ii.198 [Paulina to all] *When I have said, cry woe!* ▶ **DISCOURSE MARKERS**, p.127

said, well well done **Oth** II.i.164 [Iago to himself, of Cassio taking Desdemona's hand] *Ay, well said;* **AC** IV.iv.28; **2H4** III.ii.267; **2H6** III.ii.8; **Per** III.ii.86; **RJ** I.v.86

sail (n.) **1** ship, vessel **Oth** I.iii.37 [Messenger to First Senator, of the size of the Ottoman fleet] *Of thirty sail;* **AC** II.vi.24 [Antony to Pompey] *Thou canst not fear us … with thy sails;* **KJ** III.iv.2

2 fleet, squadron, flotilla **Per** I.iv.61 [Lord to Cleon] *We have descried … / A portly sail of ships*

3 voyage, passage, sailing **Tem** V.i.316 [Prospero to Alonso] *I'll … promise you … sail so expeditious, that shall catch / Your royal fleet far off*

4 surging power, full swell **H5** I.ii.275 [King Henry to Ambassador] *I will … / Be like a king, and show my sail of greatness*

sain (v.) [archaism] said **LL** III.i.81 [Armado to Mote, of the word 'envoy'] *it is an epilogue or discourse to make plain / Some obscure precedence that hath tofore been sain* ▶ **ARCHAISMS**, p.22

saint (v.) be saintly, play the saint **PassP** XVIII.44 [Pilgrim] *Think women still to strive with men, / To sin and never for to saint*

sainted (adj.) **1** saintly, angelic, of holy character **Mac** IV.iii.109 [Macduff to Malcolm] *Thy royal father / Was a most sainted king;* **AW** III.iv.7; **MM** I.iv.34

2 made a saint, from heaven **WT** V.i.57 [Leontes to Paulina, of Hermione] *make her sainted spirit / Again possess her corpse*

Saint Martin's summer Indian summer [feast of St Martin on 11 November] **1H6** I.ii.131 [Pucelle to all] *Expect Saint Martin's summer, halcyon days*

sake, for the Lord's [cry of a prisoner calling for alms through a cell window] in jail **MM** IV.iii.18 [Pompey alone, of the men he has met in prison] *all great doers in our trade, and are now 'for the Lord's sake'*

sake, for your on your account, because of you **Oth** I.iii.193 [Brabantio to Desdemona] *For your sake … / I am glad at soul I have no other child*

salary (n.) reward, fee, payment **Ham** III.iii.79 [Hamlet to himself] *this is hire and salary, not revenge*

sale-work (n.) ready-made goods **AY** III.v.43 [Rosalind as Ganymede to Phebe] *I see no more in you than in the ordinary / Of nature's sale-work* [i.e. of inferior quality]

Salic, Salique (adj.) name of a law stating that the French crown could be passed on only by males **H5** I.ii.11 [King Henry to Canterbury] *unfold / Why the law Salic that they have in France / Or should or should not bar us in our claim;* **H5** I.ii.91

sallet (n.) **1** salad **AW** IV.v.15 [Clown to Lafew, of Helena] *she was the sweet-marjoram of the sallet;* **AW** IV.v.13; **2H6** IV.x.8; **KL** III.iv.126

2 [= salad] tasty bit **Ham** II.ii.440 [Hamlet to First Player] *there were no sallets in the lines* [i.e. no vulgarity]

3 light round helmet **2H6** IV.x.10 [Cade alone] *many a time, but for a sallet, my brain-pan had been cleft with a brown bill* ▶ **WEAPONS**, p.491

sally (n.) sudden attack against an enemy, sortie **1H4** II.iii.53 [Lady Percy to Hotspur] *thou hast talked / Of sallies;* **1H6** IV.iv.4; **TC** V.iii.14

sally (v.) burst out, make a sudden attack **AW** IV.i.2 [First Lord to all, of Parolles] *When you sally upon him*

salt (n.) **1** salt tears **KL** IV.vi.196 [Lear to Gentleman] *this would make a man a man of salt;* **Cor** V.vi.93

2 vigour, liveliness, spirit **MW** II.iii.43 [Shallow to Page] *we have some salt of our youth in us*

salt (adj.) **1** salt-water, sea **MW** I.i.20 [Shallow to Evans] *The luce is the fresh fish. The salt fish is an old coat*

2 salted, preserved, dried **AC** II.v.17 [Charmian to Cleopatra] *your diver / Did hang a salt fish on his hook*

3 stinging, bitter, biting **TC** I.iii.371 [Ulysses to Nestor, of Achilles] *we were better parch in Afric sun / Than in the pride and salt scorn of his eyes*

4 [of a cold] bitter, intense, heavy **Oth** III.iv.51 [Othello to Desdemona] *I have a salt and sorry rheum offends me;* **CE** III.ii.135

5 lascivious, lustful, lecherous **Tim** IV.iii.86 [Timon to Timandra] *Make use of thy salt hours;* **AC** II.i.21; **MM** V.i.398; **Oth** II.i.233, III.iii.401

salt-butter (adj.) cheap-living, mean, avaricious **MW** II.ii.265 [Falstaff to Ford as Brook, of Ford] *Hang him, mechanical salt-butter rogue!*

saltier (n.) malapropism for 'satyr' **WT** IV.iv.325 [Servant to Shepherd, of the herdsmen] *that have made themselves all men of hair: they call themselves Saltiers*

saltness (n.) [unclear meaning] maturing power; piquancy; vigour **2H4** I.ii.98 [Falstaff to Lord Chief Justice] *Your lordship … have yet some smack of age in you, some relish of the saltness of time*

saltpetre (n.) substance used for making gunpowder [potassium nitrate] **1H4** I.iii.59 [Hotspur to King Henry] *This villainous saltpetre should be digged*

salt-wayed (adj.) with salt-filled courses **Luc** 1231 [of Lucrece's eyes] *Who in a salt-wayed ocean quench their light* [in some editions: *salt-waved*]

salute (v.) **1** greet, welcome, address **CE** IV.iii.1 [Antipholus of Syracuse alone] *There's not a man I meet but doth salute me;* **AY** III.ii.46; **KJ** II.i.30; **R2** III.ii.6; **TC** IV.ii.19; **TNK** III.i.23

2 approach, greet, make contact with **Tit** II.i.5 [Aaron alone] *the golden sun salutes the morn;* **KJ** II.i.590

3 pay respects to, make a formal visit to **TG** I.iii.41 [Panthino to Antonio] *gentlemen … / Are journeying to salute the Emperor, / And to commend their service to his will*
4 affect, act upon, excite **H8** II.iii.103 [Anne to Old Lady, of her advancement] *Would I had no being, / If this salute my blood a jot*

salvage (n.) variant form of 'savage' **Tem** II.ii.57 [Stephano to Caliban] *Do you put tricks upon's with salvages and men of Ind* [F]

salve (n.) healing ointment **LL** IV.iii.287 [Dumaine to Berowne, of breaking their oaths] *Some salve for perjury*; **LL** III.i.70; **Sonn** 34.7, 120.12

salve (v.) **1** heal, remedy, make good **Cor** III.ii.70 [Menenius to Coriolanus] *Come, go with us, speak fair. You may salve so*; **1H4** III.ii.155; **Sonn** 35.7
2 make more acceptable, soften down, account for **MA** I.i.294 [Claudio to Don Pedro, of his love for Hero] *I would have salved it with a longer treatise*

samingo (int.) [unclear meaning] type of drinking refrain [Latin 'mingo' = urinate] **2H4** V.iii.75 [Silence singing] *Do me right, / And dub me knight: / Samingo*

sampire, samphire (n.) variety of marine plant **KL** IV.vi.15 [Edgar to Gloucester, of the cliff birds] *Halfway down / Hangs one that gathers sampire* ☞ **PLANTS**, p.330

sample (n.) example, exemplar, model **Cym** I.i.48 [First Gentleman to Second Gentleman, of Posthumus] *A sample to the youngest* [courtiers]

sampler (n.) piece of embroidery **Tit** II.iv.39 [Marcus to Lavinia, of Philomela] *she but lost her tongue / And in a tedious sampler sewed her mind*

sanctified (adj.) **1** consecrated, holy **AW** I.i.139 [Parolles to Helena] *virginity … should be buried in highways out of all sanctified limit*; **Lover** 233; **Oth** III.iv.122
2 sanctimonious, hypocritical, deceiving **Ham** I.iii.130 [Polonius to Ophelia, of Hamlet's vows] *Breathing like sanctified and pious bawds*; **AY** II.iii.13

sanctimonious (adj.) holy, sacred, consecrated **Tem** IV.i.16 [Prospero to Ferdinand, of Miranda] *If thou dost break her virgin-knot before / All sanctimonious ceremonies may … be ministered*

sanctimony (n.) **1** sanctity, holiness, religious fervour **TC** V.ii.142 [Troilus to Ulysses, of Cressida] *if vows are sanctimony, / If sanctimony be the gods' delight … / This is not she*; **AW** IV.iii.49
2 sacred bond, religious commitment **Oth** I.iii.350 [Iago to Roderigo] *If sanctimony and a frail vow … be not too hard for my wits*

sanctity (n.) **1** holiness, saintliness; or: sainthood, saints **2H4** IV.ii.21 [Prince John to and of Archbishop] *The very opener and intelligencer / Between the grace, the sanctities, of heaven / And our dull workings*
2 true devotion, sacred intensity **TN** III.iv.352 [Antonio to Second Officer, of Viola as Cesario] *I … / Relieved him with such sanctity of love*

sanctuarize (v.) give sanctuary to, shelter **Ham** IV.vii.126 [Claudius to Laertes, of a church] *No place, indeed, should murder sanctuarize*

sanctuary (n.) holy place, church, religious place of safety **R3** III.i.42 [Cardinal Bourchier to Buckingham] *God in heaven forbid / We should infringe the holy privilege / Of blessed sanctuary*; **3H6** IV.iv.31; **TNK** III.i.62

sand (n.) grain of sand **Cym** V.v.120 [Arviragus to Belarius, of disguised Innogen as Fidele] *One sand another / Not more resembles that sweet rosy lad*

sand-blind (adj.) half-blind, dim-sighted **MV** II.ii.68 [Gobbo to Launcelot] *Alack, sir, I am sand-blind!*; **MV** II.ii.32

sanded (adj.) sandy-coloured **MND** IV.i.119 [Theseus to Hippolyta] *My hounds are bred out of the Spartan kind; / So flewed, so sanded*

sanguine (adj.) **1** blood-red, deep red **1H6** IV.i.92 [Basset to King, of the red rose] *the sanguine colour of the leaves*; **Cym** V.v.365

2 red-faced, ruddy-hued **Tit** IV.ii.96 [Aaron to Chiron and Demetrius] *ye sanguine shallow-hearted boys*; **1H4** II.iv.238

sans (prep.) without **AY** II.vii.167 [Jaques to all] *Sans teeth, sans eyes, sans taste, sans everything*; **KJ** V.vi.16; **LL** V.ii.415; **TC** I.iii.94; **Tem** I.ii.97; **Tim** IV.iii.123

sap (n.) vital fluid, life-blood **R3** IV.iv.277 [Queen Elizabeth to King Richard, of her daughter] *A handkerchief, which … did drain / The purple sap from her sweet brother's body*

sapego (n.) ☞ serpigo (n.)

sapient (adj.) wise, learned, erudite **KL** III.vi.22 [Lear to Fool] *Thou sapient sir, sit here*

sapless (adj.) feeble, sluggish, lacking vigour **1H6** IV.v.4 [Talbot to John Talbot] *When sapless age and weak unable limbs / Should bring thy father to his drooping chair*

sarcenet, sarsanet (adj.) of thin silk, light, flimsy **1H4** III.i.245 [Hotspur to Lady Percy] *you … givest such sarcenet surety for thy oaths*; **TC** V.i.28

sate (v.) satiate, glut, satisfy **Ham** I.v.56 [Ghost to Hamlet] *So lust … / Will sate itself in a celestial bed* [F; Q2 *sort*]

satiate (adj.) satiated, glutted, gorged **Cym** I.vii.48 [Iachimo to Innogen] *The cloyed will - / That satiate yet unsatisfied desire*

satiety (n.) **1** excess, over-abundance **Tim** I.i.170 [Timon to Jeweller, of his jewel] *A mere satiety of commendations*; **Venus** 19
2 wearisome gratification, tedious satisfaction **Oth** II.i.222 [Iago to Roderigo] *to … give satiety a fresh appetite*

satire (n.) satirist, derider **Sonn** 100.11 [to his Muse] *my love's sweet face survey, / If Time have any wrinkle graven there, / If any, be a satire to decay* [i.e. an attacker of the process of decay]

satirical (adj.) ironic, ridiculous, incongruous **E3** III.iii.75 [King Edward to King John] *So is the other [salutation] most satirical*; **E3** II.i.112

satisfaction (n.) **1** removal of doubt, resolved state of mind **WT** I.ii.31 [Hermione to Leontes, of all being well in Bohemia] *this satisfaction / The by-gone day proclaimed*; **AW** V.iii.100; **KL** I.ii.92
2 recompense, compensation, atonement **3H6** V.v.14 [Edward to Prince] *what satisfaction canst thou make / For bearing arms*; **Ham** IV.v.209
3 payment [of a debt] **CE** IV.i.5 [Second Merchant to Angelo] *make present satisfaction*

satisfy (v.) **1** provide with information, reassure, convince **JC** IV.ii.10 [Brutus to Pindarus, of Cassius] *if he be at hand / I shall be satisfied*; **Cym** III.v.93; **JC** III.ii.1; **Mac** V.i.33; **TS** IV.ii.4
2 atone, do penance, make amends **Cym** V.iv.15 [Posthumus alone] *to satisfy … take / No stricter render of me than my all*
3 appease, content, comfort **3H6** II.v.104 [Son to himself] *How will my mother for a father's death / Take on with me and ne'er be satisfied!*

sauce (v.) **1** spice, season, flavour **Tim** IV.iii.301 [Timon to Apemantus, of poison] *To sauce thy dishes*; **Cor** I.ix.52; **Cym** IV.ii.50; **TC** I.ii.23; **Tim** IV.iii.24
2 rebuke, berate, sting **AY** III.v.69 [Rosalind as Ganymede to Silvius, of Phebe] *I'll sauce her with bitter words*
3 make things hot for, charge extortionately **MW** IV.iii.11 [Host to Bardolph, of the Germans] *I'll sauce them*

saucily (adv.) presumptuously, cheekily, impudently **KL** I.i.20 [Gloucester to Kent, of Edmund] *this knave came something saucily to the world*; **KL** II.iv.40; **Luc** 1348

sauciness (n.) insolence, rudeness, impertinence **Tit** II.iii.81 [Lavinia to Tamora, of Bassianus] *Great reason that my noble lord be rated / For sauciness*; **AW** IV.v.64; **2H4** II.i.111; **KJ** V.vii.133

saucy (adj.) **1** insolent, impudent, presumptuous, defiant **TN** I.v.189 [Olivia to Viola as Cesario] *I heard you were saucy at my gates*; **Cym** V.v.326; **2H6** IV.x.34; **Mac** III.v.3; **Oth** I.i.129; **RJ** I.v.83;
2 lecherous, lascivious, lustful **AW** IV.iv.23 [Helena to Widow] *When saucy trusting of the cozened thoughts / Defiles the pitchy night*; **2H4** II.iv.126; **MM** II.iv.45

savage *(adj.)* **1** fierce, ferocious, wild **AY** II.vi.6 [Orlando to Adam] *If this uncouth forest yield anything savage, I will either be food for it or bring it for food to thee;* **AC** III.xiii.128; **3H6** I.i.224; **MV** V.i.78; **WT** III.iii.55

2 uncivilized, wild, ungoverned **MA** IV.i.59 [Claudio to Hero] *you are more intemperate in your blood / Than Venus, or those pampered animals / That rage in savage sensuality*

3 uncultivated, wild, rough **H5** III.v.7 [Dauphin to all] *Our scions, put in wild and savage stock*

4 boorish, uncivil, unsociable **TC** III.iii.125 [Agamemnon to Patroclus, of Achilles] *worthier than himself / Here tend the savage strangeness he puts on*

savagery *(n.)* wilderness, wildness of growth **H5** V.ii.47 [Burgundy to King Henry and the French King, of the weeds which have grown in France] *the coulter rusts / That should deracinate such savagery*

save *(v.)* **1** keep, preserve, maintain **AW** II.i.178 [King to Helena] *what impossibility would slay / In common sense, sense saves another way* [i.e. it makes sense nonetheless] **☛** **POLITENESS**, p.340

2 prevent, avoid, avert **3H6** V.iv.11 [Queen to all] *the ship splits on the rock, / Which industry and courage might have saved;* **Cym** V.iii.27; **1H4** V.iv.56; **TC** III.iii.241; **Tim** I.i.256

3 protect, make safe **1H6** V.iii.56 [Suffolk to Margaret] *So doth the swan her downy cygnets save*

4 spare, allow to live **Cym** II.iii.70 [Cloten alone] *'tis gold / Which makes the true-man killed, and saves the thief;* **JC** V.iii.38; **KL** V.iii.149

save that *(conj.)* except (that), were it not that **Sonn** 27.9 *Save that my soul's imaginary sight / Presents thy shadow to my sightless view*

save *(prep.)* except **Ham** III.iii.82 [Hamlet to himself, of his father] *And how his audit stands, who knows save heaven?*

saving *(prep.)* **1** with all respect to, without offence to **TS** II.i.71 [Gremio to Petruchio] *Saving your tale, Petruchio, … / Let us … speak too*

2 except **KJ** I.i.201 [Bastard alone] *ere answer knows what question would, / Saving in dialogue of compliment*

3 with respect to **CE** IV.i.27 [Angelo to Antipholus of Ephesus] *Saving your merry humour*

saving reverence begging pardon for, with apologies for **Cym** IV.i.5 [Cloten alone, of the bawdy pun he is about to make] *saving reverence of the word* **☛** sir-reverence *(n.)*; **POLITENESS**, p.340

savour *(n.)* **1** scent, fragrance, smell **WT** IV.iv.75 [Perdita to disguised Polixenes and Camillo, of the flowers] *these keep / Seeming and savour all the winter long;* **TS** Induction.ii.70

2 smell, stench, stink **WT** I.ii.421 [Polixenes to Camillo] *Turn then my freshest reputation to / A savour that may strike the dullest nostril / Where I arrive;* **KJ** IV.iii.112; **Tem** II.ii.51

3 flavour, nature, character **KL** I.iv.233 [Gonerill to Lear] *This admiration … is much o'the savour / Of other your new pranks*

savour *(v.)* **1** smell, reek, stink **Per** IV.vi.108 [Lysimachus to Marina] *The very doors and windows savour vilely*

2 relish, enjoy, delight [in] **KL** IV.ii.39 [Albany to Gonerill] *Filths savour but themselves;* **E3** III.iv.51

saw *(n.)* wise saying, platitude, maxim **LL** V.ii.911 [Hiems singing, of winter] *coughing drowns the parson's saw;* **AY** II.vii.157, III.v.81; **Ham** I.v.100; **KL** II.ii.158; **TN** III.iv.369

sawpit *(n.)* pit used for sawing wood **MW** IV.iv.52 [Mistress Page to all, of the children] *Let them from forth a sawpit rush at once*

say *(n.)* **1** type of fine-textured cloth **2H6** IV.vii.22 [Cade to Say] *thou say, thou serge, nay, thou buckram lord!*

2 **☛** assay *(n.)*

say *(v.)* **1** speak, utter a sound **TNK** Epilogue.2 [Speaker to audience] *I … as it is with schoolboys, cannot say*

2 deliver, report, tell **Cor** V.ii.58 [Menenius to First Watch] *I'll say an errand for you*

3 proclaim, announce, declare **TNK** IV.ii.78 [Messenger to Theseus, of one of Arcite's knights] *by his face, a prince. / His very looks so say him;* **TN** IV.ii.8

4 speak the words as an ordinary utterance **2H6** III.ii.293 [King to Queen] *Had I but said, I would have kept my word; / But when I swear, it is irrevocable*

5 finish speaking, speak one's mind, make one's point **KJ** I.i.235 [King Philip to Hubert] *When I have said, make answer to us both;* **AC** III.ii.34; **Tim** II.ii.169 **☛** **DISCOURSE MARKERS**, p.127

6 speak the truth, speak to the point **Ham** V.i.26 [First Clown to Second Clown, responding to his views about Ophelia's Christian burial] *Why, there thou sayst* **☛** **DISCOURSE MARKERS**, p.127

saying *(n.)* **1** maxim, reflection, precept **AY** III.ii.124 [Celia reading] *Tongues I'll hang on every tree, / That shall civil sayings show*

2 promising, affirmation, assertion **Tim** V.i.25 [Painter to Poet] *the deed of saying is quite out of use* [i.e. the carrying out of a promise]

'sblood *(int.)* **☛** **SWEARING**, p.435

scab *(n.)* scurvy fellow, scoundrel, villain **2H4** III.ii.268 [Falstaff to Wart] *th' art a good scab;* **TC** II.i.28; **TN** II.v.74

scaffold *(n.)* stage, platform [in a theatre] **H5** Prologue.10 [Chorus] *The flat unraised spirits that hath dared / On this unworthy scaffold to bring forth / So great an object*

scaffoldage *(n.)* theatre scaffolding, stage platform **TC** I.iii.156 [Ulysses to Agamemnon, of an actor] *To hear the wooden dialogue and sound / 'Twixt his stretched footing and the scaffoldage* [F *scaffolage*]

scald, scall, scauld *(adj.)* contemptible, vile, scabby **H5** V.i.5 [Fluellen to Gower] *the rascally, scauld, beggarly, lousy, pragging knave Pistol;* **MW** III.i.110 [Evans to Caius, of the Host] *let us … be revenge on this same scald, scurvy, cogging companion* [F *scall*]; **AC** V.ii.215; **H5** V.i.29

scale *(n.)* **1** balance, quantity, amount **Ham** I.ii.13 [Claudius to his court] *In equal scale weighing delight and dole*

2 measuring mark, graduated line, calibration **AC** II.vii.18 [Antony to Lepidus] *they take the flow o'th' Nile / By certain scales i'th' pyramid*

scale *(v.)* **1** weigh, balance, compare **Cor** II.iii.248 [Sicinius to Citizens, of Coriolanus] *Scaling his present bearing with his past*

2 weigh up [as in a scales], evaluate, appraise **MM** III.i.255 [disguised Duke to Isabella, of his plan] *by this is … the corrupt deputy scaled* [unclear meaning]

3 climb up, ascend, mount **Luc** 440 [of Lucrece] *On her bare breast … as his hand did scale*

scaled, scaling *(adj.)* scaly, covered in scales **TC** V.v.22 [Nestor to all, of soldiers opposing Hector] *like scaled schools / Before the belching whale* [Q *scaling*]

scalion *(n.)* **☛** stallion *(n.)*

scall *(adj.)* **☛** scald *(adj.)*

scaly *(adj.)* plated, armoured **2H4** I.i.146 [Northumberland to Morton] *A scaly gauntlet now with joints of steel / Must glove this hand*

scamble *(v.)* scramble, struggle, make shift **KJ** IV.iii.146 [Bastard to Hubert] *England now is left / To tug and scamble*

scambling *(n.)* scuffling, struggling, fighting **H5** V.ii.202 [King Henry to Katherine] *If ever thou beest mine … I get thee with scambling*

scambling *(adj.)* contentious, rough, quarrelsome, turbulent **H5** I.i.4 [Canterbury to Ely] *the scambling and unquiet time;* **MA** V.i.94

scamel *(n.)* [uncertain meaning] type of bird or fish **Tem** II.ii.169 [Caliban to Stephano] *sometimes I'll get thee / Young scamels from the rock*

scan *(v.)* **1** examine, carefully consider **Oth** III.iii.243 [Iago to Othello] *I would I might entreat your honour / To scan this thing no farther;* **Ham** III.iii.75; **Mac** III.iv.139

2 judge, assess, criticize **Per** II.ii.55 [Simonides to all] *Opinions's but a fool, that makes us scan / The outward habit by the inward man*

scandal (*n.*) **1** shame, discredit, disgrace **2H6** II.iv.65 [Gloucester to Duchess] *yet thy scandal were not wiped away*; **CE** V.i.15; **Ham** I.iv.38
2 disgraceful reputation, scandalous imputation **3H6** II.i.149 [Richard to Edward and Warwick, of Warwick] *Oft have I heard his praises in pursuit, / But ne'er till now his scandal of retire*; **Ham** II.i.29; **WT** I.ii.330

scandal (*v.*) **1** revile, scorn, denigrate **JC** I.ii.76 [Cassius to Brutus] *if you know / That I do fawn on men … / And after scandal them*; **Cor** III.i.44
2 discredit, disgrace, bring into ill repute **Cym** III.iv.61 [Innogen to Pisanio] *Sinon's weeping / Did scandal many a holy tear*

scandalized (*adj.*) disgraced, defamed, made a subject of scandal **TG** II.vii.61 [Julia to Lucetta, of her journey] *it will make me scandalized*; **1H4** I.iii.152

scandalled (*adj.*) scandalous, disgraceful, shameful **Tem** IV.i.90 [Ceres to Iris, of Venus and her son Cupid] *Her and her blind boy's scandalled company / I have forsworn*

scandalous (*adj.*) **1** bringing dishonour, offensive, discreditable **E3** II.i.418 [Countess to Warwick, of King Edward] *[who will] corrupt the author of my blood / To be his scandalous and vile solicitor*
2 defamatory, libellous, slanderous **E3** III.iii.170 [King Edward to the English peers] *let us … clear us of that scandalous crime*

scant (*adj.*) more chary, not so lavish, more sparing **Ham** I.iii.121 [Polonius to Ophelia] *Be something scanter of your maiden presence*

scant (*v.*) **1** neglect, stint, withhold **KL** I.i.278 [Gonerill to Cordelia] *You have obedience scanted*; **AC** IV.ii.22; **H5** II.iv.47; **MV** III.ii.112; **Oth** I.iii.264; **Sonn** 117.1
2 limit, restrict, constrain **MV** II.i.17 [Portia to Morocco] *if my father had not scanted me*; **TC** IV.iv.46
3 give out sparingly, curtail, withhold [from] **MV** V.i.141 [Portia to Antonio] *I scant this breathing courtesy*; **CE** II.ii.86; **KL** II.iv.170
4 deprive, deny, dispossess **E3** III.iii.159 [King John to the French, of the English] *but scant them of their chines of beef*; **PassP** XX.35

scant (*adv.*) scarcely, barely, hardly **RJ** I.ii.98 [Benvolio to Romeo, of Rosaline] *she shall scant show well that now seems best*

scanted (*adj.*) withheld, stinted, limited **KL** III.ii.67 [disguised Kent to Lear, of Regan's castle] *I to this hard house … return and force / Their scanted courtesy*

scantle (*n.*) ☛ cantle (*n.*)

scantling (*n.*) guideline, index, standard of measurement **TC** I.iii.341 [Nestor to Ulysses, of Hector's challenge] *the success, / Although particular, shall give a scantling / Of good or bad unto the general*

scantly (*adv.*) scantily, grudgingly, half-heartedly **AC** III.iv.6 [Antony to Octavia, of Caesar] *he hath … / Spoke scantly of me*

scape, 'scape (*n.*) **1** escape **MV** II.ii.153 [Launcelot to himself] *Here are simple scapes*; **Oth** I.iii.135; **TS** V.ii.3
2 escapade, fling, sexual wrongdoing **Luc** 747 [Lucrece to herself, of daytime] *night's scapes doth open lay*; **WT** III.iii.70

scape, 'scape (*v.*) escape, avoid **1H4** II.iv.160 [Falstaff to Prince Hal, of the recent robbery] *I have scaped by miracle* ☛ **FEW**, p.xxi

scar (*n.*) wound, cut, injury **E3** IV.vi.61 [Audley to Esquire, of Prince Edward] *this open scar / Doth end the harvest of his Audley's war*; **E3** IV.vi.55, V.i.223

scar (*v.*) wound, disfigure, maim **R3** V.v.23 [Richmond to all] *England hath long been mad and scarred herself*

scarce (*adv.*) **1** scarcely, hardly, barely, only just **Oth** V.ii.200 [Othello to Gratiano] *I scarce did know you, uncle*; **CE** III.i.23; **Cym** III.v.151; **1H6** I.i.112; **R3** I.i.21; **Tim** I.i.179
2 with difficulty, hardly possible **TN** III.iii.29 [Antonio to Sebastian] *were I ta'en here, it would scarce be answered*

scarce-bearded (*adj.*) with a beard only just emerging, juvenile **AC** I.i.21 [Cleopatra to Antony] *who knows / If the scarce-bearded Caesar have not sent / His powerful mandate to you*

scarce-cold (*adj.*) only just over, recently ended **Cym** V.v.470 [Soothsayer to Cymbeline, of the vision] *Which I made known to Lucius ere the stroke / Of yet this scarce-cold battle*

scarf (*n.*) **1** military sash, shoulder band **MA** II.i.175 [Benedick to Claudio] *like a lieutenant's scarf*; **AW** II.iii.202, 224, III.v.84, IV.iii.142, 314
2 sling **Cor** I.ix.1 [stage direction] *Enter … Martius, with his arm in a scarf*; **AY** V.ii.20

scarf (*v.*) wrap round like a scarf or sash **Ham** V.ii.13 [Hamlet to Horatio] *My sea-gown scarfed about me*

scarf up (*v.*) blindfold, cover up **Mac** III.ii.47 [Macbeth to Lady Macbeth] *Come, seeling night, / Scarf up the tender eye of pitiful day*

scarfed (*adj.*) [unclear meaning] fully decked out; under full sail; [of the hull] well-jointed **MV** II.vi.15 [Gratiano to Salerio] *The scarfed bark puts from her native bay*

scarre (*n.*) [unclear reading] scare, alarm **AW** IV.ii.38 [Diana to Bertram] *I see that men make vows in such a scarre / That we'll forsake ourselves* [F]

scatheful (*adj.*) damaging, harmful, injurious **TN** V.i.53 [Orsino to Viola as Cesario, of Antonio] *such scatheful grapple did he make / With the most noble bottom of our fleet*

scath, scathe (*n.*) harm, hurt, damage **KJ** II.i.75 [Chatillon to King Philip, of English soldiers] *To do offence and scathe in Christendom*; **2H6** II.iv.62; **R3** I.iii.316

scath, scathe (*v.*) hurt, harm, injure **RJ** I.v.84 [Capulet to Tybalt] *This trick may chance to scathe you* [F scath]

scattered (*adj.*) **1** dispersed, defeated, disunited **3H6** II.vi.93 [Warwick to Edward] *thou shalt not dread / The scattered foe that hopes to rise again*
2 disunited, distracted, divided **KL** III.i.31 [disguised Kent to Gentleman] *there comes a power / Into this scattered kingdom*
3 occasional, odd, random **AY** III.v.104 [Silvius to Phebe] *Loose now and then / A scattered smile*

scattering (*adj.*) random, haphazard, erratic **Oth** III.iii.150 [Iago to Othello, of Iago's suspicions] *nor build yourself a trouble / Out of his scattering and unsure observance*

scauld (*adj.*) ☛ scald (*adj.*)

scene (*n.*) **1** play, drama, performance **Per** IV.iv.7 [Gower alone] *in each several clime / Where our scene seems to live*; **AY** II.vii.139; **MW** IV.vi.17; **Per** IV.iv.48; **WT** IV.i.16, iv.590
2 stage, performing area **MND** III.ii.15 [Puck to Oberon, of Bottom] *The shallowest thickskin of that barren sort … / Forsook his scene*

schedule (*n.*) **1** inventory, list, itemization **TN** I.v.234 [Olivia to Viola as Cesario] *I will give out divers schedules of my beauty*; **2H4** IV.i.166; **LL** I.i.18; **MV** II.ix.55
2 document, paper, scroll **JC** III.i.3 [Artemidorus to Caesar] *Read this schedule*; **H8** III.ii.106; **Lover** 43; **Luc** 1312

scholar (*n.*) **1** learned man, erudite person [who knows Latin, the language of exorcism] **MA** II.i.235 [Benedick to Don Pedro, of Beatrice] *I would to God some scholar would conjure her*
2 pupil, student **Per** II.v.31 [Pericles to Simonides, of music] *The worst of all her scholars*; **AC** IV.xiv.102; **Per** I.iii.17

school (*n.*) **1** university **AY** I.i.5 [Orlando to Adam, of Oliver] *my brother Jaques he keeps at school*; **Ham** I.ii.113; **TC** I.iii.104
2 public building, institution **Tim** V.iv.25 [First Senator to Alcibiades, of Athens] *these great towers, trophies, and schools*
3 schooling, learning, study **LL** V.ii.71 [Princess to all] *Folly, in wisdom hatched, / Hath wisdom's warrant and the help of school … / to grace a learned fool*
4 medical faculty **AW** I.iii.235 [Countess to Helena] *the schools, / Embowelled of their doctrine*

5 shoal of fish **TC** V.v.22 [Nestor to all, of soldiers opposing Hector] *like scaled schools / Before the belching whale* [F *sculs*]

school (*v.*) **1** control, correct, teach wisdom to **Mac** IV.ii.15 [Ross to Macduff's wife] *I pray you school yourself*
  2 instruct how to act, teach a part to **TS** IV.iv.9 [Pedant as Vincentio to Tranio as Lucentio, of Biondello] *'Twere good he were schooled*

school-doing (*n.*) training, instruction, discipline **TNK** V.iv.68 [Pirithous to Palamon] *the hot horse … / Forgets school-doing*

schooling (*n.*) admonition, reproof, counsel **MND** I.i.116 [Theseus to Egeus and Demetrius] *I have some private schooling for you both*

science (*n.*) **1** knowledge, learning **MM** I.i.5 [Duke to Escalus] *your own science / Exceeds … the lists of all advice / My strength can give you;* **AW** V.iii.103
  2 area of knowledge, field of learning **TS** II.i.57 [Petruchio to Baptista, of Hortensio as Licio and Katherina] *To instruct her fully in those sciences*

scion (*n.*) shoot, graft, limb **WT** IV.iv.93 [disguised Polixenes to Perdita] *we marry / A gentler scion to the wildest stock* [F *Sien*]; **H5** III.v.7; **Oth** I.iii.329

scoff (*n.*) taunt, scorn, mockery **1H6** III.ii.113 [Bedford to himself] *They that of late were daring with their scoffs*

scold (*n.*) abusive woman, quarreller **KJ** II.i.191 [Queen Eleanor to Constance] *Thou unadvised scold;* **TS** I.ii.185

scolding (*adj.*) clamouring, brawling, chiding **JC** I.iii.5 [Casca to Cicero] *I have seen tempests, when the scolding winds / Have rived the knotty oaks*

sconce (*n.*) **1** [jocular] head, pate, bonce **Ham** V.i.100 [Hamlet to Horatio] *knock him about the sconce;* **CE** I.ii.79, II.ii.34; **Cor** III.ii.99
  2 shelter, screen, guard **CE** II.ii.37 [Dromio of Syracuse to Antipholus of Syracuse] *An you use these blows long I must get a sconce for my head* [pun: 34, sense 1]
  3 fort, military work **H5** III.vi.71 [Gower to Fluellen, of military actions] *at such and such a sconce, at such a breach*

sconce (*v.*) ☛ *ensconce* (*v.*)

scope (*n.*) **1** goal, prospect, purpose, aim **Ham** III.ii.229 [Second Player, as Queen, to her King] *An anchor's cheer in prison be my scope;* **1H4** III.i.165; **R2** III.iii.112; **Tim** I.i.75
  2 range, reach, extent **Ham** I.i.68 [Horatio to Marcellus and Barnardo, of the Ghost] *in the gross and scope of mine opinion;* **KJ** V.ii.122; **MM** III.i.73; **Tim** I.i.75
  3 opportunity, liberty, free course of action **MM** I.iii.35 [Duke to Friar Thomas] *'twas my fault to give the people scope;* **2H6** III.i.176; **JC** IV.iii.107; **MM** V.i.232; **R2** III.iii.141; **Sonn** 29.7
  4 room, space, range **R2** III.iii.140 [King Richard to Aumerle, as if to his own heart] *I'll give thee scope to beat* [pun: 141, sense 3]
  5 circumstance, course **KJ** III.iv.154 [Cardinal Pandulph to Lewis the Dauphin, of King John and the people] *No scope of nature … / But they will pluck away his natural cause / And call them meteors, prodigies and signs*

scorch (*v.*) slash with a knife, gash **Mac** III.ii.13 [Macbeth to Lady Macbeth] *We have scorched the snake, not killed it;* **CE** V.i.183

score (*n.*) **1** reckoning, account, debt **Mac** V.vi.91 [Seyward to Malcolm, of Young Seyward] *They say he parted well, and paid his score;* **AW** IV.iii.219, V.iii.56; **TS** Induction.ii.21
  2 tavern-bill, alehouse tally **2H6** IV.vii.69 [Cade to all, of when he is king] *all shall eat and drink on my score* [i.e. at my expense]; **2H4** II.i.23; **RJ** II.iv.135
  3 ☛ **NUMBERS**, p.299

score and tally method of notching a piece of wood as a means of debt-keeping; when split in two between lender and debtor, the scores on the two pieces of wood would tally **2H6** IV.vii.32 [Cade to Say] *our forefathers had no other books but the score and the tally*

score (*v.*) **1** mark up, chalk up, add to the tally **TS** Induction.ii.22 [Sly to Lord] *score me up for the lyingest knave in Christendom;* **AW** IV.iii.219; **1H4** II.iv.26; **Sonn** 122.10
  2 make a mark for, chalk up a score for **Oth** IV.i.127 [Othello to himself, of Cassio] *Have you scored me?* [or: sense 3]
  3 wound, scar, cut **AC** IV.vii.12 [Scarus to Antony, of the enemy] *Let us score their backs;*

scoring (*n.*) charging to an account; also: cutting, wounding **1H4** V.iii.31 [Falstaff alone] *Though I could scape shot-free at London, I fear the shot here, here's no scoring but upon the pate*

scorn (*n.*) **1** mockery, taunt, insult, act of derision **1H6** II.iv.77 [Suffolk to Richard] *Turn not thy scorns this way;* **Ham** III.i.70; **1H6** IV.vi.49; **LL** V.ii.854; **TC** IV.v.30; **TNK** V.i.88
  2 object of scorn, target of mockery **CE** IV.iv.101 [Antipholus of Ephesus to Adriana] *thou art … confederate with a damned pack / To make a loathsome abject scorn of me;* **1H6** IV.vi.49; **TNK** V.i.88
  3 folly, foolishness **Ham** III.ii.23 [Hamlet to the Players] *show … scorn her own image* [i.e. whatever causes scorn]

scorn, take think it a disgrace, consider it an indignity **1H6** IV.iv.35 [Somerset to Lucy, of York] *I … take foul scorn to fawn on him by sending*

scorn, think disdain, despise, consider it beneath one's dignity **2H6** IV.ii.12 [Holland to Bevis] *The nobility think scorn to go in leather aprons;* **Cym** IV.iv.53; **LL** I.ii.62

scorn (*v.*) **1** mock, jeer, express disdain [at] **RJ** I.v.57 [Tybalt to himself, of Romeo] *dares the slave / Come hither … / To fleer and scorn at our solemnity?;* **Cor** II.iii.221; **KJ** I.i.228; **LL** IV.iii.145; **MV** III.i.51
  2 refuse with contempt, disdain to offer **Cor** III.i.267 [Sicinius to all, of Coriolanus] *He hath resisted law, / And therefore law shall scorn him further trial*

scornful (*adj.*) scorned, contemptible, derided **E3** I.ii.7 [Countess to herself] *To be the scornful captive to a Scot;* **Luc** 520

scot (*n.*) payment, contribution, small amount **1H4** I.iii.213 [Hotspur to Worcester, of King Henry] *if a scot would save his soul he shall not [have his prisoners]*

scot and lot [type of local taxation] in full, thoroughly **1H4** V.iv.113 [Falstaff, alone] *'twas time to counterfeit, or that hot termagant Scot had paid me, scot and lot too*

scotch (*n.*) cut, gash, wound **AC** IV.vii.10 [Scarus to Antony] *I have yet / Room for six scotches more*

scotch (*v.*) slash, cut, gash **Cor** IV.v.193 [First Servingman to Second Servingman, of Coriolanus and Aufidius] *Before Corioles he scotched him and notched him*

scour (*n.*) rub clean, restore to brightness **2H6** III.ii.199 [Suffolk to all, of Warwick] *here's a vengeful sword, rusted with ease, / That shall be scoured in his rancorous heart*

scour (*v.*) **1** clear out, quickly remove, cleanse **H5** II.i.53 [Nym to Pistol] *If you grow foul with me … I will scour you with my rapier;* **1H4** III.ii.137; **H5** I.i.34; **Mac** V.iii.56
  2 beat, punish, scourge **CE** I.ii.65 [Dromio of Ephesus to Antipholus of Syracuse, of Dromio's mistress] *If I return I shall be post indeed, / For she will scour your fault upon my pate*
  3 go in haste, move quickly, hurry **long E3** II.ii.203 [King Edward to Audley] *Scour to Newhaven;* **WT** II.i.35

scourge (*n.*) punishment, retribution **Ham** IV.iii.6 [Claudius to his attendants] *th'offender's scourge is weighed, / But never the offence*

scouring (*n.*) hostile roving about, aggressive movement **Tim** V.ii.15 [First Senator to other Senators] *fearful scouring / Doth choke the air with dust*

scout (*v.*) **1** mock, deride, ridicule **Tem** III.ii.122 [Stephano singing] *Flout 'em and scout 'em* [F *cout*]
  2 keep a look-out, watch out **TN** III.iv.173 [Sir Toby to Sir Andrew, of Viola as Cesario] *Scout me for him at the corner of the orchard*

screech-owl (*n.*) barn-owl [thought to be a bird of ill omen] **3H6** II.vi.56 [Edward to Warwick] *Bring forth that fatal screech-owl to our house;* **2H6** I.iv.17, III.ii.327; **TC** V.x.16

screen (*n.*) division, discrepancy, separation **Tem** I.ii.107 [Prospero to Miranda, of Antonio] *To have no screen between this part he played / And him he played it for*

screw (*v.*) **1** twist, force, contort **TNK** V.i.111 [Palamon praying to Venus, of an old man] *the aged cramp / Had screwed his square foot round*
2 wrench, force, wrest **TN** V.i.121 [Orsino to Olivia] *I partly know the instrument / That screws me from my true place in your favour*

scrimer (*n.*) fencer, swordsman **Ham** IV.vii.99 [Claudius to Laertes, of the French] *the scrimers of their nation*

scrip (*n.*) **1** bag, pouch, wallet **AY** III.ii.158 [Touchstone to Corin, as they leave] *though not with bag and baggage, yet with scrip and scrippage*
2 script, text **MND** I.ii.3 [Bottom to Quince, of their company] *You were best to call them … according to the scrip*

scrippage (*n.*) contents of a scrip [an invented word to parallel 'baggage'] **AY** III.ii.158 [Touchstone to Corin, as they leave] *though not with bag and baggage, yet with scrip and scrippage*

scripture (*n.*) letter, writing, composition **Cym** III.iv.82 [Innogen to Pisanio] *The scriptures of the loyal Leonatus / All turned to heresy?*

scrivener (*n.*) professional scribe, clerk, notary **R3** III.vi.1 [stage direction] *Enter a Scrivener;* **TS** IV.iv.59

scroyle (*n.*) scoundrel, ruffian, wretch **KJ** II.i.373 [Bastard to King John and King Philip] *these scroyles of Angiers flout you*

scrubbed (*adj.*) short, undersized, stubby **MV** V.i.162 [Gratiano to Nerissa, of her ring] *I gave it to a youth … a little scrubbed boy;* **MV** V.i.261

scruple (*n.*) **1** tiny amount, last ounce **TN** II.v.2 [Fabian to Sir Toby] *If I lose a scruple of this sport, let me be boiled to death with melancholy;* **AW** II.iii.220; **MA** V.i.93; **MM** I.i.37; **MV** IV.i.327; **TC** IV.i.71
2 suspicion, misgiving, doubt **2H4** I.ii.131 [Falstaff to Lord Chief Justice] *the wise may make some dram of a scruple;* **H8** II.i.158; **Mac** IV.iii.116; **MM** I.i.64; **TC** IV.i.57
3 scrupulousness, introspective doubt **Ham** IV.iv.40 [Hamlet alone] *whether it be … some craven scruple;* **R2** V.v.13
4 objection, difficulty, doubt **Mac** II.iii.126 [Banquo to all] *Fears and scruples shake us;* **Cym** V.v.182; **1H6** V.iii.93; **H8** II.iv.150, IV.i.31

scrupulous (*adj.*) **1** quibbling, cavilling, distrustful **AC** I.iii.48 [Antony to Cleopatra] *Equality of two domestic powers / Breed scrupulous faction*
2 hesitating, troubled with doubts **3H6** IV.vii.61 [Hastings to Edward] *Away with scrupulous wit!*

scud (*v.*) move briskly, run swiftly **Venus** 301 [of Adonis' horse] *Sometime he scuds far off*

scul (*n.*) ☞ school (*n.*) 5

scullion (*n.*) **1** menial, lackey, domestic servant **2H4** II.i.57 [Page to Hostess] *Away, you scullion!;* **Ham** II.ii.585
2 ☞ stallion (*n.*)

scurril (*adj.*) scurrilous, coarse, vulgar **TNK** V.i.147 [Emilia praying to Diana] *thine ear - / Which ne'er heard scurril term;* **TC** I.iii.148

scurrility (*n.*) bawdry, indecent language **LL** V.ii.54 [Nathaniel to Holofernes] *so it shall please you to abrogate scurrility;* **LL** V.i.4

scurrilous (*adj.*) offensively facetious, coarsely abusive **E3** I.i.93 [Prince Edward to Lorraine] *I hold thy message but as scurrilous*

scurvy (*adj.*) **1** contemptible, despicable, wretched **KL** IV.vi.172 [Lear to all] *like a scurvy politician seem / To see the things thou dost not;* **AW** III.ii.321; **MW** I.iv.107; **Oth** I.ii.6; **TC** V.iv.3; **Tem** II.ii.152
2 worthless, wretched, disagreeable **TNK** II.i.322 [Palamon to Gaoler] *Thou bringest such pelting scurvy news continually*

scurvy-valiant (*adj.*) supremely worthless, heartily contemptible **TC** II.i.44 [Thersites to Ajax] *Thou scurvy-valiant ass*

scuse (*n.*) excuse **MV** IV.i.441 [Portia as Balthasar to Bassanio, of his ring] *That 'scuse serves many men to save their gifts;* **Oth** IV.i.79

scut (*n.*) short tail [as of a deer] **MW** V.v.18 [Falstaff to Mistress Ford] *My doe with the black scut!* [with bawdy pun]

scutcheon (*n.*) escutcheon, painted shield **LL** V.ii.561 [Nathaniel as Alexander] *My scutcheon plain declares that I am Alisander;* **AC** V.ii.135; **1H4** V.i.140

'sdeath (*int.*) ☞ **SWEARING**, p.435

sea (*n.*) river estuary **E3** III.iii.3 [King Edward to all] *We … had direction how to pass the sea*

sea-bank (*n.*) seashore **Oth** IV.i.134 [Cassio to Iago] *I was the other day talking on the sea-bank* ☞ **bank** (*n.*) 1

sea-boy (*n.*) ☞ sea-son (*n.*)

sea-coal (*adj.*) mined coal of high quality brought by sea **2H4** II.i.86 [Hostess to Falstaff] *Thou didst swear to me … by a sea-coal fire;* **MW** I.iv.8

sea-gown type of robe with a high collar, short sleeves, and mid-leg length **Ham** V.ii.13 [Hamlet to Horatio] *My sea-gown scarfed about me* ☞ **CLOTHING**, p.79

seal (*n.*) **1** authentication, confirmation, attestation **MA** IV.i.164 [Friar to Leonato] *my observations, / Which with experimental seal doth warrant / The tenor of my book;* **Ham** III.ii.406
2 pledge, promise, token, sign **AC** III.xiii.125 [Antony to Cleopatra, of her hand] *this kingly seal / And plighter of high hearts!;* **AW** I.iii.127; **H5** IV.i.159; **MM** IV.i.6; **MND** III.ii.144; **Oth** II.iii.334

seal (*v.*) **1** confirm, ratify, approve **MV** I.iii.168 [Antonio to Shylock] *I will seal unto this bond;* **Cor** II.iii.107; **Cym** III.vii.57; **Ham** IV.vii.1; **3H6** III.ii.57; **TC** III.iii.231
2 accomplish, carry out, fulfil **TNK** I.i.92 [Valerius to Palamon and Arcite, of Theseus] *who is at hand to seal / The promise of his wrath;* **CE** I.i.9; **Tim** V.iv.54; **TNK** II.i.87
3 make final arrangements, come to an agreement **2H4** IV.iii.128 [Falstaff to Bardolph, of Shallow] *shortly will I seal with him;* **AC** III.ii.3, IV.xiv.49; **Ham** IV.iii.58
4 make by seal, put one's name to, agree **MV** I.iii.149 [Antonio to Shylock] *I'll seal to such a bond;* **2H6** V.ii.77; **MV** I.iii.168; **TN** II.v.92
5 mark [as if by a seal], designate **Ham** III.i.75 [Hamlet to Horatio, of his soul] *Sh'hath sealed thee for herself;* **R3** I.iii.228
6 put a seal in a particular place **LL** V.ii.9 [Princess to her ladies, of the King's letter] *he was fain to seal on Cupid's name*
7 [unclear usage] seal up close, forestall, prevent **WT** I.ii.337 [Camillo to Leontes, of keeping Hermione] *thereby for sealing / The injury of tongues in courts and kingdoms / Known and allied to yours* [F] ☞ forseal (*v.*)

seal under (*v.*) become security for, set one's seal to **MV** I.i.77 [Portia to Nerissa, of the Scottish lord] *I think the Frenchman became his surety and sealed under for another*

seal up (*v.*) **1** sew up, complete, make perfect **1H6** I.i.130 [Third Messenger to all, of Talbot's battle] *Here had the conquest fully been sealed up*
2 confirm, ratify, put beyond doubt **2H4** IV.v.104 [King Henry IV to Prince Henry] *at my death / Thou hast sealed up my expectation* [i.e. confirmed my fears]
3 make up, decide **AY** IV.iii.59 [Rosalind as Ganymede reading Phebe's letter to Ganymede, of Silvius] *by him seal up thy mind*

seal at arms seal bearing a coat of arms **E3** IV.v.74 [Charles to King John] *I hope your highness will not so disgrace me / And dash the virtue of my seal at arms*

sealed (*adj.*) certified, authenticated [through a wax seal] **TS** Induction.ii.87 [First Servingman to Sly, of his supposed wife] *she brought stone jugs and no sealed quarts;* **Ham** I.i.86

sea-like (*adj.*) in sea-going trim; or: like a stormy sea **AC** III.xiii.171 [Antony to Cleopatra] *our severed navy too / Have knit again, and fleet, threatening most sea-like*

sealing day *(n.)* day for confirming a contract, wedding-day **MND** I.i.84 [Theseus to Hermia] *by the next new moon - / The sealing day betwixt my love and me*

seam *(n.)* grease, fat **TC** II.iii.183 [Ulysses to Agamemnon, of Achilles] *the proud lord, / That bastes his arrogance with his own seam*

sea-maid *(n.)* mermaid, sea-nymph **MM** III.ii.102 [Lucio to disguised Duke, of Angelo] *a sea-maid spawned him;* **MND** II.i.154

sea-marge *(n.)* margin of the sea, coast **Tem** IV.i.69 [Iris to Ceres] *thy sea-marge, sterile and rocky-hard*

sea-margent *(n.)* seashore, edge of the sea **Per** IV.i.26 [Dionyza to Marina] *On the sea-margent / Walk with Leonine* [Q *marre it*]

sea-mark *(n.)* prominent landmark used as a guide for sailors, beacon **Cor** V.iii.74 [Coriolanus to Young Martius] *stick i'th'wars / Like a great sea-mark;* **Oth** V.ii.266

search *(n.)* search-party **Oth** I.i.159 [Iago to Roderigo] *Lead to the Sagittary the raised search*

search *(v.)* **1** probe, explore, examine **AY** II.iv.40 [Rosalind as if to Silvius] *searching of thy wound, / I have by hard adventure found mine own;* **JC** V.iii.42; **TC** II.ii.16; **TG** I.ii.116; **Tit** III.i.262

2 perceive, penetrate, discover **3H6** V.ii.18 [Warwick alone, of his eyes] *as piercing as the midday sun, / To search the secret treasons of the world*

3 seek, seek out, look for **Cym** V.v.11 [Pisanio to Cymbeline, of the soldier] *He hath been searched among the dead and living*

searcher *(n.)* official appointed to view and report on corpses **RJ** V.ii.8 [Friar John to Friar Laurence] *the searchers of the town … / Sealed up the doors*

searching *(adj.)* **1** piercing, wounding, sharp **2H6** III.ii.311 [Suffolk to Queen] *Would curses kill … / I would invent as bitter searching terms*

2 finding out weak spots, penetrating, stirring **2H4** II.iv.27 [Hostess to Doll, of canary] *that's a marvellous searching wine*

searecloath *(n.)* ☞ cerecloth *(n.)*

seared *(adj.)* **1** withered, wilting, declining **Lover** 14 *Some beauty peeped, through lattice of seared age;* **Cym** I.iv.6; **MM** II.iv.9

2 branded, stigmatized, vilified **AW** II.i.173 [Helena to King] *Seared otherwise, ne worse of worst* [unclear construction]

sea-room *(n.)* space at sea to manoeuvre a ship **Per** III.i.45 [First Sailor to all] *But sea-room, an … I care not* [i.e. what happens to the weather]

sear up *(v.)* wrap up in a shroud, seal up **Cym** I.ii.47 [Posthumus to Innogen, of any future wife] *sear up my embracements from a next / With bonds of death!*

seasick *(adj.)* weary of sea travel, tired of voyaging, **RJ** V.iii.118 [Romeo alone, to himself] *Thou desperate pilot, now at once run on / The dashing rocks thy seasick weary bark*

sea-son *(n.)* sea-boy, ship's boy **2H4** III.i.27 [King Henry IV alone, as if to sleep] *give thy repose / To the wet sea-son* [F *sea-boy;* Q *season*]

season *(n.)* **1** time, due time, occasion **Ham** I.iv.5 [Horatio to Hamlet and Marcellus] *It then draws near the season / Wherein the spirit held his wont to walk;* **Cym** II.iii.47, V.v.402; **TC** I.iii.87

2 opportunity, favourable moment **AC** V.i.49 [Caesar to all] *I will tell you at some meeter season;* **Ham** III.ii.265; **2H4** IV.ii.79; **LL** V.ii.63; **Luc** 166; **MV** V.i.107

3 while, short period of time **E3** III.iv.16 [King Edward to Audley] *here a season let us breathe ourselves;* **Cym** IV.iii.22; **R3** I.iv.61

4 time of year, weather conditions **AW** V.iii.32 [King to Bertram] *I am not a day of season* [i.e. showing a sunny or a wintry mood]; **KL** III.iv.32; **MM** II.ii.168

5 age [duration of life] **Cym** III.iv.174 [Pisanio to Innogen] *with what imitation you can borrow / From youth of such a season*

6 age [period of history], time **Mac** IV.ii.17 [Ross to Macduff's wife, of Macduff] *He … best knows / The fits o'the season*

7 seasoning, flavour, preservative **MA** IV.i.140 [Leonato to Friar, of Hero] *the wide sea / Hath … salt too little which may season give / To her foul tainted flesh;* **Mac** III.iv.140

season *(v.)* **1** bring to maturity, ripen **Ham** I.iii.81 [Polonius to Laertes, of the advice he has just given] *My blessing season this in thee!;* **TNK** I.iii.56

2 moderate, temper, control **Ham** I.ii.192 [Horatio to Hamlet, telling him of the Ghost] *Season your admiration for a while*

3 modify, soften, alleviate **Ham** II.i.28 [Polonius to Reynaldo] *as you may season it in the charge*

4 turn into, make **Ham** III.ii.219 [First Player, as King, to his Queen] *And who in want a hollow friend doth try / Directly seasons him his enemy*

5 prepare, make fit **Ham** III.iii.86 [Hamlet to himself, of Claudius] *When he is fit and seasoned for his passage;* **Tim** IV.iii.86

6 imbue, infuse, fill **TNK** V.i.149 [Emilia praying to Diana] *lend thine ear … to my petition / Seasoned with holy fear*

7 fortify, temper, strengthen **E3** III.iv.49 [King Edward to Audley, of Prince Edward] *This is the day … / To season his courage;* **Cym** I.vii.9

8 preserve, keep **TN** I.i.31 [Valentine to Orsino, of Olivia's actions and tears] *all this to season / A brother's dead love;* **AW** I.i.46; **RJ** II.iii.68

9 gratify, delight, tease **MV** IV.i.97 [Shylock to all, of slaves] *let their palates / Be seasoned with such viands?*

season, of in season, at the appropriate time **MM** II.ii.85 [Isabella to Angelo] *Even for our kitchens / We kill the fowl of season*

season, of the [of male deer] in the rutting season, on heat **MW** III.iii.150 [Ford to Mistress Ford] *I warrant you, buck - and of the season too, it shall appear*

season, out of *(adj./adv.)* **1** inopportune, inappropriate, ill-timed **CE** I.ii.68 [Antipholus of Syracuse to Dromio of Ephesus] *these jests are out of season*

2 inopportunely, inappropriately, inconveniently **CE** II.ii.48 [Dromio of Syracuse to Antipholus of Syracuse] *Was ever any man thus beaten out of season;* **KL** II.i.118

seasoned *(adj.)* established, settled, mature **Lover** 18 [of a handkerchief] *That seasoned woe had pelleted in tears;* **Cor** III.iii.64

seat *(n.)* **1** throne **H5** I.ii.270 [King Henry to Ambassador] *We never valued this poor seat of England;* **Cor** I.i.134; **3H6** II.vi.100; **R2** II.i.41; **R3** III.vii.168; **TC** I.iii.31

2 estate **H5** III.v.47 [French King to his nobles] *For your great seats, now quit you of great shames;* **Cym** V.v.60; **1H4** V.i.45; **MV** I.i.171

3 residence, dwelling-place, habitat **Tim** IV.ii.45 [Flavius alone, of Timon] *He's flung in rage from this ingrateful seat / Of monstrous friends*

4 resting place, region, abode **Cym** V.iv.69 [Second Brother, to music] *from stiller seats we came;* **Sonn** 105.14

5 situation, position, location **Mac** I.vi.1 [King to all] *This castle hath a pleasant seat;* **R3** III.iii.12

6 position, place, status **R3** I.iii.111 [Queen Margaret to herself, as if to Queen Elizabeth] *Thy honour, state, and seat is due to me;* **3H6** III.iii.10

seat *(v.)* settle, establish **H5** I.ii.62 [Canterbury to King Henry] *Charles the Great … did seat the French / Beyond the river Sala*

seated *(adj.)* **1** firmly placed, fixed **Mac** I.iii.135 [Macbeth to himself] *why do I yield to that suggestion / Whose horrid image doth … make my seated heart knock at my ribs*

2 located, situated **Luc** 1144 [Lucrece as if to the nightingale] *Some dark deep desert seated from the way*

sea-wing *(n.)* means of flight by sea **AC** III.x.19 [Scarus to Enobarbus, of Antony] *Claps on his sea wing*

second *(n.)* **1** supporter, helper, champion **Tem** III.iii.105 [Antonio to Sebastian] *I'll be thy second;* **Cor** I.iv.43; **KL** IV.vi.195; **WT** II.iii.27

2 supporting action, act of assistance **Ham** IV.vii.152 [Claudius to Laertes] *this project / Should have a back or second;* **Cor** I.viii.15

3 (plural) reinforcements, reserves, back-up **Cym** V.iii.90 [Posthumus to First Captain, of himself] *Who had not now been drooping here if seconds / Had answered him*

4 second-rate material, something of inferior quality **Sonn** 125.11 *take thou my oblation … / Which is not mixed with seconds*

second (*adj.*) using a deputy, surrogate, proxy **TC** II.iii.139 [Agamemnon to all, of Achilles' response] *In second voice we'll not be satisfied;* **1H4** I.iii.163; **2H4** V.ii.90

second (*v.*) **1** support, assist, reinforce **2H6** IV.ix.35 [King to all, of Cade] *now is York in arms to second him;* **AY** III.iii.11; **Cor** V.vi.57; **Cym** V.ii.14; **H8** III.ii.60; **MA** V.i.2

2 support, confirm, corroborate **Cor** IV.vi.63 [Messenger to Sicinius] *The slave's report is seconded*

secondary (*n.*) deputy, agent, second-in-command **MM** I.i.46 [Duke to Angelo] *Escalus, / Though first in question, is thy secondary;* **KJ** V.ii.80

secret (*n.*) private affair, confidence **LL** I.i.226 [Costard to King, in response to 'No words!'] *Of other men's secrets, I beseech you*

secret (*adj.*) **1** hidden, obscure, abstruse **Per** III.ii.31 [Cerimon to First Gentleman, of physic] *through which secret art*

2 magical, mystical, occult **Mac** IV.i.47 [Macbeth to Witches] *you secret, black, and midnight hags;* **Tem** I.ii.77

secret-false (*adj.*) secretly disloyal, covertly inconstant **CE** III.ii.15 [Luciana to Antipholus of Syracuse] *Be secret-false* ☛ false (*adj.*) 2

sect (*n.*) **1** faction, cabal, party **KL** V.iii.18 [Lear to Cordelia] *we'll wear out … packs and sects of great ones;* **Tim** III.v.30

2 class, kind, sort **MM** II.ii.5 [Provost alone, of Claudio's offence] *All sects, all ages smack of this vice, and he / To die for it;* **2H4** II.iv.37

3 cutting, offshoot, branch **Oth** I.iii.328 [Iago to Roderigo, of lust] *whereof I take this, that you call love, to be a sect or scion*

sectary (*n.*) **1** devotee, disciple, adherent **KL** I.ii.149 [Edgar to Edmund] *How long have you been a sectary astronomical?*

2 follower of a heretical sect **H8** V.iii.70 [Gardiner to Cranmer] *you are a sectary*

secure (*adj.*) **1** carefree, free from anxiety, unguarded **H5** IV.Chorus.17 [Chorus] *secure in soul, / The confident and overlusty French / Do the low-rated English play at dice;* **Ham** I.v.61; **Oth** III.iii.198, IV.i.71

2 over-confident, unsuspecting, too self-confident **MW** II.ii.285 [Ford alone] *Page is an ass, a secure ass;* **E3** IV.iii.23; **1H6** II.i.11; **R2** V.iii.42; **TC** II.ii.15; **TNK** I.i.154

3 free [from], safe [from], untouched [by] **3H6** IV.iv.33 [Lady Grey to Rivers, of sanctuary] *There shall I rest secure from force and fraud* **Tit** II.i.3

secure (*v.*) **1** keep safe, protect, guard **Ham** I.v.113 [Horatio to Marcellus, of Hamlet] *Heavens secure him;* **Cym** IV.iv.8; **2H6** V.ii.76; **Tem** II.i.315

2 make over-confident, keep unsuspecting **KL** IV.i.20 [Gloucester to Old Man] *Our means secure us*

3 take comfort, free from care **Oth** I.iii.10 [Duke to Senators] *I do not so secure me in the error* [i.e. take comfort in the inconsistency]; **Tim** II.ii.181

secure (*adv.*) safely, free from anxiety **1H6** III.ii.19 [Charles to all] *once again we'll sleep secure in Rouen;* **1H4** I.iii.129; **3H6** II.v.50

securely (*adv.*) **1** confidently, without misgiving, fearlessly **R2** I.iii.97 [King Richard to Mowbray] *Securely I espy / Virtue with valour couched in thine eye;* **KJ** II.i.374; **Luc** 89; **MW** II.ii.232

2 over-confidently, carelessly, heedlessly **TC** IV.v.73 [Achilles to Agamemnon, reacting to ''Tis done like Hector'] *But securely done;* **R2** II.i.266

security (*n.*) over-confidence, carelessness **Mac** III.v.32 [Hecat to the Witches] *you all know security / Is mortals' chiefest enemy;* **2H4** I.ii.44; **H5** II.ii.44; **JC** II.iii.6; **R2** III.ii.34

sedge (*n.*) variety of grassy plant, rush **MA** II.i.186 [Benedick alone, of Claudio] *poor hurt fowl, now will he creep into sedges;* **TG** II.vii.29; **TS** Induction.ii.50 ☛ PLANTS, p.330

sedged (*adj.*) made from sedges, woven from reeds **Tem** IV.i.129 [Iris to the nymphs] *With your sedged crowns*

sedgy (*adj.*) bordered with rushes, reed-covered **1H4** I.iii.97 [Hotspur to King Henry] *on the gentle Severn's sedgy bank*

seditious (*adj.*) turbulent, tempestuous, violent **CE** I.i.12 [Duke to Egeon] *the mortal and intestine jars / 'Twixt thy seditious countrymen and us*

see (*v.*) **1** meet, see each other **TC** IV.iv.56 [Cressida to Troilus] *When shall we see again?;* **Cym** I.ii.55; **H8** I.i.2

2 see to, manage, attend to **AC** V.ii.364 [Caesar to Dolabella] *see / High order in this great solemnity;* **KL** V.iii.285; **R2** II.i.217; **TS** I.ii.144

see for (*v.*) look out for **RJ** V.i.35 [Romeo alone, as if to Juliet] *I will lie with thee tonight. / Let's see for means;* **Oth** II.i.75

seed (*v.*) mature, yield fruit **E3** IV.iv.138 [Audley to Prince Edward] *First bud we, then we blow, and after seed;* **Luc** 603

seeded (*adj.*) run to seed, seasoned, matured **TC** I.iii.316 [Ulysses to Nestor] *the seeded pride / That hath to this maturity blown up / In rank Achilles*

seedness (*n.*) action of sowing **MM** I.iv.42 [Lucio to Isabella] *from the seedness the bare fallow brings / To teeming foison*

seeing (*n.*) appearance, observing, beholding **WT** V.ii.17 [First Gentleman to Autolycus, of the reunion between Leontes and Camillo] *the wisest beholder that knew no more but seeing could not say if th'importance were joy or sorrow*

seek (*v.*) seek help from, resort to **Luc** 293 [of Lucrece's eye] *with a pure appeal seeks to the heart*

seeking (*n.*) suit, petition **Cor** I.i.186 [Martius to Menenius, of the citizens] *What's their seeking?*

seek through (*v.*) try, test, put to trial **Cym** IV.ii.160 [Arviragus to Belarius] *I would revenges, / That possible strength might meet, / would seek us through*

seel (*v.*) [falconry: sewing up a bird's eyelids, as part of taming] sew up, close up, blind **AC** III.xiii.112 [Antony to Cleopatra] *the wise gods seel our eyes;* **AC** V.ii.146; **Oth** I.iii.266; **Oth** III.iii.208

seeling (*adj.*) [falconry] concealing, screening **Mac** III.ii.46 [Macbeth to Lady Macbeth] *Come, seeling night, / Scarf up the tender eye of pitiful day*

seely (*adj.*) miserable, pathetic; or: simple-minded **R2** V.v.25 [Richard alone] *like seely beggars*

seem (*v.*) **1** have the look [of], give the appearance [of] **H8** V.i.86 [stage direction] *Lovell seems to stay;* **Mac** I.ii.48; **Per** I.ii.78, IV.iv.7

2 arrange, contrive, try speciously **Per** I.i.122 [Pericles alone] *How courtesy would seem to cover sin;* **Oth** III.i.28

seemer (*n.*) make-believer, pretender, one who assumes a behaviour **MM** I.iii.54 [Duke to Friar Thomas] *Hence shall we see … what our seemers be*

seeming (*n.*) **1** appearance, look, aspect **Cym** III.iv.55 [Innogen to Pisanio] *All good seeming … shall be thought / Put on for villainy;* **Oth** I.iii.109; **Sonn** 102.1; **TNK** II.vi.76, 117; **WT** IV.iv.75

2 deceptive appearance, two-faced behaviour, pretence **MM** II.iv.150 [Isabella to Angelo] *Seeming, seeming! / I will proclaim thee;* **H8** II.iv.108; **MA** IV.i.54; **MM** II.iv.15, III.ii.37

3 demeanour, outward behaviour **Oth** III.iii.207 [Iago to Othello, of Desdemona] *She that so young could give out such a seeming;* **Ham** III.ii.97; **2H4** V.ii.129; **KL** III.ii.56; **Oth** I.i.233; **TC** I.iii.157

4 plausibility, likelihood, credibility **Cym** V.v.453 [Cymbeline to Soothsayer, of the latter's interpretation] *This hath some seeming*

seeming (*adj.*) apparent, convincing in appearance **Sonn** 138.11 *O love's best habit is in seeming trust;* **AC** II.ii.214; **1H4** IV.iii.83; **MM** IV.ii.148; **RJ** III.iii.112; **TC** I.i.41 ☛ summer-seeming (*adj.*); well-seeming (*adj.*)

seeming (*adv.*) **1** seemingly, becomingly **AY** V.iv.67 [Touchstone to Audrey] *Bear your body more seeming;* **Lover** 327

  2 apparently, ostensibly, to outward appearance **Luc** 1514 [of a painting of Sinon] *He entertained a show so seeming just;* **Ham** I.v.46

seen, well well-versed, with good qualifications **TS** I.ii.132 [Hortensio to Petruchio, of putting himself forward as a schoolmaster] *Well seen in music*

seethe (*v.*) **1** reduce by boiling, dissipate by overheating **Tim** IV.iii.432 [Timon to Bandits, of drinking wine] *Till the high fever seethe your blood to froth*

  2 boil with urgency, bubble, be in a ferment **TC** III.i.40 [Pandarus to Servant] *my business seethes*

segregation (*n.*) dispersal, scattering, breaking up **Oth** II.i.10 [Second Gentleman to Montano] *A segregation of the Turkish fleet*

seigniory (*n.*) lordship, domain, dominion **E3** I.i.3 [King Edward to Artois] *Thou shalt retain as great a seigniory;* **R3** IV.iv.36

seised, seized (*v.*) possessed **Ham** I.i.89 [Horatio to Marcellus and Barnardo, of old Fortinbras] *his lands / Which he stood seised of*

seize, seize upon (*v.*) [legal] take possession of, take hold of **MV** IV.i.350 [Portia as Balthasar to Shylock, of an alien] *The party 'gainst the which he doth contrive / Shall seize one half his goods;* **Oth** V.ii.362 [Lodovico to Gratiano] *keep the house / And seize upon the fortunes of the Moor, / For they succeed on you;* **MA** V.iv.53

seizure (*n.*) grasping of hands, clasp, hold **TC** I.i.58 [Troilus to Pandarus, of Cressida's hands] *to whose soft seizure / The cygnet's down is harsh;* **KJ** III.i.241

seld (*adv.*) seldom, rarely **TC** IV.v.150 [Ajax to all, of making requests to Hector] *As seld I have the chance;* **PassP** XIII.7

seldom (*adj.*) rare, infrequent, uncommon **1H4** III.ii.58 [King Henry to Prince Hal] *my state, / Seldom, but sumptuous, showed like a feast;* **Sonn** 52.4; **Tim** II.ii.145

seld-shown (*adj.*) seldom-seen, rarely in the public eye **Cor** II.i.205 [Brutus to Sicinius] *Seld-shown flamens / Do press among the popular throngs*

select (*adj.*) superior, refined, cultivated **Ham** I.iii.74 [Polonius to Laertes, about wearing appropriate clothes] *And they in France of the best rank and station / Are of a most select and generous chief in that*

self (*adj.*) same, selfsame, identical, exact **KL** I.i.69 [Regan to Lear] *I am made of that self mettle as my sister;* **AC** V.i.21; **3H6** III.i.11; **MV** I.i.148; **R2** I.ii.23; **Tit** IV.ii.122

self, one sole, one and the same, a single **TN** I.i.40 [Orsino to Valentine, of Olivia's feelings] *all supplied and filled ... with one self king*

self-abuse (*n.*) self-deception, self-delusion **Mac** III.iv.141 [Macbeth to Lady Macbeth] *My strange and self-abuse / Is the initiate fear that wants hard use* ➤ **abuse** (*n.*) 1

self-admission (*n.*) self-admiration, self-centredness **TC** II.iii.164 [Ulysses to Agamemnon, of Achilles] *He ... carries on the stream of his dispose ... / In will peculiar and in self-admission*

self-affected (*adj.*) self-loving, egotistical, conceited **TC** II.iii.236 [Diomedes to all, of Ajax] *[if he were] strange, or self-affected*

self-assumption (*n.*) self-importance, arrogance, egotism **TC** II.iii.123 [Agamemnon to Patroclus, of Achilles] *we think him ... in self-assumption greater / Than in the note of judgement*

self-born (*adj.*) selfsame, identical **WT** IV.i.8 [Time to audience] *it is in my power ... in one self-born hour / To plant and o'erwhelm custom* [i.e. one and the same hour]

self-borne (*adj.*) carried for one's own cause; or: carried by oneself **R2** II.iii.80 [Berkeley to Bolingbroke] *what pricks you on / To ... fright our native peace with self-borne arms*

self-bounty (*n.*) innate generosity, inner virtue **Oth** III.iii.198 [Iago to Othello] *I would not have your free and noble nature, / Out of self-bounty, be abused*

self-covered (*adj.*) self-concealing, with the self covered over **KL** IV.ii.62 [Albany to Gonerill] *Thou changed and self-covered thing* [i.e. by the fiend within]

self-danger (*n.*) endangering oneself, putting oneself in jeopardy **Cym** III.iv.148 [Pisanio to Innogen] *if you could ... but disguise / That which, t'appear itself, must not yet be / But by self-danger*

self-drawing (*adj.*) spun from within oneself **H8** I.i.63 [Norfolk to Buckingham, of Wolsey] *spider-like, / Out of his self-drawing web*

self-endeared (*adj.*) in love with herself **MA** III.i.56 [Hero to Ursula, of Beatrice] *She is so self-endeared*

self-explication (*n.*) being able to explain it to oneself **Cym** III.iv.8 [Innogen to Pisanio, of his demeanour] *a thing perplexed / Beyond self-explication*

self-figured (*adj.*) self-made, formed by oneself **Cym** II.iii.118 [Cloten to Innogen, of the parties to lower marriages] *to knit their souls ... in self-figured knot*

self-gracious (*adj.*) coming from one's own gracious self **AW** IV.v.71 [Lafew to Countess, of the King's suggestion] *which ... his majesty out of a self-gracious remembrance did first propose*

self instant (*adj.*) individually present, self-contained **E3** IV.iv.54 [Prince Edward to Audley, of a man] *His hand, his foot, his head hath several strengths; / And being all but one self instant strength*

self-mettle (*n.*) one's own vigorous activity **H8** I.i.134 [Norfolk to Buckingham] *Anger is like / A full hot horse, who being allowed his way, / Self-mettle tires him*

self-sovereignty (*n.*) self-control, self-discipline **LL** IV.i.36 [Boyet to Princess] *Do not curst wives hold that self-sovereignty / Only for praise' sake, when they strive to be / Lords o'er their lords*

self-subdued (*adj.*) unresisting, offering no opposition **KL** II.ii.120 [Oswald to Cornwall, of disguised Kent] *got praises of the King / For him attempting who was self-subdued*

self-substantial (*adj.*) using substance from one's own body **Sonn** 1.6 *thou contracted to thine own bright eyes, / Feed'st thy light's flame with self-substantial fuel*

self-unable (*adj.*) inadequate personal, poor and subjective **AW** III.i.13 [Second Lord to Duke, of an outside observer] *That the great figure of a council frames / By self-unable motion*

sell (*v.*) **1** exchange, trade, give up **2H6** III.i.92 [York to himself, of the loss of France] *I will remedy this gear ere long, / Or sell my title for a glorious grave*

  2 ➤ buy and sell

semblable (*n.*) **1** likeness, fellow, match **Ham** V.ii.118 [Hamlet to Osrick, of Laertes] *his semblable is his mirror* [i.e. he is matched only by his reflection]

  2 fellow-man, anything of the same nature **Tim** IV.iii.22 [Timon alone] *His semblable, yea himself, Timon disdains*

semblable (*adj.*) similar, like, comparable **AC** III.iv.3 [Antony to Octavia] *thousands more / Of semblable import;* **2H4** V.i.58

semblably (*adv.*) seemingly, similarly, in the same fashion **1H4** V.iii.21 [Hotspur to Douglas, of Blunt] *Semblably furnished like the King himself*

semblance (*n.*) **1** appearance, outward show **MW** IV.ii.62 [Mistress Page to Falstaff] *If you go out in your own semblance, you die;* **CE** V.i.349; **2H6** III.ii.162; **KJ** IV.iii.4; **KL** V.iii.185; **RJ** I.v.74

  2 likeness, image, depiction **MA** V.i.239 [Claudio as if to Hero] *thy image doth appear / In the rare semblance that I loved it first;* **1H6** V.iii.193; **Luc** 1246, 1759; **MV** III.iv.20

semblative (*adj.*) resembling, looking like **TN** I.iv.34 [Orsino to Viola as Cesario, of her qualities] *all is semblative a woman's part*

sempster (*n.*) one who sews [as a profession], tailor **TNK** III.v.45 [Second Countryman to all] *Cicely, the sempster's daughter*

senator (*n.*) ➤ ROMAN HISTORY, p.377

seniory (*n.*) seniority R3 IV.iv.36 [Queen Margaret to all] *If ancient sorrow be most reverend, / Give mine the benefit of seniory* [or: seigniory, 'sovereignty'] [F *seigneurie*; Q *signorie*]

senna (*n.*) variety of shrub [producing a drug which can cause vomiting and bowel evacuation] Mac V.iii.55 [Macbeth to Doctor] *What rhubarb, senna, or what purgative drug / Would scour these English hence?* [F *cyme*]

sennet (*n.*) ☞ STAGE DIRECTIONS, p.417

sennight, se'nnight, seven-night (*n.*) [seven night] week AY III.ii.306 [Rosalind to Orlando] *If the interim be but a se'nnight;* WT I.ii.17 [Leontes to Polixenes, asking him to stay longer] *One sev'n-night longer;* MA II.i.333; Mac I.iii.22

sense (*n.*) **1** senses, sensation, organs of sense TC I.iii.252 [Aeneas to and of Agamemnon] *I bring a trumpet ... / To set his sense on the attentive bent;* AW I.ii.60; H5 II.iii.46; MM II.ii.169; TC I.i.59; TNK I.i.15

2 ability to respond to sensation, physical perception 2H4 IV.v.158 [Prince Henry to King Henry IV] *I spake unto this crown as having sense;* Cym III.ii.59; Ham IV.v.157; Oth I.iii.63; TC II.i.21, IV.iv.4

3 feeling, sensibility, capacity to feel Ham V.i.70 [Hamlet to Horatio] *The hand of little employment hath the daintier sense;* AW I.i.221; Cym II.ii.32; H5 IV.i.228; Mac I.vi.3; MM II.ii.142

4 perception, awareness, discernment, appreciation Oth III.iii.335 [Othello to Iago, of Desdemona] *What sense had I of her stolen hours of lust?;* AW I.iii.167, III.iv.39; 2H4 IV.iii.33; LL V.ii.259; Oth I.ii.64

5 mind, power of reason, wits TNK III.ii.29 [Gaoler's Daughter alone] *let not my sense unsettle;* Cym V.iv.149; Ham V.i.244; JC III.ii.17; TC IV.v.54; WT V.iii.72

6 common sense, natural feeling, reasonableness MM V.i.61 [Duke to all, of Isabella] *Her madness hath the oddest frame of sense;* MM II.ii.142, V.ii.430

7 opinion, view, judgement MM IV.iv.27 [Angelo alone, of Claudio] *his riotous youth with dangerous sense / Might ... have ta'en revenge;* Oth V.ii.287

8 interpretation, construction, signification MM I.iv.65 [Lucio to Isabella, of the law used by Angelo] *Under whose heavy sense your brother's life / Falls into forfeit;* TC I.iii.385

9 intuition, instinct Ham III.iv.193 [Hamlet to Gertrude] *in despite of sense and secrecy*

sense, to the to the quick Oth V.i.11 [Iago to himself, of Roderigo] *I have rubbed this young quat almost to the sense*

senseless (*adj.*) **1** lacking human sensation, incapable of feeling 2H6 IV.i.77 [Lieutenant to Suffolk] *thou ... / Against the senseless winds shalt grin in vain;* Cym I.iv.7; JC I.i.35; PassP XX.21; R2 III.ii.23; RJ I.iv.36

2 unconscious, insensible, oblivious Cym I.i.66 [Innogen to Cymbeline] *I am senseless of your wrath;* Cym II.iii.52; E3 III.iii.202; TG III.i.143; Tim II.i.1; WT IV.iv.606

3 lacking in sense, stupid, foolish TS I.ii.36 [Petruchio to Hortensio, of Grumio] *A senseless villain;* AW II.i.124; Cym V.iv.148; E3 IV.iii.23

senseless-obstinate (*adj.*) unreasonably stubborn, irrationally unyielding R3 III.i.44 [Buckingham to Cardinal Bourchier] *You are too senseless-obstinate*

sensible (*adj.*) **1** sensitive, responsive, capable of feeling KJ III.iv.53 [Constance to Cardinal Pandulph, of herself] *being not mad, but sensible of grief;* CE IV.iv.26; Cor I.iii.86; JC I.iii.18; LL IV.iii.313; Tem II.i.178

2 evident, perceptible by the senses, affecting the senses Mac II.i.36 [Macbeth alone, as if to a dagger] *Art thou not, fatal vision, sensible / To feeling as to sight?* Ham I.i.57; MV II.viii.48, ix.89

3 endowed with good sense, perceptive, responsible TS V.ii.18 [Petruchio to Widow] *You are very sensible, and yet you miss my sense;* 2H4 I.ii.197; LL V.ii.259; Oth II.iii.296

sensibly (*adv.*) **1** as a feeling person, with a sensitive body Cor I.iv.55 [Lartius to First Soldier, of Martius] *O noble fellow! / Who sensibly outdares his senseless sword;* Tit IV.ii.121

2 acutely, intensely, feelingly Ham IV.v.152 [Claudius to Laertes, of Polonius' death] *And am most sensibly in grief for it* [Q2; F *sensible*]

3 with common sense, intelligently LL III.i.111 [Mote to Armado, of Costard's broken shin] *I will tell you sensibly* [also: as a feeling person]

sentence (*n.*) **1** maxim, wise saying, precept MV I.ii.10 [Portia to Nerissa, of her words] *Good sentences, and well pronounced;* AW I.iii.74; E3 II.i.411; MA II.iii.233; Oth I.iii.214

2 pronouncement, authoritative decision KL I.i.170 [Lear to Kent] *with strained pride, / To come betwixt our sentence and our power* [Q; F *sentences*]

sententious (*adj.*) **1** full of wise remarks, ready with acute observations, pithy AY V.iv.61 [Duke Senior to all, of Touchstone] *he is very swift and sententious;* LL V.i.3

2 malapropism for 'sentences' RJ II.iv.206 [Nurse to Romeo, of Juliet] *she hath the prettiest sententious of it, of you and rosemary*

sentinel (*v.*) stand guard over, keep watch during Luc 942 [Lucrece as if to time] *Time's glory is ... / To wake the morn and sentinel the night*

separable (*adj.*) which causes separation, with divisive power Sonn 36.6 *In our two loves there is but one respect, / Though in our lives a separable spite*

sepulchre (*v.*) **1** place in a sepulchre, bury TG IV.ii.114 [Silvia to Proteus, of Julia's love] *in hers sepulchre thine;* Luc 805

2 serve as a burial-place for KL II.iv.127 [Lear to Regan] *I would divorce me from thy mother's tomb, / Sepulchring an adult'ress*

sequel (*n.*) sequence, series, order of succession R3 III.vi.4 [Scrivener alone] *mark how well the sequel hangs together;* H5 V.ii.326

sequence (*n.*) **1** proper lineal order, order of succession R2 II.i.199 [York to King Richard] *how art thou a king / But by fair sequence and succession?;* KJ II.i.96

2 appropriate order, correct precedence Tim V.i.206 [Timon to First Senator] *Tell Athens, in the sequence of degree, / From high to low throughout*

sequent (*n.*) follower, attendant LL IV.ii.137 [Holofernes to Nathaniel, of Berowne] *here he hath framed a letter to a sequent of the stranger Queen's*

sequent (*adj.*) **1** following, ensuing, consequent KL I.ii.106 [Gloucester to Edmund] *nature finds itself scourged by the sequent effects;* AW II.ii.51; Ham V.ii.54; MM V.i.370; TC IV.v.65; TNK I.i.60

2 sequential, successive, one after another Oth I.ii.41 [Cassio to Othello] *The galleys / Have sent a dozen sequent messengers ... at one another's heels* [F; Q *frequent*]; Sonn 60.4

sequester (*n.*) sequestration, removal, withdrawal Oth III.iv.40 [Othello to Desdemona] *This hand of yours requires / A sequester from liberty*

sequester (*v.*) separate, remove, cut off Tit II.iii.75 [Bassianus to Tamora] *Why are you sequestered from all your train;* TC III.iii.8

sequestered (*adj.*) separated, cut off from its fellows AY II.i.33 [First Lord to Duke Senior] *a poor sequestered stag*

sequestration (*n.*) **1** separation, cessation, severance Oth I.iii.341 [Iago to Roderigo, of Othello and Desdemona's love] *It was a violent commencement, and thou shalt see an answerable sequestration*

2 seclusion, removal, withdrawal H5 I.i.58 [Canterbury to Ely, of King Henry] *never noted in him ... / Any retirement, any sequestration, / From open haunts and popularity*

3 imprisonment, isolation; also: loss of property 1H6 II.v.25 [Mortimer to Gaolers] *This loathsome sequestration have I had*

sere (*n.*) trigger-catch [of a gun] Ham II.ii.324 [Hamlet to Rosencrantz and Guildenstern] *the clown shall make those laugh whose lungs are tickle o'th' sere* [i.e. ready to go off]

sere *(adj.)* dried up, withered, parched **Mac** V.iii.23 [Macbeth to himself] *my way of life / Is fallen into the sere, the yellow leaf* [or: *sere* as *(n.)*, withered state]; **CE** IV.ii.19; **E3** I.ii.151, V.i.169

serge *(n.)* type of woollen fabric **2H6** IV.vii.22 [Cade to Say] *thou say, thou serge, nay, thou buckram lord!*

sergeant *(n.)* **1** sheriff's officer, enforcer, arresting officer **Ham** V.ii.330 [Hamlet to all] *this fell sergeant, Death, / Is strict in his arrest;* **CE** IV.ii.55, 60

2 officer [in an army] **H8** I.i.198 [Brandon to Sergeant, of arresting Buckingham] *Your office, sergeant;* **1H6** II.i.1; **Mac** I.ii.3

serious *(adj.)* formal, important, solemn **TNK** I.iii.74 [Emilia to Hippolyta, of her friend's choice of dress] *I followed / For my most serious decking*

serpigo *(n.)* type of spreading skin disease **TC** II.iii.73 [Thersites to Patroclus] *Now the dry serpigo on the subject ... confound all* [F *sapego*]; **MM** III.i.31

servant *(n.)* **1** devotee, one who gives dedicated service, lover **1H6** I.ii.111 [Charles to Pucelle] *Let me thy servant and not sovereign be;* **LL** V.ii.277; **R3** I.ii.206; **TC** IV.iv.124; **TG** II.iv.104; **TNK** III.vi.147

2 follower, retainer, attendant **1H6** IV.i.80 [Richard to King, of Vernon] *This is my servant*

servant *(v.)* put in service, make submissive **Cor** V.ii.79 [Coriolanus to Menenius] *My affairs / Are servanted to others*

serve *(v.)* **1** provide, supply, furnish **Tim** I.ii.236 [Apemantus to Timon, of the lords] *Serving of becks and jutting-out of bums;* **CE** IV.iv.14; **Luc** 166

2 suffice, be enough, do [for] **Tim** III.iv.58 [Lucius' Servant to Flavius] *this answer will not serve;* **Cor** II.iii.14; **1H4** VI.i.132; **2H6** II.i.103; **LL** I.ii.108; **MW** IV.ii.72

3 provide opportunity [to], be favourable [to], favour **3H6** IV.vii.77 [Edward to all] *If fortune serve me, I'll requite this kindness;* **3H6** III.iii.236; **JC** IV.iii.221; **RJ** IV.i.39; **Tim** V.i.42; **TS** I.i.38

4 be of use, render service, be an advantage [to] **Cym** IV.i.2 [Cloten alone, of Posthumus] *How fit his garments serve me!;* **Ham** III.iii.46, iv.77; **2H6** III.i.119; **TG** IV.iv.159; **TNK** V.v.73

5 suit, allow, afford **Cym** V.v.393 [Cymbeline to all] *But nor the time nor place / Will serve our long inter'gatories;* **1H6** V.iv.164

6 enter into service; or: await employment **H8** I.ii.37 [Norfolk to King Henry, of the clothiers] *danger serves among them*

7 be a servant, serve God **MV** I.iii.88 [Antonio to Shylock, of Jacob's strategy with the sheep] *This was a venture, sir, that Jacob served for*

serve in *(v.)* supply, provide, deal out **Tim** IV.iii.481 [Timon to Flavius] *All I kept were knaves, to serve in meat to villains;* **MV** III.v.54; **TS** III.i.14

serve one's turn meet one's need, answer one's requirements **TC** III.i.72 [Pandarus to Helen, of her witty response] *that shall not serve your turn;* **LL** I.i.285; **Tim** II.i.20; **TS** V.ii.62

service *(n.)* **1** action, performance **AW** IV.v.26 [Clown to Lafew] *I would cozen the man of his wife and do his service;* **AW** III.vi.47, 56; **Cym** IV.i.12; **H5** III.vi.3, 70; **TNK** V.iii.32

2 employment, situation as a servant **Tim** IV.iii.507 [Timon to Flavius] *Thou mightst have sooner got another service;* **Cym** IV.ii.372; **H8** V.iv.81; **Tem** II.i.154; **TN** II.v.153

3 military service, affairs of war **AW** I.ii.27 [King to Bertram, of Bertram's father] *He did look far / Into the service of the time;* **H5** IV.iii.119

4 respect, duty, esteem **KL** I.i.28 [Edmund to Kent] *My services to your lordship;* **3H6** III.ii.43

5 course, order of dishes [of a meal] **Ham** IV.iii.23 [Hamlet to Claudius] *Your fat king and your lean beggar is but variable service* [F, Q2; Q1 *seruices*]

6 table preparations for a meal **Mac** I.vii.1 [stage direction] *Enter a Sewer and divers Servants with dishes and service*

serviceable *(adj.)* **1** faithful, loyal, devoted, ready to serve **E3** V.i.110 [Salisbury to King Edward] *my worthless self / With forty other serviceable knights;* **TG** III.ii.70

2 diligent, subservient, ready to do anything **KL** IV.vi.252 [Edgar to dead Oswald] *a serviceable villain;* **Cym** III.ii.15; **TS** I.i.211

servile *(adj.)* **1** subordinate, controlled [by] **MM** III.i.9 [disguised Duke to Claudio] *thou art, / Servile to all the skyey influences;* **Luc** 295; **Venus** 112, 1161

2 befitting a slave, slavish, cringing **KL** III.ii.21 [Lear to the storm] *yet I call you servile ministers;* **R2** III.ii.185

3 as a prisoner, as a slave **1H6** V.iii.58 [Suffolk to Margaret] *if this servile usage once offend*

servility *(n.)* slavery, servitude, captivity **1H6** V.iii.113 [Margaret to Suffolk] *To be a queen in bondage is more vile / Than is a slave in base servility*

serving *(n.)* means, agency, assistance **Cym** III.iv.172 [Pisanio to Innogen, of her male disguise] *you, in their serving ... 'fore noble Lucius / Present yourself* [i.e. with their help]

serving-creature *(n.)* [derisive term for] serving-man **RJ** IV.v.114 [First Musician to Peter] *will I give you the serving-creature*

servingman *(n.)* male servant, male attendant **KL** III.iv.82 [Edgar as Poor Tom to all, of himself] *A servingman, proud in heart and mind*

servitor *(n.)* **1** servant **3H6** III.iii.196 [Warwick to Queen] *henceforth I am thy true servitor;* **Luc** 285; **Oth** I.iii.40; **R3** IV.iii.52; **Tit** I.i.355

2 mercenary, soldier **E3** III.i.45 [Polonian Captain to King John] *I bring these servitors to fight for thee;* **E3** V.i.178; **1H6** II.i.5

sessa, sesey, sese *(int.)* [cry of encouragement used in hunting, fencing] be off, off you go **TS** Induction.i.5 [Sly to Hostess] *let the world slide. Sessa;* **KL** III.iv.97, vi.73 ➤ **SOUNDS**, p.410

session, sessions *(n.)* judicial assembly, trial, court **H8** II.iv.66 [Campeius to Queen Katherine] *It's fit this royal session do proceed;* **MM** V.i.368; **Oth** I.ii.86; **Sonn** 30.1; **WT** II.ii.201, III.ii.1

set *(n.)* **1** setting, cycle, revolution **Oth** II.iii.125 [Iago to Montano, of Cassio] *He'll watch the horologe a double set, / If drink rock not his cradle* [i.e. twice round the clock]

2 setting, sunset **Mac** I.i.5 [Third Witch to First and Second Witches, of meeting again] *That will be ere the set of sun;* **H5** IV.i.265; **R3** V.iii.19

3 [cards, tennis] series of games **Tit** V.i.100 [Aaron to Lucius, of Tamora] *As sure a card as ever won the set;* **KJ** V.ii.107; **LL** V.ii.29

set *(adj.)* **1** formal, ceremonial, secretary **R3** III.vi.2 [Scrivener alone] *Here is the indictment ... / Which in a set hand fairly is engrossed*

2 formally seated, arranged in a position of state **1H4** I.iv.427 [Prince Hal to Falstaff] *Well, here I am set;* **R2** I.iii.7; **Venus** 18

3 carefully composed, deliberately expressed **TN** I.v.83 [Malvolio to Olivia, of fools like Feste] *these set kind of fools;* **AY** II.vii.17

4 seated, sitting down **H8** III.i.74 [Queen Katherine to Campeius and Wolsey] *I was set at work / Among my maids;* **Lover** 39; **TG** II.i.80

5 fixed, rigid, closed **Tem** III.ii.9 [Stephano to Caliban] *Thy eyes are almost set in thy head;* **TN** V.i.196

6 focused [on], fixed [on], wrapped up [in] **Tim** V.i.115 [Flavius to Senators, of Timon] *he is set so only to himself / That nothing but himself which looks like man / Is friendly with him*

set *(v.)* **1** value, rate, esteem **TN** V.i.188 [Sir Andrew to Viola as Cesario] *I think you set nothing by a bloody coxcomb;* **Ham** IV.iii.64; **R2** I.iii.293; **RJ** V.iii.301; **Sonn** 88.1; **Tim** III.ii.31

2 rate, stake, gamble **Mac** III.i.112 [First Murderer to Macbeth] *I would set my life on any chance / To mend it or be rid on't;* **1H4** IV.i.46; **JC** V.i.74; **MND** III.i.127

3 direct, put, make come **Ham** III.iv.18 [Gertrude to Hamlet] *I'll set those to you that can speak;* **MM** IV.iii.153; **Sonn** 83.2; **Tim** II.ii.162

4 set up, plan, arrange **1H4** I.ii.106 [Falstaff to Prince Hal] *Now shall we know if Gadshill have set a match!*

5 set an activity to be followed **2H6** IV.ii.83 [Smith to Cade, of the Clerk] *We took him setting of boys' copies* [i.e. giving boys passages for copying out]

6 compare, match, weigh up **2H6** IV.x.45 [Iden to Cade] *Set limb to limb, and thou art far the lesser*

7 close, shut **KJ** V.vii.51 [King John to Bastard] *thou art come to set mine eye!* [i.e. after death]

8 compose a tune, write the music **TG** I.ii.81 [Lucetta to Julia] *your ladyship can set*

9 challenge, put down a stake against **KL** I.iv.122 [Fool to Lear] *Set less than thou throwest*; **R2** IV.i.57

10 clench **Cor** I.iii.65 [Valeria to Volumnia and Virgilia, of Young Martius] *he did so set his teeth*

set abroad (*v.*) set afoot, initiate, start up **Tit** I.i.195 [Titus to Marcus] *should I ... set abroad new business for you all?*

set against (*v.*) be hostile to, make an attack on **MND** III.ii.146 [Helena to Lysander and Demetrius] *you all are bent / To set against me for your merriment*

set apart (*v.*) discard, abandon, cast aside **KJ** III.i.159 [King John to Cardinal Pandulph, of the Pope] *all reverence set apart / To him and his usurped authority*

set down (*v.*) **1** resolve, decide, determine **R3** III.iv.42 [Derby to all] *We have not yet set down this day of triumph*; **Cor** IV.v.141; **Ham** III.i.170; **1H4** I.i.35

2 log, make note, put on record **Ham** I.v.107 [Hamlet alone] *meet it is I set it down / That one may smile, and smile, and be a villain*; **TC** IV.v.61; **Tim** IV.iii.119; **TNK** III.ii.17

3 settle down **3H6** IV.iii.2 [First Watchman to all] *The King by this is set him down to sleep*

4 [of the strings of a musical instrument] slacken, loosen **Oth** II.i.194 [Iago to himself] *I'll set down the pegs that make this music*

5 encamp, lay siege **Tim** V.iii.9 [Soldier alone, of his captain] *Before proud Athens he's set down by this*; **AW** I.i.117; **Cor** I.ii.28 ☛ sit down (*v.*)

set forth (*v.*) **1** praise, commend, extol **MV** III.v.85 [Jessica to Lorenzo] *I'll set you forth*

2 display, show, exhibit **Mac** I.iv.7 [Malcolm to King, of Cawdor] *he ... set forth / A deep repentance*

set forward (*v.*) go forward, set out, go forth **Cym** V.v.480 [Cymbeline to all] *Set we forward*; **KJ** IV.iii.19

set in (*v.*) put in [his word], join in, intervene **TNK** IV.i.14 [First Friend to Gaoler] *Pirithous ... set in too*

set off (*v.*) **1** enhance, show to advantage, display by contrast **2H4** I.ii.13 [Falstaff to Page] *If the Prince put thee into my service for any other reason than to set me off*; **Cym** I.vii.170, III.iii.13; **Tem** III.i.2; **TNK** V.iii.28

2 take away, remove, set aside [from] **2H4** IV.i.143 [Westmorland to Mowbray, of their demands] *You shall enjoy them, everything set off / That might so much as think you enemies*; **1H4** V.i.88

set on (*v.*) **1** encourage, urge, incite **MM** V.i.246 [Duke to Escalus] *There is another friar that set them on*; **Cor** III.i.37; **1H6** IV.iv.8; **MA** V.i.234; **MND** III.ii.231; **Tem** V.i.255

2 go forward, advance, proceed **H5** V.Chorus.14 [Chorus, of King Henry] *solemnly see him set on to London*; **Cym** V.v.485; **2H4** I.iii.109; **H8** II.iv.241; **JC** I.ii.11; **MM** III.i.64

3 place on the fire **Tim** II.ii.73 [Fool to Servants, of his mistress] *She's e'en setting on water to scald such chickens as you are*

set out (*v.*) pick out, send forth **Tim** V.iv.57 [Alcibiades to Senators, of his and Timon's enemies] *Whom you yourselves shall set out for reproof*

set to (*v.*) set [a broken limb] **1H4** V.i.131 [Falstaff alone] *Can honour set to a leg?*

set up (*v.*) set spinning **Cor** IV.v.156 [First Servingman to Second Servingman, of Coriolanus] *He turned me about with his finger and his thumb as one would set up a top*

set up one's rest (*n.*) [in primero] venture one's final stake, stake all **AW** II.i.135 [Helena to King] *you set up your rest 'gainst remedy*; **CE** IV.iii.26; **KL** I.i.123; **MV** II.ii.96; **RJ** IV.v.6, V.iii.110

setter (*n.*) informant, insider, confederate **1H4** II.ii.49 [Poins to all, of Gadshill] *'tis our setter*

setting (*n.*) **1** putting, placing, sitting **AW** IV.iii.109 [Second Lord to Bertram, of Parolles] *his setting i'th' stocks*

2 fixed look, settled expression **Tem** II.i.233 [Sebastian to Antonio] *The setting of thine eye and cheek proclaim / A matter from thee*

setting-down (*n.*) siege, besieging, encampment **Mac** V.iv.10 [Seyward to Malcolm, of Macbeth] *the confident tyrant / Keeps still in Dunsinane and will endure / Our setting down before't* ☛ set down (*v.*) 5

settle (*v.*) establish, set up, give a home to **TNK** III.vi.307 [Theseus to Palamon and Arcite] *When ye return, who wins, I'll settle here* [i.e. in Athens]

settled (*adj.*) **1** calm, steadfast, composed **Sonn** 49.8 *love converted from the thing it was / Shall reasons find of settled gravity*; **Ham** IV.vii.79; **MM** III.i.93; **WT** V.iii.72

2 steady, steadfast, staunch **TNK** II.ii.100 [Pirithous to Theseus, of one of Palamon's knights] *a settled valour ... runs through his body*

3 fixed, established **1H6** II.v.106 [Mortimer to Richard] *thy uncle is removing hence, / As princes do their courts when they are cloyed / With long continuance in a settled place*

4 deep-rooted, firmly implanted **1H6** V.v.4 [King to Suffolk, of Margaret] *Her virtues ... / Do breed love's settled passions in my heart*; **R2** I.i.201; **WT** IV.iv.521

5 not flowing, still, congealed **2H4** IV.iii.102 [Falstaff alone, of blood] *which ... cold and settled, left the liver white and pale*; **2H6** III.ii.160; **RJ** IV.v.26

seven-night (*n.*) ☛ sennight (*n.*)

several (*n.*) **1** (plural) details, particulars, individual points **TC** I.iii.180 [Ulysses to all, of Patroclus' imitations] *All our abilities ... / Severals and generals of grace exact*; **H5** I.i.86

2 (plural) individuals, persons **WT** I.ii.226 [Leontes to Camillo, of Hermione persuading Polixenes to stay] *Not noted, is't, / But ... By some severals / Of headpiece extraordinary?*

several (*adj.*) **1** separate, different, distinct **1H6** II.i.30 [Talbot to all] *better far ... / That we do make our entrance several ways* ☛ FEW, p.xxi; STAGE DIRECTIONS, p.417

2 various, sundry, respective, individual **Per** II.iii.109 [Simonides to his servants] *conduct / These knights unto their several lodgings*; **AW** I.i.74; **2H4** IV.ii.61; **LL** V.ii.124; **Tem** III.i.89; **WT** IV.iv.186

3 [of land] private, enclosed, restricted **LL** II.i.209 [Katharine to Boyet] *My lips are no common, though several they be*; **Sonn** 137.9

severally (*adv.*) separately, individually **Tim** II.ii.193 [Timon to Servants] *I will dispatch you severally*; **Cym** V.v.398; **JC** III.ii.10; **TC** IV.v.274; **TNK** I.v.16; **TS** IV.i.165 ☛ STAGE DIRECTIONS, p.417

severed (*adj.*) parted, opened **MV** III.ii.118 [Bassanio to all, of Portia's portrait] *Here are severed lips / Parted with sugar breath*

severity (*n.*) punishment, strictness, sternness **1H6** II.iii.46 [Talbot to Countess] *you have aught but Talbot's shadow / Whereon to practise your severity*

sewer (*n.*) supervisor, chief servant, master of ceremonies **Mac** I.vii.1 [stage direction] *Enter a Sewer and divers Servants*

'sfoot (*int.*) ☛ SWEARING, p.435

shade (*n.*) **1** shadow, unreal image, unsubstantial semblance **Sonn** 53.3 [of shadows] *every one hath, every one, one shade*; **Sonn** 43.8, 11

2 shadow, phantom, spirit **E3** IV.iv.139 [Audley to Prince Edward] *as a shade / Follows the body, so we follow death*; **MW** V.v.38

3 (plural) the underworld, Hades **TNK** III.i.78 [Palamon to Arcite] *brave souls in shades / That have died manly*

4 covered place, sheltered spot **TC** I.iii.51 [Nestor to Agamemnon] *flies flee under shade*; **Cym** III.iv.193

shade (*v.*) hide, conceal, cover up **LL** IV.iii.41 [King to himself, hiding his letter to the Princess] *Sweet leaves, shade folly*

shadow (*n.*) **1** image, likeness, portrait, semblance **TG** IV.ii.122 [Proteus to Silvia, of her picture] *to your shadow will I make true love*; **AW** V.iii.305; **2H4** I.i.193; **1H6** II.iii.35; **MV** II.ix.66; **R3** IV.iv.83

2 reflection, reflected image **Tim** II.ii.55 [Apemantus to Varro's Servant] *Dost dialogue with thy shadow?*; **AC** V.vii.100; **JC** I.ii.58; **KJ** II.i.498; **Sonn** 53.10; **TNK** II.i.157

3 imitation, copy, duplicate **1H4** V.iv.29 [King Henry to Douglas, of himself] *So many of his shadows thou hast met, / And not the very King*

4 illusion, unreal image, delusion **Luc** 460 [of Lucrece's hallucinations] *Such shadows are the weak brain's forgeries*; **Ham** II.ii.259; **RJ** I.iv.11; **Sonn** 43.5, 43.6, 61.4, 67.8; **TG** III.i.177

5 spirit, phantom, spectre, ghost **MND** III.ii.347 [Puck to Oberon] *Believe me, King of shadows, I mistook*; **AC** IV.iv.27; **Cym** V.iv.97; **R3** I.iv.53; **Sonn** 53.2; **Tit** I.i.103

6 shade, seclusion, place of retirement **Venus** 191 [Venus to Adonis] *I'll make a shadow for thee of my hairs*; **Sonn** 43.5

7 shelter, roof **Per** IV.ii.107 [Bawd to Boult, of Veroles] *I know he will come in our shadow* [i.e. come into our house]

8 shade from the sun **Venus** 176 [of Venus and Adonis] *where they lay the shadow had forsook them*

9 fictitious name, invented man **2H4** III.ii.134 [Falstaff to Shallow, of Shadow] *Prick him, for we have a number of shadows fill up the muster-book*

shadow *(v.)* **1** conceal, hide, screen from view **Mac** V.iv.5 [Malcolm to all, of using branches as camouflage] *thereby shall we shadow / The numbers of our host*; **Tit** II.i.130

2 portray, paint, depict **E3** II.i.56 [King Edward alone, of Lodowick] *I will acquaint him with my passion, / Which he shall shadow with a veil of lawn*

3 shelter, give protection to **KJ** II.i.14 [Arthur to Austria, of King Richard's children] *Shadowing their right under your wings of war*

shadowed *(adj.)* shaded, darkened; also [heraldry] faintly drawn **MV** II.i.2 [Morocco to Portia, of his complexion] *The shadowed livery of the burnished sun*

shadowing *(adj.)* foreshadowing, ill-boding, darkening **Oth** IV.i.40 [Othello to Iago] *Nature would not invest herself in such shadowing passion without some instruction*

shadowy *(adj.)* shady, shaded **TG** V.iv.2 [Valentine alone] *This shadowy desert*; **KL** I.i.64

shaft *(n.)* [long and slender] arrow **MV** I.i.140 [Bassanio to Antonio] *when I had lost one shaft, / I shot his fellow of the self-same flight*; **2H4** III.ii.46; **MW** III.iv.24; **RJ** I.iv.19; **TN** I.i.36 ☞ **bolt** *(n.)*

shag *(adj.)* shaggy, with long rough hair **Venus** 295 [of Adonis' horse] *fetlocks shag and long*

shag-eared *(adj.)* ☞ shag-haired *(adj.)*

shag-haired *(adj.)* having shaggy hair, rough-haired **Mac** IV.ii.83 [Macduff's son to Murderer] *thou shag-haired villain!*; **2H6** III.i.367

shake *(n.)* shaking, shock, blow **Per** III.iii.5 [Cleon to Pericles] *Your shakes of fortune ... yet glance / Full wonderingly on us*

shake *(v.)* **1** seize, grasp, move **KL** III.vii.76 [First Servant to Regan] *If you did wear a beard upon your chin / I'd shake it on this quarrel* [i.e. attack you if you were a man]

2 tremble, quake, shiver **Sonn** 73.3 *those boughs which shake against the cold* [i.e. in anticipation of the cold]; **TNK** Prologue.5

3 [unclear meaning] nod, make a sign with [in approval] **2H6** IV.i.55 [Suffolk to the Lieutenant] *Hast thou not ... thought thee happy when I shook my head?*

shake off *(v.)* abandon, cast off, discard **Tim** I.i.104 [Timon to Messenger] *I am not of that feather to shake off / My friend when he must need me*

shake up *(v.)* abuse violently, scold, lambaste **AY** I.i.26 [Orlando to Adam, of Oliver] *thou shalt hear how he will shake me up*

shale *(n.)* shell, husk, outer case **H5** IV.ii.16 [Constable to Dauphin, of the English army] *your fair show shall suck away their souls, / Leaving them but the shales and husks of men*

shallow *(n.)* shallow part **E3** III.iii.2 [King Edward to all] *We found the shallow of this River Somme*

shallow *(adj.)* naive, gullible, lacking in depth of character **Tem** II.ii.141 [Trinculo to Stephano, of Caliban] *this is a very shallow monster*; **AW** I.iii.42; **2H4** II.iv.232; **LL** V.ii.305; **R3** II.ii.18, V.iii.220

shallowly *(adv.)* naively, gullibly; or: rashly **2H4** IV.ii.118 [Prince John to Archbishop, Hastings, and Mowbray] *Most shallowly did you these arms commence*

shalt *(v.)* ☞ **VERB FORMS**, p.481

shambles *(n.)* meat-market, slaughter-house **Oth** IV.ii.65 [Othello to Desdemona, of her honesty] *As summer flies are in the shambles*; **3H6** I.i.71

shame *(n.)* **1** disgrace, dishonour, affront **RJ** IV.i.74 [Friar to Juliet] *thou wilt undertake / A thing like death to chide away this shame*; **KJ** II.i.168; **R2** I.i.175; **TN** V.i.61

2 modesty, decorum, seemliness **Cym** V.iii.22 [Posthumus to Lord, of the youths] *With faces ... fairer / Than those for preservation cased, or shame*

shame *(v.)* be ashamed, be embarrassed **Mac** II.ii.64 [Lady Macbeth to Macbeth] *My hands are of your colour; but I shame / To wear a heart so white*; **AY** IV.iii.136; **Ham** III.ii.154; **3H6** I.i.231; **Luc** 1143; **TNK** I.ii.6

shame-faced, shamefast *(adj.)* modest, retiring, shy **3H6** IV.viii.52 [Edward to the soldiers, of the King] *Seize on the shame-faced Henry*; **R3** I.iv.140

shank *(n.)* **1** leg **Cym** V.v.9 [Posthumus alone] *My conscience, thou art fettered / More than my shanks and wrists*; **AY** II.vii.162; **KL** II.ii.35

2 shin-bone **RJ** IV.i.83 [Juliet to Friar, of being in a charnel-house] *with dead men's rattling bones, / With reeky shanks and yellow chapless skulls*

shape *(n.)* **1** appearance, aspect, visible form **Ham** I.iv.43 [Hamlet to Ghost] *Thou comest in such a questionable shape*; **AW** I.i.60; **LL** V.ii.288; **MA** III.i.55; **TC** I.iii.385; **TG** V.iv.110

2 shaping up, taking shape **1H4** I.i.58 [Westmorland to King Henry, of the two sides] *by discharge of their artillery, / And shape of likelihood, the news was told*

3 figure, posture, attitude **Ham** IV.vii.88 [Claudius to Laertes] *in forgery of shapes and tricks*

4 disguise, appearance, identity **TNK** II.ii.21 [Arcite alone] *I am resolved another shape shall make me* [i.e. bring me success]

5 role, part [to play] **Ham** IV.vii.149 [Claudius to Laertes] *Weigh what convenience ... / May fit us to our shape*; **H8** I.i.196

shape *(v.)* **1** create, fashion, bring about **Oth** III.iii.147 [Iago to Othello] *my jealousy / Shapes faults that are not*; **2H4** IV.iv.58; **JC** IV.iii.275

2 give shape to, make out **Oth** II.i.55 [Cassio to Montano, of a sighted ship] *My hopes do shape him for the Governor*

3 be suitable, fit, accord **Cym** V.v.347 [Belarius to Cymbeline, of the children] *The more of you 'twas felt, the more it shaped / Unto my end of stealing them*

4 confer, provide, create **Tit** IV.iv.57 [Saturninus to all] *Nor age nor honour shall shape privilege*

shapeless *(adj.)* **1** unshapely, ugly, unsightly **LL** V.ii.303 [Rosaline to Princess, of their visitors] *Disguised like Muscovites in shapeless gear*; **CE** IV.ii.20; **Luc** 973

2 aimless, without guidance, desultory **TG** I.i.8 [Valentine to Proteus] *Wear out thy youth with shapeless idleness*

shaping *(adj.)* imaginative, inventive, creative **MND** V.i.5 [Theseus to Hippolyta] *Lovers and madmen have ... / Such shaping fantasies*

shard *(n.)* **1** broken pottery, pot fragments **Ham** V.i.227 [Priest to Laertes, of Ophelia] *Shards, flints, and pebbles should be thrown on her*

2 cow-pat, patch of dung; or: scaly wing [as of a beetle] **AC** III.ii.20 [Enobarbus to Agrippa, of Lepidus' relation to Caesar and Antony] *They are his shards, and he their beetle*

shard-borne *(adj.)* born in dung; or: borne on scaly wings **Mac** III.ii.42 [Macbeth to Lady Macbeth] *The shard-borne beetle, with his drowsy hums*

sharded (*adj.*) living in dung; or: with scales **Cym** III.iii.20 [Belarius to Guiderius and Arviragus] *shall we find / The sharded beetle*

share (*v.*) take, receive, have [as one's share] **R3** V.iii.269 [Richmond to his soldiers] *if I thrive, the gain of my attempt / The least of you shall share his part thereof;* **Sonn** 47.8

share from (*v.*) receive at the expense of **H5** IV.iii.32 [King Henry to all] *I would not lose so great an honour / As one man more methinks would share from me;* **TC** I.iii.367

shark up (*v.*) [like a shark] gather together indiscriminately, collect hastily and uncritically **Ham** I.i.98 [Horatio to Marcellus and Barnardo, of young Fortinbras' actions] *Sharked up a list of lawless resolutes*

sharp (*n.*) high-pitched note, shrill sound **RJ** III.v.28 [Juliet to Romeo] *It is the lark that sings so out of tune, / Straining harsh discords and unpleasing sharps*

sharp (*adj.*) **1** severe, harsh, merciless **TC** V.ix.10 [Agamemnon to all] *our sharp wars are ended;* **Tit** I.i.140
　2 angry, irritable, irascible **CE** IV.iv.48 [Luciana to all, of Antipholus of Ephesus] *how fiery and how sharp he looks!*
　3 high-pitched, shrill, out-of-tune **TG** I.ii.91 [Lucetta to Julia, of the contents of a letter compared to a tune] *it is too sharp*
　4 witty, sharp-witted, discerning **CE** II.i.92 [Adriana to Luciana] *If voluble and sharp discourse be marred*
　5 ardent, keen, fervent **MM** II.iv.161 [Angelo to Isabella] *Fit thy consent to my sharp appetite;* **H8** V.iii.74; **TG** III.ii.67
　6 [falconry] famished, hungry, starving **TS** IV.i.176 [Petruchio alone, of Katherina] *My falcon now is sharp and passing empty;* **Luc** 422; **Venus** 55
　7 subtle, delicate, acute **1H6** II.iv.17 [Warwick to all] *in these nice sharp quillets of the law;* **H8** II.i.14; **LL** V.i.3

sharp-looking (*adj.*) hungry-looking **CE** V.i.241 [Antipholus of Ephesus to Duke, of Pinch] *A needy, hollow-eyed, sharp-looking wretch*

sharp-provided (*adj.*) quick and ready, sharply equipped **R3** III.i.132 [Buckingham aside to Hastings, of York] *With what a sharp-provided wit he reasons!*

she (*n.*) lady, woman, girl **TN** I.v.230 [Viola as Cesario to Olivia] *you are the cruellest she alive;* **AY** III.ii.10; **Cym** I.iv.29; **H5** II.i.76; **Sonn** 130.14; **WT** IV.iv.346

shealed (*adj.*) ☞ shelled (*adj.*)

shearman (*n.*) one who shears excess material from woollen cloth **2H6** IV.ii.125 [Stafford to Cade] *thy father was a plasterer; / And thou thyself a shearman*

sheathing (*n.*) being fitted with a sheath **TS** IV.i.121 [Grumio to Petruchio] *Walter's dagger was not come from sheathing*

sheaved (*adj.*) made of straw; gathered up like a sheaf **Lover** 31 [of the woman's hair] *some untucked descended her sheaved hat*

shed (*v.*) spill, upset **AW** IV.iii.106 [Second Lord to Bertram, of Parolles] *he weeps like a wench that had shed her milk* ☞ sheed (*v.*)

sheed (*v.*) shed **Luc** 1549 [Lucrece to herself, of a painting] *look, how listening Priam wets his eyes, / To see those borrowed tears that Sinon sheeds;* **Sonn** 34.13 [Q]

sheen (*n.*) brightness, shining, radiance **Ham** III.ii.166 [First Player] *thirty dozen moons with borrowed sheen;* **MND** II.i.29

sheep (*n.*) fool, dolt, idiot **Ham** V.i.114 [Hamlet to Horatio] *They are sheep and calves which seek out assurance in that*

sheep-biter (*n.*) thievish fellow, shifty individual **TN** II.v.5 [Sir Toby to Fabian, of Malvolio] *Wouldst thou not be glad to have the niggardly, rascally sheep-biter come by some notable shame?*

sheep-biting (*adj.*) thieving, sneaking, shifty **MM** V.i.351 [Lucio to disguised Duke] *Show your sheep-biting face*

sheepcote (*n.*) building where sheep shelter **AY** IV.iii.78 [Oliver to Celia and Rosalind disguised] *A sheepcote fenced about with olive trees;* **AY** II.iv.81; **KL** II.iii.18; **WT** IV.iv.775

sheep-hook (*n.*) shepherd's crook **WT** IV.iv.417 [Polixenes to Florizel] *Thou a sceptre's heir, / That thus affects a sheep-hook?*

sheepskin (*n.*) [descriptive of a] drum [the skin of a sheep being used for the making of drumheads] **E3** II.ii.48 [King Edward to Lodowick, of the drum] *Poor sheepskin, how it brawls with him that beateth it!* [Q2; Q1 shipskin]

sheer (*adj.*) **1** pure, translucent, unadulterated **R2** V.iii.60 [King Henry to York] *Thou sheer immaculate and silver fountain*
　2 taken alone, unaccompanied by food **TS** Induction.ii.22 [Sly to Lord, of Marian Hacket] *If she say I am not fourteen pence on the score for sheer ale*

sheeted (*adj.*) shrouded, wrapped in a winding-sheet **Ham** I.i.115 [Horatio to Barnardo and Marcellus] *The graves stood tenantless / And the sheeted dead / Did squeak and gibber in the Roman streets*

shelf (*n.*) sandbank, shoal **3H6** V.iv.23 [Queen to all] *[We will] keep our course ... / From shelves and rocks that threaten us with wrack;* **Luc** 335

shelled, shealed (*adj.*) deprived of a shell, without a shell **KL** I.iv.195 [Fool to Gonerill, of Lear] *That's a shelled peascod* [i.e. nothing remaining]

shelly (*adj.*) shell-like, shell-covered **Venus** 1034 [of a snail] *whose tender horns being hit, / Shrinks backward in his shelly cave with pain*

sheltered (*adj.*) concealed, hidden, disguised **R3** III.v.33 [Buckingham to Richard, of Hastings] *he was the covert'st sheltered traitor*

shelving (*adv.*) slopingly, projecting out, with an overhang **TG** III.i.115 [Duke to Valentine, of a chamber] *built so shelving that one cannot climb it*

shelvy (*adj.*) gently shelving, sloping; or: made of sandbanks **MW** III.v.13 [Falstaff alone] *I had been drowned but that the shore was shelvy and shallow*

she-Mercury (*n.*) woman messenger **MW** II.ii.77 [Falstaff to Mistress Quickly] *Be brief, my good she-Mercury*

shend (*v.*) ☞ shent (*v.*)

shent (*v.*) **1** [from obsolete verb 'shend'] blamed, rebuked, reproached **TN** IV.ii.104 [Feste to Malvolio] *I am shent for speaking to you;* **Cor** V.ii.94; **Ham** III.ii.405; **MW** I.iv.36
　2 insult, disgrace, shame **TC** III.iii.78 [Agamemnon to Patroclus, of Achilles] *He shent our messengers* [F sent; Q sate]

sherris-sack, sherris (*n.*) white wine from Xeres (Spain), sherry-wine **2H4** IV.iii.95 [Falstaff alone] *A good sherris-sack hath a twofold operation in it*

shew (*v.*) eschew, avoid, shirk **Per** I.i.137 [Pericles alone] *those men / Blush not in actions blacker than the night / Will shew no course to keep them from the light* [Q]

shield (*v.*) forbid [as exclamation] **RJ** IV.i.41 [Paris to Friar] *God shield I should disturb devotion!;* **AW** I.iii.163; **MM** III.i.144

shift (*n.*) **1** expedient, measure, arrangement [especially as 'make shift' = contrive] **AW** IV.iii.36 [Lafew to Parolles, of Lafew's displeasure] *You have made shift to run into't;* **Tit** IV.i.71 [Marcus to all, of writing without hands] *Cursed be that heart that forced us to this shift;* **2H4** II.i.155, II.ii.21; **2H6** IV.viii.30; **MV** I.ii.85
　2 evasion, subterfuge, device **AC** III.xi.63 [Antony to Cleopatra] *I must ... dodge / And palter in the shifts of lowness* [i.e. appropriate to someone who has a low position]
　3 stratagem, contriving, trick **E3** I.i.76 [King Edward to Lorraine, of the King of France] *His lame unpolished shifts are come to light;* **CE** III.ii.190; **Luc** 920; **Mac** II.iii.38; **Tit** IV.ii.175; **TS** Induction.i.124
　4 stratagem, tactic, way **KJ** IV.iii.7 [Arthur alone] *I'll find a thousand shifts to get away;* **E3** III.i.172; **1H6** I.ii.75; **3H6** III.ii.108; **Venus** 690

shift, for a as a makeshift, for lack of a better alternative **MA** II.iii.79 [Don Pedro to Balthasar] *thou singest well enough for a shift* [i.e. for the lack of a better alternative]

shift (*v.*) **1** provide, look out, take care **Tem** V.i.256 [Stephano to Trinculo and Caliban] *Every man shift for all the rest;* **MW** I.iii.31

2 escape, flee, slip [away] CE V.i.168 [Messenger to Adriana] *shift and save yourself;* Mac II.iii.142

3 change, exchange, swap AC V.ii.152 [Cleopatra to Caesar] *should we shift estates, yours would be mine;* 2H6 II.iv.107

4 change [clothes] KL V.iii.184 [Edgar to Albany] *to shift / Into a madman's rags;* Cym I.iii.1; 2H4 V.v.22

shifting (*adj.*) cheating, deceitful, evasive Luc 930 [Lucrece as if to time] *injurious shifting Time* [also: moving]

shine (*n.*) shining quality, radiance Per I.ii.124 [Pericles to Helicanus] *Thou showedst a subject's shine*

shining (*adj.*) brightly lit, illuminated LL I.i.90 [Berowne to King, of namers of the stars] *Have no more profit of their shining nights / Than those that walk and wot not what they are* [i.e. nights lit up by the stars]

shiny (*adj.*) moonlit, bright AC IV.ix.3 [Sentry to the watch] *The night / Is shiny*

ship (*v.*) dispatch, send, consign Ham V.i.73 [First Clown, singing] *age … hath shipped me into the land*

shipboard, to on board ship WT IV.iv.650 [Camillo to Perdita] *you may … to shipboard / Get undescried*

shipping (*n.*) voyage, sailing, passage 1H6 V.v.87 [King to Suffolk] *Take therefore shipping;* TS V.i.37

ship-tire (*n.*) fashionable head-dress shaped like a ship MW III.iii.53 [Falstaff to Mistress Ford] *Thou hast the right arched beauty of the brow that becomes the ship-tire*

ship-wracked, -wrackt (*adj.*) ship-wrecked CE I.i.115 [Egeon to Duke, of the ship] *Gave healthful welcome to their ship-wrack'd guests* ☛ wrack (*v.*) 1

shipwracking (*adj.*) causing shipwreck Mac I.ii.26 [Captain to King] *the sun 'gins his reflection, / Shipwracking storms and direful thunders* ☛ wrack (*n.*) 2

shive (*n.*) slice Tit II.i.87 [Demetrius to Aaron] *easy it is / Of a cut loaf to steal a shive*

shiver (*n.*) fragment, splinter, piece R2 IV.i.288 [Richard, as to the mirror] *cracked in an hundred shivers;* TC II.i.37

shiver (*v.*) smash to pieces, fragment KL IV.vi.51 [Edgar to Gloucester] *Thou'dst shivered like an egg;* Luc 1763

shivered (*adj.*) shattered, broken, splintered E3 III.iv.74 [stage direction] *Edward in triumph, bearing in his hand his shivered lance*

shivering (*adj.*) shattering, splintering MND I.ii.28 [Bottom, declaiming] *The raging rocks / And shivering shocks*

shock (*v.*) repel with force, throw into confusion KJ V.vii.117 [Bastard to all, of future invaders] *Come the three corners of the world in arms / And we shall shock them!*

shoeing-horn (*n.*) shoe-horn; person used as a tool, hanger-on TC V.i.52 [Thersites alone, of Menelaus] *a thrifty shoeing-horn in a chain*

shog, shog off (*v.*) go away, be gone, get along H5 II.i.42 [Nym to Pistol] *Will you shog off?;* H5 II.iii.42 [Nym to Bardolph] *Shall we shog?;*

shoon (*n.*) [archaism] shoes Ham IV.v.26 [Ophelia singing] *And his sandal shoon;* 2H6 IV.ii.175 ☛ ARCHAISMS, p.22

shoot (*n.*) **1** shot, act of shooting 3H6 III.i.7 [First Keeper to Second Keeper] *my shoot is lost;* LL IV.i.10; Luc 579

2 outgrowth, offshoot, sprouting WT I.ii.128 [Leontes to Mamillius] *Thou want'st a rough pash and the shoots that I have / To be full like me*

shoot (*v.*) send forth, throw, let fly KL II.iv.222 [Lear to Gonerill] *I do not bid the thunder-bearer shoot* [i.e. Jove]; AW V.iii.11

shoot out (*v.*) appear suddenly, come up, emerge AW II.iii.8 [Parolles to Bertram and Lafew, of the King's cure] *'tis the rarest argument of wonder that hath shot out in our latter times*

SHIPS

Terms for the masts, sails, rigging and other parts of a sailing ship are common in Shakespearian English, and several continue to be used in modern sailing. A number have a figurative as well as a literal use, as when Romeo enthuses about his rope-ladder to Nurse: 'Which to the high topgallant of my joy / Must be my convoy in the secret night' (RJ II.iv.186). The first two scenes of *The Tempest* are an important location for nautical terminology.

Term	Example	Gloss
beak	Tem I.ii.196	prow
boresprit, bowsprit	Tem I.ii.200	pole extending from the bow which holds the lower edge of a sail
bowling, bowline	TNK IV.i.147	rope attached to the edge of a sail, to keep it steady
cabin	Tem I.ii.197	[as in modern English]
course	TNK III.iv.10	sail attached to the lower yards of a ship
gallant	E3 III.i.73	flag flown on the rear mast
main-course	Tem I.i.35	main sail
mainmast	WT III.iii.90	principal mast in a multi-masted ship
mainsail	TNK IV.i.148	principal sail of a ship
maintop	Cym IV.ii.320	top of the mainmast; or: platform near the top of the mainmast
poop	AC II.ii.197	highest deck at the stern of a ship
sail	Tem I.ii.147	[as in modern English]
tackling	TNK IV.i.144	rigging
top	TNK IV.i.149	platform at the top of a mast
topgallant	RJ II.iv.186	platform at the head of a topmast
topmast	Tem I.i.34	section of mast fitted to the top of the lower mast
topsail	Tem I.i.5	sail set above the lower course of sails
waist	Tem I.ii.197	middle of a ship; or: middle of the upper deck
yard	Tem I.ii.200	crossbar on a mast which supports a sail

shop (*n.*) workshop, workroom **Cor** I.i.131 [Menenius to Citizens, as the belly addressing the other body parts] *I am the storehouse and the shop / Of the whole body;* **JC** I.i.27; **LL** IV.iii.57

shore (*n.*) **1** limit, border, bound **MM** III.ii.240 [Escalus to disguised Duke, of Claudio] *I have laboured for the poor gentleman to the extremest shore of my modesty*
2 bank, edge **JC** I.i.101 [Cassius to Brutus] *The troubled Tiber chafing with her shores;* **JC** I.i.47, 60; **MW** III.v.13
3 waterside dump, sewage channel **Per** IV.vi.174 [Marina to Boult] *Empty ... common shores of filth*

shore (*v.*) **1** put ashore, return to the land **WT** IV.iv.831 [Autolycus alone, of Polixenes' treatment of the Clown and Shepherd on his ship] *If he think it fit to shore them again*
2 ☞ **shear** (*v.*)

short (*adj.*) **1** wanting, insufficient, inadequate **AW** V.iii.176 [Lafew to Bertram] *Your reputation comes too short for my daughter;* **LL** IV.iii.239; **Per** I.i.8; **Tim** I.i.100
2 controlled, confined, restrained **Ham** IV.i.18 [Claudius to Gertrude, of Hamlet] *us, whose providence / Should have kept short ... / This mad young man*
3 curt, brief, terse **AY** III.v.138 [Phebe to Silvius, of her letter to Rosalind as Ganymede] *I will be bitter with him and passing short*

short (*v.*) **1** break, fail to keep, fall short of **Cym** I.vii.200 [Iachimo to Innogen, of his treasures] *I shall short my word / By length'ning my return*
2 shorten **PassP** XIV.30 *good day, of night now borrow; / Short night, to-night, and length thyself to-morrow*

shorten (*v.*) **1** reduce, diminish, cut back **Cor** I.ii.23 [Aufidius to all, of their plans] *By the discovery / We shall be shortened in our aim* [i.e. we must lower our sights]
2 make ineffective, undermine, subvert **KL** IV.vii.9 [Kent to Cordelia] *Yet to be known shortens my made intent*
3 omit, ignore, leave out **MA** III.ii.92 [Don John to Don Pedro, of Hero] *circumstances shortened, ... the lady is disloyal*

shortness (*n.*) directness, straightforwardness, brevity **TS** IV.iv.39 [Baptista to Pedant as Vincentio] *Your plainness and your shortness please me well*

shot (*n.*) **1** cannonfire, firing, salvoes **E3** III.i.149 [Mariner to King John, of the navies] *by their admiral / Our admiral encountered many shot;* **1H6** I.iv.13; **KJ** V.v.5
2 armed soldier, gunner, marksman **1H6** I.iv.53 [Talbot to all, of the French] *a guard of chosen shot I had;* **2H4** III.ii.267; **R3** IV.iv.89
3 darting, shooting; or: wound, pain **Cym** I.ii.20 [Innogen to Posthumus] *I shall here abide the hourly shot / Of angry eyes*
4 tavern bill, reckoning **TG** II.v.5 [Launce to Speed] *a man is ... never welcome to a place till some certain shot be paid;* **Cym** V.iv.157
5 ☞ **loose shot**

shot-free (*adj.*) scot-free, without paying the bill; also: unwounded, unpunished **1H4** V.iii.30 [Falstaff alone] *Though I could scape shot-free at London, I fear the shot here*

shotten (*adj.*) spawned, that has shot its roe **1H4** II.iv.125 [Falstaff to all] *If manhood ... be not forgot upon the face of the earth, then am I a shotten herring* [i.e. a thin, emaciated herring]

shough (*n.*) [pron: shok] shaggy-haired Icelandic dog **Mac** III.i.93 [Macbeth to Murderers] *Shoughs, water-rugs, and demi-wolves are clept / All by the name of dogs*

shoulder (*v.*) thrust unceremoniously aside, push roughly **R3** III.vii.127 [Buckingham to Richard, of England] *Her royal stock ... almost shouldered in the swallowing gulf / Of dark forgetfulness*

shoulder-clapper (*n.*) someone who claps you on the shoulder, arresting officer **CE** IV.ii.37 [Dromio of Syracuse to Adriana, of the officer] *A backfriend, a shoulder-clapper*

shouldering (*n.*) pushing with the shoulder, jostling **1H6** IV.i.189 [Exeter alone] *no simple man that sees ... / This shouldering of each other in the court*

shoulder-piece (*n.*) armour covering the shoulder **TNK** IV.ii.127 [Messenger to Theseus, of a knight's arms] *to the shoulder-piece / Gently they swell* ☞ **BODY-ARMOUR**, p.48

shoulder-shotten (*adj.*) with a dislocated shoulder **TS** III.ii.54 [Biondello to Tranio as Lucentio, of Petruchio's horse] *swayed in the back and shoulder-shotten*

shout forth (*v.*) acclaim, hail, welcome with shouts **Cor** I.ix.49 [Martius to all] *you shout me forth / In acclamations hyperbolical*

shove by (*v.*) thrust aside, push aside **Ham** III.iii.58 [Claudius alone] *Offence's gilded hand may shove by justice* [F; Q2 *showe*]

shove-groat (*adj.*) shove-halfpenny, shovel-board **2H4** II.iv.187 [Falstaff to Bardolph, of Pistol] *Quoit him down, Bardolph, like a shove-groat shilling* [i.e. the type of coin pushed in a game]

shovel-board (*n.*) wide coin used as a counter in the game of shovel-board **MW** I.i.145 [Slender to all] *two Edward shovel-boards* [i.e. from the reign of Edward VI]

show (*n.*) **1** appearance, exhibition, display **MV** II.vii.20 [Morocco to himself] *A golden mind stoops not to shows of dross;* **1H4** V.iv.94; **2H6** I.i.239; **JC** I.i.34; **Oth** I.i.52; **RJ** V.i.48
2 spectacle, display, ceremony **Cor** III.iii.36 [Coriolanus to all] *Throng our large temples with the shows of peace;* **AC** V.ii.362; **H3** IV.i.10; **LL** V.ii.305; **Per** II.iii.56; **TS** I.i.47
3 pretence, fabrication, deception **Mac** I.vii.81 [Macbeth to Lady Macbeth] *Away, and mock the time with fairest show;* **Cym** V.v.54; **Per** IV.iv.23
4 vision, apparition, manifestation **Cym** V.v.429 [Posthumus to Lucius] *methought / Great Jupiter ... / Appeared to me, with other spritely shows*
5 view, sight **Tem** V.i.63 [Prospero to charmed Gonzalo] *Mine eyes, ev'n sociable to the show of thine* [i.e. responsive to the sight of your eyes]; **R2** III.iii.71
6 dumb-show, miming **Ham** III.ii.148, 152 [also in stage direction at 145] [Ophelia to Hamlet] *Belike this show imports the argument of the play ... Will 'a tell us what this show meant?*

show (*v.*) appear, look [like], present [as] **KL** IV.vi.14 [Edgar to Gloucester] *The crows and choughs ... / Show scarce so gross as beetles;* **AC** III.iii.20; **2H4** II.ii.6; **RJ** I.v.48; **Tim** I.ii.132; **TNK** III.v.25

showing (*n.*) **1** appearance, bearing **Ham** V.ii.108 [Osrick to Hamlet, of Laertes] *of very soft society and great showing*
2 visible form, printed form, visual representation **AW** II.iii.21 [Parolles to Lafew] *If you will have it in showing* [i.e. before your eyes]

showplace (*n.*) place for public spectacles, theatrical arena **AC** III.vi.12 [Caesar to Agrippa and Maecenas, of Antony and Cleopatra's ceremony] *I'th' common showplace*

shrew (*n.*) vexatious person, troublesome individual [of either sex] **TN** I.iii.44 [Sir Andrew to Maria] *Bless you, fair shrew;* **CE** IV.i.51; **LL** V.ii.46; **TS** [title]

shrew (*v.*) ☞ **beshrew** (*v.*)

shrewd (*adj.*) **1** harsh, hard, severe **KJ** V.v.14 [Lewis the Dauphin to Messenger] *Ah, foul, shrewd news!;* **AC** IV.ix.5; **AY** V.iv.170; **2H6** II.iii.41; **MA** II.i.17; **TNK** IV.iii.33
2 harmful, dangerous, injurious **R2** III.ii.59 [King Richard to Aumerle] *For every man that Bolingbroke hath pressed / To lift shrewd steel against our golden crown*
3 malicious, nasty, vicious **AW** III.v.67 [Widow to Helena, of Diana] *This young maid might do her / A shrewd turn;* **2H4** II.iv.206; **MW** II.ii.216
4 shrewish, bad-tempered, difficult **TS** I.i.177 [Tranio to Lucentio, of Bianca] *Her elder sister is so curst and shrewd;* **MND** III.ii.323; **TS** I.ii.59, 69, 89
5 wily, cunning, mischievous **MND** II.i.33 [Fairy to Puck] *you are that shrewd and knavish sprite / Called Robin Goodfellow;* **AW** IV.v.61; **1H6** I.ii.123; **JC** II.i.158; **LL** V.ii.12
6 knowing, artful, smart **R3** II.iv.35 [Queen Elizabeth to York] *Go to, you are too shrewd;* **H8** I.iii.7

7 ominous, telling; or: bitter, vexatious **MV** III.ii.243 [Portia to herself] *There are some shrewd contents in yond same paper;* **Oth** III.iii.426

shrewdly *(adv.)* **1** seriously, mightily, very much **AW** III.v.88 [Mariana to Helena, of Parolles] *He's shrewdly vexed at something;* **AW** V.iii.232; **H5** III.vii.148; **JC** III.i.146; **TC** III.iii.228; **WT** V.i.102

2 sharply, severely **Ham** I.iv.1 [Hamlet to Horatio and Marcellus] *The air bites shrewdly* [F; Q2 *shroudly*, Q1 *shrewd*]; **H5** III.vii.47

3 maliciously, wickedly, mischievously **TN** V.i.350 [Olivia to Malvolio] *This practice hath most shrewdly passed upon thee* [or: cunningly]

shrewishly *(adv.)* like a woman, shrilly, sharply **TN** I.v.155 [Malvolio to Olivia, of Viola as Cesario] *he speaks very shrewishly*

shrieve *(n.)* sheriff **AW** IV.iii.184 [Parolles to First Soldier, of Dumaine] *he was whipped for getting the shrieve's fool with child;* **2H4** IV.iv.99

shrift *(n.)* **1** confession **RJ** IV.ii.15 [Nurse to Capulet, of Juliet] *See where she comes from shrift with merry look;* **MM** IV.ii.201; **RJ** I.i.159, II.iv.177, v.66

2 absolution **RJ** II.iii.52 [Friar to Romeo] *Riddling confession finds but riddling shrift;* **3H6** III.ii.107

3 confessional, place for hearing confession **Oth** III.iii.24 [Desdemona to Cassio, of Othello] *His bed shall seem a school, his board a shrift*

shrike *(n./v.)* variant spelling of 'shriek' **TC** II.ii.98 [Priam to all] *What shrike is this?* [Q]

shrill-gorged *(adj.)* shrill-sounding, with high-pitched voice **KL** IV.vi.58 [Edgar to Gloucester] *The shrill-gorged lark so far / Cannot be seen or heard*

shrink *(v.)* **1** shiver, recoil, draw back **TC** III.iii.141 [Ulysses to Achilles, of Ajax] *As if his foot were on brave Hector's breast, / And great Troy shrinking* [F; Q *shriking*]; **AY** II.i.9; **1H6** IV.i.37; **R2** II.ii.32

2 shrivel up, wither away **Tit** III.i.246 [Lucius to all, of Martius' and Quintus' heads] *that this sight should make so deep a wound / And yet detested life not shrink thereat!;* **Tim** III.ii.7

3 bring low, diminish, curtail **Tim** III.ii.62 [Lucius to Strangers] *Timon is shrunk indeed*

4 yield, withdraw, give way **1H6** IV.vii.5 [Talbot to Servant, of John Talbot] *he perceived me shrink and on my knee;* **1H6** IV.v.31

5 draw back, pull in **E3** I.i.138 [King Edward as if to King David] *I will make you shrink your snaily horns*

shrinking *(adj.)* shivering, shuddering, wincing with cold **Cym** IV.iv.30 [Belarius to Arviragus and Guiderius] *to be ... / The shrinking slaves of Winter*

shrive *(v.)* hear confession, grant absolution, forgive **RJ** II.iv.179 [Romeo to Nurse, of Juliet] *she shall at Friar Laurence' cell / Be shrived and married;* **CE** II.ii.218; **1H6** I.ii.119; **MV** I.i.125

shriver *(n.)* father confessor **3H6** III.ii.108 [George aside to Richard, of Edward] *When he was made a shriver, 'twas for shift* [pun: seducer]

shriving *(adj.)* for confession and absolution **Ham** V.ii.47 [Hamlet to Horatio] *Not shriving time allowed;* **R3** III.ii.114

shroud *(n.)* **1** protection, shelter **AC** III.xiii.71 [Thidias to Cleopatra, of Caesar] *put yourself under his shroud*

2 sail-rope **3H6** V.iv.18 [Queen to all] *[is not] The friends of France our shrouds and tacklings?;* **H8** IV.i.72; **KJ** V.vii.53

shroud *(v.)* hide, conceal, shelter **LL** IV.iii.135 [King to Longaville and Dumaine] *I have been closely shrouded in this bush;* **3H6** III.i.1, IV.iii.41; **R3** I.i.2; **Tem** II.ii.40

shrow *(n.)*, **shrowd** *(adj.)*, **shrowdly** *(adv.)* variant spellings of 'shrew' *(n.)*, 'shrewd' *(adj.)*, 'shrewdly' *(adv.)*

shrug *(v.)* [shrug shoulders to] express disbelief **Cor** I.ix.4 [Cominius to Martius] *Where great patricians shall attend and shrug*

shuffle *(v.)* **1** spirit, smuggle, remove secretly **MW** IV.vi.29 [Fenton to Host, of Caius and Anne] *he shall ... shuffle her away*

2 shift, shamble along **Cym** V.v.105 [disguised Innogen to Lucius] *your life ... / Must shuffle for itself*

3 behave evasively, act shiftily **MW** II.ii.24 [Falstaff to Pistol] *I myself sometimes ... am fain to shuffle, to hedge, and to lurch*

shuffling *(n.)* trickery, deceit, evasiveness **Ham** III.iii.61 [Claudius alone, of heaven] *There is no shuffling;* **Ham** IV.vii.136

shun *(v.)* **1** refuse, avoid, refrain from **Cym** I.v.42 [Posthumus to Frenchman, of himself] *rather shunned to go even with what I heard*

2 look to escape, seek safety in flight **Cor** I.iii.32 [Volumnia to Virgilia, of Martius] *the Volsces shunning him*

shunless *(adj.)* unavoidable, inescapable, certain **Cor** II.ii.110 [Cominius to all, of Coriolanus' entry into the city] *which he painted / With shunless destiny* [i.e. with the blood that was unavoidably destined to flow]

shut up *(v.)* **1** prevent, bar, close off **3H6** IV.iii.20 [First Watchman to all, of Warwick reaching Edward] *Unless our halberds did shut up his passage*

2 conclude [a speech], wind up **Mac** II.i.16 [Banquo to Macbeth, of the King] *he ... shut up / In measureless content*

3 enclose, store up, put away **Tim** IV.iii.281 [Timon to Apemantus] *Were all the wealth I have shut up in thee, / I'd give thee leave to hang it*

4 embody, sum up, include **TC** I.iii.58 [Ulysses to and of Agamemnon] *In whom ... the minds of all / Should be shut up*

shy *(adj.)* wary, cautious, reserved **MM** III.ii.124 [Lucio to disguised Duke] *A shy fellow was the Duke;* **MM** V.i.54

sib *(adj.)* kin, related **TNK** I.ii.72 [Palamon to Arcite, of Creon] *The blood of mine that's sib to him*

sibyl *(n.)* prophetess, fortune-teller, wise woman **Oth** III.iv.70 [Othello to Desdemona, of her handkerchief] *A sibyl ... / In her prophetic fury sewed the work* ☛ **ROMAN HISTORY**, p.377

sick *(adj.)* **1** longing, pining, avid **2H4** V.vi.133 [Falstaff to Shallow] *I know the young King is sick for me;* **AW** I.i.16; **H8** II.ii.81; **MM** II.iv.103; **MW** III.ii.26; **TN** III.i.45 ☛ **fancy-sick** *(adj.)*

2 ailing, needing cure **JC** II.i.268 [Portia to Brutus] *You have some sick offence within your mind;* **AW** IV.ii.35

3 ill through excess, surfeited **Tim** IV.iii.177 [Timon alone] *That nature, being sick of man's unkindness, / Should yet be hungry!* **R2** II.ii.84

4 infected, contaminated **Tim** IV.iii.111 [Timon to Alcibiades, of Jove] *Will o'er some high-viced city hang his poison / In the sick air* [or: ailing]

5 full of loathing, full of repugnance **MND** II.i.212 [Demetrius to Helena] *I am sick when I do look on thee;* **MA** II.i.5

6 envious, resentful, malicious **TC** I.iii.132 [Ulysses to all] *every step, / Exampled by the first pace that is sick / Of his superior, grows to an envious fever;* **H8** I.ii.82

7 pale, wan, of a sickly hue **RJ** II.ii.8 [Romeo to himself, of the moon] *Her vestal livery is but sick and green*

8 unhappy, hurt, downcast **H8** V.v.74 [King Henry to all, of being thanked by Queen Anne] *She will be sick else*

sick *(v.)* sicken, fall ill **2H4** IV.iv.128 [Clarence to all] *a little time before / That our great-grandsire, Edward, sicked and died*

sickleman *(n.)* harvester using a sickle **Tem** IV.i.134 [Iris to the reapers] *You sunburned sicklemen*

sickly *(adj.)* **1** weak, feeble, dying **JC** V.i.86 [Cassius to Messala, of birds of prey] *do ... downward look on us, / As we were sickly prey*

2 of sickness, invalid **AW** II.iii.110 [King to Bertram, of Helena] *Thou knowest she has raised me from my sickly bed;* **Ham** III.iii.96; **2H4** I.i.147

sickly over *(v.)* cover with a sickly hue, make pallid **Ham** III.i.85 [Hamlet alone] *the native hue of resolution / Is sicklied o'er with the pale cast of thought* [F; Q2 *sickled*]

sick-thoughted *(adj.)* love-sick, infatuated **Venus** 5 [of Adonis] *Sick-thoughted Venus makes amain unto him*

sicle, sickle *(n.)* shekel **MM** II.ii.149 [Isabella to Angelo, of how to bribe him] *Not with fond sicles of the tested gold* [F *sickles*]

side (*n.*) frame, compass, limit **Cym** III.i.51 [Cymbeline to Cloten, of Caesar's ambition] *it did almost stretch / The sides o'th' world;* **AC** I.ii.193, iii.16; **WT** IV.iv.475

side (*v.*) take sides with, join **Cor** IV.ii.2 [Sicinius to Brutus, of Coriolanus] *The nobility … have sided / In his behalf;* **Cor** I.i.191

side-piercing (*adj.*) heart-rending, heart-breaking, harrowing **KL** IV.vi.85 [Edgar to himself, of Lear] *O thou side-piercing sight*

side-sleeve (*n.*) ➤ **CLOTHING**, p.79

siege (*n.*) **1** onslaught, storm, assail **RJ** V.iii.237 [Friar to Capulet, of his action towards Juliet] *to remove that siege of grief from her;* **Sonn** 65.6

2 rank, status, standing **Oth** I.ii.22 [Othello to Iago] *I fetch my life and being / From men of royal siege;* **Ham** IV.vii.75

3 seat, chair, place **MM** IV.ii.95 [Provost to disguised Duke] *upon the very siege of justice*

4 excrement, ordure, dung **Tem** II.ii.104 [Stephano to Trinculo] *How cam'st thou to be the siege of this mooncalf?*

sien (*n.*) ➤ **scion** (*n.*)

sieve (*n.*) basket, hold-all, container [especially for market produce] **TC** II.ii.72 [Troilus to Hector] *the remainder viands / We do not throw in unrespective sieve / Because we now are full*

sift (*v.*) **1** question carefully, examine closely **1H6** III.i.24 [Gloucester to Winchester] *if thy thoughts were sifted;* **Ham** II.ii.58

2 discover by examining, find out by questioning **R2** I.i.12 [John of Gaunt to King Richard, of Bolingbroke's accusation] *As near as I could sift him on that argument*

sight (*n.*) **1** eye **Venus** 183 [of Adonis] *His louring brows o'erwhelming his fair sight;* **Cor** II.i.197; **Luc** 104; **MND** II.i.183; **Per** I.i.75; **Phoen** 35

2 outward appearance, external show **Per** I.i.124 [Pericles alone, of a hypocrite] *The which is good in nothing but in sight*

3 sighting, presence in one's sight **Tim** I.i.250 [Timon to his visitors] *I am joyful of your sights*

4 visor **2H4** IV.i.119 [Mowbray to Westmorland, of Mowbray's father and Bolingbroke] *Their eyes of fire sparkling through sights of steel*

sight, in visibly, conspicuously **LL** V.ii.136 [Rosaline to Katharine and Maria] *wear the favours most in sight* [i.e. conspicuously]

sight-hole (*n.*) hole to see through **1H4** IV.i.71 [Worcester to Hotspur] *[we] / Must … stop all sight-holes*

sightless (*adj.*) **1** invisible, unseen, hidden **Mac** I.vii.23 [Macbeth alone] *heaven's cherubin, horsed / Upon the sightless curriers of the air, / Shall blow the horrid deed in every eye;* **Mac** I.v.47

2 unsightly, ugly, offensive **KJ** III.i.45 [Constance to Arthur] *If thou [wert] … / Full of unpleasing blots and sightless stains*

3 dark, black, impenetrable **Luc** 1013 [Lucrece to herself] *Poor grooms are sightless night, kings glorious day*

sightly (*adv.*) appropriately, handsomely, pleasingly **KJ** II.i.143 [Bastard to Blanche, of King Richard's lion-skin cloak, worn by Austria] *It lies as sightly on the back of him / As great Alcides' shows upon an ass*

sign (*n.*) **1** outward appearance, external demeanour **Cym** I.vi.28 [First Lord to Cloten, of Innogen] *She's a good sign, but I have seen small reflection of her wit;* **LL** V.ii.469

2 token, witness, attestation **E3** IV.i.7 [Mountford to Salisbury, of his swearing allegiance to King Edward] *In sign whereof receive this coronet;* **Cor** I.ix.26; **R3** I.iii.280

3 mere semblance, token symbol, show **R3** IV.iv.90 [Queen Margaret to Queen Elizabeth] *I called thee … / A sign of dignity;* **MA** IV.i.31; **Oth** I.i.158

4 banner, standard, ensign **H5** II.ii.192 [King Henry to all] *The signs of war advance!;* **JC** V.i.14

5 publicity sign, advertisement **2H4** II.iv.244 [Falstaff to Doll, of why Prince Harry loves Poins] *'a … wears his boots very smooth like unto the sign of the leg* [i.e. like one showing outside a boot-maker's shop]

sign (*v.*) **1** mark distinctively, bear a signature **KJ** IV.ii.222 [King John to and of Hubert] *A fellow by the hand of nature marked, / Quoted, and signed to do a deed of shame;* **JC** III.i.206

2 display, signify, advertise **H8** II.iv.108 [Queen Katherine to Wolsey] *You sign your place and calling, in full seeming, / With meekness and humility*

3 augur, bode, signify **AC** IV.iii.15 [Fourth Soldier to all, of the music] *It signs well, does it not?*

signal (*n.*) sign, indication, token **1H6** II.iv.121 [Warwick to Richard] *in signal of my love to thee;* **H5** V.Chorus.21; **2H6** III.iii.28

signet (*n.*) seal [of authority], signet ring **Ham** V.ii.49 [Hamlet to Horatio] *I had my father's signet in my purse;* **1H6** II.ii.206

significant (*n.*) sign, signal, indication **1H6** II.iv.26 [Richard to all] *In dumb significants proclaim your thoughts;* **LL** III.i.128

signify (*v.*) report, make known, declare **Ham** III.ii.314 [Hamlet to Guildenstern] *signify this to the doctor;* **2H6** III.i.283; **LL** II.i.33; **MV** V.i.51; **TC** IV.v.155; **Tim** III.iv.39

signor, signior (*n.*) ➤ **ADDRESS FORMS**, p.8

signory (*n.*) **1** estate, domain, territory **R2** III.i.22 [Bolingbroke to Bushy and Green] *you have fed upon my signories;* **2H4** IV.i.109; **R2** IV.i.89

2 [Italian] state, province, territory **Oth** I.ii.18 [Othello to Iago] *My services, which I have done the signory;* **Tem** I.ii.71

silence (*v.*) force to remain in silence, keep under restraint **2H4** V.ii.97 [Lord Chief Justice to King Henry V] *imagine me taking your part, / And in your power soft silencing your son;* **H8** I.i.97

silent (*n.*) time of silence **2H6** I.iv.15 [Bolingbroke to Duchess] *the silent of the night … / That time best fits the work we have in hand*

silly (*adj.*) **1** helpless, defenceless, vulnerable **3H6** II.v.43 [King alone] *shepherds looking on their silly sheep;* **E3** II.i.18; **2H6** I.i.223; **3H6** I.i.243; **TG** IV.i.72; **Venus** 1098

2 feeble, frail, weak **1H6** II.iii.21 [Countess to and of Talbot] *this is a child, a silly dwarf!*

3 foolish, stupid, ludicrous **E3** IV.v.55 [King John to Philip, of the French] *at once dispatch / This little business of a silly fraud;* **LL** III.i.73; **PassP** IX.5

4 simple, lowly, humble **TN** II.iv.46 [Orsino to Viola as Cesario, of a song] *It is silly sooth;* **Cym** V.iii.86; **Luc** 1345; **WT** IV.iii.27

5 trifling, trivial, scanty **3H6** III.iii.93 [Warwick to Oxford, of the succession] *threescore and two years - a silly time / To make prescription for a kingdom's worth*

silly-ducking (*adj.*) foolishly bowing, ridiculously obsequious **KL** II.ii.101 [Cornwall to all] *twenty silly-ducking observants*

silver (*adj.*) white-haired **2H6** V.ii.47 [Young Clifford to himself, as if to Clifford] *Wast thou ordained … to achieve / The silver livery of advised age*

silverly (*adv.*) with a silvery appearance **KJ** V.ii.46 [Lewis the Dauphin to Salisbury, of his tears] *Let me wipe off this honourable dew / That silverly doth progress on thy cheeks*

simile (*n.*) comparison, observation, saying **AW** V.ii.24 [Clown to Lafew, of Parolles] *I do pity his distress in my similes of comfort* [F *smiles*]

simony (*n.*) trading in ecclesiastical appointments **H8** IV.ii.36 [Katherine to Griffith, of Wolsey] *Simony was fair play*

simple (*n.*) **1** ingredient, element, constituent **AY** IV.i.16 [Jaques to Rosalind as Ganymede] *a melancholy of mine own, compounded of many simples;* **Luc** 530; **RJ** V.i.40

2 medicinal herb, medicine **Ham** IV.vii.143 [Laertes to Claudius] *all simples that have virtue;* **KL** IV.iv.14; **MW** I.iv.61

simple (*adj.*) **1** common, ordinary, average, humble **AC** V.ii.337 [First Guard to Dolabella] *A simple countryman;* **1H6** IV.i.187; **2H6** I.iii.72; **KL** IV.vi.153; **MV** II.ii.149; **WT** IV.iv.740

2 foolish, silly, stupid **RJ** II.v.38 [Nurse to Juliet, of Romeo] *you have made a simple choice;* **CE** III.ii.16; **3H6** I.ii.59, III.i.82; **Oth** IV.iv.19; **TS** V.ii.160

3 uninformed, ignorant, unintelligent **Ham** I.ii.97 [Claudius to Hamlet] *An understanding simple and unschooled*

4 unmixed, without addition, plain **MW** III.v.28 [Falstaff to Bardolph, of whether his sack should contain eggs] *Simple of itself;* **Phoen** 44; **Sonn** 125.7

5 sincere, honest, open, innocent **Oth** I.i.108 [Roderigo to Brabantio] *In simple and pure soul I come to you;* **2H6** III.i.54; **Venus** 795

6 basic, minimal, small **3H6** IV.ii.16 [Warwick to George, of Edward] *but attended by a simple guard;* **AW** II.i.75; **MV** III.ii.81

simple though I stand here as sure as I stand here; or: though who am I to say so **MW** I.i.203 [Slender to Evans, of Shallow] *He's a justice of peace in his country, simple though I stand here*

simple-answered (*adj.*) strait in reply, direct in answer **KL** III.vii.43 [Regan to Gloucester] *Be simple-answered, for we know the truth*

simpleness (*n.*) **1** unpretentiousness, unaffected behaviour, unassuming simplicity **AW** I.i.43 [Countess to Lafew, of Helena's virtues] *In her they are the better for their simpleness;* **MND** V.i.83

2 integrity, honesty, honour **Oth** I.iii.244 [Desdemona to Duke] *let me find a charter in your voice / T'assist my simpleness;* **MA** III.i.70

3 idiocy, stupidity, foolishness **RJ** III.iii.78 [Friar to Romeo, for not hiding] *What simpleness is this!*

simple-time (*n.*) summer-time [when aromatic herbs used as medicines (simples) were available] **MW** III.iii.68 [Falstaff to Mistress Ford, of young dandies] *that ... smell like Bucklersbury in simple-time* ☛ **simple** (*n.*)

simplicity (*n.*) **1** sincerity, unpretentiousness, artlessness **MND** V.i.104 [Theseus to Hippolyta] *tongue-tied simplicity / In least speak most, to my capacity*

2 innocence, harmlessness, guilelessness **MND** I.i.171 [Hermia to Lysander] *By the simplicity of Venus' doves ... / Tomorrow truly will I meet with thee*

3 naivety, foolishness, artlessness **LL** V.ii.78 [Maria to Rosaline] *To prove, by wit, worth in simplicity;* **LL** V.ii.52; **MV** I.iii.40; **Sonn** 66.11

simply (*adv.*) **1** completely, absolutely, totally **AY** V.i.186 [Celia to Rosalind] *You have simply misused our sex in your love-prate*

2 poorly, inadequately, weakly **AY** III.ii.361 [Rosalind to Orlando, of his appearance] *for simply your having in beard is a younger brother's revenue* [i.e. for having so little beard]

3 as is, without dowry **MW** III.iv.70 [Page to Host, of Fenton as a suitor for Anne] *If he take her, let him take her simply*

simular (*n.*) pretender, hypocrite, false claimant **KL** III.ii.54 [Lear to disguised Kent, as if to criminals] *Hide thee ... thou simular of virtue / That art incestuous*

simular (*adj.*) simulated, pretended, fake; or: plausible **Cym** V.v.200 [Iachimo to Cymbeline] *my practice so prevailed, / That I returned with simular proof enough*

simulation (*n.*) dissimulation, concealment, disguised meaning **TN** II.v.135 [Malvolio to himself, of the message in the letter] *This simulation is not as the former*

since (*adv.*) **1** recently, of late **Tem** V.i.223 [Boatswain to all] *but three glasses since;* **AC** I.iii.1

2 ago **Tem** I.ii.53 [Prospero to Miranda] *twelve year since, / Thy father was the Duke of Milan;* **AW** I.ii.71; **MND** III.ii.275

since (*conj.*) when **2H6** III.i.9 [Queen to King, of Gloucester] *We know the time since he was mild and affable*

since for (*conj.*) because of **TS** I.i.1 [Lucentio to Tranio] *since for the great desire I had / To see fair Padua*

since that (*conj.*) since, as **Mac** IV.iii.106 [Macduff to Malcolm, as if to Scotland] *When shalt thou see thy wholesome days again, / Since that the truest issue of thy throne / By his own interdiction stands accused*

sinew (*n.*) **1** muscle **TC** V.viii.12 [Achilles to dead Hector] *Here lies thy heart, thy sinews, and thy bone;* **Cor** V.vi.45; **Ham** I.v.94; **H5** II.ii.36; **3H6** II.iii.4; **Tem** IV.i.260

2 nerve **H5** III.i.7 [King Henry to all] *Stiffen the sinews;* **KL** III.vi.96; **TC** III.iii.304; **TG** III.ii.78; **Venus** 903

3 strength, force, power **KJ** V.i.63 [Lewis the Dauphin to English nobles] *knit your sinews to the strength of mine;* **1H4** IV.iv.17; **JC** I.ii.108; **TC** I.iii.143

4 mainstay, support, main strength **TN** II.v.75 [Fabian to Sir Toby] *patience, or we break the sinews of our plot;* **H5** I.ii.224; **MM** III.i.223

sinew (*v.*) join strongly, knit, bind **3H6** II.vi.91 [Warwick to Edward, of England and France] *So shalt thou sinew both these lands together* [F *sinow*]

sinewed (*adj.*) ☛ treble-sinewed (*adj.*); well-sinewed (*adj.*)

sinewy (*adj.*) muscular, well-developed, brawny **Venus** 99 [Venus to Adonis, of Mars] *Whose sinewy neck in battle ne'er did bow;* **AW** II.i.59; **AY** II.ii.14; **TC** II.iii.245

sinfully (*adv.*) without having repented of sins **H5** IV.i.144 [disguised King Henry to Williams] *if a son ... do sinfully miscarry upon the sea*

sing (*v.*) **1** anticipate trouble, see storm-clouds brewing **MW** III.ii.33 [Ford alone, of the way things are developing] *A man may hear this shower sing in the wind*

2 make music with; entice, make advances to **TC** V.ii.10 [Ulysses to Troilus, of Cressida] *She will sing any man at first sight* [pun: 11, have sex with]

3 declaim in verse **KJ** IV.iii.150 [Bastard to King John, of Peter of Pomfret's words] *sung, in rude harsh-sounding rhymes*

singing-man (*n.*) professional musician belonging to a royal chapel or cathedral **2H4** II.i.88 [Hostess to Falstaff] *when the Prince broke thy head for liking his father to a singing-man of Windsor*

single (*adj.*) **1** individual, particular **Tim** II.ii.134 [Timon to Flavius] *Perchance some single vantages you took / When my indisposition put you back;* **Cym** IV.v.13; **Ham** III.iii.11; **H8** I.i.41; **Mac** I.iii.139; **MV** I.iii.142

2 solitary, lone, unaccompanied **Tem** I.ii.433 [Ferdinand of himself, to Prospero] *A single thing, as I am now* [or: helpless]

3 poor, feeble, slight, trivial **2H4** I.ii.185 [Lord Chief Justice to Falstaff] *Is not ... your wit single;* **Cor** II.i.35; **3H6** V.i.43; **H8** I.i.15; **Mac** I.vi.16

4 unaided, single-handed, sole **KL** V.iii.103 [Albany to Edmund] *Trust to thy single virtue;* **2H6** I.iii.206

single (*v.*) [hunting] single out, pick out **3H6** II.iv.1 [Richard to Clifford] *I have singled thee alone;* **LL** II.i.28; **Tit** I.i.117; **Venus** 693

single forth (*v.*) [hunting] select from a herd, separate from other people **3H6** II.i.12 [Richard to Edward, of York] *I ... watched him how he singled Clifford forth;* **Tit** II.iii.69

single (*adv.*) alone, by oneself **Tem** V.i.248 [Prospero to all] *At picked leisure ... single I'll resolve you*

singleness simplicity, shallowness, silliness **RJ** II.iv.64 [Romeo to Mercutio] *O single-soled jest, solely singular for the singleness!*

single-soled (*adj.*) thin, poor, worthless **RJ** II.iv.64 [Romeo to Mercutio] *O single-soled jest, solely singular for the singleness!*

singly (*adv.*) **1** by another person, by a single individual **Cor** II.ii.85 [Cominius to all, of Coriolanus] *The man I speak of cannot in the world / Be singly counterpoised*

2 uniquely, solely; or: truly, sincerely **Tim** IV.iii.526 [Timon to Flavius] *Thou singly honest man*

singular (*adj.*) unmatched, preeminent, outstanding **Cym** III.iv.123 [Pisanio to Innogen] *some villain ... singular in his art;* **Luc** 32; **RJ** II.iv.64; **WT** IV.iv.144

singularity (*n.*) **1** individuality, distinctiveness, personal qualities **Cor** I.i.276 [Sicinius to Brutus, of Martius] *Let's hence and hear ... in what fashion, / More than his singularity, he goes / Upon this present action* [i.e. leaving aside his personal qualities]

2 rarity, curiosity, noteworthy object **WT** V.iii.12 [Leontes to Paulina] *your gallery / Have we passed through, not without much content / In many singularities*

3 singular behaviour, odd conduct **TN** II.v.147 [Malvolio reading the letter] *Put thyself into the trick of singularity*

singule *(v.)* set apart, distinguish **LL** V.i.76 [Armado to Holofernes] *We will be singuled from the barbarous* [Q1; F *singled*]

sinister *(adj.)* **1** left **TNK** V.iii.76 [Emilia to herself] *On the sinister side the heart lies;* **AW** II.i.44; **MND** V.i.161; **TC** IV.v.128 ☛ **dexter** *(adj.)*

2 illegitimate, erroneous, irregular **H5** II.iv.85 [Exeter to French King, of the English claim] *'Tis no sinister nor no awkward claim*

3 malicious, adverse, impolite **TN** I.v.168 [Viola as Cesario to Olivia] *I am very comptible, even to the least sinister usage*

4 unjust, unfair, underhand **MM** III.ii.232 [disguised Duke to Escalus, of Claudio] *He professes to have received no sinister measure from his judge*

sink *(n.)* cesspool, waste pit, sewer **H5** III.v.59 [Constable to all, of King Henry] *He'll drop his heart into the sink of fear;* **Cor** I.i.120; **2H6** IV.i.71; **TC** V.i.71

sink *(v.)* **1** fail, fall down, give way **JC** IV.ii.27 [Brutus to Lucilius, of insincere men compared to horses] *like deceitful jades / Sink in the trial*

2 be ruined, give up, perish **TNK** II.i.121 [Palamon to Arcite] *two souls ... so they grow together, / Will never sink;* **AC** III.vii.15; **Oth** II.iii.203; **Per** IV.vi.118

sink-apace, sinke-a-pace *(n.)* ☛ cinquepace *(n.)*

sinking-ripe *(adj.)* ready to sink **CE** I.i.78 [Egeon to Duke] *The sailors ... left the ship, then sinking-ripe, to us*

sinner *(n.)* cause of sin, instiller of wickedness **Tim** I.ii.57 [Apemantus to Timon, of water] *Here's that which is too weak to be a sinner*

sinow *(v.)* ☛ sinew *(v.)*

sip *(v.)* drink, propose a toast **WT** IV.iv.62 [Shepherd to Perdita, of his wife's treatment of guests] *She would to each one sip*

sir *(n.)* **1** man, person, individual **KL** IV.iv.74 [Fool to Lear] *That sir which serves and seeks for gain;* **Cym** I.vii.175, V.v.145; **Tem** V.i.69; **WT** IV.iv.608

2 gentleman, lord, gallant, master **TN** III.iv.74 [Malvolio alone, of the letter's requirements] *in the habit of some sir of note;* **AC** V.i.120; **Oth** II.i.171; **WT** I.ii.212 ☛ **ADDRESS FORMS**, p.8

sire *(n.)* father **3H6** II.ii.135 [Queen to Richard] *thou art neither like thy sire nor dam;* **E3** V.i.118; **3H6** II.ii.155; **Tim** IV.i.14; **Tit** V.i.50

sirrah *(n.)* ☛ **ADDRESS FORMS**, p.8

sir-reverence *(n.)* save your reverence **CE** III.ii.93 [Dromio of Syracuse to Antipholus of Syracuse, of the kitchen wench] *such a one as a man may not speak of without he say 'sir-reverence';* **RJ** I.iv.42 [Q] ☛ **POLITENESS**, p.340

SINGING

It is a commonplace that songs use a distinctive language, the selection and ordering of words being conditioned by the rhythmical demands of the line, the repetitive character of the verses, and the nature of the subject-matter – nostalgic, romantic, convivial, etc. The word *willow*, for example, is associated with sadness and unrequited love, as in the Wooer's description of the Gaoler's Daughter's singing: 'she sung / Nothing but "Willow, willow, willow"' (**TNK** IV.i.82).

The vocabulary of Shakespearian songs is notable in two respects, neither of which is easily treatable within an A–Z section. We find the addition of *a* or another word as an extra syllable to satisfy the needs of the metre in a line.

Item	Location	Example
-a	**TNK** III.v.61	*The George Alaw came from the south,* *From the coast of Barbary-a;* *And there he met with brave gallants of war,* *By one, by two, by three-a.*
and-a	**Oth** II.iii.84	*King Stephen was and-a worthy peer*
a-down	**Ham** IV.v.172	*You must sing 'A-down a-down, and you call him a-down-a'*
down-a, down-a	**TNK** IV.iii.11	*[of a song] the burden on't was 'down-a, down-a'*

And there is the use of nonsense words, such as *heigh*, *derry*, and *nonny*, to fill up a line or form a line in a chorus. They are often repeated, as in the Gaoler's Daughter's 'Hey, nonny, nonny, nonny' (**TNK** III.iv.21) or the Pages' 'With a hey, and a ho, and a hey nonino' (**AY** V.iii.16).

Item	Location	Example
derry ... down	**TNK** III.v.138	*Ladies, if we have been merry,* *And have pleased ye with a derry,* *And a derry, and a down,* *Say the schoolmaster's no clown*
heigh	**WT** IV.iii.2	*When daffodils begin to peer,* *With heigh, the doxy over the dale*
hey ding a ding ding	**AY** V.iii.19	*When birds do sing, hey ding a ding ding,* *Sweet lovers love the spring*
hey-ho	**AY** II.vii.181	*Then hey-ho, the holly,* *This life is most jolly*
hey non nony	**Ham** IV.v.167	*They bore him barefaced on the bier,* *Hey non nony, nony, hey nony*

sister (n.) ☞ **FAMILY**, p.168

sistering (adj.) acting like a sister; matching, corresponding **Lover** 2 *a hill whose concave womb reworded, / A plaintful story from a sist'ring vale*

sit (v.) **1** lodge, live, stay **MW** I.iii.8 [Falstaff to Host] *I sit at ten pounds a week* [i.e. it costs me ten pounds a week to stay here]

2 sit in conference, meet for a discussion **Per** II.ii.92 [Simonides to Knights] *we sit too long on trifles;* **H5** V.ii.80; **R3** III.i.173

3 hold an inquest **Ham** V.i.4 [Second Clown to First Clown, of Ophelia] *The crowner hath sat on her*

sit down (v.) begin a siege, encamp, blockade **AC** III.xiii.168 [Antony to Cleopatra] *Caesar sits down in Alexandria;* **Cor** IV.vii.28

sit there there you are **2H6** II.i.124 [Gloucester to Simcox] *Then, Saunder, sit there, the lyingest knave in Christendom*

sith (conj.) since **TS** I.i.208 [Tranio to Lucentio, of taking on his identity] *sith it your pleasure is*

sith (prep.) since **3H6** II.i.106 [Warwick to all, of York's death] *I come to tell you things with them befallen*

sith that (conj.) since **KL** II.iv.234 [Regan to Lear, of his knights] *sith that both charge and danger / Speak 'gainst so great a number*

sithence (adv.) since, subsequently **Cor** III.i.47 [Coriolanus to Brutus, of the Citizens] *Have you informed them sithence?*

sithence (conj.) since **AW** I.iii.115 [Steward to Countess, of Helena's thoughts] *which I held my duty speedily to acquaint you withal, sithence ... it concerns you*

sitting (n.) meeting, audience, interview **WT** IV.iv.558 [Camillo to Florizel, of writing down how he is to behave towards Leontes] *The which shall point you forth at every sitting / What you must say*

sixpenny (adj.) petty, paltry, puny **1H4** II.i.75 [Gadshill to Chamberlain] *I am joined with ... no long-staff sixpenny strikers*

size (n.) **1** kind, type, length **WT** IV.iv.193 [Servant to Clown, of Autolycus] *He hath songs for man or woman, of all sizes*

2 bounds, limit, confine **AC** V.ii.97 [Cleopatra to Dolabella, of imagining someone like Antony] *It's past the size of dreaming*

3 allowance, ration, quota **KL** II.iv.170 [Lear to Regan] *'Tis not in thee ... to scant my sizes*

size (v.) quantify, measure [for size] **Ham** III.ii.180 [Second Player, as Queen, to her King] *And as my love is sized, my fear is so* [i.e. according to the amount of my love]

sized (adj.) ☞ blood-sized (adj.); over-sized (adj.)

skains-mate (n.) [unclear meaning] cut-throat fellow **RJ** II.iv.151 [Nurse to Romeo, of Mercutio] *I am none of his skains-mates*

skiff (v.) go in a skiff [= small boat] **TNK** I.iii.37 [Hippolyta to Emilia, of Theseus and Pirithous] *they have skiffed / Torrents*

skilfully (adv.) knowledgeably, shrewdly, cleverly **LL** II.i.240 [Maria to Boyet] *Thou ... speakest skilfully*

skill (n.) **1** cause, reason, ground **WT** IV.iv.152 [Florizel to Perdita] *I think you have / As little skill to fear as I have purpose / To put you to't*

2 discernment, discrimination, capacity to perceive **KL** IV.vii.66 [Lear to Cordelia] *all the skill I have / Remembers not these garments;* **MND** II.ii.125; **WT** II.i.166

3 judgement, knowledge, common sense **TNK** V.ii.51 [Gaoler's Daughter to Gaoler] *If I have any skill* [i.e. if I know anything about it]

skill (v.) matter, make a difference, be of importance **TN** V.i.284 [Feste to Olivia] *a madman's epistles are no gospels, so it skills not much when they are delivered;* **2H6** III.i.281; **TS** III.ii.131

skill-contending (adj.) of competitive debating **Luc** 1018 [Lucrece as if to her own words] *Busy yourselves in skill-contending schools*

skillet (n.) saucepan, stew-pan, cooking pot **Oth** I.iii.269 [Othello to all] *Let housewives make a skillet of my helm*

skill-less, skilless (adj.) ignorant, unaware, unacquainted [with] **Tem** III.i.53 [Miranda to Ferdinand] *How features are abroad / I am skill-less of;* **TN** III.iii.9

skimble-skamble (adj.) nonsensical, incoherent, rubbishy **1H4** III.i.148 [Hotspur to Mortimer, of Glendower] *Sometime he angers me / With telling me of ... such a deal of skimble-skamble stuff*

skin (v.) cover up, cover with skin **Ham** III.iv.148 [Hamlet to Gertrude, of her false interpretation of his behaviour] *It will but skin and film the ulcerous place;* **MM** II.ii.136

skin-coat (n.) coat made of skin, hide **KJ** II.i.139 [Bastard to Austria] *I'll smoke your skin-coat an I catch you right!*

skip (v.) **1** pass over, fail to see, ignore **TNK** III.i.52 [Arcite to Palamon] *Honour and honesty / I cherish and depend on, howsoe'er / You skip them in me*

2 jump over, avoid, pass by **TNK** V.i.87 [Palamon praying to Venus] *the polled bachelor, / Whose youth ... / Have skipped thy flame*

3 jump into action, spring up **Tim** IV.iii.226 [Apemantus to Timon] *Will these moist trees ... page thy heels / And skip when thou pointest out?*

skipper (n.) light-brain, frivolous wretch **TS** II.i.332 [Gremio to Tranio as Lucentio] *Skipper, stand back, 'tis age that nourisheth*

skipping (adj.) **1** frivolous, flighty, frolicsome **1H4** III.ii.60 [King Henry to Prince Hal] *The skipping King, he ambled up and down;* **LL** V.ii.756; **MV** II.ii.174; **TN** I.v.193

2 runaway, fugitive; or: lightly armed **Mac** I.ii.30 [Captain to King, of the battle] *justice ... / Compelled these skipping kerns to trust their heels*

skirmish (n.) fight, clash, fracas **1H6** III.i.86 [stage direction] *Enter Servingmen ... in skirmish with bloody pates;* **1H6** III.i.92

skirmish (v.) do battle, wage war **1H6** III.i.104 [stage direction, of Gloucester's and Winchester's men] *They begin to skirmish again;* **1H6** I.ii.34, iii.70

skirr (v.) **1** scour, search quickly through **Mac** V.iii.35 [Macbeth to Seyton] *Send out more horses, skirr the country round*

2 scurry, flee, hasten **H5** IV.vii.59 [King Henry to a herald, of the French army] *we will come to them, / And make them skirr away as swift as stones*

skirt (n.) **1** one of four pieces of cloth forming the lower part of a long coat **MW** I.i.27 [Evans to Shallow, of Slender] *If he has a quarter of your coat, there is but three skirts for yourself*

2 (plural) outlying parts, borders, outskirts **AY** V.iv.156 [Jaques de Boys to all, of Duke Frederick] *to the skirts of this wild wood he came;* **AY** III.ii.325; **Ham** I.i.97

skirted (adj.) wearing a long coat **MW** I.iii.79 [Falstaff to Nym and Pistol] *Falstaff will learn the humour of the age ... myself and skirted page*

skittish (adj.) changeable, fickle, inconstant **TC** III.iii.134 [Ulysses to Achilles] *How some men creep in skittish Fortune's hall;* **TN** II.iv.18

skyey (adj.) coming from the sky, planetary **MM** III.i.9 [disguised Duke to Claudio] *thou art, / Servile to all the skyey influences*

skyish (adj.) lofty, sky-reaching **Ham** V.i.249 [Laertes to all] *the skyish head / Of old Olympus*

sky-planted (adj.) from a heavenly location, positioned in the skies **Cym** V.iv.96 [Jupiter to all, of himself] *whose bolt ... / Sky-planted, batters all rebelling coasts*

slab (adj.) coagulated, congealed, viscous **Mac** IV.i.32 [Third Witch to Witches] *Make the gruel thick and slab*

slack (adj.) less attentive, remiss, lax **TS** I.ii.272 [Tranio as Lucentio to Hortensio, of repaying Petruchio] *I shall not be slack;* **KL** I.iii.10

slack (v.) **1** slacken, reduce, slow down **RJ** IV.iii.3 [Paris to Friar, of Capulet's wish for Paris' early marriage] *I am nothing slow to slack his haste;* **Luc** 425 [or: slake]; **TC** III.iii.24

2 reduce to inactivity, quieten down **Per** III.Chorus.1 [Gower alone] *Now sleep y-slacked hath the rout* ☞ **ARCHAISMS**, p.22

3 put off, neglect, postpone **MW** III.iv.108 [Mistress Quickly alone, of her errand to Falstaff] *What a beast am I to slack it!*

4 neglect, be remiss [to] **Oth** IV.iii.86 [Emilia to Desdemona, of husbands] *Say that they slack their duties*; **KL** II.iv.240

slake (*v.*) abate, moderate, decrease **Luc** 1677 [Lucrece to Collatine] *no flood by raining slaketh*; **3H6** I.iii.29; **Luc** 425 [in some editions: *slacketh*]

slander (*n.*) **1** dishonour, disgrace, disrepute **CE** IV.iv.65 [Adriana to Antipholus of Ephesus] *Free from these slanders and this open shame*; **AY** IV.i.55; **R2** I.i.113, iii.241; **R3** I.iii.230, III.iii.12
  2 slanderer, disgraceful rogue **H5** III.vi.78 [Gower to Fluellen, of men like Pistol] *you must learn to know such slanders of the age*; **MA** V.i.207

slander (*v.*) misuse, disgrace, bring into disrepute **MA** II.iii.43 [Balthasar to Don Pedro] *tax not so bad a voice / To slander music any more than once*; **Cym** III.v.77; **Ham** I.iii.133

slanderous (*adj.*) disgraceful, shameful, discreditable **KJ** III.i.44 [Constance to Arthur] *If thou … wert grim, / Ugly and slanderous to thy mother's womb*; **Luc** 1001

slaughterman, slaughter-man (*n.*) executioner, slayer, murderer **Cym** V.iii.49 [Posthumus to Lord, of the Britons] *each one the slaughter-man of twenty*; **1H6** III.iii.75; **3H6** I.iv.169; **Tit** IV.iv.58

slave (*n.*) **1** fellow, rascal, rogue, villain **Tem** I.ii.344 [Prospero to Caliban] *Thou most lying slave*; **AC** II.v.79; **CE** II.ii.2; **2H4** II.iv.223; **Oth** V.ii.289; **TC** I.iii.193
  2 hireling, lackey, menial, servant **Tem** I.ii.270 [Prospero to Ariel, of Sycorax] *Thou, my slave … was then her servant*; **AC** V.ii.209; **R3** II.i.105; **Tem** I.ii.313

slave (*v.*) enslave, bring into subjection **KL** IV.i.67 [Gloucester to Edgar as Poor Tom, as if to the heavens] *the superfluous and lust-dieted man / That slaves your ordinance*

sleave (*n.*) [of silk] strands, threads, skein **Mac** II.ii.37 [Macbeth to Lady Macbeth] *Sleep that knits up the ravelled sleave of care*

sleave-silk (*n.*) silk thread for embroidery **TC** V.i.28 [Thersites to Patroclus] *thou idle immaterial skein of sleave-silk* [F *Sleyd silke*; Q *sleiue silke*] ☛ sleded (*adj.*)

sledded (*adj.*) carried by sleds **Ham** I.i.63 [Horatio to Marcellus and Barnardo, of King Hamlet] *He smote the sledded Polacks on the ice* [unclear reading; poleaxe (*n.*)]

sleded, sleided (*adj.*) finely divided, filamented **Per** IV.Chorus.21 [Gower alone, of Marina] *she weaved the sleded silk* [Q]; **Lover** 48 ☛ sleave-silk (*n.*)

sleek (*adj.*) oily, fawning, unctuous **H8** III.ii.241 [Wolsey to all] *how sleek and wanton / Ye appear in everything may bring my ruin!*

sleep upon (*v.*) disregard, ignore, pay no attention to **H8** II.ii.41 [Lord Chamberlain to Norfolk and Suffolk, of Wolsey] *Heaven will one day open / The King's eyes, that so long have slept upon / This bold bad man*; **Tim** III.v.44

sleepy (*adj.*) **1** sleep-inducing, soporific **WT** I.i.13 [Archidamus to Camillo] *We will give you sleepy drinks, that your senses … may, though they cannot praise us, as little accuse us*
  2 dreamlike, soporific, incoherent **Tem** II.i.215 [Sebastian to Antonio, of what the latter is saying] *It is a sleepy language, and thou speak'st / Out of thy sleep*

sleevehand, sleeve-hand (*n.*) sleeve cuff, wristband **WT** IV.iv.211 [Servant to Clown, of Autolycus] *you would think a smock were a she-angel, he so chants to the sleevehand and the work about the square on't*

sleeveless (*adj.*) futile, fruitless, unproductive **TC** V.iv.8 [Thersites alone, of Cressida] *the dissembling luxurious drab of a sleeveless errand*

sleided (*adj.*) ☛ sleded (*adj.*)

sleight (*n.*) cunning, trickery, crafty deceit **Mac** III.v.26 [Hecat to Witches, of a vaporous drop] *distilled by magic sleights / Shall raise such artificial sprites*; **3H6** IV.ii.20

slender (*adj.*) slight, trifling, insignificant **TG** I.iii.6 [Panthino to Antonio] *other men, of slender reputation*; **Ham** III.ii.209; **TS** IV.iv.60

slenderly (*adv.*) poorly, inadequately, to a slight extent **KL** I.i.293 [Regan to Goneril, of Lear] *he hath ever but slenderly known himself*

slickly (*adv.*) smoothly, sleekly, neatly **TS** IV.v.80 [Grumio to Curtis, of the servants] *Let their heads be slickly combed*

'slid (*int.*) ☛ SWEARING, p.435

sliding (*n.*) sinfulness, lapse, moral fall **MM** II.iv.115 [Angelo to Isabella, of Claudio] *proved the sliding of your brother / A merriment*

slight (*adj.*) **1** worthless, insignificant, good-for-nothing **JC** IV.i.12 [Antony to Octavius, of Lepidus] *This is a slight unmeritable man*; **Cor** V.ii.100; **Cym** V.iv.64; **JC** IV.iii.37; **LL** IV.iii.463; **Oth** III.iii.271
  2 light, insubstantial, lacking solidity **Sonn** 45.1 [of the elements] *The other two, slight air and purging fire*
  3 weak, foolish, unwise **Cym** III.v.35 [Cymbeline to Queen, of Innogen's behaviour] *We have been too slight in sufferance* [i.e. we have been too tolerant]
  4 offhand, dismissive, contemptuous **Tim** II.i.17 [Senator to Caphis, of Timon] *Importune him for my moneys. Be not ceased / With slight denial*

slight (*v.*) throw contemptuously, slide scornfully **MW** III.v.8 [Falstaff alone, of John and Robert] *The rogues slighted me into the river* [F; Q *slided*]

slight off (*v.*) dismiss with contempt, put off disdainfully **JC** IV.iii.5 [Cassius to Brutus, of Lucius Pella] *my letters, praying on his side … was slighted off*

'slight (*int.*) ☛ SWEARING, p.435

slightly (*adv.*) **1** without much attention, neglectfully **TC** III.iii.166 [Ulysses to Achilles, of time as a host] *That slightly shakes his parting guest by th'hand*; **R3** III.vii.19; **TNK** I.i.28
  2 easily, with little effort **H8** II.iv.112 [Queen Katherine to Wolsey] *You have, by fortune and his highness' favours, / Gone slightly o'er low steps*; **MV** V.i.167

slightness (*n.*) triviality, paltriness, trifling **Cor** III.i.148 [Coriolanus to Brutus, of divided sovereignty in the state] *it must omit / Real necessities, and give way the while / To unstable slightness*

slime (*n.*) rich earth, mud, soil **AC** I.iii.69 [Antony to Cleopatra] *By the fire / That quickens Nilus' slime, I go from hence / Thy soldier-servant*

slip (*n.*) **1** seedling, sprig, shoot, cutting **Mac** IV.i.27 [Third Witch to Witches] *slips of yew / Slivered in the moon's eclipse*; **AW** I.iii.141; **2H6** III.ii.214; **MM** III.i.145; **Tit** V.i.9; **WT** IV.iv.85
  2 leash, lead, tether **H5** III.i.31 [King Henry to all] *I see you stand like greyhounds in the slips*
  3 lapse, error in conduct, fault **Tit** II.iii.86 [Lavinia to Bassianus, of Saturninus] *these slips have made him noted long* [or: letting go, as of a leash]
  4 counterfeit coin; also: evasion **RJ** II.iv.48 [Mercutio to Romeo, responding to 'What counterfeit did I give you?'] *The slip*

slip (*v.*) **1** fail to hold, be broken off **TNK** II.ii.44 [Third Countryman to the others, of the Schoolmaster] *The matter's too far driven between him / And the tanner's daughter to let slip now*
  2 fail to keep, allow to pass by **Mac** II.iii.44 [Macduff to Macbeth] *I have almost slipped the hour*
  3 err, sin, transgress **MM** II.ii.65 [Isabella to Angelo, of Claudio] *You would have slipped like him*; **MM** V.i.469
  4 leave unasserted, pass over **3H6** II.ii.162 [Edward to Queen, of his claim to the crown] *Hadst thou been meek, our title still had slept; / And we, in pity for the gentle King, / Had slipped our claim until another age*
  5 let go of, allow to leave, unleash **TS** V.ii.52 [Tranio to Petruchio] *Lucentio slipped me like his greyhound*; **Cym** IV.iii.22

slip, let let go, allow to leave, unleash **JC** III.i.273 [Antony alone, of Caesar's spirit] *Shall … / Cry havoc and let slip the dogs of war*; **Cor** I.vi.39; **1H4** I.iii.272

slipper *(adj.)* slippery, shifty, unreliable **Oth** II.i.235 [Iago to Roderigo, of Cassio] *a slipper and subtle knave*

slippery *(adj.)* **1** fickle, treacherous, uncertain **Cor** IV.iv.12 [Coriolanus alone] *O world, thy slippery turns;* **AC** I.ii.186
 2 faithless, unchaste, difficult to hold on to **WT** I.ii.273 [Leontes to Camillo] *Ha'not you seen … / My wife is slippery?*
 3 swiftly passing, fleeting **2H4** III.i.24 [King Henry IV alone, of waves] *hanging them / With deafing clamour in the slippery clouds*

slipshod, slip-shod *(adj.)* wearing slippers **KL** I.v.11 [Fool to Lear] *Thy wit shall not go slipshod*

sliver *(n.)* [split piece of] branch, bough, limb **Ham** IV.vii.173 [Gertrude to Claudius and Laertes] *an envious sliver broke*

sliver *(v.)* cut off [a piece], split off, tear away **Mac** IV.i.28 [Third Witch to Witches] *slips of yew / Slivered in the moon's eclipse;* **KL** IV.ii.34

slobbery *(adj.)* slimy, muddy, sloppy **H5** III.v.13 [Britaine to all] *I will sell my dukedom / To buy a slobbery and a dirty farm*

slop, slops *(n.)* large loose breeches, baggy trousers **MA** III.ii.33 [Don Pedro to Claudio] *a German from the waist downward, all slops;* **2H4** I.ii.29; **RJ** II.iv.44 ☛ **CLOTHING**, p.79

slough *(n.)* outer skin **2H6** III.i.229 [Queen to all, of a snake] *With shining checkered slough;* **TN** II.v.144

slovenly *(adj.)* nasty, disgusting, foul **1H4** I.iii.43 [Hotspur to King Henry] *a slovenly unhandsome corpse*

slovenry *(n.)* slovenliness, negligence, neglect **H5** IV.iii.114 [King Henry to Montjoy] *time hath worn us into slovenry*

slow *(adj.)* **1** heavy, gloomy, dejected **TG** IV.ii.62 [disguised Julia to Host, of the music] *it makes me have a slow heart*
 2 reluctant, unwilling, slowly given **Ham** I.ii.58 [Polonius to Claudius, of Laertes] *He hath, my lord, wrung from me my slow leave;* **RJ** IV.i.3
 3 not readily moved, easy-going **TS** II.i.240 [Petruchio to Katherina] *thou art … / But slow in speech*

slow-gaited *(adj.)* slow-moving, sluggish **LL** III.i.53 [Mote to Armado, of Costard] *he is very slow-gaited*

slubber *(v.)* **1** smear, stain, soil **Oth** I.iii.224 [Duke to Othello] *be content to slubber the gloss of your new fortunes with this more stubborn … expedition*
 2 be careless with, rush through **MV** II.viii.39 [Salerio to Solanio, quoting Antonio] *Slubber not business for my sake, Bassanio*

slug *(n.)* sluggard, lazy fellow **R3** III.i.22 [Prince Edward to all] *what a slug is Hastings that he comes not;* **CE** II.ii.203

slug-abed *(n.)* lazy-bones **RJ** IV.v.2 [Nurse to Juliet] *Fie, you slug-abed!* ☛ **abed** *(adv.)*

sluggardized *(adj.)* like a sluggard, made lazy **TG** I.i.7 [Valentine to Proteus] *living dully sluggardized at home*

sluice *(n.)* floodgate **Venus** 956 [of Venus' eyelids] *who, like sluices, stopped / The crystal tide*

sluice *(v.)* send water through, draw water from; screw **WT** I.ii.194 [Leontes to himself, of a husband] *holds his wife by th'arm, / That little thinks she has been sluiced in's absence*

slumbery *(adj.)* slumbering, sleepy, drowsy **Mac** V.i.11 [Doctor to Gentlewoman, of Lady Macbeth's sleepwalking] *slumbery agitation*

sluttery *(n.)* **1** sluttishness, squalor, filthiness **MW** V.v.46 [Pistol as Hobgoblin to all] *Our radiant Queen hates sluts and sluttery*
 2 slut, hussy **Cym** I.vi.44 [Iachimo to Innogen] *Sluttery … / Should make desire vomit emptiness*

sly *(adj.)* stealthy, furtive, quietly moving **R2** I.iii.150 [King Richard to Mowbray] *The sly slow hours shall not determinate / The dateless limit of thy dear exile*

slyly *(adv.)* stealthily, secretly, quietly **R3** IV.iv.3 [Queen Margaret alone] *in these confines slyly have I lurked*

smack *(n.)* **1** taste, quantity, mouthful **AW** II.iii.223 [Lafew to Parolles, of the latter being wiser] *thou hast to pull at a smack o'th'contrary* [i.e. you have to swallow some of your own folly before you can become wise]
 2 smattering, superficial knowledge **AW** IV.i.15 [First Lord to all, of Parolles] *he hath a smack of all neighbouring languages*
 3 suggestion, trace, hint **2H4** I.ii.97 [Falstaff to Lord Chief Justice] *Your lordship … have yet some smack of age in you*

smack *(v.)* **1** have a taste, like the flavour **MV** II.ii.15 [Launcelot alone] *my father did something smack* [i.e. for women]
 2 show the characteristics, savour the taste **KJ** I.i.209 [Bastard alone, of obsequiousness] *whether I smack or no;* **KJ** I.i.208
 3 have an air, have a flavour **KJ** II.i.396 [Bastard to King John and King Philip, of his advice] *Smacks it not something of the policy?*

small *(n.)* lower leg **LL** V.ii.639 [Boyet to all, of Armado as Hector] *he is best indued in the small*

small *(adj.)* **1** slender, slim **Per** IV.Chorus.22 [Gower alone, of Marina] *With fingers long, small, white as milk;* **TG** II.iii.20
 2 weak, poor **3H6** V.i.64 [Edward to Richard] *the city being but of small defence, / We'll quickly rouse the traitors* ☛ **beer / ale, small**
 3 high-pitched, fluting, thin **MW** I.i.45 [Slender to Evans, of Anne] *She … speaks small like a woman;* **Cor** III.ii.114; **MND** I.ii.46

small *(adv.)* little, not much **Luc** 1273 [Lucrece to Maid, of her maid's tears] *it small avails my mood*

small and small, by little by little, by degrees, gradually **R2** III.ii.198 [Scroop to King Richard] *I play the torturer, by small and small / To lengthen out the worst that must be spoken*

smallness *(n.)* softness, gentleness, high pitch **TNK** IV.i.58 [Wooer to Gaoler, of hearing a voice] *and by the smallness of it / A boy or woman*

smart *(n.)* suffering, grief, sorrow **Cym** V.iv.42 [Sicilius, to music, as if to Jove] *Thou shouldst have … shielded him / from this earth-vexing smart;* **H8** II.i.166

smart *(adj.)* biting, stinging, painful **Ham** III.i.50 [Claudius to himself] *How smart a lash that speech doth give my conscience;* **2H6** III.ii.325

smart *(v.)* suffer, feel pain **1H6** IV.vi.42 [John Talbot to Talbot] *The sword of Orleans hath not made me smart*

smatch *(n.)* taste, relish, smack **JC** V.v.46 [Brutus to Strato] *Thy life hath had some smatch of honour in it*

smatter *(v.)* prattle, chatter, babble away **RJ** III.v.171 [Capulet to Nurse] *Smatter with your gossips, go!*

smile *(n.)* trace, sign, hint **TNK** IV.ii.30 [Emilia alone, of Palamon] *Of all this sprightly sharpness not a smile*

smile *(v.)* **1** make something happen by smiling **TN** III.ii.74 [Maria to Sir Toby, of Malvolio] *He does smile his face into more lines than is in the new map with the augmentation of the Indies;* **LL** V.ii.465; **Per** V.i.138
 2 laugh at, mock, sneer at **KL** II.ii.80 [disguised Kent to all] *Smile you my speeches as I were a fool?* [F *Smoile;* Q *smoyle*]

smilet *(n.)* slight smile **KL** IV.iii.19 [Gentleman to disguised Kent, of Cordelia] *those happy smilets / That played on her ripe lip*

smilingly *(adv.)* with a smile, experiencing some happiness **KL** V.iii.197 [Edgar to Albany, of Gloucester] *his flawed heart … / Burst smilingly*

smirch *(v.)* smear, discolour, spread on **AY** I.iii.110 [Celia to Rosalind] *with a kind of umber smirch my face*

smirched *(adj.)* marked, soiled, stained **MA** III.iii.133 [Borachio to Conrade] *like the shaven Hercules in the smirched worm-eaten tapestry;* **H5** III.iii.117; **MA** V.i.131

smite *(v.),* past forms **smote, smit 1** strike, hit (often, with great force) **MW** III.i.114 [Evans to Caius, of the Host] *I will smite his noddles;* **AC** V.ii.171; **Cor** III.i.317; **Ham** I.i.63; **LL** IV.iii.26; **Tem** IV.i.172
 2 injure, harm, do damage to **Tim** II.i.23 [Senator to Caphis, of Timon] *my reliances on his fracted dates / Have smit my credit*

smock (*n.*) woman's undergarment, shift, slip, chemise **MA** II.iii.134 [Leonato to Claudio, of Beatrice during the night] *there will she sit in her smock;* **AC** I.ii.169; **AW** II.i.30; **1H6** I.ii.119; **MW** III.v.82; **TNK** V.ii.82

smoke (*n.*) mist, fog, vapours **Mac** I.v.49 [Lady Macbeth alone] *Come, thick night, / And pall thee in the dunnest smoke of hell;* **1H6** II.ii.27; **Sonn** 34.4

smoke (*v.*) **1** spread like mist, grow misty **KJ** V.iv.34 [Melun to Pembroke, Salisbury, and Bigot, of the night] *whose black contagious breath / Already smokes about the burning crest / Of the … day-wearied sun*
2 give off steam [i.e. blood] **Mac** I.ii.18 [Captain to King, of Macbeth] *his brandished steel, / Which smoked with bloody execution;* **KL** V.iii.221
3 expose, smoke out; suspect, scent **AW** IV.i.27 [Parolles to himself, of the Lords] *They begin to smoke me;* **AW** III.vi.96
4 perfume, fumigate, deodorize **MA** I.iii.55 [Borachio to Don John] *I was smoking a musty room*
5 disinfect, sanitize; beat, thrash **KJ** II.i.139 [Bastard to Austria] *I'll smoke your skin-coat an I catch you right!*
6 burn, suffer severely **Tit** IV.ii.110 [Aaron to Demetrius, of the baby] *This maugre all the world will I keep safe, / Or some of you shall smoke for it in Rome*

smoking (*adj.*) steaming hot, sending up spray **R3** I.ii.94 [Anne to Richard, of Anne's husband] *Queen Margaret saw / Thy murderous falchion smoking in his blood;* **Cor** I.iv.11; **3H6** II.iii.21

smooth (*adj.*) **1** pleasant, welcome, gratifying **1H4** I.i.66 [King Henry to Westmorland, of Blunt] *he hath brought us smooth and welcome news;* **2H4** I.Induction.40
2 plausible, glib, apparently amiable **2H6** III.i.65 [Buckingham to all, of Gloucester's faults] *Which time will bring to light in smooth Duke Humphrey*

smooth (*v.*) **1** gloss over, make less noticeable, camouflage **3H6** III.i.48 [King to himself] *Warwick … smooths the wrong;* **R2** I.iii.240
2 adopt a flattering manner, make a plausible show, conciliate **R3** I.iii.48 [Richard to all] *I cannot … smooth, deceive, and cog;* **2H6** II.ii.22; **Per** I.ii.78
3 indulge, humour, allay, flatter **Tit** IV.iv.96 [Tamora to Saturninus, of Titus] *I can smooth and fill his aged ears;* **KL** II.ii.73; **Tit** V.ii.140
4 defend, gild, speak well of **RJ** III.ii.98 [Juliet as if to Romeo] *what tongue shall smooth thy name / When I … have mangled it?*

smooth-faced (*adj.*) plausible, bland, glib, deceitful **LL** V.ii.817 [Katharine to Dumaine] *I'll mark no words that smooth-faced wooers say;* **KJ** II.i.573

smoothing (*adj.*) flattering, plausible, ingratiating **2H6** I.i.154 [Cardinal to all, of Gloucester] *let not his smoothing words / Bewitch your hearts;* **Luc** 892; **R3** I.ii.168

smooth-pate, smoothy-pate (*n.*) cropped-head [of a Puritan city tradesman] **2H4** I.ii.36 [Falstaff to Page, of tradesmen] *The whoreson smoothy-pates do now wear nothing but high shoes and bunches of keys at their girdles* [Q; F smooth-pate]

smote (*v.*) ☞ smite (*v.*)

smother (*n.*) suffocating smoke **AY** I.ii.276 [Orlando alone] *Thus must I from the smoke into the smother* [i.e. out of the frying pan into the fire]

smother up (*v.*) conceal, hide, cover up **Cor** II.i.203 [Brutus to Sicinius] *Stalls, bulks, windows / Are smothered up*

smug (*adj.*) **1** neat, spruce, trim **KL** IV.vi.199 [Lear to Gentleman] *I will die bravely, / Like a smug bridegroom;* **MV** III.i.42
2 placid, tranquil, smooth-running **1H4** III.i.98 [Hotspur to all] *here the smug and silver Trent shall run / In a new channel*

smutch (*v.*) smudge, dirty, blacken **WT** I.ii.121 [Leontes to Mamillius] *hast smutched thy nose?*

snaffle (*n.*) bridle-bit **AC** II.ii.67 [Antony to Caesar] *The third o'th' world is yours, which with a snaffle / You may pace easy;* **E3** I.ii.28

snaily (*adj.*) snail-like **E3** I.i.138 [King Edward as if to King David] *I will make you shrink your snaily horns* [i.e. pull back your horns]

snaky (*adj.*) twisting, winding, sinuous; also: deceitful **MV** III.ii.92 [Bassanio to himself] *those crisped snaky golden locks, / Which make such wanton gambols with the wind*

snatch (*n.*) **1** hasty grab, quick theft **Tit** II.i.95 [Aaron to Demetrius and Chiron] *it seems some certain snatch or so / Would serve your turns*
2 snap, bite **KJ** IV.i.116 [Arthur to Hubert, of the blinding iron] *like a dog that is compelled to fight, / Snatch at his master that doth tarre him on*
3 catch, hesitation, jerkiness **Cym** IV.ii.105 [Belarius to Arviragus, of Cloten] *the snatches in his voice*
4 quibble, equivocation, nitpicking **MM** IV.ii.6 [Provost to Pompey] *leave me your snatches*

snatcher (*n.*) raider, thief, robber **H5** I.ii.143 [King Henry to Canterbury, of the Scots] *We do not mean the coursing snatchers only*

sneak-up (*n.*) cringing villain, creeping rascal **1H4** III.iii.84 [Falstaff to Hostess] *The Prince is … a sneak-up* [Q sneakeup; F sneak-cup]

sneap (*n.*) snub, reproof, rebuke **2H4** II.i.121 [Falstaff to Lord Chief Justice] *I will not undergo this sneap without reply*

sneaped (*adj.*) nipped, frost-bitten **Luc** 333 [Tarquin to himself, of obstacles] *Like little frosts that sometime threat the spring … / And give the sneaped birds more cause to sing*

sneaping (*adj.*) nipping, biting, sharp **WT** I.ii.13 [Polixenes to Leontes] *may blow / No sneaping winds at home;* **LL** I.i.100

sneck up (*v.*) buzz off, go hang **TN** II.iii.92 [Sir Toby to Malvolio] *Sneck up!*

snip (*n.*) snatch, scrap, shred **LL** III.i.20 [Mote to Armado] *keep not long in one tune, but a snip and away*

snipe (*n.*) [type of bird] dupe, gull, fool **Oth** I.iii.379 [Iago alone, of Roderigo] *If I would time expend with such a snipe*

snipped-taffeta, snipt-taffeta (*n.*) glossy silk fabric with irregular cuts, slashed-silk **AW** IV.v.1 [Lafew to Countess, of Parolles] *a snipped-taffeta fellow*

snort (*v.*) snore **1H4** II.iv.513 [Peto to Prince Hal, of Falstaff] *Fast asleep behind the arras, and snorting like a horse*

snorting (*adj.*) snoring **Oth** I.i.91 [Iago to Brabantio] *Awake the snorting citizens with the bell*

snow-broth (*n.*) melted snow **MM** I.iv.58 [Lucio to Isabella, of Angelo] *a man whose blood / Is very snow-broth*

snuff (*n.*) **1** resentment, huff, pique **LL** V.ii.22 [Katharine to Rosaline] *You'll mar the light by taking it in snuff* [i.e. taking offence]; **KL** III.i.26
2 smouldering candle-end, burnt-out wick **AW** I.ii.59 [King to Bertram, reporting Bertram's father] *Let me not live … to be the snuff / Of younger spirits;* **Cym** I.vii.87; **KL** IV.vi.39

snuff, in in need of snuffing out; also: in a rage **MND** V.i.243 [Demetrius to Theseus, of the candle in the lantern] *it is already in snuff*

so (*adv.*) average, middling, so-so **LL** I.i.222 [Costard to King, of Don Armado] *if he say it is so, he is, in telling true – but so* [second instance]

so (*conj.*) **1** provided that **AY** II.iii.30 [Adam to Orlando, of where Orlando should go] *No matter whither, so you come not here*
2 even though **AC** II.v.94 [Cleopatra to Messenger, of his telling a lie about Antony's marriage] *I would thou didst, / So half my Egypt were submerged*

soaking (*adj.*) quick to absorb, ready to assimilate **WT** I.ii.224 [Leontes to Camillo] *For thy conceit is soaking, will draw in / More than the common blocks*

soar (*n.*) highest point, summit **E3** II.i.87 [King Edward to Lodowick] *every ornament that thou wouldst praise, / Fly it a pitch above the soar of praise*

sob (*n.*) respite, rest, breather [given to a horse] **CE** IV.iii.24 [Dromio of Syracuse to Antipholus of Syracuse, of the officer] *the man, sir, that when gentlemen are tired gives them a sob and rests them*

sober (*adj.*) **1** sedate, staid, demure, grave **JC** IV.ii.40 [Cassius to Brutus] *this sober form of yours hides wrongs;* **AC** V.ii.54; **Luc** 1542; **MV** II.v.35, III.ii.78; **Tim** III.v.21
   2 serious, sincere, not playful **MA** I.i.160 [Claudio to Benedick] *I pray thee speak in sober judgement;* **AY** V.ii.66
   3 moderate, reasonable, with no undue haste **2H4** IV.iii.79 [Prince John to Westmorland] *we with sober speed will follow you*
   4 subdued in colour, somber **TS** I.ii.130 [Hortensio to Petruchio, of himself] *disguised in sober robes;* **Sonn** 132.8

sober-blooded (*adj.*) calm, passionless, impassive **2H4** IV.iii.86 [Falstaff alone, of Prince John] *this same young sober-blooded boy doth not love me*

sober-suited (*adj.*) sedately dressed **RJ** III.ii.10 [Juliet alone] *Come, civil night, / Thou sober-suited matron*

sociable (*adj.*) sensitive, responsive, sympathetic **Tem** V.i.63 [Prospero to charmed Gonzalo] *Mine eyes, ev'n sociable to the show of thine* [i.e. responsive to the sight of your eyes]

society (*n.*) **1** companionship, fellowship, association **Cym** IV.ii.12 [Innogen to all] *Society is no comfort / To one not sociable;* **AY** III.ii.249; **2H4** V.i.63; **LL** IV.ii.157; **Mac** III.i.42; **MW** III.iv.8
   2 disposition, manners, social graces **Ham** V.ii.108 [Osric to Hamlet, of Laertes] *of very soft society*
   3 groups of people, companions **Mac** III.iv.3 [Macbeth to all] *Ourself will mingle with society / And play the humble host;* **Cym** I.vii.167
   4 gathering, company, group **H8** I.iv.14 [Sands to all, of the ladies] *They are a sweet society of fair ones*

sod (*adj.*) soaked, sodden, steeped **Luc** 1592 [of Lucrece] *Her eyes, though sod in tears, looked red and raw;* **LL** IV.ii.22

sod (*v.*) boil, stew [from 'seethe'] **TNL** I.iii.21 [Hippolyta to Pirithous] *women / That have sod their infants in … The brine*

sodden (*adj.*) **1** boiled, stewed up **H5** III.v.18 [Constable to all, of the English] *Can sodden water … / Decoct their cold blood to such valiant heat?;* **TC** III.i.41
   2 diseased, rotten, limp **Per** IV.ii.18 [Bawd to Boult, of his girls] *they are so pitifully sodden*

sodden-witted (*adj.*) stew-brained, limp-minded, alcohol-crazed **TC** II.i.42 [Thersites to Ajax] *Thou sodden-witted lord, thou hast no more brain than I have in mine elbows*

so-forth (*n.*) such-and-such, you know what **WT** I.ii.218 [Leontes to himself, of people around him] *They're here with me already: whispering, rounding, 'Sicilia is a so-forth'*

soft (*adj.*) **1** sociable, pleasing, pleasant **Ham** V.ii.108 [Osric to Hamlet, of Laertes] *of very soft society;* **Oth** III.iii.261
   2 tender, compassionate, kind **H5** III.iii.48 [Governor to King Henry] *We yield our town and lives to thy soft mercy;* **Cor** III.iii.82; **Oth** I.iii.82; **TC** II.ii.11; **Tem** V.i.142
   3 weak, faint, soft-hearted **MV** III.iii.14 [Shylock to Antonio] *I'll not be made a soft and dull-eyed fool;* **3H6** II.ii.57

soft (*adv.*) **1** [used as a command] not so fast, wait a moment **MA** V.i.194 [Don Pedro to Claudio] *But, soft you, let me be;* **Tem** I.ii.450 [Prospero to Ferdinand] *Soft, sir! One word more;* **AC** II.ii.87; **Ham** III.i.88; **1H4** II.i.37; **Oth** V.ii.334; **RJ** I.i.195 **☞ ATTENTION SIGNALS**, p.26
   2 gently, calmly, not so forcefully **2H4** V.ii.97 [Lord Chief Justice to King Henry V] *imagine me taking your part, / And in your power soft silencing your son;* **AW** IV.iii.322

soft and fair gently, not so fast **MA** V.iv.72 [Benedick to Friar] *Soft and fair, Friar*

soft-conscienced (*adj.*) soft-headed, easy-going, lacking real convictions **Cor** I.i.35 [First Citizen to all, of Martius' actions] *Though soft-conscienced men can be content to say it was for his country*

softly (*adv.*) slowly, gently **Per** IV.i.49 [Dionyza to Marina] *Pray walk softly;* **AY** III.ii.317; **Ham** IV.iv.8; **JC** V.i.16; **TS** I.ii.235; **WT** IV.iii.110

softly-sprighted (*adj.*) mild-tempered, gentle-spirited **MW** I.iv.23 [Mistress Quickly to Simple, of Slender] *A softly-sprighted man, is he not?* **☞** sprite (*n./v.*)

soho, so-ho (*int.*) **☞ SOUNDS**, p.410

soil (*n.*) **1** blemish, stain, tarnish **H8** I.i.26 [Queen Katherine to Wolsey, of King Henry] *Whose honour heaven shield from soil!;* **Ham** I.iii.15; **LL** II.i.47; **MA** III.ii.5; **TC** II.i.149; **Tim** III.v.16
   2 country, homeland, nation **1H6** I.v.29 [Talbot to the English] *Renounce your soil* [alternative reading: *style*]

soiled (*adj.*) fully fed with fresh fodder; lively, skittish **KL** IV.vi.122 [Lear to all] *The fitchew nor the soiled horse goes to't / With a more riotous appetite*

soilure (*n.*) soiling, staining, defilement **TC** IV.i.57 [Diomedes to Paris, of Helen] *He merits well to have her, that doth seek her, / Not making any scruple of her soilure*

sojourn (*n.*) visit, temporary stay **KL** I.i.47 [Lear to all, of France and Burgundy] *Long in our court have made their amorous sojourn*

sojourn (*v.*) **1** pause, reside, stay for a while **KL** II.iv.198 [Regan to Lear] *You will return and sojourn with my sister;* **Cym** I.v.22; **KJ** I.i.103; **R3** III.i.62; **RJ** III.iii.169; **TG** IV.i.19
   2 travel, journey, go to stay **MND** III.ii.171 [Demetrius to Lysander, of Hermia] *My heart to her but as guestwise sojourned*

sojourner (*n.*) guest, lodger, visitor **Per** IV.ii.132 [Bawd to Boult, of Marina] *Report what a sojourner we have*

sol (*n.*) [musical scale] soh **LL** IV.ii.99 [Holofernes singing] *Ut, re, sol, la, mi, fa*

sola (*int.*) **☞ SOUNDS**, p.410

solace (*v.*) **1** take comfort, be happy, cheer [oneself] **RJ** IV.v.47 [Lady Capulet to all, of Juliet] *But one thing to rejoice and solace in;* **Cym** I.vii.86; **R3** II.iii.30
   2 entertain, amuse, divert **LL** IV.iii.353 [Berowne to all, of the ladies] *We will with some strange pastime solace them*

sold (*adj.*) made commercial, as if for sale **Mac** III.iv.32 [Lady Macbeth to Macbeth] *The feast is sold / That is not often vouched*

sold (*v.*) **☞** buy and sell

solder (*v.*) unite, interlink, fasten **E3** II.i.232 [Countess to King Edward, of her beauty] *it is soldered to my life;* **AC** III.iv.32; **Tim** IV.iii.389

soldier (*n.*) dedicated person, committed individual **Per** IV.i.8 [Dionyza to Leonine] *be / A soldier to thy purpose;* **Cym** III.iv.185

soldieress (*n.*) female soldier **TNK** I.i.85 [Second Queen to Hippolyta] *Most dreaded Amazonian … soldieress*

soldiership (*n.*) soldierly qualities, military skill **Mac** V.iv.16 [Macduff to all] *put we on / Industrious soldiership*

sole (*adj.*) **1** unique, unrivalled, singular **Phoen** 2 *Let the bird of loudest lay / On the sole Arabian tree, / Herald sad and trumpet be;* **KJ** IV.iii.52; **Sonn** 36.7
   2 mere, simple, alone **Mac** IV.iii.12 [Malcolm to Macduff, of Macbeth] *whose sole name blisters our tongues*

sole (*adv.*) uniquely, singularly, incomparably **TC** I.iii.244 [Aeneas to Agamemnon] *what the repining enemy commends, / That breath fame blows; that praise, sole pure, transcends*

solely (*adv.*) **1** wholly, entirely, altogether **AW** I.i.100 [Helena to herself, of Parolles] *I … / Think him a great way fool, solely a coward;* **Mac** I.v.68; **MV** II.i.13; **RJ** II.iv.64
   2 alone, by oneself **WT** II.i.17 [Leontes to Servant] *Leave me solely;* **H5** II.Chorus.4; **TS** II.i.117

solemn (*adj.*) **1** formal, ceremonious, stately **Mac** III.i.14 [Macbeth to Banquo] *Tonight we hold a solemn supper;* **Tit** II.i.112; **TS** III.ii.100
   2 impressive, breathtaking, awe-inspiring **Venus** 1057 [of nature seeming to bleed with Adonis] *This solemn sympathy poor Venus noteth*

3 dark, sombre, gloomy **Ham** I.ii.78 [Hamlet to Gertrude] *Nor customary suits of solemn black*
4 sorrowful, mournful, melancholic **LL** V.ii.118 [Boyet to Princess, of the King's party] *in this spleen ridiculous appears, / To check their folly, passion's solemn tears*

solemnity (*n.*) **1** celebration, jubilation, festivity **MND** IV.i.184 [Theseus to all] *We'll hold a feast in great solemnity;* **KJ** II.i.555; **MM** III.i.217; **MND** IV.i.133; **RJ** I.v.57; **TG** V.iv.162
2 ritual, ceremony, celebration **TNK** I.i.221 [Pirithous to Theseus] *the feast's solemnity / Shall want till your return*
3 solemn occasion, special ritual **AC** V.ii.364 [Caesar to Dolabella] *see / High order in this great solemnity*

solemnly (*adv.*) ceremoniously, with ritual celebration **H5** V.Chorus.14 [Chorus, of King Henry] *solemnly see him set on to London;* **MND** IV.i.87; **R2** IV.i.318; **R3** I.ii.213

sol-fa (*v.*) sing a scale, make a tune **TS** I.ii.17 [Petruchio to Grumio, of wringing his ears] *I'll try how you can sol-fa and sing it*

solicit (*n.*) entreaty, solicitation, wooing **Cym** II.iii.46 [Queen to Cloten] *frame yourself / To orderly solicits* [F *solicity*]

solicit (*v.*) **1** urge, move, incite, prevail upon **E3** I.ii.4 [Countess as if to Montague] *solicit / With vehement suit the king in my behalf;* **Cor** V.i.73; **Ham** V.iii.352; **1H6** V.iii.190; **Mac** IV.iii.149; **TN** III.i.106
2 court, chase after, pursue **AW** III.v.15 [Widow to Diana] *you have been solicited by a gentleman;* **AW** III.v.68; **Cor** II.iii.199; **E3** II.ii.183
3 beg pardon, make intercession **Oth** V.ii.28 [Othello to Desdemona] *If you bethink yourself of any crime / Unreconciled as yet to heaven and grace, / Solicit for it straight*

soliciting (*n.*) importuning, entreaty, urging [not necessarily immoral] **Mac** I.iii.129 [Macbeth to himself] *This supernatural soliciting / Cannot be ill, cannot be good;* **Ham** II.ii.126

solicitor (*n.*) advocate, instigator, go-between **LL** II.i.29 [Princess to Boyet] *we single you / As our best-moving fair solicitor;* **E3** II.i.418; **Oth** III.iii.27

solicity (*n.*) ➤ solicit (*n.*)

solidare (*n.*) ➤ **MONEY**, p.286

solidity (*n.*) solid body [i.e. the Earth] **Ham** III.iv.50 [Hamlet to Gertrude] *this solidity and compound mass*

solus (*adv.*) alone, on one's own **H5** II.i.42 [Nym to Pistol] *I would have you solus* ➤ **LATIN**, p.643

some (*n.*) someone, a person, one **Per** V.i.9 [Helicanus to Gentlemen] *there is some of worth would come aboard;* **R2** IV.i.267

something (*adv.*) **1** somewhat, rather **Ham** III.ii.352 [Hamlet to Rosencrantz] *the proverb is something musty* ➤ **FEW**, p.xxi
2 a little, to some extent **MM** I.i.61 [Angelo to Duke] *we may bring you something on the way;* **LL** II.i.55; **Tim** IV.iii.56

sometime (*adj.*) former, previous **KL** I.i.120 [Lear to Cordelia] *my sometime daughter;* **Cor** IV.i.23; **Ham** I.ii.8; **Sonn** 64.3

sometime (*adv.*) **1** formerly, at one time, once **Per** II.i.138 [Pericles to Fishermen, of his armour] *it was sometime target to a king;* **Cor** I.ix.81; **Cym** V.v.334; **Ham** III.i.114; **1H6** V.i.31; **MW** IV.v.27
2 sometimes, now and then **AC** IV.xiv.2 [Antony to Eros] *Sometime we see a cloud that's dragonish;* **2H6** II.iv.42; **3H6** II.ii.30; **JC** II.i.251; **KL** II.ii.19; **Venus** 277

sometimes (*adj.*) sometime, former, at one time **R2** I.ii.54 [Duchess of Gloucester to John of Gaunt] *Thy sometimes brother's wife;* **R2** V.i.37, v.75

sometimes (*adv.*) formerly, once, at one time, previously **MV** I.i.163 [Bassanio to Antonio, of Portia] *Sometimes from her eyes / I did receive fair speechless messages;* **Ham** I.i.49; **H8** II.iv.181; **Per** I.i.35; **R3** IV.iv.274

somewhat (*n.*) something **Tit** IV.i.9 [Titus to Young Lucius, of Lavinia] *somewhat doth she mean*

somewhither (*adv.*) ➤ **HITHER, THITHER, AND WHITHER**, p.224

son (*n.*) ➤ **FAMILY**, p.168

sonance (*n.*) sound, note **H5** IV.ii.33 [Constable to Dauphin] *let the trumpets sound / The tucket sonance* [F *Sonuance*]

song (*n.*) poem, set of verses, composition **Sonn** 102.14 *I would not dull you with my song;* **Sonn** 17.12

song of good life drinking song **TN** II.iii.34 [Feste to Sir Toby] *Would you have a love song, or a song of good life?* ➤ **good life**

sonnet (*n.*) **1** song, lyric **TN** III.iv.22 [Malvolio to Olivia] *it is with me as the very true sonnet is: 'Please one and please all'*
2 sonnet-writer **LL** I.ii.177 [Armado alone] *I am sure I shall turn sonnet*

sonneting (*n.*) sonnet-composition **LL** IV.iii.156 [Berowne to all] *none but minstrels like of sonneting!*

sonties (*n.*) ➤ **SWEARING**, p.435

soon (*adv.*) quickly, in a short time **Per** IV.i.3 [Dionyza to Leonine] *Thou canst not do a thing in the world so soon / To yield thee so much profit*

soon-speeding (*adj.*) quick-acting, rapidly working **RJ** V.i.60 [Romeo to Apothecary, of poison] *such soon-speeding gear / As will disperse itself through all the veins*

soopstake (*adv.*) swoopstake (*adv.*)

sooth (*n.*) **1** truth **MV** I.i.1 [Antonio to Salerio and Solanio] *In sooth I know not why I am so sad;* **H5** III.vi.140; **TN** II.iv.46; **TS** I.ii.256; **WT** IV.iv.173 ➤ **SWEARING**, p.435
2 flattery, ingratiation, appeasement **R2** III.iii.136 [King Richard to Aumerle, of Bolingbroke's sentence of banishment] *that e'er this tongue of mine .... should take it off again / With words of sooth!*
3 flattery, sycophant, sweet-talk **Per** I.ii.44 [Helicanus to Pericles] *Signor Sooth here does proclaim peace*

sooth (*adj.*) true **Mac** V.v.40 [Macbeth to Messenger] *If thy speech be sooth;* **H8** II.iii.30; **Mac** I.ii.36

sooth (*adv.*) truly **WT** IV.iv.344 [disguised Polixenes to Florizel] *Sooth, when I was young / And handed love as you do;* **TN** II.i.9; **WT** I.ii.17 ➤ **DISCOURSE MARKERS**, p.127

soothe (*v.*) **1** humour, encourage, indulge **CE** IV.iv.77 [Adriana to Pinch] *Is't good to soothe him in these contraries?;* **KL** III.iv.171; **R3** I.iii.297
2 flatter, praise, sweet-talk **Cor** II.ii.71 [Coriolanus to Brutus] *You soothed not, therefore hurt not;* **Cor** III.i.69
3 gloss over, smooth over **3H6** III.iii.175 [Lewis to Warwick, of Edward's letter] *to soothe your forgery and his, / Sends me a paper to persuade me patience?*

soothe up (*v.*) flatter, humour, play up to **KJ** III.i.121 [Constance to Austria] *Thou art perjured too, / And soothest up greatness*

soother (*n.*) flatterer, sycophant, adulator **1H4** IV.i.7 [Hotspur to Douglas] *I do defy / The tongues of soothers*

soothing (*n.*) **1** flattery, adulation, sweet-talk **Cor** I.ix.44 [Martius to all] *let courts and cities be / Made all of false-faced soothing*
2 reassurance, heartening **E3** III.i.7 [Lorraine to King John] *To lay aside unnecessary soothing*

soothing (*adj.*) flattering, sweet-talking **PassP** I.11 *O, love's best habit is a soothing tongue* ➤ **smoothing** (*adj.*)

soothsay (*v.*) tell the future, prophesy, make predictions **AC** I.ii.52 [Iras to Charmian] *you cannot soothsay*

soothsayer (*n.*) foreteller of events, prophet **JC** I.ii.19 [Brutus to Caesar] *A soothsayer bids you beware the ides of March;* **AC** I.ii.2; **Cym** V.v.427

sop (*n.*) piece of bread or cake steeped in liquid [before being eaten] **R3** I.iv.159 [Second Murderer to First Murderer, of throwing Clarence into a vat of wine] *make a sop of him;* **KL** II.ii.28; **TC** I.iii.113; **TS** III.ii.172

sophister (*n.*) sophist, cunning reasoner, clever debater **2H6** V.i.191 [Queen to all] *A subtle traitor needs no sophister*

sophisticated (*adj.*) removed from the simple state, no longer natural **KL** III.iv.102 [Lear to Edgar as Poor Tom] *Here's three on's are sophisticated* [i.e. by wearing clothes]

sore (*n.*) **1** affliction, suffering, sorrow **Tim** IV.iii.7 [Timon alone] *nature, / To whom all sores lay siege*

2 four-year-old buck **LL** IV.ii.58 [Holofernes to Nathaniel and Dull, of a deer] *Some say a sore* [pun: 58, hurt]

sore (*adj.*) **1** severe, harsh, heavy **Ham** V.ii.223 [Hamlet to Laertes] *I am punished with a sore distraction;* **Cym** III.vi.13; **Ham** I.i.75; **KL** III.v.21; **Per** IV.ii.32; **Tem** III.i.11

2 serious, grievous, grave **MV** V.i.307 [Gratiano to all] *I'll fear no other thing / So sore as keeping safe Nerissa's ring;* **Cym** IV.i.23; **H5** I.ii.26

3 violent, harsh, dreadful **Mac** II.iv.3 [Old Man to Ross] *this sore night / Hath trifled former knowings*

sore (*adv.*) seriously, greatly, very much **2H4** IV.iii.76 [Prince John to all] *I hear the King my father is sore sick;* **Cym** IV.ii.225; **RJ** I.iv.19; **TC** V.v.14; **Venus** 702; **WT** V.iii.49

sore-betrayed (*n.*) grievously deceived person **Lover** 328 *all that borrowed motion seeming owed, / Would yet again betray the sore-betrayed*

sorel (*n.*) three-year-old buck **LL** IV.ii.59 [Holofernes to Nathaniel and Dull, of a 'sore' deer] *put 'L' to sore, then sorel jumps from thicket*

sorely (*adv.*) **1** severely, intensely, very greatly **KL** II.iv.296 [Gloucester to all] *the bleak winds / Do sorely ruffle;* **AW** III.vi.40; **H8** IV.i.14; **WT** V.i.18

2 heavily, grievously, profoundly **Mac** V.i.50 [Doctor to Gentlewoman, of Lady Macbeth] *The heart is sorely charged*

sorrow (*n.*) mourning, lamentation **Tit** III.i.119 [Titus to Lavinia, of her brothers] *Witness the sorrow that their sister makes;* **H8** IV.ii.28; **WT** V.i.2; **Venus** 963

sorrow (*adj.*) sorry **Cym** V.v.297 [Cymbeline to Guiderius] *I am sorrow for thee*

sorrowed (*adj.*) sorrowful, regretful, crestfallen **Tim** V.i.147 [Second Senator to Timon, of the state] *[it] send forth us to make their sorrowed render*

sorrow-wreathen (*adj.*) folded in grief **Tit** III.ii.4 [Titus to Marcus] *unknit that sorrow-wreathen knot*

sorry (*adj.*) **1** sorrowful, painful, sad, pitiable **Mac** II.ii.20 [Macbeth to Lady Macbeth, of his bloodstained hands] *This is a sorry sight;* **CE** V.i.121; **H8** II.iv.26; **Mac** III.ii.9; **WT** II.i.123

2 awful, wretched, vile **Oth** III.iv.51 [Othello to Desdemona] *I have a salt and sorry rheum offends me* [F; Q *sullen*]

sort (*n.*) **1** class, level, social rank **H5** IV.vii.133 [King Henry to Fluellen, of Williams] *It may be his enemy is a gentleman of great sort;* **AY** I.i.156; **3H6** V.v.87; **MA** I.i.31; **MM** IV.iv.15; **Per** IV.ii.34

2 pack, crowd, gang **R2** IV.i.245 [Richard to all] *Mine eyes ... can see a sort of traitors here;* **2H6** II.i.162; **3H6** II.ii.97; **MND** III.ii.13, 21; **R3** V.iii.317

3 way, manner **Cor** I.iii.2 [Volumnia to Virgilia] *express yourself in a more comfortable sort;* **2H4** IV.v.200; **JC** I.ii.204; **MV** I.i.98; **MW** I.i.97; **Tim** II.ii.186

4 kind, variety, type **MV** I.i.88 [Gratiano to Antonio] *There are a sort of men whose visages / Do cream and mantle;* **Tem** II.i.106

5 assigned portion, allotted measure **JC** II.i.283 [Portia to Brutus] *Am I your self / But ... in sort or limitation*

6 lot [item drawn from a receptacle in a lottery] **TC** I.iii.376 [Ulysses to Nestor] *by device let blockish Ajax draw / The sort to fight with Hector*

sort (*v.*) **1** suit, be fitting, be appropriate **3H6** V.v.26 [Prince to and of Richard] *His currish riddles sorts not with this place;* **Ham** I.i.109; **3H6** II.i.208; **Luc** 1221; **MND** I.i.236; **R3** V.iii.174

2 choose, find, arrange **1H6** II.iii.26 [Talbot to Countess] *I'll sort some other time to visit you;* **3H6** V.vi.85; **Luc** 899; **MV** V.i.132; **R3** II.ii.148; **TG** III.ii.92

3 place, classify, put in the same class **Ham** II.ii.267 [Hamlet to Rosencrantz and Guildenstern] *I will not sort you with the rest of my servants*

4 associate, keep company with **Venus** 689 [Venus to Adonis, of the hunted hare] *Sometime he ... sorteth with a herd of deer;* **LL** I.i.250

5 correspond [to], be in agreement, conform [to] **TG** I.iii.63 [Antonio to Proteus, of Valentine] *My will is something sorted with his wish*

6 turn out, fall out, come about **MA** V.iv.7 [Antonio to Leonato] *I am glad that all things sort so well;* **2H6** I.ii.107; **MA** IV.ii.238; **MND** III.ii.352; **TS** IV.iii.43

7 fashion, frame, adapt **2H6** II.iv.68 [Gloucester to Duchess] *I pray thee sort thy heart to patience*

sort out (*v.*) arrange, contrive, prepare **RJ** III.v.109 [Lady Capulet to Juliet, of Capulet] *who, to put thee from thy heaviness, / Hath sorted out a sudden day of joy*

sortance (*n.*) agreement, correspondence, accord **2H4** IV.i.11 [Archbishop to Hastings and Mowbray, of Northumberland] *Here doth he wish his person, with such powers / As might hold sortance with his quality*

sot (*n.*) blockhead, idiot, dolt **Cym** V.v.178 [Iachimo to Cymbeline, of Posthumus] *his description / Proved us unspeaking sots;* **CE** II.ii.203; **KL** IV.ii.8; **MW** III.i.106; **Tem** III.ii.94; **TN** V.i.194

sot (*v.*) besot, make foolish **E3** II.i.81 [King Edward to Lodowick] *[write] To one that shames the fair and sots the wise*

sotted (*adj.*) turned into a fool, besotted **TNK** IV.ii.45 [Emilia alone] *I am sotted, / Utterly lost*

sottish (*adj.*) stupid, foolish, ludicrous **AC** IV.xv.78 [Cleopatra to all] *Patience is sottish*

soul (*n.*) **1** driving force, animating principle **Ham** II.ii.90 [Polonius to Claudius and Gertrude] *since brevity is the soul of wit;* **1H4** IV.i.50; **MND** II.i.182; **Tim** III.i.65; **TN** III.iii.56

2 inner conviction, personal impulse **MM** I.i.17 [Duke to Escalus, of Angelo] *we have with special soul / Elected him our absence to supply;* **TC** I.iii.285

3 conscience, heart, inner being **Oth** I.ii.31 [Othello to Iago] *My parts, my title, and my perfect soul / Shall manifest me rightly;* **KJ** V.i.10; **Sonn** 136.1; **TC** IV.v.111

4 real nature, essence **TC** IV.i.53 [Paris to Diomedes] *Even in the soul of sound good-fellowship;* **H5** IV.i.238

soul, half a halfwit, cretin, simpleton **Mac** III.i.82 [Macbeth to Murderers] *I made good to you ... all things else that might / To half a soul and to a notion crazed / Say, 'Thus did Banquo'*

soul-fearing (*adj.*) terrifying, petrifying **KJ** II.i.383 [Bastard to King John and King Philip, of firing their cannon] *Till their soul-fearing clamours have brawled down / The flinty ribs of this contemptuous city*

sound (*adj.*) **1** healthy, robust, uninfected **KJ** IV.ii.26 [Salisbury to King John, of his second coronation] *It ... / Makes sound opinion sick and truth suspected*

2 wholesome, beneficial **KJ** III.iv.26 [Constance as if to death] *Sound rottenness!*

3 free from error, orthodox **H8** V.iii.81 [Gardiner to Cromwell] *Ye are not sound*

4 unbroken **TN** I.iv.33 [Orsino to Viola as Cesario] *Thy small pipe / Is ... shrill and sound*

5 large, severe, serious **TNK** III.iv.8 [Gaoler's Daughter alone, of a ship] *There's a leak sprung, a sound one*

sound (*v.*) **1** sound out, question, examine **Ham** III.ii.374 [Hamlet to Rosencrantz and Guildenstern] *You would sound me from my lowest note to the top of my compass;* **Ham** II.i.42, III.i.7; **JC** II.i.141; **Tim** II.i.13

2 find out, ascertain, sound out **MW** II.i.219 [Ford alone] *I have a disguise to sound Falstaff;* **Cym** IV.ii.204; **2H4** IV.i.51; **1H6** I.i.63; **R2** I.i.8

3 cry out, declare, proclaim **TS** II.i.192 [Petruchio to Katherina] *Thy virtues spoke of, and thy beauty sounded;* **H8** V.ii.12; **JC** I.ii.142; **Luc** 717; **Per** III.Chorus.36; **RJ** III.ii.126

4 resound, ring, echo **2H4** I.iii.74 [Hastings to Lord Bardolph, of King Henry] *his coffers sound / With hollow poverty and emptiness*

5 pronounce, articulate, enunciate **2H6** IV.i.37 [Suffolk to Whitmore] *Thy name is Gualtier, being rightly sounded;* **JC** I.ii.144

6 inform with a call **Tim** IV.iv.1 [Alcibiades to Trumpeter] *Sound to this coward and lascivious town / Our terrible approach*

7 swoon, faint, pass out **Tit** V.i.119 [Aaron to Lucius, of Tamora] *She sounded almost at my pleasing tale;* **AY** V.ii.26; **Lover** 308 ➤ **swound** (v.)

sound (adv.) soundly, heartily, vigorously **MW** IV.iv.60 [Mistress Ford to all, of Falstaff] *Let the supposed fairies pinch him sound*

sounding (n.) **1** playing, making music **RJ** IV.v.139 [Peter to Third Musician] *musicians have no gold for sounding* [also: jingling]

2 sounding out, gauging depth, investigation **RJ** I.i.150 [Montague to Benvolio, of Romeo] *So far from sounding and discovery*

soundless (adj.) **1** noiseless, without sound **JC** V.i.36 [Brutus to Antony, of leaving Hybla bees stingless] *and soundless, too; / For you have stolen their buzzing*

2 beyond the ability to sound, unfathomable **Sonn** 80.10 [of a rival poet] *he upon your soundless deep doth ride*

soundly (adv.) **1** severely, strongly, dearly, in full **Tem** IV.i.263 [Prospero to Ariel, of Caliban, Stephano, and Trinculo] *Let them be hunted soundly;* **Tem** II.ii.77; **TNK** III.vi.52

2 thoroughly, properly, in full **RJ** IV.v.110 [Peter to First Musician, of their refusing to play] *I will then give it you soundly*

sour (adj.) bitter, harsh, painful **R2** IV.i.240 [Richard to all] *you Pilates / Have here delivered me to my sour cross;* **2H6** III.i.301; **3H6** V.vii.45; **LL** I.i.300; **R2** V.vi.20

sour (v.) give a morose expression, make sullen **Venus** 185 [of Adonis] *Souring his cheeks, cries 'Fie, no more of love!';* **R2** II.ii.169

souse (v.) swoop down on, beat away **KJ** V.ii.150 [Bastard to Lewis the Dauphin, of King John] *like an eagle o'er his eyrie towers / To souse annoyance that comes near his nest*

soused (adj.) preserved, pickled **1H4** IV.ii.12 [Falstaff alone] *If I be not ashamed of my soldiers, I am a soused gurnet*

south (n.) south wind [believed to bring storms, and plague-carrying mists] **Cor** I.iv.30 [Martius to his troops] *All the contagion of the south light on you;* **AY** III.v.50; **2H4** II.iv.358

south-fog (n.) contagion brought by the south wind **Cym** II.iii.130 [Cloten to Innogen, of Posthumus] *The south-fog rot him!*

sovereign (adj.) **1** excellent, excelling, superlative **LL** II.i.44 [Maria to Princess, of Longaville] *A man of sovereign parts he is esteemed;* **CE** III.i.168; **Cor** II.i.111; **1H4** I.iii.56; **Sonn** 153.8; **Venus** 28

2 leading, principal, outstanding **1H4** III.ii.161 [King Henry to Prince Hal] *Thou shalt have charge and sovereign trust herein* [or: trust of the King]

3 overpowering, unmitigated, extreme **AC** V.i.41 [Caesar to all] *let me lament / With tears as sovereign as the blood of hearts;* **KL** IV.iii.42

SOUNDS

People, animals, and objects all make noises that do not easily fall under the heading of vocabulary, but when they are written down on the page they pose similar issues of comprehension to conventional words. Authors always have a problem representing such noises, especially if they want their versions to have some immediacy of recognition, and some of the coinages used by Shakespeare have attracted not a little discussion about their exact usage, as a consequence, and are still open to interpretation.

Item	Location	Gloss
Noises and calls made by people		
do, de, do, de, do, de	KL III.iv.56	teeth chattering
hem	2H4 II.iv.29	unclear: hiccough, clearing of the throat
illo, ho, ho	Ham I.v.115–16	falconer's cry to bring a hawk down
hillo, ho, ho		
loo [= *halloo*]	TC V.vii.10	call of encouragement to a dog
rah tah tah	2H4 III.ii.274	gun drill noises
sa, sa, sa, sa	KL IV.vi.203	hunting cry
sese, sessa, sesey	KL III.vi.73	'off you go' in hunting, fencing
so-ho	TG III.i.189	hunting cry when a hare is started
sola	MV V.i.39	sound of a post horn
sola	LL IV.i.150	hunting cry
thas	2H4 III.ii.264	unintelligible military drill command
Noises made by animals		
tereu	PassP XX.14	nightingale in pain
tirra-lyra	WT IV.iii.9	lark song
wheak	Tit IV.ii.145	pig being killed
Noises made by objects		
bounce	2H4 III.ii.275	bang [of a gun]
hewgh	KL IV.vi.92	sound made by an arrow through the air

sovereignly *(adv.)* supremely, outstandingly, superlatively **WT** I.ii.323 [Camillo to Leontes, of Hermione] *So sovereignly being honourable*

sovereignty *(n.)* **1** pre-eminence, greatest excellence **TG** II.vi.15 [Proteus alone, of Julia] *Whose sovereignty so oft thou hast preferred;* **LL** IV.iii.232; **Luc** 36
  2 royal dignity, kingly authority **Cym** III.v.6 [Cymbeline to Lucius] *To show less sovereignty ... must needs / Appear unkinglike;* **H8** I.ii.150
  3 potency, efficacy, effectiveness **AW** I.iii.219 [Helena to Countess, of her father's prescriptions] *collected / For general sovereignty*
  4 control [of yourself], powers **Ham** I.iv.73 [Horatio to Hamlet, of the danger in following the Ghost] *Which might deprive your sovereignty of reason*

sow *(n.)* ingot, block, bar **TNK** V.iii.120 [Theseus to Emilia, of Palamon] *Alcides was / To him a sow of lead*

sowl *(v.)* pull, lug, seize roughly **Cor** IV.v.207 [Third Servingman to First Servingman, of Coriolanus] *He'll ... sowl the porter of Rome gates by th'ears*

Sowter *(n.)* [shoemaker, cobbler] name of a stupid hound **TN** II.v.120 [Fabian to Sir Toby, of Malvolio finding a scent] *Sowter will cry upon't for all this, though it be as rank as a fox*

space *(n.)* **1** space of time, while **AY** IV.iii.152 [Oliver to Rosalind and Celia disguised] *after some small space;* **AC** II.i.31; **AW** II.i.159, iii.180, IV.i.87; **KL** V.iii.54; **TNK** V.iii.129
  2 distance, separation **AW** I.i.218 [Helena alone] *The mightiest space in fortune nature brings / To join like likes*
  3 freedom from captivity; or: possession of property **KL** I.i.56 [Gonerill to Lear] *I love you ... / Dearer than eyesight, space, and liberty*
  4 ☛ mean space

span *(n.)* **1** hand breadth [from tip of thumb to tip of little finger, when the hand is extended] **AY** III.ii.127 [Celia reading, of a man] *the stretching of a span / Buckles in his sum of age* [i.e. life is so short;] **TC** II.ii.31
  2 span of life **Tim** V.iii.3 [Soldier alone, reading Timon's epitaph] *Timon is dead, who hath outstretched his span*

span *(v.)* measure out, delimit, determine **H8** I.i.223 [Buckingham to all] *My life is spanned already*

span-counter *(n.)* game in which counters were thrown to fall within a hand-span of the opponent's **2H6** IV.ii.148 [Cade to Stafford, of Henry V] *in whose time boys went to span-counter for French crowns*

spangle *(v.)* adorn brightly, add glitter to **Tim** III.vi.91 [Timon to Lords, of himself] *stuck and spangled with your flatteries;* **TS** IV.v.31

spaniel *(adj.)* obsequious, slavish, submissive **JC** III.i.43 [Caesar to Metellus] *sweet words, / Low-crooked curtsies and base spaniel fawning*

spaniel *(v.)* fawn upon, follow [like a spaniel] **AC** IV.xii.21 [Antony alone] *The hearts / That spanieled me at heels* [F *pannelled*]

spaniel-like *(adj.)* fawningly, slavishly, like a tame dog **TG** IV.ii.14 [Proteus alone, of Silvia] *spaniel-like, the more she spurns my love / The more it grows and fawneth on her still*

spare *(adj.)* **1** frugal, spartan, abstemious **H5** II.ii.131 [King Henry to Scroop, of other men] *are they spare in diet;* **AY** III.ii.18
  2 lean, thin, gaunt **2H4** III.ii.262 [Falstaff to Shallow] *O, give me the spare men;* **JC** I.ii.200

spare *(v.)* **1** omit, avoid, refrain [from] **Tim** IV.iii.139 [Timon to Phrynia and Timandra] *Spare your oaths;* **Cor** I.i.254; **Cym** II.iv.65; **KL** IV.ii.21; **Oth** II.iii.193; **R3** I.iii.113
  2 avoid, shun, keep away from **MND** II.i.142 [Titania to Oberon] *I will spare your haunts;* **WT** III.ii.42
  3 stop, desist **Tem** II.i.27 [Alonso to Gonzalo] *I prithee, spare*
  4 avoid offending, refrain from causing distress to **MM** II.iii.33 [disguised Duke to Juliet] *we would not spare heaven as we love it*
  5 practise economy in, be niggardly about **H8** V.iii.166 [King Henry to Cranmer] *you'd spare your spoons*

6 be free [at court], not needed **TNK** III.vi.129 [Arcite to Palamon] *every day discourse you into health, / As I am spared*

sparing *(n.)* economy, thrift, saving **RJ** I.i.218 [Romeo to Benvolio, of his love's chastity] *and in that sparing makes huge waste*

sparing *(adj.)* **1** forbearing, considerate, moderating **R3** III.vii.193 [Buckingham to Richard] *I give a sparing limit to my tongue*
  2 niggardly, frugal, miserly **Venus** 1147 [Venus to dead Adonis, of love] *It shall be sparing, and too full of riot*

sparingly *(adv.)* with restraint, discreetly, in a reserved way **R3** III.v.92 [Richard to Buckingham, of any reference to Edward's bastardy] *touch this sparingly, as 'twere far off;* **H5** I.ii.240

spark *(n.)* young blade, man about town, dude **AW** II.i.41 [Parolles to and of the Lords] *Good sparks and lustrous;* **AW** II.i.25

sparkle *(v.)* send out sparks **KJ** IV.i.114 [Arthur to Hubert, of the blinding iron] *it perchance will sparkle in your eyes*

spavin *(n.)* swelling of a horse's leg-joint **TS** III.ii.52 [Biondello to Tranio as Lucentio, of Petruchio's horse] *sped with spavins;* **H8** I.iii.12

speak *(v.)* **1** give an account of, report, describe **H8** IV.ii.32 [Katherine to Griffith, of Wolsey] *give me leave to speak him;* **Ham** III.ii.29; **1H4** V.ii.57; **H8** IV.i.61, ii.47; **KJ** III.i.39
  2 address, talk to, call upon **3H6** V.iv.24 [Queen to all] *As good to chide the waves as speak them fair;* **Tem** II.i.211
  3 proclaim, show, reveal **Tim** I.i.32 [Poet to Painter, of someone in his picture for Timon] *How this grace / Speaks his own standing!;* **Mac** IV.iii.159; **TNK** IV.ii.129
  4 declare itself, be announced **Ham** V.ii.196 [Hamlet to a Lord, of Claudius] *If his fitness speaks, mine is ready* [i.e. I am at his convenience;] **Cor** III.ii.41
  5 find language for, say in words about **Cor** II.ii.101 [Cominius to all, of Coriolanus] *I cannot speak him home*
  6 reprove, admonish, rebuke **KL** I.iii.26 [Gonerill to Oswald, of Lear] *I would breed from hence occasions ... / That I may speak*
  7 encounter, fight, exchange blows **Cor** I.iv.4 [Messenger to Martius, of the two sides] *They lie in view, but have not spoke as yet;* **AC** II.ii.169, vi.25

speak for *(v.)* demand, call for, cry out for **KL** I.iv.242 [Gonerill to Lear, of his men's behaviour] *The shame itself doth speak / For instant remedy*

speak holiday speak entertainingly; or: talk in a refined way **MW** III.ii.62 [Host to Page, of Fenton] *he speaks holiday*

speak of *(v.)* organize, order, sort out **MV** II.iv.5 [Salerio to all] *We have not spoke us yet of torchbearers*

speak on *(v.)* speak of **2H4** II.ii.61 [Poins to Prince Henry] *I am well spoke on*

speak out *(v.)* declare, manifest, display **H8** II.iv.140 [King Henry as if to Queen Katherine] *If thy rare qualities ... could speak thee out*

speak to bear witness to, attest, support **H8** II.iv.166 [King Henry to all, of Wolsey] *I speak my good lord Cardinal to this point*

speak with *(v.)* bring news to, talk to **H5** III.vi.84 [Fluellen to Gower, of King Henry] *I must speak with him from the pridge*

special *(adj.)* particular, specific, distinctive **E3** I.i.26 [Artois to King Edward, of the French] *that's the special ground of their contempt;* **AW** II.ii.6; **LL** I.i.150

specialty *(n.)* **1** obligation, bond, requirement **TC** I.iii.78 [Ulysses to all] *The specialty of rule hath been neglected*
  2 sealed contract, special agreement **TS** II.i.126 [Petruchio to Baptista] *Let specialties be therefore drawn between us;* **LL** II.i.165

speciously *(adv.)* malapropism for 'specially' **MW** III.iv.105 [Mistress Quickly alone] *I'll be as good as my word - but speciously for Master Fenton;* **MW** IV.v.102

spectacle *(n.)* thing to be seen, sight **TC** IV.iv.13 [Pandarus to himself, of Troilus and Cressida] *What a pair of spectacles is here!*

spectacle (v.) fit with spectacles, give glasses **Cor** II.i.198 [Brutus to Sicinius, of Coriolanus] *the bleared sights / Are spectacled to see him*

spectacles (n.) **1** instruments of vision, eyes **Cym** I.vii.37 [Iachimo to Innogen] *can we not / Partition make with spectacles so precious / 'Twixt fair, and foul?*; **2H6** III.ii.112

2 eye-glasses **2H6** V.i.165 [King to Salisbury] *wilt thou on thy deathbed play the ruffian, / And seek for sorrow with thy spectacles?* [or: sense 1]

spectatorship (n.) presentation to onlookers, display before spectators **Cor** V.ii.63 [Menenius to First Watch] *some death more long in spectatorship*

speculation (n.) **1** power of knowing, faculty of intelligence **Mac** III.iv.94 [Macbeth to Banquo's ghost] *Thou hast no speculation in those eyes / Which thou dost glare with*

2 power of sight, vision **TC** III.iii.109 [Achilles to Ulysses] *speculation turns not to itself / Till it hath travelled*

3 looking on, spectating, observation **H5** IV.ii.29 [Constable to Dauphin] *Though we upon this mountain's basis by / Took stand for idle speculation*

4 observer, watcher, agent **KL** III.i.24 [disguised Kent to Gentleman, of Albany and Cornwall's servants] *Which are to France the spies and speculations / Intelligent of our state*

speculative (adj.) seeing, observing, capable of vision **Oth** I.iii.267 [Othello to all] *light-winged toys / Of feathered Cupid seel with wanton dullness / My speculative and officed instruments*

speech (n.) conversation, talk, discourse **Mac** III.vi.1 [Lennox to a Lord] *My former speeches have but hit your thoughts*; **Ham** V.i.290

speed (n.) **1** success, fortune, good luck **TNK** I.iii.5 [Hippolyta to Pirithous, of Theseus] *Speed to him*; **E3** III.i.3; **1H4** III.i.184; **Oth** II.i.67; **TNK** I.iii.12

2 assistance, aid, protector **RJ** V.iii.121 [Friar to himself] *Saint Francis be my speed!*; **AY** I.ii.197; **TG** III.i.292

3 fate, lot, fortune **TS** II.i.138 [Baptista to Petruchio, of Katherina] *Well mayst thou woo, and happy be thy speed*; **Cym** III.v.162; **WT** III.ii.143

speed (v.) **1** meet with success, prosper, flourish **TG** IV.iv.104 [disguised Julia alone, of Proteus] *I would not have him speed*; **AC** II.iii.36; **AW** III.vii.44; **JC** I.ii.88; **KL** I.ii.19; **Tim** III.ii.63 **☛ POLITENESS**, p.340

2 fare, manage, get on **KJ** IV.ii.141 [Bastard to King John] *How I have sped among the clergymen / The sums I have collected shall express*; **Cym** V.iv.185; **1H6** II.i.48; **MV** V.i.115; **MW** II.ii.254; **TS** II.i.274

3 survive, succeed, prosper **E3** IV.ii.23 [King Edward to First Poor Man] *how do you imagine then to speed?*; **Cor** V.i.62; **E3** IV.iii.56

4 deal with, bring to an end, defeat **MV** II.ix.72 [Arragon, reading the portrait's schedule] *So be gone; you are sped*; **RJ** III.i.91; **TS** III.ii.52, V.ii.184

5 further, carry out, expedite **MM** IV.v.10 [Friar Peter to Duke, of the Duke's proposal] *It shall be speeded well*

6 travel speedily, make a hasty expedition **H8** I.ii.151 [Surveyor to King Henry] *before your highness speed to France*; **Sonn** 51.2

speeding (n.) **1** success, good fortune **Per** II.iii.115 [Simonides to Knights] *Tomorrow all for speeding do their best*; **TS** II.i.294

2 lot, fortune **PassP** XVII.16 *O cruel speeding, fraughted with gall*

speeding (adj.) effective, rapidly working, successful **H8** I.iii.40 [Lovell to Lord Chamberlain and Sands, of French-influenced Englishmen] *The sly whoresons / Have got a speeding trick to lay down ladies*

speken (v.) [archaism] speak **Per** II.Chorus.12 [Gower alone, of Pericles] *each man / Thinks all is writ he speken can* [i.e. everything he says is as true as the gospel] **☛ ARCHAISMS**, p.22

spell backward misrepresent, distort, conjure up a bad image of **MA** III.i.61 [Hero to Ursula, of Beatrice] *I never yet saw man … / But she would spell him backward*

spelling (adj.) incantatory, which work spells **1H6** V.iii.31 [Richard to Pucelle] *Unchain your spirits now with spelling charms*

spell-stopped (adj.) spellbound, mesmerized, transfixed **Tem** V.i.61 [Prospero to all] *There stand, / For you are spell-stopped*

spend (v.) **1** use up, wear out, exhaust, bring to an end **RJ** III.ii.130 [Juliet to Nurse, of her tears] *Mine shall be spent … for Romeo's banishment*; **Cym** V.iv.104; **2H4** III.ii.117; **R3** I.iii.124; **Sonn** 107.14; **Tim** III.v.22

2 expend, express, give vent to **2H6** V.ii.27 [York to himself] *On sheep or oxen could I spend my fury*; **Cor** II.i.50; **1H6** I.ii.16; **MND** III.ii.74; **Oth** I.ii.48; **Tim** I.ii.134

3 expend, employ, exert **Luc** 1457 [of a painting of Hecuba] *On this sad shadow Lucrece spends her eyes*; **AW** V.i.8; **Sonn** 80.3

4 waste, pass unprofitably **TC** IV.v.139 [Aeneas to Paris] *How have we spent this morning!*

5 be wasted, go by, pass by **R3** III.ii.88 [Derby to Hastings] *The day is spent* [i.e. it is getting on]

spend one's mouth [hunting] bark, bay, give tongue **Venus** 695 [Venus to Adonis, of hounds scenting a hare] *Then do they spend their mouths*; **H5** II.iv.70; **TC** V.i.87

sphere (n.) **1** celestial globe in which a heavenly body was thought to move, orbit **AC** IV.xv.10 [Cleopatra to all] *O sun, / Burn the great sphere thou mov'st in*; **AW** I.i.88; **1H4** V.iv.64; **KJ** V.vii.74; **MND** II.i.7; **TN** III.i.107 **☛ COSMOS**, p.102

2 globe, earth, world **Tim** I.i.69 [Poet to Painter, of people at the foot of Fortune's hill] *all kind of natures, / That labour on the bosom of this sphere*

3 place in the heavens **TC** I.iii.90 [Ulysses to all] *the glorious planet Sol / In noble eminence enthroned and sphered / Amidst the other*

4 star, planet **Lover** 23 [of the woman] *Sometimes her levelled eyes their carriage ride, / As they did batt'ry to the spheres intend*

5 (plural) orbits [of the eye], sockets **Ham** I.v.17 [Ghost to Hamlet] *Make thy two eyes like stars start from their spheres*; **Sonn** 119.7; **TNK** V.i.114

sphered (adj.) puffed out into the shape of a sphere, rounded, **TC** IV.v.8 [Ajax to trumpeter] *Blow, villain, till thy sphered bias cheek / Outswell the colic of puffed Aquilon*

spherical (adj.) of the spheres [stars], planetary **KL** I.ii.123 [Edmund alone] *as if we were … knaves, thieves, and treachers by spherical predomination* [F; Q spirituall]

sphery (adj.) star-like, heavenly, celestial **MND** II.ii.105 [Helena to herself] *What wicked and dissembling glass of mine / Made me compare with Hermia's sphery eyne?*

spice (n.) touch, trace, dash **Cor** IV.vii.46 [Aufidius to Lieutenant, of Coriolanus' faults] *As he hath spices of them all*; **H8** II.iii.26; **WT** III.ii.182

spicery (n.) spices **R3** IV.iv.424 [King Richard to Queen Elizabeth, of her daughter's womb] *that nest of spicery*

spigot (v.) wooden peg, tap [in a barrel] **MW** I.iii.19 [Pistol to Bardolph] *Wilt thou the spigot wield?*

spill (v.) destroy, overthrow **Luc** 1801 [Lucretius to Collatine, of Lucrece] *I did give that life / Which she … hath spilled*; **Ham** IV.v.20; **KL** III.ii.8

spilth (n.) spillage, slopping, upset **Tim** II.ii.165 [Flavius to Timon] *when our vaults have wept / With drunken spilth of wine*

spin (v.) gush, spurt, spray **H5** IV.ii.8 [Dauphin to Constable, of the horses] *That their hot blood may spin in English eyes*

spinner (n.) spider, cranefly, daddy-longlegs **MND** II.ii.21 [First Fairy, singing] *Hence, you longlegged spinners, hence*; **RJ** I.iv.62

spinster (n.) domestic woman, one who stays at home spinning **TN** II.iv.44 [Orsino to Viola as Cesario, of a song] *The spinsters … / Do use to chant it*; **H8** I.ii.33; **TNK** I.iii.23

spirit (n.) **1** disposition, temperament, frame of mind **JC** II.i.167 [Brutus to all] *We all stand up against the spirit of Caesar*; **3H6** V.iv.47; **JC** IV.i.33; **Sonn** 86.5; **Tim** III.i.35; **TS** Induction.ii.15

2 (plural) sentiments, faculties, traits of character **Oth** III.iv.62 [Othello to Desdemona, of his father] *his spirits should hunt / After new fancies*; **Ham** III.ii.68; **2H4** V.iv.125; **Tim** V.iv.74

3 life-supporting substance thought to be carried by the blood, animating essence **TC** III.iii.106 [Achilles to Ulysses, of the eye] *That most pure spirit of sense;* **2H4** IV.iii.108; **TC** I.i.59 ☞ **vital** *(adj.)*

4 intuition, perception, discernment **MV** V.i.70 [Lorenzo to Jessica] *your spirits are attentive;* **2H4** I.i.92; **LL** II.i.1

5 (plural) vital power, energy, vigour **MA** IV.i.110 [Don John to Don Pedro and Claudio, of the revelations about Hero] *These things … / Smother her spirits up*

6 courage, resolution, valour **TNK** V.iii.56 [Emilia to herself, of the trumpets] *Hark how yon spurs to spirit do incite / The princes to their proof*

7 hostility, anger, rage **Tim** III.v.103 [First Senator to Alcibiades, of his friend] *not to swell our spirit, / He shall be executed presently*

8 troublesome devil, high-spirited fiend **1H4** II.iv.361 [Falstaff to Prince Hal] *could the world pick thee out three such enemies again, as … that spirit Percy*

spirituality *(n.)* spiritual body, ecclesiastical estate **H5** I.ii.132 [Canterbury to King Henry] *we of the spirituality / Will raise your highness such a mighty sum*

spirt up *(v.)* sprout, shoot up, germinate **H5** III.v.8 [Dauphin to all] *Shall a few sprays of us … / Spirt up so suddenly into the clouds*

spit *(n.)* implement for cooking meat over a fire **MA** II.i.232 [Benedick to Don Pedro, of Beatrice] *She would have made Hercules have turned spit* [i.e. performed a very menial job]

spital *(n.)* hospital **H5** V.i.77 [Pistol alone] *News have I that my Doll is dead i'th' spital;* **H5** II.i.71

spital-house *(n.)* hospital inmates **Tim** IV.iii.40 [Timon alone] *She, whom the spital-house and ulcerous sores / Would cast the gorge at*

spite *(n.)* **1** annoyance, vexation, irritation **MND** III.ii.420 [Lysander alone] *I'll find Demetrius and revenge this spite;* **2H6** V.i.213; **Luc** 1600; **RJ** II.i.27; **TG** IV.ii.67; **TN** V.i.126

2 malice, ill-will, hatred **Ham** I.v.188 [Hamlet to himself] *The time is out of joint. O, cursed spite, / That ever I was born to set it right!;* **3H6** IV.vi.19; **RJ** I.i.78, v.62, IV.i.31; **Sonn** 37.3

3 irritate, mortify, vex **Mac** III.i.110 [Second Murderer to Macbeth] *I am reckless what I do / To spite the world;* **TS** IV.iii.11

spite of, in spite of *(prep.)* in defiance of **1H6** II.iv.106 [Somerset to Richard, of red roses] *these my friends in spite of thee shall wear;* **KJ** III.iv.9

spite of spite whatever happens, come what may **3H6** II.iii.5 [Warwick alone] *spite of spite, needs must I rest awhile;* **CE** II.ii.198

spite of spite, in despite everything, against all odds **KJ** V.iv.5 [Salisbury to Pembroke] *Faulconbridge, / In spite of spite, alone upholds the day*

spitting *(adj.)* piercing, penetrating, impaling **H8** II.iv.183 [King Henry to all] *This respite … entered me, / Yea, with a spitting power*

splay *(v.)* sterilize, spay **MM** II.i.219 [Pompey to Escalus] *Does your worship mean to geld and splay all the youth of the city?*

spleen *(n.)* **1** temper, spirit, passion [part of the body seen as the source of both gloomy and mirthful emotions] **E3** III.i.146 [Mariner to King John, of the navies] *Both full of angry spleen;* **TS** Induction.i.135 [Lord alone, of his men] *Haply my presence / May well abate the over-merry spleen;* **Cor** IV.v.94; **Oth** IV.i.89; **PassP** VI.6; **R3** V.iii.351; **TC** II.ii.129

2 irritability, malice, bad temper **H8** II.iv.89 [Wolsey to Queen Katherine] *I have no spleen against you;* **JC** IV.iii.47; **KJ** II.i.68; **R3** II.iv.64; **RJ** III.i.157; **TC** II.ii.197

3 eagerness, spirits, impetuosity **E3** I.i.160 [Prince Edward to King Edward] *As cheerful sounding to my youthful spleen / This tumult is;* **1H6** IV.vi.13; **KJ** II.i.448, V.vii.50

4 amusement, delight, merriment **LL** III.i.74 [Armado to Costard] *thou enforcest laughter; thy silly thought, my spleen;* **LL** V.ii.117; **TC** I.iii.178; **TN** III.ii.64

5 impulse, caprice, whim **1H4** V.ii.19 [Worcester to Vernon] *A hare-brained Hotspur, governed by a spleen;* **AY** IV.i.197; **MND** I.i.146; **TS** III.ii.10; **Venus** 907

spleenative *(adj.)* ☞ **splenetive** *(adj.)*

spleenful *(adj.)* passionate, furious, hot-headed **2H6** III.ii.128 [Warwick to King, of the people] *Myself have calmed their spleenful mutiny;* **Tit** II.iii.191

spleeny *(adj.)* hot-headed, over-emotional **H8** III.ii.99 [Wolsey to himself, of Anne] *Yet I know her for / A spleeny Lutheran*

spleet *(v.)* split, break up **AC** II.vii.122 [Caesar to Antony] *mine own tongue / Spleets what it speaks* ☞ **split** *(v.)*

splenitive, spleenative *(adj.)* of angry temperament, hot-headed **Ham** V.i.257 [Hamlet to Laertes] *I am not splenitive and rash*

splinter *(v.)* put in a splint, secure, bind up **Oth** II.iii.314 [Iago to Cassio, of Desdemona and Othello] *This broken joint between you and her husband, entreat her to splinter;* **R3** II.ii.118

split *(v.)* break up, split in two **E3** III.i.169 [Mariner to King John] *the reeling vessels split;* **3H6** V.iv.10; **JC** IV.iii.48; **Per** II.Chorus.32; **Tem** I.i.58; **TN** I.i.9 ☞ **spleet** *(v.)*

splitted *(adj.)* split in two, broken apart **2H6** III.ii.411 [Suffolk to Queen] *Even as a splitted bark so sunder we*

splitting *(adj.)* capable of causing ships to be split asunder **2H6** III.ii.97 [Queen to King] *The splitting rocks cowered in the sinking sands*

spoil *(n.)* **1** plundering, pillaging, despoiling **H5** III.iii.25 [King Henry to citizens of Harfleur] *We may as bootless spend our vain command / Upon th'enragèd soldiers in their spoil;* **Cor** II.i.209; **H5** III.iii.32; **2H6** IV.vii.125; **MV** V.i.85; **Sonn** 65.12

2 plunder, booty **E3** I.ii.64 [Countess to all] *Ye will not hence till you have shared the spoils;* **Cor** II.ii.122; **KJ** III.i.115; **Lover** 154; **TC** IV.v.62; **Tit** IV.iv.64

3 slaughter, destruction, ruination **3H6** V.iv.80 [Queen to her followers, of the enemy] *yonder is the wolf that makes this spoil;* **Cor** II.ii.118; **1H6** IV.iv.26; **JC** III.i.206, V.iii.7; **R3** IV.iv.290

4 [hunting] piece of the kill [given to a hound to stimulate its desire to hunt further] **AW** IV.iii.15 [Second Lord to First Lord, of Bertram and Diana] *this night he fleshes his will in the spoil of her honour*

spoil *(v.)* **1** plunder, pillage, sack **E3** I.i.128 [Montague to Edward] *Newcastle [is] spoiled and lost;* **AC** III.vi.25; **H5** IV.v.53

2 ruin, destroy, bring to an end **H5** IV.v.17 [Constable to Orleans] *Disorder that hath spoiled us, friend us now!;* **CE** V.i.37; **H8** I.ii.175; **TS** V.i.99

3 devastate, ravage, impoverish **KL** V.iii.276 [Lear to all] *I am old now / And these same crosses spoil me;* **TS** III.ii.53

4 seize by force, carry off, take away **3H6** II.ii.14 [Clifford to King] *Whose hand is that the forest bear doth lick? / Not his that spoils her young before her face*

5 badly injure, seriously hurt **Oth** V.i.54 [Cassio to Iago] *I am spoiled, undone by villains!*

spoiling *(n.)* mutilation, disfiguring, marring **TNK** V.iii.59 [Emilia to herself] *yet may Palamon wound Arcite to / The spoiling of his figure*

spongy, spungy *(adj.)* **1** rainy, damp, soggy, moisture-filled **Tem** IV.i.65 [Iris to Ceres] *Thy banks with pionèd and twillèd brims, / Which spongy April at thy hest betrims;* **Cym** IV.ii.349

2 soaked with drink, drunken **Mac** I.vii.71 [Lady Macbeth to Macbeth, of the King] *What cannot you and I … put upon / His spongy officers*

spoon *(n.)* christening spoon [given as a gift] **H8** V.iv.39 [Man to Porter] *The spoons will be the bigger;* **H8** V.iii.167

spoon *(v.)* let run [with little or no sail] **TNK** III.iv.9 [Gaoler's Daughter alone, of a ship] *Spoon her before the wind*

spoonmeat, spoon-meat *(n.)* soft food served on a spoon **CE** IV.iii.60 [Dromio of Syracuse to Antipholus of Syracuse] *expect spoonmeat, or bespeak a long spoon*

sport *(n.)* **1** recreation, amusement, entertainment **AC** I.i.47 [Antony to Cleopatra] *What sport tonight?* ☞ **FEW**, p.xxi

2 exercise, athletic pastime **Tem** III.i.1 [Ferdinand alone] *There be some sports are painful;* **AC** IV.xv.32

3 sexual recreation, intercourse, amorous dalliance **Oth** II.iii.17 [Iago to Cassio, of Desdemona] *she is sport for Jove;* **Oth** II.i.221, IV.iii.96; **Venus** 124

4 subject of sport **LL** IV.i.100 [Boyet to Princess, of Armado] *one that makes sport / To the prince;* **AW** IV.v.63; **MW** IV.iv.13

sport (*v.*) **1** make merry, take pleasure (in) **E3** II.i.235 [King Edward to Countess, of her beauty] *But thou mayst lend it me to sport withal;* **Tem** IV.i.74; **Venus** 154

2 amuse, entertain, divert **3H6** II.v.34 [King alone, of a shepherd's life] *So many hours must I sport myself;* **WT** II.i.60

sportful (*adj.*) **1** sporting, recreational, not in earnest **TC** I.iii.335 [Nestor to Ulysses, of Hector's challenge] *Though't be a sportful combat, / Yet in this trial much opinion dwells*

2 playful, frolicsome, wanton **TS** II.i.255 [Petruchio to Katherina] *let Kate be chaste and Dian sportful;* **3H6** V.i.18; **TN** V.i.363

sporting-place (*n.*) place of recreation **2H4** IV.ii.105 [Hastings to Archbishop, of their soldiers] *Each hurries toward his home and sporting-place*

sportive (*adj.*) **1** amorous, wanton, sexual **R3** I.i.14 [Richard alone] *I ... am not shaped for sportive tricks;* **Sonn** 121.6

2 light-hearted, full of amusement **AW** III.ii.106 [Helena alone, as if to Bertram] *I ... drive thee from the sportive court*

spot (*n.*) **1** stain, blemish, blot **AC** IV.xii.35 [Antony to Cleopatra] *the greatest spot / Of all thy sex;* **AW** V.iii.206; **KJ** V.ii.30, vii.107; **Luc** 1053

2 mark **JC** IV.i.6 [Antony to Lepidus, of Publius] *with a spot I damn him*

3 fault, vice, crime **Tim** IV.iii.343 [Timon to Apemantus, of being a leopard] *thou wert german to the lion, and the spots of thy kindred were jurors on thy life* [also: spots on the skin]

4 piece of embroidery **Cor** I.iii.53 [Valeria to Virgilia, of Virgilia's sewing] *A fine spot, in good faith*

spot (*v.*) stain, blemish, blot **Sonn** 95.3 [of shame] *Doth spot the beauty of thy budding name*

spotted (*adj.*) **1** stained, blemished **R2** III.ii.134 [King Richard to Scroop, of his lords] *Terrible hell / Make war upon their spotted souls for this;* **Luc** 721; **MND** I.i.110; **TC** V.iii.18; **Tit** I.iii.74; **WT** I.ii.328

2 person deemed guilty, one marked out for death **Tim** V.v.35 [Second Senator to Alcibiades] *And by the hazard of the spotted die / Let die the spotted* [second instance]

3 embroidered, patterned **Oth** III.iii.432 [Iago to Othello] *a handkerchief, / Spotted with strawberries*

spousal (*n.*) married union, state of wedlock **H5** V.ii.354 [Queen Isabel to King Henry and French King] *So be there 'twixt your kingdoms such a spousal*

spousal (*adj.*) marriage, nuptial, matrimonial **Tit** I.i.340 [Saturninus to all, of himself and his bride in the Pantheon] *There shall we consummate our spousal rites*

spout (*n.*) water-spout **TC** V.ii.174 [Troilus to Ulysses] *the dreadful spout, / Which shipmen do the hurricano call*

sprag (*adj.*) pronunciation of 'sprack': smart, active, alert **MW** IV.i.77 [Evans to Mistress Page, of William] *He is a good sprag memory* ☞ **WELSH**, p.649

sprawl (*v.*) writhe, struggle, thrash about **3H6** V.v.39 [Richard to Prince] *Sprawlest thou?* [i.e. in pain]; **Tit** V.i.51

spray (*n.*) branch, limb, offshoot **2H6** II.iii.45 [Suffolk to all, of Gloucester] *Thus droops this lofty pine and hangs his sprays;* **H5** III.v.5; **3H6** II.vi.50

spread (*v.*) **1** cover, envelop, enfold **TNK** I.i.64 [Theseus to First Queen] *Not Juno's mantle fairer than your tresses, / Nor in more bounty spread her* [i.e. covered her no more fully]

2 lay the table **CE** II.ii.196 [Luciana to Dromio of Syracuse] *go bid the servants spread for dinner;* **2H4** V.iii.8

spright (*n./v.*) ☞ sprite (*n./v.*)

sprightful, spriteful (*adj.*) spirited, animated, lively **KJ** IV.ii.177 [King John to himself, of Bastard] *Spoke like a sprightful noble gentleman!*

sprightfully, spritefully (*adv.*) spiritedly, in a lively manner **R2** I.iii.3 [Lord Marshal to Aumerle] *The Duke of Norfolk, sprightfully and bold*

sprighting, spriting (*n.*) activities as a spirit **Tem** I.ii.298 [Ariel to Prospero] *I will ... do my spriting gently*

sprightly, spritely (*adj.*) **1** cheerful, light-hearted, bright **AC** IV.vii.15 [Antony to Scarus] *I will reward thee / Once for thy sprightly comfort;* **AC** IV.xiv.52; **Cym** III.vii.47; **TC** II.ii.191

2 ghostly, spectral, supernatural **Cym** V.v.429 [Posthumus to Lucius] *methought / Great Jupiter ... / Appeared to me, with other spritely shows*

sprightly, spritely (*adv.*) cheerfully, merrily, in a lively way **WT** IV.iv.53 [Florizel to Perdita, of his guests] *Address yourself to entertain them sprightly*

spring (*n.*) **1** first moment, dawn, break **MND** II.i.82 [Titania to Oberon] *never since the middle summer's spring / Met we on hill, in dale, forest, or mead;* **2H4** IV.iv.35

2 sapling, shoot, young growth **Venus** 656 [Venus to Adonis, of solicitude] *This canker that eats up Love's tender spring;* **Luc** 869, 950; **Venus** 127

3 closing device, locking mechanism **Cym** II.ii.47 [Iachimo to himself] *To th'trunk again, and shut the spring of it*

spring, latter youthful old age **1H4** I.ii.156 [Prince Hal to Falstaff] *Farewell, the latter spring!*

spring (*v.*) spring up, rise up, multiply **KL** IV.iv.17 [Cordelia to Doctor, as if to the herbs of the earth] *All you unpublished virtues of the earth, / Spring with my tears!;* **3H6** II.vi.17

springe (*n.*) snare, trap **Ham** V.ii.300 [Laertes to Osrick] *as a woodcock to mine own springe;* **Ham** I.iii.115; **WT** IV.iii.34

springhalt (*n.*) [of horses] disease causing twitching of the hind legs **H8** I.iii.13 [Sands to Lord Chamberlain, of the effect of France upon the English] *One would take it ... the spavin / Or springhalt reigned among 'em*

springing (*adj.*) growing, sprouting, developing **Venus** 417 [Venus to Adonis] *If springing things be any jot diminished, / They wither in their prime*

sprite, spright (*n.*) **1** spirit, ghost, supernatural being **WT** II.i.26 [Mamillius to all, of a story] *I have one / Of sprites and goblins;* **CE** II.ii.199; **Mac** II.iii.76; **TC** III.ii.31; **Tem** II.ii.114

2 spirit, feeling, frame of mind **Mac** IV.i.126 [First Witch to Witches, of Macbeth] *Come, sisters, cheer we up his sprites;* **Luc** 121; **Venus** 181

3 spirit, soul **Luc** 1728 [of Lucrece] *Her contrite sighs unto the clouds bequeathed / Her winged sprite*

sprite, spright (*v.*) torment, haunt [as if by a spirit] **Cym** II.iii.138 [Innogen to Pisanio, of Cloten] *I am sprited with a fool*

spriteful, spritefully, spritely, spriting ☞ sprightful (*adj.*); sprightfully (*adv.*); sprighting (*n.*); sprightly (*adj./adv.*)

spruce (*adj.*) **1** brisk, lively, smart **TS** IV.i.101 [Grumio to Servants] *Now, my spruce companions*

2 over-elegant, smart **LL** V.i.13 [Holofernes to Nathaniel, of Armado] *He is too picked, too spruce, too affected;* **LL** V.ii.407

spungy (*adj.*) ☞ spongy (*adj.*)

spur (*n.*) **1** eagerness, alacrity, enthusiasm **Tim** III.vi.66 [Timon to Lords] *Each man to his stool, with that spur as he would to the lip of his mistress*

2 root of a tree, main root **Tem** V.i.47 [Prospero alone] *Have I ... by the spurs plucked up / The pine and cedar;* **Cym** IV.ii.58

spur, on the at a gallop **JC** V.iii.29 [Pindarus to Cassius] *Titinius is enclosed round about / With horsemen, that make to him on the spur*

spurn (*n.*) **1** contemptuous treatment, scornful rejection **Ham** III.i.73 [Hamlet alone] *the spurns / That patient merit of th'unworthy takes;* **Tim** I.ii.138

2 hurt, blow, knock **Tit** III.i.101 [Titus to all] *that which gives my soul the greatest spurn / Is dear Lavinia*

spurn (*v.*) **1** reject, scorn, despise, treat with contempt **TG** IV.ii.14 [Proteus alone, of Silvia] *the more she spurns my love / The more it grows and fawneth on her still;* **Cor** V.iii.165; **Cym** V.v.294; **KJ** III.i.142; **Mac** III.v.30; **R3** I.iv.201

2 kick, strike, stamp [on], dash **MV** I.iii.128 [Antonio to Shylock] *I am as like … / To spit on thee again, to spurn thee too;* **CE** II.i.83; **Cym** IV.i.18; **JC** III.i.46; **KJ** II.i.24; **MND** III.ii.225

spurn against / at (*v.*) kick out at, treat with contempt **E3** I.i.50 [King Edward to Artois, of the French] *That spurn against my sovereignty in France;* **Luc** 880 [Lucrece as if to opportunity] *'Tis thou that spurn'st at right, at law, at reason;* **Ham** IV.v.6; **2H4** V.ii.89; **JC** II.i.11; **Luc** 1026; **Venus** 311

spurring (*n.*) ability to use spurs **Tim** IV.iii.154 [Timon to Phrynia and Timandra, of disease] *And mar men's spurring* [possibly with bawdy pun]

spy (*n.*) **1** [of eyes] observer, watcher, witness **Tem** V.i.259 [Trinculo to all] *If these be true spies which I wear in my head*

2 [unclear meaning] opportunity to spy, watch-keeping **Mac** III.i.129 [Macbeth to Murderers] *Within this hour … / I will … / Acquaint you with the perfect spy o'th' time*

spy (*v.*) perceive, observe, behold **1H6** I.i.127 [Third Messenger to all, of Talbot] *His soldiers, spying his undaunted spirit;* **3H6** IV.vi.28

squadron (*n.*) army detachment, body of soldiers **AC** III.ix.1 [Antony to Enobarbus] *Set we our squadrons on yond side o'th' hill;* **E3** IV.iv.50; **1H6** IV.ii.23; **JC** II.ii.20; **Oth** I.i.22

squander (*v.*) scatter, disperse, dissipate **MV** I.iii.21 [Shylock to Bassanio, of Antonio] *he hath … other ventures he hath squandered abroad* [or: send recklessly]

squandering (*adj.*) random, stray, accidental **AY** II.vii.57 [Jaques to Duke Senior] *the squandering glances of the fool*

square (*n.*) **1** type of measuring instrument, especially for right angles **AC** II.iii.6 [Antony to Octavia] *I have not kept my square* [i.e. kept to the straight line]; **1H4** II.ii.12

2 rule, canon; or: proper constitution, normal condition **KL** I.i.74 [Regan to Lear] *the most precious square of sense possesses*

3 square piece of material covering the chest, embroidered breast-piece **WT** IV.iv.212 [Servant to Clown, of Autolycus] *you would think a smock were a she-angel, he so chants to the sleevehand and the work about the square on't*

4 formation, squadron, body of troops **H5** IV.ii.26 [Constable to Dauphin, of the English army] *our peasants, / Who in unnecessary action swarm / About our squares of battle*

5 affairs, proceedings **AC** III.xi.40 [Antony to Eros, of Octavius] *He … no practice had / In the brave squares of war* [or: sense 4]

square, by the accurately, exactly, with great precision **LL** V.ii.474 [Berowne to Boyet, of the Princess] *Do not you know my lady's foot by the square;* **WT** IV.iv.336

square, out of abnormal, disordered, deviant **TNK** IV.iii.94 [Doctor to Wooer, of their plan for the Gaoler's Daughter] *This may … reduce what's now out of square in her into their former law and regiment*

square (*adj.*) **1** good, sturdy, sound **TNK** V.i.111 [Palamon praying to Venus, of an old man] *the aged cramp / Had screwed his square foot round*

2 right, fair, just **Tim** V.iv.36 [First Senator to Alcibiades] *it is not square to take, / On those that are, revenges* [i.e. those still alive]

3 true, accurate, justified **AC** II.ii.190 [Maecenas to Enobarbus, of Cleopatra] *She's a most triumphant lady, if report be square to her*

4 broad, wide **Per** V.i.108 [Pericles to himself, of Thaisa compared to Marina] *My queen's square brows*

square (*v.*) **1** quarrel, fall out, disagree **AC** III.xiii.41 [Enobarbus to himself] *Mine honesty and I begin to square;* **AC** II.i.45; **MND** II.i.30; **Tit** II.i.100, 124

2 judge, measure, appraise **TC** V.ii.135 [Troilus to Ulysses] *do not give advantage / To stubborn critics, apt, without a theme / For depravation, to square the general sex / By Cressid's rule*

3 base, form, shape **AW** II.i.150 [Helena to King] *with us that square our guess by shows*

4 regulate, direct, adapt **Tit** III.ii.31 [Titus to Marcus and Lavinia] *how franticly I square my talk;* **MM** V.i.479

5 rule, direct, influence **WT** V.i.52 [Leontes to Paulina] *O that ever I / Had squared me to thy counsel!;* **WT** III.iii.40

squarer (*n.*) brawler, swaggerer, quarrelsome person **MA** I.i.75 [Beatrice to Messenger, of Benedick] *Is there no young squarer now that will make a voyage with him to the devil?*

squash (*n.*) **1** unripe pea-pod **TN** I.v.152 [Malvolio to Olivia, of the age of Viola as Cesario] *as a squash is before 'tis a peascod*

2 youngster, youth **WT** I.ii.160 [Leontes to Hermione, of Mamillius] *How like, methought, I then was to this kernel, / This squash, this gentleman*

squeny, squiny (*v.*) make squint **KL** IV.vi.138 [Lear to Gloucester] *Dost thou squiny at me?;* **KL** III.iv.112

squier (*n.*) ➤ **square** (*n.*) **1**

squiny (*v.*) ➤ **squeny** (*v.*)

squire (*n.*) **1** gentleman below a knight in rank, attendant on a knight or nobleman **H5** IV.viii.77 [Exeter to King Henry] *other lords and barons, knights and squires;* **AC** IV.iv.14; **1H4** I.ii.24; **KL** I.iv.237, III.ii.88

2 lad, fellow, youngster **WT** I.ii.171 [Leontes to Polixenes, of Mamillius compared to Florizel] *So stands this squire / Officed with me;* **MND** II.i.131

3 young lover, beau, gallant **MA** I.iii.48 [Don John to Borachio, of Claudio] *A proper squire!*

4 [contemptuous] servant, follower, attendant **Cym** II.iii.122 [Cloten to Innogen, of Posthumus] *a squire's cloth*

5 [contemptuous] fellow **1H6** IV.i.23 [Talbot to all, of Falstaff] *This dastard … / Like to a trusty squire did run away;* **Oth** IV.ii.144 ➤ **mountain-squire** (*n.*)

squire-like (*adv.*) like an attendant, submissively **KL** II.iv.209 [Lear to all, of France] *I could as well be brought / To knee his throne and, squire-like, pension beg*

squirility (*n.*) ➤ **scurrility** (*n.*)

-st (*ending*) ➤ **VERB FORMS**, p.481

stable (*adj.*) **1** constant, immutable, firm **E3** IV.v.78 [Charles to King John] *rather let me leave to be a prince / Than break the stable verdict of a prince*

2 steady, poised, self-possessed **TN** IV.iii.19 [Sebastian alone, of Olivia being mad] *if 'twere so, / She could not sway her house … / With such a smooth, discreet, and stable bearing*

stableness (*n.*) stability **Mac** IV.iii.92 [Malcolm to Macduff] *verity, temperance, stableness … / I have no relish of them*

stablish (*v.*) variant of 'establish' ➤ **ELISION**, p.146

stablishment (*n.*) confirmed possession, settlement **AC** III.vi.9 [Caesar to all, of Antony and Cleopatra] *Unto her / He gave the stablishment of Egypt*

staff (*n.*) **1** (plural 'staves') spear, lance **MA** V.i.135 [Claudio to Don Pedro, of Benedick] *give him another staff;* **AY** III.iv.40; **2H4** IV.i.118; **KJ** II.i.318; **Mac** V.vi.28; **R3** V.iii.65;

2 handle, shaft [of a weapon] **TNK** IV.ii.115 [Pirithous to Theseus, of one of Palamon's knights] *He wears a well-steeled axe, the staff of gold*

3 baton, rod of office **Mac** V.iii.48 [Macbeth to Seyton] *give me my staff* [or: sense 1]

4 stanza, verse **LL** IV.ii.103 [Holofernes to Nathaniel, of the letter] *Let me hear a staff, a stanze, a verse*

staff, set in one's make oneself at home, take up abode **CE** III.i.51 [Dromio of Ephesus to Luce] *shall I set in my staff?*

stage (*n.*) platform, dais, stand **Ham** V.ii.390 [Fortinbras to all] *Bear Hamlet like a soldier to the stage;* **Ham** V.ii.372; **TNK** V.iv.123

stage (v.) put on stage, put on public display **AC** V.ii.217 [Cleopatra to Iras] *The quick comedians / Extemporally will stage us*; **AC** III.xiii.30; **MM** I.i.68

stagger (v.) **1** hesitate, waver, vacillate **TNK** IV.i.10 [First Friend to Gaoler] *the Duke / Methought stood staggering*; **AY** III.iii.45; **MM** I.ii.164
2 make stagger, cause to reel **R2** V.v.109 [Richard to Exton] *That hand shall burn in never-quenching fire / That staggers thus my person*

staggers (n.) **1** horse disease marked by a staggering movement **TS** III.ii.53 [Biondello to Tranio as Lucentio, of Petruchio's horse] *spoiled with the staggers*
2 unsteadiness, reeling, giddiness **Cym** V.v.233 [Posthumus to himself] *How comes these staggers on me?*; **AW** II.iii.162

staid (adj.) balanced, settled, calm **Cym** III.iv.10 [Innogen to Pisanio] *Put thyself / Into a haviour of less fear, ere wildness / Vanquish my staider senses*

stain (n.) **1** disgrace, shame **1H6** IV.i.45 [King to Falstaff] *Stain to thy countrymen*; **Cor** I.x.18; **1H4** III.i.181; **MM** III.i.203
2 pollution, defilement **Tim** V.i.171 [Timon to First Senator, of Alcibiades] *Giving our holy virgins to the stain / Of contumelious, beastly, mad-brained war*
3 object stained with blood [as of a martyr] **JC** II.ii.89 [Decius to Caesar] *great men shall press / For tinctures, stains, relics, and cognizance*
4 hint, tinge, dash **AW** I.i.110 [Helena to Parolles] *You have some stain of soldier in you*; **TC** I.ii.26

stain (v.) **1** corrupt, spoil, taint **AW** II.i.120 [King to Helena] *we must not / So stain our judgement or corrupt our hope*; **Ham** IV.iv.57; **KJ** IV.ii.6; **Sonn** 109.11
2 eclipse, belittle, put in the shade **AC** III.iv.27 [Antony to Octavia] *I'll raise the preparation of a war / Shall stain your brother*; **R2** III.iii.66; **Tim** I.i.16
3 obscure, hide, blot out **Sonn** 35.3 *Clouds and eclipses stain both Moon and Sun* [also: sense 1]

stained (adj.) **1** full of disgrace, dishonouring **1H6** III.iii.57 [Pucelle to Burgundy] *wash away thy country's stained spots*; **Luc** 1059, 1316
2 blood-stained, discoloured with dirt **KJ** II.i.357 [Bastard to King John and King Philip] *Back to the stained field*; **1H4** V.iv.12
3 dyed black **TNK** I.i.25 [stage direction] *Enter three Queens in black, with veils stained*

staining (adj.) disgraceful, dishonourable, shameful **AW** III.vii.7 [Widow to Helena] *would not put my reputation now / In any staining act*

stair (n.) ladder **RJ** II.iv.185 [Romeo to Nurse] *my man shall ... bring thee cords made like a tackled stair*

stake (n.) **1** place of execution **KL** II.i.61 [Gloucester to Edmund, of Edgar] *Bringing the murderous coward to the stake*
2 [bear-baiting] post to which a bear is chained **2H6** V.i.144 [York to Clifford, of Warwick and Salisbury] *Call hither to the stake my two brave bears*

stake, at the [bear-baiting] under attack; or [gambling]: at risk **AW** III.iii.148 [King to Bertram] *My honour's at the stake*; **JC** IV.i.48; **TN** III.i.115

stale (n.) **1** [falconry] decoy, lure, stalking-horse **Tem** IV.i.187 [Prospero to Ariel] *The trumpery in my house, go bring it hither / For stale to catch these thieves*; **TS** III.i.88
2 dupe, sap, laughing-stock **1H6** III.iii.260 [Warwick alone, of Edward] *Had he none else to make a stale but me?*; **CE** II.i.101; **MW** II.iii.27; **Tit** I.i.307; **TS** I.i.58
3 prostitute, wanton, harlot **MA** IV.i.63 [Don Pedro to Leonato, of Hero] *To link my dear friend to a common stale*; **MA** II.ii.23
4 urine **AC** I.iv.62 [Caesar to Lepidus, as if to Antony] *Thou didst drink / The stale of horses and the gilded puddle / Which beasts would cough at*

stale (adj.) **1** ancient, long-standing, antiquated **TNK** V.iv.11 [Palamon to his knights] *we come towards the gods ... not halting under crimes / Many and stale*; **Lover** 268
2 past the time, no longer of value **Luc** 1362 *now 'tis stale to sigh, to weep, and groan*
3 worn-out, hackneyed, faded **2H4** II.iv.127 [Doll to Pistol] *you basket-hilt stale juggler, you!*; **WT** V.i.13
4 unfresh, old, deteriorating **RJ** II.iv.130 [Mercutio to Romeo, of Nurse] *a hare ... in a lenten pie, that is something stale and hoar ere it be spent* [also: (n.) sense 3]
5 worn out, past the prime of life **Cym** III.iv.52 [Innogen to Pisanio] *Poor I am stale, a garment out of fashion*; **TNK** V.i.85

stale (v.) **1** make stale, wear out **AC** II.ii.240 [Enobarbus to Maecenas and Agrippa, of Cleopatra] *Age cannot wither her, nor custom stale / Her infinite variety*; **Cor** I.i.90; **JC** I.ii.73, IV.i.38
2 depreciate, make cheap, lower the dignity of **TC** II.iii.189 [Ulysses to Agamemnon, of Ajax] *[he] Must not so stale his palm, nobly acquired, ... / By going to Achilles* [F, Q *staule*]

stalk (v.) move stealthily [as if hunting game] **Luc** 365 [of Tarquin] *Into the chamber wickedly he stalks*

stalk on (v.) move stealthily in concealment [as by using a stalking-horse to catch game] **MA** II.iii.94 [Claudio to himself, of Benedick] *stalk on, stalk on, the fowl sits*

stalking-horse (n.) horse behind which a hunter hides, to stalk game **AY** V.iv.103 [Duke Senior to Jaques, of Touchstone] *He uses his folly like a stalking-horse*

stall (n.) stand in front of a shop displaying goods for sale **Cor** II.i.202 [Brutus to Sicinius] *Stalls, bulks, windows / Are smothered up*

stall (v.) **1** install, place, appoint **E3** III.i.30 [King John to all, of King Edward] *we hear the Emperor conjoins, / And stalls him in his own authority*; **R3** I.iii.205
2 keep close, place, stow away **AW** I.iii.120 [Countess to Steward, of Helena's thoughts] *Stall this in your bosom*
3 dwell, live, settle **AC** V.i.39 [Caesar to all, of him and Antony] *We could not stall together / In the whole world*
4 [hunting] bring to a stand, come within range of **PassP** XVIII.2 [Pilgrim] *When as thine eye hath ... stalled the deer that thou shouldst strike*

stall (v.) tether, settle as in a stable **Venus** 39 *The steed is stalled up*

stalling (n.) stall accommodation, living quarters **AY** I.i.9 [Orlando to Adam] *the stalling of an ox*

stallion (n.) **1** prostitute, hooker, whore **Ham** II.ii.585 [Hamlet alone] *a very drab, / A stallion!* [Q1 *scalion*; Q2 *stallyon*; F *scullion*]
2 ☛ **staniel** (n.)

stammer (v.) describe poorly, undervalue **TNK** II.i.27 [Gaoler's Daughter to Gaoler, of Palamon and Arcite] *I think fame but stammers 'em*

stamp (n.) **1** impression, mark, imprint **Ham** III.iv.169 [Hamlet to Gertrude] *For use almost can change the stamp of nature*; **Cor** I.vi.23; **Cym** V.v.367; **1H4** IV.i.4; **MV** II.ix.39; **R3** I.iii.255
2 coin, impression [of the monarch's head] made on a coin **E3** II.i.256 [Countess to King Edward] *He that doth clip or counterfeit your stamp / Shall die*; **Cym** V.v.24; **Mac** IV.iii.153; **MM** II.iv.46; **MW** III.iv.16

stamp (v.) **1** press, impress, coin **TNK** I.i.216 [Theseus to Hippolyta] *I stamp this kiss upon thy current lip*; **E3** II.i.259; **Oth** II.i.236
2 authenticate, endorse, validate **MA** I.i.6 [Antonio to Leonato, of the news being good] *As the event stamps them*; **Cor** V.ii.22
3 make an impression of, mint, conceive **Cym** II.iv.157 [Posthumus alone, of his father] *[he] was I know not where / When I was stamped*

stamped (adj.) marked [as with a stamp], imprinted **R3** I.i.16 [Richard alone] *I ... am rudely stamped*

stanch (adj.) ☛ **staunch** (adj.)

stanch (*v.*) satisfy, quench, allay **Tit** III.i.14 [Titus to Tribunes and Senators] *Let my tears stanch the earth's dry appetite*

stanchless, staunchless (*adj.*) unquenchable, insatiable, incapable of being satisfied **Mac** IV.iii.78 [Malcolm to Macduff] *there grows / In my most ill-composed affection such / A staunchless avarice*

stand (*n.*) **1** [hunting] standing-place, hiding-place **MW** V.v.227 [Falstaff to all] *you have ta'en a special stand to strike at me;* **Cym** II.iii.69, III.iv.110; **3H6** III.i.3; **LL** IV.i.10

2 post, position, station **3H6** IV.iii.1 [First Watchman to all] *each man take his stand;* **MM** IV.vi.10

3 stop, pause, standing still **RJ** I.v.50 [Romeo to himself, of Juliet] *The measure done, I'll watch her place of stand;* **MV** V.i.77; **TC** III.iii.252

stand (*v.*) **1** be, appear **RJ** III.iii.166 [Friar to Romeo, before telling him his options] *here stands all your state;* **AW** II.i.112; **2H4** I.iii.15; **2H6** II.i.187; **MV** I.i.136; **TS** I.ii.52

2 continue, remain, wait, stay put **Mac** III.i.4 [Banquo alone, as if to Macbeth, of his becoming king] *It should not stand in thy posterity;* **E3** IV.ii.83; **1H6** I.iii.11; **3H6** II.iii.25; **KJ** III.i.89; **TNK** III.ii.20

3 stop, halt **MA** III.iii.25 [Dogberry to Second Watchman] *you are to bid any man stand, in the Prince's name;* **Cor** V.vi.127; **Cym** V.iii.88; **E3** II.i.346; **Ham** I.i.142; **TG** IV.i.3

STAGE DIRECTIONS

Several of the words and phrases used in stage directions continue to be used in modern theatre; but a number are typical of the period, in some cases relating to the particular configuration (insofar as this can be deduced) of the Elizabethan theatre.

Item	Example	Gloss
Speech		
aside	**Ham** III.i.50	speech not heard by other characters on stage
Movement directions		
above	**TNK** II.i.48	in the gallery or upper stage
aloft	**AC** IV.xv.1	on the upper stage
aloof	**TNK** V.i.137	to one side, a short distance away
apart	**Mac** I.iii.126	to one side, away from the others
aside	**AC** II.vii.57	to one side, away from the others
below	**AC** IV.xv.6	on the lower stage
break in	**2H6** I.iv.40	burst on to the stage
brought out	**KL** II.ii.138	brought on to the stage
enter	**KJ** I.i.1	one or more characters come on to the stage
exeunt	**H8** V.v.76	more than one character leaves the stage
exit	**KL** I.ii.118	a character leaves the stage
in	**Cor** III.i.228	into the dressing-room at the back of the stage
manent	**Cor** I.i.250 [F only]	characters remain on stage
off	**AY** I.ii.209	off-stage
severally, several ways	**Cym** III.iv.195	in different directions [said of people arriving or leaving]
top, on the	**Tem** III.iii.19	on the upper stage
within	**TNK** V.iii.77	behind the stage façade [i.e. 'outside']
Events		
alarum, alarums	**H5** IV.iv.1	a call to arms
excursions *excursion, in an*	**2H6** V.ii.72	a bout of fighting across the stage
Music		
cornet	**AW** I.ii.1	fanfare [as played by cornets, a horn-like wind instrument]
drum	**1H6** I.ii.1	drummer
flourish	**1H6** I.i.1	fanfare of horns or trumpets, usually accompanying an entrance or exit
hautboys	**H8** I.iv.1	woodwind double-reed instrument resembling an oboe
sennet	**AC** II.vii.17	trumpet call signalling a procession
trump, trumpet	**KL** V.iii.109	trumpeter
tucket	**AC** I.iii.213	personal trumpet call

4 stand still, stop, cease moving **Ham** V.i.252 [Hamlet to all] *Conjures the wandering stars, and makes them stand;* **Cor** II.ii.119; **MND** III.ii.424; **TNK** III.vi.93, 107

5 make a stand, be resolute [on a point] **RJ** II.iv.33 [Mercutio to Benvolio] *these fashion-mongers ... who stand so much on the new form;* **CE** V.i.31; **1H4** I.ii.139; **MW** II.i.215

6 be placed, set, arrange **TNK** IV.ii.50 [Emilia alone, of the pictures of Palamon and Arcite] *Stand both together;* **Tim** IV.iii.363

7 dwell on, waste time with, rely upon **MW** III.iii.117 [Mistress Page to Mistress Ford] *never stand 'you had rather' and 'you had rather'!*

8 waste time, delay, wait **JC** V.iii.43 [Cassius to Pindarus] *Stand not to answer;* **3H6** IV.viii.23; **TG** V.ii.44

9 act as, be, hold good as **2H4** III.ii.215 [Bullcalf to Bardolph] *stand my friend;* **Cor** II.iii.189; **E3** IV.v.91; **KL** I.i.39; **Tit** I.i.20; **TS** IV.iv.21

10 stand in, impersonate, represent **KL** I.iv.141 [Fool to Lear, of a lord] *Do thou for him stand;* **LL** V.ii.505; **Tim** V.i.35

11 depend, remain dependent, continue **KL** V.i.69 [Edmund alone] *my state / Stands on me to defend;* **Ham** I.i.119

12 accord, agree, hold good, be compatible **Cor** II.iii.84 [Coriolanus to Fourth Citizen] *if it may stand with the tune of your voices that I may be consul;* **AY** II.iv.88; **2H4** IV.i.182; **3H6** III.iii.38; **MA** V.iv.29

13 make a stand [against], fight, resist **Cym** V.iii.60 [Posthumus to Lord] *Who dares not stand his foe;* **AW** I.ii.15; **Cor** III.i.245; **E3** IV.vi.29; **1H6** I.i.123; **JC** III.i.89

14 withstand, endure, stand up to **KL** III.vii.53 [Gloucester to all] *I am tied to the stake, and I must stand the course;* **AC** I.i.74, iv.20; **2H4** II.ii.35; **Tim** V.i.5; **TS** I.ii.111

stand by (*v.*) **1** stay close, be near at hand **AC** III.xi.41 [Cleopatra to all] *Ah, stand by*

2 stand aside, draw back **MA** IV.i.21 [Claudio to Friar] *Stand thee by*

3 support, uphold, maintain **TN** III.i.9 [Viola as Cesario to Feste] *So thou mayst say ... the Church stands by thy tabor, if thy tabor stand by the church*

stand for (*v.*) **1** defend, uphold, protect, support **Cor** II.ii.39 [Menenius to the assembly, of Coriolanus] *it remains, / ... To gratify his noble service that / Hath thus stood for his country;* **Cor** IV.vi.45; **Cym** III.v.57; **H5** I.ii.101; **MM** III.i.9; **WT** III.ii.44

2 represent, serve, uphold **Cor** II.i.219 [Sicinius to Brutus] *Doubt not / The commoners, for whom we stand*

3 be a candidate for, offer for election **Cor** II.iii.186 [Brutus to Citizens, of Coriolanus] *his worthy deeds did claim no less / Than what he stood for*

4 take the place of, serve in lieu of **R2** II.iii.67 [Bolingbroke to Ross and Willoughby] *Evermore thank's the exchequer of the poor, / Which till my infant fortune comes to years / Stands for my bounty*

5 be acceptable as, be valid as **TS** Induction.ii.123 [Page as Sly's wife to Sly, of staying out of Sly's bed] *I hope this reason stands for my excuse*

stand in (*v.*) stand on, insist on the need for **Tit** IV.iv.105 [Saturninus to Aemilius, of Lucius] *if he stand in hostage for his safety, / Bid him demand what pledge will please him best*

stand off (*v.*) **1** stand back, draw back **TNK** III.vi.89 [Palamon to Arcite] *Stand off then* [i.e. take up your fighting position]

2 stand out, be plain **H5** II.ii.103 [King Henry to Scroop, of his guilt] *the truth of it stands off as gross / As black and white*

3 be distinguishable, differ, remain separate **AW** II.iii.119 [King to Bertram] *our bloods ... yet stands off / In differences so mighty*

stand on (*v.*) **1** insist on, demand, call for **RJ** III.iii.89 [Romeo to Friar] *I stand on sudden haste;* **H5** V.ii.94; **2H6** III.i.261; **JC** II.ii.13; **MW** II.i.207; **R2** IV.i.33

2 give (oneself) over to **CE** I.ii.80 [Antipholus of Syracuse to Dromio of Ephesus] *I shall break that merry sconce of yours / That stands on tricks when I am undisposed*

stand out (*v.*) **1** not take part, not be involved **Cor** I.i.239 [Martius to Lartius] *What, art thou stiff? Stand'st out?*

2 resist, hold out, refuse to yield **R2** I.iv.38 [Green to King Richard] *for the rebels which stand out in Ireland, / Expedient manage must be made*

stand to (*v.*) **1** maintain, uphold, be steadfast in **Cor** III.i.207 [Brutus to Sicinius] *let us stand to our authority;* **2H4** II.i.4; **H8** II.iv.86; **RJ** IV.iv.145; **TC** I.ii.130

2 stand by, side with, support **Cor** V.iii.200 [Coriolanus to Aufidius] *Stand to me in this cause;* **2H4** II.i.62; **3H6** II.iii.51

3 come forward, set to work **Tem** III.iii.50 [Alonso to Gonzalo] *I will stand to and feed;* **Mac** II.iii.32

stand to it (*v.*) **1** swear to it, insist upon it **AY** I.ii.63 [Touchstone to Rosalind] *I'll stand to it the pancakes were naught;* **1H4** III.iii.160

2 fight stoutly, get down to business **Mac** III.iii.15 [First Murderer to all, attacking Banquo] *Stand to't!;* **AW** III.ii.40

3 be steadfast, stand firm, make a stand **Cor** IV.vi.10 [Brutus to Sicinius] *We stood to't in good time;* **AW** II.i.29

stand under (*v.*) suffer, endure, bear the weight of **H8** V.i.112 [Cranmer to King Henry] *There's none stands under more calumnious tongues / Than I myself;* **MW** II.ii.280

stand up (*v.*) confront boldly, make a stand **JC** II.i.167 [Brutus to all] *We all stand up against the spirit of Caesar;* **Cor** II.iii.14; **KL** III.vii.79

stand up for (*v.*) defend, support, champion **AC** I.i.191 [Antony to Enobarbus, of Pompey] *who, high in name and power, / Higher than both in blood and life, stands up / For the main soldier*

stand upon (*v.*) **1** make an issue of, insist upon, bother about **MW** II.ii.19 [Falstaff to Pistol] *You stand upon your honour;* **AC** II.i.50; **Cor** II.ii.148; **2H4** I.i.36; **Tit** I.iii.124; **WT** IV.iv.166

2 make advantageous, profit from, make the most of **E3** IV.iii.9 [Charles to Villiers] *are not all occasions / That happen for advantage of our foes / To be accepted of and stood upon?*

3 concern, be of importance to **CE** IV.i.68 [Angelo to Antipholus of Ephesus] *Consider how it stands upon my credit;* **R3** IV.ii.57

4 depend on, rely upon, hinge on **2H4** III.i.143 [Falstaff to Shallow, of Wart] *his apparel is built upon his back, and the whole frame stands upon pins;* **MND** I.i.139

5 be the duty of, be incumbent upon **R2** II.iii.137 [Ross to York, of Bolingbroke] *It stands your grace upon to do him right;* **Ham** V.ii.63

stand with (*v.*) accompany, go along with, attend **E3** II.ii.74 [Lodowick to King Edward] *the drum that stroke the lusty march / Stands with Prince Edward*

standard (*n.*) **1** flag, ensign **R3** V.iii.265 [Richmond to his soldiers] *Advance your standards;* **2H6** I.i.254; **LL** IV.iii.343; **R3** V.iii.349

2 ensign, flagbearer, standard-bearer **Tem** III.ii.15 [Stephano to Caliban] *thou shalt be my lieutenant, monster, or my standard* [pun: 16, person capable of standing]

stander (*n.*) supporter, sustainer, prop **TC** III.iii.84 [Achilles to Patroclus, of honours] *when they fall, as being slippery standers* [i.e. not giving a firm foothold]

stander-by (*n.*) bystander, onlooker, spectator **TC** IV.v.190 [Nestor to Hector] *I have said unto my standers-by;* **R3** I.iii.209

standing (*n.*) **1** continuing existence, duration **WT** I.ii.431 [Camillo to Polixenes, of Leontes' folly] *will continue / The standing of his body* [i.e. as long as he lives]

2 status, position, stature **Tim** I.i.32 [Poet to Painter, of someone in his picture for Timon] *How this grace / Speaks his own standing!*

3 not ebbing or flowing **TN** I.v.154 [Malvolio to Olivia, of Viola as Cesario] *'Tis with him in standing water between boy and man* [i.e. at the turn of the tide]

standing (*adj.*) **1** stagnant, not flowing **Tem** V.i.33 [Prospero alone] *Ye elves of hills, brooks, standing lakes;* **KL** III.iv.127; **Tem** II.i.225

2 standing on end, upright, upended **1H4** II.iv.243 [Falstaff to Prince Hal] *you vile standing tuck!*

standing-bowl *(n.)* bowl standing on a pedestal **Per** II.iii.65 [Simonides to Thaisa, of Pericles] *we drink this standing-bowl of wine to him;* **H8** V.v.1

staniel *(n.)* inferior kind of hawk; kestrel **TN** II.v.112 [Sir Toby to Fabian, of Malvolio] *with what wing the staniel checks at it!* [F *stallion*]

stanze *(v.)* stanza **LL** IV.ii.103 [Holofernes to Nathaniel, of the letter] *Let me hear a staff, a stanze, a verse*

stanzo *(n.)* stanza, verse **AY** II.v.16 [Jaques to Amiens] *Come, more, another stanzo*

staple *(n.)* fibre, texture, material **LL** V.i.17 [Holofernes to Nathaniel, of Armado] *He draweth out the thread of his verbosity finer than the staple of his argument*

star *(n.)* **1** planet **RJ** II.ii.15 [Romeo to himself, of Juliet's eyes] *Two of the fairest stars in all the heaven*
2 pole-star, lodestar, guiding star **MA** III.iv.51 [Margaret to Beatrice] *there's no more sailing by the star;* **Sonn** 116.7
3 fate, fortune, destiny [as determined by the stars] **TNK** V.i.69 [Palamon to his knights] *Our stars must glister with new fire;* **3H6** IV.vi.22; **KL** II.i.22; **R2** IV.i.21 ☞ **COSMOS**, p.102
4 sphere, fortune, rank **TN** II.v.139 [Malvolio reading the letter] *In my stars I am above thee;* **Ham** I.iv.32, II.ii.141

star-blasting *(n.)* bad influence of the stars **KL** III.iv.57 [Edgar as Poor Tom to Lear] *Bless thee from whirlwinds, star-blasting, and taking!* [F; Q *starre-blusting*]

Star-Chamber *(n.)* supreme court of justice **MW** I.i.2 [Shallow to Evans] *I will make a Star-Chamber matter of it;* **E3** II.ii.163

star-crossed *(adj.)* thwarted by a malign star **RJ** Prologue.6 [Chorus] *A pair of star-crossed lovers take their life*

stare *(n.)* state of amazement, horror-struck condition **Tem** III.iii.96 [Gonzalo to Alonso] *why stand you / In this strange stare?*

stare *(v.)* **1** glare, glower, look madly **JC** IV.iii.40 [Brutus to Cassius] *Shall I be frighted when a madman stares?*
2 stand on end **JC** IV.iii.278 [Brutus to Caesar's Ghost] *Art thou ... some devil, / That mak'st my blood cold, and my hair to stare?*

star-gazer *(n.)* astrologer, almanac-writer **Venus** 509 [Venus to Adonis] *the star-gazers, having writ on death, / May say, the plague is banished by thy breath*

staring *(n.)* insulting stare, glaring, gawping **MW** V.v.158 [Evans to all, of Falstaff] *given to ... swearings and starings*

staring *(adj.)* glaring, wild, truculent **Venus** 1149 [Venus to dead Adonis, of love] *The staring ruffian shall it keep in quiet*

stark *(adj.)* rigid, stiff [as in death] **1H4** V.iii.40 [Prince Hal to Falstaff] *Many a nobleman lies stark and stiff;* **Cym** IV.ii.209; **RJ** IV.i.103

starkly *(adv.)* stiffly, rigidly, set fast **MM** IV.ii.64 [Claudio to Provost] *guiltless labour / When it lies starkly in the traveller's bones*

starred *(adj.)* born under a star **WT** III.ii.98 [Hermione to Leontes, of her baby] *Starred most unluckily*

start *(n.)* **1** starting up, immediate reaction, sudden movement **TN** II.v.57 [Malvolio to himself, of Sir Toby] *Seven of my people, with an obedient start, make out for him*
2 outburst, eruption, fit, reaction **KL** I.i.299 [Regan to Gonerill, of Lear's behaviour] *Such unconstant starts are we like to have from him;* **1H4** III.ii.125; **2H6** IV.viii.42; **Mac** III.iv.62
3 advantage, edge, upper hand **MW** V.v.159 [Falstaff to all] *You have the start of me;* **JC** I.ii.130; **MV** II.ii.5; **TNK** II.ii.8

start, on the without warning, with sudden appearance **AW** III.ii.49 [Countess to Lords, of joy and grief] *the first face of neither on the start / Can woman me unto't*

starts, by / in in fits and starts **TN** II.ii.21 [Viola alone, of Olivia] *she did speak in starts, distractedly;* **AC** IV.xii.7; **H5** Epilogue.4

start *(v.)* **1** jump, recoil, flinch **Mac** I.iii.50 [Banquo to Macbeth, on seeing the Witches] *why do you start, and seem to fear;* **2H6** II.iv.35; **H8** III.ii.113; **Luc** 1639; **R3** III.v.7; **Tem** IV.i.139
2 startle, alarm, disturb **TC** V.ii.104 [Cressida to Diomedes] *one cannot speak a word / But it straight starts you;* **AW** V.iii.232; **E3** II.ii.47; **Mac** V.v.15; **Oth** I.i.102; **TN** IV.i.58
3 jump away, swerve, turn aside **Ham** III.ii.317 [Guildenstern to Hamlet] *start not so wildly from my affair;* **1H6** IV.vii.12; **R3** III.iv.85
4 fly off, move off **CE** II.i.30 [Adriana to Lucinda] *How if your husband start some otherwhere?;* **2H4** I.i.46
5 [hunting] raise from cover **1H4** I.iii.196 [Hotspur to all] *the blood more stirs / To rouse a lion than to start a hare!*
6 hurry, rush, hasten **MA** IV.i.158 [Friar to all, of Hero] *I have marked / A thousand blushing apparitions / To start into her face;* **1H4** I.iii.214; **KL** IV.iii.31; **Luc** 1037
7 raise up, call up **JC** I.ii.146 [Cassius to Brutus] *'Brutus' will start a spirit as soon as 'Caesar'*

starting *(n.)* **1** removal, displacement, breaking away **Cym** V.v.372 [Cymbeline to Arviragus and Guiderius] *after this strange starting from your orbs, / You may reign in them now!*
2 startle reaction, flinching, recoiling **Mac** V.i.43 [Lady Macbeth as if to Macbeth, while sleepwalking] *You mar all with this starting*

starting *(adj.)* bounding, eager, energetic **TC** IV.v.2 [Agamemnon to Ajax] *With starting courage, / Give with thy trumpet a loud note to Troy*

starting-hole *(n.)* bolt-hole, loophole, evasion **1H4** II.iv.258 [Prince Hal to Falstaff, of his lying] *what starting-hole canst thou now find out, to hide thee from this open and apparent shame?*

startingly *(adv.)* in fits and starts, disjointedly **Oth** III.iv.79 [Desdemona to Othello] *Why do you speak so startingly and rash?*

start-up *(n.)* upstart, opportunist, climber **MA** I.iii.61 [Don John to Borachio, of Claudio] *That young start-up hath all the glory of my overthrow*

starve *(v.)* **1** die, perish **CE** II.i.88 [Adriana to Luciana, of her husband] *I at home starve for a merry look;* **Cym** I.v.165; **1H4** I.ii.20; **1H6** III.iii.48; **2H6** I.i.133; **H8** V.iii.132
2 bring to death, kill off **RJ** I.i.219 [Romeo to Benvolio, of Rosaline] *beauty, starved with her severity*
3 withhold [from], diet, be sparing with **MND** I.i.222 [Hermia to Lysander] *We must starve our sight / From lovers' food till morrow deep midnight;* **LL** II.i.11
4 show hunger, reflect starvation **RJ** V.i.70 [Romeo to Apothecary] *Need and oppression starveth in thy eyes*
5 destroy, wither, waste away **Tim** I.i.252 [Apemantus to Alcibiades] *Aches contract and starve your supple joints!;* **Per** I.iv.38; **TG** IV.iv.151

starve out *(v.)* endure in fierce cold **TC** V.x.2 [Aeneas to all] *here starve we out the night*

starved *(adj.)* **1** frozen-stiff, near-perished with cold **2H6** III.i.343 [York to himself, of his fellow lords] *I fear me you but warm the starved snake;* **Tit** III.i.250
2 meagre, insubstantial, wanting **TC** I.i.95 [Troilus alone, of the quarrel over Helen] *It is too starved a subject for my sword*
3 scrawny, lean, emaciated **2H4** III.ii.293 [Falstaff alone, of Shallow] *This same starved justice hath done nothing but prate to me of the wildness of his youth*

starveling *(n.)* **1** starved individual, emaciated being **E3** IV.vi.37 [Philip to King John, of Prince Edward and his men] *Some twenty naked starvelings with small flints;* **1H4** II.i.70
2 skinny individual, lanky fellow **1H4** II.iv.240 [Falstaff to Prince Hal] *you starveling*

state *(n.)* **1** condition, circumstances, situation, state of affairs **2H6** IV.ix.31 [King to all] *Thus stands my state, 'twixt Cade and York distressed;* **CE** II.i.95; **H8** V.i.127; **JC** I.iii.71; **KL** II.ii.167; **Tim** II.ii.130
2 status, rank, position **3H6** IV.i.68 [Lady Grey to all] *it pleased his majesty / To raise my state to title of a queen;* **AY** V.iv.172; **Cym** V.v.98; **3H6** II.ii.152; **Mac** IV.ii.66; **TN** I.v.267
3 persons of rank, nobility, court, council of state **Cym** III.iv.38 [Pisanio to Innogen] *Kings, queens, and states;* **Ham** V.ii.219; **TC** IV.ii.67, v.264; **Tim** I.ii.1

4 splendour, magnificence, stateliness, dignity **LL** V.ii.590 [Holofernes to Mote] *Keep some state in thy exit, and retire;* **Cym** III.iii.78; **2H4** III.i.13; **Per** III.i.63; **R2** V.i.18; **Tim** IV.ii.35

5 ceremony, celebration **RJ** IV.iii.8 [Juliet to Lady Capulet] *We have culled such necessaries / As are behoveful for our state tomorrow*

6 kingship, majesty, sovereignty **H5** I.ii.274 [King Henry to Ambassador] *tell the Dauphin I will keep my state;* **2H4** V.ii.99; **3H6** III.iii.93; **H8** II.iv.228; **KJ** II.i.97; **KL** I.i.149

7 ruler, sovereign, monarch **KJ** II.i.395 [Bastard to King John and King Philip, of his advice] *How like you this wild counsel, mighty states?*

8 throne, chair of state **1H4** II.iv.371 [Falstaff to Prince Hal] *This chair shall be my state;* **Cor** V.iv.21; **H8** I.iv.85; **KJ** III.i.70; **Mac** III.iv.5; **TN** IV.v.44

9 [also: cloth of state] canopy over a chair of state **H8** II.iv.1 [stage direction] *The King takes place under the cloth of state;* **H8** I.iv.1, V.iii.1

10 government, ruling body, administration **H8** I.i.101 [Norfolk to Buckingham, of Wolsey] *The state takes notice of the private difference / Betwixt you and the Cardinal;* **AC** I.iv.41; **Ham** I.i.101; **JC** I.ii.159; **KJ** IV.ii.8; **Tem** I.ii.70

11 estate, property, wealth, means **MV** III.ii.259 [Bassanio to Portia] *I told you / My state was nothing;* **1H4** IV.i.46; **Luc** 45; **Tim** I.i.70, ii.196; **TNK** IV.iii.66; **TS** I.ii.90

12 welfare, well-being, prosperity **WT** IV.iv.445 [Perdita to Florizel] *Of your own state take care;* **AC** II.ii.43; **2H6** III.ii.284, IV.x.21

13 bearing, demeanour, bodily form **LL** IV.iii.183 [Browne to all] *When shall you hear that I / Will praise a hand, a foot, a face … in state*

14 stately phrasing, high-flown expressions **TN** II.iii.142 [Maria to Sir Toby, of Malvolio] *he is … an affectioned ass that cons state without book*

state-statue (*n.*) image of a statesman **H8** I.ii.88 [Wolsey to King Henry, of not taking action for fear of criticism] *We should take root here where we sit, / Or sit state-statues only*

station (*n.*) **1** stance, bearing, posture **AC** III.iii.19 [Messenger to Cleopatra, of Octavia] *Her motion and her station are as one;* **Ham** III.iv.59

2 place to stand in, spot to see from **Cor** IV.v.32 [Third Servingman to Coriolanus] *take up some other station;* **Cor** II.i.207

statist (*n.*) statesman, politician, man of affairs **Cym** II.iv.16 [Posthumus to Philario] *Statist though I am none;* **Ham** V.ii.33

statua (*n.*) statue **R3** III.vii.25 [Buckingham to Richard, of the citizens] *like dumb statuas or breathing stones, / Stared each on other* [F *statue*]

statue (*n.*) ☞ statute (*n.*) 1

stature (*n.*) height **Per** V.i.108 [Pericles to himself, of Thaisa compared to Marina] *her stature to an inch*

statute (*n.*) **1** law, decree, regulation **MA** III.iii.77 [Dogberry to Verges] *any man that knows the statutes* [F *Statues*]; **Cor** I.i.82; **MM** V.i.318

2 bond securing a debt with the debtor's land; legal security **Ham** V.i.102 [Hamlet to Horatio, of a lawyer] *a great buyer of land, with his statutes;* **Sonn** 134.9

statute-cap (*n.*) woollen cap ordered (by an Act of 1571) to be worn on Sundays and holy days by all below a certain social rank **LL** V.ii.281 [Rosaline to all, of the King and his friends] *better wits have worn plain statute-caps* ☞ **CLOTHING**, p.79

staunch, stanch (*adj.*) water-tight, steadfast, firm **AC** II.ii.120 [Caesar to Antony] *if I knew / What hoop should hold us staunch*

staunch (*v.*) ☞ stanch (*v.*)

stave (*n.*) staff, rod **TN** V.i.281 [Feste to Olivia, of Malvolio] *he holds Beelzebub at the stave's end* [i.e. keeps him at bay] ☞ staff (*n.*) 1

stay (*n.*) **1** staying, remaining, continued presence **1H6** IV.vi.40 [Talbot to his son, of the benefits of the latter's leaving the battle] *All these, and more, we hazard by thy stay;* **Sonn** 15.9; **TG** I.iii.75; **Tim** III.vi.34, 116

2 support, prop **3H6** II.i.69 [Edward to Richard, as if to York] *Now thou art gone, we have no staff, no stay;* **1H6** II.v.13; **KJ** V.vii.68; **R3** II.ii.74; **TC** V.iii.60

3 set-back, obstacle, delay **KJ** II.i.455 [Bastard to himself, of Hubert's suggestion] *Here's a stay / That shakes the rotten carcass of old death / Out of his rags!;* **Luc** 328

stay (*v.*) **1** wait (for), await **CE** III.i.36 [Dromio of Ephesus to Dromio of Syracuse] *My master stays in the street;* **H8** I.iii.63; **KJ** II.i.58; **R2** I.iii.5; **Tit** IV.iii.42; **TS** V.iii.59

2 linger, tarry, delay **CE** IV.i.87 [Dromio of Syracuse to Antipholus of Ephesus] *there's a bark of Epidamnum / That stays but till her owner comes aboard;* **AW** V.iii.69; **1H4** IV.i.75; **3H6** I.iv.110; **MV** IV.i.239; **TG** III.i.366

3 delay, defer, postpone **H8** III.ii.33 [Surrey to all] *the Cardinal did entreat his holiness / To stay the judgement o'th' divorce*

4 remain, continue, endure **Sonn** 92.3 *And life no longer than thy love will stay / For it depends upon that love of thine;* **AC** II.ii.181; **E3** IV.vii.59; **3H6** II.i.187; **Sonn** 48.3

5 keep, make to stay, allow to remain **AY** I.iii.65 [Duke Frederick to Celia, of Rosalind] *we stayed her for your sake;* **2H6** I.i.73; **TG** II.ii.15

6 stay put on, maintain a presence on **Venus** 894 [of Venus' senses] *Like soldiers, when their captain once doth yield, / They basely fly and dare not stay the field*

7 detain, confine, keep **H8** I.i.5 [Buckingham to Norfolk] *An untimely ague / Stayed me a prisoner in my chamber;* **AY** I.i.7; **JC** II.ii.75; **RJ** V.iii.187; **Tit** II.iii.181; **TS** IV.ii.83

8 stop, prevent, end **3H6** II.v.95 [King to himself, of the killings he has seen] *O that my death would stay these ruthful deeds!;* **LL** III.i.90; **R3** III.vii.96; **RJ** V.iii.12, iii.251; **TS** Induction.i.132

9 stop, halt, come to a standstill **KJ** III.i.78 [King Philip to Constance] *the glorious sun / Stays in his course;* **AY** II.i.54, III.i.319; **RJ** IV.iii.57; **TNK** V.i.101

10 dissuade, stop, prevent **1H6** I.v.2 [Talbot alone] *Our English troops retire, I cannot stay them;* **AY** I.i.125; **2H4** IV.i.121; **JC** IV.vii.126; **Luc** 323; **MV** III.ii.24

11 retain, keep back, withhold **2H6** III.ii.136 [King to himself, as if to God] *O Thou that judgest all things, stay my thoughts;* **2H6** III.i.105; **Venus** 331

12 stay in hiding, remain hidden **2H6** IV.x.6 [Cade alone] *now am I so hungry that, if I might have a lease of my life for a thousand years, I could stay no longer*

13 stay away, delay, be absent **TS** III.ii.109 [Petruchio to all, of Katherina] *I stay too long from her;* **2H6** III.i.94

14 put up with, endure, abide **MV** IV.i.343 [Shylock to Portia as Balthasar] *I'll stay no longer question;* **RJ** I.i.212

15 hold, support, prop [up] **KJ** V.vii.55 [King John to Bastard] *My heart hath one poor string to stay it by;* **KJ** III.iv.138

stay for (*v.*) wait for, await **TC** III.ii.3 [Man to Pandarus, of Troilus] *he stays for you to conduct him thither;* **JC** I.iii.125; **MV** III.iv.82; **R3** I.iii.5; **R3** IV.iv.163; **TNK** V.ii.24

stay on / upon (*v.*) wait for, await **Cor** V.iv.7 [Menenius to Sicinius] *our throats are sentenced and stay upon execution;* **AC** I.ii.116; **CE** V.i.20; **Ham** III.ii.116; **Mac** I.ii.148; **MM** IV.i.46

stead (*n.*) advantage, help, benefit **1H6** IV.vi.31 [Talbot to John Talbot] *The help of one stands me in little stead* [i.e. is of little help to me]

stead (*v.*) help, assist, benefit **Oth** I.iii.335 [Iago to Roderigo] *I could never better stead thee than now;* **AW** III.vii.41; **MM** I.iv.17; **RJ** II.iii.50; **Tem** I.ii.165; **TS** I.ii.263

stead up (*v.*) keep, maintain, fulfil, carry out [on behalf of someone] **MM** III.i.251 [disguised Duke to Isabella, of Mariana] *we shall advise this wronged maid to stead up your appointment, go in your place*

steal (*v.*) hide furtively, conceal stealthily **TS** III.ii.139 [Lucentio to Tranio, of Bianca] *'Twere good methinks to steal our marriage*; **Ham** III.ii.98

steal on (*v.*) creep by, move stealthily **R3** V.iii.86 [Derby to Richmond] *The silent hours steal on*

stealers ☞ pickers and stealers

stealing (*adj.*) stealthily moving, gliding quietly by **Ham** V.i.71 [First Clown, singing] *age with his stealing steps / Hath clawed me in his clutch*; **R3** III.vii.167

stealth (*n.*) **1** stealing away, furtive journey, clandestine act **MND** III.ii.310 [Helena to Hermia, of Demetrius] *I told him of your stealth unto this wood*; **KL** I.ii.11; **MM** I.ii.153; **Sonn** 77.7; **TN** I.v.286
2 stealing, theft **Tim** III.iv.29 [Hortensius to Lucius' Servant] *I know my lord hath spent of Timon's wealth, / And now ingratitude makes it worse than stealth*; **KL** III.iv.90

steel (*n.*) **1** armour **Ham** I.iv.52 [Hamlet to Ghost] *dead corse, again in complete steel*; **2H6** III.ii.234; **3H6** I.i.58
2 weapon of steel, sword **3H6** II.v.132 [Queen to King, of Edward and Richard] *bloody steel grasped in their ireful hands*; **H8** II.i.76; **JC** III.ii.178; **R2** III.ii.59

steel (*v.*) **1** turn to steel, harden **H5** IV.i.282 [King Henry alone, praying] *O God of battles, steel my soldiers' hearts*; **2H4** I.i.116; **R2** V.ii.34; **Venus** 375
2 make firm, give strength **TNK** IV.ii.149 [Theseus to Emilia, of the knights] *You have steeled 'em with your beauty*
3 engrave, inscribe, make a permanent image of **Sonn** 24.1 *Mine eye hath played the painter and hath steeled / Thy beauty's form in table of my heart* ☞ stell (*v.*)

steeled (*adj.*) **1** hardened like steel, toughened **H5** II.ii.36 [Scroop to King Henry] *service shall with steeled sinews toil*; **Sonn** 112.8
2 steel-clad, armed with steel **E3** III.iii.219 [King Edward to all] *thus our steeled battles shall be ranged*; **1H6** I.i.85
3 hardened, inflexible, callous **MM** IV.ii.84 [disguised Duke alone] *seldom when / The steeled gaoler is the friend of men*

steely (*adj.*) hard as steel **E3** III.iv.80 [Prince Edward to all] *war's devouring gulfs and steely rocks*; **AW** I.i.102

steep (*n.*) ☞ step (*n.*) **1**

steep-down (*adj.*) precipitous, sheer **Oth** V.ii.278 [Othello as if to devils] *Wash me in steep-down gulfs of liquid fire!*

steep-up (*adj.*) precipitous, virtually perpendicular, sudden **PassP** IX.5 [of Cytherea] *Her stand she takes upon a steep-up hill*; **LL** IV.i.2; **Sonn** 7.5

steepy (*adj.*) steep, precipitous, difficult to ascend **Sonn** 63.5 *age's steepy night*; **Tim** I.i.78

stell (*v.*) portray, display, delineate **Luc** 1444 [of a painting of Troy] *To this well-painted piece is Lucrece come, / To find a face where all distress is stelled* ☞ steel (*v.*)

stelled (*adj.*) starry, stellar, heavenly **KL** III.vii.60 [Gloucester to Regan] *The sea … would have buoyed up / And quenched the stelled fires*

stem (*n.*) prow, bows **Cor** II.ii.105 [Cominius to all, of Coriolanus compared to a ship] *men obeyed / And fell beneath his stem*; **Per** IV.i.64

stem (*v.*) cut through, make headway against **3H6** II.vi.36 [Edward to all] *a sail, filled with a fretting gust, / [doth] Command an argosy to stem the waves*; **JC** I.ii.109

step (*n.*) **1** limit, distance, reach **MND** II.i.69 [Titania to Oberon] *Why art thou here / Come from the farthest step of India* [Q1; F steepe]
2 action, movement, coming and going **TS** II.ii.138 [Lucentio to Tranio, of Hortensio as Licio] *Doth watch Bianca's steps so narrowly*

step in (*v.*) move forward, go along **TS** I.ii.82 [Hortensio to Petruchio, of his plan for a wife for him] *since we are stepped thus far in, I will continue that I broached in jest*

step into (*v.*) come into the path of, put oneself into the power of **Tim** III.v.12 [Alcibiades to Senators] *a friend of mine … in hot blood / Hath stepped into the law*

stepdame, step-dame (*n.*) stepmother **Cym** I.vii.1 [Innogen alone] *A father cruel, and a step-dame false*; **Cym** II.i.57; **MND** I.i.5; **TC** III.ii.192

sterling (*n.*) valid currency, legitimate tender **R2** IV.i.263 [Richard to all] *if my word be sterling yet in England*; **Ham** I.iii.107

sterling (*adj.*) genuine, real, legal **2H4** II.i.119 [Lord Chief Justice to Falstaff, of repaying the Hostess for debt and villainy] *the one you may do with sterling money and the other with current repentance* [i.e. with hard cash]

stern (*n.*) guiding position, centre of control **1H6** I.i.177 [Winchester alone] *I intend to … sit at chiefest stern of public weal* [i.e. governing with greatest power]

stern (*adj.*) **1** cruel, malevolent, harsh **3H6** II.i.103 [Edward to Warwick, of York] *Is by the stern Lord Clifford done to death*; **E3** II.i.422; **3H6** I.i.239
2 coarse, rough, rugged **2H6** III.ii.213 [Suffolk to Warwick] *Thy mother took into her blameful bed / Some stern untutored churl*

sternage (*n.*) sterns [of a fleet of ships] **H5** III.Chorus.18 [Chorus] *Grapple your minds to sternage of this navy*

stew (*n.*) **1** brothel, house of ill-repute **R2** V.iii.16 [Percy to King Henry, of Henry's son] *he would unto the stews*; **Cym** I.vii.152; **2H4** I.ii.52
2 cauldron, saucepan **MM** V.i.317 [disguised Duke to Escalus] *I have seen corruption boil and bubble / Till it o'errun the stew* [also: brothel]

stew (*v.*) soak, steep, saturate **Ham** III.iv.94 [Hamlet to Gertrude] *Stewed in corruption*

steward (*n.*) controller of a household's domestic affairs **KL** I.iii.1 [stage direction] *Enter Gonerill and Oswald, her steward*

stewed (*adj.*) drenched, soaked, steeped **KL** II.iv.30 [disguised Kent to Lear] *came … a reeking post, / Stewed in his haste*

stewed prune prostitute, bawd, whore **1H4** III.iii.111 [Falstaff to Hostess] *There's no more faith in thee than in a stewed prune*; **2H4** II.iv.142; **MM** II.i.87

stick (*v.*) **1** be placed, be fixed **TNK** V.iii.54 [Emilia to herself, of Palamon] *Those darker humours that / Stick misbecomingly on others*; **AC** V.ii.79; **MM** IV.i.60; **Tim** II.i.30; **TNK** IV.i.84, V.i.44
2 place, fix, settle **AW** V.iii.45 [Bertram to King, of Lafew's daughter] *I stuck my choice upon her* [i.e. fix]; **AW** II.i.94
3 pierce, stab, wound **Mac** III.i.49 [Macbeth alone] *Our fears in Banquo / Stick deep*; **AW** III.vi.40; **AY** I.i.230; **Mac** IV.iii.85; **TC** III.ii.193
4 slaughter, kill [by stabbing] **TG** I.i.101 [Speed to Proteus, of Julia being compared to a sheep] *If the ground be overcharged, you were best stick her* [with bawdy pun]
5 decorate, adorn **Tim** III.vi.91 [Timon to Lords, of himself] *stuck and spangled with your flatteries*; **TNK** V.iii.81, V.i.137
6 shine out, stand out, be prominent **2H4** II.iii.19 [Lady Percy to Northumberland, of Percy's honour] *it stuck upon him as the sun / In the grey vault of heaven*; **Cor** V.vi.73
7 hesitate, linger, think twice **PassP** XVIII.51 [Pilgrim, of his mistress] *She will not stick to round me on th'ear*; **Cor** II.iii.15; **Ham** IV.v.94; **2H4** I.ii.22; **H8** II.ii.125; **Sonn** 10.6
8 persist, stand firm, be steadfast **E3** II.i.317 [King Edward to Warwick] *Thou wilt not stick to swear what thou hast said*

stick off (*v.*) shine out, stand out; or: stand firm **Ham** V.ii.251 [Hamlet to Laertes] *Your skill shall, like a star … / Stick fiery off indeed*

sticking place (*n.*) place on a device at which something is held fast [such as a stringed instrument or crossbow] **Mac** I.vii.60 [Lady Macbeth to Macbeth] *screw your courage to the sticking place*

stickler-like (*adv.*) like a tournament umpire **TC** V.viii.18 [Achilles to Myrmidons, of the effect of night] *stickler-like, the armies separates*

stiff *(adj.)* **1** stout, strong, tough **Cor** I.i.159 [Menenius to First Citizen] *make you ready your stiff bats and clubs*
 2 grave, formidable, weighty **AC** I.ii.101 [Messenger to Antony] *This is stiff news*
 3 disabled, incapacitated, unable to join in **Cor** I.i.239 [Martius to Lartius] *What, art thou stiff? Stand'st out?*
 4 unresponsive, unbending, stubborn **KL** IV.vi.278 [Gloucester to Edgar] *how stiff is my vile sense*
 5 unsupple, unathletic; or: lethargic, sluggish **Cym** III.iii.32 [Guiderius to Belarius] *your stiff age*

stiff-borne *(adj.)* obstinately followed, stubbornly pursued **2H4** I.i.177 [Morton to Northumberland, of dangers to Percy] *none of this … could restrain / The stiff-borne action*

stiffly *(adv.)* strongly, stoutly **Ham** I.v.95 [Hamlet alone] *And you, my sinews, grow not instant old, / But bear me stiffly up* [F; Q2 *swiftly*]

stigmatic *(n.)* misshapen individual, person marked by physical deformity **2H6** V.i.215 [Young Clifford to Richard] *Foul stigmatic;* **3H6** II.ii.136

stigmatical *(adj.)* deformed, disfigured, ugly **CE** IV.ii.22 [Adriana to Luciana, of Antipholus of Syracuse] *He is … / Stigmatical in making, worse in mind*

still *(adj.)* **1** silent, quiet **3H6** II.i.122 [Clifford to King] *the wound that bred this meeting here / Cannot be cured by words; therefore be still;* **CE** IV.ii.17; **2H6** III.ii.207; **LL** I.ii.175; **Oth** V.ii.46; **Sonn** 85.1
 2 quiet, calm, subdued **AC** II.vi.121 [Enobarbus to Menas] *Octavia is of a holy, cold, and still conversation;* **AC** IV.xi.1; **AY** V.iv.105; **Cym** V.iv.69; **LL** I.i.14; **MW** IV.ii.101
 3 impassive, inscrutable **AC** IV.xv.28 [Cleopatra to Antony] *Your wife Octavia, with her modest eyes / And still conclusion*
 4 at rest, in repose **TNK** II.ii.130 [Messenger to Theseus, of one of the knights] *stout-hearted, still, / But when he stirs, a tiger*
 5 constant, continual, perpetual **Tit** III.ii.45 [Titus to Lavinia, of her dumb gestures] *And by still practice learn to know thy meaning;* **R3** IV.iv.230
 6 lethargic, indolent, sluggish **TNK** IV.ii.28 [Emilia alone, of Palamon] *He's … a still temper*

still *(v.)* quieten, calm, hush **Sonn** 143.14 *If thou turn back and my loud crying still;* **1H6** II.ii.16

still *(adv.)* **1** constantly, always, continually **Ham** II.ii.187 [Polonius to himself, of Hamlet] *Still harping on my daughter* ☞ **FEW**, p.xxi
 2 ever, now [as before] **1H4** III.iii.171 [Falstaff to Hostess] *thou seest I am pacified still*

still and anon ☞ anon, still and

still an end repeatedly, time and again, over and over **TG** IV.iv.59 [Proteus to disguised Julia, of Launce] *A slave that still an end turns me to shame!*

still as *(conj.)* whenever **JC** I.ii.241 [Casca to Brutus, of Caesar being offered a crown] *still as he refused it, the rabblement hooted*

still-breeding *(adj.)* always reproducing, perpetually generating **R2** V.v.8 [Richard alone, of his brain and soul] *these two beget / A generation of still-breeding thoughts*

still-closing *(adj.)* always coming together [after being divided] **Tem** III.iii.65 [Ariel to Alonso, Sebastian, and Antonio, of their swords] *with bemocked-at stabs / Kill the still-closing waters*

still-discordant *(adj.)* always disagreeing, perpetually quarrelling **2H4** I.Induction.19 [Rumour alone] *The still-discordant wavering multitude*

stillitory *(n.)* still, distilling chamber **Venus** 443 [Venus to Adonis] *from the stillitory of thy face excelling / Comes breath perfumed*

stillness *(n.)* restraint, sobriety, quietness of behaviour **Oth** II.iii.185 [Othello to Montano] *The gravity and stillness of your youth / The world hath noted*

still-piecing *(adj.)* always reconstituting itself **AW** III.ii.110 [Helena alone, of bullets] *That … move the still-piecing air* [F *still-peering*]

still-pining *(adj.)* perpetually tormented **Luc** 858 [Lucrece to herself, of a sick miser] *like still-pining Tantalus he sits*

still-soliciting *(adj.)* always begging, forever looking for favours **KL** I.i.231 [Cordelia to Lear, of what she lacks] *A still-soliciting eye and such a tongue / That I am glad I have not*

still-stand *(n.)* standstill, cessation of movement **2H4** II.iii.64 [Northumberland to Lady Northumberland and Lady Percy] *'Tis with my mind / As with the tide swelled up unto his height, / That makes a still-stand, running neither way*

still-vexed always beset, perpetually plagued **Tem** I.ii.229 [Ariel to Prospero] *Thou called'st me up at midnight to fetch dew / From the still-vexed Bermoothes*

stilly *(adv.)* quietly, in a hushed manner **H5** IV.Chorus.5 [Chorus] *The hum of either army stilly sounds*

sting *(n.)* urging of lust, inflaming of passion **AY** II.vii.66 [Duke Senior to Jaques] *As sensual as the brutish sting itself;* **MM** I.iv.59; **Oth** I.iii.327

stint *(v.)* **1** cease, stop short **RJ** I.iii.59 [Juliet to Nurse] *And stint thou too, I pray thee;* **Per** IV.v.42; **RJ** I.iii.49; **Tit** IV.v.86
 2 limit, hold back, restrain **Tim** V.iv.83 [Alcibiades to Senators] *Make war breed peace, make peace stint war;* **H8** I.ii.76; **TC** IV.v.93

stir *(n.)* **1** acting, stirring, activity **Mac** I.iii.144 [Macbeth to himself] *chance may crown me / Without my stir;* **JC** I.iii.127
 2 movement, motion, agitation **Cym** I.iv.12 [Pisanio to Innogen, of Posthumus] *the fits and stirs of's mind;* **Venus** 283
 3 event, happening, activity **Luc** 1471 [Lucrece as if to Hecuba, of Helen] *Show me the strumpet that began this stir;* **AC** I.iv.82; **R2** II.iii.51

stir *(v.)* **1** move, rouse, excite **Mac** V.v.12 [Macbeth to himself] *my fell of hair / Would at a dismal treatise rouse and stir / As life were in't;* **AC** I.i.43; **Cym** IV.ii.38; **Sonn** 21.2
 2 rise in revolt, make a disturbance **Cor** III.i.53 [Sicinius to Coriolanus] *You show too much of that / For which the people stir*
 3 bestir, move, get going **KL** I.i.126 [Lear to all] *Who stirs? [i.e. somebody move!]*
 4 move about, go, travel **KL** I.ii.167 [Edmund to Edgar] *If you do stir abroad, go armed*

stir up *(v.)* provoke, agitate, rouse **Tim** III.iv.54 [Flavius to Servants] *You do yourselves but wrong to stir me up*

stirring *(n.)* liveliness, animation, vivacity **TNK** IV.ii.29 [Emilia alone, of Palamon] *No stirring in him, no alacrity*

stirring *(adj.)* busy, bustling, active **CE** III.i.99 [Balthasar to Antipholus of Ephesus] *If … you offer to break in / Now in the stirring passage of the day;* **TC** II.iii.136

stitchery *(n.)* needlework, embroidery **Cor** I.iii.70 [Valeria to Virgilia] *Come, lay aside your stitchery*

stithy *(n.)* smithy, anvil, forge **Ham** III.ii.94 [Hamlet to Horatio] *my imaginations are as foul / As Vulcan's stithy* [Q2; F *Stythe*]

stithy *(v.)* forge, hammer out **TC** IV.v.255 [Hector to Achilles] *by the forge that stithied Mars his helm*

stoccado, stoccata *(n.)* fencing] thrust, lunge **MW** II.i.207 [Shallow to Page, on fencing] *In these times you stand on distance, your passes, stoccadoes;* **RJ** III.i.73

stock *(n.)* **1** tree, family-tree, ancestry **1H6** II.v.41 [Mortimer to Richard] *sweet stem from York's great stock;* **Cym** I.vii.128; **2H6** III.ii.213; **Luc** 1063; **RJ** I.v.58
 2 stem, trunk, tree **Cym** V.v.143 [Posthumus alone, reading] *branches, which … shall after revive, be jointed to the old stock*
 3 stocking **TN** I.iii.128 [Sir Andrew to Sir Toby, of his leg] *it does indifferent well in a dun-coloured stock;* **TG** III.i.302; **TS** III.ii.64 ☞ nether-stock *(n.)*; **CLOTHING**, p.79
 4 senseless person, stupid individual **TS** I.i.31 [Tranio to Lucentio] *Let's be no stoics nor no stocks* ☞ flouting-stock *(n.)*; pointing-stock *(n.)*
 5 dowry, wedding endowment **TG** III.i.301 [Launce to Speed] *What need a man care for a stock with a wench* [pun: 302, stocking]

6 [fencing] thrust with the dagger-point **MW** II.iii.23 [Host to Caius, in answer to 'Vat be you all … come for?'] *to see thee pass … thy stock*

stock (*v.*) put in the stocks **KL** II.iv.183 [Lear to all] *Who stocked my servant?* [F; Q *struck*]; **KL** II.ii.130

stockfish (*n.*) dried cod **1H4** II.iv.241 [Falstaff to Prince Hal] *you stock-fish*; **MM** III.ii.103; **Tem** III.ii.70

stockish (*adj.*) blockish, wooden, stupid **MV** V.i.81 [Lorenzo to Jessica] *naught so stockish, hard, and full of rage / But music for the time doth change his nature*

stock-punished (*adj.*) punished by being put in the stocks **KL** III.iv.128 [Edgar as Poor Tom to Gloucester, of himself] *whipped from tithing to tithing and stock-punished* [Q *stock-punisht*; F *stocked, punished*]

stoic (*n.*) pleasure-despiser, over-rigorous person **TS** I.i.31 [Tranio to Lucentio] *Let's be no stoics nor no stocks*

stolen (*adj.*) secret, stealthy, clandestine **RJ** V.iii.233 [Friar to Prince, of Romeo and Juliet] *their stolen marriage day / Was Tybalt's doomsday*; **Oth** III.iii.335

stomach (*n.*) **1** appetite, desire [for food] **1H4** II.iii.43 [Lady Percy to Hotspur] *what is it that takes from thee / Thy stomach*; **AW** III.ii.16; **2H4** IV.iv.107; **Per** VI.i.28; **Tem** II.i.109; **TS** IV.i.144

2 wish, inclination, desire **H5** IV.iii.35 [King Henry to all] *he which hath no stomach to this fight, / Let him depart*; **AC** II.ii.54; **JC** I.ii.298; **MV** III.v.82; **TC** IV.v.264; **TS** I.ii.192

3 spirit, courage, valour, will **AW** III.vi.58 [Bertram to Parolles, of retrieving his drum] *if you have a stomach, to't*; **2H4** I.i.129; **Tem** I.ii.157

4 feelings, temper, state of mind **MA** II.i.355 [Don Pedro to all, of Benedick] *in despite of his quick wit and his queasy stomach*; **1H6** IV.i.141

5 anger, resentment, vexation **1H6** I.iii.90 [Mayor alone] *these nobles should such stomachs bear!*; **2H6** II.i.53; **KL** IV.iii.75; **TG** I.i.68; **Tit** III.i.232; **TNK** III.i.104

6 pride, obstinacy, stubbornness **H8** IV.ii.34 [Katherine to Griffith, of Wolsey] *He was a man / Of an unbounded stomach, ever ranking / Himself with princes*; **TS** V.ii.175

7 element of courage, exercise of valour **Ham** I.i.100 [Horatio to Barnardo and Marcellus, of young Fortinbras' planned action] *some enterprise / That hath a stomach in't*

stomach (*v.*) resent, take offence at **AC** III.iv.12 [Octavia to Antony, of Caesar's remarks] *if you must believe, / Stomach not all*

stomacher (*n.*) piece of clothing used by women under their bodice to help cover the chest **WT** IV.iv.226 [Autolycus singing] *Golden coifs and stomachers / For my lads to give their dears*; **Cym** III.iv.85 ☞ **CLOTHING**, p.79

stomaching (*n.*) cherishing bitterness, feeling resentful **AC** II.ii.9 [Lepidus to Enobarbus] *'Tis not a time / For private stomaching*

stomach-qualmed (*adj.*) taken sick, fallen ill **Cym** III.iv.192 [Pisanio to Innogen] *if you are sick at sea, / Or stomach-qualmed at land*

stone (*n.*) **1** mineral substance used as a mirror **KL** V.iii.260 [Lear to all, of Cordelia] *If that her breath will mist or stain the stone*

2 precious stone, gem **Cym** II.iv.40 [Posthumus to Iachimo, of Innogen's ring] *Sparkles this stone as it was wont*; **3H6** III.i.63; **MM** II.ii.150

3 thunderbolt **Oth** V.ii.232 [Othello to all] *Are there no stones in heaven / But what serve for the thunder?* ☞ stone of sulphur; thunder-stone

4 testicle **MW** I.iv.109 [Caius to himself, of Evans] *I will cut all his two stones* [i.e. castrate him]; **RJ** I.iii.54; **Tim** II.ii.114

stone (*v.*) turn to stone, harden **Oth** V.ii.63 [Othello to Desdemona] *Thou dost stone my heart*

stone-bow (*n.*) type of cross-bow which shoots stones, catapult **TN** II.v.45 [Sir Toby to Sir Andrew and Fabian, of Malvolio] *O for a stone-bow to hit him in the eye!*

stone of sulphur thunderbolt **Cym** V.v.240 [Pisanio to Innogen] *The gods throw stones of sulphur on me* ☞ thunder-stone

stonish (*v.*) ☞ astonish (*v.*)

stony (*adj.*) pitiless, unfeeling, obdurate **2H6** V.ii.51 [Young Clifford to himself] *My heart is turned to stone, and while 'tis mine / It shall be stony*

stool (*n.*) chamber-pot, commode **TC** II.i.41 [Ajax to Thersites] *Thou stool for a witch!*

stool-ball (*n.*) type of bat-and-ball game, with a stool in place of a wicket **TNK** V.ii.72 [Gaoler's Daughter to Wooer] *play at stool-ball*

stoop (*n.*) ☞ stoup (*n.*)

stoop (*v.*) **1** kneel, submit, bow down **1H6** III.i.171 [King to Richard] *Stoop then and set your knee against my foot*; **2H6** IV.viii.47; **3H6** I.i.108; **Luc** 574; **MM** II.iv.182; **R2** III.i.19

2 [falconry] swoop, descend swiftly **Cym** V.iv.116 [Sicilius to all] *the holy eagle / Stooped, as to foot us*; **Cym** V.iii.42; **H5** IV.i.105; **TS** IV.i.177

stooping (*adj.*) submissive, humble, kneeling **R2** III.iii.48 [Bolingbroke to Northumberland, of his desire not to do battle with King Richard] *My stooping duty tenderly shall show*

stop (*n.*) **1** obstruction, obstacle, hindrance **LL** I.i.70 [King to Berowne, of distractions] *These be the stops that hinder study quite*; **Oth** V.ii.262

2 pause, hesitation, breaking off **Oth** III.iii.119 [Othello to Iago] *these stops of thine affright me more*; **KJ** IV.ii.239; **R2** V.ii.4

3 [in managing a horse] pulling-up, sudden checking of a career **MND** V.i.120 [Lysander to Theseus, of Quince] *he knows not the stop*; **Cym** V.iii.40

4 means of closing a finger-hole in a wind instrument **Ham** III.ii.368 [Hamlet to Guildenstern] *these are the stops*; **2H4** I.Induction.17; **MA** III.ii.55

5 note [produced by closing a finger-hole in a wind instrument] **Ham** III.ii.81 [Hamlet to Horatio, of people like Horatio] *they are not a pipe for Fortune's finger / To sound what stop she please*; **Luc** 1124

6 full-stop, period, full point **MV** III.i.15 [Salerio to Solanio, interrupting his flow] *Come, the full stop*; **MND** V.i.120

7 filling up, plugging, sealing **2H6** III.i.288 [Cardinal to all, of rebellion in Ireland] *A breach that craves a quick expedient stop!*

stop (*v.*) **1** block, hinder, impede, obstruct **AC** III.xiii.181 [Antony to Cleopatra] *I'll … send to darkness all that stop me*; **2H4** IV.i.65; **KJ** II.i.562; **Sonn** 44.2

2 stop up, close (up), shut **AW** V.ii.10 [Parolles to Clown] *you need not to stop your nose*; **CE** III.ii.172; **Cor** V.iii.5; **LL** IV.iii.312; **TNK** III.vi.173; **Venus** 331

3 stopper, fasten, shut **MW** III.v.103 [Falstaff to Ford as Brook] *I suffered … to be stopped in, like a strong distillation*

4 fill, cram, stuff **2H4** I.i.78 [Northumberland to Morton, of his allies] *Stopping my greedy ear with their bold deeds*; **2H4** I.i.41; **R2** II.i.17

5 staunch, close up, prevent from bleeding **MV** IV.i.255 [Portia as Balthasar to Shylock, of Antonio] *Have by some surgeon … / To stop his wounds*; **R3** V.v.40

6 silence, put a stop to **KJ** II.i.558 [King John to King Philip, of Constance] *I trust we shall … in some measure satisfy her so / That we shall stop her exclamation*

stople (*v.*) stop up, close up, plug **KL** V.iii.153 [Albany to Gonerill] *Shut your mouth, dame, / Or with this paper shall I stople it* [Q; F *stop*]

store (*n.*) **1** abundance, plenty, surplus, quantity **Cym** I.v.94 [Posthumus to Iachimo] *I do nothing doubt you have store of thieves*; **CE** III.i.34; **2H6** III.i.169; **3H6** IV.i.57; **JC** IV.i.30; **TS** III.ii.185

2 possessions, belongings, property, fortune **1H4** II.ii.88 [Falstaff to Travellers] *I would your store were here*; **2H6** III.i.115

3 available money, resources, means **TN** III.iii.46 [Antonio to Sebastian] *your store, / I think, is not for idle markets*

4 group, company, assembly **RJ** I.ii.22 [Capulet to Paris, of the guests invited to the feast] *and you among the store, / One more, most welcome*

5 increasing the population, begetting children **Sonn** 11.9 *Let those whom Nature hath not made for store … barrenly perish;* **Sonn** 14.12

store *(v.)* populate, supply with children **Oth** IV.iii.84 [Emilia to Desdemona, of unfaithful women] *as many to th'vantage as would store the world they played for* ➤ **new-store** *(v.)*

stored *(adj.)* well supplied, rich, plentifully provided **Cor** II.i.17 [Brutus to Menenius, of Coriolanus] *He's poor in no one fault, but stored with all;* **KJ** V.iv.1; **Per** I.i.78

story *(n.)* **1** account, recital, narrative **Sonn** 88.6 *I can set down a story / Of faults concealed, wherein I am attainted*

2 book of history, historical record **AC** III.xiii.46 [Enobarbus to himself] *he … earns a place i'th' story*

3 narrative shown in the arras tapestry **Cym** II.ii.27 [Iachimo to himself] *the contents o'th' story* [or: room]

4 practical joke, theme for mockery **MM** I.iv.30 [Isabella to Lucio] *make me not your story*

story *(v.)* give an account of, portray **Luc** 106 [of Tarquin and Lucrece] *He stories to her ears her husband's fame;* **Cym** I.v.32; **Venus** 1013

stoup *(n.)* cup, flagon, jug, tankard **Ham** V.ii.261 [Claudius to all] *Set me the stoups of wine upon that table;* **Ham** V.i.60; **Oth** II.iii.27; **TN** II.iii.13

stout *(adj.)* **1** brave, valiant, resolute **1H4** V.iv.92 [Prince Hal to dead Hotspur] *This earth that bears thee dead / Bears not alive so stout a gentleman;* **1H6** I.i.106; **2H6** IV.ix.26; **3H6** IV.vii.30; **H8** IV.ii.12; **TNK** IV.ii.77

2 proud, haughty, arrogant **2H6** I.i.185 [Salisbury to York and Warwick, of the Cardinal] *As stout and proud as he were lord of all;* **Cor** III.ii.78; **TN** II.v.164

3 firm, bold, determined **KJ** IV.ii.173 [King John to Bastard] *adverse foreigners affright my towns / With dreadful pomp of stout invasion*

stoutness *(n.)* obstinacy, stubbornness, intractability **Cor** III.ii.127 [Volumnia to Coriolanus] *Let / Thy mother rather feel thy pride than fear / Thy dangerous stoutness;* **Cor** V.vi.27

stover *(n.)* fodder grass, hay, straw **Tem** IV.i.63 [Iris to Ceres] *Thy … flat meads thatched with stover*

stow *(v.)* **1** put away, put under cover **Oth** I.ii.62 [Brabantio to Othello] *Where hast thou stowed my daughter?;* **Luc** 119

2 [as of a ship] fill up with cargo **TNK** II.ii.32 [Second Countryman to First Countryman, of his wife] *Clap her aboard tomorrow night and stow her*

straggler *(n.)* vagabond, wanderer, roving vagrant **R3** V.iii.328 [King Richard to his army, of the enemy] *Let's whip these stragglers o'er the seas again*

straight *(adj.)* strong, muscular, strapping **Cym** III.i.38 [Cloten to Queen, of Caesar] *to owe such straight arms*

straight *(adv.)* straightaway, immediately, at once **Ham** IV.iv.31 [Hamlet to Rosencrantz] *I'll be with you straight* ➤ **FEW**, p.xxi

straight-pight *(adj.)* with a tall figure, with erect bearing **Cym** V.v.164 [Iachimo to Cymbeline, of Italian women] *for feature, laming … straight-pight Minerva*

straightway *(adv.)* straightaway **AC** III.xi.20 [Antony to attendants] *To the seaside straightway!;* **Tem** V.i.235

strain *(n.)* **1** quality, character, disposition **MW** III.iii.174 [Mistress Page to Mistress Ford, of Falstaff] *I would all of the same strain were in the same distress;* **Cym** IV.ii.24; **KL** V.iii.41; **MW** II.i.82; **TC** II.ii.155; **Tim** IV.iii.214

2 trait, feature, tendency **LL** V.ii.755 [Berowne to ladies] *love is full of unbefitting strains*

3 vocal effusion, lyrical outpouring **TC** II.ii.114 [Hector to Troilus, of Cassandra] *do not these high strains / Of divination in our sister work / Some touches of remorse?*

4 [unclear meaning] strand; extreme degree; pang, stress **Sonn** 90.13 *And other strains of woe, which now seem woe;* **MA** V.i.12

strain *(v.)* **1** stretch, make extra effort **1H6** I.v.10 [Talbot to himself] *My breast I'll burst with straining of my courage;* **Tim** I.i.147, V.i.225

2 constrain, force, press **MV** IV.i.181 [Portia as Balthasar to Shylock] *The quality of mercy is not strained;* **KJ** III.iii.46; **MA** IV.i.250; **RJ** II.iii.15

3 urge, press, encourage **Oth** III.iii.248 [Iago to Othello, of Desdemona and Cassio] *Note if your lady strain his entertainment / With any strong or vehement importunity*

4 embrace, hold, hug **H8** V.i.46 [Second Gentleman to First Gentleman, of Queen Anne] *Our King has all the Indies in his arms … when he strains that lady*

5 transgress, go beyond, exceed **Venus** 888 [of hounds and a boar] *They all strain court'sy who shall cope him first;* **WT** III.ii.49

6 overstate, exaggerate, stretch the meaning **1H4** IV.i.75 [Hotspur to Worcester] *You strain too far*

strain at *(v.)* have difficulty in accepting, have a problem with **TC** III.iii.112 [Ulysses to Achilles, of his book] *I do not strain at the position … but at the author's drift*

strained *(adj.)* **1** forced, artificial, feigned **TNK** III.iii.43 [Palamon to Arcite] *Away with this strained mirth;* **Sonn** 82.10

2 unnatural, excessive, exorbitant **2H4** I.i.161 [Lord Bardolph to Northumberland] *This strained passion doth you wrong;* **KL** I.i.169

3 refined, purified, distilled **TC** IV.iv.23 [Troilus to Cressida] *I love thee in so strained a purity / That the blest gods … take thee from me;* **TC** IV.v.169

strait *(n.)* cramped passage, confined path **TC** III.iii.154 [Ulysses to Achilles] *honour travels in a strait so narrow, / Where one but goes abreast*

strait *(adj.)* **1** stringent, strict, harsh **Tim** I.i.100 [Messenger to Timon, of Ventidius] *His means most short, his creditors most strait;* **1H4** IV.iii.79; **2H6** III.ii.258

2 strict, rigorous, scrupulous **MM** II.i.9 [Escalus to and of Angelo] *Whom I believe to be most strait in virtue*

3 mean, niggardly, stingy **KJ** V.vii.42 [King John to all] *I beg cold comfort; and you are so strait / And so ingrateful you deny me that*

4 narrow, cramped, confined **Cym** V.iii.11 [Posthumus to Lord] *the strait pass was dammed / With dead men;* **Cym** V.iii.7

5 tight, close-fitting, narrow **TNK** III.vi.86 [Palamon to Arcite, of the armour] *Is not this piece too strait?* [Q *streight*]; **H5** III.vii.52

strait *(adv.)* stringently, strictly, harshly **2H6** III.ii.20 [King to all] *Proceed no straiter 'gainst our uncle Gloucester / Than … / He be approved in practice culpable*

straited *(adj.)* at a loss, nonplussed, hard put **WT** IV.iv.351 [disguised Polixenes to Florizel] *you were straited / For a reply*

straitly *(adv.)* strictly, firmly, stringently **R3** I.i.85 [Brakenbury to Richard and Clarence] *His majesty hath straitly given in charge / That no man shall have private conference … with his brother*

straitness *(n.)* severity, strictness, rigour **MM** III.ii.244 [disguised Duke to Escalus, of Angelo] *If his own life answer the straitness of his proceeding, it shall become him well*

strand, strond *(n.)* shore, land, region **Luc** 1436 [of Trojans in a painting of Troy] *from the strand of Dardan where they fought;* **1H4** I.i.4; **2H4** I.i.62; **MV** I.i.171; **TS** I.i.167

strange *(adj.)* **1** remarkable, startling, abnormal, unnatural **Tem** V.i.228 [Alonso to all, of the happenings] *They strengthen / From strange to stranger;* **AC** V.ii.98; **Ham** I.i.69; **KL** II.i.76; **MV** IV.i.21; **TS** Induction.i.41

2 rare, singular, exceptional **R2** V.v.66 [Richard alone] *love to Richard / Is a strange brooch in this all-hating world;* **AC** II.ii.160; **1H4** III.i.161; **LL** IV.iii.353; **Tim** I.i.4

3 special, particular, very great **Tem** III.iii.88 [Prospero to Ariel] *with good life / And observation strange, my meaner ministers / Their several kinds have done;* **MV** IV.i.20

4 foreign, alien, from abroad **Cym** I.vii.191 [Iachimo to Innogen, of his treasures] *I am something curious, being strange, / To have them in safe stowage;* **Cym** I.vii.54; **H8** V.iv.34; **KJ** V.i.11; **LL** IV.ii.129; **TC** III.ii.8, iii.12

5 unfamiliar, unknown, not previously experienced **Tim** IV.iii.57 [Alcibiades to Timon] *I know thee well; / But in thy fortunes am unlearned and strange;* **MM** V.ii.194; **RJ** III.ii.15

6 of another person, not one's own **MA** V.iv.49 [Benedick to Claudio] *some such strange bull leaped your father's cow;* **RJ** II.i.25; **Sonn** 53.2

7 aloof, distant, reserved **RJ** II.ii.102 [Juliet to Romeo] *I should have been more strange;* **JC** I.ii.35; **MV** I.i.67; **TC** II.iii.236; **TN** II.v.164; **TS** I.i.85

8 diffident, pretending, coy **MA** II.iii.45 [Don Pedro to Balthasar] *It is the witness still of excellency / To put a strange face on his own perfection*

9 reluctant, unwilling, hesitant **2H4** I.i.94 [Northumberland to Morton] *I see a strange confession in thine eye*

strange *(adv.)* without recognition, as if a stranger **CE** V.i.296 [Egeon to Antipholus and Dromio of Ephesus] *Why look you strange on me?*

strange, make it affect indifference, pretend to be unwilling **TG** I.ii.102 [Lucetta to herself, of Julia] *She makes it strange*

strange-achieved *(adj.)* [unclear meaning] specially obtained; procured abroad **2H4** IV.v.73 [King Henry IV to princes, of fathers] *they have engrossed and pilled up / The cankered heaps of strange-achieved gold*

strange-disposed *(adj.)* given over to unusual happenings **JC** I.iii.33 [Cicero to Casca] *it is a strange-disposed time*

strangely *(adv.)* **1** like a stranger, distantly, in an unfriendly manner **2H4** V.ii.63 [King Henry V to his brothers] *You all look strangely on me;* **H8** III.ii.11; **Sonn** 49.5, 110.6; **TC** III.iii.39, 71; **TNK** II.i.246

2 as a stranger, as a foreigner **WT** II.iii.181 [Leontes to Antigonus, of the baby] *I do in justice charge thee ... / That thou commend it strangely to some place*

3 unaccountably, surprisingly, unusually **Tem** III.iii.41 [Francisco to all, of the spirits] *They vanished strangely;* **Cym** V.v.272; **H8** V.iii.94; **MA** III.ii.120; **Tem** V.i.160

4 admirably, wonderfully, marvellously **Tem** IV.i.7 [Prospero to Ferdinand] *thou / Hast strangely stood the test;* **Tem** V.i.314

5 very greatly, extremely **H8** IV.ii.112 [Katherine to Capuchius] *The times and titles now are altered strangely / With me since first you knew me;* **Mac** IV.iii.150

strangeness *(n.)* estrangement, disaffection, coldness, aloofness **Venus** 310 [of the jennet] *She puts on outward strangeness, seems unkind;* **2H6** III.i.5; **Oth** III.iii.12; **TC** II.iii.125, III.iii.45; **TN** IV.i.14

stranger *(n.)* foreigner, alien, outsider **MV** III.ii.237 [Gratiano to Nerissa, of Jessica] *cheer yond stranger; bid her welcome;* **CE** IV.ii.9; **2H6** I.iii.77; **H8** II.ii.100; **KJ** V.ii.27; **MND** I.i.219

stranger *(adj.)* foreign, alien **R2** I.iii.143 [King Richard to Bolingbroke] *You ... tread the stranger paths of banishment;* **AW** I.iii.106; **KJ** V.i.11; **LL** IV.iii.137; **Luc** 99

stranger *(v.)* make a stranger to, disown, alienate **KL** I.i.204 [Lear to Burgundy, of Cordelia] *Dowered with our curse and strangered with our oath*

strangle *(v.)* quench, eclipse, stifle **Mac** II.iv.7 [Ross to Old Man] *dark night strangles the travelling lamp;* **1H4** I.ii.201; **Sonn** 89.8; **TN** V.i.145; **WT** IV.iv.47

strappado *(n.)* type of torturing instrument **1H4** II.iv.233 [Falstaff to all] *an I were at the strappado ... I would not tell you on compulsion*

stratagem *(n.)* **1** scheme, device, cunning plan **2H4** II.iv.20 [Francis to Will, of the plan to fool Falstaff] *It will be an excellent stratagem;* **AW** III.vi.32; **H5** IV.viii.107; **RJ** III.v.210; **Tit** II.iii.5

2 soldierly action, well commanded engagement **E3** III.iii.195 [Audley to Prince Edward] *draw forth bloody stratagems in France;* **AW** III.vi.59; **E3** IV.iv.129

3 deed of violence, bloody act **2H4** I.i.8 [Northumberland to Lord Bardolph] *Every minute ... / Should be the father of some stratagem;* **AW** IV.i.49; **3H6** II.v.89; **MV** V.i.85

straw *(n.)* trivial matter, trifle **WT** III.ii.109 [Hermione to Leontes, of life] *I prize it not a straw;* **Ham** IV.iv.26, v.6; **KJ** III.iv.128

strawy *(adj.)* like straw, worthless as straw **TC** V.v.24 [Nestor to all, of Hector] *there the strawy Greeks ... / Fall down before him* [Q; F *straying*]

stray *(n.)* **1** stray animal **2H6** IV.x.24 [Cade to himself, of Iden] *Here's the lord of the soil come to seize me for a stray;* **H5** I.ii.160

2 stragglers, remnants **2H4** IV.ii.120 [Prince John to guards, of the rebel army] *pursue the scattered stray*

stray *(v.)* lead astray, distract, cause to wander **CE** V.i.51 [Abbess to Adriana, of Antipholus of Ephesus] *Hath not else his eye / Strayed his affection in unlawful love*

straying *(adj.)* winding, twisting, rambling **TNK** I.v.15 [Third Queen to First and Second Queens] *This world's a city full of straying streets;* **LL** V.ii.758

stream *(n.)* current, flow, drift **Oth** II.iii.59 [Iago alone] *My boat sails freely both with wind and stream;* **CE** I.i.87; **2H4** V.ii.34; **H8** III.ii.364

streamer *(n.)* banner, pennant, standard **TNK** V.i.59 [Arcite praying to Mars] *to thy laud / I may advance my streamer*

strength *(n.)* **1** troops, forces, resources, followers **2H6** III.i.380 [York to himself] *from Ireland come I with my strength;* **AC** II.i.17; **1H6** I.i.139, IV.i.73; **KJ** II.i.388; **KL** II.i.111

2 validity, forcefulness, cogency **TC** V.ii.115 [Thersites to himself, of Cressida] *A proof of strength she could not publish more*

3 mental capacity, intellectual power **MM** I.i.7 [Duke to Escalus] *your own science / Exceeds ... the lists of all advice / My strength can give you*

4 recovery, return to full health **Cor** I.iii.79 [Virgilia to Valeria, of an expectant mother] *I will wish her speedy strength*

strengthless *(adj.)* weak, delicate, puny **Venus** 153 [Venus to Adonis] *Two strengthless doves will draw me through the sky*

stretch *(v.)* **1** strain to the utmost, maximally exert **Cor** V.vi.45 [Aufidius to First Conspirator, of Coriolanus] *my sinews shall be stretched upon him;* **JC** IV.i.44; **KL** II.ii.102; **Per** V.i.52

2 stand upright, draw oneself up to full height **H8** I.ii.204 [Surveyor to King Henry, of Buckingham] *He stretched him, and ... did discharge a horrible oath*

3 open wide, extend **2H6** III.ii.171 [Warwick to Suffolk, of dead Gloucester] *his nostrils stretched with struggling;* **H5** II.ii.55, III.i.15

stretched *(adj.)* **1** strained, dislocated, tortured **Sonn** 17.12 *So should ... your true rights be termed a poet's rage / And stretched metre of an antique song*

2 strained, forced, affected **TC** I.iii.156 [Ulysses to Agamemnon, of an actor] *To hear the wooden dialogue and sound / 'Twixt his stretched footing and the scaffoldage*

stretched-out *(adj.)* extended to full length, exceptionally long-lasting **TC** I.iii.61 [Ulysses to Nestor] *thou most reverend for thy stretched-out life*

stretch-mouthed *(adj.)* wide-mouthed **WT** IV.iv.198 [Servant to Clown] *some stretch-mouthed rascal would ... mean mischief*

strew *(v.)* **1** scatter, broadcast, spread about **MM** I.iii.15 [Duke to Friar Thomas, of his supposed going to Poland] *For so I have strewed it in the common ear*

2 scatter, be spread over **KJ** I.i.216 [Bastard alone, of deceit] *For it shall strew the footsteps of my rising* [i.e. facilitate my rise]

strewing (*n.*) (plural) things to be scattered **Cym** IV.ii.285 [Belarius to Guiderius] *The herbs … / Are strewings fitt'st for graves;* **TNK** II.i.21

strewment (*n.*) strewn flowers [on a grave] **Ham** V.i.229 [Priest to Laertes, of Ophelia] *here she is allowed … / Her maiden strewments*

strict (*adj.*) **1** strained, forced, absolute **Tim** III.v.24 [First Senator to Alcibiades] *You undergo too strict a paradox, / Striving to make an ugly deed look fair*
2 tight, close, pressing **Venus** 874 [of Venus running through bushes] *She wildly breaketh from their strict embrace*
3 harsh, cruel, unrelenting **Per** III.iii.8 [Dionyza to Pericles, of Thaisa] *That the strict fates had pleased you had brought her hither*

stricture (*n.*) self-constraint, rigour; or: strictness, severity **MM** I.iii.12 [Duke to Friar Thomas, of Angelo] *A man of stricture and firm abstinence*

stride (*v.*) **1** go beyond, step over **Cym** III.iii.35 [Guiderius to Belarius] *a debtor that not dares / To stride a limit*
2 bestride, sit astride, straddle **Cor** I.ix.70 [Coriolanus to Cominius] *I mean to stride your steed;* **Mac** I.vii.22

strife (*n.*) striving, endeavour, strong effort **AW** Epilogue.4 [King to all] *we will pay / With strife to please you;* **MM** III.ii.222; **RJ** II.ii.152; **Tim** I.i.38

strike (*n.*) measure [of variable value - usually, a bushel] **TNK** V.ii.63 [Gaoler's Daughter to Gaoler, of a horse's dowry] *Some two hundred bottles, / And twenty strike of oats*

strike (*v.*), past form **stroke, strook** **1** fight, engage in fighting **TNK** II.i.308 [Palamon to Gaoler, of Arcite and Emilia] *Yet in the field to strike a battle for her;* **Cor** I.vi.4; **H5** II.iv.54
2 beat, sound, strike up **E3** II.ii.73 [Lodowick to King Edward] *the drum that stroke the lusty march;* **Cor** II.ii.74; **KL** V.iii.82; **R3** IV.iv.149; **TC** V.x.30; **WT** V.iii.98
3 touch, beset, affect **AC** V.ii.359 [Caesar to all] *High events as these / Strike those that make them* [i.e. those whose actions have caused them]
4 steal, rob, thieve **1H4** II.i.78 [Gadshill to Chamberlain] *Burgomasters and great O-yeas, … such as will strike sooner than speak* [or: deliver a blow]
5 have an evil influence, do harm **Ham** I.i.163 [Marcellus to Horatio, of Christmas night] *then no planets strike;* **Cor** II.ii.111; **WT** I.ii.201
6 [of sails] lower, take down [especially before a mightier vessel] **3H6** V.i.52 [Warwick to Richard] *I had rather chop this hand off … / Than bear so low a sail to strike to thee;* **2H4** V.ii.18; **3H6** III.iii.5; **R2** II.i.266
7 [hunting, of a prey] thrust, stab, pierce **Tit** II.i.118 [Aaron to Demetrius and Chiron, of Lavinia] *Single you thither then this dainty doe, / And strike her home by force* [with bawdy pun]

strike off (*v.*) cancel [as by a pen-stroke], erase, remove **TC** II.ii.7 [Priam to all, reporting Nestor on the war] *Deliver Helen, and all damage else … / Shall be struck off;* **AW** V.iii.56; **Oth** III.iv.175; **TC** III.iii.29

strike the vessels [unclear meaning] tap the casks; fill the cups; clink the glasses; bang the drums **AC** II.vii.95 [Antony to all] *Strike the vessels, ho!*

striker (*n.*) highwayman, footpad, robber **1H4** II.i.75 [Gadshill to Chamberlain] *I am joined with … no long-staff sixpenny strikers* [i.e. who would hold someone up for sixpence]

string (*n.*) stringed instrument **R2** V.v.46 [Richard alone] *here have I the daintiness of ear / To check time broke in a disordered string*

stripe (*n.*) stroke of a whip, lash, weal **Tem** I.ii.345 [Prospero to Caliban] *Thou most lying slave, / Whom stripes may move, not kindness;* **AC** III.xiii.152

strive (*v.*) compete, contend, vie **KL** IV.iii.16 [Gentleman to disguised Kent, of Cordelia] *patience and sorrow strove / Who should express her goodliest;* **AW** I.iii.164; **Cym** II.iv.73; **Venus** 968

stroke (*n.*) **1** blow, attack, assault **Cor** III.iii.79 [Sicinius to all, of Coriolanus] *Opposing laws with strokes;* **Cor** III.iii.97, IV.i.26; **Mac** V.iv.20
2 first blow, initial action **Cym** V.v.469 [Soothsayer to Cymbeline, of the vision] *Which I made known to Lucius ere the stroke / Of yet this scarce-cold battle*
3 affliction, blow, misery **KL** IV.i.64 [Gloucester to Edgar as Poor Tom] *thou whom the heavens' plagues / Have humbled to all strokes;* **Tim** IV.i.23
4 ☛ past tense of *strike* (*v.*)

strong (*adj.*) **1** great, serious **TNK** III.i.17 [Arcite alone, of Emilia] *She takes strong note of me* [i.e. pays a lot of attention]; **E3** IV.vi.27; **Sonn** 111.10
2 powerful, vivid, intense **Tem** II.i.212 [Antonio to Sebastian] *My strong imagination sees a crown / Dropping upon thy head*
3 forceful, persuasive, influential **Per** IV.ii.33 [Pander to Bawd] *the gods will be strong with us for giving o'er*
4 severe, oppressive, grievous **RJ** III.i.190 [Prince to Montague] *I'll amerce you with so strong a fine*
5 flagrant, barefaced; or: resolute, determined **R2** V.iii.58 [King Henry to all] *O, heinous, strong, and bold conspiracy!;* **2H6** IV.i.108; **KL** II.i.76; **Tim** IV.iii.46
6 certain, convincing, persuasive **AW** IV.iii.54 [First Lord to Second Lord, of the basis for the news of Helena] *The stronger part of it by her own letters;* **Per** II.iv.34

strongly (*adv.*) greatly, powerfully, violently **Tem** V.i.17 [Ariel to Prospero, of the King's company] *Your charm so strongly works 'em;* **Tem** IV.i.144

strook (*v.*) struck [past tense of 'strike'] **Luc** 1842 [of Brutus] *he strook his hand upon his breast* [Q] ☛ strike (*v.*)

strossers (*n.*) trousers **H5** III.vii.52 [Dauphin to Constable] *in your strait strossers* [i.e. the bare skin of the legs]

strow (*v.*) strew, scatter **Cym** IV.ii.287 [Belarius to dead Cloten and supposedly dead Innogen] *These herblets shall* [wither], *which we upon you strow* [F *strew*]

stroy (*v.*) destroy **AC** III.xi.54 [Antony to Cleopatra] *what I have left behind / 'Stroyed in dishonour*

struck (*adj.*) **1** marked, provided, beset **TS** II.i.353 [Gremio to Baptista] *Myself am struck in years, I must confess;* **R3** I.i.92
2 stricken, wounded **1H4** IV.ii.19 [Falstaff alone] *a commodity of warm slaves … such as fear the report of a caliver worse than a struck fowl*

strumpet (*n.*) harlot, prostitute, whore **AW** V.iii.290 [Diana to King] *I am no strumpet;* **AC** I.i.13; **1H6** I.v.12; **Oth** IV.i.96; **R3** III.iv.71; **Tit** V.iii.189

strumpet (*v.*) make a whore, pervert, debauch **Sonn** 66.6 *maiden virtue rudely strumpeted;* **CE** II.ii.153

stubborn (*adj.*) **1** resistant, hostile, antagonistic **TC** V.ii.134 [Troilus to Ulysses] *do not give advantage / To stubborn critics;* **H8** II.iv.122; **MM** V.i.477; **MV** IV.i.32
2 stiff, intractable, unyielding **LL** IV.iii.53 [Longaville to himself, of his letter to Maria] *I fear these stubborn lines lack power to move;* **H8** V.iii.23
3 uncompromising, unyielding, obstinate **TN** V.i.359 [Fabian to Olivia] *myself and Toby / Set this device against Malvolio here, / Upon some stubborn and uncourteous parts / We had conceived against him*
4 difficult, demanding, exacting **Oth** I.iii.225 [Duke to Othello] *You must … be content to slubber the gloss of your new fortunes with this more stubborn … expedition*

stuck (*n.*) [fencing] thrust, lunge **Ham** IV.vii.160 [Claudius to Laertes, of Hamlet] *If he by chance escape your venomed stuck*

stuck-in (*n.*) [fencing] thrust, lunge **TN** III.iv.269 [Sir Toby to Sir Andrew, of Viola as Cesario] *he gives me the stuck-in with such a mortal motion*

stud (*v.*) adorn with studs, emboss **TS** Induction.ii.41 [Lord to Sly, of horses] *Their harness studded all with gold and pearl*

studied (*adj.*) **1** deliberate, carefully planned, intentional TNK II.ii.4 [Arcite alone] *'twas a studied punishment;* H8 III.ii.168; WT III.ii.173

2 prepared, equipped, fitted AC II.vi.47 [Antony to Pompey] *I ... am well studied for a liberal thanks;* MV II.ii.183

3 experienced, skilled, practised 2H4 II.ii.7 [Poins to Prince Henry, of small beer] *a prince should not be so loosely studied as to remember so weak a composition*

4 [theatre] learned by heart, committed to memory Mac I.iv.10 [Malcolm to King, of Cawdor] *He died / As one that had been studied in his death*

studious (*adj.*) heedful, devoted, diligent 1H6 II.v.97 [Mortimer to Richard] *be wary in thy studious care*

study (*n.*) **1** aim, object, purpose KL I.i.276 [Gonerill to Cordelia] *Let your study / Be to content your lord;* AY V.ii.74

2 effort, endeavour KJ IV.ii.51 [Pembroke to King John, of his safety] *for the which myself and them / Bend their best studies;* H8 III.i.174

3 pursuit, concern, occupation 1H4 I.iii.225 [Hotspur to Northumberland and Worcester] *All studies here I solemnly defy*

4 reflection, reverie, musing 2H4 I.ii.116 [Falstaff to Lord Chief Justice, of apoplexy] *It hath it original from much grief, from study;* MA IV.i.223

5 preparation, learning, memorizing [of a part] TNK III.v.120 [Schoolmaster to Theseus] *The body of our sport, of no small study;* MND I.ii.63

study (*v.*) **1** deliberate, meditate, reflect [on] R2 V.v.1 [Richard alone] *I have been studying how I may compare / This prison where I live unto the world;* AC V.ii.10; 2H6 I.i.88; LL V.ii.826; MM II.iv.7; Tem II.i.83

2 endeavour, take pains, make an effort 3H6 IV.iii.40 [Warwick to Edward] *[you] know not ... how to study for the people's welfare;* 1H6 III.i.111

3 learn by heart, commit to memory Ham II.ii.538 [Hamlet to First Player] *You could for a need study a speech;* AY III.ii.267; TN I.v.171; TS II.i.256

stuff (*n.*) **1** substance, composition, quality, essence Tem IV.i.156 [Prospero to Ferdinand] *We are such stuff / As dreams are made on;* AC V.ii.97; Cym V.v.255; H8 III.ii.137; MV I.i.4; TS Induction. ii.137

2 matter, notion, idea Ham II.ii.311 [Rosencrantz to Hamlet] *there was no such stuff in my thoughts;* Tim V.i.82

3 rubbish, nonsense Cym V.iv.146 [Posthumus alone] *such stuff as madmen / Tongue;* Mac III.iv.59; Tem II.i.258; TNK IV.iii.17, V.ii.66; TS IV.iii.87

4 material, cloth H8 III.ii.126 [King Henry to Norfolk, of what he found in Wolsey's papers] *an inventory, thus importing / The several parcels of his plate, his treasure, / Rich stuffs*

5 equipment, stores, supplies Tem I.ii.164 [Prospero to Miranda, of the help given by Gonzalo] *Rich garments, linens, stuffs, and necessaries*

6 baggage, belongings, luggage CE IV.iv.156 [Antipholus of Syracuse to Dromio of Syracuse] *away, to get our stuff aboard;* CE IV.iv.147, V.i.409

7 stock-in-trade, merchandise 2H4 II.iv.63 [Doll to Hostess, of Falstaff] *There's a whole merchant's venture of Bordeaux stuff in him* [i.e. wine]; LL IV.iii.274

8 people, rabble MM III.ii.4 [disguised Duke to himself, of Elbow and Pompey] *O heavens, what stuff is here?;* Cym I.vii.125

9 ☞ put stuff to

stuffed (*adj.*) **1** full, complete, proven, stored up RJ III.v.182 [Capulet to Lady Capulet, of Paris] *Stuffed, as they say, with honourable parts;* MA I.i.52; WT II.i.185

2 clogged, obstructed, oppressed Mac V.iii.44 [Macbeth to Doctor] *Canst thou not ... / Cleanse the stuffed bosom of that perilous stuff / Which weighs upon the heart?*

3 filled with a head-cold, clogged MA III.iv.57 [Beatrice to Hero] *I am stuffed, cousin*

stupefied (*adj.*) lacking the ability to feel, grown insensible WT II.i.165 [Leontes to Lords] *if you - or stupefied / Or seeming so in skill – cannot or will not / Relish a truth like us, inform yourselves / We need no more of your advice*

sturdy (*adj.*) disobedient, defiant, uncompromising 3H6 I.i.50 [King to all, of York] *look where the sturdy rebel sits*

sty (*v.*) confine as in a sty, coop up Tem I.ii.342 [Caliban to Prospero] *here you sty me / In this hard rock*

style (*n.*) **1** mode of address, formal title 1H6 IV.i.50 [Gloucester to all, of Burgundy] *What means his grace that he hath changed his style?;* AW II.iii.194; 1H6 IV.vii.72, 74; 2H6 I.i.109, iii.46; MW II.ii.271

2 title, name 1H6 I.v.29 [Talbot to the English] *Renounce your style* [F: *Soyle*]

style (*v.*) **1** call, name, designate TNK V.i.60 [Arcite praying to Mars] *I may ... by thee / Be styled the lord o'th' day*

2 appoint, order, assign TNK I.i.83 [Second Queen to Hippolyta, of Theseus] *Born to uphold creation in that honour / First Nature styled it in* [i.e. the position of honour that nature first gave to created things] [Q *stilde*]

stythe (*n.*) ☞ stithy (*n.*)

sub-contracted (*adj.*) already betrothed, engaged a second time KL V.iii.87 [Albany to Regan, of Gonerill] *she is sub-contracted to this lord*

subdue (*v.*) **1** get the better of, bring down, reduce KL III.iv.67 [Lear to disguised Kent, of Edgar as Poor Tom] *Nothing could have subdued nature / To such a lowness but his unkind daughters*

2 control, overcome Cor I.i.173 [Martius to Citizens] *Your virtue is / To make him worthy whose offence subdues him* [i.e. whose crime is punishable by law]

3 persuade, convince, prevail over Oth II.iii.330 [Iago alone] *'tis most easy / Th'inclining Desdemona to subdue / In any honest suit*

subdued (*adj.*) overcome, overwhelmed, subjugated Oth I.iii.247 [Desdemona to Duke, of Othello] *My heart's subdued / Even to the very quality of my lord;* AC IV.xiv.74; Oth V.ii.344; Tem I.ii.490; TNK I.ii.232

subduement (*n.*) someone overcome in a fight TC IV.v.187 [Nestor to Hector] *I have ... seen thee scorning forfeits and subduements*

subject (*n.*) **1** subjects, people [of a state] MM III.ii.130 [Lucio to disguised Duke] *the greater file of the subject held the Duke to be wise;* Ham I.i.72, ii.33; MM II.iv.27, V.i.14; Per II.i.48; WT I.i.37

2 subordinate, junior, underling KL V.iii.61 [Albany to Edmund] *I hold you but a subject of this war, / Not as a brother*

3 object, thing, creature RJ III.v.210 [Juliet to Nurse] *alack, that heaven should practise stratagems / Upon so soft a subject as myself;* Cor II.i.80; 2H4 I.i.61

4 [unclear meaning] entity with a real-world existence MM V.i.450 [Isabella to Duke] *Thoughts are no subjects*

subjection (*n.*) duty as a subject, obedience KJ V.vii.105 [Bastard to Prince Henry] *I do bequeath my faithful services / And true subjection everlastingly;* Cym IV.iii.19; H5 IV.i.142

submission (*n.*) compliance, deference, obedience 1H4 III.ii.28 [Prince Hal to King Henry] *I may ... / Find pardon on my true submission;* 1H6 II.ii.52; MW IV.v.10; RJ III.i.72

submissive (*adj.*) of submission, of surrender 1H6 IV.vii.53 [Charles to Lucy] *On what submissive message art thou sent?*

suborn (*v.*) bribe, corrupt, persuade [someone] to commit perjury Oth III.iv.149 [Desdemona to Emilia] *I find I had suborned the witness;* CE IV.iv.80; 2H4 IV.i.90; 1H6 V.iv.21; Mac II.iv.24; MM V.i.304

subornation (*n.*) aiding and abetting, inducement to do wrong, instigation E3 II.i.445 [Warwick to Countess] *An evil deed, done by authority, / Is sin and subornation;* 1H4 I.iii.161; 2H6 III.i.45, 145; Luc 919

suborned (*adj.*) bribed, corrupted Sonn 125.13 *thou suborned informer*

subscribe (*v.*) **1** concur, consent, give assent 1H6 II.iv.44 [Somerset to Vernon, of the number of roses] *If I have fewest, I subscribe in silence;* 2H6 III.i.38; KL III.vii.64; MM II.iv.89

2 sign, endorse, support E3 IV.iii.14 [Villiers to Charles, requesting a passport for Salisbury] *Will't please your highness to subscribe, or no?;* AC IV.v.14; Ham V.ii.52; H5 V.ii.328

3 make acknowledgement of, admit to TC II.iii.146 [Ajax to Agamemnon, of Achilles being a better man than Ajax] *Will you subscribe his thought, and say he is?*

4 submit, yield, give in TC IV.v.105 [Ulysses to Agamemnon] *Hector in his blaze of wrath subscribes / To tender objects*

5 write one down as, proclaim to be MA V.ii.54 [Benedick to Beatrice, of Claudio] *I will subscribe him a coward*

subscribe for (*v.*) **1** vouch for, answer on behalf of AW IV.v.30 [Lafew to Clown] *I will subscribe for thee, thou art both knave and fool;* AW III.vi.77; MA I.i.38

2 put down for [a sum of money], pledge R2 I.iv.50 [King Richard to Green, of his regents] *They shall subscribe them for large sums of gold*

subscribe to (*v.*) **1** concur with, give assent to Tit IV.iii.129 [Demetrius to Aaron] *we will all subscribe to thy advice;* TS I.i.81

2 make acknowledgement of, admit to AW V.iii.96 [Bertram to Lafew] *when I had subscribed / To mine own fortune;* TG V.iv.146

3 sign, endorse, put one's name to E3 IV.iii.48 [Charles to Villiers] *Give me the paper; I'll subscribe to it;* LL I.i.23; Per II.v.70

subscription (*n.*) obedience, allegiance; or: approval, support KL III.ii.18 [Lear to the storm] *You owe me no subscription*

subsidy (*n.*) special tax assessment 3H6 IV.viii.45 [King to Exeter, of his subjects] *I have not … much oppressed them with great subsidies;* 2H6 IV.vii.20

subsist (*v.*) continue, remain, stay Cor V.vi.73 [Coriolanus to Lords] *I am … still subsisting / Under your great command*

substance (*n.*) **1** real thing, genuine article MV III.ii.129 [Bassanio to all, of Portia's portrait] *this shadow / Doth limp behind the substance;* 1H6 II.iii.37; 2H6 I.i.13; MW II.ii.201; TG IV.ii.120, iv.198

2 property, wealth, possessions, treasure MW I.iii.34 [Pistol to Falstaff, of Ford] *He is of substance good;* CE I.i.24; H8 III.ii.326; TC I.iii.324

substantial (*adj.*) **1** real, of substance, not imaginary RJ II.ii.141 [Romeo alone] *all this is but a dream, / Too flattering-sweet to be substantial*

2 effective, thorough, forceful 2H4 IV.i.171 [Archbishop to Westmorland] *All members of our cause … / Acquitted by a true substantial form*

substitute (*n.*) subordinate, deputy, underling 1H6 V.iii.5 [Pucelle alone, to the spirits] *You speedy helpers that are substitutes;* 2H4 IV.ii.28, vi.6; MM III.i.189, IV.ii.178; R3 III.vii.180

substitute (*v.*) delegate, depute, commission 2H4 I.iii.84 [Hastings to Lord Bardolph, of King Henry's army] *who is substituted 'gainst the French / I have no certain notice*

substractor (*n.*) detractor, slanderer, calumniator TN I.iii.32 [Sir Toby to Maria, of Sir Andrew's description] *they are scoundrels and substractors that say so of him*

subtle, subtile (*adj.*) **1** crafty, cunning, wily Tit I.i.395 [Marcus to Titus] *How comes it that the subtle Queen of Goths / Is of a sudden thus advanced in Rome?;* 2H6 II.i.103; MW III.i.93; TC IV.iv.86; Tem II.i.47; TG IV.ii.92

2 tricky, deceptive, treacherous Cor V.ii.20 [Menenius to First Watch] *Like to a bowl upon a subtle ground;* Tit II.iii.198

3 refined, rarefied, very fine Tem II.i.44 [Adrian to all, of the island] *It must needs be of subtle, tender, and delicate temperance;* Tim IV.iii.431

4 fine, thin, slender TC V.ii.154 [Troilus to Ulysses, of the division in Cressida] *the spacious breadth of this division / Admits no orifex for a point as subtle / As Ariachne's broken woof to enter*

subtle-covetous (*adj.*) craftily avaricious Tim IV.iii.511 [Timon to Flavius] *Is not thy kindness subtle-covetous*

subtle-potent (*adj.*) powerfully refined TC III.ii.22 [Troilus alone, of being with Cressida] *some joy too fine, / Too subtle-potent*

subtlety (*n.*) **1** clever effect, ingenious contrivance Tem V.i.124 [Prospero to all] *You do yet taste / Some subtleties o'th' isle* [also: sugar dessert]

2 cunning, crafty stratagem Per II.v.43 [Pericles to himself, of Thaisa's letter] *'Tis the King's subtlety to have my life*

subtle-witted (*adj.*) cunning, wily, slyly intelligent 1H6 I.i.25 [Exeter to all, of Henry V] *shall we think the subtle-witted French … / By magic verses have contrived his end?*

subtly, subtilly (*adv.*) deceitfully, treacherously, deceptively RJ IV.iii.25 [Juliet alone] *What if it be a poison which the Friar / Subtly hath ministered to have me dead;* H5 IV.i.251; TC III.iii.232

suburbs (*n.*) (plural) parts of a city lying outside the walls [reputed for lawlessness] MM I.ii.95 [Pompey to Mistress Overdone] *All houses in the suburbs of Vienna must be plucked down;* H8 V.iv.71; JC II.i.285

subversion (*n.*) destruction, overthrow, ruin 2H6 III.i.208 [King to all, as if to Gloucester] *these great lords … / Do seek subversion of thy harmless life*

subvert (*v.*) destroy, overthrow, raze 1H6 II.iii.64 [Talbot to Countess, of his troops] *With which he … subverts your towns;* E3 III.iii.49

succeed (*v.*) **1** follow on, ensue, come after KL I.ii.142 [Edmund to Edgar, of a writer] *the effects he writes of succeed unhappily;* 2H6 II.iv.2; Oth II.i.187; Per I.iv.104

2 proceed, result, issue naturally Per I.i.115 [Antiochus to Pericles] *hope, succeeding from so fair a tree / As your fair self*

3 pass through inheritance, devolve Oth V.ii.363 [Lodovico to Gratiano] *seize upon the fortunes of the Moor, / For they succeed on you;* AW III.vii.23

4 inherit, come into possession of, be heir to MM II.iv.123 [Isabella to Angelo, of Claudio] *only he / Owe and succeed thy weakness*

succeeding (*n.*) consequence, result, outcome AW II.iii.190 [Parolles to Lafew, of Lafew's words] *not to be understood without bloody succeeding*

success (*n.*) **1** result, outcome, issue 3H6 II.ii.74 [Clifford to King, of the battle] *The Queen hath best success when you are absent;* AW III.vi.74; Cor V.i.63; E3 III.ii.27; KL V.iii.192; TC II.ii.118

2 fortune, destiny TG I.i.58 [Valentine to Proteus] *let me hear … / Of thy success in love;* Cor I.vi.7

3 succession, lineage, inheritance 2H4 IV.ii.47 [Hastings to Prince John] *success of mischief shall be born;* WT I.ii.394

4 course of events, process of time MA IV.i.232 [Friar to Leonato] *doubt not but success / Will fashion the event in better shape*

successantly (*adv.*) in succession, one after another Tit IV.iv.113 [Saturninus to Tamora, of Titus] *Then go successantly, and plead to him* [F; Q1 *successantly*] ⮞ **incessantly** (*adv.*)

successfully (*adv.*) likely to succeed AY I.ii.143 [Celia to Le Beau, of Orlando] *yet he looks successfully*

succession (*n.*) **1** transmission, being passed on CE III.i.105 [Balthasar to Antipholus of Ephesus] *For slander lives upon succession*

2 behaving in the same way, following the same course of action AW III.v.23 [Mariana to Diana] *so terrible shows in the wrack of maidenhead, cannot for all that dissuade succession* [stop others from doing the same thing]

3 inheritance, birthright Sonn 2.12 *this fair child of mine … / Proving his beauty by succession thine;* Tem II.i.154

4 successors, heirs Cym III.i.8 [Lucius to Cymbeline] *Cassibelan … / And his succession, granted Rome a tribute;* Cym III.iii.102

5 future [occupation as actors] Ham II.ii.350 [Hamlet to Rosencrantz, of the child players] *their writers do them wrong to make them exclaim against their own succession*

successive *(adj.)* **1** next in descent, legitimate, succeeding **2H6** III.i.49 [Suffolk to Queen, of Gloucester] *next the King he was successive heir;* **Sonn** 127.3

2 hereditary, lineal, by right of succession **Tit** I.i.4 [Saturninus to his followers] *Plead my successive title with your swords*

successively *(adv.)* by right of succession, through inheritance **2H4** IV.v.201 [King Henry IV to Prince Henry, of the crown] *thou the garland wearest successively;* **R3** III.vii.135

succour *(n.)* **1** help, assistance, aid **H8** V.v.52 [Man to Porter, of a woman in the crowd] *I might see from far some forty truncheoners draw to her succour*

2 reinforcements, military assistance **2H6** III.i.285 [Post to all, of the revolt in Ireland] *Send succours;* **H5** III.iii.45; **1H6** IV.iv.23

succour *(v.)* help, assist, aid **E3** III.iv.46 [King Edward to Audley, of Prince Edward] *I will not have a man … sent forth to succour him;* **E3** III.iv.32, IV.ii.5; **Tit** IV.iv.80

suck *(v.)* take milk from **Tit** IV.ii.177 [Aaron to the baby] *I'll make you … suck the goat*

sucked *(adj.)* drained, empty, wanting **AY** IV.iii.127 [Rosalind as Ganymede to Oliver, of Orlando's encounter with Oliver] *did he leave him there, / Food to the sucked and hungry lioness?*

sucking *(adj.)* unweaned, suckling **MND** I.ii.77 [Bottom to Quince, of his part in the play] *I will aggravate my voice so that I will roar you as gently as any sucking dove*

sudden *(adj.)* **1** swift, rapid, prompt **1H6** IV.v.11 [Talbot to John Talbot] *I'll direct thee how thou shalt escape / By sudden flight;* **Ham** I.v.68; **1H6** V.v.99; **H8** V.iii.20; **JC** III.i.19; **KJ** IV.i.27

2 hasty, impulsive, impetuous **3H6** V.v.86 [Edward to George, of Richard] *He's sudden if a thing comes in his head;* **Cor** III.i.250

3 immediate, early, prompt **R3** III.iv.43 [Derby to all, of the coronation] *Tomorrow … is too sudden;* **Oth** IV.ii.189; **RJ** III.v.109

4 unexpected, unpredictable, unlooked for **KJ** V.vi.26 [Hubert to Bastard, telling him of King John's illness] *that you might / The better arm you to the sudden time*

5 unpremeditated, extempore, unrehearsed **H8** V.iii.122 [King Henry to Gardiner] *You were ever good at sudden commendations;* **1H6** III.i.6

6 unpredictable, prone to sudden violence **Oth** II.i.263 [Iago to Roderigo, of Cassio] *he's rash and very sudden in choler;* **AY** II.vii.152; **2H4** IV.iv.34; **Mac** III.iii.59; **R2** II.i.35

7 sharp, caustic, biting **TG** IV.ii.12 [Proteus alone, of Silvia] *notwithstanding all her sudden quips*

sudden, of / on / upon a / the **1** suddenly **AC** I.ii.83 [Cleopatra to Charmian, of Antony] *on the sudden / A Roman thought hath struck him;* **TS** I.i.144 [Tranio to Lucentio] *is it possible / That love should of a sudden take such hold?;* **Cor** I.iv.52; **2H4** IV.ii.80; **H8** IV.ii.96; **RJ** II.iii.46; **Tit** I.i.396

2 soon, at an early date **Cor** II.i.213 [Sicinius to Brutus, of Coriolanus] *On the sudden / I warrant him consul*

sudden-bold *(adj.)* hastily presumptious **LL** II.i.107 [Princess to King] *I am too sudden-bold*

suddenly *(adv.)* **1** immediately, at once, without delay **MW** IV.i.6 [Mistress Quickly to Mistress Page] *Mistress Ford desires you to come suddenly;* **AY** II.ii.19; **1H4** III.iii.5; **LL** II.i.110; **Luc** 1683; **R3** IV.iv.451

2 extempore, spontaneously, off the cuff **1H6** III.i.5 [Winchester to Gloucester, of any accusation] *Do it without invention, suddenly;* **2H6** III.i.128; **H8** III.i.70

sue *(v.)* **1** beg, plead, beseech **KL** I.i.29 [Kent to Edmund] *I must love you and sue to know you better;* **AC** I.iii.33; **AW** II.i.62; **LL** V.ii.427; **MW** II.i.160; **Tim** III.v.95

2 pay court, act as a suitor **LL** III.i.186 [Berowne alone] *What? I love? I sue? I seek a wife?;* **TG** II.i.130

3 initiate, institute, prosecute **H8** III.ii.341 [Suffolk to Wolsey] *a writ be sued against you*

sue one's livery institute a suit to obtain possession of lands **R2** II.iii.128 [Bolingbroke to York] *I am denied to sue my livery here;* **1H4** IV.iii.62; **R2** II.i.203

sued-for *(adj.)* begged for, entreated, petitioned **Cor** II.iii.207 [Sicinius to Citizens, of Coriolanus] *Of him … bestow / Your sued-for tongues?*

suffer *(v.)* **1** allow, permit, let **Tit** IV.iv.83 [Tamora to Saturninus] *The eagle suffers little birds to sing;* **Cym** I.ii.101; **1H6** V.iv.127; **RJ** II.iv.152; **Tem** III.i.62; **Venus** 388

2 put up with, tolerate, do nothing about **R2** II.i.164 [York to King Richard] *how long / Shall tender duty make me suffer wrong?;* **1H4** V.i.139; **2H6** III.ii.262; **KL** I.ii.51; **R2** II.i.269; **TS** II.i.31

3 undergo, sustain, endure **Tem** I.ii.401 [Ariel singing to Ferdinand, of his father] *Nothing of him that doth fade, / But doth suffer a sea-change;* **Ham** V.ii.112; **H8** I.ii.51; **KL** II.iv.44; **TN** II.iv.98

4 bear, endure, stand **KL** III.iv.141 [Gloucester to Lear] *My duty cannot suffer / T'obey in all your daughters' hard commands;* **AW** II.ii.38; **Cym** I.v.52; **Sonn** 58.5

5 hold up, stand up, remain valid **TN** II.v.127 [Malvolio to himself] *there is no consonancy in the sequel that suffers under probation*

6 perish, be destroyed, collapse **Tem** II.ii.35 [Trinculo to himself, of Caliban] *This is … an islander that hath lately suffered by a thunderbolt;* **AC** III.xiii.34; **Mac** III.ii.16; **MM** II.ii.106; **Per** IV.iv.23

7 injure, wound, hurt **2H6** V.i.153 [Richard to Clifford, of a dog at a bear-baiting] *being suffered with the bear's fell paw* [or, with comma after 'suffered': allowed]

8 be wronged, be abused **Per** IV.iv.23 [Gower alone] *See how belief may suffer by foul show!*

sufferance *(n.)* **1** distress, suffering, hardship **H8** II.iii.15 [Anne to Old Lady, of losing pomp] *'tis a sufferance panging / As soul and body's severing;* **2H4** V.iv.25; **JC** II.i.115; **Oth** I.iii.23; **TC** I.i.30; **Tim** IV.iii.269

2 endurance, forbearance, patience **MV** I.iii.107 [Shylock to Antonio] *sufferance is the badge of all our tribe;* **Cor** III.i.24; **Cym** III.v.35; **H5** II.vi.123; **JC** I.iii.84; **MA** I.iii.9

3 permission, consent, acquiescence, say-so **3H6** I.i.234 [Queen to King] *Thou hast … given unto the house of York such head / As thou shalt reign but by their sufferance;* **AY** II.ii.3

4 reprieve, pardoning, respite **H5** II.ii.46 [Scroop to King Henry, of an offender] *Let him be punished, … lest example / Breed, by his sufferance, more of such a kind*

suffered *(adj.)* undergone, sustained, endured **Tem** I.ii.231 [Ariel to Prospero, of the mariners] *with a charm joined to their suffered labour, / I have left asleep*

suffering *(adj.)* long-suffering, patient, submissive **JC** II.i.130 [Brutus to all] *such suffering souls / That welcome wrongs*

suffice *(v.)* **1** satisfy, nourish, provide for **KJ** I.i.191 [Bastard alone] *when my knightly stomach is sufficed;* **AW** III.v.10; **AY** II.vii.132; **Luc** 1112; **Sonn** 37.11

2 satisfy, content, be enough [for] **TC** II.iii.66 [Thersites to Patroclus, responding to 'Why am I a fool?'] *it suffices me thou art;* **LL** II.i.167; **Tit** I.i.112; **TS** III.ii.105

sufficiency *(n.)* competence, ability, capability **Oth** I.iii.222 [Duke to Othello, of the person in charge in Cyprus] *we have there a substitute of most allowed sufficiency;* **MA** V.i.29; **MM** I.i.8; **WT** II.i.185

sufficient *(adj.)* able, capable, competent **TS** IV.iv.91 [Biondello to Lucentio] *Take … some sufficient honest witnesses;* **2H4** III.ii.93; **MM** II.i.260; **MV** I.iii.17; **Oth** IV.i.267; **TNK** II.i.156

sufficing *(adj.)* sufficient, enough, adequate **AC** IV.xiv.117 [Antony to Diomedes] *Draw thy sword, and give me / Sufficing strokes for death*

suffigance *(adj.)* malapropism for 'sufficient' **MA** III.v.47 [Dogberry to Leonato] *It shall be suffigance*

suffrage (*n.*) vote, approval, consent Tit I.i.221 [Titus to Tribunes] *I ask your voices and your suffrages;* **Cor** II.ii.136; **Per** II.iv.41; **Tit** IV.iii.19

sugared (*adj.*) **1** flattering, honeyed, ingratiating 1H6 III.iii.18 [Pucelle to all] *By fair persuasions, mixed with sugared words;* **R3** III.i.13
2 sweetly tempting, outwardly attractive Tim IV.iii.260 [Timon to Apemantus] *and never learned / The icy precepts of respect, but followed / The sugared game before thee*

suggest (*v.*) **1** tempt, prompt, incite R2 III.iv.75 [Queen Isabel to Gardener] *what serpent hath suggested thee / To make a second Fall of cursed man?;* **AW** IV.v.43; **H5** II.ii.114; **Luc** 37; **Sonn** 144.2; **TG** III.i.34
2 present ideas, make suggestions TNK IV.iii.91 [Doctor to Wooer, of the Gaoler's Daughter's companions] *let them ... appear with tokens, as if they suggested for him* [i.e. were making proposals on Palamon's behalf]
3 [of an idea] insinuate [to], make hints [to] Cor II.i.237 [Brutus to Sicinius, of Coriolanus] *We must suggest the people in what hatred / He still hath held them;* **Cor** II.i.245

suggestion (*n.*) temptation, instigation, prompting towards evil Mac I.iii.133 [Macbeth to himself] *why do I yield to that suggestion / Whose horrid image doth unfix my hair;* **AW** III.v.17; **1H4** IV.iii.51; **2H4** IV.iv.45; **H8** IV.ii.35; **KJ** III.i.292

suing (*adj.*) persistently entreating, importuning, chasing TNK IV.iii.54 [Gaoler's Daughter to herself] *th'other [woman] curses a suing fellow and her garden-house*

suit (*n.*) **1** formal request, entreaty, petition Ham I.ii.43 [Claudius to Laertes] *You told us of some suit* **☛** FEW, p.xxi
2 wooing, courtship MA II.i.324 [Leonato to Don Pedro, of Beatrice] *she mocks all her wooers out of suit;* **Cym** V.v.185; **LL** V.ii.275; **MV** I.ii.97, II.vii.73; **Venus** 206
3 court attendance, personal retinue MM IV.iv.15 [Angelo to Escalus, of the Duke] *Give notice to such men of sort and suit / As are to meet him;* **Lover** 234
4 clothing, dress, garb TN V.i.232 [Viola as Cesario to Sebastian] *If spirits can assume both form and suit / You come to fright us;* **AY** II.vii.44, IV.i.78, 80; **1H4** I.ii.71

suits, in all in all respects TS Induction.i.104 [Lord to Servant, of Bartholomew] *see him dressed in all suits like a lady* [also: garments]

suit (*v.*) **1** dress, clothe, equip Cym V.i.23 [Posthumus alone] *I'll ... suit myself / As does a Briton peasant;* **AY** I.iii.114; **H5** IV.ii.51; **KL** IV.vii.6; **Sonn** 132.12; **TN** V.i.231
2 match, compare, equate MA V.i.7 [Leonato to Antonio] *such a one whose wrongs do suit with mine;* **H5** I.ii.17; **Mac** II.i.60; **TN** I.ii.51
3 act in accordance with, conform to Tim II.ii.26 [Caphis to Timon] *with your other noble parts you'll suit / In giving him his right*

suited (*adj.*) dressed up, set out, adapted MV II.v.60 [Lorenzo to Jessica, of Launcelot] *how his words are suited;* **MA** V.i.215

suitor (*n.*) petitioner, supplicant, entreater JC II.iii.11 [Artemidorus alone, of his letter to Caesar] *as a suitor I will give him this;* **AW** V.iii.151; **Cor** I.i.58; **3H6** III.i.19; **R3** I.iii.64; **TNK** III.i.114

sullen (*n.*) (plural) sullenness, gloomy mood, sulks R2 II.i.139 [King Richard to all, of John of Gaunt] *let them die that age and sullens have*

sullen (*adj.*) **1** gloomy, dismal, melancholy, mournful R2 I.iii.265 [John of Gaunt to Bolingbroke] *The sullen passage of thy weary steps;* **2H4** I.i.102; **KJ** I.i.28; **R2** I.iii.227; **RJ** IV.v.88; **Sonn** 71.2
2 dull, drab, sombre 2H6 I.i.5 [Duchess of Gloucester to Gloucester] *Why are thine eyes fixed to the sullen earth;* **1H4** I.ii.210; **Sonn** 29.12

sullied (*adj.*) tarnished, blemished, polluted Ham I.ii.129 [Hamlet alone] *O that this too too sullied flesh would melt* [reading of Q1, Q2 *sallied;* F *solid*]; **Sonn** 15.12

sully (*n.*) blemish, stain, flaw Ham II.i.39 [Polonius to Reynaldo] *You laying these slight sullies on my son* [F; Q2 *sallies*]

sully (*v.*) dim, stain, tarnish 1H4 II.iv.73 [Prince Hal to Francis] *your white canvas doublet will sully;* 1H6 IV.iv.6; TNK I.ii.5

sulphur (*n.*) **1** fire, fiery substance, hellfire TNK V.iv.64 [Pirithous to Palamon] *a spark, / Or what fierce sulphur else*
2 lightning Cor V.iii.152 [Volumnia to Coriolanus] *to charge thy sulphur with a bolt / That should but rive an oak* **☛** stone of sulphur

sulphur (*adj.*) fiery, hellish E3 III.i.121 [King John, as if to the French forces] *the sulphur battles of your rage*

sum (*n.*) **1** summary, gist, essence 2H4 I.i.131 [Morton to Northumberland] *The sum of all / Is that the King hath won;* **AC** I.i.18; **Per** III.Chorus.33
2 amount of money Tim III.iv.93 [Timon to Servants, of his creditors] *Cut my heart in sums*

sum (*v.*) audit, count up, enumerate Sonn 2.11 *this fair child of mine / Shall sum my count*

sumless (*adj.*) incalculable, immeasurable, beyond estimation H5 I.ii.165 [Canterbury to King Henry, of the bottom of the sea] *With sunken wrack and sumless treasuries*

summer (*n.*) **☛** Saint Martin's summer

summer (*adj.*) joyful, pleasant, happy R3 IV.iii.13 [Tyrrel alone, of the Princes] *Their lips were four red roses on a stalk, / Which in their summer beauty kissed each other;* **Cym** III.iv.12; **WT** IV.iii.11

summer (*v.*) nurture, care for, tend [during summer] H5 V.ii.303 [Burgundy to King Henry] *maids, well summered and warm kept, are like flies at Bartholomew-tide*

summer-leaping (*adj.*) delighting in the summertime E3 II.i.108 [King Edward to Lodowick] *To music every summer-leaping swain / Compares his sun-burnt lover when she speaks*

summer-seeming (*adj.*) befitting the summer-time [of life: early manhood] Mac IV.iii.86 [Macduff to Malcolm] *This avarice / Sticks deeper, grows with more pernicious root / Than summer-seeming lust* **☛** seeming (*adj.*)

summon (*v.*) call to a meeting [to discuss terms] Cor I.iv.7 [Lartius to trumpeter] *Summon the town*

summoner (*n.*) court-officer who ensures attendance KL III.ii.59 [Lear to disguised Kent, as if to a criminal addressing the storm] *cry / These dreadful summoners grace*

sumpter (*n.*) pack-horse, drudge KL II.iv.211 [Lear to all, of Oswald] *Persuade me rather to be slave and sumpter / To this detested groom*

sun (*n.*) sunrise, dawn, daybreak TNK II.iv.51 [Theseus to all] *you must be ready ... / Tomorrow by the sun, to do observance / To flowery May*

sun, in the out in the open, free from care AY II.v.36 [All, singing] *Who doth ambition shun, / And loves to live i'th' sun*

sun of, get the attack with the sun in their eyes LL IV.iii.345 [Berowne to all, of the ladies] *be first advised / In conflict that you get the sun of them* [with bawdy pun]

sun to sun, from from sunrise to sunset Cym III.ii.69 [Pisanio to Innogen, of the miles to be covered] *One score 'twixt sun and sun;* **R2** IV.i.55

sunburnt (*adj.*) of dark complexion, not fair-skinned [and therefore unattractive] MA II.i.294 [Beatrice to Claudio] *I am sunburnt;* **TC** I.iii.282

sunder (*v.*) **1** separate, split up, part MND V.i.131 [Quince to all, of Snout] *that vile wall which did these lovers sunder;* **AW** II.v.86; **2H6** III.ii.411; **3H6** IV.i.23; **MV** III.ii.120; **TNK** V.iv.100
2 cut, divide, put an end to TC V.x.27 [Troilus to all, as if to Achilles] *No space of earth shall sunder our two hates;* **RJ** V.iii.100

sunder, in asunder, apart, into pieces CE V.i.250 [Antipholus of Ephesus to Duke] *gnawing with my teeth my bonds in sunder;* 3H6 I.iii.15

sundered (*adj.*) separated, kept apart 1H6 IV.iii.42 [Richard to Lucy] *Vexation almost stops my breath / That sundered friends greet in the hour of death;* R3 V.iii.101

sundry (*adj.*) many, different, various E3 IV.iv.28 [Audley to Prince Edward, of Philip's pendants] *their device of antique heraldry, / Quartered in colours, seeming sundry fruits*

sun-expelling (*adj.*) protecting against the sun [to preserve facial beauty] TG IV.iv.150 [disguised Julia to Silvia, of Julia] *she ... threw her sun-expelling mask away*

sup (*v.*) **1** have supper 2H6 I.iv.79 [York to servingman] *Invite my lords of Salisbury and Warwick / To sup with me tomorrow night* ☛ FEW, p.xxi
2 provide supper for LL V.ii.689 [Berowne to Dumaine, of Armado as Hector] *if 'a have no more man's blood in his belly than will sup a flea*
3 give the last daily feed to TS Induction.i.26 [Lord to First Huntsman, of the hounds] *sup them well*

super-dainty (*adj.*) supremely excellent TS II.i.188 [Petruchio to Katherina, of descriptions of her] *my super-dainty Kate* [pun: 189] ☛ dainty (*adj.*)

superficial (*adj.*) of surface qualities, of outward gifts 1H6 V.v.10 [Suffolk to King, of Margaret] *this superficial tale / Is but a preface of her worthy praise*

superfinical (*adj.*) ☛ finical (*adj.*); super-serviceable (*adj.*)

superfluity **1** spare availability, additional instance 2H4 II.ii.17 [Prince Henry to Poins] *What a disgrace is it to me ... to bear the inventory of thy shirts, as, one for superfluity, and another for use!* [i.e. for change of wear]
2 excess, indulgence, immoderate living MV I.ii.7 [Nerissa to Portia] *superfluity comes sooner by white hairs, but competency lives longer*

superfluous (*adj.*) **1** extravagant, wasteful, immoderate AW I.i.104 [Helena to herself] *full oft we see / Cold wisdom waiting on superfluous folly;* Ham IV.v.97; H8 I.i.99; Per I.iv.54
2 having too much, over-supplied, overflowing KL II.iv.260 [Lear to Regan] *Our basest beggars / Are in the poorest thing superfluous;* KL IV.i.66
3 needlessly concerned, unnecessary 1H4 I.ii.11 [Prince Hal to Falstaff] *I see no reason why thou shouldst be so superfluous to demand the time of the day* [also: immoderate]

superflux (*n.*) superfluity, superabundance, surplus possessions KL III.iv.35 [Lear to himself, of the behaviour of rich to poor] *That thou mayst shake the superflux to them*

supernal (*adj.*) celestial, heavenly, divine KJ II.i.112 [King Philip to King John, of the origin of France's right] *From that supernal judge that stirs good thoughts*

superscript (*n.*) address, heading, opening LL IV.i.60 [stage direction, of Boyet] *He reads the superscript;* LL IV.ii.130

superscription (*n.*) address, direction [on a letter] Tim II.ii.81 [Page to Apemantus] *read me the superscription of these letters;* 1H6 IV.i.53

super-serviceable (*adj.*) offering service beyond what is needed, officious KL II.ii.16 [disguised Kent to Oswald, describing him] *super-serviceable ... rogue* [F; Q *superfinicall*]

superstitious (*adj.*) loving to the point of idolatry, excessively devoted H8 III.i.131 [Queen Katherine to Campeius and Wolsey, of herself] *Still met the King ... / Been, out of fondness, superstitious to him*

superstitiously (*adv.*) paying special attention; or: with irrational belief WT III.iii.39 [Antigonus to baby Perdita, of his dream] *Dreams are toys: / Yet for this once, yea superstitiously, / I will be squared by this*

super-subtle (*adj.*) extra-refined, specially delicate Oth I.iii.351 [Iago to Roderigo, of Othello's marriage to Desdemona] *a frail vow betwixt an erring barbarian and a super-subtle Venetian*

supervise (*n.*) perusal, reading, sight Ham V.ii.23 [Hamlet to Horatio, of the letter sent to the King of England] *on the supervise*

supervise (*v.*) look over, read through, peruse LL IV.ii.120 [Holofernes to Nathaniel, of Berowne's letter to Rosaline] *Let me supervise the canzonet*

supervisor (*n.*) onlooker, spectator, observer Oth III.iii.392 [Iago to Othello] *Would you, the supervisor, grossly gape on?* [Q1; F *supervision*]

supping (*n.*) taking supper CE IV.iii.65 [Antipholus of Syracuse to Courtesan] *What tellest thou me of supping?*

supplant (*v.*) get rid of, root out Tem III.ii.49 [Stephano to Trinculo] *I will supplant some of your teeth;* R2 II.i.156

suppliance (*n.*) pastime, diversion Ham I.iii.9 [Laertes to Ophelia, of Hamlet's love] *The perfume and suppliance of a minute*

suppliant (*adj.*) ☛ supplyant (*adj.*)

supplication (*n.*) petition, written request 2H6 IV.iv.1 [stage direction] *Enter the King with a supplication;* 2H6 I.iii.3, IV.iv.8; Tit IV.iii.106

supply (*n.*) reinforcement(s), support, relief KJ V.iii.9 [Messenger to King John, of French reinforcements] *the great supply / That was expected by the Dauphin here / Are wracked;* Cym V.iii.16; 1H4 IV.iii.3; 2H4 I.iii.28; 1H6 I.i.159; 3H6 III.iii.237

supply (*v.*) **1** fill up, take [the place of], occupy, substitute Oth III.iii.17 [Cassio to Desdemona] *I being absent and my place supplied;* 3H6 IV.vi.50; MM I.i.18
2 fill, contribute to Tim III.i.19 [Flaminius to Lucullus, of his empty box] *which ... I come to entreat your honour to supply;* Tim III.ii.36
3 reinforce, support, strengthen Mac I.ii.13 [Captain to King] *The merciless Macdonwald ... from the Western Isles / Of kerns and galloglasses is supplied*
4 maintain, provide for, sustain Tim IV.ii.47 [Flavius alone, of Timon] *Nor has he with him to supply his life*
5 satisfy, fulfil, gratify [sexually] MM V.i.210 [Mariana to Angelo] *This is the body / That ... did supply thee at thy garden-house;* Oth IV.i.28

supplyant, suppliant (*adj.*) ready to supply, making up the deficiency Cym III.viii.14 [First Senator to all, of the legions] *whereunto your levy / Must be supplyant* [F *suppliant*]

supplyment (*n.*) continuing with a supply, ongoing provision Cym III.iv.181 [Pisanio to Innogen] *I will never fail / Beginning, nor supplyment*

support (*v.*) endure, bear, sustain Oth I.iii.256 [Desdemona to Duke, of Othello] *I a heavy interim shall support / By his dear absence*

supportable (*adj.*) bearable, endurable, sustainable Tem V.i.145 [Prospero to Alonso, of the loss of his daughter] *supportable / To make the dear loss*

supportance (*n.*) support, propping up, reinforcement R2 III.iv.32 [Gardener to First Man] *Give some supportance to the bending twigs;* TN III.iv.291

supposal (*n.*) estimate, opinion, notion Ham I.ii.18 [Claudius to his court] *Young Fortinbras, / Holding a weak supposal of our worth*

suppose (*n.*) **1** supposition, belief, impression Tit I.i.443 [Tamora to Saturninus, of Titus] *Lose not so noble a friend on vain suppose;* TS V.i.106
2 expectation, hope; purpose, intention TC I.iii.11 [Agamemnon to all] *we come short of our suppose so far / That ... yet Troy walls stand*

suppose (*v.*) **1** guess at, speculate about Sonn 57.10 *Nor dare I question ... / Where you may be, or your affairs suppose;* 1H6 IV.i.186
2 consider, regard, deem 2H4 I.i.202 [Morton to Northumberland, of the Archbishop] *Supposed sincere and holy in his thoughts*
3 presume to be true, believe to be a fact Sonn 93.1 *So shall I live, supposing thou art true;* CE III.i.101

supposed (*adj.*) **1** pretended, false, counterfeit **MW** IV.iv.60 [Mistress Ford to all, of Falstaff] *Let the supposed fairies pinch him sound;* **KL** V.iii.110; **Tim** V.i.13; **TS** II.i.400

2 imagined, fancied **Luc** 455 [of Lucrece woken by Tarquin] *heedfully doth view / The sight which makes supposed terror true;* **Luc** 377

3 malapropism for 'deposed' **MM** II.i.148 [Pompey to Escalus] *I'll be supposed upon a book*

supposing (*n.*) imagination, creative thinking **Per** V.Chorus.21 [Gower alone] *In your supposing once more put your sight*

supposition (*n.*) **1** notion, opinion, belief **MA** IV.i.236 [Friar to Leonato, of Hero] *The supposition of the lady's death / Will quench the wonder of her infamy;* **AW** IV.iii.291; **CE** III.ii.50

2 doubt, uncertainty, question **MV** I.iii.17 [Shylock to Bassanio, of Antonio] *his means are in supposition*

supreme (*n.*) supreme ruler, king, highest in authority **Venus** 996 [of Venus and death] *She clepes him … / Imperious supreme of all mortal things;* **Luc** 780 ➤ co-supreme (*n.*)

sur-addition (*n.*) surname, additional title **Cym** I.i.33 [First Gentleman to Second Gentleman, of Posthumus] *gained the sur-addition Leonatus* ➤ addition (*n.*) 1

surance (*n.*) assurance, guarantee, pledge **Tit** V.ii.46 [Titus to disguised Tamora] *Now give some surance that thou art Revenge*

surcease (*n.*) cessation, termination, completion **Mac** I.vii.4 [Macbeth alone] *If the assassination / Could trammel up the consequence, and catch / With his surcease success*

surcease (*v.*) cease, stop, leave off **RJ** IV.i.97 [Friar to Juliet, of taking the potion] *no pulse / Shall keep his native progress, but surcease;* **Cor** III.ii.121; **Luc** 1766

sure (*adj.*) **1** certain, definite, reliable **Tim** III.iv.49 [Flavius to all] *If money were as certain as your waiting, / 'Twere sure enough;* **CE** II.ii.194; **Ham** IV.v.13; **2H6** II.i.200; **KL** IV.vi.210

2 harmless, innocuous, unable to cause damage **Per** I.i.168 [Thaliard to Antiochus, of Pericles] *I'll make him sure enough;* **1H4** V.iii.47; **Tit** II.iii.133, 187

3 safe, secure, free from danger **TG** V.i.12 [Eglamour to Silvia, of the forest] *If we recover that, we are sure enough;* **MW** IV.ii.5

4 loyal, trustworthy, steadfast **Cor** I.i.170 [Martius to Citizens] *You are no surer, no, / Than is the coal of fire upon the ice;* **Cym** I.vii.139; **1H4** III.i.1; **MA** I.iii.63

5 betrothed, joined, bound **AY** V.iv.132 [Hymen to Touchstone and Audrey] *You and you are sure together;* **LL** V.ii.285; **MW** V.v.216

sure (*adv.*) **1** securely, safely, well **2H6** III.i.188 [Cardinal to his men] *take away the Duke and guard him sure;* **2H4** II.i.24; **JC** I.iii.318, IV.i.47; **Tim** III.iii.40; **Tit** V.ii.76, 164

2 surely, assuredly, certainly **AY** V.iv.35 [Jaques to all] *There is sure another flood toward;* **AY** III.v.11; **Cor** III.i.271; **Cym** V.v.260; **2H6** V.i.13; **Tem** II.i.320

surely (*adv.*) certainly, doubtless, assuredly **TS** I.i.248 [Sly to Lord, of the play] *A good matter, surely*

surety (*n.*) **1** guarantee, ratification, warrant **TC** V.ii.60 [Diomedes to Cressida, of her promise] *Give me some token for the surety of it;* **1H4** III.i.245; **2H4** I.i.191; **H5** V.ii.364; **KJ** III.i.282; **TC** I.iii.220

2 person undertaking a legal responsibility in relation to another, guarantor **Tem** I.ii.476 [Miranda to Prospero, of Ferdinand] *I'll be his surety;* **AW** IV.iv.3, V.iii.108; **MV** I.i.77, V.i.254; **R2** IV.i.159

3 security, confidence, stability **TC** II.ii.14 [Hector to Priam] *The wound of peace is surety;* **KJ** V.vii.68

4 certainty, fact **Oth** I.iii.384 [Iago alone, of his suspicions] *I know not if't be true / But I … / Will do as if for surety*

surety (*v.*) go bail for, act as a guarantor for **Cor** III.i.177 [Patricians to all, of Coriolanus] *We'll surety him;* **AW** V.iii.295

surety-like (*adv.*) like a guarantor, proxy-like **Sonn** 134.7 [of his friend] *He learned but surety-like to write for me*

surfeit (*n.*) **1** excess, over-indulgence **MM** I.ii.125 [Claudio to Lucio] *surfeit is the father of much fast;* **Cor** IV.i.46; **TNK** II.i.140, IV.iii.69

2 sickness brought on by excess **R3** I.iii.196 [Queen Margaret to all] *Though not by war, by surfeit die your king;* **AC** I.iv.27; **KL** I.ii.119; **Tim** IV.iii.228; **TN** II.iv.98; **TNK** I.i.190

surfeit (*v.*) **1** feed to excess, overindulge, glut **MV** I.ii.5 [Nerissa to Portia] *they are as sick that surfeit with too much as they that starve with nothing;* **Cor** I.i.15; **2H4** I.iii.88; **MM** V.i.102; **Oth** II.i.50; **TN** I.i.2

2 become sick through having too much **TG** III.i.220 [Valentine to Proteus, of woe] *excess of it will make me surfeit;* **Luc** 139; **MV** III.ii.114; **Sonn** 75.13

surfeited (*adj.*) overfilled, intemperate, saturated **Mac** II.ii.5 [Lady Macbeth alone] *the surfeited grooms / Do mock their charge with snores*

surfeiter (*n.*) profligate, libertine, debaucher **AC** II.i.33 [Pompey to Menas, of Antony] *I did not think / This amorous surfeiter would have donned his helm / For such a petty war*

surfeiting (*n.*) feeding to excess, overindulgence **2H4** IV.i.55 [Archbishop to Westmorland] *we are all diseased, / And with our surfeiting and wanton hours / Have brought ourselves into a burning fever*

surfeit-swelled (*adj.*) swollen through over-indulgence **2H4** V.v.53 [King Henry V to and of Falstaff] *So surfeit-swelled, so old, and so profane*

surfeit-taking (*adj.*) over-indulging **Luc** 698 *So surfeit-taking Tarquin fares this night*

surge (*n.*) heavy wave, violent sea **Per** III.i.1 [Pericles alone] *The god of this great vast rebuke these surges*

surgeon (*n.*) doctor, physician **Oth** II.iii.247 [Othello to Montano] *for your hurts myself will be your surgeon;* **KL** IV.vi.193; **MND** V.i.302; **MV** IV.i.254; **Per** IV.vi.10; **RJ** III.i.94

surly (*adj.*) **1** imperious, haughty, arrogant **TN** II.v.145 [Malvolio reading the letter] *Be opposite with a kinsman, surly with servants;* **H5** I.ii.202; **JC** I.iii.21

2 gloomy, dismal, stern **Sonn** 71.2 *you shall hear the surly sullen bell*

surmise (*n.*) **1** idea, imagining, conjecture **E3** III.ii.44 [Woman to all] *such like surmises / Strike many Frenchmen cold unto the heart;* **2H4** I.iii.23; **Luc** 83; **Mac** I.iii.140; **Tit** II.iii.219

2 reflection, imagining, contemplation **Luc** 1579 [of Lucrece] *from the feeling of her own grief brought / By deep surmise of others' detriment*

surmise (*v.*) imagine, suppose, conjecture **Ham** II.ii.108 [Polonius to Claudius and Gertrude] *Now gather, and surmise;* **2H6** III.ii.347

surmised (*adj.*) imagined, hoped-for, intended **TC** I.iii.17 [Agamemnon to all, of their war efforts] *trial did draw / Bias and thwart, not answering the aim … / That gave't surmised shape*

surmount (*v.*) excel, surpass, outshine **LL** V.ii.667 [Armado to audience] *This Hector far surmounted Hannibal;* **1H4** V.iii.191; **R2** II.iii.64; **Sonn** 62.8

surprise (*n.*) **1** taking by surprise, catching unawares **MW** V.v.123 [Falstaff to all] *the sudden surprise of my powers*

2 alarm, terror [caused by a fearful event] **Per** III.ii.16 [First Gentleman to Cerimon, of being affected by the storm] *Pure surprise and fear / Made me to quit the house*

surprise (*v.*) **1** attack, capture, seize **2H6** IV.viii.57 [Cade to himself, of the rebels] *I see them lay their heads together to surprise me;* **1H6** V.iii.40; **Tit** IV.i.51

2 take prisoner, capture [especially: suddenly, unexpectedly] **3H6** IV.ii.25 [Warwick to George, of Edward] *I intend but only to surprise him;* **1H4** I.i.92; **2H6** IV.ix.8; **3H6** IV.iv.9; **Tit** I.i.287; **TN** I.iv.25

3 astonish, bewilder, perplex **WT** III.i.10 [Cleomenes to Dion] *the ear-deaf'ning voice o'th' oracle … so surprised my sense / That I was nothing;* **Tim** V.i.154; **Tit** II.iii.211

4 take off guard **LL** V.ii.84 [Boyet to ladies] *You'll be surprised*

sur-reined (*adj.*) over-ridden, overworked, worn out **H5** III.v.19 [Constable to all] *sodden water, / A drench for sur-reined jades*

surrender (*n.*) giving up, resignation [of power] **KL** I.i.304 [Gonerill to Regan, of Lear] *this last surrender of his will but offend us*

surrender (*v.*) abdicate, resign, give up the throne **R2** IV.i.156 [Bolingbroke to all] *Fetch hither Richard, that in common view / He may surrender*

survey (*v.*) **1** see, note, perceive **Mac** I.ii.31 [Captain to King] *the Norweyan lord, surveying vantage … / Began a fresh assault*

2 inspect, look over, examine carefully **1H6** I.iii.1 [Gloucester to servingman] *I am come to survey the Tower this day*

surveyor (*n.*) **1** superintendent, land agent, estate supervisor **H8** I.i.222 [Buckingham to all] *My surveyor is false*; **H8** I.i.115, ii.172, II.i.19

2 guardian, supervisor, overseer **2H6** III.i.253 [Suffolk to Queen, of Gloucester] *were't not madness … / To make the fox surveyor of the fold?*

suspect (*n.*) suspicion, mistrust, doubt **2H6** III.ii.139 [King to himself, as if to God] *If my suspect be false, forgive me*; **CE** III.i.87; **3H6** IV.i.141; **R3** I.iii.88; **Sonn** 70.3; **Tim** IV.iii.515

suspected (*adj.*) doubted, regarded with suspicion **AW** I.iii.176 [Countess to Helena] *truth should be suspected*

suspense (*n.*) suspicion, doubt, uncertainty **2H6** III.i.140 [King to Gloucester] *'tis my special hope / That you will clear yourself from all suspense* [F *suspence*]

suspicion (*n.*) anxiety, apprehension, trepidation **3H6** V.vi.11 [Richard to King] *Suspicion always haunts the guilty mind*; **3H6** V.vii.13

suspiration (*n.*) deep sighing, intense breathing **Ham** I.ii.79 [Hamlet to Gertrude] *windy suspiration of forced breath*

suspire (*v.*) breathe **2H4** IV.v.34 [Prince Henry to himself, of a feather lying by King Henry IV's 'gates of breath'] *Did he suspire, that light and weightless down / Perforce must move*; **KJ** III.iv.80

sustain (*v.*) **1** receive, undergo, experience **Cym** I.v.112 [Posthumus to Iachimo] *I doubt not you sustain what you're worthy of*; **Tim** V.i.199

2 endure, withstand, support **AC** I.iii.17 [Cleopatra to Charmian] *It cannot be thus long; the sides of nature / Will not sustain it*

3 take up a position, have a place **Oth** V.ii.258 [Othello to Gratiano] *I have a weapon: / A better never did itself sustain / Upon a soldier's thigh*

4 provide for, furnish with necessities **KL** III.iii.5 [Gloucester to Edmund, of Lear] *charged me … neither to speak of him, entreat for him, or any way sustain him*

sustaining (*adj.*) life-supporting, nourishing **KL** IV.iv.6 [Cordelia to Doctor, of Lear] *Crowned with … all the idle weeds that grow / In our sustaining corn*; **Tem** I.ii.218

sutler (*n.*) provision-seller to the army **H5** II.i.106 [Pistol to Nym] *I shall sutler be / Unto the camp*

swabber (*n.*) deckhand, sailor who washes the deck **Tem** II.ii.45 [Stephano to himself, singing] *The master, the swabber, the boatswain, and I*; **TN** I.v.196

swaddling clouts (*n.*) ☞ swathing clothes (*n.*)

swag-bellied (*adj.*) pendulous-bellied, with a hanging paunch **Oth** II.iii.73 [Iago to Cassio] *Your Dane … and your swag-bellied Hollander … are nothing to your English*

swagger (*v.*) **1** force by blustering language, bully **TC** V.ii.139 [Thersites to himself, of Troilus] *Will he swagger himself out on's own eyes?*; **KL** IV.vi.238; **Oth** I.iii.273

2 quarrel, squabble, behave in an insolent way **H5** IV.vii.123 [Williams to King Henry] *a rascal that swaggered with me last night*; **2H4** II.iv.71

swaggerer (*n.*) quarreller, blusterer, squabbler **2H4** II.iv.73 [Hostess to Drawer, of Pistol] *I must live among my neighbours; I'll no swaggerers*; **AY** IV.iii.15

swaggering (*n.*) blustering, bullying, quarrelling **TN** V.i.396 [Feste singing] *By swaggering could I never thrive*; **2H4** II.iv.69

swain (*n.*) **1** [contemptuous] rustic, yokel, fellow **2H6** IV.i.50 [Suffolk to Lieutenant] *Obscure and lousy swain*; **E3** I.ii.145; **1H6** V.iv.37; **LL** I.i.177; **Luc** 1504; **TS** II.ii.204

2 rustic, country person, shepherd **3H6** II.v.22 [King alone] *it were a happy life / To be no better than a homely swain*; **PassP** XVII.29; **WT** IV.iv.9, 30

3 man, youth, young fellow **WT** IV.iv.388 [disguised Polixenes to Florizel] *Soft, swain, awhile, beseech you*; **AY** II.iv.86; **WT** IV.iv.168, 363

4 lover, wooer, sweetheart **TG** IV.iv.39 [Musicians' song, of Silvia] *all our swains commend her*; **E3** II.i.108; **TC** III.i.171; **TG** V.iv.12

swart, swarth (*adj.*) swarthy, dusky, of dark complexion **CE** III.ii.106 [Dromio of Syracuse to Antipholus of Syracuse, of the kitchen wench] *Swart like my shoe*; **1H6** I.ii.84; **KJ** III.i.46; **Tit** II.iii.72; **TNK** IV.ii.27

swart-complexioned (*adj.*) dark-faced, black-looking **Sonn** 28.11 *So flatter I the swart-complexioned night*

swarth (*n.*) swathe, strip, chunk **TN** II.iii.142 [Maria to Sir Toby, of Malvolio] *that cons state without book and utters it by great swarths*
☞ swath (*n.*) 2

swarth (*adj.*) ☞ swart (*adj.*)

swasher (*n.*) swashbuckler, braggart, boaster **H5** III.ii.29 [Boy alone, of Pistol, Nym, and Bardolph] *I have observed these three swashers*

swashing (*adj.*) **1** swaggering, blustering, dashing **AY** I.iii.118 [Rosalind to Celia] *We'll have a swashing and a martial outside*
2 ☞ washing (*adj.*)

swath (*n.*) **1** swathing in infant clothes, swaddling-clothes **Tim** IV.iii.253 [Timon to Apemantus, comparing Apemantus' dog-like nature] *like us from our first swath*

2 swathe, sweep of a scythe **TC** V.v.25 [Nestor to all, of Hector] *there the strawy Greeks … / Fall down before him, like the mower's swath* ☞ swarth (*n.*)

swathing-clothes / clouts (*n.*) swaddling clothes, cloths for wrapping round a new-born baby **Ham** II.ii.382 [Hamlet to Rosencrantz and Guildenstern, of Polonius] *That great baby … is not yet out of his swathing clouts* [F; Q1, Q2 *swaddling clouts*]; **Cym** I.i.59; **1H4** III.ii.112

sway (*n.*) **1** power, dominion, rule **R2** IV.i.205 [Richard to all] *I give … / The pride of kingly sway from out my heart*; **1H4** V.i.57; **JC** I.iii.3; **Mac** I.v.68; **MV** IV.i.190; **RJ** IV.i.10

2 controlling influence, guiding power, direction **TS** V.ii.162 [Katherina to Widow, of women] *seek for rule, supremacy, and sway*; **KJ** II.i.578; **KL** II.v.185, IV.vii.20; **Lover** 108; **MM** I.iii.43

3 position of authority, powerful office **3H6** IV.vi.32 [George to Warwick] *thou art worthy of the sway*; **KL** I.i.136; **TC** I.iii.60

sway (*v.*) **1** control, rule, direct, govern **1H6** III.ii.135 [Talbot to Burgundy, of Bedford] *A gentler heart did never sway in court*; **Cor** II.i.196; **3H6** II.vi.14; **JC** II.i.20; **MA** IV.i.199; **TN** IV.i.51

2 be controlled, be directed **Mac** V.iii.9 [Macbeth to all] *The mind I sway by and the heart I bear / Shall never sag with doubt*

3 move, proceed, progress **TN** II.iv.31 [Orsino to Viola as Cesario, of a younger wife] *So sways she level in her husband's heart*

4 [of an instrument] guide, make yield, manipulate **Sonn** 128.3 *when thou gently sway'st / The wiry concord that mine ear confounds*

sway on (*v.*) advance, move ahead **2H4** IV.i.24 [Mowbray to Archbishop, of the King's forces] *Let us sway on and face them in the field*

swayed (*adj.*) [of horses] strained, with a spinal depression **TS** III.ii.54 [Biondello to Tranio as Lucentio, of Petruchio's horse] *swayed in the back* [F *Waid*]

swear (*v.*) promise, vow, pledge **2H6** V.i.182 [Salisbury to King] *It is great sin to swear unto a sin*; **AY** V.iv.98; **Mac** IV.ii.48

swear down (*v.*) reduce to silence by swearing, put down by

swearing CE V.i.227 [Antipholus of Ephesus to Duke] *There did this perjured goldsmith swear me down*

swear out (*v.*) renounce, abjure, abandon LL II.i.104 [Princess to King] *I hear your grace hath sworn out house-keeping* ➤ forswear (*v.*) 2

swear over (*v.*) [unclear usage] swear in opposition to, disavow, deny WT I.ii.424 [Camillo to Polixenes, of Leontes] *Swear his thought over / By each particular star in heaven and / By all their influences*

swearing (*n.*) act of swearing, moment of oath-taking AC I.iii.31 [Cleopatra to Antony] *those mouth-made vows / Which break themselves in swearing!*; TN V.i.267

sweat (*n.*) sweating-sickness [type of plague] 2H4 Epilogue.29 [Epilogue] *Falstaff shall die of a sweat*; MM I.ii.82

sweat (*v.*) **1** make great efforts, exert oneself strongly Tim III.ii.26 [Servilius to himself, of Lucius] *I have sweat to see his honour*
2 use the sweating-tub [as a cure for for venereal disease] TC V.x.56 [Pandarus alone] *Till then I'll sweat, and seek about for eases*

sweep (*n.*) parade, progress, promenade Tim I.ii.129 [Apemantus to himself, of the masque] *what a sweep of vanity comes this way!*

sweep (*v.*) **1** strut, parade, move majestically 3H6 V.i.76 [Warwick to all] *lo, where George of Clarence sweeps along*; AY II.i.55; 2H6 I.iii.75
2 prepare, clear [a way] Ham III.iv.205 [Hamlet to Gertrude, of Rosencrantz and Guildenstern] *They must sweep my way*; AC III.xi.17

sweet (*n.*) **1** sweetness, pleasure, delight RJ II.Chorus.14 [Chorus, of Romeo and Juliet] *Tempering extremities with extreme sweet*; RJ I.i.194; Sonn 8.2, 12.11, 19.7, 95.4, 99.2, 14
2 sweet-scented flower, fragrant plant R3 IV.iv.10 [Queen Elizabeth as if to the Princes] *My unblown flowers, new-appearing sweets!*; AW II.iv.42; E3 II.i.159; Ham V.i.239
3 sweet-tasting foodstuff R2 II.i.13 [John of Gaunt to York] *the last taste of sweets, is sweetest last*
4 lover, sweetheart Cym I.vi.80 [Queen to Pisanio, of Innogen] *I have given him that, / Which if he take, shall quite unpeople her / Of liegers for her sweet* [i.e. remove all those who represent her husband]
5 delightful time, pleasant part WT IV.iii.3 [Autolycus singing] *When daffodils begin to peer ... then comes in the sweet o'the year*
6 ➤ ADDRESS FORMS, p.8

sweet (*adj.*) **1** perfumed, scented, fragrant TS Induction.i.47 [Lord to Huntsmen] *burn sweet wood to make the lodging sweet*; MND II.i.252; RJ V.iii.1, 14; Tit II.iv.6; WT IV.iv.249
2 attractive, pleasing LL IV.iii.266 [King to Berowne] *Ethiops of their sweet complexion crack*; Luc 1385
3 smooth, unctuous, oily Tim I.i.253 [Apemantus to all] *That there should be small love amongst these sweet knaves, / And all this courtesy!*
4 wanton, lecherous; or: with a sweet tooth TG III.i.319 [Speed reading from Launce's paper, of his love's vices] *She hath a sweet mouth*

sweet (*v.*) sweeten, make pleasing, fumigate E3 II.ii.100 [King Edward to Prince Edward] *Let's with our colours sweet the air of France*

sweet-faced (*adj.*) good-looking, handsome CE V.i.419 [Dromio of Ephesus to Dromio of Syracuse] *I see by you I am a sweet-faced youth*

sweetheart (*n.*) ➤ ADDRESS FORMS, p.8

sweeting (*n.*) **1** sweetheart, darling, dearest Oth II.iii.246 [Othello to Desdemona] *All's well now, sweeting*; TN II.iii.40; TS IV.iii.36 ➤ ADDRESS FORMS, p.8
2 sweet-flavoured variety of apple RJ II.iv.78 [Mercutio to Romeo] *Thy wit is a very bitter sweeting*

sweetly (*adv.*) delightfully, charmingly, pleasingly TNK III.v.21 [Schoolmaster to all] *And sweetly, by a figure, trace and turn*; TNK II.ii.57, III.v.29

sweetness (*n.*) delight, pleasure, charm TNK IV.ii.13 [Emilia alone, of Arcite] *What an eye, / Of what a fiery sparkle and quick sweetness, / Has this young prince!*; MM II.iv.45

sweet-seasoned (*adj.*) filled with sweetness, gently falling Sonn 75.2 *So are you ... as sweet-seasoned showers are to the ground*

sweet-suggesting (*adj.*) sweetly tempting, seductive, irresistable TG II.vi.7 [Proteus alone] *O sweet-suggesting Love*

swell (*v.*) exalt, magnify, puff up AW II.iii.126 [King to Bertram] *Where great additions swell's*

swelling (*adj.*) **1** billowing, rising up TNK V.i.4 [Theseus to all] *the altars / In hallowed clouds commend their swelling incense / To those above us*
2 swollen [with pride], arrogant Oth II.iii.51 [Iago alone] *Three else of Cyprus, noble swelling spirits*; 1H6 III.i.26
3 tearful, overflowing, brimming with tears 1H4 III.i.195 [Mortimer to Lady Mortimer] *that pretty Welsh / Which thou pourest down from these swelling heavens*
4 magnificent, grand, resplendent Mac I.iii.127 [Macbeth to himself] *Two truths are told / As happy prologues to the swelling Act / Of the imperial theme*; H5 Prologue.4; MV I.i.124
5 inflated with anger, feeling strong emotion Tit V.iii.13 [Aaron to Lucius] *The venomous malice of my swelling heart*; R2 I.i.201; R3 II.i.52

sweltered (*adj.*) oozing, dripping [in the manner of sweat] Mac IV.i.8 [First Witch to Witches] *Sweltered venom, sleeping got, / Boil thou first i'the charmed pot*

swerve (*v.*) go astray, err, be wrong TC III.ii.182 [Cressida to Troilus] *If I be false, or swerve a hair from truth*; Cym V.iv.129; WT IV.iv.371

swerving (*n.*) lapse, transgression, error AC III.xi.50 [Antony to Eros] *I have offended reputation, / A most unnoble swerving*

swift (*adj.*) quick-witted, sharp, ready TS V.ii.54 [Petruchio to Tranio] *A good swift simile, but something currish*; AY V.iv.61

swift-starting (*adj.*) quick-spreading, rapidly moving E3 IV.vi.19 [King John alone] *swift-starting fear / Hath buzzed a cold dismay through all our army*

swill (*v.*) **1** drink greedily, gulp down R3 V.ii.9 [Richmond to all, of King Richard] *Swills your warm blood like wash*
2 wash, bathe, drench H5 III.i.14 [King Henry to all, of a rock] *Swilled with the wild and wasteful ocean*

swim (*v.*) **1** float, sail JC V.i.67 [Cassius to Brutus] *blow wind, swell billow, and swim bark*; AY IV.i.33
2 move gracefully, glide, undulate TNK III.v.28 [Schoolmaster to dancers] *Swim with your bodies*

swine (*n.*) wild boar TNK III.vi.12 [Palamon alone] *I lay fatting like a swine*; TNK II.i.103

swine-drunk (*adj.*) drunk as a pig, excessively drunk AW IV.iii.249 [Parolles to First Soldier, of Dumaine] *he will be swine-drunk*

swing (*n.*) driving force, thrusting power TC I.iii.207 [Ulysses to all, of a battering-ram] *the great swing and rudeness of his poise* [F; Q *swinge*]

swing (*v.*) beat, thrash, wallop MW V.v.182 [Slender to Page, of the boy he thought was Anne] *If it had not been i'th' church, I would have swinged him, or he should have swinged me*

swinge (*v.*) beat, thrash, flog TG III.i.370 [Launce alone, of Speed] *Now will he be swinged for reading my letter*; 2H4 V.iv.19; KJ II.i.288; MM V.i.130; TG II.i.77; TS V.ii.103

swinge-buckler (*n.*) swashbuckler, swaggering ruffian 2H4 III.ii.20 [Shallow to Silence] *you had not four such swinge-bucklers in all the Inns o'Court again*

swinish (*adj.*) coarse, gross; or: comparing [one] to pigs Mac I.vii.67 [Lady Macbeth to Macbeth, of the King's attendants] *in swinish sleep*; Ham I.iv.19

SWEARING

Under the heading of 'swearing' we include any emphatic expressions in which the speaker makes an invocation to affirm something or to make something happen. In this sense it is more narrowly focused than the notion of 'bad language', which includes a wider range of intensifying expressions, some of which are mild (such as *verily*), some much stronger (such as *whoreson*), and some very strong or rude (such as *figo*). Several items permit varied amounts of force, such as *beshrew* ('curse', 'devil take'), which is mild when used by Theseus in **TNK** II.iv.63 but strong when used by Richard in **R2** III.ii.204. Intensifiers of this kind are illustrated in the A–Z section.

The description of swearing is massively complicated by the influence of expurgators during the period. The 'Act to restrain Abuses of Players' of 1606 made it illegal for players to 'jestingly or prophanely speak or use the holy Name of God or of Christ Jesus, or of the Holy Ghost or of the Trinity', on pain of a severe (£10) fine for each offence. The late plays were obviously affected by this law, as well as performances of the earlier plays, and large-scale but erratic expurgation affected the First Folio (1623), as seen in any comparison with earlier Quarto texts (e.g. *before God* often replaced by *trust me*).

Modern editions, having restored original text as much as possible, provide evidence of a remarkable number of swearing expressions. This is chiefly a reflection of the range of characters in the plays – lords and peasants, old and young, men and women – whose swearing habits range from princely affirmations of honour ('by the honour of my blood') to servants' allusions to horse diseases ('bots on't'), and include many special usages, such as the clown's comic use of ''th'name of me' upon encountering Autolycus (**WT** IV.iii.50), the puritan oath 'by yea and no' used by Falstaff in his affected letter to Prince Hal (**2H4** II.ii.124), the fashionable swearing of gallants on items of clothing (Slender's 'by these gloves', **MW** I.i.142), and the delicate nature of ladylike oaths – specifically as noted by Hotspur, who takes his wife to task for swearing 'like a comfit-maker's wife – "Not you, in good sooth!", and "As true as I live!", and "As God shall mend me!", and "As sure as day!"' (**1H4** III.i.241–4).

You can swear 'by' virtually anything you hold dear, and these expressions range from the most sacred notions of Christianity to quite everyday notions of human behaviour and the environment. In the Roman plays, the Christian God is replaced by members of the Classical pantheon. In terms of formal construction, the commonest locution uses an introductory 'by' followed by the sworn phrase, but there are several other types of construction. These are grouped below in relation to the entities sworn by. No indication is given of frequency in the list, so it is important to note that some items are very common indeed, such as *marry*, *sooth*, and *faith*, and others are very restricted – sometimes even to individuals, who have their 'favourite' swear-words or versions of swear-words, such as Coriolanus' swearing by Jove (**Cor** III.i.86) or Dr Caius' French pronunciation as represented in 'by Gar' (**MW** I.iv.106).

Item	Example	Gloss [where needed]

God and his attributes

Item	Example	Gloss [where needed]
God, afore / 'fore	R2 II.i.200	before God
God-a-mercy	TC V.iv.31	thank God
God, by	1H4 II.i.37	
God, 'th'name of	Ham II.i.76	
God, O	Ham V.ii.338	
God bless us	MND V.i.312	
God help	CE IV.iv.127	
God mend me, so	AY IV.i.174	amend, save
God save me	2H4 II.i.153	
God shall mend me, as	1H4 III.i.243	amend, save
God shall mend my soul	RJ I.v.79	amend, save
God warn us	AY IV.i.69	[unclear] protect; warrant
God warrant us	MND V.i.311	preserve
God willing	Ham I.v.186	
God's bodkin	Ham II.ii.527	dear body
God's body	1H4 II.i.27	
God's bread	RJ III.v.176	
God's lid, by	TC I.ii.211	eyelid
God's liggens, by	2H4 V.iii.64	[unclear] lidkins = dear eyelids
God's light	2H4 II.iv.128	
God's love, for	Ham I.ii.195	
God's me	1H4 II.iii.97	save me
God's mercy	AW I.iii.144	
God's my life	MND IV.i.202	
God's my life	MA IV.ii.68	

(continues)

SWEARING – *continued*

Item	Example	Gloss [where needed]
God's name, a	TS I.ii.192	in God's name
God's peace	H5 IV.iii.31	
God's sake, for	2H4 II.iv.183	
God's sonties, by	MV II.ii.40	saints
good Father	RJ IV.iv.21	
Got's lords and his ladies	MW I.i.219	☞ WELSH, p.649
perdy	Ham III.ii.302	by God [French: par Dieu]
perdie	CE IV.iv.69	by God [French: par Dieu]

Shortening to 'Od / 'Ud

'Od's heartlings	MW III.iv.56	dear heart
'Od's lifelings	TN V.i.181	dear life
'Od's me	MW I.iv.60	save me
'Od's my little life	AY III.v.43	may God save my little life
'Od's my will	AY IV.iii.18	as God is my will
'Od's nouns	MW IV.i.23	wounds
'Od's pittikins	Cym IV.ii.293	dear pity
'Od's plessed will	MW I.i.245	blessed will ☞ WELSH, p.649
Ud's pity	Oth IV.iii.74	

Softened forms

Cock, by	Ham IV.v.62	God [often with bawdy pun]
cock and pie, by	MW I.i.283	God and the service book
Cock's passion	TS IV.i.105	God's passion
Cox my passion	AW V.ii.40	God's my passion
Gar, by	MW I.iv.105	French pronunciation of 'God'
gogs-wounds, by	TS III.ii.159	God's wounds

With 'God' omitted

'sblood	Ham II.ii.365	God's blood
'sdeath	Cor I.i.215	God's death
bodykins	MW II.iii.40	God's little body
death	H8 I.iii.13	God's death
'sfoot	TC II.iii.5	God's foot
mercy o'me	H8 V.iv.66	God have mercy on me
mercy on's	WT III.iii.68	God have mercy on us
mercy, so help you	Ham I.v.169	God's mercy
'slid	MW III.iv.24	God's eyelid
'slight	TN II.v.32	God's light
'swounds	Ham II.ii.573	God's wounds
zounds	Oth I.i.87	God's wounds

Christ

Chrish, by	H5 III.ii.85	☞ SCOTTISH, p.648
fut	KL I.ii.131	[unclear]'sfoot = Christ's foot
Gis, by	Ham IV.v.59	Jesus
Jesu	2H4 III.ii.32	
Jesus	2H4 III.ii.214	
Jesu Maria	RJ II.iii.65	
Lord	Tem I.ii.411	

SWEARING – *continued*

Item	Example	Gloss [where needed]
Lord, by the	**1H4** I.ii.39	
Lord, good	**CE** IV.i.48	
Lord, goodly	**MV** III.v.45	good Lord
Lord warrant us	**AY** III.iii.4	protect
Rood, by the	**Ham** III.iv.15	cross
Rood, by the Holy	**R3** III.ii.75	holy cross

Mary

halidom, by my	**TG** IV.ii.132	what I hold holy; or: Our Lady
holidam, by my	**RJ** I.iii.44	what I hold holy; or: Our Lady
holidame, by my	**TS** V.ii.98	what I hold holy; or: Our Lady
'Lady, by	**Tit** IV.iv.48	Our Lady
Lady, by'r	**Ham** II.ii.424	Our Lady
lakin, by'r	**MND** III.i.12	Our Lady
marry	**AY** I.ii.25	Mary
Mary, by holy	**H8** V.ii.32	
mother, by God's	**3H6** III.2.103	
mother, God's blest	**H8** V.i.153	
Mother of our Lord, by the holy	**R3** III.vii.2	

Saints

Anne, by Saint	**TN** II.iii.113	mother of the Virgin Mary
Charity, by Saint	**Ham** IV.v.59	[not a saint's name]
Francis, holy Saint	**RJ** II.iii.61	
John, by Saint	**R3** I.i.138	
Patrick, by Saint	**Ham** I.v.136	keeper of spirits in purgatory
Paul, by Saint	**R3** I.ii.36	
Paul, by holy	**R3** I.iii.45	
Paul, by the apostle	**R3** V.iii.217	

Other Christian notions

christendom, by my	**KJ** IV.i.16	
devil's name, a	**TS** IV.iii.92	in the devil's name
faith	**Ham** I.v.135	
faith, by my	**AY** IV.i.19	
faith, in	**Ham** V.ii.133	
faith, good	**Cym** IV.ii.302	in good faith
faith, in good	**Ham** V.i.45	
fay, by my	**Ham** II.ii.264	faith
fecks, i'	**WT** I.ii.120	in faith
good-year, what the	**MA** I.iii.1	what the devil [origin possibly: evil preventing a good year]
grace, for love of	**Ham** III.iv.145	
grace to boot	**WT** I.ii.80	heaven help us
heaven, by	**Ham** I.i.49	
mass	**Ham** V.i.55	
mass, by	**MA** IV.ii.49	
mass, by the	**Ham** II.i.50	
soul, by my	**MA** V.i.262	
soul, by my father's	**H5** III.ii.87	
soul, upon my	**TNK** II.iv.16	
vengeance, what the	**Cor** III.i.261	what the hell

(continues)

SWEARING – *continued*

Item	Example	Gloss [where needed]

Non-Christian religions

Apollo, by	KL I.i.160	
Castor, by	TNK III.vi.136	
gods, the	Cor II.iii.53	
Hercules, by	AC III.vii.67	
Jacob's staff, by	MV II.v.35	
Janus, by	Oth I.ii.33	
Jove	AY II.iv.55	
Jove that thunders, by	AC III.xiii.85	
Juno, by	KL II.iv.21	
Jupiter, O	AY II.iv.1	
Jupiter, by	KL I.i.178	
Mars, by th'helm of	TNK I.iv.17	
Mars his gauntlet, by	TC IV.v.177	
Mars's altar, by	TNK I.i.62	
Pluto, by	TC V.ii.105	
Pluto and hell!	Cor I.iv.36	
Venus' hand, by	TC IV.i.23	

➤ **GODS**, p.620

Human being or attributes

body o'me	H8 V.ii.21	my body, my life
complexion, good my	AY III.ii.188	cf. modern: pardon my blushes
death, upon my	1H4 V.iv.150	
death on my state	KL II.iv.107	
hand, by this	Ham V.ii.252	
me, afore	Per II.i.80	before me
me, fore	AW II.iii.25	before me
me, 'th'name of	WT IV.iii.50	
life, on / upon my	MW I.i.37	
live, as true as I	1H4 III.i.243	
whip me	3H6 III.ii.28	treat me as a criminal
whip the gosling	Per IV.ii.81	confound the little goose
yea and no, by	2H4 II.ii.124	

Human values

fidelity, by my	MW IV.ii.144	
forsooth	1H6 IV.i.157	in truth, truly
honesty, by mine	TG II.v.1	
honour, by mine	AY I.ii.58	
honour, on / upon mine	MM I.i.63	
loves, of all	MND II.ii.160	by all love, for love's sake
sooth	TN II.i.9	[truth] truly, indeed
sooth, good	TS III.ii.115	in good truth
sooth, in good	1H4 III.i.240	in good truth
troth	MW I.iv.139	in faith
troth, by my	AY I.ii.84	by my faith
troth, good	H8 II.iii.33	in good faith

(continues)

SWEARING – *continued*

Item	Example	Gloss [where needed]

Part of the body or clothing

Item	Example	Gloss [where needed]
beard, by my	TG IV.i.10	
gloves, by these	MW I.i.142	
hand, by my	2H6 V.iii.29	
hand, by this	2H4 II.ii.42	
hand of a soldier, by the	AW III.vi.66	
hat, by this	MW I.i.157	
head / heel, by my	RJ III.i.34–5	
hilts, by these	1H4 II.iv.202	of swords
honour of my blood, by the	2H4 IV.ii.55	
hood, by my	MV II.vi.51	of a mask
sword, by this	H5 II.i.96	
troth and maidenhead, by my	H8 II.iii.23	faithful virginity
white glove, by this	LL V.ii.411	
white hand of my lady, by the	H5 III.vii.90	
will, by my	LL II.i.99	

Environment

Item	Example	Gloss [where needed]
clouds, by yond	Cor III.i.50	
day, as sure as	1H4 III.i.244	
day, by this	2H4 III.ii.73	
elements, by th'	Cor I.x.10	
light, by this	KJ I.i.259	
light, by this good	TNK II.i.320	
north pole, by the	LL V.ii.690	
world, by the	LL V.i.99	

Diseases, human or animal

Item	Example	Gloss [where needed]
bots on't	Per II.i.119	horse worms
murrain on it, a	Cor I.v.3	plague, pestilence
pox	Ham III.ii.262	venereal disease, plague
pox, a	1H4 I.ii.47	
pox on it, a	Cym II.i.17	also: a pox on him [etc.]

switch *(n.)* twig, thin shoot H8 V.iv.8 [Porter to servants within] *Fetch me a dozen crab-tree staves ... these are but switches to 'em* [i.e. compared to them]

swits and spurs [switches] at full speed, in hot haste RJ II.iv.68 [Romeo to Mercutio] *Swits and spurs, swits and spurs!* [i.e. make your horse (= wit) go faster]

Switzer *(n.)* Swiss guard Ham IV.v.99 [Claudius to his guards] *Where is my Switzers?* [Q *Swissers*]

swoln *(adj.)* variant spelling of 'swollen' Venus 325 *All swoln with chafing, down Adonis sits*

swoon *(v.)* faint JC I.i.246 [Casca to Brutus, of Caesar] *he swooned, and fell down;* 2H4 IV.v.232; LL V.ii.392; MM II.iv.24; R3 IV.i.35; WT IV.iv.13 ➤ swoond *(v.)*; swound *(v.)*; swown *(v.)*

swoond *(v.)* variant spelling of 'swoon' or 'swound' AC IV.ix.26 [Sentry to Second Watch, of whether Enobarbus is sleeping] *Swoonds rather* [F] ➤ swoon *(v.)*; swound *(v.)*

swooning *(adj.)* shown by fainting, marked by loss of the senses TC III.ii.21 [Troilus alone, of being with Cressida] *Swooning destruction, or some joy too fine* [F, Q *Sounding*]

swoopstake *(adv.)* indiscriminately [taking all stakes at once] Ham IV.v.144 [Claudius to Laertes] *is't writ in your revenge / That, swoopstake, you will draw both friend and foe* [reading of F, Q2 *soopstake*; Q1 *Swoop-stake-like*]

sword *(n.)* soldier, sword-wielder KL V.iii.33 [Edmund to Captain] *to be tender-minded / Does not become a sword;* Cor II.ii.99

sworder *(n.)* sword-fighter, gladiator 2H6 IV.i.137 [Suffolk to soldiers] *A Roman sworder and banditto slave / Murdered sweet Tully;* AC III.xiii.31

sworn *(adj.)* **1** bound by an oath of loyalty Cym II.iv.125 [Posthumus to Philario, of Innogen] *her attendants are / All sworn, and honourable;* H8 I.ii.191

2 sworn to secrecy, confirmed by oath **AW** III.vii.9 [Helena to Widow] *to your sworn counsel I have spoken*

sworn brother ☛ brother, sworn

swort *(n.)* pronunciation of 'sword' or 'sort' [= outcome] **MW** I.i.39 [Evans to Shallow] *It is petter that friends is the swort, and end it* [F *Sword*] [i.e. make friends replace the sword; or: have friendship the result] ☛ **WELSH**, p.649

swound *(v.)* faint, swoon **RJ** III.ii.56 [Nurse to Juliet, of Tybalt's body] *I swounded at the sight;* **Cor** V.ii.64, 97 [F]; **Ham** V.ii.302; **KJ** V.vi.22; **Luc** 1486 ☛ swoon *(v.)*; swoond *(v.)*

'swounds *(int.)* ☛ **SWEARING**, p.435

swown *(v.)* variant spelling of 'swoon' **3H6** V.v.45 [Edward to Richard, of Queen] *Doth she swown?* [F *swowne*] ☛ swoon *(v.)*

sycamore *(n.)* variety of fig tree **Oth** IV.iii.38 [Desdemona, singing] *The poor soul sat sighing by a sycamore tree* ☛ **PLANTS**, p.330

sympathize *(v.)* **1** agree, be in accord **TC** IV.i.26 [Diomedes to Aeneas] *We sympathize*

2 respond to, match, answer to **R2** V.i.46 [Richard to Queen Isabel] *the senseless brands will sympathize / The heavy accent of thy moving tongue*

3 capture, represent fittingly, express with feeling **Sonn** 82.11 *Thou truly fair, wert truly sympathised, / In true plain words*

sympathize with *(v.)* resemble, be like, have an affinity with **H5** III.vii.143 [Constable to Orleans, of the English] *the men do sympathize with the mastiffs in robustious and rough coming on;* **1H4** V.i.7; **Luc** 113; **TC** I.iii.52

sympathized *(adj.)* **1** in which all have shared, consisting of corresponding elements **CE** V.i.398 [Abbess to Duke] *this sympathized one day's error*

2 matched, paired, partnered **LL** III.i.49 [Mote to Armado, of Costard as messenger] *A message well sympathized*

sympathy *(n.)* **1** accord, agreement, harmony **Tit** III.i.148 [Titus to Marcus] *O, what a sympathy of woe is this;* **2H6** I.i.23; **MND** I.i.141; **MW** II.i.7; **Oth** II.i.223; **RJ** III.iii.86

2 equivalence of rank, corresponding status **R2** IV.i.33 [Fitzwater to Aumerle] *If that thy valour stand on sympathy / There is my gage*

synod *(n.)* assembly, council, gathering **CE** I.i.13 [Duke to Egeon] *It hath in solemn synods been decreed;* **AC** III.x.5; **Cor** V.ii.66; **Cym** V.iv.89; **Ham** II.ii.492; **TNK** I.i.176

ta *(pron.)* dialect form of 'thou' **2H4** II.i.55 [Hostess to Falstaff] *thou wot, wot ta?*

table *(n.)* **1** writing tablet, memo pad, notebook **Ham** I.v.98 [Hamlet alone] *from the table of my memory / I'll wipe away all trivial fond records;* **Cym** III.ii.39; **Ham** I.v.107; **2H4** IV.i.199; **Sonn** 122.1; **TG** II.vii.3
2 tablet, surface, paintbook **AW** I.i.94 [Helena alone, of Bertram] *to … draw / His arched brows, his hawking eye, his curls, / In our heart's table;* **KJ** II.i.503; **Sonn** 24.2
3 intimate, confidante **2H4** II.iv.261 [Poins to Prince Henry, of Bardolph] *look whether the fiery trigon his man be not lisping to his master's old tables*
4 dinner table, dinner party **MW** IV.ii.152 [Ford to all, of his search for Falstaff] *If I find not what I seek … Let me for ever be your table sport;* **Cor** II.i.77
5 [palmistry] area between various lines on the palm **MV** II.ii.147 [Launcelot to Gobbo, of his hand] *If any man in Italy have a fairer table which doth offer to swear upon a book, I shall have good fortune!*
6 (plural) backgammon **LL** V.ii.326 [Berowne to all, of Boyet] *when he plays at tables, chides the dice / In honourable terms*

table *(v.)* tabulate, list, itemize **Cym** I.v.6 [Iachimo to all, of Posthumus] *the catalogue of his endowments had been tabled by his side*

table-book *(n.)* notebook, memo pad, memorandum book **LL** V.i.16 [stage direction, of Nathaniel] *He draws out his table-book;* **Ham** II.ii.136; **WT** IV.iv.595

tablet *(n.)* document presented within special covers **Cym** V.iv.109 [Jupiter to the spirits, of Posthumus] *This tablet lay upon his breast*

tabor *(n.)* type of small drum, especially used in revelling **Tem** IV.i.175 [Ariel to Prospero] *Then I beat my tabor;* **Cor** I.vi.25; **LL** V.i.147; **MA** II.iii.14; **TN** III.i.2; **WT** IV.iv.184

taborer *(n.)* player of a tabor **TNK** III.v.23 [Second Countryman to all] *Where's the taborer?;* **Tem** III.ii.153; **TNK** III.v.1 ☛ **tabor** *(n.)*

taborin, tabourine *(n.)* type of drum [narrower and longer than a tabor] **AC** IV.viii.37 [Antony to trumpeters] *Make mingle with our rattling tabourines;* **TC** IV.v.275 [Agamemnon to drummers] *Beat loud the taborins*

tack about *(v.)* change course, run against the wind **TNK** III.iv.10 [Gaoler's Daughter alone, of a ship] *Up with a course or two, and tack about*

tackle *(n.)* **1** [of a ship] rigging and sails **KJ** V.vii.52 [King John to Bastard] *The tackle of my heart is cracked and burnt;* **AC** II.ii.214; **Cor** IV.v.64; **3H6** V.iv.15
2 things, equipment, gear **TNK** II.ii.55 [Third Countryman to the others] *every man to's tackle*

tackled *(adj.)* made of rope **RJ** II.iv.185 [Romeo to Nurse] *my man shall … bring thee cords made like a tackled stair*

tackling *(n.)* rigging [of a ship], tackle **3H6** V.iv.18 [Queen to all] *[is not] The friends of France our shrouds and tacklings?;* **R3** IV.iv.234; **TNK** IV.i.144 ☛ **SHIPS**, p.397

ta'en *(v.)* ☛ **take** *(v.)*

taffety *(adj.)* finely dressed, showy, overdressed **AW** II.ii.21 [Clown to Countess, of his answer] *As fit as … your French crown for your taffety punk*

tag *(n.)* rabble, riffraff, mob **Cor** III.i.247 [Cominius to Coriolanus] *Will you hence / Before the tag return*

tag-rag *(adj.)* raggedly dressed; riff-raff, rabble **JC** I.ii.256 [Casca to Cassius, of Caesar] *If the tag-rag people did not clap him and hiss him*

tail *(n.)* ☛ **come cut and long tail**

tailor *(int.)* ☛ **EXCLAMATIONS**, p.158

tailor's-yard *(n.)* ☛ **yard** *(n.)* 1

taint *(n.)* **1** fault, blemish, flaw **AC** V.i.30 [Maecenas to all, of Antony] *His taints and honours / Waged equal with him;* **Ham** II.i.32; **Mac** IV.iii.124

2 discredit, doubt, dispute **KL** I.i.221 [France to Lear] *your fore-vouched affection / Fall into taint*

3 disgracing, dishonouring, discrediting **TC** I.iii.374 [Ulysses to Nestor, of Achilles] *If he were foiled, / Why then we did our main opinion crush / In taint of our best man*

4 corruption, infection, contamination **H8** V.iii.28 [Gardiner to the Councillors] *Commotions, uproars, with a general taint / Of the whole state*

taint (*v.*) **1** sully, infect, stain **Ham** I.v.85 [Ghost to Hamlet] *Taint not thy mind ... / Against thy mother aught;* **CE** III.ii.13; **Cor** IV.vii.38; **1H6** IV.v.46; **H8** III.ii.332; **TC** III.ii.232

2 tinge, affect, touch **1H6** V.iii.183 [Margaret to Suffolk] *a pure unspotted heart, / Never yet taint with love, I send the King*

3 disparage, denigrate, belittle **TN** V.i.136 [Viola as Cesario to Olivia, of loving Orsino] *Punish my life, for tainting of my love;* **Oth** II.i.259

4 impair, harm, injure **TN** III.i.66 [Viola alone] *wise men, folly-fallen, quite taint their wit;* **TN** V.i.355

5 spoil, go rotten **TN** III.iv.131 [Maria to Sir Toby and Fabian, of Malvolio] *pursue him now, lest the device take air, and taint*

6 lose vigour, become weak, wither **Mac** V.iii.3 [Macbeth to all] *Till Birnan Wood remove to Dunsinane / I cannot taint with fear;* **MM** IV.iv.4

tainted (*adj.*) **1** infected, diseased **TN** III.iv.13 [Maria to Olivia, of Malvolio] *for sure the man is tainted in's wits;* **MM** I.ii.43; **MV** IV.i.114

2 corrupted, dishonourable, depraved **MV** III.ii.75 [Bassanio to himself] *In law, what plea so tainted and corrupt, / But being seasoned with a gracious voice, / Obscures the show of evil?;* **AW** III.ii.87

3 disgraced, discredited, dishonoured **H8** IV.ii.14 [Griffith to Katherine, of Wolsey] *a man sorely tainted* [or: sense 2]

4 tinged, unnaturally touched **3H6** III.i.40 [King to himself] *Nero will be tainted with remorse*

taintingly (*adv.*) [probable error for] tauntingly **Cor** I.i.108 [Menenius to First Citizen, of the belly] *it taintingly replied / To th'discontented members* [F]

tainture (*n.*) tainting, staining, defilement **2H6** II.i.183 [Queen to Gloucester, of the Duchess's plotting] *see here the tainture of thy nest*

take (*v.*) **1** strike, hit, catch **H5** IV.i.210 [Williams to disguised King Henry] *I will take thee a box on the ear;* **H5** II.i.49, IV.vii.124; **R3** I.iv.156; **TS** III.ii.162

2 catch, receive, get **1H4** V.ii.22 [Worcester to Vernon, of Hotspur] *his corruption being taken from us;* **2H4** II.iv.294

3 make use of, seize on **TS** II.i.206 [Katherina to Petruchio, of his play on words] *Well ta'en, and like a buzzard;* **Tem** II.i.82

4 take away, detract, lessen **Ham** I.iv.20 [Hamlet to Horatio, of Claudius' behaviour] *and indeed it takes / From our achievements*

5 take in, comprehend, understand **WT** I.ii.12 [Leontes to Camillo, of Hermione persuading Polixenes to stay] *Was this taken / By any understanding pate but thine?;* **MND** V.i.90; **PassP** IV.10, XI.12

6 captivate, delight, enrapture **Tem** V.i.314 [Alonso to Prospero, of Prospero's story] *which must / Take the ear strangely;* **Per** IV.iv.3; **WT** I.ii.40, III.ii.36, IV.iv.119

7 bewitch, take possession of, take into one's power **AC** IV.ii.37 [Antony to Enobarbus] *the witch take me if I meant it thus!;* **Ham** I.i.164; **MW** IV.iv.30

8 win favour, gain acceptance, become popular **AW** III.v.51 [Diana to Helena, of Bertram] *He's bravely taken here*

9 make an impression **Cor** II.i.106 [Cominius to all, of Coriolanus] *His sword, ... / Where it did mark, it took from face to foot* [or: sense 20]

10 accept, receive, escape with **TNK** III.vi.267 [Arcite to Theseus] *'tis worse to me than begging / To take my life so basely*

11 assume, pretend, feign **Ham** II.i.13 [Polonius to Reynaldo, of Laertes] *Take you as 'twere some distant knowledge of him*

12 swear, take an oath **KJ** I.i.110 [Robert Faulconbridge to King John, of his father and Bastard] *he ... took it on his death / That this, my mother's son, was none of his;* **R2** V.iii.11

13 put up with, accept **Ham** II.ii.573 [Hamlet alone, of being insulted] *I should take it;* **2H4** I.ii.168; **KL** II.ii.98

14 accept, believe, trust **KL** IV.vi.142 [Edgar to himself, of Lear's behaviour] *I would not take this from report*

15 suppose, conceive, come to believe, **Sonn** 137.4 *Yet what the best is, take the worst to be;* **AW** II.i.90

16 measure, estimate, gauge **AC** II.vii.17 [Antony to Lepidus] *they take the flow o'th' Nile / By certain scales i'th' pyramid;* **Tim** I.ii.149

17 encounter, approach, tackle **Cor** V.i.51 [Menenius to Sicinius, of Coriolanus] *He was not taken well* [i.e. at the right moment]

18 overtake, encounter, meet up with **CE** III.i.175 [Angelo to Antipholus of Syracuse] *I thought to have ta'en you at the Porpentine;* **H5** IV.i.213

19 catch out, take by surprise **LL** I.ii.112 [Armado to Mote] *I do love that country girl that I took in the park with the rational hind Costard;* **MW** III.ii.36

20 conquer, overthrow, destroy **TC** V.v.26 [Nestor to all, of Hector] *Here, there, and everywhere, he leaves and takes;* **Cor** III.i.111

21 take refuge in, go into, enter [for safety] **CE** V.i.94 [Abbess to Adriana, of Antipholus of Syracuse] *He took this place for sanctuary;* **CE** V.i.36; **TC** V.iv.19

22 ☛ head, take the; heels, take my; order, take; truce, take; wall, take the

take all all or nothing, victory or death! **AC** IV.ii.8 [Enobarbus to Antony] *I'll strike, and cry 'Take all'*

take away (*v.*) clear the table **Tit** III.ii.81 [Titus to Servants] *Come, take away*

take down (*v.*) **1** humble, lower, cut down to size **RJ** II.iv.147 [Nurse to Romeo, of Mercutio] *An 'a speak anything against me, I'll take him down*

2 swallow, consume, ingest **Tim** III.iv.53 [Flavius to Servants, of their masters] *they could ... take down th'interest into their glutt'nous maws*

take hands ☛ FAREWELLS, p.170

take head from rebel against, rush away from **KJ** II.i.579 [Bastard alone, of the world] *This sway of motion, this commodity, / Makes it take head from all indifference*

take heel take to one's heels, run away **Cym** V.iii.67 [Posthumus alone, of those saving their skins] *Took heel to do't*

take in (*v.*) conquer, subdue, overcome **Cor** III.ii.59 [Volumnia to Coriolanus] *to take in a town with gentle words;* **AC** I.i.23, III.xiii.83; **Cor** I.ii.24; **Cym** III.ii.9; **WT** IV.iv.574

take in hand acknowledge, recognize, undertake **Luc** 1235 [of Lucrece and her maid] *One justly weeps; the other takes in hand / No cause but company of her drops' spilling*

take it affirm, swear, take an oath **MW** II.ii.12 [Falstaff to Pistol, of a lost fan] *I took't upon mine honour thou hadst it not*

take me with you I don't understand you **1H4** II.iv.447 [Falstaff (as Hal) to Prince Hal (as King)] *I would your grace would take me with you;* **RJ** III.v.141

take off (*v.*) **1** reduce, diminish, lessen **AW** II.i.89 [King to Lafew] *we with thee / May spend our wonder too, or take off thine;* **TC** II.i.207

2 kill, remove, put to death **Cym** V.v.47 [Cornelius to Cymbeline, of the Queen] *Your daughter ... she had / Ta'en off by poison;* **Mac** V.vi.110

take on (*v.*) **1** behave, act; *or:* rage, rant **MW** III.v.36 [Mistress Quickly to Falstaff, of Mistress Ford] *She does so take on with her men;* **3H6** II.v.104; **MND** III.ii.258; **TS** III.ii.213

2 assume a role, carry on **CE** V.i.243 [Antipholus of Ephesus to Duke, of Pinch] *This pernicious slave ... took on him as a conjuror;* **2H4** IV.ii.60

take out (*v.*) **1** copy, imitate, replicate **Oth** III.iii.293 [Emilia alone, of Desdemona's handkerchief] *I'll have the work ta'en out;* **Oth** III.iv.176, IV.i.150

2 study, learn; also: draw forth **TNK** II.ii.35 [Third Countryman to First Countryman, of his wife] *do but put / A fescue in her fist, and you shall see her / Take a new lesson out*

3 lead out for a dance **H8** I.iv.95 [King Henry to Anne] *I were unmannerly to take you out / And not to kiss you*

take peace make peace **H8** II.i.85 [Buckingham to Lovell] *There cannot be those numberless offences / 'Gainst me that I cannot take peace with*

take to (*v.*) **1** have recourse to, take oneself off to **Per** III.iv.10 [Thaisa to Cerimon] *A vestal livery will I take me to;* **H5** III.ii.110

2 subsist on, use as a resource **TG** IV.i.41 [Second Outlaw to Valentine] *have you anything to take to?*

take up (*v.*) **1** settle, make up, resolve **TN** III.iv.284 [Sir Toby to Fabian, of Sir Andrew] *I have his horse to take up the quarrel;* **AY** IV.iv.47, 95; **Tit** IV.iii.92

2 take on, handle, cope with **Cor** III.i.243 [Menenius to Coriolanus, of the Plebeians] *I could myself / Take up a brace o'th' best of them;* **2H4** I.iii.73

3 occupy, fill up **Cor** III.ii.116 [Coriolanus to Volumnia] *schoolboys' tears take up / The glasses of my sight;* **WT** III.iii.87

4 keep out, block, prevent **H8** I.i.56 [Buckingham to Norfolk, of Wolsey] *with his very bulk / Take up the rays o'th' beneficial sun, / And keep it from the earth*

5 raise up, let rise **Tit** I.i.460 [Tamora to Saturninus, of kneeling Titus] *Take up this good old man*

6 recruit, enlist, levy **2H4** II.i.186 [Lord Chief Justice to Falstaff] *you are to take soldiers up in counties as you go;* **2H4** IV.ii.26

7 arrest, seize, apprehend **MA** III.iii.172 [Borachio to Conrade] *We are likely to prove a goodly commodity, being taken up of these men's bills* [also: sense 8]; **AW** II.iii.206

8 take possession of, seize hold of **2H6** IV.vii.118 [Dick to Cade] *when shall we go to Cheapside and take up commodities upon our bills?*

9 rebuke, scold, reprimand **Cym** II.i.4 [Cloten to Lords] *a whoreson jackanapes must take me up for swearing;* **TG** I.ii.135

take upon (*v.*) **1** profess, pretend, affect [oneself] **TC** I.ii.140 [Pandarus to Cressida, of Helen and Troilus] *she takes upon her to spy a white hair on his chin;* **Cym** V.v.182; **2H4** II.ii.108; **TS** IV.ii.109

2 assume the burden of, undertake the study of [for oneself] **KL** V.iii.16 [Lear to Cordelia] *we'll … take upon's the mystery of things*

3 undertake a role, assume a responsibility [for oneself] **1H6** I.ii.71 [Reignier to all, of Pucelle] *She takes upon her bravely at first dash;* **Cym** V.v.183

taken (*adj.*) undertaken, set in train **AW** III.iv.12 [Steward reading Helena's letter, of Bertram] *His taken labours bid him me forgive*

taking (*n.*) **1** state, fright, agitation **Luc** 453 [of Lucrece woken by Tarquin] *she in worser taking … heedfully doth view / The sight;* **MW** III.iii.168

2 attack of disease, seizure **KL** III.iv.57 [Edgar as Poor Tom to Lear] *Bless thee from whirlwinds, star-blasting, and taking!*

taking (*adj.*) infectious, contagious, pernicious **KL** II.iv.159 [Lear to Regan, of Gonerill] *Strike her young bones, / You taking airs, with lameness!*

taking-off (*n.*) killing, elimination, removal **KL** V.i.65 [Edmund alone, of Albany] *devise / His speedy taking-off;* **Mac** I.vii.20

taking up (*n.*) dealing, bargaining, agreement **2H4** I.ii.39 [Falstaff to Page, of tradesmen] *if a man is through with them in honest taking up*

tale (*n.*) **1** talking, discourse **1H4** V.ii.90 [Hotspur to all, of King Henry] *I thank him that he cuts me from my tale;* **RJ** II.iv.92; **Venus** 74

2 remark, statement, utterance **TS** V.ii.24 [Hortensio to Petruchio] *My widow says thus she conceives her tale*

3 false rumour, story, tittle-tattle **TNK** III.iii.38 [Arcite to Palamon] *Else there be tales abroad;* **MND** III.ii.133; **TS** II.i.215

tale, in a in agreement, unanimous, in accord **MA** IV.ii.30 [Dogberry to Sexton, of Conrade and Borachio] *they are both in a tale*

talent (*n.*) **1** [unclear meaning] wealth, treasure, riches **Cym** I.vii.80 [Iachimo to Innogen, of heaven's bounty] *In you … beyond all talents* [also: desire; natural endowment]; **Lover** 204

2 variant form of 'talon' **LL** IV.ii.64 [Dull to Nathaniel, of Holofernes] *If a talent be a claw, look how he claws him with a talent* [first instance]

3 ☞ **MONEY**, p.286

talker (*n.*) someone of words but not deeds **H8** II.ii.77 [King Henry to Wolsey] *have great care / I be not found a talker*

tall (*adj.*) **1** brave, valiant, bold **TN** I.iii.18 [Sir Toby to Maria, of Sir Andrew] *He's as tall a man as any's in Illyria;* **H5** II.i.65; **MW** II.i.210; **R3** I.iv.154; **TNK** IV.i.82; **WT** V.ii.160

2 large, fine, grand **KL** IV.vi.18 [Edgar to Gloucester] *yon tall anchoring bark;* **MV** III.i.5; **R2** II.i.286; **Sonn** 80.12

3 good, fine, capable **TS** IV.iv.17 [Tranio as Lucentio to Biondello] *Th' art a tall fellow;* **MND** V.i.143

4 long, high **H8** I.iii.30 [Lovell to Lord Chamberlain, of French-influenced fashion] *tall stockings*

tallow (*n.*) fat **1H4** II.iv.160 [Falstaff to Lord Chief Justice, of himself] *A wassail candle, my lord, all tallow;* **CE** III.ii.101; **MW** V.v.14

tallow-catch (*n.*) [unclear meaning] dripping-pan [placed under roasting meat] **1H4** II.iv.224 [Prince Hal to Falstaff] *thou whoreson obscene greasy tallow-catch*

tallow-face (*n.*) [contemptuous] face as pale as wax **RJ** III.v.157 [Capulet to Juliet] *You tallow-face!*

tally (*n.*) ☞ score and tally

tame (*adj.*) **1** submissive, resigned, habituated **KL** IV.vi.221 [Edgar to Gloucester, of himself] *A most poor man made tame to fortune's blows* [F; Q *lame*]; **KJ** IV.ii.262; **Sonn** 58.7

2 familiar, habitual, customary **TC** III.iii.10 [Calchas to all] *sequest'ring from me all / That time, acquaintance, custom, and condition / Made tame and most familiar to my nature*

3 petty, decoy [attracting people into a card game] **2H4** II.iv.94 [Falstaff to Hostess, of Pistol] *He's no swaggerer, hostess, a tame cheater*

4 domesticated, as pets **AW** II.v.45 [Lafew to Bertram, of people like Parolles] *I have kept of them tame*

tame (*v.*) [= *attame*] break into, pierce, broach **H5** I.ii.173 [Ely to King Henry, of Scotland as a weasel sucking the eggs of the eagle England] *To 'tame and havoc more than she can eat*

tamed (*adj.*) [of a cask] tapped, pierced **TC** IV.i.63 [Diomedes to Paris, of Menelaus] *He … would drink up / The lees and dregs of a flat tamed piece*

tang (*n.*) sting, sharp edge **Tem** II.ii.49 [Stephano to himself, singing of Kate] *For she had a tongue with a tang*

tang (*v.*) ring out, utter resoundingly **TN** II.v.146 [Malvolio reading the letter] *Let thy tongue tang arguments of state*

tangle (*v.*) trap, snare, enmesh, hold fast **TG** III.ii.68 [Proteus to Thurio, of Silvia] *You must lay lime to tangle her desires;* **AY** III.v.44; **1H6** II.ii.22; **Venus** 67

tanling (*n.*) sun-tanned child **Cym** IV.iv.29 [Belarius to Arviragus and Guiderius] *to be still hot Summer's tanlings*

tap (*v.*) work as a tapster **MW** I.iii.10 [Host to Falstaff, of Bardolph] *he shall tap*

taper (*n.*) candle **JC** II.i.35 [Lucius to Brutus] *The taper burneth in your closet;* **Cym** II.ii.19; **LL** V.ii.267; **MW** IV.iv.49; **Oth** I.i.142; **Tit** I.i.327

taper-light (*n.*) candle-light **Per** I.Chorus.16 [Gower alone, of life] *I might / Waste it for you like taper-light;* **KJ** IV.ii.14

taphouse, tap-house (*n.*) tavern, alehouse **MM** II.i.199 [Froth to Escalus] *I never come into any room in a taphouse but I am drawn in*

tapster (*n.*) inn waiter, drawer of ale **Tim** IV.iii.216 [Apemantus to Timon] *Thou gavest thine ears, like tapsters that bade welcome;* **AY** III.iv.28; **2H4** I.ii.172; **LL** I.i.41; **MM** II.i.188; **Venus** 849

tardiness (*n.*) reserve, reticence, hesitancy **KL** I.i.235 [France to Lear, of Cordelia's behaviour] *a tardiness in nature* [i.e. a natural reluctance]

tardy (*adj.*) dull, slow-witted, reluctant **JC** I.ii.296 [Cassius to Brutus, of Casca] *he puts on this tardy form*

tardy (*v.*) delay, retard, hold back **WT** III.ii.160 [Leontes to all] *the good mind of Camillo tardied / My swift command*

tardy (*adv.*) inadequately **Ham** III.ii.25 [Hamlet to the Players] *this overdone, or come tardy off* [i.e. carried out badly]

tardy, take catch unawares, take by surprise **R3** IV.i.51 [Derby to Dorset] *Be not ta'en tardy by unwise delay*

tardy-apish (*adj.*) slow in copying, always behind in imitating **R2** II.i.22 [York to John of Gaunt, of Italy] *Whose manners still our tardy-apish nation / Limps after in base imitation*

tardy-gaited slow-moving, sluggish **H5** IV.Chorus.20 [Chorus] *The confident and over-lusty French … chide the cripple tardy-gaited night*

targe (*n.*) shield **Cym** V.v.5 [Cymbeline to all, of the soldier] *whose naked breast / Stepped before targes of proof;* **AC** II.vi.39; **LL** V.ii.549 ➤ WEAPONS, p.491

target (*n.*) light round shield **E3** III.iii.199 [Artois to Prince Edward] *take thy steel, wear it on thy arm;* **AC** IV.viii.31; **Cor** IV.v.123; **1H4** II.iv.197; **3H6** II.i.40; **Per** II.i.138 ➤ WEAPONS, p.491

tarre (*v.*) incite, provoke, arouse **TC** I.iii.391 [Nestor to Ulysses, of Achilles and Ajax] *pride alone / Must tarre the mastiffs on, as 'twere their bone;* **Ham** II.ii.352; **KJ** IV.i.116

tarriance (*n.*) **1** delay, procrastination, lingering **TG** II.vii.90 [Julia to Lucetta] *I am impatient of my tarriance*
2 waiting, abiding **PassP** VI.4 *Cytherea … / A longing tarriance for Adonis made*

tarry (*v.*) **1** stay, remain, linger **TG** II.iii.34 [Panthino to Launce] *you'll lose the tide, if you tarry any longer;* **CE** IV.iii.39; **H5** IV.vi.15; **JC** V.v.30; **Mac** V.v.48; **TN** IV.i.18
2 stay for, wait for, allow time for **2H4** III.ii.188 [Falstaff to Shallow] *I will go drink with you, but I cannot tarry dinner;* **TC** I.i.15
3 await, expect, anticipate **MW** IV.v.18 [Host to Falstaff, of Simple] *Here's a Bohemian-Tartar tarries the coming down of thy fat woman*

tarrying (*n.*) waiting, delaying, lingering **TC** II.iii.255 [Ulysses to all] *There is no tarrying here* [i.e. no point in staying]

tart (*adj.*) sour, severe, grim **AC** II.v.38 [Cleopatra to Messenger] *so tart a favour / To trumpet such good tidings?;* **KL** IV.ii.87

tartly (*adv.*) sourly, grouchily, with a bitter demeanour **MA** II.i.3 [Beatrice to all, of Don John] *How tartly that gentleman looks!*

task (*n.*) ➤ attask (*v.*)

task (*v.*) **1** test, try out, challenge **1H4** IV.i.9 [Hotspur to Douglas] *task me to my word;* **KJ** III.i.148; **LL** V.ii.126; **Sonn** 72.1
2 set a task [for], employ **Cor** I.iii.37 [Volumnia to Virgilia, of Martius] *Like to a harvest-man that's tasked to mow / Or all or lose his hire;* **Tem** I.ii.192
3 impose a tax upon **1H4** IV.iii.92 [Hotspur to Blunt, of King Henry] *In short time after he deposed the King, / Soon after that deprived him of his life, / And in the neck of that tasked the whole state*
4 take to task, censure, chastise **LL** II.i.20 [Princess to and of Boyet] *now to task the tasker* ➤ tax (*v.*) 1

task of (*v.*) occupy, engage, make demands on **MW** IV.vi.30 [Fenton to Host, of Caius and Anne] *he shall … shuffle her away, / While other sports are tasking of their minds*

tasking (*n.*) offering of a challenge **1H4** V.ii.50 [Hotspur to Vernon, of Prince Hal] *How showed his tasking?*

tassel (*n.*) ornamental fringe **TC** V.i.29 [Thersites to Patroclus] *thou tassel of a prodigal's purse* [F *tassell;* Q *toslell*]

tassel-gentle (*n.*) male peregrine falcon **RJ** II.ii.159 [Juliet to Romeo] *O for a falconer's voice, / To lure this tassel-gentle back again!*

taste (*n.*) **1** trial, testing, proof **KL** I.ii.45 [Edmund to Gloucester, of Edgar's supposed letter] *I hope … he wrote this but as an essay or taste of my virtue;* **2H4** II.iii.52
2 measure, degree, slight way **JC** IV.i.34 [Antony to Octavius, of controlling his horse] *in some taste, is Lepidus but so*

taste (*v.*) **1** try out, test, put to the proof **TN** III.i.76 [Sir Toby to Viola as Cesario] *Taste your legs, sir; put them in motion;* **KJ** III.i.148 [F]; **TC** III.ii.89; **Tim** III.i.79; **TN** III.iv.239
2 act as taster, make trial [as if by taste] **TNK** V.v.23 [Palamon to his knights] *E'en he that led you to this banquet shall / Taste to you all;* **KJ** V.vi.28

taste of (*v.*) partake of, savour of **2H4** IV.i.190 [Mowbray to Hastings] *every idle, nice, and wanton reason, / Shall to the King taste of this action*

tattered (*adj.*) **1** jagged, with pointed projections; or: dilapidated, battered **R2** III.iii.52 [Bolingbroke to Northumberland] *from this castle's tattered battlements / Our fair appointments may be well perused* [F; Q1,2 *tottered*]
2 torn, ragged **Sonn** 2.4 *Thy youth's proud livery so gazed on now, / Will be a tottered weed of small worth held* [Q *totter'd*]; **Sonn** 26.11

tattling (*n.*) prattle, chatter, idle talk **MW** IV.i.24 [Evans to Mistress Quickly] *Peace your tattlings*

tattling (*adj.*) gossiping, tale-telling, rumour-mongering **MW** III.iii.86 [Mistress Ford to Falstaff, of Mistress Page] *She's a very tattling woman*

tawdry-lace (*n.*) silk necktie, coloured neckerchief **WT** IV.iv.248 [Mopsa to Clown] *you promised me a tawdry-lace and a pair of sweet gloves*

tawny (*adj.*) **1** brown-skinned **Tit** V.i.27 [Second Goth to Lucius, reporting Aaron's words to the baby] *Peace, tawny slave;* **AC** I.i.6
2 yellowish brown **Tem** II.i.57 [Antonio to Sebastian] *The ground, indeed, is tawny*

tax (*n.*) charge, accusation, censure **AW** II.i.170 [Helena to King] *Tax of impudence;* **Tim** I.i.48

tax (*v.*) **1** censure, blame, take to task, disparage **MA** I.i.42 [Leonato to Beatrice] *you tax Signor Benedick too much;* **AW** V.iii.122; **AY** II.ii.337; **KL** III.i.16; **MM** II.iv.79; **TC** I.iii.197 ➤ task (*v.*) 4
2 order, tell, command **MA** II.iii.42 [Balthasar to Don Pedro] *tax not so bad a voice / To slander music any more than once;* **TC** V.i.38

taxation (*n.*) **1** criticism, censure, slander **AY** I.ii.80 [Celia to Touchstone] *you'll be whipped for taxation one of these days*
2 demand for money, financial claim **TN** I.v.202 [Viola as Cesario to Olivia] *I bring … no taxation of homage*

taxing (*n.*) criticism, censure, reproof **AY** II.vii.86 [Jaques to Duke Senior] *my taxing like a wild-goose flies*

teach (*v.*) **1** give direction to, lecture **Cor** II.i.247 [Sicinius to Brutus, of Coriolanus] *his soaring insolence / Shall teach the people*
2 show, point out to **MM** II.iv.19 [Angelo to Servant, of Isabella] *Teach her the way*

teachy (*adj.*) ➤ tetchy (*adj.*)

tear (*v.*) break, shatter, burst **R2** III.i.24 [Bolingbroke to Bushy and Green] *you have … / From my own windows torn my household coat*

tear-distained (*adj.*) tear-stained **Luc** 1586 [of Lucrece] *round about her tear-distained eye / Blue circles streamed*

tediosity (*n.*) tediousness, bother, trouble **TNK** III.v.2 [Schoolmaster to all] *What tediosity and disinsanity / Is here among ye!*

tedious (*adj.*) **1** laborious, painstaking, wearyingly intricate **2H6** III.i.340 [York to himself] *My brain … / Weaves tedious snares to trap mine enemies;* **1H4** III.i.45; **Mac** III.iv.137; **Tit** II.iv.39
2 painful, irksome, harrowing **AY** III.iv.314 [Rosalind to Orlando, of a rich man] *knowing no burden of heavy tedious penury;* **R2** II.iii.75
3 ➤ brief and the long / tedious, the

teem (*v.*) **1** produce, bring forth **Tim** IV.iii.180 [Timon alone, of the earth] *Whose womb unmeasurable and infinite breast / Teems and feeds all;* **H5** V.ii.51; **Mac** IV.iii.176

2 be made pregnant, conceive **Oth** IV.i.245 [Othello to Lodovico, of Desdemona] *If that the earth could teem with woman's tears, / Each drop she falls would prove a crocodile*

3 give birth, have a child **KL** I.iv.278 [Lear to the goddess Nature, of Gonerill] *If she must teem, / Create her child of spleen*

teeming (*adj.*) pregnant, prolific, overfull **R2** II.i.51 [John of Gaunt to York, of England] *this teeming womb of royal kings;* **1H4** III.i.25; **MM** I.iv.43; **Sonn** 97.6

teeming-date (*n.*) child-bearing age **R2** V.ii.91 [Duchess of York to York] *Is not my teeming-date drunk up with time?*

teen (*n.*) trouble, grief, suffering **Venus** 808 [Adonis to Venus] *My face is full of shame, my heart of teen;* **LL** IV.iii.162; **Lover** 192; **R3** IV.i.96; **RJ** I.iii.14; **Tem** I.ii.64

teeth, from one's in a pretended way, without conviction **AC** III.iv.10 [Antony to Octavia, of Caesar] *When the best hint was given him, he not took't / Or did it from his teeth*

teeth, in the to my face, in direct opposition **CE** II.ii.22 [Antipholus of Syracuse to Dromio of Syracuse] *dost thou jeer and flout me in the teeth?*

teeth and forehead of, to the in the very face of, confronting face-to-face **Ham** III.iii.63 [Claudius alone] *Even to the teeth and forehead of our faults*

tell (*v.*) **1** count out, number, itemize **H8** II.i.91 [Buckingham to Lovell, of King Henry] *May he live / Longer than I have time to tell his years;* **E3** II.i.136; **3H6** II.i.163; **KL** III.ii.91; **TNK** III.v.80

2 spell out, narrate, recount **LL** II.i.17 [Princess to Boyet] *I am less proud to hear you tell my worth;* **3H6** III.iii.92

3 tell the time on **R3** V.iii.277 [King Richard to Ratcliffe] *Tell the clock there* [i.e. count the strokes]; **Tem** II.i.294

4 communicate, make known **CE** II.i.48 [Dromio of Ephesus to Adriana, of his master] *He told his mind upon mine ear;* **KL** II.iv.53; **Sonn** 93.12

5 say, assert, put it about **Cor** II.i.58 [Menenius to Brutus and Sicinius, of their supporters] *they lie deadly that tell you have good faces*

6 disclose, reveal, explain **3H6** III.i.48 [King to himself, of Edward] *Warwick tells his title, smoothes the wrong;* **AW** IV.iii.159; **KL** I.i.208; **Per** I.Chorus.38

7 rebuke, admonish, reprove **Cor** IV.ii.48 [Menenius to Volumnia, of Brutus and Sicinius] *You have told them home* [i.e. given them a piece of your mind]

tell out (*v.*) count out, reckon up **Tim** III.iv.95 [Timon to Servants, of his bills] *Tell out my blood*

temper (*n.*) **1** frame of mind, temperament, disposition **Cor** V.ii.90 [Aufidius to Coriolanus] *You keep a constant temper;* **1H4** III.i.164; **2H4** II.i.79; **H5** V.ii.146; **RJ** III.i.115; **TNK** III.i.66

2 quality, constitution, condition **E3** IV.vii.47 [Prince Edward to Audley] *the soft temper of a Frenchman's sword;* **1H4** V.ii.93; **1H6** II.iv.13; **2H6** V.ii.70; **H8** II.iii.11; **R2** IV.i.29

3 self-control, self-restraint, moderation **MM** II.ii.185 [Angelo alone] *Never could the strumpet … / Once stir my temper;* **AC** I.i.8

4 mental balance, stable mind **KL** I.v.44 [Lear to himself, as if to heaven] *Keep me in temper*

temper (*v.*) **1** blend, mix, concoct, compound **Ham** V.ii.322 [Laertes to Hamlet, of Claudius] *It is a poison tempered by himself;* **AY** I.ii.12; **Cym** V.v.250; **MA** II.ii.19; **RJ** III.iii.115, v.97

2 mould, shape, work, bring [to a particular character] **H5** II.ii.118 [King Henry to Scroop, of a devil] *he that tempered thee bade thee stand up;* **2H4** IV.viii.127; **R3** I.i.65; **TC** II.iii.251; **TG** III.ii.64; **Tit** IV.iv.109

3 soften, moisten, mix [with] **2H6** III.i.311 [Cardinal to York] *Th'uncivil kerns of Ireland are in arms / And temper clay with blood of Englishmen;* **KL** I.iv.301; **Tit** V.ii.198

4 harden, toughen **Tem** III.i.63 [Ariel to Alonso, Sebastian, and Antonio] *The elements, / Of whom your swords are tempered* [or: sense 2]

5 moderate, soften, tone down **RJ** II.Chorus.14 [Chorus, of Romeo and Juliet] *Tempering extremities with extreme sweet*

temper with (*v.*) conform to, be moulded by **3H6** IV.vi.29 [Warwick to King] *few men rightly temper with the stars* [i.e. conform to what the stars determine]

temperality (*n.*) malapropism for 'temper' **2H4** II.iv.23 [Hostess to Doll] *methinks now you are in an excellent good temperality*

temperance (*n.*) **1** self-control, calm behaviour, moderation **KL** IV.vii.24 [Gentleman to Cordelia, of Lear] *I doubt not of his temperance;* **AC** V.ii.48; **Ham** III.ii.7; **H8** I.i.124; **MM** III.ii.227

2 chastity **AC** III.xiii.121 [Antony to Cleopatra] *Though you can guess what temperance should be, / You know not what it is;* **Luc** 884

3 temperateness, climate, mildness **Tem** II.i.45 [Adrian to all, of the island] *It must needs be of subtle, tender, and delicate temperance* [pun: 46, woman's name]

temperate (*adj.*) **1** self-restrained, abstemious, gentle-natured **TS** II.i.287 [Petruchio to Baptista, of Katherina] *She is not hot, but temperate as the morn;* **Tem** I.ii.132

2 calm, moderate, composed **KJ** II.i.195 [King Philip to Constance] *Pause, or be more temperate;* **Mac** II.iii.105; **TC** I.iii.147

temperately (*adv.*) steadily, calmly, moderately **Ham** III.iv.141 [Hamlet to Gertrude] *My pulse as yours doth temperately keep time;* **Cor** II.i.216, III.iii.67

tempered (*adj.*) **1** temperate, controlled, brought to the right quality **MM** V.i.470 [Escalus to Angelo, of Angelo's transgression] *both in the heat of blood / And lack of tempered judgement afterward*

2 in such a mood, of this disposition **TC** V.iii.1 [Andromache to Hector] *When was my lord so much ungently tempered*

tempering (*n.*) softening, moulding **Venus** 565 *What wax so frozen but dissolves with temp'ring*

temple (*n.*) **1** church **MA** III.iii.155 [Borachio to Conrade, of Claudio and Hero] *he would meet her … next morning at the temple*

2 human body [i.e. temple in which the Holy Spirit lives] **Ham** I.iii.12 [Laertes to Ophelia] *as this temple waxes*

temporal (*adj.*) secular, civil, worldly **MV** IV.i.187 [Portia as Balthasar to Shylock, of a king] *His sceptre shows the force of temporal power;* **H5** I.i.9; **H8** II.ii.71, iii.13; **MM** II.ii.155; **Tem** I.ii.110

temporary (*adj.*) in temporal affairs, of this world's doings **MM** V.i.145 [Friar Peter to Duke, of Friar Lodowick] *Not scurvy, nor a temporary meddler*

temporize (*v.*) **1** compromise, conform, become amenable **Cor** IV.vi.17 [Menenius to Sicinius, of Coriolanus] *All's well, and might have been much better if / He could have temporized;* **MA** I.i.253

2 negotiate, come to terms, effect a compromise **TC** IV.iv.6 [Cressida to Pandarus] *If I could temporize with my affection;* **KJ** V.ii.125

temporizer (*n.*) delayer, procrastinator, someone who plays for time **WT** I.ii.302 [Leontes to Camillo] *I hate thee, / Pronounce thee … a hovering temporizer*

tempt (*v.*) **1** try, test, make trial of **KJ** IV.iii.84 [Hubert to Salisbury] *I would not have you … tempt the danger of my true defence;* **AC** I.iii.11; **H8** I.ii.55; **JC** I.iii.53; **TC** IV.v.95; **WT** II.ii.50

2 persuade, entice, invite **R3** I.iv.12 [Clarence to Keeper] *Gloucester … tempted me to walk / Upon the hatches;* **2H6** III.ii.114

3 risk, venture out to, dare to encounter **TC** V.iii.34 [Hector to Troilus] *tempt not yet the brushes of the war*

tenable (*adj.*) kept secret, retained, kept back **Ham** I.ii.248 [Hamlet to Horatio and the sentinels, of the ghostly vision] *If you have hitherto concealed this sight, / Let it be tenable in your silence still*

tench (*n.*) type of freshwater fish [with red spots on its skin] **1H4** II.i.16 [Second Carrier to First Carrier] *I am stung like a tench.* [First Carrier] *Like a tench!*

tend (*v.*) **1** attend, wait on, serve **Tem** I.ii.47 [Miranda to Prospero] *Had I not / Four or five women once that tended me?*; **AC** II.ii.212; **Ham** III.ii.216; **Sonn** 57.1; **TC** II.iii.125

2 await, wait in expectation **Ham** I.iii.83 [Polonius to Laertes] *Your servants tend*; **Ham** IV.iii.44; **KL** II.iv.97

3 serve, promote, sustain **2H6** I.i.202 [Salisbury to York and Warwick] *cherish Duke Humphrey's deeds / While they do tend the profit of the land*

4 attend, listen, pay attention **Tem** I.i.6 [Boatswain to Mariners] *Tend to th' Master's whistle!*

5 relate, refer, be relevant **JC** I.ii.315 [Cassius alone, of letters about Brutus] *all tending to the great opinion / That Rome holds of his name*; **JC** III.ii.59; **R2** II.i.232; **Sonn** 103.11

6 ⟩⟨ attend (*v.*)

tend on / upon (*v.*) serve, follow, wait upon, escort **AW** II.i.207 [King to Helena] *whence thou camest, how tended on*; **2H6** III.ii.304; **KL** II.i.94, iv.258; **Mac** I.v.39; **Sonn** 53.2

tendance (*n.*) **1** attention, care, solicitude **Tim** I.i.59 [Poet to Painter, of Timon's fortune] *Subdues and properties to his love and tendance / All sorts of hearts*; **Cym** V.v.53; **H8** III.ii.149

2 retinue, people in attendance **Tim** I.i.83 [Poet to Painter, of Timon's associates in his poem] *his lobbies fill with tendance*

tender (*n.*) **1** offer, offering **Ham** I.iii.99 [Ophelia to Polonius, of Hamlet] *He hath, my lord, of late made many tenders / Of his affection to me*; **E3** II.i.315; **KJ** V.vii.106; **LL** II.i.171; **MA** II.iii.178; **MND** III.ii.87

2 proposal of marriage, offer of betrothal **MW** I.i.193 [Shallow to Slender] *there is as 'twere a tender ... made afar off by Sir Hugh*; **RJ** III.iv.12, v.185

3 care, concern, solicitude **KL** I.iv.206 [Gonerill to Lear] *the tender of a wholesome weal*; **1H4** V.iv.48

tender (*adj.*) **1** young **R3** V.iii.96 [Derby to Richmond] *thy brother, tender George*; **3H6** II.ii.28; **R3** III.i.28, IV.i.4, iv.342, 385

2 immature, undeveloped, inexperienced **AY** I.i.121 [Charles to Oliver, of Orlando] *Your brother is but young and tender*; **R2** II.iii.42; **TG** III.i.34; **Venus** 1091

3 thoughtful, considerate, solicitous **3H6** IV.vi.66 [King to Somerset] *what youth is that, / Of whom you seem to have such tender care?*; **Cym** V.v.87; **WT** II.iii.127

4 meek, submissive, spineless **Cym** IV.ii.126 [Guiderius to Belarius and Arviragus, of Cloten] *why should we be tender, / To let an arrogant piece of flesh threat us*

5 sensitive [to], easily hurt [by] **Cym** III.v.40 [Queen to Cymbeline, of Innogen] *She's a lady / So tender of rebukes that words are strokes*

6 pitiable, pathetic, moving **TC** IV.v.106 [Ulysses to Agamemnon] *Hector in his blaze of wrath subscribes / To tender objects*

7 weak, faint, delicate **Luc** 695 [of the replete hound] *Unapt for tender smell*

8 mild, soft, gentle **Tem** II.i.44 [Adrian to all, of the island] *It must needs be of subtle, tender, and delicate temperance*; **Cym** V.iv.140

9 fond of comfort, attached to the easy life **AW** IV.v.51 [Clown to Lafew, of 'the house with the narrow gate'] *the many will be too chill and tender [to enter it]*

tender (*v.*) **1** offer, give, present **H8** II.iii.66 [Anne to Lord Chamberlain] *I do not know / What kind of my obedience I should tender*; **AW** I.iii.231; **LL** II.i.230; **Tim** V.i.13; **Tit** V.iii.156; **WT** IV.iv.792

2 feel concern for, hold dear, care for **2H6** III.i.277 [Cardinal to Suffolk] *I tender so the safety of my liege*; **CE** V.i.132; **Ham** IV.iii.40; **R2** I.i.32; **R3** IV.iv.405; **TN** V.i.124

3 rate, esteem, regard **RJ** III.i.70 [Romeo to Tybalt, of the name Capulet] *which name I tender / As dearly as mine own*; **AY** V.ii.67; **Ham** I.iii.107; **H8** II.iv.116; **Tem** II.i.275; **TNK** V.i.25

4 grant, consent to **TNK** II.i.14 [Gaoler to Wooer] *I tender my consent*; **Luc** 534

5 look after, take care of **TS** Induction.i.14 [Lord to First Huntsman] *tender well my hounds*

tender down (*v.*) offer, proffer, present **Tim** I.i.56 [Poet to Painter] *You see how all conditions ... tender down / Their services to Lord Timon*; **MM** II.iv.180

tender-dying (*adj.*) dying young **1H6** III.iii.48 [Pucelle to Burgundy] *As looks the mother on her lowly babe / When death does close his tender-dying eyes*

tender-hefted (*adj.*) [*haft* = handle] set in a delicate bodily frame; tender-hearted, gentle **KL** II.iv.166 [Lear to Regan] *Thy tender-hefted nature shall not give / Thee o'er to harshness* [F; Q *teder hested*]

tenderly (*adv.*) carefully, attentively, gently **TNK** II.i.19 [Gaoler to Gaoler's Daughter] *look tenderly to the two prisoners* [i.e. look after them well]

tender-smelling (*adj.*) with a sensitive sense of smell **LL** V.ii.563 [Berowne to Boyet, of Nathaniel's portrayal of Alexander] *Your nose smells 'no' in this, most tender-smelling knight*

tending (*n.*) attendance, attention, care **Mac** I.v.35 [Lady Macbeth to Messenger, of another messenger] *Give him tending*

tenement (*n.*) land held by a tenant, landholding **R2** II.i.60 [John of Gaunt to York, of England] *Is now leased out ... / Like to a tenement or pelting farm*

tenor, tenour (*n.*) **1** substance, content, matter, drift **1H4** IV.iv.7 [Sir Michael to Archbishop, of letters] *I guess their tenor*; **AY** IV.iii.12; **H5** V.ii.72; **H8** I.ii.206; **JC** IV.iii.169; **TC** II.i.90

2 meaning, purpose, intention **TNK** III.vi.133 [Theseus to Palamon and Arcite] *you, that 'gainst the tenor of my laws / Are making battle*; **1H4** V.v.5; **MV** IV.i.232; **TNK** I.i.90

3 synopsis, digest, summary [of a performance] **TNK** III.v.122 [Schoolmaster to Theseus] *To speak before thy noble grace this tenor* [Q *tenner*] ⟩⟨ tenure (*n.*)

tent (*n.*) **1** (plural) encampment **JC** V.iii.10 [Pindarus to Cassius] *Mark Antony is in your tents*

2 fabric hung over and around a bed **TS** II.i.345 [Gremio to Baptista, of his possessions] *Costly apparel, tents, and canopies*

3 probe, insert [for exploring wounds] **TC** II.ii.16 [Hector to Priam, of doubt] *the tent that searches / To th'bottom of the worst*; **Cym** III.iv.117

tent (*v.*) **1** lodge, encamp, take up residence **Cor** III.ii.116 [Coriolanus to Volumnia] *The smiles of knaves / Tent in my cheeks*

2 probe, explore, investigate **Ham** II.ii.595 [Hamlet alone, of Claudius] *I'll tent him to the quick*

3 treat with a tent [linen for cleansing wounds]; cure, remedy **Cor** III.i.235 [Menenius to Coriolanus] *'tis a sore upon us / You cannot tent yourself*; **Cor** I.ix.31

tented (*adj.*) covered with tents, full of tents **Oth** I.iii.85 [Othello to all] *these arms of mine ... have used / Their dearest action in the tented field*

tenth (*n.*) tax, levy [amounting to a tenth of one's income] **1H6** V.v.93 [King to Suffolk] *For your expenses ... / Among the people gather up a tenth*

tenure (*n.*) **1** [legal] condition for holding property **Ham** V.i.98 [Hamlet to Horatio, of the skull of a lawyer] *Where be ... his tenures*

2 [legal] statement, account, summary **Luc** 1310 [of Lucrece's letter] *Here folds she up the tenure of her woe* [Q] [or: tenor] ⟩⟨ tenor (*n.*)

tercel (*n.*) male hawk **TC** III.ii.51 [Pandarus to Troilus and Cressida] *the falcon as the tercel, for all the ducks i'th' river* [i.e. the female will be as keen as the male hawk in pursuing quarry]

tereu (*int.*) ⟩⟨ **SOUNDS**, p.410

term (*n.*) **1** word, expression, utterance **RJ** I.i.212 [Romeo to Benvolio, of his love] *She will not stay the siege of loving terms*; **E3** I.ii.160; **2H4** IV.iv.104; **3H6** I.i.265; **Luc** 1706; **TN** II.iv.5

2 names, labels **MW** II.ii.281 [Ford alone] *I shall ... stand under the adoption of abominable terms*

3 state, condition, circumstance **Ham** IV.vii.26 [Laertes to Claudius] *A sister driven into desperate terms;* **Ham** III.iii.5, V.ii.240; **MM** I.i.10, II.ii.100; **TN** V.i.68
4 respect, consideration, form **MV** II.i.13 [Portia to Morocco] *In terms of choice I am not solely led / By nice direction of a maiden's eyes;* **AW** II.iii.165
5 any of four periods of activity within the legal year [Michaelmas, Hilary, Easter, Trinity] **AY** III.ii.321 [Rosalind to Orlando, of lawyers] *they sleep between term and term;* **2H4** V.i.73

termagant (*adj.*) savage, violent, turbulent **1H4** V.iv.112 [Falstaff alone] *'twas time to counterfeit, or that hot termagant Scot had paid me*

termed (*adj.*) named, called **2H6** IV.ii.31 [Cade to all] *We John Cade, so termed of our supposed father*

termination (*n.*) expression, utterance, sentence ending **MA** II.i.228 [Benedick to Don Pedro, of Beatrice] *If her breath were as terrible as her terminations*

termless (*adj.*) indescribable, beyond words **Lover** 94 [of the man] *His phoenix down began but to appear ... on that termless skin*

terrene (*adj.*) earthly, human, in this world **TNK** I.iii.14 [Emilia to Pirithous] *in our terrene state petitions are not / Without gifts understood;* **AC** III.xiii.153

terrible (*adj.*) terrifying, frightning, inspiring dread **Tim** V.iv.2 [Alcibiades to Trumpeter] *Sound to this coward and lascivious town / Our terrible approach*

territory (*n.*) dependency, dominion **KJ** I.i.10 [Chatillon to King John, of King Philip's claim] *To this fair island and the territories*

terror (*n.*) power to inspire dread **MM** I.i.19 [Duke to Escalus, of Angelo] *we have ... / Lent him our terror*

tertian (*n.*) type of fever with attacks every third day **H5** II.i.114 [Hostess to Pistol and Nym, of Falstaff] *he is so shaked of a burning quotidian tertian that it is most lamentable to behold*

test (*n.*) evidence, attestation, testimony **Oth** I.iii.107 [Duke to Brabantio, of Othello charming Desdemona] *To vouch this is no proof, / Without more wider and more overt test*

testament (*n.*) will, last will and testament **1H6** I.v.17 [Pucelle to the French] *Help Salisbury to make his testament;* **AW** V.iii.197; **AY** I.i.69; **JC** III.ii.131

tester, testril (*n.*) sixpenny piece **2H4** III.ii.268 [Falstaff to Wart] *there's a tester for thee;* **MW** I.iii.82; **TN** II.iii.32 ➤ **MONEY**, p.286

testern (*v.*) give a sixpence [tester] as a tip **TG** I.i.142 [Speed to Proteus] *you have testerned me*

testimony (*n.*) warrant, acknowledgement, assurance **LL** IV.ii.2 [Nathaniel to Holofernes, of hunting] *done in the testimony of a good conscience*

testimony (*v.*) justify in the light of evidence, vindicate **MM** III.ii.136 [disguised Duke to Lucio, of the Duke] *Let him be but testimonied in his own bringings-forth*

testril (*n.*) ➤ tester (*n.*)

testy (*adj.*) irritable, peevish, short-tempered **JC** IV.iii.46 [Brutus to Cassius] *Must I stand and crouch / Under your testy humour?;* **Luc** 1094; **Sonn** 140.7; **TG** I.i.58; **Venus** 319

tetchy, teachy (*adj.*) irritable, peevish, fretful **TC** I.i.98 [Troilus alone, of Pandarus and Cressida] *he's as tetchy to be wooed to woo / As she is stubborn-chaste against all suit* [F; Q *teachy*]; **R3** IV.iv.169; **RJ** I.iii.33

tetter (*n.*) scaly eruption of the skin, scurf **Ham** I.v.71 [Ghost to Hamlet] *And a most instant tetter barked about ... / All my smooth body;* **TC** V.i.20 [Q]

tetter (*v.*) cover the skin with scabs **Cor** III.i.79 [Coriolanus to First Senator] *those measles / Which we disdain should tetter us*

text (*n.*) **1** theme, subject, topic **TN** I.v.222 [Olivia to Viola as Cesario] *You are now out of your text* [i.e. straying from the point]; **KL** IV.ii.37

2 text-hand style [of handwriting] **LL** V.ii.42 [Katharine to Princess, of Rosaline's beauty] *Fair as a text B in a copy-book*

text (*v.*) engrave, write, inscribe **E3** IV.iv.130 [Prince Edward to Audley] *stratagems forepast with iron pens / Are texted in thine honourable face;* **MA** V.i.176

th' (*det.*) shortened form of 'the' **Cor** I.ix.65 [Cominius to Martius, of Martius' new name] *Bear th'addition nobly ever!;* **H8** I.i.169 [Buckingham to Norfolk, of Wolsey] *This cunning Cardinal / The articles o'th' combination drew / As himself pleased*

-th (*ending*) ➤ **VERB FORMS**, p.481

thank (*n.*) gratitude, thankfulness, appreciative thought **R2** II.iii.65 [Bolingbroke to Ross and Willoughby] *Evermore thank's the exchequer of the poor* [F *thankes*]

thanking (*n.*) word of thanks, expression of gratitude **Cym** V.v.408 [Cymbeline to all, of a soldier] *He would have ... graced / The thankings of a king;* **MM** V.i.4

thas (*int.*) ➤ **SOUNDS**, p.410

that (*conj.*) **1** if **Ham** V.ii.194 [Lord to Hamlet, of Claudius] *He sends to know if your pleasure hold to play with Laertes, or that you will take longer time*
2 when **AY** III.ii.172 [Rosalind to Celia] *I was never so be-rhymed since Pythagoras' time that I was an Irish rat*
3 with the result that **AY** III.ii.399 [Rosalind as Ganymede to Orlando, of her actions towards a suitor] *that I drave my suitor from his mad humour of love to a living humour of madness*
4 that which **Ham** I.ii.17 [Claudius to his court] *Now follows that you know*
5 to show that **TNK** III.vi.191 [Emilia to Hippolyta] *Yet that I will be woman and have pity, / My knees shall grow to th'ground*

thaw (*v.*) dissolve, soften, melt **Ham** I.ii.130 [Hamlet alone] *O that this too too sullied flesh would melt, / Thaw, and resolve itself;* **TNK** I.i.69

theft (*n.*) thief, robber **CE** IV.ii.60 [Dromio of Syracuse to Adriana, of time] *If 'a be in debt and theft*

theme (*n.*) **1** subject, subject-matter, topic of discourse **TC** IV.v.181 [Menelaus to Hector, of Helen] *Name her not now, sir; she's a deadly theme;* **CE** II.ii.190; **Cor** I.i.218; **Mac** I.iii.128; **MW** V.v.159; **Tem** II.i.6
2 reason for acting, ground of belief **TC** II.ii.200 [Troilus to Hector, of Helen] *She is a theme of honour and renown;* **AC** II.ii.48; **H8** II.iii.93; **TC** V.ii.134; **WT** I.ii.459

thence (*adv.*) ➤ **HENCE, THENCE, AND WHENCE**, p.219

theoric (*n.*) theory, academic speculation **AW** IV.iii.141 [First Lord to Bertram] *the whole theoric of war;* **H5** I.i.52; **Oth** I.i.24

there (*adv.*) ➤ **HERE, THERE, AND WHERE**, p.220

thereafter as according as, depending on **2H4** III.ii.49 [Shallow to Silence, of the price of ewes] *Thereafter as they be* [i.e. the price varies according to the quality]

therefor (*adv.*) therefore, for that **2H4** V.iii.108 [Pistol to Shallow] *lament therefor;* **H5** II.iii.6

therefore (*adv.*) for that very reason **Tit** V.ii.162 [Publius to Chiron, reacting to 'We are the Empress' sons'] *And therefore do we what we are commanded*

thews (*n.*) muscles, sinews, bodily strength **JC** I.iii.81 [Cassius to Casca] *Romans now / Have thews and limbs like to their ancestors;* **Ham** I.iii.12; **2H4** III.ii.251

thick (*adj.*) **1** deep, heavy, profound **TNK** IV.iii.48 [Doctor to Gaoler, of the Gaoler's Daughter] *'Tis not an engraffed madness, but a most thick and profound melancholy;* **Cym** I.vii.67 [or: sense 6]
2 dull, dim, poor **JC** V.iii.21 [Cassius to Pindarus] *My sight was ever thick;* **2H4** III.ii.302, IV.iii.57
3 thickset, strong, sturdy **3H6** V.vii.23 [Richard to himself] *This shoulder was ordained so thick to heave*
4 foul, nasty, dirty **AC** V.ii.211 [Cleopatra to Iras, of the Romans] *their thick breaths, / Rank of gross diet;* **TS** V.ii.142

5 confused, clouded [with suspicion] **Ham** IV.v.83 [Claudius to Gertrude] *the people muddied, / Thick and unwholesome in their thoughts*
6 quick, rapid, fast **TC** III.ii.34 [Troilus alone] *My heart beats thicker than a feverous pulse;* **Cym** V.iii.41; **Luc** 1784

thick (v.) thicken, make dense **WT** I.ii.171 [Polixenes to Leontes, of Florizel] *with his varying childness [he] cures in me / Thoughts that would thick my blood* [i.e. make me melancholic]

thick (adv.) quickly, rapidly, fast **Cym** III.ii.57 [Innogen to Pisanio] *say, and speak thick;* **AW** II.ii.41; **2H4** II.iii.24

thick-coming (adj.) coming in crowds, frequently appearing **Mac** V.iii.38 [Doctor to Macbeth, of Lady Macbeth] *she is troubled with thick-coming fancies / That keep her from her rest*

thicken (v.) grow dim, darken **Mac** III.ii.50 [Macbeth to Lady Macbeth] *Light thickens / And the crow makes wing to the rooky wood;* **AC** II.iii.28

thicket (n.) densely wooded area **3H6** IV.v.3 [Richard to Hastings and Stanley] *this chiefest thicket of the park;* **TC** II.iii.256; **TG** V.iii.11

thick-eyed (adj.) heavy-eyed, dull-sighted **1H4** II.iii.48 [Lady Percy to Hotspur] *Why hast thou ... given my treasures and my rights of thee / To thick-eyed musing*

thick-pleached (adj.) thickly hedged, with hedges made of closely interlaced branches **MA** I.ii.8 [Antonio to Leonato] *walking in a thick-pleached alley in mine orchard* ☛ **pleached** (adj.) 2

thick-ribbed (adj.) densely surrounded, compacted **MM** III.i.126 [Claudio to Isabella, of what might follow death] *the delighted spirit ... to reside / In thrilling region of thick-ribbed ice*

thick-sighted (adj.) with bad eyesight **Venus** 136 [Venus to Adonis] *Were I ... / Thick-sighted, barren, lean*

thickskin, thick-skin (n.) brutishly built, dullard, blockhead **MW** IV.v.1 [Host to Simple] *What, thick-skin?;* **MND** III.ii.13

thief (n.) villain, scoundrel, rogue, wretch **Cym** IV.ii.86 [Cloten to Guiderius] *Thou injurious thief;* **Cym** V.v.220; **1H4** III.i.229; **2H4** V.iii.56; **MA** III.iii.127; **MM** II.i.40

thievery (n.) plunder, booty, stolen property **TC** IV.iv.42 [Troilus to Cressida] *Injurious Time ... / Crams his rich thievery up*

thievish (adj.) frequented by thieves, infested with robbers **RJ** IV.i.79 [Juliet to Friar] *bid me ... walk in thievish ways*

thin (adj.) **1** flimsy, threadbare, insufficient **LL** V.ii.796 [Princess to King, of his living in a hermitage] *hard lodging and thin weeds;* **CE** III.i.70; **Oth** I.iii.108
2 thinly clad, with little covering **R3** II.i.119 [King Edward to all, of Clarence] *he did ... give himself, / All thin and naked, to the numb-cold night*
3 weak, without body, of low alcohol content **2H4** IV.iii.90 [Falstaff alone, of boys like Prince John] *thin drink doth so over-cool their blood;* **2H4** IV.iii.122

thin-belly (adj.) with lower part unpadded **LL** III.i.17 [Mote to Armado] *with your arms crossed on your thin-belly doublet like a rabbit on a spit* ☛ **great-belly** (adj.)

thing (n.) [contemptuous] being, creature, base thing **AW** IV.iii.323 [Parolles alone] *the thing I am / Shall make me live;* **Cym** I.i.16; **TNK** II.ii.51

thing, what what a thing **Cym** IV.iv.35 [Arviragus to Belarius and Guiderius] *what thing is't that I never / Did see man die* [i.e. what a terrible thing]

think (v.) **1** realize, appreciate, understand **WT** IV.iv.630 [Camillo to Autolycus] *disease thee instantly - thou must think there's a necessity in't;* **Luc** 493
2 reflect, meditate, brood **AC** III.xiii.1 [Enobarbus to Cleopatra, of her question 'What shall we do?'] *Think, and die*
3 intend, mean, propose **TS** IV.iii.188 [Petruchio to Katherina] *Look what I speak, or do, or think to do, / You are still crossing it*
4 expect, anticipate, look **TS** III.ii.184 [Petruchio to all] *I know you think to dine with me today*
5 ☛ scorn, think; **DISCOURSE MARKERS**, p.127

think for (v.) imagine, expect, suppose **TS** IV.iii.157 [Grumio to Petruchio] *the conceit is deeper than you think for*

think long feel time passing slowly, tire of waiting **Luc** 1359 [of Lucrece and her groom] *long she thinks till he return again*

think on (v.) **1** bring to mind, recall **Tim** V.i.139 [First Senator to Timon, of the senators] *who have thought / On special dignities, which vacant lie*
2 be remembered, be commemorated **Ham** III.i.143 [Hamlet to Ophelia, of any great man] *'a must build churches then, or else shall 'a suffer not thinking on* [i.e. he will be forgotten]

think on (v.) think better of, think twice about **TS** IV.iii.112 [Petruchio to Tailor, of what he will feel after being beaten] *thou shalt think on prating whilst thou liv'st*

think upon (v.) think kindly about, remember well **Cor** II.iii.55 [Menenius to Coriolanus, of the people] *You must desire them / To think upon you*

thinking (n.) thought, meditation, reflection **AW** V.iii.128 [King to all] *I am wrapped in dismal thinkings;* **H8** III.ii.134

third (v.) achieve a third of, reduce to a third **TNK** I.ii.96 [Arcite to Valerius] *Yet what man / Thirds his own worth*

thirdborough parish officer, town constable **TS** Induction.i.9 [Hostess to Sly] *I must go fetch the thirdborough* [F *Head-borough*] ☛ **headborough** (n.)

this (adv.) in this way, thus, like this **CE** I.i.76 [Egeon to Duke] *And this it was*

this, by by this time **3H6** IV.iii.2 [First Watchmen to all] *The King by this is set him down to sleep;* **AW** V.iii.134; **3H6** V.v.90; **JC** I.iii.125; **MA** III.ii.69; **Tit** III.i.109

thither (adv.) ☛ **HITHER, THITHER, AND WHITHER**, p.224

thorny-pricking (adj.) prickly, barbed, pricking like a thorn **E3** I.i.110 [King Edward to Lorraine] *Fervent desire ... / Is far more thorny-pricking than this blade*

thorough (prep.) through **JC** III.i.136 [Servant to Brutus] *Antony ... will follow / The fortunes and affairs of noble Brutus / Thorough the hazards of this untrod state*

thou (v.) use 'thou' to someone as an insult **TN** III.ii.43 [Sir Toby to Sir Andrew, of Viola as Cesario] *If thou 'thou'-est him some thrice it shall not be amiss*

thou (pron.) ☛ **THOU AND YOU**, p.450

though (adv.) ☛ what though

thought (n.) **1** intention, purpose, design **Mac** I.v.39 [Lady Macbeth alone] *Come, you spirits / That tend on mortal thoughts, unsex me here;* **E3** III.i.49; **Per** IV.Chorus.9; **Sonn** 10.9; **Venus** 551
2 melancholic reflection, anxiety, sorrow, worry **TG** I.i.69 [Proteus alone, of himself] *heart sick with thought;* **AY** IV.i.197; **Ham** III.i.85; **2H4** V.v.70; **JC** I.i.187; **TN** II.iv.111
3 imagination, conception, ability to comprehend **1H6** I.i.121 [Third Messenger to all] *valiant Talbot, above human thought, / Enacted wonders*
4 expectation, estimate, anticipation **Ham** IV.vii.87 [Claudius to Laertes, of Lamord] *So far he topped my thought*
5 train of thought **Ham** I.i.67 [Horatio to Marcellus and Barnardo] *In what particular thought to work I know not*

thought, upon a in a moment, instantly, straight away **Mac** III.iv.54 [Lady Macbeth to all, of Macbeth] *upon a thought / He will again be well*

thought is free think what you like **TN** I.iii.66 [Maria to Sir Andrew, responding to his 'do you think you have fools in hand?'] *Now, sir, 'Thought is free'*

thoughten (adj.) assured, of a mind, thinking **Per** IV.vi.106 [Lysimachus to Marina] *be you thoughten / That I came with no ill intent*

thought-executing (adj.) acting as fast as thought; or, thought-destroying **KL** III.ii.4 [Lear to the winds] *You sulphurous and thought-executing fires*

thought-sick *(adj.)* filled with dread, horror-struck **Ham** III.iv.52 [Hamlet to Gertrude, of the Earth] *Is thought-sick at the act*

thraldom *(n.)* bondage, servitude, captivity **R3** I.iv.251 [First Murderer to Clarence, of Richard] *he delivers you / From this earth's thraldom to the joys of heaven*

thrall *(n.)* slave, subject, captive **Mac** III.vi.13 [Lennox to a Lord, of the King's attendants] *That were the slaves of drink, and thralls of sleep;* **1H6** I.ii.117, II.iii.35; **Luc** 725; **R3** IV.i.45; **Sonn** 154.12

thrall *(adj.)* captive, enslaved, subject **Venus** 837 *How love makes young men thrall*

thrall *(v.)* enslave, make captive **TS** I.i.217 [Lucentio to Tranio, of Bianca] *Whose sudden sight hath thralled my wounded eye*

thralled *(adj.)* enslaved, imprisoned, held in bondage **Ham** III.iv.75 [Hamlet to Gertrude] *sense to ecstasy was ne'er so thralled;* **Sonn** 124.7

thrasonical *(adj.)* boastful, bragging, vainglorious **AY** V.ii.30 [Rosalind as Ganymede to Orlando] *Caesar's thrasonical brag;* **LL** V.i.12

thread *(v.)* trace a path through, make a way through **KL** II.i.118 [Regan to Gloucester] *Thus out of season, threading dark-eyed night;* **Cor** III.i.124; **R2** V.v.17

threaden *(adj.)* made of linen thread **H5** III.Chorus.10 [Chorus] *behold the threaden sails;* **Lover** 33

threat *(v.)* threaten **TNK** V.iii.4 [Emilia to Pirithous] *Every blow that falls / Threats a brave life;* **AC** III.v.17; **Cym** IV.ii.127; **R2** III.iii.90; **Tit** II.i.40; **Venus** 620

three *(n.)* few, hardly any, a handful **AC** III.iii.22 [Charmian to Cleopatra, of the Messenger] *Three in Egypt / Cannot make better note* ☛ **NUMBERS**, p.299

threefold *(adj.)* triple, three-part **1H4** III.i.67 [Glendower to all] *shall we divide our right / According to our threefold order taken?*

three-foot *(adj.)* three-legged **Cym** III.iii.89 [Belarius alone] *When on my three-foot stool I sit*

three-man-song *(adj.)* capable of singing three-part songs **WT** IV.iii.40 [Clown to himself, of Perdita] *She hath made me four-and-twenty nosegays for the shearers, three-man-song men all*

three-nooked *(adj.)* three-cornered **AC** IV.vi.6 [Caesar to all] *the three-nooked world / Shall bear the olive freely*

three-pile *(n.)* costly velvet [with a pile formed from three threads] **WT** IV.iii.14 [Autolycus alone] *I have … in my time wore three-pile*

three-piled *(adj.)* triple-thickness, three-threaded [i.e. very expensive or ornate] **MM** I.ii.32 [First Gentleman to Lucio, of velvet] *Thou'rt a three-piled piece;* **LL** V.ii.407

three-suited *(adj.)* allowed three suits a year; servile **KL** II.ii.14 [disguised Kent to Oswald, describing him] *beggarly, three-suited*

threne, threnos *(n.)* dirge, lament, funeral song **Phoen** 49 [of Reason] *it made this threne / To the phoenix and the dove*

thrice *(adj.)* three times **Tem** V.i.296 [Caliban to Prospero] *What a thrice double ass / Was I;* **AY** I.i.54 ☛ **NUMBERS**, p.299

thrice- *(adv.)* [intensifier] very, greatly, extremely **Tit** V.vii.112 [disguised Tamora to Titus] *send for Lucius, thy thrice-valiant son* ☛ **puissant** *(adj.)*, and following entries

thrice-driven *(adj.)* with the lightest feathers repeatedly separated; of great comfort **Oth** I.iii.229 [Othello to all, of custom] *Hath made the flinty and steel couch of war / My thrice-driven bed of down*

thrice-famed *(adj.)* most famous **TC** II.iii.240 [Ulysses to Ajax] *thy parts of nature / Thrice-famed beyond … all erudition;* **2H6** III.ii.157

thrice-noble *(adj.)* most noble **Tit** I.i.123 [Tamora to Titus] *Thrice-noble Titus, spare my first-born son*

thrice-repured *(adj.)* highly purified, extremely refined **TC** III.ii.20 [Troilus alone] *What will it be, / When that the watery palate tastes indeed / Love's thrice-repured nectar?* [Q; F *thrice reputed*] [or: *three-times purified*]

thrift *(n.)* profit, advantage, gain **Ham** III.ii.72 [Hamlet to Horatio] *thrift may follow fawning;* **Cym** V.i.15; **Ham** III.ii.193; **MV** I.i.175, iii.47; **WT** I.ii.311

thriftless *(adj.)* useless, worthless, unprofitable **TN** II.ii.39 [Viola alone] *What thriftless sighs shall poor Olivia breathe;* **Sonn** 2.8

thrifty *(adj.)* worthy, estimable; also: stingy, frugal **TC** V.i.52 [Thersites alone, of Menelaus] *a thrifty shoeing-horn in a chain*

thrill *(v.)* **1** shiver, tremble, feel a pang of emotion **1H4** II.iv.363 [Falstaff to Prince Hal, of the mention of Hal's enemies] *Doth not thy blood thrill at it?;* **KJ** V.ii.143
  2 pass like a shiver, tremble **RJ** IV.iii.15 [Juliet alone] *I have a faint cold fear thrills through my veins*

thrilled *(adj.)* pierced, deeply affected **KL** IV.ii.73 [Messenger to Albany, of Cornwall] *A servant that he bred, thrilled with remorse* [F; Q *thrald*]

thrilling *(adj.)* piercing, penetrating, bitterly cold **MM** III.i.126 [Claudio to Isabella, of what might follow death] *the delighted spirit … to reside / In thrilling region of thick-ribbed ice*

thrive *(v.)* be successful, have good fortune **1H4** I.iii.294 [Northumberland to Worcester] *We shall thrive, I trust;* **R2** I.iii.84

thriver *(n.)* aspiring person, striver, wannabe **Sonn** 125.8 *Pitiful thrivers in their gazing spent*

thriving *(adj.)* successful, satisfactory, auspicious **WT** II.ii.45 [Emilia to Paulina, of the plan to take the baby to Leontes] *your free undertaking cannot miss / A thriving issue*

throat, lie in one's be an outrageous liar **LL** IV.iii.12 [Berowne alone] *I do nothing in the world but lie, and lie in my throat;* **2H4** I.ii.81; **TS** IV.iii.129 ☛ **lie** *(n.)*

throbbing *(adj.)* with heart strongly beating, grief-stricken **2H6** IV.iv.5 [Queen to herself, of dead Suffolk's head] *Here may his head lie on my throbbing breast*

throe *(n.)* (plural) labour pains, pangs of childbirth **Cym** V.iv.44 [Mother, to music] *Lucina … took me in my throes*

throe *(v.)* agonize, torture, cost in pain [as in childbirth] **Tem** II.i.235 [Sebastian to Antonio] *a birth … / Which throes thee much to yield* [F *throwes*]

throe forth *(v.)* give painful birth to **AC** III.vii.80 [Canidius to Messenger] *With news the time's with labour and throes forth / Each minute some* [i.e. each minute yields fresh news]

throng *(v.)* crush, overwhelm **Per** I.i.102 [Pericles to Antiochus] *the earth is thronged / By man's oppression;* **Luc** 1417

throng up *(v.)* cram, fill, burden **Per** II.i.73 [Pericles to Second Fisherman] *I am … / A man thronged up with cold*

throstle *(n.)* thrush **MND** III.i.120 [Bottom singing to himself] *The throstle with his note so true;* **MV** I.ii.57

through *(adv.)* thoroughly **TC** II.iii.220 [Nestor to himself, of Ajax] *He's not yet through warm*

through *(prep.)* throughout **Cor** IV.v.90 [Coriolanus to Aufidius] *stop those maims / Of shame seen through thy country*

through, be be in agreement, see eye to eye **2H4** I.ii.38 [Falstaff to Page, of tradesmen] *if a man is through with them in honest taking up*

throughfare *(n.)* thoroughfare **MV** II.vii.42 [Morocco to himself] *the vasty wilds / Of wide Arabia are as throughfares;* **Cym** I.iii.9

throughly *(adv.)* thoroughly, fully, completely **Ham** IV.v.138 [Laertes to Claudius] *I'll be revenged / Most throughly for my father;* **E3** III.ii.23; **MV** IV.i.170; **Tem** III.iii.15; **TG** I.ii.115; **TS** IV.iv.11

through-shot *(adj.)* shot through, punctured, pierced **E3** III.i.164 [Mariner to King John] *the gushing moisture [did] break into / The crannied cleftures of the through-shot planks*

THOU AND YOU

In Old English, *thou* was singular and *you* was plural; but during the 13th century, *you* started to be used as a polite form of the singular – probably because people copied the French way of talking, where *vous* was used in that way. English then became like French, which has *tu* and *vous* both possible for singulars, giving speakers a choice. It was usual for *you* to be used by inferiors to superiors – such as children to parents, or servants to masters; and *thou* would be used in return. But *thou* was also used to express special intimacy, as when addressing God, and it was usual when the lower classes talked to each other. Upper classes used *you* to each other as a rule, even when they were closely related.

Accordingly, changing from *thou* to *you* or *you* to *thou* in a conversation always conveys a contrast in meaning – a change of attitude or an altered relationship. The potential role of *thou* as an insult, for example, is made clear by Sir Toby Belch, who advises Andrew Aguecheek to demean his enemy by calling him *thou* a few times (**TN** III.ii.43). Not all instances can be so clearly interpreted, and attitude glosses given below should be viewed as suggestive only.

The old singular/plural contrast may also still be seen, as in Hamlet's switch from 'Get thee to a nunnery', spoken to Ophelia as an individual (**Ham** III.i.137), to 'God hath given you one face, and you make yourselves another', still spoken to Ophelia, but plainly now addressing womankind as a whole (III.i.144).

Example	Location	Participants	Relationship

X and Y both use *thou*

Whither wilt thou lead me?	**Ham** I.v.1	Hamlet to Ghost	son to father
lend thy serious hearing	**Ham** I.v.5	Ghost to Hamlet	father to son
Thou needest not to be gone	**RJ** III.v.16	Juliet to Romeo	lovers
so thou wilt have it so	**RJ** III.v.18	Romeo to Juliet	lovers

X and Y both use *you*

I thank you	**TNK** II.i.150	Palamon to Arcite	cousins
I would hear you still	**TNK** II.i.165	Arcite to Palamon	cousins
Have you the lion's part written?	**MND** I.ii.62	Snug to Quince	neighbour to neighbour [as co-actors]
You may do it extempore	**MND** I.ii.64	Quince to Snug	neighbour to neighbour [as co-actors]

X uses *thou*, Y uses *you*, showing different status

Thou art e'en as just a man	**Ham** III.ii.64	Hamlet to Horatio	prince to friend
at your service	**Ham** III.ii.63	Horatio to Hamlet	friend to prince
as thou sayest	**AY** I.i.3	Orlando to Adam	master to servant
Your brother	**AY** I.i.24	Adam to Orlando	servant to master
thou swearest to me thou art honest	**AY** III.iii.22	Touchstone to Audrey	court to country
Would you not have me honest?	**AY** III.iii.25	Audrey to Touchstone	country to court

X and Y switch from *you* to *thou*, as a sign of deteriorating relationships

you must not love her	**TNK** II.i.216	Palamon to Arcite	formal between equals
I will not, as you do	**TNK** II.i.217	Arcite to Palamon	formal between equals
Thou art a traitor	**TNK** II.i.226	Palamon to Arcite	then continues with *thou* throughout the scene
why are you moved thus?	**TNK** II.i.239	Arcite to Palamon	tries to keep the peace
Thou darest not	**TNK** II.i.270	Arcite to Palamon	finally changes to *thou*

X uses *thou* and then *you*, marking a change of attitude

like a schoolboy you may overawe	**1H6** I.i.36	Gloucester [King's uncle] to Winchester [King's great-uncle]	attacking the role of the Church
thou art Protector	**1H6** I.i.37	Winchester to Gloucester	reacting to the attack

THOU AND YOU – *continued*

Example	Location	Participants	Relationship
thou lovest the flesh	**1H6** I.i.41	Gloucester to Winchester	responding in kind
Get thee to bed	**Ham** I.i.7	Barnardo to Francisco	friendly suggestion
Have you had quiet guard?	**Ham** I.i.10	Barnardo to Francisco	professional enquiry
Go thy ways to a nunnery	**Ham** III.i.130	Hamlet to Ophelia	intimate
Where's your father?	**Ham** III.i.130	Hamlet to Ophelia	suspicion

X uses *you* and then *thou*, marking a change of attitude

Example	Location	Participants	Relationship
What is your parentage	**TN** I.v.266	Olivia to Viola as Cesario	formal
I'll be sworn thou art	**TN** I.v.280	Olivia alone, thinking of Viola as Cesario	beginning to fall in love
And you are stayed for	**Ham** I.iii.57	Polonius to Laertes	father to son; a mock telling off
my blessing with thee	**Ham** I.iii.57	Polonius to Laertes	fatherly affection

Complex interaction

In **MA** IV.i.264ff., the way Benedick switches from *you* to *thou* provides an indication of his feelings and motivation during the scene. Interestingly, Beatrice always uses *you* to him, as does she to his face throughout the play. (Her one reference to him as *thee* is at III.i.111–13, when she is talking to herself.)

Benedick: *I do love nothing in the world so well as you; is not that strange?*	you	tentative
Beatrice: *As strange as the thing I know not. It were as possible for me to say I loved nothing so well as you; but believe me not, and yet I lie not; I confess nothing, nor I deny nothing. I am sorry for my cousin.*	you	proper
Benedick: *By my sword, Beatrice, thou lovest me.*	thou	first attempt at intimacy
Beatrice: *Do not swear, and eat it.*		rebuff
Benedick: *I will swear by it that you love me; and I will make him eat it that says I love not you.*	you	aggrieved reaction
Beatrice: *Will you not eat your word?*	you	proper
Benedick: *With no sauce that can be devised to it; I protest I love thee.*	thee	second attempt at intimacy
Beatrice: *Why, then, God forgive me!*		
Benedick: *What offence, sweet Beatrice?*		
Beatrice: *You have stayed me in a happy hour; I was about to protest I loved you.*	you	proper
Benedick: *And do it with all thy heart.*	thy	intimate
Beatrice: *I love you with so much of my heart that none is left to protest.*	you	proper – unusual for an affirmation of love
Benedick: *Come, bid me do anything for thee.*	thee	intimate
Beatrice: *Kill Claudio.*		
Benedick: *Ha! Not for the wide world.*		
Beatrice: *You kill me to deny it. Farewell.*	you	rebuff
Benedick [taking her by the hand]: *Tarry, sweet Beatrice.*		
Beatrice: *I am gone, though I am here; there is no love in you. Nay, I pray you, let me go.*	you	continued rebuff
…		
Benedick: *Tarry, good Beatrice. By this hand, I love thee.*	thee	intimate
Beatrice: *Use it for my love some other way than swearing by it.*		
Benedick: *Think you in your soul the Count Claudio hath wronged Hero?*	you	serious subject-matter
Beatrice: *Yea, as sure as I have a thought or a soul.*		
Benedick: *Enough, I am engaged; I will challenge him. I will kiss your hand, and so I leave you.*	you	businesslike

throw *(n.)* throwing distance, mark **Cor** V.ii.21 [Menenius to First Watch] *I have tumbled past the throw*

throw *(v.)* **1** throw off, cast, discard **MND** II.i.255 [Oberon to Puck] *there [on a bank] the snake throws her enamelled skin*
2 bestow, cast, pass on **AC** I.ii.188 [Antony to Enobarbus] *Our slippery people ... begin to throw / Pompey ... / Upon his son*

throw at *(v.)* throw dice, play dice [with] **R2** IV.i.57 [Aumerle to all] *I'll throw at all*

throw off *(v.)* brush away, discard, set aside **Tim** II.ii.139 [Flavius to Timon, of the accounts] *You would throw them off*

thrum *(n.)* unwoven end of a warp-thread on a loom **MND** V.i.278 [Bottom as Pyramus] *O Fates, come, come, / Cut thread and thrum* [i.e. cut everything]

thrummed *(adj.)* fringed with loose threads **MW** IV.ii.73 [Mistress Page to Mistress Ford, of the fat woman's clothes] *there's her thrummed hat*

thrust *(v.)* strike, pierce, stab **2H6** IV.vii.8 [Holland to himself, of Cade] *he was thrust in the mouth with a spear, and 'tis not whole yet*

thrust at / in *(v.)* make a thrust, lunge, stab [at] **RJ** III.i.89 [stage direction] *Tybalt under Romeo's arm thrusts Mercutio in* [Q1]; **1H4** II.iv.195

thrusting on *(n.)* imposition, forcing, insinuation **KL** I.ii.126 [Edmund alone] *as if ... all that we are evil in [was] by a divine thrusting-on*

thumb *(n.)* bite one's thumb

thumb-ring *(n.)* small ring used for sealing documents **1H4** II.iv.324 [Falstaff to Prince Hal] *When I was about thy years ... I could have crept into any alderman's thumb-ring*

thump *(v.)* make a bang [as of a cannon] **LL** III.i.63 [Mote to Armado, of being shot at Costard] *Thump then, and I flee*

thunder-darter *(n.)* wielder of thunderbolts **TC** II.iii.10 [Thersites alone, as if to Jove] *thou great thunder-darter of Olympus*

thunder-master *(n.)* lord of thunder; Jove **Cym** V.iv.30 [Sicilius, to music] *No more thou thunder-master show / thy spite on mortal flies*

thunder-stone *(n.)* thunderbolt **Cym** IV.ii.271 [Arviragus singing] *[Fear no more] ... th' all-dreaded thunder-stone*; **JC** I.iii.49

thwart *(adj.)* perverse, obstinate, stubborn **KL** I.iv.280 [Lear to the goddess Nature, of any child of Gonerill's] *it may live / And be a thwart disnatured torment to her*

thwart *(v.)* cross, traverse, go over **Per** IV.iv.10 [Gower alone] *Pericles Is now again thwarting the wayward seas*

thwart *(adv.)* adversely, untowardly, detrimentally **TC** I.iii.15 [Agamemnon to all, of their war efforts] *trial did draw / Bias and thwart, not answering the aim*

thwarting *(adj.)* malign, adverse, perverse **3H6** IV.vi.22 [King to Warwick] *that the people ... / May not be punished with my thwarting stars, ... / I here resign my government to thee*

Tib *(n.)* [type name for] strumpet, harlot, whore **AW** II.ii.21 [Clown to Countess, of his answer] *As fit as ... Tib's rush for Tom's forefinger*; **Per** IV.vi.164

'tice *(v.)* shortened form of 'entice' **Tit** II.iii.92 [Tamora to Demetrius and Chiron, of Bassianus and Lavinia] *These two have 'ticed me hither*

tickle *(adj.)* insecure, precarious, unstable **2H6** I.i.214 [York to himself, of lost regions of France] *the state of Normandy / Stands on a tickle point now they are gone*

tickle *(v.)* **1** move easily, affect readily **Ham** II.ii.324 [Hamlet to Rosencrantz and Guildenstern] *the clown shall make those laugh whose lungs are tickle o'th' sere* [reading of F; Q1 *tickled*]; **TC** V.ii.57
2 beat, flog, rain blows on **TN** V.i.190 [Sir Andrew to Viola as Cesario, of Sir Toby] *if he had not been in drink, he would have tickled you othergates than he did*; **TC** V.ii.180; **TNK** II.ii.28
3 tingle, run in a thrilling way **KJ** III.iii.44 [King John to Hubert, of his blood] *Which else runs tickling up and down the veins*

4 flatter, gratify, please **Cor** I.i.258 [Sicinius to Brutus, of Martius] *Such a nature, / Tickled with good success*; **Cym** I.ii.16; **1H4** II.iv.433

tickle up *(v.)* gratify, give pleasure, arouse **TNK** IV.i.137 [Gaoler's Daughter to First Friend, of Palamon] *he'll tickle it up / In two hours, if his hand be in*

tickle your catastrophe [catch phrase] make your bottom tingle **2H4** II.i.58 [Page to Hostess] *I'll tickle your catastrophe!*

tickle *(adv.)* insecurely, precariously, unstably **MM** I.ii.171 [Lucio to Claudio] *thy head stands so tickle on thy shoulders*

tickle-brain *(n.)* type of strong drink **1H4** II.iv.390 [Falstaff to Hostess] *peace, good tickle-brain*

tickled *(adj.)* vexed, irritated, provoked **2H6** I.iii.148 [Buckingham to Cardinal, of the Duchess] *She's tickled now; her fume needs no spurs*

tickling *(n.)* flattery, gratifying, pleasing **TN** II.v.22 [Maria to all, of Malvolio] *here comes the trout that must be caught with tickling*

tickling *(adj.)* **1** flattering, alluring, diverting **KJ** II.i.573 [Bastard alone] *That smooth-faced gentleman, tickling commodity*
2 aroused, titillated, excited **TC** IV.v.61 [Ulysses to Nestor] *these encounterers ... [that] wide unclasp the tables of their thoughts / To every tickling reader!* [F; Q *ticklish*]

tick-tack *(n.)* type of backgammon in which scoring is by placing pegs in holes **MM** I.ii.189 [Lucio to Claudio] *thy life, who I would be sorry should be thus foolishly lost at a game of tick-tack* [with bawdy pun]

tiddle-taddle *(n.)* tittle-tattle, idle gossip, chatter **H5** IV.i.70 [Fluellen to Gower] *there is no tiddle-taddle nor pibble-pabble in Pompey's camp*

tide *(n.)* **1** season, date, time [of year] **TC** V.i.78 [Diomedes to Achilles] *I have important business, / The tide whereof is now*; **KJ** III.i.86; **RJ** III.v.177; **Tim** I.ii.55
2 course, stream, passage **JC** III.i.257 [Antony alone, as if to Caesar's body] *Thou art the ruins of the noblest man / That ever lived in the tide of times*

tide *(v.)* [= betide] come, befall **MND** V.i.200 [Flute as Thisbe to Bottom as Pyramus] *Tide life, tide death, I come without delay* [i.e. whether life or death happens]

tidy *(adj.)* good-looking, handsome; also: fat, plump **2H4** II.iv.226 [Doll to Falstaff] *Thou whoreson little tidy Bartholomew boar-pig*

tie *(v.)* **1** oblige, constrain, force **TS** I.i.209 [Tranio to Lucentio] *I am tied to be obedient*; **Cor** II.i.63; **Luc** 818; **R2** I.i.63
2 bring into subjection, put in bondage **H8** IV.ii.36 [Katherine to Griffith, of Wolsey] *one that by suggestion / Tied all the kingdom*
3 ratify, approve, authorize **H8** III.ii.250 [Wolsey to all, of the seal given to him] *the King ... / Tied it by letters patents*

tie over *(v.)* restrict, confine, limit **H5** V.ii.307 [King Henry to Burgundy] *This moral ties me over to time and a hot summer*

tie to *(v.)* stipulate, specify, confirm **Cym** III.viii.15 [First Senator to the tribunes] *the words of your commission / Will tie you to the numbers and the time / Of their despatch*

tight *(adj.)* **1** water-tight, seaworthy, shipshape **Tem** V.i.224 [Boatswain to all, of their ship] *Is tight and yare and bravely rigged*; **TS** II.i.372
2 skilled, deft, adept **AC** IV.iv.15 [Antony to Eros, of Cleopatra] *my queen's a squire / More tight at this than thou*

tightly *(adv.)* soundly, properly, thoroughly **MW** II.iii.59 [Host to Caius, of Evans] *He will clapper-claw thee tightly* [F; Q *titely*] ➤ **titely** *(adv.)* **1**

tike *(n.)* cur, mongrel **KL** III.vi.69 [Edgar as Poor Tom to all] *bobtail tike, or trundle-tail* [Q; F *tight*]

tile *(n.)* ➤ wash a tile

tillage *(n.)* tilling, cultivation **Sonn** 3.6 *where is she so fair whose uneared womb / Disdains the tillage of thy husbandry?*

till anon ➤ anon, till

till that *(conj.)* until **Ham** IV.vii.181 [Gertrude to Claudius and Laertes, of Ophelia] *Till that her garments, heavy with their drink, / Pulled the poor wretch … / To muddy death*

tilly-fally, tilly-vally *(int.)* nonsense, fiddlesticks **2H4** II.iv.81 [Hostess to Falstaff] *Tilly-fally, Sir John, ne'er tell me;* **TN** II.iii.77 [Sir Toby to all] *Tilly-vally! 'Lady'!* ☛ **EXCLAMATIONS**, p.158

tilt *(n.)* lance-charge, joust, combat **2H6** I.iii.49 [Queen to Suffolk] *in the city Tours / Thou rannest a tilt in honour of my love;* **1H6** III.ii.51; **TG** I.iii.30

tilt *(v.)* joust, fight [with lances], thrust **RJ** III.i.158 [Benvolio to Prince, of Tybalt] *he tilts / With piercing steel at bold Mercutio's breast;* **CE** IV.ii.6; **1H4** II.iii.95; **LL** V.ii.483; **Oth** II.iii.177; **Per** I.iii.1

tilter *(n.)* jouster, tournament competitor **MM** IV.iii.15 [Pompey alone] *Master Forthright the tilter;* **AY** III.iv.39

tilth *(n.)* **1** labour of cultivation, agricultural work, husbandry **MM** I.iv.44 [Lucio to Isabella, of Juliet and Claudio] *her plenteous womb / Expresseth his full tilth and husbandry*

2 agriculture, tilled land **Tem** II.i.155 [Gonzalo to Alonso, of the imaginary commonwealth] *bound of land, tilth, vineyard, none* [or: agricultural work]

3 crop, harvest **MM** IV.i.75 [disguised Duke to Mariana and Isabella] *our tilth's to sow* [F *Tithes*]

tilt-yard *(n.)* tournament ground **2H6** I.iii.57 [Queen to Suffolk, of the King] *His study is his tilt-yard;* **2H4** III.ii.311

timbered *(adj.)* made of wood, constructed **Oth** II.i.48 [Cassio to Montano, of Othello] *His bark is stoutly timbered;* **Ham** IV.vii.22

time *(n.)* **1** (the) world, (the) age, society **Ham** III.i.70 [Hamlet alone] *For who would bear the whips and scorns of time;* **Cor** II.ii.118; **Mac** I.v.61, vii.81; **R3** IV.iv.416; **Sonn** 11.7

2 times, present day, present state of affairs **TS** IV.iii.95 [Tailor to Petruchio, of making a dress] *According to the fashion and the time;* **AC** III.vi.82; **Ham** I.v.188; **KJ** I.i.207; **Mac** V.vi.104; **TS** IV.iii.69

3 lifetime, life **1H6** IV.vi.9 [John Talbot to Talbot] *To my determined time thou gavest new date;* **Cym** III.iii.73; **3H6** I.iv.45; **KL** I.ii.47; **R2** I.i.177; **RJ** IV.i.60

4 age, years **TG** II.vii.48 [Julia to Lucetta] *To be fantastic may become a youth / Of greater time than I shall show to be;* **Cym** I.i.43; **LL** I.ii.17; **MV** I.i.129; **WT** V.i.141

5 past time, history **JC** III.i.257 [Antony alone, as if to Caesar's body] *Thou art the ruins of the noblest man / That ever lived in the tide of times;* **H5** II.iv.83

6 time to come, future days **KJ** IV.iii.54 [Pembroke to all, of Arthur's apparent murder] *Shall give a holiness, a purity, / To the yet-unbegotten sin of times*

7 circumstance, particular occasion **Ham** IV.vii.110 [Claudius to Laertes] *love is begun by time;* **CE** III.i.43; **MM** III.ii.208; **R2** V.v.48; **TC** I.iii.313; **Tim** II.i.45

8 right moment, favourable opportunity **LL** V.ii.63 [Rosaline to Princess, of Berowne] *I would make him … wait the season, and observe the times;* **AC** II.vi.23; **CE** I.i.8; **3H6** I.iv.108; **Tem** II.i.140; **Tim** II.ii.196

9 time interval, specific period of time **R2** V.v.58 [Richard alone] *So sighs, and tears, and groans / Show minutes, times, and hours* [i.e. quarter-hours, half-hours]

10 seasonal cycle **R2** I.iii.220 [John of Gaunt to King Richard] *ere the six years … / Can change their moons, and bring their times about*

11 time to be born, delivery **H8** V.i.22 [Gardiner to Lovell, of Queen Anne's baby] *I pray for heartily, that it may find / Good time, and live*

12 allotted limit, prescribed term **JC** V.i.105 [Brutus to Cassius] *I do find it cowardly … / For fear of what might fall, so to prevent / The time of life;* **1H6** IV.vi.9

13 use of time, experience, occasion **Cym** IV.ii.108 [Arviragus to Belarius, of Cloten] *I wish my brother make good time with him, / You say he is so fell* [i.e. come out of the encounter well]

14 passing of time, while **AC** III.ii.60 [Caesar to Octavia] *the time shall not / Outgo my thinking on you;* **AY** II.iv.92; **Tit** IV.iii.42

15 rhythm, tempo, measure **R2** V.v.43 [Richard alone] *How sour sweet music is / When time is broke;* **R2** V.v.46

time, for the for the time being, at present **TS** I.i.17 [Lucentio to Tranio] *for the time I study / Virtue*

time, in good **1** at the right moment **R3** II.i.45 [Buckingham to all] *in good time, / Here comes Sir Richard Ratcliffe and the Duke;* **CE** II.ii.70; **Cor** IV.vi.10; **KL** II.iv.245; **RJ** I.ii.44; **TG** I.iii.44 ☛ **happy time, in**

2 what a question!, how dare you! **WT** IV.iv.165 [Mopsa to Dorcas, of her rude remark about her kissing] *Now, in good time!;* **MW** III.i.75

3 very well **MM** III.i.181 [Provost to disguised Duke, of being asked to leave] *In good time*

4 indeed **TS** II.i.195 [Katherina to Petruchio, responding to his 'Myself am moved to woo thee for my wife'] *Moved, in good time!* ☛ **DISCOURSE MARKERS**, p.127

time, keep be restrained, keep control **Oth** IV.i.92 [Iago to Othello] *But yet keep time in all*

time, upon a once upon a time **Cym** V.v.153 [Iachimo to Cymbeline] *Upon a time, unhappy was the clock / That struck the hour*

time *(v.)* measure rhythmically, accompany regularly **Cor** II.ii.108 [Cominius to all, of Coriolanus] *He was a thing of blood, whose every motion / Was timed with dying cries*

time enough in time, soon enough **CE** IV.i.41 [Antipholus to Angelo, of the chain] *bear it with you lest I come not time enough*

time of day daily greeting **2H6** III.i.14 [Queen to King, of Gloucester] *in the morn, / When everyone will give the time of day* [i.e. say good morning]

time was, when once upon a time **Tem** II.ii.136 [Stephano to Caliban] *I was the Man i'th' Moon when time was*

time-beguiling *(adj.)* which whiles away the time **Venus** 24 [Venus to Adonis, of kissing] *A summer's day will seem an hour but short, / Being wasted in such time-beguiling sport*

timeless *(adj.)* untimely, premature, ill-timed **RJ** V.iii.162 [Juliet to herself, of Romeo] *Poison, I see, hath been his timeless end;* **1H6** V.iv.5; **2H6** III.ii.187; **R2** IV.i.5; **R3** I.ii.117; **TG** III.i.21

timely *(adj.)* early, premature **TNK** II.i.82 [Arcite to Palamon] *the graces of our youths must wither / Like a too timely spring;* **CE** I.i.139

timely *(adv.)* **1** early, in good time **Mac** III.iii.7 [First Murderer to all] *Now spurs the lated traveller apace / To gain the timely inn;* **Cym** I.vii.97; **Mac** II.iii.43

2 early, prematurely **PassP** X.3 *Bright orient pearl, alack, too timely shaded;* **AC** II.vi.51

timely-parted *(adj.)* naturally departed, who has died a natural death **2H6** III.ii.161 [Warwick to Suffolk] *Oft have I seen a timely-parted ghost*

time-pleaser *(n.)* time-server, follower of fashion **TN** II.iii.141 [Maria to Sir Toby, of Malvolio] *he is … but a time-pleaser;* **Cor** III.i.45

timorous *(adj.)* **1** fearful, apprehensive, doubting **1H6** IV.ii.46 [Talbot to all] *A little herd of England's timorous deer;* **1H6** IV.ii.40; **TNK** I.iii.3; **Venus** 881

2 causing fear, terrifying, dreadful **Oth** I.i.76 [Iago to Roderigo, of his calling aloud] *with like timorous accent and dire yell, / As when … the fire / Is spied in populous cities* [or: sense 1]

tinct *(n.)* **1** colour, hue, tint **Ham** III.iv.92 [Gertrude to Hamlet] *such black and grained spots / As will not leave their tinct;* **Cym** II.ii.23

2 [alchemy] tincture, elixir **AC** I.v.37 [Cleopatra to Alexas, of Antony] *that great medicine hath / With his tinct gilded thee;* **AW** V.iii.102

tincture *(n.)* **1** tinge, hint, flavour **Sonn** 54.6 *the perfumed tincture of the roses*

2 colour, glow, brightness **WT** III.ii.203 [Paulina to all, of Hermione] *If you can bring / Tincture or lustre in her lip*

3 token infused with blood [as of a martyr] **JC** II.ii.89 [Decius to Caesar] *great men shall press / For tinctures, stains, relics, and cognizance*

tinder-like *(adj.)* quick-tempered, inflammable, volatile **Cor** II.i.47 [Menenius to Brutus and Sicinius, of himself] *hasty and tinder-like upon too trivial motion*

tinker *(n.)* vagabond, beggar, rascal **2H6** III.ii.277 [Suffolk to and of Salisbury] *he was the lord ambassador / Sent from a sort of tinkers to the King*

tipstaff *(n.)* court officer **H8** II.i.55 [stage direction] *Enter Buckingham from his arraignment, tipstaves before him*

tire *(n.)* **1** head-dress, ornament for the head, raiment **TG** IV.iv.182 [disguised Julia alone, of Silvia's picture] *If I had such a tire this face of mine / Were full as lovely as is this of hers*; **AC** II.v.22; **MA** III.iv.12; **MW** III.iii.53; **Sonn** 53.8
2 fittings, furnishings, trappings **Per** III.ii.21 [First Gentleman to Cerimon] *having / Rich tire about you*

tire *(v.)* **1** feed greedily, prey ravenously **Venus** 56 *as an empty eagle ... / Tires with her beak on feathers, flesh and bone*; **Cym** III.iv.96; **3H6** I.i.269
2 be exercised, be actively engaged **Tim** III.vi.4 [Lucullus to Lucius, of Timon's motives] *Upon that were my thoughts tiring when we encountered*
3 exhaust, tire out; or: attire, clothe **Cym** III.vi.2 [Innogen alone] *I have tired myself*

tired *(adj.)* attired, equipped with trappings **LL** IV.ii.126 [Holofernes to Nathaniel, of imitation] *So doth ... the tired horse his rider*

tire-valiant *(n.)* fine head-dress **MW** III.iii.53 [Falstaff to Mistress Ford] *Thou hast the right arched beauty of the brow that becomes ... the tire-valiant*

tiring *(n.)* hair-dressing **CE** II.ii.106 [Dromio of Syracuse to Antipholus of Syracuse, of a hairy man] *to save the money that he spends in tiring*

tiring *(adj.)* exhausted, worn out from riding hard **2H4** I.Induction.37 [Rumour alone] *The posts come tiring on*

tiring-house *(n.)* dressing-room, theatrical green room **MND** III.i.4 [Quince to Bottom] *this hawthorn brake [shall be] our tiring-house*

tirra-lyra *(n.)* onomatopoeic representation of the sound of the lark **WT** IV.iii.9 [Autolycus singing] *The lark, that tirra-lyra chants* ➤ **SOUNDS**, p.410

tirrits *(n.)* malapropism combining 'terrors' and 'fits' **2H4** II.iv.200 [Hostess to all] *I'll forswear keeping house afore I'll be in these tirrits and frights!*

tisick *(n.)* consumptive cough, infection of lungs and throat **TC** V.iii.101 [Pandarus to Troilus] *a whoreson rascally tisick so troubles me*

tissue *(n.)* [type of] rich cloth, sumptuous fabric **AC** II.ii.204 [Enobarbus to Agrippa and Maecenas, of Cleopatra's pavilion] *cloth-of-gold of tissue*; **E3** II.i.446

titely *(adv.)* **1** quickly, speedily, swiftly **E3** III.i.77 [Mariner to King John, of the English fleet] *titely carried with a merry gale*
2 ➤ tightly *(adv.)*

tithe *(n.)* tenth part **Ham** III.iv.98 [Hamlet to Gertrude, of Claudius] *A slave that is not twentieth part the tithe / Of your precedent lord* [F; Q2 *kyth*] ➤ tilth *(n.)* 3

tithe *(adj.)* tenth **TC** II.ii.19 [Hector to Priam, of the war dead] *Every tithe soul 'mongst many thousand dismes / Hath been as dear as Helen*

tithe *(v.)* levy a tax, collect church revenue **KJ** III.i.154 [King John to Cardinal Pandulph, of the Pope] *no Italian priest / Shall tithe or toll in our dominions*

tithed *(adj.)* of one person in ten **Tim** V.iv.31 [Second Senator to Alcibiades] *By decimation and a tithed death ... take thou the destined tenth*

tithe-pig *(n.)* pig given as part of a tithe **RJ** I.iv.79 [Mercutio to Romeo, of Queen Mab] *sometime comes she with a tithe-pig's tail*

tithe-woman *(n.)* tenth woman **AW** I.iii.82 [Clown to Countess] *We'd find no fault with the tithe-woman if I were the parson*

tithing *(n.)* parish **KL** III.iv.128 [Edgar as Poor Tom to Gloucester, of himself] *whipped from tithing to tithing*

title *(n.)* **1** [legal] right, claim, entitlement **3H6** III.iii.145 [Lewis to Queen] *if your title to the crown be weak*; **AW** IV.iv.25; **E3** I.i.65; **2H6** I.iii.46; **KJ** II.i.562; **TNK** III.i.112 ➤ untitled *(adj.)*
2 possession, lordship, dominion **Mac** IV.ii.7 [Macduff's wife to Ross, of Macduff] *to leave his babes, / His mansion and his titles*; **1H6** III.iii.26; **KJ** I.i.13; **TNK** V.iv.17
3 name, label, designation **WT** IV.iv.834 [Autolycus alone, of the name of rogue] *I am proof against that title*; **AW** II.iii.116; **H8** I.i.98; **MW** V.v.219; **R3** IV.iv.340; **WT** II.i.94

title-leaf *(n.)* title-page of a book **2H4** I.i.60 [Northumberland to Lord Bardolph, of Morton] *this man's brow, like to a title-leaf, / Foretells the nature of a tragic volume*

titler *(n.)* person asserting a right, claimant **TNK** V.iii.83 [Servant to Emilia] *The two bold titlers at this instant are / Hand to hand at it*

tittle *(n.)* jot, speck, particle **LL** IV.i.83 [Boyet reading Armado's letter to Jaquenetta] *What shalt thou exchange for ... tittles? Titles*

to *(prep.)* **1** according to **TNK** V.iii.47 [Emilia to herself, of Palamon] *his brow ... alters to / The quality of his thoughts*
2 as **JC** III.i.143 [Brutus to Cassius, of Antony] *I know that we shall have him well to friend*
3 for **MW** I.i.181 [Page to all] *we have a hot venison pasty to dinner*
4 compared to **Ham** I.v.52 [Ghost to Hamlet, of Claudius] *a wretch whose natural gifts were poor / To those of mine!*
5 in accordance with **AW** II.iv.41 [Parolles to Helena, of Bertram] *The great prerogative and rite of love ... he does acknowledge, / But puts it off to a compelled restraint*
6 in addition to **KJ** I.i.144 [Bastard to Queen Eleanor, of Robert Faulconbridge] *[if I], to his shape, were heir to all this land* [first instance]

to it, to't to the test, to death **Ham** V.ii.56 [Horatio to Hamlet] *So Guildenstern and Rosencrantz go to't*; **Cor** I.i.227; **TG** IV.iv.4

toad-spotted *(adj.)* spotted like the toad [as if with poison] **KL** V.iii.136 [Edgar to Edmund] *thou art ... / A most toad-spotted traitor*

toast *(n.)* piece of hot toast, sop **TC** I.iii.45 [Nestor to Agamemnon, of a boat in a storm] *Either to harbour fled / Or made a toast for Neptune*; **MW** III.v.3

toast-and-butter *(n.)* milksop, wimp, pampered individual **1H4** IV.ii.20 [Falstaff alone, of his soldiers] *I pressed me none but such toasts-and-butter*

toaze *(v.)* tease, get out, extract **WT** IV.iv.730 [Autolycus to Shepherd] *Think'st thou, for that I insinuate, to toaze from thee thy business, I am therefore no courtier?*

tod *(n.)* bush, bushy tuft **TNK** IV.ii.104 [Pirithous to Theseus, of the hair of Palamon's first knight] *thick-twined like ivy tods* [Q *tops*]

tod *(v.)* produce a tod [c.28 pounds/12 kg] of wool **WT** IV.iii.31 [Clown to himself] *every 'leven wether tods, every tod yields pound and odd shilling*

todpole *(n.)* tadpole **KL** III.iv.124 [Edgar as Poor Tom to Gloucester, of himself] *that eats ... the todpole*

tofore *(adv.)* [archaism] earlier, beforehand **LL** III.i.81 [Armado to Mote, of 'envoy'] *it is an epilogue or discourse to make plain / Some obscure precedence that hath tofore been sain*; **Tit** III.i.292 ➤ **ARCHAISMS**, p.22

toge *(n.)* toga **Cor** II.iii.114 [Coriolanus alone] *Why in this wolvish toge should I stand here* [F *tongue*]

toged *(adj.)* toga-wearing, robed **Oth** I.i.25 [Iago to Roderigo, of Cassio] *bookish theoric, / Wherein the toged consuls can propose / As masterly as he* [Q1; F *tongued*]

together *(adv.)* **1** without a break, whole **Cor** I.iii.60 [Valeria to Volumnia and Virgilia, of Young Martius] *I looked upon him o'Wednesday half an hour together;* **AY** III.v.64

2 all at once, at the same time **TNK** III.ii.31 [Gaoler's Daughter alone] *O state of nature, fail together in me*

3 against each other **Cor** I.i.230 [Cominius to Martius, of Aufidius] *You have fought together*

toil *(n.)* net, snare, trap **Ham** III.ii.355 [Hamlet to Rosencrantz and Guildenstern] *you would drive me into a toil?;* **AC** V.ii.346; **E3** III.iv.44; **JC** II.i.206; **LL** IV.iii.3

toil *(v.)* exhaust, tire out, fatigue **2H6** I.i.81 [Gloucester to all] *did my brother Bedford toil his wits / To keep by policy what Henry got?;* **Ham** I.i.72; **MND** V.i.74; **R2** IV.i.96

token *(n.)* **1** sign, evidence, mark **KL** V.iii.247 [Edgar to Edmund] *Send / Thy token of reprieve;* **AW** V.iii.85; **CE** IV.i.56; **KJ** I.i.87; **TNK** V.i.61, 133

2 signal, indication **MW** IV.vi.44 [Fenton to Host, of Caius taking Anne by the hand] *on that token, / The maid hath given consent to go with him*

3 omen, portent, prodigy **JC** I.iii.55 [Casca to Cassius, of the storm] *the most mighty gods by tokens send / Such dreadful heralds to astonish us*

4 emblem, badge, coar-of-arms **TNK** III.i.37 [Palamon to and of Arcite] *the voidest of honour / That e'er bore gentle token*

5 keepsake, present, memento **TC** I.ii.280 [Pandarus to Cressida, of what he will bring her] *a token from Troilus;* **AW** V.iii.68; **Ham** II.ii.144; **LL** V.ii.423; **TC** V.ii.60; **TNK** IV.iii.91

token *(v.)* betoken, represent, be a sign of **AW** IV.ii.63 [Diana to Bertram] *what in time proceeds / May token to the future our past deeds*

tokened *(adj.)* shown by marks, spotted, blotchy **AC** III.x.9 [Scarus to Enobarbus, of how the fight is going] *On our side like the tokened pestilence*

toll *(v.)* **1** levy a toll, exact a payment **KJ** III.i.154 [King John to Cardinal Pandulph, of the Pope] *no Italian priest / Shall tithe or toll in our dominions;* **2H4** IV.v.76

2 enter for sale in the toll-book [tax register] of a market **AW** V.iii.148 [Lafew to King] *I will buy me a son-in-law in a fair, and toll for this*

tombless *(adj.)* without a tombstone, lacking a memorial **H5** I.ii.230 [King Henry to all, of what should happen to him if he fails] *lay these bones in an unworthy urn, / Tombless, with no remembrance over them*

tomboy *(n.)* harlot, prostitute **Cym** I.vii.122 [Iachimo to Innogen] *partnered / With tomboys hired with that self exhibition / Which your own coffers yield!*

Tom o'Bedlam *(n.)* madman, deranged person **KL** I.ii.134 [Edmund to himself] *My cue is … a sigh like Tom o'Bedlam* ☛ Bedlam *(n./adj.)*

tongs *(n.)* type of simple metal musical instrument **MND** IV.i.29 [Bottom to Titania] *Let's have the tongs and the bones*

tongue *(n.)* **1** speech, expression, language, words, voice **KL** I.i.78 [Cordelia to herself] *I am sure my love's / More ponderous than my tongue;* **E3** II.i.307; **1H6** IV.v.47; **KJ** V.vi.8; **MA** IV.i.315; **Tim** I.i.178

2 (plural) foreign language **TG** IV.i.32 [Second Outlaw to Valentine] *Have you the tongues?* [i.e. can you speak foreign languages?]; **MA** V.i.160

3 spokesman, voice **KJ** II.ii.47 [Pembroke to King John, of himself] *that am the tongue of these / To sound the purposes of all their hearts*

4 ☛ bite one's tongue *(v.)*

tongue *(v.)* **1** reproach, censure, berate **MM** IV.iv.23 [Angelo alone, of Isabella] *But that her tender shame / Will not proclaim against her maiden loss, / How might she tongue me?* ☛ out-tongue *(v.)*

2 speak, babble about, utter **Cym** V.iv.147 [Posthumus alone] *such stuff as madmen / Tongue*

tongueless *(adj.)* dumb, silent, mute **WT** I.ii.92 [Hermione to Leontes] *One good deed dying tongueless / Slaughters a thousand waiting upon that;* **R2** I.i.105

tonight *(adv.)* last night, this past night **E3** I.ii.126 [King Edward to Countess] *I dreamed tonight of treason;* **Cym** II.i.33; **KJ** IV.ii.165; **MV** II.v.18; **Per** III.ii.75; **RJ** I.iv.50

too *(adv.)* **1** anyway, in any case **Cym** V.iii.68 [Posthumus alone, of those saving their skins] *Took heel to do't, / And yet died too!*

2 very **CE** I.i.2 [First Merchant to Antipholus of Syracuse] *Lest that your goods too soon be confiscate*

tool *(n.)* **1** weapon, sword **Cym** V.iii.9 [Posthumus to Lord, of the Romans] *having work / More plentiful than tools to do't;* **Luc** 1039; **RJ** I.i.30

2 penis **H8** V.iv.34 [Porter to Man] *Or have we some strange Indian with the great tool come to court*

tooth *(n.)* **1** fangs **Mac** III.ii.15 [Macbeth to Lady Macbeth, of the snake] *our poor malice / Remains in danger of her former tooth;* **Mac** III.iv.30

2 taste for pleasure, sweet tooth **AW** II.iii.41 [Lafew to Parolles] *I'll like a maid the better whilst I have a tooth in my head;* **H8** I.iii.48

3 appetite, taste, hunger **KJ** I.i.213 [Bastard alone, of himself] *to deliver / Sweet, sweet, sweet poison for the age's tooth*

toothdrawer *(n.)* tooth-extractor, dentist **LL** V.ii.616 [Berowne to Holofernes, of a brooch] *worn in the cap of a toothdrawer*

tooth-picker *(n.)* tooth-pick **MA** II.i.244 [Benedick to Don Pedro] *I will fetch you a tooth-picker*

top *(n.)* **1** summit, peak, epitome, perfect example **Tem** III.i.38 [Ferdinand to Miranda, of her] *the top of admiration;* **MM** II.ii.76

2 head **Cym** IV.ii.354 [Lucius to all, of Cloten] *what trunk is here? / Without his top?;* **AW** I.i.43; **KL** II.iv.158; **MA** II.ii.13

3 platform at the top of a mast **TNK** IV.i.149 [Gaoler to Second Friend] *Up to the top, boy* ☛ SHIPS, p.397

4 ☛ STAGE DIRECTIONS, p.417

top *(v.)* **1** surpass, exceed, outstrip **Mac** IV.iii.57 [Macduff to Malcolm] *Not in the legions / Of horrid hell can come a devil more damned / In evils to top Macbeth;* **Cor** II.i.19; **Ham** IV.vii.87

2 prune, lop, cut back **Per** I.iv.9 [Dionyza to Cleon, of their griefs] *like to groves, being topped, they higher rise*

3 tighten, pull tight on **TNK** IV.i.147 [Gaoler's Daughter to all] *The wind's fair; top the bowling*

4 screw, copulate with **Oth** V.ii.137 [Othello to Emilia, of Desdemona] *Cassio did top her;* **Oth** III.iii.393

top / tops of, in *(prep.)* at the highest level of, at the peak of, in the forefront of **3H6** V.vii.4 [Edward to all] *What valiant foemen … / Have we mowed down in tops of all their pride;* **Lover** 55 [of the woman's letters] *in top of rage the lines she rents;* **AC** V.i.43

top of, in the *(prep.)* above, superior to, higher than **Ham** II.ii.437 [Hamlet to First Player] *whose judgements in such matters cried in the top of mine*

topfull, topful *(adj.)* brimful, over-full **Mac** I.v.40 [Lady Macbeth alone] *fill me from the crown to the toe top-full / Of direst cruelty;* **KJ** III.iv.180

topgallant *(n.)* summit, top platform **RJ** II.iv.186 [Romeo to Nurse, of a rope-ladder] *Which to the high topgallant of my joy / Must be my convoy in the secret night* ☛ SHIPS, p.397

topless *(adj.)* supreme, paramount **TC** I.iii.152 [Ulysses to Agamemnon, of Patroclus] *Sometime … / Thy topless deputation he puts on*

topmast *(n.)* section of mast fitted to the top of the lower mast **Tem** I.i.34 [Boatswain to the Mariners] *Down with the topmast!* ☛ SHIPS, p.397

top-proud *(adj.)* showing the highest degree of pride **H8** I.i.151 [Buckingham to Norfolk, of Wolsey] *this top-proud fellow*

topsail *(n.)* ☛ SHIPS, p.397

torcher (n.) light-giver, torch-carrier **AW** II.i.162 [Helena to King] *Ere twice the horses of the sun shall bring / Their fiery torcher his diurnal ring*

torch-staff (n.) staff holding a torch **H5** IV.ii.44 [Grandpré to all, of the English army] *The horsemen sit like fixed candlesticks, / With torch-staves in their hand*

tortive (adj.) contorted, tortuous, twisting **TC** I.iii.9 [Agamemnon to all, of a pine tree] *knots … divert his grain / Tortive and errant from his course of growth*

torture (v.) torment, afflict, plague **MW** III.ii.36 [Ford to himself, of Falstaff] *I will take him, then torture my wife*

toss (v.) 1 stir up, disturb, toss about **Tit** IV.i.41 [Titus to Young Lucius, of Lavinia] *what book is that she tosseth so?*; **1H4** II.iii.82
2 carry aloft, impale **2H6** V.i.11 [York to himself, of his sceptre] *On which I'll toss the flower-de-luce of France*; **3H6** I.i.244
3 throw, fling [into battle] **1H4** IV.ii.63 [Falstaff to Prince Hal, of the soldiers] *good enough to toss*

tosspot (n.) drunkard, sot, tippler **TN** V.i.400 [Feste singing] *But when I came unto my beds … / With tosspots still had drunken heads*

total (adj.) completely, entirely, totally **Ham** II.ii.455 [Hamlet to First Player, quoting lines about Pyrrhus] *Head to foot / Now is he total gules*

tottered (adj.) ☛ tattered (adj.)

tottering (adj.) 1 wavering, vacillating, fluctuating **TNK** V.iv.20 [Second Knight to Palamon] *with our patience anger tottering fortune*
2 tattered, ragged, frayed **KJ** V.v.7 [Lewis the Dauphin to all, of close of the day's battle] *And wound our tottering colours clearly up* [also: waving to and fro]

touch (n.) 1 trait, quality, feature **Mac** IV.ii.9 [Macduff's wife to Ross, of Macduff] *He wants the natural touch*; **AY** III.ii.148, V.iv.27; **Cor** IV.i.49; **TC** III.iii.175; **Tim** I.i.37, 39
2 sense, feeling, intuition, hint **H8** V.i.13 [Gardiner to Lovell] *give your friend / Some touch of your late business*; **TC** IV.ii.96; **Tem** V.i.21
3 factor, reason, motive **AC** I.ii.181 [Antony to Enobarbus] *The death of Fulvia, with more urgent touches, / Do strongly speak to us*
4 act, action, deed **MND** III.ii.70 [Hermia to Demetrius, of Lysander] *hast thou killed him sleeping? O, brave touch!*;
5 hit **Ham** V.ii.280 [Laertes to Hamlet, during their duel] *A touch, a touch. I do confess't*; **LL** V.i.56
6 touchstone, test, proof **1H4** IV.iv.10 [Archbishop to Sir Michael] *Tomorrow … is a day / Wherein the fortune of ten thousand men / Must bide the touch* [i.e. have their quality tested]; **E3** III.iii.141; **R3** IV.ii.8; **Tim** IV.iii.391
7 fingering, handling, skill in playing **MV** V.i.67 [Lorenzo to Musicians] *With sweetest touches pierce your mistress' ear*; **Ham** III.ii.364; **MV** V.i.57; **R2** I.iii.165; **TG** III.ii.79
8 depth of feeling, mental pain, pang **Cym** I.i.66 [Innogen to Cymbeline] *I am senseless of your wrath; a touch more rare / Subdues all pangs*; **AW** I.iii.113
9 ☛ keep touch

touch (v.) 1 affect, concern, regard, relate to **H5** II.ii.174 [King Henry to the traitors] *Touching our person seek we no revenge*; **1H6** IV.i.118; **KL** V.i.25; **LL** I.i.187; **R3** I.iii.261; **TS** I.i.114
2 refer to, treat of, deal with **R3** III.vii.4 [Richard to Buckingham] *Touched you the bastardy of Edward's children?*; **AC** II.ii.24; **JC** III.i.7; **R3** III.v.92, vii.4; **TC** II.ii.195
3 affect, move, stir **H8** II.i.52 [Suffolk to Norfolk, of Wolsey] *His curses and his blessings / Touch me alike*; **AC** II.ii.145; **AW** I.iii.105; **MM** II.ii.70; **MV** IV.i.25; **Sonn** 42.4
4 achieve, accomplish, attain **H8** III.ii.223 [Wolsey alone] *I have touched the highest point of all my greatness*; **AC** V.ii.329; **Ham** II.i.12; **MND** II.i.125
5 diagnose, ascertain **AY** II.vii.95 [Orlando to Duke Senior] *You touched my vein at first*

6 test the quality [of], put to the test **Tim** III.iii.6 [Servant to Sempronius, of other lords] *They have all been touched and found base metal*; **CE** II.i.111; **Cor** II.iii.190; **KJ** III.i.100; **MM** I.i.35; **Tim** IV.iii.5
7 threaten, endanger, imperil **JC** II.i.154 [Decius to all] *Shall no man else be touched but only Caesar?*; **AW** II.i.110; **Cor** III.i.123; **KJ** V.vii.2; **R3** II.iv.25
8 wound, hurt, injure **R3** I.i.112 [Richard to Clarence, of his imprisonment] *this deep disgrace in brotherhood / Touches me deeper than you can imagine*; **Cym** V.iii.10; **MM** V.i.233; **Oth** II.iii.214; **R3** II.iii.26; **Tit** IV.iv.36
9 stain, taint, infect **CE** IV.i.72 [Angelo to Antipholus of Ephesus, on being arrested] *This touches me in reputation*; **AY** III.iii.336; **Ham** IV.v.207; **H8** II.iv.155; **MM** V.i.51; **Tim** III.v.19
10 finger, sound, play on **E3** II.ii.56 [King Edward to Lodowick] *bid the drummer learn to touch the lute*; **JC** IV.iii.255; **TS** III.i.62
11 touch off, fire off **H5** III.Chorus.33 [Chorus alone] *the nimble gunner / With linstock now the devilish cannon touches*; **H5** IV.vii.175
12 reach, rise to, go as far as **Tim** I.i.14 [Jeweller to Merchant, of a jewel for Timon] *If he will touch the estimate* [i.e. pay the asking price]
13 land at, arrive at, visit **WT** V.i.138 [Florizel to Leontes, of Polixenes] *By his command / Have I here touched Sicilia*; **R2** II.i.288; **TC** II.ii.77

touching (adj.) affecting, moving, grievous **JC** IV.iii.149 [Cassius to Brutus, of Portia's death] *O insupportable and touching loss!*

touching (prep.) concerning **Cym** III.v.101 [Pisanio to Cloten, of Innogen] *This paper is the history of my knowledge / Touching her flight*

touchstone (n.) type of stone used for testing the quality of a gold or silver alloy **Per** II.ii.37 [Thaisa to Simonides] *gold that's by the touchstone tried*

tourney (v.) take part in a tournament **Per** II.i.145 [First Fisherman to Pericles, of Thaisa] *wilt thou tourney for the lady?*; **Per** II.i.110

touse (v.) tear, rip, rend **MM** V.i.309 [Escalus to disguised Duke] *We'll touse you / Joint by joint*

toward (adj.) 1 docile, compliant, obliging **TS** V.ii.181 [Vincentio to all] *'Tis a good hearing when children are toward*; **PassP** IV.13; **Venus** 1157 ☛ froward (adj.) 1
2 promising, bold, future **3H6** II.ii.66 [Clifford to the Prince, of his resolution to fight for the crown] *that is spoken like a toward prince*

toward (adv.) impending, forthcoming, in preparation **Tim** III.vi.61 [Sempronius to other Lords] *Here's a noble feast toward*; **AY** V.iv.35; **2H4** IV.iv.195; **KL** IV.vi.209; **MND** III.i.72; **TS** I.i.68

toward (prep.) towards **Ham** I.iv.69 [Horatio to Hamlet, of the Ghost] *What if it tempt you toward the flood*

towardly (adj.) dutiful, helpful, friendly **Tim** III.i.34 [Lucullus to Flaminius] *I have observed thee always for a towardly prompt spirit*

towards (adv.) at hand, approaching, imminent **E3** IV.iv.108 [Third Herald to Prince Edward] *arm thy soul for her long journey towards*; **RJ** I.v.122

tower (v.) [falconry] mount up to a great height, circle, soar **Luc** 506 [of Tarquin's sword] *like a falcon towering in the skies*; **2H6** II.i.10; **KJ** II.i.350, V.ii.149; **Mac** II.iv.12

town of war (n.) ☛ war, town of (n.)

toy (n.) 1 whim, caprice, trifling matter **Ham** I.iii.6 [Laertes to Ophelia] *For Hamlet, and the trifling of his favour, / Hold it a fashion and a toy in blood*; **AY** III.iii.70; **1H6** IV.i.145; **2H4** II.iv.164; **TG** I.ii.82; **TNK** II.i.35
2 fancy, fantastic thought **E3** IV.iii.83 [King John to Charles] *all are frivolous fancies, toys, and dreams*; **Ham** I.iv.75; **Oth** I.iii.265, III.iv.152; **R3** I.i.60
3 trinket, trifle, trivial ornament **TN** III.iii.45 [Antonio to Sebastian] *Haply your eye shall light upon some toy / You have desire to purchase*; **AC** V.ii.166; **KJ** I.i.232; **R3** III.i.114; **TNK** I.iii.71; **WT** IV.iv.317

4 piece of nonsense, foolish affair **WT** III.iii.38 [Antigonus to baby Perdita] *Dreams are toys;* **TS** II.i.395, IV.iii.67

5 foolish dislike, silly aversion **TNK** V.iv.66 [Pirithous to Palamon] *the hot horse, hot as fire, / Took toy at this*

6 flimsy being, insubstantial thing **MW** V.v.42 [Pistol as Hobgoblin to all] *silence, you airy toys*

7 foolish story, old wives' tale **MND** V.i.3 [Theseus to Hippolyta] *I never may believe … these fairy toys*

toy (*v.*) flirt, dally, make amorous sport **Venus** 34 [of Adonis] *With leaden appetite, unapt to toy;* **Venus** 106

trace (*n.*) path, way; or: team [of horses, linked by traces] **TNK** I.ii.60 [Palamon to Arcite] *Either I am / The fore-horse in the team, or I am none / That draw i'th' sequent trace* [i.e. following the leader]

trace (*v.*) **1** imitate, pursue, follow in one's footsteps **Ham** V.ii.119 [Hamlet to Osrick, of Laertes] *who else would trace him;* **1H4** III.i.45; **TNK** I.i.102

2 follow on from, come from **Mac** IV.i.152 [Macbeth to himself, of Macduff] *I will … give to the edge o'the sword / His wife, his babes, and all unfortunate souls / That trace him in his line;* **H8** III.ii.45

3 range over, pass through, traverse **MA** III.i.16 [Hero to Ursula] *As we do trace this alley up and down;* **MND** II.i.25

4 tread a measure, dance some steps **TNK** III.v.21 [Schoolmaster to all] *And sweetly, by a figure, trace and turn*

tract (*n.*) **1** continuance, duration, course of events **H8** I.i.40 [Norfolk to Buckingham] *the tract of everything / Would by a good discourser lose some life / Which action's self was tongue to*

2 course, process, track **R3** V.iii.20 [Richmond to all, of the sun] *the bright tract of his fiery car* [F; Q *track*]; **Sonn** 7.12

3 trace, trail, evidence of passage **Tim** I.i.51 [Poet to Painter, of his poem] *flies an eagle flight, bold and forth on, / Leaving no tract behind*

tractable (*adj.*) compliant, manageable, governable **TC** II.iii.149 [Agamemnon to Ajax, of Ajax compared to Achilles] *you are … altogether more tractable;* **H8** I.ii.64

trade (*n.*) **1** traffic, passage, coming and going **R2** III.iii.156 [King Richard to Aumerle] *the King's highway, / Some way of common trade;* **2H4** I.i.174; **H8** V.i.36

2 business, dealings **TN** III.i.73 [Sir Toby to Viola as Cesario] *My niece is desirous you should enter, if your trade be to her;* **Ham** III.ii.341

3 regular line of work, recognized business **Per** IV.ii.36 [Pander to Bawd] *Neither is our profession any trade; it's no calling;* **MM** III.i.152

4 course of action, practice **KL** IV.i.38 [Edgar to himself] *Bad is the trade that must play fool to sorrow*

trade (*v.*) cross, come and go **MV** III.iv.54 [Portia to Balthasar, of garments] *Bring them … / Unto the traject, to the common ferry / Which trades to Venice*

traded (*adj.*) practised, expert, experienced **KJ** IV.iii.109 [Salisbury to all, of Hubert's supposed villainy] *long traded in it;* **TC** II.ii.65

trade-fallen (*adj.*) out-of-work, unemployed, bankrupt **1H4** IV.ii.28 [Falstaff alone, of those in his command] *revolted tapsters, and ostlers trade-fallen*

trader (*n.*) trading ship, merchant vessel **MND** II.i.127 [Titania to Oberon, of the mother of her attendant] *Full often hath she … sat with me on Neptune's yellow sands / Marking th'embarked traders on the flood*

traduce (*v.*) defame, slander, calumniate, dishonour **AC** III.vii.13 [Enobarbus to Cleopatra, of Antony] *He is already / Traduced for levity;* **AW** II.i.172; **Ham** I.iv.18; **H8** I.ii.72; **Oth** V.ii.350

traducement (*n.*) slander, calumny, defamation **Cor** I.ix.22 [Cominius to Martius] *'Twere … a traducement, / To hide your doings*

traffic (*n.*) **1** trade, commerce, business, merchandise **TS** I.i.12 [Lucentio to Tranio, of his father] *A merchant of great traffic through the world;* **CE** I.i.15; **Tem** II.i.151; **Tim** I.i.240; **TN** III.iii.35; **WT** IV.iii.23

2 dealings, employment, business **1H6** V.iv.164 [Suffolk to Reignier] *this is in traffic of a king;* **E3** V.i.230; **RJ** Prologue.i.12

3 trade, deal, carry on **Luc** 131 *Despair to gain doth traffic oft for gaining*

traffic with (*v.*) traffic in, trade illicitly, pervert **Tim** I.i.162 [Timon to Painter] *dishonour traffics with man's nature*

trafficker (*n.*) trading ship, merchant vessel **MV** I.i.12 [Salerio to Antonio] *your argosies with portly sail … / Do overpeer the petty traffickers / That curtsy to them*

tragedian (*n.*) actor, strolling player [not only of tragedy] **Ham** II.ii.328 [Rosencrantz to Hamlet] *the tragedians of the city;* **AW** IV.iii.260

trail (*n.*) [hunting] scent, track **AC** V.ii.349 [First Guard to Dolabella] *This is an aspic's trail;* **Ham** II.ii.47; **MW** IV.ii.186

train (*n.*) **1** retinue, following, entourage **KL** I.iv.249 [Lear to his attendants] *Call my train together!;* **Ham** V.ii.356; **2H4** V.ii.93; **H8** IV.i.37; **KL** I.iv.260; **Tem** V.i.301

2 set of dependents, group of people **E3** III.ii.24 [First Citizen to First Frenchman] *We that have charge and such a train as this* [i.e. who have to look after these people]

3 stratagem, wile, lure **Mac** IV.iii.118 [Malcolm to Macduff] *Devilish Macbeth / By many of these trains hath sought to win me / Into his power*

train (*v.*) **1** lure, entice, decoy **Tit** V.i.104 [Aaron to Lucius, of Quintus and Martius] *I trained thy brethren to that guileful hole;* **CE** III.ii.45; **1H4** V.ii.21; **1H6** I.iii.34; **KJ** III.iv.175; **LL** I.i.71

2 draw on, induce, tempt **TC** V.iii.4 [Hector to Andromache] *You train me to offend you*

train up (*v.*) bring up, rear, educate **Cym** III.iii.82 [Belarius alone, of Guiderius and Arviragus] *though trained up thus meanly*

traitorly (*adj.*) traitorous, treacherous **WT** IV.iv.787 [Autolycus to Clown, of the Shepherd and the Clown] *But what talk we of these traitorly rascals*

traject (*n.*) ferry **MV** III.iv.53 [Portia to Balthasar, of Bellario's garments] *Bring them … / Unto the traject, to the common ferry / Which trades to Venice* [F, Q *Tranect*]

trammel (*v.*) entangle, catch up [as in a fishing net] **Mac** I.vii.3 [Macbeth alone] *If the assassination / Could trammel up the consequence, and catch / With his surcease success*

tranced (*adj.*) in a trance, lost in grief, stunned **KL** V.iii.216 [Edgar to Albany, of Kent] *there I left him tranced*

tranect (*n.*) ➼ traject (*n.*)

transform (*v.*) change in form, metamorphose **CE** II.ii.204 [Dromio of Syracuse to Antipholus of Syracuse] *I am transformed, master;* **2H4** II.ii.68

translate (*v.*) **1** transform, change, alter **MND** III.i.112 [Quince to Bottom] *Thou art translated!;* **Cor** III.ii.188; **Ham** III.i.113; **2H4** IV.i.47; **Sonn** 96.8; **Tim** I.i.75

2 explain, interpret **Ham** IV.i.2 [Claudius to Gertrude] *These profound heaves / You must translate;* **TC** IV.v.112

translation (*n.*) expression, rendering, communication **LL** V.ii.51 [Katharine to Princess, of Dumaine's letter] *A huge translation of hypocrisy*

transmigrate (*v.*) pass into a new life; or: decompose, rot **AC** II.vii.45 [Antony to Lepidus, of the crocodile] *the elements once out of it, it transmigrates*

transmutation (*n.*) change of condition **TS** Induction.ii.19 [Sly to Lord] *Am not I … by education a cardmaker, by transmutation a bear-herd*

transport (*v.*) **1** carry off, move along **Cor** I.i.73 [Menenius to Citizens] *You are transported by calamity;* **Cor** II.i.216; **KL** I.iv.217

2 carry away, captivate, enrapture **TNK** I.i.55 [Theseus to First Queen] *I was transported with your speech;* **Tem** I.ii.76; **TNK** I.i.187

3 remove from the world, put to death **MM** IV.iii.66 [disguised Duke to Provost, of Barnadine] *to transport him in the mind he is / Were damnable*

transportance (n.) transportation, conveyance **TC** III.ii.10 [Troilus to Pandarus, of Cressida as the Elysian fields] *give me swift transportance to those fields*

transported (adj.) carried off, taken away **MND** IV.ii.4 [Starveling to Quince, of Bottom] *Out of doubt he is transported*

transpose (v.) change, alter, transform **Mac** IV.iii.21 [Malcolm to Macduff] *That which you are my thoughts cannot transpose;* **MND** I.i.233

trans-shape (v.) transform, transmute, alter the shape of **MA** V.i.164 [Don Pedro to Benedick, of Beatrice] *Thus did she … trans-shape thy particular virtues*

trapically (adv.) ☛ tropically (adv.)

trapped (adj.) adorn with trappings, deck out **Tim** I.ii.182 [Second Servant to Timon] *Four milk-white horses, trapped in silver;* **TS** Induction.ii.40

trappings (n.) ornaments, embellishments, bits and pieces **TN** V.i.8 [Feste to Orsino, of Olivia] *we are some of her trappings*

trash (n.) **1** rubbish, stuff, paraphernalia **2H6** I.iv.40 [York to the Guards] *Lay hands upon these traitors and their trash;* **JC** I.iii.108
2 dirty money **JC** IV.iii.26 [Brutus to Cassius] *shall we now … sell the mighty space of our large honours / For so much trash;* **JC** IV.iii.74
3 worthless person, disreputable individual **Oth** V.i.85 [Iago to all, of Bianca] *I do suspect this trash / To be a party in this injury*

trash (v.) [hunting] rein in, keep in check, hold back **Tem** I.ii.81 [Prospero to Miranda, of people in court] *who t'advance, and who / To trash for over-topping;* **Oth** II.i.294 [F *trace*]

travail, travel (n.) **1** labour, effort, exertion [often overlapping with sense 2] **1H6** IV.iv.102 [Richard to all] *Is all our travail turned to this effect?;* **E3** IV.ii.44; **Sonn** 27.2, 79.6; **TC** I.i.71, II.ii.4
2 journeying, travel [often overlapping with sense 1] **AY** II.iv.71 [Rosalind as Ganymede to Corin, of Celia as Aliena] *Here's a young maid with travail much oppressed;* **CE** I.i.140; **R2** I.iii.262; **Tem** III.iii.16; **TNK** Prologue.29
3 movement, motion, passage **TN** II.v.52 [Malvolio to himself] *after a demure travel of regard* [i.e. a serious look at everyone]
4 suffering, torment, distress **CE** V.i.401 [Abbess to Duke] *Thirty-three years have I but gone in travail;* **MA** III.iv.5
5 labour, pain of childbirth **Per** III.i.14 [Pericles alone] *make swift the pangs / Of my queen's travails!;* **H8** V.i.71; **Per** III.Chorus.52

travail, travel (v.) **1** labour, make effort, work hard [for] [often overlapping with sense 2] **AW** II.iii.157 [King to Bertram] *Obey our will which travails in thy good;* **Tim** V.i.15
2 travel, journey [often overlapping with sense 1] **Sonn** 34.2 [as if to the sun] *make me travail forth without my cloak;* **AY** IV.i.26; **Sonn** 63.5
3 be on tour **Ham** II.ii.329 [Hamlet to Rosencrantz, of the players] *How chances it they travel?*

travel-tainted (adj.) travel-stained **2H4** IV.iii.36 [Falstaff to Prince John] *travel-tainted as I am*

traverse (v.) **1** [fencing] pierce, stab, run through **MW** II.iii.22 [Host to Caius, in answer to 'Vat be you all … come for?'] *to see thee traverse*
2 [unclear meaning] take aim, about turn **Oth** I.iii.365 [Iago to Roderigo] *Traverse!;* **2H4** III.ii.264

traverse (adv.) crosswise, transversely **AY** III.iv.38 [Celia to Rosalind, of Orlando's oaths] *He … breaks them bravely, quite traverse, athwart the heart of his lover*

traversed (adj.) placed crosswise, laid across the shoulders **Tim** V.iv.7 [Alcibiades to Senators, of himself and others] *Have wandered with our traversed arms* [i.e. with our weapons inactive; or: with arms dispiritedly crossed]

tray-trip (n.) type of dicing game [depending on the throw of game a three] **TN** II.v.183 [Sir Toby to Maria] *Shall I play my freedom at tray-trip and become thy bondslave?* ☛ trey (n.)

treacher (n.) traitor, deceiver, cheat **KL** I.ii.123 [Edmund alone] *knaves, thieves, and treachers* [F; Q *Trecherers*]

treacherously (adv.) despicably, contemptibly, in a cowardly manner **3H6** II.i.72 [Edward as if to Clifford, of York] *treacherously hast thou vanquished him*

tread (v.) mate, pair up **LL** V.ii.894 [Ver singing, of spring] *When turtles tread, and rooks, and daws*

tread down (v.) trample on, crush, repress **KJ** III.i.216 [Constance to all] *Keep my need up, and faith is trodden down;* **KJ** III.i.58

tread out (v.) treat with contempt, crush, spurn **H5** III.vii.92 [Constable to Orleans, of Orleans swearing by the white hand of his lady] *Swear by her foot, that she may tread out the oath* [or: dance away]

tread upon (v.) press down on, thrust against **Tim** III.i.73 [First Stranger to Second and Third Strangers, of Lucius] *He ne'er drinks / But Timon's silver treads upon his lip*

treason (n.) treachery, betrayal, deceitfulness **Per** IV.Chorus.14 [Gower alone, of envy] *Marina's life / Seeks to take off by treason's knife*

treasure (n.) money, ready cash **Tim** II.ii.210 [Flavius to Timon, of the Senators] *now they are at fall, want treasure*

treasury (n.) **1** money, wealth, riches **KL** IV.vi.43 [Edgar to himself] *I know not how conceit may rob / The treasury of life;* **H5** I.i.165; **2H6** I.iii.129; **WT** IV.iv.347
2 treasure-house **Sonn** 136.5 *Will will fulfil the treasure of thy love;* **E3** II.ii.194

treatise (n.) story, tale, narrative **Venus** 774 [Adonis to Venus] *Your treatise makes me like you worse and worse;* **MA** I.i.294; **Mac** V.v.12

treaty (n.) entreaty, proposal for agreement, proposition **AC** III.xi.62 [Antony to Cleopatra, of Caesar] *I must / To the young man send humble treaties;* **Cor** II.iii.53; **H8** I.i.165; **KJ** II.i.481

treble over (v.) make three times greater, increase threefold **Tem** II.i.225 [Antonio to Sebastian, of the latter heeding him] *which to do / Trebles thee o'er*

treble-dated (adj.) living three times as long as man **Phoen** 17 *thou treble-dated crow … / 'Mongst our mourners shalt thou go*

treble-sinewed (adj.) strengthened three times over **AC** III.xiii.177 [Antony to Cleopatra] *I will be treble-sinewed*

trembling (adj.) frightening, fearful, disturbing **H8** I.ii.95 [King Henry to Wolsey, of the taxation] *A trembling contribution!*

trench (v.) **1** divert by means of a trench **1H4** III.i.108 [Worcester to all, of the river] *a little charge will trench him here*
2 gouge, cut, gash **Venus** 1052 [of Adonis's injury] *the wide wound that the boar had trenched / In his soft flank*

trenchant (adj.) sharp, cutting, keen-edged **Tim** IV.iii.116 [Timon to Alcibiades] *Let not the virgin's cheek / Make soft thy trenchant sword*

trenched (adj.) **1** deep, severe, entrenched **Mac** III.iv.26 [First Murderer to Macbeth, of Banquo] *safe in a ditch he bides, / With twenty trenched gashes on his head*
2 cut, carved, engraved **TG** III.ii.7 [Duke to Thurio] *a figure / Trenched in ice*

trencher (n.) plate, platter, serving dish **TG** IV.iv.9 [Launce alone, of his dog and Silvia] *he steps me to her trencher and steals her capon's leg;* **AC** III.xiii.117; **Cor** IV.v.52; **2H6** IV.i.57; **RJ** I.v.2; **TS** V.i.151

trencher-friend (n.) friend for free meals, sponger, parasite **Tim** III.vi.96 [Timon to Lords] *You fools of fortune, trencher-friends*

trenchering (n.) plates, platters, serving dishes **Tem** II.ii.179 [Caliban singing] *Nor scrape trenchering, nor wash dish*

trencher-knight (n.) hero of the dinner-table, valiant eater **LL** V.ii.464 [Browne to all, of Boyet] *some trencher-knight … / Told our intents before*

trencher-man (n.) hearty eater, good feeder, man of appetite **MA** I.i.47 [Beatrice to Messenger, of Benedick] *he is a very valiant trencher-man*

trenching (*adj.*) cutting, wounding, scarring 1H4 I.i.7 [King Henry to all, of England] *No more shall trenching war channel her fields*

trespass (*n.*) wrong, offence, injustice, crime TNK III.i.77 [Palamon to Arcite] *I will forgive / The trespass thou hast done me;* AC II.i.40; 2H6 III.i.132; 3H6 V.i.92

trey (*n.*) [gambling] three LL V.ii.232 [masked Berowne to masked Princess, of her three sweet words] *Nay then, two treys* ☞ tray-trip (*n.*)

trial (*n.*) **1** action of testing, putting to the proof JC IV.ii.27 [Brutus to Lucilius, of insincere men compared to horses] *like deceitful jades / Sink in the trial;* Cym III.vi.11; TC I.iii.14
  2 evidence, proof, grounds MA II.ii.37 [Borachio to Don John, of Claudio and Don Pedro being told about Hero's supposed infidelity] *They will scarcely believe this without trial*

trial-fire (*n.*) testing fire, ordeal by fire MW V.v.84 [Mistress Quickly as Queen of Fairies to all, of Falstaff] *With trial-fire touch me his finger-end*

tribulation (*n.*) trouble-maker, pest, mischief-maker H8 V.iv.61 [Porter to Man, of boys] *no audience but the tribulation of Tower Hill ... are able to endure*

tribunal (*n.*) raised platform, elevated rostrum, dais AC III.vi.3 [Caesar to all, of Antony] *on a tribunal silvered, / Cleopatra and himself ... / Were publicly enthroned*

tribunal plebs malapropism for 'tribuni plebis' [= 'tribunes of the people'] Tit IV.iii.92 [Clown to Titus] *I am going with my pigeons to the tribunal plebs*

tribune (*n.*) ☞ ROMAN HISTORY, p.377

tributary (*n.*) ruler who pays tribute JC I.i.33 [Marullus to Cobbler, of Caesar] *What tributaries follow him to Rome;* AC III.xiii.96

tributary (*adj.*) paying a tribute, contributory RJ III.ii.103 [Juliet to herself, of her tears] *Your tributary drops belong to woe;* Tit I.i.162, III.i.268; Venus 1045

tribute (*n.*) payment, money [acknowledging esteem] Ham II.ii.320 [Hamlet to Rosencrantz and Guildenstern] *his majesty shall have tribute of me*

trice (*n.*) **1** brief period, moment, instant KL I.i.216 [France to Lear, of Cordelia] *This is most strange, / That she ... should in this trice of time / Commit a thing so monstrous;* Tem IV.ii.123
  2 single pull Cym V.iv.168 [First Gaoler to Posthumus, of the hangman's rope] *it sums up thousands in a trice* [also: sense 1]

trick (*n.*) **1** habit, characteristic, typical behaviour AW III.ii.8 [Clown to Countess] *I knew a man that had this trick of melancholy;* Ham IV.vii.187; 2H4 I.ii.216; LL V.ii.416; Tem I.ii.210; WT II.iii.100
  2 way, knack, skill LL V.ii.465 [Berowne to all, of Boyet] *Some carry-tale ... knows the trick / To make my lady laugh;* Cym III.iii.86; Ham V.i.89; H8 I.iii.40; TNK II.ii.71; TS IV.ii.57
  3 peculiarity, idiosyncrasy, distinguishing trait KJ I.i.85 [Queen Eleanor to King John, of Bastard] *He hath a trick of Coeur-de-lion's face;* AW I.i.95; 1H4 II.iv.397, V.iv.11; KL IV.vi.106; TN II.v.146
  4 practice, custom, current fashion MM V.i.502 [Lucio to Duke, of his earlier accusation] *I spoke it but according to the trick;* Cym III.iii.15
  5 skill, feat, achievement Ham IV.vii.88 [Claudius to Laertes] *in forgery of shapes and tricks*
  6 bauble, trifle, whim TS IV.iii.67 [Petruchio to Haberdasher, of a cap] *A knack, a toy, a trick, a baby's cap;* Cor IV.iv.21; Ham IV.iv.61; MM III.i.117; WT II.i.51
  7 misconception, delusion, fancy Oth IV.ii.128 [Iago to Desdemona, of Othello's behaviour to Desdemona] *How comes this trick upon him?*

trick up (*v.*) decorate, adorn, dress up H5 III.vi.74 [Gower to Fluellen, of men like Pistol's boasts about the wars] *which they trick up with new-tuned oaths*

tricked (*adj.*) [heraldry] delineated, spotted Ham II.ii.455 [Hamlet to First Player, quoting lines about Pyrrhus] *horridly tricked / With blood of fathers*

tricking (*n.*) costumes, ornamentation, decking out, costumery MW IV.iv.77 [Mistress Page to Ford] *Go get us properties / And tricking for our fairies*

tricksy (*adj.*) full of tricks, cleverly playful Tem V.i.226 [Prospero to Ariel] *My tricksy spirit!;* MV III.v.64

trifle (*n.*) **1** fiction, illusion, trick Tem V.i.112 [Alonso to Prospero] *Whe'er thou beest ... some enchanted trifle to abuse me*
  2 small token, insignificant sign Tim I.ii.207 [Timon to Second Lord, of a gift] *Here, my lord, a trifle of our love*

trifle (*v.*) **1** waste, squander, spend idly H8 V.iii.178 [King Henry to all] *we trifle time away;* MV IV.i.295
  2 make trivial, render insignificant Mac II.iv.4 [Old Man to Ross] *this sore night / Hath trifled former knowings*

trifling (*n.*) frivolity, foolish conduct Ham I.iii.5 [Laertes to Ophelia] *For Hamlet, and the trifling of his favour, / Hold it a fashion*

trigon (*n.*) triangle of the zodiac 2H4 II.iv.260 [Poins to Prince Henry, of Bardolph] *the fiery trigon his man* [i.e. consisting of the three fiery signs] ☞ COSMOS, p.102

trill (*v.*) roll, flow, stream KL IV.iii.12 [Gentleman to disguised Kent, of Cordelia] *now and then an ample tear trilled down / Her delicate cheek*

trim (*n.*) **1** display, array, show Lover 118 [of the man's trappings] *their purposed trim / Pieced not his grace but were all graced by him*
  2 trappings, equipment, outfit Cor I.ix.61 [Cominius to all, of Martius] *My noble steed ... I give him, / With all his trim belonging* [i.e. the trappings that go with it]; AC IV.iv.22; 1H4 IV.i.113
  3 adornment, frill Cym III.iv.166 [Pisanio to Innogen] *forget / Your laboursome and dainty trims;*
  4 readiness to sail, full preparedness CE IV.i.91 [Dromio of Syracuse to Antipholus of Ephesus] *The ship is in her trim;* Tem V.i.236

trim, in the in fine condition, in good order H5 IV.iii.115 [King Henry to Montjoy] *our hearts are in the trim* [also: fashionable]

trim (*adj.*) **1** fine, excellent, smart MND III.ii.157 [Helena to Lysander and Demetrius] *A trim exploit, a manly enterprise;* Cor I.ix.61; H8 I.iii.38; LL V.ii.363; TC IV.v.33; Tit V.i.96
  2 glib, suave, slick MA IV.i.315 [Beatrice to Benedick] *men are only turned into tongue, and trim ones too*

trim (*v.*) **1** dress, attire, make [oneself] ready TG IV.iv.158 [disguised Julia to Silvia] *I was trimmed in Madam Julia's gown;* Per I.iv.27
  2 tidy up, make ready, prepare TC V.i.42 [Achilles to Thersites] *help to trim my tent;* Tit V.i.93

trim up, trim (*v.*) **1** decorate, array, deck out RJ IV.iv.25 [Capulet to Nurse, of Juliet] *Go and trim her up;* Tem V.i.294 [Prospero to Caliban, of his cell] *trim it handsomely;* E3 IV.iv.16; 2H4 I.iii.94; TS Induction.ii.38
  2 arrange, fix up, put right AC V.ii.340 [First Guard to Caesar, of Charmian] *I found her trimming up the diadem / On her dead mistress*

trim (*adv.*) well, effectively, finely RJ II.i.13 [Mercutio to Benvolio, of Cupid] *he that shot so trim*

trimmed (*adj.*) finely dressed, decked out 3H6 II.i.24 [Richard to Edward, of the morning] *How well resembles it the prime of youth, / Trimmed like a younker prancing to his love!*

trinkets (*n.*) bits and pieces, paraphernalia 2H6 I.iv.52 [Buckingham to Jourdain, Southwell, and Bolingbroke] *We'll see your trinkets here all forthcoming*

trip (*n.*) [wrestling] foot movement which causes an opponent to fall TN V.i.165 [Orsino to Viola as Cesario] *thine own trip shall be thy overthrow*

trip (*v.*) **1** move, run along, skip AY V.i.61 [Touchstone to Audrey] *Trip, Audrey, trip* [i.e. look lively]

2 dance, step lightly **Per** II.iii.102 [Simonides to Pericles] *you knights of Tyre / Are excellent in making ladies trip*

3 overthrow, catch out, point out fault in **Cym** V.v.35 [Cornelius to Cymbeline, of the Queen] *her women / Can trip me, if I err;* **2H4** V.ii.87

tripartite (*adj.*) triple, three-part **1H4** III.i.76 [Mortimer to all] *our indentures tripartite are drawn*

tripe-visaged (*adj.*) tripe-faced, flabby **2H4** V.iv.8 [Doll to First Beadle] *thou damned tripe-visaged rascal*

triple (*adj.*) **1** one of three **AC** I.i.12 [Philo to Demetrius, of Antony] *you shall see in him / The triple pillar of the world transformed / Into a strumpet's fool* [i.e. one of three triumvirs]

2 third **AW** II.i.108 [Helena to King, of one of her father's prescriptions] *He bade me store up as a triple eye, / Safer than mine own two*

triplex (*n.*) [music] triple time **TN** V.i.35 [Feste to Orsino] *the triplex, sir, is a good tripping measure*

tripping (*adj.*) light-footed, nimble **TN** V.i.36 [Feste to Orsino] *the triplex, sir, is a good tripping measure*

tripping (*adv.*) light-footedly, with nimble dance-steps **TC** III.iii.211 [Ulysses to Achilles] *all the Greekish girls shall tripping sing*

tristful (*adj.*) sad, sorrowful, dismal **Ham** III.iv.51 [Hamlet to Gertrude] *With tristful visage* [F; Q2 *heated*]; **1H4** II.iv.386

triumph (*n.*) **1** public festivity, pageant, display of celebration, tournament **MND** I.i.19 [Theseus to Hippolyta] *I will wed thee ... / With pomp, with triumph, and with revelling;* **Cym** IV.ii.192; **3H6** V.vii.43; **Oth** II.ii.4; **Per** II.ii.1; **R2** V.iii.14

2 triumphal procession into Rome **JC** V.i.108 [Cassius to Brutus] *if we lose this battle, / You are contented to be led in triumph / Thorough the streets of Rome?;* **AC** IV.xii.33, V.i.66, ii.109; **JC** I.i.31; **Tit** I.i.113

3 festival illumination, triumphal light **1H4** III.iii.40 [Falstaff to Bardolph] *thou art a perpetual triumph*

4 high point, joy of the moment **RJ** II.vi.10 [Friar to Romeo] *These violent delights have violent ends / And in their triumph die, like fire and powder*

5 trump-card **AC** IV.xiv.20 [Antony to Eros, of Cleopatra] *she ... has / Packed cards with Caesar, and false-played my glory / Unto an enemy's triumph* [also: victory]

triumph (*v.*) exult, gloat, glory **3H6** I.iv.63 [York to and of his enemies] *So triumph thieves upon their conquered booty;* **Cor** II.i.170; **3H6** I.iv.114, II.iv.8, V.vi.93

triumphant (*adj.*) triumphal, glorious, celebrating a great victory **R3** IV.iv.333 [King Richard to Queen Elizabeth] *Bound with triumphant garlands will I come;* **AC** II.ii.189, III.i.10; **Cor** V.v.3; **1H6** I.i.22; **RJ** V.iii.83

triumphantly (*adv.*) as in a festive pageant, with great celebration **MND** IV.i.88 [Oberon to Titania] *thou and I [will] ... / Dance in Duke Theseus' house triumphantly*

triumpher (*n.*) victor, conqueror, general [given a Roman procession of welcome] **Tit** I.i.173 [Marcus to all, of Titus] *Gracious triumpher in the eyes of Rome!;* **Tim** V.i.194

triumviry, triumphery (*n.*) triumvirate, threesome **LL** IV.iii.51 [Browne to himself, as if to Longaville] *Thou makest the triumviry* [F *triumphery*]

trivial (*adj.*) slight, poor, insubstantial **2H6** III.i.241 [Suffolk to all, of Gloucester] *we have but trivial argument, / More than mistrust, that shows him worthy death*

Trojan (*n.*) ☞ Troyan (*n.*)

troll (*v.*) sing out, sing merrily **Tem** III.ii.118 [Caliban to Stephano] *Will you troll the catch / You taught me but while-ere?*

troll-my-dame (*n.*) type of game in which balls are rolled [trolled] through hoops **WT** IV.iii.85 [Autolycus to Clown, of the supposed robber] *A fellow ... that I have known to go about with troll-my-dames*

troop (*n.*) company, retinue, band of followers **2H6** I.iii.75 [Queen to Suffolk, of the Duchess of Gloucester] *She sweeps it through the court with troops of ladies;* **AC** IV.xiv.53; **R3** IV.vi.96; **Tit** II.iii.56

troop with (*v.*) go along with, be associated with, accompany **RJ** I.v.48 [Romeo to himself, of Juliet] *So shows a snowy dove trooping with crows;* **KL** I.i.132

trophy (*n.*) **1** token of victory, evidence of valour **JC** I.i.69 [Flavius to Marullus, of the statues] *let no images / Be hung with Caesar's trophies;* **H5** V.Chorus.21, V.i.68; **Lover** 218; **Tit** I.i.391

2 memorial, monument **Ham** IV.v.214 [Laertes to Claudius, of Polonius] *No trophy, sword, nor hatchment o'er his bones;* **Cor** I.iii.41; **Tim** V.iv.25

tropically (*adv.*) figuratively, like a trope [a figure of speech] **Ham** III.ii.247 [Hamlet to Claudius, who has asked the name of the play] *The Mousetrap. Marry, how? Tropically* [F, Q2; Q1 *trapically*]

trot (*n.*) old woman, hag **MM** III.ii.47 [Lucio to Pompey] *What say'st thou, trot?;* **TS** I.ii.78

troth (*n.*) **1** truth, good faith **Luc** 1059 [Lucrece as if to Collatine] *thou shalt not know / The stained taste of violated troth;* **Cym** V.v.274; **H8** II.iii.34; **LL** IV.iii.141; **MND** II.ii.42; **TC** IV.v.168 ☞ SWEARING, p.435

2 ☞ plight one's troth

troth-plight (*n.*) engagement, act of betrothal **WT** I.ii.278 [Leontes to Camillo, of Hermione] *say / My wife's a hobby-horse, deserves a name / As rank as any flax-wench that puts to / Before her troth-plight* ☞ plight (*v.*)

troth-plight (*adj.*) engaged, betrothed **H5** II.i.18 [Bardolph to Nym, of Hostess] *you were troth-plight to her;* **WT** V.iii.151

troublesome (*adj.*) **1** annoying, irritating, vexatious **KJ** IV.ii.19 [Pembroke to King John, of his second coronation] *in the last repeating troublesome, / Being urged at a time unseasonable*

2 full of affliction, crisis-torn **Cym** IV.iii.21 [Cymbeline to all] *The time is troublesome*

troublous (*adj.*) troubled, disturbed, confused **3H6** II.i.158 [Richard to Warwick] *in this troublous time what's to be done?;* **2H6** I.i.22; **R3** II.iii.9 ☞ giddy (*adj.*) 4

troudle-tail (*n.*) ☞ trundle-tail (*n.*)

trow (*v.*) **1** know, guess, imagine **AY** III.ii.173 [Celia to Rosalind] *Trow you who hath done this?;* **1H6** II.i.41; **LL** V.ii.279; **TS** I.ii.162

2 think, expect, believe **TS** I.i.4 [Petruchio to himself, of Hortensio] *I trow this is his house;* **2H6** II.iv.38; **3H6** V.i.85

3 believe, give credence to, accept as true **KL** I.iv.121 [Fool to Lear] *Learn more than thou trowest;* **H8** I.i.184

4 hope, trust, suppose **CE** III.i.54 [Antipholus of Ephesus to Luce] *You'll let us in, I trow* [F *hope*]

5 think, be sure **1H6** V.i.56 [Winchester alone] *Winchester will not submit, I trow;* **R2** II.i.218 ☞ DISCOURSE MARKERS, p.127

Troyan, Trojan (*n.*) **1** merry fellow, good companion **1H4** II.i.70 [Gadshill to Chamberlain] *there are other Troyans that thou dreamest not of;* **LL** V.ii.672

2 fellow, knave **H5** V.i.18 [Pistol to Fluellen] *Dost thou thirst, base Troyan;* **LL** V.ii.634

truant (*n.*) **1** negligent student, remiss practitioner, absentee **1H6** II.iv.7 [Suffolk to Richard] *I have been a truant in the law*

2 rogue, knave, rascal **MA** III.ii.17 [Don Pedro to Claudio, of Benedick] *Hang him, truant!*

truant (*v.*) play truant, be unfaithful **CE** III.ii.17 [Luciana to Antipholus of Syracuse, of Adriana] *'Tis double wrong to truant with your bed / And let her read it in thy looks at board*

truce, take come to terms, negotiate **KJ** III.i.17 [Constance to Salisbury] *With my vexed spirits I cannot take a truce;* **RJ** III.i.157; **Venus** 82

truckle-bed (*n.*) low-lying bed on castors, trundle-bed **RJ** II.i.39 [Mercutio as if to Romeo] *I'll to my truckle-bed;* **MW** IV.v.6

trudge (*v.*) go away, depart, leave **RJ** I.iii.35 [Nurse to Lady Capulet] *'Twas no need, I trow, / To bid me trudge;* **E3** II.ii.32

trudge about (*v.*) [of menials] walk about, tramp round **RJ** I.i.34 [Capulet to Servant] *trudge about / Through fair Verona*

true (*adj.*) **1** loyal, firm, faithful in allegiance **1H4** II.ii.27 [Falstaff, as if alone] *A plague upon it when thieves cannot be true one to another!;* **Cym** IV.iii.18; **1H6** III.i.165; **H8** II.ii.38; **R2** V.iii.97; **Tit** V.iii.101
2 constant, faithful in love **KJ** II.i.124 [Constance to Queen Eleanor] *My bed was ever to thy son as true / As thine was to thy husband;* **Ham** IV.v.122; **KL** I.i.107; **MV** II.vi.55; **Sonn** 105.9; **TC** IV.iv.57
3 honourable, virtuous, sincere **MND** II.ii.138 [Helena to Lysander] *I thought you lord of more true gentleness;* **AY** III.ii.208; **Luc** 748; **RJ** III.iii.124; **Tit** V.iii.106
4 honest, upright, law-abiding **1H4** II.ii.91 [Prince Hal to Poins] *The thieves have bound the true men;* **LL** I.i.299; **MA** III.iii.50; **MM** IV.ii.40; **Tim** IV.iii.459; **Venus** 724
5 reliable, trustworthy, dependable **WT** I.ii.309 [Leontes to Camillo] *if I / Had servants true about me;* **AC** II.ii.51,vi.99; **Sonn** 48.2; **TC** I.iii.238; **Tit** V.i.102
6 legitimate, rightful, honourable **JC** III.i.241 [Brutus aside to Cassius] *Caesar shall / Have all true rites and lawful ceremonies;* **KJ** III.iv.147; **TNK** V.i.159
7 inherent, authentic, genuine **RJ** II.iii.12 [Friar alone] *mickle is the powerful grace that lies / In plants, herbs, stones, and their true qualities*
8 true to father's likeness, authentic, genuine **KL** I.ii.8 [Edmund alone] *my shape as true / As honest madam's issue*
9 correct, accurate, exact **LL** V.ii.35 [Rosaline to Princess, of Berowne's verses] *The numbers true*
10 well-proportioned, clean-cut, good-looking **Sonn** 62.6 *no face so gracious as is mine, / No shape so true*
11 true to one's promise, faithful to one's undertaking **R2** II.i.192 [York to King Richard, of Bolingbroke] *And is not Harry true?* [i.e. in accepting exile]; **Cor** V.iii.191; **Cym** III.v.155
12 [unclear meaning] skilful, of high quality; honest, justified **KJ** IV.iii.84 [Hubert to Salisbury] *I would not have you ... tempt the danger of my true defence*

true (*adv.*) **1** steadily, reliably, surely **3H6** III.i.13 [George aside to Richard, of Edward] *how true he keeps the wind!*
2 legitimately, honourably, rightfully **KJ** II.i.130 [Constance to Queen Eleanor, of Arthur] *His father never was so true begot*
3 truthfully, honestly **LL** V.ii.364 [Rosaline to Princess] *Madam, speak true!*

true-divining (*adj.*) capable of foretelling the truth **Tit** II.iii.214 [Martius to Quintus] *To prove thou hast a true-divining heart*

true-fixed (*adj.*) firmly established, immovable, unwavering **JC** III.i.61 [Caesar to all, of the north star] *Of whose true-fixed and resting quality / There is no fellow in the firmament*

truepenny (*n.*) honest fellow, trusty chap **Ham** I.v.150 [Hamlet to the unseen Ghost] *Art thou there, truepenny?*

trull (*n.*) drab, trollop, whore **Tit** II.iii.191 [Tamora alone, of Lavinia] *Now will I ... let my spleenful sons this trull deflower;* **AC** III.vi.95; **1H6** II.ii.28; **3H6** I.iv.114

truly (*adv.*) **1** faithfully, loyally, constantly **Oth** I.i.44 [Iago to Roderigo] *all masters / Cannot be truly followed;* **Cym** III.v.114
2 fairly, justly, rightly **TNK** II.i.259 [Palamon to Arcite] *I deal but truly*

truly-falsely with faithful heart but incorrect speech **H5** V.ii.189 [King Henry to Katherine] *thy speaking of my tongue, and I thine, most truly-falsely, must needs be granted to be much at one*

trump (*n.*) **1** trumpet **Tim** I.ii.112 [Timon to all] *What means that trump?;* **1H6** I.iv.80; **Oth** III.iii.348; **TC** III.iii.210
2 trumpeter **1H6** IV.ii.1 [stage direction] *Enter Talbot, with trump and drum* ➤ STAGE DIRECTIONS, p.417

trumpery (*n.*) fancy garments, showy rubbish, worthless finery **WT** IV.iv.594 [Autolycus to himself] *I have sold all my trumpery;* **Tem** IV.i.186

trumpet (*n.*) **1** trumpeter; herald, announcer **3H6** V.i.16 [Edward to the trumpeter] *Go, trumpet, to the walls and sound a parle;* **Ham** I.i.151; **H5** IV.ii.59; **1H6** IV.iii.1; **KJ** I.i.198; **TC** IV.v.6 ➤ STAGE DIRECTIONS, p.417
2 trumpet-call **Oth** II.i.174 [Iago to all, of Othello] *I know his trumpet*

truncheon (*n.*) **1** military baton, staff of office **MM** II.ii.61 [Isabella to Angelo] *The marshal's truncheon;* **Ham** I.ii.204; **Oth** II.i.264; **TC** V.iii.53
2 thick club, stout cudgel **2H6** IV.x.47 [Iden to Cade] *Thy leg a stick compared with this truncheon* [i.e. his own leg]

truncheon (*v.*) cudgel, beat with a truncheon **2H4** II.iv.138 [Doll to Pistol] *An captains were of my mind, they would truncheon you out*

truncheoner (*n.*) club-wielder, cudgel-carrier **H8** V.iv.51 [Man to Porter] *I might see from far some forty truncheoners*

trundle-tail (*n.*) dog with a trailing tail, curly-tailed dog **KL** III.vi.69 [Edgar as Poor Tom to all] *bobtail tike, or trundle-tail* [Q; F *Troudle-taile*]

trunk (*n.*) body, form, frame **KL** I.i.177 [Lear to Kent] *If ... / Thy banished trunk be found in our dominions;* **Tem** I.ii.86; **Tim** IV.iii.230; **WT** I.ii.435

trunk (*adj.*) full, puffed, wide **TS** IV.iii.137 [Tailor reading, of a gown] *With a trunk sleeve*

truss up (*v.*) hang, string up **TNK** III.iv.17 [Gaoler's Daughter alone] *Now my father ... is trussed up in a trice / Tomorrow morning*

trust (*n.*) trustee, guardian, custodian **1H6** IV.iv.20 [Lucy to Somerset, of Talbot] *You, ... the trust of England's honour, / Keep off aloof*

trust (*v.*) **1** believe, accept, give credence to **TS** IV.iv.67 [Tranio to Lucentio, of the man he has seen] *If he be credulous and trust my tale*
2 depend, be sure, rely **Cor** V.iii.124 [Volumnia to Coriolanus] *Trust to't* [i.e. depend upon it]

trust me believe me **MW** IV.ii.189 [Mistress Page to Mistress Ford, of Ford and Falstaff] *Trust me, he beat him most pitifully;* **MW** II.i.30, III.i.103, ii.46; **TG** I.i.44; **Tit** I.i.264 ➤ DISCOURSE MARKERS, p.127

truster (*n.*) **1** creditor, believer **Ham** I.ii.172 [Hamlet to Horatio] *Nor shall you do my ear that violence / To make it truster of your own report / Against yourself*
2 creditor, lender **Tim** IV.i.10 [Timon alone, of bankrupts] *out with your knives / And cut your trusters' throats*

trusting (*n.*) acceptance, belief [in] **AW** IV.iv.23 [Helena to Widow] *When saucy trusting of the cozened thoughts / Defiles the pitchy night*

trustless treacherous, untrustworthy, unreliable **Luc** 2 [of Tarquin] *Borne by the trustless wings of false desire*

truth (*n.*) **1** loyalty, allegiance, faithfulness **Cym** III.ii.7 [Pisanio alone, of Innogen] *She's punished for her truth;* **Cor** V.vi.22; **3H6** IV.viii.29; **H8** II.iv.98; **KJ** I.i.169; **TC** IV.iv.106
2 virtue, integrity, uprightness **MM** III.i.166 [disguised Duke aside to Claudio, of Isabella] *having the truth of honour in her*
3 abstract principle, general rule **TC** II.ii.190 [Hector to all] *Hector's opinion / Is this in way of truth*

truth, for truly, honestly **3H6** III.iii.120 [Lewis to Warwick, of Edward] *Tell me for truth the measure of his love / Unto our sister*

try (*n.*) test, trial **Tim** V.i.9 [Poet to Painter, of Timon] *Then this breaking of his has been but a try for his friends?*

try (*v.*) **1** prove, ascertain, find out **Cym** I.vi.21 [Queen to Cornelius, of his drugs] *To try the vigour of them;* **AW** I.iii.242; **Ham** II.ii.159; **1H6** I.ii.89; **JC** III.i.292; **RJ** IV.i.3
2 put to the test, test the goodness [of] **Tim** III.vi.3 [Lucius to Lucullus, of Timon] *I think this honourable lord did but try us this other day;* **AC** III.xii.26; **E3** II.i.274; **H8** V.iii.146; **MM** II.iii.22; **R2** I.i.184

3 contest, decide, fight out **AY** I.ii.191 [Duke to Orlando and Charles] *You shall try but one fall;* **Ham** IV.iv.63; **2H4** II.ii.43; **2H6** II.iii.53; **Mac** V.vi.71; **WT** V.ii.131

4 experience, undergo, endure **TNK** III.ii.25 [Gaoler's Daughter alone] *Should I try death by dozens*

5 judge the case **AY** IV.i.185 [Rosalind as Ganymede to Orlando] *Time is the old justice ... and let Time try*

6 try for, aim at, aspire to **AC** II.vi.34 [Caesar to Pompey] *what may follow, / To try a larger fortune;* **PassP** XI.3

7 refine, purify **MV** II.ix.63 [Arragon, reading the portrait's schedule] *The fire seven times tried this*

8 [nautical] adjust sails so that the ship's bow is into the wind, lie to **Tem** I.i.35 [Boatswain to Mariners] *Bring her to try with main-course*

9 ➤ conclusions, try

tub (*n.*) sweating-tub [for curing venereal disease] **Tim** IV.iii.87 [Timon to Timandra, of her clients] *Season the slaves / For tubs and baths;* **MM** III.ii.54 ➤ powdering-tub (*n.*)

tub-fast (*n.*) fasting while being treated for venereal disease in a sweating-tub **Tim** IV.iii.88 [Timon to Timandra] *bring down rose-cheeked youth / To the tub-fast and the diet* [F *Fubfast*]

tuck (*n.*) rapier, long slender sword **TN** III.iv.220 [Sir Toby to Viola as Cesario] *Dismount thy tuck;* **1H4** II.iv.243 ➤ **WEAPONS**, p.491

tucket (*n.*) personal trumpet call **AW** III.v.1 [stage direction] *A tucket afar off* ➤ **STAGE DIRECTIONS**, p.417

tuft (*n.*) **1** clump, small group, thicket **R2** II.iii.53 [Percy to Northumberland] *There stands the castle by yon tuft of trees;* **AY** III.v.75; **WT** II.i.34

2 bunch, cluster **MW** V.v.70 [Mistress Quickly as Queen of Fairies to all] *Honi soit qui mal y pense write / In emerald tufts*

tug (*v.*) contend, vie, strive in opposition **3H6** II.v.11 [King alone, of the sea and wind] *Both tugging to be victors;* **2H6** III.ii.173; **WT** IV.iv.494

tugged (*adj.*) battered, mauled, knocked about **Mac** III.i.111 [First Murderer to Macbeth, of himself] *tugged with fortune*

tuition (*n.*) care, safe-keeping, protection **MA** I.i.260 [Claudio to Benedick, completing 'I commit you'] *To the tuition of God*

tumble (*v.*) **1** have sexual intercourse with **AC** I.iv.17 [Caesar to Lepidus, of Antony] *Let's grant it is not / Amiss to tumble on the bed of Ptolemy;* **Ham** IV.v.63; **WT** IV.iv.12

2 perform acrobatic feats **TNK** III.v.36 [Schoolmaster to the man dressed as a baboon] *be sure / You tumble with audacity and manhood*

3 [bowling] overshoot, move too far **Cor** V.ii.21 [Menenius to First Watch] *I have tumbled past the throw*

tumbler (*n.*) acrobat **LL** III.i.185 [Berowne alone, of Cupid] *And I to ... wear his colours like a tumbler's hoop*

tumbling-trick (*n.*) acrobatic feat **TS** Induction.ii.136 [Sly to Lord] *Is not a comonty a Christmas gambold or a tumbling trick?*

tun (*n.*) **1** barrel, large cask **1H4** II.iv.436 [Prince Hal (as King) to Falstaff (as Hal), of Falstaff] *a tun of man is thy companion;* **Cor** IV.v.102; **MW** II.i.60

2 chest, box, case **H5** I.ii.256 [Ambassador to King Henry, of the Dauphin] *He therefore sends you, meeter for your spirit, / This tun of treasure*

tun-dish (*n.*) [brewing] type of funnel fitting into the bung-hole of a cask [tun] **MM** III.ii.162 [Lucio to disguised Duke, of why Claudio is to die] *For filling a bottle with a tun-dish* [i.e. for having had sexual intercourse]

tune (*n.*) **1** state of mind, mood **KJ** III.iii.26 [King John to Hubert] *I had a thing to say, / But I will fit it with some better tune;* **Cor** II.iii.84; **KL** IV.iii.39; **MA** III.iv.37; **TC** III.iii.300; **TG** I.ii.89

2 sound, tone, voice **Cym** V.v.238 [Cymbeline to all] *The tune of Innogen!;* **Sonn** 141.5

3 fashionable speech, jargon **Ham** V.ii.186 [Hamlet to Horatio] *the tune of the time;* **MM** III.ii.46

tune, in a in unison, in harmony **AY** V.iii.13 [Second Page, to all] *both in a tune, like two gypsies on a horse*

tune (*v.*) **1** play **TG** IV.ii.25 [Thurio to the Musicians] *Let's tune, and to it lustily awhile;* **LL** IV.iii.166; **TG** III.ii.85

2 sing, utter, sound out **Luc** 1465 [Lucrece as if to Hecuba] *I'll tune thy woes with my lamenting tongue;* **Luc** 1107; **TG** IV.iv.6; **Venus** 74

tuneable (*adj.*) tuneful, musical, melodious **MND** IV.i.123 [Theseus to Hippolyta, of his hounds] *A cry more tuneable / Was never hallooed to;* **MND** I.i.184

tuned (*adj.*) harmonious, melodious, musical **AC** V.ii.84 [Cleopatra to Dolabella, of Antony] *his voice was propertied / As all the tuned spheres*

tup (*v.*) copulate with, screw **Oth** I.i.90 [Iago to Brabantio] *an old black ram / Is tupping your white ewe*

turfy (*adj.*) turf-covered, grassy **Tem** IV.i.62 [Iris to Ceres] *Thy turfy mountains*

Turk (*n.*) infidel, heathen, pagan **Oth** II.i.113 [Iago to Emilia and Desdemona, of his remarks] *it is true, or else I am a Turk* ➤ turn Turk

Turlygod (*n.*) [unclear meaning] nonsense name used by Edgar pretending to be mad **KL** II.iii.20 [Edgar alone, as a beggar] *Poor Turlygod!*

turmoiled (*adj.*) harassed, worried, troubled **2H6** IV.x.15 [Iden to himself] *who would live turmoiled in the court, / And may enjoy such quiet walks as these?*

turn (*n.*) **1** need, requirement, purpose [especially in the phrase 'serve one's turn' = meet one's need] **TC** III.i.72 [Pandarus to Helen, of her witty response] *that shall not serve your turn;* **TS** III.ii.131 [Tranio to Lucentio, of a man to stand as Vincentio] *It skills not much, we'll fit him to our turn;* **AC** II.v.58; **Ham** V.iii.181; **LL** I.i.285; **Tim** II.ii.20; **TS** IV.ii.62

2 act, action, deed **Oth** V.ii.206 [Gratiano to dead Desdemona, of her father] *Did he live now, / This sight would make him do a desperate turn*

3 change, inconstancy, vicissitude **Cor** IV.iv.12 [Coriolanus alone] *O world, thy slippery turns!*

4 winding path, twisting street, sidestreet **TNK** I.ii.28 [Arcite to Palamon] *The cranks and turns of Thebes*

5 [unclear meaning] turning-point; trick, game; occasion, proper time **Tim** V.i.45 [Timon to himself, of the Painter and the Poet] *I'll meet you at the turn*

turn (*v.*) **1** change, transform, alter **1H6** V.iv.59 [Pucelle to all] *Will nothing turn your unrelenting hearts?;* **1H6** III.iii.85; **2H6** II.i.175; **LL** IV.iii.260; **MA** III.ii.119; **MV** III.ii.246

2 become, transform, change [into] **RJ** II.iii.17 [Friar alone] *Virtue itself turns vice;* **AY** III.iii.24

3 adapt, alter, modify **AY** II.v.3 [Amiens, singing] *Who loves to lie with me, / And turn his merry note / Unto the sweet bird's throat;* **Luc** 1539

4 turn away, face the other way **TNK** V.i.31 [Palamon to Arcite] *Before I turn, let me embrace thee*

5 return, come back **AY** III.i.7 [Duke Frederick to Oliver] *turn thou no more / To seek a living in our territory;* **Oth** IV.i.254; **R3** IV.iv.185; **Tit** V.ii.141

6 send, drive, dispatch **R2** IV.i.39 [Fitzwater to Aumerle] *I will turn thy falsehood to thy heart;* **AY** III.i.18; **Cor** III.i.96; **JC** III.i.34

7 direct, point, refer **MW** III.iv.2 [Fenton to Anne, of her father] *no more turn me to him;* **JC** I.ii.56

8 spin round, whirl about, go round and round **KL** IV.vi.23 [Edgar to Gloucester] *I'll look no more, / Lest my brain turn;* **CE** III.ii.154; **TNK** I.ii.11

9 become sour, curdle **Tim** III.i.55 [Flaminius alone] *Has friendship such a faint and milky heart / It turns in less than two nights?*

10 bring, put **TG** IV.iv.59 [Proteus to disguised Julia, of Launce] *A slave that still an end turns me to shame!;* **MW** V.v.86

turn away (*v.*) send away, dismiss from service **MW** I.iii.4 [Falstaff to Host] *I must turn away some of my followers*; **MW** III.iii.28; **TN** I.v.16

turn back (*v.*) **1** redound, lead, come back **WT** IV.iv.829 [Autolycus alone, of his new opportunity] *who knows how that may turn back to my advancement?*
    2 turn tail, retreat, withdraw **3H6** I.iv.4 [York alone] *all my followers to the eager foe / Turn back and fly*; **3H6** II.i.184
    3 go back, return alive **JC** III.i.21 [Cassius to Brutus, of their plan] *If this be known, / Cassius or Caesar never shall turn back, / For I will slay myself*

turn head turn and face the enemy, make a bold front **H5** II.iv.69 [Dauphin to French King] *Turn head, and stop pursuit*

turn off (*v.*) **1** reject, repudiate, send away **AC** III.vi.94 [Maecenas to Octavia] *Only th'adulterous Antony ... turns you off*
    2 perform with skill, accomplish **LL** V.ii.507 [Costard to Berowne, of the pageant] *We will turn it finely off*

turn on the toe pirouette **LL** V.ii.114 [Boyet to Princess, of the King's party] *The fourth turned on the toe, and down he fell*

turn Turk change completely, become a renegade [as if in religion, from Christian to infidel] **Ham** III.ii.285 [Hamlet to Horatio] *if the rest of my fortunes turn Turk with me*; **MA** III.iv.50

turned-forth (*n.*) castaway, reject, discard **Tit** V.iii.108 [Lucius to all, of Rome] *I am the turned-forth ... / That have preserved her welfare in my blood*

turning (*adj.*) facing the other way, retreating **E3** III.iv.27 [Artois to King Edward, of Prince Edward] *narrowly beset / With turning Frenchmen*

turpitude (*n.*) wickedess, vileness, depravity **TC** V.ii.114 [Cressida to herself] *Minds swayed by eyes are full of turpitude*

turtle (*n.*) turtle-dove, lover **WT** IV.iv.154 [Florizel to Perdita] *so turtles pair, / That never mean to part*; **LL** IV.iii.210; **MW** II.i.75, III.iii.39; **TC** III.ii.176; **TS** II.i.207

tush (*n.*) tusk **Venus** 617 [Venus to Adonis, of a boar] *Whose tushes never sheathed he whetteth still*; **Venus** 624

tush (*int.*) ☞ **EXCLAMATIONS**, p.218

twain (*n.*) two **Ham** III.iv.157 [Gertrude to Hamlet] *thou hast cleft my heart in twain*; **Ham** II.ii.238; **Tem** IV.i.104 ☞ **NUMBERS**, p.299

twain (*adj.*) separated, not united, estranged **RJ** III.v.241 [Juliet alone, of Nurse] *Thou and my bosom henceforth shall be twain*; **Sonn** 36.1

twain (*adv.*) of separate minds, at variance **TC** III.i.99 [Pandarus to Helen, of Paris and Cressida] *they two are twain*

twangling (*adj.*) twanging, resounding, jingling **Tem** III.ii.138 [Caliban to Stephano] *a thousand twangling instruments / Will hum about mine ears*; **TS** II.i.158

tway (*n.*) two **H5** III.ii.115 [Jamy to Fluellen and Macmorris] *I wad full fain hear some question 'tween you tway*

twenty, and [ballad catch phrase, used as an intensifier] and many more **MW** II.i.182 [Shallow to Page] *Good even and twenty*; **AY** IV.i.108; **TN** II.iii.49; **TNK** V.ii.107 ☞ **NUMBERS**, p.299

twig (*n.*) stratagem for entrapping **AW** III.vi.100 [First Lord to all] *I must go look my twigs* ☞ lime-twig (*n.*)

twiggen-bottle (*n.*) bottle cased in wickerwork **Oth** II.iii.143 [Cassio to Montano, of Roderigo] *I'll beat the knave into a twiggen-bottle* [F; Q *wicker*]

twilled (*adj.*) [unclear meaning] tangled, woven with sticks **Tem** IV.i.64 [Iris to Ceres] *Thy banks with pioned and twilled brims*

twink (*n.*) twinkling, winking of an eye **Tem** IV.i.43 [Prospero to Ariel, of the latter's next action] *with a twink*; **TS** II.i.303

twinkle (*v.*) reflect, send, return **1H6** V.iii.63 [Suffolk to himself, of the sun] *Twinkling another counterfeited beam*

twinned (*adj.*) indistinguishable, identical, closely linked **Cym** I.vii.35 [Iachimo to Innogen] *the twinned stones / Upon the numbered beach*; **Tim** I.ii.67

twire (*v.*) twinkle, peep out, shine out **Sonn** 28.12 *When sparkling stars twire not thou gild'st th'even*

twist (*n.*) plaited thread, twined fibre **Cor** V.vi.96 [Aufidius to Lords, of Coriolanus] *Breaking his oath and resolution like / A twist of rotten silk*

twit (*v.*) taunt, upbraid, reproach **TG** IV.ii.8 [Proteus alone, of Silvia] *She twits me with my falsehood to my friend*; **2H6** III.i.178

'twixt (*prep.*) between **Ham** IV.v.205 [Claudius to Laertes, of Laertes' friends] *they shall hear and judge 'twixt you and me*

two or three several **Per** II.iv.17 [stage direction] *Enter two or three Lords* ☞ **NUMBERS**, p.299

type (*n.*) **1** mark, sign, indication **H8** I.iii.31 [Lovell to Lord Chamberlain, of the fashion of French-influenced Englishmen] *tall stockings, / Short blistered breeches, and those types of travel*
    2 emblem, symbol, insignia **E3** III.iii.175 [King Edward to Prince Edward] *[I] dub thee with the type of chivalry*; **R3** IV.iv.245
    3 title, stamp, distinguishing mark **3H6** I.iv.121 [York to Queen] *Thy father bears the type of King of Naples*; **Luc** 1050

tyrannically (*adv.*) outrageously, vehemently, violently **Ham** II.ii.339 [Rosencrantz to Hamlet, of the child players] *that ... are most tyrannically clapped for't*

tyrannous (*adj.*) cruel, pitiless, oppressive **R3** IV.iii.1 [Tyrrel alone, of killing the Princes] *The tyrannous and bloody act is done*; **Ham** II.ii.458; **KL** III.iv.144; **RJ** I.i.170

tyranny (*n.*) cruelty, barbarity, unmerciful violence **1H6** II.iii.39 [Countess to Talbot] *I will chain these legs and arms of thine / That hast by tyranny ... / Wasted our country*; **Cor** V.iii.43; **2H4** IV.v.86; **1H6** IV.ii.17; **MV** IV.i.13; **R3** III.vii.9

tyrant (*n.*) **1** pitiless ruffian, cruel villain **R3** I.iii.184 [Rivers to all, of Rutland's murder] *Tyrants themselves wept when it was reported*; **Cym** I.ii.15; **2H4** I.Induction.14; **MA** I.i.158; **RJ** III.i.75
    2 usurper **3H6** III.iii.206 [Warwick to Queen, of Edward] *I'll ... force the tyrant from his seat by war*; **3H6** III.iii.69, IV.iv.29

tyrant (*adj.*) cruel, violent, rapacious **Phoen** 10 *From this session interdict / Every fowl of tyrant wing* [i.e. bird of prey]

'ud (*n.*) shortened form of 'God' ☛ **SWEARING**, p.435

umber (*n.*) brown-coloured earth **AY** I.iii.110 [Celia to Rosalind] *I'll … with a kind of umber smirch my face*

umbered (*adj.*) shadowed, shadowy **H5** IV.Chorus.9 [Chorus] *Fire answers fire, and through their paly flames / Each battle sees the other's umbered face*

umbrage (*n.*) shadow, pale semblance **Ham** V.ii.119 [Hamlet to Osrick, of Laertes] *who else would trace him, his umbrage, nothing more*

umpire (*n.*) arbitrator, mediator, adjudicator **TNK** I.iii.45 [Hippolyta to Emilia] *Theseus cannot be umpire to himself;* **1H6** II.v.29; **MW** I.i.129; **RJ** IV.i.63

unable (*adj.*) **1** weak, feeble, impotent **TS** V.ii.168 [Katherina to Widow and Bianca] *come, you froward and unable worms;* **1H6** IV.v.4
2 inadequate, insufficient, incompetent **KL** I.i.60 [Gonerill to Lear] *A love that makes breath poor and speech unable*

unaccommodated (*adj.*) not possessed of clothes, unprovided with comforts **KL** III.iv.103 [Lear to Edgar as Poor Tom] *Unaccommodated man is no more but such a poor, bare, forked animal as thou art*

unaccustomed (*adj.*) unusual, strange, unfamiliar **RJ** III.v.67 [Juliet to herself, of Lady Capulet] *What unaccustomed cause procures her hither?;* **1H6** III.i.93; **JC** II.i.199; **RJ** V.i.4

unacquainted unfamiliar, strange, unusual **KJ** V.ii.32 [Salisbury to Lewis the Dauphin, of the treaty with the French] *To … follow unacquainted colours here;* **KJ** III.iv.166

unactive (*adj.*) inactive, slothful, sluggish **Cor** I.i.97 [Menenius to Citizens, of the belly] *it did remain / I'th' midst o'th' body, idle and unactive*

unadvised (*adj.*) rash, foolhardy, thoughtless, unconsidered **RJ** II.ii.118 [Juliet to Romeo, of their love] *It is too rash, too unadvised, too sudden;* **E3** IV.iv.112; **KJ** II.i.191, V.ii.132; **Luc** 1488; **Tit** II.i.38

unadvised (*adv.*) **1** accidentally, inadvertently, thoughtlessly **TG** IV.iv.119 [disguised Julia to Silvia] *I have unadvised / Delivered you a paper*
2 unadvisedly, without proper deliberation **KJ** II.i.45 [Constance to King Philip] *Stay for an answer to your embassy, / Lest unadvised you stain your swords with blood*

unagreeable (*adj.*) disagreeable, unsuited, uncongenial **Tim** II.ii.45 [Flavius to Caphis and other Servants, of repaying money] *The time is unagreeable to this business*

unaneled (*adj.*) unanointed by a priest, without extreme unction **Ham** I.v.77 [Ghost to Hamlet] *Cut off even in the blossoms of my sin, / Unhouseled, disappointed, unaneled*

unapt (*adj.*) **1** not inclined, unwilling, not prone **Cor** V.i.53 [Menenius to Sicinius] *We … are unapt / To give or to forgive;* **1H4** I.iii.2; **Venus** 34
2 unfit, not suited **1H6** V.iii.133 [Reignier to Suffolk] *I am a soldier and unapt to weep / Or to exclaim on fortune's fickleness;* **Luc** 695; **TS** V.ii.165

unaptness (*n.*) inaptitude, unreadiness, unwillingness **Tim** II.ii.136 [Timon to Flavius] *that unaptness [was] made your minister / Thus to excuse yourself*

unarm (*v.*) disarm, remove armour **TC** V.iii.3 [Andromache to Hector] *Unarm, unarm, and do not fight today;* **AC** IV.xiv.35; **TC** I.i.1, ii.274, III.i.147, V.iii.25, 35

unattainted (*adj.*) dispassionate, detached, unprejudiced **RJ** I.ii.84 [Benvolio to Romeo, of Rosaline] *with unattainted eye / Compare her face with some that I shall show*

unattempted (*adj.*) untempted, unseduced, unapproached **KJ** II.i.591 [Bastard alone, of commodity] *for my hand, as unattempted yet, / Like a poor beggar raileth on the rich*

unauspicious *(adj.)* inauspicious, discouraging, unpromising **TN** V.i.111 [Orsino to Olivia] *You uncivil lady, / To whose ingrate and unauspicious altars / My soul the faithfull'st offerings have breathed out*

unavoided *(adj.)* unavoidable, inevitable, inescapable **R3** IV.iv.218 [King Richard to Queen Elizabeth] *All unavoided is the doom of destiny;* **1H6** IV.v.8; **R2** II.i.268

unawares *(adv.)* without warning, by surprise, unexpectedly **3H6** IV.viii.63 [Richard to all, of Warwick] *take the great-grown traitor unawares;* **1H6** III.ii.39 ➤ **unwares** *(adv.)*

unawares, at unexpectedly **3H6** IV.ii.23 [Warwick to George] *we … / At unawares may beat down Edward's guard;* **3H6** IV.iv.9; **TC** III.ii.36

unbacked *(adj.)* unbroken, untrained, undisciplined **Tem** IV.i.176 [Ariel to Prospero, of Stephano, Trinculo, and Caliban] *like unbacked colts, they pricked their ears;* **Venus** 320

unbanded without a coloured hat-band **AY** III.ii.364 [Rosalind to Orlando] *your bonnet [should be] unbanded*

unbarbed *(adj.)* uncovered, unprotected, bare **Cor** III.ii.99 [Coriolanus to Volumnia] *Must I go show them my unbarbed sconce?* [i.e. as a sign of respect]

unbated *(adj.)* **1** unabated, undiminished, fresh **MV** II.vi.11 [Gratiano to Salerio] *Where is the horse that doth untread again / His tedious measures with the unbated fire / That he did pace them first?*
2 not blunted, without a button on the point **Ham** V.ii.311 [Laertes to Hamlet, of his sword] *Unbated and envenomed;* **Ham** IV.vii.137

unbend *(v.)* slacken, weaken, undermine **Mac** II.ii.45 [Lady Macbeth to Macbeth] *You do unbend your noble strength, to think / So brain-sickly of things*

unbent *(adj.)* **1** unfrowning, not wrinkled; submissive **Luc** 1509 [of a painting of Sinon] *A brow unbent that seemed to welcome woe*
2 [archery] not bent, not prepared to release an arrow **Cym** III.iv.110 [Innogen to Pisanio] *Why hast thou gone so far, / To be unbent when thou hast ta'en thy stand*

unbewailed *(adj.)* unbemoaned, without lamentation **AC** III.vi.85 [Caesar to Octavia] *let determined things to destiny / Hold unbewailed their way*

unbid *(adj.)* unbidden, unwelcome, uninvited **3H6** V.i.18 [Warwick to all, of Edward's arrival] *O, unbid spite!*

unbitted *(adj.)* unbridled, unrestrained, compelling **Oth** I.iii.327 [Iago to Roderigo] *we have reason to cool … our unbitted lusts*

unbless *(v.)* deprive of a blessing, deny happiness to **Sonn** 3.4 *Thou dost beguile the world, unbless some mother*

unblest *(adj.)* out of favour, disapproved of **TNK** I.ii.53 [Palamon to Arcite] *Or let me know / Why mine own barber is unblest*

unblown *(adj.)* unopened, not yet blooming, immature **R3** IV.iv.10 [Queen Elizabeth as if to the Princes] *My unblown flowers* [Q; F *unblow'd*] ➤ **blown** *(adj.)* 1

unbodied *(adj.)* abstract, conceptual, formless **TC** I.iii.16 [Agamemnon to all, of their war efforts] *not answering the aim / And that unbodied figure of the thought / That gave't surmised shape*

unbolt *(v.)* unfold, explain, open out **Tim** I.i.53 [Poet to Painter] *I will unbolt to you*

unbolted *(adj.)* unsifted, unkneaded, lumpy **KL** II.ii.63 [disguised Kent to Cornwall, of Oswald] *I will tread this unbolted villain into mortar*

unbonneted *(adv.)* **1** bare-headed; recklessly **KL** III.i.14 [Gentleman to disguised Kent, of Lear] *unbonneted he runs*
2 bare-headed; with all modesty **Oth** I.ii.23 [Othello to Iago] *my demerits / May speak, unbonneted, to as proud a fortune / As this that I have reached*

unbookish *(adj.)* ignorant, ill-educated, unlearned **Oth** IV.i.101 [Iago to himself, of Othello] *his unbookish jealousy must construe / Poor Cassio's smiles … / Quite in the wrong*

unborn *(adj.)* not existing, without being **Cor** III.i.129 [Coriolanus to Brutus, of the Citizens' accusations] *All cause unborn* [i.e. without any justification]

unbosom *(v.)* disclose, reveal, express from the heart **LL** V.ii.141 [Princess to Katharine, of the King's party] *Their several counsels they unbosom shall / To loves mistook*

unbounded *(adj.)* unrestrained, uninhibited, uncontrollable **TNK** I.ii.63 [Palamon to Arcite, of Creon] *A most unbounded tyrant*

unbraced *(adj.)* unfastened, not laced up, loose **Ham** II.i.78 [Ophelia to Polonius, of Hamlet] *his doublet all unbraced;* **JC** I.iii.48, II.i.262

unbraided *(adj.)* untarnished, not shop-soiled, new **WT** IV.iv.205 [Clown to Servant, of Autolycus] *Has he any unbraided wares?*

unbreathed *(adj.)* unpractised, inexperienced, inexpert **MND** V.i.74 [Philostrate to Theseus, of the rustics] *now have toiled their unbreathed memories / With this same play against your nuptial*

unbreeched *(adj.)* not dressed in breeches **WT** I.ii.155 [Leontes to Hermione] *methoughts I did recoil / Twenty-three years, and saw myself unbreeched, / In my green velvet coat*

unbruised *(adj.)* **1** unmarked, uncrushed, undamaged **KJ** II.i.254 [King Philip to Hubert, of a French retreat] *With unhacked swords and helmets all unbruised;* **MA** V.iv.109; **TC** Prologue.14
2 undamaged by the world **RJ** II.iii.33 [Friar to Romeo] *where unbruised youth with unstuffed brain / Doth couch his limbs, there golden sleep doth reign*

unbuild *(v.)* pull down, demolish, dismantle **Cor** III.i.197 [First Senator to Sicinius] *To unbuild the city and to lay all flat*

unburden, unburthen *(v.)* reveal, disclose; or: unload **MV** I.i.133 [Bassanio to Antonio] *from your love I have a warranty / To unburthen all my plots and purposes;* **2H6** III.i.156

uncandied *(adj.)* thawed, dissolved, melted **TNK** I.i.107 [Third Queen to Emilia] *by hot grief uncandied* ➤ **discandy** *(v.)*

uncapable *(adj.)* incapable, unable [to do something] **MV** IV.i.5 [Duke to Antonio, of Shylock] *an inhuman wretch, / Uncapable of pity;* **Oth** IV.ii.228

uncase *(v.)* take off outer garments, undress **TS** I.i.204 [Lucentio to Tranio, of changing identities] *Uncase thee, take my coloured hat and cloak;* **LL** V.ii.698

uncertainty *(n.)* mystery, puzzle, enigma **CE** II.ii.194 [Antipholus of Syracuse to himself, of Adriana's approach] *Until I know this sure uncertainty, / I'll entertain the offered fallacy*

uncharge *(v.)* be unable to accuse, acquit of blame **Ham** IV.vii.66 [Claudius to Laertes, of Hamlet] *no wind of blame shall breathe, / But even his mother shall uncharge the practice / And call it accident*

uncharged *(adj.)* unattacked, unassailed **Tim** V.iv.55 [Alcibiades to Senators] *Descend, and open your uncharged ports*

unchary *(adv.)* carelessly, incautiously, unguardedly **TN** III.iv.198 [Olivia to Viola as Cesario] *I have said too much unto a heart of stone, / And laid mine honour too unchary on't*

unchecked *(adj.)* **1** uncontradicted, undisputed **MV** III.i.2 [Salerio to Solanio, of the news] *it lives … unchecked that Antonio hath a ship of rich lading wracked*
2 unlimited, boundless opportunities for **Tim** IV.iii.446 [Timon to Bandits] *The laws … in their rough power / Has unchecked theft*

uncheerful *(adj.)* cheerless, joyless, desolate **Luc** 1024 [Lucrece to herself] *In vain I rail … / At Time, at Tarquin, and uncheerful Night*

unchild *(v.)* make childless, deprive of children **Cor** V.vi.153 [Aufidius to all, of Coriolanus] *in this city he / Hath widowed and unchilded many a one*

uncivil *(adj.)* uncivilized, barbarous, unrefined E3 II.ii.58 [King Edward to Lodowick] *we think it an uncivil thing / To trouble heaven with such harsh resounds;* E3 I.ii.12; 2H6 III.ii.310; R2 III.iii.102; TG V.iv.17; TN IV.i.52

unclasp *(v.)* reveal, display, divulge TN I.iv.13 [Orsino to Viola as Cesario] *I have unclasped / To thee the book even of my secret soul;* 1H4 I.iii.186; MA I.i.302; TC IV.v.60; TNK V.i.172; WT III.ii.165

unclean *(adj.)* impure, corrupted, bad AW I.i.40 [Countess to Lafew] *where an unclean mind carries virtuous qualities*

uncleanly *(adj.)* **1** unclean, dirty, filthy AY III.ii.47 [Corin to Touchstone, of kissing hands] *that courtesy would be uncleanly if courtiers were shepherds;* AY III.ii.65; Oth III.iii.138
  2 offensive, foul KJ IV.iii.112 [Salisbury to all] *all you whose souls abhor / Th'uncleanly savours of a slaughter-house;* KJ IV.i.7

unclew *(v.)* unwind, undo; ruin Tim I.i.172 [Timon to Jeweller, of the jewel] *If I should pay you for't as 'tis extolled, / It would unclew me quite*

uncoined *(adj.)* unalloyed, genuine; also: not yet in circulation [among women] H5 V.ii.152 [King Henry to Katherine] *take a fellow of plain and uncoined constancy*

uncolted *(adj.)* deprived of a horse 1H4 II.ii.38 [Prince Hal to Falstaff] *thou art not colted, thou art uncolted* [pun on 'colt' = trick]

uncomeliness *(n.)* unseemly behaviour, improper conduct MW II.i.55 [Mistress Ford to Mistress Page, of Falstaff] *he ... gave such orderly and well-behaved reproof to all uncomeliness*

uncomfortable *(adj.)* **1** comfortless, inconsolable, heartbreaking RJ IV.v.60 [Capulet to himself, of Juliet's supposed death] *Uncomfortable time, why camest thou now / To murder, murder our solemnity!*
  2 comfortless, disquieting, uneasy E3 IV.v.18 [King John to Charles] *the under earth is as a grave, / Dark, deadly, silent, and uncomfortable*

uncomprehensive *(adj.)* fathomless, boundless, immeasurable TC III.iii.198 [Ulysses to Achilles] *The providence that's in a watchful state ... / Finds bottom in th'uncomprehensive deeps*

unconfinable *(adj.)* limitless, boundless, infinite MW II.ii.20 [Falstaff to Pistol] *thou unconfinable baseness*

unconfirmed *(adj.)* inexperienced, uninstructed, ignorant MA III.iii.114 [Borachio to Conrade] *thou art unconfirmed;* LL IV.ii.18

unconsidered *(adj.)* ignominious, unrespected, disregarded TNK I.ii.31 [Arcite to Palamon] *Perceive you none that do arouse your pity / But th'unconsidered soldier?*

unconstant *(adj.)* changeable, fickle, unpredictable 3H6 V.i.102 [George to Richard] *I will henceforth be no more unconstant;* KJ III.i.243; KL I.i.299

uncontemned *(adj.)* unscorned, undespised H8 III.ii.10 [Suffolk to all, of Wolsey] *Which of the peers / Have uncontemned gone by him*

uncontrolled *(adj.)* not subject to control, never dominated Venus 104 [Venus to Adonis, of Mars] *Over my altars hath he hung ... his uncontrolled crest*

uncounted *(adj.)* uncountable, innumerable 2H4 I.Induction.18 [Rumour alone, of the public] *the blunt monster with uncounted heads*

uncouple *(v.)* release pairs of hunting dogs for the chase Venus 674 [Venus to Adonis] *Uncouple at the timorous flying hare;* E3 I.ii.91; MND IV.i.106; Tit II.ii.3

uncourteous *(adj.)* discourteous, unfriendly TN V.i.359 [Fabian to Olivia] *myself and Toby / Set this device against Malvolio here, / Upon some stubborn and uncourteous parts / We had conceived against him*

uncouth *(adj.)* unfamiliar, strange, unknown Tit II.iii.211 [Quintus to Martius] *I am surprised with an uncouth fear;* AY II.vi.6; Luc 1598

uncovered *(adj.)* **1** bare-headed, with hat in hand [in respect] 2H6 IV.i.130 [Suffolk to First Gentleman] *rather let my head / Stoop to the block ... / Than stand uncovered to the vulgar groom*
  2 barefaced, naked, glaring MA IV.i.301 [Beatrice to Benedick] *with public accusation, uncovered slander*

uncropped *(adj.)* uncut, not plucked AW V.iii.324 [King to Diana] *If thou beest yet a fresh uncropped flower*

uncrossed *(adj.)* uncancelled, undeleted, not obliterated Cym III.iii.26 [Belarius to Guiderius and Arviragus] *Such gain the cap of him that makes him fine, / Yet keeps his book uncrossed* [i.e. his debts are not crossed out]

unction *(n.)* **1** ointment, oil Ham IV.vii.140 [Laertes to Claudius] *I bought an unction of a mountebank*
  2 balm, salve, soothing ointment Ham III.iv.146 [Hamlet to Gertrude] *Lay not that flattering unction to your soul*

unctuous *(adj.)* oily, greasy, fatty Tim IV.iii.196 [Timon alone, of earth's produce] *Whereof ingrateful man with liquorish draughts / And morsels unctuous greases his pure mind*

uncuckolded *(adj.)* with a faithful wife AC I.ii.74 [Iras to Charmian] *it is a deadly sorrow to behold a foul knave uncuckolded* ☛ **cuckold** *(n./v.)*

uncurable *(adj.)* incurable, hopeless, irretrievable 2H6 V.ii.86 [Young Clifford to King and Queen] *uncurable discomfit / Reigns in the hearts of all our present parts*

uncurbed *(adj.)* unrestrained, free, unchecked H5 I.ii.245 [King Henry to Ambassador] *with frank and with uncurbed plainness / Tell us the Dauphin's mind* ☛ **curbed** *(adj.)*

uncurrent *(adj.)* **1** unacceptable, not legally current, worthless Ham II.ii.426 [Hamlet to one of the players] *like a piece of uncurrent gold;* TN III.iii.16
  2 exceptional, aberrant, out of the ordinary WT III.ii.48 [Hermione to Leontes] *With what encounter so uncurrent I / Have strained t'appear thus* [i.e. what limits of behaviour have I exceeded that I should now find myself on trial]

undeaf *(v.)* restore hearing to R2 II.i.16 [John of Gaunt to York, of King Richard] *My death's sad tale may yet undeaf his ear*

undeck *(v.)* unclothe, remove the rich garments from R2 IV.i.249 [Richard to all] *To'undeck the pompous body of a king*

undecked *(adj.)* unadorned, not decked out E3 I.ii.150 [Countess to King Edward] *The ground, undecked with nature's tapestry, / Seems barren*

undeeded *(adj.)* without any deeds performed Mac V.vi.30 [Macduff alone, as if to Macbeth] *Either thou, Macbeth, / Or else my sword with an unbattered edge / I sheathe again undeeded*

under *(adv.)* down, in a bad way, in a low position AW I.i.192 [Helena to Parolles] *The wars hath so kept you under*

underbear *(v.)* endure, suffer, put up with KJ III.i.65 [Constance to Salisbury] *get thee gone / And leave those woes alone which I alone / Am bound to underbear*

underbearing *(n.)* enduring, coping with R2 I.iv.29 [King Richard to Aumerle, of Bolingbroke] *the craft of smiles and patient underbearing of his fortune*

underborne *(adj.)* trimmed at the bottom MA III.iv.20 [Margaret to Hero, of the Duchess of Milan's gown] *round underborne with a bluish tinsel*

undercrest *(v.)* bear [as if on a crest], live up to Cor I.ix.71 [Coriolanus to Cominius] *I mean ... / To undercrest your good addition*

under fiend *(n.)* devil from hell, fiend from under the earth Cor IV.v.95 [Coriolanus to Aufidius] *I will fight / Against my cankered country with the spleen / Of all the under fiends*

undergarnished *(adj.)* adorned underneath E3 I.ii.159 [Countess to King Edward] *like a cloak doth hide / From weather's waste the undergarnished pride* [i.e. the sumptuous garments under the cloak]

undergo (*v.*) **1** undertake, carry out, perform **Tim** III.v.24 [First Senator to Alcibiades] *You undergo too strict a paradox, / Striving to make an ugly deed look fair;* **Cym** I.v.137, III.v.111; **JC** I.iii.123; **WT** II.iii.163

2 support, sustain, bear **Ham** I.iv.34 [Hamlet to Horatio, of a person's virtues] *As infinite as man may undergo;* **MM** I.i.23

3 bear, ensure, suffer **Cym** III.ii.7 [Pisanio alone, of Innogen] *[she] undergoes … such assaults / As would take in some virtue*

4 fall under, experience, face up to **MA** V.ii.53 [Benedick to Beatrice] *Claudio undergoes my challenge*

undergoing (*adj.*) sustaining, resolute, of endurance **Tem** I.ii.157 [Prospero to Miranda, of her smile] *which raised in me / An undergoing stomach*

underhand (*adj.*) secret, unobtrusive, inconspicuous **AY** I.i.131 [Oliver to Charles, of Orlando's wish to wrestle] *I … have by underhand means laboured to dissuade him from it*

under-honest (*adj.*) less than honourable **TC** II.iii.123 [Agamemnon to Patroclus, of Achilles] *we think him over-proud / And under-honest*

undermine (*v.*) dig underneath; also: overthrow **AW** I.i.118 [Parolles to Helena] *Man setting down before you will undermine you and blow you up*

underminer (*n.*) sapper; also: overthrower **AW** I.i.119 [Helena to Parolles] *Bless our poor virginity from underminers and blowers-up!*

under-peep (*v.*) peep from under **Cym** II.ii.20 [Iachimo to himself, of Innogen] *the flame o'th' taper … would under-peep her lids*

underprop (*v.*) prop up, support, uphold **Luc** 53 [of Lucrece] *Within whose face beauty and virtue strived / Which of them both should underprop her fame;* **E3** III.iv.90; **KJ** V.ii.99

underskinker (*n.*) under-wine-waiter, under-tapster **1H4** II.iv.23 [Prince Hal to Poins] *I give thee this penny-worth of sugar, clapped even now into my hand by an underskinker*

understand (*v.*) **1** stand under the force of [with pun on 'comprehend'] **TG** II.v.27 [Launce to Speed] *I'll but lean, and my staff understands me;* **CE** II.i.49, 54; **TN** III.i.77

2 come to an understanding, arrive at agreement **MW** I.i.128 [Evans to all] *Now let us understand*

3 be informed about, learn about **H8** V.ii.9 [Butts to himself, of what he has seen] *the King / Shall understand it presently*

4 use their brains **H8** I.iii.32 [Lovell to Lord Chamberlain, of French-influenced Englishmen] *They must … understand again like honest men* [also: use their legs]

understanding (*n.*) **1** knowledge, awareness **KL** IV.v.28 [Regan to Oswald] *I speak in understanding*

2 intellect, intelligence, brain **TNK** III.v.6 [Schoolmaster to all] *the very plum-broth / And marrow of my understanding laid upon ye* [i.e. the very best of my intellect]

undertake (*v.*) **1** ensure, guarantee, vouch for **Tit** I.i.439 [Tamora to Saturninus] *on mine honour dare I undertake / For good Lord Titus' innocence in all;* **LL** IV.ii.155

2 take charge of, have responsibility for **H8** II.i.97 [Lovell to Buckingham, of Vaux] *Who undertakes you to your end*

3 take responsibility, commit oneself to an enterprise **KL** IV.ii.13 [Gonerill to Edmund, of Albany] *It is the cowish terror of his spirit / That dares not undertake*

4 approach, make overtures to, commit to deal with **TN** I.iii.55 [Sir Andrew to Sir Toby, of Maria] *I would not undertake her in this company;* **MW** III.v.115

5 take on, fight with, engage in combat with **Cym** I.i.26 [Second Lord to Cloten] *It is not fit your lordship should undertake every companion that you give offence to;* **TN** III.iv.243

6 assume, take on, feign **TS** IV.ii.107 [Tranio as Lucentio to Pedant, of Vincentio] *His name and credit shall you undertake*

undertaker (*n.*) **1** person who takes on a task **Oth** IV.i.210 [Iago to Othello, of Cassio] *let me be his undertaker* [i.e. let me deal with him]; **TN** III.iv.309

2 champion, helper, upholder **TNK** I.i.74 [First Queen to Theseus, of a god] *[who will] press you forth / Our undertaker*

underwork (*v.*) undermine, seek to overthrow **KJ** II.i.95 [King Philip to King John, of England] *thou hast underwrought his lawful king*

under-world (*n.*) earth, terrestrial world **TNK** IV.ii.24 [Emilia alone] *Fame and honour … sing / To all the under world*

undescried (*adj.*) unseen, unobserved, undiscovered **WT** IV.iv.651 [Camillo to Perdita] *you may … to shipboard / Get undescried*

undeserver (*n.*) one who deserves nothing, unworthy person **H8** III.ii.175 [Wolsey to King Henry] *For your great graces / Heaped upon me, poor undeserver;* **2H4** II.iv.370

undetermined (*adj.*) unresolved, undecided, unsettled **KJ** II.i.355 [Bastard to King John and King Philip, of death] *now he feasts, mousing the flesh of men, / In undetermined differences of kings*

undinted (*adj.*) unmarked by blows, without dents **AC** II.vi.39 [Pompey to Triumvirs] *To … bear back / Our targes undinted*

undiscernible (*adj.*) indiscernible, undiscoverable **MM** V.i.365 [Angelo to Duke] *To think I can be undiscernible*

undisposed (*adj.*) not in the mood, indisposed **CE** I.ii.80 [Antipholus of Syracuse to Dromio of Ephesus] *I shall break that merry sconce of yours / That stands on tricks when I am undisposed*

undistinguishable (*adj.*) unrecognizable, undetectable, impossible to pick out **MND** II.i.100 [Titania to Oberon] *the quaint mazes in the wanton green / For lack of tread are undistinguishable;* **MND** IV.i.186

undistinguished (*adj.*) **1** indistinct, confused, inarticulate **Lover** 20 [of the woman] *shrieking undistinguished woe*

2 ➤ indistinguishable (*adj.*)

undo (*v.*) **1** ruin, destroy, wipe out **H8** III.ii.210 [Wolsey alone] *This paper has undone me;* **AW** IV.i.71; **Cor** I.i.62; **H5** V.ii.133; **LL** V.ii.425; **R2** IV.i.202

2 bring to naught **2H4** Epilogue.4 [Epilogue] *If you look for a good speech now, you undo me;* **2H4** III.ii.112; **Tim** III.ii.48, IV.iii.212; **WT** V.ii.56

3 ruin, impoverish, bankrupt **AY** V.iv.45 [Touchstone to all] *I have undone three tailors* [i.e. by not paying them]

4 eliminate, abolish, do away with **KL** IV.vi.69 [Gloucester to Edgar as Poor Tom] *So distribution should undo excess*

5 unravel, solve, explain **Per** I.i.118 [Antiochus to Pericles] *If … our secret be undone*

6 destroy the reputation of **Tit** IV.ii.75 [Chiron to Aaron, of Tamora] *Thou hast undone our mother*

undone (*adj.*) ruined, destroyed, brought down **MA** IV.i.308 [Beatrice to Benedick, of Hero] *She is wronged, she is slandered, she is undone* ➤ **FEW**, p.xxi

undoubted (*adj.*) **1** put beyond doubt, not in question **KJ** II.i.369 [Hubert to King John and King Philip, of their arguments over who is king] *till it be undoubted, we do lock / Our former scruple in our strong-barred gates*

2 absolute, assured, true **1H6** III.iii.41 [Pucelle to Burgundy] *undoubted hope of France;* **3H6** V.vii.6

undoubtful (*adj.*) certain, positive, definite **MM** IV.ii.134 [Provost to disguised Duke, of Barnadine] *his fact … came not to an undoubtful proof*

unduteous (*adj.*) undutiful, unfilial, disloyal **MW** V.v.219 [Fenton to all, of his marriage to Anne] *this deceit loses the name of craft, / Of disobedience, or unduteous title*

uneared (*adj.*) unsown, unploughed, untilled **Sonn** 3.5 *where is she so fair whose uneared womb / Disdains the tillage of thy husbandry?*

unearthed (*adj.*) unburied; or: dug out, disclosed **TNK** V.i.52 [Arcite praying to Mars] *whose havoc in vast field / Unearthed skulls proclaim*

uneasy *(adj.)* **1** not easy, hard, difficult **Tem** I.ii.452 [Prospero to himself, of Ferdinand meeting Miranda] *this swift business / I must uneasy make;* **WT** IV.ii.48

2 uncomfortable, causing discomfort **2H4** III.i.10 [King Henry IV alone, of people sleeping] *in smoky cribs, / Upon uneasy pallets*

uneath *(adj.)* with difficulty, not easily, hardly **2H6** II.iv.8 [Gloucester to his men, of the Duchess] *Uneath may she endure the flinty streets*

uneffectual *(adj.)* ineffectual, ineffective, useless **Ham** I.v.90 [Ghost to Hamlet] *The glow-worm … 'gins to pale his uneffectual fire*

unequal *(adj.)* unjust, unfair, undeserved **AC** II.v.101 [Messenger to Cleopatra] *To punish me for what you make me do / Seems much unequal;* **2H4** IV.i.100

uneven *(adj.)* irregular, erratic **RJ** IV.i.5 [Friar to Paris, of the marriage arrangements] *Uneven is the course. I like it not;* **1H4** I.i.50; **MM** IV.iv.2; **R2** II.ii.120

unexecuted *(adj.)* unused, idle, out of action **AC** III.vii.44 [Enobarbus of Antony, of the army] *you … leave unexecuted / Your own renowned knowledge*

unexperienced *(adj.)* in ignorance, lacking in knowledge **TS** IV.i.74 [Grumio to Curtis, of the untold parts of the story] *and thou return unexperienced to thy grave*

unexperient *(n.)* inexperienced person, innocent **Lover** 318 *th'unexperient gave the tempter place*

unexpressive *(adj.)* inexpressible, beyond words **AY** III.ii.10 [Orlando alone, of Rosalind] *The fair, the chaste, and unexpressive she*

unfair *(v.)* deprive of beauty, make ugly **Sonn** 5.4 *Those hours* [will] *… that unfair which fairly doth excel*

unfallible *(adj.)* infallible, not mistaken **1H6** I.ii.59 [Bastard to all, after describing Pucelle] *Believe my words, / For they are certain and unfallible*

unfathered *(adj.)* **1** unnaturally conceived, illegitimate **2H4** IV.iv.122 [Gloucester to all] *The people … do observe / Unfathered heirs and loathly births of nature;* **Sonn** 97.10

2 have one's legitimacy rejected, become fatherless **Sonn** 124.2 *If my dear love were but the child of state, / It might for Fortune's bastard be unfathered*

unfeared *(adj.)* not feared, unfrightening **TNK** I.ii.64 [Palamon to Arcite, of Creon's successes] *Makes heaven unfeared*

unfee'd *(adj.)* not rewarded with a fee, unpaid **KL** I.iv.128 [Fool to Lear] *like the breath of an unfee'd lawyer*

unfeeling *(adj.)* incapable of feeling, insensible **2H6** III.ii.145 [King to himself, of dead Gloucester] *Fain would I … with my fingers feel his hand unfeeling*

unfeignedly *(adv.)* genuinely, sincerely, honestly **AW** II.iii.242 [Parolles to Lafew] *I most unfeignedly beseech your lordship to make some reservation of your wrongs;* **E3** IV.i.41; **TNK** IV.iii.67

unfellowed *(adj.)* unmatched, unequalled, unrivalled **Ham** V.ii.141 [Osrick to Hamlet, of Laertes] *in his meed he's unfellowed*

unfelt *(adj.)* **1** intangible, not supported by solid evidence **R2** II.iii.61 [Bolingbroke to Ross and Willoughby] *All my treasury / Is yet but unfelt thanks;* **Luc** 828

2 not experienced **Mac** II.iii.133 [Malcolm to Donalbain] *To show an unfelt sorrow is an office / Which the false man does easy;* **R3** I.iv.80

unfenced *(adj.)* with walls removed, unprotected **KJ** II.i.386 [Bastard to King John and King Philip, of attacking the men of Angiers] *Even till unfenced desolation / Leave them as naked as the vulgar air*

unfirm *(adj.)* **1** weak, feeble, lacking in strength **2H4** I.iii.73 [Hastings to Lord Bardolph, of King Henry's army] *So is the unfirm King / In three divided;* **JC** I.iii.4

2 unsteady, flighty, capricious **TN** II.iv.33 [Orsino to Viola as Cesario] *Our fancies are more giddy and unfirm … / Than women's are*

3 unstable, not compact, of loose consistency **RJ** V.iii.6 [Paris to Page, of the soil] *Being loose, unfirm, with digging up of graves*

unfold *(v.)* **1** display, reveal, show **Cym** II.iii.95 [Innogen to Cloten] *I shall unfold equal discourtesy / To your best kindness;* **2H6** II.i.161; **Luc** 1146; **MND** I.i.146; **Oth** III.iii.241; **WT** IV.i.2

2 identify, disclose, reveal **Ham** I.i.2 [Francisco to Barnardo] *Stand and unfold yourself;* **KL** I.i.280; **Oth** IV.ii.140, V.i.21

3 relate, recount, narrate **MW** II.ii.212 [Falstaff to Ford as Brook] *To what purpose have you unfolded this to me?;* **Cym** V.v.313; **2H6** III.ii.117

unfolded *(adj.)* exposed, revealed, unmasked **AC** V.ii.170 [Cleopatra to Caesar, of Seleucus] *must I be unfolded / With one that I have bred?*

unfolding *(n.)* exposition, proposal, proposition **Oth** I.iii.242 [Desdemona to Duke] *To my unfolding lend your prosperous ear*

unfolding *(adj.)* rising, morning [telling the shepherd that it is time to release his sheep from the fold] **MM** IV.ii.196 [disguised Duke to Provost] *th'unfolding star calls up the shepherd*

unfool *(v.)* make less of a fool, remove the name of fool from **MW** IV.ii.109 [Ford to Page] *have you any way then to unfool me again?*

unforfeited *(adj.)* unviolated, unbroken **MV** II.vi.7 [Salerio to Gratiano] *ten times faster Venus' pigeons fly / To seal love's bonds new-made than they are wont / To keep obliged faith unforfeited*

unfought *(adj.)* without being met in battle **E3** III.iii.139 [Philip to King John, of the English] *night approaching, they might escape unfought*

unfriended *(adj.)* deprived of a friend, friendless **KL** I.i.203 [Lear to Burgundy, of Cordelia] *Will you with those infirmities she owes, / Unfriended, … / Take her;* **TNK** V.iii.141

unfurnish *(v.)* deprive, divest, take away **WT** V.i.122 [Leontes to Paulina, of Florizel] *When I shall see this gentleman thy speeches / Will bring me to consider that which may / Unfurnish me of reason*

unfurnished *(adj.)* **1** unprepared, unready **RJ** IV.ii.10 [Capulet to himself, of the forthcoming wedding] *We shall be much unfurnished for this time*

2 unprepared, unequipped, unprotected **H5** I.ii.148 [King Henry to Canterbury, of Edward III] *the Scot on his unfurnished kingdom / Came pouring*

3 unfinished, defective **MV** III.ii.126 [Bassanio to all, of the artist who painted the eyes in Portia's portrait] *Having made one, / Methinks it should have power to steal both his / And leave itself unfurnished* [i.e. lacking the other]

4 deprived, not provided [with] **Tit** II.iii.56 [Bassianus to and of Tamora] *Unfurnished of her well-beseeming troop?*

5 lacking tapestries, without the usual fittings **R2** I.ii.68 [Duchess to John of Gaunt, of Pleshey] *what shall good old York there see / But empty lodgings and unfurnished walls*

ungalled *(adj.)* uninjured, unharmed, unhurt **CE** III.i.102 [Balthasar to Antipholus of Ephesus] *that supposed by the common rout / Against your yet ungalled estimation;* **Ham** III.ii.281

ungartered *(v.)* untied, not wearing a garter [a sign of a lovesick man] **AY** III.ii.363 [Rosalind to Orlando] *your hose should be ungartered;* **TG** II.i.69

ungenerative *(adj.)* lacking the power of generation, impotent **MM** III.ii.105 [Lucio to disguised Duke, of Angelo] *he is a motion ungenerative* [F *generatiue*]

ungenitured *(adj.)* lacking genitals, sterile, impotent **MM** III.ii.163 [Lucio to disguised Duke, of Angelo] *This ungenitured agent*

ungentle *(adj.)* **1** unmannerly, discourteous, impolite **JC** II.i.242 [Portia to Brutus] *You stared upon me with ungentle looks;* **AC** V.i.60; **AY** V.ii.75

2 unkind, callous, inconsiderate **3H6** II.iii.6 [Edward to himself] *Smile, gentle heaven, or strike, ungentle death!;* **2H6** III.ii.290

3 harsh, violent, cruel **WT** V.i.153 [Leontes to Florizel] *th'fearful usage, / At least ungentle, of the dreadful Neptune;* **WT** III.iii.33

4 unchivalrous, ungentlemanly **CE** IV.ii.21 [Adriana to Luciana, of Antipholus of Syracuse] *He is … / Vicious, ungentle*

ungently *(adv.)* unkindly, roughly, rudely **Tem** I.ii.445 [Miranda to herself] *Why speaks my father so ungently;* **JC** II.i.237; **TC** V.iii.1

ungird *(v.)* take off, remove, put off **TN** IV.i.14 [Feste to Sebastian] *ungird thy strangeness*

ungored *(adj.)* uninjured, unharmed **Ham** V.ii.244 [Laertes to Hamlet] *To keep my name ungored* [Q2; F *ungorg'd*]

ungot *(adj.)* unbegotten, unborn **MM** V.i.142 [Friar Peter to Duke, of Angelo and Isabella] *[he] is as free from touch or soil with her / As she from one ungot*

ungotten *(adj.)* unbegotten, not yet conceived **H5** I.ii.288 [King Henry to Ambassador] *some are yet ungotten and unborn / That shall have cause to curse the Dauphin's scorn*

ungoverned *(adj.)* uncontrolled, unchecked, violent **KL** IV.iv.19 [Cordelia to Doctor, of Lear] *Lest his ungoverned rage dissolve the life*

ungracious *(adj.)* **1** wicked, without grace, profane **R2** II.iii.88 [York to Bolingbroke] *that word 'grace' / In an ungracious mouth is but profane;* **Ham** I.iii.47; **1H4** I.iv.434; **KL** IV.vi.275

2 inconsiderate, graceless, unmannerly **TN** IV.i.46 [Olivia to Sir Toby] *Ungracious wretch, / Fit for the mountains and the barbarous caves;* **TC** I.i.91

ungravely *(adv.)* derisively, displaying ridicule **Cor** II.iii.224 [Sicinius to Citizens, of Coriolanus] *Th'apprehension of his present portance, / Which most gibingly, ungravely, he did fashion*

unhacked *(adj.)* unused, with no gashes **AC** II.vi.38 [Pompey to Triumvirs] *To part with unhacked edges*

unhair *(v.)* take the hair from **AC** II.v.64 [Cleopatra to Messenger] *I'll unhair thy head!*

unhaired *(adj.)* beardless, youthful **KJ** V.ii.133 [Bastard to Lewis the Dauphin, of the French invasion] *This unhaired sauciness and boyish troops, / The King doth smile at* [F *un-heard*]

unhallowed *(adj.)* **1** unholy, wicked, sacrilegious **RJ** V.iii.54 [Paris to Romeo] *Stop thy unhallowed toil;* **Tit** II.iii.210, V.iii.189, III.i.4

2 without saying prayers, without devotion **2H6** II.i.84 [King to Simpcox] *Let never day nor night unhallowed pass, / But still remember what the Lord hath done*

unhandsome *(adj.)* **1** inappropriate, faulty, unfitting **AY** V.iv.197 [Rosalind, of herself as Epilogue] *it is no more unhandsome than to see the lord the prologue*

2 inadequate, inexpert, falling short **Oth** III.iv.147 [Desdemona to Emilia] *unhandsome warrior as I am*

unhappily *(adv.)* **1** unfavourably, censoriously, critically **H8** I.iv.89 [King Henry to Wolsey] *You are a churchman, or … I should judge now unhappily*

2 evilly, disastrously, wretchedly **KL** I.ii.143 [Edmund to Edgar, of a writer] *the effects he writes of succeed unhappily*

3 uncomfortably near the truth **Ham** IV.v.13 [Gentleman to Gertrude, of Ophelia's speech] *Though nothing sure, yet much unhappily*

unhappiness *(n.)* **1** misfortune, mishap, bad luck **MA** II.i.320 [Leonato to Don Pedro, of Beatrice] *she hath often dreamt of unhappiness and waked herself with laughing*

2 evil, wrong-doing, perniciousness **R3** I.ii.25 [Anne to dead Henry VI, of Richard's possible child] *And that be heir to his unhappiness!*

unhappy *(adj.)* **1** unlucky, unfortunate, ill-fated **CE** I.ii.40 [Antipholus of Syracuse alone, of his mother and brother] *I … / In quest of them unhappy*

2 hapless, miserable, wretched **KL** IV.vi.228 [Oswald to Gloucester] *Thou old unhappy traitor;* **TNK** IV.ii.64

3 objectionable, harsh, bad-tempered **TS** II.i.139 [Baptista to Petruchio, of wooing Katherina] *be thou armed for some unhappy words*

4 trouble-causing, bringing misfortune **LL** V.ii.12 [Katharine to Rosaline, of Cupid] *a shrewd unhappy gallows;* **Luc** 1565

unhappy *(v.)* make unhappy, make unfortunate **R2** III.i.10 [Bolingbroke to Bushy and Green, of King Richard] *A happy gentleman in blood and lineaments, / By you unhappied and disfigured clean*

unhatched *(adj.)* **1** evolving, still in course of development **Oth** III.iv.137 [Desdemona to Emilia, of Othello] *some unhatched practice … / Hath puddled his clear spirit*

2 unmarked, unhacked; or: undrawn **TN** III.iv.230 [Sir Toby to Viola as Cesario, of Sir Andrew] *He is knight dubbed with unhatched rapier* [i.e. not on the battlefield]

unheart *(v.)* dishearten, discourage, dispirit **Cor** V.i.50 [Menenius to Sicinius, of Coriolanus] *to bite his lip / And hum at good Cominius much unhearts me*

unheedful *(adj.)* careless, heedless, irresponsible **TG** II.vi.11 [Proteus alone] *Unheedful vows may heedfully be broken;* **1H6** IV.iv.7

unheedfully *(adv.)* heedlessly, carelessly, inattentively **TG** I.ii.3 [Lucetta to Julia, of Julia falling in love] *so you stumble not unheedfully*

unheedy *(adj.)* unheedful, headstrong, reckless **MND** I.i.237 [Helena to herself, of Cupid] *Wings and no eyes figure unheedy haste*

unhidden *(adj.)* clear-cut, undisputed, manifest **H5** I.i.86 [Canterbury to Ely, of King Henry] *The severals and unhidden passages / Of his true titles to some certain dukedoms*

unhoped *(adj.)* unexpected, unforeseen, unanticipated **3H6** III.iii.172 [Queen to Lewis, of her news] *such as fill my heart with unhoped joys*

unhoused *(adj.)* **1** unsheltered, unprotected, open to the elements **Tim** IV.iii.230 [Apemantus to Timon, of wild animals] *whose bare unhoused trunks … / Answer mere nature*

2 unconfined, unconstrained, independent **Oth** I.ii.26 [Othello to Iago] *I would not my unhoused free condition / Put into circumscription and confine*

unhouseled *(adj.)* without the Eucharist, without communion **Ham** I.v.77 [Ghost to Hamlet] *Cut off even in the blossoms of my sin, / Unhouseled*

unhurtful *(adj.)* harmless, innocuous, incapable of causing injury **MM** III.ii.156 [disguised Duke to Lucio] *you imagine me too unhurtful an opposite*

unimproved *(adj.)* undisciplined, uncensored; or: not turned to use, not raised in quality **Ham** I.i.96 [Horatio to Marcellus and Barnardo, of young Fortinbras] *Of unimproved mettle hot and full*

unintelligent *(adj.)* oblivious, unaware, ignorant **WT** I.i.14 [Archidamus to Camillo] *your senses, unintelligent of our insufficience*

union *(n.)* large pearl **Ham** V.ii.266 [Claudius to all, of himself] *in the cup an union shall he throw* [F; Q2 *Vnice, Onixe*]; **Ham** V.ii.320

unity *(n.)* reconciliation, concord, harmony **R3** IV.iv.379 [Queen Elizabeth to King Richard] *The unity the King … made / Thou hadst not broken*

unjointed *(adj.)* disconnected, confused, incoherent **1H4** I.iii.64 [Hotspur to King Henry, of a lord] *This bald unjointed chat of his*

unjust *(adj.)* **1** dishonest, untrustworthy, crooked **WT** IV.iv.670 [Autolycus alone] *this is the time that the unjust man doth thrive;* **1H4** III.iii.127, IV.ii.27; **TC** V.i.85; **WT** IV.iv.670

2 unfaithful, false [to honour] **MM** III.i.241 [disguised Duke to Isabella, of Angelo] *His unjust unkindness;* **3H6** V.i.106; **TG** IV.iv.165; **TNK** II.i.248

3 inaccurate, incorrect, inexact **Sonn** 138.9 *But wherefore says she not she is unjust?* [or: unfaithful]

unjustice *(n.)* injustice **Tit** IV.iv.18 [Saturninus to all, of Titus' letters] *blazoning our unjustice everywhere*

unkennel (_v._) reveal, bring to light, expose MW III.iii.153 [Ford to his companions, of Falstaff] _I'll warrant we'll unkennel the fox_; Ham III.ii.91

unkind (_adj._) **1** hostile, cruel, harsh 2H6 IV.ix.19 [King to the former rebels] _Henry, though he be infortunate, / Assure yourselves, will never be unkind_; 2H6 III.ii.87; TS V.ii.135; Venus 204
2 unnatural, abnormal, aberrant 1H6 IV.i.193 [Exeter alone] _when envy breeds unkind division_; TC III.ii.147
3 lacking in family affection, with no respect for kinship Tit V.iii.47 [Saturninus to Titus, of killing Lavinia] _What hast thou done, unnatural and unkind?_ [also: unnatural]; KL III.iv.68; Tit I.i.89

unkindly (_adv._) cruelly, harshly; also: unnaturally Tit V.iii.103 [Lucius to all] _Lastly myself, unkindly banished_; JC III.ii.181

unkindness (_n._) **1** offence, ill-will, umbrage JC IV.iii.157 [Brutus to Cassius, of the wine] _In this I bury all unkindness_; AW II.v.32; TS IV.iii.163
2 ingratitude, unthankfulness, lack of appreciation KL III.ii.16 [Lear to the storm] _I tax not you, you elements, with unkindness_; Mac III.iv.41
3 unnatural behaviour, abnormal conduct R2 II.i.133 [John of Gaunt to King Richard] _thy unkindness be like crooked age_; MM II.iv.166

unking (_v._) depose, dethrone, deprive of kingship R2 V.v.37 [Richard alone] _by and by / Think that I am unkinged by Bolingbroke_

unkinged (_adj._) deposed, dethroned, deprived of kingship R2 IV.i.219 [Richard to all] _'God save King Henry,' unkinged Richard says_

unkinglike (_adj._) not regal, not befitting a king Cym III.v.7 [Cymbeline to Lucius] _To show less sovereignty … must needs / Appear unkinglike_

unknit (_v._) untie, undo, unravel Cor IV.ii.31 [Sicinius to Volumnia, of Coriolanus] _I would he had … not unknit himself / The noble knot he made_

unknown (_adj._) **1** obscure, little-known TC III.iii.125 [Ulysses to Achilles, of his book] _I … apprehended here immediately / The unknown Ajax_
2 not having had sexual intercourse [with] Mac IV.iii.126 [Malcolm to Macduff] _I am yet / Unknown to woman_

unlaid (_adj._) not driven out by an exorcist, not prevented from walking Cym IV.ii.278 [Guiderius singing, to the supposedly dead Innogen] _Ghost unlaid forbear thee!_

unlaid ope not laid open, undisclosed, unrevealed Per I.ii.89 [Pericles to Helicanus, of Antiochus] _To keep his bed of blackness unlaid ope_

unlettered (_adj._) illiterate, unread LL I.i.244 [King reading Armado's letter to him, of Costard] _That unlettered small-knowing soul_

unlicensed (_adj._) without permission, lacking the assent Per I.iii.16 [Helicanus to Lords, of Pericles] _Why … unlicensed of your loves / He would depart_

unlike (_adj._) **1** unlikely, incredible, unbelievable Cym V.v.355 [Cymbeline to Belarius, Arviragus, and Guiderius] _The service that you three have done is more / Unlike than this thou tell'st_; MM V.i.52
2 unlikely, improbable, doubtful TNK I.i.187 [Hippolyta to Queens] _Though much unlike / You should be so transported_

unlimited (_adj._) allowing changes in the location of action; or: all-inclusive Ham II.ii.398 [Polonius to Hamlet, of the players' productions] _poem unlimited_

unlineal (_adj._) not of the same family, of different descent Mac III.i.62 [Macbeth alone, of the sceptre in his hand] _Thence to be wrenched with an unlineal hand, / No son of mine succeeding_

unlived (_adj._) deprived of life Luc 1754 [Lucretius as if to dead Lucrece] _If in the child the father's image lies, / Where shall I live now Lucrece is unlived?_

unlooked (_adj._) unexpected, unanticipated, unforeseen R3 I.iii.213 [Queen Margaret to all] _God, I pray Him, / That none of you may live his natural age, / But by some unlooked accident cut off!_

unlooked-for (_adj._) **1** unexpected, unanticipated, unforeseen 3H6 V.i.14 [Warwick to Somerville, of new arrivals] _Belike, unlooked-for friends_; KJ II.i.79, 560; RJ I.v.30
2 undesirable, unwelcome, disagreeable 3H6 III.ii.131 [Richard alone, of the future children standing between him and the crown] _the unlooked-for issue_

unluckily (_adv._) **1** unsuccessfully, disastrously 2H4 Epilogue.11 [Epilogue, of the play] _I meant indeed to pay you with this, which, if like an ill venture it come unluckily home, I break_
2 ominously, inauspiciously JC III.iii.2 [Cinna to himself] _things unluckily charge my fantasy_

unlucky (_adj._) unfortunate, lamentable, disastrous Oth V.ii.337 [Othello to Lodovico] _When you shall these unlucky deeds relate / Speak of me as I am_

unmake (_v._) undo, destroy, make incapable Mac I.vii.54 [Lady Macbeth to Macbeth, of the time and place to kill the King] _their fitness now / Does unmake you_

unmanned (_adj._) [falconry] untrained; also: without a husband RJ III.ii.14 [Juliet alone] _Hood my unmanned blood, bating in my cheeks_

unmannered (_adj._) ill-mannered, rude, insolent TS IV.i.152 [Petruchio to servants] _You heedless joltheads and unmannered slaves!_; R3 I.ii.39

unmannerly (_adv._) inappropriately, improperly, insultingly Mac II.iii.113 [Macbeth to all, of the King's attendants] _their daggers / Unmannerly breeched with gore_

unmastered (_adj._) uncontrolled, unrestrained Ham I.iii.32 [Laertes to Ophelia, warning her not to yield to Hamlet] _or your chaste treasure open / To his unmastered importunity_

unmeet (_adj._) **1** unfitting, unsuitable, improper 2H6 I.iii.162 [Suffolk to all, of the choice of regent] _York is most unmeet of any man_; LL IV.iii.111; MA IV.i.180; PassP XVI.13 ❧ meet (_adj._)
2 unready, unfit, ill-equipped MM IV.iii.65 [disguised Duke to Provost, of Barnardine] _A creature unprepared, unmeet for death_

unmellowed (_adj._) not matured in age, showing no grey hairs TG II.iv.68 [Valentine to Duke, of Proteus] _His head unmellowed, but his judgement ripe_

unmeritable (_adj._) unworthy, undeserving, lacking in merit JC IV.i.12 [Antony to Octavius, of Lepidus] _This is a slight unmeritable man_; R3 III.vii.154

unmitigable (_adj._) implacable, unappeasable, uncompromising Tem I.ii.276 [Prospero to Ariel, of Sycorax] _in her most unmitigable rage_

unnatural (_adj._) **1** against natural feeling, not in accord with kinship 3H6 I.i.218 [Queen to King] _thou hast proved so unnatural a father!_; 1H6 III.iii.50; 3H6 V.i.86; KL I.i.77; Tem V.i.79
2 abnormal, monstrous, aberrant Mac V.i.67 [Doctor to Gentlewoman] _unnatural deeds / Do breed unnatural troubles_; 3H6 II.v.90; KL I.i.219; RJ V.iii.152

unnaturally (_adv._) illegitimately, against normal practice 3H6 I.i.193 [King to Warwick] _my son, / Whom I unnaturally shall disinherit_

unnaturalness (_n._) conduct against natural feeling, behaviour not in accord with kinship KL I.ii.143 [Edmund to Edgar, of a writer] _the effects he writes of succeed unhappily, as of unnaturalness between the child and the parent_

unnerved (_adj._) weak, drained of strength Ham II.ii.472 [First Player to all present, of Priam] _Th'unnerved father falls_

unnoble (_adj._) ignoble, dishonourable, disgraceful AC III.xi.50 [Antony to Eros] _I have offended reputation, / A most unnoble swerving_

unnoted (*adj.*) hardly noticeable, not particularly observed **Tim** III.v.21 [Alcibiades to Senators, of his friend] *with such sober and unnoted passion / He did behove his anger*

unnumbered (*adj.*) innumerable, countless, uncountable **JC** III.i.63 [Caesar to all] *The skies are painted with unnumbered sparks;* **KL** IV.vi.21

unordinate (*adj.*) inordinate, excessive, intemperate **Oth** II.iii.298 [Cassio to Iago] *Every unordinate cup is unblessed and the ingredience is a devil* [Q1; F *inordinate*] ☞ **inordinate** (*adj.*)

unowed (*adj.*) unowned, vacant **KJ** IV.iii.147 [Bastard to Hubert] *England now is left / To tug and scamble and to part by th'teeth / The unowed interest of proud-swelling state* [also: not owed]

unpanged (*adj.*) undistracted by pain, untormented **TNK** I.i.169 [Second Queen to Theseus] *when could grief / Cull forth, as unpanged judgement can, fittest time*

unparagoned (*adj.*) unsurpassable, matchless, not able to be excelled **Cym** II.ii.17 [Iachimo to himself, of Innogen] *Rubies unparagoned;* **Cym** I.v.77

unpartial (*adj.*) impartial, detached, neutral **H8** II.ii.105 [Campeius to Wolsey, of the King's marriage] *you ... are joined with me their servant / In the unpartial judging of this business*

unpathed (*adj.*) uncharted, unexplored, untravelled **WT** IV.iv.564 [Camillo to Florizel] *a wild dedication of yourselves / To unpathed waters*

unpaved (*adj.*) without stones [testicles], castrated **Cym** II.iii.29 [Cloten to Musicians, of their music not affecting Innogen] *it is a vice in her ears, which ... the voice of unpaved eunuch to boot, can never amend*

unpeaceable (*adj.*) quarrelsome, contentious, noisily argumentative **Tim** I.i.274 [Second Lord to Apemantus] *Away, unpeaceable dog*

unpeople (*v.*) empty of people, depopulate **3H6** I.i.126 [King to all, of refusing to leave his throne] *first shall war unpeople this my realm;* **AC** I.v.78; **Cym** I.vi.79; **Luc** 1741; **MM** III.ii.164

unpeopled (*adj.*) devoid of people, lacking retinue, without servants **LL** II.i.88 [Boyet to Princess, of the King] *He rather means to lodge you in the field [than] ... let you enter his unpeopled house;* **R2** I.ii.69

unperfect (*adj.*) imperfect; not word perfect, unskilled **Sonn** 23.1 *an unperfect actor on the stage*

unperfectness (*n.*) imperfection, defect, flaw **Oth** II.iii.288 [Cassio to Iago] *one unperfectness shows me another*

unpicked (*adj.*) not gathered, unenjoyed **2H4** II.iv.363 [Falstaff to all] *Now comes in the sweetest morsel of the night, and we must hence and leave it unpicked*

unpinked (*adj.*) unadorned, lacking ornamentation **TS** IV.i.119 [Grumio to Petruchio] *Gabriel's pumps were all unpinked i'th' heel*

unpitied (*adj.*) pitiless, ruthless, unmerciful **MM** IV.ii.12 [Provost to Pompey] *you shall have ... an unpitied whipping*

unplausive (*adj.*) disapproving, displeased, censurious **TC** III.iii.43 [Ulysses to all, of Achilles] *'tis like he'll question me / Why such unplausive eyes are bent* [F; Q *vnpaulsiue*]

unpolicied (*adj.*) outwitted in intrigue, diminished in statecraft **AC** V.ii.307 [Cleopatra to the asp] *That I might hear thee call great Caesar ass / Unpolicied!*

unpolished (*adj.*) primitive, rudimentary, defective **E3** I.i.76 [King Edward to Lorraine, of the King of France] *His lame unpolished shifts are come to light*

unpossessing (*adj.*) unable to inherit property **KL** II.i.66 [Edmund to Gloucester, as if Edgar to Edmund] *Thou unpossessing bastard*

unpossible (*adj.*) impossible **R2** II.ii.125 [Bushy to Bagot and Green] *For us to levy power / Proportionable to the enemy / Is all unpossible* [F: *impossible*]

unpractised (*adj.*) inexperienced, naive, innocent **TC** I.i.12 [Troilus to Pandarus] *I am ... skilless as unpractised infancy*

unpregnant (*adj.*) unready, uninclined, unreceptive **MM** IV.iv.18 [Angelo alone] *This deed ... makes me unpregnant / And dull to all proceedings*

unpregnant of (*adj.*) unresponsive to, unmoved by **Ham** II.ii.565 [Hamlet alone] *unpregnant of my cause*

unprepared (*adj.*) unplanned, introduced without special preparation **KJ** II.i.560 [King John to King Philip, of the marriage] *Go we as well as haste will suffer us / To this unlooked-for, unprepared pomp*

unprevailing (*adj.*) unavailing, ineffective, unsuccessful **Ham** I.ii.107 [Claudius to Hamlet] *We pray you throw to earth / This unprevailing woe*

unprizable (*adj.*) **1** inestimable, beyond price **Cym** I.v.87 [Iachimo to Posthumus, of Innogen] *your brace of unprizable estimations, the one is but frail and the other casual*
2 worthless, of little value **TN** V.i.52 [Orsino to Viola as Cesario, of Antonio] *A baubling vessel was he captain of ... unprizable*

unprized-precious (*adj.*) highly valued though offered for no price, priceless **KL** I.i.259 [France to Lear] *Not all the dukes of waterish Burgundy / Can buy this unprized-precious maid of me*

unproper (*adj.*) not solely one's one, shared with another **Oth** IV.i.68 [Iago to Othello] *There's millions now alive / That nightly lie in those unproper beds / Which they dare swear peculiar*

unproperly (*adv.*) improperly, unfittingly, against all propriety **Cor** V.iii.54 [Volumnia to Coriolanus] *I ... unproperly / Show duty as mistaken all this while*

unproportioned (*adj.*) immoderate, inordinate, inappropriate **Ham** I.iii.60 [Polonius to Laertes] *Give thy thoughts no tongue, / Nor any unproportioned thought his act*

unprovide (*v.*) make unready, unequip, unresolve **Oth** IV.i.204 [Othello to Iago, of Desdemona] *I'll not expostulate with her, lest her body and beauty unprovide my mind again*

unprovided (*adj.*) **1** unprepared, unprotected, undefended **KL** II.i.51 [Edmund to Gloucester, of Edgar] *in fell motion / With his prepared sword he charges home / My unprovided body;* **3H6** V.v.63; **R3** III.ii.73
2 unprepared for death, not ready to meet God **H5** IV.i.169 [disguised King Henry to Williams, of soldiers] *if they die unprovided, no more is the King guilty of their damnation than he was before*
3 unprepared, not properly dressed **TS** III.ii.98 [Baptista to Petruchio, of Petruchio's clothing] *were we ... sadder that you come so unprovided*

unpublished (*adj.*) undisclosed, concealed, not divulged **KL** IV.iv.16 [Cordelia to Doctor, as if to the herbs of the earth] *All you unpublished virtues*

unpurged (*adj.*) not cleansed, unpurified [by the sun] **JC** II.i.266 [Portia to and of Brutus] *tempt the rheumy and unpurged air, / To add unto his sickness*

unpurposed (*adj.*) unintentional, unwitting, unthinking **AC** IV.xiv.84 [Antony to Eros] *Do it at once, / Or thy precedent services are all / But accidents unpurposed*

unqualitied (*adj.*) unmanned, beside himself, bereft of all capacities **AC** III.xi.44 [Iras to Cleopatra, of Antony] *He's unqualitied with very shame*

unqueened (*adj.*) removed from the position of queen **H8** IV.ii.171 [Katherine to Patience] *although unqueened, yet like / A queen ... inter me*

unquestionable (*adj.*) irritable when spoken to, impatient when questioned **AY** III.ii.359 [Rosalind to Orlando, of his appearance] *an unquestionable spirit, which you have not*

unquestioned (*adj.*) unconsidered, unexamined, not inquired into **MM** I.i.54 [Duke to Angelo] *Our haste ... leaves unquestioned / Matters of needful value*

unquiet (*adj.*) disturbed, disordered, restless **2H4** I.ii.152 [Lord Chief Justice to Falstaff, of the exploit at Gad's Hill] *You may thank th'unquiet time for your quiet o'erposting that action*

unquietly (*adv.*) restlessly, uneasily, with great disquiet **KL** III.i.2 [Gentleman to disguised Kent, of himself] *One minded like the weather, most unquietly*

unraised (*adj.*) ordinary, humdrum, unimaginative **H5** Prologue.9 [Chorus] *The flat unraised spirits that hath dared / On this unworthy scaffold to bring forth / So great an object*

unready (*adj.*) undressed, unclothed **1H6** II.i.39 [stage direction] *Enter, several ways, the Bastard, Alençon, Reignier, half ready and half unready;* **1H6** II.i.39

unreasonable (*adj.*) lacking the faculty of reason, irrational **RJ** III.iii.111 [Friar to Romeo] *Thy wild acts denote / The unreasonable fury of a beast;* **3H6** II.ii.26

unreasoned (*adj.*) not to be thought about, undebated **TNK** I.ii.98 [Palamon to Arcite, of the point he has just made] *Leave that unreasoned*

unrecalling (*adj.*) irrevocable, undoable, irreversible **Luc** 993 [Lucrece as if to time, of Tarquin] *ever let his unrecalling crime / Have time to wail the abusing of his time*

unreclaimed (*adj.*) unreformed, uncorrected, untamed **Ham** II.i.34 [Polonius to Reynaldo] *A savageness in unreclaimed blood*

unreconciliable (*adj.*) unreconcilable, in perpetual conflict **AC** V.i.47 [Caesar to all, of Antony] *our stars, / Unreconciliable*

unrecuring (*adj.*) incurable, terminal, allowing no recovery **Tit** III.i.90 [Marcus to Lucius and Titus, of Lavinia hiding] *as doth the deer / That hath received some unrecuring wound*

unremovable (*adj.*) immovable, firm, constant **KL** II.iv.89 [Gloucester to Lear, of Cornwall] *You know … / How unremovable and fixed he is*

unremovably (*adv.*) irremovably, immovably **Tim** V.i.222 [First Senator to Second Senator, of Timon] *His discontents are unremovably / Coupled to nature*

unreputed (*adj.*) insignificant, inconspicuous, insubstantial **E3** II.i.437 [Warwick to Countess] *An unreputed mote, flying in the sun*

unrespected (*adj.*) of little value, lacking real interest **Sonn** 43.2 [of the poet's eyes] *all the day they view things unrespected*

unrespective (*adj.*) 1 inattentive, heedless, negligent **R3** IV.ii.29 [King Richard to himself] *I will converse with … unrespective boys*
2 undiscriminating, making no distinction, all-inclusive **TC** II.ii.72 [Troilus to Hector] *the remainder viands / We do not throw in unrespective sieve / Because we now are full*

unrest (*n.*) uneasiness, anxiety, apprehension **RJ** I.v.120 [Romeo to Benvolio, reacting to 'The sport is at the best'] *The more is my unrest*

unreverend (*adj.*) irreverent, impertinent, impudent **TG** II.vi.14 [Proteus alone, of Julia] *fie, unreverend tongue, to call her bad;* **KJ** I.i.227; **MM** V.i.303

unreverent (*adj.*) irreverent, disrespectful, unseemly **TS** III.ii.111 [Tranio as Lucentio to Petruchio] *See not your bride in these unreverent robes;* **1H6** III.i.49; **R2** II.i.123

unrighteous (*adj.*) insincere, wicked, unjust **Ham** I.ii.154 [Hamlet alone, of his mother's grief] *the salt of most unrighteous tears*

unripe (*adj.*) immature, youthful, inexperienced **Venus** 524 [Adonis to Venus] *Measure my strangeness with my unripe years;* **PassP** IV.9

unroll (*v.*) strike off the roll, remove from the list **WT** IV.iii.119 [Autolycus to himself, of the Clown] *If I make not this cheat bring out another … let me be unrolled* [i.e. from the official list of rogues]

unroosted (*adj.*) dislodged from a position, driven from a perch **WT** II.iii.74 [Leontes to Antigonus, of Paulina] *thou art woman-tired, unroosted / By thy Dame Partlet here*

unrough (*adj.*) beardless, unbearded **Mac** V.ii.10 [Lennox to Cathness, of the English army] *there is Seyward's son / And many unrough youths that even now / Protest their first of manhood*

unruly (*adj.*) disorderly, violent, unscrupulous **KJ** III.iv.135 [Cardinal Pandulph to Lewis the Dauphin] *A sceptre snatched with an unruly hand / Must be as boisterously maintained as gained*

unsanctified (*adj.*) unholy, wicked, ungodly **KL** IV.vi.273 [Edgar to dead Oswald] *the post unsanctified / Of murderous lechers;* **Mac** IV.ii.81

unsatiate (*adj.*) ☞ insatiate (*adj.*)

unsatisfied (*adj.*) 1 unsatisfiable, insatiable **H8** IV.ii.55 [Griffith to Katherine, of Wolsey] *though he were unsatisfied in getting*
2 people unaware of the facts **Ham** V.ii.334 [Hamlet to Horatio] *Report me and my cause aright / To the unsatisfied*

unsay (*v.*) take back, withdraw, retract **E3** II.i.432 [Warwick to Countess] *mark how I unsay my words again;* **1H4** I.iii.75; **H8** V.i.175; **R2** IV.i.9

unscanned (*adj.*) unthinking, unconsidered, thoughtless **Cor** III.i.311 [Menenius to Brutus, of the Tribunes' rage] *it shall find / The harm of unscanned swiftness*

unsealed (*adj.*) lacking formal confirmation, without legal ratification **AW** IV.ii.30 [Diana to Bertram] *your oaths / Are … poor conditions but unsealed*

unseam (*v.*) split in two, rip up, undo the seam of **Mac** I.ii.22 [Captain to King, of Macbeth killing Macdonwald] *he unseamed him from the nave to the chops*

unseasonable (*adj.*) 1 unsuitable, inappropriate, unwelcome **KJ** IV.ii.20 [Pembroke to King John, of his second coronation] *in the last repeating troublesome, / Being urged at a time unseasonable*
2 not in the hunting season **Luc** 581 [Lucrece to Tarquin] *He is no woodman that doth bend his bow / To strike a poor unseasonable doe*

unseasoned (*adj.*) 1 unseasonable, inopportune, badly timed **MW** II.ii.163 [Ford as Brook to Falstaff] *this unseasoned intrusion;* **2H4** III.i.101
2 unready, immature, raw **AW** I.i.69 [Countess to Lafew, of Bertram] *'Tis an unseasoned courtier*

unseconded (*adj.*) unsupported, unsustained **2H4** II.iii.34 [Lady Percy to Northumberland, of Percy] *him did you leave, / Second to none, unseconded by you*

unsecret (*adj.*) lacking in secrecy, unconfidential **TC** III.ii.123 [Cressida to Troilus] *Who shall be true to us / When we are so unsecret to ourselves?*

unseeming (*adj.*) not seeming, not appearing **LL** II.i.156 [Princess to King, of wronging her father] *In so unseeming to confess receipt / Of that which hath so faithfully been paid*

unseen (*adj.*) unknown, unnoticed, unobserved **CE** I.ii.38 [Antipholus of Syracuse, comparing himself to a drop of water] *falling there to find his fellow forth, / Unseen, inquisitive, confounds himself*

unseminared (*adj.*) emasculated, deprived of virility **AC** I.v.11 [Cleopatra to Mardian] *'Tis well for thee / That, being unseminared, thy freer thoughts / May not fly forth of Egypt*

unsettle (*v.*) become unsettled, be disturbed **TNK** III.ii.29 [Gaoler's Daughter alone] *let not my sense unsettle*

unsettled (*adj.*) 1 disturbed, troubled; also: unresolved, unfixed **TNK** V.iii.106 [Theseus to all] *our sister is in expectation, / Yet quaking and unsettled;* **AW** II.v.63; **H8** II.iv.64
2 discontented, dissatisfied, restless **KJ** II.i.66 [Chatillon to King Philip, of English soldiers] *all th'unsettled humours of the land*

unsevered (*adj.*) inseparable, intimate, united **Cor** III.ii.42 [Volumnia to Coriolanus] *Honour and policy, like unsevered friends, / I' th' war do grow together*

unsex (*v.*) take away one's sex; here: remove all feminine qualities **Mac** I.v.39 [Lady Macbeth alone] *Come, you spirits / That tend on mortal thoughts, unsex me here*

unshape (v.) deform, disfigure, destroy **MM** IV.iv.18 [Angelo alone] *This deed unshapes me quite*

unshaped (adj.) uncontrolled, poorly formed **Ham** IV.v.8 [Gentleman to Gertrude, of Ophelia's speech] *the unshaped use of it doth move / The hearers to collection*

unshrubbed (adj.) bare, empty, treeless **Tem** IV.i.81 [Ceres to Iris] *with each end of thy blue bow dost crown / My bosky acres and my unshrubbed down*

unshunned (adj.) unshunnable, unavoidable **MM** III.ii.57 [Lucio to Pompey] *An unshunned consequence*

unsifted (v.) untried, inexperienced, unskilled **Ham** I.iii.102 [Polonius to Ophelia, of Hamlet's attentions] *You speak like a green girl, / Unsifted in such perilous circumstance*

unsinewed (adj.) weak, feeble, slight **Ham** IV.vii.10 [Claudius to Laertes] *reasons, / Which may to you perhaps seem much unsinewed*

unsisting (adj.) [unclear meaning] unassisting; or: unshifting **MM** IV.ii.86 [disguised Duke alone, of knocking] *That wounds th'unsisting postern with these strokes*

unskilful (adj.) undiscerning, ignorant, uneducated **Ham** III.ii.25 [Hamlet to Players] *though it make the unskilful laugh;* **Oth** I.iii.27

unskilfully (adv.) ignorantly, foolishly, in an uninformed way **MM** III.ii.138 [disguised Duke to Lucio] *you speak unskilfully*

unsmirched (adj.) unstained, untainted, spotless **Ham** IV.v.121 [Laertes to Claudius] *the chaste unsmirched brows*

unsorted (adj.) unsuitable, unfit, badly chosen **1H4** II.iii.13 [Hotspur alone, reading a letter] *the time itself unsorted*

unsought (adj.) unsearched, uninvestigated **CE** I.i.136 [Egeon to Duke, of Ephesus] *loath to leave unsought / Or that or any place that harbours men*

unsounded (adj.) unfathomed, unexplored, with unrevealed depths **2H6** III.i.57 [Suffolk to King] *Gloucester is a man / Unsounded yet and full of deep deceit;* **Luc** 1819; **TG** III.ii.81

unspeak (v.) retract, renounce, take back **Mac** IV.iii.123 [Malcolm to Macduff] *I … / Unspeak mine own detraction*

unspeakable (adj.) indescribable, inexpressible, beyond description **Tit** I.i.259 [Saturninus to Romans, of Titus' offerings] *when I do forget / The least of these unspeakable deserts;* **WT** IV.ii.40

unspeaking (adj.) unable to speak out, incapable of speech **Cym** V.v.178 [Iachimo to Cymbeline, of Posthumus] *his description / Proved us unspeaking sots*

unsphere (v.) remove [a star] from its sphere **WT** I.ii.48 [Hermione to Polixenes] *you would seek t'unsphere the stars with oaths* ➥ **sphere** (n.) 1

unspotted (adj.) unblemished, unstained, pure **2H6** III.i.100 [Gloucester to Suffolk] *A heart unspotted is not easily daunted;* **H5** IV.i.156

unsquared (adj.) badly fitting, unsuitable, unbecoming **TC** I.iii.159 [Ulysses to Agamemnon, of Patroclus] *when he speaks, / 'Tis … with terms unsquared*

unstaid (adj.) **1** unsteady, unsettled, vacillating **TN** II.iv.18 [Orsino to Viola as Cesario, of lovers] *Unstaid and skittish in all motions else*

2 unrestrained, unregulated, unchecked **R2** II.i.2 [John of Gaunt to York, of King Richard] *wholesome counsel to his unstaid youth*

3 immodest, undignified, indecorous **TG** II.vii.60 [Julia to Lucetta] *how will the world repute me / For undertaking so unstaid a journey?*

unstained (adj.) unmitigated, unaffected, no longer stained with hatred **KJ** II.i.16 [Arthur to Austria] *I give you welcome … with a heart full of unstained love*

unstanched (adj.) **1** unquenchable, insatiable, unable to be satisfied **3H6** II.vi.83 [Richard to all, of dead Clifford] *the villain whose unstanched thirst / York and young Rutland could not satisfy*

2 not made staunch [water-tight]; loose, promiscuous **Tem** I.i.47 [Gonzalo to all] *the ship were … as leaky as an unstanched wench*

unstate (v.) **1** strip position from, deprive of standing, dispossess **AC** III.xiii.30 [Enobarbus to himself] *like enough, high-battled Caesar will / Unstate his happiness*

2 deprive of rank and estate, give up everything **KL** I.ii.99 [Gloucester to Edmund] *I would unstate myself to be in a due resolution*

unsteadfast (adj.) unsteady, precarious, not firm **1H4** I.iii.191 [Worcester to Northumberland and Hotspur] *to o'er-walk a current roaring loud / On the unsteadfast footing of a spear*

unstuffed (adj.) unclogged by troubles **RJ** II.iii.33 [Friar to Romeo] *where unbruised youth with unstuffed brain / Doth couch his limbs, there golden sleep doth reign*

unsubstantial (adj.) lacking in material substance, intangible **KL** IV.i.7 [Edgar alone] *Welcome, then, / Thou unsubstantial air that I embrace!*

unsuitable (adj.) unfashionable, old-fashioned, passé **AW** I.i.155 [Parolles to Helena, of virginity] *richly suited but unsuitable*

unsured (adj.) insecure, uncertain, doubtful **KJ** II.i.471 [Queen Eleanor to King John, of a marriage between Lewis the Dauphin and Blanche] *by this knot thou shalt so surely tie / Thy now unsured assurance to the crown*

unswayed (adj.) unwielded, uncontrolled, lacking direction **R3** IV.iv.469 [King Richard to Derby] *Is the sword unswayed?;* **Sonn** 141.11 ➥ **sway** (v.) 1

unswear (v.) abjure, retract, repudiate **E3** II.i.327 [King Edward to Warwick] *Think'st that thou canst unswear thy oath again?;* **Oth** IV.i.31

unsworn (adj.) not subject to vows **MM** I.iv.9 [Francisca to Isabella] *you are yet unsworn*

untainted (adj.) **1** unblemished, unsullied, pure **2H6** III.ii.232 [King to all] *What stronger breastplate than a heart untainted!;* **Luc** 1710; **R3** III.i.7; **Sonn** 19.11

2 unaccused, not denounced **R3** III.vi.9 [Scrivener alone] *within these five hours Hastings lived, / Untainted, unexamined*

untaught (adj.) **1** uninstructed, uneducated, uncultivated **1H4** I.iii.42 [Hotspur to King Henry, of a lord] *as the soldiers bore dead bodies by, / He called them untaught knaves;* **RJ** V.iii.214

2 natural, spontaneous **Cym** IV.ii.178 [Belarius alone, of Arviragus and Guiderius] *'Tis wonder / That an invisible instinct should frame them / To … honour untaught;* **MM** II.iv.29

untempering (adj.) unsoftening, without fostering tenderness **H5** V.ii.222 [King Henry to Katherine] *thou dost [love me], notwithstanding the poor and untempering effect of my visage* ➥ **temper** (v.) 3

untender (adj.) ungentle, unkind; or: unyielding **KL** I.i.106 [Lear to Cordelia] *So young, and so untender?*

untendered (adj.) unpaid, not offered, outstanding **Cym** III.i.10 [Lucius to Cymbeline, of the tribute] *which … lately / Is left untendered*

untent (v.) remove from a tent **TC** II.iii.166 [Agamemnon to Ulysses, of Achilles] *Why will he not … / Untent his person*

untented (adj.) too deep to be cleansed with lint [tent], undressed **KL** I.iv.297 [Lear to Gonerill] *Th'untented woundings of a father's curse / Pierce every sense about thee!*

unthink (v.) remove from one's thoughts **H8** II.iv.104 [Wolsey to Queen Katherine] *I do beseech / You … to unthink your speaking*

unthought-of (adj.) despised, poorly thought of **1H4** III.ii.141 [Prince Hal to King Henry, of himself] *your unthought-of Harry*

unthought-on (adj.) unexpected, unforeseen, fortuitous **WT** IV.iv.535 [Florizel to Camillo] *th'unthought-on accident is guilty / To what we wildly do*

unthrift (n.) spendthrift, squanderer, wastrel **Sonn** 9.9 *Look what an unthrift in the world doth spend;* **R2** II.iii.121; **Sonn** 13.13; **Tim** IV.iii.313

unthrift (*adj.*) unthrifty, spendthrift, prodigal **MV** V.i.16 [Lorenzo to and of Jessica] *with an unthrift love did run from Venice*

unthrifty (*adj.*) **1** prodigal, profligate, wasteful **R2** V.iii.1 [King Henry to all] *Can no man tell me of my unthrifty son?*; **MV** I.iii.173; **Sonn** 4.1

2 wasteful of the chance to increase **WT** V.ii.109 [First Gentleman to other Gentlemen] *Our absence makes us unthrifty to our knowledge*

3 harmful, pernicious, unfortunate **RJ** V.iii.136 [Friar to Balthasar] *O much I fear some ill unthrifty thing*

untimbered (*adj.*) lacking a strong wooden frame; unsound, frail **TC** I.iii.43 [Nestor to Agamemnon] *Where's then the saucy boat, / Whose weak untimbered sides but even now / Co-rivalled greatness?*

untimely (*adj.*) premature, coming before its time **RJ** IV.v.28 [Capulet to all, of Juliet] *Death lies on her like an untimely frost*; **E3** V.i.156; **R2** V.vi.52; **R3** II.iii.35; **RJ** V.iii.234

untimely (*adv.*) **1** prematurely, too soon, before due time **Mac** V.vi.55 [Macduff to Macbeth] *Macduff was from his mother's womb / Untimely ripped*; **E3** V.i.206; **3H6** V.v.62; **R3** I.ii.22; **RJ** I.iv.111; **TNK** IV.ii.69

2 inopportunely, at a bad time **E3** III.i.184 [Mariner to King John, of the navies] *We have untimely lost, and they have won*; **KL** III.vii.97

untirable (*adj.*) tireless, inexhaustible, indefatigable **Tim** I.i.11 [Merchant to Jeweller, of Timon] *A most incomparable man, breathed, as it were, / To an untirable and continuate goodness*

untitled (*adj.*) with no right to rule, illegal **Mac** IV.iii.104 [Macduff to Malcolm] *O nation miserable, / With an untitled tyrant* ➤ **title** (*n.*) **1**

unto (*prep.*) **1** [gambling] against **R2** III.iv.26 [Queen Isabel to her ladies, of the gardeners] *My wretchedness unto a row of pins / They will talk of state*

2 in relation to **Ham** IV.vii.180 [Gertrude to Claudius and Laertes, of Ophelia in the brook] *like a creature native and indued / Unto that element*

3 to **TNK** V.i.76 [Palamon to his knights, of Venus] *we … implore / Her power unto our party*

unto … ward (*prep.*) towards **1H6** III.iii.30 [Pucelle to all, of the English] *Their powers are marching unto Paris-ward*

untoward (*adj.*) **1** stubborn, difficult, perverse **TS** IV.v.79 [Hortensio alone as if to Petruchio, of the widow] *if she be froward, / Then hast thou taught Hortensio to be untoward*

2 unmannerly, improper, unseemly **KJ** I.i.243 [Lady Faulconbridge to Bastard] *thou most untoward knave*

untowardly (*adv.*) unluckily, unfavourably, wretchedly **MA** III.ii.119 [Don Pedro to Claudio and Don John] *O day untowardly turned!*

untraded (*adj.*) unconventional, unaccustomed, unfamiliar **TC** IV.v.178 [Hector to Menelaus] *Mock not that I affect th'untraded oath*

untread (*v.*) retrace, go back upon **Venus** 908 [of Venus] *She treads the path that she untreads again*; **KJ** V.iv.52; **MV** II.vi.10

untreasure (*v.*) rob, empty [of a treasure] **AY** II.ii.7 [First Lord to Duke Frederick, of Celia's attendants] *They found the bed untreasured of their mistress*

untried (*adj.*) unexamined, unexplored, not ascertained **WT** IV.i.6 [Time to audience] *I slide / O'er sixteen years, and leave the growth untried / Of that wide gap*

untrimmed (*adj.*) **1** unadorned, lacking ornament **Sonn** 18.8 *every fair from fair sometime declines, / By chance, or nature's changing course untrimmed* [also: unbalanced]

2 [unclear meaning] unbedded, virgin **KJ** III.i.209 [Constance to Lewis the Dauphin, of Blanche] *The devil tempts thee here / In likeness of a new, untrimmed bride* [or: sense 1]

untrod (*adj.*) unprecedented, untraversed **JC** III.i.136 [Servant to Brutus] *Antony … will follow / The fortunes and affairs of noble Brutus / Thorough the hazards of this untrod state*

untrue (*adj.*) false, deceptive, deceiving **Lover** 170 [of the woman] *For further I could say this man's untrue, / And knew the patterns of his foul beguiling*; **KJ** III.iv.148

untrue (*adv.*) untruly, unfaithfully **Sonn** 72.10 *That you for love speak well of me untrue*

untrussing (*n.*) undoing the points attaching hose to doublet, dropping one's breeches **MM** III.ii.169 [Lucio to disguised Duke] *Claudio is condemned for untrussing*

untruth (*n.*) disloyalty, unfaithfulness, infidelity **R2** II.ii.101 [York to all, of King Richard] *I would to God - / So my untruth had not provoked him to it - / The King had cut off my head with my brother's*

untuneable (*adj.*) unsuitable, disagreeable; or: unmelodious **TG** III.i.208 [Proteus to Valentine, of his news] *they are harsh, untuneable, and bad*; **AY** V.iii.41

untuned (*adj.*) **1** out-of-tune, disordered, disturbed **R2** I.iii.134 [King Richard to Bolingbroke and Mowbray] *roused up with boisterous untuned drums*; **KL** IV.vii.16

2 disagreeable, distressing, rude **E3** I.ii.8 [Countess to herself] *to be wooed with broad untuned oaths*

untutored (*adj.*) badly brought up, untaught, inexperienced **3H6** V.v.32 [George to Prince] *Untutored lad, thou art too malapert*; **2H6** III.ii.213; **PassP** I.3; **Sonn** 138.3

untwind (*v.*) untwine, untwist the spinning of **2H4** II.iv.194 [Pistol to all] *let grievous, ghastly, gaping wounds / Untwind the Sisters Three!*

unvalued (*adj.*) **1** unimportant, of no position, insignificant **Ham** I.iii.19 [Laertes to Ophelia, of Hamlet] *He may not, as unvalued persons do, / Carve for himself*

2 invaluable, of great worth **R3** I.iv.27 [Clarence to Keeper] *I saw … / Inestimable stones, unvalued jewels*

unvexed (*adj.*) untroubled, unmolested, unimpeded **KJ** II.i.253 [King Philip to Hubert, of a French retreat] *with a blessed and unvexed retire*

unvulnerable (*adj.*) invulnerable, unassailable **Cor** V.iii.73 [Coriolanus to Young Martius] *thou mayst prove / To shame unvulnerable*

unwappered (*adj.*) unexhausted, fresh, energetic **TNK** V.iv.10 [Palamon to his knights] *we come towards the gods / Young and unwappered*

unwares (*adv.*) unawares, unknowingly, unintentionally **3H6** II.v.62 [Son to himself] *It is my father's face, / Whom in this conflict I, unwares, have killed* ➤ **unawares** (*adv.*)

unwedgeable (*adj.*) unsplittable, incapable of being cleft **MM** II.ii.116 [Isabella to Angelo, of the heavens] *with thy sharp and sulphurous bolt / Splits the unwedgeable and gnarled oak*

unweighed (*adj.*) hasty, thoughtless, ill-judged **MW** II.i.21 [Mistress Page alone, of Falstaff's letter] *What an unweighed behaviour hath this Flemish drunkard picked … out of my conversation*

unweighing (*adj.*) thoughtless, injudicious, undiscriminating **MM** III.ii.132 [Lucio to disguised Duke, of the Duke] *A very superficial, ignorant, unweighing fellow*

unwholesome (*adj.*) **1** harmful, damaging, noxious **Luc** 870 [Lucrece to herself] *Unwholesome weeds take root with precious flowers*; **Cor** IV.vi.132; **H5** II.iii.54; **MW** III.iii.37; **TC** II.iii.119; **Tem** I.ii.322

2 corrupted, infected, diseased **Ham** IV.v.83 [Claudius to Gertrude] *the people muddied, / Thick and unwholesome in their thoughts* [i.e. infected with suspicion]; **Per** IV.ii.19

3 impaired, defective, flawed **Oth** IV.i.121 [Cassio to Iago, of his intelligence] *do not think it so unwholesome*

unwit (*v.*) deprive of wits, make crazy **Oth** II.iii.176 [Iago to Othello, of the quarrel between Cassio and Montano] *As if some planet had unwitted men*

unwitnessed (*adj.*) unconfirmed, unsupported, unverified [by] **Venus** 1023 [Venus to love] *Trifles unwitnessed with eye or ear / Thy coward heart with false bethinking grieves*

unwonted (*adj.*) unusual, unaccustomed, abnormal **Tem** I.ii.498 [Miranda to Ferdinand, of Prospero] *This is unwonted / Which now came from him;* **MM** IV.ii.113

unwrung (*adj.*) not rubbed sore, not chafed **Ham** III.ii.252 [Hamlet to Claudius] *Our withers are unwrung*

unyoke (*v.*) **1** separate, disjoin, unlink **KJ** III.i.241 [King Philip to Cardinal Pandulph, of the treaty] *shall these hands ... / Unyoke this seizure*
2 stop working, cease labouring **Ham** V.i.52 [First Clown to Second Clown] *tell me that, and unyoke* [i.e. have done with it]

unyoked (*adj.*) unbridled, unrestrained, rampant **1H4** I.ii.194 [Prince Hal alone, of his companions] *I ... will awhile uphold / The unyoked humour of your idleness*

up (*adv.*) **1** up in arms, in rebellion, in revolt **2H6** III.i.283 [Post to all] *from Ireland am I come amain, / To signify that rebels there are up;* **1H4** III.ii.120; **2H4** I.i.189, IV.ii.2, 167
2 in a state of forceful action, exerting power **Cor** III.i.109 [Coriolanus to Senators] *when two authorities are up, / Neither supreme, how soon confusion / May enter*
3 roused, agitated, angry **RJ** III.i.133 [Benvolio to Romeo] *The citizens are up*
4 shut up, in prison, in custody **AC** III.v.11 [Eros to Enobarbus, of Lepidus] *so the poor third is up, till death enlarge his confine*
5 hidden, concealed, shut up **Cym** II.iv.97 [Iachimo to Posthumus, of Innogen's jewel] *now 'tis up again*

up and down (*adv.*) exactly, completely, in every respect **Tit** V.ii.107 [Titus to disguised Tamora, of her true self] *For up and down she doth resemble thee;* **MA** II.i.105; **TG** II.iii.27

upcast (*n.*) [bowls] accident, chance; or: throw, pitch **Cym** II.i.2 [Cloten to Lords] *I kissed the jack upon an upcast*

upheave (*v.*) raise, lift up **Venus** 482 [of Venus] *Her two blue windows faintly she upheaveth* ➤ **heaved-up** (*adj.*)

uphoard (*v.*) hoard, heap up, amass **Ham** I.i.137 [Horatio to Ghost] *Or if thou hast uphoarded in thy life / Extorted treasure*

uphold (*v.*) maintain, sustain, keep intact **KJ** V.iv.5 [Salisbury to Pembroke] *Faulconbridge, / In spite of spite, alone upholds the day*

uplifted (*adj.*) brandished, raised up **R2** II.ii.50 [Green to Queen Isabel] *The banished Bolingbroke ... with uplifted arms is safe arrived*

up-locked (*adj.*) locked-up, hidden safely away **Sonn** 52.2 *So am I as the rich, whose blessed key / Can bring ... his sweet up-locked treasure*

upmost (*adj.*) uppermost, topmost **JC** II.i.24 [Brutus alone, of an ambitious young man] *when he once attains the upmost round*

upon (*prep.*) **1** against **Mac** IV.iii.131 [Malcolm to Macduff] *My first false speaking / Was this upon myself*
2 as a result of **JC** IV.iii.150 [Cassius to Brutus, of Portia's death] *Upon what sickness?*
3 on account of **AC** II.ii.219 [Enobarbus to Agrippa and Maecenas, of Cleopatra] *The city cast / Her people out upon her*
4 on the side of **KL** II.i.26 [Edmund to Edgar, of Cornwall] *Have you nothing said / Upon his party 'gainst the Duke of Albany?*
5 owing to **Cor** II.i.220 [Sicinius to Brutus, of the commoners' attitude to Coriolanus] *they / Upon their ancient malice will forget / With the least cause these his new honours*
6 towards **JC** IV.iii.276 [Brutus to himself, of the Ghost] *It comes upon me*

up-pricked (*adj.*) pricked up, alert **Venus** 271 [of Adonis' horse] *His ears up-pricked*

uprear (*v.*) upraise, lift up **2H4** IV.i.212 [Archbishop to Mowbray] *this land ... hangs resolved correction in the arm / That was upreared to execution;* **Sonn** 49.11

upreared (*adj.*) standing on end **2H6** III.iii.171 [Warwick to Suffolk, of dead Gloucester] *His hair upreared*

uprightly (*adv.*) in an upright way, justly, honourably **E3** IV.iii.31 [Villiers to Charles, of obedience to the prince] *In all things that uprightly he commands*

uprise (*n.*) rising, dawn **AC** IV.xii.18 [Antony alone] *O sun, thy uprise shall I see no more*

uproar (*n.*) public disturbance, outbreak of disorder **1H6** III.i.75 [Warwick to King] *An uproar, I dare warrant, / Begun through malice of the Bishop's men*

uproar (*v.*) throw into turmoil, reduce to confusion **Mac** IV.iii.99 [Malcolm to Macduff] *had I power, I should ... / Uproar the universal peace*

uprouse (*v.*) arouse, get up, leave one's bed **RJ** II.iii.36 [Friar to Romeo] *Thou art uproused with some distemperature*

upshoot (*n.*) [archery] final shot, determining shot **LL** IV.i.137 [Costard to Boyet, of Maria] *Then will she get the upshoot by cleaving the pin* [with bawdy pun]

upshot (*n.*) **1** remaining stroke, final shot [as in archery, determining the result] **E3** III.iv.120 [King Edward to all, of Calais] *Now lies it on an upshot;* **TN** IV.ii.69
2 result, conclusion, outcome **Ham** V.ii.378 [Horatio to the Ambassadors and Fortinbras] *in this upshot*

upspring (*adj.*) newly introduced, trendy; or: a type of wild dance **Ham** I.iv.9 [Hamlet to Horatio] *The King doth wake tonight and takes his rouse / Keeps wassail, and the swaggering upspring reels*

up-staring standing on end **Tem** I.ii.213 [Ariel to Prospero] *The King's son Ferdinand, / With hair up-staring*

up-swarm (*v.*) raise up in swarms **2H4** IV.ii.30 [Prince John to Archbishop, of the people] *You ... / Have here up-swarmed them*

up-till (*prep.*) up against **PassP** XX.10 [of a nightingale] *She ... / Leaned her breast up-till a thorn*

upward (*n.*) crown, top part **KL** V.iii.134 [Edgar to Edmund] *from th'extremest upward of thy head*

upward (*adj.*) upturned, looking upwards **JC** V.iii.93 [Brutus to Messala] *Titinius' face is upward;* **Tim** IV.iii.191

urchin (*n.*) **1** hedgehog **Tit** II.iii.101 [Tamora to Demetrius] *Ten thousand swelling toads, as many urchins, / Would make such fearful and confused cries*
2 spirit in hedgehog form, goblin **Tem** I.ii.326 [Prospero to Caliban] *Urchins / Shall ... / All exercise on thee;* **MW** IV.iv.48

urchin-show (*n.*) goblin apparition, spirit vision **Tem** II.ii.5 [Caliban alone, of Prospero's spirits] *But they'll [not] / Fright me with urchin-shows*

urchin-snouted (*adj.*) with nose like a hedgehog **Venus** 1105 *this foul, grim, and urchin-snouted boar*

ure (*v.*) accustom, inure, habituate **E3** I.i.159 [King Edward to Prince Edward] *thou must begin ... [to] ure thy shoulders to an armour's weight*

urge (*v.*) **1** press, insist on, state emphatically **3H6** I.i.98 [Clifford to Warwick, of the York threat] *Urge it no more;* **H5** V.ii.94; **JC** II.i.155; **Luc** 475; **MV** V.i.206; **R2** V.v.5
2 entreat with, plead with **KJ** II.i.475 [Queen Eleanor to King John, of France and an alliance] *Urge them while their souls / Are capable of this ambition;* **JC** II.i.243; **Tim** III.ii.12
3 solicit, force, press forward **KJ** I.i.258 [Lady Faulconbridge to Bastard, of being seduced by King Richard] *Which was so strongly urged past my defence*
4 bring forward, advocate, represent **Tim** III.ii.42 [Servilius to Lucius, of Timon] *If his occasion were not virtuous, / I should not urge it half so faithfully;* **AC** II.ii.50; **Cor** V.i.10; **MV** I.i.144; **Venus** 787
5 state formally, present, propose **1H4** V.ii.52 [Vernon to Hotspur] *I never in my life / Did hear a challenge urged more modestly;* **AY** V.iv.5; **H8** V.iii.48; **RJ** I.v.109
6 provoke, incite, impel **JC** IV.iii.35 [Cassius to Brutus] *Urge me no more, I shall forget myself;* **CE** II.ii.47; **H5** V.ii.144; **TG** IV.iii.27
7 stimulate, excite, tempt **Sonn** 118.2 *With eager compounds we our palate urge*

urging (*n.*) pressing on the attention, bringing forward **R3** I.iv.108 [Second Murderer to First Murderer] *The urging of that word judgement hath bred a kind of remorse in me;* **CE** V.i.350; **R2** III.i.4

urinal (*n.*) medical vessel for holding urine **TG** II.i.37 [Speed to Valentine] *these follies … shine through you like the water in an urinal;* **MW** III.i.13, 80

usage (*n.*) treatment, handling, conduct **Tit** I.i.269 [Saturninus to Tamora] *Princely shall be thy usage every way;* **1H6** V.iii.58; **3H6** IV.v.6; **TN** I.v.169

usance (*n.*) interest on a loan **MV** I.iii.105 [Shylock to Antonio] *you have rated me / About my moneys and my usances;* **MV** I.iii.42, 138

use (*n.*) **1** usual practice, habit, custom **Oth** IV.i.276 [Lodovico to Iago, of Othello striking Desdemona] *Is it his use?;* **Ham** III.iv.169; **JC** II.ii.25; **Mac** I.iii.136; **R3** IV.iv.230; **TG** V.iv.1

2 activity, practice, enterprise **TNK** II.iv.7 [Arcite to Theseus, of his sporting skills] *[my father] to these gentle uses gave me life;* **Cym** IV.iv.7; **Tim** II.i.20; **TNK** II.i.105

3 need, requirement **Tim** II.i.20 [Senator to Caphis, of Timon] *tell him / My uses cry to me;* **Tim** V.i.204

4 opportunity, benefit, advantage **H8** III.ii.420 [Wolsey to Cromwell] *make use now, and provide / For thine own future safety* [i.e. take the present opportunity]

5 end, outcome, resolution **KL** IV.ii.36 [Albany to and of Gonerill] *She … must wither / And come to deadly use*

6 trust, possession, tenure **AC** I.iii.44 [Antony to Cleopatra] *my full heart / Remains in use with you;* **MV** IV.i.380

7 profit, interest, premium **Venus** 768 [Venus to Adonis] *gold that's put to use more gold begets;* **KL** I.iv.129; **MA** II.i.256; **MM** I.i.40; **Sonn** 6.5; **TN** III.i.49

use (*v.*) **1** be accustomed, make a habit [of] **AY** II.iii.23 [Adam to Orlando, of Oliver] *he means / To burn the lodging where you use to lie;* **Cor** III.i.114; **MW** IV.ii.52; **RJ** III.v.190; **TC** II.i.47; **Tem** II.i.178

2 treat, deal with, manage **H5** III.ii.123 [Fluellen to Macmorris] *you do not use me with that affability as in discretion you ought to use me;* **AW** I.ii.42; **Ham** V.i.285; **KL** I.v.14; **TC** IV.iv.120; **TS** I.ii.31

3 make use of, engage [in], practise [with] **AC** II.vi.132 [Enobarbus to Menas] *We have used our throats in Egypt;* **KL** I.iv.168; **R3** V.iii.199; **Tim** I.i.83, III.ii.51

4 present, conduct, behave **H8** III.i.176 [Queen Katherine to Campeius and Wolsey] *pray forgive me / If I have used myself unmannerly*

5 keep company with, entertain **Mac** III.ii.10 [Lady Macbeth to Macbeth] *Why do you keep alone … / Using those thoughts which should indeed have died / With them they think on?*

6 permit, allow, tolerate **3H6** IV.viii.60 [Edward to all] *The sun shines hot; and, if we use delay, / Cold biting winter mars our hoped-for hay* [i.e. if we hesitate]

7 satisfy, fulfil, engage in **AC** II.vi.128 [Enobarbus to Menas] *Antony will use his affection where it is*

8 frequent, hang out at, visit regularly **TC** V.i.92 [Thersites alone, of Diomedes] *he … uses the traitor Calchas his tent*

use the person of represent, stand in place of **2H4** V.ii.73 [Lord Chief Justice to King Henry V] *I then did use the person of your father*

use thy freedom do what you want, do your own thing **TNK** II.i.254 [Palamon to Arcite, advising him how to behave] *Let that one say so, / And use thy freedom*

used (*adj.*) customary, usual, accustomed **Per** I.ii.3 [Pericles alone, of melancholy] *my so used a guest*

ushering (*n.*) organization of ceremony **LL** V.ii.328 [Berowne to all, of Boyet] *in ushering / Mend him who can*

usually (*adv.*) habitually, routinely, regularly **2H6** IV.vii.35 [Cade to Say] *thou hast men about thee that usually talk of a noun and a verb*

usurer (*n.*) money-lender, one who charges excessive interest **KL** III.ii.91 [Fool alone] *When usurers tell their gold i'the field;* **KL** IV.vi.164; **RJ** III.iii.123; **Sonn** 4.7

usuring (*adj.*) expecting ample interest, looking for maximum return **Tim** IV.iii.512 [Timon to Flavius] *Is not thy kindness subtle-covetous, / A usuring kindness;* **Tim** III.v.111

usurp (*v.*) **1** supplant, oust, impersonate **TN** I.v.179 [Olivia to Viola as Cesario, of whether she is the lady of the house] *If I do not usurp myself, I am*

2 assume, take on, adopt **TS** Induction.i.129 [Lord alone, of Page] *I know the boy will well usurp the grace … of a gentlewoman*

3 take wrongful possession of, misappropriate **KL** IV.ii.28 [Gonerill alone, of her husband] *A fool usurps my bed;* **Ham** I.i.46; **KL** V.iii.315; **Tem** I.ii.454; **TN** I.v.180

usurp on / upon take wrongful possession of, misappropriate **Per** III.ii.80 [Cerimon to Gentlemen] *Death may usurp on nature many hours;* **Tit** III.i.267 [Titus to Marcus, of sorrow] *would usurp upon my wat'ry eyes / And make them blind with tributary tears;* **Ham** III.ii.269

usurpation (*n.*) encroachment, intrusion, trespass **2H4** I.i.63 [Northumberland to Lord Bardolph, of Morton's face] *So looks the strand whereon the imperious flood / Hath left a witnessed usurpation*

usurped (*adj.*) false, counterfeit, disguising **Oth** I.iii.337 [Iago to Roderigo] *defeat thy favour with an usurped beard;* **TN** V.i.247

usurping (*adj.*) false, made into a wig **LL** IV.iii.257 [Berowne to King] *It mourns that painting and usurping hair / Should ravish doters with a false aspect*

usury (*n.*) way of dealing with money, financial practice **Cym** III.iii.45 [Belarius to Guiderius and Arviragus] *Did you but know the city's usuries;* **MM** III.ii.5

ut (*n.*) [musical scale] doh **LL** IV.ii.99 [Holofernes singing] *Ut, re, sol, la, mi, fa;* **TS** III.i.74

utensil (*n.*) **1** distinctive feature, functional organ **TN** I.v.235 [Olivia to Viola as Cesario, of her beauty] *It shall be inventoried, and every particle and utensil labelled to my will*

2 household goods, domestic furnishing; or: implement [for magic] **Tem** III.ii.97 [Caliban to Stephano, of Prospero] *He has brave utensils*

utis (*n.*) clamour, din; or: festivity, jollification **2H4** II.iv.19 [Francis to Will] *By the mass, here will be old utis*

utmost (*adj.*) **1** maximum, largest number of **JC** IV.iii.212 [Brutus to Cassius] *we have tried the utmost of our friends;* **2H4** I.i.65

2 last, final **CE** IV.i.28 [Angelo to Antipholus of Ephesus] *here's the note / How much your chain weighs to the utmost carat*

utter (*v.*) **1** emit, exhale, discharge **MND** IV.ii.38 [Bottom to all] *eat no onions nor garlic; for we are to utter sweet breath;* **JC** I.ii.243; **WT** IV.iv.186

2 offer for sale, dispense, make available **RJ** V.i.67 [Apothecary to Romeo, of deadly poisons] *Mantua's law / Is death to any he that utters them;* **LL** II.i.16, V.ii.316; **WT** IV.iv.321

3 [unclear meaning] commemorate, express, voice **MA** V.iii.20 [Balthasar, singing] *Graves yawn and yield your dead, / Till death be uttered*

utterance, at to the uttermost, to the very last, at any cost **Cym** III.i.73 [Cymbeline to Lucius, of the honour received from Caesar] *Which he to seek of me again, perforce, / Behoves me keep at utterance*

utterance, to the to the bitter end, to the death **Mac** III.i.71 [Macbeth to himself, of Banquo's children becoming kings] *Rather than so, come fate into the list / And champion me to the utterance!*

uttermost (*n.*) latest time, last moment **JC** II.i.213 [Brutus to all] *By the eighth hour; is that the uttermost?*

vacancy *(n.)* **1** empty space, nothingness **Ham** III.iv.118 [Gertrude to Hamlet] *you do bend your eye on vacancy;* **AC** II.ii.221

2 spare time, leisure **AC** I.iv.26 [Caesar to Lepidus, of Antony] *If he filled / His vacancy with his voluptuousness*

vacant *(adj.)* lacking, devoid, deficient **H8** V.i.125 [Cranmer to King Henry] *I with mine enemies / Will triumph o'er my person, which I weigh not, / Being of those virtues vacant;* **Sonn** 77.3

vade *(v.)* fade, pass away, disappear **Sonn** 54.14 [of youth] *When that shall vade, my verse distils your truth;* **PassP** XIII.2

vaded *(adj.)* faded, made pale, with lost brightness **PassP** XIII.8 *As vaded gloss no rubbing will refresh;* **PassP** X.1

vagabond *(adj.)* drifting, meandering, wandering **AC** I.iv.45 [Caesar to Lepidus, of the people] *This common body, / Like to a vagabond flag upon the stream, / Goes to and back*

vagary *(n.)* wandering, displacement, roaming about **TNK** IV.iii.72 [Doctor to Gaoler and Wooer, of the Gaoler's Daughter] *[her senses] are now in a most extravagant vagary*

vagram *(adj.)* malapropism for 'vagrant'; or: mispronunciation of 'fragrant' **MW** III.i.24 [Evans alone, singing] *a thousand vagram posies*

vagrom *(adj.)* vagrant, vagabond [malapropism of 'vagrant'] **MA** III.iii.25 [Dogberry to Second Watchman] *you shall comprehend all vagrom men*

vail *(n.)* **1** setting, going down **TC** V.viii.7 [Achilles to Hector] *Even with the vail and dark'ning of the sun / To close the day up, Hector's life is done*

2 [textiles: remnant of cloth, leftover of material] tip, gratuity, perk **Per** II.i.152 [Second Fisherman to Pericles, of the help the fishermen have provided] *There are ... certain vails*

vail *(v.)* **1** lower, bow down, cast down [as in submission] **1H6** V.iii.25 [Pucelle alone] *Now the time is come / That France must vail her lofty-plumed crest;* **Cor** III.i.98; **E3** II.i.17; **MV** I.i.28; **Per** II.iii.42; **TS** V.ii.175

2 let fall, yield, surrender **LL** V.ii.297 [Boyet to and of ladies] *Dismasked, their damask sweet commixture shown, / Are angels vailing clouds;* **R3** IV.iv.348

3 lower, direct downwards **MM** V.i.20 [Isabella to Duke] *Vail your regard / Upon a wronged ... maid*

4 do homage, pay respect, show devotion **Per** IV.Chorus.29 [Gower alone, of Marina] *She would ... / Vail to her mistress Dian*

vailed *(adj.)* lowered, downcast **Ham** I.ii.70 [Gertrude to Hamlet] *Do not for ever with thy vailed lids / Seek for thy noble father in the dust*

vain *(n.)* deceptive, false, idle [in using words] **CE** III.ii.27 [Luciana to Antipholus of Syracuse] *'Tis holy sport to be a little vain*

vain *(adj.)* **1** foolish, silly, stupid **CE** III.ii.188 [Antipholus of Syracuse alone] *there's no man is so vain / That would refuse so fair an offered chain;* **2H4** V.v.46; **KL** IV.ii.61; **LL** V.ii.756; **Tem** I.ii.174; **TG** IV.iii.17

2 worthless, idle, useless, empty **3H6** I.ii.27 [Richard to York] *Your oath ... is vain and frivolous;* **R3** I.iii.240, IV.iv.82; **Tit** I.i.443

vain, for in vain, to no purpose **MM** II.iv.12 [Angelo alone] *an idle plume / Which the air beats for vain*

vainglory, vain-glory *(n.)* **1** undue vanity, unwarranted pride **Cym** IV.i.7 [Cloten alone] *it is not vain-glory for a man and his glass to confer in his own chamber;* **H8** III.i.127

2 showy event, ostentatious activity **Tim** I.ii.247 [Apemantus to Timon] *What needs these feasts, pomps, and vainglories?;* **TC** III.iii.259

vainly *(adv.)* **1** uselessly, fruitlessly, ineffectively **RJ** V.iii.125 [Friar to Balthasar] *What torch is yond that vainly lends his light / To grubs and eyeless skulls?*

2 wrongly, falsely, in error **Sonn** 138.5 *Thus vainly thinking that she thinks me young*

vainness (*n.*) boasting, ostentation, vanity **H5** V.Chorus.20 [Chorus, of King Henry] *Being free from vainness and self-glorious pride;* **TN** III.iv.346

valance (*n.*) drapery making up the border of a bed canopy **TS** II.i.347 [Gremio to Baptista, of his possessions] *Valance of Venice gold in needlework*

valanced (*adj.*) fringed [with a beard] **Ham** II.ii.422 [Hamlet to one of the players] *thy face is valanced since I saw thee last* [Q1, Q2; F *valiant*]

vale (*n.*) valley, lowland **AC** IV.xi.3 [Caesar to all] *To the vales, / And hold our best advantage*

valiant (*adj.*) worthy, fine, hearty **MA** I.i.47 [Beatrice to Messenger, of Benedick] *he is a very valiant trencher-man*

validity (*n.*) **1** value, worth, estimation **KL** I.i.81 [Lear to Regan, of her land] *No less in space, validity, and pleasure / Than that conferred on Gonerill;* **AW** V.iii.192; **RJ** III.iii.33; **TN** I.i.12
  2 strength, robustness, stamina **Ham** III.ii.199 [First Player, as King, to his Queen, of purpose] *Of violent birth, but poor validity*

valley (*n.*) indentation, hollow [e.g. in the upper lip, or beneath the lower lip] **WT** II.iii.100 [Paulina to all, of the baby's features] *the valley, / The pretty dimples of his chin and cheek*

valuation (*n.*) appreciation of merit, estimation of worth **Cym** IV.iv.49 [Belarius to Arviragus and Guiderius] *since of your lives you set / So slight a valuation;* **2H4** IV.i.187

value (*n.*) worth, estimation, valuation **Cym** I.v.13 [Iachimo to all, of Posthumus and Innogen] *he must be weighed rather by her value than his own;* **Tim** I.i.82

value (*v.*) **1** consider, appraise, take into account **1H4** III.ii.177 [King Henry to Prince Hal] *Our business valued, some twelve days hence / Our general forces at Bridgnorth shall meet;* **1H4** V.ii.59
  2 estimate, reckon, number **3H6** V.iii.14 [Richard to Edward] *The Queen is valued thirty thousand strong*
  3 consider equal in value [to] **LL** II.i.137 [King to Princess] *One part of Aquitaine is bound to us, / Although not valued to the money's worth;* **H8** I.i.88

valued (*adj.*) showing value, discriminating **Mac** III.i.94 [Macbeth to Murderers] *The valued file / Distinguishes the swift, the slow, the subtle*

vambrace (*n.*) ☞ **vantbrace** (*n.*)

vane (*n.*) weathervane; inconstant person **LL** IV.i.96 [Princess to Boyet, of Armado] *What vane? What weathercock?*

vanish (*v.*) leave, depart from, be expelled **E3** IV.iv.79 [Prince Edward to Herald] *That such base breath should vanish from my lips*

vanity (*n.*) **1** worthlessness, futility, unprofitable way of life **1H4** I.ii.82 [Falstaff to Prince Hal] *I prithee trouble me no more with vanity;* **H4** IV.v.120; **RJ** I.i.178, II.vi.20
  2 foolishness, absurdity, inanity **Tim** I.ii.129 [Apemantus to himself, of the masque] *what a sweep of vanity comes this way!;* **H8** I.i.85; **KJ** V.vii.13
  3 trifling display, light-hearted show **Tem** IV.i.41 [Prospero to Ariel, of Ferdinand and Miranda] *I must / Bestow upon the eyes of this young couple / Some vanity of mine art*
  4 trifle, folly, vain thing **H8** II.iii.69 [Anne to Lord Chamberlain] *nor my wishes / More worth than empty vanities;* **H8** I.i.54; **R2** III.iv.86
  5 fop, dandy, dude **H8** I.iii.38 [Lord Chamberlain to Lovell, of French-influenced Englishmen] *What a loss our ladies / Will have of these trim vanities!*

vant (*n.*) van, front line **AC** IV.vi.9 [Caesar to all] *Go charge Agrippa / Plant those that have revolted in the vant*

vantage (*n.*) **1** right moment, suitable opportunity **Mac** I.ii.31 [Captain to King] *the Norweyan lord, surveying vantage … / Began a fresh assault;* **Cor** V.vi.54; **Cym** I.iv.24; **3H6** I.iv.59; **MM** IV.vi.11; **Tim** II.ii.134 ☞ **advantage** (*n.*) 1
  2 advantageous position, place of vantage, superiority **2H4** II.iii.53 [Lady Percy to Northumberland, of the rebels] *If they get*

ground and vantage of the King, / Then join you with them like a rib of steel;* **Ham** V.ii.384; **H5** III.vi.142; **MND** I.i.102; **TC** V.viii.9; **TNK** III.i.122 ☞ **advantage** (*n.*) 2
  3 advantage, benefit, advancement, profit **R2** I.iii.218 [John of Gaunt to King Richard, of Bolingbroke's reduced banishment] *little vantage shall I reap thereby;* **AC** III.vii.33; **KJ** II.i.550; **Mac** I.iii.112; **MM** II.ii.74; **R3** I.iii.309 ☞ **advantage** (*n.*) 3
  4 helpful position, beneficial location **2H4** II.i.77 [Falstaff to Hostess] *I think I am as like to ride the mare if I have any vantage of ground to get up*

vantage, of / to the in addition, as well, besides **Ham** III.iii.33 [Polonius to Claudius] *o'erhear / The speech, of vantage;* **Oth** IV.iii.83

vantage (*v.*) benefit, aid, help **E3** II.i.325 [Warwick to King Edward] *If nothing but that loss may vantage you;* **E3** IV.iv.13; **Sonn** 88.12

vantbrace, vambrace (*n.*) armour to protect the fore-arm **TC** I.iii.297 [Nestor to Aeneas] *I'll … in my vantbrace put this withered brawn* [F; Q *vambrace*] ☞ **BODY-ARMOUR**, p.48

vaporous (*adj.*) misty, damp-filled, foggy **MM** IV.i.57 [disguised Duke to Isabella and Mariana] *The vaporous night approaches;* **Luc** 771; **Mac** III.v.24

vapour (*n.*) **1** exhalation, steamy emission, mistiness **Ham** II.ii.303 [Hamlet to Rosencrantz and Guildenstern] *a foul and pestilent congregation of vapours;* **2H4** IV.iii.97; **1H6** II.ii.27; **Venus** 1166
  2 mist, cloud, fog **CE** I.i.90 [Egeon to Duke] *the sun … / Dispersed those vapours that offended us;* **AC** IV.xiv.3; **2H4** II.iv.359; **Luc** 550, 782; **Venus** 184
  3 smoke **E3** III.ii.58 [Third Frenchman to all, of the burning cities] *as the leaking vapour in the wind / Turned but aside*
  4 hot steamy breath **Venus** 274 [of Adonis' horse] *His nostrils drink the air, and forth again, / As from a furnace, vapours doth he send*
  5 empty manifestation, worthless emanation **Tim** III.vi.97 [Timon to and of Lords] *Cap-and-knee slaves, vapours, and minute-jacks!;* **3H6** V.iii.12

vara (*adv.*) dialect form of 'very' **LL** V.ii.487 [Costard to Berowne, of only three Worthies] *it is vara fine, / For every one pursents three*

variable (*adj.*) varied, diverse, different **MV** II.viii.13 [Solanio to Salerio] *I never heard a passion so confused … and so variable;* **Cor** II.i.204; **Cym** I.vii.134; **Ham** III.i.173, IV.iii.23

variance (*n.*) falling out, disagreement, discord **AC** II.vi.127 [Enobarbus to Menas, of Caesar and Antony] *that which is the strength of their amity shall prove the immediate author of their variance*

varlet (*n.*) **1** knave, rogue, rascal, ruffian **MW** IV.ii.96 [Mistress Page to Mistress Ford, of Falstaff] *Hang him, dishonest varlet!;* **Cor** V.ii.74; **1H4** II.ii.23; **2H4** V.iii.12; **KL** II.i.25; **TC** V.iv.2
  2 manservant, page, attendant **TC** V.i.15 [Thersites to Patroclus] *Thou art thought to be Achilles' male varlet;* **TC** I.i.1

varletry (*n.*) mob, menials, ruffians **AC** V.ii.56 [Cleopatra to Proculeius] *Shall they … show me to the shouting varletry / Of censuring Rome?*

varletto (*n.*) [mock-Italian] varlet, rascal, rogue **MW** IV.v.60 [Host to Bardolph] *Where be my horses? Speak well of them, varletto*

varnish (*n.*) finish, polish, gloss **LL** I.ii.43 [Armado to Mote] *being a gentleman and a gamester] They are both the varnish of a complete man*

varnished (*adj.*) embellished, decked out, adorned **MV** II.ix.49 [Arragon to himself] *how much honour [would be] / Picked from the chaff and ruin of the times / To be new varnished*

vary (*n.*) variation, vacillation, shifting **KL** II.ii.77 [disguised Kent to Cornwall, of Oswald] *Renege, affirm, and turn their halcyon beaks / With every gale and vary of their masters* [i.e. follow every whim of their master]

vary (*v.*) **1** express in fresh words, verbalize anew **H5** III.vii.32 [Dauphin to Orleans, of his horse] *the man hath no wit that cannot ... vary deserved praise on my palfrey;* **LL** I.i.282

2 bring novelty to, cause to change **LL** IV.iii.98 [Berowne to himself] *Once more I'll mark how love can vary wit*

vassal (*n.*) **1** servant, slave, subject **2H4** IV.v.176 [Prince Henry to King Henry IV] *make me as the poorest vassal is;* **AC** V.ii.29; **AW** I.iii.154; **2H6** IV.i.111; **LL** IV.i.67; **Tem** I.ii.374

2 wretch, creature, slave **LL** I.i.246 [King reading Armado's letter to him, of Costard] *That shallow vassal;* **R3** I.iv.198

vassal (*adj.*) **1** subject, servile, subordinate **R2** III.iii.89 [King Richard to his opponents, of God's armies] *they shall strike / Your children yet unborn and unbegot, / That lift your vassal hands against my head;* **H5** III.v.51; **Luc** 608

2 submissive, abject, yielding **E3** II.i.398 [Warwick to Countess] *The lion doth ... grace his foragement by being mild / When vassal fear lies trembling at his feet;* **1H4** III.ii.124; **LL** IV.iii.222; **Sonn** 141.12

vassalage (*n.*) **1** humble people, low subjects **TC** III.ii.36 [Troilus alone] *all my powers do their bestowing lose, / Like vassalage at unawares encountering / The eye of majesty*

2 servitude, subjection, total allegiance **Sonn** 26.1 *Lord of my love, to whom in vassalage / Thy merit hath my duty strongly knit*

vast (*n.*) **1** great expanse, immense space, waste **Per** III.i.1 [Pericles alone] *The god of this great vast rebuke these surges;* **WT** II.i.29

2 long deserted period, empty space of time **Tem** I.ii.327 [Prospero to Caliban, of spirits] *for that vast of night that they may work*

vast (*adj.*) boundless, extensive, widespread **Tit** IV.i.53 [Titus to Lavinia, of her rape] *Forced in the ruthless, vast, and gloomy woods?;* **KJ** IV.iii.152; **R3** I.iv.37; **Tit** V.ii.36

vastidity (*n.*) vastness, immensity, enormity **MM** III.i.72 [Isabella to Claudio] *Though all the world's vastidity you had* [F *Through*]

vastly (*adv.*) like a wasteland, in desolation **Luc** 1740 [of Lucrece's body lying in blood] *Who like a late-sacked island vastly stood / Bare and unpeopled in this fearful flood*

vasture (*n.*) vastness, immensity, extent **E3** II.i.403 [Warwick to Countess] *can one drop of poison harm the sea, / Whose hugy vastures can digest the ill*

vasty (*adj.*) vast, immense, spacious **1H4** III.i.50 [Glendower to Hotspur] *I can call spirits from the vasty deep;* **H5** Prologue.12, II.ii.123, iv.105; **MV** II.vii.41

vault (*n.*) **1** roof, covering, ceiling **KL** V.iii.257 [Lear to all] *Had I your tongues and eyes I'd use them so / That heaven's vault should crack;* **TNK** I.i.54

2 sky **Tem** V.i.43 [Prospero alone] *'twixt the green sea and the azured vault;* **Mac** II.iii.93

3 wine-cellar, liquor storeroom **Tim** II.ii.164 [Flavius to Timon] *when our vaults have wept / With drunken spilth of wine*

vaultage (*n.*) vault, cavern, chamber **H5** II.iv.124 [Exeter to Dauphin] *caves and womby vaultages of France / Shall chide your trespass*

vaulting (*adj.*) rising and falling **2H6** III.ii.94 [Queen to King] *The pretty vaulting sea refused to drown me*

vaulty (*adj.*) **1** resembling a vault, arched, domed **RJ** III.v.22 [Romeo to Juliet] *The vaulty heaven so high above our heads;* **KJ** V.ii.52

2 empty, cavernous, sepulchral **KJ** III.iv.30 [Constance as if to death] *I will ... put my eyeballs in thy vaulty brows;* **Luc** 119

vaunt (*n.*) **1** boast, bragging assertion **2H6** III.i.50 [Suffolk to Queen, of Gloucester] *by reputing of his high descent ... / And such high vaunts of his nobility*

2 beginning, outset, first part **TC** Prologue.27 [Prologue, of the wars] *our play / Leaps o'er the vaunt and firstlings of those broils*

vaunt (*v.*) **1** boast, brag, crow **2H6** I.iii.82 [Queen to Suffolk, of the Duchess] *She vaunted 'mongst her minions t'other day / The very train of her worst wearing gown / Was better worth than all my father's lands*

2 show off, display proudly **Luc** 41 [of Tarquin] *envy ... that meaner men should vaunt / That golden hap which their superiors want*

3 exult, rejoice, revel **Sonn** 15.7 [of men as plants] *Vaunt in their youthful sap;* **R3** V.iii.289

vaunt-currier (*n.*) forerunner, announcer, herald **KL** III.ii.5 [Lear to the storm] *Vaunt-curriers of oak-cleaving thunderbolts* [F *Vauntcurriors*; Q *vaunt-currers*]

vaunter (*n.*) boaster, braggart, show-off **Tit** V.iii.112 [Lucius to all] *you know I am no vaunter, I*

vaunting (*n.*) boasting, bragging **JC** IV.iii.52 [Brutus to Cassius] *make your vaunting true*

vaunting (*adj.*) boastful, bragging, loud-mouthed **H5** II.iii.4 [Pistol to Nym] *rouse thy vaunting veins!;* **1H4** V.iii.41

vaward (*n.*) **1** [military] vanguard, foremost division **1H6** I.i.132 [Third Messenger to all, of Falstaff] *He, being in the vaward ... / Cowardly fled;* **Cor** I.vi.53; **E3** III.iii.220; **H5** IV.iii.131

2 foremost part, front line, vanguard **2H4** I.ii.178 [Falstaff to Lord Chief Justice] *we that are in the vaward of our youth ... are wags too;* **MND** IV.i.104

veal (*n.*) [unclear usage] Dutch pronunciation of 'well'; or: version of Dutch 'viel' = plenty **LL** V.ii.247 [masked Katharine to masked Longaville] *'Veal', quoth the Dutchman* [with pun on 'veal' and '-ville']

vegetive (*n.*) plant, vegetable **Per** III.ii.35 [Cerimon to First Gentleman] *the blest infusions / That dwells in vegetives*

vehemency (*n.*) vehemence, forcefulness, fervour **MM** V.i.109 [Duke to Isabella, of Angelo] *with such vehemency he should pursue / Faults proper to himself;* **H8** V.i.148

veil (*v.*) conceal, hide, disguise **MM** IV.vi.4 [Isabella to Mariana] *I am advised ... to veil full purpose;* **JC** I.ii.37

vein (*n.*) **1** state of mind, motive, mood **R3** IV.ii.115 [King Richard to Buckingham] *I am not in the giving vein today;* **AY** II.vii.95; **CE** II.ii.20, IV.iv.78; **LL** IV.iii.72; **TC** II.iii.198

2 style, manner **1H4** II.iv.380 [Falstaff to Prince Hal] *I must speak in passion, and I will do it in King Cambyses' vein;* **MND** I.ii.36

3 right line, proper course to follow **MM** II.ii.70 [Lucio aside to Isabella, of Angelo] *touch him; there's the vein*

velure (*n.*) velvet **TS** III.ii.59 [Biondello to Tranio as Lucentio, of Petruchio's horse] *with ... a woman's crupper of velure*

velvet (*n.*) piece of velvet fabric **1H4** II.ii.2 [Poins to Prince Hal, of Falstaff] *he frets like a gummed velvet* [i.e. one which wears out quickly]; **MM** I.ii.34

velvet-guard (*n.*) [someone who wears] velvet trimming **1H4** III.i.250 [Hotspur to Lady Percy, of her oaths] *leave ... such protest of pepper-gingerbread, / To velvet-guards, and Sunday citizens* ☛ guard (*n.*) 5

vendible (*adj.*) **1** saleable, marketable, sought-after **AW** I.i.153 [Parolles to Helena, of virginity] *Off with't while 'tis vendible*

2 marriageable **MV** I.i.112 [Gratiano to Antonio] *silence is only commendable / In a neat's tongue dried and a maid not vendible*

venerable commanding esteem, deserving of great respect **TN** III.iv.354 [Antonio to Second Officer, of Viola as Cesario] *to his image, which methought did promise / Most venerable worth, did I devotion*

venereal (*adj.*) displaying the character of Venus, associated with sexual desire **Tit** II.iii.37 [Aaron to Tamora, of his appearance and behaviour] *these are no venereal signs*

veney (*n.*) [fencing] bout, turn **MW** I.i.265 [Slender to Anne] *three veneys for a dish of stewed prunes*

venge (*v.*) avenge, revenge **3H6** II.i.87 [Richard to Edward, as if to York] *I'll venge thy death;* **Cym** I.vii.91; **1H6** III.iv.42; **KL** IV.ii.80; **R2** I.ii.36; **RJ** III.v.86

vengeance (*n.*) **1** harm, mischief, damage **Tit** II.iii.113 [Tamora to Demetrius, of Lavinia and Bassianus] *This vengeance on me had they executed;* **AY** IV.iii.49

    2 ☛ **SWEARING**, p.435

vengeance of fie on, a plague on **MW** IV.i.57 [Mistress Quickly to Evans, mistaking 'genitive case'] *Vengeance of Jenny's case!*

vengeance (*adj.*) formidable, tremendous, terrific **TNK** II.ii.71 [First Countryman to the others, of Arcite] *This fellow has a vengeance trick o'th' hip*

vengeance (*adv.*) exceedingly, intensely, tremendously **Cor** II.ii.5 [First Officer to Second Officer, of Coriolanus] *he's vengeance proud*

venom (*adj.*) venomous, poisonous, spiteful **CE** V.i.69 [Abbess to Adriana] *The venom clamours of a jealous woman;* **3H6** II.ii.138; **Luc** 850; **R2** II.i.19; **R3** I.iii.290

venomed (*adj.*) poisoned, venomous **Ham** IV.vii.160 [Claudius to Laertes, of Hamlet] *If he by chance escape your venomed stuck;* **R2** I.i.171; **TC** V.iii.47; **Venus** 916

venomous (*adj.*) **1** harmful, injurious, hurtful **Cor** IV.i.23 [Coriolanus to Menenius] *Thy tears are salter than a younger man's / And venomous to thine eyes*

    2 embittered, rancorous, malignant **Tit** V.iii.13 [Aaron to Lucius] *The venomous malice of my swelling heart;* **TC** IV.ii.12

vent (*n.*) **1** aperture, opening **2H4** I.Induction.2 [Rumour alone] *which of you will stop / The vent of hearing when loud Rumour speaks?;* **Luc** 310, 1040; **TC** V.iii.82

    2 emission, discharge, seepage **AC** V.ii.347 [Dolabella to Caesar, of Cleopatra] *Here, on her breast, / There is a vent of blood*

    3 airing, utterance, telling **AW** II.iii.201 [Lafew to Parolles] *Thou didst make tolerable vent of thy travel;* **Venus** 334

    4 [of a hunted animal] scent **Cor** IV.v.230 [First Servingman to Second Servingman, of war] *It's sprightly walking, audible, and full of vent*

vent (*v.*) **1** utter, express, air, proclaim **Tem** I.ii.280 [Prospero to Ariel] *thou didst vent thy groans;* **AY** II.vii.41; **Cor** I.i.207; **Cym** I.iii.4; **KL** I.i.165; **TN** IV.i.15

    2 get rid of, cast out **Cor** I.i.223 [Martius to Messenger, of the Volscian rising] *we shall ha' means to vent / Our musty super-fluity*

    3 discharge, excrete, defecate **Tem** II.ii.104 [Stephano to Trinculo, of Caliban] *Can he vent Trinculos?*

ventage (*n.*) finger-hole [of an instrument] **Ham** III.ii.365 [Hamlet to Guildenstern] *Govern these ventages with your fingers and thumb*

venter (*v.*) ☛ venture (*v.*)

ventricle (*n.*) cavity within the brain **LL** IV.ii.69 [Holofernes to Nathaniel and Dull, of his literary gifts] *These are begot in the ventricle of memory*

venture (*n.*) **1** deal, enterprise, business, expedition **MV** I.iii.88 [Antonio to Shylock, of Jacob's strategy with the sheep] *This was a venture, sir, that Jacob served for;* **2H4** Epilogue.11; **MV** I.iii.20

    2 risky enterprise, hazardous attempt **2H4** Epilogue.7 [Epilogue] *But to the purpose, and so to the venture;* **Mac** I.iii.90

    3 cargo, consignment, goods **MV** I.i.42 [Antonio to Salerio] *My ventures are not in one bottom trusted;* **2H4** II.iv.62; **JC** IV.iii.222; **MV** I.i.15

    4 prostitute **Cym** I.vii.123 [Iachimo to and of Innogen] *to be partnered ... with diseased ventures*

venture, at a without proper thought, recklessly **2H4** I.i.59 [Lord Bardolph to Northumberland, of a gentleman] *He ... / Spoke at a venture* [F *aduenture*]

venture, venter (*v.*) run a risk, take a chance, dare to act **KL** IV.ii.20 [Goneril to Edmund] *If you dare venture in your own behalf;* **2H4** I.i.183; **TNK** II.v.2; **Venus** 628

venturous (*adj.*) adventurous, daring, bold **2H6** III.ii.9 [Suffolk to Murderers, of killing Gloucester] *I will reward you for this venturous deed;* **1H6** II.i.45; **H8** I.ii.54

venue (*n.*) [fencing] sword-thrust, assault, thrust **LL** V.i.56 [Armado to Mote, of his comments] *a quick venue of wit*

Ver (*n.*) [personification of] spring, springtime **TNK** I.i.7 [Boy singing to all] *Primrose, first-born child of Ver;* **LL** V.ii.880

verbal (*adj.*) talkative, verbose, vocal **Cym** II.iii.105 [Innogen to Cloten] *You put me to forget a lady's manners, / By being so verbal*

verdict (*n.*) **1** opinion, judgement, view **1H6** III.i.63 [Richard to himself, imagining the lords talking to him] *Must your bold verdict enter talk with lords?*

    2 decision, pledge, final word **1H6** II.iv.48 [Vernon to all] *Giving my verdict on the white rose side;* **E3** IV.v.78

    3 unanimous decision, agreed judgement **Cor** I.i.11 [First Citizen to all] *Is't a verdict?*

verdour (*n.*) ☛ verdure (*n.*)

verdure, verdour (*n.*) sap, vitality, vigour, freshness **TG** I.i.49 [Valentine to Proteus, of a lover] *Losing his verdure even in the prime;* **Tem** I.ii.87; **Venus** 507

verge (*n.*) **1** rim, band, encircling edge **R3** IV.i.58 [Anne to herself, of the crown] *the inclusive verge / Of golden metal*

    2 [unclear meaning] limit, bound; rim of metal; sphere of jurisdiction **R2** II.i.102 [John of Gaunt to King Richard] *encaged in so small a verge*

    3 ☛ hallowed verge

verify (*v.*) **1** confirm, substantiate, prove correct **3H6** I.iv.126 [York to Queen] *the adage must be verified;* **H5** III.ii.69; **1H6** I.ii.32; **MA** V.i.208

    2 support, back up, bolster **Cor** V.ii.17 [Menenius to First Watch] *I have ever verified my friends ... with all the size that verity / Would without lapsing suffer* [F; sometimes emended to 'varnished']

    3 come true, be fulfilled **1H6** V.i.30 [Exeter to himself] *that will be verified / Henry the Fifth did sometime prophesy*

verily (*adj.*) true, certain, right **Tem** II.i.326 [Gonzalo to Alonso] *There was a noise, / That's verily*

verily (*adv.*) in truth, truly, indeed **Cor** I.iii.93 [Valeria to Virgilia] *Verily I do not jest with you;* **AY** IV.iii.26; **H8** II.iii.18; **TG** IV.iv.14; **TNK** V.iv.33; **WT** I.ii.11 ☛ **SWEARING**, p.435

verity (*n.*) **1** truth, truthfulness, veracity **Mac** IV.iii.92 [Malcolm to Macduff] *justice, verity ... / I have no relish of them;* **AY** III.iv.22; **Cor** V.ii.18; **Ham** V.ii.115; **H8** I.ii.159; **TNK** III.v.104

    2 truth, reality, actuality **Mac** III.i.8 [Banquo as if to Macbeth, of the Witches] *by the verities on thee made good;* **MM** IV.iii.125

versal (*adj.*) malapropism for 'universal' **RJ** II.iv.201 [Nurse to Romeo, of Juliet] *she looks as pale as any clout in the versal world*

very (*adj.*) **1** [intensifying] thorough-going, absolute **TN** I.iii.22 [Maria to Sir Toby, of Sir Andrew] *He's a very fool and a prodigal;* **Cym** V.iv.202 [First Gaoler alone] *there are verier knaves desire to live;* **TS** V.ii.64 [Baptista to Petruchio, of Katherina] *I think thou hast the veriest shrew of all;* **AC** III.x.7; **2H4** III.ii.217; **MV** III.ii.223; **TN** V.i.55; **WT** I.ii.66

    2 true, real, genuine **Tem** II.ii.103 [Stephano to Trinculo] *Thou art very Trinculo indeed;* **1H4** V.v.30; **MW** III.iv.17; **Oth** II.i.227; **Sonn** 74.6; **TG** II.ii.41

    3 mere, alone **Cym** II.iv.9 [Philario to Posthumus] *Your very goodness, and your company, / O'erpays all I can do;* **3H6** V.iii.12; **TC** III.iii.131

    4 proper, correct, appropriate **KL** V.iii.232 [Albany to all, of receiving Kent] *The time will not allow the compliment / Which very manners urges*

vesper (*n.*) evening, eventide **AC** IV.xiv.8 [Antony to Eros, of signs in the sky] *They are black vesper's pageants*

VERB FORMS

Two present-tense verb-endings from Middle English are still to be found in the Early Modern period: *-est* for the 2nd person singular following *thou* (as in *thou goest*); and *-th* or *-eth* for the 3rd person singular (as in *she goeth*). Both were reducing in frequency, and in due course the *-est* form would disappear (modern: *you go*), and the *-(e)th* form be entirely replaced by *-s* (modern: *she goes*).

In Shakespearian English, the verbs which most commonly take the *-th* ending are *hath* (*has*), *doth* (*does*), and *saith* (*says*). The factors governing the choice of this ending are not entirely understood. Context is important: *-(e)th* is used in many formal proclamations, and it is often found in stage directions; but there are some curious mixtures ('Enter Douglas; he fighteth with Falstaff, who falls down as if he were dead', **1H4** V.iv.76). The demands of the metre are also important, *-eth* giving the poet the option of an extra syllable: a rhythmical contrast with the same verb can be seen at the beginning of Cleon's speech, 'Who wanteth food and will not say he wants it' (**Per** I.iv.11).

The most distinctive verbs, both in Shakespearian and in modern English, are *be*, *have*, *do*, and the set of auxiliary verbs known as the *modals*, such as *can*, *may*, *would*, and *shall*. The chief differences between then and now are shown below.

be

Item	Modern	Description	Example
art	are	2nd person singular, present tense	**MND** III.i.140 *Thou art as wise as thou art beautiful*
beest, be'st	be	2nd person singular, present tense [usually in a clause beginning with *if*]; also a dialect usage	**H5** V.ii.201 *If ever thou beest mine*
be	are	3rd person plural, present tense	**KL** I.v.31 *Be my horses ready?*
been	are	3rd person plural, present tense [archaic]	**Per** II.Chorus.28 *when men been*
wast	were	2nd person singular, past tense	**RJ** II.iv.74 *Thou wast never with me* [Q *wert*]
wert	were	2nd person singular, past tense	**2H4** III.ii.162 *I would thou wert a man's tailor*

have

Item	Modern	Description	Example
ha'	have	☞ ELISION, p.146	
hast	have	2nd person singular, present tense	**Tem** I.i.19 *remember whom thou hast aboard*
hath	have	3rd person singular, present tense	**MW** III.iv.100 *A kind heart he hath*
hadst	had	2nd person singular, past tense	**MW** V.iii.281 *where thou hadst this ring*

do

Item	Modern	Description	Example
dost	do	2nd person singular, present tense	**TN** III.iv.31 *Why dost thou smile so*
doth	does	3rd person singular, present tense	**1H4** III.iii.92 *How doth thy husband?*
didst	did	2nd person singular, past tense	**TS** Induction.i.87 *thou didst it excellent*
didest	did	2nd person singular, past tense [rare]	**Ham** IV.vii.56 *Thus didest thou*

Modals

Item	Modern	Description	Example
canst	can	2nd person singular	**R3** III.v.1 *canst thou quake*
'ce	shall	dialect use	**KL** IV.vi.240 *I'ce try*
'chill	will	dialect use	**KL** IV.vi.235 *'Chill not let go*
'choud	should	dialect use	**KL** IV.vi.238 *And 'choud ha' bin zwaggered*
mayst	may	2nd person singular	**R3** I.iii.203 *Long mayst thou live*

(continues)

VERB FORMS – *continued*

Item	Modern	Description	Example
mought	might	[in the sense of 'could']	**3H6** V.ii.45 *That mought not be distinguished*
's	shall	dialect or colloquial	**RJ** I.iii.10 *thou's hear our counsel*
shalt	shall	2nd person singular	**3H6** I.ii.36 *thou shalt to London*
shouldst	should	2nd person singular	**Oth** III.iii.378 *thou shouldst be honest*
'st	will	dialect	**Cor** I.i.124 *you'st hear the belly's answer*
wilt	will	2nd person singular	**TG** I.i.11 *Wilt thou be gone?*
wolt	will	[=*wilt*] dialect	**Per** IV.i.62 *wolt out?*
woo	would	2nd person singular	**Ham** V.i.271 *Woo't weep?*
wot	will	[=*wilt*] dialect	**2H4** II.i.54 *Thou wot, wot thou*
wouldst	would	2nd person singular	**MV** II.ii.111 *Wouldst thou aught with me?*

vessel *(n.)* body, frame **JC** V.v.13 [Clitus to Dardanius, of Brutus] *Now is that noble vessel full of grief;* **AY** II.iv.6; **LL** I.i.261; **Oth** IV.ii.82; **RJ** I.i.15; **WT** III.iii.20

vestal *(n.)* woman vowed to chastity, virgin, priestess **Luc** 883 [Lucrece as if to opportunity] *Thou mak'st the vestal violate her oath;* **AC** III.xii.31; **CE** IV.iv.73; **MND** II.i.158; **Per** IV.v.7; **Venus** 752

vestal *(adj.)* **1** as a virgin priestess **Per** III.iv.10 [Thaisa to Cerimon] *A vestal livery will I take me to;* **TNK** V.i.150
   2 virgin **RJ** II.ii.8 [Romeo to himself, of the moon] *Her vestal livery is but sick and green;* **RJ** III.iii.38

vesture *(n.)* garment, clothing, garb, costume **JC** III.ii.197 [Antony to all] *what weep you when you but behold / Our Caesar's vesture wounded?;* **Cor** II.i.226; **MV** V.i.64; **Oth** II.i.64; **TG** II.iv.158

vex *(v.)* afflict, trouble, torment **Tit** V.i.62 [Aaron to Lucius] *'Twill vex thy soul to hear what I shall speak;* **1H6** I.iv.13; **3H6** II.vi.68; **KL** III.iv.58; **RJ** III.v.95; **Sonn** 135.3

vexation *(n.)* **1** agitation, disturbance, turmoil **Oth** I.i.73 [Iago to Roderigo, of Brabantio's joy] *throw such chances of vexation on't, / As it may lose some colour;* **MND** IV.i.68
   2 torment, affliction, mortification **Cor** III.iii.140 [Sicinius to Plebeians, of Coriolanus] *Give him deserved vexation*
   3 anguish, grief, affliction **1H6** IV.iii.41 [Richard to Lucy] *Vexation almost stops my breath*

vexed *(adj.)* **1** troubled, distressed, grieved **KJ** III.i.17 [Constance to Salisbury] *With my vexed spirits I cannot take a truce*
   2 stormy, turbulent, blustery **KL** IV.iv.2 [Cordelia to Doctor, of Lear] *As mad as the vexed sea* [F; Q *vent*]

vext *(adj.)* vexed **Tem** IV.i.158 [Prospero to Ferdinand] *I am vext*

via, fia *(int.)* **1** come / go on, hurry up **MV** II.ii.9 [Launcelot alone] *'Fia!' says the fiend; 'Away!' says the fiend;* **LL** V.i.142; **MW** II.ii.149
   2 forward, onward **3H6** II.i.181 [Warwick to Edward, of the size of their army] *Will but amount to five and twenty thousand, / Why, via!;* **LL** V.ii.112

vial *(n.)* phial, small bottle, flask **TNK** I.v.5 [Song] *Sacred vials filled with tears;* **AC** I.iii.64; **Ham** I.v.62; **R2** I.i.17; **RJ** V.i.93; **WT** III.iii.122

viand *(n.)* (usually plural) food, victuals, foodstuff **Per** II.iii.31 [Thaisa to herself] *All viands that I eat do seem unsavoury;* **AC** III.xi.73; **Cor** I.i.98; **Cym** V.v.156; **3H6** II.v.52; **MV** I.i.97

vice *(n.)* **1** (usually capitalized) buffoon, stage jester **TN** IV.ii.123 [Feste, singing] *In a trice, like to the old Vice;* **Ham** III.iv.99; **1H4** II.iv.441; **2H4** III.ii.308; **R3** III.i.82 ☞ **CONTEMPORARY FIGURES**, p.629
   2 grip, grasp **2H4** II.i.21 [Fang to Hostess, of Falstaff] *An I but fist him once, an 'a come but within my vice* [F; Q *view*]
   3 screw **MA** V.ii.21 [Benedick to Margaret, of a buckler] *you must put in the pikes with a vice* [with bawdy pun]

vice *(v.)* force, constrain, press hard **WT** I.ii.416 [Camillo to Polixenes, of Leontes] *As he had … been an instrument / To vice you to't, that you have touched his queen / Forbiddenly*

vicegerent *(n.)* **1** official acting in place of a ruler during his absence **E3** IV.i.38 [Percy to King Edward] *from … the lord viceregent / I bring this happy tidings of success*
   2 deputy, second-in-command **LL** I.i.216 [King reading Armado's letter to him] *the welkin's viceregent*

viceroy *(n.)* substitute ruler, deputy monarch **Tem** III.ii.109 [Stephano to Trinculo and Caliban] *Trinculo and thyself shall be viceroys*

vicious *(adj.)* **1** defective, faulty, bad **Ham** I.iv.24 [Hamlet to Horatio, of certain men who have] *some vicious mole of nature in them;* **Oth** III.iii.144
   2 blameworthy, reprehensible, shameful **Cym** V.v.65 [Cymbeline to all, of the Queen] *It had been vicious / To have mistrusted her;* **H8** I.ii.117
   3 caused by vice, immoral, depraved **KL** I.i.227 [Cordelia to Lear, of the cause of her situation] *It is no vicious blot, murder or foulness*

victual *(n.)* (usually plural) provisions, supplies, food and drink **E3** IV.ii.4 [King Edward to Derby, of Calais] *neither victuals nor supply of men / May come to succour this accursed town;* **Cym** III.vii.13; **E3** IV.ii.21, 31; **MA** I.i.46

victual *(v.)* supply, furnish, provide [with food] **AY** V.iv.189 [Jaques to Touchstone] *thy loving voyage / Is but for two months victualled;* **1H6** I.v.14

victualler *(n.)* inn-keeper, tavern-owner **2H4** II.iv.341 [Hostess to Falstaff, of allowing meat to be sold in Lent] *All victuallers do so*

vie *(v.)* **1** stake, venture, wager **AC** V.ii.98 [Cleopatra to Dolabella] *Nature wants stuff / To vie strange forms with fancy*
   2 [cards] raise the stakes, add to a total **TS** II.i.302 [Petruchio to all, of Katherina's supposed behaviour] *kiss on kiss / She vied so fast*
   3 offer in competition, display in rivalry **Per** IV.Chorus.33 [Gower alone] *With dove of Paphos might the crow / Vie feathers white*

view *(n.)* **1** sight, range of vision **JC** I.i.74 [Flavius to Marullus, of Caesar] *Who else would soar above the view of men;* **TC** III.iii.241 [also: sense 2]
   2 inspection, examination **TN** II.ii.19 [Viola alone, of Olivia] *She made good view of me;* **TC** IV.v.232
   3 presence, meeting, sight **AC** II.ii.172 [Caesar to Antony] *And do invite you to my sister's view*

viewless *(adj.)* invisible, unseeable **MM** III.i.127 [Claudio to Isabella] *To be imprisoned in the viewless winds*

vigour *(n.)* power, efficacy, effect **Ham** I.v.68 [Ghost to Hamlet, of the poison] *And with a sudden vigour it doth posset;* **Cym** I.vi.21; **MM** II.ii.184; **Tem** I.ii.486; **Venus** 953

vild *(n./adj.)* ☞ **vile** *(n./adj.)*

vildly *(adv.)* ➤ vilely *(adv.)*

vile, vild *(n.)* **1** lowly person, person of humble birth 2H4 III.i.15 [King Henry IV alone, as if to sleep] *why liest thou with the vile / In loathsome beds*

2 worthless person, one not deserving of praise Tim I.i.15 [Poet reciting to himself] *When we for recompense have praised the vile*

vile, vild *(adj.)* **1** degrading, ignominious, worthless KL III.ii.71 [Lear to disguised Kent] *The art of our necessities … can make vile things precious;* 1H4 III.ii.87; 1H6 V.iii.112; KL III.iv.138; LL IV.iii.274; MV II.iv.6

2 despicable, disgusting, abhorrent AW II.i.174 [Helena to King] *Extended / With vildest torture let my life be ended;* AC V.ii.313; 1H6 V.iv.16; JC I.iii.111; KJ III.i.138

3 shameful, contemptible, wretched 2H4 I.ii.17 [Falstaff to Page] *I will inset you neither in gold nor silver, but in vile apparel;* H5 IV.Chorus.50; JC IV.iii.71; KL IV.vi.278; Tim IV.iii.466; TN III.iv.356

4 lowly, of humble birth H5 IV.iii.62 [King Henry to all, of those who may die in the battle] *be he ne'er so vile, / This day shall gentle his condition*

vile-drawing *(adj.)* attracting towards evil KJ II.i.577 [Bastard alone, of commodity] *this advantage, this vile-drawing bias* [no hyphen in F]

vilely, vildly *(adv.)* shamefully, wretchedly, meanly 2H4 II.ii.6 [Prince Henry to Poins] *Doth it not show vilely in me to desire small beer?;* JC IV.iii.131; MV I.ii.81; WT IV.iv.22

villagery *(n.)* villages MND II.i.35 [Fairy to Puck] *Are not you he / That frights the maidens of the villagery*

villain *(n.)* **1** serf, servant, bondman AY II.ii.3 [Duke Frederick to all] *some villains of my court / Are of consent and sufferance in this* [i.e. have been accomplices]; CE I.ii.19; Luc 1338; RJ III.i.94; Tem I.ii.309; Tit IV.iii.73

2 scoundrel, rogue, rascal CE I.ii.96 [Antipholus of Syracuse alone] *The villain is o'er-raught of all my money;* LL I.ii.140; MW IV.v.65; TC III.ii.31; TN I.v.93; WT I.ii.136

villain *(adj.)* lowly, boorish, base Cym IV.ii.71 [Cloten to departing Belarius and Arviragus] *[are you] Some villain mountaineers?*

villain-like *(adv.)* like a serf; or: like a rogue KL V.iii.99 [Edmund to Albany] *What in the world he is / That names me traitor, villain-like he lies*

villainous *(adv.)* villainously, vilely, detestably Tem IV.i.249 [Caliban to Stephano and Trinculo] *apes / With foreheads villainous low*

villain-slave *(n.)* villainous wretch R3 IV.iv.144 [Queen Elizabeth to King Richard] *thou villain-slave*

villainy *(n.)* **1** coarseness, boorishness, discourtesy MA II.i.126 [masked Beatrice to masked Benedick, of Benedick] *the commendation is not in his wit, but in his villainy*

2 shaming practice, discrediting activity MW II.i.91 [Mistress Ford to Mistress Page, of Falstaff] *I will consent to act any villainy against him*

villiago *(n.)* villain, scoundrel, rogue 2H6 IV.viii.45 [Clifford to the rebels, of the French] *Crying 'Villiago!' unto all they meet*

vindicative *(adj.)* vindictive, punitive, revengeful TC V.v.107 [Ulysses to Agamemnon, of Troilus] *he in heat of action / Is more vindicative than jealous love*

vinegar *(adj.)* sour, bitter, crabby MV I.i.54 [Solanio to Antonio, of certain people] *of such vinegar aspect / That they'll not show their teeth in way of smile*

vinewed *(adj.)* mouldy, rotten, decaying TC II.i.14 [Ajax to Thersites] *Speak, then, you vinewd'st leaven* [F *whinid'st;* Q *vnsalted*]

viol *(n.)* type of stringed instrument played with a bow Per III.ii.89 [Cerimon to a servant] *The viol once more!;* Per I.i.82; R2 I.iii.162 ➤ bass viol *(n.)*

viol-de-gamboys *(n.)* viola da gamba TN I.iii.23 [Sir Toby to Maria, of Sir Andrew] *He plays o'the viol-de-gamboys*

violent *(adj.)* **1** extreme, intense, utmost Cor IV.vi.74 [Menenius to Sicinius, of Coriolanus] *He and Aufidius can no more atone / Than violent'st contrariety*

2 rushed, hasty, impetuous WT III.i.17 [Dion to Cleomenes, of their journey to the oracle] *The violent carriage of it / Will clear or end the business*

violent *(v.)* rage with violence, seethe, rampage TC IV.iv.4 [Cressida to Pandarus] *The grief … violenteth in a sense as strong / As that which causeth it* [Q; F *no lesse*]

virgin *(v.)* remain a virgin, stay chaste Cor V.iii.48 [Coriolanus to Virgilia, of his kiss] *my true lip / Hath virgined it e'er since*

virginal *(adj.)* **1** typical of a virgin Per IV.vi.54 [Bawd to Marina, of Lysimachus] *without any more virginal fencing, will you use him kindly?*

2 of young girls 2H6 V.ii.52 [Young Clifford to himself, of his revenge] *tears virginal / Shall be to me even as the dew to fire;* Cor V.ii.41

virginal *(v.)* move the fingers up and down [as if playing a virginal] WT I.ii.125 [Leontes to himself, of Hermione and Polixenes] *Still virginalling / Upon his palm?*

virginals *(n.)* small keyboard instrument TNK III.iii.34 [Palamon to Arcite] *Play o'th' virginals?* [with bawdy pun]

virgin-knot *(n.)* maidenhead, virginity Tem IV.i.15 [Prospero to Ferdinand, of Miranda] *If thou dost break her virgin-knot before / All sanctimonious ceremonies may … be ministered*

virtue *(n.)* **1** quality, accomplishment, ability 1H6 I.i.9 [Gloucester to all, of Henry V] *Virtue he had, deserving to command;* AW I.i.60; Cor I.i.172; MND III.i.133; Per II.i.146; TNK II.v.23

2 essence, heart, soul Tim III.v.8 [Alcibiades to Senators] *For pity is the virtue of the law;* MND IV.i.168; Tem I.ii.27

3 courage, valour, bravery 1H4 II.iv.115 [Falstaff to all] *A plague of all cowards! … Is there no virtue extant?* AC V.viii.17; Cor III.i.73; 2H4 I.iii.170; KL V.iii.103; TNK III.vi.81

4 power, capability, efficacy, property MV V.i.199 [Portia to Bassanio] *If you had known the virtue of the ring;* Cym I.vi.23; Ham IV.v.157; LL V.ii.348; Mac IV.iii.156; RJ II.iii.9

5 worth, value, excellence TC I.iii.30 [Agamemnon to all] *what hath mass or matter by itself / Lies rich in virtue and unmingled*

6 goodness, benevolence, kindness AW I.i.8 [Lafew to Bertram, of the King] *He … must of necessity hold his virtue to you*

7 authority, jurisdiction, power 2H4 IV.i.161 [Hastings to Westmorland] *Hath the Prince John a full commission, / In very ample virtue of his father*

8 virtuous self, honour, excellency H8 III.i.103 [Queen Katherine to Campeius and Wolsey] *Holy men I thought ye … two reverend cardinal virtues;* TC III.iii.169; Tim III.v.7

9 chastity, sexual purity KL III.ii.54 [Lear to disguised Kent, as if to criminals] *Hide thee … thou simular of virtue / That art incestuous*

virtuous *(adj.)* **1** potent, powerful, efficacious Oth III.iv.107 [Cassio to Desdemona, of Othello] *by your virtuous means I may again / Exist and be a member of his love;* MND III.ii.367

2 showing fine qualities, praiseworthy AY I.iii.79 [Duke Frederick to Celia, of Rosalind] *thou wilt show more bright and seem more virtuous / When she is gone;* AY II.iii.5; 2H4 IV.v.76

3 capable of producing great growth, beneficial MM II.ii.168 [Angelo alone] *I … / Do as the carrion does, not as the flower, / Corrupt with virtuous season*

4 arising from virtuous practice, justifiable, well-warranted Tim III.ii.41 [Servilius to Lucius, of Timon] *If his occasion were not virtuous, / I should not urge it half so faithfully*

virtuously *(adv.)* steadfastly, strongly, powerfully Tim I.ii.229 [First Lord to Timon] *We are so virtuously bound*

visage *(n.)* **1** face, countenance 2H6 V.i.69 [King to Iden, of Cade] *let me view his visage* ➤ FEW, p.xxi

2 outward appearance, aspect, air **TNK** V.iv.127 [Theseus to Palamon] *The visages of bridegrooms we'll put on;* **Ham** III.i.47, iv.51; **Oth** I.i.50; **TN** III.ii.61

visaged *(adj.)* featured, looking **TNK** V.iii.41 [Emilia to herself] *Arcite is gently visaged* [i.e. of a gentle countenance]

vision *(n.)* sight, object of sight, display **WT** I.ii.270 [Leontes to Camillo, of Hermione's behaviour] *to a vision so apparent rumour / Cannot be mute*

visit *(v.)* **1** punish, deal with **KJ** II.i.179 [Constance to Queen Eleanor, of Arthur] *Thy sins are visited in this poor child;* **H5** IV.i.171; **MV** III.v.12
2 supply, furnish, provide **TG** I.i.60 [Valentine to Proteus, of being sent his news] *And I likewise will visit thee with mine*
3 afflict with sickness, strike down with disease **LL** V.ii.422 [Berowne to Rosaline, of his friends being in love] *These lords are visited;* **1H4** IV.i.26

visitating *(adj.)* visiting, attending, observing **TNK** I.i.146 [First Queen to Theseus] *our lords / Lie blistering 'fore the visitating sun*

visitation *(n.)* **1** visit **H8** I.i.179 [Buckingham to Norfolk] *Charles the Emperor ... here makes visitation;* **MM** III.ii.230; **R3** III.vii.106; **Tem** III.i.32; **Tim** I.i.220; **WT** I.i.6
2 forceful onset, violence, buffeting **2H4** III.i.21 [King Henry IV alone] *the visitation of the winds, / Who take the ruffian billows by the top*

visitor *(n.)* parish visitor [of the sick], charity worker **Tem** II.i.12 [Antonio aside to Sebastian, of Gonzalo and Alonso] *The visitor will not give him o'er so*

visor *(n.)* mask **LL** V.ii.385 [Rosaline to Berowne] *Which of the visors was it that you wore?;* **LL** V.ii.271; **MA** II.i.86; **Per** IV.iv.44; **R3** II.ii.28; **RJ** I.v.23

visored *(adj.)* masked **LL** V.ii.158 [stage direction] *Enter ... the King and the rest of the lords disguised like Russians and visored*

vital *(adj.)* life-supporting, animating **2H6** III.ii.41 [King to all, of Suffolk] *Came he right now to sing a raven's note, / Whose dismal tune bereft my vital powers;* **2H4** IV.iii.108 ☞ spirit *(n.)* 3

vizament *(n.)* malapropism for 'advisement' [consideration] **MW** I.i.36 [Evans to Shallow] *Take your vizaments in that*

vizard *(n.)* mask, visor **1H4** II.ii.51 [Bardolph to all] *on with your vizards;* **E3** I.i.77; **1H4** I.ii.126; **H8** IV.ii.83; **Mac** III.ii.34; **MW** IV.iv.68

vizard *(v.)* cover with a mask; conceal, hide **TC** I.iii.83 [Ulysses to all] *Degree being vizarded, / Th'unworthiest shows as fairly in the mask*

vizarded *(adj.)* masked, visored, disguised **MW** IV.vi.40 [Fenton to Host, of the people present] *they must all be masked and vizarded*

vizard-like *(adj.)* like a mask, expressionless **3H6** I.iv.116 [York to Queen] *thy face is vizard-like*

vlouting-stock, -stog *(n.)* dialect form of 'flouting-stock' [= laughing-stock, object of derision] **MW** III.i.108 [Evans to Caius, of the Host] *He has made us his vlouting-stog;* **MW** IV.v.74 [Evans to Host] *You are wise, and full of gibes and vlouting-stocks* ☞ **WELSH**, p.649; stock *(n.)* 4

voice *(n.)* **1** vote, official support **Ham** III.ii.349 [Rosencrantz to Hamlet] *you have the voice of the King himself* ☞ **FEW**, p.xxi
2 support, approval, good word **Ham** I.iii.68 [Polonius to Laertes] *Give every man thine ear, but few thy voice;* **JC** II.i.146; **MND** I.i.54; **MW** I.iv.151; **TC** V.iii.74
3 authoritative opinion, judgement **Ham** V.ii.243 [Laertes to Hamlet] *I have a voice and precedent of peace;* **H8** II.ii.86; **MW** I.iii.42; **TC** I.iii.187, IV.v.70
4 talk, rumour, opinion **H8** IV.iii.11 [Griffith to Katherine, of how Wolsey died] *Well, the voice goes, madam;* **H8** V.iii.175; **Oth** I.iii.223; **TN** I.v.249
5 shout of acclamation, cry of applause **TC** I.iii.382 [Ulysses to Nestor, of the prospect of Ajax defeating Hector] *We'll dress him up in voices;* **Tit** I.i.233

voice *(v.)* **1** vote, elect, appoint **Cor** II.iii.233 [Sicinius to Citizens, of Coriolanus] *your minds ... made you against the grain / To voice him consul*
2 talk about, acclaim, praise **Tim** IV.iii.82 [Timandra to and of Timon] *Is this th'Athenian minion whom the world / Voiced so regardfully?*

void *(adj.)* **1** empty, lacking, devoid **2H6** IV.vii.59 [Lord Say to Cade] *[I] hope you are not void of pity;* **TNK** III.i.36
2 uncrowded, unfrequented, roomy **JC** II.iv.37 [Soothsayer to Portia] *I'll get me to a place more void*

void *(v.)* **1** empty, clear out, discharge **MV** I.iii.114 [Shylock to Antonio] *You, that did void your rheum upon my beard;* **H5** III.v.52
2 leave, withdraw, quit **H5** IV.vii.57 [King Henry to a herald, of the French lords] *bid them come down, / Or void the field*

void up *(v.)* bring up, regurgitate, disgorge **Tim** I.ii.135 [Apemantus to himself] *We ... spend our flatteries to drink those men / Upon whose age we void it up again*

voiding lobby antechamber, waiting-room **2H6** IV.i.61 [Suffolk to the Lieutenant] *in our voiding lobby hast thou stood / And duly waited for my coming forth*

volley *(v.)* utter, express, proclaim **AC** II.vii.110 [Enobarbus to all] *The holding every man shall beat as loud / As his strong sides can volley*

voluble *(adj.)* **1** fluent, eloquent, articulate **LL** II.i.76 [Rosaline to Princess, of Berowne] *So sweet and voluble is his discourse;* **LL** III.i.64
2 glib, facile, persuasive **Oth** II.i.231 [Iago to Roderigo, of Cassio] *a knave very voluble*
3 changeable, inconstant, mutable **TNK** I.ii.67 [Palamon to Arcite, of Creon] *deifies alone / Voluble chance*

volume, by the to a great extent, a large number of times **Cor** III.iii.33 [Coriolanus to Menenius] *an hostler, that for th'poorest piece / Will bear the knave by th'volume*

voluntary *(n.)* volunteer **KJ** II.i.67 [Chatillon to King Philip, of English soldiers] *Rash, inconsiderate, fiery voluntaries;* **TC** II.i.97

voluntary *(adj.)* willing, ready, enthusiastic **Oth** IV.i.27 [Iago to Othello, of knaves] *Who having by their own importunate suit / Or voluntary dotage of some mistress / Convinced or supplied them*

vor *(v.)* dialect version of 'warn' **KL** IV.vi.240 [Edgar to Oswald, adopting a country accent] *keep out, che vor' ye* [i.e. I warrant you]

votaress *(n.)* woman under vow, votary, devotee [of an order] **Per** IV.Chorus.4 [Gower alone, of Thaisa] *Unto Diana there's a votaress;* **MND** II.i.123, 163

votarist *(n.)* vow-taker, religious, nun / monk **MM** I.iv.5 [Isabella to Francisca] *the sisterhood, the votarists of Saint Clare;* **Oth** IV.ii.188; **Tim** IV.iii.27

votary *(n.)* **1** devotee, disciple, worshipper [of] **TG** III.ii.58 [Duke to Proteus] *You are already Love's firm votary;* **Sonn** 154.5; **TG** I.i.52
2 someone bound by a special vow **LL** II.i.37 [Princess to Lords] *Who are the votaries ... / That are vow-fellows with this virtuous Duke?;* **LL** IV.ii.136, V.ii.872

vouch *(n.)* **1** formal statement, attestation, express declaration **H8** I.i.157 [Buckingham to Norfolk, of declaring Wolsey treasonous] *I'll ... make my vouch as strong / As shore of rock;* **MM** II.iv.156
2 approval, testimony, witness **Oth** II.i.144 [Desdemona to Iago, of a deserving woman] *One that ... did justly put on the vouch of very malice itself?*
3 warrant, guarantee, formal confirmation **Cor** II.iii.116 [Coriolanus alone] *To beg of Hob and Dick that does appear / Their needless vouches?*

vouch *(v.)* **1** make good, uphold, support **TNK** V.iv.107 [Theseus to Palamon] *our master Mars / Hath vouched his oracle;* **Tit** I.i.363
2 guarantee, assure, warrant **Ham** V.i.106 [Hamlet to Horatio, of a lawyer] *Will his vouchers vouch him no more of his purchases* [pun: voucher *(n.)*, sense 2]
3 pledge, praise, commend **Mac** III.iv.33 [Lady Macbeth to Macbeth] *The feast is sold / That is not often vouched*

vouched *(adj.)* guaranteed, attested, certified **Tem** II.i.63 [Sebastian to Antonio, of rare events being beyond belief] *As many vouched rarities are*

voucher *(n.)* **1** piece of evidence, circumstance **Cym** II.ii.39 [Iachimo to himself, of Innogen's mole] *Here's a voucher, / Stronger than ever law could make*

    2 [legal] warrantor of someone's right to property **Ham** V.i.103 [Hamlet to Horatio, of a lawyer] *a great buyer of land, with his ... double vouchers* [*double* = two such warrantors; pun: 106, *vouch* (*v.*), sense 2]

vouchsafe *(v.)* **1** allow, permit, grant **Ham** III.ii.304 [Guildenstern to Hamlet] *vouchsafe me a word with you;* **Cym** II.iii.38; **H8** II.iii.71; **JC** III.i.130; **MW** II.ii.39; **Tem** I.ii.423 ☛ **POLITENESS**, p.340

    2 be pleased to accept, graciously receive **Tim** I.i.156 [Poet to Timon] *Vouchsafe my labour;* **JC** II.i.313

    3 deign, condescend **AC** V.ii.160 [Cleopatra to Caesar] *thou vouchsafing here to visit me*

    4 cope with, sustain, be prepared to bear **H8** II.iii.43 [Old Lady to Anne, of accepting a husband lower than king] *If your back / Cannot vouchsafe this burden*

vouchsafed *(adj.)* well-bestowed, kindly granted **TN** III.i.86 [Viola as Cesario to Olivia] *My matter hath no voice, lady, but to your own most pregnant and vouchsafed ear*

vow-fellow *(n.)* person bound by the same vow **LL** II.i.38 [Princess to Lords] *Who are the votaries ... / That are vow-fellows with this virtuous Duke?*

vox *(n.)* proper voice, right manner of speaking **TN** V.i.293 [Feste to Olivia, of reading Malvolio's letter frantically] *you must allow vox*

vulgar *(n.)* **1** common people, ordinary folk **LL** I.ii.48 [Mote to Armado, of one more than two] *Which the base vulgar do call three;* **H5** IV.vii.75; **JC** I.i.70; **WT** II.i.94

    2 familiar, ordinary, everyday **E3** II.i.315 [King Edward to Warwick] *These are the vulgar tenders of false men;* **Cor** IV.vii.21; **Ham** I.ii.99; **1H4** III.ii.41; **1H6** III.ii.4; **TN** III.i.121

    3 vernacular, everyday language **AY** V.i.46 [Touchstone to William] *abandon - which is in the vulgar 'leave';* **LL** IV.i.70

vulgar *(adj.)* **1** public, general, common **2H4** I.iii.90 [Archbishop to all] *An habitation giddy and unsure / Hath he that buildeth on the vulgar heart;* **CE** III.i.100; **Cor** II.i.207; **KJ** II.i.387

    2 generally known, commonly acknowledged **KL** IV.vi.210 [Gentleman to Edgar, of the impending battle] *Most sure and vulgar;* **AC** III.xiii.119

    3 cheap, common to all, plebeian **Ham** I.iii.61 [Polonius to Laertes] *Be thou familiar, but by no means vulgar*

    4 low-born, humble, menial **2H6** IV.i.130 [Suffolk to First Gentleman] *rather let my head / Stoop to the block ... / Than stand uncovered to the vulgar groom*

vulgarly *(adv.)* publicly, openly, in front of the world **MM** V.i.160 [Friar Peter to Duke, of Angelo] *So vulgarly and personally accused*

vulgo *(adv.)* [unclear meaning] popularly, commonly; in everyday speech **TN** I.iii.39 [Sir Toby to Maria] *Castiliano, vulgo - for here comes Sir Andrew Agueface!*

vulture *(adj.)* ravenous, devouring, rapacious **Venus** 551 [of Venus approaching Adonis] *Whose vulture thought doth pitch the price so high / That she will draw his lips' rich treasure dry*

wafer-cake *(n.)* type of thin, lightweight cake **H5** II.iii.48 [Pistol to Hostess] *men's faiths are wafer-cakes* [i.e. are extremely fragile]

waft *(v.)* **1** beckon, wave [at], signal **Tim** I.i.73 [Poet to Painter, of Timon] *Whom Fortune with her ivory hand wafts to her;* **CE** II.ii.118; **MV** V.i.11

2 carry, convey, transport [over the sea] **2H6** IV.i.117 [Whitmore to Suffolk] *Come, Suffolk, I must waft thee to thy death;* **2H6** IV.i.115; **3H6** III.iii.253, V.vii.41

3 turn derisively, direct scornfully **WT** I.ii.372 [Polixenes to Camillo, of Leontes] *Wafting his eyes to th'contrary*

waft over *(v.)* carry across, transport **KJ** II.i.73 [Chatillon to King Philip, of English soldiers] *the English bottoms have waft o'er*

waftage *(n.)* passage, conveyance by water **CE** IV.i.96 [Dromio of Syracuse to Antipholus of Ephesus] *A ship you sent me to, to hire waftage;* **TC** III.ii.9

wafture *(n.)* waving, gesture, flourish **JC** II.i.246 [Portia to Brutus] *with an angry wafture of your hand / Gave sign for me to leave you*

wag *(n.)* fellow, lad, mischievous boy **1H4** I.ii.16 [Falstaff to Prince Hal] *I prithee sweet wag* [also: habitual joker]; **1H4** I.ii.23, 44; **2H4** I.ii.179; **MA** V.i.16; **TG** V.iv.86

wag *(v.)* **1** go off, depart, go on one's way **MW** II.i.212 [Host to all] *Shall we wag?;* **MW** I.iii.6, II.iii.64, 88

2 talk foolishly, utter silly remarks **MA** V.i.16 [Leonato to Antonio] *Bid sorrow wag, cry 'hem!' when he should groan* [F *sorrow, wagge*]

3 move, stir, rouse **Ham** V.i.263 [Hamlet to all] *Until my eyelids will no longer wag;* **AY** II.vii.23; **Cym** IV.ii.173; **2H4** V.iii.34; **MV** IV.i.76; **Tit** V.ii.87

wage *(v.)* **1** risk, venture upon, engage in **Oth** I.iii.30 [First Senator to Duke] *We must not think the Turk is so unskilful ... / To wake and wage a danger profitless;* **1H4** IV.iv.20; **KJ** I.i.266

2 stake, hazard **Cym** I.v.129 [Posthumus to Iachimo] *I will wage against your gold, gold to it;* **Ham** V.ii.145; **KL** I.i.156

3 compete, be a rival to, measure up to **Per** IV.ii.29 [Pander to Bawd] *the commodity wages not with the danger*

4 struggle, do battle, vie **KL** II.iv.204 [Lear to all] *I ... choose / To wage against the enmity o'th' air;* **AC** V.i.31

5 pay, recompense, reward **Cor** V.vi.40 [Aufidius to Conspirators, of Coriolanus] *He waged me with his countenance*

waggish *(adj.)* playful, mischievous, impish **MND** I.i.240 [Helena to herself] *As waggish boys in game themselves forswear, / So the boy love is perjured everywhere;* **Cym** III.iv.159

waggon, wagon *(n.)* carriage, coach **AW** IV.iv.34 [Helena to Widow and Diana] *Our wagon is prepared;* **Tit** V.ii.51; **WT** IV.iv.118

waggoner, wagoner *(n.)* driver, charioteer **RJ** I.iv.67 [Mercutio to Romeo, of Queen Mab] *Her wagoner, a small grey-coated gnat;* **RJ** III.ii.2; **Tit** V.ii.48

wagtail *(n.)* [contemptuous form of address] tail-wagger, bower and scraper **KL** II.ii.65 [disguised Kent to Oswald] *you wagtail!*

wail *(v.)* bewail, lament, grieve [for] **3H6** V.iv.1 [Queen to all] *wise men ne'er sit and wail their loss;* **3H6** II.iii.26; **Luc** 1508; **R2** II.ii.22; **Sonn** 9.4

wailful *(adj.)* plaintive, disconsolate, wistful **TG** III.ii.69 [Proteus to Thurio, of Silvia] *You must ... tangle her desires / By wailful sonnets*

wain-rope *(n.)* waggon-rope **TN** III.ii.57 [Sir Toby to Fabian, of Sir Andrew and Viola as Cesario] *I think oxen and wain-ropes cannot hale them together*

wainscot *(n.)* wooden panelling **AY** III.iii.79 [Jaques to Touchstone and Audrey, of Martext] *This fellow will but join you together as they join wainscot*

waist *(n.)* **1** girdle, belt **1H6** IV.iii.20 [Lucy to Richard] *Spur to the rescue of the noble Talbot, / Who now is girdled with a waist of iron;* **KJ** II.i.217; **MM** III.ii.38

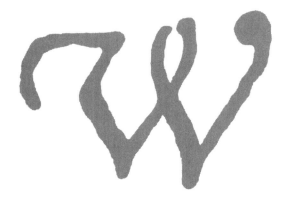

2 middle [of the upper deck], centre **Tem** I.ii.197 [Ariel to Prospero, of the ship] *Now on the beak, / Now in the waist* ➤ **SHIPS**, p.397

wait (*v.*) be in attendance, do service **RJ** I.iii.104 [Servingman to Lady Capulet] *I must hence to wait;* **1H4** I.ii.69; **2H6** IV.vi.62; **LL** V.ii.401

wait on / upon (*v.*) **1** accompany, attend **3H6** III.iii.42 [Queen to Lewis] *impatience waiteth on true sorrow;* **Tim** II.ii.40 [Timon to lords] *I'll wait upon you instantly;* **Ham** II.ii.265; **H5** II.ii.110; **MW** I.i.244; **Tem** I.ii.389
2 follow in escort, attend **KJ** V.vii.98 [Bastard to Prince Henry] *you … / With other princes that may best be spared, / Shall wait upon your father's funeral*
3 go on before, proceed ahead of **1H6** I.i.45 [Bedford to the heralds] *wait on us*
4 attend to, pay attention to, not ignore **Tit** IV.i.121 [Titus to Marcus] *Lucius and I'll go brave it at the court. … and we'll be waited on*
5 depend on, be subject to **MW** III.ii.70 [Page to Host] *The wealth I have waits on my consent*
6 follow, obey, pay attention to **Ham** III.iv.71 [Hamlet to Gertrude] *the blood … waits upon the judgement*

waiting-gentlewoman (*n.*) lady-in-waiting **1H4** I.iii.54 [Hotspur to King Henry, of a lord] *To see him … talk so like a waiting-gentlewoman*

wake (*n.*) **1** festival, revel, fete **WT** IV.iii.99 [Clown to Autolycus, of the supposed robber] *He haunts wakes, fairs, and bear-baitings;* **KL** III.vi.73; **LL** V.ii.318
2 state of wakefulness **KL** I.ii.15 [Edmund alone] *a whole tribe of fops / Got 'tween asleep and wake;* **KL** III.ii.34

wake (*v.*) **1** remain awake, stay up **Ham** I.iv.8 [Hamlet to Horatio] *The King doth wake tonight and takes his rouse;* **Sonn** 61.13
2 urge, arouse; or: trouble, disturb **MA** V.i.102 [Don Pedro to Antonio and Leonato] *we will not wake your patience;* **Mac** III.vi.31; **R2** I.iii.132

wake out (*v.*) cause to come out through staying awake **Cym** III.iv.103 [Pisanio to Innogen, of her command to kill her] *I'll wake mine eye-balls out first* [i.e. I'll stay awake until my eyes drop out]

waked (*adj.*) awakened, aroused, roused **Oth** III.iii.360 [Othello to Iago] *Thou hadst been better have been born a dog / Than answer my waked wrath!*

waking (*adj.*) awake, wakeful **Tem** II.i.213 [Sebastian to Antonio] *art thou waking?;* **2H6** III.ii.227; **H8** I.iv.23; **TC** I.i.35

walk (*n.*) **1** garden path, walkway **JC** III.ii.248 [Antony to all, of Caesar's bequests] *he hath left you all his walks;* **2H6** II.ii.3, IV.x.16; **3H6** V.ii.24; **Sonn** 89.9; **Tit** II.i.114
2 area of a forest under the supervision of a forester **MW** V.v.26 [Falstaff to Mistresses Ford and Page] *I will keep … my shoulders for the fellow of this walk*

walk (*v.*) **1** exercise, take out walking **MW** II.ii.289 [Ford alone] *I will rather trust … a thief to walk my ambling gelding … than my wife with herself*
2 walk aside, withdraw to duel **RJ** III.i.74 [Mercutio to Tybalt] *you ratcatcher, will you walk?*

walk in (*v.*) come in, enter **MW** I.i.262 [Anne to Slender] *I pray you, sir, walk in*

wall, take the take the inside position, keep to the cleaner side of a path **RJ** I.i.11 [Sampson to Gregory] *I will take the wall of any man or maid of Montague's*

wall (*v.*) shut off, block, impede **1H6** IV.ii.24 [General to Talbot] *On either hand there there are squadrons pitched / To wall thee from the liberty of flight*

wallet (*n.*) **1** protruding lump, bulging growth **Tem** III.iii.47 [Gonzalo to Alonso, of mountaineers] *whose throats had hanging at 'em / Wallets of flesh*

2 bag, knapsack **TC** III.iii.145 [Ulysses to Achilles] *Time hath … a wallet at his back, / Wherein he puts alms for oblivion*

wall-eyed with glaring eyes **Tit** V.i.44 [Lucius to Aaron] *wall-eyed slave;* **KJ** IV.iii.49

wall-newt (*n.*) lizard on the wall **KL** III.iv.124 [Edgar as Poor Tom to Gloucester, of himself] *that eats … the wall-newt*

wan (*v.*) grow pale, turn pale **Ham** II.ii.551 [Hamlet alone, of the First Player] *all his visage wanned* [Q2 *wand;* F *warm'd*]

wand (*n.*) rod, staff **MV** I.iii.81 [Shylock to Antonio] *The skilful shepherd peeled me certain wands;* **2H6** I.ii.28; **H8** IV.i.37

wandering (*adj.*) **1** [astrology] having its own motion **MND** IV.i.97 [Oberon to Titania] *We the globe can compass soon, / Swifter than the wandering moon;* **Ham** V.i.252; **2H6** IV.vi.16
2 lost, straying from the correct path **Sonn** 116.7 [of love] *It is the star to every wand'ring bark*
3 straying, erring, disloyal **1H6** III.iii.76 [Pucelle to Burgundy] *return, thou wandering lord*

waned (*adj.*) faded, diminished [in beauty] **3H6** IV.vii.4 [Edward to all] *I shall interchange / My waned state for Henry's regal crown;* **AC** II.i.21

wanion, with a with a vengeance, with a plague **Per** II.i.17 [First Fisherman to Third Fisherman] *Come away, or I'll fetch thee with a wanion*

wanny (*adj.*) wan, pallid, pale **RJ** IV.i.100 [Friar to Juliet, of taking the potion] *The roses in thy lips and cheeks shall fade / To wanny ashes* [F *many*]

want (*n.*) **1** lack, shortage, dearth **3H6** V.ii.8 [Warwick alone] *my want of strength … shows, / That I must yield my body to the earth;* **Cor** III.ii.69; **1H6** I.i.69; **2H6** III.ii.348; **KL** I.i.230; **R2** III.iv.16
2 absence, non-appearance, non-attendance **1H4** IV.i.44 [Hotspur to Worcester, of Northumberland] *His present want / Seems more than we shall find it*
3 need, requirement, necessity **Tim** II.ii.33 [Caphis to Timon] *If you did know, my lord, my master's wants;* **AC** III.xii.30; **Cym** IV.iii.31; **Tim** IV.iii.92

want (*v.*) **1** lack, need, be without **AY** III.ii.23 [Corin to Touchstone] *he that wants money, means, and content is without three good friends* ➤ **FEW**, p.xxi
2 miss, feel the loss of **Oth** III.iii.339 [Othello to Iago] *He that is robbed, not wanting what is stolen, / Let him not know't, and he's not robbed at all*
3 fall short, be deficient **AW** I.i.9 [Lafew to Bertram, of the King's goodness] *whose worthiness would stir it up where it wanted;* **AC** II.ii.80; **Cym** IV.iii.20; **KJ** I.i.435
4 require, demand, need **LL** V.ii.866 [King to Browne, of their waiting time] *it wants a twelvemonth and a day;* **MM** IV.iii.103

wanting (*n.*) needs, wants **AY** II.vii.127 [Duke Senior to Orlando] *take upon command what help we have / That to your wanting may be ministered*

wanton (*n.*) **1** libertine, seducer **E3** II.i.275 [Countess to King Edward] *try the wife of Salisbury, / Whether she will hear a wanton's tale or no;* **Luc** 401; **MW** II.ii.55; **RJ** I.iv.35
2 mistress, paramour, lover **Oth** IV.i.71 [Iago to Othello] *To lip a wanton in a secure couch*
3 harlot, whore **MA** IV.i.42 [Claudio to Leonato, of Hero] *Not to knit my soul to an approved wanton*
4 wilful creature, obstinate individual **MND** II.i.63 [Oberon to Titania] *Tarry, rash wanton!;* **KL** II.iv.119; **LL** III.i.193; **TG** V.ii.10
5 young rogue, scamp, rascal **E3** IV.iv.122 [Prince Edward to Third Herald, of his words to Philip] *So tell the courtly wanton;* **RJ** II.ii.177
6 spoilt child, pampered baby, weakling **KJ** V.i.70 [Bastard to King John, of Lewis the Dauphin] *A cockered silken wanton;* **Cym** IV.ii.8; **Ham** V.ii.293; **R2** V.iii.10

wanton (*adj.*) **1** carefree, light-hearted, frolicsome, playful **1H4** IV.i.103 [Vernon to Hotspur, of Prince Hal and his companions] *Wanton as youthful goats;* **H8** III.ii.359; **LL** V.ii.756; **RJ** II.vi.19; **TNK** II.i.150; **WT** I.ii.126

2 casual, gentle **RJ** II.vi.19 [Friar to himself] *A lover may bestride the gossamers / That idles in the wanton summer air;* **2H4** IV.i.189; **LL** IV.iii.102; **MV** III.ii.93; **TC** IV.v.220; **TNK** II.ii.17

3 unrestrained, undisciplined, boisterous, uncontrolled **MV** V.i.71 [Lorenzo to Jessica] *do but note a wild and wanton herd ... of youthful and unhandled colts;* **Cor** II.i.209; **Ham** II.i.22; **2H4** IV.i.55; **R2** V.i.101; **TNK** V.i.86

4 gay, lively, cheerful **TS** Induction.i.45 [Lord to Huntsmen, of his room] *hang it round with all my wanton pictures;* **KJ** III.iii.36

5 sexually hot, passionate, sportive **Oth** II.iii.16 [Iago to Cassio, of Othello and Desdemona] *He hath not yet made wanton the night with her;* **AW** II.vii.18; **LL** IV.iii.56; **TC** Prologue.10, III.iii.222; **TN** III.i.19

6 lascivious, lewd, obscene **3H6** I.iv.74 [Queen to York, of his sons] *The wanton Edward, and the lusty George;* **1H6** III.i.19; **R3** I.i.17; **Tem** IV.i.95; **TNK** V.i.148; **Venus** 809

7 [jocularly] naughty, wicked, mischievous **TNK** II.i.201 [Emilia to Woman, of her risque remark] *Thou art wanton;* **Luc** 401

8 cruelly irresponsible, badly behaved **KL** IV.i.36 [Gloucester to Old Man] *As flies to wanton boys are we to the gods*

9 merciless, cruel, pitiless **H8** III.ii.241 [Wolsey to all] *how sleek and wanton / Ye appear in everything may bring my ruin!*

10 equivocal, ambiguous, uncontrollable **TN** III.i.15 [Viola as Cesario to Feste] *They that dally nicely with words may quickly make them wanton*

11 luxuriant, flourishing, lush, profuse in growth **R2** I.iii.214 [Bolingbroke to King Richard] *Four lagging winters and four wanton springs;* **1H4** III.i.207; **Mac** I.iv.35; **MND** II.i.99; **Sonn** 97.7

12 feminine; or: child-like **TNK** IV.ii.124 [Messenger to Theseus, of one of the knights] *He's white-haired, / Not wanton white* [i.e. very light blond]; **2H4** I.i.148

wanton (*v.*) play, sport, frolic **WT** II.i.18 [First Lady to Mamillius] *you'd wanton with us, / If we would have you;* **Tit** II.i.21; **TS** Induction.ii.51; **Venus** 106

wanton (*adv.*) lasciviously, lewdly **Ham** III.iv.184 [Hamlet to Gertrude] *Pinch wanton on your cheek*

wantonly (*adv.*) playfully, frolicsomely, unrestrainedly **Sonn** 54.7 *The canker-blooms ... play as wantonly, / When summer's breath their masked buds discloses*

wantonness (*n.*) **1** foolish behaviour, caprice, whims **1H4** V.ii.68 [Vernon to Hotspur, of Prince Hal] *England did never owe so sweet a hope / So much misconstrued in his wantonness;* **Ham** III.i.146; **KJ** IV.i.16; **TC** III.iii.137

2 libertine, seducer, womanizer **E3** III.iv.113 [King Edward to all, as if to King John] *I hope / Thou know'st King Edward for no wantonness;* **E3** III.iii.156

3 lust, lasciviousness, promiscuity **MW** IV.iv.7 [Ford to Mistress Ford] *I rather will suspect the sun with cold / Than thee with wantonness;* **LL** V.ii.74; **MW** IV.ii.197

wantons, play the dally, trifle, sport **R2** III.iii.164 [King Richard to Aumerle] *shall we play the wantons with our woes*

want-wit (*adj.*) senseless, stupid, ridiculous **MV** I.i.6 [Antonio to Salerio and Solanio] *such a want-wit sadness makes of me / That I have much ado to know myself*

wappened (*adj.*) [unclear meaning] worn-out, weary, exhausted [perhaps sexually] **Tim** IV.iii.39 [Timon alone, of gold] *That makes the wappened widow wed again*

war, town of (*n.*) garrison town, fortified town **Oth** II.iii.207 [Othello to all] *In a town of war / Yet wild*

war (*v.*) make war, fight, do battle **H5** III.i.25 [King Henry to all] *Be copy now to men of grosser blood, / And teach them how to war*

ward (*n.*) **1** [fencing] defensive posture, parrying movement **Tem** I.ii.472 [Prospero to Ferdinand] *Come from thy ward!;* **1H4** I.ii.186, II.iv.190; **TC** I.ii.259; **TNK** V.iii.63; **WT** I.ii.33

2 guard, protection, defence **LL** III.i.130 [Armado to Costard, of giving him a coin] *the best ward of mine honour is rewarding my dependants;* **MW** II.ii.238; **Sonn** 48.4

3 cell [in a prison] **Ham** II.ii.246 [Hamlet to Rosencrantz and Guildenstern] *there are many confines, wards, and dungeons;* **MM** IV.iii.61, V.i.10; **Tim** III.iii.38

4 catch inside a lock; lock **Luc** 303 [of Tarquin and Lucrece's door locks] *Each one by him enforced, retires his ward;* **Tim** III.iii.38

5 person under someone's protection, minor **RJ** I.v.41 [Capulet to Cousin Capulet, of Lucentio] *His son was but a ward two years ago;* **E3** II.i.288; **KL** I.ii.74 ☞ ward, in

6 custody, imprisonment **2H6** V.i.112 [York to all, of his sons] *ere they will have me go to ward, / They'll pawn their swords of my enfranchisement*

7 type of political administrative district **1H4** III.iii.114 [Falstaff to Hostess] *Maid Marian may be the deputy's wife of the ward to thee*

ward, in as a ward, under guardianship **AW** I.i.5 [Bertram to Countess, of the King] *to whom I am now in ward* ☞ ward (*n.*) 5

ward (*v.*) protect, defend, guard **R3** V.iii.255 [Richmond to his soldiers] *God will in justice ward you as his soldiers;* **TC** I.ii.267; **Tit** III.i.193

warden (*adj.*) made from a variety of baking pear **WT** IV.iii.44 [Clown to himself] *I must have saffron to colour the warden pies*

warder (*n.*) **1** staff, truncheon, baton **R2** I.iii.118 [stage direction] *King Richard throws his warder into the lists;* **2H4** IV.i.123; **R2** I.iii.118

2 guard, sentry, watchman **1H6** I.iii.3 [Gloucester to servingmen, of the Tower] *Where be these warders that they wait not here?*

ware (*adj.*) **1** aware, conscious, sensible **RJ** I.i.124 [Benvolio to Lady Montague, of Romeo] *he was ware of me;* **AY** II.iv.52; **RJ** II.ii.103; **TC** IV.ii.55

2 wary, cautious, guarded **AY** II.iv.53 [Touchstone to Rosalind] *I shall ne'er be ware of mine own wit till I break my shins against it* [pun: 52, sense 1]

warm (*adj.*) **1** warmed, well-aired **Tim** IV.iii.224 [Apemantus to Timon] *thinkest / That the bleak air, thy boisterous chamberlain, / Will put thy chin on warm?*

2 well-to-do, affluent, comfortably off **1H4** IV.ii.17 [Falstaff alone] *I press ... such a commodity of warm slaves as had as lief hear the devil as a drum*

warn (*v.*) **1** summon, send for, officially call **KJ** II.i.201 [Hubert to all] *Who is it that hath warned us to the walls?;* **R3** I.iii.39

2 challenge, confront, defy **JC** V.i.5 [Octavius to Antony, of the enemy] *They mean to warn us at Philippi here*

warp (*v.*) **1** turn, twist, change **AY** II.vii.188 [Amiens, singing, of the winter wind] *thou the waters warp* [i.e. freeze]

2 go wrong, go astray **AY** III.iii.80 [Jaques to Touchstone and Audrey] *one of you will prove a shrunk panel and ... warp*

3 deviate, turn away, diverge **MM** I.i.14 [Duke to Escalus] *There is our commission, / From which we would not have you warp*

4 distort, pervert, deform **AW** V.iii.49 [Bertram to King, of a woman's face] *Which warped the line of every other favour*

5 reduce, shrink, lessen **WT** I.ii.365 [Polixenes to Camillo] *methinks / My favour here begins to warp*

warped (*adj.*) twisted, distorted **MM** III.i.145 [Isabella to and of Claudio] *such a warped slip of wilderness;* **MM** I.vi.52

war-proof (*n.*) valour tested in war **H5** III.i.18 [King Henry to all] *you noblest English, / Whose blood is fet from fathers of war-proof!*

warrant (*n.*) **1** assurance, pledge, guarantee **1H6** V.iii.143 [Reignier to Suffolk] *Upon thy princely warrant I descend;* **CE** I.i.69; **Cym** I.v.56; **E3** IV.i.39; **2H4** I.iii.40; **Oth** III.iii.20

2 licence, sanction, authorization **TG** III.i.10 [Duke to Proteus] *Upon this warrant shall you have access / Where you with Silvia may confer;* **Cor** III.i.274; **Mac** II.iii.142; **MW** IV.ii.195; **Per** IV.ii.123; **R3** I.iii.341

3 token, sign, evidence, proof **MA** III.ii.101 [Don John to Claudio] *Wonder not till further warrant;* **MM** II.iv.137

warrant, of allowed, warranted, justifiable **Ham** II.i.38 [Polonius to Reynaldo] *I believe it is a fetch of warrant. / You laying these slight sullies on my son* [F; Q2 *wit*]

warrant, out of illegal, unlawful, banned **Oth** I.i.79 [Brabantio to Othello] *a practiser / Of arts inhibited, and out of warrant*

warrant (*v.*) **1** assure, promise, guarantee, confirm **CE** I.i.140 [Egeon to Duke, of his sons] *happy were I in my timely death / Could all my travels warrant me they live* ➤ FEW, p.xxi; **DISCOURSE MARKERS**, p.127

2 authorize, sanction, license **MM** II.iv.59 [Angelo to Isabella, of his previous remarks] *I'll not warrant that;* **TNK** I.i.177

3 act as a pledge for, give an assurance about **Tit** I.i.275 [Lavinia to Saturninus] *true nobility / Warrants these words in princely courtesy;* **CE** IV.iv.3; **Tem** I.i.45

4 justify, defend, stand up for **TC** I.ii.97 [Troilus to all, of the abduction of Helen] *We fear to warrant in our native place!*

5 tell, assure, give good grounds to **1H4** II.iv.398 [Falstaff (as King) to Prince Hal] *That thou art my son ... a foolish hanging of thy nether lip, that doth warrant me;* **1H6** II.v.95

6 protect, preserve, keep safe **AY** III.iii.4 [Audrey to Touchstone, reacting to 'Doth my simple feature content you?'] *Your features, Lord warrant us!* ➤ SWEARING, p.435

warranted (*adj.*) justified, legitimate, rightful **Mac** IV.iii.137 [Malcolm to Macduff] *the chance of goodness / Be like our warranted quarrel!;* **AW** II.v.4; **MM** III.ii.135 ➤ well-warranted (*adj.*)

warrantise, warrantize (*n.*) authorization, surety, guarantee **1H6** I.iii.13 [Gloucester to his men, of the Tower] *Break up the gates; I'll be your warrantize;* **Sonn** 150.6

warranty (*n.*) authorization, permission, sanction **MV** I.i.132 [Bassanio to Antonio] *from your love I have a warranty / To unburden all my plots and purposes;* **Ham** V.i.223; **Oth** V.ii.60

warren (*n.*) hunting park, land used for breeding game **MA** II.i.197 [Benedick to Don Pedro, of Claudio] *as melancholy as a lodge in a warren*

warrener (*n.*) keeper of a rabbit warren **MW** I.iv.26 [Simple to Mistress Quickly, of Slender] *He hath fought with a warrener*

wash (*n.*) kitchen swill, hogwash **R3** V.ii.9 [Richmond to all, of King Richard] *Swills your warm blood like wash*

wash (*v.*) make damp, moisten, wet **MND** II.i.104 [Titania to Oberon] *the moon, the governess of floods ... washes all the air*

wash a tile labour in vain, work to no purpose **TNK** III.v.41 [Schoolmaster to all] *We have ... washed a tile*

washing (*adj.*) swashing, slashing **RJ** I.i.62 [Sampson to Gregory] *remember thy washing blow* [F; Q4 *swashing*]

waspish-headed (*adj.*) peevish, irascible, spiteful **Tem** IV.i.99 [Iris to Ceres, of Venus] *Her waspish-headed son has broke his arrows*

wassail (*n.*) drinking-party, carousal, revels **AC** I.iv.56 [Caesar to Lepidus, as if to Antony] *Leave thy lascivious wassails;* **Ham** I.iv.9; **2H4** I.ii.160; **LL** V.ii.318; **Mac** I.vii.64

waste (*n.*) **1** wasting, devastation, ravages **E3** I.ii.159 [Countess to King Edward] *like a cloak doth hide / From weather's waste the undergarnished pride*

2 wasteland, wild domain **2H4** I.iii.62 [Lord Bardolph to Hastings, of someone who stops a building project] *[who] leaves his part-created cost / A ... waste for churlish winter's tyranny*

3 desolate time or place **Ham** I.ii.198 [Horatio to Hamlet] *In the dead waste and middle of the night* [reading of Q1 *vast*, Q1,F *wast*]

4 [legal] damage to property by a tenant **MW** IV.ii.200 [Mistress Page to Mistress Ford, of Falstaff] *If the devil have him not in fee simple, with fine and recovery, he will never ... in the way of waste, attempt us again* [i.e. by way of attacking our virtue]

5 lavish spending, extra expenditure **AC** IV.vi.16 [Caesar to Maecenas, of the army] *they have earned the waste*

waste (*v.*) **1** pass, spend, while away **MND** II.i.57 [Puck to Fairy] *A merrier hour was never wasted;* **AY** II.iv.92; **MV** III.iv.12; **Per** IV.iv.1; **Tem** V.i.303; **Venus** 24, 583

2 consume, use up **JC** II.i.59 [Lucius to Brutus] *March is wasted fifteen days;* **AY** II.vii.135; **Cym** V.v.52; **2H4** IV.i.213

3 squander, wear away, lay waste to **CE** II.i.90 [Adriana to Luciana, of her husband's treatment of her beauty] *he hath wasted it*

4 lay waste, ravage, devastate **E3** III.iii.21 [Prince Edward to King Edward] *Some of their strongest cities we have won ... / And others wasted;* **2H4** IV.v.216; **1H6** II.iii.40; **3H6** III.iii.125

5 efface, wipe out, destroy **2H4** IV.v.215 [King Henry IV to Prince Henry] *action hence borne out / May waste the memory of the former days;* **Luc** 959

wasted (*adj.*) **1** spent, consumed, burnt-out **MND** V.i.365 [Puck to himself] *Now the wasted brands do glow*

2 laid waste, ravaged, ruined **Tit** V.i.23 [Second Goth to Lucius] *I earnestly did fix mine eye / Upon the wasted building*

wasteful (*adj.*) **1** destructive, devastating, ruinous **H5** III.i.14 [King Henry to all, of a rock] *Swilled with the wild and wasteful ocean;* **Mac** II.iii.111; **Sonn** 55.5

2 causing the body to waste away, wasting **AY** III.ii.313 [Rosalind to Orlando, of the priest who lacks Latin] *lacking the burden of lean and wasteful learning*

wasting (*adj.*) destructive, devastating, ravaging **1H6** III.iii.46 [Pucelle to Burgundy, of France] *the cities and the towns defaced / By wasting ruin of the cruel foe*

watch (*n.*) **1** watchmen, officers, street patrol **1H4** II.iv.474 [Hostess to Prince Hal] *The sheriff and all the watch are at the door;* **1H4** II.iv.468; **JC** II.i.16; **MA** III.iii.6; **R2** V.ii.9; **RJ** V.iii.158

2 watcher, watchman, observer **Luc** 928 [Lucrece as if to time] *Base watch of woes*

3 sleepless state, wakefulness **Ham** II.ii.148 [Polonius to Claudius and Gertrude, of Hamlet] *Fell ... into a fast, / Thence to a watch;* **Cym** III.iv.42; **RJ** II.iii.31; **Sonn** 148.10; **TC** I.ii.264

4 time interval, period of time **Oth** II.i.124 [Roderigo to Brabantio] *At this odd-even and dull watch o'th' night;* **R2** V.v.52

5 dial, clock face **R2** V.v.52 [Richard alone] *mine eyes, the outward watch / Whereto my finger, like a dial's point / Is pointing;* **PassP** XIV.14

6 signal, watchword, call **Mac** II.i.54 [Macbeth alone, of the wolf] *Whose howl's his watch*

watch (*v.*) **1** stay awake, keep vigil **Mac** V.i.1 [Doctor to Gentlewoman] *I have two nights watched with you;* **Ham** III.ii.282; **2H6** I.i.247; **KJ** IV.i.30; **RJ** IV.iv.9; **TG** III.i.136

2 keep the watch, keep guard, be on the look-out **Ham** I.ii.242 [Hamlet to Horatio] *I will watch tonight;* **Cor** II.iii.126; **1H6** II.i.7; **KL** II.i.20; **Oth** II.iii.50, 55; **TS** IV.ii.59

3 be on the watch for, look out for **JC** IV.iii.247 [Varro to Brutus] *we will stand and watch your pleasure;* **2H6** II.iv.7; **TS** III.ii.143

4 keep watch on, look out over **1H6** I.i.161 [Third Messenger to Bedford] *The Earl of Salisbury ... hardly keeps his men from mutiny, / Since then, so few, watch such a multitude*

5 keep in view, catch in the act **MW** V.v.103 [Page to Falstaff] *I think we have watched you now;* **2H6** I.iv.41, 54

6 [falconry, in taming a hawk] prevent from sleeping, keep awake **TS** IV.i.181 [Petruchio alone, of taming Katherina] *to watch her, as we watch these kites / That bate and beat and will not be obedient;* **Oth** III.iii.23

watch-case (*n.*) [unclear meaning] receptacle containing a watch; place for keeping watch **2H4** III.i.17 [King Henry IV alone, as if to sleep] *why ... leavest the kingly couch / A watch-case, or a common 'larum-bell?* [i.e. a place of restlessness]

watcher (*n.*) one who stays wide-awake **Mac** II.ii.71 [Lady Macbeth to Macbeth] *Get on your nightgown, lest occasion call us / And show us to be watchers;* **TG** II.iv.133

watchful *(adj.)* wakeful, unsleeping, vigilant JC II.i.98 [Brutus to Cassius] *What watchful cares do interpose themselves / Betwixt your eyes and night?;* 2H4 IV.v.26; R3 III.vii.76; TG I.i.31

watching *(n.)* wakefulness, sleeplessness, vigilance RJ IV.iv.8 [Nurse to Capulet] *you'll be sick tomorrow / For this night's watching;* MA II.i.344; Mac V.i.10; Oth III.iii.282; R2 II.i.78

water *(n.)* **1** tears Oth IV.ii.103 [Desdemona to Emilia] *answers have I none, / But what should go by water;* MM IV.iii.145 [disguised Duke to Isabella] *Command these fretting waters from your eyes;* 1H4 III.i.90; 3H6 V.iv.75; KJ IV.iii.107; Lover 291; MV II.ii.44

2 lustre, sheen, quality Per III.ii.100 [Cerimon to all, of Thaisa] *The diamonds / Of a most praised water doth appear;* Tim I.i.18; TN IV.ii.62

3 urine 2H4 I.ii.2 [Falstaff to Page] *what says the doctor to my water?;* TN III.iv.102

4 water-newt KL III.iv.124 [Edgar as Poor Tom to Gloucester, of himself] *that eats … the wall-newt and the water*

5 ☞ cast the water

water-gall *(n.)* rainbow-like halo Luc 1588 [of Lucrece] *These water-galls in her dim element / Foretell new storms to those already spent*

waterish *(adj.)* abounding in water; also: wishy-washy, watered down KL I.i.258 [France to Lear] *Not all the dukes of waterish Burgundy / Can buy this … maid of me*

water-rug *(n.)* rough-haired water-dog Mac III.i.93 [Macbeth to Murderers] *Shoughs, water-rugs, and demi-wolves are clept / All by the name of dogs*

water-standing *(adj.)* flooded with tears 3H6 V.vi.40 [King to Richard] *many an orphan's water-standing eye … / Shall rue the hour that ever thou wast born*

waterwork *(n.)* watercolour, distemper [imitating tapestry] 2H4 II.i.144 [Falstaff to Hostess] *the story of the Prodigal, or the German hunting, in waterwork*

watery *(adj.)* **1** made of water-drops, aqueous Tem IV.i.71 [Iris to Ceres] *Whose wat'ry arch and messenger am I* [i.e. the rainbow]

2 moist, clammy, salivating TC III.ii.19 [Troilus alone] *What will it be, / When that the watery palate tastes indeed / Love's thrice-repured nectar?*

wave *(v.)* **1** waver, vacillate, alternate Cor II.ii.16 [First Officer to Second Officer, of Coriolanus and the people] *If he did not care whether he had their love or no, he waved indifferently* [i.e. he would have wavered impartially]

2 move up and down, incline Cor III.ii.77 [Volumnia to Coriolanus] *waving thy head* [i.e. as a token of repentance]

wavering *(adj.)* inconstant, fickle, capricious 2H4 I.Induction.19 [Rumour alone] *The still-discordant wavering multitude;* E3 II.ii.92

wawl *(v.)* yell, howl, bawl KL IV.vi.181 [Lear to Gloucester] *the first time that we smell the air / We wawl and cry*

wax *(n.)* ☞ man of wax

wax *(v.)* **1** grow, become, turn 2H6 IV.x.19 [Iden to himself] *I seek not to wax great by others' waning;* CE I.i.92; Ham I.iv.87; H5 V.i.80; Tim III.iv.11; Tit III.i.221

2 grow, increase, enlarge Ham I.iii.12 [Laertes to Ophelia, of the body] *as this temple waxes / The inward service of the mind and soul / Grows wide withal;* Cor II.ii.97; LL V.ii.10

waxen *(adj.)* written on wax, perishable, quickly worn away H5 I.ii.234 [King Henry to all, of his grave] *Not worshipped with a waxen epitaph* [i.e. not even a perishable epitaph will be on his grave]

waxen *(v.)* increase, grow MND II.i.56 [Puck to Fairy] *the whole choir hold their hips and laugh, / And waxen in their mirth*

waxing *(adj.)* incoming, growing, increasing Tit III.i.95 [Titus to all, of himself] *Who marks the waxing tide grow wave by wave*

way *(n.)* **1** course, passage Mac V.iii.22 [Macbeth to himself] *my way of life / Is fallen into the sere, the yellow leaf*

2 journey, expedition, outing 3H6 V.iii.21 [Edward to all, of their journey] *willingness rids way* [i.e. makes the journey seem short]; Cym IV.ii.149

3 path, track, trail 3H6 III.ii.176 [Richard to and of himself] *like one lost in a thorny wood … / Seeking a way and straying from the way;* TS IV.i.2

4 direction, route, path H5 I.ii.207 [Canterbury to all] *many arrows loosed several ways / Come to one mark* [i.e. from different places]

5 entrance, access, path CE IV.iii.91 [Courtesan alone, of Antipholus] *Belike his wife … / On purpose shut the doors against his way;* JC IV.iii.39

6 best path, course of action CE IV.iii.92 [Courtesan alone, of Antipholus] *My way is now to hie home to his house;* R3 I.i.78; TNK II.i.127

7 opportunity, scope Cor IV.iv.25 [Coriolanus alone, of Aufidius] *If he give me way, / So shall I do his country service;* AW III.vi.2; H8 III.ii.16; KL II.iv.293; MM V.i.236

8 calling, vocation, profession H8 I.iii.61 [Sands to Lord Chamberlain and Lovell, of Wolsey] *Men of his way should be most liberal*

9 ☞ give way; great way; keep your way

way, by the on the way, on the journey Cym III.ii.60 [Innogen to Pisanio] *by th'way / Tell me how Wales was made so happy*

way, on one's pregnant, with child LL V.ii.670 [Costard to Armado, of Jaquenetta] *She is two months on her way*

way of, in *(prep.)* of the nature of, as a point of TC II.ii.190 [Hector to all] *Hector's opinion / Is this in way of truth*

ways, come thy / your come along TC III.ii.43 [Pandarus to Cressida] *come your ways; an you draw backward, we'll put you i'th' fills;* AW II.i.93; AY I.ii.196; MM III.ii.76; TN II.v.1 ☞ DISCOURSE MARKERS, p.127; FAREWELLS, p.170

ways, go thy / your 1 get along, be off Ham III.i.129 [Hamlet to Ophelia] *Go thy ways to a nunnery;* AW IV.v.54; MW II.ii.134 ☞ DISCOURSE MARKERS, p.127; FAREWELLS, p.170

2 carry on, go ahead H8 II.iv.133 [King Henry to departed Queen Katherine] *Go thy ways, Kate;* TS V.v.23

3 well done TS V.ii.187 [Hortensio to departed Petruchio] *Now go thy ways, thou hast tamed a curst shrew;* TS V.ii.180

wayward *(adj.)* **1** perverse, unreasonable, awkward CE IV.iv.4 [Antipholus of Ephesus to Officer] *My wife is in a wayward mood today;* R2 II.i.142; TG I.i.57

2 changeable, capricious, erratic Per V.i.88 [Marina to Pericles] *wayward fortune did malign my state*

3 hostile, contrary, antagonistic Per IV.iv.10 [Gower alone] *Pericles / Is now again thwarting the wayward seas*

waywarder *(n.)* obstinate, wilful, self-willed AY IV.i.150 [Rosalind as Ganymede to Orlando] *The wiser, the waywarder*

waywardness *(n.)* perversity, wrong-headedness, capriciousness KL I.i.297 [Gonerill to Regan, of Lear] *must we look from his age to receive … the unruly waywardness that infirm and choleric years bring with them*

weak *(adj.)* **1** of little worth, wanting, deficient MND V.i.417 [Puck to audience, of the play] *this weak and idle theme;* H5 III.vi.130; H8 I.ii.82; MA II.i.54; Oth III.iii.440

2 weakening, debilitating, enfeebling AY II.vii.133 [Orlando to Duke Senior, of Adam] *Oppressed with two weak evils, age and hunger*

3 contemptible, despicable, dishonourable RJ II.iv.167 [Nurse to Romeo, of playing Juliet false] *it were an ill thing to be offered to any gentlewoman, and very weak dealing*

weak-built *(adj.)* on poor foundation, ungrounded Luc 130 [of Tarquin] *weak-built hopes persuade him to abstaining*

weaken *(v.)* lower, reduce, lessen TNK V.iv.52 [Pirithous to Palamon, of Arcite's black horse] *which some will say / Weakens his price* [i.e. because horses of a single dark colour were thought to be bad-tempered]

WEAPONS

Weapons terminology can be grouped into four types: (i) terms for swords and daggers, especially in relation to fencing, and their accompanying carrying apparatus (a key reference is Osric's conversation with Hamlet in **Ham** V.ii.143ff.); (ii) terms for attacking weapons of war, as used by foot-soldiers or in jousting; (iii) terms for shields; and (iv) terms for guns, both hand-held and mounted.

Swords, daggers, and trappings

backsword	2H4 III.ii.63	sword-like stick with a basketwork hilt, used in fencing practice
baldric	TNK IV.ii.86	belt worn from one shoulder across the chest and under the opposite arm, used for carrying a weapon, bugle, etc.
basket-hilt	2H4 II.iv.127	sword hilt consisting of a steel lattice in a basket shape for protecting the hand
bilbo	MW I.i.150	flexible sword from Bilbao
bodkin	Ham III.i.76	sharply pointed dagger
carriage	Ham V.ii.148	looped strap attached to a sword belt, from which a sword may be hung
chape	AW IV.iii.142	metal plate covering the point of a dagger
curtle-axe	AY I.iii.115	short broad sword used for slashing and cutting; cutlass
dagger	Ham V.ii.143	[as in modern English]
dudgeon	Mac II.i.46	dagger hilt
falchion	KL V.iii.274	curved broad sword with the edge on the outer side
foil	Ham II.ii.321	light sword specially blunted for use in fencing
girdle	Ham V.ii.148	waist-belt for attaching a sword
half-sword	1H4 II.iv.159	small-sized sword
hanger	Ham V.ii.148	loop or strap attached to a sword belt, from which a sword may be hung
hilt	Ham V.ii.149	[as in modern English]
long sword	MW II.i.209	heavy two-handed sword with a long cutting blade
pilcher	TN III.i.33	scabbard
poniard	Ham V.ii.147	type of short dagger
rapier	Ham II.ii.342	light sharp-pointed sword used for thrusting; the sign of a gentleman
scabbard	TN III.iv.268	[as in modern English]
scimitar	MV II.i.24	short curved sword with a single edge, from the East
sheath	RJ V.iii.170	[as in modern English]
sword	Ham V.ii.158	[as in modern English]
two-hand sword	2H6 II.i.47	heavy sword wielded with both hands
tuck	TN III.iv.220	light sharp-pointed sword used for thrusting; rapier
whinyard	E3 I.ii.33	type of short sword

Long-handled weapons

battle-axe	Tit III.i.168	[as in modern English]
bill	2H6 II.iv.17	handle ending in a hooked blade [of varying design]
charging-staff	TNK IV.ii.140	lance used in jousting
halberd	CE V.i.185	handle ending in a combination of axe-blade and spearhead
lance	Per II.ii.50	metal-ended shaft used by a charging horseman
partisan	Ham I.i.141	handle ending in a broad spearhead, usually with one or more projections at the side
pick	E3 I.ii.52	pike
pike	H5 IV.i.40	handle ending in a spearhead
spear	1H6 I.i.138	[as in modern English]

Shields and parts

buckler	1H4 I.iii.227	small round shield
pike	MA V.ii.21	central spike in a buckler
shield	LL V.ii.549	[as in modern English]
targe	Cym V.v.5	light shield
target	Ham II.ii.321	light shield, smaller than a targe

(continues)

WEAPONS – continued

Guns

basilisk	H5 V.ii.17	large brass cannon, firing heavy shot of c.200 lb / c.100 kg
caliver	1H4 IV.ii.19	lightweight musket
cannon	AY II.vii.154	mounted gun of several kinds and sizes, each type firing shot of a particular weight
culverin	1H4 II.iii.55	small cannon with a long barrel, firing shot of c.8–16 lb / c.4–8 kg
demi-cannon	TS IV.iii.88	small cannon firing shot of c.30 lb / c.15 kg
gun	1H4 I.iii.55	[as in modern English]
mortar-piece	H8 V.iv.46	short high-firing cannon with a large bore
murdering-piece	Ham IV.v.96	mortar which scatters lethal projectiles
musket	AW III.ii.108	early form of rifle
pistol	MW IV.ii.47	[as in modern English]

weal 1 state, community, commonwealth **Cor** III.i.175 [Sicinius to and of Coriolanus] *A foe to th'public weal;* **Cor** I.iii.180; **1H6** I.i.177; **KL** I.iv.206; **Mac** III.iv.75, V.ii.27

2 welfare, well-being, prosperity **RJ** III.ii.51 [Juliet to Nurse] *Brief sounds determine of my weal or woe;* **Cor** I.i.149; **Ham** III.iii.14; **1H6** III.ii.92, V.i.27; **KJ** IV.ii.65

wealsman (n.) public servant, one devoted to the well-being of the state **Cor** I.i.51 [Menenius to Brutus and Sicinius] *Meeting two such wealsmen as you are*

wealth (n.) well-being, welfare, prosperity **MV** V.i.249 [Antonio to Portia, of Bassanio] *I once did lend my body for his wealth;* **Ham** IV.iv.27

wean (v.) **1** separate, detach, alienate **Tit** I.i.214 [Titus to Saturninus] *I will restore to thee / The people's hearts, and wean them from themselves* [i.e. reconcile them to making a more mature decision]

2 bring up, train **LL** V.ii.250 [masked Katharine to masked Longaville, of a calf] *Take all and wean it*

wear (n.) fashion, vogue, trend **AY** II.vii.34 [Jaques to all, of Touchstone] *A worthy fool: motley's the only wear!;* **AW** I.i.202; **MM** III.ii.70

wear (v.) **1** wear out, weary, tire **AW** V.i.4 [Helena to Widow and Diana] *To wear your gentle limbs in my affairs;* **AY** II.iv.34; **Venus** 506

2 pass, waste, run out **Tim** I.i.3 [Painter to Poet, of the world] *It wears, sir, as it grows;* **MW** V.i.7; **TS** III.ii.110

3 fashion, adapt, conform **TN** II.iv.30 [Orsino to Viola as Cesario] *Let still the woman take / An elder than herself; so wears she to him;* **Lover** 291

4 possess, enjoy, have **Cym** I.v.85 [Iachimo to Posthumus, of Innogen] *You may wear her in title yours;* **MA** V.ii.82; **Mac** III.iii.33

5 have, experience **Tim** IV.iii.483 [Flavius to Timon] *Ne'er did poor steward wear a truer grief / For his undone lord than mine eyes for you*

6 be the fashion, be trendy **AW** I.i.156 [Parolles to Helena, of virginity] *like the brooch and the toothpick, which wear not now*

wear out (v.) **1** outlive, survive, outlast **AC** IV.xiv.133 [First Guard to Antony] *you may not live to wear / All your true followers out;* **KL** V.iii.17

2 pass, spend **Luc** 123 [of Tarquin] *long he questioned / With modest Lucrece, and wore out the night*

wearing (n.) **1** clothing, dress, garments **Oth** IV.iii.15 [Desdemona to Emilia] *Give me my nightly wearing;* **WT** IV.iv.9

2 possession, having, enjoyment **Tim** V.i.140 [First Senator to Timon] *special dignities, which vacant lie / For thy best use and wearing*

wearing, worst most unfashionable, least stylish **2H6** I.iii.83 [Queen to Suffolk, of the Duchess] *The very train of her worst wearing gown / Was better worth than all my father's lands*

weary (adj.) wearisome, tedious, long-drawn-out **MM** I.iv.25 [Lucio to Isabella, of Claudio] *Not to be weary with you, he's in prison;* **Ham** I.ii.133; **Oth** III.iv.172

weasand, wezand (n.) throat, windpipe, gullet **Tem** III.ii.92 [Caliban to Stephano, of Prospero] *There thou mayst ... cut his weasand with thy knife*

weather (n.) tempest, storm **KJ** IV.ii.109 [King John to Messenger, of his news] *Pour down thy weather*

weather, in the in an exposed situation, open to the elements **MV** II.ix.29 [Arragon to himself] *the martlet / Builds in the weather on the outward wall*

weather, keep the keep to the windward side **TC** V.iii.26 [Hector to Cassandra and Andromache] *Mine honour keeps the weather of my fate* [i.e. has the advantage over fate]

weather, make fair appear friendly, be conciliatory **E3** I.ii.23 [King David to Lorraine] *we with England will ... never make fair weather*

weather-fend (v.) defend from the weather, shelter **Tem** V.i.10 [Ariel to Prospero] *In the line-grove which weather-fends your cell*

weaved-up (adj.) woven together, intertwined **R2** IV.i.228 [Richard to Northumberland] *must I ravel out / My weaved-up follies?*

web and the pin, pin and web disease of the eye, cataract **WT** I.ii.291 [Leontes to Camillo, of Hermione and Polixenes] *all eyes / Blind with the pin and web but theirs;* **KL** III.iv.111

wedding-dower (n.) ☛ **dower** (n.) 1

wedge (n.) ingot **R3** I.iv.26 [Clarence to Keeper] *Methoughts I saw ... / Wedges of gold*

wedge (v.) cleave, split [as with a wedge] **TC** I.i.37 [Troilus to Pandarus] *my heart, / As wedged with a sigh, would rive in twain*

wee away (v.) ☛ **oui away** (v.)

weed (n.) **1** (plural) garments, dress, clothes **MA** V.iii.30 [Don Pedro to Claudio] *let us hence, and put on other weeds;* **Cor** II.iii.153; **KL** IV.vii.7; **TG** II.vii.42; **TN** V.i.270; **WT** IV.iv.1

2 garment, piece of clothing **Cor** II.iii.220 [Sicinius to Citizens, of Coriolanus] *With what contempt he wore the humble weed;* **Luc** 196; **MND** II.i.256; **Per** IV.i.13; **Sonn** 2.4, 76.6

weed (v.) [debated usage] weed out, root out **TG** III.ii.49 [Proteus to Duke, of slandering Valentine to Silvia] *say this weed her love from Valentine*

weedy (adj.) made of weeds **Ham** IV.vii.174 [Gertrude to Claudius and Laertes, of Ophelia] *down her weedy trophies and herself / Fell*

week, in by the hopelessly caught, trapped **LL** V.ii.61 [Rosaline to Princess, of Berowne] *O that I knew he were but in by th'week*

ween (*v.*) think, intend, expect, be minded **H8** V.i.135 [King Henry to Cranmer] *Ween you of better luck ... than your Master;* **1H6** II.v.88

weepingly (*adv.*) tearfully, with many tears **Lover** 207 [of gifts to the woman] *Their kind acceptance, weepingly beseeched*

weeping-ripe (*adj.*) ready to weep, on the point of tears **LL** V.ii.274 [Rosaline to all] *The King was weeping-ripe for a good word;* **3H6** I.iv.172

weet (*v.*) know **AC** I.i.39 [Antony to Cleopatra] *I bind ... the world to weet / We stand up peerless*

weigh (*v.*) **1** balance [as in scales], poise, match **2H4** II.ii.171 [Prince Henry to Poins] *in everything the purpose must weigh with the folly;* **H8** I.i.11; **LL** V.ii.26; **Mac** IV.iii.90; **R2** III.iv.84; **Tim** I.i.150
2 consider, take into account **H8** II.iv.197 [King Henry to all] *I weighed the danger which my realms stood in;* **AC** II.vi.32; **Ham** I.iii.17; **JC** II.i.108; **Sonn** 120.8 [or: sense 3]; **WT** III.ii.42
3 judge, rate, assess the value of **2H4** V.ii.102 [King Henry V to Lord Chief Justice] *You are right justice, and you weigh this well;* **MM** II.ii.126; **TC** IV.v.81
4 weigh anchor, heave up the anchor **TNK** IV.i.145 [Gaoler's Daughter to all] *Come, weigh, my hearts, cheerily!*

weigh out (*v.*) make amends for, compensate for **H8** III.i.88 [Queen Katherine to Campeius and Wolsey] *They that must weigh out my afflictions ... live not here* [also: take into account]

weighing (*adj.*) ☛ **well-weighing** (*adj.*)

weight (*n.*) burden of sorrow, sadness, affliction **KL** V.iii.321 [Edgar to all] *The weight of this sad time we must obey*

weighty (*adj.*) rigorous, severe, harsh **Tim** III.v.102 [First Senator to Alcibiades] *If after two days' shine Athens contain thee, / Attend our weightier judgement*

welfare (*n.*) being well, remaining healthy **Sonn** 118.7 *I ... sick of welfare found a kind of meetness*

welked (*adj.*) twisted, ridged, convoluted **KL** IV.vi.71 [Edgar to Gloucester, of the imagined fiend] *he had ... / Horns welked and waved like the enridged sea* [Q *welk't*; F *wealk'd*]

welkin (*n.*) sky, firmament, heavens **MND** III.ii.356 [Oberon to Puck] *The starry welkin cover thou anon / With drooping fog;* **KJ** V.v.2; **R3** V.iii.342; **Tem** I.ii.4; **TN** II.iii.55; **TS** Induction.ii.44

welkin, out of one's out of one's element, none of one's business **TN** III.i.56 [Feste to Viola as Cesario] *Who you are and what you would are out of my welkin - I might say 'element'*

welkin (*adj.*) heavenly blue **WT** I.ii.136 [Leontes to Mamillius] *Look on me with your welkin eye*

well (*adj.*) fine, all right, satisfactory **TS** IV.i.155 [Katherina to Petruchio] *The meat was well, if you were so contented;* **Sonn** 103.10

well (*adv.*) **1** easily, clearly, readily **2H6** III.ii.185 [Warwick to Suffolk, of Gloucester] *'tis well seen he found an enemy*
2 clearly, plainly, frankly **Tim** I.ii.158 [Flavius to himself, of Timon] *There is no crossing him in's humour, / Else I should tell him well*
3 in a state of happiness, in bliss **AC** II.v.33 [Cleopatra to Messenger] *we use / To say the dead are well;* **WT** V.i.30

well-a-day (*n.*) lamentation, grief, sorrowing **Per** IV.iv.49 [Gower alone, of Pericles] *our scene must play / His daughter's woe and heavy well-a-day* ☛ **REGRETS**, p.367

well-advised (*adj.*) **1** prudent, sensible, thoughtful **KJ** III.i.5 [Constance to Salisbury] *Be well advised, tell o'er thy tale again;* **R3** IV.iv.515; **Tit** IV.ii.10 ☛ **advised** (*adj.*) 3
2 in one's right mind, sane, rational **LL** V.ii.434 [Princess to King, of being disguised] *were you well advised?;* **CE** II.ii.223

well-a-near (*int.*) alas, alack **Per** III.Chorus.51 [Gower alone, of Thaisa] *The lady shrieks and, well-a-near, / Does fall in travail with her fear* ☛ **REGRETS**, p.367

well-apparelled (*adj.*) well-dressed, nicely adorned **RJ** I.ii.27 [Capulet to Paris] *well-apparelled April on the heel / Of limping winter treads* ☛ **apparel** (*n.*)

well-appointed (*adj.*) well-equipped, properly fitted out **2H4** IV.i.25 [Archbishop to Mowbray, of Westmorland] *What well-appointed leader fronts us here?;* **2H4** I.i.190; **H5** III.Chorus.4 ☛ **appoint** (*v.*) 1

well-beseeming (*adj.*) fine-looking, well-ordered **1H4** I.i.14 [King Henry to all] *Those opposed eyes ... / Shall now, in mutual well-beseeming ranks, / March all one way;* **Tit** II.iii.56 ☛ **ill-beseeming** (*adj.*)

well-breathed (*adj.*) strong in wind, well-exercised **Venus** 678 [Venus to Adonis] *on thy well-breathed horse keep with thy hounds* ☛ **breathed** (*adj.*)

well-compact (*adj.*) well-formed, nicely put together **KL** I.ii.7 [Edmund alone, of himself and his brother] *my dimensions are as well-compact* ☛ **compact** (*adj.*) 2

well-dealing (*adj.*) fair-dealing, conducting business well **CE** I.i.7 [Duke to Egeon] *the rancorous outrage of your Duke / To merchants, our well-dealing countrymen*

well-disposed (*adj.*) ☛ **disposed** (*adj.*) 1, 2

well-divided (*adj.*) well-balanced, evenly shared **AC** I.v.53 [Cleopatra to Alexas, of Antony] *O well-divided disposition!*

well-entered (*adj.*) well-trained, duly initiated **AW** II.i.6 [First Lord to King] *'Tis our hope ... / After well-entered soldiers, to return* [i.e. after having become experienced]

well-favoured (*adj.*) good-looking, attractive in appearance **TN** I.v.154 [Malvolio to Olivia, of Viola as Cesario] *He is very well-favoured;* **KL** I.iv.251; **MA** III.iii.14; **MW** II.ii.260; **Per** IV.i.86; **TG** II.i.47 ☛ **hard-favoured** (*adj.*)

well-forwarning (*adj.*) giving an accurate early warning, truth-predicting **2H6** III.ii.85 [Queen to King] *well-forwarning wind / Did seem to say 'Seek not a scorpion's nest, / Nor set no footing on this unkind shore'?*

well-found (*adj.*) **1** of proven merit, of established reputation, commendable **AW** II.i.102 [Helena to King, of her father] *In what he did profess, well found;* **TNK** II.iv.27
2 commendable, meritorious, laudable **Cor** II.ii.42 [Menenius to all, of Cominius] *last general / In our well-found successes*

well-graced (*adj.*) full of pleasing qualities, well-favoured **R2** V.ii.24 [York to Duchess of York] *After a well graced actor leaves the stage* ☛ **graced** (*adj.*) 1

well-hallowed (*adj.*) well-blessed, well-consecrated **H5** I.ii.294 [King Henry to Ambassador] *I am coming on ... to put forth / My rightful hand in a well-hallowed cause*

well-knit (*adj.*) strongly built, well-constructed **LL** I.ii.71 [Armado to Mote] *O well-knit Samson!*

well-known (*adj.*) certain, clear, apparent **KJ** I.i.60 [Bastard to King John, of Robert and him having the same mother] *That is well known*

well-liking (*adj.*) thriving, healthy, in good condition **LL** V.ii.268 [Rosaline to all, of the King and his friends] *Well-liking wits they have* ☛ **liking** (*n.*) 3

well-lost (*adj.*) lost in a good cause **AW** I.iii.243 [Helena to Countess] *I'd venture / The well-lost life of mine on his grace's cure* [i.e. it would be worthwhile to risk my life]

well met ☛ **GREETINGS**, p.206

well-minded (*adj.*) right-minded, well-disposed, loyal **3H6** IV.viii.27 [King to George] *Well-minded Clarence, be thou fortunate!*

well-respected (*adj.*) well-considered, duly regarded **1H4** IV.iii.10 [Vernon to Douglas] *If well-respected honour bid me on, / I hold as little counsel with weak fear / As you* ☛ **respect** (*v.*) 1

well said ☛ **said, well**

well-seeming (*adj.*) attractively looking, presenting a plausible appearance **MM** III.i.224 [disguised Duke to Isabella, of Mariana] *she lost … her combinate husband, this well-seeming Angelo;* **RJ** I.i.179 ☛ seeming (*adj.*)

well-sinewed (*adj.*) well-strengthened, strongly prepared **KJ** V.vii.88 [Bastard to Salisbury, of Lewis the Dauphin withdrawing] *He will the rather do it when he sees / Ourselves well-sinewed to our defence*

well-spoken (*adj.*) refined, courteous, eloquent **R3** I.i.29 [Richard alone] *I cannot prove a lover / To entertain these fair well-spoken days*

well to live (*adj.*) well-to-do, well-off, prosperous **MV** II.ii.48 [Gobbo to Launcelot, of himself] *an honest exceeding poor man and … well to live;* **WT** III.iii.117

well-warranted (*adj.*) highly approved, most justified **MM** V.i.252 [Duke to Angelo] *my noble and well-warranted cousin* ☛ warranted (*adj.*)

well-weighing (*adj.*) heavy, weighty, significant **AW** IV.iii.176 [First Soldier to Parolles, reading about Dumaine] *[is it] possible with well-weighing sums of gold to corrupt him to a revolt* [also: influential]

well-willer (*n.*) well-wisher, one who offers good will **MW** I.i.66 [Evans to Shallow] *I beseech you be ruled by your well-willers;* **TNK** III.v.115

well-wished (*adj.*) accompanied by good wishes, much loved **MM** II.iv.27 [Angelo alone] *The general, subject to a well-wished king*

wen (*n.*) swelling, tumour, lump **2H4** II.ii.100 [Prince Henry to Poins, of Falstaff] *I do allow this wen to be as familiar with me as my dog*

wench (*n.*) girl, lass **TNK** II.i.178 [Emilia to Woman] *That's a good wench* ☛ FEW, p.xxi; ADDRESS FORMS, p.8

wenching (*adj.*) someone who hangs around with women **TC** V.iv.33 [Thersites alone, of Troilus and Diomedes] *What's become of the wenching rogues?*

wenchless (*adj.*) lacking in women **Per** IV.ii.5 [Pander to Boult] *We lost too much money this mart by being too wenchless*

wench-like (*adj.*) girlish, womanish, effeminate **Cym** IV.ii.230 [Guiderius to Arviragus] *do not play in wench-like words with that / Which is so serious*

wend (*v.*) direct, betake [oneself] **MM** IV.iii.144 [disguised Duke to Isabella] *Wend you with this letter*

weraday (*int.*) well-a-day, alas **RJ** IV.v.15 [Nurse calling out, on finding Juliet dead] *O weraday that ever I was born!* ☛ REGRETS, p.367

wert (*v.*) ☛ VERB FORMS, p.481

westward (*adv.*) over in the west, in the west country **WT** IV.iv.288 [Autolycus to Mopsa, of a ballad] *There's scarce a maid westward but she sings it*

wet (*v.*) 1 weep for, lament with tears **Tem** II.i.129 [Sebastian to Alonso, of his daughter's absence] *you … hath cause to wet the grief on't*
2 [unclear meaning] bequeath, bestow; suffuse, steep **2H4** IV.iv.104 [King Henry IV to all] *Will Fortune never come with both hands full, / But wet her fair words still in foulest terms?* [Q; F write]

wether (*n.*) sheep, ram **MV** IV.i.114 [Antonio to Bassanio] *I am a tainted wether of the flock, / Meetest for death;* **PassP** XVII.18; **Tim** IV.iii.12; **WT** IV.viii.31

wharf (*n.*) river bank **AC** II.ii.218 [Enobarbus to Agrippa and Maecenas] *A strange invisible perfume hits the sense / Of the adjacent wharfs;* **Ham** I.v.33

what (*pron.*) ☛ look what; WHAT AND WHAT-, p.495

what though what of it, never mind **KJ** I.i.169 [Bastard to Queen Eleanor, of being her grandson] *by chance but not by truth; what though?;* **MW** I.i.256 ☛ DISCOURSE MARKERS, p.127

wheak (*int.*) ☛ SOUNDS, p.410

wheel (*n.*) [unclear meaning] song refrain; or: spinning-wheel **Ham** IV.v.173 [Ophelia to Laertes] *how the wheel becomes it*

wheels, on running smoothly, providing an easy life **TG** III.i.307 [Launce to Speed, of his love's virtues] *Then may I set the world on wheels, when she can spin for her living*

wheel (*v.*) turn to face in a new direction, circle round **TC** V.vii.2 [Achilles to Myrmidons] *Attend me where I wheel*

wheeling (*adj.*) roving, wandering, drifting **Oth** I.i.137 [Roderigo to Brabantio, of Desdemona] *Tying her duty, beauty, wit, and fortunes / In an extravagant and wheeling stranger*

whe'er (*conj.*) [whether] if **Ham** II.ii.517 [Polonius to all, of the First Player] *Look whe'er he has not turned his colour*

Wheeson (*adj.*) Whitsun **2H4** II.i.87 [Hostess to Falstaff] *Thou didst swear to me … upon Wednesday in Wheeson week*

whelk (*n.*) pimple, pustule **H5** III.vi.100 [Fluellen to King Henry, of Bardolph] *his face is all bubukles, and whelks, and knobs*

whelm (*v.*) overwhelm, drown, sink **MW** II.ii.133 [Pistol to himself, of Mistress Quickly] *She is my prize, or ocean whelm them all!*

whelp (*n.*) 1 cub, young **Cym** V.iv.138 [Posthumus alone, reading] *a lion's whelp*
2 [term of abuse] pup, son of a bitch **Tem** I.ii.283 [Prospero to Ariel, of Caliban] *A freckled whelp*

when (*conj.*) ☛ whenas (*conj.*)

when (*int.*) ☛ EXCLAMATIONS, p.158

when that (*conj.*) for the time when **AY** IV.iii.117 [Oliver to Rosalind and Celia disguised, of a lioness] *Lay couching … with catlike watch / When that the sleeping man should stir*

whenas, when as (*conj.*) 1 when, at the time when **E3** III.ii.42 [Woman to all] *the time will shortly come / Whenas a lion .. / Shall carry hence the fleur-de-lis of France*
2 whereas **3H6** V.vii.34 [Richard to himself, of kissing the infant prince] *so Judas kissed his master, / And cried 'All hail!' when as he meant all harm*

whence (*adv.*) ☛ HENCE, THENCE, AND WHENCE, p.219

whencesoever (*adv.*) from somewhere or other, from whatever place **R2** II.iii.22 [Northumberland to Bolingbroke, of Harry Percy] *It is my son … / Sent from my brother Worcester whencesoever*

whensoever (*adv.*) whenever **Ham** V.ii.197 [Hamlet to a Lord, of Claudius] *If his fitness speaks, mine is ready, now or whensoever*

where (*adv.*) ☛ HERE, THERE, AND WHERE, p.220

where (*conj.*) 1 whereas **TNK** III.vi.160 [Arcite to Theseus, of Palamon] *Where this man calls me traitor, / Let me say thus much*
2 whether **JC** V.iv.30 [Antony to all] *see where Brutus be alive or dead*

whereabout (*adv.*) about what, on what business **1H4** II.iii.107 [Hotspur to Lady Percy] *I must not have you henceforth question me / Whither I go, nor reason whereabout*

where-through (*adv.*) through which **Sonn** 24.11 [of eyes] *thine for me / Are windows to my breast, where-through the Sun / Delights to peep*

whet on (*v.*) encourage, incite, egg on **2H6** III.i.33 [King to Queen] *whet not on these furious peers;* **3H6** I.ii.37; **KJ** III.iv.181

whether (*pron.*) which of the two **MW** III.ii.3 [Mistress Page to Robin] *Whether had you rather, lead mine eyes, or eye your master's heels?*

whetstone (*n.*) shaped stone used for sharpening [whetting] tools **AY** I.ii.52 [Celia to Rosalind, of Touchstone] *Nature … hath sent this natural for our whetstone: for always the dullness of the fool is the whetstone of the wits*

whey-face (*n.*) milk-face, pasty-face **Mac** V.iii.17 [Macbeth to Servant, of the approaching army] *What soldiers, whey-face?*

whiffler *(n.)* armed processional attendant H5 V.Chorus.12 [Chorus, of the sea] *Which like a mighty whiffler fore the King / Seems to prepare his way*

while *(n.)* **1** space of time, interval 1H6 I.iv.54 [Talbot to all, of the French] *a guard of chosen shot I had / That walked about me every minute while* [i.e. at intervals of a minute]
    2 times, age 1H4 II.iv.127 [Falstaff to all] *God help the while*; JC I.iii.82

while, the meanwhile, in the meantime Tem III.i.24 [Miranda to Ferdinand] *I'll bear your logs the while; AY II.v.28*

while-ere *(adv.)* a while before, a short time ago Tem III.ii.119 [Caliban to Stephano] *Will you troll the catch / You taught me but while-ere?*

whiles *(n.)* meantime, meanwhile TS III.i.22 [Bianca to Hortensio as Licio] *play you the whiles*

whiles *(conj.)* while 1H6 IV.iii.52 [Lucy alone, of the English lords] *Whiles they each other cross, / Lives, honours, lands, and all hurry to loss*

whilst, the in the meantime, meanwhile Cym IV.ii.254 [Arviragus to Belarius] *We'll say our song the whilst*

whinyard *(n.)* short sword E3 I.ii.33 [King David to Lorraine, of the Scots soldiers] *never shall [they] ... from their buttoned tawny leathern belts / Dismiss their biting whinyards* ⚔ **WEAPONS**, p.491

whip *(v.)* **1** dash, hurry, hasten LL V.ii.309 [Princess to ladies] *Whip to our tents, as roes runs o'er the land; MA I.iii.56*

WHAT AND WHAT-

What and its derivatives had a wide range of interrogative and exclamatory uses, many of which are still found today; the chief difference in Shakespearian English is their reference to people as well as things, where today we would use *who*. *Whatever* shows very little other difference, apart from the way its elements can be split as *what ... ever*. *Whatsoever* is generally equivalent to *whatever*, and is still found in emphatic use in modern English (though not in the *-e'er* form). Syntactic usage occasionally varies, as in 'As if that whatsoever god who leads him' (Cor II.i.211) and 'what and if / His sorrows have so overwhelmed his wits?' (Tit IV.iv.9), where modern English drops the *and* – 'what if'. The examples below distinguish uses of the compound forms as adjective and conjunction.

Item	Location	Example	Gloss
what			
what	AY II.iv.85	*What is he that shall buy his flock and pasture?*	who
what	KL V.iii.98	*What in the world he is / That names me traitor*	whoever
what	2H4 I.ii.114	*What tell you me of it?*	why, what for
what	Mac III.iv.125	*[Macbeth] What is the night? [Lady Macbeth] Almost at odds with morning*	how much time has passed?
what though (conj.)	2H6 I.i.158	*What though the common people favour him*	what happens if, what does it matter if
what though (as elliptical sentence)	AY III.iii.46	*here we have no temple but the wood ... But what though?*	so what?, what if it is so?
what-			
whatever, whate'er	AY II.vii.110	*But whate'er you are ... in this desert inaccessible*	whoever
what ... ever	Oth III.iii.466	*to obey shall be in me remorse, / What bloody business ever*	whatever
whatsoever, whatsoe'er (adj.)	2H6 IV.x.29	*rude companion, whatsoe'er thou be*	whatever
whatsoever, whatsoe'er (conj.)	MM IV.ii.117	*Whatsoever you may hear to the contrary*	whatever
whatsoever, whatsoe'er (conj.)	R3 III.iv.65	*doom th'offenders: whatsoever they be*	whoever
whatsomever, whatsome'er (adj.)	Ham I.ii.249	*And whatsomever else shall hap tonight*	whatever
whatsomever, whatsome'er (conj.)	AC II.vi.97	*All men's faces are true, what-some'er their hands are*	whatever
whatsomever, whatsome'er (conj.)	AW III.v.50	*Whatsome'er he is*	whoever

⚔ **WHO AND WHO-**, p.497

2 ☞ SWEARING, p.435

whipping-cheer (*n.*) whipping fare, good flogging **2H4** V.iv.5 [First Beadle to others, of Hostess] *she shall have whipping-cheer*

whipster (*n.*) wretch, degenerate, good-for-nothing **Oth** V.ii.242 [Othello to himself] *every puny whipster gets my sword*

whipstock (*n.*) whip-handle **TNK** I.ii.86 [Valerius to Palamon and Arcite, of Creon] *He broke his whipstock*; **Per** II.ii.50; **TN** II.iii.26

whir (*v.*) whirl, rush along, carry **Per** IV.i.20 [Marina to herself] *This world to me is as a lasting storm, / Whirring me from my friends*

whirligig (*n.*) spinning top, roudabout **TN** V.i.374 [Feste to Malvolio] *thus the whirligig of time brings in his revenges*

whisper (*v.*) speak secretly with, talk confidentially to **H8** I.i.179 [Buckingham to Norfolk, of Emperor Charles] *he came / To whisper Wolsey*; **TC** I.iii.250

whist (*adj.*) silent, quiet, still **Tem** I.ii.378 [Ariel singing to Ferdinand] *kissed / The wild waves whist*

whistle (*v.*) whisper, speak in private **WT** IV.iv.245 [Clown to Mopsa and Dorcas] *Is there not milking-time, when you are going to bed, or kiln-hole, to whistle of these secrets*

whistle, go carry on to no purpose, waste [one's] time **TNK** III.v.39 [Fourth Countryman to all] *We may go whistle*; **WT** IV.iv.693

whistling (*n.*) calling, watching out for **KL** V.ii.29 [Gonerill to Albany] *I have been worth the whistling* [i.e. you've finally decided to come to meet me]

whit, no not at all, not in the least **JC** II.i.149 [Metellus to all, of Cicero] *Our youths and wildness shall no whit appear, / But all be buried in his gravity*

white (*n.*) [archery] white ring at the centre of a target **TS** V.ii.185 [Petruchio to Lucentio, of Bianca] *'Twas I won the wager, though you hit the white*

white (*adj.*) **1** ready for harvesting, ripening **KL** III.iv.113 [Edgar as Poor Tom to all, of Gloucester, imagined as a devil] *He ... mildews the white wheat*
2 fresh, unsmoked **KL** III.vi.31 [Edgar as Poor Tom to all] *Hoppedance cries in Tom's belly for two white herring*

white (*adv.*) [unclear meaning] clearly, lacking colour **2H4** I.ii.213 [Falstaff to Lord Chief Justice] *I would I might never spit white again* [i.e. spit healthily]

white and black, under in black-and-white, written down **MA** V.i.292 [Dogberry to Leonato] *which indeed is not under white and black ... the offender, did call me ass*

whitebeard (*n.*) old man, patriarch, old-timer **R2** III.ii.112 [Scroop to King Richard] *Whitebeards have armed their thin and hairless scalps* [QQ *White beards*; F *White beares*]

white-haired (*adj.*) fair-haired **TNK** IV.ii.123 [Messenger to Theseus, of one of the knights] *He's white-haired, ... such a manly colour / Next to an auburn*

white-livered (*adj.*) lily-livered, cowardly, feeble-spirited **H5** III.ii.32 [Boy alone] *For Bardolph, he is white-livered and red-faced*; **R3** IV.iv.464

whitely (*adj.*) pale-complexioned, light-skinned **LL** III.i.193 [Berowne alone, of Rosaline] *A whitely wanton with a velvet brow* [F *whitly*]

whither (*adv.*) ☞ HITHER, THITHER, AND WHITHER, p.224

whiting-time (*n.*) whitening time, time for clothes-bleaching **MW** III.iii.123 [Mistress Page to Mistress Ford] *it is whiting-time*

whitly (*adj.*) ☞ whitely (*adj.*)

whitster (*n.*) linen-bleacher, whitener of clothing **MW** III.iii.13 [Mistress Ford to John and Robert, of the basket] *carry it among the whitsters in Datchet Mead*

whittle (*n.*) clasp-knife, carving knife **Tim** V.i.178 [Timon to First Senator, of Alcibiades' army] *There's not a whittle in th'unruly camp / But I do prize it at my love before / The reverend'st throat in Athens*

who (*pron.*) ☞ WHO AND WHO-, p.497

whole (*adj.*) **1** healthy, well, in sound condition **JC** II.i.327 [Brutus to Ligarius, of the conspiracy] *A piece of work that will make sick men whole*; **AC** IV.viii.11; **2H6** IV.vii.8
2 unbroken, sound, intact **Mac** III.iv.21 [Macbeth to First Murderer, of Fleance's escape] *I had else been perfect, / Whole as the marble*; **MND** III.ii.209
3 well, good **AW** V.iii.37 [King to Bertram] *All is whole*

wholesome (*adj.*) **1** good, beneficial, advantageous **H8** III.ii.99 [Wolsey to himself, of Anne] *Yet I know her for / A spleeny Lutheran, and not wholesome to / Our cause*; **H8** I.i.45; **Oth** I.i.146
2 reasonable, sensible, rational **Ham** III.ii.324 [Guildenstern to Hamlet] *make me a wholesome answer*; **Cor** I.i.80; **Ham** III.ii.329; **KL** II.iv.139; **Oth** III.i.45
3 sound, firm, in good condition **Mac** IV.iii.105 [Macduff to Malcolm, of Scotland] *When shalt thou see thy wholesome days again*; **Ham** I.v.70, III.ii.269, iv.66; **MW** V.v.59; **Per** IV.vi.22
4 profitable, valuable, promoting well-being **H8** I.i.113 [Norfolk to Buckingham] *Bosom up my counsel; / You'll find it wholesome*; **Cor** II.i.65, iii.59
5 good, nutritious, fit to eat **R2** III.iv.46 [First Man to the Gardener, of England as a garden] *her wholesome herbs*; **CE** V.i.104; **Cor** I.i.17
6 good for the health, health-giving, salubrious **Ham** I.i.163 [Marcellus to Horatio, of the Christmas season] *The nights are wholesome*; **KL** I.iv.206; **MW** IV.ii.70

wholesome-profitable (*adj.*) beneficial to well-being **LL** V.ii.745 [King to Princess] *to wail friends lost / Is not by much so wholesome-profitable / As to rejoice at friends but newly found*

whoo-bub (*n.*) hubbub, confused yelling **WT** IV.iv.611 [Autolycus to himself] *the old man come in with a whoo-bub against his daughter and the King's son* [F]

whoop, hoop (*v.*) **1** shout with astonishment, make an outcry **H5** II.ii.108 [King Henry to all, of treason and murder] *Working so grossly in a natural cause / That admiration did not whoop at them*
2 howl, hoot, jeer **Cor** IV.v.81 [Coriolanus to Aufidius, of the Roman nobles] *who ... suffered me by th'voice of slaves to be / Whooped out of Rome*

whooping (*n.*) exclaiming, excited shouting **AY** III.ii.187 [Celia to Rosalind] *out of all whooping* [i.e. beyond the power of exclamation]

whore (*n.*) whoring, fornication **Tim** IV.iii.142 [Timon to Phrynia and Timandra] *Be strong in whore*; **Tim** IV.iii.169

whoremaster (*n.*) fornicator, lecher, one who deals with whores **MM** III.ii.33 [Elbow to disguised Duke, of Angelo] *The deputy cannot abide a whoremaster*; **1H4** II.iv.456; **Tim** II.ii.108

whoremaster (*adj.*) lecherous, fornicating, licentious **KL** I.ii.126 [Edmund alone] *An admirable evasion of whoremaster man*

whore-masterly (*adj.*) lecherous, having the character of a whoremaster **TC** V.iv.7 [Thersites alone, of Diomedes] *that Greekish whore-masterly villain*

whoremonger (*n.*) fornicator, lecher, one who deals with whores **MM** III.ii.34 [Elbow to disguised Duke, of Pompey] *If he be a whoremonger*

whoreson (*n.*) [son of a whore; serious or jocular term of abuse] fellow, bastard **RJ** IV.v.20 [Capulet to Second Servingman] *A merry whoreson, ha!*; **H8** I.iii.39; **KL** I.i.22

whoreson (*adj.*) [abusive intensifier, serious or jocular] bastard, wretched, vile **1H4** II.iv.135 [Prince Hal to Falstaff] *you whoreson round man*; **Cym** II.i.14; **2H4** I.ii.14; **LL** IV.iii.202; **TG** IV.iv.41; **TS** IV.i.141 ☞ SWEARING, p.435

wide (*adj.*) **1** full, extensive, far-reaching **Oth** I.iii.107 [Duke to Brabantio, of Othello charming Desdemona] *To vouch this is no proof, / Without more wider and more overt test* [F; Q *certain*]
2 distant, removed, moving astray [from] **MW** III.i.54 [Shallow to Evans, of Caius] *I never heard a man ... so wide of his own respect*
3 wide of the mark, mistaken **TC** III.i.85 [Pandarus to Paris, of his guess] *no such matter, you are wide*; **TNK** III.iii.45

4 confused, disoriented **KL** IV.vii.50 [Cordelia to all, of Lear] *still far wide!*

wide *(adv.)* **1** in error, mistakenly **MA** IV.i.60 [Hero to Claudio] *Is my lord well, that he doth speak so wide?*; **Sonn** 140.14

2 astray, into a lax state **Ham** I.iii.14 [Laertes to Ophelia] *but as this temple waxes / The inward service of the mind and soul / Grows wide withal*

wide-chopped *(adj.)* wide-jawed, big-mouthed **Tem** I.i.55 [Antonio to Sebastian, of the Boatswain] *This wide-chopped rascal* ◆ chaps *(n.)* 1

wide-enlarged *(adj.)* widespread; or: greatly endowed **AY** III.ii.139 [Celia reading] *Heaven Nature charged / That one body should be filled / With all graces wide-enlarged*

wide-skirted *(adj.)* with wide-borders, widely spread out **KL** I.i.65 [Lear to Gonerill] *all these bounds ... / With plenteous rivers and wide-skirted meads*

wide-stretched *(adj.)* widely extended, extensive, sweeping **H5** II.iv.82 [Exeter to French King] *the crown, / And all wide-stretched honours that pertain ... / Unto the crown of France*

widow-dolour *(adj.)* widow's sorrow **R3** II.ii.65 [Girl to Queen Elizabeth] *Our fatherless distress was left unmoaned: / Your widow-dolour likewise be unwept!*

widowhood *(n.)* estate settled upon a widow, widow's rights **TS** II.i.124 [Petruchio to Baptista, of Katherina] *for that dowry I'll assure her of / Her widowhood*

wield *(v.)* express, utter, speak **KL** I.i.55 [Gonerill to Lear] *I love you more than word can wield the matter*

wife *(n.)* woman **TN** V.i.134 [Viola as Cesario to Olivia, of loving Orsino] *More by all mores than e'er I shall love wife*; **H5** V.Chorus.10; **KJ** III.i.89

wight *(n.)* [archaism] person, human being **Oth** II.iii.88 [Iago singing, of King Stephen] *He was a wight of high renown*; **H5** II.i.57; **LL** I.i.175; **MW** I.iii.34; **Per** I.Chorus.39; **Sonn** 106.2 ◆ ARCHAISMS, p.22

wild *(n.)* wilderness, waste land **MV** II.vii.41 [Morocco to himself] *the vasty wilds / Of wide Arabia*; **MV** III.ii.182

wild *(adj.)* **1** erratic, irregular, unruly **TNK** III.iii.24 [Palamon to Arcite, of 'mad lodging ... in the wild woods'] *Yes, for them / That have wild consciences*; **2H4** V.ii.123; **MW** III.iv.8

2 rash, reckless, careless **WT** II.i.182 [Leontes to Antigonus, of Hermione's guilt] *in an act of this importance 'twere / Most piteous to be wild*; **Cor** IV.i.36; **1H6** IV.iv.7

3 agitated, disturbed, upset **Ham** V.ii.388 [Horatio to Fortinbras, of recounting events] *let this same be presently performed, / Even while men's minds are wild*

4 savage, fierce, cruel **2H6** V.ii.59 [Young Clifford to himself] *Meet I an infant of the house of York, / Into as many gobbets will I cut it / As wild Medea young Absyrtus did*

5 furious, mad, infuriated **AC** V.ii.154 [Cleopatra to Caesar] *The ingratitude of this Seleucus does / Even make me wild*

6 delirious, ecstatic, passionately elated **Per** V.i.223 [Pericles to all] *I am wild in my beholding* [i.e. over what I can see]

7 wanton, flighty, frivolous **AC** I.ii.51 [Iras to Charmian] *you wild bedfellow*; **CE** III.i.110

8 daring, irregular, audacious **KJ** II.i.395 [Bastard to King John and King Philip, of his advice] *How like you this wild counsel*

wilderness *(n.)* wildness of character, licentiousness **MM** III.i.145 [Isabella to and of Claudio] *a warped slip of wilderness*

wildfire *(n.)* flaming gunpowder; also: will o' the wisp; type of eruptive disease **1H4** III.iii.39 [Falstaff to Bardolph, of Bardolph's face] *a ball of wildfire*; **Luc** 1523

wildly *(adv.)* naturally, without cultivation **Cym** IV.ii.180 [Belarius alone, of Arviragus and Guiderius] *valour / That wildly grows in them*

wildness *(n.)* madness, distraction, frenzy **Ham** III.i.40 [Gertrude to Ophelia] *I do wish / That your good beauties be the happy cause / Of Hamlet's wildness*; **Cym** III.iv.9

WHO AND WHO-

Who and its derivatives present a less complex scenario than *what*. Most interrogative uses are the same in Shakespearian as in modern English, the chief difference being the sense of 'whoever' illustrated below. *Whoever* itself differs only in the use of a contracted form, *whoe'er*, a contraction also seen in *whosoe'er*.

Grammatical usage of *who* shows two other points of difference from modern English. There is wider use of this form after a preposition, where standard English today would use *whom*: for example, Edgar asks 'To who?' (**KL** V.iii.246) and Hamlet 'Between who?' (**Ham** II.ii.195). And the semantic range of *who* is wider, including abstract concepts, objects, and animals: among the entities that are qualified as 'who' are the world, 'who of itself is peised well' (**KJ** II.i.575); a golden casket, 'who this inscription bears' (**MV** II.vii.4); a drop of water, 'Who, falling there to find his fellow forth' (**CE** I.ii.37); and a lion, 'Who glazed upon me' (**JC** I.iii.21).

Item	Location	Example	Gloss
who	**Oth** 3.3.156	*Who steals my purse, steals trash*	whoever, anyone who
who	**Mac** I.iii.108	*Who was the Thane lives yet*	the person who
whoever, whoe'er (conj.)	**1H6** I.iii.7	*Whoe'er he be, you may not be let in*	whoever
whoso	**1H6** III.iv.39	*whoso draws a sword 'tis present death*	whoever, anyone who
whosoever, whosoe'er	**TNK** IV.ii.155	*whosoever wins / Loses a noble cousin*	whoever, anyone who
whomsoever (conj.)	**TC** II.i.63	*whomsoever you take him to be, he is Ajax*	whoever
whose ... soever	**R3** IV.iv.225	*Whose hand soever lanched their tender hearts*	of whoever

◆ WHAT AND WHAT-, p.495

wile *(n.)* trick, delusion, illusion **CE** IV.iii.10 [Antipholus of Syracuse alone, of his experiences] *these are but imaginary wiles* [i.e. existing in my imagination only]

wilful *(adv.)* wilfully, deliberately **Sonn** 51.13 *But love, for love, thus shall excuse my jade / Since from thee going he went wilful slow*

wilful-blame *(adj.)* wilfully blameworthy, at fault for being too obstinate **1H4** III.i.171 [Worcester to Hotspur] *you are too wilful-blame* ☛ blame *(adj.)*

wilful-negligent *(adj.)* deliberately negligent, at fault for being too negligent **WT** I.ii.255 [Camillo to Leontes] *In your affairs … / If ever I were wilful-negligent, / It was my folly* ☛ negligent *(adj.)*

wilful-opposite *(adj.)* stubbornly hostile, at fault for being too antagonistic **KJ** V.ii.124 [Cardinal Pandulph to Bastard] *The Dauphin is too wilful-opposite* ☛ opposite *(adj.)*

will *(n.)* **1** desire, wish, liking, inclination **RJ** III.v.23 [Romeo to Juliet] *I have more care to stay than will to go*; **AW** IV.iv.30; **Cym** I.vii.8; **H8** I.ii.13; **Mac** II.i.18; **MW** II.i.154

2 lust, sexual desire, passion **Luc** 495 [Tarquin to Lucrece] *Will is deaf, and hears no heedful friends*; **AC** III.xiii.3; **Ham** III.iv.89; **MM** II.iv.164; **Oth** III.iii.230; **RJ** II.iii.24

3 wilfulness, self-will, determination **TG** II.vi.12 [Proteus alone] *he wants wit that wants resolved will / To learn his wit t'exchange the bad for better*; **Per** III.iii.30; **TC** I.iii.120, II.iii.164

4 intent, purpose, design **KL** I.i.43 [Lear to Cornwall and Albany] *We have this hour a constant will to publish / Our daughters' several dowers*; **Cor** I.ix.18; **Ham** IV.v.127; **2H6** I.iii.141; **TNK** III.vi.229, IV.ii.87

5 emotion, distractedness, agitation **Luc** 1299 *What wit sets down is blotted straight with will*

will *(v.)*, past form **would** **1** desire, wish, want **AY** I.ii.242 [Rosalind to Celia, of Orlando] *I'll ask him what he would*; **Ham** V.ii.241 [Laertes to Hamlet] *I stand aloof, and will no reconcilement*; **1H6** IV.ii.5; **3H6** I.i.102; **KJ** I.i.1; **TC** IV.v.19; **Tit** V.i.160

2 command, order, direct **1H6** I.iii.10 [First Warder to Gloucester's servingman] *We do no otherwise than we are willed*; **AW** I.iii.219; **1H6** II.iii.11; **2H6** V.i.80; **H8** II.i.18

3 require, demand, need **1H6** II.ii.54 [Bedford to Talbot, refusing to accompany him] *'tis more than manners will*; **Cor** II.i.234

4 decree, determine, decide [to] **Tim** IV.iii.110 [Timon to Alcibiades] *when Jove / Will o'er some high-viced city hang his poison / In the sick air*

willed *(adj.)* [debated reading] self-willed, deliberate, premeditated **TC** I.iii.340 [Nestor to Ulysses, of Hector's challenge] *Our imputation shall be oddly poised / In this willed action* [F *wild*; Q *vilde*] ☛ wild *(adj.)*

willing *(adj.)* **1** dynamic, energetic **TNK** II.i.122 [Palamon to Arcite] *A willing man dies sleeping and all's done* [i.e. an active man would die as peacefully as in his sleep]

2 voluntary, taken up willingly **Tim** IV.iii.243 [Apemantus to Timon] *Willing misery / Outlives incertain pomp*

willow *(adj.)* made of leaves from the willow tree [a symbol of the grief felt by a deserted or unrequited lover] **TN** I.v.257 [Viola as Cesario to Olivia] *[I would] Make me a willow cabin at your gate*; **3H6** III.iii.228 ☛ PLANTS, p.330

willow *(int.)* ☛ SINGING, p.402

wilt *(v.)* ☛ VERB FORMS, p.481

wimpled *(adj.)* blindfolded **LL** III.i.176 [Browne alone, of Cupid] *This wimpled, whining, purblind, wayward boy*

win *(v.)* **1** gain advantage [over], get the better [of] **H8** V.i.58 [Suffolk to King Henry, of playing primero] *I did never win of you before*; **AC** II.iv.9; **Cym** I.ii.52; **2H4** IV.iii.66; **KJ** II.i.569; **MA** V.i.82

2 win over, prevail upon **Cym** I.i.6 [Queen to Posthumus] *So soon as I can win th'offended king*

3 earn, deserve, merit **TNK** I.ii.18 [Palamon to Arcite, of a soldier] *honour and golden ingots, / Which though he won he had not* [i.e. did not receive the reward he had earned]

win upon *(v.)* prevail over, overcome **Cor** I.i.218 [Martius to Menenius, of the rabble] *It will in time / Win upon power*

winch *(v.)* wince, flinch, recoil **KJ** IV.i.80 [Arthur to Hubert, of being blinded] *I will not stir, nor winch, nor speak a word*

Winchester goose *(contemptuous)* groin swelling caused by venereal disease **1H6** I.iii.53 [Gloucester to Winchester] *Winchester goose! I cry a rope, a rope!*; **TC** V.x.55

wind *(n.)* **1** breath **2H4** I.ii.184 [Lord Chief Justice to Falstaff] *Is not your voice broken, your wind short*; **1H4** II.ii.13; **3H6** II.i.82, III.i.85; **MV** I.i.22

2 sighing, lamenting breath **TC** IV.iv.52 [Pandarus to himself] *Rain, to lay this wind, or my heart will be blown up by the root*

3 ☛ blow wind in the breech

wind, allow the go down-wind **AW** V.ii.8 [Clown to Parolles] *Prithee, allow the wind*

wind, break one's gasp for breath, lose one's breath **Tim** V.iv.12 [Alcibiades to Senators] *pursy insolence shall break his wind / With fear and horrid flight* [also: fart]

wind, have in the scent, detect **AW** III.vi.107 [Bertram to Second Lord, of Parolles] *this same coxcomb that we have i'th' wind* [i.e. that we have the scent of]

wind, keep the stay downwind of a quarry [so as to maintain a scent] **3H6** III.ii.13 [George aside to Richard, of Edward] *how true he keeps the wind!*

wind, recover the [in hunting] get to the windward side **Ham** III.ii.354 [Hamlet to Rosencrantz] *why do you go about to recover the wind of me* [i.e. the quarry is allowed to scent the hunter]

wind, stop in your hold your breath, shut up **CE** I.ii.53 [Antipholus of Syracuse to Dromio of Ephesus] *Stop in your wind, sir*

wind of, have the [hunting] stay downwind of; stay in a safe position in relation to **Tit** IV.ii.12 [Aaron to all, of their seats] *My son and I will have the wind of you*

wind *(v.)* **1** scent, get wind of **Tit** IV.i.96 [Titus to Marcus, of Tamora as a mother-bear] *if she wind ye once*

2 sound, blow **1H6** II.iii.60 [stage direction] *He winds his horn*; **MA** I.i.222; **Tit** II.ii.11; **TNK** III.i.96, 108; **TS** Induction.i.14

3 insinuate, pursue a devious course **MV** I.i.154 [Antonio to Bassanio] *You … herein spend but time / To wind about my love with circumstance*; **Cor** III.iii.64; **KL** I.ii.98

4 [horsemanship] make wheel about **1H4** IV.i.109 [Vernon to Hotspur] *To turn and wind a fiery Pegasus*; **JC** IV.i.32

5 go, wend, take oneself **AY** III.iii.93 [Touchstone singing, to Sir Oliver Martext] *Wind away, / Be gone*

wind up *(v.)* **1** occupy, fill up, take up **H5** IV.i.272 [King Henry alone, of a wretched slave] *Winding up days with toil, and nights with sleep*

2 prepare for action, set in readiness **Mac** I.iii.36 [Witches chanting] *The charm's wound up*

3 put in tune, put in order, harmonize **KL** IV.vii.16 [Cordelia to the gods, of Lear] *Th'untuned and jarring senses O wind up / Of this child-changed father*

wind-changing *(adj.)* changing with the direction of the wind, fickle **3H6** V.i.57 [Edward to Warwick] *Wind-changing Warwick now can change no more*

windgall *(n.)* soft tumour on a horse's leg **TS** III.ii.52 [Biondello to Tranio as Lucentio, of Petruchio's horse] *full of windgalls*

winding-sheet *(n.)* burial cloth, shroud **3H6** I.i.129 [King to all, of his father and grandfather] *their colours … / Shall be my winding-sheet*; **3H6** II.v.114

windlass *(n.)* circuit made to intercept game while hunting; roundabout way **Ham** II.i.65 [Polonius to Reynaldo] *With windlasses and with assays of bias*

window *(n.)* **1** shutter **1H6** III.i.84 [Mayor to all] *Our windows are broke down in every street*; **JC** III.ii.260

2 (plural) eyelids **Cym** II.ii.22 [Iachimo to himself, of Innogen's eyes] *now canopied / Under these windows*; **AC** V.ii.315; **R3** V.iii.117; **RJ** IV.i.100

3 opening, hole; wound R3 I.ii.12 [Anne to dead Henry VI] *these windows that let forth thy life*

window *(v.)* put in a window, place on display AC IV.xiv.72 [Antony to Eros] *Wouldst thou be windowed in great Rome*

windowed *(adj.)* full of holes KL III.iv.31 [Lear to himself, as if to wretches everywhere] *Your looped and windowed raggedness*

windows' tops *(n.)* topmost windows, upper windows R2 V.ii.5 [Duchess of York to York] *rude misgoverned hands from windows' tops / Threw dust and rubbish*

windring *(adj.)* winding, wandering Tem IV.i.128 [Iris to the nymphs] *You nymphs … of the windring brooks*

wind-swift *(adj.)* swift as the wind RJ II.v.8 [Juliet alone] *therefore hath the wind-swift Cupid wings*

windy *(adj.)* windward, situated towards the wind [so that scent will travel away from the follower] TN III.iv.163 [Fabian to Sir Andrew] *Still you keep o' the windy side of the law*; MA II.i.290

wing *(n.)* **1** flight, manner of flying AW I.i.201 [Helena to Parolles] *the composition that your valour and fear makes in you is a virtue of a good wing* [i.e. able to fly swiftly]
2 flank, force at the side of the main body of troops 1H6 IV.i.43 [Talbot to all] *Out, some light horsemen, and peruse their wings*

wing, hold a *(falconry)* take a course, maintain a course 1H4 III.ii.30 [King Henry to Prince Hal] *let me wonder … / At thy affections, which do hold a wing / Quite from the flight of all thy ancestors*

wing *(v.)* **1** furnish with troops, have a wing protected [by] R3 V.iii.301 [King Richard to Norfolk] *we will follow / In the main battle, whose puissance on either side / Shall be well winged with our chiefest horse*
2 put on wings; hoist sail E3 III.i.84 [King John to all, of his navy] *How are they prepared / To wing themselves against this flight of ravens?*

winged *(adj.)* impelled, incited, raised up [as if in flight] 3H6 I.i.267 [King to Exeter, of York] *Whose haughty spirit, winged with desire, / Will cost my crown*

wing-led *(adj.)* [unclear meaning] led on in organized formation Cym II.iv.24 [Posthumus to Philario, of the British discipline] *Now wing-led with their courages*

wink *(n.)* **1** closing of the eyes, shutting, sleep WT I.ii.317 [Leontes to Camillo, of Polixenes] *thou, / His cupbearer … mightst bespice a cup / To give mine enemy a lasting wink*; Tem II.i.290
2 blink WT V.ii.108 [First Gentleman to other Gentlemen] *Every wink of an eye some new grace will be born*
3 least bit, smallest amount Tem II.i.246 [Antonio to Sebastian, of the latter's hopes] *even / Ambition cannot pierce a wink beyond*

wink *(v.)* **1** shut one's eyes H5 II.i.6 [Nym to Bardolph] *I dare not fight, but I will wink and hold out mine iron*; CE III.ii.58; 2H6 II.i.104; Luc 553; TG II.iv.96; WT III.iii.100
2 [of the eyes] close, shut Cym V.iv.188 [Posthumus to First Gaoler] *none want eyes to direct them the way I am going, but such as wink, and will not use them*; RJ III.ii.6
3 fail to look, connive Mac I.iv.53 [Macbeth to himself] *The eye wink at the hand*; Tim III.i.44
4 blink LL I.ii.51 [Mote to Armado] *here is three studied ere ye'll thrice wink*; TN V.i.88
5 sleep, doze, nod off LL I.i.43 [Berowne to King, of their state] *not be seen to wink of all the day*; Tem II.i.220
6 shrink away, wince, flinch Venus 90 [of Adonis] *He winks, and turns his lips another way* [or: sense 4]

wink at *(v.)* ignore, disregard, overlook H5 II.ii.55 [King Henry to all] *If little faults … / Shall not be winked at*

wink on *(v.)* give someone a significant glance, invite with a look H5 V.ii.301 [Burgundy to King Henry, of Katherine] *I will wink on her to consent*

winking *(n.)* shutting the eyes Cym V.iv.192 [First Gaoler to Posthumus] *I am sure hanging's the way of winking*; Ham II.ii.137; H5 V.ii.300; KJ IV.ii.211

winking *(adj.)* **1** closed, shut KJ II.i.215 [King John to Hubert, of the French armies] *Confronts your city's eyes, your winking gates* [or: opening and closing]
2 with closed eyes Cym II.iv.89 [Iachimo to Posthumus, of Innogen's room] *Her andirons … were two winking Cupids / Of silver*
3 with closed petals Cym II.iii.23 [Song] *winking Mary-buds begin to ope their golden eyes*

winter *(adj.)* aged, venerable 2H6 V.iii.2 [York to all, of Salisbury] *That winter lion*

wintered *(adj.)* worn in winter AY III.ii.101 [Touchstone to Rosalind] *Wintered garments must be lined*

winter-ground *(v.)* [of plants] cover so as to protect from winter harshness Cym IV.ii.229 [Arviragus to Belarius and Guiderius, as if to the supposedly dead Innogen] *To winter-ground thy corse*

winterly *(adj.)* harsh, cheerless, unpleasant Cym III.iv.13 [Innogen to Pisanio, of the letter] *If't be summer news, / Smile to't before: if winterly, thou need'st / But keep that count'nance still*

wipe *(n.)* mark, brand, scar Luc 537 [Tarquin to Lucrece, of her disgrace if she resists] *Worse than a slavish wipe or birth-hour's blot*

wisdom *(n.)* **1** knowledge, learning, science KL IV.iv.8 [Cordelia to Doctor, of Lear] *What can man's wisdom / In the restoring his bereaved sense?*
2 good sense, judgement Ham V.i.259 [Hamlet to Laertes] *have I in me something dangerous, / Which let thy wisdom fear* [Q1, Q2 *wisedome*; F *wiseness*]
3 [political] caution, prudence, judgement Ham IV.vii.8 [Laertes to Claudius] *As by your safety, greatness, wisdom*

wise *(n.)* manner, way, fashion E3 I.i.31 [King David to Lorraine, of the Scots soldiers] *never shall [they] … hang their staves of grained Scottish ash / In peaceful wise upon their city walls*; E3 V.i.137

wise *(adj.)* **1** discreet, sensible, prudent TNK II.iv.65 [Theseus to Emilia] *you have a servant / That, if I were a woman, would be master; / But you are wise*; Tim III.i.31
2 informed, well-aware, knowledgeable Tim III.i.40 [Lucullus to Flaminius] *thou art wise, and thou knowest well enough … that this is no time to lend money*; Oth I.i.122

wise woman, wisewoman *(n.)* fortune-teller, witch, sorceress MW IV.v.54 [Host to Falstaff] *Was there a wise woman with thee?*; MW IV.v.23; TN III.iv.102

wish *(n.)* (plural) good wishes TNK V.i.17 [Theseus to Palamon and Arcite] *betwixt ye / I part my wishes*

wish *(v.)* **1** hope, desire AW I.iii.207 [Helena to Countess] *if yourself … / Did ever … / Wish chastely and love dearly*; Cym IV.ii.108; Sonn 56.14
2 wish for, support AC I.iv.42 [Caesar to Lepidus] *It hath been taught us from the primal state / That he which is was wished until he were* [i.e. the man who wants power is supported until he gets it]
3 entreat, invite LL V.ii.400 [Browne to Rosaline] *I will wish thee never more to dance*
4 commend, recommend TS I.i.111 [Gremio to Hortensio, of a good teacher for Bianca] *I will wish him to her father*; TS I.ii.59

wished *(adj.)* longed-for, desired E3 III.iv.81 [Prince Edward to all] *I bring my fraught unto the wished port*; 2H6 III.ii.113; PassP XIV.22

wishful *(adj.)* longing, yearning, wistful 3H6 III.i.14 [King to himself] *To greet mine own land with my wishful sight*

wishtly *(adv.)* fixedly, intently, steadfastly R2 V.iv.7 [Exton to a Man, of King Henry] *he wishtly looked on me* [Q1, 2; F *wistly*]

wist *(v.)*, past form of **wit** knew for certain 1H6 IV.i.180 [Richard to Warwick, of the King] *An if I wist he did*

wistly (*adv.*) intently, attentively, earnestly **E3** II.ii.88 [King Edward to himself, of Prince Edward's eyes] *looking wistly on me;* **E3** III.iv.121; **Luc** 1355; **PassP** VI.12; **Venus** 343

wit (*n.*) **1** intelligence, wisdom, good sense **Ham** II.ii.90 [Polonius to Claudius and Gertrude] *since brevity is the soul of wit* ☛ FEW, p.xxi; mother-wit (*n.*); want-wit (*n.*)
2 mental sharpness, acumen, quickness, ingenuity **AY** V.i.28 [William to Touchstone] *I have a pretty wit* ☛ FEW, p.xxi
3 reasoning, thinking, deliberation **3H6** IV.vii.61 [Hastings to Edward] *Away with scrupulous wit!;* **MM** IV.i.62
4 cunning plan, ingenious design **TN** I.ii.62 [Viola to Captain] *shape thou thy silence to my wit;* **KL** I.ii.179
5 mind, brain, thoughts **KJ** III.iv.102 [Constance to King Philip, of her tidied hair] *I will not keep this form upon my head / When there is such disorder in my wit;* **CE** II.ii.38; **Luc** 290
6 lively person, sharp-minded individual **Venus** 850 [of the sound of insects] *Soothing the humour of fantastic wits;* **Sonn** 59.13

wit, to [legal] that is to say **AY** V.i.51 [Touchstone to William] *thou perishest ... or, to wit, I kill thee;* **3H6** V.vi.51

wits, also **five wits** faculties of the mind (common wit, imagination, fantasy, estimation, memory) or body (the five senses) **MA** I.i.61 [Beatrice to Leonato, of Benedick] *four of his five wits went halting off, and now is the whole man governed with one;* **RJ** I.iv.47, II.iv.72; **Sonn** 141.9; **TN** IV.ii.86

wit (*v.*) know, be aware, realize **Per** IV.iv.31 [Gower alone] *Now please you wit / This epitaph is for Marina writ;* **1H6** II.v.16

witch (*n.*) enchanter, magician, wizard **Cym** I.vii.166 [Iachimo to Innogen, of Posthumus] *he is ... such a holy witch / That he enchants societies into him*

witch (*v.*) bewitch, charm, enchant **2H6** III.ii.116 [Queen to King] *How often have I tempted Suffolk's tongue ... / To sit and witch me;* **1H4** IV.i.110; **2H6** III.ii.119; **3H6** III.ii.150; **Tim** V.i.153

witching (*adj.*) witchcraft-practising, spell-casting **Ham** III.ii.395 [Hamlet alone] *'Tis now the very witching time of night*

with (*prep.*) **1** against **3H6** I.iv.21 [York alone] *I have seen a swan ... spend his strength with overmatching waves*
2 by **WT** V.ii.61 [Third Gentleman to all, of Antigonus] *he was torn to pieces with a bear*
3 by virtue of **1H6** I.ii.85 [Pucelle to Dauphin, of Our Lady] *With those clear rays which she infused on me / That beauty am I blessed with which you may see* [first instance]
4 like **Ham** III.ii.143 [Hamlet to Ophelia, of any great man] *'a suffer not thinking on, with the hobby-horse, whose epitaph is 'For O ... the hobby-horse is forgot!'*

withal (*adv.*) **1** in addition, moreover, as well **1H4** IV.iii.103 [Hotspur to Blunt, of King Henry] *he ... drove us to seek out / This head of safety, and withal to pry / Into his title* ☛ WITHAL AND -WITHAL, p.501
2 nevertheless, notwithstanding **TS** III.ii.25 [Tranio as Lucentio to Katherina and Baptista, of Petruchio] *Though he be merry, yet withal he's honest* ☛ WITHAL AND -WITHAL, p.501
3 with this / it, by this / it **CE** III.i.113 [Antipholus of Ephesus to Balthasar] *This woman that I mean, / My wife ... / Hath oftentimes upbraided me withal* ☛ WITHAL AND -WITHAL, p.501

withal (*prep.*) with **AY** III.ii.300 [Rosalind as Ganymede to Orlando] *I'll tell you who Time ambles withal, who Time trots withal, who Time gallops withal, and who he stands still withal.*

withdraw (*v.*) turn aside, stand apart **R3** IV.iv.8 [Queen Margaret alone] *Withdraw thee, wretched Margaret!;* **Ham** III.ii.353

wither out (*v.*) cause to dwindle, make less **MND** I.i.6 [Theseus to Hippolyta, of the moon] *She lingers my desires, / Like to a stepdame ... / Long withering out a young man's revenue*

withers (*n.*) [of a horse] ridge between the shoulder-blades **1H4** II.i.6 [First Carrier to Ostler, of his horse] *poor jade is wrung in the withers;* **Ham** III.ii.252

withhold (*v.*) **1** restrain, hold back, keep in check **AC** III.vi.79 [Caesar to Octavia] *Your letters did withhold our breaking forth;* **TC** V.iii.51
2 detain, keep in possession **MND** II.i.26 [Puck to Fairy, of Titania and her attendant] *she perforce withholds the loved boy;* **Venus** 612

within (*adv.*) ☛ STAGE DIRECTIONS, p.417

within (*prep.*) among **1H6** IV.i.140 [King to all, of the French] *If they perceive ... that within ourselves we disagree*

without (*adv.*) externally, on the outside **Ham** IV.iv.28 [Hamlet to Captain] *th'imposthume ... / That inward breaks, and shows no cause without / Why the man dies;* **Cym** I.v.8; **Sonn** 146.12; **TC** III.iii.97; **Tim** V.iv.39

without (*conj.*) **1** unless **MA** III.iii.77 [Dogberry to Verges, of detaining the Prince] *any man that knows the statutes, he may stay him ... not without the Prince be willing*
2 beyond **Cor** III.i.144 [Coriolanus to Brutus] *one part does disdain with cause, the other / Insult without all reason*
3 outside **RJ** III.iii.17 [Romeo to Friar] *There is no world without Verona walls*

without-door (*adj.*) outward, surface, public **WT** II.i.69 [Leontes to Lords, of Hermione] *Praise her but for this her without-door form*

witless (*adj.*) stupid, foolish, crazy **TNK** II.i.5 [Gaoler's Daughter alone, of Palamon] *To be his whore is witless;* **MND** I.ii.258

witness (*n.*) evidence, sign **Mac** II.ii.47 [Lady Macbeth to Macbeth] *wash this filthy witness from your hand;* **MA** III.iii.44

witness, with a without a doubt, and no mistake **TS** V.i.107 [Gremio to all] *Here's packing, with a witness, to deceive us all*

witness (*v.*) **1** bear witness to, attest, testify to **CE** V.i.220 [Antipholus of Ephesus to Duke] *That goldsmith there ... / Could witness it;* **AW** V.iii.200; **Cym** IV.iv.67; **MA** I.i.36; **MND** V.i.25
2 be a sign of, foreshadow, betoken **Sonn** 26.4 *To thee I send this written ambassage / To witness duty* [or: sense 1]; **MM** IV.iii.93; **R2** II.iv.22

witnessed (*adj.*) visible, evident, attested **2H4** I.i.63 [Northumberland to Lord Bardolph, of Morton's face] *So looks the strand whereon the imperious flood / Hath left a witnessed usurpation*

wit-old (*adj.*) cuckold **LL** V.i.58 [Mote to Armado, of his wit] *Offered by a child to an old man - which is wit-old*

wit-snapper (*n.*) wisecracker, smart aleck **MV** III.v.45 [Lorenzo to Launcelot] *what a wit-snapper are you!*

wittily (*adv.*) ingeniously, cleverly, resourcefully **Venus** 471 [of Adonis and Venus] *sharply he did think to reprehend her, / Which cunning love did wittily prevent*

wittingly (*adv.*) deliberately, knowingly, intentionally **3H6** II.ii.8 [King to Queen] *Nor wittingly have I infringed my vow*

wittol (*n.*) compliant cuckold, man who accepts his wife's infidelity **MW** II.ii.284 [Ford alone, of names] *But Cuckold! Wittol!*

wittolly (*adj.*) cuckoldy; also: half-witted **MW** II.ii.259 [Falstaff to Ford as Brook, of Ford] *They say the jealous wittolly knave hath masses of money*

witty (*adj.*) **1** clever, quick, intelligent **Oth** II.i.130 [Desdemona to Iago, of a woman] *How if she be black and witty?;* **3H6** I.i.43; **Tit** IV.ii.29
2 intelligent, ingenious, sensible **MND** V.i.164 [Demetrius to Theseus, of the Wall] *It is the wittiest partition that ever I heard discourse;* **TN** I.v.32
3 crafty, cunning, wily **R3** IV.ii.42 [King Richard to himself] *The deep-revolving witty Buckingham / No more shall be the neighbour to my counsels;* **MA** V.ii.25
4 with all one's wits at the ready **TC** III.ii.29 [Pandarus to Troilus] *You must be witty now* [also: amusing]

wiving (*n.*) marriage, marrying, taking a wife **Cym** V.v.167 [Iachimo to Cymbeline, of Italian women] *that hook of wiving, / Fairness, which strikes the eye*

woe *(n.)* pitiable creature, mournful sight **RJ** V.iii.179 [First Watchman to other members of the Watch, of dead Romeo, Juliet, and Paris] *We see the ground whereon these woes do lie*

woe *(adj.)* sorry, sorrowful, sad **Ham** III.i.161 [Ophelia alone] *O, woe is me / T'have seen what I have seen, see what I see!;* **AC** IV.xiv.133; **2H6** III.ii.73; **Sonn** 71.8, 90.13; **Tem** V.i.139 ☛ **REGRETS**, p.367

woeful *(adj.)* full of woe, sorrowful, mournful **AY** II.vii.149 [Jaques to all] *the lover … with a woeful ballad;* **2H6** III.ii.342

wold *(n.)* rolling hills, upland **KL** III.iv.115 [Edgar as Poor Tom to all] *S'Withold footed thrice the 'old*

wolvish *(adj.)* wolfish **KL** I.iv.305 [Lear to Goneril, of Regan] *She'll flay thy wolvish visage;* **E3** III.iii.79

wolvish-ravening *(adj.)* devouring like a wolf **RJ** III.ii.76 [Juliet as if to Romeo] *Wolvish-ravening lamb!*

woman *(v.)* **1** make behave like a woman, weep **AW** III.ii.50 [Countess to Lords, of joy and grief] *the first face of neither on the start / Can woman me unto't*

2 be in the company of a woman **Oth** III.iv.191 [Cassio to Bianca, of Othello] *[I] think it no addition … / To have him see me womaned*

womanhood *(n.)* gentle womanliness, female modesty **Tit** II.iii.174 [Lavinia to Tamora] *'Tis present death I beg, and one thing more / That womanhood denies my tongue to tell*

womanly *(adj.)* womanish, feeble, fearful **Mac** IV.ii.78 [Macduff's wife to herself] *Why then, alas, / Do I put up that womanly defence / To say I have done no harm?*

woman-post *(n.)* female carrier of dispatches **KJ** I.i.218 [Bastard to himself, of Lady Faulconbridge] *What woman-post is this?*

woman-queller *(n.)* ☛ queller *(n.)*

woman-tired *(adj.)* henpecked, torn apart by a woman **WT** II.iii.74 [Leontes to Antigonus, of Paulina] *thou art woman-tired, / unroosted / By thy Dame Partlet here*

womb *(n.)* belly, paunch **RJ** V.iii.45 [Romeo as if to Juliet's tomb] *Thou detestable maw, thou womb of death;* **2H4** IV.iii.22

womby *(adj.)* womb-like, hollow, cavernous **H5** IV.iv.124 [Exeter to Dauphin] *caves and womby vaultages of France / Shall chide your trespass*

wonder *(n.)* **1** feeling of wonder, astonishment, marvelling **TN** IV.iii.3 [Sebastian alone] *though 'tis wonder that enwraps me thus, / Yet 'tis not madness;* **H5** II.ii.110; **JC** I.iii.60; **LL** IV.ii.113; **MA** V.v.70; **Mac** III.ii.111

2 object of fascination, target of astonishment **2H6** II.iv.46 [Duchess to Gloucester] *I … / Was made a wonder and a pointing-stock;* **1H6** IV.vii.48; **TC** III.iii.242; **Tim** IV.iii.463

3 surprise, astonishment, amazement **TS** III.ii.190 [Petruchio to all, of leaving so suddenly] *Make it no wonder;* **MA** IV.i.237

4 miracle, prodigy, marvel **Tem** I.ii.428 [Miranda to Ferdinand, responding to his 'wonder' and 'maid'] *No wonder, sir, / But certainly a maid;* **TS** II.i.402, V.ii.105

5 special power, miraculous quality **CE** III.ii.30 [Antipholus of Syracuse to Luciana] *what your name is else I know not, / Nor by what wonder you do hit of mine;* **Oth** III.iv.97

6 calamity, disaster, tragedy **Ham** V.ii.357 [Horatio to Fortinbras] *If aught of woe or wonder;* **2H6** II.iv.69

7 grief, distress; or: bewilderment **Ham** IV.v.90 [Claudius to Gertrude, of Laertes] *Feeds on his wonder* [F; Q2 *this wonder* = astonishing course of events]

WITHAL AND -WITHAL

Withal and its derivatives (sometimes spelled with a final *-ll*) are chiefly used as adverbs expressing various kinds of additive meaning - usually positive ('in addition'), occasionally negative ('nevertheless'). The simple form is also used as a preposition, but as it is only found at the end of a construction, in place of *with*, it would perhaps be better referred to as a *postposition*.

Although *herewithal* and *therewithal* had been used in English since the 14th century, examples of *wherewithal* are recorded only from the mid-16th century. *Henry VIII* provides an early instance of the noun use – the only form to have survived into modern English.

Item	Location	Example	Gloss
withal (adv.)	**MV** IV.i.447	*Let his deservings, and my love withal, / Be valued*	in addition, moreover, as well
withal (adv.)	**MA** I.ii.19	*I will acquaint my daughter withal, that she be the better prepared for an answer*	in spite of all, nevertheless, notwith-standing
withal (adv.)	**KL** I.ii.102	*I will … convey the business as I shall find means, and acquaint you withal*	therewith, with this / it
withal (prep.)	**MW** II.i.81	*I'll entertain myself like one that I am not acquainted withal*	with
herewithal (adv.)	**E3** V.i.197	*And herewithal I render to your hands / These prisoners*	herewith, along with this, besides this
therewithal (adv.)	**TG** IV.iv.82	*give her that ring, and therewithal / This letter*	therewith, along with that, besides that
therewithal (adv.)	**CE** IV.iii.9	*[a tailor] showed me silks … / And therewithal took measure of my body*	thereupon, forthwith, that being done
wherewithal (pron.)	**R2** V.i.55	*Northumberland, thou ladder where-withal / The mounting Bolingbroke ascends my throne*	whereby, with which
wherewithal (n.)	**H8** I.iii.59	*has wherewithal*	what is needed

☛ **HERE, THERE, AND WHERE**, p.220

wonder (v.) **1** marvel [at], be astonished [at] **MA** I.iii.10 [Don John to Conrade] *I wonder that thou … goest about to apply a moral medicine to a mortifying mischief*; **TG** V.iv.170 [Valentine to Duke] *you will wonder what hath fortuned*; **3H6** V.vi.74; **MA** III.iii.113; **MV** III.iii.8; **Sonn** 123.10; **TN** III.iv.149

2 stare in curiosity, look in fascination **TN** I.v.190 [Olivia to Viola as Cesario] *I … allowed your approach rather to wonder at you than to hear you*; **Luc** 1845

3 wonder at, be curious about, guess at **Luc** 1596 [of Collatine and Lucrece] *Like stood like old acquaintance in a trance … wondering each other's chance*

wondered (adj.) to be wondered at, performing such wonders **Tem** IV.i.123 [Ferdinand to Prospero] *So rare a wondered father and a wise*

wonderful (adj.) amazing, astonishing, extraordinary **JC** I.iii.14 [Cicero to Casca, of the storm] *Why, saw you anything more wonderful?*; **E3** IV.iv.11; **TS** IV.iii.15

wonderful (adv.) wonderfully, remarkably, incredibly **TS** I.i.69 [Tranio to Lucentio, of Katherina] *That wench is stark mad or wonderful froward*

wondering (n.) admiring, marvelling **2H6** I.i.34 [King to and of Queen] *her grace in speech … / Makes me from wondering fall to weeping joys*

wonderingly (adv.) with wonder, with amazement **Per** III.iii.7 [Cleon to Pericles] *Your shakes of fortune … glance / Full wonderingly on us*

wonder-wounded (adj.) awestruck, wonder-struck **Ham** V.i.253 [Hamlet to all] *Conjures the wandering stars, and makes them stand / Like wonder-wounded hearers*

wondrous (adj.) unbelievable, bizarre, strange **TS** III.ii.94 [Petruchio to all, of their stares] *As if they saw some wondrous monument*; **KJ** IV.ii.184

wondrous (adv.) wonderfully, extraordinarily, marvellously **Cor** II.i.34 [Menenius to Brutus] *your helps are many, or else your actions would grow wondrous single*

wont (n.) custom, habit, practice **Ham** I.iv.6 [Horatio to Hamlet and Marcellus] *It then draws near the season / Wherein the spirit held his wont to walk*; **2H6** III.i.2

wont (v.) be accustomed, used [to], be in the habit of **AY** II.ii.9 [Second Lord to Duke Frederick, of Touchstone] *at whom so oft / Your grace was wont to laugh* ☞ **FEW**, p.xxi

wonted (adj.) accustomed, usual, customary **Ham** III.i.41 [Gertrude to Ophelia, of Hamlet] *bring him to his wonted way again*; **E3** IV.v.5; **1H6** III.i.32; **3H6** II.v.49; **H8** V.ii.102; **MND** I.i.113

woo (v.) **1** win over, persuade, coax **AY** I.iii.131 [Celia to Rosalind, of Touchstone] *Leave me alone to woo him*; **E3** II.i.344

2 entreat, plead with, implore **E3** II.i.172 [King Edward to Lodowick, of the Countess] *I shall woo her to cut off my head*

wood (adj.) mad, wild, furious **1H6** IV.vii.35 [Bastard to all] *the young whelp of Talbot's, raging wood*; **MND** II.i.192; **Venus** 740

woodbine (n.) **1** honeysuckle **MA** III.i.30 [Ursula to Hero, of Beatrice] *who even now / Is couched in the woodbine coverture*; **MND** II.i.251 ☞ **PLANTS**, p.330

2 bindweed, convolvulus **MND** IV.i.41 [Titania to Bottom] *So doth the woodbine the sweet honeysuckle / Gently entwist* ☞ **PLANTS**, p.330

woodcock (n.) type of game bird, thought to be easily tricked or snared; simpleton **AW** IV.i.89 [First Lord to Second Soldier, of Parolles] *We have caught the woodcock*; **3H6** I.iv.61; **LL** IV.iii.80; **MA** V.i.152; **TN** II.v.83; **TS** I.ii.158

wooden (adj.) spiritless, dull, stupid **1H6** V.iii.89 [Suffolk to himself, of the King] *Tush, that's a wooden thing!* [also possible: referring to the matter in hand, i.e. 'stupid business']

woodman (n.) hunter, huntsman **Cym** III.vii.1 [Belarius to Guiderius] *You … have proved best woodman*; **Luc** 580; **MM** IV.iii.160; **MW** V.v.27

woof (n.) cross-threads in a web; web **TC** V.ii.155 [Troilus to Ulysses, of the division in Cressida] *the spacious breadth of this division / Admits no orifex for a point as subtle / As Ariachne's broken woof to enter*

wooingly (adv.) enticingly, alluringly, temptingly **Mac** I.vi.6 [Banquo to King] *The temple-haunting martlet, does approve / By his loved mansionry that the heaven's breath / Smells wooingly here*

woollen (adj.) in coarse woollen clothes **Cor** III.ii.9 [Coriolanus to Nobles, of the Plebeians] *my mother … was wont / To call them woollen vassals*

woollen, lie in the sleep in rough blankets **MA** II.i.27 [Beatrice to Leonato] *I had rather lie in the woollen*

woolward (adj.) wearing wool next to the skin **LL** V.ii.707 [Armado to all] *I go woolward for penance*

woosel (n.) ☞ ousel (n.)

word (n.) **1** remark, speech, utterance **LL** V.ii.19 [Rosaline to Katharine, of her remark] *What's your dark meaning … of this light word?*; **3H6** V.v.27

2 declaration, affirmation, proclamation **AC** II.ii.48 [Caesar to Antony] *You were the word of war* [debated reading]

3 maxim, saying, adage, motto **Ham** IV.v.107 [Messenger to Claudius, of antiquity and custom] *The ratifiers and props of every word*; **Per** II.ii.21

4 word of God **2H4** IV.ii.10 [Prince John to Archbishop] *Turning the word to sword, and life to death*; **MW** III.i.41; **R2** V.v.13

5 (plural) speech, talk, utterance **Mac** III.vi.21 [Lennox to a Lord] *from broad words … / Macduff lives in disgrace*

6 (plural) angry exchanges, altercations, recriminations **3H6** II.ii.177 [Edward to Queen] *These words will cost ten thousand lives this day*

7 (plural) empty rhetoric, vain talk **H8** V.iii.72 [Gardiner to Cranmer] *Your painted gloss discovers, / To men that understand you, words and weakness*

word, at a **1** in a word, once and for all, in short **Cor** I.iii.110 [Virgilia to Valeria] *No, at a word, madam*; **2H4** III.ii.288; **MA** II.i.101; **MW** I.i.100 ☞ **DISCOURSE MARKERS**, p.127

2 without more ado, at once, forthwith **JC** I.ii.265 [Casca to Brutus, of Caesar] *if I would not have taken him at a word, I would I might go to hell among the rogues*; **MW** I.iii.14

word, with a in brief, in short **1H4** II.iv.251 [Prince Hal to Falstaff, of the robbery] *Then did we two set on you four, and, with a word, out-faced you from your prize* [or: with a single shout] ☞ **DISCOURSE MARKERS**, p.127

word (v.) **1** speak, utter, say **Cym** IV.ii.240 [Guiderius to Arviragus] *I cannot sing: I'll weep, and word it with thee*; **AC** IV.xiii.9

2 represent in words, give a reputation **Cym** I.v.14 [Iachimo to all, of Posthumus] *This matter of marrying his king's daughter … words him … a great deal from the matter* [i.e. greater than he merits]

work (n.) **1** deed, doing, action **KJ** II.i.93 [King Philip to King John] *This toil of ours should be a work of thine*; **H8** V.i.18; **TC** I.iii.18

2 fort, barricade **H8** V.iv.57 [Man to Porter, of boys] *I was fain to draw mine honour in, and let 'em win the work*

3 (plural) fortifications, defences, ramparts **Oth** III.ii.3 [Othello to Iago] *I will be walking on the works*

4 embroidery, needlework **Oth** IV.i.151 [Bianca to Cassio, of Desdemona's handkerchief] *I must take out the work*; **Oth** III.iv.176

work (v.), past form **wrought** **1** bring about, arrange, effect **RJ** V.iii.245 [Friar to Prince, of his potion's effect on Juliet] *it wrought on her / The form of death*; **Cym** V.v.55; **2H4** IV.iv.119; **2H6** I.iii.65; **KL** IV.vii.96; **R2** IV.i.4

2 perform, do, carry out **Tim** I.i.199 [Timon to Apemantus, of a painting] *Wrought he not well that painted it?*; **Cym** V.iii.55; **2H6** V.i.70; **Mac** II.i.19; **Tem** V.i.53

3 affect, stir, act upon **Tem** V.i.17 [Ariel to Prospero, of the King's company] *Your charm so strongly works 'em*; **Mac** I.iii.149; **Tem** IV.i.144; **WT** V.iii.58

4 happen, proceed, come about **MM** III.ii.30 [disguised Duke to the Officer, of Pompey] *Correction and instruction must both work / Ere this rude beast will profit;* **Ham** III.iv.206
5 act upon, continue with **Ham** I.i.67 [Horatio to Marcellus and Barnardo] *In what particular thought to work I know not*
6 act, behave, conduct oneself **Ham** IV.vii.20 [Claudius to Laertes, of the common people] *Who ... / Work like the spring that turneth wood to stone;* **MM** III.ii.201
7 persuade, urge **JC** I.ii.162 [Brutus to Cassius] *What you would work me to, I have some aim;* **Ham** IV.vii.62; **Oth** V.ii.341
8 practise, proceed, plot **Mac** III.i.81 [Macbeth to Murderers] *[I] passed in probation with you / How you were borne in hand, how crossed, the instruments, / Who wrought with them*
9 work for, plan, try to arrange **MM** IV.ii.132 [Provost to disguised Duke, of Barnadine] *His friends still wrought reprieves for him;* **H8** III.ii.311
10 work on, manipulate **3H6** II.i.170 [Warwick to Richard and Edward, of the Queen and her supporters] *Have wrought the easy-melting King like wax;* **JC** I.ii.306
11 activate, galvanize, make work **Sonn** 27.4 [after going to bed] *then begins a journey in my head / To work my mind*
12 run, toss about, rage **Per** III.i.48 [First Sailor to Pericles] *The sea works high*
13 embroider, make, sew **TNK** II.i.181 [Emilia to Woman] *Canst not thou work such flowers in silk;* **KJ** IV.i.43

work out (*v.*) preserve to the end, manage to maintain **2H4** I.i.182 [Lord Bardolph to Northumberland] *We all ... / Knew that we ventured on such dangerous seas / That if we wrought out life 'twas ten to one*

work to (*v.*) bring about, arrange, effect **Oth** V.ii.319 [Cassio to Othello, of Iago and Desdemona's handkerchief] *he dropped it for a special purpose / Which wrought to his desire*

work upon (*v.*) practise on, work upon, act on **Oth** I.iii.106 [Brabantio to all, of Othello and Desdemona] *with some dram conjured ... / He wrought upon her;* **Luc** 235; **Tim** III.i.60

working (*n.*) **1** operation, action, activity **LL** I.i.9 [Mote to Armado, of distinguishing sadness and melancholy] *By a familiar demonstration of the working* [i.e. the operation of the two emotions]
2 perception, mental operation, insight **2H4** IV.ii.22 [Prince John to and of Archbishop] *The very opener and intelligencer / Between the grace, the sanctities, of heaven / And our dull workings*
3 aim, endeavour, performance **AY** I.ii.190 [Orlando to Charles, of himself] *his will hath in it a more modest working;* **2H4** V.ii.90
4 effort, exertion, labour **2H4** IV.iv.41 [King Henry IV to Clarence, of Prince Henry] *being moody, give him time and scope, / Till that his passions, like a whale on ground, / Confound themselves with working*

working, in being used, being worked upon [by the world] **Ham** II.i.40 [Polonius to Reynaldo] *a thing a little soiled i'th' working*

working (*adj.*) moving, full of emotion **H8** Prologue.3 [of the play's topic] *Sad, high, and working, full of state and woe*

working-day (*adj.*) workaday, everyday, humdrum **AY** I.iii.12 [Rosalind to Celia] *O, how full of briars is this working-day world!*

working-house (*n.*) workhouse, place of industry **H5** V.Chorus.23 [Chorus] *In the quick forge and working-house of thought*

workman (*n.*) craftsman, skilled worker **Tim** IV.iii.437 [Timon to Bandits] *Do villainy, do, since you protest to do 't, / Like workmen;* **AC** IV.iv.18; **AW** II.v.18; **Cym** IV.i.6; **Tim** V.i.29

workmanly (*adv.*) skilfully, with great artistry **TS** Induction.ii.59 [Third Servingman to Sly, of a painting of Daphne] *So workmanly the blood and tears are drawn*

workyday (*adj.*) ordinary, commonplace, everyday **AC** I.ii.55 [Charmian to Soothsayer, of Iras] *tell her but a workyday fortune*

world (*n.*) **1** whole of mankind, human race, mass of society **TN** II.iv.80 [Orsino to Viola as Cesario] *my love, more noble than the world, / Prizes not quantity of dirty lands;* **Sonn** 148.6
2 times, life, state of affairs **2H6** IV.ii.8 [Holland to Bevis] *I say it was never merry world in England since gentlemen came up;* **JC** I.ii.304; **TN** III.i.95
3 large number, multitude **1H6** II.ii.48 [Talbot to Burgundy] *when a world of men / Could not prevail with all their oratory;* **1H6** IV.iv.25

world, go to the get married **AW** I.iii.18 [Clown to Countess] *if I may have your ladyship's good will to go to the world;* **MA** II.i.294

world, it is a it's a marvel, it's a great thing **MA** III.v.34 [Dogberry to Leonato, of Verges' insights] *it is a world to see!;* **TS** II.i.304

world away, thus runs the ☞ runs the world away, thus

worldling (*n.*) citizen of the world, world's inhabitant **2H4** V.iii.99 [Pistol to Falstaff] *A foutre for the world and worldlings base!;* **AY** II.i.48

worldly (*adj.*) of this world, of the earth **Tit** V.ii.65 [Titus to disguised Tamora] *we worldly men / Have miserable, mad, mistaking eyes* [i.e. men not from the underworld]

worm (*n.*) **1** serpent, snake **Cym** III.iv.36 [Pisanio to Innogen, of slander] *whose tongue / Outvenoms all the worms of Nile;* **AC** V.ii.243; **2H6** III.ii.263; **Mac** III.iv.28; **MM** III.i.17; **MND** III.ii.71
2 germ, microbe, bug **MA** III.ii.25 [Leonato to Don Pedro, of Benedick's toothache] *Where is but a humour or a worm;* **TN** II.iv.110

wormwood (*n.*) **1** absinthe plant, known for its bitter taste **RJ** I.iii.27 [Nurse to Lady Capulet, of weaning Juliet] *I had then laid wormwood to my dug;* **E3** III.iii.72; **Luc** 893
2 bitter substance, bitterness **Ham** III.ii.191 [Hamlet to himself, of the Player Queen's remarks] *That's wormwood;* **LL** V.ii.836 ☞ **PLANTS**, p.330

worn (*adj.*) worn out, exhausted, spent **2H6** II.iv.69 [Gloucester to Duchess] *These few days' wonder will be quickly worn;* **Cor** III.i.6; **TN** II.iv.34; **WT** V.i.141

worn-out (*adj.*) past, bygone, departed **Luc** 1350 [of Lucrece's groom] *this pattern of the worn-out age / Pawned honest looks, but laid no words to gage*

worried (*adj.*) maltreated, harassed, savaged **H5** I.ii.220 [Canterbury to all] *If we ... / Cannot defend our own doors from the dog, / Let us be worried*

worse (*adj.*) evil, harmful, wicked **KL** IV.vi.218 [Gloucester to all] *Let not my worser spirit tempt me again;* **Tem** IV.i.27

worship (*n.*) **1** esteem, honour, renown **AC** IV.xiv.86 [Eros to Antony] *that noble countenance / Wherein the worship of the whole world lies;* **1H4** III.ii.151; **H8** I.i.39; **KL** I.iv.263
2 honour, distinction, repute **R3** I.i.66 [Richard to Clarence, of Woodville] *that good man of worship;* **KJ** IV.iii.72; **WT** I.ii.314
3 sovereignty, supremacy **Cor** III.i.142 [Coriolanus to Brutus] *This double worship, / Where one part does disdain with cause, the other / Insult without all reason* [i.e. respect paid to two authorities]
4 dignified ease, comfortable dignity **3H6** IV.iii.16 [Third Watchman to all] *give me worship and quietness*
5 ☞ **ADDRESS FORMS**, p.8

worship (*v.*) esteem, honour, renown **Tem** V.i.298 [Caliban to Prospero, of Stephano] *What a thrice double ass / Was I to ... worship this dull fool*

worshipfully (*adv.*) respectfully, with due honour, with proper regard **R3** III.iv.39 [Richard to Prince Edward and Hastings] *His master's child, as worshipfully he terms it*

worst (*n.*) **1** weakest, least powerful **WT** II.iii.61 [Paulina to Leontes, of Hermione] *I ... would by combat make her good, so were I / A man, the worst about you*
2 lowest, most despicable **Tim** IV.iii.276 [Timon to Apemantus] *If thou hadst not been born the worst of men, / Thou hadst been a knave and flatterer*

worst (*adj.*) wicked, evil, corrupt **Tim** III.v.117 [Alcibiades alone] *'Tis honour with worst lands to be at odds* [F *most*]

worsted (*adj.*) made of woollen fabric [inferior to silk] **KL** II.ii.15 [disguised Kent to Oswald, describing him] *filthy-worsted-stocking knave*

wort (*n.*) **1** sweet unfermented beer **LL** V.ii.233 [masked Berowne to masked Princess, adding to her three sweet words] *Metheglin, wort, and malmsey*
　　2 [pun on Evans' pronunciation of 'word'] cabbage **MW** I.i.115 [Falstaff to Evans] *Good worts? Good cabbage!*

worth (*n.*) **1** worthiness, value, excellence **MA** IV.i.216 [Friar to Leonato] *what we have we prize not to the worth / Whiles we enjoy it*; **1H6** V.iii.151; **Sonn** 62.8
　　2 means, resources, wherewithal **KL** IV.iv.10 [Cordelia to Doctor, of Lear] *He that helps him, take all my outward worth*; **RJ** II.v.32; **TN** III.iii.17
　　3 rank, standing, dignity **1H6** IV.vii.86 [Lucy to all, of the Talbots] *And give them burial as beseems their worth*; **JC** III.ii.222; **WT** V.i.213
　　4 pennyworth, fill **Cor** III.iii.26 [Brutus to Sicinius, of Coriolanus] *He hath been used ... to have his worth / Of contradiction* [i.e. to give as good as he gets]

worth (*adj.*) worthy of, deserving, meriting **H8** III.ii.134 [King Henry to Norfolk, of Wolsey] *His thinkings are below the moon, not worth / His serious considering*

worth (*v.*) become of, happen to, fall on **TNK** III.vi.249 [Emilia to Theseus, of Palamon and Arcite] *all the longing maids that ever loved 'em ... / [shall] Despise my cruelty, and cry woe worth me*

worthily (*adv.*) justly, deservedly, rightly **CE** I.i.100 [Egeon to Duke, of receiving no pity from the gods] *had the gods done so, I had not now / Worthily termed them merciless to us*

worthless (*adj.*) unworthy, contemptible, ignoble **JC** V.i.61 [Cassius to and of Octavius] *A peevish schoolboy, worthless of such honour*; **1H6** IV.iv.21

worthy (*n.*) thing of worth, distinction, excellence **TG** II.iv.164 [Valentine to Proteus, of Silvia] *whose worth makes other worthies nothing*; **LL** IV.iii.234

worthy (*adj.*) **1** of worth, of value, deserving **JC** I.ii.50 [Cassius to Brutus] *this breast of mine hath buried / Thoughts of great value, worthy cogitations*; **1H6** V.v.11; **MW** IV.iv.88; **WT** IV.iv.171
　　2 deserved, justified, warranted **AW** IV.iii.5 [First Lord to Second Lord, of Bertram] *He has much worthy blame laid upon him*; **JC** IV.ii.8; **R2** V.i.68; **R3** I.ii.87
　　3 estimable, admirable, heroic **Cor** II.ii.120 [Menenius to Cominius, of Coriolanus] *Worthy man!*
　　4 good, sensible, shrewd **2H6** III.i.235 [Cardinal to all, of Gloucester] *That he should die is worthy policy*

worthy (*v.*) make worthy, give honour to **KL** II.ii.119 [Oswald to Cornwall, of disguised Kent] *he ... put upon him such a deal of man / That worthied him* [i.e. people would think him worthy]

wot (*v.*) **1** learn, know, be told **E3** III.iii.76 [King Edward to King John] *Yet wot how I regard thy worthless taunts* ☛ FEW, p.xxi
　　2 [dialect] wilt **2H4** II.i.55 [Hostess to Falstaff] *thou wot, wot ta?*
☛ VERB FORMS, p.481

would (*v.*) ☛ will (*v.*)

wound (*n.*) incision, most painful part **KJ** V.vi.21 [Bastard to Hubert] *Show me the very wound of this ill news*

wounded (*adj.*) damaged, tainted, tarnished **AC** III.x.35 [Enobarbus to all] *I'll yet follow / The wounded chance of Antony*; **Ham** V.ii.338

woundless (*adj.*) invulnerable, that cannot be hurt **Ham** IV.i.44 [Claudius to Gertrude] *slander ... may miss our name / And hit the woundless air*

wrack (*n.*) **1** destruction, ruin **Mac** V.v.51 [Macbeth to all] *Blow wind, come wrack*; **AW** III.ii.22; **Cym** I.vii.84; **E3** IV.ii.85; **Per** IV.Chorus.12; **R3** I.ii.127

2 wreck, loss, shipwreck **Tem** I.ii.26 [Prospero to Miranda] *The direful spectacle of the wrack*; **H5** I.ii.165; **KJ** III.i.92; **MV** III.i.95; **TN** V.i.263; **Venus** 454

wrack (*v.*) **1** wreck, shipwreck, lose at sea **Tem** I.ii.236 [Ariel to Prospero] *the King's ship wracked*; **3H6** V.v.23; **KJ** V.iii.11; **Mac** I.iii.28; **MV** III.i.3; **Per** II.Chorus.32
　　2 destroy, ruin, dishonour **Ham** III.i.113 [Polonius to Ophelia, of Hamlet] *I feared he did but trifle / And meant to wrack thee*
　　3 overthrow, ruin, wipe out **R3** IV.i.96 [Duchess of York to all] *Eighty odd years of sorrow have I seen, / And each hour's joy wracked with a week of teen*
　　4 work with disastrous result **Cor** V.i.16 [Menenius to Brutus and Sicinius] *A pair of Tribunes that have wracked for Rome*

wrackful (*adj.*) destructive, devastating, damaging **Sonn** 65.6 *how shall summer's honey breath hold out / Against the wrackful siege of batt'ring days*

wrack-threatening (*adj.*) threatening dishonour **Luc** 590 [Lucrece to Tarquin, of his sighs] *Beat at thy rocky and wrack-threatening heart*

wrangle (*v.*) dispute, contest, argue over **Tem** V.i.174 [Miranda to Ferdinand] *for a score of kingdoms you should wrangle*; **MW** II.i.80

wranglere (*n.*) quarreller, arguer; also: opponent, disputant **H5** I.ii.265 [King Henry to Ambassador, of the Dauphin and himself] *he hath made a match with such a wrangler*; **TC** II.ii.76

wrangling (*adj.*) quarrelsome, disputatious, argumentative **TS** III.i.4 [Hortensio as Licio to Lucentio as Cambio] *wrangling pedant*; **1H6** II.iv.6; **3H6** II.ii.176

wrap (*v.*) beset, envelop, surround [by] **Luc** 456 [of Lucrece] *Wrapped and confounded in a thousand fears*

wrap in (*v.*) entangle, catch, involve **Luc** 636 [Lucrece to Tarquin] *how are they wrapped in with infamies / That from their own misdeeds askance their eyes!*

wrastle (*v.*) variant form of 'wrestle' **KJ** V.ii.41 [Lewis the Dauphin to Salisbury] *great affections wrastling in thy bosom* [F]

wreak (*n.*) revenge, vengeance, retribution **Tit** IV.iii.34 [Marcus to all] *Take wreak on Rome for this ingratitude*; **Cor** IV.v.88; **Tit** IV.iv.11

wreak (*v.*) **1** revenge, requite, pay back **Venus** 1004 [Venus as if to death, of the boar] *Be wreaked on him*
　　2 inflict, deliver, bestow **RJ** III.v.101 [Juliet to Lady Capulet, of Tybalt and Romeo] *To wreak the love I bore my cousin / Upon his body that hath slaughtered him!*

wreakful (*adj.*) vengeful, retributive; relentless **Tit** V.ii.32 [disguised Tamora to Titus, of easing his mind] *By working wreakful vengeance on thy foes*; **Tim** IV.iii.230

wreathe (*v.*) fold, intertwine **TG** II.i.18 [Speed to Valentine] *you have learned ... to wreathe your arms, like a malcontent*

wrench (*v.*) twisting, sudden movement **H8** I.i.167 [Buckingham to Norfolk, of the treaty] *like a glass / Did break i'th' wrenching* [or: rinsing]

wrest (*n.*) [music] implement for tuning **TC** III.iii.23 [Calchas to all, of Troy] *Antenor ... is such a wrest in their affairs* [i.e. the foundation of harmony]

wrest (*v.*) **1** distort, twist, strain **2H6** III.i.186 [Buckingham to all, of Gloucester] *He'll wrest the sense and hold us here all day*; **H5** I.ii.14; **MV** IV.i.212
　　2 twist, pervert, warp **MA** III.iv.30 [Margaret to Hero] *an bad thinking do not wrest true speaking, I'll offend nobody*
　　3 wring out, derive, deduce **Tit** III.ii.10 [Titus to Lavinia, of her dumb gestures] *I of these will wrest an alphabet*

wrested (*adj.*) seized, snatched away, taken by force **KJ** IV.iii.154 [Bastard to Hubert] *vast confusion waits ... / The imminent decay of wrested pomp*

wretchedness (*n.*) humble people, the poor, the lowly **MND** V.i.85 [Hippolyta to Theseus] *I love not to see wretchedness o'ercharged*

wring *(v.)* **1** writhe, struggle, twist [as if in pain] **Cym** III.vii.51 [Belarius to Arviragus and Guiderius, of disguised Innogen] *He wrings at some distress;* **MA** V.i.28

2 wrack, rack, press down **Tit** IV.iii.49 [Titus to Marcus] *we are … wrung with wrongs more than our backs can bear*

3 rub, bruise, press **1H4** II.i.6 [First Carrier to Ostler, of his horse] *poor jade is wrung in the withers;*

4 cause to weep, force tears from **Tem** I.ii.135 [Miranda to Prospero, of the events in his story] *It is a hint / That wrings mine eyes to't*

wringing *(n.)* **1** squeezing, pressing, gripping **Venus** 421 [Adonis to Venus] *You hurt my hand with wringing*

2 aches and pains **H5** IV.i.229 [King Henry alone, of being king] *subject to the breath / Of every fool, whose sense no more can feel / But his own wringing!*

wrinkle *(n.)* frown, disapproving look **R2** II.i.170 [York to King Richard] *Or bend one wrinkle on my sovereign's face;* **Luc** 562

wrinkled *(adj.)* frowning, furrowed **R3** I.i.9 [Richard alone] *Grim-visaged war hath smoothed his wrinkled front*

writ *(n.)* **1** document, missive, letter **Ham** V.ii.51 [Hamlet to Horatio] *Folded the writ up;* **Tit** II.iii.264

2 written authority, formal order, warrant **KL** V.iii.243 [Edmund to Albany] *my writ / Is on the life of Lear and on Cordelia;* **2H6** V.iii.26

3 [archaism] gospel, holy writ **AW** II.i.138 [Helena to King] *holy writ in babes hath judgement shown, / When judges have been babes;* **Oth** III.iii.321; **Per** II.Chorus.12; **R3** I.iii.336 ☞ **ARCHAISMS**, p.22

4 writing, text **2H6** I.iv.56 [York to Buckingham] *let's see the devil's writ*

5 plays written according to traditional rules of drama; also: a district of the city subject to a sheriff's legal order [i.e. less suitable for theatres] **Ham** II.ii.400 [Polonius to Hamlet, of the players] *For the law of writ and the liberty, these are the only men*

write *(v.)* **1** claim, bear, exhibit **AW** II.iii.60 [Lafew to Parolles] *I'd give bay curtal and his furniture / My mouth no more were broken than these boys', / And writ as little beard*

2 call oneself, claim to be **2H4** I.ii.26 [Falstaff to Page, of Prince Henry] *he'll be crowing as if he had writ man ever since his father was a bachelor;* **AW** II.iii.197

3 sign, designate, call **MW** I.i.9 [Slender to Evans, of Shallow] *a gentleman born … who writes himself Armigero*

writhled *(adj.)* wrinkled, shrivelled, withered **1H6** II.iii.22 [Countess to and of Talbot] *It cannot be this weak and writhled shrimp*

written *(adj.)* preserved, engraved, fixed **Mac** V.iii.42 [Macbeth to Doctor] *Canst thou not … / Raze out the written troubles of the brain*

wroath *(n.)* ☞ wroth *(n.)*

wrong *(n.)* **1** dishonour, discredit, harm **MW** III.iii.195 [Mistress Page to Ford] *You do yourself mighty wrong;* **1H4** I.iii.74; **1H6** II.v.22; **H8** II.iv.100; **MM** I.ii.40; **Tem** I.ii.444

2 insult, offence, slight **1H6** III.iv.42 [Basset to Vernon] *I'll … crave / I may have liberty to venge this wrong;* **KL** IV.ii.14, 51; **MND** III.ii.361; **Tim** III.v.33; **Tit** IV.iv.1; **TS** IV.iii.2

3 wrong-doing, wrongful gain, unjust claim **KJ** II.i.168 [Constance to Queen Eleanor, of the cause of Arthur's tears] *His grandam's wrongs, and not his mother's shames;* **2H4** V.vi.46; **H5** I.ii.27; **Mac** IV.iii.33

4 wrong course of action **MW** V.v.186 [Page to Slender] *you took the wrong*

wrong *(v.)* **1** discredit, dishonour, injure, disgrace **1H6** II.i.16 [Bedford to all, of the Dauphin] *How much he wrongs his fame … / To join with witches;* **MW** IV.ii.145

2 put in the wrong, do injustice to, injure **MW** III.iii.156 [Page to Ford] *You wrong yourself too much;* **MA** II.i.218

wrong-incensed *(adj.)* inflamed with wrath, kindled with rage **R3** II.i.52 [King Edward to Richard, of the lords] *these swelling, wrong-incensed peers*

wroth *(n.)* misfortune, grief, ruin **MV** II.ix.78 [Arragon to Portia] *I'll keep my oath, / Patiently to bear my wroth* [F, Q *wroath*]

wrought *(v.)* ☞ work *(v.)*

wry *(v.)* err, lapse, go wrong **Cym** V.i.5 [Posthumus alone] *how many / Must murder wives much better than themselves / For wrying but a little?*

wry-necked *(n.)* having a crooked neck [of the player] **MV** II.v.29 [Shylock to Jessica] *the vile squealing of the wry-necked fife*

yard *(n.)* **1** yard measure **TS** IV.iii.111 [Petruchio to Tailor] *I shall so bemete thee with thy yard;* **1H4** II.iv.242; **LL** V.ii.666; **RJ** I.ii.40 ➤ clothier's yard; mete-yard *(n.)*

2 crossbar on a mast which supports a sail **Tem** I.ii.200 [Ariel to Prospero] *On the topmast, / The yards, and boresprit would I flame distinctly* ➤ **SHIPS**, p.397

yare *(adj.)* **1** [nautical] manageable, easy to manoeuvre, ready for sea **Tem** V.i.224 [Boatswain to all, of their ship] *Is tight and yare and bravely rigged;* **AC** III.vii.38

2 quick, deft, adept **TN** III.iv.220 [Sir Toby to Viola as Cesario] *be yare in thy preparation;* **AC** III.xiii.131; **MM** IV.ii.55

yare *(adv.)* quick, without delay, right now **Tem** I.i.6 [Boatswain to Mariners] *Yare, yare!;* **AC** V.ii.282; **Tem** I.i.34

yarely *(adv.)* quickly, briskly, lively **Tem** I.i.3 [Master to Boatswain] *Fall to't, yarely, or we run ourselves aground;* **AC** II.ii.216

yas *(n.)* ➤ eyas *(n.)*

yaw *(v.)* move unsteadily, wander about **Ham** V.ii.114 [Hamlet to Osrick, of Laertes] *but yaw neither in respect of his quick sail* [i.e. still be slow by comparison with his speed]

yawn *(v.)* open wide, gape **JC** II.ii.18 [Calphurnia to Caesar] *graves have yawned and yielded up their dead;* **Cor** III.ii.11; **Ham** III.ii.396; **H5** IV.vi.14; **MA** V.iii.19; **Oth** V.ii.102

yawning *(adj.)* sleep-inducing, lulling **Mac** III.ii.43 [Macbeth to Lady Macbeth] *The shard-borne beetle, with his drowsy hums, / Hath rung night's yawning peal*

y-clad *(adj.)* [archaism] decked out, clothed **2H6** I.i.33 [King to and of Queen] *Her words y-clad with wisdom's majesty* ➤ **ARCHAISMS**, p.22

yclept *(v.)* [archaism] called **LL** I.i.234 [King reading Armado's letter to him, of the garden] *It is yclept thy park;* **LL** V.ii.594 ➤ clepe *(v.)*

ye *(pron.)* you [singular or plural] **AY** II.vii.136 [Orlando to Duke Senior] *I thank ye, and be blessed for your good comfort!;* **1H6** III.ii.66 [Talbot to French lords] *Will ye, like soldiers, come and fight it out?*

yea *(adv.)* ➤ **RESPONSES**, p.373

yea-forsooth *(adj.)* always agreeing, fawning, sycophantic **2H4** I.ii.35 [Falstaff to Page, of his tailor] *A rascally yea-forsooth knave*

yearn *(v.)* grieve, make mourn, move with pity **MW** III.v.41 [Mistress Quickly to Falstaff, of Mistress Ford's distress] *it would yearn your heart to see it;* **H5** IV.iii.26

years *(n.)* **1** age **R2** I.iii.171 [Mowbray to Richard] *I am ... / Too far in years to be a pupil now;* **2H6** II.iii.28; **KJ** II.i.424; **LL** V.ii.465; **Oth** I.ii.60; **RJ** III.v.46

2 maturity, experience [coming through age] **CE** III.i.90 [Balthasar to Antipholus of Ephesus, of Adriana] *Her sober virtue, years, and modesty;* **R2** II.iii.66

yeast *(n.)* foam, froth, spume **WT** III.iii.91 [Clown to Shepherd, of the ship] *swallowed with yeast and froth*

yeasty *(adj.)* frothy, superficial, trivial **Ham** V.ii.187 [Hamlet to Horatio] *a kind of yeasty collection* [F; Q2 *histy*]

yell *(n.)* outcry, yelping, full cry **Venus** 688 [Venus to Adonis, of the hunted hare hiding from hounds] *To stop the loud pursuers in their yell*

yellow *(n.)* **1** [colour of] jealousy **WT** II.iii.106 [Paulina as if to Nature, of the baby's character] *if thou hast / The ordering of the mind too, 'mongst all colours / No yellow in't*

2 (plural) jaundice [as found in horses] **TS** III.ii.52 [Biondello to Tranio as Lucentio, of Petruchio's horse] *rayed with the yellows*

yellow *(adj.)* sallow, pasty-faced; or: jealous **Cym** II.iv.166 [Posthumus alone] *This yellow Iachimo*

yellowing *(adj.)* yelping, bellowing **Tit** II.iii.20 [Tamora to Aaron, of the hounds] *Let us sit down and mark their yellowing noise*

yellowness *(n.)* jealousy **MW** I.iii.93 [Nym to Pistol, of Page] *I will possess him with yellowness*

yeoman *(n.)* **1** man who owns property but is not a gentleman; land-holding farmer **KL** III.vi.10 [Fool to Lear] *tell me whether a madman be a gentleman or a yeoman;* **1H4** IV.ii.15; **2H4** II.i.3; **H5** III.i.25; **3H6** I.iv.123

2 keeper of the wardrobe **TN** II.v.39 [Malvolio to himself] *The lady of the Strachy married the yeoman of the wardrobe*

3 [term of abuse] commoner, plebeian **1H6** II.iv.81 [Somerset to Suffolk] *We grace the yeoman by conversing with him;* **1H6** II.iv.85, II.iv.95

yeoman's service good and faithful service **Ham** V.ii.36 [Hamlet to Horatio, of his good handwriting] *now / It did me yeoman's service*

yerk *(v.)* thrust, strike, beat **Oth** I.ii.5 [Iago to Othello, of Roderigo] *Nine or ten times / I had thought t'have yerked him here under the ribs;* **H5** IV.vii.78

yesternight *(n.)* last night **JC** II.i.238 [Portia to Brutus] *yesternight at supper / You suddenly arose and walked about;* **Ham** I.ii.189; **1H4** I.i.36; **MA** IV.i.81; **TC** I.i.34; **Tit** IV.vii.152

yesty *(adj.)* [as of yeast] foaming, frothy **Mac** IV.i.52 [Macbeth to Witches] *though the yesty waves / Confound and swallow navigation up*

yet, as yet *(adv.)* still **R2** II.iv.3 [Captain to Salisbury] *And yet we hear no tidings from the King;* **Lover** 75 [the woman to the reverend man] *I might as yet have been a spreading flower;* **Ham** I.iii.55; **2H6** IV.ix.49; **H8** II.iv.204; **MW** II.ii.136; **R3** I.iv.123

yield *(v.)* **1** agree [to], consent [to], comply [with] **Cor** II.ii.52 [First Senator to the Tribunes] *We do request ... / Your loving motion toward the common body / To yield what passes here;* **2H6** I.i.125

2 concede, acknowledge, grant **Tim** I.ii.193 [Flavius to himself, of Timon] *Nor will he know his purse, or yield me this, / To show him what a beggar his heart is;* **AC** II.v.28; **1H6** II.iv.42

3 give, grant, return **Tem** I.ii.309 [Prospero to Miranda] *Caliban ... who never / Yields us kind answer*

4 give back to, return to **Cym** I.vii.210 [Innogen to Iachimo, of the trunk] *it shall safe be kept, / And truly yielded you*

5 bring forth, produce **Per** V.iii.48 [Pericles to Thaisa, of Marina's birth at sea] *she was yielded there;* **AY** II.iii.64; **Tem** II.i.235

6 hand over, give up, deliver **Tem** III.ii.60 [Caliban to Stephano, of Prospero] *I'll yield him thee asleep*

7 reward, repay, thank **AC** IV.ii.33 [Antony to the servants, of their service] *the gods yield you for't!*

8 communicate, deliver, represent **TN** III.ii.3 [Fabian to Sir Andrew, of his reason for leaving] *You must needs yield your reason;* **Ham** IV.v.11; **Tem** II.i.235

9 express an opinion about, comment on **AW** III.i.10 [Second Lord to Duke] *The reasons of our state I cannot yield*

10 render, make, cause to be **JC** I.iii.156 [Cassius to Casca, of Brutus] *the man entire / Upon the next encounter yields him ours*

11 ☞ 'ild *(v.)*

yield the ghost *(v.)* give up the spirit, die **1H6** I.i.67 [Bedford to the Messenger, of Henry V] *These news would cause him once more yield the ghost* ☞ ghost *(n.)* 1

yield up *(v.)* give up, surrender, relinquish **1H6** I.i.65 [Gloucester to the Messenger] *Is Rouen yielded up?*

yielded *(adj.)* surrendered, conceded **KJ** V.ii.107 [Lewis the Dauphin to Cardinal Pandulph, of the English submission] *And shall I now give o'er the yielded set?* [i.e. the set of cards already won]

yielder *(n.)* one who gives up, conceder **MND** III.ii.30 [Puck to Oberon] *From yielders all things catch*

yielding *(n.)* consent, compliance, agreement **KJ** II.i.474 [Queen Eleanor to King John] *I see a yielding in the looks of France;* **Cym** I.v.102; **Ham** I.iii.23; **LL** I.i.118; **RJ** II.ii.105

yoke *(n.)* **1** servitude, state of subjection **JC** I.iii.84 [Cassius to Casca] *Our yoke and sufferance show us womanish;* **Tit** I.i.72, 114, IV.i.108

2 pair, couple, brace **MW** II.i.163 [Page to Ford, of Nym and Pistol] *these that accuse him [Falstaff] in his intent towards our wives are a yoke of his discarded men;* **2H4** III.ii.37

3 horn, antler **MW** V.v.107 [Mistress Page to Page, of Falstaff's horns] *Do not these fair yokes / Become the forest better than the town?*

yoke *(v.)* **1** associate, link, join, couple **Cym** IV.ii.51 [Arviragus to Belarius and Guiderius, of disguised Innogen] *Nobly he yokes / A smiling with a sigh;* **Cor** III.i.57; **Cym** IV.ii.19; **3H6** IV.i.23, IV.vi.49

2 conquer, tame, bring under subjection **Tit** I.i.30 [Marcus to Saturninus and Bassianus, of Titus] *He ... / Hath yoked a nation strong*

3 submit, subject **Luc** 1633 [Lucrece to Collatine, quoting Tarquin's words] *Unless thou yoke thy liking to my will*

yoked *(adj.)* joined in marriage, wedded **Oth** IV.i.66 [Iago to Othello] *Think every bearded fellow that's but yoked / May draw with you*

yoke-devil *(n.)* companion-devil, asssociate in evil **H5** II.ii.106 [King Henry to all] *Treason and murder ever kept together, / As two yoke-devils sworn to either's purpose*

yoke-fellow *(n.)* fellow-worker, comrade, partner **H5** II.iii.51 [Pistol to Bardolph, Nym, and Boy] *Yoke-fellows in arms, / Let us to France;* **H5** IV.vi.9; **KL** III.vi.37

yoking *(adj.)* embracing, enfolding, enclosing **Venus** 592 [of Venus and Adonis] *on his neck her yoking arms she throws*

yon *(adv.)* ☞ YON WORDS, p.507

YON WORDS

The *yon* series of words in English always carry the suggestion that an object is some distance away but visible. *Yond* and *yonder* are used both as an adverb of place and as a demonstrative word before a noun (a determiner); *yon* has only determiner function. The senses are 'over there' or 'in that place' (for the adverb) and 'that [one] over there' (for the determiner).

Item	Location	Example	Gloss
yon (det.)	**Ham** I.i.168	*yon high eastward hill*	that (one) over there
yond (adv.)	**Tem** I.ii.410	*say what thou seest yond*	there
yond (det.)	**1H6** II.i.33	*I'll to yond corner*	that (one) over there
yonder (adv.)	**AY** I.i.24	*Yonder comes my master*	in that place, over there
yonder (det.)	**MND** III.ii.61	*yonder Venus in her glimmering sphere*	that (one) over there

☞ HITHER, THITHER, AND WHITHER, p.224

yond (*adv.*) over there **Tem** I.ii.410 [Prospero to Miranda] *say what thou seest yond* ☛ **YON WORDS**, p.507

yond (*det.*) that [one] over there **AY** II.iv.58 [Celia to all] *one of you question yond man* ☛ **YON WORDS**, p.507

yonder (*adv.*) there **AY** I.i.24 [Adam to Orlando] *Yonder comes my master* ☛ **YON WORDS**, p.507

yore, of of old, formerly, in times long past **Sonn** 68.14 [of his friend] *him as for a map doth Nature store, / To show false Art what beauty was of yore*

you (*pron.*) ☛ **THOU AND YOU**, p.450

young (*adj.*) **1** immature, inexperienced, raw **Mac** III.iv.143 [Macbeth to Lady Macbeth] *We are yet but young in deed;* **AY** I.i.51; **Cym** I.v.41; **TS** II.i.231

 2 in good condition, strong **TS** II.i.232 [Petruchio to Katherina] *I am too young for you*

young days, of so from such an early age **Ham** II.ii.11 [Claudius to Rosencrantz and Guildenstern, of Hamlet] *being of so young days brought up with him*

younger (*n.*) younger son **MV** II.vi.14 [Gratiano to Salerio] *How like a younger or a prodigal / The scarfed bark puts from her native bay*

younger (*adj.*) earlier, former, previous **1H4** V.i.71 [Worcester to King Henry] *violation of all faith and troth / Sworn to us in your younger enterprise*

youngest (*adj.*) latest, most recent **E3** II.ii.115 [King Edward alone, of the Countess] *The register of all rarieties / Since leathern Adam till this youngest hour*

youngling (*n.*) **1** stripling, youngster, beginner **TS** II.i.330 [Gremio to Tranio as Lucentio] *Youngling, thou canst not love so dear as I;* **PassP** XI.3; **Tit** II.i.73, IV.ii.92

 2 young, offspring **E3** III.i.119 [King John, as if to the French forces] *be like the field of bears / When they defend their younglings*

youngly (*adv.*) in youth, early in life **Cor** II.iii.235 [Brutus to Citizens, of Coriolanus] *How youngly he began to serve his country;* **Sonn** 11.3

younker (*n.*) **1** fashionable young man, fine young gentleman **3H6** II.i.24 [Richard to Edward, of the morning] *Trimmed like a younker prancing to his love!*

 2 greenhorn, juvenile, prodigal child **1H4** III.iii.79 [Falstaff to Hostess] *will you make a younker of me?*

zany *(n.)* stooge, clown's assistant, mimic **TN** I.v.84 [Malvolio to Olivia, of fools like Feste] *I take these wise men … no better than the fools' zanies;* **LL** V.ii.463

zeal *(n.)* ardour, fervour; or: loyalty, devotion **R2** I.i.47 [Mowbray to King Richard] *Let not my cold words here accuse my zeal;* **2H4** IV.ii.27, V.v.14; **TC** IV.iv.121; **Tim** IV.iii.519

zealous *(adj.)* earnest, fervent, ardent **R3** III.vii.93 [Buckingham to Lord Mayor] *So sweet is zealous contemplation;* **E3** III.iv.95; **KJ** II.i.19, 428; **Sonn** 27.6

zenith *(n.)* highest point (in fortunes), summit, peak **Tem** I.ii.181 [Prospero to Miranda] *by my prescience / I find my zenith doth depend upon / A most auspicious star*

zephyr *(n.)* mild breeze, gentle wind [especially from the west] **Cym** IV.ii.172 [Belarius alone, of Arviragus and Guiderius] *they are as gentle / As zephyrs blowing below the violet*

zir *(n.)* dialect variant of 'sir' **KL** IV.vi.244 [Edgar to Oswald, adopting a country accent] *'Chill pick your teeth, zir;* **KL** IV.vi.235

zo *(adv.)* dialect form of 'so' **KL** IV.vi.239 [Edgar to Oswald, adopting a country accent] *'twould not ha' bin zo long as 'tis by a vortnight*

zodiac *(n.)* **1** belt of the celestial sphere within which the sun, moon, and planets appear to move, divided into twelve equal domains [signs] named after constellations **Tit** II.i.7 [Aaron alone] *the golden sun … / Gallops the zodiac in his glistering coach*
   2 year, calendar course of the zodiac **MM** I.ii.167 [Claudio to Lucio] *nineteen zodiacs have gone round*

zone, burning inter-tropical domain encircling the earth **Ham** V.i.278 [Hamlet to Laertes, of piling earth on them] *till our ground, / Singeing his pate against the burning zone, / Make Ossa like a wart!*

zounds *(int.)* God's wounds ☛ **SWEARING**, p.435

zwagger *(v.)* dialect form of 'swagger' ☛ swagger *(v.)*

Shakespearian Circles, Synopses, and Dramatis Personae

ORDER OF PLAYS

The diagrams in this section display the circles within which people move during a play, so that their relationships to each other, either individually or in groups, can be better understood.

The conventional method of character listing makes it virtually impossible to get a sense of the social world which people inhabit. Typically, characters are presented in a list with a minimum of structure: the more important people tend to appear towards the top; the most obvious groupings (e.g. families, countries) may be identified; and there may be a short description of the way one character relates to another (e.g. through blood or occupation). But no list, no matter how much it describes its characters, is as clear or as insightful as a diagram.

Diagrams of relationships can be of many different kinds. Family relationships are normally shown using lines in the form of a family tree. Our approach makes use of this convention, but also extends it to include all social relationships, such as the relationship between servant and master, or leader and supporter. Lines are also used to identify discourse relationships – showing which people routinely associate with each other and talk to each other.

In society, people move in certain circles, which overlap and interact in different ways. These circles are the core of the following diagrams. Specific family and social or occupational relationships (e.g. the church, London citizenry, travelling players) are shown grouped within circles of interaction. The implication is that the people within a circle are most likely to associate with others in their circle during the course of a play. Lines of connection between circles identify important points of contact between different groups. Overlaps between circles are intentional, and point to relationships where people have a more specific influence on each other.

Our intention was to capture the important permanent relationships linking the characters. In certain plays (such as the English histories) some selectivity was essential to avoid the diagrams becoming excessively complex, and we focused on what we felt to be the important connections. The 'other sons' of Edward III, for example, are not included in the circles for *Richard II*. Similarly, we did not include most of the relationships between characters arising out of the plot, such as 'X killer of Y'. The diagrams, therefore, do not tell the story of the play. For those who wish to be reminded of the story, a plot synopsis is given in each case.

TYPOGRAPHICAL CONVENTIONS

Roman SMALL CAPITALS are used to identify that part of a person's name which is used as the character name in the corpus text of the play; Roman lower-case is used for other names/titles which belong to a character.
　Examples: DUKE of Venice. Michael CASSIO.

Non-speaking characters are shown in Roman lower-case.
　Examples: Officers. Lords.

A name in square brackets identifies someone who is not actually in a play, but has a relevant relationship to someone who is.
　Example: [Henry IV] in *Henry VI*.

Italic lower-case is used to show a relationship between characters.
　Examples: *daughter, supporter*.

Sans serif upper-case is used to label the identity of a circle.
　Examples: **THE ENGLISH COURT. THE PLAYERS**.

Lines are used to express different types of relationships.

——————　a mutual relationship within a circle of characters, e.g. spouses

————▶　clarifies the direction of a relationship between characters, e.g. servant of

— — — —　a historical relationship which helps explain the identity of a character by referring to someone who is not in the play

Abbreviation
sib = sibling (brother/sister relationship)

All's Well That Ends Well

DRAMATIS PERSONAE

(as conventionally listed)

BERTRAM, Count of Rossillion, a ward of the King of France
The COUNTESS of Rossillion, Bertram's mother
HELENA, a young girl brought up by the Countess
PAROLLES, Bertram's friend
Rynaldo, STEWARD in the Countess's household
Lavatch, CLOWN in the Countess's household
A Page in the Countess's household

The KING of France
LAFEW, an old Lord
The brothers Dumaine, two French LORDS: later
    Captains serving the Duke of Florence
Other LORDS
Two French SOLDIERS
A GENTLEMAN, Astringer to the Court of France
A Messenger

The DUKE of Florence
WIDOW Capilet of Florence
DIANA, the Widow's daughter
MARIANA, a friend of the Widow

Lords, attendants, soldiers, citizens

Following his father's death, Bertram, the young Count of Rossillion, leaves home to attend the court of the ailing King of France, along with his friend Parolles. Helena, the Countess's ward, is in love with Bertram, and reveals her affection to the Countess, who is sympathetic. She gives Helena permission to visit Paris in an attempt to cure the King of his ailment using a drug devised by Helena's father, a physician.

Lafew, a lord at court, persuades the King to see Helena, and he is cured by her medicine. As a reward, she is offered a husband of her choice, and she chooses Bertram. He rejects her for her lack of social standing, but then accepts her rather than suffer the King's anger. He decides to leave for Florence and the Tuscan wars, along with Parolles, abruptly sending Helena back home.

In a letter to Helena, Bertram vows that he will be her husband only if she can get the ring from his finger and prove she is pregnant with his child. Helena then leaves home secretly, ostensibly on a pilgrimage, but in fact going to Florence, where Bertram has acquitted himself well in the war. There she discovers he is trying to seduce Diana, the daughter of the widowed hostess of her inn. She reveals her identity to Diana and the widow, and hatches a plan with them. Diana tells Bertram she will sleep with him, on condition that he gives Diana his ring. Helena will actually take Diana's place, giving Bertram her ring in return.

In the meantime, several lords are trying to persuade Bertram that Parolles is a braggart and coward – an impression earlier conveyed by both Lafew and the Countess. They persuade Parolles to go behind enemy lines to retrieve a drum he has left behind. On his way, they pretend to be enemy soldiers, kidnap him, and blindfold him. In his interrogation, he readily betrays and vilifies his compatriots.

Peace is concluded, and Bertram returns to Rossillion, where the King is visiting. Everyone believes that Helena is dead, and there is a proposal that Bertram should marry Lafew's daughter. Bertram gives Lafew his ring, but the King recognizes it as the one he himself gave Helena, and Bertram is arrested. Diana obtains entrance to the gathering and tells her story, which is shown to be true when Helena reveals herself. Bertram professes his love for Helena and they are reunited.

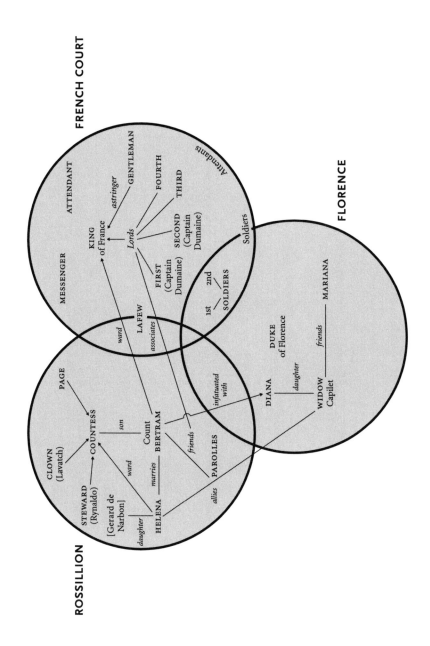

Antony and Cleopatra

Antony, Octavius Caesar, and Lepidus are a triumvirate ruling the Roman Empire; but Antony prefers to spend his time at leisure in Egypt as a consort to Queen Cleopatra rather than in Rome. News of his wife's death, and of a threatened revolt by young Pompey, motivates his return, much to Cleopatra's disapproval.

A meeting takes place between Caesar, Lepidus, and Antony, at which they acknowledge the importance of maintaining their alliance. As a sign of good faith, Antony agrees to marry Octavia, Caesar's widowed sister. Cleopatra receives news of this arrangement with great anger, to the discomfiture of the messenger who brings it.

The triumvirs and Pompey meet and agree a peace, which they celebrate with a drunken feast. Following the successful campaign of Antony's general Ventidius in Parthia, Antony and Octavia leave Rome. However, it is not long before Antony receives news of Caesar's increasing disaffection, and of renewed wars by Pompey. He allows Octavia to return to Rome to attempt a reconciliation. But he then returns to Egypt, and to Cleopatra, which incenses Caesar further. Lepidus meanwhile has been arrested for conspiracy, leaving the stage clear for a confrontation between Caesar and Antony.

Antony ignores advice from his officer and friend Enobarbus not to meet the Romans at sea, and is defeated near Actium, following the flight of Cleopatra and the Egyptian fleet. Caesar sends Thidias to negotiate with Cleopatra, but Antony has him whipped and sent back to Rome. Enobarbus then deserts Antony for Caesar, leaving his personal treasure behind; but when Antony generously sends this after him, Enobarbus is consumed with grief, and dies.

Caesar and Antony continue their conflict. Antony has some success by land, but the Egyptian fleet once again loses at sea, and he charges Cleopatra with betrayal. In an attempt to win back his affection, she takes herself and her maids off to her burial monument, sending him word that she is dead. Grief-stricken at the news, Antony asks his servant Eros to kill him, but Eros kills himself rather than carry out the task. Antony then attempts to kill himself, wounding himself grievously, only to hear that Cleopatra is still alive. He is carried to her monument, where he dies in her arms.

Antony's follower Decretas informs Caesar of his death, and Proculeius is sent to bring Cleopatra to Rome. Cleopatra knows she will be made a public spectacle there, and attempts to kill herself, but is prevented. She has a meeting with Caesar, where she feigns total submission, but her attempt to conceal some of her wealth is revealed by her treasurer Seleucus. Arrangements to take her to Rome are made, but she manages to have a clownish rustic smuggle in a basket of figs containing asps, and she and her maids all die from their bite.

DRAMATIS PERSONAE
(as conventionally listed)

Mark ANTONY
Octavius CAESAR | triumvirs
LEPIDUS

DEMETRIUS
PHILO
Domitius ENOBARBUS
VENTIDIUS
SILIUS
EROS
CANIDIUS
SCARUS
DECRETAS | Antony's friends and followers

MAECENAS
AGRIPPA
TAURUS
DOLABELLA
THIDIAS
GALLUS
PROCULEIUS | Caesar's friends and followers

Sextus POMPEY
MENECRATES
MENAS
VARRIUS | Pompey's friends

CLEOPATRA, Queen of Egypt
CHARMIAN
IRAS
ALEXAS
MARDIAN
DIOMEDES
SELEUCUS | Cleopatra's attendants

OCTAVIA, Caesar's sister

MESSENGERS
A SOOTHSAYER
ATTENDANTS
SERVANTS
SOLDIERS
A BOY
A schoolmaster, Antony's AMBASSADOR
A SENTRY and WATCH
GUARDS
An EGYPTIAN
A CLOWN

Cleopatra's ladies, eunuchs, servants, soldiers, captains, officers

CLEOPATRA'S
ATTENDANTS

Servants

CLOWN

MESSENGERS

IRAS

Charmian
maids

servant

DIOMEDES

CLEOPATRA
Queen of Egypt

eunuch

MARDIAN
Eunuchs

Ladies

ALEXAS
attendant

treasurer

SELEUCUS

GUARDS

SOLDIERS

lovers

SOOTHSAYER

ANTONY'S FRIENDS
AND FOLLOWERS

ATTENDANTS

EROS
servant

SCARUS

SILIUS
officer

VENTIDIUS

PHILO

generals

CANIDIUS

Mark
ANTONY

trusted
friend

MESSENGERS

DECRETAS

DEMETRIUS

Domitius
ENOBARBUS

GUARDS

[FULVIA]
spouse

SOLDIERS

CAESAR'S FRIENDS
AND FOLLOWERS

marries

SERVANTS

MESSENGERS

AGRIPPA

OCTAVIA

BOX

sib

DOLABELLA

TAURUS

SENTRY

Octavius
CAESAR

GUARDS

GALLUS

THIDIAS

MAECENAS

SOLDIERS

SECOND WATCH

PROCULEIUS

FIRST WATCH

THE
TRIUMVIRATE

enemy
of Rome

MENECRATES

LEPIDUS

VARRIUS

POMPEY

MENAS

As You Like It

Duke Senior, banished and usurped by his brother, Duke Frederick, now lives in the Forest of Arden with his noblemen. Senior's daughter Rosalind has been allowed to remain at court with Frederick's daughter Celia, but she suddenly incurs Frederick's displeasure, and is banished. Celia decides to run away with her, and they leave for Arden with Rosalind disguised as a man, and accompanied by Touchstone, a clown. Rosalind changes her name to Ganymede, and Celia to Aliena.

Before they leave, Rosalind falls in love with one of the sons of Rowland de Boys – Orlando, who is ruled and hated by his elder brother, Oliver. Orlando foils Oliver's plan to have him killed in a match against the Duke's chief wrestler, Charles, by defeating the champion. Orlando is then advised by Le Beau to leave the court, and he flees to Arden with an old servant Adam. They are starving when they encounter Duke Senior, who takes them in, delighted to discover that Orlando is the son of his old friend Sir Rowland.

Rosalind and Celia observe two shepherds Corin and Silvius talking, and learn of Silvius's love for Phebe, a shepherdess. They buy pastures and herds from them, and decide to live as shepherds. Touchstone spends much time in the company of Audrey, a country wench who is loved by William, eventually wooing her himself. Jaques, a melancholy nobleman of Duke Senior's company, becomes fascinated by Touchstone, and spends much time talking to him.

Orlando leaves love messages for Rosalind all over the forest, which in due course she sees. When the two girls meet Orlando again, 'Ganymede' persuades Orlando to treat 'him' as his Rosalind, so that he may practise wooing. Frederick, believing Celia and Rosalind to have fled with Orlando, sends Oliver after his brother, threatening to take the De Boys lands if Oliver returns without him.

Oliver is saved from a lion by Orlando, and the two brothers are reconciled. Oliver relates the story to the two girls, and falls in love with Celia. Phebe has fallen for Ganymede, which causes some confusion until Rosalind reveals herself. Phebe then agrees to marry Silvius. Rosalind is reunited with her father, and marries Orlando. Oliver marries Celia. Touchstone marries Audrey.

The third son of Sir Rowland, Jaques, arrives to announce that Frederick had intended to invade the forest with an army, but on his way he met a religious man who converted him from his harsh ways, and he has now begun a religious life. Jaques decides to join him. Duke Senior has his lands and crown restored.

DRAMATIS PERSONAE
(as conventionally listed)

DUKE SENIOR, a banished duke

AMIENS | noblemen in attendance on him
JAQUES |

DUKE FREDERICK, his brother, the usurper

LE BEAU, a courtier

CHARLES, a wrestler

OLIVER |
JAQUES | sons of Sir Rowland de Boys
ORLANDO |

ADAM | servants of Oliver
DENNIS |

THE CLOWN, alias TOUCHSTONE

SIR OLIVER MARTEXT, a country vicar

CORIN | shepherds
SILVIUS |

WILLIAM, a country youth, in love with Audrey

ROSALIND, daughter of Duke Senior, later disguised as GANYMEDE

CELIA, daughter of Duke Frederick, later disguised as ALIENA

PHEBE, a shepherdess

AUDREY, a country wench

A masquer representing HYMEN

Lords, pages, and attendants

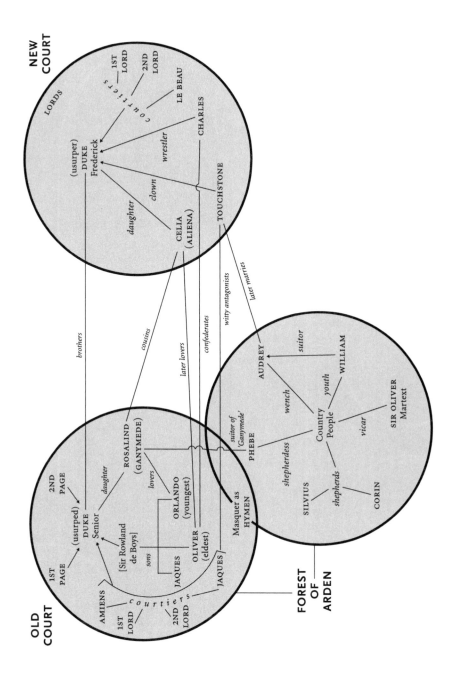

NEW COURT

LORDS

1ST LORD

2ND LORD

c o u r t i e r s

LE BEAU

(usurper)
DUKE
Frederick

CHARLES

wrestler

clown

daughter

CELIA
(ALIENA)

TOUCHSTONE

witty antagonists

later marries

brothers

cousins

later lovers

confederates

OLD
COURT

2ND
PAGE

1ST
PAGE

(usurped)
DUKE
Senior

ROSALIND
(GANYMEDE)

daughter

lovers

ORLANDO
(youngest)

[Sir Rowland
de Boys]

sons

JAQUES

OLIVER
(eldest)

AMIENS

1ST
LORD

2ND
LORD

JAQUES

c o u r t i e r s

Masquer as
HYMEN

FOREST
OF
ARDEN

AUDREY

suitor

WILLIAM

wench

youth

Country
People

SIR OLIVER
Martext

vicar

*suitor of
'Ganymede'*

PHEBE

shepherdess

SILVIUS

shepherds

CORIN

The Comedy of Errors

Because of recent enmity, no Syracusan is allowed in Ephesus. A Syracusan merchant Egeon, searching for his wife and twin boys separated and lost at sea, has been found there and arrested. The Duke is sympathetic, so gives him a day to find a way of paying his fine before the death penalty has to be carried out.

Antipholus and servant Dromio of Syracuse (S) arrive in Ephesus, on their travels. They are instantly mistaken by the townsfolk to be Antipholus and servant Dromio of Ephesus (E). Antipholus (E) meets Dromio (S), who denies knowledge of money given to him earlier. Adriana, the wife of Antipholus (E) sends Dromio (E) to find his master. Adriana and Luciana encounter Antipholus and Dromio (S). Antipholus (S) does not recognize Adriana, and Dromio (S) denies the received instructions from her. Adriana insists they both accompany her home, and they think they are going mad.

Antipholus (E) meanwhile arrives home with merchant Balthasar and goldsmith Angelo, who is making a gold chain for Adriana. Dromio (S) and kitchen-maid Luce refuse to let them in, much to the annoyance of Dromio (E), so Antipholus (E) goes to a tavern instead. Inside the house, Antipholus (S) has fallen in love with Adriana's sister Luciana, much to her amazement; and Dromio (S) is awed by a kitchen-maid who claims him as hers.

Antipholus (S) meets Angelo, who gives him the chain, proposing to return later for the money. Angelo, being himself pressed for a debt, later meets Antipholus (E) and asks for his money. When Antipholus (E) denies having had the chain, Angelo has him arrested until he pays the amount. Antipholus (E) sends Dromio (S) to Adriana for the money, which she immediately sends.

Dromio (S) brings the money to Antipholus (S). They meet a Courtesan with whom Antipholus (E) had dined and who asks for the return of a ring Antipholus (E) had taken, but Antipholus (S) of course denies knowledge of it. Dromio (E) meets the arrested Antipholus (E), who asks for the money to obtain his release, but Dromio (E) obviously does not have it. Adriana arrives with Dr Pinch, who tries to conjure the supposed madness out of Antipholus (E). Both he and Dromio (E) resist and they are arrested and taken away. Adriana and the others then immediately meet Antipholus (S) and Dromio (S) with

swords drawn, and, confused by their sudden liberty, flee from them.

Angelo meets Antipholus (S), sees the chain, and prepares to fight him. On the arrival of Adriana and the others, Antipholus and Dromio (S) run into a priory for safety. The abbess Æmilia discusses his supposed madness with Adriana, but refuses to let her enter the priory. Adriana decides to complain to the Duke, who is nearby for Egeon's execution, that she has been unable to see her supposed husband. Antipholus (E) and Dromio (E) appear and also complain to the Duke. All parties tell what has happened from their own points of view. Egeon recognizes Antipholus (E) as his son, but Antipholus does not know him. Æmilia then brings out Antipholus and Dromio (S), and all is revealed. Egeon recognizes Æmilia as his wife. The Duke forgives Egeon. The two pairs of twins are reunited.

DRAMATIS PERSONAE
(as conventionally listed)

Solinus, DUKE of Ephesus
EGEON, a merchant of Syracuse
Æmilia, Lady ABBESS at Ephesus, and Egeon's wife
ANTIPHOLUS OF EPHESUS ⎤ twin brothers, sons of
ANTIPHOLUS OF SYRACUSE ⎦ Egeon and Æmilia
DROMIO OF EPHESUS ⎤ twin brothers, bondsmen
DROMIO OF SYRACUSE ⎦ to the Antipholus twins
ADRIANA, wife of Antipholus of Ephesus
LUCIANA, her sister
Luce (also referred to as Nell), Adriana's kitchen-maid
BALTHASAR, a merchant
ANGELO, a goldsmith
Doctor PINCH, a schoolmaster
FIRST MERCHANT
SECOND MERCHANT
An OFFICER
A COURTESAN
A MESSENGER

Gaoler, officers, headsman, and other attendants

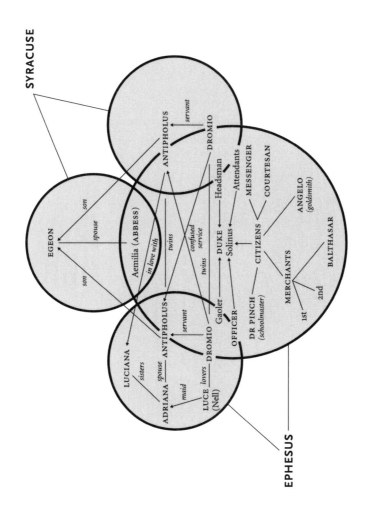

Coriolanus

DRAMATIS PERSONAE

(as conventionally listed)

CAIUS MARTIUS, afterwards Caius Martius
    Coriolanus
TITUS LARTIUS ⎤ Roman generals against the Volsces
COMINIUS ⎦
MENENIUS AGRIPPA, friend of Coriolanus
SICINIUS VELUTUS ⎤ Tribunes of the People,
JUNIUS BRUTUS ⎦ opposed to Coriolanus
A Crowd of Roman Citizens
A Roman Herald
NICANOR, a Roman in the pay of the Volsces

VOLUMNIA, mother of Coriolanus
VIRGILIA, wife of Coriolanus
YOUNG MARTIUS, son of Coriolanus
VALERIA, friend of Virgilia
A Gentlewoman attending on Virgilia

TULLUS AUFIDIUS, General of the Volsces
A Lieutenant under Aufidius
Conspirators with Aufidius
ADRIAN, a Volsce
A Citizen of Antium
Two Volscian Guards

Roman and Volscian senators, patricians, aediles, lictors,
    soldiers, messengers, Volscian citizens, servants of
    Aufidius, and other attendants

Menenius tries to calm a mutiny among the Roman citizens over the way they have been treated by the nobles. His friend Caius Martius treats them with contempt, and the citizens disperse. Martius' attitude arouses the anger of the tribunes Sicinius and Brutus.

News arrives that the Volsces are in arms under Aufidius, who has been sent to attack Rome. Volumnia and Virgilia proudly discuss Martius' earlier feats, and are visited by Valeria, who reports Martius' arrival at the Volscian city of Corioles. The generals Cominius and Titus Lartius attack. Martius plays a major role in several skirmishes, and there is a fight between him and Aufidius, after which Corioles is captured. For his part in the battle, Martius is given the honorary title of Coriolanus.

Coriolanus returns to Rome, where he meets his family and finds himself nominated for a consulship. For the nomination to be valid, he needs to present himself humbly to the people and obtain their votes, a task which he carries out grudgingly. The people do give him their votes, but Brutus and Sicinius then portray him as the people's enemy, and they change their minds. When this is reported to Coriolanus, he cannot contain his anger; he speaks out against the people, and is accused of being a traitor. A violent confrontation forces him to leave. After being advised by his family and friends, he returns to meet the people, intending to speak mildly; but is unable to control himself in the face of their taunts, and is banished. Volumnia delivers some harsh words to the tribunes.

The Volscians meanwhile have taken up arms again. Coriolanus goes to offer his services to Aufidius, and he is made welcome. When the news of this alliance reaches Rome, there is panic, and the people begin to regret what they have done. They send supplicants to ask Coriolanus to spare Rome. He rejects the approaches of Cominius and Menenius, but eventually yields to Volumnia, Virgilia, Valeria, and Young Martius, who are received back in Rome with great joy.

Meanwhile, the popularity of Coriolanus grows among the Volscians, much to Aufidius' dismay. He meets with a group of conspirators, and when Coriolanus returns he is once again called a traitor, and killed. Aufidius immediately regrets his actions, and the Volscians prepare to give Coriolanus a noble funeral.

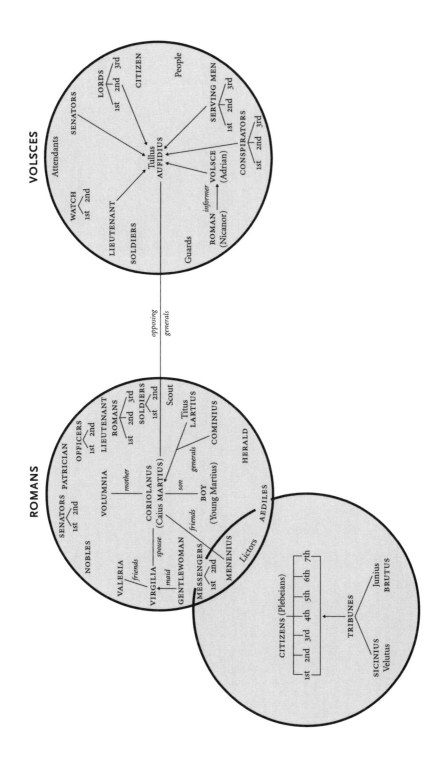

Cymbeline

Two gentlemen discuss King Cymbeline's family, and the disappearance of his two young children twenty years before. Posthumus, in love with Cymbeline's daughter Innogen, is banished because he is not thought worthy to be her husband. The Queen, Innogen's stepmother, professes to help them, but actually works to ensure his removal. The Queen's son Cloten, a laughing-stock among the lords, is also in love with Innogen. He attempts to woo her but she rejects him. The Queen asks a doctor, Cornelius, for a poison, intending to kill Innogen, and gives it to Pisanio to take to her, telling him it is a rejuvenating cordial. The doctor, distrusting the Queen, substitutes a potion that instils only a harmless temporary death-like state.

Posthumus arrives in Rome, where he meets Iachimo, who challenges Posthumus' claim that Innogen is the most faithful woman in the world. They make a wager, Iachimo betting he can seduce Innogen. He arrives at Cymbeline's court, and presses his affection on her, but she rejects him. He then explains that this was only a stratagem to confirm her reputed worthiness, and she forgives him. She agrees to give safe keeping to a large trunk of Iachimo's valuables that night. Iachimo hides inside the trunk, and while she is asleep he emerges from it to note details of her room and her body, and steals her bracelet. Back in Rome, this evidence convinces Posthumus that Innogen has been unfaithful, and he gives Iachimo her ring, condemning her and all women.

Lucius arrives at court from Rome demanding the British tribute, but without success. Posthumus writes to his servant, Pisanio, telling him of Innogen's unfaithfulness, and that he must murder her. Innogen also receives a letter from Posthumus, telling her he will meet her in Wales – actually only providing Pisanio an opportunity to kill her. Innogen insists on going there.

Pisanio knows Posthumus has been misled, and that Innogen is innocent, so when they arrive in Wales he shows his master's letter to her. He convinces her to disguise herself as a man, and find service with Lucius, also now in Wales, so that she may be near Posthumus. He gives Innogen the Queen's potion, still thinking it to be a rejuvenating cordial. Pisanio returns to England, and Cloten forces from him Innogen's whereabouts; then, dressed in Posthumus' clothes, Cloten follows her to Wales.

In the Welsh mountains, Belarius sends Guiderius and Arviragus out hunting, reflecting on their true origin as sons of Cymbeline and on his own former position in court, from where he stole them in revenge for his unjust banishment. Innogen gets lost, and takes refuge in their cave. The sons meet her, and immediately are strongly attracted to her. She feels unwell, and while the men are out she takes Pisanio's potion, falling into a death-like sleep. Guiderius meets Cloten; they quarrel, fight, and Guiderius beheads Cloten, whom Belarius later recognizes. They return to the cave, and find Innogen. Thinking her dead, they lay her on the ground in a burial ceremony, and place Cloten's headless body beside her. When she wakes, she sees Posthumus' garments and assumes it is him. She faints across the body, and is found there by Lucius, who takes her into his service as a page. She calls herself Fidele.

The Roman army advances, and Belarius's sons persuade him to let them fight. Posthumus has come as part of the Roman forces, but decides to fight for Britain, in reparation for what he has done to Innogen. Iachimo is also in the Roman army, regretting what he has done. In the battle, Cymbeline is taken but rescued by Belarius and his sons and Posthumus, and the British emerge as victors. Posthumus puts on his Roman clothes and is captured; imprisoned, he looks forward to death. While sleeping, he is visited by the spirits of his dead family and by Jupiter, who leaves him a tablet containing a prophecy.

Cymbeline knights Belarius and his sons. He learns that the Queen is dead and that she has earlier confessed her wrongdoing. Lucius commends 'Fidele' to Cymbeline, who grants her any request. She asks for the ring she sees Iachimo is wearing, and he confesses his villainy. Posthumus then reveals himself, and Fidele reveals herself to be Innogen. The disappearance of Cloten is explained, and Cymbeline reluctantly condemns Guiderius, but he is pardoned when Belarius reveals the true status of his sons. Iachimo is forgiven, the prophecy is explained, and Cymbeline makes peace with Rome.

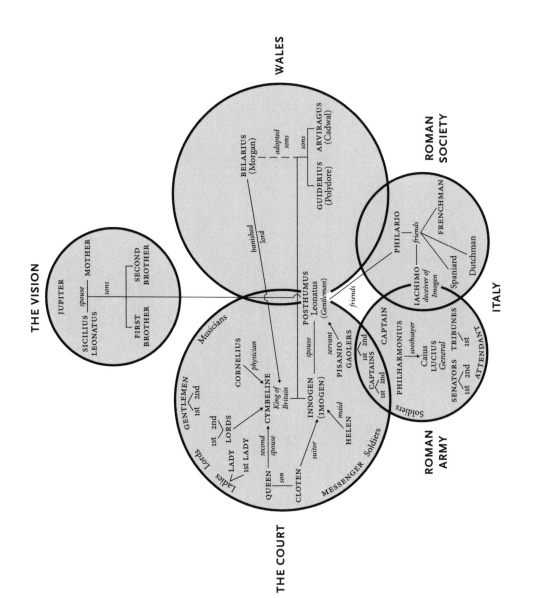

THE VISION

WALES

ROMAN SOCIETY

ITALY

ROMAN ARMY

THE COURT

JUPITER

SICILIUS LEONATUS — spouse — MOTHER

sons

FIRST BROTHER   SECOND BROTHER

BELARIUS (Morgan)

adopted sons

GUIDERIUS (Polydore)   ARVIRAGUS (Cadwal)   sons

banished lord

PHILARIO

IACHIMO — friends — FRENCHMAN   deceiver of Imogen   Spaniard   Dutchman

POSTHUMUS Leonatus (Gentleman)

friends

Musicians

CORNELIUS   physician

GENTLEMEN   1st 2nd

LORDS   1st 2nd

CYMBELINE   King of Britain

LADY   1st LADY   second spouse

Ladies   Lords

QUEEN — spouse   son — CLOTEN

INNOGEN (IMOGEN) — spouse

servant   PISANIO

GAOLERS

suitor

maid   HELEN

MESSENGER   Soldiers

Soldiers

CAPTAINS   1st 2nd

CAPTAIN

PHILHARMONIUS   soothsayer

Caius LUCIUS   General

SENATORS   1st 2nd   TRIBUNES   1st

ATTENDANT

King Edward III

Edward, having been persuaded by Artois that he has rights in France, is about to mount an expedition there, when Lorraine brings a message from the French demanding Edward's allegiance. News also arrives of fresh invasions by the Scots King David, whose gains include the castle where Warwick's daughter, the Countess of Salisbury, lives.

David and Douglas are arguing over the spoils when the English army arrives and they flee. Edward falls in love with the Countess, and asks his secretary Lodowick to write her a courtship letter on his behalf. Edward's attempt to seduce her is rebuffed. He then invokes Warwick's oath of loyalty to make him use his influence on her. Warwick reluctantly agrees, and is delighted when she maintains her opposition.

Edward, in an ill-humour at his lack of progress, is distracted by the arrival of his son, Prince Edward. He sees in his son's face his wife's image, and this makes him come to his senses. The Countess approaches him and threatens to kill herself unless he ceases his advances; but her offer is no longer required. Edward expresses respect for her courage, and leaves immediately for France.

The French King John and his son Philip greet their Bohemian and Polish allies, and are told of the arrival of the English fleet. The French are defeated at sea, but regroup on land. French citizens discuss prophecies of impending doom. The English army makes progress and they confront the French at Crécy. Edward and John parley, and Prince Edward is formally attired for his first battle. The French begin to flee, but the Prince is surrounded. Edward refuses to send him reinforcements, wishing him to prove himself. The Prince wins through, and is knighted. The English then continue their pursuit of the French.

Lord Mountford, Duke of Brittany, wishes to support Edward, and asks Salisbury to carry a symbolic coronet to him. Salisbury needs a safe-conduct to pass through the French lines, and asks his prisoner Villiers to visit Charles, Duke of Normandy, to obtain it, trusting him to return. Charles tries to dissuade Villiers from returning, but Villiers keeps his word. On his way to Calais, Salisbury is taken by the French, but Charles persuades King John to let him continue his journey.

Prince Edward and Audley find themselves surrounded, but they reject three sarcastic French offers to yield. The French army breaks up in disarray at the sight of ravens on the battlefield and the English use of flintstones as weapons – events which had previously been prophesied – and King John and Charles are taken.

Meanwhile Edward has arrived at Calais, and received the town's submission, having insisted that the citizens humble themselves. Copland arrives from England, bringing King David as a prisoner. Salisbury also arrives, bringing the allegiance of Mountford, and reports his belief that Prince Edward is defeated. However, almost immediately the Prince arrives with the French prisoners. All parties then return to England.

DRAMATIS PERSONAE

(as conventionally listed)

The English
KING EDWARD III
QUEEN Philippa, his wife
Edward, PRINCE OF WALES, their son
Earl of SALISBURY
COUNTESS of Salisbury, his wife
Earl of WARWICK, her father
Sir William MONTAGUE, Salisbury's nephew
Earl of DERBY
Lord AUDLEY
Lord PERCY
John COPLAND, an esquire, later Sir John Copland
LODOWICK, King Edward's secretary
Two Esquires
A Herald

Supporters of the English
Robert, Count of ARTOIS, and Earl of Richmond
Lord MOUNTFORD, Duke of Brittany
GOBIN de Grace, a French prisoner

The French
KING JOHN II
Prince CHARLES, Duke of Normandy, his oldest son
Prince PHILIP, his youngest son
Duke of LORRAINE
VILLIERS, a Norman Lord
The CAPTAIN of Calais
Another CAPTAIN
A MARINER
Three HERALDS
Two CITIZENS from Crécy
Three other FRENCHMEN
A WOMAN with two children
Six wealthy CITIZENS | of Calais
Six POOR Frenchmen

Supporters of the French
King of BOHEMIA
A POLONIAN CAPTAIN
Danish troops

The Scots
KING DAVID Bruce of Scotland
Sir William DOUGLAS
Two MESSENGERS

Lords, attendants, officers, soldiers, citizens, servants, etc.

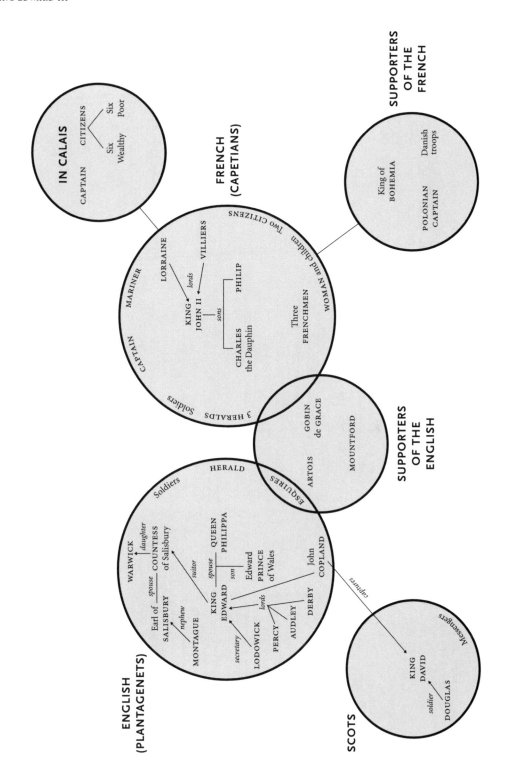

IN CALAIS

CAPTAIN   CITIZENS
Six Wealthy
Six Poor

SUPPORTERS OF THE FRENCH

King of BOHEMIA
Danish troops
POLONIAN CAPTAIN

FRENCH (CAPETIANS)

MARINER   LORRAINE
VILLIERS
lords
KING JOHN II   PHILIP
sons
CHARLES the Dauphin
Three FRENCHMEN
WOMAN and children
Two CITIZENS
CAPTAIN
3 HERALDS   Soldiers

SUPPORTERS OF THE ENGLISH

ARTOIS   GOBIN de GRACE
MOUNTFORD
ESQUIRES

ENGLISH (PLANTAGENETS)

HERALD   Soldiers
WARWICK   COUNTESS of Salisbury   *daughter*
Earl of SALISBURY   *spouse*   *suitor*   QUEEN PHILIPPA   *spouse*
nephew   MONTAGUE   KING EDWARD   *son*   Edward PRINCE of Wales
LODOWICK   *lords*   John COPLAND
PERCY   *secretary*
AUDLEY
DERBY

SCOTS

KING DAVID
DOUGLAS   *soldier*
Messengers
captures

Hamlet

Guarding the castle at Elsinore, Marcellus and Barnardo tell Horatio that they have seen the ghost of the dead King Hamlet. The ghost reappears, and they decide they must tell the dead King's son, Hamlet, about it. Hamlet is present at a reception being given by his uncle Claudius, who has just married Hamlet's mother, Gertrude. Claudius is sending ambassadors to Norway to stop a planned invasion by young Fortinbras. He gives Polonius' son Laertes permission to return to France. Hamlet reflects on the hasty marriage, and learns of the ghost's visit. That night he meets the ghost, who reveals that King Hamlet was murdered by Claudius, and Hamlet willingly agrees to be the means of revenge. He warns Horatio and the others not to speak of what has happened, even if he should behave strangely.

Polonius bids farewell to Laertes and warns his daughter Ophelia against Hamlet's courtship. Later, she tells Polonius of a strange visitation by Hamlet, and Polonius reports to the King and Queen that rejected love is the cause of Hamlet's supposed madness. Hamlet's fellow-students Rosencrantz and Guildenstern arrive, invited by the King to find out what is wrong. Polonius arranges for Ophelia to meet Hamlet where he and Claudius can observe them. Hamlet reflects to himself on the nature of life and death, then meets Ophelia. They argue about their relationship, and Hamlet, having become suspicious about being observed, tells her she should go to a nunnery. Claudius is convinced that love is not the cause of Hamlet's behaviour, and decides to send him abroad.

Meanwhile, travelling players have arrived, and Hamlet asks them to perform 'The Murder of Gonzago' before the King, so that he and Horatio can judge Claudius' guilt by his reaction. Hamlet contrasts his own inaction with the way the players can become so involved in their characters. When one of the players enacts the poisoning of a king, Claudius leaves in high emotion, much to Hamlet's jubilation. Gertrude asks to see Hamlet, and Polonius decides to hide in the room to hear what is said. On his way, Hamlet comes across Claudius alone, trying to pray for forgiveness, but decides that killing him in this state would not be fit revenge.

Hamlet arrives in his mother's room, and kills the person he discovers in hiding, thinking it to be Claudius but finding it to be Polonius. He argues fiercely with Gertrude, eventually persuading her to change her ways. The Ghost appears, restraining Hamlet's anger towards his mother, and reminding him of the need for revenge. Claudius instructs Rosencrantz and Guildenstern to take Hamlet immediately to England. Travelling to the ship, Hamlet passes the Norwegian army on its way to fight for a small patch of land, and contrasts their determination with his own lack of resolve.

Ophelia descends into madness. Laertes returns, blaming Claudius for his father's death, and is incensed to see Ophelia in this state. Claudius persuades him that Hamlet is to blame. When Claudius receives a letter from Hamlet reporting his return to Elsinore, he plots with Laertes to kill him. They arrange a duel in which Laertes' sword will be unblunted and poisoned. Claudius will also poison a drink, which he will offer Hamlet. Gertrude arrives with the news that Ophelia has drowned.

Hamlet meets Horatio on returning to Elsinore. On the way, they see two Clowns digging a grave, and Hamlet talks to the First Clown, reflecting on the skulls he finds. They discover that the grave is for Ophelia. Hamlet reveals himself to the funeral party, grappling with Laertes and proclaiming his love for Ophelia. Later, Hamlet tells Horatio how the trip to England was a subterfuge for his death, arranged by Claudius, and how he had managed to escape.

Osric enters with news of the proposed fencing match, and Hamlet accepts the challenge. With Hamlet in the lead, Gertrude toasts him, and drinks from the poisoned cup. Laertes wounds Hamlet with the poisoned rapier, and is then wounded with it by Hamlet. Before he dies, Laertes blames Claudius, and Hamlet kills the King. Hamlet, close to death, passes the Danish succession to Fortinbras, and instructs Horatio to tell his story.

DRAMATIS PERSONAE

(as conventionally listed)

GHOST of Hamlet, lately King of Denmark
Claudius, his brother, now KING of Denmark
Gertrude, QUEEN of Denmark, widow of the late King and now wife of his brother Claudius

HAMLET, son of the late King Hamlet and of Gertrude

POLONIUS, counsellor to the King
LAERTES, son of Polonius
OPHELIA, daughter of Polonius
REYNALDO, servant of Polonius

HORATIO, friend of Prince Hamlet

VOLTEMAND
CORNELIUS
ROSENCRANTZ
GUILDENSTERN } members of the Danish court
OSRICK
A LORD
GENTLEMEN

FRANCISCO
BARNARDO } soldiers
MARCELLUS

Two MESSENGERS
A SAILOR
Two CLOWNS, a gravedigger and his companion
A PRIEST
FORTINBRAS, Prince of Norway
A CAPTAIN, a Norwegian
English AMBASSADORS

FIRST PLAYER, who leads the troupe and takes the part of a king
SECOND PLAYER, who takes the part of a queen
THIRD PLAYER, who takes the part of Lucianus, nephew of the king
FOURTH PLAYER, who speaks a Prologue

Lords, attendants, players, guards, soldiers, followers of Laertes, sailors

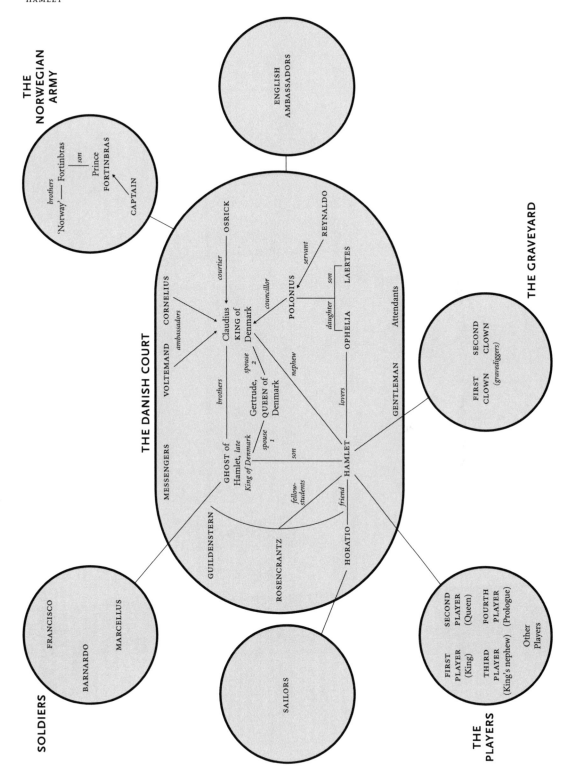

THE NORWEGIAN ARMY

brothers
'Norway' — Fortinbras
| son
Prince
FORTINBRAS
CAPTAIN

ENGLISH AMBASSADORS

SOLDIERS

FRANCISCO
BARNARDO
MARCELLUS

THE DANISH COURT

OSRICK

courtier

Claudius
KING of
Denmark

councillor

REYNALDO

servant

POLONIUS

son
LAERTES

daughter
OPHELIA

CORNELIUS

VOLTEMAND

ambassadors

MESSENGERS

brothers

Gertrude,
QUEEN of
Denmark

spouse 2

nephew

Attendants

GENTLEMAN

lovers

GHOST of
Hamlet, late
King of Denmark

spouse 1

son

HAMLET

fellow-students

friend

GUILDENSTERN

ROSENCRANTZ

HORATIO

SAILORS

THE GRAVEYARD

FIRST
CLOWN

SECOND
CLOWN

FIRST (gravediggers)

THE PLAYERS

FIRST
PLAYER
(King)

SECOND
PLAYER
(Queen)

THIRD
PLAYER
(King's nephew)

FOURTH
PLAYER
(Prologue)

Other
Players

Henry IV Part 1

DRAMATIS PERSONAE

(as conventionally listed)

The King's Party

KING HENRY IV, formerly Henry Bolingbroke, son of John of Gaunt

HENRY (or HAL), Prince of Wales, the King's eldest son

LORD JOHN OF LANCASTER, a younger son of King Henry IV

EARL OF WESTMORLAND, kinsman by law to Henry IV

SIR WALTER BLUNT

The Rebels

HENRY PERCY, Earl of Northumberland

HARRY HOTSPUR, his son

LADY PERCY (KATE), Hotspur's wife, sister of Mortimer

THOMAS PERCY, Earl of Worcester

EDMUND, LORD MORTIMER

LADY MORTIMER, Mortimer's wife, daughter of Glendower

OWEN GLENDOWER

EARL OF DOUGLAS

SIR RICHARD VERNON

RICHARD SCROOP, Archbishop of York

SIR MICHAEL, a member of the household of the Archbishop

Hal's Companions

SIR JOHN FALSTAFF

POINS

BARDOLPH

PETO

MISTRESS QUICKLY, hostess of the Tavern in Eastcheap

FRANCIS, a drawer

Vintner

At Rochester

GADSHILL

Two Carriers

Chamberlain

Sheriff and officers

Ostler

Messengers

Travellers

Lords and attendants

Soldiers

Henry IV discusses with his lords the recent fighting against the Welsh and Scots, as a result of which Hotspur has refused to yield up his prisoners. Henry regrets that Prince Hal, his son, does not match Hotspur's prowess. When Henry meets Hotspur, Northumberland, and Worcester, Hotspur still refuses to comply; all three later discuss their grievances and plan rebellion. Lady Percy tries and fails to find out from Hotspur what he is planning. The rebels then meet with Mortimer and Glendower, and plan the division of England after their victory.

Meanwhile, Prince Hal is found at leisure with Falstaff and his companions. They plan a robbery for the next day at Gadshill, but Hal and Poins secretly plan to disguise themselves in buckram suits and rob the robbers of their gains. Events take place as predicted, and later in the tavern they play out the jest on Falstaff, who over-dramatizes everything that has happened. Hal and Falstaff then role-play the forthcoming meeting between Hal and the King, in which first Falstaff and then Hal take the part of Henry. At the real meeting with the King, Hal resolves to reform, and plans for fighting the rebels are made. Falstaff and his companions also prepare to travel to the battle, and Falstaff begins to put together a fighting force which proves to be of abysmal quality.

Hotspur and his associates receive news from Northumberland that he is too sick to help them. They decide to proceed nonetheless. Blunt visits them with offers from the King, which they consider. The Archbishop of York, a sympathizer of the rebels, reflects on the balance of power between the two sides. Worcester and Vernon visit the King, who extends them an offer of peace. Through them, Hal challenges Hotspur to single combat. However, Worcester hides these offers from the other rebels, and reports Henry's defiance.

The battle of Shrewsbury begins. Several soldiers dressed in the likeness of Henry are killed by Douglas, including Blunt. Prince Hal and his brother Prince John both fight bravely, and Hal saves his father from being killed by Douglas. Hal then kills Hotspur. Falstaff, feigning death nearby, gets up when the fight is over and brings in Hotspur's body, claiming to have killed him. With the battle won, Worcester and Vernon are sent for execution, but Douglas is released. Henry then makes plans for further attacks on the rebels in the north and west.

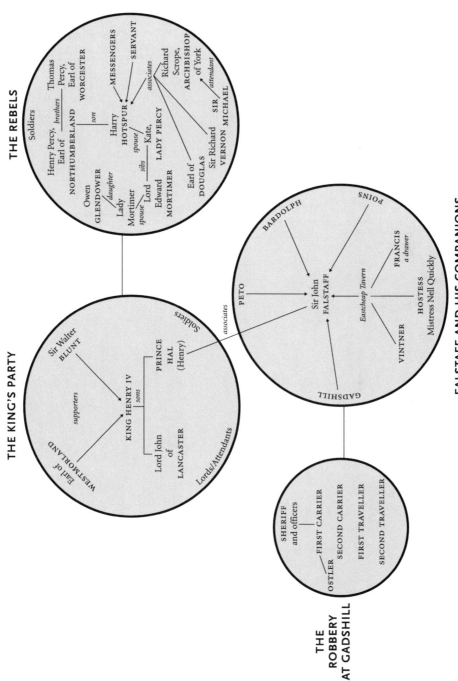

THE REBELS

Soldiers

Henry Percy, Thomas
Earl of Percy,
NORTHUMBERLAND Earl of
WORCESTER
brothers

son

Harry
Owen HOTSPUR MESSENGERS SERVANT
GLENDOWER
associates
daughter
Richard
Lady _spouse_ Kate, Scrope,
Mortimer _sibs_ LADY PERCY ARCHBISHOP
spouse Lord of York
Edward _attendant_
MORTIMER SIR
Earl of MICHAEL
DOUGLAS VERNON
Sir Richard

THE KING'S PARTY

Sir Walter
BLUNT

supporters

Earl of
WESTMORLAND

KING HENRY IV

sons

PRINCE
HAL
(Henry)

Lord John
of
LANCASTER

Lords/Attendants

Soldiers

associates

FALSTAFF AND HIS COMPANIONS

BARDOLPH

POINS

PETO

Sir John
FALSTAFF

FRANCIS
a drawer

Eastcheap Tavern

HOSTESS
Mistress Nell Quickly

VINTNER

GADSHILL

THE
ROBBERY
AT GADSHILL

SHERIFF
and officers

FIRST CARRIER

OSTLER SECOND CARRIER

FIRST TRAVELLER

SECOND TRAVELLER

Henry IV Part 2

Good and bad rumours of the outcome at the battle of Shrewsbury reach the ears of Northumberland and other rebels. When he learns the truth, and hears of the approach of the King's forces, Northumberland makes plans to join with the Archbishop of York, who is also preparing a force; but Lady Northumberland manages to dissuade her husband from joining with the Archbishop.

Falstaff, about to travel north to recruit soldiers, receives a series of rebukes from the Lord Chief Justice. Mistress Quickly tries to have him arrested for debts, but he manages to appease her. He then engages in a mixture of banter and quarrelling with Doll and Pistol. Prince Henry and Poins disguise themselves as tavern men, and spy on Falstaff. They overhear him being scornful at their expense, and then confront him. The revelry is disrupted by a call to arms.

King Henry reflects on the nature of kingship, and discusses the state of the kingdom with Warwick and Surrey. Falstaff travels north, passing through Gloucestershire, where he visits two justices, Shallow and Silence, whom he knows of old. They have assembled a number of local men for Falstaff and Bardolph to conscript, and a selection is made in which bribery proves to be a more important factor than fighting ability.

The Archbishop, Mowbray, and Hastings meet Westmorland and explain their grievances, which he agrees to put before Prince John. John agrees to see the grievances redressed, and the rebels dismiss their army. But John then arrests the rebel leaders, and has the scattered army pursued. One of the rebels, Colevile, yields to Falstaff, who then has to defend his achievement against Prince John's scepticism.

The King, now very ill, hears news of the rebel overthrow, and takes to his bed to sleep. When Prince Henry visits him, he thinks his father is dead, which causes him to reflect on the burden of kingship and take up the crown. After the Prince leaves the room, the King awakes. Seeing the crown gone, he accuses his son of wanting him dead, but the Prince resolves his fears and they are reconciled. The King dies soon after. News of his death alarms the lords, and especially the Lord Chief Justice, fearful that the Prince as King will exact retribution for previous chastisement. But Henry affirms his intention to rule wisely, and reappoints the Chief Justice.

Falstaff, on his way back to London, has stopped off again in Gloucestershire. He is drinking with Shallow and Silence when Pistol brings news of the King's death. They travel to London immediately, where Mistress Quickly and Doll have been arraigned by beadles. They wait in the street to see the King, expecting to be shown favour, but Henry firmly rejects Falstaff, who is then sent to the Fleet prison with his companions. Prince John reflects on the likelihood that the next major political event will be a French campaign.

DRAMATIS PERSONAE
(as conventionally listed)

RUMOUR, the presenter

KING HENRY IV
PRINCE HENRY, afterwards crowned King Henry V

PRINCE JOHN OF LANCASTER ⎱ sons of
Humphrey DUKE OF GLOUCESTER ⎰ Henry IV
Thomas DUKE OF CLARENCE ⎰ and brothers of Henry V

Of the King's Party
EARL OF WARWICK
EARL OF WESTMORLAND
Earl of Surrey
Sir John Blunt
GOWER
HARCOURT
The LORD CHIEF JUSTICE
A SERVANT of the Lord Chief Justice

Opposed to the King
EARL OF NORTHUMBERLAND
The ARCHBISHOP OF YORK
LORD MOWBRAY
LORD HASTINGS
LORD BARDOLPH
TRAVERS
MORTON
SIR JOHN COLEVILE

LADY NORTHUMBERLAND, Northumberland's wife
LADY PERCY, Percy's widow

'Irregular Humorists'
POINS
SIR JOHN FALSTAFF
BARDOLPH
PISTOL
PETO
Falstaff's PAGE

HOSTESS Quickly
DOLL TEARSHEET

Robert SHALLOW ⎱ country justices
SILENCE ⎰
DAVY, Shallow's servant

Ralph MOULDY ⎱
Simon SHADOW ⎰
Thomas WART ⎰ country soldiers
Francis FEEBLE ⎰
Peter BULLCALF ⎰

FANG ⎱ sergeants
SNARE ⎰
FRANCIS, WILL, and another DRAWER
FIRST BEADLE
Three GROOMS

A PORTER
A MESSENGER

Speaker of the EPILOGUE

Officers, musicians, a page, soldiers, a captain, lords, beadles

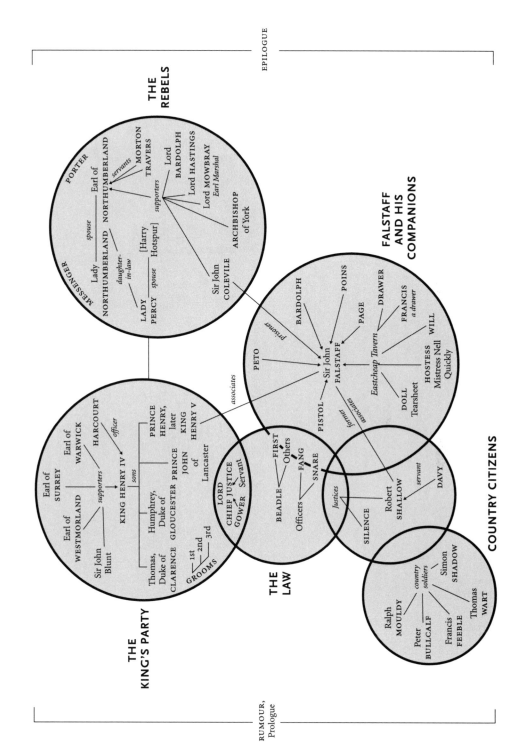

**THE
REBELS**

PORTER

MORTON
TRAVERS

servants

Earl of
NORTHUMBERLAND

Lord
BARDOLPH
Lord HASTINGS
Lord MOWBRAY
Earl Marshal

supporters

ARCHBISHOP
of York

Lady   *spouse*
NORTHUMBERLAND   NORTHUMBERLAND

MESSENGER

*daughter-
in-law*

[Harry
LADY   *spouse*   Hotspur]
PERCY

Sir John
COLEVILE

associates

**FALSTAFF
AND HIS
COMPANIONS**

BARDOLPH   POINS

PAGE

DRAWER

FRANCIS
a drawer

WILL

prisoner

PETO

Sir John
FALSTAFF

Eastcheap Tavern

HOSTESS
Mistress Nell
Quickly

DOLL
Tearsheet

PISTOL

former

associates

**THE
KING'S PARTY**

Earl of
SURREY

Earl of
WARWICK

HARCOURT   *officer*

PRINCE
HENRY,
later
KING
HENRY V

Earl of
WESTMORLAND

supporters

KING HENRY IV   *sons*

Sir John
Blunt

Humphrey,
Duke of
GLOUCESTER

PRINCE
JOHN
of
Lancaster

Thomas,
Duke of
CLARENCE

1st
2nd
3rd

GROOMS

LORD
CHIEF JUSTICE   Servant
GOWER

**THE
LAW**

BEADLE

FIRST
Others

FANG

SNARE

Officers

Justices

SILENCE

Robert
SHALLOW

servant

DAVY

COUNTRY CITIZENS

Ralph
MOULDY

*country
soldiers*

Simon
SHADOW

Peter
BULLCALF

Francis
FEEBLE

Thomas
WART

Henry V

Henry, now seen to be a wise and serious king, is assured by the Archbishop of Canterbury and the Bishop of Ely that he has a right to the French throne. His decision to take the French crown is reinforced when ambassadors from the Dauphin bring him a contemptuous present, in the form of tennis balls.

As Henry and his associates prepare for France, he arraigns Cambridge, Scroop, and Grey as traitors. Meanwhile, Nym and Pistol quarrel while they make their preparations for war, with Bardolph trying to keep the peace. They learn of Falstaff's death from the Hostess and the Boy, and bid her farewell.

The French lords discuss the arrival of the English, and receive Exeter with Henry's demands, which are rejected. Pistol and his associates try to avoid the fighting, much to the disgust of the Boy, but they are forced into the front line by Fluellen, who then enters into a discussion of military strategy with his fellow-captains Gower, Jamy, and Macmorris. Harfleur falls after Henry's assault. Pistol has a sharp encounter with Fluellen.

The French King's daughter, Katherine, has an English lesson from her maid, Alice, while the French lords discuss their impending victory over the English. They send their herald, Montjoy, to Henry, who dismisses the suggestion that he should yield. The French boastfully prepare for battle. In the English camp, Henry disguises himself as an ordinary soldier and engages in discussion with some of the men. He tries to justify the King's strategy in response to criticisms from Williams, who refuses to accept the disguised Henry's account of the King's motives. Henry and Williams agree to challenge each other, if they live to see each other again, exchanging gloves by way of recognition. Henry then reflects on the responsibilities of kingship.

The French, ebullient as ever, leave their camp for the battle of Agincourt. Henry rallies his troops, dismissing anxieties about their number. He rejects a further suggestion that he should surrender from Montjoy. The battle begins. Pistol captures a French soldier, and obtains a ransom with the help of the Boy's ability to speak French. The French lords find themselves facing defeat, but some of the French make a late rally into the English camp, and against the code of war kill the boys, much to Henry's anger. Montjoy brings news of the French surrender.

Henry sees Williams, and gets Fluellen to wear Williams' glove on his behalf, but defuses the ensuing quarrel as soon as it begins by explaining who it was that caused it. News arrives of great French losses and very few English ones. Fluellen meets Pistol, and reacts to his insults by making him eat a Welsh leek and giving him a beating.

The English and French Kings and lords meet to discuss terms of peace. While the lords work out the details, Henry woos Katherine, who eventually agrees to marry him. The French accept the English terms, and Henry looks forward to a peaceful relationship between the two countries.

DRAMATIS PERSONAE
(as conventionally listed)

CHORUS

KING HENRY THE FIFTH
DUKE OF GLOUCESTER
DUKE OF BEDFORD } brothers of the King
DUKE OF CLARENCE
DUKE OF EXETER, uncle of the King
DUKE OF YORK, cousin of the King
EARL OF SALISBURY
EARL OF WESTMORLAND
EARL OF WARWICK
EARL OF HUNTINGDON
ARCHBISHOP OF CANTERBURY
BISHOP OF ELY
RICHARD, EARL OF CAMBRIDGE }
HENRY, LORD SCROOP } conspirators against the King
SIR THOMAS GREY }
SIR THOMAS ERPINGHAM
CAPTAIN FLUELLEN
CAPTAIN GOWER } officers in the King's army
CAPTAIN JAMY
CAPTAIN MACMORRIS

JOHN BATES
ALEXANDER COURT } soldiers in the King's army
MICHAEL WILLIAMS
BARDOLPH
NYM } camp-followers in the King's army
PISTOL
BOY
HOSTESS of an Eastcheap tavern, formerly Mistress Quickly, now married to Pistol
An English Herald

CHARLES THE SIXTH, King of France
Lewis, the DAUPHIN
DUKE OF BURGUNDY
DUKE OF ORLEANS
DUKE OF BRITAINE
DUKE OF BOURBON
CHARLES DELABRETH, the Constable of France
GRANDPRÉ } French Lords
RAMBURES
THE GOVERNOR OF HARFLEUR
MONTJOY, a French Herald
AMBASSADORS to the King of England
MONSIEUR LE FER, a French soldier
ISABEL, Queen of France
KATHERINE, daughter of the King and Queen of France
ALICE, a lady attending on her

Lords, ladies
Officers, soldiers, citizens, messengers, and attendants

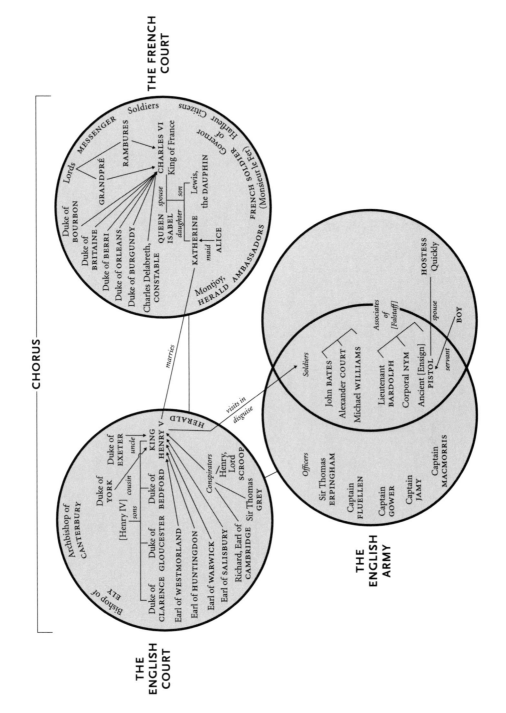

CHORUS

THE FRENCH COURT

Lords MESSENGER Soldiers
Duke of BOURBON
Duke of BRITAINE
GRANDPRÉ
Duke of BERRI
RAMBURES
Duke of ORLEANS
Duke of BURGUNDY
CHARLES VI King of France
Charles Delabreth, CONSTABLE
QUEEN ISABEL *spouse*
Lewis, the DAUPHIN *son*
KATHERINE *daughter*
ALICE *maid*
Montjoy, HERALD AMBASSADORS
Governor of Harfleur Citizens
FRENCH SOLDIER (Monsieur le Fer)

THE ENGLISH COURT

Archbishop of CANTERBURY
Bishop of ELY
Duke of YORK
Duke of EXETER *uncle*
KING HENRY V
[Henry IV] *cousin*
Duke of BEDFORD
sons
Duke of CLARENCE
Duke of GLOUCESTER
Earl of WESTMORLAND
Earl of HUNTINGDON
Earl of WARWICK
Earl of SALISBURY
Richard, Earl of CAMBRIDGE
Sir Thomas GREY
Henry, Lord SCROOP
Conspirators
HERALD
marries
visits in disguise

THE ENGLISH ARMY

Officers
Sir Thomas ERPINGHAM
Captain FLUELLEN
Captain GOWER
Captain JAMY
Captain MACMORRIS
Soldiers
John BATES
Alexander COURT
Michael WILLIAMS
Associates of [Falstaff]
Lieutenant BARDOLPH
Corporal NYM
Ancient [Ensign] PISTOL
HOSTESS Quickly
spouse
BOY
servant

Henry VI Part 1

Henry V is dead, and some of the nobles are beginning to quarrel, especially Gloucester (Protector of the young Henry VI) and the Bishop of Winchester, who is ambitious for power. News arrives of English defeats in France, and Bedford prepares to leave with reinforcements.

The French are attacking the English-held Orleans, but are beaten back. They are offered help by Joan la Pucelle, who beats the Dauphin in a duel, thereby persuading them she has a divinely inspired ability to lead France to victory. An Orleans gunner kills two English lords, spurring the English leader Talbot to fresh action. He fights Pucelle, who takes Orleans; but Talbot leads a force into the city at night, forcing the French to flee. The Countess of Auvergne tries to capture Talbot by inviting him to her castle, but he anticipates her treachery.

Back in England, Gloucester and his men arrive at the Tower but are refused their right to enter, on Winchester's orders. The two factions fight, until stopped by the Mayor. Richard Plantagenet (of York) and the Earl of Somerset (of Lancaster) argue in the Temple gardens. They ask those around them to join whoever they think is right in the argument by picking a red rose for Lancaster or a white rose for York. Richard learns about his claim to the throne from his dying uncle, Mortimer. Gloucester and Winchester continue to quarrel in front of the King, who insists on their reconciliation; they agree, though Winchester does not intend to keep his word. Henry restores Richard's titles as Duke of York, then goes to France to be crowned in Paris.

Pucelle captures Rouen, but is driven out by Talbot, aided by Burgundy. Pucelle then persuades Burgundy to change sides and return to his native France. The news of Burgundy's betrayal reaches Henry in Paris, and Talbot is sent to deal with him. Rivalry breaks out again between the York and Lancaster factions, and intended reinforcements are not sent to Talbot. As a result, though Talbot and his son fight bravely, both are killed. French fortunes begin to turn, and Pucelle uses black magic to ask for help, but the spirits refuse. York overcomes her, and she is brought to trial. She pleads for mercy, but is sent to be burned at the stake.

Henry is advised to seek peace, and to marry a French princess. Suffolk captures Margaret, daughter of Reignier, and falls in love with her; being married already, he woos her on behalf of Henry. The two countries having agreed peace, Suffolk returns to England and gives Henry a description of Margaret which convinces him that he should marry her, despite objections from other nobles. Suffolk's hope is that the Queen will come to dominate Henry, and that through her he himself will achieve a position of great power.

DRAMATIS PERSONAE

(as conventionally listed)

KING HENRY THE SIXTH
DUKE OF GLOUCESTER, Lord Protector and uncle of the King
DUKE OF BEDFORD, Regent of France and uncle of the King
DUKE OF EXETER, Thomas Beaufort, great-uncle of the King
BISHOP OF WINCHESTER, Henry Beaufort, great-uncle of the King, later a Cardinal
DUKE OF SOMERSET, John Beaufort, formerly Earl of Somerset
RICHARD PLANTAGENET, later Duke of York and Regent of France
EARL OF WARWICK
EARL OF SALISBURY
William de la Pole, EARL OF SUFFOLK
LORD TALBOT, later Earl of Shrewsbury
JOHN TALBOT, his son
EDMUND MORTIMER, Earl of March
SIR WILLIAM GLANSDALE
SIR THOMAS GARGRAVE
SIR JOHN FALSTAFF
SIR WILLIAM LUCY
WOODVILLE, Lieutenant of the Tower of London
MAYOR OF LONDON
VERNON
BASSET
A LAWYER of the Temple
A PAPAL LEGATE
MESSENGERS

WARDERS of the Tower of London
SERVINGMEN
An OFFICER
A SOLDIER
CAPTAINS
A GAOLER
WATCH

CHARLES, Dauphin and later King of France
REIGNIER, Duke of Anjou and titular King of Naples
DUKE OF ALENÇON
BASTARD OF ORLEANS
DUKE OF BURGUNDY
GENERAL of the French army at Bordeaux
MASTER GUNNER of Orleans
A BOY, son of the Master Gunner
SHEPHERD, father of Joan la Pucelle
JOAN LA PUCELLE, Joan of Arc
MARGARET, daughter of Reignier
COUNTESS OF AUVERGNE
PORTER of the Countess of Auvergne
French SERGEANT
French SENTINEL
French SOLDIER
French SCOUT

English and French heralds, soldiers, servants, officers, sentinels, gentlemen, gaolers, attendants, courtiers, the Governor of Paris, ambassadors, fiends (Joan la Pucelle's familiars)

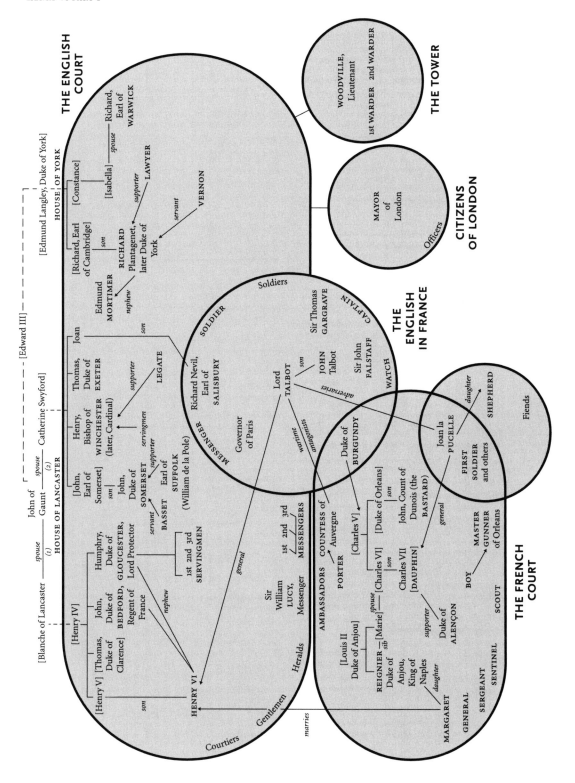

Henry VI Part 2

Suffolk has brought Queen Margaret to England on behalf of Henry, but the terms of the marriage involve a loss of territory in France, which angers the English peers. Rivalry between Gloucester (the Lord Protector) and Cardinal Beaufort emerges, and York's ambitions for the English crown are revealed. York explains his right to the throne to Salisbury and Warwick. Suffolk's intimacy with Margaret leads him to work against her rivals. Antagonism grows between York and Somerset over who should be regent in France.

The political conflict in court has its parallel in a group of petitioners. One petition is by an apprentice, Peter, against his master, Horner, for saying that York is the rightful heir. This is read by Suffolk, who brings the parties to court. A day for their single combat is assigned, at which Peter manages to defeat Horner, who confesses treason before he dies. In another incident, the King encounters a St Albans man, Simpcox, whose blindness is said to have been cured miraculously, but Gloucester shows him to be a fraud.

The Duchess of Gloucester tells her husband of dreams for their advancement, and approaches a priest, John Hume, to get black magicians to tell her the future, but she is surprised by York and Buckingham, and arrested. The affair is reported to Henry, who banishes her, and later is persuaded that Gloucester should resign as Protector. As Gloucester bids farewell to his wife, he is called to attend a meeting of parliament. There, the Queen, Beaufort, Suffolk, and York launch an attack on him, and despite Henry's sympathy he is arrested. A plot to kill him is laid, and he is murdered by Suffolk's men. After learning of the murder, Warwick confronts Suffolk, whose complicity is also suspected by the common people, and Suffolk is banished, despite the Queen's pleas. The Queen and Suffolk part in an intimate farewell. Beaufort dies. The boat taking Suffolk to France is taken by pirates, and he is killed by one of them, Whitmore.

News of an Irish rebellion arrives, and York is sent to quell it. He reveals that he has instigated a rebellion led by Jack Cade, who will test public opinion by claiming the throne under the name of Mortimer. Cade and his men begin their revolt, killing a clerk and the Staffords, and march to London, forcing the King to leave. They kill Lord Say and others, but the rebels are persuaded by Bucking-ham and Clifford to leave Cade, who flees. A starving Cade is killed by a Kentish gentleman, Iden, in his garden. York, meanwhile, has arrived back in England with an army, wishing to remove Somerset from his position. As a stratagem Henry sends Somerset to the Tower, and Buckingham is sent to report this to York, who dismisses his army. When Somerset is liberated, York is infuriated, brings in his sons to prevent his arrest by Somerset, and calls on Henry to yield his throne. Lord Clifford and his son support Henry, and Warwick and Salisbury support York. The battle of St Albans takes place, in which York kills Lord Clifford, and York's son Richard kills Somerset. The King flees, and the Yorkists plan to pursue him to London.

DRAMATIS PERSONAE

(as conventionally listed)

KING HENRY THE SIXTH
Margaret, QUEEN of England, daughter of King Reignier
DUKE OF YORK, Richard Plantagenet
EDWARD | sons of the Duke of York
RICHARD |
DUKE OF GLOUCESTER, Humphrey of Lancaster, Protector of England, uncle of the King
DUCHESS OF GLOUCESTER, Eleanor Cobham
CARDINAL BEAUFORT, Bishop of Winchester, great-uncle of the King
DUKE OF SUFFOLK, William de la Pole
DUKE OF SOMERSET, Edmund Beaufort
DUKE OF BUCKINGHAM, Humphrey Stafford
EARL OF SALISBURY, Richard Nevil
EARL OF WARWICK, Richard Nevil, son of the Earl of Salisbury
LORD CLIFFORD
YOUNG CLIFFORD, son of Lord Clifford
LORD SCALES
LORD SAY
SIR HUMPHREY STAFFORD
William Stafford, BROTHER of Sir Humphrey Stafford
SIR JOHN STANLEY
VAUX
ALEXANDER IDEN, a Kentish gentleman

JOHN HUME, a priest
JOHN SOUTHWELL, a priest
ROGER BOLINGBROKE, a conjurer
MARGERY JOURDAIN, a witch
A SPIRIT

THOMAS HORNER, an armourer
PETER THUMP, Horner's assistant
PETITIONERS
NEIGHBOURS
PRENTICES

SAUNDER SIMPCOX
WIFE of Simpcox
A MAN
MAYOR of St Albans
A BEADLE

JACK CADE
GEORGE BEVIS
JOHN HOLLAND
DICK, a butcher
SMITH, a weaver
MICHAEL
} followers of Jack Cade

A LIEUTENANT
A MASTER
A MASTER'S MATE
WALTER WHITMORE
Two GENTLEMEN, prisoners with Suffolk

MESSENGERS
SERVANTS
A HERALD
A SHERIFF
A POST
MURDERERS
COMMONS
CLERK OF CHARTHAM
A CITIZEN
A SOLDIER

Guards, soldiers, servants, attendants, falconers, aldermen, neighbours, prentices, officers, a sawyer, citizens, Matthew Gough

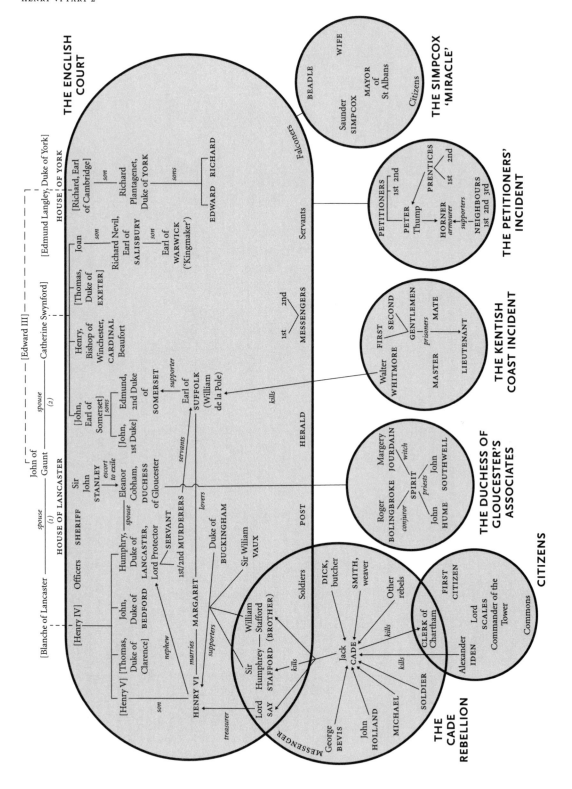

THE ENGLISH COURT

[Edmund Langley, Duke of York]

HOUSE OF YORK

[Richard, Earl of Cambridge]

son

Richard Plantagenet, Duke of YORK

sons

EDWARD RICHARD

THE SIMPCOX 'MIRACLE'

BEADLE   WIFE

Saunder SIMPCOX

MAYOR of St Albans

Citizens

[Edward III]

John of Gaunt

spouse (1)   spouse   spouse (2)
Catherine Swynford

HOUSE OF LANCASTER

[Blanche of Lancaster]

Joan

son

Richard Nevil, Earl of SALISBURY

son

Earl of WARWICK ('Kingmaker')

[Thomas, Duke of EXETER]

Henry, Bishop of Winchester, CARDINAL Beaufort

Falconers

Servants

THE PETITIONERS' INCIDENT

PETITIONERS 1st 2nd

PETER Thump

HORNER armourer

PRENTICES 1st 2nd

supporters

NEIGHBOURS 1st 2nd and 3rd

[John, Earl of Somerset]

sons

[John, 1st Duke]

Edmund, 2nd Duke of SOMERSET

supporter

Earl of SUFFOLK (William de la Pole)

kills

1st   2nd

MESSENGERS

THE KENTISH COAST INCIDENT

Walter WHITMORE

FIRST   SECOND GENTLEMEN

prisoners

MASTER   MATE

LIEUTENANT

HERALD

Sir John STANLEY

escort to exile

Eleanor Cobham, DUCHESS of Gloucester

SERVANT

1st/2nd MURDERERS

servants

THE DUCHESS OF GLOUCESTER'S ASSOCIATES

Roger BOLINGBROKE conjuror

Margery JOURDAIN witch

SPIRIT

John HUME priests John SOUTHWELL

[Henry IV]

Officers

SHERIFF

Humphrey, Duke of Gloucester, LANCASTER, Lord Protector

spouse

Duke of BUCKINGHAM

lovers

Sir William VAUX

POST

[Thomas, Duke of Clarence]

John, Duke of BEDFORD

[Henry V]

nephew

son

MARGARET

marries

supporters

HENRY VI

treasurer

Lord SAY

Sir Humphrey STAFFORD

kills

William Stafford (BROTHER)

Soldiers

MESSENGER

THE CADE REBELLION

George BEVIS

John HOLLAND

MICHAEL

SOLDIER

kills

Jack CADE

DICK, butcher

SMITH, weaver

Other rebels

kills

kills

CLERK of Chartham

Alexander IDEN

FIRST CITIZEN

Lord SCALES Commander of the Tower

Commons

CITIZENS

Henry VI Part 3

The Yorkists, following their victories, meet Henry in London. York ascends the throne, and the rival parties debate their respective rights. Henry is allowed to remain king on condition that York and his heirs receive the crown after Henry's death, much to the disgust of Henry's supporters, and the anger of Queen Margaret and Prince Edward, who vow to fight on. Three of York's sons, Edward, George, and Richard, persuade their father that he should not wait, and he agrees, but they are surprised by the arrival of the Queen's army. Rutland, York's youngest son, is killed by Clifford. York is taken, humbled, and killed by the Queen and her followers.

Warwick offers support for the Yorkist cause, and a further confrontation takes place between the two sides. The Yorkists have setbacks, but resolve to fight on. Richard defeats Clifford, who dies from his wounds. Henry reflects on the nature of kingship, and grieves over civil war as he observes a son who has killed his father and a father who has killed his son. The Yorkists win, Henry flees to Scotland, and Edward plans his coronation and the installing of Richard as Duke of Gloucester and of George as Duke of Clarence. Henry is overheard reflecting on his fate by two keepers, who seize him. He is returned to London, and imprisoned. Richard reflects on his own ambitions for the crown.

Edward, now King, receives a petition from the widowed Lady Grey for the return of her husband's lands. He agrees, in the process persuading her to marry him. Margaret arrives in France to ask for help from King Lewis. Warwick also comes to France, with a request from Edward for marriage to Lady Bona, Lewis's sister. Lewis is persuaded that Edward's offer is genuine, and agrees, much to Margaret's discomfiture. But the situation is reversed when news comes that Edward has married Lady Grey. Warwick, feeling betrayed, changes sides, and is provided with a French army.

News of the new alliance reaches Edward, and Clarence and Somerset decide to join with Warwick. Warwick captures Edward and frees Henry, who makes Warwick and Clarence joint Protectors. Lady Grey flees with her brother, Rivers. However, Richard and others manage to free Edward. Young Henry, Earl of Richmond and a Lancastrian hope, is sent abroad for his safety. Edward reaches the city of York and is allowed to enter.

Montgomery arrives in support, but refuses to join Edward if he is happy to remain as Duke. Edward reasserts his title, recaptures Henry, and confronts Warwick at Coventry. Oxford, Montague, and Somerset bring support for Warwick; but Clarence changes sides. At the battle of Barnet, Warwick is killed. The Queen's army is defeated at Tewkesbury, and the Lancastrian leaders are taken prisoner. Richard kills Prince Edward in front of the Queen, then leaves for London, where he kills Henry and plots the removal of others standing between him and the throne. Margaret is banished to France. Edward and Lady Grey are established as King and Queen. Their baby prince is welcomed by the peers, but Richard is already anticipating the baby's death.

DRAMATIS PERSONAE
(as conventionally listed)

KING HENRY THE SIXTH
Margaret, QUEEN of England, daughter of King Reignier
Edward, PRINCE OF WALES, their son
DUKE OF EXETER
DUKE OF SOMERSET
EARL OF NORTHUMBERLAND
EARL OF WESTMORLAND   } supporters of the house of Lancaster
EARL OF OXFORD
LORD CLIFFORD
SIR JOHN SOMERVILLE

DUKE OF YORK, Richard Plantagenet
EDWARD, Earl of March, later Duke of York and King Edward IV
RICHARD, later Duke of Gloucester
GEORGE, later Duke of Clarence   } sons of the Duke of York
Edmund, EARL OF RUTLAND
SIR JOHN MORTIMER
SIR HUGH MORTIMER   } uncles of the Duke of York

DUKE OF NORFOLK
MARQUESS OF MONTAGUE
EARL OF WARWICK
EARL OF PEMBROKE   } supporters of the house of York
LORD HASTINGS
LORD STAFFORD
SIR WILLIAM STANLEY
SIR JOHN MONTGOMERY

LADY ELIZABETH GREY, later wife of Edward IV and Queen of England
Prince Edward, her infant son
EARL RIVERS, brother of Lady Grey
Henry, Earl of Richmond
LEWIS THE ELEVENTH, King of France
LADY BONA, his sister

MESSENGERS
TUTOR of Edmund, Earl of Rutland
A SON who has killed his father   } at the battle of
A FATHER who has killed his son   } Towton
Two KEEPERS
A NOBLEMAN
POSTS
Three WATCHMEN
A HUNTSMAN
LIEUTENANT of the Tower of London
MAYOR of York

Soldiers, attendants, Admiral Bourbon, aldermen, Mayor of Coventry, nurse to Prince Edward (infant son of Edward IV)

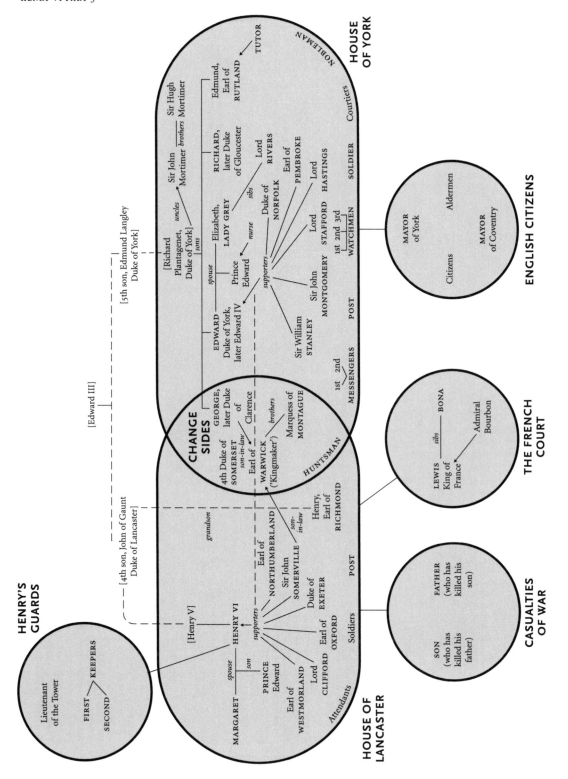

HOUSE OF YORK

TUTOR

Sir Hugh Mortimer *brothers* Sir John Mortimer

NOBLEMAN

Edmund, Earl of RUTLAND

[Richard Plantagenet, Duke of York] *uncles*

RICHARD, later Duke of Gloucester

Lord RIVERS

Courtiers

Earl of PEMBROKE

Elizabeth, LADY GREY *sons*

Lord HASTINGS

spouse *sibs*

Prince Edward *nurse* Duke of NORFOLK

Lord STAFFORD

SOLDIER

supporters

Sir John MONTGOMERY

1st 2nd and 3rd WATCHMEN

EDWARD Duke of York, later Edward IV

Sir William STANLEY

POST

ENGLISH CITIZENS

MAYOR of York   Aldermen

Citizens

MAYOR of Coventry

[5th son, Edmund Langley Duke of York]

1st 2nd MESSENGERS

CHANGE SIDES

GEORGE, later Duke of Clarence

4th Duke of SOMERSET

son-in-law Earl of WARWICK ('Kingmaker')

brothers Marquess of MONTAGUE

HUNTSMAN

THE FRENCH COURT

LEWIS King of France *sibs* BONA

Admiral Bourbon

[Edward III]

grandson

Earl of NORTHUMBERLAND

son-in-law

Henry, Earl of RICHMOND

Sir John SOMERVILLE

Duke of EXETER

POST

[4th son, John of Gaunt Duke of Lancaster]

HENRY'S GUARDS

Lieutenant of the Tower

FIRST KEEPERS SECOND

[Henry V]

HENRY VI

spouse *son*

MARGARET   PRINCE Edward

supporters

Earl of WESTMORLAND

Lord CLIFFORD

Earl of OXFORD

Soldiers

Attendants

HOUSE OF LANCASTER

CASUALTIES OF WAR

FATHER (who has killed his son)

SON (who has killed his father)

Henry VIII

Buckingham, suspicious of Wolsey's actions, is about to arraign him before the King, when Wolsey has Buckingham arrested for treason. Witnesses are called, and Buckingham is proved guilty. Despite Queen Katherine's protestations, he is sentenced to death, much to the dismay of two gentlemen who observe the proceedings. The King then hears the Queen accuse Wolsey of certain crimes, which he denies, and his claims of innocence are accepted.

Wolsey holds a party for some court friends, at which a group of masquers arrive. One of them is the King, who notices Anne Bullen. Her affirmations to an aged lady companion of hers that she would not wish to be queen are treated with cynical realism, especially when Anne is created Marchioness of Pembroke. The King makes his intentions to divorce Katherine known. At a public trial, the Queen accuses Wolsey of encouraging the King to divorce her, but the King defends him. Wolsey and Cardinal Campeius visit the Queen to persuade her to comply with Henry's wishes.

The nobles discuss their causes for complaint against Wolsey. They learn that letters from Wolsey to the Pope have been discovered which show Wolsey's personal wealth, and that Wolsey has been trying to have the King's divorce delayed in the hope of arranging a political marriage between England and France. The King challenges Wolsey with the letters, and Surrey and Norfolk read out a list of charges against him. Wolsey's servant Cromwell reports that Thomas More has been made Lord Chancellor, that Cranmer has been made Archbishop of Canterbury, and that the King has secretly married Anne.

A group of gentlemen watch the procession of the Queen's coronation pass by, and discuss the ceremony. Griffith comes to visit the sick Katherine, and tells her that the repentant Wolsey has died. Katherine has a vision as she sleeps. When she wakes she is visited by Capuchius, who has brought greetings from her nephew King Charles V. She sends Henry a letter with her last requests.

Lovell arrives with news that Queen Anne is in labour, and hears Gardiner complaining about Cranmer. King Henry calls for Cranmer, and tells him he has heard of these complaints. He gives Cranmer a ring that will save him if he is accused before the Council. The next morning, Henry notices Cranmer being kept waiting outside the Council, and later observes while he is accused of heresy. Gardiner and Cranmer quarrel, and it is decided Cranmer must be sent to the Tower. But Cranmer then shows the King's ring, and Henry, having watched all that has happened, enters and gives Cranmer his support, making him his daughter's godfather. Crowds of people gather for the christening. Cranmer predicts at Elizabeth's baptism that her future as Queen will be glorious.

DRAMATIS PERSONAE
(as conventionally listed)

KING HENRY THE EIGHTH

DUKE OF BUCKINGHAM
DUKE OF NORFOLK
DUKE OF SUFFOLK
EARL OF SURREY
LORD ABERGAVENNY
LORD SANDS (Sir Walter Sands)
LORD CHAMBERLAIN
LORD CHANCELLOR
SIR HENRY GUILFORD
SIR THOMAS LOVELL
SIR NICHOLAS VAUX
SIR ANTHONY DENNY

CARDINAL WOLSEY
THOMAS CROMWELL, in Wolsey's service, afterwards in the King's
SECRETARY to Wolsey
SERVANT to Wolsey
CARDINAL CAMPEIUS
CAPUCHIUS, ambassador from the Emperor Charles the Fifth
GARDINER, Secretary to the King, afterwards Bishop of Winchester
PAGE to Gardiner
BISHOP OF LINCOLN
THOMAS CRANMER, Archbishop of Canterbury
BRANDON
SERGEANT-AT-ARMS

SURVEYOR to the Duke of Buckingham
Three GENTLEMEN
SCRIBE
CRIER
MESSENGER to Queen Katherine
KEEPER of the Council Chamber
DOCTOR BUTTS
PORTER
Porter's MAN
GARTER KING-OF-ARMS

QUEEN KATHERINE, wife of King Henry, afterwards divorced
GRIFFITH, gentleman usher to Queen Katherine
PATIENCE, Queen Katherine's woman
GENTLEWOMAN ⎫
GENTLEMAN ⎬ attending upon Queen Katherine
ANNE BULLEN
OLD LADY, friend of Anne Bullen

Speaker of the PROLOGUE and EPILOGUE

Lords, ladies, gentlemen; bishops, priests, vergers; judges; Lord Mayor of London, aldermen, citizens; guards, tipstaves, halberdiers; scribes, secretaries; attendants, pursuivants, pages, choristers, musicians, dancers as spirits appearing to Queen Katherine

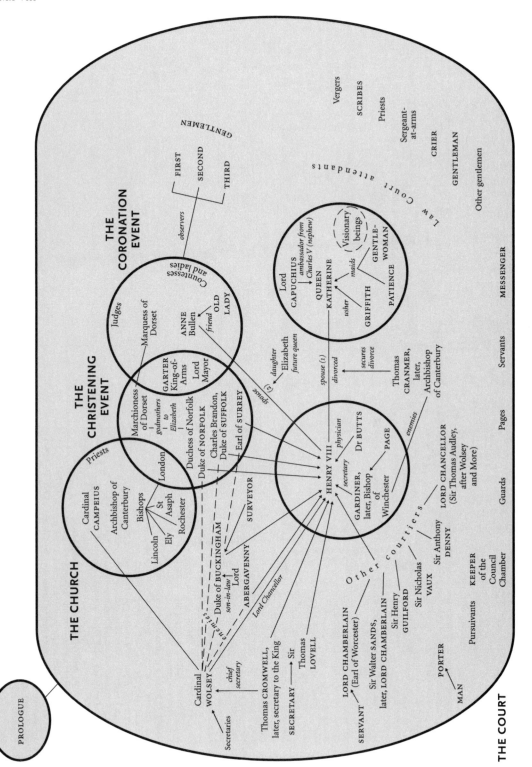

Julius Caesar

DRAMATIS PERSONAE
(as conventionally listed)

JULIUS CAESAR
CALPHURNIA, his wife

MARCUS BRUTUS
CAIUS CASSIUS
CASCA
TREBONIUS
DECIUS BRUTUS
METELLUS CIMBER
CINNA
CAIUS LIGARIUS
} conspirators against Caesar

OCTAVIUS CAESAR
MARK ANTONY
LEPIDUS
} triumvirs after Caesar's death

CICERO
PUBLIUS
POPILIUS LENA
} Senators

FLAVIUS
MARULLUS
} Tribunes of the People

LUCILIUS
MESSALA
YOUNG CATO
VOLUMNIUS
TITINIUS
VARRO
CLITUS
CLAUDIUS
DARDANIUS
} followers of Brutus and Cassius

PORTIA, Marcus Brutus's wife
ARTEMIDORUS
CINNA, a poet
PINDARUS, a servant of Cassius
LUCIUS
STRATO
} servants of Brutus

A Soothsayer
A Poet
A Cobbler
A Carpenter
A Servant of Caesar
A Servant of Antony
A Servant of Octavius
The Ghost of Caesar
Senators
Soldiers, plebeians, attendants and others

Caesar has returned in triumph from the war against Pompey, though tribunes Marullus and Flavius express their discontent to the people at the outcome. During the celebrations, a soothsayer warns Caesar to beware the Ides of March. Cassius and Brutus discuss their fears that Caesar's ambition is to become king, despite learning from Casca that he had refused the people's offer of the crown.

Casca, Cassius, and Cinna meet during a stormy night that has been full of unnatural events, and agree the need to win Brutus over to their cause, and agree the need to win Brutus over to their cause. Brutus meanwhile has been reflecting on the dangers of having Caesar crowned, so when the conspirators arrive at his house he agrees to the assassination plot. He is reluctant to reveal his intentions to his wife, Portia, but yields to her persuasion.

Caesar's wife Calphurnia, frightened by dreams and omens, tries to persuade him not to go to the Capitol. He agrees, but Decius reinterprets the omens in a favourable light, and Caesar leaves, disregarding a warning from Artemidorus on the way. When Caesar refuses to grant Metellus Cimber's suit, the conspirators kill him. Caesar's friend Mark Antony meets the conspirators, who allow him to speak at Caesar's funeral following Brutus's own speech. Brutus justifies their action to the citizens, and receives their support; but Antony's speech rouses them against the conspirators, and Brutus and Cassius flee. The angry citizens kill Cinna the poet, mistaking him for Cinna the conspirator.

Antony forms a triumvirate with Octavius Caesar and Lepidus, and they plan the deaths of the conspirators, and form an army. Brutus and Cassius join forces at Sardis, agreeing to fight together at Philippi after a fierce personal quarrel. Messala brings news of happenings at Rome, and reports that Portia has killed herself. Caesar's ghost visits Brutus at night, and warns him that he will meet him at Philippi.

The two sides parley, then the battle begins. Thinking they are defeated, Cassius orders his servant Pindarus to kill him. He does so, but it is then revealed that the news was misleading, as Brutus had gained an advantage. A further battle leads to Brutus's defeat, and he commits suicide. Antony and Octavius acknowledge Brutus's nobility, and arrange to bury him with honour.

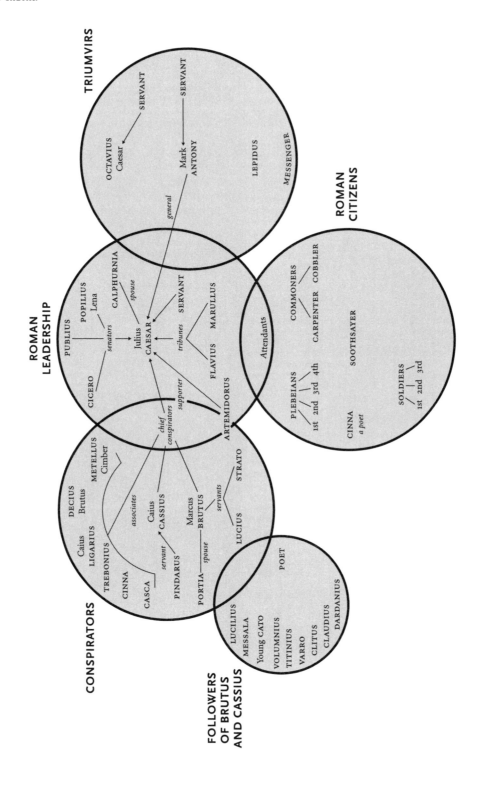

TRIUMVIRS

OCTAVIUS Caesar — SERVANT

Mark ANTONY ← SERVANT

LEPIDUS

MESSENGER

general

ROMAN LEADERSHIP

PUBLIUS

POPILIUS Lena

CALPHURNIA

spouse

senators

Julius CAESAR

SERVANT

tribunes

FLAVIUS

MARULLUS

CICERO

supporter

ARTEMIDORUS

ROMAN CITIZENS

Attendants

COMMONERS

CARPENTER COBBLER

SOOTHSAYER

PLEBEIANS
1st 2nd 3rd 4th

SOLDIERS
1st 2nd 3rd

CINNA
a poet

CONSPIRATORS

chief conspirators

METELLUS Cimber

DECIUS Brutus

associates

Caius LIGARIUS

TREBONIUS

CINNA

CASCA

servant

PINDARUS

Caius CASSIUS

Marcus BRUTUS

servants

STRATO

LUCIUS

PORTIA

spouse

FOLLOWERS OF BRUTUS AND CASSIUS

LUCILIUS

MESSALA

Young CATO

VOLUMNIUS

TITINIUS

VARRO

CLITUS

CLAUDIUS

DARDANIUS

POET

King John

King John refuses the demands of Chatillon, an ambassador from King Philip of France, to yield the English crown to young Arthur, Duke of Bretagne. John then intervenes in a dispute between Robert and Philip Faulconbridge over their inheritance. It emerges that Philip is the bastard son of King Richard. Philip gives up his share of his inheritance in return for service to John, who knights him. The English then prepare to leave for France.

The French King and his ally the Archduke of Austria are meeting to besiege Angiers when they receive news of John's arrival. The two sides parley, and then prepare to fight. Hubert of Angiers refuses to open his gates to either side until one is victor, but the matter is not resolved when after a battle both sides claim victory. The Bastard suggests that the two sides unite to attack Angiers, but Hubert forestalls this by proposing a marriage between John's niece, Blanche, and Lewis the Dauphin. The parties agree to the alliance, and they prepare for the wedding. The Bastard, angry at the way events have turned out, reflects on the madness of it all.

Constance, mother of Arthur, angrily rejects the new alliance. Cardinal Pandulph arrives from Rome, and threatens King Philip with excommunication if he allies himself with John, who is considered a heretic because of his opposition to the Church in England. Philip, after some mind-searching, complies, and the battle recommences. The French are defeated; the Bastard kills the Archduke of Austria, and Arthur is taken prisoner, to Constance's great distress. John orders Hubert to kill Arthur, but Hubert is dissuaded by Arthur's heartfelt pleas. Meanwhile, Pandulph persuades the Dauphin to continue the fight in England.

John celebrates at home with a second coronation, and tries to keep the support of Pembroke, Salisbury, and other nobles. Their fears that John is plotting Arthur's death cause John to regret his request to Hubert, and he is delighted when he learns from Hubert that Arthur is alive. But Arthur falls to his death in trying to escape from prison, and the nobles defect when they find his body, believing that John was responsible for his death.

John is forced to accept Pandulph's demands for reconciliation with Rome, in return for an assurance that he will dissuade the Dauphin from attacking. But Lewis, whose confidence has been boosted by the support of the English

nobles, refuses to do Pandulph's bidding. The French make progress, though a fleet carrying reinforcements is wrecked. The English lords learn from Melun that the Dauphin plans to kill them after his victory, so they return to John. The Dauphin sues for peace. The news arrives too late for John, who has been poisoned by a monk and dies soon after, leaving Prince Henry and the Bastard to reflect on the country's future.

DRAMATIS PERSONAE

(as conventionally listed)

The English Party
KING JOHN
PRINCE HENRY, son of King John, afterwards King Henry III
EARL OF PEMBROKE
EARL OF SALISBURY
EARL OF ESSEX
LORD BIGOT
ROBERT FAULCONBRIDGE, son of Sir Robert Faulconbridge
Philip the BASTARD, his half-brother, revealed as the son of King Richard Coeur-de-Lion
HUBERT, a citizen of Angiers and afterwards a follower of King John
JAMES GURNEY, a follower of Lady Faulconbridge
PETER OF POMFRET, a prophet
A HERALD
AN EXECUTIONER
A MESSENGER

QUEEN ELEANOR, mother of King John
BLANCHE of Spain, niece of King John
LADY FAULCONBRIDGE, widow of Sir Robert Faulconbridge

The French Party
KING PHILIP II
LEWIS THE DAUPHIN
ARTHUR, Duke of Brittaine (Brittany), nephew of King John

ARCHDUKE OF AUSTRIA (Viscount of Limoges)
MELUN, a French lord
CHATILLON, ambassador from France to King John
A HERALD
A MESSENGER

CONSTANCE, mother of Arthur

The Pope's Legate
CARDINAL PANDULPH

Lords, a sheriff, soldiers, executioners, attendants

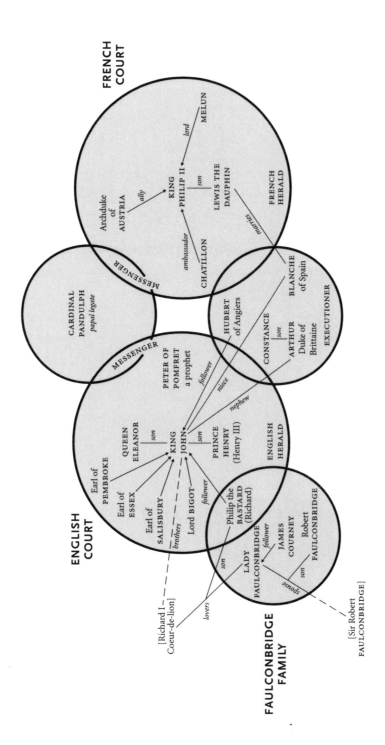

King Lear

Lear, King of Britain, in an attempt to avoid future strife, divides his kingdom between his three daughters. The two eldest, Regan (wife of Cornwall) and Gonerill (wife of Albany), respond to his request for a show of love, but Cordelia is unable to, not wanting to be hypocritical. In a fit of rage, Lear banishes her, and she leaves to marry the King of France. When his adviser Kent attempts to tell Lear he is doing wrong, he too is banished.

The Earl of Gloucester's bastard son Edmund is planning to gain his brother Edgar's lands by disinheriting him. He convinces Gloucester that Edgar is plotting against him, and then persuades his brother to flee from his father's anger. To avoid arrest, Edgar disguises himself as a mad beggar, Poor Tom. Edmund is taken into Cornwall's service.

Lear begins a series of visits to Gonerill and Regan, followed by a disguised and loyal Kent. Kent insults Gonerill's steward Oswald, and Lear takes Kent into his service. Gonerill then quarrels with Lear, who leaves her castle to go to Regan's. Kent is sent ahead, but he quarrels again with Oswald, and is put in the stocks by Regan, who supports her sister's attitude. The sisters meet together with Lear at Gloucester's castle, and tell him to dismiss some and then all of his followers. He leaves the castle in a rage, going out into a violent storm accompanied only by his Fool and Kent. Lear harangues the storm, then meets Poor Tom, whom he treats as a counsellor.

Gloucester tells Edmund of his intention to help Lear, and advises Kent to take Lear to Dover, where Cordelia and a French army are to be found. But Edmund has informed on Gloucester to Cornwall, and when Gloucester returns to his castle he is accused of being a traitor, his eyes are put out, and he is thrown out into the wilderness. In the mêlée, Cornwall is killed by a servant. Edgar encounters his blind father, and, as Poor Tom, journeys with him to Dover, where Gloucester finds Lear.

There is growing animosity between Albany and Gonerill, who is showing increasing affection to Edmund, who also has a liaison with Regan. Oswald, taking a letter from Gonerill to Edmund, encounters Gloucester, but before he can harm him he is killed by Edgar. Lear is found by Cordelia's army, and they are reconciled, but they are then taken prisoner by Edmund's soldiers, and Edmund orders them both to be killed.

Gonerill and Regan both admit their feelings for Edmund. Albany challenges Edmund, and a disguised Edgar appears to fight him. Regan dies, poisoned by Gonerill, and Gonerill takes her own life when her husband hears of her betrayal. Edmund is fatally wounded, and Edgar reveals himself. An order is sent to cancel Lear and Cordelia's execution, but it arrives too late to save Cordelia. Lear carries her in, and soon after dies of a broken heart. Albany abdicates, leaving Kent and Edgar to rule the realm; but Kent announces that he has a journey to go on like his master. Edgar reflects on the future.

DRAMATIS PERSONAE
(as conventionally listed)

LEAR, King of Britain
GONERILL, Lear's eldest daughter
REGAN, Lear's second daughter
CORDELIA, Lear's youngest daughter
DUKE OF ALBANY, husband of Gonerill
DUKE OF CORNWALL, husband of Regan
KING OF FRANCE
DUKE OF BURGUNDY

EARL OF KENT, later disguised as Caius
EARL OF GLOUCESTER
EDGAR, son of Gloucester, later disguised as Poor Tom
EDMUND, bastard son of Gloucester

OSWALD, Gonerill's steward
Lear's FOOL
Three KNIGHTS
CURAN, gentleman of Gloucester's household
GENTLEMEN
Three SERVANTS
OLD MAN, a tenant of Gloucester
Two MESSENGERS
DOCTOR, attendant on Cordelia
A CAPTAIN, follower of Edmund
HERALD
Two OFFICERS

Knights of Lear's train, servants, soldiers, attendants, gentlemen

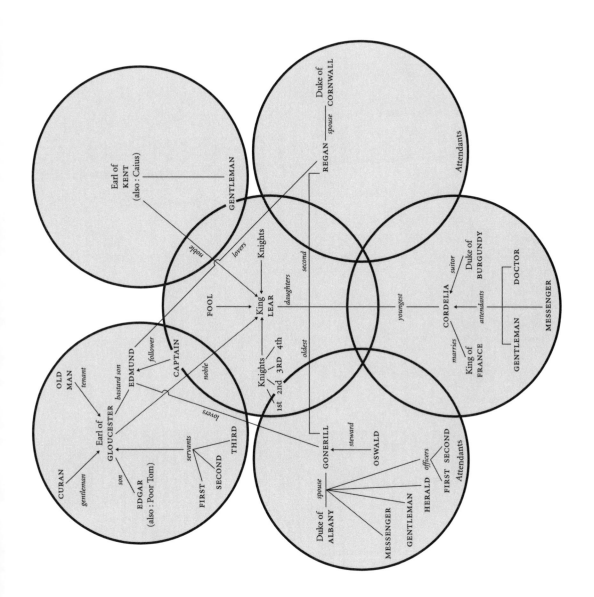

Love's Labour's Lost

DRAMATIS PERSONAE
(as conventionally listed)

KING FERDINAND OF NAVARRE
BEROWNE
LONGAVILLE } lords attending the King
DUMAINE

DON ADRIANO DE ARMADO, a Spanish braggart
MOTE, his page
HOLOFERNES, a schoolmaster
NATHANIEL, a curate
DULL, a constable
COSTARD, a swain
JAQUENETTA, a dairymaid
A FORESTER

THE PRINCESS OF FRANCE
ROSALINE
MARIA } ladies attending the Princess
KATHARINE
BOYET, a French lord
Two LORDS
MARCADE, a messenger

Lords and attendants

The King of Navarre and his three friends, Berowne, Longaville and Dumaine, swear to devote themselves to three years of study, abstaining from all distractions, particularly of the female kind, with only Armado and Costard to entertain them. They are confounded, on signing the vow, when Berowne remembers that the Princess of France and her three ladies, Rosaline, Maria, and Katharine, attended by Boyet, are on an embassy to Navarre's court.

Armado has decided to arrest Costard for being in the company of a woman, thus breaking the King's edict – the woman being Jaquenetta, with whom Armado himself is in love. The ladies arrive, and the King and his lords fall in love with them. Armado frees Costard, on condition he delivers a note to Jaquenetta; Berowne charges Costard with a letter to Rosaline; and the two letters get mixed up.

The four lords enter one by one and voice despair about their love for their particular woman, and one by one are overheard by the others. They decide to tear up their vow, and woo the ladies. They disguise themselves as Russians, but Boyet tells the ladies beforehand, and the ladies change identities with each other. The lords enter, and each woos the wrong woman. They leave, and on their return are mocked by the ladies.

Armado then approaches the schoolmaster Holofernes and curate Nathaniel to join with him, Costard, and the page, Mote, to present the Nine Worthies as entertainment to the nobles. This provides the nobles with many opportunities for comment and laughter. The mood changes when Marcade brings news that the Princess's father has died. As the ladies prepare to leave, the lords affirm that all their expressions of love were genuine, but the Princess claims that everything they said was in jest. The ladies tell the lords that, if they are serious, they must carry out certain tasks for a year, and then return to offer marriage. The lords agree. Armado then presents the learned men in a dialogue between the owl and the cuckoo, representing winter and spring, by way of conclusion.

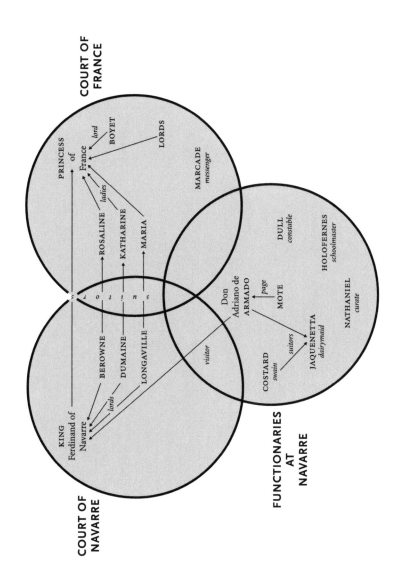

COURT OF FRANCE

PRINCESS of France

lord BOYET

LORDS

ROSALINE
ladies
KATHARINE

MARIA

MARCADE
messenger

joins

DULL
constable

HOLOFERNES
schoolmaster

Don Adriano de ARMADO

page MOTE

NATHANIEL
curate

BEROWNE

DUMAINE

LONGAVILLE

lords

visitor

KING
Ferdinand of
Navarre

COSTARD
swain

suitors

JAQUENETTA
dairymaid

FUNCTIONARIES
AT
NAVARRE

COURT OF
NAVARRE

Macbeth

Three witches anticipate a meeting with Macbeth. King Duncan hears a report of how his generals Macbeth and Banquo defeated the Norwegians and the Scottish rebels. The witches gather on a heath, and meet the generals returning from the war. They predict Macbeth will become Thane of Cawdor, and one day king, and that Banquo will be the father of kings. Macbeth is then greatly impressed when he is greeted by Ross and Angus with the title of Cawdor.

Duncan greets Macbeth with great praise, and proposes to visit him. Macbeth writes to his wife telling her what has happened and the King's plans. Lady Macbeth, seeing the opportunity, plots with her husband how they might kill Duncan when he arrives. After initial enthusiasm, Macbeth changes his mind, but Lady Macbeth persuades him to carry out the deed. He murders Duncan, making it seem that the servants were to blame, and describes the scene to his wife. She finds herself having to return the daggers he has used to Duncan's bedroom, and her hands become covered with blood too. They retire when they hear repeated knocking at the castle gates.

Macduff arrives, and has a brief exchange with the porter. He discovers the dead King, and rouses the porter. Malcolm and Donalbain, fearing blame for their father's death, flee abroad. Soon after, Ross and Macduff reflect on what has happened, and Macduff reports that Macbeth has been made King.

Macbeth is concerned about his position, very aware of the prophecies about Banquo. He arranges with a group of murderers to kill Banquo and his son Fleance; they succeed with Banquo, but Fleance escapes. At a dinner that night, where Banquo would have been the chief guest, Macbeth is terrified by the appearance of Banquo's ghost. Macbeth decides to return to the witches to discover his fate. They tell him that he should fear Macduff, that no man born of woman can hurt Macbeth, and that he will never be vanquished until Birnam Wood comes to Dunsinane. They then show a line of eight kings deriving from Banquo.

Macbeth learns that Macduff has fled to England, so he arranges the death of Macduff's wife and children. Macduff meets Malcolm, who tests Macduff's allegiance to Scotland by first painting a bleak picture of his own personality as a future king, then revealing his true character.

They agree to fight together, with English support. During the meeting, Ross brings news of the murder of Macduff's family. In Scotland, a doctor and gentlewoman observe Lady Macbeth sleepwalking, imagining she cannot cleanse her hands of Duncan's blood.

The Scottish nobles gather, and Malcolm orders his men to camouflage themselves with tree branches as they attack, thus giving the appearance of Birnam Wood approaching Dunsinane. Macbeth learns his wife has died. Fearing no man born of woman, Macbeth fights on, killing Young Seyward, but on meeting Macduff he learns of Macduff's caesarian birth. Macbeth refuses to yield, is killed by Macduff, and Malcolm is proclaimed King.

DRAMATIS PERSONAE

(as conventionally listed)

DUNCAN, King of Scotland
MALCOLM | his sons
DONALBAIN |
MACBETH, Thane of Glamis, later of Cawdor, later King of Scotland
BANQUO
MACDUFF
LENNOX
ROSS | Thanes of Scotland
MENTETH
ANGUS
CATHNESS

FLEANCE, Banquo's son
SEYWARD, Earl of Northumberland
YOUNG SEYWARD, his son
SEYTON, Macbeth's armour-bearer
SON OF MACDUFF
A Captain
An English Doctor
A Scottish Doctor
A Porter
An Old Man

LADY MACBETH

WIFE OF MACDUFF
Gentlewoman attendant on Lady Macbeth
Three Weird Sisters
Three other Witches
HECAT
Apparitions
Three Murderers
Other Murderers

Lords, gentlemen, officers, soldiers, attendants, messengers

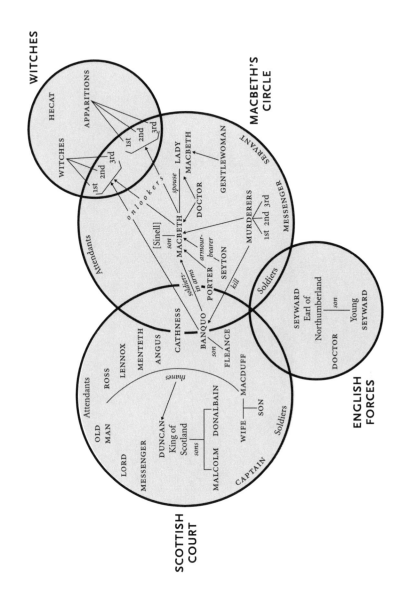

Measure for Measure

Duke Vincentio decides to transfer the government of Vienna to his deputy Angelo, assisted by Escalus, while purporting to leave on a mission. In fact he stays in the city, disguising himself as Friar Lodowick. He explains to Friar Thomas that he has left it to Angelo to implement a strict moral code on his behalf.

Angelo enthusiastically begins the strict enforcement of the laws, including the death penalty for fornication. This affects Claudio, who has made his intended wife Juliet pregnant, and he is arrested for lechery. Claudio asks his friend Lucio to approach Isabella, his sister who has just entered a convent, to intercede for him. At the same time a constable, Elbow, brings Pompey before Escalus, on suspicion of keeping a brothel.

Isabella approaches Angelo, and asks him to be merciful. Angelo refuses, but is taken with Isabella's beauty, and tells her to return. He offers to release Claudio if Isabella will sleep with him, but she refuses. Meanwhile, 'Friar Lodowick' is on his way to visit the prisoners, when he meets Juliet and hears about her and Claudio's love.

'Friar Lodowick' overhears Isabella telling Claudio of Angelo's proposal. Claudio appals her by asking her to agree. The 'Friar' intervenes, suggesting that she meet with Angelo, but that Mariana, a girl Angelo had jilted some years before, should take her place. The 'Friar' arranges a meeting between Isabella and Mariana, who agrees to the plan.

Elbow is taking Pompey to be seen by Angelo, when they encounter Lucio. Pompey asks Lucio for bail, but Lucio refuses. The 'Friar' is present, and engages Lucio in conversation, asking him what he thinks of Duke Vincentio. Lucio paints a black picture of the Duke's character. Escalus and the Provost take Mistress Overdone to prison. Escalus expresses his sympathy for Claudio to the 'Friar'.

The Provost gives Pompey a job assisting Abhorson, the executioner. Both Claudio and an unrepentent murderer, Barnardine, are due to die the next day. 'Friar Lodowick' is present when a message arrives from Angelo; but instead of it being the expected pardon, it is an instruction for Claudio to be executed early in the morning, and for the head to be brought to him. Following the 'Friar's suggestion, the head of a dead prisoner is substituted for Claudio's.

Isabella arrives expecting to be told of Claudio's release.

Instead, 'Friar Lodowick' tells her that Claudio has been executed, and that she should obtain justice from the Duke, who is about to return. Duke Vincentio then arrives in the city, and is approached by Isabella, who accuses Angelo of attempted seduction. The Duke pretends not to believe her, and has her arrested. To support her, Mariana reveals herself and affirms that she has slept with Angelo. 'Friar Lodowick' is called for, and the Duke leaves, returning as the 'Friar' to defend the women. Condemned by Angelo as a false witness, he reveals himself. Angelo admits his guilt, but is pardoned on condition that he marries Mariana. Claudio is reunited with Juliet, and the Duke proposes to Isabella.

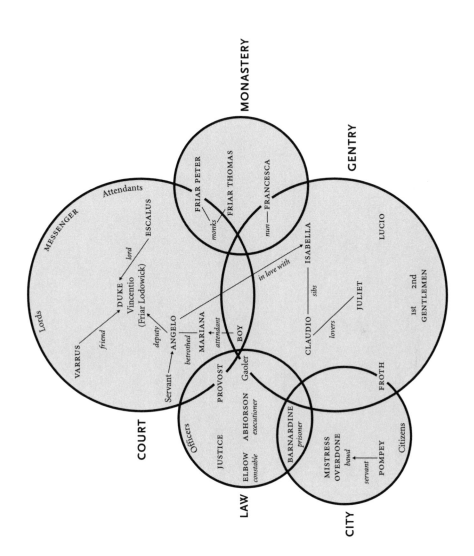

The Merchant of Venice

Bassanio, needing money to become Portia's suitor, asks his friend Antonio for a loan. Antonio's money is tied up in shipments away from Venice, so he approaches Shylock, a money-lender. Shylock agrees to lend the money, on condition that if Antonio does not pay it back by an appointed time, Shylock may cut a pound of flesh from him. Not taking him seriously, Antonio agrees. Bassanio prepares to leave, allowing his friend Gratiano to accompany him.

Launcelot Gobbo, Shylock's servant, decides to leave him, telling his father about his plan. Lorenzo, with the help of Solanio, Salerio and Gratiano, plot to help Jessica, Shylock's daughter, to escape. While Shylock is out meeting with Antonio, Jessica and Lorenzo elope with some of Shylock's money and jewels.

Meanwhile Portia is unhappy with her suitors. Her father has decreed that she must marry the man who chooses from three caskets the one containing her picture. Fortunately for Portia, the Prince of Morocco and the Prince of Arragon both fail, being seduced by the external glamour of the two incorrect caskets. When Bassanio arrives he chooses the right casket. Gratiano falls in love with Nerissa, Portia's waiting-woman.

In Venice, Solanio and Salerio hear that some of Antonio's ships are lost, and Shylock promises to redeem his bond. Another Jew, Tubal, brings him news of Antonio's loss and Jessica's new spending habits.

Portia and Nerissa give Bassanio and Gratiano rings in honour of their love, and make them vow never to be parted from them. Salerio arrives with Lorenzo and Jessica, bringing news that Antonio, unable to repay his loan, has been arrested and that Shylock is demanding his bond. Bassanio returns to Venice with money from Portia to repay the loan. Shylock refuses to listen to Antonio's pleas.

Disguised as a lawyer called Balthasar and his clerk, Portia and Nerissa travel to Venice to defend Antonio against Shylock, leaving Lorenzo and Jessica in charge of the house. At the court, the Duke of Venice hears Shylock present his case, and though he protests he accepts the legal validity of Shylock's claim. Shylock rejects the offer of money from Bassanio. 'Balthasar' arrives and agrees that Shylock must take his bond if he refuses to be merciful, but only if the pound of flesh is exactly excised and no blood is spilt. Realizing this cannot be done, Shylock tries

to leave, but because he has attempted to take the life of Antonio, his goods are confiscated and his life is in Antonio's hands. Antonio allows him to live if he agrees to become a Christian and gives his possessions as a dowry to Lorenzo and Jessica when he dies. Shylock agrees, and leaves.

By way of thanks for their work, the disguised Portia and Nerissa each ask for the rings they had given to Bassanio and Gratiano in their true identities. Reluctantly the men agree. Portia and Nerissa then return to Belmont, where Jessica and Lorenzo are waiting. When Bassanio and Gratiano arrive soon after, along with Antonio, the women trick their men into begging forgiveness for giving their rings away. They then reveal their identities at the court. Antonio learns that his ships are safe. The couples prepare for their marriage.

DRAMATIS PERSONAE

(as conventionally listed)

THE DUKE OF VENICE
THE PRINCE OF MOROCCO } suitors of Portia
THE PRINCE OF ARRAGON
ANTONIO, a merchant of Venice
BASSANIO, his friend, suitor of Portia
PORTIA, the Lady of Belmont
SHYLOCK, a Jew of Venice
GRATIANO
SALERIO } friends of Antonio and Bassanio
SOLANIO
LORENZO, in love with Jessica
NERISSA, Portia's waiting-woman
JESSICA, daughter of Shylock
TUBAL, a Jew of Venice, Shylock's friend
LEONARDO, servant of Bassanio
BALTHASAR } servants of Portia
STEPHANO

LAUNCELOT GOBBO, servant of Shylock
OLD GOBBO, father of Launcelot

Magnificoes of Venice, officers of the Court of Justice, a gaoler, servants, and other attendants

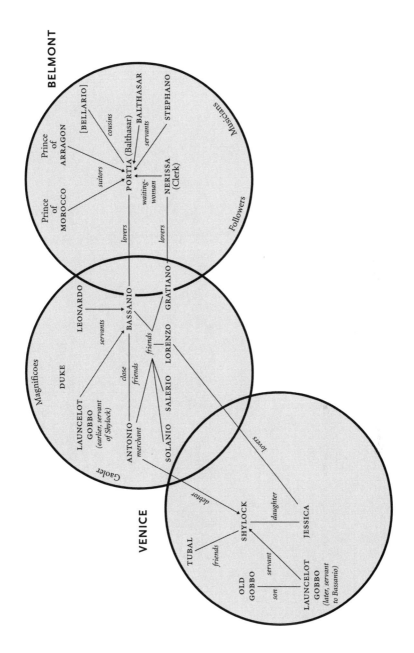

The Merry Wives of Windsor

Justice Shallow, his nephew Slender, and parson Evans are upset at the behaviour of Falstaff and his associates, Nym, Pistol, and Bardolph. Slender is one of several suitors for Anne Page, and her father's choice. Evans sends a message to Mistress Quickly, who is Doctor Caius' housekeeper and a friend of Anne, asking her to help Slender's suit. Caius is also a suitor for Anne, and her mother's choice; so when he hears of Evans' interference, Caius sends him a challenge. Fenton, a third suitor, also approaches Quickly, asking for her help to woo Anne.

Falstaff has met Mistress Ford and Mistress Page and imagines they are taken with him. He writes them both love-letters and asks Nym and Pistol to deliver them. When they refuse, Robin his page takes them. Falstaff dismisses his men, who decide to take revenge by telling Page and Ford of the letters. Page dismisses the matter, but Ford is suspicious of his wife's fidelity and decides to test it. He gets the Host of the Garter to introduce him to Falstaff as 'Master Brook'. The Host also averts the duel between Caius and Evans by directing them to different places.

The two ladies compare their letters, and decide to teach Falstaff a lesson. Mistress Quickly brings Falstaff a message from Mistress Ford, asking him to visit her. Meanwhile, 'Brook' has persuaded Falstaff to act as a go-between to Ford's wife on his behalf, and when he learns about the appointment Falstaff has already made, he is furious, and resolves to catch him. Falstaff is in the middle of expressing his love to Mistress Ford when Mistress Page brings news of Ford's approach. Falstaff escapes by hiding in a laundry basket, and he is dumped in a ditch. Ford is embarrassed in front of his friends to find no one with his wife.

Mistress Quickly brings Falstaff another invitation from Ford's wife. 'Brook' meets Falstaff and learns what happened at the previous encounter, and that a second appointment has been made. Once again Ford arrives during the meeting, but this time Falstaff escapes when the women disguise him as an old aunt. The ladies then tell their husbands what has happened, and all four decide to punish Falstaff.

The women persuade Falstaff to disguise himself as Herne the hunter, and meet them at night in Windsor Park, where they plan to frighten him by dressing everyone as fairies. Page decides to take advantage of the occasion by having Slender elope with Anne; Mistress Page makes a similar arrangement with Caius; and Fenton arranges with the Host to take Anne himself, with her approval. Falstaff is terrified by the sight of the fairies, who pinch and burn him with their tapers. Looking for Anne, Slender and Caius choose fairy boys by mistake, but Fenton finds and marries Anne. All reveal themselves to the discomfited Falstaff. Fenton and Anne return as man and wife, and the Pages accept the marriage.

DRAMATIS PERSONAE
(as conventionally listed)

GEORGE PAGE, a citizen of Windsor
MISTRESS PAGE, his wife
ANNE PAGE, their daughter
WILLIAM PAGE, their son, a schoolboy
FRANK FORD, another citizen of Windsor
MISTRESS FORD, his wife
JOHN } Ford's servants
ROBERT
SIR HUGH EVANS, a Welsh parson
DOCTOR CAIUS, a French physician and suitor for the hand of Anne Page
MISTRESS QUICKLY, Doctor Caius' housekeeper
JOHN RUGBY, Doctor Caius' servant
THE HOST OF THE GARTER INN
Several children of Windsor

FENTON, a young gentleman and suitor for the hand of Anne Page

SIR JOHN FALSTAFF
ROBIN, Falstaff's page
BARDOLPH
PISTOL } Falstaff's followers
NYM

ROBERT SHALLOW, a country Justice of the Peace
ABRAHAM SLENDER, Shallow's nephew and suitor for the hand of Anne Page
PETER SIMPLE, Slender's servant

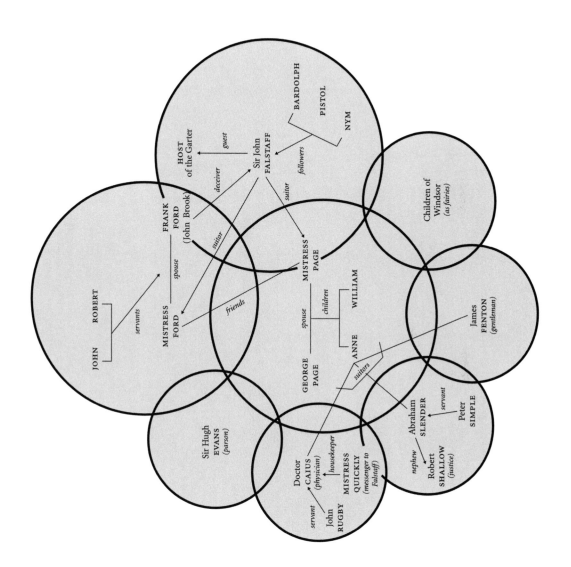

A Midsummer Night's Dream

Duke Theseus and Hippolyta are preparing for their wedding when Egeus arrives with his daughter Hermia, together with Lysander and Demetrius. Hermia and Lysander love each other; but Egeus wants Hermia to marry Demetrius (who is loved by Helena). Theseus insists that Egeus must have his way, and gives Hermia a month to marry Demetrius, or she must become a nun or die. Hermia and Lysander decide to run away and to meet in the forest. Hermia tells Helena of their plans, and she in turn tells Demetrius, in the hope that he will like her the more for telling him. Demetrius chases after the eloping couple, and Helena chases after him.

A group of tradesmen meet to discuss a play on the theme of Pyramus and Thisbe which they want to perform at Theseus' wedding. They plan to rehearse in the forest.

Oberon and Titania, the King and Queen of the Fairies, are arguing over who should have a changeling boy Titania has stolen. Titania will not give him up, so Oberon takes his revenge by having his servant Puck find a special flower whose juice he will squeeze on to Titania's eyes while she is asleep. This will make her fall in love with the first person she sees upon waking. Oberon, seeing Demetrius reject Helena, tells Puck to put the potion on Demetrius' eyes also. But Puck mistakes Lysander for Demetrius, and Lysander wakes to see Helena, with whom he falls in love; he chases after her, leaving Hermia alone.

The rustics begin their rehearsal near the place where Titania is sleeping. Puck gives Bottom an ass's head. Bottom frightens his friends away, and in doing so wakes Titania. She falls in love with him, and Bottom is treated like a lord by the fairy retinue.

Hermia, having lost Lysander, thinks Demetrius has killed him, and when he denies it she goes to look for him. Oberon is furious with Puck for his mistake and tells him to find Helena and bring her to him. Oberon squeezes the flower on to Demetrius' eyes while he sleeps. Lysander enters with Helena, begging for her love, and telling her Demetrius does not love her; Demetrius then wakes, sees Helena, and begs for her love. Hermia enters and is snubbed by Lysander, while Helena thinks all three are tricking her.

Demetrius and Lysander challenge each other to a duel. Oberon gets Puck to imitate the two men's voices, leading

them around until they fall asleep. Puck puts an antidote on Lysander's eyes so that he resumes his love for Hermia. Oberon then releases Titania from her spell, having received the changeling boy from her. Puck removes the ass's head from Bottom.

Theseus and Hippolyta arrive to hunt in the forest, along with Egeus, where they discover the sleeping lovers. They hear their story, and Theseus decrees they shall be married as they wish, despite Egeus' continuing objection. Bottom is reunited with his friends, and they rehearse their play, which has been selected as one of those to be made available as entertainment at the wedding. After supper, Theseus chooses their play, which is presented in front of an audience of all the lovers. They all retire to bed, and Oberon and Titania enter to sing and dance; Oberon blesses the three couples, and Puck is left to address the audience.

DRAMATIS PERSONAE

(as conventionally listed)

THESEUS, Duke of Athens
HIPPOLYTA, Queen of the Amazons, betrothed to Theseus
EGEUS, Hermia's father
HERMIA, Egeus' daughter, in love with Lysander
LYSANDER, loved by Hermia
DEMETRIUS, suitor of Hermia
HELENA, in love with Demetrius
PHILOSTRATE, Theseus' Master of the Revels

OBERON, King of the Fairies
TITANIA, Queen of the Fairies
PUCK, or Robin Goodfellow
PEASEBLOSSOM
COBWEB
MOTH ⎱ Fairies
MUSTARDSEED ⎰

PETER QUINCE, a carpenter; Prologue in the interlude
NICK BOTTOM, a weaver; Pyramus in the interlude
FRANCIS FLUTE, a bellows-mender; Thisbe in the interlude
TOM SNOUT, a tinker; Wall in the interlude
SNUG, a joiner; Lion in the interlude
ROBIN STARVELING, a tailor; Moonshine in the interlude

Other fairies attending on Oberon and Titania
Lords and attendants to Theseus and Hippolyta

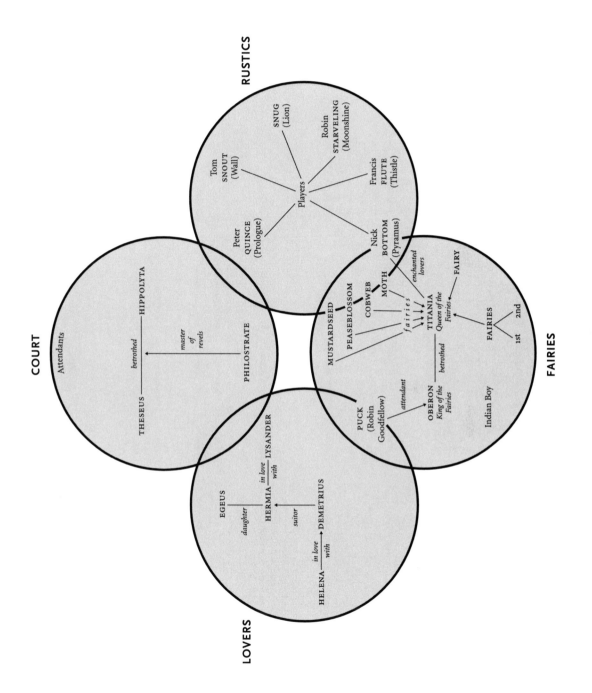

RUSTICS

SNUG
(Lion)

Robin
STARVELING
(Moonshine)

Tom
SNOUT
(Wall)

Francis
FLUTE
(Thistle)

Players

Peter
QUINCE
(Prologue)

Nick
BOTTOM
(Pyramus)

COURT

HIPPOLYTA

Attendants

betrothed

master
of
revels

THESEUS

PHILOSTRATE

FAIRIES

MUSTARDSEED

PEASEBLOSSOM

COBWEB

MOTH

enchanted
lovers

fairies

TITANIA
Queen of the
Fairies

FAIRY

FAIRIES

2nd

1st

betrothed

OBERON
King of the
Fairies

Indian Boy

PUCK
(Robin
Goodfellow)

attendant

LOVERS

LYSANDER

in love
with

EGEUS

HERMIA

daughter

suitor

in love
with

DEMETRIUS

HELENA

Much Ado About Nothing

Don Pedro and his men return after a war to stay at Leonato's house. Benedick continues a prickly relationship with Leonato's niece, Beatrice. Both solemnly declare they will never marry. Claudio falls in love with Hero, Leonato's daughter. Don Pedro agrees to woo Hero for Claudio at a reception that evening. Don John, Pedro's bastard brother, plots with his two men, Borachio and Conrade, to do some wickedness.

At the party, Claudio is told by Don John that Pedro is wooing Hero for himself, but Claudio soon learns that this is not so, and that Hero is his. Further antagonism between Beatrice and Benedick leads Pedro and the others to trick them into falling in love with each other. Leonato, Claudio and Don Pedro let Benedick overhear them speak of how much Beatrice loves him. Later, Hero and Maria let Beatrice overhear their talk about how much Benedick loves her. Both Benedick and Beatrice find they have feelings for each other, and appear love-struck to their friends.

Meanwhile, Don John arranges for Borachio to woo Hero's maid, Margaret, at Hero's window. He informs Pedro and Claudio that Hero is going to be unfaithful that night, and arranges with them to be present. They see Borachio calling Margaret 'Hero', and are taken in.

The Watch, led by Dogberry and Verges, prepare to carry out their evening duties. Borachio is overheard telling Conrade about the plot, and they are arrested. Dogberry and Verges begin an interrogation, but the time of the wedding arrives before they can reach any conclusions. There, Claudio and Pedro reveal the 'truth' about Hero. She faints, and they leave. Don John flees the estate. Leonato harangues Hero, while she protests her innocence. The priest supports her, and suggests they should pretend she has died, until the truth is discovered. Beatrice and Benedick declare their feelings for each other, and Beatrice makes Benedick vow to kill Claudio for shaming Hero.

Leonato and Antonio offer to fight with Claudio, then learn the truth from the Watch. Dogberry and Verges bring Borachio and Conrade to confess before Claudio and Pedro, and Claudio begs forgiveness. Leonato demands that Claudio mourns Hero, and in recompense marries his brother's daughter – who happens to look exactly like Hero. Claudio agrees, and at the ceremony

the real Hero is unveiled. Beatrice and Benedick stop denying their love for each other and agree to be married. As they are all about to dance, they receive news of Don John's capture.

DRAMATIS PERSONAE

(as conventionally listed)

DON PEDRO, Prince of Arragon
BENEDICK, of Padua | young lords, companions of
CLAUDIO, of Florence | Don Pedro
DON JOHN, Don Pedro's bastard brother
BORACHIO | followers of Don John
CONRADE |
LEONATO, Governor of Messina
ANTONIO, his brother, an old man
BALTHASAR, a singer
FRIAR FRANCIS, a priest

HERO, Leonato's daughter
MARGARET | attendants on Hero
URSULA |
BEATRICE, an orphan, Leonato's niece

DOGBERRY, the Constable in charge of the Watch
VERGES, the Headborough, Dogberry's partner in authority
A Sexton, and several Watchmen, under Dogberry's authority

A Boy, servant to Benedick
Attendants and musicians in Leonato's household
Messengers

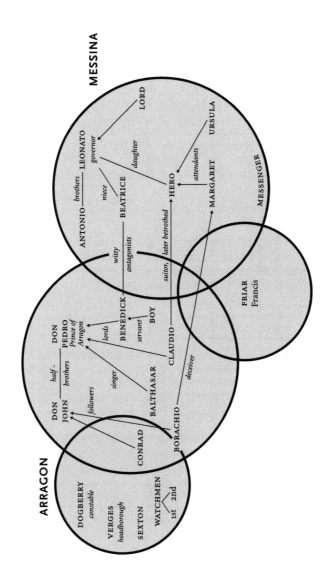

Othello

Provoked by Iago, a jealous Roderigo tells Brabantio of Othello's secret affair and marriage to Brabantio's daughter Desdemona. Othello is brought before the Duke of Venice, where he explains how he wooed Desdemona, and she is brought to the chamber to confirm her willingness to marry him. Othello is then sent to defend Cyprus against the Turks. He prepares to leave, entrusting Desdemona to his ensign, Iago. Iago tells Roderigo that he will obtain Desdemona for him, and persuades him to come to Cyprus, bringing with him his money. Iago reflects on his hatred for Othello, and plots a way to destroy him.

Cassio, Othello's lieutenant, arrives in Cyprus, followed by Iago and Desdemona, and then by Othello. The Turkish fleet is reported lost in a storm, and during the celebrations Iago persuades a reluctant Cassio to drink, then prompts Roderigo to start a fight with Cassio. Cassio becomes angry, and also attacks Montano, the Cyprus governor. Othello is roused, and removes Cassio from office. Iago advises Cassio to work his way back into Othello's affections by speaking to Desdemona.

Cassio asks Iago's wife Emilia to arrange a meeting with Desdemona, and she agrees to do what she can. Iago puts into Othello's mind the thought of Desdemona being unfaithful, and hints at Cassio's role in the infidelity. Emilia finds a handkerchief that Desdemona has dropped, and passes it to Iago. Othello's jealousy grows, and he asks Iago to prove his suspicions. Iago suggests that Desdemona has given Cassio the handkerchief. Othello asks Desdemona for it and is angered when she is unable to produce it. Cassio meanwhile has found the handkerchief in his chamber, and he asks his mistress Bianca to have it copied.

Iago arranges for Othello to overhear a conversation between himself and Cassio, joking about Cassio's mistress Bianca – but making the conversation appear to be about Desdemona. Bianca appears with the handkerchief and returns it to Cassio. This enrages Othello, and he hits Desdemona, much to the dismay of his kinsman Lodovico who has arrived from Venice with letters ordering Othello to return. Othello asks Emilia about Desdemona's unfaithfulness, but she denies any knowledge of it. He then accuses Desdemona to her face, leaving her distraught.

Iago convinces Roderigo that Cassio must die to keep Desdemona in Cyprus. Roderigo attacks Cassio, but is wounded by him. Iago wounds Cassio. Hearing Cassio's cries, Othello thinks Iago has killed him, and leaves to deal with Desdemona. Iago then kills Roderigo. Othello kills Desdemona, strangling her in her bed. Emilia discovers her body, and tells Othello that she was innocent, and that Iago had lied to him; she is stabbed and killed by Iago. Letters are revealed telling of Iago and Roderigo's plot to kill Cassio. Othello, realizing Desdemona was innocent, laments her death, then stabs Iago, but only wounds him. Lodovico gives Cassio power to rule in Cyprus, and is about to arrest Othello, when Othello commits suicide.

DRAMATIS PERSONAE

(as conventionally listed)

OTHELLO, a Moor, General in the Venetian army
DESDEMONA, his wife
CASSIO, his Lieutenant
IAGO, his Ancient
EMILIA, wife of Iago
BIANCA, mistress of Cassio
RODERIGO, in love with Desdemona

THE DUKE OF VENICE
BRABANTIO, a Venetian Senator, Desdemona's father
GRATIANO, his brother
LODOVICO, his kinsman
MONTANO, Governor of Cyprus

Senators of Venice
Gentlemen of Cyprus
Musicians
Officers
A Clown in Othello's household
A Herald
A Sailor
A Messenger
Soldiers, attendants, and servants

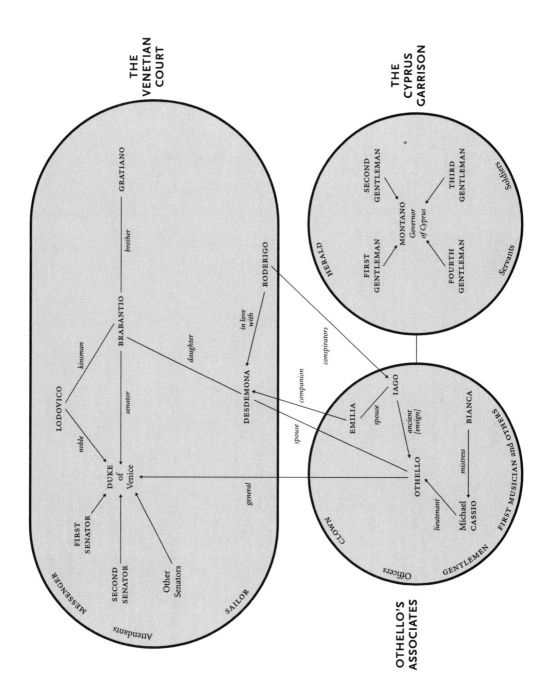

THE VENETIAN COURT

THE CYPRUS GARRISON

OTHELLO'S ASSOCIATES

Pericles

The poet Gower introduces the story and provides a commentary throughout. Antiochus has a riddle which any prince seeking the hand of his daughter has to solve, though the penalty for solving it is death, for the riddle reveals Antiochus' incest with his daughter. Pericles of Tyre interprets the riddle, but returns home, realizing his danger. Antiochus then sends Thaliard to kill him. Pericles puts his friend Helicanus in charge of Tyre, and leaves until he can safely return.

Pericles arrives at Tarsus, and brings food to the starving town. Continuing his voyage, he is shipwrecked, and washed up on the shores of Pentapolis. With the help of fishermen who rescue him, he goes to Simonides' court to enter a tournament as suitor to Thaisa. He wins her heart, but Simonides feigns disapproval to test Pericles, later approving of their marriage.

In Tyre, civil unrest is brewing, as Pericles has been away for so long. Helicanus is persuaded that, if Pericles does not return within a year, he should become lord of Tyre. Receiving this news, Pericles leaves for Tyre. In the middle of a storm, the pregnant Thaisa gives birth to Marina. Thaisa appears to die, and is put overboard in a chest. Pericles then makes for Tarsus. He leaves his daughter and her nurse Lychorida in the care of Cleon and Dionyza, and returns to Tyre. The box containing Thaisa is washed up on the shores of Ephesus. There Cerimon revives her, and, thinking she will never see Pericles again, she becomes a nun at Diana's temple.

Marina grows up to outshine Cleon's daughter, Philoten. Dionyza, jealous of Marina, tells Leonine to murder her. As he is about to kill her, Marina is captured by pirates, who take her to Mytilene and sell her to Pander and Bawd, who intend to use her as a prostitute. Cleon reluctantly agrees to pretend that Marina died naturally. Pericles, returning to Tyre, is distraught at the news.

Pander and Bawd are horrified when Marina keeps persuading her intended customers that what they are trying to do is wrong. The governor Lysimachus attempts to use her, but she makes him see the error of his ways. She persuades Boult, the servant of Pander and Bawd, to let her earn money for them by doing decent work. Pericles and Helicanus arrive in Mytilene, and are greeted by Lysimachus. Helicanus explains how Pericles has withdrawn into himself since he heard of his daughter's death. Lysimachus thinks he knows a maid who will be able to help him. Marina is brought, and makes Pericles speak to her. She reveals her name, and Pericles realizes she is his daughter.

Overcome by joy he falls asleep, whereupon he is visited by the goddess Diana, who tells him to go to her temple in Ephesus and tell his story there. He gives his blessing to a marriage between Marina and Lysimachus, and they leave for Ephesus, where Cerimon reveals the temple nun to be Thaisa. Thaisa reports that her father has died, so Pericles returns with her to Pentapolis to rule, leaving Lysimachus and Marina to rule in Tyre.

DRAMATIS PERSONAE

(as conventionally listed)

John GOWER, the presenter

ANTIOCHUS, King of Antioch
PERICLES, Prince of Tyre
DAUGHTER of Antiochus
THALIARD, a lord of Antioch
MESSENGER of Antioch

HELICANUS } lords of Tyre
ESCANES
Other LORDS of Tyre

CLEON, governor of Tarsus
DIONYZA, wife of Cleon
LORD of Tarsus

Three FISHERMEN of Pentapolis
SIMONIDES, King of Pentapolis
THAISA, daughter of Simonides
Three LORDS of Pentapolis
Five KNIGHTS
MARSHAL

LYCHORIDA, a nurse
Two SAILORS

CERIMON, a lord of Ephesus

Two SERVANTS of Ephesus
PHILEMON, servant of Cerimon
Two GENTLEMEN of Ephesus

LEONINE, servant of Dionyza
MARINA, daughter of Pericles
Three PIRATES

PANDER
BAWD
BOULT, servant of the Pander and the Bawd
Two GENTLEMEN of Mytilene
LYSIMACHUS, governor of Mytilene

SAILOR of Tyre
SAILOR of Mytilene
GENTLEMAN of Tyre
LORD of Mytilene

DIANA, goddess of chastity

Messengers, gentlemen, lords, ladies, attendants, servants, companion of Marina, priestesses, inhabitants of Ephesus

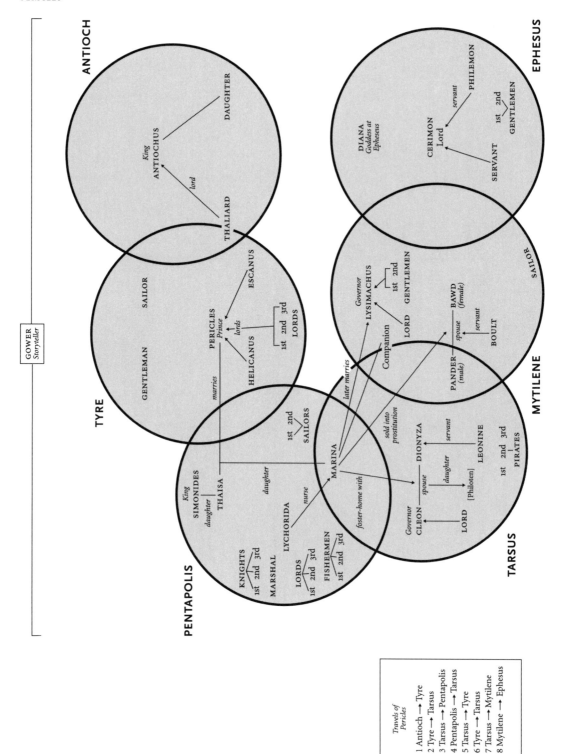

GOWER
Storyteller

Travels of Pericles

1 Antioch → Tyre
2 Tyre → Tarsus
3 Tarsus → Pentapolis
4 Pentapolis → Tarsus
5 Tarsus → Tyre
6 Tyre → Tarsus
7 Tarsus → Mytilene
8 Mytilene → Ephesus

Richard II

Richard hears a dispute between Mowbray and Bolingbroke, each accusing the other of conspiracy in the Duke of Gloucester's murder, and decides the matter must be settled by their single combat. The Duchess of Gloucester laments over her husband's death to John of Gaunt. Just as the contestants are about to fight, Richard halts the duel. He banishes Mowbray for life, then Bolingbroke for ten years, which he reduces to six after hearing Gaunt's pleas. On his deathbed, Gaunt tries to persuade Richard to reform, but is ignored. When he dies, Richard seizes his estates to help pay for his war in Ireland.

Ross, Willoughby, and Northumberland hear of Bolingbroke's return to claim his father's land, and go to join him, as do several other peers. Queen Isabel, upset at Richard's absence, is comforted by Bushy and Bagot, but they and Green decide to flee when they hear of the growing rebellion. Bolingbroke meets the English lords who are supporting him, including Harry Percy. When York arrives, he accuses Bolingbroke of treason. Bolingbroke protests his innocence, saying he has only come to claim what is rightfully his. Bushy and Green are captured and executed.

Thinking Richard dead, the Welsh army disperses. Richard then arrives, and when he learns of the extent of the rebellion, and the support for Bolingbroke, he retreats to Flint castle. Bolingbroke agrees to swear allegiance to Richard if his banishment is repealed and his lands are restored. Richard agrees, and they return to London. The Queen overhears her gardeners commenting on the political situation, and predicting Richard's deposition.

A quarrel breaks out among the peers over who was responsible for Gloucester's death, but this is broken off when York arrives with the news that Richard is willing to yield the throne. When Bolingbroke accepts the offer, the Bishop of Carlisle rebukes him, and is charged with treason. Richard is summoned, and with great grief hands his crown to Bolingbroke. Charged with various crimes, he is sent to the Tower. The Abbot of Westminster, Carlisle and Aumerle, incensed at Bolingbroke's treatment of Richard, begin to plot against Bolingbroke.

The Queen bids farewell to Richard on his way to the Tower, but he is then sent to Pomfret, while she is sent to France. York discovers that Aumerle has a document outlining the plot against Bolingbroke, recently installed as Henry IV. Horrified, York leaves to inform Henry of the conspiracy. The Duchess encourages Aumerle to reach the King first and beg forgiveness before York accuses him, which he manages to do.

Exton, having heard that Henry wishes Richard dead, sets off to Pomfret where he and his associates murder him. He brings Richard's body back to London, but is not welcomed by Henry, who banishes him. Henry then vows to go on a pilgrimage to the Holy Land to expiate his guilt.

DRAMATIS PERSONAE
(as conventionally listed)

KING RICHARD the Second
JOHN OF GAUNT, Duke of Lancaster, King Richard's uncle
Edmund of Langley, DUKE OF YORK, King Richard's uncle
HENRY BOLINGBROKE, Duke of Hereford; John of Gaunt's son; afterwards KING HENRY the Fourth
DUKE OF AUMERLE, Earl of Rutland; the Duke of York's son

THOMAS MOWBRAY, Duke of Norfolk
EARL OF SALISBURY
LORD BERKELEY
BAGOT
BUSHY } followers of King Richard
GREEN

Henry Percy, EARL OF NORTHUMBERLAND
HARRY PERCY (Hotspur), the Earl of Northumberland's son } of Bolingbroke's party

LORD ROSS
LORD WILLOUGHBY
BISHOP OF CARLISLE
SIR STEPHEN SCROOP
LORD FITZWATER
DUKE OF SURREY
ABBOT OF WESTMINSTER
SIR PIERS OF EXTON

LORD MARSHAL
CAPTAIN of the Welsh army
QUEEN ISABEL, King Richard's wife
DUCHESS OF YORK
DUCHESS OF GLOUCESTER, widow of Thomas of Woodstock, Duke of Gloucester (King Richard's uncle)
LADIES attending Queen Isabel

GARDENER
Two GARDENER'S MEN
KEEPER of the prison at Pomfret
SERVINGMAN
GROOM to King Richard

Lords, two Heralds, officers, soldiers, and other attendants

THE ENGLISH COURT

[Edward III]

BOLINGBROKE'S PARTY

RICHARD'S PARTY

1st Son — Edward (The Black Prince)

4th Son — JOHN OF GAUNT Duke of Lancaster

5th Son — Edmund of Langley Duke of YORK

6th Son — spouse [Thomas of Woodstock, Duke of Gloucester]

DUCHESS OF GLOUCESTER

DUCHESS OF YORK — spouse — Servant

son — Edward, Earl of Rutland, Duke of AUMERLE

Bishop of CARLISLE

Abbot of WESTMINSTER

son

Henry BOLINGBROKE, later KING HENRY IV

son

Lord FITZWATER

LORD MAN

Sir Piers EXTON — MAN

SERVINGMAN

Guards

Attendants

Nobles

LORD MARSHAL

HERALDS

FIRST SECOND

CAPTAIN

KEEPER

GROOM

SERVINGMAN

1st 2nd MAN — GARDENER

1st 2nd LADY

QUEEN ISABEL — spouse — RICHARD II

favourites

BUSHY BAGOT GREEN

Lord BERKELEY

Earl of SALISBURY SURREY

lords

Thomas MOWBRAY, Duke of Norfolk

Sir Stephen SCROOP

kills

antagonists

Lord ROSS

Lord WILLOUGBY

Henry Percy Earl of NORTHUMBERLAND

son

Harry PERCY (Hotspur)

Richard III

Richard puts his plan to become king into action, first turning King Edward against his brother Clarence, having Clarence imprisoned and later murdered. He then interrupts Henry VI's funeral procession to woo Lady Anne, who had been betrothed to Henry VI's son (killed by Richard at Tewkesbury), and after initial reluctance she accepts his proposal.

Richard engages in argument with Queen Elizabeth and her family, suggesting that they are to blame for the imprisonment of Clarence and Hastings. Queen Margaret warns them against Richard. King Edward, now very sick, fosters a peace between the peers, but this is disrupted when Richard shocks everyone by announcing Clarence's death. Soon after, Edward dies, leaving the lords and people apprehensive. The Duchess of York, Queen Elizabeth, and Clarence's children all grieve for the death of Edward and Clarence.

Buckingham and Richard begin to plan for the removal of the young Prince Edward and the young Duke of York. They are sent to lodge in the Tower, and no one is allowed to see them. Rivers, Grey, and Vaughan are imprisoned on Richard's instructions, and later executed.

Catesby is sent to establish if Hastings will support Richard's claim to be king. Hastings ignores Stanley's advice to flee, and rejects Richard's advances. At the Council meeting Richard reports a plot against him and arraigns Hastings, who is promptly executed. He persuades the Lord Mayor of the existence of the plot, and obtains his support to influence the people in his favour. When the Mayor arrives to ask Richard to accept the crown, Richard feigns reluctance but finally agrees.

Richard plans the death of the princes, but is angered when Buckingham shows some reserve. He sends Tyrrel to the Tower to kill the princes, and hastens the death of his wife Anne. He then brusquely rejects Buckingham's claim for his promised earldom, and Buckingham decides to desert him. Queen Margaret, Queen Elizabeth, and the Duchess of York all grieve for their lost men and children killed by Richard, but when Richard arrives he persuades an initially antagonistic Elizabeth to accept his proposal of marriage to her daughter.

Dorset flees to join Henry, Earl of Richmond, who has come to England with an army. Many join him, but Buckingham is captured and executed. The ghosts of Richard's victims visit him and Richmond the night before the battle of Bosworth, prophesying doom to Richard and success to Richmond. Richard is killed by Richmond, who takes the crown as Henry VII. He announces his marriage to Elizabeth of York, thus uniting the houses of York and Lancaster.

DRAMATIS PERSONAE

(as conventionally listed)

KING EDWARD IV
EDWARD, Prince of Wales, afterwards King Edward V } sons of King Edward
RICHARD, Duke of York
GEORGE, Duke of Clarence } brothers of King Edward
RICHARD, Duke of Gloucester, afterwards King Richard III
QUEEN ELIZABETH, wife of King Edward
DUCHESS OF YORK, mother of King Edward and his brothers
LADY ANNE, widow of Edward, Prince of Wales, the son of King Henry VI; afterwards married to Richard, Duke of Gloucester
EDWARD PLANTAGENET } children of Clarence
MARGARET PLANTAGENET
QUEEN MARGARET, widow of King Henry VI
HENRY, Earl of Richmond, afterwards King Henry VII
CARDINAL (Thomas Bourchier, Archbishop of Canterbury)
ARCHBISHOP (Thomas Rotheram, Archbishop of York)
JOHN MORTON, Bishop of Ely
DUKE OF BUCKINGHAM
DUKE OF NORFOLK
EARL OF SURREY, son of Norfolk
EARL OF OXFORD
ANTHONY WOODVILLE, Earl Rivers, brother of Queen Elizabeth
MARQUESS OF DORSET } sons of Queen Elizabeth
LORD GREY
EARL OF DERBY (also called Lord Stanley)

LORD HASTINGS
LORD LOVEL
SIR RICHARD RATCLIFFE
SIR WILLIAM CATESBY
SIR JAMES TYRREL
SIR THOMAS VAUGHAN
SIR JAMES BLUNT
SIR WALTER HERBERT
SIR WILLIAM BRANDON
SIR ROBERT BRAKENBURY, Lieutenant of the Tower
KEEPER in the Tower
CHRISTOPHER URSWICK, a priest
JOHN, another priest
TRESSEL, BERKELEY, gentlemen attending on Lady Anne
LORD MAYOR of London
SHERIFF of Wiltshire
GHOSTS of King Henry VI, Edward Prince of Wales, and other victims of Richard
HASTINGS, a Pursuivant
Scrivener
Page
Two Murderers
Lords and other attendants
Messengers, soldiers, bishops, aldermen, citizens

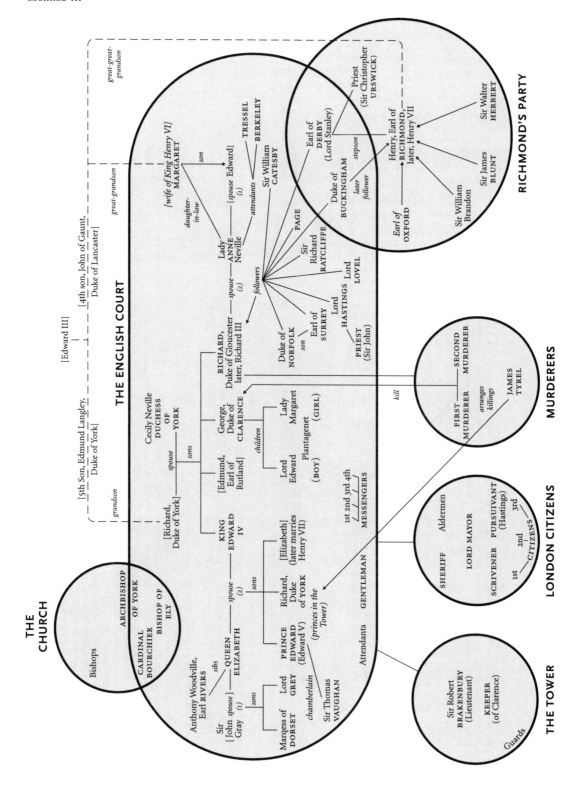

THE CHURCH

Bishops

CARDINAL BOURCHIER
ARCHBISHOP OF YORK
BISHOP OF ELY

[Edward III]

[5th Son, Edmund Langley, Duke of York]

[4th son, John of Gaunt, Duke of Lancaster]

grandson

great-grandson

great-grandson

great-great-grandson

THE ENGLISH COURT

[wife of King Henry VI] MARGARET

son

daughter-in-law

[spouse Edward] Lady ANNE Neville

TRESSEL
BERKELEY
Sir William CATESBY

attendants

spouse (1)

spouse (2)

RICHARD, Duke of Gloucester later, Richard III

followers

PAGE
Sir Richard RATCLIFFE
Lord LOVEL
Lord HASTINGS
Earl of SURREY
son
Duke of NORFOLK
PRIEST (Sir John)

Cecily Neville DUCHESS OF YORK

spouse

sons

[Richard, Duke of York]

George, Duke of CLARENCE

Lady Margaret Plantagenet (GIRL)

Lord Edward Plantagenet (BOY)

children

[Edmund, Earl of Rutland]

KING EDWARD IV

1st 2nd 3rd 4th MESSENGERS

GENTLEMAN

Attendants

Anthony Woodville, Earl RIVERS

sibs

QUEEN ELIZABETH

[John spouse] Sir Gray (1)

sons

Marqess of DORSET
Lord GREY
chamberlain
Sir Thomas VAUGHAN

spouse (2)

sons

[Elizabeth] (later marries Henry VII)

Richard, Duke of YORK

PRINCE EDWARD (Edward V)

(princes in the Tower)

RICHMOND'S PARTY

Priest (Sir Christopher URSWICK)

Sir Walter HERBERT

Earl of DERBY (Lord Stanley)

stepson

Duke of BUCKINGHAM

later follower

Earl of OXFORD

later

Henry, Earl of RICHMOND, later, Henry VII

Sir James BLUNT

Sir William Brandon

MURDERERS

SECOND MURDERER

FIRST MURDERER

arranges killings

JAMES TYREL

kill

LONDON CITIZENS

SHERIFF
Aldermen
LORD MAYOR
SCRIVENER
PURSUIVANT (Hastings)
1st 2nd 3rd CITIZENS

THE TOWER

Sir Robert BRAKENBURY (Lieutenant)

KEEPER (of Clarence)

Guards

Romeo and Juliet

An ongoing feud between the Capulets and the Montagues breaks out again on the streets of Verona. Both sides are warned by Prince Escalus that they must not further disturb the peace, on pain of death.

Romeo, love-sick for Rosaline, is comforted by his friend Benvolio. Capulet tells Paris that he may not marry his daughter Juliet until she is older. Romeo and his friends learn of a party being held by the Capulets, and decide to go to it as masquers. At the party, Tybalt sees Romeo, but is prevented from fighting him by Capulet. Romeo meets Juliet, and they instantly fall in love. After leaving the party, Romeo eludes his friends, returns to meet Juliet, and they exchange vows of love. Romeo tells Friar Laurence what has happened, and he consents to marry them.

Benvolio tells Mercutio that Tybalt has sent Romeo a challenge. Romeo joins them, and is visited by the Nurse, who is told the marriage plan. She tells Juliet, who then goes to Friar Laurence's cell, and the lovers are married. Tybalt, looking for Romeo, finds Benvolio and Mercutio. Romeo returns, and is challenged by Tybalt, but refuses to fight. Mercutio draws on Tybalt and is fatally wounded. Tybalt then fights with Romeo, and is killed. Romeo flees, and Benvolio reports what has happened to the Prince, who banishes Romeo. The Nurse tells Juliet of Romeo's banishment, and promises to bring him to her. The Friar tells a distraught Romeo he is banished, but advises him to visit Juliet secretly, then to leave for Mantua.

Capulet tells Paris he may marry Juliet in three days, and Lady Capulet brings the news to Juliet, who has just bid Romeo a hasty farewell. Juliet refuses to marry Paris, persisting in the face of her father's anger. She goes to the Friar for help, and finds Paris there arranging their marriage. After he leaves, the Friar devises a plan: he will give her a drink that will make her appear dead and thus avoid the marriage, and will write to Romeo to tell him; they can then elope to Mantua.

Juliet tells her father she will now marry Paris, and Capulet brings the wedding forward to the next day. Juliet retires, and drinks the liquid. When her 'body' is discovered, all mourn, and she is taken to the family crypt. In Mantua, Balthasar tells Romeo that Juliet is dead. He vows to lie dead next to her that night, and obtains a poi-

son from an apothecary. Friar John tells Friar Laurence that he was unable to deliver Laurence's letter to Romeo. Realizing the danger, Laurence leaves to tell Juliet what has happened.

Paris goes to Juliet's tomb to mourn her, and encounters Romeo. They fight, and Romeo kills Paris. Romeo then drinks the poison, and dies by Juliet. The Friar arrives to see Romeo dead and Juliet waking. She refuses to leave, and kills herself with Romeo's dagger. Officers arrive, and rouse the families and the Prince. The Friar explains what has happened. Montague and Capulet agree to make peace with each other.

DRAMATIS PERSONAE
(as conventionally listed)

ESCALUS, Prince of Verona

MERCUTIO, kinsman of the Prince and friend of Romeo

PARIS, a young count, kinsman of the Prince and Mercutio, and suitor of Juliet

Page to Count Paris

MONTAGUE, head of a Veronese family at feud with the Capulets

LADY MONTAGUE

ROMEO, son of Montague

BENVOLIO, nephew of Montague and friend of Romeo and Mercutio

ABRAM, servant of Montague

BALTHASAR, servant of Montague attending on Romeo

CAPULET, head of a Veronese family at feud with the Montagues

LADY CAPULET

JULIET, daughter of Capulet

TYBALT, nephew of Lady Capulet

An old man of the Capulet family

Nurse of Juliet, her foster-mother

PETER, servant of Capulet attending on the Nurse

SAMPSON
GREGORY
ANTHONY } of the Capulet household
POTPAN
A Clown
Servingmen

FRIAR LAURENCE, a Franciscan

FRIAR JOHN, a Franciscan

An Apothecary of Mantua

Three Musicians (Simon Catling, Hugh Rebeck, James Soundpost)

Members of the Watch

Citizens of Verona, maskers, torchbearers, pages, servants

Chorus

CHORUS

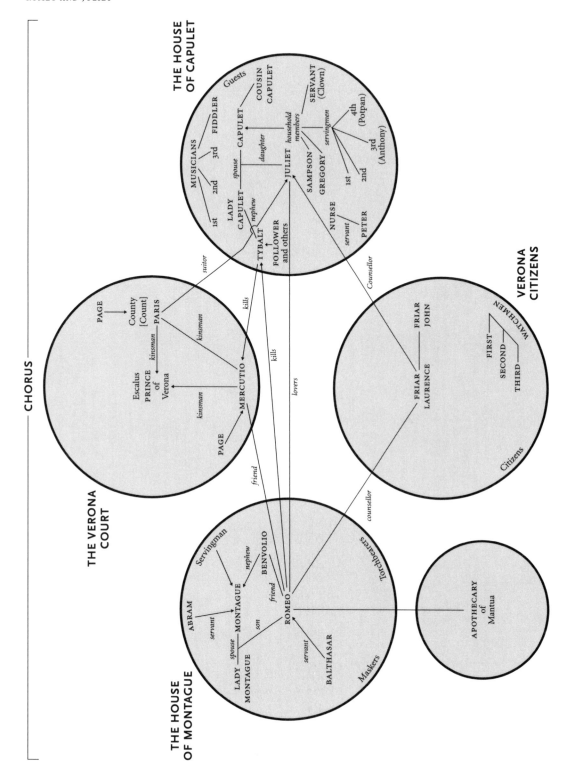

THE HOUSE OF CAPULET

Guests

COUSIN CAPULET

MUSICIANS
1st   2nd   3rd   FIDDLER

SERVANT (Clown)

CAPULET

LADY CAPULET

household members

servingmen

4th (Potpan)

3rd (Anthony)

spouse

daughter

nephew

JULIET

SAMPSON   GREGORY

1st   2nd

NURSE

servant   PETER

TYBALT

FOLLOWER and others

THE VERONA COURT

PAGE

County [Count] PARIS

kinsman

Escalus PRINCE of Verona

kinsman

MERCUTIO

kinsman

PAGE

suitor

kinsman

kills

kills

Counsellor

lovers

VERONA CITIZENS

FRIAR JOHN

FRIAR LAURENCE

WATCHMEN
FIRST
SECOND
THIRD

Citizens

counsellor

friend

THE HOUSE OF MONTAGUE

Servingman

ABRAM

servant

MONTAGUE

nephew

BENVOLIO

LADY MONTAGUE

spouse

son

friend

ROMEO

servant

BALTHASAR

Torchbearers

Maskers

APOTHECARY of Mantua

The Taming of the Shrew

A lord comes across a drunken and comatose Christopher Sly, and conceives the idea of bringing him back to his house and treating him as a nobleman when he awakes, to see what happens. The lord has his servants dress and act appropriately, and convinces Sly that he has come to his senses after a long illness. A passing troupe of players perform a play for him, during which Sly shows an occasional bored reaction.

The play begins with Lucentio arriving in Padua to study. As soon as he sees Bianca, the younger daughter of the rich merchant Baptista, he falls in love with her. Bianca is also being wooed by Gremio and Hortensio, but Baptista will not allow her to be married until a husband is found for his older daughter Katherina, 'the shrew', whose aggressive character has made this unlikely. Gremio and Hortensio decide to join forces to find a husband for Katherina. Lucentio changes identities with his servant Tranio, and gets a job as Bianca's tutor in order to be close to her.

Petruchio of Verona is visiting Hortensio, and agrees to help his friend by marrying Katherina, especially when he learns the size of her dowry. At his first meeting with her, he takes no argument from her and insists on marrying her despite her angry protestations. Baptista willingly agrees, leaving Bianca's suitors to argue their respective cases among themselves. Lucentio makes progress with Bianca in his guise as tutor.

Petruchio arrives late for his wedding, badly dressed, behaves badly during the service, and afterwards refuses to stay for the reception, despite Katherina's desire that he attend. He takes her back to his country house, where he refuses to let her eat, sleep, or dress well until she submits to his every whim.

Hortensio and Gremio see Bianca courting the tutor Lucentio and decide in disgust to court her no longer. Hortensio decides to marry a rich widow. Tranio persuades a passing schoolmaster to play the part of Lucentio's father, Vincentio, and confirm to Baptista that Lucentio has a wealthy background. Lucentio elopes with Bianca and they are married. On their way back to Padua, Katherina and Petruchio meet the real Vincentio. They arrive at Lucentio's house, but the schoolmaster and Tranio refuse to acknowledge him, calling him a villain. The real Vincentio is about to be taken off to prison when

Lucentio arrives, revealing his marriage and the identity changes. The parents accept the situation.

At a combined wedding-reception for Petruchio, Lucentio, and Hortensio, the three husbands wager among themselves which of their wives, who are in another room, will be the most obedient and come at their bidding. Katherina, now a changed person, is the only one to do so. She remonstrates with the other women, lecturing them on the merits of wifely obedience.

DRAMATIS PERSONAE

(as conventionally listed)

Induction

CHRISTOPHER SLY, a drunken tinker
The Hostess of a country alehouse
A Lord
Page, Huntsmen, and Servants attending on the Lord
A company of strolling Players

The Taming of the Shrew

BAPTISTA MINOLA, a wealthy citizen of Padua

KATHERINA, the Shrew, elder daughter of Baptista
PETRUCHIO, a gentleman of Verona, suitor for the
    hand of Katherina
GRUMIO, Petruchio's personal lackey
CURTIS, Petruchio's servant, in charge of his country
    house
A Tailor
A Haberdasher
Five other servants of Petruchio

BIANCA, the Prize, younger daughter of Baptista
GREMIO, a wealthy old citizen of Padua, suitor for the
    hand of Bianca
HORTENSIO, a gentleman of Padua, suitor for the
    hand of Bianca
LUCENTIO, a gentleman of Pisa, in love with Bianca

TRANIO, Lucentio's servant and confidant
BIONDELLO, Lucentio's second servant
VINCENTIO, a wealthy citizen of Pisa, father of
    Lucentio
A Pedant of Mantua
A Widow, in love with Hortensio
Servant attending on Baptista

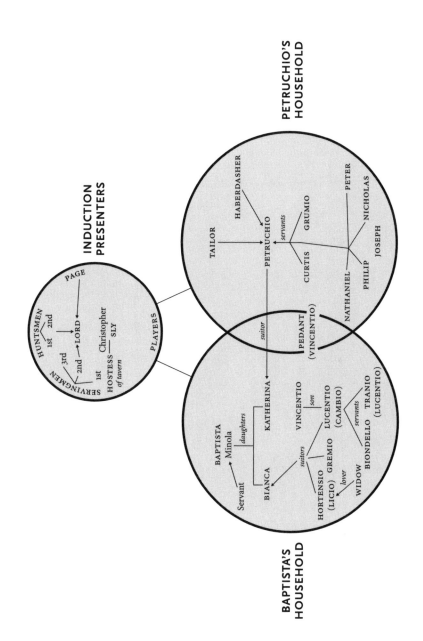

The Tempest

DRAMATIS PERSONAE

(as conventionally listed)

ALONSO, King of Naples
SEBASTIAN, his brother
PROSPERO, the rightful Duke of Milan
ANTONIO, his brother, the usurping Duke of Milan
FERDINAND, son of the King of Naples
GONZALO, an honest old councillor
ADRIAN ⎱ lords
FRANCISCO ⎰ lords
CALIBAN, a savage and deformed slave
TRINCULO, a jester
STEPHANO, a drunken butler
Master of a ship
Boatswain
Mariners
MIRANDA, daughter of Prospero
ARIEL, an airy spirit
IRIS ⎱
CERES ⎰ characters in the masque, played by Ariel and
JUNO ⎰ other Spirits
Nymphs ⎰
Reapers ⎰

Additional Spirits in the service of Prospero

A ship carrying Alonso, King of Naples, his son Ferdinand, Antonio, and other nobles, is wrecked in a storm created by the spirit Ariel, under the magic art of Prospero. Prospero's daughter Miranda, afraid for the voyagers, is told they are safe. Prospero explains to her that he is the rightful Duke of Milan, usurped by Antonio, and that they had arrived on their island many years before after being sent out to sea by some of those whom he now has in his power.

As Miranda sleeps, Ariel reports that the lords are on the island as he had commanded, with Ferdinand separated from the others. Caliban, a savage inhabitant of the island who is under the power of Prospero, expresses his hostility to Prospero, but is forced to do his bidding. Prospero gets Ariel to lead Ferdinand across the island so that he meets Miranda, and they fall in love. To test his worth, Prospero makes Ferdinand carry out menial tasks.

Alonso and the lords begin their search for Ferdinand, though they fear he has been drowned. Antonio persuades Alonso's brother Sebastian to kill the King and claim his throne, but Ariel intervenes and stops them. Caliban encounters Alonso's jester Trinculo and butler Stephano, whom he decides to serve with the aim of persuading them to kill Prospero. They get drunk, and Prospero sends Ariel to confuse and play tricks on them.

A magical banquet is placed before the lords. As they prepare to eat, Alonso, Sebastian, and Antonio are fiercely reprimanded for their past deeds by Ariel. Alonso runs off, followed by the others. Prospero brings Iris, Juno, and Ceres into a ceremony celebrating Ferdinand and Miranda's betrothal. He has Ariel and other spirits chase Caliban, Stephano, and Trinculo away through the marshes, to foil their plot against him. He then vows to give up his magical powers once he has achieved his aims, and to free Ariel, who has been begging for liberty.

Ariel leads the lords to Prospero, and they stand in a trance before him. He rouses them, and they beg forgiveness, which Prospero grants, and he is restored to his dukedom. Ferdinand and Miranda are revealed to them. Ariel leads in the sailors from their ship, and then Caliban, Trinculo, and Stephano. Caliban regrets his service to Stephano and Trinculo, and promises to behave. Prospero sets Ariel free, and finally asks the audience for his own release, through their applause.

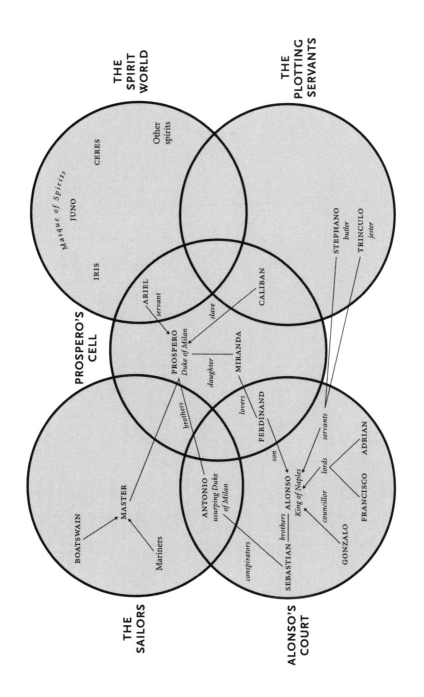

THE SPIRIT WORLD

THE PLOTTING SERVANTS

Masque of Spirits

CERES

Other spirits

JUNO

IRIS

STEPHANO
butler

TRINCULO
jester

ARIEL
servant

CALIBAN

slave

PROSPERO'S CELL

PROSPERO
Duke of Milan

MIRANDA

daughter

servants

lovers

FERDINAND

brothers

ADRIAN

son

MASTER

lords

ALONSO
King of Naples

FRANCISCO

BOATSWAIN

ANTONIO
usurping Duke
of Milan

councillor

GONZALO

Mariners

SEBASTIAN brothers

conspirators

THE SAILORS

ALONSO'S COURT

Timon of Athens

A poet, painter, and various merchants of Athens are discussing the things they have prepared for Timon, a wealthy nobleman known for his lavish entertainment. Timon arrives, displaying his generosity by paying a fine on behalf of Ventidius and offering a dowry to his servant Lucilius. Apemantus, a misanthropic observer, warns Timon about his excesses, and tells him that his friends are insincere, but Timon ignores him and throws a lavish party, giving his guests expensive gifts.

His steward Flavius expresses his concern, knowing that Timon is nearly bankrupt. A senator sends his servant to call in a debt from Timon, and other servants join in demanding that their masters' bills are paid. Flavius finally makes Timon see that he has nothing left, so Timon sends his servants to his friends to ask for help. They approach Lucullus and Lucius, both of whom offer their excuses and deny him any assistance, to the shocked disbelief of some passing strangers. Sempronius also denies him. When everyone starts pressing Timon personally for payment, he decides to hold a final feast for his friends, whom he now recognizes as false. When they arrive at his house he offers them warm water and stones, which he throws at them, driving them away. He then turns his back on Athens. His servants are dismissed, but Flavius expresses a wish to continue as Timon's steward.

Meanwhile, the Athenian captain Alcibiades has approached the senators asking for mercy to be shown to one of his men who is under sentence of death. The senators refuse to be lenient, and when Alcibiades remonstrates with them they banish him.

Timon finds himself a cave to live in near the shore, and while digging for roots discovers gold. Alcibiades with his army passes by, on his way to take revenge on Athens, and accompanied by his two mistresses, Phrynia and Timandra. Timon gives them all some gold, enabling Alcibiades to pay his soldiers, but rejects the kindness they display towards him. Apemantus arrives, and there is a bad-tempered discussion of Timon's situation and their respective characters, before Apemantus is driven away. Bandits visit Timon, and he gives them gold. Flavius also finds him, and Timon recognizes his honesty. The poet and painter come to flatter him, and are also driven away.

Senators arrive, offering Timon absolute power in Athens if he will return with them to defend the city against Alcibiades, but he refuses, and indicates his forthcoming death. The senators plead with Alcibiades, who agrees to spare the city if his enemies are punished. A soldier finds the epitaph Timon has written about himself, and brings it to Alcibiades, who reads it to all as he enters the city.

DRAMATIS PERSONAE
(as conventionally listed)

TIMON, a noble Athenian
FLAVIUS, Timon's steward

FLAMINIUS ⎫
LUCILIUS ⎬ servants of Timon
SERVILIUS ⎪
and others ⎭

ALCIBIADES, an Athenian captain

PHRYNIA ⎫ mistresses of Alcibiades
TIMANDRA ⎭

APEMANTUS, a churlish philosopher
A Fool
A Page
Three Strangers

LUCIUS ⎫
LUCULLUS ⎬ flattering lords
SEMPRONIUS ⎭

VENTIDIUS, one of Timon's false friends
Other Lords

CAPHIS ⎫
PHILOTUS ⎪
TITUS ⎬ servants of the flattering lords and of
HORTENSIUS ⎪ Timon's creditors
and others ⎭

A Poet
A Painter
A Jeweller
A Merchant
An Old Athenian
Seven Senators
Three Bandits

Soldier
Two Messengers
Cupid and Amazons in the masque
Other soldiers, officers, and attendants

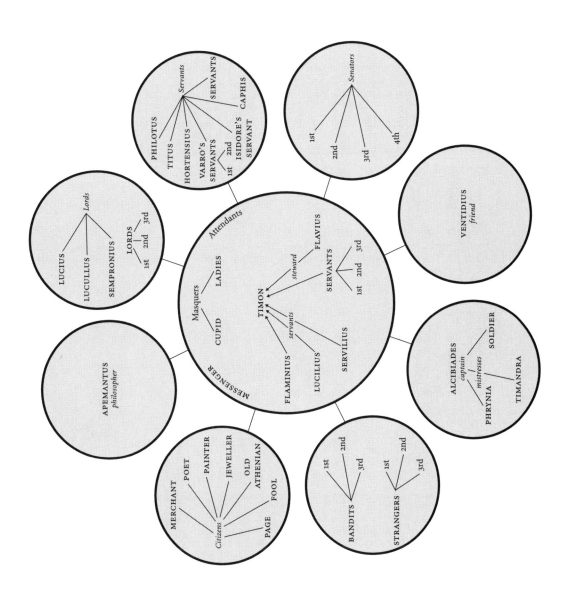

PHILOTUS
TITUS
HORTENSIUS
VARRO'S SERVANTS
1st 2nd
ISIDORE'S SERVANT
Servants
SERVANTS
CAPHIS

Senators
1st
2nd
3rd
4th

VENTIDIUS
friend

LUCIUS
LUCULLUS
SEMPRONIUS
Lords
LORDS
1st 2nd 3rd

Attendants
LADIES
Masquers
CUPID
MESSENGER
FLAMINIUS
LUCILIUS
SERVILIUS
servants
TIMON
steward
FLAVIUS
SERVANTS
1st 2nd 3rd

APEMANTUS
philosopher

ALCIBIADES
captain
SOLDIER
mistresses
PHRYNIA
TIMANDRA

MERCHANT
POET
PAINTER
JEWELLER
OLD ATHENIAN
Citizens
PAGE
FOOL

BANDITS
1st 2nd 3rd
STRANGERS
1st 2nd 3rd

Titus Andronicus

Saturninus and Bassianus are in contention for the title of emperor, but dismiss their followers on the arrival of Titus, returning victorious with his sons from war with the Goths. His prisoner Tamora pleads for the life of one of her sons, Alarbus, but Titus has him killed. Titus is offered the emperorship on behalf of the people by his brother Marcus, but he confers the title on Saturninus, who then asks for Titus' daughter Lavinia to be his wife. Because she is already betrothed to Bassianus, Titus' sons stop Saturninus taking her. Titus calls them traitors, and kills his son Mutius in the struggle.

Saturninus then claims Tamora as his bride, and she vows revenge on Titus. Aaron persuades her sons Chiron and Demetrius to ravish Lavinia. Bassianus and Lavinia discover Tamora with her Moorish lover Aaron, but before Bassianus can tell Saturninus, he is killed by Chiron and Demetrius, and his body thrown into a pit. They then rape Lavinia, removing her tongue and hands so that she cannot tell anyone what has happened to her.

Aaron leads Titus' sons Martius and Quintus to the pit where Bassianus' body lies, and traps them there. They are accused of the murder, and sentenced to death. Aaron persuades Titus that if someone removes one of their own hands and sends it to Saturninus it will save his sons' lives, but after Titus sends his own hand it is immediately returned along with the heads of his two sons. Lucius vows revenge, and leaves to raise an army from among the Goths.

Titus, apparently beginning to go mad, argues with Marcus for killing a fly. With the help of Young Lucius and Marcus, Lavinia informs them who attacked her. Planning revenge, Titus sends weapons to Tamora's sons, fires arrows with letters attached to them at Saturninus' court, then sends a Clown to Saturninus with a knife wrapped up in a letter.

Aaron is given his newborn baby, born to Tamora. Tamora wants the Moorish-looking child killed, to avoid Saturninus finding out about their affair. Aaron takes the baby away, replacing it with a white baby. The Goths capture Aaron and his baby, and Lucius (now their leader) threatens the child with death. Aaron agrees to tell Lucius the truth about events, if he spares the baby's life.

Tamora, Demetrius and Chiron disguise themselves as Revenge, Murder, and Rape, respectively, to trick Titus, whom they believe to be mad, into sending for Lucius. They think they have succeeded in fooling him, but, when Tamora leaves, Titus kills Chiron and Demetrius with Lavinia's help. He then invites Saturninus and Tamora to a parley with Lucius at a dinner, having cooked Chiron and Demetrius in a pie. He kills Lavinia, then reveals to Tamora that she has been eating her own sons, and stabs her. Saturninus kills Titus, and is then killed by Lucius.

Marcus and Lucius relate to the people what has happened, and Lucius is proclaimed Emperor. An unrepentant Aaron is sentenced to death; the Andronici are given proper burial; and Tamora's body is thrown to the animals.

DRAMATIS PERSONAE
(as conventionally listed)

SATURNINUS, newly elected Emperor of Rome
BASSIANUS, brother of Saturninus

Titus ANDRONICUS, Roman general
Marcus ANDRONICUS, Roman Tribune, brother of Titus
LUCIUS ⎤
QUINTUS ⎢ sons of Titus Andronicus
MARTIUS ⎢
MUTIUS ⎦
LAVINIA, daughter of Titus Andronicus
YOUNG Lucius, a boy, son of Lucius and grandson to Titus Andronicus
SEMPRONIUS ⎤
CAIUS ⎢ kinsmen of Titus Andronicus
VALENTINE ⎦
AEMILIUS, a noble Roman

TAMORA, Queen of the Goths, afterwards Empress of Rome
ALARBUS ⎤
DEMETRIUS ⎢ Tamora's sons
CHIRON ⎦
AARON, a Moor, and Tamora's lover

NURSE
CLOWN
MESSENGER

Senators, tribunes, Roman soldiers, attendants, Goths

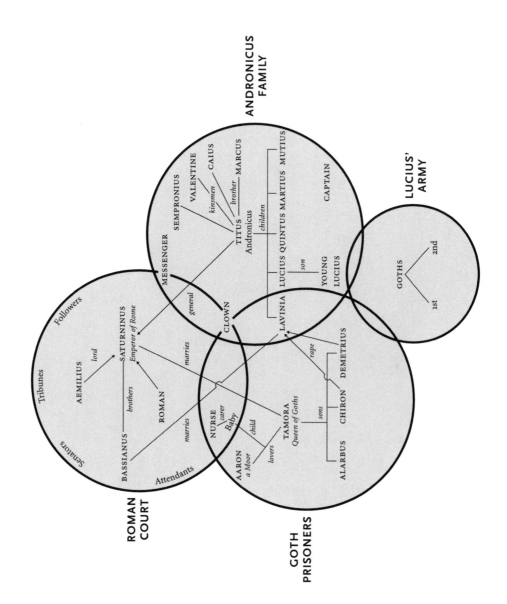

Troilus and Cressida

Troilus, the youngest son of the Trojan King Priam, is in love with Cressida, the niece of Pandarus, through whom he is hoping to arrange a meeting. While Cressida watches the nobles and soldiers pass by, Pandarus draws her attention to Troilus, and she is attracted to him. Pandarus begins to liaise between the two.

The Greek commander Agamemnon discusses the unsatisfactory military situation with Ulysses, Nestor and other leaders, noting especially the way Achilles has become proud and temperamental, along with Ajax, who spends his time exchanging insults with Thersites, a hanger-on at the camp and observer of events. Aeneas arrives with a challenge from Hector to fight any Greek in single combat. They recognize that the challenge is aimed at Achilles, but they put Ajax forward as their champion. Agamemnon and the other lords visit Achilles' tent, but Achilles refuses to speak to them. The lords heap praise on Ajax instead.

The Trojans consider the conditions of a Greek proposal for peace, which involves the return of Helen, whose abduction caused the war. They reject the proposal, ignoring Cassandra's prophecies of doom. Pandarus visits Paris to ask him to present Troilus' apologies if Priam should ask for him at supper. Paris and Helen suspect a liaison between Troilus and Cressida, though Pandarus denies it. He then brings Cressida to a secret meeting with Troilus, and they declare their mutual love, promising fidelity.

Calchas, Cressida's father, visits Agamemnon, and persuades him to release Antenor, recently taken prisoner, in exchange for Cressida. Agamemnon and the other lords treat Achilles with disdain as they pass him standing at the entrance to his tent. Ulysses explains their attitude, and makes Achilles see that his reputation is at stake. Achilles invites the Trojans to his tent after the combat next day.

Diomedes is sent to conduct Cressida to Troy. Aeneas arrives with the news at Cressida's house, where Troilus has spent the night. Accepting the inevitable, Troilus delivers her to Diomedes, after they exchange tokens and promise to be faithful. Cressida arrives at the Greek camp, where she is warmly welcomed.

Hector and Ajax fight, but agree a draw, and Ajax invites the Trojan lords to the Greek tents. When Achilles and Hector meet, they insult each other, promising to fight

next day. Troilus asks Ulysses to take him to Calchas' tent, where Cressida is staying. They observe Cressida's meeting with Diomedes, and see her become increasingly drawn to him, then giving him Troilus' token. Troilus is enraged.

Next day Hector prepares to fight, disregarding warnings from Andromache, Cassandra, and Priam. Troilus goes to the battle with the intention of killing Diomedes, but fails. Hector kills Patroclus. Achilles and his Myrmidons find Hector resting, and kill him. Troilus reports Hector's fall, and responds to an approach from Pandarus with an abrupt dismissal. Pandarus reflects gloomily on the way he has been treated, and curses the audience.

DRAMATIS PERSONAE

(as conventionally listed)

The Trojans

PRIAM, King of Troy
HECTOR
PARIS
DEIPHOBUS | sons of Priam
HELENUS, a priest
TROILUS
MARGARELON, a bastard
AENEAS | Trojan leaders
ANTENOR
PANDARUS, a lord, Cressida's uncle
CALCHAS, Cressida's father, a defector to the Greeks
ALEXANDER, Cressida's servant
ANDROMACHE, Hector's wife
CRESSIDA
CASSANDRA, Priam's daughter, a prophetess
Troilus's servants, a BOY and a MAN
Paris's SERVANT
Soldiers, attendants

The Greeks

AGAMEMNON, general commander of the Greeks
MENELAUS, King of Sparta, Agamemnon's brother
ULYSSES
ACHILLES
AJAX | Greek leaders
NESTOR
DIOMEDES
PATROCLUS, Achilles' companion
THERSITES
HELEN, Menelaus's wife, living with Paris in Troy
Diomedes' SERVANT
Soldiers, Myrmidons, attendants
Speaker of the PROLOGUE

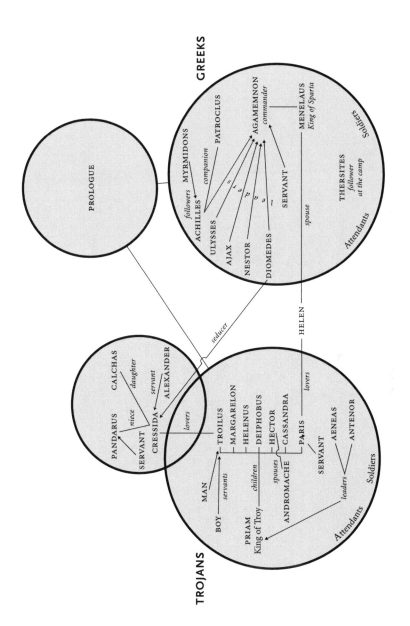

PROLOGUE

GREEKS

MYRMIDONS
followers
ACHILLES
companion
PATROCLUS
ULYSSES
AJAX
NESTOR
DIOMEDES
AGAMEMNON
commander
SERVANT
MENELAUS
King of Sparta
spouse
THERSITES
follower
at the camp
Soldiers
Attendants

Helen

seducer

TROJANS

CALCHAS
daughter
PANDARUS
niece
SERVANT
CRESSIDA
servant
ALEXANDER
lovers

BOY
MAN
servants
TROILUS
MARGARELON
HELENUS
DEIPHOBUS
HECTOR
CASSANDRA
PARIS
lovers
PRIAM
King of Troy
children
spouses
ANDROMACHE
SERVANT
AENEAS
ANTENOR
leaders
Attendants
Soldiers

HELEN

Twelfth Night

Duke Orsino of Illyria is in love with Olivia, but his advances are rejected. A shipwrecked Viola arrives on his shores, and with the help of a Captain disguises herself as a boy, calling herself Cesario, and enters Orsino's service. Orsino takes to Cesario, and sends 'him' to woo Olivia for him. Viola, however, is already falling in love with Orsino.

Cesario arrives to woo Olivia, and Olivia falls in love with 'him'. She rejects Orsino's approach, but asks Cesario to return. Orsino discusses the nature of love with Cesario, and sends 'him' again to Olivia, who confesses her love for Cesario, much to 'his' dismay. Meanwhile, Viola's twin brother Sebastian, also a casualty of the shipwreck, arrives in Illyria with the help of Antonio, a sea-captain and former enemy of Orsino. Sebastian looks around the town, and Antonio gives him his purse for safety, deciding to stay at an inn for safety.

Staying with Olivia is her uncle Sir Toby, who is encouraging Sir Andrew, his drinking-companion and source of funds, to woo Olivia. While carousing with Olivia's fool Feste late one night, they quarrel with Malvolio, her steward, and with the help of Olivia's maid Maria they decide to trick him. Maria writes a letter to Malvolio, forging Olivia's handwriting, to make Malvolio think Olivia loves him. The letter asks Malvolio to dress and behave in eccentric ways.

Toby, Andrew, and Fabian observe Malvolio opening the letter and absorbing its contents. He approaches Olivia according to the letter's instructions, and she thinks him mad. Toby arranges for him to be confined in a dark room. Later, he gets Feste to disguise himself as a priest, Sir Topas, to taunt Malvolio. Malvolio writes a letter of complaint to Olivia.

Meanwhile, Andrew prepares to leave the house, having seen Cesario apparently being more successful with Olivia, but Toby persuades him to stay, and to challenge Cesario to a duel. Sir Toby separately informs Andrew and Cesario that the other is a ferocious fighter, and they approach each other with trepidation. They are about to fight when Antonio arrives, intending to defend Cesario, whom he has mistaken for Sebastian. Antonio is arrested by officers who recognize him as Orsino's enemy. He asks for his purse from Cesario, who of course professes no knowledge of it.

Feste is sent to bring Cesario to Olivia, but encounters Sebastian instead. They meet Andrew, who strikes Sebastian, thinking him to be Cesario, and Andrew is beaten for his pains. Olivia arrives to stop a fight between Sebastian and Toby. Sebastian is immediately taken with her. Thinking him to be Cesario, she is delighted that he has finally responded to her advances, and they go off to be married.

Orsino is told by Cesario of Antonio's arrival, but when Antonio is brought before him and asserts that he has been with Cesario for some time, Orsino thinks him mad. Olivia arrives, and again rejects Orsino's advances. As he and Cesario prepare to leave, Olivia insists on Cesario staying, and calls him her husband. When Cesario denies it, she presents the priest as confirmation. Orsino is enraged, thinking Cesario has betrayed him. Toby and Andrew pass by, having just been severely beaten by Sebastian. Sebastian then arrives, and the twins delightedly recognize each other. Everyone is amazed, Viola's true identity is revealed, and she and Orsino decide to be married.

Feste delivers Malvolio's letter to Olivia, and he is brought from his cell. Fabian reveals the nature of the trick played upon him, and Malvolio leaves vowing revenge on them all. They all prepare for celebration, leaving Feste to bid the audience farewell.

DRAMATIS PERSONAE

(as conventionally listed)

ORSINO, Duke of Illyria
VALENTINE ⎤ gentlemen attending on Orsino
CURIO ⎦
First Officer
Second Officer

VIOLA, a shipwrecked lady, later disguised as Cesario
SEBASTIAN, her twin brother
CAPTAIN of the wrecked ship
ANTONIO, another sea-captain

OLIVIA, a countess
MARIA, her waiting-gentlewoman
SIR TOBY BELCH, her uncle
SIR ANDREW AGUECHEEK, Sir Toby's protégé

MALVOLIO, Olivia's steward
FABIAN, a member of her household
FESTE, her jester
A PRIEST
A SERVANT

Musicians, lords, sailors, attendants

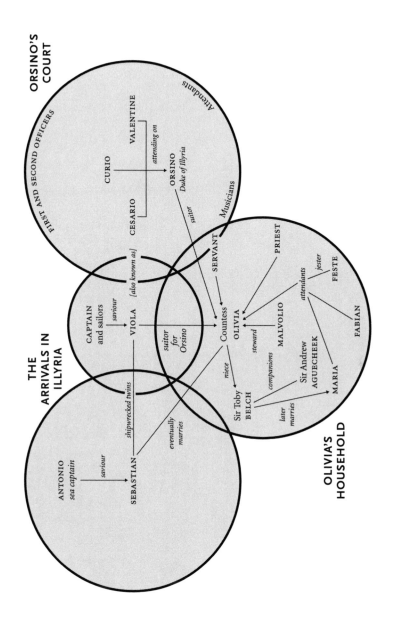

The Two Gentlemen of Verona

Valentine is leaving his friend Proteus in order to take up residence at the Duke's court in Milan; but Proteus stays in Verona to be near his love, Julia. Julia talks about falling in love with her waiting-woman Lucetta, expressing indifference, and tears up a letter from Proteus, though immediately regretting her action.

Proteus' father, Antonio, decides to send Proteus to the Duke's court, where Valentine is in love with the Duke's daughter, Silvia. Proteus leaves, professing constancy and exchanging rings with Julia. Valentine asks Proteus to help him elope with Silvia, but Proteus falls in love with her himself, and expresses his determination to have her. The two men's servants, Launce and Speed, meet and discuss the parting of Proteus from Julia. Julia decides to follow Proteus to Milan, disguising herself as a man.

Proteus informs the Duke of Valentine's plan. The Duke engages Valentine in conversation on the subject of how to reach a lady's chamber at night, makes Valentine reveal the rope-ladder and letter intended for Silvia, and promptly banishes him. On his way towards Mantua, Valentine is captured by outlaws in a forest, but he impresses them greatly and they make him their leader. Launce discusses the qualities of his own love, a milkmaid, with Speed.

The Duke, who wants Silvia to marry the wealthy Thurio, asks Proteus to use his influence with her to make her forget Valentine and notice Thurio. Julia, disguised as a page called Sebastian, arrives in Milan and is disgusted to overhear Proteus wooing Silvia on his own behalf. Silvia rejects Proteus' advances, and approaches Sir Eglamour for help to escape from Milan and reach Valentine. Proteus takes 'Sebastian' into his service. He gives her a ring and a letter to take to Silvia, who refuses it and tears up the letter, expressing sympathy for the forsaken Julia, whom 'Sebastian' describes to her.

Proteus and 'Sebastian' follow Silvia out of Milan. She is captured by the outlaws, but rescued by Proteus, who tries to force her to yield to him. Valentine, who has observed everything, comes to her aid. He tells Proteus that he can have Silvia, which causes Julia to faint. Her identity is revealed when Proteus recognizes the ring she is wearing as the one he had given her. Her fidelity rekindles his love for her.

The outlaws capture the Duke and Thurio, who have come in pursuit of Silvia, and they are brought before Valentine, who reveals his identity. Thurio claims Silvia, but immediately yields when Valentine threatens to fight him. The Duke applauds Valentine's spirit, repeals his banishment, and gives him Silvia. Valentine obtains pardon for the outlaws. All return to Milan, where marriages are planned between Valentine and Silvia and between Proteus and Julia.

DRAMATIS PERSONAE
(as conventionally listed)

THE DUKE OF MILAN
SILVIA, his daughter and the beloved of Valentine
THURIO, a foolish suitor for Silvia's hand
EGLAMOUR, Silvia's accomplice in her flight from Milan
PROTEUS ⎫ the two gentlemen of Verona
VALENTINE ⎬
JULIA, the beloved of Proteus, later disguised as SEBASTIAN, a page
ANTONIO, father of Proteus
LUCETTA, waiting-woman of Julia
SPEED, servant of Valentine
LAUNCE, servant of Proteus
PANTHINO, servant of Antonio
Host of the Inn where Julia lodges in Milan
Outlaws, led by Valentine during his banishment
Servants
Musicians
Attendants

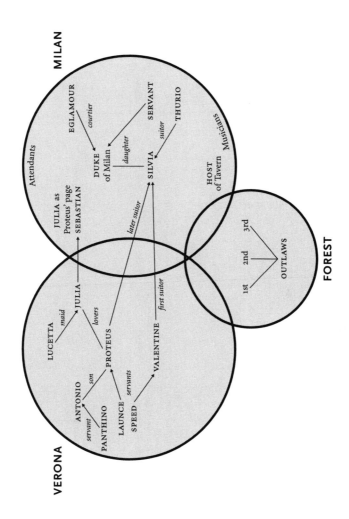

The Two Noble Kinsmen

Immediately after Theseus and Hippolyta are married, three widowed queens arrive from Thebes, begging Theseus to go to war with the tyrant Creon so that their husbands' bodies can receive proper burial. Hippolyta and her sister Emilia also plead for them, and he agrees to go off to fight. His friend Pirithous later leaves to join his campaign.

Two Theban friends, Palamon and Arcite, decry the evil in their city, but out of loyalty stay to help defend it. Following Theseus' victory, they are recognized for their prowess in battle. Almost dead, they are brought to Athens and given care, though imprisoned. Their gaoler has a daughter who falls in love with Palamon, disregarding her own suitor.

Palamon and Arcite regain their strength, and vow eternal friendship. Then Palamon sees Emilia through the prison bars, and falls in love with her. Arcite notices, sees Emilia, and also falls in love with her. They argue over her fiercely, Pirithous persuades Theseus to give Arcite his liberty, and he is banished. When Arcite encounters country people preparing for a dance to be performed before the nobles, he joins them in disguise so that he can enter the Athenian sports. He impresses everyone, and Theseus makes him a servant to Emilia.

The gaoler's daughter sets Palamon free, in the hope of winning his love. She follows him into the countryside, but loses track of him, and then gradually loses her wits. The schoolmaster, rehearsing the country people for the dance, finds he is a woman short, but the gaoler's daughter takes the place. They perform the dance in front of Theseus and Hippolyta.

Palamon, in hiding, sees Arcite in Theseus' hunting-party, and reveals himself. Arcite fetches him clothes, food and armour. They express their affection for each other, but in spite of this engage in a duel, and are disturbed by Theseus and his court. They explain who they are, and admit their love for Emilia. Theseus sentences them to death, but Hippolyta, Emilia, and Pirithous successfully beg mercy for them. Emilia cannot choose between them, so Theseus commands them to return in a month with knights, and engage in single combat. The winner will gain Emilia; the loser will be sentenced to death.

The gaoler and his friends despair over his daughter's madness. They consult a doctor, who advises that the

daughter's wooer should pretend to be Palamon. She accepts the substitution, and they go off to be married.

Palamon and Arcite return to fight for Emilia, and all three make prayers to their gods, asking for help. Emilia refuses to watch the combat. Arcite wins, and Palamon and his knights are sent for execution. The sentence is about to be carried out when Pirithous rushes in with the news that Arcite has been thrown by his horse, and is badly injured. Arcite is brought in, and yields Emilia to Palamon before he dies, affirming Palamon's original claim to her. Theseus recognizes Palamon's right to marry Emilia, and announces a period of mourning for Arcite, to be followed by Palamon and Emilia's wedding.

DRAMATIS PERSONAE

(as conventionally listed)

THESEUS, Duke of Athens
HIPPOLYTA, Queen of the Amazons, and then wife of Theseus
EMILIA, her sister
PIRITHOUS, friend of Theseus

PALAMON │ the two noble kinsmen, cousins from
ARCITE   │ Thebes

Hymen, god of marriage
A BOY
ARTESIUS, an Athenian soldier
Three QUEENS, widows of kings killed in the siege of Thebes

VALERIUS, a Theban

A HERALD
WOMAN, servant of Emilia
A GENTLEMAN
MESSENGERS
Six KNIGHTS, assisting Palamon and Arcite
A SERVANT

GAOLER, in charge of Theseus' prison
DAUGHTER of gaoler
WOOER of gaoler's daughter

Two FRIENDS of gaoler
BROTHER of gaoler
A DOCTOR

Six COUNTRYMEN, one dressed as a bavian or baboon
A SCHOOLMASTER
NELL and four other country wenches
A TABORER

Speaker of the PROLOGUE and EPILOGUE

Nymphs, attendants, countrymen, garland-bearer, hunters, maids, executioner, guard of soldiers

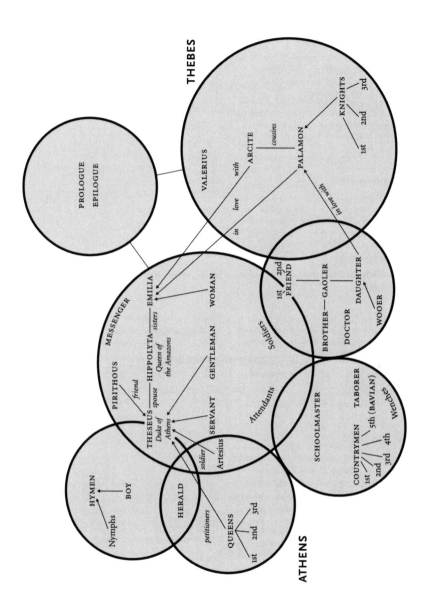

THEBES

ATHENS

PROLOGUE
EPILOGUE

VALERIUS

ARCITE

in love with

cousins

PALAMON

KNIGHTS

1st   2nd   3rd

in love with

MESSENGER

HIPPOLYTA — EMILIA

sisters

WOMAN

GENTLEMAN

Queen of
the Amazons

PIRITHOUS

friend

Soldiers

Attendants

1st 2nd
FRIEND

BROTHER — GAOLER

DOCTOR

DAUGHTER

WOOER

THESEUS

spouse

Duke of
Athens

SERVANT

SCHOOLMASTER

TABORER

COUNTRYMEN

1st 2nd 3rd 4th 5th (BAVIAN)

Wenches

Artesius

soldier

HYMEN

BOY

Nymphs

HERALD

petitioners

QUEENS

1st 2nd 3rd

The Winter's Tale

Camillo and Archidamus are discussing the long-standing friendship between Leontes and Polixenes, their respective kings. Polixenes has been staying at Leontes' court, and is persuaded by Leontes' wife Hermione (who acts at Leontes' suggestion) to stay with him longer. But Leontes then grows jealous of the affection shown to Polixenes by Hermione, and convinces himself they are having an affair. So quickly does his jealousy grow that he asks Camillo to poison Polixenes. Camillo, knowing Polixenes' innocence, informs him of Leontes' intentions, and Polixenes flees Sicilia for Bohemia, taking Camillo with him.

Leontes publicly accuses the pregnant Hermione, and puts her in prison, sending Cleomenes and Dion to the Oracle to have his course of action confirmed. After she gives birth, he overrules the opinions of his lords, and banishes the baby. One of his lords, Antigonus, is instructed to take the baby and abandon it far from Sicilia. Leontes then puts Hermione on trial, but Cleomenes and Dion bring the judgement from the Oracle, which proclaims Hermione, Polixenes, and Camillo all innocent, and predicts that Leontes will have no heir if the banished baby is not found. Leontes rejects the Oracle, only to learn that his much-loved son Mamillius has died. Hermione faints and is taken out. Leontes immediately repents. Paulina returns to say that Hermione is dead and rages against Leontes. Leontes vows perpetual sorrow.

In Bohemia, Antigonus reluctantly leaves the baby by itself, but as he starts to return home he is killed by a bear. The baby is rescued and adopted by a shepherd and his son, a clown.

The Chorus, Time, takes the play forward sixteen years. Polixenes and Camillo disguise themselves in order to be present at a sheep-shearing festival. Polixenes wants to find out what is going on with his son Florizel, who is in love with the shepherd's adopted daughter, now called Perdita. A rogue, Autolycus, after earlier picking the Clown's pockets, comes to the festival to sell his wares. Dancing and singing take place, and Florizel and Perdita plan to marry. The disguised Polixenes suggests to Florizel that his father should be told; when Florizel refuses, Polixenes reveals himself, and bans Florizel from seeing Perdita again.

With the help of Camillo the two lovers escape to Sicilia, where the now pious Leontes still visits his wife's tomb.

Leontes welcomes them, and Florizel claims they are there with their fathers' knowledge. Back in Bohemia, the shepherd decides to tell Polixenes the truth about Perdita's birth, making her eligible for marriage to Florizel, and Autolycus helps them make their way to court. They then all journey to Sicilia. When Polixenes unexpectedly arrives, the warmth of his meeting with Leontes is described by a group of gentlemen, who report the unravelling of the whole history of Perdita.

Antigonus' widow Paulina invites everyone to Hermione's tomb to view a remarkable sculpture of Hermione. Paulina, who has made Leontes vow not to remarry unless she chooses a wife for him, demonstrates that she can make the statue move. When it does, it is shown to be Hermione, who has been hidden by Paulina in the hope that Leontes would come to his senses. Perdita and Hermione are reunited. Paulina laments the loss of her husband, and Leontes matches her with Camillo. Leontes begs forgiveness from Hermione and Polixenes.

DRAMATIS PERSONAE
(as conventionally listed)

LEONTES, King of Sicilia
HERMIONE, his wife
MAMILLIUS, his son
PERDITA, his daughter
CAMILLO ⎤
ANTIGONUS ⎥ lords at the court of Leontes
CLEOMENES ⎥
DION ⎦
PAULINA, wife of Antigonus
EMILIA, a lady attending on Hermione
A Gaoler
A Mariner
Other lords and gentlemen, ladies, officers, and servants
    at the court of Leontes

POLIXENES, King of Bohemia
FLORIZEL, his son
ARCHIDAMUS, a Bohemian lord
AUTOLYCUS, a rogue

Old SHEPHERD, reputed father of Perdita
CLOWN, his son
MOPSA ⎤ shepherdesses
DORCAS ⎦
A Servant of the old Shepherd
Other Shepherds and Shepherdesses
Twelve countrymen disguised as satyrs

TIME, as Chorus

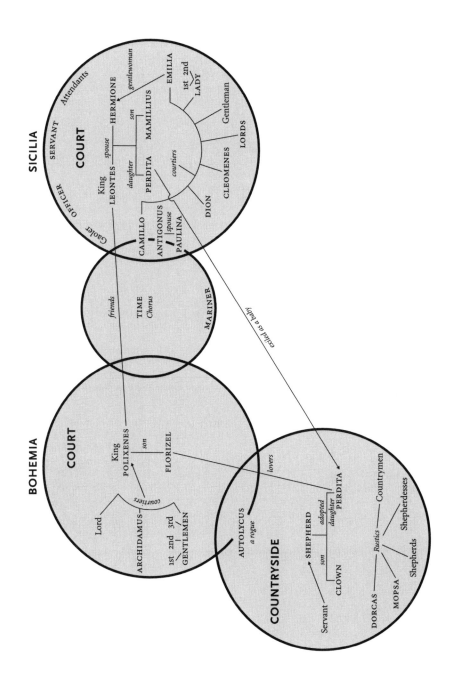

Text Chronology

We give below the order of plays as concluded by Stanley Wells and Gary Taylor in their *Complete Oxford Shakespeare*, with the addition of *King Edward III*. The dates reflect some of the conclusions arrived at by scholars about when the texts were written, which in many cases is significantly earlier than the date of first known publication or performance.

PLAYS

1589–93	The Two Gentlemen of Verona
1590–93	The Taming of the Shrew
1590–94	King Edward III [with other authors]
1590–92	Henry VI Part 3
1590–91	Henry VI Part 2
1590–91	Titus Andronicus
1591–2	Henry VI Part 1 [with other authors]
1592–3	Richard III
1592–4	The Comedy of Errors
1593–5	Love's Labour's Lost
1594–5	A Midsummer Night's Dream
1594–5	Romeo and Juliet
1594–6	Richard II
1594–6	King John
1596–7	The Merchant of Venice
1596–7	Henry IV Part 1
1597	The Merry Wives of Windsor
1597–8	Henry IV Part 2
1598–9	Much Ado About Nothing
1599	Henry V
1599	Julius Caesar
1599–1600	As You Like It
1600–1601	Hamlet
1601–2	Twelfth Night
1602–3	Troilus and Cressida
1604	Measure for Measure
1603–4	Othello
1603–5	All's Well That Ends Well
1604–7	Timon of Athens [with Thomas Middleton]
1605–8	King Lear
1606	Macbeth
1606–7	Antony and Cleopatra
1608–9	Pericles [with George Wilkins]
1608	Coriolanus
1609–10	The Winter's Tale
1610–11	Cymbeline
1610–11	The Tempest
1613	Henry VIII [with John Fletcher]
1613–15	The Two Noble Kinsmen [with John Fletcher]

POEMS

1593	Venus and Adonis
1594	The Rape of Lucrece
1598–1609	Sonnets, A Lover's Complaint
1599	The Passionate Pilgrim
1601	The Phoenix and the Turtle

List of Characters' Names

This is an alphabetical and integrated list of the proper names of all the characters which appear in the plays, and thus in the quotations we have used in the A–Z Glossary. The different lists of characters on pp.514–90 (the 'dramatis personae') enable readers to find all the characters within an individual play; the list below enables readers to find the play in which a particular character appears. But it also enables the reader to track alternative names for people, such as *Sir John Falstaff, Sir John, Jack*, and *Oldcastle*, and alternative spellings such as *Philario* and *Filario*. Names in square brackets are there to help identification; we do not relate alternatives to particular editions of the texts.

The emphasis is very much on the way the names appear in the texts themselves, so that Claudius, for example, who is referred to as 'the King' and as 'Denmark', is additionally listed as *King of Denmark* and *Denmark, King of*. We have focused our attention on characters as they actually appear in the plays (whether speaking or non-speaking, alive or dead), but we go beyond the conventional list of dramatis personae, adding the names of people who are of importance to the plot but who do not actually appear, such as Fulvia in *Antony and Cleopatra*. We exclude the names of off-stage people who are mentioned only in passing (such as the bevy of servants mentioned by Dromio in *The Comedy of Errors*). We also exclude the various attendants and servants unless they have a speaking role.

We include the following features in the list:

- A character's function, where this is specifically recognized, along with their personal name, if this is known. Examples: Abbess, Soothsayer.
- Names adopted while disguised. Examples: Ganymede, Friar Lodowick.
- Titular designations, with cross-referencing where the title is used in the play. Example: Duke of Florence, under both D and F.
- Private names of people with titles, when there is more than one of the same name, usually as given in the character list of a play. Example: the various Dukes of Buckingham.
- Terms of endearment, pet names, and other designations – given either by the characters themselves or assigned to them by other people. Examples: Nell, Plantagenet.

We provide selective information about personal relationships, shown in round brackets, when this helps to avoid confusion between characters, as in the case of the various Prince Edwards. More extensive information about character relationships is given in the play's 'circles', pp.515–91.

Character	Play	Character	Play
Aaron [the Moor]	**Tit**	Agrippa	**AC**
Abbess [Æmilia]	**CE**	Agrippa, Menenius	**Cor**
Abbot of Westminster	**R2**	Aguecheek, Sir Andrew	**TN**
Abergavenny, Lord	**H8**	Ajax	**TC**
Abhorson [Executioner]	**MM**	Alarbus	**Tit**
Abraham ☛ Abram	**RJ**	Albany, Duchess of [Gonerill]	**KL**
Abram [Abraham]	**RJ**	Albany, Duke of	**KL**
Achilles	**TC**	Alcibiades	**Tim**
Adam	**AY**	Alençon, Duke of	**1H6**
Adam	**TS**	Alexander	**TC**
Adam [Officer]	**CE**	Alexas	**AC**
Adrian	**Cor**	Alice	**H5**
Adrian	**Tem**	Alice Ford, Mistress	**MW**
Adriana	**CE**	Aliena [Celia]	**AY**
Adriano de Armado, Don	**LL**	Alonso, King of Naples	**Tem**
Æmilia [Abbess]	**CE**	Amazons, Queen of the [Hippolyta]	**TNK**
Aemilius [Emillius]	**Tit**	Ambassador, Antony's [Schoolmaster]	**AC**
Aeneas	**TC**	Ambassador, English	**Ham**
Aeschines [Escanes]	**Per**	Ambassador, French	**H5**
Agamemnon	**TC**	Ambassador, Papal	**1H6**

Character	Play
Amiens	AY
Ancient [Aunchient; Iago]	Oth
Ancient [Aunchient; Pistol]	MW, 2H4, H5
Andrew Aguecheek, Sir	TN
Andromache	TC
Andronicus, Lavinia	Tit
Andronicus, Lucius	Tit
Andronicus, Marcus	Tit
Andronicus, Martius	Tit
Andronicus, Mutius	Tit
Andronicus, Quintus	Tit
Andronicus, Titus	Tit
Andronicus, Young Lucius	Tit
Angelica [Nurse]	RJ
Angelo	CE
Angelo [Deputy]	MM
Angus	Mac
Anjou, Duke of [Reignier]	1H6
Anne Bullen [Boleyn; Marchioness of Pembroke; later, Queen of England]	H8
Anne Neville, Lady [Plantagenet; later, Queen]	R3
Anne Page	MW
Antenor	TC
Anthony	RJ
Antigonus	WT
Antioch ☛ Antiochus	
Antiochus, King of Antioch	Per
Antiope [Hippolyta]	TNK
Antipholus of Ephesus	CE
Antipholus of Syracuse	CE
Antium, Citizen of	Cor
Antonio	MA
Antonio	MV
Antonio	TG
Antonio	TN
Antonio [Duke of Milan]	Tem
Antony, Mark	AC, JC
Apemantus	Tim
Apothecary	RJ
Apparition, First	Mac
Apparition, Second	Mac
Apparition, Third	Mac
Aragon, Prince of	MV
Archbishop of Canterbury [Cardinal Bourchier]	R3
Archbishop of Canterbury [Henry Chicheley]	H5
Archbishop of Canterbury [Thomas Cranmer]	H8
Archbishop of York [Thomas Rotheram]	R3
Archbishop of York [Richard Scroop]	1H4, 2H4
Archduke of Austria [Viscount of Limoges]	KJ
Archibald [Douglas, Earl of]	1H4
Archidamus	WT
Arcite	TNK
Ariel	Tem
Armado, Don Adriano de	LL
Arragon, Prince of	MV
Arragon, Prince of [Don Pedro]	MA
Artemidorus	JC
Artesius	TNK
Arthur [Duke of Brittaine; Earl of Richmond; Arthur Plantagenet]	KJ
Artois, Count of [Robert]	E3
Arviragus [Cadwal]	Cym

Character	Play
Asmath [Asnath; Spirit]	2H6
Asnath ☛ Asmath	
Astringer [Austringer; Gentleman]	AW
Athenian, Old	Tim
Athens, Duke of [Theseus]	TNK
Attendant to Cymbeline	Cym
Audley, Lord	E3
Audrey	AY
Aufidius, Tullus	Cor
Aumerle, Duke of [Earl of Rutland]	R2
Aunchient [Ancient; Iago]	Oth
Aunchient [Ancient; Pistol]	MW, 2H4, H5
Austria, Archduke of [Viscount of Limoges]	KJ
Autolycus	WT
Auvergne, Countess of	1H6
Bagot	R2
Balthasar	CE
Balthasar	MA
Balthasar	RJ
Balthasar [servant of Portia]	MV
Balthasar [Portia]	MV
Bandit, First [Thief]	Tim
Bandit, Second [Thief]	Tim
Bandit, Third [Thief]	Tim
Banquo	Mac
Baptista Minola	TS
Bardolph [Harvey]	1H4, 2H4, H5, MW
Bardolph, Lord	2H4
Barnadine	MM
Barnardo	Ham
Bartholomew [Page]	TS
Bassanio	MV
Basset	1H6
Bassianus	Tit
Bastard [Edmund]	KL
Bastard [Margarelon; Margareton]	TC
Bastard, Philip the	KJ
Bastard of Orleans	1H6
Bates, John	H5
Bavian [Fifth Countryman]	TNK
Bawd	Per
Beadle	2H6
Beadle, First	2H4
Beatrice	MA
Beau, Philip le [King Philip IV]	E3
Beauchamp, Richard [Earl of Warwick]	2H4, H5, 1H6
Beaufort, Cardinal [Bishop of Winchester]	1H6, 2H6
Beaufort, Edmund [Duke of Somerset]	1H6, 2H6, 3H6
Beaufort, Henry [Duke of Somerset]	3H6
Beaufort, Thomas [Duke of Exeter]	H5, 1H6
Bedford, Duke of [earlier, John of Lancaster]	1H4, 2H4, H5, 1H6
Bedlam, Tom o' [Edgar]	KL
Belarius [Morgan]	Cym
Belch, Sir Toby	TN
Bellario, Doctor	MV
Benedick	MA
Benvolio	RJ
Berkeley	R3
Berkeley, Lord	R2
Berowne [Biron]	LL
Berri, Duke of	H5
Bertram, Count of Rossillion [County]	AW
Bess [Lady Elizabeth Grey; later, Queen of England]	3H6

Character	Play	Character	Play
Bevis, George	2H6	Brutus, Marcus	JC
Bianca	Oth	Buckingham, Duke of [Edward Stafford]	H8
Bianca	TS	Buckingham, Duke of [Henry Stafford]	R3
Bigot, Lord	KJ	Buckingham, Duke of [Humphrey Stafford]	2H6
Biondello	TS	Bullcalf, Peter	2H4
Biron [Berowne]	LL	Bullen, Anne [Boleyn; Marchioness of	H8
Bishop of Carlisle	R2	Pembroke; later, Queen of England]	
Bishop of Ely [John Fordham]	H5	Bum [Pompey]	MM
Bishop of Ely [John Morton]	R3	Burgh, Hubert de	KJ
Bishop of Lincoln	H8	Burgundy, Duke of	H5, 1H6
Bishop of London	H8	Burgundy, Duke of	KL
Bishop of Rochester	H8	Bushy	R2
Bishop of Saint Asaph	H8	Butcher [Dick]	2H6
Bishop of Winchester [Gardiner]	H8	Butts, Doctor	H8
Blanche of Spain	KJ	Cade, Jack	2H6
Blunt, Sir James [Captain Blunt]	R3	Cadwal [Arviragus]	Cym
Blunt, Sir John	2H4	Caesar, Julius	JC
Blunt, Sir Walter	1H4	Caesar, Octavius	JC, AC
Boatswain	Tem	Caithness [Cathness]	Mac
Bohemia, King of	E3	Caius	Tit
Bohemia, King of [Polixenes]	WT	Caius [Earl of Kent]	KL
Boleyn, Anne [Bullen; Marchioness of	H8	Caius, Doctor	MW
Pembroke; later, Queen of England]		Caius Cassius	JC
Bolingbroke, Henry [Harry; later, King	R2, 1H4, 2H4	Caius Ligarius	JC
Henry IV]		Caius Lucius	Cym
Bolingbroke, Roger	2H6	Caius Martius [Coriolanus]	Cor
Bona, Lady	3H6	Calais, Captain of	E3
Borachio	MA	Calchas	TC
Bottom, Nick [Pyramus]	MND	Caliban	Tem
Boult	Per	Calphurnia [Calpurnia]	JC
Bourbon, Admiral	3H6	Cambio [Lucentio]	TS
Bourbon, Duke of	H5	Cambridge, Earl of [Richard]	H5
Bourchier, Cardinal [Archbishop of	R3	Camillo	WT
Canterbury]		Campeius, Cardinal	H8
Boy [Edward Plantagenet]	R3	Canidius	AC
Boy [attendant to Hymen]	TNK	Canterbury, Archbishop of [Cardinal	R3
Boy [camp-follower]	H5	Bourchier]	
Boy [servant to Benedick]	MA	Canterbury, Archbishop of [Henry	H5
Boy [servant to Troilus]	TC	Chicheley]	
Boy [singer]	AC	Canterbury Archbishop of [Thomas	H8
Boy [singer]	MM	Cranmer]	
Boy [son of Master Gunner]	1H6	Caphis	Tim
Boyet	LL	Capilet, Widow	AW
Boys, Jaques de	AY	Captain [Dumaine; First / Second Lord]	AW
Boys, Oliver de	AY	Captain [in Duncan's army]	Mac
Boys, Orlando de	AY	Captain [in Edmund's army]	KL
Brabantio [Brabanzio]	Oth	Captain [Norwegian]	Ham
Brabanzio ☞ Brabantio		Captain [of a pirate ship]	2H6
Brakenbury, Sir Robert	R3	Captain [of the Welsh army]	R2
Brandon	H8	Captain [of the wrecked ship]	TN
Brandon, Sir William	R3	Captain [Polonian]	E3
Bretagne, Duke of [Britaine]	H5	Captain [Roman]	Cym
Britain, King of [Cymbeline]	Cym	Captain [Roman]	Tit
Britain, King of [Lear]	KL	Captain, First	Cym
Britaine, Duke of [Bretagne]	H5	Captain, Second	Cym
Brittaine, Duke of [Arthur]	KJ	Capuchius [Caputius]	H8
Brittany, Duke of [Lord Mountford]	E3	Capulet	RJ
Brook, John [Frank Ford]	MW	Capulet, Cousin	RJ
Brother, First (to Posthumus, as apparition)	Cym	Capulet, Lady	RJ
Brother, Second (to Posthumus, as	Cym	Caputius [Capuchius]	H8
apparition)		Cardinal Bourchier	R3
Brother of Gaoler	TNK	Cardinal Campeius	H8
Bruce of Scotland [King David]	E3	Cardinal Pandulph	KJ
Brute [Marcus Brutus]	JC	Cardinal Wolsey	H8
Brutus, Decius	JC	Carlisle, Bishop of	R2
Brutus, Junius	Cor	Carpenter	JC

Character	Play	Character	Play
Carrier, First	1H4	Cloten	Cym
Carrier, Second	1H4	Clown	AC
Casca [Caska]	JC	Clown	Oth
Caska ☞ Casca		Clown	RJ
Cassandra	TC	Clown	Tit
Cassio, Michael	Oth	Clown	WT
Cassius, Caius	JC	Clown [Feste]	TN
Catesby, Sir William	R3	Clown [Launcelot Gobbo]	MV
Catharine [Katherine]	LL	Clown [Lavatch]	AW
Catherine, Princess [Katherine]	H5	Clown [Pompey]	MM
Cathness [Caithness]	Mac	Clown [Touchstone]	AY
Catling, Simon	RJ	Clown, First [Gravedigger]	Ham
Cato, Young	JC	Clown, Second [Gravedigger]	Ham
Cawdor, Thane of [Macbeth]	Mac	Cobbler	JC
Celia [Aliena]	AY	Cobham, Eleanor [Duchess of Gloucester]	2H6
Ceres	Tem	Cobweb	MND
Cerimon	Per	Colevile, Sir John [Coleville]	2H4
Cesario [Viola]	TN	Coleville ☞ Colevile	
Chamberlain	1H4	Cominius	Cor
Chamberlain, Lord	H8	Companion to Marina	Per
Chancellor, Lord	H8	Conrad(e)	MA
Charles VI, King of France	H5	Conspirator, First	Cor
Charles VII, King of France [earlier, Dauphin]	1H6	Conspirator, Second	Cor
		Conspirator, Third	Cor
Charles Delabreth, Constable of France	H5	Constable [Dogberry]	MA
Charles the Dauphin [Duke of Normandy]	E3	Constable [Dull]	LL
Charles (wrestler to Duke Frederick)	AY	Constable [Elbow]	MM
Charmian	AC	Constable of France [Lord High Constable; Charles Delabreth]	H5
Chartham, Clerk of	2H6		
Chatillon	KJ	Constance	KJ
Chiron [Rape]	Tit	Copland, John	E3
Chorus	H5	Cordelia [later, Queen of France]	KL
Chorus	RJ	Corin	AY
Chorus [John Gower]	Per	Coriolanus [Caius Martius]	Cor
Chorus [Time]	WT	Cornelius	Cym
Cicero	JC	Cornelius	Ham
Cimber, Metellus	JC	Cornwall, Duchess of [Regan]	KL
Cinna [poet]	JC	Cornwall, Duke of	KL
Cinna [conspirator]	JC	Costard	LL
Citizen, First	Cor	Cotus [Servingman]	Cor
Citizen, First	2H6	Count Orsino [County; Duke of Illyria]	TN
Citizen, First	R3	Count of Artois [Robert]	E3
Citizen, First Rich	E3	Count of Rossillion [Bertram]	AW
Citizen, Second	Cor	Countess of Auvergne	1H6
Citizen, Second	R3	Countess of Rossillion	AW
Citizen, Second Rich	E3	Countess of Salisbury	E3
Citizen, Third	Cor	Countryman, First	TNK
Citizen, Third	R3	Countryman, Second	TNK
Citizen, Fourth	Cor	Countryman, Third	TNK
Citizen, Fifth	Cor	Countryman, Fourth	TNK
Citizen, Sixth	Cor	Countryman, Fifth [Bavian]	TNK
Citizen, Seventh	Cor	County [Bertram]	AW
Clarence, Duke of [George]	3H6, R3	County [Claudio]	MA
Clarence, Duke of [Thomas]	2H4, H5	County [Orsino]	TN
Claudio [County]	MA	County [Paris]	RJ
Claudio	MM	Court, Alexander	H5
Claudius	JC	Courtesan	CE
Claudius [King of Denmark]	Ham	Coventry, Mayor of	3H6
Cleomenes	WT	Cranmer, Thomas [later, Archbishop of Canterbury]	H8
Cleon	Per		
Cleopatra [Queen of Egypt]	AC	Creon (uncle of Palamon and Arcite; King of Thebes)	TNK
Clerk [Nerissa]	MV		
Clerk of Chartham	2H6	Cressid ☞ Cressida	
Clifford, Lord [Old Clifford]	2H6	Cressida [Cressid]	TC
Clifford, Lord [Young Clifford]	2H6, 3H6	Crier	H8
Clitus	JC	Cromwell, Thomas	H8

Character	Play
Cumberland, Prince of [Malcolm]	**Mac**
Cupid	**Tim**
Curan	**KL**
Curio	**TN**
Curtis	**TS**
Cymbeline [King of Britain]	**Cym**
Dame Eleanor [Eleanor Cobham, Duchess of Gloucester]	**2H6**
Dardanius	**JC**
Daughter of Antiochus	**Per**
Daughter of Gaoler	**TNK**
Dauphin, Charles the [later, Charles VII]	**1H6**
Dauphin, Charles the [Duke of Normandy]	**E3**
Dauphin, Lewis the [Louis]	**H5**
Dauphin, Lewis the [Louis]	**KJ**
David, King [Bruce of Scotland]	**E3**
Davy	**2H4**
de Boys, Jaques	**AY**
de Boys, Oliver	**AY**
de Boys, Orlando	**AY**
de Boys, Rowland	**AY**
Decius Brutus	**JC**
Decretas	**AC**
Deiphobus	**TC**
Demetrius	**AC**
Demetrius	**MND**
Demetrius [Murder]	**Tit**
Denmark, King of [Claudius]	**Ham**
Denmark, King of [Hamlet; Ghost]	**Ham**
Denmark, Prince of [Hamlet]	**Ham**
Denmark, Queen of [Gertrude]	**Ham**
Dennis	**AY**
Denny, Sir Anthony	**H8**
Deputy [Angelo]	**MM**
Derby, Earl of	**E3**
Derby, Earl of [Lord Stanley]	**R3**
Desdemona [Desdemon]	**Oth**
Dian ⟩ Diana	
Diana [Dian; goddess]	**Per**
Diana Capilet	**AW**
Dick [Butcher]	**2H6**
Dick [Richard of Gloucester]	**3H6**
Dighton	**R3**
Diomed ⟩ Diomedes	
Diomedes [Diomed]	**TC**
Diomedes	**AC**
Dion	**WT**
Dionyza	**Per**
Doctor	**KL**
Doctor	**TNK**
Doctor, English	**Mac**
Doctor, Scottish	**Mac**
Doctor Butts	**H8**
Dogberry [Constable]	**MA**
Dolabella	**AC**
Doll Tearsheet [Mistress Dorothy]	**2H4**
Domitius Enobarbus [Enobarb]	**AC**
Don John	**MA**
Donalbain	**Mac**
Dorcas	**WT**
Doricles [Florizel]	**WT**
Dorothy, Mistress [Doll Tearsheet]	**2H4**
Dorset, Marchioness of	**H8**
Dorset, Marquess of [Henry Grey/Gray]	**H8**
Dorset, Marquess of [Thomas Grey/Gray]	**R3**
Douglas, Earl of [Archibald]	**1H4**

Character	Play
Douglas, Sir William	**E3**
Dowsabel [Luce]	**CE**
Drawer	**2H4**
Dromio of Ephesus	**CE**
Dromio of Syracuse	**CE**
Duchess of Gloucester [Eleanor Cobham; Nell]	**2H6**
Duchess of Gloucester [Eleanor de Bohun]	**R2**
Duchess of York (mother of Aumerle)	**R2**
Duchess of York [Cicely Neville]	**R3**
Duke Frederick	**AY**
Duke of Albany	**KL**
Duke of Alençon	**1H6**
Duke of Anjou [Reignier]	**1H6**
Duke of Athens [Theseus]	**TNK**
Duke of Aumerle [Earl of Rutland]	**R2**
Duke of Bedford [earlier, John of Lancaster]	**1H4, 2H4, H5, 1H6**
Duke of Berri	**H5**
Duke of Bourbon	**H5**
Duke of Britaine	**H5**
Duke of Brittaine [Arthur]	**KJ**
Duke of Brittany [Lord Mountford]	**E3**
Duke of Buckingham [Edward Stafford]	**H8**
Duke of Buckingham [Henry Stafford]	**R3**
Duke of Buckingham [Humphrey Stafford]	**2H6**
Duke of Burgundy	**H5, 1H6**
Duke of Burgundy	**KL**
Duke of Clarence [George]	**3H6, R3**
Duke of Clarence [Thomas]	**2H4, H5**
Duke of Cornwall	**KL**
Duke of Exeter [Thomas Beaufort]	**H5, 1H6**
Duke of Exeter [Henry Holland]	**3H6**
Duke of Florence	**AW**
Duke of Gloucester [Humphrey]	**2H4, H5, 1H6, 2H6**
Duke of Gloucester, Richard [later, King Richard III]	**2H6, 3H6, R3**
Duke of Hereford [Henry Bolingbroke]	**R2**
Duke of Illyria [Orsino]	**TN**
Duke of Lancaster [John of Gaunt]	**R2**
Duke of Lorraine	**E3**
Duke of Milan	**TG**
Duke of Milan [Prospero; Antonio]	**Tem**
Duke of Norfolk [John Howard]	**R3**
Duke of Norfolk [John Mowbray]	**3H6**
Duke of Norfolk [Thomas Howard]	**H8**
Duke of Norfolk [Thomas Mowbray]	**R2**
Duke of Normandy [Prince Charles]	**E3**
Duke of Orleans	**H5**
Duke of Rambures	**H5**
Duke of Somerset [Edmund Beaufort]	**2H6**
Duke of Somerset [Henry Beaufort]	**3H6**
Duke of Somerset [John or Edmund Beaufort]	**1H6**
Duke of Suffolk	**H8**
Duke of Surrey	**R2**
Duke of Venice	**MV**
Duke of Venice	**Oth**
Duke of Vienna [Duke Vincentio]	**MM**
Duke of York [Edmund of Langley]	**R2**
Duke of York [Edward, later Edward IV]	**3H6**
Duke of York [Edward Plantagenet]	**H5**
Duke of York [Richard, son of Edward IV]	**R3**
Duke of York [Richard Plantagenet]	**1H6, 2H6, 3H6**
Duke Senior	**AY**

Character	Play	Character	Play
Duke Vincentio [of Vienna; Friar Lodowick]	MM	Edward, Prince of Wales (son of Henry VI) [Plantagenet; Ned]	3H6
Dull, Anthony	LL		
Dumaine	LL	Edward Plantagenet (son of Clarence) [Boy; Ned]	R3
Dumaine, First [First Lord; Captain]	AW		
Dumaine, Second [Second Lord; Captain]	AW	Edward Poins [Poines; Poynes; Pointz; Ned; Yedward]	1H4, 2H4, MW
Duncan, King of Scotland	Mac		
Dunois, John, Count of [Bastard of Orleans]	1H6	Egeon	CE
Dutchman	Cym	Egeus	MND
Earl Marshal [Mowbray]	2H4	Eglamour, Sir	TG
Earl of Cambridge [Richard]	H5	Egypt, Queen of [Cleopatra]	AC
Earl of Derby [Henry of Lancaster]	E3	Egyptian	AC
Earl of Derby [Lord Stanley]	R3	Elbow [Constable]	MM
Earl of Douglas	1H4	Eleanor, Queen	KJ
Earl of Essex	KJ	Eleanor Cobham [Duchess of Gloucester; Dame Eleanor; Nell]	2H6
Earl of Gloucester	KL		
Earl of Huntingdon	H5	Eleanor de Bohun [Duchess of Gloucester]	R2
Earl of Kent [Caius]	KL	Elinor, Queen	KJ
Earl of March [Edmund Mortimer]	1H6	Elizabeth, Queen [Lady Elizabeth Grey/ Gray]	3H6, R3
Earl of March [Edward, later, Edward IV]	2H6, 3H6		
Earl of Northumberland [Henry Percy, 3rd Earl]	3H6	Ely, Bishop of [John Fordham]	H5
		Ely, Bishop of [John Morton]	R3
Earl of Northumberland [Henry Percy, 1st Earl]	R2, 1H4, 2H4	Emanuel, Clerk of Chartham [Emmanuel]	2H6
		Emilia	Oth
Earl of Northumberland [Seyward / Siward]	Mac	Emilia	WT
Earl of Oxford	3H6, R3	Emilia [Emily]	TNK
Earl of Pembroke [William Herbert]	3H6	Emillius [Aemilius]	Tit
Earl of Pembroke [William Marshal]	KJ	Emily [Emilia]	TNK
Earl of Richmond [Arthur]	KJ	Emmanuel, Clerk of Chartham [Emanuel]	2H6
Earl of Richmond [later, Henry VII]	3H6, R3	Emperor of Rome [Saturninus]	Tit
Earl of Richmond [Robert, Count of Artois]	E3	Empress of Rome [Tamora]	Tit
Earl of Rutland [Edmund]	3H6	England, Harry [Henry V]	H5
Earl of Rutland [Aumerle]	R2	England, King of [Edward III]	E3
Earl of Salisbury [William de Longespée]	KJ	England, King of [Edward IV]	3H6, R3
Earl of Salisbury [John Montacute]	R2	England, King of [Edward V]	R3
Earl of Salisbury [Thomas Montacute; Plantagenet]	H5, 1H6	England, King of [Henry III]	KJ
		England, King of [Henry IV]	R2, 1H4
Earl of Salisbury [William Montacute; Plantagenet]	E3	England, King of [Henry V]	2H4, H5
		England, King of [Henry VI]	1H6, 2H6, 3H6
Earl of Salisbury [Richard Neville]	2H6	England, King of [Henry VII]	R3
Earl of Suffolk [William de la Pole]	1H6, 2H6	England, King of [Henry VIII]	H8
Earl of Surrey [Thomas Fitzalan]	2H4	England, King of [John]	KJ
Earl of Surrey [William Fitzalan]	H8	England, King of [Richard II]	R2
Earl of Surrey [Thomas Howard]	R3	England, King of [Richard III]	R3
Earl of Warwick [Richard Beauchamp]	2H4, H5, 1H6	England, Queen of [earlier, Lady Grey]	3H6
Earl of Warwick [Thomas de Beauchamp]	E3	Enobarb ☛ Enobarbus	
Earl of Warwick [Richard Neville]	2H6, 3H6	Enobarbus, Domitius [Enobarb]	AC
Earl of Westmorland [1st Earl]	1H4, 2H4, H5	Ephesus, Antipholus of	CE
Earl of Westmorland [2nd Earl]	3H6	Ephesus, Dromio of	CE
Earl Rivers	R3	Ephesus, Duke of [Solinus]	CE
Edgar [Poor Tom; Tom O'Bedlam]	KL	Epilogue	2H4
Edmond ☛ Edmund		Epilogue	TNK
Edmund [Edmond; Bastard; later, Earl of Gloucester]	KL	Epilogue	H8
		Eros	AC
Edmund [Mortimer]	1H4	Erpingham, Sir Thomas	H5
Edmund, Earl of Rutland	3H6	Escalus	MM
Edmund of Langley [Duke of York]	R2	Escalus, Prince of Verona	RJ
Edward III, King of England	E3	Escanes [Aeschines]	Per
Edward IV, King of England [earlier, Duke of York]	2H6, 3H6, R3	Essex, Earl of	KJ
		Evans, Sir Hugh	MW
Edward V, King of England [earlier, Prince Edward]	R3	Executioner	KJ
		Executioner [Abhorson]	MM
Edward, Prince of Wales (son of Edward III) [Edward Plantagenet; Ned; Black Prince]	E3	Exeter, Duke of [Thomas Beaufort]	H5, 1H6
		Exeter, Duke of [Henry Holland]	3H6
		Exton, Sir Pierce of [Piers Exton]	R2
Edward, Prince of Wales (son of Edward IV) [Ned]	3H6, R3	Fabian	TN
		Fairies, King of the [Oberon]	MND

Character	Play
Fairies, Queen of the [Titania]	MND
Fairy	MND
Fairy, First	MND
Fairy, Second	MND
Falconbridge, Lady [Faulconbridge]	KJ
Falconbridge, Lord [= Montague, in some editions]	3H6
Falconbridge, Philip [Faulconbridge; Bastard]	KJ
Falconbridge, Robert [Faulconbridge]	KJ
Falstaff, Sir John [Sir John Fastolf(e)]	1H6
Falstaff, Sir John [Sir John Oldcastle; Jack]	1H4, 2H4, H5, MW
Fang	2H4
Fastolf(e), Sir John [Sir John Falstaff]	1H6
Father who has killed his son [Soldier who …]	3H6
Faulconbridge, Lady [Falconbridge]	KJ
Faulconbridge, Philip [Falconbridge; Bastard]	KJ
Faulconbridge, Robert [Falconbridge]	KJ
Feeble, Francis	2H4
Fenton, James	MW
Fer, Monsieur Le	H5
Ferdinand	Tem
Ferdinand of Navarre, King	LL
Feste [Jester]	TN
Fidele [Innogen]	Cym
Fife, Thane of [Macduff]	Mac
Filario [Philario]	Cym
Fisherman, First	Per
Fisherman, Second [Pilch]	Per
Fisherman, Third [Patchbreech]	Per
Fitzwalter ☛ Fitzwater	
Fitzwater, Lord [Fitzwalter]	R2
Flaminius	Tim
Flavius [soldier]	JC
Flavius [steward]	Tim
Flavius [tribune]	JC
Fleance	Mac
Florence, Duke of	AW
Florizel [Doricles]	WT
Fluellen, Captain	H5
Flute, Francis [Thisbe]	MND
Fool	KL
Fool	Tim
Ford, Frank [Brook]	MW
Ford, Mistress Alice	MW
Forester	LL
Forrest	R3
Fortinbras, King of Norway [Old Fortinbras]	Ham
Fortinbras, Prince of Norway [Young Fortinbras]	Ham
France, King of	AW
France, King of	KL
France, King of [Charles VI]	H5
France, King of [Charles VII]	1H6
France, King of [John II]	E3
France, King of [Lewis XI]	3H6
France, King of [Philip II]	KJ
France, Princess of	LL
France, Princess of [Katherine]	H5
France, Queen of [Cordelia]	KL
France, Queen of [Isabel]	H5
Francis	1H4, 2H4
Francis, Friar	MA

Character	Play
Francis Flute [Thisbe]	MND
Francisca	MM
Francisco	Ham
Francisco	Tem
Frank Ford [Brook]	MW
Frederick, Duke	AY
Frenchman	Cym
Frenchman, First	E3
Frenchman, Third	E3
Friar Francis	MA
Friar John	RJ
Friar Laurence	RJ
Friar Lodowick [Duke Vincentio]	MM
Friar Peter	MM
Friar Thomas	MM
Friend of Gaoler, First	TNK
Friend of Gaoler, Second	TNK
Froth	MM
Fulvia	AC
Gabriel	TS
Gadshill	1H4
Gallus	AC
Gamekeeper, First [Keeper]	3H6
Gamekeeper, Second [Keeper]	3H6
Ganymede [Rosalind; Rose]	AY
Gaoler [Jailer]	1H6
Gaoler [Jailer]	CE
Gaoler [Jailer]	MV
Gaoler [Jailer]	TNK
Gaoler [Jailer]	WT
Gaoler, First [Jailer]	Cym
Gaoler, Second [Jailer]	Cym
Gaoler's Daughter [Jailer's]	TNK
Gardener	R2
Gardener's Man, First	R2
Gardener's Man, Second	R2
Gardiner [Bishop of Winchester]	H8
Gargrave, Sir Thomas	1H6
Garter King-of-Arms	H8
Gaunt, John of [Duke of Lancaster]	R2
General of the French Army	1H6
Gentleman [Astringer]	AW
Gentleman [attendant to Albany]	KL
Gentleman [attendant to Cordelia]	KL
Gentleman [attendant to Kent]	KL
Gentleman [attendant to Queen Katherine]	H8
Gentleman [attendant to Theseus]	TNK
Gentleman, First [as passer-by]	MM
Gentleman, First [as prisoner]	2H6
Gentleman, First [at Ephesus]	Per
Gentleman, First [attendant to Montano]	Oth
Gentleman, First [of the Bohemian Court]	WT
Gentleman, First [of the Court]	Cym
Gentleman, Second [as passer-by]	MM
Gentleman, Second [as prisoner]	2H6
Gentleman, Second [at Ephesus]	Per
Gentleman, Second [of the Court]	Cym
Gentleman, Second [Rogero, of the Bohemian Court]	WT
Gentleman, Second [attendant to Montano]	Oth
Gentleman, Third [of the Bohemian Court]	WT
Gentleman, Third [to Montano]	Oth
Gentleman, Fourth [attendant to Montano]	Oth
Gentleman Observer, First	H8
Gentleman Observer, Second	H8
Gentleman Observer, Third	H8

Character	Play	Character	Play
Gentlewoman [to Lady Macbeth]	Mac	Graziano [Gratiano]	MV
Gentlewoman [to Queen Katherine]	H8	Graziano [Gratiano]	Oth
Gentlewoman [to Virgilia]	Cor	Green [Greene]	R2
Geoffrey (father of Arthur)	KJ	Greene ☛ Green	
George [later Duke of Clarence]	3H6, R3	Gregory	RJ
George Page, Master	MW	Gregory	TS
George Stanley	R3	Gremio	TS
Gerard de Narbon (father of Helena)	AW	Grey, Lady Elizabeth [Gray; later Queen of England]	3H6
Gerrold, Master [Schoolmaster]	TNK		
Gertrude [Queen of Denmark]	Ham	Grey, Lord [Gray; Marquess of Dorset]	R3
Ghost of Banquo	Mac	Grey, Sir Thomas	H5
Ghost of Caesar	JC	Griffith	H8
Ghost of Edward, Prince of Wales	R3	Groom	R2
Ghost of Hamlet [earlier, King of Denmark]	Ham	Groom, First	2H4
		Groom, Second	2H4
Ghost of Henry VI	R3	Groom, Third	2H4
Giacomo [Iachimo]	Cym	Grumio	TS
Girl [Margaret Plantagenet]	R3	Guardsman	AC
Glamis, Thane of [later, Macbeth]	Mac	Guiderius [Polydore]	Cym
Glamis, Thane of [Sinell]	Mac	Guildenstern	Ham
Glansdale, Sir William	1H6	Guilford, Sir Henry / Harry	H8
Glendower, Owen [Owain Glyndwr]	1H4	Gurney, James	KJ
Gloucester, Duchess of [Eleanor Cobham; Nell]	2H6	Haberdasher	TS
		Hal, Prince [Harry Monmouth; later, Henry V]	1H4, 2H4
Gloucester, Duchess of [Eleanor de Bohun]	R2		
Gloucester, Duke of [Humphrey]	2H4, H5, 1H6, 2H6	Hamlet	Ham
		Hamlet, King [Ghost]	Ham
		Harcourt	2H4
Gloucester, Duke of [later, Richard III]	2H6, 3H6, R3	Harfleur, Governor of	H5
Gloucester, Duke of [Thomas of Woodstock]	R2	Harry [Henry IV]	1H4, 2H4
		Harry [Prince Hal; later, Henry V]	2H4, H5
Gloucester, Earl of (father of Edmund)	KL	Harry [Henry VI]	1H6, 3H6, R3
Gloucester, Earl of [Edmund]	KL	Harry Bolingbroke [Henry Bolingbroke]	R2
Glyndwr, Owain [Owen Glendower]	1H4	Harry England [Henry V]	H5
Gobbo, Launcelot / Lancelot	MV	Harry Hereford [Henry Bolingbroke]	R2
Gobbo, Old	MV	Harry Hotspur [Harry Percy; Hotspur]	R2, 1H4
Gobin de Grace [Gray]	E3	Harry le Roi / Roy [Henry V]	H5
Goffe, Matthew [Gough]	2H6	Harry Monmouth [Prince Hal; later, Henry V]	1H4, 2H4
Gonerill [Gonoril]	KL		
Gonoril ☛ Gonerill		Harry Percy [Henry Percy; Hotspur]	R2, 1H4
Gonzalo	Tem	Harvey [Bardolph]	1H4, 2H4, H5, MW
Goodfellow, Robin [Puck]	MND		
Goth, First	Tit	Hastings [Pursuivant]	R3
Goth, Second	Tit	Hastings, Lord [Ralph Hastings]	2H4
Goths, Queen of the [Tamora]	Tit	Hastings, Lord [William Hastings]	3H6, R3
Gough, Matthew [Goffe]	2H6	Headborough [Verges]	MA
Governor of Cyprus [Cassio]	Oth	Headsman	CE
Governor of Cyprus [Montano]	Oth	Hecat(e) [Queen of the Witches]	Mac
Governor of Cyprus [Othello]	Oth	Hector	TC
Governor of England [York]	R2	Hecuba (wife of Priam)	TC
Governor of Harfleur	H5	Helen	Cym
Governor of Messina [Leonato]	MA	Helen [Helena]	MND
Governor of Mytilene [Lysimachus]	Per	Helena [Helen]	AW
Governor of Paris	1H6	Helena [Helen]	MND
Governor of Tharsus [Cleon]	Per	Helen of Troy	TC
Governor of Vienna [Angelo]	MM	Helenus	TC
Gower, Captain	H5	Helicane ☛ Helicanus	
Gower, John [Presenter]	Per	Helicanus [Helicane]	Per
Gower, Master	2H4	Henry III, King of England [earlier, Prince Henry]	KJ
Grace, Gobin de	E3		
Grandpré	H5	Henry IV, King of England [earlier, Henry Bolingbroke]	R2, 1H4, 2H4
Gratiano [Graziano]	MV		
Gratiano [Graziano]	Oth	Henry V, King of England [Harry]	2H4, H5
Gravedigger [First Clown]	Ham	Henry VI, King of England [Harry]	1H6, 2H6, 3H6
Gravedigger [Second Clown]	Ham		
Gray, Lady Elizabeth [Grey; later Queen of England]	3H6	Henry VII, King of England [earlier, Earl of Richmond]	R3
Gray, Lord [Marquess of Dorset]	R3		

Character	Play	Character	Play
Henry VIII, King of England	H8	Innogen [Imogen; Fidele]	Cym
Henry, Prince [later, Henry III]	KJ	Iras	AC
Henry, Prince of Wales [Prince Hal; later,	1H4, 2H4	Iris	Tem
Henry V]		Isabel [Isabella]	MM
Henry Beaufort [Bishop of Winchester]	1H6	Isabel, Queen [of England]	R2
Henry Bolingbroke [later, Henry IV]	R2, 1H4, 2H4	Isabel, Queen [of France]	H5
Henry Percy [Earl of Northumberland]	1H4	Isabella [Isabel]	MM
Henry Plantagenet [King Henry V]	H5	Isidore	Tim
Henry [Lord Scrope of Masham; Lord	H5	Jack [Falstaff, Sir John; Sir John Oldcastle]	1H4, 2H4, H5,
Henry Scroop]			MW
Herald	2H6	Jailer [Gaoler]	1H6
Herald	Cor	Jailer [Gaoler]	CE
Herald	H5	Jailer [Gaoler]	MV
Herald	KL	Jailer [Gaoler]	TNK
Herald	Oth	Jailer [Gaoler]	WT
Herald	TNK	Jailer, First [Gaoler]	Cym
Herald [Montjoy]	H5	Jailer, Second [Gaoler]	Cym
Herald, English	KJ	Jailer's Daughter [Gaoler's]	TNK
Herald, First	E3	Jamy, Captain	H5
Herald, First	R2	Jaquenetta	LL
Herald, French	KJ	Jaques	AY
Herald, Second	E3	Jaques de Boys	AY
Herald, Second	R2	Jessica	MV
Herald, Third	E3	Jester [Feste]	TN
Herbert, Sir Walter	R3	Jeweller	Tim
Hereford, Duke of [Harry Hereford /	R2	Joan la Pucelle [Pucelle; Joan of Arc]	1H6
Herford; Henry Bolingbroke; later,		Joan of Arc ➤ Joan la Pucelle	
Henry IV]		John	MW
Herford ➤ Hereford		John, King of England	KJ
Hermia	MND	John II, King of France	E3
Hermione	WT	John, Prince [John of Lancaster; later,	1H4, 2H4, H5,
Hero	MA	Duke of Bedford]	1H6
Hiems	LL	John, Don	MA
Hippolita ➤ Hippolyta		John, Friar	RJ
Hippolyta [Hippolyte; Hippolita; Queen of	MND, TNK	John, Sir	R3
the Amazons]		John of Gaunt [Duke of Lancaster]	R2
Hippolyte ➤ Hippolyta		John of Lancaster [Prince John; later,	1H4, 2H4, H5,
Holland, John	2H6	Duke of Bedford]	1H6
Holofernes [Schoolmaster]	LL	John of Valois	E3
Horatio	Ham	John Falstaff, Sir [Jack; Sir John Oldcastle]	1H4, 2H4, H5,
Horner, Thomas	2H6		MW
Hortensio [Licio]	TS	John Fastolfe, Sir [Sir John Falstaff]	1H6
Hortensius	Tim	John Gower	Per
Host of the Garter	MW	John Oldcastle, Sir [Sir John Falstaff; Jack]	1H4, 2H4, H5,
Host of the Tavern	TG		MW
Hostess	TS	John Rugby	MW
Hostess [Mistress Quickly]	1H4, 2H4, H5,	Jordan, Margery [Jourdain]	2H6
	MW	Joseph	TS
Hostilius [Second Stranger]	Tim	Jourdain, Margery [Jordan]	2H6
Hotspur, Harry [Harry Percy; Henry Percy]	R2, 1H4	Julia [Sebastian]	TG
Hubert de Burgh	KJ	Juliet [Julietta]	MM
Hugh, Sir [Evans]	MW	Juliet (daughter of Capulet)	RJ
Hume, John	2H6	Julietta [Juliet]	MM
Humphrey [Duke of Gloucester]	2H4, H5, 1H6,	Julius Caesar	JC
	2H6	Junius Brutus	Cor
Huntingdon, Earl of	H5	Juno	Tem
Huntsman	3H6	Jupiter	Cym
Huntsman, First	TS	Justice	MM
Huntsman, Second	TS	Kate [Lady Percy]	1H4
Hymen	AY, TNK	Kate [Katherina; Katherine; Shrew]	TS
Iachimo [Giacomo]	Cym	Katharine [Katherine; Catherine]	LL
Iago [Ancient / Aunchient]	Oth	Katharine, Princess [Katherine; Catherine]	H5
Iden, Alexander	2H6	Katherina [Katherine; Kate; Shrew]	TS
Illyria, Duke of [Count Orsino; County]	TN	Katherine, Queen	H8
Imogen [Innogen; Fidele]	Cym	Katherine Minola [Katherina; Kate; Shrew]	TS
Indian Boy (changeling)	MND	Keeper, First [Gamekeeper]	3H6

Character	Play	Character	Play
Keeper, Second [Gamekeeper]	3H6	Knight to Lear, Fourth	KL
Keeper in the Tower	R3	Lady, First [in the masque]	Tim
Keeper of the Council Chamber	H8	Lady, First [of the Court]	Cym
Keeper of the Prison	R2	Lady, First [of the Sicilian Court]	WT
Kent, Earl of [Caius]	KL	Lady, First [to Queen Isabel]	R2
King Antiochus of Antioch	Per	Lady Macbeth [later, Queen of Scotland]	Mac
King Charles VI of France	H5	Lady, Old	H8
King Claudius of Denmark	Ham	Lady, Second [of the Court]	Cym
King Cymbeline of Britain	Cym	Lady, Second [of the Sicilian Court]	WT
King David of Scotland	E3	Lady, Second [to Queen Isabel]	R2
King Edward III of England	E3	Laena, Popilius [Lena]	JC
King Edward IV of England	3H6, R3	Laertes	Ham
King Edward V [earlier, Prince Edward]	R3	Lafeu ☛ Lafew	
King Ferdinand of Navarre	LL	Lafew [Lafeu]	AW
King Hamlet of Denmark [Ghost]	Ham	Lancaster, Duke of [John of Gaunt]	R2
King Harry [King Henry V of England]	H5	Lancaster, John of [Prince John; later,	1H4, 2H4, H5,
King Henry III of England [earlier, Prince Henry]	KJ	Duke of Bedford]	1H6
		Lancelot Gobbo [Launcelot Gobbo; Clown]	MV
King Henry IV of England [earlier, Henry Bolingbroke]	R2, 1H4, 2H4	Langley, Edmund of [Duke of York]	R2
		Lartius, Titus	Cor
King Henry V of England [King Harry]	2H4, H5	Launce	TG
King Henry VI of England	1H6, 2H6, 3H6	Launcelot Gobbo [Lancelot Gobbo; Clown]	MV
King Henry VII of England [earlier, Earl of Richmond]	R3	Laurence, Friar	RJ
		Lavatch [Clown]	AW
King Henry VIII of England	H8	Lavinia (daughter of Andronicus)	Tit
King John of England	KJ	Lawyer of the Temple	1H6
King John II of France	E3	Lear, King of Britain	KL
King Lear of Britain	KL	Le Beau	AY
King of Antioch [Antiochus]	Per	Le Fer, Monsieur	H5
King of Bohemia	E3	Legate	1H6
King of Bohemia [Polixenes]	WT	Lena, Popilius [Laena]	JC
King of Denmark [Claudius]	Ham	Lennox [Lenox]	Mac
King of Denmark [Hamlet; Ghost]	Ham	Lenox ☛ Lennox	
King of the Fairies [Oberon]	MND	Leonardo	MV
King of France	AW	Leonato [Governor of Messina]	MA
King of France	KL	Leonatus, Posthumus	Cym
King of France [Charles VI]	H5	Leonatus, Sicilius (as apparition)	Cym
King of France [Charles VII]	1H6	Leonine	Per
King of France [John II]	E3	Leontes, King of Sicilia	WT
King of France [Lewis XI]	3H6	Lepidus	JC, AC
King of Naples [Alonso]	Tem	Lewis XI, King of France [Louis]	3H6
King of Naples [Reignier]	1H6	Lewis the Dauphin [Louis]	H5
King of Navarre [Ferdinand]	LL	Lewis the Dauphin [Louis]	KJ
King of Norway [Old Fortinbras]	Ham	Licio [Hortensio]	TS
King of Norway [Sweno]	Mac	Lieutenant	2H4
King of Pentapolis [Simonides]	Per	Lieutenant	Cor
King of Scotland [David]	E3	Lieutenant of the Tower	3H6
King of Scotland [Duncan]	Mac	Lieutenant of the Tower [Woodville]	1H6
King of Scotland [Macbeth]	Mac	Ligarius, Caius	JC
King of Sicilia [Leontes]	WT	Limoges, Viscount of [Archduke of Austria]	KJ
King of Sparta [Menelaus]	TC	Lincoln, Bishop of	H8
King of Troy [Priam]	TC	Lion [Snug]	MND
King Philip II [of France]	KJ	Lodovico	Oth
King Philip IV [of France; Philip le Beau]	E3	Lodowick	E3
King Richard II of England	R2	Lodowick, Friar [Duke Vincentio]	MM
King Richard III of England [earlier, Richard Plantagenet, Duke of Gloucester]	R3	London, Bishop of	H8
		London, Mayor of	1H6
Knight, First	TNK	London, Mayor of	H8
Knight, First	Per	London, Mayor of	R3
Knight, Second	TNK	Longaville [Longueville]	LL
Knight, Second	Per	Longueville ☛ Longaville	
Knight, Third	TNK	Lord [attendant to Leonato]	MA
Knight, Third	Per	Lord [of Leontes' court]	WT
Knight to Lear, First	KL	Lord [of the Scottish Court]	Mac
Knight to Lear, Second	KL	Lord [patron of Sly]	TS
Knight to Lear, Third	KL	Lord, First [at Duke Frederick's court]	AY

Character	Play
Lord, First [at Duke Senior's court]	AY
Lord, First [at Pentapolis]	Per
Lord, First [at the French Court]	AW
Lord, First [guest of Timon]	Tim
Lord, First [of Aufidius]	Cor
Lord, First [of the Court]	Cym
Lord, Second [at Duke Frederick's court]	AY
Lord, Second [at Duke Senior's court]	AY
Lord, Second [at Pentapolis]	Per
Lord, Second [at the French Court]	AW
Lord, Second [guest of Timon]	Tim
Lord, Second [of Aufidius]	Cor
Lord, Second [of the Court]	Cym
Lord, Third [at Pentapolis]	Per
Lord, Third [at the French Court]	AW
Lord, Third [guest of Timon]	Tim
Lord, Third [of Aufidius]	Cor
Lord, Fourth [at the French Court]	AW
Lord Chamberlain [Earl of Worcester]	H8
Lord Chancellor	H8
Lord Chief Justice	2H4
Lord High Constable [of France; Charles Delabreth]	H5
Lord Marshal	H8
Lord Marshal	R2
Lord Protector [Gloucester]	1H6
Lord Protector [Richard of Gloucester]	R3
Lord Scroop of Masham, Henry [Lord Henry Scrope]	H5
Lord Scrope ☛ Lord Scroop	
Lord of York [Cardinal Wolsey]	H8
Lorenzo	MV
Lorraine, Duke of	E3
Louis XI, King of France [Lewis]	3H6
Louis the Dauphin [Lewis]	KJ
Louis the Dauphin [Lewis]	H5
Lovel, Lord	R3
Lovell, Sir Thomas	H8
Luce [Nell; Dowsabel]	CE
Lucentio [Cambio]	TS
Lucetta	TG
Luciana	CE
Lucianus [Third Player]	Ham
Lucilius	Tim
Lucilius [Lucillius]	JC
Lucillius ☛ Lucilius	
Lucio	MM
Lucius	JC
Lucius [lord]	Tim
Lucius [servant]	Tim
Lucius, Caius	Cym
Lucius, Young	Tit
Lucius (son of Andronicus)	Tit
Lucullus	Tim
Lucy, Sir William	1H6
Lychorida	Per
Lysander	MND
Lysimachus [Governor of Mytilene]	Per
Macbeth [Thane of Glamis; Thane of Cawdor; later, King of Scotland]	Mac
Macbeth, Lady [later, Queen of Scotland]	Mac
Macdonald [Macdonwald]	Mac
Macdonwald ☛ Macdonald	
Macduff [Thane of Fife]	Mac
Macduff, Son of	Mac
Macduff, Wife of	Mac

Character	Play
MacMorris, Captain	H5
Maecenas	AC
Malcolm [Prince of Cumberland; later, King of Scotland]	Mac
Malvolio	TN
Mamillius	WT
Man, First Poor	E3
Man, servant to Troilus	TC
Marcade [Mercadé]	LL
Marcellus	Ham
March, Earl of [Edmund Mortimer]	1H6
March, Earl of [Edward; later, Edward IV]	2H6, 3H6
Marcus Andronicus	Tit
Marcus Brutus	JC
Mardian	AC
Margarelon [Margareton; Bastard]	TC
Margaret	1H6
Margaret [Meg]	MA
Margaret, Queen	2H6, 3H6, R3
Margaret Page, Mistress	MW
Margaret Plantagenet [Girl]	R3
Margareton [Margarelon; Bastard]	TC
Maria	LL
Maria [Mistress Mary; Marian]	TN
Marian ☛ Maria	
Mariana	AW
Mariana	MM
Marina	Per
Mariner	E3
Mariner	WT
Mark Antony	JC, AC
Marshal	Per
Martext, Sir Oliver	AY
Martius, Caius [Coriolanus]	Cor
Martius, Young	Cor
Martius (son of Titus Andronicus)	Tit
Marullus	JC
Mary, Mistress [Maria; Marian]	TN
Masham, Lord Scrope of [Henry; Lord Henry Scroop]	H5
Master	2H6
Master Gunner	1H6
Master of the ship	Tem
Master's mate	2H6
Mayor of Coventry	3H6
Mayor of London	1H6
Mayor of London	H8
Mayor of London	R3
Mayor of Saint Albans	2H6
Mayor of York	3H6
Meg [Margaret]	MA
Melun	KJ
Menas	AC
Menecrates	AC
Menelaus [King of Sparta]	TC
Menenius Agrippa	Cor
Menteith [Menteth]	Mac
Menteth ☛ Menteith	
Mercadé [Marcade]	LL
Merchant	Tim
Merchant, First	CE
Merchant, Second	CE
Mercutio	RJ
Messala	JC
Messenger to Adriana	CE
Messenger to Albany	KL

Character	Play	Character	Play
Messenger to Antiochus	Per	Monmouth, Harry [Henry V]	1H4, 2H4
Messenger to Antony	AC	Montague	RJ
Messenger to Brutus and Sicinius	Cor	Montague, Lady	RJ
Messenger to Cade	2H6	Montague, Marquess of [= Falconbridge,	3H6
Messenger to Claudius	Ham	in some editions]	
Messenger to Cleopatra	AC	Montague, Sir William	E3
Messenger to Cominius	Cor	Montano	Oth
Messenger to Cordelia	KL	Montgomery, Sir John	3H6
Messenger to Countess of Auvergne	1H6	Montjoy [Herald]	H5
Messenger to Cymbeline	Cym	Moonshine [Starveling]	MND
Messenger to Don Pedro	MA	Moor, the [Aaron]	Tit
Messenger to French nobles	H5	Moor, the [Othello]	Oth
Messenger to Gaoler	Cym	Mopsa	WT
Messenger to Gaoler	TNK	Morgan [Belarius]	Cym
Messenger to Gloucester	2H6	Morocco, Prince of	MV
Messenger to Hastings	R3	Mortimer, Edmund, Earl of March	1H6
Messenger to Henry VI	2H6	Mortimer, Lady	1H4
Messenger to Henry VI and Queen	3H6	Mortimer, Lord Edmund	1H4
Messenger to Hotspur	1H4	Mortimer, Sir Hugh	3H6
Messenger to Katherine	H8	Mortimer, Sir John	3H6
Messenger to King David	E3	Morton	2H4
Messenger to King John	KJ	Mote	LL
Messenger to Lady Macduff	Mac	Moth	MND
Messenger to Leonato	MA	Mother (of Posthumus, as apparition)	Cym
Messenger to Lords	AW	Mouldy, Ralph	2H4
Messenger to Macbeth	Mac	Mountford, Lord Charles de [Duke of	E3
Messenger to Martius	Cor	Brittany; John]	
Messenger to Portia	MV	Mowbray, Lord [Earl Marshal]	2H4
Messenger to Provost	MM	Mowbray, Thomas [Duke of Norfolk]	R2
Messenger to rebels	2H4	Mugs [First Carrier]	1H4
Messenger to Richard and Edward	3H6	Murder [Demetrius]	Tit
Messenger to Talbot	1H6	Murderer, First	2H6
Messenger to Theseus	TNK	Murderer, First	Mac
Messenger to Timon	Tim	Murderer, First	R3
Messenger to Titus	Tit	Murderer, Second	2H6
Messenger to Venetian court	Oth	Murderer, Second	Mac
Messenger to Warwick	3H6	Murderer, Second	R3
Messenger to York	1H6	Murderer, Third	Mac
Messenger to York	3H6	Musician, First	Oth
Messenger, First, to English nobles	1H6	Musician, First [Simon Catling]	RJ
Messenger, First, to Hotspur	1H4	Musician, Second [Hugh Rebeck]	RJ
Messenger, First, to King and Queen	2H6	Musician, Third [James Soundpost]	RJ
Messenger, First, to Richard III	R3	Mustardseed	MND
Messenger, First, to Warwick	3H6	Mutius (son of Titus Andronicus)	Tit
Messenger, Second, to Brutus and Sicinius	Cor	Mytilene, Governor of [Lysimachus]	Per
Messenger, Second, to English nobles	1H6	Mytilene, Lord of	Per
Messenger, Second, to Hotspur	1H4	Mytilene, Sailor of	Per
Messenger, Second, to King and Queen	2H6	Naples, King of [Alonso]	Tem
Messenger, Second, to King David	E3	Naples, King of [Reignier]	1H6
Messenger, Second, to Richard III	R3	Nathaniel	TS
Messenger, Second, to Warwick	3H6	Nathaniel, Sir	LL
Messenger, Third, to English nobles	1H6	Navarre, King of [Ferdinand]	LL
Messenger, Third, to Richard III	R3	Ned [Edward Poins]	1H4, 2H4, MW
Messenger, Fourth, to Richard III	R3	Ned (son of Edward III) [Prince Edward]	E3
Metellus Cimber	JC	Ned (son of Edward IV) [Prince Edward]	3H6
Michael	2H6	Ned (son of Henry VI) [Prince Edward]	3H6
Michael, Sir	1H4	Ned Plantagenet (son of Clarence) [Prince	R3
Michael Cassio	Oth	Edward]	
Milan, Duke of	TG	Neighbour, First	2H6
Milan, Duke of [Prospero; Antonio]	Tem	Neighbour, Second	2H6
Minola, Baptista	TS	Neighbour, Third	2H6
Miranda	Tem	Nell	TNK
Mistress Alice Ford	MW	Nell [Eleanor Cobham, Duchess of	2H6
Mistress Margaret Page	MW	Gloucester]	
Mistress Nell Quickly [Hostess]	1H4, 2H4, H5,	Nell [Helen of Troy]	TC
	MW	Nell [Luce]	CE

Character	Play	Character	Play
Nell Quickly, Mistress	1H4, 2H4, H5, MW	Owain Glyndwr ☛ Owen Glendower	
		Owen Glendower [Owain Glyndwr]	1H4
Nerissa [Clerk]	MV	Oxford, Earl of	3H6, R3
Nestor	TC	Pacorus (son of Orodes, King of Parthia)	AC
Nevil [Earl of Warwick, Richard Beauchamp]	2H4	Page	H8
		Page	R3
Nicanor	Cor	Page	RJ
Nicholas	TS	Page	Tim
Nick Bottom [Pyramus]	MND	Page	TS
Nim [Nym]	MW, H5	Page [to Falstaff]	2H4
Nobleman	3H6	Page [to the Countess]	AW
Norfolk, Duchess of	H8	Page, First	AY
Norfolk, Duke of [John Howard]	R3	Page, Second	AY
Norfolk, Duke of [Thomas Howard]	H8	Page, Anne	MW
Norfolk, Duke of [John Mowbray]	3H6	Page, George	MW
Norfolk, Duke of [Thomas Mowbray]	R2	Page, Mistress	MW
Normandy, Duke of [Prince Charles]	E3	Page, William	MW
Northumberland, Earl of [Henry Percy, 1st Earl]	3H6	Painter	Tim
		Palamon	TNK
Northumberland, Earl of [Henry Percy, 3rd Earl]	R2, 1H4, 2H4	Pandar ☛ Pandarus	
		Pandarus [Pandar]	TC
Northumberland, Earl of [Seyward / Siward]	Mac	Pander	Per
Northumberland, Lady	2H4	Pandolf, Cardinal [Pandulph]	KJ
Norway, King of [Old Fortinbras]	Ham	Pandulph, Cardinal [Pandolf]	KJ
Norway, King of [Sweno]	Mac	Panthino	TG
Norway, Prince of [Young Fortinbras]	Ham	Papal Legate	1H6
Norwegian Captain	Ham	Paris	TC
Nurse	3H6	Paris, County	RJ
Nurse	RJ	Paris, Governor of	1H6
Nurse	Tit	Paroles ☛ Parolles	
Nym [Nim]	MW, H5	Parolles [Paroles; Tom Drum]	AW
Oberon [King of the Fairies]	MND	Patchbreech [Third Fisherman]	Per
Octavia	AC	Patience	H8
Octavius Caesar	JC, AC	Patroclus	TC
Officer	TS	Paulina	WT
Officer	TNK	Peaseblossom	MND
Officer [Adam]	CE	Pedant [of Mantua; Schoolmaster; Vincentio]	TS
Officer, First	Cor		
Officer, First	KL	Pedro, Don, Prince of Arragon	MA
Officer, First	TN	Pembroke, Earl of [William Herbert]	3H6
Officer, Second	Cor	Pembroke, Earl of [William Marshal]	KJ
Officer, Second	KL	Pembroke, Marchioness of [Anne Bullen / Boleyn; later, Queen of England]	H8
Officer, Second	TN		
Old Athenian	Tim	Pentapolis, King of [Simonides]	Per
Old Lady	H8	Percy, Harry [Hotspur]	R2
Old Man	KL	Percy, Henry [Earl of Northumberland]	R2, 1H4
Old Man	Mac	Percy, Lady	2H4
Old Man	RJ	Percy, Lady [Kate]	1H4
Oldcastle, Sir John [Sir John Falstaff; Jack]	1H4, 2H4, H5, MW	Percy, Lord	E3
		Percy, Thomas [Earl of Worcester]	1H4
Oliver de Boys	AY	Perdita [Queen of the Feast]	WT
Oliver Martext, Sir	AY	Pericles, Prince of Tyre	Per
Olivia	TN	Peter	RJ
Ophelia	Ham	Peter [Petruchio's servant]	TS
Orlando de Boys	AY	Peter [a Servingman]	TS
Orleans, Bastard of	1H6	Peter, Friar	MM
Orleans, Duke of	H5	Peter of Pomfret	KJ
Orsino, Duke of Illyria	TN	Peter Quince [Prologue]	MND
Osric(k)	Ham	Petitioner, First	2H6
Ostler	1H4	Petitioner, Second	2H6
Oswald	KL	Peto	1H4, 2H4
Othello [the Moor]	Oth	Petruccio ☛ Petruchio	
Outlaw, First	TG	Petruchio [Petruccio]	RJ
Outlaw, Second	TG	Petruchio	TS
Outlaw, Third	TG	Phebe [Phoebe]	AY
Overdone, Mistress	MM	Philario [Filario]	Cym

Character	Play
Philemon	Per
Philharmonus [Soothsayer]	Cym
Philip	TS
Philip II, King of France	KJ
Philip, Prince	E3
Philip, Queen [Philippa; Philippe; Philip]	E3
Philip Faulconbridge [later, Sir Richard Plantagenet; Bastard]	KJ
Philip le Beau [Philip IV]	E3
Philippa, Queen [Philippe; Phillip; Philip]	E3
Philippe, Queen ☞ Philippa, Queen	
Phillip, Queen ☞ Philippa, Queen	
Philo	AC
Philostrate	MND
Philoten	Per
Philotus	Tim
Phoebe [Phebe]	AY
Phrynia	Tim
Pierce of Exton ☞ Piers Exton	
Piers Exton [Sir Pierce of Exton]	R2
Pilch [Second Fisherman]	Per
Pinch, Doctor [Schoolmaster]	CE
Pindarus	JC
Pirate, First	Per
Pirate, Second	Per
Pirate, Third	Per
Pirithous	TNK
Pisanio	Cym
Pistol [Ancient / Aunchient]	MW, 2H4, H5
Plantagenet [Anne]	R3
Plantagenet [Earl of Salisbury]	1H6
Plantagenet [Prince Hal]	1H4
Plantagenet [Richard, Duke of Gloucester; later, Richard III]	R3
Plantagenet, Arthur	KJ
Plantagenet, Edward [Edward IV]	R3
Plantagenet, Edward (son of Clarence)	R3
Plantagenet, Edward (son of Edward III)	E3
Plantagenet, Edward (son of Edward IV)	R3
Plantagenet, Edward (son of Henry VI)	3H6, R3
Plantagenet, Henry [King Henry V]	H5
Plantagenet, Henry [King Henry VI]	1H6, 2H6, 3H6
Plantagenet, Margaret (daughter of Clarence)	R3
Plantagenet, Ned (Prince Edward, son of Clarence)	R3
Plantagenet, Richard [Duke of York]	1H6, 2H6, 3H6
Plantagenet, Sir Richard, [Bastard; earlier, Philip Faulconbridge]	KJ
Player, First	TS
Player, First [Player King]	Ham
Player, Second [Player Queen]	Ham
Player, Third [Lucianus]	Ham
Player, Fourth [Prologue]	Ham
Player King [First Player]	Ham
Player Queen [Second Player]	Ham
Plebeian, First	JC
Plebeian, Fourth	JC
Plebeian, Second	JC
Plebeian, Third	JC
Poet	JC
Poet	Tim
Poines ☞ Poins	
Poins, Edward [Poines; Poynes; Pointz; Ned; Yedward]	1H4, 2H4, MW
Pointz ☞ Poins	

Character	Play
Pole, William de la [Earl of Suffolk; Poole]	1H6, 2H6
Polixenes, King of Bohemia	WT
Polonian Captain	E3
Polonius	Ham
Polydore [Guiderius]	Cym
Pomfret, Peter of	KJ
Pompeius [Sextus Pompey]	AC
Pompey [Bum; Clown]	MM
Pompey, Sextus [Pompeius]	AC
Poole, William de la [Earl of Suffolk; Pole]	1H6, 2H6
Poor Tom [Edgar; Tom O'Bedlam]	KL
Popilius Lena [Popillius Lena / Laena]	JC
Popillius Lena ☞ Popilius Lena	
Porter	1H6
Porter	2H4
Porter	H8
Porter	Mac
Porter's Man	H8
Portia	JC
Portia	MV
Post from Ireland	2H6
Post to Warwick	3H6
Posthumus Leonatus	Cym
Potpan	RJ
Poynes [Edward Poins]	1H4, 2H4, MW
Prentice, First [Robin]	2H6
Prentice, Second [Will]	2H6
Prentice, Third [Tom]	2H6
Presenter [John Gower]	Per
Priam, King of Troy [Priamus]	TC
Priamus ☞ Priam	
Priest	Ham
Priest	R3
Priest	TN
Prince Charles [Duke of Normandy]	E3
Prince Edward (son of Edward III) [Prince of Wales; Edward Plantagenet; Ned]	E3
Prince Edward (son of Edward IV)[Edward Plantagenet; Ned]	3H6, R3
Prince Edward (son of Henry VI)	3H6
Prince Fortinbras	Ham
Prince Hal [Prince Henry; Harry; later, Henry V]	1H4, 2H4
Prince Henry [later, Henry III]	KJ
Prince Henry [Prince Hal; Harry; later, Henry V]	1H4, 2H4
Prince John of Lancaster	1H4, 2H4
Prince Philip	E3
Prince of Arragon	MV
Prince of Arragon [Don Pedro]	MA
Prince of Cumberland [Malcolm; later, King of Scotland]	Mac
Prince of Morocco	MV
Prince of Tyre [Pericles]	Per
Prince of Wales (Edward, son of Edward III)	E3
Prince of Wales (Edward, son of Edward IV) [Plantagenet]	3H6, R3
Prince of Wales (Henry, son of Henry IV; later, Henry V) [Prince Hal; Harry]	1H4, 2H4
Prince of Verona [Escalus]	RJ
Princess of France	LL
Prisoner	MM
Proculeius	AC
Prologue	H8
Prologue	TC

Character	Play	Character	Play
Prologue	TNK	Richard Vernon, Sir	1H4
Prologue [Fourth Player]	Ham	Richmond, Earl of	E3
Prologue [Peter Quince]	MND	Richmond, Henry, Earl of [later, Henry VII]	3H6, R3
Prospero	Tem	Rinaldo [Rynaldo]	AW
Protector, Lord [Gloucester]	2H6	Rivers, Earl [Anthony Woodville]	3H6, R3
Protector, Lord [Richard of Gloucester]	R3	Robert	MW
Proteus	TG	Robert [Count of Artois]	E3
Provost	MM	Robert Faulconbridge	KJ
Ptolemy, Queen of [Cleopatra; Egypt]	AC	Robin [Prentice]	2H6
Publius	JC	Robin	MW
Publius	Tit	Robin Goodfellow [Puck]	MND
Pucelle, Joan la [Joan of Arc]	1H6	Rochester, Bishop of	H8
Puck [Robin Goodfellow]	MND	Roderigo	Oth
Pursuivant [Hastings]	R3	Rogero [Second Gentleman]	WT
Pyramus [Bottom]	MND	Roman, First	Cor
Queen Eleanor (mother of King John) [Elinor]	KJ	Roman, Second	Cor
		Roman, Third	Cor
Queen Elizabeth (mother of Edward V)	R3	Rome, Emperor of [Saturninus]	Tit
Queen Gertrude of Denmark	Ham	Rome, Empress of [Tamora]	Tit
Queen Isabel (wife of Richard II)	R2	Romeo (son of Montague)	RJ
Queen Isabel of France	H5	Rosalind [Rose; Ganymede]	AY
Queen Katherine (wife of Henry VIII)	H8	Rosaline	LL
Queen Margaret (wife of Henry VI)	2H6, 3H6, R3	Rosaline	RJ
Queen Philippa (wife of Edward III)	E3	Rose [Rosalind; Ganymede]	AY
Queen of Britain	Cym	Rosencrantz	Ham
Queen of Egypt [Cleopatra]	AC	Ross, Lord	R2
Queen of England [earlier, Lady Grey]	3H6	Ross, Thane of	Mac
Queen of France [Cordelia]	KL	Rossillion, Count of [Bertram]	AW
Queen of Scotland [earlier, Lady Macbeth]	Mac	Rossillion, Countess of	AW
Queen of the Amazons [Hippolyta]	MND, TNK	Rowland de Boys	AY
Queen of the Goths [Tamora]	Tit	Rugby, John	MW
Queen of the Fairies [Titania]	MND	Rumour	2H4
Queen of the Feast [Perdita]	WT	Russell	1H4
Queen of the Witches [Hecat(e)]	Mac	Rutland, Earl of [Edmund]	3H6
Queen, First	TNK	Rutland, Earl of [Aumerle]	R2
Queen, Second	TNK	Rynaldo [Rinaldo]	AW
Queen, Third	TNK	Sailor	Ham
Quickly, Mistress Nell [Hostess]	1H4, 2H4, H5, MW	Sailor	Oth
		Sailor, First	Per
Quince, Peter [Prologue]	MND	Sailor, Second	Per
Quintus (son of Titus Andronicus)	Tit	Saint Albans, Mayor of	2H6
Rafe	TS	Saint Asaph, Bishop of	H8
Ragozine	MM	Salarino [Solanio]	MV
Rape [Chiron]	Tit	Salaryno [Solanio]	MV
Rambures, Duke of	H5	Salerio	MV
Ratcliffe, Sir Richard	R3	Salisbury, Countess of	E3
Rebeck, Hugh	RJ	Salisbury, Earl of [John Montacute]	R2
Regan	KL	Salisbury, Earl of [Richard Neville]	2H6
Reignier, Duke of Anjou [René]	1H6	Salisbury, Earl of [Thomas Montacute Plantagenet]	H5, 1H6
René, Duke of Anjou [Reignier]	1H6		
Revenge [Tamora]	Tit	Salisbury, Earl of [William de Longespée]	KJ
Reynaldo	Ham	Salisbury, Earl of [William Montacute Plantagenet]	E3
Richard II, King of England	R2		
Richard III, King of England [earlier, Duke of Gloucester]	2H6, 3H6, R3	Sampson	RJ
		Sands, Sir Walter [Sandys; Sir William Sands]	H8
Richard, Duke of Gloucester [later, Richard III]	R3		
		Sandys ☛ Sands	
Richard, Duke of York [Prince Richard] (son of Edward IV)	R3	Saturnine ☛ Saturninus	
		Saturninus [Saturnine; Emperor of Rome]	Tit
Richard Nevil [Earl of Salisbury]	2H6	Sawyer	2H6
Richard Nevil [Earl of Warwick]	2H6	Say, Lord [Saye]	2H6
Richard Plantagenet [Duke of Gloucester; later, Richard III]	R3	Saye ☛ Say	
		Scales, Lord	2H6
Richard Plantagenet [Duke of York]	1H6, 2H6, 3H6	Scarus	AC
Richard Plantagenet, Sir [Bastard; earlier, Philip Faulconbridge]	KJ	Schoolmaster [Ambassador]	AC
		Schoolmaster [Doctor Pinch]	CE

Character	Play
Schoolmaster [Holofernes]	LL
Schoolmaster [Master Gerrold]	TNK
Schoolmaster [Pedant]	TS
Scotland, King of [David]	E3
Scotland, King of [Duncan]	Mac
Scotland, King of [Macbeth]	Mac
Scotland, Queen of [Lady Macbeth]	Mac
Scout, French	1H6
Scribe	H8
Scrivener	R3
Scroop, Henry, Lord [Lord Henry Scrope of Masham]	H5
Scroop, Richard [Archbishop of York]	1H4
Scroop, Sir Stephen [Scroope; Stephen le Scrope]	R2
Scrope, Lord Henry, of Masham [Lord Henry Scroop]	H5
Scrope, Stephen le [Sir Stephen Scroop(e)]	R2
Scrope, William le [Earl of Wiltshire]	R2
Seacole, Francis [Sexton]	MA
Sebastian	Tem
Sebastian	TN
Sebastian [Julia]	TG
Secretary to Wolsey	H8
Seleucus	AC
Sempronius	Tim
Sempronius	Tit
Senator, First	Cor
Senator, First	Cym
Senator, First	Oth
Senator, First	Tim
Senator, Second	Cor
Senator, Second	Cym
Senator, Second	Oth
Senator, Second	Tim
Senator, Third	Tim
Senator, Fourth	Tim
Senior, Duke	AY
Sentinel, French	1H6
Sergeant, French	1H6
Sergeant-at-arms	H8
Servant to Antony	JC
Servant to Baptista	TS
Servant to Caesar	JC
Servant to Diomedes	TC
Servant to Emilia	TNK
Servant to Gloucester	2H6
Servant to Gloucester, First	KL
Servant to Gloucester, Second	KL
Servant to Gloucester, Third	KL
Servant to Hotspur	1H4
Servant to Isidore	Tim
Servant to Leontes	WT
Servant to Macbeth	Mac
Servant to Octavius	JC
Servant to Olivia	TN
Servant to Paris	TC
Servant to Shepherd	WT
Servant to Silvia	TG
Servant to Theseus	TNK
Servant to Wolsey	H8
Servant, First [to Timon]	Tim
Servant, First [to Varro]	Tim
Servant, Second [to Timon]	Tim
Servant, Second [to Varro]	Tim
Servant, Third [to Timon]	Tim

Character	Play
Servilius	Tim
Servingman	R2
Servingman, First	1H6
Servingman, First	RJ
Servingman, First	TS
Servingman, First	Cor
Servingman, Second	1H6
Servingman, Second	RJ
Servingman, Second	TS
Servingman, Second	Cor
Servingman, Third	1H6
Servingman, Third	TS
Servingman, Third	Cor
Sexton [Francis Seacole]	MA
Sextus Pompey [Pompeius]	AC
Seyton	Mac
Seyward, Earl of Northumberland [Siward]	Mac
Seyward, Young [Young Siward]	Mac
Shadow, Simon	2H4
Shallow, Robert	MW, 2H4
Shepherd	1H6
Shepherd	WT
Sheriff	1H4
Sheriff	2H6
Sheriff	KJ
Sheriff	R3
Shore, Mistress Jane	R3
Shrew [Katherina; Katherine; Kate]	TS
Shrewsbury, Earl of [Lord Talbot]	1H6
Shylock	MV
Sicilia, King of [Leontes]	WT
Sicilius Leonatus (father to Posthumus, as apparition)	Cym
Sicinius Velutus	Cor
Silence	2H4
Silius	AC
Silvia	TG
Silvius	AY
Simonides [King of Pentapolis]	Per
Simpcox, Saunder	2H6
Simpcox, Wife of	2H6
Simple, Peter	MW
Sinel(l) [Thane of Glamis]	Mac
Siward [Earl of Northumberland; Seyward]	Mac
Siward, Young [Young Seyward]	Mac
Slender, Abraham	MW
Sly, Christopher(o)	TS
Smith [Weaver]	2H6
Snare	2H4
Snout, Tom [Wall]	MND
Snug [Lion]	MND
Solanio [Salarino; Solarino; Salaryno]	MV
Solarino ⟩ Solanio	
Soldier	Tim
Soldier, First	Cor
Soldier, First	JC
Soldier, French	1H6
Soldier, Second	Cor
Soldier, Second	JC
Soldier, Third	JC
Soldier who has killed his father [Son who …]	3H6
Soldier who has killed his son [Father who …]	3H6
Solinus, Duke of Ephesus	CE
Somerset, Duke of [Edmund Beaufort]	2H6

Character	Play	Character	Play
Somerset, Duke of [Henry Beaufort]	3H6	Thisbe [Flute]	MND
Somerset, Duke of [John or Edmund Beaufort]	1H6	Thomas, Duke of Clarence	2H4
		Thomas, Friar	MM
Somerville, Sir John	3H6	Thomas Beaufort [Duke of Exeter]	1H6
Son who has killed his father [Soldier who …]	3H6	Thomas Grey, Sir	H5
		Thomas Mowbray, Sir [Duke of Norfolk]	R2
Soothsayer	AC	Thomas of Woodstock [Duke of Gloucester]	R2
Soothsayer	JC	Thump, Peter	2H6
Soothsayer [Philharmonus]	Cym	Thurio	TG
Soundpost, James	RJ	Timandra	Tim
Southwell, John	2H6	Time [Chorus]	WT
Spaniard	Cym	Timon	Tim
Sparta, King of [Menelaus]	TC	Timothy	TNK
Speed	TG	Titania [Queen of the Fairies]	MND
Spirit [Asmath / Asnath]	2H6	Titinius	JC
Stafford, Lord	3H6	Titus	Tim
Stafford, Sir Humphrey	2H6	Titus Andronicus	Tit
Stafford, William	2H6	Titus Lartius	Cor
Stanley, George	R3	Toby Belch, Sir	TN
Stanley, Lord [Earl of Derby]	R3	Tom [Ostler]	1H4
Stanley, Sir John	2H6	Tom [Prentice]	2H6
Stanley, Sir William	3H6	Tom, Poor [Tom O'Bedlam; Edgar]	KL
Starveling, Robin [Moonshine]	MND	Tom Drum [Parolles]	AW
Stefano [Stephano]	MV	Tom O'Bedlam [Poor Tom; Edgar]	KL
Stefano [Stephano]	Tem	Tom Snout [Wall]	MND
Stephano [Stefano]	MV	Topas, Sir [Feste]	TN
Stephano [Stefano]	Tem	Touchstone [Clown]	AY
Stranger, First	Tim	Tower, Lieutenant of the [Brakenbury]	R3
Stranger, Second [Hostilius]	Tim	Tranio	TS
Stranger, Third	Tim	Traveller, First	1H4
Strato	JC	Traveller, Second	1H4
Suffolk, Duke of	H8	Travers	2H4
Suffolk, Earl of [William de la Pole]	1H6, 2H6	Trebonius	JC
Sugarsop	TS	Tressel	R3
Surrey, Duke of [Thomas Holland]	R2	Tribune, First	Cym
Surrey, Earl of [Thomas Fitzalan]	2H4	Trinculo	Tem
Surrey, Earl of [Thomas Howard]	R3	Troilus	TC
Surrey, Earl of [William Fitzalan]	H8	Troy, King of [Priam]	TC
Surveyor	H8	Tubal	MV
Sweno, King of Norway	Mac	Tullus Aufidius	Cor
Sycorax (mother of Caliban)	Tem	Tutor	3H6
Syracuse, Antipholus of	CE	Tybalt	RJ
Syracuse, Dromio of	CE	Tyre, Gentleman of	Per
Taborer	TNK	Tyre, Prince of [Pericles]	Per
Tailor	TS	Tyre, Sailor of	Per
Talbot, John [Young Talbot]	1H6	Tyrrel, Sir James	R3
Talbot, Lord [Earl of Shrewsbury]	1H6	Ulysses	TC
Tamora [Queen of the Goths; Revenge]	Tit	Ursula	MA
Tarus [Taurus]	AC	Urswick, Sir Christopher	R3
Tarsus, Lord of	Per	Valentine	Tit
Taurus [Tarus]	AC	Valentine	TN
Tearsheet, Doll	2H4	Valentine [Valentinus]	TG
Thaisa	Per	Valentinus ➤ Valentine	
Thaliard [Thaliart]	Per	Valeria	Cor
Thaliart ➤ Thaliard		Valerius	TNK
Thane of Cawdor	Mac	Valois, John of	E3
Thane of Cawdor [Macbeth]	Mac	Valtemand [Voltemand]	Ham
Thane of Fife [Macduff]	Mac	Varrius	AC
Thane of Glamis [earlier, Sinell]	Mac	Varrius	MM
Thane of Glamis [later, Macbeth]	Mac	Varro	JC
Thersites	TC	Varro	Tim
Theseus, Duke of Athens	MND, TNK	Vaughan, Sir Thomas	R3
Thidias	AC	Vaux	2H6
Thief, First [Bandit]	Tim	Vaux, Sir Nicholas	H8
Thief, Second [Bandit]	Tim	Velutus, Sicinius	Cor
Thief, Third [Bandit]	Tim	Venice, Duke of	MV

Character	Play	Character	Play
Venice, Duke of	Oth	Widow	TS
Ventidius	AC	Widow Capilet	AW
Ventidius	Tim	Will	2H4
Ver	LL	Will [Prentice]	2H6
Verges [Headborough]	MA	William	AY
Vernon	1H6	William Page	MW
Vernon, Sir Richard	1H4	William Sands, Sir [Sandys; Sir Walter	H8
Verona, Prince of [Escalus]	RJ	Sands]	
Vienna, Duke of [Vincentio; Friar	MM	Williams, Michael	H5
Lodowick]		Willoughby, Lord	R2
Villiers, Lord	E3	Wiltshire, Earl of [William le Scrope]	R2
Vincentio	TS	Wiltshire, Sheriff of	R3
Vincentio [Pedant; Schoolmaster]	TS	Winchester, Bishop of [later, Cardinal	1H6, 2H6
Vincentio, Duke of Vienna [Friar Lodowick]	MM	Beaufort]	
Vintner	1H4	Winchester, Bishop of [Gardiner]	H8
Viola [Cesario]	TN	Witch, First	Mac
Violenta [in some editions; possibly Diana]	AW	Witch, Second	Mac
Virgilia	Cor	Witch, Third	Mac
Voltemand [Valtemand]	Ham	Wolsey, Cardinal [Lord of York]	H8
Volumnia	Cor	Woman	E3
Volumnius	JC	Woman, servant to Emilia	TNK
Wall [Snout]	MND	Woodstock, Thomas of [Duke of	R2
Walter	TS	Gloucester]	
Walter Sands, Sir [Sandys; Sir William	H8	Woodville, Lieutenant of the Tower	1H6
Sands]		Woodville, Anthony [Rivers]	R3
Warder, First	1H6	Wooer	TNK
Warder, Second	1H6	Worcester, Earl of [Lord Chamberlain]	H8
Wart, Thomas	2H4	Worcester, Earl of [Thomas Percy]	1H4
Warwick, Earl of [Richard Beauchamp]	2H4, H5, 1H6	Yedward [Edward Poins]	1H4, 2H4, MW
Warwick, Earl of [Richard Neville]	2H6, 3H6	Yorick	Ham
Warwick, Earl of [Thomas de Beauchamp]	E3	York, Archbishop of [Thomas Rotheram]	R3
Watch, First	AC	York, Archbishop of [Richard Scroop]	1H4, 2H4
Watch, First	Cor	York, Duchess of (mother of Aumerle)	R2
Watch, Second	AC	York, Duchess of [Cicely Neville]	R3
Watch, Second	Cor	York, Duke of [Edmund of Langley]	R2
Watchman, First	3H6	York, Duke of [Edward Plantagenet]	H5
Watchman, First	MA	York, Duke of [Edward, later Edward IV]	3H6
Watchman, First	RJ	York, Duke of [Richard Plantagenet]	1H6, 2H6, 3H6
Watchman, Second	3H6	York, Lord of [Cardinal Wolsey]	H8
Watchman, Second	MA	York, Mayor of	3H6
Watchman, Second	RJ	York, Richard, Duke of [Prince Richard]	R3
Watchman, Third	3H6	(son of Edward IV)	
Watchman, Third	RJ	Young Cato	JC
Weaver [Smith]	2H6	Young Lucius (grandson of Titus	Tit
Westminster, Abbot of	R2	Andronicus)	
Westmorland, Earl of [1st Earl]	1H4, 2H4, H5	Young Martius	Cor
Westmorland, Earl of [2nd Earl]	3H6	Young Seyward / Siward	Mac
Whitmore, Walter / Gualtier	2H6		

APPENDICES

List of Appendices

The A–Z section of this book deals with Shakespeare's general English vocabulary. Two types of information have thereby been excluded: the use of proper (as opposed to common) nouns – that is, the names of individual people, places, days, etc. which have a distinctive form or connotation compared to modern English; and vocabulary belonging to languages other than English or representing the three main Celtic-influenced dialects of English. Appendices I–XVI cover these areas.

A cross-reference to another Appendix, or to a panel in the A–Z section, is given a page reference; but no page number is given to a cross-reference within the same Appendix. The quotations used within certain themes are purely for illustration, and do not represent the range of contexts in which a word occurs.

Beings

I CLASSICAL MYTHOLOGY

Roman and Greek gods and goddesses are listed separately: ☞ p.620. For mythological locations, ☞ p.634.

Being	Location	Example	Gloss
Absyrtus	2H6 V.ii.59	[of an infant] *Into as many gobbets will I cut it / As wild Medea young Absyrtus did*	younger brother of Medea, killed by her to aid Jason's escape with the Golden Fleece
Acheron	Mac III.v.15	*at the pit of Acheron / Meet me*	the chasm or abyss of the Underworld, and the name of one of the rivers there which the souls of the dead have to cross
Achilles	E3 II.i.393	*The poets write that great Achilles' spear / Could heal the wound it made*	son of Peleus and Thetis; according to the oracle, only Achilles' spear could heal the wounds it made; character in *Troilus and Cressida*
Actaeon	MW III.ii.39	*a secure and wilful Actaeon*	hunter who encountered Artemis, goddess of chastity, while she was bathing and therefore naked: she changed him into a stag, who was pursued and killed by his own hounds
Adonis	TS Ind.ii.49	*Adonis painted by a running brook*	handsome young man loved by Aphrodite, Greek goddess of sexual love (in Roman mythology, by Venus); character in *Venus and Adonis*
Aeacides	TS III.i.50	*Aeacides / Was Ajax, called so from his grandfather*	☞ Ajax
Aeacus	2H6 I.iv.61	*Aio … Aeacida* [Latin: I proclaim … descendant of Aeacus]	son of Zeus and Aegina; an ancestor of Achilles
Aegle, Aegles	MND II.i.79	[to Titania, of Theseus] *Didst thou not … make him with fair Aegles break his faith*	daughter of Panopeus of Phocis, loved by Theseus ☞ Theseus
Aeneas	JC I.ii.112	*Aeneas, our great ancestor, / Did from the flames of Troy upon his shoulder / The old Anchises bear*	Trojan hero, son of Anchises and Aphrodite; escaped after the fall of Troy, bearing his father on his shoulders; in Roman legend, the ancestor of the Romans ☞ Anchises; Dido
Aeson	MV V.i.14	*Medea gathered the enchanted herbs / That did renew old Aeson*	father of Jason and half-brother of Pelias; magically restored to youth by Medea ☞ Jason; Medea
Agamemnon	E3 III.i.55	*we are as puissant as the force / Of Agamemnon in the haven of Troy*	commander of the Greek forces at Troy, married to Clytemnestra; character in *Troilus and Cressida*
Agenor	TS I.i.165	*sweet beauty … / Such as the daughter of Agenor had*	husband of Telephassa; father of daughter Europa, and of sons Cadmus, Phoenix, and Cilix ☞ Europa
Ajax	KL II.ii.123	*None of these rogues and cowards / But Ajax is their fool*	son of Telamon, King of Salamis, thus known as Telamonian Ajax, and sometimes Telamon or Aeacides; fought against Troy, proverbial for his size and strength; when the armour of the dead Achilles was not given to him, he went mad and killed himself; character in *Troilus and Cressida*

Being	Location	Example	Gloss
Ajax Telamonius	2H6 V.i.26	*like Ajax Telamonius, / On sheep or oxen could I spend my fury*	☛ Ajax
Alcides	TNK V.iii.119	*Alcides was / To him a sow of lead*	original name of Hercules, after his grandfather Alceus ☛ Hercules
Alecto	2H4 V.v.37	*Rouse up Revenge from ebon den with fell Alecto's snake*	one of the Furies, whose name means 'never-ceasing'
Althaea	2H6 I.i.232	*the fatal brand Althaea burnt*	mother of Meleager, whose life-span was determined by the preservation of a magic log; when Althaea burnt the log on a fire, Meleager died ☛ Meleager
Anchises	2H6 V.ii.62	*did Aeneas old Anchises bear*	father of Aeneas, who saves him from blazing Troy by carrying him out of the city on his shoulders
Anna	TS I.i.151	*as secret and as dear / As Anna to the Queen of Carthage was*	sister of Dido, to whom Dido confides her love for Aeneas ☛ Dido
Antiopa	MND II.i.80	[to Titania, of Theseus] *Didst thou not ... make him with fair Aegles break his faith, / With Ariadne, and Antiopa*	Amazon captured or abducted by Theseus; also known as Antiope ☛ Theseus
Argus	MV V.i.230	*watch me like Argus*	hundred-eyed guard of Io, a heifer; Hermes killed him to rescue Io, and Hera then transferred his many eyes to the peacock's tail
Ariachne	TC V.ii.154	*Admits no orifex for a point as subtle / As Ariachne's broken woof to enter*	weaver from Lydia, who challenged Athena to a contest; when Ariachne's work was seen to be superior, Athena destroyed it, and Ariachne hanged herself; Athena saved her, but changed her into a spider; also known as Arachne
Ariadne	TG IV.iv.164	*'twas Ariadne passioning / For Theseus' perjury*	daughter of Minos who helped Theseus find his way through the labyrinth, and then fled with him; Theseus abandoned her while she slept at Naxos ☛ Theseus
Arion	TN I.ii.15	*like Arion on the dolphin's back, / I saw him hold acquaintance with the waves*	legendary Greek musician; about to be robbed and killed by a ship's crew, he was allowed to sing one last song; dolphins then appeared, Arion leapt overboard, and was carried by one of them to safety
Ascanius	2H6 III.ii.116	*witch me, as Ascanius did / When he to madding Dido would unfold / His father's acts*	son of Aeneas and Creusa, and grandson of Priam ☛ Aeneas; Dido
Atalanta	AY III.ii.269	*You have a nimble wit; I think 'twas made of Atalanta's heels*	fleet-footed huntress who swore only to marry the suitor who could outrace her; those she defeated, she killed
Atlas	3H6 V.i.36	*Thou art no Atlas for so great a weight*	giant, sentenced by Zeus to carry the heavens on his shoulders for taking part in the struggle against the gods
Atropos	2H4 II.iv.194	*Come, Atropos, I say!*	☛ Fates
Bacchanals	MND V.i.48	*The riot of the tipsy Bacchanals*	devotees of Bacchus (Dionysus), the god of wine and inspiration
Briareus	TC I.ii.28	*he is a gouty Briareus, many hands and no use*	son of Uranus and Gaea; legendary monster with 100 arms and 50 heads who fought and defeated the Titans for Zeus
Cadmus	MND IV.i.111	*Hercules and Cadmus ... bayed the bear / With hounds of Sparta*	son of Agenor, King of Tyre; he set off in pursuit of his sister Europa, arrived in Greece, and founded Thebes
Capaneus	TNK I.i.59	*King Capaneus was your lord*	one of seven champions - the 'Seven against Thebes' - who attacked Thebes to deprive Eteocles of his kingship
Centaurs	Tit V.ii.202	*this banquet, which I wish may prove / More stern and bloody than the Centaurs' feast*	creatures with the upper half of a man and the rear legs of a horse; reputed for bestial behaviour; at Pirithous' wedding feast, one tried to violate his bride, resulting in a fatal brawl

Being	Location	Example	Gloss
Cerberus	**Tit** II.iv.51	*fell asleep, / As Cerberus at the Thracian poet's feet*	three-headed dog guarding the entrance to the Underworld, originally fifty-headed, later with three heads; charmed to sleep by Orpheus during his quest to rescue Euridice ➤ Orpheus
Charon	**TC** III.ii.9	*be thou my Charon, / And give me swift transportation*	guardian of the Underworld; ferryman who carried the souls of the dead across the River Acheron
Cimmerian	**Tit** II.iii.72	*your swart Cimmerian*	native of a mythical country where the sun was never seen
Circe	**1H6** V.iii.35	*See how the ugly witch doth bend her brows / As if, with Circe, she would change my shape*	enchantress who detained Odysseus and his followers on the isle of Aeaea, transforming Odysseus' men into swine with a magic drink
Collatine	**Luc** 33 and throughout	*why is Collatine the publisher / Of that rich jewel he should keep unknown*	husband of Lucrece; character in *The Rape of Lucrece* ➤ Lucrece
Creon	**TNK** I.i.40	*three queens, whose sovereigns fell before / The wrath of cruel Creon*	king of Thebes who gave orders that any who died attacking Thebes should be left unburied
Cressid, Cressida	**H5** II.i.73	*from the powdering tub of infamy / Fetch forth the lazar kite of Cressid's kind*	fickle daughter of Calchas, a Trojan priest; beloved by Troilus, a Trojan prince, she deserted him for Diomedes; character in *Troilus and Cressida*
Cyclops	**Ham** II.ii.487	*never did the Cyclops' hammers fall / On Mars's armour … / With less remorse than Pyrrhus' bleeding sword / Now falls on Priam*	one-eyed giants who aided Vulcan in forging armour for the gods
Daedalus	**3H6** V.vi.21	*I, Daedalus; my poor boy, Icarus*	legendary Athenian inventor who constructed the labyrinth for King Minos in Crete; escaped to Sicily with wings he had made for himself and his son Icarus
Damon	**Ham** III.ii.290	*thou dost know, O Damon dear / This realm dismantled was / Of Jove himself*	Syracusan remembered as a model of faithful friendship; Pythias, condemned to death by Dionysus, begged to be allowed home to arrange his affairs; Damon pledged his own life against Pythias' return; Dionysus, impressed by their friendship, pardoned Pythias
Daphne	**MND** II.i.231	*Apollo flies, and Daphne holds the chase*	nymph loved by Apollo; chased by the god, she was saved by being turned into a laurel, which became Apollo's sacred tree
Dardanian	**MV** III.ii.58	*The rest aloof are the Dardanian wives*	poetic name for Trojan
Deucalion	**Cor** II.i.86	*[of Martius] who … is worth all your predecessors since Deucalion*	son of Prometheus; Deucalion and his wife Pyrrha survived in an ark when Zeus flooded the world; the oracle advised them to restore the human race by throwing stones over their shoulders; these turned into human beings
Dido	**MND** I.i.173	*by that fire which burned the Carthage queen / When the false Trojan under sail was seen*	Queen of Carthage who fell in love with Aeneas when he was shipwrecked on her shores; commanded by Jupiter, Aeneas left without seeing Dido again, and she killed herself on a funeral pyre
Diomed, Diomede	**3H6** IV.ii.19	*Ulysses and stout Diomede / With sleight and manhood stole to Rhesus' tents*	Greek hero who fought in the Trojan War and even took on the gods in battle; character in *Troilus and Cressida*, where he is Cressida's lover
Enceladus	**Tit** IV.ii.92	*Enceladus / With all his threat'ning band of Typhon's brood*	giant who fought against the Olympian gods, son of Tartarus and Gaea; possible brother of Typhon
Endymion	**MV** V.i.109	*the moon sleeps with Endymion, / And would not be awaked*	young shepherd loved by Selene (the Moon); Zeus granted his wish of eternal sleep, and thus he remained forever young
Ercles	**MND** I.ii.26	*I could play Ercles rarely*	➤ Hercules
Erebus	**2H4** II.iv.153	*to th'infernal deep, with Erebus and tortures vile also*	'Darkness', son of Chaos, the place where Shades passed on their way to Hades

Being	Location	Example	Gloss
Europa	**MW** V.v.3	*Remember, Jove, thou wast a bull for thy Europa*	daughter of Agenor; she was abducted by Jove in the shape of a bull, who then swam with her on his back to Crete
Fates	**MND** V.i.277	*O Fates, come, come, / Cut thread and thrum*	a trio of goddesses who control human destiny: Atropos ('the inflexible') cuts the thread of life allotted and spun by Lachesis ('the distributor') and Clotho ('the spinner')
Furies	**MND** V.i.276	*Approach, ye Furies fell*	three goddesses: Alecto 'never-ceasing', Megaira 'grudger', and Tisiphone 'avenger of blood'; spirits of vengeance, depicted as carrying torches and covered with snakes
Gorgon	**AC** II.v.116	*Though he be painted one way like a Gorgon, / The other way's a Mars*	generally applied to Medusa, one of three monsters who had snakes in their hair, ugly faces, huge wings, and whose staring eyes could turn people to stone
Hector	**1H6** II.iii.19	*I thought I should have seen some Hercules, / A second Hector, for his grim aspect*	bravest Trojan, who led out their army to battle; the son of Priam, married to Andromache; character in *Troilus and Cressida*
Hecuba	**Ham** II.ii.556	*What's Hecuba to him, or he to her, / That he should weep for her?*	wife of Priam, King of Troy, and mother of eighteen children; after the Greeks took Troy, she saw her sons and her husband killed, and was sent into slavery
Helen	**AY** III.ii.141	*Nature presently distilled / Helen's cheek, but not her heart*	Helen, renowned for her beauty, whose abduction from the Greeks by Paris of Troy caused the Trojan War; character in *Troilus and Cressida*
Helicons	**2H4** V.iii.104	*Shall dunghill curs confront the Helicons?*	nine Muses from the slopes of Mt Helicon, daughters of Zeus and Mnemosyne, who give artistic inspiration
Hercules	**TNK** II.iv.2	*I have not seen, / Since Hercules, a man of tougher sinews*	(Roman form of Heracles) proverbial for his mythical physical strength and miraculous achievements; also referred to as Alcides and comically as Ercles ☛ Nine Worthies, p.628
Hero			☛ Leander
Hesperides	**Per** I.i.28	*Before thee stands this fair Hesperides, / With golden fruit*	daughters of the evening star (Hesper), who guard the garden of the gods where the golden apples grow
Hippolyta	**TNK** I.i.77	*Honoured Hippolyta, / Most dreaded Amazon*	queen of the Amazons; character in *The Two Noble Kinsmen*
Hydra	**H5** I.i.35	*never Hydra-headed wilfulness / So soon did lose his seat*	many-headed monster, the child of Typhon and Echnida; as each head was cut off, it grew again
Hyrcania	**Ham** II.ii.448	*The rugged Pyrrhus, like th'Hyrcanian beast*	☛ Hyrcan tiger
Hyrcan tiger	**Mac** III.iv.100	*Approach thou like ... the Hyrcan tiger*	tiger of Hyrcania (in Asia Minor), proverbial for its ferocity
Icarus	**1H6** IV.vi.55	*follow thou thy desperate sire of Crete, / Thou Icarus*	son of Daedalus, who tried to escape from Crete wearing wings made by his father; ignoring a warning, he flew too near the Sun; the wax holding the wings melted, and he fell into the Aegean Sea
Io	**TS** Ind.ii.53	*We'll show thee Io as she was a maid, / And how she was beguiled and surprised*	daughter of river-god Inachus, loved by Zeus, who turned her into a heifer to save her from the jealousy of Zeus' wife, Hera
Jason	**MV** I.i.172	*[of Portia] many Jasons come in quest of her*	son of Aeson, King of Iolcos; he was sent, leading the Argonauts, on the quest for the Golden Fleece, which he obtained with Medea's assistance ☛ Medea
Laertes	**Tit** I.i.383	*wise Laertes' son / Did graciously plead for his funerals*	father of Ulysses ☛ Ulysses
Leander	**TG** I.i.22	*story of deep love, / How young Leander crossed the Hellespont*	young man in love with Hero, priestess of Aphrodite, who lived on the opposite side of the Hellespont; each night he swam across, guided by her lamp; one night the lamp blew out in a storm, and he was drowned; Hero committed suicide by throwing herself into the sea ☛ Hellespont, p.635
Leda	**MW** V.v.7	*You were also, Jupiter, a swan for the love of Leda*	daughter of Thestius; loved by Jove, who turned himself into a swan to seduce her

Being	Location	Example	Gloss
Lichas	**AC** IV.xii.45	*Let me lodge Lichas on the horns o'th' moon*	companion to Hercules, who carried to him a poisoned tunic; after wearing the tunic, Hercules in agony threw Lichas into the sky ☛ Nessus
Limander	**MND** V.i.193	*like Limander am I trusty still*	malapropism for Leander
Medea	**MV** V.i.13	*In such a night / Medea gathered the enchanted herbs / That did renew old Aeson*	daughter of Aeetes, King of Colchis, who assisted Jason in obtaining the Golden Fleece ☛ Aeson; Jason
Meleager	**TNK** III.v.18	*do you, / As once did Meleager and the boar, / Break comely out before him*	son of Althaea, his life-span determined by an unburnt magic log; he murdered his uncles in a quarrel over the killing of a boar ravaging the fields in Calydon; in her rage Althaea burnt Meleager's log on a fire, and he died
Menelaus	**3H6** II.ii.147	*Helen of Greece was fairer far than thou, / Although thy husband may be Menelaus*	brother of Agamemnon, king of Sparta, married to Helen of Troy; character in *Troilus and Cressida*
Minos	**3H6** V.vi.22	*I, Daedalus; my poor boy, Icarus; / Thy father, Minos, that denied our course*	king of Crete, who imprisoned Daedalus and his son, Icarus, for helping Theseus escape from his labyrinth
Minotaur	**1H6** V.iii.189	*Thou mayst not wander in that labyrinth: / There Minotaurs and ugly treasons lurk*	son of Pasiphae and a bull from the sea, half bull and half human; kept in Minos' labyrinth, and killed by Theseus
Myrmidons	**TC** I.iii.378	*the great Myrmidon, / Who broils in loud applause*	band of warriors from Thessaly, who went to the Trojan War with Achilles; characters in *Troilus and Cressida*
Naiades	**Tem** IV.i.128	*You nymphs, called Naiades, of the windring brooks*	nymphs who inhabit springs, rivers, and lakes
Narcissus	**Venus** 161	*Narcissus ... died to kiss his shadow in the brook*	handsome youth who fell in love with his own reflection in a pool; he pined away and was turned into a flower
Nemean lion	**Ham** I.iv.83	*As hardy as the Nemean lion's nerve*	monstrous lion, reputably invulnerable, from the region of Nemea; its destruction was one of the twelve labours of Hercules
Neoptolemus	**TC** IV.v.142	*Not Neoptolemus so mirable ... could promise to himself / A thought of added honour torn from Hector*	son of Achilles and Deidamia, but here referring to Achilles himself ☛ Pyrrhus
Nereids	**AC** II.ii.211	*Her gentlewomen, like the Nereides, / So many mermaids, tended her i' th' eyes*	sea-nymph, one of the 50 or (in some accounts) 100 daughters of Nereus and Doris; they lived with their father in the depths of the sea
Nessus	**AC** IV.xii.43	*The shirt of Nessus is upon me*	centaur, shot by Hercules for attempting to rape Deianeira; Nessus gave her a poisonous liquid in the guise of a love-potion, which caused Hercules' death when he wore a shirt dipped in the mixture ☛ Hercules; Lichas
Nestor	**E3** III.iv.50	*if he breaketh out, Nestor's years on earth / Will make him savour still of this exploit*	Greek Trojan leader, reputed for his age and wisdom; character in *Troilus and Cressida*
Ninus	**MND** III.i.91	*I'll meet thee, Pyramus, at Ninny's tomb* [Quince] *'Ninus' tomb', man*	founder of the Assyrian city of Nineveh ☛ Pyramus
Niobe	**Ham** I.ii.149	*she followed my poor father's body / Like Niobe, all tears*	Theban heroine, daughter of Tantalus, whose seven sons and seven daughters (numbers vary in different versions) were slain by Apollo and Diana; the gods then turned her into a rock, but her eyes continued to weep in the form of a spring
Orpheus	**TG** III.ii.78	*Orpheus' lute was strung with poets' sinews*	legendary Greek poet, able to charm beasts and even stones with his music
Pandarus	**MW** I.iii.70	*Shall I Sir Pandarus of Troy become*	Trojan prince, killed by Diomedes; character in *Troilus and Cressida*, where he is Cressida's uncle and go-between
Pandion	**PassP** XX.23	*King Pandion he is dead*	King of Athens, the father of Philomela

Being	Location	Example	Gloss
Parca	H5 V.i.19	*Dost thou thirst ... / To have me fold up Parca's fatal web?*	originally, a Roman birth-goddess, later trebled, and identified with the Moerae, or Parcae, the goddesses who decide the destiny of humans ☞ Fates
Paris	1H6 V.v.104	*thus he goes, / As did the youthful Paris once to Greece, / With hope to find the like event in love*	youngest son of Priam and Hecuba; he stole Helen away from her Greek husband, Menelaus, causing the Trojan Wars; character in *Troilus and Cressida*
Pegasus	1H4 IV.i.109	*To turn and wind a fiery Pegasus*	winged horse, which sprang from the body of Medusa after her death; he brought thunderbolts to Zeus ☞ Gorgon
Pelops	TNK IV.ii.21	*a brow ... / Smoother than Pelops' shoulder*	son of Tantalus, served to the gods at a banquet; Demeter ate his shoulder, which the gods replaced by one of ivory
Penelope	Cor I.iii.83	*You would be another Penelope ... all the yarn she spun in Ulysses' absence did but fill Ithaca full of moths*	Ulysses' wife, who waited twenty years for his return from Troy; she told her suitors she had to finish weaving a shroud for Ulysses' father before she could remarry, and undid the day's work each night ☞ Ulysses
Penthesilea	TN II.iii.170	*[of Maria] Good night, Penthesilea*	Amazonian queen, who helped Priam at Troy
Perigenia	MND II.i.78	*Didst thou not lead him through the glimmering night / From Perigenia, whom he ravished*	daughter of a robber, Sinnis; loved by Theseus; also known as Perigouna
Perseus	E3 III.iii.200	*take this target, wear it on thy arm, / And may the view thereof, like Perseus' shield, / Astonish and transform thy gazing foes*	son of Zeus and Danae; advised by Athene to look at the reflection in his shield when cutting off Medusa's head, thereby avoiding being turned to stone; associated with the winged horse released by her death ☞ Pegasus
Philemon	MA II.i.86	*My visor is Philemon's roof*	peasant who, with his wife Baucis, entertained Jupiter and Mercury when they visited the Earth to test people's hospitality
Philomel, Philomela	Luc 1079	*By this, lamenting Philomel had ended / The well-tuned warble of her nightly sorrow*	daughter of Pandion, King of Athens; Tereus, her brother-in-law, raped her and cut out her tongue, but she told the tale in her embroidery; the gods turned her into a nightingale after she took her revenge ☞ Procne; Tereus
Priam	Ham II.ii.462	*the hellish Pyrrhus / Old grandsire Priam seeks*	King of Troy, son of Laomedon, husband of Hecuba; he was killed by Pyrrhus during the sack of Troy; character in *Troilus and Cressida*
Procne, Progne	Tit V.ii.194	*worse than Philomel you used my daughter, / And worse than Procne I will be revenged*	Philomel's sister, who served her son Itys in a meal to Tereus, her father, in revenge for Tereus' rape and mutilation of Philomel ☞ Philomel; Tereus
Procrus	MND V.i.195	*Not Shafalus to Procrus was so true*	mispronunciation of Procris, legendary Greek lover whose love for her husband Cephalus was tragically harmed through his jealousy ☞ Shafalus
Prometheus	Tit II.i.17	*faster bound to Aaron's charming eyes / Than is Prometheus tied to Caucasus*	Titan who stole fire from heaven to help mankind; he was punished by being chained to a rock in the Caucasus
Proserpine, Proserpina	TC II.i.32	*thou art as full of envy at his greatness as Cerberus is at Proserpina's beauty*	daughter of the corn-goddess Ceres; Hades, king of the Underworld, abducted her and made her his queen
Proteus	3H6 III.ii.192	*I can ... / Change shapes with Proteus for advantages*	old man of the sea, shepherd of Poseidon's flock; he had the ability to change his shape
Pygmalion	MM III.ii.43	*is there none of Pygmalion's images ... to be had now*	sculptor who created and fell in love with his ivory statue of a woman; Aphrodite brought her to life, and he married her
Pyramus	MND I.ii.20 and throughout	*What is Pyramus? ... A lover that kills himself, most gallant, for love*	lover of Thisbe; kept apart by their parents, they talked through a crack in their dividing wall; arriving at a rendezvous, Pyramus found Thisbe's cloak stained with blood from a lion's prey; thinking she had been killed by a lion, he committed suicide; when she found him, Thisbe killed herself with his sword

Being	Location	Example	Gloss
Pyrrhus	Ham II.ii.450	*The rugged Pyrrhus, he whose sable arms ... did the night resemble*	son of Achilles, who entered Troy in the wooden horse and killed Priam; also known as Neoptolemus
Rhesus	3H6 IV.ii.20	*Ulysses and stout Diomede ... stole to Rhesus' tents, / And brought from thence the Thracian fatal steeds*	Thracian hero, famed for his horses; after he had fought for one day in the Trojan War, Ulysses and Diomedes killed him in his tent at night, and stole the horses ➤ Thracian, p.637
Sagittary	TC V.v.14	*the dreadful Sagittary / Appals our numbers*	centaur-like being which fought in the Trojan army against the Greeks
Shafalus	MND V.i.195	*Not Shafalus to Procrus was so true*	mispronunciation of Cephalus, son of Deion ➤ Procrus
Sibyl, Sibylla	MV I.ii.100	*If I live to be as old as Sybilla, I will die as chaste as Diana unless I be obtained by the manner of my father's will*	priestess inspired by Apollo, her prophecies being written on leaves; Apollo granted her as many years of life as she could hold grains of sand in her hand; there were later said to be ten Sibyls
Sinon	Cym III.iv.60	*Sinon's weeping / Did scandal many a holy tear*	spy who alerted the Greeks inside the Trojan horse after it had been taken into the citadel of Troy
Siren	Sonn 119.2	*Siren tears / Distill'd from limbecks foul as hell within*	sea-demon of Greek mythology, half bird, half woman, whose music lured sailors to destruction on the rocky shores of her island
Sisters Three	MND V.i.328	*O sisters three, / Come, come to me*	➤ Fates
Sphinx	LL IV.iii.318	*Subtle as Sphinx*	female monster who killed people unable to answer its riddle
Tantalus	Venus 599	*That worse than Tantalus' is her annoy, / To clip Elisium and to lack her joy*	king of Sipylos in Lydia, punished in the Underworld for his crimes; he sits in a pool which recedes when he bends to drink, and the grapes over his head elude his grasp
Telamon	AC IV.xiii.2	*he's more mad / Than Telamon for his shield*	➤ Ajax
Tereus	Cym II.ii.45	*She hath been reading late, / The tale of Tereus*	legendary king of Athens, who raped and mutilated Philomel ➤ Philomel
Thersites	Cym IV.ii.252	*Thersites' body is as good as Ajax', / When neither are alive*	cowardly Greek; killed by Achilles after Thersites jeered at him for killing, then falling in love with, Penthesilea; character in *Troilus and Cressida*
Theseus	TG IV.iv.165	*'twas Ariadne passioning / For Theseus' perjury and unjust flight*	legendary king and national hero of Athens, who with Ariadne's help killed the Minotaur; he conquered the Amazons, and married their queen, Hippolyta; character in *The Two Noble Kinsmen*
Thetis	Per IV.iv.41	*The earth ... / Hath Thetis' birth-child on the heavens bestowed*	sea-nymph destined to bear a son greater than his father; she was married to Peleus, and mother of Achilles ➤ Achilles
Thisbe	MND I.ii.41 and throughout	*What is Thisbe? ... It is the lady that Pyramus must love*	➤ Pyramus
Timon	LL IV.iii.168	*To see ... critic Timon laugh at idle toys!*	nobleman from Athens; disgusted with mankind as shown in the ingratitude of his friends, he lived a life of almost total seclusion; character in *Timon of Athens*
Troilus	AY IV.i.88	*Troilus had his brains dashed out with a Grecian club*	youngest son of Priam and Hecuba; killed by Achilles; in *Troilus and Cressida*, the lover of Cressida
Typhon	Tit IV.ii.93	*Enceladus / With all his threat'ning band of Typhon's brood*	giant, half man, half animal, who fought against the Olympian gods; said to be the father of several monsters; Zeus crushed him with Mt Etna
Ulysses	Cor I.iii.84	*You would be another Penelope ... all the yarn she spun in Ulysses' absence did but fill Ithaca full of moths*	son of Laertes, who fought for ten years in the Trojan War; on his return to Ithaca, he slaughtered the suitors who were besieging his wife Penelope; in Greek, known as Odysseus

Being	Location	Example	Gloss
Aeolus	**2H6** III.ii.92	*Yet Aeolus would not be a murderer*	Greek god of the winds
Aesculapius	**MW** II.iii.25	*What says my Aesculapius?*	Roman god of healing; from Greek Asclepius
Apollo	**WT** III.i.19	*the oracle, / Thus by Apollo's great divine sealed up*	Greek sun-god, often thought of as pulling the sun across the sky in a horse-drawn chariot; god of prophecy (who spoke through the oracle at Delphi), poetry, music, archery, and healing; also known as Phoebus Apollo, or Phoebus
Astraea	**1H6** I.vi.4	*Divinest creature, Astraea's daughter*	Daughter of Zeus and Themis; Greek goddess of justice
Ate	**MA** II.i..234	*the infernal Ate*	Greek goddess of discord and vengeance
Athene	**TNK** III.v.94	*Pallas inspire me!*	Greek goddess of wisdom and learning; protectress of Athens; also known as Athena, Pallas Athena, or Pallas
Aurora	**MND** III.ii.380	*Aurora's harbinger*	Roman goddess of the dawn
Bacchanals	**AC** II.vii.102	*Shall we dance now the Egyptian Bacchanals*	☛ Bacchus
Bacchus	**LL** IV.iii.315	*Love's tongue proves dainty Bacchus gross in taste*	Roman god of wine; associated with drunken revelry; devotees, festivals, and dances were known as Bacchanals
Bel	**MA** III.iii.131	*like god Bel's priests in the old church-window*	Babylonian god, discredited by Daniel (Bible: Apocrypha; or, Daniel 14)
Bellona	**TNK** I.i.75	*the helmeted Bellona*	Roman goddess of war
Boreas	**TC** I.iii.38	*let the ruffian Boreas once enrage / The gentle Thetis*	Greek god of the north wind
Ceres	**Tem** IV.i.60	*Ceres, most bounteous lady, thy rich leas / Of wheat*	Roman goddess of crops and fruit
Cupid	**AY** IV.i.196	*wicked bastard of Venus*	Roman god of love, son of Venus and Mercury; depicted as a winged boy with curved bow and arrows, and blind-folded
Cynthia	**Venus** 728	*Cynthia for shame obscures her silver shine*	Roman goddess of the Moon; one of the identities of Diana ☛ Diana
Cytherea	**PassP** IV.1	*Cytherea ... / Did court the lad with many a lovely look*	one of the titles of the Roman goddess of beauty and love
Diana, Dian	**1H4** I.ii.25	*Let us be Diana's foresters, gentlemen of the shade, min-ions of the moon*	Roman goddess associated with the Moon, chastity, and hunting; often known as Cynthia, Luna, and Phoebe
Dictynna	**LL** IV.ii.36	*Dictynna ... A title to Phoebe, to Luna, to the moon*	one of the titles of the Roman goddess of the Moon
Dis	**Tem** IV.i.89	*dusky Dis my daughter got*	Roman god of the Underworld; another name for Pluto ☛ Pluto
Flora	**WT** IV.iv.2	*Flora / Peering in April's front*	Roman goddess of flowers, who appears with the spring
Fortune	**AY** I.ii.30	*Let us ... mock the good housewife Fortune from her wheel*	Roman goddess, often represented as a woman at a spin-ning-wheel, or controlling a rudder, and as blind
Ganymede	**AY** I.iii.122	*Jove's own page* [name adopted by Rosalind]	beautiful boy, son of a Trojan prince, taken by Jove to be cup-bearer to the gods
Graces, Three	**TC** I.ii.236	*Had I a sister were a grace*	daughters of Zeus and Hera; Greek goddesses of grace and beauty
Hecat, Hecate	**Mac** II.i.52	*Witchcraft celebrates / Pale Hecat's offerings*	Greek goddess of the Underworld; associated with magic, ghosts, witchcraft
Hermes	**H5** III.vii.17	*more musical than the pipe of Hermes*	messenger of the Greek gods, often shown wearing winged shoes; god of science and commerce, inventor of the lyre and flute

Being	Location	Example	Gloss
Hymen	**Ham** III.ii.168	*Hymen did our hands / Unite*	Greek god who led a wedding procession; associated with a torch, a crown of flowers, and a flute; also known as Hymenaeus
Hymenaeus	**Tit** I.i.328	*everything / In readiness for Hymenaeus stand*	☛ Hymen
Hyperion	**Tim** IV.iii.185	*Whereon Hyperion's quickening fire doth shine*	Greek god, son of Uranus and Gaia, who fathered the Sun (Helios), Moon (Selene), and Dawn (Eos); often, the Sun itself, associated with a horse-drawn chariot
Iris	**TNK** IV.i.87	*as Iris / Newly dropped down from heaven*	Greek goddess of the rainbow; messenger of the gods, especially of Zeus and Hera
Isis	**AC** I.ii.65	*let him marry a woman that cannot go, sweet Isis, I beseech thee*	Egyptian goddess of the Moon, fertility, and magic; wife of Osiris
Janus	**MV** I.i.50	*by two-headed Janus, / Nature hath framed strange fellows in her time*	Roman god who guards gates and doors; depicted with two faces, one at the back of his head
Jove	**Luc** 568	*She conjures him by high almighty Jove*	☛ Jupiter
Juno	**WT** IV.iv.121	*sweeter than the lids of Juno's eyes*	Roman supreme goddess, wife of Jupiter; associated with the Moon, childbirth, marriage, and female identity
Jupiter	**Cym** V.v.428	*Great Jupiter, upon his eagle backed*	Roman supreme god; associated with the heavens and the weather, especially thunder and lightning; husband of Juno; also known as Jove
Lucina	**Cym** V.iv.43	*Lucina … took me in my throes*	Roman goddess of childbirth
Luna	**LL** IV.ii.39	*Dictynna … A title to Phoebe, to Luna, to the moon*	One of the titles of the Roman goddess of the Moon ☛ Diana
Mars	**TNK** I.iv.17	*By th' helm of Mars*	Roman god of war, second only to Jupiter
Mercury	**Ham** III.iv.59	*the herald Mercury*	messenger of the Roman gods, with the attributes of Hermes; also, god of commerce ☛ Hermes
Merops	**TG** III.i.153	*Phaethon – for thou art Merops' son – / Wilt thou aspire to guide the heavenly car*	husband of Clymene; Phaethon was the son of her union with Helios ☛ Phaethon
Minerva	**Cym** V.v.164	*laming … straight-pight Minerva*	Roman goddess of wisdom, the arts, and trades
Nemesis	**E3** III.i.120	*Steer, angry Nemesis, the happy helm*	Greek goddess of vengeance, especially retribution for human folly, pride, or excessive good fortune
Neptune	**MND** II.i.126	*Full often hath she … sat with me on Neptune's yellow sands*	Roman water-god; chiefly associated with the sea and sea-weather
Pallas	**Tit** IV.i.65	*Apollo, Pallas, Jove or Mercury / Inspire me*	☛ Athena
Phaethon	**R2** III.iii.178	*down I come like glistering Phaethon*	son of Helios, the Greek sun-god, who tried to drive his chariot but was destroyed when he drove it too near Earth; symbol of pride
Phoebe	**LL** IV.ii.39	*Dictynna … A title to Phoebe, to Luna, to the moon*	One of the titles of the Roman goddess of the Moon ☛ Diana
Phoebus	**H5** IV.i.266	*like a lackey… / Sweats in the eye of Phoebus*	Latin name for Apollo as the sun-god; also called Phoebus Apollo ☛ Apollo
Pluto	**Cor** I.iv.36	*Pluto and hell!*	one of the titles of the Greek god of the Underworld, Hades ☛ Plutus
Plutus	**AW** V.iii.101	*Plutus … / That knows the tinct and multiplying medicine*	Greek god of wealth and gold; also known as Pluto
Priapus	**Per** IV.vi.4	*She's able to freeze the god Priapus*	Greek god of human and plant fertility
Proserpine, Proserpina	**TNK** IV.iii.25	*do nothing all day long but pick flowers with Proserpine*	Roman goddess of the Underworld; Hades abducted her while she was picking flowers; associated with springtime

Being	Location	Example	Gloss
Saturn	**Sonn** 98.4	*heavy Saturn laugh'd and leap'd with him*	Roman god of seed time and harvest
Tellus	**Per** IV.i.13	*I will rob Tellus of her weed* [i.e. flowers]	Roman goddess of the earth
Titan	**Venus** 177	*Titan … with burning eye did hotly overlook them*	one of the titles of the Roman sun-god, Sol
Triton	**Cor** III.i.89	*this Triton of the minnows*	minor Greek sea-god, the son of Poseidon and Amphitrite
Venus	**TNK** V.i.74	*to the goddess Venus / Commend we our proceeding*	Roman goddess of beauty and love
Vulcan	**TN** V.i.50	*As black as Vulcan in the smoke of war*	Roman god of fire, and the gods' blacksmith; his forge was under Mt Etna, and thus associated with destruction and hell

Being	Location	Example	Gloss
Amazon, Amazonian	1H6 I.ii.104	*stay thy hands; thou art an Amazon*	one of a race of warrior women, said to be descended from Ares, god of war
Anthropophagi	Oth I.iii.143	*the Cannibals that each other eat, / The Anthropophagi*	mythical race of man-eaters
Bayard	E3 III.i.58	*Bayard-like, blind, overweening Ned*	magic horse given by Charlemagne to Rinaldo (Renaud), one of the four sons of Aimon; a symbol of blind recklessness
Bevis	H8 I.i.38	*that former fabulous story, ... got credit, / That Bevis was believed*	medieval Saxon knight who conquered Ascapart, a giant, and made him his squire
Chanticleer	AY II.vii.30	*My lungs began to crow like Chanticleer*	cock in the medieval story of Reynard the Fox, such as retold in Chaucer's *Nun's Priest's Tale*
Child Roland	KL III.iv.176	*Child Roland to the dark tower came*	Charlemagne's most famous knight, as recounted in various ballads ☛ Charlemain, p.627
Colbrand	KJ I.i.225	*Colbrand the Giant, that same mighty man?*	medieval Danish champion giant, killed by Sir Guy of Warwick at Winchester
Cophetua	LL IV.i.68	*most illustrate King Cophetua set eye upon the pernicious and most indubitate beggar Zenelophon*	African king of a romantic ballad, who fell in love with a beggar-girl, Zenelophon
Corin	MND II.i.66	*in the shape of Corin sat all day / Playing on pipes of corn, and versing love / To amorous Phillida*	traditional name given to a love-sick shepherd; Phillida, the corresponding name given to his beloved
Dagonet, Sir	2H4 III.ii.271	*I was then Sir Dagonet in Arthur's show*	King Arthur's fool
Florentius	TS I.ii.68	*Be she as foul as was Florentius' love*	knight in Gower's *Confessio Amantis* who married an ugly woman in return for the answer to a riddle on which his life depended
Gargantua	AY III.ii.218	*You must borrow me Gargantua's mouth*	large-mouthed voracious giant of N. France, as described by Rabelais
Gorboduc	TN IV.ii.14	*the old hermit of Prague ... said to a niece of King Gorboduc: that that is, is*	legendary king of Britain; name of a play by Norton and Sackville, first performed in 1561
Grissel	TS II.i.288	*For patience she will prove a second Grissel*	Griselda, model of wifely patience in Chaucer's *Clerk's Tale*
Guinevere	LL IV.i.124	*when Queen Guinevere of Britain was a little wench*	legendary queen of Britain, known for her unfaithfulness to her husband
Guy, Sir	H8 V.iv.22	*I am not Samson, nor Sir Guy, nor Colbrand*	legendary hero of Warwick, whose last great act was to kill the giant Colbrand ☛ Nine Worthies, p.628
John	MW I.i.160	*What say you, Scarlet and John?*	Will Scarlet and Little John, companions of Robin Hood
Mab, Queen	RJ I.iv.53	*I see Queen Mab hath been with you*	midwife to the fairies
Maid Marian	1H4 III.iii.113	*Maid Marian may be the deputy's wife of the ward to thee*	woman loved by Robin Hood
Merlin	KL III.ii.95	*This prophecy Merlin shall make; for I live before his time*	good wizard or sage whose magic helped King Arthur; famous for his prophecies
Partlet	1H4 III.iii.51	*How now, dame Partlet the hen*	traditional name for a hen [Pertelote], as in Chaucer's *Nun's Priest's Tale*
Pendragon	1H6 III.ii.95	*stout Pendragon in his litter sick / Came to the field*	early British king, the father of Arthur
Phillida	MND II.i.68		☛ Corin

Being	Location	Example	Gloss
Pigmies	**MA** II.i.247	*I will ... do you any embassage to the Pigmies, rather than hold three words' conference with this harpy*	legendary race of dwarfs
Prester John	**MA** II.i.245	*I will ... bring you the length of Prester John's foot ... rather than hold three words' conference with this harpy*	legendary Christian king of Africa or Asia
Scarlet	**MW** I.i.160		☛ John
Sycorax	**Tem** I.ii.340	*All the charms / Of Sycorax – toads, beetles, bats light on you!*	witch, and mother of Caliban, character in *The Tempest*
Zenelophon	**LL** IV.i.69		☛ Cophetua

Name	Example	Gloss
Abel	**1H6** I.iii.40	Bible (Genesis 4): son of Adam and Eve, killed by his brother Cain
Abraham	**R3** IV.iii.38	Bible (Genesis 12): Hebrew patriarch, whose name is changed by God from Abram to Abraham (Genesis 17)
Abram	**MV** I.iii.69	☛ Abraham
Achitophel	**2H4** I.ii.34	Bible (2 Samuel 16): adviser to King David, who sided with Absalom in the conspiracy against David
Adam	**Ham** V.i.31	Bible (Genesis 2): first human being
Amaimon, Amamon	**MW** II.ii.282	name of a devil
Arthur	**H5** II.iii.9	malapropism for Abraham ☛ Abraham
Barabbas	**MV** IV.i.293	Bible (John 18): robber released instead of Christ at the Passover
Barbason	**MW** II.ii.283	name of a devil
Beelzebub	**TN** V.i.281	the Devil; or, a principal devil
Belzebub	**H5** IV.vii.135	the Devil; or, a principal devil
Bennet, Saint	**TN** V.i.36	medieval name of Benedict; here, name given to a church
Cain	**Ham** V.i.77	☛ Abel
Castiliano	**TN** I.iii.39	[unclear meaning] possibly, a name of a devil
Crispian, Crispin, Saints	**H5** IV.iii.40	Crispinus and Crispianus, martyrs under Roman emperor Diocletian; joint feast day 25 October
Daniel	**MV** IV.i.220	Bible (Daniel): influential Babylonian administrator and visionary
Deborah	**1H6** I.ii.105	Bible (Judges 4): Hebrew prophetess, judge, and army commander
Denis, Saint	**1H6** I.vi.28	first apostle of France, 3rd c.
Dives	**1H4** III.iii.31	Bible (Luke 16): rich man who feasted while the beggar Lazarus starved at his gate
Flibberdigibbet	**KL** III.iv.110	name of a devil
Francis, Saint	**RJ** II.iii.61	founder of the Franciscan order
Frater(r)etto	**KL** III.vi.6	name of a devil
George, Saint	**3H6** II.i.203	patron saint of England, 3rd c.
Golias, Goliath	**1H6** I.ii.33	Bible (1 Samuel 17): Goliath; giant, seen as a model of strength
Hagar	**MV** II.v.42	Bible (Genesis 16): bondwoman to Sarah, whose child was Ishmael, a 'wild-ass of a man'
Herod	**Ham** III.ii.14	Bible (Matthew 2): Judaean king, portrayed in medieval mystery plays as a wild and angry figure
Hoppedance, Hobbididence	**KL** III.vi.30	name of a devil
Jacob	**MV** I.iii.68	Bible (Genesis 25): Hebrew patriarch, the younger son of Isaac
Jacob, Saint		☛ DAYS AND DATES, p.630
Japhet	**2H4** II.ii.112	Bible (Genesis 10) Noah's third son, the ancestor of Europeans
Jaques, Saint	**AW** III.iv.4	Saint James; name of a pilgrim centre in Compostela, N. Spain
Jephthah	**Ham** II.ii.409	Bible (Judges 11): judge in Israel who promised God to sacrifice the first he met if he returned home victorious; this proved to be his daughter
Jeronimy, Saint	**TS** Induction.i.7	Jerome; but here a confusion with Hieronimo ☛ CONTEMPORY FIGURES, p.629
Jezebel	**TN** II.v.40	Bible (1 Kings 16): infamous wife of King Ahab
Job	**2H4** I.ii.127	Bible (Job): patriarch, seen as a symbol of destitution and patience
Joshua	**LL** V.i.120	Bible (Joshua) Israelite leader ☛ Nine Worthies, p.628
Judas	**R2** IV.i.170	Bible (Matthew 26) Judas Iscariot, betrayer of Christ
Judas Maccabaeus	**LL** V.i.121	Bible (1 Maccabees) leader of a Jewish revolt, 2nd c. BC ☛ Nine Worthies, p.628
Judith	**E3** II.i.170	Bible (Apocrypha; also, Judith); heroine who kills Assyrian general Holofernes with a sword

Name	Example	Gloss
Laban	MV I.iii.68	Bible (Genesis 30) uncle of Jacob ➤ Jacob
Lazarus	1H4 IV.ii.24	➤ Dives
Legion	TN III.iv.85	name of a devil
Lucifer	MW II.ii.282	name of a principal devil; or, the Devil
Mahu	KL III.iv.137	name of a devil
Martin, Saint	1H6 I.ii.131	patron saint of France, 4th c.
Mephostophilus	MW I.i.123	name of a devil
Modo	KL III.iv.136	name of a devil
Nicholas, Saint	1H4 II.i.62	here, as patron saint of travellers
Nicholas, Saint	TG III.i.292	here, as patron saint of scholars
Obidicut	KL IV.i.58	name of a devil
Pharaoh	MA III.iii.130	Bible (Exodus 14) Egyptian ruler
Philip, Saint	1H6 I.ii.143	Bible (Acts 21): evangelist who had four daughters who were prophets; also, ➤ DAYS AND DATES, p.630
Pilate	R2 IV.i.238	Pontius Pilate, Roman prefect of Judaea, 1st c.; interrogator of Jesus
Prodigal	MW IV.v.7	Bible (Luke 15): son who foolishly wastes his share of his father's estate
Samson	1H6 I.ii.33	Bible (Judith 13): judge, possessor of legendary strength
Sarah	E3 II.i.255	Bible (Genesis 16) Abraham's wife, seen as a model of submission to a husband ➤ Abraham
Satan	AW V.iii.259	the Devil
Smulkin	KL III.iv.134	name of a devil
Solomon	LL I.ii.168	Bible (1 Kings 1): son and successor of David; proverbial for his wisdom
Whore of Babylon	H5 II.iii.35	Bible (Revelation 17): prostitute figure, taken as a symbol of degenerate Rome, and thus of Roman Catholicism
Withold, Saint	KL III.iv.115	[possible reading] defender against harms

➤ **DAYS AND DATES**, p.630; **SWEARING**, p.435

V HISTORICAL FIGURES

Name	Example	Gloss
Alexander	Ham V.i.194	Alexander the Great; Macedonian king in 4th c. BC, known for his extensive empire ➤ Nine Worthies, below
Alisander	LL V.ii.561	old form of Alexander ➤ Alexander
Ancus Martius	Cor II.iii.238	fourth king of Rome, 7th c. BC
Antiochus the Great	Per I.Chorus.17	Antiochus III; Syrian king in 2nd c. BC
Antony, Mark	H5 III.vi.14	Roman leader in 1st c. BC; character in *Antony and Cleopatra*
Bajazeth	AW IV.i.41	Ottoman sultan in 14th c.
Bargulus	2H6 IV.i.108	Balkan pirate of Roman times
Brutus, Lucius	JC I.ii.158	Lucius Junius Brutus, founder of the Roman republic in 509 BC
Brutus, Marcus	Ham III.ii.113	Marcus Junius Brutus; 1st c. BC Roman politician, involved in the assassination of Julius Caesar; character in *Julius Caesar*
Cadwallader	H5 V.i.27	last of the British kings, 7th c.
Caesar	Ham V.i.209	Roman politician and general; character in *Julius Caesar*
Cassibelan	Cym I.i.30	British king in 1st c., brother or (III.i.5) uncle of Cymbeline
Catilines	E3 III.i.14	Catiline, a Roman noble, a conspirator against the Roman republic in 62 BC
Cato	Cor I.iv.59	Cato the Elder, 2nd c. BC Roman politician
Cato	JC V.i.101	Cato the Younger, 1st c. BC Roman politician, and opponent of Caesar
Censorinus	Cor II.iii.242	Caius Marcius Rutilus, 3rd c. BC Roman politician
Cham	MA II.i.246	khan or oriental emperor; emperor of China
Charlemain	AW II.i.77	Charlemagne, king of the Franks in 768–814; great patron of learning ➤ Nine Worthies, below
Cleitus	H5 IV.vii.43	friend and commander of Alexander, killed by him in a quarrel ➤ Alexander
Cleopatra	AY III.ii.142	Egyptian queen in 1st c. BC; character in *Antony and Cleopatra*
Clotharius	H8 I.iii.10	king of the Franks in 6th c.
Coriolanus	Tit IV.iv.68	Caius Martius, defender of the early Roman republic in 5th c. BC; character in *Coriolanus*
Cyrus	1H6 II.iii.6	Cyrus the Great, 6th c. BC, king of Persia
Darius	1H6 I.vi.25	Darius the Great, 6th c. BC king of Persia
Epicurus	JC V.i.76	Greek philosopher, 4th c. BC
Galen	Cor II.i.111	Greek physician, 2nd c.
Hannibal	1H6 I.v.21	Carthaginian general, 3rd c. BC
Hector		➤ Nine Worthies, below
Helen	1H6 I.ii.142	St Helena, 3rd c., mother of Constantine the Great
Horace	Tit IV.ii.22	Latin poet, 1st c. BC
Hostilius	Cor II.iii.239	Tullus Hostilius, third king of Rome, 7th c. BC
Julius Caesar	R2 V.i.2	➤ Caesar; Nine Worthies, below
Laura	RJ II.iv.39	lady addressed in Petrarch's love poetry ➤ Petrarch
Lucretia, Lucrece	AY III.ii.144	legendary Roman heroine, 6th c. BC, who killed herself after being raped by Tarquin; subject of *The Rape of Lucrece* ➤ Tarquin
Lycurgus	Cor II.i.52	Spartan legislator, 7th c. BC, legendary for wisdom
Machiavel	1H6 V.iv.74	Machiavelli; early 16th c. Italian political theorist, associated with stratagem and cunning
Mahomet	1H6 I.ii.140	the prophet Mohammed; founder of Islam, 7th c.
Milo	TC II.iii.244	Greek athlete, 6th c. BC, who carried an ox around the stadium at Olympia then ate it all in a single day
Mulmutius	Cym III.i.59	early British king
Nabuchadnezzar	AW IV.v.18	king of Babylon, 6th c. BC

Name	Example	Gloss
Nero	Ham III.ii.401	Roman emperor, 1st c., who slew his mother, Agrippina; supposed to have played on his lute while watching Rome burn; considered a model of cruelty
Nervii	JC III.ii.174	Belgian tribe, defeated by Caesar in 57 BC
Nine Worthies	2H4 II.iv.215	three pagans (Hector of Troy, Alexander the Great, Julius Caesar), three Jews (Joshua, David, Judas Maccabaeus), three Christians (Arthur, Charlemagne, Godfrey of Bouillon or Guy of Warwick); Hercules and Pompey the Great are (unusually) included by the players in LL V.ii
Numa	Cor II.iii.238	Numa Pompilius, second king of Rome, 716–672 BC
Ovid, Ovidius	AY III.iii.6	Latin poet; exiled to live among the Goths in AD 8
Pepin, Pippen	LL IV.i.121	king of the Franks in 8th c.
Petrarch	RJ II.iv.39	Italian poet, 14th c.
Pharamond	H5 I.ii.37	legendary king of the Salian Franks
Pippen	AW II.i.76	➤ Pepin
Plautus	Ham II.ii.399	Latin comic playwright, 2nd c. BC
Pompeion, Pompion	LL V.ii.501	malapropism for Pompey the Great
Pompey	2H6 IV.i.140	Pompey the Great; Roman politician and general, 1st c. BC ➤ Nine Worthies, above
Portia	MV I.i.166	wife of Brutus, daughter of Cato the Younger ➤ Brutus, Marcus
Priscian	LL V.i.28	Latin grammarian, 6th c.
Publicola	Cor V.iii.64	one of the first consuls of Rome, 6th c. BC
Publius	Cor II.iii.240	supposed ancestor of Caius Martius ➤ Coriolanus
Pythagoras	TN IV.ii.49	Greek philosopher and mathematician, 6th c. BC
Quintus	Cor II.iii.240	supposed ancestor of Caius Martius; in fact, Quintus Martius Rex was a later Roman administrator, 2nd c. BC ➤ Coriolanus
Rhodope	1H6 I.vi.22	Greek courtesan who became queen of Memphis, and the supposed builder of the third pyramid
Roscius	Ham II.ii.389	most famous actor of ancient Rome, 2nd c. BC
Semiramis	TS Induction.ii.38	semi-legendary Assyrian queen renowned for promiscuity, 9th c. BC
Seneca	Ham II.ii.399	Seneca the Younger, 1st c., Roman tragedian
Socrates	TS I.ii.70	Greek philosopher, 5th c. BC
Solon	Tit I.i.180	Athenian statesman, c.7th c. BC
Sylla	2H6 IV.i.84	Lucius Cornelius Sulla, Roman dictator, 2nd c. BC
Tarquin	Cor II.i.143	Tarquinius Superbus, seventh king of Rome, 6th c. BC
Tenantius	Cym I.i.31	British king, father of Cymbeline ➤ Cymbeline
Tomyris	1H6 II.iii.6	Scythian queen, 6th c. BC, who killed Cyrus the Great
Tully	2H6 IV.i.138	Marcus Tullius Cicero, Roman orator, statesman, and philosopher, 1st c. BC
Turk	2H4 III.ii.297	Sultan of Turkey
Virginius	Tit V.iii.36	character in Livy: 5th c. BC centurion who slew his daughter, either to avoid her being raped or because she had been raped
Xanthippe	TS I.ii.70	wife of Socrates, 5th c. BC
Xerxes	E3 III.i.56	king of Persia, 5th c. BC

➤ RELIGIOUS PERSONALITIES AND BEINGS, p.625

VI CONTEMPORARY FIGURES, FACTUAL AND FICTITIOUS

Name	Example	Gloss
Adam	**MA** I.i.239	Adam Bell, famous archer
Amurath	**2H4** V.ii.48	16th c. Turkish sultan, Murad III, who killed all his brothers on ascending the throne; as did his successor
Andrew	**MV** I.i.27	the *Saint Andrew*; name of a Spanish galleon captured at Cadiz in 1596
Basilisco	**KJ** I.i.244	knight character in a contemporary play, *Solyman and Perseda*
Brownist	**TN** III.ii.30	follower of Robert Browne, founder of a 16th c. religious sect advocating a new form of church government
Calipolis	**2H4** II.iv.174	mother of Muly Mahamet, character in a contemporary play by George Peele, *The Battle of Alcazar*
Cambyses	**1H4** II.iv.380	6th c. BC king of the Medes and Persians, as represented in a 16th c. play by Thomas Preston, *Cambyses*
Dowland	**PassP** VIII.5	John Dowland; English composer and musician, 16th c.
Hiren	**2H4** II.iv.155	[unclear meaning] character in a lost contemporary play by George Peele, *The Turkish Mahomet and Hyrin the Fair Greek*
Iniquity	**1H4** II.iv.441	character in morality plays
Jeronimy, Saint	**TS** Induction.i.7	Jerome; but here a confusion with Hieronimo from Thomas Kyd's *The Spanish Tragedy* ☛ p.625.
Mall, Mistress	**TN** I.iii.120	Mary; several contemporary figures possible, such as Mary Fitton, lady-in-waiting involved in a scandal of 1601
Monarco	**LL** IV.i.100	contemporary fantastical character at court
Peg-a-Ramsey	**TN** II.iii.74	spying wife in a contemporary ballad
Quinapalus	**TN** I.v.32	imaginary name for a learned authority
Ringwood	**MW** II.i.111	traditional name for an English hound
Ruffian	**1H4** II.iv.442	character of a fiend in morality plays
Sackerson	**MW** I.i.275	famous bear from the bear-baiting ring at Paris Garden, London
Solyman	**MV** II.i.26	Suleiman, 16th c. sultan who fought against Persia
Sophy	**TN** II.v.174	Shah of Persia, possibly Abbas the Great, 16th c.
Spenser	**PassP** VIII.7	Edmund Spenser; English poet, 16th c.
Termagant	**Ham** III.ii.13	noisy and overbearing character in mystery plays
Vanity	**1H4** II.iv.442	character in morality plays
Vice	**1H4** II.iv.441	buffoon character in morality plays

Times

VII DAYS AND DATES

CHRISTIAN

Name	Example	Gloss
Allhallond Eve, Allhallown	MM II.i.120	Allhallow's Eve, Hallowe'en, 31 October
Allhallowmas	MW I.i.189	All Saints' Day, 1 November
Ash Wednesday	MV II.v.26	first day of Lent
Bartholomew	2H4 II.iv.226	Saint Bartholomew's Day, 24 August
Bartholomew-tide	H5 V.ii.303	Saint Bartholomew's Day, 24 August
Black Monday	MV II.v.24	here, confusion of day after Easter with Ash Wednesday
Christmas	LL I.i.105	feast of the birth of Christ
Easter	RJ III.i.27	feast of Christ's resurrection
Hallowmas	R2 V.i.80	All Saints' Day, 1 November
Holy-rood day	1H4 I.i.52	Holy Cross day, 14 September
Lammas Eve	RJ I.iii.18	day before harvest festival, 31 July
Lammastide	RJ I.iii.16	harvest festival, 1 August
Lent, Lenten	2H4 II.iv.342	six-week penitential season before Easter
Martlemas [Martinmas]	2H4 II.ii.96	Saint Martin's Day, 11 November
Michaelmas	MW I.i.190	Saint Michael's Day, 29 September
Philip and Jacob	MM III.ii.193	Saints Philip and James, 1 May
Shrovetide	2H4 V.iii.35	three days before Ash Wednesday
Wheeson	2H4 II.i.87	dialect form of Whitsun
Whitsun	WT IV.iv.134	feast of Pentecost

ROMAN

Ides of March	JC I.ii.18	15 March (half-way point in the month)
Lupercal	JC I.i.67	15 February (purification feast in honour of Lupercus, god of shepherds)

Places

VIII LONDON

Modern locations are given, where known, using the traditional postal codes.

Location	Example	Gloss
Bridge, the	R3 III.ii.70	London Bridge, over the River Thames
Bucklersbury	MW III.iii.68	East End street with aromatic herb shops; near Mansion House, EC4
Cheapside	2H6 IV.ii.64	East End street, a main market area; near St Paul's, EC2
Clement's Inn	2H4 III.ii.13	Inn of Chancery, which trained students for the law; near the Strand, WC2
Counter-gate	MW III.iii.74	gate of the Counter [Compter], debtors' prisons in London, such as the one near Cheapside and the one in Southwark
Eastcheap	2H4 II.ii.141	East End street; near Monument, EC3
Fleet	2H4 V.v.94	debtors' prison; near Fleet Street, EC4
Gray's Inn	2H4 III.ii.31	Inn of Chancery, which trained students for the law; near Holborn, WC1
Limehouse	H8 V.iv.61	riverside area named after the lime-kilns there which processed chalk from Kent; now E14
London Stone	2H6 IV.vi.2	ancient stone, possibly Roman, once a city landmark in Cannon Street; now EC4
Lud's town	Cym III.i.33	old name for London
Lumbert Street	2H4 II.i.27	Lombard Street, a trading street for merchants; near Monument, EC3
Marshalsea	H8 V.iv.85	debtors' prison in Southwark; near Borough, SE1
Mile-end	AW IV.iii.262	area in the East End where the citizen militia drilled; Mile End Park; now E3
Moorditch	1H4 I.ii.78	filthy channel between Bishopsgate and Cripplegate; now EC2
Moorfields	H8 V.iv.33	site once used for training militia; later a popular park; near Moorgate, EC2
Newgate	1H4 III.iii.89	main prison of the City of London; near Cheapside, EC2
Paul's	R3 III.vi.3	St Paul's Cathedral; now EC4
Pie Corner	2H4 II.i.25	at the corner of Smithfield, noted for its cooking-pig shops; now EC1
Saint George's Field	2H4 III.ii.191	in Southwark, well known for its brothels; now SE1
Strachy	TN II.v.39	[unknown meaning] possibly a local house or institution
Strand	H8 V.iv.52	street of fashionable merchants; also of apprentices; now WC2
Tower Hill	H8 V.iv.61	site of the Tower scaffold, where executions drew crowds of spectators; now EC3
Turnbull Street	2H4 III.ii.295	disreputable East End street, peopled by thieves and prostitutes; now Turnmill Street, near Farringdon, EC1

Location	Example	Gloss
Albion	KL III.ii.85	poetic name for Britain
Ampthill	H8 IV.i.28	Ampthill Castle, Bedfordshire, S.C. England; Katherine of Aragon stayed there in 1533 while her marriage to Henry VIII was annulled
Banbury	MW I.i.121	Oxfordshire town, known for its rich milk cheese about an inch thick
Birnan	Mac IV.i.92	Birnam, Dunkeld, E. Scotland, near the River Tay
Brainford	MW IV.ii.71	Brentford, not far from Kew Gardens, London
Bristow, Bristol	2H6 III.i.328	city-port in S.W. England, close to the mouth of the River Severn
Britany	Cym I.v.69	early form of the name Britain
Cambria	Cym III.ii.44	medieval name for Wales
Camelot	KL II.ii.82	capital of King Arthur's legendary kingdom; possible sites include Winchester ☞ Sarum
Chartham	2H6 IV.ii.80	village near Canterbury, Kent, S.E. England
Ciceter	R2 V.vi.3	Cirencester, market town in Gloucestershire, S.W.C. England
Colebrook	MW IV.v.72	Colnbrook, near Windsor, S. England
Colmekill	Mac II.iv.33	Iona, island off the west coast of Scotland; once the traditional burial place for Scottish kings
Cotsall	MW I.i.84	Cotswold Hills; hill range mainly in Gloucestershire, S.E. England
Cotsole	2H4 III.ii.20	Cotswold ☞ Cotsall
Daintry	3H6 V.i.6	Daventry, town west of Northampton, C. England
Downs	2H6 IV.i.9	The Downs; anchorage just off the Kent coast, S.E. England
Dunsinane	Mac IV.i.92	Dunsinnan, hill west of Dundee, E. Scotland
Gallia	MW III.i.89	[someone from] France
Gaul	MW III.i.89	[unclear usage by the Host] [someone from] Wales; usually at the time, with reference to France
Gaultree Forest	2H4 IV.i.2	now Sutton-on-the-Forest, north of York, North Yorkshire, N. England
Goodwins	MV III.i.4	Goodwin Sands; treacherous sands for shipping, off the Kent coast, S.E. England
Hampton	H5 II.ii.91	Southampton; port city in Hampshire, S. England
Ha'rfordwest	R3 IV.v.10	Haverfordwest; town in Pembrokeshire, S.W. Wales
Herford	2H4 IV.i.136	Hereford; city in Herefordshire, W.C. England, on the River Wye
Holmedon	1H4 I.i.55	Humbleton, village in Northumberland, N.E. England
Hunkley, Hinckley	2H4 V.i.21	town north-east of Stratford-upon-Avon, C. England; site of a large fair
Killingworth	2H6 IV.iv.39	Kenilworth Castle, to which Henry V retired after the battle of Agincourt; between Coventry and Warwick, C. England
Kimbolton, Kymmalton	H8 IV.i.34	Kimbolton, Cambridgeshire, E.C. England; castle owned by Edward de Bohun, Duke of Buckingham; later, a manor house in which Katherine of Aragon was imprisoned
Lynn	3H6 IV.v.20	King's Lynn; port in Norfolk, E. England
Pomfret	R3 III.i.183	Pontefract, West Yorkshire, N. England; site of castle in which Richard II was imprisoned; later, a Lancastrian stronghold during the Wars of the Roses
Readins	MW IV.v.71	Reading; former county town of Berkshire, S. England
Saint Colm's Inch	Mac I.ii.64	Inchcolm; small island in the Firth of Forth, E. Scotland; site of an abbey
Saint Edmundsbury	KJ IV.iii.11	Bury St Edmunds, market town in Suffolk, E. England; site of the shrine of St Edmund and a place of pilgrimage
Sarum	KL II.ii.81	old name for Salisbury, Wiltshire, S. England; Salisbury Plain is a possible site for Camelot
Stamford	2H4 III.ii.37	market town in Lincolnshire, E.C. England, with a tradition of fairs from Anglo-Saxon times
Tewkesbury	2H4 II.iv.236	town in S.W.C. England, a mustard-making centre in Elizabethan times; Henry VI's son, Edward, killed in battle here (1471)

Location	Example	Gloss
Ware	**TN** III.ii.45	town in Hertfordshire, S.E. England; the Great Bed of Ware, famous for its size, is now in the Victoria and Albert Museum, London
Washes	**KJ** V.vii.63	The Wash; shallow inlet of the North Sea on the east coast of England
Washford	**1H6** IV.vii.63	Wexford, city in Leinster, S.E. Ireland
Winchester	**TC** V.x.55	city in Hampshire, S. England; Henry IV married in its cathedral; one Bishop of Winchester licensed brothels in Southwark, London, hence 'Winchester goose' for a prostitute

Location	Example	Gloss
Acheron	**MND** III.ii.357	one of the mythological rivers of the Underworld, traditionally black, crossed by souls after death
Adonis, gardens of	**1H6** I.vi.6	mythological garden of fertility
Afric	**Cym** I.ii.98	Africa, thought of as a desert place
Afric	**TC** I.iii.370	African
Almagne	**E3** I.i.152	Germany
Almaine	**Oth** II.iii.77	German
Andren	**H8** I.i.7	Andres, valley in Picardy, N. France
Angiers	**KJ** II.i.1	Angers, N.W. France; capital of the former province of Anjou
Antiates	**Cor** V.vi.80	people from Antium (modern Anzio), S. Italy
Aquitaine	**LL** I.i.135	region of S.W. France; acquired by England on the marriage of Henry II to Eleanor of Aquitaine, 1152
Arabia	**Cor** IV.ii.24	region of S.W. Asia (modern Saudi Arabia and nearby countries), thought of as a desert area
Arde	**H8** I.i.7	Ardres, town in Picardy, N. France; site of the Field of the Cloth of Gold, where Henry VIII and Francis I met
Ardea	**Luc** 1	capital city of the Rutuli, south of Rome
Argier	**Tem** I.ii.261	Algiers; seaport capital of Algeria, N. Africa
Aulis	**TNK** I.i.212	seaport in Boeotia, S.E. Greece [Q *Anly*]
Barbary	**Ham** V.ii.145	Barbary Coast of N. Africa, famous for swift horses and a breed of cock-pigeon
Barfleur	**E3** III.iii.20	Harfleur, Normandy, France; besieged by Henry V in 1415
Basan, Hill of	**AC** III.xiii.127	Bible (Psalms 68): area noted for cattle
Belgia	**CE** III.ii.145	Holland and Belgium
Bergomask	**MND** V.i.344	in the manner of the people of Bergamo, N. Italy
Bermoothes	**Tem** I.ii.229	Bermuda islands
Boheme	**E3** III.iv.86	☛ Bohemia
Bohemia	**WT** I.i.1	historic province of W. Czech Republic
Bretagne	**E3** I.i.133	Brittany, N.W. France
Britain	**R3** IV.iii.40	Breton, from Brittany, N.W. France
Britaine	**H5** II.iv.4	Brittany, N.W. France
British	**E3** IV.iv.75	Breton, from Brittany, N.W. France
Brittaine	**R2** II.i.278	Brittany, N.W. France
Calaber	**2H6** I.i.7	Calabria, region of S. Italy
Callice	**R2** I.i.126	Calais, port in N.W. France
Calydon	**2H6** I.i.233	region of ancient Aetolia, W.C. Greece, where the hunt for the Calydonian boar took place ☛ Meleager, p.617
Candy	**TN** V.i.58	Candia (modern Heraklion), port in Crete
Capitol	**Ham** III.ii.113	national temple in Rome where Caesar was killed
Carentan	**E3** III.iii.20	Carentine, Normandy, N. France
Champaigne	**1H6** I.i.60	Compiègne, Picardy, N.E. France
Chartreux	**H8** I.i.221	Carthusian abbey at Chartreuse, Grenoble, E. France; also, used as the name of the order
Charybdis	**MV** III.v.15	mythological whirlpool in the Straits of Messina which swallowed ships whole ☛ Scylla
Cocytus	**Tit** II.iii.236	one of the mythological rivers of the Underworld, which souls of the dead must cross
Colchos	**MV** I.i.171	Colchis, ancient region at the eastern end of the Black Sea; in mythology, home of the Golden Fleece ☛ Jason, p.616
Collatium	**Luc** 4	city of Collatine, husband of Lucrece

Location	Example	Gloss
Colossus	1H4 V.i.123	huge bronze statue of the sun-god Apollo, which bestrode the harbour entrance to the port of Rhodes
Corinth	CE I.i.88	Greek city-state; on an isthmus separating the Adriatic Sea from the Aegean
Crete	H5 II.i.70	Mediterranean island, known for its shaggy dogs
Crotoy	E3 III.iii.20	Le Crotoy, Normandy, N. France
Cydnus	Cym II.iv.71	river in Cilicia, S. Turkey, now River Tarsus; meeting-place of Cleopatra and Antony, 41 BC
Dalmatians	Cym III.i.74	people from ancient Dalmatia; Balkan region bordering the Adriatic Sea, modern S.W. Croatia; also known as Illyria, Illyricum
Dardan, Dardania	TC Prologue.13	region of which Troy was the capital ➤ Troy
Delphos	WT II.i.183	island of Delphi, C. Greece, famous for its oracle
Elysium	Cym V.iv.97	mythological location of heaven
Ephesus	Per III.ii.42	former port on west coast of Asia Minor; site of Diana's temple, one of the Seven Wonders of the Ancient World
Epidamnum	CE I.i.42	town on coast of Illyricum (Dalmatia), Adriatic Sea ➤ Dalmatians
Epidaurus	CE I.i.94	town on coast of Illyricum (Dalmatia), Adriatic Sea ➤ Dalmatians
Erebus	JC II.i.84	mythological place of darkness on the way from Earth to Hades
Ethiop, Ethiope	AY IV.iii.36	someone from Ethiopia; a stereotype of dark complexion
Ethiope	MND III.ii.257	➤ Ethiop
Europa	MA V.iv.45	Europe
Florentine	AW I.ii.1	from Florence, Tuscany, N.C. Italy
Gallia	1H6 IV.vi.15	[unclear meaning] old name for France [Gaul]
Gallian	Cym I.vii.66	from France
Goths	Tit I.i.28	warlike Germanic tribe from C. Europe, 3rd–5th c.
Guynes	H8 I.i.7	Guines, town in Picardy, N. France
Harfleur	H5 III.Chorus.17	town in Normandy, N. France; besieged by Henry V in 1415
Hellespont	Oth III.iii.453	Dardanelles; narrow strait in N.W. Turkey, connecting the Aegean Sea and the Sea of Marmara ➤ Leander, p.616
Hesperides	E3 IV.iv.29	mythological garden in the Isles of the Blest, at the western end of the Earth, where golden apples grew
Hybla	1H4 I.ii.41	town in Sicily, famed for the honey from its nearby hills
Hyrcan	Mac III.iv.100	➤ Hyrcania
Hyrcania	3H6 I.iv.155	ancient Persian region on the Caspian Sea; known for its ferocious wild animals
Iceland	H5 II.i.39	country known for its long-haired dogs
Ilion	LL V.ii.650	city of Troy ➤ Troy
Ilium	Ham II.ii.472	city of Troy ➤ Troy
Illyria	TN I.ii.2	eastern seaboard of the Adriatic and its hinterland (Dalmatia); modern Croatia ➤ Dalmatians
Ind	AY III.ii.84	➤ Indies
Inde	LL IV.iii.220	India
Indian	H8 V.iv.34	American Indian
Indies	MV I.iii.18	East Indies, thought of as a region of great wealth
Ithaca	Cor I.iii.85	island of W. Greece; home of Ulysses, where Penelope waited for his return from the Trojan Wars
Lacedaemon	Tim II.ii.156	Sparta, city-state of S. Greece
Lapland	CE IV.iii.11	province of N. Finland; known for sorcery and witchcraft
Lethe	TN IV.i.61	one of the mythological rivers of the Underworld, causing oblivion to those who drank from it
Limbo	AW V.iii.260	domain on the border of hell containing the souls of unbaptized infants and of those just people born before Christ

Location	Example	Gloss
Lô	E3 III.iii.20	Saint Lô, Normandy, N. France
Louvre	H8 I.iii.23	palace of the French kings, Paris
Marcellus	AW IV.iv.9	Marseilles, S. France
Mediterraneum	LL V.i.55	Mediterranean
Messaline	TN II.i.15	probably Marseilles, S. France
Messina	MA I.i.2	port in Sicily, S. Italy
Misena, Mt	AC II.ii.166	Mt Misenum, port in S. Italy
Mytilene	Per IV.ii.3	city in Lesbos, Greece (variously spelt in Q)
Netherland	E3 III.i.24	Holland
Nilus	AC I.ii.49	River Nile, Egypt
Olympus	TC II.iii.10	mountainous region of N. Greece; the home of the gods
Ossa	Ham V.i.279	mountain in Thessaly, N. Greece
Pannonians	Cym III.i.74	people from ancient Pannonia (in and around modern Hungary)
Paphos	Tem IV.i.93	Cyprus; favourite abode of Venus, goddess of love
Parthian	AC I.ii.101	from Parthia, ancient kingdom of W. Asia; known for skilled horsemen and archery
Pelion	MW II.i.74	mountain in Thessaly, N. Greece; the gods revenged themselves on rebellious Titans by burying them under Mt Pelion
Pentapolis	Per II.i.100	city region on N. African coast, modern Libya
Philippan	AC II.v.23	☛ Philippi
Philippi	JC IV.iii.168	battle site in Thrace, Asia Minor, where Antony defeated Brutus and Cassius
Phrygia	TN III.i.50	once the central plateau of Asia Minor and its western flank; area of Asia Minor where Troy was situated
Polonian	E3 III.i.34	from Poland
Pontic Sea	Oth III.iii.450	Black Sea
Portugal, Bay of	AY IV.i.193	sea of supposed great depth off Portugal [unclear location]
Propontic Sea	Oth III.iii.453	Sea of Marmora, Turkey
Pyrenean	KJ I.i.203	Pyrenees, mountain range between France and Spain
Rialto	MV I.iii.19	commercial exchange in Venice, N.E. Italy; also, bridge spanning the Grand Canal
Saba	H8 V.v.23	Bible (1 Kings 10): Sheba, proverbial for wealth
Sardis	JC IV.ii.28	capital of Lydia, Asia Minor; once the political centre
Scylla	MV III.v.14	rock (or sea-monster) in the Straits of Messina opposite Charybdis ☛ Charybdis
Scythian	E3 II.i.72	someone from Scythia, ancient region of E Europe; people known for pitilessness
Senoy	AW I.ii.1	Sienese; from Siena, Tuscany, C. Italy
Sestos	E3 II.ii.155	location of the temple of Aphrodite, on the Hellespont ☛ Hellespont
Sicil	2H6 I.i.6	Sicily, S. Italy
Sicilia	2H6 I.i.47	Sicily, S. Italy
Sicils	3H6 I.iv.122	Naples and Sicily (formerly, the 'Two Sicilies')
Sicyon	AC I.ii.114	town in S. Greece, where Antony's wife Fulvia stayed
Simois	Luc 1437	river flowing from Mt Ida to the plain of Troy, W. Turkey
South Sea	AY III.ii.191	South Seas, seen as a distant and unknown location
Sparta	MND IV.i.113	city of Peloponnesia, S. Greece
Stygian	TC III.ii.8	of the River Styx ☛ Styx
Styx	Tit I.i.91	the principal mythological river of the Underworld
Syracuse, Syracusa	CE I.i.1	port city in Sicily, S. Italy
Tarpeian rock	Cor III.i.212	rock in Rome, from which criminals were thrown to their deaths
Tarsus	Per I.ii.115	ancient city of Asia Minor, S. Turkey
Tartar	E3 II.i.71	someone from Tartary, C. Asia; known for pitilessness; also, a stereotype of dark complexion

Location	Example	Gloss
Tartar	CE IV.ii.32	Tartarus; underworld place of confinement for those who incurred the wrath of the gods
Taurus	MND III.ii.141	Turkish mountain range
Tenedos	TC Prologue.11	island near Troy, W. Turkey ☛ Troy
Thasos	JC V.iii.104	Thassos, island near Philippi, N. Greece
Theban	KL III.iv.150	from Thebes ☛ Thebes
Thebes	TNK I.i.42	city-state in Boeotia, S.E. Greece; associated with wisdom and learning
Thessalian	MND IV.i.121	of Thessaly ☛ Thessaly
Thessaly	AC IV.xiii.2	ancient region of N.E. Greece
Thracian	3H6 IV.ii.21	of Thrace; region of ancient N.E. Greece associated with the worship of Dionysus
Tiber	Cor II.i.46	river in Rome
Tripolis	MV I.iii.18	Tripoli; seaport capital in N. Africa (modern Libya)
Troy	TC Prologue.8	ancient city of W. Turkey, besieged for ten years during the Trojan Wars; also called Ilium, Ilion
Troyant	2H4 II.iv.162	Trojan ☛ Troy
Tunis	Tem II.i.73	former N. African state (in modern Tunisia)
Tyre, Tyrus	Per I.i.1	Mediterranean port, S.W. Lebanon
Volquessen	KJ II.i.527	Vexin, district around Rouen, N.W. France

Languages and Dialects

XI FRENCH

Most French usage appears in *Henry V*, but items occasionally appear in other plays. For grammatical abbreviations, see p.xvii.

VOCABULARY

Item	Example	Dictionary form (if different)	Translation	Item	Example	Dictionary form (if different)	Translation
à (prep.)	**H5** III.vii.62		to, at, on	*baiser (v.)*	**H5** V.ii.259		to kiss
abaissiez (v.)	**H5** V.ii.251	abaisser	lower, descend	*batailles (n. f.)*	**H5** III.v.15	bataille	battles
adieu (int.)	**MW** V.iii.5		goodbye	*belle (adj.)*	**H5** V.ii.214		beautiful
affaire (n. f.)	**MW** I.iv.50		business	*bien (adv.)*	**H5** III.iv.2		good, well
ai (v.)	**H5** III.iv.38	avoir	[I] have	*boîtier (n. m.)*	**MW** I.iv.44		case, box
ainsi (adv.)	**H5** III.iv.45		thus, in this way	*bon (adj.)*	**H5** III.iv.12		good
				bon jour (int.)	**RJ** II.iv.43		good morning, good day
air (n.m.)	**H5** IV.ii.4		air				
allons (v.)	**LL** IV.iii.359	aller	[we, let's] go	*bonne (adj.)*	**H5** IV.iv.3	bon	good
amour (n. m.)	**H5** IV.iv.40		love	*bourbier (n. m.)*	**H5** III.vii.62		mire, mud
anges (n. m.)	**H5** V.ii.111	ange	angels	*bras (n. m.)*	**H5** III.iv.18	bras	arms
anglais (n. m.)	**H5** III.iv.5		English	*brave (adj.)*	**H5** IV.iv.56		brave, courageous
Angleterre (n. f.)	**H5** III.iv.1		England				
appelé(es) (v.)	**H5** III.iv.6	appeler	called	*ça (pron.)*	**H5** III.vii.12		that, it
appelez (v.)	**H5** III.iv.5	appeler	[do you] call	*capitaine (n. m.)*	**H5** IV.iv.65		captain
appelons (v.)	**H5** III.iv.14	appeler	[we] call	*car (conj.)*	**H5** IV.iv.35		because
apprendre (v.)	**H5** III.iv.36		to learn	*ce (det.)*	**H5** III.iv.38		that, this
apprenne (v.)	**H5** III.iv.4	apprendre	[I] learn	*cents (adj.)*	**H5** IV.iv.42	cent	hundred
appris (v.)	**H5** III.iv.23	apprendre	taught	*ces (adj.)*	**H5** III.iv.51	ce	these
as (v.)	**H5** III.iv.1	avoir	[you] have	*c'est (pron. + v.)*	**H5** III.iv.17	être	it is, it's
assez (adv.)	**H5** III.iv.57		enough	*cette (det. f.)*	**H5** IV.iv.35	ce	this
au (prep. + det.)	**H5** III.vii.63	à + le	to the	*chaud (adj.)*	**MW** I.iv.49		hot, warm
aucun (adj.)	**H5** IV.iv.50		no, not any	*cher (adj.)*	**H5** V.ii.215		dear
aussi (adv.)	**TN** III.i.70		too, also	*cheval (n. m.)*	**H5** III.vii.14		horse
aussi ... que (conj.)	**H5** III.iv.35		as ... as	*chevalier (n. m.)*	**H5** IV.iv.56		knight
autre (adj.)	**H5** III.iv.53		other	*chez (prep.)*	**H5** III.vii.14		with, at
avez (v.)	**H5** III.iv.23	avoir	[you] have	*chien (n. m.)*	**H5** III.vii.62		dog
ayez (v.)	**H5** IV.iv.12	avoir	[may you] have	*ciel (n. m.)*	**H5** IV.ii.4		sky, heavens
baille (v.)	**MW** I.iv.86		give	*col (n. m.)*	**H5** III.iv.29		neck
baisant (v.)	**H5** V.ii.252	baiser	kissing	*commande (v.)*	**H5** IV.iv.34	commander	order
baisées (v.)	**H5** V.ii.255	baiser	kissed	*comme (conj.)*	**H5** III.iv.24		as
				comment (adv.)	**H5** III.iv.5		what, how

Item	Example	Dictionary form (if different)	Translation
content (adj.)	H5 IV.iv.52		happy, content
contre (prep.)	H5 IV.iv.50		against
corruptible (adj.)	H5 III.iv.49		debased
coude (n. m.)	H5 III.iv.20		elbow
couper (v.)	H5 IV.iv.35		cut
cour (n. f.)	MW I.iv.50		court
couronne (v.)	2H6 V.ii.28	couronner	crown
coutume (n. f.)	H5 V.ii.256		custom
d' (det.)	H5 III.iv.21	de	of, of the
dames (n. f.)	H5 III.iv.50	dame	ladies
de (det.)	H5 III.iv.49		of
déesse (n. f.)	H5 V.ii.215		goddess
déjà (adv.)	H5 III.iv.38		already
demoiselle(s) (n. f.)	H5 V.ii.217		young lady (ladies)
dépêche (v.)	MW I.iv.52	dépêcher	[you] hurry
des (det.)	H5 V.ii.115	de	of the
dès (prep.)	H5 III.iv.23		up [to], until
deux (adj.)	H5 III.iv.12		two
devin [= divine] (adj. f.)	H5 V.ii.215	divin	divine
devant (prep.)	H5 III.iv.51		in front of, before
diable (n. m.)	MW III.i.83		devil
Dieu (n. m.)	H5 V.ii.115		God
difficile (adj.)	H5 III.iv.24		difficult
dîner (v.)	H5 III.iv.58		to dine, have dinner
dire (v.)	H5 IV.iv.34		to say, tell
disposé (v.)	H5 IV.iv.35		disposed, prepared
distingué (adj.)	H5 IV.iv.57		distinguished
dit (v.)	H5 IV.iv.33	dire	[he] says
dit (v.)	H5 III.iv.17	dire	said
dites (v.)	H5 III.iv.15	dire	[you] tell
divine (adj. f.)	H5 V.ii.215	divin	divine
doigts (n. m.)	H5 III.iv.7	doigt	fingers
donc (adv.)	H5 V.ii.182		then
donner (v.)	H5 IV.iv.52		to give
donnerai (v.)	H5 IV.iv.42	donner	[I] will give
doute (n. m.)	H5 III.iv.36		doubt
droit (adv.)	H5 III.iv.35		correctly, well
du (prep. + det.)	H5 V.ii.214	de + le	of the
eaux (n. f.)	H5 IV.ii.3	eau	waters
échapper (v.)	H5 IV.iv.17		to escape
écolier (n. m.)	H5 III.iv.12		scholar
écoutez (v.)	H5 III.iv.15	écouter	[you] listen
écus (n. m.)	H5 IV.iv.42	écu	crowns
elle (pron.)	H5 III.iv.6		she, it
en (prep.)	H5 III.iv.1		in, on
en (pron.)	H5 III.iv.28		of it, of them
encore (adv.)	H5 IV.iv.50		again
enseigné (v.)	H5 III.iv.39	enseigner	taught
enseignez (v.)	H5 III.iv.4	enseigner	[you] teach
ensemble (adv.)	H5 III.iv.53		together
entendre (v.)	H5 V.ii.261		to understand
entre (prep.)	H5 IV.iv.56		into, between
est (v.)	H5 III.vii.62	être	is
estime (v.)	H5 IV.iv.55	estimer	consider
et (conj.)	H5 III.vii.62		and
été (v.)	H5 III.iv.1	être	been
êtes (v.)	H5 IV.iv.2	être	[you] are
excellent (adj.)	H5 III.iv.56		excellent
excusez (v.)	H5 III.iv.25	excuser	[you] excuse, pardon
fais (v.)	H5 III.iv.22	faire	[you] make
fait (v.)	MW I.iv.49	faire	makes, is
faites (v.)	H5 IV.iv.34	faire	[you] make
fausse (adj.)	H5 V.ii.216		false
faut (v.)	H5 III.iv.4	falloir	have, must, need
feu (n. m.)	H5 IV.ii.4		fire
fils (n. m.)	H5 V.ii.332		son
fin (n. f.)	2H6 V.ii.28		end
foi (n. f.)	H5 III.iv.8		faith
fois (n. f.)	H5 III.iv.53		time, occurrence
force (n. f.)	H5 IV.iv.17		strength
fort (adv.)	H5 III.iv.17		most, very
fortune (n. f.)	H5 IV.v.5		fortune, luck
français (n. m.)	H5 V.ii.186		French
franchisement (n. m.)	H5 IV.iv.52		freedom
gagné (v.)	H5 III.iv.12	gagner	gained
garçon (n. m.)	MW V.v.200		boy
garde (v.)	TN III.i.69	garder	[may he] save
gardez (v.)	H5 IV.iv.42	garder	[you] save
genoux (n. m.)	H5 IV.iv.54	genou	knees
gent (n. f.)	1H6 III.ii.14	gens	race, people
gentilhomme (n. m.)	H5 IV.iv.2		gentleman
gorge (n. f.)	H5 IV.iv.36		throat
grace, grâce (n. f.)	H5 III.iv.36		blessing, favour
grande (adj.)	MW I.iv.50	grand	great, important
grandeur (n. f.)	H5 V.ii.251		greatness

Item	Example	Dictionary form (if different)	Translation	Item	Example	Dictionary form (if different)	Translation
gros (adj.)	H5 III.iv.49		coarse, vulgar	mienne (pron. f.)	H5 V.ii.182	mien	mine
Henri (n. m.)	H5 V.ii.332		Henry	mille (adj.)	H5 IV.iv.54		thousand
héritier (n. m.)	H5 V.ii.333		heir	miséricorde (n. f.)	H5 IV.iv.12		mercy
heure (n. m.)	H5 IV.iv.35		time	moi (pron.)	H5 III.iv.25		me
heureux (adj.)	H5 IV.iv.55		fortunate	mon (det. m.)	H5 V.ii.214		my
hommes (n. m.)	H5 V.ii.115	homme	men	monde (n. m.)	H5 III.iv.52		world
honi soit qui mal y pense	MW V.v.69		shame to him who thinks evil of it	monsieur (n. m.)	AW III.vi.58		sir, mister
				montez (v.)	H5 IV.ii.2	monter	[you] climb
honneur (n. m.)	H5 III.iv.50		honour	mort (n. f.)	E3 IV.vi.40		death
içi (adv.)	H5 IV.iv.35		here	mots (n. m.)	H5 III.iv.12	mot	words
il (pron.)	H5 III.iv.4		he, it	moy [= moi] (pron.)	H5 IV.iv.13		me
ils (pron.)	H5 III.iv.48		they	n' ... pas (part.)	H5 III.iv.38	ne	not
impossible (adj.)	H5 IV.iv.17		impossible	narines (n. f.)	H5 III.vii.14	narine	nostril
impudique (adj.)	H5 III.iv.49		immodest, shameless	natifs (n. m.)	H5 III.iv.35	natif	natives
				néanmoins (adv.)	H5 III.iv.53		nevertheless
indigne (adj.)	H5 V.ii.252		unworthy	ne ... pas (part.)	H5 III.iv.36		no, not
je, j' (pron.)	H5 III.iv.4		I	noces (n. f.)	H5 V.ii.256	noce	wedding, nuptials
jour (n. m.)	H5 IV.v.2		day				
jurement (n. m.)	H5 IV.iv.50		oath, vow	non (part.)	H5 III.iv.40		no, not
la, l' (det. f.)	H5 III.iv.5		the	notre (det.)	H5 V.ii.332		our
là (adv.)	1H6 III.ii.13		there	nous (pron.)	H5 III.iv.14		we, us
laissez (v.)	H5 V.ii.250	laisser	[you] stop, leave	oeuvres (n. f.)	2H6 V.ii.28	oeuvre	works
				ongles (n. m.)	H5 III.iv.13	ongle	fingernails
langage (n. m.)	H5 III.iv.2		language	oublie (v.)	H5 III.iv.8	oublier	[I] forget
langues (n. f.)	H5 V.ii.115	langue	tongues	oublié (v.)	H5 III.iv.38	oublier	forgotten
larron (n. m.)	MW I.iv.66		thief	oui (int.)	H5 III.iv.10		yes
lavée (v.)	H5 III.vii.62	laver	washed	par (prep.)	H5 III.iv.36		by
le, l' (det. m.)	H5 III.iv.2		the	pardonne (v.)	R2 V.iii.118	pardonner	[you] pardon, forgive
leçon (n. f.)	H5 III.iv.53		lesson				
lequel (pron.)	H5 V.ii.187		which	pardonner (v.)	H5 IV.iv.41		to pardon, forgive
les (det. plural)	H5 III.iv.8		the				
leurs	H5 V.ii.256	leur	their	pardonnez (v.)	H5 V.ii.108	pardonner	[you] pardon, forgive
liberté (n. f.)	H5 IV.iv.52		liberty				
m' (pron.)	H5 III.iv.4	me	me, myself	parle (v.)	H5 III.iv.15	parler	[I] speak
ma (det. f.)	H5 III.iv.53		my	parler (v.)	H5 III.iv.5		to speak
madame (n. f.)	H5 III.iv.3		madam	parles (v.)	H5 III.iv.1	parler	[you] speak
main(s) (n. f.)	H5 III.iv.5		hand(s)	parlez (v.)	H5 V.ii.187	parler	[you] speak
mais (conj.)	H5 III.iv.8		but	pas (part.)	H5 III.iv.38		not
maison (n. f.)	H5 IV.iv.41		house	pauvre (adj.)	1H6 III.ii.14		poor
mauvais (adj.)	H5 III.iv.49		bad	paysan(s) (n. m.)	MW V.v.200		peasant(s)
me (pron.)	H5 III.iv.8		me	pense (v.)	H5 III.iv.9	penser	[I] think
méchante (adj. f.)	H5 IV.v.5		spiteful, wicked	perdu (v.)	H5 IV.v.2	perdre	lost
				père (n. m.)	H5 V.ii.244		father
meilleur (adj.)	H5 V.ii.187		better	petit (adj.)	H5 IV.iv.49		little
menton (n. m.)	H5 III.iv.31		chin	peu (n. m.)	H5 III.iv.3		little bit
mes (pron.)	H5 IV.iv.54	me	my	pied (n. m.)	H5 III.iv.46		foot
mette (v.)	MW I.iv.52	mettre	[you] put	pitié (n. f.)	H5 IV.iv.12		pity

Item	Example	Dictionary form (if different)	Translation	Item	Example	Dictionary form (if different)	Translation
pleines (adj.)	H5 V.ii.116	pleine	full	*sembable (adj.)*	H5 V.ii.111		similar, like
plus (adv.)	H5 IV.iv.56		most	*serviteur (n. m.)*	TN III.i.70		servant
point (adv.)	H5 III.iv.36		not at all	*si (conj.)*	H5 III.iv.15		if
possession (n. f.)	H5 V.ii.180		possession	*soldat (n. m.)*	H5 IV.iv.35		soldier
pour (prep.)	H5 III.iv.50		for	*son (det. m.)*	H5 III.vii.62		his, its
pourquoi (adv.)	TN I.iii.87		why	*son (n. m.)*	H5 III.iv.49		sound
prenez (v.)	H5 IV.iv.12	prendre	take, have	*sont (v.)*	H5 III.iv.9	être	[they] are
présent (n. m.)	H5 III.iv.23		present time	*souviendrai (v.)*	H5 III.iv.9	souvenir	remember
prêt (adj.)	H5 IV.iv.34		ready	*suis (v.)*	H5 IV.iv.41	être	[I] am
prie (v.)	H5 III.iv.4	prier	beg, pray	*suivez (v.)*	H5 IV.iv.65	suivre	[you] follow
princesse (n. f.)	H5 V.ii.120		princess	*supplie (v.)*	H5 IV.iv.40	supplier	[I] beseech
prisonnier (n. m.)	H5 IV.iv.51		prisoner	*sur (prep.)*	H5 IV.iv.54		on
promis (v.)	H5 IV.iv.52	promettre	promised	*temps (n. m.)*	H5 III.iv.37		time
promptement (adv.)	H5 III.iv.40		quickly, readily	*terre (n. f.)*	H5 IV.ii.3		earth, land
				tombé (v.)	H5 IV.iv.55	tomber	fallen
prononcer (v.)	H5 III.iv.51		to pronounce	*ton (det. m.)*	H5 IV.iv.18		your
prononcez (v.)	H5 III.iv.34	prononcer	[you] pronounce	*tous (adj. plural)*	H5 III.iv.22	tout	all
				tout (adj.)	H5 III.iv.52		all
propre (adj.)	H5 III.vii.62		own	*très (adv.)*	H5 IV.iv.57		very, most
puis (adv.)	H5 IV.ii.4		then	*tromperies (n. f.)*	H5 V.ii.116	tromperie	deceit
puissant (adj.)	H5 V.ii.253		powerful, mighty	*trop (adv.)*	H5 III.iv.24		too
				truie (n. f.)	H5 III.vii.63		sow
qu' (conj.)	H5 IV.iv.50		that, which, what	*tu (pron.)*	H5 III.iv.1		you
				un (det. m.)	H5 III.iv.3		a, an
qualité (n. f.)	H5 IV.iv.3		quality	*une (det. f.)*	H5 III.iv.53	un	a, an
quand (adv./conj.)	H5 V.ii.180		when	*user (v.)*	H5 III.iv.50		use
que (pron./conj.)	H5 III.iv.38		that, which, what	*vaillant (adj.)*	H5 IV.iv.57		valiant
				vais (v.)	MW I.iv.50	aller	[I] go
question (n. f.)	LL V.i.81		question, doubt	*vérité (n. f.)*	H5 III.iv.34		truth
				vert (adj.)	MW I.iv.44		green
qui (pron./conj.)	1H6 III.ii.13		who	*veux (v.)*	H5 V.ii.251	vouloir	want
réciterai (v.)	H5 III.iv.40	réciter	[I] will recite	*vie (n. f.)*	H5 IV.iv.42		life
remercîments (n. m.)	H5 IV.iv.55	remercîment	thanks	*vitement (adv.)*	H5 III.iv.13		quickly
				vivant (adj.)	H5 III.v.5		living
répétition (n. f.)	H5 III.iv.22		repetition	*vive (v.)*	E3 III.iii.165	vivre	[may he] live
retourné (v.)	H5 III.vii.62	retourner	returned	*volant (adj.)*	H5 III.vii.14		flying
rien (adv.)	H5 IV.ii.4		nothing else	*vomissement (n. m.)*	H5 III.vii.62		vomit
robe (n. f.)	H5 III.iv.46		gown				
roi (n. m.)	H5 V.ii.244		king	*votre (det.)*	TN III.i.70		your
sage (adj.)	H5 V.ii.217		wise	*vôtre (pron.)*	H5 V.ii.182		yours
sans (prep.)	LL V.i.81		without	*voudrais (v.)*	H5 III.iv.51	vouloir	[I] would like
sauf (prep.)	H5 V.ii.112		save, except	*vous (pron.)*	TN III.i.69		you
Seigneur (n. m.)	H5 III.iv.28		Lord	*vraiment (adv.)*	H5 V.ii.112		really
seigneur(s) (n. m.)	H5 III.iv.51		lord(s)				

FRENCH PRONUNCIATION

Several English words are written so as to represent the pronunciation of a French person speaking English.

French pronunciation	English word	Example
/th/ (voiceless) becomes /t/		
tank	thank	MW II.iii.65
tree	three	MW II.iii.33
troat	throat	MW I.iv.106
trot	troth	MW I.iv.60
turd	third	MW III.iii.222
/th/ (voiceless) becomes /d/		
dank	thank	MW II.iii.82
/th/ (voiced) becomes /d/		
dat	that	MW I.iv.61
de	the	MW I.iv.71
den	then	H5 V.ii.247
dere	there	MW I.iv.71
dese	these	MW I.iv.43
/f/ and /w/ become /v/		
varld	world	MW I.iv.62
vat	what	MW I.iv.43
vell	well	MW II.iii.87
ver	where	MW I.iv.112
vetch	fetch	MW I.iv.44
vill	will	MW I.iv.113
vor	for	MW II.iii.82
vorld	world	MW II.iii.28
/b/ becomes /p/		
Pible	Bible	MW II.iii.7
/g/ becomes /k/		
gown	count	H5 III.iv.47

French pronunciation	English word	Example
/j/ and /g/ becomes /zh/		
Ja(r)many	Germany	MW IV.v.80
Jarteer	Garter	MW I.iv.115
/ch/, /sh/, and /s/ are confused		
mush	much	MW III.ii.59
nursh	nurse	MW III.ii.58
shallenge	challenge	MW I.iv.106
sin	chin	H5 III.iv.33
sould	should	H5 V.ii.168
/h/ is dropped		
'ave	have	H5 V.ii.216
vowel change		
Ja(r)many	Germany	MW IV.v.80
nick	neck	H5 III.iv.30
varld	world	MW I.iv.62
final syllable change		
extra -a	green-a	MW I.iv.45
fingre	finger	H5 III.iv.10
nailès	nails	H5 III.iv.14

In the following case, the spelling change is enough to suggest a foreign accent, though there is actually little or no difference in pronunciation between the words.

wat	what	H5 V.ii.108

There are also a few instances of mock French, used by Pistol, Parolles, and Cade.

calen o custure me	[nonsensical]	H5 IV.iv.4 [Pistol]
couple a gorge	couper la gorge [= cut the throat]	H5 II.i.68 [Pistol]
mor du vinager	a pseudo oath [unclear meaning]	AW II.iii.43 [Parolles]
Basimecu	baise mon cul [= kiss my arse]	2H6 IV.vii.25 [Cade]

For grammatical abbreviations, see p.XVII.

Item	Example	Dictionary form (if different)	Translation
accommodo (v.)	2H4 III.ii.71		[I] accommodate
accusativo (n. m.)	MW IV.i.41	accusativus	in the accusative case
ad (prep.)	Tit IV.iii.54		to, for
adsum (v.)	2H6 I.iv.22		[I am] present
Aeacida (n. m.)	2H6 I.iv.61	Aeacus	Aeacus ☞ p.613
aer (n. m.)	Cym V.v.448		air
aio (v.)	2H6 I.iv.61		[I] proclaim
aliis (n. m.)	TNK III.v.132	alius	other
alit (v.)	Per II.ii.33	alo	[he] feeds, nourishes
Angliae (n. f.)	H5 V.ii.334	Anglia	of England
animis (n. m.)	2H6 II.i.24	animus	creature, being; mind, soul
antiquius (adj.)	Per I.Chorus.10	antiquus	older
apex (n. m.)	Per II.ii.30		honour, crown
Apollinem (n. m.)	Tit IV.iii.54	Apollo	Apollo ☞ p.620
arcu (n. m.)	Tit IV.ii.21	arcus	bow
armigero (adj.)	MW I.i.9	armiger	[bearing arms] esquire
artus (n. m.)	2H6 IV.i.118		joint, limb
Astraea (n. f.)	Tit IV.iii.4		Astraea ☞ p.620
audis (v.)	Tit IV.i.81	audio	[you] hear
aut (conj.)	Tit II.i.133		or
ave (int.)	E3 I.i.164		hail
bene (adv.)	LL V.i.28		well
benedicite (v.)	MM II.iii.39	benedico	[blessing] may God be with you
bis (adv.)	LL IV.ii.22		twice
bone [= bene] (adv.)	LL V.i.27		well
boni (adj.)	TNK III.v.84	bonus	good
bonum (adj.)	Per I.Chorus.10	bonus	good
brevis (adj.)	Tim I.ii.27		short
caelum (n. m.)	LL IV.ii.5	caelus	sky
candidatus (n. m.)	Tit I.i.188		candidate for office
canus [= canis] (n. m.)	LL V.ii.585	canis	dog
capite (n. nt.)	2H6 IV.vii.116	caput	head
captum (n. m.)	TS I.i.159	captus	prisoner
caret (v.)	LL IV.i.122	careo	[it is] lacking
celsa (adj.)	TS III.i.29	celsus	lofty
cita (adj.)	LL V.i.65	citus	quick, ready
coctus (v.)	LL IV.ii.22	coquo	cooked
coelestibus (n. plural)	2H6 II.i.24	coelestis	heavenly beings
coram [= quorum]	MW I.i.6	qui	of whom
cordis (n. nt.)	WT I.ii.110	cor	of the heart
credo (v.)	LL IV.ii.11		[I] believe
cucullus (n. m.)	MM V.i.261		hood
cuique (pron.)	Tit I.i.283		☞ suum cuique
cum (prep.)	H8 I.iii.34		by, with
custalorum [= custos rotulorum] (n. m.)	MW I.i.7		keeper of the rolls [= official records]
deaeque [= deae + que] (n. f.)	TNK III.v.157	dea	and goddesses
Deo (n. m.)	LL V.i.27	Deus	God
deum (n. m.)	H5 IV.viii.122	deus	god
di (n. m.)	3H6 I.iii.48	deus	gods
dii (n. m.)	TNK III.v.84	deus	gods
diluculo (n. nt.)	TN II.iii.2	diluculum	dawn
dominator (n. m.)	Tit IV.i.80		ruler, lord
domine (n. m.)	LL IV.ii.104	dominus	master, sir
ecce (part.)	1H4 II.iv.163		behold
eget (v.)	Tit IV.ii.21	egeo	[he] needs
ego (pron.)	H8 III.ii.314		I
eo (adv.)	Per I.Chorus.10		by so much more
erga (prep.)	H8 III.i.40		towards
ergo (adv.)	LL V.ii.589		therefore
est (v.)	H8 III.i.40	sum	is
et (conj.)	H5 V.ii.334		and
exegi (v.)	TNK III.v.89	exigo	[I] completed
exeunt (v.)	Ham V.ii.397	exeo	[they] go out
extinguit (v.)	Per II.ii.33	exstinguo	[he] extinguishes
facere (v.)	LL IV.ii.15	facio	make, cause
faciant (v.)	3H6 I.iii.48	facio	[they] make, cause
facile (adv.)	LL IV.ii.92		pleasantly
facit (v.)	MM V.i.261	facio	[it] makes, causes
facto (n. nt.)	TNK V.ii.35	factum	fact
fas (adj.)	Tit II.i.133		right
fatuus (adj.)	TNK III.v.42		foolish, false
Fauste (n. m.) [F facile]	LL IV.ii.92	Faustus	O Faustus
fidelicet [= videlicet] (adv.)	MW I.i.130		namely

Item	Example	Dictionary form (if different)	Translation
fides (*n. f.*)	**Per** II.ii.38		hope
fidius (*n. m.*)	**TNK** III.v.11		☞ *medius fidius*
filii (*n. m.*)	**TNK** III.v.136	filius	boys
filius (*n. m.*)	**H5** V.ii.334		boy
finem (*n. m.*)	**CE** IV.iv.39	finis	end
Franciae (*n. f.*)	**H5** V.ii.334	Francia	France
fratrum (*n. m.*)	**Tit** I.i.101	frater	brother
furor (*n. m.*)	**Tim** I.ii.27		madness
gaudeo (*v.*)	**LL** V.i.31		[I] rejoice
gelida (*adj.*)	**LL** IV.ii.92	gelidus	cool, cold, numb
gelidus (*adj.*)	**2H6** IV.i.118		cool, cold, numb
genitivo (*n. m.*)	**MW** IV.i.40	genitivus	in the genitive case
hac (*det.*)	**Per** II.ii.43	hic	this
haec (*det.*)	**MW** IV.i.38	hic	this
haeres (*n. m.*)	**H5** V.ii.334		heir
harum (*det.*)	**MW** IV.i.56	hic	of these
haud (*adv.*)	**LL** IV.ii.11		not at all
Henricus (*n. m.*)	**H5** V.ii.334		Henry
hic (*adv.*)	**MW** IV.i.38		here
hinc [= *hunc*] (*det.*)	**MW** IV.i.41		this
hoc (*det.*)	**MW** IV.i.38	hic	this
hominem (*n. m.*)	**LL** V.i.9	homo	man
homo (*n. m.*)	**1H4** II.i.96		man
honorificabilitudi-nitatibus	**LL** V.i.41		[supposed longest word in Latin] state of being honoured
horum (*det.*)	**MW** IV.i.56	hic	of these
hujus (*det.*)	**MW** IV.i.40	hic	of this
iaculis (*n. nt.*)	**Tit** IV.ii.21	iaculum	javelin
ibat (*v.*)	**TS** III.i.28	eo	[he] ran, went
idem (*pron.*)	**2H4** V.v.28		same
ignis (*n. m.*)	**1H4** III.iii.39		fire
imitari (*v.*)	**LL** IV.ii.125	imitor	imitate
imprimendum (*v.*)	**TS** IV.iv.90	imprimo	right to print
in (*prep.*)	**2H6** IV.vii.116		in
integer (*adj.*)	**Tit** IV.ii.20		upright (person)
integritas (*n. f.*)	**H8** III.i.40		integrity
intelligis (*v.*)	**LL** V.i.25	intelligo	[you] understand
intelligo (*v.*)	**LL** V.i.27		[I] understand
intrate (*v.*)	**TNK** III.v.136	intro	[you] enter
invitis (*adj.*)	**2H6** IV.i.99	invitus	unwilling [= in spite of]
Iovis (*n. m.*)	**TNK** III.v.89	Jovis	of Jove
ipse (*pron.*)	**AY** V.i.42		he
ipso (*pron.*)	**TNK** V.ii.35	ipse	by that
ira (*n. f.*)	**Tim** I.ii.27		anger
irae (*n. f.*)	**2H6** II.i.24	ira	anger
ista (*pron.*)	**3H6** I.iii.48	iste	that
Jovem (*n. m.*)	**Tit** IV.iii.54	Jovis	Jove
labras [= *labra*] (*n. nt.*)	**MW** I.i.151	labrum	lips
lapis (*n. m.*)	**MW** IV.i.29		stone
laudis (*n. f.*)	**3H6** I.iii.48	laus	fame, praise
laus (*n. f.*)	**LL** V.i.27		fame, praise
lege (*v.*)	**LL** IV.ii.103	lego	[you] read
lentus (*adj.*)	**Tit** IV.i.81		slow
leo (*n. m.*)	**Cym** V.v.446		lion
limbo (*n. m.*)	**H8** V.iv.63	limbus	border region [= limbo]
loquitur (*v.*)	**LL** IV.ii.79	loquor	[he] says, speaks
lux (*n. f.*)	**Per** II.ii.21		light
magni (*adj.*)	**Tit** IV.i.80	magnus	great
majestas (*n. f.*)	**2H6** V.i.5		majesty
manent (*v.*)	**Cor** I.i.250 [F only]		they remain ☞ STAGE DIRECTIONS, p.417
manes (*n. plural*)	**Tit** I.i.101		shades, departed spirits
manu (*n. f.*)	**LL** V.i.65	manus	with a hand
manus (*n. f.*)	**LL** V.ii.587		hand
Martem (*n. m.*)	**Tit** IV.iii.55	Mars	Mars
Mauri (*n. m.*)	**Tit** IV.ii.21	Maurus	of the Moor
me (*pron.*)	**Per** II.ii.30		me
medice (*n. m.*)	**2H6** II.i.51	medicus	physician
medius fidius (*n. m.*)	**TNK** III.v.11		by heaven!, by Jupiter!
mehercle (*int.*)	**LL** IV.ii.77		by Hercules!
melius (*adj.*)	**Per** I.Chorus.10		better
memento (*v.*)	**1H4** III.iii.30	memini	be mindful
mentis (*n. f.*)	**H8** III.i.40	mens	purpose, plan
meus (*det.*)	**H8** III.ii.314		my
mihi (*pron.*)	**Per** II.ii.21	ego	to me
minime (*adv.*)	**LL** III.i.58		by no means
minimo (*adj.*)	**TS** I.i.159	minimus	little, small
mollis (*adj.*)	**Cym** V.v.448		soft, gentle
monachum (*n. m.*)	**MM** V.i.261	monachus	monk
mons (*n. m.*)	**LL** V.1.79		mountain, hill
mori (*v.*)	**1H4** III.iii.30	morior	die
mulier (*n. f.*)	**Cym** V.v.449		woman
mulieres (*n. f.*)	**H5** I.ii.38	mulier	women
multis (*adj.*)	**TNK** III.v.132	multus	many

Item	Example	Dictionary form (if different)	Translation	Item	Example	Dictionary form (if different)	Translation
natus (adj.)	**Cym** V.v.446		born	*quae (pron.)*	**MW** IV.i.72	qui	which
ne (part.)	**H5** I.ii.38		not	*quam (conj.)*	**TS** I.i.159		as
ne, -ne (part.)	**LL** V.i.25		[particle marking a question]	*quando (conj.)*	**LL** IV.ii.92		when
nec (conj.)	**Tit** IV.ii.21		neither, nor	*quare (adv.)*	**LL** V.i.33		why
nefas (adj.)	**Tit** II.i.133		wrong	*quasi (conj.)*	**LL** IV.ii.82		as if
nihil (n. nt.)	**2H4** V.v.28		nothing	*queas (v.)*	**TS** I.i.159	queo	[you] be able
nobis (pron.)	**H5** IV.viii.122	ego	to us	*qui (pron.)*	**MW** IV.i.72		who
nominativo (n. m.)	**MW** IV.i.38	nominati-vus	in the nominative case	*quis (pron.)*	**LL** V.i.50		who
non (part.)	**H5** IV.viii.122		not	*quo (pron.)*	**Per** I.Chorus.10	qui	for which
noster (det.)	**H5** V.ii.334		our	*quod (pron.)*	**MW** IV.i.72		which
novi (v.)	**LL** V.i.9	nosco	[I] knew	*quondam (adv.)*	**LL** V.i.6		at one time [here: former]
nubibus (n. f.)	**2H6** IV.i.99	nubes	clouds	*quoniam (conj.)*	**LL** V.ii.588		since
obsque [= abs-que] (prep.)	**2H4** V.v.28		without, apart from	*quousque (adv.)*	**TNK** III.v.38		how long
occupat (v.)	**2H6** IV.i.118	occupo	seize	*ratolorum [= rotulorum] (n. f.)*	**MW** I.i.8	rotula	of the rolls [= official records]
offendendo [= defendendo] (v.)	**Ham** V.i.9	defendo	defending [here: self-defence]	*redime (v.)*	**TS** I.i.159	redimo	[you] ransom
omne (pron.)	**LL** IV.ii.32	omnis	all	*regia (n. f.)*	**TS** III.i.29		palace
omnes (adj.)	**TNK** III.v.157	omnis	all	*regina (n. f.)*	**H8** III.i.40		queen
opus (n. nt.)	**TNK** III.v.89		work	*reliquit (v.)*	**Tit** IV.iii.4	relinquo	[she] has left
ostentare (v.)	**LL** IV.ii.15	ostento	show	*respice (v.)*	**CE** IV.iv.39	respicio	[you] have regard for
patrum (n. m.)	**H8** V.iv.63	pater	of the fathers	*rex (n. m.)*	**H5** V.ii.334		king
pauca (n. plural)	**MW** I.i.114		few [words]	*Romanos (n. m.)*	**2H6** I.iv.61	Romanus	Romans
pecus (n. f.)	**LL** IV.ii.92		cattle	*ruminat (v.)*	**LL** IV.ii.93	rumino	[it] chews the cud
pedagogus (n. m.)	**TNK** III.v.109		teacher	*Salicam (adj.)*	**H5** I.ii.38	Salica	Salic [= of the Salian Franks]
pene (adv.) [F pine]	**2H6** IV.i.118		almost	*sancta (adj.)*	**2H6** V.i.5	sanctus	holy
per (pron.)	**TC** I.ii.15		by, through, across	*sanguis (n. m.)*	**LL** IV.ii.3		blood
				sapit (v.)	**LL** IV.ii.79	sapio	[he] is wise
perge (v.)	**LL** IV.ii.53	pergo	[you] proceed	*satis (adv.)*	**LL** V.i.1		enough
poli (n. m.)	**Tit** IV.i.80	polus	sky, heavens	*scelera (n. nt.)*	**Tit** IV.i.81	scelus	crimes
pompae (n. f.)	**Per** II.ii.30	pompa	triumph, contest	*scelerisque [= sceleris + que] (n. nt.)*	**Tit** IV.ii.20	scelus	and of crimes
posse (v.)	**2H6** I.iv.61	possum	be able				
praeclarissimus (adj.)	**H5** V.ii.333	praeclarus	most noble	*se (pron.)*	**Ham** V.i.9		oneself, himself, herself
precor (v.)	**LL** IV.ii.92		[I] pray, beg	*secundo (adv.)*	**TN** V.34		second
Priami (n. m.)	**TS** III.i.29	Priamus	of Priam	*semper (adv.)*	**2H4** V.v.28		always
primo (adv.)	**TN** V.34		first	*senis (n. m.)*	**TS** III.i.29	senex	of the old man
privilegio (n. nt.)	**H8** I.iii.34	privilegium	privilege, prerogative	*serenissima (adj.)*	**H8** III.i.40	serenus	most noble
proh (int.)	**TNK** III.v.11	pro	O, alas	*sic (adv.)*	**E3** III.iv.126		so, thus
provexit (v.)	**Per** II.ii.30	proveho	led on, carried along	*Sigeia (adj.)*	**TS** III.i.28		Sigeian [= Trojan]
pueritia (n. f.)	**LL** V.i.47		childishness	*signum (n. nt.)*	**1H4** II.iv.164		sign
pulcher (adj.)	**MW** IV.i.25		fair, beautiful	*Simois (n. m.)*	**TS** III.i.28		Simois ☞ p.636
purus (adj.)	**Tit** IV.ii.20		free	*sine (prep.)*	**LL** V.i.20		without

Item	Example	Dictionary form (if different)	Translation	Item	Example	Dictionary form (if different)	Translation
singulariter (adv.)	**MW** IV.i.38		singly	*tua (det.)*	**Per** II.ii.21		your [singular]
sit (v.)	**3H6** I.iii.48	sum	[it] may be, be it	*tuae (det.)*	**3H6** I.iii.48	tua	of your [singular]
solum (adj.)	**TS** IV.iv.90	solus	sole	*ubique (adv.)*	**Ham** I.v.156		everywhere
solus (adj.)	**H5** II.i.42		alone	*umbra (n. f.)*	**LL** IV.ii.92		shade
spe (n. f.)	**Per** II.ii.43	spes	hope	*vehor (v.)*	**Tit** II.i.135	veho	I am carried
spectanda (v.)	**Per** II.ii.38	specto	to be tested	*veni (v.)*	**LL** IV.i.70	venio	[I] came
steterat (v.)	**TS** III.i.29	sto	[it] stood	*venit (v.)*	**LL** V.i.30	venio	comes
stuprum (n. nt.)	**Tit** IV.i.77		rape	*verba (n. nt.)*	**MW** I.i.114	verbum	words
Stygia (n. f.)	**Tit** II.i.135	Styx	Styx ☛ p.636	*via (n. f.)*	**LL** IV.ii.14		way
sub (prep.)	**LL** IV.ii.92		in, under	*vici (v.)*	**LL** IV.i.70	vinco	[I] conquered
succedant (v.)	**H5** I.ii.38	succedo	[they] succeed	*videlicet (adv.)*	**Ham** II.i.61		that is to say, namely
sufficit (v.)	**LL** V.i.1	sufficio	[it] suffices, provides	*video (v.)*	**LL** V.i.31		[I] see
summa (adj.)	**3H6** I.iii.48	summus	highest	*vides (v.)*	**Tit** IV.i.81	video	[you] see
surgere (v.)	**TN** II.iii.2	surgo	rise	*videsne [= vides + ne] (v.)*	**LL** V.i.30	video	do you see
suum cuique (prons.)	**Tit** I.i.283	suus	to each his own	*vidi (v.)*	**LL** IV.i.70	video	[I] saw
tam (adv.)	**Tit** IV.i.81		so	*vincere (v.)*	**2H6** I.iv.61	vinco	conquer, defeat
tandem (adv.)	**TNK** III.v.38		at length, at last	*vir (n. m.)*	**LL** IV.ii.79		man
tanquam (adv.)	**LL** V.i.9		as well as, just as	*vita (n. f.)*	**Per** II.ii.21		life
tanta (adj.)	**H8** III.i.40	tantus	so great, so much	*vitae (n. f.)*	**Tit** IV.ii.20	vita	of life
tantaene [= tantae + ne] (adj.)	**2H6** II.i.24	tantus	so great, so much	*viva (adj.)*	**H8** II.i.18	vitus	live, present
				vivo (v.)	**Per** II.ii.43		[I] live
te (pron.)	**H5** IV.viii.122	tu	you [singular]	*vocativo (n. m.)*	**MW** IV.i.48	vocativus	in the vocative case
teipsum (pron.)	**2H6** II.i.51		yourself [here, in context of: heal yourself]	*vocatur (v.)*	**LL** V.i.23		[it] is called
				voce (n. f.)	**H8** II.i.18	vox	voice
tellus (n. f.)	**TS** III.i.28		land	*vos (pron.)*	**E3** III.iv.126		you [plural]
terra (n. f.)	**LL** IV.ii.7		earth, land				
terram (n. f.)	**H5** I.ii.38	terra	earth, land				
terras (n. f.)	**Tit** IV.iii.4	terra	earth, lands				
tertio (adv.)	**TN** V.i.34		third				
timor (n. m.)	**2H6** IV.i.118		fear				
tremor (n. m.)	**WT** I.ii.110		palpitations				
tu (pron.)	**JC** III.i.77		you [singular]				

As well as the errors listed above, there are also instances of mock Latin, produced by Feste (in his role as Sir Topas) and Costard.

bonos dies	**TN** IV.ii.12		good day
ad dunghill	**LL** V.i.72		[= *ad unguem* 'to the nail'] to a nicety

XIII ITALIAN AND SPANISH

For grammatical abbreviations, see p.xvii.

VOCABULARY

Item	Example	Translation	Item	Example	Translation
alla (prep.)	**TS** I.ii.25	to the	*terra (n. f.)*	**2H6** IV.vii.52	country
basta (v.)	**TS** I.i.195	enough	*ti (pron.)*	**LL** IV.ii.97	you
ben trovato	**TS** I.ii.24	well met	*tutto (adj.)*	**TS** I.ii.24	all
ben venuto	**TS** I.ii.25	welcome	*vede (v.)*	**LL** IV.ii.97	see
bona (adj.)	**2H6** IV.vii.52	good	*Venetia (n. f.)*	**LL** IV.ii.96	Venice
casa (n. f.)	**TS** I.ii.25	house	*via (int.)*	**E3** II.ii.12	away!
chi (pron.)	**LL** IV.ii.97	who			
con (prep.)	**TS** I.ii.24	with			
coragio (n. m.)	**Tem** V.i.257	courage			
cuore (n. m.)	**TS** I.ii.24	heart			
Diablo (n. m.)	**Oth** II.iii.155	Devil			
gens (n. f.)	**2H6** IV.vii.52	people			
honorato (v.)	**TS** I.ii.26	honoured			
il (det. m.)	**TS** I.ii.24	the			
mala (n. m.)	**2H6** IV.vii.52	evil			
mi (pron.)	**TS** I.i.25	me			
mio (det.)	**TS** I.ii.26	my			
molto (adv.)	**TS** I.ii.26	most			
non (part.)	**LL** IV.ii.97	not			
nostra (det.)	**TS** I.ii.25	our			
passa (v.)	**TNK** III.v.87	go by			
perdonato (v.)	**TS** I.i.25	excuse			
pretia (v.)	**LL** IV.ii.97	prize			
roba (n.f.)	**2H4** III.ii.22	material			
signor (n. m.)	**TS** I.ii.26	mister			

The motto described by Thaisa in *Pericles* II.ii.27 [Q] as 'Spanish' – *pue per doleera kee per forsa* ('more by gentleness than by force') – is actually much closer to Italian.

Q item	Probable Italian word	Translation
doleera	dolcezza	gentleness
forsa	forza	force
kee	que	than
per		by
pue	piu	more

Similarly, the utterances by Pistol (**2H4** II.iv.176 and V.v.99) are garbled mixtures of Italian and Spanish: *Si fortune me tormente sperato me contento* and *Si fortuna me tormenta, spero me contenta* ('If fortune torments me, hope contents me'). Christopher Sly (**TS** Induction.i.5) also seems to be attempting Spanish in his *paucas pallabris* ('few words', i.e. 'be brief'), elliptically but accurately uttered by Dogberry as *palabras* (**MA** III.v.15). The only other piece of Spanish is Don Armado's *fortuna de la guerra* (**LL** V.ii.528), 'the fortunes of war'.

XIV IRISH

The speech of Macmorris in *Henry V* displays a few hints of an Irish pronunciation, with its replacement of /s/ by /sh/, changes in vowel quality, and the loss of a final consonant.

Irish pronunciation	English word	First usage in H5 III.ii
be	by	106
beseeched	besieged	105
Chrish	Christ	85
ish	is	85
sa'	save	109
'tish	'tis	85
trompet	trumpet	86

XV SCOTTISH

In *Henry V*, the Scots captain Jamy is given a few features of localized pronunciation. The distinctiveness is almost entirely conveyed by variation in vowel quality, as suggested by the spelling – a contrast with the way Fluellen's Welshness is portrayed.

Scottish pronunciation	English word	First usage in H5 III.ii
bath	both	99
breff	brief	114
capten	captain	99
de	do	111
feith	faith	99
grund	ground	112
leve	leave	100
lig	lie	111
mess	mass	110
slomber	slumber	111
suerly	surely	113
theise	these	110
vary	very	99
wad	would	114

The only changes affecting consonants are in these words:

Chrish	Christ	85
lig	lie	111
sall	shall	99

Welsh pronunciation is illustrated in the characters of Fluellen in *Henry V* and Evans in *The Merry Wives of Windsor*. The majority of the distinctive features follow the same trend, but there are some exceptions. There is usually just one localized feature per word.

The most noticeable feature is that voiced consonants (those with vocal cord vibration, such as /b, d, g, v/) lose their voicing.

Welsh pronunciation	English word	First usage in H5 *or* MW	Welsh pronunciation	English word	First usage in H5 *or* MW
/b/ becomes /p/			*Tavy*	Davy	H5 IV.vii.101
Pabylon	Babylon	MW III.i.23	*tevil*	devil	MW I.i.139
pad	bad	MW III.iii.207			
pashful	bashful	H5 IV.viii.70	**/v/ becomes /f/**		
pattle	battle	H5 IV.vii.93	*aggriefed*	aggrieved	H5 IV.vii.158
pear	bear	H5 IV.viii.35	*falorous*	valorous	H5 III.ii.74
peard	beard	MW IV.ii.182	*fehemently*	vehemently	MW III.i.8
peat	beat	MW I.i.66	*fery*	very	MW I.i.46
peds	beds	MW III.i.18	*focative*	vocative	MW IV.i.49
peseech	beseech	H5 V.i.21	*prerogatifes*	prerogatives	H5 IV.i.67
petter	better	MW I.i.39			
pibble-pabble	bibble-babble	H5 IV.i.70	**/z/ becomes /s/ or /sh/**		
pid	bid	MW V.iv.3	*ass*	as	H5 V.i.4
pless	bless	MW I.i.67	*Jeshu*	Jesu	MW III.i.11 [Q only]
plows	blows	H5 IV.viii.14	*possitable*	positively	MW I.i.220
plood	blood	H5 IV.vii.105			
ploody	bloody	H5 V.i.40	**/j/ becomes /ch/**		
plue	blue	H5 III.vi.101	*Cheshu*	Jesu	H5 III.ii.61
pody	body	H5 IV.vii.105			
pold	bold	MW V.iv.2	The general pattern is clearly 'voiced becomes voiceless', hence the occasional instances of the reverse process are noteworthy. They include Evans' pronunciation of Latin as well as English.		
porn	born	H5 IV.vii.11			
poys	boys	H5 IV.vii.1			
prabble	brabble	MW I.i.51			
pragging	bragging	H5 V.i.5	**/p/ becomes /b/**		
prain	brain	MW I.i.40	*Hibocrates*	Hippocrates	MW III.i.61
prave	brave	H5 III.vi.62	*taber*	taper	MW IV.iv.67
prawls	brawls	H5 IV.viii.65	*trib*	trip	MW V.iv.1
pread	bread	H5 V.i.8			
preeches	breeches	MW IV.i.73	**/t/ becomes /d/**		
pridge	bridge	H5 III.vi.12	*tiddle-taddle*	tittle-tattle	H5 IV.i.70
prief	brief	MW I.i.134			
pring	bring	MW I.i.41	**/k/ becomes /g/**		
putter	butter	MW V.v.139	*cogscomb*	coxcomb	MW III.i.81
py	by	MW I.i.26	*hic, haec, hoc*	hig, hag, hog	MW IV.i.39
trempling	trembling	MW III.i.12	*knog*	knock	MW III.i.13
			stog	stock	MW III.i.108
/d/ becomes /t/					
digt	digged	H5 III.ii.60	**/f/ becomes /v/**		
goot	good	MW I.i.41	*vagram*	fragrant	MW III.i.24
Got	God	MW I.i.34	*vlouting*	flouting	MW III.i.108
offert	offered	H5 IV.vii.3			
tam	dam	MW I.i.139			

Welsh pronunciation	English word	First usage in H5 or MW

In a few cases, voicing stays the same and the Welshness is signalled by a change in the manner of articulation.

/ch/ becomes /s/

pinse	pinch	MW V.v.129
seese	cheese	MW V.v.139

/ch/ becomes /t/

voutsafe	vouchsafe	H5 III.ii.92

/sh/ becomes /s/

sall	shall	H5 IV.vii.23
silling	shilling	H5 IV.viii.71

/w/ becomes /v/

verefore	wherefore	MW III.i.73

There are also some cases where a consonant is omitted at the beginning of a word – usually /w/.

Sound omission

'oman	woman	MW I.i.211
'ord, 'ort	word	MW I.i.236
'ork	work	MW I.i.135
'orld	world	MW I.i.46
'udge	judge	MW I.i.171

Welsh pronunciation	English word	First usage in H5 or MW

It is unusual to show a variation in vowel quality.

louse	luce	MW I.i.17

And there is the occasional case where the spelling looks distinctive, with little difference in pronunciation.

chollors	cholers	MW III.i.11

Grammatical features

The representation of the dialect makes great use of distinctive grammatical features, such as the stereotypical discourse tag, *look you* (H5 III.ii.57). Nouns and the occasional adverb are made plural – *conjectures, disparagements, atonements, compromises* (MW I.i.28ff.), and *peradventures* (MW I.i.72). Grammatical agreement can be non-standard – *a joyful resurrections* (MW I.i.49). And words are frequently assigned to the wrong part of speech or given the wrong ending:

with as great discreetly	MW I.i.136
I will description the matter	MW I.i.200
if you be capacity of it	MW I.i.200
can you affection the 'oman	MW I.i.211
a very discretion answer	MW I.i.235
how melancholies I am	MW III.i.13
I will desires	MW III.iii.208
this is lunatics [= lunacy]	MW IV.ii.117
possitable [= positively]	MW I.i.220